THIRD EDITION

SCHROEDER'S
ANTIQUES
PRICE GUIDE

Edited by Sharon & Bob Huxford

COLLECTOR BOOKS
A Division of Schroeder Publishing Co., Inc.

The current values in this book should be used only as a guide. They are not intended to set prices, which vary from one section of the country to another. Auction prices as well as dealer prices vary greatly and are affected by condition as well as demand. Neither the Editor nor the Publisher assumes responsibility for any losses that might be incurred as a result of consulting this guide.

On the cover:
Light blonde Teddy Bear, 13″ $350.00
Beige mohair Teddy Bear, 10″ $250.00
Flow Blue wash set, $600.00-700.00
Majolica parrot pitcher, $75.00-95.00
Fiesta sauceboat $12.00-16.00
Fiesta covered casserole $38.00-42.00
Oak bentwood chair, $60.00-75.00
Painted blanket chest $1,500.00-2,000.00; Shaker box $250.00-350.00

Additional copies of this book may be ordered from:

COLLECTOR BOOKS
P.O. Box 3009
Paducah, Kentucky 42001

@$9.95 Add $1.00 for postage and handling.

Copyright: Schroeder Publishing Co., Inc., 1985
ISBN: 0-89145-281-8

Introduction

The upswing reported by antiques experts during the spring of 1983 is now being termed a national revival. Even in the most severely depressed areas of the country, auction gallery sales are up a strong 25%. This turnaround was effected by the same general economic factors that sent Wall Street rebounding, and the predictions for the coming months strongly suggest continued improvement. Money is flowing more freely and those with the capital to permit long term investing are returning from the certainty of the 16% interest-yielding money market to antiques. This is evidenced by increased activity in the sale of coins, rare stamps, jewelry, and silver, where recently finer examples have been consistently fetching prices well over their appraisals.

Strong interest is reported in English and 19th century American paintings, good antique and semi-antique Caucasian rugs, and in furniture -- Victorian and 19th century country pieces, early 19th century English styles, and country French. Early English porcelain has long been considered a sound investment, but early 19th century figure groups, cottages, and animals are much in demand as well. Interest in English pottery and Delft ware is growing.

In areas where sales indicate the affluence of middle-class America, recovery is strong. The pinch of the recession has eased, and collectibles such as photos and prints, vintage clothing, depression glass, dolls, cookie jars, country store memorabilia, American primitives, and Shaker items are selling very well. Those whose purses may not allow them to invest on a large scale, consider their's an investment in pleasure, though appreciation is often much more swiftly realized on a newly-introduced collectible than one long-established.

Experts project that the best buys for the coming year will be in glassware, silver, and American pottery. The best investments will be high quality examples from any period, which regardless of the economic climate is always a safe prediction.

This book has been compiled in an effort to report current market dealings. It should be used as only a tool to assist you in evaluating an item in question. We recommend that to become better educated and more knowledgeable you also study collectors' books, trade papers, and auction reports. Attend antique shows -- there is much to be gained by examining antiques first hand, as well as by conversing with reputable, experienced dealers.

Nearly six-hundred topics are represented in this guide, listed alphabetically, either by manufacturer or by type of product. Consult the index if you have difficulty in locating your subject. Feel free to contact dealers listed in our directory. Many will be glad to ship you the merchandise you need. Several of the newer collectors' clubs are also listed.

The Editors

Listing of Standard Abbreviations

The following is a list of abbreviations that have been used throughout this book in order to provide you with the most accurate descriptions possible in the limited space available. No periods are used after initials or abbreviations. When two dimensions are given, height is noted first. If only one dimension is listed, height will be indicated, except in the case of bowls, dishes, plates, or platters, when it will indicate diameter. The standard two letter state abbreviations apply.

For glass items, when no color is noted, glass is clear crystal. A number following the last comma in a listing refers to how many items are included in the lot price. Teapots and sugar bowls are assumed to be 'with lid', and butter dishes 'with cover'.

When condition is noted by our sources, we have noted it as well. We assume that an item that is offered for sale with no damage noted is in mint or near mint condition.

American	Am	Light	lt
Attributed to	att	Lithograph	litho
Back	bk	Made in Germany	MIG
Black	blk	Mahogany	mahog
Black and white	b/w	Mark	mk
Blue	bl	Mint condition	M
Brown	br	Mint in box	MIB
Bulbous	bulb	Mother of pearl	MOP
Cardboard	cb	Mount, mounted	mt, mtd
Cast iron	CI	Multicolor	mc
Century	C	Near mint condition	NM
Circa	ca	New England	NE
Complimentary	comp	Opalescent	opal
Composition	compo	Original	orig
Copyright	c	Otherwise	o/w
Creamer & sugar	cr/sug	Paint	pnt
Crossed	X	Patented	pat
Cup & saucer	c/s	Pedestal	ped
Dark	dk	Piece	pc
Decoration	decor	Pink	pk
Diameter	dia	Pint	pt
Double	dbl	Professional	prof
Dovetail	dvtl	Porcelain	porc
Drawer	drw	Refinished	rfn
Embossed	emb	Regarding	re
Engraved	eng	Repainted	rpt
Excellent condition	EX	Restored	rstr
Exterior	ext	Reticulated	retic
Footed	ftd	Reverse painted	rvpt
Framed	fr	Round	rnd
Good condition	G	Salt & pepper	S&P
Graduated	grad	Signed	sgn
Grain painted	grpt	Silverplated	SP
Green	gr	Small	sm
Hand colored	hc	Square	sq
Hand painted	HP	Standard	std
Handle	hdl	Turned	trn
Impressed	imp	Turquoise	turq
In the	i/t	Upholstered	uphl
Individual	ind	Very good condition	VG
Interior	int	White	wht
Iridescent	irid	Width	W
Large	lg	With	w/
Lavender	lav	Without	w/o
Leaded glass	ldgl	Yellow	yel
Length	L		

A B C Plates

Children's plates featuring the alphabet as part of the design were popular from as early as 1820 until after the turn of the century. The earliest English creamware plates were decorated with embossed letters and prim moralistic verses; but the later Staffordshire products were conducive to a more relaxed mealtime atmosphere -- often depicting playful animals and riddles, or scenes of pleasant leisure time activities. They were made around the turn of the century by American potters as well. All featured transfer prints, but color was sometimes brushed on by hand to add interest to the design. Braille plates were made for the blind, but are rather scarce, and therefore usually more valuable. You may also find an occasional bowl or mug . . . a matching set is rare.

American Sports Baseball Pitcher, br transfer.............125.00
At The Seaside, bl/wht, Roman numeral, children in boat, 7½"..35.00
Behold Him Rising, mc w/lustre rim, Meakin, 5½"...........65.00
Bowl & plate, Humpty Dumpty, mk Arlow, Ireland.............35.00
Boy & girl fishing, 8".................................35.00
Catch It Carlo, mc, boy/girl/dog.......................46.00
Children washing clothes, girl w/doll, 3 Crown, Germany, 6½"...45.00
Cowboy, Staffordshire..................................25.00
Crusoe & Friday, Staffordshire.........................65.00
Crusoe at Work, br transfer/HP, ABC border, 7¼".........70.00
Crusoe Rescues Friday, Staffordshire...................65.00
Crusoe Viewing the Island, Staffordshire, 8"...........65.00
Cup, tin, early..48.00
Dish, Bo Peep in center, ABCs & #s, glass, 7½".........40.00
Dish, children swinging, playing w/doll & horse, Germany......30.00
Dish, Dolly Dingle, hunting w/dog, china...............50.00
Franklin Maxim, For Age & Want, blk transfer, gr border, 6½"..68.00
Girl holding puppy, mother dog nearby, scolloped gold rim, 6"..35.00
Glass, clock in center, irregular edge, amethyst, 7"...........75.00
Glass, Garfield, 6"....................................45.00
Glass, rabbit, frosted, 6".............................50.00
Glass, vaseline, child's head in center, Clay Glass Works, 8"...40.00
Glass, 2 ducks w/ducklings center & emb rim, 6".............45.00
Golliwog...125.00
Harry Baiting His Line, mc, Elsmore, 5½"................65.00
Harvest Home, mc, 5½".................................55.00

He That Hath a Trade Hath an Estate, etc, w/blacksmith, 6¾"..55.00
How Wars Start, ironstone, gold letters, br pup/kitten, 6".......35.00
Hunter w/dogs, 1860s...................................38.00
Letter 'F', Staffordshire, 7"..........................45.00
London Dog Seller, Powell & Bishop.....................45.00
Man sliding downhill, mc, Staffordshire, 7½"............65.00
Nursery characters, Syracuse...........................23.00
October, family in woods, October verse, Staffordshire, 7¼".....68.00
Old Mother Hubbard, color transfer, 7".................55.00
Old Woman, Old Woman; DM McNicol, 7"...................38.00
Oriental couple, blk transfer/mc enamel, Nations o/t World, 7"..45.00
Owls at school transfer w/enamel, deaf hand signs, Aynsley, 8"..90.00
Parrot, children, dog & verse..........................25.00
Parrot, children, God, verse, Elsmore/Foster...........55.00
Playing shuttlecock, blk transfer w/mc enamel, Meakin, 7", G...65.00
Pride of the Barnyard, Staffordshire...................42.00
Punch & Judy in center, letters on border in bl, English, 7"....95.00
Sioux Indian Chief, brown, letter relief rim, 8¼"............60.00
Spoon, Rogers sterling, w/ABCs.........................35.00
Steeple Chase, Staffordshire, 7"......................40.00
The Drive, mc, couple in buggy.........................40.00
Thoroughbreds, sheep in pasture by woods, br w/gold ABCs, 6".40.00
Tin, bird in center, 8"................................40.00
Tin, bunny teacher....................................35.00
Tin, children in center, letters on border, 2" dia.........65.00
Tin, Cock Robin, 8", EX...............................65.00
Tin, Liberty..35.00
Tin, Mary & Lamb.....................................65.00
Toddy plate, blk transfer shepherd w/multicolor, hairline, 4½"..40.00
Train transfer in center, 7½".........................75.00
Two Indians in canoe fishing, 'The Candle Fish', Staffordshire...55.00
Two men on balking donkeys, Staffordshire, 7"..........65.00
Two men w/dogs & guns, stags on hill, Staffordshire, 8¼"......65.00
Village Blacksmith, blk transfer/mc enamel, Staffordshire, 5"...50.00
Zebra Hunt, Staffordshire, 8¼".......................65.00
1893 Expo, shows 3 buildings..........................75.00

Abingdon

From 1934 until 1950, the Abingdon Pottery Co. of Abingdon, Ill., made a line of art pottery with a white vitrified body, decorated with various glazes in an array of lovely colors -- matt as well as glossy, crystalline, and iridescent. Novelties, cookie jars, utility ware, and lamps were made in addition to several lines of simple yet striking art ware. Fern Leaf, introduced in 1937 featured molded vertical feathering. La Fleur, in 1939, consisted of flower pots and flower arranger bowls with rows of vertical ribbing. Classic, 1939-40, was a line of vases, many with evidence of Chinese influence. Several marks were used, most of which employed the company name. In 1950, the company reverted to the manufacture of sanitary ware that had been their mainstay before the Art Ware Division was formed.

Cookie jar, #471, Little Old Lady, solid black..............85.00
Cookie jar, #549, Hippo, black........................50.00
Cookie jar, #588, Money Bag..........................35.00
Cookie jar, #651, Train...............................65.00
Cookie jar, #653, Clock...............................45.00
Cookie jar, #662, Miss Muffet.........................60.00
Cookie jar, #663, Humpty Dumpty......................60.00
Cookie jar, #664, Pineapple...........................35.00
Cookie jar, #667D, Daisy, yellow & brown...............25.00
Cookie jar, #694, Bo Peep............................50.00
Cookie jar, #695, Mother Goose, LAL...................40.00
Cookie jar, #697D, Plaid, decorated...................35.00

Wild Animals series by B.P. Co., Tunstall, England, 'The Lion', 7½", $75.00.

G-1, oil jar, tall...............................75.00
101, vase, Classic, blue, w/sticker.........................12.00
102, vase, Beta...............................15.00
111, vase, Gamma...............................25.00
115, vase, Classic, 10"...............................10.00
116, vase, Classic, 10"...............................9.00
155, vase, Classic, lg...............................15.00
180, vase, Floral...............................25.00
202, jug, ice lip, pint...............................10.00
301, jar, Ming, w/lid...............................30.00
305, bookends, Sea Gull...............................40.00
306, ash tray, Abingdon...............................12.00

Little Old Lady cookie jar with exceptional decoration, $60.00.

312, vase, Han, pink...............................12.00
313, salad bowl, Rope...............................12.00
318, vase, Ring...............................35.00
321, bookends, Cossack/Russian...............................55.00
340, service plate, square...............................10.00
345, bowl, Chinese, oval...............................15.00
349, vase, Chalice...............................18.00
357, vase, Salon...............................40.00
366, flower pot, Egg & Dart, medium...............................10.00
374, planter bookends, Cactus...............................25.00
376, mask, male or female, large, each...............................38.00
388, Pouter Pigeon...............................25.00
3903, seated kneeling nude...............................200.00
3906, Shepherdess & Fawn...............................225.00
393, bowl, Morning Glory...............................18.00
401, teapot tile, Coolie...............................35.00
403, bowl, Chain, oval...............................20.00
407, bowl, Rose...............................15.00
410, vase, Volute, small...............................20.00
413, bowl, Wreath...............................25.00
419, bowl, Rhythm...............................15.00
441, bookends, Horsehead...............................50.00
447, candle holder, Sunburst, triple...............................25.00
456, ash tray, New Mode...............................12.00
463, vase, Star, pink...............................12.00
474, vase, Single Cornucopia, pink...............................10.00
482, vase, Double Cornucopia, pink...............................15.00

484, vase, Fan, pink...............................10.00
491, vase, flower arranger, wht...............................12.00
494, vase, Ship, blue...............................16.00
505, candle holders, Double Shell, pink, pr...............................20.00
513, vase, Swirl, pink...............................12.00
533, bowl, medium Shell, pink...............................10.00
543, bowl, Geranium...............................35.00
582D, basket, decorated...............................30.00
583, vase, Triple Cornucopia...............................18.00
613, pitcher, Grecian...............................12.00
627, cache pot...............................20.00
639, vase, Calla...............................20.00
647, urn, tall...............................35.00
657, Swordfish...............................30.00
666, jam jar set w/tray...............................25.00
668, planter, Daffodil...............................25.00
676D, wall vase...............................20.00
683, teapot, Daisy...............................30.00
690, range set, Daisy, yellow & brown...............................40.00
702, string holder, Chinese Face...............................35.00
707, planter bowl, Cradle...............................15.00
712, string holder, Mouse...............................35.00
9701, bowl, oblong, pink w/2 pink geese: 1 upright/1 feeding....30.00

Adams

Wm. Adams, whose potting skills were developed under the tutelage of Josiah Wedgwood, founded the Greengates Pottery at Tunstall, England in 1769. Many types of wares including basalt, ironstone, parian, and jasper were produced, and various impressed or printed marks were employed. Until 1800, 'Adams Co.' or 'Adams' impressed in block letters identified the company's earthenwares and a fine type of jasper similar in color and decoration to Wedgwood's. The latter mark was used again from 1845 to 1864 on parian figures. Most examples of their product found on today's market are transfer printed dinnerwares with ornate backstamps which often include the pattern name and the initials 'W.A. & S.' This type of product was made from 1820 until about 1920. After 1890, the word 'England' was included in the mark; 'Tunstall' was added after 1896. From 1914 through 1940 a printed crown with 'Adams, Estbd 1657, England', identified their products. From 1900 to 1965 they produced souvenir plates with transfers of American scenes, many of which were marketed in this country by Roth Importers of Peoria, Illinois. In 1965, the company affiliated with Wedgwood. Although there were other Adams potteries in Staffordshire, their marks incorporate either the first name initial or a partner's name, and so are easily distinguished from those of this company.

See also Spatter; Staffordshire

Adam's Rose, cup, handleless; w/saucer, late...............52.00
Adam's Rose, cup plate, 4¼"...............................45.00
Adam's Rose, deep plate, ca 1840, 9½"...............................68.00
Adam's Rose, plate, 8¾", late...............................43.00
Biscuit jar, bl/wht jasper, hunters decor, SP lid & bail.........160.00
Creamer, Shell, dk bl transfer...............................195.00
Cup & saucer, Bird Cage, dk bl transfer...............................95.00
Cup & saucer, handleless; gaudy florals, hairline...............25.00
Cup & saucer, Sower, pink transfer...............................38.00
Cup & saucer, thatched cottage, dk bl transfer...............85.00
Cup plate, blue Casino pattern, ca 1840, 5" dia, pr...............40.00
Plate, Caledonia, blk/purple transfer, 10½"...............................75.00
Plate, Cupid & Virgin, dk bl transfer, 8¾"...............................75.00
Plate, Fountain Scenery, purple/blk transfer, 7"...............35.00
Plate, man fishing, dk bl, 7"...............................45.00
Plate, milk maid, cottage, cows, dk bl, 6½"...............................55.00

Plate, Woodcock Shooting, black and white transfer with multicolor brushed-on details, advertising on back, 10½", $18.00.

Plate, Seasons, March, pink transfer, 9½"....................45.00
Plate, The Sea, Shipwreck, pink transfer, 9½"...............45.00
Platter, The Sea, Homeward Bound, pink transfer, 10"........75.00
Soup, The Sea, shipwreck, pink transfer, 9¼"................45.00
Tidbit, 2 tier, N Currier Winter Scenes, made for B Altman.....25.00
Tray, stick spatter w/gaudy florals, mk Titian Ware, 7½".......30.00

Advertising

The advertising world has always been a fiercely competitive field. In an effort to present their product to the customer, every imaginable gimmic was put into play. Colorful and artfully decorated signs and posters, thermometers, tape measures, fans, hand mirrors, and attractive tin containers -- all with catchy slogans, familiar logos, and often bogus claims -- are only a few of the many examples of early advertising memorabilia that are of interest to today's collectors.

Porcelain signs were made as early as 1890 and are highly prized for their artistic portrayal of life as it was then . . . often allowing amusing insights into the tastes, humor and way of life of a bygone era. As a general rule, older signs are made from a heavier gauge metal. Those with three or more fired on colors are especially desirable.

Tin containers were used to package consumer goods ranging from crackers and coffee to tobacco and talcum. After 1880, can companies began to decorate their containers by the method of lithography. Though colors were still subdued, intricate designs were used to attract the eye of the consumer. False labeling and unfounded claims were curtailed by the Pure Food & Drug Administration in 1906, and the name of the manufacturer as well as the brand name of the product had to be printed on the label. By 1910, color was rampant with more than a dozen hues printed on the tins or on paper labels. The tins themselves were often designed with a second use in mind -- as canisters, lunch boxes, even toy trains. As a general rule, tobacco related tins are the most desirable, though personal preference may direct the interest of the collector to peanut butter pails with illustrations of children, or talcum tins with irresistible babies or beautiful ladies. Coffee tins are popular, as are those made to contain a particularly successful or well known product.

Perhaps the most visual of the early advertising gimmics were the character logos -- the Fairbank Company's Gold Dust Twins, the goose trademark of the Red Goose Shoe Company, Nabisco's Zu Zu Clown and Uneeda Kid, the Campbell Kids, the RCA dog Nipper, and Mr. Peanut, to name only a few. Any example of these brings high prices on the market today.

Our listings are alphabetized by company name, or in lieu of that information, by word content or other pertinent description.

See also Advertising Dolls; Advertising Cards; Banks; Calendars; Cookbooks; Fans; Paperweights; Posters; Sewing Items, tape measure; Thermometers

Key:
cb-----cardboard	ps----porcelain sign
fr-----framed	sf-----self-framed
lcs-----litho on canvas sign	tc-----tin container
pp-----pre-prohibition	ts-----tin sign

A&P Coffee, medal.....................................8.00
A-C Spark Plugs, clock, electric.....................30.00
Acme, coach's whistle, The Acme Thunderer................10.00
Acorn Brand Peanut Butter, pail, orig label.............40.00
Adam Scheidt Brewery, pocket mirror, shows bottle, colorful....75.00
Adams Gum, jar......................................105.00
Adams Gum, store tins, 4: CA Fruit/Spearmint/Yuctan/Pepsin...600.00
Adams Pepsin Tutti Frutti, blotter, pack & 5 sticks, early, NM....6.00
Adams Pepsin Tutti Frutti, store dispenser tin, G.............55.00
Adams Pepsin Tutti Frutti, tin gum box, colorful, NM.........89.00
Aetna, mirror......................................20.00
Ainslie's Whiskey, pitcher, Edinburgh Castle/Natn'l Gallery......45.00
Air Float, talcum tin...............................20.00
Alcazar Cigar, tin can.............................300.00
Allen's Lung Balsam, glazed panel, cut w/cherubs/banner.....1,050.00
Alt Heidelberg, tin sign, w/boy, 19x9"..................22.00
Altes Lager Beer, tray, Bavarian waiter, 1910.............125.00
American Breeders Service, tin sign, emb steer, mc, early, NM...55.00
American Brewing & Maltin Co, plate, roses, name on bk, 10"..20.00
American Liberty Rochester Beer, tray, pre-pro.............125.00
American Line, pocket mirror, shows lg cruise ship, colorful.....35.00
American Line, tip tray, 4" dia, VG.......................85.00
American Oil, mini CI skillet, raised letters, torch logo........20.00
Angelus Marshmallows, pocket mirror, cherub w/product, horn...60.00
Angelus Marshmallows, pocket mirror, 2 cherubs w/product.....75.00
Anheuser Busch, beer crate, dated 1920....................40.00
Anheuser Busch, mirror...............................25.00
Anheuser Busch, tin sign, Dr & stork, 7x12"................50.00
Anheuser Busch, tin sign, Say When, NM...................300.00
Anheuser Busch Malt Nutrine, metal plate, bare shouldered girl..95.00
Apache Trail Cigar, tin can...........................550.00
Arcade Store, pocket mirror, redhead w/yel flower in hair.......75.00
Arctic Ice Cream, tray, polar bear.......................165.00
Arm & Hammer, bird chart, 1915, 33x44"..................150.00
Arm & Hammer, poster, boy laughs at hunter, 1910, 25x17"...250.00
Arm & Hammer Soda, blotter, pictures emblem, corner torn.....2.50
Arm & Hammer Soda, poster, bees after hunters, 1910, 25x17"225.00
Arm & Hammer Soda, sign, pictures emblem, blk/gold, 16x12"..24.50
Armour Star Hot Dogs, emb tin sign, cooks hold up hot dog...175.00
Armour's Vigoral, mug................................16.00
Arrow Brand Collars & Cuffs, mirror, ornate fr, 11x15", VG...75.00
Arthur Donaldson Pilsen Cigars, cigar box stand-up display......7.00
AT Cook Seed Specialist, pocket mirror, w/orig envelope.......38.50
Atlanta Constitution, thermometer, wood, 21x5"..............40.00
Atlas Spark Plug, wood sign, looks like rat trap.............35.00
Atwater Kent, whistle, tin, M..........................10.00
Aunt Jemima, pancake machine, 1940s, M..................350.00
Ayers Cathartic Pills, die-cut litho, Blk man/2 children, 1883...125.00
Babbitt's Soap, paper sign, 2 babies/Our Twins, 24x15", EX...150.00
Babbitt's Soap, poster, Little Lord Fauntleroy, 1890, 30x15"....95.00

Baer Bros Brushes & Paints, statue, 2 teddy bears, lg........125.00
Baer Bros Paint, display, chalkware bears w/sign, dtd 1931, 5"..45.00
Bagdad Short Cut, tobacco pocket tin, G..................42.00
Bagley Tobacco, mirror..........................20.00
Bailey's Pure Rye, tip tray.......................45.00
Baker's Chocolate, pencil sharpener, w/lady, orig paint, NM.....50.00
Baker's Chocolate, tin table, urn shape, lady on 24" base....1,350.00
Baker's Cocoa, tin canister......................45.00
Baker's Cocoa, tin sign, sf, w/Colonial lady, Breakfast Cocoa..1,000.00
Ballard's Obelisk Edible Bran, pocket mirror, w/box/lettering....23.50
Ballard's Obelisk Flour, mirror....................20.00
Banquet Ice Cream, cb sign, 25x13"................55.00
Barbarossa Beer, sign, canvas, 16x12"..............45.00
Bardahl Oil, clock, detective on face, glass/metal, 15" sq......55.00
Bartel's Beer, metal sign, rnd....................95.00
Bartel's Beer, tin sign, emb....................195.00
Bartel's Beer, tip tray, shows 'Night Watchman', pre-1920.....135.00
Bartholomay, beer tray, pre-pro..................85.00
Bartholomay, blotter, pre-pro, mc.................18.00
Bartholomay, Tam O'Shanter, tip tray, pre-pro..........150.00
Bauer & Black Mustard Plasters, tc, red/wht/bl cylinder, 3¾"....7.00
Bayuk Cigars, store tin, 3x5x7", M................20.00
Beech-Nut Chewing Tobacco, fr litho, w/John & Demijohn/pack..85.00
Beech-Nut Coffee, trial tin, Not For Sale, 4 oz, unopened.....28.00
Beechnut Gum, display rack, w/little girl, 1920s, VG.........125.00
Beeman's Gum, canister........................450.00
Belfast, tobacco tin..........................23.00
Bell Brand Chocolate, sign, tin, emb cherubs/etc...........425.00
Bell System, fan, AT&T, lg bl bell picture............25.00
Bell Telephone, paperweight, cobalt, local & long distance.....65.00
Belle of Milton Whiskey, ts, camp w/hunters/dogs, 27x39"....1,000.00
Berkley Knit Ties, cardboard, man w/tie, 8x10"..........20.00
Big Ben, pocket tin..........................18.00

Clarnico, candy or gum tin with lithographed portrait, 2" x 5", 38.00.

Bingaman & Co Jewelers, pocket mirror, Nouveau lady, G.....28.50
Birchola, tin dbl sided sign, 10x12"................25.00
Bixota, Red Wing Milling Co, pocket mirror............25.00
Black & White Scotch Whiskey, display, figural dogs, w/bottles..45.00
Black Cat Shoe Dressing, clock, w/cat, in wood case.......5,400.00
Blanke's Mojav Coffee, tin container, red w/lady on horse.....120.00
Blanke's Oak Lawn Coffee, can w/lid, 2 lb, G...........30.00
Blatz, clock, barrel man cast metal sign w/clock..........45.00

Blatz Beer, sign, girl on barrel, dtd 1933, 14x36"..........495.00
Blatz Beer, sign, Old Heidlberg girl, dtd 1933, 22x36", M....650.00
Blatz Grape, cb cluster of grapes, 10¢ a bottle...........17.50
Blue Banner Chocolates, tin sign, wood fr, 17x8".........95.00
Blue Boar Tobacco, canister, sm top................22.00
Blue Crown Spark Plugs, emb tin sign, shows plug.........65.00
Blue Jay, tin die-cut display, man skipping.............130.00
Blue Label, tobacco tin, flat pocket.................65.00
Blue Seal, cleanser tin, pictures bathtub, wash basin........10.00
Bob White, tobacco tin........................250.00
Bond Street, tobacco pocket tin...................16.00
Borated Talcum Powder, tc, girl's portrait, 1906, EX........35.00
Bouquet Coffee, tin container....................55.00
Boye Needle Co, hook display, glass tilt front, decals, 8x7x5½"..85.00
Bradley Swim Suits, fan, cb, '20s couple in suits, 13½".......4.00
Braem's Bitters, sign, metal on cb, bottle w/label, 7x13½".....30.00
Brainard & Armstrong, spool cabinet, 2 drawers..........250.00
Braumeister, tin sign, mc banner, 35x22"............68.00
Breakfast Call, coffee tin, 1 lb..................22.00
Breethem for the Breath, tc, flat, holds 12 tablets, '30s lady.....8.00
Briggs, tobacco pocket tin......................18.00
Brighton Silk Garters, oak display case, emb, ca '02, 19x12"...365.00
Brinly Rastus, emb plow stickpin..................18.00
Brown's Iron Bitters, blotter, 4 color, mother/desk/children......6.50
Brownell & Field Spices, tc, Pepper & Cayenne, 1910s, pr....462.00
Brownie Peanuts, tin container, rnd.................40.00
Buckingham Cut Plug, tobacco pocket tin, G............30.00
Buckingham Cut Plug, tobacco tin, trial size............70.00
Budweiser, clock, pocket watch, illuminated, revolving chain....175.00
Budweiser, neon sign, eagle emblem w/'A', 26½x11".........65.00
Budweiser, print, Custer's Last Fight, nameplate, 1952, 33x46"..55.00
Budweiser, print, Relief Train, 1910................125.00
Budweiser, sign, illuminated, Clydesdale draft horse team......900.00
Budweiser, tray, foxhunters, shadow of fox by fireplace.........75.00
Budweiser, tray, 1914 St Louis Levee scene.............75.00
Budweiser, 3-D sign, Clydesdales, 8x21x70"...............850.00
Buffalo, glass jar, embossed.....................200.00
Buffalo Brand Peanuts, tin container, 10 lb.............90.00
Buffalo Lager, tin sign, Toast o/t Coast, 7x17¼"..........250.00
Buffalo Peanut Butter, tin pail...................50.00
Bull Durham, paperboard, bull fight, 1909, orig fr, 35x23".....450.00
Bull Durham, pocket tc, 1910s, 4".................2,600.00
Bull Durham, sgn, paper under glass, couple kiss, umbrella...1,350.00
Bunte Candy, store jar, emb name, w/orig glass stopper........48.00
Burger Beer, sf tin sign, 18x26".................50.00
Burger Brau Beer, clock, tin, wood fr, old man w/mug, 19"....185.00
Burley Boy, pocket tin........................350.00
Burton Brewing Co, Katz Bros, sign, rvpt/chain hung, pp, 14x8".90.00
Busch Beer, poster, Victorian men & women at table, fr, 1900.195.00
Busch Ginger Ale, ps, Extra Dry, 1920s, rect, 11x21".........85.00
Buster Brown Bread, pocket mirror..................40.00
Buster Brown Cigar, cigar band, 1920s................1.00
Buster Brown Shoes, banjo, calfskin, child's, stringless........48.00
Buster Brown Shoes, pocket mirror, celluloid w/BB & Tige, G...28.50
Buster Brown Shoes, tin whistle, cylinder, BB & Tige.........15.00
Butternut Bread, cb, girl carrying bread, 7x10"............5.50
Butternut Bread, poster, baker w/loaf, mc, dtd 1935, 22x15".....8.00
Butternut Bread, sign, cb, boy w/knife, chef's outfit, 10x13".....8.00
B1 Lemon Lime Soda, sign, die-cut tin, 1940............75.00
C Shenkberg Co, Java & Mocha, lift top bin, 15x12x14".....150.00
Cadbury's Dairy Milk Chocolate, tc, butter churn, English....175.00
Camel, tip tray............................20.00
Camel Cigarettes, cardboard pack..................15.00
Camel Cigarettes, light pull.....................12.00

Camel Cigarettes, thermometer, For Mildness & Flavor, 14″, EX.17.50
Camel Cigars, tin container.............................70.00
Camel Flat 50s, tin container.........................20.00
Camel Tube Patch, tin container.......................15.00
Campbell, coffee tin, desert scene, 4 lb..............50.00
Campbell's Shag, tobacco upright pocket tin, Sherlock Holmes.100.00
Campbell's Soup, handkerchief, 7 Kids w/dog & verse, ca 1930..15.00
Campfire Marshmallows, tin container..................35.00
Canada Dry, clock, electric...........................65.00
Canuck Tobacco, tc, round corner, EX..................35.00
Capstan Cigars, sign, dbl sided porcelain, 21x14″.....75.00
Cardinal Tobacco, pocket tin, sample size............300.00
Carling Brewery, framed print, 9 Pints of the Law, old........50.00
Carlton Club, tobacco pocket tin......................65.00
Carnation Malted Milk, jar, milk glass, domed metal lid, 6x6″...65.00
Carnation Malted Milk, tin canister, red/wht flower design......45.00
Carson's Cookies, tin/glass container.................45.00
Carter's Infant Underwear, tin sign, child, brass bed, rabbit....115.00
Carter's Ink, thermometer, porcelain, 1915, 7x27″....165.00
Cascarets, paper sign, The Sleeping Gazebo, 1910s, fr, 20x16″.100.00
Casey & Kelly Brewery, tray, king holding mug, colorful, pp....260.00
Cat's Paw Heels & Soles, tin sign, 29x20″.............95.00
Cataract Beer, sign, tin litho, 1930s, 14″ dia........75.00
Cavitt's System Regulator, pocket mirror, 1¾″, EX.....9.50
Central Union, tin tobacco box........................35.00
Century Beer Schneider, tip tray, old man, woman drinking....125.00
Ceresota Flour, match holder, Ceresota boy, tin, wall hung.....90.00
Ceresota Flour, pocket mirror, boy cutting bread......55.00
Cero Fruto Cereal, litho sign, girl w/doll...........145.00
Cesco Wide Angle Vision Goggle, tin sign, w/goggle, EX........15.00
Cetacolor, oil cloth sign, Victorian woman, 1890s, 36x25″.....50.00
Champagne Velvet, beer bottle, 450 oz, 30″ w/3″ cap, G labels.150.00
Champagne Velvet, sign, man fishing, hornets after him........50.00
Champagne Velvet, sign, man has fishing line tangled in tree....50.00
Champagne Velvet Beer, sign, rvpt....................50.00
Champion Air Service, porcelain service station sign..........85.00
Charm of the West, flat tobacco pocket tin............85.00
Chase & Sanborn's, sample tin.........................16.00
Chaser Soap, sign, tin litho, 'Does the Work', sunbonnet girls..440.00
Check Cigar, tc, pictures monetary check of Rock City Cigar Co.75.00
Cheney Phonographs, emb brass sign, lyre/fiddle/instruments...225.00
Chero Cola, fr calendar, 1917, lady w/bottle, 36″....225.00
Cherry Julep, tin sign, red w/wht lettering, Drink..., 7x20″.....18.50
Cherry Smash, syrup dispenser, ruby glass............275.00
Cherry Tooth Paste, pot lid...........................35.00
Chew Walla Walla Gum, Aids Digestion, tin sign, 9x19″.......65.00
Chiclets, display, 1906...............................25.00
Chico's, counter jar, lid: Makers Baby Ruth..........350.00
Chief, rolled oat sack, 100 lbs, M....................35.00
Chief Watta Pop, sucker holder.......................125.00
Christian Feigenspan Breweries, tip tray, redhead/low-cut gown..90.00
Churchman's Cigarettes, store display box, 13x8x4½″........150.00
Cities Service, oil can, ½ gal, 1920s.................25.00
Citizen Ins Co of NJ, sign, rvpt, Greek Revival building........85.00
City Club, tobacco pocket tin, sm.....................70.00
Clarke's Teaberry Gum, gum & change tray, w/6 pkgs gum.....195.00
Clarks Mile End Spool, litho, Blk man in cotton field/product..495.00
Clarks ONT Thread, poster, w/lady, 21x14½″...........325.00
Class, cigar tin......................................45.00
Clayton's Dog Remedies, bulldog, life size, ca 1900..450.00
Cleo Cola, ts, emb, Cleopatra, 1920s, rect, 12x26″...45.00
Cleveland & Sandusky, tray, w/factory................295.00
Cleveland 'Sirups', tray, tin litho w/product, dispenser, '07....200.00
Cleveland Fruit Juice Co, tray, tin litho, w/dispenser, 1908....195.00

Liquid Force, The World's Greatest Health Drink, syrup dispenser, embossed multicolor map of the world, very rare, 14″, $2,200.00.

Climax, tobacco tin...................................25.00
Cloverine Salve, sample tin............................9.00
Clysmic, tip tray, EX................................120.00

Coca-Cola

Established in 1891, the Coca-Cola Company at once began an extensive advertising campaign that in retrospect must be considered one of the most powerful and successful promotions of all time. Coke's continuing popularity and the sheer volume of the advertising items issued by the company over the years have resulted today in creating what may well be the most collectible field of specific product memorabilia ever offered.

The first Coca-Cola drinks were only available 'on tap' at the local soda fountains. By 1894 it was available in bottles. The earliest calendars indicated that Coca-Cola was not only 'Delicious and Refreshing', but could also 'Relieve Mental and Physical Exhaustion' and 'Cure Headaches'! Coca-Cola Chewing Gum was sold from about 1908 through 1916.

Though the more familiar Coke trays are rectangular, from the 1890s until 1910 they were round or oval. Early metal signs decorated with lovely ladies in Victorian costumes are rare and fetch prices into the thousands of dollars. Yet even those later items -- door pushes, bottles, toy trucks, playing cards, blotters, rulers, paperweights and fans -- are valued by collectors today. In 1970 the company began to distribute advertising items of a markedly different nature, and most Coke buffs have adopted this year as the cut-off point to add to their collections.

Bank, vending machine, dispenses actual drink, late '50s.......90.00
Bank, vending machine, dispenses toy bottle, 1950s...........30.00
Beach ball...20.00
Blotter, 1904, Branch Factories Phila/LA/Chicago/Dallas, NM...175.00
Blotter, 1904, Pure & Healthful/5¢, hand/tap fills glass, NM.....50.00
Blotter, 1916, Pure & Healthful, 2 bottles, no price, NM.......65.00
Blotter, 1920, Refresh Yourself, 2 bottles, no price, NM.......15.00
Blotter, 1927, man & lady w/bottles, The Pause...Refreshes, EX..61.00
Blotter, 1931, Rockwell/boy & dog fishing, 'OK', EX..45.00
Blotter, 1935, boy/bike/dog, A Home Run With Three On, NM..15.00
Blotter, 1935, trainman, Feeling Fit For Duty Ahead, M..15.00
Blotter, 1936, 50th Anniv, bottle center, M...........35.00
Blotter, 1938, traffic cop, Stop for Pause/Go Refreshed, M.....7.00
Blotter, 1942, girl on stomach reads magazine, It's Swell, M.....5.00
Blotter, 1944, 3 girls w/bottles, How About A Coke, NM.......3.00

Blotter, 1960, Over 60 Million A Day, lg bottle & chart, M......3.00
Booklet, Truth About Coca-Cola, 1912.....................20.00
Bookmark, celluloid, owl reading book, M................275.00
Bookmark, 1898, celluloid, heart w/seated lady portrait, M....285.00
Bookmark, 1902, Hilda Clark, paper, G...................225.00
Bookmark, 1903, Nordica, mug & flowers at top, EX.........175.00
Bottle, amber, much embossing, dtd 1917, Dayton, O.........75.00
Bottle, br, Lexington KY..............................50.00
Bottle, hobble skirt, Christmas 1923.......................5.00
Bottle, hobble skirt, 1915..............................5.00
Bottle, straight side, 'Best By A Dam Site', Las Vegas.........50.00
Bottle, straight side, amber, Nashville, 7½″...............35.00
Bottle, straight side, Biedenharn Candy Co, w/script logo.....100.00
Bottle, 21″, M....................................125.00
Bottle carrier, cardboard, 1937.........................20.00
Bottle opener, iron, hand held.........................7.50
Calendar, 1914...................................400.00
Calendar, 1916...................................400.00
Calendar, 1926, girl w/fox stole......................250.00
Calendar, 1931, Rockwell, boy & dog...................375.00
Calendar, 1932, Rockwell, boy w/dog & bucket.............200.00
Calendar, 1935, Rockwell, boy fishing...................200.00
Calendar, 1947, girl w/skis...........................40.00
Calendar, 1950, Hospitality cover page...................40.00
Calendar, 1950, 2 months per pg, complete, M..............30.00
Calendar, 1955....................................20.00
Cardboard cut-outs, Olympic Games of 1932................35.00
Cardboard cut-outs, Toy Town, 1927....................35.00
Change purse, leather, Coke..........................30.00
Check, Coca-Cola Bottling Works, Paducah Ky, 1915 w/bldg....5.00
Cigar band, oval medallion w/bottle, scroll decor, paper, M.....55.00
Clock, Coke, 1939.................................225.00
Clock, dated 1953..................................65.00
Clock, red/maroon, 18″ dia...........................45.00
Clock, Regulator, Gilbert, 1916.......................700.00
Coupon, Lillian Russell, 1904, M.......................90.00
Cuff links, 1920s, celluloid, Coca-Cola written out, pr, NM.....26.00
Door pull, plastic, orig box w/instructions, old, M...........110.00
Fan, wicker, Waycross, GA, 1950s, EX...................50.00
First day cover, 1939, Detroit, hand w/bottle, NM............8.00
Ice pick, red advertising, VG...........................8.00
Knife, pocket; Coca-Cola, 5¢.........................20.00
Lapel pin, 5 yr service, figural bottle w/ruby...............35.00
Lapel pin/tie tac, figural bottle, 10k.....................22.50
Lighter, glass bottle................................10.00
Lock, safety; orig box, 1930..........................20.00
Map, wall hanging; 1940.............................35.00
Matchbox, Yesteryear Model T, no box, M.................45.00
Menu, 1903, Nordica, excellent color, EX................300.00
Mini 6-pack w/bottles, 1950, M........................30.00
Needle folder, 1924, lady w/glass, bottle on table, M.........35.00
Overalls, wht w/gr pin stripe, Coca-Cola.................65.00
Pencil, mechanical; stamped Coca-Cola motif, Hope, AR.......30.00
Pencil box, w/ruler, eraser, pens, 1930s..................27.50
Playing card, 1915, 1 single card, lady w/closed parasol, NM....21.00
Playing cards, girl bowler, hand offers bottle, full deck, MIB.....15.00
Playing cards, 1943, girl portrait, falling leaves, w/box, M......30.00
Playing cards, 1943, telephone operator, MIB..............30.00
Playing cards, 1943, WAC portrait, bottle w/wings, NM w/box...30.00
Playing cards, 1961, girl holds bottle & card, MIB...........15.00
Playing cards, 1963, couple sitting under tree, MIB...........10.00
Pocket mirror, 1910, Hamilton King, girl w/lg hat, oval, NM...200.00
Pocket mirror, 1911, lady w/lg flowered hat, oval, EX........195.00
Pocket mirror, 1913................................250.00

Pocket mirror, 1917, girl in country w/bottle, oval, NM........195.00
Pocket mirror, 1936, memo board, 50th Anniv, rectangular, NM.47.00
Pocket watch, old, runs good.........................175.00
Postcard, 1920s, Atlanta Bottling plant, 5 scenes, NM.........75.00
Postcard, 1930s, International delivery truck, color, M.........20.00
Postcard, 1930s, send for free opener, man/woman on couch, b/w.8.00
Radio, bottle; 1940s, working.........................200.00
Radio, figural cooler, RCA Model 5A410A................350.00
Ruler..10.00
Sandwich plate, 1930s, 7¼″ dia........................85.00
Santa, cardboard, 18″...............................20.00
Score keeper, 1906, Drink...Relieves Fatigue, EX............35.00
Sign, Drink Coca-Cola, emb bottle, sf, 5 color, '30s, 9x27″....120.00
Sign, drug store; porcelain, Candy Film, 1940s, 28x16″........50.00
Sign, flanged, Coke................................150.00
Sign, flanged, enamel, Vendu Ice Glace, 4 colors NM........125.00
Sign, metal, Christmas bottle, Delicious, etc; 1930s, 36x52″....175.00
Sign, porcelain, Drink Coca-Cola, 1920s.................130.00
Sign, porcelain, Fountain Service, 1935..................150.00
Sign, tin, carton & bottles, dtd 1939, 23x29″..............95.00
Sign, tin, fishtail design, 23x14″........................35.00
Sign, tin, It's A Natural, 1954.........................45.00
Sign, tin, shows 1916 bottle.........................150.00
Sign, tin, shows 1923 bottle..........................65.00
Sign, tin, shows 6 bottles for 25¢, dated 1939, 23x29″........95.00
Sign, Victorian lady, plummage, 1911, sm.................55.00
Stationery, Macon Bottling Co, Georgia, 1911, 1 pg, M........35.00
Stationery, Macon Ga, shows building & bottle, 1906, NM......35.00
Stationery, Waycross Ga, bottle on left, logo center, 1 pg, NM...18.00
Stationery, Waycross Ga, Exclusive Bottlers of, bottle center....18.00
Thermometer, Drink Coca-Cola in Bottles, 12″ dia...........27.50
Thermometer, Sign of Good Taste, 1940s, 8x27″............45.00
Tip tray, 1900, glass, Hilda Clark, cb insert, EX............850.00
Tip tray, 1903, Hilda Clark, NM, 6″....................750.00
Tip tray, 1909, Exposition Girl, girl at St Louis Fair, EX......225.00
Tip tray, 1912, NM................................165.00
Tip tray, 1914, Betty, oval, NM.......................120.00
Tip tray, 1914, VG.................................85.00
Tip tray, 1917, girl w/glass looks over shoulder, oval, EX......90.00
Tip tray, 1920, EX................................180.00

Tray, girl on diving board, 1939, 13″ x 10½″, $40.00.

Tray, 1903, Hilda Clark, 15x8½", M......................2,500.00
Tray, 1903, Hilda Clark, 15x8½", VG..................1,500.00
Tray, 1904, Nordica w/glass, oval, G....................210.00
Tray, 1904, Nordica w/glass, oval, M.................1,000.00
Tray, 1905, Jaunita, oval, EX, 10½x13"...............600.00
Tray, 1906, Relieves Fatigue, oval, 10½x13¼", G.....145.00
Tray, 1906, Relieves Fatigue, oval, 13¾x16½", G........1,051.00
Tray, 1908, topless, Western, NM, 12½" dia..............1,695.00
Tray, 1910, Hamilton King, girl w/hat, rectangular, EX.......325.00
Tray, 1914, Betty, rectangular, VG......................65.00
Tray, 1917, girl looks over shoulder, long rectangle, Ex......101.00
Tray, 1920, girl w/hat, oval, 13¾x16½", M..............300.00
Tray, 1921, girl in beret type hat, rectangular, EX........237.00
Tray, 1922, girl w/glass, rectangular, M................200.00
Tray, 1923, girl w/glass, rectangular, NM...............100.00
Tray, 1924, girl w/glass, brown rim, rectangular, NM......250.00
Tray, 1926, man golfer pours for seated lady, rectangular, EX..180.00
Tray, 1927, girl drinks w/straw from bottle, rectangular, NM...100.00
Tray, 1927, waiter w/3 glasses, rectangular, M..........195.00
Tray, 1929, girl w/bottle, rectangular, VG...............215.00
Tray, 1930, girl w/bottle, rectangular, EX..............100.00
Tray, 1930, telephone, VG............................115.00
Tray, 1931, Rockwell scene/boy & dog, rectangular, M......250.00
Tray, 1933, girl in bathing suit sits on wall, rectangular, NM...93.00
Tray, 1938, girl w/brimmed hat, seated w/bottle, oblong, EX....38.00
Tray, 1939, girl seated on diving board, rectangular, EX......40.00
Tray, 1942, girl talks to girl in convertible, rectangular, EX.....40.00
Tray, 1948, girl w/bottle, rectangular, NM...............37.00
Tray, 1957, birdhouse, rectangular, EX..................45.00
Tray, 1957, rooster & floral arrangement, rectangular, M......75.00
Tray, 1957, table w/bottles & sandwiches, rectangular, M......75.00
Tray, 1957, umbrella girl, rectangular, NM..............100.00
Tray, 1958, flower cart, rectangular, NM.................24.00
Tray, 1961, bottle pours into glass by flowers, rectangle, NM...10.00
Tray, 1970, Santa at the fireplace, rectangular, NM..........28.00
Truck cab header sign, 9½x50", M.....................125.00
Vending machine, 10¢ Coca-Cola......................300.00
Vienna Art Plate, Western Bottling, brunette/low gown, no fr...400.00
Wallet, blk leather, gold embossed Drink Coca-Cola, 1918......50.00
Watch fob, swastika, NM.............................125.00
Water bottle, sailing ship.............................46.00
Yo-Yo, Coca-Cola...................................25.00

Coes Wrench Co, letter opener, celluloid monkey wrench.......16.50
Coke Box Mixture, Leavitt & Pierce, tobacco tin, 4½x3½x2"...26.00
Colburn Mustard, thermometer, wood..................105.00
Colby's Clothing House, Taunton MA, mirror, dtd 1876........32.00
Coleman Lantern, funnel, copper........................6.00
Colgate, calendar on 2" pamphlet, 1899 Patriot............12.50
Colgate Cream, tin die-cut, lady & product..............165.00
Colgate's Monad Violet, sample bottle.....................8.00
Colman's Mustard, cb sign, dog & product, in fr, 24½x20"....275.00
Columbia Battery, tin sign, w/early dry cell battery........110.00
Columbia Lager, ball tap knob..........................28.00
Columbia Tool Steel Co, Clarite, pocket mirror, w/Am shield, G.12.50
Columbus Brewery, tip tray, Christopher Columbus..........135.00
Congress Beer, match holder..........................130.00
Continental Gas & Oil, pocket whetstone, bl on wht celluloid...12.50
Cook's Beer, tin sign, girl w/glass, 1938, 28x22"...........85.00
Cook's Beer, ts, horseless carriage/policeman, 1930s, 21x13"....85.00
Coon Chicken Inn, dinner plate........................120.00
Coon Chicken Inn, match holder, metal head...............75.00
Coon Chicken Inn, menu, 8"............................35.00
Coon Chicken Inn, napkin holder, chalk head...............75.00

Coon Chicken Inn, place mat...........................25.00
Coon Chicken Inn, reserved card........................5.00
Coon Chicken Inn, take-out box........................10.00
Coors Malted Milk, soda fountain canister, pottery, alum lid....130.00
Corticelli Spool Silk, lap desk, pictures lg cat logo...........65.00
Cortley Cigars, ts, man w/cigar box, 1914, 20x16"..........375.00
Counsellor Cigar, tobacco tin, old man...................25.00
Cow Brand Soda, poster, hunting dog/game bird, 1900, 17x26".200.00
CPC Peanut Butter, tin pail w/cartoon figures.............80.00
Crawford Cooking Ranges, pitcher, wht w/cobalt design & print.135.00
Cream Of Wheat, poster, fr under glass, boy & chef, 35½x25".125.00
Credo Peanut Butter, pail.............................24.00
Creme, tobacco tin, Queen's head......................125.00
Cresca Raisins, tin container, gr........................42.00
Crescent Beverages, emb tin sgn, w/crescent moon/star, 19x13"..55.00
Critic Chop Cut, tin tobacco box........................35.00
Critic Mixture, tobacco tin............................50.00
Crosman Seeds, sign, paper...........................195.00
Crusade Tobacco, paper sign, knight holding flag, 1900, 13x7"..20.00
Cuba Seal, tin tobacco pail, paper label, G................35.00
Cubanola Cigar, paper/wood sign, lady/mandolin, 1890, 32"...195.00
Culture, tobacco pocket tin, full........................30.00
Cunard Steamship Caronia, tin sign, w/deck/plane/saloon rates..300.00
Dairy Maid Baking Powder, tin container...................9.00
Dark Sweet Burley Tobacco, store canister...............150.00
Davis Baking Powder, tin container, 3 oz.................10.00
Davis Carriage Mfg Co, tin sign, carriage/horses, 1906, 7x20"..155.00
Davis Ice Cream, dish, w/lady & product.................65.00
Dead Shot Powder, tc, slain duck falling................125.00
DeLaval, book, Golden Anniv, '1st in 1878...'.............75.00
DeLaval, canvas banner, lady, 'Sooner or later...', 10 ft......850.00
DeLaval, figural tin cut-out, cow w/2 calves..............40.00
DeLaval, match holder...............................95.00
DeLaval, nameplate, brass, w/28 pat dates, 3x3½"..........22.50
DeLaval, oiler, top mk...............................35.00
DeLaval, paper litho sign, on red, 20x30"...............675.00
DeLaval, porcelain bracket sign, colorful, 27x19", NM.......325.00
DeLaval, tin sign, red, milkmaid, fancy fr, 1910..........1,000.00
DeLaval, tin sign, 16x12"............................20.00
Delaware Underwriters of NY, metal sign in wood fr, 16½x28".110.00
Detroit Fire Insurance, sign, rvpt.......................75.00
Dettmer Woolens, counter display case, mc, 1915..........95.00
Dev'lish Good Cigar, tin sign, children smoking cigars, M.....125.00
Dial, tobacco pocket tin..............................18.00
Diamond Dyes, cabinet, emb tin litho, children on Maypole...1,300.00
Diamond Dyes, cabinet, Governess, EX.................700.00
Diamond Dyes, case, rfn oak, Mansion, emb tin front, EX.....500.00
Diamond Dyes, sign, litho tin, All-American Girls, 14x28", M...750.00
Diamond Dyes, sign, litho tin over cb, Busy Day in Dollsville...700.00
Diamond Dyes, sign, tin, 1908, 28x11"..................55.00
Dicks Beer, pottery sign, mug shape, emb bird & emblem, 14".225.00
Dill's Best Slice Cut Plug, tobacco tin...................20.00
Dixie Maid, cigar tin................................40.00
Dixie Queen Tobacco, canister, blue knob top, VG..........300.00
Dixie Queen Tobacco, lunch box........................90.00
Dobler Brewing Co, tray, oval, w/3 beer wagons, 1906.......175.00
Doe-Wah-Jack, cb sign, stoves, 14", M,.................300.00
Doegler Oysters, tray...............................185.00
Dolly Dingle, Cho Malted Dairy Drink, cb stand-up w/cupid....17.50
Dolly Dingle, O'Baby Cho Dairy Drink, cb stand-up, 8x10½"...17.50
Domino Cane Sugar, sample box, empty..................10.00
Don Murano Cigars, ts, girl/low-cut pk dress, sfr, 19" round...295.00
Double Cola, thermometer, Make It Double Or Nothing, 5x17"..15.00
Dove Brand Allspice, tin container......................10.00

Dr Pepper

Calendar, 1944...45.00
Match holder, wall model, green tin.......................22.00
Mechanical pencil..9.00
Pocket mirror, Drink A Bite To Eat, 1936..................14.00
Sign, porcelain, Good For Life, colorful, 10x25", VG.........80.00
Thermometer, 10-2-4, Frosty Cold.........................40.00
Token, aluminum, early......................................75.00
Tray, girl w/2 bottles of product.........................150.00
Vienna Art plate, King Of Beverages, w/roses, EX..........155.00

Dr Brown's Soda, thermometer, wood........................95.00
Dr Caldwell's Syrup Pepsin, pocket mirror, yel box on bl......28.50
Dr Daniels' Horse & Dog Medicines, tin sign, 17x28", NM....115.00
Dr Daniels' Veterinary Medicines, cabinet...................700.00
Dr Haile's Dog Drops, sign, for indigestion, before & after.....25.00
Dr Morse's Indian Root Pills, cardboard Indian stand-up, 1920..35.00
Dr Scholl's, display cabinet, wood/tin......................75.00
Dr Shoop's Coffee, tin match holder.........................90.00
Dr Swett's, paperweight mirror...............................48.00
Duesseldorfer Beer, tray, baby holding bottle, pp...........350.00
Duffy's Pure Malt Whiskey, pocket mirror, chemist at work....55.00
Duffy's Pure Malt Whiskey, tin sign, chemist, sf, 20x30", VG...450.00
Duffy's Whiskey, mirror.....................................30.00
Duke's Mixture, paperboard, Our Comrade/soldiers, orig fr, '99.295.00
Duke's Mixture, ps, 2 little men w/suitcase, 1910, fr, 24x30"...295.00
Dukehart Brewing Co, beer mug, pre-prohibition.............175.00
Duluth Imperial Flour, tin sign, Black man w/bread, 25x18"....700.00
Dupont, paper sign, soldier on horse/buffalo, fr, 1895, 30".....250.00
Dupont, poster, hunting dog by Osthaus, 1908, fr, 33x28".....175.00
Dupont, tin sign, hunting scene............................500.00
Dupont Indian Rifle Gun Powder, tc, Indian w/rifle...........95.00
Dupont Powders, tin sf sign, 2 dogs, 1908, 22x28", VG......750.00
Dutch Boy, hanging die-cut, w/string holder & pail.........1,350.00
Dutch Boy, match holder, cutout tin........................195.00
Dutch Cleanser, ps, old lady w/stick, mc, 32x22", EX.........350.00
Dutch Java Coffee, pocket mirror, celluloid w/kissing couple....24.50
Dwights Baking Soda, litho tin, w/cow......................185.00
E Robinson's Sons Beer, tray, factory w/train & wagons, pp....325.00
E&O Pilsner, beer sign, shows city, tin, 11x9"..............25.00
Earl & Wilson, collar case, walnut, glass top, 1923, EX......235.00
East Buffalo Brewery, paperboard sign, men in tavern, 1900, fr.195.00
Edelweiss Beer, tray, lady w/red hair, pp..................110.00
Eden Washing Machine, copper sign, 23x13".................45.00
Edgworth, tobacco pocket tin...............................18.00
Edison Mazda, sign, logo/Conversation Figures ea side/lights..1,250.00
Ehert's Beer, tray, oval w/star, VG........................150.00
Ehlermann Beer, ts, founder's portrait/plant, sf, 1900, 26x18"..650.00
Eight Brothers Tobacco, pail, tin, EX......................35.00
El Moriso Cigars, cardboard sign, 5¢ Guaranteed, 10½x13½"...25.00
El Producto Cigars, store tin, sides: girl w/harp, 6x4" sq, M....20.00
El Ricardo Cigars, tip tray, Spanish conquistador portrait.....85.00
El Verso Cigars, tip tray, man dreams of girl while smoking.....55.00
Electric Cleanser, tc, 1890s................................8.00
Electrolux, bank, figural refrigerator, 4"..................35.00
Elgin Watch, paperboard sign, Father Time, wood fr, 1910, 22".150.00
Empire Brewery, ts, different working men, sf, pp, 29x22", VG.595.00

English Biscuit Tins

Carr & Co, Ice Maiden, 1892, VG..........................190.00
Carr & Co, Juvenile No 1, box w/kittens & fishbowl, 1897.....187.00
Carr & Co, Juvenile-Nursery Rhymes, box w/children, 1893....110.00
Carr & Co, Tea Caddy, 1936, VG............................170.00
Huntley & Palmers, Baronial Hall, 1887, EX..................180.00
Huntley & Palmers, Basket, 1897............................121.00
Huntley & Palmers, Bell...................................300.00
Huntley & Palmers, Ben George Box, 1868...................253.00
Huntley & Palmers, Bookstand, 1905, EX....................290.00
Huntley & Palmers, Brass Plaque, lid made to hang on wall, EX130.00
Huntley & Palmers, Bule Locket, red/gold, 1909.............85.00
Huntley & Palmers, Camera, Brownie camera type box, 1913...495.00
Huntley & Palmers, Dickens, figural set of books, 1911......209.00
Huntley & Palmers, Elves Penny-in-the-Slot Machine, 9x4".....110.00
Huntley & Palmers, Field Glass Case, 1907..................176.00
Huntley & Palmers, Globe, 1906............................260.00
Huntley & Palmers, Glove Box, gr, coach & horses on lid, EX...85.00
Huntley & Palmers, Golden Jubilee, 1887, EX................210.00
Huntley & Palmers, Grandfather Clock, hands move, 1929, NM.319.00
Huntley & Palmers, India, ornate scenes, 1894...............473.00
Huntley & Palmers, Lantern, 1911, EX......................150.00
Huntley & Palmers, Literature, 1901, VG....................210.00
Huntley & Palmers, Lizard on Log Purse....................150.00
Huntley & Palmers, Locket, 1912...........................352.00
Huntley & Palmers, Mirror, 1914, EX.......................210.00
Huntley & Palmers, Moroccan Hamper, gr, 1894, EX...........95.00
Huntley & Palmers, Seasons, 1885, VG......................130.00
Huntley & Palmers, Snakeskin Bag..........................275.00
Huntley & Palmers, Watteau, 1903, EX......................140.00
Huntley & Palmers, Wembley Exhibition, 1924................90.00
Huntley & Palmers, Windmill, w/detachable blades, 1924, EX..742.50
Huntley & Palmers, Windmill, 1924, VG.....................675.00
Huntley & Palmers, Worcester Vase, 1934, VG................180.00
McFarlane, Lang & Co; Alligator Bag........................295.00
McFarlane, Lang & Co; Anvil, 1910..........................253.00
McFarlane, Lang & Co; Bird Nest, 1910, VG..................380.00
McFarlane, Lang & Co; Chippendale, chest w/movable drawers..539.00
McFarlane, Lang & Co; Golf Bag, 1913, EX...................577.50
McFarlane, Lang & Co; Stationary Cage, 1901, VG............350.00
McFarlane, Lang & Co; Strawberry Box, 1909, G..............220.00
McVitie & Price, Blue Bird, 1911, NM.......................495.00
McVitie & Price, Footed Dresser............................395.00
McVitie & Price, Raeburn, 1910, VG.........................110.00
McVitie & Price, Roll Top Desk, 1910.......................180.00
McVitie & Price, Uncle Tom's Cabin, 1896...................170.00
Wm Crawford & Sons, Bickey House, 1933, VG................170.00
Wm Crawford & Sons, Chums, 1911, G.........................70.00
Wm Crawford & Sons, Fairy Tree, 1935.......................198.00
Wm Crawford & Sons, Globe, 1938, G........................110.00
Wm Crawford & Sons, Regency Coach, no seat & buckboard...286.00
Wm Crawford & Sons, Stage Coach, G........................260.00
Wm Crawford & Sons, Sundial, 1926..........................90.00

Evening In Paris, bottle, 7 oz..............................15.00
Evening In Paris, deodorant stick, bl bottle/metal cap, full....5.00
Ever-Ready, calendar, 1933, man shaving, 12x4".............25.00
Ever-Ready Safety Razor, clock, tin, 8 day, w/man's face, EX.2,000.00
Eversharp, wood display case, etched glass..................85.00
Ex-Lax, thermometer, porcelain, M..........................85.00
Excelsior Beer, tray, lady in sailor blouse, 2 bottles.........325.00
Extra Kettle Rendered Lard, pail, grinning pig, no lid, EX.....25.00
Fairy Soap, tip tray, EX....................................60.00
Farmer Protective Service, tin sign, Thieves Beware w/eagle.....9.00
Fast Mail, flat tobacco pocket tin..........................75.00

Fatima Cigarettes, moving picture flip book/couple dance, 1914..20.00
Favorite Stoves & Ranges, porcelain sign, w/rising sun........275.00
Favorite Stoves & Ranges, stamp holder, celluloid.............8.50
Feders Eagle Brand Stogies, tc, paper label, old, G..........20.00
Fehr's Ambrosia, tray, Grecian maiden/couple on veranda, pp..225.00
Fehr's Brewing Co, poster/fr, 2 rams on beer keg, 28x39".....295.00
Feigenspon, tin sign, curled corner, w/girl..................250.00
Ferry Seed, poster, fr, Dutch girl w/cabbage, 32x22½"........200.00
FF Adams & Co Peerless Tobacco, tin pail, EX.................35.00
Fidelity & Casualty Co, wood, gold letters, 16x24"..........130.00
Fidelity Phoenix Fire Insurance, porcelain sign..............85.00
Firestone, porcelain sign, 72x30", M.........................200.00
Fitzgerald Bros, tray, pre-pro, 2 Victorian ladies, eagle.......170.00
Fleischmann's Yeast, tin sign, 5½x8½", G.....................45.00
Flour Roses Talcum, tin container............................15.00
Flower Brand Peanut Butter, pail.............................30.00
Flying A, gasoline dealer's plaque, solid brass, 9x11½".......55.00
Folger's Coffee, 5# tin container, w/ship....................45.00
Folger's Golden Gate, ½ #, tin container, old style..........25.00
Forest & Stream Tobacco, pocket tin, w/duck..................25.00
Foster's Ice Cream, Waterloo, tray, litho of little girl, 13½"....85.00
Four Roses, clock, brass cage, glass front...................35.00
Francisco Auto Heater, tin sign, self-framed, EX.............600.00
Fredericksburg Brewery, San Jose, tray, Dutch boy w/tray, 1915.45.00
Frisco Line, pocket mirror, train running by waterfall........65.00
Frishmuth's Whittle Cut Tobacco, tc, round corner, EX.......20.00
Frostie Root Beer, door push plate...........................25.00
Full Dress, tobacco pocket tin...............................100.00
Fuller Furniture Polish, sample tin..........................15.00
Furnace Ice Cream, tray, girl holding tray, 1920s............145.00
Gallagher's, tobacco tin, pool players.......................75.00
Gambrinus Beer, tin sign, w/King Gambrinus, 14" dia.........125.00
Game Fine Cut Tobacco, store bin, 48 nickle packs, 7x11½"...300.00
Garcia Grande Cigars, display case, litho tin, 1900, 15x10x19".105.00
Garfield Tea, sign, tin, w/Pres Garfield, 28x20"............750.00
Garland Stoves, mirror......................................20.00
Garrett's Baker Rye, pocket mirror, w/nude...................60.00
Gem, clock, wood, shaving..................................1,400.00
Gem Damaskeen, clock, wood, man & baby...................1,350.00
General Electric, ash tray, figural motor....................20.00
General Electric, Big Top Circus.............................70.00
General Electric, clock, CI refrigerator, 1928...............120.00
General Electric Radio, band master figure, compo/wood......360.00
Genesse, beer tray, post-pro, Jenny Girl.....................16.00
Genesse, beer tray, post-pro, Old Fashion Goodness..........18.00
Genesse, beer tray, post-pro, 12 Horse Ale...................40.00
Genesse All Malt, ball tap knob..............................38.00
Genesse 12 Horse, ball tap knob..............................32.00
Gets It Corn Loosener, tc, girl w/shoes off, spittoon shape....125.00
Gilt Top, beer tray, pre-pro, Spokane Washington............325.00
Gin Sing, tray, Oriental girl w/drink in rickshaw, 1910.......95.00
Glendora Coffee, sample tin..................................15.00
Globe Tobacco, pocket tin, small, G..........................45.00
Globe-Wernicke, tip tray, sectional bookcase ad..............22.00
GM Hydromatic Drive, neon sign..............................250.00
Goebel Brewing, chromolitho, Tickled to Death, 1890s, 26x21".210.00
Goebel Brewing, match holder, stoneware, lg.................245.00
Gold Crumb Tobacco, tin sign, w/pouch, 1910, 7x11".........40.00
Gold Dust, display, cb Black boy, 1920s......................20.00
Gold Dust Twins, sign, twins scrubbing dishes, 1922.........150.00
Gold Flake Peanut Butter, pail...............................35.00
Gold Shore, tin tobacco box.................................100.00
Golden Dome Tea, tin container..............................45.00
Golden Grain Tobacco, paper die-cut, cowboy w/product.......250.00

Golden Knight Shaving Soap, glass mug, emb, 3x2¾".........25.00
Golden Rod tobacco, tin......................................55.00
Golden Rule Tea, 3# tin container............................40.00
Good Cheer, cigar tin..85.00
Good Luck Baking Powder, tin container.......................12.00
Goodyear, sign, porcelain blimp..............................85.00
Goodyear Tires, clock, electric Sessions.....................35.00
Goodyear Tires, tin sign, red/wht/bl/yel, 15x28".............20.00
Goodyear Zeppelin Corp, bookmark, Duralumin metal, rare.....85.00
Goorge Washington, tobacco canister.........................30.00
Granger, tobacco canister....................................18.00
Grant Batteries, sign, tin, sm...............................25.00
Granulated 54, tobacco pocket tin............................45.00
Grape Nuts, paper ad, Build Your Body, man/boy, 40x54"...1,000.00
Grape Nuts, tin sign, girl & St Bernard, G...................375.00
Grape Nuts, tin sign, girl & St Bernard, M................1,000.00
Grape Nuts Flakes, Woody Woodpecker flip movies book, 1949...8.50
Grape-Ola, ts, emb, grapes, It's Real Grape, 1920s, 14x24"....50.00
Gravely Tobacco, wooden chair................................85.00
Great Western Champagne, tin sign, w/bottles................400.00
Green River Whiskey, ash tray/matchbox holder, figural........23.00
Green River Whiskey, blotter, full color, w/Black man.........18.50
Green River Whiskey, bottle, 23".............................80.00
Green River Whiskey, bottle opener/corkscrew combo..........22.00
Green River Whiskey, brass token.............................10.00
Green River Whiskey, cb sign, mc litho, tavern/Black man/mule.165.00
Green River Whiskey, chalkware store display, man & mule....195.00
Green River Whiskey, playing cards, w/box....................55.00
Green River Whiskey, tin sign, orig wood fr, 32x42".........675.00
Green River Whiskey, tray, old Blk man w/mule, 1890s........300.00
Guasti Pure Grape Syrup, tc, bear pulls chariot/cherub, 1 gal....55.00
Gulf Brewing Co Sparkling Ale, reverse on glass/oak fr, 32x26".395.00
Ha-Ha Cigars, tc, 5x8", VG...................................55.00
Haig Scotch Whiskey, pitcher, By Appt to Her Majesty, blk trim.15.00
Half & Half, tobacco sample pocket tin.......................60.00
Hamilton Brown Shoes, tin sign, oval, Shoes Wear Longer, 19".20.00
Hamilton Watch RR Timekeeper, stamp case, celluloid.........18.00
Hamlins Wizard Oil, statue, papier mache, man/elephant, EX.1,650.00
Hand Made, tobacco canister.................................215.00
Handbag Cut Plug, tobacco tin...............................95.00
Harkert Cigar Co, tip tray, Andrew White portrait............85.00
Hartford Insurance, tin litho sign, Monarch o/t Glen, 20x24"...325.00
Hauptmans, cigar tin...22.00
Havard Beer, clock, glass....................................750.00
Hazard Powder, tin, red KY rifle, man & dog..................65.00
Heidelberg Blatz, sign, girl on barrel, plaster, 1933, NM......300.00
Heinz, jar, 6 sided, w/key logo emb top, early...............105.00
Heinz, store baked bean warmer, br glaze crock...............165.00
Heinz Apple Butter, crock...................................135.00
Heinz Vinegar, dispenser, frosted glass, 2 pc................295.00
Henderson Wild Cherry, glass pitcher.........................95.00
Hercules Coffee, tin container...............................500.00
Hermitage Cement, desk letter holder, bronze w/A Jackson/horse.10.00
Herold Smoked Sardine, tc, book form, early 1900s, 10x10x4"...75.00
Hesitator, clock, neon, bl/wht, M............................95.00
HGC, sign, emb tin, man in tuxedo, 1890s, 7x10"..............95.00
Hi-Plane, tobacco pocket tin, 1 motor, G.....................32.00
Hi-Plane, tobacco pocket tin, 2 motors, G....................20.00
Hiawatha Granulated Mixture, tobacco tin.....................40.00
Hibard, Spencer, Bartlett & Co; poster, hunter trips over dog..125.00
Hick's Capudine, tray, several cherubs.......................150.00
Hickory, tobacco pocket tin, G...............................15.00
Highest Grade Smoking Tobacco, tc, Falk Co, 4x6", EX........20.00
Hills Bros Coffee, trial size tin container...................15.00

Hiram Walker Bourbon, pitcher, McCoy Pottery, red/bl/gold.....24.00
Hires, book, recipes for Root/Ginger/Birch Beers, 1931, NM.....14.00
Hires, booklet, The Animals Trip To Town, colorful cover.....12.00
Hires, display, cut-out, boy w/package, ca 1900.............175.00
Hires, mug, Mettlach..115.00
Hires, mug, 7"..22.50
Hires, syrup bottle, box dtd 1929............................8.00
Hires, tin chalkboard, 1960s, 28x20".........................15.00
Hires, tin sign, bottle shape, 1950s, 48"....................90.00
Hires, tin/wood fr, emb drinking girl, 1920s, 16x22".........350.00
Hires, tray, Hires To Your Health...........................125.00
Hocum Coal Co, sign, enameled, hooks for 2 shovels..........24.00
Holiday Beer, clock, glass/metal, 15" sq.....................95.00
Hollier Eight Automobile, poster, w/car, 1915...............175.00
Honest Labor, tobacco pocket tin.............................30.00
Honeymoon, pocket tin..35.00
Hood's Rubbers, mirror, rnd, zodiac signs....................30.00
Hood's Sarsaparilla, booklet, Safety of the Public, dog, EX.....22.00
Hood's Sarsaparilla, calendar, 1893..........................24.00
Hood's Sarsaparilla, coloring book, 36 pg, 7x9", VG.........16.00
Horlicks Malted Milk, jar w/orig lid.........................20.00
Hoster Brewery, ts, comical monk, wood oval fr, 1900, 27x23".850.00
Hudson, neon sign, w/emblem.................................250.00
Humphrey's Witch Hazel, mirror in oak fr, stand-up, w/lady.....40.00
Hunt Pen Co, showcase, oak & glass, Nibs.....................75.00
Hunt Shoe Co, tip tray, close-up of stag.....................55.00
Hunter Cigars, ts, fox hunter on horse, colorful, 1915, 27x19".295.00
IGA Coconut, tin pail..25.00
Imported Pilsner, sign, stone litho, curled corners, emb, girl....300.00
Imported Pilsner Beer, tin sign, Dutch Girls, curled corners....195.00
Ingersol Watches, glass case, 9x13".........................125.00
Invincible Motor Insurance, ts, 1920s autos/navy ship, 20x10"...75.00
Iroquois, tip tray, pre-pro..................................75.00
IW Harper Whiskey, milk glass sign, dog inside cabin, 1900, fr.750.00
J&P Coates, sign, paper, fishing scene w/man & woman.......350.00
Jack Daniel's Old #7, silver holder for 5th, 1940s...........50.00
Jacob Ruppert's, tray, 19th century men served outdoors, pp...225.00
Java Mocha Coffee, tc, pictures factory, 1900s, G...........15.00
Jell-O, cb die-cut sign under glass, girl w/box, 22x20".......85.00
Jim Dandies, peanut tin, 10 lbs............................800.00
John Deer, quality Farm Equipment, porcelain sign, 24x72"....325.00
John Deer, tape measure, celluloid, gr/yel...................20.00
Johnson's Auto Cleaner, tc, man waxing car, 1920s............6.00
Johnston's Hot Fudge, tin dispenser..........................75.00
Jolly Tar Tobacco, clock, papier mache, 1890.............2,800.00
Jumbo Peanut Butter, bank, elephant, clear glass, sm........60.00
Jumbo Peanut Butter, glass container, hexagon fish bowl, 2#....27.50
Jumbo Peanut Butter, glass container, 1½# lantern type.......25.00
June Caprice, calendar, 1918, EX............................115.00
Justrite, cigar tin..22.00
Kardomah Tea, tc, Gibson Girl pours tea, EX..................20.00
Kato Beer, convex glass sign, w/eagle, 15" dia..............125.00
Kayo Soda, sign, emb cartoon character, 1930s, 14x29", EX....58.00
Kellogg's Corn Flakes, poster, miniature billboard, 1920s.....35.00
Kendall's Spavin Cure, sign, paper, 22x28", EX..............225.00
Kennys Maid Coffee, tin container, 4 lb....................145.00
Kentucky Club, tobacco pocket tin............................18.00
King Cole Coffee, tin container............................125.00
King Cole Tea & Coffee, sign, porcelain, king w/cup, 15x9"....620.00
Kipps Hand Made, cigar tin...................................24.00
Kirkman's Borax Soap, brass token, Admiral Dewey...........25.00
Kist, litho, lady w/bottle, sgnd Elvgren, 1940s, 16x12".......35.00
Kist Root Beer, ts, emb, Drink...Lg Bottle 5¢, 1940s, 16x26"...40.00
Knickerbocker Coffee, tc, pictures small rooster & boy, early....85.00

Kodak, beaker, glass, emb measuring sections, early..........15.00
Korby's Whiskey, tip tray, tramp steals whiskey from man.....65.00
Krak-R-Jack Biscuits, tin container..........................40.00
Krisp Peanut Butter, pail, 1#................................20.00
Lacquer Wax, sign, emb tin, '40s auto w/man/product.........165.00
Lady Churchill, cigar tin.....................................8.00
LaFendrich, thermometer, tin.................................95.00
Laflin & Rand, powder tin, man & dog.........................60.00
Laflin & Rand Powder, poster, hunter/dogs/boy, 1870s, fr, 26".750.00
Lamons Wagon Co, blotter, w/wagon, 3x6".....................13.50
LaResta, cigar pocket tin....................................18.00
Laurier 10¢ Cigar, tin sign, emb, Sir Wilred Laurier portrait....720.00
Lava Soap, pocket mirror, rnd................................18.00
Lavender Shaving Cream, free sample bank, 1910..............15.00
Lawrence Barrett Tobacco, leather pouch......................12.00
Laxative Bromo Quinine, cb stand-up Uncle Sam, '10, 45".....200.00
Legion Soap, tc, string holder, English.....................175.00
Leichtman's Ice Cream, clicker...............................12.00
Lemon Chill Cure, sign, emb tin, No Cure, No Pay, 1890s......65.00
Lewis 66 Whiskey, tip tray, man eating lobster...............60.00
Libby's Asparagus, sample tin................................30.00
Lion Gas, sign, porcelain, w/lion, 60"......................250.00
Lion Head Chewing Tobacco, litho sign, Victorian girl/bird....120.00
Lion Packing, for Steam Engines & Pumps, cb sgn, w/caged lion.45.00
Lipton Tea, needle book, figural tea box.....................10.00
Lipton Tea, tin container, Indian woman gathers leaves, 3#, M..90.00
Livery & Feed Stable, wood sign, 34x54".....................350.00

Log Cabin Syrup

Log Cabin Syrup tins have been made since the 1890s, in variations of design that can be attributed to specific years of production. Until about 1914, the log cabin tins were made with paper labels. These are quite rare and highly prized by today's collectors. Tins with colored lithographed designs were made after 1914. When General Foods purchased the Towle Company in 1927, the letters 'GF' were added to the tins.

A cartoon series, illustrated with a mother flipping pancakes in the cabin window and various children and animals declaring their appreciation of the syrup in voice balloons, was introduced in the 1930s. A Frontier Village series followed in the late 1940s. A schoolhouse, jail, trading post, doctor's office, blacksmith shop, inn and private homes were available. Examples of either series are today in the $75 to $100 range.

Bank, Towle's...35.00
Letter, invoice & price list, 1927...........................7.50
Spoon, EX...18.00
Syrup tin, bear at door......................................95.00
Syrup tin, Home Sweet Home, 12 oz............................70.00
Syrup tin, lady flipping pancakes............................95.00
Syrup tin, red, 5 lbs..65.00
Syrup tin, Savings Bank cabin, Towles......................700.00
Syrup tin, western cartoon, sm, G............................45.00
Syrup tin, 12 oz...30.00

London Life Cigarettes, sign, paper........................235.00
Long Life, tc, early plane, 2 gal, G.........................55.00
Loose-Wiles Biscuit Co, Geo Washington bust..................30.00
Loose-Wiles Biscuit Co, octagon box, Robin Hood scenes.......35.00
Lord Calvert, barometer, 12" octagon gr pnt wood fr..........85.00
Lord Calvert, plaque, rnd, emb brass, 23"....................65.00
Lowenbrau, plastic sign, shows lions, 10x14".................25.00
Lowney's Chocolate, banner, 72x36"...........................65.00

Lowney's Chocolate, dlb face sign, bronze finish, iron bracket . . 300.00
Lucky Heart Pomade, sample tin, 2 Black men 7.00
Lucky Strike, cb display, stand-up, 1948 . . . . 60.00
Lucky Strike, clock, RA Patterson 700.00
Lucky Strike, tin, flat, green 12.50
Lucky Strike Roll Cut, tobacco sample pocket tin 35.00
Luzianne Coffee, sample tin, red 30.00
Luzianne Coffee, tin container, Mammy pouring coffee, 1 lb 30.00
Mack Trucks, bill clip, brass w/picture of early teens truck 18.00
MacMillan Ring Free Motor Oil, dbl face sign, Scotsman bust . . 60.00
Magnet Beer, tin sign, rolled edges, lady & product 295.00
Maltosia, tip tray, pre-pro 40.00
Manchester Bix Sioux Biscuits, tin container, Indian decor 50.00
Manhattan Baking Powder, tin container 15.00
Manhattan Cocktail, tobacco pocket tin 20.00
Manru Coffee, tin container 33.00
Mapacuba, cigar tin 25.00
Marvel, thermometer 4.00
Maryland Club Coffee, sample tin 12.00
Maryland Club Tobacco, pocket tin, flat lid 200.00
Maryland Club Tobacco, pocket tin, flip lid 225.00
Mascot Cut Tobacco, pocket mirror, pictures dog 55.00
Master Workman, tobacco tin, flat pocket 75.00
Masury Paint Co, ts, workers in factory, fr, 1900, 29x23" . . . 1,250.00
Maxwell House Coffee, reverse pnt on glass, light-up display 150.00
Mayo Tobacco, clock, Baird Clock Co, figure 8 plaster 1,815.00
Mazda, bulb display, Parrish figural 750.00
Mazda, tin display, for 5 bulbs 125.00
McCormick Deering Farm Machinery Headquarters, ps 185.00
McLaughlin Coffee, sign, w/box, ca 1900 . . . . 65.00
McNess Cocoa, sample tin container 28.00
Meadow Gold, clock, lighted, 16" sq oak fr, M 75.00
Meadow Gold Milk, creamer, sq, miniature 7.50
Mellin's Food, cb stand-up, baby w/crepe paper dress, 24" 150.00
Mellrose Marshmallows, tin container 15.00
Mennen Talcum Powder, sample tin 8.00
Mennen Talcum Powder, sign, 7 babies on fence, ca 1900 . . . . . 165.00
Mentholatum, blotter, 6" ruled edge, '30s lady 3.00
Mentholatum, sample tin, w/girl 9.00
Merita Bread, screen door 95.00
Merrigan's Ice Cream, tray, little girl/boy on beach, 1923 . . . . . 145.00
Miles Standish Mince Meat, 30# bucket w/lid, pictures pilgrims . . 45.00
Miller High Life, tin sign, lady in moon, bottle atop world 225.00
Minard's Liniment, blotter, bl script on wht, 4x9½", VG 7.50
Minard's Liniment, die-cut, girl w/product, in oak fr, lg 125.00
Miner's & Puddlers, tin tobacco pail 75.00
Minnesota Girl Flour, pocket knife, suede case, 1915 . . . . 20.00
Mobil Flying Red Horse, ash tray 85.00
Mobil Oil, mug, red horse logo 7.50
Mobile Gas, die-cut sign, w/flying horse 85.00
Model, tobacco pocket tin 18.00
Moehn Brewery, tip tray 95.00
Monadnock Peanut Butter, tin pail 45.00
Monarch, peanut butter pail, w/lion, 2 lb 55.00
Monarch Breakfast Cocoa, tin container 20.00
Monarch Cinnamon, tin container, w/lion, 3 lb, EX 17.50
Monarch Foods, clock, electric, EX 125.00
Monarch Teenie Weenie, peanut butter pail, 2 lb 100.00
Monarch Teenie Weenie Barrel, tin container 50.00
Monarch Toffees, tin container, large 170.00
Monroe Brewery, tray, king holding goblet, pp 175.00
Monticello, tip tray, EX 75.00
Monticello Whiskey, tin sign 350.00
Morning Glow Coffee, tin container 12.00

Morton's Salt, pocket mirror 30.00
Moseman Peanut Butter, free sample tin, NM 75.00
Moses Cough Drops, sample tin 70.00
Mother's Joy Coffee, tin container 14.00
Motorola Auto Radio, cloth banner, dbl sides, 30x44" 75.00

Moxie

The Moxie Company was organized in 1884 by George Archer of Boston, Massachusetts. It was at first touted as a 'nerve food' to improve the appetite, promote restful sleep and in general to make one 'feel better'! Emphasis was soon shifted, however, to the good taste of the brew, and extensive advertising campaigns rivaling those of such giant competitors as Hires and Coca-Cola resulted in successful marketing through the 1930s. Today the term Moxie has become synonomous with courage and audacity, traits displayed by the company who dared compete with such well established rivals.

Bottle, lt gr, 10" 8.00
Bottle, orange label, 7 oz 18.00
Bottle, pop top 10.00
Bottle stopper 10.00
Box, wood, dovetailed 30.00
Candy tin 55.00
Fan, cb, mc litho, girl w/Moxie tumbler, 1924 . . . . 25.00
Fan, cb, Muriel Ostriche sitting on rock, dtd 1916 . . . . 25.00
Fan, celluloid, unfolds, word Moxie cut out of ea fold 50.00
Ice cooler, figural Moxie bottle, 36" 695.00
Lapel pin, Moxie Man, tin 40.00
Miss Moxie, wood figure holding Moxie metal ash tray, 28" 285.00
Mug, glass 40.00
Postcard, Moxie Mobile, dtd 1916, M 75.00
Sheet music 20.00
Shopping bag, w/The Three Moxie-Teers, walking bottles, sm . . . 15.00
Sign, tin, w/buildings, cars & buggies in street 1,000.00
Sign, tin, 1931, 12x18" 300.00
Soda case, tin 175.00
Sugar bowl, china, Moxie lady & floral band 65.00
Syrup dispenser, 10" 100.00
Thermometer, man pointing, red bkground 125.00
Thermometer, 12" dial, M 35.00
Tumbler, embossed 25.00
Tumbler, etched glass, wht letters 30.00

Munsing Wear, lcs, girls in undies, grandma, orig fr, '14, 36" . . 425.00
Munsing Wear, ts, little girls in undies, sf, 1905, 38x25" 950.00
Murad Cigarettes, paper sign, X-mas pack/girl, '20s, 20", EX . . . 40.00
Murray's Fruit Sherbet, rvpt syrup bottle, 11" 32.00
Musgo Gas, sign, porcelain, w/Indian, 48" 550.00
Nabisco, bowl, boy w/slicker 48.00
Namar, mirror, 14x10" 45.00
National Cash Register Co, bill spike 28.00
National Cigar, tip tray, girl holds bouquet of yel flowers 85.00
National Lead Co, Genuine Babbit, emb lead paperweight w/boy . . 9.50
National San Iran, tip tray, cowboy on horse, pre-1920 . . . . 275.00
Nature's Remedy, pocket mirror 28.00
Nature's Remedy, thermometer, porcelain, 6x25" 125.00
Near's Livestock/Poultry Products, ts, We Use..., 9x12" 12.00
Nebo Cigarettes, ts, pack figural/Nebo portrait, 1920s, 15x13" . . 150.00
Nesbitt's Orange, thermometer, w/Little Professor 40.00
Nesbitt's Orange, tin sign, wht/blk/orange/yel, 12x34", VG 20.00
New Bachelor Cigars, tin container, rnd 100.00

New England Telephone & Telegraph, hand fan, Blue Bell logo..15.00
New Factory Tobacco, tin pail, mythical figure/horse/dragon....125.00
New Scotch Snuff, sign, tin/emb battleship, early, VG.........75.00
Ney Mfg Co, tip tray, brunette in low-cut gown..............68.00
Niagara Insurance, porcelain sign, bl/wht..................100.00
Nigger Hair Tobacco, canister, cardboard...................35.00
Nigger Hair Tobacco, tin container.......................100.00
Niles Moser, cigar tin...................................25.00
North Pole Cut Plug, canister...........................400.00
North Star, tobacco tin, flat pocket.....................150.00
Nu Grape, tray, flapper girl w/bottle, 1920s.............110.00
Nusis Talcum, tin container..............................18.00
Nyal's Easem Foot Powder, tin............................10.00
O'Keefe's Stock Ale, tray, post-pro......................37.00
Ocident Flour, door pull, brass..........................35.00
Odgen's Nibs Pigtail, tobacco tin........................45.00
Old Colony, pocket tin...................................55.00
Old Dutch Cleanser, porcelain sign, lady w/broom, 22x32", VG.200.00
Old Dutch Cleanser Soap, window sign, hand w/box, lady in bk..65.00
Old English Curve Cut Tobacco, tin container.............20.00
Old Gold Cigarettes, bookmark............................18.00
Old Gold Cigarettes, flat tin............................28.00
Old Gold Cigarettes, pack, tin...........................15.00
Old Gold Leaf Rye, litho, portrait of blonde, 1900......145.00
Old Gold Leaf Rye, tray, blonde lady, 1900..............150.00
Old Gold Smoking Tobacco, tc, sq corner, 1900s, G........20.00
Old Hill Side Cut Tobacco, paperboard, old man, 1915, fr, 26".150.00
Old Master Coffee, tc, pictures artist, EX...............55.00
Old Pepper Whiskey, tray, Revolutionary War soldiers....180.00
Old Reliable Coffee, Always Good, old man/box, pocket mirror..26.00
Old Squire, tobacco pocket tin..........................100.00
Olympia Beer, tray, cavalier holding bottle, pp.........125.00
Omar Cigarettes, poster/fr, 2 men in tuxedos, 1910, 26x35"....295.00
Ontario Biscuits, sign, paper, child & product..........185.00
Opera Lights Cigarettes, cut-out cb stand-up, dtd 1892, 10x14"..48.50
Opera Soda, tin sign, lithographed, 1840................120.00
Orange Crush, dispenser, blk ceramic base...............235.00
Orange Crush, thermometer, bottle shape..................35.00
Orange Crush, tin sign, Feel Fresh, shows bottle, 17x47".....90.00
Orange Crush, tin sign, orange/bl/yel/wht/silver, 40" sq.......25.00
Orange Crush, tin sign w/thermometer, 6x18".............19.50
Orange Julep, tray, girl in swimsuit, EX................120.00
Orange Kist, tin sign, embossed, 27x10"..................35.00
Original Pin Head Cigarettes, cardboard box, 1890s, EX....25.00
Our Advertiser Tobacco, window sign, w/pack, 1905........65.00
Ovaltine, mug, Uncle Wiggily.............................25.00
Owensboro Wagons, tin/sfr, picking apples, wagons, 38x26"..1,100.00
Owl Cigars, clockwork store display, log owl w/smoking cigar...900.00
Ox-Heart Chocolate, ts, emb ox head, rectangle, 1930s, 4x24"..60.00
Oxford Chocolates, mirror................................25.00
Oxydol, celluloid pencil, w/Mammy, makers of Lava Soap....15.00
Pabst Blue Ribbon, bartender figure holds glasses, hvy metal....65.00
Pabst Bock Beer, poster, fr, litho......................125.00
Pabst Brewery, book, 1894................................35.00
Pabst Brewing Co, sign, paper under glass, 1890s, 54x32"....850.00
Pacific Shoe, mirror.....................................25.00
Pall Mall, tin sign, pictures lady, 1950s, 23x16".......145.00
Pan Peanut Butter, free sample tin.......................35.00
Papoose Cigars, ts, Indian baby, 1880s, 17x27", fair condition..400.00
Parker Hair Balsam, paper under glass, w/girl............85.00
Paul Jones, bar display, camel w/bottle between humps, 9"....20.00
Paul Jones Whiskey, ts, Kentucky Colonel, 1904, 18x27".....325.00
Pears Soap, ad, full color, naked baby by washbowl, 12x15"....25.00
Pennsylvania Fire Insurance Co, rvpt, orig fr, 13½x19½"....180.00

Pennsylvania Sugar, sample bag...........................8.00
Pennzoil, sign, porcelain, w/bell, 36"...................90.00
Pepp O'Day Bouquet, paper sign,. w/lady, Best 25¢ Perfume.....45.00

Pepsi-Cola

Pepsi-Cola was first served in the early 1890s to customers of Caleb
D. Bradham, a young pharmacist who touted his concoction to be medicinal
as well as delicious. It was first called 'Brad's Drink', and renamed Pepsi-
Cola in 1898.

Advertising doll, Santa Claus, 24", EX...................75.00
Bag dispenser, country store............................125.00
Bank, compo, cooler figural, G decals, dbl dots..........45.00
Bank, 5¢ vending machine................................60.00
Blackboard, early.......................................55.00
Blotter, dbl dot, Hits the Spot/Bigger Better/musical notes, M...45.00
Blotter, Navy girl, Sip Ahoy!, dbl dot logo, 1940s, EX....38.00
Blotter, Pepsi & Pete, sm carton, lg bottle, 5¢, M.......30.00
Calendar, 1941..60.00
Carrier, metal, holds 6 bottles.........................20.00
Clock, glass, 14".......................................75.00
Display, die-cut cardboard Santa w/bottle, N Rockwell, 20", M..200.00
Fan, Keystone Cops, 1940, M.............................20.00
Game, Number; 7 cards/envelopes, all w/dlb dot logo, M....22.00
Lighter, can shape, 1960s...............................20.00
Napkin holder, soda fountain, ceramic...................45.00
Opener, bottle shape, tin, dtd 1924......................9.0C
Pen w/bottle clasp......................................42.00
Pin, 1942, softball champs, ball pendant, M.............12.00
Pinback, celluloid, shows cooler w/5¢, has ribbon, NM....82.00
Poster, Nouveau portrait of girl w/flowers, fr, 1914, 36".....850.00
Radio, figural bottle, bakelite, from soda fountain, 1930s.....300.00
Sign, bottle, 28".......................................40.00
Sign, tin, die cut, emb 5¢ bottle......................135.00
Syrup can, 5 gal..25.00
Thermometer, tin, bottle cap logo, 1940s, 28"...........45.00
Thermometer, 1920s, lg..................................48.00
Tray, beach scene, rnd, EX..............................20.00
Tray, bottle over US map, EX...........................110.00
Tray, children singing, 1950s, M........................30.00
Tray, Coney Island, 1950s, M............................25.00
Tray, Giering's, w/shield, round, EX...................200.00
Truck, Marx, MIB..75.00
Watch fob, Delicious, Healthful, emb eagle/bottle, 1903....125.00

Peter Rabbit Peanut Butter, tin pail...................275.00
Peter's Hot Chocolate, tin dispenser, emb...............55.00
Pflueger Fishing Tackle, cardboard stand-up fish, 1930s, 20"...65.00
Philco Lazy X Radio, early puzzle w/envelope............25.00
Philip Morris, Johnny ceramic figurine w/tray, Japan, 12"....18.00
Phillies, ts, emb, America's Real Cigar, 1940, 14x20"....25.00
Phoenix Horseshoe Co, paper clip, red/bl on wht celluloid....15.00
Pickwick Coffee, can, 1 lb..............................22.00
Picobac, tobacco pocket tin.............................35.00
Piedmont, folding chair, porcelain.....................110.00
Pikes Peak Pure Lard, 4# bucket.........................14.00
Pillsbury, cb display, Join the Pillsbury Parade.........18.00

Planters Peanuts

Mr. Peanut, the dashing peanut man with the top hat, spats, monocle and cane, has represented the Planters Peanut Company from 1916 to 1961, when the company was purchased by Standard Brands. He promoted the company's product by appearing on premium give-aways, store displays, jars, scales and in special promotional events. Among the favored treasures of collectors today are the glass display jars. They come in a variety of styles; some are square, some hexagonal, some barrel shaped, and others are round. The earliest, issued in 1926, was octagonal and is usually referred to as the 'pennant' jar. Although later reproduced, these are marked 'Made in Italy' on the bottom. The original is embossed on the back panel 'Sold Only in Printed Planters Red Pennant Bags'; in a second octagonal style this embossed message was replaced with a paper label.

In 1930 a 'fishbowl' jar was introduced, and in 1932 a '4 corner peanut' jar was issued. The rarest jar of all, the 'football' jar, was also used during the early 1930s. The Planters' square jar followed in the 1930s, and was replaced by the 'barrel' jar. The six sided jar with Mr. Peanut decals and the 'pickle' jar were later. All in all more than 15 different styles were developed.

In the late 1930s, premiums such as glass and metal figural paperweights, pens, and pencils were distributed; post-war items were often made of plastic -- Mr. Peanut salt and pepper shakers, mugs and banks were popular. Today's collectors find a treasure trove of advertising memorabilia depicting that debonair, tasteful gentleman, Mr. Peanut.

Advertisement, 8 pg rotogravure, 1935, shows factories, fr.....415.00
Alarm clock, Lux, Mr Peanut....................................45.00
Ash tray, ceramic..60.00
Belt buckle..10.00
Bookmark, 1939, Mr Peanut figural, arm repaired, VG........17.00
Bowl, counter; plastic...30.00
Bowl, Mr Peanut, metal, lg.....................................12.00
Bracelet, brass chain w/4 Mr Peanuts & 2 peanuts............17.50
Champagne glass..10.00
Deep fryer...45.00
Display stand, tin, Jumbo Peanut Block, Mr Peanut/5¢, 9", VG.330.00
Figure, papier mache peanut, lg................................35.00
Jar, Barrel, all orig, M......................................200.00
Jar, Clipper...65.00
Jar, Fish Bowl, large, w/label & orig lid......................90.00

Jar, Football, peanut finial lid..............................185.00
Jar, Leap Year, tin lid EX condition, 1940.....................50.00
Jar, Octagon, Pennant 5¢ Salted Peanuts, 12"...................85.00
Jar, octagonal w/T label......................................125.00
Jar, round, frosted, orig lid..................................45.00
Jar, six sided, yellow transfer................................85.00
Jar, sq, 1934, M...70.00
Jar, Streamline, orig lid......................................45.00
Jar, 4 corner, lg blown-out peanuts on ea.....................245.00
Knife & fork, Mr Peanut, Carlton SP, pr........................30.00
Letter opener, enameled.......................................120.00
Mr Peanut, CI...1,495.00
Mr Peanut, papier mache figure w/tin scoop.....................75.00
Mr Peanut, plastic windup walker..............................125.00
Mr Peanut, rag doll...7.00
Mr Peanut, wood jtd, 8½", NM..................................225.00
Nut set, Mr Peanut, tin, 5 pc..................................25.00
Nut set, World's Fair, 1939....................................35.00
Oil funnel, 2 pc, w/fittings...................................15.00
Paint book, Mr Peanut, historical, 1949........................10.00
Paint book, 1950...10.00
Paperweight, Mr Peanut, M.....................................540.00
Peanut butter grinder, Mr Peanut...............................15.00
Pencil, mechanical; Mr Peanut floating in oil..................18.00
Pocket knife...20.00
Scale, Mr Peanut, unrstr....................................4,995.00
Scoop, tin, 5¢...95.00
Shakers, ceramic, pr...50.00
Spoon, silverplated, Mr Peanut.................................15.00
Tin, Clean & Krisp, 10 lb, M..................................350.00
Tin, Jumbo Bar, 10 lb..50.00
Tin, peanut pennant..50.00
Tin, rectangular, 1919...75.00
Tote lunch bag, insulated.......................................8.00
Whistle, Mr Peanut, plastic.....................................6.00
Wrist watch..75.00

Players, tobacco tin...28.00
Plover Brand, tea tin, slightly faded..........................35.00
Plow Boy, tobacco canister.....................................60.00
Plymouth Gin, tip tray, monk drinking..........................75.00
Polarine Oil, gas gauge, wood, Atwater Kent pat 1909, 1x17"...22.00
Poll Parrot, Bat-a-Ball...8.00
Poll Parrot Shoes, china parrot, emb ad, 1930s, 8½"............75.00
Poll Parrot Shoes, sf tin sign, 26x14".........................395.00
Polly Prim Cleanser, sign, lady w/can..........................65.00
Pontiac Gas, sign, porcelain, w/Indian, 36"...................175.00
Poor Mustard, box, fireside scene, 16x8".......................50.00
Post Toasties, sign, paper die-cut............................225.00
Postmaster, cigar tin..32.00
Postum Cereal, tin container...................................15.00
Potosi Pure Malt Beer, tray, red/wht/gold/blk..................65.00
Power Lube Motor Oil, sign, porcelain, w/tiger................225.00
President Suspenders, tip tray, w/portrait, 4¼" dia............40.00
President Taft Cigars, cigar band, 1920s........................1.50
Pride of Oregon Lard, tin bucket, EX...........................15.00
Primrose Tea, tea tile, figure playing violin..................45.00
Princess Novelty Range, hand mirror............................28.00
Proctor & Gamble Soap, tin sign...............................250.00
Prof Field's Worm Powders, emb ts, girl w/dog, 1880s, 10x13".325.00
Pure Cotton Seed Meal, Fertilizer for Tobacco, booklet, 1898....8.50
Pure Oil, metal sign, bl/wht sunburst, Be Sure w/Pure, 41" dia.100.00

Jar, barrel w/running peanut-man, peanut finial, 12", $200.00.

Pure Oil, sign, porcelain, sm...............................20.00
Puritan, tobacco pocket tin..............................80.00
Putnam Dyes, calendar, 1916, The Grand Daughter, complete...45.00
Putnam Dyes, case, Revolutionary War scene................135.00
Quaker Oats, bowl, pictures man & box....................60.00
Quaker State, sign, tin, sm..............................15.00
Queen Quality Shoes, pocket mirror.......................40.00

RCA Victor

Nipper, the RCA Victor trademark was the creation of Francis Barraud, an English artist. His pet's intent fascination with the music of the phonograph seemed to him a worthy subject for his canvas. Although he failed to find a publishing house who would buy his work, the Gramaphone Co. saw its potential and adopted Nipper to advertise their product. The company eventually became the Victor Talking Machine Co. and was purchased by RCA in 1929. Nipper's image appeared on packaged accessories, in ads and brochures. If you are very lucky you may find a life-size statue of him -- but all are not old, they have been reproduced! Except for the years between 1971 and 1981, Nipper has seen active duty, and with his image spruced up only a bit for the present day, the ageless symbol for RCA still listens intently to 'His Master's Voice'.

Advertisement, Victor records, trolley car, in fr...............125.00
Album, exercise; hardcover, Nipper emb on front, 1908........32.00
Banner, canvas, Victor Talking Machines Sold Here, 2½x10 ft..550.00
Crate, for Victor Gramaphone, w/Nipper & Gramaphone.......75.00
Cup, w/blue logo, Sterling China.........................30.00
Dog, tin w/glass eyes, 19"............................1,000.00
Easter poster, Victor Records, 1916......................20.00
Fan, Victor Records, record shape, 1915..................28.00
Mechanical pencil, figural tubes ea end, w/dog.............35.00
Needle tin, blue, lg, Victor.............................25.00
Nipper, bisque, imp Victor/Greenwood's/1909, 4", MIB........40.00
Nipper, papier mache, b/w paint, EX, 40".................745.00
Nipper, plaster, 3 ft, EX.............................1,500.00
Pocket mirror, orig....................................175.00
Puzzle, Victor Talking Machine, record shape, dtd 1908, MIB...45.00
Radio, Wing's cigarettes pack, 8x12x16".................295.00
Record duster, w/Victor dog at phonograph.................35.00

R&G Corsets, tin sign/oak fr, lady in corset, hand on chair....285.00
Rainbow Beverages, ts, emb, shows bottle, rect, 1940s, 12x27"..25.00
Raleigh's Talcum, tin container, w/circus..................15.00
Ramon's, jar, glass.....................................35.00
Ramon's Pills, thermometer, tin, 21x9"...................65.00
Raptco, tobacco tin.....................................25.00
Rawleigh's Antiseptic Salve, tc, For Man & Beast, 1x3½" dia...12.00
Reas Habana, cigar tin..................................28.00
Red Bird Cigar, box.....................................15.00
Red Crescent, cracker tin................................28.00
Red Cross Cotton, poster/fr, Blacks pick cotton, 1894, 33"....280.00
Red Goose Shoes, bank..................................125.00
Red Goose Shoes, bell, Ring for Red Goose Shoes...........20.00
Red Goose Shoes, clicker, long nose goose.................10.00
Red Goose Shoes, display, w/metal goose: lays 'gold eggs'....675.00
Red Goose Shoes, string holder, CI......................750.00
Red Indian Cut Plug, tobacco tin w/paper label.............45.00
Red Indian Motor Oil, porcelain sign, w/Indian.............350.00
Red J Tobacco, tc, pictures bird, 6x6", G.................55.00
Red Jacket, tobacco pocket tin, G........................24.00
Red Raven, match holder/ash tray, raven & bottle, Warwick.....50.00

Red Raven, tray, bird next to bottle, square, 1910...........160.00
Red Raven, tray, man & raven, VG........................125.00
Red Raven, tray, Papa has a headache, nude child w/bottle....195.00
Red Raven Splits, tip tray, World's Fair, 1904.............78.00
Red Rose Farm Feeds, emb sign, 18x24", 1963..............45.00
Red Seal, peanut butter pail, NM........................65.00
Red Seal Lye, pocket mirror, w/can, mirror has specks........22.50
Red Wing Milling, Red Wing, MN, hand mirror...............20.00
Rega Coach Oil, tc w/spout, pictures coach, early 1900s, EX....15.00
Remington, poster, blk man in cart/hunters, 1920s, 21x14"....325.00
Remington, thermometer, porcelain.......................125.00
Renner's Hi Power Malt Tonic, tin sign, red/wht/bl, 10x9".....22.00
Restorff & Bettman Shoe Dressing, store bin, Blk folk, G.......55.00
Revelation, tobacco pocket tin...........................10.00
Rexall, store candy jar, emb lettering, trade mk, M..........30.00
Rexall Drugs, thermometer, wood, lg......................125.00
Rhinelander Butter, tin sign, w/product...................65.00
Rice's Agent, cigar tin..................................45.00
Rice's Seeds, poster, Early Winningstadt Cabbage, 22x28".....175.00
Richardsons 5¢ Root Beer, barrel dispenser................350.00
Richfield Gasoline, jigsaw puzzle, Goofy Golf, MIB...........15.00
Rick's Canton Ginger, tin container.......................4.50
Rochester Beer, litho on paper, 1800s...................650.00
Rochester Great American Insurance, metal sign, eagle/shield....90.00
Rock Castle, tobacco pocket tin.........................300.00
Rock Crystal Salt, memo pad calendar, celluloid, red/bl box.....25.00
Roessle Lager, tray, 2 old men at table drinking, pp.........150.00
Roi-tan Cigars, display, tin '39 Chevy, radio premium, 4", VG...25.00

Roly Poly

The Roly Poly tobacco tins were patented on November 5, 1912, by Washington Tuttle and produced by Tindeco of Baltimore, Maryland. There were six characters in all -- Satisfied Customer, Storekeeper, Mammy, Dutchman, Singing Waiter and Inspector. Four brands of tobacco were packaged in selected characters; some tins carry a printed tobacco box on the back to identify their contents. Mayo and Dixie Queen Tobacco were packed in all six; Red Indian and U.S. Marine Tobacco in only Mammy, Singing Waiter and Storekeeper.

Of the set, the Inspector is considered the rarest, and in mint condition may fetch as much as $1,000 on today's market.

Inspector, average pitting and rusting, $550.00; in mint condition: $1,000.

Dutchman, EX...450.00
Inspector from Scotland Yard, EX................1,000.00
Mammy, Dixie Queen...............................475.00
Mammy, Mayo..600.00
Satisfied Customer, EX.............................475.00
Singing Waiter, EX..................................350.00
Storekeeper, EX......................................375.00

Rooster Snuff, glass jar, salesman's sample, unopened, 5".......25.00
Round Trip, tin tobacco box.............................100.00
Royal Crown Cola, rvpt sign & clock, 2 bottles............110.00
Royal Crown Cola, thermometers, emb bottle, 6x14", EX......17.50
Runkel's Breakfast Cocoa, tc, girl w/cocoa, early, no lid, EX....15.00
Runkel's Cocoa, tin sign, sf, court of Louis XV, 22x28", EX...600.00
Russell's Chocolates, ts, blonde girl/pk dress, 1910, 13x19"....350.00
Ryan's Beer, tip tray, Gypsy girl........................80.00
S Bolton's Sons Home Brewed Ale, tray, monks w/keg, pp, 18".175.00
S&S Cough Drops, mirror..............................18.00
SAC Mixture Tobacco, tc, lg round corner, EX.............40.00
Sailor Boy Brand, tc, 8¾x6½"............................300.00
Sanfords Inks, display, tin, 3-tier.......................95.00
Satin Skin Powder, fr ad, 1903.........................50.00
Schenley is the Name, enameled money clip..............6.50
Schlitz Beer, mug, woman sitting on globe, old...........65.00
Schneider Brewing Co, tip tray, couple drinking..........95.00
Schoenling Beer, neon sign............................100.00
Schoeny Grocers, Vienna Art Plate, metal, sexy brunette, 1905..65.00
Scholl's Axle Grease, tin, w/Blacks.....................75.00
School Boy, peanut butter pail, 2 lb....................200.00
Seabury's Quick Setting Plaster Paris Bandage, tc, 4½".......7.00
Seal of N Carolina Tobacco, wood canister/paper label, no lid...45.00
Sealtest, badge, Schmoo...............................15.00
Sealtest, cottage cheese glass, Snow White, Disney 1930s, M....20.00
Sears Roebuck, cartoon book, Santa/Christmas, 1941 premium..10.00
Seaside Gasoline, ps, 2 sided/triangular, seagull, 26".......65.00
Segar Tobacco, sign, emb paper, w/dog..................325.00
Sen-Sen Chewing Gum, box.............................15.00
Senator, tobacco tin...................................40.00
Shapleigh Hdw Co, puzzle, red celluloid, mirror size........38.50
Sharples, stick pin, celluloid w/picture...................42.50
Sharples Cream Separator, match holder, tin, shows cows/lady..195.00
Sharples Cream Separator, porcelain sign, red/wht, 11x18"......95.00
Sharps Toffee, tin container............................65.00
Shaw's Malt, tin sign, What the Dr Ordered, couple/Dr, 22x34".350.00
Sherwin Williams Paints, pocket mirror, red/wht celluloid......17.50
Shinola, shoe horn, The Wonderful Shoe Polish, litho........30.00
Short Cut Tobacco, cb sign, Turk smoking pipe, in fr, 1909...125.00
Silvertown Cords Goodrich Tires, wall mt porcelain 2 side sign..42.50
Simplex Typewriter for Boys, Santa die-cut, mid '20s, 11x5"....20.00
Sinclair, sign, porcelain, sm...........................17.00
Sinclair Household Oil, can, dinosaur on front............15.00
Sir Walter Raleigh, tobacco tin, Christmas...............25.00
Skeezix Shoes, pocket mirror, Skeezix w/different birth stones...65.00
Skoal, Copenhagen, tin chewing tobacco dispenser, rnd.......39.00
Slippery Elm Lozenge, tin container....................425.00
Smile Beverages, tin clicker, Kewpie type w/orange face, 1930s...5.00
Smith Bros, paperweight, cast iron......................45.00
Smith Premier Typewriter Ribbon, tc, early typewriter, EX......8.00
Smoke Old Virginia Cheroots, 5 for 10¢, cb sign, 6x11".......18.50
Snap Shot Gun Powder, tc, slain duck falling.............75.00
Snow King Baking Powder, tin container.................20.00
Socony Aircraft Oil, sign, porcelain.....................120.00

Sohio Oil, sign, tin, sm................................15.00
Sovereign Cigarettes, sign, litho, orig wood fr, 34x26".......175.00
Sparrow's Chocolates, ts, queen eating candy, 1915, 21x15"...325.00
Spokane Brewery, tray, elk stands by water, pp............155.00
Spring Lake Whiskey, chromolitho, woman/rose, 1890, 33x23".340.00
Squibbs Talcum Powder, tin container, baby in tub..........85.00
Squirrel Brand Peanuts, emb jar........................100.00
Squirrel Peanut Butter, 1# pail.........................80.00
St Charles Evaporated Cream, figural CI cow w/clock belly.....250.00
St Louis Plume Co, Cleaners of Ostrich Goods, pocket mirror, G.13.50
Stag, tobacco pocket tin, sm............................42.00
Standard Oil Co Mica, Axle Grease, miniature pail, 2".......85.00
Standard Oil of Indiana, sign, porcelain, 30"..............125.00
Standard Sewing Machine, wood sign, 12x72".............225.00
Stanton Beer & Ale, tray, red/gold & blk letters, 12".........36.00
Staple Mixture Tobacco, tc, lg round corner, EX...........40.00
Star Belt Lacing, emb tin litho sign, M..................75.00
Star Brand Shoes, litho/orig wood fr, Victorian lady, 32x22"...225.00
Star Plug Chewing Tobacco, envelope/coupon/leaflet, 1880.....18.00
Star Soap, fr litho, Victorian child, 1885................125.00
Star Soap, Schutz & Co, pocket mirror, paper.............12.50
Star Soap, sign, porcelain, 20x26".....................135.00
Starrett Tools, pocket mirror, tools on red celluloid.........16.50
Sterling Dark Tobacco, store canister, tin, G.............50.00
Sterling Ranges, mirror................................35.00
Stoddard Gilbert & Co, Old Green 10¢ Cigar, pocket mirror....38.50
Stroh's Beer, cardboard fan, tavern scene................70.00
Sultana Peanut Butter, pail w/lid & bail, 1#, litho of children....35.00
Sultana Spice Mills, tin container.......................12.00
Sun Crest, thermometer, bottle shaped, 16½"..............45.00
Sunoco Nu-Blue, blotter, 1940, Mickey Mouse in car, M.......15.00
Sunset Trail Cigars, tc, cowboy & cowgirl on horses.........125.00
Sunshine Biscuit, tin container, lg......................65.00
Sunshine Coffee, glass canister, emb lion, early 1900s, 1 lb.....20.00
Superior Cleanser, sample tin..........................15.00
Sweet Burley, tobacco tin, yellow w/red letters, 8x11".......85.00
Sweet Cuba Fine Cut Tobacco, canister, slant top, w/woman....95.00
Sweet Cuba Tobacco, bin, yellow.......................125.00
Sweet Cuba Tobacco, canister, br/gold..................85.00
Sweet Cuba Tobacco, cardboard store container, no lid, G......35.00
Sweet Cuba Tobacco, pie tin, EX.......................30.00
Sweet Mist Tobacco, store tin, cb w/tin top & bottom, VG......45.00
Sweet Mist Tobacco, tc, canister, children by fountain........175.00
Sweet Orr Overalls, porcelain sign, 8 men pulling on pants.....375.00
Swift's Oz Peanut Butter, tin pail.......................35.00
Tam O'Shanter, beer tray, post-pro.....................40.00
Tarzan Ice Cream Cup, poster, Tarzan rescues girl, mc, '30s, M.35.00
Teddy Bear Peanut Butter, tin pail, CJ Jones Co...........700.00
Temple Bar Tobacco, tc, pictures temple, EX..............20.00
Tenderleaf Tea, radio premiums book, 1938, w/orig mailer, M...15.00
Tetley Tea, clock, tin.................................500.00
Texaco, sign, porcelain, 36"...........................110.00
Texaco Sky Chief, enamel sign, 12x18"..................25.00
The Boston Herald, Sunday Herald, pocket mirror, w/boy, G....43.50
Three States Mixture, tin tobacco box...................35.00
Tiger Tobacco, cb store canister, red....................95.00
Tiger Tobacco, store tin, blue.........................350.00
Tiger Tobacco, tc, 4x6"...............................60.00
Times Square Tobacco, canister, New York night scene, M.....50.00
Times Square Tobacco, pocket tin......................125.00
Tip Top Stoves & Ranges, corner sign, porcelain, 20x18".......95.00
Tivoli Brewery, tray, Bavarian waiter, 1910...............135.00
Toby Ale, tin sign, 21x15"............................95.00
Tonka Smoking Mixture, tc, British military encampment scene.165.00

Tootsie Roll, porcelain sign............................295.00
Topper Porter, ball tap knob........................50.00
Toyland, peanut butter pail, 2 lb...................200.00
Train Master, cigar tin................................45.00
Travler, cigar tin.....................................25.00
Treadeasy Shoes, pull toy pig, wood, 1920s, 6"........18.00
True Blue, tin tobacco pail..........................25.00
Tuckett's Abbey, pocket tin.........................80.00
Tuckett's Marguerite Cigars, sgn, litho tin/lady by Asti, 1900...900.00
Tuxedo, tobacco pocket tin.........................25.00
Twin Oaks, casket, M...............................100.00
Twin Oaks, tobacco pocket tin.....................40.00
U-Need-A-Biscuit, tin container, 11¼x8"...........24.00
UMC Cartridges, poster, hunter & grizzly, 1920s, fr, 21x31"...550.00
Uncle Daniel Cut Tobacco, tc, flat canister...........150.00
Uncle John's Syrup, window display, 5 pc, lg.........175.00
Underwood Typewriter, bank, metal figural, 1940 NY Fair......75.00
Uniform, tin tobacco box, 4x6".....................140.00
Union Leader, cuspidor, ceramic, rectangular.........65.00
Union Leader, pocket tin............................35.00
Union Leader, tobacco canister, Sam..................25.00
Union Pacific Tea, tray, cute litle girl/kids in snow, 1905......75.00
Union Workman Chewing Tobacco, thermometer, rnd.........85.00
Union Workman Tobacco, pail, paper label, no lid........15.00
Universal Batteries, thermometer, Quality Since 1899........110.00
Universal Batteries Sales Service, tin sgn, heart shape, 20x19"...45.00
Urban's Liberty Flour, plate, pink....................16.50
Utica Club, ball tap knob...........................40.00
Vanko Cigars, tc, race horse, EX.....................40.00
Vantage Cigarettes, clock, battery op................20.00
Vaseline, Toonerville Town, cb stand-up, 1920s, 17x10".......95.00
Velvet Tobacco, canister, octagon....................50.00
Velvet Tobacco, porcelain sign, w/pocket tin, 48x12".....150.00
Velvet Tobacco, sample tin..........................55.00
Velvet Tobacco, ts, man in chair w/dog, sfr, 1910...........450.00
Viceroy Cigarettes, tin sign, lady w/package, Smoother, 1954....65.00
Victory Gums, tc, slant top dresser, English..........375.00
Victrola, Economy Furniture Co, pocket mirror, record........31.50
Volunteer Whiskey, rvpt glass sign, CW soldiers/flag, 12x16"...200.00
Vulcanol Stove Polish, tin sgn/wood fr, w/bulldog, 41x15".....145.00
Waldreys Milk, rvpt sign, early bottle.................65.00
Walter Baker Chocolate, bar dispenser, w/lady, 44x8".......200.00
Waltham Watches, envelope, mailed, lg watch/slogan, 1880.....11.00
Wampum Coffee, tin container, 2 lbs...................175.00
Ward's Lemon Crush, ts, Tempting Tang of Lemons, '20s, 19"..30.00
Washburn Crosby Flour, enameled 1" button w/slit leather bk...12.50
Washington Brand Lard, tin bucket, pictures George, EX......15.00
Waterman's Fountain Pens, sign, porcelain, 8x30".........325.00
Way-Up Tobacco, tin pail, paper label, no lid.........15.00
WE Garrett & Sons Scotch Snuff, tc, emb lid/label/stamp.......4.00
Weiland's Beer, tray, Viking woman, bear on cliff, pp, G.......175.00
Wellington, tobacco pocket tin......................65.00
Wellington Conover Pianos, mirror, w/picture..........20.00
Wesson Oil, beater jar, crockery.....................65.00
West End Brewing Co, tip tray, Victorian lady wrapped in flag..175.00
Western Union Teleg & Cable, display box w/porcelain inset....85.00
Westinghouse, Blondie/Dagwood game, appliance pcs, '40.......30.00
Westinghouse, neon sign............................135.00
Whip Cigars, 2 sided tin sign, round.................110.00
White Brothers, token, willow tree logo on copper...........5.00
White Eagle Gas, sign, porcelain, 30"................80.00
White House Coffee, tin container, ½ lb..............15.00
White House Tea, sample tc, pictures White House, EX........35.00
White Rock Table Water, tip tray, semi-nude on rock by water..80.00

Zeno Gum, display case, oak with slant front, mirror back, and glass sides, 1890s, 17½", $295.00.

White Rose Bread, tin sign, child baker w/loaf, dtd 1915......195.00
White Rose Gas, sign, man w/checkered pants, G............225.00
White Rose Petroleum Jelly, sample tin..................5.00
White Rose Whiskey, tin sign, We Sell, bottle, 1920, 34x13"...600.00
Whiterock Ginger Ale, tin sign, 13x36"................65.00
Whitman's, candy box, litho metal, pat 1923.............25.00
Whiz Car Polish, tc, car & pixies, 1905, VG.............110.00
Wiedemann Beer, cb/fr, old man w/newspaper, 1895, 21x22"...185.00
Wilbur Stock Food Co, fr litho, Blue Ribbon 12 horse team...150.00
Wilbur's Tonic, litho sign, delivery wagon/horse/drivers, '04.....95.00
Williams Shave, thermometer, wood....................110.00
Willoughby Taylor, tobacco pocket tin, G..............12.00
Wilson's Bachelor 10¢ Cigars, countertop dispenser, tin.......180.00
Witch Hazel Pile Cure, mirror, beveled, oak fr..........67.50
Wm Penn Tobacco, sign, paper.......................185.00
Woolson Spice, paper litho, dancing lesson, girl & cat, in fr.....80.00
Woolworth, tin candy container, Santa/airplane litho, 1930s, M..50.00
Worcester Salt, sign, w/longest train................350.00
World's Navy, tobacco tin...........................35.00
Wrigley's Gum, counter scales, brass.................200.00
Wrigley's Gum, Tootsie Toy van, mc logo & elf ea side, 1940s...65.00
Wrigley's Spearmint Pepsin Gum, display, gum shape, cb, 5x18"..30.00
Yale Coffee, bookmark...............................5.00
Yellow Cab Cigars, tin container, no lid...............250.00
Yoc-o-May Tobacco, tc, pocket, flat, EX...............30.00
Yocum Bros, cigar pocket tin........................18.00
Yuengling's Beer, emb tin sign, w/hand & bottle.........285.00
Yuengling's Beer, tin sign, eagle on keg, 6x13¼".........95.00
Yum-Yum Smoking Tobacco, tin pail, pictures farm boy.......425.00
Zanzibar Spices, canister, #6, nude Blacks, M...........125.00
Zatek, jar w/orig gold paint........................535.00
ZBT Baby Powder, tin container.......................3.00
Zeno Chewing Gum, tin box, early....................45.00
Zeno Gum, showcase, oak, slant front, marquee, 18½x10x8"...295.00
Zetta Bavarian Beer, tray, king w/city in bkground, pp, 13" sq..350.00
Zingo Sweets, tin container, 10 lb, old time race car/driver.....175.00
20 Grand Cigarettes, sign, cb in wood fr, pictures horse, 26"...60.00
20 Mule Team Borax, tin sign, mules, wagons, product, 33"...550.00
3 States, tobacco tin, flat oval pocket................250.00
4 Roses Whiskey, ts, fox/game birds/rifle, 1900, 48x32", G.....450.00

7-Up, bottle, salesman's sample mini, paper label/girl, 1930s.....15.00
7-Up, tin corner sign, 1947, 18x14".......................125.00

Advertising Cards

Advertising trade cards enjoyed a heyday during the last quarter of the 19th century when the printing process known as chromolithography became refined and put into popular use. The purpose of the trade card was to acquaint the public with a place of business, a product or an available service. Well known firms such as Louis Prang and Company and Currier and Ives produced quality cards which today command prices in the $40 to $60 range.

Mechanical cards are those which achieve movement through the use of a pull tab, fold out side or rotating disk. Metamorphic cards transform a person or a thing from a 'before' to an 'after' condition, which of course represented a marked improvement immediately upon use of the featured product. Both types are favored by collectors today. Another popular type, the 'hold-to-light' card, reveals its design only when viewed before a strong light.

Die-cut cards in figural forms such as the Heinz pickle series usually fall into a price range of $6 to $8.

Ayer's Cherry Pectoral, 7 pilgrims meet w/Indians..............8.00
Belgium Exposition, 1885.................................6.00
Bishop/Veitch Photographers, mc litho spider woman/new gallery.18.00
Bliss Bros Portrait & View Photographers, mc floral litho, lg....10.00
Brooklyn Bridge, between NY & Brooklyn, in color, 4x7"......3.00
Brown's Iron Bitters, lady's face looks through broken pane.....10.50
Brown's Iron Bitters, 2 pups in barrel watch cat, EX...........4.50
Brown's Vermifuge Comfits, mother in housecoat w/children......3.50

Finney's Block, 1886, 4" x 6", $9.00.

Burdock Blood Bitters, child on toboggan, VG.................7.50
Burdock Blood Bitters, girl in wht toga on grass w/dog.........8.00
Burdock Blood Bitters, maid in bl ballerina dress w/kitten......3.25
Carolina Lily, mc circle w/tipped on albumen of man...........8.00
Carter's Little Liver Pills, blackbird on branch/lake scene.......5.50
Celery Bitters, Steuben Wine Co, cavalier w/pipe.............7.00
Cheatham's Tasteless Chill Tonic, vignette of girl, AB Richard....7.50
Creme Oat Meal Toilet Soap, 1881.......................7.00
Currier & Ives, Bad Point on a Good Pointer, 1879..........50.00
Currier & Ives, Crack Trotter, 1880....................50.00

DeWitt's Photograph Studio, mc litho: children feed chicks.....14.00
Domestic Sewing Machines, child blowing bubbles.............5.00
Dr Kilmer's Swamp Root Liver & Bladder Cure, w/alligator......11.00
Dr McLane's Liver Pills, yellow roses, testimonials............7.50
Dr Pardee's Celebrated Remedy, boy pulls dolly from creek, 5"...7.50
Dr Thomas' Eclectic Oil, cat emerges from box, emb bottle......3.50
Dr White's Cough Drops, pictures children...................5.00
Easle, tipped on albumen print of woman, VG................7.00
Elgin Condensed Milk, pictures babies, 3x5½"...............10.00
Emulsion De Scott...................................9.00
Gale--Photographer, mc litho couple/old time swimsuits/lg hat....10.00
GE Gray Artist--Photographer, sm w/floral litho...............5.00
Grobecker's Pills...................................3.00
Heald & Co Portrait Photographers, mc litho couple in rowboat.12.00
Hood's, die-cut water lilly.............................5.00
Hood's Sarsaparilla, Wedding in Catland, puzzle, fr, 14½x9¾"..75.00
Hood's Sarsaparilla, 5 children look at product name, EX.......6.50
Hunt's Remedy, man beating skeleton, EX..................12.00
IU Doust--Fine Photographer, sm w/bright colored floral border...6.00
Johnson's Anodyne Liniment, girl ties scarf on dolly, VG........3.50
JW Laming, Artist/Photographer; Boston, nice graphics/colorful...7.00
Kendall's Spavin Cure, Black jockey on horse/groom, 4x6½"....12.50
Malena, remedy, 4x5½"..............................4.00
Malt Bitters, House That Jack Built, 7 illus, 3¼x5¼"..........7.50
Manhattan Biscuit Co, Indian on pkg......................5.00
Merchant's Gargling Oil, man in top hat/sick lady, menu bk......4.50
MG Gilmore Tintypes & Crayon Work, lg business card........7.00
Moore's Instantaneous Portraits, Quicker than a Wink, florals...10.00
Paris Exposition, 1878................................6.00
Paxine, child, spear, dog & bird, 4½x6"..................12.00
Perry Davis' Pain Killer, teacher at blackboard, boy/girl, VG.....3.50
Pond's Extract, obelisk in desert/hieroglyphics...............2.50
PS Ryder/Leading Photographer, floral litho w/ornate bird, lg...12.00
Quaker Bitters, girl 'Brighton Belle', Donaldson Bros, 6".......8.00
Quaker Bitters, young girl in barrel, 'Rustic Beauty', 6".......8.75
Red Star Cough Cure, lad in toga, star on chest w/sword, EX....3.50
Richmond Stove Co.................................5.00
Sanative Pills, Scottish couple..........................6.00
Shaker Extract of Roots, Steigel's syrup, 2 children/kitten......20.00
Shaker Soothing Plasters, girl, head on hands, on pink blanket...5.00
Simmon's Sarsaparilla, flowers/crane in creek, cures on bk......6.00
Smith's German Sweet Chill Cure, bear carries off piglet.......12.00
St Jacobs Oil, man in forest looks at bottle, castle, G..........3.50
Strunk's New Photograph Parlors, mc/gilt litho for 'tintyping'....15.00
Turner--Photo Artist, b/w engraving of man, back: description...15.00
Walter Wood, mower, small tear........................6.00
Wheat Bitters, man in top hat, girl & lady at outdoor table......9.00
Willard's Golden Seal Bitters, child's face/floral/fruit..........7.50

Advertising Dolls

Often the secret to finding advertising doll bargains hinges on being able to spot one. Many are unmarked. As you walk past merchandise at a flea market, can you spot trademark figures? What may look like a baby's squeeze toy may be the illusive Chiquita banana doll!

Common trademark figures used today are easy to identify: Mr. Peanut, the Jolly Green Giant and Pillsbury's Doughboy; but what about Coco Wheat's Gretchen, or Peter Pan Ice Cream's doll -- they are not marked, and haven't been sold for several years.

Browse through old magazines . . . the old ads are a good source of information. Some companies and products no longer exist, and trademark figures change through the years.

When buying dolls, condition is very important. Check cloth dolls to make sure the fabric is not torn or rotted. Remember, it is almost impossible to clean a cloth doll that has been soiled for a long time. And if it is faded, nothing can restore the color. Rubber items often disintegrate; check unpainted areas to make sure they are solid. Plastics, though they may look hopeless, usually come out looking good as new with a little soap and water.

Never pay full price for a damaged advertising doll, unless it is very rare. At least you'll have one in your collection while you watch for a better example.

Collectors often build their collections by trading. Watch for dolls offered in your area and buy several. Look for bargains, and exchange them for one you need.

New dolls and other toys are offered each month. Watch the grocery shelves, read the doll literature, and talk with fellow collectors. Many items sell for only a few months before the offer is withdrawn. Save the information relating to the advertising doll; clip ads, get extra coupons, and keep them in a scrapbook -- in time, advertising literature will add greatly to the history of your doll collection.

Arbuckle Bros Coffee, Jack & Jill, litho cloth, 1931, 14", pr...100.00
Baby Ruth Candy, flannel doll, blk oilcloth buttons/belt, 16"....20.00
Beach Nut Gum, Fruit Stripe Zebra, cloth, mc stripes, 12".......8.00
Brown's Chicken, Farmer Brown, litho cloth, wears hat, 18"....11.00
Budweiser Beer, Bud Man, cloth, removable cape............12.00
Campbell Kid, compo, redressed orig, NM, 12"..............175.00
Chesty Potato Chips, Chesty Boy, rubber squeak doll, '50s, 8"....15.00
Cracker Jack, cloth trademark boy, sewn on hat, 1974, 15".....15.00
Duncan Hines Brownie Mix, felt elf, removable clothes, 26".....17.00
Elgin Nut Margarine, KoKo Kid, cloth girl eats sandwich, 1920..57.00
Farmer's Brand, J Le Roy Farmer, litho cloth farmer, 14"......45.00
Fisk Tires, Fisk Boy, bisque, in pajamas, sucks thumb, 1914...135.00
Fletcher's Castoria, Mammy, litho cloth, 1930s, colorful, 11"....75.00
Good & Plenty Candy, Choo Charlie, bean bag engineer-boy....10.00
Hanes, Blk baby, wears Hanes sleepers, cloth & vinyl, 21"......30.00
Hires Root Beer, inflatable Black Cow, 40" long, 1976.........15.00
Hot Tamale Candies, Tamale Kid, cloth Mexican boy, 16".......5.00
Imperial Granum, litho cloth girl wears long underwear, 1918...65.00
Istrouma Flour, Humpty Dumpty, cloth, wears plaid suit, 13"....15.00
Jack Frost Sugar, Jack Frost, cloth boy w/hat & scarf, 18"......12.00
Junior Mints, Fonz Doll, cloth Henry Winkler, 1976, 16".......5.00
Kellogg's, Drooper--Banana Splits Doll, cloth, 1969, 12"........6.00
Kellogg's, Johnny Bear, stuffed cloth......................35.00
Kellogg's Corn Flakes, Mary & Her Lamb, litho cloth, 1928.....55.00
Kellogg's Rice Crispies, Snap!, baker boy, litho cloth, 1954.....15.00
Kelly Services Inc, Kelly Girl, cloth, yarn hair, w/clothes........15.00
Korn Krisp, Miss Corn Krisp, cloth, 1920s, 26"................65.00
Lion Uniform Co, heavy plastic boy in uniform, 1940s, 13".....44.00
MacDonald's Restaurant, Hamburgler, cloth, plastic cape, 17"...10.00
Minnesota Sales Co, My Dear Dolly, 21" cloth w/6" doll, 1924..65.00
Mission Macaroni Co, JP Patches, cloth clown-bum, 15"........9.00
Morton Salt, cloth girl w/product, yarn hair, Mattel, 14".......15.00
Nugget Casino, Nugget Sam, rubber prospector, '50, 12"......10.00
Pillsbury, Popie Fresh, molded vinyl dough girl, 1972..........8.00
Pioneer Seeds, Selmore/Semore, cloth man, different ea side....10.00
Plaid Stamp Co, Bonnie, plastic w/Scottish costume, 1968, 20"..15.00
Pol Parrot Shoes, Kewpie type girl, bisque, 1940s, Japan, 4"....40.00
Post Cereals, Storykin Cinderella, vinyl, 1969, 4", w/coach.......5.00
Post Crispy Critters Cereal, Linus the Lion, plush, 10".........5.00
Quaker's Quake Cereal, man flexing biceps, cloth, 1960s, 11"...10.00
Ralston Purina, Squarecrow, scarecrow w/cloth body/vinyl head..17.00
Red Barn Restaurant, Chicken Hungry, plush chicken leg, 22"..15.00
Revlon, Mrs Revlon, made by Ideal, not jointed, 1958, 19".....49.00
Rexall Drugs, baby doll, all vinyl/molded diaper & bib, 7½"......5.00
Rodkey's Flour, Rag Darling, litho cloth, printed on flour bag...65.00
Royal Crown Cola, Zippy, inflatable man w/crown.............4.00

Gilbert Giddyup, issued by Hardee's, 1971, 16", $8.00.

Sea Island Sugar, Dusty the Cowboy, litho cloth, 1930s, 8".....17.00
Seven Up, Freddie, bird squeeze toy, holds bottle, 1959, 9".....15.00
Seven Up, Undeer hand puppet, plush w/plastic horns, 10"......4.00
Simplicity, Mannequin w/pedestal, patterns, w/box, 1943, 12"....35.00
Snow Crop Orange Juice, Teddy, plush fabric/vinyl mask face.....9.00
Sunshine Animal Crackers, litho cloth circus elephant, 6x5".....45.00
Sylvania Light Bulbs, Bugs Bunny, cloth, talking, 1974, 12".....10.00
Tastykake Bakeries, Baker, litho cloth, 1974, 13"..............8.00
Thompson's Mail Order House, Dolly Dimple, cloth, 13".......45.00
Toni Permanent Wave, mkd American Character, all orig, 10"...35.00
Tropic-Ana, cloth: Hawaiian boy w/fruit on head, '77, 17".......4.00
Tru Test Paint, cloth & compo boy, Kewpie eyes, 1940s, 12".....17.00
Vanta Baby Garments, Vanta Baby, 1927, w/orig outfit, 21"....160.00
Voortman Cookies, Dutch Girl, plastic doll, Dutch outfit, 8"......5.00
Westinghouse, Kangaroo, tan plush fabric, w/baby, 1976, 18"....12.00
Westinghouse, Lotta Light, cloth: girl/braids/carries slate.......45.00
White Front Stores, Friendlee, cloth elf, red cap/shirt, 16".......7.00
WITN Television, cloth newscaster, 2 sides: 1 neat, 1 sloppy....10.00
Wurlitzer, Funmaker Sprite, cloth, green suit, 15".............8.00
Yukon Flour Mills, Peter Rabbit, cloth, face both sides, 7"......20.00
Zee Toilet Tissue, Li'l Softee, plastic, long hair, hat, 5".........5.00

African Art

These artifacts of the African nation are a unique form of folk art, of interest not only in relation to the craftsman evident in their making but because of the culture they represent.

Belt, Baule, cloth w/5 wood/gold leaf masks & shell pendants...522.00
Club, Solomon Island, wood, carved snake/human figure, 49".1,870.00
Cup, Kuba, human head, gridwork coiffure, 6"..............770.00
Figure, Dogon, cubistic form, knees bend, helmet head, 12"...495.00
Figure, Genin, rooster/grooved wings/upright tailfeathers, 15".1,430.00
Figure, male ancestor; Leti Island, post form, head atop, 46".2,750.00
Figure, Yoruba, male & female twins, 10", pr................825.00
Gong, Yaka, slit cylinder w/ferocious human head, clapper, 18".770.00
Group, Ashanti mother & children, seated, nursing baby, 16"..770.00
Heddle pulley, Ashanti, stylized female, pierced ovoid head...1,045.00

Heddle pulley, Baule, w/head w/zigzag beard, crested hair, 8"..660.00
Heddle pulley, Guro, tall neck/oval human head, antelope atop.715.00
Heddle pulley, Senufo, w/porpianong bird atop, 9"..........605.00
Mask, Bakaka, winged face w/chin & top projections, 23"....1,650.00
Mask, face; Bobo, antelope, slender snout, curving horns, 30"..935.00
Mask, face; Chokwe, open mouth/bared teeth/slit eyes, 7¾"....660.00
Mask, helmet; Mende, compressed face/slit eyes, 10".........495.00
Mask, monkey face, wood w/ptd glass eyes, orig pnt, 6½"......65.00
Mask, New Guinea cult, convex lozenge w/facial features, 10"..525.00
Mask, Punu, white face, pointed oval form, 13"...........2,310.00
Mask, tiger face, carved wood, orig pnt, 8".................35.00
Pendant, Luba, ivory w/female, hands to breasts, 4".........605.00
Plaque, Benin, bronze rectangle w/mudfish relief, 13½".....2,200.00
Staff, East African, female figure atop short shaft, 31".......935.00
Stool, Hemba, female caryatid w/upraised arms support, 20"..1,210.00

Left: mask, carved wood, Dan tribe of West Africa, 6", $75.00.
Center: mask, carved wood, Dan tribe of West Africa, 10", $50.00.
Right: female figure, carved wood, Baole tribe of West Africa, 22", $100.00.

Agata

Agata glass is a very rare and expensive type of art glass that was made at the New England Glass Co. in 1887. John Locke developed the method for achieving the characteristic mottled effect which was usually used on their lovely peachblow glass, although occasionally it was applied to opaque green. The procedure involved spraying an alcohol mixture on the surface of the glass while it was still very hot. The results produced a marbelized appearance not unlike the agate stone. Caution -- be sure to use only gentle cleaning methods!

Bowl, flared/ruffled, allover gold/raspberry to pink, 3" H.....2,000.00
Bowl, fluted top, 2x5"...................................975.00
Mustard, raspberry color, metal top.....................1,150.00
Toothpick, opaque gr...................................425.00

Tumbler, New England, blk splotches, heavy gold tracing......650.00
Vase, sq/indented sides, ruffled 4 scallop rim, New Eng, 4½"...550.00

Akro Agate

The Akro Agate Company founded in 1914 in Clarksbury, West Va., was primarily a marble factory. Not until 1932 did they start to manufacture their popular lines of children's dishes, novelty items, etc. Although not always marked, much of their ware was made in a distinctive marbled or opaque glass that is easily recognized. Some of the children's pieces were also made of clear colors. In the list that follows, colors not termed opaque or marble are clear. Items that are marked bear the circle seal with AKRO and a flying crow carrying marbles in his talons. The company closed in 1951.

General Merchandise Line

Ash tray, Hotel Lincoln, powder blue......................20.00
Flower pot, ribs & flutes, scalloped, marbleized bl/wht, 5½".....8.50
Flower pot, stacked disc, marbleized, 5½".................12.00
Jardiniere, bell shape, rectangular top, opaque yellow, 4¾".....12.00
Jardiniere, ribs & flutes, square top, cobalt, 5"............15.00
Lamp, wall; w/Akro shade................................58.00
Planter, octagonal shape, opaque wht, 7x11½".............28.00
Powder jar, apple figural, pumpkin......................150.00
Powder jar, Mexicali, w/sombrero cover, marbleized orange/wht..25.00
Puff box, Colonial lady figural, white....................28.00
Shaving mug, powder blue...............................20.00
Vase, cobalt or pumpkin, 7 darts, 8¾"...................30.00

Chiquita

Creamer, baked-on colors, 1½"...........................5.25
Creamer, opaque green, 1½".............................4.00
Creamer, opaque: lt blue, turq, lav, caramel, or yel; 1½"......7.25
Creamer, transparent cobalt, 1½".......................8.75
Cup, baked-on colors, 1½".............................4.25
Cup, opaque green, 1½"................................3.50
Cup, opaque: lt blue, turq, lav, caramel, or yellow; 1½"......7.75
Cup, transparent cobalt, 1½"..........................4.75
Plate, baked-on colors................................1.50
Plate, opaque green, 3¾"..............................2.00
Plate, transparent cobalt, 3¾"........................5.25
Saucer, opaque: lt blue, turq, lav, caramel, or yellow; 3¼".....2.25
Saucer, transparent cobalt, 3¼".......................2.75
Set, 16 pc, baked-on colors, MIB......................58.00
Set, 16 pc, opaque colors other than green, MIB.........83.00
Set, 16 pc, opaque green, MIB.........................50.00
Set, 16 pc, transparent cobalt, MIB...................115.00
Set, 22 pc, opaque green, MIB.........................69.00
Sugar, no lid, baked-on colors, 1½"...................4.25
Sugar, no lid, opaque green, 1½"......................3.75
Sugar, no lid, opaque: lt bl, turq, lav, caramel, or yel; 1½"....6.50
Sugar, no lid, transparent cobalt, 1½"................7.00
Teapot, w/lid, baked-on colors, 3"....................12.50
Teapot, w/lid, opaque green, 3".......................8.75
Teapot, w/lid, opaque: lt bl, turq, lav, caramel, or yel; 3".....15.00
Teapot, w/lid, transparent cobalt, 3".................16.00

Concentric Rib

Creamer, opaque colors other than green, 1¼".............4.75
Creamer, opaque green or white, 1¼"....................4.00
Cup, opaque colors other than green or white, 1¼".........3.00

Cup, opaque green or white, 1¼".........................2.25
Set, 7 pc, opaque colors other than green or white, MIB......27.50
Set, 7 pc, opaque green or white, MIB.......................23.00
Sugar, opaque colors other than green or white, 1¼"..........4.75
Sugar, opaque green or white, 1¼"...........................4.00
Teapot, w/lid, opaque colors other than green or white, 3½".....8.00
Teapot, w/lid, opaque green or white, 3½"...................6.50

Concentric Ring

Cereal, large, marbleized blue, 3⅜".......................28.50
Cereal, large, other opaque colors, 3⅜"...................16.00
Cereal, large, transparent cobalt, 3⅜"...................23.50
Creamer, large, marbleized blue, 1⅜".....................32.50
Creamer, large, other opaque colors, 1⅜".................11.00
Creamer, large, transparent cobalt, 1⅜".................23.50
Creamer, small, marbleized blue, 1¼".....................25.00
Creamer, small, other opaque colors, 1¼"..................9.00
Creamer, small, transparent cobalt, 1¼".................19.00
Cup, large, marbleized blue, 1⅜".........................27.50
Cup, large, opaque lavender, 1⅜".........................22.00
Cup, large, opaque pumpkin or yellow, 1⅜"................14.50
Cup, large, other opaque colors, 1⅜".....................13.00
Cup, large, transparent cobalt, 1⅜"......................23.50
Cup, small, marbleized blue, 1¼".........................28.00
Cup, small, other opaque colors, 1¼".......................9.00
Cup, small, transparent cobalt, 1¼"......................25.00
Set, large, marbleized blue, 21 pc, MIB..................440.00
Set, large, other opaque colors, 21 pc, MIB..............225.00
Set, large, transparent cobalt, 21 pc, MIB..............350.00
Set, small, marbleized blue, 16 pc, MIB..................105.00
Set, small, other opaque colors, 16 pc, MIB..............112.00
Set, small, transparent cobalt, 16 pc, MIB..............245.00
Sugar, lg, other opaque colors, 1⅞".......................17.00
Sugar, lg, transparent cobalt, 1⅞".......................31.50
Sugar, small, marbleized blue, 1¼".......................25.00
Sugar, small, other opaque colors, 1¼"....................9.00
Sugar, small, transparent cobalt, 1¼"...................19.00
Teapot, w/lid, large, marbleized blue, 3¾"...............47.50
Teapot, w/lid, large, transparent cobalt, 3¾"...........37.50
Teapot, w/lid, small, marbleized blue, 3⅜"...............53.00
Teapot, w/lid, small, other opaque colors, 3⅜"..........13.00
Teapot, w/lid, small, transparent cobalt, 3⅜"...........28.50

Interior Panel

Cereal, large, lemonade & oxblood, 3⅜"...................23.00
Creamer, large, lemonade & oxblood, 1⅜".................23.00
Creamer, small, luster pink or green, 1¼"...............21.00
Creamer, small, marbleized blue/wht, 1¼"................21.00
Creamer, small, marbleized green/wht, 1¼"...............14.00
Creamer, small, transparent green or topaz, 1¼"..........9.00
Cup, large, lemonade & oxblood, 1⅜"......................19.00
Cup, small, azure blue or yellow, 1¼"...................23.50
Cup, small, marbleized green/wht, 1¼".....................9.50
Cup, small, marbleized red/wht, 1¼"......................21.00
Cup, small, pumpkin, 1¼".................................11.50
Pitcher, small, transparent green or topaz, 2⅞"..........8.50
Plate, large, lemonade & oxblood, 4¼"...................10.00
Plate, small, marbleized blue/wht, 3¾"....................9.00
Plate, small, marbleized red/wht, 3¾".....................6.50
Saucer, large, lemonade & oxblood, 3⅛"....................6.50
Set, large, lemonade & oxblood, 21 pc, MIB..............335.00
Set, large, marbleized green/wht, 21 pc, MIB............250.00

Set, small, azure blue or yellow, 8 pc, MIB.............100.00
Set, small, luster pink or green, 8 pc, MIB..............40.00
Set, small, marbleized blue/wht, 8 pc, MIB..............105.00
Set, small, marbleized red/wht, 16 pc, MIB..............205.00
Set, small, transparent green or topaz, 8 pc, MIB........35.00
Sugar, small, cobalt, 1¼".................................9.00
Sugar, small, luster pink or green, 1¼".................20.00
Sugar, small, marbleized green/wht, 1¼".................14.50
Sugar, small, marbleized red/wht, 1¼"...................23.50
Sugar, w/lid, large, lemonade & oxblood, 1⅞"............29.00
Teapot, w/lid, large, lemonade & oxblood, 3¾"...........37.50
Teapot, w/lid, small, azure blue or yellow, 3⅜".........30.00
Teapot, w/lid, small, cobalt, 3⅜"........................16.00
Teapot, w/lid, small, luster pink or green, 3⅜".........13.50
Teapot, w/lid, small, marbleized blue/wht, 3⅜"..........31.00
Teapot, w/lid, small, marbleized green/wht, 3⅜".........20.00
Teapot, w/lid, small, marbleized red/wht, 3⅜"...........19.00
Teapot, w/lid, small, transparent green or topaz, 3⅜"....9.00
Tumbler, small, luster pink or green, 2"................23.00
Tumbler, small, transparent green or topaz, 2"...........6.00

Miss America

Creamer, forest green or marbleized orange/wht...........34.00
Cup, forest green or marbleized orange/wht...............29.00
Plate, forest green or marbleized orange/wht.............16.00
Saucer, forest green or marbleized orange/wht............10.50
Set, forest green or marbleized orange/wht, MIB.........360.00
Sugar, w/lid, forest green or marbleized orange/wht......45.00
Teapot, w/lid, forest green or marbleized orange/wht.....68.00

Octagonal

Cereal, large, green, white, or dark blue, 3⅜"............3.50
Cereal, large, lemonade & oxblood, 3⅜"...................21.00
Creamer, large, beige, pumpkin, or lt blue, closed hdl, 1½"....11.00

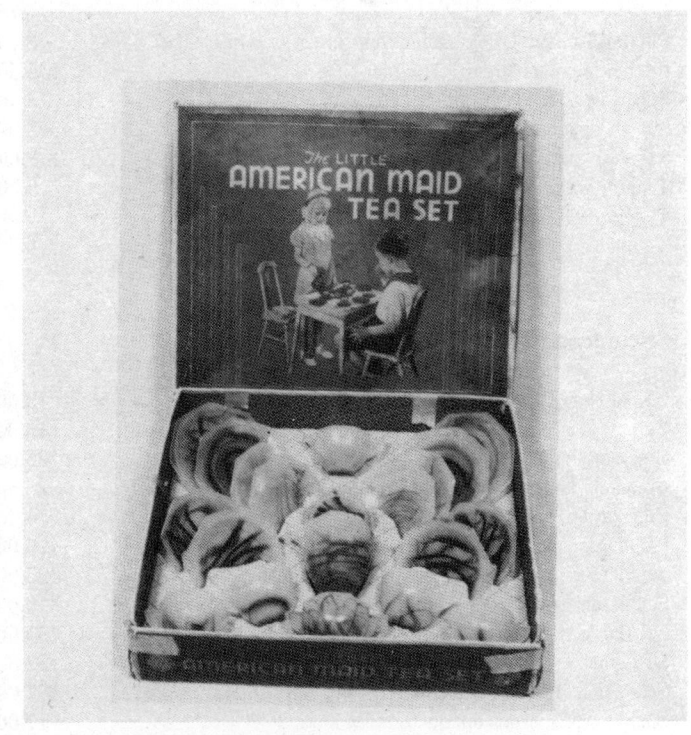

American Maid Tea Set, lemonade and oxblood, closed handles, large, 21 pieces in original box, $280.00.

Creamer, large, lemonade & oxblood, closed handle, 1½"......21.00
Cup, large, lemonade & oxblood, closed handle, 1½"..........16.00
Cup, large, pink, yel, or other opaques, closed handle, 1½".....3.00
Cup, large, pumpkin, closed handle, 1½"....................20.00
Cup, small, pumpkin, yellow, or lime green, open hdl, 1¼".....12.00
Plate, large, lemonade & oxblood, 4¼".......................9.00
Set, large, green, white, or dk blue, 21 pc, closed hdl, MIB....46.00
Set, large, lemonade & oxblood, 21 pc, closed handles, MIB...280.00
Set, large, pink/yellow/other opaques, 21 pc, closed hdl, MIB...80.00
Set, small, dk green, blue, or white, 16 pc, open hdl, MIB.....92.00
Sugar, w/lid, large, green, white, or dk blue, closed handle......4.50
Sugar, w/lid, large, lemonade & oxblood, closed handle........26.00
Teapot w/lid, large, beige/pumpkin/or lt blue, closed hdl, 3½"...15.00
Teapot w/lid, large, lemonade & oxblood, closed handle, 3½"...32.50
Teapot w/lid, small, dk green/blue/or white, open hdl, 3⅜"....13.00
Tumbler, small, dk green, blue, or white, 2"..................4.50
Tumbler, small, pumpkin, yellow, or lime green, 2"...........13.00

Raised Daisy

Creamer, yellow, 1¾"...................................26.00
Cup, blue, 1¾".......................................26.00
Cup, green, 1¾"......................................13.50
Plate, blue, 3".......................................10.00
Saucer, yellow or beige, 2½"............................7.50
Sugar, yellow, 1¾"...................................26.00
Teapot, open, blue or green, 2⅜".......................21.00
Teapot, open, yellow, 2⅜"............................28.50
Teapot, w/lid, blue, 2⅜".............................47.00
Tumbler, blue, 2"....................................31.00
Tumbler, yellow or beige, 2"..........................17.00

Stacked Disc

Creamer, opaque colors other than green or wht, 1¼".........5.50
Creamer, opaque green or white, 1¼"....................2.75
Creamer, pumpkin, 1¼".................................7.75
Pitcher, opaque colors other than green or white, 2⅞".........8.00
Pitcher, opaque green or white, 2⅞"....................5.50
Sugar, opaque colors other than green or white, 1¼"..........5.50
Sugar, opaque green or white, 1¼".....................3.00
Sugar, pumpkin, 1¼"..................................8.00
Teapot, w/lid, opaque colors other than gr or wht, 3⅜".......9.50
Teapot, w/lid, pumpkin, 3⅜"..........................13.50
Tumbler, pumpkin, 2".................................6.00

Stacked Disc & Interior Panel

Cereal, large, opaque solid colors, 3⅜"....................15.00
Cereal, large, transparent green, 3⅜".....................16.00
Creamer, large, marbleized blue, 1⅜"....................26.00
Creamer, large, transparent cobalt, 1⅜".................23.50
Cup, large, transparent green, 1⅜".....................14.00
Set, large, marbleized blue, 21 pc, MIB...................415.00
Set, large, opaque solid colors, 21 pc, MIB...............225.00
Set, large, transparent cobalt, 21 pc, MIB................310.00
Set, large, transparent green, 21 pc, MIB.................255.00
Set, small, opaque solid colors, 8 pc, MIB.................52.50
Set, small, transparent cobalt, 8 pc, MIB.................187.00
Sugar, w/lid, large, opaque solid colors, 1⅞"..............17.00
Sugar, w/lid, large, transparent cobalt, 1⅞"..............31.00
Teapot w/lid, large, marbleized blue, 3¾"................47.00

Stippled Band

Creamer, large, transparent amber, 1½".................13.00
Creamer, small, transparent amber, 1¼".................5.50
Cup, large, transparent green, 1½"....................4.50
Pitcher, small, transparent green, 2⅞".................8.00
Plate, large, transparent azure, 4¼"..................9.00
Set, large, transparent amber, 17 pc, MIB..............140.00
Set, large, transparent green, 17 pc, MIB..............75.00
Set, small, transparent green, 8 pc, MIB...............32.00
Sugar, w/lid, large, transparent amber, 1⅞".............17.00
Teapot w/lid, large, transparent green, 3¾".............15.50
Teapot w/lid, small, transparent amber, 3⅜"............11.00

Alexandrite

Alexandrite is a type of art glass introduced around the turn of the century by Thomas Webb and Sons, of England. It is recognized by its characteristic shading -- pale yellow to rose and blue. It was also produced by other companies.

Bowl, honeycomb, ruffled top, 2x4½"..................950.00
Mushroom, flower form, wide bl band, Webb............1,050.00
Toothpick, flared, fluted, Thos Webb & Son, 2⅛".........1,000.00
Toothpick, ruffled top...............................1,000.00
Toothpick, spherical w/hexagonal flared top, 2½"..........765.00
Wine, honeycomb, 4½"...............................750.00

Alhambra China

Bowl, vegetable; 9".................................45.00
Cake set, 11½" pierced hdl plate + eight 6½" plates.........250.00
Candy jar, ftd, Rococo styling, 8½".....................43.00
Creamer, triple crown mk............................40.00
Dresser set, powder, hair receiver, oval tray, HP paisley, sgn...165.00
Jug, red/gr/cream & gray, elaborate design, much gold, 8½"...135.00
Mayonnaise set, 2 pc, lg.............................41.00
Nappy, w/hdl......................................43.00
Plate, pierced hdls, 10½"............................50.00
Plate, 6"...20.00
Plate, 7½".......................................25.00
Plate, 8½".......................................30.00
Teapot, geometric gr/red, gold scroll, oval shape, 8x4½".......58.00

Almanacs

The earliest evidence indicates that almanacs were used as long ago as Ancient Egypt. Throughout the Dark Ages they were circulated in great volume and were referred to by more people than any other book except the Bible. *The Old Farmer's Almanac* first appeared in 1793 and has been issued yearly since that time. Usually more of a pamphlet than a book (only a few have had hard covers) the almanac provided planting and harvesting information to farmers, weather forecasts for seamen, medical advice, household hints, mathematical tutoring, postal rates, railroad schedules, weights and measures, 'receipts' and jokes.

Before 1800, the information was unscientific and based entirely on astrology and folklore. The first almanac in America was printed in 1639 by William Pierce Mariner; it contained data of this nature. One of the best known editions, Ben Franklin's *Poor Richard's Almanac* was introduced in 1732 and continued to be printed for twenty-five years.

By the 19th century, merchants saw the advertising potential in a publication so widely distributed, and the advertising almanac evolved. These were distributed free of charge by drugstores and mercantiles, and were usually somewhat lacking in information, containing simply a calendar, a few jokes, and a variety of ads for quick remedies and quack cures.

Today their concept and informative, often amusing text make almanacs a popular collectible that may usually be had at reasonable prices. Because they were printed in such large numbers and often saved from year to year, their prices are still low -- most fall within a range of $4 to $15. Those printed before 1860 are especially collectible.

Quite rare and highly prized are the Kate Greenaway 'Almanacks', printed in London from 1883 to 1897. These are illustrated with her drawings of children, one for each calender month.

AL Scovill & Co Farmers & Mechanics, 1871, 72 pgs...........6.00
Almanach Francais D'Ayer, 1887, man w/gout, all in French.....4.50
Almanak, 1887, Peaceful Life o/t Shakers, 34 pgs.............29.00
Am Anti-Slavery, 1839, NY & Boston, yellow cover w/woodcut...80.00
Astronomical Dairy, Nathaniel Low, 1809, sewn together/tattered.18.50
Ayer's American, 1874, blk on yellow cover, lithos/ads.........2.50
Barker's Illus, 1888, profusely illus ea page.................5.50
Beers Calendar, Andrew Beers, 1815.......................17.50
Burdock Blood Bitters, 1885, full color litho front/bk.........17.00
Burdock Blood Bitters, 1888, blk on yellow, girl & box.......17.00
Case Plow Works, American Farmers, 1895.................45.00
Clergyman's Minor, 1812..................................18.50
Columbian Calendar, Andrew Beers, 1817..................16.50
Dr Jayne's Medical, 1881, bldg/horse/buggies on red, VG.......5.00
Farmer's, Andrew Beers, 1818.............................15.50
Farmer's, Dudley Leavitt, 1817............................16.50
Farmer's, Dudley Leavitt, 1823............................16.50
Farmer's, Nathan Bassett, 1838...........................11.50
Farmer's, Robert Thomas, 1854, bk pg gone.................6.50
Farmer's, Robert Thomas, 1858............................7.50
Farmer's, Thos Spofford, 1812............................15.00
Father Abraham's, 1774, pages missing.....................65.00
GG Green, illus Cox, 1890................................22.00
Green's Dairy, 1885-1886, full color, mansion/factory/horses.....6.50
Hostetter's Illus US Almanac, 1874, 1 pg trimmed.............7.50
Isaiah Thomas's, 1807, part of front pg missing.............13.50
Isaiah Thomas's, 1902, pages missing in back, tears..........13.50
LF Atwood's Bitters, Farmer's Almanac, 1896, 48 pgs..........6.50
Medical, Warner's Safe, testimonials, cures via product, 32 pg...12.00
New England, Isaac Bickerstaff, 1805, page missing..........13.50
Oneida, Geo Perkins, 1845................................11.00
Oneida, Geo Perkins, 1849................................10.00
Prindle's, Chas Prindle, 1848.............................10.00
Temperance, Whipple & Damrell, 1839......................11.00
The 7 Wonders o/t World, 1886, full color...................4.50
United States, Chas Egelmann, 1857........................9.50
United States, David Young, 1847, bk page tattered...........10.00
United States, Hunt, 1846, bk pg torn......................11.00
Vinegar Bitters, 1872, 3 color cover, ads/poems/etc, G..........7.50
Western, Ed Prentiss, 1828...............................13.50
Western, Geo Perkins, 1842...............................10.00
Western, M Miller, 1845..................................11.00
Western Patriot, Chas Egelmann, 1837......................12.50
Western Patriot, Chas Egelmann, 1840, last pg gone..........11.00
Wm Lusk, magazine, 1837, edges tattered..................11.50
Yearly Messenger, 1827, corner tattered, front torn..........11.50

Almaric Walter

Almaric Walter was employed from 1904 through 1914 at Verreries Artistiques des Freres Daum in Nancy, France. After 1919, he opened his own business where he continued to make the same type of quality objects d'art in pate-de-verre glass as he had earlier. His pieces are signed A. Walter, Nancy H. Berge' Sc.

Figure of classical woman, lime green to dark green at the foot, signed, minor chip to base, 10½", $3,300.00.

Bookends, resting satyr figurals, by Descamps, rstr, 6¾".....2,200.00
Clock, arch flanked w/foliate panels, dish aside, 4¾" L......1,100.00
Dish, lg bee figural, sienna head, aqua wings, sgn, 6½" dia...1,760.00
Inkwell, pendant fruits, lg bee, 1 sloping sides, no top, 4¾"...450.00
Leaf w/moth, wht to bl, 4x3½"..........................1,750.00
Vase, Apple Pickers, red/yel/turq on ochre, ca 1925, 9½"....4,950.00

Aluminum

Aluminum, though being the most abundant metal in the earth's crust, always occurs in combination with other elements. Before a practical method for its refinement was developed in the late 19th century, articles made of aluminum were very expensive. After the process for commercial smelting was perfected in 1916, it became profitable to adapt the ductile, non-tarnishing material to many uses.

By the late thirties, novelties, trays, pitchers, and many other tableware items were being produced. They were often hand crafted with elaborate decoration. Russell Wright designed a line of lovely pieces such as lamps, vases, and desk accessories, that are becoming very collectible. Many that crafted the ware marked it with their company logo, and these signed pieces are attracting the most interest.

Bun warmer, spun aluminum, sgn Russel Wright.............95.00
Cake safe, spun aluminum, sgn Russel Wright...............75.00
Cigar tube, screw cap, Cuest Rey, Corona..................14.00
Crumb tray & scraper, ornate.............................8.50
Crumber, Farberware, hammered w/ornate leaf design..........6.00

Crumber & brush, hammered, #444, Rodney Kent............20.00
Ladle, 14"..4.50
Percolator, blk wood hdl, fluted pattern, ca 1920s, 11"........18.00
Percolator, w/basket, wood hdl, 1 cup.......................10.00
Powder box, Lalique mkd design on top, orig inside label, 3"...12.00
Relish, hexagonal, divided, fruit decor, scalloped, Cromwell......7.50
Silent butler, 5 petal flower & leaf, twist rod 10½" hdl, 5½".....8.00
Tea kettle, whistling, figural bakelite chef head stopper........12.00
Teapot, gooseneck spout, 2½ cups..........................11.50
Teapot, Wagner Ware, octagonal, w/wood hdl, 10x7" dia......23.00
Tray, allover hand crafted designs, 11½" dia.................9.50
Tray, etched tulips, hammered, w/hdls, Rodney Kent, 14x20"....22.00
Tray, fluted edge, roses, 11½" w/2¼" lip....................7.00
Tray, roses/flowers/scrolls in center, 13x6"..................5.00
Water pitcher, hammered, no decor, lg.......................8.00

Compote, beaded edges and scrolled devices on standard, marked Farberware, 4½" x 6½", $8.50.

Amberina

Amberina, one of the earliest types of art glass, was developed in 1883 by Joseph Locke, of the New England Glass Company. The trademark was registered by W.L. Libbey who often signed his name in script within the pontil.

Amberina was made by adding gold powder to the batch which produced glass in the basic amber hue. Part of the item, usually the top, was simply reheated to develop the characteristic deep red or fuchsia shading. Early amberina was mold-blown, but cut and pressed amberina was also produced. The rarest type is plated amberina, made by New England for a short time after 1886.

Other companies, among the Hobbs and Brockunier, Mt. Washington Glass Company, and Sowerby's Ellison Glassworks of England, made their own versions, being careful to change the name of their product to avoid infringing on Libbey's patent.

Basket, amber hdl, smooth flared rim, Libbey, 7½".........575.00
Bowl, ftd, Thumbprint, 3 amber ft/tri-con top, gold decor, 10"..400.00
Bowl, fuschia tones, flared collar, 5½" dia.................135.00
Bowl, swirl, fold-sided, applied amber decor...............100.00
Celery vase, scalloped top.................................110.00
Compote, Dia Quilt, crimped rim, New England, 4x7" dia.....500.00

Pitcher, frosted Hobnail, quatrefoil lip, Wheeling Glass Co., 7¼", $550.00.

Condiment, fern etched, incised t'prints, SP fr, 6 pc, 18"....2,000.00
Creamer, plated, ribbed, squatty.........................3,000.00
Creamer, Reverse Swirl....................................220.00
Cruet, Dia Quilted, 3 petal top, amber faceted stopper, NE, 6".300.00
Cruet, Reverse Thrumbprint, faceted stopper, 6¾"..........250.00
Cruet, Thumbprint, tri-con spout, amberina hdl/stopper........260.00
Parfait, plated, ribbed cylinder, New England, 4¾"........1,100.00
Parfait, ribbed, low hdl, 4¾"..............................225.00
Pitcher, Baby Thumbprint, reverse, sq w/sq applied hdl, 5"....275.00
Pitcher, Dia Quilt, amber hdl, New England, 7x4"...........325.00
Pitcher, Dia Quilt, sq bulbous, clear hdl, 8"...............225.00
Pitcher, hobstars, 4¾".....................................70.00
Pitcher, melon ribbed, plain top, amber strap hdl, trace gold...190.00
Pitcher, paneled w/applied amber hdl, 7½".................170.00
Pitcher, quatrefoil rim, dimpled, amber hdl, EX color, 4¾"....275.00
Pitcher, reversed coloring, sq top, bulbous, 7¾"............175.00
Pitcher, ribbed, sheared top, 7".........................105.00
Pitcher, swirl rib, amber hdl, polished pontil, 6½"..........300.00
Punch cup, melon ribbed, amber hdl, fuschia to amber shading.125.00
Punch cup, Optic, applied reeded amber hdl, polished pontil...145.00
Ramekin w/6" under plate, light ribbing, New England, 2x2¾".200.00
Spittoon, swirl, gold ruffled applied top, corset shape, 9x5"....380.00
Tumbler, Dia Quilt, New England, 3½".......................90.00
Tumbler, lemonade; w/hdl, Optic pattern, 4"................225.00
Tumbler, plated, New England, 3½"........................850.00
Tumbler, whiskey; Dia Quilt, New England, 2½"............150.00
Vase, lily form, 9½"......................................425.00
Vase, log, 9"..110.00
Vase, lovebirds on branch, panel effect, mc pnt floral, 8"......375.00
Vase, sq w/stork pattern, Joseph Locke, 4½"...............450.00
Vase, swirl w/gold enamel decor, 12"......................525.00
Vase, Thumbprint, disk ft, 5½"...........................135.00

American Encaustic Tiling Co.

A.E. Tile was organized in 1879 in Zanesville, Ohio. Until its closing in 1935, they produced beautiful ornamental and architectural tile equal to the best European imports. They also made vases, figurines and novelty items with exceptionally fine modeling and glazes.

Ash tray, w/frog, green glaze..............................25.00
Bookends, cherub motif...................................75.00
Bookends, cupid & rabbit, 1926, pr.......................57.50
Lamp base, glossy cobalt blue, Oriental shape, unmkd, 12", pr.175.00
Tile, bat motif, glossy gr................................85.00
Tile, floral relief, high gloss brown, well mkd, 6", M...........25.00
Tile, glossy cobalt w/4 relief wht lines, 3x6", 8 for............50.00
Tile, hdld vase w/flowers, high gloss br relief, 4 pc, 6" ea.....200.00
Tile, lady's profile in high relief, Dedication AET, 1892.......75.00
Tile, mc decor, matt crystalline glaze, 6" sq.................48.00
Tile, Pres Harding, bl, 3" sq.............................60.00
Tile, relief floral, high gloss lt gr, 4¼x6", pr..............15.00
Tile, sailboat, br/wht, artist sgn, oak fr, 15x9".............170.00
Tile, standing classical figures relief, br glaze, 18x6", pr......395.00
Vase, bl crystals/br at bottom, closed ear hdls, 6"...........50.00

Fountain tile, glossy aqua glaze, 12" x 8¼", $285.00.

American Indian Art

That time when the American Indian was free to practice the crafts and culture that was his heritage has always held a fascination for many. They were a people that appreciated beauty of design and colorful decoration in their furnishings and clothing; and because instruction in their crafts was a routine part of their rearing, they were well accomplished. Several tribes developed areas in which they excelled. The Navajo were weavers and silversmiths, the Zuni lapidaries. Examples of their craftsmanship are very valuable. Today, even the work of contemporary Indian artists -- weavers, silversmiths, carvers and others -- is highly collectible.

Apparel and Accessories

Before the white traders brought the Indian women cloth from which to sew their garments and beads to use for decorating them, clothing was made from skins sewn together with sinew, usually made of buffalo tendon. Porcupine quills were dyed bright colors and woven into bags and armbands, and used to decorate clothing and mocassins. Examples of early quillwork are scarce today and highly collectible.

Early in the 19th century, beads were being transported via pony pack trains. These 'pony' beads were irregular shapes of opaque glass imported from Venice. Nearly always blue or white, they were twice as large as the later 'seed' bead. By 1870, translucent beads in many sizes and colors had been made available, and Indian beadwork had become commercialized. Each tribe developed their own distinctive methods and preferred decorations, making it possible for collectors today to determine the origin of many items. Soon after the turn of the century the practice of beadwork began to diminish.

Arm bands, Assiniboin, hide/full bead, 8 pnt stars, 4x9"........50.00
Arm bands, Cree, rust cloth w/mc lg triangle beadings, 3" W...125.00
Arm bands, Nez Perce, full bead/6 hide thongs/brass rondels...115.00
Arm bands, Plains, full bead, wht w/bl/red/gr geometrics, pr....100.00
Arm bands, Sioux, full bead/cloth over hide, H devices, 2½x12".85.00
Arm bands, Sioux, full bead/hide, mc geometrics, 2¾x11½"...115.00
Arm bands, Sioux, full bead/hide, 2 dangles w/tin cones, 1900...75.00
Belt, Blackfeet, full bead/leather, berry/X/foliate, 1½x48"......100.00
Belt, Blackfeet, full bead/leather, opposing triangles, 34"......100.00
Belt, Blackfeet, full bead/leather, rectangular panels, 40" L...125.00
Belt, Blackfeet, full beaded cloth, mc w/wht hearts, 3½x41"....250.00
Belt, Blackfoot, beaded, Indian stars, gold diamonds, 35"......150.00
Belt, Crow, cloth covered hide/full bead, heart/flower, 4x44"...150.00
Belt, Crow, full bead/cloth, florals/foliate, 4¾x34"............265.00
Belt, Sioux, full bead, 6 stitch joined piping rows, 29".........155.00
Blanket strip, Blackfeet, beaded hide on cloth, 7½x58", EX...750.00
Blanket strip, N Cheyenne, full bead/hide, sinew sewn, 66" L...700.00
Breech clout, Flathead, bl trade cloth/church vestment.........75.00
Cap, woman's; Plains, blk cloth w/wht pipe beads, 1860, 10¾"..55.00
Collar & necktie, Crow, hide w/mc beading, 19" L, EX.........85.00
Dress, Navajo, 2 pc specialty rug, ea 22x41"................200.00
Dress, Paiute, buckskin, full bead shoulders. tassels/fringe.....800.00
Dress, Sioux, marriage/wedding, pink cloth/mc beaded yolk/cuff.350.00
Dress yoke, Nez Perce, full bead/cloth, sqs/rectangles, 6x36"...200.00
Dress yoke, Nez Perce, hide/mc beads/metal sequins/pelt 44"...600.00
Gauntlets, Cherokee, red felt w/line beadwork, heart/circle.....200.00
Hair decoration, Sioux, beaded/quilled hide, tin cones/fluffs....200.00
Headband, Plains, full bead w/15 Xs, tied at ends.............35.00
Headband, Plains, reptile w/full bead arrow motif, 1880, 18"....75.00
Headband, Prairie Indian, loom beaded, ca 1900..............40.00
Headband, Shoshoni, loom beaded, 2 rosettes, 1920..........40.00
Headband, Sioux, full bead/cloth, terraced X/stripe, 1½x24"....55.00
Headband, Sioux, hide/mc beads, X repeat decor, 1¾x24½"....35.00
Kilt, Tlingit, hide w/pnt totemic decor, 1880s, 32x14".........150.00
Leggings, Cree, cloth/beadings/metal sequins/yarn ties, 16".....135.00
Leggings, Crow, cloth/buffalo head beadings on blanket, 32"...250.00
Leggings, Kiowa, gr hide/stripe & X beadings/fringed, 12x32"..500.00
Leggings, squaw's; Arapaho, buckskin, pnt/beads, 1880s, 17"...195.00
Leggings, Umatilla, full beaded cloth/velvet/trade cloth trim.....275.00
Moccasins, Apache, 22" high top, cactus kicker toes, hide, EX.300.00
Moccasins, Blackfeet, floral beading on top/hide, 10".........85.00
Moccasins, Canadian, blk trade cloth, floral beading, 9½".....150.00
Moccasins, Central Plains, soft sole, floral beading, 1900......100.00
Moccasins, Cheyenne, partial beaded, mk Red Shield, worn.....85.00
Moccasins, child's; Cheyenne, partial bead, buckskin..........50.00
Moccasins, Comache, hard sole, beaded, well worn, 11½"....100.00
Moccasins, Cree, blk velvet w/mc floral beading, 9", EX.......225.00
Moccasins, Delaware, soft sole, flaps, beaded toes, 10"........85.00
Moccasins, full beaded, hard soles, 11½", VG..............200.00
Moccasins, Kiowa, 18" high top, beaded/fringed/silver buttons..650.00
Moccasins, Kiowa, 23" high top, gr hide/beading/silver buttons.850.00
Moccasins, Plains, hard sole, beaded, sinew sewn, 1890, 10"...135.00
Moccasins, Sioux, lazy stitch beading/bands/dia/ptd toe........200.00
Moccasins, Sioux, mc parfleche sole/quilled toe/top/bands, 11"..275.00

Necktie, Crow, full bead/hide, sq w/in 8 point star, 16" L......25.00
Panel, Flathead, beaded cloth, florals/butterflies, 16x13".......85.00
Roach, attached beaded headband, bone head, 2 feathers, old..200.00
Roach, dyed horsehair, recent.............................20.00
Roach, Sioux, N Plains, porcupine hair, 18½" L.............80.00
Roach, Sioux, porcupine hair, dyed outside, stick stand, 11½"..45.00
Roach, Sioux, porcupine hair, natural & red dyed, 11" L......45.00
Sash, loom beaded, pipe beads in wht/amber w/red cord edge...10.00
Sash, Navajo, woven, red w/blk trim, 5" fringe ea end, 72".....50.00
Serape, child's; Navajo, bl/vegetal gr/aniline pink, 1870, EX..6,500.00
Vest, Kootenai, moosehide w/beaded western decor, 1940.....200.00
Vest, man's: Plains Sioux, full bead on buckskin, 1880, lined...950.00

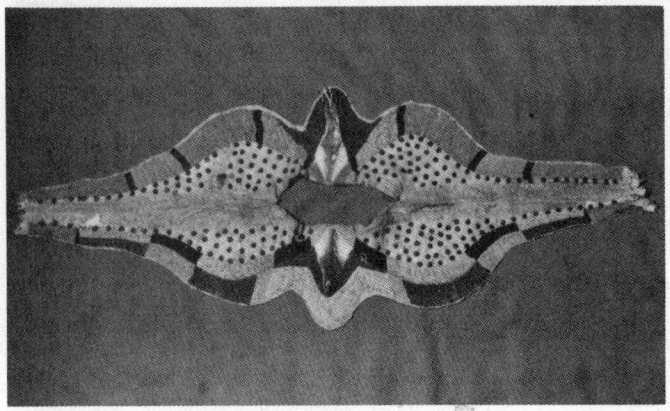

Dress yoke, beaded and sequined hide, animal pelt decor, Nez Perce tribe, ca 1870-80, 17" x 44" long, $600.00.

Arrowheads and Points

Relics of this type usually display characteristics of a general area, tribe, or a particular location. With study, those made by the Plains Indians are easily discerned from those of the West Coast. Because modern man has imitated the art of the Indian by reproducing these artifacts through modern means, use caution before investing your money in 'too good to be authentic' specimens.

Alibates flint, corner-notched, 1½".........................6.00
Antler, Mortan Co, ND, 5", EX............................16.00
Archaic, thick short stem, flint, 3½".......................12.00
Bird point, knotched, glossy flint, ¾".......................4.00
Breckenridge, br, beveled, lt serrations, Izard Co, AR, 3¾".....25.00
Clovis, Northern Plains, bifacially fluted, 3"................275.00
Clovis variant, Tennessee, glossy br flint, fluted, 3"..........165.00
Dalton, blue-gray flint, 2½".............................48.00
Dalton, serrated, eared, polished, 1¾"....................15.00
Dalton, 2¾"...55.00
Dovetail, br w/deep notches, thin base, Taylor Co, KY, 3¼"....30.00
Dovetail, St Charles, Flintridge chalcedony, 3¼"............350.00
Dovetail, tan w/speckled inclusions, well made, 3"............50.00
Duncan, Dewey Co, ND, off wht w/pink, 2⅛"..................8.00
Fluted ea side, gray/br, eared, polished sides, worn, 1¾".......35.00
Gem point, NW Coast, red agate, barbed, 1¼"..............150.00
Gem point, Rouge River, Oregon, 1⅛"....................30.00
Gem point, Texas, pebble flint, mc, 1¼".....................15.00
Hellgap type, rounded shoulders, 2¾".....................70.00
Homan, tan, deeply notched, G bars, serrated, Oregon, 1¼"....8.00
Illinois Hopewell, ovate notches, 2¾".....................35.00
Kahokia, tri-notched, serrated edge, 2"....................35.00
Kentucky, deep bevel, gray flint, sm corner notch, 2½".......35.00
Kentucky, Taylor Co, fluted ea side, gray flint/smoky quartz.....50.00

Lanceolate, stemmed; reworked tip, glossy flint, 1½".........9.00
Limestone, gray/tan, 2½"................................8.00
Mississippian, triangular, equi-sided, 1¼"................350.00
Nebo Hill, 4", EX.....................................75.00
Obsidian, California, corner-notched, 1¾"..................15.00
Paleo, gray, KY, 1¾"...................................6.00
Paleo, unfluted, tan flint, KY...........................10.00
Paleo, wht/pink, 2"...................................10.00
Perdiz, Comache Co, TX, gray, thin/serrated, 2"............50.00
Pine Tree, lt gray, lt serrations, thinned base & point, 2¾"....20.00
Rhyolite, edge damage, 2".................................1.00
Snyder, gray glossy flint, MO, EX notches, 3¼x2"...........75.00
Thebes, beveled blunt area in center, polished base, 1½".......8.00
Thebes, E-notched, slight bevel, polished base, lt gray.........90.00
Thebes, very wide base, deep notches, EX barbs, 2¾".........35.00
Trade point, iron, 1¾"...................................9.00
Trade point, iron, 3¼"..................................25.00
Trade point, metal, Upper Hidatsa Site, ND, 1830............35.00
Upper Mercer flint, wht 'lightning' lines, 2"..................6.00
War point, glossy lt gray, 2½"............................5.00
War point, triangular, Ft Ancient culture, gray, 1¾"..........2.50

Bags and Cases

The Indians used bags for many purposes and most display excellent form and workmanship. Of the types listed below, many collectors consider the pipe bag to be the most desirable form. Pipe bags were long, narrow leather and bead or quillwork creations made to hold tobacco in a compartment at the bottom and the pipe, with the bowl removed from the stem, in the top. Long buckskin fringe was used as trim, and complimented the quilled and beaded design to make the bags a masterpiece of Indian Art.

Awl, S Plains, full bead, tin cone/feather decor, 15".........265.00
Bag, Apache, full bead/hide, fringed w/flap, 6x4", EX.........400.00
Bag, Apache, hide/fringed/beaded Xs front & flap, 8½x6".....100.00
Bag, Blackfeet, beaded hide, mc/red w/wht hearts, 1885, 5x6"..135.00
Bag, Crow, full bead/cloth, mc/wht heart center/florals, 11x9"..125.00
Bag, Crow, full bead/cloth, 8 pointed star/floral, 8x6½", EX...235.00
Bag, Crow, full bead/hide, hearts/florals, pony bead hdl, 9x9"...135.00
Bag, Crow, hide & cloth/full bead/fringed, florals, 10", EX......95.00
Bag, Eastern Sioux, full bead/hide/fringe, florals, 5x6".......150.00
Bag, N Blackfeet, full bead/cloth, florals, 12x9¼"...........135.00

Bandolier bag, fully beaded on hide with stylized flowering plant, 11¾" x 10¼", $300.00.

Bag, N Blackfeet, full bead/hide/cloth, lg florals, 12x11".......175.00
Bag, Nez Perce, corn husk, pnt terrace triangle/sqs/dia, 11x9"..125.00
Bag, Nez Perce, cylinder, corn husk/mc arrows/triangles, 12x8".200.00
Bag, Nez Perce, full bead/cloth, Am flag/eagle, 11x10".......170.00
Bag, Nez Perce, full bead/cloth, 10x8¾".........155.00
Bag, Nez Perce, full beaded cloth w/elk/deer/florals, 12x15"..165.00
Bag, Nez Perce, rectangle, twined corn husk w/geometrics, 21".375.00
Bag, Nez Perce, twined husk w/grass/yarn embroidery, 22"...1,210.00
Bag, paraflesh, pnt decor, some wear, 14x25"...............45.00
Bag, paraflesh, pnt decor, 14x24", EX.....................65.00
Bag, pipe; Cheyenne, hide w/geometric beadings, 1920, 26x5"..400.00
Bag, pipe; geometrics, quill work, fringe, minor wear, 29".....225.00
Bag, pipe; Sioux, full bead/hide/geometric/quill/fringe, 29x7"...500.00
Bag, pipe; wht w/geometric beading, fringe, minor damage, 20".375.00
Bag, Shoshone, full bead/hide, sqs/triangle, 1940, 7x5"........65.00
Bag, Sioux, beaded hide/fringe/cloth, parrot/monkey decor, 11".100.00
Bag, Sioux, drawstring velvet, full bead 1 side, 11x14"........75.00
Bag, Sioux, hide/beaded ea side, mc birds/florals/etc, 14x13"...105.00
Bag, Sioux, tepee/possible, sinew sewn/beaded/quilled, 16x22"..350.00
Bag, Stony, full bead/cloth, chief/butterfly/dia, 11x10".......135.00
Bag, Stony, full bead/cloth, wolves/doe/woods, 12x11", EX....150.00
Bag, Stony, full bead/hide, wht hearts/floral/star, 7¼x5¾"....85.00
Bag, Stony, full bead/hide/fringe/cloth, bird/circle, 10½x9¾"...120.00
Bag, Stony, full beaded mc on wht cloth/hide w/fringe, 14x12".350.00
Bag, Yakima, full bead/cloth, buck/elk/florals, 13x12".......225.00
Bag, Yakima, full bead/cloth, stripes/floral on cobalt, 13x12"...175.00
Bag, Yakima, full bead/cloth w/mc florals/geometrics, 8x9"....125.00
Bag, Yakima, full beaded cloth, mc on bl, 13¾x13", EX......85.00
Bag, Yakima, string/wool, mc geometrics, corn husk style, 6"....15.00
Bandolier, Chippewa, full bead w/mc florals on wht, 1880s.....225.00
Case, Crow, pnt parfleche, ca 1890, 11x26"...............185.00
Case, Flathead, buffalo hide/pnt geometrics, 1870, 27x16".....120.00
Medicine bundle, Midi mink/cloth/beads/bells/cases w/in, 29"..450.00
Pipe, N Plains, dyed hide/beadwork bands/fringe, 17".......325.00
Pipe, Plains Sioux, fringe 3 sides/beaded bands, 1890........275.00
Pipe, Sioux, mc geometric beading w/Am flags, quill work, 33".450.00
Pouch, beaded buckskin, multicolored, 5½" L..............95.00
Pouch, Blackfeet, full bead/hide, floral/deer head, 4½".......45.00
Pouch, Crow, fringed, checkerboard beading, 6".............60.00
Pouch, full bead, quilled fringe, drops w/tin cones, feathers....310.00
Pouch, Mojave, mesh style w/beaded swastika/whirling logs, 4"...35.00
Pouch, Navajo, medicine man, hide w/68 silver buttons, strap...175.00
Pouch, Plains, beaded ea side w/leaf/flower/geometrics, 4½"...125.00
Pouch, Sioux, sinew sewn, full bead/hide, lg X on altar, 5x4"...35.00
Pouch, tobacco; Flathead, blk velvet/floral beading, 9x7".......65.00
Pouch, 1 side full bead, 1 w/multicolor beading, worn, 7".....145.00
Sheath, knife; fringed, dk & lt purple beading, w/knife.......150.00
Sheath, knife; Kiowa, mc beaded & fringed hide, w/knife, 12"..275.00
Sheath, knife; Sioux, beads/hide, La Azteca etched knife, 11"..125.00
Sheath, knife; Sioux, full bead/hide, rectangle/lines, 2x9".......50.00
Sheath, knife; Sioux, full bead/hide/tin cones, 9", w/knife......100.00
Sheath, knife; Sioux, partial bead, 1920, 7"................35.00
Sheath, knife; Sioux, pnt/fringed parfleche, geometrics, 9"......25.00
Sheath, knife; Sioux, sinew sewn/beads/tin cone/feather, knife...150.00
Tobacco pouch, Plains, fringe, 5 color geometrics, losses, 21"..175.00
Tobacco pouch, w/Strike-A-Light, front full bead, 1880s.......175.00

Baskets

Apache, multiple radiating star/flower+9 dogs at rim, 5x17"...300.00
Apache, twining, trade cloth center, 1890, 9½" dia...........75.00
Berry, vine wood coils, loop lashed narrow splints, oval/ftd.....15.00
Birch bark w/bentwood hdl & fancy lacing, 7½"+hdlx8x10"....60.00
Bowl form, simple geometrics in dk br & natural, 2¾x6" dia....55.00

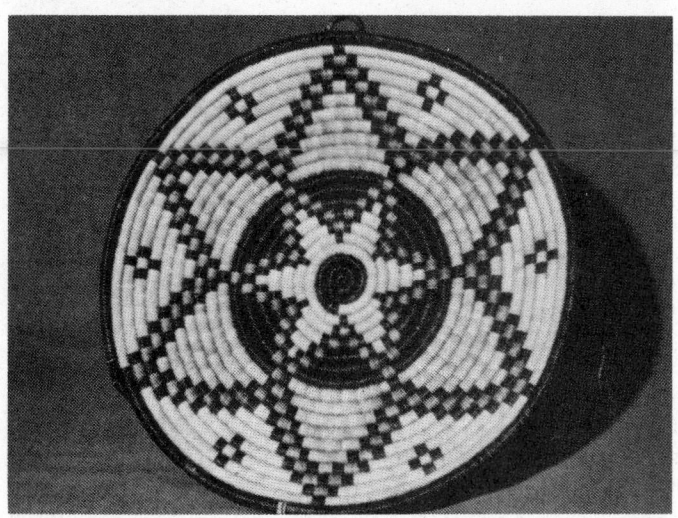

Basket, polychrome with black, white, yellow and rust in large six-pointed star, Hopi tribe, 14¾" diameter, $225.00.

CA Mission, polychrome, checkerboard at rim, 3x16"........325.00
CA Mission, tight weave/tree & wind decor/sgn, 8½".........175.00
Chemehuevi, terraced rectangle band, 1x3½".............150.00
E Indian, wrapped grass w/pine cone scales, turkey form, 11"...45.00
Flattened coil, domed lid w/finial, beaded sq decor, 8x10".....225.00
Hopi, blk/wht/yellow/rust, 6 pointed star, 14¾"...........225.00
Hopi, coiled polychrome w/lid, Mary Jane Batala, 10x10"......450.00
Hopi, plaque, blk/yellow/wht, coiled, 15½".............125.00
Hopi, plaque, coiled, mc Wedding design, 8½" dia, EX.......75.00
Hopi, woven yucca w/8 animals in br/blk, minor wear, 7x9".....90.00
Hualapai, polychrome, horizontal bands, 5¼x9½"...........75.00
Hupa, fine weave, blk/lt br/med br/natural, 5x7"...........300.00
Hupa, polychrome, fine weave, lt/dk br/naturals, 3x4½", EX...150.00
Jar, Acoma, 4 colors, 1930s, 6½x7¾", EX...............125.00
Jar, glass w/very fine woven covering & lid, 2¾"...........265.00
Jicarilla Apache, polychrome, multiple circles, 3½x10½"......125.00
Jicarilla Apache, polychrome, 4x14", EX.................400.00
Jicarilla Apache, 4 color polychrome, running W, 1900, 13x12".175.00
Kern River, 5 rows blk rectangular terraces, 4½x7¼", EX....125.00
Klamath, basketry covered pt whiskey, polychrome row decor....25.00
Klamath, boat, polychrome, rows of triangles, 5x12x13", EX...250.00
Klamath, dk br geometrics on natural, 3¾x4¾"...........25.00
Klamath, dk br/natural/red flicker quills, 2¾x4½".........45.00
Klamath, oval polychrome, porcupine quills, 2x3½x4".......35.00
Klamath, polychrome w/porcupine/flicker quills, 1900, 3½x7½".125.00
Klamath, twined 'hat', 3½x6½", EX..................125.00
Klamath, 4x10½x11½" oval, EX.....................175.00
Makah, simple geometric in red/bl, worn/faded, 2½x4½".....35.00
Makah/Nootka, covered shell, polychrome, bird/fish, 4".......35.00
Makah/Nootka, w/lid, polychrome, snake/bird/duck, 2¾x3"....60.00
Micmac, polychrome w/porcupine quills on birch bark, 5x3x6"..125.00
N Western, natural/gr reedgrass w/geometrics, snowflake on lid..60.00
Navajo, polychrome Wedding, shows use, 3x11½"...........65.00
Navajo, polychrome Wedding design, 13½" dia, EX..........95.00
NW Coast, flexible, 4 color geometrics, 4½x5".............150.00
Paiute, w/lid, polychrome, florals, 9x8½", EX.............225.00
Papago, blk vertical terraces, 5¾x5¾".................35.00
Papago, br/natural, straight sides, 4x10" dia..............35.00
Papago, br/natural design, ca 1930, minor wear, 11½".......35.00
Papago, br/natural design, flat, 11"...................35.00
Papago, gold terraced decor, 3x7", EX.................27.50
Papago, horizontal terraces, 2¾x6½", EX...............25.00
Papago, polychrome, blk/mustard/natural, 3x11¾", EX.......45.00

Papago, tray, 4 terraced designs, 2½x12½x16"............55.00
Papago, w/lid, blk terraced dia around body, 9¾x10", EX...25.00
Papago, w/lid, br/natural, 4 horses, 4"......................25.00
Papago, w/lid, diagonal rows of blk terraces, 7x8½", EX......65.00
Passamaquoddy, tight weave/bow hdls/checkerwork base, 6x10"..75.00
Penobscot, carrier, splint, dbl lid, notched hdl, 8x12x20", G....65.00
Penobscot, goose feather/ash splint, tray lid, side hdls, 28".....65.00
Penobscot, sweetgrass w/lid, polychrome/natural, 3x6¾", EX....65.00
Pima, bowl w/ft & ped, 1900, 3x6", EX.....................75.00
Pima, lg dk circle in tondo/radiating fret to rim, 5¾x16½"....275.00
Pima, polychrome, open work in geometrics, 6x11"..........175.00
Pima, storage olla, 1900, 14x12".........................350.00
Pima, thick coils w/br geometrics, reed lashed top, 8¾" dia.....60.00
Pima, 4 petal squash blossom decor, 3x13¼", EX..........300.00
Pima/Papago, w/lid, fret decor, woven of nylon thread, 2x2½"...45.00
Tukuts/Tulare, polychrome/serrated rim decor/rectangles, 6x15".200.00
Tulare/Mono, polychrome, horizontal lines, 1900, 2x5¼".......55.00
Washo, single rod split stitch, woven ped, 1900, 4x5¼".......70.00
Washo, single rod split stitch, 1900, 4x8", EX...............75.00
Washo, single rod split stitch/geometrics, 2½x4" dia..........45.00
Yavapai/Havasupai, olla w/butterfly/deer, 14x12½".........350.00

Crafts and Miscellaneous

Box, birch, florals on wht quill work, 6" dia.................50.00
Box, birch, gr leaf on wht quill work, 5" dia................45.00
Box, Navajo, w/lid, stamped silver, Knife Wing Dancer, 3"....100.00
Bronze, Montain Man, Austin Deuel, AICA, WAI, 13".......900.00
Bronze, Piegan Brave, Bob Scriver, CA, NAWA, 11x11".....1,800.00
Bronze, The Outlaw, Bob Scriver, 15"...................800.00
Canoe model, bark w/splint curlique, 1938 Pow-wow, w/paddle...10.00
Canoe model, NW Coast, figural/geometric decor, 26" L, G....750.00
Cover illus, Harper's, 1877, Sitting Bull/US Commission.......20.00
Egg tempra, Trail of Tears, Z O'Leary, Commanche, dbl mt/fr..400.00
Etching, The Mesa, Gerry Pierce, dbl matted/fr, #/sgn.........65.00
Flute, Plains, wood, 2 pc, V shape, cord & string decor.......27.50
Flute, Sioux, wood/hide fringe/pnt geometrics, 25"..........275.00
Game ball, canvas w/full beading which is incomplete, 2¼".....65.00
Horse crop, Apache, braided horsehair, dia/rattlesnake design...80.00
Ink drawing, Five Longhorns, John E Borein, matt/fr, 4½x9"...400.00
Pen & ink, Conversation, Maynard Dixon, dbl matt/fr/dt, 8x5"..400.00
Pencil drawing, Veteran, John Edward Borein, matt/fr, 9x8"....400.00
Picture frame, beads on trade cloth, shield shape, losses........18.00
Pincushion, Iroquois, rnd red cloth w/clear beads, 2¾" dia.....25.00
Print, Protected by the Spirit, Jerry Ingram, Choctaw, matt/ft...100.00
Print, Wagon & Remuda, Olaf Weighorst, sgn/#, 20x28".....300.00
Print, When Buffalo Were Plenty, c 1974, ltd ed, sgn/#........90.00
Quirt, hand woven, mc horsehair, matching strap, 16" L.......75.00
Sandpainting, Navajo, Father Sky/Mother Earth, Rosabelle Ben.150.00
Sandpainting, Navajo, still life: jars/fetish/necklace, C Nez.....100.00
Sandpainting, Navajo, Yeibichai, by Nelson Lewis, EX fr, 24"...275.00
Sandpainting, Navajo, 4 Sacred Plants/Butterflies, J&G Dick....250.00
Sandpainting, Yeibichai, Sun Verse/Corn, N Lewis, suede matt..175.00
Velvet panel, moosehair floral embroidery, Huron, early 1800s...85.00
Watercolor, buck/doe, Quincy Tahoma, Navajo, 12x10"......675.00
Watercolor, cowboy on horse, distant mtns, Wm T Zivic, 6x5"..40.00
Watercolor, Old Brave, Bert Seabourn, Cherokee, 8x14"......275.00
Wood carving, Navajo, Arrow Maker, Tom W Yazzie, 5¼x3½".100.00

Dolls

Doll, Kiowa, w/cradle, heavy bead hood, carved head/HP, EX....85.00
Female, Navajo, blk velvet dress w/mc beaded 'jewelry', 11½"...40.00
Female, Sioux, buckskin dress/mocs w/beading, yarn hair, 13½".90.00

Female, Skookum, w/infant, wool blanket/hair wigs, 11¼"......45.00
Female, w/infant, wood/cb/cloth/fibre hair, sgn Woods, 12"....45.00
Kachina, Hopi, Antelope/Deer, 15".......................175.00
Kachina, Hopi, Badger, 3rd Mesa type, 18¾"...............100.00
Kachina, Hopi, Big Head, 1st or 2nd Mesa type, 7".........200.00
Kachina, Hopi, Black Ogre, 17½"........................150.00
Kachina, Hopi, Butterfly Girl, (Palhik' Mana), 19".........175.00
Kachina, Hopi, Clown, by Cal Yestewa, corn husk horns, 9"...120.00
Kachina, Hopi, Cross Legged (Huhuwa), 9½"................40.00
Kachina, Hopi, Flower/Throwing Stick Man, 14½"............70.00
Kachina, Hopi, Hano Clown (Koshare), seated, 6¼"..........35.00
Kachina, Hopi, Havasupai (Konin), Third Messa, 14".........75.00
Kachina, Hopi, Hopi Cloud Man, 12"......................95.00
Kachina, Hopi, Kokopelli, well sculpted, sgn, 18".........300.00
Kachina, Hopi, Ogre Woman, 11¾".......................35.00
Kachina, Hopi, Owl, 28".................................250.00
Kachina, Hopi, Snake Dancers, 14½", pr..................300.00
Kachina, Hopi, Squash (Patung), 15".......................75.00
Kachina, Hopi, Wolf (Kweo), 10½".......................125.00
Kachina, Hopi, X-legged, AKA Bluebird Snare, 9½"...........25.00
Kachina, Hopi, Zuni (Sio), older, 18"....................200.00
Kachina, Hopi, Zuni Rain Priest of the North, 17"...........85.00
Kachina, Hopi, Zuni Warrior (Sip-Ikne), 17½".............150.00
Male, Sioux, hide w/cloth clothing, beaded decor, 14", EX......90.00
Pr, Paiute, hide/beaded & fringed/buckskin clothing, ea 11¾"..150.00
Pr, Sioux, hide w/buckskin/bead/fringed dress/mocs, ea 13½"...175.00

Kachina doll with 12½" diameter face mask of Tawa (Sun),
Hopi tribe, 21½" tall, $150.00.

Domestics

Bowl, Gila-Tonto/Salado, stone, 2½x5½x6½".............22.50
Cradle board, Apache, hand carved slats, sun shade, twill, 27"..130.00
Cradle board, N Ute, wicker hood/hide lace up/fringe, 28x13"..225.00
Cradle board, Nez Perce, bent bough sun shade, beaded, 1940.130.00
Cradle board, San Carlos Apache, hood/beaded hide/cloth/wood.250.00
Cradle cover, Cheyenne, full bead/hide/fringed, 1880s, 28" L...800.00
Cradle cover, Cree, cloth w/mc & metallic beads, 19" L, M....725.00
Hairpin, bone, curved/notched, 3".........................15.00
Mortar & pestle, Gila-Tonto/Salado, stone, ball pestle, 2½x6"...20.00
Paint cup, tan stone................................10.00
Spoon, blk buffalo horn................................35.00
Spoon, mountain sheep horn, 12"........................10.00
Thimble holder, natural/gr sweetgrass, loop lid finial, 1x3¾"...850.00

Cradle cover, cloth beaded in nine colors, metallic cut beads, florals on black velvet, Cree tribe, in pristine condition, 19" long, $725.00.

Jewelry

As early as 500 A.D., Indians in the Southwest drilled turquoise nuggets and strung them on cords made of sinew or braided hair. The Spanish introduced them to coral and it became a popular item of jewelry; abalone and clam shells were favored by the Coastal Indians. Not until the last half of the 19th century did the Indians learn to work with silver. Each tribe developed their own distinctive style and preferred design, which until about 1920 made it possible to determine tribal origin with some degree of accuracy. Since that time, because of modern means of communication and travel, motifs have become less distinct.

Quality Indian silver jewelry may be antique or contemporary -- age, though certainly to be considered, is not as important a factor as fine workmanship and good stones. Pre-1910 silver will show evidence of hammer marks, and designs are usually simple. Beads have sometimes been shaped from coins; stones tend to be small, and when silver wire was used, it is usually square. To insure your investment, choose a reputable dealer.

Bead, shell, rectangular, Florida..........................15.00
Belt, Kiowa, 3" leather w/11 nickle silver conchos ea 2½".....225.00
Belt, Navajo, link style button conchos, 27"................175.00
Belt, Zuni, concho w/9 mc inlaid 2½" rnds/buckle, Natachu..1,000.00
Bow guard, Navajo, tufa/sand cast openwork silver/leather band.175.00
Bracelet, Navajo, chisel split shank, stamped, 1x3/4" turq cab..105.00
Bracelet, Navajo, chisel split shank/stamped, sm Blue Gem turq..45.00
Bracelet, Navajo, hand stamped, ¾" L triangle turq cab.......105.00
Bracelet, Navajo, hand stamped, ¾x1½" crescent gr turq cab...85.00
Bracelet, Navajo, hand stamped w/18 lg/sm Royston cabs, sgn..150.00
Bracelet, Navajo, hand stamped w/5 sq turq cabs, ¾" W......100.00
Bracelet, Navajo, tufa/sand cast, sm rectangle bl turq, 1930s.....90.00
Bracelet, Navajo, twisted, ½ rnd bead, wire shank, 3 sm turq....75.00
Bracelet, Navajo, ½ rnd/twist wire shank, lg turq cab.........125.00

Bracelet, Navajo, 2 rows of 9 ea oval red coral cabs.........115.00
Bracelet, trade; copper, Ft Berthold, ND, rstr...............25.00
Bracelet, Zuni, mc inlaid 2x1½" Mudhead, sgn ARP, NM.....210.00
Bracelet, Zuni, old pawn cluster, 139 lg/med shaped turq.....325.00
Bracelet, Zuni, petit point, 98 shaped turq.................150.00
Bracelet/ring, Navajo, ea w/lg trapezoid turq cab w/cut lines....115.00
Bracelet/ring, Navajo, total of 8 coral cabs.................150.00
Buckle, Shoshone, deer/elk decor in mc on blue beads, 3x4½"..25.00
Buckle, Zuni, stamped Knife Wing Dancer+turq cab, 1½x2½"..75.00
Earrings, Zuni, mc inlay Knife Wing Dancer..................95.00
Earrings, Zuni, mc inlay Sun Face w/12 petit point turq.......45.00
Earrings, Zuni, petit point, 10 turq in floral design...........30.00
Earrings, Zuni, petit point, 23 turq, wagon wheel.............100.00
Earrings, Zuni, stars w/turq/jet/MOP/shell inlay, 1930s.........45.00
Earrings, Zuni, thunderbirds, channel inlay/turq, 1930s........70.00
Earrings, Zuni, 6 turq in ½ rnd cluster w/10 in ea dangle......65.00
Hat band, Navajo, hand stamped silver w/4 oval turq cabs......75.00
Hat band, Navajo, ½" w/hand stamping, 4 turq cabs.........100.00
Hat band, 14 sm hand stamped conchos....................30.00
Necklace, Bisbee graduated rnd disks/silver beads, 20k, 20"....175.00
Necklace, disk/barrel turq beads w/silver beads/clasps, 800k....200.00
Necklace, N Plains, dance bandolier, pony beads/cowrie shell....25.00
Necklace, Navajo, liberty head dime beads, 23"..............250.00
Necklace, Navajo, 3 lg Blue Gem turq cab pendants...........75.00
Necklace, Navajo, 3 oval turq cab pendants on silver chain......80.00
Necklace, Navajo, 8 bird beaks ea 1" to 2½" w/seed beads.....50.00
Necklace, Pueblo, 20 strands silver tubes; 3 strand earrings....100.00
Necklace, Santo Domingo, 32" strand turq beads/5 silver beads.385.00
Necklace, Sioux, dance bandolier, 24 hairpipe bone beads/hide.375.00
Necklace, Spider Mt hand cut & drilled beads, 1000+k.......250.00
Necklace, Zuni, mc wire wrap fetish on shell heshi..........125.00
Necklace, 2 strand tortoise/turq heshi+42 fetish, John Sheeka..300.00
Necklace, 43 nuggets strung w/shell heshi, 13".............175.00
Pendant, Cheyenne, loom beaded, flags/eagle, 1920...........20.00
Pin, Zuni, etched jet/MOP inlay, horse head, 1930s...........30.00
Pin, Zuni, Indian w/etched features, hand stamping, mc inlay....90.00
Pin, Zuni, 45 Persian turq in cluster, 1950s.................65.00
Ring, Navajo, 1" triangular turq cab.......................55.00
Ring, Navajo, 1 lg rnd bl turq cab, almost 1" dia.............60.00
Ring, Navajo, ½" oval Spider Mt turq cab, 1930s............75.00
Ring, Navajo, ½x¾" oval #8 spiderweb cab.................65.00

Cross, trade silver, engraved with initials, late 1700s, 3", value in excellent condition: $450.00.

Squash blossom, Hopi, 6 ea side, w/naja, Taylor............250.00
Squash blossom, Navajo, 2-strand/16 blossoms/3 Morenci turq..715.00
Squash blossom, Navajo, '40s ½ dollars/liberty head dime, 24".150.00
Squash blossom, Navajo, liberty head dollars/dimes/naja w/turq..165.00
Squash blossom, Navajo, 16 w/naja ea w/turq cab, 2-row beads..200.00
Squash blossom, Navajo, 24 fluted beads, twist wire naja......350.00
Squash blossom/earrings, 6 ea side/naja w/200 petit point turq..350.00
Trade bead, faceted, elongated, High Plains, 2¾"............12.00
Trade bead, Star Chevron, High Plains, 1800s...............14.00
Trade beads, bl/wht/gr/yellow/red/blk glass, 1700s, 28" L.......65.00
Trade silver, cross, engraved, initials, late 1700s, 3½", M.....450.00
Watch bracelet, man's; Navajo, multiple leaf/turq cab ea side....50.00

Knives and Chipped Blades

The knife was an indispensable tool to the Indian whether he was in battle, hunting game, or doing chores at the campsite. Before the white man's metal blades, all were made of chiseled bone or stone. Knife cases, fashioned of leather with intricate decorations of quilling or beadwork, were first worn suspended from the neck, and later attached to the belt.

Awl blade, metal, Upper Hidatsa Site, ND, 1830.............12.50
Bison skinner, Texas, 4¼", VG.........................65.00
Blade, bison; gray, well made, thin, Bell Co, TX, 4"..........30.00
Blade, blk flint, Ohio, 5x2".............................30.00
Blade, burrial; wide w/thin hdl, dk gray, TN, 6"............100.00
Blade, cache; Hopewell, red, oval, 4¼x3¼"................60.00
Blade, cache; ovate Adena, translucent, mc, 4¾"...........475.00
Blade, deeply beveled, round base, 5"....................60.00
Blade, draw; gray w/blue flint.........................10.00
Blade, flesher; metal, Ft Union, ND, 1830.................20.00
Blade, fracture chipped baseline, sharp tip, glossy, 2¾"......100.00
Blade, glossy gray/blue/crystals, beveled, flute-like strikes.......20.00
Blade, gray/tan/red, slight bevel, KY, 3¾"................25.00
Blade, Meadowwood, mottled chert, triangular outline, 3¼".....55.00
Blade, Paleo uniface, incurvate edge, dk flint, 3"............7.00
Blade, red w/blue flint, serrated/beveled/notched ⅓ way, 5¼"...85.00
Blade, serrated Kinney, TX, 3¾".......................55.00
Blade, sheet chalcendony, stemmed, colorful, 6¼".........90.00
Blade, skinning; curved, gray flint, IN, 4½".............20.00
Blade, skinning; gray flint, KY, 5"......................12.50
Blade, stemmed, br chert, shouldered, 3"..................7.00
Blade, stemmed Archaic-era, EX chipping, ground base, 3".....35.00
Cactus/Mescal blade, stone, 5x8¼"....................45.00
Chert, Dalton, yellow w/red, flaring ears, deep base, taper......18.00
Knife, corner tang, Texas dk flint, 6"...................750.00
Knife, gray flint, thin, 6x2½".........................25.00
Knife, gray stone, 4¼x1½"...........................20.00
Knife, gray/tan, Pike Co, AR, 2¼", EX.................12.00
Knife, lt tan stone, Columbia River, WA, 1¼"..............4.00
Knife, obsidian, Oregon's Glass Buttes, side-notched, 3".......85.00
Knife, obsidian, 4½x2".............................20.00
Knife, red flint, from MO, 3½"........................2.50
Knife, Star Co, gray, 3⅛"...........................30.00
Knife, 1 curved, 1 straight edge, striated flint, 4"............18.00

Pipes and Ceremonial Items

Pipe bowls were usually carved from soft stone, such as catlinite or pipestone, an argilaceous sedimentary rock composed mainly of clay. Granite was also used. Some ceremonial pipes were simply styled, while others were intricately designed naturalistic figurals, sometimes in bird or frog forms, called effigies. Their stems, made of wood and often covered with leather, were sometimes nearly a yard in length.

Bannerstone, ball; br w/blk bands, OH, 2nd hole underneath...200.00
Bannerstone, banded slate, IN, 4½"....................150.00
Bannerstone, crescent, polished gray hardstone.............180.00
Bannerstone, dbl notched, gray, 2¾" miniature.............135.00
Bannerstone, expanded center, good banding, IN...........200.00
Bannerstone, geniculate band slate, elongated hole, IN.......100.00
Bannerstone, pick; banded, 3½".......................150.00
Bannerstone, polished, tally mks ea end, 1½".............65.00
Bannerstone, slate w/slight banding, MI, 4¼".............50.00
Bannerstone, tube; br/blk banded slate, 4".................200.00
Bannerstone, tube; br/blk bands, polished, wide hole, 2½".....125.00
Birdstone, quartzite, drilled, MI......................50.00
Ceremonial set, Navajo, 10 Yeibichai dancers, wood, T Yazzie..600.00
Charm, Tlingit, carved ivory fish, 1880, 2x½"..............300.00
Dance bells, Ft Berthold, ND, ca 1820, pr.................20.00
Dance bustle, Sioux, butterfly type, w/feathers, 1900.........185.00
Dance club, Sioux, miniature skull cracker, 1920............20.00
Drum, Sioux, gut cover, pnt stick man decor in red..........200.00
Drum, wood w/rawhide heads, vine & rope construction, 8x16"..20.00
Fetish, Sioux, turtle, hide/beads/fringe/brass bell, 7½".........300.00
Fetish, turtle, hide/full beaded, 1880s, 2½x3".............95.00
Gorget, Adena Keel, humped, flat underneath, hardstone, 3¾".135.00
Gorget, bi-concave, OH, 3¼", EX.....................115.00
Gorget, indented, red slate, OH, 5¼", EX................250.00
Gorget, quadra-concave, OH, 3½"....................150.00
Gorget, 2 holes, 3".................................40.00
Mask, NW Coast, abalone inlay on beak, +5 hair tufts, 13"..1,850.00
Pendant, anchor, 1 drilled hole, OH, thick, 4¼", EX.........200.00
Pendant, bell shaped, banded, OH, 5¼", EX..............200.00
Pendant, gr/red slate, 4¾".............................85.00
Pendant, greenish w/blk bands, lg hole, OH, 4¼", EX.......125.00
Pendant, KY, good hole, 3½"..........................65.00

Platform pipe, made of slate, 6¾" long, $900.00.

Pipe, Arapaho, catlinite/pipestone/bead stem/brass tacks, 27"...250.00
Pipe, catlinite, from Barron Co WI, 1½x3"................200.00
Pipe, catlinite, from SD, very early, 3½" L................200.00
Pipe, catlinite, tubular, 3½" L........................200.00
Pipe, catlinite, 1½x3"..............................200.00
Pipe, Cherokee, blk steatite, 1700s, 2¼x3"...............175.00
Pipe, Chippewa, stone, pewter inlay, nude male stem, 2½".....150.00
Pipe, clay, early, historic, from VA....................15.00
Pipe, elbow, sandstone, no polish, OH, 2¼"..............85.00
Pipe, man's face effigy, stone, KY, 5½"..................350.00
Pipe, nude female in sitting position, steatite, 1650s, 4½".....500.00
Pipe, Ojibwa/Chippewa, T bowl w/heart/sq inlay, puzzle stem...450.00
Pipe, sandstone, polished, very early, OH, 3¼" L............100.00
Pipe, Sioux, Dakota, catlinite, carved florals, pierced stem.....205.00

Pipe, Sioux, T bowl, blk w/lead/pewter inlay, 7½x3½" 400.00
Pipe, trade, VA, ca 1700s, wht clay 8.00
Pipe, trade axe, brass w/wood hdl w/brass studs, 16" 225.00
Pipe, tubular, blk steatite, middle etched, tally mks, 7½" 500.00
Pipe, tubular, drilled stem hole, polished hardstone, tally mk . . . 200.00
Pipe, wood stem w/hide wrap, hardstone Indian face bowl 750.00
Pipe bowl, Sioux, L shape, pipestone/catlinite, 2½x3" 45.00
Pipe-tomahawk, N Plains, 7" steel head w/17" tiger maple hdl . . 275.00
Pipe-tomahawk, pewter inlaid w/catlinite, 8¼" 700.00
Rattle, Plains, wood hdl, buffalo horn top/brass nails, 11" 60.00
Rattle, Seminole, gourd w/shaped wood hdl, 1885, 10" 60.00
Spoon, Sioux, cow horn, beaded 55.00
Tobacco canteen, Kiowa, nickle silver w/etched deer, 3½x2½" . . 500.04
War club, Sioux, stone club head, fringed hide/horsehair/beads . 250.00

Pottery

Indian pottery nearly always is decorated in such a manner as to indicate the tribe who produced it or the pueblo in which it was made. For instance, the designs of Cochite potters were usually scattered forms from nature or sacred symbols. The Zuni preferred an ornate repetitive decoration of a closer configuration. They often used stylized deer and bird forms, sometimes in dimensional applications.

The pottery of the San Ildefonso pueblo is especially sought after by collectors today. Under the leadership of Maria Martinez and her husband Julian, experiments began about 1918 which led to the developement of the 'black on black' design achieved through exacting methods of firing the ware. They discovered that by smothering the fire at an exact temperature, the carbon in the smoke that ensued caused the pottery to become blackened. Maria signed her work from 1923 through 1926. Today a piece with her signature may bring prices in the $200 to $300 range.

Bear, Santa Clara, sgn Pula Gutierrez, 2⅛x3½" 65.00
Bowl, Acoma, polychrome, 1940s, 5¼x8" 65.00
Bowl, Chaco, blk/wht terraced lines/geometric, 950 AD, 4x8", G . 85.00
Bowl, Gila, red, w/blk on wht w/in, geometrics, 1300 AD, 7" . . . 150.00
Bowl, Gila-Tonto/Salado, plainware, 1200 AD, 3½x7½", EX 25.00
Bowl, Homolovi (Hopi), mc decor w/in w/out, rpr, 5x10" 150.00
Bowl, Hopi, buff w/wht slip, red base, blk decor, 4½x9" 85.00
Bowl, Hopi, mc Anasazi decor/tan slip, Duwakuku, 2½x5" dia . . 100.00
Bowl, Jeddito/Hopi, yellow/br/blk lines/geometrics, 3x6", rstr . . . 45.00
Bowl, Keyenta, blk on wht, 1200 AD, rpr/rst, 4¼x7½" 55.00
Bowl, Mesa Verde, blk on wht, lg dia/linear, 1150 AD, 8½", rpr . 35.00
Bowl, Mimbres, blk/wht, kill hole/crack, 1000 AD, 5x9½" 750.00
Bowl, Mimbres, dk br on wht, 1000 AD, prof rpr/rst, 5x10½" . . . 250.00
Bowl, Puerco, blk/red, fine line/terraces/dia, 950 AD, 4x8", G . . 85.00
Bowl, Reserve, blk on wht w/12 rows zigzags, 950 AD, 6x7x8" . . 125.00
Bowl, San Ildefonso, polychrome, sgn Blue Corn, 2x2¾" 250.00
Bowl, Santa Clara, redware w/incised decor, sgn T Naranjo, 6" . 350.00
Bowl, Santa Domingo, buff/orange mottle, red/blk decor, 7x10" . 85.00
Bowl, Sikyatki, polychrome, cross/feather/horn, 1400 AD, 4x9" . 250.00
Bowl, Tonto, blk/wht/rust bottom, geometrics, 1400 AD, 5x8", G 75.00
Bowl, Tonto/Salado, fingernail design/plainware, 1400 AD, 9" . . 35.00
Bowl, Tonto/Salado, thumbnail decor plainware, 1200 AD, 3x7" . 20.00
Bowl, Tusayan, blk on wht, 1100-1300 AD, 3¾x7½", EX 75.00
Bowl, Tusayan, blk/wht, rpr/rst, 4x6¾" 85.00
Bowl, Verde Valley, plainware, 1200 AD, 1 age crack, 5x9" 55.00
Bowl, Verde Valley/S Sinagua, plainware, 1200 AD, 4x10½", EX . 35.00
Bowl, Zia, br/sienna on buff, bird/foliate/florals, Lucero, 7" 65.00
Bowl, Zuni, buff w/red/wht slip, blk decor, w/hairline, 4x7" 45.00
Effigy jar, Santa Clara, mc/turtle head, Margaret/Luther, 5" . . . 250.00
Jar, Acoma, polychrome, intricate designs, 1930s, 10x12" 200.00
Jar, Acoma, polychrome, sgn R Aragon, 7x8½" 175.00
Jar, Chaco, blk/wht seed w/fine line fret/etc, 950 AD, 7x10½" . . 225.00

Jar, Gila-Tonto/Salado, plainware, 1200 AD, 5½x6", EX 25.00
Jar, Santa Clara, polychrome, water snake, Margaret/Luther, 2" . . 55.00
Jar, Santa Clara, rare sienna w/incising, Margaret Tafoya, 8" . . 1,600.00
Jar, Santa Clara, water serpent/geometric, Margaret/Luther, 5" . . 500.00
Jar, Santo Domingo, blk on creme w/orange bottom, 7x8" 175.00
Jar, South Western, red clay w/wht slip, red/blk decor, 4" 25.00
Jar, Tonto, blk on wht on red geometrics, 1400 AD, 4x6", rpr . . 50.00
Jar, Tonto, polychrome w/geometric & linear decor, 5x6½", G . 100.00
Jar, Tonto/Salado, plainware, 1200 AD, 4½x5", EX 35.00
Jar, Tularosa, blk on wht, 1100 AD, 5x5", EX 195.00
Jar, Zia, long neck, 4 color birds/floral/etc, E Medina, 8x7" . . . 150.00
Jar, Zia, mc, 4 male/female dancers, JD Medina, 12x10" 325.00

Jar, unusual sienna color with incised designs, Santa Clara, signed Margaret Tofoya, in pristine condition, 7¾" x 7½", $1,600.00.

Olla, Jeddito, blk on yellow/terraced keys, 1325 AD, 9x11", G . . 175.00
Olla, Tonto, blk/wht/rust, terraces/geometrics, 1400, 7x9", G . . . 150.00
Olla, Tularosa, blk/wht, swirl/terrace/etc, 1100 AD, 9x11" 450.00
Pitcher, Chaco, blk on wht, rows triangles/dots/lines, 2½" 50.00
Pitcher, Reserve, blk/wht, Greek Key maze/triangles, 3½", rpr . . 45.00
Pitcher, Reserve, blk/wht, tri-lobe bottom, 950 AD, 4", EX 225.00
Pitcher, Tularosa, blk/wht, 1100 AD, 3½" 155.00
Pitcher, Tularosa, blk/wht, 1100 AD, 5¾x6" 225.00
Pot, effigy; South Eastern, red clay bird, tail damaged, 5x8" 15.00
Pot, figural; Casa Grande, buff w/red/blk, 6½" 25.00
Pot, figural; Casa Grande, buff w/red/blk decor, 7¾", G 30.00
Pot, San Ildefonso, sgn Marie & Julian, 3½x5", VG 150.00
Rabbit, Santa Clara, blackware, 3" 40.00
Vase, Santo Domingo, wht w/blk & sienna decor, fire mks, 5" . . . 75.00

Tools

Awl, bone, 4¼" 20.00
Awl, trigger; polished, 6" 45.00
Awl sharpener, for bone awls, stone, 6" L 25.00
Axe, blk, ¾ grooved, 4½ lb, 7" 50.00
Axe, dk gray stone, grooved, 5 lb 50.00
Axe, Gila-Tonto/Salado, stone, prehistoric, 3x5" L 15.00
Axe, gray, polished, 8¼ lbs, 9x6" 500.00
Axe, polished granite, grooved, 3½ lb 150.00
Axe, S Indian, prehistoric, stone, 2½x3¾" 15.00
Axe, speckled stone, ¾ grooved, 6" 185.00
Axe, 6 lbs, 8" 150.00

Celt, blk, EX polish & shape, Columbia River, WA, 3½"......25.00
Celt, granite, Ohio, 3 lb..................35.00
Celt, gray, round base, MO, 3½ lbs, 8"................100.00
Celt, KY gray flint, 3 lbs, 9"..................85.00
Celt, Pike Co, AK, good bit, 5"..................30.00
Celt, polished, 9"..................150.00
Drill, br stone, 2½"..................12.00
Drill, chipped, blk obsidian, pin-shaped, 2"..................30.00
Drill, chipped, hafted base, reworked point, 2¼"..................35.00
Drill, chipped, T-base, straight, narrow shaft, 2"..................20.00
Drill, Dalton, gray, 3½"..................45.00
Drill, Flint Ridge, Ohio, 2½"..................10.00
Drill, notched, black, Columbia River area, Oregon, 1¾".......8.00
Drill, notched base, Benton Co, TN, gray/tan, 3¼"..................20.00
Drill, oval base, gray, Jasper Co, IN, 2"..................7.00
Drill, oval base, gray/tan, Jackson Co, AR, 3⅛"..................12.00
Drill, pin; dk gray, 2¾"..................8.00
Drill, pipe; gray/tan stone, 2"..................12.00
Drill, wide mid-section, long taper, 3½"..................15.00
Engraver, gray stone, 2"..................8.00
Gouge, bone, polished, 4"..................18.00
Gouge, bone, suspension hole, 7"..................40.00
Gunflint, historic Indiana site, reworked French honey flint......4.00
Hammer/maul, stone, nicely grooved, 3½x3¾"..................12.50
Needle, bone, polished, 3¼", EX..................35.00
Needle, bone, polished, 6½"..................50.00
Plummet, hematite, grooved..................40.00
Scraper, hafted; blk..................4.50
Scraper, snub-nose w/side-edge graver spur, 1¼"..................3.00
Scraper, split bone; Mortan Co, ND, 5½" L..................45.00
Side-scraper, chipped, glossy flint, working edge 1¼".........2.00
Spade, no polish, IL, 8½"..................25.00
Spade, tan, polished, flared, 8"..................200.00
Spade, tan, polished, oval, KY, 10"..................200.00
Trade axe, mk DS, rpl wood hdl, 8" blade..................45.00

Weapons

Lance, white flint, thin, 4"..................20.00
Skull cracker, grooved, round, 3 lb..................15.00
Skull crusher, full bead leather wrap wood hdl, horsehair trim...20.00
Skull crusher, Plains, beaded & pnt designs, 17"..................25.00
Spear, Adena, mottled gray flint, Ohio, 4"..................25.00
Spear, Adena, rnd shoulders, grays, 5"..................65.00
Spear, Adena, wht stem, W VA, heavy..................25.00
Spear, Agate Basin, Greene Co, MO, 3¾"..................75.00
Spear, blk stone, Ohio, 4½", VG..................25.00
Spear, br w/red, TN, 5x1¾"..................75.00
Spear, buffalo; gray flint, full base, 5"..................25.00

Spear, dovetailed, Ohio area, flintridge material, 5" long, $1,100.00.

Spear, Dalton, Sevier Co, AR, 5"..................125.00
Spear, deep notch, dk gray, KY, 3¼" L..................90.00
Spear, Dover flint, rounded base, thick/heavy, 5"..................25.00
Spear, Flint Ridge, crystals/tan/wht/bl/gray, 4"..................35.00
Spear, giant Etley, orange, MO, 6", G..................40.00
Spear, gray w/red streaks, lg notches, TN, 5"..................75.00
Spear, gray/fossils, extra, thin/translucent, 4"..................60.00
Spear, Holland, lt tan, 4", EX..................150.00
Spear, Johnson, 3"..................35.00
Spear, Montell, Texas gray flint, corner notch, 4¾"..................100.00
Spear, Paleo, even ears, wht/gray, 4½"..................50.00
Spear, Paleo, Sedalia flaring type, thick, 4¾"..................50.00
Spear, pink, 3x2"..................30.00
Spear, pink KY flint, lg ears, 4¾"..................42.00
Spear, purple w/fossils, stemmed, 4"..................40.00
Spear, Texas gray flint, 5½", EX..................85.00
Spear, white flint, Pope Co, Ill, 3"..................10.00
Tomahawk, grooved gray stone..................25.00

Weaving

Blanket, Chimayo, lt bl w/geometrics & arrows, 45x68".......105.00
Blanket, Navajo, eyedazzler, ca 1890s, 49x88", EX........1,500.00
Blanket, Navajo, Germantown eyedazzler, 1890, 77".......1,950.00
Blanket, Navajo, 3rd Phase Chief's, Germantown, 77" sq, EX.1,750.00
Blanket, saddle; Navajo, wht w/5 color stripes/arrows, 28x57"....55.00
Blanket, South West, figure w/pole/Greek Key/stripes, 28x62"..100.00
Blanket/rug, Navajo, lg X/dia, transitional, 1900, 48x68", EX...375.00
Blanket/rug, Navajo, Old Chief's 9 Spot 3 Phases, 50x67".....750.00
Blanket/rug, Navajo, transitional, wavy lines/dia, 51x68".......300.00
Mat, Huron, wild hemp/vegetal dye, pre 1900, 15x24".........40.00
Rug, Chimayo, dk bl/red w/medallion in wht/blk/orange, 52x74".150.00
Rug, Navaho, br/tan/gray/wht geometrics, very worn, 10x13 ft.1,250.00
Rug, Navajo, blue w/wht/rust, 7 panels ea w/2 diamonds, 19x31".50.00
Rug, Navajo, br w/2 terraced dia in wht/red, 1930, 17x37".....75.00
Rug, Navajo, Central Reservation, joined X/terrace, 37x54"....200.00
Rug, Navajo, Central Reservation, lg terrace dia, '60s, 45x58"..200.00
Rug, Navajo, chinle, repeated arrows w/in bands, 31x61"......150.00
Rug, Navajo, Coal Mine Mesa/Storm, Mary Yazzie, 35x58"....350.00
Rug, Navajo, crystal, banded & arrowhead design, 21x30"......45.00
Rug, Navajo, crystal, 2 rows terrace Xs, hour glass, 1955, 99"..800.00
Rug, Navajo, crystal/chinle, terraced bands w/diamonds, 28x48".325.00
Rug, Navajo, dbl Yei deities/cornstalk, Louise Randall, 21x27"..105.00
Rug, Navajo, East Reservation vegetal dye, bands/dia, 19x39"...45.00
Rug, Navajo, Fox Dance Yeibichai by Julia John, 36x62", EX..500.00
Rug, Navajo, gray/wht/dk br/tan geometrics, 50x82".........450.00
Rug, Navajo, Klagetoh, lg terraced dia/sq blocks, 46x68", EX..275.00
Rug, Navajo, Klagetoh/N Central, blk/br/red/gray/wht, 55x96"...600.00
Rug, Navajo, life on reservation pictorial, Nellie Lee, 27x47"...300.00
Rug, Navajo, Lukachukai Yei+7 deities+Rainbow God, 39x69"..300.00
Rug, Navajo, mc wide/thin bands, Caroline Thompson, 19x40"..30.00
Rug, Navajo, N Central Reservation, serrated dia, 60x40".....275.00
Rug, Navajo, natural wools, terrace dia/X decor, 1920, 40x67"..250.00
Rug, Navajo, NE Reservation, lg serrated dia w/T/swastika, 58".350.00
Rug, Navajo, NE Reservation, 2 panels w/serrated dia, 55x83"..500.00
Rug, Navajo, optical decor in rust/tan/wht, 16x24"............30.00
Rug, Navajo, outlined Coal Mine Mesa, Sue Preston, 15x36"....95.00
Rug, Navajo, overall sawtooth, red has bled, 1930, 38x57"....175.00
Rug, Navajo, pictorial w/Yei figures & birds, ca 1920, 39x76"..400.00
Rug, Navajo, Red Mesa, umber w/7 rows of 3 dia 33x43".....240.00
Rug, Navajo, red/gray/br/wht, 5 rectangles w/dia w/in, 30x44"..95.00
Rug, Navajo, serrated bands red w/br ea side, 1910, 36x57"..215.00
Rug, Navajo, single figure Yei/pictorial, 45x66"..................375.00
Rug, Navajo, Storm pattern, wool/vegetal/aniline dye, 50x76"..400.00

Rug, Navajo, tan w/2 prominent terraced/serrated bands, 16x14"..50.00
Rug, Navajo, Teec-Nos-Pos, bands/propellers/dia/triangle, 78"...450.00
Rug, Navajo, Teec-Nos-Pos, saddle/eyedazzler/tassels, 34x29"...175.00
Rug, Navajo, transitional period NE Reservation, 1900, 32x58"..150.00
Rug, Navajo, wht w/red dashes, br/gray corners, 1900, 25x28"..200.00
Rug, Navajo, wht w/simple blk/gray decor, 1955, 30x32".......70.00
Rug, Navajo, wht/gray/blk/red stripes, squares, worn, 44x57"...500.00
Rug, Navajo, Wide Ruins, wool/bands/terraced X, 38x61".....300.00
Rug, Navajo, Wide Ruins, vegetal dye, tapestry, 5x8".........65.00
Rug, Navajo, Wide Ruins, wool/fine weave/rare colors, 30x40"..600.00
Rug, Navajo, wide/thin bands/dia/checkerboard, 1940s, 22x64"..165.00
Rug, Navajo, Window Rock tapestry, Ella Yazzie, 6½x9".......35.00
Rug, Navajo, 2 Gray Hills, blk/gray/wht/br, 24x35"..........235.00
Rug, Navajo, 2 Gray Hills, by Ason Chille Begay, 41x62½"...1,000.00

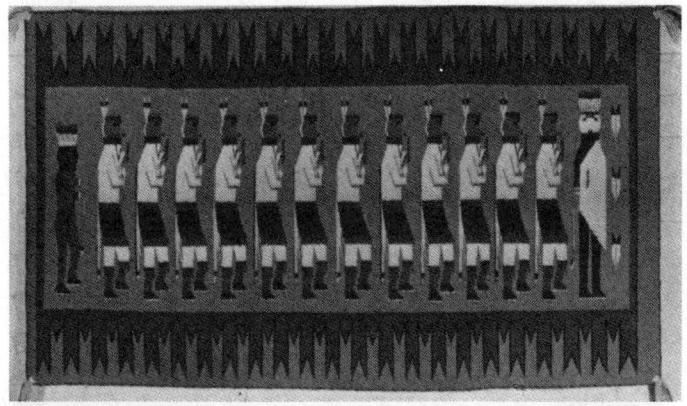

Rug, ceremonial Fox Dance Yeibichai by Julia John, Navajo, in twelve colors, pristine condition, 36" x 62½", $500.00.

Rug, Navajo, 2 Gray Hills, serrated/terraced/geometric, 23x43"..325.00
Rug, Navajo, 2 Gray Hills, sm hole in center, 43x54"........250.00
Rug, Navajo, 2 Gray Hills tapestry, 28x10½"...............475.00
Rug, Navajo, 2 Gray Hills/4 Corners, intricate design, 57x92"..900.00
Rug, Navajo, 3rd Phase Chiefs, red/blk/br/bl/wht, 52x53".....500.00
Rug, Navajo, 5 serrated dia w/in narrow bands, 1930, 16x33"..35.00
Rug, Navajo, 6 Yei, tapestry quality, by Anna Gray, 32x47½"..655.00
Rug, Navajo, 7 bands in dia pattern, natural wool, 32x60"....150.00
Rug, Navajo, 9 color Lukachukai Yei, 6 deities, 44x62"......450.00
Sampler, Navajo, rug on loom/Germantown, 1900, 8x14".....125.00
Tapestry, Navajo, Wide Ruins/serrated dia/X, MY Bai, 9x13"...135.00
Throw, Gallup, red/wht/gray/blk, 17x33"....................45.00
Throw, Gallup, 4 color arrows & stripes, ca 1940s, 28x57".....35.00
Throw, Navajo, wht/red/blk/gray, minor bleeding of red, 26x37"..25.00

Amethyst Glass

Amethyst simply describes the rich purple color of this glassware, made by many companies both here and abroad since the 19th century.

Bowl, swirl w/gold flowers, clear ft, 4¾x7½"................165.00
Canoe, Daisy & Button, scalloped edge, 3½x5x12"...........47.50
Cocktail shaker, SP top, Depression era, 12½"..............95.00
Compote, ruffled top, ped, Depression era, 6x12" dia........55.00
Decanter, glass stopper, Depression era...................45.00
Mug, birds in nest & lyre, 2¾"...........................55.00
Pitcher, w/lid, engraved grapes & vines, 9"...............75.00
Rolling pin, 15½".......................................75.00
Salt & peppers, Inverted Thumbprint, pr...................65.00

Sweetmeat, forget-me-not enameling, SP top/rim/hdl, 5¼".....120.00
Tumbler, Bull's Eye & Arched Panel, 3¾"...................35.00
Vase, brandy snifter shape, Depression era, 12"............65.00
Vase, etched holly leaves & berries, Depression era, 6".......35.00
Vase, paneled, petal top, ftd, Sandwich, 10"..............125.00

Ferner, polished flint glass in ormolu holder with classical figures, French, $145.00.

Amphora

The Amphora Porcelain Works of Teplitz, Austria, produced Art Nouveau styled vases and figurines during the latter part of the 19th century. They marked their wares with various stamps, some incorporating the name and location of the pottery with a crown or a shield.

Basket, applied 3 cherubs w/garlands, gr/gold rope trim, 12x8".675.00
Basket, candle holder top of hdl, 2 girls' heads on hdl, 10".....75.00
Basket, cobalt, reserves: portrait; buildings/steeples, 9x8"......170.00
Bowl, turkey figural, enameling/jewels, imp crown mk, 10x6"..235.00
Compote, mosaic inlay, rainbow colors, 3 zigzag columns, 6x9"..65.00
Compote, 3 vertical strap hdls, br/gold & gr roses, 9½x9".....175.00
Dish, Kate Greenaway type figural child....................165.00
Ewer, lizard hdl, porcelain glaze.........................125.00
Figurine, girl selling roses, 1920s, 8"....................70.00
Figurine, lion, 12x15"..................................195.00
Figurine, man w/lute, seated in lotus position, 13".........875.00
Figurine, peasant girl kneels by lg basket, artist sgn, 8x10"....255.00
Loving cup, portrait of woman, cobalt bisque body/hdls, Czech.155.00
Mug, Arab on horseback, sgn Stellmacher, 3"...............40.00
Vase, basketweave w/molded/applied pk roses, 4 twig hdls, 6½"..65.00
Vase, brn & tan leaf pattern, mc lg stork, bl lustre hdls, 6"....110.00
Vase, brn/beige etched, pnt medallions, hdls, artist sgnd, 8"....190.00
Vase, dragonfly & jewels, dbl hdls, 7½"...................350.00
Vase, enamel poppies, 4 hdls, sgn, 9x8"..................145.00
Vase, gilt spiderwebs/applied stone centers/butterflies, 10".....375.00
Vase, gladiator, full length, in reserve, hdls w/spouts, 9½"....105.00
Vase, gold medallions/mc enamel jewels/mc threadings, 8½", M.150.00
Vase, gold/bl basketweave, applied berry bunches/leaves, 8".....85.00
Vase, gr w/gold hdls, gold flowers, paper label, 10"........175.00
Vase, grapes in relief, sgn, 12".........................250.00
Vase, Grecian lady, sgn Stellmacher, 5"...................35.00
Vase, grotesque face near top, imp Beehive, Austria, 8".......50.00
Vase, lg tropical birds, mosaic technique, floral ground, 12"....125.00
Vase, long beak birds/water/tree in heavy enamel, dbl hdls, 7"..140.00
Vase, matt gray w/mc floral band at center & base, 9x7"......175.00

Vase, Nouveau, gr irid w/leaf decor, gold buds at neck, 11½"..235.00
Vase, pocked surface, ducks in flight/grass/moon, gr/red, 9"....220.00
Vase, 2 figural birds perched on rim.........................125.00
Vase, 3 profile men w/beards & hats, 3 king's crown hdls, 10"...90.00
Vase, 4 pillars w/bl jewels & reticulated top plaques, 7".......185.00
Wall pocket, br/tan basketweave w/mc mosaic flowers, 9".......78.00

Pitcher, smiling lion figural, in combination matt and glossy glaze, signed, 12", $850.00.

Animal Dishes with Covers

Covered animal dishes have been produced for nearly two centuries and are as varied as their manufacturers. They were made in many types of glass -- slag, colored, clear, and milk glass -- as well as china and pottery. On bases of nests and baskets you will find animals and birds of every sort. The most common was the hen.

Some of the smaller versions made by McKee, Indiana Tumbler and Goblet Company, and Westmorland Glass of Pittsburgh, Pennsylvania, were sold to food processing companies who filled them with prepared mustard, baking powder, etc. Occasionally, one will be found with the paper label identifying the product and processing company still intact.

Many of the glass versions produced during the latter part of the 19th century have been recently reproduced. As late as the 1960s, the Kemple Glass company made the rooster, fox, lion, cat, lamb, hen, horse, turkey, duck, dove, and rabbit, on split ribbed or basketweave bases. They were made in amethyst, blue, amber, and milk glass, as well as a varigated slag. Careful comparison to known examples of older glass with strict attention to detail is sometimes necessary to recognize reproductions.

Boar's head, red glass eyes, Pat May 29, 1888, Atterbury......800.00
British lion, milk glass...................................65.00
Camel, resting, head/neck/humps make up cover, 5⅜x6¼".....110.00
Cat, bl/wht, on wht ribbed base............................55.00
Cat, milk glass, sgn McKee................................125.00
Cat, on lacy base, milk glass, pat dtd......................85.00
Cat, wht, on blue ribbed base..............................20.00
Chick & egg, milk glass, 1889.............................95.00
Chick on sleigh, milk glass................................40.00

Cow on tub base, purple slag..............................42.50
Crawfish, milk glass......................................155.00
Dog, amber, on wide rib base...............................80.00
Dog, bl/wht on bl ribbed base..............................55.00
Dolphin, gravy w/lid.......................................50.00
Duck, amethyst crystal, wavy base, has eyes, 1930s.........60.00
Duck, clear, ribbed base...................................70.00
Eagle, hovering over fallen bird, round ornate clear base, ftd....95.00
Eagle on nest, milk glass..................................85.00
Fish, flat, milk glass....................................125.00
Fish on skiff, milk glass..................................45.00
Hen, 'The American', milk glass............................65.00
Hen, carmel slag, lacy base, Atterbury....................170.00
Hen, chocolate glass......................................375.00
Hen, crystal blue, slim, on oval grassy base...............80.00
Hen, dk amber, milk glass head............................145.00
Hen, gold basketweave base, mc on bisque, Staffordshire, 7x8".395.00

Boar's head with red glass eyes, marked Pat May 19, 1888, Atterbury, 5½" x 11" x 6", $800.00.

Hen, lacy base, bl cased head..............................90.00
Hen, purple slag, basketweave base, mk Dia w/H, 6½".........35.00
Hen, vaseline, 5"...65.00
Hen, wht w/bl head on wide rib base, Atterbury.............65.00
Hen on sleigh, milk glass..................................75.00
Horse on split rib base, milk glass........................85.00
Lion, milk glass, dtd on lid, Atterbury...................135.00
Lovebirds, deep blue satin glass, Westmoreland.............85.00
Owl head, basket rib base, amber...........................50.00
Pheasant, oval, frosted glass.............................130.00
Rabbit, Atterbury..155.00
Rabbit, crouching, frosted, Vallerystahl, 6"...............60.00
Rabbit, mule eared, ribbed base, milk glass w/gilt, 5½".....55.00
Rabbits, several in cabbage head, stippled leaves..........110.00
Robin on nest, milk glass, Westmoreland....................50.00
Robin on pedestal nest, blue, w/P-V France label...........25.00
Rooster, blue w/wht head, on blue ribbed base..............25.00
Rooster, milk glass, Atterbury, very lg...................120.00
Setter dog lid, opal, sgn Vallerysthal....................125.00
Snail, on strawberry, sgn Vallerystahl.....................80.00
Squirrel, amber, on fancy shaped dish......................75.00
Swan, block, w/eyes, Atterbury............................200.00

Swan, frosted, head & neck laid far back, clear base 90.00
Turkey, cobalt blue, standing, large 90.00
Turtle, snail on bk, milk glass, unsgn Vallerystahl 75.00

Antiquities

The ancient Egyptians, Romans, and the early craftsmen of India and China have left us with exquisite treasures bearing mute witness of their esthetic convictions that even a water carrier, a knife, or a rug should be created a thing of beauty.

Though time and the elements have taken their toll on the more fragile works of these ancient artisans, it is incredible that many remain intact to this day. The fragile tear and scent bottles, blown by Roman artisans from the 1st century A.D., and examples of the red or black predynastic potteries of Egypt -- though understandably quite rare -- can yet occasionally be found on the market today. Jewelry, often interred with the dead, has survived the centuries well; figurines of marble and terra cotta, ceremonial masks, earthenware vessels, and other relics such as these offer us of the 20th century the only tangible link possible to the ancient world.

Glassware

Bottle, bulbous w/flared neck, pinch decor, Syrian, 100-400 AD . 210.00
Bowl, deep w/flared rim, yellow-gr, 100 AD, 7½" 180.00
Drinking glass, ultra lite, dbl line rim etching, Roman 200.00
Ewer, flared pear form, applied rib hdl, lt gr, Syrian, 100 AD . . 230.00
Flask, good iridescence, Roman, 4½" 90.00
Jar, some iridescence, Roman, 5", EX 350.00
Tear vase, Roman 60.00
Vase, amber, ribbed/flared mouth/hdls, 3/500 AD, 6¾" 275.00
Vial, no iridescence, Roman, 4" 65.00

Jar, bluish-green, with applied zigzag and thread banding, everted base, dark green strap handles, 3rd-5th Century A.D., 4", $550.00.

Hardstone Carvings

Altar panel, dancing maenad relief, Roman 100 AD, 26", pr . . 770.00
Amulet, boar form, carved stone, Elam, 3000 BC, 1½" 935.00
Amulet of Thoth, Lapis-Lazuli, ibis headed deity, 305-30 BC . . 990.00

Egyptian bronze Ibis, on green marble base, eyes recessed, engraved plumage, 22nd-26th Dynasty, 946-525 B.C., 5¾" x 10½", $1,800.00.

Baboon, blk steatite, 19th/20th Dynasty, 1305-1080 BC, 2½" . 2,090.00
Grave relief, limestone, figure relief, Palmyra 200 AD, 17x21" . 2,640.00
Head of man, wide wig, basalt, 664-525 BC, 2" 1,045.00
Head of warrior, w/crested helmet, marble 100 AD, 6" 5,500.00
Jar, marble, squat/rnd/disk rim, Egypt, 1991-1785 BC, 3" W . . 660.00
Jar, stone, flared w/broad shoulder, Minoan, 25/1700 BC, 4½" . 330.00
Libation vessel, shallow/3 tabs/spout, 305 BC-100 AD, 15" . . 3,630.00
Plaque, grazing bull, losses, Assyrian ivory, 800 BC, 4" 9,900.00
Sarcophagus fragment, marble, 5 figure relief, 300 AD, 20x29" 10,450.00
Seal, recumbent bull, Sumerian, gr alabaster, 3200 BC, 4.4 cm . 350.00
Torso of a woman, Hellenistic, 2/100 BC, 14" 4,510.00
Volute krater, Apulian Red-figure, Gorgon masks hdls, 31" . . . 9,900.00

Pottery

Amphora, Attic Black-figure, 3 hdls, 500 BC, 5¾" 1,430.00
Animal, stylized monkey, terra cotta, Greek, 600 BC, 3½" 990.00
Chalice, Etruscan Bucchero, stem ft, 13 human heads, 600 BC 1,100.00
Cinerarium, terra cotta, lg reclining lady atop, 200 BC, 22" . . 3,410.00
Figure, goddess, Hellenistic, terra cotta, 3/200 BC, 18½" 3,850.00
Figure, goddess/bird head, Syro-Hittite, 20/1500 BC, 5½" 1,210.00
Figure, lady, Hellenistic, terra cotta/pigment, 3/200 BC, 10" . . 2,090.00
Figure, Ushabti, bl faience, 1808-946 BC, 6" 4,950.00
Figure, Ushabti, turq/bl faience, 570-525 BC, 7" 4,400.00
Head, Dionysos, terra cotta, Greek, 500 BC, 6" 495.00
Head, grotesque, terra cotta/polychrome, 200 BC, 4½" 770.00
Horse, terra cotta, head to right, blk pnt, Attic, 800 BC, 4½" . . 550.00
Horse & rider, terra cotta, 4½" 245.00
Hydria, Attic Red-figure, ogee ft/bar hdls, 500 BC, 9¼" 2,750.00
Incense stand, woman head/wings, terra cotta, Hellenistic, 6" . 1,320.00
Jar, buffware, pnt/waves & spirals, Egypt, 35/3200 BC, 5" 605.00
Jar, ovoid, red w/panels of wavy lines, 35/3200 BC, Egypt, 9" . 1,650.00
Jar, turq glaze, dbl twist hdls/heads ea side, Parthian, 14½" . . 3,300.00
Kylix, low std, band of satyrs, Attic Blk, 600 BC, 3x7½" 200.00
Lekythos, Attic Black-figure, 500 BC, 9½" 880.00
Mycenaean goddess, plaited hair, 1425-1300 BC, 4½" 825.00
Mycenean bull, terra cotta, br/red stripes, 1425-1300 BC, 3½" . 935.00
Pitcher, Etruscan Bucchero, incised bands at ft, 600 BC, 8" . . 660.00
Ram, curing horns, terra cotta, Mycenaean, 14/1200 BC, 5½" . 440.00
Rhyton, Apulian Red-figure, goat head form, 340-330 BC, 10" 3,410.00

Rhyton, form of boot, Iranian, 1000/800 BC, 7½"........1,870.00
Rhyton, Laconian hound's head, losses, Apulian, 400 BC....2,750.00
Stirrup jar, buffware w/bands, Mycenaean, 13/1200 BC........275.00

Kylix, Attic Black-figure, low standard, band of satyrs decor, 6th Century B.C., 3¼" x 7½", $200.00.

Miscellaneous

Bronze, bull's head lamp, 2 nozzles in mouth, 400 AD, 7"...2,970.00
Bronze, figure of cat, seated, 712-30 BC, 14½"..........13,750.00
Bronze, figure of Diana, losses, Roman, 300 AD, 13½".....3,300.00
Bronze, figure of man, losses, Celtic, 2/100 BC, 3½"........770.00
Bronze, figure of Osiris, 664-342 BC, 13".................6,050.00
Bronze, figure of Ptah, 712-30 BC, 7"....................1,650.00
Bronze, harness-ring, moufflon w/horns arched over 2 deities.1,320.00
Bronze, head of Osiris/crown/Upper Egypt, 946-720 BC, 6"..1,210.00
Bronze, mirror, Iranian, female form hdl, arms hold disc, 12".1,650.00
Bronze, mongoose on papyrus/paws raised, 664-324 BC, 4"..2,310.00
Bronze, rooster, detail poor, Etruscan, 400 BC, 2¼"........880.00
Bronze, satyr, leaping up, Green, 500 BC, 2¾"...........4,400.00
Bronze, stag, towering rack, Iranian, 1000 BC, 4"..........3,520.00
Bronze, strigil, sharple curved/faceted, Greco-Roman, 8½".....550.00
Earrings, gold, open triangular form, 9/800 BC, 4.6 cm......7,150.00
Earrings, gold, winged Eros forms, 200 BC, 1.5 cm.........2,310.00
Mirror, Etruscan bronze, engraved scenic, 300 BC, 11"......3,410.00
Mosaic panel, 2 interlocked pelta & knot, 200 AD, 15x28"...3,520.00
Mummy case, wood, triparte wig, gilt traces, 712-30 BC, 72".3,850.00
Necklace, gold/garnet, Hellenistic, 100 BC-100 AD, 17".....2,750.00
Pendant of baboon, wood, 712-30 BC, 2¼".................440.00
Roundel, gold, Roman, repousse Medusa, 200 AD, 1¾" dia..1,320.00

Appliances

As quaint as these old appliances may seem today, imagine how welcome each new innovation must have been when first introduced! The ice box was invented in the very early 1800s by Thomas Moore, who built a box within a box, separated by insulation to keep the block of ice from melting. Today, sans the drip pan, these lovely old boxes are refinished and used as cabinets to store everything from records to liquor.

Vintage light bulbs are another area of interest recently showing a flurry of activity. The Edison type of the 1880s had a carbon filament, double looped and self-supporting, and gave off a mellow, subdued light. The General Electric 'Mazda' bulbs introduced thirty years later, replaced their golden glow with a brilliant white illumination made possible with the new drawn metal tungsten filament, which was supported by a central glass rod. While most early bulbs had straight sides, a few were pear shaped or round; and nearly all were made with small tips on the top through which air was exhausted.

Fans of early fans are especially fond of the very early electric models

and, of course, those powered by other means such as kerosene, alcohol, or batteries.

Kitchen appliances -- toasters, food mixers, coffee makers, etc. -- that demonstrate the earlier innovations in contrast to the modern, hold lots of appeal and interest to many.

Cider press, wood, Sears................................80.00
Fan, Knapp-Monarch Co, non-oscillating, pat #5..............12.00
Ice box, oak, doors: 3 glass/1 mirror; brass trim, McCray, 66"..450.00
Ice box, ornately carved maple, 2 doors...................475.00
Ice cream freezer, Acme the 5 Minute Freezer, hand crank, blue.18.00
Juice, Sunkist #2700, electric...........................35.00
Light bulb, New Type Sunbeam, 16 candle, 1901 pat in base....35.00
Light bulb, Shelby, 16 candle, brass Thomson-Houston base....35.00
Light bulb, typical carbon, unknown manufacturer, 1901-1920...10.00
Light bulb, 16 candle, lamp, w/brass base, 1890s.............30.00
Mixer, Dormeyer, motor detaches, heavy, 1921...............30.00
Oil heater, Perfection Smokeless, graniteware.................43.00
Shake mixer, Hamilton Beach, gr porcelain, single...........185.00
Sweeper, Reeves Suction..............................28.00
Television Lightning Arrester, pat pending, gr ironstone........45.00
Toaster, electric, wire frame/exposed elements, GE X2, 1905...100.00
Toaster, fold down sides, ornate, Edison, 1914, no cord.......38.00
Toaster, pop-up, single, 1930s..........................15.00
Toaster, Samson, w/cord, late 1920s......................18.00

Electric toaster, nickle plated with blue wood knobs, Electrex, pat'd 1920-27, United Drugs Co., $35.00.

Toaster, Tee-Ten, 1920s, no cord.........................26.00
Toaster, Turnover, Westinghouse, early 1920s, w/cord..........30.00
Vacuum cleaner, bellows action, ca 1880s..................150.00

Arequipa

The Arequipa Pottery operated from 1911 until 1918 at a sanitorium near Fairfax, California. Its purpose was two-fold -- therapy for the patients, and financial support for the institution. Frederick H. Rhead was the originator and director. The ware, made from local clays, was often hand thrown, simply styled and decorated. Marks were varied, but always incorporated the name of the pottery and the state. A circular arrangement encompassing the negative image of a vase beside a tree is most common.

Bowl, leaf/branch relief, bl gloss, mk/#s, 4x9" 225.00
Bowl, lt mc mirror glaze, irid, 2 sm rim chips, 2¾x7" 140.00
Plate, br/bl border on wht, initials in center, dtd 1912, 7" 110.00
Vase, bl/gray, 5½" 150.00
Vase, incised florals, gray-plum, 1916, 3½" 250.00
Vase, thick pink/br on ribbed free form, gr/bl w/in, 7¾" 400.00

Art Deco

To the uninformed casual observer, 'Art Deco' envokes thoughts of chrome and glass, streamlined curves and aerodynamic shapes, mirrored prints of pink flamingos, and statues of slender nudes and greyhound dogs. Though the Deco movement began in 1925 at the Paris International Exposition and lasted to some extent into the 1950s, within that period of time the evolution of fashion and taste continued as it always has, resulting in subtle variations.

The French Deco look was one of opulence -- exotic inlaid woods, rich material, lush fur and leather. Lines tended toward symetrical curves. American designers adapted the concept to cover every aspect of fashion and home furnishings from inexpensive picture frames and cigarette lighters, plastic and bakelite jewelry, to high fashion designer clothing and exquisite massive furniture with squared or circular lines. Vinyl was a popular covering and chrome plated brass was used for chairs, cocktail shakers, lamps and tables. Dinnerware, glassware, theaters, and train stations, were designed to reflect the new 'Modernism'.

The Deco movement made itself apparent into the fifties in wrought iron lamps with stepped pink plastic shades and Venetian blinds. The sheer volume of production during those twenty-five years provides collectors today with fine examples of the period that can be bought for as little as $10 to $20 into the thousands. Chrome items signed 'Chase' are prized by collectors and are available at prices ranging from $15 to $20 for smaller items to $200 to $300 for larger pieces. Blue glass radios and tables with blue glass tops are high on the list of desirability in many areas.

See also Aluminum; Bronzes; Frankart; Furniture; Jewelry; Lalique

Ash tray, blk/chrome w/greyhound 12.50
Ash tray, nude, pnt metal, glass insert, 9x8" 45.00
Bookends, nude in extended bk bend, brass plated, pr 90.00
Box, cigar; metal, semi-nude on lid, 4 relief scenes, 6x6¾" 125.00
Bud vase, Lubino, gray w/molded leaves, France, 5" 145.00
Candy dish, gr satin glass, supported by 2 kneeling nudes, 7" . . 75.00
Cigarette case, blk enamel & leopard print, sgn Marathon 18.00
Clock set, nudes hold 8-sided clock, pr sticks, gr metal 125.00
Cocktail set, Chase chrome, blk banded shaker/tray/8 tumblers . . 65.00
Cocktail shaker, SP, incised rooster: pnt decor, Meriden, 13" . . . 55.00
Coffee set, chrome, blk hdls/knobs, slim pot/sugar/creamer 95.00
Decanter, nude under water/fish/bubbles, sgn Kosta, 11" 195.00
Figurine, bronzed metal, kneeling lady w/urn in headdress, 10" . . 85.00
Figurine, on knee, arms extended/ball on ea hand, marble base . 650.00
Flower frog, dancing girl, German porcelain, 8" 27.50
Lamp, bl satin glass, nude playing harp, 12x6", pr 300.00
Lamp, draped nude kneels, holds vase-form shade, Guerbe, 15" . 550.00
Lamp, draped nude seated on tall marble plinth, M LaVerrier . . 750.00
Lamp, nude lady, Dance de Lumiere, gr acid glass, 11½" 300.00
Lamp, nude sits on ped by post, chipped ice gr globe, 13¾" . . . 130.00
Lamp, seated Oriental man, gold crackle glass shade, Ronson . . . 95.00
Lamp, spelter girl & base, half moon frosted shade, Betty Beck . . 50.00

Lady, painted metal with ivory face, brass greyhound on marble base, signed Scalj, 25½" long, $1,600.00.

Lamp, upright nude holds crown aloft, frosted flame, iron, 14" . 110.00
Lamp, w/clock, kneeling lady supports arch w/lights, 1930, 18" . 150.00
Lamp, wht cube w/blk scotty 65.00
Light, hall; kneeling metal nude w/beacon, marble/mahog base . . 165.00
Mirror, banded in aluminum w/stepped device at top, 40x30" . . . 600.00
Pillow, lav satin w/lady walking greyhound 20.00
Pillow, peach satin heart w/lady's face 20.00
Plaque, copper, stylized woman, Mitzi Otten, 5x9" 880.00
Plaque, dramatic women, plaster, ABCO, by Michel, 9½", pr . . 65.00
Powder jar, Chase, brass tone w/gr enamel leaf, glass insert . . . 25.00
Powder jar, gr frosted glass, 12 leg base, clown head finial 38.50
Radio, blue mirrored glass, Troy 650.00
Smoke stand, chrome & slag glass, 2 ash trays, lighter, jar 225.00
Vase, silver w/MOP insets, enamel Celtic motif, Liberty, 8" 200.00
Vase, trumpet, frosted & clear glass, geometric base, Luce, 7" . . 375.00

Art Glass Baskets

A popular novelty and gift item during the Victorian era, these one-of-a-kind works of art were produced in just about any type of art glass in use at that time. They were never marked, since these were not true production pieces, but 'whimsies' made by glassworkers to relieve the tedium of the long work day, or as special gifts. The more decorative and imaginative the design, the more valuable the basket.

Beige w/gold traced br pods, dbl gold/br hdls, scalloped, 1892 . . 60.00
Blue, melon rib, swirled, applied twist thorn hdl 150.00
Burmese, thorn hdl, Gunderson 225.00
Cased, blue spangle, clear thorn hdl, 5x4" 135.00
Cased, br/wht w/in, rose/bl wht swirl, clear hdl w/leaf, 6" 175.00
Cased, wht, blue w/in, ruffled, dbl twist clear hdl, 5x4½" 110.00
Cobalt, applied ft, lt bl thorn hdl 75.00
Diamond pattern, blue w/clear crimp rim, thorn hdl, 5x7½" . . . 165.00
Gr, clear braided hdl, ball shaped base w/flared rim, 10" dia . . . 85.00
Lime gr to wht, crystal twist hdl w/mica flakes 175.00
Overlay, wht satin, rose w/in, scalloped camphor edge, 8" 275.00
Peppermint swirl, clear hdl & ruffle, 5½x4" 145.00
Peppermint swirl, clear thorn hdl, 6x7" 195.00
Quatrefoil/fine fluted, M-hdl, ribbon candy red/wht, 6x10" 325.00
Spatter, amber w/br/rust/wht, gold encrusted, 8x13" 245.00
Spatter, mc w/clear casing, thorn hdl, scalloped, 9x6" 180.00
Spatter, mc w/wht lining, clear hdl, 5x5½" 63.00

Spatter, petal top, clear/wht w/in, medallion pattern, 7".......195.00
Spatter, 4 dimples, wht w/in, clear thorn hdl, 7"...........195.00
Spatter, 6 point rim, wht lined, twist thorn hdl, 6¾"........125.00
Swirled pk/wht stripes, pinched rim, twist/frost thorn hdl, 7"...350.00
Tomato glass, deep ruffles, twisted clear thorn hdl/ft, 10½"....350.00

Peppermint striped with white casing, clear twist thorn handle, attributed to Sandwich, 8½", $375.00.

Art Nouveau

From the famous 'L' Art Nouveau' shop in the rue de Provence in Paris, 'New Art' spread across the continent, and belatedly arrived in America in time to add its curvilineal elements and asymetrical ornamentation to the ostentatious remains of the Rococo revival of the 1880s. Nouveau manifested itself in every facet of decorative art. In glassware, Tiffany turned the concept into a commercial success that lasted well ito the second decade of this century, and created a style that inspired other American glassmakers for decades. Furniture, lamps, bronzes, jewelry, and automobiles, were designed within the realm of its dictates.

Today's market abounds with lovely examples of Art Nouveau, allowing the collector to choose one or several areas that hold a special interest.

See also Bronzes; Jewelry; Tiffany

Pewter figural ewers after Charles Theodore Perron, sea nymphs in low and full relief, late 19th Century, 11½", pr, $385.00.

Bookends, Nouveau design, sgn Carence Crafters, pr..........55.00
Cigar holder, woman w/flowing dress.....................80.00
Crumber, SP, floral relief, swirl hdl, 11".................15.00
Desk plateau, lion/lioness at pool, bronze after Radetzky, 15"..350.00
Desk set, brass, water lily relief, 2 crystal wells, 5 lg pcs....265.00
Desk set, dore bronze, mk JB, #1659, 8 pc.................350.00
Dresser set, silver, lady w/flowing hair, lilies, brush/mirror.....225.00
Figurine, nude emerging from center of lily, German china, 5".110.00
Fire tender, dbl rod balustrade w/floral filigree, glass sqs.......525.00
Lamp, bronze dancer, mc pnt face, millefiori ball over bulb....300.00
Lamp, 3 women, arms outstretched, metal, confetti globe.......95.00
Letter holder & inkwell, brass, female figure on front........100.00
Letter opener, brass, nude w/swirling hair..................35.00
Mirror, gilt metal, figural lady, robe supports mirror, 21x14"...565.00
Mirror, table; maid w/flowing gown/child, plaster, A Piet, 27"...250.00
Perfume, clear w/metal spiderweb/insects/flowers, 6½".......85.00
Plaque, girl w/autoharp, pottery, after Walahliss, 14x19".......150.00
Shaving mug, applied crocus flowers, dtd 1904, Derby SP......38.00
Spoon, sterling, nude lady in hdl.......................125.00
Syrup pitcher, pewter, relief floral/rattan hdl, Liberty & Co.....65.00
Tazza, standing maiden standard, bronze finish, 10"..........75.00
Tray, shell, bust of maid/dragonflies, sgn, porcelain, 13".......300.00
Vase, keyhole w/semi-nude & cherub, ormolu, France........4,000.00
Wine cooler, 6 blow-outs in top, floral relief, Orvit, 8x10½"....275.00

Arts and Crafts

The Arts and Crafts movement began in England during the last quarter of the 19th century and its influence soon was felt in this country. Among it's proponents in America were Elbet Hubbard (see Roycrofters) and Gustav Stickley (see Furniture). They rebelled against the mechanized mass production of the industrial revolution, and against the cumulative influence of hundreds of years of man's changing taste. They subscribed to the theory of purification of the styles -- that designs be geared strictly to necessity. At the same time, they sought to elevate these basic ideals to the level of accepted 'art'. Simplicity was their virtue; to their critics it was a fault.

The style of furniture they promoted was squarely built of heavy oak, and so simple was its appearance that as a result many began to copy the style, which became known as 'Mission'. Soon factories had geared production toward making cheap copies of their designs. In 1915, Stickley's own operation failed, forced into bankruptcy by the machinery he so despised. Hubbard lost his life that same year on the ill-fated *Lusitania*. Within the decade, the style has lost its popularity.

Beakers, sterling, Georg Jensen, 3", pr....................130.00
Blotter & letter opener, Dirk Van Erp, patinated copper, 11½".110.00
Book, 'Craftsman Houses, a Book for Homemakers', G Stickley.100.00
Book rack, table top, sliding, w/Gustav Stickley logo, 12" L....150.00
Book rack, w/tooled copper ends, ca 1910, 8½x7¼".........35.00
Bookends, Dirk Van Erp, copper........................225.00
Catalog, L&JG Stickley Furniture, 1930s, 90 pgs.............45.00
Chafing dish, copper/silver, 3 strap ft, burner, oak base, 11"...400.00
Costumer, oak, G Stickley #52, X base, dlb set of hooks, 71"...250.00
Creamer, sterling, rolled rim on extended spout, Kalo, 3½"....100.00
Desk set, Laguna Beach, hammered copper, 4 pc............95.00
Fernery, recessed side panels/H stretchers, Stickley Bros, 32"...225.00
Inkwell, copper w/gr enamel/silver decor, A/C Shop, 3½x5"....140.00
Jardiniere, hammered copper, ruffled/2 hdls, G Stickley, 12"...500.00
Lamp, copper w/wicker shade, conical, G Stickley, 15"........375.00
Lighter, Cape Cod, brass wash/copper, Old Mission Kopperkraft..35.00
Magazine, The Craftsman, 1916.........................25.00
Magazine stand, 4 shelves w/incised trees, G Stickley, 34".....400.00
Mirror, tin w/2 bl enamel medallions, octagon fr, 16x28"......230.00

Pitcher, sterling, bulbous, tapering to ft, sgn Kalo, 8½″......340.00
Pitcher, water; sterling, hand hammered, Lebolt, 9½″........350.00
Plant stand, oak, G Stickley #41, rfn, 28″.................750.00
Server, oak, Limbert #445, 34x36x16″....................200.00
Stamp box, oak, sgn Charles Rohlfs, 1910, 5½″...........325.00
Tray, hammered copper, #346, G Stickley, 20″ dia.........375.00
Tray, hammered metal, emb bird/griffin border, bl eyes, 16½″...70.00
Umbrella stand, slat sided/copper insert, Libert brand, 30″.....160.00

Carved and stained oak drop leaf table by Chas. Rohlfs, ca 1900, 32″ wide by 4 feet extended, $9,900.00.

Aurene

Aurene, developed in 1904 by Frederick Carder of the Steuben Glass Works, is a metallic iridescent glassware similar to some of Tiffany's. Usually a rich lustrous gold, blue is also found, and ocassionally red or green. It was used alone and in combination with calcite, a cream colored glass with a calcium base, also developed by Carder. It is usually marked Aurene or Steuben, sometimes with the factory number added, etched into the glass by hand. Paper labels were also used.

Basket, blue, berry prunts ea side hdl, sgn, 12″............2,200.00
Basket, blue, berry prunts ea side hdl, sgn, 7x7″...........1,265.00
Basket, gold, berry prunts ea side hdl, sgn, 12″............1,650.00
Candlestick, blue, twist stem, sgn, 10¼″, pr...............990.00
Candlestick, blue w/purple hi-lites, swirled, sgn, 8″..........965.00
Candlestick, gold, #686, 10″, pr........................585.00
Candlestick, gold, twisted stem, sgnd, 10″.................275.00
Compote, gold, swirl stem, berry prunts, sgn, 6¾x5″........465.00
Compote, gold/calcite, Inv Teardrop stem, shape 1983, 4x6″...275.00
Compote, gold/calcite, Inv Teardrop stem, shape 1983, 5½x8″.425.00
Finger bowl/under plate, gold...........................165.00
Finger bowl/under plate, gold on calcite, ribbed.............200.00
Goblet, gold, twist shafts, Steuben, #2361, 6″, pr...........350.00
Nut dish, gold on calcite, 2½x6″........................165.00
Nut dish, gold w/pink & rose hi-lites, ruffled, 2½x6″.........175.00
Perfume, bl irid, bird form stopper, ped base, Steuben, 12″...1,300.00
Perfume, gold, conical w/flared neck/teardrop stopper, 5″......350.00
Pin dish, gold/pink irid, ruffled, fancy ft, sgn Haviland, 3½″....125.00
Rose bowl, ribbed w/scalloped edge, deep gold irid, #2651, 3″..275.00
Salt, ped, EX gold, #3067.............................140.00
Salt, ped, tapered shape, EX blue/gold irid, 1½x2¼″ dia......165.00

Finger vases, gold iridescent, signed Steuben, Aurene, 5½″, $700.00 for the pair.

Shade, gold, ribbed, 5″, pr.............................300.00
Vase, blue, baluster shape w/flared rim, sgnd Steuben, 9½″....975.00
Vase, blue, morning glory shape, 4¾″....................450.00
Vase, blue, ruffled top, ftd, sgn, 9x4″....................945.00
Vase, blue irid, flange rim, 5x4″........................595.00
Vase, blue w/gr hi-lites, cone shape, sgn, 12″..............965.00
Vase, fan, peacock bl, vines/leaves decor, sgnd, Steuben, 8″..1,400.00
Vase, gold, much pink fire, EX color, early, #210, sgnd, 3¾″..200.00
Vase, gold, sgn/#d, 2x1¼″.............................275.00
Vase, gold, stretched ruffled top, sgn, 12″................575.00
Vase, gold w/heavy bl hi-lites, Steuben, 6½″...............250.00
Vase, millefiore florets, gold/gr/wht, Steuben label, 5½″......1,750.00
Vase, stick shape, blue, sgnd & #2546 on base, 8½″.........550.00
Vase, tree stump, 3 pronged, EX gold, #2744, 6″...........425.00

Austrian Ware

From the late 1800s until the beginning of WWI, several companies were located in the area known at the turn of the century as Bohemia. They produced hard paste porcelain dinnerware and decorative items, primarily for the American trade. Today, examples bearing the marks of these firms are usually referred by collectors as Austrian ware, indicating simply the country of their origin. Of those various companies, these marks are best known: M.Z. Austria; Victoria, Carlsbad, Austria (Schmidt and Company); and O. & E.G. (Royal) Austria.

Though most of the decoration was achieved through transfer designs which were sometimes signed by the original artist, pieces marked Royal Austria were often hand painted, and so indicated alongside the backstamp.

Of these three companies, Victoria, Carlsbad, Austria, is the most valued by today's collectors.

Biscuit jar, floral decor, MZ Austria, 7″..................65.00
Biscuit jar, wht w/pink floral garlands, Victoria, 7″..........80.00
Bowl, berry; cream, lg wht/gr/pk flowers, lav scallop rim, MZ...165.00
Bowl, berry; HP floral decor, mkd O&EG, 9″................35.00
Bowl, lady & gladiator, cobalt & silver shell rim, 9″ dia.......95.00
Bowl, roses & foliage, pearlized border, gold, scalloped, 10″....95.00
Box, powder; wht w/yellow flowers, mkd O&EG, 3x4″.........35.00
Cake plate, blue, pink flowers, gold, open hdls, HP/sgnd, MZ....65.00
Candle holder, cream w/pk & gr HP florals, mkd O&EG, pr, 9″..75.00
Celery, HP roses, gold border, mkd O&EG, 12″ L............30.00
Chocolate set, HP yellow roses on shaded brown ground, 7-pc..150.00
Creamer, moose.....................................25.00
Dessert set, pink floral w/pearl lustre border, MZ Austria......95.00

Ewer, cherubs reserve, rust ground, rococo hdl, Victoria, 9"...175.00
Ewer, classical portrait, gold trim, Victoria, 12"..............250.00
Fish set, fish transfer, cobalt border, gold spatter, 3-pc, MZ....350.00
Hair receiver, ivory w/3 gold ft/rim, sgn E TenEycke, 1916, MZ..15.00
Hatpin holder, HP blue forget-me-nots, mkd O&EG, 5".........35.00
Hatpin holder, violets, MZ Austria, 5"......................35.00
Luncheon set, blk & gold geometrics/pk floral border, 6-pc.....80.00
Mug, monk portrait, MZ Austria, 7"........................65.00
Nut set, mixed floral decor, serving bowl & 6 cups, mkd O&EG..65.00
Pin dish, HP roses on cream, MZ, 6" long...................22.00
Pitcher, cider; HP fruit decor, MZ Austria, 6"................90.00
Pitcher, lilies on shaded wht to gr ground, lustre finish, 10"....90.00
Pitcher, wht satin/center red rose band/bulbous/scalloped, 10"..175.00
Plate, apple blossoms, emb leaves, gold, Mark/Gutherz, 7"......12.00
Plate, chrysanthemums, silver trim, artist sgnd, mkd O&EG, 9"..45.00
Plate, country scene, Victoria, 10"........................65.00
Plate, ea w/mc fruit, 7½", set of 4.......................45.00
Plate, game bird, pearl lustre border, MZ Austria, 9¼"........45.00
Plate, gr w/gold, fluted edge, classic scene, 6"..............10.00
Plate, grapes, gold trim, artist sgnd, mkd O&EG, 9"..........50.00
Plate, Greek goddess center, wide cobalt border, Victoria, 8"....60.00
Plate, hydrangeas, silver trim, artist sgnd, mkd O&EG, 9".....45.00
Plate, lady w/cherubs, Victoria, 9".......................50.00
Plate, lady's portrait transfer, 10" dia....................145.00
Plate, multifloral decor, reticulated border, Victoria, 10".....45.00
Plate, Napoleon w/troops, sgn Fony, gr/gold border, 9¾".....250.00
Platter, HP fish w/pink floral designs, gold trim, mkd O&EG....95.00
Ramekin & under plate, sm rosebud transfer, gold beads, O&EG.25.00
Relish, floral decor, artist sgnd, mkd O&EG, 9" L............30.00
Relish, maroon w/gold tracery, center floral, MZ, 6" L........22.00
Salt, open, HP gold decor, 3 ftd, mkd O&EG...............12.00
Salt & pepper, cream w/bl florals, Deco shape, mkd O&EG, pr..20.00
Teapot, HP floral in transfer outline, gold trim, Leonard, 8½"...40.00
Tray, bl & yel flowers, beaded border, MZ Austria, 4" L.......25.00
Tray, dresser; Madame du Barry portrait transfer............110.00
Tray, dresser; pk/yel flowers, gold edge, 9x6¾".............23.00
Tray, dresser; scattered floral decor, scalloped, MZ, 9" L......35.00
Tray, dresser; wht w/HP violets, mkd O&EG................45.00
Tray, purple floral/emb designs, gold trim, scalloped, 12" L.....60.00
Tureen, floral transfer decor, oblong shape, w/lid, mkd O&EG...55.00
Tureen, vegetable; w/lid, hdls, decorated...................35.00
Vase, mixed florals & gold, matt, scalloped ped, Victoria, 13"..185.00
Vase, 3-color floral on wht to cream, reticulated hdls, 6"......45.00

Tazza, figural female head handles, cobalt blue with multifloral and gold decor, signed, 3½" x 9½", $85.00.

Autographs

Philography is defined as the practice of studying as well as collecting autographs. And to be a successful philographer one must study. In order to fairly evaluate an autograph, you must first research your subject to determine the rarity of his signature. Age has very little to do with worth. For instance, a letter signed by Greta Garbo would fetch $1,000 to $1,200 simply because so few exist. Presidential or political signatures on letters and documents are evaluated by the significance of the contents. These two factors -- rarity and content -- are more important considerations than condition, though naturally tears, holes, etc., lessen the value of vintage documents. Forgeries exist in this field, just as reproductions abound in other areas; so before investing in a rare and expensive signature, it would be wise to check with an established reputable dealer.

Key:
ALS-----hand written letter   PLH-----personal letterhead
AQS-----autograph quotation signed   sig-----signature
DS-----document signed   SP-----signed photo
ISP-----inscribed signed photo
LH-----letterhead
LS-----signed letter, typed or written by someone else

Armstrong, Louis; ISP, full length w/horn, 1920s, smeared sig...40.00
Astaire, Fred; SP, in dancing pose, 7½x9"..................20.00
Barrymore, John; DS, RKO Studios, 1 pg, 1934............245.00
Beatles, photo, sgnd by all four, 1964, D Bailey: photographer..660.00
Beatty, Clyde; on slip of paper, 4x6".....................10.00
Bergman, Ingrid; autograph on 3x5" card....................7.00
Bernhardt, Sarah; signed postcard picture, 1906............195.00
Bernstein, Leonard; AQS, 2 bars of Fancy Free, 1960, red ink..38.00
Blackstone, Harry Jr; SP, Blackstone doing magic, 1979, 5x7"..17.00
Bolger, Ray; ISP, Garland & scarecrow dancing, b/w glossy, 11".35.00
Bryan, William Jennings; signature on card.................40.00
Buchanan, James; DS authorizing pardon:Thad Wetmore, 1860.160.00
Burns (George) & Allen (Gracie); ISP, 1940s, 5x7", M.........55.00
Burroughs, Edgar Rice; envelope from Tarzana, CA, 1935......27.00
Byrd, Richard E; signature on 5x4" paper, 1937.............22.00
Chaplin, Charles; typed legal documents re: Lita Grey's trust...750.00
Charles II, King of England; 3" sig cut from document.......265.00
Churchill, Winston; envelope addressed & sgnd, 1917........220.00
Cleveland, Grover; ALS, 1886, thanks for book he sent.......160.00
Cleveland, Rose Elizabeth; executive mansion card, dated 1885..25.00
Cobb, Ty; Centennial of Baseball stamp, sgnd...............95.00
Cole, Nat King; ISP, King Cole Trio, sgnd twice, b/w, 8x10"...125.00
Coolidge, Calvin; bank check, 1932.......................65.00
Coolidge, Calvin; 2x3" card w/orig envelope, no date.........48.00
Crawford, Joan; book, My Way Of Life, sgnd on flyleaf, 1971....30.00
Curie, Marie; sgnd pg from book, picture of her & Pierre......325.00
Dayan, Moshe; SP, in uniform...........................70.00
Dean, Dizzy; DS, Baseball Questionaire, filled in & sgnd, 1 pg...32.00
Dempsey, Jack; Dempsey's Corner Restaurant menu, sgnd......15.00
Dickens, Charles; ALS, emb stationary/Tavistock House, 1859..550.00
Dietrich, Marlene; LS, wishing Argentina Happy New Year, 1940.38.00
Dimaggio, Joe; SP, Monroe wedding/courthouse steps, b/w, 11"..65.00
Disney, Walt; sig on back of flight itinerary, late 1960s........160.00
Eddy, Nelson; LS, on his personal stationery, 1 pg...........35.00
Eisenhower, Mamie Doud; birthday card, inscribed & sgnd, 1969.25.00
Emerson, Ralph Waldo; ALS, 2 pgs, 1873.................145.00
Ferdinand I, King of Bulgaria; SP, 1947, 3½x5¼"...........55.00

Fillmore, Millard; letter, 1850............................2,970.00
Fillmore, Millard; sgnd check, dated 1849...............2,860.00
Fitzgerald, F Scott; from book flyleaf, inscribed/sgnd, 1926....250.00
Fitzsimmons, Fred; ALS, PLH, re: teaching baseball, 2 pgs.....25.00
Fonda, Henry; vintage ink signature, ca 1935, on 3x5" card....25.00
Ford, Gerald R; signature on 3x5" card....................30.00
Frost, Robert; portion of envelope w/his signature & address....38.00
Gable, Clark; bank check, Sherman Oaks, California, 1950.....170.00
Garfield, James A; 3x4" card, no date, good borders.........100.00
Geer, Will; autograph on 3x5" card........................5.00
George III, King of England; sig cut from document as king.....39.00
Gerlich, Martin; postcard picture, in uniform, sgnd...........35.00
Glenn, John H Jr; SP, in business suit, 8x10"...............40.00
Grable, Betty; ISP, sexy ¾ length semi-reclining, ca 1935......150.00
Grant, Julia D; 2x4" card, sgnd both sides, dated 8/26/1891.....50.00
Grissom, Virgil I; signature on card......................100.00
Guest, Edgar A; TLS, PLH/Detroit Free Press, 1936..........14.00
Hancock, John; DS, 1781, as Gov of Mass, professionally mtd..600.00
Harding, Florence; engraved invitation, w/emb gold seal, 4x3"...20.00
Harding, Warren G; DS, appointing Postmaster, WA, 1922....125.00
Hardy, Oliver; DS, application/Federation Radio Artists, 1939...250.00
Hearst, William Randolph; full signature, w/SL of presentation...35.00
Hepburn, Katharine; DS, 2 pgs, RKO Studios, 1934..........110.00
Hoover, J Edgar; TLS, LH/FBI, request for information, 4/5/67..25.00
Hope, Bob; autograph on 3x5" card........................5.00
Johnson, Lady Bird; book, A White House Diary, autographed...20.00
Jolson, Al; signature on page from an album................50.00
Keller, Helen; Christmas card/sgnd also by associate P Thomsan.35.00
Kipling, Rudyard; ALS on 5x4" card, both sides, 1913, M.....170.00
Kipling, Rudyard; book, The Naulahka, sgnd title page, 1892...175.00
Langtry, Lillie; signature on card.........................40.00

Lincoln, Abraham; DS, 1864, appointing Consul General.....1,300.00
Lind, Jenny; full signature from ALS......................25.00
Lloyd, Harold; ISP, bust shot, b/w, 7x9"..................150.00
Lombard, Carol; ISP, 8x10"...............................275.00
Manson, Charles; ALS, rambling discussion, April 1981.......100.00
Mantle, Mickey; book, Whitey & Mickey, sgnd on flyleaf, M.....25.00
McKinley, William; TLS, personal letterhead, 5/4/1896.........60.00
Meir, Golda; SP, 4¾x6".................................70.00
Merman, Ethel; ISP, ½ length pose, ca 1935, b/w matt, 8x11"..35.00
Mix, Tom; signature cut from document.....................30.00
Monroe, James; DS, land grant, signed as President, 1823.....200.00
Monroe, Marilyn; ISP, reclines nude, 1952, 8x10" b/w glossy.1,875.00
Monroe, Marilyn; ISP, swimsuit, ca 1955, 3½x4", tape stains...400.00
Moses, Grandma; signature on 3x5" card....................28.00
Nixon, Richard; TLS, personalized stationary, letter of thanks...80.00
Olds, Ransom Eli; signature.............................30.00
Parrish, Maxfield; ALS, 2 pgs, poetic message to 'Emily'......150.00
Picasso, Pablo; Dove of Peace stamp, mtd, multicolor signature.200.00
Pierce, Franklin; cut signature, signed in full, bold...........75.00
Pierce, Franklin; DS, re: letter to King of Siam, 1857........175.00
Pike, James A; TLS, PLH/Cathedral Church, April 1957, 8x6"...30.00
Pons, Lily; ISP, 1935, b/w, portrait quality, 8x10".........25.00
Princess Grace/Prince Ranier; SP of family, sgnd by both, b/w...45.00
Pyle, Ernie; signature on envelope, 1944..................55.00
Robinson, Edward G; typed note, EGR stationery, sgnd, 1941...35.00
Rockwell, Norman; autograph note sgnd....................40.00
Rogers, Kenny; ISP, b/w glossy, 8x11"....................10.00
Romero, Caesar; ISP, ¾ length pose, ca 1935, b/w, M........28.00
Roosevelt, Franklin D; sgnd bank check, 6/1/1944............575.00
Roosevelt, Franklin D; sig clipped from White House LS, 1935..75.00
Roosevelt, Theodore; full sig, from White House letter, 1904....65.00
Roosevelt, Theodore; TLS, personal letterhead, 11/17/1914....120.00
Ruby, Jack; Dallas bank check, sgnd in full, June 1959........125.00
Salk, Jonas; Infantile Paralysis 1st day cover, signed...........15.00
Sanburg, Carl; book, Always The Young Strangers, signed......60.00
Scott, Randolph; ISP, action scene on horseback, b/w, 8x11"...16.00
Sheridan, Ann; ISP, ¾ length pose, 1935, matte finish, 8x6"....60.00
Sherman, William T; cabinet photo, inscription & sgnd, 1889..110.00
Sinclair, Upton; signature on 3x5" card....................10.00
Smith, Kate; signature...................................5.00
Smith, Sidney; orig pencil sketch of Andy Gump, sgnd, 4x6"....40.00
Starr, Ringo; SP of the Beatles, sgnd by Ringo, 10x8".........60.00
Swanson, Gloria; autograph on 3x5" card....................7.00
Taft, William H; bank check, 12/1/1917....................250.00
Taft, William H; White House card, insc, 6/7/1911, w/envelope.150.00
Three Stooges; check from Moe Howard to Larry Fine, 1960...150.00
Truman, Harry S; TLS, Senate letterhead, 6/21/1943.........150.00
Truman, Harry S; 4x6" card, insc & sgnd, 12/30/68..........60.00
Tucker, Sophie; book, Some Of These Days, inscribed & signed.27.00
Vargas, Alberto; color print of Vargas Girl, sgnd, 8x11".......38.00
Wallace, George; ALS, PLH, discusses health & family, 1979....50.00
Wayne, John; inscription & signature on card................65.00
Williams, Tennessee; book, Moise & World of Reason, sgnd, M..45.00
Willkie, Wendell; book, One World, sgnd on flyleaf, 1943......40.00

Lincoln letter on Executive Mansion stationery, in regard to promotion of Lt. Chas. H. Thompkins who later became the first officer to receive the Medal of Honor, penned by Lincoln, March 10, 1864, $2,200.00.

Automobilia

While some automobilia buffs are primarily concerned with restoring vintage cars, others concentrate on only one area of collecting. For instance, hood ornaments were often quite spectacular. Made of chrome or nickel plate on brass or bronze, they were designed to represent the 'winged maiden' Victory, flying bats, sleek greyhounds, soaring eagles and a host of other creatures. Today they bring prices in the $75 to $200 range. R. Lalique glass ornaments go much higher!

Horns, radios, clocks, gear shift knobs and key chains with company emblems are other areas of interest. Generally, items pertaining to the classics of the thirties are most in demand. Paper advertising material, manuals and catalogues in excellent condition are also collectible.

License plate collectors search for the early porcelain on cast iron examples. First year plates -- e.g., Massachusetts, 1903; Wisconsin, 1905; Indiana, 1913 -- are especially valuable. The last of the states to issue regulation plates were South Carolina and Texas in 1917, and Florida in 1918. While many northeastern states had registered hundreds of thousands of vehicles by the 1920s making these plates relatively common, those from the southern and western states of that period are considered rare. Naturally, condition is important -- a pair in mint condition might sell for as much as $100 to $125, while a pair with the porcelain in poor condition may sometimes be had for as little as $25 to $30.

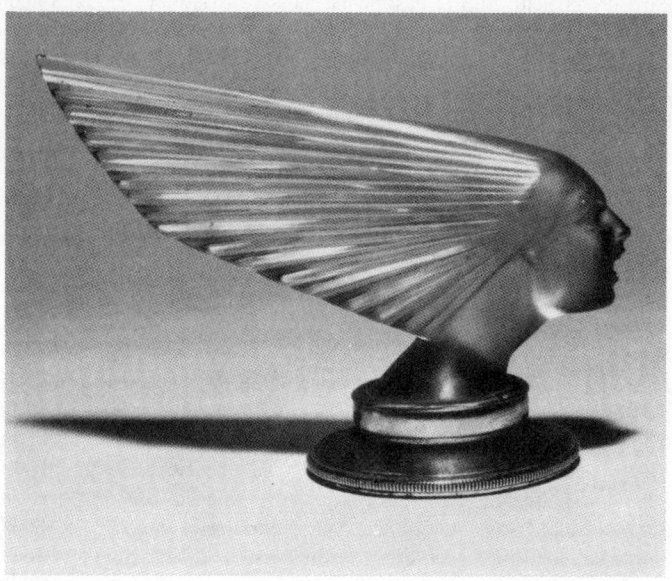

Car mascot, 'Spirit of the Wind', clear and frosted glass, signed R. Lalique, 10" long, $1,870.00.

Award plate, 1962 Ford 300-500 sales, silverplated...........25.00
Badge, Chevrolet Forge Plant............................20.00
Badge, employee; Cadillac Motor Car Division...............50.00
Badge, Ford Aircraft & Engine Division, Plant Protection......50.00
Badge, plant; Fisher Body Grand Blanc......................15.00
Badge, plant; Red Motors Inc............................25.00
Book, Audel's New Automobile Guide, 1938, 1536 pgs, 5x6½"..20.00
Book, Lee's American Auto Annual, 1900, leather cover, illus...76.00
Booklet, Schedule of Repair Charges, 1926 Model T, 20 pgs....17.50
Booklet, Traffic Truck, good pictures, 1919, 12x14".........20.00
Bottle opener, Nash script..............................15.00
Car clock, Pierce Arrow, electric, mid-'30s................100.00
Cartoon book, How To Be An Expert Driver, Ford, 1949, EX...15.00
Catalog, Chevrolet, 1937, color..........................18.00
Catalog, Ford Cars, Accessories for, 1917, 48 pgs w/pictures....8.50
Catalog, Hudson, 1939, deluxe edition, color, 23 pgs, 9x12"....30.00
Catalog, Plymouth, 1937, VG.............................10.00
Catalog, Plymouth Road King, 1939, color, 16 pgs, 9x10"......8.50
Catalog, Plymouth Sales, 1939, 9x10"....................28.00
Catalog, REO, 1922, special bodies/speed wagon chassis, illus...25.00
Catalog, REO Speedwagon, 1925, heavy duty trucks, 11 pgs....18.00
Catalog, REO Speedwagon trucks & cars, w/specs, 1921, 20 pgs.22.00
Coil, brass top, for Model T.............................25.00
Coin, 1933 Ford, Thirty Years of Progress, copper...........25.00

Coin, 1934 Chrysler, A Century of Progress In A Decade, brass..25.00
Coin, 1934 Ford, Century of Progress, brass.................25.00
Coin, 1939 Chrysler, Be Modern Buy Chrysler, brass...........35.00
Coin, 1940 Ford, 29 Millionth Ford Car, brass...............45.00
Coin, 1940 Oldsmobile, dollar size.......................25.00
Dash light cover, 1931 Ford.............................10.00
Emblem, State Farm Mutual, 1930 car.......................7.50
Gas can, Mona Motor, picture of car, tractor, cycle, 1 gal......35.00
Gas can, White Rose, picture of boy w/slate.................7.00
Gas tank straps, for 1927 Ford, pr........................25.00
Heater, motor, catalytic, used in Model Ts..................12.00
Hood ornament, Cadillac emblem (crown).....................5.00
Hood ornament, Dodge emblem, small........................3.00
Hood ornament, hand holding playing cards..................75.00
Hood ornament, lady w/flowing hair, 1942...................60.00
Hood ornament, Mack Truck bulldog.........................35.00
Hood ornament, Miller hearse emblem.......................10.00
Hood ornament, stylized wings............................25.00
Hood ornament, Whippet pup..............................30.00
Hood ornament, 1941 Dodge accessory, w/gr glass insert......85.00
Horn, brass, early, large..............................125.00
Horn, twisted brass, sm................................45.00
Horn, 1909 Buick, brass, orig bulb, works................125.00
Hubcap, Art Deco nude spinners, 14" dia, pr..............150.00
Hubcap, 1927 Nash, screw type, EX........................20.00
Instrument panel, Plymouth Floating Power, brass/chrome......15.00
Jack, Ford..10.00
Key chain, Pontiac, Indian picture 1 side/dealer info on bk......2.00
Key chain ID tag, Lincoln Zephyr V-12, celluloid............25.00
Key chain token, 50 Years Chevrolet, brass.................15.00
License plate, Hawaii, 1949, G..........................50.00
License plate, miniature, BF Goodrich, 1939, Missouri, metal....40.00
License plate, New York, 1932, orange letters on blk..........7.50
License plate, Ontario, 1913...........................150.00
License plate, Texas, 1980, TOP CAT......................10.00
License plate attachment, I Like Ike......................35.00
License plate attachment, Studebaker/Phillips 66, Mich dealer...25.00
Magazine, Buick Bulletin, 1925.........................10.00
Magazine, Ford Times, 1916, pictures & prices, 96 pgs, 9x6"...12.50
Magazine, REO Review, October 1921, 14 pgs, many photos....12.00
Manual, Whippet Six Model 98...........................25.00
Manual, 1915 Audel, instructions, illustrated..............15.00
Manual, 1925 Dodge, w/fold out lubrication chart, G.........25.00
Manual, 1926 Ford, VG.................................16.00
Manual, 1927 Chrysler '50', instructions, G................12.00
Manual, 1930 Cadillac/La Salle, for V6 auto................35.00
Manual, 1930 Ford Model A Instructions, G.................25.00
Manual, 1935 Desoto Airstream..........................25.00
Manual, 1935 Plymouth, instructions, G....................10.00
Manual, 1936 Pontiac, Auto Users Guide, VG................20.00
Manual, 1939, Plymouth, Operation & Care, VG..............10.00
Manual, 1954 Chevrolet, Truck Operator's..................15.00
Mirror, door post; for Model A truck......................25.00
Money clip, Dollar For Dollar Can't Beat Pontiac, 1935.......65.00
Moto-Meter, Boyce, pat 1913, gold lettering ea side: Willys 6..125.00
Moto-Meter, Paige, mounted on lg dogbone style cap, 8" across.75.00
Motorist Wash-up Kit, box shows couple/car, 1920, unused, M...35.00
Nameplate, Republic, w/hallmk on bk......................45.00
Nameplate, Rickenbacker 6..............................60.00
Pamphlet, GM, Diesel Engine 1939, fold-out, color, 16x12".....4.00
Paperweight, Henry Ford Centennial, brass.................45.00
Parts price list, Ford Model A & AA, June 1930, 82 pgs, illus...30.00
Pencil, mechanical; 1955 Ford..........................25.00
Pencil, 1948 Ford, bullet style, pictures sedan.............20.00

Photo, Mercedes-Benz 196, racing at Rheims in 1954, framed...20.00
Photo, 1948 Cadillac factory, 31 models back to 1904, framed...20.00
Pin, Ford, pictures early T touring, Be Wise Drive A Ford.....50.00
Pin, Ford V8, Scotty dog, Aye and Thrifty Too!..............35.00
Pin, Indian Motorcycle, winged chief's head.................50.00
Pin, Now A Cadillac For Only $1345.........................40.00
Pin, Packard Handbook of Automobile Merchandising.........15.00
Pin, Paige The Most Beautiful Car In America...............35.00
Pin, Plymouth, It's Going To Be A Great Day, 1940s, 2" dia....25.00
Pin, Plymouth, Cream Is Always At The Top, w/Dodge ribbon...25.00
Pin, Studebaker script, w/star in background................25.00
Pin, Studebaker script, w/wheel...........................20.00
Pin, Studebaker's Really Rolling...........................15.00
Pin, 1909 Minneapolis Auto Show...........................15.00
Pin, 1932 Chevrolet, Watch the Leader.....................15.00
Pin, 1941 Plymouth, Hotter Than A Firecracker.............25.00
Postcard, Plymouth Sedan, 1939, New Low Prices, color......20.00
Postcard, 1933 Ford, color................................25.00
Poster, fold-out, 1927 Pontiacs, 6 full color views, 12x30".....12.00
Program, 1970 Trans-Am Championship, w/drivers autographs...50.00
Promotional car, 1958 Edsel, all orig, 8", VG..............30.00
Promotional car, 1958 Lincoln, plastic....................55.00
Promotional car, 1959 Plymouth, plastic...................45.00
Radiator emblem, Hupmobile, blue/wht enamel..............45.00
Radiator emblem, 1925 Auburn, enameled..................50.00
Radiator emblem, 1929 Nash..............................30.00
Sign, emb tin, Mitchell Car, cars in lg tire surround, '15......325.00
Sign, porcelain, Chrysler, 1930s, 24x36"..................125.00
Sign, tin, Winter Front Radiator Shutter, 1915 auto, fr, 39"...850.00
Silverware, Ford script, from Rouge plant, old heavy SP, 3 pcs..25.00
Speedometer, AC Spark Plug Co, clock face, speed to 60 mph..58.00
Speedometer, Jones, beveled glass cracked, 1904...........25.00
Speedometer, Stewart-Warner Co, speed to 80 mph.........25.00
Stickpin, John Deere, deer & plow........................25.00
Tie clip, Chrysler Corporation Master Technician...........20.00
Tire, for Model A..50.00
Tire pump, oak handle....................................10.00
Traffic signal, 3 sided, 1920s, all orig...................375.00
Tray, serving; Ford/1934 Century of Progress Expo, metal, lg...85.00
Valve stem, metal, Model A...............................20.00
Watch fob, Dodge Brothers, mc enamel, early.............75.00
Watch fob, Indian Motorcycles, arrow w/chiefs face........85.00
Watch fob, Studebaker script wheel, leather background......50.00
Wheel cap, MG spin-off....................................5.00
Wrench, crescent, Model A, mk Ford......................40.00

Autumn Leaf

In 1933, the Hall China Company designed a line of dinnerware for the Jewell Tea Company who offered it to their customers as premiums. Although you may hear the ware referred to as 'Jewell Tea', it was officially named 'Autumn Leaf' in the 1940s. In addition to the dinnerware, frosted Libbey glass tumblers, stemware, and a tilt jug with the orange & gold bittersweet pod were available over the years, as were tablecloths, plastic covers for bowls and mixers, and metal items such as cake safes, hot pads, coasters, waste baskets, and canisters. Even shelf paper and playing cards were made to coordinate. In 1958, the International Silver Company designed silverplated flatware in a pattern they called 'Autumn'. These accessory lines are prized by collectors today.

Hall discontinued the Autumn Leaf line in 1978. At that time the date was added to the backstamp to mark ware still in stock in the Jewell warehouse.

Kitchen clock, electric, 9½" diameter, rare, $225.00.

Bake dish, Swirl, 3 pt, 8" across top.......................15.00
Baker, oval, individual....................................65.00
Baker, 2 pt..47.00
Bean pot, 1 hdl, rare....................................225.00
Bean pot, 2 hdld, 2¼ qt..................................70.00
Bottle, Jewel Food Stores 50th Anniversary, Jim Beam.......39.00
Bottle, Jewel-T Wagon, Jim Beam, empty..................85.00
Bowl, cereal; mint gold...................................8.75
Bowl, fruit...4.00
Bowl, Glassbake, middle size.............................11.00
Bowl, mixing; set of 3 in orig box, 1978..................25.00
Bowl, mixing; set of 3: 6¼", 7½", 9".....................35.00
Bowl, mixing; 6¼".......................................10.00
Bowl, mixing; 7½".......................................12.00
Bowl, mixing; 9"...13.00
Bowl, salad; 9"..12.00
Bowl, vegetable; divided.................................50.00
Bowl, vegetable; oval, w/cover...........................32.00
Bowl, vegetable; oval, 10"...............................16.00
Bowl, vegetable; round, 9", rare..........................65.00
Bud vase...165.00
Butter, 1 lb, w/cover...................................110.00
Butter, ¼ lb, square top, rare..........................275.00
Butter, ¼ lb, wings, rare...............................225.00
Cake, on Golden Ray base...............................105.00
Cake plate..12.00
Cake safe, metal, NM....................................25.00
Candy dish, on Golden Ray base, rare....................225.00
Canister, round, brown & gold...........................25.00
Canister, round, ivory plastic top........................10.00
Canister, round, metal, w/coppertone lids, set of 4, VG.....145.00
Canister, square, set of 4..............................100.00
Casserole, covered; 1½ qt, tab hdls.....................22.50
Casserole, individual; round, 4"..........................9.00
Casserole/souffle, 10 oz size, 4⅜", rare.................25.00
Cleanser can, metal....................................115.00
Clock, original works..................................300.00
Coaster, 3¼"..4.00
Coffee maker, drip, all china, 4 pc w/insert..............175.00
Coffee pot, 8 cup.......................................30.00

Coffee pot, 8 cup, fat, w/lid, 8¼".........................35.00
Coffee pot, 9 cup, gold wear.........................35.00
Cookbook, Mary Dunbar Favorite Recipes.................12.00
Cookie jar, big ear.........................65.00
Cookie jar, Tootsie.........................85.00
Cookware, 7 pc set in orig box.........................85.00
Creamer, New Style.........................8.00
Creamer, Old Style.........................15.00
Cup.........................6.00
Cup, St Denis.........................10.00
Cup & saucer.........................8.00
Custard cup.........................4.75
Drip jar, w/cover.........................12.50
Fondue set, in orig box.........................45.00
Fork, stainless steel.........................6.00
Fruit cake tin.........................3.00
Glasses, Brockway, set of 6 sm.........................66.00
Golden Ray bases, pr.........................50.00
Gravy boat.........................14.00
Hot pad, metal, red felt backing, 7".........................14.00
Knife, stainless steel.........................6.00
Marmalade, w/cover & underplate.........................45.00
Mixer cover, Mary Dunbar, plastic.........................22.00
Mug, beverage; set of 4.........................140.00
Mug, Irish Coffee.........................55.00
Mustard set, 3 pc.........................45.00
Percolator, electric, OB.........................200.00
Pickle dish.........................14.00
Picnic thermos, usual aging.........................150.00
Pie baker.........................15.00
Pitcher, beverage jug; ice lip, 5½ pt.........................20.00
Pitcher, utility; 2½ pt, 6".........................15.00
Place setting, cup/saucer/plate, Melmac.........................14.00
Plate, 10" dinner; mint gold.........................10.00
Plate, 6".........................4.00
Plate, 7" salad; mint gold.........................6.00
Plate, 8".........................8.00
Plate, 9".........................9.00
Platter, 11½".........................14.00
Platter, 13½".........................17.00
Salt & pepper shakers, casper.........................12.00
Salt & pepper shakers, range, hdld.........................15.00
Saucer.........................2.00
Saucer, St Denis, NM.........................5.00
Sifter, metal.........................85.00
Soup, coupe.........................10.50
Soup, cream.........................15.00
Spoon, stainless steel.........................6.00
Stack set, 3 bowls w/lid, in orig box.........................50.00
Sugar w/lid, New Style.........................10.00
Sugar w/lid, Old Style.........................15.00
Tablecloth, plastic, lg, still in package.........................125.00
Tablecloth, sailcloth, 54x54".........................48.00
Tablecloth, sailcloth, 54x72".........................60.00
Tea towel, pr.........................75.00
Teapot, Aladdin, 3 pc.........................30.00
Teapot, Newport, old, slight gold wear.........................100.00
Teapot, Newport, 1978, M.........................65.00
Teapot, Sunshine, long spout.........................55.00
Tid bit tray, 3 tiered.........................45.00
Tray, glass, w/wood hdls, w/part of orig label.........................110.00
Tray, glass, wooden hdls.........................85.00
Tray, metal, oval, VG.........................65.00
Tray, metal, oval, 2 small worn spots.........................30.00

Tray, red, w/AOP.........................60.00
Tumbler, frosted, 14 oz, 5½".........................14.50
Tumbler, frosted, 9 oz, 3¾".........................16.00
Tumbler, ftd, gold frost etched, 6½ oz.........................45.00
Tumbler, gold frost etched, 10 oz, flat.........................25.00
Warmer, oval.........................95.00
Warmer, round, w/orig box.........................100.00

Aviation

Aviation buffs are interested in any phase of flying -- from early developments with gliders, balloon, airships and flying machines, to more modern innovations. Books, catalogues, photos, patents, lithographs, ad cards, and posters are among the paper ephemera they treasure, alongside models of unlikely flying contraptions, propellers and rudders, insignia and equipment from WW I and II, and memorabilia from the flights of the Wright Brothers, Lindberg, Earhart and the Zepplins.

Autograph, Wrong Way Corrigan, in flyleaf of That's My Story...69.00
Book, Aeronautics Aircraft Spotters Handbook, WWII.........................40.00
Book, Flight to Everywhere, illus diary of ATC, 1944, 1st ed....25.00
Book, Lindberg's Trophies & Decorations, 1933, 64 pgs.........................35.00
Booklet, Standard Oil, about flying sm aircraft, 1930, 48 pgs....12.00
Calendar, desk; Grumman Aircraft, 18 color pages, 1943.........................15.00
Card game, New Lindy Flying Game NY to Paris, 1927.........................12.00
Control grip, from T-33 jet, gun trigger switch, sits upright.........................25.00
Extra-Seattle Times, 3/4/32, Ranson Demand Phoned to Lindy..16.00
First aid kit, Sentinel Jr Ace, shows aviator/airplanes.........................15.00
Flight plan, Deutsche Luft Hansa, 43" foldout, 1930s, colorful...14.00
Fuel gauge, Luftwaffe markings, WWII.........................45.00
Gloves, gauntlet type, leather w/wool uppers, Eaglet, 1920s.........................25.00
Goggles, blk framed, curved lense, 2 pc brn rubber mask, 1930s.55.00
Goggles, WWII Royal Air Force, tinted lenses/brass framed, RAF.85.00
Helmet, wht leather, used: some yellowing, Eaglet Co, 1920s....35.00
Jacket, WWII type A-2, orig AF US Army tag, orig AAF decal..200.00
Logbook, leather w/wing & prop symbol, 6/1934-12/1937, VG...10.00
Logbook, unissued, unused, 1943, standard to CAA regulations..10.00
Magazine, Aircraft Spotters' Guide Quarterly, complete.........................15.00
Magazine, Parks Air College, 1935, 64 pgs, illustrated.........................13.00
Manual, Flying & How To Do It, Jordanoff, 1932, sgn.........................25.00
Manual, Through the Overcast, Jordanoff, 1942.........................18.00
Manual, WWII War Dept Pictorial Aircraft Recognition, 1943...25.00
Model airplane, AAF P-38, WWII, blk rubber, 1:72 scale, EX..55.00
Model airplane, mkd PBY-5 Catalina, AAF, cardboard, dtd 1943.25.00
Model airplane, RAF Spitfire, WWII, blk rubber, 1:72 scale, EX.55.00
Needle case, paper, figural dirigible, shows airship ea side.........................14.00
Paperweight, figural airline seats, metal, Aerotec Indus, '50s.........................13.00
Paperweight, lucite w/aircraft carrier, Golden Anniv Naval, 3½"..25.00
Parachute pack survival kit, knife/fishhooks/compass/etc, 2x6"..20.00
Photo, Wrong Way Corrigan, 1938, sepia, autographed comment100.00
Pin, AAF WWII Crew member wings, sterling, pin-back, 3".........................25.00
Pin, pictures Charles Lindbergh, commemorates flight.........................15.00
Plate, w/air-brushed early jet fighter, Jackson China.........................28.00
Postcard, Lincoln Beachey/World's Most Daring Aviator, photo..35.00
Radar Indicator, Bendix, screen w/5x5" face, numerous dials....45.00
Record, actual moments in Lindbergh's Washington DC reception.9.50
Ring, Air Corps, eagles/shield/stars, sterling/10k, WWII, EX....100.00
Scarf, Charles Lindbergh, chiffon, MIB.........................25.00
Sign, Skelly Aviation Fuel.........................105.00
Sketch book, Lockheed Aircraft Design, 1940.........................25.00
Spirit of St Louis, metalcraft plane w/directions, orig box.........................225.00
Tapestry, Lindbergh, framed.........................285.00
Token, Lucky Lindbergh, gilt plated, profile/plane, 1¼".........................6.50
WWII Official Publication, Memphis Belle crew's story, illus.........................20.00

Avon

The California Perfume Company, the parent of the Avon Co., was founded in 1886. Although an 'Avon' line was introduced by the company in the mid-20s, not until 1939 did it become known as Avon Products, Inc. Collectible Avon items include not only figural bottles, containers and jars, but jewelry, awards, product samples, magazine ads, and catalogues as well.

See also California Perfume Company

Alpine Flask. 45.00
Award, Albee, 1980, yellow. 60.00
Award, Bird Plates, set. 80.00
Award, Car Glasses & Pitcher, 1971, MIB. 57.50
Award, Christmas Gift Picture Frame, 1979. . . . . .5.00
Award, Christmas Mouse, ceramic, 1980. . . . . .35.00
Award, Color-Up America Watch. 30.00
Award, Crown Performance, Regence, earrings/necklace, 1966. .110.00
Award, Diamond 4A Pin, 1961-76, MIB. 25.00
Award, Div Managers Loving Cup, 1966. . . . . .100.00
Award, Going Calling Car. .60.00
Award, Golden Slipper, slipper/labeled bottle/card/box, 1959. . . .200.00
Award, Pearl Pin, 1963-70, MIB. 10.00
Award, Pres Club Highest Award Charm Bracelet, MIB. 250.00
Award, President's Club, Lenox China Bowl, 1979, MIB. 40.00
Award, Rep's Bracelet, 5 charms, 22k gold finish, 1969, MIB. . . .42.00
Award, Retirement Pin, 1967, M. 50.00
Award, Sales Achievement Necklace, smaller size, 1977, MIB. . . .20.00
Award, Sapphire 4A Pin, 1963-76, MIB. 15.00
Award, Small Treasures Mini Collection complete w/display case. 100.00
Award, Smile Jewelry Box, music box, 1978. . . . . .40.00
Award, Sonnet Vanity Tray & Vanity Box, MIB. 28.00
Award, Sounds of Seasons Music Box, 1966. . . . . . . .65.00
Award, Spoon Set, 1969, set of 7, boxed & sleeved. 50.00
Award, Teddy Bear Cookie Jar, 1979. . . . . .35.00
Award, Tiffany Sterling Bracelet. 40.00
Award, Townhouse Canister Set, complete. 75.00
Award, Wildflower Plates, set, 1976-78. . . . . .60.00
Award, Woman of Achievement, 1969, no box. 275.00
Bay Rum Keg, 1965, MIB. .16.00
Bridal Moments, 1976-79, empty, MIB. 6.00
Bright Night Toilet Water, 1955-61, full, no box, M. 11.00
Brocade Deluxe Gift Set, 1967, MIB. 30.00
Brocade Perfume Skin Softener, glass, ball shape, 1968, MIB. . . .12.00
Bronze Washington Bust, 1979, MIB. 11.00
Cameo Glace Brooch, 1965, MIB. 15.00
Canada Goose, 1973-74, MIB. 8.00
Candid Blazer, 1977, large man. 75.00
Candlestick Cologne, silver, 1966, empty, no box, M, pr. 12.00
Cape Cod Candlesticks, 1975-1980, MIB, pr. 15.00
Cape Cod Wine Decanter, 1977-1980, MIB. 10.00
Charley Brown Children's Mug, 1969-70, MIB. 6.00
Chess Set, complete, (no chess board). 85.00
Christmas Plate, Carollers in the Snow, 1977, MIB. 20.00
Christmas Plate, Christmas on the Farm, 1973. . . . . . . .83.00
Christmas Plate, Country Church, 1974. . . . . .40.00
Christmas Plate, Skaters, 1976. . . . . .22.00
Close Harmony, barber bottle w/tip, 1963, empty, no box, M. . .12.00
Cologne Trilogy, 1969-70, full, MIB. 13.00
Cruet Cologne Set, 1973-74, empty, MIB. 8.00
Crystal Beauty Dust, 1966, empty, no box, M. 15.00
Crystalique Beauty Dust, 1972, empty, MIB. 9.00
Dutch Girl, 1973-74, empty, MIB. 7.00
Emerald Accent Serving Tray, Goblets, & Decanter, MIB. 35.00

Flowertime Sachet, green-blue cap, 1952, full, no box, M. 6.00
Fore N After Set, 1966, MIB. 20.00
Fragrance Chest, 1966, MIB. 40.00
Garden Girl, MIB. 3.50
Gavel, 1967-68, MIB. 10.00
George & Martha Washington Goblets, 1975, MIB, pr. 20.00
Golden Promise Cologne, 4 oz, 1947-56, full, no box, M. 13.00
Good Cheer box, 1957, shows age, EX. 40.00
Happy Hours box, 1958, shows age, G. 40.00
Imperial Gardens Ceramic Vase, short neck, 1973-75, MIB. . . .14.00
Island Lime After Shave Lotion, dk yel, 1966, empty, no box, M. .7.00
Jasmine Dusting Powder, 1947-50, sm nicks, empty, no box, G. .19.00
Jennifer, 1973, MIB. 45.00
Lady Slipper Soap, 1965-66, MIB. 20.00
Marine Binoculars, 1973-74, empty, MIB. 8.00
Merry Christmas Hostess Set, w/tree & salt & pepper, MIB. . . .25.00
Mickey Mouse Bubble Bath, 1969, MIB. 6.00
Mt Vernon Sauce Pitcher, 1977-79, empty, MIB. 12.00
My Pet, 1973, MIB. 35.00
NAAC McConnell Club Bottle, 1973. . . . . .80.00
NAAC 6 Year Plate, gold rimmed, 1977, MIB. 60.00
NAAC 7 Year Plate, 1978, gold rimmed, MIB. 45.00
Nearness Beauty Dust, 1959-61, full, no box, M. 18.00
Opening Play, dull gold over blue, 1968-69, empty, MIB. 12.00
Original After Shave Lotion, 4 oz, gr label, 1965, full, MIB. 6.00
Overnighter, 1958, full, no box, M. 32.50
Overnighter, 1968, full, MIB. 10.00
Persian Wood Beauty Dust, glass, 1957-60, empty, no box, M. . .10.00
President Lincoln, bronze Everest after shave, '79, empty, MIB. .11.00
President's Busts, colored, set, 1978, MIB. 85.00
President's Heads, white painted set, MIB. 160.00
Quaintance Body Powder, 1948-56, 5 oz, empty, no box. 12.00
Quaintance Powder Sachet, 9/10 oz, large printed, 1948, MIB. . .20.00
Rapture Pin, 1964, MIB. 20.00
Rapture Soap, 1965-68, full, MIB. 17.50
Royal Jasmine Bath Oil, 1957-59, 8 oz, full, no box. 20.00
Scentiments Cream Sachet & Soap, 1969, full, MIB. 10.00
Scimitar, 1968-69, MIB. 24.00
Sea Trophy, Windjammer, 1972, empty, MIB. 7.00
Sentimental Doll Adorable Abigail, 1979-80, empty, MIB. . . .10.00
Skip-A-Rope, Sweet Honesty, 1975-77, empty, MIB. 8.00
Spicy After Shave Lotion, 2 oz, 1965-67, full, no box, M. . . .17.50
Stein, large, 1976-79, MIB. 25.00
Stein, Sporting Stein Decanter, large, 1978. . . . . .27.00
Structured for Men, 1969, full, MIB. 15.00
Tag Alongs, 1967, full, MIB. 12.00
Tall Pony Post, 1966-67, MIB. 13.00
Tribute Shaving Set, 1964-65, MIB. 35.00
Tug-A-Brella, 1978-80, MIB. 10.00
Victorian Fashion Figurine, aqua/blue, 1973-74. . . . . . . .30.00
Viking Horn, 1966, MIB. 17.50
Western Roundup Ceramic Stein, 1980-82, MIB. 38.00
Wild Country Body Powder, 1967-68, full, MIB. 12.00

Baccarat

The Baccarat Glass company was founded in 1765 near Luneville, France, and continues to this day to produce quality crystal tableware, vases, perfume bottles, and figurines. The firm became famous for the high quality millefiori and caned paperweights produced there from 1845 until about 1860. Examples of these range from $300 to as much as several thousand. Since 1953, they have resumed the production of paperweights on a limited edition basis. These are listed later, in the Paperweight section.

Blotter frame, rectangular, cut cane/bust of Massillion, 4½"..1,210.00
Bowl, cut crystal, diamond point pattern, sgn, 6"..............60.00
Breakfast set, Gold Grape, 43 pcs.......................1,800.00
Cellarette/music box, 4 decanters/12 glasses, rosewood w/inlay..990.00
Decanter, emb swirl, rose tiente, matching stopper, 9¾"......110.00
Goblet, emb swirl, rose tiente, 4½".........................55.00
Goblet, Francois Villon....................................30.00
Goblet, gr to clear, sgnd..................................90.00
Perfume, Guerlain...45.00
Perfume, swirl, rose, 6½".................................75.00
Rose bowl, engraved, w/cameos of ladies in pink............125.00
Sugar bowl, w/lid, emb swirl, rose tiente, 4¾".............95.00
Tray, dresser; rose tiente swirl, 8½x12"...................85.00
Tray, emb swirl, rose tiente, scalloped, 11¼" dia..........88.00
Tumbler, ftd, amberina, flattened diamond, 5x3¼"...........57.00

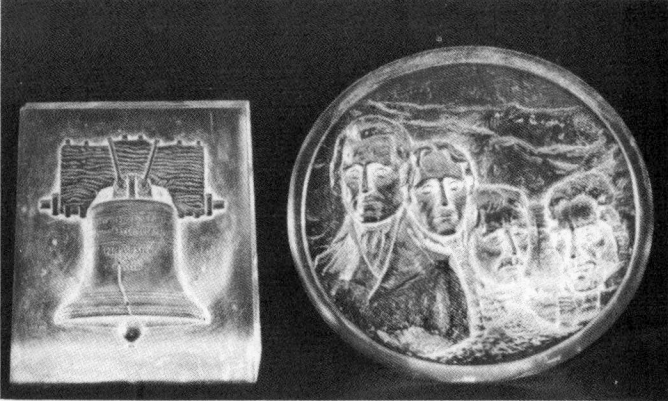

Left: Sculptured plaque, Liberty Bell, inscribed and acid stenciled Baccarat, 10" x 8½", $400.00.
Right: Sculptured plaque, Mt. Rushmore, signed J. Goy, inscribed and acid stenciled Baccarat, 14" x 12", $650.00.

Badges

The breast badge came into general usage in this country about 1840. Since most are not marked and styles have changed very little to the present day, they are often diffcult to date. The most reliable clue is the pin and catch. One of the earliest types, used primarily before the turn of the century, involved a 't-pin' and a 'shell' catch. In a second style, the pin was hinged with a small square of sheet metal, and the clasp was cylinderical. From the late 1800s until about 1940, the pin and clasp were made from one continuous piece of thin metal wire. The same type, with the addition of a flat back plate, was used a little later. There are exceptions to these findings, and other types of clasps were also used. Hallmarks and inscriptions may also help pinpoint an approximate age.

Badges have been made from a variety of materials, usually brass or nickle silver, but even solid silver and gold were used on special order. They are found in many basic shapes and variations -- stars with five to seven points, shields, discs, ovals, and octagonals being most often encountered.

Of prime consideration to collectors, however, is the title and/or location appearing on the badge. Those with designations of positions no longer existing (City Constable, for example) and names of early western states and towns are most valuable.

Key: pt-------point

Bailiff, Muncipal (misspelled Municipal) Court/eagle top, old.....25.00
Baker Construction Co, porcelain heavy duty truck, hat badge...15.00
Bus driver, Dodson's Line, porcelain bus cap badge...........15.00
Chief, Hollywood, Knickerbocker House Detective.............20.00

Chief Deputy Sheriff, Arizona, seal center, gold, eagle top.....100.00
Chief Jailer, Galveston Sheriff Dept, brass..................75.00
Chief of Police, med size, enamel seal, LA format............32.50
City Marshall, Hamilton, nickeled silver, shield sunburst......50.00
Civil Defense Special Officer, Kansas, shield, rimless, 1950s.....12.00
Commander, Police Reserve, CA 7-point star..................45.00
Constable, star w/sm diamond in center, brass, bl letters.......75.00
Deputy Bailiff, seal of Municipal Court Chicago, 5-pt star......40.00
Deputy Marshall, South Hutchison, eagle shield, very old......75.00
Deputy Police, Indian Creek, NY............................45.00
Deputy Sheriff, Kauai, silver w/blue enameling..............20.00
Deputy Sheriff, Passaic Co, NJ, mkd.......................45.00
Deputy Sheriff, purse size, 5-point star w/ball tips..........18.50
Deputy Sheriff, 6-point star, ball tips, early...............30.00
Detective, 7-pt star, Pacific Electric......................25.00
Fire Dept, McAllen, Texas.................................20.00
Honorary Deputy Sheriff, LA shape, gilded..................23.50
Lieutenant, Tucson Police, gold color, city seal center, 1950s...85.00
Lieutenant Police, gold clam shell, Arizona seal center........85.00
Patrolman, Guam, #63, lg nickeled shield....................40.00
Paul Central Cab Co, porcelain taxi hat badge...............15.00
Piaute Tribal Council, Nevada.............................55.00
Police, Brawley, CA, hallmark, hat piece....................42.50
Police, Chicago, before 1910, large star....................85.00
Police, Examiner of Chauffeurs, Hawaii, nickeled, cut-out star...25.00
Police, Minnesota, #9 med size nickled shield...............22.50
Police, New Jersey, nickeled shield, cut-out #s..............33.50
Police, nickled, numbered, typical.........................20.00
Police, NY State Seal, eagle atop, ca 1920, lg size...........28.00
Police, Wabash Railway Co, silver color/blk lettering..........25.00
Police, Wisconsin, sunburst w/eagle atop, enamel ring/seal......28.50
Police Reserve, Bedford, nickeled silver shield/enamel center....45.00
Police Reserve, Chicago, 6-pt star, city seal, early 1900s.....50.00
Police Rivere Du Loup, silver shield, no seal, Canadian, 1930s...20.00
Policia y Transito, Mexican Traffic Police, gold color w/seal.....35.00
Sargeant, Crow Indian Reservation, nickeled, rare............40.00
Sargeant, Florida, pointed shield w/gilt, #d................30.00
Sargeant, Police, lg gold clam shell, Arizona seal center, EX...100.00
Secret Service, Mexico, bronze/enamel, eagle w/snake in beak...30.00
Security, Ford Plant, med size sunburst, nickeled............15.00
Security Officer, US Rubber, Michigan......................20.00
Set, cap & breast, matching #s, nickled w/copper #, '05........55.00
Sheriff, Arizona, gold, eagle top, raised star, bl letters......125.00
Sheriff, Lincoln County, star.............................75.00
Sheriff, purse size, nickled..............................18.50
Special Constable, Ottawa Prov Secret Service, shield, old......50.00
Special Police, Bethlehem Steel Co, nickle shield, lg, old......25.00
Special Police, Florida, nickeled, 1910....................32.50
Technician, Victoria Police #340, nickeled silver/gold/enamel....40.00
Trooper, Idaho, 6-pt star, ball tips, nickle/enamel, '80........45.00
Trooper, LA, EX lg, nickled w/enameled letters..............50.00
US Forest Reserve Ranger, Dept of Interior, current..........20.00
US Liberty Loan Committee, sm brass shield w/eagle, mk, 1917..65.00
US Post Office, hat badge................................20.00

Banks

Still banks were manufactured from as early as 1800, and were intended to inspire thriftiness through amusing character themes, charming animal figures, and areas of special interests. They were made in virtually every kind of material existant: wood, glass, ceramics, and metal. Among the most prominent manufacturers were J. & E. Stevens Company of Cromwell, Connecticut, and A.C. Williams Company of Revanna, Ohio. Stevens was the first company to design and market a mechanical bank in 1890. During the years of the Civil War, people hoarded coins to the extent that silver became scarce. The paper money issued to alleviate this situation was regarded with distrust, and the hoarding continued. This created a natural market for the new mechanical banks, and their complex, often amusing actions made saving money fun. It is estimated that more than 250 designs were patented, some as late as 1935. Others who manufactured mechanical banks were Shephard Hardware of Buffalo, New York; Kilgore Manufacturing Company of Westville, Ohio; Kyser and Rex of Philadelphia, Pennsylvania; and the Mechanical Novelty Works of New Britain, Connecticut. Each attempted to outdo the other in producing the more complex mechanism. Sensitive balances, rotating wheels, springs, and levers interacted one with another to produce animation of every description.

Popular concepts of the day dictated design. Buildings, such as Victorian domes with gingerbread trim, gave way to early 20th century skyscrapers. Comic strip characters were immortalized in cast iron banks, and political and patriotic themes aptly reflected the state of the Union.

Registering banks were designed to divulge the total amount of the money as it was deposited. Some would accomodate only one denomination; others had seperate slots for different sized coins.

Advertising banks have a two fold interest -- both bank collectors and those who like antique advertising find them appealing.

Because many old banks are so valuable, reproductions are common. Some of these restrikes were themselves made over forty years ago, so some study is required to be able to recognize the originals.

Condition is judged by the percentage of the remaining original paint, and whether all parts are present, original, and in working order. Rarity is a factor in evaluating worth, but those with an especially popular design may bring the higher prices. Some of the banks listed here are identified by C for Cranmer, G for Griffeth, and W for Whiting, standard references used by many collectors.

Key: NPCI--nickle plated cast iron   EPCI--electroplated cast iron

Advertising

Bosco Food Drink, litho tin can, 2¾", EX...................50.00
Buick Fireball Eight, ball shape, litho tin, 4½", NM..........75.00
Buster Brown Mustard, tin can/litho paper label, 2½", EX......50.00
Campbell Kids, W-45.....................................150.00
Chevrolet, Symbol of Savings, globe figural, litho tin, 4½"......90.00
Dr Oetker Biskets, can, litho paper on cardboard, 4½", NM....45.00
General Electric, refrigerator, W-237, NM...................65.00
Gerber Orange Juice, litho tin can, 2¾", NM.................25.00
Good Year, Zeppelin Airship Dock, duraluminum/felt base, 7" L.80.00
High Lindens Coffee, litho tin can, 3", EX..................27.00
Kool/Raleigh Cigarettes, litho tin can, rectangular, 2¾", EX....35.00
Liberty Bell, litho tin hat-shaped can, 4" dia, EX.............30.00
Masons Extract of Herbs, can: litho paper/cardboard, 3", EX....50.00
Meadow Gold Butter, litho tin can, 2½", VG.................45.00
Mobil Oil, baseball figural, plastic & glass, 3½", EX..........20.00
Nugget Saves Money, litho tin can, 3½", EX................325.00
Peacock Sliced Dried Beef, litho tin can, 2¾", EX............40.00
Pearl White Plunder, litho tin can, 1½", G..................75.00
Red Goose School Shoes, ptd CI goose, W-215, 4", VG........80.00
Red Goose Shoes, ptd CI goose, W-212, 4½", G.............125.00
Sanford's Writing Fluid, can: litho paper/cardboard, 3", EX.....25.00
Snow's Minced Clams, tin can, litho paper label, 2", EX........40.00

Mechanical

Always Did 'Spise A Mule, ptd CI, Stevens, 10" L, EX........475.00
Archie, bust of man, ptd aluminum, EX....................70.00

Bad Accident...475.00
Bear, arms around vertical stump, ptd CI, 5¼", EX..........425.00
Billie Grin...250.00
Bismark Bank, figural pig, ptd CI, some restoration, G.......650.00
Boy Bust, ptd aluminum, G..............................90.00
Bull Dog, standing, ptd CI, 7" L, EX......................900.00
Calumet, lg..80.00
Cannon & Octagonal Fort, ptd CI, replaced trap & trigger, G..825.00
Charlie McCarthy, sits on chest, ptd pot metal, 5¾", VG......60.00
Chief Big Moon, Indian gives frog fish, no coin return cover...550.00
Clown, in globe, CI....................................300.00
Clown Bust, dots on hat, ptd aluminum, EX.................80.00
Clown Bust, figure on hat, ptd aluminum, EX...............120.00
Creedmore, JE Stevens Co, missing coin return cover........250.00
Darktown Battery, CI, 10"..............................700.00
Darky in Cabin, G-39..................................225.00
Dinah, ptd aluminum, EX...............................130.00
Dog, Speaking Dog, trap missing, G orig pnt, 7x8"..........450.00
Dog on Turntable, orig coppertone, 3x5x5", VG.............200.00
Doll's Head, baby coming out of egg figural, ptd CI, 7¾", NM.500.00
Eagle & Eaglets, CI, G-78, 8"..........................275.00
Elephant, Gar-Ru, die cast, 4¾", G.......................20.00
Elephant, w/howdah, ptd CI, Hubley, gray, 5½", EX..........130.00
Elephant, w/howdah, ptd CI, Hubley, wht, 5½", NM..........250.00
Elephant, w/3 dots, porcelainized CI, 4¾", EX..............225.00
Elephant, w/3 stars, ptd CI, 4¾", G......................100.00
First National Duck Bank, Disney, tin, semi-mechanical........95.00
Football, figural boy kicks coin, ptd CI, English, 10" L, G...1,050.00
Fortune Teller Savings Bank............................750.00
Frog on Rock, mouth opens, orig G pnt, w/orig key..........140.00
Greedy Nigger Boy, ptd CI, EX..........................360.00
Hall's Excelsior, building figural/ptd CI, rpl man, 5¼", EX....110.00
Hawaiian Statehood Commemorative, dtd 1960, EX pnt.......135.00
Home Bank, building figural, litho tin, 5¼", EX.............130.00
Hoopla Bank, trap missing, old pnt, 8x8", VG..............400.00
Hunter, w/pilgrim type hat, ptd CI & tin, 10" L, G...........200.00
Joe Socko, figural fighters, litho tin, 3½x2¼" base, EX.......400.00
Jolly Nigger, plastic, EX................................25.00
Jolly Nigger, ptd CI, EX................................120.00
Jolly Nigger High Hat, ptd CI, G.........................200.00
Kanter's Baby Telephone, litho tin figural wall phone, 10", EX..85.00
Keene Savings Bank, building figural/litho tin, Wilkins, 6", EX.360.00
Key, figural large key, ptd CI, 5¾", VG...................345.00
Kiltie Bank..650.00
Little Joe, ptd CI, EX..................................130.00
Little Joe High Hat, ptd CI, EX..........................350.00
Little Moe, ptd CI, VG.................................400.00
Locomotive, figural, Safety, NPCI, 6" L, EX................800.00
Locomotive, figural, Safety, NPCI, 6" L, G.................425.00
Minstrel, relief face at top, litho tin, German, 7", EX........130.00
Monkey, sitting, arms raise, dump coins in mouth, early tin...225.00
Monkey & Parrot......................................225.00
Mule Entering Barn, CI, 5¼"............................340.00
New Bank, building figural, ptd CI, 6x4¼", EX.............625.00
New Bank, variation, building figural, ptd CI, 5¾x4½", EX....575.00
Organ Grinder..250.00
Pig in Chair, w/orig nickel plated coin tray................550.00
Pineapple..50.00
Rabbit, eats lettuce, mechanical ears, w/orig key, pnt poor.....100.00
Rooster, crowing, CI, G-231............................195.00
Santa by Chimney, G-236...............................700.00
Scotsman, relief man on front, litho tin, 7", EX.............525.00
Scottish Highlander, figural man, ptd pot metal, 8", EX.......95.00
Smyth X-Ray Bank, CI, 5¼" L, no finish.................1,300.00

Sparskytt, ptd aluminum, 9¾″ L, G........................55.00
Squirrel & Tree Stump, G-251...........................450.00
Surly Bruin, ptd CI, 6¼″, VG...........................190.00
Sweet Thrift...85.00
Tammany, CI w/orig pnt, pat 1785, no trap, 7″..........150.00
Tank & Cannon, ptd aluminum, tank 8¼″ L, EX...........300.00
Tank & Cannon, ptd CI, tank 8″ L, EX..................425.00
Tank & Cannon, ptd CI, wood base added: 10¾x7¼″, EX....275.00
Teddy & the Bear, CI, 7″..............................700.00
Trenton Trust Roebling, lady in chair, ptd CI, 6x4″ base, NM..900.00
Trick Pony, EX..450.00
Uncle Sam...425.00
William Tell, Australian, ptd tin & aluminum, 14½″ L, G.....625.00
William Tell, ptd CI, 10½″ L, EX......................450.00
Wireless Bank, building figural, ptd CI/litho tin/wood, 5″, EX...130.00

Registering

Beehive Savings Bank, figural hive, nickel plated CI, 5½″, VG...85.00
Lucky Savings, tin, tone rings for coins, auto open at $10.....125.00
Popeye, dime register, flat metal, 1929...................35.00
Uncle Sam's Register Bank, sheet metal/orig pnt, 6¼″........30.00

Still

A Good Turn For The Blind, English, ptd CI/litho tin/glass, G..470.00
Acorn, rockingham on yellowware, minor chips at slot, 3″.....40.00
Administration Building/Columbian Expo, NPCI, Saks, 5″, VG...50.00
Amish boy, holding pig, sits on bale of hay................65.00
Apple, W-299, ptd CI, 3½″, EX.........................650.00
Auto, W-157, ptd CI, 6¼″ L, G.........................360.00
Auto w/people, W-159..................................395.00
Bank, C-372, tin.......................................45.00
Bank Building, figural, rpr Indian on roof, ptd CI, 9″, EX.....100.00
Bank Building, W-242, ptd CI, 3¼″, rpt..................10.00
Bank Building, W-305, ptd CI, mica on face, 5½″, EX.......250.00
Bank Building, W-306, ptd CI, 4¼″, G...................75.00
Bank Building, W-307, ptd CI, 3½″, EX..................80.00
Bank Building, W-366, japanned & ptd CI, 5½″, EX.........40.00
Bank Building, W-403, japanned CI, 3¼″, VG..............70.00
Bank Building, W-412, ptd CI, 5¾″, rpt.................25.00
Bank Building, W-413, ptd CI, 4½″, EX..................30.00
Bank Building, W-414, ptd CI, 3¾″, EX..................50.00
Bank Building, W-421, ptd CI, 5″, rpt..................40.00
Bank Building, W-423, ptd CI, 4″, rpt..................15.00
Bank Building, W-441, State, japanned & ptd CI, 8¾″, EX....320.00
Bank Building, W-442, State, japanned & ptd CI, 3″, EX.....80.00
Bank Building, W-443, State, japanned & ptd CI, 6″, EX.....85.00
Bank Building, W-444, State, japanned & ptd CI, 5½″, EX....110.00
Barrel with Arms, W-151, ptd CI, 3¾″, rstr..............90.00
Baseball on Three Bats, W-220, ptd CI, 5″, VG...........325.00
Baseball Player, full figure, CI, very worn old red/gold paint....105.00
Battleship Maine, W-142, small........................195.00
Battleship Oregon, W-144, ptd CI, 5″ L, VG.............220.00
Bear, ptd pot metal, head opens, 5½″ L, EX..............85.00
Bear, W-246, stealing pig, brass, 5½″..................50.00
Bear, W-246, stealing pig, CI.........................775.00
Bear, W-331, Teddy, ptd CI, 4″ L, G....................80.00
Beehive, W-169, japanned & ptd CI, 7¼″, EX.............225.00
Ben Franklin, bust, W-313, pot metal, 5¼″, EX...........30.00
Bill-E-Grin, aluminum.................................65.00
Billiken, W-48, Good Luck, ptd CI, 6½″, rstr.............55.00
Billiken, W-51, ptd CI, 4¼″, EX........................25.00
Bird on Stump, W-209, ptd CI, 5″, G...................180.00

Bear, C-227, cast iron still bank with gold paint, 5½″, $65.00.

Boat, When My Fortune Ship Comes In, W-249............900.00
Boy Scout, ptd CI, W-14, 6″, G.........................50.00
Buffalo, recumbent, wht clay mk Savings Bank, bl/blk/br, 6½″...35.00
Buffalo, W-208, ptd CI, 4½″ L, VG.....................45.00
Building, W-320, octagonal, tower shape, japanned CI, 6½″, EX.60.00
Building, W-381, ptd CI, 5½″, EX......................300.00
Building, W-388, EPCI, 3½″, G..........................35.00
Buster Brown & Tige, W-2, ptd CI, 5″, VG...............100.00
Buster Brown & Tige, W-83, w/horseshoe, EX.............150.00
Buster Brown & Tige Cashier, W-398, ptd CI, 5″, EX......450.00
Butler, ptd CI, W-4, heavily pitted, 6″, rstr............300.00
Camel, W-201, ptd CI, 7¼″, rpt........................130.00
Camel, W-202, ptd CI, 4¾″, rpt.........................35.00
Captain Kidd, W-130..................................130.00
Captain Kidd, W-38, ptd CI, 5½″, G....................180.00
Cash Register, Crescent, variation, 4 slots, ptd CI/steel, 5½″...100.00
Cash Register, Crescent, 4 slots, ptd CI, pressed steel, 6″, G....90.00
Cash Register, National/Your Savings, nickeled iron, 6¾″, VG...90.00
Cash Register, National/Your Savings, NPCI/electroplated, EX..200.00
Cash Register, NPCI, 4 slots, ptd CI, 4¾″, VG...........160.00
Cat, W-247, w/ball, ptd CI, 5¾″ L, rstr................110.00
Cat, W-248, seated, ptd CI, 4″, EX....................100.00
Cat, W-53, on tub, ptd CI, 4″, rpt.....................90.00
Charlie Chaplin, figural, beside glass container, 4″, M......325.00
Chest, C-349...45.00
Chest of drawers, agate ware, red/yellow swirl, 5¾″, G......325.00
City Bank, W-400, Paying Teller, ptd CI, 5½″, VG.........150.00
Clock, W-217, w/rpl pendulum, ptd CI, 5¾″, VG..........150.00
Clock, W-224, A Money Saver, ptd CI, 3½″, VG............25.00
Clown, W-29, ptd CI, 6″, VG............................90.00
Clown, W-38, w/crooked hat, ptd CI, 7″, VG.............875.00
Cow, W-188, ptd CI, 4½″ L, VG..........................90.00
Cow, W-200, ptd CI, 5¼″ L, EX.........................110.00
Crystal Bank, W-243, ptd CI & glass, 4¼″, VG............35.00
Daisy Safe, W-319, ptd CI, 2″, G........................40.00
Dandy Candy Savings, tin cylinder: litho man, figural hat, 8″...260.00
Deer, W-195, ptd CI, 6¼″, EX...........................40.00
Deer, W-196, ptd CI, 9½″, over-varnished...............45.00
Dispenser, cigarette machine, Penny Smoke, 1¢, works......240.00
Dispenser, for chocolate cigarettes, litho tin, window, 6″, EX...310.00
Dog, C-197, aluminum..................................35.00
Dog, W-102, English Bull, seated, ptd CI, 4″, VG.........130.00
Dog, W-103, Spitz, ptd CI, 4½″ L, G...................210.00

Dog, W-106, w/pack, ptd CI, 5½" L, G.....................25.00
Dog, W-107, Bird Dog, ptd CI, 5½" L, VG................45.00
Dog, W-110, Scotty, seated, ptd CI, 5", EX................70.00
Dog, W-111, Pug, seated, ptd CI, 4", G....................60.00
Dog, W-113, I Hear A Call, w/pack on back, ptd CI, 8" L, EX..60.00
Dog, W-115, Lost Dog, japanned CI, 5½", VG.............525.00
Dog, W-261, Basset Hound, ptd CI, 3¼", G.............750.00
Dog, W-336, Puppy on Cushion, ptd CI, 7½" L, EX.......140.00
Dog, W-337, Puppy Dog, ptd CI, 5", EX...................225.00
Dog, W-392, w/wash tub, ptd CI & pressed tin, 3" L, G......250.00
Dog, W-54, on tub, ptd CI, 4", VG.......................90.00
Dog finial, on flattened sphere, wht clay w/Albany slip, 4¾"....125.00
Dolphin, ptd CI, W-6, 4¼", VG..........................210.00
Donald Duck, as sailor by life saver, compo, 1938...........125.00
Donkey, W-197, ptd CI, 6½", G...........................40.00
Donkey, W-198, ptd CI, 5", EX............................30.00
Donkey, W-216, ptd CI, 5" L, EX.........................300.00
Double Combination Safe Deposit, CI, 90% orig paint, 5x6"...85.00
Dreadnought Bank, W-363, ptd CI, broken & rpr, 7¼", EX...100.00
Dutch Boy, ptd CI, W-25, 6½", G........................400.00
Dutch Boy, ptd CI, W-36, 6", EX.........................100.00
Dutch Girl, ptd CI, W-35, 5½", EX.......................130.00
Elephant, W-55, on bench on tub, ptd CI, 4¼", G...........70.00
Elephant, W-59, on tub, ptd CI, 5¼", EX..................70.00
Elephant, W-60, on tub................................65.00
Elephant, W-64, ptd CI, 5" L, EX.........................70.00
Elephant, W-68, ptd CI, 4¼" L, EX.......................25.00
Elephant, W-69, ptd CI, 3¼" L, EX.......................55.00
Elephant, W-73, GOP, ptd CI, 4½" L, G...................120.00
Elephant, W-75, on wheels, ptd CI, 4" L, G................140.00
Ferry Boat, W-148, ptd CI, 7½" L, G.....................210.00
Fireman, W-9...165.00
Football Player, ptd CI, W-12, 6", rstr....................160.00
Foxy Grandpa, ptd CI, W-23, screw missing, 5½", EX........170.00
Frog, amber & green on wht clay, sm flakes on base, 4".......65.00
General Butler, W-294, ptd CI, 6½", EX.................1,200.00
General Pershing, W-312, EPCI, 8", EX....................85.00
General Sherman, on horse, W-88........................575.00
Girl, leaning on tree stump, figural, ptd pot metal, 4¾", EX...400.00
Give Billy a Penny, W-22...............................325.00
Give Me A Penny, ptd CI, W-19, 5¾", EX..................270.00
Gollywog, ptd CI, W-3, 6¼", EX.........................290.00
Goose, W-211, ptd CI, 5", rstr..........................100.00
Graf Zeppelin, ptd CI, 6½" L, VG........................130.00
Hat, W-167, WWI, pressed steel, 3¾" dia, VG...............60.00
Hat, W-258, Grandpa's Hat, ptd CI, 2¼", VG...............300.00
Hat, W-259, Pass Around The Hat, Lincoln high-hat, 2¼", G...60.00
Head, 2-faced Blk, small................................85.00
Hen on nest, yellowware, br base w/spotted hen, 3½".........95.00
Home Bank, figural building, W-333, ptd CI, 4¼", EX........180.00
Home Savings Bank, W-345, building figural, ptd CI, 3½", G..100.00
Horse, W-56, on tub, ptd CI, 5¼", VG....................130.00
Horse, W-76, on oval base, ptd CI, 5¼", rstr................45.00
Horse, W-77, prancing, ptd CI, 4½" L, EX..................25.00
Horse, W-78, prancing on oblong base, ptd CI, 7½", G........70.00
Horse, W-82, Beauty, ptd CI, 5¾" L, EX...................70.00
Horse, W-85, My Pet, ptd CI, 5" L, G.....................130.00
Horse, W-87, on wheels, ptd CI, minor rust on wheels, 5", EX.180.00
Horseshoe, Good Luck, ptd CI, W-83, 4¼", EX..............150.00
Horseshoe Wire Bank, W-239, ptd CI & pressed steel, 3¼", EX.60.00
House, tin, paneled windows/doors, worn pnt, dents, 4½"......65.00
House, w/porch, W-404, ptd CI, 3", EX....................70.00
House, 2 chimneys, round stoop, Rockingham glaze, chip, 3¾".135.00
Indian, W-291, two-faced, ptd CI, 4¼", VG................800.00

Indian, W-39, ptd CI, 6", VG...........................170.00
Indian Chief, bust, pot metal...........................45.00
Indian Family, W-289, CI, 5" L, no paint.................445.00
Keg, stoneware w/Albany slip, 3¼".......................20.00
Kitten, sitting, W-335, ptd CI, 5", EX...................120.00
Kodak Bank, W-315, NPCI, 5" L, EX.....................225.00
Lamb, W-192, ptd CI, 4¼" L, G..........................65.00
Liberty Bell, W-274, ptd CI, musical, 6", VG..............825.00
Liberty Bell, W-281, Sesquicentennial, EPCI, 4", VG.........55.00
Life Saver, litho tin can: sailor boy, figural hat, 5", VG......40.00
Linemar, Color TV Bank, tin litho, 4", EX................100.00
Lion, W-57, on tub w/cord in mouth, ptd CI, 5½", EX.......125.00
Lion, W-58, on tub, ptd CI, 5½", poor condition............75.00
Lion, W-61, on tub, ptd CI, 4¼", G......................140.00
Lion, W-89, ptd CI, 6½" L, rstr..........................25.00
Lion, W-90, ptd CI, 5" L, EX.............................25.00
Lion, W-92, ptd CI, 5½" L, VG...........................45.00
Lion, W-93, ptd CI, 5½" L, poor condition.................45.00
Lion, W-94, ptd CI, 3¾" L, EX..........................100.00
Lion, W-95, on wheels, ptd CI, 5" L, EX..................200.00

Lion, C-231, cast iron still bank with gold paint, 4" x 5", $40.00

Lucy Atwell Fairy House, tin...........................250.00
Mail Box, W-116, ptd CI, 5¼", EX.......................70.00
Mail Box, W-121, ptd CI, 4¼", VG.......................45.00
Mail Box, W-122, ptd CI, 3½", G........................30.00
Mail Box, W-124, eagle at top, 4"......................100.00
Main Street Street Car, W-164, ptd CI, rpl wheels, 6½" L, VG.280.00
Mammy, W-17, w/spoon, ptd CI, 5¾", G..................120.00
Mammy, W-20, ptd CI, 5¼", EX.........................170.00
Man on Bale of Cotton, ptd CI, W-37, with trap, 5", VG.....1,000.00
Mary & Her Little Lamb, ptd CI, repainted, W-1............170.00
Middy Bank, japanned CI, W-26, incomplete, 5¼", VG.......130.00
Moody & Sankey, W-266, ptd CI, 5¼", VG.................800.00
Mulligan the Cop, ptd CI, W-8, 6", EX...................120.00
Mutt & Jeff, ptd CI, W-13, 5¼", rpt.....................130.00
Old South Church, W-450, ptd CI, paper label, 9¾", EX......975.00
Our Kitchener Bank...................................145.00
Owl, W-203, ptd CI, 4¼", EX...........................375.00
Owl, W-204, on stump, Be Wise/Save Money, ptd CI, 5", EX...110.00
Parlor Stove, W-138, 7"...............................100.00
Parrot, figural, pot metal, head opens, 4", EX.............180.00

Pig, W-179, seated, ptd CI, orig tag, 3″, EX..............25.00
Pig, W-182, Deckers Iowana, ptd CI, 4½″ L, G..........90.00
Pig, W-184, ptd CI, 4¼″ L, EX........................70.00
Pinocchio, by barrel, composition, 1939................65.00
Pirate, holds pistol, sitting on chest, pot metal.............45.00
Plymouth Rock, W-292, ptd CI, 4″ L, G................800.00
Poor Weary Willie, figural bum, German, litho tin, 5″, EX.....140.00
Porky Pig, figural, standing next to barrel, ptd CI, 5″ L, VG...55.00
Possum, W-205, ptd CI, 4¾″ L, EX....................250.00
Potato, The Pingree Bank, W-301, CI, 5½″ L, no paint.......600.00
Presto Still, W-427, ptd CI, 3½″, G....................10.00
Professor Pug Frog, W-230, ptd CI, 3¼″, EX............300.00
Rabbit, W-100, sitting, ptd CI, 4¾″, VG................120.00
Rabbit, W-199, standing on 4 ft, ptd CI, 6½″, G.........200.00
Rabbit, W-96, seated, ptd CI, 3½″, rpt.................65.00
Rabbit, W-97, on base, 2¼″..........................865.00
Rabbit, W-98, sitting upright, ptd CI, 5″, VG...........75.00
Radio, W-137, ptd CI/pressed steel, orig Kenton label, 4½″, EX.70.00
Rhino, W-252, ptd CI, 5¼″ L, VG.....................275.00
Rocket Bank, Mercury, Merchants National, cast aluminum, 8″...7.50
Rooster, W-186, Polish, ptd CI, rpr foot, 5½″, EX..........475.00
Rooster, W-187, ptd CI, 5″, EX........................65.00
Round Wire Bank, W-242, ptd CI & pressed steel, 4¼″, G.....55.00
Rumplestiltskin, ptd CI, W-49, 6″, G...................260.00
Safe, W-346, Arabian, japanned CI, 4½″, EX.............40.00
Safe, W-347, japanned & ptd CI, 4½″, VG...............50.00
Safe, W-348, ptd CI, 5½″, EX.........................160.00
Safe, W-349, Japanese, japanned & ptd CI, 5½″, EX.......80.00
Safe, W-350, Young America, japanned & ptd CI, 4½″, EX....60.00
Safe, W-351, The Roller, japanned & ptd CI, 3¾″, EX.......70.00
Safe, W-374, Sport, japanned & ptd CI, 3″, EX............50.00
Safe, W-435, Metropolitan, ptd CI, 6″, G................140.00
Sailor, ptd CI, W-16, 5½″, G.........................100.00
Santa, W-238, at chimney, ptd lead, 4¼″ L, G............200.00
Santa, W-31, with tree, ptd CI & wire, 7½″, rstr..........210.00
Santa, w/pack, pot metal.............................125.00
Save & Smile Money Box, ptd CI, W-46, 4¼″, EX.........340.00
Save Your Pennies, brass filigree, combination lock, 3½″.......25.00
Saving Sam, figural man in business suit, ptd metal, 5″, EX...260.00
Seal, W-199, ptd CI, 4¼″ L, EX......................250.00
Share Cropper, ptd CI, W-18, 5½″, VG.................65.00
Shell, W-385, 1½″..................................65.00
Shell Out, W-293, ptd CI, 5″ L, rpt...................130.00
Singer Sewing Machine, tin litho, 5½″.................600.00
Smiling Jim & Peaceful Bill, W-314, bust, EPCI, 4″, EX......550.00
Soldier, WWI, W-40, NM.............................300.00
State House, W-271, ptd CI, 6½″, VG..................700.00
Statue of Liberty, W-268, ptd CI, 9½″, EX..............375.00
Statue of Liberty, W-269, ptd CI, 6¼″, EX.............55.00
Stollwerck Savings, litho tin & glass, rectangular, 6¼″, EX....400.00
Stove, W-130, ptd CI & pressed steel, 4½″, EX...........50.00
Sweet Thrift Bank, litho tin & glass, drawer opens, 6″, EX....300.00
Tabernacle Savings, W-228, NP & EPCI, minor rust, 5″ L, VG.525.00
Tank, WWI, W-161, ptd CI, 6″ L, G...................100.00
Tank, WWI, W-162, ptd CI, 4½″ L, G..................100.00
Tank, WWI, W-163, CI, 6½″ L, no paint................60.00
Teddy Roosevelt, W-309, ptd CI, 5¼″, some rstr, EX.......150.00
Three Monkeys, W-236, ptd CI, 3½″, VG................140.00
Trolley Car, W-265, ptd CI, 4¼″ L, rstr................140.00
Turkey, W-193, ptd CI, 3½″, EX......................55.00
Turkey, W-194, ptd CI, 4¼″, EX......................400.00
Two-Faced Devil, ptd CI, W-41, 4¼″, EX...............550.00
Two-Faced Woman, ptd CI, W-43, large, 4½″, EX.........130.00
Two-Faced Woman, ptd CI, W-44, small, 3¼″, EX.........70.00

Yellow Cab, W-158, ptd CI, wire grill, 7¼″ L, VG...........600.00
Young Negro, ptd CI, W-42, 4½″, VG...................130.00

Barber Shop Collectibles

Even for the stranger in town, the local barber shop was easy to find, its location vividly marked with the traditional red and white striped barber pole that for centuries identified such establishments. As far back as the 12th century, the barber has had a place in recorded history. At one time, he not only groomed the beards and cut the hair of his gentlemen clients, but was known as the 'blood letter' as well -- hence the red stripe for blood and the white for the bandages. Many early barbers even pulled teeth! Later, laws were enacted that divided the practices of barbering and surgery.

The Victorian barber shop reflected the charm of that era with fancy barber chairs upholstered in rich wine colored velvet; rows of bottles made from colored art glass held hair tonics and shaving lotion. Backbars of richly carved oak with bevelled mirrors lined the wall behind the barber's station.

During the late 19th century, the barber pole with a blue stripe added as a patriotic gesture to the standard red and white came into vogue.

Today, the barber shop has all but disappeared from the American scene, replaced by modern unisex salons. Collectors search for the barber poles, the fancy chairs, and the tonic bottles of an era gone but not forgotten.

See also Razors; Shaving Mugs

Barber pole, wht porcelain, wind-up motor, Koch, 40x10″.....500.00
Blade dispenser, wall; Blue Blades Gillette, much advertising....85.00
Bottle, bulbous w/ringed neck, sapphire bl w/enamel decor, 7″..140.00
Bottle, burmese type w/gr painted vine, bulbous w/long neck...100.00
Bottle, clear frosted w/HP scene, inverted cone shape, 8¼″....200.00
Bottle, clear w/opal swirls, square, collared mouth, 8¼″........50.00
Bottle, cranberry, square w/fern pattern, w/opal decor, 8¼″....190.00
Bottle, electric blue w/enamel decor, barrel shape, 7½″......310.00
Bottle, emb lady on label under glass......................260.00
Bottle, emerald gr w/enamel decor, corseted shape, 8″.......400.00
Bottle, fluted, Coinspot, blue opal, tooled mouth, 7″..........80.00
Bottle, frosted cone w/pnt lav palm tree decor, 1880s, 8″......200.00
Bottle, gold trim Pompeian Hair Message label under glass, 9″.100.00
Bottle, hobnail, electric blue, 7¾″........................65.00
Bottle, hobnail, lt gr opaque glass, nickel plated stopper, NM....30.00
Bottle, hobnail, lt lav opaque glass, ribbed neck, 7″, NM......75.00

Milk glass globe trade sign, with 'Hair Bobbing' and woman's head, 12½″, $195.00.

Bottle, hobnail, red glass, 3 hob rings on neck, w/stopper, 9"..100.00
Bottle, honeycomb, amber opal.........................135.00
Bottle, label under glass: Lavern's Rose Tonic, w/stopper, 9"...75.00
Bottle, Lilac Toilet Water, w/orig dispenser top, lilac label.....20.00
Bottle, Loetz type, irid w/purple streaks, 7"................130.00
Bottle, Mary Gregory type on amethyst, tooled mouth/pontil, 8".260.00
Bottle, mc paper label: man w/mandolin, lady w/parrot, 9", NM..75.00
Bottle, milk glass, ribbed, label w/rvpt under glass, 12".......260.00
Bottle, milk glass w/HP Toilet Water/flowers, aqua neck, 9"....100.00
Bottle, milk glass w/painted leaf decor, round, tooled mouth.....50.00
Bottle, opaque blue, applied lip, pontil, 10½"..............125.00
Bottle, ornate, w/reverse painted label under glass, 8", EX.....255.00
Bottle, paneled, deep amethyst, applied lip, 7"..............95.00
Bottle, paneled, sapphire blue, applied lip, residue, 7½".......60.00
Bottle, seaweed pattern, square, blue opal..................95.00
Bottle, stars & stripes, cranberry/wht, 1880s, 7"............315.00
Bottle, stars & stripes, electric bl w/wht decor, 7"...........200.00
Bottle, tall bell shape, gr w/enamel decor, tooled mouth, 9".....50.00
Bottle, Violet Sec Water, crown on dispensing cap, eagle label...20.00
Bottle, yel w/opal stripe decor, segmented body flutes, 7¼".....70.00
Bottle, 5 graduating bulging rings, gr w/decor, sheared mouth..400.00
Catalog, Buerger Bros, 1929, w/ornate order blanks, 10 pgs, NM..5.00
Catalog, Koch's Barber Chairs & Accessories, #39, 1927, 19 pgs.22.00
Chair, Koch's, oak & brass w/gr tufted velvet uphl..........1,650.00
Chair, Koken, 4 ft, rnd bk, oak w/tufted leather, rstr.......2,500.00
Chair, Koken hydraulic, carved oak/leather/ornate, rstr, 1900s.1,800.00
Display case, wood base/slant front, etched Auto Strop Safety....60.00
Magazine, Barber's Journal, 1925, ads/articles, some color, VG..24.00
Photo, interior barber shop, much detail of rarities, 7x10"......35.00
Pole, ball ea end, swelled center w/ball turning, 41".........295.00
Pole, porcelain, revolving, w/orig milk glass globe on top......350.00
Pole, trn wood, alligatored rpt, age cracks, 65".............120.00
Postcard, 3 barbers shave customers, mug rack, dtd 1941, NM..12.00
Shaving basin, shell, gr stipes, pk/yel flowel, La Francaise.....248.00
Shaving bowl, paperweight base, mk Ed Lyons/Barber/1902.....50.00
Shaving brush, copper/metal, w/button to push out soap, 1887...15.00
Shoe shine stand, Koken, oak/marble/brass w/velvet uphl, dbl.1,750.00
Sign, emb tin, pole & Ask For Wildroot, 1940s, 12x36".......35.00
Sign, metal, pole/stars, Modern Service, 3 color stripes, 48"....105.00
Sign, porcelain on steel, Look Better/Feel Better, w/pole, 48"..110.00
Water heater, copper w/brass lid & spigot, early 1900s........45.00

Barometers

Barometers are instruments designed to measure the weight or pressure of the atmosphere in order to anticipate approaching weather changes. Those

Charles X, verre eglomise in multicolors on white ground, second quarter of the 19th Century, 34", $550.00.

made around the turn of the century -- earlier in England and on the continent -- were beautifully housed in period cases of mahogany, rosewood, walnut, or cherry, often with brass trim. These quality pieces bring high prices on today's market.

C Barkham, mahog veneer/line inlay/convex mirror/spirit level..375.00
Eugene Dietzgen, brass, pocket watch form, 3¼" dia.........65.00
Fitzroy, 1870....................................1,350.00
Gally Manchester, Geo III, carved/inlaid mahog wheel, ornate...350.00
Louis Phillippe, brass mt/inlay mahog cistern, 1850s, 41".....275.00
Oak veneer w/parquetry inlay, late Geo III, 44"............3,500.00
Ship's, mahogany/ivory/brass, orig gimbal ring, mid-1800s, VG..875.00
Victorian, shell inlaid mahogany wheel, 1850s, 39"..........350.00

Basalt

Basalt is a type of black unglazed pottery developed by Josiah Wedgwood and copied by many other companies during the late 18th and early 19th century. It was also called 'Egyptian Black'.
  See also Wedgwood

Figurine, bulldog, standing, w/glass eyes, 2¼x4"............85.00
Plaque, mother & child, sgn Mayer, 4½" dia...............390.00

Baskets

Basket weaving is a craft as old as ancient history. Baskets have been used to harvest crops, for domestic chores, and to contain the catch of fishermen. Materials at hand were utilized, and baskets made in one region are often distinguishable simply by analyzing the natural fibers used in their construction. Early Indian examples were made of corn husks or woven grasses. Willow splints, straw, rope, and paper are only a few of the materials that have been used. Until the invention of the veneering machine in the late 1800s, splint was made by water soaking a split log until the fibers were softened and flexible. Long strips were pulled out by hand, and while still wet and pliable, woven into baskets in either a cross-hatch or hexagonal weave.

Most hand crafted baskets on the market today were made between 1860 and the early 1900s. Factory baskets, with a thick, wide splint cut by machine, are of little interest to collectors.

The more popular baskets are those designed for a specific purpose, rather than the more commonly found utility baskets that had multiple uses. Among the most costly forms are the Nantucket Lighthouse baskets, which were basically copied from those made there for centuries by Aboriginal Indians. They were designed in the style of whale oil barrels, and named for the south Shoal Nantucket Lightship, where many were made during the last half of the 19th century. Cheese baskets, used to separate curds from whey, herb gathering baskets, and finely woven Shaker miniatures are other highly prized examples of the basket weaver's art.
  See also Sewing; Shaker

Bentwood, worn orig velvet cover, PA, 4½"+hdlx6x12"........45.00
Bushel, factory made, attached hdls, late 1800s...............75.00
Buttocks, splint, br & yellow stripes, 7"+hdlx11x14", VG......85.00
Buttocks, splint, fine weave w/good color, 3½"+hdlx6½x7"...165.00
Buttocks, splint, good age, traces of red stain, 8"+hdlx16" sq..125.00
Buttocks, splint, good age & color, 7"+hdlx12x7", VG........95.00
Buttocks, splint, good age/color/condition, 6½x11x11½"......135.00
Buttocks, splint, not too old, 4"+hdlx6½x6½"..............70.00
Buttocks, splint, sq mouth, br/natural design, 11x12"+hdl....145.00
Buttocks, splint, sq mouth, some wear, 6¾"+hdlx11x14".....135.00
Buttocks, splint, worn, 5½"+hdlx9½x10"..................50.00
Buttocks, splint, worn br varnish, 10"+hdlx14x17"..........155.00

Buttocks, splint, worn/weathered, oval, 8"+wood hdlx15x13"....80.00
Buttocks, splint, 3¾"+hdlx5½x6", EX................135.00
Cheese, splint, 8x24" dia.........................385.00
Compote, stripped & unstripped willow, geometrics, 1850s, 9x7".80.00
Field, oblong, indented #, upper NY state.............50.00
Gathering, splint, blue over wht pnt, 4"+hdlx13x20".........45.00
Gathering, splint, KY, 13x23", NM..................300.00
Gathering, splint, worn, 7"+hdlx14x23½"..............115.00
Gathering, wood w/webb shoulder strap, 13x13¾x12¼".......25.00
Hickory strips in fine weave, minor rim wear, 4½"+hdlx10"...135.00
Long needle pine, thread constructed & decorated, 4x2½".....25.00
Market, splint, bentwood hdl, EX....................65.00
Market, splint, nailed rim, bentwood hdl, 9"+hdl, 12x20".....20.00
Melon rib, splint, good age, 3¾"+hdlx6x7", EX..........135.00
Melon rib, splint, minor wear, 4¾"+bent sapling hdlx10x12"...75.00
Miniature, all leather, blk paint, 4¼x8¼".............120.00
Miniature, buttocks, fine weave, wide hdl, 3¾x4¼".......125.00
Miniature, buttocks, old worn blk finish, 2¼"+hdlx4".......175.00
Miniature, buttocks, well woven, minor wear, 4x4½".......105.00
Miniature, fine splint w/lid, some wear, 4"+hdlx4½x4½".....60.00
Miniature, splint, bottom mkd 1890, 2½"+hdlx3½" dia......125.00
Nantucket, sm rim hdls, 7½" dia...................440.00
Nantucket, willow/ash, minor breaks, 6x13" dia..........715.00
Nantucket, willow/ash, 4¾x12" dia.................690.00
Oriental export, pnt florals, worn, 3x5½"..............75.00
Picket fence, rpl bottom, rpt, 30x20"................160.00
Rye straw, good age & color, rim wear, 4¼x12"..........35.00
Rye straw, open rim hdls, worn, 8x15" dia.............65.00
Rye straw, 8x12".............................35.00
Rye straw w/lid, side hdls missing, 10x20" dia..........55.00
Splint, bentwood rim hdls, old patina, 13½x23x35", VG.....85.00
Splint, bentwood swivel hdl, 9¾x13" dia.............100.00
Splint, EX rim detail, 7½"+hdlx11x14"...............115.00
Splint, good age/color, minor wear, 5x8" dia...........50.00
Splint, good color, minor wear, 5½"+bentwood hdlx10½" dia..90.00
Splint, hickory, 1890, 17"x22" L..................245.00
Splint, lg bentwood rim hdls, 12x18"...............105.00
Splint, minor wear, 8"+hdlx16"....................55.00
Splint, minor wear, 8½x11½x12½"..................40.00
Splint, oak, flat bottom, w/hdl, early 1900s, 13½" dia......85.00
Splint, open hand-holds in rim, worn, 13x21"...........55.00

Splint, oval w/bentwood rim hdls, some wear, 11½x22x28"....55.00
Splint, rectangular, bentwood rim hdls, G age, color, 13x18"...105.00
Splint, rectangular w/integral hdls, 6x14x11"............70.00
Splint, red/bl/natural, 8"+hdlx11¾" dia...............75.00
Splint, red/blk pnt detail, w/lid, some wear, 12x15" dia......65.00
Splint, rim hdls, minor wear, 10x22"................65.00
Splint, rim hdls, some wear, 8x20".................60.00
Splint, rnd ea side, circular weave, w/twist hdl & lid, lg.....225.00
Splint, round, good design, some wear, 10"+hdlx16" dia.....85.00
Splint, sq device woven under hdl, 19½" including hdl......115.00
Splint, swing hdl, Nantucket style, 15x10"............200.00
Splint, w/kick-up & bentwood swivel hdl, 8x15" dia.......135.00
Splint, wood bottom, 9½"+bentwood hdlx12½x9½".......45.00
Splint, wood swivel hdl, 10½x17½", EX.............135.00
Splint, 11"+hdlx16x30".........................55.00
Splint, 2 tone br/natural, 7½"+bentwood hdlx12½x20".....40.00
Splint, 8"+hdlx10x16".........................50.00
Splint & sweetgrass, Maine, w/lid, 1900s, 9x5½".........45.00
Splint/reed, zinc reinforcement, 8x15x25".............35.00
Willow, bentwood hdl, dtd 1879, 19x13½x9½"...........65.00
Woven vine, worn, 11"+bentwood hdlx16" dia...........15.00

Batchelder

Ernest Batchelder first gained experience in the field of ceramics working in the production of insulators in the Boston area during the 1850s. He was granted a patent for an improved style with an altered shoulder line that resulted in a more efficient water shed. By the 1870s, he had moved to Los Angeles, California, where he founded the Batchelder Tile Company. Early examples of the company's art tiles are scarce today. During the 1930s and forties the company produced dinnerware, though never on a large scale. By the late 1950s, the firm had dissolved.

Bookends, tiles with brass mounts marked 'Potter Studio', 5¼", $85.00 for the pair.

Bowl, Kineloa, bl-gr, flared top, gr interior, mkd, 4x7"........95.00
Ginger jar, w/lid, Kineloa, 6"....................150.00
Tile, blue wash, grapes, 3x3"....................30.00
Tile, classical floral motif in relief, unglazed, mkd, 4".......40.00
Tile, pr peacocks, 5½"........................65.00
Tile, relief grapes/leaves, unglazed bl wash ground, mk, 7x12"..100.00
Vase, dk bl gloss w/heavy gray drip, full body, 6¾".......120.00

Battersea

Battersea is a term that refers to enameling on copper or other metal. Though originally produced at Battersea, England, in the mid-18th century, the craft was later practiced throughout the Staffordshire district. Boxes

Splint gizzard basket, 4½" plus handle, 8½" in diameter, $170.00.

are the most common examples -- some are figurals, and many bear an inscription.

Box, Innocence, w/lamb, 1¼x1¾"......................500.00
Box, patch; gr base, laurel wreath, crown, eagle, X standards...145.00
Box, pink w/wht lid, lady in bonnet, minor cracks, 1½" dia....135.00
Box, snuff; bird form, I Will Never Change, 1½", EX........975.00
Box, snuff; bird form w/floral sprig on bottom, 1½", EX.....725.00
Box, Take This For a Kiss, lovebirds, 1770, 2", EX.........500.00
Salt celler, rnd w/rural scenes in gold, 3 ft, 2½", pr, EX.....550.00
Scent bottle, fruit form, dolphin stopper, chain, 3", EX......750.00
Tie backs, lady beside pedestal, 'Sacred to Friendship', pr......80.00

Pot de Creme with cover, each piece with two figures and landscape reserves, blue with gold decor, minor roughage, 3¼", $300.00.

Bauer

Originally founded in Paducah, Kentucky, in 1885, the J.A. Bauer Company moved to Los Angeles where it was re-established in 1909. Until the 1920s, their major products were terra cotta garden ware, flower pots, and stoneware and yellowware bowls. During prohibition, they produced crocks for home use.

A more artful form of product began to develop with the addition of designer Louis Ipsen to the staff in 1915. Some of his work -- a line of molded vases, flower pots, bowls, etc. -- was awarded a bronze medal at the Pacific International Exposition the following year.

After the Depression, the first of many dinnerware lines was tested on the market. Their initial pattern, Plain Ware, was well accepted and led the way to the introduction of the most popular dinnerware in their history and with today's collectors -- Ringware. It was produced from 1932 into the early 1960s, in solid colors of jade green, royal blue, Chinese yellow, light blue, organge-red, and in very limited quantities, black or white. It's simple pattern was a design of closely spaced concentric ribs, either convex or concave. Over the years more than one hundred shapes were available.

Some were made in limited quantities, resulting in rare items to whet the appetites of Bauer buffs today.

Other popular patterns were Modern, made during the mid-30s in turquoise, burgandy, orange, yellow, white, rust, green, and blue; Smooth, made in 1936 in pastels as well as a dark tan; Speckware, made in 1946; and Monterey Moderne, made in 1948.

After WWII, a flood of foreign imports drastically curtailed their sales, and the pottery began a steady decline that ended in failure in 1936.

Ash tray, metal holder, 1 ea: red, orange, gr, yellow, dk bl......35.00
Bowl, batter.....................................20.00
Bowl, batter; Ring, 2 qt, orange/red, #37.............45.00
Bowl, beating; Ring, 1 qt, dk bl, #31................36.00
Bowl, fruit; Monterey, 3 ft, orange/red..............30.00
Bowl, fruit; Monterey, 3 ft, turq, 10"..............25.00
Bowl, mixing....................................20.00
Bowl, nesting; Ring, orange/red, #90/8".............22.00
Bowl, salad; #409, turquoise, 11½"................25.00
Bowl, vegetable; Ring, orange/red, oval, #54/10"......34.00
Butter dish, rectangular, yellow....................27.00
Butter dish, Ring, round w/lid, orange/red, #96.......61.00
Candle holder, Monterey, turq, #417, ea.............12.00
Candlestick, Monterey, Vapore 1-lite, turq, 2½x5"......8.00
Carafe, w/6 handleless mugs.......................85.00
Casserole, Ring, w/lid, orange/red, #36, 7½".........41.00
Coffee server, Ring, metal hdl w/raffia, dk bl, 8 cup, #94.....35.00
Coffee server, Ring, metal hdl w/raffia, lt bl, 8 cup, #94......29.00
Coffee server, Ring, 6 cup, lt bl, #93...............24.00
Coffee server, Ring, 8 cup/wood hdl, orange/red, #94.........41.00
Cookie jar, swirl design, blue speckles, 'Cookies'............39.00
Custard cup, Ring, dk bl, #34.......................6.00
Custard cup, Ring, lt bl, #34........................5.00
Gravy boat, Ring, oval w/under tray, orange/red, #99.........36.00
Lug soup, Ring, w/lid, dk bl, #52, 5½"...............41.00
Mug, Ring, Barrel, orange........................20.00
Pitcher, Ring, 1 qt, orange/red, #12.................29.00
Pitcher, Ring, 1½ pt, orange/red, #12................24.00
Pitcher, Ring, 2 qt, lt bl, #12.....................28.00
Planter, ivory, sgn, oval, 13" L...................29.00
Plate, Ring, lt bl, #61, 10½".......................22.00
Plate, Ring, lt bl, #61, 9".........................11.00
Plate, Ring, lt bl, #63, 6".........................6.00
Platter, Ring, oval, dk bl, #73, 12"................24.00

Gravy boat, Ringware, in yellow glaze, 11" long, $22.50.

Platter, Ring, oval, lt bl, #73.............................22.00
Pudding dishes w/metal holders, Mission, 6 assorted..........45.00
Relish plate, Ring, sectioned, orange/red, 10½"..............38.00
Sherbet, Ring, dk bl, #83....................................30.00
Stacking jar, Ring, green.....................................7.50
Stacking jar, Ring, orange...................................12.50
Stacking jar, Ring, yellow....................................9.00
Sugar bowl, Ring, no lid, orange/red, #40.....................8.00
Tumbler, Ring, lt bl, 12 oz, #26.............................16.00
Tumbler, Ring, wood hdl, 6 oz, dk bl.........................15.00
Vase, blk Santa Maria Indian shape, rare....................125.00
Vase, fan shape, yellow, sgn, 4¼x5½", pr.....................28.00

Bavaria

Bavaria, Germany, was long the center of that country's pottery industry; in the 1800s, many firms operated in and around the area. China ware vases, novelties, and table accessories were decorated with transfer prints as well as by hand by artists who sometimes signed their work. The examples here are marked with 'Bavaria' and the logos of some of the various companies who were located there.

Bowl, bl w/swans on lake transfer, gold scallop rim, ftd, 7".....46.00
Bowl, grape decor, sgn Koch, 10".............................45.00
Bowl, pink w/yellow roses, 9"................................16.00
Cake plate w/6 sm plates, gr grapes, HP, open hdls, 9".......59.00
Coffee server, gold/lav leaf, Royal Heidelberg, 6¾"..........20.00
Coffee set, allover geometrics, Winterlong/Marletlenthen, 3 pc...24.00
Cup & saucer, Queen's Rose, Tirschenreuth....................15.00
Dresser set, ballerina figurals, puff jar & 2 perfumes, pink.....195.00
Fish set, fleur de lis relief, gold rim, Mignon, 22½" platter....350.00
Gravy w/attached under plate, florals/emb scrolls, J Haviland....10.00
Hair receiver, red roses, gr leaves, ZS&S....................25.00
Nappy, open gold hdls, HP flowers, sgn Noels, ZS&Co, 5x8"....25.00
Plate, grapes, sgn Koch, G&C, 8½"............................35.00
Plate, grapes, sgn Koch, 6", pr..............................35.00
Plate, salad; Queen's Rose, Tirschenreuth.....................8.00
Plate, Schumann, Dresden, reticulated border, flowers, 10½"....38.00
Platter, mc floral band/fruit basket border, Gimble Bros, 14½"..12.00
Powder jar, HP, sgn Esther Gardner, pearl finish.............30.00
Tea set, 6-sided, pk roses/gold trim, pot/creamer/sugar, ZS&Co..95.00
Teapot, barrel form, ivory w/flowers & leaves, Fine China, 9"....12.00
Vegetable dish w/lid, Tirschenreuth Queen's Rose, 8½".......45.00

Bowl with floral reticulated rim, central fruit and flower transfer, gold trim, 13" diameter, $145.00.

Beer Cans

When the flat top can was first introduced in 1934, it came with printed instructions on how to use the triangular punch opener. Cone top cans, which are rare today, were patented in 1935 by the Continental Can Company. By the 1960s, aluminum cans with pull tabs had made both types obsolete.

The hobby of collecting beer cans has been rapidly gaining momentum over the past ten years. Series types such as South African Brewery, Lion, and the Cities Series by Schmit and Tucker are especially popular.

Condition is an important consideration when evaluating market price. Grade 1 must be in like new condition, with no rust. However, the triangular punch hole is acceptable. Grade 2 cans may have slight scratches or dimples, but must be free of rust. For Grade 3, light rust, minor scratching, and some fading may be acceptable. Grade 4 cans have the same defects, but are in much worse condition. Cans in less than excellent condition devaluate sharply.

In the listing that follows, cans are arranged alphabetically by brand name, not by brewery.

A-1 Phoenix Suns, 1974-75, bank top.........................5.00
Ace Hi Malt Liquor, 7 oz, flat top..........................65.00
Alpen Brau, Potosi...2.50
Amana..8.00
Beckers, 11 oz, flat top.....................................4.00
Black Label, Carling, blk can...............................10.00
Canadian Ace Beer, quart, Chicago, IL, cone top.............50.00
Chief Oshgosh..9.00
Clyde Cream Ale, 12 oz, Enterprise Brewery, MA, cone top...235.00
Colt 45, Phoenix Suns, 1975-76, bank top.....................2.00
Colt 45, Phoenix Suns, 1976-77, bank top.....................2.00
E&B Special, cone top, NM...................................58.00
F&S Beer..10.00
Gambrinus, Ohio State, 1974, straight steel..................2.50
Gettleman, crimped steel.....................................2.00
Gilt Edge..5.00
Grace Bros Beer, 8 oz, Santa Rosa, California, flat top.....55.00
Hamms Sunburst, flat top, 1955...............................2.50
Happy Hops, 12 oz, 1944, Grace Brewery, flat top...........250.00
Hawkeye, BCCA, Canvention Can 1975...........................2.50
Historical Brewery Series, Breweries of Chicago, 6 can set....6.00
Holiday Bock, red..7.00
Hoosier Beer, 12 oz, South Bend, Indiana, cone top.........190.00
Innsbrau..10.00
Iron City, Penn State, Numero Uno............................2.50
Iron City New Jersey Series, Barnegat Light House............5.00
Iron City New Jersey Series, Map of New Jersey...............5.00
Iron City New Jersey Series, Passaic Falls...................3.00
Iroquois Draft, flat top.....................................2.00
Katz, w/Cat...10.00
Keg, Baltimore..13.00
King Snedly...2.00
Krueger Cream Ale, quart, Newark, New Jersey, cone top.....145.00
Metz..6.00
Nat'l Lager, flat top..4.00
National Bohemian, 12 oz, Baltimore, cone top...............55.00
Old Crown Bock...2.00
Old Dutch, Assoc...2.00
Old Tavern..16.00
Olde Frothingslosh, red......................................4.00
Original $1000 Natural Process B.............................12.00
Pearl, mc, crimped steel.....................................2.50
Pearl Premium Light, 8 oz, mc, straight steel................2.00

Pfeiffer, black shoe soles...................................13.00
Price Chopper..2.00
Red Cap Ale...15.00
Red Top Beer..5.00
Red Top Extra Pale, 12 oz, yellow label, red letters, cone top...55.00
Regal Select Draft..18.00
Reidenbach, straight steel.................................5.00
Richbrau..6.00
Royal 58..8.00
Schlitz Lager, 12 oz, Milwaukee, Wisconsin, cone top........135.00
Schmidt, BCCA, Canvention Can, 1976......................2.00
Shell, mc...2.00
Tam O'Shanter Ale, 12 oz, American Brewery, cone top......140.00
Utica Club Pilsner, quart, West End Brewery, NY, cone top....165.00
Walters, Pueblo, 16 oz....................................2.50
Waynesboro, PA, Fire Dept, 4 can set.....................3.00
West Virginia...4.00
Yankee, 16 oz, New York, NY, flat top....................100.00
9 0 5, red can w/stripes..................................10.00

Belleek

Belleek is a very thin translucent porcelain that takes its name from the district in Ireland where it originated in 1857. The glaze is a creamy ivory color with a pearl-like luster. Tablewares, baskets, figurines, and vases have been produced; Shamrock, Tridacna, Echinus and Lotus are but a few of the many patterns.

It is possible to date an example to within twenty to thirty years of manufacture by the mark. Pieces with an early stamp often bring prices nearly double that of a similar but later piece. With some variation, the marks have always incorporated the wolfhound, castle, harp, and shamrock. Three of these were in black, used from 1863 until 1946, and three were in green, used from 1946 until the present.

See also Collector Plates

For American Belleek, see Lenox; Ott and Brewer; Willets

Aberdeen, vase, applied flowers, 3rd blk mk, facing pr, 6".....180.00
Aberdeen, vase, no color, 2nd gr mk, 7"...................135.00
Basket, 2 strand, rope edge, 6½" dia...................1,000.00
Basket, 3 strand, Shamrock, floral decor, sm.............450.00
Basket, 3 strand, trefoil shape, 5".......................300.00
Basket, 4 strand, Bird's Nest, w/flowers, 4" dia..........500.00
Basket, 4 strand, Shamrock, 5" wide......................350.00
Blarney, plate, pink & gold trim, 2nd blk mk, 6"..........90.00

Cheese dish, cottage form, ochre roof, 3rd black mark, 4¼" x 7", $900.00.

Boat, spoon rest, 1st blk mk, 4" L........................275.00
Box, heart shape w/lid, gr trim, 2nd blk mk..............220.00
Cake plate, 4 strand weaving, pearl, 9¼".................750.00
Celtic, cup & saucer, 3rd blk mk.........................235.00
Cherub box, 3rd gr mk.....................................95.00
Cherub cornucopia, 1st blk mk, 7"......................1,850.00
Cleary, creamer, pk rope hdl, 2nd blk mk.................45.00
Cleary, spill vase, 1st blk mk, 4".......................200.00
Cone, cup & saucer, rust w/gilt, 2nd blk mk, rare.........155.00
Cone, plate, yellow center, 2nd blk mk, 6"...............45.00
Echinus, bowl on coral, 2nd blk mk, 3x5".................275.00
Fermanagh, vase, yel luster w/in, gr mk w/R..............30.00
Figurine, Affection, 1st blk mk, 14"...................1,800.00
Figurine, boy w/basket on shoulder.......................185.00
Figurine, Cavalier w/dueling pistol, 1900, 15"...........495.00
Figurine, dog, 2nd gr mk..................................65.00
Figurine, dog, 3rd gr mk, 3"..............................35.00
Figurine, girl w/basket, 1st blk mk, 9"..................950.00
Figurine, girl w/basket, 3rd blk mk......................240.00
Figurine, greyhound, 3rd blk mk..........................615.00
Figurine, leprechaun, discontinued gr mk.................55.00
Figurine, leprechaun, no color, 3rd blk mk, 5"...........240.00
Figurine, leprechaun, 2nd blk mk.........................265.00
Figurine, lighthouse tower, dtd, 1st blk mk..............420.00
Figurine, Meditation, 2nd gr mk, 15".....................700.00
Figurine, pig, 2nd blk mk, 2¼"...........................165.00
Figurine, swan, discontinued gr mk.......................45.00
Grasses, cup & saucer, 1st imp mk, #897..................150.00
Grasses, plate, irid colors, gold edge, impressed 1st blk mk, 6"..45.00
Grasses, tea plate, lustre color, 1st imp mk, 6"..........75.00
Grasses, teacup & saucer, 1st gr mk......................45.00
Grasses, teapot, pearl lustre, 1st blk mk................490.00
Harp & Shamrock, cup & saucer, 3rd blk mk...............83.00
Harp & Shamrock, teacup & saucer, 1st gr mk.............50.00
Harp & Shamrock, teapot, 2nd blk mk.....................235.00
Harp & Shamrock, teapot, 2nd gr mk......................75.00
Hawthorne, cup & saucer, pk/br/gold trim, 1st blk mk....135.00
Hawthorne, pitcher, ftd, aqua trim, 1st blk mk, 7".......450.00
Heart dish, scalloped, pk trim, 2nd blk mk...............70.00
Heart dish, 3rd blk mk...................................55.00
Hexagon, cup & saucer, 2nd blk mk.......................85.00
Hexagon, plate, gr trim, mkd: Robinson & Cleaver, Belfast, 6"..55.00
Hexagon, plate, gr trim, 2nd blk mk, 6"..................45.00
High Lily, creamer & sugar, 2nd blk mk..................80.00
High Lily, cup & saucer, 2nd blk mk......................85.00
Honeysuckle, vase, pink w/in, 1st blk mk, 7".............950.00
Institute, cup & saucer, 1st blk mk......................125.00
Institute, plate, 1st blk mk/reg mk 1871, 4 no-show flakes, 8"..125.00
Institute, saucer, 1st blk mk............................35.00
Institute, sucier, 1st blk mk, raised pad registry mk.....590.00
Ivy, cream jug, 3rd blk mk...............................45.00
Ivy, creamer & sugar, 1st blk mk, pr....................150.00
Ivy, stump spill, bright gr leaves, 2nd blk mk...........185.00
Ivy, sugar, lav/bl-gr lustre, 1st blk mk, 1¾"............95.00
Ivy, sugar, yellow trim, large, 2nd blk mk...............68.00
Ivy, trunk stump, 1st blk mk, 6½".......................160.00
Lace, cake plate, 2nd blk mk.............................48.00
Lifford, creamer, pink trim, gr mk w/R...................35.00
Lily, creamer & sugar, wht/gr, 2nd blk mk, pr...........150.00
Limpet, cup & saucer, demitasse, eggshell, 3rd blk mk....55.00
Limpet, cup & saucer, 3rd blk mk.........................70.00
Limpet, saucer, pk, 3rd blk mk...........................12.50
Limpet, sugar & creamer, orange trim, 3rd blk mk........88.00
Limpet, teapot, long spout, 3rd blk mk..................295.00

Lotus, creamer & sugar, 3rd blk mk........85.00
Mask, cup & saucer, yel lustre hdl & interior, 3rd blk mk.....85.00
Mask, tea cup & saucer, 3rd blk mk........65.00
Masque, cream jug, 1st blk mk, 4½".........290.00
Nautilus, creamer, 1st blk mk.............275.00
Nautilus, vase, 1st blk mk................300.00
Neptune, bread plate, pk trim, 2nd blk mk, 10"......85.00
Neptune, cake plate, gr trim, 2nd blk mk.....135.00
Neptune, cake plate, pink, 2nd blk mk.....150.00
Neptune, cake plate, plain, 2nd blk mk.....90.00
Neptune, cup & saucer, pk trim, 2nd blk mk.....80.00
Neptune, cup & saucer, wht, 2nd blk mk.....70.00
Neptune, cup & saucer & 8" plate, 3rd blk mk.....110.00
Neptune, dejeuner set, pink, 1st blk mk.....1,900.00
Neptune, plate, gr trim, 2nd blk mk, 5¾".....32.00
Neptune, sugar, 2nd blk mk................50.00
Neptune, teapot, pk trim, 2nd blk mk.....345.00
Neptune, teapot, 2nd blk mk..............385.00
New Shell, butter dish, 3rd blk mk........45.00
New Shell, cup & saucer, pk trim, 3rd blk mk.....50.00
New Shell, cup & saucer, 1st gr mk........35.00
New Shell, plate, pk shells all around, 1st gr mk, 7".....55.00
New Shell, plate, pk trim, 3rd blk mk, 8".....40.00
New Shell, saucer, pink tint, 3rd blk mk.....15.00
Nut cup, 1st gr mk.......................30.00
Plate, Sycamore leaf, 2nd blk mk..........45.00
Prince of Wales, compote, 3 horse base, 1st blk mk, 9½"...2,250.00
Princess, vase, 3rd blk mk, 9"............950.00
Rathmore, creamer, yel lustre hdl, 3rd gr mk, 4".....25.00
Rathmore, vase, 3rd blk mk...............125.00
Ribbon, vase, applied florals, no color, 3rd blk mk.....245.00
Seahorse, salt stand, turq w/pink & gold trim, 1st blk mk, 4"..550.00
Seahorse/Trumpet, vase, dk br gilded horse, 1st blk mk, 5"....590.00
Shamrock, bowl, basketweave, blk mk, 2x3½".....45.00
Shamrock, bread plate, twig hdls in br, 3rd blk mk, 10½".....125.00
Shamrock, butter tub w/lid, lustre w/in, 3rd blk mk.....95.00
Shamrock, creamer, br twig hdl, 3rd blk mk.....75.00
Shamrock, cup & saucer, demitasse; 3rd blk mk.....68.00
Shamrock, cup & saucer, harp hdl, 3rd blk mk.....95.00
Shamrock, cup & saucer, tall, 3rd gr mk.....36.00
Shamrock, cup & saucer, tea; very thin, 1st gr mk.....39.00
Shamrock, cup & saucer & 8" plate, low cup/saucer, 3rd blk mk.85.00
Shamrock, ewer, 2nd gr mk................50.00
Shamrock, honey pot, 2nd blk mk, 6".......535.00
Shamrock, honey pot, 3rd blk mk, 6½".....245.00
Shamrock, marmalade jar, 1st gr mk........60.00
Shamrock, milk pitcher, 3rd blk mk, 4½".....65.00
Shamrock, mustard w/lid, barrel, 3rd blk mk, 3½".....80.00
Shamrock, nut bowl, 2nd gr mk............30.00
Shamrock, plate, 2nd blk mk, 8"..........33.00
Shamrock, plate, 3rd blk mk, 6¾".........28.00
Shamrock, plate, 3rd blk mk, 8"..........32.00
Shamrock, plate, 4 twig hdls, 3rd blk mk, 6".....32.00
Shamrock, saucer, 3rd blk mk.............15.00
Shamrock, sugar & creamer, 3rd gr mk, lg.....60.00
Shamrock, tea set, basketweave, gr/br trim, 2nd blk mk, 3 pc..325.00
Shamrock, teapot, long spout, 3rd blk mk.....195.00
Shamrock, teapot, short spout, 2nd blk mk.....165.00
Shamrock, teapot, small size, 3rd blk mk, rare.....175.00
Shamrock, toy; sugar & creamer, 3rd blk mk.....90.00
Shamrock, vase, gr mk, 6"................45.00
Shell, bowl, 1st blk mk, 5½".............125.00
Shell, creamer, gr trim, 2nd blk mk, 5".....325.00
Shell, plateau bowl, purple coral base, in holder, 1st blk mk...465.00

Dragon charger, circa 1863-90, black printed mark, 15" diameter, $900.00.

Shell, salt, 3rd blk mk..................28.00
Shell, teapot, vivid color, 1st blk mk/registry mk.....1,250.00
Shell, toy; creamer, pink trim, 2nd blk mk.....67.50
Shell on coral ped, 2nd blk mk, 8½".......490.00
Sidney, plate, gr trim, 2nd blk mk, 6"......70.00
Snail, tea plate, gold/turq/pk trim, 1st blk mk, 7¼".....85.00
Swan, cream jug, 2nd blk mk, lg..........190.00
Swan, creamer, wht, 2nd blk mk...........100.00
Sydney, plate, pink trim, 2nd blk mk, 6".....55.00
Thistle, cup & saucer, 2nd blk mk........85.00
Tridacna, creamer, #101, pk/gold trim, 1st blk mk.....85.00
Tridacna, cup & saucer, pink & gold trim, 2nd blk mk.....90.00
Tridacna, cup & saucer, pink trim, 2nd blk mk.....85.00
Tridacna, cup & saucer, wht, 3rd blk mk.....65.00
Tridacna, plate, pink trim, 1st blk mk, 6¾".....65.00
Tridacna, plate, pink trim, 3rd blk mk, 7¾".....45.00
Tridacna, tea plate, gold/yel lustre trim, 1st blk mk, 6½".....45.00
Tridacna, tea set, pearl, w/2 c/s, tray, 2nd blk mk.....1,550.00
Tridacna, tea set, pk trim, w/2 c/s, tray, 2nd blk mk.....1,850.00
Tridacna, teapot, pk trim, 2nd blk mk.....285.00
Tridacna, teapot w/under plate, individual, 1st blk mk.....225.00
Tumbler, fan, yellow trim, 3rd blk mk.....85.00
Tumbler, round, yellow interior, 2nd blk mk.....95.00
Undine, creamer, 1st blk mk.............150.00
Vase, amphora, yellow trim, 2nd blk mk, 13".....850.00
Vase, applied flowers & leaves, fluted, gr mk, 8".....125.00
Vase, Marine, unusual epergne-like shape, last gr mk.....250.00
Vase, spill; cornucopia on rock, 3rd blk mk.....110.00
Vase, spill; fish, 1st blk mk, 7".........365.00
Vase, Vine, 2nd blk mk, 13x5½"...........500.00
Wall pocket, swan, gilded, 1st blk mk, 9".....1,650.00

Bells

The earliest form of the bell, the crotal or closed mouth, is most familiar to us today as the sleigh bell. Rattles, hollow forms containing stones or seed pods, are also of this type of construction. Gongs, most often associated with the Orient, have no clapper and must be struck to sound. The more common forms of bells are made with a flaring shape and a freely moving interior clapper that causes the bell to ring when it is swung.

Bells come in many shapes, and serve many uses. They have been used throughout history to sound an alarm, call a congregation, announce dinnertime, or signal a victory. School bells called children in from recess, and cow bells made the herd easier to locate. Bells have been made in brass, glass, china, bronze, and cast iron, in simple as well as elaborately embossed forms, and in amusing figurals.

Brass, fish handle is 5″ long.............................45.00
Brass, raised Assyrian figures, 6½x5¼″ dia, heavy...........110.00
Brass, Tutonic heads emb each side, ornate, 4x3″ dia.........75.00
Brass & Capo Di Monte, w/relief figural, sgn/#d, 9¼″.........45.00
Brass w/worn silvering, wood hdl, 6″......................20.00
Bronze, French, dtd 1552, Prpheus/Armorial, 4¼″...........990.00
Canadian beaver, bronze figural..........................35.00
Church warden's, cast bronze/trn wood hdl, 1732, 14″.......125.00
Colonial type, bronze, 1913, 4½″.........................25.00
Cow, brass/mixed metals, handmade.......................25.00
Dinner, Dutch silver, faceted baluster hdl, 1838, 7″........495.00
Farm, Crystal Metal, Upright #1, w/yoke, iron...............200.00
Gong, brass, w/in ornate framework, hammer ea side, 7x5½″...125.00
Hemony, bear & shield figural hdl, brass, 8x4¾″............180.00
Lady holds up hat, full skirted dress, brass, 5x3¼″.........100.00
Lady in hoop skirt, brass figural, 5¾″....................75.00
Lady w/pleated bonnet, French porcelain, figural............80.00
Marie Antoinette w/butterfly net, bronze..................165.00
Old woman carries pot, brass figural, feet form clapper, 5x2″....75.00
Pairpoint, amethyst w/latticino hdl.......................95.00
Pheasant atop plated bell, on ornate iron base, pat 1856, 1863.125.00
Pomade seller, brass figural, head/clapper 1 pc, nodder, 4x2½″.200.00
RAF Victory, V on hdl, emb heads: Stalin, Roosevelt, Churchill..60.00
Ruby flashed souvenir...................................60.00
Saddle, brass, triple mtd, orig clappers, Fort Ross..........85.00
Saignelegier Chiantel Foundeur, 1878, clapper rpl, 5″.......25.00
School, brass w/wooden hdl..............................70.00
School, bronze w/wood hdl, 6½″.........................36.00
Sleigh, brass, #5 to #12, 19 on orig leather strap...........125.00

Sleigh, brass, engraved, string of 23, orig leather............150.00
Sleigh, nickel plated iron, 25 on orig leather strap, G.........80.00
Storks in nests, 2 fish hdl, brass, 4¾x4″..................75.00
Trolley car, gong-type, cast iron..........................75.00
Wedding, clear w/opaque & vaseline loops, English, 11½″....400.00
Wedding, cranberry Dia Quilt, cream opaque hdl, 10x6½″.....235.00
Wedding, opal mauve irid/Dia Quilt, Cristal d'Albret, '60, 15″..175.00

Bennett

The firm of Edwin Bennett was established in 1846 in Baltimore, Maryland. They produced stoneware, majolica, and Rockingham glazed pitchers and teapots in designs such as Rebecca at the Well, an adaptation of an earlier model by S. Alcock & Company, Staffordshire. Underglaze slip decorated art ware was attempted in 1895, called Albion Ware. A variety of marks were used; some contained Bennett's full name, but usually only his initials were incorporated.

Shaving mug, man in relief, br glaze, 4″...................365.00
Vase, Albion, tigers stalk antelopes, KD Berg, 1897, 4″, VG...450.00
Vase, pillow; Albion, 2 squirrels, gr/br, AH Brinton, '95, 8″....950.00
Wash set, wht ironstone w/strawberry blooms, 8 pcs, M......1,200.00

Bennington

Although the term has become a generic one for the mottled brown ware produced there, Bennington is not a type of pottery, but rather a town in Vermont where two important potteries were located. The Norton Company, founded in 1793, produced mainly redware and salt glazed stoneware; only during a brief partnership with Fenton (1845-47) was any Rockingham attempted. The Norton Company endured until 1894, operated by succeeding generations of the Norton family.

Fenton organized his own pottery in 1847. There he manufactured not only redware and stoneware, but many other artistic types as well -- graniteware, scroddled ware, flint enamel, a fine parian, and vast amounts of their famous Rockingham. Though from an esthetic standpoint his work rated highly among the country's finest ceramic achievements, he was unsuccessful economically. His pottery closed in 1858.

It is estimated that only one in five Fenton pieces were marked, and although it has become a common practice to link any fine piece of Rockingham to this area, careful study is vital to distinguish Bennington's from the similar wares of many other American and Staffordshire potteries. Although the practice was without the permission of the proprietor, it was nevertheless a common occurrence for a potter to take his molds with him when moving from one pottery to the next. So particularly well received designs were often reproduced at several locations. Of eight known Fenton marks, four are variations of the '1849' impressed stamp -- 'Lyman Fenton Co., Fenton's Enamel Patented, 1849, Bennington, Vermont'. These are generally found on examples of Rockingham and flint enamel. A raised, rectangular scroll with 'Fenton's Works, Bennington, Vermont', was used on early examples of porcelain. From 1852 to 1858, the company operated under the title of the United States Pottery Company. Three marks -- the ribbon mark with the initials USP; the oval with a scrollwork border and the name in full; and the plain oval with the name in full -- were used during that period.

Among the more sought after examples are the bird and animal figurines, novelty pitchers, figural bottles, and all of the more finely modeled items. Recumbent deer, cows, standing lions with one forepaw on a ball, and opposing pairs of poodles with baskets in their mouths and 'coleslaw' fur were made in Rockingham, flint enamel, and occasionally in parian.

See also Stoneware
    Key: c/s----cobalt on salt glaze

Tower bell, white brass, supported in cast iron swivel arbor standard, by Meneely and Co., West Troy, New York, 1899, $1,100.00.

Vase, dog and rabbit figurals, in a rare belleek made by Fenton, 5", $285.00 for either vase.

Bill of sale, Edward Norton & Co, Bennington, Vt.............50.00
Bottle, coachman, rockingham, no mk, 9¼"...............400.00
Bottle, coachman, rockingham, 1849 mk, prof repr, 10½".....450.00
Bottle, coachman, rockingham, 1849 mk, 10½"............750.00
Cake crock, stylized flower, c/s, J&E Norton, 1½ gal, hairline..200.00
Candlestick, flint enamel, minor flakes under base, 6½".......475.00
Candlestick, flint enamel, sm base flake, 7¾"...............475.00
Candlestick, flint enamel, 9½", M.....................525.00
Candlestick, rockingham, rpr, 8¼"......................300.00
Churn, bird on fancy leaf, c/s, E & LP Norton, 5 gal, G-EX....425.00
Churn, elaborate floral, c/s, 5 gal, M....................725.00
Churn, flower front & side, c/s, Norton & Fenton, 6 gal, M....475.00
Cooler, houses/stag/flower basket/fences/etc, c/s, 5 gal, VG....4,000.00
Creamer, cow, flint enamel...........................450.00
Flask, book; flint enamel, 'Departed Sprits', 6", VG.........475.00
Flower pot, rockingham, acanthus leaves, no base, 7", G......50.00
Flower pot w/attached saucer, emb cattails, dk br glaze, 8".....60.00
Frame, rockingham, 2" Wx10¾" dia....................475.00
Jar, birds, (pr/Xed), c/s, J Norton & Co, ovoid, 2 gal, EX.....900.00
Jar, bold leaf, c/s, E & LP Norton, 1 gal, age line in rear.......50.00
Jar, chicken pecking, fancy/deep bl; c/s, J&E Norton, 4 gal...1,350.00
Jar, elaborate floral, c/s, E & LP Norton, 6 gal, hairlines.....300.00
Jar, fancy floral, c/s, J&E Norton, 1½ gal, EX..............175.00
Jar, fancy flower basket, c/s, J&E Norton, 2 gal, bk line.......400.00
Jar, flower w/4 buds, c/s, J&E Norton, 2 gal, chip on ear......100.00
Jar, flowers, drooping; c/s, Norton & Fenton, ovoid, 2 gal....200.00
Jar, stylized flower, c/s, J&E Norton, 2 gal, rear hairline......125.00
Jar, triple flowers, c/s, Julius Norton, w/lid, 1½ gal, EX......175.00
Jar, w/lid, stylized flower, c/s, E & LP Norton, 2 gal, EX.....135.00
Jug, bird on branch is blurred, c/s, imp J&F Norton, 11¼"....195.00
Jug, bird on mound, incised, c/s, L Norton & Co, 1 gal, EX...800.00
Jug, bird on stump, c/s, J&E Norton, 1 gal, front crack......325.00
Jug, butterfly, c/s, Julius Norton, ovoid, 2 gal, EX...........275.00
Jug, compote w/lg flower, c/s, J&E Norton, 2 gal, minor lines..450.00
Jug, dbl birds on twig, c/s, J Norton & Co, 4 gal, EX........600.00
Jug, double flower, c/s, J&E Norton, 2 gal, filled base chip....150.00
Jug, fancy floral, c/s, J&E Norton, 3 gal, EX...............275.00
Jug, fancy stylized flower, c/s, J Norton & Co, 3 gal, M......325.00
Jug, flower, c/s, J&E Norton, 2 gal, hairline in hdl...........175.00
Jug, flower w/leaf, c/s, J&E Norton, 2 gal, hairlines.........135.00
Jug, lg flower/dbl leaf, c/s, L Norton & Son, ovoid, 3 gal, M...250.00
Jug, log, c/s, E & LP Norton, 4 gal, hole in front/hairlines.....225.00
Jug, peacock on stump, c/s, J&E Norton, 3 gal, EX.........700.00
Jug, simple floral, sm E Norton & Co, 11".................125.00
Jug, simple leaf decor, mk Norton & Fenton, 14"...........285.00

Jug, stylized flower, c/s, E & LP Norton, 2 gal, M...........175.00
Mug, rockingham, w/hdl, 3⅛", M.....................130.00
Pie plate, rockingham, 10", M.........................130.00
Pitcher, hound hdl, emb stag & doe, hairline, rim flake, 8½"..400.00
Snuff jar, toby, w/lid, flint enamel, sgn, 4½"..............675.00
Snuff jar, toby, w/lid, not flint, 4½"....................575.00
Soap dish, rockingham, 3 pcs, sq finial, 1849 mk, 4x6"......425.00
Vase, parian, bl/wht, 8", pr..........................150.00
Vase, tulip, flint enamel, 9", M.......................700.00
Wholesale price list, E & LP Norton, 1880, in fr............170.00

Beswick

James Wright Beswick operated a pottery in Longston, England, in the early 1890s, where he produced fine dinnerware as well as ornamental ceramics. Collectors of Beswick today are most interested in the figurines made since 1936 by a later generation Beswick firm, John Beswick, Ltd. They specialize in reproducing authentic breeds of animals in accurate detail in a fine bone china body. Their Fireside Series includes models of dogs, cats, elephants, horses, the Huntsman, and an Indian figure, all of which measure up to 14" in height. The Connoisseur line is modeled after the likenesses of famous racing horses.

Beatrix Potter's characters, and some of Walt Disney's, are charmingly recreated, and appeal to adults as well as children. Other items, such as character tobys, have also been produced.

The Beswick name is stamped on each piece. The firm was absorbed by the Doulton group in 1973.

Toby mug, 5", $55.00.

Beatrix Potter, Cecily Parsley, 1965........................30.00
Beatrix Potter, Mrs Tiggy Winkle, 1948...................50.00
Beatrix Potter, Ribby, 1951............................50.00
Beatrix Potter, Tom Kitten, 1948........................30.00
Figurine, bird on sunflower, #929.......................35.00
Figurine, Cardinal, #927, 6"...........................20.00
Figurine, cat, wht, #1030.............................30.00
Figurine, collie, Lockinvar of Lady Park, 5½x7¼"..........40.00
Figurine, giraffe....................................45.00
Figurine, Golden Retriever............................50.00
Figurine, horse, wht w/gray dappling, 6".................36.00
Figurine, male mallard duck, wings up, 6x8"..............40.00
Figurine, polar bear, walking, ice bl/gray, paper label, 7x10"....60.00

Figurine, Siamese cat, #1071............................25.00
Shakers, Mr Micawber & Sairey Gamp, pr..................35.00
Teapot, Peggotty, sgnd.................................45.00
Toby pitcher, Tony Weller, #281.........................60.00
Vase, cobalt gloss w/blown-out palm trees, gilt trim, #1070......85.00
Vase, pastel tones, 6¼"................................25.00

Big Little Books

The first Big Little Book was published in 1933, and copyrighted in 1932, by the Whitman Publishing Company of Racine, Wisconsin. Its hero was Dick Tracy. The concept was so well accepted that others soon followed Whitman's example, and though the 'Big Little Book' phrase became a trademark of the Whitman Company, the formats of his competitors -- Saalfield, Goldsmith, Van Wiseman, Lynn, and World Syndicate -- were exact copies. Today's Big Little Book buffs collect them all.

These hand-sized sagas of adventure were illustrated by full page cartoons on the right hand page, and the story narration on the left. Colorful cardboard covers contained hundreds of pages, usually totaling over an inch in thickness. Big Little Books originally sold for 10¢ at the dime store; as late as the mid-1950s, when the popularity of comic books caused sales to decline signaling an end to production, their price had risen to a mere 20¢.

Their appeal was directed toward the pre-teens who bought, traded, and hoarded Big Little Books. Because so many were stored in attics and closets, many have survived. Among the super heroes are G-Men, Flash Gordon, Tarzan, the Lone Ranger, and Red Ryder; and in a lighter vein, Blondie and Dagwood, Mickey Mouse, Little Orphan Annie, and Felix the Cat.

In the early to mid-30s, Whitman published several Big Little Books as advertising premiums for the Coco Malt Company, who packed them in boxes of their cereal. These are highly prized by today's collectors, as are Disney stories and super hero adventures.

Ace Drummond, 1935, M...............................25.00
Air Fighters of America, 1941, Bob Jenny art, EX...........20.00
Alice in Wonderland, movie version, 1934, G..............12.00
Allen Pike of the Parachute Squad, EX...................20.00
Alley Oop, Jungles Moo, VG..........................18.00
Andy Panda's Vacation, 1946, EX......................15.00
Apple Mary & Denny, 1936, EX........................15.00
Arizona Kid, 1936, EX...............................17.00
Beasts of Tarzan, #1410, Whitman, 1937................20.00
Believe It or Not, 1931, G..............................9.00
Big Chief Wahoo, #1443, Whitman, VG..................15.00
Billy the Kid...6.00
Billy the Kid's Pledge, 1940, VG.......................7.00
Black Silver, 1937, Vallely art, G.......................7.00
Blondie, Bounding Baby Dumpling, 1940, NM.............30.00
Blondie, Bumsteads Carry On, 1939, VG.................15.00
Blondie, Papa Knows Best, 1945, EX....................23.00
Blondie & Dagwood In Hot Water, 1946, EX..............23.00
Border Eagle, 1938, VG..............................12.00
Brad Turner, Trans-Atlantic Flight, 1939, VG.............10.00
Bringing Up Father, EX..............................20.00
Bronco Peeler, the Lone Cowboy, 1937, G................12.00
Brown Bomber, movie, Joe Louis, 1936, EX...............35.00
Buccaneer, The; 1938, movie version, Fredric March, NM......10.00
Buck Rogers, Coco Malt giveaway......................30.00
Buck Rogers, Doom Comet, 1935, VG....................35.00
Buck Rogers, Fiend of Space, VG.......................28.00
Buck Rogers, Fiend of Space, 1940, NM..................50.00
Buck Rogers, Overturned World, NM.....................60.00
Buck Rogers, Planetoid Plot, NM........................55.00
Buck Rogers, Super Dwarf of Space, NM..................58.00
Bugs Bunny, Masked Marvel, NM.......................30.00

Bugs Bunny, Pirate Loot, 1947, VG......................17.00
Bugs Bunny, Risky Business, 1948, VG...................18.00
Bugs Bunny, Trouble at Diamond Island, EX...............7.00
Bullets Across the Border.............................10.00
Call of the Wild, movie, Clark Gable, 1935, M.............60.00
Captain Marvel, Return of Scorpion, VG..................40.00
Captain Midnight, and the Secret Squadron, 1941, EX.......25.00
Captain Midnight, Sheik Jomak Khan, NM.................25.00
Chandu the Magician, movie, Bela Lugosi, 1935, VG.........15.00
Charlie Chan of the Honolulu Police, 1939, G..............15.00
Charlie McCarthy & Edgar Bergen, 1938, VG..............10.00
Chester Gump, Pole to Pole Flight, #1402, Whitman.........12.00
Chuck Malloy Railroad Detective On Streamliner, 1938, VG....12.00
Convoy Patrol, 1942, VG...............................8.00
Cowboy Lingo, 1938, VG.............................15.00
Dan Dunn, On Trail of Wu Fang, EX.....................20.00
Dan of the Lazy L, 1939, VG............................8.00
David Copperfield, movie, WC Fields, 1934, EX............25.00
Detective Higgins, 1938, EX...........................13.00
Dick Tracy, and His G-Men, #1439, 1941, EX..............25.00
Dick Tracy, Crooks in Disguise, 1939, EX.................30.00
Dick Tracy, on Voodoo Island, 1944, EX..................30.00
Dick Tracy, Out West, 1933, G.........................22.00
Dick Tracy, Phantom Ship, 1940, #1434, EX...............30.00
Dick Tracy, Special FBI Operative, 1936, EX...............30.00
Dick Tracy, Super-Detective, 1939, #1488, VG.............20.00
Dick Tracy, Yogee Yamma, #1412, Whitman, 1946..........30.00
Doctor Doom, Faces Death At Dawn, 1937, G..............12.00
Dog Stars of Hollywood, movie scenes, 1930s, NM.........35.00
Don Winslow of the Navy, Great War Pilot, 1940, NM........30.00
Donald Duck, Forgets To Duck, 1939, EX.................25.00
Donald Duck, Gets Fed Up, 1940, EX....................35.00
Donald Duck, Sees Stars, 1941, NM.....................50.00
Donald Duck, Silly Symphony, 1937, EX..................20.00
Draftee of the US Army, #1416, Whitman, 1943............10.00
Erik Noble..6.00
Felix the Cat, 1936, VG..............................14.00
Flame Boy, and the Indians' Secret.....................10.00
Flash Gordon, Forest Kingdom of Mongo, G...............30.00
Flash Gordon, Monsters of Mongo, NM...................70.00
Flash Gordon, Perils of Mongo, 1940, EX.................60.00
Flash Gordon, Red Sword Invaders, VG..................25.00
Flash Gordon, Tyrant of Mongo, 1941, EX................45.00
Flash Gordon, Water World of Mongo, EX.................50.00
Flash Gordon, Witch Queen of Mongo, VG................30.00
Flying Sky Clipper, EX................................10.00
Freckles, The Lost Diamond Mine, 1937, VG...............12.00
Freddie Bartholomew, The Story of; soft cover, 1935, G......15.00
G-Man, and the Radio Bank Robbers, 1937, VG............20.00
G-Man, In Action, 1940, VG...........................17.00
G-Man, Vs the Fifth Column, G.........................15.00
G-Men, On the Job, 1935, G...........................10.00
G-Men, On the Trail..................................10.00
G-Men, Vs the Red X, VG.............................15.00
Gang Busters in Action, 1938, Vallely art, VG..............8.00
Gang Busters Smash Through, 1942, Russell Stamm art, EX....15.00
Gene Autry, Cowboy Detective, 1940, G...................9.00
Gene Autry, Gunsmoke Reckoning, EX...................25.00
Gene Autry, Hawk of the Hills, NM......................23.00
Gene Autry, Law of the Range, VG.......................8.00
Gene Autry, Red Bandit's Ghost, 1949, VG................18.00
Gentleman Joe Palooka, 1940, Saalfield, NM..............35.00
Ghost Avenger, 1943, VG.............................18.00
Go Into Your Dance, movie, Jolson, 1935, EX..............35.00

Great Expectations, movie version, 1934, VG............15.00
Green Hornet Returns, 1941, NM.....................45.00
Guns in the Roaring West, 1937, VG.................11.00
Hall of Fame of the Air, 1936, VG..................15.00
Inspector Wade Solves Mystery of Red Aces, 1937, NM.......10.00
Jackie Cooper, Movie Star of Skippy & Sooky, Whitman, 1933..20.00
Jane Arden, Vanished Princess, 1938, VG...............9.00
Jane Withers, Keep Smiling.........................10.00
Jaragu of the Jungle, 1937, G......................15.00
Jim Starr, of the Border Patrol....................10.00
John Carter of Mars, EX............................45.00
Jr G-Men...10.00
Jungle Jim, Vampire Woman, #1139, Whitman, 1937..........35.00
Just Kids, Mysterious Stranger, 1935, NM.............30.00
Ken Maynard, Western Justice.......................10.00
Kit Carson, color cover, G...........................8.00
Laughing Dragon of Oz, Frank Baum.................27.50
Law of the Wild, movie w/Rin Tin Tin Jr, 1935, VG........9.00
Li'l Abner Among The Millionaires, 1939, EX...........32.00
Little Lord Fauntleroy.............................15.00
Little Miss Muffet, 1936, EX.......................20.00
Little Orphan Annie, and Sandy, 1933, EX............20.00
Little Orphan Annie, in the Thieves Den, 1944, NM.......25.00
Little Orphan Annie, Million Dollar Formula, 1935, VG.......10.00
Lone Ranger, and His Horse Silver, EX................30.00
Lone Ranger, Black Shirt Highwayman, 1939, Vallely art, NM...35.00
Lone Ranger, Great Western Span, 1942, VG...........10.00
Lone Ranger, Menace of Murder Valley, 1938, EX.........20.00
Lone Ranger, Red Renegades, 1939, EX................30.00
Lone Ranger, Red Renegades, 1939, G.................10.00
Lone Ranger, Secret Killer, 1937, VG................22.00
Lone Ranger, Secret Weapon, #1428, EX...............25.00
Lone Ranger, Vanishing Herd, 1936, VG...............10.00
Mac of the Marines in Africa, 1936, VG..............12.00
Mickey Mouse, Dude Ranch Bandit, 1940, VG...........18.00
Mickey Mouse, Foreign Legion, VG...................20.00
Mickey Mouse, Magic Lamp, EX.......................30.00
Mickey Mouse, On Sky Island, NM....................40.00
Mickey Mouse, Stolen Jewels, 1949, NM...............25.00
Moon Mullins & Kayo, 1933, VG......................12.00
Mr District Attorney on the Job, 1941, G............15.00
O'Shaughnessy's Boy, movie, Berry & Cooper, 1935, Lynn, EX..45.00
Our Gang, 1942, Vallely art, EX....................25.00
Peggy Brown, & the Jewel of the Fire, 1943, VG.........10.00
Peggy Brown, Mystery Basket, Vallely art, EX.........12.00
Perry Wincle and the Rinkeydinks, 1937, VG...........10.00
Phantom, Desert Justice, VG........................17.00
Phantom, Return of; NM.............................35.00
Pioneers, 1933, blue cover, VG.......................8.00
Popeye, and the Deep Sea Mystery, EX................25.00
Popeye, Castor Oyl Detective, NM...................38.00
Popeye, Queen Olive Oyl, 1946, VG..................18.00
Porky Pig & Petunia, EX............................20.00
Radio Patrol Safeblowers, 1937, VG.................14.00
Range Busters, 1942, Vallely art, VG................12.00
Rangers of the Rio Grand, NM.......................13.00
Red Hot Holsters, 1938, EX.........................13.00
Red Ryder, Code of the Range, 1941, G...............10.00
Red Ryder, Code of the West, NM....................35.00
Red Ryder, Fighting Westerner, 1940, EX.............30.00
Red Ryder, Hoofs of Thunder, M.....................40.00
Red Ryder, Squaw Tooth Rustlers, 1941, VG...........15.00
Red Ryder, War on the Range, 1945, G.................8.00
Roy Rogers, King of Cowboys, 1943, EX...............19.00

Roy Rogers, Mystery Of Howling Mesa, 1948, EX.........19.00
Roy Rogers, Robin Hood of the Range, G..............10.00
Skippy, The Story of; soft cover, 1934, G...........12.00
Smilin' Jack & the Stratosphere Ascent, 1937, G........20.00
Smitty, Lost Among Indians, NM.....................20.00
Snow White & Seven Dwarfs, 1938, Walt Disney, EX.......20.00
Spike Kelly of the Commandos, 1943, EX..............20.00
Tailspin Tommy, Air Race, Saalfield, 1940, NM.........30.00
Tailspin Tommy, Hooded Flyer, 1937, EX..............15.00
Tailspin Tommy, Hunting Pirate Gold, 1935, EX.........18.00
Tailspin Tommy, Lost Transport, 1940, NM............30.00
Tailspin Tommy, Payroll Mystery, 1933, spine taped, G......10.00
Tale of Two Cities, Ronald Coleman movie, 1935, VG.......15.00
Tarzan, Lord of the Jungle, 1946, EX................20.00
Tarzan, New Adventures, VG.........................25.00
Tarzan, Revenge of; 1938, VG.......................19.00
Tarzan Escapes, 1936, EX...........................30.00
Terry and the Pirates, original, 1935, VG............20.00
Terry and the Pirates, War in Jungle, 1946, VG........17.00
Texas Kid, The; 1937, NM...........................12.00
The Shadow & the Ghost Makers, #1195, Whitman.........25.00
Three Musketeers, 1935, G..........................16.00
Tim Tyler's Luck, Adventure in Ivory Patrol, 1937, G......10.00
Tiny Tim in the Big World, 1934, NM.................20.00
Tom Mix, Hoard of Montezuma, 1937, Henry Vallely art, EX....20.00
Tom Mix, On Barbary Coast, M.......................40.00
Tom Mix, Range War, #1166, Whitman, 1937............30.00
Tom Mix, Terror Trail, 1934, movie scenes, EX.........25.00
Tom Sawyer, 1934, VG...............................12.00
Two Gun Montana, 1936, VG..........................12.00
Uncle Ray's Story Of The United States, 1934, VG........9.00
Wash Tubbs in Pandemonia, 1932, G...................8.00
Wells Fargo..10.00
Westward Ho!, movie scenes, John Wayne, 1935, EX.......50.00
Wheels of Destiny, movie, Ken Maynard, 1934, EX........20.00
Zip Saunders, 1939, EX.............................15.00

Bing and Grondahl

In 1853, brothers M.H. and J.H. Bing formed a partnership with Frederick Vilhelm Grondahl in Copenhagen, Denmark. Their early wares were porcelain plaques and figurines, designed by the noted sculptor Thorvaldsen of Denmark. Dinnerware production began in 1863, and by 1889 their underglaze color 'Copenhagen Blue' had earned them worldwide acclaim.

They are perhaps most famous today for their Christmas plates, the first of which were made in 1895. The plate was titled 'Behind the Frozen Window', and the series has continued to the present with annual editions. A second series commemorating Mother's Day was added in 1969.

See also Collector Plates

Coffee pot, blue, 10".............................55.00
Dish, shell form, hermit crab figural on end, sgn, 7½"........70.00
Figurine, blacksmith, #2225, 11½"..................265.00
Figurine, duck, #1548..............................38.00
Figurine, Earache, #2206...........................45.00
Figurine, fisherman & his family, #2025, 13".......250.00
Figurine, girl & sheep, sgn Locher, #2010, 6½x10½"....275.00
Figurine, goat, #1699, 6"..........................65.00
Figurine, Mary the Doll, 1st edition...............200.00
Figurine, mother, child on lap, one beside chair, #2262, 8"....160.00
Figurine, penguin, #1823, 3".......................60.00

Figurine, penguin, standing; #1821, 3"......................65.00
Figurine, The Kissers........................185.00
Vase, Christmas 1918, bl/wht, 7½".................125.00

Fisherman and his family, #2025, 13", $250.00.

Birdcages

Birdhouse, 2 doors/2 windows/staircase/tin roof, early 1900s.....90.00
Brass, Osborne Mfg Co...........................45.00
Brass, 4 milk glass accessories, brass & iron stand, Hendrix....135.00
Brass wire dome top w/steeple, compote base.................65.00
Delft, pnt allover w/birds/flowers, bl/gold/gr/br, sgn.........1,500.00
Mansion, Victorian, 3 chimneys, windows, wood.............260.00
Parrot cage, brass wire, tin bottom.......................38.00
Wood, barrel form w/overhanging roof, round base, old pnt.....85.00

Birdcage, wooden slat construction, circa 1930, 20" x 14" x 19½", $425.00.

Bisque

Bisque is a term referring to unglazed earthenware or porcelain that has been fired only once. During the Victorian era, bisque figurines became very popular. Most were highly decorated in pastels and gilt, and demonstrated a fine degree of workmanship in the quality of their modeling. Few were marked.

See also Heubach; Piano Babies; Snow Babies

Box, trinket; blk/tan dog w/long chain on lid, 9"..............85.00
Bust, lady w/flowing gown & shawl, florals, 21"..............220.00
Figurine, Black boy eats from sack/girl holds pk bow, 3½", pr.275.00
Figurine, Black boy on potty, holding watermelon slice, 4¼"....55.00
Figurine, Black boy sits on stump, plays accordian, 4½"......115.00
Figurine, boy, bkwards on chair/top hat/wood cigar, German, 7".85.00
Figurine, boy & girl on common base, German Grafenthal, 15".175.00
Figurine, boy in tan/blk bath tub, German, 4x3¾".............80.00
Figurine, child in shawl & bonnet, 'Grandma', German, 10".....85.00
Figurine, Colonial couple, pastels, 12", pr..................60.00
Figurine, girl, bl dress/bead trim/dog at side/cats in lap, 8".....200.00
Figurine, girl w/letter, hand over heart, sgn Bauer, 13½"......375.00
Figurine, minstrel man, EX detail, 7"......................70.00
Figurine, pug dog, tan w/blk markings, 4½".................50.00
Figurine, trapeze artists, swinging figures, 6¼", pr...........275.00
Figurine, Victorian boy in sailor hat & girl, German, 13½", pr.375.00
Figurine, wild boar, decorated, German, 4x7"...............165.00
Figurine, wolf in red jacket, bl pants, yel shirt, bow tie, 5".....50.00
Figurine, 2 cherubs w/flower basket, sgn Colbert, 10x18"......325.00
Humidor, lady's head, br skin/blk hair, w/bandana, 5x3½"......85.00
Match holder, wall; maid w/cat in shuttered window, 4½x2¾"...32.00
Potty girl w/fan, wearing cap, bl/wht/maroon, 4¼".............55.00
Vase, well w/girl in lg hat feeding rooster, figural, gr/lav.......95.00

Busts, excellent detail, no markings, 8", for the pair: $135.00.

Black Americana

Black memorabilia is without a doubt a field that encompasses the most widely exploited ethnic group in our history. But within this field there are many levels of interest: arts and achievements such as folk music and literature; caricatures in advertising, souvenirs, toys, and fine art; and legitimate research into the days of their enslavement and enduring struggle for equality. The list is endless.

In the listing below are some with a derogatory conotation. Thankfully, these are from a bygone era, and represent the mores of a culture that existed nearly a century ago. They are included only to convey the fact that they are a part of this growing area of collecting interest.

See also Posters, minstrel

Ash tray, ceramic, baby on pot eating watermelon, Japan, 4x3"..14.00
Ash tray, head figural w/lg bobbing tongue, mc underglaze, EX..35.00
Ash tray, majolica, lg clam shell w/boy smoking pipe, 4x4", EX..35.00
Aunt Jemima face mask, Ask Your Grocer, 11x13"..........75.00
Automated picture, Black boy changes expression, Hoyt Life..1,225.00
Bank, tin mechanical, X-legged minstrel tips hat, mc, 7", EX..700.00
Bellhop, floor standing, metal, orig paint..................295.00
Bowl, Cream of Wheat, Rastus w/bowl & steam locomotive, EX..75.00
Brush, horsehair, figural bellboy, mc ptd wood, 8", M.........12.00
Brush, horsehair, figural ptd wood Mammy w/neck ribbon, 7"...15.00
Card stand, figural butler, mc painted wood, 34", VG.........175.00
Clock, Dixie Boy, Lux, mc wood face/shoulders, eyes move, EX.495.00
Coaster, glass, mc decal: man playing sax, 3" dia.............6.00
Cocktail napkin, cloth, 'Forbidden Fruit', Blks dancing, mc.....10.00
Coffee grinder, maple, w/drawer, picture of boy, Austria, 5".....65.00
Cookie jar, Aunt Jemima, plastic........................55.00
Creamer & sugar, Aunt Jemima, celluloid, yellow............39.00
Cup & saucer, Coon Chicken Inn, mc face on both, Syracuse, M.95.00
Darning egg, wood, painted Black face w/gr & red hat, 5½"....12.00
Doll, Aunt Jemima, oil cloth............................28.00
Doll, Aunt Jemima, plastic, mc, ca 1948, 11½", G............35.00
Figurine, Amos & Andy, plaster/ptd bl/red/blk/gr, 12", EX, pr..225.00
Figurine, bisque egg w/baby hatching, 2", M................24.00
Figurine, boy on pot w/melon slice, bisque, Japan, 3½", EX....20.00
Figurine, dog chases boy up tree, German bisque, detailed, 4½".55.00
Game, mirror w/lady's picture, roll balls into mouth, 1890, 2"...42.00
Game, Watch On De Rine, 1931, litho: 3 eating melon, M.....175.00
Humidor, Picaninny Girl Tobacco, girl w/pigtails, majolica......275.00
Illustration, Little Black Sambo, mc, FB Peat, sgnd/dtd 1931....45.00
Label, Black Joe Juice Grapes, dk blue & yel, M..............2.00
Lawn figurine, girl w/cute expression, wood, 1930s............18.00
Lighter, CI boy's head w/cigar in mouth, electric/110V, 6", EX.295.00
Make-up, 5" tube/Dk Creole, w/orig box, both picture minstrel...12.00
Map, Henrico County, Virginia, 1853, lists # of slaves, etc.....300.00
Match holder, boys/melon/cotton CI figural, 1884 Cotton Expo..75.00
Mug, figural Mammy head, 3 color chalkware, lg features, 2", M.28.00
Mug, frosted glass, enamel singing Blk, song on verso, 5", M....22.00
Mug, Mammy, scarf wrapped head, lg eyes, HP, Japan, 5"......14.00
Napkin, Coon Chicken Inn, wht linen w/green lettering, 17x16"..18.00
Napkin holder, Coon Chicken Inn, face figural, plaster, EX, 6".125.00
Noisemakers, colorful tin, 2 crank, 1 bell, set of 3 for.........20.00
Nut dish, Brazil nut shape, ceramic, hi-glaze boy figure, 6x9"...50.00
Paperweight, blk glass, gator w/boy in mouth, mc, 5x2", EX....42.00
Pen wipe, small Black Mammy, blk felt w/worn wht linen......40.00
Pencil sharpener, figural head, metal, gross features, Germany...36.00
Perfume, Golliwog, blk lucite hair, w/orig label, 5", M.........54.00
Pincushion, Mammy mc chalkware figural, orig stuffed skirt, 6"..24.00
Pipe, boy eating banana, Meerschaum.....................285.00
Pitcher, ironstone, transfer: 9 musicians, captions, 1870, EX...650.00
Planter, mc underglaze, boy w/lg bass, mkd Japan, 4".........18.00
Plaque, chalkware, umbrella kids, mc paint, 8", pr...........25.00
Plate, glass, Currier/Ives Balking Mule pressed pattern, 1880....60.00
Plate, man/woman talk old-type phone, cupid on line, mc china.125.00
Print, American Beauty, boy smelling rose, dtd 1904, 8x10"....65.00
Print, The Fortune Teller, Harry Roseland, 1890s, framed....395.00
Recipe box, Aunt Jemima, celluloid, yellow.................55.00
Recipe box, red plastic w/Aunt Jemima face, mkd Fosta, VG....40.00
Salt & pepper, Aunt Jemima/Uncle Mose, shiny, F&F Mold, 5"...13.00
Salt & pepper, 3 color printed on wood, Liza & Rastus, 2½".....8.00
Sheet music, My Nappy Headed Coon, 1896.................10.00
Sign, O'Baby Malt Chocolate Drink, cardboard, boy/bottle, 14"..80.00
Sign, Restrooms: White--Colored, reverse painted on glass.....125.00
Sign, We Serve Colored: Carry-Out Only, paper, 1931..........55.00
Sign, White Only--Cotton Belt Route, paper, 1929............55.00

Spice set, Aunt Jemima, celluloid, yellow, set of 6............95.00
Spoon, Florida, w/Black boy & alligator....................95.00
Spoon, Sunny South, w/Sonny Jim's face, sterling silver.......75.00
Spoon rest, mc Chef, nodder, Lefton's orig label, 4½".........35.00
Swizzle sticks, Zulu-Lulu, brn plastic, on orig yel/red card.....20.00
Tablecloth, printed cotton/fancy Mammys/fruit border, '30s, EX..42.00
Tea towel, linen, embroidered Mammy at old stove, 18x30", EX.22.00
Tea towel, 3 houses, fancy couple dance, check border, 2 sides..24.00
Thermometer, Diaper Diana, shows little girl, dtd 1955, 5", EX..22.00
Thermometer, pressed wood, Black boy....................16.50
Timer, figural maid w/spoon, chalkware, timer in hand, EX.....25.00
Tin container, Nigger Hair Tobacco, NM..................115.00
Toothpaste, Darkie, wht/blk tube, w/orig gr/blk/wht box, EX.....10.00
Toothpick, boy's head, German porcelain, brn/blk/red, 2½".....25.00
Towel holder, Mammy/arms come out to hold roll, mc ptd wood.65.00
Tumbler, glass, decal: boy w/dog, No Dogs Allowed sign, 7", EX.15.00
Valentine, penny; lady all dressed up, full color, VG..........15.00

Painted cast iron figural with brass tip tray and matchbook holder, 35", $275.00.

Black Cat

The main producer of 'Black Cat' collectibles was the Shafford Company, although occasionally pieces will be found bearing the marks of other firms. Wood & Sons, Ltd., in Burlsem, England, produced an 8" figural teapot as part of a novelty line marketed in this country by Fondeville of New York. Other items have been found marked 'Wales', 'Empress', and 'Napco Ceramics, Japan'. 'Black Cat' collectors usually prefer to limit their 'litter' to those kittens with a shiny black glaze and styling similar to the Shafford cats.

Ash tray, head w/mouth open..........................12.50
Bank, green eyes, w/lock & key, mkd Napco Tommy, 7".......75.00
Creamer, yellow eyes, paw up, 6".......................12.50
Cruet, pr..20.00
Decanter, w/2 cordials, green eyes......................35.00
Decanter, 7½".....................................12.00
Decanter, 9".......................................22.00
Figurine, green eyes, 2"..............................4.00
Figurine, mother & 2 kittens, 3 pc, rhinestone eyes..........17.50
Figurine, yellow eyes, long body, 5½"....................8.00
Marmalade, double head, center hdl, gr edge, w/lid & spoon....30.00
Match holder, ash tray set, 4 pc........................18.00
Mug, green eyes, 2".................................6.00

Pitcher, 6¼"...16.00
Planter, cat beside cup.............................6.00
Salt & pepper, green eyes, 4", pr.................12.50
Salt & pepper, yellow eyes, long bodies, 10", pr....12.50
Salt & pepper, 2½", pr............................9.00
Spice set, 9 pcs in wooden rack, blk cats w/yel eyes..........55.00
Strainer spoon, green eyes........................20.00
Teapot, green eyes, 5½".........................15.00
Teapot, green eyes, 9"..........................20.00
Teapot, yel eyes, lifted paw pours, sleepy cat sugar on top......18.00
Teapot, yel eyes, 6"............................17.00
Utensil holder, green eyes.......................25.00

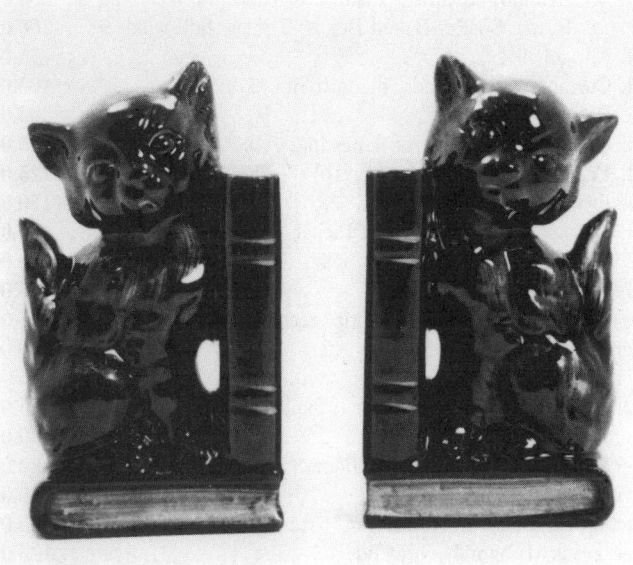

Bookends with pen well at back, 6¾" x 3" x 2", $15.00.

Black Glass

Black glass, sometimes called black milk glass, is a term used to describe a type of colored glass. When held to a strong light, color can be seen through most items. Each glass house had its own formula, so colors may vary, but the most common hue is a deep purple.

Occasionally, it was decorated with silver, gold, enamel, or coralene. It was sometimes etched or given a satin finish, either by the glass house or by firms which specialized in decorating. Often, more than one of these devices was used. Crystal, jade, colored, or milk glass was combined with the black as an accent.

Black glass has been made by many companies since the 17th century. Contemporary glass houses produced black glass during the Depression, seldom signing their product. It is still being made today.

Ash tray, Carnegie National Bank, 1902-28, Tiffin, 6".........25.00
Ash tray, metal cat figural hdl.....................20.00
Ash tray, turtle figural, Westmoreland................15.00
Basket, Tiffin, 11"..............................50.00
Bon bon, rolled up hdls, Mt Pleasant................13.75
Bon bon, stem ft, dolphin hdl.....................38.00
Bottle vase, Art Deco, w/applied gr/gold spirals, Warren, 9".....25.00
Bowl, Art Deco, 4x6½"..........................20.00
Bowl, ftd, Mt Pleasant, 9"........................32.50
Bowl, Molly, Imperial, 9".........................15.00
Bowl, rolled rim, satin glass, Tiffin, 2x6½"...........30.00
Box w/hdls, silver decor, 6½" dia...................50.00

Bud vase, 9¾"..................................32.00
Candle bowl, notched rim, hobnail base, for 5 sm candles, 6½"..25.00
Candle holder, Swan, New Martinsville, pr............30.00
Candle holder, Tiffin, 2x4", pr.....................30.00
Candlestick, Diamond Quilted, #414/1, Imperial, pr....25.00
Candlestick, double stem, Mt Pleasant, pr............40.00
Candy dish, w/hdl, gold trim, red flowers............22.00
Centerpiece bowl, gold parrots w/in, Tiffin..........55.00
Cigarette lighter, Cape Cod, Imperial...............115.00
Cocktail shaker, silver overlay golfers, sgn Hayes, 14"....195.00
Compote, HP red poppies w/in, Tiffin, 10"...........68.50
Compote, jelly; sm enamel florals on lid.............18.00
Creamer & sugar, Diamond Quilted, Imperial..........25.00
Creamer & sugar, Fancy Square, New Martinsville.......24.00
Creamer & sugar, Mayfair, Fostoria................18.00
Creamer & sugar, Mt Pleasant.....................28.00
Cup & saucer, Mt Pleasant........................14.50
Cuspidor, Tiffin................................100.00
Elephant, 1929.................................16.00
Flower pot, 4"..................................7.50
Lamp, Scotty dog figure, frosted shade w/blk dog.......75.00
Pencil pup, Cambridge............................9.00
Plate, hdld, Mayfair, Fostoria.....................15.00
Plate, luncheon; New Martinsville #34...............4.00
Plate, plain pattern, 8".........................10.00
Plate, 10½" square, 2 hdld, Mt Pleasant.............27.00
Plate, 7" octagonal...............................3.50
Plate, 8", Molly, Imperial.........................6.00
Plate, 8", scalloped, Mt Pleasant...................8.75
Rose bowl, Mt Pleasant...........................14.50
Server, center hdl, LE Smith......................25.00
Server, center hdl, Mt Pleasant....................37.00
Shakers, HP yel roses w/gr leaves, 3", pr............20.00
Sherbet, Mt Pleasant..............................9.95
Spittoon, hand; 3"..............................24.00

Window box with classic figures in relief, 3¾" x 3½" x 8", $30.00.

Sugar, scalloped, dlb hdl.........................10.00
Tray, clover shape, Cambridge, 7"..................15.00
Tumbler, New Martinsville #34.....................14.00
Vase, bird in tree, HP, Tiffin, 8"..................40.00
Vase, blown-out chrysanthemums, 5¼"...............90.00
Vase, blown-out poppies & thistles, 8½x8"...........35.00
Vase, dancing ladies, LE Smith....................40.00
Vase, flat flared, ftd, gold thistle trim, 8"..........75.00
Vase, Greek Key, 6"..............................15.00
Vase, pilgrim shape, raised rnd base, wht beading, stork, 9"....150.00
Vase, poppies, coralene, Tiffin, 5½"................30.00
Vase, poppies, coralene, Tiffin, 8"................50.00
Vase, scalloped, 5"...............................8.00

Blown Glass

Blown glass is rather difficult to date; 18th and 19th century examples vary little as to technique or style -- it ranges from primitive to the sophisticated. But the metallic content of very early glass caused tiny imperfections that are obvious upon examination, and these are often indicative of age.

In America, Stiegel introduced the English technique of using a patterned, part-size mold, a practice which was generally followed by many glasshouses after the Revolution. From 1820 to about 1850, glass was blown into full size 3-part molds.

See also specific categories

Beaker, pale amber, flared folded lip, 6½"....................25.00
Bottle, case; ½ post, applied lip, engraved tulips, 8", G.......45.00
Bottle, case; ½ post, gr, pnt label 'Rutae', sickness, 8"........45.00
Bottle, globular, aqua, iron pontil, applied bulb lip, 11".......125.00
Bottle, globular, clear, applied flared lip, Midwestern, 3"......30.00
Bottle, globular, clear, Midwestern, 3¼"......................35.00
Bottle, globular, lt gr, 18 vertical melon ribs, sick, 7".......135.00
Bottle, globular, lt gr w/applied lip, minor sickness, 2¾"......255.00
Bottle, pinch, ½ post, EX impression swirl ribs, cobalt, 10"....105.00
Bottle, scent, wht looping & applied rigaree, 2¾", G...........55.00
Bottle, 16 tight swirl ribs/base w/16 faint vertical ribs, 12".....110.00
Bowl, clear w/applied flared base, folded rim, 12x12".........125.00
Creamer, cobalt, threaded neck/swirl rib lower ½, 1835, 4"....425.00
Creamer, free blown, applied/crimp hdl, triangle rim, 3".......150.00
Creamer, opaque wht, applied ft & hdl, 5"....................145.00
Cruet, hollow hdl & stopper, early, 9".......................50.00
Cruet, 18 swirled ribs, flared lip, scratches, 7"..............135.00
Decanter, pillar mold, matching stopper, sick, 10"............45.00
Decanter, rib mold/3 applied rings, minor sickness, 8"+stopper..30.00
Decanter, 3 applied rings, frosted base w/scratched eagle, 7"....15.00
Fish bowl, clear, applied flaring ft, folded rims, 14x13".......85.00
Flask, aqua, w/label 'carried in Rev War & War of 1812', 6"....45.00
Flask, lt gr, 24 vertical ribs, flared lip, 5¼"................20.00
Flip, clear w/copper wheel engraved basket of flowers, 5".....105.00
Flip, clear w/copper wheel engraved rim, 3¾"................60.00
Flip, fluted base, copper wheel engraved rim, 6¼"............85.00
Flip, w/polka dot pattern of bubbles, clear, 8"...............35.00
Flip, 3 mold, clear, 5½"...................................75.00
Float ball, green, 11" dia..................................22.00
Goblet, clear, applied ft & baluster stem, 5¼"...............25.00
Hanging lamp, aqua, in tin frame w/tooling, 15".............675.00
Hat, clear w/swirled ribs & ground pontil, 6x9".............85.00
Hat, mold blown, in-folded rim, rough pontil, 2½"...........165.00
Jar, preserving; aqua, folded lip, 8½".......................25.00
Jar, tin lid, 10"...35.00
Pitcher, lily pad, aqua, applied threads/hdl, folded rim, 6¼"....25.00
Pitcher, swirl mold, applied hdl, 8¼"......................200.00
Pitcher, 3 mold, applied hdl, 5½"..........................150.00
Rolling pin, opalescent, 15"...............................40.00
Tumbler, aqua, fluted base, 4½"...........................45.00
Tumbler, clear, applied ft, panel-cut bowl, 4¼".............12.00
Tumbler, deep aqua, 16 rib broken swirl, minor sickness, 4"....135.00
Tumbler, 16 swirled ribs, honey amber, Mantua, 3"...........135.00
Vase, clear, applied ft/fold-over rim, ground pontil, 6½".......135.00
Wine, lt gr, folded rim on applied ft, 3¾"...................40.00

Blue and White Stoneware

Blue and white stoneware -- much of which was decorated with such in-mold designs as grazing cows and Dutch children -- was made by practically every American pottery from the turn of the century until the mid-1930s. Crocks, pitchers, wash sets, rolling pins, and canisters are only a few of the items that may be found in this type of 'country' pottery that has become one of today's popular collectibles.

Roseville, Brush-McCoy, Uhl Co., and Burley Winter were among those who produced it, but very few pieces were ever signed.

Naturally, condition must be a prime consideration, especially if one is buying for resale; pieces with good, strong color and a fully molded pattern bring premium prices. Normal wear and signs of age are to be expected, since this was utility wear and received heavy use in busy households.

In the listings that follow, crocks and jars are without lids unless noted otherwise.

Batter jar, Apple Blossom & Basketweave, 8x7" dia..........125.00
Batter jar, Wildflower, pinched spout, bl band, lid, 8x7" dia....150.00
Bean pot, Swirl, 'Boston Baked Beans' 2 sides, hdl, w/lid, 9"...200.00
Bowl, Apricot, 9½"......................................75.00
Bowl, Currants & Diamonds, piecrust rim, 5x9½" dia.........100.00
Bowl, Daisy & Lattice, 9"................................65.00
Bowl, Diamond Point, set of 4 nesting....................165.00
Bowl, Feathers, double ring, 5½x10½" dia................125.00
Bowl, Flying Bird, 5x7½" dia, G.........................150.00
Bowl, Reverse Pyramids/Reverse Picket Fence, 5x10½".......55.00
Bowl, Wedding Band, 3½x7¼", EX.........................60.00
Bowl, Wildflower, 10"...................................55.00
Butter crock, adv, bail hdl/orig grip, recessed lid, 7x4" dia....125.00
Butter crock, Apricots, orig lid.........................125.00
Butter crock, Butterfly.................................95.00
Butter crock, Cows, stencil decor, w/bail.................85.00
Butter crock, Cows & Columns..........................180.00
Butter crock, Cows & Fence, leaf/flower bands, lid & hld, 5"..250.00
Butter crock, Daisy....................................80.00
Butter crock, Daisy & Trellis, 3x4".....................125.00
Butter crock, Dragonfly, orig lid.......................125.00
Butter crock, Dutch stencil on gray, no lid, bail...........95.00
Butter crock, Eagle, w/lid, NM.........................275.00
Butter crock, Indian Swastika..........................110.00
Butter crock, Peacock.................................225.00
Butter crock, Scroll, w/lid & hdl.......................90.00
Butter crock, Wildflower..............................85.00
Canister, 'Coffee', Snowflake, 6½"......................110.00
Canister, 'Coffee', Wildflowers........................110.00
Canister, 'Sugar'.....................................110.00
Canister, plain.......................................85.00
Canister, spice; Basketweave, w/lid, 5"..................135.00
Canister, spice; Basketweave, 3½"......................110.00
Chamber pot, Wildflower on Bowtie, w/lid................100.00
Chamber pot, Wildflower stencil, sponged rim, cup shape, 6"..100.00
Coffee pot, shell pattern, hearts on unglazed section, M......200.00
Coffee pot, Swirl, w/orig liner.........................500.00
Cookie jar, Basketweave, Put Your Fist In, orig lid, 7½"....200.00
Cooler, Apple Blossom, chain/rope bands, brass spigot, 17"...525.00
Cooler, blue letters, w/lid, 1 gal.......................95.00
Cooler, elk & polar bear, orig spigot, no lid, 9½x14".......375.00
Crock, berry/cereal; Flying Bird, 2x4" dia.................75.00
Crock, milk; Daisy & Lattice, G color, little wear, 4x8" dia....110.00
Crock, pickle; Heart Band, Heinz logo, br glaze w/in, 8x8" dia..200.00
Crock, pickle; pickle adv, bl bands, bail hdl, lid, 12x9" dia....125.00
Cup, Paneled Fir Tree, spurs on applied hdl, 3½x3" dia......65.00
Custard cup, Fishscale, 5x2½" dia.......................75.00
Footwarmer, Logan Pottery, w/hdl, pat applied, 12½".......125.00
Grease jar, Flying Bird, w/lid...........................250.00
Measuring cup, Spearpoint & Flower, 6x6¾"...............150.00
Meat tenderizer, Wildflower............................175.00
Mug, Basketweave and Apple Blossoms....................75.00

Mug, Felko...85.00
Mug, Flying Bird, M..............................125.00
Mug, scuttle, swirl blue, 6x4″ dia.............300.00
Pitcher, advertising, 'Merry Christmas from...', 7″, EX.........195.00
Pitcher, Alpine, beer, 10½″......................400.00
Pitcher, American Beauty Rose, emb petals top/bottom, 10x7″..195.00
Pitcher, Apricot.................................125.00
Pitcher, Basketweave & Morning Glory, rope hdl, 9x6½″ dia...150.00
Pitcher, Beaded Panels w/Open Rose, hot water, 10x8″ dia....150.00
Pitcher, Bowtie...................................85.00
Pitcher, boy & girl kissing.....................125.00
Pitcher, Butterfly, 4½″..........................165.00
Pitcher, Butterfly, 9x7″.........................135.00
Pitcher, Castle & Fishscale, 8″, M..............155.00
Pitcher, Cattail, rnd hdl, 7½″, EX..............110.00
Pitcher, Cattail, sq hdl, 7″, M.................150.00
Pitcher, Cherry & Leaves, w/advertising, 6″, M..225.00
Pitcher, Cherry Band, 8½″.......................150.00
Pitcher, Columns & Arches, brick wall ground, ornate hdl, 9″..225.00
Pitcher, Cosmos.................................150.00
Pitcher, Cows....................................175.00
Pitcher, Daisy...................................175.00
Pitcher, Doe & Fawn, bulbous base w/scroll, 8½x6″ dia.......175.00
Pitcher, Dutch Boy & Girl, w/dog................145.00
Pitcher, Eagle, M................................325.00
Pitcher, Good Luck..............................120.00
Pitcher, Grape w/Rickrack, waffle ground, 8x6″ dia..........100.00
Pitcher, hunting scene..........................235.00
Pitcher, Indian Boy & Girl......................225.00
Pitcher, Iris, quilted dia band, flared rim, incurved body, 9″....175.00
Pitcher, Leaping Deer, in leaf medallion, 8½x6″ dia.........175.00
Pitcher, Old Fashioned Garden Rose, straight sides, 10x7″ dia..150.00
Pitcher, Peacock, M.............................400.00
Pitcher, Pine Cone, straight sides, 9½x5¾″ dia...............175.00

Pitcher, Apricot, 8″, $125.00.

Pitcher, Swan/leaf & flower medallion ea side, bead hdl, 8½″..175.00
Pitcher, Wildflower, bulbous.....................140.00
Pitcher, Windmill & Bush, 7″, M.................125.00
Pitcher, 3 Bluebirds raised ea side, bl bands, 9x7″ dia......150.00
Roaster, double; Chain Link, ear hand holds, 9x11″ dia.......95.00
Roaster, Grooved Band, lid w/button finial, 9x16″ dia.......95.00
Roaster, Swirl, 8x15½″..........................225.00

Roaster, Wildflower, w/lid, 8½x12″ dia..........125.00
Rolling pin, Swirl, orig wood hdls, 13x3″ dia...225.00
Rolling pin, Wildflower.........................155.00
Rolling pin, Wildflower, w/advertising..........200.00
Salt crock, Apricot, w/pottery lid, M...........125.00
Salt crock, Blackberry, deep pattern, 5½x5½″ dia...........110.00
Salt crock, Butterfly, orig lid.................125.00
Salt crock, Daisy, orig lid.....................135.00
Salt crock, Eagle, orig lid, M..................275.00
Salt crock, Flying Bird, orig lid/mushroom finial, 6″......300.00
Salt crock, Grapevine on Fence, diffused color, orig lid, 6″....155.00
Salt crock, Peacock, w/pottery lid..............300.00
Soap dish, Beaded Rose...........................85.00
Soap dish, Cat's Head, 5″ dia...................150.00
Soap dish, cut-out corners, diffused color, 3½x4¾″..........90.00
Soap dish, Flower Cluster w/Fishscale, M.........95.00
Soap dish, Indian in war bonnet, beaded snake rim..........175.00
Soap dish, Lion.................................125.00
Soap dish, Rose w/Beaded Medallion, M............95.00
Spittoon, Peacock, brick foundation design, 9x10″ dia......250.00
Spittoon, Poinsettia & Basketweave, bl glazed w/in, 9x9¾″ dia..95.00
Teapot, Swirl, pulled ears/dbl bail hdl, relief disks rim, 9″....450.00
Toothpick holder, Swan figural, 3¼x4″ dia........50.00
Wash set, Feather & Swirl, pitcher 12x8½″ dia, bowl 14″ dia..300.00
Wash set, Fishscale & Rose, bowl & pitcher......250.00
Waste pot, Fleur de Lis & Scrolls, w/lid, bail hdl, 13″.......175.00

Blue Bird China

Made from 1910 to 1934, Blue Bird china is lovely ware decorated with flying blue birds among pink flowering branches. It was inexpensive dinnerware, and reached the height of its popularity in the second decade of this century. Several potteries produced it; shapes differ from one manufacturer to another, but with only minor variations, the decal remains the same.

Among the backstamps, you'll find W.S. George, Cleveland, Carrolton, Homer Laughlin, and Limoges China of Sebring, Ohio . . . and there are others.

Bowl, berry; master............................16.00
Bowl, fruit; 6″..................................5.00
Bowl, soup; 7½″.................................10.00
Bowl, 8″ round.................................15.00
Bowl, 9½″ oval.................................12.00
Butter w/cover.................................60.00
Casserole, w/lid...............................50.00
Creamer..10.00
Pickle dish, 7″.................................9.00
Pitcher, milk..................................50.00
Platter, 15½″..................................18.00
Sugar w/lid....................................15.00
Syrup pitcher, 4¼″.............................16.00

Blue Ridge

Blue Ridge dinnerware was produced by Southern Potteries of Erwin, Tennessee, from the late 1930s until 1956, in eight basic styles and over four hundred different patterns, all of which were hand decorated under the glaze. Vivid colors lit up floral arrangements of seemingly endless variation, fruit of every sort from simple clusters to lush assortments, barnyard fowl, peasant figures, and unpretentious textured patterns.

Although it is these dinnerware lines for which they are best known, collectors prize the artist signed plates from the forties and the limited line of character jugs made during the fifties most highly.

Chocolate set with peasant figures decor, 3-pc, $110.00.

Antique Leaf, ash tray......................................10.00
Antique Leaf, custard..2.75
Antique Leaf, plate, dinner.................................3.50
Apple Jack, berry bowl.......................................2.50
Apple Jack, bowl, 9"..7.00
Apple Jack, plate, dinner...................................3.50
Apple Jack, plate, 6"..1.50
Beaded Apple, plate, 10"....................................4.50
Betty, bowl, fruit, 5½"..1.75
Betty, bowl, tab hdl, 6"......................................3.50
Betty, creamer...4.50
Betty, cup & saucer..6.00
Betty, flat soup, 8"...4.00
Betty, plate, 6½"..1.50
Betty, plate, 9½"..4.00
Betty, platter, 14"..8.00
Betty, saucer..1.00
Betty, vegetable, oval, 9"...................................8.00
Bittersweet, bowl, oval vegetable, 9¼"....................8.50
Bittersweet, bowl, round vegetable, 9", pinhead nick.....5.00
Bittersweet, bowl, Skyline shape, 5".......................2.00
Bittersweet, creamer & sugar, Skyline shape.............10.00
Bittersweet, cup, Skyline shape............................2.50
Bluebell Bouquet, plate, 6".................................2.00
Bluebell Bouquet, plate, 9½"...............................5.50
Bountiful, bowl, fruit, 5¼"...................................3.50
Bountiful, bowl, open vegetable, 9".......................9.00
Bountiful, bowl, soup, 8"....................................4.50
Bountiful, cup & saucer.....................................9.00
Bountiful, plate, 10"...4.50
Bountiful, plate, 6"..2.50
Bountiful, plate, 6½" square...............................3.00
Bountiful, platter, oval, 11½"..............................8.00
Cantata, bowl, fruit, sm....................................1.75
Cantata, bowl, round vegetable, 9½".....................9.00
Cantata, cup..5.00
Cantata, plate, 10½"...6.00
Cantata, plate, 6"..1.75
Cantata, saucer..1.50
Carnival, bowl, fruit, Candlewick shape..................2.50
Carnival, flat soup, Candlewick shape, 8"................3.50
Carnival, plate, Candlewick shape, 6"....................2.00
Carnival, plate, Candlewick shape, 9"....................3.50
Caroline Sky, bowl, oval vegetable, Woodcrest shape.....8.00

Caroline Sky, creamer, Woodcrest shape....................4.50
Caroline Sky, cup, Woodcrest shape.......................3.75
Caroline Sky, cup & saucer, Woodcrest shape.............5.50
Caroline Sky, gravy boat, Woodcrest shape...............8.00
Caroline Sky, plate, Woodcrest shape, 6".................1.75
Caroline Sky, plate, Woodcrest shape, 9".................4.50
Caroline Sky, sugar w/lid, Woodcrest.....................7.50
Chintz, bowl, Colonial blank, 5"...........................3.00
Chintz, coaster, 4" round.................................12.00
Chintz, creamer, Colonial blank...........................4.00
Chintz, cup & saucer, Colonial blank......................5.00
Chintz, plate, Colonial blank, 10".........................5.00
Chintz, plate, Colonial blank, 6"..........................2.00
Chintz, plate, Colonial blank, 7"..........................3.00
Chintz, platter, oval, Colonial blank, 15"................10.00
Chintz, round vegetable, Colonial blank, 9"...............5.00
Chintz, sugar w/lid, Colonial blank........................5.00
Chintz, vegetable, Colonial blank, oval, 9"...............5.00
Cosomi, cake plate, 10¼"...................................7.00
Country Garden, bowl, 9"..................................10.00
Crabapple, berry, lg...8.50
Crabapple, bowl, fruit; 5¼".................................2.00
Crabapple, bowl, soup; 8"..................................5.00
Crabapple, creamer..4.00
Crabapple, cup...3.00
Crabapple, plate, 10"...4.50
Crabapple, plate, 6"..2.00
Crabapple, platter, 12".......................................7.00
Crabapple, saucer..1.00
Crabapple, sugar w/lid.......................................5.00
Delicious, creamer & sugar w/lid..........................10.00
Delicious, plate, 10"...3.00
Delicious, saucer...1.00
Field Daisy, butter w/lid...................................12.00
Field Daisy, plate, 8¼"......................................3.50
Flower Fantasy, gravy.......................................8.00
Glamour, gravy...8.50
Glamour, vegetable, round, 9"..............................8.00
Greenbriar, bowl, fruit; Piecrust shape....................3.00
Greenbriar, cup & saucer, Piecrust shape.................6.00
Greenbriar, plate, Piecrust shape, 9".....................4.50
Greenbriar, saucer, Piecrust shape.........................2.50
Hilda, plate, 6"...1.00
Mardi Gras, saucer..1.00
Mountain Ivy, bowl, fruit....................................2.00
Mountain Ivy, creamer..4.00
Mountain Ivy, creamer & sugar, demitasse, Astor shape...14.00
Mountain Ivy, cup & saucer.................................6.00
Mountain Ivy, flat soup......................................4.00
Mountain Ivy, plate, 10".....................................6.00
Mountain Ivy, plate, 6½".....................................2.00
Mountain Ivy, platter, 13½"..................................7.00
Mountain Ivy, sugar w/lid...................................6.50
Mountain Nosegay, plate, 9".................................5.00
Nocturne, berry, sm..3.50
Nocturne, cereal..4.50
Nocturne, cup...3.50
Nocturne, flat soup..5.50
Nocturne, gravy liner, oval, 7½"...........................10.00
Nocturne, plate, 10"..5.50
Nocturne, plate, 6"...1.25
Nocturne, plate, 9"...4.50
Painted Daisy, sugar, demitasse............................5.00
Petal Point, plate, 9¼"......................................2.50

Platter, turkey & Fall motif, huge.........................40.00
Poinsetta, bowl, 5¼".............................2.00
Poinsetta, bowl, 8".............................3.00
Poinsetta, bowl, 9".............................7.00
Poinsetta, creamer.............................3.00
Poinsetta, cup.............................3.00
Poinsetta, gravy.............................6.00
Poinsetta, plate, 10".............................3.50
Poinsetta, plate, 14".............................8.00
Poinsetta, plate, 6".............................1.50
Poinsetta, platter, 13".............................5.00
Poinsetta, saucer.............................1.00
Poinsetta, sugar w/lid.............................5.00
Quilted Fruit, creamer & sugar w/lid.............................17.50
Quilted Fruit, cup & saucer.............................5.50
Quilted Fruit, plate, dinner.............................5.00
Quilted Fruit, plate, 6".............................1.50
Red Onions, plate, 9½".............................5.00
Ridge Daisy, child's set, 16 pcs.............................450.00
Rosalinde, plate, 10¼".............................6.00
Rosalinde, platter, 11¾".............................9.00
Rose Marie, sugar w/lid, large.............................10.00
Roundelay, creamer.............................2.50
Roundelay, plate, 7½".............................2.00
Roundelay Green, cup & saucer.............................3.50
Roundelay Green, plate, 10½".............................3.50
Roundelay Green, platter, 10¾".............................4.00
Roundelay Green, vegetable, round, 8¾".............................4.50
Sculptured Fruit, pitcher, 6⅝".............................24.00
Shoo Fly, bowl, vegetable, 8¾".............................6.50
Shoo Fly, bowl, 5¼".............................2.00
Shoo Fly, creamer.............................2.50
Shoo Fly, cup & saucer.............................3.50
Shoo Fly, plate, 7".............................1.75
Shoo Fly, plate, 9¼".............................2.50
Shoo Fly, platter, oval, 11½".............................6.00
Silhouette Blue, creamer.............................3.00
Silhouette Blue, sugar w/lid.............................4.50
Silhouette Blue, vegetable, round, 9".............................6.50
Silhouette Gray, creamer.............................3.25
Silhouette Gray, cup & saucer.............................3.50
Silhouette Gray, plate, 10½".............................3.50
Skyline, sugar w/lid, unusual pattern.............................6.00
Spray, bowl, cereal, Piecrust shape.............................3.00
Spray, cup & saucer, Piecrust.............................5.50
Spray, plate, Piecrust shape, 6".............................1.50
Spray, plate, Piecrust shape, 9".............................3.50
Stanhome Ivy, bowl, fruit, 5½".............................1.50
Stanhome Ivy, cup.............................4.00
Stanhome Ivy, cup & saucer.............................5.00
Stanhome Ivy, gravy.............................6.00
Stanhome Ivy, plate, Skyline shape, 6".............................1.50
Stanhome Ivy, plate, Skyline shape, 9".............................3.50
Strawberry, cereal/lug soup.............................4.00
Strawberry, saucer.............................1.00
Summertime, leaf celery, oval.............................22.00
Sunny, creamer.............................4.00
Sunny, plate, 6¼".............................1.50
Sunny, plate, 9½".............................3.00
Sunny Spray, bowl, 8¾".............................6.50
Sunny Spray, cup & saucer.............................3.50
Tralee Rose, pitcher, 6½".............................28.00
Verna, relish, 10".............................20.00
Waltz Time, creamer, ped.............................12.00

Weathervane, coupe soup.............................4.00
Weathervane, cup.............................5.50
Weathervane, cup & saucer.............................7.00
Weathervane, pepper shaker.............................5.00
Weathervane, plate, 6".............................2.00
Weathervane, plate, 9½".............................6.00
Whirligig, bowl, fruit.............................1.75
Whirligig, creamer & sugar, open style, large.............................17.50
Whirligig, cup & saucer.............................5.00
Whirligig, flat soup.............................4.00
Whirligig, plate, 10½".............................5.00
Wild Cherry, bowl, sauce, Colonial shape.............................2.00
Wild Cherry, cup & saucer, Colonial shape.............................4.00
Wild Cherry, plate, Colonial shape, 6".............................6.00
Wild Cherry, plate, Colonial shape, 9".............................4.00
Woodcrest Cattails, bowl, 9¼" round.............................7.00
Yellow Mums, bowl, hdls, 6".............................3.50
Yellow Mums, plate, 10".............................4.50
Yellow Mums, plate, 8".............................2.50
Zinna, vase, colored, 7¾".............................28.00

Boch Freres

Founded in the early 1840s in La Louviere, Boch Freres Keramos became the foremost producer of art pottery in Belgium. Though primarily they served a localized market, in 1844 they earned international recognition for some of their sculptural works on display at the International Exposition in Paris.

In 1907, Charles Catteau of France was appointed head of the art department. Before that time the firm had concentrated on developing glazes and perfecting elegant forms. The style they pursued was traditional, favoring the re-creation of established 18th century ceramics. Catteau brought with him to Boch Freres the New Wave, or Art Nouveau influence in form and decoration. His designs won him world-wide acclaim at the Exhibition d'Art Decoratif in Paris in 1925, and it is for his work that Boch Freres is so highly regarded today. He occasionally signed his work as well as that of others who, under his direct supervision, carried out his preconceived designs. He was associated with the company until 1950, and lived the remainder of his life in Nice, France, where he died in 1966.

The Boch Freres Keramos factory continues operations today, pro-

Vase, symetrical mosaic and floral pattern in blue, turquoise, and orange on cream crackle, signed, 12½", $300.00.

ducing bathroom fixtures and other utilitarian wares.

A variety of marks were used, all incorporating some combination of 'Boch Freres', 'Keramis', 'BFK', or 'Ch Catteau'.

Plate, Napoleon, bl/wht, w/battlefield scene..................65.00
Vase, Art Deco w/roosters, mk Gres Keramis..............200.00
Vase, bl w/flying birds, bulbous, rolled lip..................150.00
Vase, cream w/yel top band w/abstract flowers; blk lines, 9½"...60.00

Boehm

Boehm sculptures were the creation of Edward Marshall Boehm, a ceramic artist who coupled his love of the art with his love of nature to produce figurines of birds, animals, and flowers in lovely background settings accurate to the smallest detail. Sculptures of historical figures, and those representing the fine arts, were also made, and along with many of the bird figurines have established secondary market values many times their original price.

His first pieces were made in the very early 1950s, in Trenton, New Jersey, under the name of Osso Ceramics. Mr. Boehm died in 1969, and the firm has since been managed by his wife. Today, known as Edward Marshall Boehm, Inc., the private family-held corporation produces not only porcelain sculptures, but collector plates as well. Both limited and non-limited editions of their works have been issued.

Examples are marked with various backstamps, all of which have incorporated the Boehm name since 1951. 'Osso Ceramics' in upper case lettering was used in 1950 and 1951.

Figurine, Adios, horse, bisque wht, sgn Ed Boehm..........1,500.00
Figurine, American Goldfinch, #400-39, sm chip on leaf........95.00
Figurine, American Redstarts, 1958......................950.00
Figurine, angel kneeling on cushion, EX detail, all wht, 7½"....60.00
Figurine, Bengal Tiger, decor/bisque, 20x14"................2,200.00
Figurine, Black Capped Chickadee, Male w/Holly Leaves, #428.140.00
Figurine, Black-Headed Grosbeak........................1,150.00
Figurine, Black-Throated Blue Warbler....................1,300.00
Figurine, Blue Grosbeck, #489, ca 1977..................605.00
Figurine, Blue Heron, 4½"..............................160.00
Figurine, Blue-Throated Hummingbird.....................500.00
Figurine, Bob White Quail, pr..........................1,200.00
Figurine, Bobolink w/Corn Stubble.......................775.00
Figurine, Boxer Dog, lg...............................750.00
Figurine, Cactus Wren................................1,800.00
Figurine, Catbird....................................1,400.00
Figurine, Chick, yellow, 1950s.........................225.00
Figurine, Cocker Spaniel, br/wht........................450.00
Figurine, Cupid w/Harp; Cupid w/Horn, pr................500.00
Figurine, Don Quixote................................120.00
Figurine, Downy Woodpecker...........................1,100.00
Figurine, Eastern Bluebirds w/Rhododendrons, pr..........6,000.00
Figurine, Egret......................................850.00
Figurine, Fledgling Baby Bluebird.......................325.00
Figurine, Fledgling Bluejay............................225.00
Figurine, Fledgling Chickadee..........................250.00
Figurine, Fledgling Crested Flycatcher, gray base...........500.00
Figurine, Fledgling Kingfisher..........................225.00
Figurine, Fledgling Magpie.............................285.00
Figurine, Fledgling Red Poll, 4".........................250.00
Figurine, Fledgling Woodthrush.........................235.00
Figurine, Giselle.....................................120.00
Figurine, Green Jays, pr..............................2,600.00
Figurine, Hummingbird, #440..........................412.00
Figurine, Indigo Bunting, #429.........................330.00

Pair of Mearns Quail with Cactus and Tiger Beetle, Boehm hallmark #467, limited edition of 350, $1,400.00.

Figurine, La Pieta Madonna, sgn, 1958...................600.00
Figurine, Madonna La Pieta, bisque, 4½".................95.00
Figurine, Mearns Quail w/Cactus, pr.....................1,400.00
Figurine, Mergansers.................................1,850.00
Figurine, Mockingbirds, pr............................3,200.00
Figurine, Morning Doves, 13¾".........................825.00
Figurine, Neptune on Seahorse, 1953.....................2,500.00
Figurine, Northern Waterthrush.........................1,050.00
Figurine, Nuthatch w/Ivy & Moneywort, #469..............265.00
Figurine, Old Meadowlark, decor/bisque..................1,100.00
Figurine, Ovenbird..................................1,100.00
Figurine, Polo Player, #206, 14".........................2,400.00
Figurine, Prothonotary Warbler.........................500.00
Figurine, Rabbits, male & female, 1950s, pr...............325.00
Figurine, Red-Winged Blackbirds w/Cattail, pr.............3,600.00
Figurine, Ring-Necked Pheasants, pr.....................700.00
Figurine, Road Runner...............................2,700.00
Figurine, Robin w/Daffodils...........................3,250.00
Figurine, Rufous Hummingbirds........................1,800.00
Figurine, Sugarbirds.................................4,250.00
Figurine, Swallows w/Marsh Marigolds, decor/bisque........2,100.00
Figurine, Swan Lake.................................120.00
Figurine, The Nutcracker.............................120.00
Figurine, Tree Sparrow...............................500.00
Figurine, Varied Thrush & Parrot Tulip...................1,950.00
Figurine, Verdins....................................800.00
Figurine, Woodcock.................................600.00
Figurine, Yellow-Throated Warbler......................500.00
Figurine, Young American Bald Eagle....................950.00

Bohemian Glass

The term 'Bohemian glass' has come to refer to a type of glass developed in Bohemia in the late 6th century at the Imperial Court of Rudolf II, the Hapsburg Emperor. The popular artistic pursuit of the day was stone carving, and it naturally followed to transfer familiar procedures to the glass making industry.

During the next century, a formula was discovered that produced a glass with a fine crystal appearance which lent itself well to deep, intricate engraving, and the art was further advanced.

Although many other types of art glass were made there, collectors today use the term Bohemian glass to most often indicate clear glass overlaid with color, through which a design is cut or etched. Red on crystal was used most often, but other colors may also be found. Another type of Bohemian glass involves cutting through and exposing three layers of color in patterns that are often very intricate. Items such as these are sometimes further decorated with enamel work.

Covered jar, cupids and floral etchings, deep star-like cuttings, amber and clear, 12¼", $800.00.

Butter dish, ruby, deer & castle............................65.00
Candle holder, amber, heron & floral, 3½", pr..............60.00
Candlesticks, ruby, deer, step rings, U-drop prisms, pr.......200.00
Candy dish, ruby, bird & castle............................85.00
Chalice, ruby, deer & pine trees.........................185.00
Cologne bottle w/stopper, ruby, vintage, 7"................60.00
Compote, cobalt, floral cutting, sterling ped, 6x8"........150.00
Cruet, ruby, deer & castle, 5½"...........................50.00
Cruet, ruby, deer & pine tree, w/matching stopper...........65.00
Decanter, ruby, Vintage, clear stopper, 10"................60.00
Decanter, ruby w/engraved foliage/birds/monkey, 15½"........65.00
Decanter, ruby w/grape leaves, figure w/goblet, stopper........80.00
Ewer, ruby, triple dia & oval, 10"........................80.00
Finger bowl, ruby, vintage................................50.00
Mustard w/lid, ruby, deer & castle........................50.00
Toothpick, ruby, flying bird..............................18.00
Tumbler, ruby, deer & trees etching, 5"...................44.00
Vase, ftd, amber, deer & castle scene, 1860s, 8"...........47.50
Vase, ftd, ruby/wht/clear cut overlay/buildings in reserve, 5"....350.00
Vase, ruby, dove & castle, 6½"............................60.00
Wine, ruby, giraffe/lion/elephant/water buffalo/etc, set of 6.....400.00
Wine set, ruby, deer & castle, decanter+6 stemmed wines.....150.00

Bookends

Though a few were produced before 1880, bookends became a necessary library accessory and a popular commodity after the printing industry was revolutionized by Mergenthaler's invention, the linotype. Books became abundantly available at such affordable prices that almost every home suddenly had need for bookends. They were carved from wood, cast in iron, bronze, or brass, or cut from stone. Today's collectors may find such designs as ships, animals, flowers and children. Patriotic themes, art reproductions, and those with Art Nouveau and Art Deco styling provide a basis for a diverse and interesting collection.

Basket of nuts & fruit, CI, orig gold pnt, 5½x5", pr............30.00
Boy fishing, wht metal, pr................................25.00
Cape Cod Fisherman, dtd 1928, iron, pr....................25.00
Dogs, recumbent, head up, EX detail, CI, 6" L, pr...........65.00
Dying Gladiator, bronze finish, pr........................38.00
Galleons, bronze, pr.....................................35.00
Geo Washington bust, metal/ivory head/marble base, J-RVHL, pr.35.00
German Shephard, CI, pr..................................18.00
Golfer swinging club, Deco, gold metal, 5x4", pr...........250.00
Horse head, w/bridle, SP, EX detail & finish, pr............65.00
Innocence, weighted copper, pr............................21.00
Knute Rockne, iron, 1930, pr.............................65.00
Lady holds skirt outstretched, Deco, silver on bronze, 11", pr..185.00
Lady w/wings, Art Nouveau, CI, pr.........................65.00
Lindbergh bust, pr......................................45.00
Mahog w/line inlay, emb brass lion head, planter insert, pr.....55.00
Minute Man, worn gr pnt on CI, 1900s, 5½", pr..............25.00
Pouter pigeons, solid crystal, 6", pr......................60.00
Sailing ships, iron, pr...................................18.00
Scottie dogs, iron, pr...................................28.00
Scottie dogs, mc tiered onyx base, pr......................85.00
Sea horses, McClelland Barclay, 1932, pr...................75.00
Soapstone, Oriental man on water buffalo, 7½", pr...........50.00
St George & the Dragon, iron, pr..........................25.00
Teddy Roosevelt, pr.....................................35.00
The Thinker, copper finished pot metal, mk JB2176, 1930s, pr..35.00

Bells of San Juan, Capestrano, Claycraft Pottery Co, pair, $120.00.

Bootjacks and Bootscrapers

Bootjacks were made from metal or wood -- some were fancy figural shapes, others strictly business! Their purpose was to facilitate the otherwise awkward process of removing one's boots. Bootscrapers were handy gadgets that provided an effective way to clean the soles of mud and such.

Bootjack, beetle, hand forged iron, late 1800s, 12½".........40.00
Bootjack, bull w/horns, 10¼"..............................28.00
Bootjack, cricket, CI, 11½"...............................18.00
Bootjack, cricket, 9"...................................15.00
Bootjack, dolphin ea side, scraper top, CI, 1850s..........150.00
Bootjack, Mussleman's Plug Tobacco........................84.00

Naughty Nellie bootjack, cast iron with the original red, white and blue paint, 1800s, at auction: $770.00.

Bootjack, Naughty Nellie, CI, 9¾".........................20.00
Bootjack, pistol-shape, The American Bulldog Bootjack, CI, 8"..88.00
Bootjack, Try Me, CI, 12".............................38.00
Bootscraper, CI, G scrollwork detail, 6½".................25.00
Bootscraper, dachshund, CI, 20½" L....................65.00
Bootscraper, forged iron, conical finials, mortised, 1700s.......85.00
Bootscraper, griffins, EX detail, rnd reticulated base, 15".......40.00
Bootscraper, silhouette of scottie, cast edge detail, 8½x10".....25.00
Bootscraper, standing horse, sgn JW, CI, 1870s, 9½x9".......135.00
Bootscraper, terrier, bronze, w/monogram...................28.00
Bootscraper, terrier, CI...............................85.00
Bootscraper, witch on broomstick, CI, orig pnt, 1900........250.00

Bootscraper, figural male atop, cast iron, 14", $95.00.

Bottles and Flasks

As far back as the first century B.C., the Romans preferred blown glass containers for their pills and potions. Though you're not apt to find many of those, you will find bottles of every size, shape and color made to hold perfume, ink, medicine, soda, spirits, vinegar, and many other liquids.

American business firms preferred glass bottles in which to package their commercial products, and used them extensively from the late 18th century on. Bitters bottles contained 'medicine' -- actually herb flavored alcohol -- and judging from the number of these found today, their contents found favor with many! Because of a heavy tax imposed on the sale of liquor in 17th century England by King George, who hoped to curtail alcohol abuse among his subjects, bottlers simply added 'curative' herbs to their brew and thus avoided taxation. Since gin was taxed in America as well, the practice continued in this country. Scores of brands were sold; among the most popular were Dr. H.S. Flint & Co. Quaker Bitters, Dr. Kaufman's Anti-Cholera Bitters, and Dr. J. Hosetter's Stomach Bitters. Most bitters bottles were made in shades of amber, brown and aquamarine. Clear glass was used, to a lesser extent, as were green tones. Blue, amethyst, red-brown, and milk glass examples are rare.

Perfume or scent bottles were produced abroad by companies all over Europe from the late 16th century on. Perfume making became such a prolific trade that as a result beautifully decorated bottles were fashionable. In America, they were produced in great quantities by Stiegel in 1770, and by Boston and Sandwich in the early 19th century. Cologne bottles were first made in about 1830, and toilet water bottles in the 1880s. Rene Lalique produced fine scent bottles from as early as the turn of the century. The earliest were one-of-a-kind creations with silver casings. He later designed bottles for the Coty Perfume Company, with a different style for each Coty fragrance. (See also Lalique)

Spirit flasks from the 19th century were blown in specially designed molds that produced various motifs including political subjects, railroad trains, and symbolic devices. The most commonly used colors were amber, dark brown and green.

From the 20th century, early pop and beer bottles are very collectible, as are nearly every extinct commercial container.

Bottles may be dated by the methods used in their production. For instance, a rough pontil indicates a date before 1845. The iron pontil, used from then until about 1860, left a metalic residue on the base of the bottle which is evident upon examination. A seam that reaches from base to lip marks a machine-made bottle from after 1903, while an applied or hand finished lip points to an early mold-blown bottle. The Industrial Revolution saw keen competition between manufacturers, and as a result scores of patents were issued. Many concentrated on various types of closures; the crown bottle cap, for instance, was patented in 1892. If a manufacturer's name is present, consulting a book on marks may help you date your bottle.

Key:
bk----back   gp----graphite pontil
bt----blob top   grd----ground pontil

See also Advertising, various brands such as Coca-Cola; Lalique; Medical Collectibles

Flasks

Book, wht clay w/bl glaze, emb decor & History Holland, 4x5"..15.00
BP & B, yellow-gr, ½ pint................................35.00
Calabash, hunter & fisherman, aqua, quart...................35.00
Chestnut, Coin Spot, gold/yellow, shear mouth/pontil scar, 5¾".450.00
Chestnut, 10 Diamond pattern, gold/yel, pontil scar, 5½"....1,125.00
Columbian Jubilee, w/sailing ship, amber, pint................75.00
Corn For The World, amber, 8¼".........................400.00
Cornucopia, amber, pint.................................85.00
Cornucopia, Coventry CT, deep olive gr, pint.................85.00
Dancer & soldier, clear, Chapman, Baltimore MD, pint.......125.00
Eagle, facing right on shield & rock pile, aqua, pint..........85.00
Eagle & clasped hands, aqua, pint.........................42.00
Flora Temple, aqua, pint................................175.00
For Pike's Peak, old rye, aqua, pint.......................35.00
Frank Tea & Spice Co, aqua, 5¼"..........................6.00
Gemel, Nailsea-type, lt bl w/wht loops, ftd, 1850s, 8¾".......160.00
Girl For Joe, girl on bicycle, aqua, pint....................60.00
Granite Glass Co, bk: Stoddard NH, sheared top, olive, pint....125.00

Isabella GW, sheaf of wheat, pint..............................85.00
Jenny Lind Lyre, aqua, pint..................................95.00
KCCNE, olive amber, pint...................................195.00
Keene, Masonic, tooled lip, pontil, pint......................225.00
Legendary Grandfather, broken swirl pattern, reddish amber.....95.00
Louisville GW, w/eagle, aqua, ½ pint.........................75.00
Lowell RR, olive, ½ pint....................................110.00
Ludlow, olive amber, blown w/applied lip, 5¼"................65.00
Nailsea type, boot figural, clear w/wht loops, 1850s, 9¼"....130.00
Nailsea type, fat ovoid, wht w/rose loops, 6¼"..............180.00
Nailsea type, ovoid, golden amber w/wht lace decor, 1860s, 5"..150.00
Nailsea type, teardrop, sea gr w/wht loops, 1850s, 8¾".......160.00
Pikes Peak, traveler & hunter, yel-amber.....................600.00
Pottery, figure of man & horse both sides, pint..............215.00
PU Benjamin Co/Natchez, clear, lt haze, ½ pt, 6"............35.00
Ravenna, w/anchor & rope, ring top, aqua, pint...............115.00
Ravenna Glass Works, ring top, yellow-gr, pint...............150.00
Ravenna Travelers Companion, pontil, amber, quart............225.00
Scroll, violin shape, aqua, 9"...............................250.00
Sheaf of Wheat, olive amber, Westford Glass, pint.............60.00
South Carolina Dispensary, w/palm tree, aqua, pint............48.00
Springfield GW Cabin, aqua, ½ pint..........................50.00
Stag & tree, aqua, pint......................................50.00
Stoddard NH in panel, eagle facing left, pontil, amber, pint....80.00
STRA in 5-pt star, bk: plain; ring, collared top, amber, ½ pt....80.00
Success To RR, eagle, olive, pint............................100.00
Success To The Railroad, horse & cart both sides, aqua, pint..120.00
Summer & winter, aqua, ½ pint..............................70.00
Travelers Companion, w/sheaf, amber, quart...................90.00
Union, clasped hands/shield, bk: eagle w/banner; pint.........48.00
Union, side mold, ball & cannon on bk, aqua, 7½"...........80.00
Warranted Flask, amethyst, 7½"...............................8.00
Washington, w/sheaf of wheat, aqua, pint....................115.00
Washington & Albany, aqua, ½ pint..........................110.00
Will You Take A Drink?/Will A Duck Swim?, aqua, pint.......160.00
Zanesville City Glass Works in oval panel, ring top, amber.....82.00

Miscellaneous

Beer, Buffalo Brewing Co, emb horseshoe/buffalo, amber, 12"...10.00
Beer, Falstaff Lemp, St Louis, shield, crown top, aqua, 9".......5.00
Beer, Geo Young California Pop Beer, pat 1872, amber, 10½"..45.00
Beer, Gutsch Brewing Co, 13 under bottom, red, 8½".........15.00

John Root's Bitters, Buffalo, aquamarine, 10¼", $250.00.

Beer, Independent Co of Pittsbrugh (misspelled), lt amber, 9"...14.00
Beer, John Ryan, All XXX Star 1866, blob top, cobalt, 8¼"....24.00
Beer, Kessler Malt Extract, squat body, crown top, amber.......5.00
Beer, Lake Erie Bottling Works/Toledo in circle, aqua, 10½"...8.00
Beer, M Mayer, This Bottle Not To Be Sold, aqua, 9".........6.00
Beer, Nebraska Brewing/Oakland around shoulder, amber, bt, 9"..8.00
Beer, Robert Portner Brewing Co, amber, 7¼"................17.00
Beer, Teikoku, Japanese writing, graduated collar/ring, amber....5.00
Beer, Wisconsin Select Beer, aqua, 9¼"....................6.00
Bitters, Alpine, hdld jug, vertical ribs, yel-gr, gold letters......240.00
Bitters, Asparagin Co, clear to aqua, 11"...................33.00
Bitters, Atwood's Quinine Tonic Bitters, aqua, 8½"..........40.00
Bitters, Baker's Orange, sq w/roped corners, golden yel, 10½"..70.00
Bitters, Bird, Phila Proprietor, clear, 4¾"..................45.00
Bitters, Boston Malt Bitters, round, green, 9½".............24.00
Bitters, Brown's Celebrated Indian Herb, Indian queen figural..750.00
Bitters, Burdock Blood, Canadian type, early ABM, clear, 8½"..10.00
Bitters, Caracas, dk green, 8¼"...........................37.00
Bitters, Caroni, amber, pint...............................9.00
Bitters, Corn Juice, flask shaped, aqua, quart...............59.00
Bitters, Dr Brown's Berry, aqua or clear, 8¼".............35.00
Bitters, Dr CW Roback's, barrel, deep golden amber, 9¾"....170.00
Bitters, Dr Hoeletter's Stomach, amber.....................15.00
Bitters, Dr Sim's Anti-Constipation, amber, 6½"............65.00
Bitters, Dr Sweet Strengthening, long tapered top, aqua, 8¼"...35.00
Bitters, Fer-Kina Galeno, machine-made brn beer type, 10"....14.00
Bitters, Fish, figural fish, clear, tooled mouth, 11½".........375.00
Bitters, Goff's, label, Camden NH on bottle, aqua...........10.00
Bitters, Greeley's Bourbon Bitters, barrel, olive, sq mouth.....195.00
Bitters, Greer's Eclipse, Louisville Ky, amber, 9"............85.00
Bitters, Hansard's Hop, crock, tan & gr, 8"................30.00
Bitters, Hi Hi Bitter Co, triangular shape, amber, 9½".......68.00
Bitters, Imperial Russian Tonic, rope design sides, aqua, 9¼"..55.00
Bitters, Johnson's Calisaya, tapered top, amber, 10".........30.00
Bitters, Kelly's Old Cabin, cabin figural, olive amber, 9"....450.00
Bitters, Lord Bros/Dr Mandrake Baxto's, amber, 12".........20.00
Bitters, Mariani Coco Bitters, green, 7½".................18.00
Bitters, Mohica, bk: Roth & Co SF; ringed top, amber, 9"....125.00
Bitters, National, ear of corn figural, golden amber, 12½"....250.00
Bitters, National, patent 1867 on bottom, amber, 12¼"......185.00
Bitters, Old Homestead Wild Cherry, cabin shape, amber, 10"..170.00
Bitters, Original Pocahontas, barrel shape, aqua, 9½".......1,225.00
Bitters, Oswego, amber, 7¼".............................39.00
Bitters, Pineapple pattern on bottle, lt amber, 9¼".........100.00
Bitters, Poor Man's Family Bitters, ringed top, aqua, 6½"....25.00
Bitters, Royal Pepsin Stomach Bitters, amber, 8½"..........65.00
Bitters, Simon's Centennial, bust of G Washington, amber, 10".850.00
Bitters, Steketees Blood Purifying, amber, 9½".............40.00
Bitters, Suffolk, pig, yellow amber, dbl collared mouth, 10"...320.00
Bitters, William Allen's Congress, emerald gr/rectangular, 10"..540.00
Cologne, Art Deco, blk w/gold decor, atomizer, 2x3".........50.00
Cologne, bl glass w/atomizer, Duray, 1920s-'30s, 4".........20.00
Cologne, clear, swirled, 3⅛".............................40.00
Cologne, cranberry, crystal stopper, wht enamel, gold trim, 5"...95.00
Cologne, cranberry w/clear ball stopper, enamel florals, 7x3"...150.00
Cologne, figural lady, German porcelain, 4½"...............45.00
Cologne, gr w/crystal stopper, Irice, West Germany..........65.00
Cologne, Le Golli Wogg, Black man.........................24.00
Cologne, monument shape, brick design, cobalt, 1870s, 11¾"..300.00
Cologne, pressed glass, w/atomizer, 1920s, 3½"............25.00
Cologne, round, opaque bl milk glass, tooled mouth, 1870s, 9"..90.00
Cologne, round, tapered, Sandwich type, opal bl, 1870s, 10¾".200.00
Cologne, round, vertical ribs & beads, milk glass, 1870s, 6"...55.00
Cologne, seahorse, applied rigaree, clear w/wht swirls, 2½"...110.00

Price's Patent Candle Co. Topper Ltd, cobalt, $50.00.

Cologne, violin shape, aqua, rolled mouth, 1850s, 5¼"........65.00
Cologne, violin shape, cobalt blue, 1850s, 5½"..............600.00
Cologne, 12-sided, Sandwich type, purple-blue, 1870s, 7¼"....180.00
Cosmetics, Creme Simon, milk glass, sheared top, 2½".........4.00
Cosmetics, De Vry's Dandero-off Hair Tonic, clear, 6½".........9.00
Cosmetics, Dr Koch's Toilet Articles, ring top, clear, 5¼".......6.00
Cosmetics, Hagans Magnolia Balm, beveled corners/ring top, 5"..10.00
Cosmetics, Hyacinthia Hair Dressing, rectangular, aqua, 6"......15.00
Cosmetics, Mineralava Face Finish, clear, 5¼"................6.00
Cosmetics, Pompeian Massage Cream, amethyst, 2¾"...........4.00
Figural, bull fighter, milk glass, tooled mouth, 6½"............35.00
Figural, fat man w/cape, sapphire blue, 1890s, 9¾".........330.00
Figural, fluted ped w/bust of Grant as lid, red amber & clear...170.00
Figural, grandfather clock, milk glass, Europe, 1890s, 12"......45.00
Figural, Grant's Tomb, milk glass w/metal Grant cover, 10"....175.00
Figural, Liberty Bell, milk glass, ground mouth, 3"............55.00
Figural, monk, milk glass, tooled mouth, 9¼"...............130.00
Figural, Oriental seated man, milk glass w/metal head, 5½".....50.00
Figural, seated bear, applied face, blk slag glass, 10¾".......410.00
Figural, Statue of Liberty, milk glass w/metal lady, 15½"......210.00
Ink, Bourne Derby, crock, brown, 8½"......................6.00
Ink, cabin figural, clear, ground mouth, 1870s, 3¼".........325.00
Ink, Cardinal, aqua...................................30.00
Ink, Carter, cathedral, cobalt, qt.........................45.00
Ink, George W Williams & Co, cone, aqua, 2½".............25.00
Ink, Harrison's Columbian, open pontil, cobalt, 1½x1½"......115.00
Ink, Hooker's, sheared top, round, aqua, 2"................10.00
Ink, Keene Umbrella Ink, 8-sided, open pontil, green.........40.00
Ink, Moore & Son, sheared top, aqua, 1¾".................10.00

Ink, Octagon Ink, mushroom shaped, pontil, aqua............25.00
Ink, pitkin-type, yellow amber, swirled to left, 1820s, 1½".....240.00
Ink, Union Ink Co, ring top, aqua, 2¼"...................18.00
Medicine, Acker's Elixir/The Great Health Restorer, amber, 6½"..6.00
Medicine, Allen's Nerve/Bone Liniment, sq collar, round, aqua....5.00
Medicine, Anodyne For Infants, Dr Groves/Phila, rect, 5¼"......6.00
Medicine, Barry's Tricopherous, aqua, w/pontil, 6"..........11.00
Medicine, Bism Subnitr, clear, 5¼".......................10.00
Medicine, Brant's Indian Pulmonary Balsam, vert panels, aqua...50.00
Medicine, Bromo Seltzer, cobalt, 4".......................1.50
Medicine, Bumstead's Worm Syrup, Philadelphia, aqua, 4½"....10.00
Medicine, Burnett's Cocaine, 1864-1900, ringed top, clear......12.00
Medicine, Butler's Balsam of Liverwort, pontil, aqua, 4¼"......15.00
Medicine, Caldwell's Syrup Pepsin, aqua, rectangular, 3"........4.00
Medicine, Cary Gum Tree Cough Syrup, lime green, 7½"......15.00
Medicine, Chamberlain's Colic/Cholera/Diarrhea, aqua, 4½".....5.00
Medicine, Christie's Magnetic Fluid, flared top, aqua, 4¾".....10.00
Medicine, Cod Liver Oil, fish figural, 9½".................13.00
Medicine, Cone Asthma Conqueror Co, clear, 8".............6.00
Medicine, D Evan's Camomile Pills, pontil, aqua, 3¾".........25.00
Medicine, Dana's Sarsaparilla, sunken panels, aqua, 9".........12.00
Medicine, Dill's Balm of Life, rectangular, clear, 6"...........4.00
Medicine, Dolton's Sarsaparilla & Nerve Tonic, aqua, 9".......15.00
Medicine, Dr Alexander, bk: Lung Healer, sq collar, aqua, 6½"...6.00
Medicine, Dr Birney's Catarrah All Power, clear, 2¼".........4.00
Medicine, Dr Cumming's Vegetine, aqua, 9¾"..............6.00
Medicine, Dr Doyen Staphylase Du, amethyst, 8"............6.00
Medicine, Dr E Bricker's Tonic for Fever/Chills, aqua, 6"......33.00
Medicine, Dr Evan's Teething Syrup, flare lip/pontil/aqua, 2"....20.00
Medicine, Dr Harrison's Chalybeste Tonic, teal blue, 7¾".....20.00
Medicine, Dr Harter's Iron Tonic, amber, 9¼".............12.00
Medicine, Dr McLean's Liver & Kidney Balms, aqua, 8¾".....10.00
Medicine, Dr McMunn's Elixir of Opium, pontil, round, aqua, 4".15.00
Medicine, Fenning's Fever Curer, rectangular, aqua, 6½"......6.50
Medicine, Ferro China Melaro Tonico, 3 sides w/emb lions, gr...25.00
Medicine, Frog Pond Chill & Fever Tonic, cobalt, 7".........12.00
Medicine, Gray's Syrup of Red Spruce Gum, sunken panels, aqua.4.00
Medicine, John Hart Co, heart shape, golden amber, dbl collar..75.00
Medicine, Moore's Revealed Remedy, amber, 8¾"...........10.00
Medicine, OK Plantation, triangular, amber, 11"...........200.00
Medicine, Osgood's India Cholagogue, NY, w/pontil, 5¼".....20.00
Medicine, Paine's Celery Compound, aqua, 10"..............9.00
Medicine, Pawnee Indian Ta-Ha, price 25¢, aqua, 8½"........15.00
Medicine, Racine de Guimauve, cut glass, blue, 9¼".........28.00
Medicine, Ridgway's Acme Liniment, amber, 8".............12.50
Medicine, Royal Gall Remedy, machine made, dk amber, 7"....10.00
Medicine, Sanford's Radical Cure, med bl, 7½"..............30.00
Medicine, Skoda's Wolefirlle Discovery, aqua, 9"............25.00
Medicine, Sloan's Liniment, full, in orig box, 5"............9.00
Medicine, Walker's Tonic, Free Sample, clear, 3¼"..........28.00
Medicine, Warner's Safe Cure, emb safe, amber, 10".........35.00
Medicine, Warner's Safe Cure, London, emb safe, dk gr, 7¼"...50.00
Medicine, Wood's Great Peppermint Cure, aqua, 5½".........6.00
Medicine, Wyeth's Safe & Sulphur Compound..............10.00
Milk, cobalt ½ pt, Sherman College Inn, VG...............125.00
Milk, Voegell, baby face...............................20.00
Mineral water, A Schroth Superior, round w/paneled base, bl...270.00
Mineral water, Congress & Empire Spring Co, emerald gr, 9"...25.00
Mineral water, Geyser Water, Hammond LA, aqua, sq, 9", M....25.00
Mineral water, Hammond Co, amber, round, very lt haze, 12"...15.00
Mineral water, Improved, blob top, graphite pontil, bl, 6¼"....30.00
Mineral water, Missisquoi, olive, 9¾"....................30.00
Mineral water, Saratoga Red Spring, emerald gr, 1870s, 9½"....50.00
Mineral water, Saratoga Spring, emb star, golden amber, 9¼"...50.00

Mineral water, Vermont Spring Saxe & Co, green 14.00
Mineral water, Washington Spring, Washington's face, gr, 6¼" . .95.00
Pickle, cathedral, w/label, lt blue, 9½" 20.00
Pickle, plain, paneled corner, tapered neck, yel, 7¼x2" sq 15.00
Poison, dagger on front, sq, pouring lip, aqua, 5" 10.00
Poison, Do Not Take, N written backwards, 4¼" 18.00
Poison, Durfee Embalming Fluid Co, amethyst, 8¾" 18.00
Poison, Frederia: vertical, flask type, hobnail cover, ½ pint 27.00
Poison, Lray, label, emb ribs on edges, amber, 3½" 15.00
Poison, Owl Poison Ammonia, label, 3-cornered, cobalt, 5¼" . . .25.00
Poison, Poisonous across shoulder, oval, ribbed front, 6½" 6.00
Poison, Rat Poison horizontal around bottle, clear, 2½" 17.00
Poison, Syr:Fer:Iodid, cobalt, 7" 66.00
Poison, Tinct Nux Vom, label, green, 6" 13.00
Poison, vertical: Not To Be Taken, wide ribbing, cobalt, 6¾" . . .11.00
Poison, Wyeth Poison vertical in back, cobalt, 2¼" 9.00
Soda, A M'Farland, Phila, squat, gr, w/pontil 26.00
Soda, Bay City Soda Water Co, star symbol, blue, 7" 15.00
Soda, Celery Cola, C on bottom, amber, 7½" 6.00
Soda, Chadsey & Bro, 2" hollow letters, bt, gp, cobalt, 7½" 33.00
Soda, Dearborn, 83 3rd Ave NY, bt, green, 7" 30.00
Soda, H Sanders, Savannah GA, amber, 8½" 25.00
Soda, Haddock & Sons, torpedo shape, yel-olive, 1850, 6" 225.00
Soda, Hutchinson, WW Lake, Jackson Miss, aqua, 7" 12.50
Soda, JA Dearborn, sapphire bl, round, heavy collar, 7" 220.00
Soda, Johann Hoff, amber 10.00
Soda, L&B in hollow letters, bt, gp, green, 7¼" 35.00

Figural ceramic pretzel flask, 5½" x 3½", $95.00.

Soda, Life Preserver, clear, 7" 9.00
Soda, Muff Co, label, marble in center of neck, aqua, 7¼" 8.00
Soda, Nova Kola, This Bottle Not To Be Sold, clear, 7¾" 6.00
Soda, Ozo-Ola The Happy Drink, clear, 7½" 4.00
Soda, RC&T New York, gp, aqua, 7½" 40.00
Soda, Seitz Bros/Easton PA, bk: lg S, bt, green, 7¼" 25.00
Soda, Sietz & Bro, Easton Pa, squat, pontiled, cobalt 75.00
Soda, Stolen From Eureka Bottling Works, aqua, 6¾" 35.00
Soda, Superior, eagle/shield/flags, cobalt, 1850s, 8¼" 240.00
Soda, Union Glass Work/Phila, bt, gp, green, 7" 20.00
Spirits, Cutter Hotaling, coffin type, 1886, amber 85.00
Spirits, Daniel Schaeffer's Log Cabin Whiskey 50.00

Spirits, Duffy Malt Whiskey Co, pat Aug 1886, amber, 10½" 15.00
Spirits, Eagle Liqueur Distilleries, olive, 7¾" 45.00
Spirits, Imperial Wedding Whiskey Blend, amethyst, 8" 10.00
Spirits, John Hart & Co each side, amber, 7¼" 30.00
Spirits, Old Henry Rye in script, ring top, aqua, 9½" 10.00
Spirits, Pedro, 1880, bt, amber, quart 70.00
Spirits, Rebecca At The Well, pontil, amethyst, 8" 55.00
Spirits, Teakettle Old Bourbon, San Francisco, amber, quart . . .150.00
Vinegar, Champion's, aqua, tower shape neck, 14½" 30.00

Boxes

Boxes have been used by civilized man since ancient Egypt and Rome. Down through the centuries, specifically designed containers have been made from every conceivable material. Precious metals, papier mache, battersea, oriental lacquer, and wood have held riches from the treasuries of kings, snuff for the fashionable set of the last century, China tea, and countless other commodities.

See also Jewelry Boxes

Band, courting scenic wallpaper on cardboard, 12x15x18" 325.00
Band, wallpaper/cb, 'Clayton's Ascent' w/balloon, 13x20x16", G.625.00
Band, wallpaper/1800s newspaper, Hannah Davis, 15x20x16" . . .495.00
Bentwood, branded label on lid, worn blk pnt, 9¾" dia 55.00
Bentwood, dk bl w/lt blue beneath, 4¼x8¾" 105.00
Bentwood, finger constructed lid, orig sponging, oval, 7x9x12" .225.00
Bentwood, laced finger built, orig pnt w/foliage, 12" dia 355.00
Bentwood, old worn blue pnt, lid cracked, 4¼x13" 195.00
Bentwood, old worn red pnt, 3½x7½" .75.00
Bentwood, rpt, shows peddler selling brooms to lady, 11" W . . .125.00
Bentwood, traces of wallpaper cover, Hannah Davis, 9¾" oval . . .45.00
Bentwood, wrought iron hdl on trn ears, worn pnt, 7x12" 55.00
Bible, oak, English, floral carving, has till, rpr, 11x16x26" 160.00
Birch, relief carved w/stylized compote & vines, 9½" L 175.00
Blackball, mahog w/2 drw, wire nail construction, 4¾x6x8¾" . . .50.00
Blackball, walnut, dvtl, 3 dvtl drw, orig brass, 7x10" 115.00
Bride's, bentwood, orig floral, decoupage engraving, 8x18x11" . .325.00

Bride's box, German inscription around edge, hand painted soldier on horseback, mid-1800s, 7" x 16¾" x 10½", $595.00.

Bride's, bentwood, orig pnt w/couple on swing/inscription, 18″	375.00
Bride's, pine, unpntd w/tulips/stylized flowers, 7x10x17″, G	325.00
Bride's, pine w/laced seams/mc florals/scene w/couple/verse, 18″	495.00
Butternut, base drw w/2 trn pulls, lift top, sq nails, 6x12″	75.00
Curly maple, blk striping w/printed house/garden, 3½″ L	80.00
Desk, table top, mahog/ornate inlay/fitted interior/fall front	425.00
Dome top, dvtl pine/poplar, grpt worn, iron lock/hdls, 24″	325.00
Dome top, pnt w/dots/hearts/stripes on bird's eye maple, 11″ L	450.00
Dome top, poplar, dvtl, dtd 1882, rfn, incomplete hasp, 20″ L	95.00
Dome top, poplar w/orig bl & freehand florals, 11x14x25″	500.00
Dome top, tooled leather, wrought iron lock/hdl, 4x6x11″	95.00
Dome top, tulip wood/orig br graining/line inlay, 10x20x10″	475.00
Elmwood w/oyster veneer/inlay, Wm & Mary, 19″ L	900.00
Grpt, w/blue beneath, base/lid moldings, 11x6x6″	155.00
Grpt over pnt, dvtl, base & lid moldings, till w/lid, 6x7x11″	155.00
Ivory, etched/stained, Baroque, 10½″ L	400.00
Knife, Federal, inlaid mahogany, serpentine front, 14x9″	450.00
Knife, walnut, dvtl canted sides w/cut-out divider, trn hdl	95.00
Lady's shoe figural, wood, 2 tone, inlaid brass buttons, 1877	150.00
Leather over poplar, brass stud trim, iron/brass lock, 18″ L	30.00
Oak, panel sides, trn ft, cut-out lid slot, 8½x12¾x8″	190.00
Patch, bl, lid reads Remember the Giver, English, 1¼″ oval	275.00
Patch, lavender w/cherub, 'Summer', mirror w/in, English 1½″	300.00
Patch, puce w/floral medallion, Esteem the Giver, English, 1½″	220.00
Pine, dvtl, sliding lid, worn grpt, 7½x10″	65.00
Pine, mahog lid, orig varnish w/gold & blk striping, 5x7x11″	40.00
Pine, orig br vinegar grain, dvtl, 12″ L	275.00
Pine, orig flame grain imitates mahog w/line inlay, 17″ L	80.00
Pine, overall twig art decor bird/moon/star, incomplete, 29″ W	95.00
Pine, primitive, dvtl, worn finish, 12x23x13″	85.00
Pine, primitive, panel front, iron side hdls, 35″ W	35.00
Pine, salmon w/brushed decor, 1 board top split, 8x12x6″	350.00
Pine, 2 pnt medallions+7 on sides w/deer/squirrel/men, 12″ L	775.00
Pipe, cherry, 1 drw, scalloped top, red rpt, w/3 clay pipes	150.00
Poplar, base/lid molding, orig grpt bird's eye maple, 6x7x10″	195.00
Poplar, scalloped crest w/hanging hole, glass insert, 12x6″	245.00
Poplar, sliding lid, dvtl, compass flower decor, 4x9x14″, G	350.00
Sewing, Geo II parquetry inlaid burl walnut, 1740, 14″ L	500.00
Snub nose wood plane form, mahog, locking device, 4″ L	75.00
Spice, poplar, sliding lid, 4 part interior, 3x5x9″	65.00
Turned poplar, orig red/yellow grpt good, 8¼″	525.00
Wallpaper on cb w/wood lid/base, 1855 paper lining, 2¾x3¾″	75.00
Walnut, dvtl, applied rope-like molding, alligatored, 5½x9x12″	60.00
Walnut, dvtl, sliding lid, varnish, 3x3½x14″	60.00

Boyd's Crystal Art Glass

In 1978, Bernard C. Boyd and his son bought the Degenhart factory in Cambridge, Ohio, acquiring fifty of Elizabeth Degenhart's glass molds with the 'D in heart' trademark removed. Many are used by Boyd, who also produces the Louise doll, the pony Joey, and the elephant Zack. These are issued each month in a new and different color of crystal as well as slag or 'marble' glass.

Candy Dish, Dawn, February 1980	27.50
Candy Dish, Deep Purple, March 1979	9.00
Candy Dish, Ice Green, October 1979	10.50
Candy Dish, Rubina, May 1979	20.00
Chick, 1″, Butterscotch	17.50
Chick, 1″, Candy Swirl	15.00
Chick, 1″, Cobalt	10.00
Chick, 1″, Crown Tuscan	10.00
Chick, 1″, Deep Purple, March 1979	12.50

Chick, 1″, Delphenium	10.00
Chick, 1″, Firefly	14.00
Chick, 1″, Frosty Blue	15.00
Chick, 1″, Furr Green	10.00
Chick, 1″, Heather, January 1980	10.00
Chick, 1″, Ice Green, October 1979	12.50
Chick, 1″, Impatience	15.00
Chick, 1″, John's Surprise, December 1980	15.00
Chick, 1″, Marigold	17.50
Chick, 1″, Old Ivory, April 1981	10.00
Chick, 1″, Peanut Butter	15.00
Chick, 1″, Royalty	17.50
Chick, 1″, Rubina, May 1979	12.50
Chick, 1″, Shamrock Slag	15.00
Chick, 1″, Walnut Slag	15.00
Chick, 1″, Willow Blue	14.00
Hen, 3″, Cobalt Blue, October 1981	10.00
Hen, 3″, Dawn, February 1980	14.50
Hen, 3″, Deep Purple, March 1979	10.00
Hen, 3″, Furr Green, August 1981	14.00
Hen, 3″, Heather, January 1980	12.50
Hen, 3″, Ice Green, October 1979	13.50
Hen, 3″, Lavender, March 1982	10.00
Hen, 3″, Old Ivory Slag, April 1981	15.00
Hen, 3″, Pink Champagne, August 1979	12.50
Hen, 3″, Pippin Green, April 1982	10.00
Hen, 3″, Rubina, May 1979	15.00
Hen, 5″, Apricot	20.00
Hen, 5″, Candy Swirl	18.50
Hen, 5″, Chocolate	18.50
Hen, 5″, Cobalt Blue, October 1981	15.00
Hen, 5″, Deep Purple, March 1979	15.00
Hen, 5″, Delphinium, March 1981	6.00
Hen, 5″, Furr Green, August 1981	17.50
Hen, 5″, Heather, January 1980	17.50
Hen, 5″, Lavender, March 1982	15.00
Hen, 5″, Lemon Ice, September 1979	18.50
Hen, 5″, Mardi Gras, May 1981	20.00
Hen, 5″, Old Ivory Slag, April 1981	18.00
Hen, 5″, Persimmon	18.50
Hen, 5″, Pink Champagne, August 1979	17.50
Hen, 5″, Pippin Green, April 1982	11.00
Hen, 5″, Rubina, May 1979	22.50
Hen, 5″, Snow, January 1982	10.00
Hen, 5″, Vacation Swirl, June 1982	16.00
Joey Horse, Candy Swirl, 1980	20.00
Joey Horse, Chocolate, 1980	35.00
Joey Horse, Delphinium, March 1981	10.00
Joey Horse, Firefly, 1980	15.00
Joey Horse, Flame, 1980	15.00
Joey Horse, Furr Green, August 1981	10.00
Joey Horse, Impatient, 1980	15.00
Joey Horse, Mardi Gras, May 1981	10.00
Joey Horse, Old Ivory, April 1981	10.00
Joey Horse, Persimmon, 1980	20.00
Joey Horse, Willow Blue, 1980	15.00
Joey Horse, Zack Boyd Slag, 1980	15.00
Kitten, Delphinium, March 1981	10.00
Kitten, Furr Green, August 1981	12.00
Kitten, Lavender 'N Lace, March 1982	10.00
Kitten, Lemon Ice, September 1979	12.00
Kitten, Mardi Gras, May 1981	12.00
Kitten, Old Ivory, April 1981	10.00
Kitten, Pink Champagne, August 1979	25.00

Kitten, Snow, January 1982...........................10.00
Lamb, 5″, Rubina, May 1979.........................20.00
Logo, Blue Chiffon...................................25.00
Louise, Cobalt Blue, October 1981...................12.00
Louise, Delphinium, March 1981......................12.00
Louise, Furr Green, August 1981.....................12.00
Louise, Heather, January 1980.......................25.00
Louise, Ice Green, October 1979.....................55.00
Louise, Lavender 'N Lace, March 1982................12.00
Louise, Mardi Gras, May 1981........................14.00
Louise, Old Ivory, April 1981.......................14.00
Louise, Pink Champagne, August 1979.................25.00
Louise, Snow, hand painted, January 1982............17.50
Louise, Snow, January 1982..........................10.00
Owl, Apricot..15.00
Owl, Black Walnut...................................25.00
Owl, Blue Chiffon, February 1980....................12.50
Owl, Cobalt Blue....................................12.00
Owl, Dark Chocolate.................................12.00
Owl, Deep Purple....................................15.00
Owl, Delphinium, March 1981.........................10.00
Owl, Dogwood..12.00
Owl, Furr Green, August 1981........................12.00
Owl, Heather, January 1980..........................12.50
Owl, Ice Blue.......................................12.00
Owl, Ice Green, October 1979........................12.50
Owl, Lavender 'N Lace, March 1982....................8.00
Owl, Lemon Ice......................................15.00
Owl, Mardi Gras, May 1981...........................12.00
Owl, Old Ivory, April 1981..........................10.00
Owl, Peach Whisper, August 1979.....................12.50
Owl, Pink Champagne, August 1979....................12.50
Owl, Rubina..9.00
Robin, 5″, Apricot..................................20.00
Robin, 5″, Chocolate................................20.00
Robin, 5″, Deep Purple, March 1979..................10.00
Robin, 5″, Delphinium, March 1981...................17.50
Robin, 5″, Heather, January 1980....................17.50
Robin, 5″, Impatient................................18.50
Robin, 5″, Mardi Gras...............................20.00
Robin, 5″, Persimmon................................20.00
Robin, 5″, Snow, January 1982.......................10.00
Turkey, 5″, Chocolate...............................18.50
Turkey, 5″, Cobalt Blue, October 1981...............10.00
Turkey, 5″, Heather, January 1980...................18.00
Turkey, 5″, Ice Blue................................18.50
Turkey, 5″, Ice Green, October 1979.................17.50
Turkey, 5″, Impatient...............................18.50
Turkey, 5″, Lemon Ice, September 1979................18.50
Turkey, 5″, Snow, January 1982......................10.00
Turkey, 5″, Willow Blue.............................18.50
Zack Elephant, Cobalt Blue, October 1981............12.00
Zack Elephant, Crown Tuscan, 1982...................14.00
Zack Elephant, December '82 Swirl,1983..............14.00
Zack Elephant, Delphinium, March 1981...............14.00
Zack Elephant, Flame, 1981..........................50.00
Zack Elephant, Furr Green, 1981.....................14.00
Zack Elephant, Golden Delight, 1982.................14.00
Zack Elephant, Lavender, 1982.......................14.00
Zack Elephant, Mardi Gras, 1981.....................15.00
Zack Elephant, Old Ivory Slag, April 1981...........10.00
Zack Elephant, Old Ivory Surprise, 1981.............15.00
Zack Elephant, Pippin Green, 1982...................14.00
Zack Elephant, Sandpiper, 1981......................14.00

Bradley and Hubbard

The Bradley and Hubbard Mfg. Company was a firm who produced metal accessories for the home. They operated during the early part of this century, and their products reflected both the Arts and Crafts and Art Nouveau influence.

Their logo was a device with a triangular arrangement of the company name containing a smaller triangle and an Aladdin lamp.

Book rack, expandable brass..........................30.00
Bookend, sailboat.. ....12.00
Bookends, Lincoln Memorial, bronze, pr...............48.00
Bookends, ships, bronze, pr..........................30.00
Bookends, w/lions, pr................................35.00
Candle holder, dragon hdl, brass, sgn, 3¾x5¾″........20.00
Desk set, brass w/classic border design, 4 pcs.......85.00
Hatpin holder, dbl, center hdl, horse & rider w/horn, brass.....95.00
Inkwell, bronze, w/insert............................35.00
Inkwell, copper w/porcelain liner, w/blotter.........40.00
Inkwell, dbl, brass w/milk glass inserts.............80.00
Inkwell, letter rack & paper clip combo, Deco styling, brass.....70.00
Lamp, #5, brass urn base, w/hdls, 12″ glass etched shade......365.00
Lamp, banquet; etched shade, brass & onyx std, wired.......350.00
Lamp, desk; 4 caramel slag panes w/2″ Greek Key border, 15″.250.00
Lamp, table; wicker, w/wicker & cloth shade, 17″.........195.00
Lamp, table/piano; 12″ decor red satin ball shade, brass, 63″.1,095.00
Lamp, wht/gr slag glass in 8 panel shade, orig brass base.....565.00
Lamp, 15″ shade w/gr & red panel ldgl, heavy overlay.......325.00
Lamp, 8 panel caramel slag shade, pot metal fr/std, 1907, 19″..400.00
Lamp, 8 panels ribbed amber glass w/leaf & vine overlay, 22″..350.00
Lamp base, desk; #256, brass, curved Bryant sockets, sgn.....100.00
Lamp fixture, oil; 3 arm pull-down, ornate.................250.00
Letter holder, brass.................................12.00
Letter rack, dbl, brass, center hdl, horseman/hurdles/horn.....125.00
Mirror, wall hanging, bevel glass, ornate, 13½x10½″.........50.00
Plaque, gypsy, mc on iron............................55.00
Smoking stand, orig glass insert....................125.00
Wall bracket, for night lamp, ornate iron, 1881.............38.00
Wall sconce, filigree w/face, beveled mirror, 3 lite, prisms......120.00

Brass

Brass is an alloy consisting essentially of copper and zinc in variable proportions. It is a medium that has been used for both utilitarian items and objects of artistic merit. Today, with the inflated price of copper and the popular use of plastics, almost anything made of brass is collectible.

Basin, spun, hanging loop, imp FW Haydens Pat, 3½x10¾″....20.00
Bed warmer, bird/floral engraving, wood hdl, 40″...........440.00
Bed warmer, floral engraving, trn hdl w/flame pnt, 12x44″.....540.00
Bowl, spun, iron rim hdls, minor dents, 5x10″..............40.00
Bucket, spun, label on bottom, 9x13½″.....................50.00
Bucket, spun, mk Hayden's Pat 1851, 8x12″.................45.00
Bullet, Take A Shot, opens to 4 shot cups, Germany..........28.00
Chestnut roaster, trn wood hdl, 9″ dia, 22″ hdl...........125.00
Crumb tray & sweeper.................................22.50
Dipper, wrought iron hdl, 20″ L......................35.00
Dish cross w/shell detail, late, 11½″....................60.00
Easel, Victorian, turned, late 1800s, 72″................450.00
Kettle, dvtl w/wrought iron bale hdl, rpr, dented, 11x15″....100.00
Kettle, spun, iron bale, stamped E Muler & Co, rim split, 11″...65.00
Kettle, spun, wide wrought iron hdl, 5½x11½″ dia...........45.00

Sundial, male figure holding ring pierced with arrow, circa 1900, 28″, $350.00.

Kettle, spun, wrought iron hdl, label: HW Hayden's Pat, 20½″.130.00
Pan, hammered, wrought iron rim hdls, 3″+hdlx9¼″ dia.......55.00
Pastry cutter, pinch fluter end, handmade, 6¼″...............45.00
Sauce pan, cast w/wrought iron hdl, 5½″ dia, 6¾″ hdl........18.00
Shoehorn, ca 1800s, lg....................................65.00
Spout lamp, hanging, Middle Eastern, old pnt worn, 6″+hanger.25.00
Tea kettle, gooseneck spout, trn wood hdl, att Dutch, 8½″.....45.00
Tinder box, w/candle holder/flint/steel/kindling/fabric, 4″......475.00
Tray, incised floral/animals/people, raised rim, 26½″ dia........50.00

Brayton Laguna

Dish, crescent shape, wht w/blk & red enamel flowers..........8.00
Figurine, advertising, sun bathers w/life preserver, c 1943.......45.00
Figurine, family group: father, mother, child, c 1943, 8½″......18.00
Figurine, man pushing cart, ink stamp mk, 6″...............40.00
Figurine, Pluto, WDP....................................50.00

Peasant lady with baskets, hand-incised, signed, 8½″, $22.00.

Bread Plates

Bread trays have been produced not only in glass -- crystal, colors, milk glass, and goofus -- but in metal and pottery as well. Those considered most collectible were made during the last quarter of the 19th century from pressed glass with well detailed embossed designs, many of them portraying a particularly significant historical event. A great number of these plates were sold at the 1876 Philadelphia Centennial Exposition by various glass manufacturers who exhibited their wares on the grounds. Among the themes depicted were the Declaration of Independence, the Constitution, McKinley's memorial 'It is God's Way', Remberance of Three Presidents, the purchase of Alaska, and various presidential campaigns. These are to mention only a few.

Actress, Miss Neilson.................................65.00
Ashman 25.00
Barley, 11¾x9½″..................................21.00
Be Industrious, Iowa City...........................60.00
Button & Daisy, amber, open handle..................38.00
Columbia, clear, rim flakes.........................125.00
Columbus..30.00
Constitution.....................................35.00
Crying Baby......................................38.50
Cupid & Venus...................................30.00
Do Unto Others..................................36.00
Elaine..110.00
Faith, Hope & Charity.............................50.00
Fan & Ball, 10½x5″...............................16.00

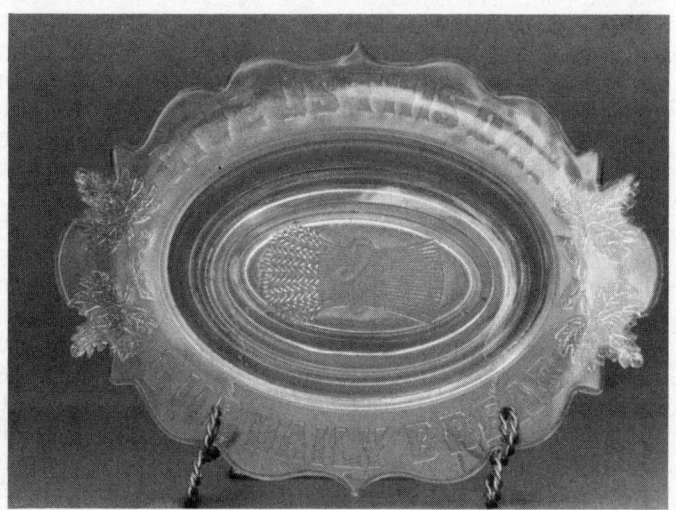

Sheaf of wheat, Give Us This Day, 13″ x 9½″, $65.00.

Frosted Lion, 10½″................................55.00
Frosted Stork, frosted center, w/101 border..............49.50
Garfield Drape, head in center........................45.00
George Washington, First in War..., clear................75.00
Golden Rule......................................35.00
Good Luck.......................................40.00
Grant, square....................................30.00
Hand 20.00
It Is Pleasant To Labor, For Those We Love..............55.00
Jenny Lind......................................35.00
John Mitchell, w/some gold.........................175.00
Knight's of Labor, vaseline.........................95.00
Last Supper, w/frosted border.......................50.00
Later Double Vine, 10¾″............................26.00
Liberty & Freedom, w/Federal eagle, 1776, scalloped.........95.00

Liberty Bell, signers..............................78.00	Cased, blue Herringbone, pink w/in, very heavy frame.........350.00
Lord's Supper, Findlay.............................30.00	Cased, coral to wht, pleats, Webb; Greenaway figural fr........700.00
Lotus...35.00	Cased, pinks/wht w/in, crimped/undulating amber rim, 6x11"...175.00
Maple Leaf, vaseline, 11"..........................28.00	Cased, rose shading to wht, simple SP holder................75.00
McKinley, oval...................................20.00	Cobalt overlay w/gold florals, wht w/in, compote stand, 14"....425.00
One Hundred One................................35.00	Crackle glass, gr, ornate SP fr w/figural birds...............155.00
Palmette Variant, blue or amber.....................22.00	Cranberry bowl, in fancy SP holder, 8"....................285.00
Paneled Forget-Me-Not............................22.00	Cranberry to pk w/enamel florals, SP holder.................225.00
Philadelphia State House, 12½" dia...................125.00	Cranberry-rose w/gold/wht florals, gr cased, Webb, Indian fr....700.00
Pioneer White Wings Flour..........................30.00	Cut glass, elaborate Pairpoint fr, 8".......................140.00
Pleat & Panel....................................25.00	Milk glass, Challinor, in orig SP holder....................225.00
Reaper, 13x8"...................................48.00	Milky blue w/hobs, ruffle top, ornate SP stand, S&W, 9x10"...350.00
Saxon..15.00	Mt Washington on Pairpoint base, cream w/gold, purple w/in...845.00
Scroll w/Flowers.................................30.00	Opaque yellow w/floral/butterfly, ruffled/pleated, Webb, 11"...350.00
Sheraton, amber.................................30.00	Overlay mahog red to custard, frilly applied rim, star decor....105.00
State House, amber...............................150.00	Peachblow, fluted/frilly, gold decor, New Martinsville, sgn fr...500.00
Teddy Roosevelt, w/many dancing bears..............95.00	Peachblow, glossy/cased, ruffled/fluted, Van Bugh mk fr......325.00
Thousand Eye...................................20.00	Peppermint stick, SP fr w/warrior head medallions, Pairpoint...135.00
Three Presidents, clear & frosted....................65.00	Satin, bl w/frilled camphor rim, SP fr w/loops, ornaments, 9¾".150.00
Transcontinental Railroad..........................65.00	Tree of Life, milk glass, Challinor, SP Meriden holder........285.00
US Grant, blue...................................35.00	
Victoria, Diamond Jubilee, gilt center................35.00	
Washington Centennial, Washington's head, First in War......110.00	
Waste Not, Want Not, apple green...................37.50	

Bride's Baskets

Victorian brides were showered with gifts, as brides have always been; one of the most popular gift items was the bride's basket. Art glass inserts from both European and American glass houses, some in lovely clear color with dainty enameled florals, others of Peachblow, Vasa Murrhina, satin or cased glass, were cradled in complimentary silverplated holders. While many of these holders were simply engraved or delicately embossed, others such as those from Pairpoint and Wilcox were wonderfully ornate, often with figurals of cherubs or animals. The bride's basket was no longer in fashion after the turn of the century.

Bristol Glass

Bristol is a type of semi-opaque opaline glass whose name was derived from the area in England where it was first produced. Similar glass was made in France, Germany, and Italy. In this country it was made by the New England Glass Company, and to a lesser extent by its contemporaries. During the 18th and 19th century, Bristol glass was imported in large amounts and sold cheaply, thereby contributing the the demise of of the earlier glass houses here in America. It is very difficult to distinguish the English Bristol from other opaline types. Style, design, and decoration serve as clues to it's origin; but only those well educated in the field can spot these subtle variations.

Mt. Washington mother-of-pearl glass in three colors, $950.00.

Bl opal, lattice, pleats/flutes; 4 ftd fr, leaf ornaments, 13"......185.00	
Bristol, pink to rose, cased, ruffled, pnt florals w/in, 10½".....135.00	
Cased, bl shaded to wht, deeply fluted/ruffled; Pairpoint fr.....275.00	

Revolving silverplated frame, decanters with enameled birds and florals, 15½", $485.00.

Cologne, wht w/birds & flowers, 10"......................75.00	
Compote, cobalt, cased & cut, 6".........................175.00	
Ewer, wht w/cupid scene, 17"............................80.00	
Figurine, couple in carriage pulled by 2 wht horses, 4x6"......350.00	

Figurine, rider on horseback, blown, 2¼x3¼"...............60.00	Cigarette tin, Princess Mary's Xmas gift to troops, 1914........60.00
Mantle lustre w/8 prisms, bl/gold decor, 10¾", pr...........295.00	Creamer, Queen Victoria Jubilee, 1887, glass, 3½"............65.00
Pitcher, bl base w/wht body, floral decor, crimp top, 10"......45.00	Cup & saucer, com Great War 1914-18, crest w/map/flags/dove..32.00
Plate, HP bl/wht horses, artist sgn, 14"...................375.00	Cup & saucer, cor King Geo/Queen Elizabeth, portrait, Radfords.30.00
Punch set, blue, 15 pc, some minor expert repairs..........225.00	Cup & saucer, cor Queen Elizabeth, bone china, Royal Albert..25.00
Sweetmeat, duck among foliage, pk/wht w/in, 5x3"..........100.00	Cup & saucer, cor Queen Elizabeth, portraits, Windsor, 1953...28.00
Tumbler, wht w/HP pk roses............................15.00	Cup & saucer, Princess Margaret birth, Paragon.............60.00
Vase, bl w/HP flower, bulbous, 5"........................24.00	Dish, cor King Geo VI/Queen Elizabeth, Grindley, 5" sq........25.00
Vase, frosted, HP poppies/gilt decor, ped base, 9½", M, pr....145.00	Dish, Queen Elizabeth, glass w/blk/wht photo, 4½" dia........20.00
Vase, gr, gold overlay enamel, fluted, 12½"................50.00	Humidor, cor queen Elizabeth, portrait/flags, Sandland, 5¼"....45.00
Vase, gr w/enameling & jewels, 10"......................110.00	Loving cup, Prince & Princess of Wales, 3 griffin hdls, ltd ed..350.00
Vase, gr w/HP roses, 18"..............................125.00	Medal, Queen Victoria 1897 Jubilee, silver, 2¼", in box........95.00
Vase, ped ft, mc bird & branch on pink, 8½"...............32.50	Mug, com King Geo VI/Queen Elizabeth Canada/USA visit, Soho.35.00
Vase, pk, ruffled rim, w/floral enameling, 6"...............35.00	Mug, com Royal Visit to Canada '59, mc leaf w/portraits, Wood..40.00
Vase, pk overlay, wht heron in panel, flowers, ped ft, 15x5"....200.00	Mug, cor Edward VIII, portrait, mfg Soho, Solian Ware, 1937...30.00
Vase, relief lizard w/in flowering vines on wht ground, 15½"...150.00	Mug, cor Queen Elizabeth, portrait/crown, Queen Anne, 4½"...35.00
Vase, rust/beige w/bl birds, bulbous, 10¾"................95.00	Mug, cor Queen Elizabeth, portrait/date, mfg Empire, 1953....35.00
Vase, wht w/floral enameling, crimped, 7¼"...............45.00	Mug, Geo V/Queen Mary, 1935.........................27.50
Vase, wht w/HP birds/flowers, 11½", pr..................150.00	Mug, Prince Charles' Investiture, red/gr decor, Adams, 3¼"....18.00
Vase, wht w/yellow/gr enamel florals, 9".................25.00	Mug, Queen Elizabeth Silver Jubilee, '52-77, Chudleigh, rare....45.00
Vase, yel to gr, HP floral, 13".........................85.00	Mug, Queen Elizabeth Silver Jubilee, portrait, Czech...........20.00
	Piggy bank, Queen Elizabeth II/Prince Philip, mc/gold, 4½"....18.00

British Royal Commemoratives

British souvenir items have been made to commemorate coronations as well as other notable occasions involving the royal families for many years. Bells, thimbles, postcards, mugs, plates, and spoons are the most common.

Key: com----commemorative   cor----coronation

Ash tray, cor Edward VIII, mfd Lancaster, 1937.............22.00	Pin tray, cor Queen Elizabeth, mfg Royal Winton, 1953........12.00
Ash tray, cor Edward VIII, sepia portrait, mfg Wedgwood......25.00	Pin tray, HM Edward VIII, mfg Meakin, 6x4"................25.00
Ash tray, cor Edward VIII, sq w/ruffled rim, Meakin, 4½"......22.00	Plate, com King Geo/Queen Elizabeth, Canada/USA visit, 9"....30.00
Ash tray, Queen Elizabeth, Wedgwood, 1953, 4½" dia........22.00	Plate, cor King Geo/Queen Elizabeth, bl w/gold trim/portraits....35.00
Basket, cor King Geo/Queen Elizabeth, clear glass, 1937......55.00	Plate, King Geo/Queen Elizabeth, mfg Shelly, 1937, 9".......32.00
Beaker, cor Edward VIII, portrait/inscription, Moyott..........28.00	Plate, Queen Elizabeth Silver Jubilee, Liverpool Rd Pot, 9"....25.00
Beaker, King Geo/Queen Elizabeth, Solian Ware, Soho, '37, 4"..18.00	Plate, Queen Victoria center portrait, gold rim, 9½".........100.00
Biscuit tin, Queen Elizabeth Silver Jubilee, portrait, 4x10"......28.00	Plate & cup & saucer, Queen Elizabeth, mfg Meakin, 1953.....45.00
Bookmark, SP, portraits King Geo/Queen Elizabeth, Canada, '39.28.00	Postcard, J Beagles #410E, King Geo/Queen Mary in open landau.3.00
Bust, cor Queen Elizabeth, parian/gold trim, Foley, 5½".......60.00	Postcard, Tuck #3966, Queen Mary, Silver Jubilee portrait.......3.00
Candy dish, cor Edward VIII, bone china, Royal Chelsea........20.00	Postcard, valentine; Duchess of York/Princess Elizabeth, #3C1....3.00
Candy dish, King Geo/Queen Elizabeth, mfg Meakin, 1937, 5½".15.00	Spoon, cor Edward VII/Queen Alexander, SP w/portraits, 1902..25.00
	Spoon, Queen Victoria 1897 Jubilee, sterling/gw, elaborate, 6"..145.00
	Teapot, child's; Royal Princesses, mc portraits w/blue, 2¾".....45.00
	Teapot & stand, cor Queen Elizabeth, gold w/portrait, Sudlow...65.00
	Tin, cor Queen Elizabeth/Prince Philip, bl/gold, Scribbans, 9"...18.00
	Tin, portrait of Royal Princesses, mfg for Riley's Toffee, 5".....30.00
	Tumbler, cor King Geo/Queen Elizabeth, glass w/portraits/flags..12.00

Broadsides

Webster defines the term as simply a large sheet of paper printed on one side. During the 1800s, the broadside was the most practical means of mass communication. By the middle of the century they had become elaborate and lengthy with information, illustrations, portraits, and fancy border designs.

Advertising appearance of Two Headed Girl, 1869, 12x24"......75.00
Confession & dying words of murderer, dtd 1793, 23x26"......55.00
Newspaper, Spanish Am war, posted in office windows, 1899....15.00
Political, Alf M Landon photo, From Typical Prairie St, KS.....45.00
Political, Deserters Not Entitled to Vote, J Cessna, 1865.......50.00
Political, Garfield & Arthur, PA meeting, 1880, 19x24".........55.00
Political, Geo B McClellan, Liberty keeps Gen from Wht House..60.00
Political, How Shall the Soldiers Vote, 1864.................35.00
Political, John Tyler, Pres Tyler's Address to...US, 15".......260.00
Public sale, dtd 1864, 16x20"...........................25.00

Tumbler, Coronation of King George VI and Queen Elizabeth; Myott, Staffordshire, 4¼", $32.00.

Bronzes

Thomas Ball, George Bessell, and Leonard Volk were some of the earliest American sculptors who produced figures in bronze for home decor during the 1840s. Pieces of historical significance were the most popular, but by the 1880s a more fanciful type of artwork took hold. Some of the fine sculptors of the day were Daniel Chester French, Augustus St. Gaudens and John Quincy Adams Ward.

Bronzes enjoyed the height of their popularity at the turn of the century. The American West was portrayed to its fullest by Remington, Russell, James Frazier, Hermon MacNeil, and Solon Borglum. Animals of every specie were modeled by A.P. Proctor, Paul Bartlett, and Albert Laessele, to name but a few.

Art Nouveau and Art Deco influenced the medium during the twenties, evidenced by the works of Allen Clark, Harriet Freshmuth, E.F. Sanford and Bessie P. Vonnoh.

Be aware that recasts abound, and while often esthetically satisfactory, they are not original and should be priced accordingly. In much the same manner as prints are evaluated, the original castings made under the direction of the artist are the most valuable. Later castings from the original mold are worth less. A recast is not made from the original mold. Instead, a rubber like substance is applied to the bronze, peeled away, and filled with wax. Then, using the same 'lost wax' procedure as the artist uses on completion of his original wax model, a clay like substance is formed around the wax figure and the whole fired to vitrify the clay. The wax of course melts away, hence the term 'lost wax'. Recast bronzes loose detail and are somewhat smaller than the original due to the shrinkage of the clay mold.

Female Water Carrrier, after Edouard Drouot, circa 1900, signed, 38½", $1,800.00.

Appeal to the Great Spirit, CH Humphriss, 29".........3,500.00
Arab, standing, w/falcon, Pilet, 15½".....................1,300.00
Arab on horseback, Barye, sgn, 27¾x33"...............3,500.00
Baccante in flowing robes w/2 putti, Mathurin Moreau, 19"...1,320.00
Ballerina, arm outstretched, after K Lorenzl, 11½"........440.00
Barbary stallion near fence, PJ Mene, 11½x16½"...........850.00
Battling Stags, elk in combat, PJ Mene, 11¼x24"........2,250.00
Boxer, allegorical, H Galdenbeck, Aktien-Gesellschaft, 19"....700.00
Buffalo, Bruno Zoick, 9½x16".............................750.00
Bull, I Bonheur, sgn, 19x22".............................1,800.00
Bull, PJ Mene, 2½x4"....................................495.00
Bust, Athena, after Villanis, Societe Des Bronzes, 26".......935.00
Bust, Indian Brave, Max Bachmann, 22½"................1,150.00
Bust, lady in lg plumed hat, Ernest Rancoulet, 26".........850.00
Bust, maiden, 'Capture' Villanis, 24½"..................1,320.00
Bust, woman emperor, Flemish, early 1600s, 6½"...........550.00
Bust, woman: Lalou, after Finn-Haekon Frolich, 1899, 25"...1,100.00
Bust, 2 lovers, H Vohburge, 5"...........................275.00
Centaur and a god w/bow & arrow, A Barye, 17x19".......2,700.00
Ceres, w/cornucopia, F Rhigetti F Romae, 1791, 9¾".......935.00
Cheval De Marly, horse & trainer, after Coustou, 22½"......550.00
Clodin, after Claude-Michael, late 1800s, 24".............1,210.00
Comedy, after V Rousseau, 22"...........................935.00
Cupid, running, drawing bow, Elias de Witte, 1600s, 4¼"...1,650.00
Dancer, ivory head/arms/legs, Barthelemy, France, 9½"....1,650.00
Dancer, mk Deronno, marble socle (losses), nude, 20".......250.00
Dancer, Starlight, after Chiparus, parcel silver/ivory, 23"....4,950.00
Dancing Neapolitan Boy, after F Duret, Delafontaine, 38"...4,400.00
Dantas, Indian bust, Fonderia Sommez Napoli, on gr marble...795.00
Diana, after Bruno Zach, attended by hound, 1925, 14".......990.00
Diana, after Luca Madrassie, attended by hound, 27".......1,800.00
Diana, after Mathurin Moreau, red marble plinth, 25".......990.00
Dog, seated, foundry pattern, wht/red/blk worn pnt, 5½".....65.00
Dogs, three; PJ Mene, 7½x14¼"........................1,000.00
Duke Lorenzo, after Michaelangelo, seated warrior, 12".....550.00
Elk, PJ Mene, 14½x28"..................................900.00
Equestrian struggle, knights/steeds, French, late 1800s, 13" L..550.00
Eros, after Laurent, kneeling w/butterfly, 17"...........2,860.00
Fallen Sparrow, Commalera, sgn, French foundry mk, 2x4"....450.00
Female, classical style, partial drape, in chair w/book, 9½"....950.00
Female, seated allegorical, holds sm lamp, Richard, 10"......400.00
Female, standing, pins hair/holds mirror, Guilbert, 30".....1,400.00
Female fencer, after Fritz Preiss, parcel ivory, 7".........880.00
Fisherboy by pond, inscribed Joliveaux, 20"..............715.00
Franz Josef of Austria, standing figure, gilt bronze, 15".....825.00
Horse, elaborate bridle/tasseled blinders, Gechter, 17" L.....1,320.00
Horse, trotting; PJ Mene, 11¼x14½".....................1,300.00
Horse & hound, greeting playfully, P Lenordez, 10½" L.....880.00
How-Kola cowboy, Carl Kuba, 20½x16½"................2,750.00
Huntsman on horseback, 2 dogs, after PJ Mene, 30" L.....13,750.00
Indian Chief, standing, Carl Kauba, 1900, polychrome, 26"...6,000.00
Japanese warrior, standing, 14½".........................850.00
Japanese warrior on horseback, Oriental, 12¾x15".........1,500.00
Kaiser Karl of Austria, standing, 10"....................275.00
Kaiser Wilhelm II, standing, Gladenbeck & Sohn Berlin, 28"...935.00
Kitchen scene, Austrian, cold pnt, Franz Bergman mk, 6".....660.00
L'Amour, after Chaudet, youth w/butterfly, 19x23".........2,750.00
L'Ideal, nude stands facing garden wall, Picault, 41".......3,190.00
Les Amis De Toujours, after Chiparus, ivory/polychrome, 11".3,300.00
Lion, A Barye, 9¾x18½"................................1,300.00
Lion, recumbent; after Barye, F Barbedienne Fondeur, 13"....550.00
Macaw snatching at insect on limb below, Paurot, 14".......1,100.00
Male, w/staff, seated, Jean Bulio, dtd 1860, A Vetu, 28".....1,500.00
Mexican ranchero on rearing horse, Carl Kuba, 7½".........500.00

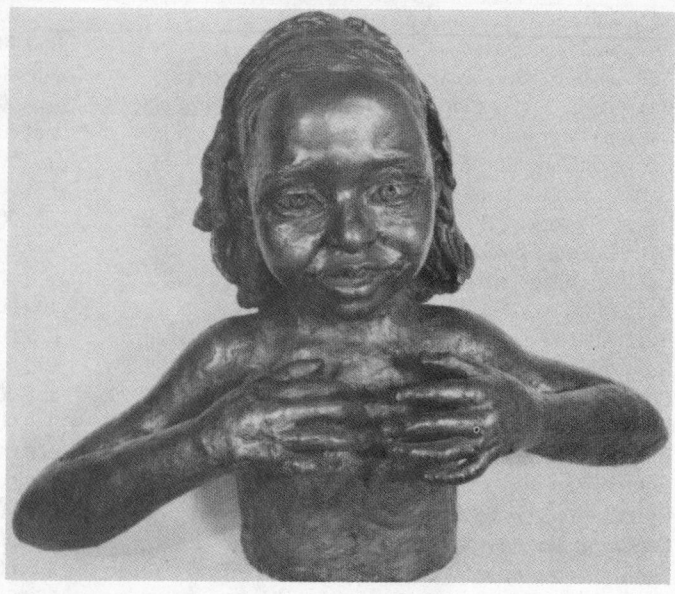

Young Girl at Puberty, Jacob Ebstein, #1 of 6, 16″, $5,000.00.

Moroccan Falconer, PJ Mene, 25″ 2,000.00
Napoleon on horseback, inscribed E Fremiet, 13″ 1,430.00
Nude, drapery on left arm, w/mask, Stundl, Austria, 19″ 990.00
Nude, shielding face w/Xd arms, after Mario Korbel, 9½″ 350.00
Nude, standing, classical, Etinne M Falconet, dtd 1757, 23″ . .1,300.00
Nude, standing female, ivy wreath, outstretched arms, 21″ 1,100.00
Nude, w/marceled hair, reaching out to child, Bouraine, 22″ . . .770.00
Nude male, standing w/sword, Louis Gossin, 33½″ 1,200.00
Pan w/pipes, after Delesalle, 13½″ 1,200.00
Panther, reclining, after Barye, F Barbedienne Fondeur, 7½″ . .400.00
Passage De Gue, Par Levasseur (Hors Concours), 29″ 1,210.00
Pastorale Watteau, standing female w/lute, A Gaudez, 27″ 1,750.00
Pax, after Antoine Bofill, olive branch/plowshare/helmet, 39″ . .1,980.00
Peasant couple, parcel gilt, she w/harvest; he w/staff, 14″ 800.00
Plough & the Sword, standing male, E Boisseau, 24½″ 750.00
Psyche, after M Moureau, seated on rocks, swivel base, 21″ . .1,100.00
Rabbit, sign Route de la Casserole, inscribed Cain, 3¾″ 385.00
Roman warrior, standing, E Picalut, 20″ 900.00
Roman warrior on horseback, E Picault, 20″ 1,600.00
Russian figure, standing, Alexandrovitch, 18″ 900.00
Satyr w/youth on his shoulders offering grapes, French, 12″ 440.00
Serenade, E Picault, standing troubador w/lute, 29″ 2,500.00
Shepherd in cloak w/staff & hound, Geo Omerth, gilt/ivory, 11″ .635.00
Shepherdess w/lamb, Geo Omerth, (losses), gilt/ivory, 11″ 495.00
Signing of the Magna Carta, Devaulx, 16¾x20″ 1,900.00
Soldier w/musket, Picault, 29½″ .2,300.00
Spirit of Spring, Moreau Math, 32″ 4,950.00
Stag against tree, PJ Mene, 13½x14½″ 800.00
The Two Furrows, after Emile-Louis Picault, 38″ 2,310.00
Three figures in grape harvest, after Clodion, 19¼″ 1,100.00
Two clam pickers, after Debut, 41½″ 2,530.00
Two lovers, Gautherin, mk Thiebaut Freres Fouderu, 32″ 2,200.00
Two monkeys preening, Sandoz, Cire/CV Alsuani/Perdue, 13″ .1,100.00
Urn, lg bird in tree & fox relief, E Sanglan #9879, 14″ 425.00
Valkyrie, after L Chalon, on rearing horse, 30″ 2,640.00
Venus De Milo, Barbedienne foundry mk, 1880, 28″ 950.00

Brownies by Palmer Cox

Created by Palmer Cox in 1883, the Brownies charmed children through the pages of books and magazines, as dolls, on their dinnerware, in advertising material, and on souvenirs. Each had his own personality -- among them The Bellhop, The London Boby, The Chairman, and Uncle Sam -- but the oversized triangular face with the startled expression, the protruding tummy, and the spindle legs were characteristics of them all.

They were inspired by the Scottish legends related to Cox as a child by his parents, who were of English descent. His introduction of the Brownies to the world was accomplished by a poem called *The Brownies Ride.* Books followed in rapid succession -- thirteen in the series, all written as well as illustrated by Palmer Cox.

By the late 1890s, the Brownies were active in advertising. They promoted such products as games, coffee, toys, patent medicines, and rubber boots. 'Greenies' were the Brownies first cousins, created by Cox to charm and to woo through the pages of the advertising almanacs of the G.G. Green Company of New Jersey. Perhaps the best known endorsement in the Brownie's career was for the Kodak Brownie, which became so popular and sold in such volume that their name became synonomous with this type of camera.

Book, Another Brownie Book, 1890, sm spine chip 22.00
Book, Brownies, Their Book 45.00
Book, Brownies & Prince Florimel, 1918, 1st edition 45.00
Book, Brownies & The Farmer, 1902, G 18.00
Book, Brownies at Home, 1893 . . . . .55.00
Book, Brownies through the Union, VG 37.50
Book, Queer People, Donohue 28.00
Book, Queerier Queers 25.00
Creamer, Brownie decor, no mk, 4½″ 65.00
Cup & saucer, various scenes, Cook & Hancock 100.00
Decalcomania Album #4, 9 pgs decals, NM 35.00
Desk seal, hollow head of Brownie, silver w/ruby eyes 175.00
Doll, cloth, handmade, early 1900s .65.00
Doll, composition, cotton jacket & pants, 32″ 1,250.00
Doll, Sailor, compo, 8½″ 175.00
Doll, Soldier, paper on wood, in wood base, 1892, 12″ 35.00
Fork, child's; w/Brownie 15.00
Game, Alphabet, w/Brownies, Parker Bros, 1893 . . . . .115.00
Game, Jack Straw, Parker Bros, depicts Brownies 12.00
Game, Lotto, w/Brownies on box cover 25.00
Ladies' Home Journal page w/Brownies 10.00
Napkin ring, silverplate 50.00
Napkin ring, w/enamel Brownies 125.00
Paint book, Whitman #669-10, c 1949 . . . . .25.00
Plate, Brownies decor, porcelain, 7″ 28.50
Plate, Brownies w/in scalloped rim, pr in center, Limoges, 8″ 85.00
Plate, 2 Brownies & billy goat, Staffordshire 28.00
Print, litho of all Brownies, in fr 50.00
Ruler, w/Brownies, Mrs Winslow's soothing syrup, +syrup bottle .35.00
Shakers, w/Brownie decor, Mt Washington, 2¾″ 350.00
Spoon, demitasse; enameled Brownie 29.00
Stamps, rubber, w/various Brownies, set of 12 . . . . .85.00
Stickpin, w/Brownie 34.00
Thimble holder, Brownie on rectangular base, SP 45.00
Toy, papier mache/compo nodding head figure, Germany, 5½″ . .40.00
Toy, tin suitcase 'Teenie Weenie', dtd 1922, Brownie decor 35.00
Watch fob, figural Brownie, sterling .95.00

Brush

George Brush began his career in the pottery industry in 1901, working for the J.B. Owens Pottery Co. in Zanesville, Ohio. He left the company in 1907 to go into business for himself, only to have fire completely destroy his pottery less than one year after it was founded.

Brush became associated with J.W. McCoy in 1909, and for many years served in capacities ranging from General Manager to President. (From 1911 until 1925, the firm was known as The Brush-McCoy Pottery Co; see that section for information.) After McCoy died, the family withdrew their interests, and in 1925 the name of the firm was changed to The Brush Pottery.

The era of hand decorated art pottery had passed for the most part, and would soon be completely replaced by the production of commercial lines. Of all the wares bearing the later Brush script mark, their figural cookie jars are the most collectible.

See also Brush-McCoy

Cookie Jars

Antique Touring Car	37.50
Boy w/Balloons	25.00
Chick in Nest	35.00
Cinderella Pumpkin	42.00
Circus Horse	42.00
Clown, w/yellow pants	45.00
Clown Head	25.00
Cookie House	30.00
Covered Wagon	35.00
Cow, w/cat on back	40.00
Davey Crockett	60.00
Dog w/Basket	35.00
Donkey & Cart	38.00
Elephant, w/monkey on back	80.00
Elephant in Baby Bonnet	55.00
Fish	32.00
Formal Pig	50.00
Granny	32.00
Happy Bunny, wht w/pastels	48.00
Hen on Basket	32.00
Hill Billy Frog	100.00
Hobby Horse	40.00

Clown, yellow shirt, brown pants, and green bow, 12″, $50.00.

Humpty Dumpty, w/beanie & bow tie	50.00
Humpty Dumpty, w/peaked hat	45.00
Laughing Hippo	45.00
Little Angel	35.00
Little Boy Blue	60.00
Little Girl	35.00
Nite Owl	40.00

Old Clock	32.00
Old Shoe	32.00
Peter Pan	40.00
Pumpkin	45.00
Puppy Police	35.00
Raggedy Ann	35.00
Red Riding Hood	40.00
Sitting Hippo	45.00
Sitting Pig	35.00
Smiling Bear	35.00
Squirrel in Top Hat	50.00
Squirrel on Log	32.00
Stylized Owl	38.00
Stylized Siamese	38.00
Teddy Bear, feet apart	40.00
Teddy Bear, feet together	35.00
Treasure Chest	27.00

Miscellaneous

Bowl, Bittersweet, 4½x8″	12.00
Bowl, Bronze Line, ftd, free form open work top, 4½x9½″	9.00
Cornucopia, Bittersweet, 4″	7.50
Planter, bird, #246, USA	6.00
Planter, house, gr glaze, #887, USA	12.00

Vase, Vestal line, brown and yellow with lady's head medallions, 8¼″, $45.00.

Planter, turtle, #205, USA	4.00
Vase, Deco styling, #579, 6″	4.00
Vase, Oriental pagoda, #225, 7½″	6.50
Vase, Princess, w/hdls, 12″	10.00
Wall pocket, horse, blk/wht	17.50
Wall pocket, Western horse	20.00

Brush McCoy

The Brush-McCoy Pottery was formed in 1911 in Zanesville, Ohio, an alliance between George Brush and J.W. McCoy. Brush's original pottery had been destroyed by fire in 1907; McCoy had operated his own business there since 1899.

After the merger, the company expanded and produced not only their staple commercial wares, but also fine art ware. Lines such as Navarre, Venetian, Persian, Oriental, and Sylvan were of a fine quality equal to that of their larger competitors. Because very little of the ware was marked, it is often mistaken for Weller, Roseville, or Peters and Reed.

In the twenties, after a fire in Zanesville had destroyed the manufacturing portion of that plant, all production was contained in their Roseville (Ohio) plant #2. A stoneware type of clay was used there, and as a result, the artware lines of Jewell, Zuni-Art, King Tut, Florastone, and Panel-Art are so distinctive that they are more easily recognizable. Examples of these lines are unique and very beautiful -- also quite rare and highly prized!

The Brush-McCoy Pottery operated under that name until after J.W. McCoy's death, when it became the Brush Pottery. The Brush-Barnett family retained their interest in the pottery until 1981, when it was purchased by the Dearborn Company.

See also Brush

Florastone, bowl, #55, straight sides, 2½x4½" 45.00
Florastone, jardiniere, 7" 65.00
Florastone, vase, #007, full body, 6" 65.00
Jar, cereal, grapes on trellis 75.00
Jetwood, bowl, #01, 2½x7½" 55.00
Jetwood, candlestick, #30, 7", pr 140.00
Jetwood, candlestick, #32, 10¼", pr .165.00
Jetwood, vase, 10½x4¼" 225.00
Jewell, bud vase, 10" 55.00
Jewell, vase, #052 . . . . .45.00

Onyx jug, music box in base, brown glaze, teardrop form, 10", $50.00.

Krakle-Kraft, vase, w/dragon motif, 8" 140.00
Krakle-Kraft, vase, 8" 50.00
Majolica, jardiniere, br w/blue amaryllis, 8" 70.00
Majolica, vase, gr w/rose amaryllis, 4½" 12.50
Moderne, vase, #0159, blue 20.00
Moderne KolorKraft, jardiniere, Deco style, cobalt, 10" 30.00
Navarre, bowl, lady w/flowing hair, 4½x8" 200.00
Navarre, vase, narrow w/flaring body, ½ circle hdls, 9" 250.00
Navarre, vase, 7" 115.00
Onyx, bottle, teardrop, w/hdl, gr, 10" .50.00
Onyx, candlestick, dk br, 10½", pr 65.00

Onyx, jardiniere, arches alternate w/sq devices, bl/gr, 8½" 30.00
Onyx, Jug Time clock, br, 7" 65.00
Onyx, vase, br, 4" 15.00
Onyx, vase, wide body, disc hdls, br, 6x9" 30.00
Pompeian, vase, modeled floral, gr inlay, #171, 6x4¾" 40.00
Sylvan, vase, bulbous top, gr glaze, 10" 35.00
Vase, bluebirds, stylized trees, cylinder, semi-matt, 13" 100.00
Vase, stick w/wide base, 2x2¼" 140.00
Vestal, vase, bl/wht w/draped lady, 10½" 35.00
Zuniart, bottle base w/flared rim, 8¾" 60.00
Zuniart, bowl, 2x7" 45.00
Zuniart, candlestick, #32, 10", pr 135.00
Zuniart, jardiniere, #240, 9" 150.00
Zuniart, vase, 10x5" 135.00

Buffalo Pottery

The founding of the Buffalo Pottery in Buffalo, New York in 1901, was a direct result of the success achieved by John Larkin through his innovative methods of marketing 'Sweet Home Soap'. Choosing to omit 'middle-man' profits, Larkin preferred to deal directly with the consumer, and offered premiums as an enticement for sales. The pottery soon proved a success in its own right and began producing advertising and commemorative items for other companies, as well as commercial tableware.

In 1905, they introduced their Blue Willow line, after extensive experimentation resulted in the development of the first successful underglaze cobalt achieved by an American company.

Between 1905 and 1909, a line of pitchers and jugs were hand decorated in historical, literary, floral, and outdoor themes. Twenty-nine styles are known to have been made. These have been found in a wide array of color variations.

Their most famous line was Deldare Ware, the bulk of which was made from 1908 to 1909. It was hand decorated after illustrations by Cecil Aldin. Views of English life were portrayed in detail through unusual use of color against the natural olive green cast of the body. Today, the 'Fallowfield Hunt' scenes are more difficult to locate than 'Scenes of Village Life in Olden Days'. A Deldare calendar plate was made in 1910. These are very rare and are valued highly by collectors. The line was revived in 1923 and dropped again in 1925. Every piece was marked 'Made at Ye Buffalo Pottery -- Deldare Ware Underglaze'. Most are dated, though date has no bearing on the value.

Emerald Deldare, made with the same olive body and on standard Deldare Ware shapes, featured historical scenes and Art Nouveau decorations. Most pieces are found with a 1911 date stamp. Production was very limited due to the intricate, time consuming detail. Needless to say, it is very rare and extremely desirable.

Abino Ware, most of which was made in 1912, also used standard Deldare shapes, but its colors were earthy and the decorations more delicately applied. Sailboats, windmills, and country scenes were favored motifs. These designs were achieved by overpainting transfer prints, and were often signed by the artist. The ware is marked 'Abino' in hand printed block lettering. Production was limited, and as a result, examples of this line are scarce today. Prices only slightly trail those of Emerald Deldare Ware.

The many uncatalogued items that have been found over the years indicate that Buffalo Pottery decorators were free to use their own ideas and talents to create many beautiful one-of-a-kind pieces.

Deldare

Bowl, cereal; Ye Olden Days, 6½" 225.00
Bowl, nut; Ye Lion Inn, sgn A Wade, 1909, 3¾" H 425.00
Bowl, Ye Village Tavern, sgn L Striessel, 1908, 3¾x9" 385.00
Creamer, Breaking Cover, sgn Gerhardt, 1908, 2¾" 225.00
Creamer, Scenes of Village Life 150.00

Emerald Deldare tray, 'Dr. Syntax Mistakes a Gentleman's House for an Inn', 13¾″ x 10¼″, $1,950.00.

Creamer & sugar, Scenes of Village Life, sgn	350.00
Cup & saucer, Ye Olden Days, sgn E Harker	200.00
Humidor, Ye Lion Inn, 1924, NM	650.00
Match holder, Fallowfield Hunt, artist sgn, 3½x6½″	425.00
Mug, Breakfast at the Three Pigeons, 4½″	325.00
Mug, Fallowfield Hunt, Breaking Cover, 4½″	325.00
Mug, Fallowfield Hunt, sgn A Wade, 1908, 2¼″	400.00
Mug, Ye Lion Inn, sgn W Foster, 1909, 4½″	275.00
Mug, Ye Lion Inn, 3¾″	275.00
Pin tray, Olden Days	275.00
Pitcher, milk; Fallowfield Hunt, sgn Striessel, 6″	475.00
Pitcher, Old English Village, octagonal, 10″	550.00
Pitcher, tankard; Emerald, To Becky's Hand He Gave..., 12″	950.00
Pitcher, tankard; The Great Controversy, 1908	800.00
Plate, chop; An Evening At Ye Lion Inn, 14″	435.00
Plate, chop; Emerald, Dr Syntax Sells Grizzle, 13½″	1,350.00
Plate, Emerald, Dr Syntax Loses His Way, 9¼″	750.00
Plate, Emerald, Dr Syntax Loses His Wig, 9¼″	750.00
Plate, Emerald, Introduction to Courtship, 9¼″	750.00
Plate, Emerald, Misfortune At Tulip Hall, sgn Stuart, 8½″	425.00
Plate, Emerald, The Garden Trio, 9¼″	900.00
Plate, Fallowfield Hunt, Breaking Cover, 10″	185.00
Plate, Fallowfield Hunt, The Start, sgn Delaney, 9¼″	150.00
Plate, Fallowfield Hunt, To The Death, Delaney, 8½″	145.00
Plate, Ye Olden Times, 9½″	145.00
Plate, Ye Town Crier, A Wade, 8½″	120.00
Plate, Ye Village Gossips, 1909, 10″	185.00
Powder jar, Ye Village Street, w/lid	325.00
Saucer, Ye Olden Days, sgn L Newman, 1908, 6″	75.00
Soup plate, Breaking Cover, 9″	250.00
Soup plate, Village Street, 9″	200.00
Sugar, Scenes of Village Life	150.00
Tea tile, Traveling In Ye Olden Days, sgn MHB, 6″ dia	225.00
Tray, card; Emerald, Dr Syntax Robbed of His Property	500.00
Tray, dresser; Dancing Ye Minuet, artist sgn, 9x12″	500.00
Tray, Heirloom, 13½″ L	550.00
Tray, relish; Ye Olden Times, artist sgn, oval, 12″	350.00
Vase, village scene, no title, sgn GHS, 1925, 7″	300.00

Miscellaneous

Child's dish, Campbell Kids, boy & girl w/doll, sgn, 7¾″	60.00
Game set, sgn RH Beck, 7 pcs	250.00

Mug, Saturn Night the Buffalo Club, 1911	35.00
Pitcher, Cinderella, sgn, NM	375.00
Pitcher, Gloriana, bl/wht	450.00
Pitcher, John Paul Jones	475.00
Pitcher, Pilgrim	550.00
Pitcher, Rip Van Winkle	475.00
Pitcher, Sailor	495.00
Pitcher, souvenir of New Bedford, w/various views, 1907, 6″	475.00
Plate, Christmas, 1954	45.00
Plate, Christmas, 1955	45.00
Plate, Christmas, 1958	40.00
Plate, Faneuil Hall, 10″	35.00
Plate, souvenir; Wanamakers Store, 1911, 4½″	100.00
Plate, Wild Ducks, 1907, 9½″	45.00
Platter, Deer at Stream	75.00
Platter, fish decor, sgn Beck, lg	75.00

Pitcher, John Alden and Priscilla, 1908, 9″, $750.00.

Burmese

Burmese glass is opaque, in soft shades of yellow shading to pink. It was patented in 1885 by Frederick Shirley of the Mt. Washington Glass Co. The formula he developed contained gold which reacted with the fire to produce the delicate pink blush. It was made in both a glossy and satin finish. Some pieces were decorated by hand or gilded.

Similar glass was later produced by Webb in England; it was reissued by Gunderson-Pairpoint, and again in 1978 by Bryden at the Sagamore Pairpoint factory.

Basket, ruffled crimp leaf rim, bark hdl, Gunderson, 7½″	295.00
Bowl, crimped, floral enamel, Webb's Queen's Ware, 2½x4½″	550.00
Bowl, crimped/ruffled, Gunderson, 2¼x7½″	150.00
Bowl, tightly crimped rim, refired yellow edge, acid, 4½″	210.00
Condiment set, ribbed, acid finish, 3 pc in Pairpoint holder	1,400.00
Creamer, glossy, reed hdl, sm	125.00
Creamer, satin finish, Mt Washington, 3½″	240.00
Fairy lamp, Clarke clear cup, ruffled sgn Webb top, 6¾″ dia	595.00
Fairy lamp, 5 part, ruffled, mk Clarke, 24″	1,900.00
Hat, glossy, 2″	85.00
Mug, shell hdl, floral raised base, Gunderson, 4½″	180.00
Pitcher, fern arbor w/dedication monogram/1886, strap hdl, 9″	800.00
Pitcher, hobnail, smooth at top, satin, dtd/Mt Washington, 10″	950.00
Plate, acid finish, Mt Washington, 12″	250.00
Plate, acid finish, pansies decor, Mt Washington, 8″	550.00

Rose bowl, acid, mc floral/buds on branch, Webb's Queen's, 4"..475.00
Rose bowl, gold hdls & ptd ivy, verse by Dickens..........1,685.00
Rose bowl, 8 crimp top, orange berries, unsgn Webb, 2½x2¾"..325.00
Salt shaker, ribbed, satin, Mt Washington, 4".............250.00
Set, 2 cruets/2 shakers, shiny/ribbed, in SP Pairpoint holder..1,850.00
Toothpick, bulge bottom, sq top, satin, Mt Washington, 2¾"...200.00
Toothpick, dainty florals, fig shape......................550.00
Toothpick, sq top, acid finish, 2½x2½"....................150.00
Tumbler, Diamond Quilted..................................285.00
Tumbler, Gunderson, 5"...................................125.00

Condiment set, ribbed, acid finish, 4 pieces in silverplated holder signed Rogers, $1,750.00.

Vase, allover swirls of millefiori/scrolls, 11¾"..........1,500.00
Vase, ball form, incurvate fluted rim, enamel ivy, Webb, 2½"...165.00
Vase, ball shape/flared & ruffled, acid, unsgn Webb, 3x3"....195.00
Vase, bulb/stick neck, decor/matt, sgn Webb, 10x5½".......1,195.00
Vase, bulb/stick neck, EX color, Webb, 12x5½".............1,400.00
Vase, bulb/stick neck/swirled panels: millefiori/scroll, 12"...1,500.00
Vase, convex sides, gr leaves/red buds, acid, Webb, 4½".....345.00
Vase, daisies/butterfly/verse, stick neck, Mt Washington, 12"..2,000.00
Vase, fish/seaweed/gold fishnet decor, acid finish, 9½".....3,000.00
Vase, flared/ruffled, floral, Queen's Ware, acid, Webb, 4x2½...225.00
Vase, folded petal top, gold vines/berries, Webb's Queen's, 4"..550.00
Vase, pear shape w/stick neck, Mt Washington, 12½".........950.00
Vase, ped ft, gold leaves/berries, Queen's Ware, Webb, 4x2½".325.00
Vase, ped ft, ruffled top & base, unsgn Webb, 4½x2¾".......200.00
Vase, petal top, gr leaves/red berries, acid, Webb, 3½x3"...325.00
Vase, ptd floral decor, applied lemon hdls, 5"............795.00
Vase, ribbed w/flared top, satin finish, 4"...............150.00
Vase, rnd/fluted/flared ruffled collar, decorated, Webb, 3½"...350.00
Vase, ruffled, Webb's Queen's Brumese, satin finish, 3½"....375.00
Vase, scalloped, #59 in 1885 Mt Washington catalog, 6".....295.00
Vase, stick neck, enamel floral, Webb's Queen's Burmese, 7½".700.00
Vase, w/hdls, ribbon top, Gunderson, 6½x4"...............275.00
Vase, 5 scallops, good color, American, 3"................225.00

Butter Molds and Stamps

The art of decorating butter began in Europe during the reign of Charles II. This practice was continued in America by the farmer's wife who sold her homemade butter at the weekly market to earn extra money during hard times. A mold or stamp with a special design, hand carved either by her husband or a local craftsman, not only made her product more attractive, but helped identify it as hers. The pattern became the trademark of Mrs. Smith, and all who saw it knew that this was her butter, 'for butter or worse'. It was usually the rule that no two farms used the same mold within a certain area, thus the many variations and patterns available to the collector today.

The most valuable of the collectible molds are those which have animals, birds, or odd shapes. The most sought after motifs are the eagle, cow, fish, and rooster. These works of early folk art are quickly disappearing from the market.

Molds

Acorns & oak leaf, unfinished, late, 3¾" dia................30.00
Acorns & oak leaf, 4¼"....................................65.00
Cow, rectangular, hinged case, 5x6¾".....................125.00
Cow, rectangular, removable hinged fr, 6x9½".............295.00
Cow, 3¾"..185.00
Elm leaves, cluster of four, rnd..........................65.00
Flower, 4 petals, brass latches, 5½x6"....................25.00
Flower & leaves, primitive, 5" dia........................40.00

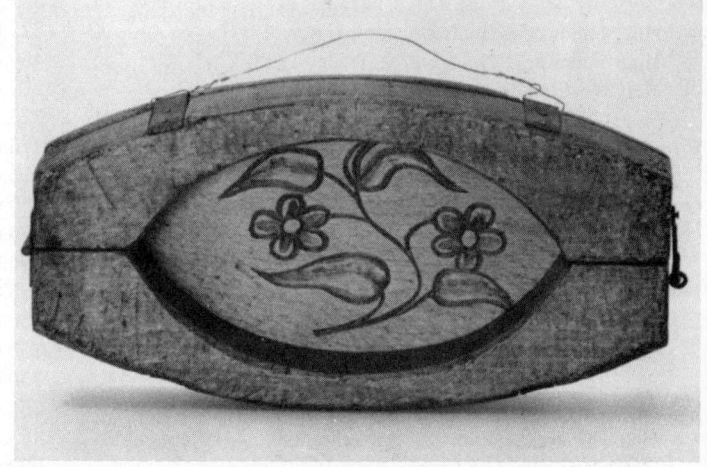

Butter mold with florals, 3 parts, hinged, 10" long, $140.00.

Hex sign, simple, rectangular mortised/pinned case, 5x8".....35.00
House design, 1 side on ea of 4 panels, minor crack, 5x4x3"...155.00
Leaf, in hexagonal stave constructed case w/pewter bands, 5x4"..30.00
Leaf, simple design, 4¼" sq...............................65.00
Miniature, simple flower, 1½" dia.........................15.00
Miniature, strawberry....................................65.00
Pineapple, 4½"...40.00
Scrolls/foliage/hearts/etc, 5 parts, pin held, 5x6x4".....345.00
Sheaf of wheat, rectangular, 4¼x7".......................110.00
Sheaf of wheat, 3½".......................................65.00
Sheaf of wheat & 2 leaves, cased, 4½" dia.................40.00
Stars, 4, chip carved, scrubbed finish, 5x9"..............75.00
Swan, simple, 4½"...45.00
Tulips, chip carved edge, trn hdl, 4" dia................205.00

Stamps

Acorn, 1 pc w/trn hdl, 3" dia.............................75.00
Bell shaped, ribbed sides, deer in base, 1 pc, 4½x5"......250.00

Christian lamb w/cross & banner, cracks, 3¼" dia........195.00
Compass stars, 4, primitive carving, paddle form, 3½x9"......240.00
Cow, hand carved, 1700s.................................250.00
Eagle, head right, EX carving, trn hdl, 4½", EX............625.00
Eagle, 3½"...195.00
Flower, deeply carved, stylized, trn hdl, minor wear, 4" dia.....45.00
Flowers, leaves & stars, stylized design, 4" dia.............125.00
Foliage, well carved, trn hdl, minor worm holes, 4" dia.......55.00
Geometric star, sq carved hdl w/Maltese cross, 4¾" dia.......115.00
Lollipop, compass star/rickrack edge, taper hdl w/heart, 10"....685.00
Paddle form, chip carving 3 surfaces/whittled hdl, 4½" L......65.00
Pineapple, deeply carved, semicircle, no hdl, 3¼x7"........175.00
Pineapple, simple carving, hdl missing, 3½" dia.............65.00
Pineapple, stylized, 1 pc w/trn hdl, age cracks, 4¾" dia.......85.00
Pinweel, 1¾" dia, 5" L.................................48.00
Plant w/3 leaves, 1 pc w/trn hdl, 3" dia..................45.00
Sheaf of wheat, EX carving, crimped, trn hdl, 4½" dia........85.00
Sheaf of wheat, threaded hdl, 3¾" dia...................20.00
Sheaf of wheat, w/air holes, oval, 5x3½".................125.00
Spade shape w/simple chip carved motif, worn pnt, 4½" L.....45.00
Star flower, screw in handle, 3½".......................35.00
Star flower, simple, trn hdl, 3¼" dia....................35.00
Sunflower flowerhead, 1 pc w/trn hdl, crack, 4" dia.........175.00
Thistle blossom, single, 1 pc w/trn hdl, 4"................45.00
Thistle blossoms, inserted trn hdl, 5" dia.................275.00
Tulip, deeply carved, stylized, carved hdl, 4½" dia..........225.00
Tulip, stylized, carved hdl, almond shaped, 4½x9"..........195.00
Tulip, stylized, G carving, 1 pc, trn hdl, 3½"..............175.00
Tulip & star flower, stylized, carved hdl, worm holes, 5½".....155.00

Buttonhooks

Buttonhooks were made from around the mid-1800s, when high button shoes made of stiff leather became fashionable, and continued to be used to some extent until 1935. They were made of bone, brass, iron, or silver -- simple utilitarian no-nonsense styles, fold-up styles with jeweled gold handles, combination styles with built-in gadgets -- all designed to ease the struggle of buttoning high top shoes, long kid gloves, and stiffly starched collars.

While most do have a hook end, some were made with a wire loop instead. Study the construction, since quality workmanship is an important worth-assessing factor, in addition to the more obvious elements of material and design.

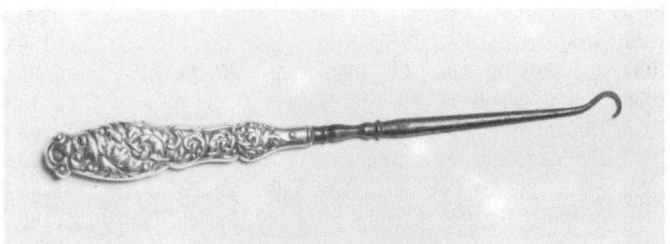

Art Nouveau relief decoration, sterling silver, 7½", $23.00.

Advertising, Spats.......................................5.00
Brass, handmade, 3¾"..................................22.00
FL George, Derry, NH, metal.............................10.00
Folding, shoe horn/hook combo, Physical Culture Shoes........8.00
Leg w/high button shoe, simulated ivory...................25.00
Mother of pearl, 4"......................................8.50
Simulated ivory w/dainty flowers, 5½"...................7.50
Tortoise hdl, 4¾"......................................9.00

C. D. Kenny

C.D. Kenny was determined to be a successful man, and he was. Between 1890 and 1934, he owned 75 groceries in 15 states. He accomplished this success in two ways: fair business dealings and premium give-aways. These ranged from trade cards and advertising mirrors to tin commemorative plates and kitchen items; there were banks and toys, clocks and tins. Today's collectors are finding hundreds of these items, all marked with Kenny's name.

Bank, stein, mustard yellow, 4"...........................45.00
Figurine, 3 cats in a hat, china...........................20.00
Jar, Norwood Coffee, 1 lb, orig tin lid, M..................20.00
Match holder, Black man's face & collar, majolica............75.00
Match holder, 3 cats in top hat...........................75.00
Pig bank, Austria.......................................90.00
Plate, tin, child in red coat holding muff, 9"...............75.00
Plate, tin, coffee ad, Holly Girl w/doll....................95.00
Stickpin, oval w/lady's portrait..........................40.00
Tip tray, America's Pride................................60.00
Tip tray, Chean Tea....................................65.00
Tip tray, raising Am flag at Valley Forge...................65.00
Toothpick, china, elephant...............................30.00
Toothpick, china, Oriental girl beside holder................30.00

Calendar Plates

Calendar plates were popular advertising give-aways most popular from about 1906 until the late twenties. They were decorated with colorful underglaze decals of lovely ladies and handsome men, flowers, animals, and birds -- and, of course, the 12 months of the year of their issue.

During the late thirties they came into vogue again, but never to the extent they were originally.

Those with exceptional detailing, or those with scenes of a particular activity are most desirable -- so are any from before 1906.

Sailing ships and windmills decorate this 1910 calendar plate, with advertising, 9", $25.00.

1906, flowers, months in panels, PA advertising, 9"...........37.50
1907, Santa Claus in sleigh, holly berries, 9¼"...............35.00
1908, roses decor..20.00
1908, Victorian lady driving auto, West End Pottery...........35.00
1909, cherries & white berries, 7½".........................30.00
1909, girl in bl dress, 10".................................35.00
1909, red breasted bird, scenes of seasons..................25.00
1910, carnations, McNicol...................................28.00
1910, floral scenes..20.00
1910, Gibson girl center, calendars around edge.............32.00
1910, girl w/horse...35.00
1911, Gibson girl decal....................................35.00
1911, open touring car, Buffalo............................35.00
1911, pk flowers, Hagerstown advertising, 7½"..............25.00
1911, pk flowers under calendar center, MD ad, 7½".........27.00
1912, balloons, advertising................................37.00
1912, bi-plane transfer, advertising.......................37.00
1912, football, basketball, etc, advertising...............45.00
1912, scenic, White River Tavern, Hartford, VT, 8¼"........32.00
1915, Black boy eating watermelon.........................125.00
1916, eagle w/shield, American flag........................29.00
1916, Indian maid bust.....................................30.00
1924, game birds & dog, Maine advertising..................32.00
1936, fishing boat scene, bl/wht...........................55.00

Calendars

Calendars are collected for their colorful prints, often attributed to a well recognized artist of the period. Advertising calendars from the turn of the century often have a double appeal when representing a company whose products are themselves collectible.

Chicago Rock Island and Pacific Railroad calendar, issued in 1888, in unused condition, $100.00.

1889, Hood's Sarsaparilla, EX but soiled....................25.00
1891, Hood's Sarsaparilla, no pad..........................12.00
1892, Hood's Sarsaparilla, center pad, 8 children, round, EX....12.00
1893, Hood's Sarsaparilla, boy/girl hugging, complete, sm, NM...18.00
1894, Hood's Sarsaparilla, lady w/hat, complete, NM........48.00
1897, Hood's Sarsaparilla, Coupon Calendar, girl w/hat, NM.....18.00
1900, Hood's Sarsaparilla, pad incomplete..................40.00
1903, Fairbanks Fairy.....................................125.00
1903, Hoods, corner wear, fold mk..........................25.00
1903, Maud Humphrey, Butterfly Time.......................100.00
1904, Blatz Brewery, Victorian girl drinking, 18x27".......175.00
1904, Metropolitan Life, perpetual desk calender, mc celluloid...25.00
1905, Howard Chandler Christy, girl in bl dress w/rose, 19½"..45.00
1905, Howard Chandler Christy, 3 month pg, Arbutus.........27.00
1906, Brown & Bigelow, George Washington...................15.00
1906, Wales Goodyear Rubber, American litho, EX............40.00
1907, advertising, boy/girl on barrel, puppies in harness...45.00
1907, Brilliant, King of Metal Polishes, Victorian lady........15.00
1909, DeLaval, in orig mailing tube, M....................375.00
1909, Dicken's, A Shuman, EX...............................25.00
1909, Peter's Brand, hunters, dog on point w/puppies, 14x27"..295.00
1909, Prudential Life Ins, Victorian lady in color.........15.00
1910, Wrigley Gum, 3 children & cat........................60.00
1911, Bradley Fertilizers, EX..............................20.00
1911, Hood's Sarsaparilla, complete........................45.00
1912, Frank Coe Fertilizers, Rus Bon Heur Horse Fair, EX.....15.00
1912, The Store, cardboard die-cut girl w/dog & flowers, 21"....95.00
1913, Dodge Publishing, art calender, MIB..................25.00
1915, Dodge Publishing, Friendship Calender, MIB...........25.00
1915, Hercules Powder Co, ducks flying, mounted, 16½x32½".250.00
1917, Chero Cola, brunette w/bottle, wood fr, 36x20".......295.00
1917, Hood's Sarsaparilla, complete........................45.00
1917, Peter's Brand, hunting dogs in field, 28x14".........275.00
1920, Edison Mazda, M Parrish, small, complete pad, EX.....245.00
1922, Edison Mazda, M Parrish, cropped, w/frame............145.00
1922, Savage Stevens, mountain goat on mountain, 14x28"....245.00
1923, Peter's Brand, hunter/dog discover porcupine, 30x15"...275.00
1924, Remington, old hunter paints decoys, fr, 21x33".......850.00
1925, Peter's Brand, mallards fly over marsh, 30x15".......395.00
1928, RA Fox, Good Ship Adventure, 46x26"..................85.00
1929, Boy Scout, Norman Rockwell, Brown & Bigelow, 16x33"..50.00
1929, Calendar of Cheer, Parrish, ribbon tied, clowns/lanterns...70.00
1930, Color Symphonies, Milton Bradley, incomplete.........45.00
1930, Edison Mazda, Maxfield Parrish, w/fr, 10x20".........260.00
1932, DeLaval, 6 beautiful pictures, 9x15", M..............35.00
1933, Winchester, western.................................295.00
1937, Brown & Bigelow, Twilight, lg.......................150.00
1937, Travelers Insurance Co, John Rogers groups, EX........25.00
1938, Dionne Quints.......................................18.00
1938, Dupont Ammunition...................................65.00
1939, Dionne Quints, M in wrapper..........................20.00
1939, Penn RR, Art Deco style, Grif Teller, 29x29".........55.00
1940, Brown & Bigelow, Evening Shadows, Maxfield Parrish, lg.180.00
1941, Esquire, Vargas, EX.................................100.00
1941, Hudson's Bay Co, frontiersman, 18x30", M.............15.00
1942, Brown & Bigelow, Silent Night, Maxfield Parrish, med...125.00
1943, Brown & Bigelow, Perfect Day, Maxfield Parrish, 22x48".325.00
1944, Brown & Bigelow, Eventide, med......................100.00
1946, Brown & Bigelow, Valley of Enchantment, M Parrish, med.70.00
1948, Brown & Bigelow, Christmas Morning, M Parrish.......100.00
1948, Esquire, w/orig envelope.............................18.00
1951, Brown & Bigelow, Twilight Hour, Maxfield Parrish......100.00
1953, Brown & Bigelow, Peaceful Night, Maxfield Parrish, lg...100.00
1953, Ford Motor Co 50th Anniversary, 7 Rockwells..........49.00

1953, Poll Parrot shoes, advertising. 9.00
1956, Brown & Bigelow, Misty Morn, Maxfield Parrish, lg. 125.00
1958, Brown & Bigelow, Sunlight, Maxfield Parrish, med. 100.00
1958, Playboy w/cover. 75.00
1962, Rouge-Topper. 10.00
1963, Brown & Bigelow, Peaceful Country, M Parrish, lg. 75.00

California Faience

In 1916, Chauncey R. Thomas and William Victor Bragdon formed an association in Berkley, which by 1924 they called the California Faience Company. They produced simple art ware for the tourist trade, primarily from red clay with a monochromatic matt glaze, although occasionally a piece may be found with a glossy finish. They also made decorative tile, hand pressed into molds designed to create an intaglio effect. The depressions were filled in with colors while the ridges between were left unglazed.

Never a large company, two kilns were used and only a few workers were ever employed. Except for some tile made for the 1932 Chicago World's Fair, production stopped at the onset of the Depression.

The art ware was marked with the incised company name, the tiles with an ink stamp.

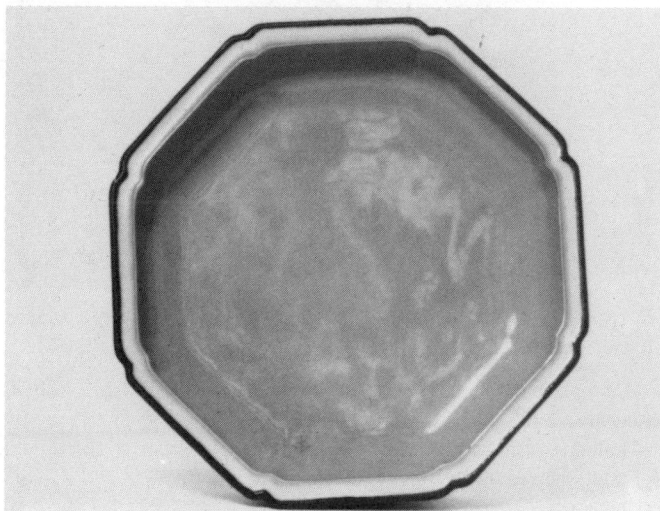

Bowl, black with aqua interior, 11½", $125.00.

Bowl, incurvate rim, dk bl, sm inside chip, 3½x10", VG. 50.00
Bowl, scalloped, dk glossy bl w/lighter bl interior, mk, 2x6". 90.00
Bowl, twin duck flower frog, blue gloss. 250.00
Candlestick, lg base, bl/purple high glaze, 7" pr. 200.00
Console bowl, w/candlesticks, maroon & blk. 175.00
Tile, Mission Bldg, 7 colors, 5½" dia. 300.00
Tile, ship, 5½". 350.00
Vase, bl/gr high glaze, 4½". 80.00
Vase, bl/turq gloss, 6½". 150.00
Vase, blue high gloss, 3¾". 75.00
Vase, rose, 5x3½". 110.00

California Perfume Company

D.H. McConnell, Sr., founded the California Perfume Company (C.P. Company; C.P.C) in 1886, in New York City. He had previously been a salesman for a book company, which he later purchased. His door-to-door sales usually involved the lady of the house, to whom he presented a complimentary bottle of inexpensive perfume. Upon determining his perfume to be more popular than his books, he decided that the manufacture of perfume might be more lucrative. He bottled toiletries under the name 'California Perfume Company', and a line of household products called 'Perfection' until 1929, when 'Avon Products, Inc.' appeared on the label. In 1939, the C.P.C. name was entirely removed from the product.

The success of the company is attributed to the door-to-door sales approach and 'money back' guarantee offered by his first 'Depot Agent', Mrs. P.F.E. Albee, known today as the 'Avon Lady'.

The company's containers are quite collectible today, especially the older, hard-to-find items. There are hundreds of local clubs throughout the world that are supported by the National Association of Avon Collectors Organization and the Western World Avon Collectors Clubs. Those wishing to join may contact Dick Pardini, listed in the Directory under California.

American Ideal Perfume, 'Introductory Size', in wood box, M. . .225.00
Ariel Toilet Water, 2 oz, 1930-1935, M. 100.00
Baby Set, 3 piece in box, 1923, M. .175.00
Bandoline Hair Dressing, 1923, M. 60.00
Bay Rum, 4 oz, 1908, M. 135.00
Boudoir Manicure Set, 4 pc, w/booklet, 1929, M. 165.00
California Tooth Tablet, 1896-1905, M. 85.00
CPC Sample Case, basketweave w/label, 1915, M. 100.00
Cut Glass Perfume, 1915, M. 200.00
Daphne Talcum Powder, 4 oz can, 1923, M. 65.00
Depilatory, 1 oz, 1915, M. 90.00
Eau De Quinine, 6 oz, 1923, M. 90.00
Gentleman's Shaving Set, 7 pieces, in box, 1917, M. 400.00
Gertrude Recordon's Introductory Facial Treatment Set, M. . . .275.00
Juvenile Set, 1915, M. 425.00
Lavender Salts, green glass, 1910, M. 250.00
Lemonal Cleansing Cream, jar, 1926, M. 55.00
Liquid Shampoo, 6 oz, 1923, M. 80.00
Little Folks Set, 4 bottles, 1937, M. .130.00
Lotus Cream, 12 oz, 1917, M. 150.00
Massage Cream, jar, 1916, M. 110.00
Mission Garden Compact, 1925, M. 30.00
Narcissus Perfume, 1 oz, 1925, M. 110.00
Natoma Rose Perfume, ½ oz, 1916, M. 110.00
Perfection, Auto Lustre, 1 pt, 1930, M. 30.00
Perfection, Baking Powder, 1 lb can, 1931, M. 25.00
Perfection, Coloring, ½ oz bottle, 1934, M. 15.00
Perfection, Coloring Set, 5 bottles in box, 1920, M. 250.00
Perfection, Coloring Set, 5 bottles in tin box, 1941, M. 65.00
Perfection, Flavoring Set, 5 bottles in tin box, 1941, M. 60.00
Perfection, Furniture Polish, 12 oz, 1936, M. 20.00
Perfection, Kwick Cleaning Polish, 8 oz, 1922, M. 35.00
Perfection, Laundry Crystals, in box, 1931, M. 30.00
Perfection, Liquid Shoe White, sample, ½ oz, 1935, M. 40.00
Perfection, Liquid Shoe White, 4 oz, 1935, M. 25.00
Perfection, Liquid Spots Out, 4 oz, 1925, M. 35.00
Perfection, Machine Oil, 3 oz, ribbed side, 1945, M. 25.00
Perfection, Mending Cement, tube, 1933, M. 7.00
Perfection, Mothicide, 1 lb can, 1925, M. 40.00
Perfection, Olive Oil, 1 pt can, 1931, M. 25.00
Perfection, Powdered Cleaner, 10 oz, 1934, M. 20.00
Perfection, Prepared Starch, 6 oz, 1931, M. 25.00
Perfection, Savoury Coloring, 4 oz, 1941, M. 15.00
Perfection, Silver Cream Polish, ½ lb can, 1931, M. 20.00
Perfume Sample Set, 1931, M. 300.00
Powder Sachets, 1890s, M. 90.00
Radiant Nail Powder, 1923, M. 45.00
Rose Pomade, jar, 1914, M. 55.00
Shampoo Cream, 4 oz jar, 1908, M. 75.00
Sweet Sixteen Face Powder, 1916, M. .45.00
Tooth Wash, 1915, M. 100.00

Trailing Arbutus Face Powder, 1925, M....................30.00
Vernafleur Toilet Soap, 3 bars in box, 1936, M.............55.00
Violet Almond Meal, 1923, M..........................50.00

Calling Cards, Cases, and Receivers

The practice of announcing one's arrival with a calling card, borne by the maid to the mistress of the house, was a social grace of the Victorian era. Different messages were related by turning down one corner or another -- condolences, a personal visit, or a goodbye. The custom was forgotten by WWI.

Fashionable ladies and gents carried their personally engraved cards in elaborate cases made of such materials as embossed silver, mother-of-pearl with intricate inlay, tortoise shell, and ivory. Card receivers held cards left by visitors who called while the mistress was out or 'not receiving'.

Calling cards with fringe, die-cut flaps that cover the name, or an unusual decoration are worth about $3.00 to $4.00, while plain cards usually sell for around $1.00.

Card case, English sterling marked N.M. (Nathaniel Mills), hinged lid, circa 1820, 3¾" x 2½", $375.00.

Cases

Coin silver, sgn, early, ornate, in orig box.................125.00
Honey agate, w/G gold scrolls & fittings, sm sapphires, 3¼"....275.00
Inlay, sm pcs ivory, silver & malachite, geometric design, 3".....55.00
Silver w/gw interior, dragons/man & lady relief, 3½x2½".....125.00
Sterling, engraved bamboo & florals, 3½x2½"..............85.00
Sterling, Victorian, w/monogram, English..................50.00

Receivers

Blown cut crystal, stemmed base.........................25.00
Cherub figural pushes holder on rectangle base, SP...........55.00
Lady figural, cast metal, gr paint, Deco....................85.00
Milk glass, Jewish star, Victorian........................22.00
Silverplate, Simpson, Hall & Miller; 3 ball ft, 6¾"...........55.00
Silverplate, Wilcox; upright, ornate......................75.00
Tray, iron, imprinted advertising.........................18.00

Camark

The Camden Art and Tile Company of Camden, Arkansas, was organized in 1926. John Lesell and his wife were associated with the company only briefly before he died that same year. After his death, his wife stayed on and continued to decorate wares very similar to those he had made for Weller. Le-Camark closely resembled Weller LaSa; Lessell was almost a duplication of Marengo. Perhaps the most outstanding was a mirror black line with luster decoration. Naturally, examples of these lines are very rare.

The company eventually became known as Camark, and began production of commercial ware of the type listed below.

Demitasse cup and saucer, maroon glaze, $8.00.

Basket, wht w/bird on hdl, #34..........................22.50
Pitcher, Iris, pink, 13"................................45.00
Vase, bulbous w/sm neck & flaring collar, hdls, gr/br/tan, 4".....8.00
Vase, matt yellow, ribbed, w/eggshell crackle finish, 13"........50.00
Vase, pink matt w/bl drip, 6"...........................18.00
Vase, pink w/gr drip glaze, 4½"........................15.00
Vase, yel, ribbed, 13".................................36.00
Wall pocket, bl, 7"...................................25.00
Wall pocket, 4 openings, rose & gray.....................40.00

Cambridge Glass

The Cambridge Glass Company began operations in 1901, in Cambridge, Ohio. They made primarily crystal dinnerware and well designed accessory pieces until the 1920s, when they introduced the concept of color that was to become so popular on the American dinnerware market.

Always maintaining high standards of quality and elegance, they produced many lines that became best sellers; through the twenties and thirties they were recognized as the largest manufacturer of this type of glassware in the world.

Of the various marks the company used, the 'C in triangle' is the most familiar. Production stopped in 1958.

#1066, cobalt; cigarette holder, oval......................75.00
#1066, cobalt; cigarette holder/ash tray, individual, #3400/144...95.00
#1066, cobalt; juice, ftd...............................18.50
#1066, cobalt; sherbet, 4".............................12.50
Achilles, sherbet, tall.................................22.00

Achilles, tea, ftd, 12 oz...................................25.00
Adonis, compote, #3500/148, 6″........................26.00
Adonis, relish, 3 part, #3500/69, 6½″..................19.00
Apple Blossom, blue; relish, 5 part, #3400/67............85.00
Apple Blossom, crystal; goblet, water, #3130, w/gold......25.00
Apple Blossom, crystal; plate, hdld, #3400/8, 11½″.......17.50
Apple Blossom, crystal; plate, w/gold, 6″...............10.00
Apple Blossom, crystal; sherry cocktail, #3130, w/gold......25.00
Apple Blossom, green; bowl, hdld, #3400/1185, 10″........47.50
Apple Blossom, green; relish, 5 part, #3400/67...........40.00
Apple Blossom, green; tray, hdld, #3400/1186, 12″........39.50
Apple Blossom, yellow; bon bon, #3400/1179..............17.00
Apple Blossom, yellow; champagne, #3130.................20.00
Apple Blossom, yellow; cup & saucer.....................20.00
Apple Blossom, yellow; goblet, water, #3130..............25.00
Apple Blossom, yellow; goblet, wine, #3130..............39.50
Apple Blossom, yellow; juice, ftd, 4″...................25.00
Apple Blossom, yellow; mayonnaise, liner & ladle.........95.00
Apple Blossom, yellow; plate, #3400, 8½″................9.50
Apple Blossom, yellow; server, center hdl...............50.00
Apple Blossom, yellow; water, ftd, 4¾″.................27.50
Blossom Time, crystal; bowl, 2 hdld, #325, gold trim, 5½″....14.00
Caprice, amber; cup & saucer...........................25.00
Caprice, amber; nut dish, ftd, individual................6.00
Caprice, blue; ash tray, #216, 5″......................21.00
Caprice, blue; ash tray, shell, 3 toes, 3″, #34..........11.00
Caprice, blue; ball jug, #183, 80 oz...................260.00
Caprice, blue; bon bon, 2 hdld, diamond shape, 6″........19.00
Caprice, blue; bowl, belled, #62, 12½″.................42.50
Caprice, blue; bowl, flared, 3 toe, #54, 10½″...........52.00
Caprice, blue; bowl, shallow, 4 toe, #81, 11″...........77.00
Caprice, blue; bowl, square, 12″.......................45.00
Caprice, blue; bowl, 2 hdld, oval, 4 toe, #66, 11″.......65.00
Caprice, blue; bowl, 4 toe, #62, 12½″.................45.00
Caprice, blue; bowl, 4 toe, low, cupped, 10½″...........55.00
Caprice, blue; candlesticks, Alpine, #70, w/prisms, pr....50.00
Caprice, blue; candlesticks, keyhole, 2 light, pr.........85.00
Caprice, blue; candlesticks, small, #7, pr..............32.00
Caprice, blue; candy, covered, 3 ftd, #165, 6″..........80.00
Caprice, blue; celery relish, 3 part, #124, 8½″.........35.00

Helitrope bud vase, 10″, $40.00.

Caprice, blue; champagne, #3000S......................30.00
Caprice, blue; cigar box..............................25.00
Caprice, blue; cigarette box, covered, #207, 3½x2¼″....35.00
Caprice, blue; cigarette holder, triangular, #204, 3x3″...25.00
Caprice, blue; cup & saucer...........................37.50
Caprice, blue; goblet, water, 9 oz, #300...............29.00
Caprice, blue; mayonnaise, 2 hdld, ftd, on ringed tray....85.00
Caprice, blue; nut dish, #C37, 3″.....................14.00
Caprice, blue; pickle, 2 hdld, #102, 9″................37.50
Caprice, blue; plate, Alpine, 8½″.....................26.00
Caprice, blue; plate, buffet, 4 toe, Alpine, 14″.........40.00
Caprice, blue; plate, 4 toes, 15″.....................70.00
Caprice, blue; plate, 8″, M...........................21.00
Caprice, blue; relish, 2 part, 2 hdld, Alpine, #120, 6½″....26.00
Caprice, blue; relish, 3 part, #C124, 8½″..............42.50
Caprice, blue; relish, 3 part, #122...................32.00
Caprice, blue; rose bowl, 4 toe, #235.................77.00
Caprice, blue; sugar, #38.............................17.00
Caprice, blue; sugar, #41.............................15.00
Caprice, blue; tumbler, #310, flat, 12 oz..............40.00
Caprice, blue; tumbler, balloon top, #184, 12 oz........35.00
Caprice, blue; tumbler, ftd, #300, 10 oz...............27.00
Caprice, blue; tumbler, ftd, #300, 12 oz...............30.00
Caprice, crystal; almond basket, 2 hdld, #93...........20.00
Caprice, crystal; ash tray, 4″, #215..................10.00
Caprice, crystal; bon bon, square, 2 hdld, 6″...........7.00
Caprice, crystal; bowl, ftd, 11″......................15.00
Caprice, crystal; bowl, 2 hdld oval, #65, 11″..........26.00
Caprice, crystal; bowl, 4 toes, #62, 13″...............30.00
Caprice, crystal; candle holder, 2½″, #67, pr..........25.00
Caprice, crystal; candlestick, 3 light, tri-level, pr.....50.00
Caprice, crystal; candy, covered, #165.................30.00
Caprice, crystal; candy, 2 hdld, 6″....................7.00
Caprice, crystal; candy, 2 hdld, 7¼″...................9.00
Caprice, crystal; cigarette box, w/lid, #207............21.00
Caprice, crystal; creamer & sugar, individual, #40......16.00
Caprice, crystal; creamer & sugar on tray, #30.........25.00
Caprice, crystal; cup, #17............................6.00
Caprice, crystal; ice bucket, #201, w/hdl..............35.00
Caprice, crystal; relish, 3 part, 8″...................11.00
Caprice, crystal; rose bowl, 4½x3½″...................70.00
Caprice, crystal; smoke set: #207 box w/lid & 4 #213 ftd trays...32.00

Footed Carmen bowl, with gold encrusted Rosepoint decoration, 5¼″x 12½″, $350.00.

Caprice, crystal; spiral cornucopia...........................18.00
Caprice, crystal; sugar, #38...............................10.00
Caprice, crystal; sugar, #41................................9.00
Caprice, crystal; tumbler, #300, 5 oz......................17.00
Caprice, crystal; tumbler, flat, 5 oz, 3½"..................10.00
Caprice, crystal; tumbler, ftd, #300, 12 oz................12.00
Caprice, mandarin gold; ash tray, #214, 3".................16.00
Caprice, mandarin gold; sherbet, #3175.....................10.00
Caprice, moonlight; bowl, belled, #62, 12".................45.00
Caprice, moonlight; bowl, mayonnaise; small, #129..........20.00
Caprice, moonlight; plate, low ftd, #131, 8"...............30.00
Caprice, pink; console set: 11" bowl #855/4" candlesticks #627..25.00
Caprice, pink; server, center hdl..........................20.00
Cascade, crystal; bowl, 2 hdld, 6½"........................10.00
Cascade, crystal; plate, 6¾"................................5.00
Cascade, crystal; plate, 8½"................................7.00
Cascade, crystal; sherbet, molded, 4"......................10.00
Cascade, crystal; tumbler, molded, ftd, 5 oz...............10.00
Cascade, green; creamer & sugar on tray....................28.50
Chantilly, candy dish, covered, 3 part, silver knob........70.00
Chantilly, champagne, #3600, 6 oz..........................18.00
Chantilly, cocktail, #3775, 3 oz...........................29.00
Chantilly, cordial, #3600, 1 oz............................30.00
Chantilly, goblet, water, #3600, 10 oz.....................25.00
Chantilly, ice bucket......................................70.00
Chantilly, mayonnaise, no ladle, #3900/19..................29.00
Chantilly, mayonnaise, w/ladle, #3900/19...................35.00
Chantilly, shaker, ball shape, sterling top, #3400.........18.00
Chantilly, vase, keyhole, 10"..............................45.00
Chrysanthemum, pink; tumbler, #1630, 12 oz.................16.00
Crown Tuscan, ash tray, shell, #34, 3"......................8.00
Crown Tuscan, bowl, flying nude, 12½" L...................195.00
Crown Tuscan, bowl, oval, 4 ftd, #SS31, 8".................85.00
Crown Tuscan, bud vase, ftd, #274, 10".....................18.00
Crown Tuscan, candy, covered, 3 part, #3500/57.............26.50
Crown Tuscan, compote, nude stem, 8"......................150.00
Crown Tuscan, ivy ball, ring stem..........................49.00
Crown Tuscan, plate, shell, #2, 7".........................25.00
Crown Tuscan, plate, torte; w/enameled roses & gilding, 14"..75.00
Crown Tuscan, relish, 3 part...............................12.00
Crown Tuscan, sandwich plate, seashell, #7, 14"............45.00
Crown Tuscan, shell, 3 toed, small.........................20.00
Crown Tuscan, shell flower holder, #46, 7½"................55.00
Crown Tuscan, vase, ped, gold trim 'Candlelight', 8½"......40.00
Crown Tuscan, waste bone dish...............................4.00
Decagon, amber; almond, individual, ftd.....................8.00
Decagon, amber; candelabra, #638...........................15.00
Decagon, amber; cream soup w/liner.........................10.00
Decagon, amber; goblet, water, #3130.......................14.00
Decagon, amber; ice bucket, hdld...........................28.00
Decagon, amber; plate, 6¼"..................................3.00
Decagon, amber; server, center hdld........................18.00
Decagon, amber; sherry cocktail, #3077.....................11.00
Decagon, amber; sherry cocktail, #3130.....................14.00
Decagon, amber; syrup, ftd.................................35.00
Decagon, amber; tray, 2 hdld, #167.........................12.00
Decagon, amber; tumbler, ftd, #3077, 10 oz.................11.00
Decagon, black; saucer, mkd, #865...........................5.00
Decagon, blue; bowl, oval vegetable, 9½"...................45.00
Decagon, blue; creamer......................................9.50
Decagon, blue; cup & saucer................................12.50
Decagon, blue; juice, ftd, #3130...........................14.50
Decagon, blue; plate, salad; mkd, #597, 8¼"................13.00
Decagon, blue; plate, 6"....................................6.00

Decagon, blue; plate, 8½"...................................9.50
Decagon, blue; sherbet, low, #3130.........................12.50
Decagon, green; bon bon, 2 hdld, 7¼".......................15.00
Decagon, green; bowl, 2 hdld, 6"............................8.50
Decagon, green; champagne, #3077, 6 oz.....................11.00
Decagon, green; cream soup & plate.........................17.50
Decagon, green; creamer, cup shape..........................6.00
Decagon, green; creamer & sugar, mkd, #1096................20.00
Decagon, green; creamer & sugar, mkd, #979.................25.00
Decagon, green; cup & saucer, #866..........................8.50
Decagon, green; cup & saucer, mkd, #865....................16.00
Decagon, green; ice bucket.................................32.00
Decagon, green; plate, 7"...................................3.50
Decagon, green; plate, 8¼"..................................7.50
Decagon, green; plate, 9".................................10.00
Decagon, green; platter, oval, 12½"........................25.00
Decagon, green; sandwich server, center hdl................25.00
Decagon, green; sherbet, #3077, 6 oz........................9.00
Decagon, green; sugar, #520.................................7.00
Decagon, green; tumbler, ftd, #3077, 10 oz.................13.50
Decagon, green; tumbler, ftd, #3077, 5 oz...................9.00
Decagon, lt blue; candlestick, #627, 4", pr................30.00
Decagon, lt blue; mayonnaise, ftd..........................45.00
Decagon, lt blue; plate, grill, 10"........................28.00
Decagon, lt blue; plate, 7½"................................7.50
Decagon, lt blue; sandwich server, center hdl..............30.00
Decagon, lt blue; tumbler, ftd, #3077, 10 oz...............15.00
Decagon, pink; berry, 5¼"...................................9.50
Decagon, pink; bon bon, 2 hdld, 7¼"........................15.00
Decagon, pink; bowl, oval vegetable, 10½"..................25.00
Decagon, pink; bowl, round, 8".............................20.00
Decagon, pink; cordial goblet, #3077, 1 oz.................14.00
Decagon, pink; creamer & sugar, #979, sgnd.................16.00
Decagon, pink; cup, sgnd....................................6.00
Decagon, pink; cup & saucer.................................8.50
Decagon, pink; cup & saucer, mkd, #865.....................16.00
Decagon, pink; ice bucket, #851............................30.00
Decagon, pink; plate, 6"....................................4.00
Decagon, pink; plate, 7½"...................................5.50
Decagon, pink; plate, 8¼"...................................7.00
Decagon, pink; sauce boat & under plate....................79.50
Decagon, pink; server, center hdl..........................18.00
Decagon, pink; snack bowl, center hdl, unlisted............35.00
Diane, crystal; ball jug..................................175.00
Diane, crystal; candle holder, 2 light, keyhole, pr........45.00
Diane, crystal; candlestick, 2 light, fleur-de-lis, pr.....55.00
Diane, crystal; cheese & cracker, 2 pc, #3400/6............47.50
Diane, crystal; cigarette holder...........................65.00
Diane, crystal; claret, #3122..............................28.00
Diane, crystal; cup & saucer, #3400........................32.50
Diane, crystal; hurricane lamp, #1604.....................275.00
Diane, crystal; ice bucket.................................55.00
Diane, crystal; mandarin gold; bowl, mkd, #3400/1, 13".....62.00
Diane, crystal; marmalade, open, #147......................35.00
Diane, crystal; mayonnaise & liner, #1532..................45.00
Diane, crystal; mayonnaise & liner, #3400..................47.00
Elaine, cocktail, #3035, 3 oz..............................23.00
Elaine, goblet, #3035, 9 oz................................15.00
Elaine, goblet, water, #3121...............................18.00
Elaine, ice bucket, #1402..................................55.00
Elaine, sherbet, tall, #3035, 6 oz.........................14.00
Elaine, sherry cocktail, #3121.............................16.50
Euclid, cocktail, #3750, 3½ oz.............................17.00
Euclid, cordial, #3750, 1 oz...............................19.00

Crown Tuscan seashell cornucopia, 10″, $90.00.

Euclid, wine, #3750, 3 oz.................................17.00
Everglades, crystal; candlestick, #33....................30.00
Everglades, crystal; creamer, flat........................12.00
Everglades, crystal; plate, tulip; #31, 17″..............58.00
Everglades, crystal; plate, tulip; 16″....................37.00
Everglades, green; vase, frosted, #21, 7½″..............35.00
Everglades, lt blue; bowl, belled, #8, 12″..............76.00
Farber Ware, bowl, divided, green, w/orig label.........15.00
Farber Ware, bowl, divided, ruby.........................20.00
Farber Ware, candy dish, hdld, amber....................15.00
Farber Ware, cocktail set, shaker & 6 goblets, amethyst.......58.00
Farber Ware, compote, amber, 5½″........................29.00
Farber Ware, compote, amethyst, 5½″.....................29.00
Farber Ware, compote, cobalt, 5½″.......................30.00
Farber Ware, compote, nude, amber......................39.00
Farber Ware, compote, nude, amethyst...................39.00
Farber Ware, relish bowl, covered, amethyst.............30.00
Farber Ware, salt & pepper, ball, amethyst..............18.00
Farber Ware, tray, 3 part, #3500/112, amber.............40.00
Georgian, carmen; tumbler, #319, 12 oz..................15.00
Georgian, forest green; tumbler, #319, 9 oz..............8.00
Georgian, mandarin gold; sherbet, #3175................10.00
Georgian, mandarin gold; tumbler, #319, 9 oz............8.00
Gloria, crystal; cup & saucer, #3400/54.................27.50
Gloria, crystal; decanter set, ball, 8 pc................245.00
Gloria, crystal; goblet, water, #3130....................25.00
Gloria, crystal; mayonnaise set, 3 pc, #3400/11.........55.00
Gloria, crystal; plate, dinner; #3400/63, 9½″...........40.00
Gloria, crystal; plate, tea/salad; #3400/61, 7½″.........13.50
Gloria, crystal; sandwich tray, center hdl, #3400/10.....45.00
Gloria, mandarin gold; goblet, #1066, 11 oz.............23.00
Gloria, mandarin gold; plate, #3400, 8½″................15.00
Gloria, pink; plate, #3400, 8½″..........................15.00
Gloria, shaker, crystal top, amber ft, #3400/77.........25.00
Jefferson, mandarin gold; goblet, #1401, 10 oz, w/label........17.00
Lorna, pink; plate, decorated, sgnd, 8½″.................8.00
Lorna, pink; relish, 3 hdld, #3400/91, 8″...............28.00
Martha, crystal; bowl, ftd, cupped, 9½″.................15.00
Martha, crystal; candlesticks, #494, 4″, pr.............32.00
Martha, crystal; candy, covered, 3 toe, strawberry finial........27.00
Martha, crystal; compote, etched Blossom Time, gold trim......52.00
Martha, crystal; compote, 7″............................18.00

Martha, crystal; creamer & sugar on tray, individual, w/gold.....30.00
Martha, crystal; cup & saucer............................15.00
Martha Washington, carmen; sherbet, tall, #1401, 6 oz........14.00
Martha Washington, cobalt; sherbet, tall, #1400..............11.00
Martha Washington, green; urn, w/cover, #41...............32.00
Martha Washington, Heather Bloom; compote, low, 5½″........32.00
Martha Washington, pink; candy, covered, 3 pc, #43..........27.00
Martha Washington, pink; creamer, ftd....................20.00
Mt Vernon, crystal; cocktail, #26, 3½ oz.................8.00
Mt Vernon, crystal; goblet, water........................7.25
Mt Vernon, crystal; ice bucket, #92......................32.00
Mt Vernon, crystal; plate, 6¼″..........................4.50
Mt Vernon, crystal; relish, 2 part, hdld, #101, 8″.........15.00
Mt Vernon, crystal; relish/celery, 5 part, 12″, #104........21.00
Mt Vernon, crystal; tumbler, #59, 14 oz.................9.00
Mt Vernon, crystal; tumbler, ftd, #20, 12 oz.............10.00
Mt Vernon, crystal; tumbler, ftd, #22, 3 oz..............9.00
Nude stem, claret, carmen...............................125.00
Nude stem, claret, emerald..............................110.00
Nude stem, cocktail, amethyst............................70.00
Nude stem, cocktail, carmen.............................120.00
Nude stem, cocktail, crystal w/ebony foot & stem.........82.00
Nude stem, cocktail, emerald gr..........................82.50
Nude stem, cocktail, mandarin gold.......................82.50
Nude stem, cocktail, mocha..............................95.00
Nude stem, cocktail, royal blue.........................120.00
Nude stem, compote, amethyst top.........................60.00
Nude stem, ivy bowl, royal blue w/crystal stem...........200.00
Portia, crystal; cheese & cracker, #3400................50.00
Portia, crystal; cup, #3400.............................20.00
Portia, crystal; iced tea, #3121........................25.00
Portia, crystal; iced tea, #3130........................17.50
Portia, crystal; plate, #3400, 8½″......................12.00
Portia, crystal; sherbet, tall, #3121...................15.00
Portia, crystal; sugar, #3400/68........................16.00
Ramshead, amethyst; candlestick, pillar stem, 4½″........25.00
Ramshead, crystal; candy, covered, gadroon, round, 6½″......47.00
Rose Point, amber; cocktail, pressed....................55.00
Rose Point, amber; sherbet, pressed.....................44.00
Rose Point, carmen; goblet, water; pressed..............75.00
Rose Point, crystal; basket, #3500/52, 6″..............195.00
Rose Point, crystal; bowl, #3400/45, 11″................56.00
Rose Point, crystal; bowl, #3900/28, 11½″...............55.00
Rose Point, crystal; bowl, ftd oval, #3400/1240.........70.00
Rose Point, crystal; butter w/cover, #3400/52..........220.00
Rose Point, crystal; cake plate, 3 toe, 12″.............75.00
Rose Point, crystal; candle holder, #3900/67, 5″, pr....95.00
Rose Point, crystal; candy, covered, hound..............95.00
Rose Point, crystal; candy, covered, 3 part.............55.00
Rose Point, crystal; champagne, #3121...................27.00
Rose Point, crystal; cheese & cracker, #3400/6, 11½″.....67.00
Rose Point, crystal; cheese & lid, very rare...........795.00
Rose Point, crystal; cocktail, #3121, 3 oz..............40.00
Rose Point, crystal; cordial, #7966, rare..............125.00
Rose Point, crystal; creamer, #3900/44.................24.00
Rose Point, crystal; creamer & sugar, #3500/14.........50.00
Rose Point, crystal; creamer & sugar, individual, #3500/15.....45.00
Rose Point, crystal; cruet, w/stopper, #3900/100.......135.00
Rose Point, crystal; cup & saucer, #3400/54............38.00
Rose Point, crystal; goblet, #3121, 10 oz..............25.00
Rose Point, crystal; iced tea, #3121...................29.00
Rose Point, crystal; mayonnaise w/under plate, #3900/129.....32.00
Rose Point, crystal; plate, #3400, 7½″.................14.00
Rose Point, crystal; plate, #3500, 8″..................15.00
Rose Point, crystal; plate, rolled edge, #3900/166, 14″........42.00

Rose Point, crystal; plate, 2 hdld, #3400, 7″ 17.00
Rose Point, crystal; platter, rectangular, 2 hdld, 15¾″ 95.00
Rose Point, crystal; relish, #3900/125, 9″ 37.00
Rose Point, crystal; relish, divided, 3 part, #3400/91 . . . . .27.50
Rose Point, crystal; relish, 2 part, 2 hdld, #3400/90, 6″ 28.00
Rose Point, crystal; salt & pepper, #3400/77 . . . . .43.00
Rose Point, crystal; saucer, #3400/54 . . . . .7.00
Rose Point, crystal; sherbet, low, #3121 . . . . .21.00
Rose Point, crystal; sherbet, tall, #3121, 6 oz 23.00
Rose Point, crystal; sugar, #138 . . . . .22.00
Rose Point, crystal; sugar, #3400/68 . . . . .24.00
Rose Point, crystal; tray, #3500/112, 15″ 175.00
Rose Point, crystal; tray, w/5 relish inserts, #3500/67, 12″ 295.00
Rose Point, crystal; tumbler, flat, 4¾″ 45.00
Rose Point, crystal; tumbler, iced tea; #3121 . . . . .25.00
Rose Point, crystal; vase, bud; #274, 10″ 55.00
Rose Point, crystal; wine, #3121, w/gold 75.00
Rose Point, cyrstal; creamer & sugar, #138 . . . . .45.00
Rose Point, royal blue; iced tea, pressed 75.00
Roselyn, crystal; relish, 2 part, #3400/90, 6″ 11.00
Tally Ho, amber; ice bucket, #1402/52, w/gold hdl 47.00
Tally Ho, amethyst; salt & pepper, #1402/116, glass tops, pr 40.00
Tally Ho, carmen; bowl, flat rim, 12″ 35.00
Tally Ho, carmen; bowl, 2 hdld, #72, 10½″ 30.00
Tally Ho, carmen; punch mug, #78, 6 oz 20.00
Tally Ho, carmen; relish, 2 part, #90, 6″ 22.00
Tally Ho, crystal; jug, #49, 88 oz 45.00
Tally Ho, crystal; punch mug, #1402/78, 6 oz 12.00
Tally Ho, royal blue; sherry cocktail, #10, 3 oz 25.00
Valencia, crystal; relish set, 6 pc, #3500 . . . . .110.00
Wildflower, ball jug, 80 oz 175.00
Wildflower, bon bon, ftd, hdld, #3500 .14.00
Wildflower, bowl, oval, 4 toe, #3400/1240, 12″ 35.00
Wildflower, candlestick, keyhole, 4″, pr 50.00
Wildflower, candy, covered, #3500/57 .44.00
Wildflower, cheese & cracker, gold encrusted 39.00
Wildflower, cornucopia, ruffled 65.00
Wildflower, creamer & sugar, #3400 . . . . .22.00
Wildflower, creamer & sugar, individual, #3500 . . . . .19.00
Wildflower, creamer & sugar, individual, Gadroon 32.00
Wildflower, goblet, cocktail; #3121 . . . . .16.00
Wildflower, goblet, water; #3121 . . . . .18.00
Wildflower, ice bucket, gold encrusted .55.00
Wildflower, iced tea, #3121 . . . . .25.00
Wildflower, pink; server, 3 part, 9 sided, center hdl, unlisted . . .155.00
Wildflower, sherbet, tall, #3121 . . . . .14.00
Wildflower, sherry cocktail, #3121 . . . . .18.00
Wildflower, vase, #797 flip, 8″ 65.00
Wildflower, vase, gold edge on rim & ft, #1299, 11″ 89.00

Cambridge Pottery

The Cambridge Art Pottery operated in Cambridge, Ohio, from 1900 until 1909. During that time several lines of art ware were developed under the direction of C.B. Upjohn, an established ceramic artist of the period.

Their standard brown-glazed line was Terrhea, examples of which are often found bearing the signature of the artist responsible for the underglaze decoration. Oakwood was a second brown-glazed line, without the slip painting. Other lines were Acorn, introduced in 1904; and Otoe, a matt green ware (introduced in 1907) that utilized already existing shapes from earlier wares. However, their most successful product was a line of cookware called Guernsey, made from a red-brown clay with a white-glazed interior. Sales proved to be so profitable that by 1908 all art ware was discontinued in favor of its exclusive production. By the following year, the firm elected to change the name of their pottery to The Gurnsey Earthenware Company. Marks varied, but all incorporate a device comprised of the letters 'CAP', with the co-joined 'AP' most often contained within a larger scale 'C'.

Baking cup, Gurnsey 4.50
Ewer, sgnd Terrhea, some crazing 230.00
Tile, high relief floral, majolica type glaze, 6x6″, pr 15.00
Vase, br glaze w/florals, artist sgnd, 9″ 160.00
Vase, brown glaze w/dog portrait, AV Lewis, 9″ 675.00
Vase, standard br glaze w/florals, 5½″ .225.00

Piggy bank, 3¼″ x 6″, $75.00.

Cameo

The technique of glass carving was perfected 2,000 years ago in ancient Rome and Greece. The most famous ancient example of cameo glass is the Portland Vase, made in Rome around 100 A.D. After glass blowing was developed, glassmakers devised a method of casing several layers of colored glass together, often with a light color over a darker base, to enhance the design. Skilled carvers meticulously worked the fragile glass to produce incredibly detailed classic scenes. In the 18th and 19th centuries, Oriental and Near Eastern artisans used the technique more extensively. European glassmakers revived the art during the last quarter of the 19th century. In France, Galle and Daum produced some of the finest examples of modern times, using as many as five layers of glass to develop their designs, usually scenics or subjects from nature. Hand carving was supplemented by the use of the copper engraving wheel, and acid was used to cut away the layers more quickly.

In England, Thomas Webb and Sons used modern machinery and technology to eliminate many of the problems that plagued early glass carvers. One of Webb's best known carvers, George Woodall, is credited with producing over 400 pieces. Woodall was trained in the art by John Northwood, famous for reproducing the Portland Vase in 1876.

Cameo glass became very popular during the late 1800s, resulting in a market that demanded more than could be produced, due to the tedious procedures involved. In an effort to produce greater volume, less elaborate pieces with simple floral or geometric designs were made, often entirely acid etched with little or no hand carving. While very little cameo glass was made in this country, a few pieces were produced by James Gillender, Tiffany, and the Libbey Glass Company. Though some continued to be made on a limited scale into the 1900s, for the most part, inferior products caused a marked reduction in its manufacture by the turn of the century.

See also specific manufacturers.

Perfume, bamboo/leaves, red, silver top/chain, English, 5"....2,000.00
Perfume, lay-down; devil's face relief, ivory/br, English, 5"....1,400.00
Perfume, lay-down; palm fronds, wht/citron, English, 9½"....1,500.00
Perfume, lay-down; wht/rose florals, butterfly, English, 3¾"....600.00
Perfume, red w/wht floral, silver screw top, English, 2½".....600.00
Perfume, turq w/wht flowers & leaves, hinged silver lid, 3½"...695.00
Shade, wht w/lav/bl/orange floral band, Veilleruse/Charder, 5"..500.00
Spoon, serving; wht to amber hdl, porcelain bowl insert, 8" L..500.00
Vase, allover leaves & butterfly, deep blue, English, 9".....2,000.00
Vase, birds on branches, blk/gray, ped base/hdls, Ver-art, 12"..450.00
Vase, bl cluthra glass, sgn DeGue, 9½"....................550.00
Vase, blossoms, 2 color peachblow, English, 7"...........2,000.00
Vase, blue, wht seashells at top, florals on body, English, 9"..2,700.00
Vase, cream w/bl flowers, English, late 1800s, 3½"..........520.00
Vase, daisies & leaves, gray & pk w/lav & gr, Arsall, 10½".....650.00
Vase, fern leaves, wht cut to blue, English, 5"..............800.00
Vase, florals in pinks, 4 sided, tapering, Pantin, 8½".........450.00
Vase, irid mottle w/poppies/butterflies, Pantin, mk CP, 10½"...975.00
Vase, lt br foliage on tan, Cristallerie de Pantin, 14".........850.00
Vase, mottle gr/wht/stippled, trees/pond, 1 cut, Fernandez, 6"..600.00
Vase, ped ft, jelly fish/seaweed, gr cut to ochre, Bensop......1,300.00
Vase, pink w/3 cherubs in branch fr/butterfly, E Michel, 4¾"...900.00
Vase, pk frost w/purple house scene, De Veau, 4x2½".......400.00
Vase, sailboats, 3 acid cuts, br/yel on frost, sgn Michel, 8½"...750.00
Vase, spray of wildflower blossoms, turq/wht, English, 5".....900.00
Vase, wht to red, dogwood flowers, English, 1¾", EX........450.00

Unsigned cameo vase with florals and lattice base, clear green over green satin, wheel worked, 7¼", $175.00.

Camphor Glass

The term 'camphor glass' refers to a type of acid-finished lusterless glassware, so named for its resemblance to gum camphor.

Bowl, fluted, polished pontil, 10"........................125.00
Candy dish, w/lid, Deco, filigree gilt base/trim, 3 ftd..........18.00
Elephant, GOP on side.................................38.00
Powder jar, parrots on lid..............................18.00
Slipper, mk Gillinder Centennial........................15.00
Toothpick holder, Baby Mine, Sandwich...................85.00
Vase, nude on front, 8½"..............................27.50
Vase, wht w/blue enameling, 10½"......................40.00

Canary Lustre

Canary lustre was produced from the late 1700s until about the mid-19th century in the Staffordshire district of England. The body of the ware was of yellow clay, with a yellow overglaze; and, more often than not, copper or silver lustre trim was added. Decorations were usually black printed transfers, though occasionally hand painted polychrome designs were also used.

Mug, gaudy decor....................................400.00
Pitcher, red/blk/silver resist scroll staff & leaf decor, 5"......475.00
Plate, lady & young boy transfer, red rim, 5½".............195.00
Toothpick holder, wht enamel daisies, gold leaves & base band..65.00

Candleholders

The earliest type of candlestick, called a pricket, was constructed with a sharp point on which the candle was impaled. The socket type, first used in the 16th century, consisted of the socket and a short stem, with a wide drip pan and base. These were made from sheets of silver or other metal; not until late in the 17th century were candlesticks made by casting. By the 1700s, styles began to vary from the traditional fluted column or baluster form, and became more elaborate. A Rococo style with scrolls, shellwork, and naturalistic leaves and flowers came into vogue that afforded the individual silversmith the opportunity to exhibit his skill and artistry. The last half of the 18th century brought a return to classic fluted columns with neo-classic motifs. Because they were made of thin sheet silver, weighted bases were used to add stability.

The Rococo styles of the Regency period were heavily encrusted with applied figures and flowers. Candelabra with six to nine branches became popular. By the Victorian era, when lamps came into general use, there was less innovation and more adaptation of the earlier styles.

Candelabra, cut glass/bronze std, 7-lite, 3 tiers/prisms, 21".....225.00
Candelabra, pink glass, 3-lite, pr.........................60.00
Candelabra, pressed glass, 4-lite, Waterford style, 19", pr......250.00
Candle holder, wood w/4 trn columns holding tin collar, 7½"..155.00
Candle holder, wrought iron/tin, 2-lite, chain to hang, 8x7".....60.00
Candle sconce, punched tin, crimped edge reflector, 13", G.....30.00
Candlestand, wrought iron, tri-ft base, arm adjusts, 42"......1,750.00
Candlestick, amber glass, baluster/6 panels/flare base, 6", pr...35.00
Candlestick, beehive, push-up, 1800s, 11", pr..............155.00
Candlestick, brass, baluster stem screws in sq base, early, 6"...350.00
Candlestick, brass, English, 1690, 6¼".....................225.00
Candlestick, brass, heavy w/G detail, threaded, 1850s, 4", pr....90.00
Candlestick, brass, push-up, beehive/dia detail, 1880s, 9", pr....90.00
Candlestick, brass, push-up, newly burnished, old, 10", pr.....135.00
Candlestick, brass, push-up, Victorian, 7"..................65.00
Candlestick, brass, Queen Anne, scalloped base, 7½"........255.00
Candlestick, brass, Queen Anne, scalloped base, 8"..........300.00
Candlestick, brass, Queen Anne, 7¼", pr..................500.00
Candlestick, brass, Spanish 1700s, drip plate/dome ft, 13", pr..935.00
Candlestick, brass, Victorian, push-up, beehive/dia, 11", pr.....200.00
Candlestick, clear flint glass, hexagonal, 7"................35.00
Candlestick, clear glass, 6 sided, 7", pr....................25.00
Candlestick, electric bl glass, 6 panels, flared base, 6", pr......50.00
Candlestick, hog scraper, iron, push-up, lip reattached, 4½"....50.00
Candlestick, hog scraper, iron, push-up mk Shaw's, rpr, 7".....55.00
Candlestick, hog scraper, iron w/push-up & lip hanger, 6¼"....95.00
Candlestick, hog scraper, iron w/worn tin plate/brass ring, 8"...150.00
Candlestick, hog scraper, iron w/worn tin plating, push-up, 6"...75.00
Candlestick, hog scraper, tin w/push-up mk Ryton & Walton, 7".85.00
Candlestick, hog scraper, tin/brass ring & push-up, 7½", pr....620.00

Candlestick, Louis XVI ormolu/vase socket/fluted stem, 10″, pr.	385.00
Candlestick, pricket; bronze, Italian, 1600s, 18½″, pr.	1,430.00
Candlestick, wrought iron spiral w/wood base, push-up, 7″	90.00
Chamber stick, brass, stem threads into base, 4″	50.00
Chamber stick, brass w/push-up, minor dents, 4½″	30.00
Chamber stick, tin w/push-up, 4″	20.00
Chamber stick, tin w/wrought iron push-up, handleless, 3¾″	50.00
Chandelier, 6 S-curve arms/punched dbl conical center, 32″ dia.	250.00
Lantern, tin/4 panes, 9″	85.00

Three rams' heads form the socles, and three panthers with tails entwined around tall standards form the bases of these cast metal candlesticks, 10″, $100.00 for the pair.

Candlewick

Candlewick crystal was made by the Imperial Glass Corporation, a division of Lenox Inc., Bellaire, Ohio. It was introduced in 1936, and though never marked except for paper labels, is easily recognized by the beaded crystal rims, stems, and handles inspired by the tufted needlework called candlewicking, practiced by our pioneer women.

During its production, more than 741 items were designed and produced. In September, 1982, when Imperial closed its doors, 34 pieces were still being made.

Identification numbers and mold numbers used by the company help collectors recognize the various styles and shapes. Most of the pieces are from the #400 series, though other series numbers were also used. Stemware was made in eight styles -- five from the #400 series made from 1941 to 1962, one from #3400 series made in 1937, another from #3800 series made in 1941, and the eighth style from the #4000 series made in 1947.

In the listing that follows, some #400 items lack the mold number because that information was not found in the company files.

A few pieces have been made in color, or with a gold wash, and at least two lines, Valley Lily and Floral, utilized Candlewick with floral patterns cut into the crystal. These are scarce today. Other rare items include gifts such as the desk calender, made by the company for its employees and customers; the dresser set comprised of a mirror, clock, puff jar, and cologne; and the chip and dip set.

Ash tray, nesting, 3 pc, round	10.00
Ash tray, oblong, 4½″	4.50
Bell, 4″	15.00
Bowl, baked apple; rolled edge, 6″	12.00
Bowl, banana; 10″	17.50
Bowl, basket; 2 up-turned sides, 5″	14.00

Bowl, belled, 14″	25.00
Bowl, bon bon; hdld, 5″	15.00
Bowl, bouillon; 3 hdld	12.50
Bowl, center piece; flared, 11″	19.00
Bowl, covered vegetable; 8″	18.50
Bowl, cream soup; 5″	12.00
Bowl, divided, deep 2 hdls, 10″	18.50
Bowl, finger; #3400	10.00
Bowl, flared, 10½″	20.00
Bowl, float; 12″	17.50
Bowl, fruit; 6½″	12.00
Bowl, heart; w/hdl, 10″	19.00
Bowl, heart; w/hdl, 6″	15.00
Bowl, heart; 5½″	8.00
Bowl, heart; 9″	18.00
Bowl, lily; bead rim, ftd, 7½″	15.00
Bowl, lily; 4 ft, 7″	18.00
Bowl, mint; w/hdl, 6″	12.00
Bowl, oval, flared, 12″	20.00
Bowl, oval, 11″	20.00
Bowl, pickle/celery; 8½″	12.00
Bowl, punch base, belled, 10″	10.00
Bowl, relish; divided, 7″ square	14.00
Bowl, relish; 5 part, 13½″	23.00
Bowl, round, 7″	9.00
Bowl, round, 9″	12.00
Bowl, salad; 10½″	20.00
Bowl, square, 5″	9.50
Bowl, square, 7″	10.00
Bowl, 3 ftd, 6″	10.00
Bowl, 3 ftd, 8½″	12.00
Butter w/cover, round, 5½″	18.00
Candle holder, flower, 6″	10.00
Candle holder, hdld w/bowl base, 5″	12.00
Candle holder, mushroom	8.50
Candle holder, 2-lite	12.00
Candle holder, 3-lite on circular bead center	15.00
Candy box, square, round lid, 6½″	17.50
Cheese & cracker set, 2 pc round, indent plate, cheese compote	30.00
Cigarette holder, bead ft, 3″	10.00
Coaster, w/spoon rest	7.50
Compote, 10″, ftd fruit, crimped	22.50
Compote, 11″	15.00
Compote, 4½″	10.00
Compote, 5½″, low, plain stem	12.00
Compote, 8″, bead stem	17.50
Console set, 3 pc, 14″ oval bowl, two 3-lite candle holders	52.50
Creamer, plain ft	6.00
Cup, after dinner	12.00
Cup, punch	4.00
Cup, tea	7.50
Deviled egg server, center handle, 12″	55.00
Ice tub, 5½″ deep, 8″ dia	18.50
Jam set, 5 pc, oval tray w/2 marmalade jars w/ladles	37.50
Mayonnaise, w/7″ liner	17.50
Mayonnaise set, 3 pc, hdld tray/hdld bowl/ladle	20.00
Mirror, round, standing, 4″	40.00
Oil, 4 oz, bulbous bottom	17.50
Party set, 2 pc, plate w/indentation for cup	10.00
Pitcher, 14 oz, short, round	20.00
Pitcher, 16 oz, no ice lip	20.00
Pitcher, 64 oz	32.50
Pitcher, 80 oz	35.00
Plate, 10″, dinner	13.00

Plate, 11", cake, tall, bead ft 20.00
Plate, 12" 15.00
Plate, 12", service 15.00
Plate, 12½", oval 17.50
Plate, 14", 2 hdld 20.00
Plate, 17", cupped edge 30.00
Plate, 17", torte 22.00
Plate, 4½" 4.00
Plate, 6", canape w/off center indent 3.50
Plate, 7½", 2 hdld 7.50
Plate, 8½", 2 hdld crimped 8.50
Plate, 8¼", crescent salad 9.00
Plate, 9", luncheon 8.50
Plate, 9", oval salad 13.00
Platter, 16" 23.00
Punch set, bowl w/12 cups & ladle 120.00
Salad fork & spoon, set 12.00
Salt & pepper, individual, pr 4.00
Salt spoon, 3 bead hdl 2.50
Sauce boat w/plate, set 45.00
Snack jar, w/cover, bead ft 25.00
Stem, #3400, low sherbet 12.00
Stem, #3400, 1 oz, cordial, graduated beads 20.00
Stem, #3400, 5 oz, ftd juice tumbler 17.50
Stem, #3800, brandy 17.50
Stem, #3800, champagne/sherbet 15.00
Stem, #3800, claret 17.50
Stem, #400, 5 oz, tall sherbet, bead ft 14.00
Stem, #400, 5 oz, wine, bead ft 16.50
Stem, 7 oz, parfait 13.00
Strawberry set, 2 pc, 7" plate & sugar dip bowl 12.00
Tid bit set, 3 pc, nesting heart 20.00
Tray, 11½", center hdld party 27.50
Tray, 13½", 2 hdld celery 25.00
Tray, 5¼x9¼", condiment 14.50
Tumbler, #3400, 9 oz, ftd 14.00
Tumbler, #3800, 12 oz 15.00
Tumbler, #400, 12 oz, bead ft 12.50
Tumbler, #400, 5 oz, bead ft juice 10.00
Tumbler, #400, 7 oz, old fashioned 12.00
Vase, 10", bead ft, straight sides 20.00
Vase, 5¾", miniature bud, bead ft 15.00
Vase, 6" dia 55.00
Vase, 8", fan w/bead handle 15.00
Vase, 8½", hdld, pitcher shape 20.00

Candy Containers

Figural glass candy containers have been made in hundreds of designs from as early as 1876, when Independence Hall and the Liberty Bell inspired patriotic candy containers for our country's centennial year celebration. From then until the 1940s, hundreds of designs have been made -- locomotives, comic characters, suitcases, telephones, submarines, lanterns, and automobiles are only a sampling of the figural containers. When full they held tiny colored candies; empty they became a toy or a bank. While many were made in clear glass, a few from around 1910 were produced in milk glass, sometimes trimed with gilt. During the late twenties, green, amber, blue, and pink were made. Many had tin and paper parts, and some were partially painted.

Among the better known manufacturers were West Bros., Cambridge, L.E. Smith, Victory, and Jeanette Glass. Values hinge on the condition of the paint and parts, and whether or not the closure is the original.

Papier mache containers were also made in figural form; most are marked 'Made in Germany'. Many of this type were made for special holidays -- bun-nies and eggs for Easter, turkeys for Thanksgiving, and black cats and jack-o'-lanterns for Halloween.

The numbers in our listings refer to a standard reference series, *An Album of Candy Containers*, Vols 1 and 2, by Jennie Long, who assisted us with this section.

Airplane, P-38 . . . . 125.00
Amos & Andy 360.00
Baby on log, papier mache, early 50.00
Barney Google, by barrel bank 425.00
Barney Google, on ped 150.00
Baseball Player by Barrel 415.00
Battleship, Victory Glass Co 20.00
Bird on Mount, with pewter whistle 400.00
Black Cat for Luck 485.00
Boston Bean Pot, with closure 40.00
Bulldog, #2 . . . . 15.00
Bulldog, rnd base 27.00
Cabin Cruiser, variety A 12.00
Camera, original version, complete 275.00
Candelabra 30.00
Carpet Sweepers, Baby or Dolly 350.00
Charlie Chaplin, Borgfeldt 95.00
Charlie Chaplin, LE Smith 450.00
Chevrolet Station Wagon, 1938 . . . . 20.00
Chick in Eggshell Auto 275.00
Chicken, nodding head, compo, mk German 30.00
Clown, pressed paper, 10½" 40.00
Clown on Horse 150.00
Colorado Boat, complete 225.00
Colorado Boat, glass only 40.00
Coupe, long hood, variation A 75.00
Coupe, wheel on side in glass, tin wheels 450.00
Dog by Barrel, without closure 150.00
Don't Park Here 125.00
Donkey Pulling Cart, original version 50.00
Duck, papier mache w/wire legs, on stump, Germany, 3½" 15.00
Duck on Rectangular Basket 35.00
Duckling, #30 . . . . 75.00
Dutch Windmill 45.00
Easter egg, papier mache, HP, lg 22.00
Electric Iron 20.00
Express Wagon, tin wheels, West Bros 400.00

Spirit of Goodwill, $85.00.

Felix by Barrel...450.00
Felix on Pedestal...600.00
Fire Engine, bottom closure, 4 solid tires, dtd Nov 24, 1914...100.00
Fire Engine, Little Boiler.................................75.00
Gas Pump...90.00
Greyhound Bus, tin wheels...............................165.00
Happifats on Drum, original version, with slotted closure.....225.00
Happifats on Drum, original version, without closure.........200.00
Hen & chicks, papier mache, HP, Germany, 1917, 3x2".......10.00
Hen on nest, papier mache, orig label, 1924, 7x6"..........45.00
Hen on Sagging Basket...................................35.00
Horn, Trumpet, milk glass...............................40.00
Horn, 3 Valve...65.00
House of Glass (Cottage).................................100.00
Jack-O'-Lantern, straight eyes..........................75.00
Jackie Coogan, metal closure, clear/frosted, c 1925, 5".....800.00
Jitney Bus..240.00
Kewpie by Barrel..65.00
Kiddie Kar...165.00
Ladder Truck, two firemen, tin wheels....................150.00
Lantern, tin top w/bail, 2¼"............................12.00
Lantern, Victory Glass Co, brass cap.....................20.00
Lawn Swing..575.00
Liberty Bell, amber, aqua, or green; orig screw closure.......45.00
Lincoln Zephyr, 1936, glass wheels......................25.00
Lincoln Zephyr, 1936, tin wheels........................75.00
Locomotive, paper closing...............................20.00
Man on Motorcycle, no tin closure......................300.00
Mr Rabbit w/Hat.......................................950.00
Mug, Necco Sweets......................................11.00
Oak Bucket...11.00
Orange, papier mache, early.............................30.00
Owl, good paint...80.00
Pail, w/hdl, mk Ball......................................8.00
Passenger Plane..150.00
Phonograph, glass record...............................250.00
Phonograph, tin record, complete........................250.00
Pig, papier mache, green.................................55.00
Pocket Watch, no fob....................................90.00
Pocket Watch w/Fob....................................125.00
Pumpkin Head Policeman................................600.00
Pumpkin Head Witch....................................500.00
Rabbit, Basket on Arm, 4½"..............................85.00
Rabbit, papier mache, sitting on haunches, glass eyes, 5½".....22.50
Rabbit, papier mache, standing lady/gent, 6", pr.............34.00
Rabbit, Paws Together...................................75.00
Rabbit, Peter; Millstein, orig version, w/orig paper closure.....25.00
Rabbit Begging, screw bottom............................45.00
Rabbit Crouching.......................................85.00
Rabbit Family, VG......................................525.00
Rabbit in Egg Shell, gilded, #48.........................85.00
Rabbit Nibbling Carrot...................................30.00
Rabbit Pushing Chick in Cart............................275.00
Rabbit Pushing Wheelbarrow.............................125.00
Rabbit Running on Log..................................110.00
Rabbit Wearing Apron, w/baby...........................625.00
Rabbit with Layed-Back Ears.............................65.00
Radio, Tune In..85.00
Rapid Fire Gun..275.00
Rapid Transit Bus, VG..................................600.00
Revolver, mercury glass, Pat Pending, lg..................30.00
Rocking Horse, no rider.................................275.00
Rooster, Crowing.......................................125.00
Rooster, papier mache w/wire legs, on stump, MIG, 4".......15.00

Safe, mk Penny Trust Co, milk glass/gold decor, orig closure....45.00
Safety First, by Smith...................................450.00
Safety First by Barrel...................................400.00
Salt & pepper shakers, anchor base, sgn Van Style Specialties...40.00
Santa Claus, Banded Coat...............................125.00
Santa Claus by Square Chimney, small....................235.00
Santa Claus Leaving Chimney............................65.00
Santa Claus w/Double Cuff..............................65.00
Santa Claus w/Plastic Head.............................35.00
Santa's Boot, w/wrap-around label, paper cap.............22.50
Skookum..250.00
Soldier by Tent, damaged.............................1,700.00
Soldier on Monument..................................400.00
Sparkplug..65.00
Spirit of Goodwill Airplane.............................85.00
Spirit of St Louis, complete original....................225.00
Spirit of St Louis, glass only...........................40.00
Statue of Liberty, 5¾"...............................1,500.00
Steam Engine, #1028, mk Victory Glass Co...............20.00
Stop & Go...275.00
Stretch Neck Cat, VG...................................450.00
Suitcase, milk glass, gilt trim...........................85.00
Suitcase, Variation A, clear glass........................20.00
Swan Boat...475.00
Tank, Victory Glass Co, cardboard closure................20.00
Toonerville Trolley......................................700.00
Top, #1, large...60.00
Top, mk USA ½ oz avor, #2 variation....................35.00
Trunk, clear glass......................................130.00
Trunk, milk glass.......................................150.00
Turkey...65.00
Ugly Duckling..75.00
Uncle Sam by Barrel...................................375.00
Willy's Jeep, orig paper.................................18.00
Windmill, pewter top...................................475.00
Windmill, teddy top....................................475.00
World Globe, glass only.................................50.00
World Globe, with stand................................250.00

Canes

Fancy canes and walking sticks were once the mark of a gentleman. Hand carved examples are collected and admired as folk art from the past, and the glass canes that never could have been practical, as unique whimseys of the glass blower's profession.

Canes
Bamboo, dog's head hdl w/glass eyes, label: Cross, London, 34".35.00
Blown glass, aqua w/red/wht/bl/yellow swirl, 59".............285.00
Blown glass, clear w/red/wht/orange swirl, 50½"............205.00

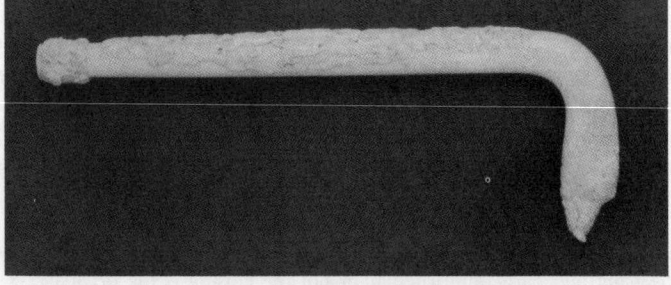

Carved ivory cane handle, boar's head tip, hounds chasing stags down side, acanthus leaves, and wild beasts; late 1800s, 13", $1,320.00.

Inlaid sterling silver hdl, dtd 1914, w/orig cloth sleeve, 36".....90.00
Ivory hdl, carved eagle/shield, gold tooled ferrule, 35½".......230.00
Sawblade housed in slot, Holtzapffel, London, 38"..........295.00
Whale ivory lady's hand/cuff hdl, whalebone shaft, 1860, 32".1,265.00

Walking Sticks

Ebony, w/ivory knob, emb brass eagle on anchor.............75.00
Expanded grip, bludgeon end, Colonial period..............40.00
Geometrics, bold art carving, 35".........................45.00
Gnarled sapling, carved face on top, 37"..................50.00
Gnarled sapling, carved w/2 nude's backs, 38"............35.00
Gnarled sapling, root head man in hat, 35"...............45.00
Lady's leg cast metal hdl, leather washer shaft...........70.00
Mastiff's head, carved ivory, 1800s......................100.00
Oriental, carved bamboo w/insects/snail relief............55.00
Rosewood, mk Sterling silver knob, 35"...................35.00
Shape of cross w/applied porcelain buttons, 40"..........20.00

Canton

From the last part of the 18th century until late in the 1900s, dinnerware was made in and around Canton, China, expressly for western export. This pattern, whose name was borrowed from the city of its manufacture, is decorated in blue on a white ground with a scene containing a bridge, willow trees, birds, and a teahouse. It is completed with various border designs, usually a solid band accompanied by scalloped lines.

Basket, oval, reticulated, 8½x7½x3"........................275.00
Bowl, elongated oval, lemon peel glaze, shallow, 10¼".......150.00
Bowl, fruit; reticulated, oval, 10".........................325.00
Bowl, octagonal, 1800s, 8¼x11".............................150.00
Bowl, oval, shallow, 10⅛" L................................150.00
Bowl, oval, 1800s, 6½x8¾", pr..............................225.00
Bowl, rectangular, 8¾"......................................100.00
Bowl, reticulated, 8½" oval................................295.00
Bowl, scalloped, no mk, ca 1890, shallow, 5¾"...............40.00
Bowl, scalloped rim, eggshell glaze, 9½"...................285.00
Bowl, soup; scalloped, 8¾", set of 4.......................150.00
Bowl, soup; straight edge, 1800s, 8½", set of 10...........325.00
Bowl, sq w/notched corners, 1800s, 10" W...................250.00
Bowl, sq w/shaped rims, 1800s, 9" W, pr....................300.00
Bowl, w/dome lid; rectangular w/canted corners, 10½".......275.00
Bowl, w/lid, berry finial, 9" L............................225.00
Bowl, w/strainer & lid, octagonal, 1800s, 7" dia...........300.00
Cider jug, barrel form, twined hdl, foo puppy lid finial, 9½"....625.00
Creamer, bulbous, 4", VG....................................75.00
Creamer, 5x3"...100.00
Dish w/lid, marquise shaped, 11" L.........................210.00
Ginger jar, early, 10x8"...................................410.00
Hot water dish, oblong octagonal, 1800s, 13½".............300.00
Hot water dish w/cover, octagonal, 1800s, rpr, 10" W.......300.00
Hot water plate, 1800s, 9"................................190.00
Master salt, open, 1800s, 2¾x3½" L........................275.00
Pitcher, helmet form, strap hdl, 6".......................220.00
Plate, 1840s, 6"...30.00
Plate, 1840s, 7½"..50.00
Plate, 1840s, 8½"..60.00
Plate, 9"..65.00
Platter, canted corners, 11"..............................160.00
Platter, canted corners, 12"..............................200.00
Platter, canted corners, 9½"..............................110.00
Platter, octagonal, late 1800s, 18½"......................300.00
Platter, octagonal, 9½x12¾"...............................160.00

Left: marquise shaped covered vegetable dish, blossom finial, 19th century, 11" long, $245.00.
Right: cider jug, barrel form, foo puppy finial, early 19th century, 9½", $625.00.

Platter, reticulated border, 8¼x9½"........................100.00
Posset pot, intertwined strap hdl, berry finial, 3¼", 3 for......270.00
Sauce boat, sm flake on hdl, 7½"..........................100.00
Sauce boat, 1800s, 7½" L..................................125.00
Teapot, domed lid, minor glaze chips on hdl, 9"...........375.00
Toddy jug w/lid, star crack on base, 1800s, 8"............300.00
Tray, cartouch, 1800s, 5½x7½".............................90.00
Tray, octagonal, 1800s, 7x10".............................110.00
Tureen, 6" dia w/8" L under plate.........................325.00
Tureen w/lid, boar's head hdls, 4½x12"....................550.00
Vase, Ku-form, 1800s, 15", pr...........................1,200.00

Capo-Di-Monte

Established in 1743 near Naples, and sponsored by Charles II, King of Naples, Capo-Di-Monte produced soft paste porcelain figurines and dinnerware, usually marked with a 'crown over N' device, though a fleur-de-lys was used on occasion. The factory was closed throughout the 1760s, but reopened in 1771 in the city of Naples. There, both hard and soft paste porcelains were made, sometimes decorated with applied florals in high relief. This technique, and their marks as well, were blatantly copied. As a result, this type of encrusted decoration is often referred to today as Copo-Di-Monte. The original factory closed in 1821. Some of their molds were purchased by the Docceia Porcelain factory in Florence, which continues to operate to the present time.

Nearly all wares of this type on the market today are of fairly recent manufacture. Capo-Di-Monte type wares have been made in Hungary and Germany, as well as France and Italy. Many of these pieces continue to bear the 'crown over N' gold stamp.

Key: C/N-----'crown over N' mark

Box, angel musicians, decorated interior, sgnd, 5½x3" dia.....139.00
Box, shaped top & sides, relief figures, 13½x17x14½".......1,250.00
Cache pot, woman & cherub, castle scene, Toulan, 9½".......180.00
Coffer, relief Bacchic panels w/putti at corners, in wood, 18".2,475.00
Compote, shell form, scroll base, classic design, 6½x13".....115.00
Cup & saucer, demitasse, cherubs & florals in relief on gold.....30.00
Demitasse pot, ftd tray, 6 c/s, sgn P, Capo di Monte, Italy.....250.00
Figurine, African Crowned Crane, sgn Armani, 14"..........265.00

Figurine, boy kneels w/camera, girl sits on wall, C/N, 9″......120.00
Figurine, boy on stump w/fishing pole, C/N, 5¾″.............85.00
Figurine, Cyrano de Bergerac, minor roughage, 6″...........60.00
Figurine, gypsy w/tambourine, parrot on shoulder, 5″.........70.00
Figurine, lady & gentleman from 1700s, common base, C/N, 8″..85.00
Figurine, Last Cab, Armani, 17″ L.....................285.00
Figurine, 2 cherubs w/flower garland, 13″.................625.00
Perfume, cherub in garden, bl crown, old mk, 3″...........95.00
Sauce tureen w/under plate, putti & shells, mc relief, 6″ dia....100.00
Tureen w/lid & under plate, 28 figure relief, C/N mk, 15″ dia..250.00

Footed vase, typical decoration, early underglaze mark, 5¾″ x 2¾″, $165.00.

Carlton

Carlton Ware was the product of Wiltshaw and Robinson, who operated in the Staffordshire district of England from about 1890. During the 1920s, they produced ornamental ware with enameled and gilded decorations such as flowers and birds, often on a black background. In 1958, the firm was renamed Carlton Ware Ltd. Their trademark was a crown over a circular stamp with 'W & R, Stoke on Trent' surrounding a swallow. 'Carlton Ware' was sometimes added by hand.

Biscuit jar, floral on salmon, integral ft, sgn.................75.00
Bowl, w/hdls; beige w/florals & gilt w/in & w/out, 9x13″......110.00
Box, Rouge Royal, flying duck, irises, pearlized w/in, 5x4″.....120.00
Compote, spider in web/dragonfly/butterfly, Rouge Royal, 4x9″..160.00
Ginger jar, Rouge Royal, 7″...........................45.00
Jam, w/leaf cover, Rouge Royal, oval.....................50.00
Pitcher, gr w/florals, 6″.............................40.00
Pitcher, pewter lid, tan w/florals & gilt, 6½″...............85.00
Tray, pin; pink blown-out w/lav & dk pk flowers.............18.00
Vase, enamel decor, Derf Royale, 5½″...................50.00

Carnival Collectibles

Carnival items from the early part of this century represent the lighter side of an America that was alternately prospering and sophisticated, or devastated by war and domestic conflict. But whatever the country's condition, the carnival's thrilling rides and shooting galleries were a sure way of letting it all go by . . . at least for an evening.

Catalog, HC Evans, Chicago, unusual carnival games, etc, 80 pg.75.00
Game, doll, weighted canvas from ball toss, worn pnt, 11″......15.00
Game, 8 men w/hand carved heads, Phila Toboggan, 1913...4,000.00
Kewpie doll, plaster w/water paint color, 12½″..............40.00
Knockdown figure, owl, EX carving, concave rayed eyes, 15″...265.00
Shooting gallery figure, CI bird, wht pnt, 4″.................47.50
Shooting gallery figure, man w/sword/horsebk, CI, J Smith, 6″..185.00
Shooting gallery target, plate steel, kicking donkey, 24x30″....850.00
Shooting gallery targets, row of 8, orig mt, 6 stars, 2 birds.....185.00

Carnival Glass

Carnival glass is pressed glass that has been coated with a sodium solution and fired to give it an exterior luster.

First made in America in 1905, it was produced until the late 1920s and had great popularity in the average American household; for unlike the costly art glass produced by Tiffany, Carnival glass could be mass produced at a small cost.

Colors most found are marigold, green, blue, and purple, but others exist in lesser quantities and include white, clear, red, aqua opalescent, peach opalescent, ice blue, ice green, amber, lavender, and smoke.

Companies mainly responsible for its production in America include the Fenton Art Glass Company, Williamstown, West Virginia; the Northwood Glass Company, Wheeling, West Virginia; the Imperial Glass Company, Bellaire, Ohio; the Millersburg Glass Company, Millersburg, Ohio; and the Dugan Glass Company (Diamond Glass), Indiana, Pennsylvania.

In addition to these major manufacturers, lesser producers included the U.S. Glass Company, the Cambridge Glass Company, the Westmoreland Glass Company, and the McKee Glass Company.

Carnival glass has been highly collectible since the 1950s, and has been reproduced for the last twenty-five years. Several national and state collector's organizations exist, and many fine books are available on old Carnival glass, including *The Standard Encyclopedia of Carnival Glass* by Bill Edwards.

Acorn (Millersburg), compote, rare, either amethyst or green..1,050.00
Acorn Burrs (Northwood), bowl, flat, 5″, amethyst.............50.00
Acorn Burrs (Northwood), covered butter, marigold...........125.00
Acorn Burrs (Northwood), covered sugar, amethyst...........130.00
Acorn Burrs (Northwood), creamer or spooner, marigold........90.00
Acorn Burrs (Northwood), punch bowl & base, blue..........750.00
Acorn Burrs (Northwood), tumbler, marigold.................50.00
Acorn Burrs (Northwood), water pitcher, amethyst............570.00

Age Herald (Fenton), bowl, 9¼″, scarce, amethyst...........865.00
Age Herald (Fenton), plate, 10″, scarce.................910.00
Amaryllis (Northwood), small compote, amethyst.........120.00
Amaryllis (Northwood), small compote, blue.............140.00
Amaryllis (Northwood), small compote, marigold.........195.00
Amaryllis (Northwood), whimsey, flattened, amethyst........175.00
Apothecary Jar, small size, marigold....................50.00
Apple Blossom Twigs (Dugan), bowl, amethyst............58.00

Apple Blossom Twigs (Dugan), bowl, peach opalescent.........65.00
Apple Blossom Twigs (Dugan), plate, blue...................125.00
Apple Blossom Twigs (Dugan), plate, pastel................155.00
Apple Blossoms (Dugan), bowl, 7½″, white...................60.00
Apple Blossoms (Dugan), plate, 8¼″, amethyst..............120.00
Apple Blossoms (Dugan), plate, 8¼″, peach opalescent.......165.00
Apple Panels (English), creamer, green....................36.00
Apple Panels (English), sugar, open, marigold.............30.00
Apple Tree (Fenton), tumbler, blue........................52.00
Apple Tree (Fenton), water pitcher, white................425.00
April Showers (Fenton), vase, amethyst....................55.00
April Showers (Fenton), vase, pastel......................65.00
Arched Panels, tumbler, marigold..........................50.00
Arcs (Imperial), bowl, 8½″, green.........................45.00

Arcs (Imperial), bowl, 8½″, white.........................60.00
Arcs (Imperial), compote, smoke...........................60.00
Asters, bowl, 6″, marigold................................48.00
Astral, shade, marigold...................................45.00

Aurora, bowl, 8½″, marigold...............................50.00
Aurora, bowl, 8½″, pastel.................................70.00
Autumn Acorns (Fenton), bowl, 8¾″, amethyst...............42.00
Autumn Acorns (Fenton), bowl, 8¾″, red...................675.00
Autumn Acorns (Fenton), plate, rare, amethyst............900.00
Autumn Acorns (Fenton), plate, rare, blue................850.00
Aztec (McKee), creamer, clambroth........................150.00
Aztec (McKee), rose bowl, clambroth......................250.00
Aztec (McKee), sugar, marigold...........................100.00
Aztec (McKee), tumbler, rare, marigold...................500.00
Baby Bathtub (US Glass), miniature piece, pastel..........75.00
Balloons (Imperial), cake plate, smoke....................90.00
Balloons (Imperial), compote, marigold....................55.00
Balloons (Imperial), vase, marigold.......................65.00
Banded Diamonds (Crystal), bowl, 10″, marigold............90.00

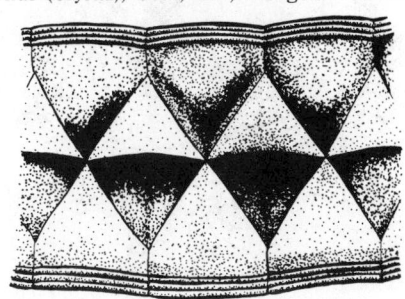

Banded Diamonds (Crystal), bowl, 5″, amethyst.............65.00
Banded Diamonds (Crystal), tumbler, rare, marigold.......450.00
Banded Drape (Fenton), tumbler, white.....................80.00
Banded Drape (Fenton), water pitcher, green..............450.00
Banded Panels (Crystal), open sugar, amethyst.............45.00
Banded Portland (US Glass), puff jar, marigold............60.00
Barber Bottle (Cambridge), green, complete...............420.00
Basket (Northwood), either shape, footed, aqua opalescent.....400.00
Basketweave (Fenton), open edge hat, marigold.............35.00

Basketweave (Fenton), spittoon whimsey, blue...........2,750.00
Basketweave (Fenton), vase whimsey, blue, rare...........325.00
Beaded Acanthus (Imperial), milk pitcher, smoke..........150.00
Beaded Bullseye (Imperial), vase, 8″, smoke...............65.00
Beaded Cable (Northwood), candy dish, blue................70.00
Beaded Cable (Northwood), rose bowl, amethyst.............65.00
Beaded Hearts (Northwood), bowl, amethyst.................60.00
Beaded Panels (Imperial), powder jar w/lid, marigold......50.00
Beaded Shell (Dugan), bowl, ftd, 9″, marigold.............68.00

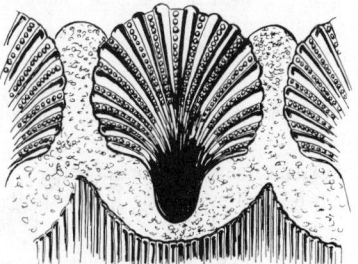

Beaded Shell (Dugan), covered butter, amethyst...........175.00
Beaded Shell (Dugan), creamer, marigold...................75.00

Beaded Shell (Dugan), mug, blue..........................185.00
Beaded Spears (Crystal), pitcher, rare, amethyst.............250.00
Beaded Spears (Crystal), tumbler, rare, marigold.............75.00
Beaded Swirl (English), compote, blue......................55.00
Beaded Swirl (English), milk pitcher, marigold...............60.00
Beads & Bars (US Glass), spooner, marigold.................50.00
Berry Basket, matching shakers, pair, marigold..............65.00
Berry Basket, one size, marigold..........................45.00
Big Fish (Millersburg), banana bowl, rare, amethyst........1,500.00

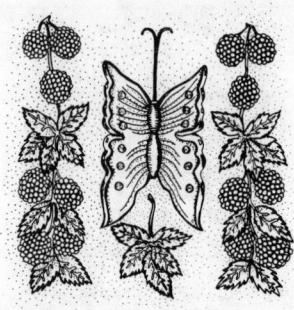

Big Fish (Millersburg), bowl, tri-cornered, green.............900.00
Big Fish (Millersburg), bowl, various shapes, marigold........365.00
Bird Of Paradise (Northwood), bowl, advertising, amethyst.....195.00
Bird Of Paradise (Northwood), plate, advertising, amethyst.....220.00
Blackberry (Northwood), bowl, ftd, 9″, marigold.............47.00
Blackberry (Northwood), compote, amethyst.................65.00
Blackberry Block (Fenton), pitcher, marigold................250.00
Blackberry Block (Fenton), tumbler, white..................200.00
Blackberry Spray (Fenton), bon bon, blue...................40.00
Blackberry Spray (Fenton), compote, marigold...............35.00
Blackberry Spray (Fenton), hat shape, aqua opalescnet.........95.00
Blackberry Wreath (Millersburg), plate, 8″, rare, green........850.00
Blocks & Arches (Crystal), pitcher, rare, marigold............150.00
Blocks & Arches (Crystal), tumbler, rare, amethyst...........85.00
Blossom & Spears, plate, 8″, marigold.....................45.00
Blossoms & Band (Imperial), wall vase, complete, marigold.....42.00
Blueberry (Fenton), pitcher, scarce, marigold...............400.00
Blueberry (Fenton), tumbler, scarce, blue..................85.00
Bo Peep (Westmoreland), ABC plate, rare, marigold..........450.00
Bo Peep (Westmoreland), mug, scarce, marigold.............190.00
Boggy Bayou, see Panelled Diamond & Bows
Border Plants (Dugan), bowl, flat, 8½″, amethyst............50.00
Border Plants (Dugan), bowl, ftd, 8½″, peach opal...........85.00
Briar Patch, hat shape, amethyst.........................45.00
Brocaded Summer Gardens, center bowl, ftd, pastel..........100.00
Brocaded Summer Gardens, rose bowl, pastel...............70.00
Brocaded Summer Gardens, wine, pastel...................45.00
Broken Arches (Imperial), bowl, 8½″, amethyst.............50.00
Broken Arches (Imperial), punch bowl & base, marigold.......290.00
Brooklyn, bottle w/stopper, marigold......................70.00
Bubble Berry, shade, pastel.............................60.00
Bull Dog, paperweight, marigold.........................250.00
Bull's Eye & Loop (Millersburg), vase, rare, 11″, amethyst.....175.00
Bull's Eye & Spearhead, wine, marigold....................48.00
Butterflies & Bells (Crystal), compote, amethyst.............125.00
Butterflies & Waratah (Crystal), compote, large, amethyst......250.00
Butterfly, pin tray, marigold............................35.00
Butterfly & Berry (Fenton), bowl, ftd, 10″, blue.............80.00
Butterfly & Berry (Fenton), bowl whimsey, blue............1,350.00
Butterfly & Berry (Fenton), covered butter, amethyst.........240.00

Butterfly & Berry (Fenton), covered sugar, green.............190.00
Butterfly & Berry (Fenton), pitcher, white..................650.00
Butterfly & Berry (Fenton), spooner, amethyst..............160.00
Butterfly & Berry (Fenton), vase, marigold.................55.00
Butterfly & Fern (Fenton), pitcher, green..................475.00
Butterfly & Fern (Fenton), tumbler, blue...................50.00
Butterfly & Tulip (Dugan), bowl, ftd, 10½″, scarce, marigold...375.00
Butterfly & Tulip (Dugan), bowl, whimsey shape, rare, marigold.850.00
Butterfly Bower (Crystal), cake plate, stemmed, amethyst.......175.00
Butterfly Bower (Crystal), compote, marigold...............80.00
Butterfly Bush (Crystal), compote, large, marigold...........110.00
Buttress (US Glass), pitcher, rare, marigold................300.00
Buzz Saw (Cambridge), cruet, small, 4″, rare, green.........375.00
Cane (Imperial), bowl, 10″, pastel.......................45.00
Cane (Imperial), wine, marigold.........................50.00
Cane & Daisy Cut (Jenkins), basket, hdld, rare, pastel........190.00
Cane & Daisy Cut (Jenkins), vase, marigold................90.00
Cannonball Variant, pitcher, marigold.....................250.00
Cannonball Variant, tumbler, marigold....................60.00
Capitol (Westmoreland), bowl, ftd, small, amethyst...........65.00
Capitol (Westmoreland), mug, small, marigold..............75.00
Captive Rose (Fenton), bon bon, marigold.................40.00
Captive Rose (Fenton), bowl, 10″, amethyst...............50.00
Captive Rose (Fenton), compote, blue....................48.00
Captive Rose (Fenton), plate, 7″, pastel..................135.00
Carolina Dogwood (Westmoreland), plate, rare, milk glass opal..290.00
Cartwheel #411 (Heisey), compote, marigold...............40.00
Cartwheel #411 (Heisey), goblet, marigold.................60.00
Cathedral, bowl, 10″, marigold..........................40.00
Cathedral, butter dish, marigold.........................185.00
Cathedral, chalice, 7″, blue............................115.00
Cathedral, compote, blue...............................55.00
Cathedral Arches (English), punch bowl, one piece, marigold...250.00
Chatham (US Glass), candlestick, marigold, pr..............75.00
Chatham (US Glass), compote, marigold...................65.00
Checkerboard (Westmoreland), punch cup, marigold.........75.00
Checkerboard (Westmoreland), tumbler, marigold, rare.......600.00
Checkerboard (Westmoreland), wine, marigold, rare.........250.00
Checkers, butter, marigold.............................140.00
Checkers, plate, 7″, marigold...........................50.00
Cherry (Dugan), bowl, flat, 5″, marigold..................30.00
Cherry (Dugan), bowl, 8½″, ftd, amethyst................75.00
Cherry (Dugan), cruet, rare, white.......................500.00
Cherry (Millersburg), bowl, 4″, amethyst.................50.00
Cherry (Millersburg), covered butter, green................165.00
Cherry (Millersburg), creamer, marigold..................65.00
Cherry (Millersburg), milk pitcher, rare, green.............525.00
Cherry (Millersburg), plate, 6″, rare, marigold.............425.00
Cherry (Millersburg), tumbler, green.....................250.00
Cherry & Cable (Northwood), bowl, 5″, scarce, marigold......45.00
Cherry & Cable (Northwood), butter, rare, marigold.........350.00
Cherry & Cable Intaglio (Northwood), bowl, 10″, marigold.....36.00
Cherry Blossoms (Fenton), pitcher, blue..................95.00

Cherry Chain (Fenton), bon bon, marigold.................37.00
Cherry Chain (Fenton), bowl, 7½″, green.................70.00
Cherry Chain (Fenton), plate, 7″, blue.................110.00
Cherry Smash (US Glass), bowl, 8″, marigold.................50.00
Cherry Smash (US Glass), butter, marigold.................110.00
Cherry Smash (US Glass), tumbler, marigold.................135.00
Chrysanthemum (Fenton), bowl, 10″, ftd, green.................90.00
Chrysanthemum (Fenton), bowl, 9″, flat, pastel.................90.00
Circle Scroll (Dugan), compote, scarce, amethyst.................125.00
Circle Scroll (Dugan), spooner, marigold.................150.00
Circle Scroll (Dugan), sugar, amethyst.................350.00
Circle Scroll (Dugan), vase whimsey, rare, marigold.................120.00
Classic Arts (English), powder jar, marigold.................175.00
Classic Arts (English), rose bowl, marigold.................160.00
Classic Arts (English), vase, 7″, Egyptian, marigold.................145.00
Cleopatra, bottle, marigold.................100.00
Coal Bucket (US Glass), one size, marigold.................90.00
Cobblestones (Dugan), bowl, 9″, marigold.................55.00
Coin Dot (Fenton), basket whimsey, rare, blue.................85.00
Coin Dot (Fenton), pitcher, rare, marigold.................295.00
Coin Dot Variant (Westmoreland), compote, marigold.................60.00
Coin Dot Variant (Westmoreland), rose bowl, amethyst.................75.00
Coin Spot (Dugan), compote, green.................62.00
Colonial (Imperial), candlesticks, marigold, pr.................185.00
Colonial (Imperial), vase, marigold.................38.00
Colonial Lady (Imperial), vase, rare, amethyst.................300.00
Columbia (Imperial), vase, amethyst.................48.00
Columbus, plate, 8″, marigold.................38.00
Compote Vase, stemmed shape, blue.................60.00
Concave Flute (Westmoreland), rose bowl, green.................65.00
Concave Flute (Westmoreland), vase, amethyst.................60.00
Concord (Fenton), bowl, 9″, amber.................95.00
Concord (Fenton), plate, 10″, rare, marigold.................300.00
Corn Bottle (Imperial), one size, marigold.................285.00
Cornucopia (Fenton), candlestick, 5″, marigold, pr.................75.00
Cosmos (Millersburg), bowl, 5″, green.................55.00
Cosmos (Millersburg), plate, 6″, green.................65.00
Cosmos & Cane, bowl, 5″, white.................70.00
Cosmos & Cane, covered butter, marigold.................175.00
Cosmos & Cane, covered sugar, marigold.................125.00
Cosmos & Cane, tumbler, marigold.................85.00
Cosmos Variant (Fenton), plate, 10″, rare, amethyst.................110.00
Country Kitchen (Millersburg), covered butter, rare, marigold...400.00
Country Kitchen (Millersburg), creamer, amethyst.................325.00
Country Kitchen (Millersburg), vase whimsey, rare, marigold....400.00
Crab Claw (Imperial), bowl, 10″, marigold.................45.00

Crab Claw (Imperial), tumbler, scarce, marigold.................95.00
Crackle (Imperial), bowl, 5″, green.................15.00
Crackle (Imperial), pitcher, dome base, marigold.................85.00
Crackle (Imperial), plate, amethyst.................45.00
Crackle (Imperial), punch cup, marigold.................10.00
Crucifix (Imperial), candlestick, rare, marigold, each.................400.00

Cut Ovals (Fenton), bowl, 7″, pastel.................70.00
Cut Ovals (Fenton), candlesticks, marigold, pr.................65.00
Cut Sprays, vase, 9″, peach opalescent.................60.00
Dahlia (Dugan), bowl, 5″, ftd, marigold.................40.00
Dahlia (Dugan), spooner, amethyst.................100.00
Dahlia (Dugan), sugar, white.................250.00
Dahlia (Fenton), twist epergne, one lily, marigold.................250.00
Dahlia & Drape (Fenton), tumble-up, complete, ice blue.................185.00
Daisy & Cane (English), decanter, rare, marigold.................75.00
Daisy & Cane (English), spittoon, rare, blue.................185.00
Daisy & Plume (Northwood), candy dish, amethyst.................55.00
Daisy & Plume (Northwood), rose bowl, blue.................75.00
Daisy Basket (Imperial), one size, smoke.................60.00
Daisy Chain, shade, marigold.................45.00
Daisy In Oval Panels (US Glass), sugar, marigold.................50.00
Daisy Web (Dugan), hat, rare, peach opalescent.................68.00
Dandelion (Northwood), mug, blue opalescent.................650.00
Dandelion (Northwood), tumbler, blue.................90.00
Dandelion (Northwood), vase whimsey, rare, amethyst.................650.00
Diamond & File, bowl, 7″, marigold.................35.00
Diamond & Rib (Fenton), funeral vase, 17″, marigold.................275.00
Diamond Band (Crystal), float set, amethyst.................300.00
Diamond Band (Crystal), open sugar, marigold.................38.00
Diamond Checkerboard, bowl, 5″, marigold.................25.00
Diamond Checkerboard, butter, marigold.................70.00
Diamond Checkerboard, cracker jar, marigold.................75.00
Diamond Daisy, plate, 8″, marigold.................40.00
Diamond Flutes (English), parfait, marigold.................40.00
Diamond Ovals (English), open sugar, marigold.................35.00
Diamond Pinwheel (English), butter, marigold.................65.00
Diamond Point, basket, rare, blue.................385.00
Diamond Point Columns (Imperial), butter, marigold.................65.00
Diamond Point Columns (Imperial), plate, 7″, marigold.................35.00
Diamond Point Columns (Imperial), spooner, marigold.................40.00
Diamond Prisms (English), compote, marigold.................45.00
Diamonds (Millersburg), pitcher, amethyst.................185.00
Diamonds (Millersburg), pitcher oddity, no spout, green.................250.00
Diamonds (Millersburg), tumbler, amethyst.................50.00
Dog, ash tray, marigold.................65.00
Dotted Daisies, plate, 8″, marigold.................65.00
Double Dolphins (Fenton), bowl, ftd, 9″, pastel.................110.00
Double Dolphins (Fenton), cake plate, center hdl, pastel.................70.00
Double Dolphins (Fenton), fan vase, pastel.................65.00
Double Scroll (Imperial), bowl, pastel.................65.00
Double Scroll (Imperial), candlestick, green, pr.................60.00
Double Star (Cambridge), pitcher, scarce, marigold.................350.00
Double Star (Cambridge), tumbler, scarce, marigold.................60.00
Dragon & Lotus (Fenton), bowl, ftd, 9″, amethyst.................67.00
Dragon & Lotus (Fenton), plate, 9½″, rare, marigold.................570.00
Dragon's Tongue (Fenton), bowl, 11″, scarce, marigold.................285.00
Dragon's Tongue (Fenton), shade, peach opalescent.................75.00
Dragonfly, shade, pastel.................48.00
Eagle Furniture (Northwood), plate, amethyst.................175.00
Embroidered Mums (Northwood), bowl, marigold, 9″.................48.00
Embroidered Mums (Northwood), stemmed bon bon, pastel....115.00
Emu (Crystal), bowl, 10″, rare, amber.................450.00
Emu (Crystal), bowl, 5″, rare, marigold.................60.00
English Button Band (English), creamer, marigold.................38.00
Engraved Floral (Fenton), tumbler, green.................85.00
Engraved Grapes (Fenton), pitcher, squat, marigold.................80.00
Engraved Grapes (Fenton), tumble-up, marigold.................135.00
Engraved Grapes (Fenton), vase, 8″, pastel.................50.00
Exchange Bank (Northwood), plate, 6″, amethyst.................200.00
Fancy Cut (English), miniature pitcher, rare, marigold.................125.00

Fancy Flowers (Imperial), compote, green.................110.00
Fans (English), pitcher, marigold......................60.00
Fantail (Fenton), bowl, 9″, ftd, blue...................35.00
Fantail (Fenton), compote, marigold...................45.00
Farmyard (Dugan), bowl, 10″, rare, amethyst............2,600.00
Fashion (Imperial), bowl, 9″, smoke...................47.00
Fashion (Imperial), butter, amethyst..................185.00
Fashion (Imperial), punch bowl & base, marigold.........70.00
Fashion (Imperial), rose bowl whimsey, rare, marigold........55.00
Feather Stitch (Fenton), bowl, 10″, amethyst...........75.00
Feather Swirl (US Glass), butter, marigold.............110.00
Feather Swirl (US Glass), vase, marigold...............50.00
Feathered Arrow (English), bowl, 8½″, marigold.........40.00
Fentonia Fruit (Fenton), bowl, ftd, 10″, blue..........150.00
Fentonia Fruit (Fenton), pitcher, rare, marigold.........375.00
Fentonia Fruit (Fenton), tumbler, rare, blue...........150.00
Fern (Fenton), bowl, 7″, rare, blue..................800.00
Fern (Northwood), bowl, 6½″, green..................50.00
Fern (Northwood), compote, pastel...................80.00
Fern (Northwood), hat, rare, marigold................52.00
Fern Brand Chocolates (Northwood), plate, amethyst.........175.00
Field Flower (Imperial), milk pitcher, rare, marigold.........165.00
Field Flower (Imperial), pitcher, scarce, blue...........290.00

Field Flower (Imperial), tumbler, scarce, amber...........90.00
Field Thistle (US Glass), butter, marigold.............125.00
Field Thistle (US Glass), spooner, marigold, rare...........70.00
Field Thistle (US Glass), vase, marigold...............60.00
File & Fan, bowl, 6″, ftd, marigold..................38.00
File & Fan, compote, aqua opalescent................100.00
Fine Cut Rings (English), celery, marigold.............58.00
Fine Cut Rings (English), oval bowl, marigold...........40.00
Fine Cut Rings (English), stemmed cake stand, marigold.......70.00
Fine Rib (Northwood & Fenton), bowl, 5″, green.........36.00
Fine Rib (Northwood & Fenton), compote, peach opalescent....50.00
Fish Net (Dugan), epergne, amethyst.................285.00
Five Hearts (Dugan), bowl, 8¾″, dome base, marigold.......48.00
Flannel Flower (Crystal), cake stand, amethyst...........175.00
Fleur De Lis (Jenkins), vase, green..................225.00
Flickering Flames, shade, pastel....................45.00
Floral & Grape (Dugan), pitcher, marigold.............95.00
Floral & Grape (Dugan), tumbler, amethyst.............35.00
Floral & Grape Variant (Fenton), pitcher, marigold.........95.00
Floral & Grape Variant (Fenton), tumbler, blue..........30.00
Floral & Optic (Imperial), bowl, ftd, 10″, peach opalescent....150.00
Floral & Optic (Imperial), cake plate, ftd, pastel..........50.00
Floral Fan, etched vase, marigold...................42.00
Florentine (Imperial), hat vase, pastel................85.00
Flower & Beads, plate, 7½″, 6 sided, amethyst..........110.00
Flower & Beads, plate, 8½″, round, marigold...........75.00
Flower Basket, one size, marigold...................48.00

Flowering Dill (Fenton), hat, green..................42.00
Flowering Dill (Fenton), hat, red...................220.00
Flute (British), sherbet, mkd 'British', marigold..........45.00
Flute (Millersburg), punch bowl & base, marigold.........150.00
Flute (Millersburg), sugar, green....................90.00
Flute (Northwood), butter, amethyst.................165.00
Flute (Northwood), creamer or sugar, amethyst..........85.00
Flute (Northwood), ring tree, rare, marigold............175.00
Flute (Northwood), tumbler, 3 varieties, green..........70.00
Flute & Cane (Imperial), champagne, rare, marigold.......120.00
Flute & Cane (Imperial), punch cup, marigold...........28.00
Flute #3 (Imperial), amethyst spooner................95.00
Flute #3 (Imperial), covered butter, marigold...........175.00
Flute #3 (Imperial), punch bowl & base, marigold.........275.00
Footed Drape (Westmoreland), vase, white.............50.00
Footed Prism Panels (English), vase, blue.............85.00
Formal (Dugan), vase, jack-in-pulpit, rare, amethyst.......100.00
Forty-Niner (Imperial), pitcher, squat, marigold.........250.00
Forty-Niner (Imperial), tumbler, marigold.............75.00
Four Flowers Variant (Westmoreland), bowl, 8½″, ftd, green....75.00
Four Hundred Seventy Four (Imperial), cup, amethyst.......40.00
Four Hundred Seventy Four (Imperial), sugar, marigold......60.00
Four Hundred Seventy Four (Imperial), tumbler, green.......65.00
French Knots (Fenton), hat, blue...................42.00
Frosted Block (Imperial), compote, clambroth...........120.00
Frosted Block (Imperial), covered butter, marigold.........67.00
Frosted Block (Imperial), pickle dish, hdld, rare, marigold.....40.00
Frosted Buttons (Fenton), bowl, 10″, ftd, pastel.........175.00
Frosted Ribbon, tumbler, marigold..................27.00
Frosty, bottle, marigold.........................25.00
Fruit & Flowers (Northwood), banana plate, 7″, rare, green....110.00
Fruit & Flowers (Northwood), bon bon, stemmed, marigold.....38.00
Fruit & Flowers (Northwood), bowl, 5″, amethyst.........32.00
Fruit & Flowers (Northwood), fruit bowl, 10″, marigold......56.00
Fruit Jar (Ball), one size, marigold..................65.00
Fruit Salad (Westmoreland), punch bowl & base, rare, marigold.650.00
Garden Mums (Northwood), bowl, 10″, blue............75.00
Garden Mums (Northwood), plate, 7″, handgrip, marigold.....70.00
Garden Mums (Northwood), plate, 7″, regular, green.......110.00
Garden Path (Dugan), bowl, 5″, peach opalescent.........47.00
Garden Path (Dugan), compote, rare, marigold..........175.00
Gay 90's (Millersburg), tumbler, amethyst, rare..........975.00
Georgia Belle (Dugan), card tray, ftd, rare, peach opalescent....80.00
Georgia Belle (Dugan), compote, ftd, marigold..........65.00
Goddess Athena, epergne, rare, green...............1,800.00
Gold Fish, bowl, marigold.......................70.00
Golden Cupids (Crystal), bowl, 5″, rare, pastel..........75.00
Golden Grapes (Dugan), bowl, 7″, marigold...........36.00
Golden Harvest (US Glass), wine, marigold............28.00
Golden Honeycomb (Imperial), bon bon, amber..........60.00
Golden Honeycomb (Imperial), bowl, 5″, marigold........25.00
Golden Honeycomb (Imperial), creamer or sugar, marigold....32.00
Golden Oxen, mug, marigold.....................48.00
Golden Wedding, bottle, small, marigold..............16.00
Good Luck (Northwood), bowl, 8¾″, amethyst..........135.00
Good Luck (Northwood), plate, 9″, marigold...........210.00
Gooseberry Spray, bowl, 10″, marigold...............50.00
Gooseberry Spray, compote, blue...................125.00
Graceful (Northwood), vase, amethyst...............70.00
Grape, Heavy (Dugan); bowl, 5″, rare, amethyst.........55.00
Grape, Heavy (Imperial); bowl, 9″, blue..............56.00
Grape, Heavy (Imperial); fruit bowl w/base, marigold......195.00
Grape, Heavy (Imperial); nappy, marigold.............35.00
Grape, Heavy (Imperial); plate, 6″, marigold...........50.00
Grape (Fenton's Gr & Cable), bowl, 8½″, marigold.......42.00

Grape (Fenton's Gr & Cable), plate, ftd, 9", green............160.00
Grape (Imperial), bowl, 5", marigold......................18.00
Grape (Imperial), compote, amethyst......................55.00
Grape (Imperial), cup & saucer, pastel....................60.00
Grape (Imperial), fruit bowl, 8¾", amethyst...............50.00
Grape (Imperial), fruit bowl, 8¾", red....................65.00
Grape (Imperial), plate, 12", green......................80.00
Grape (Imperial), plate, 8½", ruffled, marigold...........58.00
Grape (Imperial), punch cup, amber......................30.00
Grape (Imperial), rose bowl, rare, marigold..............175.00
Grape (Imperial), tray, center hdl, marigold...............38.00
Grape (Imperial), tumbler, marigold......................15.00
Grape (Imperial), water bottle, rare, marigold............125.00
Grape (Imperial), wine, pastel...........................30.00
Grape (Northwood's Gr & Cable), bon bon, amethyst.......45.00
Grape (Northwood's Gr & Cable), bowl, ftd, 9", green.....65.00
Grape (Northwood's Gr & Cable), bowl, 5½", flat, pastel....50.00
Grape (Northwood's Gr & Cable), butter, pastel...........275.00
Grape (Northwood's Gr & Cable), candlesticks, marigold, pr....150.00
Grape (Northwood's Gr & Cable), compote, covered, amethyst..410.00
Grape (Northwood's Gr & Cable), compote, open, amethyst....475.00

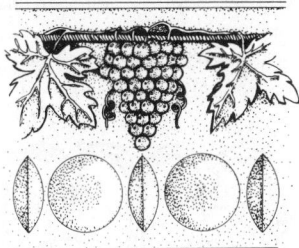

Grape (Northwood's Gr & Cable), cookie jar w/lid, amethyst....265.00
Grape (Northwood's Gr & Cable), cup & saucer, rare, marigold.400.00
Grape (Northwood's Gr & Cable), ice cream bowl, 11", green...250.00
Grape (Northwood's Gr & Cable), ice cream sherbet, marigold...35.00
Grape (Northwood's Gr & Cable), nappy, green..............65.00
Grape (Northwood's Gr & Cable), orange bowl, ftd, marigold...135.00
Grape (Northwood's Gr & Cable), pin tray, marigold.........105.00
Grape (Northwood's Gr & Cable), pitcher, standard, marigold...270.00
Grape (Northwood's Gr & Cable), punch cup, amethyst........35.00
Grape (Northwood's Gr & Cable), scalloped bowl, 5½", pastel..58.00
Grape (Northwood's Gr & Cable), shot glass, amethyst......150.00
Grape (Northwood's Gr & Cable), sugar w/lid, pastel........170.00
Grape (Northwood's Gr & Cable), sweetmeat w/lid, marigold....875.00
Grape (Northwood's Gr & Cable), sweetmeat whimsey, marigold.400.00
Grape (Northwood's Gr & Cable), tumbler, jumbo, marigold....54.00
Grape (Northwood's Gr & Cable), tumbler, regular, marigold....40.00
Grape & Cherry (English), bowl, 8½", rare, marigold.........65.00
Grape & Gothic Arches (Northwood), bowl, 10", blue.........60.00
Grape & Gothic Arches (Northwood), bowl, 5", marigold......24.00
Grape & Gothic Arches (Northwood), butter, green..........185.00
Grape & Gothic Arches (Northwood), pitcher, amethyst......375.00
Grape & Gothic Arches (Northwood), sugar w/lid, green......95.00
Grape & Gothic Arches (Northwood), tumbler, blue..........50.00
Grape Arbor (Dugan), bowl, ftd, 11", amethyst.............75.00
Grape Arbor (Northwood), hat, blue......................125.00
Grape Arbor (Northwood), tumbler, marigold...............45.00
Grape Delight (Dugan), nut bowl, 6 ftd, amethyst...........75.00
Grape Delight (Dugan), rose bowl, 6 ftd, amethyst..........65.00
Grape Leaves (Northwood), bowl, 8¾", marigold............60.00
Grape Leaves (Northwood), bride's basket, complete, amethyst.235.00
Grape Wreath (Millersburg), bowl, 5", green...............55.00
Grape Wreath (Millersburg), ice cream bowl, 10", marigold....125.00
Grapevine Lattice (Fenton), pitcher, rare, marigold.........220.00
Greek Key (Northwood), plate, 9", rare, marigold...........185.00

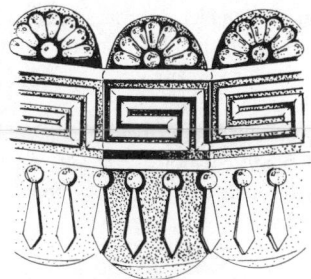

Greek Key (Northwood), tumbler, rare, green..............128.00
Hand Vase (English), one shape, 8", amethyst.............300.00
Harvest Flower (Dugan), tumbler, marigold...............120.00
Harvest Poppy, compote, amethyst.......................50.00
Hatchet (US Glass), one shape, marigold.................145.00
Heart & Horseshoe (Fenton), bowl, 8½"..................495.00
Heart & Trees (Fenton), bowl, 8¾", marigold.............145.00
Heart & Vine (Fenton), bowl, 8½", marigold...............38.00

Heart & Vine (Fenton), plate, 9", rare, amethyst...........225.00
Hearts & Flowers (Northwood), bowl, 8½", blue............58.00
Hearts & Flowers (Northwood), compote, marigold..........36.00
Heavy Diamond (Imperial), bowl, 10", marigold............32.00
Heavy Diamond (Imperial), sugar, marigold...............28.00
Heavy Heart (Higbee), tumbler, marigold.................75.00
Heavy Prisms (English), celery vase, 6", amethyst..........90.00
Heavy Vine, atomizer, marigold.........................65.00
Heisey #357, tumbler, marigold.........................42.00
Heisey #357, water bottle, marigold.....................75.00
Hobnail, Miniature; tumbler, 2½".......................48.00
Hobnail (Millersburg), creamer, rare, marigold............275.00
Hobnail (Millersburg), spittoon, rare, marigold............600.00
Hobnail Panels (McKee), vase, 8¾", clambroth............65.00
Hobstar (Imperial), berry, bowl, 10", pastel...............45.00
Hobstar (Imperial), creamer, marigold...................40.00
Hobstar (Imperial), fruit bowl w/base, amethyst...........85.00
Hobstar & Cut Triangles (English), bowl, green............58.00
Hobstar & Feather (Millersburg), dessert, stemmed, marigold...650.00

Hobstar & Feather (Millersburg), punch cup, scarce, marigold...26.00
Hobstar & Fruit (Westmoreland), bowl, 6", rare, peach opal.....90.00

Hobstar Band (Imperial), tumbler, 2 shapes, rare, marigold......54.00
Hobstar Flower (Northwood), compote, scarce, amethyst........65.00
Hobstar Panels (English), creamer......................45.00
Hobstar Reversed (English), butter, marigold................58.00
Hobstar Reversed (English), frog & holder, marigold..........50.00
Hobstar Whirl (Whirlagig), compote, 4½″ tall, amethyst.......58.00
Holly, Panelled (Northwood); bon bon, ftd, green.............57.00
Holly, Panelled (Northwood); bowl, green...................65.00
Holly (Fenton), bowl, 10″, marigold.......................36.00

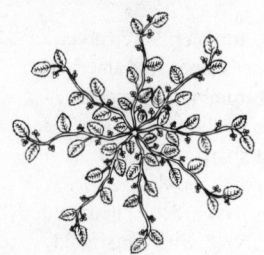

Holly (Fenton), compote, 5″, blue.........................36.00
Holly (Fenton), hat, amethyst............................32.00
Holly & Berry (Dugan), bowl, 9″, peach opalescent..........60.00
Holly & Berry (Dugan), gravy boat, hdld, blue..............62.00
Holly & Berry (Dugan), nappy, marigold....................42.00
Holly Sprig or Whirl (Millersburg), bowl, 7″, ruffled, green.....60.00
Holly Sprig or Whirl (Millersburg), deep sauce, rare, amethyst..175.00
Homestead, shade, marigold.............................40.00
Honeycomb & Clover (Fenton), bon bon, marigold............38.00
Honeycomb & Clover (Fenton), compote, green...............57.00
Horn of Plenty, bottle, marigold..........................56.00
Horses Heads (Fenton), bowl, 7½″, flat, marigold............57.00

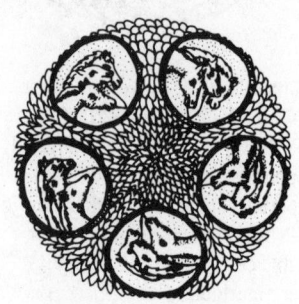

Horses Heads (Fenton), rose bowl, ftd, pastel...............195.00
Horseshoe, shot glass, marigold.........................42.00
Hourglass, bud vase, marigold...........................46.00
Humpty-Dumpty, mustard jar, marigold...................75.00
Ice Crystals, bowl, ftd, pastel...........................85.00
Ice Crystals, candlesticks, pastel, pr.....................160.00
Idyll (Fenton), vase, rare, amethyst......................375.00
Illinois Daisy (English), bowl, 8″, marigold.................40.00
Illinois Daisy (English), cookie jar w/lid, marigold...........55.00
Illusion (Fenton), bon bon, marigold......................47.00
Illusion (Fenton), bowl, blue............................90.00
Intaglio Daisy (English), bowl, 7½″, marigold...............48.00
Intaglio Feathers, cup, marigold.........................25.00
Intaglio Ovals (US Glass), bowl, 7″, pastel.................65.00
Intaglio Ovals (US Glass), plate, 7½″, pastel...............80.00
Interior Panels, mug, marigold..........................75.00
Interior Poinsettia (Northwood), tumbler, rare, marigold......465.00
Interior Rays (Westmoreland), covered butter, marigold........65.00
Interior Rays (Westmoreland), jam jar, marigold.............40.00
Inverted Coin Dot (Northwood & Fenton), pitcher, marigold...225.00
Inverted Coin Dot (Northwood & Fenton), rose bowl, marigold...47.00
Inverted Feather (Cambridge), covered butter, rare, marigold..250.00
Inverted Feather (Cambridge), punch cup, rare, green.........65.00

Inverted Feather (Cambridge), sugar, marigold..............190.00
Inverted Strawberry, bowl, 5″, amethyst...................50.00
Inverted Strawberry, candlesticks, rare, marigold, pr.........250.00
Inverted Strawberry, powder jar, rare, green................130.00

Inverted Strawberry, spooner, rare, marigold...............90.00
Inverted Strawberry, table set, 2 pcs, stemmed, rare, amethyst..575.00
Inverted Thistle (Cambridge), bowl, 5″, rare, amethyst.........85.00
Inverted Thistle (Cambridge), bowl, 9″, rare, green...........200.00
Jacob's Ladder, perfume, marigold.......................47.00
Jacobean Ranger (Czechoslovakian & English), wine, marigold...28.00
Jewelled Heart (Dugan), bowl, 5″, peach opalescent..........65.00

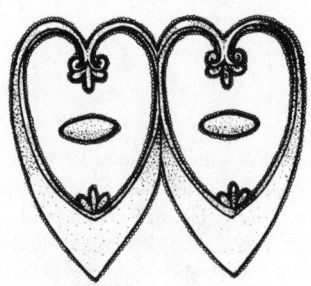

Jewelled Heart (Dugan), tumbler, rare, marigold.............100.00
Jewels (Imperial), candlesticks, red, pr....................210.00
Kangaroo (Australian), bowl, 9½″, amethyst................97.00
Kitten, miniature paperweight, rare, marigold...............250.00
Kittens, bottle, pastel.................................52.00
Kittens (Fenton), bowl, 4″, scarce, marigold................118.00

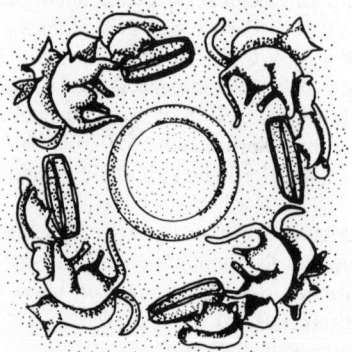

Kittens (Fenton), cup & saucer, scarce, marigold............252.00
Kittens (Fenton), plate, 4½″, scarce, marigold..............128.00
Kiwi (Australian), bowl, 10″, rare, marigold................135.00
Kokomo (English), rose bowl, ftd, green...................60.00
Lacy Dewdrop (Westmoreland), bowl, covered, pastel.........240.00
Lacy Dewdrop (Westmoreland), goblet, pastel...............150.00
Lady's Slipper, one shape, rare, marigold..................250.00
Lattice & Daisy (Dugan), bowl, 5″, marigold................30.00

Lattice & Daisy (Dugan), tumbler, marigold..................40.00
Lattice & Leaves, vase, 9½″, marigold..................50.00
Lattice & Points (Dugan), vase, amethyst..................42.00
Lattice & Prisms, cologne w/stopper, marigold..................55.00
Lattice & Sprays, vase, 10½″, marigold..................40.00
Laurel, shade, pastel..................40.00
Laurel Band, tumbler, marigold..................42.00
Laurel Leaves (Imperial), plate, amethyst..................55.00
Leaf & Beads (Northwood & Dugan), bowl, 9″, marigold........70.00
Leaf & Beads (Northwood & Dugan), candy dish, ftd, white....130.00
Leaf & Beads (Northwood & Dugan), rose bowl, ftd, green......67.00
Leaf Chain (Fenton), bon bon, marigold..................35.00
Leaf Chain (Fenton), plate, 9¼″, blue..................85.00
Leaf Column (Northwood), vase, green..................40.00
Leaf Swirl (Westmoreland), compote, amethyst..................55.00
Leaf Swirl (Westmoreland), compote, teal..................58.00
Leaf Swirl & Flower (Fenton), vase, marigold..................45.00
Leaf Tiers (Fenton), bowl, 5″, ftd, marigold..................30.00
Leaf Tiers (Fenton), butter, ftd, marigold..................175.00
Leaf Tiers (Fenton), creamer, ftd, marigold..................82.00
Lined Lattice (Dugan), vase, 7″, white..................60.00
Lion (Fenton), bowl, 7″, scarce, marigold..................85.00
Lion (Fenton), plate, 7½″, rare, marigold..................320.00
Little Beads, bowl, 8″, peach opalescent..................45.00
Little Beads, compote, small, marigold..................26.00
Little Daisies (Fenton), bowl, 8″, rare, blue..................245.00
Little Darling, bottle, marigold..................52.00
Little Flowers (Fenton), bowl, 5½″, vaseline..................50.00

Little Flowers (Fenton), bowl, 9¼″, blue..................85.00
Little Stars (Millersburg), plate, 7¾″, rare, green..................275.00
Long Hobstar, bowl, 8½″, marigold..................45.00
Long Hobstar, punch bowl & base, clambroth..................135.00
Long Horn, wine, marigold..................35.00
Long Leaf (Dugan), bowl, ftd, peach opalescent..................58.00
Long Thumbprint (Dugan), bowl, 8¾″, amethyst..................38.00
Long Thumbprint (Dugan), butter, marigold..................60.00
Lotus & Grape (Fenton), bon bon, blue..................42.00
Lotus & Grape (Fenton), bowl, 7″, flat, green..................50.00
Lotus Land (Northwood), bon bon, amethyst..................80.00
Louisa (Westmoreland), candy dish, ftd, green..................65.00
Louisa (Westmoreland), rose bowl, marigold..................52.00
Lovebirds, bottle w/stopper, marigold..................130.00
Lucky Bell, bowl, 8¾″, rare, marigold..................65.00

Luster, tumbler, marigold..................40.00
Lustre & Clear (Fenton), fan vase, blue..................50.00
Lustre & Clear (Imperial), butter dish, marigold..................65.00
Lustre & Clear (Imperial), pitcher, marigold..................195.00
Lustre & Clear (Imperial), vase, ftd, 8″, amethyst..................110.00
Lustre & Clear (Lightolier), shade, marigold..................40.00
Lustre Flute (Northwood), hat, green..................36.00
Lustre Flute (Northwood), nappy, marigold..................30.00
Lustre Flute (Northwood), punch bowl & base, green........150.00
Lustre Flute (Northwood), punch cup, amethyst..................24.00
Lustre Flute (Northwood), sugar, amethyst..................55.00
Lustre Rose (Imperial), berry bowl, 5″, marigold..................20.00
Lustre Rose (Imperial), bowl, 9″, ftd, green..................58.00
Lustre Rose (Imperial), butter, amethyst..................75.00

Lustre Rose (Imperial), fernery, blue..................75.00
Lustre Rose (Imperial), pitcher, amethyst..................97.00
Lustre Rose (Imperial), tumbler, amber..................50.00
Lutz (McKee), mug, ftd, marigold..................45.00
Magpie (Australian), bowl, 10″, amethyst..................56.00
Malaga (Dugan), bowl, 9″, scarce, marigold..................70.00
Many Fruits (Dugan), punch bowl w/base, marigold..................200.00
Many Fruits (Dugan), punch cup, green..................35.00
Many Prisms, perfume w/stopper, marigold..................65.00
Many Stars (Millersburg), bowl, 9″, ruffled, scarce, marigold....325.00
Maple Leaf (Dugan), bowl, 4½″, stemmed, green..................40.00

Maple Leaf (Dugan), butter, amethyst..................125.00
Maple Leaf (Dugan), tumbler, blue..................40.00
Massachusetts (US Glass), vase, marigold..................150.00
May Basket (English), basket, 7½″, smoke..................56.00
Mayflower, bowl, 7½″, amethyst..................40.00
Mayflower, shade, marigold..................30.00
Maypole, vase, 6¼″, green..................56.00
Melon Rib (Imperial), candy jar w/lid, marigold..................30.00
Melon Rib (Imperial), shakers, marigold, pr..................50.00
Memphis (Northwood), bowl, 10″, green..................100.00
Memphis (Northwood), fruit bowl w/base, amethyst..................240.00
Memphis (Northwood), sugar, amethyst..................50.00
Mikado (Fenton), compote, large, marigold..................95.00
Milady (Fenton), pitcher, blue..................500.00
Miniature Shell, candle holder, clambroth, each..................75.00

Mirrored Peacocks, tumbler, rare, marigold...................90.00
Mitered Diamond & Pleats (English), bowl, 4½", blue..........30.00
Mitered Ovals (Millersburge), vase, rare, amethyst...........1,800.00
Moonprint (English), bowl, 8¼", marigold....................45.00
Moonprint (English), cheese keeper, rare, marigold...........135.00
Moxie, bottle, rare, pastel.................................78.00
Multi-Fruits & Flowers (Millersburg), tumbler, green.........750.00
Napolean, bottle, pastel...................................70.00
Narcissus & Ribbon (Fenton), wine bottle w/stopper, marigold..485.00
Near Cut Souvenir (Cambridge), mug, rare, marigold..........175.00
Near Cut Souvenir (Cambridge), tumbler, rare, marigold......210.00
Nesting Swan (Millersburg), bowl, 10", round or ruffled, green..235.00
Nippon (Northwood), bowl, 8½", marigold.....................48.00
Nippon (Northwood), plate, 9", marigold....................100.00
Northern Star (Fenton), bowl, 7", marigold..................28.00
Northwood Jack-In-The-Pulpit, vase, amethyst................48.00
Northwood Jester's Cap, vase, blue.........................58.00
Northwood's Lovely, bowl, 9", leaf & beads exterior, marigold..85.00
Number 270 (Westmoreland), compote, amethyst...............70.00
Octagon (Imperial), sugar, green...........................76.00
Octagon (Imperial), wine, marigold.........................25.00
Octet (Northwood), bowl, 8½", marigold......................48.00
Oklahoma (Imperial), tumble-up, complete, marigold..........175.00
Olympus, shade, marigold...................................50.00
Open Rose (Imperial), bowl, ruffled, amber.................45.00
Open Rose (Imperial), fruit bowl, 10", marigold.............38.00
Open Rose (Imperial), plate, 9", green......................85.00
Optic & Buttons (Imperial), cup & saucer, rare, marigold.....185.00
Optic & Buttons (Imperial), goblet, marigold................58.00
Optic Flute (Imperial), bowl, 10", marigold.................40.00
Optic 66 (Fostoria), goblet, marigold......................45.00
Orange Peel (Westmoreland), custard cup, scarce, marigold....26.00
Orange Peel (Westmoreland), punch cup, teal.................35.00
Orange Tree (Fenton), butter, blue.........................150.00

Orange Tree (Fenton), goblet, large, marigold...............90.00
Orange Tree (Fenton), powder jar w/lid, marigold............70.00
Orange Tree & Scroll (Fenton), tumbler, marigold............45.00
Orange Tree/Orchard (Fenton), pitcher, marigold.............320.00
Oriental Poppy (Northwood), tumbler, amethyst...............45.00
Oval & Round (Imperial), bowl, 9", marigold.................30.00
Owl Bank, one size, marigold...............................38.00
Owl Bottle, one shape, clear...............................65.00
Palm Beach (US Glass), bowl, 9", marigold...................50.00
Palm Beach (US Glass), tumbler, marigold...................100.00
Palm Beach (US Glass), vase whimsey, amethyst...............120.00
Panelled Cruet, one size, marigold.........................95.00

Panelled Dandelion (Fenton), tumbler, amethyst..............58.00
Panelled Diamond & Bows (Fenton), vase, 14", green..........38.00
Panelled Smocking, sugar, marigold.........................47.00
Panelled Thistle (Higbee), tumbler, marigold................95.00
Pansy (Imperial), oval pickle dish, marigold................28.00

Pansy (Imperial), sugar, amethyst..........................40.00
Panther (Fenton), bowl, 5", ftd, marigold...................55.00
Pastel Panels (Imperial), mug, stemmed, pastel..............85.00
Pastel Panels (Imperial), pitcher, pastel...................320.00
Peach (Northwood), spooner, white..........................125.00

Peach (Northwood), tumbler, blue...........................80.00
Peach & Pear (Dugan), banana bowl, marigold................70.00
Peacock, Fluffy (Fenton); tumbler, marigold................45.00
Peacock, Strutting (Westmoreland); creamer, amethyst........65.00
Peacock (Millersburg), bowl, 9", marigold...................165.00
Peacock (Millersburg), ice cream bowl, 10", rare, marigold...350.00
Peacock & Dahlia (Fenton), bowl, 7½", marigold..............50.00
Peacock & Grape (Fenton), bowl, 7¾", flat or ftd, marigold...38.00
Peacock & Grape (Fenton), bowl, 7¾", flat or ftd, red.......575.00
Peacock & Urn (Fenton), compote, amethyst..................45.00
Peacock & Urn (Northwood), bowl, 9", marigold...............65.00
Peacock At The Fountain (Dugan), tumbler, amethyst..........75.00

Peacock At The Fountain (Northwood), sugar, amethyst........90.00
Peacock At The Fountain (Northwood), tumbler, green.........475.00
Peacock Tail (Fenton), bon bon, green......................40.00
Peacock Tail (Fenton), hat, marigold.......................32.00
Peacocks On Fence (Northwood), bowl, 8¾", marigold..........80.00
Pebble & Fan (English), vase, 11¼", rare, blue..............450.00
Perfection (Millersburg), tumbler, rare, amethyst...........400.00
Persian Garden (Dugan), berry bowl, 5", amethyst............58.00
Persian Garden (Dugan), plate, 6", rare, marigold...........90.00
Persian Medallion (Fenton), bon bon, blue..................50.00

Persian Medallion (Fenton), hair receiver, marigold............60.00
Petal & Fan (Dugan), bowl, 8½″, marigold..................50.00
Petals (Dugan), banana bowl, amethyst.....................90.00
Petals (Dugan), compote, marigold.........................45.00
Peter Rabbit (Fenton), plate, 10″, rare, marigold........1,675.00
Pillow & Sunburst (Westmoreland), bowl, 7½″, amethyst......54.00
Pin-Ups (Australian), bowl, 8¾″, rare, marigold...........90.00
Pine Cone (Fenton), plate, 6½″, blue......................54.00
Pineapple (English), bowl, 7″, amethyst...................56.00
Pineapple (English), sugar, stemmed, marigold.............50.00
Pinwheel (Dugan), bowl, 6″, peach opalescent..............57.00
Pinwheel (English), bowl, 8″, rare, marigold..............65.00
Plaid (Fenton), bowl, 8¾″, blue...........................58.00
Plain Jane (Imperial), basket, marigold...................60.00
Plain Petals (Northwood), nappy, scarce, amethyst.........85.00
Plume Panels, vase, 12″, red.............................350.00
Poinsettia (Northwood), bowl, 8½″, flat or ftd, amethyst......175.00
Pond Lily (Fenton), bon bon, blue.........................52.00
Poppy (Millersburg), salver, rare, marigold..............900.00
Poppy Show (Northwood), plate, 9″, rare, marigold........260.00
Premium (Imperial), candlesticks, amethyst, pr............95.00
Premium (Imperial), under plate, 14″, marigold............65.00
Pretty Panels (Fenton), tumbler, handled, pastel..........70.00
Pretty Panels (Northwood), tumbler, green.................70.00
Primrose (Millersburg), ice cream bowl, 9″, scarce, marigold....160.00
Prism, tray, 3″, marigold.................................45.00
Prism & Cane (English), bowl, 5″, rare, marigold..........42.00
Prism & Daisy Band (Imperial), compote, marigold..........35.00
Prism & Daisy Band (Imperial), vase, marigold.............28.00
Prism Band (Fenton), tumbler, decorated, white............60.00
Prisms (Westmoreland), compote, 5″, scarce, aqua.........125.00
Propeller (Imperial), bowl, 9½″, rare, marigold...........80.00
Propeller (Imperial), vase, stemmed, rare, marigold.......75.00
Proud Puss (Cambridge), bottle, marigold..................80.00
Pulled Loop (Dugan), vase, green..........................35.00
Puzzle (Dugan), bon bon, stemmed, amethyst................48.00
Quartered Block, creamer, marigold........................50.00
Question Marks (Dugan), bon bon, amethyst.................48.00
Question Marks (Dugan), compote, peach opalescent.........75.00
Quill (Dugan), tumbler, rare, marigold...................375.00
Ragged Robin (Fenton), bowl, 8¾″, scarce, blue...........60.00
Raindrops (Dugan), bowl, 9″, marigold.....................50.00
Rambler Rose (Dugan), pitcher, blue......................170.00
Rambler Rose (Dugan), tumbler, amethyst...................35.00
Ranger (Imperial), creamer, marigold......................40.00
Ranger (Imperial), sugar, marigold.......................140.00
Raspberry (Northwood), bowl, 9″, marigold.................45.00
Raspberry (Northwood), tumbler, ice green................350.00
Rays & Ribbons (Millersburg), bowl, 9½″, ruffled, green...55.00
Red Panels (Imperial), shade, red........................160.00
Regal Swirl, candlestick, marigold, each.................55.00
Rex, tumbler, marigold....................................55.00
Rib & Panel (Fenton), vase, marigold......................45.00
Ribbed Elipse, mug, rare, clambroth.......................90.00
Ribbed Swirl, tumbler, marigold...........................56.00
Ribbon & Leaves, sugar, small, marigold...................48.00
Ribbon Tie (Fenton), bowl, 8¾″, green.....................60.00
Ribbon Tie (Fenton), plate, flat, 9½″, blue..............285.00
Robin (Imperial), mug, old only, marigold.................40.00
Roll, shakers, marigold, each.............................40.00
Roll, tumbler, marigold...................................38.00
Roman Rosette (US Glass), goblet, 6″, rare, clear.........90.00
Rosalind (Millersburg), bowl, 10″, scarce, marigold......150.00
Rose Bouquet, creamer, marigold...........................54.00

Rose Garden (Norway), bowl, 6″, rare, amethyst............75.00
Rose Garden (Norway), butter, rare, marigold.............120.00
Rose Panels (Australian), compote, large, marigold.......120.00
Rose Show (Northwood), bowl, 8¾″, aqua opalescent........475.00
Rose Spray (Fenton), compote, pastel......................80.00
Rosetime, vase, marigold..................................68.00
Rosettes (Northwood), bowl, 9″, dome base, amethyst.......85.00
Round-Up (Dugan), bowl, 8¾″, marigold.....................54.00
Royalty (Imperial), punch bowl w/base, marigold..........125.00
Ruffled Rib (Northwood), vase, 14″, marigold..............60.00
Rustic (Fenton), vase, green..............................35.00
S-Band (Australian), compote, marigold....................50.00
S-Repeat (Dugan), tumbler, marigold.......................45.00
Sailboats (Fenton), bowl, 6″, marigold....................28.00
Sailboats (Fenton), wine, blue...........................210.00
Sailboats (Fenton), wine, marigold........................30.00
Satin Swirl, atomizer, clear..............................65.00
Scale Band (Fenton), bowl, peach opalescent...............40.00
Scale Band (Fenton), plate, dome base, 7″, marigold.......45.00
Scales (Westmoreland), bowl, 10″, teal....................46.00
Scales (Westmoreland), plate, 9″, amethyst................95.00
Scotch Thistle (Fenton), compote, blue....................45.00
Scroll (Westmoreland), pin tray, marigold.................45.00
Scroll Embossed (Imperial), plate, 9″, amethyst...........97.00
Seagulls, bowl, 6½″, scarce, marigold.....................65.00

Seaweed (Millersburg), bowl, 10½″, ruffled, scarce, blue.......195.00
Shell (Imperial), bowl, 9″, marigold......................38.00
Shell (Imperial), plate, 8½″, amethyst...................145.00
Shell & Jewel (Westmoreland), sugar w/lid, amethyst.......56.00
Ship & Stars, plate, 8″, marigold.........................30.00
Silver & Gold, tumbler, marigold..........................25.00
Silver Queen (Fenton), pitcher, marigold.................175.00
Silver Queen (Fenton), tumbler, marigold..................45.00
Singing Birds (Northwood), bowl, 5″, blue.................42.00

Singing Birds (Northwood), butter, amethyst..............295.00
Singing Birds (Northwood), creamer, marigold..............80.00
Single Flower (Dugan), bowl, 8″, peach opalescent.........50.00
Single Flower Framed (Dugan), bowl, 8¾″, green............80.00
Six Petals (Dugan), bowl, 8½″, marigold...................38.00
Six Petals (Dugan), hat, green............................50.00
Skater's Shoe (US Glass), one shape, marigold.............90.00
Ski-Star (Dugan), banana bowl, amethyst..................120.00

Ski-Star (Dugan), bowl, 10″, marigold.....................58.00
Small Blackberry (Northwood), compote, green............57.00
Small Rib (Dugan), rose bowl, stemmed, amber..............48.00
Small Thumbprint, creamer, marigold......................60.00
Smooth Panels (Imperial), tumbler, pastel................42.00
Smooth Rays (Northwood & Dugan), plate, 9″, marigold.....60.00
Smooth Rays (Westmoreland), bowl, dome base, 7½″, teal.....75.00
Smooth Rays (Westmoreland), compote, green...............70.00
Snow Fancy (McKee), bowl, 5″, green......................40.00
Soda Gold (Imperial), candlestick, 3½″, pastel, each..........40.00
Soda Gold Spears (Dugan), bowl, 8½″, marigold............38.00
Soda Gold Spears (Dugan), plate, 9″, clear...............160.00
Southern Ivy, wine, marigold.............................38.00
Souvenir Bell (Imperial), one shape, lettering, marigold.......170.00
Sowerby Flower Block (English), flower frog, marigold.........60.00
Spiderweb (Northwood & Dugan), vase, 8″, pastel...........75.00
Spiderweb & Treebark (Dugan), vase, 6″, pastel............60.00
Spiralled Diamond Point, vase, 6″, marigold..............38.00
Split Diamond (English), sugar, open, marigold...........40.00
Spring Basket (Imperial), hdld basket, 5″, smoke...........48.00
Springtime (Northwood), bowl, 9″, amethyst..............110.00
Springtime (Northwood), butter, green...................235.00
Springtime (Northwood), tumbler, rare, marigold..........68.00
Stag & Holly (Fenton), rose bowl, ftd, marigold.........185.00
Star & File (Imperial), bon bon, marigold................30.00
Star & File (Imperial), pitcher, marigold...............185.00
Star & File (Imperial), rose bowl, amber.................90.00
Star & File (Imperial), vase, hdld, pastel...............40.00
Star Center (Imperial), bowl, 8½″, marigold..............31.00
Star Medallion (Imperial), compote, marigold.............38.00
Star Medallion (Imperial), handled celery, pastel...........65.00
Star Medallion (Imperial), tumbler, green................45.00
Star of David (Imperial), bowl, 8¾″, scarce, marigold........60.00
Star of David & Bows (Northwood), bowl, 8½″, green.........70.00
Star Spray (Imperial), bride's basket, complete, amber opal.....85.00
Starbright, vase, 6½″, blue..............................42.00
Stars & Bars, wine, marigold.............................40.00
Stars & Stripes (Old Glory), plate, 7½″, rare, marigold......95.00
Stippled Petals (Dugan), bowl, 9″, peach opalescent..........56.00

Stippled Rambler Rose (Dugan), nut bowl, ftd, marigold.......60.00
Stippled Rays (Fenton), bowl, 9″, marigold...............30.00
Stippled Rays (Fenton), sugar, blue......................35.00
Stippled Rays (Northwood), compote, green................60.00
Stippled Strawberry (Jenkins), tumbler, marigold............75.00
Stork & Rushes (Dugan), bowl, 10″, amethyst..............50.00
Stork & Rushes (Dugan), mug, marigold....................30.00
Stork & Rushes (Dugan), tumbler, blue....................38.00
Strawberry (Fenton), bon bon, amethyst...................45.00
Strawberry (Millersburg), bowl, 10″, scarce, green...........175.00
Strawberry (Northwood), bowl, 5″, amethyst...............30.00
Strawberry (Northwood), plate, handgrip, 7″, marigold........75.00
Strawberry Intaglio (Northwood), bowl, 5½″, marigold........25.00
Strawberry Scroll (Fenton), tumbler, rare, blue.............275.00
Stream of Hearts (Fenton), bowl, 10″, ftd, marigold..........60.00
Stretched Diamond (Northwood), tumbler, rare, marigold.....290.00
Studs (Imperial), tray, large, marigold..................60.00

Sunflower & Diamond (English), vase, blue................90.00
Sunk Diamond Band (US Glass), tumbler, rare, white.........70.00
Sweetheart (Cambridge), tumbler, rare, marigold...........600.00
Swirl (Northwood), candlestick, marigold, each............30.00
Swirl (Northwood), mug, rare, marigold...................65.00
Swirled Flute (Fenton), vase, 12″, green.................40.00
Swirled Ribs (Northwood), tumbler, amethyst..............70.00
Sword & Circle, tumbler, rare, marigold..................85.00
Sydney (Fostoria), tumbler, rare, marigold...............375.00
Taffeta Lustre (Fostoria), console bowl, 11″, rare, green......150.00
Target (Fenton), vase, 7″, marigold......................32.00
Ten Mums (Fenton), bowl, 11″, amethyst...................92.00

Ten Mums (Fenton), tumbler, scarce, marigold.............70.00
Thin Rib & Drape (Fenton), vase, 14″, green..............48.00
Thistle (English), vase, 6″, marigold....................30.00
Thistle (Fenton), compote, blue..........................58.00
Thistle & Lotus (Fenton), bowl, 7″, green................58.00
Thistle & Thorn (English), plate, ftd, 8½″, marigold.........130.00
Three Diamonds (Dugan), vase, 10″, peach opal.............75.00
Three Fruits (Northwood), bon bon, stemmed, marigold.......46.00

Three Fruits (Northwood), bowl, 9″, amethyst.............50.00
Three-In-One (Imperial), bowl, 8¾″, green................36.00
Thumbprint & Oval (Imperial), vase, 5½″, rare, amethyst......175.00
Thunderbird (Australian), bowl, 9½″, marigold............67.00
Tiger Lily (Imperial), pitcher, amethyst.................265.00

Tiger Lily (Imperial), tumbler, amethyst.................47.00
Tobacco Leaf (US Glass), champagne, clear................90.00
Towers (English), hat vase, marigold.....................37.00

Tree Bark (Imperial), bowl, 7½", marigold..................18.00
Tree Bark (Imperial), candlestick, 4½", marigold, pr..........30.00
Tree of Life (Imperial), pitcher, marigold....................60.00
Tree Trunk (Northwood), vase, 12", amethyst..................45.00
Triands (English), butter, marigold..........................60.00
Trout & Fly (Millersburg), bowl, 8¾", various shapes, marigold. 375.00
Tulip & Cane (Imperial), wine, 2 sizes, rare, marigold........45.00
Twins (Imperial), bowl, 5", pastel...........................28.00
Two Flowers (Fenton), bowl, 10", ftd, green..................78.00
Two Flowers (Fenton), rose bowl, rare, marigold..............95.00
Two Fruits (Fenton), divided bowl, 5½", scarce, blue.........85.00
US Diamond Block (US Glass), compote, peach opalescent......75.00
Valentine (Northwood), bowl, 10", rare, marigold.............165.00

Victorian, bowl, 12", rare, amethyst........................175.00
Vineyard (Dugan), pitcher, amethyst.........................295.00
Vineyard (Dugan), tumbler, white............................165.00
Vineyard Harvest (Australian), tumbler, rare, marigold.......97.00
Vining Leaf & Variant (English), vase, rare, marigold........250.00
Vining Twigs (Dugan), bowl, 7½", pastel.....................47.00
Vintage (Dugan), powder jar w/lid, amethyst.................150.00
Vintage (Fenton), bowl, 10", green..........................60.00
Vintage (Fenton), compote, blue.............................42.00
Vintage (Fenton), punch bowl w/base, marigold...............190.00
Vintage (Millersburg), bowl, 9", rare, marigold.............475.00
Vintage (US Glass), wine, marigold..........................40.00
Vintage Banded (Dugan), mug, smoke..........................45.00
Waffle Block (Imperial), fruit bowl w/base, clambroth........90.00
Waffle Block (Imperial), plate, 12", any shape, marigold.....77.00
Waffle Block (Imperial), shakers, marigold, pr...............75.00
Waffle Weave, inkwell, marigold.............................85.00
War Dance (English), compote, 5", marigold..................65.00
Washboard, creamer, 5½", marigold...........................42.00
Water Lily (Fenton), bon bon, marigold......................35.00
Water Lily (Fenton), bowl, 10", ftd, blue...................45.00
Water Lily & Cattails (Fenton), bowl, 5", amethyst...........50.00
Water Lily & Cattails (Fenton), butter, marigold............140.00

Water Lily & Cattails (Northwood), pitcher, marigold.........285.00
Water Lily & Cattails (Northwood), tumbler, marigold.........95.00
Water Lily & Dragonfly, float bowl, 10½", marigold..........90.00
Western Daisy (Westmoreland), bowl, milk glass opalescent.....167.00
Wheels (Imperial), bowl, 9", marigold.......................45.00
Whirling Leaves (Millersburg), 3-cornered bowl, 10", vaseline...450.00
Whirling Star (Imperial), bowl, 9", marigold................35.00
Whirling Star (Imperial), punch cup, marigold...............20.00
Wide Panel (Northwood/Fenton/Imperial), compote, marigold....36.00
Wide Panel (Northwood/Fenton/Imperial), lemonade, hdld, white. 75.00
Wide Rib (Dugan), vase, aqua opalescent.....................87.00
Wild Berry, jar w/lid, marigold.............................75.00
Wild Blackberry (Fenton), bowl, 8½", scarce, green..........58.00
Wild Loganberry (Westmoreland), goblet, peach opalescent.....100.00
Wild Rose (Northwood), bowl, 6", ftd, open edge, green.......42.00
Wild Strawberry (Dugan), bowl, 10½", amethyst...............135.00
Windflower (Dugan), bowl, 8½", blue.........................47.00

Windflower (Dugan), plate, 9", marigold.....................70.00
Windmill (Imperial), bowl, 9", vaseline.....................125.00
Windmill (Imperial), milk pitcher, green....................95.00

Windmill (Imperial), tumbler, amethyst......................58.00
Wine & Roses (Fenton), wine, aqua...........................90.00
Winged Heavy Shell, vase, 3½", pastel.......................95.00
Wishbone (Northwood), bowl, 9", ftd, green..................90.00

Wishbone (Northwood), tumbler, scarce, amethyst...........135.00
Wishbone & Spades (Dugan), plate, 10½″, rare, peach opal....600.00
Woodlands, vase, 5″, rare, marigold......................75.00
Woodpecker (Dugan), wall vase, marigold..................38.00
Wreath of Roses (Dugan), spittoon whimsey, rare, marigold....100.00
Wreath of Roses (Fenton), bon bon, stemmed, amethyst.......48.00
Wreath of Roses Variant (Fenton), compote, green...........60.00
Wreathed Bleeding Hearts (Dugan), vase, 5¼″, marigold......70.00
Wreathed Cherry (Dugan), oval bowl, 5″, peach opalescent.....60.00

Wreathed Cherry (Dugan), spooner, amethyst................95.00
Zig Zag (Millersburg), 3-cornered bowl, 10″, marigold........285.00
Zip Zip (English), flower frog holder, marigold...............54.00
Zipper Stitch (English), tray/decanter/4 cordials, marigold......750.00
Zippered Heart (Imperial), bowl, 9″, amethyst..............110.00

Carousel Figures

Who can forget the dazzle of the merry-go-round -- lights blinking, animals prancing proudly by to the waltzes that bellowed from the band organ . . .

Gustav Dentzel, a German woodworker, created one of the first carousels in America in 1867. By the turn of the century, his animals had evolved from horses with a military bearing to fanciful creatures in various postures with garlands of flowers, exotic saddles, and other adornment. Dentzel was followed in the business by his son, William, and both are noted for the exacting perfection of their carving and painting. The Philadelphia Toboggan Company, established in 1903, is famous today for its superior chariot designs. William F. Mangels, together with his head carver Marcus Charles Illions, produced some of the most exquisite carousel animals made after 1910. The largest carousels were produced by the Artistic Carousel Manufacturers of Brooklyn -- Terry and Solomon Goldstein. Other builders whose works are highly valued are Allan Herschell, who later with his brother-in-law formed the Herschell-Spillman Company; American Merry-Go-Round and Novelty Company; Charles Dore of the New York Carousel Manufacturing Company; and Charles Parker.

Until the 1930s, carousels were found in nearly every fair and amusement park in the country. One by one, as they fell into disrepair, many have

been dismantled and junked, or sold at auction. Today, these hand carved creatures are respected examples of American folk art, and often bring prices well into the thousands.

Although Dentzel is considered the master carver, Spillman and Parker animals are also very valuable.

AH----Allan Herschell	PR-----paint removed
C/B----Carmel-Borelli	PTC----Philadelphia Toboggan Co.
OR-----outside row	R2----row two
PP----park paint	S&G----Stein & Goldstein

Camel, C/B, OR Coney Island, mc jewels, fancy straps/fabric.11,500.00
Camel, PTC, R2, EX....................................9,000.00
Cat, Dentzel, Phila style, bird in mouth, ribbons/ornate, rstr.14,300.00
Chariot side, Carretta for PTC, Phila style/angel/birds, PP....3,740.00
Chicken, English, dbl seater, running, ca 1915, rstr.........2,860.00
Deer, AH, Co Fair, real antlers/tassels/jewels, PP...........3,850.00
Deer, Dentzel, Phila style, eagle bk saddle, real antlers, PP...5,500.00
Donkey, Dentzel, Phila style, lifelike/expressive, 1912, rstr....6,710.00
Giraffe, AH, CO Fair, jewels/fancy tasseled trappings, PR/rstr..9,020.00
Goat, Dentzel, Phila style, eagle bk of saddle, rstr.........6,600.00

Goat with twin eagle saddle, carved by Salvatore Cernigliaro, Gustav A. Dentzel's shop, circa 1904, 56½″ x 67″, $10,175.00.

Horse, AH, OR jumper, Co Fair, jewelled/canteen on saddle..3,520.00
Horse, AH, OR Trojan jumper, Co Fair, cropped mane, rstr.3,520.00
Horse, AH, Trojan lead, Co Fair, hatchet/shield/bearskin, rstr.5,830.00
Horse, Carmel, OR stander, EX mane, tassels, 60x58″.....12,000.00
Horse, Dentzel, OR row lead Phila stander, lady/eagles, rstr.11,550.00
Horse, Dentzel, OR stander, EX stylized trappings, rstr.....10,890.00
Horse, Dentzel, OR stander 'sweet face', eagle saddle, PR...11,500.00
Horse, Illions, OR jumper, Coney Island style, cropped/jewels.4,620.00
Horse, Looff, OR stander, eagle head on saddle, rpt, 57x56″...600.00
Horse, Looff jumper, stationary machine, 1880, 72″ L, VG...1,750.00
Horse, Muller, med flying mane prancer, PP, 57x56″, EX....4,600.00
Horse, Muller, OR Phila jumper, EX carved/fabric/tassel, rstr.10,540.00
Horse, Parker, inner row jumper/Co Fair, jewelled on left....6,050.00
Horse, PTC, OR lead stander/PTC shield/jewel/wolf head/PR.10,175.00
Horse, PTC, OR lead stander eagle/EX trappings, PR......18,150.00
Horse, PTC, OR stander, animal behind saddle, PP, 58x55″..7,000.00
Horse, PTC, OR stander, PP, 1 leg loose o/w EX, 61″......7,500.00
Horse, PTC, OR stander, windblown, Father Time/jewels, PR.9,900.00
Horse, PTC prancer, PP, blk w/simple trappings, 56x56″, EX.3,650.00
Horse, S&G, OR jumper Co Isle warhorse, cropped tail, rstr.15,400.00

Lion, AH, Co Fair style, primitive detail, PP, 1918.........8,800.00
Lion, C/B, Coney Island, multi-jewelled, 1912, PR........22,000.00
Lion, Dentzel, Phila style, leaf saddle/2 monkeys/leaves, PR..19,800.00
Ostrich, Dentzel, Phila style/hi-relief allover feathers, rstr....11,000.00
Pig, Dentzel, Phila style, detailed saddle/blanket, 1912, rstr...9,350.00
Polar bear, AH, Co Fair, massive/jewels/tassels, PP........28,600.00
Polar bear, Herschell, park paint, 1918.................28,600.00
Rabbit, Dentzel, Phila style, deep fur/ribbon, rstr.........15,950.00
Shield, Dentzel, Phila style, lights/lg jester head...........2,530.00
Shield, PTC, lighted, bevelled mirror/wood, cherub head atop..825.00
Tiger, Dentzel, Phila style, ornate saddle, massive, PR.....16,500.00
Tiger, Dentzel, Phila style, PR, rpr, unrstr.............16,500.00
Zebra, PTC, OR, PP, EX, 57″......................13,500.00

Carpet Balls

Carpet balls are glazed china spheres, decorated with intersecting lines or other simple designs, that were used for indoor games in the British Isles during the early 1800s.

Black w/allover blk dots w/frilly wht circles, 3¼″.............60.00
Brown w/brown dots in frilly reserves, 3¼″, EX..............65.00
Gr & wht sponged, 3½″................................95.00
Pink w/pink dots in wht stars, 3¼″, M...................70.00
Plaid, blk/red/yellow on wht, 3⅛″ dia, G.................68.00
Purple stripes, 3″, VG................................45.00
Stick spatter, raspberry & wht.........................85.00
Wht, 2½″, EX.....................................50.00
Wht, 3¼″, EX.....................................50.00
Wht bull's eye w/in wide dk bl band w/in 2 bl stripes, 2″, EX...40.00
Wht w/bl 8 petaled flowers w/wht centers, 3½″, VG..........60.00
Wht w/gr & pink sponging, EX..........................65.00
Wht w/3 bands of blk lines Xing ea other at right angles, 3¼″..60.00
Wine stripes, 2¾″, M................................65.00
Yellow stripes, 3½″, M...............................60.00
Yellow w/yellow dots in frilly wht reserves, 3¼″, EX..........70.00

Cartoon Art

Collectors of cartoon art are interested in many forms of original art -- animation cels; sports, political or editorial cartoons; syndicated comic strip panels; and caricature.

To produce even a short animated cartoon strip, hundreds of original drawings are required, each showing the characters in slightly advancing positions. Called 'cels' because those made prior to the 1950s were made from a celluloid material, collectors often pay hundreds of dollars for a frame from a favorite movie. Background paintings, model sheets, storyboards, and preliminary sketches are also collectible -- so are comic book drawings executed in India ink, and signed by the artist. Daily 'funnies' originals, especially the earlier ones portraying super heroes, and Sunday comic strips, the early as well as the later ones, are collected. Cartoon art has become recognized and valued as a novel yet valid form of contemporary art.

Animation Cell--Full Color

Chip & Dale; w/knapsacks, 1960s, WDS, 4x9″, EX............99.00
Cinderella; w/scarf on head, ¾ figure, WDS, 4x5½″, EX......150.00
Fun & Fancy Free; Bongo Bear, full pose, WDS, 1947, EX....126.00
Lady & the Tramp; Tony Italian Chef w/accordian, WDS, 5x7″..77.00
Lady & the Tramp; Tramp/full pose, WDS, 4½x5″, EX......151.00
Peter Pan; Wendy: ¾ pose, WDS, 1953, 3x6″, EX..........150.00

Walt Disney cel from Pinocchio, 1939, on original watercolor ground, 12″ x 8″, $770.00.

Pinocchio; Jiminy Cricket, WDS, 1940, matted, full pose, 5x6″.399.00
Sleeping Beauty; Flora & Merryweather, WDS, 7x8″, EX.....121.00
The Hockey Champ; Donald Duck, WDS, '39, 3½x5½″, VG...225.00
3 Little Pigs drag tied-up wolf, WDS, 4½x10½″, EX........165.00

Comic Books

Captain America #209, pgs 15/30, India ink, sgnd, 10x15″, EX..55.00
Disney's Comics Stories #64, ink, 1 pg, C Barks sgnd......1,485.00
Magnus Robot Fighter #21, pg 12/14/16, India ink, R Manning.122.00
My Secret Marriage #5, Kisses Of Forgiveness, 8 pgs, India ink..65.00
Planet Comics #50, Life on Other Worlds, splash pg, Anderson.298.00
Disney's Comics/Stories #65, D Duck/nephews, ½ pg, sgn....1,485.00
X-Men #14, pg 2, India ink, J Kirby/J Gavin, 12x18″, EX......55.00

Daily Newspaper Comic Strip

Big Ben Bolt, 2/25/61, Ben/woman/ship, ink/shading, 5x18″, VG.24.00
Conan the Barbarian, 6/4/1979, India ink, 4x14″, E Chan, EX..18.00
Dick Tracy, 1/13/48, Tracy/Shoulders, India ink, 6x20″, EX....101.00
Flintstones, 4/9/1962, Fred/Barney, India ink, 6x20″, EX......22.00
Thimble Theatre, 8/10/57, India ink, Popeye/Sweetpea, 5x18″...20.00

Storyboard

Cinderella, King/Grand Duke, opaque watercolor, WDS, 7x10″..77.00
Cinderella, 4 watercolor castle scenes, mounted, 1950, WDS...120.00
Fantasia, Hippo Ballerinas, bl pencil, WDS, 5½x7″, EX........82.00
Fantasia, 2 Pastoral Symphony backgrounds, pencil, WDS, VG.110.00
Sleeping Beauty, Aurora asleep/castle tower, tempera, 7x9″, EX.399.00
Snow White, Grumpy & Doc, red/blk pencil, WDS, 7x8″, EX...132.00

Sunday Newspaper Comics

Bringing Up Father, ½ pg, 10/24/20, ink/watercolor, 12x16″....99.00
Bunky/Barney Google, 7/11/43, India ink, Laswell, 17x22″, EX.100.00
Casey Ruggles, 8/12/51, India ink, Warren Tufts, 15x21″, EX..250.00
Lambert the Sheepish Lion, 9/9/56, sgnd Floyd Gottfredson, fr.110.00
Tailspin Tommy, 7/9/1933, ink/watercolor, 22x29″, EX........111.00

Cartoon Books

'Books of cartoons' were printed during the first decade of the 20th century, and remained popular until the advent of the modern comic book in the late thirties. Cartoon books, printed both in color as well as black and white, were merely reprints of current newspaper comic strips. The books, ranging from thirty to seventy pages and in sizes from 3½″ x 8″ up to 11″ x 17″, were usually bound with cardboard covers, and were often distributed as premiums in exchange for coupons saved from the the daily paper. One of the largest of the companies who printed these books was Cupples and Leon, producers of nearly half of the two hundred titles on record. Among the most popular sellers were Mutt and Jeff, Bringing Up Father, and Little Orphan Annie.

Bringing Up Father, #13, NM...................35.00
Buster Brown & His Dog Tige, 1906, EX...................60.00
Hans & Fritz, G...................35.00
Mutt & Jeff Cartoons, #6, M...................65.00
Nebbs, by Sol Hess, color cover, RR edition, 30¢, 1928, 48 pgs..45.00
Ralph in Action 'Tween the Decks o/t Merrimac, Dec 19, 1896..25.00

Bringing Up Father, Series #21, $35.00.

Cash Registers

Cash registers are being restored, rebuilt, and used as they were originally intended, in businesses ranging from eating establishments to antique stores. Their brass and marble construction has made them almost impervious to aging, and with just a bit of polish and shine they bring a bit of the grand Victorian era into modern times.

Antique cash registers are categorized as either restored or unrestored. A restored register is one where the cabinet has been stripped, polished, and lacquered. Indicators are free of dust, dirt and visible signs of wear; key stems are rust-free, plated or painted; and key checks and rings are 'like new' used originals. The drawer has been stripped and revarnished, and the rails are in good condition. All mechanisms are completely reworked, broken parts are replaced, oiled, and working perfectly. Prices for registers in unrestored condition vary greatly. Those with major parts missing, are worth considerably less.

National #0, brass, EX orig............................1,000.00
National #1, brass, extended base, EX orig...............1,000.00
National #12, EX orig...................800.00
National #130, EX orig...................600.00
National #2, walnut w/ornate inlaid MOP, EX orig..........1,200.00
National #211, brass or bronze, EX orig...................800.00

National #216, EX orig...................700.00
National #235, detail adder, EX orig...................500.00
National #250, EX orig...................550.00
National #3, brass, detail adder, EX orig...................500.00
National #310, EX orig...................450.00
National #313, EX restoration, fully working...................975.00
National #317, EX orig...................450.00
National #33, EX orig...................450.00
National #332, EX orig...................250.00
National #346, EX orig...................250.00
National #347, 2 drawers side-by-side, EX orig...................650.00
National #348, EX orig...................250.00
National #35, EX orig...................550.00
National #356, EX orig...................300.00
National #416, crank hdl, wood or brass base, EX orig.......400.00
National #421, crank hdl, wood or brass base, EX orig.......400.00
National #441, crank hdl, wood or brass base, EX orig.......400.00

National, #313, in excellent restored condition, $975.00.

National #442, crank hdl, wood or brass base, EX orig........400.00
National #442-E, electric, not illuminated, EX orig..........500.00
National #451, crank, EX orig...................450.00
National #452-E, electric, not illuminated, EX orig...................600.00
National #5, brass, EX orig...................750.00
National #50, candy store type, EX orig...................450.00
National #512, 2 drawers side-by-side, EX orig...................900.00
National #52¼, extended base, EX orig...................750.00
National #522-E, 2 drawers side-by-side, EX orig...................900.00
National #542, manual, single drawer, EX orig...................750.00
National #562, electric, single drawer, EX orig...................750.00
National #57, EX orig...................450.00
National #592, 2-4 drawers, counter base, EX orig...........400.00
National #592-E, multiple drawer, floor model, EX orig.......900.00
National #6, brass, wooden or brass base, EX orig...................850.00
National #7, EX orig...................550.00
National #9, EX orig...................500.00
National #92, EX orig...................500.00

Cast Iron

In the mid-1800s, the cast iron industry was raging in the United States. It was a medium recognized as extremely adaptable for uses ranging from ornamental architectural filigree to actual building construction. It could be cast into any conceivable design from a mold that could be reproduced over and over, at a relatively small cost. It could be painted to give an entirely versatile appearance. Furniture with openwork designs of grapevines and leaves and intricate lacy scrollwork was cast for gardens, as well as inside use. Figural doorstops of every sort, bootjacks, trivets, and a host of other useful and decorative items were made before the 'ferromania' had run its course.

Bird figure, G detail, ½ relief, 5″ L........................30.00
Can opener, bull's head & tail, 6½″........................35.00
Can opener, fish, 5″ L....................................45.00
Cat, realistic pnt worn, 1900s, 12½″......................175.00
Chair, lawn; vintage, wht pnt, early 20th C, set of 4.........100.00
Cookie board, eagle w/shield, 5½″.........................200.00
Cookie board, pineapple, repro mk Va Metal Crafters, 4½x6″...20.00
Cookie board, 12 sections, birds/flowers/turkey/etc, 5x6″.......70.00
Cookie mold, bird on branch, oval, 3½x5″..................200.00
Cookie mold, lyre, 4x6″...................................105.00
Cookie mold, urn w/hdl impression, 4x3″....................25.00
Dog, sitting, front legs extended, blk/wht w/red collar, 4½″.....40.00
Eagle, rough casting, 30½″ W..............................85.00
Eagle, spread wings, stylized features, 15″ wide..............45.00
Eagle & snow bird, 6½″ W, pr..............................55.00
Fountain & well, emb dolphins/cattails, 30x19x20″..........195.00
Frog, gr/wht pnt, 3″ L....................................50.00
Frog, worn gr pnt, 5½″...................................25.00
Garden chair, lyre backs, ornate, early 20th C repro, set of 6...600.00
Gate, 8 vertical bars w/arrowheads, 20x30″..................55.00
Griddle, bale hdl, mk 5½, 14¼″ dia........................20.00
Gypsy kettle w/lid, rpl wire hdl, 10″......................35.00
Hitching post, horse head w/flowing mane/loose bit, Silberzahn.375.00
Hitching post, seated dog, EX detail, fluted std, CI, 83″.....4,100.00
Hitching post, stylized horse's head w/simple detail, 54″, VG...345.00
Kettle, 3 short legs, removable bale, rusty, 10x18½″...........20.00
Lizzard w/very long curled tail, CI, 8″....................65.00
Medallion, bust of Abraham Lincoln relief, bronze finish, 11″...30.00
Muffin pan, makes 12, 16x11″..............................28.00
Muffin pan, w/6 semispherical sections, 4½x6¾″.............15.00
Porringer, mk Kenrick, 5½″................................55.00
Rabbit, old gray rpt, 12″.................................115.00
Rabbit, sgn Kramer Bros, old wht pnt, 10½″.................85.00
Rooster, crowing, 7¾″....................................35.00
Shaving mirror, Jenny Lind/flag/shield, rpt, worn, 21″........95.00
Skillet, 3 short legs, 4½x10″dia, 9″ hdl...................25.00

Figural box, caricature head of man with hat lid, 4¼″, $65.00.

Spider pan, 3 short legs, 5½″ dia, 4¾″ hdl..................25.00
Stove plate, emb w/hearts/tulips/inscription/1756, 26x28½″.....225.00
Table, cabriole legs w/maids/leaves/paw ft, ornate, 24″ dia.....150.00
Table, garden; vintage, wht pnt, early 20th C, 15″............50.00
Umbrella stand, dog w/crossed canes in back, ornate ftd tray...265.00
Urn, serrated rim, pnt rusted, 27x21″......................85.00

Castor Sets

Castor sets became popular during the early years of the 18th century, and continued to be used through the late Victorian era. Their purpose was to hold various condiments for table use. The most common type was a circular arrangement with a center handle on a revolving pedestal base, and held at least shakers, a mustard pot, and oil and vinegar bottles. Some had extras; a few were equipped with a bell for calling the servant. Frames were made of silver or plated, and some were of pewter. Though most bottles were of pressed glass, some of the designs were cut, and occasionally colored glass with enameled decorations was used.

Revolving silverplated signed holder, with five etched glass condiments, 16″, $125.00.

Blue, Baby Thumbprint w/florals; emb Wilcox fr w/tongs.......215.00
Blue, Daisy & Button w/V, Beatty; ftd emb Derby fr w/tongs....135.00
Clear w/stork in rushes decor; replated Webster fr & tongs......85.00
Clear/vaseline, Daisy & Button, swivel fr, 5 pc, Pairpoint.......165.00
Cranberry, Thumbprint; ftd galleried fr w/tongs, Meriden.......195.00
Cranberry to clear Inverted Hobnail/fancy 2 hdl Webster fr, 7″.225.00
Dbl cranberry inserts, gold encrusted; ftd SP holder..........395.00
Etched ivory on clear, 5 bottles............................72.50
Flint glass, cut & etched, 5 bottles; 12″ SP plate............150.00
Green w/florals; ornate Meriden frame......................210.00
Honeycomb, 5 clear bottles; Meriden fr....................165.00
Pewter fr, 5 octagonal bottles, flint, mold blown.............140.00
Puffed Quilt, pk, metal hdl/salt & pepper/mustard lids, 1890....195.00
Revolving, 5 floral cut bottles; ped fr w/loop bail, 17″........150.00
Twist knob to reveal 6 bottle compartments, fish/flowers, 22″...375.00

Catalina Island

Founded on the eastern shore of Catalina Island in 1927 by William Wrigley, Jr., the primary product of the Catalina Pottery Company was tiles, both architectural and decorative. By the late twenties, art ware such as vases, lamps, and accessories for the home were being produced from native clays, with glazes formulated from locally mined metallic oxides. Mandarin Yellow, Catalina Blue, Turquoise, Descanso Green, Toyan Red, Pearl White, Obsidian Black, Sea Foam, and Monterey Brown comprised the pallate of color, which was also employed in the developement and manufacture of their Avalonware dinner services, introduced during the early thirties.

After 1932, the native brown clay was replaced by a white-burning clay of a more durable nature, a step that held dire consequences for the formerly lucrative business. Higher costs of raw material, and the added expense of transporting it to the island, necessitated the sale of the pottery in 1937 to a mainland firm, Gladding, McBean and Company.

The company marked their wares in several ways -- Catalina or Catalina Island, either impressed or with a paper label. Hand thrown pieces were incised by hand. Items marked Catalina Pottery are from a line made by Gladding, McBean and Company after 1937, called Catalina Art Pottery.

Key:
C----Catalina   CI----Catalina Island
CP----Catalina Pottery

Ash tray, hat; ivory, mk CP.............................16.00
Ash tray, Siesta, wht w/pnt decor.......................125.00
Bowl, blue gloss, 3x6".................................35.00
Bowl, celadon green, leaf shape, ftd, 10"...............10.00
Bowl, ivory, CI, 14½" dia..............................35.00
Bowl, salad; Sunkist, gr, CP, 10".......................50.00
Candlestick, 2 hdls, cobalt............................30.00
Console bowl, w/2 lily pad candle holders, matt gr, 17" dia....150.00
Mermaid on shell, turquoise/br, dtd 1937................95.00
Mug, yellow...6.00
Planter, girl's head, hands hold flowers, mc scarf, mk C, 7"....25.00
Tile, geometric design, 4 color, unmkd, corner fleck, 4x4"....25.00
Tray, gr w/pk lining, scalloped, oval, CP, 14"..........15.00
Tray bowl, Starlight, ivory w/blue interior, 15½".......10.00
Vase, green, w/hdls, bulbous base, 8x8".................30.00

Plate, yellow rim band, polychrome underwater scene, signed Catalina Island, 10½", $150.00.

Vase, green w/yellow interior, flared, 7"................10.00
Vase, sea shell, textured ivory, pink w/in, CP/C355, 6x10"....26.00
Vase, turq, ivory w/in, flared w/bulbous body, 11".......85.00

Vase, turq w/ivory interior, satin gloss, CI, MI USA, 7½"....30.00
Vase, wht w/green interior, leaf shape, 8"...............10.00
Vase, wht w/green interior, tulip shape, 6"..............8.00
Wall pocket, basketweave decor, orange..................65.00

Vase, wine with light blue rim and interior, with sticker: Catalina Pottery, 10¾", $95.00.

Catalogs

Catalogs are not only intriguing to collect on their own merit, but for the collector who is interested in a specific area, they are often the only remaining source of background information available, and as such offer a wealth of otherwise unrecorded data.

The mail order industry can be traced as far back as the mid-1800s. Even before Aaron Montgomery Ward began his career in 1872, Laacke and Joys of Wisconsin, and the Orvis Company of Vermont, both dealers in sporting goods, had been well established for many years. The E.C. Allen Company sold household necessities and novelties by mail on a broad scale in the 1870s. By the end of the Civil War, sewing machines, garden seed, musical instruments, even medicine, were available throughout the country through catalog sales. In the 1880s, Macy's of New York issued a 127 page catalog; Sears and Spiegel followed suit in about 1890.

Craft and art supply catalogs were first available about 1880, and covered such varied fields as china painting, stenciling, wood burning, brass embossing, hair weaving, and shellcraft. Today, some collectors confine their interests not only to craft catalogs in general, but often to one subject only. Examples may range from $1 to as much as $25 for the larger, color illustrated versions.

A 20th century enterprise, Johnson, Smith and Company, has produced catalogs since 1914. Their merchandise tends toward books and novelties, such as magic tricks, magnetic lodestones, fireworks, and puzzles. By the late twenties their catalogs contained nearly 800 pages, in both soft and hard cover editions, and retained this large size until late in the forties. The company still exists, and continues to offer novelties similar to those from earlier times. Reproductions of their 1929 catalog are currently available.

American Flag Mfg Co, 1918, flags & decorations, color, 24 pgs.25.00
American Sawmill Machinery Co, #22, 208 pgs, 1921.........48.00
Anderson Carriage Co, Detroit, MI, 1907, 127 pgs, illustrated...65.00
Arts & Gems, Schumann, clothbound, 64 pgs, 1891..........15.00
Beckley Ralston Co, motorcar/boat/cycle accessories, 1914......22.00

Blue Ribbon Foods, premium catalog, 1905...................6.00
Bradley Bonded Warehouse Inc, #101, arm/navy surplus, 64 pgs.25.00
Brown Jaspers, Inc; St Paul, hotel/restaurant supplies, 1930....75.00
Brown-Camp Co, #63, wholesale hdw, 1377 pgs, 1952........40.00
Butler Bros, Our Drummer, Santa edition, 1916, 248 pgs, 9x13".45.00
Case & Co, Harford, Conn, school desks, 1888, 24 pgs, 9x6"...25.00
Catalog of US Stamps, Specialized, 472 pgs, 1941............10.00
Charles May Jewelers Supplies for Clock/Watchmakers........35.00
Combined catalogs sporting goods/trade journal, 1929, 436 pgs.125.00
Come-Packet Furniture, 1911, 31 pgs......................12.50
Crusader Bicycles..9.00
Cutler Hdw Co, knives, sporting goods, etc, 614 pgs, 1951.....32.00
DeMoulin Bros & Co, #137, novelty trick items, 184 pgs, 1909..37.50
Diamond Products, Bottles of Every Description, Ill Glass, '30...25.00
Edison Cylinder Records, 'Gold Moulded', records to Feb 1906..15.00
EV Roddin, 1896, watches, jewelry, etc, 209 pgs............45.00
Farwell, Ozmun, Kirk Co, #1741, hdw, 3000 pgs, 1941.......65.00
Grangle Blue Book, 1913, costumes, emblem pins, 52 pgs......25.00
Groban Supply Co, war surplus, 52 pgs, 1953...............12.00
H Channon Co, camping equip, tents, etc, 116 pgs, 1912-13....12.50
Hapgood Plow Co, 1892, 40 pgs..........................10.00
Hardware & Ship Chandlery, Bushnell Co, 1901, 371 pgs, illus..45.00
Henderson Ames, K of P costumes, #68K, 1900, 16 pgs......15.00
Henderson Bros, 1907, carriages & wagons, 14 pgs, illus, 3x6"..17.00
Hudson Automobiles, 1939, deluxe edition, color illus, 23 pgs...30.00
HW Knight & Son, wht metal, brass, 24 pgs, 1908...........9.00
I&M Hats, Chicago, 1907, beautiful cover illus, 29 pgs, 11x16"..35.00
Isaac Walker Hardware, 1925, 539 pgs....................55.00
JI Mott Iron Works, 1890, CI statues, street lamps, 9x12".....32.00
Johnson Smith Co, novelties, 571 pgs, 1938...............38.00
Joseph Hagn, jewelry/watches/gifts, 1932, 708 pgs..........30.00
Keystone Jewelry & Watches, 1892......................45.00
Knape & Vogt Mfg Co, hardware, 132 pgs, cloth binding, 1925..15.00
Knapp & Spencer, #41, wholesale hdw, 512 pgs, 1941........35.00
Levey Printing Co, Bank Stationers, 96 pgs, 1936...........25.00
Lowell Machine Shop, cotton machines, 75 pgs, 1904.........25.00
Macey, 1906, prices & illustrations......................75.00
Macy's Christmas, 1907, toys/phonographs/leaded glass, 448 pgs.35.00
Matthai-Ingram Co, sheet metal goods, 250 pgs, 1890........60.00
May & Malone Red Book, jewelry, etc, 410 pgs, 9x12", 1941...38.00
Moline Plow Co, #26, McDonald Pitless Scales, 24 pgs, 1915....16.50
Montgomery Wards, #69, 1901..........................68.00
Murray's Horse Drawn Vehicles, 1906, 162 pgs, 8x10".......40.00
Myers Hydropneumater Pumps, 1917......................12.00
Northrup Seed Co, 1902, 80 pgs, inserts..................40.00
NY Belting & Packing Co, rubber specialties, 221 pgs, 1924.....8.00
Parlin & Orendorff, 1900, #59, plows/cultivators/etc, 552 pgs...100.00
Pittsburgh Glass, Wallace & MacAffe Co, 1880, 16x20, 8 pgs.....8.00
Poole Pianos...4.00
Ranger Bicycles..8.00
Rexall Store Premium, 1915.............................10.00
Rogers & Hamilton, artistic plated ware, 65 pgs, 9x12", 1897...70.00
Sargent & Greenleaf, key locks & door bolts, 1895...........15.00
Sears & Roebuck, 1908, large............................7.00
Sears Lighting Fixtures, 1922, 128 pgs....................25.00
Sears Modern Plumbing & Heating, 1926, 56 pgs............7.50
Shapleigh Hardware Catalog, #300, 1935, 2546 pgs..........75.00
Sharples Cream Separators, 1905, 24 pgs, 3½x6"...........10.00
Spiegel Furniture, early 1900s, prices & illustrations.........75.00
Thayer & Chandler, Brass Crafts, 16 pgs, 1910.............25.00
Thayer & Chandler Pyrography, supplement #66, 1900, 8 pgs....9.00
Thoms Wilson Co, 1917, sporting goods, 100 pgs, EX........10.00
Thurston Manual Training Supplies, hdw for cabinetmakers, '22..15.00
Victor Talking Machine Co, Victor Records, 1922............15.00

Western Auto Supply, auto accessories, 130 pgs, 1928.........9.00
Wilson Chemical Co, dinnerware, lamps, etc, 20 pgs, 1923......10.00
Wisconsin Deluxe Co, novelties, premiums, etc, 70 pgs, 1945....25.00
Wright & Wilhelmy Co, 1937, hardware, 1288 pgs............45.00
Youth's Companion, premiums, asst mdse, 48 pgs, 11x16", 1892.40.00
Youth's Companion, premiums, 1891......................15.00

Caughley Ware

The Caughley Coalport Porcelain Manufactory operated from about 1775 until 1799 in Caughley, near Salop, Shropshire, in England. The owner was Thomas Turner, who gained his potting experience from his association with the Worcester Pottery Company. The wares he manufactured in Caughley are often referred to as 'Salopian'. He is most famous for his blue printed earthenwares, particularly the Blue Willow pattern, designed for him by Thomas Minton.

For a more detailed history, see Coalport.

Cup & saucer, handleless, Salopian, blk/polychrome stag.......145.00
Punch bowl, Fisherman pattern, ca 1785, 10⅜" dia.........440.00

Celluloid

Celluloid was patented in 1869 by John W. Hyatt, who developed the formula by mixing pulp from the cotton plant with solvents and camphor. Although others claimed to have made the product earlier, it was ruled that Hyatt's celluloid was different enough to protect his patent rights. Today, celluloid is a generic term for all early plastics. World War II marked the end of its usefullness.

Earlier pieces have a creamy color with striations meant to imitate the texture of ivory or bone. Trademarks were not generally added until the 20th century when the color and weight became lighter, with little or no striations. During the twenties, tints were sometimes added; relief designs and gilding were popular decorative treatments.

The term 'French Ivory' was used until it was outlawed in 1920 by a bill which curtailed the practice of deceptive trademarks and advertising. Items bearing this mark are especially collectible. Other trade names were DuPont Pyralin, Windsor Arch Amerith, and Acwalit.

Baby rattle, ornate decor, 1910...........................20.00
Bookmark, parrot, mc...................................15.00
Box, collar & cuff; holly & berries........................37.50
Box, glove; scenic cover, ca 1910.........................35.00
Box, handkerchief; etched florals.........................14.00
Box, jewelry; dk brown, relief design, ca 1925, 2x8".........16.00
Box, necktie; allover emb flowers, 'Neckties', 12½" L.........48.00
Calendar, 'Diary', 1926, 3".............................12.00
Clock, dresser..25.00
Compact, lg..20.00
Dice, set in box.......................................90.00
Dresser set, in fancy satin lined box, 4 pcs................20.00

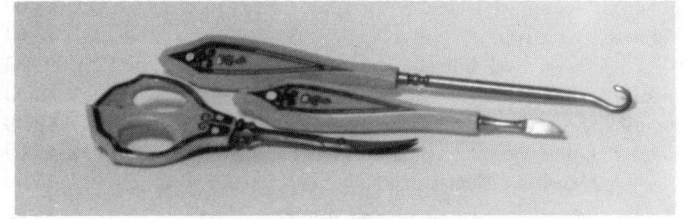

Set, scissors, buttonhook and manicure tool, enamel decorated, 3 pieces, $18.00.

Dresser set, leaping deer Deco design in green, 4 pc.........28.00
Envelope, stamp holder for Travelers Ins Co, Hartford, 2½"....15.00
Fan, folding, yellow ribbon, 4x6".......................20.00
Letter opener, George Washington head, White House on blade.18.00
Mirror, pocket; emb flowers, beveled mirror, w/hdl, sm........26.00
Set, frame: 9x6"; Wilcox clock, not working................24.00
Set, 2 brushes, nail file & buffer w/holder, Ambassador........28.00
Stamp box, double, figural dog on lid, 1½".................42.00

Ceramic Arts Studio, Madison, Wisconsin

The work of the Ceramic Arts Studio has recently begun to attract a following of fascinated collectors, and for apparent reason. Though sold from 1938 until about 1952 as knick-knacks and novelty items, the workmanship is far superior to most Japanese imports, and the original often complex designs are distinctively American.

Many pieces are marked, but even unmarked items become easily recognized after only a brief study of their distinctive styling and glaze colors. Those that are marked carry the black ink underglaze stamp: 'Ceramic Arts Studio, Madison, Wisc'. Do not confuse this mark with 'Ceramic Art' or 'Arts Studio', which have both been used by American and Japanese companies on other novelty ware.

Bell, Dance Hall Girl, decorated long gown, 6½"............45.00
Bud vase, Oriental figure playing mandolin, 6½".............35.00
Candle holder, 5" lady kneels w/candle holder cups, pr........95.00
Candle holder/planter, angels, Hear/See/Speak No Evil, 3 pc...150.00
Ewer, jasperware, wht raised ballerina, Wedgwood bl, 4".......45.00
Figurine, Arabesque & Attitude, dancers, wall hang, pr, 9½"....25.00
Figurine, Archibald the Dragon, gr, 7"....................45.00
Figurine, baby skunk, blk & wht, 2"......................20.00
Figurine, Bo Peep & Lamb, pr...........................15.00
Figurine, Bruce & Beth, modern dancers, pr................22.00
Figurine, Collie dog, standing, lt br, 2½"................18.00
Figurine, colt, pk & blk, 8"...........................45.00
Figurine, Columbine & Harlequin, blk & wht attire, pr, 8".....60.00
Figurine, Dutch boy & girl, dancing, pr, 5"...............45.00
Figurine, Fire, lady w/maroon swirled fire-type gown, 11½".....45.00
Figurine, Harem girl, reclining, 6"......................18.00
Figurine, Harem girl, sitting, 4½".......................18.00
Figurine, Harlequins, pink/blk, Michelle & Maurice, pr........85.00
Figurine, Indian Family, 4 pcs in 8" L canoe..............150.00
Figurine, Jester, lutist, wht/blk/gr, 12".................55.00
Figurine, Lady Rowena, on horse, gr & blk, 8½"............55.00
Figurine, lion & lioness, bronze & br, 5½", pr.............55.00
Figurine, Lover boy & girl, red & blk attire, pr...........45.00
Figurine, Oriental boy & girl, 6", pr....................22.00
Figurine, rooster, stylized, pk & blk, #481, 7"............45.00
Figurine, seahorse & seaweed, gr & lt gr, 4", pr...........35.00
Figurine, St George, on horse, gr & blk, 10½".............55.00
Figurine, Sultan on pillow, 5".........................18.00
Figurine, Tom-Tom....................................18.00
Figurine, Tragedy & Comedy, grey holding blue masks, pr.....95.00
Figurine, Water Lady, waves form dress, gr finish, 12".......55.00
Figurine, Zora & Zorina, blue draped clothing, pr...........60.00
Planter, Lotus, Oriental woman, 7¾"....................45.00
Planter, Manchu, Oriental man, 7".....................45.00
Planter, masked Harlequin w/mask planter................35.00
Planter, Space Bowl, turq & blk, #471, 5½"..............45.00
Plate, Paul Bunyan, Wisconsin souvenir, lav glaze, 5½".......45.00

Salt & pepper, boy wearing turban rides alligator, pr..........30.00
Salt & pepper, cheese & mouse, pr.......................18.00
Salt & pepper, Chirp & Twirp, canaries, pr................16.00
Salt & pepper, dog & dog house, gr & br, pr...............20.00
Salt & pepper, donkey 'Dem' & elephant 'Rep', pk & gray, pr...40.00
Salt & pepper, leprechaun & mushroom, pk & bl, pr..........18.00
Salt & pepper, mushrooms, pr...........................30.00
Salt & pepper, Oriental boy & girl, 3"...................14.00
Salt & pepper, Oriental boy & girl, 4½".................18.00
Salt & pepper, ox & Conestoga wagon, br & wht, pr.........20.00
Salt & pepper, Paul Bunyan & sm tree, pr.................25.00
Salt & pepper, penguins w/blue hats, pr..................30.00
Salt & pepper, pigs: girl in tutu, boy w/sailor hat, pr.......30.00
Salt & pepper, polar bear & cub, pr.....................45.00
Shelf sitters, Maurice & Michele, green, pr................25.00
Shelf sitters, Oriental boy & girl, 6", pr.................18.00
Shelf sitters, Pierrot & Pierette, 7", pr..................55.00
Vase, African Lady/African Man, brn & wht matt, 8" each, pr...60.00
Vase, Becky...25.00
Wall hangers, shadow dancers, 8", pr....................25.00
Wall hangers, Zor & Zorina, 9", pr......................20.00

Knight and lady on horseback, 8¼" x 7½", $80.00.

Chalkware

Chalkware figures were a popular commodity from approximately 1860 until 1890. They were made from gypsum, or plaster of Paris, formed in a mold and then hand painted in oils or watercolors. Items such as animals and birds, figures, banks, toys, and religious ornaments modeled after more expensive Staffordshire wares, were often sold door to door. Their origin is attributed to Italian immigrants.

Today, regarded as a form of folk art, 19th century American pieces bring prices in the hundreds of dollars. Carnival chalkware from this century is also collectible, especially figures that are personality related.

Bank, dog w/snake in mouth, worn orig pnt, 20th C, 4½".....135.00
Bank, horse w/ptd harness, 20th C, 4½".................65.00
Bank, peach form, faded peach color, 3"................110.00

Church, reticulated, windows with colored glass inserts, holds single candle; Pennsylvania, 19th century, 18″ x 9½″, $1,045.00.

Bird, water damage/rpr, orig red/bl/gr/blk pnt, 4″ 90.00
Cat, recumbent, nodder, worn orig pnt, sm holes, 8½″ 400.00
Cat, recumbent, yellow/blk decor worn, 10″ L 155.00
Cat, seated, blk smoked coat, face orig red/yel/blk, 15″, EX . .2,400.00
Cat, seated, orig red/blk/yel paint, 15″, G 2,000.00
Cat, seated, pnt worn, touch up rpr, 6″ 120.00
Child in armchair, repaired 100.00
Deer, recumbent, worn br/red pnt, 5½″ 185.00
Dog, bank, legs open/basket in mouth, orig sponging, late, 10″ .260.00
Dog, seated, good detail, worn orig blk/yellow/red pnt, 8″ 195.00
Dog, seated, open front legs, orig pnt faded, 6″ 225.00
Dog, seated, orig decor fairly worn, 7½″ 95.00
Dog, seated, red/blk decor, 6½″ 225.00
Dog, sitting, open front legs, basket swing from mouth, 6″, G . .330.00
Dog, standing, open front legs, orig br & wht w/dots, 8″, G 400.00
Dog, standing, open front legs, worn orig pnt, 8″, G 350.00
Dove, lt yellow w/blk eyes, orig pnt, 8¼″, pr, G 850.00
Ewe w/lamb, recumbent, orig red/blk/yellow/gr, rpr, 6x9″ 170.00
Fruit basket w/pr lovebirds, pnt only G, 7¾″ 325.00
Garniture, fruit & foliage, some wear but G orig color, 14″ 600.00
Girl, wearing bloomers, worn pnt, rpr base, 9½″ 100.00
Lamb, gr on base, red/yellow in face, 5¼″, G 350.00
Lamb, recumbent, worn w/traces of old pnt, chips, 4¾″ 65.00
Parrot, on ball, orig decor G, rpr to base, 7¾″ 200.00
Pig, bank, br varnish, gr base, minor wear, late, 6½″ 115.00
Poodle, standing, open legs, no pnt, rpr, 7″ 65.00
Rabbit, seated, red/blk decor, 5¼″ 225.00
Rooster, good orig paint, red & blk, 6¾″ 425.00
Rooster, pnt worn, 6¾″ 150.00

Champleve

Champleve, enameling on brass, differs from cloisonne in that the design is depressed or incised into the metal, rather than being built up with wire dividers as in the cloisonne procedure. The cells, or depressions, are filled in with color, and the piece is then fired.

Inkstand, dbl w/lids, scalloped alabaster base/bronze ft, 8″ L . . .400.00
Salt dish, ball ftd under plate, spoon; cut glass insert 58.00
Urn, bird head hdls, flowers in 5 colors, 9½x7″, pr 165.00
Urn, 2 bands of flowers, foo dog hdls, 7½x12″ 325.00

Vase, applied hoo bird head hdls, flowers in 5 colors, 9½″ 265.00
Vase, champleve on bronze, Chinese, EX quality, 10″ 80.00
Vase, dia shape, rust/turq, Tokagawa Royal Crest, 1840, 12″ . . .300.00
Vase, dragon hdls, much enameling, 14″ 190.00

Inkwell with hinged lid, attached tray with open handles, 3½″ x 5½″, $165.00.

Chelsea

The Chelsea Porcelain Works operated in London from the middle of the 18th century, making porcelains of the finest quality. In 1770 it was purchased by the owner of the Derby Pottery and for about twenty years operated as a decorating shop. Production periods are indicated by trademarks: 1745-1750, incised triangle, sometimes with 'Chelsea' and the year added; early fifties, raised anchor mark on oval pad; 1752-1756, small painted red anchor, only rarely found in blue underglaze; 1756-1769, gold anchor; 1769-84, Chelsea Derby mark, the script 'D' containing a horizontal anchor. Many reproductions have been made -- be suspicious of any anchor mark large than ¼″.

Fig leaf dishes with floral sprays over puce veining, red anchor mark, 8″, $1,210.00 for the pair.

Bowl, sunflower form, lid is center w/br seeds, 1775, 5".......330.00
Dish, leaf form, floral sprays, grapevine relief, 9¾" L........900.00
Dish, leaf form w/fruit relief, pnt flowers, 1765, 8½" L........500.00
Figurine, English lady, 18th C clothes, gold anchor mk, 6"....275.00
Plate, Japan pattern, scalloped, red anchor mk, 9½"........400.00
Plate, Kakiemon, Chinese pheasant/shrubbery, red anchor, 9"..650.00
Platter, leaves/insects/fruit, Hans Sloane, red anchor mk, rpr..1,250.00
Scent bottle, apple figural/stem stopper, 1750s, 3"..........1,250.00
Scent bottle, boy & bagpipe, seated figural, flame atop, 2¾"..1,100.00
Scent bottle, cupid by rose tree, ca 1765, minor rpr, 2½".....600.00
Scent bottle, cupid figural, head stopper, gold mtd, 2¾".....1,250.00
Scent bottle, wht vase w/flowers, butterfly atop, 1760, 3".....1,700.00
Seal, cupid w/heart, runs from dragon, Malgre Ton Envie, ¾"..150.00
Seal, seated dove, 1755, no seal, ⅝"....................150.00
Vase, grapes in relief in panels, lavender, hand trn, hdls.......66.00
Vase of flowers, floral HP/molded scroll; w/flowers, 1760, 10"..400.00

Chelsea Dinner Ware

Made from about 1830 to 1880 in the Staffordshire district of England, this white dinner ware is decorated with lustre embossings in the grape, thistle, sprig, or fruit and cornucopia patterns. The relief designs vary from lavender to blue, and the body of the ware may be porcelain, ironstone, or earthenware. Because it was not produced in Chelsea as the name would suggest, dealers often prefer to call it 'Grandmother's Ware'.

Grape, bowl, 7"..40.00
Grape, coffee pot...140.00
Grape, creamer & sugar....................................75.00
Grape, cup & saucer w/hdl.................................22.00
Grape, plate, copper lustre trim, 3¾"....................20.00
Grape, plate, w/hdls, 9".................................25.00
Grape, plate, 7"...12.00
Grape, plate, 8½".......................................17.00
Grape, vegetable, oval...................................22.00

Chelsea Keramic Works

Established in 1872 in Chelsea, Massachusetts, by several members of the Robertson family who later formed the Dedham Pottery, this firm is most noted for its experiments in attempting to re-create the ancient Oriental oxblood-red glaze. They succeeded in this in 1885, and also developed several other outstanding glazes as a result of their perseverance. One was their Oriental crackle glaze which they ultimately used in the manufacture of the very successful Dedham dinnerware.

Though their very early art ware utilized a redware body, by the late 1870s it was replaced with yellow or buff burning clay. A line called Bourg-la-Reine, underglaze slip painting primarily on blue or green backgrounds, was produced, though not to any great extent. Other pieces were designed in imitation of those of metal craftsmen, even to the extent that surfaces were 'hammered' to further enhance the effect. Occasionally, live flora were pressed into the damp vessel walls to leave a decorative impression.

The pottery closed in 1889. Early wares were not marked; those made from 1875 to 1880 were marked with either two or three lines containing 'Chelsea Keramic Art Works, Robertson and Son', or the 'C-KA-W' cipher which was used up to 1889. A paper label was used for a short time on the crackle ware.

Pitcher, ducks in relief, olive gr, sgn Robertson & Son, 9".....400.00
Plaque, cows in forest relief, green gloss, sgn HCR, 10½x8"...625.00
Tile, man w/knife, pineapple, tree, gr, Robertson & Son, 4x7"..350.00

Vase, moss gr/honey br, 4x4¼"...........................85.00
Vase, thick mottled br on red, wide mouth/squat, CKAW, 3"...170.00
Vase, w/hdl, ringed neck, rnd flat form/scroll ft, green, 8½"....225.00

Children's Books

Children's books, especially those from the Victorian era, are charming collectibles. Colorful lithographic illustrations that once delighted little boys in long curls, and tiny girls in long stockings and lots of ribbons and lace, have lost none of their appeal.

A Child's Garden of Verses, Stevenson, EB Barry illus, 1920....20.00
Alice's Adventures in Wonderland, Tenniel illus/Lothrop, 1898...40.00
Animal Pictures & Stories, Grand Union Tea Co, 200 illus, 1896.30.00
Beauty & Beast, R Tuck, 1895, color: cover/4 plates, 10½x8"....8.00
Chanticleer & the Fox, G Chaucer, B Cooney illus, Crowell, '58.45.00
Daddy Jake & Runaway/Stories by Uncle Remus, Century, 1889.125.00
Father Tuck's Apple Pie/Dolly Dear ABC, R Tuck & Sons, 1899.45.00
Father Tuck's Sunny Day Series, color: cover & 2 plates, 1901...8.00
Favorite Uncle Remus, The; Chandler, AB Frost illus, 1948.....25.00
Girls & Boys Book of Sports, 11 woodcuts/1 color, 1840, NM..100.00
Goldilocks, Pop-Up Book, 1934...........................75.00
Gypsy's Year at the Golden Crescent, SE Phelps, 1880s, G.....20.00
Happy Prince/Other Tales, Crane plates/Hood vignettes, 1888..375.00
Jack & Bean Stalk, Chapbook, Turner & Fisher, 1840s, 4x6"...50.00
Jungle Book, 2 vols, JL Kipling illus, London, 1894, 1st ed....120.00
Kellogg's Funny Jungleland, moving pictures, 1909, color, 9x7"..24.00
Knave of Hearts, Parish illus, New York, 1925, 1st ed........325.00
Little Bears Friend, EH Minarik, Sendak illus, 1st ed, 1960, M..80.00
Little Black Sambo, Pop-Up Book, 1934....................95.00
Little Lord Fauntleroy, C Scribner's Sons, 1914, 24 illus......20.00
Pandora & Circus Palace, M Parrish frontispiece, Colliers......20.00
Popeye, Pop-Up Book, Hag o/t 7 Seas, 1935...............150.00
Rebecca/Sunnybrook Farm, KD Wiggin, Grosset/Dunlap, 1903..100.00
Rip Van Winkle, Arthur Rackham illus, Lippincott, 1867, M....75.00
Robinson Crusoe, EB Smith illus, Riverside Press, 1909........45.00

The House That Jack Built, W.B. Conkey, 1898, $35.00.

Sinbad the Sailor, Chapbook, 9 woodcuts/1 color, 1840s, 4x6"..40.00
Swinehers, The; HC Anderson, 1st ed/1958, E Bleguad illus, M..45.00
Tam-O'-Shanter, R Burns, G Cruikshank illus, London, 1884....75.00
Tarzan, Jungle Tales of; Burroughs, McClurg, 1st ed, 1919, M..695.00
Tarzan & Foreign Legion, Burroughs, ERB Inc, 1st ed, 1947, M.30.00
Tarzan & Leopard Men, Burroughs, ERB Inc, 1st ed, 1935, M.185.00
Tarzan & Castaways, Burroughs, Canaveral Press, 1st ed, 1965..18.00

Tarzan Lord o/t Jungle, Burroughs, McClurg, 1st ed, 1928, M..770.00
Tarzan o/t Apes, Burroughs, McClurg, 1st edition, 1914, M...3,950.00
Tarzan the Invincible, Burroughs, ERB Inc, 1st ed, 1931, M...115.00
Treasure Island, Wyeth illus, New York, 1911, 1st ed........100.00
Where Wild Things Are, M Sendak, 1964, Harper & Row.....100.00
Wonderful Wizard of Oz, Denslow illus, Hill Co, 1900, 1st ed.1,600.00

Children's Things

Nearly every item devised for adult furnishings has been reduced to child's size -- furniture, dishes, sporting goods, even some tools. All are very collectible.

During the late 17th and early 18th centuries, miniature china dinnerware sets were made both in China and in England. They were not intended primarily as children's playthings, however, but instead were made to furnish miniature rooms and cabinets that provided a popular diversion for the adults of that period. By the 19th century, the emphasis had shifted, and most of the small scaled dinnerware and tea sets were made for children's play.

Late in the 19th century and well into the 20th, toy pressed glass dishes were made, many in the same pattern as full scale glassware. Today, these toy dishes often fetch prices in the same range as those for the 'grown-ups'!

The earliest cradles made in America were box-shaped structures with crude rockers and very little trim. The idea of 'field' or 'slave' cradles is said to have originated with European peasants. Walkers have been used for about 200 years, and construction methods have varied, including a round type utilizing a wooden frame on coasters, with a padded ring to support the child under his arms; and a vertical pole model with ball bearings and a padded angle arm that rotated to allow the child to move in circles. Early hobby horses either rocked or jumped via steel band springs, and were often decked out with leather saddles and reigns. Some were painted, while others had realistic plush coats.

Toy sewing machines, first available in the early 1900s, have become popular collectibles today. One of the companies that made these working machines was Kay-an-EE, located in Germany. Many models were made, all of which, with some variations, were capable of sewing a chain stitch. They were made until after World War II, when plastic began to replace metal as the material used in toy production.

China

Bowl, Blue Willow, Made in Japan, 3½"......................13.00
Bowl, duck w/red boots & hat, bl bands, Roseville Juvenile......40.00
Cake plate, Blue Willow, Made in Japan, 5¼".................14.00
Casserole, covered, bl/yel/gr pagoda transfer, England, 5½"...42.00
Casserole, open, bl bird/floral branch, bl band, Noritake, 6"....40.00
Chamber stick, pink flowers with brown trim, Nippon.........85.00
Chocolate set, otter scene, yel-beige ground, Noritake, for 4....370.00
Coffee set, ea pc w/lady's portrait, set for 4, German, MIB.....95.00
Creamer, blue/wht, Water Hen, mkd Caason's England, 3"......23.00
Creamer, Buster Brown/Tige, w/gold, scalloped, Germany, 2¾"..32.00
Creamer, dog sitting/colored bands, Roseville Juvenile.........40.00
Creamer, duck w/red boots & hat, bl bands, Roseville Juvenile...40.00
Creamer, figural tan lustre sitting elephant, mc decor, Japan....10.00
Creamer, Girls w/Pets, bl/wht, Charles Allerton & Sons, 3".....13.00
Creamer, Jack & Jill verse & scene, Germany, 1¾"...........10.00
Creamer, Kate Greenaway scenes, Cleve-ron China USA, 2½"...22.00
Creamer, Mary/lamb mc transfer, Brentleigh Ware, Staffordshire..5.50
Creamer, Mickey Mouse on tan lustre, Made in Japan, 2".......8.00
Creamer, pig motif/colored band, Roseville Juvenile..........100.00
Cup, blue/wht, Water Hen, mkd Caason's England, 2".........12.00
Cup, Chinaman face figural, braid hdl, gold trim, Japan.......15.00
Cup, dog sitting/colored band, Roseville Juvenile............43.00

Cup, Dutch children on tan lustre, Made in Japan.............2.50
Cup, Girls w/Pets, brn/wht, Charles Allerton & Sons, 2".......10.00
Cup, Kate Greenaway scenes, mkd Cleve-ron China USA, 2"....18.00
Cup, Mickey Mouse on tan lustre, Made in Japan, 1¼".........6.00
Cup, rabbit, standing, wears jacket; bl bands, Roseville.........75.00
Cup, Simple Simon verse & scene, Germany, 1¾".............7.50
Cup & saucer, bl/blk trim/girl & stroller silhouette, Noritake.....10.00
Cup & saucer, Buster Brown/Tige, w/gold, scalloped, Germany...40.00
Cup & saucer, mc Mary/lamb, Brentleigh Ware, Staffordshire.....7.00
Cup & saucer, wht/shaded pk, St Nicholas/old auto, Germany....26.00
Egg whip, Blue Onion, star shape, wood hdl, Germany, 4½"....65.00
Feeding dish, children w/animals, Nippon, rising sun mk........75.00
Feeding dish, Dutch girl w/puppy, Nippon, rising sun mk.......65.00
Feeding set, 2 sailors, dish & cup, Nippon, rising sun mk......80.00
Fish set, cobalt rim, wht center w/fish, 7 pc, Austria.........195.00
Gravy boat, Blue Willow, Made in Japan....................19.00
Gravy boat, blue/wht, kite scene, England, 3¼".............99.00
Gravy boat, wht w/blue marble effect, mkd England, 1½"......30.00
Grill plate, Blue Willow, Made in Japan, 5".................20.00
Gum holder, dog on edge of small round dish, Noritake........45.00
Meat tenderizer, Blue Onion, wood hdl, Germany, 7".........85.00
Mug, br transfer Naomi & daughter-in-law, Staffordshire.......30.00
Mug, chidren playing, white ground, Nippon.................55.00
Mug, Franklin maxim, w/tree feller, leaf end hdl, 3".........110.00
Mug, red transfer of youth w/flute, 2½", G.................45.00
Mug, young men in garden, purple lustre rim, canary lustre, G...55.00
Pitcher, rabbit sitting/gr bands, Juvenile by Roseville, 3½".....42.00
Plate, Baby Bunting, creamware, rolled edge, unmkd Roseville...55.00
Plate, bl/yel/gr pagoda transfer, England, 4½"..............10.00
Plate, blue/wht, Punch & Judy, England, 5¾"..............18.00
Plate, blue/wht, Scenes of England, DeGout Castle, 3".........18.00
Plate, Dutch children on tan lustre, Made in Japan............2.50
Plate, Girls w/Pets, Charles Allerton & Sons, England, 5¼"......6.50
Plate, Mickey Mouse, tan lustre rim, Made in Japan, 3¼"......5.00
Plate, purple Maidenhair Fern, Ridgway's Stroke-on-Trent, 4½"...7.00
Plate, rabbit sitting, gr bands, Roseville, 7"................40.00
Plate, Santa Claus, rolled edge, Roseville Juvenile, mk Rv, 8"..150.00
Plate, This Little Pig verse, mother & child pigs, Germany......4.50
Plate, 3 Kate Greenaway scenes, mkd Cleve-ron China USA, 6"..12.00
Platter, Blue Willow, Made in Japan, 6"....................8.00
Platter, blue/wht, Chas Dicken's scenes, Ridgway's, 8".........30.00
Platter, Colonial couple silhouette, open hdls, Made in Japan.....6.50
Platter, Gaudy Ironstone, blues & oranges, England, 6"........33.00
Platter, wht w/bl marble effect, deep well, mkd England, 4½"...29.00
Rolling pin, Blue Onion, wood hdls, Germany, 8".............160.00
Salt box, Blue Onion, wall hanging, Germany, 4¼"...........110.00
Set, allover swan/lake/sunset, Made in Japan, 4 place.........40.00
Set, bluebird on floral branch, lt bl band, Noritake, for 4......175.00
Set, cobalt w/ladies portraits, gold trim, Germany, for 4......250.00
Set, House That Jack Built, various scenes, Germany, for 6....180.00
Soap dish, pink roses on white w/gold, Nippon...............55.00
Soup, blue/wht, Scenes of England, DeGout Castle, 3½".......23.00
Soup, purple Maidenhair Fern, Ridgway's Stroke-on-Trent, 4½"..11.00
Sugar, open, Old Mother Goose verse & scene, Germany, 1¼"..10.00
Sugar w/lid, Blue Willow, Made in Japan, 2¾"...............8.50
Sugar w/lid, blue/wht, Punch & Judy, England, 4½".........23.00
Sugar w/lid, Chinaman sits w/hands over ears, hat lid, Japan....37.00
Sugar w/lid, Dutch children on tan lustre, Made in Japan.......4.50
Sugar w/lid, figural tan lustre elephant, Made in Japan, 2¼"....12.00
Sugar w/lid, Girls w/Pets, brn/wht, Charles Allerton & Sons.....16.00
Sugar w/lid, Mickey Mouse on tan lustre, Made in Japan, 2¾"...10.00
Sugar w/lid, wht/pk, St Nicholas & hot air balloon, Germany....30.00
Tea set, Little May, 21 pcs.............................195.00
Teapot, blue ground, girl & stroller silhouette, Noritake, 3½"...35.00

Teapot, Blue Willow, Made in Japan, 3¾"................40.00
Teapot, bluebird on floral branch, lt bl band, Noritake, 3½"....40.00
Teapot, Buster Brown/Tige, w/gold, scalloped, Germany, 5¾"..150.00
Teapot, Colonial couple silhouette, gold trim, Made in Japan.....7.50
Teapot, Dutch children on tan lustre, Made in Japan..........9.00
Teapot, figural sitting Chinaman, lid is hat, Japan, 3½".......50.00
Teapot, figural tan lustre elephant, mc decor, Made in Japan....16.00
Teapot, Gaudy Ironstone, blue & orange, England, 4½".......65.00
Teapot, Girls w/Pets, brn/wht, Charles Allerton & Sons, 5"....27.00
Teapot, mc Mary & lamb scene, Brentleigh Ware, Staffordshire..26.00
Teapot, Mickey Mouse, on tan lustre, Made in Japan, 3¾".......20.00
Teapot, Taffy Was A Welshman verse, boy & dog, Germany.....29.00
Teapot, wht & shaded pk, St Nicholas/dirigible, Germany, 5½"..80.00
Teapot, wht w/silhouette children, Victoria Czecho-Slovakia.....15.00
Tureen, Blue Willow, Made in Japan, 4½"................17.00
Tureen, blue/wht, Chas Dicken's scenes, Ridgway's, w/lid, 4¾"..45.00
Tureen, purple Maidenhair Fern, Ridgway's Stroke-on-Trent, 4"..29.00
Vegetable, blue/wht, Scenes of England, Leclad's Bridge, 3¾"...70.00
Vegetable, covered, blue/wht, kite scene, England, 3½".......99.00
Wash set, Christmas Holly decor, 8½" pitcher, 10" dia bowl..325.00
Waste bowl, Gaudy Ironstone, blues & oranges, England, 2¾"..47.00

Glassware

ABC plate, Full Standing Dog, 6" dia....................45.00
ABC plate, Hey Diddle Diddle, 6" dia...................35.00
Acorn, butter w/lid...............................145.00
Amazon, creamer................................18.50
Angel in Ring, castor set, 5 crystal bottles, pewter holder......99.00
Arched Panel, pitcher, amber, Westmoreland..............75.00
Austrian, butter w/cover, crystal, Greentown, 2¼"..........170.00
Austrian, creamer, chocolate, Greentown, 3¼"............230.00
Austrian, spooner, canary, Greentown, 3"................148.00
Baby Thumbprint, cakestand, clear, United States Glass, 2"....75.00
Banded Ring, castor set, 4 bottles, pewter holder...........62.00
Banded Swirl, chamberstick, blue, 2¼".................37.00
Bead & Scroll, creamer, 3".........................55.00
Beaded Swirl, table set, crystal, 4 pc..................148.00
Beautiful Lady, banana stand, crystal...................40.00
Block, creamer, amber, 3"..........................50.00
Block, creamer, blue milk glass......................88.00
Block, sugar w/lid, crystal, 4½".....................89.00

Dish, holly and berries, embossed 'Merry Christmas', on sapphire blue, manufactured by Sowerby, 6¼", $85.00.

Braided Belt, spooner, opaque wht w/enamel floral, 2½".......99.00
Button Panel, butter w/cover, D&M....................45.00
Button Panel, creamer, D&M........................25.00
Button Panel #44, sugar w/lid, clear w/mint gold, 4½"........80.00
Buzz Saw, butter w/cover, crystal, Cambridge, 2¼"..........28.00
Buzz Saw, table set, crystal, 4 pc, Cambridge............100.00
Cat & Dog, cup & saucer, amber.....................80.00
Chateau, punch bowl.............................225.00
Chateau, punch cup..............................30.00
Chimo, punch bowl..............................200.00
Chimo, punch cup...............................25.00
Clear & Diamond Panels, butter w/cover, crystal, 2½".........47.00
Clear & Diamond Panels, creamer, green, 2¾"............30.00
Clear & Diamond Panels, spooner, blue, 2¼".............33.00
Clear & Diamond Panels, sugar w/lid, crystal, 3½".........36.00
Cloud Band, sugar w/lid, milk glass, enamel decor, Gillinder.....95.00
Colonial, pitcher, crystal, 3¼".......................16.00
Colonial, punch bowl, crystal, 3¼"...................37.00
Colonial #2630, spooner, crystal, Cambridge, 2"...........18.00
Colonial #2630, table set, olive gr, Cambridge, 4 pc.........160.00
Column, candlestick, crystal, 4¾"....................53.00
Daisy & Star, banana stand, crystal...................40.00
Dewdrop, butter w/cover, crystal, Columbia, 2½"...........99.00
Dewdrop, table set, blue, Columbia, 4 pc...............415.00
Diamond Ridge, creamer, crystal, Duncan & Miller #48, 2½"....73.00
Doyle #500, butter w/cover, crystal, 2¼"................50.00
Doyle #500, mug, amber, 2".........................35.00
Doyle #500, tray, blue, 6½".........................44.00
Drum, mug, crystal, 2½"..........................30.00
Dutch Kinder, candlestick, blue milk glass, 3"............115.00
English Hobnail, condiment, gr, cruet/shaker/open salt/tray.....70.00
Fernland #2635, spooner, emerald green, Cambridge, 2¼".....35.00
Fernland #2635, table set, cobalt, 4 pc, Cambridge..........177.00
Fine Cut, master berry, crystal, 1¾"...................60.00
Fine Rib, candlestick, crystal, ring hdl, 4"...............40.00
Fish set, crystal, alphabet rim, fish center, Federal, 7 pc......650.00
Flattened Diamond & Starburst, punch bowl..............18.00
Flattened Diamond & Starburst, punch cup...............7.00
Flute, berry set, crystal w/mint gold, 7 pc...............200.00
Fluted, chamberstick, cobalt, 2".....................80.00
Frances Ware, water set, frosted w/amber, Hobbs Brockunier...388.00
Galloway, water set, blush, 7 pc.....................163.00
Grapevine w/Ovals, butter w/cover, crystal, McKee, 1½"........75.00
Grapevine w/Ovals, creamer, blue, McKee, 2"............50.00
Grapevine w/Ovals, spooner, crystal, McKee, 1¾"..........35.00
Hawaiian Lei, cake plate, crystal.....................40.00
Hawaiian Lei, table set, crystal, 4 pc..................100.00
Hickman, condiment set, gr, cruet/shaker/open salt/3x5" tray....70.00
Hobnail w/Thumbprint Base, sugar w/lid, blue, Doyle, 4".......80.00
Hobnail w/Thumbprint Base, tray, blue, Doyle, 7¼".........40.00
Horizontal Threads, butter w/cover, crystal, 1¾"...........50.00
Horizontal Threads, sugar w/lid, ruby flashed, 3¼".........48.00
Ice cream set, crystal, alphabet rim, 7 pc...............350.00
Inverted Strawberry, master berry, crystal, Cambridge, 1½".....60.00
Inverted Strawberry, punch set, crystal, 7 pc, Cambridge.......165.00
Lacy & Beads, chamberstick, cobalt, 2"................78.00
Lamb, spooner, milk glass, 2".......................120.00
Lamb, sugar w/lid, lamb finial, crystal, 4"...............100.00
Liberty Bell, creamer, crystal, Gillinder, 2½".............70.00
Liberty Bell, mug, milk glass, 2"....................200.00
Lion, butter w/cover, head finial, crystal, Gillinder, 4¼".......65.00
Lion, table set, crystal w/frosted head, 4 pc, Gillinder........460.00
Little Ladders, banana stand, crystal...................40.00
Long Diamond, sugar w/lid, crystal, US Glass, 3¾"..........95.00

Menagerie, butter w/cover, turtle, blue, Bryce Higbee, 2¼"....750.00
Menagerie, sugar w/lid, bear, crystal, Bryce Higbee, 4¼"......250.00
Michigan, table set, crystal w/red & gr flashing, US Glass.....385.00
Monk, stein set, crystal, 4" tankard w/four 2" steins........182.00
Nearcut, pitcher, crystal, Cambridge, 3¼"....................28.00
Nursery Rhyme, berry set, crystal, 7 pc, US Glass...........170.00
Nursery Rhyme, individual berry.............................20.00
Nursery Rhyme, punch bowl, blue milk glass.................250.00
Nursery Rhyme, punch bowl, blue transparent...............350.00
Nursery Rhyme, punch bowl, clear..........................125.00
Nursery Rhyme, punch bowl, cobalt, US Glass, 3¼".........410.00
Nursery Rhyme, punch cup, blue milk glass, US Glass, 1¼".....42.00
Nursery Rhyme, punch cup, blue transparent..................60.00
Nursery Rhyme, punch cup, clear.............................20.00
Nursery Rhyme, punch set, milk glass, 7 pc, US Glass........270.00
Nursery Rhyme, tumbler.....................................20.00
Oval Star, butter w/cover, crystal w/mint gold, Indiana Glass....23.00
Oval Star, punch set, crystal w/mint gold, 7 pc, Indiana Glass..127.00
Oval Star, spooner, clear..................................10.00
Palm Leaf Fan, banana stand, crystal.......................40.00
Pattee Cross, berry set, crystal, 7 pc, US Glass...........100.00
Pattee Cross, punch cup....................................30.00
Pattee Cross, tumbler, crystal, US Glass, 1¾"..............13.00
Pattee Cross, tumbler, crystal w/mint gold, US Glass, 1¾"....17.50
Peacock Feather, cake stand, crystal, US Glass, 3"..........79.00
Peacock Feather, creamer, crystal, US Glass, 2"............47.00
Pennsylvania, creamer, green, small foot chip..............25.00
Pennsylvania, spooner, green, US Glass, 2½"................72.00
Pennsylvania, sugar w/lid, crystal w/EX gold, US Glass, 4"....77.00
Pert, creamer, crystal, 3¼"................................82.00
Rex, punch bowl...75.00
Rex, punch cup..25.00
Rexford, cake stand.......................................25.00
Ribbon Candy, cake stand, green, 3½".......................52.00
Rooster, nappy, crystal, King Glass.......................105.00
Rooster, table set, crystal, 4 pc, King Glass.............468.00
Sandwich Ivy, creamer, crystal, 2¼".......................75.00
Sandwich Ivy, sugar, open, amethyst, 3¼"..................95.00
Sawtooth, creamer, crystal, 3½"...........................30.00
Sawtooth Band, butter w/cover, red flashed, Heisey, 3½"....215.00
Sawtooth Band, spooner, crystal, Heisey, 2¼"..............47.00
Sawtooth Variation, creamer & sugar w/lid, crystal.........73.00
Stippled Diamond, butter w/cover, blue, 2¼"...............105.00
Stippled Diamond, spooner, crystal, 2"....................58.00
Stippled Diamond, sugar w/lid, amber, 3¼"................110.00
Stippled Raindrop & Dewdrop, creamer, cobalt, 2¼".........94.00
Stippled Raindrop & Dewdrop, spooner, crystal, 2¼".........55.00
Stippled Vines & Beads, butter w/cover, crystal, 2¼".......72.00
Stippled Vines & Beads, creamer, teal or amber, 2½".......90.00
Stippled Vines & Beads, spooner, sapphire blue, 2"........93.00
Sultan, creamer, chocolate, McKee, 2½"...................255.00
Sultan, spooner, green, McKee, 2½"........................75.00
Sultan, sugar w/lid, crystal & frosted, McKee, 4½".......107.00
Sweetheart, sugar w/lid...................................35.00
Tappan, butter w/cover, crystal, McKee, 3"................28.00
Thousand Eye, mug, vaseline, 2½"..........................25.00
Thumbelina, punch bowl....................................50.00
Thumbelina, punch cup......................................8.00
Tokyo, cakestand, gr opal.................................22.00
Tulip & Honeycomb, butter w/cover, crystal, Federal, 3½"....37.00
Tulip & Honeycomb, casserole, oval, covered, crystal, 3¼"....73.00
Tulip & Honeycomb, creamer................................18.00
Tulip & Honeycomb, dish, low, covered, crystal, 2½".......44.00
Tulip & Honeycomb, punch set, crystal, 7 pc, Federal......79.00

Tulip & Honeycomb, spooner................................15.00
Tulip & Honeycomb, sugar w/lid............................20.00
Twin Snowshoes, creamer...................................18.00
Twin Snowshoes, sugar w/lid, crystal, US Glass, 3¼".......65.00
Twist #137, butter, frosted, Albany Glass, 3½"............57.00
Twist #137, creamer, blue opal, Albany Glass, 2½".........88.00
Twist #137, spooner, vaseline opal, Albany Glass, 2½".....84.00
Twist #137, sugar w/lid, crystal, Albany Glass, 3¾".......16.00
Two Band, sugar w/lid, crystal, 3¾".......................45.00
Wee Branches, cup, crystal, 1¾"...........................38.00
Wee Branches, mug, blue, 2"...............................42.00
Wee Branches, sugar w/lid, crystal, 2¾"...................59.00
Wheat Sheaf #500, punch cup, milk glass, Cambridge, 1¼"....20.00
Wheat Sheaf #500, wine jug, crystal, Cambridge, 4¼".......55.00
Whirligig, creamer..15.00
Whirligig, punch bowl.....................................20.00
Whirligig, punch cup.......................................8.00
Whirligig, punch set, crystal, 7 pc, US Glass.............65.00
Whirligig, spooner..13.50
Whirligig, sugar w/lid, crystal, US Glass, 3¼"............19.00
Wild Rose, butter w/cover, milk glass, decorated, Greentown....82.00
Wild Rose, candlestick, crystal, 4¼".......................78.00
Wild Rose, punch cup, crystal, 1¼".........................23.00
Wild Rose, punch set, blue milk glass, Greentown..........255.00
Wild Rose, punch set, milk glass, Greentown...............195.00
Wooden Pail, creamer, clear, Bryce Brothers, 2½"..........55.00

Miscellaneous

Armchair, ladderback, 2 slats/trn finials, rpr woven seat, 23"...115.00
Armchair, primitive spindleback, worn red pnt, woven seat, 24"..55.00
Baby bed, Jenny Lind, birch, needs rfn, 20x37½"...........150.00
Bench, Sheraton, bamboo trn legs, rockers, scroll arms, 33" W.400.00
Blocks, set of 36, hand colored lithos: English history, 1800s....75.00
Blocks, wood w/chromolitho paper alphabet/children playing.....80.00
Blocks, 1½", in orig wood 9½x13" box, 1890s...............225.00
Chair, corner, primitive, late, rfn, needs seat, 19½".........85.00
Chair, Empire side, mahog, vase splat, new rush seat, rpr, 28"..65.00
Chair, ladderback arm, 3 curved slats, splint seat, 22"......65.00
Chair, soda fountain, copper.............................125.00
Chair, Windsor, bamboo, plank seat, 5 spindle, rfn, 22¼"....125.00
Cook stove, cast steel, w/plates/lifter/pans, 'Pet', 7x9".....60.00
Cook stove, CI, 17x17"...................................380.00
Cradle, birch/pine hood, partially dvtl, old red, rpr, 39" L...285.00
Cradle, primitive w/traces of old pnt, rpl rockers, 35½".....95.00
Dress, wool, cape flannel w/cotton lining, wool bonnet, Amish...45.00
Dressing table, poplar, country, 1 drw, mirror in lyre fr, rpr....55.00
Highchair, ladderback, 2 slat, simple finials, splint seat........195.00
Highchair, ladderback, 2 slat, worn rpt, new splint seat, 32"...105.00
Highchair/stroller combination, cane seat, EX.............245.00
Hobby horse, metal on wood fr, 26".......................145.00
Hobby horse, wood, old pnt, harness & saddle, 27x33"......270.00
Hobby horse, wood, worn orig dapple gray pnt, losses, 54"....445.00
Hobby horse, wood/worn orig dapple gray pnt/worn saddle, 42".300.00
Horn, tin, orig red/bl japanning, wht pnt w/clown faces, 24"....20.00
Ice cream freezer, White Mountain Junior, early 1900s, 6½x5".125.00
Ice cream freezer, wood bucket, 7½".......................125.00
Ice tongs, 6", metal......................................35.00
Ink box, slanted hinged lid, orig bottle, English, 4½" long......60.00
Lap desk, mahogany, closes: suitcase form, fitted w/in, 6x8x4"...225.00
Noah's Ark, 9 carved animals, orig pnt, 7¼"...............250.00
Noise maker, wood, well trn parts, brass fittings, 8".......65.00
Phonograph, floor model, Mary Lu.........................210.00
Quilt, Amish, doll size, simple design, contemporary, 32".....55.00

Electric 'Empire' stove, tin and enamel, 14" x 15", $65.00.

Rattle, silver, mermaid figural w/6 bells, Spanish, 1600s, 3"....550.00
Rattle, silver, octagon w/whistle finial, 7 bells, 1700s, 7"......275.00
Rattle, silver/gilt, crowned lion figural, 1600, 2½"...........880.00
Rattle, sterling silver punch head/hanging bells/MOP end.......75.00
Rattle, 2 color gold, mk IR, London, 1810, bells/teether, 5"..2,420.00
Ride on toy, elephant, plush w/leather/metal saddle, 28x30"....600.00
Rocker, Country Sheraton, rpl paper rush seat, rockers added...60.00
Rocker, ladderback arm, rpl cane seat, worn orig red pnt, 1876.95.00
Rocker, rustic cottage furniture of bent saplings, worn pnt......75.00
Rolling pin, wood, 10"....................................10.00
Sewing box, hinged front, English walnut, satin lined, 15x12".1,000.00
Sewing machine, treadle, Stitch Well, 30".................400.00
Shirt, boy's, printed calico w/MOP buttons, 1880s............18.00
Shoe horn, sterling silver punch head, plated blade, small......65.00
Sled, wood w/metal fittings, orig striping/florals, 47", G.........95.00
Sled, wood w/orig gr pnt, wood runners resemble fish, 12x25"..205.00
Sled, wood w/steel runners, red pnt, 21" L..................25.00
Stool, Windsor, pnt w/striping, worn uphl, 11½".............125.00
Toy, bell w/in CI wheels w/heart spokes, 3¾"................50.00
Wagon, flat bed, mortised, 16" & 18" iron spoke wheels, 41" L.85.00
Wagon, orig pnt faded, paper coverings on wheels, 11x18".....35.00

Christmas Collectibles

Christmas past . . . lovely mementos from long ago attest to the ostentatious Victorian celebrations of the season.

St. Nicholas, better known as Santa, has changed much since 300 A.D. when the good Bishop Nicholas showered needy children with gifts and kindnesses. During the early 18th century, Santa was portrayed as the kind gift giver to well behaved children, and the stern switch-bearing disciplinarian to those who were bad. In 1822, Clement Clark Moore, a New York poet, wrote his famous 'Night Before Christmas', and the Santa he described was jolly and jovial -- a loveable old elf who was stern with no one. Early Santas wore robes of yellow, brown, blue, green, red, or even purple. But Thomas Nast, who worked as an illustrator for Harper's Weekly, was the first to depict Santa in a red suit instead of the traditional robe, and to locate him the entire year at the North Pole headquarters.

Today's collectors prize early Santa figures, especially those in robes of fur or mohair, or those dressed in an unusual color.

Some early examples of Christmas memorablia are the pre-1870 ornaments from Dresden, Germany. These cardboard figures -- angels, gondolas, umbrellas, dirigibles, and countless others -- sparkled with gold and silver trim. Late in the 1870s, blown glass ornaments were imported from Germany. There were over 6,000 recorded designs -- carrots and cucumbers, clown faces and angel heads, butterflies and stars -- all painted inside with silvery colors. From 1890 through 1910, blown glass spheres were often decorated with beads, tassels, and tinsel rope.

Christmas lights, made by Sandwich and some of their contemporaries, were either pressed or mold-blown glass, shaped into a form similar to a water tumbler. They were filled with water and then hung from the tree by a wire handle; oil floating on the surface of the water served as fuel for the lighted wick.

Kugels are glass ornaments that were made as early as 1820 and as late as 1890. Ball shaped examples are more common than the fruit and vegetable forms, and have been found in sizes ranging from 1" to 14" in diameter. They were made of thick glass with heavy brass caps, in cobalt, green, gold, silver, and occasionally in amethyst.

Although experiments involving the use of electric light bulbs for the Christmas tree occured before 1900, it was 1903 before the first manufactured socket set was marketed. These were very expensive and often proved a safety hazard. In 1921, safety regulations were established and products were guaranteed safety approved. The early bulbs were smaller replicas of Edison's household bulb. By 1910, G.E. bulbs were rounded with a pointed end, and until 1919 all bulbs were hand blown. The first figural bulbs were made around 1910 in Austria. Japan soon followed, but their product was never of the high quality of Austrian wares. American manufacturers produced their first machine-made figurals after 1919. Today, figural bulbs, especially character related examples, are very popular collectibles.

Bubble lights were popular from about 1945 to 1960 when miniature lights were introduced. These tiny lamps dampened the public's enthusiasm for the bubblers, and manufacturers stopped providing replacement bulbs.

Bulbs

Andy Gump...45.00
Bell..10.00
Betty Boop..45.00
Bird, painted milk glass, 3", M.......................14.00
Bird, rnd body, milk glass w/deep bl decor............16.50
Cat, playing mandolin, painted milk glass, 4", M......24.00
Cat & fiddle..65.00
Dick Tracy..45.00
Dirigible, w/Am flags ea side, minor pnt wear, 3" L...50.00
Father Christmas......................................22.00
Fish..35.00
Grape cluster, painted milk glass, 4", M..............14.00
House, snow-covered, painted milk glass, 3", M........15.00
Kayo..45.00
Lantern...4.50
Lemon..7.50
Lion in suit, milk glass, 4"..........................15.00
Pear..5.00
Rose..18.00
Santa, head, milk glass, 2 sided, large...............22.50
Santa, head, oval, w/holly, painted milk glass, 4", M.24.00
Santa, head, painted milk glass, 2", M................20.00
Santa, holding sack, painted milk glass, 3", M........20.00
Santa, holding tree, painted milk glass, 2", M........20.00
Santa, std base, working, 5"..........................65.00
Santa, std base, working, 9".........................110.00
Santa, w/pack, 2 sided................................22.00
Smitty, EX..35.00
Snowman...10.00
Woman in a Shoe.......................................35.00

Ornaments

Airplane, blown w/fiber glass wings, paper propeller, 4".......85.00
Angel, wax w/orig hair & fiberglass wings & dress, 4", EX.....75.00
Baby chick w/bonnet, 6"..145.00
Baby doll, blown, 3"..50.00
Basket, glass, old, 1"...4.50
Basket, wire trim, 5"...45.00
Basket of fruit, blown glass, early, 3½".............................65.00
Bass fiddle, blown glass w/tinsel, early, 7½".......................38.00
Bird, blown glass, on clip, Germany, 4"............................28.00
Bird, celluloid..10.00
Bird, mercury glass, clip-on...12.50
Bird house w/birds, silver w/mc decor, 2¾".......................35.00
Blowfish, rnd & fat, frosted, blown, rare.........................150.00
Boat, blown glass, early, 3¼".......................................65.00
Bowling pin, glass, early...27.00
Boy character doll, Germany, 3"....................................85.00
Boy's head figural, blown glass......................................25.00
Bug, on round shape, blown glass, early, 2½"......................85.00
Bugle, blown glass..18.00
Bust of Indian, red/blk pnt, 4"....................................175.00
Butterfly, on triangular shape, blown glass, early, 2½".........30.00
Cabbage, blown glass...42.00
Cat head figural, blown glass..65.00
Charlie Chaplin, sm hole in chin, 3½".............................160.00
Cherub on geometric, soft tin/paper scrap, flat...................65.00
Christmas tree, blown, wht, on clip, 3"............................45.00
Christmas tree, blown glass, clip on, early, 4"...................40.00
Clown, blown glass..30.00
Clown, full figure, magenta, minor wear, 3¼"......................8.00
Clown, playing a banjo, blown glass, early, 4½"...................50.00
Clown, silver w/mc decor, 4¼".......................................25.00
Clown face, blown, 3½"...50.00
Clown face, blown glass, early, 4"..................................75.00
Clown face, silver w/red, yellow & blk decor, 3¾"...............32.50
Clown in the moon, pnt face, blown, 3½"..........................160.00
Clown playing drum, blown glass....................................35.00
Cockatoo, silver w/angel hair tail, red/gr, 6¼"....................7.00
Corn, blown glass...38.00
Couple dancing, wooden compo, old, M.............................35.00
Dog on ball, blown, 3½"..65.00
Dog on ball, silver/gr, blown, 3"...................................65.00
Doll's head, glass eyes, sm clip connection chip, pnt G, 2¾"...30.00
Doll's head, pnt face & eyes, 2½"..................................30.00
Double face, indent w/glass eyes, 4½".............................175.00
Duck, blown glass...30.00
Elephant, blown glass...110.00
Father Christmas, holding a tree, blown glass, early, 3½".......30.00
Father Christmas, holding a tree, blown glass, early, 4½".......48.00
Father Christmas head, blown glass.................................30.00
Fish, blown glass, early, 4½".......................................38.00
Fish, silver w/polychrome decor, 3¼"..............................21.00
Foxy Grandpa, blown legs..200.00
Girl, full figure, 4", M...105.00
Gnome, blown, 4"...60.00
Gondola, blown glass/wire/tinsel/Father Christmas, 7"..........45.00
Grapes...10.00
Guitar, silver w/magenta trim, minor wear, 5¼"....................5.00
Heart, blown glass, early, 3".......................................26.00
Heart, w/pansy, blown glass, early, 4".............................30.00
Hot air balloon, tinsel wire supports, glass/paper scrap Cupid....35.00
House, snow-covered, blown glass, early, 2¼"......................25.00
Ice skater, magenta costume trimmed in cotton/glitter, 6".......40.00

Ornament, crepe paper bell with Santa's face, hanging paper ropes, circa 1890s, 3" bell, $135.00.

Icicle, silver w/mc spirals & snow, 6", pr..........................15.00
Kugel, gold glass w/fancy CI holder, German, 12"................265.00
Kugel, gold w/nickel clip, minor fading, 5".......................30.00
Kugel, silver, brass clip, minor fading, 5"........................25.00
Kugel, silver, 11"..60.00
Kugel, silver mercury glass grapes w/orig brass cap, heavy, 3"..100.00
Lantern candle holders for tree, colored glass lenses, tin, 5"....55.00
Man in Moon, blown glass...30.00
Man in Moon, pnt face, blown, 3½".................................110.00
Mandolin, blown glass, early, 3"...................................18.00
Mushroom, blown glass, clip on, early, 3¾".......................28.00
Mushrooms, 2 on clip, blown glass.................................20.00
Ovoid shape w/church, blown glass, early, 4".....................45.00
Owl, blown, 4"...85.00
Owl, blown glass, clip on, early, 6"...............................58.00
Owl, on ball, pink, blown, 3".......................................85.00
Owl, silver w/gold wash, pink/bl decor, angel hair tail, 6½"....22.50
Parrot, blown glass, on clip, spun glass tail, Germany, 6½".....45.00
Peach, blown glass, painted, early, 3¾"...........................38.00
Peacock, blown glass, angel hair wings............................35.00
Peacock, mother & baby, on clip, blown glass.....................30.00
Peacock, silver w/red/gr/blk, angel hair tail, spring clip, 6"....5.00
Peacock on ball, blown glass..65.00
Pine cone, blown glass...6.00
Rabbit eating carrot, blown glass...................................85.00
Rose, large, blown glass, early, 4¼"...............................28.00
Santa, chenille, compo face, HP, holding tree, w/hook, 3".......10.00
Santa, dbl faced..25.00
Santa, face, blown, 3"...85.00
Santa, head, blown glass w/mica decor, early, 2¾"...............50.00
Santa, in airship, glass/plaster/tinsel trim, 7".................120.00
Santa, in wire swing, 2 feather trees, scrap face/paper, 5½"...205.00
Santa, mechanical whiskers, 6"......................................65.00
Santa, red, blown glass, full figure................................30.00
Santa, w/tree, silver w/red decor, wht sanding, some wear, 4½"..15.00
Santa, wht/gold, blown glass, full figure..........................35.00
Santa in gold coat, blown glass....................................40.00
Santa on ball, blown glass..65.00
Santa on pine cone, blown glass....................................45.00
Set, cardboard houses, Made in Japan, 12 in G orig box.......25.00

Spider on web, beaded................................45.00
Swan, long crooked neck, silver w/red/gr, angel hair, 4"........45.00
Teapot, blown glass, early, 2½".......................20.00
Towle, silver, Partridge in Pear Tree, 1st edition, no box......425.00
Towle, 1972, sterling...............................125.00
Tree, silver w/wht snow, tin clip, mk Germany, 3¾"..........12.00
Tree, tin, enameled, 1912, w/orig box, 4"................38.00
Tree top, tier of blown glass balls/tinsel/glitter bells, 12".......45.00
Tree top angel, emb printed/gilded paper, wht angel hair, 9"....40.00
Victorian girl, 5", G...............................75.00
Violin, red w/wht decor, minor wear....................3.50

Miscellaneous

Bank, mc porcelain, baby/fireplace/stockings, old, 6x4½", M....24.00
Book, pop-up; Christmas on Stage.......................20.00
Book, Santa Claus Visit, Donahue, 1905.................12.50
Bowl, plate & mug, Rudolph the Reindeer decor............25.00
Candle cup top, blown glass fruit, early, 4"................85.00

Santa doll, composition face, circa 1890s, 19½", $235.00.

Candle holders, poinsettia, tin, 3" dia, pr.................35.00
Candy container, cardboard box, Santa painting doll, '40s, M...15.00
Candy container, Father Christmas/chimney, glass/tin base, 5"..125.00
Candy container, Santa, pressed cardboard, pack on back......35.00
Candy pail, Merry Christmas, tin litho, Norton Bros, 1898....200.00
Card, Santa w/bag, toys, etc, 14½x10", M...............100.00
Christmas light, emerald gr, expanded 12 dia w/folded rim, 3"...75.00
Christmas light, green, hobnail pattern, 4", pr..............40.00
Christmas light, lt bl dia quilt, pontil, flared rim, 3½"..........75.00
Christmas light, milk glass, bell w/2 Santa faces............14.00
Christmas light, milk glass, lg oval w/2 Santa faces...........14.00
Christmas light, puce, pontil, expanded dia, folded rim, 3"....125.00
Father Christmas, brass clockworks in chest, glass eyes, 20"..1,575.00
Father Christmas, compo figure/cb sleigh/fur beard, German, 7".95.00
Father Christmas, papier mache figure, orig sprig, 9".........75.00
Fence, for tree, wicker & wood, 24x36".................70.00
Fence, ornate CI, Victorian...........................175.00
Fence, wood, folding, pnt gr, 6 ft L....................15.00
Fence, wood picket w/gate, fourteen 7" posts & 12" sections...185.00
House, cotton/compo Santa alongside, cb w/mica roof, '20s, 4"..38.00
Light, tree shaped, pierced tin, Noval, 10"................25.00
Lights, complete set of comic character figurals.............325.00

Lights, for tree, Scrappy w/his friends, 1930s..............150.00
Lights, Mickey Mouse, by Noma, orig box................150.00
Lights, plastic stars, electric, 1950s, 25 on card............22.50
Lights, Popeye, in orig box, 1930s.....................150.00
Pitcher, china, Santa face on spout & hdl................80.00
Print, Santa in sleigh w/reindeer, Victorian, 11x19".........100.00
Sampler, 'Holly & Mistletoe', on old stretcher, 27x38".......130.00
Santa, bisque, pre-1900, old repair on arm, 6"............30.00
Santa, candy cane holder, bisque, Made in Japan, 4½"........15.00
Santa, cardboard & folding crepe paper, opens to 20", M......15.00
Santa, celluloid windup, Occupied Japan................60.00
Santa, climbs into chimney on roof, compo/HP, 1920s, 2½"....28.00
Santa, cloth & chenille, compo head, HP, 6"..............20.00
Santa, cloth face, straw filled, early, 31", G..............110.00
Santa, compo, HP, 5"..............................35.00
Santa, compo w/felt coat, holds tree, German, 5", G.........85.00
Santa, doll, printed cloth, ES Peeke, 1886...............250.00
Santa, gr cloth w/gold ladder, Teem bottle cap buckle, adv.....45.00
Santa, holding sm feather tree, mk German, 9".............90.00
Santa, in sleigh, papier mache, 'Morris for Quality', 21x24"....190.00
Santa, on skis, bisque, Japan, miniature.................18.00
Santa, on skis, 2 ice skaters, cast lead, 3" Santa, USA.........60.00
Santa, papier mache, pre 1920, 12"....................120.00
Santa, papier mache, sitting in decorated wreath............45.00
Santa, papier mache face, automated, electric, 55"..........220.00
Santa, plaster, 1930s, 2"............................12.00
Santa, plaster face, early, 8".........................65.00
Santa, pulling sleigh, bisque, Germany, sm...............35.00
Santa, silver/blue, Occupied Japan, 3".................15.00
Santa, straw stuffed, buckram/pnt face, early, 2 ft..........350.00
Santa, stuffed, cloth head/pnt features/fiber beard, 24".......150.00
Santa, Thos Nast design printed cloth, w/pipe/toys, 15".......235.00
Santa, tin windup, made in Great Britain, 4½".............50.00
Santa, wax figural, mk Gurley, 3".....................10.00
Santa, 1940s compo, 5"............................25.00
Santa face, pressed cardboard, deep relief, pnt, 18x11x6".......95.00
Santa face, wall plaque, pressed paper/chicken feathers, 20".....35.00
Santa mask, full head, 1920s.........................45.00
Santa's boot, papier mache, red, 6"....................20.00
Snowman, cotton, Occupied Japan, 6"..................12.00
Spoon, hdl: Santa goes down chimney/bowl: fireplace, demitasse.75.00
Spoon, sterling, Santa hdl, nativity in bowl, teaspoon........195.00
Tree, feathers, in orig box, 36".......................225.00
Tree, feathers, Made in Germany, orig box, 60"............385.00
Tree, feathers, red beads on end of limbs, weighted base, 72"..475.00
Tree, feathers, w/tin candle clips, 32".................150.00
Tree, feathers, wht w/red berries, 29"..................85.00
Tree, red wood tub mk Germany, w/glass acorns/rnd balls, 10"..40.00
Tree, wht goose feathers w/red berries/wood pot, 15".........65.00
Tree stand, blk iron, pat 1890s.......................25.00
Tree stand, iron cylinder on wood board, picket fence, 7x12"...90.00
Tree stand, musical, Germany, 'Silent Night', orig box, 10".....75.00
Tree stand, musical, Symphonion Gloriosa, 6⅛" disks, walnut.1,000.00
Tree stand, musical, VG...........................275.00
Tree stand, wood, 3 trn legs/trn cylinder, pnt, 1890s, 20x16"...85.00

Cincinnati Art Pottery

The Cincinnati Art Pottery was established in 1879 by T.J. Wheatley along with several others, primarily, it is felt, to generate funds to augment his further experimentation with the underglaze decorated Cincinnati Faience. It was this type of ware that was produced there until 1882, when Wheatley withdrew his interests and the firm actually began to utilize the title 'Cincinnati Art Pottery'.

During the years that followed, several other artware lines were successfully developed. Hungarian Faience was a light glazed line depending on its in-mold modeling for decoration. The resulting patterns were painted in contrasting colors, often highlighted with gold tracing. Portland Blue Faience imitated the rich blue of the famous Portland vase, and it, too, was often highlighted with gold.

But their most famous product was an ivory line featuring flowers painted in natural colors and elaborate gold scrollwork. The ware is often marked 'Keyonta', either in block letters or with a circular device containing a turtle, the Indian translation of the line's name.

Ewer, wht/bl w/bl/orange floral, heavy gold decor, 12".........90.00

Circus Collectibles

The 1890s -- the Golden Age of the circus. Barnum and Bailey's parades transformed mundane city streets into an exotic never-never land inhabited by trumpeting elephants with gold jeweled headgear, strutting by to the strains of the caliope that issued from a fine red and gilt painted wagon extravagantly decorated with wood carved animals of every description. It was an exciting experience -- is it any wonder that collectors today treasure the mementos of that golden era?

Posters that once whetted interest and stirred imaginations are today avidly sought, and though rarely signed by the artist, often carry the name of the printer or lithographer. Among them, many consider the work of the Strobridge Lithograph Company to be the finest. Other early printing companies were Gibson and Company Litho, Erie Litho, and Enquirer Job Printing Company.
   Key:
   lm----linen mount

Autograph, Clyde Beatty, 4x6" slip of paper.................10.00
Cat's head carving, worn old pnt, 12x12"...................300.00
Head, smiling man, carved pine/glass eyes, G pnt, 1800s, 8x5".175.00
Magazine & program, Ringling Bros/Barnum & Bailey, 1948.....9.00
Photos, 1930s circus troupe, glossies, 12x20", 4 for.........145.00
Poster, Barnum & Bailey, circus train & cars, French Tour, lm.275.00
Poster, Christy Bros, Big 5 Ring Wild Animal Show..........275.00
Poster, Cole Bros, boy/girl on giant hippo, 1930s, 28x40", EX.65.00
Poster, Cole Bros, circus trains unloading, 1930s, 20x30", M....95.00
Poster, Ringling Bros, Story of Hunt, 1914, Strobridge, lm, NM.275.00
Poster, Ringling Bros Barnum/Bailey, charging Hippo, '43, 30"..35.00
Poster, Ringling Bros Barnum/Bailey, Horses/Fete of Garlands..125.00
Poster, Sparks Railroad circus w/tiger, wild animals, 40x54"...200.00
Poster, The Baileys, big top/crowds, Donaldson, 1910, 20x30"...65.00
Wagon panel, carved/pnt, horse/banner, att Dentzel, 56x20"...650.00

Clambroth

Clambroth is a term that refers to a type of glass popular during the Victorian period. It was semi-opaque and gray- white in color, said to resemble the broth of the clam.

Cologne w/stopper, 5".....................................15.00
Creamer, Swan...55.00
Lamp, sq stepped base, fluted stem, petal font, 12"..........200.00
Rolling pin, wood hdls, 21"..............................35.00
Shaving mug...35.00
Syrup, applied hdl, pewter top w/hinged lid, 6¾"...........200.00
Vase, pebbeled panels in globular base, flared mouth, 7".......15.00

Clarice Cliff

Between 1928 and 1935, in Burslem, England, as the director and part owner of Wilkinson and Newport Pottery Companies, Clarice Cliff and her 'paintresses' created a body of hand painted pottery whose influence is felt to the present time.

The name for the oevre was Bizarre Ware, and the predominant sensibility, style, and appearance was Deco. Almost all pieces are signed and include pattern names, such as Fantasque, Crocus, Inspiration, Persian, Applique, Gay Day, My Garden, Delicia, etc. Clarice Cliff died in 1972, shortly after the Victoria and Albert Museum showed her work in retrospect, and collectors, primarily in England, began seeking and admiring her work.

Basket, Celtic Harvest, cream/gold/flowers/fruit, mkd, 9x6x12"..275.00
Bowl, bl parrots relief, mc, low..........................95.00
Bowl, brown leaves, 10"..................................45.00
Bowl, Crocus, deep, 8" dia...............................75.00
Bowl, Secret, 8"...100.00
Bowl, vegetable; Charlotte, bl, Royal Staffordshire..........13.50
Centerpiece, Water Lily, 9".............................95.00
Comport, Bizarre, star motif in center, 11"................200.00
Creamer, Gay Day, mkd, 4x3" dia.........................65.00
Ewer, cream, ringed body w/Deco florals, 8x4"..............75.00
Honey pot, Art Deco, orange, cream, yellow & tan, 4x3¾"....125.00
Honey pot, beehive, orange/yel/cream/tan, w/lid, mkd, 4x3"....118.00
Jam jar, Celtic Harvest, nickel plate lid, 4¾x4"............95.00
Jar, covered; geometric, cylindrical, Bizarre Ware, 3½".......120.00
Jug, aqua & gold floral on cream, gr band, Deco shape, 3¾"...55.00
Jug, Bizarre Ware, My Garden, 7½x5".....................175.00
Jug, Celtic Harvest, cream & gold, mc fruit/flowers, mkd, 10"..175.00
Jug, cream w/mc florals, squarish form, 4¾x3x5½".........140.00
Jug, Fantasque, mc stylized florals, 4x5" dia...............150.00
Jug, lt gray body w/bl & tan trees & shrubs, 6¾x5" dia......110.00
Jug, My Garden, red/br drip w/floral hdl, 7½x5"...........175.00
Jug, orange flowers on cream, sq Deco shape, 5x5¼".........135.00
Pitcher, Bizarre, chicken, 6"............................75.00
Pitcher, Bizarre, octagonal w/trees & hills, 8"............135.00
Plate, dinner; Devonshire, Royal Staffordshire.............12.00
Plate, Islands, Bizarre Ware, 10".........................30.00
Plate, Mutiny on Bounty, Royal Staffordshire...............24.00
Salt & pepper, Bizarre, 2½", w/matching mustard pot, 2".....130.00
Sugar shaker, Bizarre, gr & blue florals on cream, 5x2¼".....125.00
Sugar shaker, My Garden, 6".............................50.00
Sweetmeat, floral relief, SP lid, rim, hdl, 4x3½"...........125.00
Teapot, Chelsea, pink, Wilkinson.........................28.00
Toothbrush beaker, Fantasque............................85.00
Tray, sandwich; relief deco floral ends, gray ground, 6x12".....65.00
Tray, SP center hdl, mk Bizarre, 5½x11½".................75.00
Tray, stylized sunflower, 8½x10".........................95.00
Vase, Bizarre, ribbed, flowers/willow trees, bulbous, 8"........95.00
Vase, Bizarre, 5 color circular stripes, 6½x4¾"...........195.00
Vase, branches & violet flowers, 6"......................70.00
Vase, florals in relief, multi on blue & cream, 8½x6¾".......175.00
Vase, gr/tan/bl florals on cream, Deco styling, 6½x3½".......135.00
Vase, My Garden, mc flowers, 12".........................150.00
Vase, My Garden, mc flowers, 5"..........................40.00
Vase, parakeets in relief, Art Deco, 12½x4¾".............195.00
Vase, relief Deco flowers on lt gray, bl at top, 6x3½".........55.00
Wall plaque, lady's face, bisque gray, 9½x6½".............165.00
Wall pocket, dolphin, 5½"...............................50.00
Wall pocket, w/bird, 8x6½"..............................75.00

Clewell

Charles Walter Clewell was a metal worker who perfected the technique of plating an entire ceramic vessel with a thin layer of copper or bronze treated with an oxidizing agent to produce a natural deterioration of the surface. Through trial and error, he was able to control the degree of patina achieved. In the early stages, the metal darkened, and if allowed to develop further, formed a natural turquoise blue or green corrosion. He worked alone in his small Akron, Ohio, studio from about 1906, buying undecorated pottery from several Ohio firms, among them Weller, Owens, and Cambridge.

His work is usually marked. Clewell died in 1965, having never revealed his secret process to others.

Ash tray, riveted copper, dark patina........................85.00
Bud vase, #344-6, EX patina, 7½".......................145.00
Bud vase, G patina, 7½"................................120.00
Chalice, bronze, gr patina, sgn C in circle, #503-21ZX, 6".....350.00
Vase, bl/gr patina, #322-12, 9".........................150.00
Vase, bl/gr patina, baluster, EX color allover, #430-2-6, 18½"..575.00
Vase, good color, stress lines in bronze only, bulbous, 3½".....70.00
Vase, gr orange patina, elongated teardrop, 9"..............200.00
Vase, gr patina: shoulder/base; elongated gourd, #44-2-6, 15"..425.00
Vase, gr pottery w/incised design, molded hdls, sgn/#.........90.00
Vase, rich patina, sgn/#d, 5"...........................110.00
Vase, tapered cylinder, bl patina, #368-2-9, 6¾".............140.00
Vase, w/hdls, #408-2-6, EX patina, 6"....................200.00

Vase, copper corn figural, 4¾", $185.00.

Clews

Brothers Ralph and James Clews were potters who operated in Cobridge, in the Staffordshire district, from 1817 to 1835. They are best known for their blue and white transfer printed earthenwares, which included American Views, Moral Maxims, Picturesque Views, and English Views. A series called *Three Tours of Dr. Syntax* contained nearly eighty different scenes, with each piece bearing a descriptive title. Two other popular series were *Don Quixote,* with twenty prints, and *Pictures of Sir David Wilkie,* with twelve.

Both printed and impressed marks were used, often incorporating the pattern name as well as the pottery.

Cup & saucer, Christmas Eve, dk bl transfer, lg..............200.00
Cup & saucer, Coronation, dk bl...........................85.00
Pepper pot, Coronation, dk bl transfer....................200.00
Plate, cup; Errand Boy, dbl transfer, dk bl, 3½"............225.00

Plate, Dr Syntax Painting a Portrait, bl/wht, 10"...........195.00
Plate, Dr Syntax Star Gazing, dk bl, 9"...................180.00
Plate, Dr Syntax Taking Possession of His Living, dk bl, 10"...195.00
Plate, Dr Syntax Turned Nurse, dk bl, 8".................180.00
Plate, Escape of the Mouse, Wilkie Series, dk bl, 10", M....195.00
Plate, Knighthood Conferred on Don Quixote, dk bl, 10"......175.00
Plate, Meeting of Sancho & Dapple, dk bl, 9", VG...........130.00
Plate, Moral Maxims, blk transfer, ca 1830s, 7"............50.00
Plate, Sancho Panza Hoisted in Blanket, Don Quixote, 10"....175.00
Plate, States, dk bl, 10½"..............................220.00
Platter, Dr Syntax Copying the Wit of Widow, dk bl, 10¾"....350.00
Platter, Teresa Panza and the Messenger, dk bl, 14½".......495.00
Platter, Valentine, Wilkie Series, dk bl, 15"..............425.00
Sugar bowl, Water Girl, dk bl...........................250.00
Teapot, Water Girl, dk bl..............................295.00
Waste bowl, child & dog in cradle, dk bl, 5½".............125.00
Waste bowl, Christmas Eve, Wilkie Series, dk bl, 6½".......285.00

Clifton

Clifton Art Pottery, of Clifton, New Jersey, was organized in 1905, and until 1911 when they turned to the production of wall and floor tile, made art ware of several varieties.

The founders were Fred Tschirner and William A. Long. Long had developed the method for underglaze slip painting that had been used at the Lonhuda Pottery in Steubenville, Ohio, in the 1890s.

Crystal Patina, the first art ware made by the small company, utilized a fine white body and flowing, blended colors, the earliest a green crystalline. Indian Ware, copied from the pottery of the American Indians, was decorated in black geometric designs on red clay. Robin's Egg Blue, pale blue on the white body; and Tirrube, a slip decorated matt ware were also produced.

Bud vase, crystalline, 1906, 6¾".........................85.00
Bud vase, pear form, wht w/flambe gr/yellow w/in, crystals, 6"..275.00
Jug, red clay w/br Indian decor, mkd/#230/4 Mile, AZ, 4½"....110.00
Pitcher, Indian Ware, dk br on red clay, 4½"..............67.50
Pot, Indian Ware, 1 hdl, 5¾" dia.........................55.00
Teapot, Crystal Patina, 5¾"............................72.00
Teapot, Indian Ware, sm................................55.00
Vase, cr/br, gr crystals, integral rim to shoulder hdls, 7".....120.00
Vase, Crystal Patina, 8½"..............................75.00
Vase, crystalline, 1907, sgn CS, 9"......................80.00
Vase, Indian Ware, #213, can neck/bulbous base, 2¾".......32.00
Vase, Indian Ware, bulbous base, 12"....................250.00
Vase, Indian Ware, bulbous base, 4½"....................65.00
Vase, Indian Ware, cream/rust points w/blk outlines, 6".....65.00
Vase, Indian Ware, long neck, bulbous, sgn, 12"...........250.00
Vase, wht crystalline, widens from tiny neck, mk/1906, 6¾"...100.00

Clocks

In the early days of our country's history, clock makers were influenced by styles imported from Europe and Germany. They copied their cabinets and re-constructed their movements. But needed materials were in short supply; modifications had to be made. Of necessity was born mainspring motive power and spring clocks. Wooden movements were made on a mass production basis as early as 1808. Before the middle of the century, metal movements had been developed.

Today's collectors prefer clocks from the 18th and 19th centuries, with pendulum regulated movements.

Bracket clocks made during this period utilized the shorter pendulum improvised in 1658 by Fromentiel, a prominent English clock maker. These smaller square-face clocks usually were made with a dome top fitted with a handle or a decorative finial. The case was usually walnut or ebony, and was often decorated with pierced brass mountings. Brackets were often mounted on the wall to accomodate the clock, hence the name.

The banjo clock was patented in 1802 by Simon Willard. It derived its descriptive name from its banjo-like shape. A similar but more elaborate style was called the lyre clock.

Twentieth century novelty clocks, such as the animated examples in the listings that follow, are becoming very popular collectibles, as their values indicate.

Key: pnd----pendulum   T&S----time and strike

A Redier, mantel, ebonized calendar on paper rolls, 13x10"....500.00
A Smith, water bracket, wood w/repousse brass reservoir, 27"..200.00
Aaron Willard, banjo, mahog/gilt, eagle atop/rvpt w/ships, 41".1,500.00
Aaron Willard, banjo, mahog/gilt acorn finial/rvpt, rstr, 39"....900.00
Aaron Willard, shelf, mahog, Federal, rvpt matt, 31"........3,200.00
Aaron Willard, shelf, mahog, scroll cornice/rvpt/8 day/paw ft..2,600.00
Aaron Willard, shelf, mahog, scroll top/brass urn finial, 38".10,000.00
Aaron Willard, shelf, mahog/rvpt, gilt eagle atop/paw ft, 33"..2,300.00
Alarm, Baby Ben, repeat alarm, blk dial, nickel case..........30.00
Alarm, Big Ben, repeat alarm, nickle case, ca 1927............25.00
Alarm, Old Reliable, 8 day, Wards..........................35.00
American Clock Co, crystal regulator, battery, 13½".........850.00
Animated, bird in cage, ball revolves, bird is pnd, Japan......200.00
Animated, cottage w/Swiss scene, tin/plastic, 4x5"............30.00
Animated, couple on seesaw, E Engslier.......................8.00
Animated, driver w/whip, coach & horse, United Metal Goods...90.00
Animated, early bird pulls worm from ground, farm scene.....200.00
Animated, fish, electric, Sessions..........................35.00
Animated, God Bless America, tin, #s are stars, 7½x5¼".......85.00
Animated, man at anvil, color..............................55.00
Animated, mouse, eyes move, HP, wood pnd, German, 7½x4"...35.00
Animated, racing car, man w/flag, Jaz Clock.................55.00
Animated, Roy Rogers alarm, desert scene...................85.00
Animated, Snow White, dwarf head moves, house shape, 5¾x4".27.50
Animated, soldier, Germany, wood, weight driven, 11x6½".....22.00
Animated, The Fame, spirit of '76, 2 drummers/fife player.....100.00
Animated, windmill & Dutch scene, Sessions, 9¾x6¾x3".......60.00
Anniversary, 400 day, disc pnd, glass dome.................150.00

Leroy and Files, Paris, mantel clock, circa 1800s, 17", $250.00.

Ansonia, blk mahog, schoolhouse, 8 day/time...............450.00
Ansonia, carriage, brass/glass case w/ormolu mts, 15"........400.00
Ansonia, carriage, dbl enameled face, 10"..................600.00
Ansonia, Diana..900.00
Ansonia, dresser, Royal Bonn case, 6¼"....................140.00
Ansonia, Excelsior, lg ornate crystal regulator............1,600.00
Ansonia, Fisherman, swinger..............................1,500.00
Ansonia, Huntress, swinger...............................1,500.00
Ansonia, mantel, allegorical panel, rnd urn form, 17½".......200.00
Ansonia, mantel, Crystal Palace, #1 Extra, glass dome/pnd, 17".850.00
Ansonia, mantel, cut glass pnd, mirror sides/cherubs, 1876....425.00
Ansonia, mantel, figure in 18th century garb/allegorical panel...200.00
Ansonia, Marquis, crystal regulator.......................1,200.00
Ansonia, Patricia, figural.................................750.00
Ansonia, Portico, crystal regulator........................450.00
Ansonia, Prompt, 8 day, weight, blk walnut................1,100.00
Ansonia, Royal Bonn china w/porcelain dial, lt bl w/florals.....650.00
Ansonia, Santa Fe, 8 day, weight, mahog..................1,800.00
Attleboro, shelf, carved oak Cylon, panel glass w/rvpt, 23½"...170.00
Auguste Leroy, carriage, engraved gilt brass case, 4¾".......825.00
Austrian, enamel/mtd, gilt metal, jewels/carved figures, 8"....605.00
Banjo, Howard type, blk/gold door, throat glasses, 29½".....500.00
Banjo, mahog, Fed, acorn finial, rvpt panel w/eagle, 33".....600.00
Banjo, mahog, Fed, rvpt panels/acorn finial, weight drive, 30".1,100.00
Banjo, mahog/gilt wood/rvpt Constitutions Escape, 1820, 30".1,200.00
Becker, Vienna regulator, 2 weight, T&S, fancy.............650.00
Birge & Fuller, dbl steeple, fusee movement, 27½".........1,500.00
Birge & Fuller, dbl steeple, twin candle wagon spring, 26"...2,500.00
Birge & Mallory, shelf, 3 part, eagle crest, 8 day/weight, 39"...750.00
Boston, brass/glass crystal reg, tandem wind, 8 day/T&S.......450.00
Brewster/Ingraham, mahog beehive, etch/cut lower glass, 8 day.450.00
Campignon, travelling, repeat/alarm, gilt metal/paw ft/floral...1,320.00
Carriage, alarm, floral engraved, lever movement, 4¾".......330.00
Carriage, brass & Limoges enamel, girl/cupid, 3"..........1,750.00
Carriage, brass/Limoges enamel putti/birds, columns, 6½", G.1,600.00
Carriage, champleve enamel flowers, round dial/columns, 5"..3,575.00
Carriage, enamel face, beveled glass, dtd 1901 w/in, 2½".....375.00
Carriage, enamel sgn face, beveled glass, dtd 1878, 4½".....425.00
Carriage, enamel vignettes w/lovers ea side, 1890, miniature..2,750.00
Carriage, enameled numerals on alabaster face, brass, 4½"....375.00
Carriage, lever movement, striker/alarm, columns/foliage ft.....880.00
Carriage, 8 day, hour & ½ hour, French, late 1800s, 7½"....850.00
Carriage, 8 day time/alarm, repeater, retailed by Tiffany, 6½".1,100.00
Cartier, desk, beveled crystal arch w/gold enamel/diamond, 8".7,700.00
Cartier, desk, gold/agate/sapphire/diamond/champleve, 7".....4,400.00
Cartier, diamonds in hands, gold/enamel/agate, miniature......770.00
Cuckoo, carved, hunting scene, Black Forest, 3 weight, 40"..1,200.00
Cuckoo, house atop, trees side & bottom, water mill, deer, 11".125.00
Cuckoo, walnut, German, ornate carving, pnd, 3 weight, 31"...600.00
Daniel Balch, shelf, mahog, Fed, brass weights/pnd, 28x12"..8,000.00
Daniel Pratt, Jr; shelf, mahog veneer, strike/time, 28x19"......400.00
Delft, mantel, porcelain, bl/wht florals, 11¾"...............450.00
Delphine-Barrois, carriage, brass, 30 hr, 4½"...............200.00
Dent, gilt metal architectural pnd, 2 columns/paw ft, 15".....1,320.00
Derry Mfg Co, banjo, mahog/eagle finial/rvpt throat/door, 42".1,300.00
Drocourt, carriage, brass repeater/detached lever movement, 5".660.00
E Couaillet, carriage, brass repeater, for Tiffany, 5¼".......1,500.00
E Currier, mahog/gilt, lyre form, eagle atop, rvpt panel, 39"..3,500.00
E Howard, mahog/rvpt throat panel & oval, pnd, 1850, 52"..1,870.00
EF Caldwell, carved ivory hinged face, turq carving, cast base.1,760.00
EF Caldwell, etched rnd glass face, 2 figural griffin supports..1,650.00
Eli Terry, shelf, mahog, ½ rnd columns/rvpt, paw ft, 38x18"...550.00
Elmer Stennes, girandole/eagle atop/EX rvpt throat/door, 47".1,800.00
EN Welch, Arditti, Gales perpetual dbl dial calendar........1,250.00

Cartel clock, gilt bronze with enamel dial, inscribed J. Berth, d/A Paris, mounted on velvet backing, late 19th century, 37", $1,760.00.

EN Welch, mahog, 8 day weight ogee, T&S, rvpt............300.00
EN Welch, regulator, 8 day time/strike, Verdi model.........450.00
EN Welch, shelf, oak, 8 day, ½ hr strike/alarm, rvpt door, 21".160.00
EN Welch, shelf, rosewood, Gerster 'patti', 8 day/time/strike..1,300.00
F Kroeber, Angel Swing, walnut mantel, 1876..............500.00
F Kroeber, mantel, bl w/gold base/top, 8 day time/strike......350.00
Figural, carved marble 3 Graces holding clock sphere, 34"...3,575.00
Figural, classical maid resting against malachite socle, 23"....2,640.00
Figural, Empire style, bronze female holding watch, 7"........175.00
Figural, marble/ormolu, Perseus & Adromeda by Gregoine, 33".950.00
Figural, 3 putti on blk orb, gilt base, French, 32".........5,500.00
Forrestville, 8 day weight ogee, T&S, crotch mahog/mirror.....475.00
French, bracket, Bouille-style, circle face/pnd/keys, 24", G....825.00
French, carriage, sold by Tiffany, 8 day brass, fluted, 6".......450.00
French, carriage, time, 8 day, SP case w/porcelain dial.......325.00
French, crystal regulator, mercury pnd, porcelain dial.......425.00
French, gold dore bronze, cherub on globe, 14x10"........1,325.00
French, Japy Freres, gallery, 10" dial, 8 day/time, blk case.....250.00
French, mantel, figural boy w/flute, girl, bronze, 15"........250.00
French, mantel, figural surmount/columns/Sevres inserts.......395.00
French, picture fr, gold leaf, silk thread suspension, T&S......375.00
Frodsham & Baker, bracket, burl walnut/metal mts, 32".....3,000.00
G Marsh, shelf, acanthus/floral, eagle crest, 8 day/wood works..450.00
Germany, Delft scenes w/windmill, 8 day, 8½x8½"............75.00
Germany, miniature kitchen w/clock below, handmade, pnd.....65.00
Germany, porcelain w/HP windmill scenes, pnd/8 day,.........75.00
Germany, tin w/porcelain face/brass works, litho house/lake......55.00
Germany, 6 nursery rhymes in color, 8 day/pnd, early 1900s...100.00
Gilbert, Boston, oak gingerbread, 8 day, T&S, alarm.........160.00
Gilbert, rosewood, pointed top cottage, 8 day, T&S, rvpt......150.00

Gilbert, store regulator, 8 day, time......................325.00
Gilbert, 8 day T&S, oak kitchen, Concord pat case..........175.00
Gubelin, carriage, gilt metal neo-classic mts on tortoise, 9½"...210.00
Gustaf Becker, wall, 14 day, 2 weight, T&S, box cabinet, 1895.395.00
H Welton & Co, pillar & scroll shelf, inlaid mahog, Fed, 32"...900.00
Haig & Haig, wall, pnd, illuminated, MIB..................35.00
Henry Terry, shelf, acanthus ½ columns/flame finial, 42".....800.00
Horace Tifft, banjo, mahog veneer w/blk/gilt rvpt glasses, 29"..900.00
IBM, International Time Recording Master, #685.............275.00
Ingraham, kitchen, Capitol, 8 day, embossed oak............300.00
Ingraham, mantel, rosewood, Ionic-style, 8 day.............185.00
Ingraham, mantel, 8 day T&S, pnd, 10x11".................90.00
Ingraham, oak, gingerbread, 8 day/time/strike/alarm...........175.00
Ingraham, oak schoolhouse, drop octagon, 8" dial, 8 day/time..250.00
Ingraham, rosewood, cottage, 8 day/time/strike, rnd top.......160.00
Ingraham, rosewood, cottage, 8 day/time/strike/alarm, octagon..175.00
Ingraham, store regulator, advertising.....................400.00
Ithaca, #1 regulator, shelf model, calendar.................1,800.00
Ithaca, dlb dial, calendar, HB Horton, iron case, 30 day, 21".2,400.00
Ithaca, Pony Model, mahog veneer, perpetual calendar, 18"....275.00
Japanese, brass/iron lantern w/alarm, 1800, no weights, 11"..1,650.00
Jefferson Golden Hour, glass face/gold #s, 'mystery', electric.....75.00
Jerome, Argyle, shelf, 8 day/T&S, rvpt glass................110.00
Jerome, bracket wall, Empire, 8 day, rvpt door floral face.....225.00
JJ Beals & Son, banjo, inlaid mahog, Federal, rvpt, 33½".....800.00
Joe Louis, boxing theme................................100.00
John P Creed, girandole, mahog/rvpt throat/door glass, 43"....100.00
Johnson, mahog, 8 day weight ogee, T&S, mirror lower glass...325.00
Julias P Fries, water level, #78, brass/CI/glass, 7x19x10"......250.00
Junghan, Diana, swinger................................650.00
Junghan, elephant, swinger, orig jewel bar, 1910............700.00
Junghan, Statue of Liberty, swinger.......................475.00
Lendan, Nixon as Superman, 9" dia.......................75.00
Lenzkirsch, wall, 14 day T&S, 1890......................650.00
Louis Phillippe, mantle, boullework, ivory face, lyre pnd, 16"...550.00
Lux, Beer Drinkers, animated............................150.00
Lux, Black Cat.......................................175.00
Lux, Blue Bird..35.00
Lux, Bulldog w/Kittens.................................50.00
Lux, Calico Horse, yellow...............................160.00
Lux, Clown w/Seals, moving ball, carved wood, 7x5¾".......265.00
Lux, Dixie Boy, original tie.............................400.00
Lux, dresser, ballerina scene, not animated, rare............185.00
Lux, Lovebirds..65.00
Lux, Old Lady at the Spinning Wheel, alarm, animated........100.00
Lux, Organ Grinder w/Monkey, animated...................200.00
Lux, Quail, full size, 8-day, pendulette....................95.00
Lux, Red Bobbing Bird.................................45.00
Lux, Rudolph...55.00
Lux, Ship's Wheel, blue................................125.00
Lux, Showboat, paddle wheel revolves.....................185.00
Lux, Woody Woodpecker................................200.00
Mantel, Charles X, ormolu, eagle/draped female, 1800s, 17"..1,100.00
Mantel, French, coral/blk enamel gilt metal mtd, 11".........500.00
Mantel, Louis XV ormolu mt, scrolls/foliage, boulle inlay, 26".1,870.00
Mantel, Louis XVI, gilt bronze, trellis work surmount, 23"...1,800.00
Mantel, Louis XVI ormolu/bronze draped lion pelt case, 7"....660.00
Mantel, Louis XVI type, HP porcelain dial/acanthus leaves, 22".900.00
Mantel, mahog, carriage clock form, lever movement, 8½".....440.00
Mantel, mahog w/satinwood inlay, Georgian style, 12"........225.00
Morbier, ornate, 8 day/T&S, weight, 2 minute repeat.......1,100.00
Moulignie, carriage, 8 day/T&S, engraved case, 6½".........650.00
New Haven, banjo, clipper ship, 8 day....................275.00
New Haven, banjo, mahog, eagle finial, rvpt throat, pnd, 41"...450.00

New Haven, banjo, Waring label, 8 day time, rvpt, mahog, 40".450.00
New Haven, banjo, 8 day T&S, pnd, eagle, mahog, 33"......350.00
New Haven, brass, figural lily pad w/frog in relief.............185.00
New Haven, mantel, Deco onyx/red marble strips/terminals, 7"...70.00
New Haven, regulator, mahog, 8 day, miniature...............95.00
New Haven, schoolhouse, 1929.........................300.00
Norris North, pillar & scroll shelf, mahog case, 30½".......1,200.00
Novelty, HP Oriental scene, wood/brass works, early '30s, 16"..100.00
Phineas Deming, mantel, curly maple/rvpt, pillar/scroll, 29"...9,250.00
Planchon A Paris, calender, treasure chest w/figural, 13".....850.00
Postal Telegraph, gallery wall, 1920s, lg..................35.00
Raingo Fres, gilt bronze/marble garniture, 7 lite/3 pc........2,750.00
Regulator, walnut w/arch, trn columns, European, 1900, 46"...650.00
Regulator, walnut w/architectural ped w/female mask, 33".....350.00
Regulator, walnut/pine/weight driven/trn pilasters, 33"........325.00
Samuel Marti, lyre, Fr porcelain frame w/fruit swag, 22".....3,200.00
Sawin, banjo, weight driven/alarm, crotch gr mahog, 39".....1,750.00
Sebastian Franz, painting of church, clock in steeple, 32"....4,000.00
Sessions, banjo, 8 day, rvpt ship, orig pnd, 42".............450.00
Sessions, clipper ship, wood/chrome electric, G.............50.00
Sessions, mantel, architectural 8 day, ½ hr strike, gong, 11"....85.00
Sessions, oak case, porcelain face, 9½x9½".................125.00
Sessions, shelf, 8 day T&S, pnd, walnut case, 9½"...........95.00
Seth Thomas, #1 Extra wall regulator, walnut, 8 day/T&S....1,800.00
Seth Thomas, brass/glass crystal reg/mercury pnd/8 day, T&S...475.00
Seth Thomas, mantel, 'rosewood' grain architectural 8 day, 14".150.00
Seth Thomas, mantel, bronze, Gothic case, 8 day, 14".......175.00
Simon Willard, mahog/rvpt panels, eagle atop, 1815, 35"...10,000.00
Standard Electric Time Co, master, lg pnd, oak case, 65".....300.00
Stennis, NH, mirror, weight, time only, prison sgn...........950.00
Stephen Rimbault, bracket, Geo III, musical, ornate, 29".....6,600.00
Sydenham, Cowes, congreve-type rolling ball brass, 16"......2,750.00

Tall Case

Aaron Willard, mahog/inlay, pierce crest/3 brass finials, 100".4,950.00
Cherry, Chpndl, John Filber, swan neck ped w/rosettes, 98"..4,100.00
Cherry, Federal, broken swan ped, waisted, 101"..........1,430.00
Cherry, Federal, shaped crest w/brass finials, ¼ columns, 89".2,310.00
Dutch Rococo, walnut, 2nd dial, moon phase, pnd, 1775.....1,430.00
Elnathan Tabler, mahog/inlay, Federal, shaped crest, 86".....7,150.00
Empire, fruitwood, ormolu mt/inlaid, ½ columns, 1825, 94"....605.00
Herschede, 9 tube chime, moon phase, mahog case, 96"....12,500.00
J Bryan, mahog, swan neck crest/columns, 64"............1,870.00
Mahog, calendar/strike, 3 brass finials, Geo III............1,800.00
Mahog/inlay, Fed, swan neck hood w/3 finials, waisted, 72"...3,740.00
Nichols Goddard, cherry/mahog/inlay, Federal, 80".........2,000.00
Poplar, primitive, orig wood works w/2nd hand, rfn, 70½"....925.00
Rice, NY, mahog/flowerhead inlay, Federal, moon phase, 94".3,600.00
Thos Braf Guilford, arched hood/columnar supports.........950.00
Walnut, Federal, swan ped w/3 trn finials, moon phases/date..3,740.00

Theodore Starr, carriage, Limoges enamel/brass, putti/birds...1,760.00
Tiffany, carriage, brass repeater w/calendar dial/alarm, 6"....1,900.00
Tiffany, Fr, 8 day/T&S, bl/wht china beehive, sgn...........395.00
Time Setter, Agnew dressed in red/wht/blue, orig box.........68.00
Union Clock, mantel, glass door, 13"....................200.00
Vienna, regulator wall, 2 weights, blk forest carved case, 47"...750.00
Wag on the Wall, curly maple, deer pntd on arch dial, 60"....600.00
Waltham, banjo, 8 day/weight driven/stop wind, orig rvpt, EX.1,500.00
Waltham, Chronometer, 8 day, gimballed, mahog/brass sgn box.625.00
Waltham, girandole banjo, mahog/gilt eagle atop, rvpt panels.1,400.00

Waterbury, carriage, wht face, glass all sides, 4½".........250.00
Waterbury, mantel, brass/bevel glass 3 sides, 10"...........300.00
Waterbury, marine engine room, oak, time, 8 day...........225.00
Waterbury, marine engine room, oak case, 30 hr...........150.00
Waterbury, pressed oak, eagle finial, dbl dial calendar, 29"...700.00
Waterbury, ship's bell, brass, spoked wheel, 4" dial, 8 day....300.00
Westclox, Art Deco, celluloid, light flashes w/alarm...........60.00
Western Union, regulator................................350.00
WS Walker, carriage, brass repeater, detached lever, 6".......715.00
WS Walker, carriage, repeater, canted corners, 1900, 5½"....650.00

Cloisonne

Cloisonne is a method of decorating metal with enameling. Fine metal wires are soldered onto the metal body following the lines of a predetermined design. The resulting channels are filled in with enamels of various colors, and the item is fired. The final step is a smoothing process that assures even exposure of the wire pattern.

The art is predominately Oriental, and has been practiced continuously, except during war years, since the 16th century. The most excellent examples date from 1865 until the turn of the century.

The early 20th century export variety is usually light weight, and the workmanship inferior. Modern wares are of good quality and are produced in Taiwan as well as China.

Several variations of the basic art include plique a jour, achieved by removing the metal body after firing, leaving only the transparent enamel work; foil cloisonne, using transparent or semi-translucent enameling over a layer of embossed silver foil covering the metal body of the vessel; wireless cloisonne, made by removing the wire dividers prior to firing; and cloisonne executed on ceramic, wood, or lacquer rather than metal.

Bowl, bulb, flowering branches on lt bl fretwork, 8" dia......120.00
Bowl, candy; rnd on short base, bl w/gold scrolls/florals, 5"....120.00
Bowl, peonies/flying bird, lt gr w/bl/yel, scalloped, 9" dia......330.00
Bowl, royal bl w/gold clouds/peonies/flying bird, 3½x10".......345.00
Bowl, scalloped, gr w/bl/yel peonies, flying bird, 3x9".........275.00
Bowl, w/lid & ped, vases w/cherry blossoms, scrolls, 5x4½"....130.00
Bowl, wht w/mc peony/leaves/cloud scrolls, short ped, 3½x10"..400.00
Box, apple; cloud/scrolls/peony, pk/yel on bl, 4x3½"..........95.00

Vase, goldstone effect in ground, with dragon decor, Japanese, 6½", $350.00.

Box, blk, ornate lotus design, long life symbol, domed, 5x4"...425.00
Box, dragon decor on cover, very early, 5" dia..............170.00
Box, egg; clouds/peony/bird, beige w/gold/bl/lav, 5½x3½".......85.00
Box, egg; red w/gold clouds, wht/bl prunus/birds, 3x5".........60.00
Box, mc peonies/butterfly on royal bl, divider w/in, 8" dia.....360.00
Box, rnd on short base, mc florals/butterfly on bl, 4x8" dia....350.00
Box, stamp; hinged, 3½x1½".................................40.00
Box, view of Fuji on red, brocade lined, mk Ando, 5x4x2".....330.00
Cache pot, hexagon, floral medallions w/jardiniers on bl, 10"...300.00
Candlestick, rust colored, 6", pr..........................165.00
Charger, crane standing among lily pads, Japanese, 12".......265.00
Charger, mums/tiger lily on blk center, mc border, 1875, 10"..625.00
Compote, scalloped, bl w/mc florals, 5½x9½"................250.00
Cup, saki; blk & wht......................................22.00
Ducks, male & female on separate bases, flowers/birds, 3x4x5".340.00
Humidor, foo dog finial, 7x5½", EX........................350.00
Incense pot, reticulated, peony/leaves, 4x2½"................45.00
Jar, bulbous, champleve lotus/leaf, 24k gold wash, 5x6".......250.00
Jar, lotus/leaf in champleve, 24k gold wash, 6½x5"..........335.00
Jar, repousse, EX details, 5"..............................365.00
Jar, rose; noir/gold flecked w/butterflies, Japan, 1800s, 5"....125.00
Jar, 8 panels: 4 goldstone & flowers/4 fierce faces, 4".......175.00
Match holder & ash tray, ftd, bl w/dragons/flowers, 6½x5"....165.00
Mirror, lotus flowers, mc/lt bl, engraved glass, ped ft, 18"....465.00
Pendant, gourd shape vase w/lid, peony flower, 1x1½"........150.00
Pendant, purse shape, bl w/goldfish, 1¾x2"..................35.00
Pot, relief work, holds enamel flowers, 2½x3½"..............40.00
Table, rosewood, Ming style, w/cloisonne insert: foo lion, 14"..250.00
Teapot, flowers/Tao Tieh masks, fancy spout/hdl, 6¼x5".....185.00
Vase, aqua foil w/lg prunus in purple/pk, Japan, 12".........225.00
Vase, baluster, wht/yellow mums on gr goldstone, 1900, 36"..1,760.00
Vase, beige w/panel of flowers/plants/feathers, dbl gourd, 15"..625.00
Vase, bird in cherry tree on pink, pink florals, 18x7½".....2,200.00
Vase, blk w/yellow dragon, 5".............................135.00
Vase, cloud scrolls, yel dragon, red flames, 8½"............250.00
Vase, clouds/pk cherry blossoms on lt gr, straight sides, 8"...275.00
Vase, flat ovoid w/flared neck, bird head hdls, bl ground, 12"..150.00
Vase, flowering prunus tree on royal bl, 12", pr............480.00
Vase, flowers/fruit/bushes in reserve, dbl gourd, 9½".......365.00
Vase, intricate florals/animals, Japanese, 12", pr...........910.00
Vase, iris blossoms/buds, blk ground, 25"................1,150.00
Vase, lime gr w/gold clouds, 5 claw mc dragon, bl waves, 11"..185.00
Vase, lt bl w/rnd & fan reserves w/florals/birds, 1880, 9½"...375.00
Vase, ovoid, multicolor lilies on blue, minor cracks, 24", pr..1,430.00
Vase, ovoid, sparrows in wisteria/iris on blk, 58", G.......4,510.00
Vase, ovoid, 2 dragons, gr/gray/red on blk, 1900s, 38".....2,090.00
Vase, pk/wht peony, flying bird on med gr, 10", pr..........340.00
Vase, royal bl w/prunus tree, flowers, baluster, 6½x12", pr....475.00
Vase, sparrows in iris/wisteria boughs on bl, 1890s, 46", G...2,000.00
Vase, 2 bands/3 sections, magnolia in purple/wht, 10", pr....375.00
Vase, 2 panels of deer/geese, mc florals, bulb/taper neck, 7½"..175.00
Vase, 4 panels w/goldstone, many colors, EX detail, Japan, 6"..175.00

Clothing and Accessories

'Second-hand' or 'vintage'? It's all a matter of opinion. But these days it's considered good taste -- downright fashionable -- to wear clothing from Victorian to World War II vintage. Jackets with padded shoulders from the thirties are 'trendy'. Jewelry from the Art Deco era is just as beautiful and often less expensive than current copies. Victorian blouses on models with Gibson Girl hair styles are pictured in leading fashion magazines -- but why settle for new, when the genuine article can be bought for the same price with exquisite lace that no reproduction can rival.

Where once the 'style' of the day was so strictly obeyed, today -- in New York and the larger cities of California and Texas, in particular -- nothing well designed and constructed is 'out of style'. And though in recent days costumes by such designers as Chanel, Fortuny, and Lanvin may bring four-figure prices at fine auction houses, as a general rule, prices are very modest considering the wonderful fabrics one may find in vintage clothing, many of which are no longer available. Cashmere coats, elegant furs, and sequined or beaded gowns can be bought for only a small fraction of today's retail.

Though some are strictly collectors, many do buy their clothes to wear. Care must be given to alterations, and gentle cleaning methods employed to avoid damage that would detract from their value.

Key:
cap/s----cap sleeves   plt----pleated
emb----embroidery   s/s----short sleeves
hm----handmade   3/4/s----three-quarter sleeves
lgth----length
l/s----long sleeves
n/s----no sleeves

Apron, child's; calico, reversible...........................15.00
Apron, embroidered/appliqued sunbonnet ladies..............15.00
Apron, Vict, tucking/crochet insert, scalloped crochet hem, M...28.00
Apron, wht calico...17.00
Bag, blk crepe w/rhinestone closure, '40s....................6.00
Bathing dress w/bloomers, blk cotton, 1910.................30.00
Bathing slippers, blk canvas..............................16.00
Bathing suit, striped tank type...........................16.50
Bathing suit, wool, man's, 1920s..........................20.00
Bathing suit, 2 pc, blk Edwardian.........................28.00
Bed jacket, pk taffeta, 1930s.............................15.00
Bed jacket, rayon satin w/lace, 1930s.....................18.50
Blazer, man's; wool, dbl breasted, pointed lapel, '40s.......10.00
Bloomers, gym, blk.......................................18.00
Bloomers, top, cap; blk taffeta w/wht braid trim, Victorian.....30.00
Bloomers, wht cotton, 1" lace insert/hem trim, hm buttonholes..10.00
Blouse, blue voile w/cross stitching, 1920s.................34.00
Blouse, Chinese kimono type sleeves, silk brocade...........40.00
Blouse, Chinese kimono type sleeves, silk brocade, embroidered.95.00
Blouse, eyelet, cotton lined, s/s, peplum style..............12.00
Blouse, hand embroidery, cut work, egg shell silk...........40.00
Blouse, sheer lace/embroidery; puff ¾/s, front buttons........25.00
Blouse, Victorian, cream silk & lace.......................70.00
Bodice, bl silk velvet & taffeta, 1900......................45.00
Bodice, blk & bl silk, 1840s..............................20.00
Bodice, blk lace, wht lining, heavy beading/sequins, hi collar....30.00

Shoes, leather with pearls on bows, turn of the century, $35.00 for the pair.

Bodice, blk net over satin, lace sleeve, V neck, beads/tassels....25.00
Bodice & skirt, cotton, lace collar w/silk bow & palmette......125.00
Bodice & skirt, silk, bone stays, leg-o'-mutton sleeves, Vct.....150.00
Bonnet, checked homespun.............................30.00
Bow tie, clip on, '40s....................................2.00
Breeches, gray twill, Montgomery Ward label, 1940s...........15.00
Camisole, lace trim, stays...............................45.00
Camisole & panty 2 in 1 combination, button crotch, lacy......35.00
Cap, baby's; Irish crochet...............................25.00
Cape, blk brocade, 3" neck band, 2" tassels at hem, jet beads...55.00
Cape, blk moire, scalloped, w/fox collar, 1920s.............30.00
Cape, blk velvet, long, 1930s...........................45.00
Cape, blk velvet w/long jet bead collar trim.................35.00
Cape, shoulder length, blk velvet w/allover beading, 1890......40.00
Cape, silk, lined, pointed collar, braid trim, bone buttons......40.00
Cape jacket, blk/red w/heavy beading, feathers at edge, 1880s...45.00
Cardigan, copper beads, flower design front/waist/cuffs, lined....25.00
Cardigan, orlon w/sequins & pearls front & collar, '50s........25.00
Cardigan, wht beads on bl in flower design, neck & cuffs......25.00
Choker, wht & blk ostrich feathers.......................15.00
Christening gown, crochet inserts, eyelet, w/tucked slip, 1900....80.00
Christening gown, ornate tucks/embroidery, Victorian, w/slip.....75.00
Christening gown, w/lacy slip............................27.00
Cloak, br w/blk satin neck ruffle, knotted fringe, 1850s, 38"....95.00
Coat, blk wool, puff sleeves, ornate passamenterie trim, 1905...135.00
Coat, br velvet w/gray fur collar/cuffs, short front, pleated.......75.00
Coat, evening; blk satin w/fox collar, 1920s................30.00
Coat, evening; blk velvet, 1930s.........................70.00
Coat, evening; floor length, wht knit, Woolf Bros............75.00
Coat, frock, man's.....................................35.00
Coat, navy pea, 1940s.................................25.00
Coat/cape, navy silk blend, 1920s.......................70.00
Collar, gray & gold bugle beads, 1920s....................35.00
Collar, needlepoint lace, elaborate, Victorian, 8" wide, EX......35.00
Corset cover, wht lace trim.............................100.00
Crinoline, net, 1950s..................................5.00
Drawers, fine muslin w/embroidered flounce, flared...........18.00
Drawers, lawn w/alecon lace trim, split flared legs...........18.00
Dress, baby's; beige silk...............................14.00
Dress, baby's; crochet.................................30.00
Dress, baby's; long calico print.........................40.00
Dress, bias lace, 3 pc, floor length, 1930s.................75.00
Dress, blk crepe, beaded velvet collar & cuffs..............25.00
Dress, blk lace/satin applique, flares knee to floor, n/s, '30......75.00
Dress, blk silk velvet, long, matching capelet, 1920s.........75.00
Dress, br panne velvet, long skirt/drop waist/drape neck, '20s....75.00
Dress, br striped silk, 1 pc, 1860s.......................75.00
Dress, carnival beading on sleeves, and bottom half skirt.......90.00
Dress, charcoal felt w/rhinestones, 1950s..................15.00
Dress, chiffon, completely beaded, s/s, underslip, EX.........275.00
Dress, coarse woven, striped, 1860s.....................110.00
Dress, coral cut velvet, floor lenth, 1930s.................50.00
Dress, crepe, V neck, lg pads, s/s, full calf-lgth skirt, '40s......17.50
Dress, crepe, V neck/jewel clip/cap/s, bead belt/jacket, '30......35.00
Dress, crepe bk satin, l/s, deep V w/inset, tiered skirt, 1918.....65.00
Dress, evening; gold crepe, 1930s.......................40.00
Dress, evening; plum silk velvet, bat-wing sleeves...........65.00
Dress, evening; silver wool knit, Italian...................50.00
Dress, evening; wht satin bias, n/s, 1930s.................50.00
Dress, flapper, allover beaded beige/wht w/red cherries.......250.00
Dress, flapper, bl w/beading............................140.00
Dress, girl's, gr calico w/bustle.........................40.00
Dress, l/s, long train, blk w/sm floral, 1850s...............45.00
Dress, linen, wht/gr emb edge, ¾/s w/cuff/6 panel skirt, '10....28.00

Fortuny velvet robe, blue-gray with gilt stenciled foliate medallions, satin lining, with Fortuny label, 40" long, auction estimate: $2,000.00

Dress, linen, 2 pc, passamenterie trim.....................95.00
Dress, long, lace w/silk slip, V front & back, cap/s, '30s.......65.00
Dress, lounging; floral, pads, zips, full skirt, E Pearson.........20.00
Dress, net lace w/silk underdress, s/s, draped skirt, '20s.......50.00
Dress, pleated gray silk w/beading front & bk...............90.00
Dress, Quaker's, blk, 1800s............................100.00
Dress, satin, gored skirt, chiffon yoke & l/s, '30s............25.00
Dress, silk velvet, rnd neck/bias skirt & sleeve trim, '30s......26.00
Dress, tea; wool paisley, 1870s.........................70.00
Dress, traveling; plum color, w/train, handmade, 1890s, M.....200.00
Dress, w/bustle, br silk taffeta, 2 pc, 1880................75.00
Dress, w/jacket, navy & cream silk, Deco, 1920s............65.00
Dress, w/jacket, silk pongee, 1925......................25.00
Dress, wedding; bl wool, Amish, 3 pc....................40.00
Dress, wedding; ecru silk, high neck, 1913, floor length.......75.00
Dress, wedding; flapper style, wht satin, 1920s.............95.00
Dress, wedding; silk, high neck, tiered skirt, 1900s..........225.00
Dress, wht w/lace inserts, early 1900s, fancy...............30.00
Dress, wool challis, ruffled sleves, 1860s, M...............70.00
Dress, 2 pc, cotton crochet, 1930s......................35.00
Dress, 2 pc, ruffled train, voile.........................125.00
Dress, 2 pc, teal wool knit, 1950s.......................30.00
Dress, 2 pc br velvet/taffeta, Xed front overskirt, bustle bk.....125.00
Duster, lady's, linen..................................35.00
Formal, bl taffeta w/lace & sequin appliqued bodice, 1950s......15.00
Formal, pk faille w/net petticoat, fabric rose at waist, '50s......10.00
Fur boa, Kalinsky, 5 skins..............................25.00
Fur boa, red fox......................................28.00
Fur cape, monkey, ¾ length............................300.00
Fur cape, ocelot, short................................75.00
Fur cape, Samoli leopard, by Jones of W VA..............2,200.00
Fur cape, squirrel.....................................45.00
Fur coat, blk Persian lamb, Tailored Woman label............70.00
Fur coat, blk seal, dbl breasted.........................70.00
Fur coat, Bokara Kurl, blk, matching stole, 1930s............45.00
Fur coat, br seal w/mink collar, 42" L....................300.00
Fur coat, buffalo....................................135.00
Fur coat, dk br mouton, full cut, full length, fully lined.......325.00
Fur coat, imitation, charcoal w/striped satin lining, '50s.......30.00
Fur coat, raccoon, lady's, 1930s.......................200.00

Fur coat, raccoon, man's...145.00
Fur coat, sheared possum, 1930s...............................150.00
Fur coat, Siberian squirrel, gray, new lining..............1,500.00
Fur collar, leopard, Peter Pan.................................25.00
Fur collar, raccoon, 39".......................................12.00
Fur collar, silver fox...22.00
Fur collar, wht, wide w/high neck, fancy buttons, 1920s........16.00
Fur hat, beaver, high top, in orig box, 1860, M...............65.00
Fur hat, mink tails..25.00
Fur hat, w/chin strap, mink, lady's............................18.00
Fur jacket, blk Persian lamb, waist length, mink collar, ¾/s...65.00
Fur jacket, br beaver, 2 pockets, shawl collar................175.00
Fur jacket, lynx dyed fox, ¾ length, full sleeves, 1940s......480.00
Fur jacket, mouton, br...70.00
Fur muff, black seal, pocket in bottom, satin ruffles, tassel...35.00
Fur muff, blk Persian lamb, zipper compartment................10.00
Fur muff, Bokara Kurl, blk.....................................15.00
Fur muff, fox..25.00
Fur muff, lt br sheared beaver, B Altman.......................30.00
Fur muff, mink, 4 skins..20.00
Fur muff, red fox, full tail & face............................30.00
Fur neckpiece, black seal, 17" L...............................25.00
Fur neckpiece, mink, 50" L.....................................35.00
Fur neckpiece, mouton, processed imitation 5 skin mink, 1960s..75.00
Fur stole, mink, honey beige, full skinned, deep collar.......250.00
Gloves, kid leather, cream, long...............................20.00
Gloves, knit, '50s..2.50
Gloves, wht African kid skin, short.............................7.50
Handkerchief, blk lace w/silk center............................4.00
Hat, afternoon; wht straw, Schiaparelli-Paris label, 1930s.....22.00
Hat, blk velvet, wide blk satin ribbon, jeweled buckle, '20s...26.00
Hat, blk/purple velvet, blk plumes, 1918.......................35.00
Hat, br velvet, 4 rows wide br ribbon ruching trim, '20s.......26.00
Hat, child's; felt w/velvet piping on brim, 1880s..............18.00
Hat, child's; straw, w/Shirley Temple label....................14.00
Hat, felt, pearl trim, Sax 5th Ave label & box.................20.00
Hat, gr felt cloche, ribbon trim...............................22.00
Hat, horsehair, w/flowers......................................25.00
Hat, lacy straw cloche...23.00
Hat, man's; Fedora, blk..15.00
Hat, over size natural straw, lily-of-valley flowers...........36.00
Hat, rust velvet cloche..25.00
Hat, salmon w/velvet flowers, braid trim, narrow rim, 1920s....30.00
Hat, straw boater..32.00
Hat, straw bonnet, lady's, 1860s...............................20.00
Hat, top hat, collapsible, silk................................60.00
Hat, Victorian, sm beaded material.............................12.00
Jacket, Battenburg..150.00
Jacket, evening; wht satin w/wht fur cuffs.....................75.00
Jacket, red/blk velvet, w/boa, 1920s...........................45.00
Jacket, smoking; blk brocade, silk lined, frog trim............36.50
Jacket, tailored, padded shoulders, cuffs, button on pocket....20.00
Jacket, velvet w/shirred sleeves...............................40.00
Knickers, wht linen..35.00
Neck scarf, blk satin w/wht thread trim, fully ruffled, 1850s..18.00
Negligee, wht satin & lace, ca 1940............................30.00
Night cap, pink crochet, silk lining, satin bows................6.00
Nightgown, peach satin, ca 1940................................25.00
Nightgown, pk rayon satin w/lace trim, ca, 1930s...............35.00
Nightgown, w/bedjacket, rayon w/sm flowers, lace trim..........30.00
Nightgown, wht cotton, 6½" filet crochet yoke, tatted hem......18.00
Nightgown, wht dimity, 3½" crochet yoke, gathered drop waist...18.00
Parasol, blk chantilly lace over silk, French ivory hdl/top...150.00
Parasol, blk satin w/8" lace, lg lace butterflies, carved hdl..65.00

Parasol, blk silk, embroidered roses, ruffled, brass fr/tassel...30.00
Parasol, blk silk & lace, red lining, carved hdl, Victorian, M..95.00
Parasol, child's; blk lace, ivory silk lined, ivory hdl.......125.00
Parasol, dk gr satin w/blk lace trim, branch hdl...............45.00
Petticoat, beige w/rose striped border.........................20.00
Petticoat, br & gold calico print.............................110.00
Petticoat, calico prints, reversible..........................135.00
Petticoat, flannel w/aqua stripes..............................36.00
Petticoat, tucked/tatted edge & insert/drawstring waist, M.....60.00
Petticoat, wht, 4 panel, dust ruffle w/sm lace trim, long......30.00
Petticoat, wht, 6 panel, scallop dust ruffle, 2 tucks..........22.00
Petticoat, wht fancy eyelet w/ribbon trim......................55.00
Petticoat, wht w/pk feather stitching..........................26.00
Purse, lizard, gold clasp.......................................5.50
Scarf, man's; rayon...4.50
Shawl, blk w/heavy allover floral embroidery, tied fringe, lg.245.00
Shawl, chantilly lace, blk, 1800s..............................95.00
Shawl, pk wool, 12" wool fringe, 24x69"........................25.00
Shawl, rayon, openwork design, 10" fringe, 72x38"..............30.00
Shell, irid sequins, dangle beads, lined.......................25.00
Shirt, Hawaiian print, s/s, rayon..............................17.00
Shoes, lady's, high buttoned, wht..............................30.00
Shoes, lady's; blk cloth & leather, high button Victorian......20.00
Shoes, lady's; blk leather, high top, lace to calf.............45.00
Shoes, lady's; br leather, ties, ca 1935.......................38.00
Shoes, lady's; high button, gray, EX...........................50.00
Shoes, pumps, blk w/silver thread design, Vogue, 2½" heel......10.00
Shoes, pumps, leather, 2½" heel, open toe, '40s................10.00
Shoes, turtoise lucite, Deco...................................15.00
Skirt, bl velvet w/embroidered border, long, very early........60.00
Skirt, blk satin w/wht gores, 40" L............................25.00
Skirt, br cotton w/embroidered hem w/velvet applique, 37"......40.00
Skirt, cotton, full, calf length, flowered, '50s...............10.00
Skirt, gr printed satin, velvet/lace hem trim, lined, 40" L....40.00
Spats, br suede, button, G.....................................12.00
Stockings, hand knit, 1860s....................................16.00
Suit, long skirt, boned jacket, silky w/lace trim, hm, Vict...150.00
Suit, lt wt wool, cuffs, peplum, calf length, shoulder pads....35.00
Suit, sailor; little boy's, Lord & Taylor......................15.00
Suit, wool crepe, window pane check............................50.00
Suit, 2 pc wool, leg-o'-mutton/s, plt skirt/slight train, 1900.147.00
Suitdress, faille, rhinestone trim, 2 pcs......................55.00
Sunbonnet, brown calico..22.50
Suspenders, men's; MIB..2.00
Sweater, V neck, allover sequins, l/s, lined wool..............25.00
Sweater, w/school letter, 1920s................................30.00
Tap pants, peach crepe, 1920...................................15.00
Teddy, pink organdy, sm tucks in front, scalloped legs, lace...15.00
Trousers, men's; dlb pleats/cuffs, tan gabardine...............8.00
Vest, tuxedo, '20s...15.00
Waist, Victorian, wht eyelet...................................60.00

Cluthra

The name Cluthra is derived from the Scottish word 'clutha', meaning cloudy. Glassware by this name was first produced by J. Couper and Sons, England. Frederick Carder developed Cluthra glass while at the Steuben Glass Works. It is found in both solid and shaded colors, and is characterized by a spotty appearance resulting from small air pockets trapped between its two layers.

Bowl vase, lavender, sgn Steuben, #6415, 4x7¾".................550.00
Dish, ruffled, shaded wht to lt gr, Steuben, 8½" dia..........225.00

Vase, mottled light amethyst, acid marked Steuben within fleur-de-lys, 10¼", $715.00.

Place setting, pink, Steuben, wine/goblet/bowl/8" plate.......1,200.00
Rose bowl, sgn Degue France.............................95.00
Vase, classical form, pk, #2683, Steuben, 8½".............650.00
Vase, gourd form, wht, Kimball, 4".......................150.00
Vase, gr to wht, wide base, 3" top diameter, 5".............260.00
Vase, lime gr, trapered triangle, Steuben mk, 11"..........600.00
Vase, mottled orange/wht, sgn K/30142-7, Durand, 6".......400.00
Vase, ovoid, lt amethyst, sgn Steuben/fleur-de-lys, 10½"......715.00
Vase, pink, sgnd Steuben, 10x10½"......................800.00
Vase, rose, Steuben, 5½"................................165.00
Vase, shaded bl/orange/br, Kimball, 4"...................185.00
Vase, strawberry, classical shape, #2683 Steuben, 8½".......550.00
Vase, wht, sgn Kimball, 6".............................125.00
Vase, yellow, bulbous, sgn Kimball, 7"..................160.00

Coalport

In 1745 in Caughley, England, Squire Brown began a modest business fashioning crude pots and jugs from clay mined in his own fields. Tom Turner, a young potter who had apprenticed his trade at Worcester, was hired in 1772, to plan and oversee the construction of a 'proper' factory. Three years later he bought the business, which he named Caughley Coalport Porcelain Manufactory. Though the dinnerware he produced was meant to be only everyday china, the hand painted florals, birds, and landscapes used to decorate the ware were done in exquisite detail and in a wide range of colors. In 1780 Turner introduced the Willow pattern, which he produced using a newly perfected method of transfer printing. (Wares from the period between 1775 to 1799 are termed 'Caughley' or 'Salopian' -- see section on Caughley.)

John Rose purchased the Caughley factory from Thomas Turner in 1799, adding that holding to his own pottery he had built two years before in Coalport. (It is from this point in the pottery's history that the wares are termed 'Coalport'.) The porcelain produced there before 1814 was unmarked, with very few exceptions. After 1820, some examples were marked with a '2' with an oversize top loop. The term 'Coalbrookdale' refers to a fine type of porcelain decorated in floral bas relief, similar to the work of Dresden.

After 1835, highly decorated ware with rich ground colors imitated the work of Sevres and Chelsea, even going so far as to copy their marks.

From about 1895 until about 1920, the mark in use was 'Coalport' over a crown, with 'England, A.D. 1750', indicating the date claimed as the founding, not the date of manufacture.

From the 1920s until 1945, 'Made in England' over a crown, and 'Coalport' below, was used. Later, 'Coalport' again got top billing, over a smaller crown, with 'Made in England' in a curve below.

In 1926 the Coalport Company moved to Shelton in Staffordshire, and today belongs to a group headed by the Wedgwood Company.

Bowl, cabbage leaf, 3x6"................................35.00
Box, egg form, Blue Willow pattern, 3x4¼"................85.00
Box, patch; rnd w/floral petal top, bl roses/leaf, 1x2¼".........30.00
Dish, 3 compartment, center hdl, jeweled, EX quality, 10" dia..125.00
Jar, gr top & base trim, 4 lg enamel reserves+1 on lid, 5½"...150.00
Mug, Salopian, 3 Graces, 4¾".............................375.00
Mustache cup w/saucer, dk bl bamboo & birds on wht, 1880s...85.00
Plate, girl, donkey & child, by Hancock, red/gold border, 10"..225.00
Tea set, cobalt floral/vignettes, orange/gold, pot+6 c/s, 1870...295.00
Teapot w/lid, pr of teacups & saucers, portrait/jewels, 1903....400.00
Vase, w/lid, ped ft, HP River Derwent, sgn Hancock, 10"......215.00

Cobalt Glass

Cobalt glass is characterized by its deep transparent blue color obtained by mixing cobalt oxide and alumina to the batch. It may be found in free blown, mold blown, and pressed glassware.

Biscuit jar, Arches pattern w/enamel decor, SP lid & bail......175.00
Box, enamel floral, hinged, brass fittings, 3" dia.............70.00
Candlestick, encrusted gold bands, 9½", pr.................120.00
Celery vase, Arch pattern, cascade base, wafer connector, 11"..475.00
Compote, applied ft, 8 ribs, folded lip, tooled scallops, 4"......50.00
Ewer, melon rib, fluted top, mc enamel/gold, pontil, 9¼".......70.00
Ewer, w/enamel decor, 8½"...............................65.00
Hat, blown 3 mold, 2¼"..................................275.00
Pitcher, blown, applied ft/hdl, 4½", G....................35.00
Pomade jar, Little Cavalier, mk ETS & Co NY, translucent bl..650.00
Spittoon, very old......................................60.00
Sugar, paneled, hexagonal, flint, 1840s, 5"................600.00
Water set, 7 pc+ice bucket, wht sailboat/gulls decor.........100.00
Whiskey taster, 6 panels, 2½".............................50.00

Coffee Grinders

In Grandma's day the task of choosing the brand of coffee she preferred was simple. She bought the whole beans in bulk from a wooden barrel, had them ground to order, or ground them at home to suit herself. There were patented grinders of every description to make the task a simple one.

As methods of packaging food progressed, coffee became available ready- ground in sealed bags, and is the American way, Grandma threw her coffee grinder out. But today, early Americana collectors search for those that managed to survive the eviction. Those with dates; original paint and decals; fancy ironwork trim; unusual wood, brass, or pewter hoppers; and those bearing the manufacturers trademark bring the highest prices.

Arcade, #25, w/glass jar & orig top, M...................75.00
Arcade Telephone mill, wall hung, pat 1898, EX...........350.00
Aroma #9, tin/iron, wall hanging, red/blk.................65.00
Challenge Fast Grinder, CI, wood, tin drawer, 1 pound size.....45.00
Chas Parker, #700....................................600.00
Chas Parker, Meriden Ct, wall mt tin cover, iron crank hdl.....55.00
Crystal #3, CI base, 18"..............................60.00
Enterprise, #1, counter model, blk cast iron, crank, 13"......260.00
Enterprise, #7, pat 1873, red pnt/florals/eagle finial, 23"......595.00
Enterprise, countertop, iron, 1873......................110.00
Enterprise, sliding riveted lid, wood drawer, all orig, 25"......400.00
Enterprise, 6 ft.....................................395.00
Golden Rule...195.00
Hand wrought, butterfly tabs hold grinder, sq nails, 1700s, 8"..215.00
Henry Troemner, 2 foliate CI wheels, ornate base, 1885, 61"...880.00
Hobart, electric, aluminum hopper.......................150.00
John C Dell & Sons, 33" wheels, brass hopper, 1884 pat, 66"..900.00

Landers, Frary & Clark; iron clamp-on, orig red & label 65.00
LF & Co, New Britain, CT, table model 195.00
Maple, dovetailed, w/hdl, tin tray & spout 55.00
National Elgin, w/eagle top 350.00
Parker, tin & iron, mtd on wood, #60 . . . . 55.00
Star Model, CI, 5 ft 375.00
Wood, w/porcelain knobs, dvtl edges, 8½x7½", EX 40.00
Wood & CI, closed lid bowl, grooved construction, 1900, 6½" . . 75.00
Wood & CI, open bowl, grooved construction, 5x7½x7¾" 80.00

Coin Operated Machines

Slot machines may be the fastest appreciating collectible on the market today. Legal in about half of the states, many are bought, restored, and used for home entertainment. The rate of appreciation has been estimated at 20% per year to 5% monthly. Older machines from the turn of the century, and those with especially elaborate decoration and innovative accessories are most desirable, often bringing prices in excess of $5,000.

Vending machines sold a product or a service. They were already in common usage by 1900, selling gum, cigars, matches, and a host of other commodities.

For one penny, arcade machines would entertain you with flip cards, test your strength, or tell your fortune!

The coin operated phonograph of the early 1900s paved the way for the jukeboxes of the twenties. Seeburg was first on the market with an automatic 8-tune phonograph. By the 1930s, Wurlitzer was the top name in the industry, with dealerships all over the country. As a result of the growing ranks of competitors, the forties produced the most beautiful machines made. Wurlitzers from this era are probably the most popularly sought after models on the market today. The model 1015 of 1946 is considered the all time classic, and often brings prices in excess of $4,500.

Juke Boxes

AMI, Model A 1,200.00
Empress 800.00
Gabels, 1932 . . . . 650.00
Mills, paddle wheel changer, walnut case, frosted glass, '30s . . 1,295.00
Mills De Luxe, EX rstr 800.00
Mills Empress, 1939, EX 3,000.00

Wurlitzer juke box, #1015, in mint restored condition, $4,500.00.

Rock-Ola #1426, orig 1,750.00
Rock-Ola #1426, 1947, M rstr 2,000.00
Rock-Ola B, multi-selector 660.00
Rock-Ola Commando, needs rstr 3,500.00
Rock-Ola Princess 225.00
Rock-Ola Rocket 700.00
Seeburg #147 Trashcan 800.00
Seeburg #9800 Hi-Tone 800.00
Seeburg #9800 Low Tower, 1941, EX 1,800.00
Seeburg Bookcase #200 LU-3, oak 250.00
Seeburg H-148, rstr 1,000.00
Seeburg LPC1, Select-O-Matic 350.00
Seeburg Symphonion, w/wall speaker, 1947, rstr 1,200.00
Seeburg Symphonola Regal, 55" 1,000.00
Wurlitzer #1015, bubble tubes, glazed front, G orig, 58" 2,750.00
Wurlitzer #1015, EX 4,200.00
Wurlitzer #1015, rstr 4,500.00
Wurlitzer #1080, rstr 4,800.00
Wurlitzer #1100, rstr, 60" 2,350.00
Wurlitzer #1550, EX 650.00
Wurlitzer #412, EX orig 900.00
Wurlitzer #580 speaker, EX orig 8,600.00
Wurlitzer #600, orig 1,400.00
Wurlitzer #600, rstr 2,000.00
Wurlitzer #700, orig 1,650.00
Wurlitzer #71, counter top, rstr 3,500.00
Wurlitzer #780, rstr 3,500.00
Wurlitzer #850, early, EX 5,500.00
Wurlitzer #950, orig 9,000.00

Slot Machines

Bally Ray's Track Horse Race console slot, 1936, M rstr 9,500.00
Bally 25¢ Reliance 3,000.00
Caille Ben Hur, EX 3,000.00
Caille Sphinx, EX orig 1,800.00
Caille 25¢ Nude Front, skill button, all orig 2,500.00
Caille 25¢ Superior Jackpot Bell, 4 reel, VG orig 1,600.00
Caille 5¢ Centaur upright, American, EX orig 11,500.00
Caille 5¢ New Century Puck, w/music, rstr 11,200.00
Caille 5¢ Superior, 3 reel/jackpot, rstr, 24" 1,400.00
Columbia 5¢ 575.00
English pub, penny slot 350.00
Groetchen 5¢ Club Columbia Bell, 1940 . . . . 850.00
Groetchen 5¢ Columbia Standard Bell, 1937, G 750.00
Jennings $1 floor model light-up, w/jackpot, M 2,900.00
Jennings $1 Wild Indian 2,000.00
Jennings Airplane Chief, EX 1,150.00
Jennings 1¢ Little Duke, single jackpot, small coin head, VG . . 1,600.00
Jennings 1¢ Little Duke, tall coin head, VG orig 1,600.00
Jennings 1¢ Little Duke, w/side gumball vendor, EX orig 1,800.00
Jennings 1¢ Silver Club, rstr 1,300.00
Jennings 10¢ Standard Chief, deluxe light-up, rstr 1,200.00
Jennings 25¢ Dutch Boy, flat face, EX 1,995.00
Jennings 25¢ Governor Bell, silver $ jackpot, brass Indian . . . 1,450.00
Jennings 5¢ Fey Twin Jak Pot Revamp Bell, G orig 1,400.00
Jennings 5¢ Operator Bell 1,100.00
Jennings 5¢ Peacock 1,300.00
Jennings 5¢ Sun Chief, light-up style 1,200.00
Jennings 5¢/25¢ Challenger 1,500.00
Midget 5¢ dice machine, Vendet Co, 1932 . . . . 200.00
Mills $1 Golden Falls, w/jackpot, rstr 2,700.00
Mills Dewey, EX 6,500.00
Mills Dewey, musical, in orig musical cabinet, VG rstr 12,500.00

Mills Gooseneck Silent Skyscraper, VG orig............... 1,500.00
Mills Jumbo Parade, floor model, free game feature, 1930s.....975.00
Mills Silver Dollar Hi-Top............................. 1,600.00
Mills 1¢ QT, chrome, EX orig........................... 1,600.00
Mills 1¢ Skyscraper, EX orig........................... 1,400.00
Mills 10¢ Black Cherry................................. 985.00
Mills 10¢ Extraordinary, gold award token payoff, G........ 1,200.00
Mills 10¢ Extraordinary, table model, gold award, twin jp..... 1,500.00
Mills 10¢ Golden Falls................................. 1,050.00
Mills 10¢ Hi-Top, EX orig.............................. 1,000.00
Mills 10¢ Midas Touch, CI/chrome/formica trim............. 500.00
Mills 25¢ High-Top.................................... 1,075.00
Mills 5¢ Big Six, rstr................................. 8,100.00
Mills 5¢ Dial, ½ size, scores points, airplanes/side vendor.... 1,200.00
Mills 5¢ Extraordinary, VG orig......................... 1,750.00
Mills 5¢ FOK escalator vendor, token pay out, fortune telling. 1,500.00
Mills 5¢ Golden Falls, hand load jackpot front, G orig...... 1,250.00
Mills 5¢ High-Top, guaranteed jackpot................... 950.00
Mills 5¢ High-Top, w/bonus & jackpot................... 1,050.00
Mills 5¢ High-Top Bonus, rstr.......................... 1,500.00
Mills 5¢ Lion Head, chrome plated/HP, rstr............... 1,650.00
Mills 5¢ Operators Bell, Chas Fey jackpot front, side vendor..2,500.00
Mills 5¢ Poinsettia, EX orig............................ 1,095.00
Mills 5¢ The Owl, 1 wheel upright, carved oak w/owl/foliage..7,500.00
Mills 5¢ War Eagle, 3 reel/dbl jackpot, G orig, 26"........ 1,815.00
Mills 50¢ Operators Bell, poinsettia front, G orig........... 1,200.00
Pace 10¢ Comet, twin jackpot.......................... 1,100.00
Pace 5¢ All Star Comet Bell............................ 1,200.00
Pace 5¢ Comet....................................... 1,100.00
Pace 5¢ Fancy Front, 1932............................. 1,050.00
Pace 5¢ Kitty, VG orig................................ 2,800.00
Pace 5¢ Rocket...................................... 1,450.00
Pace 50¢ Deluxe Comet, 1940, VG...................... 1,000.00
Pachinko, counter top, gives Japanese revenue stamps......... 95.00
Rockola 5¢ Roberts Black Front, 3 reel w/jackpot, rstr, 24"..1,250.00
Rockola 5¢ Roberts Blue Front, 3 reel/jackpot, rstr, 24".....1,100.00

Starlite 5¢ Aristocrat.................................. 675.00
Vendent Midget 5¢ 2 reel............................. 1,700.00
Watling 25¢ Coin Front............................... 2,800.00
Watling 25¢ Roll-a-Top, Cherry Front, all orig, 100% rstr....4,000.00
Watling 5¢ Blue Seal, 3 reel/twin jackpot, rstr, 24"........ 1,500.00
Watling 5¢ Operator's Bell CI, 3 reel/payout, rstr, 23½".....1,210.00

Trade Stimulators

Buckley 1¢ Ball Gum, cigarette reel...................... 340.00
Burnham & Mills Ball Gum, rstr......................... 750.00
Cent-A-Smoke, cigarette reel........................... 350.00
Columbus A, gum, hourglass, CI......................... 295.00
Daval Reel Spot, rpt.................................. 260.00
Deval Free Play, 5¢, 3 reels, counter, sm, G orig........... 225.00
Deval Reel 21, 5¢ counter blackjack...................... 350.00
Gem Gumball.. 250.00
Griswald Black Cat, early, M........................... 950.00
Groetchen Zepher, no gum mechanism, rstr................ 125.00
JD Latimer, Game-O'-Skill, wood penny toss, early.......... 550.00
Lucky Coins... 125.00
Marvel, cigarette reels, token payout, VG.................. 250.00
Marvel, Groetchen, 1¢ gumball & token reward 3 reel, VG..... 180.00
Marvel, 5¢, cigarette reels, token payout, VG.............. 250.00
Mercury DeLuxe 1¢, cigarette reels, token payout........... 245.00
Mill's Dial, w/side vendor............................. 1,200.00
Mill's Target Practice................................. 550.00
Penny Pack... 400.00
Pick-A-Pack, Garden City, 1¢ & 5¢, windmill.............. 750.00
Play Write, lottery type, 3 reels, VG..................... 180.00
Red Man, Jennings, 5¢ pinball.......................... 350.00
Rockola, hold & draw, 1934............................ 695.00
Signal, Automatic Amusement Co, 5¢ pinball, 1930, VG...... 220.00
Triangle Penny Drop, CI, early.......................... 850.00

Miscellaneous

ABT Rol-let, 5¢, pinball type, EX........................ 325.00
Ace, gumball.. 95.00
Acorn, gumball, 1¢, w/sm pinball game built in............. 50.00
Advance, gumball, football globe........................ 150.00
Advance, gumball, rnd globe............................ 125.00
Aromint, cigar lighter................................ 200.00
Atlas, baseball machine................................ 2,200.00
Baby Grand 10¢ Black Jack, gumball machine.............. 140.00
Bales, peanut vendor, L-shaped oak...................... 300.00
Bally Champion, sm payout pinball, M.................... 400.00
Bally Hi-Hand....................................... 400.00
Bally Hoo, pinball, tilted wood case/glass top, 31".......... 60.00
Bally Sparkplug, 5¢ counter payout horserace.............. 1,700.00
Bangtail Horse Race.................................. 850.00
Basketball Game, 1¢, flip ping-pong balls into basket........ 225.00
Bennet, cigar vendor................................. 800.00
Booze Barometer, 5¢, M............................... 125.00
Brandt Automatic Cashier, ornate cast sides/bk, pat 1924..... 200.00
Buckley Point Maker.................................. 450.00
Buckley Track Odds................................... 2,000.00
Buckley Treasure Chest Digger, rstr...................... 1,050.00
Caille, Correct Weight 1¢ scales, oak cabinet.............. 1,500.00
Caille Eureka, strength/electricity floor model machine, rstr...2,550.00
Callie Mascot, stength/shock, floor model, iron legs, rstr.....1,850.00
Career Fortune Telling Machine......................... 800.00
Challenger Duck shoot, 1¢, rstr......................... 14.00
Challenger Target Shoot, 1¢, gun shoots 10 steel balls........ 30.00

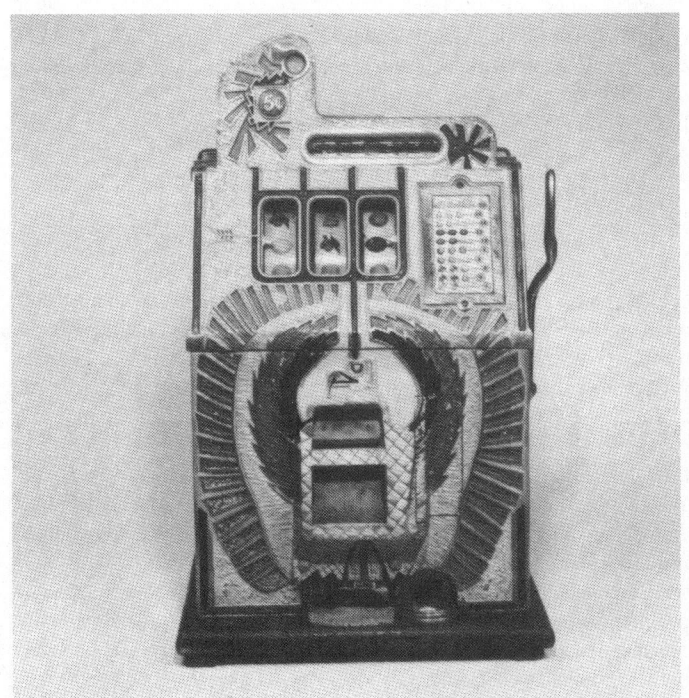

Mill's 5¢ War Eagle slot machine, three reels, double jackpot, in good original condition, $1,815.00.

Change machine, change for quarter.....................60.00
Chester Pollard, 25¢ football game......................950.00
Columbus, 25¢ vendor....................................345.00
Columbus A, candy vendor, rpl locks/globe, rstr........150.00
Columbus A, gold paint, lg orig globe..................225.00
Columbus B-Mor, candy/nut #32, 1932....................325.00
Columbus M...150.00
Columbus MB..155.00
Columbus 14, gumball, red..............................265.00
Columbus 21, hex globe.................................295.00
Cop & Robber, Pulver, EX...............................600.00
Cottlieb 1¢ Strength Tester, counter top, 1930s.......225.00
Dixie Cup, 1¢ cup dispenser, pat 12/15/13.............500.00
Donkey in the Gold Mine Fortune Teller..............2,200.00
Elm City, cigar vendor, oak, orig, working condition.1,800.00
Exhibit Supply, Hercules Grip Tester, floor model, oak & iron..850.00
Exhibit Supply, iron claw digger, rstr..............1,250.00
Exhibit Supply, Kiss-O-Meter..........................850.00
Exhibit Supply, Model D card vendor...................400.00
Exhibit Supply, Radiogram, card vending machine.......550.00
Exhibit Supply, screen test camera....................425.00
Exhibit Supply, Striking Clock, arcade, floor model.1,100.00
Exhibit Supply, tiger tail puller, strength tester..2,700.00
Exhibit Supply, 1¢ arcade card machine, metal case.....90.00
Exhibit Supply, 1¢ Radio Love Message, card machine...700.00
Fields Four Jaks, VG..................................575.00
Fortune machine, 1¢...................................225.00
Gayton Novelty, penny drop, oak, EX...................300.00
Gem, 5¢ candy & gum machine, counter model............135.00
Globe Novelty Co Lighthouse, arcade, floor model...1,200.00
Gottlieb Grip Tester, 1¢, metal counter top, 2 way tester...150.00
Grandma Fortune Teller, full size, 25¢ play, rstr...2,500.00
Grandma Solor Horoscope, rstr.........................700.00
Groetchen Skill Jump, 1¢, 32x21".....................295.00
Groetchen Sparks, 1¢, rstr...........................325.00
Hart 1¢, gumball, 1940s................................60.00
Hawkeye, vendor, w/decal..............................125.00
Hershey, 1¢ vendor....................................165.00
Horrible Monster, arcade machine, 5¢, 20x31"..........350.00
Ideal, cigar lighter..................................225.00
International Vending Co, match vendor.................450.00
Jenning 1¢ Target Practice, Indian decor..............550.00
Jergens Lotion, 1¢, holds bottle, unrstr...............10.00
Jockey, Mills Co 5¢ counter gambling machine, VG orig..3,500.00
Keeneys Scramball, 5¢, balls roll down ramps..........100.00
Keep 'Em Bombing, Smak-A-Jap Penny Drop, 1¢, 1943.....585.00
Kotex, vendor, 5¢, 1930, G orig........................90.00
Log Cabin Duplex, 1925................................125.00
Master, gumball, 1923, rpt............................140.00
Master, 1¢ peanut vendor, gr/tan porcelain............160.00
Master, 1¢ vendor, 1923...............................135.00
Master, 1¢ vendor, 1924...............................225.00
Match dispenser, box matches, 'Matches 1¢' in CI front...265.00
Mercury Grip Tester, 1¢, rpt..........................125.00
Metropolitan, arcade, 2¢ card dispenser, 2 slot, 20 cards...180.00
Midget Baseball 1¢, counter top skill game............250.00
Mills, Baseball Pintable, professional................450.00
Mills, Firefly Shocker, EX............................300.00
Mills, Lollipop Scale, 1¢, G orig...................1,500.00
Mills, Old Mill, arcade, floor model..................500.00
Mills, Perfume Vender, 1¢, rstr.....................2,500.00
Mills, Pneumatic Puncher............................2,500.00
Mills, tab gum, 1¢, no lock............................25.00
Mills, vertical puncher.............................2,500.00

Mills, Wizard Fortune Teller..........................395.00
Mills, Wow, pinball, 5¢ counter top...................200.00
Mills, 1¢ perfume vendor, CI, rstr.................2,500.00
Mills, 1¢ Target Practice.............................275.00
Mutoscope, Raise the Devil, floor model.............1,100.00
Mutuscope, Career Pilot...............................795.00
Mystic Ray, 25¢ card vending machine, rstr............895.00
Mystic Ray Fortune Teller.............................750.00
Nickel Nudger, change making device, 1930s.............20.00
Northwestern gumball, 1931............................110.00
Northwestern 5¢, gumball, 1949.........................50.00
OK 5¢, Pinball, 1930s, 32½"............................80.00
Penny King, 1930......................................125.00
Perfume machine, metal................................200.00
Perfume machine, wood.................................300.00
Pilot, gum vendor, cast, 1902.........................300.00
Pool table, sm..850.00
Pulver, gum vendor, Yellow Kid mannequin, EX........1,800.00
Regal, candy/gumball/peanut vendor.....................45.00
Remington Type-O-Meter................................300.00
Ro-Bo the Mechanical Salesman, gumball w/mannequin..1,250.00
Safe Driver Reaction, catch nickel before it drops....145.00
Saratoga Sweepstakes, 1¢ counter horse race, EC Evans Co..2,000.00
Shermack, stamp vendor, sm.............................40.00
Silver King, peanut machine............................65.00
Silver King, peanut machine, red light on top.........125.00
Simmons A, cast iron vendor...........................135.00
Skill crane digger....................................625.00
Sparkplug 5¢ horse race, counter gambling, 1934, G..2,400.00
Stamps & razor blade vendor, 10¢, orig red/wht/bl......80.00
Stereoptican, oak.....................................250.00
Test Your Strength, 5¢ counter arcade, 'P Bachagullupi'..1,600.00
Totalizer, basketball game............................200.00
Turtle Soup, jar type penny drop.......................30.00
UG Grandbois, drop-in ringlet coin insert, rare.......240.00
UG Grandbois, gumball.................................150.00
UG Grandbois, notched globe base ring, rare...........195.00
Universal, floor vendor, 1902.......................2,500.00
Watling, Guess Your Weight, scale.....................325.00
Zipper Skill, 1¢ counter top, wood, ball skill game...190.00
Zoom Payout Skill Game, 1¢, battleships/planes........300.00
1933 World's Fair Jig Saw Pinball, 10¢ coin slide.....450.00

Collector Plates

After a period of reduced activity in the market of limited edition plates, a renewed enthusiasm, brought on perhaps by full-scale publicity effected through direct mailing, magazines, and national television, has established what many collectors optimistically regard as a solid secondary market. As a result, values of choice issues are steadily appreciating; first editions usually prove the best investment. In the listings that follow, they are indicated by the letters FE.

Two of the earliest manufacturers of Christmas plates were Bing and Grondahl, who issued their first plate in 1895, and the Royal Copenhagen Porcelain Manufactory who followed with their series in 1908. In this country, Frankoma Pottery began producing limited edition plates in 1965. Today they have been joined by well over 100 manufacturers and marketing organizations world-wide. Only a few are listed here to represent some of the more familiar companies.

There are several specific publications and many other sources of information available to keep today's collector aware of the current market trends.

America The Beautiful

1969, US Capitol..................................40.00
1970, Mount Rushmore.............................40.00
1971, Statue of Liberty...........................39.00
1972, Monument Valley.............................40.00

American Commemorative

1973, Southern Landmarks, Monticello..............96.00
1973, Southern Landmarks, Williamsburg............94.00
1974, Southern Landmarks, Beauvoir................89.00
1974, Southern Landmarks, Cabildo.................87.00
1975, Southern Landmarks, Hermitage...............79.00
1975, Southern Landmarks, Oak Hill................70.00

American Express

1976, Four Freedoms/Rockwell, Freedom from Fear...........38.00
1976, Four Freedoms/Rockwell, Freedom from Want..........38.00
1976, Four Freedoms/Rockwell, Freedom of Speech..........38.00
1976, Four Freedoms/Rockwell, Freedom of Worship.........38.00

American Historical

1972, Aviation, Amelia Earhart....................58.00
1972, Aviation, Charles Lindbergh.................40.00
1972, Bicentennial, A New Dawn....................60.00
1972, Bicentennial, Turning Point.................60.00
1976, Gen Douglas MacArthur.......................30.00

American Rose Society

1975, All-American Rose, Arizona.................110.00
1975, All-American Rose, Oregold................110.00
1975, All-American Rose, Rose Parade............110.00
1976, All-American Rose, America................102.00
1976, All-American Rose, Cathedral..............102.00
1976, All-American Rose, Seashell...............102.00
1976, All-American Rose, Yankee Doodle..........110.00
1977, All-American Rose, Double Delight..........94.00
1977, All-American Rose, First Edition...........99.00
1977, All-American Rose, Prominent...............95.00
1978, All-American Rose, Charisma................75.00
1978, All-American Rose, Color Magic.............75.00

Anri

1972, Ferrandiz Birthday, Boy or Girl, each.....150.00
1972, Ferrandiz Christmas, Christ in the Manger.175.00
1972, Ferrandiz Christmas, Finishing Cradle, FE.235.00
1972, Mother's Day, Alpine Mother & Children.....50.00
1972, Mother's Day, Children Play House..........140.00
1972, Wedding, Boy & Girl Embracing.............175.00
1973, Ferrandiz Birthday, Boy...................200.00
1973, Ferrandiz Birthday, Girl..................150.00
1973, Ferrandiz Christmas, Christmas............225.00
1973, Ferrandiz Christmas, Shepherd & Sheep.....165.00
1973, Mother's Day, 1973, Mother & Child........120.00
1973, Wedding, Wedding Scene.....................90.00
1974, Father's Day, Alpine Father & Children.....85.00
1974, Ferrandiz Birthday, Boy or Girl, each.....150.00
1974, Ferrandiz Christmas, Holy Night...........135.00

1974, Mother's Day, Mother Holding Child.........130.00
1975, Ferrandiz Christmas, Flight into Egypt.....120.00
1975, Mother's Day, Mother & Dove................110.00
1976, Ferrandiz Christmas, Mary & Joseph.........100.00
1976, Mother's Day, Mother & Child...............100.00

Artists Of The World

1976, Children of the World/DeGrazia, Los Ninos..........1,400.00
1976, Don Ruffin, Navajo Lullaby.................88.00
1976, Holiday Series/DeGrazia, Festival of Lights.........365.00
1977, Children of the World/DeGrazia, White Dove.........260.00
1977, Don Ruffin, Through the Years.............157.00
1977, Game Birds/Larry Toschik, Mallards/Whistling In........80.00
1977, Holiday Series/DeGrazia, Bell of Hope.....276.00
1978, Children of the World/DeGrazia, Flower Girl.........310.00
1978, Don Ruffin, Child of the Pueblo............78.00
1978, Game Birds/Larry Toschik, Maytime/Gambel Quail.......45.00
1978, Holiday Series/DeGrazia, Little Madonna...344.00
1979, Children of the World/DeGrazia, Flower Boy.........247.00
1979, Don Ruffin, Colima Madonna.................50.00
1979, Holiday Series/DeGrazia, The Nativity.....224.00
1980, Children of the World/DeGrazia, Little Cocopah Girl.....190.00
1980, Holiday Series/DeGrazia, Little Pima Drummer........188.00
1981, Children of the World/DeGrazia, Beautiful Burden......170.00
1981, Children of the World/DeGrazia, Merry Little Indian.....205.00
1981, Holiday Series/DeGrazia, A Little Prayer..178.00
1982, Children of the World/DeGrazia, Wondering.........140.00
1982, Holiday Series/DeGrazia, Blue Boy.........170.00

B & J Art Designs

1978, Yesterday's Children/Jan Hagara, Lisa & Jumeau Doll.....95.00
1979, Yesterday's Children/Jan Hagara, Adrianne & Bye-lo Baby.78.00
1980, Yesterday's Children/Jan Hagara, Lydia & S Temple Doll..63.00
1981, Yesterday's Children/Jan Hagara, Melanie, S O'Hara Doll..60.00

Bareuther

1967, Christmas, Stiftskirche, FE...............115.00
1968, Christmas, Kapplkirche.....................36.00
1968, Danish Church, Roskilde Cathedral, FE.....25.00
1969, Christmas, Christkindlemarkt...............24.00
1969, Father's Day, Castle Neuschwanstein.......50.00
1969, Mother's Day, Mother & Children............75.00
1970, Father's Day, Castle Pfalz................20.00
1970, Mother's Day, Mother & Children...........25.00
1971, Mother's Day, Mother & Children...........20.00
1971, Thanksgiving, First Thanksgiving..........30.00
1972, Christmas, Christmas in Munich............50.00
1972, Thanksgiving, Harvest.....................20.00
1974, Father's Day, Wurzburg Castle.............40.00

Belleek

1970, Christmas, Castle Caldwell, FE............120.00
1971, Christmas, Celtic Cross...................50.00
1972, Christmas, Flight of the Earls............55.00
1973, Christmas, Tribute to Yeats...............60.00
1974, Christmas, Devenish Island...............175.00
1978, Irish Wildlife, A Leaping Salmon..........70.00
1979, Irish Wildlife, Hare at Rest..............70.00
1980, Irish Wildlife, Hedgehog..................67.00

Bing & Grondahl

1895, Christmas, Frozen Window......................3,750.00
1896, Christmas, New Moon..........................2,050.00
1897, Christmas, Sparrow...........................1,275.00
1898, Christmas, Roses & Star........................775.00
1899, Christmas, Crows.............................2,000.00
1900, Christmas, Church Bells.........................785.00
1901, Christmas, Three Wise Men......................400.00
1902, Christmas, Gothic Church Interior.................385.00
1903, Christmas, Expectant Children...................285.00
1904, Christmas, Frederiksberg Hill....................145.00
1905, Christmas, Christmas Night......................160.00
1906, Christmas, Sleighing to Church..................100.00
1907, Christmas, Little Match Girl.....................135.00
1908, Christmas, St Petri Church.......................95.00
1909, Christmas, Yule Tree...........................105.00
1910, Christmas, The Old Organist.....................105.00
1910, Easter Plaque.................................130.00
1911, Easter Plaque..................................90.00
1912, Easter Plaque..................................90.00
1913, Christmas, Bringing Home the Tree................98.00
1913, Easter Plaque.................................100.00
1914, Easter Plaque..................................85.00
1915, Christmas, Dog Outside.........................140.00
1915, Easter Plaque..................................65.00
1915, Julilee (5 year cycle), Frozen Window............200.00
1918, Christmas, Fishing Boat........................100.00
1920, Easter Plaque..................................75.00
1920, Jubilee (5 year cycle), Church Bells.............120.00
1921, Christmas, Pigeons.............................72.00
1925, Easter Plaque..................................64.00
1925, Jubilee (5 year cycle), Dog Outside Window.......210.00
1926, Christmas, Churchgoers.........................80.00
1930, Easter Plaque.................................175.00
1930, Jubilee (5 year cycle), The Old Organist.........240.00
1931, Christmas, Christmas Train.......................98.00
1933, Easter Plaque.................................220.00
1934, Easter Plaque.................................550.00
1935, Easter Plaque.................................700.00
1935, Jubilee (5 year cycle), Little Match Girl..........1,000.00
1936, Christmas, Royal Guard, Amalienborg.............90.00
1940, Jubilee (5 year cycle), Three Wise Men..........2,000.00
1941, Christmas, Horses.............................315.00
1945, Jubilee (5 year cycle), Amalienborg Castle.......300.00
1948, Christmas, Watchman...........................90.00
1950, Jubilee (5 year cycle), Eskimos.................275.00
1954, Christmas, Snowman...........................110.00
1955, Jubilee, Dybbol Mill...........................275.00
1957, Christmas, Christmas Candles...................140.00
1960, Christmas, Village Church.......................200.00
1960, Jubilee, Kronborg Castle........................200.00
1963, Christmas, Christmas Elf........................125.00
1965, Christmas, Bringing Home the Tree...............60.00
1965, Jubilee, Churchgoers..........................125.00
1969, Mother's Day, Dog & Puppies...................490.00
1970, Jubilee, Amalienborg Castle......................35.00
1975, Jubilee, Horses Enjoying Meal....................50.00
1980, Jubilee, Yule Tree.............................60.00

Dave Grossman Designs

1976, Margaret Keane, Balloon Girl.....................35.00
1976, Tom Sawyer Series/Rockwell, Whitewashing Fence.......77.00

1977, Margaret Keane, My Kitty........................30.00
1977, Tom Sawyer Series/Rockwell, First Smoke............60.00
1977, Tom Sawyer Series/Rockwell, Take Your Medicine.......48.00
1978, Margaret Keane, Bedtime........................25.00
1978, Tom Sawyer Series/Rockwell, Lost in Cave...........46.00

Franklin Mint, Crystal

1970, Rockwell Christmas, Bringing Home The Tree.........385.00
1971, Rockwell Christmas, Under the Mistletoe............175.00
1972, Rockwell Christmas, The Carolers.................165.00
1973, Buffet Annual, Gazelle.........................260.00
1973, Rockwell Christmas, Trimming the Tree............175.00
1974, Buffet Annual, Panda..........................245.00
1974, Rockwell Christmas, Hanging the Wreath...........175.00
1975, Buffet Annual, Giraffe.........................245.00
1975, Rockwell Christmas, Home for Christmas...........180.00
1976, Buffet Annual, Lion...........................240.00
1977, American Sweetheart Rockwell, Youngsters at Play.....160.00
1977, American Sweethearts/Rockwell, Teenagers Together....160.00
1977, Buffet Annual, Rhinoceros......................240.00
1977, Crystal Annual, Snowflake......................200.00
1977, Rockwell's Thanksgiving, Old-Fashioned Thanksgiving....220.00
1978, American Sweethearts/Rockwell, Bride & Groom.......160.00
1978, American Sweethearts/Rockwell, Graduation Day......160.00
1978, American Sweethearts/Rockwell, Proud Parents.......160.00
1979, American Sweethearts/Rockwell, Retirement Kiss......120.00

Franklin Mint, Porcelain

1976, Hans Christian Andersen, Princess & the Pea, FE......75.00
1976, Hans Christian Andersen, Steadfast Tin Soldier........75.00
1976, Hans Christian Andersen, The Little Mermaid..........75.00
1977, Hans Christian Andersen, The Snow Queen...........75.00
1977, Hans Christian Andersen, The Tinder Box............75.00
1977, Hans Christian Andersen, Thumbelina..............75.00
1977, Mark Twain, Stealing a Kiss......................45.00
1977, Mark Twain, Trading Lives.......................40.00
1977, Mark Twain, Traveling the River..................45.00
1977, Mark Twain, Whitewashing the Fence...............55.00
1978, Grimm's Fairy Tales, Sleeping Beauty...............42.00
1979, Grimm's Fairy Tales, Hansel & Gretel...............42.00
1979, Grimm's Fairy Tales, Shoemaker & the Elves..........42.00

Goebel

1971, Hummel Annual, Heavenly Angel..................875.00
1972, Hummel Anniversary, Hear Ye....................90.00
1973, Hummel Annual, Globe Trotter...................200.00
1974, Goebel Wildlife Series, Robin....................60.00
1974, Hummel Annual, Goose Girl.....................120.00
1975, Goebel Mother's Series, Rabbits..................35.00
1975, Goebel Wildlife Series, Blue Titmouse..............45.00
1975, Hummel Anniversary, Stormy Weather.............300.00
1975, Hummel Annual, Ride Into Christmas..............100.00
1976, Goebel Mother's Series, Cats....................45.00
1976, Goebel Wildlife Series, Barn Owl.................50.00
1976, Hummel Annual, Apple Tree Girl.................85.00
1977, Hummel Annual, Apple Tree Boy.................150.00
1978, Hummel Annual, Happy Pastime.................110.00
1979, Hummel Annual, Singing Lesson..................70.00
1980, Hummel Anniversary, Spring Dance...............190.00
1980, Hummel Annual, Schoolgirl.....................80.00
1981, Hummel Annual, Umbrella Boy..................100.00

Gorham

1971, Four Seasons Annual Set of 4/Rockwell, Boy & His Dog.475.00
1971, Pewter Bicentennial, Burning of Gaspee...............35.00
1972, China Bicentennial, The 1776 Plate..................32.00
1972, Four Seasons Annual Set of 4/Rockwell, Young Love....193.00
1972, Silver Bicentennial, Burning of the Gaspee...........500.00
1973, Four Seasons Annual Set of 4/Rockwell, Ages of Love...325.00
1973, Moppets Christmas, Christmas March, FE..............35.00
1973, Moppets Mother's Day, FE..........................30.00
1973, Silver Bicentennial, Boston Tea Party................575.00
1974, Christmas/Rockwell, Tiny Tim......................72.00
1974, Four Seasons Annual Set of 4/Rockwell, Grandpa & Me..160.00
1974, Moppets Christmas, Decorating the Tree.............22.00
1974, Moppets Mother's Day.............................20.00
1975, Boy Scout Plates/Rockwell, Our Heritage.............60.00
1975, Christmas/Rockwell, Good Deeds....................65.00
1975, Four Seasons Annual Set of 4/Rockwell, Me & My Pal...190.00
1975, Irene Spencer, Dear Child.........................100.00
1975, Moppets Christmas, Bringing Home the Tree...........15.00
1976, American Artists, Apache Mother & Child.............50.00
1976, Boy Scout Plates/Rockwell, A Scout Is Loyal...........50.00
1976, China Bicentennial, 1776 Bicentennial...............33.00
1976, Christmas/Rockwell, Christmas Trio.................59.00
1976, Four Seasons Annual Set of 4/Rockwell, Grand Pals....200.00
1976, Irene Spencer, Promises to Keep...................50.00
1976, Presidential/Rockwell, Eisenhower..................35.00
1976, Presidential/Rockwell, Kennedy....................55.00
1977, Boy Scout Plates/Rockwell, A Good Sign.............35.00
1977, Boy Scout Plates/Rockwell, The Scoutmaster..........56.00
1977, Christmas/Rockwell, Yuletide Reckoning.............32.00
1978, Christmas/Rockwell, Planning Christmas Visits.........25.00
1980, Boy Scout Tribute/Rockwell, Beyond the Easel.........45.00

Haviland-Parlon

1971, Tapestry I, Unicorn in Captivity....................185.00
1972, Christmas Madonnas, Raphael.....................155.00
1972, Tapestry I, Start of the Hunt......................75.00
1973, Christmas Madonnas, Feruzzi......................98.00
1973, Tapestry I, Chase of the Unicorn..................125.00
1974, Christmas Madonnas, Raphael.....................90.00
1974, Tapestry I, End of the Hunt......................115.00
1975, Christmas Madonnas, Murillo......................58.00
1975, Mother's Day, Mother & Child.....................80.00
1975, Tapestry I, Unicorn Surrounded...................70.00
1976, Christmas Madonnas, Botticelli....................58.00
1976, Tapestry I, Brought to the Castle..................55.00
1977, Christmas Madonnas, Bellini......................48.00
1977, Tapestry II, Lady & Unicorn, FE...................75.00
1978, Tapestry II, Sight................................48.00
1979, Tapestry II, Sound...............................50.00
1980, Tapestry II, Touch...............................85.00
1981, Tapestry II, Scent...............................59.00

Knowles

1978, Gone with the Wind Collection, Scarlett.............235.00
1979, Gone with the Wind Collection, Ashley..............125.00

Reco

1977, World of Children/John McClelland, Rainy Day Fun.....210.00
1978, World of Children/John McClelland, When I Grow Up....80.00

1979, Mother Goose/John McClelland, Mary Mary...........250.00
1979, World of Children/John McClelland, You're Invited.......75.00
1980, Mother Goose/John McClelland, Little Boy Blue.........95.00
1980, World of Children/John McClelland, Kittens for Sale.....50.00
1981, Mother Goose/John McClelland, Little Miss Muffet........25.00

Reed & Barton

1970, Audubon, Pine Siskin.............................175.00
1970, Christmas Carols, Partridge in a Pear Tree...........210.00
1971, Audubon, Red-Shouldered Hawk....................75.00
1971, Christmas Carols, We Three Kings of Orient Are........75.00
1972, Christmas Carols, Hark! The Herald Angels Sing........65.00

River Shore

1976, Famous Americans/Rockwell-Brown, Lincoln...........385.00
1977, Famous Americans/Rockwell-Brown, Triple Self-Portrait..120.00
1978, Famous Americans/Rockwell-Brown, Peace Corps........70.00
1978, Famous Americans/Rockwell-Brown, Spirit of Lindbergh...50.00

Royal Bayreuth

1972, Christmas, Carriage in the Village..................75.00
1973, Christmas, Snow Scene...........................20.00
1973, Mother's Day, Consolation.......................48.00
1974, Mother's Day/Leo Jansen, Young Americans...........125.00
1975, Mother's Day/Leo Jansen, Young Americans II..........98.00
1976, Mother's Day/Leo Jansen, Young Americans III.........70.00
1977, Mother's Day/Leo Jansen, Young Americans IV.........60.00

Royal Copenhagen

1908, Christmas, Madonna & Child....................1,800.00
1909, Christmas, Danish Landscape.....................150.00
1917, Christmas, Our Saviour's Church..................95.00
1924, Christmas, Star Over the Sea.....................100.00
1934, Christmas, Hermitage Castle......................125.00
1940, Christmas, The Good Shepherd....................360.00
1943, Christmas, Flight into Egypt......................495.00
1948, Christmas, Nebodo Church........................225.00
1951, Christmas, Christmas Angel.......................410.00
1958, Christmas, Sunshine over Greenland................155.00
1964, Christmas, Fetching the Tree......................89.00
1968, Christmas, The Last Umiak........................34.00

Rockwell Society

1974, Christmas, Scotty Gets His Tree...................140.00
1975, Christmas, Angel with Black Eye...................90.00
1976, Christmas, Golden Christmas.....................55.00
1976, Mother's Day, A Mother's Love...................110.00
1977, Heritage, Toy Maker............................260.00
1977, Mother's Day, Faith.............................68.00
1978, Heritage, The Cobbler..........................125.00
1978, Mother's Day, Bedtime..........................95.00
1979, Heritage, Lighthouse Keeper's Daughter.............98.00
1980, Heritage, Ship Builder..........................60.00

Royal Delft De Porceleyne Fles

1915, Christmas: 10" dia, Christmas Bells...............6,250.00
1915, Christmas: 7" dia, Christmas Star................3,620.00
1916, Christmas: 10" dia, Star-Floral Design..............720.00

1918, Christmas: 10" dia, Shepherd......................375.00
1921, Christmas: 10" dia, Canal Boatman................425.00
1925, Christmas: 10" dia, Towngate in Delft............460.00
1926, Christmas: 7" dia, Bell Tower....................225.00
1927, Christmas: 10" dia, Sailboat.....................475.00
1929, Christmas: 7" dia, Church Spire..................325.00
1930, Christmas: 10" dia, Church Entrance, Delft.......350.00
1932, Christmas: 10" dia, Fireplace....................438.00
1932, Christmas: 7" dia, Bell Tower....................300.00
1938, Christmas: 10" dia, Interior Scene...............488.00
1955, Christmas: 9" dia, Christmas Star................175.00
1956, Christmas: 10" dia, Landscape....................325.00
1956, Christmas: 9" dia, Christmas Bells...............340.00
1956, Christmas: 9" dia, Flower Design.................137.00
1957, Christmas: 9" dia, Christmas Star................137.00
1958, Christmas: 9" dia, Christmas Star................137.00
1961, Christmas: 10" dia, Village Scene................363.00
1961, Christmas: 7" dia, Snow Landscape................163.00
1967, Christmas: 10" dia, Tower in Amsterdam...........388.00
1967, Christmas: 7" dia, Mill in Hazerswoude...........163.00
1971, Christmas: 7" dia, Towngate at Zierikzee.........125.00
1973, Christmas: 10" dia, De Waag in Alkmaar...........413.00
1977, Christmas: 7" dia, Dromedaris Tower..............150.00

Royal Devon

1975, Christmas/Rockwell, Downhill Daring...............75.00
1975, Mother's Day/Rockwell, Doctor & Doll.............100.00
1976, Christmas/Rockwell, The Christmas Gift............85.00
1976, Mother's Day/Rockwell, Puppy Love.................75.00
1977, Christmas/Rockwell, The Big Moment................80.00
1977, Mother's Day/Rockwell, The Family.................70.00
1978, Christmas/Rockwell, Puppets for Christmas.........35.00
1978, Mother's Day/Rockwell, Mother's Day Off...........70.00
1979, Christmas/Rockwell, One Present Too Many..........35.00
1979, Mother's Day, Mother's Evening Out................32.00
1980, Christmas/Rockwell, Gramps Meets Gramps...........33.00
1980, Mother's Day/Rockwell, Mother's Treat............33.00

Royal Doulton

1973, Mother's Day/Edna Hibel, Colette & Child.........485.00
1974, Commedia Del Arte/LeRoy Neiman, Harlequin........100.00
1974, Mother's Day/Edna Hibel, Sayuri & Child..........170.00
1975, Mother's Day/Edna Hibel, Kristina & Child........120.00
1976, Commedia Del Arte/LeRoy Neiman, Pierrot..........90.00
1976, Mother's Day/Edna Hibel, Marilyn & Child.........110.00
1977, Commedia Del Arte/LeRoy Neiman, Columbine........80.00
1977, Mother's Day/Edna Hibel, Lucia & Child...........90.00
1978, Mother's Day/Edna Hibel, Kathleen & Child........85.00
1980, Portraits of Innocence/Masseria, Panchito.......200.00
1981, Portraits of Innocence/Masseria, Adrien.........120.00

Rosenthal

1907, Christmas.......................................5,000.00
1914, Christmas, Christmas Song........................350.00
1921, Christmas, Christmas in the Mountains............200.00
1930, Christmas, Group of Deer Under the Pines.........225.00
1936, Christmas, Nurnberg Angel.......................195.00
1942, Christmas, Marianburg Castle....................300.00
1947, Christmas, The Dillingen Madonna................985.00
1948, Christmas, Message to the Shepherds.............875.00
1951, Christmas, Star of Bethlehem....................450.00

1954, Christmas, Christmas Eve........................195.00
1971, Wiinblad Christmas, Maria & Child.............1,500.00
1972, Wiinblad Christmas, Caspar......................685.00
1973, Wiinblad Christmas, Melchior....................545.00
1976, Oriental Gold/Edna Hibel, Yasuko.............1,000.00
1976, Wiinblad Crystal, The Madonna...................380.00
1977, Oriental Gold/Edna Hibel, Mr Obata..............535.00
1977, Wiinblad Crystal, The Annunciation..............275.00
1978, Oriental Gold/Edna Hibel, Sakura................460.00
1979, Oriental Gold/Edna Hibel, Michio................495.00

Schmid

1971, B Hummel Christmas, Angel........................70.00
1972, B Hummel Christmas, Angel with Fire..............38.00
1972, B Hummel Mother's Day, Playing Hooky, FE........40.00
1972, Peanuts Christmas, Snoopy on Sleigh.............60.00
1972, Peanuts Mother's Day, Linus, FE.................20.00
1973, B Hummel Christmas, Nativity...................230.00
1973, B Hummel Mother's Day, Little Fisherman.........75.00
1973, Disney Christmas, Sleigh Ride.................300.00
1973, Peanuts Christmas, Christmas Eve at Doghouse....90.00
1973, Peanuts Mother's Day, Mom?.....................20.00
1974, B Hummel Christmas, Guardian Angel.............35.00
1974, B Hummel Mother's Day, Bumblebee...............35.00
1974, Disney Christmas, Trimming the Tree............45.00
1974, Disney Mother's Day, Flowers for Mother........60.00
1974, Peanuts Christmas, Christmas at Fireplace......50.00
1974, Peanuts Mother's Day, On Parade................30.00
1975, B Hummel Christmas, Christmas Child............35.00
1975, Disney Christmas, Caroling.....................20.00
1975, Disney Mother's Day, Snow White................30.00
1975, Peanuts Christmas, Woodstock Santa Claus.......20.00
1975, Raggedy Ann Christmas, Gifts of Love, FE.......50.00
1976, B Hummel Christmas, Sacred Journey.............50.00
1976, Disney Christmas, Building A Snowman...........15.00
1976, Disney Mother's Day, Minnie Mouse & Friends....25.00
1976, Raggedy Ann Christmas, Raggedy Ann Skates......25.00
1977, B Hummel Christmas, Herald Angel...............45.00
1977, Ferrandiz Mother & Child, Orchard Mother & Child.....140.00
1977, Raggedy Ann Christmas, Decorating the Tree.....13.00
1978, Disney Special, Mickey at 50...................50.00
1978, Ferrandiz Mother & Child, Pastoral Mother & Child....100.00
1979, Ferrandiz Mother & Child, Avian Mother & Child.......100.00
1979, Ferrandiz Mother & Child, Floral Mother........95.00
1980, Country Pride/Lowell Davis, Surprise in the Cellar....38.00
1980, Disney Special, Happy Birthday Pinocchio.......18.00
1981, Country Pride/Lowell Davis, Bustin' with Pride.......35.00
1981, Country Pride/Lowell Davis, Duke's Mixture......35.00
1981, Country Pride/Lowell Davis, Plum Tuckered Out.......38.00

Veneto Flair

1971, Bellini, Madonna...............................450.00
1971, Christmas, Three Kings.........................160.00
1971, Wildlife, Deer.................................450.00
1972, Birds, Owl.....................................100.00
1972, Christmas, Shepherds............................90.00
1972, Wildlife, Elephant.............................275.00
1973, Birds, Falcon...................................55.00
1973, Christmas, Christ Child.........................55.00
1973, Goddess, Pomona................................125.00
1973, Wildlife, Puma..................................65.00
1974, Birds, Mallard..................................60.00

1974, Christmas, Angel....................................55.00
1974, Goddess, Diana....................................75.00
1974, Wildlife, Tiger....................................50.00

Comic Books

Public acceptance of the cartoon book as an enjoyable form of entertainment caused printing companies to experiment with size and format, and by the early 1930s the comic book as we know it today had evolved —7" x 9" paper back books stapled together and selling for 10¢. Each unfolded a new saga of adventure as experienced by detective extraordinare Dick Tracy; super-heroes like Batman and Robin, Superman and Wonderwoman, Tarzan, and The Lone Ranger; or the science fictional characters Flash Gordon and Captain Midnight.

Today first issues in excellent condition may bring prices as high as $300 or over. Rarity, age, and quality of art work are prime factors in determining comic book values.

Ace #84, G....................................10.00
Action, #29, Oct 1940, Superman & more, G....................................30.00
Action, #67, G....................................22.00
Adventure, #64, July 1941, VG....................................38.00
Adventure, #99, G....................................21.00
Adventures In 3-D, #1, Nov 1953, Powell art, w/glasses, EX.....28.00
Air Fighters, #1, Nov 1941, 1st issue, EX....................................115.00
Air Fighters V2, #9, G....................................12.00
All American, #24, G....................................38.00
All American, #67, EX....................................28.00
All Good Comics, 1944, 128 pgs, EX....................................28.00
All Star, #47, VG....................................39.00
All Star, #52, April-May 1950, VG....................................60.00
All Star, #55, Oct-Nov 1950, VG....................................40.00
All Winners, #18, Summer 1946, 1st Series, VG....................................50.00
All Winners, #21, Winter 1946-7, last issue, VG....................................137.00
All-Flash, #19, VG....................................20.00
All-Flash, #6, Sept-Oct 1942, VG....................................41.00
All-Flash, #8, Jan-Feb 1943, VG....................................38.00
All-Flash, #9, March-April 1943, EX....................................50.00
Amazing #1, Fall 1944, VG....................................75.00
Amazing Mystery Funnies V2, #12, Dec 1939, VG....................................115.00
Amazing Mystery Funnies V2, #8, G....................................23.00
Amazing Spider-Man, #5, EX....................................71.00
Amazing Spider-Man, #8, Jan 1964, M....................................57.00
Amazing Spider-Man, #9, EX....................................22.00
Amazing-Man, #16, Oct 1940, VG....................................40.00
Amazing-Man, #9, Feb 1940, EX....................................89.00
America's Best, #15, EX....................................20.00
America's Greatest, #8, Summer 1943, 100 pgs, last issue, EX...40.00
America's Greatest, #8, Summer 1943, 100 pgs, last issue, VG...29.00
Animal, #17, VG....................................16.00
Animal, #25, NM....................................28.00
Animal Fables, #1, VG....................................11.00
Avengers, #2, Nov 1963, Avengers by Kirby, EX....................................50.00
Avengers, #3, VG....................................39.00
Barker, #2, VG....................................4.00
Barker, #9, EX....................................3.00
Batman, #12, Aug-Sept 1942, EX....................................133.00
Batman, #15, Feb-Mar 1943, VG....................................95.00
Batman, #30, EX....................................112.00
Batman, #7, Oct-Nov 1941, Batman vs Joker, G....................................66.00
Batman, #76, VG....................................23.00
Big Shot, #10, Feb 1941, EX....................................27.00
Big Shot, #13, NM....................................25.00

Big Shot, #16, Aug 1941, EX....................................20.00
Big Shot, #31, EX....................................11.00
Big 3, #1, Fall 1940, EX....................................67.00
Big 3, #1, Fall 1940, VG....................................38.00
Black Cat, #24, NM....................................33.00
Black Terror, #15, EX....................................13.00
Blackhawk, #24, EX....................................23.00
Blackhawk, #40, G....................................11.00
Blondie, FB #29, VG....................................7.00
Blue Beetle, #12, June 1942, EX....................................25.00
Blue Beetle, #18, EX....................................19.00
Blue Beetle, #42, EX....................................20.00
Blue Ribbon, #5, July 1940, VG....................................36.00
Boy, #17, G....................................11.00
Boy, #3, April 1942, Crimebuster origin, G....................................67.00
Boy Commandos, #13, EX....................................10.00
Bulletman, #2, Fall 1941, 4 complete stories, EX....................................85.00
Bulletman, #2, Fall 1941, 4 tales, VG....................................51.00
Captain Aero V4, #3, LB Cole cover, EX....................................17.00
Captain America, #20, G....................................34.00
Captain America, #22, Jan 1943, EX....................................88.00
Captain America, #29, Aug 1943, EX....................................82.00
Captain America, #49, EX....................................52.00
Captain America, #60, G....................................25.00
Captain Battle, #3, EX....................................18.00
Captain Battle Jr, #1, VG....................................33.00
Captain Easy, FC #24, VG....................................38.00
Captain Fearless, #1, VG....................................21.00
Captain Marvel, #33, EX....................................26.00
Captain Marvel, #5, Dec 1941, G....................................45.00
Captain Marvel, #68, EX....................................18.00
Captain Marvel Jr, #10, VG....................................22.00
Captain Midnight, #10, VG....................................22.00
Cat-Man, #3, July 1941, VG....................................32.00
Choice, #1, VG....................................26.00
Comic Cavalcade, #10, Spring 1945, 100 pgs, VG....................................30.00
Comic Cavalcade, #3, Summer 1943, 100 pgs, EX....................................79.00
Comics On Parade, #31, Captain & Kids, VG....................................14.00
Comics On Parade, #7, VG....................................25.00
Crack, #38, EX....................................10.00
Crackajack Funnies, #15, VG....................................24.00
Crime Suspenstories, #12, G....................................33.00
Crime Suspenstories, #24, VG....................................17.00
Curly Kayoe, #1, VG....................................8.00
Daredevil, #2, June 1964, Marvel Comics, EX....................................49.00
Daredevil Comics, #18, Aug 1943, Lev Publications, EX....................................57.00
Daring, #10, G....................................27.00
Detective, #153, EX....................................30.00
Detective, #53, July 1941, EX....................................67.00
Detective, #54, Aug 1941, VG....................................41.00
Detective, #56, Oct 1941, EX....................................50.00
Detective, #82, EX....................................30.00
Detective, #93, VG....................................24.00
Dick Tracey, FC #96, VG....................................12.00
Doll Man, #18, EX....................................15.00
Donald Duck, #26, VG....................................33.00
Dynamic, #1, Oct 1941, VG....................................49.00
Exciting, #32, G....................................12.00
Extra, #3, EX....................................15.00
Fairy Tale Parade, #321, VG....................................5.00
Fairy Tale Parade, FC #50, EX....................................25.00
Famous Funnies, #108, VG....................................12.00
Famous Funnies, #11, G....................................26.00
Famous Funnies, #195, G....................................3.00

Famous Funnies, #209, Dec 1953, Frazetta cover, M.........108.00
Fantastic, #15, EX.........31.00
Fantastic Four, #20, NM.........46.00
Fantastic Four, #4, May 1962, FF vs Sub-Mariner by Kirby, EX..75.00
Fantastic Four, #9, EX.........71.00
Feature, #29, Feb 1940, EX.........50.00
Feature, #44, VG.........22.00
Feature, #75, EX.........13.00
Feature, #90, EX.........6.00
Fight, #14, Aug 1941, EX.........20.00
Fight, #5, May 1940, EX.........35.00
Fight, #50, NM.........18.00
Fight, #54, G.........7.00
Flame, #7, VG.........24.00
Flash, #23, Nov 1941, VG.........49.00
Flash, #58, EX.........33.00
Flash Gordon, #1, Oct, 1950, G.........24.00
Funnies, #13, VG.........21.00
Funnies, #62, VG.........16.00
Green Hornet, #36, VG.........14.00
Green Hornet, #4, EX.........36.00
Green Lantern, #13, VG.........37.00
Green Lantern, #2, Winter 1942, EX.........169.00
Green Lantern, #3, Spring 1942, EX.........130.00
Green Lantern, #5, Fall 1942, VG.........81.00
Green Mask, #3, VG.........14.00
Happy Houlihans, #1, EC, EX.........27.00
Harold Teen, FC #2, VG.........22.00
Haunt of Fear, #10, EX.........49.00
Hello Pal, #1, G.........15.00
Heroic, #11, G.........9.00
Hit, #38, VG.........8.00
House of Terror, #1, Oct 1953, 3-D, glasses attached, EX.........51.00
Hulk, #5, EX.........60.00
Human Torch, #13, EX.........71.00
Human Torch, #6, Winter 1942, EX.........121.00
Human Torch, #9, Fall 1942, VG.........115.00
Ibis, #6, VG.........21.00
Incredible Hulk, #3, Sept 1962, 1st series, VG.........44.00
Incredible Science Fiction, #30, July-Aug 1955, VG.........24.00
Jim Hardy, Single Series #27, G.........6.00
Journey Into Mystery, #85, Oct 1962, Thor/Loki by Kirby, EX..44.00
Jumbo, #10, Oct-Nov 1939, EX.........133.00
Jumbo, #11, Dec-Jan 1939-40, Sheena & more, EX.........77.00
Jungle, #32, EX.........22.00
Jungle, #9, Sept 1940, Kaanga, Camilla, & more, EX.........57.00
Jungle, #91, EX.........11.00
Keen Detective Funnies V2, #9, EX.........55.00
Kid Komics, #4, 1944, VG.........42.00
Kid Komics, #8, EX.........61.00
Leading, #1, Winter 1941-2, orig of 7 Soldiers of Victory, EX..295.00
Leading, #13, VG.........18.00
Leading, #7, Summer 1943, EX.........46.00
Looney Tunes, #12, EX.........25.00
Looney Tunes, #30, VG.........15.00
Looney Tunes & Merrie Melodies, #25, VG.........14.00
Looney Tunes & Merrie Melodies, #3, Jan 1942, VG.........40.00
M.D., #1, EX.........18.00
M.D., #4, VG.........12.00
Mad, #16, EX.........27.00
Mad, #8, VG.........17.00
Magic, #8, March 1940, EX.........30.00
Martin Luther King & Montgomery Story, M.........10.00
Marvel, #25, VG.........55.00

Marvel Family, #21, EX.........12.00
Marvel Family, #74, EX.........10.00
Marvel Mystery, #15, Jan 1941, EX.........175.00
Marvel Mystery, #23, G.........35.00
Marvel Mystery, #27, Jan 1942, EX.........82.00
Marvel Mystery, #53, EX.........103.00
Merry-Go-Round, 1944, 130 pgs, VG.........9.00
Military, #41, EX.........28.00
Miracle, #1, Feb 1940, G.........20.00
More Fun, #103, EX.........55.00
Mystery Men, #2, Sept 1939, EX.........116.00
Mystery Men, #9, EX.........62.00
National, #37, EX.........25.00
National, #37, VG.........13.00
New Comics, #9, Oct 1936, EX.........80.00
New Funnies, #72, EX.........23.00
New Funnies, #8, VG.........7.00
Our Gang, #1, 1942, 1st issue, Walt Kelly art, EX.........170.00
Our Gang, #22, Carl Barks & Walt Kelly art, VG.........16.00
Our Gang, #26, EX.........18.00
Our Gang, #7, VG.........22.00
Panic, #60, VG.........4.00
Panic, #9, EX.........7.00
Phantom, HH #26, EX.........9.00
Picture Stories From Bible, #1, EX.........10.00
Piracy, #3, VG.........15.00
Planet, #36, May 1945, EX.........66.00
Planet, #48, May 1947, G.........26.00
Plastic Man, #18, EX.........45.00
Pogo, #13, VG.........12.00
Police, #43, EX.........50.00
Popeye & Wimpy, #17, 1940.........55.00
Popular, #85, EX.........23.00
Popular, #9, Oct 1936, EX.........63.00
Porky Pig, #78, VG.........13.00
Prince Valiant Feature Book, #26, 1941, EX.........194.00
Prize, #50, VG.........8.00
Psychoanalysis, #1, G.........12.00
Raggedy Ann & Andy, #12, EX.........15.00
Rangers, #20, G.........11.00
Rangers of Freedom, #4, April 1942, G.........26.00
Rangers of Freedom, #5, June 1942, VG.........31.00
Real Fact, #5, Nov-Dec 1946, EX.........50.00
Remember Pearl Harbor, 1942, EX.........46.00
Science, #1, Feb 1940, VG.........75.00
Scoop, #2, VG.........18.00
Sensation, #11, Nov 1942, VG.........24.00
Sensation, #12, VG.........33.00
Sensation, #38, VG.........12.00
Sensation, #45, VG.........13.00
Sensation, #77, EX.........24.00
Shadow V2, #5, VG.........8.00
Sheena, #1, Spring 1942, 1st issue, VG.........100.00
Shock Suspenstories, #7, VG.........33.00
Silver Streak, #17, VG.........23.00
Silver Surfer, #1, Aug 1968, 1st issue w/origin, EX.........26.00
Smash, #31, EX.........33.00
Smash, #78, VG.........7.00
Smash, #9, April 1940, VG.........21.00
Smilin' Jack, FC #58, G.........13.00
Smilin' Jack, Four Color, #14, 1942, VG.........37.00
Space Adventures, #13, Blue Beetle, EX.........17.00
Sparkler, #1, Jim Hardy, G.........12.00
Speed, #2, VG.........25.00

Speed, #39, VG................................16.00
Speed, #41, VG................................12.00
Spirit, #2, VG.................................21.00
Spirit, #3, VG.................................15.00
Star Spangled, #3, Dec 1941, Star Spangled Kid & more, G....40.00
Star Spangled, #35, EX.........................19.00
Star Spangled, #68, VG..........................8.00
Startling, #12, EX.............................18.00
Strange Tales, #102, Nov 1962, EX...............17.00
Strange Tales, #106, EX........................19.00
Strange Tales Annual, #1, EX...................27.00
Sub-Mariner, #11, Fall 1943, Schomburg cover, EX.........110.00
Sub-Mariner, #3, Fall 1941, Schomburg cover, EX..........261.00
Sub-Mariner, #9, Spring 1943, Wolverton art, EX..........110.00
Super Animal 3-D, glasses attached, NM.....................60.00
Super Magician V1, #6, EX.......................9.00
Super Mystery V4, #4, EX.......................12.00
Superman, #10, 4 stories, G.....................67.00
Superman, #20, Jan-Feb 1943, VG................76.00
Superman, #3, Winter 1940, 4 stories, EX.......444.00
Superman, #86, G..............................15.00
Superman, #93, VG.............................15.00
Supersnipe V1, #9, G............................8.00
Swamp Thing, #1, VG............................4.00
Tales From The Crypt, #28, VG..................23.00
Tales From The Crypt, #43, VG..................18.00
Tales of Suspense, #41, May 1963, Iron Man by Kirby, EX.....25.00
Tales To Astonish, #27, Jan 1962, 1st Ant-Man by Kirby, VG..106.00
Tales To Astonish, #36, Oct 1962, EX...........72.00
Target, #10, Nov 1940, Spacehawk story by Wolverton, EX....215.00
Target V2, #11, Wolverton, EX..................50.00
Tarzan, #4, EX................................40.00
Tarzan, #5, EX................................29.00
Terry & Pirates, FC #44, VG....................40.00
Terry Toons, #4, VG...........................12.00
Tessie the Typist, #1, Wolverton, EX...........20.00
The Funnies, #2, Nov 1936, early comic strip reprints, G......25.00
Thrilling, #30, EX.............................17.00
Thrilling, #62, EX.............................23.00
Tillie Toiler, FC #8, EX........................23.00
Top-Notch, #2, Jan 1940, G.....................20.00
Tor, #3, EX...................................34.00
Two Fisted Tales, #29, VG......................10.00
Two Fisted Tales, #30, EX......................40.00
Two Fisted Tales, #40, EX......................13.00
Uncle Sam, #7, VG.............................28.00
Uncle Scrooge, #4, VG..........................30.00
USA, #17, EX..................................75.00
USA Is Ready, EX..............................17.00
Valor, #1, VG.................................11.00
Vault Of Horror, #26, EX.......................33.00
Vault Of Horror, #34, EX.......................33.00
Walt Disney Comics, #107, VG...................12.00
Walt Disney Comics & Stories, #149, EX.........18.00
Walt Disney Comics & Stories, #80, VG..........23.00
Wambi, #5, EX..................................7.00
Weird, #4, EX.................................60.00
Weird, #8, Nov 1940, EX........................33.00
Weird Fantasy, #13(#1), May-June 1950, EC, 1st issue, EX.....220.00
Whiz, #27, VG.................................20.00
Whiz, #33, Aug 1942, EX........................34.00
Whiz, #66, EX.................................13.00
Wings, #122, EX...............................16.00
Wings, #18, VG................................15.00

Wings, #58, EX................................18.00
Wings, #9, May 1941, EX........................22.00
Wonder Comics, #1, May 1944, EX................49.00
Wonder Comics, #11, G..........................13.00
Wonder Comics, #15, EX.........................20.00
Wonder Woman, #39, EX..........................30.00
Wonderworld, #12, April 1940, EX...............42.00
World's Finest, #32, VG........................25.00
World's Finest, #4, Winter 1941, 100 pgs, VG...82.00
World's Finest, #42, VG........................17.00
World's Finest, #7, Fall 1942, 100 pgs, VG.....55.00
Wow, #10, EX..................................31.00
Wow, #26, EX..................................16.00
Wow, #5, Spring 1942, VG.......................27.00
X-Men, #2, Nov 1963, EX........................58.00
X-Men, #4, EX.................................33.00
X-Men, #8, EX.................................27.00
Xmas, #4, 196 pgs, EX..........................38.00
Yankee, #1, Sept 1941, Yankee Doodle Jones origin, VG......40.00
Young Allies, #10, VG..........................24.00
Young Allies, #18, VG..........................28.00
Zip, #38, VG..................................11.00

Compasses

Bronze, pocket, mk US Engineer Corps, WWII..............15.00
Frye & Shaw, surveyor's, cased, 1840, 18x9x4¾"...........500.00
Nautical, in orig wood box, 1835......................225.00
Taylor Usanite, nickel hunting case, mk Eng Dep USA, 1918....35.00
Traveling, in folding wood case w/Kleininger fecit, 2x3¾"......160.00

Gimballed wet-card brass compass, Observator Rotterdam, 1880s, 12"
diameter, $330.00.

Cookbooks

Cookbooks from the 19th century, though often hard to find, are a
delight to today's collectors both for their quaint formats and printing
methods, as well as for their outmoded, often humorous views on nutrition.
Recipes required a 'pinch' of salt, butter 'the size of an egg' or 'a walnut',
or a 'handful' of flour.

Collectors sometimes specialize in cookbooks issued as advertising
premiums. Especially desirable are the figurals that were shaped like a jar,
a slice of bread, or some other form pertinent to the product. Others with

unique features such as illustrations by well known artists or references to famous people or places are priced in accordance.

Cookbooks written earlier than 1874 are the most valuable, and when found command prices as high as $200; figurals usually sell in the $10 to $15 range.

Key: Cb-----Cookbook

A Thousand Ways to Please a Husband, 1911 . . . . .20.00
Aristos Flour, 1911, 30 pgs 60.00
Armstrong, table-top stove book, 1918 .25.00
Baker's Chocolate Choice Receipts, Columbian Expo 8.50
Betty Crocker, McGraw Hill, 1950 . . . . .9.00
Betty Crocker Guide to Easy Entertaining, 1st ed/1st print 12.00
Choice Recipes for Clever Cooks, 1924 .15.00
Elsie the Cow, 1952 . . . . .9.00
Encyclopedia of Cooking, Mary Margaret McBride, 12 vols, '58 . .50.00
Enterprise Mfg Cookbook, 1906 . . . . .9.00
Fine Old Dixie Recipes, mammy on wood cover, illus, 1930s 55.00
Happy Home, radio & TV show, 1956, 94 pgs 3.00
Hood's, tooth powder ad on bk, 64 pg, 4x6" 10.00
Hood's #3, 32 pgs, 7x4½", scarce 14.00
Hood's High Street, 32 pg, 4½x7" 15.00
Jack Benny & Mary Livingston, Jello recipes, 1937 . . . . .10.00
Jane Astor, NY 30.00
Ladies' Delight, AP Ordway, Sulphur Bitters, 1886 . . . . .11.00
Larkin Housewives Cb, 1916 . . . . .10.00
Lowney, Maria Willett Howard, w/ad on cover, 1907 . . . . .20.00
Lowney's Chocolate, 1908 . . . . .14.00
Majestic Cook Book, B Joseph, Sole Agent Majestic Ranges 8.00
Modern Women of America Cb, 1913, Anna Claire Van Galder . .10.00
New American Cb, 1946 . . . . .10.00
New Butterick Cookbook, 1924 . . . . .15.00
New England, 1906 . . . . .17.00
Our Kitchen Treasures, AWO Dallas, Texas, spiral, 300+ pgs . . .10.50
Ralston Mother Goose Recipe Book, illus Burd, 1919 . . . . .5.00
Recipes for Clever Cooks, 1925 . . . . .15.00
Rumford Baking Powder, 1906, girl w/wheat on cover, colorful . .10.00
Rumford Receipt Book, 1905 . . . . .20.00
Swansdown, book & tube cake pan, 1923 . . . . .17.00
White House Cook Book, 1911 . . . . .30.00
100 Delicious Foods from 4 Basic Recipes, Pillsbury, 1926 . . . . . .5.00

White House Cookbook, 1908, in used condition, 9¾" x 7", $25.00.

Cookie Jars

The appeal of the cookie jar is universal; folks of all ages, both male and female, love to collect 'em! The early thirties heavy stoneware jars of a rather nondescript nature, quickly gave way to figurals of every type imaginable. Those from the mid- to late thirties were often decorated over the glaze with 'cold paint', but by the early forties underglaze decorating resulted in cheerful, bright, permanent colors and cookie jars that still have a new look forty years later.

The jars listed here were made by companies other than those represented by other sections.

See also specific manufacturers

Albert Apple, Pee Dee Co, figural boy w/apple shaped body 30.00
Andy 35.00
Baby Elephants, American Bisque, boy & girl, pr 45.00
Baby Pig, American Bisque, wears diaper, sitting, holds rattle 35.00
Bear with Cookie, Royalware 20.00
Beehive, American Bisque 25.00
Bird, American Bisque 25.00
Bo-Peep, Napco, long yel braids, apron w/blue trim, bl/wht hat . .15.00
Boots, American Bisque 35.00
Boy Pig, American Bisque 25.00
Casper, Harvey Productions, USA 40.00
Castle Tower, mk Cardinal 3100 USA 15.00
Cat on Beehive 22.00
Cheerleaders, American Bisque 32.00
Chef, bl & wht striped pants, hands in pockets, small 25.00
Chef, black face, Pearl China 75.00
Chef, holds salad bowl, yellow skirt-like apron, EX quality 36.00
Chef, wht clothes, blue eyes, crude design 25.00
Chef, yel & wht clothes, red neckerchief, blk hair 25.00
Chef, yel shirt, blk spoon, mustache & goatee, American Bisque . .35.00
Chef Pig, wears chef hat, standing behind stove 12.00
Churn, American Bisque Co 12.00
Churn Boy, blue & yellow clothes, American Bisque Co 36.00
Clock, American Bisque 20.00
Clown, American Bisque, mkd USA, pastel colors 18.00
Coffee Pot, American Bisque, hammered metal look, bail hdl 10.00
Coffee Pot, American Bisque, w/pine cones 20.00
Collegiate Owl, American Bisque, 1940s 25.00
Cookie Monster, Muppets, California Originals 20.00
Cookie Safe, mk Cardinal 309 USA 15.00
Cookie Trolley, Treasure Craft 20.00
Cookie Truck, American Bisque 35.00
Cow, Doranne of California, sits w/milk can between legs 25.00
Cow, w/suspenders, flower on collar, red/blk trim, Am Bisque 20.00
Davey Crockett, Regal China 60.00
Dog in Basket 18.00
Donald Duck, embossed, blk, Walt Disney Productions 25.00
Donald Duck, embossed, tan, Walt Disney Productions 35.00
Donald Duck & J Carioca, turnabout, Disney, very good paint . . .50.00
Donald Duck & Nephew, Walt Disney Productions 35.00
Donkey & Cart, American Bisque 35.00
Duck, Doranne of California, sits w/basket of corn between ft 25.00
Duck, red shawl, orange & blk trim 26.00
Dutch Boy, holds sailboat, American Bisque Co 20.00
Dutch Girl, blue dress, American Pottery Guild, sm rim chip 20.00
Elf Bakery Tree Stump, Twin Winton, elf finial 15.00
Elf Head, bright orange hat, very large, slight paint loss 15.00
Elf's School House, California Originals, red roof lid, unmkd 15.00
Fancy Cat, yel clothes, blue bow tie, tiny nicks on ear tips 15.00
Farmer Pig, patch on pants, American Bisque Co 25.00

Howdy Doody, ivory and maroon, with blue eyes, 9", $175.00.

Gold Buddha, Twin Winton, full figure.....................25.00
Granny, American Bisque.................................25.00
Horse, sitting; American Bisque, mk USA...................25.00
Horse & Cart, American Bisque...........................25.00
Humpty-Dumpty, bl jacket/orange vest/yel pants, Maddux of CA..28.00
Jack in the Box, American Bisque..........................25.00
Kittens & Ball of Yarn, American Bisque, kitten finial..........18.00
Kittens in Old Fashioned Shoe, yel, mk Maurice of Calif USA...15.00
Lamb, American Bisque....................................20.00
Lamb, Twin Winton, For Good Little Lambs Only, unmkd......20.00
Lion, Belmont...25.00
Majorette Head, gold details.............................65.00
Mickey & Minnie, turnabout, EX paint.....................55.00
Monk, Thou Shall Not Steal, Twin Winton...................18.00
Mother Goose, Doranne of California, red, mk C J 16 USA.....20.00
Noah's Ark, mk Twin Winton Calif USA.....................15.00
Pelican, California Originals, baby pelican finial, unmkd........15.00
Penquin, wearing tux, Deco look, Japan....................18.00
Pig Boy, American Bisque.................................28.00
Pig in Polk, American Bisque Co..........................25.00
Pig Lady, American Bisque................................28.00
Popeye..150.00
Rabbit in Hat, American Bisque...........................30.00
Rag Doll, American Bisque................................35.00
Raggedy Ann...20.00
Red Riding Hood, Pottery Guild of America.................35.00
Rooster, American Bisque, unmkd.........................22.00
Rooster, American Bisque, white ball-shape body............15.00
Sad Iron, American Bisque, iron is lid, rooster on oval base.....25.00
Saddle w/Blackboard, American Bisque.....................45.00
Sailor Mouse, brightly colored, Twin Winton................25.00
Sandman Cookies, American Bisque, mk 801 USA............30.00
Seal on Igloo, American Bisque, seal finial, igloo base.........30.00
Sleeping Cat, white & tan, good quality....................20.00
Snow White, dwarfs encircle skirt at bottom, WDP...........20.00
Soldier, American Bisque.................................25.00
Spaceship, American Bisque, Cookies Out Of This World......40.00
Star Wars R2D2, USA....................................40.00
Stella Strawberry, PD & Co...............................40.00
Teapot, American Bisque, Martha & George, mk USA.........18.00
Teddy Bear, American Bisque.............................30.00

Telephone, Sierra Vista, old fashioned wall-type, wht & blk.....25.00
Thumper, Walt Disney Productions.........................45.00
Tomato, Pantry Parade Co, red w/green stem finial...........12.00
Topo Gigio, w/display box................................30.00
Train Engine, American Bisque............................32.00
Treasure Chest, Sierra Vista..............................12.00
Turnabout Bear, EX paint.................................30.00
Umbrella Kids, American Bisque, mk USA 739...............35.00
Walrus, Twin Winton, circus ruffle on neck, yel trimmed hat....18.00
Windmill, Fredricksburg Art Pottery, red trim, mk FAPCo......18.00
Winnie the Pooh, Walt Disney Productions..................45.00
Witch...20.00
Yarn Doll, American Bisque...............................30.00
Yogi Bear, Hanna Barbera Productions.....................30.00

Coors

The firm that became known as Coors Porcelain Company in 1920, was founded in 1908 by John J. Herold, originally of the Roseville Pottery in Zanesville, Ohio. Though still in business today, they are best known for their art ware vases and Rosebud dinnerware produced there before 1939.

Bowl, mixing; nest of 4, medium blue, M..................40.00
Cake plate, Rosebud, orange..............................25.00
Cookie jar, bulbous w/twisted hdls, yellow.................32.50
Custard, Rosebud.......................................10.00
Mug, miniature, 1½".....................................12.50
Plate, Rosebud, 7", 4 for.................................22.50
Platter, Rosebud, red, 13"................................15.00
Shaker, Rosebud, slender shape, aqua.....................15.00
Table tile, thermo porcelain, floral decor, 11".............15.00
Vase, Colorado State Fair, 1939...........................35.00
Vase, hdls, bl w/out, wht w/in, 8".........................35.00
Vase, rope hdls, wht, 12"................................60.00
Vase, tan/turq, 12".....................................40.00
Vase, w/hdls, turq/wht ribbed, 8".........................40.00
Water server, Rosebud, yellow, w/stopper..................15.00

Bean pot, Rosebud, $32.50.

Copper

Hand-crafted copper was made in America from early in the 18th century until about 1850, with the center of its production in Pennsylvania. Examples have been found signed by such notable coppersmiths as Kidd, Buchanan, Babb, Bently, and Harbeson.

Of the many utilitarian items made, tea kettles are the most desirable. Early examples from the 18th century were made with a dovetailed joint which was hammered and smoothed to a uniform thickness. Pots from the 19th century were seamed.

Coffee pots were made in many shapes and sizes, and along with mugs, kettles, warming pans, and measures are easiest to find. Stills, ranging in sizes of up to 50 gallon, are popular with collectors today.

Tea kettle, hand seamed, dovetailed and joined at the bottom, goose-neck spout, acorn final, signed, 10½", $155.00.

Bed warmer, floral engraving on lid, trn wood hdl, 12" dia.....300.00
Bowl, hammered, old, 3½x12" dia.........................60.00
Coffee pot, slant sides, tin lid, copper ring finial, 1850........75.00
Dipper, dvtl bowl, wrought iron hdl w/hook finial, rpr, 5x17"....40.00
Footwarmer, dtd 1818 on top, from Norway, EX.............135.00
Frying pan, tin lined, oblong/curved wrought iron hdl, 10x16"...85.00
Funnel, filter, brass thumb stop, 4x7".....................25.00
Gridiron, American, EX hdl, late 1700s....................95.00
Hot water bottle, oval w/brass ring hdl & cap, 6¾x10¼".......55.00
Kettle, jelly; w/lid & loop hdls, 6x12"....................65.00
Kettle, rivets down side, no hdls, brass hdl on lid, 13x13".....115.00
Mug, w/lead lining, 2 hdls, 1800s, 9½".....................8.50
Pan, egg poaching; tin lined, Middle Eastern, 20" dia........45.00
Pan, primitive, ring hanger, 1½x11¾".....................22.00
Pan, 12½" L forged iron hdl, mid 1800s, 5½x10"..........110.00
Porringer, English, Balwin, late 1700s, EX.................125.00
Pot, bail hdls, hand wrought/hand hammered, early 1800s, 12".115.00
Pot, tined interior, hand formed throughout, American, 1800s...95.00
Sauce pan, brass hdl, tinned w/in, sgn NY, miniature, 2".......20.00
Sauce pan, dvtl, 8" wrought copper hdl, 7" dia..............70.00
Sauce pan, dvtl, 9" wrought copper hdl, 8" dia..............95.00
Still, brass spigot, Sanitary #3, works, 1800s, 20"..........300.00
Taster, slim wrought iron hdl, 9¾".......................95.00
Tea kettle, Am, bottom to fit stove top, swivel strap hdl.......195.00
Tea kettle, conical/whistles, strap hdl/spout filler, Revere.......85.00
Tea kettle, dvtl, goose neck, acorn finial, minor dents, 10"....135.00
Tea kettle, dvtl, goose neck, brass acorn finial/hdl, 11".......165.00

Tea kettle, dvtl, swing hdl, hammered, F Wickman, 14"......250.00
Tea kettle, dvtl side & base, gooseneck spout, rigid hdl........95.00
Tea kettle, English, fixed hdl, oval, dvtl, 1850, 1½ pts........110.00
Tea kettle, oval, 10¼".................................75.00
Tea kettle, Scandinavian, scarce sm size, 1 qt..............110.00
Tea kettle, scroll iron fr suspension/base w/burner, 1882, 13"...85.00
Teapot, cylindrical w/iron goose neck/hdl, dvtl, rpr, 9½".......80.00
Tray, pierced edge, engraved, mkd Royalty Copperware, 16" dia.68.00
Wash boiler, tin lid, 12x23x12½".........................50.00

Copper Lustre

Copper lustre is a term referring to a type of pottery made in Staffordshire after the turn of the 19th century. It is finished in a metallic rusty-brown glaze resembling true copper. Pitchers are found in abundance, ranging from simple styles with dull bands of color, to those with fancy handles and bands of embossed polychromed flowers. Bowls are common; goblets, mugs, teapots, and sugar bowls much less so. It's easy to find, but not in good condition. Pieces with hand painted decoration and those with historical transfers are the most valuable.

Beaker, bl band w/applied floral band w/mc enameling, 3¼"....45.00
Bowl, gold decor, blue band, 6¼x3¼".....................52.00
Creamer, bl band w/emb child & dog in garden, 3½".........25.00
Creamer, gr band w/florals, 4".........................25.00
Creamer, mask spout, floral/bird decor, minor flaking, 5½"....30.00
Creamer, pink lustre neck/flowers, HP copper base, trim, 3"...22.00
Creamer, wht band w/bl stripes/emb copper foliage, 6¾".......45.00
Creamer, yel bkbround, 'LaFayette Crowned at Yorktown', 4"..500.00
Cup & saucer, bl bands, mk England, #10/199, 1½"; 2½" dia..12.00
Goblet, gr band w/lustre decor scene w/boats, 4".............37.00
Goblet, peach color band w/2 wht reserves of enamel flowers....45.00
Mug, w/yellow band, early, 2¾x2½" dia....................45.00
Pitcher, canary band w/wht ovals, red lady/child, 5"..........55.00
Pitcher, coaching scene, Gray's Pottery, 2¼"...............12.00
Pitcher, enameled ovals of gr/bl/orange, rim flakes, 8"........30.00
Pitcher, rust band w/emb mc cherubs/ram, 6¾".............30.00
Pitcher, water; Adam Buck print/HP trim, 1850.............250.00
Pitcher, wht band w/chariots, minor damage, 9".............75.00

Teapot, elaborate multifloral enamel decor, footed, fancy spout and handle, 8", $295.00.

Salt, footed, tan band w/blue dots & lustre foliage, 2x3″ 40.00
Salt, ftd, putty band w/lustre foliage & bl blossoms, 2x3″ 45.00
Salt, wht band w/pink & purple lustre house, pr. 95.00
Shaker, wht band w/gr/orange floral enamel, 3½″ 55.00
Spill holder, pink/purple band w/house, stains, 4½″ 50.00

Coralene Glass

Coralene is a unique type of art glass easily recognized by the tiny grains of glass that form its decoration. Lacy allover patterns of seaweed, geometrics, and florals were used, as well as solid forms such as fish, plants, and single blossoms. It was made by several glass houses, both here and abroad.

Cologne, seaweed, opaque w/bl decor, 6¾″ 220.00
Mug, amber w/orange seaweed beading, turq hdls, 2″ 200.00
Tumble-up, cranberry w/snowflake pattern, w/tumbler 200.00
Tumbler, seaweed pattern, shaded pink, 4″ 150.00
Vase, bl to wht w/overall yel coral-like beading, 4″ 300.00
Vase, coral beading on frost, w/enamel decor, 8″ 300.00
Vase, cranberry, 3 clear scroll ft, scalloped top, floral, 10″ 295.00
Vase, doughnut form, mc florals & gr leaves on rose, 'Pat', 8″ . .200.00

Pitcher, shaded yellow cased in white with gold seaweed decor, 8¾″, $495.00.

Cordey

The Cordey China Company was founded in Trenton, New Jersey, in 1942, by Boleslaw Cybis. They produced figurines, vases, lamps, and similar wares, much of which was marketed through gift shops both nationwide and abroad.

Cordey figurines and busts were characterized by old world charm, Rococo scrolls, delicate floral appliques, ruffles, and lace. Cybis developed his own formula for a porcelain composition which he called 'Papka', and was the first ceramist in America to use real lace dipped in liquified clay to add dimension to his work. After each piece was hand trimmed and painted it was assigned a number, either impressed or imprinted in the base, and was marked the second time to indicate the artist decorator.

After Cybis developed a true porcelain body in the early 1960s, he founded the Cybis studio where excellent limited edition porcelain figurines

were produced. For a few years both types of ware were made concurrently, then Cordey was phased out.

See also Cybis

Ash tray, #8019. . . . . .20.00
Bust, #4050, blk top hat, orange turban, lace scarf, cape, 7″. . . .85.00
Bust, #4140, lady w/lace around collar, elaborate hair, 12″. 100.00
Bust, #5001, Junior Prom figure, 1 leaf broken, 5¾″. 35.00
Bust, #5004, Chantillon figure, 6¼″. 40.00
Bust, #5007, lady. 65.00
Bust, #5011, girl w/gold roses in hair, JD, 6″. 45.00
Bust, #5013-164, lady, 6″. 70.00
Bust, #5013-36, lady, blue scroll encircling base, 5½″. 85.00
Bust, #5020, French gentleman, 6½″. 50.00
Bust, #5026, lace wrap, pink roses, wide hat, 7½″. 55.00
Bust, #5027, Jr Miss, bl shawl, 7½″. 65.00
Bust, #5034, Colonial man, feathered hat. 46.00
Bust, #8037, Victorian man/top hat, wht, minor damage, 16″. . .125.00
Candlestick, #7032, 8¼″, pr. 85.00
Figurine, #300 & #303, male & female, 16″, pr. 225.00
Figurine, #3004, lady w/lace/roses, gold trim, 6¾″. 80.00
Figurine, #305, Grape Harvester, 16″. 90.00
Figurine, #306, lady, scrolled base, 15¾″. 110.00
Figurine, #4087D, lace trim jabot/cuffs, w/cane/bouquet, 16″. . .135.00
Figurine, #5037, ¾ figure, roses on hat, lace skirt, 9½″. 90.00
Figurine, #5041, Monsieur, 11″. .120.00
Figurine, #5050, lady w/lg hat, roses & lace, sgnd, 7½″. 70.00
Figurine, #5059, girl of Sophisticated Group, 10¾″. 75.00
Figurine, #5061, Dubarry, 14″. .225.00
Figurine, #5084, Madame, 11¾″. 120.00
Figurine, #5090, male, full color, fine detail, 11″. 95.00
Figurine, #6023, bird in stump, yel/blk, ornate flowers, 9″. 100.00
Lamp, figurines #5041 & 5084, on brass bases, ornate, pr. 225.00
Lamp, gold scrolls/swirls, 3 legs, knobby stem, ball body, 9″. . . .30.00
Lamp, Marie Antoinette/Louis XVI, pr. 145.00
Lamp, w/figurine #5026 on base, 21″. 75.00
Shoe. 55.00
Swan, #7066, ornate vase, festooned neck, EX detail, 8¾″. . . .290.00
Vase, Oriental lady in relief, #7090, 8¾″. 100.00
Wall mask, face. 150.00

Bust, French gentleman, original sticker, 6½″, $50.00.

Cosmos

Cosmos, sometimes called Stemless Daisy, is a patterned glass tableware produced from 1894 through 1915 by Consolidated Lamp and Glass Company. Relief molded flowers on a fine cross-cut background were painted in soft colors of pink, blue, and yellow. Though nearly all were made of milk glass, a few items may be found in clear glass, with the designs painted on. In addition to the tableware, lamps were also made.

Butter dish...200.00
Cologne bottle, EX decor..............................150.00
Creamer, pink band....................................140.00
Lamp, clear w/pnt flowers, miniature...................60.00
Lamp, kerosene banquet, 24"...........................475.00
Lamp, milk glass w/pk band, 15".......................410.00
Pickle castor...335.00
Pickle castor insert w/orig SP collar, pk band, EX....135.00
Pitcher, water; pink band, 9".........................175.00
Shakers, pk band, 3", pr...............................85.00
Sugar w/lid, pink band................................185.00
Water set, pk band, 7 pc..............................495.00

Butter dish, 8", $200.00.

Coverlets

The Jacquard loom, made in the early 1800s in France, made possible the production of intricately woven coverlets in various designs. They were made of wool, both dyed and natural, from patterns punched into paper cards that indicated the colors of woof and warp necessary to develop the motif.

Soon after 1820, the Jacquard loom was brought to this country, and by 1840 was standard equipment for every professional weaver. Pictorial designs once reserved for the wealthy became available at modest prices. The old geometrics were replaced by florals, eagles, and elaborate medallion patterns. The new process enabled the weaver to sign and date his work, though not all names refer to the artist. It was also a common practice to weave the new owner's name into the corner of the coverlet.

In America the earliest pattern-woven coverlets were made around 1820 at the Colonel Rutger's Works of Brunswick, New Jersey. Often used to cover the dead for burial, they became known as 'corpse coverlets'. Usually buried with the departed, true examples of this type of coverlet are rarely found today.

Angels, jacquard, 1 pc, red/blk, Victorian, M................225.00
Bird & rose border, sgn corners, 1839, 2 pc single weave, G...150.00
Central medallion, vintage border, 4 color, label, 1 pc single...285.00
Central star medallion, red/bl/gr/wht, 1 pc single jacquard......200.00
Checkerboard in bl/red/wht, 2 pc dbl, sm holes/rpr............95.00
Crossed roses devices/stars, eagle corners, bl/wht, 1852........775.00
Deer/eagle/capitol dome, bl/wht, 2 pc dbl, Ithica, 1845.......1,300.00
Deer/eagles/capitol dome, Ithica Factory/'45, bl/wht, 2 pc dbl..1,300.00
Eagle & Liberty borders, sgn, 1833, 2 pc dbl, 74x87".........475.00
Eagle border, floral medallion, 1833, 2 pc dlb, 80x92".......350.00
Eagles in spandrels of design, 5 colors, 1 pc single, worn.....155.00
Five patch sq, dbl weave, red/bl/wht, 2 pc, 72x80"...........275.00
Floral, bird border, navy/beige, jacquard, sgn 1848, 92x73"....385.00
Floral, bl/wht, 1 pc dbl weave jacquard, fringed, 82x92"......185.00
Floral, blue/wht, 2 pc dbl weave jacquard, 72x84"............205.00
Floral, dbl rows of bldgs, red/bl/wht, 2 pc jacquard, 72x82"...300.00
Floral, flower basket border, 3 color, 1 pc single, 1852......245.00
Floral, vintage border, sgn corners, 1847, 2 pc single........350.00
Floral, 2 pc single weave jacquard, bl/wht, worn, 70x90".....150.00
Floral & star medallions, urn w/flower border, 1849, 1 pc, G...300.00
Floral devices & notched circles, 2 pc single, 4 color, 1839....185.00
Floral medallions, bird borders, 1837, bl/wht, 2 pc single.....575.00
Governor's Garden, bl/wht, 1840s........................200.00
Jacquard, dlb, red stars/gold & bl leaves/tan border, sgn/dtd....750.00
Leaf medallions, vintage border, 2 pc, red/wht/navy/teal, worn..150.00
Lg central floral medallion, 4 colors, 1 pc single, minor wear...125.00
Lovebirds, 2 eagles, positive front/negative bk, 3 color, VG...1,000.00
Medallions alternate w/Xs, 2 pc jacquard, bl/wht, 1833, 72x82".155.00
Overshot, bl/red/wht, 2 pc, minor wear, 70x94"..............200.00
Overshot, br/wht/dk rose, worn, 60x90"....................100.00
Overshot, gr/wht/pumpkin, fringe, minor wear, 2 pc, 80x92"...150.00
Overshot, red, 2 shades bl, wht, 2 pc, 68x90"...............300.00

One-piece single weave Jacquard, central star medallion; red, blue, green, and white, 80" x 96", $200.00.

Pine tree & snow flakes, bl/red/wht, 2 pc dbl weave, worn, 82".250.00
Pinwheels in bl/red on wht, overshot, 2 pc, 82x88", G.......125.00
Rose medallion, bird/house borders dtd 1842, 2 pc dbl, worn...200.00
Rose medallion, bl/red/wht, 2 pc dbl jacquard, 80x86".......350.00
Rose medallion, bl/red/wht, 2 pc single jacquard, 90" sq......200.00
Rose medallion, dtd 1839, bl/wht single jacquard.........250.00
Rose medallion w/rose border, navy/beige, sgn 1847, 90x75"...495.00
Snowflake & pine tree, bl/wht, 2 pc dbl, worn/stains, 76x84"...105.00
Snowflake & pine tree, bl/wht, 2 pc dbl, 74x97"...........325.00
Snowflake & pine tree border, red/wht/bl, 2 pc dbl, worn.....235.00
Snowflake design, 2 pc single weave, minor wear, 72x80".....150.00
Star flower medallions, vintage border, 2 pc single jacquard...300.00
Star/flower center, bird border, 1848, bl/red/wht, 2 pc dbl, G...150.00
Tulip medallions, vining tulip border, dtd 1852, 2 pc single....350.00
Vases w/flowers w/scroll leaf border, red/wht, single weave.....300.00
Vintage & birds, 2 pc dbl weave jacquard, bl/wht, worn, 84"...225.00
Vintage border, bl/red/wht, 1862, 2 pc single weave jacquard...300.00
Vintage border, floral wreaths w/4 rose medallions, 2 pc.......225.00
Washington/horses/eagles/1869/etc, 4 colors, 2 pc single, G....145.00

Cowan

Guy Cowan opened a small pottery near Cleveland, Ohio, in about 1912, where he made tile and art ware on a small scale from the natural red clay available there. He developed distinctive glazes -- necessary, he felt, to cover the dark red body. After the war and a temporary halt in production, Cowan moved his pottery to Rocky River, where he made a commercial line of art ware utilizing a highly fired white porcelain. Although he acquiesced to the necessity of mass production, every effort was made to insure a product of highest quality. Fine artists, among them Waylande Gregory, Thelma Frazier Winter, and Viktor Schreckengost, molded figurines which were often produced in limited editions, some of which sell today for upwards of $1,000. Most of the ware was marked 'Cowan' or 'Lakewood', not to be confused with the name of the 1927 mass produced line called 'Lakeware'. Falling under the crunch of the Great Depression, the pottery closed in 1931.

Vase, exotic foliage decor, signed Waylande Gregory, 1930, 10", $600.00.

Ash tray, bird figural, pk, sgn.........................37.50
Bookend, Sunbonnet Girls, ivory, pr....................250.00
Bookend, unicorn, green hi-glaze, pr...................250.00
Bowl, B-6, w/S-6 candle holders, Etruscan, blue, 3 pc........110.00
Bowl, bl lustre, 2¼x7¼"..............................25.00
Bowl, blue lustre, #538, 11¾x4½x3¼"..................47.00
Bowl, console, pink w/in, cream w/out, 3x12".............20.00
Bowl vase, Lakeware 1928-31, blue/gr, 2¾" opening, 3½".....18.00
Bud vase, seahorse, #725, pink, 7¼"....................30.00
Candelabra, #751, ivory, oval, pr......................45.00
Candle holder, bl lustre, 6x3½", pr....................30.00
Candle holder, bulbous, ivory, #681, 3¾", pr...........18.00
Candle holder, bulbous, ivory, #692, 2¼", pr...........15.00
Candle holder, Byzantine, Guava yellow, pr.............275.00
Candle holder, flower shape, ivory, #735, 4¼", pr.......30.00
Candle holder, seahorse, ivory, #716, 4", pr...........20.00
Candle holder, tulip, ivory, #940, 4", pr..............24.00
Candy compote, seahorse, gr/ivory, #724, 3½"...........22.00
Candy dish, #951, gr/ivory, 2½".......................20.00
Cigarette holder, seahorse, ivory.....................20.00
Compote, lt gr w/in, buff w/out, 4x9".................24.00
Flower frog, #686, ivory, 6½".........................100.00
Flower frog, #698, ivory, by Walter Sinz, 6½"..........135.00
Flower frog, nude, #680..............................110.00
Jardiniere, Alice in Wonderland on turq, Waylands, 12", rpr..2,200.00
Sculpture, Russian peasant, tan crackle glaze, A Blazys, #d....350.00
Soap dish, seahorse base, bl, sgn, 4".................30.00
Strawberry planter, Oriental red, 8"..................90.00
Teapot, wht, 7¼".....................................60.00
Vase, Art Deco 6 sides, gr w/gold specks, 6"............35.00
Vase, bl gloss w/gr mushrooms, full body, 5¼"..........85.00
Vase, bl lustre, ribbed, 11½".........................40.00
Vase, center divider, V-783, pink, 6".................45.00
Vase, fan shape, seahorses at base, blue lustre, 7"......50.00
Vase, matt gr crystalline, 11".......................95.00
Vase, nasturtium, dk gr, 2 hdls, Logan Medal Award, 1924.....60.00
Vase, orange lustre, #591, 7½".......................36.00
Vase, seahorse, #715B, wht, no mk, 8".................35.00
Vase, spotted gr & pink shades to all pink, 4¾x4½".........60.00

Cracker Jacks

F.W. Ruekeim and his brother Louis, German immigrants who settled in Chicago, Illinois, in 1871, opened a small popcorn stand and from this unpretentious inception founded a giant confectionary industry that has continued to flourish until the present day. It was during the 1893 Columbian Exposition that they introduced their famous product, Cracker Jacks. Though first marketed in wax-lined tin containers, a specially designed wax-sealed box was in use by the turn of the century. The sailor boy and his dog, Bingo, were created in 1916, and with only slight modifications are still in use as the familiar Cracker Jack logo.

In 1910 and 1911, the boxes carried coupons redeemable for premiums. The first toys were packed inside the boxes in 1912. Since then about 10,000 different prizes -- more than 16 billion in all -- have been distributed. At one time, toys were imported from Hong Kong and Japan, but all are now made in America. In addition to the toy prizes, collectors also value early advertisements and cartons.

Cast Metal

Angelus horse & wagon, 3-D, gold or silver, CJ, 2½".........85.00
Angelus thimble, aluminum w/red paint fill, CJ............42.00
Animals w/shoes, tools, pipe, etc, no mk, about 1"............2.50
Cars, trolleys, trains, bikes, etc, no mk, about 1"............3.75

Coin set, Presidential; 31 pc, aluminum, CJ................10.00
Dollhouse items: lantern, tray, mug, candle, etc, no mk.......12.00
Stand-up flats w/base, colored, not game piece, no mk........17.50
Stud button, crossed bats & ball, 'Pitcher'................48.00
Tootsie toy series, boats, cars, animals, 1-3", CJ.............8.25
Wings, Air Corps, blk or silver, CJ, 3"...................35.00

Paper

Ad, from comic book...........................10.00
Ad, Saturday Evening Post, 1918-1920..................22.00
Book, CJ Animals to Color.........................48.00
Book, CJ Birds to Color..........................48.00
Book, CJ Riddles Book: Boy & Dog, RWB...............28.00
Book, CJ Riddles Book: Jester, RYBK.................30.00
Book, drawing; CJ.............................40.00
Book, Jackie's Friends, miniature, CJ, ea..............38.00
Book, Stories of the Presidents, series of 6 mini books, CJ.....38.00
Book, Uncle Sam's Famous National Songs, CJ............38.00
Bookmark, bulldog, CJ..........................9.25
Card, riddle; series of 20, CJ......................12.00
Cards, baseball; score counter, CJ...................95.00
Cards, baseball; 1906 & 1907 series, CJ...............32.00
Hat, overseas vendor cap, RWB, CJ...................68.00
Letter heads & envelopes, 1900-1920, CJ...............60.00
Mask, Halloween, 10" or 12".......................37.50
Movies, pull tab for 2nd picture, CJ, about 3"...........48.00
Post card, bear series, 1907, CJ, ea.................14.00
Puzzles: envelope w/metal puzzle, series of 15, CJ, ea.......22.00
Spinner w/string, rectangle, CJ.....................22.00
Spinner w/string, 1½" round, CJ....................22.00
Toy, jumping frog, CJ..........................10.00

Plastic

Baseball players & spacemen, 3-D, CJ.................8.50
Fob, alphabet letter, CJ.........................5.00
Nosco, rocking base, animals & people, CJ..............4.50
Nosco, stand-up semi-flat animals & people, CJ...........1.75
Railroad train engine & cars, plastic, 3-D, CJ, about 2".......9.50

Tin

Angelus truck, ad on ea side, 1½", CJ................28.00
Bank, book shape, Vol 1, gr, 2", CJ..................48.00
CJ Band, gold or silver, Hummer, 1¾" dia..............34.00
CJ Show, circus animals in cage, RBY, 1¾"..............34.00
Clicker, Noisy Cracker Jack, tear-shape, CJ, 2"...........17.50
Comic characters, oval stand-ups, CJ, 2"...............47.50
Die-cut, boy & dog, RBW, 2"......................22.00
Die-cut, boy & dog, w/bend over tabs in place, CJ..........48.00
Doll dish, silver/gold, CJ, 1¾"....................25.00
Doll plate, silver, CJ, 2".........................25.00
Horse & wagon..............................15.00
Knife, Our Boy Sailor, 2¾".......................90.00
Lunch box.................................14.00
Model T Ford, NY 1916 #999, B & W, CJ, 2"............58.00
Pocket watch, silver/gold, CJ, 1½"..................32.00
Sulky, 2 wheels, 5" w/stick, CJ....................10.00
Top, Fortune Teller, CJ.........................45.00
Tops, variety of types.........................22.00
Train engine & tender #512, RBW, CJ, 2"..............35.00
Tray, toy; w/picture of package, large, CJ..............60.00
Two toppers, CJ.............................45.00

Whistle, 'Life Saver', CJ, 1¼" dia...................42.00
Whistle, close end w/fingers, ID etched, CJ..............37.50
Whistle, close end w/fingers, ID in relief, CJ.............22.00
Whistle, enameled twin tune, CJ, 2½"................37.50

Crackle Glass

Crackle glass (or craquelle) was made during the 1800s in America as well as abroad. The name is derived from the crackled texture of the ware, achieved either by plunging the hot glass into cold water, or by rolling it in small particles of broken glass which fuse to the surface upon reheating.

Basket, applied ornate hdl, 9x6"...................30.00
Basket, clear w/vaseline, applied hdl, scalloped, 8x7½".......85.00
Goblet, gr/gold snake stem, lg.....................65.00
Pitcher, amberina, bulbous, rnd mouth, amber hdl, 7¾".....200.00
Pitcher, jug type, ice bl w/amber hdl, 2 qt.............125.00
Rose bowl, bl/wht, miniature.....................68.00
Vase, amber, blown, dimpled, 5½"..................17.50
Vase, applied bl flowers, 18".....................35.00
Vase, cranberry, 7½", pr.........................90.00

Pitcher, clear with green handle and finial, 10", $50.00.
Tumbler, footed, 5½", $12.00.

Cranberry

Cranberry glass is named for its resemblence to the color of cranberry juice. It was made by many companies, both here and abroad, becoming popular in America soon after the Civil War. It was made in both free-blown ware as well as mold-blown. Today, cranberry glass is being reproduced, and it is sometimes difficult to distinguish the old from the new. Ask a reputable dealer if you are unsure.

Bell, clear hdl, green clapper, 12x5½"...............185.00
Biscuit jar, panel molded, clear ball lid finial, 7½".........115.00
Bowl, applied crystal feet, fluted edges, flint, old, 4x6" dia....100.00
Bowl, ruffled, 9½" dia.........................95.00
Bowl, 3 clear ft/berry pontil/berries & 3 fans at top, 5½"......265.00
Bud vase, ruffled top..........................98.00
Chalice w/lid, portrait of girl, enameled, 16"............275.00

Condiment set, 3 bottles, SP crescent moon fr, 5½x7"........150.00
Cruet, clear ft/hdl/faceted stopper, gold flowers, 7"..........135.00
Cruet, cranberry bubble stopper, cut star base, 10½"........195.00
Cruet, Inverted Thumbprint, clear reed hdl/cut stopper, 6".....95.00
Decanter, cut to clear, w/mushroom stopper.................225.00
Decanter, enamel wht flowers/gold leaves, cut stopper, 9½"....125.00
Dish, clear applied rim decor, in 7" dia SP fr, 2x4½"........95.00
Ewer, bottle form, enamel flowers, clear hdl, 8½x4½".......165.00
Ferner, in brass holder w/cherubs hdls, King Tut ft, 4x10".....265.00
Finger bowl, Thumbprint, in orig basket w/leaves holder.......95.00
Finger bowl, w/plate, gold vines/butterfly/pk florals, Webb.....375.00
Finger bowl, w/under plate, hexagonal......................55.00
Jar w/lid, 4 clear berry prunts & ball finial, 5x3½"..........110.00
Nappy, ftd, clear hdl, ruffled serrated rim, pnt floral, 5½".....48.00
Pitcher, clear hdl, 7½"..................................200.00
Pitcher, jug type, clear hdl, pt...........................135.00
Pitcher, tankard; Invert T'print, decor, clear/braided hdl, 9"....295.00
Pitcher, yel florals, gold leaves/trim, clear applied hdl, 4".......95.00
Pitcher, 3 clear ft & hdl, 6½"...........................155.00
Planter, rectangular, w/crystal thorn ft, 2¾x2¼x7"..........175.00
Rose bowl, threaded, gold trim, ruffled, 3"..................55.00
Shade, Hobnail, fluted top, 4" fitter......................135.00
Sugar shaker, cut panels w/blocks at top, 5½".................68.00
Sweetmeat, crystal ruffled rim/applied shells, SP basket, 5¾"...110.00
Syrup, Spanish Lace....................................97.50
Tumbler, enamel decor, inside ribs, blown...................18.00
Tumbler, gold enameling w/bl roses........................38.00
Urn, w/lid; sanded gold leaves, enamel floral, ped base, 11"....300.00
Vase, bulbous, ruffled top, 5½", pr.........................50.00
Vase, crystal leaves at top & base, 8½"....................110.00
Vase, flattened oval, gold scroll ft, 2 cupids, 6x4"...........225.00
Vase, gold enameled leaf decor, 9"........................50.00
Vase, Jack-in-Pulpit, clear ft & stem, 12½x5"...............145.00
Vase, ribbed, pinched near top & base, wht pnt florals, 3½"....35.00
Vase, sanded gold leaves, wht pnt floral, bl dots, 8¾", pr.....375.00
Vase, slender neck, flared rim, 7x4"........................45.00
Vase, wht lilies of valley decor, gold trim, stick neck, 10¾"....125.00
Watering can, clear spout/hdl, gold flowers, butterflies, 8½"....600.00
Wine, stars cut overall & on border, clear stem & ft, 6 for.....325.00

Box, enameled florals, gold leaves; hinged lid and ormolu foot, 3¼", $195.00.

Crown Devon

Crown Devon was the trade name of S. Fielding and Company, Ltd., an English firm founded about 1879. They produced majolica, earthenware, and pottery mugs, vases, and kitchenware. In the 1930s they manufactured an exceptional line of Art Deco vases that have recently been much in demand.

Biscuit jar, w/hdls, SF & Co, mk Pendant..................75.00
Condiment set on tray, gray w/pk/lav florals, S&P, mustard pot..50.00
Cookie jar, Chef, bl/wht striped pants, w/rolling pin & spoon....35.00
Humidor, ships, lustre/enamel, sgn........................95.00
Jam jar, gray w/florals, matching spoon, 4½x3½"............40.00
Pitcher, beige w/pk & bl floral in wide center band, SP lid.....90.00
Pitcher, John Peel relief, 1925, 9".........................25.00
Urn, w/lid; coral to ivory w/garlands & rose baskets, 9¼".......80.00

Crown Milano

Crown Milano was introduced in 1884 by the Mt. Washington Glass Company. When the company merged with Pairpoint in 1894, it continued to be one of their best sellers. It is an opaque, highly decorated ware, with gold or colored enamels in intricate designs on pale backgrounds, nearly always in a satin finish. Many pieces are marked 'CM' with a crown.

Jam jar, enameled florals, silverplated lid and handle, 3½", $750.00.

Biscuit jar, cream w/mottling, heavy gold threads, melon ribs..1,150.00
Biscuit jar, enamel floral on acid, SP top/bail, sgn, 7"........950.00
Biscuit jar, heavy gold florals, SP top, paper label, 6½".......850.00
Biscuit jar, pebbles, starfish, jewels, blown-out..............1,250.00
Biscuit jar, squat, Fuji mums, plated lid, sgnd...............650.00
Box, hinged cover, florals, gold, brass collar, sgnd...........600.00
Calling card tray, 2 sides rolled, fan shape, bird decor/gold.....135.00
Cockle shell salt, white w/florals, shaker top, 2¾"...........495.00
Ewer, HP relief gold decor, twisted rope hdl, unmkd, 13"....1,100.00
Ewer, lt gr w/gr & gold water lilies, dolphin hdl, sgnd.......1,950.00
Ewer, rnd/flattened, shepherd/flock; verso church, rope hdl...2,500.00
Ewer, sheep scenic, rope twist hdl, sgn, #504, 10".........1,350.00
Lamp, melon base, metal ft w/leaves/acorns, w/shade, 18".....550.00
Marmalade, pastel pansies, silverplated lid w/butterfly.........895.00
Mustard, florals, plated lid & handle.....................650.00

Pickle castor, floral enameling, elegant ftd stand w/fork, 10″..1,050.00
Sugar shaker, melon rib, floral enameled, 2½x3½″..........400.00
Sweetmeat, sgn Mt Washington, worn lid..................450.00
Tray, spray of lilacs, 2 rolled edges, scallops, shiny, 7½″.....345.00
Tumbler, florals & gold.................................385.00
Vase, allover floral/scroll in lav, Colonial boy & girl, 13¾″....1,100.00
Vase, frolicking cherubs, gold scrolls, stick neck, 13″........2,450.00
Vase, stick neck, bulbous base, gold floral, sgn, 9″..........1,200.00
Vase, 4 mallards fly over gold wheat, Frank Guba, shiny, 17″.3,750.00

Cruets

Cruets, containers made to hold oil or vinegar, are usually bulbous with tall narrow throats and a stopper. During the 19th century and for several years after, they were produced in abundance, in virtually every type of glassware available.

Alabama, orig stopper....................................55.00
Alaska, green w/gold, clear stopper, rare..................255.00
Argonaut Shell, custard, w/EX gold, not orig stopper........265.00
Balder..20.00
Beaded Grape, green, orig stopper........................95.00
Bellaire Basketweave, blue w/clear stopper................95.00
Bevelled Diamond & Star, clear, w/orig stopper............25.00
Blazing Cornucopia, cranberry eyes, orig stopper, M........85.00
Block..20.00
Block & Fan, large......................................29.50
Block w/Stars...16.00
Broken Column, w/orig stopper............................80.00
Bubble Lattice on Panelled Sprig, clear opal..............95.00
Cathedral, amber, w/orig stopper.........................55.00
Clear Circle, w/orig stopper.............................45.00
Cord Drapery, amber, w/orig stopper.....................285.00
Cranberry, clear hdl, faceted stopper, 5¾″................95.00
Cranberry Swirl, tri-cornered spout, clear stopper.......125.00
Cut Log, orig stopper, 5½″...............................45.00
Daisy & Button, amber w/amber stopper...................100.00
Daisy & Button, blue....................................90.00
Daisy & Button w/Crossbars, clear........................28.00
Daisy & Fern, blue opal, orig stopper.....................95.00
Daisy & Fern, clear to opal..............................55.00
Daisy & Fern, vaseline opal, applied rib hdl, clear stopper......65.00
Dewey, amber, w/orig stopper............................100.00
Dewey, green, w/orig stopper............................135.00
Diamond Ridge, clear, Duncan.............................65.00
Dice & Block, amber, orig stopper........................75.00
Esther, green & gold, w/stopper.........................125.00
Fancy Loop, clear, Heisey................................80.00
Fluted Scroll, vaseline opal w/enamel decor, clear stopper.....135.00
Forget-Me-Not, milk glass, 4¼″...........................35.00
Frosted Wild Rose w/Bowknot, orig stopper...............125.00
Grape & Gothic Arches, w/nutmeg stain stopper............75.00
Herringbone, blown, blue opal, clear stopper..............85.00
Hobb's Hobnail, vaseline opal, w/clear stopper...........215.00
Hobnail, blue, w/clear stopper, old......................110.00
Hobnail, cranberry opal.................................200.00
Hobnail w/Bars, blue, w/clear stopper....................75.00
Hobnail w/Ribbed Base, rubena..........................145.00
Intaglio, blue opal......................................95.00
Intaglio, clear opal.....................................70.00
Inverted Thumbprint, blown, clear, 4¾″...................27.00
Inverted Thumbprint, blue, w/blown clear stopper..........95.00
Jackson, vaseline opal...................................95.00

Cranberry with clear twisted rope handle and neck band, clear faceted stopper, 5½″, $195.00.

Jeweled Heart, apple green, w/vaseline pattern glass stopper....125.00
Leaf Bracket, chocolate, Greentown, w/stopper...............95.00
Louis XV, custard, not orig stopper.......................145.00
Nestor, sapphire blue, w/orig blue cut glass stopper..........135.00
New Hampshire..23.00
Palm Leaf Fan...24.00
Panelled Diamond Block..................................28.00
Panelled Heather..24.00
Peacock & Feather.......................................25.00
Petticoat, vaseline......................................90.00
Portland..22.00
Pressed Diamond, amber w/amber stopper.................65.00
Queen Anne, clear, Heisey................................65.00
Queen Anne, Sahara, Heisey..............................95.00
Ribbed Thumbprint, green, clear stopper..................95.00
Royal Crystal...20.00
Rubena Verde..250.00
Seaweed, clear opal.....................................95.00
Shoshone, green, orig stopper............................75.00
Spatter, ruby & wht, clear base & hdl, 10″................135.00
Star in Bull's Eye, orig stopper..........................20.00
Stars & Bars, amber, orig stopper.........................80.00
Strigil...19.00
Stripe, vaseline opal, jug shape.........................145.00
Sturbridge, bl to wht, pk rigaree, wht stopper & applied hdl....115.00
Swirl, cranberry opal, w/orig stopper....................195.00
Tiny Optic, green, decorated, orig stopper.................85.00
Tokyo, apple green w/EX opalescence, orig stopper..........85.00
Twist Oceanic, Sahara, Heisey............................85.00

Cup Plates

In the early 1800s, it was the fashion to pour hot beverages from the cup into a deep saucer to cool before drinking. The cup plate was used as a coaster for the cup. While many companies made them, Sandwich was probably the largest manufacturer of the type called 'lacy'. Those made by Midwestern firms are identified by techniques, characteristics, and peculiarities of design attributed to that area.

Cup plates range in size from 2⅞″ up to 4″ on occasion. Early plates were simply styled, but by 1820 designs had become quite intricate. Hearts, spoked devices, wheat sheaves, and stars were popular patterns. Backgrounds became 'stippled', and eventually they took on the characteristics that are today known as 'lacy'.

Many cup plates portray historical events. Bunker Hill, Harrison's log cabin, statesmen, and presidents were featured. Others depict anchors, harps, beehives, and eagles. Condition is as always an important factor; though it is the rule, rather than the exception, that one must expect a certain amount of edge roughness, due to the intricate nature of the molds. More important in determining value is scarcity of design and color.

In these listings, numbers (computer sorted) refer to *American Cup Plates* by Ruth Webb Lee and James A. Rose.

See also Staffordshire; Pairpoint

Bunker Hill, emerald gr, probably Sandwich 475.00
Hairpin, clear, 3¾″ 15.00

Heart Variant, LR-212, $16.00.

LR-100A 35.00
LR-108, clear, rim chips, 3¾″ 25.00
LR-109 . . . . 14.00
LR-11, clear, rim chips, 2¾″ 10.00
LR-120, VG 48.00
LR-129, EX 40.00
LR-129, rim chips 18.00
LR-130, EX rare, VG 175.00
LR-136, clear, scarce, 3½″ 30.00
LR-136A, clear, edge flakes, 3½″ 18.00
LR-145C 22.00
LR-154A, 3¼″ 27.50
LR-156A, EX 50.00
LR-158B 48.00
LR-160A, 3¼″ 17.50
LR-162A, M 45.00
LR-164A, EX 35.00
LR-172B 20.00
LR-174, EX 35.00
LR-178B, clear, minor flakes, 3¼″ 18.00
LR-178B, gr tint 24.00
LR-179, rare, EX 65.00
LR-180A, clear, sm edge flakes, 3¼″ 15.00
LR-187, rare, G 80.00
LR-191B, clear, 3″ 12.00
LR-211, EX rare, VG 215.00
LR-22, 4¾″, EX 30.00
LR-223, EX 40.00

LR-243, 3½″ 22.50
LR-245 . . . . 30.00
LR-246, sm rim chips, 3½″ 12.50
LR-255 . . . . 25.00
LR-255, opal, 3½″ 40.00
LR-237 . . . . 22.00
LR-257A 40.00
LR-262 . . . . 20.00
LR-269C, EX 35.00
LR-270, rare, VG 55.00
LR-271 . . . . 22.00
LR-272, lt opal, 43 scallops, 3½″ 45.00
LR-275, clear, 3½″ 10.00
LR-276 . . . . 17.00
LR-281B, clear, 3″ 5.00
LR-285, M 45.00
LR-29, 1 scallop underfilled, VG 26.00
LR-300, 4″ 15.00
LR-313 . . . . 14.00
LR-313, gr tint, rare 85.00
LR-316, EX rare, 4 scallops tipped, G 140.00
LR-322, VG 20.00
LR-324 . . . . 12.00
LR-329 . . . . 19.00
LR-331 . . . . 25.00
LR-333 . . . . 12.00
LR-339 . . . . 15.00
LR-367A, rim chips, 3″ 15.00
LR-37 . . . . 48.00
LR-39, 3½″ 17.50
LR-390A 12.00
LR-391 . . . . 12.00
LR-396, EX 15.00
LR-41, clear, 3¼″ 27.00
LR-425, clear, 3½″ 22.50
LR-427 . . . . 15.00
LR-430 . . . . 22.00
LR-440 . . . . 18.00
LR-440, unlisted, 51 even scallops, opal 125.00
LR-440A 20.00
LR-440B, clear, 3½″, rare 18.00
LR-440B, opal, very rare, 3½″ 105.00
LR-440B, Sweetheart, cobalt, scarce 175.00
LR-441A, clear, 3″ 12.50
LR-447 . . . . 17.00
LR-448 . . . . 45.00
LR-458, clear, 12 hearts, sm edge chips, 3½″ 12.50
LR-465 . . . . 18.00
LR-465G 28.00
LR-465L, fiery opal 95.00
LR-467B, EX 25.00
LR-476 . . . . 16.00
LR-477 . . . . 35.00
LR-477A 17.00
LR-502, Sunburst, apple green, 3″ 60.00
LR-509, Sunburst, cobalt blue, lacy, rim chip, 3″ 75.00
LR-520 . . . . 18.00
LR-522, Sunburst, amber, lacy, rim chips, 3¼″ 55.00
LR-532 . . . . 18.00
LR-547, pebbly, EX 15.00
LR-563 . . . . 10.00
LR-564 . . . . 22.00
LR-565 . . . . 22.00
LR-565B 22.00

LR-565B, Henry Clay, electric blue, rim chips, 3½".........65.00
LR-575, fire polished, scarce, EX.............................75.00
LR-590..31.00
LR-593, 2 rim bubbles, 3¼".......................................35.00
LR-594..27.00
LR-595..55.00
LR-61..125.00
LR-61, fiery opal, rim check & chips, 3¼"......................150.00
LR-610, EX...45.00
LR-610A..12.00
LR-610B, Ship, sapphire blue, lacy, badly chipped, 3½"......70.00
LR-619..24.00
LR-624, scarce, 4"..30.00
LR-629, 3½"..15.00
LR-637, rim flakes, very rare, VG.............................255.00
LR-640..14.00
LR-641..15.00
LR-643..15.00
LR-65, clear, 3¼", scarce...25.00
LR-655, pebbly, 3 scallops tipped, VG.........................250.00
LR-659, milky..29.00
LR-66, EX..80.00
LR-660..17.00
LR-665, sm rim flakes, 3½".......................................40.00
LR-670-A, rim chips, 3½"..20.00
LR-671, opal, rare, 3½"..225.00
LR-676B, rim chips, 3¾"...28.00
LR-677..42.00
LR-679..22.00
LR-680..22.00
LR-69, VG..68.00
LR-691, scarce, 3¼"..35.00
LR-693..65.00
LR-803, 4½"...17.50
LR-890..12.00
LR-90, opaque opal, rare, 3¾".....................................95.00
LR-95, EX..40.00
LR-95, opaque opal, rare, 3½".....................................75.00
LR-97, minor edge roughness, VG.................................48.00
LR-98, 1 tiny nick, rare...68.00
Maid of the Mist, lt gr, probably Mid-Western...............275.00
Pinwheel Peacock Eye center, 3¼".................................10.00
Plume & Diamond rim, clear, edge flakes, 4".....................12.00
Rayed Peacock Eye, rim chips, 5¼"................................17.50
Star & Diamond, clear, Sandwich, some edge roughness......45.00
Sunburst, blue, lacy, minor rim flakes, unlisted..............80.00
Thirteen heart, opal, rim chips, 3½".............................20.00

Custard

As early as the 1880s, custard glass was produced in England. Migrating glassmakers brought the formula for the creamy ivory ware to America. One of them was Harry Northwood, who in 1898 founded his company in Indiana, Pennsylvania, and introduced the glassware to the American market. Soon other companies were producing custard, among them Heisey, Tarentum, Fenton, and McKee. Not only dinnerware patterns, but souvenir items were made. Today, custard is the most expensive of the colored pressed glassware patterns. The formula for producing the luminous glass contains uranium salts which imparts the cream color to the batch and causes it to glow when it is examined under a black light. Although not true custard in the strictest sense, the blue opaque version of Northwood's Chrysanthemum Sprig is listed here also.

See also specific manufacturers

Maple Leaf, tumbler, gold and green trim, 4", $90.00.

Apple & Fan, creamer, tankard, souvenir, ½ pint............65.00
Argonaut Shell, berry, small...................................45.00
Argonaut Shell, bowl, fruit; 5x10½" dia.....................125.00
Argonaut Shell, butter base only.............................175.00
Argonaut Shell, butter dish..................................260.00
Argonaut Shell, creamer..95.00
Argonaut Shell, pitcher, water; EX gold & enamel...........325.00
Argonaut Shell, spooner..95.00
Argonaut Shell, tumbler, w/good gold..........................82.50
Beaded Cable, rose bowl..90.00
Beaded Circle, butter dish....................................175.00
Beaded Circle, sugar w/lid, EX gold & enamel.................165.00
Beaded Shell, mug, sgn N..60.00
Beaded Swag, bowl, 4½"..30.00
Butterfly & Berry, vase, pink decor, 9".........................50.00
Cherry & Scale, butter, nutmeg stain.........................210.00
Cherry & Scale, pitcher.......................................325.00
Cherry & Scale, tumbler, nutmeg trim...........................55.00
Chrysanthemum Sprig, blue; celery............................825.00
Chrysanthemum Sprig, blue; creamer...........................360.00
Chrysanthemum Sprig, blue; cruet, EX gold....................675.00
Chrysanthemum Sprig, blue; spooner...........................340.00
Chrysanthemum Sprig, blue; toothpick.........................400.00
Chrysanthemum Sprig, blue; tumbler, M gold...................207.00
Chrysanthemum Sprig, bowl, berry; lg, oval...................225.00
Chrysanthemum Sprig, butter w/cover..........................275.00
Chrysanthemum Sprig, compote, ftd, plain......................85.00
Chrysanthemum Sprig, compote, jelly; EX gold & enamel......95.00
Chrysanthemum Sprig, creamer.................................100.00
Chrysanthemum Sprig, pitcher, water; w/EX gold & enamel....285.00
Chrysanthemum Sprig, shakers, pr.............................100.00
Chrysanthemum Sprig, spooner.................................125.00
Chrysanthemum Sprig, sugar, w/lid............................200.00
Chrysanthemum Sprig, tumbler, EX gold & enamel, 4".........75.00
Chrysanthemum Sprig, vinegar cruet...........................150.00
Cut Block, sugar, individual...................................35.00
Delaware, creamer, individual, w/EX rose decor................57.00
Delaware, pin tray, rose decor.................................60.00
Delaware, sauce, blue trim.....................................45.00
Delaware, tumbler, bue decor...................................60.00
Diamond w/Peg, creamer, rose decor, souvenir..................50.00
Diamond w/Peg, cup, w/red rose & gold..........................35.00
Diamond w/Peg, mug, w/red rose & gold, 3"......................50.00

Diamond w/Peg, sugar w/lid, roses decor/souvenir St Louis Fair.105.00
Diamond w/Peg, toothpick..................................50.00
Diamond w/Peg, tumbler, souvenir Reading PA, some gold.....40.00
Diamond w/Peg, water set, rose decor, 8″ pitcher+6 tumblers..325.00
Diamond w/Peg, wine, souvenir............................75.00
Diamond w/Peg, wine, stemmed, w/roses decor, not souvenir....50.00
Doric Column, candlestick, Cambridge, pr.................125.00
Drape, vase, nutmeg stain, Northwood, 12″................45.00
Everglades, tumbler, EX gold & enamel, gold rim...........110.00
Fan, table set, EX gold, 4 pc............................550.00
Festoon, pitcher, water; Northwood.......................55.00
Fine Cut & Roses, rose bowl, pinched top, nutmeg stain, 4″....85.00
Flute, dish, ruffled, ftd................................135.00
Geneva, berry set, oval, w/red & gr decor, 7 pc...........365.00
Geneva, bowl, master berry; gr/gold, oval.................95.00
Geneva, bowl, master berry; w/red & green decor, round.....125.00
Geneva, creamer, red/gr decor............................65.00
Geneva, jelly compote....................................75.00
Geneva, sauce, ftd.......................................35.00
Geneva, spooner, no decor................................45.00
Geneva, spooner, w/red & green decor.....................65.00
Geneva, sugar w/lid, w/red & green.......................120.00
Geneva, tumbler, w/gr & gold trim........................60.00
Georgia Gem, berry, sm...................................25.00
Georgia Gem, breakfast creamer & sugar, no decor..........75.00
Georgia Gem, butter w/cover..............................110.00
Georgia Gem, creamer.....................................40.00
Georgia Gem, cruet, orig stopper, gr trim................165.00
Georgia Gem, hair receiver, souvenir.....................50.00
Georgia Gem, pitcher, water; gr w/enamel florals, not souvenir..165.00
Georgia Gem, sugar.......................................45.00
Grape, berry, individual; on ped, Northwood..............45.00
Grape, plate, hexagonal, Northwood, 8″...................45.00
Grape & Cable, breakfast creamer & sugar, nutmeg stain.....110.00
Grape & Cable, sauce, on ped, nutmeg stain...............45.00
Grape & Cable, water set, nutmeg stain, 6 pc.............700.00
Grape & Gothic Arches, goblet, nutmeg stain..............50.00
Grape & Gothic Arches, rose bowl, ftd....................90.00
Grape & Gothic Arches, spooner, nutmeg stain.............70.00
Grape & Gothic Arches, sugar, open, worn gold............75.00
Grape & Gothic Arches, water set, nutmeg stain, 5 pc......325.00
Grape Arbor, vase, ruffled top, nutmeg stain, edge flake, 4″.....65.00
Hat, not souvenir, 2¾x4½″................................55.00
Honeycomb, wine..75.00
Intaglio, berry, small, ftd..............................50.00
Intaglio, bowl, fruit; green decor, ftd, lg..............200.00
Intaglio, butter w/cover, w/EX gold & blue...............235.00
Intaglio, compote, jelly; ftd, small.....................100.00
Intaglio, creamer, G gold/green..........................65.00
Intaglio, cruet, w/gr & gold trim........................275.00
Intaglio, pitcher..300.00
Intaglio, salt shaker, gold & gr decor...................85.00
Intaglio, spooner..35.00
Intaglio, sugar w/lid, decorated.........................120.00
Intaglio, table set, green decor, 4 pc...................445.00
Intaglio, tumbler, M gold & gr decor.....................55.00
Inverted Fan & Feather, berry, large.....................250.00
Inverted Fan & Feather, butter dish......................275.00
Inverted Fan & Feather, compote, jelly...................250.00
Inverted Fan & Feather, salt shaker......................125.00
Inverted Fan & Feather, spooner..........................110.00
Inverted Fan & Feather, tumbler, EX decor................85.00
Ivorina Verde, spooner, w/gold...........................80.00
Jackson, bowl, master berry..............................97.50

Jackson, pitcher, water..................................195.00
Jackson, shakers, w/goofus decor, pr.....................125.00
Jackson, tumbler...40.00
Lion, plate, w/green stain...............................75.00
Lotus & Grape, bon-bon, 2 hdls, pk stain.................30.00
Louis XV, berry bowl, gold trim, sm......................40.00
Louis XV, butter dish....................................175.00
Louis XV, creamer..75.00
Louis XV, cruet..125.00
Louis XV, master berry...................................175.00
Louis XV, pitcher, water.................................225.00
Louis XV, salt & pepper shakers, w/trace of gold, pr......165.00
Louis XV, spooner..80.00
Louis XV, sugar w/lid....................................125.00
Louis XV, table set, sugar & lid/butter & lid/creamer/spooner...450.00
Louis XV, tumbler..60.00
Louis XV, water set, EX gold, 7 pc.......................550.00
Maple Leaf, bowl, master berry...........................350.00
Maple Leaf, butter w/cover...............................185.00
Maple Leaf, creamer, gold & enamel decor.................80.00
Maple Leaf, spooner, w/good gold.........................85.00
Maple Leaf, sugar w/lid, gold & enamel decor.............140.00
Maple Leaf, table set, w/gold & enamel, 4 pc.............495.00
Maple Leaf, tumbler, M...................................90.00
Peacock & Dahlia, plate, gr stain........................95.00
Peacock & Urn, individual ice cream, nutmeg stain.........65.00
Peacock & Urn, master ice cream, nutmeg stain............250.00
Plate, lion, gr stain, 7½″...............................125.00
Poinsettia Lattice, bowl, satin w/dusty rose decor.......215.00
Punty Band, creamer, souvenir, Heisey....................32.00
Ring & Beads, creamer, individual, souvenir..............20.00
Ring Band, bowl, master berry, no decor..................50.00
Ring Band, butter, EX decor..............................170.00
Ring Band, creamer, souvenir.............................28.00
Ring Band, pitcher, State Fair, 1906.....................215.00
Ring Band, salt shaker, old lid..........................45.00
Ring Band, spooner, rose decor...........................85.00
Ring Band, sugar, w/lid, rose decor......................125.00
Ring Band, syrup, rose decor.............................275.00
Ring Band, tumbler, souvenir.............................65.00
Ring Band, water set, 7 pcs..............................595.00

Ring Band, pitcher, floral enameling, 7½″, $240.00.

Sawtooth Band, custard cup, no handles, Heisey, 2¼x2½".....55.00
Sawtooth Band, match holder...........................40.00
Smocking, bell...42.00
Vermont, celery dish, bl trim, floral center...............48.00
Victoria, spooner......................................58.00
Wild Bouquet, creamer................................115.00
Winged Scroll, berry set, 5 pc.........................240.00
Winged Scroll, card dish w/rolled edges..................85.00
Winged Scroll, cigarette holder, no gold................120.00
Winged Scroll, creamer.................................75.00
Winged Scroll, spooner, open, 2 hdls...................125.00
Winged Scroll, toothpick, gold decor...................110.00
Winged Scroll, tumbler.................................90.00

Cut Glass

The earliest documented evidence of commercial glass cutting in the United States was in 1810; the producers were Bakewell and Page of Pittsburgh. These first efforts resulted in simple patterns with only a moderate amount of cutting. By the middle of the century, glass cutters began experimenting with a thicker glass which enabled them to use deeper cuttings, though patterns remained much the same. This period is usually referred to as Rich Cut. Using three types of wheels -- a flat edge, a mitered edge, and a convex edge -- facets, mitres, and depressions were combined to produce various designs.

In the late 1870s, a curved mitre was developed which greatly expanded design potential. Patterns became more elaborate, often covering the entire surface.

The Brilliant Period of cut glass covered a span from about 1880 until 1915. Because of the pressure necessary to achieve the deeply cut patterns, only glass containing a high grade of metal could withstand the process. For this reason, and the amount of hand work involved, cut glass has always been expensive.

Bowl, allover cutting, 4x8"..............................85.00
Bowl, banana; Cosmos & Caning, 7½x11"..................60.00
Bowl, berry; hobstar & fan, serrated rim, 8"............160.00
Bowl, cane, lg fans, X-hatching, dbl hobstar base, 3¾x9"......155.00
Bowl, central hobstar/hobstar band w/fan/X-hatch edging, 10"..300.00
Bowl, elongated dia, rnd corners; cane, straw hobs, 10" L.....80.00
Bowl, flat base/cutting beneath, allover deep cut, Hoare, 10"...390.00
Bowl, floriform, Cosmos, 10".............................125.00
Bowl, flowers w/15 petals cutting, heavy, oval, 7½"..........45.00
Bowl, fruit; buzz star w/fine cut dia panels, 8" dia...........110.00
Bowl, grape vintage & chain of hobstars, unsgn Tuthill, 6".....250.00
Bowl, hobstar & caning, 8" dia...........................50.00
Bowl, hobstar & wheat, J Hoare, 1853, oval, 10½" L........550.00
Bowl, hobstar & wheat, shallow oval, 11½" L...............90.00
Bowl, hobstar & wheat, 8¼" sq..........................225.00
Bowl, hobstar & wheat, 9"..............................125.00
Bowl, hobstars/fans/X-hatching, serrated rim, shallow, Clarke...175.00
Bowl, Lotus pattern, sgn Egginton, low, 7"................125.00
Bowl, pinwheel & fan, sgn Clarke, 2x8"...................160.00
Bowl, pinwheel cutting, paper label, Thatcher Bros, 3½x7½"..120.00
Bowl, primroses, engraved berries/leaves, Pitkin/Brooks, 7".....60.00
Bowl, sawtooth & pineapple plume, deep, 9" dia............150.00
Bowl, sawtooth edge, fan & pinwheel, 7" dia...............65.00
Bowl, serrated/scalloped, pinwheels & fans, star base, 3x8"....180.00
Bowl, star & waffle, rim chip, 9¼".......................50.00
Bowl, star cutting, 8".................................110.00
Bowl, straw dia, minor rim chips on points, 9½"............60.00
Bowl, straw dia & fan, 3 sections.......................110.00
Bowl, sunburst cutting, 9"..............................180.00
Bowl, thistle & butterfly, 10" dia........................125.00

Teapot, ball form with floral design, signed Sinclair, 5½", $3,000.00.

Bowl, 3 lg sunbursts w/floral garland, silver rim, 9"..........160.00
Bowl, 5 lobed edge, 3x5"...............................100.00
Bowl, 8 sides w/Harvard variant, base: frosted floral, 10".....150.00
Bowl w/tray (chip), Russian cut, rectangular, 9x11"; 13x11"..1,700.00
Box, dresser; lg hobstar on top w/expanding rays, hinged lid...140.00
Box, handkerchief; intaglio flowers on hinged lid, sq.........310.00
Bucket, pinwheel & star, 5½x7".........................110.00
Butter dish, faceted hdl, flower/leaves/cane/hobnail, etc......285.00
Butter dish, Harvard & florals, domed top.................295.00
Butter dish, hobstar, allover cutting.....................200.00
Butter tub, cane, straw hobs, panels w/floral, cane base, 4½"..90.00
Candy dish, divided, w/hdls; bevels, prisms, hobstars, 9¼".....145.00
Candy dish, star & button, Averbeck, 6"...................42.50
Candy dish, star & floral, sgn Hoare, 6" dia...............60.00
Canoe, hobstars, 11"..................................235.00
Carafe, hobstars, dia points, notched prims, ray base, 7x6".....95.00
Carafe, stars, fans, bull's eyes, sgn Clarke, 8"............135.00
Carafe, straw & fan, 32 ray base, notched panel neck, 8".....85.00
Carafe, water; cranberry to clear, straw dia/fan, heavy, 6½"...325.00
Carafe, 24 ray base, notched neck, allover cutting, 7x6½".....95.00
Celery dish, allover hobstars, 11½" L....................80.00
Celery dish, brilliant cut, 5x11".........................125.00
Champagne, honeycomb w/engraved vintage band, 4½", set of 8.70.00
Cheese & cracker, dbl lozenge..........................200.00
Cheese dish, hobstar/straw/dia/fans/star block panels, 5½x8"...295.00
Chip-n-dip, 2 tier, floral rim, star base, 5" center compote.....165.00
Clock, rose bud, McKanna CG Co, 4x5½"..................115.00
Compote, buzz star & fan, zipper ped, 8".................125.00
Compote, cobalt cut to clear, 17".......................450.00
Compote, cranberry to clear, twist stem, flowers/leaves, 8x7"...125.00
Compote, gr/clear, ferns/flowers/thumbprint, clear stem, 7x8"..175.00
Compote, hobstar & blazed leaf, 32 point hobstar base........320.00
Compote, hobstar & diamonds, 12"......................175.00
Compote, hobstars, notched rim, 16 pt base, 6"............60.00
Compote, honeycomb w/engraved vintage band, 6x9½".......90.00
Compote, pineapple/dia, 8½"...........................200.00
Compote, star cutting, 5x5½"...........................65.00
Compote, strawberry dia/fan, shallow, 3x6"...............145.00
Compote, teardrop stem, brilliant period, 9¼x6"............255.00
Compote, teardrop stem, chain 5 ptd zipper stars/hobstars, 8"..265.00
Compote, teardrop stem w/thumbprints, wheel cut flowers, 8x6"..60.00
Compote, vesicas/hobstars/straw dia, w/4" center uncut, 3x8"...225.00
Creamer, stars, fans & dia, ray base, 4½"................30.00
Creamer & sugar, allover cut, hobstars/flashed stars/fans......125.00
Creamer & sugar, hobstar & notched prisms, pr.............90.00
Creamer & sugar, 24 ray base, notched hdls/rims, floral cut....125.00

Cruet, buzz star & dia, 6"..60.00
Cruet, fan cutting, faceted stopper, 6".........................60.00
Cruet, hobstars w/in pinwheels, X-hatching, ray base, 6"........45.00
Decanter, allover hobstars, fans, vesicas, facet stopper, 9".....165.00
Decanter, basketweave, honeycomb neck, notched hdl, 13"....650.00
Decanter, cane pattern, 16 pt base, lg faceted stopper, 8", VG...85.00
Decanter, Harvard, floral, bowling pin shape, 13½"...........435.00
Decanter, silver repousse/pierced foliate overlay, 9"..........625.00
Dish, diamond, shallow rectangular, 10½" L, pr..............150.00
Dish, divided boat; cut/etched floral, rope/star band, 7x5½"....100.00
Dish, heart shape, hobstars/vesica w/star center/fan, 8x1½".....95.00
Dish, 4 pt, leaves & 12 petal flower, dbl notched hdls, 7"......60.00
Ferner, hobstars & fluted fans, 4x7¾".........................85.00
Goblet, balloon shape, 3 color enamel decor w/ruby jewels......75.00
Ice bucket, brilliant cut, sgn w/maple leaf, 6"................275.00
Ice bucket, overall cutting, 7x5"..............................295.00
Inkwell, sterling lid, repousse decor, mk Dominick & Hall, 2½".115.00
Jam jar w/under plate, sterling cover/ladle, panel cut, 3x5½"....75.00
Knife rest, barbell shape, stars on end, 3½"...................28.00
Knife rest, pattern cut on both ends, 4½".....................50.00
Knife rest, tapered ends, fan w/X-hatch dia...................30.00
Lamp, bun font, trumpet std w/fruit relief/putti/birds, 29".....750.00
Lamp, leaf & diamond, brass fittings, electric, 14½".........225.00
Loving cup, 3 hdls, repousse sterling top, notched prism.....325.00
Muffineer, corset shape, allover cut, repousse sterling top.....200.00
Napkin ring, hobstars..70.00
Nappy, ring hdl, fans, X-hatching, 7" dia.....................40.00
Nappy, ring hdl, scalloped/serrated, G cutting, heavy, 6".......38.00
Nappy, w/hdl, hobstar & dia, 2¼x6½".........................40.00
Nappy, w/hdl, prisms & flash stars, 6"........................45.00
Perfume, dbl, lay-down, ornate sterling caps, 4½"...........125.00
Perfume, globular, pinwheels, sgn Clarke, 7½x4½"...........145.00
Petit-fors stand, Conner's Split Square, 7x3"................290.00
Pitcher, buzz star & fan, 8".................................150.00
Pitcher, floral & leaf, stenciled Pitkin Brooks, 10½".........200.00
Pitcher, hobstar, 9"...200.00
Pitcher, pinwheel & X-hatch, 7".............................65.00
Pitcher, star medallions enclosing hobstars, flat form, 8"....250.00

Pitcher, sterling mount, 10".................................250.00
Pitcher, sunburst...350.00
Pitcher, tankard; pinwheels, notched hdl, rayed base, 9½".....95.00
Pitcher, tankard; zipper & rosettes..........................185.00
Pitcher, waffle, 7"...65.00
Pitcher, White Rose, sgn Irving, w/4 tumblers................275.00
Plate, Daisy & Button, 7", set of 10.........................270.00
Plate, sgn Tuthill, 7"......................................87.50
Powder jar w/lid, 5" dia....................................115.00
Punch bowl, ftd, allover hobnail cut, 6½x10"................450.00
Punch bowl & stand, six 6 point stars/sunburst fan/etc, 9x12"..400.00
Punch bowl & stand, 9x9"...................................150.00
Punch cup, Russian bowl w/hobstar ft........................90.00
Rose bowl, strawberry diamond & star, miniature.............145.00
Rose bowl, swirl cutting, bulbous, 7".......................280.00
Salesman's sample, nappy, 2 hdls, M.........................85.00
Salt & peppers, etched leaves, sterling bases & tops, 2½", pr...30.00
Salt & peppers, panel & notch, pr...........................15.00
Salt & peppers, pinwheel cutting, brass lids, 2½", pr.........30.00
Salt & peppers, prism cut, sterling lids, 3", pr..............22.00
Spooner, hobstars, pinwheels................................50.00
Spooner, honeycomb w/engraved vintage band, 9x10"..........50.00
String holder, sterling top, Brunswick type cutting...........200.00
Sugar bowl, brilliant cut, Pitkin & Brooks...................35.00
Teapot, ball form, floral design, sgn Sinclair, 5½"........3,000.00
Toothpick, faceted bulb base, dia pts, fans in scalloped rim....35.00
Tray, allover cutting, 8x5".................................75.00
Tray, Harvard pattern, intaglio cut flowers, scalloped, 11x6½"..75.00
Tray, hobstars/notched prisms radiate from center, heavy, 12"..575.00
Tray, ice cream; cane, 17¾x10", EX.........................300.00
Tumble-up, ruby cut to clear, florals & fluted bands..........95.00
Tumbler, buzz star, dbl fan, 3¾"...........................20.00
Tumbler, daisy & leaves.....................................20.00
Tumbler, floral etch top, 1¼" cane band at base, flared, 4"....25.00
Tumbler, intaglio butterflies/flowers, deep cut leaves........45.00
Tumbler, pineapple & fan....................................15.00
Tumbler, pineapple pattern, 4"..............................20.00
Tumbler, pinwheel & leaves..................................20.00
Tumbler, sgn Clarke..50.00
Urn, oval body w/pleated drapery cut panels, ftd, 8", pr......175.00
Vase, allover brilliant cutting, ftd, 18"....................575.00
Vase, cobalt/clear, rose & leaf pattern, vertical ribs, 8".....125.00
Vase, corset shape, scalloped/serrated, long hobs/dia pts, 15"..300.00
Vase, gr/clear, basketweave on 4 stars in sq, Honesdale, 18"...900.00
Vase, hobstar/straw dia, sq ft, incurvate neck, flare rim, 14"...525.00
Vase, Lotus pattern, sgn Eggington, 11½x4¾"...............170.00
Vase, ped base, bulbous, straw dia & fan, 10"...............125.00
Vase, pinwheels, diamonds, stars & fans, 12"...............250.00
Vase, sawtooth rim, X-hatch dia, rib points, knopped stem, 8"..100.00
Vase, sweet pea, ruffled rim, brilliant cutting...............165.00
Vase, trumpet/ftd, fine quality, very heavy, 15"............395.00
Whiskey, floral, 2½"......................................15.00
Wine, claret; hobstars, X-hatching, 24 ray base, 4½", 4 for...125.00
Wine, dbl teardrop stem, 5½", set of 8.....................225.00
Wine, ray base, 8 panel baluster std, hobstars/dia pt/X-hatch...25.00
Wine, Rhine; cobalt to clear, Arcadia, 7½".................325.00

Cut Velvet

Cut Velvet glassware was made during the late 1800s. It is characterized by the effect achieved through the application of relief molded patterns,
either ribbing or diamond quilting, which allows its white inner casing to
show through the outer pastel layer.

**Punch bowl, green cut to clear, on stand, circa 1900, minor
restoration, 12" x 12", $1,500.00.**

Vase, ribbed, rose with white casing, 5", $175.00.

Rose bowl, Dia Quilt, bl, 4 crimp top, 3¼x3½"............170.00
Rose bowl, Dia Quilt, rose/wht lining, 8 crimp top, 3½x3".....195.00
Vase, Dia Quilt, deep rose/wht lining, 7x3"................175.00
Vase, Dia Quilt, green, tall shaped collar on bulb, 6½".......135.00

Cybis

Boleslaw Cybis was a graduate of the Academy of Fine Arts in Warsaw, Poland, and was well recognized as a fine artist by the time he was commissioned by his government to paint murals in the Polish Pavillion's Hall of Honor at the 1939 World's Fair. With the outbreak of World War II, the Cybises found themselves stranded in the United States, and founded an artists' studio, first in Astoria, New York, and later in Trenton, New Jersey, where they made fine figurines and plaques with exacting artistry and craftsmanship entailing extensive hand work. The studio still operates today producing exquisite porcelains on a limited edition basis.

Adoration, color.....................................385.00
Alexandra Elephant..................................350.00
Alice, closed.......................................375.00
Allegra, closed.....................................350.00
Angleface Rose, closed..............................400.00
Appaloosa, horse, 9¼" L.............................220.00
Ariel, closed.......................................400.00
Azalea, closed......................................400.00
Baby Owl..100.00
Ballerina Cynthia...................................395.00
Ballerina Karina....................................325.00
Ballerina Kristina..................................375.00
Ballerina on Cue, white, 1970.......................450.00
Beatrice, closed..................................1,750.00
Begonia, pink, closed.............................1,250.00
Betty Blue..300.00
Big Top Circus Dog..................................250.00
Blue Moon Rose, closed..............................650.00
Bunny Bon Bon..50.00
Cactus Dahlia, closed...............................900.00
Carousel, Sugar Plum..............................1,200.00

Chelsea Kitten......................................135.00
Christmas Rose......................................300.00
Christopher...450.00
Clematis, closed....................................250.00
Colts, Darby & Joan, closed.........................475.00
Court Jester......................................1,750.00
Cybele, 1970..485.00
David...245.00
Desdemona...2,000.00
Dogwood, lg...900.00
Dormouse, Maximillian, closed.......................265.00
Drummer Boy Nickey..................................300.00
Duckling, Baby Brother, closed......................120.00
Easter Egg, 1983....................................300.00
Edith, closed.......................................345.00
Elephant Alexander..................................225.00
Elizabeth Ann, closed...............................250.00
Emily Ann...200.00
Eros..225.00
Eskimo Head...235.00
First Flight..150.00
Fleurette w/Morning Glories.........................750.00
Free Spirit...800.00
Frolic & Gambol...................................2,000.00
Funny Face..235.00
Grandpa Dixon Rose................................1,200.00
Great White Buffalo, decor/bisque.................2,000.00
Guinivere, closed.................................1,750.00
Hamlet..1,500.00
Hanzel & Gretal, pr.................................500.00
Harp Seal...75.00
Heart box, made for Bicentennial....................75.00
Heidi...235.00
Holiday Child.......................................215.00
Indian Boy Head.....................................450.00
Iris, lg stem, closed...............................400.00
Jamie, Boy w/Chick, closed..........................325.00
Jane Eyre...1,300.00
Jason, closed.......................................275.00
Jeannie with the Light Brown Hair...................475.00
Jeremy, closed......................................325.00
Jessica, closed.....................................325.00
King Arthur.......................................1,100.00
Lady MacBeth, closed..............................1,250.00
Little Blue Heron...................................600.00
Little Bo Peep, closed..............................365.00
Little Boy Blue, closed.............................425.00
Little Match Girl...................................300.00
Little Miss Muffet, closed..........................300.00
Little Red Riding Hood..............................175.00
Lucy Lockett..240.00
Madonna, Mother of Love.............................250.00
Madonna, Queen of Angels............................265.00
Madonna Angelica....................................300.00
Magnolia Watson, closed.............................600.00
Male Jogger, 1970...................................295.00
Mandy Lamb, closed..................................125.00
Marigold, lg Stem w/Vase............................325.00
Match Girl..225.00
Melissa...300.00
Mr Fluffytail, ca 1965-71, 7¾"......................148.00
Mr Snowball..45.00
Muffet, closed......................................135.00
Mushroom Jack-O'-Lantern............................350.00

Nancy & Ned, Boy on Sleigh............................400.00
Noah..1,500.00
Oceania, Sea King Steed, closed.......................1,500.00
Orchid, Pink, closed....................................750.00
Orchid, Yellow, closed..................................750.00
Pandora...200.00
Pat-a-Cake, closed......................................120.00
Peace Rose, lg Stem, closed.............................300.00
Peony, closed...800.00
Peter Pan, 1970...350.00
Pink Lotus, closed....................................1,000.00
Pinto Pony, 8½″ long....................................220.00
Pip...700.00
Plato Pig...200.00
Polyanna..300.00
Poppy Pony..500.00
Priscilla...975.00
Queen Esther..2,000.00
Raffles the Raccoon, 6½″................................159.00
Rapunzel, pink..550.00
Rebecca...310.00
Rumples, Pensive Clown, closed..........................550.00
Rusty & Johnny, closed..................................400.00
Satin, decorated horse head...........................1,650.00
Sharmaire, the sea Nymph..............................1,550.00
Small Brown Buffalo.....................................150.00
Small White Buffalo.....................................175.00
Squirrel High Rise......................................600.00
Suzanne, Girl w/Kitten..................................350.00
Tiffin, closed..300.00
Tropicana Rose, closed..................................975.00
Victoria..400.00
Walrus..110.00
Wee Willie Winkie.......................................210.00
Wendy...200.00
Wind Flower, closed.....................................350.00
Wood Wren w/Dogwood, closed.............................400.00

Ring Neck Pheasant, 1960, 15″ x 21″, $450.00.

Czechoslovakian Collectibles

Czechoslovakia came into being as a country in 1918. Located in the heart of Europe, it was a land with the natural resources necessary to support a glass industry that dates back to the mid-14th century. This ware has recently captured the attention of today's collectors, and for good reason.

There are beautiful vases – cased, ruffled, applied with rigaree or silver overlay -- fine enough to rival those of the best glasshouses. Czechoslovakian art glass baskets are quite as attractive as Victorian America's, and the elegant cut glass perfumes made in colors as well as clear crystal are unrivaled. There are also pressed glass perfumes, molded in lovely Deco shapes, of various types of art glass. Some are overlaid with gold filigree set with 'jewels'. Jewelry, lamps, and fine art pottery are also included in the field. More than thirty-five marks have been recorded.

Basket, clear with yellow and orange spatter, signed, 7″, $65.00.

Baby's dish, w/children & animals, 5″.......................25.00
Bottle, amethyst, opal hobnail, 5½″ dia....................85.00
Bowl w/under plate, ruby cut to clear, Vintage.............25.00
Bud vase, blue w/enameled flowers, 8½″.....................37.00
Bud vase, red, enamel Deco, 8½″............................35.00
Christmas ornament, red cone...............................4.00
Creamer, blue & wht Delft type............................15.00
Creamer, cow figural, orange spotted......................22.50
Creamer, moose figural....................................35.00
Creamer, woodpecker figural...............................27.00
Dish, red apple figural, w/cover, sgnd....................12.00
Dish, tomato figural, covered, red, sgnd..................12.00
Figurine, dog, blue glass, miniature......................15.00
Lamp, reverse painted scenic, 12″........................180.00
Perfume, cut glass, pink, 2½″.............................45.00
Perfume, cut glass, w/dropper, ornate, 6½x4½″.............65.00
Pitcher, lt blue, cobalt hdl, Deco, 7″....................35.00
Planter, bald fat man.....................................22.50
Rosary box, w/rosary......................................15.00
Salt & pepper, cut glass, pink, large, pr.................90.00
Salt jar, blue & wht Dutch scene..........................45.00
Tea set, gold lustre, 7 pc................................45.00
Tumble-up, wht w/allover reserves of mc blossoms on bl, blk ft..72.00
Vase, cottage scene, high glaze, 9″.......................95.50
Vase, cranberry w/delicate pink hdls, Deco, 7″............90.00
Vase, end-of-day, tall w/slender neck.....................35.00
Vase, fan, lt gr, mottled bottom, red/yel, 7½″............85.00
Vase, pink, yel casing, purple & red overlay, Deco, 7″....85.00
Wall pocket, Amphora, 9″..................................78.00
Wall pocket, bird...22.50
Wall pocket, bird house...................................12.00
Wall pocket, dk br side, striped turq/pink/wht w/garlands, 6½″...9.00
Wall pocket, matt bl/br/yellow, bird, 7″..................12.00
Wine set, amber, Deco, 7 pc..............................135.00

D'Argental

D'Argental cameo glass was produced in France from the 1870s until about 1920, in the Art Nouveau style. Browns and caramels were used to compliment florals and scenic designs developed through acid cuttings.

Bowl, flat ovoid, wide mouth, wild roses, red/amber, 12″ dia...800.00
Bowl, medium blue w/dk blue clematis, squatty shape, sgnd, 4″.195.00
Candy dish w/lid, florals, red/purple/yel, sgn, 4x5″...........575.00
Egg, amber to burgandy, thistles & butterflies, 5″..........1,300.00
Sealing wax light, w/wicks, cap & metal top, floral cameo, 7″...550.00
Vase, allover florals, red/purple on yel, 10″...............1,000.00
Vase, flowers/pods/leaves, red/gr/lav, 3 cuts, St Louis, 4″.....500.00
Vase, pastoral scene w/shepherd/sheep/dog, multi-layered, 14″.2,500.00
Vase, raspberries on bulging cylinder w/disk ft, 11¾″........440.00
Vase, red crocus, cameo w/enamel, 4¾″....................440.00
Vase, rose cameo, 3 cuttings, unusual shape, 9″............850.00
Vase, trees/house, br/rust on wht, 3 cuttings, 7x4¼″.........700.00
Vase, village roof top w/stork in chimney, in cameo, 10″.....1,500.00

Vase, sailboats and mountains, greens and beige, signed, 3½″, $650.00.

Daum Nancy

Daum was an important producer of French cameo glass, operating from the late 1800s until after the turn of the century. They used various techniques -- acid cutting, wheel engraving, and hand work -- to create beautiful scenic designs and nature subjects in the Art Nouveau manner. Marked examples are much in demand and command very high prices.

Bowl, br aspen leaves on yel to lav, 5x11½″................925.00
Bowl, controlled bubbles, tri-con rim, 3½x6½″..............250.00
Bowl, poppies, leaves w/gilt, silver flower mold rim, 9″.......440.00
Bowl, relief grapes w/in; pate-de-verre snail hdls, 4¾x8″....27,500.00
Bowl, underwater plants w/in, aqua/br/olive, 14¾″ dia.......1,500.00
Bowl, winter scenic w/trees, 1 cutting/enamel, 2½x5¾″.......700.00
Bowl, yellow w/berry & leaf decor, sgnd, 6″...............500.00
Bowl, 3 applied ft, ferns, 4 colors, sgn, 6″ W.............975.00
Candlestick, swirl, clear molded crystal, sgn, 4″, pr..........75.00
Cup & saucer, Clair de Lune............................475.00
Lamp, lobed domed shade/base in cameo w/pnt floral, 16½″..2,970.00
Perfume, br to yel cameo, bl enamel bachelor buttons, 5″.....600.00
Rose bowl, lake & trees, cut & enameled, 3x3¼″............600.00
Rose bowl, lt bl w/gondola/Venice scene, 1 cut/enamel, 2½x3″.750.00
Rose bowl, winter scene, 4 pinch top, 1 cut/enamel, 2¾x3″....650.00
Salt, sailing ship, woods/farmhouse in cameo, X Lorraine......475.00
Toothpick, winter scenic cameo, EX detail & color, 2″........475.00
Torchere, mottled glass/wrought iron, pine cone std, 6 ft.....1,320.00

Tumbler, summer forest scene in cameo...................540.00
Tumbler, wht frost/yel leaves/shrubbery, 1 cut/enamel, 5x2½″..650.00
Vase, amethyst w/gold, thistle flowers, in cameo, 8″..........700.00
Vase, dk maroon w/gold & wht bkground, 5 color cameo 9″...1,500.00
Vase, Dutch landscape/verso tulips, cut/enameled, 7¾″........750.00
Vase, floral cameo in 5 colors, 11¼″....................1,650.00
Vase, forest scene, fall cameo, flat oval shape, sgnd, 4″......575.00
Vase, forest/lake, gr/apricot cameo, ovoid, 6½″..............770.00
Vase, frost w/pk, gr mottle, rain & trees, 1 cut/enamel, 7½″..1,900.00
Vase, frosted opal w/floral cameo, inverted bulb shape, 10″..1,400.00
Vase, gilt/enamel intaglio scrolling leafage, ped ft, 6½″........440.00
Vase, incurvate top, dk maroon base, 5 color cameo, 9″.....1,500.00
Vase, lake & trees, 4 color cameo, 7¾″....................875.00
Vase, landscape w/sailboats on lake, cameo, beaker form, 9¼″.450.00
Vase, mountains/blossoms, blue/wht/gr cameo, 11½″........1,500.00
Vase, opal w/Delft style enamel decor, 3″..................200.00
Vase, ovoid, Deco cutting, 4″..........................325.00
Vase, purple cut to wht w/pnt violets, X Lorraine, sq, 4¾″.....875.00
Vase, raspberries, 3 color cameo, slim w/sm neck/ft, 8¼″......575.00
Vase, sailing ships, 4 cuttings, 15″.....................1,950.00
Vase, scenic w/lake & tree, 4 color cameo, 7¾″.............900.00
Vase, snow cameo enamel details, stick form, 2½x1″.........595.00
Vase, snow on tree branches, cameo, 7½″..................575.00
Vase, snowflake bkgd, cut/enamel bird/flowers, flared top, 7″..1,500.00
Vase, summer scene, blue, cameo w/enamel detail, 12″.........900.00
Vase, summer scene, lime w/gr, 1 cut/enamel, 3½x1¼x2¾″....650.00
Vase, sweet peas on milk ground, cameo/enamel accents, 5″...520.00
Vase, thistles, red/yel, 4″.............................325.00
Vase, translucent peach etched w/lappets, sgn, 18″..........880.00
Vase, winter scenic, 1 cutting/enamel, low/bulbous, 4½″......885.00

Lamp, landscape in Chinese red and brown over mottled apricot, signed in cameo 'Daum, Nancy', with croix de Lorraine, 17¾″, $3,080.00.

Davenport

W. Davenport and Company were Staffordshire potters operating in that area from 1793 to 1887, producing earthenware, creamware, porcelain, and ironstone. Many different stamps, all with 'Davenport', were used to mark the various types of ware.

Cup & saucer, pink lustre, imp mk, set of 6 . . . . .250.00
Plate, cattle by stream, lavender, Feb 1836, 8½" 45.00
Plate, Legend of Montrose, anchor mk, 9" 50.00
Plate, Waverly Scott's Illus, dtd 1852, 10½" 70.00

De Vez

De Vez was a type of acid-cut French cameo glass produced by Cristallerie de Pantin in Paris around the turn of the century.

Vase, boat & village w/in leaf fr, 10" 1,500.00
Vase, boat scene w/men, peach on cream, 3 cuttings, 7x2½" . . .900.00
Vase, brass base w/leaves, gold w/bl/rose, bird/flowers, 19" . . .1,800.00
Vase, gold w/gr trees/mtns/shore cut to rose, cylinder, 8x3" 800.00
Vase, landscape w/castle/mtn/lake, yellow/bl-blk, 7¾" 790.00
Vase, mtn & lake, bl w/gr, 3 cuttings, 11½" 1,000.00
Vase, mtn & lake, yel/red & br, 10" 1,000.00
Vase, mtn landscape, cylinder neck, rnd base, 6" 700.00
Vase, mtn scene w/lake/birds/trees, 3 cuttings, 11½" 1,000.00
Vase, mtns/village/water, red/blk/yel/bl, 6" 800.00
Vase, river & mtns, lt bl w/gr, 13" 1,100.00
Vase, river w/swans in cameo, festooned colonnade, 7¾" 900.00
Vase, spruce trees/birds/mtns, sunset effect, mc cameo, 8" 850.00
Vase, water/trees/mtns/village, in 4 colors, 6" 800.00
Vase, yel w/bl to rose, 3 cuttings, island/mtns, 4¾x2" 500.00
Vase, yel w/bl/rose scene, sailboat w/mtns, 3 cuts, 9¾" 900.00

Vase, mountain scene, water lilies in foreground, three cuttings in four colors, signed, 9½", $1,600.00.

De Vilbiss

Perfume bottles, atomizers, and dresser accessories marketed by the De Vilbiss Company are appreciated by collectors today for the various types of lovely glassware used in their manufacture, as well as for their pleasing shapes. Those most preferred are marked with the etched De Vilbiss signature.

Advertising, serving tray, w/Oriental lady, 13¼x10½" 25.00
Brochure, advertising, perfumizers & lights, color, 12 pgs 10.00

Atomizer, Steuben glass insert, brass foot and fittings, signed De Vilbiss, 9½", $125.00

Perfume, amber etched, w/atomizer, 7" 65.00
Perfume, amber opal w/etching on gr base, no atomizer, 7½" . . .45.00
Perfume, aqua w/blk butterflies, orig bulb 85.00
Perfume, Art Deco, gold w/blk trim, w/atomizer, 6¼" 35.00
Perfume, Art Deco, rose w/gold, w/atomizer bulb, sgn, 5" 55.00
Perfume, Art Deco w/gold overlay lattice, w/atomizer, 4" 30.00
Perfume, bl glass, orig sticker, w/atomizer, 1920s, 4" 22.50
Perfume, blk w/gold design, no atomizer, 6" 25.00
Perfume, blk w/goldstone effect, w/atomizer, sgn 70.00
Perfume, gr glass, brass top w/decor, slender shape, 6" 65.00
Perfume, ivory w/gold trim/fleur-de-lis finial, by Lenox 50.00
Perfume, marigold carnival, w/atomizer, sgn, 6" 30.00
Perfume, orange opaque, gold plated top, mesh bulb, sgnd, 6" . .45.00
Perfume, satin striped w/pnt florals, w/atomizer, orig label 65.00
Perfume, vaseline, quilted, w/atomizer 50.00
Vase, fan shape, gr w/gold tropical birds, 8¾" 150.00

Decanters

Ceramic whiskey decanters were brought into prominence in 1955 by the James Beam Distilling Company. Few other companies besides Beam produced these decanters during the next ten years or so; however, other companies did eventually follow suit, so that today there are at least twenty prominent companies and several on a lesser scale that make these decanters. They vary in size from miniatures (approximately 2 oz.) to gallons. Values range from a few dollars to more than $3,000 per decanter. A mint condition decanter is one with no chips or cracks and all labels intact. Whether a decanter is full or not has no bearing on the value, nor does a missing federal tax stamp. It is advisable to empty the contents of a ceramic decanter, otherwise the thin inner glaze could crack, allowing the contents to seep through the porous body, thus ruining the decanter.

Beam

Casino Series, Barney's Slot Machine, 1978 . . . . .30.00
Casino Series, Golden Gate, 1969 . . . . .59.00
Casino Series, Harold's Club, Man in Barrel #2, 1958 . . . . .227.00
Casino Series, Harold's Club, Pinwheel, 1965 . . . . .62.00
Casino Series, Harold's Club, VIP, 1972 . . . . .38.00
Casino Series, Harrah's, grey, 1963 . . . . .765.00

Club, Akron, 1973. . . . . .24.00
Club, California Mission, 1970. . . . . .20.00
Club, Camellia City, 1979. . . . . .30.00
Club, Milwaukee Stein, 1972. . . . . .80.00
Club, Pennsylvania Dutch, 1974. . . . . .17.00
Club, Twin Bridges, 1971. . . . . .56.00
Convention, #2, Ahaheim, dtd 18-25th. 64.00
Convention, #2, Anaheim, dtd June 20-23rd, 1972. . . . . .100.00
Convention, #3, Detroit, 1973. . . . . .25.00
Convention, #4, Lancaster, 1974. . . . . .117.00
Convention, #5, Sacramento, 1975. . . . . .16.00
Customer, Marina City, 1962. . . . . .34.00
Customer, Poulan Chain Saw, 1979. . . . . .24.00
Customer, Zimmerman, Bell, 1976. . . . . .11.00
Customer, Zimmerman, Oatmeal China Jug, 1966. . . . . .53.00
Customer, Zimmerman, Two Handled Jug, 1965. . . . . .96.00
Executive, 1956, Royal Gold Round. 133.00
Executive, 1957, Royal Di Monte. 70.00
Executive, 1960, Blue Cherub. 130.00
Executive, 1961, Golden Chalice. 65.00
Executive, 1962, Flower Basket. 51.00
Executive, 1963, Royal Rose. 46.00
Executive, 1964, Gold Diamond. 51.00
Executive, 1965, Marble Fantasy. 66.00
Executive, 1967, Prestige. 14.00
Executive, 1968, Presidential. 11.00
Executive, 1969, Sovereign. 9.00
Executive, 1971, w/case. 10.00
Executive, 1976, w/case. 13.00
Foreign Series, Australia, Galah, 1980. . . . . .18.00
Foreign Series, Australia, Sydney Opera House, 1978. . . . . .26.00
Foreign Series, Fiji Island, 1971. . . . . .6.00
Foreign Series, New Zealand Kiwi Bird, 1974. . . . . .8.00
Opera Series, Aida. 272.00
Opera Series, Carmen. .347.00
Opera Series, Madame Butterfly. 563.00
Opera Series, Mesphistopheles. 246.00
Opera Series, Nutcracker. 250.00
People Series, Buffalo Bill, 1971. . . . . .7.00
People Series, Charlie McCarthy, 1976. . . . . .36.00
People Series, John Henry, 1972. . . . . .57.00
People Series, Mortimer Snerd, 1976. . . . . .33.00
People Series, Paul Bunyan, 1970. . . . . .8.00
Political, Campaigner Donkey, 1960. . . . . .17.00
Political, Clown Donkey or Elephant, 1968. . . . . . . .7.00
Political, Donkey, 1960. .13.00
Political, Elephant, 1964. . . . . .13.00
Political, Miami Beach Elephant w/Plate, 1972. . . .916.00
Political, San Diego Elephant, 1972. . . . . .21.00
Political, Washington DC Republican Dinner, 1972. . . . . .730.00
Regal China, Antique Trader, 1968. . . . . .5.00
Regal China, Ivory Ash Tray, 1955. . . . . .21.00
Regal China, New Hampshire Golden Eagle, 1971. . . . . .40.00
Sport Series, Bing Crosby 29th, 1970. . . . . .6.00
Sport Series, Bing Crosby 33rd, 1973. . . . . .32.00
Sport Series, Hawaiian Open, Menehune, 1975. . . . .15.00
Sport Series, Kentucky Derby, 100th, 1974. . . . . . .10.00
State, Colorado, 1959. . . . . .39.00
State, Kansas, 1960. . . . . .57.00
State, Michigan, 1972. . . . . .8.00
State, Montana, 1963. . . . . .78.00
State, New Jersey, blue, 1963. . . . . .63.00
State, Pennsylvania, 1967. . . . . .8.00
State, Washington, 1975. . . . . .15.00

State, West Virginia, 1963. . . . . .239.00
Trophy Series, Doe, 1963. . . . . .30.00
Trophy Series, Fox, green coat, 1965. . . . . .34.00
Trophy Series, Ram, 1958. . . . . .125.00
Trophy Series, Sailfish. .31.00
Trophy Series, St Bernard, 1979. . . . . .52.00
Wheels Series, Bobby Unser Olsonite Eagle, 1975. . . . . .42.00
Wheels Series, Circus Wagon, 1979. . . . . .28.00
Wheels Series, Ernie's Flower Cart, 1976. . . . . . . .30.00
Wheels Series, Ford Fire Chief. 54.00
Wheels Series, Harold's Club Covered Wagon, 1974. . . . . .23.00
Wheels Series, Jewel Tea Van, 1976. . . . . .95.00
Wheels Series, Model T Ford, black. 50.00
Wheels Series, Oldsmobile, 1972. . . . . .81.00
Wheels Series, Stutz Bearcat, 1977. . . . . .40.00
Wheels Series, Vendome Drummers Wagon, 1975. . . . . .65.00

Brooks

Animal Series, African Lion, 1980. . . . . .41.00
Animal Series, Beaver, 1972. . . . . .8.00
Animal Series, Brahma Bull, 1971. . . . . .15.00
Animal Series, Charolais, 1972. . . . . .14.00
Animal Series, Clydesdale, 1972. . . . . .13.00
Animal Series, Moose, 1972. . . . . .23.00
Automotive Series, Duesenberg, 1971. . . . . .28.00
Automotive Series, Ford Mustang Indy Pace Car, 1979. . . . . .23.00
Automotive Series, Ontario Racer #10, 1970. . . . . .22.00
Automotive Series, Pontiac Indy Pace Car, 1980. . . . . .25.00
Automotive Series, 1962 Corvette Mako Shark, 1979. . . . . .24.00
Bird Series, Canadian Honker, 1975. . . . . .16.00
Bird Series, Macaw, 1980. . . . . .51.00
Bird Series, Owl #2, Eagle, 1978. . . . . .85.00
Bird Series, Owl #3, Snowy, 1979. . . . . .39.00
Bird Series, Owl #4, Scops, 1980. . . . . .54.00
Bird Series, Turkey, White, 1971. . . . . .25.00
Fish Series, Maine Lobster, 1970. . . . . .24.00
Heritage China Series, Christmas Tree, 1979. . . . . .35.00
Heritage China Series, Phonograph, 1970. . . . . . . .18.00
Heritage China Series, Telephone, 1971. . . . . .15.00
Heritage China Series, Ticker Tape, 1970. . . . . .9.00
Institutional Series, American Legion, Denver, 1977. . . . . .23.00
Institutional Series, Club Bottle #2, Birthday Cake, 1971. . . . . .7.00
Institutional Series, Club Bottle #3, USA Map, 1972. . . . . .15.00
Institutional Series, FOE Eagle, 1979. . . . . .24.00
Institutional Series, Fresno Grape, w/no gold, rare. 40.00
Institutional Series, Fresno Grape, 1970. . . . . .8.00
Institutional Series, Horseshoe Club, Horseshoe, 1970. . . . . .10.00
Institutional Series, Iowa Statehouse, 1971. . . . . . .39.00
Institutional Series, Kachina #1, Morning Singer, 1971. . . . . .161.00
Institutional Series, Kachina #2, Hummingbird, 1973. . . . . .59.00
Institutional Series, Kachina #3, Antelope, 1974. . . . . .69.00
Institutional Series, Kachina #4, Maiden, 1975. . . . . .26.00
Institutional Series, Katz Cat, Philharmonic, 1970. . . . . .8.00
Institutional Series, Liquor Square, 1972. . . . . .7.00
Institutional Series, Maine Lighthouse, 1971. . . . . . .22.00
Institutional Series, NH Statehouse, 1969. . . . . . . .11.00
Institutional Series, Nugget Classic, 1970. . . . . . . .12.00
Institutional Series, Saddle, silver, 1972. . . . . .26.00
Institutional Series, Shrine, Clown, 1978. . . . . .21.00
Institutional Series, Slot Machine, 1971. . . . . .21.00
Institutional Series, Walgreen Drugs, 1973. . . . . . . .20.00
People Series, Betsy Ross, 1975. . . . . .12.00
People Series, Clown #1, Smiley, 1979. . . . . .30.00

People Series, Clown #2, Cowboy, 1979 .28.00
People Series, Clown #3, Pagliacci, 1979 . . . . .35.00
People Series, Clown #4, Keystone Cop, 1980 . . . . .33.00
People Series, Clown #5, Cuddles, 1980 . . . . .35.00
People Series, Clown #6, Tramp, 1980 . . . . .37.00
People Series, Dakota Cowboy, 1975 .43.00
People Series, Dakota Cowgirl, 1976 .25.00
People Series, Iowa Farmer, 1977 . . . . .60.00
People Series, Sea Captain, 1971 . . . . .11.00
People Series, Stonewall Jackson, 1974 . . . . .25.00
People Series, West Virginia Mountain Lady, 1972 . . . . .19.00
People Series, West Virginia Mountain Man, 1970 . . . . .88.00
Sport Series, Badger #1, Boxer, 1973 .16.00
Sport Series, Bareknuckle Fighter, 1971 . . . . .8.00
Sport Series, Bluejay, Creighton Univ, 1975 . . . . .20.00
Sport Series, Bucking Bronco, 1973 . . . . .13.00
Sport Series, Gopher, Minnesota Hockey Player, 1975 . . . . .16.00
Sport Series, Greensboro Open, Club & Ball, 1977 . . . . .41.00
Sport Series, Minnesota & Michigan Jug, 1974 . . . . .22.00
Sport Series, Razorback Hog, 1969 . . . . .20.00
Sport Series, Trojan Horse, 1974 . . . . .17.00
Transportation Series, Riverboat, Delta Belle, 1969 . . . . .8.00
Transportation Series, Snowmobile, 1972 . . . . .13.00
Transportation Series, Train, Casey Jones #1, 1980 . . . . .44.00

Cyrus Noble

Animal Series, Bear & Cubs, 1st edition, 1978 . . . . .137.00
Animal Series, Beaver & Kit, Nevada edition, 1978 . . . . .38.00
Animal Series, Beaver & Kit, 1st edition, 1978 . . . . .108.00
Animal Series, Buffalo Cow & Calf, Nevada edition, 1977 . . . . . .89.00
Animal Series, Elk, Bull, 1980 . . . . .50.00
Animal Series, Moose & Calf, 1st edition, 1977 . . . . .115.00
Animal Series, Mountain Lion & Cubs, Nevada edition, 1977 . . . .86.00
Animal Series, Mountain Lion & Cubs, 1st edition, 1977 . . . . . .125.00
Animal Series, Mountain Sheep, 1st edition, 1978 . . . . .139.00
Carousel Series, Horse, Black Flyer, 1979 . . . . .44.00
Carousel Series, Horse, White Charger, 1979 . . . . .27.00
Carousel Series, Lion, 1979 . . . . .33.00
Carousel Series, Tiger, 1979 . . . . .38.00
Dancers, Oklahoma, 1978 . . . . .32.00
Dancers, South of the Border, 1978 . . . . .26.00
Delta Saloon, set 296.00
Mine Series, Assayer, 1972 . . . . .185.00
Mine Series, Bartender, 1971 . . . . .174.00
Mine Series, Blacksmith, 1974 . . . . .41.00
Mine Series, Burro, 1973 . . . . .69.00
Mine Series, Gambler, 1974 . . . . .43.00
Mine Series, Gambler's Lady, 1976 . . . . .41.00
Mine Series, Landlady, 1977 . . . . .26.00
Mine Series, Middle of Piano Trumpeter, 1978 . . . . .47.00
Mine Series, Miner's Daughter, 1975 .38.00
Mine Series, Music Man, 1977 . . . . .30.00
Mine Series, Snowshoe Thompson, 1972 . . . . .200.00
Mine Series, The Mine, 1978 . . . . .42.00
Mine Series, Violinist, 1976 . . . . .34.00
Mine Series, Whiskey Drummer, 1975 . . . . .40.00
Olympic Skater, 1980 . . . . .41.00
Owl in Tree, 1980 . . . . .40.00
Sea Animal Series, Harp Seal, 1979 .50.00
Sea Animal Series, Penguin Family, 1978 . . . . .52.00
Sea Animal Series, Sea Turtle, 1979 .53.00
Sea Animal Series, Seal Family, 1978 . . . . .30.00
Sea Animal Series, Walrus Family, 1978 . . . . .45.00

Lionstone

Animal-Safari Series, Lion & Cub, 1977 . . . . .29.00
Animal-Safari Series, Zebras, 1977, mini 11.00
Bicentennial Series, Betsy Ross, 1975 . . . . .26.00
Bicentennial Series, George Washington, 1975 . . . . .20.00
Bicentennial Series, Mecklenburg, 1975 . . . . .35.00
Bicentennial Series, Molly Pitcher, 1975 . . . . .20.00
Bicentennial Series, Paul Revere, 1975 . . . . .18.00
Bicentennial Series, Valley Forge, 1975 . . . . .25.00
Bird Series, Blue Bird, Eastern, 1972 .24.00
Bird Series, Blue Bird, Western, 1972 .17.00
Bird Series, Blue Jay, 1971 . . . . .24.00
Bird Series, Canada Goose, 1980 . . . . .58.00
Bird Series, Capistrano Swallow w/silver bell, 1972 . . . . .51.00
Bird Series, Cardinal, 1972 . . . . .35.00
Bird Series, Owls, 1973 . . . . .35.00
Bird Series, Roadrunner, 1969 . . . . .30.00
Buccaneer, 1973 . . . . .32.00
Car Series, Turbo Car STP, red, 1972 . . . . .25.00
Cherry Valley, Gold, 1971 . . . . .25.00
Circus Clowns Series, #1, Monkey Business, 1978 . . . . .35.00
Circus Clowns Series, #3, Say It With Music, 1978 . . . . .28.00
Circus Clowns Series, #4, Salty Tails, 1978 . . . . .28.00
Circus Clowns Series, #6, Lampy, 1979 . . . . .28.00
Circus Series, Giraffe Necked Lady, 1973 . . . . .14.00
Circus Series, Strong Man, 1973 . . . . .14.00
European Workers Series, Silversmith, 1974 . . . . .25.00
Firefighter Series, #2, with child, 1974 . . . . .102.00
Firefighter Series, #4, Emblem, 1978 .31.00
Old West Series, Annie Christmas, 1969 . . . . .21.00
Old West Series, Bar Scene w/nude & frame, 1970 . . . . .550.00
Old West Series, Bartender, 1969 . . . . .32.00
Old West Series, Belly Robber, 1969 .16.00
Old West Series, Blacksmith, 1973 . . . . .25.00
Old West Series, Camp Cook, 1969 .30.00
Old West Series, Camp Follower, 1969 . . . . .20.00
Old West Series, Dancehall Girl, 1973 . . . . .67.00
Old West Series, Gold Panner, 1969 .42.00
Old West Series, Indian Bust #2, 1980 . . . . .33.00
Old West Series, Indian Weaver, 1976 . . . . .26.00
Old West Series, Indian--Casual, 1969 . . . . .11.00
Old West Series, Indian--Proud, 1969 . . . . .15.00
Old West Series, Jesse James, 1969 .14.00
Old West Series, Judge Roy Bean, 1973 . . . . .28.00
Old West Series, Madame, 1969 . . . . .41.00
Old West Series, Rain Maker, 1976 . . . . .25.00
Old West Series, Wells Fargo Man, 1969 . . . . .15.00
Oriental Workers Series, Basket Weaver, 1974 . . . . .31.00
Oriental Workers Series, Tea Vendor, 1974 . . . . .31.00
Police Association Convention, 1980 .21.00
Rose Parade, 1973 . . . . .26.00
Sports Series, Backpacker, 1980 . . . . .36.00
Sports Series, Basketball Players, 1974 . . . . .24.00
Sports Series, Boxers, 1974 . . . . .19.00
Sports Series, Fisherman, 1980 . . . . .38.00
Sports Series, Football Players, 1974 .23.00
Sports Series, Golfer, 1974 . . . . .25.00
Sports Series, Hockey Players, 1974 .21.00

McCormick

Bicentennial Series, Betsy Ross 31.00
Bicentennial Series, Jefferson 20.00

Bicentennial Series, John Paul Jones...................26.00
Bicentennial Series, Paul Revere.....................34.00
Bicentennial Series, Spirit of '76, 1976.............83.00
Entertainer Series, Elvis #1, 1978...................82.00
Entertainer Series, Elvis #2, 1979...................36.00
Entertainer Series, Elvis #3, 1980...................41.00
Entertainer Series, Elvis Bust, white, 1978..........23.00
Entertainer Series, Elvis Designer #1...............215.00
Entertainer Series, Elvis--Aloha....................111.00
Entertainer Series, Elvis--Gold, 1979...............231.00
Entertainer Series, Elvis--Silver, 1980.............134.00
Entertainer Series, Tom T Hall, 1980.................39.00
Football Mascots, Baylor Bears, 1972.................28.00
Football Mascots, New Mexico Lobo....................34.00
Football Mascots, SMU Mustangs, 1972.................25.00
Football Mascots, TCU Horned Frogs, 1972.............30.00
Football Mascots, Washington Cougars, 1974...........13.00
Frontiersman Series, Davy Crockett, 1975.............19.00
Frontiersman Series, Jim Bowie, 1975.................16.00
Frontiersman Series, Kit Carson, 1975................18.00
Great American Series, Sam Houston, 1977.............21.00
Lobsterman, 1979.....................................25.00
Mikado, 1980..258.00
Shrine Series, Jester Mirth King, 1972...............42.00
Sports Series, Johnny Rodgers #2, 1973...............99.00
Sports Series, Kansas City Chiefs, 1969..............34.00

Ski Country

Bicentennial Series, Birth of Freedom, 1976..........87.00
Christmas Series, Bob Cratchit w/Tiny Tim, 1977......51.00
Circus Series, Circus Lion, 1975.....................35.00
Circus Series, Clown Bust, 1974......................37.00
Circus Series, Jenny Lind, blue......................75.00
Circus Series, PT Barnum, 1976.......................35.00
Customer Specialties Series, Bonnie, 1974............30.00
Customer Specialties Series, Mill River Country Club, 1977.....38.00
Customer Specialties Series, Oregon Cave Man, 1974...........23.00
Domestic Animal Series, Charlois Bull, 1974..........50.00
Domestic Animals Series, Basset Hound, 1978..........54.00
Fish Series, Muskie, 1977............................29.00
Indian Series, Arizona Ceremonial Eagle Dancer, 1978.......179.00
Indian Series, Cigar Store Indian, 1974..............29.00
Indian Series, Lookout, 1977.........................80.00
State Bird Series, Baltimore Oriole, 1975............47.00
Waterfowl Series, Duck--King Elder, 1977.............50.00
Waterfowl Series, Goose & Chicks--Canadian, 1980.....48.00
Waterfowl Series, Penguin Family, 1978...............41.00
Wild Life Series, Brown Bear, 1974...................29.00
Wild Life Series, California Condor, 1973............40.00
Wild Life Series, Kangaroo, 1974.....................31.00
Wild Life Series, Mountain Goat, 1975................44.00
Wild Life Series, Owl--Northern Snowy, 1972.........110.00
Wild Life Series, Peacock, 1972......................93.00
Wild Life Series, Peregrine Falcon, 1980.............67.00
Wild Life Series, River Otter, 1979..................48.00
Wild Life Series, Skunk Family, 1978.................43.00
Wild Life Series, Woodpecker--Gila, 1972.............79.00

Wild Turkey

Turkey #2, Female, 1972.............................200.00
Turkey #3, On The Wing, 1973.........................97.00
Turkey #5, With Flags, 1975..........................41.00

Turkey #6, Striding, 1976............................24.00
Turkey #8, Strutting, 1978...........................39.00
Turkey Lore, #2......................................38.00
Turkey Lore, #3......................................42.00

Decoys

American colonists learned the craft of decoy making from the Indians who used them to lure birds out of the sky as an important food source. Early models were carved from wood such as pine, cedar, balsa, etc., and a few were made of canvas or papier mache. There are 2 basic types of decoys: water floaters and shorebirds (also called 'stick-ups'). Within each type are many different species, ducks being the most plentiful since they migrated along all four of America's great waterways. Market hunting became big business around 1880, resulting in large scale commercial production of decoys which continued until about 1910, when such hunting was outlawed by the Migratory Bird Treaty.

Today, decoys are among the most collectible American folk art. The most valuable are those carved by such artists as Laing, Crowel, Ward, and Wheeler, to name only a few.

Each area, such as Massachusetts, Connecticut, Maine, the Illinois River, and the Delaware River produces decoys with distinctive regional characteristics. Examples of commercial decoys produced by well known factories -- among them Mason, Stevens, and Dodge -- are also prized by collectors. Though mass produced, these nevertheless required a certain amount of hand carving and decorating.

Well carved examples, especially those of rare species, are appreciating rapidly, and those with original paint are more desirable.

Key:

RP----repaint   OP----original paint
WOP----worn original paint OWP----original working paint
ORP----old repaint   WRP----working repaint

Black Breasted Plover, EX wings/feathers, John Dilley......12,500.00
Black Duck, cork/wood, worn OP, Charlie Jonier, 17½".......200.00
Black Duck, feeding, balsa w/pine head, Chas Wheeler.......1,100.00
Black Duck, hollow, WOP, rpr, glass eyes, wing carving, Anger.130.00
Black Duck, hollow/tack eyes, WRP, Ohio origin, 14".........25.00
Black Duck, Mason's Premier, snaky head, OP, EX........2,900.00
Black Duck, Nathan Cobb............................7,000.00

Hand carved Canadian Goose, exceptional wing detail, original paint, circa 1920, 14" x 20", $295.00.

Black Duck, oversize; hollow, turned head/OP, Cramner, 20″....85.00
Black Duck, punched feathers/glass eyes/OP, by C Rollins......55.00
Black-Bellied Plover, Geo Boyd.........................2,400.00
Blue Winged Teal, Mason's Detroit grade...................475.00
Blue Winged Teal, Mason's Premier, worn.................325.00
Bluebill, primitive w/folk art appeal, carved eyes, OP, 11″.......95.00
Bluebill, traces of OP, att Jim Kelly, 12¼″................55.00
Bluebill drake, Mason's Challenge, glass eyes, RP, 14″........175.00
Bluebill drake, Mason's Standard, glass eyes/OP/G rpr, 13½″...185.00
Bluebill drake, OP, rusted tack eyes, Ira Hudson..........1,000.00
Bluebill drake, worn WRP, cracks, primitive, 13½″..........45.00
Bluebill drake bobtail, chunky body, glass eyes, WRP, Gardner..30.00
Bluebill hen, bold stylized carving/OP/glass eyes, Quebec, 17″...50.00
Bluebill hen, glass eyes, OP, contemporary, L Smith, Canada....30.00
Bluebill hen, Nathan Cobb.............................6,000.00
Bluebill hen, worn RP, relief carved detail, Sherman Hendrick...35.00
Bluebills, pr, Mason's Premier, OP w/rpt, rstr...............600.00
Bluewing Teal drake, contemporary, unused, Eastern Shore, MD.80.00
Bluewing Teal hen, sleeper, glass eyes, OP, sgn Chas Moore '81.95.00
Bobtail Michigan Coot, WRP, cracks/damage, 13¼″..........20.00
Brant, balsa, preening, carved wing tops, WRP, Ira Hudson..1,900.00
Brant, belligerent, Nathan Cobb.......................2,800.00
Brant, carved V split tail, sgn N for Nathan Cobb..........2,200.00
Brant, hollow, Charles Birch..........................3,300.00
Brant, hollow carved, swimmer, eye detail, V tail, Cobb.....19,500.00
Brant, hollow carved, V split tail, Nathan Cobb..........10,500.00
Brant, Mason's Challenge, OP w/wear, rpr.................1,100.00
Brant goose, balsa body/pine head, OP, glass eyes, Wildfowler...95.00
Bufflehead, glass eyes, OP, sgn Chas Moore '78, 7¾″..........65.00
Bufflehead drake, OP, A J Mallory, 10½″...................95.00
Bufflehead drake, tack eyes, old RP, Hoppers Island, 9″........45.00
Bufflehead drake, worn WRP, 12¾″......................55.00
Canada Goose, canvas w/straw stuffing, homemade, rpr, 30″.....65.00
Canada Goose, Dave Watson...........................2,600.00
Canada Goose, hollow, OP w/wear, split, Dave Watson.......2,600.00
Canada Goose, laminated body, 1 pc carved head, Schmitz, 21″.75.00
Canada Goose, OP, glass eyes, HG Smith Decoys, 23″ L......245.00
Canada Goose, OP, turned head, Capt Harry Jobes, 1980, 15″..70.00
Canada Goose, pine, hollow, 2 pc neck/head, worn RP, 23″....150.00
Canada Goose, preening, stylized carving/OP/glass eyes/LJR....260.00
Canada Goose, primitive, wrought iron ft, rpl head, RP, 26″ L..85.00
Canada Goose, relief feathers, 2 part head/neck, OP, Ackerman.125.00
Canada Goose, swimmer, carved wings on back, Ira Hudson..1,600.00
Canada Goose, WOP, canvas/slats, Capt Bailey............2,800.00
Canada Goose, WOP, Walter Brady.....................5,400.00
Canvasback, hollow/laminated/tack eye, worn WRP, shot scars...58.00
Canvasback bobtail, brass tack eyes/WRP, Detroit River, 17″....35.00
Canvasback drake, glass eyes, well carved, worn WRP, 15″.....65.00
Canvasback drake, high head/glass eyes/WRP, rpr, 14½″.......65.00
Canvasback drake, hollow w/glass eyes, worn RP, cracks, 16″...55.00
Canvasback drake, OP good, balsa body, sleepy, Ward Bros..1,200.00
Canvasback drake, w/keel, WP, glass eyes, Dodge Factory, 15″.135.00
Canvasback drake bobtail, rpr bill, WRP, glass eyes, Mich, 15″..35.00
Canvasback hen, balsa body, wood keel, OP, Wildfowler, 15″....40.00
Canvasback hen, OP/glass eyes, worn, 1950s, Ackerman, 19″....45.00
Cork body w/carved wood head & keel, WP, tack eyes, Sharron.45.00
Dowitcher, feeder, EX feathering, sgn Maggioni, 1971.......3,600.00
Dowitcher, spring plumage, EX wings/feathering, John Dilley..8,000.00
Eider drake, from Lowell's Cove, Orrs Island, Maine.......2,600.00
Eider drake, OP, glass eyes, contemporary, 14″..............85.00
Eider drake, WOP, Gouldsboro, Maine, 1870, EX........10,500.00
Folding, cardboard w/wire rods, orig canvas bag, Johnson's, EX..35.00
Goldeneye, old RP, glass eyes, Northern NY, 14½″...........65.00
Goldeneye drake, OP/glass eyes, AJ Mallory, 15″............40.00

Goldeneye drake, simple wing tip carving, WRP/glass eyes, 14″..40.00
Goldeneye drake, tack eyes, WRP, iron keel, att Peterson, 14″..35.00
Goldeneye drake, WOP, rpt eyes, age cracks, Ontario, 14¼″....35.00
Goldeneye hen, worn WRP/glass eyes, Ontario, 15″............35.00
Goldeneyes, pr, trn heads, Ward Bros...................3,200.00
Goose, canvas covered, WOP, rpt patch, Geo Boyd, EX......3,250.00
Goose, primitive carving, blk/wht WRP, bill damaged, 16½″.....75.00
Goose, primitive carving from 1 log, weathered pnt, 44x35″....300.00
Greenwing Teal, OP, Paul Gibson, MD, 12¾″ L..............65.00
Greenwing Teal drake, Ward Bros.......................3,000.00
Greenwing Teal hen, Ward Bros........................2,800.00
Hooded Merganser hen, Ira Hudson.....................7,000.00
Hooded Merganzer, flying stick-up, sheet metal wings/OP, 18″..45.00
Hugh Eider drake, OP, from Lowell's Cove, Maine, 24″ L....3,000.00
Loon, root head/tack eye, old blk rpt, 12″.................135.00
Mallard, pr, balsa, trn heads, Ward Bros.................3,400.00
Mallard, standing, CI foot, Charles Schoenheider, Sr.......11,000.00
Mallard drake, head to right, AE Crowell..................200.00
Mallard drake, OP, contemporary, by Paul Gibson, 17″........40.00
Mallard drake, OP+varnish, hollow, Chas Walker..........1,200.00
Mallard drake, OP/glass eyes, contemporary, by Snow, 17½″....35.00
Mallard drake, OP/glass eyes/simple carving, DWS, 17½″.......30.00
Mallard drake, Victor factory, 15½″......................25.00
Mallard drake, wood silhouette by JW Reynolds Co, hinged, OP.95.00
Mallard drake, WOP/glass eyes, Ontario, 16¼″.............35.00
Mallard hen, glass eyes, WOP, 18″......................105.00
Mallard hen, stamped feathers/glass eyes, Cecil Rollins, 18″....50.00
Mallard hen, swimmer; well carved/pntd, hollow, Gerlach, 21″...45.00
Mallards, pr, Mason's Premiere........................525.00
Mallards, pr, Ward Bros, ca 1951, balsa.................3,400.00
Marganser hen, Mason's Premiere, OP/minor rpr..........2,600.00
Merganser, sgn Marvin Schmitz, contemporary, 7½″..........45.00
Morning dove, papier mache, OP, clothespin fasteners, 8″......15.00
Pintail, Mason's Premier grade.........................700.00
Pintail, Mitchell Fulcher.............................3,000.00
Pintail, pr, hollow, trn head/wing detail, OP, Whittington.....1,400.00
Pintail drake, glass eyes, sgn Chas Moore, '78, orig pnt, 10″....45.00
Pintail drake, glass eyes, WOP, sgn Jerry Hutchings, 14¼″....230.00
Pintail drake, head to right, OP, Ward Bros, 1938..........6,000.00
Pintail drake, OP, neck & tail glued rpr, sgn M Mitchell, 18″...95.00
Pintail drake, OP w/some overpnt, mk Mitchell Fulcher......3,000.00
Pintail drake, partial rpt by L Ward, worn, 1942..........1,600.00
Pintail drake, standing, CI ft, Charles Schoenheider, Sr......8,750.00
Pintail hen, OP, Ward Bros...........................2,200.00
Plover, shorebird, glass eyes, sgn Perkins, 8½″.............45.00
Redbreasted Merganser, preening; hollow, OP, glass eyes, 1950..75.00
Redbreasted Merganser drake, glass eyes/OP, Wildfowler.......45.00
Redbreasted Merganser drake, hollow, EX OP, Mark English...850.00
Redbreasted Merganser drake, hollow, WOP, Forked River.....875.00
Redbreasted Merganser drake, stylized carving/OP, modern.....40.00
Redhead, hollow body, cleaned down to traces of OP, 1890-'20..60.00
Redhead drake, canvas body, glass eyes, WRP, Reeves, 15½″...95.00
Redhead drake, glass eyes, worn ORP, style of Kellie, 12¼″....45.00
Redhead drake, hollow, glass eyes old WRP, part recarved, 15″.65.00
Redhead drake, OP, Keyes Chadwick, EX structurally.......1,800.00
Redhead drake, WRP, nailed rpr, att Sam Barnes, 16¼″......65.00
Redhead hen, hollow, OP w/average wear, neck split, Graham.2,400.00
Redheads, pr, Mason's Premiere, OP....................2,400.00
Ringbill drake, carved detail/glass eyes/OP, contemporary, DWS..50.00
Ringbill drake, WRP, glass eyes, Michigan, 15″.............35.00
Ringbill hen, glass eyes/OP, 12¾″......................45.00
Robin Snipe, Mason's, glass eyes, OP, EX...............3,200.00
Robin Snipe, WOP, hit by shot, tail carving, rpr bill.........625.00
Ruddy Duck drake, glass eyes, OP, sgn Dave Fried, 10½″......65.00

Seagull, stick-up, relief carved wings/glass eyes/OP, 17"........40.00
Shorebird, glass eyes, branded P (Perkins), contemporary, 6"....55.00
Shorebird, glass eyes, cracks, worn, pnt traces, 11" L.........95.00
Shorebird, glass eyes, OP, stamped Stevens, contemporary, 6"...35.00
Shorebird, sheet metal, wings up, G detail, OP, 10" W........95.00
Sickle Bill Curlew, Mason's, OP, EX...................11,000.00
Snow Goose, feeder stick-up, laminated/glass eyes/OP, 23x27"...50.00
Swan, hollow, WRP, rpr, Creeds, VA....................1,100.00
Swan, hollow carved, OP w/average wear, Charlie Birch......6,500.00
Swan, mk Torch Lake Swan, Wm DeMott Stull, '77, OP, 6½"...45.00
Swan, relief carved, 1 pc, well formed head/glass eyes/OP, 25"..110.00
Teal, carved body/root head, WOP, 8" L..................140.00
Trumpeter Swan, Maryland, sgn Capt Harry Jobes, 1980, 21¾".435.00
Turkey hen, stick up, hollow compo/wood/glass eyes, 27"......150.00
White Marlin, dtd Feb 1943, sgn Ira Hudson.............1,750.00
White Winged Scoter, w/mussel in mouth, Maine, G structure.2,100.00
Widgeon drake, WOP, rpr, Lem & Lee Dudley............2,000.00
Widgeon hen, rectangular brand of Elmer Crowell.........2,800.00
Wood Duck drake, glass eyes, stenciled spray pnt, Haskin, 16"..65.00
Wood Duck drake, Mason Premiere head/challenge body, rpr.6,000.00
Yellowlegs, carved wing tips, WOP, bill broken, Dave Watson.2,400.00
Yellowlegs, Charles Clark, NM......................2,000.00
Yellowlegs, head to right, split tail, EX feathering, Crowell...13,500.00
Yellowlegs, OP w/minor wear, split tail, John Dilley.........1,750.00
Yellowlegs, semi-flat, OP, Ben Franklin Torrey, 1870........450.00
Yellowlegs, WOP, losses, EX feather paint, Ira Hudson......2,100.00

Dedham

Originally founded in Morrisville, Pennsylvania, as the Chelsea Keramic Works, the name was changed to Dedham Pottery in 1895, after the firm relocated in Dedham, near Boston, Massachusetts. The move was effected to make use of the native clay deemed more suitable for the production of the popular dinnerware designed by Hugh Robinson, founder of the company. The ware utilized a gray stoneware body with a crackle glaze and simple cobalt border designs of flowers, birds, and animals. Decorations were brushed on by hand using an ancient Chinese method which suspended the cobalt within the overall glaze. There were thirteen standard patterns, among them Magnolia, Iris, Butterfly, Duck, Polar Bear, and the Rabbit, the latter of which was chosen to represent the company on their logo. On the very early pieces the rabbits face left; decorators soon found the reverse position easier to paint, and the rabbits were turned to the right.

In addition to the standard patterns, other designs were produced for special orders. These and artist signed pieces are highly valued by collectors today.

The firm was operated by succeeding generations of the Robertson family until it closed in 1943.

Basin, Rabbit, shallow, glaze imperfection, 10½"............150.00
Bowl, Grape, 9" dia, VG.............................350.00
Bowl, Polar Bears, 6", VG...........................400.00
Bowl, whipped cream; Turtle band/wide rim, minor chips, 8"...525.00
Charger, Rabbit, 1920, 12".........................260.00
Cup & saucer, Snow Tree pattern, 4" dia, VG.............190.00
Dish w/lid, Rabbit, flat wide rim/shallow lid, 9½", G.........450.00
Mug, Rabbit, hairline..............................110.00
Pitcher, Day/Night, 5", EX..........................450.00
Pitcher, Rabbit, cylindrical w/angled hdl, 9", VG...........600.00
Plate, Bird-in-Potted-Orange-Tree, minor imperfections, 8½"...110.00
Plate, Chestnut, fair glaze, 8½".......................100.00
Plate, Chestnut, 1 w/chip, 6", set of 4.................280.00
Plate, Dolphin, 8¾", G.............................260.00
Plate, Iris, 6", G..................................65.00

Plate, Lotus, fair glaze, 8½".........................65.00
Plate, Moth, 8½", G...............................215.00
Plate, Polar Bear, minor chips/imperfections, 8½"..........200.00
Plate, Rabbit, fair glaze, 10".......................110.00
Plate, Rabbit, 6", G................................85.00
Plate, Rabbit, 7½", G..............................90.00
Plate, Rabbit, 8½", VG.............................95.00
Plate, Rabbit, 9¾", EX............................175.00
Plate, Turtle alternating w/scenic border, (crack), 10".......475.00
Relish dish, 12 Rabbit border, oblong, rim blemish, 9".......275.00
Tray, Rabbit, rectangular, bubbled glaze, 9¾"............210.00

Charger, Rabbit decor, rolled-in rim, 13", $1,250.00.

Degenhart

The Crystal Art Glass factory in Cambridge, Ohio, opened in 1947 under the private ownership of John and Elizabeth Degenhart. John had previously worked for the Cambridge Glass Company, and was well known for his superior paperweights. After his death in 1964, Elizabeth took over management of the factory, hiring several workers from the defunct Cambridge Company, including Zack Boyd. Boyd was responsible for many unique colors, some of which were named for him. From 1964 to 1974, more than twenty-seven different moulds were created, most of them resulting from Elizabeth Degenhart's work and creativity, and over 145 official colors were developed. Elizabeth died in 1978, requesting that the ten moulds she had built while operating the factory were to be turned over to the Degenhart Museum. The remaining moulds were to be held by the Island Mould and Machine Company, who, complying with her request, removed the familiar 'D in heart' trademark.

The factory was eventually bought by Zack's son, Bernard Boyd. He also acquired the remaining Degenhart moulds, to which he added his own logo.

Baby Shoe, Chocolate Creme..........................20.00
Basket Toothpick, Blue Milk Glass.....................20.00
Basket Toothpick, Opalescent.........................20.00
Beaded Oval Toothpick, Amberina, not mkd..............20.00
Beaded Oval Toothpick, Bittersweet....................30.00
Beaded Oval Toothpick, Cobalt Carnival, not mkd..........40.00
Beaded Oval Toothpick, Fawn.........................17.50

Beaded Oval Toothpick, Lavender Blue.....................20.00	Chick, 2″, Caramel, not mkd..........................50.00
Beaded Oval Toothpick, Lt Pink........................15.50	Chick, 2″, Crystal..................................15.00
Beaded Oval Toothpick, Old Custard, not mkd.........25.00	Chick, 2″, Lemon Custard............................50.00
Beaded Oval Toothpick, Royal Crown Tuscan............20.00	Chick, 2″, Lt Powder Blue...........................25.00
Beaded Oval Toothpick, Sapphire.......................20.00	Chick, 2″, Pistachio................................22.00
Beaded Oval Toothpick, Vaseline.......................17.50	Chick, 2″, Vaseline, not mkd........................15.00
Bell, 1776-1976; Butterscotch.........................25.00	Colonial Drape Toothpick, Amethyst..................15.00
Bell, 1776-1976; Charcoal.............................12.00	Colonial Drape Toothpick, Blue Milk Glass...........22.50
Bell, 1776-1976; Cobalt...............................12.00	Colonial Drape Toothpick, Lt Custard................15.00
Bell, 1776-1976; Frosty Caramel.......................20.00	Colonial Drape Toothpick, Sapphire..................15.00
Bell, 1776-1976; Heatherbloom.........................20.00	Daisy & Button Salt, Amberina.......................20.00
Bell, 1776-1976; Mauve................................12.00	Daisy & Button Salt, Blue Milk Glass................20.00
Bell, 1776-1976; Medium Green.........................12.00	Daisy & Button Salt, Crown Tuscan...................25.00
Bell, 1776-1976; Mint, crystal........................12.00	Daisy & Button Salt, Crystal, not mkd...............12.00
Bell, 1776-1976; Old Lavender.........................12.00	Daisy & Button Salt, Vaseline, not mkd..............12.00
Bell, 1776-1976; Pink Lady............................15.00	Daisy & Button Salt, White Milk Glass, not mkd......12.00
Bell, 1776-1976; Red Carnival.........................30.00	Daisy & Button Toothpick, Baby Blue Slag............25.00
Bell, 1776-1976; Rose Marie...........................13.00	Daisy & Button Toothpick, Cobalt Carnival...........50.00
Bell, 1776-1976; Sapphire.............................10.00	Daisy & Button Toothpick, Lime Ice..................20.00
Bird Salt w/Cherry, Brown Sparrow Slag................15.00	Daisy & Button Toothpick, Royal Crown Tuscan........25.00
Bird Salt w/Cherry, Brownie...........................15.00	Daisy & Button Toothpick, Vaseline..................20.00
Bird Salt w/Cherry, Caramel Custard...................25.00	Dog, April Green....................................12.00
Bird Salt w/Cherry, Ebony.............................25.00	Dog, Baby Green.....................................15.00
Bird Salt w/Cherry, Forest Green......................12.50	Dog, Bittersweet Slag...............................25.00
Bird Salt w/Cherry, Lavender Blue.....................25.00	Dog, Delft..15.00
Bird Salt w/Cherry, Lavender Marble...................30.00	Dog, Dk Dapple Gray Slag............................20.00
Bird Salt w/Cherry, Powder Blue Slag..................30.00	Dog, Gray Slag......................................20.00
Bird Salt w/Cherry, Spring Green......................15.00	Dog, Gray Tomato....................................20.00
Bird Toothpick, Rose Marie............................20.00	Dog, Ivory..12.00
Bow Slipper, Blue Milk Glass..........................20.00	Dog, Mosser White...................................15.00
Bow Slipper, Caramel..................................30.00	Dog, Old Lavender...................................15.00
Bow Slipper, Cobalt, not mkd..........................20.00	Forget-Me-Not Toothpick, Baby Green.................20.00
Bow Slipper, Crystal..................................15.00	Forget-Me-Not Toothpick, Bittersweet, not mkd.......30.00
Bow Slipper, Milk Blue................................20.00	Forget-Me-Not Toothpick, Blue Bird #2...............17.50
Bow Slipper, Mint Green Opaque........................20.00	Forget-Me-Not Toothpick, Bluebell...................15.00
Bow Slipper, Rose Marie...............................15.00	Forget-Me-Not Toothpick, Bluejay....................17.50
Bow Slipper, Ruby, not mkd............................30.00	Forget-Me-Not Toothpick, Brown Sparrow..............20.00
Bow Slipper, Sapphire, not mkd........................15.00	Forget-Me-Not Toothpick, Clear January Blizzard.....17.50
Buzz Saw Wine, Crown Tuscan...........................35.00	Forget-Me-Not Toothpick, Cobalt.....................17.50
Buzz Saw Wine, Dk Green...............................20.00	Forget-Me-Not Toothpick, Cobalt Carnival, not mkd...20.00
Buzz Saw Wine, Lt Custard.............................30.00	Forget-Me-Not Toothpick, Crystal....................15.00
Buzz Saw Wine, Vaseline...............................15.00	Forget-Me-Not Toothpick, Heatherbloom...............20.00
Candy Dish, Amberina..................................25.00	Forget-Me-Not Toothpick, Lavender...................20.00
Candy Dish, Amethyst, not mkd.........................25.00	Forget-Me-Not Toothpick, Old Custard, not mkd.......30.00
Candy Dish, Crown Tuscan, no mk.......................25.00	Forget-Me-Not Toothpick, Peach, clear...............15.00
Candy Dish, Dk Green..................................20.00	Forget-Me-Not Toothpick, Peach, opaque..............17.50
Candy Dish, Nile Green................................30.00	Forget-Me-Not Toothpick, Pearl Gray.................20.00
Cat Slipper, Amberina, no mk..........................20.00	Forget-Me-Not Toothpick, Persimmon..................12.50
Cat Slipper, Autumn...................................20.00	Forget-Me-Not Toothpick, Powder Blue Slag...........20.00
Cat Slipper, Bloody Mary..............................50.00	Forget-Me-Not Toothpick, Royal Crown Tuscan.........20.00
Cat Slipper, Caramel..................................25.00	Forget-Me-Not Toothpick, Royal Violet...............20.00
Cat Slipper, Crystal Green............................20.00	Forget-Me-Not Toothpick, Shamrock...................15.00
Cat Slipper, Gray/Brown Slag, not mkd.................30.00	Forget-Me-Not Toothpick, Smoke Heather..............15.00
Cat Slipper, Ivorene..................................20.00	Forget-Me-Not Toothpick, Spring Green...............17.50
Cat Slipper, Mint Green Opal..........................30.00	Forget-Me-Not Toothpick, Toffee.....................20.00
Cat Slipper, Olive Green, not mkd.....................20.00	Forget-Me-Not Toothpick, Tomato.....................35.00
Cat Slipper, Orange Slag Opal, not mkd................25.00	Gypsy Pot, Amethyst.................................15.00
Cat Slipper, Sea Foam.................................20.00	Gypsy Pot, Bittersweet..............................35.00
Cat Slipper, Tiger....................................20.00	Gypsy Pot, Bloody Mary..............................50.00
Cat Slipper, Vaseline.................................20.00	Gypsy Pot, Caramel..................................40.00
Cat Slipper, Willow Green, not mkd....................25.00	Gypsy Pot, Diochromatic Green.......................45.00
Chick, 2″, Amethyst, not mkd..........................15.00	Gypsy Pot, Jade.....................................35.00
Chick, 2″, Bittersweet................................40.00	Gypsy Pot, Lemon Opal...............................20.00
Chick, 2″, Bloody Mary, not mkd.......................50.00	Gypsy Pot, Old Opal Custard.........................35.00

Hands, Amethyst....................................8.00
Hands, Crown Tuscan.............................17.50
Hands, Sapphire...................................8.00
Hat, Amethyst....................................15.00
Hat, Ruby..18.00
Hat, Sapphire....................................17.50
Hat, Vaseline, not mkd...........................15.00
Heart & Lyre Cup Plate, Amber, not mkd...........10.00
Heart & Lyre Cup Plate, Amethyst, not mkd........10.00
Heart & Lyre Cup Plate, Blue Milk Glass, not mkd...15.00
Heart & Lyre Cup Plate, Cobalt, not mkd..........12.00
Heart & Lyre Cup Plate, Crown Tuscan.............25.00
Heart & Lyre Cup Plate, Green, not mkd...........10.00
Heart & Lyre Cup Plate, Opalescent, not mkd......12.00
Heart & Lyre Cup Plate, Peach, clear, not mkd....10.00
Heart & Lyre Cup Plate, Pink, not mkd............10.00
Heart Box, April Green...........................22.00
Heart Box, Caramel Custard Slag..................30.00
Heart Box, Crystal...............................15.00
Heart Box, Custard...............................25.00
Heart Toothpick, Amberina........................17.50
Heart Toothpick, Amethyst........................15.00
Heart Toothpick, Blue Milk Glass.................22.50
Heart Toothpick, Crystal Green...................12.50
Heart Toothpick, Gray Tomato.....................17.50
Heart Toothpick, Opalescent......................17.50
Heart Toothpick, Peach, opaque...................15.00
Heart Toothpick, Royal Crown Tuscan..............20.00
Heart Toothpick, White Milk Glass................15.00
Hen, 3", Baby Blue...............................30.00
Hen, 3", Brown Sparrow Slag......................25.00
Hen, 3", Caramel Custard.........................45.00
Hen, 3", Crown Tuscan............................30.00
Hen, 3", Crystal.................................20.00
Hen, 3", Dk Green................................25.00
Hen, 3", Sapphire................................20.00
Hen, 3", Sparrow.................................25.00
High Boot, Crystal, not mkd......................20.00
Hobo Shoe, Blue & White Slag.....................20.00
Hobo Shoe, Brown Sparrow Slag....................20.00
Hobo Shoe, Caramel Custard Slag..................20.00
Jewel Box, Amethyst..............................20.00
Jewel Box, Baby Green............................25.00
Jewel Box, Caramel Custard.......................35.00
Jewel Box, Frosty Jade...........................30.00
Jewel Box, Green Lavender........................35.00
Jewel Box, Lt Chocolate Creme....................35.00
Michigan Beaded Oval Toothpick, Amberina.........25.00
Michigan Beaded Oval Toothpick, Crown Tuscan.....22.50
Michigan Beaded Oval Toothpick, Ruby Red.........30.00
Mini Pitcher, Blue Milk Glass....................20.00
Mini Pitcher, Chocolate Creme....................20.00
Mini Pitcher, Crown Tuscan.......................20.00
Mug, child's; Lt Chocolate Slag..................25.00
Owl, Amber.......................................32.50
Owl, Amethyst....................................25.00
Owl, Antique Blue................................35.00
Owl, Apple Green.................................40.00
Owl, Baby Green..................................50.00
Owl, Blue & White................................50.00
Owl, Blue Green Marble...........................60.00
Owl, Bluejay.....................................45.00
Owl, Buttercup...................................50.00
Owl, Chad's Blue.................................50.00

Owl, Cobalt......................................45.00
Owl, Crown Tuscan................................35.00
Owl, Daffodil....................................40.00
Owl, Dk Caramel.................................100.00
Owl, Dk Helitrope...............................100.00
Owl, Dk Sapphire Blue............................30.00
Owl, Fog...40.00
Owl, Frosty Jade.................................40.00
Owl, Heatherbloom................................75.00
Owl, Honey Amber, 1974...........................20.00
Owl, Lt Bittersweet..............................75.00
Owl, Mission Green...............................40.00
Owl, Old Lavender................................45.00
Owl, Orchid......................................45.00
Owl, Peach, clear................................25.00
Owl, Pearl Gray..................................40.00
Owl, Pigeon Blood................................30.00
Owl, Pink Lady...................................40.00
Owl, Red Carnival...............................125.00
Owl, Rose Marie..................................25.00
Owl, Sahara Sand.................................50.00
Owl, Sapphire, 1970..............................20.00
Owl, Shamrock Green..............................30.00
Owl, Teal..25.00
Owl, Vaseline....................................32.00
Owl, Willow Blue, old............................30.00
Plate, Face; Amberina............................45.00
Plate, Face; Sapphire............................35.00
Pooche, Bittersweet Slag.........................35.00
Pooche, Caramel Slag.............................25.00
Pooche, Crystal..................................15.00
Pooche, Fawn.....................................20.00
Pooche, Gray Marble Opal.........................30.00
Pooche, Gray Tomato..............................30.00
Pooche, Green Caramel Slag.......................30.00
Pooche, Gunmetal Blue............................20.00
Pooche, Henry's Blue.............................20.00
Pooche, Opal to Clear............................25.00
Pooche, Sahara Sand..............................35.00
Pooche, Sapphire.................................15.00
Pottie Salt, Amethyst............................10.00
Pottie Salt, Blue Milk Glass.....................20.00
Pottie Salt, Chocolate Creme.....................15.00
Pottie Salt, Crown Tuscan........................20.00
Pottie Salt, Henry's Blue........................15.00
Pottie Salt, Honey...............................12.50
Pottie Salt, White Milk Glass....................12.00
Priscilla, Amber.................................60.00
Priscilla, Blue Willow...........................60.00
Priscilla, Daffodil..............................90.00
Priscilla, Degenhart Green.......................80.00
Priscilla, Delft Blue............................80.00
Priscilla, Ebony.................................80.00
Priscilla, Fawn..................................75.00
Priscilla, Ice Blue Carnival.....................85.00
Priscilla, Jade..................................85.00
Priscilla, Orchid................................80.00
Priscilla, Periwinkle............................60.00
Priscilla, Pink..................................80.00
Priscilla, Powder Blue...........................95.00
Priscilla, Smokey Blue...........................60.00
Priscilla, Snow White............................80.00
Priscilla, Tomato Red...........................130.00
Priscilla, Vaseline..............................65.00

Robin Covered Dish, Amberina	35.00
Robin Covered Dish, Lemon Custard	50.00
Seal of Ohio Cup Plate, Blue Milk Glass, not mkd	20.00
Seal of Ohio Cup Plate, Custard, decal	25.00
Seal of Ohio Cup Plate, Opalescent to Clear, not mkd	20.00
Skate Shoe, Amberina	25.00
Skate Shoe, Cobalt Carnival	30.00
Skate Shoe, Sapphire, not mkd	30.00
Texas Boot, Amethyst	15.00
Texas Boot, Baby Green	20.00
Texas Boot, Chocolate	25.00
Texas Boot, Sapphire	15.00
Tomahawk, Amber	15.00
Tomahawk, Lt Pink	28.00
Tomahawk, Sapphire, no mk	18.00
Turkey, 5″, Amethyst	50.00
Turkey, 5″, Blue Milk Glass, not mkd	60.00
Turkey, 5″, Crown Tuscan	75.00
Turkey, 5″, Gray Slag, not mkd	80.00

Delft

Old Delft ware, made as early as the 16th century, was originally a low-fired earthenware coated with a thin opaque tin glaze with painted-on polychrome designs. It was not until the last half of the 18th century, however, that the ware became commonly referred to as Delft, acquiring the name from the Dutch village that had become the major center of its production.

English potters also produced Delft, though with noticeable differences, both in shape and decorative theme.

In the early part of the 18th century, the German potter, Bottger, developed a formula for porcelain; in England, Wedgwood began producing creamware -- both of which were much more durable. Unable to compete, one by one the Delft potteries failed. Soon, only one remained. In 1876, De Porcelyne Fles reintroduced Delft ware on a hard white body with blue and white decorative themes reflecting the Dutch countryside, windmills by the sea, and Dutch children. This type continues to be produced and can be found today in nearly any gift shop.

Ash tray, chrome top, ink mk HP/Delft, #912, 4½″	15.00
Bottle, Pilgrim's; bl/wht, man in scroll reserve, Dutch, 9″	450.00
Bowl, florals in 5 colors, 1750s, prof rpr, 3½x8″	95.00

Novelty windmill with silver blades, $195.00.

Bowl, 3 pc w/lid, bl/wht foliage/coiled fish on lid, 5¾x7½″	200.00
Candlestick, flared nozzle pierced/pntd florals, Bristol, 2½″	275.00
Charger, English, 4 color flower basket, 1750, stapled, 13½″	175.00
Charger, Holland, bl/wht florals/ochre rim, sgn Duyn, 13½″	275.00
Charger, portrait of Wm of Orange, sgn WR on front, 14″	1,540.00
Creamer, cow, Hersey Park	12.00
Drug jar, Balsamic w/angel head label, London, 7″	750.00
Pitcher, sunflower in 3 colors, prof rpr, 4¼″	85.00
Plaque, lg basket of flowers, bl/wht, velvet fr, 1700s, 16″	750.00
Plaque, Rembrandt portrait, bl/wht, 1800s, 15½″	225.00
Plate, bl/wht florals w/ochre rim, hatchet & X mk, 1760, 9″, G	145.00
Plate, bl/wht Oriental decor w/yellow rim, 1800s, 8¾″	125.00
Plate, Bristol, rooster, rust/yel/bl w/purple trees, 1700s, 8″	675.00
Plate, Bristol, rooster in 3 colors/trees in 2, 1750s, 9″, G	675.00
Plate, Dutch, bl/wht floral, lattice w/oval border, 1740, 8¾″	135.00
Plate, Dutch, bl/wht flowering branch, 1750, 13¾″	250.00
Plate, Dutch, bl/wht reserves w/flowers, 5 around 1, 1740, 9″	215.00
Plate, Dutch, brush stroke bl/wht flower basket, 1690, 12½″	475.00
Plate, Dutch, peacock & florals w/allover stylized plants, 12¾″	475.00
Plate, Dutch, 2 swans in water/allover florals, 1740, 16″	500.00
Plate, floral center, bl/wht, att Lambeth, 1750s, 10″	325.00
Plate, Oriental decor, red/bl/gr, 1800s, 8¾″	225.00

Depression Glass

Other than coins and stamps, colored glassware produced during the Depression era is probably the most sought-after collectible in the field today. There are literally thousands of collectors in the United States and Canada buying, selling, and trading 'Depression Glass' on today's market.

Depression Glass is defined by Gene Florence, author of several best-selling books on the subject, as 'the inexpensive glassware made primarily during the Depression era in the colors of amber, green, pink, blue, red, yellow, white, and crystal'. This glass was mass produced and sold through five-and-dime stores and mail-order catalogs, and given away as premiums with gas and food products.

The listings in this book are far from being complete. If you want a more thorough presentation of this fascinating glassware, we recommend *The Collector's Encyclopedia of Depression Glass* by Gene Florence. This beautiful full color volume contains thousands of descriptions and prices. It is available at your favorite bookstore or public library.

Adam, Jeannette Glass Co., 1932-1934

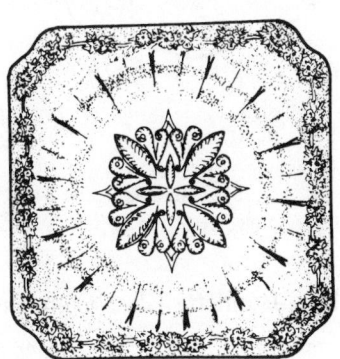

Ash tray, 4½″, pink	19.50
Bowl, 5¾″ cereal, green	20.00
Bowl, 9″, covered, pink	37.50
Butter dish & cover, green	217.50
Candlesticks, 4″, delphite blue, pr	87.50
Coaster, 3¼″, green	12.00

Cup, round, yellow...95.00
Pitcher, 32 oz, round base, pink.......................35.00
Plate, 9″ square dinner, green.........................14.00
Platter, 11¾″, green...12.00
Salt & pepper, 4″, footed, pink.......................42.50
Sugar, pink...9.50
Tumbler, 5½″ iced tea, green..........................25.00

American Pioneer, Liberty Works, 1931-1934

Bowl, 10⅜″ console, pink................................35.00
Candy jar w/cover, 1½ lb, pink.......................60.00
Cup, amber..21.00
Goblet, 4″, 3 oz wine, crystal.........................17.50
Lamp, 8½″ tall, green.....................................67.50
Mayonnaise, 4¼″, pink...................................37.50
Pitcher, 5″ covered urn, pink..........................97.50
Plate, 8″, green...6.00
Sherbet, 3½″, pink..10.00
Sugar, 3½″, amber..35.00
Tumbler, 4″, 8 oz, pink...................................15.00
Whiskey, 2¼″, 2 oz, crystal............................30.00

American Sweetheart, Macbeth Evans, 1930-1934

Bowl, 18″ console, monax..............................277.50
Bowl, 3¾″ flat berry, pink...............................22.50
Creamer, footed, pink..7.50
Plate, 10¼″ dinner, monax..............................13.50
Plate, 15½″ server, monax.............................152.50

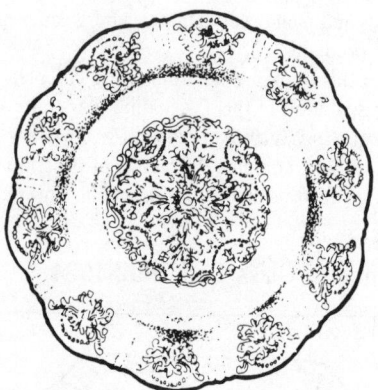

Platter, 13″ oval, pink.....................................17.50
Sherbet, 3¾″, footed, pink..............................11.50
Sugar, open, ftd, pink.......................................7.50
Tidbit, 3 tier, 8″, 12″, & 15½″, monax..........150.00
Tumbler, 4½″, 10 oz, pink...............................40.00

Anniversary, Jeannette Glass Company, 1947-1949

Bowl, 4¾″ berry, crystal....................................1.50
Butter dish w/cover, pink................................40.00
Candlestick, 4¾″, crystal, pr..........................12.50
Cup, pink..4.50
Plate, 9″ dinner, pink..4.50
Relish dish, 8″, crystal......................................4.50
Sherbet, ftd, crystal..2.50

Sugar, pink...4.50
Vase, wall pin-up, pink...................................15.00
Wine glass, 2½ oz, crystal................................5.50

Aunt Polly, U.S. Glass Co., Late 1920s

Bowl, 4½″ berry, blue..6.00
Butter dish w/cover, blue...............................147.50
Candy, w/cover, 2 handled, blue......................47.50
Creamer, green or iridescent...........................16.50
Plate, 8″ luncheon, blue....................................8.50
Sherbet, blue...8.50
Tumbler, 3½″, 8 oz, blue.................................13.50

Avocado "Sweet Pear," No. 601, Indiana Glass Co., 1923-1933

Bowl, 6″ footed relish, green...........................18.50
Bowl, 9½″, 3¼″ deep, pink.............................57.50
Cup, footed, pink..26.50
Pitcher, 64 oz, pink..300.00
Plate, 10¼″ 2 hdld cake, green.......................32.50
Sherbet, pink..47.50

Sugar, footed, pink...25.00
Tumbler, green...99.50

Beaded Block, Imperial Glass Co., 1927-1930s

Bowl, 4½″ round lily, red................................57.50
Bowl, 7½″ round, plain edge, green..................7.50
Bowl, 8½″ large berry, yellow.........................17.50
Bowl, 8¼″ celery, amber...................................9.50
Candlesticks, 1¾″, pink, pr............................25.00
Candy jar w/cover, 6¼″, green.......................29.50

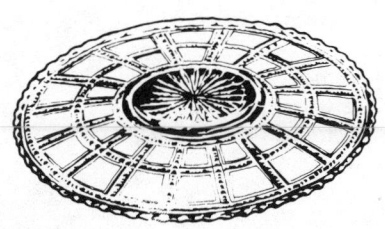

Cup, 4 styles, yellow.........................6.00
Goblet, 5½" wine, clear.......................6.00
Ice bucket, green...........................27.50
Pitcher, 7½", 68 oz, bulbous, pink...........40.00
Plate, 7¾" square, amber......................5.00
Plate, 8" luncheon, yellow....................3.75
Salt & pepper, ftd, pink....................42.50
Saucer, 5¾", with cup ring, green.............7.00
Saucer, 5¾", with cup ring, yellow............7.50
Sherbet, not stemmed, cone, green.............3.00
Stemmed jelly, 4½", flared top, green.........8.50
Sugar, amber..............................10.00
Sugar, three different styles, yellow.........9.50
Tumble-up night set, 3" tumbler bottle & tumbler, 6" high, gr..47.50
Tumbler, 4", 5 oz, footed, pink..............11.50
Vase, 6" bouquet, pink........................8.50
Whiskey, 2½", green..........................12.50

"Bubble," "Bullseye," "Provincial," Anchor Hocking Glass Co., 1934-1965

Bowl, 7¾" flat soup, lt blue..................8.00
Bowl, 8⅜" large berry, pink...................3.00
Bowl, 9" flanged, lt blue....................37.50
Candlesticks, crystal, pr....................10.00
Cup, pink.................................27.50
Pitcher, 64 oz, ice lip, crystal.............32.50

Platter, 12" oval, lt blue....................8.50
Saucer, pink...............................17.50
Tidbit, 2 tier, ruby red....................16.50
Tumbler, 16 oz lemonade, ruby red...........13.50

Cameo, "Ballerina" or "Dancing Girl," Hocking Glass Co., 1930-1934

Bowl, 11", 3 leg console, pink...............17.50
Bowl, 8¼" large berry, green.................24.50
Cake plate, 10½" flat, green.................57.50
Candy jar, 4", w/cover, pink................350.00
Cocktail shaker, metal lid, crystal.........325.00
Creamer, 4¼", green.........................16.00
Domino tray, 7", w/3" indentation, green.....67.50
Goblet, 4" wine, green......................47.50
Goblet, 6" water, pink.....................110.00
Pitcher, 8½", 56 oz water, green.............37.50

Plate, 8" luncheon, yellow....................4.50
Plate, 9½" dinner, pink.....................30.00
Platter, 12", closed handles, yellow.........13.50
Saucer, 6", (sherbet plate), pink...........45.00
Sherbet, 4¾", green.........................22.50
Sugar, 3¼", yellow...........................9.50
Tumbler, 3¾", 5 oz juice, green.............18.50

Tumbler, 5¼", 15 oz, pink...................85.00
Tumbler, 6¼", 15 oz footed, green..........150.00
Vase, 8", green.............................18.50

Cherry Blossom, Jeannette Glass Co., 1930-1939

Bowl, 8½" round berry, yellow..............350.00
Bowl, 9" oval vegetable, pink...............17.50
Butter dish w/cover, green..................75.00
Coaster, pink...............................11.50
Creamer, delphite...........................16.00
Mug, 7 oz, green...........................137.50

Pitcher, 8", 42 oz flat, pattern at top, green.......37.50
Plate, 9" dinner, green.....................17.50
Platter, 13" divided, pink..................35.00
Salt & pepper, scalloped bottom, pink......925.00
Tumbler, 3¾", 4 oz ftd, round or scalloped, delphite........16.00
Tumbler, 4¼", 9 oz flat, pattern at top, green.......16.50

Chinex Classic, Macbeth-Evans, Late 1930s-Early 1940s

Bowl, 9" vegetable, browntone................9.50
Butter dish, ivory..........................50.00
Creamer, ivory...............................4.50
Plate, 9¾" dinner, castle decor..............6.00

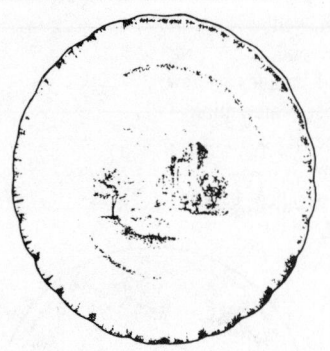

Sherbet, low footed, decal decorated........................9.00
Sugar, open, browntone..................................4.00

Circle, Hocking Glass Co., 1930s

Bowl, 4½", pink or green................................3.00
Cup, 2 styles, pink or green.............................2.50
Decanter, handled, pink or green........................16.50
Goblet, 4½" wine, pink or green..........................4.00
Goblet, 8 oz water, pink or green........................6.50
Pitcher, 80 oz, pink or green...........................17.50
Plate, 9½" dinner, pink or green.........................6.00
Sherbet, 5¾", pink or green..............................4.50
Tumbler, 8 oz water, pink or green.......................4.50

Cloverleaf, Hazel Atlas Glass Co., 1930-1936

Bowl, 4" dessert, green.................................12.50
Bowl, 8", green..42.50
Candy dish w/cover, yellow..............................95.00
Creamer, 3¾" footed, black.............................12.50
Plate, 8" luncheon, pink................................5.00
Salt & pepper, pr, green...............................22.50
Sugar, footed, 3¾", green...............................7.50
Tumbler, 5¾", 10 oz ftd, yellow........................22.50

Colonial, "Knife and Fork," Hocking Glass Co., 1934-1936

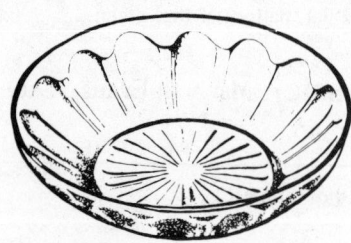

Bowl, 10" oval vegetable, green.........................18.50
Bowl, 4½" cream soup, pink.............................28.50

Butter dish w/cover, green.............................42.50
Cup, pink..6.00
Goblet, 3¾", 1 oz cordial, green.......................23.00
Goblet, 5¾", 8½ oz water, pink.........................20.00
Pitcher, 7¾", 68 oz, ice lip or none, pink.............35.00
Plate, 10" dinner, green...............................39.50
Salt & pepper, green, pr..............................107.50
Tumbler, 15 oz lemonade, pink..........................27.50
Tumbler, 4", 9 oz water, royal ruby....................27.50
Whiskey, 2½", 1½ oz, green..............................9.00

Colonial Fluted, "Rope," Federal Glass Co., 1928-1933

Bowl, 4" berry, green...................................4.00
Bowl, 7½" large berry, green............................9.00
Plate, 6" sherbet, green................................1.50
Sherbet, green...4.50

Sugar, green...3.50
Sugar cover, green.....................................7.50

Columbia, Federal Glass Co., 1938-1942

Bowl, 10½" ruffled edge, crystal.......................12.50
Bowl, 5" cereal, crystal................................7.50
Cup, crystal...3.50
Plate, 11¾" chop, crystal...............................5.50

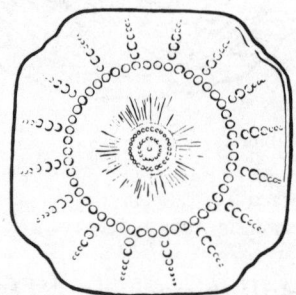

Plate, 9½" luncheon, crystal............................3.50
Snack plate, crystal..................................12.50
Tumbler, crystal.......................................8.00

Cornation, "Banded Fine Rib," "Saxon," Hocking Glass Co., 1936-1940

Bowl, 4¼" berry, pink...................................3.00
Bowl, 8", no handles, green............................20.00
Cup, ruby red..4.50
Pitcher, 7¾", 68 oz, pink.............................125.00
Plate, 8½" luncheon, green.............................12.00

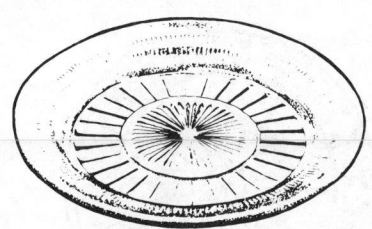

Tumbler, 5″, 10 oz footed, green.........................25.00
Tumbler, 5″, 10 oz footed, pink..........................8.50

Cube, "Cubist," Jeannette Glass Co., 1929-1933

Bowl, 4½″ dessert, green..................................5.00
Bowl, 6½″ salad, ultramarine............................30.00
Butter dish w/cover, pink...............................45.00
Pitcher, 8¾″, 45 oz, green.............................147.50

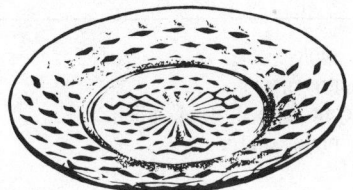

Powder jar & cover, 3 legs, pink........................12.00
Sherbet, footed, green...................................6.00
Sugar, 3″, green...5.50
Tumbler, 4″, 9 oz, pink.................................21.50

Cupid, Paden City Glass Co., 1930s

Bowl, 11″ console, green................................35.00
Bowl, 8½″ oval footed, pink............................32.50
Cake plate, 11¾″, blue.................................35.00
Candy w/lid, footed, 4¾″, pink........................37.50
Creamer, 5″, footed, blue.............................32.50
Mayonnaise, 6″ dia, fits on 8″ plate, pink.............40.00
Tray, 10¾″ oval, footed, green........................37.50

"Daisy," Number 620, Indiana Glass Co., crystal, 1933; amber, 1940; green and milk, 1960-80s

Bowl, 6″ cereal, green...................................6.00
Bowl, 7¼″ deep berry, amber............................10.00
Creamer, footed, crystal.................................4.50
Plate, 10½″ grill, green.................................4.00
Plate, 11½″ cake or sandwich, amber.....................8.50
Plate, 7½″ salad, amber..................................5.50
Platter, 10¾″, green.....................................5.00

Sherbet, footed, amber...................................7.00
Tumbler, 9 oz footed, amber............................12.50

Diamond Quilted, "Flat Diamond," Imperial Glass Co., Late 1920s-Early 1930s

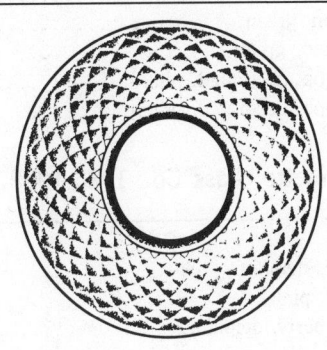

Bowl, 4¾″ cream soup, blue.............................12.50
Bowl, 7″ crimped edge, pink.............................5.50
Candlesticks, blue, pr.................................22.50
Compote & cover, 11½″, pink...........................37.50
Creamer, blue...9.50
Goblet, 1 oz cordial, pink..............................5.50
Ice bucket, blue.......................................55.00
Mayonnaise set, ladle, plate, 3 ftd dish, pink.........17.50
Pitcher, 64 oz, pink...................................27.50
Plate, 14″ sandwich, pink...............................8.50
Plate, 8″ luncheon, blue...............................10.00
Punch bowl & stand, green.............................257.50
Tumbler, 12 oz footed, green...........................12.50
Tumbler, 9 oz water, pink...............................6.50
Vase, fan, dolphin hdls, blue..........................32.50

Diana, Federal Glass Co., 1937-1941

Ash tray, 3½″, green.....................................3.00
Bowl, 11″ console fruit, crystal.........................5.00
Bowl, 5½″ cream soup, pink...............................5.00
Candy jar & cover, round, amber.........................22.50
Cup, pink..3.50
Plate, 9½″ dinner, pink..................................5.50
Platter, 12″ oval, amber.................................7.50
Salt & pepper, crystal, pr.............................17.50
Sherbet, pink..5.00
Sugar, open oval, amber..................................3.50

Dogwood, "Apple Blossom," "Wild Rose," Macbeth-Evans Glass Co., 1929-1932

Bowl, 5½″ cereal, yellow................................45.00
Bowl, 8½″ berry, pink..................................32.50
Cake plate, 11″, heavy solid foot, pink...............152.50
Creamer, 3¼″, thick, pink..............................13.50

Pitcher, 8″, 80 oz, decorated, pink......................127.50
Plate, 12″ salver, pink.................................18.50
Plate, 8″ luncheon, green..............................5.00
Sherbet, low footed, green.............................47.50
Tumbler, 4″, 10 oz, decorated, pink....................22.50
Tumbler, 5″, 12 oz, decorated, green...................67.50

Doric, Jeannette Glass Co., 1935-1938

Bowl, 4½″ berry, delphite..............................27.50
Bowl, 5½″ cereal, pink.................................16.00
Bowl, 8¼″ large berry, delphite.......................77.50
Bowl, 9″ oval vegetable, green.........................12.50
Butter dish w/cover, pink..............................55.50
Candy dish, 3 part, green..............................5.50
Cup, pink..5.50
Pitcher, 6″, 36 oz flat, green.........................27.50
Plate, 7″ salad, pink..................................12.50
Plate, 9″ grill, green.................................10.00

Relish tray, 4x8″, green...............................9.50
Salt & pepper, pink, pr................................24.00
Sherbet, footed, delphite..............................5.00
Sugar, green...9.50
Sugar cover, green.....................................15.00
Tray, 10″ handled, green...............................9.50
Tumbler, 4″, 10 oz ftd, pink...........................18.00

Doric and Pansy, Jeannette Glass Co., 1937-1938

Bowl, 4½″ berry, pink..................................6.00
Bowl, 8″ large berry, pink.............................17.50
Butter dish w/cover, ultramarine.......................625.00
Creamer, crystal.......................................57.50

Plate, 7″ salad, ultramarine...........................27.50
Tray, 10″ handled, ultramarine.........................17.50

English Hobnail, Westmoreland Glass Co., 1920s-1970s

Bowl, cream soup, pink.................................13.50
Candlesticks, 3½″, green, pr...........................30.00
Candy dish, ½ lb, cone shaped, w/lid, green............45.00
Candy dish, 3 feet, pink, w/lid........................57.50
Egg cup, pink..25.00
Goblet, 6¼″, 8 oz, cobalt..............................34.00
Marmalade & cover, pink................................32.50
Pitcher, 39 oz, pink...................................120.00
Plate, 5½″ or 6½″ sherbet, cobalt......................7.00
Plate, 8″ round or square, cobalt......................14.00
Salt & pepper, round or square bases, pink, pr.........67.50
Salt dip, 2″ footed, w/place card holder, turq.........24.00
Tumbler, 5″, 12 oz iced tea, green.....................17.50
Whiskey, 3 oz, pink....................................16.50

Fire-King Dinnerware, "Philbe," Hocking Glass Co., 1937-1938

Bowl, 5½″ cereal, pink or green........................30.00
Candy jar, 4″, w/cover, blue...........................157.50
Cookie jar w/cover, blue...............................350.00
Cookie jar w/cover, pink or green......................200.00
Goblet, 7¼″, 9 oz, pink or green.......................117.50
Plate, 11½″ salver, blue...............................32.50
Plate, 8″ luncheon, crystal............................12.00
Sugar, 3¼″, footed, pink or green......................45.00

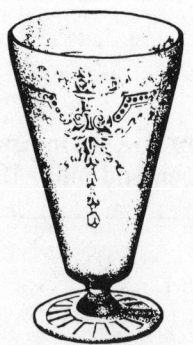

Tumbler, 3½″ footed juice, crystal.....................30.00
Tumbler, 5¼″, 10 oz footed, pink or green..............40.00
Tumbler, 6½″, 15 oz footed iced tea, blue..............35.00

Fire-King Oven Glass, Anchor Hocking Glass Corporation, 1941-1950s

Baker, 2 qt, blue...10.00
Bowl, measuring; 16 oz, blue.........................15.00
Bowl, 5¼" cereal or deep dish pie plate, blue................8.50
Bowl, 8½" utility, blue.................................8.50
Casserole, 10 oz, tab handle cover, blue..............12.00
Casserole, 2 qt, knob handle cover, blue..............15.00
Cup, 8 oz, dry measure, no spout, blue................25.00

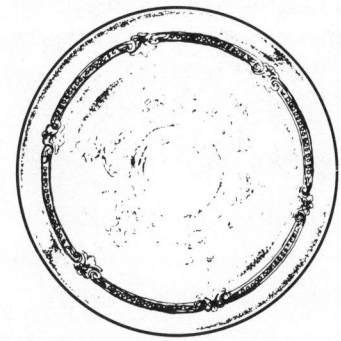

Nurser, 4 oz, blue.....................................12.00
Pie plate, 10¼" juice saver, blue.....................35.00
Pie plate, 9", blue.....................................8.00
Refrigerator jar & cover, 4½x5", blue.................7.50
Roaster, 8¾" blue.....................................25.00

Floragold, "Louisa," Jeannette Glass Co., 1950s

Bowl, 9½" deep salad, iridescent......................25.00
Bowl, 9½" ruffled, iridescent..........................6.50
Butter dish & cover, round, iridescent................35.00
Candy, 5¼" long, 4 feet, iridescent....................4.50
Coaster or ash tray, 4", iridescent....................4.50
Cup, iridescent...4.00
Plate, 8½" dinner, iridescent........................16.50
Platter, 11¼", iridescent............................13.50
Salt & pepper, w/plastic tops, iridescent.............35.00
Sugar, iridescent.......................................5.00
Sugar lid, iridescent...................................7.50
Tumbler, 11 oz, footed, iridescent...................12.50
Tumbler, 15 oz, footed, iridescent...................42.50

Floral, "Poinsetta," Jeannette Glass Co., 1931-1935

Bowl, 4" berry, delphite...............................25.00
Butter dish w/cover, pink............................67.50

Candlesticks, 4", green, pr...........................62.50
Canister set, coffee/tea/cereal/sugar, 5¼", jadite, each........25.00
Ice tub, 3½" high, oval, pink.......................375.00
Pitcher, 10¼", 48 oz lemonade, pink................160.00
Pitcher, 8", 32 oz footed cone, green................25.00
Plate, 9" dinner, delphite...........................95.00
Plate, 9" dinner, pink...............................11.00
Platter, 10¾" oval, green............................12.50
Salt & pepper, 4", footed, green, pr.................35.00
Sherbet, pink..8.50
Tray, 6" square, closed handles, green...............10.00
Tumbler, 4½", 9 oz flat, green......................157.50
Tumbler, 5¼", 9 oz footed lemonade, green...........27.50
Vase, 3 legged rose bowl, green.....................387.50

Floral and Diamond Band, U.S. Glass Co., Late 1920s

Bowl, 4½" berry, green.................................5.00
Butter dish w/cover, pink............................85.00
Creamer, 4¾", green or pink..........................10.00
Plate, 8" luncheon, green............................12.50
Sherbet, pink..4.00
Sugar, 5¼", green......................................8.50

Florentine No. 1, "Old Florentine," "Poppy No. 1," Hazel Atlas Glass Co., 1932-1935

Ash tray, 5½", pink...................................24.00
Bowl, 8½" large berry, green.........................15.00
Butter dish w/cover, yellow.........................135.00
Creamer, ruffled, pink...............................22.50
Cup, blue...57.50
Cup, pink..6.50
Pitcher, 6½", 36 oz, footed, yellow..................40.00

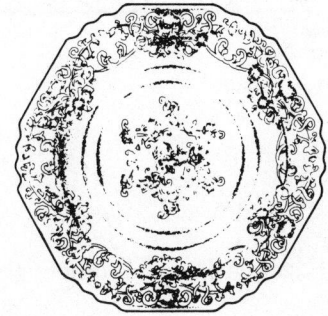

Plate, 10" grill, green.................................7.50
Sherbet, 3 oz, footed, green...........................5.50
Sugar, yellow..9.50
Sugar cover, yellow...................................13.50
Tumbler, 3¼", 5 oz footed, green......................8.50

Florentine No. 2, "Poppy No. 2," Hazel Atlas Glass Co., 1934-1937

Bowl, 4¾" cream soup, pink............................9.00
Bowl, 6" cereal, yellow..............................21.00
Bowl, 9" flat, green.................................16.50
Butter dish w/cover, green...........................82.50
Compote, 3½" ruffled, blue...........................45.00
Custard cup or jello, green..........................42.50
Pitcher, 7½", 48 oz, pink............................97.50

Pitcher, 8″, 76 oz, green...72.50
Plate, 10″ dinner, pink..12.00
Platter, 11″ oval, yellow..13.50
Relish dish, 10″, 3 part, green...............................12.00
Sherbet, footed, amber..39.50
Sugar, yellow..8.50
Sugar cover, yellow...14.50
Tumbler, 3½″, 5 oz juice, pink................................8.00

Forest Green, Anchor Hocking Glass Co. Corporation, 1950-1957

Bowl, batter; green...6.00
Bowl, 7¼″ salad, green...6.50
Cup, green..2.50
Mixing bowl set, 3 piece, green..............................17.50
Pitcher, 3 qt round, green......................................20.00
Plate, 10″ dinner, green...8.50
Punch bowl w/stand, green.....................................20.00
Punch cup, green..2.00
Sugar, flat, green...4.50
Tumbler, 5 oz, green...2.00
Vase, 9″, green..5.00

"Fortune," Hocking Glass Co., 1937-1938

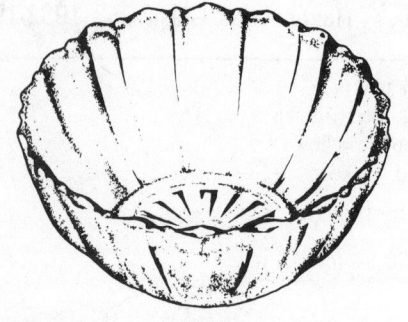

Bowl, 4″ berry, pink...2.50
Bowl, 5¼″, rolled edge, pink....................................4.00
Candy dish w/cover, flat, pink.................................13.50
Cup, pink..3.00
Plate, 8″ luncheon, pink..4.00
Tumbler, 4″, 9 oz water, pink....................................4.50

"Fruits," Hazel Atlas and other glass companies, 1931-1933

Bowl, 5″ cereal, green..12.00
Pitcher, 7″ flat bottom, green..................................40.00
Plate, 8″ luncheon, pink or green...............................4.00

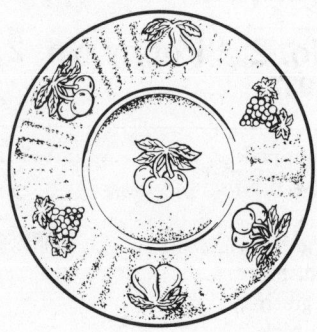

Sherbet, pink...5.50
Tumbler, 5″, 12 oz, green..35.00

Georgian, "Lovebirds," Federal Glass Co., 1931-1936

Bowl, 7½″ large berry, green...................................39.50
Creamer, 4″, footed, green.......................................9.50
Cup, green..7.50
Plate, 9¼″ dinner, green..16.50
Platter, 11½″ closed handle, green...........................45.00
Sugar, 3″, ftd, green..8.50
Sugar, 4″, footed, green..9.00
Sugar cover for 3″, green..22.50
Sugar cover for 4″, green..32.50
Tumbler, 4″, 9 oz flat, green....................................35.00

Harp, Jeannette Glass Co., 1954-1957

Cake stand, 9″, ice blue or shell pink........................12.50
Cup, crystal..4.50
Plate, 7″, crystal..3.50
Saucer, crystal...2.00
Vase, 6″, crystal...9.50

Heritage, Federal Glass Co., Late 1930s-1960s

Bowl, 5″ berry, pink...15.00
Bowl, 8½″ large berry, blue or green........................57.50
Cup, crystal..3.50
Plate 9¼″ dinner, crystal...6.50
Saucer, crystal...2.00
Sugar, open footed, crystal.......................................9.50

Hex Optic, "Honeycomb," Jeannette Glass Co., 1928-1932

Bowl, 10″ mixing, pink or green...............................18.00
Bowl, 7½″ large berry, pink or green..........................5.00

Butter dish w/cover, rectangular 1 lb size, pink or green........35.00
Pitcher, 5″, 32 oz, sunflower motif in bottom, pink............12.50

Plate, 8″ luncheon, pink or green...................................4.50
Refrigerator stack set, 3 pc, pink..................................30.00
Sugar, 2 styles of hdls, pink or green...............................4.00
Tumbler, 4¾″, 7 oz, footed, pink...................................5.00
Whiskey, 2″, 1 oz, pink or green...................................3.50

Hobnail, Hocking Glass Co., 1934-1936

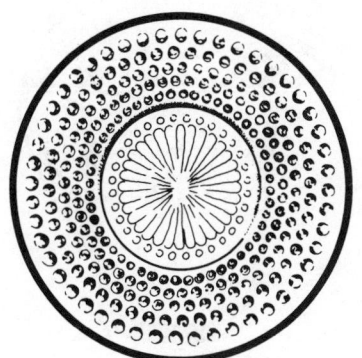

Bowl, 7″ salad, crystal.................................2.00
Cup, pink...2.00
Decanter w/stopper, 32 oz, crystal.......................12.50
Goblet, 10 oz water, crystal...........................4.50
Pitcher, 18 oz milk, crystal...........................12.50
Plate, 8½″ luncheon, pink............................2.00
Sherbet, pink.......................................2.50
Tumbler, 15 oz iced tea, crystal........................5.00
Whiskey, 1½″ oz, crystal.............................4.00

Holiday, "Buttons and Bows," Jeannette Glass Co., 1947-1949

Bowl, 8½″ large berry, pink.........................14.50
Butter dish w/cover, pink............................35.00
Cake plate, 10½″, 3 legged, pink.....................55.00
Pitcher, 6¾″, 52 oz, pink...........................25.00
Platter, 11½″ oval, pink............................10.00
Sugar, pink..6.00
Sugar cover, pink...................................8.50
Tumbler, 4″, 10 oz flat, pink........................14.50

Homespun, "Fine Rib," Jeannette Glass Co., 1939-1940

Bowl, 4½″, closed handles, pink or crystal...............4.50
Butter dish w/cover, pink or crystal...................40.00

Cup, pink or crystal...................................4.00
Pitcher, 96 oz, pink or crystal........................27.50
Platter, 13″, closed handles, pink or crystal.............8.50
Sugar, footed, pink or crystal........................6.00
Tumbler, 6½″, 15 oz, footed, pink or crystal...........13.50

Indiana Custard, "Flower and Leaf Band," Indiana Glass Co., 1930s & 1950s

Bowl, 5¾″ cereal, ivory.............................12.50
Bowl, 8¾″ large berry, ivory.........................20.00
Cup, ivory...29.00
Plate, 7½″ salad, ivory.............................8.50
Platter, 11½″ oval, ivory...........................22.50

Saucer, ivory.......................................6.00
Sugar, ivory..8.50
Sugar cover, ivory..................................13.50

Iris, "Iris and Herringbone," Jeannette Glass Co., 1928-1932, 1950s, 1970s

Bowl, 11″ ruffled fruit, crystal.......................8.50
Bowl, 7½″ soup, iridescent...........................20.00
Butter dish w/cover, crystal.........................30.00
Candlesticks, iridescent, pr.........................22.50
Creamer, ftd, crystal................................7.00
Cup, demitasse, iridescent...........................50.00
Goblet, 4″ wine, crystal............................12.50
Goblet, 5¾″, 8 oz, iridescent.......................22.50
Pitcher, 9½″, footed, crystal........................20.00
Plate, 9″ dinner, iridiscent.........................17.50
Saucer, demitasse, iridescent........................60.00
Sherbet, 2½″ footed, crystal........................13.50
Sugar, iridiscent....................................6.00
Sugar cover, iridescent..............................6.00
Tumbler, 4″ flat, crystal...........................47.50
Vase, 9″, pink or green.............................40.00

Jubilee, Lancaster Glass Co., Early 1930s

Bowl, 9″ handled fruit, yellow.......................32.50
Creamer, yellow.....................................16.50
Cup, yellow..11.50
Goblet, 6¼″, 12½ oz, yellow........................25.00
Plate, 13″ sandwich, yellow..........................20.00
Plate, 8¾″ luncheon, yellow.........................8.50

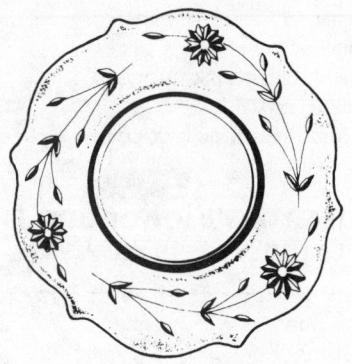

Saucer, yellow...3.00
Sugar, yellow..16.00

Lace Edge, "Open Lace," Hocking Glass Co., 1935-1938

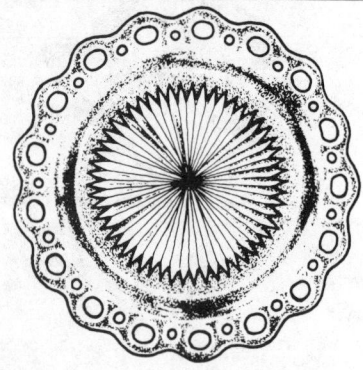

Bowl, 10½", 3 legs, pink...............................125.50
Bowl, 7¾", ribbed, pink................................30.00
Candy jar w/cover, ribbed, pink........................32.50
Plate, 10½" dinner, pink...............................17.50
Plate, 13", 4 part solid lace, pink....................17.50
Relish dish, 7½", 3 part, deep, pink...................37.50
Sugar, pink..14.50
Tumbler, 5", 10½ oz, footed, pink......................40.00

Lake Como, Anchor Hocking Glass Co., 1934-1937

Bowl, 9¾" vegetable, white w/blue scene.................5.00
Creamer, footed, white w/blue scene....................8.50
Cup, regular, white w/blue scene.......................6.50
Cup, St Denis, white w/blue scene......................7.50
Plate, 9¼" dinner, white w/blue scene..................9.50
Salt & pepper, white w/blue scene, pr.................22.50
Sugar, footed, white w/blue scene......................8.50

Laurel, McKee Glass Co., 1930s

Bowl, 9" large berry, poudre blue......................17.50
Bowl, 9¾" oval vegetable, ivory........................15.00
Platter, 10¾" oval, jade green.........................13.50
Salt & pepper, ivory, pr...............................35.00
Sherbet, ivory..9.50
Sugar, tall, jade green.................................7.50
Tumbler, 5", 12 oz, flat, ivory........................27.50

Lincoln Inn, Fenton Glass Co., Late 1920s

Bowl, 5" fruit, red.....................................6.00
Bowl, 9¼", footed, blue................................13.50
Creamer, red...16.50
Goblet, wine, blue.....................................13.50
Pitcher, 7¼", 46 oz, blue.............................350.00
Plate, 9¼", red...8.50

Salt & pepper, green, pr...............................77.50
Sugar, red...16.50
Tumbler, 7 oz, footed, blue............................13.50
Vase, 12", footed, blue................................60.00

Lorain, "Basket," No. 615, Indiana Glass Co., 1929-1932

Ash tray, 6" square, green.............................77.50
Bowl, 10" oval vegetable, green........................13.50
Bowl, 7¼" salad, yellow................................40.00
Butter dish w/cover, amber.............................60.00

Cup, green..8.50
Cup, pink...6.00
Jello mold, 2¼" high, amber.............................8.50
Pitcher, 8½", 80 oz, amber.............................50.00
Plate, 10½" dinner, blue...............................37.50
Plate, 10¼" dinner, yellow.............................40.00
Plate, 10¼" relish, pink................................8.50
Salt & pepper, 3½" flat, green.........................55.00
Saucer, green...3.50
Sherbet, footed, green.................................13.50
Sherbet, 2 styles, blue.................................9.50
Sugar, amber..6.50
Sugar cover, amber.....................................24.50
Tumbler, 4¼", 9 oz, green..............................17.50
Tumbler, 4¾", 9 oz, footed, yellow.....................21.50
Tumbler, 5½", 10 oz, footed, amber.....................19.50

Manhattan, "Horizontal Ribbed," Anchor Hocking Glass Co., 1938-1941

Bowl, 8", closed handles, pink............................12.50
Bowl, 9½" fruit, crystal................................15.00
Candy dish w/cover, crystal.............................20.00

Compote, 5¾", pink.....................................10.00
Pitcher, 42 oz, pink...................................25.00
Plate, 8½" salad, pink..................................6.50
Salt & pepper, 2", square, crystal, pr.................13.50
Tumbler, 10 oz, footed, green...........................5.50
Wine, 3½", crystal......................................7.50

Mayfair, Federal Glass Co., 1934

Bowl, 10" oval vegetable, green........................13.50
Bowl, 5" sauce, amber...................................4.00
Bowl, 6" cereal, crystal................................6.00
Creamer, footed, amber..................................9.00
Plate, 9½" dinner, amber................................9.50
Plate, 9½" grill, green.................................7.50
Platter, 12" oval, amber...............................12.50
Sugar, footed, green....................................8.50
Tumbler, 4½", 9 oz, crystal.............................6.50

Mayfair, "Open Rose," Hocking Glass Co., 1931-1937

Bowl, 10" vegetable, blue..............................40.00
Bowl, 5" cream soup, pink..............................30.00
Butter dish w/cover, pink..............................45.00
Cake plate, 10" footed, green..........................50.00
Celery dish, 9" divided, green........................100.00
Cup, blue..35.00
Goblet, 4", 3½ oz cocktail, pink.......................52.50
Pitcher, 6", 37 oz, pink...............................32.50
Plate, 8½" luncheon, blue..............................25.00
Salt & pepper, flat, blue, pr.........................175.00

Sherbet, 3" footed, pink...............................12.50
Sugar, footed, pink....................................15.00
Sugar lid, pink...8.50
Tumbler, 4¾", 11 oz water, yellow.....................157.50
Vase, blue...65.00
Whiskey, 2¼", 1½ oz, pink..............................57.50

Miss America, (Diamond Pattern), Hocking Glass Company, 1935-1937

Bowl, 4½" berry, green..................................7.00
Bowl, 8¾", straight deep fruit, pink..................37.50
Candy jar w/cover, 11½", crystal......................47.50
Compote, 5", pink......................................15.00
Goblet, 3¾", 3 oz wine, crystal.......................14.00
Pitcher, 8½", 65 oz w/ice lip, pink...................92.50
Plate, 10¼" dinner, pink..............................17.50

Plate, 8½" salad, green................................8.00
Platter, 12¼" oval, crystal...........................10.00
Salt & pepper, pr, pink...............................42.50
Sugar, pink...12.50

Moondrops, New Martinsville, 1932-1940

Ash tray, blue or red.................................27.50
Bowl, 13" console, with 'wings', blue or red..........57.00
Bowl, 6¾" soup, blue or red...........................10.00
Bowl, 9½", 3 legged, ruffled, blue or red.............17.50
Bowl, 9¾", 2-hdld oval, colors other than red or blue.25.00
Butter dish w/cover, colors other than red or blue...225.00
Candle holder, 5½" sherbet style, red or blue, pr.....19.50
Candlesticks, 5¼" triple light, red or blue, pr.......65.00
Compote, 11½", colors other than red or blue..........17.50

Cup, red or blue.......................................9.00
Decanter, 11¼" large, colors other than red or blue..37.50
Goblet, 4", 4 oz wine, red or blue....................15.00
Goblet, 6¼", 9 oz water, red or blue..................17.50
Mug, 5¼", 12 oz, colors other than blue or red........15.00
Pitcher, 6¾", 22 oz small, red or blue...............125.00
Plate, 7¼" salad, red or blue..........................6.00
Plate, 9½" dinner, colors other than blue or red......12.50
Platter, 12" oval, red or blue........................17.50
Tumbler, 3¼", 3 oz footed juice, red or blue..........11.50
Tumbler, 4¾", 9 oz handled, blue or red...............13.50

Moonstone, Anchor Hocking Glass Corporation, 1941-1946

Bowl, cloverleaf, crystal w/opal hobnails..............8.50
Bowl, 5½" berry, crystal w/opal hobnails...............7.00
Bowl, 7¾" flat, crystal w/opal hobnails................8.00

Cigarette jar w/cover, crystal w/opal hobnails.................14.50
Creamer, crystal w/opal hobnails............................6.00
Goblet, 10 oz, crystal w/opal hobnails.......................14.50
Plate, 8″ luncheon, crystal w/opal hobnails..................8.50
Sherbet, footed, crystal w/opal hobnails.....................6.00
Sugar, footed, crystal w/opal hobnails.......................6.00
Vase, 5½″ bud, crystal w/opal hobnails......................8.50

Mt. Pleasant, "Double Shield," L.E. Smith Co., 1920s-1934

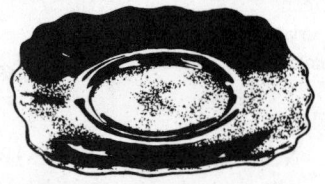

Bowl, bon bon, rolled up handles, pink or green..............9.50
Bowl, 8″, 2-hdld, square, blk amethyst......................16.50
Creamer, scalloped edges, pink or green.....................8.50
Cup, cobalt..7.50
Plate, 10½″ cake, w/solid hdls, cobalt......................20.00
Sherbet, scalloped edges, black amethyst...................11.00
Sugar, scalloped edges, pink or green.......................9.50

New Century, incorrectly "Lydia Ray," Hazel Atlas Glass Co., 1930-1935

Ash tray/coaster, 5½″, green or crystal......................25.00
Bowl, 8″ large berry, green or crystal........................9.50
Butter dish w/cover, green or crystal.......................47.50
Cup, green or crystal..4.50
Goblet, 2½ oz wine, green or crystal........................11.50
Plate, 10″ grill, green or crystal............................7.50
Platter, 11″ oval, green or crystal..........................10.00

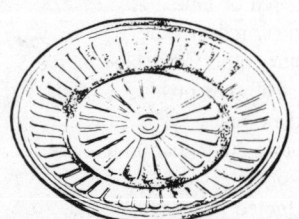

Saucer, green or crystal.....................................2.00
Sherbet, 3″, green or crystal................................5.00
Sugar, green or crystal......................................5.00
Sugar cover, green or crystal................................8.50
Tumbler, 4¾″, 9 oz footed, green or crystal.................10.50
Tumbler, 5¼″, 12 oz, green or crystal.......................13.50
Whiskey, 2½″, 1½ oz, green or crystal........................6.00

Newport, "Hairpin," Hazel Atlas Glass Co., 1936-1940

Bowl, 4¾″ cream soup, amethyst..............................8.50
Bowl, 8¼″ large berry, cobalt..............................22.50
Cup, cobalt..6.50
Plate, 8½″ luncheon, cobalt.................................6.00

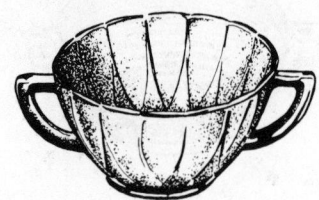

Platter, 11¾″ oval, amethyst...............................18.00
Saucer, cobalt..2.50
Tumbler, 4½″, 9 oz, cobalt.................................20.00

Normandie, "Bouquet and Lattice," Federal Glass Co., 1933-1940

Bowl, 8½″ large berry, amber...............................10.00
Cup, amber...5.50
Plate, 9¼″ luncheon, pink...................................8.50
Platter, 11¾″ pink...14.00
Salt & pepper, pink, pr....................................45.00
Sherbet, iridescent...7.00

Sugar, amber..5.00
Sugar lid, amber...57.50
Tumbler, 4″, 5 oz juice, pink..............................25.00
Tumbler, 5″, 12 oz iced tea, amber.........................15.00

No. 610, "Pyramid," Indiana Glass Co. 1928-1932

Bowl, 9½″ oval, green......................................22.50
Creamer, yellow..24.00
Pitcher, green..167.50
Relish tray, 4 part, hdld, pink............................27.50
Sugar, yellow..24.50
Tray for creamer & sugar, yellow...........................40.00
Tumbler, 11 oz footed, pink................................32.50

No. 612, "Horseshoe," Indiana Glass Company, 1930-1933

Bowl, 8½" vegetable, green...............................16.00
Bowl, 9½" large berry, yellow.............................25.00
Butter dish w/cover, green..............................500.00
Cup, yellow...7.50
Pitcher, 8½", 64 oz, yellow............................200.00
Plate, 11" sandwich, yellow.............................11.50
Plate, 9½" luncheon, green..............................7.50
Saucer, yellow...3.50
Sugar, open, green.....................................10.00

No. 618, "Pineapple & Floral," Indiana Glass Co., 1932-1937

Ash tray, 4½", crystal.................................13.00
Bowl, 10" oval vegetable, amber.........................15.00
Bowl, 6" cereal, crystal................................18.50
Creamer, diamond shaped, crystal.........................6.50
Cup, red..7.00
Plate, 11½", indentation, crystal........................20.00

Platter, 11½" relish, divided, crystal....................14.00
Saucer, red..3.00
Sugar, diamond shaped, crystal...........................6.50
Tumbler, 5", 12 oz, crystal.............................27.50

Old Cafe, Hocking Glass Co., 1936-1938, 1940

Bowl, 5½" cereal, ruby red...............................8.50
Bowl, 9", closed hdls, crystal...........................7.50
Cup, ruby red..6.00
Pitcher, 6", 36 oz, crystal.............................47.50
Plate, 10" dinner, pink................................12.50
Tumbler, 3" juice, pink.................................4.00

Old English, "Threading," Indiana Glass Co., Late 1920s

Bowl, 9½" flat, all colors.............................22.50
Candlesticks, 4", all colors, pr........................22.50

Candy jar, 9¾", 2 hdls, all colors......................25.00
Compote, 3½" tall, 7" across, all colors.................12.50
Goblet, 5¾", 8 oz, all colors...........................17.50
Plate, indent for compote, all colors...................17.50
Sherbet, all colors...................................14.50
Tumbler, 4½" footed, all colors.........................12.50
Vase, 12" footed, all colors...........................30.00

Ovide, incorrectly "New Century," Hazel Atlas Glass Co., 1930-1935

Bowl, 8" large berry, decorated white....................13.50
Cup, decorated white...................................5.50

Plate, 9" dinner, decorated white........................7.50
Salt & pepper, black, pr...............................20.00
Saucer, decorated white.................................3.00

Oyster and Pearl, Anchor Hocking Glass Corporation, 1938-1940

Bowl, 5¼" heart, one hdl, white w/fired on gr or pink.........5.00
Bowl, 6½", deep, hdld, royal ruby.......................12.50
Candle holder, 3½", crystal or pink, pr..................15.00
Plate, 13½" sandwich, royal ruby........................25.00

"Parrot," Sylvan, Federal Glass Co., 1931-1932

Bowl, 8" large berry, green.............................47.50
Butter dish w/cover, green.............................227.00
Creamer, footed, amber.................................22.50
Cup, amber..22.50
Plate, 9" dinner, amber................................25.00
Platter, 11¼" oblong, green.............................27.50
Salt & pepper, green, pr...............................177.50
Saucer, amber..8.50
Sherbet, footed cone, amber............................15.00
Sherbet, footed cone, blue.............................75.00
Sugar, green..20.00
Sugar cover, green.....................................85.00
Tumbler, 5¾", footed, heavy, amber......................89.50

Patrician, "Spoke," Federal Glass Co., 1933-1937

Bowl, 4¾" cream soup, green...........................15.00
Bowl, 8½" large berry, amber.........................25.00
Butter dish w/cover, crystal..........................67.50
Cup, pink...7.50
Jam dish, green.....................................25.00
Pitcher, 8", 75 oz, pink.............................97.50
Plate, 10½" dinner, amber............................5.00

Salt & pepper, amber or crystal, pr...................40.00
Saucer, pink...5.00
Sherbet, amber or crystal.............................9.00
Sugar, green...7.00
Sugar cover, green...................................40.00

"Peacock Reverse," Line 412, Paden City Glass Co., 1930s

Bowl, 4¾" square, red or blue........................20.00
Candlesticks, 5¾" square base, red or blue, pr........72.50
Cup, red or blue....................................25.00
Plate, 5¾" sherbet, red or blue......................16.50
Saucer, red or blue.................................10.00
Sugar, 2¾" flat, red or blue.........................47.50
Tumbler, 4", 10 oz flat, red or blue..................42.50

"Petalware," Macbeth-Evans Glass Co., 1938-1940

Bowl, 8¾" large berry, cobalt........................32.50
Bowl, 8¾" large berry, cremax or monax w/fired on decor......15.00

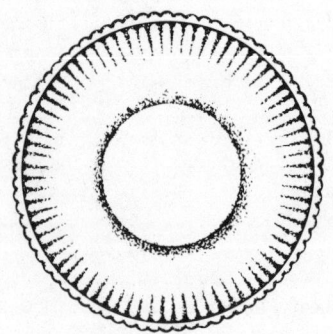

Pitcher, 80 oz, pink or crystal.......................20.00
Plate, 9" dinner, pink or crystal......................3.00
Platter, 13" oval, cremax or monax w/fired on decor....12.50
Sherbet, 4½", low footed, cobalt.....................19.50
Sherbet, 4½", low footed, cremax or monax w/fired on decor...7.50
Sugar, footed, cremax or monax w/fired on decor.......7.50

Princess, Hocking Glass Co., 1931-1935

Ash tray, 4½", green................................50.00
Bowl, 4½" berry, pink...............................10.00
Bowl, 9" octagonal salad, yellow.....................67.50
Butter dish w/cover, pink............................65.00
Candy dish w/cover, green............................35.00
Cookie jar w/cover, blue............................400.00
Creamer, oval, yellow................................9.50
Cup, pink...6.50
Pitcher, 8", 60 oz, green............................37.50
Plate, 9½" dinner, pink.............................11.00
Platter, 12", closed handles, green..................12.50
Relish, 7½" divided, amber..........................47.50
Salt & pepper, green, 4½", pr........................37.50

Spice shakers, 5½", green, pr........................27.50
Sugar, green..8.50
Sugar cover, green..................................12.50
Tumbler, 5¼", 13 oz iced tea, amber..................25.00
Vase, 8", pink......................................17.50

Queen Mary (Prismatic Line), "Vertical Ribbed," Hocking Glass Co., 1936-1940

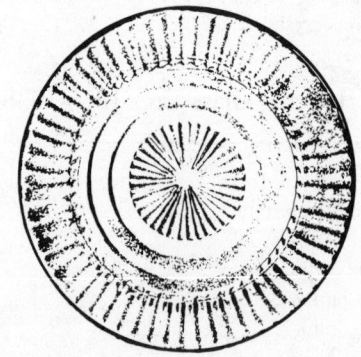

Bowl, 5½", 2 hdls, pink..............................4.00
Butter dish/preserve dish, w/cover, crystal...........20.00
Candlesticks, 4½" double branch, ruby red, pr.........27.50
Cigarette jar, 2x3" oval, pink........................5.50
Compote, 5¾", pink..................................5.00
Cup, 2 sizes, pink...................................5.00
Plate, 12" relish, 3 sections, pink...................8.50

Plate, 9¾″ dinner, crystal............................6.50
Plate, 9¾″ dinner, pink.............................17.50
Relish tray, 14″, 4 part, pink or crystal.................8.50
Salt & pepper, crystal, pr...........................12.50
Saucer, pink......................................1.50
Sherbet, footed, crystal.............................3.50
Sugar, oval, pink..................................4.50
Tumbler, 4″, 9 oz water, pink........................5.50

Raindrops "Optic Design," Federal Glass Co., 1929-1933

Bowl, 4½″ fruit, green..............................2.00
Creamer, green....................................4.50
Salt & pepper, green, pr............................37.50
Sherbet, green....................................3.50
Sugar, green......................................3.50
Sugar cover, green................................20.00
Tumbler, 3″, 4 oz, green............................3.00

Ribbon, Hazel Atlas Glass Co., Early 1930s

Bowl, 4″ berry, green..............................2.00
Bowl, 8″ large berry, green..........................6.00
Creamer, footed, black.............................9.00
Plate, 8″ luncheon, black...........................8.00

Salt & pepper, green, pr............................15.00
Sugar, footed, green...............................3.00
Tumbler, 6½″, 13 oz...............................6.50

Ring, "Banded Rings," Hocking Glass Co., 1927-1932

Bowl, 8″ large berry, green..........................6.00
Butter tub or ice bucket, crystal.....................8.50

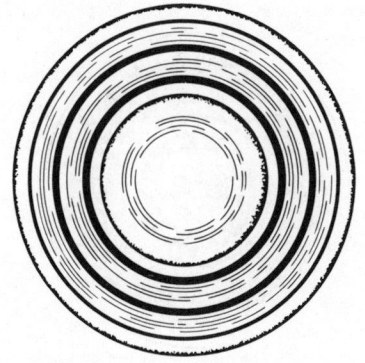

Creamer, footed, crystal decorated....................4.50
Pitcher, 8″, 60 oz, green...........................15.00
Plate, 8″ luncheon, crystal decorated.................2.50
Salt & pepper, 3″, crystal decorated, pr..............22.50
Sherbet, 4¾″, footed, crystal decorated...............6.00
Tumbler, 4¼″, 9 oz, green..........................4.50
Tumbler, 5½″ footed water, green....................8.50
Whiskey, 2″, 1½ oz, green..........................5.00

Rock Crystal, "Early American Rock Crystal," McKee Glass Co., 1920s & 1930s

Bon bon, 7½″, scalloped edge, red...................37.50
Bowl, 12″ oblong celery, colors other than red or crystal......27.00
Bowl, 12½″ footed center bowl, cobalt...............137.50
Bowl, 5″ finger bowl w/7″ plate, plain edge, red.........35.00
Bowl, 9″ salad, scalloped edge, crystal...............17.50
Butter dish w/cover, crystal........................197.00
Candelabra, 2-lite, cobalt, pr.......................75.00
Candlestick, 8½″, colors other than crystal or red, pr.........75.00
Creamer, flat, scalloped edge, crystal................20.00
Pitcher, ½ gal, 7½″ high, crystal...................95.00
Plate, 10½″ dinner, scalloped edge, lg center design, red......62.50
Plate, 7½″, plain edge or scalloped, crystal............6.50
Punch bowl & stand, 14″, crystal...................265.00
Salt & pepper, 2 styles, crystal, pr..................40.00

Sandwich server, center hdld, colors other than red or crystal...30.00
Spooner, crystal..................................27.50
Stemware, 3 oz wine, red...........................37.50
Stemware, 8 oz large footed goblet, crystal.............13.50
Sugar, 10 oz, open, colors other than red or crystal.........20.00
Syrup, w/lid, crystal...............................52.50
Tumbler, 9 oz, concave or straight, red................37.50
Vase, cornucopia, crystal...........................35.00

Rosemary, "Dutch Rose," Federal Glass Co., 1935-1937

Bowl, 10″ oval vegetable, green.....................15.00
Bowl, 6″ cereal, pink.............................10.00

Cup, pink...4.50
Plate, dinner, green...............................10.00
Platter, 12" oval, amber............................9.50
Sugar, footed, pink................................7.50
Tumbler, 4¼", 9 oz, amber.........................10.00

Roulette, "Many Windows," Hocking Glass Co., 1935-1939

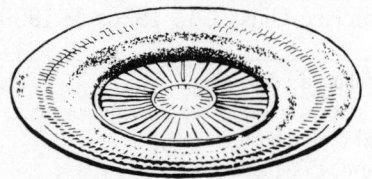

Bowl, 9" fruit, pink, green or crystal.....................8.50
Pitcher, 8", 64 oz, pink, green, or crystal...............22.50
Plate, 12" sandwich, pink, green, or crystal..............7.50
Plate, 8½" luncheon, pink, green, or crystal..............4.00
Tumbler, 4¼", 9 oz water, pink, green or crystal..........12.50
Tumbler, 5½", 10 oz footed, pink, green, or crystal........9.50
Whiskey, 2½", 1½ oz, pink, green, or crystal..............6.50

Royal Lace, Hazel Atlas Glass Co., 1934-1941

Bowl, 10", 3 leg, rolled edge, pink.......................25.00
Bowl, 11" oval vegetable, blue...........................35.00
Bowl, 4¾" cream soup, green or blue......................22.50
Butter dish w/cover, crystal.............................52.50
Candlestick, rolled, edge, green, pr.....................50.00
Cookie jar w/cover, pink.................................37.50
Creamer, footed, blue....................................25.00
Cup, green...14.00
Pitcher, 48 oz, straight sides, pink.....................40.00
Plate, 10" dinner, green.................................17.50

Saucer, green...5.00
Sherbet, in metal holder, amethyst.......................25.00
Sugar, blue..22.50
Sugar lid, blue..77.50
Tumbler, 5¼", 12 oz, pink................................20.00

Royal Ruby, Anchor Hocking Glass Co., 1938-1960s, 1977

Bowl, 11½" salad, red....................................18.00
Bowl, 7½" soup, red.......................................9.50
Creamer, footed, red......................................7.50

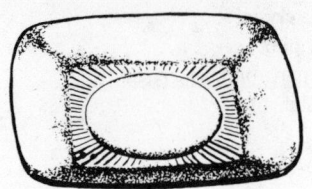

Cup, round or square, red.................................3.50
Goblet, ball stem, red....................................6.50
Pitcher, 22 oz, tilted or upright, red...................20.00
Plate, 13¾", red...12.50
Plate, 9 or 9¼" dinner, red...............................7.50
Saucer, round or square, red..............................1.50
Sugar, footed, red..7.50
Sugar lid, red..7.50
Tumbler, 9 oz water, red..................................5.00
Vase, 4" ball shaped, red.................................4.50

"S" Pattern, "Stippled Rose Band," Macbeth- Evans Glass Co., 1930-1933

Creamer, thick or thin, crystal w/trim...................5.50
Pitcher, 80 oz, crystal, Am Sweetheart shape............47.50
Pitcher, 80 oz, pink or green, Dogwood shape...........495.00
Plate, 13" heavy cake, crystal..........................47.50
Plate, 8" luncheon, deep red............................50.00
Plate, 8" luncheon, yellow or amber......................2.50
Sugar, thick & thin, crystal w/trim......................5.50
Tumbler, 3½", 5 oz, crystal w/trim.......................4.50

Sandwich, Hocking Glass Co., 1939-1964, 1977

Bowl, 6" cereal, desert gold.............................6.00
Bowl, 7" salad, forest green............................30.00
Bowl, 8¼" oval, crystal..................................5.00
Butter dish, low, crystal...............................32.50
Creamer, forest green...................................14.50
Pitcher, 6" juice, crystal..............................45.00

Plate, 12″ sandwich, crystal..........7.50
Plate, 9″ dinner, desert gold..........4.00
Punch bowl & stand, crystal..........30.00
Sherbet, footed, crystal..........6.00
Sugar, no cover, forest green..........14.50
Sugar w/cover, crystal..........12.50
Tumbler, 9 oz footed, desert gold..........20.00
Tumbler, 9 oz water, crystal..........6.50

Sandwich, Indiana Glass Co., 1920s-1980s

Bowl, 6″, pink or green..........3.50
Bowl, 8¼″, pink or green..........10.00
Butter dish w/cover, domed, pink or green..........157.50
Candlesticks, 3½″, pink or green, pr..........15.00
Creamer, pink or green..........6.50
Cup, pink or green..........4.50
Decanter w/stopper, pink or green..........77.50
Pitcher, 68 oz, pink or green..........80.00
Plate, 8¼″ luncheon, pink or green..........4.50
Sandwich server, center hdl, pink or green..........27.50
Saucer, pink or green..........2.50
Sherbet, 3¼″, pink or green..........5.00
Sugar, large, open, pink or green..........8.50
Tumbler, 12 oz footed iced tea, pink or green..........22.50
Tumbler, 3 oz footed cocktail, pink or green..........15.00
Wine, 3″, 4 oz, pink or green..........17.50

Sharon, "Cabbage Rose," Federal Glass Co., 1935-1939

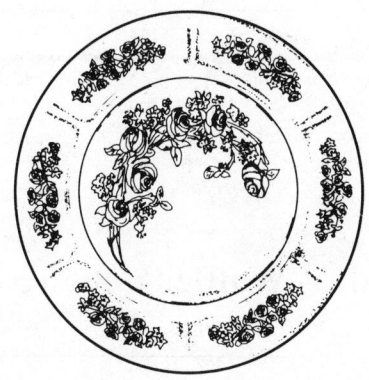

Bowl, 10½″ fruit, green..........22.50
Bowl, 5″ berry, amber..........6.00
Bowl, 8¼″ large berry, pink..........16.00
Butter dish w/cover, pink..........42.50
Cake plate, 11½″ footed, green..........45.00
Candy jar w/cover, amber..........35.00
Creamer, footed, pink..........12.00
Cup, green..........10.00
Jam dish, 7½″, amber..........25.00
Pitcher, 80 oz, w/ice lip, pink..........105.00
Plate, 9½″ dinner, amber..........9.50
Salt & pepper, pink, pr..........37.50
Saucer, green..........5.50
Sherbet, footed, green..........20.00
Sugar, amber..........6.50
Sugar lid, amber..........16.50

Sierra, "Pinwheel," Jeannette Glass Co., 1931-1933

Bowl, 5½″ cereal, pink..........6.00
Bowl, 9¼″ oval vegetable, green..........40.00
Butter dish w/cover, pink..........45.00
Creamer, green..........12.50
Cup, pink..........6.00
Pitcher, 6½″, 32 oz, green..........62.50
Platter, 11″ oval, pink..........12.50
Salt & pepper, green, pr..........27.50

Spiral, Hocking Glass Co., 1928-1930

Bowl, 8″ large berry, pink or green..........6.50
Cup, pink or green..........3.50
Ice or butter tub, pink or green..........13.50
Plate, 8″ luncheon, pink or green..........2.00
Salt & pepper, pink & green, pr..........16.00
Saucer, pink or green..........1.00
Sugar, flat or footed, green or pink..........4.00
Tumbler, 5″, 9 oz water, pink or green..........3.50

Starlight, Hazel Atlas Glass Co., 1938-1940

Bowl, 5½″ cereal, pink..........3.50
Cup, crystal..........2.50
Plate, 6″ bread & butter, crystal..........2.00
Plate, 8½″ luncheon, pink..........3.50

Relish dish, pink..........4.50
Sherbet, crystal..........3.50
Sugar, oval, crystal..........3.00

Strawberry or "Cherryberry," U.S. Glass Co., Early 1930s

Bowl, 6½″ deep salad, pink or green..........10.00
Butter dish w/cover, cherry motif..........137.50
Butter dish w/cover, pink or green..........125.00
Compote, 5¾″, crystal..........8.50

Creamer, 4½", large, pink or green.........................15.00
Pickle dish, 8¼" oval, pink or green.......................9.00
Pitcher, 7¾", cherry motif................................127.50
Pitcher, 7¾", crystal.....................................150.00
Plate, 7½" salad, pink or green............................8.50

Swirl, "Petal Swirl," Jeannette Glass Co., 1937-1938

Bowl, 10" footed, closed hdls, ultramarine..................22.50
Bowl, 5¼" cereal, pink.....................................5.00
Butter dish w/cover, pink.................................130.00
Candle holders, single branch, delphite, pr................77.50
Creamer, footed, ultramarine...............................9.50
Cup, delphite..5.00
Plate, 9¼" dinner, ultramarine............................11.00
Sherbet, low footed, pink..................................5.50
Tumbler, 4½", 9 oz, pink.................................10.00
Tumbler, 9 oz footed, ultramarine.........................20.00

Tea Room, Indiana Glass Co., 1926-1931

Bowl, 7½" banana split, pink..............................32.50
Bowl, 9½" oval vegetable, green...........................39.50
Creamer & sugar on tray, 3½", pink........................50.00
Cup, pink...17.50
Parfait, pink...32.50
Plate, 8¼" luncheon, pink or green........................20.00
Relish, divided, green....................................16.00

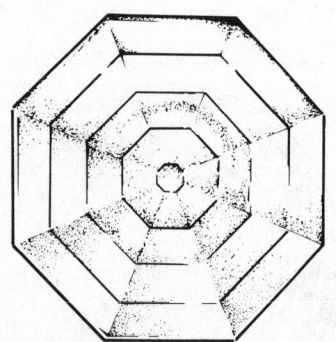

Sherbet, low, flared edge, pink...........................18.00
Sugar, 4", green..12.50
Sugar, 4½" footed, pink...................................12.00
Sundae, footed, ruffled top, green........................27.50
Tumbler, 11 oz footed, green..............................27.50
Tumbler, 8½ oz flat, pink.................................37.50
Vase, 6", ruffled or straight edge, pink..................30.00

Twisted Optic, Imperial Glass Co., 1927-1930

Bowl, 4¾" cream soup, all colors...........................5.50
Bowl, 6½" cereal, amber....................................7.50
Candlesticks, 3", all colors, pr..........................10.00
Candlesticks, 3", green, pr...............................15.00
Creamer, green...7.50
Cup, amber...6.00
Gravy boat & platter, amber...............................97.50
Pitcher, 64 oz, all colors................................17.50
Plate, 7" salad, all colors................................2.00
Plate, 8" luncheon, all colors.............................2.00
Plate, 9" dinner, pink....................................10.00

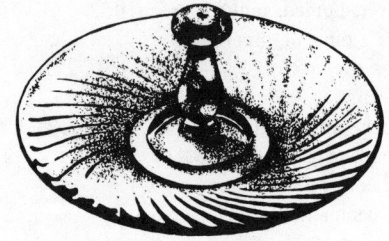

Sandwich server, center hdl, all colors...................12.50
Sandwich server, center hdl, green........................15.00
Saucer, amber..4.00
Sherbet, all colors..4.00
Sugar, all colors..4.50
Sugar, green...7.00
Tumbler, 4½", 9 oz, all colors.............................4.50

Vitrock, "Flower Rim," Anchor Hocking Glass Co., 1934-1937

Bowl, 4" berry, white......................................3.00
Bowl, 5½" cream soup, white................................7.50
Creamer, oval, white.......................................3.00
Plate, 8¾" luncheon, white.................................2.00
Plate, 9" soup, white......................................3.50
Platter, 11½", white......................................12.00
Sugar, oval, white...3.00

Waterford, "Waffle," Hocking Glass Co., 1938-1944

Bowl, 8¼" large berry, crystal.............................6.00
Butter dish w/cover, crystal..............................20.00
Creamer, oval, pink..7.50
Goblet, 5½", Miss America style, crystal..................22.50
Pitcher, 42 oz tilted juice, crystal......................15.00

Plate, 13¾" hdld sandwich, pink...........................8.50
Plate, 9½" dinner, crystal.................................5.00
Relish, 13¾", 5 part, crystal.............................12.50
Sherbet, footed, crystal..................................2.50
Sugar, crystal..2.50
Sugar cover, oval, crystal................................2.50
Tumbler, 4¾", 10 oz footed, crystal.......................6.00

Windsor, "Windsor Diamond," Jeannette Glass Co., 1936-1946

Bowl, 10½" salad, crystal.................................5.00
Bowl, 7x11¾" boat shape, green............................20.00
Bowl, 8", 2 handled, pink.................................10.00
Butter dish, crystal.....................................22.50
Compote, pink...7.50
Cup, green..7.00
Pitcher, 6¾", 52 oz, pink................................18.50
Plate, 15½" serving, crystal..............................5.00
Plate, 9" dinner, pink or green...........................9.50
Salt & pepper, pink, pr..................................27.50
Sugar w/cover, green.....................................17.50
Tray, 8½x9¾", w/handles, pink............................18.50
Tumbler, 4", 9 oz, red...................................50.00
Tumbler, 4" footed, crystal...............................4.50

Derby

William Duesbury operated in Derby, England, from about 1755, purchasing a second establishment, The Chelsea Works, in 1769. During this period fine porcelains were produced which so impressed the King that in 1773 he issued the company the Crown Derby patent. In 1810, several years after Duesbury's death, the factory was bought by Robert Bloor. The quality of the ware suffered under the new management, and the main Derby pottery closed in 1848. Within a short time the work was revived by a dedicated number of former employees who established their own works on King Street, in Derby.

The earliest known Derby mark was the crown over a script 'D'; however this mark is rarely found today. Soon after 1782, that mark was augmented with a device of crossed batons and six dots, usually applied in underglaze blue. During the Bloor period the crown was centered within a ring containing the words 'Bloor' above and 'Derby' below the crown, or with a red printed stamp -- the crowned Gothic 'D'. The King Street plant produced figurines that may be distinguished from their earlier counterparts by the presence of an 'S' and 'H' on either side of the crown and crossed batons.

In 1876, a new pottery was constructed in Derby, and the owners revived the earlier company's former standard of excellence. The Queen bestowed the firm the title Royal Crown Derby in 1890; it still operates under that name today.

See also Royal Crown Derby

Vase, enamel and gilt scrolled foliate decor on pink, 12", $1,500.00.

Bough pot w/lid, HP floral panel, scroll ft/hdls, Bloor, 9" L....500.00
Figurine, King & Queen, mc, 10", pr......................800.00
Plate, florals/leaves in vibrant color, red mk, 1800-1820, 10"...325.00
Plate, King's pattern, ca 1825, 8½", set of 12..............850.00

Documents

Documents are collected for their historical significance. Those of a military nature are especially valued.

Account, firewood etc, Boston, 1743, hand written/laid paper....40.00
Act, English, re Preservation of Game, w/masthead, 1770......35.00
Act, Queen Victoria, re merchant navy, 44 pp/masthead, 1850...25.00
Bond, obligation, two 8x12" sheets, 1 blank, handmade paper...50.00
Deed, handwritten, re property transfer, 1721, in fr..........65.00
Deed to land in KY, 1818, handwritten & printed, 17½x20½"..25.00
Document, English, re land/money, fancy penwork/vellum, 1667..85.00
Document, printed w/script insertions, re manor rent, 1658.....50.00
Document, re 'good lawful money', sgn/seal tag, wax seal, 1675..95.00
Indenture, English, in Latin on vellum, 16th century, 9x13"....120.00
Indenture, English, re sundry goods/money, vellum w/seal, 1635..85.00
Indenture, English, vellum, seal tag/sgn, 1670, 9x21".........95.00
Indenture, English, vellum, w/3 wax seals/sgns, 1756, 29x34"....70.00
Indenture, English, vellum/ink/2 seals, re property, 1790, 31"...65.00
Legal bond, manuscript, NC, 1792, 2 signatures, 8x5".........8.00
Legal bond, manuscript, NC, 1792, 3 signatures, 8x5½".......10.00
Pay paper, Revolutionary War, 1781, 7½x6"..................18.00
Receipt, Confederate, penned script, 5x8"...................19.00
Receipt, manuscript, w/prices for purchases, VA, 1860, 7½x6"...8.00
Slave, printed bond/hand completed, AL, 1839, sale of male....47.00
Tax receipt, printed form/hand completed, 1853, 7½x3".......9.00
Warrant, English, sgn Sir Wm Savile, vellum, 1645, 7½x5".....40.00

Doll Furniture

Little girls have always loved their dolls, and loving parents have bought them steamer trunks, cupboards, bureaus, and beds -- everything a child needed to make her doll comfortable. Some were lovingly hand crafted and rather primitive, while other pieces were commercially made. All make charming collectibles.

Armchair, ladderback, primitive, trn finials, splint seat, 12"....65.00
Armoire, Eastlake bamboo style, ca 1885, minor damage......225.00

Bed, dk wood, wood beads at top, canopy, ornate, 20x13x18"..125.00
Bed, half crown, Victorian, 23" L........................140.00
Bed, iron, ornate, woven metal springs, 1910, 19x12", EX....225.00
Bed, mahog, well turned posts, shaped head/ft boards, 23x13"..155.00
Bed, Murphy; chestnut, 2 doors/2 drw in wardrobe, 15x10½"..225.00
Bed, primitive, open lattice sides/applied star on hdbd, 22" L..25.00
Bed, walnut, turned posts, rails, spindles, 15x12x15"........125.00
Bureau, walnut, 3 drw, 2 mock drw, oval mirror, 16x10x28"...325.00
Cabinet, hoosier; ptd gr wood, w/flour sifter, bread board, 17"..300.00
Cabinet, 2 doors above 2 drawers, dtd 1909, 9½"............75.00
Carriage, pnt wood, 3 wheel, Ludlow, 1886, hood folds, 39"...250.00
Carriage, pnt wood, 4 wheel, fringed canopy, 27"...........275.00
Carriage, pnt wood, 4 wheel, Ludlow, canopy, 1874, 35".....385.00
Carriage, wicker, 4 wheels, pivot mtd cotton parasol, 28"....250.00
Chair, oak, back folds down, old, 23x13x7½"...............225.00
Chair, rocking; oak, ornate trim on top back, old, 28x12x15"...75.00
Chair, side; ladderback, primitive, trn posts, paper seat, 11"...20.00
Chair, spindle bk, orig red pnt w/yellow striping, 10".......25.00
Chair, walnut, red velvet & upholstery, old, 15x8x8".........150.00
Chest, Empire, curly cherry/walnut, scrolled ft, 12½x11".....375.00
Chest, oak, 10½x7x6½"..................................35.00
Chest, tiger maple, 3 drw/wooden knobs/scalloped galley, 6"...240.00
Chest of drws, oak, 5 long drw/pilasters ea side, 13".........110.00
Chest of drws, poplar, 2 nailed drws, scalloped crest, 19".....85.00
Chest of drws, poplar w/pnt & transfers/porcelain knobs, 17"..110.00
Cradle, pine, orig pnt w/stenciled stag, etc, worn, 11½".......155.00
Cradle, poplar, primitive, worn dk finish, 12¾"..............25.00
Cradle, poplar w/worn orig graining imitation oak, 19½", G....55.00
Cradle, walnut, Jenny Lind, four poster, old, 22x17x24"......325.00
Cupboard, kitchen; 2 door, 2 drw below, old, 9½x7½x4"......75.00
Cupboard, pine w/plywood doors, orig brass latch, rfn, 23x16"..45.00
Cupboard, pine/poplar, open shelves, orig pnt decor, 12x7½"..170.00
Cupboard, pine/trn ft, 4 nailed drw/glass doors, sq nails, 22"...350.00
Cupboard, walnut, 1 dvtl drw/door, scalloped crest, 14x11".....85.00
Cupboard, wood/high bk, 4 tin utensils, orig pnt/decoupage, 9"..35.00
Cupboard, 2 pc, pine, dbl doors, drw, open shelves, red, 17"...300.00
Desk, Davenport; oak, 3 drw, spindle gallery, 7½x4¼x12½"...625.00
Desk, Governor Winthrop, bracket ft, ivory trim, 1810, 12x10".450.00
Desk, roll top; oak/chestnut, 6 drw, 15x18x9"...............275.00
Desk, rounded lid, floral rope inlay, French legs, 15½x12"...850.00

Dresser, oak/brass, tilt mirror, serpentine top drawer, 26".....185.00
Dresser, pine, 1 drw/ 2 doors, mirror, old, sticker dtd 1905....125.00
Dresser, white, flower trim, oval mirror, old, 19x12x5½"......150.00
Dresser, 3 drw & mirror, orig red pnt, 18"..................40.00
Dry sink, pine/buttermilk paint, 2 doors, primitive, 7½x8".....225.00
Fainting couch, wine velvet/upholstery, rfn, old, 16x12x12"....150.00
Highchair, w/tray, foot rest, old, 29x9x9"..................125.00
Highchair, w/tray, old, 18x7x9"...........................85.00
Ice box, oak, nickeled brass, 3 doors, works, complete, 16½"..500.00
Ironing board, oak, 13x16½"..............................26.00
Picnic table, oak, 2 attached benches, 17½x13½x7½"........150.00
Secretary, Dutch Marquetry, shaped front, bun ft, 1840, 33"..3,000.00
Sofa, Empire, mahogany/horsehair, all orig, 1840, 19½x39½"..750.00
Stroller, Paris Mfg, all orig, early........................365.00
Swing/chair, Victorian, braided straw/bent wood/scrolls, 24"...195.00
Table, turtle top, carved skirt & bow legs, Victorian, 5".......90.00
Table, walnut, octagonal, walnut burl top, ornate base, 4½"...110.00
Trunk, wood w/marbleized paper cover/brass studs, JF Mehrman.50.00
Washstand, 1 drw, 2 doors below, towel bar, old, 16x13x6"....195.00

Dollhouses and Furnishings

Dollhouses were introduced commercially in this country late in the 1700s by Dutch craftsmen who settled in the East. By the middle of the 1800s, they had become meticulously detailed, divided into separate rooms, and lavishly furnished to reflect the opulence of the day. Originally intended for the amusement of adults of the household, by the latter 1800s their status had changed to that of a child's toy. Though many early dollhouses were lovingly hand fashioned for a special little girl, those made commercially by such companies as Bliss and Schoenhut are highly valued.

Furniture and furnishings in the Biedermeir style featuring stenciled Victorian decorations often sell for several hundred dollars each. Other early pieces made of pewter, porcelain, or papier mache are also quite valuable. Certainly less expensive, but very collectible none-the-less, is the quality hallmarked plastic furniture produced during the forties by Renwal and Acme, and the 1960s Petite Princess line produced by Ideal.

Furnishings

Armchair, fabric uphl, trn legs, 4x2".......................10.00
Armchair, gr velvet uphl, 4x2"............................20.00
Armchair, print uphl, wood legs, rolled arms, Germany, 3x2¾"...8.50
Armchair, wood, straight bk, 4⅛".........................5.00
Armchair, wood w/padded seat, Germany label, '30s, 4x3"......12.50
Armoire, oak, Victorian, 7x3"............................80.00
Ash tray, floor standing, wire/wood, Strombecker.............9.00
Baby bed, Arcade.......................................22.00
Baby stroller, red/yellow, Ideal...........................25.00
Baby swing, Renwal.....................................12.00
Basket, woven, mini......................................1.00
Bathroom set, pnt wood, curved tub, 2" ped sink, toilet, '20s...12.50
Bathroom set, 6 pcs, Renwal..............................20.00
Bathtub, blue, Renwal....................................5.00
Bathtub, lavender, Tootsie Toy...........................12.00
Bathtub, toilet w/lift lid, sink, hamper, Tootsie Toy...........28.00
Bathtub, wht w/blk faucet, Renwal........................6.00
Bed, dbl; Victorian, oak, 4¾" hdbd, 2¾" ftbd...............45.00
Bed, twin; br frame/wht stenciled spread, Renwal.............6.00
Bed, twin; chest & mirrored vanity, Renwal..................17.50
Bed, twin; rnd head & ft board, pink, Tootsie Toy, 1¼x3¼".....6.50
Bedroom commode, oak, Victorian.........................125.00
Bellows, brass, sgn England, 3½".........................12.00
Bookcase, 2 top shelves, lift front, 2 doors open, wood, 4¾"...25.00

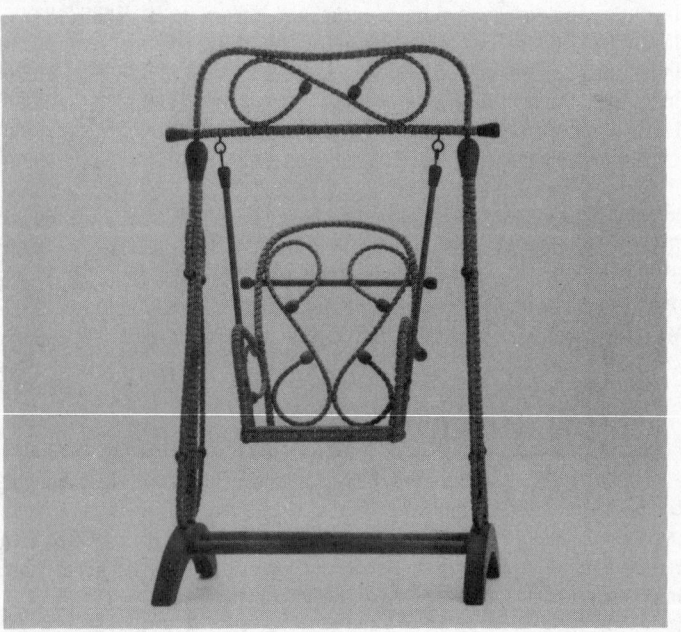

Doll swing, braided wicker wrapped wood, 24" x 14½", $125.00.

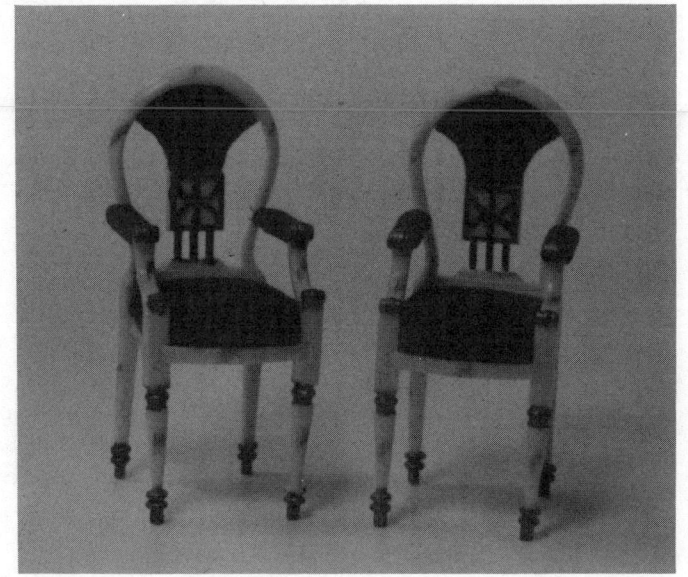

Petite Princess, host dining chairs, #4413-1, mint in box, $17.50.

Bookends, horsehead, w/books, Petite Princess..............2.00
Buffet, drawer opens, br w/stencil, Renwal, M.................6.00
Buffet, wood, mirror top, Victorian.........................175.00
Buggy, lead filigree, 5″....................................15.00
Bureau, w/mirror & 3 tiers of drws, 1 opens, stenciled, Renwal..7.00
Bureau, 5 tiers of drws, 2 open, stenciled...................7.00
Bureau w/mirror, 2 drws pull out, pnt wood, 5″...............9.50
Carpet sweeper, red w/bl hdl................................8.00
Cedar chest, lift top, Strombecker...........................9.50
Chair, arm; bl velvet rolled arms & bk, mk Germany, '20s, 3½″.30.00
Chair, fancy, mahog, rung bk w/padded seat, 4¾″.............10.00
Chair, fancy, stained wood w/rush seat, 4x2″.................8.00
Chair, iron, fancy bk, curved legs, worn red pnt, 3¾″.......10.00
Chair, lavender, Tootsie Toy...............................10.00
Chair, oak w/padded seat, 5″................................8.50
Chair, occasional; wire/wood, Strombecker..................10.00
Chair, parlor; overstuffed, wht w/stencil decor, Renwal......5.00
Chair, parlor; velvet padded seat, fancy rung bk, wood, 4½″..6.00
Chair, plastic, bentwood seat/open bk/curved arms/pad seat, 3″.28.00
Chair, side; Tootsie Toy...................................12.00
Chair, wing; Lynnfield......................................9.00
Chair, wood w/cane seat, curved ft legs, 3½″.................6.00
Chandelier, brass/glass, 6 arms w/bulbs/ruffled shades, MIG....490.00
Chest, 3 drws, varnished wood, 3½x4x2″.....................12.50
Chest, 5 drws, metal pulls/pine, top shelf removes, 4¼″.....16.00
Clock, alarm; Strombecker...................................5.50
Clock, Grandfather; Schoenhut..............................12.50
Clock, Grandfather; Strombecker.............................6.50
Clock, hall type, pnt br w/brass pendulum, ca 1900, 7½″.....18.00
Clock, mantel, Strombecker.................................12.50
Closet, wood w/pewter knob, mirror door, fancy top, 4¾x2¾″...35.00
Clothes hamper, lavender, Tootsie Toy.......................8.00
Coffee set, brass, orig package, Petite Princess.............2.50
Couch, red w/br legs, Renwal................................6.00
Couch, studio; Schoenhut...................................25.00
Couch, wood/red pnt, '40s, 2½x6½″...........................4.00
Couch & chair, Strombecker.................................15.00
Decanter, bisque, Petite Princess...........................1.50
Dining room, wood, 1920s, closet/table/4 chairs/server......50.00
Dining room server, marble top, 4½x5½″.....................175.00
Dining room table w/leaves, 6 chairs, wood, Victorian.......195.00

Dining table, rnd, Tootsie Toy.............................22.00
Dining table w/2 leaves, 6 chairs w/cane seats, fancy, German....90.00
Doll, open/close eyes, celluloid, Italy......................6.00
Doll, pntd features & outfit, Renwal.........................6.50
Doll cradle, wood, hood/rockers............................20.00
Dolls, father, mother, girl, boy, folding, Renwal...........75.00
Dresser, swinging mirror, blk metal, fancy legs, French, 2¾″....22.00
Dresser, swinging mirror, Tootsie Toy......................25.00
Dry sink, top drw & door below opens, Sturbridge, 3¼″.......12.00
Fireplace, paper w/'bricks', mantel, mk Whitehouse, 3½x4¾″...15.00
Fruit bowl, pewter, German..................................3.00
Heater, bathroom; portable, Strombecker.....................5.00
Hutch, 3 shelves, br w/stencil, Renwal, M...................5.00
Ironing board, Renwal......................................6.00
Lamp, boudoir; w/shade, bird base, Petite Princess..........3.00
Lamp, floor; candelabrum, brass w/red shades, Petite Princess...15.00
Lamp, floor; wood/wire, Strombecker.........................7.50
Lamp, library; brass w/gr shade.............................3.00
Lamp, table; gr shade, Grecian figure, Petite Princess......3.50
Lamp, table; solid brass/glass shade, 2½″..................12.50
Lamp, table; Tiffany style, Tootsie Toy....................10.00
Lamp, table; wood w/shade, '20s, 1¾″........................2.50
Loveseat, curved arms/bk, open work seat, metal, French, 1½″..22.00
Medicine chest, Tootsie Toy................................15.00
Night stand, Strombecker....................................5.00
Ottoman, Schoenhut..12.50
Piano, baby grand; Renwal..................................10.00
Piano, baby grand; Schoenhut...............................30.00
Piano, pine w/paper keys, 4x4″.............................15.00
Piano, wood, Victorian, 5½x4½″............................145.00
Piano bench, brown, Renwal..................................2.00
Piano bench, wht pnt wood, 1½x3″............................4.00
Piano stool, wood, Victorian...............................25.00
Picture in frame, lg, Petite Princess.......................2.50
Pitcher, bisque, Petite Princess............................1.50
Pitcher & wash bowl..5.00
Plant stand, wood, base shelf, 2″ dia top...................8.00
Plant stand, 5 steps, mahog stained wood, 4½″..............12.50
Planter, brass, Petite Princess.............................7.50
Plate in holder, orig package, Petite Princess..............2.00
Potty chair, pink, table top removes, Renwal, VG............4.50
Potty chair w/tray, Marx....................................6.00
Radiator, CI, 8 ribs, 2½x2″................................35.00
Radio, console; door opens, knobs, trn legs, mahog stain, 3¼″..18.00
Radio, console; walnut, Strombecker........................12.50
Radio, table; Diamond K, Strombecker.......................16.00
Refrigerator, Strombecker...................................8.50
Rocker, all wood, Strombecker, EX..........................25.00
Rocker, oak, padded seat, 4¾″...............................8.50
Rocker, Tootsie Toy..17.50
Rug, hooked, 3″ dia...4.50
Sandbox, yellow & orange awning, Liddle Kiddles.............5.00
Scales, bathroom; Strombecker...............................4.00
Scales, lavender, Tootsie Toy..............................10.00
Secretary bookcase, doors & drws open, Marx................15.00
Set, china, 3¾″ L sofa w/arms/armchair/str chair/chest, Japan..25.00
Set, pine w/padded seats, mk Germany, 5″ sofa+4 chairs, 3½″..35.00
Settee, iron, fancy bk & arms, 1¾x4½″......................25.00
Settee & 2 armchairs, wicker, 12″.........................100.00
Sewing machine, Renwal.....................................15.00
Sideboard, 2 doors open/trn legs/fancy top, mahog stained, 3¾″.22.00
Sink, counter top, Schoenhut................................6.50
Sink, lavender, Tootsie Toy................................12.00
Sink, Strombecker...8.00

Sink, Tootsie Toy...............................28.00
Sink, wht w/blk faucet, Renwal........................5.50
Sofa, pnt CI, rolled arms, rnd bk, curved legs, Arcade, 7" L...35.00
Sofa, pnt CI, slanted arms, curved bk, 3¾" L.........28.00
Statue, Negro jockey w/horse ring in hand.............15.00
Stool, kitchen; Strombecker..........................4.00
Stool, Tootsie Toy, ¾".................................4.00
Stove, CI w/silver pnt, 2 burners/hood, mk Daisy, 4¼"........22.50
Stove, gas; pnt CI, mk Geneva/Champion, 4 legs, 3½x3x1½"...28.00
Stove, kitchen; cast metal, Arcade...................25.00
Stove, kitchen; wht w/blk fixtures, Renwal..............6.00
Stove, oven door opens, wht w/stencil & red fixtures, Renwal.....8.00
Stove, Strombecker...................................8.00
Stove, Tootsie Toy.................................30.00
Table, blk open work metal, fancy legs, French, 2½" dia top....18.00
Table, card; legs fold, red, Renwal...................10.00
Table, clear, Petite Princess, 3½".......................5.00
Table, corner; 3 lift up shelves, trn legs, mahog stain, 2¾"......9.00
Table, dining; gateleg, mahog stain, 5¼" L, 5" W.........18.00
Table, dining; w/4 chairs, Strombecker...............22.50
Table, end; br w/2 sm false drw, Renwal...............2.00
Table, end; Schoenhut...............................6.50
Table, kitchen; 4 chairs, pnt blk....................15.00
Table, parlor; curved ends, trn legs, mahog stained, 2¾x4½"...18.50
Table, parlor; ped base, fancy legs, pine, 3½" dia top........6.50
Table, rnd; w/2 wire & wood chairs, Strombecker.........12.00
Table, rnd; w/4 wire/wood chairs, Strombecker...........20.00
Table, trestle; dk pine, Sturbridge, 2¼x5¼x2¼"..........9.00
Table, 2 chairs, stove, cabinet (doors open), Tootsie Toy......28.00
Table & chair, carved wood, 6".......................30.00
Tables, 3 stacking, Strombecker.......................8.00
Tea cart, sides drop, base shelf, wheels turn, mahog stain, 3"...28.00
Tea cart, Strombecker................................8.00
Tea set, metal, 2" hdl tray, teapot/creamer/sugar, German.....12.50
Telephone stand, lyre, Petite Princess.................4.00
Television, turn dial to change cb pictures, Ideal........14.00
Toilet, china w/wood top, 2¼"........................40.00
Toilet, lavender, Tootsie Toy........................12.00
Toilet, sink, tub, Strombecker.......................12.00
Toilet, wht w/blk, seat & lid lifts, Renwal.............5.50
Tray, serving; galleried edge, mahog wood, 1½x2¼"........4.00
Tricycle, red/yellow, moving parts, Renwal.............7.50
Urn, bisque, Petite Princess.........................1.50
Vanity, brown, w/mirror & 2 drawers that open, Renwal.......7.00
Vase, brass..1.25
Vase w/flowers, orig package, Petite Princess...........1.50
Victrola, top lifts, 4 legs, Tootsie Toy, 2"..............8.50
Wardrobe, 2 doors open, 5¼x4x1¼"....................28.00
Washboard, Rub-A-Dub..............................2.00
Washer w/wringer, Renwal...........................12.00
Waste basket, broom, dustpan, Strombecker.............7.00

Houses

Bathroom, tin, ornate, functional, w/5" bisque doll..........550.00
Bliss, Adirondack House, unmkd, rare.................325.00
Bliss, center hinged, VG lithograph, needs some work, 15x6½"..250.00
Bliss, Stable, litho paper/wood, 2 stalls/hayloft/animals, 18"...385.00
Bliss, Victorian 3-story, ornate lithograph decor, 1890s......720.00
Classroom, 6 grpt dbl desks+schoolmaster's w/figures, 1865...450.00
Colonial, center hall, metal w/G paint, 30x40"............40.00
Georgian Revival, wood, 7 rooms, staircase, electric, 30x48"...150.00
Georgian style, pntd wood, 31½x24"...................300.00
Kitchen, tin, asstd plates/pans/etc, orig pnt/stencil, 7x9x4"....200.00

Bliss house, mint condition with original curtains, 12½", $650.00.

Litho tin, Colonial style, w/Disney playroom...............35.00
McLoughling, paper litho fold-up, 17x10x5"..............400.00
Paper on wood, glass windows, fireplace, stove, 22x24".......85.00
Patisserie, French, 5 story/compo/slate roof, glass dome, 20".1,540.00
Pnt wood, glass windows, 4 fireplaces, 24x24".............100.00
Tri-ang, Tudor style, late, 16x14".....................100.00
Tri-ang, wood sides/cardboard roof/tin front, late, 18x17"......45.00
Wood, hinged front, orig lithographic cover worn, 9½".......55.00
Wood/paper, Victorian, glass windows, 4 fireplaces, 20x24"...290.00
12 rooms, completely furnished, w/25 dolls, European, 54"..19,800.00

Dolls

Collecting dolls of any sort is one of the most rewarding hobbies in the United States. The rewards are in the fun, the search and the finds -- plus there is a built-in factor of investment. No hobby, be it dolls, glass, or anything else, should be based completely on investment, but any collector should ask: 'Can I get my money back out of this item if I should ever have to sell it?'. Many times we buy on impulse, rather than with logic, which is understandable; but by asking this question we can save ourselves a lot of 'buyer's remorse', which we have all experienced at one time or another.

Since we want to learn to invest our money wisely while we are having fun, we must become aware of defects which may devaluate a doll. In bisque, watch for eye chips, hairline cracks and chips, or breaks on any part of the head. Composition should be clean, not crazed or cracked. Vinyl and plastic should be clean, with no pen or crayon marks. Though a quality replacement wig is acceptable for bisque dolls, composition and hard plastics should have their originals, in uncut condition. Original clothing is a must, except in bisque dolls, since it is unusual to find one in its original costume. However, they should be well-dressed and ready for your collection.

A price guide is only that -- a guide. It suggests the average price for each doll. Bargains can be found for less than suggested values; and 'unplayed-with' dolls in their original boxes may cost more. Dealers must become aware of condition so that they do not overpay and therefore over-price their dolls -- a common occurence across the country. Quantity does not replace quality, as most find out in time. A faster turnover of sales with a smaller margin of profit is far better than being stuck with an item that does not sell because it is over-priced. It is important to remember that prices are based on condition and rarity.

Barbie dolls are priced mint in box.

For a more thorough study of the subject, we recommend you refer to the many lovely doll books written by authority Pat Smith, available a your favorite bookstore or public library.

Key:

bjtd----ball-jointed

blb----bent limb body

bsk----bisque

c/m----closed mouth

hh----human hair

hp----hard plastic

jtd----jointed

MIG----Made In Germany

NC----no clothes

o/c----open closed

OC----original clothes

P/E----pierced ears

ptd----painted

pwt----paperweight eyes

RpC----replaced clothes

ShHd----shoulder head

ShPl----shoulder plate

SkHd----socket head

str----straight

trn----turned

Armand Marseille

A 1 M, SkHd, closed dome, 11".........................275.00
A 3 M, SkHd, 1915, c/m, intaglio eyes, mkd MIG, 18"......1,800.00
A 3/0 M, SkHd, mkd MIG/Armand Marseille, 14".........250.00
A 3/0 M, SkHd, mkd MIG/Armand Marseille, 18".........325.00
A 3/0 M, SkHd, mkd MIG/Armand Marseille, 22½".........375.00
A 3/0 M, SkHd, mkd MIG/Armand Marseille, 26".........525.00
A 4/0 M/MIG, ShPl, turned, 16½"....................275.00
A 6M/DRGM 3748 30, ShPl, hair eyebrows, mkd 1374, 20"....400.00
A 6M/DRGM 3748 30, ShPl, hair eyebrows, mkd 1374, 26"....550.00
A 7/0 M/MIG, ShPl, boy, 14"........................325.00
A 8/0 M, SkHd, side glance eyes, 13"................1,100.00
A 8/0 M/MIG, ShPl, 13"............................185.00
A 8/0 M/MIG, ShPl, 16"............................300.00
A 8/0 M/MIG, ShPl, 21"............................400.00
A 8/0 M/MIG, ShPl, 24"............................495.00
A 8/0 M/MIG, ShPl, 28"............................695.00
A 980 M 16/Germany, mechanical, eyes & tongues move, 26".1,400.00
Alma/10/0/Germany, ShPl, 12"......................175.00
Alma/10/0/Germany, ShPl, 18"......................295.00
Alma/10/0/Germany, ShPl, 26"......................450.00
AM, SkHd, black, 12"..............................550.00
AM DEP/Germany/9, ShPl, 12".......................175.00
AM DEP/Germany/9, ShPl, 26".......................450.00
AM Germany, SkHd, Oriental, voice box, 10".........500.00
AM Germany/12, flange neck, 1907, 16"..............465.00
AM 2 DEP, SkHd, 16"...............................350.00
Armand Marseille, SkHd, 18½"......................295.00
Baby Gloria/Germany 3, ShPl, 16"..................600.00
Baby Phyllis, cloth body, 1915, 4/240/MIG, 12"....450.00
Baby/O/Betty/DRGM, 1912, ShPl & SkHd, MIG, 12"....195.00
Baby/O/Betty/DRGM, 1912, ShPl & SkHd, MIG, 17"....295.00
Beauty/MIG, ShPl, 1898, mkd AM, 12"...............195.00
Beauty/MIG, ShPl, 1898, mkd AM, 20"...............325.00
Beauty/MIG, ShPl, 1898, mkd AM, 26"...............425.00
Dutch couple, ptd bisque, orig costumes, 6", pr....150.00
Floradora, Germany, ShPl, mkd 16/0 Germany/body, 6".......145.00
Floradora/A 2/0x M/MIG, SkHd, closed dome, 19½".........375.00
Floradora/A 3/0 M, SkHd, mkd MIG/Armand Marseille, 14"....250.00
Floradora/A 3/0 M, SkHd, mkd MIG/Armand Marseille, 18"....325.00
Floradora/A 3/0 M, SkHd, mkd MIG/Armand Marseille, 22½"..375.00
Floradora/A 3/0 M, SkHd, mkd MIG/Armand Marseille, 26"...525.00
Floradora/A 4/0 M/MIG, ShPl, turned, 16½"..............275.00
Floradora/A 6M/DRGM 3748 30, ShPl, mkd 1374, 26".......550.00
Floradora/A 6M/DRGM 3748 30, ShPl, mkd 1874, 20".......400.00
Floradora/A 8/0 M/MIG, ShPl, 13"......................185.00
Floradora/A 8/0 M/MIG, ShPl, 16"......................300.00

Floradora/A 8/0 M/MIG, ShPl, 21"......................400.00
Floradora/A 8/0 M/MIG, ShPl, 24"......................495.00
Floradora/A 8/0 M/MIG, ShPl, 28"......................695.00
GB/AM 3-04, SkHd, closed dome, c/m, 18"..............1,300.00
Googly, A11/0/M/Germany/DRGM, SkHd, painted eyes, 7½"....650.00
Googly, mkd AM, 9"..................................700.00
Googly, ptd bsk, Just Me, SkHd, c/m, Reg/A 310 3/0 M, 12"...695.00
Googly, ptd bsk, Just Me, SkHd, c/m, Reg/A 310 3/0 M, 9"....450.00
Googly, 253 M, Nobbikid, SkHd, 1915, US Pat Germany, 10".825.00
Googly, 253 M, Nobbikid, SkHd, 1915, US Pat Germany, 7½".650.00
Indian, AM/7/0, mkd Germany, SkHd, 9½"..............365.00
Indian, mkd AM 8/0, 12"............................425.00
Indian, mkd AM/xGermany 4/0, SkHd, 11"..............425.00
Kiddiejoy, AM 375/6, 1918, o/m, Germany, 18".........900.00
Kiddiejoy, AM 375/6, 1918, o/m, Germany, 9"..........265.00
Kiddiejoy, 372/A 1 M, ShPl, closed dome, 1926, Germany, 9"..265.00
Kiddiejoy/1/0, closed dome baby, mkd Germany, 18".........900.00
Kiddiejoy/1/0, closed dome baby, mkd Germany, 9"..........265.00
Lilly/3/0/Germany, ShPl, 12"........................175.00
Lilly/3/0/Germany, ShPl, 16"........................250.00
Lilly/3/0/Germany, ShPl, 20"........................300.00
Lilly/3/0/Germany, ShPl, 26"........................450.00
Mabel 5 Germany/Armand Marseille, ShPl, turned, SkHd, 20"..375.00
Mabel/0, ShPl, mkd Germany, 12".....................175.00
Mabel/0, ShPl, mkd Germany, 18".....................275.00
Mabel/0, ShPl, mkd Germany, 22".....................350.00
Mabel/0, ShPl, mkd Germany, 26".....................475.00
My Companion, 1911, mkd AM Germany, 18".............325.00
My Playmate, 1903, closed dome & mouth, 18".........500.00
New Born Baby, mkd LA&S 1914/G45520 4/Germany, 12"....285.00
New Born Baby, mkd LA&S 1914/G45520 4/Germany, 18"....400.00
Otto Gans/A 11 M, SkHd, baby, 26"...................995.00
Puppet baby in a blanket, mkd AM, 8"................225.00
Queen Louise/7/Germany, SkHd, 1910, 12".............195.00
Queen Louise/7/Germany, SkHd, 1910, 16".............275.00
Queen Louise/7/Germany, SkHd, 1910, 22".............400.00
Queen Louise/7/Germany, SkHd, 1910, 30".............850.00
Rosebud/A 3/0 M, ShPl, 1902, 18"....................385.00
Rosebud/A 3/0 M, ShPl, 1902, 26"....................550.00
Rosland/A 0 M, 1910, 18"...........................395.00
Special/Germany, SkHd, 1904, 12"....................195.00
Special/Germany, SkHd, 1904, 16"....................295.00
Special/Germany, SkHd, 1904, 20"....................395.00
Special/Germany, SkHd, 1904, 26"....................600.00
The Dollar Princess/Germany/A 3½ M, SkHd, 26".........725.00
1894 AM/0 DEP/MIG, SkHd, black, 15"..................485.00
1894 AM/2/0/DEP, SkHd, black, 12"...................325.00
1894 AM/8/0 DEP/MIG, ShPl, 1901, 12"................225.00
1894 AM/8/0 DEP/MIG, ShPl, 1910, 17"................350.00
1894 AM/8/0 DEP/MIG, ShPl, 1910, 22"................375.00
1894 AM/8/0 DEP/MIG, ShPl, 1910, 26"................675.00
248/Fany/A 2/0 M, SkHd, mkd DRGM, also #230-9".......900.00
248/Fany/A 2/0 M, SkHd, mkd DRGM, 16"..............3,500.00
248/Fany/A 2/0 M, SkHd, mkd DRGM, 20"..............4,750.00
248/Fany/A 2/0 M, SkHd, mkd DRGM, 24"..............6,000.00
3/H/41 K/AM, SkHd baby, 16".........................450.00
3200/AM 10/0x DEP, musical jestor, 1900, 10".........350.00
341, flange or SkHd, My Dream Baby, c/m, 13".........375.00
341, flange or SkHd, My Dream Baby, c/m, 13", black....575.00
341, flange or SkHd, My Dream Baby, c/m, 21".........625.00
341, flange or SkHd, My Dream Baby, c/m, 21", black....825.00
341, flange or SkHd, My Dream Baby, c/m, 9"..........195.00
341, flange or SkHd, My Dream Baby, c/m, 9", black.....295.00
351/AM OK/Germany, SkHd, My Dream Baby, o/m, 14"......325.00

351/AM OK/Germany, SkHd, My Dream Baby, o/m, 18"......500.00
351/AM OK/Germany, SkHd, My Dream Baby, o/m, 25".....995.00
351/AM OK/Germany, SkHd, My Dream Baby, o/m, 7".......165.00
352/Germany, SkHd, 1914, mkd AM, 12".................285.00
352/Germany, SkHd, 1914, mkd AM, 18".................400.00
352/Germany, SkHd, 1914, mkd AM, 23".................595.00
353 12/OK, SkHd, Oriental, mkd Am/Germany, 12"........795.00
353 12/OK, SkHd, Oriental, mkd Am/Germany, 16".......1,400.00
353 12/OK, SkHd, Oriental, mkd Am/Germany, 9".........550.00
370, ShPl, o/m, kid body, 15"........................250.00
370, ShPl, o/m, kid body, 17"........................275.00
370, ShPl, o/m, kid body, 21"........................325.00
370, ShPl, o/m, kid body, 24"........................385.00
370/AM, 2-1/2 DEP/MIG, ShPl, brown tones, 22".........500.00
390, SkHd, o/m, 12"..................................175.00
390, SkHd, o/m, 18"..................................295.00
390, SkHd, o/m, 23"..................................365.00
390, SkHd, o/m, 30"..................................895.00
390, SkHd, o/m, 40"................................1,600.00
390/A 2M, talker, (mama), SkHd, 17"..................325.00
390/DRGM 246 1/A 3-1/2 M, SkHd, MIG/AM, 24"..........385.00
390N, SkHd, o/m, 11".................................185.00
390N, SkHd, o/m, 22".................................350.00
5/6/3/2K, closed dome baby, o/m, 16".................450.00
560/DRGM 232, SkHd, toddler, 1924, Armand Marseille, 15"..475.00
560/DRGM 232, SkHd, toddler, 1924, Armand Marseille, 20"..695.00
560/DRGM 232, SkHd, toddler, 1924, Armand Marseille, 9"..250.00
640/A 3 M/Germany, ShPl, 1909, ptd eyes, 22".........650.00
975 M/Germany, SkHd, baby, Armand Marseille, 14".....350.00
975 M/Germany, SkHd, baby, Armand Marseille, 20".....595.00
975 M/Germany, SkHd, baby, Armand Marseille, 25"...1,200.00
975 M/Germany, SkHd, baby, Armand Marseille, 9"......225.00

Arranbee

Baby, 13" head, o/c eyes, o/m, dimples, cloth/compo hands....295.00
Boy, Nancy Lee mold, compo, mohair wig, all orig, 1939, 14"...76.00
My Angel, hair rooted in vinyl head, o/c eyes, walker, 8".......97.00
Nancy Lee/Nanette, hp, long blonde braids, o/c eyes, 1950, 14".98.00
Nurser baby, #7770 w/14k pacifier, 14"................1,750.00
Raving Beauty, hp, o/m, felt tongue, o/c eyes, braids, 18"......104.00
Snuggle, plush/compo, molded hair, o/c eyes, 1941, 16".......32.00

Barbie Dolls and Related Dolls

Allen, 1963, painted hair................................45.00
Allen, 1964, bendable legs..............................100.00
Barbie, 1959, #1, blonde, holes in feet for holder...........800.00
Barbie, 1959, #1, brunette, holes in feet for holder.........850.00
Barbie, 1959, #2, blonde, same as #1 but no holes in feet....450.00
Barbie, 1959, #2, brunette, same as #1 but no holes in feet....500.00
Barbie, 1960, #3, blonde, brown eye liner, heavy vinyl body...100.00
Barbie, 1960, #3, blonde, ponytail & curly bangs, bl eyeliner...110.00
Barbie, 1960, #3, brunette, pony tail & soft curly bangs.......110.00
Barbie, 1960, #4, blonde, braided ponytail/curly bangs........100.00
Barbie, 1960, #4, brunette, braided ponytail/curly bangs.......110.00
Barbie, 1961, #5, various color ponytail/bangs, hollow body....80.00
Barbie, 1962, bubble cut hair (various colors)...............70.00
Barbie, 1963, Fashion Queen, w/3 wigs & wig stand..........100.00
Barbie, 1964, Miss Barbie, 'sleepy' eyes, 3 wigs/lawn swing....350.00
Barbie, 1964, swirl ponytail, any color hair...............90.00
Barbie, 1965, Color Magic, bendable legs/changeable hair color.200.00
Barbie, 1965, 1st bendable leg, Dutch boy hairstyle..........100.00
Barbie, 1965, 1st bendable leg, side part short hair.........200.00

Barbie, 1966, Twist 'N Turn..............................50.00
Barbie, 1967, standard..................................50.00
Barbie, 1967, Twist 'N Turn..............................50.00
Barbie, 1968, Spanish Talking...........................100.00
Barbie, 1968, Talking...................................75.00
Barbie, 1968, Twist 'N Turn..............................50.00
Barbie, 1969, Living....................................55.00
Barbie, 1969, Spanish Talking...........................100.00
Barbie, 1969, Talking Barbie............................75.00
Barbie, 1969, Twist 'N Turn..............................50.00
Barbie, 1970, standard, pink & green swimsuit.............50.00
Barbie, 1971, Dramatic New Living........................55.00
Barbie, 1971, Hair Happenin's, Sears limited edition, rare....250.00
Barbie, 1971, Live Action Barbie Doll.....................65.00
Barbie, 1971, Live Action Barbie On Stage.................75.00
Barbie, 1971, Malibu....................................20.00
Barbie, 1971, Talking...................................75.00
Barbie, 1971, Twist 'N Turn..............................50.00
Barbie, 1971, With Growin' Pretty Hair...................70.00
Barbie, 1972, Busy Barbie With Holdin' Hands.............80.00
Barbie, 1972, Talking Busy Barbie With Holdin' Hands.....80.00
Barbie, 1972, Walk Lively...............................75.00
Barbie, 1972, Ward's Anniversary........................150.00
Barbie, 1972, With Growin' Pretty Hair, rarer than 1971 issue..100.00
Barbie, 1973, Quick Curl................................35.00
Barbie, 1973, Quick Curl w/extra outfit, store promotional.....55.00
Barbie, 1974, Newport...................................55.00
Barbie, 1974, Sun Valley, ski costume....................45.00
Barbie, 1974, Sweet Sixteen.............................35.00
Barbie, 1974, Sweet Sixteen, w/promotional outfit on card.....40.00
Barbie, 1975, Free Moving...............................35.00
Barbie, 1975, Gold Medal, Olympic Sports.................25.00
Barbie, 1975, Gold Medal, Skater........................35.00
Barbie, 1975, Gold Medal, Skier.........................35.00
Barbie, 1975, Gold Medal, Winter Sports..................25.00
Barbie, 1976, Ballerina, 1st issue, hair pulled back.........30.00
Barbie, 1976, Ballerina Barbie On Tour, dept store special.....40.00
Barbie, 1976, Beautiful Bride, sold in most stores...........30.00
Barbie, 1976, Beautiful Bride, 1st issue, dept store special.....65.00
Barbie, 1976, Deluxe Quick Curl.........................25.00
Barbie, 1976, Super Star, 1st issue, w/extra hair comb........35.00
Barbie, 1976, Super Star, 2nd issue, w/extra necklace.........30.00
Barbie, 1978, Ballerina, 2nd issue, heavier make-up, side curl...20.00
Barbie, 1978, Ballerina Barbie On Tour re-issue, 3 costumes....30.00
Black Francie, 1967, 1st issue, lt brn eyes/red oxidized hair....200.00
Black Francie, 1967, 2nd issue, dark eyes/dk brn hair.........175.00
Brad, 1969, Talking.....................................45.00
Brad, 1971, bendable leg................................40.00
Buffy & Mrs Beasley, 1968...............................50.00
Cara, 1973, Quick Curl, from Canada......................35.00
Cara, 1975, Free Moving.................................35.00
Cara, 1976, Ballerina...................................30.00
Cara, 1976, Deluxe Quick Curl...........................25.00
Casey, 1967, twist & turn waist, blonde or brunette..........65.00
Chris, 1967, Bendable Posable...........................40.00
Chris, 1967, very long dark hair.........................50.00
Christie, Super Star....................................30.00
Christie, 1969, New Talking.............................50.00
Christie, 1969, Twist...................................50.00
Christie, 1970, Talking.................................50.00
Christie, 1971, Live Action.............................65.00
Curtis, 1975, Free Moving, only issued for 1 year............40.00
Fluff, 1971, Living.....................................55.00
Francie, 1966, bendable leg.............................50.00

Francie, 1966, straight leg.....................................60.00
Francie, 1967, Twist 'N Turn.............................50.00
Francie, 1969, Twist 'N Turn.............................55.00
Francie, 1970, Hair Happenin's, twist 'n turn, w/4 hairpieces....65.00
Francie, 1970, Twist 'N Turn.............................55.00
Francie, 1970, With Growin' Pretty Hair.................65.00
Francie, 1971, Malibu......................................25.00
Francie, 1971, Twist 'N Turn, no bangs, blonde or brunette....150.00
Francie, 1972, Busy Francie With Holdin' Hands.................80.00
Francie, 1973, Quick Curl.................................35.00
Ginger, 1976, Growing Up.................................30.00
Jamie, 1970, Walking......................................75.00
Julia, 1969, Talking......................................45.00
Julia, 1969, Twist 'N Turn, 2-piece nurse's uniform...........55.00
Julia, 1970, Twist 'N Turn, nurse's dress.................55.00
Kelley, 1973, Quick Curl.................................50.00
Kelley, 1974, Yellowstone................................75.00
Ken, 1961, 1st issue flocked hair, w/trunks/sandals/towel.......65.00
Ken, 1961, 2nd issue flocked hair.........................55.00
Ken, 1962, painted hair...................................50.00
Ken, 1964, bendable leg..................................100.00
Ken, 1969, bendable leg...................................45.00
Ken, 1969, Spanish Talking...............................55.00
Ken, 1969, Talking..45.00
Ken, 1970, bendable leg...................................40.00
Ken, 1971, Live Action....................................50.00
Ken, 1971, Live Action Ken On Stage......................65.00
Ken, 1971, Malibu, each...................................15.00
Ken, 1972, Busy...65.00
Ken, 1972, Malibu...15.00
Ken, 1972, Talking Busy...................................75.00
Ken, 1972, Walk Lively....................................65.00
Ken, 1973, Malibu...15.00
Ken, 1973, Mod Hair.......................................20.00
Ken, 1974, Malibu...15.00
Ken, 1974, Sun Valley, ski outfit.........................50.00
Ken, 1975, Free Moving....................................30.00
Ken, 1975, Gold Medal Skier...............................35.00
Ken, 1976, Now-Look Ken, long hair........................20.00
Ken, 1976, Super Star Ken, 1st issue, w/extra gift ring........20.00
Ken, 1979, Sport Star Ken, Canadian.......................30.00
Ken, 1980, Golden Night Ken, Canadian.....................25.00
Ken, 1981, Jogging Ken, Canadian..........................20.00
Midge, 1963, closed mouth, red, brunette or blonde hair.......55.00
Midge, 1963, unusual skin coloring & no freckles............120.00
Midge, 1963, w/teeth, side-glance eyes, unusual.............110.00
Midge, 1965, bendable leg, last issue of Midge.............100.00
Miss America, Blonde Quick Curl, from Canada...............45.00
Miss America, Blonde Quick Curl, offered at most stores.......25.00
Miss America, Brunette Quick Curl, w/longer hair & twist waist..85.00
Miss America, 1972, Walk Lively, Kellogg Co promotional......40.00
PJ, 1969, New 'N Groovy Talking...........................70.00
PJ, 1969, Twist 'N Turn....................................55.00
PJ, 1971, Live Action PJ Doll.............................65.00
PJ, 1971, Live Action PJ On Stage.........................75.00
PJ, 1972, Malibu..20.00
PJ, 1975, Free Moving.....................................35.00
PJ, 1976, Deluxe Quick Curl...............................25.00
Pretty Pairs, 1970, Angie 'N Tangie.......................90.00
Pretty Pairs, 1970, Lori 'N Rori..........................90.00
Pretty Pairs, 1970, Nan 'N Fran...........................90.00
Ricky, 1965, painted hair.................................65.00
Skipper, 1964, varied colors of hair......................45.00
Skipper, 1965, 1st bendable leg...........................55.00

Skipper, 1967, re-issued bendable leg, rare only when MIB......75.00
Skipper, 1968, Twist 'N Turn..............................45.00
Skipper, 1969, New Twist 'N Turn..........................45.00
Skipper, 1970, New Living.................................45.00
Skipper, 1970, Twist......................................45.00
Skipper, 1971, Malibu.....................................15.00
Skipper, 1973, Pose 'N Play, comes in bag, mint in package....15.00
Skipper, 1973, Quick Curl.................................30.00
Skipper, 1975, Growing Up.................................20.00
Skooter, 1964, various hair coloring......................50.00
Skooter, 1966, bendable leg...............................65.00
Stacey, 1968, Talking.....................................50.00
Stacey, 1968, Twist 'N Turn...............................45.00
Stacey, 1969, Twist 'N Turn...............................50.00
Steffie, 1972, Busy Steffie With Holdin' Hands.................85.00
Steffie, 1972, Busy Talking Steffie With Holdin' Hands........100.00
Steffie, 1972, Walk Lively................................75.00
Tiff, 1972, hard to find.................................125.00
Todd, 1966, plaid cap & shorts............................50.00
Todd, 1967, Bendable Posable..............................40.00
Truly Scrumptious, 1969, standard........................225.00
Truly Scrumptious, 1969, Talking.........................225.00
Tutti, 1966, blonde or brunette...........................45.00
Tutti, 1966, Me & My Dog play set........................150.00
Tutti, 1966, Melody In Pink play set.....................150.00
Tutti, 1966, Night Night Sleep Tight play set.................75.00
Tutti, 1966, Tutti & Tod Sundae Treat play set..............175.00
Tutti, 1966, Walking My Dolly play set....................75.00
Tutti, 1967, Bendable Posable.............................40.00
Tutti, 1967, Cookin' Goodies play set....................125.00
Tutti, 1967, Swing-a-Ling play set.......................175.00
Tutti, 1975, Night Night Sleep Tight set, European re-issue.....45.00
Tutti, 1975, Swing-a-Ling play set, European re-issue.........45.00
Tutti, 1975, Walking My Dolly play set, European re-issue......45.00
Twiggy, 1967, Casey w/more make-up & short hair, twist waist...75.00

Barbie Accessories and Related Accessories

Barbie & Francie Color Magic Fashion Set.................110.00
Barbie & Ken Little Theatre, #0490 (1963 booklet)..........100.00
Barbie & Skipper's Schoolroom, 1964 Sears Christmas catalog..150.00
Barbie Baby-Sits, #953 (1962 booklet)....................125.00
Barbie Hot Rod, Irwin Corporation.........................75.00
Barbie Lawn Swing & Planter, Go Together Furniture.........50.00
Barbie Mix 'N Match Set, 1962, purchased at JC Penney......300.00
Barbie Queen Size Bed, by Suzy Goose, M...................30.00
Barbie Round the Clock Gift Set, #1013 (1964 booklet).......375.00
Barbie Sparkling Pink Gift Set, #1011 (1963 booklet)........250.00
Barbie Sports Car, Irwin Corporation......................60.00
Barbie stand, #1, for dolls with holes in feet.............60.00
Barbie stand, #2..50.00
Barbie stand, #3..40.00
Barbie Twinkle Town Set..................................275.00
Barbie Vanity & Bench, by Suzy Goose, w/throw rug, M........15.00
Barbie Wedding Party Gift Set, #1017 (1964 booklet)........400.00
Barbie's Dining Room Furniture Set, Go Together Furniture....50.00
Barbie's Dream Kitchen & Dinette, #4095 (1964 booklet)......75.00
Barbie's Four Poster Bed Outfit, by Suzy Goose, M...........15.00
Barbie's Mountain Ski Cabin, #4283, Sears Exclusive, M.......15.00
Barbie's Music Box Piano & Bench, by Suzy Goose, M.........125.00
Barbie's New Restyled Dream House, #4092..................50.00
Chris Gift Set, 1967 Sears Christmas catalog..............175.00
Clothes, Barbie In Japan, #0821, (1963 booklet)............50.00
Clothes, Business Appointment, #1424......................65.00

Clothes, Campus Sweetheart, #1616.........................45.00
Clothes, Candy Striper Volunteer, #0889, (1963 booklet).......25.00
Clothes, Dog Show, #1929, (1965 booklet)...................75.00
Clothes, Drum Major, #0775, (1963 booklet)................25.00
Clothes, Easter Parade, #971 (#1 1958 booklet).............125.00
Clothes, Gold 'N Glamour, #1647 (1964 booklet).............30.00
Clothes, Ken In Mexico, #0820, (1963 booklet)..............35.00
Clothes, Masquerade Party, #0944 (1963 booklet)............20.00
Clothes, Miss Astronaut, #1641, (1964 booklet)............100.00
Clothes, Nighty-Negligee, #965, (1958 booklet).............20.00
Clothes, Pink Formal, Sears Exclusive.....................50.00
Clothes, Plantation Belle, (1958 booklet)..................35.00
Clothes, Poor & Rich Cinderella, #6872, (1963 booklet).......40.00
Clothes, Solo In The Spotlight, #982, (#2 1958 booklet).......35.00
Clothes, Sophisticated Lady, #993 (1963 booklet)...........45.00
Clothes, Tuxedo, #787, (1961 booklet).....................35.00
Clothes, Wedding Day Set, #972, (1961 booklet)............45.00
Francie & Her Swingin' Separates, #1042, 1966 Sears special..275.00
Skipper Dream Room, #4094 (1964 booklet)..................75.00
Skipper Jeweled Bed, by Suzy Goose, M....................30.00
Skipper On Wheels Gift Set, #1032 (1964 booklet)..........225.00
Skipper Party Time Gift Set, #1021 (1964 booklet)..........200.00
Skipper Swing-A-Rounder Gym Set, #1179 (1972 booklet).....275.00
Skooter Cut 'N Button Gift Set, 1967 Sears Christmas catalog..175.00
Talking Barbie Pink Premiere Gift Set, #1596 (1969 booklet)...275.00
Tutti & Todd Dutch Bedroom Furniture Set, by Suzy Goose...150.00
Tutti Playhouse, #3306 (1966 booklet), doll included, M.......50.00

Barbie's Round the Clock Gift Set, #1013, 1964, $375.00.

Belton

Concave head, 2/3 hole, EX bisque, o/c or c/m w/wig, 10".....950.00
Concave head, 2/3 hole, EX bisque, o/c or c/m w/wig, 13"...1,100.00
Concave head, 2/3 hole, EX bisque, o/c or c/m w/wig, 15"...1,200.00
Concave head, 2/3 hole, EX bisque, o/c or c/m w/wig, 16"...1,350.00
Concave head, 2/3 hole, EX bisque, o/c or c/m w/wig, 17"...1,550.00
Concave head, 2/3 hole, EX bisque, o/c or c/m w/wig, 20"...1,850.00
Concave head, 2/3 hole, EX bisque, o/c or c/m w/wig, 22"...1,950.00
Concave head, 2/3 hole, EX bisque, o/c or c/m w/wig, 23"...2,150.00
Concave head, 2/3 hole, EX bisque, o/c or c/m w/wig, 26"...2,400.00
Concave head, 2/3 hole, EX bisque, o/c or c/m w/wig, 8".....600.00

Bisque, Unmarked

All bsk, bonnet doll, c/m, pwt eyes, arms move, 4"............85.00
All bsk, French, set glass eyes, o/m, mohair, 5".............500.00
All bsk, French #208-8, glass eyes, OC, wig, 9½".............550.00
All bsk, o/c eyes, orig wig, movable limbs, OC, #6343, 7"....400.00
All bsk blonde/hair band, pnt eyes, o/c mouth/jtd arms, 4½"....65.00
All bsk girl, molded blonde hair/ribbon, jtd arms, dressed, 7"...95.00
Boy, c/m, pnt eyes, cloth body, rpr/rpl, 17"................175.00
Boy, set eyes, o/m, mohair, bsk/cotton, RpC, 10½"...........125.00
Boy, wht head/hands, cotton body, lace trimmed 2 pc suit, 8"..150.00
Bride, set glass eyes, o/m, Gibson hh wig, 30"..............750.00
C/m, felt body, pnt eyes, mohair, bsk head/hands, 12".......300.00
Character, o/c eyes, dimple in chin, o/m, p/e, bjtd, 18".......550.00
Character, stationary eyes, hh, comp bjtd, #390N, 24".......495.00
Character toddler, Kestner type, no mk, 13"................410.00
Compo flapper body, set eyes, mohair, o/m, underwear, 8¼"..125.00
Dutch girl, all bsk, carries wood yoke/2 bsk buckets, 2½"......25.00
Fashion, S 7½H, o/m, pwt eyes, p/e, kid body/ft, 19".........975.00
Flapper body, mohair braids, glass eyes, German dress, 7"....125.00
Googlie, #210, colored/comp toddler body, intaglio eyes, 6½"..675.00
Googlie, #293, all bsk, o/c eyes, swivel head/limbs, OC, 5"....585.00
Googlie, #914, papier mache body, o/c eyes, o/m, OC, 8".....725.00
Japanese girl, all bsk, molded hair, jtd arms/legs, OC, 5½"....50.00
Molded hair/eyes, cotton body/rpl bsk arms/china legs, 10½"...125.00
Queen Louise, o/m, set eyes, hh, bjtd, flapper, '20s, 23".....500.00
Robinson Crusoe, mohair, set eyes, o/m, molded boots, 11"....350.00
ShHd, molded hair/pnt eyes, c/m, cloth w/bsk limbs, 3¾".....100.00
ShPl, glass eyes, o/m, hh, ball bsk arms, kid body, 20".......350.00
Trn ShHd, c/m, o/c eyes, hh, orig pate, kid, ½ bsk arms, 26"..995.00

Bru

Closed mouth, all kid body, bisque lower arms; Bru, 16".....6,500.00
Closed mouth, all kid body, bisque lower arms; Bru, 18".....7,400.00
Closed mouth, all kid body, bisque lower arms; Bru, 21".....8,300.00
Closed mouth, all kid body, bisque lower arms; Bru, 26".....9,500.00
Closed mouth, kid/wood body, bsk lower arms; Bru Jne, 12"..5,000.00
Closed mouth, kid/wood body, bsk lower arms; Bru Jne, 14"..6,600.00
Closed mouth, kid/wood body, bsk lower arms; Bru Jne, 16"..8,500.00
Closed mouth, kid/wood body, bsk lower arms; Bru Jne, 20".10,000.00
Closed mouth, kid/wood body, bsk lower arms; Bru Jne, 25".14,500.00
Closed mouth, kid/wood body, bsk lower arms; Bru Jne, 28".15,500.00
Closed mouth, kid/wood body, bsk lower arms; Bru Jne, 32".17,500.00
Closed mouth, kid/wood body, bsk lower arms; Bru Jne, 36".22,000.00
Closed mouth, mkd Bru, circle dot, 16"....................7,400.00
Closed mouth, mkd Bru, circle dot, 19"...................11,500.00
Closed mouth, mkd Bru, circle dot, 23"...................14,500.00
Closed mouth, mkd Bru, circle dot, 26"...................16,000.00
Closed mouth, mkd Bru, circle dot, 28"...................17,300.00
Closed mouth, socket head on compo body; Bru, R, 14".....3,800.00
Closed mouth, socket head on compo body; Bru, R, 17".....5,000.00
Closed mouth, socket head on compo body; Bru, R, 22".....5,800.00
Closed mouth, socket head on compo body; Bru, R, 25".....6,500.00
Closed mouth, socket head on compo body; Bru, R, 28".....7,000.00
Open mouth, comp walker's body, throws kisses, 18"........3,000.00
Open mouth, comp walker's body, throws kisses, 22"........3,500.00
Open mouth, comp walker's body, throws kisses, 26"........5,000.00
Open mouth, nursing (Bebe), high color, late SFBJ, 12".....1,800.00
Open mouth, nursing (Bebe), high color, late SFBJ, 15".....2,800.00
Open mouth, nursing (Bebe), high color, late SFBJ, 18".....3,500.00
Open mouth, nursing Bru (Bebe), early, EX bsk, 12"........4,500.00
Open mouth, nursing Bru (Bebe), early, EX bsk, 15"........7,500.00
Open mouth, nursing Bru (Bebe), early, EX bsk, 18"........8,500.00
Open mouth, socket head on compo body; Bru, R, 14".......2,500.00

French bisque head, Bru Jne, swivel head and paperweight eyes, pierced ears, original mohair wig, open-close mouth, kid body with bisque lower arms, 18", $7,150.00.

Open mouth, socket head on compo body; Bru, R, 17".....3,200.00
Open mouth, socket head on compo body; Bru, R, 22".....5,000.00
Open mouth, socket head on compo body; Bru, R, 25".....5,800.00
Open mouth, socket head on compo body; Bru, R, 28".....6,200.00
Open mouth, socket head on compo body; Bru, R, 32".....7,200.00

Bye-Lo

Frozen bisque, on bk w/arms & legs raised, 3½"............400.00
O/c eyes, 16" mk head..................................995.00
Orig body, celluloid hands, o/c eyes, 9½".................395.00
Orig body, celluloid hands, 12½"........................550.00
Putnam, Grace; o/c eyes, celluloid hands, 12"............650.00
Putnam, Grace; 14" head, cloth body, o/c eyes, antique clothes.495.00
Salt & pepper shakers, 1 on bk, other on stomach, pr........550.00

China, Unmarked

Biedermeier, braided wig, cotton body, china arms/legs, 6".....350.00
Black hair/11 curl, pnt eyes, rpl kid arms, RpC, 23".......450.00
Blk, hair full at sides, pnt eyes, stone bsk hands/ft, 8".......150.00
Blk, rare hairdo, china hands, OC, 11½"..................250.00
Blk Godey style hair, mk #5, twill body, OC, 19"...........125.00
Blk hair, early style, apple cheeks, fancy dress, 18"..........250.00
Blk hair, flat top, cotton body/spoon hands, RpC, CW era, 15".250.00
Blk hair/pnt bl eyes, bisque lower arms/legs, NC, German, 9"....50.00
Blonde, china arms/legs, sawdust filled body, 15", EX..........75.00
Blonde, open mouth w/teeth, 13".........................225.00
Boy, blk hair, rpl hands/shoes, prof rpr, 23"...............125.00
Braided bun hairdo, 1830s, 19"..........................700.00
Godey type, Philippine outfit, yarn hair, beads, 10½".........125.00

Cloth

Bed doll, pnt face, blonde pigtail, 5 ft.....................25.00
Black boy, dressed/felt shoes/cloth hair, 1930s, 20"..........120.00
Black boy in knickers, high button shoes, 1890s, 14"........140.00
Boy, ink features, applied ears, wears 1½ yr clothes..........75.00
Geisha, pnt silk screen features, 15"......................125.00
Harlequin clown, hand sewn features, 1925, 20"..............40.00
Lenci type, elaborate dress, 10½", EX.....................35.00

Mechanical o/c mouth, mohair, 12"......................175.00
Mr & Mrs Peter Rabbit, 1930s, 15", pr....................65.00
Pressed pnt face, '20s style mouth, mohair, OC, 22"..........35.00
Topsy-turvy, felt features/yarn hair/dressed, 1930, 13".........85.00

Composition, Unmarked

Baby, molded hair, o/c mouth/2 pnt teeth, cotton body, 14", VG.45.00
Dollhouse type, wire body/lead ft, clothed, 3"...............15.00
Dutch girl, molded hair, decal eyes, OC, 1920s, 10"..........85.00
Liberty Boy, movable head/limbs, WWI, rpr, 12".............85.00
Man Friday, all compo, red/br w/blk plush hair, 8½"..........75.00
Negro, bent limb baby, pnt eyes, blk hair, 9½", G............35.00
Toddler, all compo, can sit, pnt hair/booties, wool diaper, 9"....45.00
Toddler, 2 faced: o/c eyes/crying; OC, minor damage, 17".....125.00

Effanbee

Airman, 1919, 16".....................................100.00
Alyssa, 1958-1962, 24"................................175.00
America's Children, 1936-1940, 21".....................300.00
Americana Collection, 1975-1977, ea.....................55.00
Anchor's Aweigh Boy & Girl, 1979-1980, ea...............45.00
Anne of Green Gables, 1935, 14".........................85.00
Anne Shirley, 1935-1939, 15"...........................100.00
Aunt Dinah, 1915, 14".................................150.00
Auto Train Hostess, 1979...............................65.00
Babette, 1980..45.00
Baby & Big Sister, 1940, 9"............................95.00
Baby Blanche, 1918, 15"..............................100.00
Baby Blue, 1919, 12".................................100.00
Baby Bright Eyes, 1916, 11"............................85.00
Baby Bright Eyes Jr, 1915, 11".........................85.00
Baby Bunting, 1917, 16"..............................198.00
Baby Catherine, 1918, 12"............................125.00
Baby Cuddle, 1967-1968, 16"...........................45.00
Baby Cupcake, 1963-1964, 12"..........................25.00
Baby Daintie, 1918, 16"...............................96.00
Baby Face, 1967-1969, 1973-1976, 15"...................44.00
Baby Face Collection, 1977, ea..........................55.00
Baby Peaches, 1965, 15"...............................44.00
Baby Pink, 1919, 12".................................100.00
Baby Wonder, 1935, 16"...............................96.00
Babyette, 1942, 10".................................135.00
Barbara Lee, 1924, 29"...............................252.00
Barbara Lou, 1936, 21"...............................298.00
Beautee-Skin Baby, 1944, 17"..........................66.00
Belle Telle, 1962....................................77.00
Betsy Ross, 1976-1978................................75.00
Betty Bounce, 1913-1915, 11"..........................78.00
Betty Lee, 1924, 21".................................198.00
Billy Boy, 1915, 11"..................................85.00
Blue Danube, 1978...................................76.00
Blue Heaven Collection, 1977-1978, ea...................45.00
Bobby Ann, 1913, 12".................................65.00
Bobby Bounce, 1913, 11"..............................76.00
Bride, 1938-1943, 21"................................152.00
Bubbles, Charlotte, 1924, 20".........................176.00
Bubbles, Walking, 1926, 14"..........................178.00
Butterball, 1963, 1969-1981, 12".......................25.00
Button Nose, Betty, 1943, 8"...........................77.00
Buttons Monk, 1923, 12"..............................96.00
Candy Ann, 1954, 20".................................75.00
Candy Kid, 1954, 12".................................56.00

Candy Land Collection, 1973, ea............................55.00
Castle Garden, 1979-1980.............................67.00
Catherine, 1926, 16″...............................165.00
Champagne Lady, 1957..............................96.00
Charlie, 1966-1967, 13″.............................47.00
Charlie McCarthy, 1937, 21″.........................278.00
Cherries Jubilee, 1979..............................75.00
Christening Baby, 1918, 25″.........................128.00
Cinderella, 1952, 18″...............................152.00
Cinderella for Disney, 1977-1978....................105.00
Clippo Clown, 1937, 14″.............................96.00
Coquette, Miss, 1912-1918, 12″......................120.00
Country Bumpkin Collection, 1977, ea.................55.00
Country Cousins, 1974, ea...........................55.00
Cream Puff Collection, 1980, ea.....................45.00
Cupcake, 1963, 12″.................................26.00
Daffy Dot Collection, 1972, ea......................55.00
Denise, Bebe, 1981.................................56.00
Dolly Dumpling, 1918, 14″..........................126.00
Duchess, 1976-1978.................................75.00
DyDee Darlin', 1967-1969, 1971, 16″.................77.00
DyDee Kin, 1933-1940, 13″...........................76.00
Educational Doll, 1971-1979, 20″...................100.00
Ella, 1938, 24″....................................98.00
Emerald Isle, 1979.................................75.00
Emily Ann, 1937, 14″...............................96.00
Florence, 1938, 31″...............................155.00
Flowergirl, 1973 on, 11″............................44.00
Frontier Women, 1977-1979..........................66.00
Gay Nineties, 1979.................................65.00
Gigi, 1979-1980....................................57.00
Ginger Curls, 1938, 21″...........................154.00
Gloria Ann, 1936, 21″.............................295.00
Grumpy, Lady, 1918, 14″...........................178.00
Half Pint, 1966-1980, 11″...........................47.00
Heartbeat Baby, 1942, 17″.........................155.00
Historical Dolls, 14″.............................398.00
Honey, 1950s, 18″.................................105.00
Honey Walker, 1949-1955, 21″.......................127.00
Honey-kins, 1954, 12″..............................48.00
Hourglass Look, 1978-1979..........................65.00
Howdy Doody, 1947, 20″.............................98.00
Ingenie, 1979-1980.................................56.00
Jack, 1979-1981....................................65.00
Jan Carol, 1929, 24″..............................200.00
Jill, 1979-1981....................................66.00
Judy, 1928, 18″....................................85.00
Kilroy, 1940, 14″..................................98.00
Lady Ascot, 1981...................................48.00
Lady Snow, 1979....................................75.00
Lamkin, 1930, 16″.................................276.00
Lil' Darlin', 1947, 16″.............................62.00
Lil' Sweetie, 1967, 16″.............................75.00
Lili, 1980...46.00
Little Gumdrop, 1967, 14″...........................58.00
Little Lady, 1939-1946, 15″........................105.00
Little Lady, 1939-1946, 27″........................300.00
Little Lady Birthday Doll, 1941, 21″...............200.00
Little Walter, 1912, 16″...........................105.00
Liza Lee, 1937, 14″................................98.00
Love & Learn Set, 1965, 22″.........................65.00
Lovums, 1928, 22″.................................166.00
Lucinda, 1952, 1959, 18″..........................154.00
Lynn, 1969, 14″....................................45.00

Ma Chere, 1976.....................................76.00
Madame DuBerry, 1977-1978..........................75.00
Mae Starr, 1928, 29″..............................327.00
Maid Marion, 1978.................................105.00
Marietta, 1938, 27″...............................115.00
Martha Washington, 1976-1977.......................78.00
Marvel-Tot, 1934, 16″..............................98.00
Mary Jane, 1959, 32″..............................148.00
Mary Lou, 1924, 20″...............................200.00
Mary Sue, 1927, 26″...............................155.00
Mickey, 1952-1962, 16″.............................98.00
Mickey Baby, 1939-1949, 15″........................115.00
Miss Glamour Girl, 1942, 21″.......................155.00
Most Happy Family, 1957-1961, set for..............125.00
My Fair Baby, 1958-1969, 18″.......................67.00
Naughty Eyes, 1927, 16″............................95.00
Nun, 1914, 12″.....................................77.00
Old Fashioned Baby, 1979-1980......................45.00
Over the Rainbow, 1973, ea.........................55.00
Patriciakin, 1932,14″.............................198.00
Patsy, Limited Edition............................252.00
Patsy, Wee; 1930, 6″..............................225.00
Patsy, 1926, 1930s, 1940s, 14″....................195.00
Patsy Ann, Music Box, 1939, 18″...................300.00
Patsy Fluff, 1932, 14″............................198.00
Peaches & Cream, 1965, ea..........................55.00
Peggy Lou, 1936, 21″..............................300.00
Pimbo, 1940, 14″...................................96.00
Polka Dottie, 1954, 21″...........................147.00
Poochie, 1937, 14″................................125.00
Prairie Nights, 1976, ea...........................45.00
Precious New Born, 1962, 16″.......................46.00
Pun'Kin, 1966-1980, 11″............................45.00
Rainbow Parfait Collection, 1979, ea...............45.00
Red Riding Hood, 1936, 9″..........................97.00
Ringbearer, 1973 on, 11″...........................56.00
Robin Hood, 1978...................................75.00
Romper Babies, 1918, 15″...........................98.00
Ruby, 1980...76.00
Sewing Kit Dolls, 1942, 5½″.......................100.00
Skippy, Limited Edition...........................176.00
Southern Belle, 1976...............................75.00
Strawberry Patch Collection, 1972, ea..............55.00
Sugar Pie, 1959, 1963, 1969, 22″...................88.00
Suzette, 1939, 11″................................102.00
Suzie Sunshine, 1960-1981, 18″.....................50.00
Sweethearts, The; 1918, 16″, ea...................125.00
Three Pigs, 1934, 10″, ea.........................150.00
Thum'kin, 1965-1966, 24″...........................64.00
Tintair, 1951-1952, 14″............................75.00
Tiny Tubber, 1955-1981,............................28.00
Toddle Tot, 1958-1970, 13″.........................26.00
Topaz, 1981..75.00
Turquoise, 1981....................................76.00
Uncle Sam, 1914, 16″..............................178.00
WC Fields, 1929, 18″..............................327.00
WC Fields, 1929, 22″..............................400.00
Winkie, 1963, 16″..................................37.00
Yesterday's Collection, 1977, ea...................45.00

Germany

All bsk, jtd arms/legs, mohair, pnt eyes, 4½″...............45.00
All bsk, pnt eyes, molded hair, lace clothes, #5360-0, 6″.......75.00

American School Boy, ShHd, molded hair, bsk/cloth, rpr, 13".. 350.00
Baby, #11001/I, pnt eyes, all bsk, 6½"................... 125.00
Baby, all pink pnt bsk, molded blonde hair, 3½", VG......... 35.00
Boy, ShHd, bsk, molded blonde hair, cloth body, 1870, 16"... 110.00
Boy, SkHd, set eyes, o/m, mohair, stick body, 11".......... 175.00
Bsk, o/c eyes/lashes, compo bjtd, dressed, #63, 24".......... 560.00
Bsk, PM 914, o/c eyes, compo 5 pc toddler, wig, 11"........ 525.00
Bsk head, glass eyes, teeth, sgn P Sch, jtd compo, 14"....... 160.00
Bsk head, o/c glass eyes/teeth/tongue/compo blb, #152-11, 20". 260.00
Bsk head/cb torso/crude 5 pc body, set eyes, o/m, #11/0, 13".. 125.00
Bsk head/glass eyes, c/m, p/e, jtd compo, 1900, 15"......... 625.00
Bsk LHK, o/c eyes, hh, solid wrists, crepe costume, 18"...... 650.00
Character, bald w/brush mks, intaglio eyes, o/c mouth, 10".... 500.00
Character, pwt eyes, o/m, hh, comp bjtd, #410-4, 20"...... 1,895.00
Dream Baby #A.341, 8½" bsk head, o/c eyes, o/m, 10"...... 325.00
Flapper, glass eyes, mohair, OC, 7½"..................... 150.00
Nodder, all bsq, molded clothes, hand holes for flowers, 3".... 45.00
O/c eyes, o/m, bsk hands/kid body, OC, #273, 14".......... 250.00
O/c glass eyes, o/m, jtd (except wrists) bsk/compo, LHK/2, 17". 140.00
O/c glass eyes, o/m w/teeth, mk GB, jtd compo body, 24"..... 200.00
Set eyes, o/m, mohair, bsk/cotton, #12/0, 13".............. 150.00
Set eyes, rpl wig, o/m, kid body/rpl hands/RpC, #14/0, 17".... 150.00
Special, set eyes, o/m, hh, bjtd, rpl hand/shoes, 21"......... 475.00

Half Dolls

Arms away, rose in hand, china, #5237, 4½"............... 165.00
Arms extended, flowers in hair, china, orig skirt/base, 5¾".... 135.00
Bathing beauty, arms away, pink, bisque, German............ 65.00
Bisque, arms away, #3705, 4⅛"......................... 110.00
Blonde curly hair, pink top w/sleeves/rose, arms on waist, 3".... 35.00
Br hair/pink bodice w/gold insert/wht sleeves, German #17234... 65.00
Carmen, gr bodice, lustre shawl & hat, German #74503, 4".... 85.00
Colonial lady, arms away, molded bust, tiny waist, 3¼"....... 145.00
Colonial lady, rose in hand on hair, 1 arm away, chemise, 3"... 95.00
Dk bl bodice, German #5023, 2½"........................ 40.00
Doll, 3½", w/4" legs attached, pincushion body, German #7983. 75.00
Flapper, bl dress, gray lid lines, German #74507, 4".......... 85.00
Flapper, fancy hat, low neck, pnt earrings, w/fan, Japan, 3½".. 350.00
Flapper, lg rose at side, pink bodice, hands at waist, 3¼"...... 35.00

Flapper doll, on original pincushion skirt, arms away from body, 6",
$250.00.

Flapper, orange lustre dress/gr hat, German #14506, 3¾"..... 100.00
Flapper, red bodice, bracelets, lined eyes, German #5848, 1¾".. 50.00
Flapper, wht dress/bl trim/gloves/necklace, German #6716, 4". 160.00
Goebel, red lid lines, blue beads, German #1806, 3½"........ 75.00
Green picture hat, 1 open arm, 1 away, china, #14910, 3¾".... 85.00
Heubach, 1 arm away at breast/1 to rose/fancy coif, #15542, 5". 150.00
Japanese lady on base, bl/wht hat, hands to chest, dressed, 5"... 40.00
Lady in gr bodice/pink collar/orange hat, German #13432, 3½". 100.00
Lady w/fan, 1 hand to face, blonde w/bl headband, Japan, 3¼".. 30.00
Lady w/pearl necklace, blonde in bl bodice, Japan, 2¾"....... 30.00
Marie Antoinette coif, arms away, hands curved to bust, 3¼"... 100.00
Old fashioned lady, gr dress, gray hair, Foreign #15144, 4½".. 55.00
Open arms behind head, mohair hair, German, 2¼".......... 110.00
Powder box, 2 pc, HP Japan, Colonial lady w/mirror, flowers.... 45.00
Red hat w/bl plume, holds fan, German #345, 3¾", VG....... 35.00
Sitting, bl hat & blouse, legs show, orig skirt/cushion, 2½"..... 25.00
Spanish lady, 1 arm to waist/1 to face, orig dress, Japan, 7½"... 60.00

Handwerck

#28 F/0/2, o/c eyes, hh, compo bjtd, 21"................. 400.00
#99, 21"... 400.00
#99 DEP, o/c eyes, jtd compo, p/e, 22".................. 425.00
ShHd, o/m/teeth, #26.139-3HO, 19½".................... 375.00

Heubach

All bsk, Chin-Chin, 4"................................ 225.00
Black boy, c/m/teeth, kinky molded hair, 12".............. 1,200.00
Boy, #6-6894, c/m, intaglio eyes, molded hair, sailor, 19".... 2,200.00
Boy, #7602/insignia, c/m pouty, intaglio eyes, jtd compo, 11". 1,200.00
Character, almond pwt eyes, ShHd, o/m, mk sunburst, 14½". 1,200.00
Character, o/m, o/c eyes, hh, comp bjtd, mk in sq, 16"...... 1,400.00
Compo & wood ball jtd body, o/c mouth, mk sunburst, 16".. 1,300.00
Googly glass eyes/5 pc papier mache/watermelon mouth, 7"... 1,600.00
Nurser baby, #7770 w/14k pacifier, 14".................. 1,400.00
Papier mache body, o/c eyes, o/m, #320-16/0, 9"........... 275.00
Toddler boy, orig wig, glass eyes, o/c mouth/teeth, 18"...... 2,400.00

Heubach-Koppelsdorf

Bl o/c eyes, o/m, comp bjtd body, #250, dressed, 18"........ 325.00
Blk character toddler, bsk/compo bjtd/set eyes, o/m, p/e, 14".. 475.00
Boy, ShHd, #1900-0, kid body, 20"...................... 350.00
Bsk, set eyes, o/m, RpC/arms/hh wig, 17"................. 295.00
Bsk head, o/c eyes, o/m, German 275.4/0, jtd compo body, 17". 325.00
Toddler, 12½" head, o/c eyes, 5 pc body, #267-5 DRGM, 18". 575.00

Horsman

Chubby Baby Ruthie, cloth w/vinyl head/limbs, cryer, 20"..... 20.00
Gold Medal Doll, 1 pc vinyl body/legs, o/c eyes, 1953, 26"... 145.00
Mary Poppins, 12"..................................... 35.00
Peggy, vinyl, 1 pc, jtd arms, rooted hair, o/c eyes, 25"....... 95.00
Ruthie Walker, brown vinyl on plastic body, o/c eyes, 13"..... 15.00
Tynie Baby, o/c eyes, c/m, bsk/cloth body/celluloid hands, 13". 450.00

Ideal

Evel Knievel & rescue set, 7".......................... 12.00
Fanny Brice, all orig, 12½"............................ 250.00
Fanny Brice as Baby Snooks, rpl outfit, 1939.............. 130.00
Mortimer Snerd, all orig, 12½"......................... 250.00
Patsy, orig clothes, EX................................ 195.00

Jumeau

Closed mouth, mkd EJ (incised) Jumeau, 10″	3,000.00
Closed mouth, mkd EJ (incised) Jumeau, 14″	4,000.00
Closed mouth, mkd EJ (incised) Jumeau, 16″	4,500.00
Closed mouth, mkd EJ (incised) Jumeau, 19″	5,000.00
Closed mouth, mkd EJ (incised) Jumeau, 21″	5,600.00
Closed mouth, mkd Tete Jumeau, 10″	2,200.00
Closed mouth, mkd Tete Jumeau, 14″	2,600.00
Closed mouth, mkd Tete Jumeau, 16″	2,800.00
Closed mouth, mkd Tete Jumeau, 19″	3,300.00
Closed mouth, mkd Tete Jumeau, 21″	3,600.00
Closed mouth, mkd Tete Jumeau, 23″	3,700.00
Closed mouth, mkd Tete Jumeau, 25″	4,100.00
Closed mouth, mkd Tete Jumeau, 28″	5,200.00
Closed mouth, mkd Tete Jumeau, 30″	5,500.00
Depose/Tete Jumeau, swivel head, earrings, long curls, 18″	3,700.00
Depose/Tete Jumeau, swivel head, earrings, long curls, 28″	5,000.00
E 6 J/Jumeau, swivel head, inset eyes, kid body, 16″	4,500.00
E 6 J/Jumeau, swivel head, inset eyes, kid body, 20″	5,000.00
EJ/Depose Brevete, swivel head, inset eyes, 'mama/papa', 16″	4,500.00
Jumeau 1907, SkHd, applied ears, o/m, 18″ cir, 32″	2,900.00
Jumeau 1907, swivel head, o/m, o/c eyes, pierced ears, 18″	1,300.00
Jumeau 1907, swivel head, o/m, o/c eyes, pierced ears, 23″	1,800.00
Jumeau 1909, swivel head, o/m, inset eyes, pierced ears, 21″	1,500.00
Long face, closed mouth, 21″	10,000.00
Long face, closed mouth, 25″	12,000.00
Long face, closed mouth, 30″	14,000.00
Open mouth, mkd Tete Jumeau, 10″	750.00
Open mouth, mkd Tete Jumeau, 14″	1,200.00
Open mouth, mkd Tete Jumeau, 16″	1,400.00
Open mouth, mkd Tete Jumeau, 19″	1,700.00
Open mouth, mkd Tete Jumeau, 21″	2,000.00
Open mouth, mkd Tete Jumeau, 23″	2,300.00
Open mouth, mkd Tete Jumeau, 25″	2,500.00
Open mouth, mkd Tete Jumeau, 28″	2,800.00
Open mouth, mkd Tete Jumeau, 30″	3,000.00
Open mouth, mkd 1907 Jumeau, 14″	750.00
Open mouth, mkd 1907 Jumeau, 17″	1,200.00
Open mouth, mkd 1907 Jumeau, 20″	1,400.00
Open mouth, mkd 1907 Jumeau, 25″	2,200.00
Open mouth, mkd 1907 Jumeau, 28″	2,500.00
Open mouth, mkd 1907 Jumeau, 32″	2,900.00
Phonograph in body, o/m, 20″	2,400.00
Phonograph in body, o/m, 25″	2,850.00
Portrait Jumeau, closed mouth, 16″	4,500.00
Portrait Jumeau, closed mouth, 20″	5,400.00
211/Jumeau, swivel head, o/m, inset eyes, Screamer, 17″	12,000.00

Kammer and Reinhardt

#101, boy or girl w/glass eyes, 12″	2,000.00
#101, boy or girl w/glass eyes, 16″	3,800.00
#101, boy or girl w/glass eyes, 20″	4,500.00
#101, boy or girl w/glass eyes, 9″	1,300.00
#101, boy or girl w/painted eyes, 12″	1,500.00
#101, boy or girl w/painted eyes, 16″	1,900.00
#101, boy or girl w/painted eyes, 20″	2,850.00
#101, boy or girl w/painted eyes, 9″	1,000.00
#109, rare, w/glass eyes, 15″	7,500.00
#109, rare, w/glass eyes, 18″	12,000.00
#109, rare, 15″	6,500.00
#109, rare, 18″	10,000.00
#112, rare, w/glass eyes, 15″	7,500.00

#112, rare, w/glass eyes, 18″	12,000.00
#112, rare, 15″	7,200.00
#112, rare, 18″	9,500.00
#114, rare, w/glass eyes, 15″	5,200.00
#114, rare, w/glass eyes, 18″	6,500.00
#114, rare, 15″	3,600.00
#114, rare, 18″	4,200.00
#115, closed mouth, 15″	2,500.00
#115, closed mouth, 18″	3,000.00
#115, closed mouth, 22″	3,400.00
#115, open mouth, 15″	1,400.00
#115, open mouth, 18″	2,000.00
#115, open mouth, 22″	2,500.00
#115a, closed mouth, 15″	2,500.00
#115a, closed mouth, 18″	3,000.00
#115a, closed mouth, 22″	3,400.00
#115a, open mouth, 15″	1,400.00
#115a, open mouth, 18″	2,000.00
#115a, open mouth, 22″	2,500.00
#116, closed mouth, 15″	2,000.00
#116, closed mouth, 18″	2,500.00
#116, closed mouth, 22″	3,200.00
#116, open mouth, 15″	1,000.00
#116, open mouth, 18″	1,900.00
#116, open mouth, 22″	2,300.00
#116a, closed mouth, 15″	2,000.00
#116a, closed mouth, 18″	2,500.00
#116a, closed mouth, 22″	3,200.00
#116a, open mouth, 15″	1,000.00
#116a, open mouth, 18″	1,900.00
#116a, open mouth, 22″	2,300.00
#117, closed mouth, 18″	3,800.00
#117, closed mouth, 24″	5,000.00
#117, closed mouth, 30″	6,200.00
#117a, closed mouth, 18″	3,800.00
#117a, closed mouth, 24″	5,000.00
#117a, closed mouth, 30″	6,200.00
Dolly face, open mouth, mold #400-403-109, etc, 16″	425.00
Dolly face, open mouth, mold #400-403-109, etc, 20″	500.00
Dolly face, open mouth, mold #400-403-109, etc, 24″	625.00
Dolly face, open mouth, mold #400-403-109, etc, 28″	725.00
Dolly face, open mouth, mold #400-403-109, etc, 38″	1,450.00
Dolly face, open mouth, mold #400-403-109, etc, 40″	2,000.00

Lenci

Boy, greek peasant w/flute & wicker basket on back, 17″	600.00
Boy, in blk felt w/bagpipe, 10″, M	395.00
Boy, in br/red felt suit, 10″, M	395.00
Boy, mountain climber w/knapsack, all orig, 18″	495.00
Boy, ptd features, all felt, original, 9″	225.00
Boy, RpC, 17″	300.00
Boy, w/leggets, all orig, 20″	550.00
Girl, all orig, missing shoes, 12″	395.00
Girl, crimped curl wig, tagged, all orig, 18″	450.00
Girl, in rust felt dress, shoes & bows, all orig, 18″	550.00
Girl, pink felt/organdy dress, shoes, hat, 20″	550.00
Girl, pink/bl felt dress, shoes, 19″	525.00
Girl, red mohair wig, orig gr felt/organdy dress, 32″	550.00
Girl, RpC, 12″	150.00
Little Lulu, Georgene Novelties, all orig, 14″, EX	175.00
Sisters, swivel neck, looking at ea other, orig, 13″	1,504.00

Lenci, rare glass eyes, original 1870s style dress, carrying a poodle, 19½", $1,540.00.

Madame Alexander

African, hp, 1966-1971, 8"................................350.00
Agatha, Portrette, Cissette, 1968, 11"....................485.00
Agnes, cloth/felt, 1930s...................................450.00
Alice in Wonderland, cloth, 1930 & 1933, 16".............350.00
Alice in Wonderland, hp, with trousseau, Maggie, 14"........700.00
Amanda, hp, 1961 Americana Group, Wendy Ann, 8".......600.00
American Babies, cloth, 16-18".............................175.00
Amish Boy or Girl, hp, Wendy Ann, 1966-1969, 8"...........450.00
Annabelle, hp, Maggie, 1952, 15"..........................165.00
Annie Laurie, compo, Wendy Ann, 1937, 14"................285.00
Artie, plastic/vinyl, Smarty, sold through FAO Schwarz, 12"....275.00
Babbie, cloth, long thin legs, after K Hepburn/Little Minister...395.00
Babs Skater, hp, Margaret, 18"............................385.00
Babsie Baby, compo/cloth, moving tongue..................150.00
Baby Betty, compo, 1935-1936, 10-12".....................150.00
Baby Clown, hp, painted face, Wendy Ann, 1955, 8".......1,200.00
Baby Jane, compo, 1935, 16"...............................700.00
Baby Precious, cloth/vinyl, 1975 only, 14".................95.00
Bad Little Girl, cloth, blue dress, 1964, 16"..............125.00
Ballerina, compo, Wendy Ann, 1936-1938, 11"..............185.00
Barbara Jane, cloth/vinyl, 1952, 29"......................350.00
Beau Art Dolls, hp, 1953, 18".............................700.00
Belgium, compo, Tiny Betty, 1935-1938, 7"................145.00
Belle Brummel, cloth......................................700.00
Birthday Party, hp, Wendy Ann, 1955, 8"..................275.00
Bitsey, compo, 11"..125.00
Blue Boy, cloth, 16"......................................350.00
Blue Danube, hp, Wendy Ann, 1953, 8"....................600.00
Bo Peep, Little; hp, Wendy Ann, 1955, 7½"................350.00
Bonnie Toddler, cloth, hp head, vinyl limbs, 1951, 18"....200.00
Bride, compo, Little Betty, 1936-1941, 9".................200.00
Bride, hp, Margaret/Maggie, 21"...........................400.00
Bride, plastic/vinyl, 1973-1976, 14"......................185.00
Bridesmaid, hp, Elise, 1957, 16½".........................265.00

Butch McGuffey, compo/cloth, 1940........................175.00
Carmen Portrait, compo, Tiny Betty, 7"....................225.00
Carmen Portrait, compo, Wendy Ann, 1937-1939, 21".......950.00
Caroline, vinyl, in riding habit, 1961, 15"................425.00
Carreen, compo, Wendy Ann, 1937, 14"....................200.00
Cathy, compo, Wendy Ann, 1939, 17".......................450.00
Charity, hp, Wendy Ann, Americana Group, 1961, 8"........600.00
Cheri, hp, Margaret, 1954, 18"............................700.00
Cherry Twins, hp, Wendy Ann, 1957, 8"....................450.00
Cherub Babies, cloth......................................350.00
China, hp, bend knees, Wendy Ann, 1972, 8"...............145.00
Cinderella, compo, Princess Elizabeth, 16"................395.00
Cinderella, hp, Lissy Classic, 1966, 12"................1,400.00
Cissette, hp, in street dress, 1957-1963, 11".............165.00
Clover Kid, compo, 7".....................................185.00
Colonial, compo, Tiny Betty, 1937-1938, 7"...............185.00
Colonial, hp, Wendy Ann, 1962-1964, 8"...................600.00
Cornelia, cloth/felt, 1930s...............................425.00
Country Cousins, cloth, 30"...............................300.00
Cousin Karen, hp, Wendy Ann, 1956, 8"....................600.00
Cowboy, hp, Wendy Ann, 1967-1969, 8".....................650.00
Curly Locks, hp, Wendy Ann, 1955, 7½"....................600.00
Cynthia, hp, Black Margaret, 1952, 23"....................750.00
Czechoslovakia, hp, Wendy Ann, bend knees, 1972, 8"......145.00
David Copperfield, cloth Dicken's character, 16"..........500.00
David Quack-a-field or Twistail, cloth/felt, 1930s........350.00
Davy Crockett Boy, hp, Wendy Ann, 1955, 8"...............475.00
Day of Week Dolls, compo, Little Betty, 1936-1938, 9".....245.00
Dearest, 12" Baby...125.00
Debutant, hp, Maggie, 1953, 18"...........................700.00
Degas, compo, portrait, 1945, 21".........................950.00
Dicksie & Ducksie, cloth/felt, 1930s......................400.00
Dionne Quints, cloth body/compo, 14", each...............450.00
Dionne Quints, compo baby, wig & sleep eyes, 11", each....275.00
Dolls of the Month, compo, Tiny Betty, 1936, 7-8".........185.00
Doris Keene, compo, Little Betty, 1936, 9"................195.00
Dressed for Opera, hp, Margaret, 18"......................700.00
Dude Ranch, hp, Wendy Ann, 1955, 8"......................295.00
Easter Doll, hp, Wendy Ann, 1968, 8"...................1,200.00
Edwardian, hp, Margaret, 1953, 18"........................700.00
Egyptian, compo, Little Betty, 1936, 9"...................250.00
Elaine, hp, Cissy, 1954, 18"..............................700.00
Elise, hp, vinyl arms, 1961-1962, 17".....................175.00
Elizabeth Monroe...225.00
Emily, cloth/felt, 1930s..................................375.00
Eskimo, hp, Wendy Ann, w/Maggie Mixup face, 8"..........595.00
Eva Lovelace, compo, Tiny Betty, 1935, 7"................195.00
Fairy Princess, compo, Wendy Ann, 11"....................275.00
Fairy Queen, hp, Margaret, 18"............................450.00
First Communion, hp, Wendy Ann, 1957, 8".................350.00
Fisher Quints, hp/vinyl, Little Genius, 1964, 7", set......450.00
Flora McFlimsey, compo, Princess Elizabeth, 22"..........495.00
Flowergirl, hp, Cissy, 1954, 15"..........................250.00
French Flowergirl, hp, Wendy Ann, 1956, 8"...............450.00
Funny, cloth, 1963, 18"....................................95.00
Gainsbourgh, hp, Cissy, 1957, 20".........................600.00
Garden Party, hp, Margaret, 1953, 18".....................700.00
Gardening, hp, Wendy Ann, 1955, 8".......................250.00
Gibson Girl, hp, Cissette, 1962, 10"....................1,200.00
Ginger Rogers, compo, Wendy Ann, 1940-1945, 14".........450.00
Glamour Girls of 1953, hp, Margaret-Maggie, 18"..........700.00
Godey, hp, Maggie, 1953, 18"..............................550.00
Godey, plastic/vinyl, Coco, 1966, 21"...................2,000.00
Godey Lady, hp, Margaret, 14".............................700.00

Going to See Grandma, hp, Wendy Ann, 1955, 8"...........275.00
Gold Rush, hp, Cissette, 1963, 11"...................1,200.00
Goldilocks, compo, Tiny Betty, 1938, 7"..............185.00
Good Fairy, hp, Margaret, 14".......................450.00
Goya, hp/vinyl arms, Jacqueline, 1968, 21".........575.00
Graduation, hp, Lissy, 12"..........................650.00
Grave Alice, cloth, 18".............................350.00
Greek Boy, hp, Wendy Ann, 1965-1968, 8".............450.00
Greek Girl, hp, Wendy Ann, bend knees, 1968-1972, 8"......145.00
Gretel, compo, Tiny Betty, 1937, 7".................185.00
Groom, compo, 18-21"................................495.00
Guardian Angel, hp, Wendy Ann, 1954, 8"...........1,200.00
Hansel, hp, Wendy Ann, 1955, 7½"...................350.00
Heidi, compo, Tiny Betty, 7".........................185.00
Hello Baby, 22".....................................125.00
Helping Mama, hp, Wendy Ann, 1955, 8"...............275.00
Hiawatha, hp, Wendy Ann, 1967-1969, 8"..............450.00
Highland Fling, hp, Wendy Ann, 1955, 8".............275.00
Hilda, compo, Margaret, 1946, 18"...................650.00
Honeybun, 1951, 19".................................125.00
Honeyette Baby, compo/cloth, 1950...................125.00
Huggums, Big; 1963-1979, 25".........................85.00
Ice Capades, Jacqueline...........................1,700.00
Ice Skater, hp, Wendy Ann, 1954-1956, 8"............275.00
Indian Boy or Girl, hp, Wendy Ann, 1966, 8".........500.00
Irish, Cissette, 1963, 10"........................1,200.00
Irish, hp, Wendy Ann, bend knees, 1964-1972, 8".........145.00
Jack & Jill, compo, Little Betty, 1939 only, 9".....250.00
Jacqueline in Riding Habit..........................900.00
Jane Withers, compo, closed mouth, 1937, 12"........725.00
Janie, Baby; 1972, 20".............................150.00
Jenny Lind, hp, Cissette, 1969, 11".................650.00
Jogo-slav, compo, Tiny Betty, 1935-1937, 7".........145.00
Judy, hp/vinyl arms, Jacqueline, 1962, 21"..........950.00
Juliet, hp, Wendy Ann, 1955, 8"...................1,000.00
June Wedding, hp, Wendy Ann, 1956, 8"...............275.00
Karen Ballerina, compo, Margaret, 1947, 15".........350.00
Kate Greenaway, compo, Princess Elizabeth, 13"......350.00
Kathy Cry Dolly, vinyl, 1957, 11"....................95.00
Kitty Baby, compo, 1941, 21".........................125.00
Little Audrey, vinyl, 1954..........................185.00
Little Cherub, compo, 11"...........................165.00
Little Colonel, compo, 1953, 13"....................475.00
Little Lady Doll, hp, Maggie Mixup, 1960, 8"........600.00
Little Women, cloth, Meg/Jo/Amy/Beth, 1933, 16".....400.00
Little Women, compo, Wendy Ann, 13-15"..............400.00
Madame Doll, hp/vinyl arms, Coco, 1966, 21".......2,000.00
Madelaine Du Bain, compo, Wendy Ann, 1937-1939.......450.00
Maggie Mixup, hp, Angel, 1961, 8".................1,200.00
Maggie Mixup, hp/vinyl, Elise body, 1960, 16½"......350.00
Maggie Teenager, hp, 1951, 15"......................295.00
Mama Kitten, 18"....................................125.00
Marcella Dolls, compo, dressed '30s fashions, 1936, 24"......285.00
Margot, hp, Cissette, 1961, 10".....................425.00
Mary Cassatt Baby, cloth/vinyl, 1969, 14"...........185.00
Mary Ellen, rigid vinyl, 1954, 31"..................425.00
Mary Rose Bride, hp, Margaret, 1941, 17"............275.00
Matinee, hp, Wendy Ann, 1955, 8"....................275.00
McGuffey, Ana; compo, Princess Elizabeth, 1937, 25".......425.00
McGuffey, Ana; hp, Wendy Ann, 1956, 8"..............600.00
Melanie, hp/vinyl arms, Coco, 1966, 21"...........2,000.00
Melinda, hp, Cissette, 1968, 11"....................485.00
Milly, plastic/vinyl, Polly, 1968, 17"..............275.00
Miss Muffet, hp, Wendy Ann, bend knees, 1965-1972, 8"......145.00

Nat, Little Men, hp, Maggie, 1952...................650.00
Nina Ballerina, hp, Margaret, 1951, 15".............300.00
Old Fashioned Girl, compo, Betty, 13"...............225.00
On Train, hp, Wendy Ann, 1955, 8"...................275.00
Pamela, hp, Lissy, takes wigs, 1962, 12"............300.00
Patty, plastic/vinyl, Melinda, 1965, 18"............250.00
Penny, cloth/vinyl, 1952, 42".......................400.00
Peter Pan, hp, Margaret, 1953, 15".................400.00
Picnic Day, hp, Margaret, 18".......................750.00
Playing in the Garden, hp, Wendy Ann, 1955, 8"......275.00
Polly, plastic/vinyl, Maria, in ballgown, 1965, 17"......275.00
Polly Put The Kettle On, compo, Tiny Betty, 1937, 7"......185.00
Prince Charming, compo, Margaret, 1947, 16".........500.00
Princess Ann, hp, Wendy Ann, 1957, 8"...............600.00
Princess Rosetta, compo, Wendy Ann, 17".............500.00
Queen Alexandrine, compo, Wendy Ann, 1939, 21"......950.00
Rainy Day, hp, Wendy Ann, 1955, 8".................275.00
Rebecca, compo, Wendy Ann, 1940, 21"................375.00
Red Riding Hood, hp, Wendy Ann, 1955, 7½"..........475.00
Renoir, hp/vinyl arms, Elise, 1963, 18".............475.00
Renoir Child, plastic/vinyl, Nancy Drew, 1967, 12"......400.00
Riley's Little Annie, plastic/vinyl, Mary Ann, 1967, 14"......600.00
Rosebud, cloth/vinyl, 1952-1953, 16-19".............125.00
Royal Evening, hp, Margaret, 1953, 18"..............600.00
Rusty, cloth/vinyl, 1967, 20".......................275.00
Ruth, compo, Tiny Betty, 1935-1939, 7"..............145.00
Scarlett O'Hara, compo, Little Betty, pre-movie: 1936-1938, 9".275.00
Scarlett O'Hara, hp, Lissy, 1963, 12".............1,400.00
School Girl, hp, Wendy Ann, 1955, 8"................275.00
Shari Lewis, 1959, 14"..............................325.00
Simone, hp/vinyl arms, Jacqueline, 1968, 21", w/trunk......950.00
Skater's Waltz, Cissy, 1955, 14-18".................450.00
Sleeping Beauty, compo, Princess Elizabeth, 1938, 15-16"......350.00
Sleeping Beauty, 1959, 21"..........................500.00
Slumbermate, compo/cloth, 21".......................200.00
Snow White, Disney Crest Colors, #1455, 1967, 14"......425.00
Sonja Henie, compo, 1939, 13-15"....................275.00
Sound of Music, full set of 7 dolls, large size, 1967-1970.....1,800.00
Southern Belle, hp, Lissy, 1963, 12"..............1,400.00
Special Girl, cloth/compo, 1942, 23-24".............325.00
Story Princess, hp, Wendy Ann, 1956, 8".............600.00
Sugar Darlin', cloth/vinyl, 1956, 24"...............125.00
Sweet Violet, hp, Cissy, 1951-1954, 18".............325.00
Swimming, hp, Wendy Ann, 1955, 8"...................200.00
Timmy Toddler, plastic/vinyl, 1960, 30".............275.00
Tinkerbelle, hp, Cissette, 1969, 11"................500.00
Tippy Toe, cloth, 16"...............................350.00
Tweedle-Dum & Tweedle-Dee, cloth, 14", each.........400.00
Victorian, hp, Margaret, 1953, 18".................600.00
Walking Her Dog, hp, Wendy Ann, 1955, 8"............275.00
Washington, Martha; President's Ladies, 1976........350.00
Wendy Angel, hp, Wendy Ann, 1954, 8"..............1,200.00
White Rabbit, cloth/felt............................350.00
Yugoslavia, hp, Wendy Ann, bend knees, 1968-1972, 8"......145.00
Zorina Ballerina, compo, Wendy Ann, 1937, 17".......600.00

Papier Mache

Hemp hair, kid body, mended, set glass eyes, 20"....350.00
Home made cotton body, mohair, c/m, 21".............150.00
Horned w/wig, set glass eyes, c/m, 22"..............300.00
Molded center part hair w/nape curls, 20"...........150.00
Molded hat/nape curls, wood hands/ft, 15½"..........250.00
Set glass eyes, rpl wig, mended body, 34"...........250.00

ShPl/ball head/mohair/glass eyes/compo hands, 12".........150.00
ShPl/hands/ft, orig pnt/wig, straw filled, 32"...............300.00

Schoenhut

Boy, pouty, c/m, ptd eyes, mk head/incised body, 16"........495.00
Boy, pouty/walker, ptd eyes, c/m, mohair, sailor, 16½".......595.00
Boy, rpt, rpl wig/suit, 14"................................300.00
Bride, pouty, orig, 19"................................1,150.00
Girl, br hair, bl checked pleated dress, 14", MIB..........1,300.00
Girl, o/c eyes, orig red hair, mk, sailor dress, 16"..........495.00
Girl, pouty character, w/trunk, rpr finger, 16"..........1,200.00
Milkmaid, orig outfit, 8"................................350.00

SFBJ

Bebe Parisiana, 1902, bsk head, c/m, inset eyes, 16".......1,700.00
Celestine, bsk SkHd on mache, o/m, inset eyes, 18".........900.00
SkHd, fully jtd mache/wood body, o/m, o/c eyes, 30"........1,800.00
Tete Jumeau, pierced ears, o/c eyes/lashes, o/m, 18".......1,400.00
11, compo w/bsk swivel head, c/m, inset eyes, 16"..........700.00
20, molded ptd shoes & eyes, 5 pc body, Paris/12, 10"......300.00
203, 1900 bsk head on compo, o/c mouth, inset eyes, 20"...1,500.00
215, bsk swivel on compo, c/m, inset eyes, 15"............1,500.00
223, bsk, closed dome, o/m 8 teeth, molded hair, 17"......1,500.00
227, brown swivel closed dome head, animal skin wig, 15"...1,900.00
227, brown swivel closed dome head, animal skin wig, 18"...2,200.00
227, closed dome, o/m, inset eyes, ptd hair, 15"..........1,800.00
228, toddler, c/m, inset eyes, mache body, 16"...........1,900.00
229, swivel head, o/c mouth, inset eyes, compo, 18".......2,200.00
229, wood walker, o/c mouth, inset eyes, 18".............1,850.00
230, pierced ears, compo walker, o/m, inset eyes, 16"......1,200.00
230, SkHd, pierced ears, o/m, o/c eyes, 23"..............1,700.00
235, closed dome, molded hair, o/c mouth & eyes, 16".....1,700.00
235, closed dome, molded hair, o/c mouth & eyes, 8"........750.00
236, laughing Jumeau, o/m, o/c eyes, double chin, 12"......800.00
236, laughing Jumeau, o/m, o/c eyes, double chin, 20".....1,600.00
238, swivel head, o/m, inset eyes, compo body, Paris 6, 15"..3,500.00
239, Poulbot, c/m, street urchin, red wig, 14"...........3,900.00
239, Poulbot, c/m, street urchin, red wig, 17"...........4,500.00
245, boy, large glass eyes, googly, ptd shoes, o/c mouth, 12".4,500.00
245, boy, large glass eyes, googly, ptd shoes, o/c mouth, 8"..3,800.00
247, toddler, o/c mouth/2 inset teeth, 16"...............2,000.00
247, toddler, o/c mouth/2 inset teeth, 20"...............2,800.00
247, toddler, o/c mouth/2 inset teeth, 24"...............3,200.00
247, twirp, o/c eyes & mouth/2 teeth, SkHd, 21"..........2,800.00
251, 1099 character baby, o/c mouth, eyes, hair lashes, 16"..1,500.00
251, 1099 character baby, o/c mouth, eyes, hair lashes, 18"..1,800.00
252, character, pouty, c/m, inset eyes, mache body, 18"....3,000.00
252, character, pouty, c/m, inset eyes, mache body, 22"....5,500.00
257, 1900 toddler, o/c mouth, inset eyes, 16"............1,600.00
266, bsk head, closed dome, o/c mouth, character, 20".....1,800.00
301, bsk SkHd on compo, o/m, inset eyes, 16".............595.00
301, bsk SkHd on compo, o/m, inset eyes, 22".............895.00
301, bsk SkHd on compo, o/m, inset eyes, 30"............1,300.00
60, French WWI nurse, 5 pc body, SFBJ/13/0, 8½".........250.00
60, SkHd, compo w/straight legs, o/m, curved arms, 15"....500.00
60, SkHd, mache/compo 1 pc body, plunger cryer, o/m, 11"..450.00
60 Kiss-Blower, cryer walker, 22".....................1,450.00

Shirley Temple

Look-alike, 22" compo/cloth, o/c eyes, o/m/teeth, hh.........200.00
Look-alike, 24" all compo/tin eyes, teeth, long curls, VG......200.00

Outfit, #9540, pants/jacket/straw hat, 1950s, MIB.............35.00
Outfit, #9716, dress/panties, MIB.........................30.00
Outfit, #9718, cowgirl dress/boots/hat, MIB..................50.00
Outfit, #9750, shirt/shorts, MIB..........................20.00
Outfit, #9756, red stripe dress/pocketbook.................30.00
Outfit, #9757, orange print dress/pocketbook................30.00
Outfit, #9760, pants/jacket/straw hat, MIB.................35.00
Outfit, #9768, violet dress/underpants/pocketbook, MIB.......30.00
Outfit, #9771, dress/jacket/shoes/socks/pocketbook/hat, MIB.....45.00
11" compo, orig dress, wig, undies, flirty eyes, EX..........595.00
12" vinyl, 1957, script pin, pocketbook, extra dress, 1957, M..140.00
13" compo, all orig, in Shirley trunk.....................500.00
13" compo, dress not tagged.............................275.00
13" compo, tagged bl/wht dress w/pin, 1930s, all orig.........360.00
15" vinyl, RpC, Ideal..................................150.00
16" compo, Our Little Girl, w/pin, all orig, tagged, M.........500.00
16" vinyl, Rebecca, Ideal, 1972.........................150.00
17" compo, copy of Curly Top, EX........................575.00
17" vinyl, flirty eyes..................................175.00
18" compo, w/pin, all orig.............................550.00
18" vinyl, orig clothes, Ideal, EX.......................175.00
19" compo, all orig, EX................................575.00
19" vinyl, flirty eyes, all orig, 1957....................200.00
22" compo, tagged pink dance dress, all orig, Ideal, VG......600.00
25" compo, sailor suit, EX.............................725.00
27" compo, flirty eyes, sailor dress, w/pin, in box, EX........795.00
7" compo, Japan, M...................................100.00
8" vinyl, Stowaway, Ideal, 1982........................30.00

Simon and Halbig

AW, SkHd, o/m; SH/13, 21".............................450.00
Baby Blanche, SkHd, o/m baby; S&H, 16"..................495.00
Baby Blanche, SkHd, o/m baby; S&H, 21"..................695.00
CM Bergmann, SkHd, o/m, 1895; Halbig/S&H5, 30".........850.00
CM Bergmann, SkHd, o/m, 1897, S&H6, 12"...............175.00

Simon and Halbig, Kammer and Reinhardt, #46, human hair, sleep eyes, pierced ears, ball-jointed wood and composition, in original dress, 17½", $1,100.00.

CM Bergmann, SkHd, o/m; Simon & Halbig, 3½, 18″ 450.00
Elenore, SkHd, o/m; CMB/Simon & Halbig, 18″ 550.00
G68, SkHd, flirty eyes, 1908; S&H/K*R, 16″ 500.00
Handwerck, SkHd, o/m, 1893; 16″ 375.00
Handwerck, SkHd, o/m, 1895; G/S&H/1, 16″ 375.00
Handwerck, SkHd, o/m; G/Halbig, 4, 26″ 600.00
S&H3, all bisque, c/m, inset eyes, molded on shoes, 6″ 285.00
SkHd, 2 teeth, tongue; K*R/Simon & Halbig, 116a-38, 17″ . . . 1,800.00
10, SkHd, o/m; G/Halbig/S&H, 16″ 400.00
10, SkHd, o/m; G/Halbig/S&H, 19″ 475.00
10, SkHd, o/m; G/Halbig/S&H, 22″ 500.00
10½, SkHd, o/m, flirty o/c eyes; S&H, 18″ 950.00
100, SkHd, o/m; Simon & Halbig/S&C/G, 15″ 395.00
100, SkHd, o/m; Simon & Halbig/S&C/G, 22″ 500.00
101, SkHd, c/m; Simon & Halbig/K*R, 16″ 1,900.00
1059, SkHd, swivel on ShPl, wood w/kid fashion, o/m; 19″ . . . 1,400.00
109, SkHd, o/m, 1895; Handwerck/G/Halbig, 23″ 500.00
114, SkHd, c/m; Simon & Halbig K*R/L, 14″ 3,000.00
114, SkHd, c/m; Simon & Halbig K*R/L, 20″ 4,400.00
114, SkHd, c/m; Simon & Halbig K*R/L, 9″ 1,500.00
115, SkHd, c/m, 1912; K*R, Simon & Halbig, 16″ 2,400.00
115a, SkHd, c/m pouty; K*R/Simon & Halbig, 15″ 2,500.00
1159, SkHd, adult body, 1905; G/Simon & Halbig/S&H7, 14″ . . 750.00
1159, SkHd, adult body, 1905; G/Simon & Halbig/S&H7, 18″ . 1,200.00
1159, SkHd, adult body, 1905; G/Simon & Halbig/S&H7, 24″ . 1,600.00
116a, SkHd, c/m; K*R/Simon Halbig, 17″ 2,500.00
117, SkHd, c/m, 1919; Simon & Halbig/K*R, 16″ 3,300.00
117, SkHd, c/m, 1919; Simon & Halbig/K*R, 20″ 4,200.00
117a, SkHd, c/m; K*R/Simon & Halbig, 16″ 3,300.00
117a, SkHd, c/m; K*R/Simon & Halbig, 20″ 4,200.00
117n, SkHd, c/m; Simon & Halbig/K*R, 20″ 3,900.00
119, SkHd, o/m, 13/Handwerck 5/Halbig, 16″ 400.00
120, SkHd, o/m; SH, 28″ 2,500.00
121, SkHd, o/c mouth/teeth, flirty o/c eyes, 1920; K*R, 16″ . . 1,200.00
121, SkHd, o/c toddler, 16″ 1,400.00
121, SkHd, o/m, 1920; K*R/Simon & Halbig, 14″ 400.00
121, SkHd, o/m, 1920; K*R/Simon & Halbig, 19″ 525.00
122, SkHd, 1920; K*R/Simon & Halbig, 14″ 450.00
126, SkHd, o/c mouth; SH, 23″ 1,500.00
126, SkHd, o/m; Simon & Halbig/K*R, 14″ 425.00
126, SkHd, o/m; Simon & Halbig/K*R, 19″ 575.00
127, SkHd, o/m; K*R, Simon & Halbig, 18″ 425.00
128, SkHd, o/m; K*R/Simon & Halbig, 14″ 425.00
128, SkHd, o/m; K*R/Simon & Halbig, 19″ 575.00
1296, SkHd, 1911; FS&Co/Simon & Halbig, 14″ 475.00
1329, SkHd, o/m, olive; G/Simon & Halbig/SH, 14″ 1,600.00
151, SkHd, o/c mouth, ptd eyes; S&H/1, 16″ 4,000.00
156, SkHd, 1925, S&H, 18″ 450.00
156, SkHd, 1925, S&H, 22″ 500.00
159, SkHd, o/m; Simon & Halbig, 16″ 400.00
179, SkHd, o/m; Simon & Halbig S11H DEP, 20″ 2,100.00
1848, SkHd, o/m; Jutta Simon & Halbig, 16″ 485.00
191, SkHd, o/m; Bergmann/CB, 18″ 450.00
1923, SkHd, o/m; SH Sp 53/4/G, 14″ 325.00
1923, SkHd, o/m; SH Sp 53/4/G, 21″ 475.00
1923, SkHd, o/m; SH Sp 53/4/G, 26″ 650.00
246, SkHd, o/m, 1900, K*R/Simon & Halbig, 18″ 450.00
282, SkHd, o/m; S H, 14″ 375.00
282, SkHd, o/m; S H, 18″ 450.00
282, SkHd, o/m; S H, 22″ 500.00
383, SkHd, flapper body; S H, 14″ 900.00
402, SkHd, o/m; K*R SH, 16″ 400.00
403, SkHd, o/c mouth; K*R, Simon & Halbig, 20″ 1,200.00
403, SkHd, o/m, walker; K*R SH, 21″ 750.00

409, SkHd, o/m; S&H, 24″ 550.00
409, SkHd, o/m; S&H, 26″ 650.00
409, SkHd, o/m; S&H, 30″ 800.00
48m SkHd, o/m, 1905; Simon & Halbig/K*R, 27″ 650.00
50, SkHd, c/m; Simon & Halbig, 16″ 950.00
50, SkHd, o/m, 1900; K*R/Simon & Halbig, 14″ 375.00
53, SkHd, c/m, brown bsk; Simon & Halbig/K*R, 16″ 1,200.00
530, SkHd, o/m; G/Simon & Halbig, 21″ 450.00
540, SkHd, o/m; G/Halbig/S&H, 16″ 1,000.00
540, SkHd, swivel on bsk shoulder plate, o/m; S&H, G, 16″ . . 400.00
550, SkHd, o/m; Simon & Halbig/S&H, 16″ 400.00
570, SkHd, o/m, walking, head turns; G/Halbig S&H, 18″ 700.00
570, SkHd, o/m; Halbig S&H/G, 18″ 475.00
576, SkHd, o/m; Simon & Halbig, 16″ 400.00
612, SkHd, o/m; MIG/S&H/CM Bergmann, 16″ 400.00
670, SkHd, o/m; Simon & Halbig, 16″ 400.00
70, SkHd, o/m, 1896, Halbig/K*R, 26″ 650.00
719, SkHd, c/m; S&H DEP, 16″ 1,800.00
719, SkHd, swivel, shoulder plate, c/m; S&H, DEP, 20″ 2,200.00
739, SkHd, c/m, brown; S 5 H DEP, 14″ 1,400.00
739, SkHd, c/m, brown; S 5 H DEP, 18″ 2,000.00
759, SkHd, o/m, brown; S 10 H DEP, 20″ 850.00
769, SkHd, S&H DEP, 17″ 1,600.00
905, SkHd, swivel on shoulder plate, c/m; S H, 21″ 2,800.00
908, SkHd, swivel on shoulder plate, c/m; S H, 16″ 2,200.00
929, SkHd, c/m; S&H, DEP, 20″ 1,800.00
929, SkHd, c/m; S&H, DEP, 25″ 2,800.00
939, o/c eyes, o/m, S16H, 30″ 2,900.00
939, SkHd, c/m; S 11H DEP, 17″ 1,800.00
939, SkHd, c/m; S 11H DEP, 23″ 2,500.00
940, SkHd, closed dome, o/c mouth; S 2 H, 26″ 2,600.00
940, SkHd, swivel on shoulder plate, o/c mouth; S 2 H, 14″ . . 1,400.00
945, SkHd, c/m; S 2 H DEP, 16″ 2,000.00
99, SkHd, o/m, 1899, 11½ Handwerck/Halbig, 16″ 400.00

Steiner

A series boy, c/m, wool pants/velvet jacket, pwt eyes, 20″ . . . 3,400.00
A-15, o/c eyes, o/m, p/e, hh, Fr bjtd, pull string/voice, 23″ . . . 2,500.00
A5 Paris, blue pwt eyes, 12″ 1,500.00
A7-8 Le Parisien, blue pwt eyes, earrings, o/m, hh, 15″ 1,400.00
Bourgoin, blue lever-op eyes, orig body, 18″ 3,500.00
Bourgoin, c/m, blue pwt eyes, str wrists, early, 14½″ 2,200.00
Wire-eyed, o/m w/2 row teeth, p/e, hh, Fr bjtd, OC, 18″ 3,200.00

Jules Steiner, swivel head mechanical walker, hands move, late 1870s, 14½″, $1,430.00.

Vogue

Brook Shields. 12.00
Cracker Jack, 12". 16.00
E Wilkens Baby Dear, 12", MIB. 25.00
Gen MacArthur, compo, orig outfit, 1940s. 165.00
Ginny, bent knee, hard plastic, vinyl head, heart dress, 1963. . . .80.00
Ginny, Bride, straight leg walker. 125.00
Ginny, Davy Crockett, bent leg walker, 1955. . . . . .85.00
Ginny, Dolls from Far-away Lands, #1864, dtd 1972, MIB. 14.00
Ginny, Majorette, bent leg walker, 1956. . . . . .100.00
Ginny, Pioneer Girl, 1977. . . . . .15.00
Ginny, Spanish outfit, red/blk, purple box, 1970s. 20.00
Jill, compo, MIB, 10". 125.00
Sassoon Ginny, blonde, 1981. . . . . .12.00
Toddles, orig, 8", EX. 125.00
Welcome Home Baby Turns Two, MIB. 85.00

Wax, Poured Wax

Boudoir, poured head/hands/legs, mohair, pnt eyes, 18". 65.00
Poured, pw eyes, earrings, compo hands/ft, 20". 500.00
ShHd, compo pate, o/c glass eyes, c/m, cloth body, 19". 150.00
Wax/papier mache, horned, rpl wig, ray eyes/compo hands, 22".250.00
Wax/papier mache, mohair, set glass eyes, much rpr, 19". 250.00
Wax/papier mache/cloth, molded hair, pnt eyes, 35". 350.00

Miscellaneous

ABG, 17" hd, o/c eyes, p/e, hh, jtd compo, EX dress, 34". . .1,295.00
ABG #1361-55, character toddler, set eyes/pierced nostril, 23". .795.00
American Character, Sweet Sue, 15". 65.00
American Character, Sweet Sue, 1950s, 17", MIB. 210.00
American Character, Tiny Tears. 45.00
Amish, girl, dressed, sawdust filled, 1900, 12½". 185.00
Amish, girl, multi-layered body/sewn on shoes/dress, 1935, 18".180.00
Austrian, boy w/staff, all felt, sgn, 8". 10.00
Averill, Georgene; Bonnie Babe, o/c eyes, 13½" head, 20". . .1,295.00
Baby Dear, orig, pnt eyes, 12". .125.00
Baby Dear, pnt eyes, 18". 175.00
Baby Phyllis, 9" bsk head, o/c eyes, cloth/compo, dressed, 12".595.00
Bergman, CMB; o/c eyes, o/m, mohair, rpl hands/ft, bjtd, 32". .750.00
Black boy, compo head/pnt eyes/hair/cloth body/hm clothes, 24".80.00
Borgfeldt Co, Mickey Mouse, stuffed cloth, 12". 550.00
Burkeman, Mildred; artist porcelain head, Blk character, 26". . .375.00
Cameo, Kewpie Gal, MIB. 18.00
Cameo, Miss Peep, 15". 45.00
Campbell Kid, mk EIH 1913, cotton/compo, rpl arms, 13", G. . .95.00
Campbell Kid, shoulder head boy. 295.00
Carlton, Carole; Katherine Hepburn, artist, 13½". 150.00
Celluloid, character, flirty eyes, chunky, all orig. 100.00
Chad Valley, Bambino, glass eyes, 18". 400.00
Chatty Baby, colored compo, 2 teeth, toddler, 19". 225.00
Chemtoy, John Travolta, 1977, 12". 14.00
Clothespin, cloth covered, dressed w/bonnet, sewn on features. . .25.00
Clown on wood stick, celluloid child's face, stuffed hood, 10". . .95.00
COD, o/c eyes, hh, bsk/compo bjtd, old dress, 18". 485.00
Colored Dream Baby, compo bent limbs, o/c eyes, 9", EX. 650.00
CP Catterfelder Puppenfabrik, o/c eyes, tongue retracts, 25". . .695.00
D&KM, ShPl, glass eyes, o/m w/teeth, bsk/kid/china/cloth, 12". . .55.00
DCI in heart, girl, celluloid, pnt eyes, EX costume, EX. 25.00
Deanna Durbin, orig clothes, light crazing, 18". 275.00
Deans Rag Book Co, Minnie Mouse, English, 1930s, 7". 350.00
Dearest One, 17". 75.00

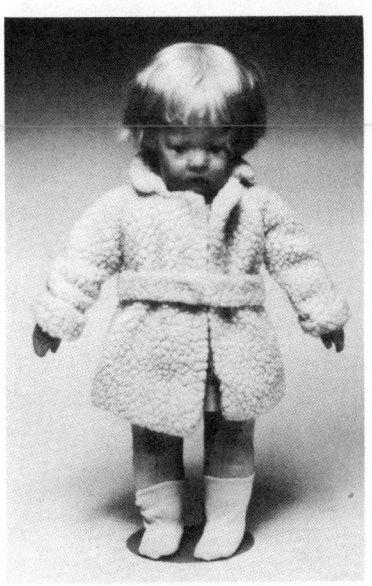

Kathe Kruse, painted cloth, original mohair, circa 1910-1928, 17", $880.00.

DEP, o/c eyes, comp jtd, hh, custom costume, 18½". 695.00
DEP S 7½.H.1009, fashion, pwt eyes/p/e/hh, ShPl/swivel, 19". .975.00
Dewees Cochran, American Girl. .795.00
Dewees Cochran, Cindy, latex, all orig. 695.00
Dondi, blk molded hair, o/c eyes, plastic, overalls, mk V, 14". . .25.00
Dopey, compo/cloth all orig, 12", VG. 85.00
Dressel, bsk ShHd, teeth, glass eyes, 21". 150.00
Dressel, bsk socket head, glass eyes, o/m w/teeth, 1914, 23". . .300.00
Dressel, Cuno/Otto, set eyes, o/m, mohair, OC, 25". 450.00
Eegee, Howdy Doody, vinyl head/hands, cloth body, 17½". 18.00
Eegee, Little Miss Sunbeam, blonde w/bl o/c eyes, 17". 18.00
Fabrication Francaise Al & Co Limoges A6, pwt, p/e, 17". 685.00
Felix the Cat, Pat Sullivan, swivel head/spool arms/legs, 8". . . .225.00
Fess Parker, plastic, made for dashboard, MIB. 15.00
FG in scroll, Fr Gaultier, c/m, pwt eyes, compo jtd, hh, 14". .1,495.00
French, compo head, o/c eyes, o/m, cloth body, 15". 195.00
French, swivel ShHd, glass eyes, o/c mouth, jtd kid body, 14". .600.00
French, young lady, swivel ShHd, glass eyes, c/m, p/e, 15". . . .700.00
Frozen Charlotte, blk, mended leg, 2". 215.00
Frozen Charlotte, bsk, molded bonnet, arms jtd, 3". 30.00
Frozen Charlotte, detailed molded hair, 2". 20.00
Fulper, boy, set eyes, EX bsk, prof rpt compo body, hh, 26½".695.00
Furga, plastic, older face, o/c eyes, all orig, 22". 60.00
Furga, redhead w/long braids, wht dress, hula hoop, 14". 45.00
Furga, short wht hair, o/c eyes, CW dress w/hoop, plastic, 14". .45.00
GBRK, #165, o/m, wig, bjtd body, dressed, 21". 395.00
Georgene Novelties, Nancy, all orig, 15". 195.00
Georgene Novelties, Sluggo, w/tag, 14", M. 225.00
Georgene Novelties, Tubby, all orig, 12". 165.00
Goebel, bsk, o/c eyes, o/m, wig, comp bjtd, dressed, 21". 350.00
Goebel, o/c eyes, o/m, hh, RpC, ballerina, 14". 250.00
Hallmark, Annie Oakley, MIB. 5.00
Hallmark, Betsy Ross, Bicentennial, MIB. 45.00
Hallmark, Chief Joseph, MIB. 5.00
Hallmark, Indian Maiden, MIB. 5.00
Handwerck, bsk head, o/c eyes, teeth, pierced ears, jtd, 14½". .240.00
Handwerck, bsk/jtd compo, o/c glass eyes, #119-12¾", 24". . . .225.00
Handwerck, o/c eyes, o/m, comp bjtd body, dressed, 25". 450.00
Hanna, S, pb in star, H 4, bjtd compo, jtd wrists, teeth, 22". .1,450.00
Harmus #8, bsk, o/m, stationary eyes, mohair, bjtd, 21". 695.00
Hug-A-Bye Baby, 22", MIB. 75.00
Indian, set eyes, o/m, crude 5 pc body, Indian suit, 6½". 125.00
Izannah walker, orig outfit, 1873, 24½", G. 2,200.00
Japan, all bsk girl, molded hair/eyes/slippers, clothed, 5". 45.00

Bru, signed Paul Girard, French bisque head Bebe, paperweight eyes, pierced ears, human hair wig, composition body, redressed, 18½″, $3,500.00.

Japan, bsk/compo bent limb, molded hair, pnt eyes, c/m, 5½″...85.00
Japan, character, bsk/compo, o/c eyes, o/m, mk H in dia, 13″...90.00
Japan, chubby girl, all bsk toddler, 3¾″.....................25.00
JDK #237 MIG 41, toddler, set eyes, 17″.....................410.00
JDK #260 character, bsk, o/c eyes, hh, bjtd, dressed, 20″......995.00
JUTTA, baby, o/c eyes/lashes, compo body, hh, 23″.........695.00
Katsuraningye, Oriental, compo w/6 wigs, OC/box, 6″.........125.00
Kewpie, compo, key wind, crawling baby....................80.00
Kewpie, compo, 14″......................................65.00
Kley & Hahn, #568-12, o/c mouth & eyes, 2 teeth, 19″......695.00
Kley & Hahn, 16″ bsk hd character baby/jtd wrists/flirty, 24″...895.00
Knickerbocker, Minnie Mouse, stuffed, in polka dot dress, 11″..475.00
Knickerbocker, Pinocchio, jtd, orig Disney Prod, compo, 14″....75.00
Knickerbocker, Raggedy Ann, 12″, MIB.....................10.00
LHK, o/c eyes, hh, bsk/Fr bjtd body, solid wrists, 18″.........985.00
Limbach, bsk w/Fr bjtd body, pwt eyes, p/e, hh, EX dress, 16″.600.00
Little Annie Rooney, compo, all orig, 16″...................550.00
Little Orphan Annie, compo, w/lg plaster Sandy.............225.00
Madame Hendron, Indian Boy, minor damage, 13″...........65.00
Magic Skin Baby, blk, hard plastic head w/molded hair, OC, 14″.50.00
Mama Katzenjammer, compo, mechanical, cloth dress, 9″.....225.00
Mattel, Donny Osmond, 12″...............................15.00
Mattel, Marie Osmond Modeling doll w/sewing patterns, 30″.....45.00
Mattel, Robin Williams as Mork, talking, cloth, 17″...........12.00
MB Japan, toddler, bsk head/o/c eyes/o/m/dimple, rpl legs, 17″.200.00
MB Japan, toddler, o/m, set eyes, mohair, 5 pc body, RpC, 12″.175.00
Mego, Coppertone Candi, w/scent, 1980, 11½″..............12.00
Mego, Diana Ross, 12″...................................25.00
Mego, Growing Hair Cher, 1976, 12¼″.....................15.00
Mego, Tennille, 12¼″....................................15.00
Melitta, 16″ bsk head, o/c eyes/teeth, 5 pc baby body, 26″...1,500.00
Milliner's, papier mache head/kid body/wooden limbs, OC, 7½″.175.00
Minerva, metal head/cloth, glass eyes, c/m, molded hair, 16″...75.00
Momma Katzenjammer, compo, mechanical, 1920s, 9″.......225.00
Morimura Bros, set eyes, o/m, rprs, 30″....................600.00
Morimura Bros, toddler character, mk MB in circle 2/4, 15″...295.00
Morimura Bros, toddler character, o/m/tongue, set eyes, 17″...325.00

Nesbet, Peggy; Belly Dancer..............................16.00
Nesbet, Peggy; Danish Lady..............................20.00
Nesbet, Peggy; King Henry VIII...........................40.00
Nesbet, Peggy; Prince Chas in Royal Regiment of Wales.......45.00
Nesbet, Peggy; Princess Diana & Prince Charles Wedding, sgn.135.00
Nesbet, Peggy; Santa in America, 7½″.....................50.00
Nesbet, Peggy; Swedish Lady.............................20.00
Nippon, all bsk girl, mohair, pnt features, lace clothes, 4½″....55.00
Nippon, Baby Bud, molded swimsuit, pnt look-to-left eyes, 3¾″..65.00
Nippon, bsk head/molded hair, pnt eyes, c/m, 5 pc toddler, 5½″.65.00
Nippon, bsk Oriental character/o/c eyes/5 pc toddler, 13″.....625.00
Nippon, pnt eyes, c/m, bald, 5 pc baby, 7″..................85.00
Patty Cake Sings, MIB....................................30.00
Paul Revere Pottery, glass eyes, o/m, sgn #2, compo blb, 12″..150.00
Poir, Eugenie; French, mohair, RpC, 18″...................350.00
Poir, Eugenie; girl, dressed in felt, all orig, 19″............275.00
R/A, set eyes, o/m, stick figure, bjtd, rpl wig, 15″...........175.00
Rata, plastic, long blk braids, flirty eyes, all orig, EX..........35.00
Reinecke, Otto; 14½″ bsk head, o/m/teeth/tongue, toddler, 22″.675.00
Revelo, 10″ bsk head, o/c eyes, compo 5 pc baby, 14″.......695.00
RID, bsk, o/m, pwt eyes, p/e, hh, bjtd, OC, 20″...........2,000.00
Saroff, Adolph Hitler, 12″................................125.00
Saroff, Joseph Stalin, 12″................................110.00
Saroff, Mussolini, 12″...................................110.00
Schmidt, Bruno; bsk, o/c eyes, p/e, hh, bjtd, dressed, 20″....525.00
Schoenau & Hoffmeister, #1909 7½, red dress, 25″.........395.00
Schoenau & Hoffmeister, #1909-6, o/c eyes, jtd compo, 24″....395.00
SHPB in star, colored bsk/compo, stationary eyes, hh, 14″....525.00
Snookums, compo, all orig, 1¾″..........................25.00
Sun Rubber, So-Wee, by Ruth E Newton, w/accessories, '50s....45.00
Superman, w/cape, wood jointed, 1940s, 13″..............450.00
Sweetheart Tanzpuppe, plastic, windup, German outfit, MIB.....25.00
Switzerland, bsk/compo, o/m, set glass eyes, cute clothes, 10″.175.00
Taylor, Mason; wood, fully ftd, metal ft, ca 1879, 12″........500.00
Uneeda, Angel, cardboard wings.........................15.00
Uneeda, Purdy, in snowsuit, 15″..........................35.00
Unis France, #301, o/c eyes/lashes, o/m, p/e, bjtd, voice, 21″.1,500.00
Waltershausen, Bergman; pw eyes, o/m, rpl shoes, 25″.......450.00
Wax/papier mache, hi-fashion, mohair, c/m, o/c eyes, 19″, G...300.00
Whimsie Monk, 21″, VG.................................45.00
Whimsie Zake, no clothes, 22″, G.........................30.00
Wislizenus, Adolf; o/c eyes/lashes, hh, jtd compo, 23½″......395.00
Wood, carved head, pnt eyes/hair, kid body/hands/ft, 15″......950.00
Wood, jtd, Queen Anne, w/plastic dome, parrot & cage, 3″....300.00
Zapf, rubber, sexed boy, o/c eyes, molded wig, o/m, new, 14″...50.00
Zeller, Fawn; Ms Kentucky, 25″..........................350.00

Door Knockers

Door knockers, those charming precursors of the door bell, come in an intriguing array of shapes and styles -- the very rare ones come from England. Cast iron examples made in this country were often produced in forms similar to the more familiar doorstop figures.

Acanthus leaf design, CI, 7″.............................25.00
Arm & Hammer advertising, brass.........................35.00
Bear standing by tree trunk, brass, 3½″...................35.00
Brass, simple scroll, no bkplate, Victorian, 9½″.............25.00
Cast iron, foliage detail, 8½″.............................10.00
Cat, high arched back, bronze, English, 1900, 3½″..........25.00
Cowboy boot w/horseshoe, brass, weighs about 1#, 1900.......17.00
Flower basket, knocks against openwork patterned plate, CI.....35.00
Fox head, w/knocking ring in mouth, CI, EX detail, 5½″.......65.00

Basket of flowers, painted cast iron, 4" x 3", $32.50.

Lady's head, CI, 1840s, 8"	75.00
Owl, knocks against grooved plate, CI, orig colors	35.00
Parrot, cast iron, colorful	25.00
Victorian, ornate, CI, mk Akedrick & Sons, Eng reg mk, 9½"	15.00
Warrior's head, brass, 1920s, lg	30.00
Woodpecker, brass	25.00

Doorknobs

Decorative doorknobs are found in Bennington type pottery, fancy Victorian brass, glass, and hand painted porcelain. Just about any interesting old knob is collectible.

Bennington type, on shank, pr	22.00
Brass, ornate, pr	15.00
China, HP florals, gold trim, pr	50.00
Cut glass, mushroom form, teardrop w/in, straw/dia, 2", pr	45.00
French porcelain, pr	28.00
French porcelain, w/scenic decor, pr	35.00
Grotesque figure, bronze, English, 1900, 4½"	30.00
Parrot sitting on branch	20.00
Porcelain, wht, 2¼" dia	4.00
Wood, carved w/bust of Washington, 2¼", pr	40.00

Doorstops

Although introduced in England in the mid-1800s, cast iron doorstops were not made to any great extent in this country until after the Civil War. Once called 'door porters', their function was to keep doors open to provide better ventilation. They have been produced in many shapes and sizes, both dimensional and flat backed, and in the past few years have become a popular yet affordable collectible. While cast iron examples are the most common, brass, wood, and chalk were also used. An average price is in the $40 to $50 range, though some are valued at more than $100. Doorstops retained their usefullness and appeal well into the thirties.

Black Geo Washington, flat back, 9½", NM	140.00
Blue House, cottage figural on base, orig blue coloring	65.00
Campbell's Kid w/teddy bear, CI	185.00
Cat, Hubley, sitting, full figure, orig pnt, 9", M	165.00

Cat, seated; G orig pnt, early 1900s, 10"	110.00
Cat, sgn NUYDEA in dia, full figure, 13"	235.00
Cat on pillow, flat back, orig pnt	95.00
Cat w/arched back, old rpt, 10¾"	65.00
Cats, pr dressed in clothes, flat back, 7½"	175.00
Coach, bronze, flat back, comp Midwest Chandelier Co, 7"	110.00
Coach w/horses, 9x19", EX	140.00
Cornucopia w/fruit, CI, rpt, 7½"	45.00
Cottage, Ann Hathaway; 2 pc casting, EX	180.00
Cottage, flat back, orig pnt	70.00
Cottage, Irish; oblong, cast iron, good detail	65.00
Deer, full antlers, flat bk	95.00
Diamond Back Rattler, realistic rattle & orig paint, 1880s	275.00
Dog, Airdale, CI w/worn pnt, 8½"	95.00
Dog, Boston Bull, blk/wht, 5", VG	65.00
Dog, Boston Bull, CI, old worn pnt, 9¾"	70.00
Dog, facing pr, on mound w/stump/flowers, flat back, 4¾x5½"	75.00
Dog, German Shepherd, facing side, full figure, 9½", EX	125.00
Dog, Russian Wolfhound, 7½x11½", M	140.00
Dog, Scotty, full figure, facing front, 8½x10½", EX	110.00
Dog, Scotty, Hubley #391, sitting, blk w/red collar, solid, 5"	50.00
Dog, Scotty, sad expression, flat back, sgn Wilton, 7½"	80.00
Dog, Setter, EX orig pnt, 3x4½"	40.00
Drummer, flute player, w/flag, orig pnt, 6", M	75.00
Ducks, pr, Hubley, flat back, 8½", EX	180.00
Eagle on perch, spread wings	165.00
Elephant, flat back, Bradley & Hubbard, 10½x11½", M	160.00
Elephant, full figure, trunk up, tusks, 8", M	90.00
Elephant, gathering coconuts/tree, flat back, 13", VG	150.00
Fisherman, full figure, EX orig pnt, 11"	120.00
Flower basket, flat back, M orig pnt, 3"	35.00
Flower basket, Hubley, orig pnt, 10½"	75.00
Flower basket, narcissus, Hubley #266, 7½", EX	75.00
Frog on mushroom, full figure, 4½", EX	115.00
Fruit bowl, Hubley #465, orig pnt, 7", EX	100.00
Geisha girl, w/mandolin, on pillow, full figure, 6½", EX	200.00
Gnome, full figure, red cap/gr jacket/gr pants, 13½", EX	250.00
Golfer, Hubley, 7½", M	225.00
Horse, Hubley, #345, full figure, M orig pnt, 10½"	135.00

Santa Maria, mint original paint on cast iron, marked Toledo, Ohio, A.W. Reiser, 12½" x 11", $50.00.

Jenny Lind, flat back, 9″, EX...........................145.00
Knight in armour, flat back, orig pnt, sgn, 7″, M.............80.00
Lady, holding hat & flowers, flat back, 11″, EX.............85.00
Lady, in canoe, flat back, 4½x9¾″, EX...................120.00
Lilies, Hubley, orig pnt, 10½″, VG......................100.00
Lion, fighting snake; CI w/orig blk/gold pnt, 9½x6x2″........65.00
Lion, standing; CI w/orig gold pnt, 11½x8½x4″...........135.00
Little Red Riding Hood & Wolf, 7½x9″, M.................235.00
Mammy, full figure, Hubley, red dress/bl bandana, 12″, M.....250.00
Mammy, full figure, Hubley, red dress/bl bandana, 8½″.......120.00
Mayflower, CI w/EX orig pnt, 12x10″.....................40.00
Organ grinder & monkey, iron, 9½″.......................85.00
Parrot, flat back, orig pnt, 8″, M........................47.50
Parrot, on tree stump, never pntd, 6½″...................20.00
Peacock, CI...100.00
Penguin, Hubley #463, top hat & bow tie, 10″.............190.00
Peter Rabbit, flat back, in tux/hat, 10½″, EX.............195.00
Peter Rabbit, red sweater, bl pants, 8¼″.................80.00
Pheasant, Hubley #458, flat back, orig pnt, 8½″...........120.00
Pirate, flat back, 13½″, EX.............................95.00
Policeman w/baton, rpt................................120.00
Poppy vase, Hubley, flat back, 10½″, EX.................85.00
Rooster, flat back, 7″, EX..............................75.00
Rose vase, Hubley, #441, M orig pnt, 10″.................85.00
Sambo, derby hat/cigar, hand in pocket, 3¼″, VG...........90.00
Ship, sgn 1928, flat back, 4″...........................12.00
Shoe, lady's high button, CI, step down base, 6x9½″.........95.00
Spanish lady w/fan, orig polychrome, CI, 9x5x2¼″...........65.00
Squirrel on tree stump, flat back, 9½″, M................175.00
Stagecoach, flat back, G orig pnt, 7″....................50.00
Turtle, Winton, full figure, 9x7½″, EX...................100.00
Windmill, flat back, orig pnt, M.........................65.00

Dorflinger

C. Dorflinger and Sons, Inc., was a glass company that operated in White Plains, Pennsylvania, from the 1880s until about 1921.

Bell, Kalana Lily, etched, 6″.............................85.00
Bowl, ambrosia; ftd, Prince of Wales, hobstar ft, 7x9″......375.00
Bowl, Mitre & Silver Diamonds, 9″ dia...................210.00
Compote, gold border, 7x5½″...........................150.00
Cruet, #80, blank #429................................110.00
Dessert, stem, rnd ft, floral etched crystal...............175.00
Master salt, paperweight; Parisian cutting................85.00
Tumbler, ftd, funnel form, Kalana Lily, 5½″................45.00
Vase, frosted w/internal lustre, gold decor, 10x7″.........600.00
Vase, frosted w/internal lustre, gold decor, 12x5″.........600.00
Vase, Kalana Geranium, shouldered, 7½″..................75.00
Vase, Kalana Pansy, waisted, 6″.........................65.00

Doulton and Royal Doulton

The range of wares produced by the Doulton Company since its inception in 1815 has been vast and varied. Their earliest wares produced in the tiny pottery in Lambeth, England, were salt glaze pitchers, plain and fancy figural bottles -- all utility-type stoneware geared to the practical need of everyday living.

The original partners, John Doulton and John Watts, saw the potential for success in the manufacture of drain and sewage pipes, and during the 1840s concentrated on this highly lucrative type of commercial ware. Watts retired from the company in 1854, and Doulton began experimenting with a more decorative style of product. As time went by, many glazes and decorative effects were developed, among them Faience, Impasto, Silicon, Carrara, Marqueterie, Chine, and Rouge Flambe. Tiles and architectural terra cotta were an important part of their manufacture. Late in the 19th century, at the original Lambeth location, fine art ware was decorated by such notable artists as Hannah and Arthur Barlow, George Tinworth, and J.H. McLennan. Stoneware vases with incised animal drawings, gracefully shaped urns with painted scenes, and cleverly modeled figurines rivaled the best of any competitor.

In 1882 a second factory was built in Burslem, which continues even yet to produce the famous figurines, character jugs, series ware, and table services so popular with collectors today. Their Kingsware line, made from 1899 to 1946, featured flasks and flagons with drinking scenes, usually on a brown glazed ground, some of which were limited editions, while others were commemorative and advertising items.

The Gibson Girl series, twenty-four plates in all, was introduced in 1901. It was drawn by Charles Dana Gibson, and is recognized by its blue and white borders and central illustrations, each scene depicting a humorous or poignant episode in the life of 'The Widow and Her Friends'. Dickensware, produced from 1911 through the early 1940s, featured illustrations by Charles Dickens, with many of his famous characters.

The Robin Hood series was introduced in 1914, and the Shakespeare series #1, portraying scenes from the bard's plays, was made from 1914 until World War II. The Shakespeare series #2 ran from 1906 until 1974, and was decorated with featured characters.

The Nursery Rhymes series was produced first in earthenware in 1903, and later in bone china. In 1933 a line of decorated children's ware, the Bunnykins series, was introduced and continues to be made to the present day. About 150 'bunny' scenes have been devised, the earliest and most desirable being those signed by the artist Barbara Vernon.

The value of a figurine is appreciated by age, because of a limited production run, or by exceptional color and detail. Those signed by the artist, marked 'Potted' (indicating pre-1939 origin), or those bearing the title of the figure and date of production, are also more valuable. After 1920, wares were marked with a lion -- with or without a crown -- over a circular 'Royal Doulton'.

Animals

Alsation, #1117, small....................................85.00
Bulldog, #1044, brindle, 3″................................89.00
Bulldog pup, #K2, 1¾″...................................30.00

Elephant, Rouge Flambe, 5¾″ x 8″, $225.00.

Carin, #1035, small.............................40.00
Cat, flambe, #9................................45.00
Cat, Lucky Cat, #K12, 2¾"......................45.00
Chatcull Bear, #2659..........................175.00
Chatcull White Tailed Deer, #2658.............175.00
Cocker Spaniel, #1000, large, black...........195.00
Cocker Spaniel, #1002.........................168.00
Cocker Spaniel, #1037, brown/wht, small........50.00
Cocker Spaniel, #1108, blk/wht, large.........195.00
Cocker Spaniel, #1188, brown, small............65.00
Cocker Spaniel & Pheasant, #1029, 3¾"..........50.00
Collie, #1057, large..........................275.00
Collie, #1058, medium..........................65.00
Collie, #1059, small...........................95.00
Dachshund, #1140...............................97.00
Dalmation, #1113, medium.......................65.00
Dalmation, #1114, small........................75.00
Dragon, flambe................................400.00
Drake, #137, flambe............................48.00
Drake, #806, mini..............................25.00
Drake, mallard; #956..........................195.00
Duck, #112, flambe.............................33.00
Duck, #395, flambe............................395.00
Duck on Rock..................................125.00
Elephant, flambe, dated 1930, 7" long.........225.00
English Setter, #1049, large..................275.00
English Setter, #1051, small...................85.00
Fox, #14, flambe, sitting......................45.00
Fox, #29B, flambe, lying.......................33.00
Fox, lying, #147..............................125.00
Fox, small, lying..............................35.00
Frog, flambe, 2"..............................135.00
Gold Crested Wren, #2613......................125.00
Horse, #2571..................................175.00
Kingfisher, #2573.............................125.00
Kingfisher on Rock, #131......................125.00
Llama, #2665, 6½".............................125.00
Monkey, flambe, 2"............................150.00
Nyala Antelope, #2664.........................145.00
Penguin, flambe, 6"............................50.00
Pheasant, large, #2545........................250.00
Rabbit, #113, flambe, ear up...................45.00
Rabbit, #1157, flambe, sitting.................45.00
Rabbit, #2593, lying, 7"......................175.00
Rabbit, #656A, flambe, lying...................33.00
Rooster, white.................................75.00
Scottish Terrier, #1016........................59.00
Sealyham, #1032...............................135.00
Sealyham, #1098................................89.00
Springer Spaniel, #2516.......................115.00

Character Jugs

Apothecary, large..............................52.00
Apothecary, miniature..........................21.00
Arriet, large, A..............................175.00
Arriet, miniature, A...........................70.00
Arriet, small, A...............................80.00
Arriet, tiny.................................175.00
Arry, large....................................75.00
Arry, miniature, A.............................70.00
Arry, small....................................85.00
Arry, tiny....................................175.00
Auld Mac, small, A.............................55.00

Fortune Teller, miniature character jug, 2½", $285.00.

Auld Mac, tiny................................180.00
Beefeater, lg, 'GR'...........................115.00
Ben Franklin, small............................30.00
Blacksmith, large..............................52.00
Bootmaker, large...............................52.00
Captain Hook, large...........................345.00
Captain Hook, small...........................250.00
Captain Morgan, miniature......................35.00
Captain Morgan, small..........................45.00
Cardinal, large...............................135.00
Cardinal, miniature............................60.00
Cardinal, small, A.............................70.00
Cardinal, tiny................................200.00
Cavalier, large, A............................125.00
Cavalier, small................................70.00
Dick Turpin, large, gun handle, mask up.......130.00
Dick Turpin, large, horse handle, mask down....63.00
Dick Turpin, miniature, horse handle, mask down..30.00
Dick Turpin, miniature, mask up................45.00
Dick Turpin, small, gun handle, mask up........65.00
Dick Turpin, small, horse handle, mask down....40.00
Dick Whittington, large.......................350.00
Drake, small, A................................75.00
Farmer John, large............................165.00
Farmer John, small, A..........................75.00
Fat Boy, miniature.............................60.00
Fat Boy, small.................................85.00
Fat Boy, tiny..................................93.00
Fortune Teller, miniature.....................285.00
Fortune Teller, small.........................325.00
Friar Tuck....................................360.00
Gardener, large................................75.00
Gardener, miniature............................35.00
Gardener, small................................50.00
Gladiator, large..............................495.00
Gladiator, miniature..........................335.00
Gladiator, small..............................295.00
Gondolier, large..............................525.00
Gondolier, miniature..........................350.00
Gone Away, large...............................70.00

Gone Away, miniature	30.00
Gone Away, small	40.00
Granny, large	52.00
Granny, small	28.00
Guardsman, large	52.00
Gulliver, large	550.00
Gulliver, small	325.00
Gunsmith, large	52.00
Isaac Walton, large	60.00
Jarge, small	150.00
Jester, small	110.00
Jockey, large	175.00
John Barleycorn, miniature	58.00
John Barleycorn, small	75.00
John Peel, large	135.00
John Peel, miniature	45.00
John Peel, small	60.00
John Peel, tiny	225.00
Johnny Appleseed, large	250.00
Lord Nelson, large	285.00
Lumberjack, large	60.00
Lumberjack, small	35.00
Mikado, small	250.00
Mine Host, large	60.00
Mine Host, miniature	30.00
Mine Host, small	40.00
Mr Micawber, miniature	50.00
Mr Micawber, small	90.00
Mr Micawber, tiny	110.00
Mr Pickwick, large, A	155.00
Mr Pickwick, miniature	55.00
Mr Pickwick, small, A	70.00
Mr Pickwick, tiny	215.00
Night Watchman, large	52.00
Old Charley, large	100.00
Old Charley, miniature	21.00
Old Charley, miniature, A	45.00
Old Charley, small	28.00
Old Charley, small, A	55.00
Old King Cole, small	110.00
Paddy, large	125.00
Paddy, miniature	50.00
Paddy, small	55.00
Paddy, tiny	95.00
Parson Brown, large	120.00
Parson Brown, large, A	130.00
Parson Brown, small	60.00
Parson Brown, small, A	65.00
Pied Piper, large	65.00
Pied Piper, miniature	35.00
Pied Piper, small	40.00
Punch & Judy Man, miniature	350.00
Punch & Judy Man, small	335.00
Robin Hood, large	145.00
Robin Hood, miniature	59.00
Robin Hood, small	65.00
Robin Hood, small, A	70.00
Robinson Crusoe, miniature	23.00
Robinson Crusoe, small	35.00
Sairey Gamp, large, A	60.00
Sairey Gamp, miniature, A	30.00
Sairey Gamp, tiny	90.00
Sam Johnson, large	240.00
Sam Johnson, small	165.00

Sam Weller, miniature, A	50.00
Sam Weller, tiny	100.00
Sancho Panza, large	60.00
Sancho Panza, miniature	23.00
Sergeant Buz Fuz, small	110.00
Simon the Cellarer, large	120.00
Simon the Cellarer, large, A	125.00
Simon the Cellarer, small, A	65.00
Sir Francis Drake, large	135.00
Smuggler, large	65.00
Smuggler, small	45.00
St George, large	110.00
Tam O'Shanter, large	65.00
Tam O'Shanter, miniature	30.00
Tam O'Shanter, small	45.00
Toby Philpots, large	125.00
Toby Philpots, miniature	45.00
Toby Philpots, small	60.00
Tony Weller, extra large size	210.00
Tony Weller, large	125.00
Tony Weller, miniature	45.00
Tony Weller, small	60.00
Touchstone, large	215.00
Town Crier, miniature	115.00
Town Crier, small	110.00
Trapper, large	65.00
Trapper, small	35.00
Ugly Duchess, miniature	230.00
Ugly Duchess, small	275.00
Uncle Tom Cobbleigh, large	310.00
Vicar of Bray, large, A	168.00
Viking, large	120.00
Viking, miniature	110.00
Viking, small	60.00
Walrus & Carpenter, large	80.00
Walrus & Carpenter, miniature	35.00
Walrus & Carpenter, small	45.00
Yachtsman, large	80.00

Figurines

A La Mode, #2544	160.00
A'Courting	395.00
Abdullah, #2104	625.00
Adrienne, #2152, rose dress, ca 1964, 8"	130.00

Joan, HN 1422, 1930-1949, $350.00.

Affection..95.00	Cissie, #1809, 5½"..................................70.00
Afternoon Tea, #2164...........................185.00	Clarinda, #2724....................................110.00
Alexandra, sgnd by M Doulton...............195.00	Clarissa...110.00
Alice, #2158, pale gr dress, 4½"...............85.00	Clemency...350.00
Anna, #2802...65.00	Clothilde, #1598..................................450.00
Antoinette...125.00	Coachman..400.00
Apple Maid..275.00	Cobbler, #1706....................................227.00
Ascot, #2356......................................130.00	Collinette..340.00
At Ease...153.00	Columbine, #1296................................725.00
Autumn Breezes, #1911.........................150.00	Coppelia, #2115...................................575.00
Autumn Breezes, #1913.........................145.00	Coralie...125.00
Autumn Breezes, #1934, red dress, 7½"......105.00	Country Lass..98.00
Babie, #1679, 4¼"..................................70.00	Cradle Song..390.00
Bachelor..225.00	Cup of Tea, #2322..................................75.00
Ballerina...233.00	Cymbals, #2699....................................650.00
Balloon Man, #1954..............................125.00	Dainty May, #M67.................................275.00
Balloon Seller.....................................325.00	Dainty May, #1639................................350.00
Bather, #687.......................................525.00	Dancers of the World, Balinese.................475.00
Beachcomber......................................175.00	Dancers of the World, Breton....................450.00
Beat You To It.....................................265.00	Dancers of the World, Chinese..................450.00
Bed Time, #1978, 5½"..............................45.00	Dancers of the World, NA Indian...............475.00
Bedtime Story.......................................95.00	Dancers of the World, Polish....................450.00
Beggar, #2175......................................550.00	Dancers of the World, West Indian.............475.00
Belle, #2340...30.00	Dancing Eyes......................................175.00
Belle of the Ball, #1997..........................225.00	Dancing Years.....................................275.00
Bess...225.00	Daphne...135.00
Biddy, #1513, ca 1940-50, 5¾".................150.00	Darling, #1985, 5¼"................................55.00
Blithe Morning, #2021............................160.00	Daydreams...110.00
Blithe Morning, #2065............................175.00	Debbie...75.00
Boatman, #2417...................................115.00	Deidre, #2020......................................270.00
Bon Appetit..150.00	Delight, old mark, artist sgnd MT..............195.00
Bride, #2166.......................................176.00	Delphine..275.00
Bridesmaid, #M12.................................210.00	Derrick..600.00
Bridesmaid, #M30.................................200.00	Diana, #1986, 5¾"..................................70.00
Bridesmaid, #2148................................230.00	Dimity, #2169......................................295.00
Bridesmaid, #2196, wht dress w/pk trim, 5"...60.00	Dinky Do, #1678, 4¾"..............................35.00
Bridesmaid, #2874.................................50.00	Dorcas, #1558......................................195.00
Bridget...250.00	Doreen..525.00
Broken Lance......................................450.00	Dreamweaver, #2283.............................150.00
Bunny...75.00	Drummer Boy, #2679..............................270.00
Buttercup, #2309....................................75.00	Easter Day, #2039.................................238.00
Butterfly, #720....................................900.00	Eleanor of Provence..............................595.00
Calumet, #1689....................................500.00	Elegance...125.00
Camellia, #2222....................................240.00	Elfreda...450.00
Captain, #2260.....................................190.00	Eliza, #2543..165.00
Carmen, #2545.....................................132.00	Emma...65.00
Carolyn, #2112, ca 1955, 7".....................200.00	Enchantment..99.00
Carpet Seller......................................190.00	Ermine Coat, #1981, ca 1945-60, 7"............175.00
Carrie..65.00	Eugene, #1520.....................................525.00
Cavalier, #2716....................................129.00	Evelyn..335.00
Celeste, #2237, ca 1960-65, 7½"................150.00	Fair Lady...75.00
Cellist, #2226......................................400.00	Fair Maiden, #2211.................................50.00
Centurion, #2726..................................133.00	Fairy, #1379..310.00
Charmian, #1569...................................650.00	Falstaff, #2054......................................95.00
Chief, #2892.......................................135.00	Family Album......................................265.00
Child of Williamsburg, #2154, 5½"...............55.00	Faraway, #2133....................................200.00
Child Study, #604B................................250.00	Fat Boy, #2096....................................250.00
Chloe, #M10..225.00	Fat Boy, #555......................................300.00
Chloe, #M9...190.00	Fiddler, #2171......................................600.00
Chloe, #1767.......................................240.00	Fiona, #2694..85.00
Choir Boy...85.00	First Waltz...195.00
Christine, #2792...................................140.00	Fleur...135.00
Christmas Morn......................................95.00	Flower Seller's Children, #1206.................450.00
Christmas Parcels.................................150.00	Flute, #2483..950.00

Forty Winks, #1974..............................185.00
Francine, #2422..................................68.00
French Horn, #2795.............................750.00
Friar Tuck, #2143..............................450.00
Gaffer...350.00
Gay Morning, #2135.............................225.00
Geisha...550.00
Genevieve, #1962, 7"...........................165.00
Genie, #2989....................................70.00
Geraldine......................................105.00
Giselle, #2140.................................270.00
Golden Days, #2274.............................145.00
Gollywog, #2040................................323.00
Good King Wenceslas............................275.00
Good Morning, #2671............................130.00
Gossips..295.00
Grace..125.00
Grand Manner...................................210.00
Granny's Shawl, #1647..........................350.00
Greta, #1485...................................198.00
Griselda.......................................399.00
Guy Fawkes.....................................850.00
Gwynneth, #1980................................235.00
Gypsy Dance, #2157.............................345.00
Gypsy Dance, #2230.............................235.00
Harlequinade, #635...........................1,150.00
Harmony, #2824..................................98.00
Heart to Heart.................................325.00
Helen, #1572...................................575.00
Helen of Troy..................................700.00
Henrietta Maria................................595.00
Her Ladyship...................................250.00
Hilary...135.00
Huntsman, #2492................................148.00
Hurdy Gurdy, #2796.............................750.00
Invitation.....................................125.00
Irene, #1697...................................425.00
Ivy, #1768, 4¾".................................60.00
Jack...175.00
Jane, #2806....................................100.00
Janet, #M75....................................225.00
Jean, #2032....................................165.00
Jennifer, #1484................................375.00
Jennifer, #2392................................100.00
Jester, wht, dtd 1927..........................130.00
Jovial Monk....................................150.00
Judge, matte...................................175.00
Judith, #2189..................................250.00
Julia, #2705....................................75.00
June, #M71.....................................375.00
June, #1691....................................250.00
Kate Hardcastle, #2028, pink skirt, ca 1949, 8".425.00
Kathleen, #1252................................475.00
Katrina, #2237.................................270.00
La Sylphide, #2138.............................325.00
Lady Anne Neville..............................750.00
Lady April, #1958, ca 1940-1959................275.00
Lady Charmain, #1948, 8".......................175.00
Lady Charmain, #1949...........................183.00
Lady Clare.....................................650.00
Lady Fayre, #1265..............................410.00
Lady Pamela....................................150.00
Lambing Time, #1890............................130.00
Lasyphide......................................400.00

Laurianne......................................135.00
Lavinia, #1955, 5"..............................70.00
Leading Lady, #2269............................130.00
Leisure Hour...................................380.00
Lights Out, #2262, ca 1965-69, 5¼".............225.00
Lily, #1798, ca 1935-45, 5¼"...................130.00
Linda..115.00
Lisa, #2310, blue..............................100.00
Little Boy Blue.................................85.00
Little Bridesmaid, #1433, ca 1945-50...........143.00
Little Land, #67.............................1,500.00
Long John Silver...............................445.00
Loretta, #2335.................................100.00
Lorna...75.00
Lucy Anne......................................160.00
Lucy Lockett, #524.............................750.00
Lunchtime, #2485...............................140.00
Lute, #2431....................................950.00
Margaret, #1989................................250.00
Margaret of Anjou, #2012.......................500.00
Marie, #1370, 4¾"...............................45.00
Marietta, #1341................................660.00
Marietta, #1446................................600.00
Mary Jane, #1990...............................350.00
Mary Mary, #2044, 5"...........................155.00
Mask Seller, #2103.............................125.00
Masque...115.00
Masquerade, #2259..............................220.00
Master Sweep, #2205............................595.00
Matilda..595.00
Maureen, #1770.................................225.00
Mayor, #2280...................................360.00
Maytime..260.00
Meditation, #2330..............................145.00
Melanie, #2271.................................125.00
Mendicant......................................250.00
Midenette, #2090...............................210.00
Milkmaid.......................................110.00
Minuet, #2019..................................210.00
Miss Demure....................................150.00
Mother's Help..................................150.00
My Pet...130.00
Nell Gwynn, #1882..............................475.00
Nina, matte....................................125.00
Officer of the Lines, #2734....................126.00
Old Balloon Seller, #1315, ca 1960, 8".........100.00
Old King, #3134................................295.00
Olga...195.00
Olivia...300.00
Omar Khayyam...................................125.00
Once Upon A Time, #2047........................250.00
Orange Lady, #1759.............................200.00
Orange Lady, #1953.............................200.00
Owd Willum, #2042..............................250.00
Paisley Shawl, #M4, dated 1934.................225.00
Paisley Shawl, #1987, 8½"......................225.00
Pantalettes, #M15..............................235.00
Parisian, #2245................................115.00
Parson's Daughter..............................225.00
Past Glory, #2484..............................178.00
Patricia, #M28, dated 1934.....................265.00
Patricia, #1414................................375.00
Pearly Boy, #2035..............................170.00
Peggy, #2038....................................75.00

Left: Gypsy Dance, HN 2230, 7″, $235.00.
Right: Polka, HN 2156, 7½″, $240.00.

Penelope, #190[1] 270.00
Pensive Moments..................................135.00
Perfect Pair, #581................................700.00
Pirate King, #2901................................325.00
Pirate Maid......................................350.00
Pirouette, #2216.................................225.00
Poke Bonnet, #612................................800.00
Polka..240.00
Polly Peachum, #549..............................235.00
Polly Peachum, #620..............................350.00
Polly Peachum, #694, 'Potted By'.................295.00
Premiere...125.00
Priscilla, #1340.................................190.00
Professor, #2281.................................135.00
Prue, #1996, ca 1950, 7″.........................275.00
Puppetmaker, #2253...............................425.00
Queen Elizabeth, #2878...........................415.00
Queen of Sheba...................................700.00
Regal Lady.......................................150.00
Repose...150.00
Reverie, #2308...................................190.00
Rhapsody...130.00
River Boy..148.00
Robin, #M39......................................300.00
Rocking Horse..................................1,500.00
Romance, #2430...................................132.00
Roseanna...325.00
Rosebud..425.00
Rowena...350.00
Ruth...350.00
Sailor's Holiday, #2442..........................155.00
Santa Claus, #2725...............................135.00
Schoolmarm, #2223................................127.00
Sea Harvest......................................158.00
Shepherd...160.00
Shore Leave......................................155.00
Silks & Ribbons, #2017............................93.00
Simone...118.00
Sir Walter Raleigh, #1751........................450.00
Skater...350.00
Sleepy Scholar, #16............................2,200.00
Southern Belle, #2229............................100.00
Spring Flowers...................................300.00
Spring Morning, #1922............................190.00
St George..230.00
Stayed at Home, #2207, ca 1965, 5¼″.............170.00
Stitch In Time, #2352............................110.00
Stop Press, #2683................................140.00

Suitor...350.00
Summer...345.00
Sunday Best, #2206...............................160.00
Susan, #2056.....................................275.00
Suzette, #2026, ca 1950, 7½″.....................250.00
Sweet & Twenty, #1298............................250.00
Sweet Anne, #M5..................................195.00
Sweet Anne, #1496, ca 1950, 7½″.................175.00
Sweet Lavender...................................350.00
Symphony, #2287..................................295.00
T'Zu-Hsi...700.00
Teenager, #2203..................................210.00
Tildy..325.00
Tinkerbell, #1677, 4¾″...........................40.00
To Bed, #1805....................................105.00
Tootles, #1680, 4¾″..............................90.00
Top O' The Hill, #1833...........................180.00
Top O' The Hill, #1834, 7″.......................95.00
Town Crier, #2119................................220.00
Toymaker...450.00
Treasure Island..................................140.00
Twilight...165.00
Vanity, #2475, 5¼″...............................75.00
Veneta...120.00
Veronica, #1517..................................200.00
Veronica, miniature..............................330.00
Victoria, #2471, 6½″.............................135.00
Victorian Lady, 7¾″..............................200.00
Viola D'Amore....................................600.00
Vivienne, #2073..................................225.00
Wardrobe Mistress................................335.00
Wayfarer...135.00
Wedding Couple, English version, pr..............800.00
Wendy, #2109, 5″..................................50.00
Williamsburg Lady.................................75.00
Willy Won't He, #2150............................250.00
Winter...338.00
Wistful, #2396...................................160.00
Yeoman of the Guard, #2122.......................600.00
Young Love.......................................495.00
Young Master, #2872..............................169.00

Toby Jugs

Cap'n Cuttle, seated, A..........................175.00
Double X, seated.................................300.00
Mr Micawber, seated, A...........................175.00
Old Charley, seated..............................185.00
Sam Weller, seated, A............................175.00

Miscellaneous

Ash bowl, Sairey Gamp.............................65.00
Ash tray, Bateman Character, Laughing Caddie......35.00
Ash tray, Old Charlie.............................75.00
Ashpot, Farmer John...............................90.00
Baron jug, Bradley's Eastern Figures, Morrisan Ware, 7½″....145.00
Bowl, Barkis, 6″..................................50.00
Bowl, Chang, veined wht/multi drip, scrip mk, Noke, 9½″ dia..800.00
Bowl, Coach Scene, dated 1919, small..............25.00
Bowl, Dickens Ware, Sam Weller, sgnd Noke, 8″.....85.00
Bowl, Dickens Ware, 3 characters, ftd, 7¾″ dia...145.00
Bowl, Dr Johnson At Temple Bar, oval, A Australian Reg, 10¾″.65.00
Bowl, Gaffers, scene int, ext stone wall decor, ped, 8x3¾″.....105.00

Bowl, Juliet, square, large....................................95.00
Bowl, Oliver Asks For More..................................80.00
Bowl, Robin Hood the King of the Archers, octagonal, 6½"....45.00
Bowl, shell, flambe, Bernard Moore, 4" dia....................50.00
Bowl, Under the Greenwood Tree, Robin meets Friar Tuck, 8"..95.00
Bowl, 3 ftd, gilt trim.......................................97.50
Box, covered, Tony Weller, square...........................70.00
Bunnykins, mug, sterling overlay, sgn Barbara Vernon........45.00
Bunnykins, set, mug/plate/6" rnd bowl/8" oval bowl, '70s.....20.00
Candle holder, Kingsware, Pickwickians, 3x3"................145.00
Candlestick, Dickens Ware, Fagin/Sam Weller, 1st line, pr, 7"..350.00
Candlestick, Gleaner's, pr..................................105.00
Candlestick, Kingsware, Pickwickians, 3x3".................145.00
Chamberstick, deep, w/landscape scenes, blotchy glaze, 6¼"...85.00
Charger, Dickens Ware, Tony Weller, sgnd Noke...............90.00
Cheese dish, Geneva, flow blue.............................140.00
Coffee pot, Welsh Ladies, pewter insert at top, small........110.00
Creamer, Coaching Days, coaching scene.....................30.00
Creamer, Kingsware, Granny, Heart's Content, sterling spout...185.00
Creamer, Welsh ladies......................................80.00
Creamer & sugar, Fox Series, dated 1930....................75.00
Cup & saucer, Coaching Days, riding scene..................40.00
Cup & saucer, demitasse; cobalt w/gold decor, sgnd For Tiffany..69.00
Cup & saucer, Dickens Ware, Fagin, Mr Micawber on 3" saucer.70.00
Cup & saucer, Fat Boy & Sam Weller, relief, dated 1938......95.00
Cup & saucer, Gaffers, gentlemen in country setting..........50.00
Cup & saucer, Robin Hood, 2¾", 6" dia......................65.00
Cup & saucer, The Kirkwood................................24.50
Dish, Zunday Zmocks series, rectangular, 6¾x9½"............88.00
Flask, Kingsware, Dewars, Sporting Life....................260.00
Inkwell, stoneware, hinged, monkey.........................250.00
Jar, tobacco; Tavern Scenes, 2 men at table, 6"............110.00
Jardiniere, Babes in Woods, young woman w/basket on bridge..450.00
Jardiniere, dk bl rim/base, 4" floral tapestry, Slater's, 9x7"...135.00
Jardiniere, pierced rim, tapestry w/floral, Slater's pat, 9x6"...175.00
Jardiniere & ped, Silicon, brn w/bl jasper, 1884, 30½", M.....15.00
Jug, Dickens Ware, Sam Weller, mkd, miniature, 2¼x1½" dia..88.00
Jug, Dogberry Watch, Shakespearean, set of 3, largest 9½"....345.00
Jug, flow blue, Watteau, 7x8".............................125.00
Jug, Huntsman..60.00
Jug, ice; Coaching Days, riding scene, 9".................145.00
Jug, Kingsware, Drink Wisely, sgn Noke, medium............90.00
Jug, wine; 'Watson & Co', stoneware, narrow spout, 1920s.....125.00
Lamp, Ermine Coat...335.00
Loving cup, Captain Cook, limited edition, black, 11".......175.00
Loving cup, Dutch Ladies, miniature.......................120.00
Loving cup, Kingsware, Huntsman, 7x4".....................295.00
Match holder, Dickens Ware, Sam Weller, 3¼"................70.00
Match stand, Bill Sykes & Micawber........................200.00
Menu holder, rabbit, flambe...............................200.00
Mug, Coach Scene, small....................................35.00
Mug, Rex, Rustic England, country scene: cottage/dogs, 5"....45.00
Mug, 3 different scenes, 3 hdld, small flake on inner rim, 6½"..75.00
Mustard pot, Mr Micawber..................................115.00
Pitcher, Dickens character, Fagin, 2½".....................80.00
Pitcher, Diversions of Uncle Toby, 2 men/quarterstaff, 4"....50.00
Pitcher, Egyptian relief, Sphinx spout, 10"................79.00
Pitcher, fine ribbed w/applied florals, cobalt/br bands, 5½"...70.00
Pitcher, fine ribbed w/applied flowers, cobalt/br bands, 7"....95.00
Pitcher, flambe, scene: man tied to street sign, 6½"........90.00
Pitcher, Gallant Fishers, Gallant Fishers Life Is Best, 6½"...115.00
Pitcher, hot water; Zunday Zmocks series, 7x4"............155.00
Pitcher, hunting scene after G Morland, Holbein glaze, 6½"...115.00
Pitcher, Kings Ware, Parson Jones, 8¼"....................145.00

Pitcher, monk scene, sgn Noke, 7¼"........................115.00
Pitcher, Neptune figural spout, Lambeth, 1870-71 mk, 5½".....45.00
Pitcher, Old Curiosity Shop, mkd A, dated 1951.............145.00
Pitcher, Old London, Garrick at St John's Gate, sgn Nun, 6¾".150.00
Pitcher, Old Sea Dogs, 6".................................69.00
Pitcher, Romeo, small......................................85.00
Pitcher, scene of children playing on beach, 3½"...........45.00
Pitcher, Shakespearean Knights/Sir Andrew Aguecheek, 7".....120.00
Pitcher, Shylock, tall....................................120.00
Pitcher, stoneware, America...............................185.00
Pitcher, tankard; Morrisan................................135.00
Pitcher, tapestry blue/wht/gold...........................110.00
Pitcher, tudor; Night Watchman, 2 different figures, 8".....130.00
Pitcher, w/horse, rider, dogs, mkd Morland................225.00
Pitcher, water; Green King Suffolk Ales...................110.00
Pitcher, Wedlock Is A Ticklish Thing......................125.00
Pitcher, Westcott; Wiltshire Moonrakers, 4½".................95.00
Place setting, Chelsea Rose, 5 pc.........................125.00
Planter, brown flowered, mkd Lord Desborough 1935, 3½x8"...65.00
Plaque, terra cotta, religious, George Tinworth, 9".........190.00
Plaque, wall; Jackdaw of Rheims, Bishop & Abbot & Prior, 15".185.00
Plate, allover bl florals, 2 red & gr peacocks, 10½"........40.00
Plate, American Views, Pikes Peak, railroad scene, 10".......75.00
Plate, American Views, US Capital, Washington, DC, 10".......55.00
Plate, Bobbie Burns, I Ha'e A Wife, 6¼"....................35.00
Plate, Castles & Churches series, Hurstmonceaux Castle, 10"...45.00
Plate, Chang Writes A Book, Willow pattern story............55.00
Plate, chop; Treasure Island, LJ Silver with treasure map, 13"..135.00
Plate, Coaching Days, coaching scene/changing horses, 10"....65.00
Plate, Coaching Days, riding scene/riders jumping fences, 10"..65.00
Plate, Cottage, rack plate.................................15.00
Plate, Dickens series, Bill Sykes, early version, 10".......75.00
Plate, Dickens series, Old Peggotty, early version, 10".....75.00
Plate, Dickens series, Tony Weller, early version, 10".......75.00
Plate, dinner; The Kirkwood...............................22.50
Plate, dogs series, Scottie, 10"..........................55.00
Plate, Don Quixote/The Blanket Tossing, fruit border, 10"....70.00
Plate, Egyptian Pottery, Egyptian series, 10".............75.00
Plate, El Cobler, sitting outside shop, Roger Solem, 10".....65.00
Plate, English Old Scenes, The Gipsies, family at campfire, 10"..65.00
Plate, English Old Scenes, The Gipsies, family w/donkey, 10"..65.00
Plate, flambe, Laughing Cavalier Sung, 10"................175.00
Plate, French scene, sgn HJ Plant, 10¼"..................200.00
Plate, Gaffers, elderly gentlemen in country setting........45.00
Plate, Gaffers, man w/basket & walking stick, 8½"..........45.00
Plate, Gaffers, man w/umbrella by country house, 8½".......45.00
Plate, Gaffers, 10".......................................90.00
Plate, George Washington..................................55.00
Plate, Gibson Girl Series, A Quiet Dinner w/Dr Bottles, 10"..85.00
Plate, Gibson Girl Series, And Here Winning New Friends, 10"..85.00
Plate, Gibson Girl Series, Message from Outside World........70.00
Plate, Gibson Girl Series, Mrs Diggs is Alarmed, 10".......85.00
Plate, Gibson Girl Series, She Becomes a Trained Nurse, 10"..85.00
Plate, Gibson Girl Series, She Contemplates the Cloister.....85.00
Plate, Gibson Girl Series, She Longs For Seclusion, 10".....85.00
Plate, Gibson Girl Series, They All Go Skating, 10".........85.00
Plate, Gibson Portrait series, hearts/lovers knots border, 10"..130.00
Plate, Historic England, Sir Francis Drake/Plymouth Hoe, 10"..60.00
Plate, Jackdaw of Rheims, And of That Terrible Curse He Took.65.00
Plate, Loch Ness painted scenic, 9".......................30.00
Plate, luncheon; Cavalier, sgnd Noke on back side..........40.00
Plate, Maple Tree Series, tree scene/verse around border, 10"..75.00
Plate, monk in wine cellar, Wembley advertising piece, 6¼"...30.00
Plate, Mother Goose, crown on lion mk.....................25.00

Biscuit jar, elephant ear handles, marked Burslem, 7½", $135.00.

Plate, North Wales scene, JH Plant, 10¼"...................200.00
Plate, Nursery Rhymes, Old Mother Hubbard, 7"..............20.00
Plate, Old English Inns/The Kings Head, Chigwell, 10".........45.00
Plate, Professionals Series, Admiral, earthenware, 10".........65.00
Plate, Professionals Series, Bookworm, rare, 10".............85.00
Plate, Professionals Series, Doctor, earthenware, 10".........65.00
Plate, Professionals Series, Falconer, earthenware, 10".........65.00
Plate, Professionals Series, Hunting Man, earthenware, 10".....65.00
Plate, Professionals Series, Jester, earthenware, 10"..........65.00
Plate, Professionals Series, Mayor, earthenware, 10"..........65.00
Plate, Professionals Series, Mayor, translucent china, 10"......40.00
Plate, Professionals Series, Parson, earthenware, 10".........65.00
Plate, Professionals Series, Squire, earthenware, 10".........65.00
Plate, Robert Burns, scene of Scotsman w/thistle border........70.00
Plate, Robin Hood, Under the Greenwood Tree, 10"............90.00
Plate, Robin Hood, Under the Greenwood Tree, 13½".........160.00
Plate, Rochester Castle, early version, 10"..................55.00
Plate, Shakespearean Knights, Sir Andrew Aguecheek, 10".....65.00
Plate, St Mary's Aisle, Dryburgh, 10".....................30.00
Plate, Tavern Scenes, men around table, 10"................50.00
Plate, Temple pattern, 8", pr..........................35.00
Plate, Timber Wagon, logging scene, 10"..................45.00
Plate, Titian Ware, bird & leaf design....................55.00
Pot, oval, Welsh ladies, bone china, small.................95.00
Salt, bean pot form, ad Watson & Co, English pub, 1⅜x2".....95.00
Salt dish, 2 cupids, 5"..............................450.00
Saucer, Old English Inns, small, A......................18.00
Soap dish, stoneware, Wright's Coalter Dragonfly............85.00
Spittoon, stoneware, cobalt, ornate, patented, 8"..........125.00
Sugar w/lid, Kingsware, Granny, The Cup That Cheers, 4x4"...165.00
Tankard, Oliver Twist..............................140.00
Tazza, Harlem Art Deco Temple, Liberty Co, 9"............175.00
Tea caddy, Sir Roger DeCoverley, Mr Spectator Reads Invitation.85.00
Tea pot stand, Shylock..............................65.00
Tea set, Jackdaw of Rheims, teapot/creamer/sugar...........185.00
Teapot, Coach Scene, small...........................110.00
Teapot, Dutch scene, windmill finial, imp #38, mk D1886, 9½".300.00
Teapot, Kingsware, Granny, Heart's Content, sterling spout/lid..275.00
Teapot, self-pouring, dated 1886......................140.00
Thimble, Dorcas..................................39.00
Thimble, Dreema..................................60.00

Thimble, Royal Spa, ornate top, sterling, dated 1929.........85.00
Tobacco jar, Tavern Scenes, 6"........................110.00
Toothpick, Dutch Series Ware, 2-hdl loving cup shape, 1½"....74.00
Toothpick, Gleaners................................45.00
Toothpick, Milkmaid...............................60.00
Tray, Coaching Scene, 8½x6½".......................85.00
Tray, Minstrels, 2 in center, instruments border, 7x8".........55.00
Tray, Old English Inns, Fighting Cocks, St Albans, 5½x4"......22.00
Vase, Artful Dodger, 3¼"............................85.00
Vase, Babes in Woods, full figured lady w/little girl, 9".......300.00
Vase, Babes in Woods, girls w/pixie, 8¼"................285.00
Vase, Babes in Woods, mother & child, 10"...............365.00
Vase, Babes in Woods, woman on rock pile, 9x7"...........300.00
Vase, Babes in Woods, woman walking in snow, 9x7".........300.00
Vase, Burslem, yel/orange/br, scenic, Holbein Ware, 6".......100.00
Vase, celadon shoulder/neck, bands of tapestry, Slater, 8¾"....270.00
Vase, Coaching Scene, bone china, 9"...................180.00
Vase, cobalt blue w/hallmkd silver rim, Lambeth............125.00
Vase, cobalt top/base, 3" tapestry band w/florals, MS, 6", pr...100.00
Vase, Dickens Ware, Alfred Jingle, w/hdl, 5½"..............88.00
Vase, Dickens Ware, Barnaby Rudge, 4¾".................70.00
Vase, Dickens Ware, Fagin, mkd, miniature, 2¾x2¼".........88.00
Vase, Dickens Ware, Mr Micawber, 6"....................80.00
Vase, Dickens Ware, Sydney Carton, 7"..................138.00
Vase, Dutch scene, miniature, ca 1904...................85.00
Vase, Egyptian desert scene, gr mk, 4½"..................150.00
Vase, fish design, sgnd FM, 8½".....................1,000.00
Vase, flambe, heavy silver overlay, hallmkd & #d, 10", VG.....75.00
Vase, ftd, 3½" cobalt base band & tapestry body, florals, 12"..270.00
Vase, Gaffers series, w/hdls, 5½"......................75.00
Vase, Gallant Fishers, sgnd Noke.......................75.00
Vase, impasto, 1879, 8".............................59.00
Vase, incised/applied mosaic, turq/br/gold ft, S498/S, 8½", pr..180.00
Vase, King's Ware, Dutchman, 4".......................105.00
Vase, Orlando, square, small...........................75.00
Vase, ornate, flowers, cobalt/gold, Slaters Pat, 5¾"..........60.00
Vase, red leaves, yel-gr glaze, artist sgnd, ca 1902, 7x5½".....85.00
Vase, Rosalind, ca 1912.............................110.00
Vase, silicon, Persian motif, reticulated top, sgn EDL, 14".....140.00
Vase, stoneware, amber Crackle Ware, 9".................59.00
Vase, stoneware, blue, 4"............................29.00
Vase, stoneware, incised, pressed beads, Lambeth/A Barlow, 9".325.00
Vase, stoneware, irises/strapwork, Simmance, 1902, 19", pr....770.00
Vase, stylized leaves/scrolls, sgn AL, imp RD Lambeth, 9", pr..160.00
Vase, Sydney Carton, 2 hdld, small.....................110.00
Vase, tan w/blue beadwork, 1890s, Doulton Silicon, 6½", pr...140.00
Vase, Trotty Veck, 2 hdld, small.......................105.00
Vase, veined Sung, pumpkin shape, 6"...................550.00
Vase, wood cut scene of castle in landscape, #1614 flambe, 6".125.00
Wine barrel, crest & grape leaves, Doulton-Watts, 1840, 12"...300.00

Dresden

Today, the term Dresden is used to indicate the porcelains that were produced in Meissen and Dresden, Germany, from the very early 18th century, well into the next. John Bottger, a young alchemist, discovered the formula for the first true porcelain in 1708, while being held a virtual prisoner at the palace in Dresden because of the King's determination to produce a superior ware. Two years later, a factory was erected in nearby Meissen, with Bottger as director. There, fine tableware, elaborate centerpieces, and exquisite figurines with applied details were produced. In 1731, to distinguish their product from the wares of such potters as Sevres, Worcester, Chelsea, and Derby, Meissen adopted their famous crossed swords trademark. During the next century, several potteries were producing porcelain in the 'Meissen style' in Dresden itself. Their wares were marked with their own logo and the Dresden indication. Those listed here are from that era. See the Meissen section for examples with the crossed swords marking.

Basket, applied pk/bl flowers, reticulated, ftd, loop hdl, 7".....125.00
Basket, applied roses/children, gr leaves, 4 ft, bl X mk, 7"......85.00
Basket, pierced, 7 cherubs at base w/floral festoons, 14½".....275.00
Boot, allover floral, gold, gold w/in rim, lamb/Dresden mk, 5"...45.00
Cache pot, twig hdls, ribbed, scalloped, HP roses, 1870.......155.00
Candlestick, dbl, applied roses, gold, F/Crown W mk, pr, 5"...250.00
Centerpiece, applied florals, tree stem, 4 dancers, 1900, 22"...275.00
Centerpiece, lattice bowl/base/mc florals, three figures, 18"..1,000.00
Clock, applied flowers/cherub atop/lady & bird ea side, 14"..1,430.00
Cup & saucer, demitasse; ea on 6 ft, wht w/applied mc flowers..125.00
Cup & saucer, HP flowers, gold trim, ca 1870................85.00
Cup & saucer, 18th century courtesans, HP, miniature, 1¼"....95.00
Figurine, Cupid as Engineer, after Meissen series............125.00
Figurine, Dame De La Courde Francois I, C Thieme, 1872, 8".465.00
Figurine, dancing lady, wht dress/flowers/lace, 7"............190.00
Figurine, lady in 1700s costume by marble ped w/book, 27", G.330.00
Figurine, lady w/lantern & lg basket, X swords, 8"..........200.00
Figurine, man & lady dancing, applied roses, Crown mk, 6"....350.00
Figurine, mother & daughter sit, read book, bl mk, 7".......350.00
Group, 7 musicians/dancers, scalloped base, lace/gold, 13½"..1,400.00
Letter holder, wht w/sm red/bl floral, gold trim, sgn Dresden....95.00
Loving cup, reserve w/nymphs in woodlands, 3 gold hdls, 5½".550.00
Plaque, Daphne, by Wagner, in ornate gilt-wood fr, plaque: 5".440.00
Plate, emb gold scrolls, flowers, mk Dresden, 9".............40.00
Plate, lady in garden w/2 cupids, gold relief, 8½"..........125.00
Plate, molded floral border, figures & oxcarts on pink, 10".....40.00
Plate, woman & child, mk Dresden, Crown RK, 8½".........40.00
Ramekin w/lid & under plate, garlands of mc florals, gold, pr....85.00
Tea caddy, lacy gold top, panels w/couple or florals, 5¼x3½"..130.00
Urn w/lid, HP, molded florals, females on hdls, cherubs, 21"...825.00
Urn w/lid, sq plinth, hdls, acanthus/floral, Crown RK, 19".....535.00
Vase, HP female portraits in garden, sgn Wagner, 15", pr....1,320.00
Vase, mc florals & gold, 3 hdls, old mk, 7½x5".............150.00
Vase, w/lid, bottle form, figural scenics/scale panels, 13½".....115.00
Vase, w/lid, on stand, romantic scene on black, rstr, 19", pr...330.00
Vase, w/lid, reserve w/HP hunting scene, bulbous, cobalt, 24".1,250.00

Covered urn, courting couple in reserve, signed with co-joined AR in script, fraudulent Meissen mark, 1850-80, 10", $650.00.

Dresser Accessories

Dresser sets, ring trees, figural or satin pincushions, manicure sets -- all those lovely items that graced milady's dressing table -- were at the same time decorative as well as functional. Today they appeal to collectors for many reasons. The Victorian era is well represented by repousse silver backed mirrors and brushes, and pincushions that were used to display ornamental pins for the hair, hats, and scarves. The hair receiver -- similar to a powder jar, but with an opening in the lid -- was used to hold the lovely strands of hair retrieved from milady's comb or brush. These were wound around the finger and tucked in the opening to be used later for hair jewelry and pictures, many of which survive to the present day. (See Hair Weaving)

Celluloid dresser sets were popular during the late 1800s and early 1900s. Some included manicure tools, pill boxes, and button hooks, as well as the basic items. Because celluloid tends to break rather easily, a whole set may be hard to find today.

With the current interest in anything Art Deco, sets from the thirties and forties are especially collectible. These may be made of crystal, bakelight, or silver, and the original boxes just as lavishly appointed as their contents.

Dresser set, Fin de Siecle period, paste jewels, in chased brass, mint condition, $400.00.

Box, made of horn, w/deer, sm...........................65.00
Brush, clothes; Art Nouveau, sterling....................28.00
Brush, clothes; man's, old, mkd Real Ebony, Made In Japan....45.00
Comb, tortoise shell, solid top w/gold inlay................75.00
Jar, cobalt w/gold & yel enamel, Deco decor, hinged lid, 3x4"..115.00
Jar, gr w/pk/wht floral enamel, ormolu ft, 3¼x3¾"..........100.00
Jar, vaseline opal w/gr & gold enameling, hinged lid, 3¾".....95.00
Mirror & brush set, green jasperware: ladies/cupids, brass......110.00
Perfume caddy, beveled glass 4 sides & top, claw ft, 4 bottles..300.00
Perfume w/atomizer/cologne/trinket, pk w/silver flashing, Deco...85.00
Powder jar/nail buffer/case, Dominick & Haff, sterling/floral....120.00
Set, amber Pyralin, Labelle, jewelry box/buffer in stand+6 pcs..110.00
Set, celluloid, lt & dk gr, 12 pc in blk leather case, 1915......45.00
Set, tortoise shell look, gold & gr decor, 14 pcs.............75.00

Duncan and Miller

The firm that became known as the Duncan and Miller Glass Company in 1900, was organized in 1874, a partnership between George Duncan, his sons Harry and James, and his son-in-law Augustus Heisey, in Pittsburgh, Pennsylvania. John Ernest Miller was hired as their designer. He is credited with creating the most famous of all Duncan's glassware lines, Three Face. (See Pattern Glass) The George Duncan and Sons Glass Company, as it was titled, was only one of eighteen companies that merged in 1891 with U.S. Glass. Soon after the Pittsburgh factory burned in 1892, the association was dissolved and Heisey left the firm to set up his own factory in Newark, Ohio. Duncan built his new plant in Washington, Pennsylvania, where he continued to make pressed glassware in such notable patterns as Bagware, Amberette, Duncan Flute, Button Arches, and Zippered Slash.

The firm was eventually sold to U.S. Glass in Tiffin, Ohio and officially closed in August, 1955.

In addition to the early pressed dinnerware patterns, today's Duncan and Miller collectors enjoy searching for opalescent vases in many patterns and colors, frosted 'Satin Tone' glassware, acid etched designs, and lovely stemware such as the Rock Crystal cuttings. Milk glass was made in limited quantity and is considered a good investment.

Ruby glass, Ebony (a lovely opaque black glass popular during the twenties and thirties), and of course the glass animal and bird figurines are all highly valued examples of the art of Duncan and Miller.

#112 Caribbean, divided salad, blue 65.00
#112 Caribbean, flower bowl centerpiece, blue 45.00
#112 Caribbean, goblet, 8½ oz, crystal 23.00
#112 Caribbean, punch cup, w/amber hdl 8.00
#112 Caribbean, punch cup, w/crystal hdl 6.00
#112 Caribbean, punch cup, w/red hdl 8.00
#112 Caribbean, punch set, bowl/plate, 12 cups/ladle, crystal . . . 119.00
#112 Caribbean, punch set, bowl/plate, 16 cups/ladle, red hdl . . 220.00
#115 Canterbury, bowl, crimped, bl opal, 9″ 50.00
#115 Canterbury, bowl, crimped, crystal, 10½″ 25.00
#115 Canterbury, bowl, gardenia; pink opal, 7½″ 17.00
#115 Canterbury, bowl, oval, crystal, 10″ 25.00
#115 Canterbury, candy w/cover, 3 part, crystal, w/HP orchids . . . 35.00
#115 Canterbury, candy w/cover, 3 part, 3 hdld, ruby, 8″ 39.00
#115 Canterbury, candy w/lid, wisteria, 9¼″ 50.00
#115 Canterbury, candy w/lid, 3 part, pk opal 38.00
#115 Canterbury, celery & relish, 3 part, crystal, 10½″ 18.00
#115 Canterbury, compote, crystal, 5x7½″ 22.00
#115 Canterbury, compote, vaseline 35.00
#115 Canterbury, creamer & sugar, regular, crystal 15.00
#115 Canterbury, cup & saucer, crystal 10.00
#115 Canterbury, nappy, hdld, pink opal, 7½″ 29.00
#115 Canterbury, plate, crystal, 6½″ 7.00
#115 Canterbury, rose bowl, crystal, 5″ 15.00
#115 Canterbury, sauce, crystal 4.00
#115 Canterbury, sugar, crystal, 3″ 8.00
#115 Canterbury, top hat, pink opal, 3″ 14.00
#115 Canterbury, vase, crimped, pink opal, 4″ 25.00
#115 Canterbury, vase, oval, pink opal, 3½″ 20.00
#115 Canterbury, vase, violet; crimped, blue opal, 3½″ 20.00
#115 Canterbury, vase, violet; crimped, pink opal, 3½″ 20.00
#117 Three Feathers, bowl, oval, blue opal, 12″ 68.00
#117 Three Feathers, vase, cornucopia, pink opal, 8″ 59.00
#118 Hobnail, basket, pink opal, 12″ 125.00
#118 Hobnail, bon bon, diamond shape, ftd, hdld, pink opal, 6″ . 29.00
#118 Hobnail, bowl, crimped, blue opal, 12″ 53.00
#118 Hobnail, bowl, crimped, pink opal, 12″ 53.00
#118 Hobnail, bowl, oval, blue opal, 12″ 53.00
#118 Hobnail, candlestick, blue opal, 6″, pr 25.00
#118 Hobnail, champagne, saucer style, crystal 6.00
#118 Hobnail, cocktail, crystal, 4¼″ 3.50
#118 Hobnail, cologne, pink, w/stopper 24.00
#118 Hobnail, creamer & sugar, individual, crystal 28.00
#118 Hobnail, creamer & sugar, milk glass, w/label 39.00
#118 Hobnail, creamer & sugar, regular, crystal 19.00

#118 Hobnail, cup, crystal 7.00
#118 Hobnail, goblet, crystal 9.00
#118 Hobnail, goblet, milk glass, 9 oz 17.00
#118 Hobnail, goblet, pink opal, 9 oz 25.00
#118 Hobnail, ivy ball, cobalt blue, 4″ 49.00
#118 Hobnail, ivy ball, crystal, 5″ 20.00
#118 Hobnail, ivy ball, gold, 4″ 29.00
#118 Hobnail, liner, pink opal, 17″ 40.00
#118 Hobnail, plate, crystal, 6″ 6.00
#118 Hobnail, plate, crystal, 7½″ 7.00
#118 Hobnail, plate, sandwich; crystal, 12″ 20.00
#118 Hobnail, puff box & cover, crystal 14.00
#118 Hobnail, puff box & cover, pink 17.00
#118 Hobnail, puff box w/cover, green 30.00
#118 Hobnail, punch cup, blue opal 18.00
#118 Hobnail, punch ladle, pink opal 50.00
#118 Hobnail, shaker, ftd, ornate lid, crystal, pr 27.00
#118 Hobnail, sherbet, low, crystal, 6 oz 7.50
#118 Hobnail, sugar, individual, blue opal 14.00
#118 Hobnail, top hat, crystal, 3½″ 14.00
#118 Hobnail, top hat, pink opal, 2½″ 30.00
#118 Hobnail, tray, oval, 2 hdld, crystal, 12″ 18.00
#118 Hobnail, tumbler, crystal, 10 oz, 5″ 9.00
#118 Hobnail, tumbler, crystal, 13 oz, 5½″ 10.00
#118 Hobnail, vase, crimped, blue opal, 6″ 41.00
#118 Hobnail, vase, flared, crystal, 8″ 19.00
#118 Hobnail, vase, flip; crimped, pink opal, 7½″ 79.00
#118 Hobnail, vase, violet; crimped, crystal, 4″ 15.00
#118 Hobnail, vase, violet; ftd, blue opal, 4″ 35.00
#118 Hobnail, vase, violet; ftd, green, 4″ 29.00
#122 Sylvan, bon bon, 5½″ 8.00
#122 Sylvan, tray, mint; hdld, crystal, 7½″ 8.00
#126 Venetian, vase, ruby 39.00
#127 Murano, flower arranger, blue opal, oval, 12½″ 50.00
#127 Murano, flower arranger, crystal satin, 5½″ 39.00
#127 Murano, flower arranger, oval, crystal, 8″ 25.00
#127 Murano, vase, crown, pink opal, 7″ 63.00
#127 Murano, vase, flared, pink opal, 7″ 59.00
#130 Sanibel, bowl, salad; shallow, pink opal 75.00
#130 Sanibel, bowl, salad; shallow, yellow opal 85.00
#130 Sanibel, nut dish, cranberry/pink 30.00
#130 Sanibel, plate, salad; blue opal, 8½″ 28.00
#130 Sanibel, plate, salad; yellow opal, 8½″ 34.00
#130 Sanibel, relish, 2 compartments, pink opal, 8½″ 29.00
#130 Sanibel, sweetmeat, pink opal, 8″ 29.00
#130 Sanibel, tray, mint; pink opal, 7″ 23.00
#30 Pall Mall, spooner 19.00
#301 Teardrop, ash tray, individual 5.00
#301 Teardrop, bowl, divided, 5¾″ 3.00
#301 Teardrop, bowl, oblong, 7″ 4.00
#301 Teardrop, bowl, 3 part oblong, 10¾″ 10.00
#301 Teardrop, butter w/cover, metal, ¼# 12.00
#301 Teardrop, candlestick, cone, pr 12.00
#301 Teardrop, cheese & cracker 38.00
#301 Teardrop, creamer, 3½″ 4.00
#301 Teardrop, goblet, 9 oz, #5301, 7″ 14.00
#301 Teardrop, juice, ftd 9.50
#301 Teardrop, marmalade w/cover 22.00
#301 Teardrop, mayonnaise w/under plate 18.00
#301 Teardrop, mustard w/cover 15.00
#301 Teardrop, nappy, 2 hdld, 5″ 5.00
#301 Teardrop, nut dish, 2 section, hdld, #301, 6″ 8.00
#301 Teardrop, plate, 14″, light use 20.00
#301 Teardrop, plate, 6″ hdld 6.00

#301 Teardrop, salt & pepper, 3"..........................15.00
#301 Teardrop, saucer champagne, 5 oz, #5301..............13.00
#301 Teardrop, sugar, large.............................8.00
#301 Teardrop, tumbler, stemmed, 5¾"....................8.00
#301 Teardrop, tumbler, 12 oz..........................12.50
#301 Teardrop, vase, 8½".............................20.00
#40 Spiral Flutes, bowl, flanged, green, 7½"............15.00
#40 Spiral Flutes, bowl, flanged, green, 8½"............15.00
#40 Spiral Flutes, bowl, green, 5"......................5.00
#40 Spiral Flutes, bowl, rimmed, green, 6¾".............8.00
#40 Spiral Flutes, finger bowl, pink....................6.50
#40 Spiral Flutes, finger bowl w/liner, green..........10.00
#40 Spiral Flutes, goblet, green.......................10.00
#40 Spiral Flutes, iced tea, flat, rose, 5½"...........15.00
#40 Spiral Flutes, plate, crystal, 6"...................3.50
#40 Spiral Flutes, plate, green, 6".....................3.00
#40 Spiral Flutes, plate, green, 7½"....................5.00
#40 Spiral Flutes, plate, green, 8½"....................4.00
#40 Spiral Flutes, plate, pink, 8½".....................7.00
#40 Spiral Flutes, saucer, green........................3.00
#40 Spiral Flutes, sugar, green.........................8.00
#40 Spiral Flutes, vase, green, 6½"....................12.00
#40 Spiral Flutes, vase, green, 8¾"....................15.00
#41 Sandwich, bowl, flower; crimped, crystal, 11".......30.00
#41 Sandwich, bowl, fruit; flared, crystal, 12".........25.00
#41 Sandwich, bowl, grapefruit; crystal w/yel flat rim, 7".......15.00
#41 Sandwich, bowl, shallow, crystal, 1¾x11½"..........33.00
#41 Sandwich, cake stand, crystal, 13".................45.00
#41 Sandwich, candlestick, crystal, 4", pr.............25.00
#41 Sandwich, candy, covered, ftd, crystal, 8".........57.00
#41 Sandwich, candy, 2 pt, 1 hdl, crystal, 5½".........20.00
#41 Sandwich, cocktail, crystal, 4¼"...................12.00
#41 Sandwich, compote, low, ftd, green, 5x6" dia........25.00
#41 Sandwich, condiment set, crystal, 5 pc.............55.00
#41 Sandwich, creamer & sugar, crystal, large..........32.00
#41 Sandwich, creamer & sugar, crystal, small..........23.00
#41 Sandwich, creamer & sugar on tray, crystal, small....27.50
#41 Sandwich, cruet w/stopper, crystal, 4".............15.00
#41 Sandwich, cup, crystal.............................10.00
#41 Sandwich, cup & saucer, crystal....................12.00
#41 Sandwich, deviled egg tray, crystal................50.00
#41 Sandwich, finger bowl & plate, green...............20.00
#41 Sandwich, fruit, crystal, 5".......................7.50
#41 Sandwich, goblet, crystal, 9 oz, 6".................8.00
#41 Sandwich, goblet, green, 9 oz......................16.00
#41 Sandwich, goblet, water...........................12.50
#41 Sandwich, hat, crystal, 4¼".......................40.00
#41 Sandwich, ice cream................................6.00
#41 Sandwich, iced tea, ftd, crystal, 12 oz, 5½".......9.00
#41 Sandwich, juice, ftd, crystal, 5 oz................9.00
#41 Sandwich, mayonnaise, ftd, w/under plate & ladle, crystal...27.50
#41 Sandwich, pitcher, ice lip, crystal, ½ gal.........70.00
#41 Sandwich, plate, crystal, 12".....................37.00
#41 Sandwich, plate, crystal, 8"......................11.00
#41 Sandwich, plate, green, 8"........................12.00
#41 Sandwich, relish, 2 part, crystal, 7".............15.00
#41 Sandwich, relish, 3 pt, oval, crystal, 10".........30.00
#41 Sandwich, relish, 4 pt, 2 hdld, crystal, 10½"......30.00
#41 Sandwich, salad dressing set, crystal, 13".........45.00
#41 Sandwich, saucer champagne, crystal, 5 oz...........7.00
#41 Sandwich, tray, oval, crystal, 8½"................14.00
#41 Sandwich, tumbler, straight, crystal, 10 oz, 4½"...10.00
#41 Sandwich, tumbler, straight, crystal, 10 oz, 5¼"...10.00
#41 Sandwich, wine, 4¼"................................9.50

#42 Mardi Gras, creamer, 3" to top of lip..............22.50
#42 Mardi Gras, pitcher, water; w/pewter top...........90.00
#42 Mardi Gras, punch cup..............................8.00
#42 Mardi Gras, sugar w/lid, large....................28.00
#42 Mardi Gras, vase, trumpet, 8".....................17.50
#48 Diamond Ridge, bowl, fruit; ftd, 9½x12½" dia.......95.00
#48 Diamond Ridge, punch cup, mold mark on hdl.........8.00
#5326 Indian Tree, juice, ftd, 5 oz, 4¾"..............21.00
Ash tray, duck, floral decor & gold beak, 5" long......18.00
Basket, needle etched florals, 10"....................38.00
Block, rose bowl, 5¼".................................29.00
First Love, candle holder, 2 lite, pr.................50.00
First Love, candlestick, 4"...........................35.00
First Love, champagne, 5 oz, #5111½...................17.00
First Love, compote, 5"...............................32.00
First Love, cup.......................................22.00
First Love, cup & saucer, Canterbury blank............27.50
First Love, flower bowl, flared, 12"..................20.00
First Love, goblet, 10 oz, #5111½.....................20.00
First Love, plate, 6", Canterbury blank...............7.50
First Love, plate, 7¾", Canterbury blank..............13.00
First Love, plate, 8¾", Canterbury blank..............18.00
First Love, saucer champagne, 5 oz, #5111½............20.00
Radiance, red; pitcher w/8 flat tumblers.............375.00
Rememberance, liquor cocktails, #5115.................17.00
Swan, crystal, W&F, 12"...............................45.00
Swan, crystal, 8" long................................18.00
Swan, lt gr, W&F, 12" W...............................95.00
Swan, narrow forest gr, crystal neck, 7½".............30.00
Swan, Pall Mall, chartreuse, w/candle holder in center, 7"......28.00
Swan, Pall Mall, chartreuse, 10½".....................40.00
Swan, Pall Mall, chartreuse, 3½"......................25.00
Swan, Pall Mall, crystal, 10".........................30.00
Swan, Pall Mall, crystal, 3½".........................23.00
Swan, Pall Mall, ruby, 3½"............................29.00
Swan, ruby & crystal, 12".............................60.00
Swan, ruby stained, crystal neck, 7½".................15.00
Swan, ruby w/crystal neck, 7".........................38.00
Swan, solid, 5".......................................22.00
Swan, spread wind, blue opal, 12"....................135.00
Swan, swag back, pink opal...........................155.00

Figurine, Heron, crystal, 6¾" x 2½", $85.00.

Swan, Sylvan #122, blue opal, 12".........................145.00
Swan, Sylvan #122, blue opal, 7"...........................52.00
Swan, Sylvan #122, pink opal, 12".........................145.00
Swan, Sylvan #122, pink opal, 7"...........................52.00
Swirl, cornucopia, 14"....................................35.00

Durand

Durand Art Glass was a division of Vineland Glass Works, in Vineland, New Jersey. Created in 1924, it was geared specifically toward the manufacture of fine hand crafted art ware. Iridescent, opalescent, and cased glass was used to create such patterns as King Tut, reminiscent of Tiffany and Steuben. Production halted in 1931, after the death of Victor Durand.

Atomizer, King Tut, lt gr, unsgnd.......................250.00
Bowl, blue irid, rolled rim, sgn, deep, 14"..............800.00
Bowl, centerpiece; fluted, blue & wht trim, 14" dia......185.00
Bowl, orange to gold irid, 4x10".........................445.00
Compote, gold w/bl hi-lites, sgn/#d, 6½x7¾"..............400.00
Compote, King Tut, gold/bl, stem & inside gold, 6".......750.00
Cup & saucer, red & wht feathered.......................400.00
Jar, wht w/gr & gold feather design at bottom, gr finial, sgnd.2,300.00
Lamp base, boudoir; threaded gold.......................150.00
Plate, amber w/blue trim, unsgnd, 8½".....................75.00
Plate, black cut to clear w/silver overlay rim, 14"......195.00
Plate, blue & wht scalloped rim, unsgnd, 11"............100.00
Plate, blue w/wht pulled feather center, unsgnd, 8".....250.00
Plate, cobalt w/opal pulled feathers, X hatch pontil, 7½"....225.00
Plate, cranberry, feathered, Emil Larson................210.00
Plate, gr w/pulled feather center, unsgnd, 8"...........285.00
Plate, ruby, paneled, hand blown, 8½"...................150.00
Plate, ruby w/wht pulled feather center, cut rim, unsgnd, 8½"..230.00
Rose bowl, King Tut, blue irid, 5½".....................650.00
Rose bowl, King Tut, orange, sgnd V Durand..............450.00
Rose bowl, Moorish crackle cranberry & wht, 2¾".........175.00
Shade, cylinder, gold, wht pulled feather/gold threads, 7", pr...190.00
Shade, feather pattern, ruffled, 6½x4¾".................210.00
Sherbet, gr w/wht pulled feather design, unsgnd.........160.00
Tumbler, sgn Larson......................................85.00
Vase, ambergris w/3 engraved thistle plants, 4".........125.00
Vase, amethyst, paneled, bl applique on rim & stem, 6¾"....200.00
Vase, bl banded irid, bulbous/sm neck, glass liner, sgn, 16x8"..750.00
Vase, bl irid, bulbous w/rnd panel ft, 7"...............425.00
Vase, bl irid, wide mouth, can neck, angle shoulder, #30139-14.625.00
Vase, bl irid w/allover random threading, sgn, #1710-6, 5".....750.00
Vase, bl irid w/wht pulled leaves, urn shape, sgn, 4½x4"......675.00
Vase, blue aurene w/hanging hearts & vine, #198, 12½"......975.00
Vase, clear blue w/pulled feather design, sgnd, pr, 8"..........900.00
Vase, cobalt w/yel ft, opal pulled feathers, #20120-12, 11½"...900.00
Vase, cut overlay, cobalt to clear, 4"..................400.00
Vase, dk bl irid, sgn & #d, 10½".......................575.00
Vase, gold, intaglio cut, #20161-8, sgn................1,200.00
Vase, gold & irid orange, simple shape, sgn, 8".........400.00
Vase, gold banded irid, bulbous/sm neck, sgn, 4½x4".....325.00
Vase, gold bullet form w/in scrolled metal holder, unsgn, 12"...350.00
Vase, gold lustre w/gr vines & leaf, 7½"................575.00
Vase, gold w/opaque & gr feathers & threading, 8¾"......400.00
Vase, gold/gr lustre, vines/leaves, 7½".................575.00
Vase, gr & clear crackle glass, bulbous, rare, 8".....3,400.00
Vase, gr leaves & veins on irid wht, orange w/in, unsgn, 8½"..200.00
Vase, gr transparent, cut floral design, unsgnd, 4¼"....200.00
Vase, gr w/opaque wht leaves & veins, gold w/in, unsgn, 9"....500.00
Vase, gr w/wht pulled feather, cut flowers at rim, unsgnd, 10"..450.00

Vase, King Tut, gold & cobalt, 10".......................650.00
Vase, King Tut, gr w/gold, pk/lav hi-lites, sgn, 12½", pr.....2,000.00
Vase, King Tut, gr w/pattern, gold lined, sgn, 4½".......675.00
Vase, King Tut, irid gr & bl w/gold, 6".................900.00
Vase, King Tut, red-orange w/blue decor, sgnd, 10¼"....1,750.00
Vase, King Tut, red-orange w/blue decor, unsgnd, 10¼"....1,450.00
Vase, King Tut, silver, fluted top, gold liner, 4¼".....375.00
Vase, King Tut, wht w/blue, unsgnd, 9¼".................250.00
Vase, orange irid, pulled feather trim, unsgnd, 10½"....300.00
Vase, orange irid, threading, 7", EX....................350.00
Vase, orange irid w/gr scrolled waves, 5"...............375.00
Vase, orange irid w/gr vines, orange throat, sgnd, 8x8"...775.00
Vase, ruby crystal, wht pulled feathers, sgn, 8".........450.00
Vase, ruby cut to clear, sgnd V Durand, 12".............625.00
Vase, ruby irid, ribbed, w/gold liner, unsgnd, 8½".......900.00
Vase, silver/wht/blue crackle, unsgnd, 9½"..............700.00
Vase, threaded fan, gray w/dk bl & gr lustre, 10½".......350.00
Vase, Venetian style w/applied amber art work, rare, 6".....500.00

Durant Kilns

The Durant Pottery Company operated in Bedford Village, New York, in the early 1900s. Its founder was Mrs. Clarence Rice, who was aided by L. Volkmar to whom she assigned the task of technical direction. (See also Volkmar) The art ware and tableware they produced was simple in form, relying on the unique glaze treatments developed by Volkmar. The creative aspects of the work were carried on almost entirely by Volkmar himself, with only a minimal crew to help with production. After Mrs. Rice's death in 1919, the pottery was purchased by Volkmar, who chose to drop the Durant name by 1930.

The ware was marked simply 'Durant' and dated prior to 1919, after which a stylized 'V' was added.

Bowl vase, footed, bl crackle gloss, 4x7"................75.00
Compote, turquoise/plum, 2½x6".........................200.00
Vase, flared, heavy cobalt, Volkmar, 6x7½".............325.00

Easter Eggs

Blown glass, emb 'Easter Greetings', 6".................35.00
Blown glass, hand painted, 4".........................30.00

Blown milk glass, orange poppy decoration, 7", $20.00.

Blown glass, 2″ 10.00
Blown glass, 6″ 20.00
Papier mache, ca 1908, lg 15.00

Epergnes

A popular item during the Victorian era, epergnes were fancy center-pieces often consisting of several tiers of vases (called lilies), candle holders, or dishes, or a combination of components. They were made in all types of art glass, and some were set in ornate plated frames.

Bl opal, 3 lily, deep pleated 10¾″ bowl, 17¾″ H 325.00
Bl opal, 4 lily, pleated bowl & center lily, allover threaded 350.00
Cranberry, single lily, crystal rigaree 135.00
Cranberry, 10″ ruffled bowl, center lily w/eng floral, 18″ 350.00
Cranberry opal, 12″ fluted bowl/3 lilies/2 canes w/baskets 650.00
Emerald gr, 3 lilies, applied rigaree, 10″ base dia, 22″ 350.00
Frosted glass dolphin support sunflower bowls w/trumpets, 20″ .400.00
Hobnail, bl opal, triple lily, 9x6½″ 65.00
Lavender opal, single lily, w/metal holder, Victorian 185.00
Miniature, 1 lily, lt olive w/florals, blown 95.00
Pk/opal/clear, 3 lily, sq folded bowl, crystal rigaree, 21″ 295.00
Sapphire bl w/applied rigaree, 3 lilies, 20″ 195.00
Shaped mirror base w/peachblow peaches, one yel lily, 14½″ .2,850.00
Vaseline, cranberry ruffled top, ornate brass holder, single 95.00
Vaseline opal, ruffled center lily/bowl/6 hanging lilies, 16″ 425.00

Silver nine-vase floral epergne, Martin Hall and Co., London, 1934, 187 ozs., 16 dwts., 23″, $3,000.00.

Erphila

Rather difficult to find, these fine porcelain novelty items were made for only a short time in Bavaria, Germany. They are marked with a stamp 'Erphila, Germany' in a rectanglar reserve.

Cigarette box, lady/dog/child, yellow/blk 35.00
Dresser doll, bl gown, blk hair 75.00
Figurine, Pinscher pup, sitting, gray/wht blend, 2¾″ 12.00
Figurine, 2 German Shepherds, standing, 4½x4½″ 45.00
Flower frog, water buffalo 35.00
Pitcher, milk; figural toucan bird 45.00
Planter, flowers & roses on vase & base plate, 4x3½″ 40.00
Teapot, begging dog figural, 8″ 55.00
Teapot, Dachshund figural 38.00
Teapot, elephant figural, sitting/front legs form spout, 8½″ 45.00
Teapot, gray elephant figural, trunk upraised, 8¾″ 58.00
Teapot, pink pig w/blk ears & spots, figural, 7¼″ 65.00
Toby, Mrs Gamp, w/sticker: R 1886, Erphila, Czech, 5¾″ 45.00
Toothpick, character figure, sgn 47.00

Eskimo Artifacts

While ivory carvings made from walrus tusks or whale teeth have been the most emphasized articles of the Eskimo art, basketry and woodworking are other areas in which these Alaskan Indians excell. Their designs are effected through the application of simple yet dramatic lines and almost stark decorative devices. Though not pursued to the extent of American Indian art, the unique work of this northern people is beginning to attract the serious attention of today's collectors.

Arrowhead, walrus tusk, pre-1900, 3″ 25.00
Awl, iron, 5″; w/ivory seal head, 19th century 250.00
Basket, Aleut, mc yarn lg & sm terraced diamonds, 11x10″ dia .150.00
Basket, baleen, flared, openwork weave, ivory fox atop, 3″ . . .1,980.00
Basket, baleen, rnd sides, domed lid/ivory seal head knob, 5″ .2,475.00
Basket, Tlingit, twine/spruce root, rye grass decor, w/lid, 6″ 880.00
Belt, twined, rye grass, silk thread florals, mtd in fr, 23″ 880.00
Bird, carved gray stone, sgn, 6¾″ 50.00
Bone tool, 1 point at right angle to shaft, 13½″ 85.00
Bow drill, ivory, engraved w/hunters/caribou/seals/etc, 12″ 825.00
Box handle, ivory, much engraving, 5″ 150.00
Button, ivory, stylized whale, 1¾″ 75.00
Buttons, ivory, lot of 8 assorted 50.00
Calendar, for week, fox head plugs into fish w/7 holes 100.00
Child's jacket, cap & boots, seal skin 400.00
Crib board, 2 carved animal heads, unique, 20th century, 12″ .1,000.00
Cup scraper, walrus ivory, prehistoric, 4¼″ 45.00
Drum handle, large fragment, Punuk culture, ivory 50.00
Figurine, duck, ivory, prehistoric, 3½″ .350.00
Figurine, Eskimo & 4-dog team chasing rabbit, ivory, 9½″ 850.00
Figurine, head & torso, ivory, classic Okvik, 2″ 250.00
Figurine, man wrestling lg seal, blk soapstone, sgn, 8x11″ 950.00
Figurine, sailing schooner, ivory, 20th century, 5½″ 450.00
Figurine, seal, on carbonized ivory bone base, 2½″ 45.00
Float plug, ivory, prehistoric, lg 40.00
Float plug, ivory, prehistoric, small 15.00
Game, ivory pegs, fish/fishing scenes, w/compartment, 15″ 200.00
Harpoon finger rest, ivory tooth, excellent form, ¾″ 65.00
Harpoon head, walrus ivory, dug from old campsites, 4″ 35.00
Harpoon toggle, Okvik, ivory, fine engraving, 4½″ 350.00
Harpoon toggles & dart, set of five, miniature, early historic 150.00
Hat, twined/spruce root weave, sea mammal pigmented decor . . .770.00
Mallet, ivory, seal shaped hdl, minor age cracks, 8″ 55.00
Moccasins, cuffed, long ties, florals on blk cloth, soft sole 100.00
Napkin ring, fossil ivory w/carved bear, 20th century 75.00
Needle case, ivory, carved in form of seal, 4″ 1,045.00
Net gauge, bone, pegged, good form, 9½″ 125.00
Okvik fragment, ivory, fine example engraving 100.00

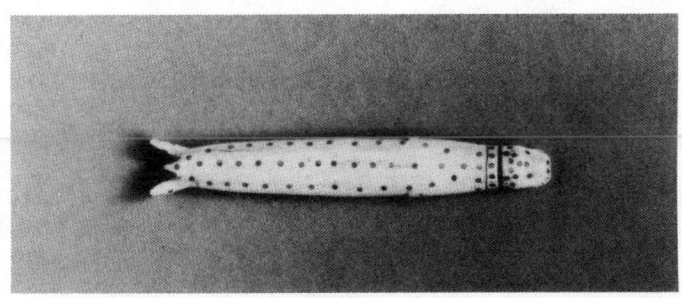

Ivory needle case, seal-form with engraved features, 4″ long, $1,045.00.

Parka, fur, decorated, 19th century, man size.............1,000.00
Pin, fossil ivory, walrus head carving, 20th century...........45.00
Pipe, Haida, argillite, thunderbird w/bird-headed bear, 4″...1,320.00
Pipe, ivory, bear head carving, 20th century, 5½″...........450.00
Pouch, Tlingit, twined/woven spruce root/zig zag decor, 7″.....300.00
Pull, ivory seal head, bead eyes, 1½″.....................350.00
Rudimentary torso, ivory, prehistoric, 3″.................100.00
Salt & pepper shakers, polar bears, carved ivory, 2½″.......120.00
Sewing tool, ivory, good form, 4¼″.......................100.00
Spoon, blubber; wood, early 1800s, 9″.....................20.00
Staff, North West Coast, wood, wolf head hdl, blk/red pnt, 32″.495.00
Tool, ivory, well engraved, prehistoric, 8½″.................150.00
Tool, pointed spoon, ivory, 5½″..........................100.00
Tooth, carved human face & whaling effigy, 1″.............550.00
Tooth, Nunivak Island, engraved human & seal face, 1½″....200.00
Totem pole, relief bears w/mask & fish/sea mammal, 185″....4,675.00
Tusk, primitive engraving of dog sled/harpooning whale, 13″ L.150.00
Whale eardrum, 5½″.....................................200.00
Whistle, ivory, 2½″.....................................35.00

Fans

The Japanese are said to have invented the fan. From there it went to China, and Portuguese traders took the idea to Europe. Though usually considered milady's accessory, even the gentlemen in 17th century England carried fans! More fashionable than practical, some were of feathers and lovely hand-painted silks with carved ivory or tortoise sticks -- some French fans had peepholes. There are mourning fans, calendar fans, and those with advertising. All are collectible!

Advertising, Jardin Danse, Wm Morris, NY Roof, 25 stick.......35.00
Advertising, Maxwell/Chrysler, lady driving...................20.00
Advertising, photo supplies, Victorian designs, ca 1909.........35.00
Chantilly lace, blk, knights/horses, boat, 26″...............195.00
Chinese, bl/gr cloisonne landscapes on silver filigree, 8″ L.....450.00
Chinese, HP, circular, w/orig holder, 1873...................50.00
Chinese, ivory & painted feathers, 1800s, 18x25″............75.00
Chinese, ivory brise w/carved figures, 1800.................250.00
Chinese Mandarin, embroidered silk, gold figural sticks, 1880....90.00
Court scene HP vignette, gold embossed, ivory struts w/mirror..200.00
Cut paper, HP figural decor w/florals, ivory leaves/silver mts.....60.00
English, HP silk, Brussels lace, orig box....................170.00
Fabric, wht w/embroidered florals & peacock.................25.00
French, HP, ivory sticks w/silver inlay, 1850................150.00
French, HP ivory brise, minor stick rpr, 1800...............150.00
French, map/jack of clubs/etc, ivory sticks, 1770, 11″ L, G.....750.00
French, painted, w/trompe l'oeil decor, 1770s...............750.00
French, sgn Duvelleroy, print w/wood sticks, 1870...........120.00
French, silk, painted balloon scenes, late 1700s.............950.00
German, HP lady/iris, silk/sequins/MOP sticks/gold inlay, 1850..300.00
Lace, black, 14″, M....................................45.00

Linen, HP reserve w/couple, silver mts/sequins, English, 1800..200.00
Net & lace w/ivory slats, 14x26″, G.......................50.00
Oil cloth, blk, circular, folds into hdl, 9½″..................22.00
Oil cloth, blk w/HP flowers, 25″..........................40.00
Paper, HP classical decor, MOP leaves w/gold decor, bird hdl..300.00
Paper, HP figural decor, carved ivory leaves, 1800s...........50.00
Paper, HP figural decor ea side, gilt decor on ivory leaves, G....45.00
Paper, HP romatic decor both sides, carved ivory leaves, rpr....45.00
Paper, HP royal riverside party, carved/silvered ivory leaves.....50.00
Plumes, blk w/wrist ribbon, 13½x22″, G...................75.00
Plumes, br w/gray slats & wrist ribbon, 12x19″..............50.00
Plumes, flamingo color, 17″ spread........................30.00
Plumes, ostrich, blk, 12″................................35.00
Plumes, ostrich, net & lace, tortoise frame, 18″.............25.00
Plumes, ostrich, orange, w/tortoise struts..................100.00
Pressed fiber leaves w/spangles, carved ivory struts, 8x15″.....60.00
Russian, tortoise w/shaded ostrich feathers, 1870............120.00
Satin, beige, bone struts, 23″............................40.00
Silk, blk w/pnt scene, sgn Le Martre, tortoise sticks, Tiffany....150.00
Tortoise shell spokes, pique work, ivory tips, early Victorian....315.00
Vellum, HP nymphs/satyrs/cupids, carved ivory sticks, 20″, fr...895.00
World's Columbian Expo, 1893, JW Green, w/buildings, 13½″...65.00

Farm Collectibles

Country living in the 19th century entailed plowing, planting, and harvesting; gathering eggs and milking; making soap from rendered lard on butchering day; and numerous other tasks performed with primitive tools of which we in the 20th century have had little first-hand knowledge.

Apple butter stirring stick, 36″ long.......................12.50
Auger, hollow, Stearns & Co, 6¾″ blade...................26.00
Barley fork head, wrought iron, flat tine tips, early, 14″........16.00
Barn lantern, wood fr w/glass sides/door/tin top/candle socket...170.00
Barrel spigot, 8″.......................................4.00
Bee smoker, sheet copper, fabric bellows, copper spout........50.00
Bell, for animal, cast brass, 3″ bell-mouth dia...............17.50
Bench, splayed legs, old gray paint finish, 19x49″............55.00
Birdhouse, wren's, hanging, cream-glazed pottery, 11″ tall......87.50
Buggy step, CI...9.00
Bull nose ring, polished solid copper, 3″ dia.................6.50
Calf weaner, forged iron, 1700s..........................22.00
Calf weaner, frame & prong type, tinned metal...............8.00
Catalog, Allison-Chalmers Model WD tractor.................15.00
Catalog, Huber Tractor & Threshing Machinery, early..........25.00
Catalog, P&O Plows, 1920s..............................15.00
Cheese-tester, wood hdl, tapered steel blade, 15″ long........40.00
Chicken snatcher, homemade long wire w/hook end/wood hdl...12.50

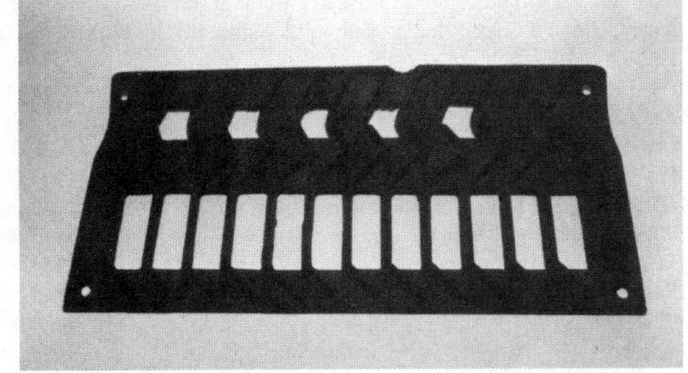

Corn sheller, patented Feb. 28, 1875, cast iron, $75.00.

Conestoga wagon ax-holder, wrought iron, sturdy, ornate.......90.00
Corn planter, wood hdl, 32"..............................15.00
Corn sheller, iron, pat Feb 28, 1875.....................75.00
Corn sheller, 2 part, metal teeth, 1700s................220.00
Digger, post-hole; clamshell shovels, split hdl.........25.00
Egg basket, wire, not collapsible, 9"...................18.00
Egg scale, flip-up leaves, yellow paint, metal..........13.00
Engine, Fairbanks-Morse, gasoline, used on spray rigs, ca 1918.150.00
Feed sack, colorful label print, woven cotton...........10.00
Fence wire stretcher & splicer, Hayes, 18" long.........45.00
Flax breaker, hand carved hardwood, hdld, 19" long......45.00
Frame support joint, from barn, auger holes & broad axe mks...13.50
Grain measure, double, wood staved, ½ & 1 peck sizes.......67.50
Grain measure, metal, traces orig red paint.............25.00
Grain scoop, NE, hand cut, 18th century, 1 pc pine, w/hdl.....125.00
Hames, brass ends, 26", pr..............................15.00
Hay fork, all wood, 60" L...............................90.00
Hay fork, wood, 43½"....................................75.00
Hay knife, sawtooth edge, two wooden hdls...............12.50
Hay rake, all wood, rpr hdl, 72"........................20.00
Hay rake, all wood, 64".................................65.00
Haylift, rope sliding, for moving bales from wagon to loft, CI....50.00
Hinges, barn door, CI, hinged at shaped section, 32", pr.......45.00
Hinges, barn door, wrought iron, 29" L, pr.............110.00
Hinges, ram's horn design, wrought iron, 9½" long, pr.....50.00
Hitching post, horse head, CI, ca 1800s, detailed, orig post....200.00
Hog ringer, to put rings in nose, iron, mkd Hill's, pat 1872.....18.00
Hog scraper, wood hdl, iron scraper, 7½"................15.00
Hog trimmer, to trim snouts, iron, 1870s................25.00
Horse anchor, iron, RR spike in cannon ball, ca 1800s.........30.00
Horse anchor, iron block w/orig brass studded leather strap.....45.00
Horse bit w/rings, iron, 7" L............................4.00
Horse collar, leather, weathered........................17.50
Implement seat, American Harrow Co, CI, EX..............65.00
Implement seat, Champion, CI, EX........................30.00
Implement seat, Ideal, CI, figural decorations..........87.50
Implement seat, Jones Rake, CI, EX......................60.00
Implement seat, Taylor, CI, EX..........................80.00
Implement seat, Walter A Wood, CI, EX...................50.00
Implement seat, Worchester Buckeye, CI, EX..............90.00
Kettle, rendering; CI, paw ft, steer heads, corn, Kenwood, 36"..470.00
Kettle, sugar; for cooking cane, iron, orig Kelly......250.00
Lantern, wood w/chipped carved detail, weathered/damaged, 12".65.00
Maiden's yoke, chains & hooks, red paint, 38" long......40.00
Manual, Fordson tractor, 1923...........................12.00
Maple syrup pot, black tin, spout filter, 4¾"...........85.00
Milk jug, heavy tin, brass bands, bail, Shaker type.....65.00
Milk pail, tin, bail, lid, tinner made..................35.00
Milking stool, hand cut half-moon shape hickory, 3 legs.......75.00
Milking stool, primitive, made from tree trunk & branches.....55.00
Milking stool, 3 legged, hand made, splay legs, early 1800s.....95.00
Millstone, 18" dia......................................18.00
Ox yoke key, wrought iron, 6"...........................8.50
Parts list, Fordson tractor, 1926.......................8.00
Parts list, Oliver Tractor Implements...................20.00
Plow, dbl oxen, man-guided, cast iron, 1850s...........125.00
Post winch, for hauling hay to top of barn, CI, pat 1986......35.00
Pulley, single wheel haymow type, CI w/hardwood wheel, 12"....13.00
Pump, high pressure, used on horse-drawn spray rigs, iron, 21".150.00
Pump, iron, emb: Red Jacket Mfg Co, Davenport, Iowa, #1A....45.00
Repairs list, Deer & Mansur, 1919.......................20.00
Sale bill, 1937 Iowa farm, fold marks, typical listings.......14.00
Sap spigot, CI, used in maple sugar trees...............45.00
Sausage press, Enterprise, CI, orig pnt/stencil, 28"....35.00

Seeder, hand; CI gears, no straps.......................35.00
Shovel, grain; all wood, orig stenciled label indistinct, rpr......85.00
Shovel, grain; all wood, 34"...........................195.00
Shovel, grain; all wood, 46"...........................125.00
Shovel, made from 1 pc wood, wrought iron edge, rfn, 55"..95.00
Sign, Farm Produce/Farm Prices, 13½x38¾"...............87.50
Single tree, trace chain hook, 24" L....................8.00
Spray rig, horse drawn, CI axles, CI & forged wheel, 1890s...100.00
Wagon side, old bl pnt w/wht/red striping, 12¾x33", pr....40.00
Wagon wheels, wood w/iron rims, worn old red, set of 4.......35.00
Winnowing sieve, splint bottom, 1700s, 24" dia.........260.00
Yoke, adjustable bentwood collars & lg iron ring, 32" L.......40.00

Fenton

Frank and John Fenton were brothers who founded the Fenton Art Glass Company in 1906 in Martin's Ferry, Ohio. The venture was first only a decorating shop using blanks purchased from other companies. This operation soon proved unsatisfactory, and by 1907 they had constructed their own glass factory in Williamstown, West Virginia. John left the company in 1909, and organized his own firm in Millersburg.

The Fenton Company produced over 150 patterns of carnival glass. They also made custard, chocolate, opalescent, and stretch glass; and during the fifties manufactured the colored glassware so popular during that era. Free-hand, or off-hand pieces introduced in 1925 were made without molds, and because the process proved to be unprofitable, the line was discontinued by 1927. Even their newer glassware made in the past twenty-five years is already regarded as collectible. Various paper labels have been used since the 1920s; only since 1967 has the logo been stamped into the glass.

See also Carnival Glass; Collector Plates; Custard Glass

Aqua Crest, nappy, 5½"..................................15.00
Aqua Crest, plate, 8½"..................................15.00
Aqua Crest, vase, #189, 10".............................85.00
Aqua Crest, vase, 6"....................................35.00
Ash tray, ruby, #9176, 9"...............................25.00
Basket, Colonial gr, crimped/fluted, elongated t'prints, 8x8".....40.00
Bicentennial planter, chocolate.........................25.00
Bicentennial plate, Eagle, chocolate....................25.00
Big Cookies, hat basket, ruby...........................98.00
Bowl, Chinese yellow, #1504A............................65.00
Bowl, Mandarin red, orig blk glass stand, 3½x8".........60.00
Bowl, periwinkle bl, ftd, 7"............................67.50
Bubble Optic, vase, gold, fluted, wht interior, 12"....185.00
Burmese, basket, ruffled, gr maple leaf decor, 5x7½"....80.00
Burmese, bud vase, w/roses decor, 6½"...................30.00
Burmese, creamer, tan & gr autumn leaves, 4½"...........40.00
Burmese, Empress vase..................................100.00
Burmese, Mandarin vase.................................150.00
Burmese, vase, bulbous, short base, autumn leaves, 7½"......80.00
Burmese, vase, decorated, sgn, 4x5".....................40.00
Burmese, vase, undecorated, Beaded Melon, 6"............25.00
Cactus, cruet, aqua blue opal, orig stopper.............55.00
Candle holder, jade, #848, pr...........................20.00
Candlestick, Mandarin red, 10"..........................75.00
Candlestick, ruby cut, 10".............................175.00
Candy box, apple green, #6080, 6" dia..................100.00
Candy box, milk glass w/bl/yellow HP butterflies, #8288.......75.00
Candy dish, 3 fruits w/basketweave, serrated rim, bl opaque.....30.00
Candy w/lid, jade gr, #835, 9½".........................33.00
Cased, bowl, hexagonal, turq, 5x8½".....................45.00
Cased, shell bowl, lilac................................75.00
Cased, vase, lilac, #7255, 8"...........................85.00

Chou Ting light, #8407, ruby irid.........................50.00
Cigarette lighter, #9198, ruby.........................30.00
Coin Dot, bowl, cranberry opal, #203.....................50.00
Coin Dot, bowl, cranberry opal, 10″ dia....................40.00
Coin Dot, bowl, cranberry opal, 3¾″......................45.00
Coin Dot, creamer, cranberry opal, #421, 4″.............42.00
Coin Dot, cruet, cranberry opal, 6″......................45.00
Coin Dot, decanter, cranberry opal, 8″..................60.00
Coin Dot, pitcher, cranberry opal, 5½″...................33.00
Coin Dot, pitcher, Fr opal, scalloped.....................125.00
Coin Dot, student lamp, honey amber opal, #1401, 21″......285.00
Coin Dot, top hat, cranberry opal, 3¼″..................35.00
Coin Dot, tumbler, Fr opal..............................17.50
Coin Dot, water set, Fr opal, crimp pitcher+six 9 oz tumblers..150.00
Coin Spot, iced tea tumbler, gr opal, #1352.............20.00
Coin Spot, syrup, clear opal, ring neck, early.............75.00
Coin Spot, table lamp, blue opal, 23″, pr..................225.00
Coin Spot, vase, cranberry opal, ruffled top, 8x8″.........95.00
Daisy & Button, box, vanity; amber......................22.00
Daisy & Button, hat, amber, Olde Virginia Glass............30.00
Dancing Ladies, vase, fan shape, clear/frosted, 4¾″..........30.00
Diamond Lace, epergne, Emerald Crest, Fr opal, 4 pc........125.00
Diamond Lace, epergne, Silver Crest, milk glass, 4 pc, lg.....65.00
Diamond Lace, vase, fan form, ftd, blue opal, 6″...........45.00
Diamond Lace, 10″ bowl w/3″ candlestick, Fr opal...........35.00
Diamond Lace, 9″ bowl & 4½″ candlesticks, Fr opal..........35.00
Diamond Optic, cup & saucer, ruby......................25.00
Diamond Optic, goblet, pink, 7″..........................18.50
Diamond Optic, goblet, water; cobalt.....................30.00
Diamond Optic, jug, ruby overlay, squat, 5½″.............100.00
Diamond Optic, plate, ruby, 7½″..........................9.00
Diamond Optic, shaker, ruby, single......................45.00
Diamond Optic, shakers, amber, pr.......................45.00
Diamond Optic, sherbet, ruby............................25.00
Diamond Optic, tumbler, ftd, ruby.......................25.00
Diamond Optic, vase, dolphin, ruby, 5″...................40.00
Diamond Optic, vase, rolled edge, ruby, 7″...............35.00
Dolphin, bon bon, green, #1621.........................20.00
Dolphin, candlestick, gold, 3½″..........................11.00
Dolphin, candlestick, pink, 3½″..........................12.50
Dolphin, candlestick, ruby, #1623, 3½″, pr...............35.00
Dolphin, compote, Grecian gold stretch, ruffled top...........75.00
Dolphin, vase, jadite, dolphin hdl.......................26.00
Dot Optic, creamer, cranberry opal, squat, 4″.............30.00
Dot Optic, hat, cranberry opal, 3x4″.....................75.00
Dot Optic, hat, Fr opal, 2¾″............................35.00
Dot Optic, miniature lamp, cranberry opal...............100.00
Ebony Crest, bowl, 9″...................................30.00
Emerald Crest, fan vase, 4¼″...........................15.00
Epergne, milk glass, 2 pc, 11″...........................45.00
Fairy light, Heart, springtime green......................40.00
Fairy light, owl, bl milk, satin finish....................25.00
Fairy light, owl, lime sherbet, #5108....................20.00
Fairy light, owl, rosalene...............................25.00
Figurine, alley cat, amethyst carnival....................67.50
Figurine, butterfly on stand, lime sherbet................20.00
Georgian, ash tray, ruby, 1934.........................15.00
Georgian, cup & saucer, ruby...........................16.00
Georgian, goblet, ruby, 5½″.............................65.00
Georgian, mug, pink, 4″.................................30.00
Georgian, shakers, amber, pr...........................45.00
Georgian, shakers, cobalt, pr...........................65.00
Georgian, shakers, ruby, pr............................60.00
Georgian, water goblet, ruby............................15.00

Vase, Free-Hand, deep purple with multicolor spatter, 5″ x 6½″, $395.00.

Gold Crest, bride's basket, deep pk cased w/wht, fancy SP fr...125.00
Gold Crest, epergne, 11″ bowl, frog, 5″ lily, 8″.............70.00
Gold Crest, epergne, 5 pcs, 17″........................175.00
Gold Crest, vase, #1808, triangle, orig label, 8″..........50.00
Gold Crest, vase, crimped, 4½″.........................15.00
Gold Crest, vase, milk glass, 2″........................32.00
Grape & Cable, tobacco jar, blue marble, #9188...........50.00
Hanging Hearts, basket, bl.............................65.00
Hanging Hearts, vase, custard, dbl crimp, '76, 6½″........50.00
Hobnail, banana bowl, milk glass........................35.00
Hobnail, basket, bl opal w/clear hdl, 9″..................40.00
Hobnail, basket, cranberry, 4½″.........................55.00
Hobnail, basket, cranberry opal, 10″.....................70.00
Hobnail, basket, cranberry opal, 8″......................65.00
Hobnail, basket, Fr opal, 4½″...........................25.00
Hobnail, basket, lt gr, 7″...............................48.00
Hobnail, bon bon, ruffled, cranberry opal, 6″.............25.00
Hobnail, bowl, crimped, topaz opal, 4¼x10″..............80.00
Hobnail, bowl, ftd, scalloped, plum opal, 8″..............95.00
Hobnail, cake plate, ftd, milk glass, 13″.................45.00
Hobnail, cake plate, ftd, topaz opal, 13″................125.00
Hobnail, candle bowl, blue marble.......................20.00
Hobnail, candlestick, plum opal, style similar to #283.......40.00
Hobnail, cat slipper, Colonial green.....................20.00
Hobnail, cat slipper, orange............................25.00
Hobnail, cat slipper, ruby..............................27.50
Hobnail, cat slipper, vaseline opal......................12.00
Hobnail, champagne, French opal........................14.00
Hobnail, champagne set, bl opal, ruffled bowl & stand, 10 pc...125.00
Hobnail, cologne, cranberry opal........................40.00
Hobnail, cologne, lt aqua opal, matching stopper..........29.00
Hobnail, cologne lamp base, brilliant blue, Paulux label.......65.00
Hobnail, compote w/lid, lt gr, 8½″......................53.00
Hobnail, compote, plum opal, dbl crimp..................60.00
Hobnail, cornucopia, topaz opal, 4¼″....................30.00
Hobnail, cruet, blue opal, large, w/orig stopper............45.00
Hobnail, cruet, blue opal, small.........................25.00
Hobnail, cruet, cranberry opal, 6″.......................55.00
Hobnail, cruet, Fr opal.................................20.00
Hobnail, epergne, bl opal, 10″..........................45.00
Hobnail, epergne, topaz opal, miniature..................30.00
Hobnail, epergne, 3 lily, aqua opal, 10″..................42.00
Hobnail, fruit bowl, collared base, milk glass, lg...........25.00

Hobnail, goblet, bl opal, #3845, 9 oz.........................15.00
Hobnail, iced tea, cranberry opal..........................30.00
Hobnail, iced tea, topaz...................................26.00
Hobnail, lamp, cranberry, 26".............................150.00
Hobnail, mustard, topaz opal, 3 pc.........................65.00
Hobnail, oil cruet, cranberry opal, 5½"....................48.00
Hobnail, oil fount, Colonial blue, 7" dia, similar to #255.......60.00
Hobnail, pitcher, blue opal, 5½"...........................38.00
Hobnail, pitcher, Fr opal, squat, 4½"......................38.00
Hobnail, pitcher, Fr opal, squat, 5¼"......................40.00
Hobnail, pitcher, plum opal, 5½"...........................95.00
Hobnail, pitcher, water; cranberry opal, #389, 80 oz.........200.00
Hobnail, plate, Fr opal, 8"................................10.00
Hobnail, powder jar w/lid, Fr opal, 4".....................13.00
Hobnail, punch set, w/7 qt bowl, topaz, 14 pcs.............300.00
Hobnail, rose bowl, vaseline, 4½"..........................14.00
Hobnail, shakers, blue opal, pr............................34.00
Hobnail, shakers, clear opal, #3806, pr....................35.00
Hobnail, shakers, Fr opal, pr..............................34.00
Hobnail, syrup jug, #3762, turq, 12 oz.....................60.00
Hobnail, top hat, Fr opal, 2¼".............................20.00
Hobnail, tumbler, blue opal, flat, 3½".....................10.00
Hobnail, tumbler, blue opal, flat, 4¼".....................15.00
Hobnail, tumbler, blue opal, ftd, 4½"......................15.00
Hobnail, tumbler, clear opal, 5 oz.........................10.00
Hobnail, tumbler, clear opal, 9 oz.........................12.00
Hobnail, tumbler, Fr opal, flat, 3½".......................10.00
Hobnail, tumbler, Fr opal, flat, 6¼".......................14.00
Hobnail, vanity bottle, bl opal, #3986, 1953..............125.00
Hobnail, vase, bl opal, bulbous, 5".......................33.00
Hobnail, vase, bl opal, 4"................................20.00
Hobnail, vase, bl opal, 8"................................55.00
Hobnail, vase, clear opal, 4"..............................9.00
Hobnail, vase, cranberry opal, lg ruffled top, 5½".........58.00
Hobnail, vase, cranberry opal, triangle, 5½"...............38.00
Hobnail, vase, cranberry opal, 4"..........................24.00
Hobnail, vase, fan shape, vaseline, 7½x10¾"................30.00
Hobnail, vase, Fr opal, #3858, dbl crimped, 8"............45.00
Hobnail, vase, Fr opal, miniature..........................10.00
Hobnail, vase, gr opal, #389, 4"...........................30.00
Hobnail, vase, lime opal, 3"...............................21.00
Hobnail, vase, orange, ftd, 19"............................35.00
Hobnail, vase, pink opal, 8"...............................65.00
Hobnail, vase, topaz opal, ruffle top, 6".................40.00
Hobnail, vase, topaz opal, tri-con top, 4¼"................30.00
Hobnail, water set, bl opal, squat jug w/6 tumblers........140.00
Hobnail, water set, cranberry opal, ruffled top, 9 pcs.....250.00
Hobnail, water set, topaz opal, 7 pc.......................95.00
Hobnail, Wrisley cologne bottle/powder box, Fr opal, wood top..48.00
Ivory Crest, tulip vase, #1923.............................32.00
Ivory Crest, vase, 8"......................................30.00
Ivy, vase, #1925, dk gr over milk glass, 6"...............65.00
Ivy ball, cranberry overlay w/milk glass ft, 8½"...........70.00
Ivy ball, footed, green/milk glass.........................65.00
Jar, macaroon; ebony......................................135.00
Jar, macaroon; jade gr, wicker hdl, 'Big Cookies'..........55.00
Lamb's Tongue, salt and pepper, pink, rare, pr.............75.00
Lamp, Gone With The Wind, Beaded Melon, ca 1949, 10"....160.00
Lamp, hurricane; lime opal swirl w/milk glass bases, 11", pr....160.00
Lavabo, milk glass, 3 pc...................................50.00
Leaf Tiers, plate, #1790, Fr opal, 3 toed, 12"............75.00
Lincoln Inn, plate, gr, 8"..................................5.00
Lincoln Inn, sherbet, green, 4¼"............................7.50
Lotus & Grape, bon bon, Persian blue.......................30.00

Madonna, vase, milk glass..................................25.00
Ming, biscuit jar w/hdl....................................70.00
Ming, vase, pink, #184, 11½"...............................55.00
Paperweight, large egg, sgnd/dated '76, 4x3"...............65.00
Peach Blow, vase, crimped, #1923...........................45.00
Peach Crest, basket, Beaded Melon, milk glass hdl..........85.00
Peach Crest, bowl, 8 part crimp, 10".......................48.00
Peach Crest, candlestick, #1523, pr........................35.00
Peach Crest, creamer, #1924................................17.50
Peach Crest, epergne, single lily, 10".....................75.00
Peach Crest, pitcher, Beaded Melon, 6".....................40.00
Peach Crest, shell bowl....................................58.00
Peach Crest, top hat, 3½"..................................27.00
Peach Crest, vase, crimped, 8".............................35.00
Peach Crest, vase, cupped, pk w/in, 5½"....................35.00
Peach Crest, vase, dbl crimp, 4"...........................22.00
Peach Crest, vase, petticoat, Beaded Melon, 6".............35.00
Peach Crest, vase, Tulip, ca 1942, pr......................75.00
Pitcher, rose overlay, 1943................................45.00
Plate, Backward C, rose pastel, 9".........................35.00
Plate, Christmas, blue satin, 1978.........................10.00
Plate, Mandarin/flame red, 3 row open edge, 9"............140.00
Plate, Valentine, 1st edition, Romeo & Juliet, carnival, 1972....40.00
Plated Amberina, candy jar, #1680, w/lid, 7".............125.00
Plated Amberina, vase, #1651, 7"...........................75.00
Plymouth, cocktail shaker, amber...........................35.00
Polka Dot, vase, cranberry, #2255..........................60.00
Rib Optic, gr opal...18.00
Rib Optic, pitcher, gr opal, cobalt hdl....................85.00
Rib Optic, tumbler, opal, 12 oz............................18.00
Rib Optic, vase, lily form, Fr opal, 8"....................25.00
Rib Optic, vase, lily form, lime opal, 8"..................25.00
Rib Optic, wine bottle, cranberry opal, #396..............110.00
Ring, water pitcher, gr opal w/blk hdl, rare..............150.00
Rosalene, bon bon, butterfly, w/hdls.......................35.00
Rosalene, bowl, Ogee, 3 pc.................................88.00
Rosalene, candlestick, water lily, pr......................50.00
Rosalene, candy w/lid, ftd, water lily, #8480, 7".........65.00
Rosalene, Chessie box.....................................250.00
Rosalene, compote w/cover..................................55.00
Rosalene, swan, open back..................................25.00
Rose, candy box w/lid, #9284, Colonial blue................47.50
Rose, candy box w/lid, Colonial green, #9284...............47.50
Rose, compote, orange, #9223, 6½"..........................35.00
Rose, student lamp, amber, #9208, 19".....................225.00
Rose, vase, oval, 4 toed, milk glass, #9251................25.00
Rose bowl, blk, dbl crimp, 7"..............................85.00
September Morn, blk, nymph & frog..........................200.00
September Morn, in #848 candle holder, ruby................95.00
Silver Crest, basket, Bead & Melon, wht over gr, wht hdl.......50.00
Silver Crest, basket, low..................................30.00
Silver Crest, cake stand, Holly Sprig pattern..............28.00
Silver Crest, cake stand, 13"..............................40.00
Silver Crest, candlesticks, #680, pr.......................25.00
Silver Crest, compote, 7"..................................15.00
Silver Crest, dessert, deep, #680..........................10.00
Silver Crest, fruit bowl, sq, ftd..........................60.00
Silver Crest, pitcher, lg..................................95.00
Silver Crest, plate, 8¼"...................................15.00
Silver Crest, punch set, complete.........................180.00
Silver Crest, server w/center hdl, 12½"....................20.00
Silver Crest, tidbit, 2 tier, 12½" & 8½" plates............25.00
Silver Crest, vase, #7262, sq throat, 12".................50.00
Silver Crest, vase, 3¾"....................................12.00

Silver Crest, vase, 6½"...............................10.00
Silvertone, console set, amethyst, #1004 bowl+#1010 candles...95.00
Snow Crest, bowl, cranberry Spiral Optic, 10½"............85.00
Snow Crest, vase, blue, 6".............................6.00
Snow Crest, vase, emerald, 9½".........................40.00
Snow Crest, vase, pinched, emerald, 8".................65.00
Spiral, vase, Fr opal, #186, 8".......................25.00
Spiral, vase, lime opal, #186, 8".....................25.00
Spiral, vase, violet; Fr opal, #1923, 4½" sq..........28.00
Spiral Optic, hat, Fr opal, 4x6"......................75.00
Spiral Optic, lamp, cranberry opal, #183, 22".........225.00
Spiral Optic, vase, Fr opal, 6¾".......................20.00
Stretch, bon bon, green, #363.........................35.00
Stretch, cup & saucer, blue, #1502....................45.00
Stretch, fan vase, Florent, gr........................30.00
Stretch, fan vase, pink, #857, 8".....................25.00
Stretch, lemon server, topaz..........................25.00
Stretch, pitcher, blue, #222..........................95.00
Stretch, plate, topaz, 6".............................20.00
Stretch, sherbet w/under plate, blue, #604............35.00
Swirl, cruet, amethyst, orig paper label, orig stopper.........35.00
Swirl, cruet, cranberry, orig paper label, orig stopper.........35.00
Swirl, rose bowl, bl opal, pinched top................35.00
Swirl, tumbler, bl opal...............................15.00
Swirl, water pitcher, bl opal, 10"....................85.00
Thumbprint, basket, Colonial green, #4438.............45.00
Thumbprint, bud vase, ftd, ruby, 18"..................37.50
Thumbprint, handkerchief vase, orange, #4454, 9"......35.00
Tobacco jar, black, #9188.............................75.00
Tray, leaf shape; Fr opal, 8½"........................30.00
Tumble-up, amber......................................22.00
Tumble-up, bl opal....................................66.00
Tumble-up, marigold...................................55.00
Vasa Murrhina, basket, autumn orange, 11".............85.00
Vasa Murrhina, basket, gr/blue, #6437, 11"............100.00
Vasa Murrhina, vase, blue mist, 4"....................50.00
Vasa Murrhina, vase, rose w/aventurine gr, #6454, 4"........60.00
Vase, black rose, crimped.............................45.00
Vase, blue opal, #547, miniature......................39.00
Vase, cranberry, blown, ruffled top, 8"...............70.00
Vase, cranberry Optic, spiral, ca 1939, 9½x4½"........95.00
Vase, cranberry overlay, draped, w/sticker, 7".........15.00
Vase, Dancing Girl, Peking blue, w/lid, 12"...........500.00
Vase, freehand, hanging hearts, Chinese ivory w/bl ft, 1926....550.00
Vase, Old Mill Stream, #7257, 10".....................45.00
Vase, opaline, peach w/wht flowers, trumpet form, 8"........35.00
Vase, peacock, bl satin...............................35.00
Vase, peacock, Mandarin red...........................125.00
Vase, peacock, periwinkle blue........................110.00
Vase, rose overlay, #192, 8¾".........................28.00
Vase, swans/cattails/water lily, blown/bulbous, custard, 8½"......95.00
Vase, Venetian red slag, #857, 1920s..................110.00
Velva Rose, tray, center hdl, 10".....................70.00
Vintage, ferner, ftd, chocolate.......................125.00
Water Lily & Cattails, basket, lavender satin, #8434.........40.00
Water Lily & Cattails, berry bowl, bl opal, 1908, 9" dia......50.00
Water Lily & Cattails, bowl, bl opal, 10½" sq.........55.00

Ferrandiz

Artist Jaun Ferrandiz designs the figurines, bells, ornaments, music boxes, and bells that are sculpted by carvers at the world's most renowned woodcarving workshop, Anri, in St. Ulrich, Italy. Discontinued or retired editions often bring many times their original price on the secondary market. See also Collector Plates

Adoration, 3"..100.00
Basket of Joy, 3"....................................60.00
Blessing, 6"...140.00
Bouquet, 3"..50.00
Camel, 3"..65.00
Camel, 6"..200.00
Camel Guide, 3"......................................45.00
Carole, 3"...45.00
Courting, 6"...275.00
Dove Girl, 6"..90.00
Driver, 6"...100.00
Drummer Boy, 1979, 6"................................145.00
First Blossom, 3"....................................50.00
First Blossom, 6"....................................120.00
Flight into Egypt, 3"................................90.00
Flight into Egypt, 6"................................170.00
Flower Girl, 3"......................................55.00
Freedom Bound, dtd, 3"...............................85.00
Friend, 6"...120.00
Friendship, dtd, 3".................................250.00
Friendship, 6".......................................168.00
Gardener, 3"...50.00
Gift, 3"...65.00
Girl & Egg, 3".......................................45.00
Girl & Egg, 6".......................................115.00
Girl w/Dove, 6"......................................100.00
Girl w/Rooster, 3"...................................65.00
Good Shepherd, 10"...................................200.00
Good Shepherd, 20"...................................825.00
Good Shepherd, 3"....................................45.00
Good Shepherd, 6"....................................110.00
Happy Strummer, 3"...................................55.00
Happy Strummer, 6"...................................120.00
Happy Wanderer, 3"...................................45.00
Happy Wanderer, 6"...................................100.00
Happy Wanderer, 6", unusual, w/hearts on vest.............150.00
Harmony, 3"..45.00
Have You Heard, 3"...................................75.00
Helper, 6"...150.00
High Riding, 10".....................................200.00
Hiker, 6"..120.00
Hurdy Gurdy, 3"......................................55.00
Introduction, 6".....................................140.00
Jesus, 6"..55.00
Joseph, 6"...80.00
Journey, 3"..75.00
Kitchen Time, 3".....................................50.00
Leading the Way, 6"..................................195.00
Little Mother, 3"....................................70.00
Little Mother, 6"....................................175.00
Love Gift, 3"..45.00
Love Gift, 6"..125.00
Love Letter, 3"......................................75.00
Love Letter, 6"......................................125.00
Merry Melody, 6".....................................120.00
Mother & Child, 3"...................................55.00
Mother & Child, 6"...................................135.00
Path Finder, 6"......................................150.00
Prayer, 6"...140.00
Proud Mother, 6".....................................150.00
Quintet, 10"...200.00

Quintet, 20"...825.00
Quintet, 3"..45.00
Quintet, 6"...100.00
Reverence, 6"..110.00
Riding in the Rain, 10"................................425.00
Romeo, 6"..165.00
Slalom Skier, 8"......................................250.00
Sleeper, 6"...140.00
Small Talk, 6"...100.00
Spreading the Word, 6"................................150.00
Spring Arrival, 3"......................................45.00
Spring Arrival, 6"......................................95.00
Spring Bride, 3".......................................40.00
Stepping Out, 3"......................................50.00
Stolen Kiss, 6".......................................375.00
Stray, The; 3"...45.00
Summertime, 3".......................................60.00
Summertime, 6".......................................150.00
Talking to the Animals, 10"...........................290.00
Talking to the Animals, 20"...........................825.00
Talking to the Animals, 3".............................45.00
Thanksgiving, 6".....................................140.00
Tracker, 3"..75.00
Tracker, 6"...240.00
Trumpeter, 3"...55.00
Trumpeter, 6"..150.00
Wanderlust, 6".......................................100.00
Weary Travelers, 3"...................................50.00
Weary Travelers, 6"..................................100.00

Fiesta

Fiesta is a line of dinnerware produced by the Homer Laughlin China Company of Newell, West Virginia, from 1936 until 1973. It was made in eleven different solid colors, with over fifty pieces in the assortment. The pattern was developed by Frederic Rhead, an English Stoke-on-Trent potter who was an important contributor to the art pottery movement in this country during the early part of the century. The design was carried out through the use of a simple band of rings device near the rim. Fiesta Red, a strong red-orange glaze color, was made with depleted uranium oxide. It was more expensive to produce than the other colors, and sold at higher prices. Today's collectors still pay premium prices for Fiesta Red pieces.

During the fifties the color assortment was gray, rose, chartreuse, and dark green. These colors are relatively harder to find, and along with Fiesta Red and medium green, new in 1959, command the higher prices.

Fiesta Kitchen Kraft was introduced in 1939; it consisted of seventeen pieces of kitchenware such as pie plates, refrigerator sets, mixing bowls, and covered jars, in four popular Fiesta colors.

As a final attempt to adapt production to modern-day techniques and methods, Fiesta was restyled in 1969. Of the original colors, only Fiesta Red remained. This line, called Fiesta Ironstone, was discontinued in 1973.

Two types of marks were used, an ink stamp on machine-jiggered pieces, and an indented mark molded into the hollow ware pieces.

In the listings below, 'original colors' indicates only five of the original six -- ivory, light green, cobalt, turquoise, and yellow. Red values are listed separately.

Ash tray, original colors...............................22.00
Ash tray, red & '50s colors............................28.00
Bowl, dessert, 6"; '50s colors.........................16.00
Bowl, dessert, 6"; original colors......................12.50
Bowl, dessert, 6"; red.................................20.00
Bowl, footed salad; original colors....................100.00

Bowl, footed salad; red...............................135.00
Bowl, fruit, 11½".....................................80.00
Bowl, fruit, 4¾"; '50s colors..........................10.00
Bowl, fruit, 4¾"; medium green.......................30.00
Bowl, fruit, 4¾"; original colors........................8.00
Bowl, fruit, 4¾"; red...................................12.00
Bowl, fruit, 5½"; medium green.......................18.00
Bowl, fruit, 5½"; original colors........................9.00
Bowl, fruit, 5½"; red & '50s colors.....................13.00
Bowl, individual salad.................................35.00
Bowl, individual salad; medium green..................40.00
Bowl, unlisted; yellow.................................35.00
Candle holders, bulb; original colors..................30.00
Candle holders, bulb; red.............................40.00
Candle holders, tripod; original colors.................95.00
Candle holders, tripod; red...........................125.00
Carafe, original colors.................................62.00
Carafe, red...90.00
Casserole, French; yellow............................120.00
Casserole, medium green..............................85.00
Casserole, original colors..............................42.00
Casserole, red & '50s colors...........................58.00
Coffee pot, '50s colors................................70.00
Coffee pot, demitasse; original colors..................85.00
Coffee pot, demitasse; red...........................100.00
Coffee pot, original colors.............................45.00
Coffee pot, red..58.00
Comport, sweets; original colors.......................20.00
Comport, sweets; red..................................32.00
Comport, 12"; original colors..........................42.00
Comport, 12"; red.....................................60.00
Creamer, individual; red...............................50.00
Creamer, individual; yellow............................27.50
Creamer, original colors................................6.50
Creamer, red, medium green & '50s colors...............12.00
Creamer, stick handle; original colors..................12.00
Creamer, stick handle; red.............................15.00
Cup & saucer, demitasse; '50s colors...................75.00
Cup & saucer, demitasse; original colors................24.00
Cup & saucer, demitasse; red..........................32.50
Cup & saucer, original colors...........................15.00
Cup & saucer, red & '50s colors........................18.50
Egg cup, '50s colors...................................40.00
Egg cup, original colors................................20.00
Egg cup, red..30.00
Gravy boat, original colors.............................16.00
Gravy boat, red & '50s colors..........................20.00
Marmalade, original colors.............................70.00
Marmalade, red.......................................85.00
Metal handle for 13" chop plate........................25.00
Metal holder for marmalade............................25.00
Mixing bowl, #1, original colors........................25.00
Mixing bowl, #2, original colors........................23.00
Mixing bowl, #3, original colors........................27.00
Mixing bowl, #4, original colors........................29.00
Mixing bowl, #6, original colors........................40.00
Mixing bowl, #7, original colors........................45.00
Mixing bowl, #8, any color.............................85.00
Mug, original colors...................................22.50
Mug, red, medium green & '50s colors...................45.00
Mustard, original colors................................50.00
Mustard, red..80.00
Nappy, 8½"; original colors............................13.00
Nappy, 8½"; red & '50s colors.........................18.50

Nappy, 9½″; original colors................................18.00
Nappy, 9½″; red..23.00
Pitcher, disc; chartreuse..................................55.00
Pitcher, disc; original colors.............................28.00
Pitcher, disc; red...38.00
Pitcher, disc; rose, dk gr & gray..........................45.00
Pitcher, ice lip; original colors..........................32.00
Pitcher, ice lip; red......................................50.00
Pitcher, jug, 2 pt; original colors........................23.00
Pitcher, jug, 2 pt; red & '50s colors......................32.00
Plate, chop, 13″; '50s colors..............................22.00
Plate, chop, 13″; original colors..........................12.50
Plate, chop, 13″; red......................................16.00
Plate, chop, 15″; '50s colors..............................26.00
Plate, chop, 15″; original colors..........................15.00
Plate, chop, 15″; red......................................20.00
Plate, compartment, 10½″; '50s colors......................20.00
Plate, compartment, 10½″; original colors..................12.00
Plate, compartment, 10½″; red..............................17.50
Plate, compartment, 11½″...................................22.00
Plate, deep; original colors...............................11.50
Plate, deep; red or '50s colors............................18.00
Plate, 10″; medium green...................................22.00
Plate, 10″; original colors.................................9.50
Plate, 10″; red & '50s colors..............................14.00
Plate, 6″; original colors..................................3.00
Plate, 6″; red, medium green & '50s colors..................4.50
Plate, 7″; original colors..................................4.50
Plate, 7″; red, medium green & '50s colors..................6.00
Plate, 9″; original colors..................................6.00
Plate, 9″; red, medium green & '50s colors.................10.00
Platter, original colors...................................11.50
Platter, red & '50s..20.00
Relish, multicolored.......................................57.50
Salt & peppers, original colors............................10.00
Salt & peppers, red & '50s colors..........................16.00
Soup, cream; '50s colors...................................22.00
Soup, cream; original colors...............................15.00
Soup, cream; red...20.00
Soup, onion; original colors..............................130.00
Soup, onion; red..150.00
Sta Brite tableware, 6 place settings......................45.00
Sugar, w/lid, '50s colors..................................14.50
Sugar, w/lid, original colors...............................9.50
Sugar, w/lid, red & medium green...........................20.00
Syrup, original colors.....................................80.00
Syrup, red..120.00
Teapot, large; original colors.............................50.00
Teapot, large; red & '50s colors...........................70.00
Teapot, medium; medium green..............................125.00
Teapot, medium; original colors............................40.00
Teapot, medium; red & '50s colors..........................56.00
Tom & Jerry, wht w/lettering...............................13.50
Tray, figure-8; cobalt.....................................30.00
Tray, figure-8; turquoise..................................50.00
Tray, figure-8; yellow.....................................65.00
Tray, utility; original colors.............................13.00
Tray, utility; red...20.00
Tumbler, juice; original colors............................13.50
Tumbler, juice; rose & red.................................15.00
Tumbler, 10 oz; red..28.00
Tumbler, 10 oz; regular colors.............................21.50
Vase, bud; original colors.................................24.00
Vase, bud; red...35.00

Left: Carafe, original colors, $62.00.
Right: Ice-lip pitcher, original colors, $32.00.

Vase, 10″; original colors................................175.00
Vase, 10″; red..225.00
Vase, 12″; original colors................................190.00
Vase, 12″; red..250.00
Vase, 8″; original colors.................................150.00
Vase, 8″; red...200.00

Kitchen Kraft

Cake plate, other than red.................................24.00
Cake plate, red..30.00
Casserole, individual; other than red......................50.00
Casserole, individual; red.................................65.00
Casserole, 7½″; other than red.............................55.00
Casserole, 7½″; red..65.00
Casserole, 8½″; other than red.............................60.00
Casserole, 8½″; red..70.00
Fork...30.00
Jar, large; other than red................................125.00
Jar, large; red...135.00
Jar, medium; other than red...............................110.00
Jar, medium; red..130.00
Jar, small; other than red................................100.00
Jar, small; red...125.00
Jug...135.00
Pie plate, 10″; in frame...................................50.00
Pie plate, 10″; other than red.............................28.00
Pie plate, 10″; red..35.00
Pie plate, 9″; other than red..............................25.00
Pie plate, 9″; red...32.00
Platter, in frame..70.00
Platter, without frame.....................................50.00
Salt & peppers, other than red.............................40.00
Salt & peppers, red..50.00
Server...38.00
Spoon, other than red......................................30.00
Spoon, red...38.00
Stack set..80.00
Stack set, lid only..25.00

Finch, Kay

Kay Finch and her husband Braden operated a small pottery in Corona Del Mar, California, from 1939 until the mid-1960s. The company remained small, employing from twenty to forty local residents who Kay trained in all but the most requiring tasks, which she herself performed. The company produced animal and bird figurines, most notably dogs, Kay's favorites. Figures of 'Godey' type ladies were also made, as were dinnerware and tiles. Most pieces were marked with her name -- incised, ink stamped, or painted.

Figurine, lady w/muff.....................................38.00
Plaque, w/dog...12.00

Rooster figure, purple, blue, green and ivory, 11″, $60.00.

Findlay Onyx

Findlay, Ohio, was the location of the Dalzell, Gilmore, and Leighton Glass Company, one of at least sixteen companies that flourished there between 1886 and 1901. Their most famous ware, Onyx, is very rare. It was produced in 1889, in several colors -- cream, rose, raspberry, and amber among them – developed by layering two or three compatible shades together. Lustre trapped between the layers accented the dainty pattern. Heavy losses were incurred in the manufacturing process, and it was made for only a short time.

Celery, custard...500.00
Salt shaker, cream, single................................245.00

Covered jar, cream, 5¾″, $425.00.

Sugar shaker. custard....................................300.00
Sugar w/lid, custard, EX.................................425.00
Toothpick, custard......................................200.00
Tumbler, 3½″...250.00
Vase, custard w/silver, 4″...............................225.00

Fire Fighting Collectibles

Fire fighting collectibles from the early 19th century reflect the feeling of pride the men had in their brigades and in their roll as volunteer fire fighters. Dress uniforms and fancy helmets recall the charisma of the unit on parade. The leather buckets; blown glass, liquid-filled fire extinguishers; and brass hatchets serve as reminders of their heroism and dedication to their calling.

In the 1860s, volunteer units were replaced by municipal fire departments. Equipment evolved from horse-drawn wagons and bucket brigades to fire engines and water wagons with hoses. Today, many collectors find a fascination with these fire fighting relics of the past.

Axe, wood hdl, red/blk decor, G..........................25.00
Badge, crossed wrenches w/owners name....................45.00
Badge, emb steam engine/hooks/ladders/hose, silver look, early..55.00
Badge, gold, hat shield form w/high eagle helmet............230.00
Bag, salvage; cloth w/stencil, VG........................60.00
Banner, 'Welcome' w/fireman, 68x72″, G..................130.00
Banner, parade; w/trumpet/axe/hat/etc....................95.00
Bell, Fire Chief's; faceted, jeweled lights in top, hood mt......135.00
Belt, blk leather, mustard/wht letters: Wakefield #1 WA........85.00
Belt, parade, blk leather w/wht: Beverly Fair Play 3, keeper.....95.00
Belt, parade, leather, Newton, w/keeper..................35.00
Belt, parade, Wm Penn Fire Assoc, blk w/red & wht letters.....65.00
Book, Fires & Firefighters, John V Morris, 1st edition, G.......55.00
Book, Romance of Firefighting, Robert S Holzman, 1956.......35.00
Box, fire alarm; Gamewell, w/key, 1924, rstr................150.00
Box, fire alarm; Gamewell, working, 1935..................75.00
Box, fire alarm; Horni, cottage, rebuilt...................125.00
Box, Gamewell, Fire Alarm Telegraph Station, cottage w/light..175.00
Broadside, constitution, bylaws & rules of order, 1866, 20″.....45.00
Broadside, Eastern Fire Ins Co, Atlantic City, 20x25″..........20.00
Broadside, Howard & Davis Fire Engines...................150.00
Broadside, Silsby Mfg Co, color, 18x23″...................475.00
Broadside, St Paul Fire & Marine Ins Co, calendar for 1909....55.00
Bucket, leather, blk w/lg oval w/orange/blk letters, needs rpr...175.00
Bucket, leather, blk w/red interior pnt late addition, VG........85.00
Bucket, leather, blk/yellow name & date, 1783, hdl rpl, o/w G..110.00
Bucket, leather, gr pnt w/blk & wht scrolls, dtd 1828, pr......450.00
Bucket, leather, HP Mercury w/trumpet/name/slogan/1806, G...550.00
Bucket, leather, HP spread wing phoenix/flames/slogan........450.00
Bucket, leather, Masonic design on mustard w/name, pnt poor...85.00
Bucket, leather, pnt X arrows, imp Tilley, worn, 12″..........200.00
Button, brass, w/hand tub, lot of 9.......................37.50
Button, w/steamer & city ID, lot of 6.....................22.50
Cane, presentation, wood w/GP 'L' hdl w/inscription, 1895.....300.00
Catalog, Fire Dept Supplies & Equip NE Fire Appliance Co, '29.75.00
Catalog, Woodhouse Mfg Co, 1931.........................50.00
Certificate, engraving w/hand tub, hose cart, etc, dtd 1843......75.00
Certificate, exempt, dtd 1914, in fr, 25½x31½″.............85.00
Chamber, air expansion, copper/brass, dvtl, 13″, G...........80.00
Chemical Fire Cart, ca 1900.............................650.00
Clamp, hose; wood w/iron mountings, red pnt, VG............190.00
Coat, dress; long navy wool w/30 brass buttons, w/hat, 1900....50.00
Extinguisher, Am La France, w/mounting bracket, 24″, G.......75.00
Extinguisher, glass keg, Hazeltons High Pressure, amber, full...130.00
Extinguisher, Manville Fire Ext, w/contents................60.00

Fire bucket, decorated with painting of Mercury, owner's name, dated 1806, leather, minor restoration, $550.00.

Extinguisher, Phoenix Dry Chem, w/contents 65.00
Extinguisher, Pyrene Fire Ext, hand held, brass w/hanger, 14" . .35.00
Extinguisher, solid copper/brass, refurbished 85.00
Gong, brass on iron bk panel, 11" dia .150.00
Hat front, leather, Fire Warden, very early 200.00
Hat front, leather shield HP w/coat of arms/etc, 8", G 100.00
Hat front, St John Fire Dept, leather, pr 35.00
Hat shield, presentation, leather, 9½", G 225.00
Helmet, aluminum, mk HFD, pnt blk, Cairns 25.00
Helmet, aluminum, pnt red/blk, 'Memphis-2-Fire Dept', Cairns . . .45.00
Helmet, aluminum blk, H&L-1 LFD, made by Cairns 35.00
Helmet, aluminum wht, 'Chaplain-EPFD', Cairns 65.00
Helmet, blk pnt leather, tooled, brass serpent holder, Cairns . . .650.00
Helmet, fiberglass, w/liner, 'Ladder-1-AFD', w/face shield 25.00
Helmet, fiberglass wht, 'Miss Birmingham-Fire Prevention' 25.00
Helmet, hi-eagle, rose border on rim, Winship & Co, VG 125.00
Helmet, hi-eagle chief's, badge center front, SF Hayward Co 75.00
Helmet, hi-eagle leather, on hat ft: Libery E&H-1-FJM, Cairns . .175.00
Helmet, hi-eagle parade, tooled hat ft w/stitching/cut stars 275.00
Helmet, hi-eagle parade, torch atop, pnt red, leather front 325.00
Helmet, hi-eagle parade, 64 combs, wht w/tooled hat front/1891 .150.00
Helmet, jockey style, G 200.00
Helmet, jockey style hi-eagle, red w/brass eagle: Cairns 150.00
Helmet, leather, #28 on front, w/liner/eye shield, Cairns 95.00
Helmet, leather, running fireman holder, by Cairns, dtd 1879 . . .250.00
Helmet, leather fire hat w/hi-eagle holder, vines at brim 175.00
Helmet, leather w/brass trim/blk pnt, mk Cairns & Bro, 14½" . . .70.00
Helmet, parade, wht, hi-eagle front holder, leather letters, G . . .205.00
Helmet, presentation hi-eagle leather, badge dtd 1910 . . . . .225.00
Horn, SP, floral engraved/emb birds/figures, 1877, 22" 395.00
Hydrant, CI, emb: Mueller Co/Chattanooga/Pat'd, orig paint 100.00
Lamp, candle, hook/ladder, brass/tin, curved clear front panel . .275.00
Lantern, Dietz, brass, bell bottom w/telescoping shield, EX 45.00
Lantern, Dietz King, copper/brass/tin w/iron hanging bracket . . .130.00
Lantern, Dietz King, solid brass, clear globe, pat Aug 17/07 . . . .300.00
Lantern, Dietz King, tin w/copper base, pat Aug 07, G 100.00
Lantern, presentation Chief type hand, White/pat 1874, 19" 700.00
Lantern, Rayo, metal, oil, 17" w/hdl 25.00
Lantern, wrist; clear lens, nickeled, orig oil burner, 19" 250.00
Name plate, steam engine; #754, 1882, brass/nickle, 7x9" 275.00

Name plate, steam engine; Portland-2, brass, fr w/badges/etc . . .500.00
Nozzle, brass, AJ Morse, Boston, 17" 85.00
Nozzle, brass, mk AJ Morse & Son, 14", pr 45.00
Nozzle, brass, rubber grips/control valve, 1920s, 26" 160.00
Nozzle, brass w/brass hdls, Poweron P-4-A Am LaFrance, 10" . .25.00
Nozzle, brass w/flow control, 7½", G 30.00
Nozzle, brass w/shut off, mk Boston Woven Hose Co, 8" 20.00
Nozzle, chrome plated brass, control valve/leather hdls, 10" 110.00
Nozzle, fog; Rockwood Sprinkler Co, 10" 50.00
Photo, Boston fireman, framed oval w/matt, 14¾x12½" 25.00
Photo, ladder truck w/7 firemen, early motorized apparatus 40.00
Pin-back, Arcade Hook & Ladder Co, w/torch/axe/ladder, 1909 . .20.00
Pipe, brass/copper, Boyd & Sons, 36" L 115.00
Pipe, copper/brass play, red cord wrap, Allen FD Supply, 30" . . .65.00
Punch, Gamewell paper tape punch & take up reel, 1" tape 200.00
Repeater, Gamewell, 6 stations/weights/power supply, 40½" 800.00
Salvage bag, w/name/1870, orig drawstring, 54x21", EX 80.00
Sign, pnt blk w/gold: Hose 1, sgn Evans, 13"x9½ ft 275.00
Siren, w/red light combination, Sterling Siren Co, 1928 . . . . .80.00
Torch, parade; brass on wood pole w/oil burner font, 63" 175.00
Torch, parade; fireman's axe form, wood/tin, 38" 600.00
Torch, parade; nickel over brass on trn wood hdl, 29", G 200.00
Torch, parade; wood w/oil font, blk pnt/simulated flames, 21" . .110.00
Transmitter, Gamewell, brass mechanism/bevel glass door/oak . . .950.00
Truck, pumper, ca 1872, G 3,750.00
Trumpet, brass w/presentation plate dtd 1909, 23½" 250.00
Trumpet, parade; SP, cord/tassel, muster badge attached, 17" . .325.00
Trumpet, parade; SP w/cord, 20" 225.00
Trumpet, presentation grade, SP w/florals/medallions, 23" 650.00
Trumpet, speaking; brass, ca 1870, 18½" 350.00

Fire Marks

During the early 18th century, insurance companies used fire marks -- signs of insurance -- to indicate to the volunteer fire fighters which homes were covered by their company. Handsome rewards were promised to the brigade that successfully extinguished the blaze, so competition was fierce between rivals, and sometimes resulted in an altercation at the scene to settle the matter of which brigade would be the one to fight the fire!

Fire marks were originally made of cast iron or lead; later examples were sometimes tin or zinc. They were used abroad as well as in this country, and those from England tended to be much more elaborate.

When municipal fire departments were organized in the mid- to late 1860s, the volunteer departments and fire marks became obsolete.

Eagle Fire Insurance Co, copper, oval w/eagle/rose/shamrocks . .500.00
Fire Assoc of Phila, CI, relief FA w/hydrant & hose, 11½x7½" .175.00
Fire Association of Phila, CI oval, 12x16" 225.00
German, blk pnt on tin w/gold eagle, 'Thuringia', 5x7", G 25.00
Guardian, copper, emb female, 9x8½", VG 110.00
Hartford, tin 115.00
Liverpool & London & Globe 90.00
Royal Ins Co, copper 100.00
Sun, copper, English 40.00
United Firemans, CI, old 145.00

Fireplace Implements

In the colonial days of our country, fireplaces provided heat in the winter, and were used year round to cook food in the kitchen. The implements that were a necessary part of these functions were varied and have become treasured collectibles today, many put to new use in modern homes as decorative accessories. Gypsy pots may hold magazines; copper and brass kettles, newly polished and gleaming, contain dried flowers or green plants. Firebacks, highly ornamental iron panels that once reflected heat and protected masonry walls, are now sometimes used as wall decorations.

By Victorian times, the cookstove had replaced the kitchen fireplace, and many of these early utensils were already obsolete. But as a source of heat and comfort, the fireplace continued to be used for several more decades.

Andirons, brass, lemon finials, rstr iron log rests, 1700s......340.00
Andirons, brass, scalloped skirt/lg ball finials/ball ft, 1800.....325.00
Andirons, brass, trn w/ball finials, spur on legs, 1700s, 18"....250.00
Andirons, brass w/spurred arch supports, ball ft, Federal, 12"..150.00
Andirons, brass/wrought iron, ball finial/spur arch, 1800, 14"...660.00
Andirons, brass/wrought iron, Federal, lemon finial, 15".....1,045.00
Andirons, brass/wrought iron, J Davis, 1800, 16"...........715.00
Andirons, Hessian soldier w/sword, CI, 1800, 19½".........825.00
Andirons, seated cats w/eye holes, CI, no supports, 16".......30.00
Andirons, seated dogs w/foliage scroll bases, CI, 14"........50.00
Andirons, wrought iron, ram's horn finials, 14"...........115.00
Andirons, wrought iron knife blade, penny ft, brass balls, 15"..185.00
Bellows, orig pntd shell/foliage, brass nozzle, top split, 18"....100.00
Bellows, turtle bk, orig pnt/stencil, leather G, brass nozzle......85.00
Bread peel, wrought iron, diamond faceted hdl, 44" long.......75.00
Broiler, revolving, hand wrought, ca 1780, 14" dia.........240.00
Broiler, rotating, 3 ftd, unusual 9" square top, 19" overall.....185.00
Crane, hand forged iron, 1700s, 24" L................95.00
Crane, wrought iron, hook on end, 43"................95.00
Fender, brass w/reticulated design, 6x36".............50.00
Fender, Geo III, engraved brass bow front, early 1800s, 54" L..350.00
Fire dog, wrought iron, dog form w/4 legs, 1700s, 7x12".....175.00
Grate, floral molded bkplate, serpentine firebox, steel/CI......650.00
Grate, serpentine, floral engraved brass, Federal, 31x39".....850.00
Griddle, hanging, 1 pc arm w/crane hook, early 1700s, 13" dia.225.00
Hanging pan, spouted, w/hanging ring, 11" dia...........65.00
Hearth broom, trn hdl, red/blk graining w/striping, 28" hdl.....60.00
Kettle tipper, wrought iron, 19"...................85.00
Lid lifter, wood hdl, thimble ferrule, 4½" hook, 5½" hdl.......50.00
Mantle, pine, country, simple pilasters/shelf, stripped, 54" W....85.00
Screen, Victorian style, brass, fan shape, 28"...........250.00
Shovel, wrought iron, knob hdl, 27"................45.00
Stove plate, CI w/2 arch panels/urn of tulips/heart, 1762, 24"..770.00

Cast iron fireplace surround, designed by Hector Guimard, circa 1900, 35½", $1,430.00.

Toaster, flip style, 12" across, 21" hdl................89.00
Toaster, w/2 sets of sq bars across, 3 ftd, dk wood 18" hdl....185.00
Tongs, wrought iron, sm brass finial, 19" L.............15.00
Tongs, wrought iron, 25" L.....................25.00
Tools, iron/brass, lemon finials, shovel & tongs, 33".......150.00
Trammel, sawtooth, hand wrought, 1750s, 9½" open........130.00
Trivet, CI, 3 ftd, 5½x7½" dia...................49.00
Trivet, wrought iron, 3 lg ft, 4x7" dia...............60.00
Trivet, 3 legs, rnd top w/3 arrow prongs, 6½x9" dia........45.00

Fischer

Fine porcelain has been produced in the Herend area of Hungary since the late 18th century. In 1839 Moritz Fischer founded a pottery that continues today to produce hard paste porcelain dinnerware, vases, and figurines similar to those of Sevres and Meissen.

Charger, red decor w/gold tracing, 13" dia..............345.00
Jar, allover multicolor florals, gold traced, 9½"..........250.00
Mug, lustre flowers all over, gold trim, 5½"............100.00
Pitcher, mc flowers, gold trim, reticulated top, 13".........435.00
Pitcher, reticulated, cobalt w/floral reserves, gold trim........450.00
Tray, shell shape, reticulated, polychrome/gold, 8½x13½".....215.00
Vase, Chinese Bouquet, gold/enamel, flat sides, sgn/#d, 13"....245.00
Vase, reticulated flowers at neck, floral body, gold trim, 11"...240.00
Vase, reticulated mc pansies, 4 dk bl ring top hdls, Emil, 10"..200.00
Wine jug, gold w/bl & yellow florals, 11"..............325.00

Fishing Collectibles

Fishing as a sport was unheard of in America before 1800. During the 19th century one patent after another was issued for various reels, rods, and arificial plugs. Today's collector may choose to specialize in one area only . . . some search for wooden plugs, while others are interested in the products of one specific manufacturer.

Early plugs from around the turn of the century were made almost entirely of wood, with the exception of a few crude attempts at molding plastic, by James Heddon, Shakespeare, Rhodes, and Pflueger, to note the most successful. A considerable amount of hand work was involved; some plugs were sprayed with several layers of high quality enamel to achieve finishes such as 'silver flash' or 'frog scale', and often glass eyes were added to give the finished lure a realistic appearance. Metal propellors or blades were an added attraction, but whether they were more successful at attracting the fish or a potential buyer in a very competitive market is debatable.

Fishing gear as a collectible is a hobby only newly established, so market values are variable. Older plugs are most valuable; condition is very important, and original cartons add to net worth.

Book, Determined Angler, pocket volume, 1900...........20.00
Catalog, 1937 Wright & McGill, 68 pgs, EX.............10.00
Creel, tight woven wicker, leather strap/bait tray, EX.........80.00
Decoy, bass, wood w/5 tin fins & tail, pnt details, 1930s, 5½"...65.00
Decoy, carved wood w/metal fin/tack eyes/pnt, 6"..........32.00
Decoy, cut-out & bent sheet copper/pnt details, 1930s, 6"......48.00
Decoy, jigsaw cut-out, w/lead weight, tack eyes, pnt, 9".......35.00
Decoy, Northern Pike, deep gills, 5 tin fins, trn tail, 11".......70.00
Decoy, Northern Pike, pnt wood w/tin fins & tail, 1930s, 9".....58.00
Decoy, perch, wood w/metal fins, tack eyes, orig pnt, 14".......75.00
Decoy, pike, carved wood w/metal fins/glass eyes/pnt, 10" Collectibles.55.00
Decoy, pike, modern, carved wood/metal fins/orig pnt, 11".......40.00
Decoy, primitive, wood w/metal fins, tack eyes, 7¾"..........18.00
Decoy, tin tail, 2 lg fins, pnt dots, glass insert eyes, 8"........45.00

Decoy, carved wood with metal fins, painted green and yellow, 6", $48.00.

Decoy, tin tail, 4 fins, cut-out mouth, tack eyes, striped, 8".....45.00
Decoy, wood w/copper fins & tail, worn wht pnt/polka dots, 8½".35.00
Decoy, wood w/metal fin, worn old rpt, 15"...................95.00
Decoy, wood w/tack eyes, weighted belly, glued tail, 15½".....85.00
Fish spear, no hdls, iron, 3 barbed prongs..................30.00
Lure, Arbogast, Hawaiian Wiggler, ca 1930...................7.00
Lure, Arbogast, Hula Popper, ca 1948.......................6.00
Lure, Arbogast, Jitterbug, plastic, ca 1937.................6.00
Lure, Arbogast, Jitterbug, wood, ca 1937..................14.00
Lure, Arbogast, Weedless Kicker, frog or silver finish, 1929.....14.00
Lure, frog, wood w/glass bead eyes, primitive, 4¾" L.........28.00
Lure, Harry F Drake, Sea-bait, ca 1932, red & wht...........17.00
Lure, Heddon, #200 Surface Bait, red/wht/blue..............42.00
Lure, Heddon, #50 Artistic Minnow, yel w/feathers or bucktail...50.00
Lure, Tony Accetta, Jugolet, ca 1941.......................6.00
Lure, Torpedo Ray, ice fishing, wood......................12.50
Minnow bucket, polished copper, extra lg..................190.00
Mold, CI, for making lead sinkers, hinged..................25.00
Net float, aqua glass, SH Davis Co, pat Jan 16, 1877, 5x3x3½".65.00
Reel, AF Meisselbach, NJ, #2605..........................50.00
Reel, fly; Shakespeare, Model HB.........................25.00
Reel, Hendryx, pat 1876-88..............................200.00
Reel, Horricks Ibson 'Shark'.............................12.00
Reel, Pleuger Akron, #1893, bait casting...................18.00
Reel, Ramsbottom, YB...................................185.00
Reel, Shakespeare, 1914.................................10.00
Reel, Shakespeare Criterion #1960.........................8.00
Reel, Sunnybrook Union Hardware #8010....................5.00
Reel, Wm Slote, NY, wood, rnd, brass plate, 2 wood knobs.....60.00
Rod, bamboo, Winchester.................................85.00
Rod, fly; South Bend, split bamboo, #359, 9 ft.............165.00
Rod, fly; split bamboo, 1927, 9 ft, rstr, pr................140.00
Rod & reel, Winchester.................................140.00
Speargun head, bronze, 5" arrow w/upward flair tail..........18.50

Flags

One of the earliest American flags was displayed in 1775. Called 'Continental Colors', it consisted of a red field with a 'Union Jack' and six white stripes. During the Revolution other designs and mottos, such as the rattle snake 'don't tread on me' flag, made symbolic statements pertinent to the times.

Soon after the United States was declared an independent nation, the Union Jack was replaced by stars, representing the free states. Since then, as our country expanded, so did the number of stars, with various arrangements of circles and rows having been used. Of most interest to serious collectors of American flags are those with thirty-seven stars or less, and those which are hand stitched. Design, size, construction, scarcity, and condition are factors to be considered in arriving at a fair market price. Reproductions or commemorative flags have little or no value.

Larger American Flags of All Sewn Construction (4 ft. fly and up; ordinary star patterns)

49-48   star..5.00-25.00
46-44   star.......................................25.00-55.00
43 star, rare.......................................Negotiable
42-38   star......................................55.00-100.00
37-34   star.....................................100.00-200.00
33 stars or less................................200.00 and up

Larger All Printed American Flags (over 2x3 ft.; silk most preferred)--50%-75% of above listing.

Smaller All Printed American Flags (up to 2x3 ft.; silk most preferred)--20%-50% of above listing.

Printed 'Flaglets' (5"x7" or less). Most have 37 stars or less, usually printed on glazed muslin, and are latter day commemoratives.......1.00-5.00

American Flags of Unusual or Special Design ('great star' patterns, wreath patterns, etc.)--150%-200% of above prices for ordinary patterns.

American Flags of Proven Historical Significance (military, political, etc.)--Negotiable--some priced just slightly above the norm, but potentially the highest priced category of American flags.

13 Star American Flags/Naval Ensigns--Priced according to above listings, by age.

Florence Ceramics

Figurines marked 'Florence Ceramics' were produced in the forties and fifties in Pasadena, California. The quality of the ware and the attention given to detail are prompting a growing interest among today's collectors. These lovely ladies, gents, and figural groups are nearly always identified by the name incised in the base.

Louis XV and Madam Pompadour, 12", $250.00 for the pair.

Amber 75.00
Amelia 60.00
Belle 45.00
Beth 35.00
Camille, 8½″ 65.00
Charmaine, minor lace damage, 9″ 65.00
Grace, 8″ 65.00
Irene, gray dress, gold/red neck muff, 5¾″ 38.00
Kay, 6″ 45.00
Lillian, 7½″ 60.00
Melanie 65.00
Oriental man w/musical instrument, 10½″ 65.00
Rhett, wht clothing, 9″ 60.00
Sarah, green glaze 50.00
Story Book Hour, mother & child, one base 150.00
Sue 38.50
Victor & Charmaine, each 9″, pr 125.00
Wall vase, 7″ 22.00

Flow Blue

Flow Blue ware was produced by many Staffordshire potters, among the most familiar were Meigh, Podmore and Walker, Samuel Alcock, Ridgway, John Wedge Wood (who often signed his work Wedgwood), and Davenport. It was popular from about 1825 through 1860, and again from 1880 until the turn of the century. The name describes the blurred or flowing affect of the cobalt decoration, achieved through the introduction of a chemical vapor into the kiln. The body of the ware is ironstone, and Oriental motifs were favored. Later issues were on a lighter body, and often decorated with gilt.

La Belle bowl, flower handles, gold trim, 12″, $145.00.

Abbey, teapot, Geo Jones 69.00
Alaska, creamer, Grindley 65.00
Albany, butter pat, Grindley 18.00
Albany, cereal, deep, Grindley 45.00
Albany, cup & saucer, coffee; Grindley 48.00
Albany, pie plate 12.00
Albany, plate, Grindley, 7¾″ 18.00
Albany, sauce dish, Johnson Bros 15.00
Albion, plate, 1882, 9″ 20.00
Amoy, plate, 10½″ 52.00
Amoy, plate, 8½″ 42.00
Amoy, soup plate, Davenport, 10½″ 95.00

Amoy, sugar bowl, Davenport 195.00
Amoy, sugar w/lid, Davenport, 7½″ 300.00
Amoy, vegetable, rectangular, Davenport, 8x5¾″ 145.00
Amoy, wash pitcher, Davenport 475.00
Andorra, gravy boat 75.00
Anemone, pitcher, dragon hdl, Bishop & Stenier 100.00
Anemone, soup plate, Minton, 10½″ 85.00
Anemone, soup tureen & tray, rnd, Minton 850.00
Arabesque, cup, Mayer 40.00
Arabesque, gravy boat, Mayer 115.00
Arabesque, plate, Mayer, 9½″ 65.00
Argyle, cup & saucer 45.00
Argyle, pitcher 105.00
Argyle, plate, dinner; Grindley 58.00
Argyle, plate, luncheon; Grindley 32.00
Argyle, plate, pie; Grindley 30.00
Argyle, sauce, Johnson 20.00
Argyle, sauce boat, Johnson 75.00
Argyle, sauce tureen, w/lid, rnd 150.00
Argyle, vegetable w/lid 185.00
Ashburton, bone dish, Grindley, EX 35.00
Ashburton, plate, Grindley, 1891, 10″ 30.00
Ashburton, platter, 16″ 85.00
Asiatic Pheasant, plate, Adams, 11″ 90.00
Aster, jardiniere, lg 195.00
Astoria, bowl, Johnson Bros, 10″ dia 65.00
Ayr, butter pat, Corn, EX 20.00
Ayr, platter, W & E Corn, 10″ 40.00
Balmoral, hot water dish w/cork 250.00
Baltic, bowl, cereal; Grindley 30.00
Bamboo, plate, edge rough, Alcock, 10½″ 70.00
Basket, coffee saucer, lg 30.00
Basket, cup & saucer 95.00
Beauty Roses, sugar & creamer, Grindley, 1914, pr 69.00
Belmont, bowl, covered vegetable; Ford 155.00
Belmont, plate, 7½″ 22.50
Bisley, bowl, 6¾″ 15.00
Bisley, plate, 6″ 12.00
Blue Rose, berry bowl, Grindley, 6″ 35.00
Bombay, bowl, 8″ 50.00
Botanical, toothbrush holder w/lid 185.00
Brunswick, cup & saucer 39.00
Brush Stroke, child's teapot 250.00
Brush Stroke, cup plate, Dimmock 40.00
Brush Stroke, mug, grape leaf design, base chip 95.00
Brush Stroke, pitcher, copper lustre, tea leaf type, Allerton 115.00
Burleigh, chop plate, round, Burgess & Leigh, 13½″ 95.00
Burleigh, plate, 9½″ 27.00
Byzantium, bowl, Cauldon, 9″ 32.00
Cabul, vegetable, rnd; Edwards 135.00
California, plate, Wedgwood, 8″ 42.00
California, plate, Wedgwood, 9½″ 48.00
Cambridge, milk pitcher, New Wharf, 1891 . . . . 170.00
Candia, sauce, Cauldon, set of 6 . . . . 75.00
Canton, plate, Edwards, 10½″ 80.00
Canton, plate, Maddock, 7¾″ 35.00
Cashmere, custard cup, scalloped, Francis Morley 45.00
Cashmere, plate, 6½″ 48.00
Cecil, pitcher, Grimwade, 6½″ 100.00
Celtic, platter, Grindley, 12½x8½″ 70.00
Ceylon, cup & saucer, Furnival 45.00
Chapoo, cup & saucer, demitasse; John Wedge Wood 95.00
Chapoo, plate, John Wedge Wood, 9½″ 70.00
Chapoo, platter, 14″ 195.00

Chapoo, sauce dish, John Wedge Wood....................45.00
Chapoo, saucer, John Wedge Wood.......................35.00
Chapoo, vegetable w/lid, rectangular....................395.00
Charger, cherubs decor...................................130.00
Chatsworth, platter.....................................130.00
Chinese, plate, Dimmock, 7¾".............................35.00
Chinese, sauce tureen, Dimmock.........................175.00
Chrysanthemum, tea cup & saucer, 1855...................65.00
Chusan, plate, Clementson, 10½"..........................95.00
Chusan, saucer, PW Co...................................25.00
Circassia, soup, 10½"....................................65.00
Circassia, teapot.......................................195.00
Clarence, platter, Wood & Sons, 10¾" oval...............35.00
Clifton, plate, 10".....................................37.50
Clifton, water pitcher, Grindley, lg....................220.00
Coburg, plate, 10½"......................................85.00
Coburg, platter, 18"....................................275.00
Colonial, plate, 9", Meakin.............................30.00
Colonial, vegetable w/lid, rnd; Meakin..................140.00
Colonna, soap dish, 3 pcs...............................45.00
Conway, bowl, New Wharf, 9" dia.........................44.00
Conway, plate, 10"......................................39.00
Conway, plate, 9", New Wharf Pottery....................32.00
Conway, platter, oval, 10½x8"...........................45.00
Conway, saucer, New Wharf...............................18.00
Countess, plate, Grindley, 8"...........................30.00
Country Scenes, berry set, master+6 sm berries.........225.00
Cows, plate, Wedgwood & Co, 9½".........................50.00
Crawford Cooking Range, advertising pitcher, Wood & Sons...135.00
Crumlin, vegetable w/lid, Myott & Sons, hairline in lid, 9¾"....85.00
Dainty, bone dish, Maddock..............................45.00
Dahlia, gravy boat, E Challinor, under rim chip.........95.00
Delamere, cereal bowl, Alcock, under rim chip, 6½"......18.00
Delamere, plate, Henry Alcock, 8½"......................35.00
Delft, plate, 10".......................................37.50
Delft, sauce tureen w/lid, oval, Wood & Sons............65.00
Denton, butter dish, Grindley..........................100.00
Devon, bowl, serving; rnd, Meakin.......................75.00
Devon, cup & saucer.....................................45.00
Dorothy, bowl, covered vegetable; Corn..................75.00
Duchess, gravy & under plate, Grindley..................40.00
Duchess, plate, 7"......................................22.00
Dunbarton, bone dish, New Wharf Pottery, set of 8......190.00
Dundee, creamer, Ridgways...............................05.00
Eclipse, platter, Johnson Bros, 14".....................95.00
Elgar, cake plate, Upper Hanley, 10¼"...................25.00
Elgar, creamer & sugar, Upper Hanley...................125.00
Elgar, plate, Upper Hanley, 7"..........................10.00
Elgar, plate, Upper Hanley, 8"..........................12.00
Elgar, platter, oval, sm, Upper Hanley..................15.00
Elgar, vegetable, oval, Upper Hanley....................15.00
Elsa, plate, W & E Corn, 9".............................42.00
Elsie, tureen, w/lid, 6 ft, Wedgwood & Co..............165.00
Fairy Villas, bowl, Adams, 10"..........................75.00
Fairy Villas, bowl, covered vegetable; W Adams.........220.00
Fairy Villas, butter dish cover only, Adams, 2¾x5½".....45.00
Fairy Villas, cup & saucer, rpr rim chip, Adams.........30.00
Fairy Villas, pitcher, W Adams & Co, 9"................185.00
Fairy Villas, plate, 9".................................34.00
Fairy Villas II, individual vegetable, Adams, 5½x4x1"...28.00
Fairy Villas III, plate, Adams, 7¾".....................28.00
Fairy Villas III, soup plate w/flange, Adams, 9".......40.00
Fern, cup & saucer......................................85.00
Florence, chocolate pot, Bennett, 1890.................200.00

Florentine, platter, 13"................................55.00
Florida, bone dish, Johnson.............................20.00
Florida, bowl, mush; Grindley...........................85.00
Florida, bowl, open, Grindley, 8".......................35.00
Florida, cup, Johnson...................................30.00
Florida, gravy boat, Grindley...........................40.00
Florida, gravy boat, Johnson............................40.00
Florida, plate, Johnson, 7".............................25.00
Florida, plate, Johnson, 9".............................30.00
Florida, platter, Grindley, 10".........................40.00
Florida, sauce dish, Grindley...........................18.00
Flower, platter, Heath, 13½"...........................135.00
Formosa, bowl, soup; Mayer..............................85.00
Formosa, plate, Mayer, 9½"..............................80.00
Formosa, platter, Mayer, 15¾x12".......................275.00
Formosa, vegetable dish, open, Mayer, 12¾x10¼".........185.00
Gainsborough, compote, ped base, fluted edge, Ridgways, 2x9"..145.00
Gainsborough, plate, 9".................................20.00
Geisha, cup & saucer, Meakin............................40.00
Geisha, plate, Meakin, 9"...............................40.00
Geisha, tureen, Upper Hanley Pottery...................250.00
Geneva, tureen tray w/hdls, Doulton, 12½", EX..........125.00
Genevese, teapot, sq form, EM & Co, 5¾"................135.00
Georgia, platter..95.00
Gironde, bone dish, Grindley, EX........................30.00
Gironde, platter, Grindley, 10x15", EX..................90.00
Gladys, bowl, New Wharf Pottery, 8" dia.................50.00
Gothic, plate, Furnival, 7¼"............................30.00
Granada, sugar, no lid, Alcock..........................45.00
Grecian Statue, butter dish drainer only, Brownfield....65.00
Hindustan, platter, Maddock, 13½"......................110.00
Hofburg, gravy boat.....................................35.00
Hofburg, sugar w/lid....................................90.00
Holland, plate, Cauldon, England, 8"....................32.00
Holland, plate, Johnson Bros, 9"........................40.00
Honc, bowl, Petros Regout, Holland, 3¼x6", EX..........125.00
Hong Kong, plate, Meigh, 7¼"............................60.00
Hong Kong, sugar w/lid, Meigh..........................245.00
Hudson, gravy boat, J&G Meakin..........................45.00
Idris, plate, Grindley, 10".............................28.00
Idris, platter, pin nick on edge, 12"...................30.00
India, saucer, Villeroy & Boch..........................12.00
Indian, sauce tureen/under plate, inside rim chip, Pratt...195.00
Indian Jar, cup, Furnival...............................45.00
Indian Jar, cup & saucer, paneled, Furnival.............78.00
Indian Jar, plate, Furnival, pin head nick, 7½".........35.00
Indian Jar, plate, glaze worn, Furnival, 9".............45.00
Indian Jar, platter, Furnival..........................300.00
Irene, gravy boat.......................................38.00
Iris, cup & saucer, demitasse; Royal Potteries, Staffordshire...20.00
Iris, plate, Royal Potteries, Staffordshire, 10¼".......35.00
Italian Urn, plate, 10".................................35.00
Janette, bone dish......................................32.00
Japan, plate, Fell, 6½".................................35.00
Japanese, milk pitcher, henna/yellow over pnt, W&R, hairline....95.00
Jaqueminot Rose, berry, sm..............................12.00
Jenny Lind, bowl, 8"....................................32.50
Keele, sauce, Grindley, 6"..............................20.00
Kelvin, bowl, Meakin, 7"................................47.00
Kelvin, creamer, Meakin.................................85.00
Kenworth, cup & saucer, Johnson Bros....................45.00
Kinshan, cup & saucer, minor base chip, EC & Co.........70.00
Kinshan, plate, EC & Co, 11¼"...........................95.00
Kyber, plate, Adams, 9".................................70.00

Kyber, plate, 10"...45.00
Kyber, platter, Adams, 17¾"..............................325.00
Kyber, platter, 7¼x10"......................................110.00
Kyber, saucer, Meir...38.00
La Belle, banana boat, sm leg flake....................225.00
La Belle, bowl, Wheeling Pottery Co, 11" long.........110.00
La Belle, cereal, deep.......................................45.00
La Belle, chop plate, 14½"..................................55.00
La Belle, creamer..125.00
La Belle, pitcher, milk; Wheeling Pottery Co..........120.00
La Belle, plate, 9"..38.00
La Belle, snack plate, Wheeling Pottery Co.............95.00
La Belle, syrup jug, orig lid, sgnd......................135.00
Lahore, plate, Phillipson, 9½".............................80.00
Lahore, teapot, Thos Phillips & Son, 1840............175.00
Lakewood, cup & saucer, demitasse; Wood & Son.....52.00
Lancaster, cup & saucer.....................................55.00
Lancaster, plate, dinner.....................................47.00
Lancaster, plate, New Wharf Pottery, 9"...............32.00
Lancaster, saucer, New Wharf Pottery..................12.00
Lancaster, soup dish, New Wharf..........................50.00
Le Pavot, platter, Gindley, 14½".........................45.00
Libertas Prussia, bowl, 9" long............................30.00
Lily, biscuit jar, Adderly...................................85.00
Linda, creamer, Maddock.....................................65.00
Linda, cup & saucer..55.00
Linda, sauce boat w/lid, 8¾" plate & ladle, Maddox, 4 pc.....150.00
Livingstone, cup & saucer...................................48.00
Lobelia, coffee pot, red mk 1845, EX....................265.00
Lois, bowl, New Wharf, 8"...................................55.00
Lois, platter..38.00
Lois, sauce dish, New Wharf................................24.00
Lonsdale, creamer, Ridgways, sm base chip, 4¼".....75.00
Lorne, plate, Grindley, 8"...................................25.00
Lorne, waste bowl, Grindley................................45.00
Lorraine, sauce tureen, Wood & Sons.....................55.00
Lotus, sauce...15.00
Lotus, vegetable, oval; Grindley, 10¾x8½"............70.00
Lozere, creamer...50.00
Lugano, sauce dish, Ridgeways.............................10.00
Lugano, soup, Ridgeways.....................................45.00
Lugano, vegetable dish, Ridgeways.......................55.00
Lusitania, plate, 10"...25.00
Luzerne, sauce dish, Mercer................................16.00
Mabel, bowl, oval serving; Allertons.....................60.00
Madras, gravy boat...55.00
Madras, platter, Alcock, 13½"............................165.00
Madras, platter, Alcock, 18½"............................190.00
Madras, relish, Doulton......................................65.00
Madras, teapot, JT, minor rpr............................395.00
Manilla, cup, Walker...45.00
Manilla, cup & saucer, handleless; Podmore Walker & Co.....65.00
Manilla, plate, PW Co, 10"..................................85.00
Manilla, plate, PW Co, 9½".................................75.00
Manilla, teapot, PW Co.....................................295.00
Marechal Neil, platter, 16".................................68.00
Marechal Neil, sugar bowl w/lid, Grindley.............100.00
Marechal Neil, teapot, Grindley..........................250.00
Marguerite, compote, Grindley............................165.00
Maria, plate, 10"...65.00
Marie, cake stand w/ped ft, Grindley....................110.00
Marie, pitcher, Grindley, 5¾", EX........................95.00
Marie, plate, 8¾"...25.00
Marie, soup, 9"...35.00

Marquis, berry dish, sm.....................................20.00
Marquis, plate, Grindley, 6"................................15.00
Martha, bone dish, B&B Co..................................50.00
Martha Washington, cup & saucer........................50.00
Martha Washington, plate, 9"..............................38.00
Meissen, bowl, open, Libertas, 10".......................55.00
Melbourne, berry bowl, 5½".................................25.00
Melbourne, butter pat, Grindley...........................16.00
Melbourne, creamer...75.00
Melbourne, cup & saucer, Grindley.......................35.00
Melbourne, gravy boat..75.00
Melbourne, platter, 10".......................................55.00
Melbourne, platter, 16".....................................100.00
Melbourne, salad plate.......................................25.00
Melbourne, soup, flat...30.00
Melbourne, sugar w/lid.......................................80.00
Melbourne, tureen w/cover, Grindley, 8½"..............95.00
Melbourne, vegetable, oval, 10"...........................60.00
Melbourne, vegetable, oval, 9".............................50.00
Melbourne, vegetable w/lid, 9" dia......................150.00
Melbourne, waste bowl, 5¾".................................70.00
Melrose, soup tureen, oval, Doulton, 12" L...........165.00
Melville, platter, 14"...28.00
Mongolia, gravy boat w/attached liner, Johnson Bros.....52.00
Montana, pitcher, 7"...130.00
Morning Glory, rose bowl, inside rim chip, Hughes, 6" dia.....40.00
Morning Glory w/Lustre, creamer.........................195.00
Morning Glory w/Lustre, cup & saucer...................95.00
Mug, Indian portrait, name in script, gold trim, 4¼".....50.00
Muriel, gravy..45.00
Nankin, mitten relish, Mellon & Venables...............55.00
Navy, cup & saucer, Till.....................................58.00
Navy, sauce dish, Till..15.00
Navy, soup plate, Till..75.00
Nelson, plate, New Wharf Pottery, 9"....................40.00
Ning Po, plate, 9½"...55.00
Non Pareil, bowl, cereal; 6".................................28.00
Non Pareil, cake plate, closed hdls.......................50.00
Non Pareil, creamer, Burgess & Leigh...................125.00
Non Pareil, cup & saucer, Burgess & Leigh..............75.00
Non Pareil, flanged soup, Burgess & Leigh, lg.........38.00
Non Pareil, plate, Burgess & Leigh, 6¾".................20.00
Non Pareil, plate, Burgess & Leigh, 8½".................45.00
Non Pareil, platter, Burgess & Leigh, 15x13".........175.00
Normandy, butter pat..24.00
Normandy, saucer, Johnson Bros..........................12.00
Normandy, vegetable w/lid, oval, Johnson Bros......225.00
Normandy, waste bowl..55.00
Olympia, bowl, Grindley, 9".................................30.00
Oregon, plate, Longport, 7¼"..............................60.00
Oriental, plate, Ridgways, 5¾".............................25.00
Oriental, platter, Ridgways................................200.00
Ormonde, platter, Meakin, 12½x9".........................70.00
Osborne, butter pat...20.00
Osborne, creamer & sugar, Grindley.....................285.00
Osborne, creamer & sugar, Ridgways....................145.00
Osborne, plate, Grindley, 8"................................27.00
Osborne, saucer, Grindley.....................................8.00
Osborne, vegetable dish w/cover, Ridgway.............135.00
Oxford, creamer & sugar, Johnson Bros.................190.00
Oyama, pitcher, Doulton, 6½", EX.........................75.00
Pansy, bowl, England, 10"...................................45.00
Peach, bone dish, Royal.....................................20.00
Peach, plate, Johnson Bros, 10"...........................48.00

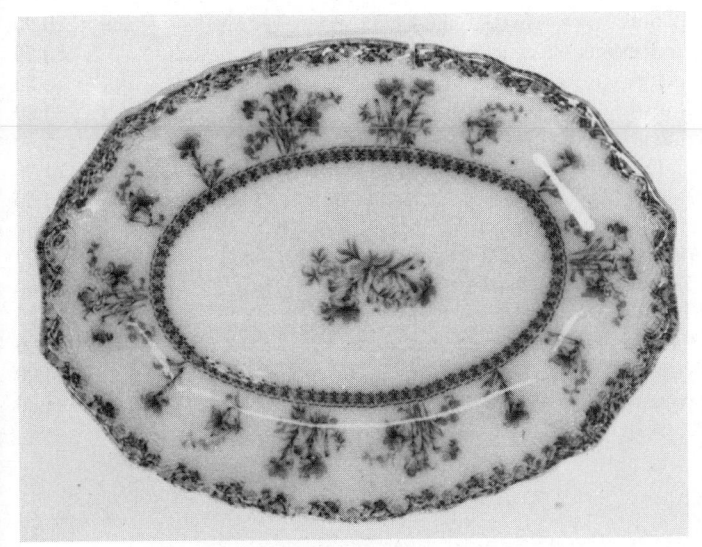

Louise platter by New Warf, 16", $125.00.

Pekin, plate, 10"...35.00
Pekin, soup, W&S, 9½"..40.00
Pelew, plate, Challinor, 9"...................................65.00
Pelew, plate, Challinor, 9½"..................................75.00
Persian, platter, Johnson Bros...............................110.00
Persian Moss, cup & saucer, demitasse.........................14.00
Poppy, platter, 18"...125.00
Portman, butter pat..15.00
Princeton, butter pat, Johnson Bros..........................16.00
Princeton, sauce ladle, Johnson Bros.........................75.00
Princeton, soup plate, flanged, 9"...........................27.00
Punch bowl, leaf hdls, scenic/floral, gold, Sabraon, 6x10½"....225.00
Raleigh, gravy boat..39.00
Rebecca, saucer, G Jones & Sons..............................23.00
Regout's Flower, bowl, Maastricht, 3x6"......................45.00
Rhine, vegetable w/lid, 8 sided.............................100.00
Rhoda Gardens, plate, Hackwood, edge roughage, 9½".........65.00
Richmond, butter base..30.00
Richmond, creamer, Johnson Bros..............................75.00
Richmond, plate, Johnson Bros, 10"...........................35.00
Richmond, plate, Johnson Bros, 7"............................15.00
Richmond, plate, Johnson Bros, 9"............................25.00
Richmond, platter, Johnson Bros, 12½"........................45.00
Richmond, soup, Johnson Bros, 7½"............................25.00
Rock, cup & saucer, handleless...............................95.00
Romance, sauce dish, 5".....................................35.00
Rose, plate, Grindley, 9"....................................40.00
Rose, sauce boat, Grindley...................................50.00
Roseville, cup & saucer, sm nick, Maddock....................35.00
Roseville, platter, Maddock, 11½x16", EX....................115.00
Savoy, sauce tureen under plate, Johnson Bros................25.00
Scinde, butter dish w/lid, sm hairline, Alcock..............285.00
Scinde, cup & saucer, handleless, style #10.................115.00
Scinde, plate, Alcock, 6"....................................45.00
Scinde, plate, Alcock, 7¼"...................................55.00
Scinde, platter, 16".......................................325.00
Scinde, sauce dish, Alcock...................................54.00
Seaweed, plate, 8½"...56.00
Segapore, platter, G Phillips, 1846, 18"....................200.00
Seville, bowl, New Wharf, 6".................................20.00
Seville, gravy boat, Wood....................................30.00
Seville, vegetable bowl, oval, Wood, 11".....................60.00
Shanghai, bowl, oval; Grindley, 9"...........................75.00

Shanghai, cup & saucer, Grindley.............................45.00
Shanghai, gravy, Grindley....................................75.00
Shanghai, plate, Furnival, 10"...............................75.00
Shanghai, plate, Grindley, 10"...............................50.00
Shanghai, plate, Grindley, 5¾"...............................28.00
Shanghai, plate, Grindley, 9"................................45.00
Shanghai, platter, Grindley, 12"............................110.00
Shanghai, platter, Grindley, 16"............................135.00
Shanghai, soup bowl, 8".....................................35.00
Shapoo, plate, 8½"..25.00
Shapoo, toothbrush box w/lid, Hughes........................215.00
Shell, plate, Challinor, 9¾"................................65.00
Shell, platter, octagonal, Challinor, 1842-67, 15¾x12"......165.00
Shell, wash bowl & pitcher, hairline, Challinor.............350.00
Simla, plate, Elsmore & Foster, 9½", EX.....................55.00
Simla, sugar w/lid, unmkd...................................150.00
Sobraon, sauce tureen under plate, 7¼x5½"...................95.00
Somerset, plate, 10"..39.00
Spinach, cup w/hdl, Libertas................................30.00
Spinach, plate, Libertas, 7½"...............................40.00
Spinach III, bowl, Luneville, 8"............................60.00
Spinach III, cup & saucer, Luneville France.................50.00
Splendid, bowl, Societe Ceramique, Maastricht, 9"...........40.00
St Louis, bone dish...20.00
St Louis, butter pat, Johnson Bros..........................20.00
Stanley, butter pat, Johnson Bros...........................14.00
Stregis, pitcher, New Wharf, 6½"............................50.00
Sydney, cup & saucer..48.00
Tankard, ftd, scenic, sgn John Gilpin, 6½".................135.00
Tea set, child's; simple floral band, 10 pcs...............205.00
Temple, cup & saucer, handleless; P Walker & Co.............85.00
Temple, plate, Podmore Walker, 9"...........................65.00
Temple, plate, Podmore Walker, 9¾"..........................85.00
Temple, plate, PW & Co, 7½", EX.............................50.00
Temple, plate, under rim chip, PW Co, 10"...................60.00
Temple, sauce dish..28.00
Tivoli, sauce tureen w/under tray, Meigh....................275.00
Togo, butter pat, 4 for.....................................60.00
Togo, milk pitcher, 1 qt....................................45.00
Togo, plate, ca 1900, 9"....................................35.00
Tonquin, bowl, soup; W Adams & Sons........................125.00
Tonquin, cup plate, Heath...................................48.00
Tonquin, platter, edge roughage, Heath, 10½x13½"...........275.00
Tonquin, sauce tureen lid only, Heath.......................65.00
Tonquin, saucer, pinhead under rim, Heath...................35.00
Touraine, bacon dish..45.00
Touraine, berry bowl, 5¾"...................................25.00
Touraine, bone dish, Alcock.................................35.00
Touraine, bowl, oval; Stanley, 9½"..........................83.00
Touraine, butter pat..28.00
Touraine, butter w/cover, bottom crazed....................200.00
Touraine, creamer..138.00
Touraine, cup & saucer, demitasse; gold trim...............145.00
Touraine, cup & saucer, lg..................................65.00
Touraine, cup & saucer, sm..................................60.00
Touraine, milk pitcher.....................................325.00
Touraine, plate, Stanley, 6½"...............................22.00
Touraine, plate, Stanley, 9"................................38.00
Touraine, plate, 10"..75.00
Touraine, platter, 12¾".....................................95.00
Touraine, platter, 15".....................................125.00
Touraine, shortcake dish, 7½"...............................45.00
Touraine, soup, rimmed......................................45.00
Touraine, sugar w/lid......................................125.00

Touraine, teapot..................................325.00
Touraine, vegetable w/lid, 9½"....................225.00
Touraine, waste bowl..............................85.00
Troy, plate, Meigh, 7½"...........................45.00
Troy, saucer, Meigh...............................25.00
Tulip & Sprig, creamer, Walker, 5½"..............185.00
Tulip & Sprig, cup & saucer, Walker...............65.00
Tulip & Sprig, sauce dish, Walker, 5¼"............30.00
Tulip & Sprig, vegetable dish w/lid, hairline, Walker, 6x11"....300.00
Unique, gravy boat................................20.00
Vase of Flowers, bowl, Royal Doulton, 3½x8".......60.00
Vermont, platter, Burgess & Leigh, 12"............75.00
Vermont, soup ladle, Burgess & Leigh.............135.00
Verona, bowl, Meakin, 9"..........................20.00
Versailles, vegetable w/lid, Furnival, sm under lid chip........95.00
Victoria, vegetable, open, 10" dia................43.00
Virginia, bowl, Maddock, 7".......................25.00
Virginia, saucer, Maddock.........................17.00
Wagon Wheel, mug..................................65.00
Waldorf, bowl, New Wharf, 2x9¼"...................70.00
Waldorf, bowl, New Wharf, 3x10", EX...............85.00
Waldorf, creamer, New Wharf, 3¾".................100.00
Waldorf, cup & saucer, NWP........................55.00
Waldorf, egg platter, NWP, 10¾"...................55.00
Waldorf, pitcher, 1 qt, New Wharf.................50.00
Waldorf, plate, 9½"...............................45.00
Waldorf, platter, New Wharf.......................75.00
Waldorf, saucer...................................15.00
Waldorf, vegetable, open, 9" dia..................55.00
Warwick Pansy, cake plate w/hdl, 10", EX..........55.00
Warwick Pansy, chocolate cup & saucer.............45.00
Warwick Pansy, teapot, child's; minor prof rstr..125.00
Washington, coffee pot, T Walker.................180.00
Watteau, soup, 9½"................................35.00
Watteau, vegetable w/lid, Doulton................165.00
Waverly, bone dish, Grindley, lg..................48.00
Waverly, cup......................................50.00
Whampoa, cup & saucer, Mellor & Venables..........75.00
Whampoa, mug, Mellon & Venables, ca 1850, 3".....125.00
Wild Rose, creamer, Warwick.......................90.00
Wild Rose, pitcher, Warwick, 7"..................155.00
Willow, mush cup & saucer, line in hdl...........125.00
Windsor, bowl & pitcher, 1890....................400.00
Windsor, platter, CH & H Tunstall, 14"............35.00
Yedo, bowl, covered vegetable; Ashworth..........250.00
York, cup & saucer................................30.00

Flue Covers

When spring house cleaning started and the heating stove was taken down for the warm weather season, the unsightly hole where the stove pipe joined the chimney was hidden with an attractive flue cover. They were made with a colorful litho print behind glass with a chain for hanging. Although scarce today, some scenes were actually reverse painted on the glass itself. The most popular motifs were florals, children, and lovely ladies. Square, rectangular, or diamond shapes are more valuable than oval or round covers, especially when Victorian ladies or children are pictured. Occasionally flue covers were made in sets of three -- one served a functional purpose, while the other two were added to provide a more attractive wall arrangement. They range in size from 7-8" to 13-14", but 9" is the average.

Advertising, Hesse Meats, Cleveland, w/Hereford picture, chain...26.00
Blue Willow motif on tin..........................20.00

Chinese boy w/umbrella, old China shoes, w/hanger (no chain)...25.00
Four maidens among mushrooms & butterflies, pastels.........50.00
Girl, brass rim w/chain, Victorian, 7½"...........38.00
Horse head..35.00
Kitten, rnd, lg...................................35.00
Little girls peeling apples, kitchen scene, tinsel trim, 12"......25.00
Maiden w/water scene in center, dk bl around rim, Belgium.....30.00
Maidens in garden, mk Germany, M..................58.00
Portrait of blond child w/red cap, 8½"............20.00
Two girls in boat on lake w/swans.................40.00
Two Victorian ladies..............................40.00
Victorian children w/long curls...................55.00
Victorian scenic, 9¼".............................40.00
Woman bathing child, metal fr w/emb griffins, lg..........35.00

Victorian, lady reading book, under glass, 8", $36.00.

Folk Art

That the creative energies of the mind ever spark innovations in functional utilitarian channels as well as toward playful frivolity is well documented in the study of American folk art. While the average early settler rarely had free time to pursue art for its own sake, his creative energy exemplified itself in fashioning useful objects carved or otherwise ornamented beyond the scope of pure practicality. After the advent of the industrial revolution, the pace of everyday living became more leisurely, and country folk found they had extra time. Not accustomed to sitting idle, many turned to carving, painting, or weaving. Whirligigs, imaginative toys for the children, and whimsies of all types resulted. Though often rather crude, this type of early art represents a segment of our heritage, and as such has become a valued collectible.

Baskets, decoys, frakturs, samplers, trade signs, weathervanes, and wood carvings are specialized areas of folk art dealt with in other sections; see those specific headings.

Cut work, fine detail, rvpt mat, peafowl/cherubs/etc, 12x14"....425.00
Deer, wrought iron, primitive PA Dutch, 6½" L....295.00
Doorstop, reclining cat, wood/brass tack eyes/leather ears, 8"...110.00
Horse, cut from 1 pc pine, pntd, tack eyes, 1900s, 14".......95.00
Stand, triangle shelves w/wood cotton spool dividers, 58"......55.00
Theorem on paper, basket of fruit/foliage, veneer fr, 12x15"....185.00

Theorem on velvet, floral bouquet, 15½x21½".............150.00
Twig art, easle, table top, blk/gold pnt, 19x10x8"...........25.00
Twig art, stand, triangle base w/applied sapling swirls, 22"......65.00
Wall shelf, sculptural birds, smoke finish, 19th century, sm.....450.00
Whirligig, airplane, 1 prop, wood/wire/tin, ca 1930s, 21x24x7"...70.00
Whirligig, bearded old man in hat pumping water, wood/tin....185.00
Whirligig, Black dancer w/vane arms, sheet metal/pnt, rpr, 12".125.00
Whirligig, fife/drum/flag/Liberty Bell, wood/sheet metal, 31"....150.00
Whirligig, Indian in canoe, wood w/metal oars, old rpt, 16".....65.00
Whirligig, mountain man, old paint, minor damage, 18½".......25.00
Whirligig, sailor boy w/metal cap/ribbons, by Chase, 14"......325.00
Whirligig, Uncle Sam in red/wht/bl/blk pnt, 10".............375.00

Fostoria

The Fostoria Glass Company was built in 1887 at Fostoria, Ohio, but by 1891 it had moved to Moundsville, West Virginia. During the next two decades they produced many lines of pressed patterned tableware and lamps. Their most famous pattern, American, was introduced in 1915, and has been produced continuously since that time, in well over 200 different pieces. From 1920 to 1925, top artists designed tablewares in colored glass -- canary (vaseline), amber, blue, orchid, green, and ebony -- in pressed patterns as well as etched designs. By the late thirties Fostoria was recognized as the largest producer of handmade glassware in the world. The company continues in operation today, making the same quality glassware for which it became famous.

#2433, bowl, tripod, azure, 12"..........................75.00
#2433, candlestick, tripod, pr..........................35.00
#2433, compote, mint, topaz...........................30.00
#2635, Madonna, crystal..............................60.00
#2635, Madonna, silver mist, 10".......................50.00
Acanthus, amber; bouillon.............................16.50
Acanthus, amber; cup.................................18.00
Acanthus, amber; lemon dish...........................20.00
Acanthus, amber; sweetmeat...........................10.00
Acanthus, green; baker, 9½"...........................45.00
Acanthus, green; cereal, 6"...........................22.50
Acanthus, green; creamer.............................25.00
Acanthus, green; gravy & under plate....................70.00
Acanthus, green; plate, 6".............................8.00
Acanthus, green; platter, 12"..........................38.00
Acanthus, green; sugar...............................24.00
Acanthus, green; wine................................35.00
American, ash tray, oval..............................11.00
American, ash tray, square, 3"..........................5.00
American, ash tray, topper, 1".........................22.00
American, basket, wicker hdl..........................135.00
American, bell, table.................................40.00
American, bitters bottle, plain, w/sleeve.................45.00
American, bitters bottle, pr engraved Orange & Angostura.....100.00
American, bon bon, 1 hdl, 4"...........................9.00
American, bon bon, 3 toe, 7"..........................14.00
American, bottle, cologne.............................75.00
American, bowl, canoe, 12"............................21.00
American, bowl, centerpiece; flat, 26"..................160.00
American, bowl, console, ftd, 10"......................20.00
American, bowl, covered, 5½"..........................25.00
American, bowl, cupped, 7"............................47.00
American, bowl, deep, 10" dia..........................30.00
American, bowl, deep, 8½x5"...........................42.50
American, bowl, flared, 5¼"............................8.00
American, bowl, ftd, 7¼"..............................10.00

American, bowl, master almond, 3¾".....................22.00
American, bowl, rolled edge, 11½".......................25.00
American, bowl, tri-cornered, 11".......................20.00
American, bowl, 3 toe, 10½" dia........................25.00
American, bowl, 4½".....................................7.00
American, bowl, 5½".....................................8.50
American, bowl, 6½"....................................14.00
American, bowl, 7½"....................................21.00
American, bowl, 8" dia, on 6½" ped.....................50.00
American, box, cigar; w/lid............................40.00
American, box, cigarette; w/lid........................40.00
American, butter, ¼#..................................22.00
American, butter w/cover, 1 lb.........................85.00
American, cake plate, 2 hdld, 10"......................25.00
American, cake plate, 3 ftd, 12".......................25.00
American, cake salver, round ped......................75.00
American, cake salver, square ped......................90.00
American, candlestick, twin, #2056½, pr................55.00
American, candlestick, 1 light, octagonal ft, 6", pr.........45.00
American, candy, covered, tall, 5"......................22.00
American, candy, covered, 6¾".........................22.00
American, celery, oval, 10"............................18.00
American, celery, tall, 6".............................45.00
American, cheese & cracker set.........................40.00
American, coaster, 3¾".................................6.00
American, cocktail, ftd, 3 oz...........................9.00
American, compote, cheese............................18.00
American, compote, jelly; covered......................25.00
American, compote, mint; covered......................40.00
American, compote, stemmed, 5".......................10.00
American, compote, wedding; open......................45.00
American, cookie w/cover.............................249.00
American, cordial, stemmed............................90.00
American, cream soup.................................40.00
American, creamer & open sugar, no hdl, lg...............20.00
American, creamer & open sugar, w/hdls, large............20.00
American, creamer & sugar on tray, individual.............25.00
American, creamer & sugar on tray, regular...............25.00
American, creamer & sugar w/lid, large...................37.50
American, cruet, w/stopper, 5 oz, 6¼"...................30.00
American, cruet, w/stopper, 7 oz, 7"....................35.00
American, cup...10.00
American, cup, ftd......................................8.50
American, cup & saucer................................14.00
American, cup & saucer, ftd............................16.00
American, custard, flared, flat...........................9.00
American, decanter, cordial; sterling trimmed stopper, 10 oz...150.00
American, decanter, plain, w/stopper, 24 oz..............85.00
American, decanter, plain, w/stopper in SP tantalus, 24 oz, pr..265.00
American, decanter, Rye, 24 oz.........................90.00
American, floating garden, oval, 11½"...................70.00
American, goblet, fruit; hexagonal ft, 4¾"................12.00
American, goblet, hexagonal bottom, 10 oz...............12.50
American, goblet, round bottom, 9 oz....................10.00
American, goblet, wine; hexagonal ft, 4¼"................13.00
American, hat, 2½"....................................12.00
American, ice cream insert, hdld.......................25.00
American, ice cream saucer, 5½".......................28.00
American, ice tub, 6".................................55.00
American, iced tea, ftd, 12 oz.........................16.00
American, jug, cupped, no ice lip, 4 pint................80.00
American, jug, milk; pink..............................35.00
American, jug, straight, ice lip, 4 pint..................80.00
American, jug, ½ gal, #2056...........................65.00

American, jug, 3 pint, #2056.........................80.00	American, tumbler, old fashioned; 7 oz...............14.00
American, juice, ftd, 4¾".............................8.00	American, tumbler, water; flat, flared...............13.50
American, ketchup bottle...........................135.00	American, tumbler, water; flat, regular..............11.00
American, lemon dish w/cover.......................30.00	American, tumbler, whiskey.........................15.00
American, marmalade, covered, 2 pc.................52.50	American, urn, square, ftd, 6½"......................25.00
American, mayonnaise, ftd, 2 pc....................40.00	American, urn, square, ftd, 7½"......................32.00
American, mayonnaise set, 3 pc......................37.50	American, urn, square, 6½"...........................18.00
American, mug, Tom & Jerry, 5½ oz.................25.00	American, vase, bud; cupped, 6"......................10.00
American, mustard pot, 3 pc.........................35.00	American, vase, bud; ftd, cupped, 8".................21.00
American, mustard w/lid.............................30.00	American, vase, bud; ftd, flared, 6".................12.00
American, nappy, square, hdld, 4"....................7.50	American, vase, bud; ftd, flared, 8".................21.00
American, nappy, tri-cornered, 4"....................7.50	American, vase, bud; square ftd, 7½"................30.00
American, nappy, 1 hdl, 5" dia.......................7.00	American, vase, cupped, plain rim, 10½".............75.00
American, old fashioned, 3¼".......................14.00	American, vase, flared, flat, 7½"...................20.00
American, olive, canoe, 8¾".........................10.00	American, vase, flared, flat, 9½"...................37.00
American, olive, oval, 6"............................8.00	American, vase, flared, ftd, 9½"....................25.00
American, oyster cocktail............................8.00	American, vase, square ftd, 7½"....................30.00
American, pickle, oval, 8"..........................14.00	American, vase, straight, 12".......................110.00
American, pickle jar, SP lid.......................110.00	American, wine, hexagonal ft.........................12.00
American, pin tray..................................45.00	Arcady, crystal; bowl, flared, flat, 11".............30.00
American, plate, bread & butter......................8.00	Baroque, blue; bowl, 2 hdld, oval, 8½"..............22.00
American, plate, dinner; 9½".......................18.00	Baroque, blue; candlestick, 3 light, pr.............65.00
American, plate, salad; 7½".........................10.00	Baroque, blue; cocktail, ftd........................25.00
American, plate, sandwich; 12".......................25.00	Baroque, blue; compote, jelly, covered..............70.00
American, plate, sandwich; 9".......................22.50	Baroque, blue; compote, 5½"........................22.50
American, plate, torte; cupped, 14".................25.00	Baroque, blue; cup & saucer.........................29.00
American, plate, torte; cupped, 18"................125.00	Baroque, blue; lustre w/prism, 8", pr..............135.00
American, plate, torte; oval, 14"...................40.00	Baroque, blue; mayonnaise, 2 part...................29.00
American, plate, 8½"...............................12.00	Baroque, blue; plate, 7"............................13.50
American, platter, 10½".............................45.00	Baroque, blue; plate, 9¼"..........................49.00
American, platter, 12"..............................50.00	Baroque, blue; tray, hdld, 10"......................29.00
American, punch bowl w/base, 14" dia...............175.00	Baroque, crystal; bowl, hdld, #2484.................15.00
American, relish, canoe, 12"........................15.00	Baroque, crystal; bowl, hdld, #2496, 10½"...........17.00
American, relish, divided, 10¼" square..............45.00	Baroque, crystal; bowl, rolled edge, 11"............18.00
American, relish, oval, 3 part, 9½".................29.00	Baroque, crystal; candelabra/bobeche/prism, 2 lite, #2484, pr....75.00
American, relish, rectangular, 9½x6½"...............45.00	Baroque, crystal; candelabra/bobeche/prism, 3 lite, #2484......65.00
American, rose bowl, 3½"...........................15.00	Baroque, crystal; candle holder, double light.......12.00
American, rose bowl, 5"............................25.00	Baroque, crystal; candle holder, 1 light, 4".........8.00
American, salt & pepper.............................20.00	Baroque, crystal; candle holder, 1 light, 5½"........8.00
American, salt & pepper on tray, individual.........27.00	Baroque, crystal; cheese tray.......................17.00
American, salt dip..................................8.50	Baroque, crystal; creamer & sugar...................12.00
American, sauce boat, 6¾x5".........................55.00	Baroque, crystal; cup & saucer......................15.00
American, server, center hdl........................35.00	Baroque, crystal; iced tea, flat....................29.00
American, sherbet, round bottom, regular, 5 oz.......5.50	Baroque, crystal; plate, dinner.....................15.00
American, sherbet, tall, hexagonal bottom, 5 oz......8.50	Baroque, crystal; relish, 3 part, 12"...............28.00
American, sugar shaker, old top....................125.00	Baroque, crystal; sherbet, low.......................9.00
American, sugar w/lid, 2 hdld.......................22.00	Baroque, crystal; tumbler, old fashioned............17.00
American, sundae, 6 oz..............................8.00	Baroque, topaz; bowl, flared, 12"...................22.00
American, syrup, brown hdl..........................85.00	Baroque, topaz; bowl, flared, 13"...................32.00
American, syrup, drip cut, chrome top & plastic hdl..55.00	Baroque, topaz; bowl, 2 hdld, 8"....................38.00
American, syrup, Sani cut, ivory hdl................60.00	Baroque, topaz; candlestick, 5¼", pr...............35.00
American, syrup, Sani cut, mahogany hdl.............60.00	Baroque, topaz; compote, mint.......................30.00
American, tankard, hdld beer; 12 oz.................40.00	Baroque, topaz; compote, open jelly.................30.00
American, tidbit, 2 tier............................50.00	Baroque, topaz; compote, w/lid, ftd.................29.00
American, toothpick.................................35.00	Baroque, topaz; creamer.............................11.50
American, top hat, 2"...............................24.00	Baroque, topaz; ice bucket..........................45.00
American, top hat, 3"...............................32.00	Baroque, topaz; plate, torte; 14"...................20.00
American, top hat, 4"...............................40.00	Baroque, topaz; sweetmeat...........................15.00
American, tray, muffin; 2 hdld, 10".................35.00	Baroque, topaz; tidbit, 3 toe, 8"...................15.00
American, tray, round, hdld, 7½"...................18.00	Beverly, amber; candle holder, 3"...................30.00
American, tumbler, ftd, 5 oz........................12.00	Beverly, amber; creamer, large......................18.00
American, tumbler, ftd, 9 oz........................16.00	Beverly, amber; cup & saucer, AD....................15.00
American, tumbler, iced tea; flat, flared...........17.50	Beverly, amber; cup & saucer, footed................16.00
American, tumbler, iced tea; flat, regular..........16.00	Beverly, amber; goblet, cordial, #5397..............30.00

Beverly, amber; goblet, wine, #5397.............25.00
Beverly, amber; plate, torte; footed.............45.00
Beverly, amber; salt & pepper, #5000.............65.00
Beverly, amber; tray w/center handle, 11".............25.00
Beverly, green; champagne, tall.............17.00
Beverly, green; compote, #2327, 7½".............35.00
Beverly, green; cream soup.............13.00
Beverly, green; creamer.............18.00
Beverly, green; plate, 3¾".............8.00
Beverly, green; tankard, water, #5000.............260.00
Buttercup, cocktail.............15.00
Buttercup, cup, #2337.............13.00
Buttercup, cup, #2350½.............8.00
Camelia, claret, 3½ oz.............10.00
Camelia, plate, 6".............6.50
Century, bon bon, 3 toe.............14.00
Century, creamer & sugar, 4".............15.00
Century, goblet, water; 10½ oz.............15.00
Century, Tricornes, 3 toe, 7½".............14.00
Chintz, bon bon, ftd.............22.50
Chintz, bowl, flared, flat, 11".............32.50
Chintz, bowl, 2 hdld, 4 toes, 10½".............35.00
Chintz, bowl, 2 hdld, 8½".............35.00
Chintz, candle holder, 1 light.............17.50
Chintz, candlestick, 1 light, 4", pr.............22.50
Chintz, candlestick, 3 light, 5½", pr.............50.00
Chintz, candy, 3 part, covered.............60.00
Chintz, celery, oval, 10½".............32.00
Chintz, champagne, saucer type, 5½".............15.00
Chintz, cheese & cracker set, 2 pc.............50.00
Chintz, cheese compote.............20.00
Chintz, claret, 5¼".............24.00
Chintz, cocktail, 5".............24.00
Chintz, compote, 5".............22.50
Chintz, cordial, #6025, 3¾".............32.00
Chintz, creamer & sugar, individual.............37.50
Chintz, creamer & sugar, large.............30.00
Chintz, creamer & sugar on tray, individual.............45.00
Chintz, cup & saucer.............24.00
Chintz, goblet, 9 oz, 7½".............22.00
Chintz, ice bucket w/tongs.............65.00
Chintz, juice, ftd, 5 oz.............13.50
Chintz, mayonnaise set, 3 pc.............45.00
Chintz, oil & stopper.............57.50
Chintz, plate, #2496, 7½".............12.00
Chintz, plate, torte; 14".............45.00
Chintz, plate, 8½".............20.00
Chintz, plate, 9½".............37.50
Chintz, relish, divided, 2 hdld, 6".............22.00
Chintz, relish, 3 part, 10".............29.00
Chintz, relish, 3 part, 2 hdld, 12".............40.00
Chintz, salt & pepper, large.............80.00
Chintz, sandwich tray, C-hdld.............40.00
Chintz, sherbet, 6 oz, #6026, 4¼".............17.00
Chintz, tidbit, ftd.............22.50
Chintz, tumbler, ftd, 12 oz.............18.00
Chintz, vase, ftd, 7½".............65.00
Chintz, wine, 5½".............25.00
Coin Glass, amber; candy, covered, 13".............60.00
Coin Glass, amber; nappy, hdld.............12.00
Coin Glass, amber; pitcher, qt.............40.00
Coin Glass, amber; vase, flared, 8".............20.00
Coin Glass, crystal; bowl, oval, 9".............32.50
Coin Glass, crystal; candlestick, 4½", pr.............25.00

Coin Glass, ruby; candlestick, 4½", pr.............35.00
Colony, blue milk glass; bowl, oval, 7".............16.50
Colony, blue milk glass; tray, oval, 8¼".............15.00
Colony, crystal; bowl, deep, flared, 10½".............25.00
Colony, crystal; bowl, deep, round, 8¼".............30.00
Colony, crystal; bowl, oval, ftd, 11".............35.00
Colony, crystal; bowl, rolled edge, 14".............32.50
Colony, crystal; bowl, rolled edge, 9".............32.50
Colony, crystal; bowl, 2 hdld, 8¼".............22.50
Colony, crystal; candlestick, 3¼", pr.............15.00
Colony, crystal; candlestick, 7", pr.............45.00
Colony, crystal; champagne, Colonial Dame, crystal/gr.............10.00
Colony, crystal; compote, covered, low, 6½".............45.00
Colony, crystal; compote, covered, tall, 9½".............45.00
Colony, crystal; compote, open, 8x10½".............80.00
Colony, crystal; creamer & sugar, individual.............10.00
Colony, crystal; creamer & sugar, large.............12.50
Colony, crystal; creamer & sugar on tray, individual.............30.00
Colony, crystal; cruet w/stopper.............40.00
Colony, crystal; cup & saucer.............8.50
Colony, crystal; goblet, water.............10.00
Colony, crystal; goblet, water; Colonial Dame, crystal/gr.............15.00
Colony, crystal; goblet, wine.............12.00
Colony, crystal; juice, ftd, Colonial Dame.............5.00
Colony, crystal; lily pond, 13".............35.00
Colony, crystal; nappy, round, 4½".............5.00
Colony, crystal; parfait glass, ftd.............17.00
Colony, crystal; plate, 6".............2.50
Colony, crystal; plate, 7½".............6.00
Colony, crystal; relish, 3 part, 11".............25.00
Colony, crystal; relish, 3 part, 2 hdld, 13".............20.00
Colony, crystal; salt & pepper, regular.............25.00
Colony, crystal; sherbet, low.............6.00
Colony, crystal; tray, muffin; 2 hdld.............32.00
Colony, crystal; tray, sandwich; C-hdld.............30.00
Colony, crystal; tumbler, water; flat.............15.00
Colony, crystal; vase, sweetpea, 6".............27.00
Colony, milk glass; candy, covered, 6½".............35.00
Colony, pink milk glass; candy, covered, 6½".............45.00
Corsage, champagne.............18.00
Corsage, cocktail, oyster.............18.00
Corsage, compote, ftd.............22.00
Corsage, creamer, large.............17.50
Corsage, cup & saucer.............25.00
Corsage, goblet, cocktail.............22.50
Corsage, goblet, water.............22.50
Corsage, relish, 2 part.............22.00
Corsage, sherbet, tall.............19.50
Corsage, sugar, large.............17.50
Fairfax, amber; almond, individual, #2374.............7.00
Fairfax, amber; bowl, cereal; 6".............8.00
Fairfax, amber; candy, covered, 3 part, #2331.............21.00
Fairfax, amber; cocktail, #5097, 3 oz.............11.00
Fairfax, amber; cream soup.............7.00
Fairfax, amber; creamer & sugar, flat.............15.00
Fairfax, amber; creamer & sugar, ftd, large.............11.00
Fairfax, amber; cup & saucer, demitasse.............17.00
Fairfax, amber; juice, ftd, #5000, 5 oz.............7.00
Fairfax, amber; pickle, divided, oval, 9".............15.00
Fairfax, amber; pickle, oval, 9".............15.00
Fairfax, amber; plate, 6".............2.00
Fairfax, amber; plate, 7¼".............4.50
Fairfax, amber; plate, 9½".............9.00
Fairfax, amber; sherbet, low, #877.............5.50

Fairfax, amber; sweetmeat, 2-hdld..........................15.00
Fairfax, amber; tankard, water; #5000.....................130.00
Fairfax, amber; tumbler, ftd, #877, 2 oz....................5.00
Fairfax, amber; vase, #5000, 9¾"..........................50.00
Fairfax, blue; almond, individual, #2374...................12.00
Fairfax, blue; ash tray, 2½"...............................15.00
Fairfax, blue; ash tray, 4"................................20.00
Fairfax, blue; ash tray, 5"................................25.00
Fairfax, blue; bon bon.....................................27.00
Fairfax, blue; bowl, #2394, 12"............................40.00
Fairfax, blue; bowl, combination...........................45.00
Fairfax, blue; bowl, 5"....................................12.00
Fairfax, blue; butter w/cover.............................125.00
Fairfax, blue; candy w/cover, 3 toes.......................37.00
Fairfax, blue; celery, oval, 11½"..........................25.00
Fairfax, blue; celery, 8¾".................................12.00
Fairfax, blue; champagne, #5298 blank, 6"..................24.00
Fairfax, blue; cigarette box w/cover.......................39.00
Fairfax, blue; coaster......................................6.00
Fairfax, blue; cocktail, #4095, 2½ oz......................17.00
Fairfax, blue; creamer & sugar, ftd, large.................28.00
Fairfax, blue; creamer & sugar w/tray.....................125.00
Fairfax, blue; cup & saucer, bouillon......................11.00
Fairfax, blue; cup & saucer, demitasse.....................22.00
Fairfax, blue; cup & saucer, ftd...........................14.00
Fairfax, blue; goblet, iced tea, #5298, 6".................24.00
Fairfax, blue; iced tea, ftd, 5"...........................18.50
Fairfax, blue; jelly, 3 toes...............................35.00
Fairfax, blue; mint..25.00
Fairfax, blue; pickle, oval, 9"............................18.00
Fairfax, blue; plate, lemon, hdld...........................7.00
Fairfax, blue; plate, 6"....................................4.00
Fairfax, blue; plate, 7"....................................5.00
Fairfax, blue; plate, 8¾"..................................12.00
Fairfax, blue; relish, 8½".................................10.00
Fairfax, blue; salt & pepper, individual, #2111............12.00
Fairfax, blue; sherbet, low, #5298.........................17.00
Fairfax, blue; sugar lid...................................60.00
Fairfax, blue; sugar pail..................................47.00
Fairfax, blue; tumbler, ftd, #4095, 10 oz..................17.00
Fairfax, blue; tumbler, ftd, #6016, 10 oz..................10.00
Fairfax, blue; vase, #4128, 5¼"............................35.00
Fairfax, blue; vase, blown, 3".............................25.00
Fairfax, blue; whiskey, #5298..............................25.00
Fairfax, green; almond, individual, #2374...................8.00
Fairfax, green; almond, master; #2374......................35.00
Fairfax, green; bon bon, 2 hdld............................15.00
Fairfax, green; bouillon, 2 hdld, w/liner..................11.50
Fairfax, green; bouillon cup................................6.00
Fairfax, green; bowl, cereal; 6"...........................14.00
Fairfax, green; bowl, finger...............................10.00
Fairfax, green; bowl, oval vegetable; 10½".................28.00
Fairfax, green; bowl, oval vegetable; 9"...................22.50
Fairfax, green; bowl, round, 9¼"...........................27.50
Fairfax, green; bowl, whip cream; 2 hdld...................18.00
Fairfax, green; bowl, 3 toe, 12"...........................18.00
Fairfax, green; bowl, 5"....................................5.00
Fairfax, green; butter w/cover.............................88.00
Fairfax, green; celery, oval, 11"..........................14.00
Fairfax, green; champagne, #6017, 6 oz.....................12.50
Fairfax, green; cocktail...................................14.00
Fairfax, green; compote, #5098, blown, rare................40.00
Fairfax, green; confection box w/cover, #2380..............30.00
Fairfax, green; cream soup w/liner.........................12.00

Fairfax, green; creamer & sugar, flat......................27.00
Fairfax, green; creamer & sugar, ftd.......................14.00
Fairfax, green; cruet, #2375, w/cut stopper................60.00
Fairfax, green; cup & saucer, demitasse....................22.50
Fairfax, green; cup & saucer, ftd...........................7.00
Fairfax, green; goblet, water; #6017.......................14.00
Fairfax, green; gravy boat w/under plate...................60.00
Fairfax, green; iced tea, ftd, #5098........................9.00
Fairfax, green; mayonnaise bowl, ftd.......................18.00
Fairfax, green; parfait, #5098.............................14.00
Fairfax, green; plate, grill; 10¼".........................12.00
Fairfax, green; plate, 6"...................................3.00
Fairfax, green; plate, 8¾"..................................6.00
Fairfax, green; sandwich server, C-hdl.....................18.00
Fairfax, green; sauce boat plate...........................10.00
Fairfax, green; server, C-hdld.............................12.00
Fairfax, green; sherbet, #6202.............................10.00
Fairfax, green; sherry, #6017, 3½".........................12.50
Fairfax, green; shrimp icer, w/insert, #945½...............18.00
Fairfax, green; soup, flat rim, Pioneer.....................7.50
Fairfax, green; sweetmeat, 2 hdld..........................15.00
Fairfax, green; tankard, water; #5000.....................120.00
Fairfax, green; tray, lemon; 2 hdld........................12.00
Fairfax, green; tumbler, #6017, 9 oz........................7.00
Fairfax, green; tumbler, ftd, #5099, 9 oz...................7.00
Fairfax, green; wine, #6017, 2½ oz.........................15.00
Fairfax, orchid; creamer & sugar, ftd......................18.00
Fairfax, orchid; cup & saucer..............................11.00
Fairfax, orchid; plate, 10"................................16.00
Fairfax, orchid; plate, 6"..................................3.00
Fairfax, orchid; relish, 2 part, 8½".......................10.00
Fairfax, orchid; sauce boat & under plate..................45.00
Fairfax, pink; almond, individual, #2374....................9.00
Fairfax, pink; baker, 9½"..................................25.00
Fairfax, pink; bouillon & liner............................14.00
Fairfax, pink; bowl, icer..................................12.00
Fairfax, pink; candy, covered, 3 toes......................45.00
Fairfax, pink; champagne, #5299, 6"........................19.00
Fairfax, pink; compote, #2400, 8"..........................25.00
Fairfax, pink; creamer & sugar, individual.................17.00
Fairfax, pink; creamer & sugar w/tray......................75.00
Fairfax, pink; cup & saucer, demitasse.....................17.00
Fairfax, pink; cup & saucer, ftd............................7.00
Fairfax, pink; goblet, iced tea; #5298 blank, 6"...........18.00
Fairfax, pink; goblet, water; #5298, 5¼"...................18.00
Fairfax, pink; goblet, water; #5298, 8¼"...................25.00
Fairfax, pink; goblet, wine; #5298.........................35.00
Fairfax, pink; gravy boat w/under plate....................40.00
Fairfax, pink; juice, ftd, #5298 blank.....................18.00
Fairfax, pink; mint..20.00
Fairfax, pink; nut set, #2374, ftd master w/6 individual...40.00
Fairfax, pink; oil, ftd, w/stopper........................110.00
Fairfax, topaz; celery, 11½"...............................15.00
Fairfax, topaz; compote, #5299, 6".........................15.00
Fairfax, topaz; cream soup..................................9.00
Fairfax, topaz; goblet, water; #5299.......................15.00
Fairfax, topaz; mayonnaise, ftd............................20.00
Fairfax, topaz; mint.......................................15.00
Fairfax, topaz; oil, ftd, w/stopper.......................110.00
Fairfax, topaz; plate, 7½"..................................5.00
Fairfax, topaz; sugar, individual...........................5.00
Fairfax, topaz; tumbler, water; #5299......................12.00
Florentine, creamer & sugar, ftd...........................25.00
Florentine, cup & saucer...................................15.00

Florentine, plate, 7".........................6.00
Florentine, plate, 9".........................14.00
Fuchsia, tumbler, ftd, 5 oz.....................18.00
Garland, tumbler, hdld, #869, 12 oz.............19.00
Glacier, ice bucket............................30.00
Glacier, jug, w/ice lip........................45.00
Heirloom, blue opal; bon bon, #2729/135.........30.00
Heirloom, blue opal; candlestick, #2183/34......16.50
Heirloom, blue opal; candlestick, #2726/311, 3", pr.........27.00
Heirloom, blue opal; flower float, #2183/415....40.00
Heirloom, blue opal; nappy, grip hdl............30.00
Heirloom, crystal opal; bon bon, 8¾"............22.00
Heirloom, green opal; bowl, #1514/208, 10"......36.00
Heirloom, pink opal; basket, #2720/126..........34.00
Heirloom, pink opal; candle holder, 3½x9".......25.00
Heirloom, pink opal; florette, #2720/170........30.00
Heirloom, ruby opal; bowl, #2183/168, 7".........33.00
Heirloom, yellow opal; bowl, #2720/168, 7".......32.00
Hermitage, amber; cocktail, cone, 3½ oz.........10.00
Hermitage, amber; old fashioned, 7 oz...........10.00
Hermitage, blue; cocktail, cone, 3½ oz..........15.00
Hermitage, blue; old fashioned, #2449...........15.00
Hermitage, crystal; cocktail, cone, 3½ oz........8.00
Hermitage, crystal; cup & saucer.................7.00
Hermitage, crystal; goblet, water................7.00
Hermitage, crystal; mustard w/lid, #2449........27.50
Hermitage, crystal; oil w/stopper, 3 oz, #2449...30.00
Hermitage, crystal; plate, #2449, 6".............6.00
Hermitage, crystal; vase, flared, 6"............11.00
Hermitage, green; vase, #2449, 6"...............25.00
Hermitage, topaz; candlestick, 6", pr...........60.00
Hermitage, topaz; cocktail, cone, 3½ oz.........12.00
Hermitage, topaz; goblet, water.................25.00
Hermitage, topaz; mustard, 3 pc.................25.00
Hermitage, topaz; plate, 7¼"....................6.50
Hermitage, topaz; vase, flared, 6"..............30.00
Hermitage, wisteria; bowl, icer; w/4 oz wisteria insert.........45.00
Hermitage, wisteria; cocktail, cone, ftd, 3½ oz.........12.00
Hermitage, wisteria; juice, ftd.................14.00
Hermitage, wisteria; sherbet, low, 7 oz.........12.50
Hermitage, wisteria; tumbler, ftd, 10 oz, 4¼"...18.00
Jamestown, amber; goblet, wine...................9.00
Jamestown, amber; iced tea, 6"..................7.50
Jamestown, amber; juice, ftd.....................6.00
Jamestown, amethyst; goblet, 9½ oz.............10.50
Jamestown, amethyst; plate, 8"..................6.50
Jamestown, blue; goblet, wine...................15.00
Jamestown, blue; iced tea, ftd..................14.00
Jamestown, green; goblet, water, 5¾"............6.00
Jamestown, green; iced tea, 6"..................7.50
Jamestown, green; plate, 8".....................4.00
Jamestown, green; sherbet.......................4.00
Jamestown, green; wine, 4½".....................6.00
Jamestown, pink; iced tea, 6"...................7.50
Jamestown, ruby; goblet, 9½ oz.................15.00
June, blue; bowl, finger; blown.................35.00
June, blue; bowl, fruit; 5".....................29.00
June, blue; cream soup & liner..................39.00
June, blue; cup & saucer........................47.00
June, blue; cup & saucer, demitasse.............75.00
June, blue; goblet, cocktail....................47.00
June, blue; goblet, water; 8¼"..................35.00
June, blue; ice bucket.........................125.00
June, blue; oyster cocktail.....................27.00

June, blue; pitcher, water.....................495.00
June, blue; plate, 7½"..........................12.50
June, blue; salt shaker.........................60.00
June, blue; server, C-hdld, 11".................55.00
June, blue; sherbet, low........................24.00
June, blue; sugar lid only.....................175.00
June, blue; sugar w/lid........................210.00
June, blue; tray, service, rare................275.00
June, blue; vase, 8"...........................195.00
June, crystal; champagne, low...................15.00
June, crystal; cheese dish......................20.00
June, crystal; cocktail.........................28.00
June, crystal; cup & saucer, demitasse..........35.00
June, crystal; goblet...........................28.00
June, crystal; plate, 7½".........................6.00
June, crystal; salt & pepper....................65.00
June, pink; candle holder, mushroom.............25.00
June, pink; cream soup..........................15.00
June, pink; cup.................................23.00
June, pink; cup & saucer, ftd...................35.00
June, pink; finger bowl & under plate...........35.00
June, pink; grapefruit insert...................45.00
June, pink; plate, 6"............................6.00
June, pink; plate, 7½" salad.....................8.00
June, pink; plate, 8¾", lt use.................12.50
June, pink; relish, 2 part......................18.00
June, pink; saucer...............................6.00
June, pink; sugar, large........................27.50
June, pink; under plate, 6".......................9.50
June, pink; whiskey, 2½ oz......................39.00
June, topaz; bouillon cup.......................22.00
June, topaz; bowl, console; 3 leg, #2375........39.00
June, topaz; cream soup & plate.................39.00
June, topaz; cup & saucer.......................29.00
June, topaz; cup & saucer, demitasse............49.00
June, topaz; goblet, claret.....................49.00
June, topaz; goblet, cocktail...................35.00
June, topaz; goblet, cordial....................69.00
June, topaz; goblet, water......................25.00
June, topaz; goblet, wine.......................42.00
June, topaz; mint...............................35.00
June, topaz; parfait............................39.00
June, topaz; plate, 10¼", lt use...............39.00
June, topaz; plate, 6"...........................6.00
June, topaz; plate, 7½"..........................8.00
June, topaz; plate, 8¾".........................12.00
June, topaz; plate, 9½" dinner..................23.00
June, topaz; sherbet, low.......................25.00
June, topaz; sweetmeat..........................22.00
June, topaz; tumbler, water, 5¼"................24.00
Kashmir, blue; plate, 8¾".........................7.00
Lafayette, cobalt blue; plate, 2 hdl, 13".......29.00
Lafayette, crystal; pickle, 2 hdl, 2 part, sterling decor.........7.00
Lafayette, crystal; plate, 6¼"...................3.00
Lafayette, green; relish, 3 part, 3 hdl.........16.00
Lafayette, ruby; plate, torte; 14"..............55.00
Lafayette, ruby; relish, divided, 2 hdl, 9".....15.00
Lafayette, ruby; tray, 2 hdl, 10½"..............12.00
Lafayette, topaz; creamer & sugar...............16.00
Lafayette, topaz; pickle, 2 part, 2 hdl.........16.00
Lafayette, topaz; plate, lemon; 2 hdl, 7".........5.00
Lafayette, topaz; plate, 9".......................7.00
Lafayette, wisteria; plate, 7½".................12.50
Lafayette, wisteria; plate, 8½".................15.00

Laurel, champagne...11.00
Laurel, goblet, water..15.00
Lido, ice bucket...65.00
Lido, plate, #2496, 8½″......................................9.00
Lido, tidbit, 3 toes...15.00
Manor, bowl, ftd, #2470½, 10½″..............................35.00
Manor, goblet, #6003..18.00
Manor, goblet, #6007..25.00
Manor, icer, w/liner..15.00
Mayfair, crystal; ash tray..................................10.00
Mayfair, green; relish, 4 part..............................20.00
Mayfair, green; tray, sandwich; C-hdld......................22.00
Mayfair, pink; ash tray, round, #2419, 4″....................8.00
Mayfair, pink; bowl, cereal; #2419, 6″.......................6.00
Mayfair, pink; bowl, oval vegetable; #2419, 10″.............20.00
Mayfair, pink; creamer & sugar, #2419.......................19.00
Mayfair, pink; cup & saucer..................................7.00
Mayfair, pink; cup & saucer, ftd, #2419......................8.00
Mayfair, pink; jelly, 2 hdld, #2419, 6″......................9.50
Mayfair, pink; lemon dish, 2 hdld, #2419, 6¼″...............10.00
Mayfair, pink; pickle dish, #2419, 9″........................9.00
Mayfair, pink; plate, bread & butter, #2419..................4.00
Mayfair, pink; plate, 9″, #2419, NM.........................10.00
Mayfair, pink; plate, #2419, 11″............................14.00
Mayfair, pink; sauce boat w/attached liner..................25.00
Mayfair, topaz; compote, mint...............................30.00
Mayfair, topaz; creamer & sugar, ftd, #2419.................20.00
Mayfair, topaz; relish, 2 part, #2419, 9″...................12.00
Mayfair, topaz; relish, 4 part..............................25.00
Mayfair, topaz; sauce boat w/stand..........................35.00
Mayflower, goblet, 9 oz, #6020..............................15.00
Mayflower, plate, 7½″, #2560................................12.00
Mayflower, sherbet, low, 6 oz, #6020........................12.00
Meadow Rose, bowl, flared, flat, 11″........................45.00
Meadow Rose, bowl, flat, #2496, 12″.........................37.00
Meadow Rose, cake plate, 2 hdld, #2496, 10″.................28.00
Meadow Rose, candlestick, duo, #2496, pr....................42.50
Meadow Rose, champagne, saucer style, #6016, 5½″...........22.50
Meadow Rose, cheese tray, 11″...............................22.50
Meadow Rose, cocktail.......................................25.00
Meadow Rose, compote, mint, covered.........................50.00
Meadow Rose, creamer & sugar, ftd, #6016....................32.00
Meadow Rose, goblet, 10 oz, #6016, 7½″.....................22.50
Meadow Rose, iced tea, 6″...................................22.00
Meadow Rose, mayonnaise, 3 pc...............................45.00
Meadow Rose, plate, torte; #2496, 14″.......................37.00
Meadow Rose, plate, 2 hdld, 10½″...........................30.00
Meadow Rose, relish, 3 part, 2 hdld, 10″....................45.00
Meadow Rose, relish, 5 part, #2419, 13x9″...................45.00
Meadow Rose, salt shaker....................................45.00
Meadow Rose, sandwich server, C-hdld........................35.00
Meadow Rose, sherbet, tall, w/orig brown label..............20.00
Meadow Rose, sherry cocktail................................14.00
Meadow Rose, tankard, water; #5000.........................235.00
Meadow Rose, tumbler, ftd, 5 oz, #6016, 4¾″................18.00
Meadow Rose, tumbler, iced tea..............................22.50
Midnight Rose, candlestick, #2470½.........................25.00
Midnight Rose, pickle, 9″...................................20.00
Midnight Rose, sugar...8.00
Minuet, green; bowl, fruit; #2419, 5″........................5.00
Minuet, topaz; tumbler, ftd, 10 oz..........................16.00
Mystic, green; cordial, Spiral Optic........................35.00
Navarre, blue; goblet, #6016, 10 oz, w/label................24.00
Navarre, blue; saucer champagne, #6016......................21.00

Navarre, crystal; bon bon, 3 toes...........................25.00
Navarre, crystal; bowl, 2 hdld, 4 toes, 10½″...............35.00
Navarre, crystal; cake plate, 10″...........................30.00
Navarre, crystal; candlestick, trindle, #2496, 3″, pr.......60.00
Navarre, crystal; candlestick, 1 light, 4″, pr..............30.00
Navarre, crystal; candlestick, 2 light, 4½″, pr............50.00
Navarre, crystal; candlestick, 3 light, 5½″................35.00
Navarre, crystal; celery, oval, 12″.........................28.00
Navarre, crystal; compote, #2400, 6½″......................30.00
Navarre, crystal; compote, 5½″.............................25.00
Navarre, crystal; cordial, 1 oz.............................30.00
Navarre, crystal; creamer & sugar...........................32.00
Navarre, crystal; creamer & sugar, individual...............25.00
Navarre, crystal; cup & saucer..............................25.00
Navarre, crystal; goblet, #6016, 10 oz......................21.00
Navarre, crystal; juice, ftd................................22.00
Navarre, crystal; nappy, hdld, ftd..........................15.00
Navarre, crystal; nappy, triangular, 1 hdld, 5″.............16.00
Navarre, crystal; oyster cocktail, #6016....................23.00
Navarre, crystal; pickle, oval, 9″..........................20.00
Navarre, crystal; plate, torte; 14″.........................35.00
Navarre, crystal; plate, 2 hdld, 10½″......................25.00
Navarre, crystal; plate, 7½″...............................15.00
Navarre, crystal; plate, 9½″...............................25.00
Navarre, crystal; relish, square, 2 part, 6″................16.00
Navarre, crystal; relish, 3 part............................40.00
Navarre, crystal; sherbet, low..............................18.50
Navarre, crystal; sugar, large..............................17.00
Navarre, crystal; tankard, water; #5000....................225.00
Navarre, crystal; tumbler, ftd, #6016, 13 oz................21.00
New Garland, topaz; cocktail, #4220.........................16.00
New Garland, topaz; gravy boat w/liner......................42.50
New Garland, topaz; sherbet, #4220, 4½″....................12.00
Oak Leaf, bowl, whipped cream, #2375.........................8.00
Oak Leaf, ice bucket..36.00
Oak Leaf, plate, cracker, #2368, 11½″......................14.00
Oak Leaf, plate, 7½″ dia....................................6.00
Oak Leaf, under plate, #2283, 7″............................6.00
Paradise, orchid; bowl, ftd, #2315, 11″.....................75.00
Paradise, orchid; candy, covered, #2380.....................75.00
Paradise, orchid; compote, #2362, 11″.......................80.00
Paradise, rose; compote, twist stem.........................40.00
Pioneer, amber; bouillon cup & saucer, ftd...................8.00
Pioneer, amber; butter w/cover..............................62.50
Pioneer, amber; cream soup & plate...........................9.00
Pioneer, amber; creamer & sugar, flat.......................14.00
Pioneer, amber; cup, flat....................................4.00
Pioneer, amber; cup & saucer, flat...........................7.00
Pioneer, amber; plate, 10½″................................15.00
Pioneer, amber; plate, 7″....................................3.00
Pioneer, amber; plate, 9½″..................................8.00
Pioneer, amber; relish, 3 part...............................9.00
Pioneer, amber; server, center hdld.........................18.00
Pioneer, green; bouillon cup & saucer........................8.00
Pioneer, green; bowl, rolled edge, 3 ftd....................12.00
Pioneer, green; candlestick, 3¼″............................8.00
Pioneer, green; cheese stand................................15.00
Pioneer, green; compote, mint...............................18.00
Pioneer, green; cup & saucer, demitasse.....................10.00
Pioneer, green; egg cup.....................................10.00
Pioneer, green; plate, canape................................8.00
Pioneer, green; plate, 7½″..................................3.00
Pioneer, orchid; plate, 7¼″.................................6.00
Priscilla, amber; creamer...................................11.00

Priscilla, green; bouillon cup	7.00
Priscilla, green; creamer	7.00
Priscilla, green; custard, ftd	7.50
Priscilla, green; egg cup	35.00
Priscilla, green; jug, #2321	61.00
Queen Anne, candlestick, blue, 9", pr	75.00
Queen Anne, compote, clear bowl, gr high stem & ft	110.00
Rambler, champagne, #6012, 5½ oz	11.00
Rambler, tumbler, ftd, #6012, 13 oz	14.00
Rogene, cocktail, 4½"	25.00
Rogene, goblet	22.00
Rogene, oyster cocktail, #837	16.00
Romance, candlestick, #2324, 3½"	14.50
Romance, candlestick, duo, #6023, pr	65.00
Romance, champagne	18.00
Romance, cocktail	25.00
Romance, creamer	17.00
Romance, cup & saucer	19.00
Romance, goblet, cocktail	19.00
Romance, goblet, water	19.00
Romance, goblet, wine	25.00
Romance, iced tea, ftd, 6"	19.50
Romance, juice tumbler, 5 oz	25.00
Romance, plate, 7"	6.00
Romance, relish, 3 part, 2 hdld, 12"	32.50
Romance, sherbet, 6 oz	12.00
Romance, sherry cocktail, 3½ oz	16.00
Romance, sugar	17.00
Romance, tumbler, ftd, 12 oz	18.00
Royal, amber; bowl, deep, 12"	23.50
Royal, amber; centerpiece bowl, rolled, 11"	15.00
Royal, amber; creamer, ftd	12.00
Royal, amber; plate, 7½"	7.00
Seascape, blue opal; plate, buffet; 14"	45.00
Seascape, blue opal; relish, 3 part	37.50
Seascape, pink opal; relish, 3 part, 11½"	40.00
Seville, amber; bowl, fruit; 5"	10.00
Seville, amber; pitcher, water; #5084	225.00
Seville, amber; plate, 8¼"	10.00
Seville, green; compote, #2327, 7"	39.00
Shirley, creamer	10.00
Shirley, goblet, #6017, 9 oz	13.00
Shirley, relish, 3 part, 10"	25.00
Sunray, crystal; cigarette box w/cover	22.50
Sunray, crystal; cigarette jar, w/cover	25.00
Sunray, crystal; coaster	6.00
Sunray, crystal; cocktail, #2510, 3¾"	8.00
Sunray, crystal; compote, Glacier decoration, mint	18.00
Sunray, crystal; cream soup, #2510	10.00
Sunray, crystal; creamer, regular size	8.00
Sunray, crystal; creamer & sugar, individual	16.00
Sunray, crystal; creamer & sugar on tray, individual	30.00
Sunray, crystal; cup & saucer	11.00
Sunray, crystal; goblet, water	14.00
Sunray, crystal; ice bucket	35.00
Sunray, crystal; jug, w/ice lip	40.00
Sunray, crystal; mayonnaise, Glacier decoration, 3 pc	40.00
Sunray, crystal; mayonnaise bowl w/ladle	15.00
Sunray, crystal; mayonnaise w/under plate	16.00
Sunray, crystal; nappy, flared, hdld, 5"	6.00
Sunray, crystal; pickle, 2 part, 2 hdls, Glacier decoration	12.00
Sunray, crystal; plate, 6"	5.00
Sunray, crystal; plate, 7"	6.00
Sunray, crystal; relish, 3 part, 3 hdld	10.00
Sunray, crystal; rose bowl, 3¼"	14.00
Sunray, crystal; tumbler, ftd, 13 oz	7.00
Sunray, ruby; bowl, round, 3 toe, 7¼"	15.00
Sunray, ruby; sweetmeat, triangle	12.50
Sunray, yellow; sherbet	10.00
Trojan, amber; relish, 2 part, 8½"	12.00
Trojan, amber; server, C-hdld	25.00
Trojan, pink; creamer & sugar	350.00
Trojan, topaz; bon bon	22.00
Trojan, topaz; bowl, hdld, 9"	45.00
Trojan, topaz; bowl, whip cream	22.00
Trojan, topaz; cake plate, 2 hdld, 10"	20.00
Trojan, topaz; candlestick, scroll, 5", pr	65.00
Trojan, topaz; candy, covered, 3 toes	150.00
Trojan, topaz; champagne, 6"	17.00
Trojan, topaz; cocktail	27.00
Trojan, topaz; cordial	55.00
Trojan, topaz; cream soup & liner	35.00
Trojan, topaz; creamer & sugar, individual	95.00
Trojan, topaz; cup, ftd	16.00
Trojan, topaz; cup & saucer	20.00
Trojan, topaz; finger bowl	22.00
Trojan, topaz; goblet, water, 8¼"	27.00
Trojan, topaz; ice bucket w/bail	95.00
Trojan, topaz; iced tea, 6"	22.00
Trojan, topaz; oil, ftd, w/stopper	325.00
Trojan, topaz; oyster cocktail	22.00
Trojan, topaz; parfait	49.00
Trojan, topaz; plate, soup; 7½"	7.00
Trojan, topaz; plate, 7½"	7.00
Trojan, topaz; plate, 9½", light use	17.00
Trojan, topaz; relish, 2 part, 8½"	25.00
Trojan, topaz; salt & pepper	95.00
Trojan, topaz; sherbet	18.50
Trojan, topaz; sweetmeat	22.00
Trojan, topaz; tumbler, water; 5¼"	16.00
Trojan, topaz; vase, blown, 8"	150.00
Trojan, topaz; whip cream pail	125.00
Trojan, topaz; wine, 6"	20.00
Vernon, amber; baker, 9", slight stain near edge	30.00
Vernon, amber; bowl, ftd, #2394	35.00
Vernon, amber; platter, oval, 12¼", shows use	35.00
Vernon, blue; bowl, grapefruit; no liner, tiny nick on rim	45.00
Vernon, green; bouillon	15.00
Vernon, green; sugar	15.00
Vernon, orchid; server, center hdld	45.00
Vernon, orchid; sugar	15.00
Versailles, blue; candlestick, 4", pr	37.00
Versailles, blue; cordial	85.00
Versailles, blue; cup & saucer	32.00
Versailles, blue; goblet, water; 8¼"	32.00
Versailles, blue; jug, 7"	475.00
Versailles, blue; plate, #2375, 6"	9.50
Versailles, blue; plate, 10¼", light use	39.00
Versailles, blue; plate, 8¾"	8.00
Versailles, blue; sherbet, low, #5298	25.00
Versailles, green; bowl, 5"	15.00
Versailles, green; candle holder, mushroom, pr	47.00
Versailles, green; candlestick, 3", pr	40.00
Versailles, green; cocktail, goblet	33.00
Versailles, green; creamer	18.00
Versailles, green; oyster cocktail	23.00
Versailles, green; sugar pail	125.00
Versailles, green; tumbler, water, 5¼"	23.00

Versailles, pink; bowl, berry; 5"...........................13.00
Versailles, pink; bowl, grapefruit.........................75.00
Versailles, pink; bowl, 2 hdld, 6", NM.....................14.00
Versailles, pink; candlesticks, 2", pr.....................25.00
Versailles, pink; cup & saucer.............................15.00
Versailles, pink; cup & saucer, ftd........................25.00
Versailles, pink; iced tea, 6".............................27.50
Versailles, pink; mint, 3 toes.............................33.00
Versailles, pink; parfait..................................42.00
Versailles, pink; plate, 6".................................4.00
Versailles, pink; plate, 7¼"................................5.00
Versailles, pink; tumbler, ftd, 5¼"........................21.00
Versailles, topaz; baker, #2375, 9"........................39.00
Versailles, topaz; bowl, cereal; 6"........................25.00
Versailles, topaz; bowl, oval vegetable; 9¼"...............40.00
Versailles, topaz; celery, oval, 11½"......................32.50
Versailles, topaz; champagne, 6"...........................19.00
Versailles, topaz; claret..................................35.00
Versailles, topaz; cocktail................................33.00
Versailles, topaz; compote, #2400, 6"......................25.00
Versailles, topaz; compote, #5299..........................50.00
Versailles, topaz; creamer.................................20.00
Versailles, topaz; cup & saucer, #2375.....................19.00
Versailles, topaz; cup & saucer, demitasse; #2375..........26.00
Versailles, topaz; finger bowl.............................18.00
Versailles, topaz; finger bowl, w/liner....................20.00
Versailles, topaz; ice bucket & tongs......................90.00
Versailles, topaz; jelly, 3 toes, 6½"......................45.00
Versailles, topaz; plate, #2375, 10½"......................39.00
Versailles, topaz; plate, soup; 7½".........................7.00
Versailles, topaz; plate, torte; 14".......................45.00
Versailles, topaz; plate, 6"................................4.50
Versailles, topaz; plate, 7½"...............................6.00
Versailles, topaz; platter, oval, 15½".....................55.00
Versailles, topaz; server, center hdld.....................45.00
Versailles, topaz; tumbler, iced tea.......................25.00
Vesper, amber; bowl, rolled edge, #2329, w/orig amber frog.....35.00
Vesper, amber; centerpiece, 11"............................25.00
Vesper, amber; compote, #2327, 7"..........................35.00
Vesper, amber; cream soup, #2350...........................18.00
Vesper, amber; goblet, #5093...............................15.00
Vesper, amber; plate, 10½".................................20.00
Vesper, green; bowl, 3 ftd, #2375, 12".....................39.00
Vesper, green; sugar.......................................14.00
Vesper, green; tray, lunch, center hdl, #2287, 12".........26.00
Vesper, green; wine, 5½"...................................35.00
Virginia, goblet, water; #661..............................20.00
Virginia, sherbet, #661....................................14.00
Willowmere, bowl, 13"......................................27.50
Willowmere, candlestick, 4", pr............................35.00
Willowmere, claret goblet..................................35.00
Willowmere, creamer & sugar, footed........................35.00
Willowmere, cruet & stopper...............................125.00
Willowmere, plate, 14".....................................25.00

Fraktur

Fraktur is a German style of black letter text type. To collectors, the fraktur is a type of hand-lettered document used by the people of German decent who settled in the area of Pennsylvania and New Jersey. These documents recorded births, baptisms, and marriages, and were used as bookplates and as certificates of honor. They were elaborately decorated with colorful folk art borders of hearts, birds, angels, and flowers. Examples by recognized artists, and those with an unusual decorative motif, bring prices

well into the thousands of dollars. Frakturs made in the late 1800s, after the invention of the printing press, provided the writer with a prepared text that he needed only to fill in with the appropriate names and dates -- the decoration was left to his own discretion. The next step in the evolution of machine printed frakturs combined woodblock printed decorations along with the text which the 'artist' sometimes enhanced with color. By the late 1800s, even the coloring was done by machine.

The vorschrift was a handwritten example prepared by a fraktur teacher to demonstrate his skill in lettering and decorating. These are often considered to be the finest of frakturs. Those dated before 1820 are most valuable.

The practice of fraktur art began to diminish after 1830, but hung on even into the early years of this century among the Pennsylvania Germans ingrained with such customs.

Key:

hc----hand color	p/wc-----printed & watercolored
p/i----------pen and ink	wc--------watercolor

Birth Record

Baptismal, wc, full length lady/man, Rev Young, 1849, 9x7"..2,420.00
Chain of hearts w/verse above/dbl heart, wc, 1793, 13x15"...1,100.00
Drawing, wc/cut-work tulips/compass star, 1807, 7x6".......1,375.00
Elaborate compass-drawn circle w/2 pillar supports, 1863, 9x7".525.00
Ewers of flowers ea side, strap-work letters, wc, 1793, 7x10"..3,575.00
Heart reserve, parrot/tulip/heart border, Trevits/1811, 13x16".2,970.00
Heart/crown/floral wc border, wove paper, 1774, 12x15".....1,870.00
P/wc, angels in robes hold wreaths, Peters, 15½x12"........275.00
P/wc, drawn lions/flowers/foxes/etc, pub Speyer, 1788, 13x15".1,980.00
P/wc, kings w/tulips/mermaids/parrots, Speyer, 1752, 13x15"..1,980.00
P/wc, 10 Commandment border, Geo Mentz, 1805, 17x15"....275.00
Pen/ink/wc, corner hearts, English verse, 1791+2 dates, 8"....135.00
Pen/ink/wc, floral wreaths/cornucopias/etc, 1806, 11x18", G...350.00
Pen/ink/wc, octagon center w/verse/crucifix, 1835, 11", G.....125.00
Printed in Harrisburg by Peters, hc, 14x18"................45.00
Printed in Reading by Kebler, 1860, hc, 17x19".............65.00
Printed w/Christ's Baptism, Egelmann, 1821, 11x9½".........135.00
Printed/hc, baptism of Christ/Sermon on Mount, 1813, 12x14".100.00
Wc, calligraphy/strap-work, floral border, Stony Creek artist...2,750.00
Wc, heart reserve, drapery at top, Stony Creek artist, 1812...4,125.00
Wc, on laid paper, 2 facing angels/dotted wings, 1786, 8x12".8,250.00
Wc, orbs/pine trees/etc, Mt Pleasant artist, 1822, 9x7".....2,640.00
Wc, paired birds, strap-work/calligraphy, Earl Township artist.2,310.00
Wc, pr lg birds on flowering urns, 1816, 8½x10"...........2,200.00
Wc, red winged X leg angel, birds ea side, 1791, 12x15"....2,970.00
Wc/cut-work center panel w/birds/flowers/etc, 1815, 10x12"....935.00

Bookplate, wc, laid paper, Elisabeth/1781 w/religious figure....700.00
Drawing, man, red/bl robes w/book, calligraphy, wc, 4".......275.00
Drawing, wc, portraits, man/wife w/verse, 1841, fr, 9½x7", pr.6,600.00
Drawing, wc stylized portrait of Commodore Decatur, 7½x5½".525.00
Drawing, 2 birds perched on lg flowering tulip plant, 4x4".....495.00
House blessing, wc, calligraphy/flowers/etc, Engelhard, 12x9".1,650.00
Letter, keystone w/vine borders, calligraphy, 1823, 9x7".......715.00
Merit reward, lg stylized flower w/rows of buds, 4½x2½"......350.00
Merit reward, wc, 2 peafowls flank crown, 4½x6"............770.00
Printed/wc, Procession to the Cross, early 1800s, 18x14".....275.00
Religious, wc, concentric text, hearts/birds/stars, 15x12"....1,760.00
Religious, wc, text w/rows of hearts/tulips/stars, Brubacher....4,510.00
Uninscribed, wc, 2 pr unicorns, late 1800s, 13x16".........2,310.00
Valentine, hearts w/#d verse, pen/ink/wc, 17" square.........375.00

Vorschrift, scrolls/tulips in pots, 1810, losses, 8x10″, pr.......770.00
Vorschrift, wc, lg strap-work letters/calligraphy, 1824, 7x8″.....770.00
Vorschrift, wc/laid paper, lg lettering w/floral sprays, 1815....2,310.00

Watercolor and cutwork, 'When My Jesus Comes', signed Johannes Aiter, Southeastern Pennsylvania, March 29, 1778, 12½″ x 14½″, $4,125.00.

Frames

Styles in picture frames have changed with the fashion of the day, but those that especially interest today's collectors are the deep shadow boxes made of fine woods such as walnut or cherry, those with Art Nouveau influence, and the oak frames decorated with molded gesso and gilt from the Victorian era.

Art Deco, glass, blk/gray w/silver trim, metal corners, 5½x7″.....8.00
Art Deco, glass, ivory, gold/blk leaf, Decorative Arts, 10x12″....17.50
Cast iron, easel type, gilded, inner border pk enamel, 5½x7″....40.00
Cast iron, easel type, openwork scrolls, gilt finish, 4x5½″.......45.00

Criss-cross at corners with oak leaf trim, gilt inner frame, 12½″ x 15″, $22.00; with accompanying 8″ x 10″ print, $35.00.

Compact style, brass, holds 2 photos, open: 3x4½″...........22.00
Criss cross, walnut, gold liner, corner leaves, 13x15″.........22.00
Criss cross, walnut, leaf corners, 13x17″.....................16.00
Dutch silver, triptych, center arched, chased medallions, 15″..1,340.00
Easel, brass w/tin bk, floral fretwork crest, 1890s, 3x5″.......22.00
Ivory, carved w/florals, oval, 1800s, 5½″.....................45.00
Ivory, reticulated, carved dragons, easel type, 3½x3″.........125.00
Mahogany veneer, blk ebonized stripe, 1″ W, 7x8½″.........45.00
Pine, beveled, orig br/red sponging, minor wear, 1¾″ W, 10x8″.95.00
Poplar, beveled, orig blk pnt/yel stencil, 1¾″ W; 13x17″.....135.00
Poplar, ½ turnings w/corner blocks, grpt, 12x23″.............45.00
Rococo, easel bk, oval w/pierced leaves/scrolls, 8½x11″........40.00
Shadowbox, walnut w/gilt liner, 16x19″, VG.................35.00
Shadowbox, wide deep walnut, opening 4¾x6¼″, pr...........36.00
Tiger oak, extra wide ogee, wavy glass, wood bk, for 16x20″....65.00
Tin, 5″ wide sides, old ornamentation missing, 13x15″........190.00
Tortoise shell faced easel, ca 1880, 3½x4½″.................24.00
Walnut, black liner, deep set, 15x17″.......................35.00
Walnut, gilt liner, semi-deep, 17½x22″.....................28.00
Walnut jigsaw work, holds 3 oval pictures, folk art, 16x20″....115.00

Franciscan

Franciscan Ware was developed by Gladding McBean and Company at their site in Glendale, California. First introduced in 1934, it has been made in many lovely patterns that are today attracting the attention of collectors interested in modern American dinnerware. Perhaps the best known of their early lines is Swirl, or Coronado, as it was officially named. It was made in more than sixty shapes and fifteen colors. El Patio and El Patio Neuvo were two other early lines, also made in simple shapes and in solid colors. In 1937, the first of their hand-decorated lines was introduced, and in 1940, they began producing the embossed patterns with under the glaze hand decoration that has become typical of Franciscan wares since that time.

The first mark, used in the late thirties, was a large 'F' within a double-walled square. In the forties, a two-line Franciscan mark was adopted. It was replaced in 1947 by a circular device -- 'Franciscan Ware' centered by 'Made In California USA'.

The company is still in business today, owned by the Interpace Corporation, and continues to produce dinnerware on a large scale.

Apple

Bone dish, large...9.00
Bowl, soup/cereal.......................................7.00
Bowl, vegetable; medium................................17.00
Butter pat...3.00
Creamer..10.00
Cup & saucer..11.50

Nested bowls, largest 8¾″, $75.00 for the set.

Cup & saucer, demitasse.............................8.00
Egg cup...8.00
Fruit/sauce.......................................5.00
Plate, bread & butter.............................5.00
Plate, chop......................................25.00
Plate, dinner....................................10.00
Plate, luncheon...................................9.00
Plate, salad......................................7.00
Platter, 12″.....................................18.00
Platter, 14″.....................................24.00
Salt & pepper, rosebud, pr.......................12.50
Sauce boat w/liner...............................25.00
Saucer..3.50
Sugar, open......................................10.00
Sugar w/lid......................................17.50

Ballet

Cup & saucer.....................................12.50
Plate, bread & butter.............................6.00
Plate, dinner....................................10.00
Plate, salad......................................7.50

Coronado

Bowl, cereal; coral...............................4.50
Candle holders, w/orig sticker, ivory, pr........25.00
Carafe, orange...................................13.00
Coffee pot, AD, yellow, satin....................35.00
Cream soup, burgandy gloss.......................12.00
Cream soup & liner, coral gloss..................10.00
Cream soup liner, burgundy gloss..................5.00
Creamer, turq.....................................4.00
Cup & saucer, demitasse, coral gloss.............12.00
Cup & saucer, ivory...............................6.00
Gravy boat, attached under liner, ivory..........15.00
Jam jar, square...................................7.00
Plate, ivory, 8½″.................................5.00
Plate, ivory, 9½″.................................6.00
Plate, serving; coral, 11½″......................10.00
Plate, turq, 6½″..................................3.00
Plate, yellow, 10½″...............................8.00
Platter, yellow, 12½″............................12.50
Relish, oval, burgundy gloss......................5.00
Salt & peppers, turq, pr..........................8.00
Sherbet, ivory....................................4.00
Sugar, open, yellow gloss.........................6.00
Sugar w/lid, coral gloss..........................6.50
Teapot, white....................................18.00
Teapot, yellow...................................35.00
Vase, ivory.......................................8.00
Vase, pumpkin shape, yellow......................20.00

Desert Rose

Ash tray, rose petal, small......................10.50
Bowl, cereal.....................................10.50
Bowl, mixing; 3 nested...........................65.00
Bowl, soup.......................................12.50
Butter, oblong, ¼ lb.............................17.50
Candle holder, pr................................27.50
Cigarette box....................................37.50
Creamer & sugar w/lid............................27.50
Jam jar w/lid....................................27.50

Pitcher, pint....................................15.00
Pitcher, water...................................32.00
Plate, chop; 11½″................................19.50
Relish, 3 part...................................17.50
Shakers, large, pr...............................27.50
Shakers, lg pepper mill & salt shaker, pr........47.50
Shakers, rose bud, small, pr.....................22.50
Sherbet...9.50
Soup cup, large, w/liner.........................18.50
Teapot...32.50
Tidbit, 3 tier...................................32.50
Tumbler, 14 oz...................................12.50

El Patio

Bowl, cereal; lettuce gr gloss, 5½″...............7.00
Cream soup, hdld, lettuce gr gloss................9.00
Cup & saucer, demitasse; pretzel hdl, w/orig label...........10.50
Cup & saucer, lettuce gr gloss....................7.50
Plate, lettuce gr gloss, 8¼″......................4.50
Plate, lettuce gr gloss, 9¼″......................5.50
Platter, oval, lettuce gr gloss, 13″.............13.00
Shakers, lettuce gr gloss, pr.....................9.00
Sugar w/lid, lettuce gr gloss.....................8.00

Heritage

Butter dish w/lid................................20.00
Chop plate, lg...................................40.00
Creamer & sugar..................................32.00
Fruit..12.00
Gravy boat.......................................30.00
Plate, bread & butter.............................9.00
Plate, salad.....................................11.00
Platter, sm......................................30.00
Relish, divided..................................28.00
Salt & pepper, pr................................20.00
Vegetable, divided...............................30.00
Vegetable, rectangular...........................22.50

Indigo

Cup & saucer.....................................26.50
Plate, bread & butter............................15.00
Plate, dinner....................................20.00
Plate, salad.....................................17.50
Soup, rimmed.....................................22.00

Ivy

Bowl, 5″..4.00
Bowl, 6″..5.00
Bowl, 8″...10.00
Cup & saucer......................................7.50
Nut bowl, w/brass hdl............................12.00
Plate, dinner.....................................5.00
Sauce boat w/liner...............................23.00
Sugar w/lid......................................10.00
Tumbler, 12 oz....................................8.00

Medallion Blue

Cup & saucer.....................................13.50
Plate, bread & butter.............................4.50

Plate, dinner.....................................8.50
Plate, salad......................................6.00

Midnight Mist

Coffee pot.......................................60.00
Cup & saucer....................................25.00
Gravy w/attached under plate....................50.00
Plate, dinner....................................20.00
Plate, salad.....................................16.00

Silver Pine

Cup & saucer....................................15.00
Plate, bread & butter.............................7.50
Plate, dinner....................................13.50
Plate, salad.....................................10.00

Miscellaneous

Place setting, Cameo, 5 pc.......................85.00
Place setting, Concord, 5 pc....................125.00
Place setting, Golden Leaves, 5 pc...............85.00
Place setting, Somerset, 5 pc....................85.00

Francisware

Francisware, produced by Hobbs, Brockunier and Company of Wheeling, West Virginia, in the 1880s, is a clear or frosted tableware with amber stained rim bands. The most often found pattern is Hobnail, but a Swirl design was also made.

Hobnail, clear; berry, small, 4" dia...............30.00
Hobnail, clear; berry, small, 4" sq...............25.00
Hobnail, clear; creamer..........................50.00
Hobnail, clear; pitcher, 8½".....................145.00
Hobnail, clear; spooner..........................45.00
Hobnail, clear; tumbler..........................35.00
Hobnail, frosted; bowl, 7½" sq...................68.00
Hobnail, frosted; celery.........................80.00
Hobnail, frosted; creamer........................70.00

Frosted Hobnail sugar bowl, $75.00.

Hobnail, frosted; creamer & sugar w/lid.........145.00
Hobnail, frosted; decanter......................155.00
Hobnail, frosted; pitcher, 8½"..................180.00
Hobnail, frosted; salt & peppers, pr.............75.00
Hobnail, frosted; sauce, ruffled, square.........25.00
Hobnail, frosted; spooner........................70.00
Hobnail, frosted; sugar w/lid....................75.00
Hobnail, frosted; syrup.........................125.00
Hobnail, frosted; table set, 4 pcs..............360.00
Hobnail, frosted; toothpick......................50.00
Hobnail, frosted; tray, ice cream; 14x9½".......225.00
Hobnail, frosted; waste bowl.....................70.00
Swirl, frosted; celery tray, 12x7"...............75.00
Swirl, frosted; finger bowl, w/amber rim.........25.00
Swirl, frosted; salt & peppers, pr...............75.00
Swirl, frosted; sugar w/lid......................85.00
Swirl, frosted; toothpick........................95.00
Swirl, frosted; tray, oval, 12½x6¾"..............35.00
Swirl, fruit bowl, 9", w/12 sm sauce dishes.....375.00

Frankart

During the 1920s, Frankart Inc. of New York City produced a line of metal accessories such as lamps, bookends, and ash trays in a green patina finish. Animals and bird figurals were used, but their nudes were the most popular. Many pieces were marked 'Frankart', with the patent number and date of manufacture.

Ash tray, stylized gazelle leaps oval gr glass tray, 5½", VG.....75.00
Cigarette box, 2 back-to-back nudes, gr glass box atop, 87942..425.00
Lamp, silhouette; nude kneels under 7" glass disc shield, 11"..525.00
Lamp, 2 nudes kneel/embrace 8" crackle glass globe, 9", VG..435.00
Smoker set, nude w/urn walks on sq pottery ash tray, 12", NM.455.00
Smoking stand, nude w/ash bowl (missing) on brass ball, rpt....250.00
Vase, upright nude embraces removable frosted vase, 10", NM..375.00
Wall sconce, nude sits atop floral work, pan missing, rpt, 12"..250.00
Wall sconce, nude w/pan sits on floral work, 93876, 12", NM..435.00

Frankoma

The Frank Pottery, founded in 1933 by John Frank, became known as Frankoma in 1934. The company produced decorative figurals, vases, and such, marking their ware from 1936-38 with a pacing leapord 'Frankoma' mark. These pieces are highly sought. The entire operation was destroyed by fire in 1938 and new molds were cast -- some from surviving pieces -- and a similar line of production was pursued.

The body of the ware was changed in 1954 from a honey tan to a red brick clay, and this, along with the color of the glazes (over forty have been used) helps determine the period of production.

A Southwestern theme has always been favored in design as well as in color selection. In 1965 they began to produce a limited edition series of Christmas plates, followed by a bottle vase series in 1969. Considered very collectible are their political mugs, bicentennial plates, Teenagers of the Bible plates, and the Wildfire series. Their ceramic Christmas cards are also very popular items with today's collectors.

Frankoma celebrated their 50th Anniversary in 1983. On September 26, of that same year, Frankoma was again destroyed by fire. Because of a fire-proof wall, master molds of all 1983 production items were saved, allowing plans for rebuilding to begin immediately. 'Grand Opening' was celebrated in July, 1984.

Ash tray, Texas shape, Robin Egg Blue, #459................5.00
Ash tray/candle holder, Wagon Wheel, no mk...............20.00

Bowl, #105, black, 3".................................12.00
Bowl, leaf form, #226, Redbud......................9.50
Candle holder, double, Brown Satin, #304, pr.............12.00
Canister, 'Flour', #25F.............................25.00
Chocolate set, Mayan, pitcher+6 8-oz cups, ivory, sgn, '30s...115.00
Christmas card, 1947................................75.00
Christmas card, 1949................................55.00
Christmas card, 1953................................60.00
Christmas card, 1954................................65.00
Christmas card, 1958................................50.00
Christmas card, 1959................................65.00
Christmas card, 1960................................50.00
Christmas card, 1966................................45.00
Christmas card, 1967................................35.00
Christmas card, 1971................................25.00
Christmas card, 1972................................17.50
Christmas card, 1973................................16.00
Christmas card, 1975................................80.00
Christmas card, 1976................................13.50
Christmas card, 1980.................................8.00
Cookie jar..12.00
Cornucopia, #222, Prairie Green.....................25.00
Cornucopia, #57, Peach Glow, 9½" L..................25.00
Creamer & sugar, Wagon Wheel, old mk................10.00
Dealer's sign, 8" curved strip, Prairie Gr, Frankoma....15.00
Donkey mug, 1975, Autumn Yellow.....................15.00
Donkey mug, 1976, Centennial Red....................15.00
Donkey mug, 1977, Carter/Mondale, Dusty Pink........10.00
Donkey mug, 1978, Woodland Moss.....................10.00
Donkey mug, 1979, Brown Satin........................8.50
Donkey mug, 1980, Terra Cotta........................8.00
Elephant mug, 1968, White...........................75.00
Elephant mug, 1969, Nixon/Agnew, Flame..............70.00
Elephant mug, 1970, Blue............................22.50
Elephant mug, 1971, Black...........................50.00
Elephant mug, 1972, Prairie Green...................24.50
Elephant mug, 1973, Nixon/Agnew, Desert Gold........32.00
Elephant mug, 1974, Coffee..........................12.50
Elephant mug, 1975, Autumn Yellow...................10.50
Elephant mug, 1976, Centennial Red..................15.00
Elephant mug, 1977, Carter/Mondale, Dusty Pink.......9.50
Elephant mug, 1978, Woodland Moss...................10.00
Elephant mug, 1979, Brown Satin......................8.50
Elephant mug, 1980, Terra Cotta......................8.00
Elephant mug, 1981, Reagan/Bush, Celery Green........9.00
Flower arranger, Gracetone #68, Brown, 4½" cube.....10.00
Flower bowl, blk, #88, 15" L.........................14.50
Flower holder, Cross, Wht Sand, no mk, 6½"..........20.00
Honey pot, beehive w/bee finial, Desert Gold, 4½"...20.00
Mask, Comedy, blk...................................15.00
Mug, Uncle Sam toby, Bicentennial Blue, #600, 1976...12.00
Pitcher, #835, 8"...................................10.00
Pitcher, juice; w/lid, Prairie Green, 7"............20.00
Pitcher, juice; w/lid & 2 cups, Prairie Green, #93..10.00
Pitcher, snail, miniature, Prairie Green.............8.00
Pitcher, Woodland Moss, #81, 1 qt...................10.00
Planter, blk foot, #55, 4"..........................15.00
Planter, swan, Redbud, #228, 5x8"...................25.00
Plate, Bible Teenagers, 1972, Jesus the Carpenter, White Sand.120.00
Plate, Bible Teenagers, 1972, Jesus/Carpenter, Desert Gold.....20.00
Plate, Bible Teenagers, 1974, David the Musician, Desert Gold..22.00
Plate, Bible Teenagers, 1975, Jonathan the Archer, Desert Gold.20.00
Plate, Bible Teenagers, 1976, Dorcas the Seamstress, Des Gold..35.00
Plate, Bible Teenagers, 1977, Peter the Fisherman, Desert Gold.20.00

Plate, Bible Teenagers, 1978, Martha the Homemaker, Gold....20.00
Plate, Bible Teenagers, 1979, Daniel the Courageous, Gold.....17.00
Plate, Bible Teenagers, 1980, Ruth the Devoted, Desert Gold...16.00
Plate, Bible Teenagers, 1981, Joseph the Dreamer, Desert Gold.15.00
Plate, Bible Teenagers, 1982, Mary the Mother, Desert Gold....15.00
Plate, Bicentennial, 1972, 'Provocations', Prairie Gr or Gold...125.00
Plate, Bicentennial, 1972, 'Provocations', White Sand..........25.00
Plate, Bicentennial, 1972, States misspelled 'Statis'..........125.00
Plate, Bicentennial, 1973, 'Patriots/Leaders', White Sand......25.00
Plate, Bicentennial, 1974, 'Battles For Independence', White....25.00
Plate, Bicentennial, 1975, 'Victories For Independence', White...25.00
Plate, Bicentennial, 1976, 'Symbols Of Freedom', White Sand...25.00
Plate, Christmas, 1965, Good Will Towards Men.............220.00
Plate, Christmas, 1966, Joy To The World.................85.00
Plate, Christmas, 1967, Gifts For The Christ Child........60.00
Plate, Christmas, 1968, Flight Into Egypt.................32.50
Plate, Christmas, 1969, Laid In A Manger.................35.00
Plate, Christmas, 1970, King Of Kings....................20.00
Plate, Christmas, 1971, No Room In The Inn...............20.00
Plate, Christmas, 1972, Seeking The Christ Child..........20.00
Plate, Christmas, 1973, The Annunciation.................20.00
Plate, Conestoga....................................50.00
Plate, Mason's commemorative, 1849-1949, 10"........23.00
Plate, Oral Roberts.................................17.00
Plate, Postman's, 1952..............................80.00
Plate, Wildlife series, complete set of 7............150.00
Sculpture, coyote...................................15.00
Sculpture, gardener boy, 7".........................90.00
Sculpture, gardener girl, 5¾".......................80.00
Sculpture, Indian maiden............................15.00
Sculpture, mare & colt, white, 12"..................15.00
Sculpture, puma, reclining, wht.....................15.00
Sculpture, puma, sitting, wht.......................15.00
Swan, #229, middle..................................45.00
Trivet, ATR Oklahoma, Arrows to Atoms, Desert Gold, 1957....20.00
Trivet, Bicentennial Liberty Bell, dates on face, Wht Sand, 6"...10.00
Trivet, Cherokee Alphabet, Peach Glow....................9.00
Tumbler, juice; Prairie Green, wht clay, 3", set of 4.........25.00
Vase, bottle; turq blue Chinese, #14, 1938, 10".........35.00
Vase, bowl; Blue Gray Jade, #35, 1933-42, 3x6".........22.50
Vase, Cactus, #206, Prairie Green...................25.00
Vase, cockatoo, yellow, ca 1936.....................75.00
Vase, collector; V-1, Prairie Gr/blk base, sgn John Frank, 15"...85.00
Vase, collector; V-10-B, Morning Glory Blue, sgn JF, 11½".....25.00
Vase, collector; V-10-C, Coffee, 1978, sgn JF, 11½".....25.00
Vase, collector; V-11-B, Morning Glory Blue, 1979, 11½".....25.00
Vase, collector; V-11-C, Coffee, wht int, 1979, sgn JF, 11½"....25.00
Vase, collector; V-12, Black w/Terra Cotta, 1980, sgn JF, 13"...30.00
Vase, collector; V-13, Black w/Terra Cotta, 1982, sgn JF, 13"...30.00
Vase, collector; V-14, Flame & Blk, 1982, sgn JF, 11"........45.00
Vase, collector; V-2, Turquoise Bl, 1970, sgn John Frank, 12"..50.00
Vase, collector; V-3, red & blk, 1971, sgn John Frank, 12".....65.00
Vase, collector; V-4, Terra Cotta & blk, sgn John Frank, 12"....60.00
Vase, collector; V-5, Flame, blk base, wht int, Grace Lee, 13"...60.00
Vase, collector; V-6, Celadon, blk base, sgn Grace Lee, 13".....70.00
Vase, collector; V-7, Desert Gold, Coffee base/stopper, sgn JF...50.00
Vase, collector; V-8, Freedom Red/Wht, red stopper, JF, 13"....60.00
Vase, collector; V-9, wht w/blk base & stopper, sgn JF, 1977....50.00
Vase, cornucopia, Desert Gold, #56, 7"..............18.00
Vase, cylinder, black w/combed effect, 8"...........15.00
Vase, fan, shell, blk, #54..........................12.50
Vase, flower girl, #700.............................65.00
Vase, free form, Desert Gold, #6, 7".................6.00
Vase, Gracetone, Pink Champagne.....................12.00

Vase, snail, #31, Osage Brown.........................12.00
Vase, Wagon Wheel, Desert Gold, #94, 7"..................15.00
Wall mask, Indian, blk...................................8.00
Wall pocket, Acorn, any color, 5½"......................20.00
Wall pocket, Peter Pan, #100............................25.00
Wall pocket, Phoebe, red, #130..........................27.00

Shrine goblet, Rochester, N.Y.; Pittsburgh, Pennsylvania; dated 1911, 5" x 3¾", $110.00.

Cup, Indian head relief, china, Pittsburgh, 1903, 3¼".........45.00
Goblet, scimitar & moon, silver swords, wheat stalks, 1908......75.00
Hat, w/brass scarab & denim zipper case, old.................49.00
Mug, Atlantic City, 1904....................................60.00
Mug, glass, silver fish hdl, relief Nouveau lady/ship, 1904......65.00
Pin, lapel; 32nd, sterling..................................10.50
Plate, bandaged Shriner center, camels/oasis border, Shenango..48.00
Plate, Los Angeles, May 1906, 6"...........................25.00
Tumbler, milk glass w/gold Syria sword/star/etc, 1915.........55.00

Flower girl, figural vase, blue, brown and yellow, 6", $65.00.

Fraternal Organizations

Fraternal memorabilia is a vast and varied field. Emblems representing the various organizations have been used to decorate cups, shaving mugs, plates, and glassware. Medals, swords, documents, and other ceremonial paraphernalia from the 1800s and early 1900s are especially prized.

Elks

Ash tray, tin, stag on bottom, Grand Lodge Reunion, 1916, 4"..60.00
Mirror, brass fr, oval, w/emblem at top.....................55.00
Pin-back, Elks Reunion Denver 1906, enamel clock, 3 pc, metal.20.00
Print, lady w/elk, How I Love an Elk, sepia, 1907, oak fr.......35.00
Stein, pewter/relief elk/#1 NY 1913, red glass base/logo, ½ L...102.00

Masons

Books, History of Freemasonry, Klegg, leather bound, 7 vols...125.00
Champagne, New Orleans, Neptune & alligators, 1910..........65.00
Clock, New Haven, Knights Templer on lower glass, ogee, 26".500.00
Cup, red flashed, Temple, World's Fair, 1893...............25.00
Jigger, glass lined sterling...............................29.00
Loving cup, Niagara Falls, 1905............................85.00
Mug, Atlanta 1914 Convention, rat w/cap & basket, 5½".......45.00
Plate, glass, Los Angeles, 1906, 6".........................40.00
Shaving mug...95.00
Spoon, sterling, ornate....................................65.00
Watch charm, gold, Santa Fe, 1866..........................25.00

Shrine

Candlestick, cut crystal, 1901, pr........................100.00
Champagne, buildings, man on camel, man w/camera, 1911.....95.00
Champagne, Pittsburgh Shrine, 1909, ornate stem w/daggers...100.00

Miscellaneous

FOA, shaving mug...95.00
Knights of Columbus, shaving mug...........................95.00
Odd Fellows, plate, w/symbols, bl/yel spatterware, 7".......70.00
Odd Fellows, podium, wht & dk wood, applied cross, etc.......18.00
Royal Order of Moose, shaving mug..........................95.00
Royal Order of Moose, watch fob, dbl tooth.................75.00

Fraunfelter

Charles Fraunfelter organized his company in Zanesville, Ohio, in 1915. It was known as the Ohio Pottery Company until 1923. During this period their main product was a line of utilitarian articles for chemical laboratories made of hard paste porcelain. In 1918 they used the same body to produce a brown and white line called 'Petrascan'. By 1920 a line of hotel ware was added. The company organized in 1923 and became known as the Fraunfelter China Company; but after the death of Fraunfelter in 1925, the business fell into hard times and eventually closed altogether in 1939.

Teapot, green and white, 3", $12.50.

Candlesticks, pearlized, sgn, 8½", pr......................36.00
Coffee pot, yel w/silver decor, 4 pcs, all china...............55.00
Teapot, 5"...30.00

Fruit Jars

As early as 1829, canning jars were being manufactured for use in the home preservation of foodstuffs. For the past fifteen years, they have been sought as popular collectibles. At the last estimate, over 4,000 fruit jars and variations were known to exist. Some are very rare, perhaps one-of-a-kind examples, known to have survived to the present day. Among the most valuable are the black glass jars, the amber Van Vliet, and the cobalt Millville. These often bring prices in excess of $500 when they can be found. Aside from condition, values are based on age, rarity, and special features.

A B C, aqua pt..345.00
A R S, fancy script, aqua qt..............................55.00
ABGA Mason Improved, gr qt..............................2.50
Airtight, wax sealer, barrel shape, 1877, gr qt...............75.00
All Right, aqua qt, pat Jan 28th 1868, orig lid..............145.00
Almy, aqua qt...100.00
American, Eagle & Flag, gr qt............................120.00
Anchor Hocking Lightening, glass top, 1937, clear qt..........4.00
Atlas, Mason's Patent, olive gr pt.........................20.00
Atlas E-Z Seal, amber qt.................................27.50
Atlas E-Z Seal, aqua ½ gal...............................5.00
Atlas Strong Shoulder Mason, lt bl pt.......................10.00
Ball (printed) Perfect Mason, deep aqua pt...................3.50
Ball Mason, erased root, yellow gr qt.......................20.00
Ball Perfect Mason, dk olive gr ½ gal......................35.00
Baltimore Glass Works, aqua qt, stopper neck...............250.00
Banner, Pat Feby 9th 1864, Reisd Jan 22 1867, aqua qt......100.00
Beaver, chewing log, clear qt.............................20.00
Bloeser Jar, aqua qt, orig clamp, EX......................120.00
Boldt Mason Jar, zinc lid, bl-gr qt.........................15.00
Burlington, BG Co R'd 1875, clear ½ gal....................80.00
Canadian King, glass lid & full wire bail, clear qt.............6.00
Canton Domestic Fruit Jar, clear pt.......................125.00
Champion Syrup & Refining Co, Indpls, aqua qt.............25.00
Clark's Peerless, wire bail & glass lid, 1882, bl qt............15.00
Clarke Fruit Jar Co, aqua ½ gal..........................60.00
Cohansey, in arch, aqua pt...............................30.00
Cohansey Glass Mf'g Co Pat MCH 20 77, aqua qt...........125.00
Columbia, clear pt......................................20.00
Crown, w/crown, amber qt...............................50.00
Crown Imperial, w/crown, ½ gal sun amethyst...............20.00
Cunningham & Co Pittsburg, aqua ½ gal, pontiled...........250.00
Cunningham & Ithsem Pittsburg, aqua ½ gal, wax seal.......35.00
Darling, ADM, aqua qt..................................30.00
Darling Imperial, ADM, aqua ½ gal........................50.00
Decker Dependable Food, JE Decker & Son, Mason City, cl qt...3.00
Dexter, aqua ½ gal......................................35.00
Doolittle Patented Dec 3 1910, on lid, clear qt...............20.00
E G Co Imperial, aqua qt................................20.00
Eagle, aqua qt...120.00
Electric, glass lid & wire bail, rnd, aqua qt..................20.00
Erased Western Pride, aqua qt............................32.50
Eureka Pat'd Dec 27th 1864, aqua qt......................75.00
Excelsior Improved, aqua ½ gal...........................60.00
F & A Co, pontiled, aqua qt.............................175.00
Flaccus Co, EC Trade Mark, elk & floral design, milk glass.....90.00
Fruit Commonwealth Jar, clear ½ gal.......................90.00
Fruit Keeper, G C Co, aqua pt............................42.50

Woodbury, 'WCW' monogram, blue, ½ gallon, $35.00.

G J CO, monogram, aqua qt..............................22.50
Gem, w/maltese cross, aqua qt.............................3.00
Gilchrist, zinc lid, dome opal liner, wide mouth, aqua-gr qt......6.00
Globe, amber qt..50.00
Glocker Trade Mark Sanitary Pat 1911 Others Pending, aqua qt.25.00
Hahne & Co Newark NJ, w/star, pt.........................45.00
Haines Improved March 1st 1870, aqua qt..................75.00
Hamilton Glass Works, Clamp Jar ½ gal, aqua..............200.00
Hamilton No 3 Glass Works, aqua ½ gal...................250.00
Hartell's Glass Air Tight Cover Pat Oct 19 1858, aqua pt.....150.00
Hawley Glass Co, aqua pt................................20.00
Helmes Railroad Mills, amber qt...........................12.00
Hero Improved, whittle mk, tin insert, aqua qt...............30.00
Hilton's Pat Mar 10th 1868, aqua qt......................285.00
Ideal Imperial, aqua qt..................................25.00
Ivanhoe, 4 under bottom, clear, 4½"........................6.00
Jewel Jar, block letters, in fr, clear qt.....................65.00
JM Clark & Co, amber qt.................................45.00
Johnson & Johnson New Brunswick NJ USA, amber qt........22.50
Joshua Wright, Phila, pontil, barrel type..................225.00
Kalamazoo, The Jay B Rhodes, wax seal, 1875, qt.............8.00
Kerr Wide Mouth Mason, clear ½ pt........................11.50
King Pat Nov 2 1869, qt................................140.00
Kline's Patent Oct 27 63, on blown stopper, aqua qt.........125.00
LaFayette, in script, aqua qt..............................95.00
LaFayette, w/profile, aqua qt............................750.00
Leader, aqua qt..30.00
Mason's, sheared top, black, 7¼".........................250.00
Mason's Patent Nov 30th 1858, CFJ Co monogram, aqua pt.....5.00
Mason's Union, w/shield, aqua qt..........................50.00
Millville Atmospheric Fruit Jar, aqua pt....................40.00
Newark, zinc top, clear qt.................................7.00
Newmark Special Extra Mason Jar, w/fleur de lys, aqua pt......25.00
Patented Oct 19 1858, on lid, aqua qt......................40.00
Pearl, aqua qt..30.00
Princess, fancy shield, glass top & wire bail, clear qt..........16.00
Queen, aqua qt...15.00
RAG, monogram, aqua qt.................................42.50
Red Mason's, emb key, Patent Nov 30th 1858, zinc lid, aqua pt.12.00
Sanitary, glass lid, wire bail, 1900, aqua qt..................13.50
Smalley Full Measure AGS Quart, amber qt...................50.00

Telephone Jar, full wire bail, glass top, gr qt 17.50
Trade Mark Bee Hive, aqua qt 130.00
Trade Mark Lightning Reg US Patent Office, apple gr qt 125.00
Trade Mark Lightning Reg US Patent Office, cornflower bl pt . . .40.00
Van Vliet, glass top & iron band w/screw, aqua qt 50.00
Yeoman's Fruit Bottle, wax seal, sm mouth, 1855-1870, aqua 35.00

Fry

Henry Fry established his glassworks in 1901 in Rochester, Pennsylvania. There until 1933 when it was sold to the Libbey Company, he produced glassware of the finest quality. In the early years they produced beautiful cut glass, and when it began to wane in popularity, Fry turned to the manufacture of occasional pieces and oven glassware. He is perhaps most famous for the opalescent pearl glass called 'Foval'. It was made in combination with crystal or colored trim, and because it was in production for only a short time in 1926 and 1927, it is hard to find.

Collectors of depression era glassware look for the opalescent reamers and opaque green kitchenware made during the early thirties.

Bowl, pineapple & wheels cutting, sgnd, 8" 95.00
Candlestick, Foval, Delph bl/wht, 12", pr 350.00
Candlestick, Foval, wht w/bl threading & wafer, 10½", pr 185.00
Compote, Foval, opal w/bl stem, 7x6" 125.00
Compote, Foval, opal w/gr stem, 6¾x6" 100.00
Creamer & sugar, Foval, pearl w/cobalt handles 175.00
Cruet, Foval, cobalt handle, orig stopper 85.00
Cup & saucer, Foval, bl hdl 85.00
Decanter, Foval, opal w/cobalt hdl, ftd, 9" 160.00
Pitcher, clear crackle w/gr hdl, +4 mugs 65.00
Pitcher, crackle glass, applied bl hdl, knob on lid, lg 80.00
Pitcher, lemonade; Foval, bl hdl & lid finial, 10½" 165.00
Tea set, Foval, pot & 4 cup/saucers 395.00
Vase, Foval, Delph bl/wht, ped ft, 9¾" 395.00
Vase, Foval, opaline w/jade gr ft, rolled rim, 7½" 200.00
Whiskey taster, jade gr w/opal hdl 90.00

Fulper

The Fulper Pottery was founded in 1899 after nearly a century of producing utilitarian stoneware under various titles and managements. Not until 1909 did Fulper venture into the art pottery field. Vasekraft, their first art line, utilized the same heavy clay body used for their utility ware. Shapes were severe, unadorned, and rather ungraceful. But the glazes they developed were used with such flair and imagination, alone and in unexpected combined harmony, that each piece was truly a work of art. In contrast to the Vasekraft line, graceful Oriental shapes were produced to compliment the important 'famille rose' glaze developed by W.H. Fulper, Jr. Other designs were developed with an Art Deco influence.

During WWI, doll's heads and Kewpies were made as a substitute for imports. Figural perfume lamps and powder boxes were made both in bisque and glazed ware. Although the plant was in operation until 1935, the most prized examples pre-date 1930. Much of the ware was marked with a vertical 'Fulper' in line reserve, although a horizontal mark as well as a 'Vasekraft' paper label was also used.

Basket, handmade, applied roses, twist hdl, wht glaze, 6x12" . . .165.00
Bookends, lion's mask, pr 195.00
Bottle, musical, glossy streak tan/blk, loop hdl, stopper, 9" 125.00
Bottle, musical, 3 sides pinched, bl/olive mirror lustre, 10" 130.00
Bowl, blue crystalline, #4012, 12" dia .95.00

Bowl with applied rose, green crystalline glaze, 4½" x 7", $185.00.

Bowl, gold-bronze drip w/in, 3 ft, 2x6¼" 45.00
Bowl, gr w/br flambe, 9" 65.00
Bowl, matt bl w/bl/gr crystals, glaze flake w/in, 2½x9" 45.00
Bowl, modeled rim decor, gr/br flambe, 11" 200.00
Bowl, mottled blue/matt/scalloped/ribbed, collar ft, early, 9" 115.00
Bowl, ped ft, bl flambe, 10" 135.00
Bowl, roll edge, purple drip on rose matt, flambe w/in, 9½" 45.00
Bowl, rose, 13" 75.00
Bowl, rose/leaves in full relief, wht, vertical stamp, 3½x7" 75.00
Bowl, royal bl, 2½x9" 50.00
Bowl, scalloped, rolled pierced bk, gr/yel/bl, oval, 9½x11½" . . .300.00
Bowl, variegated cobalt, early, 3½x9½" 75.00
Box, powder; figural lady 135.00
Candle holder, gr w/gold, crystalline, pr 75.00
Candlestick, bl crystal, 8" 90.00
Candlestick, blue drip glaze, w/hdl, 2½" 25.00
Candlestick, hooded, w/hdl, bl/purple, 7" 95.00
Candlestick, wisteria, low, w/hdl 45.00
Cat, green/ochre, repaired ear, horizontal block mk, 3x8½" 490.00
Chamberstick, dk gr, vertical mk 42.00
Chamberstick, olive over bright blue 38.00
Compote, gr crystalline leopard skin, ink stamp, 6x10" 165.00
Decanter, musical, dk tan/blk, indented sides, silver top, 8½" . . .50.00
Dish, open shell, pink, mk C, 1½x5½" .10.00
Flower frog, frog, br/gr 45.00
Flower frog, lily pad 20.00
Flower frog, marsh motif, w/figural duck 95.00
Flower frog, pelican, br/gr semi-matt, 7¼" 130.00
Flower frog, penguin 185.00
Ginger jar, gr crystalline, 7 sides, 8x7" 145.00
Humidor, matt blk, 7x7½" 180.00
Jug, gr w/silver overlay golf/polo/hunt scenes, musical, 8½" 95.00
Jug, pinched sides, powder bl crystalline, w/music box 160.00
Lamp base, bl streaked glaze, orig fittings, 14" 150.00
Lamp base, sea gr crystalline, dlb hdls, bulbous, 24" 275.00
Mug, green glaze 35.00
Mug, Prang, lg 35.00
Pitcher, green, coiled, 6¼" 65.00
Planter, belted, streaked bl/gr/cream drip on tan mirror, 3x7" . . .55.00
Powder jar, Deco lady 120.00
Vase, angle hdls, rolled rim on bulb, rose over gr, 6" 65.00
Vase, bl crystalline, #425, 12" 145.00
Vase, bl crystalline, ball shape w/3 hdls below collar, 8" 125.00

Vase, bl flambe, #26, 6″ 65.00
Vase, bl w/rust/cream crystalline, bottle form, 8″ 100.00
Vase, bl/red crystalline, classic shape, 10¾″ 115.00
Vase, blk crystalline over gold, rim to shoulder hdls, 7½″ 150.00
Vase, blk/br/bl/cream, incurvate rim, straight sides, 5″ 85.00
Vase, bowl; cobalt, imp mk, 5x7″ 70.00
Vase, br on turq drip, sgn, 3¾″ 55.00
Vase, br w/bl crystalline, squat pear, rim to width hdls, 6″ 100.00
Vase, br/cream/bl flambe, bottle form, tiny base chip, 5½″ 30.00
Vase, br/gr crystalline, gourd shape, 8″ 85.00
Vase, br/gray/yel flambe, 4″ 45.00
Vase, buckle, bl shaded drip, crystalline, 4x7¼″ 65.00
Vase, buttress, gr/br flambe, 8″ 200.00
Vase, buttress, mirror blk to butterscotch, 8½″ 120.00
Vase, copper dust, hdld, 5x6″ 225.00
Vase, cream/bl/blk flambe, orange jewel decor, 7″ 115.00
Vase, crystalline gr, pntd 'Fulper', baluster form, 33″ 1,100.00
Vase, cylinder, texture grape/bl/lav semi matt/bl/gray rim, 6″ ..47.50
Vase, Deco hdls, leopard skin crystalline, 6½″ 135.00
Vase, flared rnd bottom/long hdls/gr crystal/copper dust, 9″ ..225.00
Vase, glossy blk drip over shaded br base, bulb w/can neck, 5″ ..60.00
Vase, gr drip over br, #531, 5x6″ 60.00
Vase, gr gloss w/dk br flambe drip over br speckle, #531, 5″ 65.00
Vase, gr w/many crystals, w/hdls, 6x5″ 70.00
Vase, gr/cream crystals, wide ribs, rim design, bulbous, 7½″ ..175.00
Vase, gray over tan, 6¾″ 75.00
Vase, gunmetal & leopard skin, hdld, 5x6″ 115.00
Vase, mc glaze w/crystals/gr/br/gray, can w/rolled-in rim, 7″ ..155.00
Vase, mirror blk, crystals, hdld, 9″ 175.00
Vase, molded design, gr & blue, flattened sphere, 3¼x5½″ 75.00
Vase, mustard, elephant hdls, 4½″ 55.00
Vase, pillow, fan shape, blue lava glaze, small hdls, 7″ 45.00
Vase, pink/gr/bl semi gloss, squat pear w/akimbo rim hdls, 5″ ..70.00
Vase, purple streaks, semi-gloss, 9″ 125.00
Vase, sm neck, wide shoulder, heavy bl crystalline, 6¾″ 140.00
Vase, speckled bl matt, w/hdls, 7″ 48.00
Vase, tan leopard skin, crystalline, 8 sided, 8x7″ 285.00
Vase, thrown, Kraft, leopard skin w/crystal, vertical mk, 12½″ .315.00
Vase, wht w/bl drip glaze, 6″ 65.00
Vase, wisteria, 3″ 35.00
Vase, 7 sided, cream gloss w/purple/br crystalline drip, 9″ ...130.00
Wall pocket, green, #855, 7½″ 95.00

Furniture

From the cabinetmaker's shop of the early 1800s, with apprentices and journeymen who learned every phase of the craft at the side of the master carpenter, the trade had evolved by the mid-century to one with steam-powered saws and turning lathes and workers who specialized in only one operation.

By 1870 the industrial revolution had been accomplished and large factories in the East and Midwest turned out increasingly elaborate styles, ornately machine carved and heavily inlaid. Rococo, Egyptian, and Renaissance Revival furniture lent themselves well to factory production. Eastlake offered a welcome respite from Victorian frumpery, and a return to quality hand crafting. All of these styles remained popular until the turn of the century.

As early as 1880, factories began using oak; early mail-order catalogs offered oak furniture simply styled and lighter in weight, since long-distance shipping was often a factor.

Mission, or Craftsman, a style introduced around 1890, was simple to the extreem. Stickley and Hubbard were two of its leading designers.

Other popular Victorian styles were Colonial Revival, Cottage, Bentwood, and Windsor. Prices are as variable as the styles.

Key:
Am----American	hdw----hardware
brd----board	Hplwht----Hepplewhite
c&b----claw & ball	NE----New England
Chpndl----Chippendale	ped----pediment
dbl----double	prim----primitive
do----door	pt----part
drwr----drawer	QA----Queen Anne
dvtl----dovetail	refn----refinished
Emp----Empire	repr----repaired
Fr----French	rept----repaint
ft----feet	rnd----round
ftbd----footboard	str----straight
Geo----Georgian	trn----turning
grpt----grain painted	Vict----Victorian
hbbd----headboard	wal----walnut

/----over (example: 1 door/2 drawers----1 door over 2 drawers)

Bed

Brass, tubular w/trn fittings, posts mtd w/Fr pottery 3,000.00
Cherry, Fed, 4 post tester, scalloped hdbd, 62″ 1,200.00
Curly maple, Fed, 4 post w/leaf finials, scroll hdbd 750.00
Day, mahog, Charles X, bkrest adjusts, not uphl, 64″ L 1,320.00
Day, oak, Louis XV, scrolled ends/cabriole legs, 64″ L 550.00
Maple, 4 poster, hdbd carved w/Am eagle, 47x82x52″ 1,900.00
Rope, birch, pine hdbd rpl, altered rails, sq posts, 37x80x52″ ..210.00
Rope, maple w/minor curl, poplar hdbd, trn posts & rails, 56″ ..225.00
Rope, poplar, cannon ball posts, trn blanket rail, hdbd decor ..200.00
Rope, poplar, single, trn posts, shaped hd/ftbd, rfn 275.00
Rosewood, Rococo, shaped hd/ftbd, 45″ 660.00
Rosewood parquetry, French, laid w/floral in MOP, 53″ 495.00
Rosewood/laminated, Belter, 4 part form, carved ornaments ..16,000.00
Walnut, Nouveau, organic bands at edge, 67″, 2 side tables .28,600.04
Walnut, sq posts w/trn ft/finials, wide hd/ftbds w/rolled edge ..400.00

Bed, French, 19th century, kingwood with 'Vernis Martin' painted panel in footboard, 58″ x 58½″ x 76″, $1,250.00.

Bench

Bucket, pine, primitive, shaped sides, scalloped ft, 17x68″ 350.00
Bucket, pine, primitive wide brd w/base shelf, 28x28x18″ 180.00
Bucket, poplar, primitive, 3 shelf/canted sides/crest, 46x38″ ..400.00

Country, trn ft, mortised fr, rope holes, spindle bk, 75"......230.00
Mammy's, poplar, 1 board plank seat, scroll arms, rpl, 61".....400.00
Pine, cut out legs, scalloped aprons, 16x48"................115.00
Pine, primitive, cut out ft, late wire nails, grpt, 96" L........105.00
Pine, primitive, worn br pnt, 18x9x60".....................135.00
Pine, shaped cut out legs mortised through top, worn pnt, 60".225.00
Settle, arrowback, trn legs, scroll arms, plank seat, pnt, 78"....810.00
Settle, English Country, pine w/yew seat, curved/panel bk, 82"..375.00
Settle, oak, floral carved top rail/scroll arms, Stuart, 42½".....600.00
Settle, pine, panel base w/lift lid, high back w/arms, grpt.....925.00
Settle, plank seat, scroll arms, spindle bk, worn/rpr, 109".....300.00
Settle, pnt w/stencil decor, country, baby guard, 54"........2,150.00
Shaker, bucket, pine, in old yellow, Handcock, 71".........3,250.00
Water, ash w/poplar bk boards, scalloped sides & bk, 35x49".....450.00
Water, pine, cut out hearts/dia in front apron addition, 70" L..140.00
Water, poplar, bootjack ends, sq nails, worn/losses, 36" L......95.00
Windsor, bamboo trn, scroll arms, arrow spindles, rfn/rpl, 87"..575.00

Bookcase

Bookcase cabinet, mahog, Deco, Joubert et Petit, 39x94"....3,300.00
Breakfront, burl walnut, astragal do, compass inlay.........6,000.00
Mahog, Geo III, dentil mold cornice/2 shelves/bracket ft, 46"...450.00
Mahog, Geo III, over chest of drw, 80x65"................7,000.00
Mahog, Geo III, pr glaze do/slant front/4 grad drw, 88x42"...3,000.00
Mahog, Geo III, slant front, leaf carved cartouch, 96x42"....4,000.00
Mahog, Regency, 3 open shelves/pr do, trn ft, 48x39".......1,100.00
Mahog/inlay, Fed, 2 pt, 2 Gothic arch do/drw/2 do, 88x48"...1,500.00
Mahog/inlay, Geo III, 2 glaze do/roll cylinder/2 do, 91x44"..11,000.00
Maple/bird's eye, Eastlake, bamboo gallery/sides, Horner, 56".1,045.00

Bureau

Cabinet, walnut/ebony/Biedermeier/2 part/pierce gallery/3 drw.1,320.00
Mahog, block front w/shell/gadroon carving, c/b ft, 34x40"...2,100.00
Mahog, Geo II, slant front/4 grad drw, fitted w/in, 38x36"....1,760.00
Mahog, Sheraton, 4 drw bowfront, porringer top, 40x42"....3,500.00
Walnut, German Neoclassic, slant front, 1 short/long drw, rstr.1,210.00
Walnut/laburnum, Italian Rococo slant front/canted/concave...1,430.00

Bureau Bookcase

Burl walnut w/inlay, Geo I, 74x30½"....................3,850.00
Gilt/red lacquer/Geo I/mirror do/drop front/3 drw, 82".......6,000.00
Mahog, Geo II/swan neck ped/open fret, 94x44"...........5,000.00
Mahog, Geo III, broken swan crest/slant front.............7,000.00
Mahog, Geo III, dentil moulding/pr glaze do.............2,200.00
Mahog, Vict, 2 do/drw/2 do/plinth base, 85x52"...........1,000.00
Mahog/parcel gilt/Geo III/2 mirror do/slant lid, 84"..........6,000.00
Two pt/mirror do/slant front/2 short+2 drw, 82"...........6,500.00
Walnut, QA, arch crest w/urn, shaped mirror do, 88x33"....3,630.00

Cabinet

Am Renaissance, gilt bronze mt/gilt incised/ebony inlay, 71" W.825.00
Bar, mahog, Deco, silver cloth padded mount on drop front....440.00
Cabinet on chest, burl walnut/inlay, Wm & Mary, 67x42"....6,000.00
Drafting, mahog, trefoil outset corners/2 slides/2 grilled do...1,400.00
Elmwood/oak/inlay, 2 do/2 drw, German Baroque, 45x47".....990.00
Gilt-bronze mtd inlaid rosewood, Renaissance, 44".........1,320.00
Gilt-bronze mtd inlaid walnut, panel do+2 glaze ea side......660.00
Gilt-bronze mtd thuyawood Continental Neoclassic, 63x57"...2,750.00
Inlaid walnut, Biedermeier, 1 drw/panel arch, 65x38"........880.00
Mahog, Geo III, superstructure w/fret supports, 56x25".....1,250.00

Mahog, Wm IV, brass mtd, mirror bk, trn support, 52½x32"..950.00
Rosewood, gilt incised/pnt/inlay Eastlake, Herter, 68x66".....1,650.00
Tortoise shell/ebony, on stand, Italian Baroque, ormolu pulls..2,750.00
Tortoise shell/ebony inlay/ormolu Minerva/8 drw, Italian, 34"..3,025.00
Vitrine, gilt wood, Louis XV style, Vernis Martin, 70x26"....1,100.00
Vitrine, gilt wood, Louis XVI style, D form, carve heads, 56".1,540.00
Vitrine, rosewood, Deco, central bevel glass do, mirror w/in....550.00
Walnut, carved, Vict, 67x30"..........................550.00
Walnut, Fr Renaissance, carved figures/column/etc, 60x45"...3,025.00
Walnut, Vict, bronze/porcelain HP do mts, 45x75".........2,750.00
Walnut, Vict Arts & Crafts, pntd panel, 1870, 81x69".......3,190.00
Walnut, 2 do w/enamel does/foliage on ivory, 1935, 36x59".3,025.00
Walnut/fruitwood inlay, Dutch Rococo, glaze do/4 drw, 77"....220.00
Walnut/oak, French Renaissance, 2 carved drw/do, 37x48"...3,300.00

Candlestand

Birch, Country Hplwht, spider legs, octagon 15x22" top......375.00
Birch, octagonal molded top, cabriole legs, pnt, 26x11"......275.00
Cherry, QA, oval tilt top, tripod w/snake ft, 28x19"........900.00
Cherry, tilt top 17x23", spider legs, tripod base, rfn.........325.00
Curly maple, Chpndl, oblong top, ring/vase std, tripod, 27x14".450.00
Curly maple, Fed, 22" tilt top/vase std/arch tripod, 27".......650.00
Curly maple/cherry, Fed, tilt top/trn std/arch tripod, 29x26"....600.00
Mahog, Chpndl, 21" tilt top/bird cage/trn std/tripod, 27".....2,500.00
Mahog, oval 16x24" tilt top w/edge inlay, snake ft/trn column..475.00
Mahog/inlay, Fed, 26" tilt top, ring/vase std/tripod, 28".......750.00
Maple, Chpndl, 13" circle top, ring/vase std/tripod/snake ft.....350.00
Maple, cut out X member base, trn column, rnd 16" top......175.00

Cellaret

Mahog, Fed, box case/leaf carved tripod, 32x17"..........1,000.00
Mahog, sarcophagus form, carved pineapples/paw ft........6,600.00
Mahog/inlay, canted rectangle, c/b ft, 19x19".............770.00

Chair

Arm, bannister back, Centennial period, rpt, rpl rush seat.....325.00
Arm, bannister back, trn finials, shaped crest w/heart, rpt......600.00
Arm, Chinese Chpndl, pierced splat bk, mahog fr/velour uphl...770.00
Arm, curly maple, Fed, open arm, bowed crestrail/rstr........500.00
Arm, Flemish scroll, cane seat/bk, 1900s, blk rpt.............50.00
Arm, Ji Chi Mu, disk w/dragon, footrest, 18th/19th century....770.00
Arm, laminated rosewood, pierced foliate crest/scroll sides....1,100.00
Arm, mahog, Geo II, pierced bk/drop seat/cabriole legs, c/b ft.1,250.00
Arm, mahog/caned fr, Regency, padded arms/seat/bk.........880.00
Arm, mahog/caned seat, Fed, carved crestrail, trn/reed legs....500.00
Arm, mahog/ormolu sphinx supports, Restauration, uphl.....1,980.00
Arm, maple, Chpndl, rush seat, shaped crest/pierced splat.....700.00
Arm, oak, carved panel bk/scroll arm/loose seat, Stuart, rstr....250.00
Arm, Oriental, hardwood, revolving tubular headrest, 1800s...1,430.00
Arm, Oriental, reclining, tubular headrest, leg support........715.00
Arm, ormolu/wrought iron, Charles X, campaign, leather bkrest.935.00
Arm, rosewood, floral crest/scroll arms, satin tufted oval bk....825.00
Arm, rosewood, tufted shield bk/floral crest/serpentine/uphl.....950.00
Arm, walnut, Italian Baroque, pad bk, uphl seat, rpr, rst, pr....605.00
Arm, walnut, Italian Renaissance, padded bkrest, trn legs, pr..1,540.00
Arm, walnut, Italian Rococo, uphl cartouch bk/seat, 1750......605.00
Arm, walnut, Jules Leleu, scroll arms, block cushions.........500.00
Arm, walnut, Louis XV, cartouch bk, cabriole legs, rstr, pr...1,760.00
Arm, walnut, Louis XV, cartouch bk/leaf carving............3,575.00
Arm, walnut, Louis XV, cartouch uphl bk/arms, cabriole legs..1,590.00
Arm, walnut inlay/fruitwood, Dutch Rococo, open bk, pr.......825.00

Lolling chair, American Chippendale, walnut, cabriole front legs with claw and ball feet, $2,750.00.

Arm, wingback, Hplwht, uphl, reproduction................205.00
Barcelona, by Marcel Breuer for Knoll, imitation suede, pr...1,430.00
Captain's, orig pnt, flame graining, worn....................205.00
Club, Ebene de Macassar & leather, French, 1930, Deco.....935.00
Corner, cherry, Chpndl, horseshoe bk/vase splats/apron w/drw..800.00
Corner, mahog Chpndl, 2 vase splats, for chamber pot, damage.265.00
Corner arm, mahog, Geo II, scrolled top rail/baluster splats...1,100.00
Deck, aluminum, Troy Sunshade Co, reclining bk, pr.........990.00
Ladderback arm, mahog, Geo III/4 pierced slats/serpentine seat.385.00
Ladderback arm, sausage trn bk posts/finials/shaped arms.....585.00
Ladderback arm, spool trn/3 slat bk+trn rung/rpl splint seat...275.00
Ladderback arm rocker, simple, 4 slats, worn finish, no seat...125.00
Ladderback arm rocker, slender turnings, 5 grad slats, rfn.....250.00
Ladderback arm rocker, 4 slat bk/EX finials/trn arms/new seat..175.00
Ladderback arm rocker, 4 slats, simple trn, shaped arms, rfn...130.00
Ladderback side, 3 slat, trn finials, dk w/rpl rush seat.........35.00
Library arm, Geo III style, leather uphl mahog...............500.00
Lolling, mahog/inlay, Federal, shaped uphl bk/seat...........550.00
Made from branches & roots of laurel.......................65.00
Parlor, carved mahog shield bk, rose/scroll/leafy crest/sides...1,700.00
Parlor, rosewood, J&J Meeks, Stanton Hall, needlepoint uphl.2,300.00
Potty, pine, wing back, lift lid, sliding do in bk, grpt, 40"......305.00
Rocker, Boston; old rpnt w/red/blk graining/stencil...........90.00
Rocker, Boston; orig pnt w/flame grain, glued break, rpr......135.00
Rocker, strap metal, after Winfield rocker of 1851............660.00
Shaker, armchair rocker, #7, woven bk, rfn, no label..........375.00
Shaker, child's ladderback, 2 slats, trn finials, rfn, 25".........220.00
Shaker, ladderback, 3 slat/trn finials/tape seat, mk #3.........300.00
Shaker, ladderback, 3 slats, trn finials, rfn, rpl seat..........135.00
Shaker, ladderback, 3 slats, trn finials, worn splint seat.......140.00
Shaker, ladderback rocker, orig finish w/stencil label, #7......375.00
Shaker, rocker, Bro Gregory type, spindle back, old finish.....375.00
Shaker, side, Canterbury, light weight, cane seats, pr........6,000.00
Side, arrowback, bamboo trn, curved crests, worn grpt, rpr, pr..110.00
Side, bannister back, maple, old finish, rpl rush seat.........375.00
Side, bannister back, sausage trn/trn posts/finials, new seat.....325.00
Side, bannister back w/heart cut-out, rpt, rpl rush seat.......425.00
Side, bannister maple, QA, bk/inverted crestrail..............350.00
Side, cherry, Chpndl, pierce splat/drop in seat...............600.00
Side, cherry, QA, oxbow crest/solid vase splat/rush seat.......650.00
Side, Chinese, wht marble plaque w/in carved bkrest, 1800s, pr.935.00
Side, ebonized/brass mtd, Regency, lyre splat, cane seat, pr...1,210.00
Side, Fed, balloon bk w/splat, pnt w/eagle/floral, pr..........350.00
Side, gilt-bronze mtd ebonized, ca 1870, pr.................715.00

Side, Hong Mu, concave splat, pierced scrollwork, cane seat....300.00
Side, mahog, Chpndl, shaped crest/pierced Gothic splat, pr....900.00
Side, mahog, Chpndl, shell/leaf crest/pierced splat, c/b ft.....1,500.00
Side, maple, Country QA, EX turnings/shaped crest, rpr/rpl....200.00
Side, maple, Country QA, rush seat, vase splat, rockers added..325.00
Side, maple, QA, shaped crest/balloon horsehair seat, EX....2,300.00
Side, maple, 3 arch slat bk/rush seat, Delaware Valley, 1750...415.00
Side, oak, assymetrical leaf groups, Nouveau, Busquets, pr....1,500.00
Side, oak, Chas Rohfs, pierce carved tall plank bks, pr......3,300.00
Side, oak, G Stickley, spindle bk & ea side, slip seat.......1,320.00
Side, plank seat, ½ spindle bk, orig pnt w/fruit..............65.00
Side, pnt, Louis XIII, molded frame/uphl, pr.................715.00
Side, pnt decor worn, plank seat, trn legs, spindle bk.........85.00
Side, rosewood, carved/pierced fr around uphl bk, Belter.....1,100.00
Side, rosewood, fruit carved crest, scroll bk fr, Belter........880.00
Side, walnut, Chpndl, cabriole legs/duck ft/shaped crests, pr..2,000.00
Side, walnut, Italian Neoclassic, open bk/lyre, uphl seat, pr...1,980.00
Side, walnut, Italian Rococo, cartouch uphl bk, carved, pr....1,210.00
Side, walnut, Spanish Rococo, solid seat/open backrests, pr...220.00
Windsor, arm, high bow back/trn legs/shaped seat/scroll arms...525.00
Windsor, arm, low horseshoe bkrest w/applied crest, pr........700.00
Windsor, arm, splay base, trn legs, knuckle arms, re-grpt.....1,050.00
Windsor, bow back arm, oval seat, knuckle arms, rpt, rpr......450.00
Windsor, bow back arm, S arm support, shaped seat, new pnt..575.00
Windsor, bow back arm, saddle seat/knuckle arms, W Cox, rpr1,000.00
Windsor, comb back arm, 1770.........................8,500.00
Windsor, continuous arm, 9 spindle, saddle seat, 1800, pr....1,000.00
Windsor, country, bamboo base, shaped seat, 7 spindle, pnt....200.00
Windsor, fan back arm, 7 spindle, simple arms, rfn..........650.00
Windsor, fan back side, splayed trn legs/saddle seat, new rpt...450.00
Windsor, fan back side, 7 spindle, dk br over orig pnt finish...750.00
Windsor, fan back side, 9 spindle, saddle seat, rpr..........350.00
Windsor, rocker, comb back, blk pnt, 1800..................700.00
Windsor, side, bamboo, cage type back, rfn, rpr............210.00
Windsor, side, bamboo, 9 spindle, modern paint w/striping.....175.00
Windsor, side, step down/bamboo trns/shape seat/6 spindle, pnt.185.00
Windsor, writing arm, plank seat/drw, shaped writing surface...935.00
Wing back arm, mahog, Chpndl, serpentine bk, rpr..........600.00
Wing back pine, high back wing, primitive, rfn..............170.00

Chair Set

Arm, mahog fr/uphl, Adams wheel bk, circle arms, set of 4...8,250.00
Bamboo trn/plank seat, ½ spindle bk, floral decor, 6 for.....1,050.00
Federal pnt/decorated, 2 arm+8 side.....................2,000.00
Mahog, att Nathan Margolis, heart bk w/swags/slats, 8 for....3,300.00
Mahog, carved/inlay, att J Seymour, 1800, 3 slats, 4 for......4,000.00
Mahog, Chpndl, interlace vase splat, c/b ft, 2 arm+6.......5,300.00
Mahog, Chpndl style, pierced & carved crest, 10 for........3,200.00
Mahog, Fed, sq bk/leaf carved splat/slip seat, 4 for.........2,500.00
Mahog, Geo II, acanthus/rosette carved/c/b ft, 8 for.......10,000.00
Mahog, Geo III, open carved shield bk, serpentine seat, 10..6,600.00
Mahog, Geo III, pierce ribbon/scroll bk, uphl seat, set of 7...4,675.00
Mahog, Regency, reed/scroll top rail, 6 side+2 arm........7,150.00
Mahog, Regency, spiral X bar, panel top rail, 5 side+2 arm..3,000.00
Mahog, scroll on scroll legs, scroll uphl bk, set of 4........1,000.00
Mahog/brass mts, Regency, caned seat, trn X bar, set of 6...2,860.00
Oak, Yorkshire, 5 shape splats/rush seat, set of 4...........500.00
Pnt/decor/cane seat, Fed, set of 6.......................3,850.00
Pnt/parcel gilt, Geo III style, set of 4....................825.00
Pnt/parcel gilt, Portuguese Rococo, caned bk/floral decor, 6..1,650.00
Pnt/parcel gilt/Italian Neoclassic/bk open w/griffins, 6 for...1,980.00
Rosewood, Vict, carved open bk/uphl seat/baluster legs, 4......770.00
Rosewood/laminated, Belter, foliate crest/scroll frame, 3.....5,250.00

Shaker, ladderback side, Canterbury, NH, no seats, set of 4....260.00
Walnut, Geo I, scroll bk w/vase splats/balloon seat, 8 for.....5,000.00
Walnut, Italian Neoclassic, foliate splat/uphl seat, 6..........220.00

Chest

Apothecary, pine, 24 nailed drws, rpl drw runners, rfn, 59x49".850.00
Birch, Country Hplwht, 4 dvtl drw/curved base/orig brass, rfn...925.00
Birch/maple, Fed, 2 short+3 grad drw w/fan spandrels, 42x42".800.00
Blanket, butternut, dvtl, wrought iron hdw, rope hdls, 38" W...200.00
Blanket, oak/pine, geometric molded & pntd, 1670, 54" L..1,980.00
Blanket, PA decor of vines, flowers, inscription, 1802, 48" L.7,600.00
Blanket, pine, dvtl/trn ft/3 drw/till, orig sponge grpt, 49" L....850.00
Blanket, pine, 6 brd, dvtl drw/till, worn rpt, 44" W..........370.00
Blanket, pine, 6 brd, scroll ft, pnt w/smoke grain, till........325.00
Blanket, pine w/grpt, lift top, 1800, 20x50"................350.00
Blanket, poplar, dvtl, fancy bracket ft, w/till, 37" W.........275.00
Blanket, poplar, dvtl w/till, single wide brds, grpt, 38" W....250.00
Blanket, poplar, trn ft/till/dvtl/orig urn of flowers pnt, 39"......945.00
Blanket, walnut, PA stars/fan inlay in arch, ogee ft, 54" W..2,900.00
Blanket, walnut, 3 arches w/pnt flowers/horse/rider, 50" W...1,300.00
Burl walnut/ebonized, rnd corners/2 do+4 short drw/5, 52"..1,760.00
Cherry, Country, scallop base, 5 dvtl drw w/shaped fronts, 38"..425.00
Cherry, Country Empire, trn ft, 4 dvtl drw w/trn pulls, 45x42"..275.00
Cherry, Country Empire, trn ft, 4 edge beaded drw, 43x41"....375.00
Cherry, Fed, 4 grad drw/shaped apron/bracket ft, 38x42".....750.00
Curly maple, Chpndl, 6 grad drw, 57x40"................6,325.00
Immigrant's, pine, dvtl/strap hdls/till, orig grpt, 1801, worn.....275.00
Mahog, Chpndl, 4 drw serpentine, beaded frame, 32x35x20"..7,500.00
Mahog, Fed, 3 cockbead drw/valance apron/bracket ft, 35x44"..600.00
Mahog, Geo III, bow front, 2 short+2 long drws, 31x33"....1,430.00
Mahog, Hplwht, bow front, 4 dvtl drw, rpl brasses, rfn, 38x24"..700.00
Mahog/inlay, Geo III, bow front, 2 short+3 grad drw, 33x36".2,420.00
Maple, Chpndl, dvtl case w/7 dvtl drw, orig brass, 52x44"....1,650.00
Mule, pine, 6 board, scalloped base w/2 dvtl drw, rpt/rpl, 38"..750.00
Mule, pine/maple, 2 false+2 dvtl drw, lift lid, rpl ft, 43x38"..1,000.00
Mule, poplar, 2 dvtl drw+ 2 false, high ft, rpr, 45x44".......450.00
Mule, poplar, 6 brds, scalloped apron, 2 drw+2 false, 43x40"..550.00
Oak, floral/butterfly inlay, Dutch Rococo, serpentine, 32x40".1,430.00
Oak, flower/rosette carved, scroll ft, rstr, 1600s, 32x68" W..1,320.00
Oak, lunette/flower carved front, late 1600s, 22x44".........700.00
Oak, Wm & Mary, 2 part, 2 short/3 long drws, 42x42".....1,250.00
On chest, burl walnut/inlay, Geo II, 2 short+3 drw/3, 59"..2,250.00
On chest, mahog, Geo III, 2 short+3/3 drw, rstr, 77x42".....5,000.00
On chest, mahog/pine, Geo III, 2 short+3grad drw/3, 74x40".3,740.00
On stand, inlaid walnut, QA, 2 short+2 drw/1 long+2 short..2,000.00
Pine, bracket ft, 6 overlapping drws w/early dvtl, rpt, 41"....1,025.00
Shaker, blanket, pine, bracket ft/dvtl case/till, rpr, 20x38".....325.00
Shaker, pine, 5 nailed drws, orig grpt, 25x67"...............500.00
Shaker, walnut, 2 dvtl drw, on 8 rollers, 26x40x18".........475.00
Shaker, 4 dvtl drw w/edge beading, rpl pulls, rfn, rpr, 30x46"..300.00
Spice, pine, 15 short drw/2 long, smoke grained, 17x18"....1,500.00
Walnut, Chpndl, 3 short/5 grad drw, 62x40"..............4,000.00
Walnut, Country, cut out ft/scalloped apron/3 drw, 39x45".....135.00
Walnut, Country Vict, cut out ft/crest, 5 dvtl drw, 40x43"....245.00
Walnut, Italian Rococo/serpentine/2 drw/cabriole legs, 38x50".3,025.00
Walnut, 3 dvtl drw w/porcelain pulls, shaped crest, rfn, 30"....125.00
Walnut/brass mt, Dutch Baroque, inlay/burl panel, 3 drw, rstr.1,430.00
Walnut/pine, German Neoclassic, 3 drw/attached columns/ball ft.715.00

Commode

Elmwood/brass mt/Regence Provincial/shape front/3 drw......3,025.00
Fruitwood, German Neoclassic, concave/canted/3 drw........3,300.00

Gilt-bronze mtd mahog Louis XVI style, 67" W...........2,530.00
Mahog, bronze mtd/inlay, Louis XV, 2 drw, 35x50", pr......3,000.00
Mahog, Geo III, serpentine/3 drw/shaped stiles, 40" W......17,000.00
Mahog/gilt mt/Louis XVI/marble top/2 drw/2 do, 37x60"....10,000.00
Mahog/ormolu mt, Louis Phillipe, marble top/3 drw.........1,430.00

Cupboard

Corner, cherry/poplar, 2 glazed do/2, brass latches orig, 82"..2,400.00
Corner, English pine, scalloped apron, 1 panel do/1, rstr, 83"..475.00
Corner, hanging, pine, dvtl, do removes/pintel hinges, 24x24"..325.00
Corner, pine, Chpndl, 2 glaze do/2 panel do/bracket ft, 82x47".800.00
Corner, pine, Country English, panel do/butterfly shelves, 82"..650.00
Corner, pine/poplar, 2 pc, brilliant orig grpt, glaze do/do.....5,500.00
Corner, poplar, panel do/wide molded cornice, old red, 45x34"..400.00
Corner, walnut, Chpndl, glazed do/panel do/bracket ft, 79x36"..800.00
Corner, 1 pc, scallop base/reed trim, 12 pane do, rpt, 38" W.1,350.00
Hanging, cherry, dvtl case, panel do w/3 drw w/in, 23x20".....895.00
Hanging, grpt imitates quarter sawed oak, panel do, 25x16"....65.00
Hanging, pine, rosemulled decor, reproduction, 18x14x8"......85.00
Hanging, poplar, 1 dvtl drw, board & batten drw, grpt, 19x10".360.00
Hanging, poplar do w/5 raised panels, rpr, rfn, 31x21"........175.00
Jelly, pine/poplar, 2 panel do/cut out ft, worn grpt, 51x43"....250.00
Jelly, poplar, raised panel do, dvtl gallery is rpl, 36".........225.00
Korean, elm, burlwood panels, brass mts/hdls, w/stand, 58x22".770.00
Pewter, pine, dvtl case w/panel do in base, rpr, rfn, 80x50"....550.00
Pewter, pine, 1 pc, open, alterations, rfn, 76x43"...........400.00
Pine, Chpndl, pr arch do/pr do in base, 1760-70, 81x38".....1,870.00
Pine, Country, dry sink well, nailed construction, 74"........335.00
Pine, English, panel do/2 dvtl drw, ventilated, grpt, 69x38"....500.00
Pine, primitive, wide board do, battens w/in, pnt, 48x36"......270.00
Pine, primitive, 1 panel do over 1 in base, pnt, 1750, 74x43".1,250.00
Pine, scallop top w/2 shelves, board/batten do, rfn, 77x32"....750.00
Pine, 2 panel do/1 drw, grpt, pnt fish on do, 1835, 65x50"...1,760.00
Pine w/unusual grpt decor, hutch top/panel do, 78x43"......2,310.00
Poplar, 2 pc, 2 glazed do/base w/2 panel do/2 drw, rfn, 80x48".990.00
Shaker, apothecary, walnut, 1 pc, 21 dvtl base drw, 80x38x13".600.00
Shaker, hanging, chestnut, shelves w/in, rfn, rpl, 51x40".......150.00
Shaker, jelly; pine/poplar, 1 brd ends/panel do/2 drw/orig red...500.00
Shaker, pine, 1 brd do/inset battens, shelves/do w/in, 33x21"...375.00
Shaker, poplar, paneled do/beveled cornice, rfn, 65x48".......445.00
Shaker, top only, poplar, 4 drw/panel do, rfn, 48x42x12".....200.00
Walnut, panel do/base w/43 dvtl apothecary drws, 89x56"....4,200.00
Walnut, 2 pc/panel do/pie shelf/3 dvtl drw, 1848, 81x50"....1,175.00

Desk

Bureau plat, gilt-bronze mtd tulipwood Louis XV, 48" W.....1,430.00
Bureau plat, gilt-bronze tulipwood parquetry mahog, 44", G..2,750.00
Davenport, mahog, Regency, swivel top/brass gallery, 31x14".3,000.00
Davenport, mahog, Vict, ¾ brass gallery, 3 drw, 43x20".....1,250.00
Drop front, cherry, Chpndl, fan carved w/in/4 drw, 44x36"..2,420.00
Drop front, cherry, Hplwht, inlay: compass star/dia/line, rpr...1,150.00
Drop front, cherry, tiger maple drw front/scrolled apron, 43"..950.00
Drop front, cherry/inlay, Chpndl, 4 grad drw, c/b ft, 43x38"..1,500.00
Drop front, mahog, Chpndl, oxbow front, 4 grad drw, 45x41".2,970.00
Drop front, mahog, Chpndl, 4 drw/reed ¼ columns, 41x34"..4,000.00
Drop front, maple, Chpndl, fan carve prospect flap/3 drw, 41"1,200.00
Drop front, maple, Chpndl, fitted w/in/4 grad drw, 42x35"..2,000.00
Drop front, oak, G Stickley, fitted w/in, paper label, 44x30"..1,100.00
Drop front, walnut, Country, 3 dvtl drw, 45x43".............500.00
Drop front, walnut, w/bookcase, urn finial/pr do/4 drw, 86"...5,200.00
Drop front, walnut, 4 drw/bracket ft, 1780, 36x44".........2,000.00
Lady's, mahog, Fed, 3 short drw/2 do, base w/4 drw, 53x41".1,500.00

Bureau plat, Louis XV, fruitwood with ormolu mounts and serpentine tooled leather insert, 5 drawers, cabriole legs, 57" wide, $1,200.00.

Mahog, Chpndl, serpentine front/bracket ft, 44x42"........6,500.00
Mahog, Geo II, slide/frieze drw, kneehole w/4 drw+3 ea side.3,200.00
Mahog, Geo III, 2 ped supports w/carved hinged do, 65x34".18,000.00
Mahog, Vict, 3 top drw w/3 drw ea side ped, bracket ft, 54"..2,500.00
Mahog, Vict, 3 top drw+3 in both ped, ornate brass, 42x23".3,500.00
Partner's, Hong Mu, 3 sections, 2 drw/pr ped, 34x30x71"....4,950.00
Partner's, walnut, Geo III, 4 drw+3 in ea ped, rstr, 72x41".12,500.00
Plantation, Country Hplwht, pine/poplar, new grpt, 72x34".....350.00
Satinwood, table/curve superstructure, Geo III Carlton House.8,000.00
Shaker, red stain/pine/butternut drw front, fold out surface.....400.00
Walnut, Eastlake, dbl ped ea w/3 drw, inset Minton tiles, 45"..900.00
Wooton, walnut Rotary, ¾ gallery/cylinder front, 57x56".....3,000.00

Dresser

Oak, Geo II, 2 pt, 2 shelves/arched apron w/3 drw, 70x74"...3,500.00
Oak, Geo III, Welsh, superstructure w/shelves, 72x56".......3,000.00
Oak, Geo III Provincial/3 frieze drw/baluster support, 32x64".2,000.00
Oak, Welsh Provincial, 2 shelves/3 drw/3 do, 75x59"........2,500.00
Oak w/inlay, Geo II, 3 drws/shape apron/cabriole leg, 72" W..3,200.00
Oak w/inlay, Georgian, 3 shelves w/do ea side/3 drw, 87x75"..5,500.00
Satinwood, Geo III, 3 frieze drw/3 drw ea side, arch apron..16,000.00

Dry Sink

Pine, wide boards/sq nail/central pull out bin/pr side do, lg.....500.00
Pine, wide brd ends, panel doors, dvtl well removes, 1830s...1,350.00
Pine/poplar, 3 raised panel do, high bk top w/drw & crest.....900.00
Poplar, sm side drw, 2 do, sq nails, rfn, rpr, 33" W..........275.00

Dumbwaiter, mahog, Chpndl, 3 rnd tier, tripod/c/b ft..........800.00
Dumbwaiter, mahog, 2 rnd tier, poke galleries, ornate legs...2,250.00
Etagere, mahog, Regency, 3 rectangles/slim trn legs, 43x17"...525.00
Etagere, rosewood, Am Rococo, central marble shelf, 80x56".2,200.00

Highboy

Cherry, QA, flat top/2 short+4 grad drw/1+3, 76x44"......2,500.00
Cherry, QA, flat top/5 grad drw/1+2 short, fan carving, 78"..7,500.00
Curly maple, QA, shell/fan on base, hidden drw, flat top, 69".2,850.00
Maple, QA, cabriole legs/scalloped skirt, orig brass, rfn, 69"..6,000.00
Maple, QA, 5 grad dvtl drw/1+3, cabriole legs/duck ft, 75"...9,500.00
Maple/pine, QA, flat top/4 grad drw/3 short/cabriole legs, 69".3,500.00
Oak/inlay, QA, flat top/2 short+3 grad drw/2, carved, 62".....900.00

Walnut, QA, flat top/3 short+3 long/1 long+2, 41x69"......7,400.00
Walnut/maple/inlay, Wm & Mary, base w/6 trumpet legs, 63".1,500.00

Linen Press

Cherry, Fed, 2 pt, 2 do/stepback 2-drw/3, 91"...............500.00
Grpt, 2 pt, cornice removes, 3 do/3+2 drw, 86x62".........850.00
Mahog, Fed, 2 pt, detachable cornice/pr do/4 drw.........1,500.00
Mahog, Geo III, 2 do/2½ drw/2, 77x22x51"................200.00

Lowboy

Burl walnut, Wm & Mary, 3 drw/trumpet legs/ball ft.........900.00
Curly maple, QA, 1 long/3 short drw/cut-out apron, rfn......1,100.00
Mahog, Chpndl, 1 lg+3 sm drw/foliage/shell/c/b ft, 36"......2,300.00
Mahog, Chpndl style, shell carve drw & apron, c/b ft.........725.00
Mahog, Geo I, 3 frieze drw, cabriole legs, pad ft, 29".......700.00
Walnut, QA, fan carved drw +2 below, rstr, 28x33"........2,000.00

Lowboy, Queen Anne style, mahogany, cabriole legs with modified Spanish feet, 41" wide, $700.00.

Parlor Suite

Joseph Meeks, 66" sofa, 2 arm ch+4 side ch.............19,000.00
Mahog/laminated, Belter, Fountain Elms, 4 pcs............28,500.00
Rosewood, J&J Meeks, Stanton Hall, 10 pcs...............21,000.00
Rosewood, Rococo, 3 oval bk settee+2 armchairs...........990.00
Rosewood, Rococo Revival, carved crests, 7 pc............4,500.00
Rosewood/gilt bronze mtd, Louis Phillippe, 10 pc...........1,500.00

Pie Safe

Pine, screen do/drw, yel pnt, mortised/pegged, 1850s, 37x40".2,000.00
Pntd w/pierced tin panels front & sides, 2 do/drw/2 do, 82"..1,100.00
Poplar, dvtl drw/2 do ea w/3 punched tin panels, rpt, 75x42"..200.00
Poplar, high legs, nailed drw, do & sides w/12 tin panels, 60"..525.00
Poplar, 2 short drw/2 do ea w/3 tin panels, ea side tin, 52"....395.00
Walnut, sq corner posts/panel sides/do w/3 tin panels, 60".....225.00

Secretary

Bookcase, mahog, Chpndl style, 79x35"...................800.00
Bookcase, mahog, flat top/2 glaze do/secretary drw/3, 86"...3,250.00
Bookcase, mahog/fan inlay, Geo III, arch glaze do/drop/3 drw.8,800.00
Bookcase, oak, side-by-side, bow glass curio, claw ft.........750.00

Bookcase, walnut, QA, arch panel do, fitted, 78″..........9,900.00
Breakfront, mahog/inlay, Geo III, glaze do/secretaire drw, 92″.6,000.00
Cherry, bonnet top/flame finial, blind front, rfn, 85x36″.....2,500.00
Cherry, Co Empire, 2 pc, glaze do/drw/drop leaf, 75x30″....3,200.00
Cherry, Fed, flat top/dbl blind do/Fr ft base/orig brass, 84″...6,500.00
Mahog, Chpndl, 2 do/slant front/4 grad drw/c/b ft, 92x46″....3,000.00
Mahog, Dutch Neoclassic, marble top/shutter, fitted, 62x41″..2,750.00
Mahog, Hplwht, inlay top/drw facing, bracket ft, 4 drw, 80″..9,500.00
Mahog, Sheraton Hplwht transition, 2 do/3 drw, 1810, 50x38″.750.00
Mahog/ormolu/gilt metal mt, Russian Neoclassic, 2 pt, 66x34″.1,650.00

Settee

Burl walnut, Geo II, 2 chair bk, acanthus scroll legs/paw ft..11,000.00
Geo II crewel work mtd on Geo III style settee, 1850s......8,000.00
Gilt wood, Rococo, 2 chair bk w/floral/cartouch...........1,980.00
Mahog, Federal, carved swags/fluted panels, reed legs, 78″...2,250.00
Mahog, Geo III, Chinese Chpndl style open 2 chair bk, 45″.3,630.00
Mahog, Geo III, arch bk/scroll arms/serpentine seat, 82″.....2,860.00
Mahog fr w/Geo III needlepoint uphl, scroll arm/loose seat....7,000.00
Parcel gilt/wht pnt, Geo III, uphl bk/arms/loose seat, 70″.....8,000.00
Rosewood, Portuguese Rococo, 3 chair bk, ornate, 77″.....2,750.00
Rosewood, Regency, scroll arms, spiral top rail, brass ft, 75″.1,750.00
Rosewood, Vict, triple bk w/pierced rose/scroll fr, 70″......2,310.00
Satinwood/polychrome, Regency, panel top rail, scroll arms..2,250.00
Walnut, Continental Neoclassic, open bk, lyre splats, 34″ L...525.00
Windsor, bow back, pnt blk, arch crest, tapered spindles, 79″.3,300.00
Windsor, 35 bamboo trn spindles, plank seat, 1800, 65″.....2,000.00

Shelf

Hanging, cherry, well cut ends/4 grad shelves, 42x30″........750.00
Hanging, pine, worn bl pnt, 9x17x50″....................295.00
Hanging, 3 shelves w/trn dividers, orig bl pnt, 22x21″.........85.00
Pine, scalloped ends/3 shelves/crest, 1900s................150.00
Vict, oak, w/mirror/lift top compartment, 26x14″...........145.00
Walnut, tombstone ends, 4 shelf, 37x31″...................90.00

Sideboard

Credenza, walnut, 2 drw/2 do/paw ft, Italian Baroque, 54″ W.1,430.00
Credenzina, walnut, Italian Renaissance style, drw/2 do/paw ft..550.00
Mahog, French Deco, bow front w/2 do w/bronze mts, 78″ L...605.00
Mahog, Geo III, concave frieze drw/arch apron w/cellaret, 80″.1,430.00

Sideboard, Empire, mahogany, projecting cushion drawers over two paneled cupboard doors flanked by stiles, 61″ wide, $700.00.

Mahog, Geo III/inlay, 2 tambour sliding do atop, 102″.......3,300.00
Mahog/flame grain veneer, Empire, w/butler's desk, 72″ L....1,050.00
Mahog/inlay, Fed, arch bkbrd w/drws/2 ped/curve front, 76″....800.00
Mahog/inlay, Fed, serpentine/brass gallery/bowed drw, 74″....900.00
Mahog/inlay, Geo III, serpentine front/brass splash rail, 86″..4,000.00
Mahog/shell inlay, Geo III, gallery w/drw/4 frieze+2 drw, 84″.3,000.00
Rosewood, Deco, serpentine/4 do, central parquetry panel, 92″.550.00
Rosewood, Rococo, open scroll crest, 2 shelves/2 do, 48″ W...495.00
Satinwood/mahog, bow front, frieze drw+2 ea side, 64″ L....1,700.00

Sofa

Mahog, Chpndl, uphl camel bk/scroll arms/seat, 85″.........3,300.00
Mahog, Chpndl, uphl camel bk/scroll arms/curve seat, 90″....4,125.00
Mahog, classical, carved crest/acanthus/paw ft, uphl, 89″.......660.00
Mahog, Fed, crest rail w/sq w/carved swags, reed legs, 75″...2,500.00
Mahog, Geo III, arched bk, enclosed arms, spade ft, uphl.....700.00
Mahog/uphl, Sheraton, carved crest/center panel, 77″........3,900.00

Stand

Butternut, 4 serpentine tiers/trn legs & posts, acorn finials.....165.00
Cherry, Country Hplwht, dvtl drw, 2 brd 18″ sq top.........325.00
Cherry w/2 curly maple drw front, top 17x18″, rfn...........250.00
Corner, 3 tier, spool trns & finials, shaped shelves, 21x33″....275.00
Country Empire, 2 ogee drw, drop leaf top, veneer/graining....160.00
Country Sheraton, trn legs, dvtl drw, 1 brd 19″ top, pnt......400.00
Curly maple, burl edge on dvtl drw, trn legs, top 18x20″.....425.00
Curly maple, shoe ft, mortised, base shelf, 1 board 14x20″ top.270.00
Library, pnt/parcel gilt, Italian Rococo, 39″.................385.00
Mahog, Continental Neoclassic, rnd marble top, 3 ftd, 13″ dia..440.00
Maple/poplar, trn/octagonal legs, dvtl drw/1 brd top, orig pnt...190.00
Oriental, burlwood panel/shaped apron/5 scroll ft, 13″.......1,320.00
Oriental, hardwood, 2 tier, rectangular, scroll ft, 31x12x16″....250.00
Pine/poplar, Country Sheraton, reed apron edge, 20″ top.....300.00
Poplar/Country Hplwht, dvtl drw/2 brd 24″ top removes, rpt...350.00
Poplar/pine, trn legs, dvtl drw, orig grpt, by Rupp, 30x20″ sq..550.00
Shaker, Country Hplwht, walnut, 1 dvtl drw, 1 brd top, 28x18″.250.00
Shaker, maple/pine, 2 dvtl drw, rfn, rpr, 29x20x20″..........175.00
Shaker, wallnut, 1 drw, 2 brd 19″ sq top, old finish, sq legs...250.00
Walnut, Country, tripod base w/spider legs, 2 brd shaped top....90.00

Stool

Caned/pntd, shell carvings, Italian rococo, mid-1800s, pr.......825.00
Decorated w/primitively applied fruit/shell, 1900s, 7x12x7″......55.00
Pine, primitive, cut-out ft mortised through top, pnt, 6x7x13″...75.00
Pine, primitive, rfn, 7x8½x12″............................40.00
Pine, sq nail construction, old varnish, 6x6x13″..............40.00
Pine, well scalloped ft, shaped top, damage, rpr, 9x7x14″.......45.00
Tabouret, pnt, Italian Neoclassic, uphl seat, carved, pr........880.00
Tabouret, pnt, Louis XV, rectangle seat, cabriole legs........400.00
Tabouret, walnut, Italian Baroque, X form, foliate/eagle decor.2,200.00

Table

Architect's, mahog, Geo II, w/candle arms, hinged top.......2,750.00
Bedside, inlaid fruitwood/1 drw/cabriole legs, 27x22x16″.....1,320.00
Birch, Windsor, trn legs, 4 gate legs, rnd drop leaves, 54x60″..875.00
Birch/cherry, Country Hplwht Pembroke, X stretcher, dvtl drw..900.00
Birch/pine, Country Hplwht drop leaf, open: 36x43″.........400.00
Blond wood/glass, Robsjohn-Gibbings, shaped glass/3 prongs..1,320.00
Breakfast, kingwood/inlay, Regency, tilt top, center ped, 56″..2,475.00
Breakfast, mahog, Regency, trn ped/4 curved reed legs, 54″..1,100.00

Breakfast, mahog/inlay, Geo III, tilt top w/reed X band, 58"..2,750.00
Card, birch, Fed, bellflower inlaid legs, rstr, 34"...........1,000.00
Card, bird's eye maple/mahog/inlay, Federal, 36"...........1,980.00
Card, mahog, Chpndl, applied molding on apron & top.......575.00
Card, mahog, Chpndl, flame grain veneer apron, inlay, 18x36".750.00
Card, mahog, Chpndl, serpentine, scalloped apron, rosettes...1,250.00
Card, mahog, Fed, D top w/inlay, reed legs, 38"...........800.00
Card, mahog, QA, outset corners, 1 drw, cabriole legs, 31"...1,000.00
Card, mahog/inlay, Fed, D top w/serpentine front, 36" L.....500.00
Center, fruitwood, Nouveau, Marjorelle, 2 ridged legs, 45" L...605.00
Center, gilt-bronze kingwood/mahog Louis XVI type, 30" dia...550.00
Center, pnt/parcel gilt/carved, Italian Neoclassic, marble top..1,980.00
Center, walnut, Dutch Baroque, oval, baluster legs, 40x58"...6,500.00
Center, walnut, frieze w/drws, Italian Baroque, rpr, 60x29".....825.00
Center, walnut, Italian Renaissance, 7 columns, 54x30" top...2,475.00
Center, walnut, Louis XV, cabriole legs, top: 46x26".........1,100.00
Chamber, mahog, Fed, extends/case w/2 drw/trn legs, 37x42".1,200.00
Chinese export, blk laquer/gilt floral decor/39" dia/tripod.....1,320.00
Chinese export, occasional, blk laquer/decor, Vict, nest of 4..1,540.00
Console, carved giltwood, Italian Rococo, foliage/strap-work...1,650.00
Console, Italian Rococo carved/gilt gesso, marble 21x14" top...715.00
Console, oak, Louis XV style, marble top/serpentine frieze, pr.1,100.00
Console, pnt/parcel gilt, curving front/marble top, Venetian...1,430.00
Console, rosewood/marble/ornate apron/base ornament, Belter.2,530.00
Console, rosewood/Rococo, pierce/carve apron, Roux, 34x78".4,400.00
Console, wrought iron, Restauration, D travatine top, 40x19"...770.00
Demilune, satinwood, female supports w/paw ft, Geo III, 48"..3,500.00
Dining, cherry, Chpndl, drop leaves, c/b ft, 50"...........3,600.00
Dining, cherry, Fed, 2 pt, ea D shape w/drop leaf, open: 63".1,200.00
Dining, mahog, Geo II style, 2 column ped, extended 124"...1,750.00
Dining, mahog, Geo III, D end, sq tapered legs, 110".......2,970.00
Dining, mahog, Geo III, 2 ped ea w/4 reeded legs, 42" L.....700.00
Dining, mahog, Geo III, 3 peds ea w/curving tripod, 152"...5,500.00
Dining, mahog/inlay, Geo III, D form ends+2 leaves, 86½"..1,430.00
Dining, mahog/ormolu casters, Louis XVI style, oval, 56x46"..1,540.00
Dining, rosewood, extension, broken lyre base, Deco, 114"...3,410.00
Dining, rosewood, French Deco, 1935, extension, open: 109".1,100.00
Dressing, burl walnut, QA, carved apron/cabriole legs/3 drw..3,000.00
Dressing, Geo I inlaid burl walnut, angular cabriole legs, 30".3,000.00
Dressing, gilt metal mtd tulipwood inlay Louis XV, 58" W....1,100.00
Dressing, mahog, Geo III, serpentine top w/3 frieze drw, 36".1,650.00
Dressing, oak, Geo II, frieze drw/trn legs/pad ft, 1750, 27" W..500.00
Drop leaf, Cherry, Fed, skirt w/drw, 36" L.................350.00
Drop leaf, mahog, Empire, well trn legs, 2 swing supports, 54".200.00
Drop leaf, mahog, QA, swing leg, duck ft, cut down, 13x30"...250.00
Drop leaf, mahog/cherry, Fed, trn legs/ball ft, 42"...........600.00
Drop leaf, maple, QA, swing/cabriole legs, rpr, open: 26x42".1,250.00
Drop leaf, oak, Chas Rohfs, organic carving, brass nail heads.9,900.00
Drop leaf, oak, Dutch Baroque, oval top open: 45x78½".....3,025.00
Drop leaf, oak, gate leg, Dutch Baroque, end drw/baluster legs.825.00
Drop leaf, walnut, Wm & Mary, baluster trn supports, 60" L..1,450.00
Drop leaf breakfast, mahog, Federal, leaf carved tripod/paw ft..500.00
Drum, mahog, Geo III, leather inset revolving 27" top/tripod.1,650.00
Drum, mahog/inlay, Regency, leather 36" top/4 frieze drw....770.00
Games, gate leg, walnut, Italian Rococo, serpentine top, drw..880.00
Games, mahog, Hplwht, inlaid checkerboard in ivory/rosewood..470.00
Games, MOP inlay, Middle Eastern, 1800s, 34" W...........1,650.00
Games, Tunbridge ware/inlaid rosewood, Regency, 17" W....1,980.00
Games, walnut, Eastlake, octagonal/inlay checkerboard/urns/etc.450.00
Hutch, maple, dvtl drw, 1 brd pine seat, 2 brd top, rfn, 44"...950.00
Hutch, pine 3 brd rectangle top, compartment under lid, 83".1,200.00
Hutch, pine 3 brd top w/rnd corners, old red stain, 49½" dia.2,100.00
Hutch, poplar, end cut-out/sides mortised, marred, rpt, 65" L..375.00
Japanese, silver lacquer w/fish, some wear, 1900s, 11x16x37"...935.00

Lacquer wood free form base w/shaped glass top, 1957, 64"..1,430.00
Library, mahog, Geo III, octagon w/sq ped, revolves, 45"....8,000.00
Library, oak, Chas Rohfs, Nouveau scrolls/carving, 72" L...24,000.00
Library, oak, G Stickley, spindle side, label/decal, 52" L...3,740.00
Occasional, mahog, Geo III, shaped galleried sq top, 13" W..495.00
Occasional, satinwood/inlay, Geo III, top: 27x19"...........1,980.00
Oriental, marble inset, MOP inlay birds/flowers, 18x25x50"...1,650.00
Oriental, rectangle w/open panel frieze, scroll ft, 15x17x36"...550.00
Pembroke, cherry, Fed, shaped leaves w/ovolo corners, 35" L..800.00
Pembroke, mahog, Fed, line inlay, shaped leaves, 29".......1,800.00
Pembroke, mahog, Fed, 1 drw, rstr, 29" L.................600.00
Pier, mahog, Empire, acanthus/cornucopia/paw ft, 36x36"....2,310.00
Pine, Country Hplwht Pembroke, part scrubbed/old red, 36" L.400.00
Pool, pewter inlay, tag: Proust/Les Billars de Haute Precision.3,080.00
Refectory, elmwood/Continental Rococo/4 drw in frieze, 107".1,870.00
Refectory, Jacobean oak, fluted frieze/blauster legs, 1600s..2,750.00
Refectory, oak, Continental Baroque, fan carving, 95" L......220.00
Refectory, Stuart oak, draw leaf, carved frieze, 1650s, 82" L...330.00
Refectory, walnut, Spanish Baroque carved, 4 drw, 93" L....1,870.00
Refectory, walnut/oak/Continental Baroque/spiral legs, 108" L.1,430.00
Sawbuck, pine, curved legs, 2 board top/breadboard ends, 57"..250.00
Sewing, curly maple, Fed, D form sides/drw/medial shelf, 25" L.800.00
Shaker, Pembroke, Co Hplwht, rpl top 21x41", 10" leaves.....375.00
Shaker, sorting; inside chamfer/mortised apron, 30x20x26"...1,000.00
Shaker, walnut, 1 drw, 2 board rpl top w/crack, rfn, 28x28x30".375.00
Shaker, work; cherry/poplar/pine, trn legs/4 dvtl drw, 72x35".1,350.00
Side, blk lacquer/incised Orientals/scenics allover, 55" L.....2,200.00
Side, fruitwood parquetry mt, Louis XV, rstr, 21x13".........935.00
Side, gilt wood/marble, Geo II, foliate frieze, att Kent........2,860.00
Side, giltwood, Italian Neoclassic, marble top, rstr, 35x52".....110.00
Side, Hong Mu, frieze carved w/dragons, hoof ft, 1800s, 48".1,320.00
Side, mahog, Geo III, bell flower/scroll brackets, 60" L......6,600.00
Side, parcel gilt/faux marble, Geo II style, lg center scroll...3,520.00
Side, pine, Fed, 1 frieze drw/sq taper legs/box stretcher, 17"...200.00
Side, thuyawood/inlay, Geo III, demi lune, 34", pr..........4,950.00
Side, walnut, Louis XIII, spiral legs, trn knob on stretcher....3,757.00
Side, walnut/pine, inlay, Continental Baroque, rstr, 50" L.....450.00
Sofa, mahog/inlay, Regency, drop, pr frieze drw, 36x26".....2,200.00
Tavern, maple, QA, scrolled apron, rpl top: 25x30".........625.00
Tavern, maple/pine, Country QA, 1 brd top 23x28" is split...1,500.00
Tavern, maple/pine, QA, rectangle extends/drw/box stretcher...800.00
Tavern, maple/pine, splay leg/oval top/box stretcher, 1750....1,500.00
Tavern, pine, English QA, triangular apron, 3 brd 32" dia top..650.00
Tavern, pine/maple, oval top/box stretcher, 1750, 29".......2,250.00
Tavern, pine/maple, oval top/trn legs/box stretcher, rstr, 32"...700.00
Tea, ashwood, QA, carved shell apron, tray top, ornate......1,650.00
Tea, mahog, Chpndl, tilt top, shaped corners/tripod/c/b ft......900.00
Tea, mahog, Chpndl, 31" tilt top/bird cage/leaf carved/c/b/ft.6,500.00
Tea, Oriental, hardwood w/burl panel, pierced/carved scrolls....825.00
Temple, Walnut, Chinese style, John Widdicomb, 51" L......990.00
Tilt top, mahog, Geo II, circular spindle gallery 30" dia......1,760.00
Tilt top, mahog, tripod w/cabriole legs/trn column, 27" dia....300.00
Tilt top, mahog/satinwood inlay/Geo III/3 legs/pad ft, 34" dia.1,250.00
Trestle, walnut, Italian Baroque, 2 frieze drw, iron stretcher...715.00
Trestle, walnut, Italian Renaissance, 2 frieze drw, 83" L....2,750.00
Work, Chinese export, gold decor/blk lacquer, 1850, 25".....700.00
Work, mahog, Empire, hinged top/fitted w/in, top: 20x14".....500.00
Work, mahog/inlay, Fed, D drop leaves/2 drw/paw casters, 22".250.00
Work, rosewood, Rococo, lift top/gaming board/drws, 21" W...400.00
Work, walnut/inlay/parcel gilt/ormolu mt, Italian Neoclassic...2,475.00
Writing, oak, Louis XV Provincial/1 drw/cabriole legs, 30x20"..770.00
Writing, oak/frieze drw/Continental/baluster legs, 20x30" top...550.00
Writing, satinwood/inlay/Geo III/kidney shape/lyre sides, 36"..1,760.00
Writing, walnut, Italian Baroque, lozenges inlay, carving......880.00

Tete a Tetes, carved rosewood, joined by a turned standard and triangular hinged top table, 66″, $2,500.00.

Writing, walnut, Louis XV, frieze drw+2 ea side...........1,980.00
Writing, walnut/brass mt, Louis XVI style, 2 drw, 40x24″.....1,210.00

Wardrobe

Armoire, pine, 2 do/panels/geometrics, German Baroque.....1,980.00
Armoire, pine/pnt, Louis XV, 93x57″.....................1,200.00
Pine, Country Beidermier, corner ornament, scallop do fr, 72″.150.00
Shaker, open type, orig label, pine, wht pnt over orig, 75x46″..200.00
Shaker, poplar, imitation mahog graining, 2 base drw, 48″.....350.00

Washstand

Commode, inlay walnut/fruitwood marquetry, Italian Neoclassic..110.00
Commode, walnut/brass mts, Italian, swag carved apron, 3 drw..220.00
Corner, mahog, high gallery, cut out for bowl, false drws, rfn...200.00
Corner, pine, Fed, pierced for basin/soap dish/medial shelf.....250.00
Country Sheraton, cut out for bowl, gallery, orig grpt/stripes...265.00
Mahog, Sheraton, cut-out top/shaped gallery, base drw, rough..250.00
Shaker, pine/poplar, 1 dvtl base drw, rpl top w/gallery, rfn.....275.00

G. Argy-Rousseau

Gabriel Argy-Rousseau produced both fine art glass and quality commercial ware in 1918, in Paris, France. He favored Art Nouveau as well as Art Deco, and in the twenties produced a line of vases in the Egyptian manner, made popular by the discovery of King Tut's tomb. One of the most important types of glass he made was pate de verre. Most of his work is signed.

Dish, molded vine/berries, mottled gold, sgn, 4″.............475.00
Vase, ferns, ovoid shape, gray/bl/aqua mottle, 6″, EX.........850.00
Vase, inverted trumpet, fluted sides, gr/ochre in clear, 8″......440.00
Vase, The Apple Pickers, sgn, 1925, 9½″.................4,950.00
Vase, 3 dia form flowerheads, yellow/orange, sgn, 6¼″........950.00

Galle

Emile Galle was one of the most important producers of cameo glass in France. His firm, founded in Nancy in 1874, produced beautiful cameo in the Art Nouveau style during the 1890s, using a variety of techniques. He also produced glassware with enameled decoration, as well as some fine pottery -- animal figurines, table services, vases, and other objects d' art.

In the mid-1880s, he became interested in the various colors and texture of natural woods, and as a result began to create furniture which he used as yet another medium through which to express his art. Marquetry was the primary method Galle used in decorating his furniture -- prefering landscapes, Nouveau floral and fruit arrangements, butterflies, squirrels, and other forms from nature. It is for his furniture and his cameo glass that he is best known today.

Cameo

Bowl, fern fronds, gray & gr w/lime overlay, silver ped, 8½″...700.00
Bud vase, flower laden leafy vines, gray/yellow/lavender, 13″...770.00
Bud vase, landscape, gray/gr to ochre, rnd w/stick neck, 9½″..700.00
Bud vase, wild flowers, rose/grape, rnd w/slim neck, 8½″......800.00
Egg, bl/yel/br leaves on frost, 7½″.......................2,000.00
Ewer, grapevine, foil inclusions, clear applied vine hdls, 7½″.3,300.00
Flagon, florals, yellow/rust, squat rectangle w/can neck, 4″.....700.00
Flagon, waisted sphere, pendant lily, fire polished, 4¼″.....1,100.00
Lamp base, violets on salmon w/gr leaves, sgn, 15″...........700.00
Pilgrim flask, gr/bl mtns & lake/br trees on gold/wht, 9″.....1,950.00
Powder box, trailing tendrils/leaves, chartreuse/dk gr, 4″ dia...700.00
Salt, open; orange floral on clear, 1½x2¾″.................350.00
Vase, autumn leaves/beetle, internal decor, inscription, 13″...2,000.00
Vase, berries/tendrils, purple/br w/gr overlay, 16″...........1,100.00
Vase, blk w/bl hi-lites, red wheel-carved lilies, bronze ft, 8″....900.00
Vase, blossom/pods, straight w/trefoil lip, mauve/gr, 11½″.....770.00
Vase, blossoming branches, gray/pink/rose/gr, 6¾″...........900.00
Vase, blossoms/pods, baluster form, gray/pink to olive, 13″...1,100.00
Vase, blown out red hyacinths, creamy gold ground, 12½″...5,000.00
Vase, bridge/trees, gray-orange/gr-ochre overlay, 10¾″.......2,200.00
Vase, brown fuchsia on frosted ground, sgnd, 23¼″.........2,500.00
Vase, chrysanthemum, puce/gr on gray, bulb base, 11¾″.....1,200.00
Vase, clematis, mold blown cylinder, dbl overlay, 9¾″.......2,500.00
Vase, clematis/leaves, gray/salmon, fire polished, 6¾″........825.00
Vase, crocus/leaves, yellow/red, low bulb form, 4″............770.00
Vase, daisies w/applied centers, sgn E Galle, 5½″............550.00
Vase, dragonfly/pond w/lotus, yellow w/bl-violet overlay, 15″...1,800.00
Vase, exotic floral, gr w/maroon overlay & ft, polished, 16″...1,500.00
Vase, fern fronds, ovoid w/pulled lip, partial polish, 13¾″.....715.00
Vase, florals, disk ft/inverted tear drop, yellow/red, 8″........880.00
Vase, florals, pink/yellow/apricot/gr/lime, EX detail, 12½″....1,700.00
Vase, fuschia blossoms, gray/purple, 15¼″.................825.00
Vase, gr cased/gr & rust inclusions/leaf cut/appliques, 11″....4,400.00
Vase, hydrangea, smoke-pink/purple overlay, 25″...........1,760.00
Vase, hydrangea, stick w/bun ft, frost/lavender/olive, 23¼″...1,320.00
Vase, irises, gray/purple, fire polished, 13″................1,500.00
Vase, lake scene, frost w/violet overlay, polished, 14″.......2,100.00
Vase, lake scene, yellow-gray/blue overlay, 24½″...........4,400.00
Vase, landscape, yellow/bl-gr, slim w/ped ft, 8″.............1,320.00
Vase, landscape, yellow/dk br/lt br, sgn, 21″...............2,090.00
Vase, leafy vines, yellow w/purple overlay, 9½″.............800.00
Vase, lotus pads/blossoms, expanded base, gray/bl, 10″.......900.00
Vase, molded w/leafy branches, w/paper label, 9¾″, G.......900.00
Vase, morning-glory vines, frost/wht/mauve, 13½″...........1,100.00
Vase, orchids, internal mottled, bl & gr w/br & gr overlay, 6″.1,500.00
Vase, pear w/ft, floral/applied tendril/bud/foil inclusion, 8″....1,760.00
Vase, pendant berry branches, yellow/cherry red, cylinder, 10″..900.00
Vase, pendant orchids, gray-yellow w/ochre overlay, 7½″.....1,100.00
Vase, pendant wisteria, slim form, gray-yellow/violet, 28″...2,090.00
Vase, Pilgrim flask, floral/leaves, part fire polish, 8½″.......1,540.00
Vase, primrose, flat sphere, internal flecks, intaglio sgn, 6″....750.00

Bowl, scenic in scrolled cartouch, white with gold trim, multicolor decor, signed 'E. Galle, Nancy', 8″ x 5″, $495.00.

Vase, red leaves, banjo shape, 2 cut layers, golden ground, 7″..650.00
Vase, river landscape, salmon to gray/gr & br, flared, 9½″.....880.00
Vase, spider/berries, cut & enameled, sgn Emile Galle, 7″....1,500.00
Vase, thistle, peach w/gr decor, 16″.....................1,210.00
Vase, trumpet vines, yellow w/red, maroon overlay, ovoid, 14″.1,100.00
Vase, water lilies/dragonfly, yellow w/bl & gr overlay, 20″.....3,500.00
Vase, wintergreen, orange w/gr ft, part polished, 17″.......1,400.00
Vase, wisteria, candlestick, cream w/purple overlay & ft, 24″..1,100.00

Enameled Glass

Bowl, spring blossoms/leafage, sgn intaglio, 6½″............550.00
Vase, water lilies in 2 shades of lav w/yellow, 11″...........995.00

Furniture

Etagere table, 2 shelves inlaid w/florals/butterfly, rstr, 45″....1,760.00
Nest of 4 tables, inlaid w/scenic/cottage/boat/gulls, 28x23″....3,000.00
Nest of 4 tables, inlaid w/tulips/irises/butterflies.............3,025.00
Sewing table, fruitwood marquetry, florals, shaped top, 20″...1,540.00
Table, inlaid w/squirrel, curving sides, 25″ L..............1,500.00
Table, 2 rectangular tiers inlaid w/iris/dragonfly, 28x28″ L....2,500.00

Gambling Memorabilia

Apron, dealer's, to steal chips, w/letter of explanation, 1920.....76.00
Ball knocker, under sleeve roulette operator cheat device, NM..416.00
Bingo outfit, w/ballboard/cage/balls/cards/etc.................45.00
Book, Canfield, Alexander Gardiner, 3rd ed, 1930, 350 pgs, NM.61.00
Book, Fools of Fortune, JP Quinn, 1st ed, 1890, illus, EX......55.00
Book, Hills Vest Pocket Hoyle, Ogilvie Co, 132 pgs, 1900......10.00
Book, Hoyle's Games Improved, 1843, pocket ed, emb, gilt pgs.109.00
Book, Protection, The Sealed Book, J Meyer, 127 pgs, 1911....90.00
Broadside, Fletcher Co, for benefit of Delaware, 1861, 6x17″....26.00
Card shaver, shear type, cheating device.................1,200.00
Card trimmer, German silver base, 2½″ ivory hdl, brass, M....921.00
Cardpress, wood dividers/hdl/screw, lt wood, dovetailed, NM.....50.00
Cash box, for traveling game, lid w/long piano hinges, 17x11″...21.00
Catalog, Mason & Co, Aristocratic Club Line, 60 pgs, 1930s, M.165.00
Chip rack, lg wood rack, 12 rows, G......................50.00

Chip rack, stainless steel, 14 rows, removable bill box, M.......65.00
Crap layout, full sz, from 'The Flamingo Club', Nevada Co, NM.105.00
Dagger, carved ivory hdl, leather sheath/brass trim, 1830s, 9″..121.00
Diana layout, under glass/brass corners/wood bk, all orig, M..1,235.00
Dice boat, wood, w/gr felt lining, for extra dice, 4x8x3″, NM....72.00
Dice cup, carved burl walnut, ribbed interior, early 1800s, 3″....50.00
Dice cup, carved wood, ribbed int, 4″, w/2 bone dice, 1860s....72.00
Dice cup, leather embossed Pour La Roblesse, 4″, NM.......41.00
Dice jiggler, pull dome down: jiggle trapped dice, 3½x2″ dia....25.00
Dice stick, 3 pcs, wood, combination pull/card flip tool, 36″.....32.00
Faro layout, folding w/felt top, Spades, Ball Co, G...........450.00
Faro layout, straight board, clubs, walnut trim, early, NM.....531.00
Flyer, consolidated lotteries of Delaware, 1860, 4 pg, 8x11, NM.31.00
Gambling license, Virginia City, 1885, $25, sgnd Chief Police....95.00
Hazard horn, turned wood, many individual pieces, 6½″, NM..275.00
Horse race wheel, roulette type, German silver spin, 5″ dia.....57.00
Lottery ticket, Old Kentucky, $1/$100,000, Feb 28 1923, 8x3″..24.00
Magazine, Poker Chips, Vol 1/#1, June 1896, poker articles....250.00
Magnetic switch plate, cheating device, w/dummy screw, 4x5″, M.50.00
Pan dealing shoe, wood, chips section, spins to deal, 13x4x5″..75.00
Paperweight, 5 tiny bone dice, advertising, brass base, 1902.....95.00
Penny flip game, Fields 4 Jacks 5¢ pocket payout, 4 jackpots..525.00
Poker chip, MOP, bevelled perimeter, monogram/$100, 3 for...232.00
Poker chip, MOP, ornate emb front/bk, Oriental woman 1 side..50.00
Poker chips, custom mahog case w/silver mts, 7x9½x9″.......275.00
Postcard, cowboys gambling, going for guns, color, ca 1900, EX.20.00
Poster, Sins o/t Fathers, devil, suits in corners, mc, 1920s......75.00
Put & take top, sterling silver, 1¼″, NM...................80.00
Roulette ball, old, composition, for full sz roulette wheel.......21.00
Roulette wheel, Geo Mason & Co, w/laydown & ivory ball....1,500.00
Roulette wheel, pnt wood, 48″...........................150.00
Sleeve holdout, arm pressure style, much brass.............650.00
Suit markers, solid brass, suit shape/3 cards decor, set of 4.....21.00

Games & Puzzles

Among the most popular 19th century games attracting collectors today are the board games and their components which are hand-carved and painted, often with great attention to detail. Near the last decade of the century, commercially marketed games were introduced, some by companies who are still working. As is true today, many Victorian games were instructional and educational as well as entertaining. Colorfully lithographed boxes and game parts add to their appeal, and subject matter often exhibits customs and attitudes of a bygone era.

Puzzles were invented in 1760 by an English map-maker whose intention it was to facilitate the teaching of geography. By the mid-1850s, both America and Europe were producing children's puzzles. The earliest examples were made of wood, and were hand-cut. Die-cut cardboard puzzles were first manufactured in the 1890s, and 'adult' puzzles came into vogue. Although wood continued to be used, plywood replaced solid wood during the twenties and thirties, and interlocking pieces made them easier to construct.

Hand-colored, hand-cut, or special-interest 19th century puzzles are favorites of today's collectors; character-related and quality wooden puzzles are also very desirable.

Games

Alphabet Game, w/Brownies, Parker Bros, 1893.............115.00
Board, bl/wht, hand carved, Canadian, 1890s, 23x16″.........235.00
Board, pine w/applied edge, red/blk on natural, 19″ sq.......435.00
Board, wormy curly maple, dk br/blk stain, 16″.............90.00

Cats & Mice, McLoughlin Bros, lithographed, folding board....125.00
Chess set, handmade ambergris/brass, 15 pc w/board, 1800...1,685.00
Chessmen, pnt carved wood comical figures, set of 32, 3¼".....65.00
Corner Grocery, Parker Bros, 1887.........................75.00
Dominoes, dbl set, ivory, wood case w/ivory inlay & portrait....155.00
Dominoes, Embossing Co, dtd 1874, in box, EX...............20.00
Dominoes, ivory/ebony, in beech box w/sliding lid, 7".........20.00
Dominoes, ivory/ebony, in mahog case w/chip carving, 2¾x5"...35.00
Donkey Party, linen, Milton Bradley, 1932.................20.00

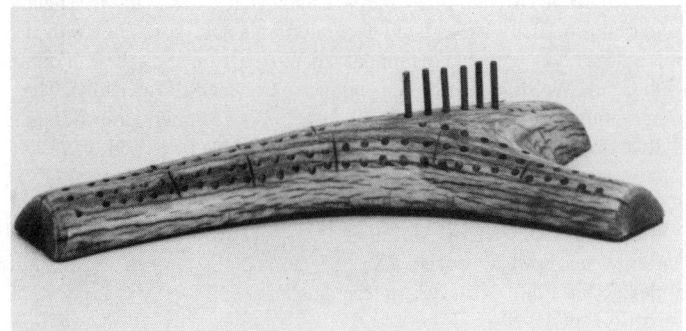

Cribbage set, made of horn with wire pegs, 9½", $48.00.

Farmer Jones' Pigs, McLoughlin.........................110.00
Fish Pond, orig box, 1890s............................65.00
Flying 4 Airplane Race...............................115.00
Game of Battle, McLoughlin, cannons/tents/etc, 65 pcs, VG...285.00
Game of Fish Pond, Milton Bradley, #4324A................15.00
Game of Golden Egg, Singer...........................115.00
Game of Jack Straws, Milton Bradley Co..................15.00
Grandma's Geography Game, McLoughlin..................30.00
Great Automobile Card Game, Touring...................25.00
Hopla, Bavaria......................................35.00
How Silas Popped the Question........................15.00
Jack Sprat & His Merry Wife, Parker Bros, 1880s...........35.00
Jolly Game of Old Maid, Parker Bros...................25.00
Lotto, McLoughlin Bros, 1898..........................48.00
Magic box, 2 dice w/in, only one removes, old pnt, 6½".......100.00
Magnetic Jack Straws, 1891...........................20.00
Marja, Fortune Teller, 1930...........................15.00
Marx target game, tin litho, 1930s, orig box, 10x10".........20.00
Merican Roll Game, Louis Marx & Co, MIB................35.00
Messanger Game, M Singer, early.......................25.00
MJ & CIE Automobile Jeu De Course, French, car race, 1905..275.00
Moon Mullins Automobile Race.........................50.00
Peter Coddle Tells of His Trip to Chicago, Parker Bros.......25.00
Picture Lotto, cards illus w/animals/birds/etc, 1800s, in bag....75.00
Pit, World's Liveliest Party Game, Parker Bros, orig box......25.00
Poppin' Ball, Parker Bros.............................45.00
Progressive Angling, 1886, poles/hooks/fish, in box..........85.00
Santa Claus' Panorama, Milton Bradley, in G orig box.......650.00
Sir Hinkle Funny Duster, 1903.........................35.00
Steeple Chase, Milton Bradley, #44449, 1909..............45.00
Tell It To The Judge, Parker Bros, Eddie Cantor, 1936.......15.00
The Nebbs, Bradley..................................45.00
Uncle Sam's Mail Game, McLoughlin Bros, orig box, 1893, G...55.00
Uncle Wiggily, Milton Bradley, 1954....................16.00
Visit to Camp, McLoughlin............................45.00
20th Century Limited, train on box lid, Parker Bros.........65.00

Puzzles

Clark Gable.......................................15.00

Puzzle 'Dissected Outline Map of the United States of America', Milton Bradley Co., complete with original box, $65.00.

Fallowfield Hunt, wood, 141 pcs..........................45.00
Hood's Sarsaparilla, Rainy Day, advertising, 10x15"...........95.00
Locomotive, 1900, orig box.............................65.00
Map of United States, Parker Bros, copyright 1915, orig box....22.00
Ocean liner, McLoughlin, prof framed, cover on reverse, 1896..175.00
Picture cubes, McLoughlin, 6 puzzles, 4 sheets, paper on wood.450.00
Popeye, 4 picture puzzles, orig box, 1932..................65.00
Ship that Sank in Victory, wood, 511 pcs..................35.00
Singer Sewing Machines, Indian, premium, complete in pkg.....24.00
The Gold Eagle, Bismark's, wood box, 1880................22.00
USA, Parker Bros, 1915...............................15.00
White Sewing Machines & Bicycles, advertising, 12½x16".....125.00

Gas Globes and Panels

Gas globes and panels, once a common sight, have vanished from the countryside, but are being sought by collectors as a unique form of advertising memorabilia. Early globes from the 1920s, now referred to as 'one-piece globes', were made of molded milk glass, and were globular in shape. The gas company name was etched or painted on the glass. Few of these were ever produced, and this type is valued very highly by collectors today.

A new type of pump was introduced in the early 1930s, the old 'visible' pumps replaced by 'electric' models. Globes were changing at the same time. By the mid-thirties, a 5-piece globe consisting of a pair of inserts, two retaining rings, and a metal body were being produced in both 15" and 16½" sizes. These were prone to damage and were made for only a few years. A third type, used in the thirties and forties, consisted of a glass frame retainer with two milk glass inserts. Occasionally, textured glass in red, yellow, or blue was used; these are rare today, and very valuable.

The most recently manufactured gas globes, used since the late 1940s, are made with a plastic body that contains two 13½" glass lenses.

Type 1, Plastic Body, Glass Inserts--1940s-1950s

Apco Diesel, plastic body or frame.......................55.00
Apco Premium, plastic body............................45.00
Apco Regular, plastic body.............................45.00
Champlin, iron cross, globe, plastic frame.................75.00
Conoco, plastic, 3 pc, 13½" face........................75.00
Fleetwing, plastic, 3 pc, 13½" face.....................125.00
Sinclair Dino, plastic body, glass inserts.................45.00
Sinclair Dino Supreme, globe............................75.00

Texaco, plastic body, glass inserts.........................70.00
Texaco Diesel Chief, inserts, 3 pc, plastic body, 13½".........60.00

Type 2, Glass Frame, Glass Inserts--1930s-1940s

American Gas, glass body...............................175.00
Atlantic, mirror border, gill type, 3 pc, 13½" face...........175.00
Atlantic, sign, regular type, 3 pc, 13½" face..............150.00
Atlantic Hi-Arc, Gill Band, glass body....................175.00
Barnsdall, glass, 3 pc, 13½" face.......................165.00
Champlin, iron cross, glass frame.......................175.00
Cities Service, cloverleaf, glass, 3 pc, 13½" face size........350.00
Conoco, glass, 3 pc, 13½" face.........................165.00
Dixie Power to Pass, gill type, 3 pc, 13½" face.............180.00
Fleetwing, F-W, glass, 3 pc, 13½" face...................200.00
Gulf, glass, 3 pc, 12½" face...........................165.00
Hudson, plastic body, glass inserts.....................120.00
Imperial Refineries, glass body........................175.00
Inreco Texas, glass, 3 pc.............................175.00
Kanotex Aviation, 3 pc, 13½".........................350.00
Mobilgas Special, glass, 3 pc, 13½"....................165.00
Pemco Premium, glass body...........................175.00
Phillips, glass, 3 pc, 13½" face........................150.00
Pure, glass, 3 pc, 13½".............................150.00
Richfield, glass, 3 pc, 13½" face.......................185.00
Road King, 3 pc, 13½", glass..........................225.00
Save X, glass, 3 pc, 13½" face.........................150.00
Simpson's Premium Ethyl, all glass globe..................155.00
Sinclair, HC, glass, 3 pc, 13½" face.....................155.00
Sinclair Dino, globe, glass body........................100.00
Sinclair HC, glass fr & inserts, red middle circle............180.00
Sinclair Power X, insert, 3 pc, 13½" glass frame............160.00
Skelly, glass, 3 pc, 13½" face.........................150.00
Texaco, glass, 3 pc, 13½" face........................150.00
Texaco Star, globe, glass frame........................165.00
Tower Gasoline, glass frame, 13½".....................275.00
Tydol Flying A, globe, glass frame......................175.00
Zepher, glass, 3 pc, 13½" face........................145.00

Type 3, Metal Frame, Glass Inserts--1920s-1930s

Atlantic, crossed arrows, metal fr, 16½" face..............250.00
California Richfield, metal fr, 15" face...................325.00
Cities Service Koolmotor, 15" metal.....................300.00
Dixie, metal fr, 15" face, rare.........................275.00
Essolene, metal fr, 16½".............................200.00
Gulf Coast, metal fr, 15" face.........................235.00
Mobilgas, flying horse, metal banded, 17"................275.00
Mobilgas Special, w/picture Pegasus, insert, 16½", pr........150.00
Once-Always, Cities Service, metal.....................300.00
Pan Am, metal fr, glass inserts........................300.00
Peerless, metal fr, 15" face...........................245.00
Purol, w/arrow, metal fr, 15".........................400.00
Richfield, w/bird, metal fr, 15" face....................300.00
Richfield Hi-Octane, metal, 15".......................300.00
Service, w/spartan, metal fr, 15"......................300.00
Sunoco, metal fr, glass inserts........................220.00
Tydol Ethyl, metal body.............................250.00

Type 4, One Piece Glass Globes, No Inserts, Co. Name Etched, Raised or Enameled--1914-1931

Gold Crown Standard, globe...........................200.00
Shells..175.00

Sinclair Aircraft...................................1,200.00
Sinclair Gas......................................700.00
Skelly, 1 pc......................................600.00
Standard Oil Crown, blue, 'Solite' raised letters, VG.........450.00

Gaudy Dutch

Inspired by Oriental Imari wares, Gaudy Dutch was made in England from 1800 to 1820. It was hand-decorated on a soft paste body with rich underglaze blues accented in orange, red, pink, green, and yellow. It differs from Gaudy Welsh in that there is no lustre (except on Water Lily). There are seventeen patterns, some of which are: War Bonnet, Grape, Dahlia, Oyster, Urn, Butterfly, Carnation, Single Rose, Double Rose, and Water Lily.

Butterfly, milk pitcher, 4", M........................1,000.00
Butterfly, tea bowl & saucer, EX......................650.00
Butterfly, tea bowl & saucer, saucer glued/chips............60.00
Carnation, plate, 8¼", EX...........................475.00
Carnation, saucer, minor wear & hairline.................155.00
Carnation, tea bowl & saucer, M......................500.00
Carnation, tea bowl & saucer, worn decor................185.00
Double Rose, plate, 10", VG.........................425.00
Double Rose, plate, 7", M...........................425.00
Double Rose, saucer, hairline........................55.00
Double Rose, soup plate, minor rim flake, enamel worn, 8¼"...80.00
Double Rose, sugar w/lid, worn, sm chips, 5½".............150.00
Double Rose, tea bowl & saucer, M.....................450.00
Double Rose, teapot, hairlines/chips/prof lid rpr, 6¼".......250.00
Double Rose, waste bowl, minor wear, 3x5½".............375.00
Grape, dessert plate, 8", set of 4, VG..................800.00
Grape, plate, 7", M................................425.00
Grape, soup plate, 10", set of 4, 1 w/hairline, others G......950.00
Grape, tea bowl & saucer, minor stains/flakes.............175.00
Grape, tea bowl & saucer, set of 6, EX.................1,300.00
Grape, tea bowl & saucer, worn decor..................185.00
Grape, toddy, some wear on leaves, 5¼".................235.00
Oyster, plate, 10", minor scratches....................325.00
Oyster, soup plate, underglaze bl floral border, 8½", EX.....450.00
Primrose, toddy plate, 4¾", G........................350.00
Single Rose, creamer, wide mouth, stained...............275.00
Single Rose, plate, dbl border, 10", M..................525.00
Single Rose, plate, worn/faded, 10"....................90.00
Single Rose, plate, 7", M............................410.00
Single Rose, plate, 8½", hairline......................110.00
Single Rose, plate, 8¼", M..........................450.00
Single Rose, tea bowl & saucer, flakes..................200.00
Single Rose, tea bowl & saucer, hairline/rpr..............80.00
Sunflower, creamer, hairline in spout, stain/wear, 4½".......100.00
Sunflower, milk jug, 4½", VG........................550.00
Sunflower, plate, 8¼", VG..........................460.00
Sunflower, tea bowl & saucer, hairline in cup/flakes.........105.00
Urn, plate, 5", M..................................525.00
Urn, plate, 7¼", VG...............................305.00
Urn, plate, 8¼", EX...............................475.00
War Bonnet, creamer, minor wear, 4½".................350.00
War Bonnet, plate, minor hairlines/stains/wear, 8¼".........225.00
War Bonnet, sugar bowl, 5¼", EX.....................750.00
War Bonnet, tea bowl & saucer, ea pc hairlines/rpr..........90.00
War Bonnet, teapot, chip on inner rim of lid, 6"............850.00
Water Lily, tea bowl & saucer, EX.....................725.00
Zinnia, plate, imp Riley, minor enamel flaking, 8½".........400.00

Gaudy Ironstone

Gaudy Ironstone was produced in the mid-1800s in Staffordshire, England. Some of the ware was decorated in much the same colors and designs as Gaudy Welsh, while other pieces were painted in pink, orange, and red, with black and light blue accents. Lustre was used on some designs, omitted on others. The heavy ironstone body is its most distinguishing feature.

Gaudy Ironstone teapot, floral decor, 9¼", $350.00.

Cheese dish, cobalt bird, orange flowers, Lo Sol Ware, England . 95.00
Dish, serving; ped ft, open hdl, no mk 75.00
Pitcher, bl w/mc flowers/birds/trees, reg mk, 6" 85.00
Pitcher, mc floral, sea serpent hdl, octagonal, 5¾" 125.00
Pitcher, milk; pagoda & palm tree 100.00
Plate, cobalt leaves w/strawberries, 12 sided, minor rpr, 8" 75.00
Plate, Oriental decor, lion & unicorn mk, 9¼" 50.00
Plate, pinwheel 125.00
Plate, thistle border in red/gr/yellow/blk, 10" 18.00
Teapot, cr/sug, Lustre Band 235.00

Gaudy Welsh

Gaudy Welsh was an inexpensive hand decorated ware made in both England and Wales from 1820 until 1860. It is characterized by its colors -- principally underglaze blue, orange-rust, and copper lustre -- and by its bold uninhibited patterns. Accent colors may be yellow and green; pink lustre may be present, since lustre applied to the white areas develops pink rather than the copper affected over dark colors. The body of the ware may be heavy ironstone, creamware, earthenware, or porcelain; even style and shapes vary considerably. Patterns, while usually floral, are also sometimes geometric, and may have trees and birds.

Biscuit plate, Tulip, 9" 65.00
Compote, floral decor w/purple luster w/out & w/in, 6x10" 200.00
Cup & saucer, Onion 25.00
Cup & saucer, Oyster, set of 6 . . . . 150.00
Cup & saucer, Tulip 50.00
Jug, oyster, 4½" 70.00
Mug, child's; Grape II 46.00
Mug, w/frog, 4" 170.00

Mustard jar, 3" 40.00
Plate, strawberry, gold trim, 10" 75.00
Plate, Tulip, 6" 40.00
Plate, Tulip, 9" dia 55.00
Platter, Morning Glory, octagonal, ironstone, minor wear, 12" . . . 85.00
Sugar, ftd, Tulip 85.00
Sugar, Tulip, 6¾" 80.00
Sugar w/lid, 2 hdls, Tulip 75.00
Tea set, Morning Glory, pot, sug/cr, 6 c/s 750.00
Tea tile 70.00
Teapot, Cornflower 125.00
Teapot w/lid, ornate, Tulip 135.00
Waste bowl, Tulip, minor rim hairline, 3½x6½" 40.00

Gaudy Welsh pitcher in the Deiniolen pattern, 6", $235.00.

Geisha Girl

Geisha girl porcelains have only recently attracted a following in the collectible market. They were made primarily for export in dinnerware, tea sets, and vases, in several patterns featuring Geisha girls in various daily pursuits. Some were entirely hand painted, others were hand decorated over decals or with stencils. Pieces were bordered in one of many bright colors -- red, yellow, blue, green, or brown -- and collectors generally prefer to match border colors when re-assembling a matching set.

Bowl, dessert; bl lady, 5¼", set of 6 . . . . 35.00
Bowl, hdld, rust w/gold trim, 7x13" 45.00
Chocolate pot, red lady, 10" 65.00
Chocolate set, 9 pcs 125.00
Cracker jar, cobalt, M 45.00
Creamer, orange, 3¾" 8.50
Cup & saucer 8.00
Cup & saucer, demitasse 40.00
Hair receiver, rust 25.00
Hatpin holder, orange border 45.00
Match holder, rust 25.00
Mayonnaise set, 3 pc, Nippon 45.00
Mustard, 3 pc, rust 35.00
Nut bowl, ftd, 6" 16.00
Pitcher, bulbous melon shape, rust, small 20.00

Geisha Girl bowl, blue border, 9″, $25.00.

Pitcher, milk; Satsuma style, 6″...........................60.00
Plate, gold border, Nippon, 6″, set of 6...................35.00
Powder box & hair receiver, red trim, pr..................45.00
Powder jar...28.00
Saucer, blue border..2.50
Shakers, old Chinese mk, 2½″, pr..........................15.00
Shakers, red border, tall, pr...............................12.00
Tea set, orange border, 6 c/s.............................175.00
Teapot, dk orange, 1 cup...................................30.00
Teapot, orange, 1½ cup....................................36.00
Teapot, orange, 4 cup......................................45.00
Toothpick holder..22.00

German Porcelain

The porcelain listed in this section is marked simply 'Germany'. Products of other German manufacturers are listed under specific name. The Pink Pigs series referred to in the listing are very collectible, though produced by an anonymous maker.

Bathing beauty, mermaid coming out of shell, souvenir, glazed...75.00
Bathing beauty, reclining, gr suit/cap, #5834................75.00
Bathing beauty, reclining mermaid, 3½″.....................75.00
Bathing beauty, sitting on shell, blue suit/cap, glazed, #4901....65.00
Bathing beauty, standing, bl suit, bisque, #5685.............75.00
Bowl, gold w/blk trim, orange/yellow poppies, 3 crown mk, 10″.125.00
Bowl, pk roses, pearlized finish, hdld, artist sgnd, 4½x5″......20.00
Bust, Victorian children, grown-up dress, German, 4¾″, pr....85.00
Cache pot, allover sm bl flowers, gold, PB Wurttenburg, 5½″...23.00
Candle holders for birthday cake, circus figures, set of 12......85.00
Chocolate pot, lady's portrait, gold trim, 9¾x3½″............95.00
Chocolate pot, lav/wht w/pk/wht roses, satin finish, 9¾″.......90.00
Condiment set, 3 quail figurals, grasses holder, anchor mk, 4″..155.00
Elfinware, box, heart shaped, sm...........................45.00
Elfinware, pen stand, ornate, HP...........................25.00
Elfinware, perfume, Coronet stopper, pr....................55.00
Elfinware, salt, wheelbarrow figural.......................45.00
Elfinware, salt & peppers, pr..............................50.00
Elfinware, stamp box.......................................22.00

Elfinware, swan, yellow, 2″................................15.00
Elfinware, toothpick, 2″...................................23.00
Figurine, girl, deer, bunnies, bisque/gold/gr/wht, 12″......295.00
Figurine, man w/long coat, lady w/shawl, bl/wht, 1800s, 5″, pr..160.00
Figurine, News Vendor, Scheibe Kister, 1834, 5¼″...........100.00
Figurine, Red Riding Hood, bisque..........................85.00
Figurine, shepherd holding pipe, 2 sheep, 16½″.............65.00
Golden Bears, bear coming out door of log cabin............65.00
Golden Bears, bear looking in outhouse at farmer...........75.00
Golden Bears, bear on gr dish looks at ball................60.00
Golden Bears, 2 wht bears driving auto, 3½x4½″.............65.00
Gravy boat, rooster shape, HP orange/gr/yellow, sgn, 4x8″......39.00
Pink Pigs, by boot, souvenir, 3″...........................75.00
Pink Pigs, by cradle w/baby pig, Hush-a-bye Baby..., 3½″.......95.00
Pink Pigs, by top hat, 2″..................................65.00
Pink Pigs, by tub, 2½″.....................................65.00
Pink Pigs, gr cup, sm pg crawling out......................65.00
Pink Pigs, in gr car, 1 driving, 2 ride in bk, 3½x2¼x4½″.......85.00
Pink Pigs, lg outhouse, 1 w/in, 1 peeking in...............60.00
Pink Pigs, match holder, pig sits on dice, red devil, 3½″......85.00
Pink Pigs, one sitting in pot..............................55.00
Pink Pigs, one w/binoculars................................50.00
Pink Pigs, one w/Boston Bean pot...........................45.00
Pink Pigs, pig looking in outhouse, devil seated w/in, 4½″.....150.00
Pink Pigs, reclining on rim of horseshoe ash tray..........70.00
Pink Pigs, seated in train engine, 4½″ L..................125.00
Pink Pigs, smoking pipe, 3¼″...............................85.00
Pink Pigs, sq bale, 1 peers out of hole, 1 atop............60.00
Pink Pigs, wearing chef's costume, holds frying pan, basket.....80.00
Pink Pigs, 2 in a 7″ canoe, ea wearing hat.................60.00
Pink Pigs, 2 in boat, Over the Rowing Sea..................55.00
Pink Pigs, 2 in open suitcase..............................70.00
Pink Pigs, 2 on see-saw atop pouch bank....................55.00
Pink Pigs, 2 pigs in car, 4½″ L...........................100.00
Pink Pigs, 2 sitting before upturned hat...................60.00
Pink Pigs, 2 sitting in open purse, 3½x5″..................85.00
Pink Pigs, 3 by oval dish, Souvenir of Jamestown Expo, 1907...75.00
Pink Pigs, 3 w/oval gr basin...............................55.00
Pitcher, lav, HP pk & wht flowers, branch hdl, raised mold, 8″..50.00
Plate, castle scene, Give Us This Day...around rim, 2 hdld, 9″..25.00
Plate, w/hdls, HP grapes/mums, gold trim, artist sgn, 10″......55.00
Stamp pad, cat's head w/sponge in mouth, mkd, 2x4½x2½″....60.00
Sugar & creamer, HP pink roses w/br/gold, mk JS............58.00
Vase, tapestry, scenic, 7″.................................65.00

Figural coffee pot, head is lid, cucumber spout, 11¼″, $385.00.

Goebel

F.W. Goebel founded the Hummelwork Porcelain Manufactory in 1871, located in Rodental, West Germany. They produced porcelain figurines, plates, and novelties, the most famous of which are the Hummel figurines (these are listed in a separate section). There were many other series produced by Goebel -- Disney characters, birds, animals, and the Friar Tuck Monks that are especially popular.

See also Collector Plates; Hummel

Ash tray, Friar Tuck Monks, full bee mk...................20.00
Ash tray/match holder, parrot sits on edge, mc.............25.00
Bank, Friar Tuck Monks, current mk........................15.00
Bank, Friar Tuck Monks, stylized bee mk...................27.50
Bottle, liquor; Friar Tuck Monks, full bee mk.............65.00
Bowl, raised orange chicken w/mc tail, Crown mk, Lotte Sund...25.00
Calendar, Friar Tuck Monks, full bee......................48.00
Candle holder, flying angel child, dbl, wall hung, Crown mk.....15.00
Candle holder, seated angel rings bell, Crown mk, M Spotl..17.00
Candle holder, seated angel w/fir tree, Crown mk, M Spotl......17.00
Candle holder, seated angel w/heart, Crown mk, M Spotl, sm....17.00
Christmas ornament, angel holding sm tree, mc, last bee mk....12.00
Christmas ornament, Mrs Claus w/hands in muff, mc, last bee mk.8.50
Christmas ornament, red Santa, 1st edition, 1978...........11.00
Christmas ornament, Santa, frosted glass, last bee mk.........10.00
Christmas ornament, Santa, multi-color, 1st ed, 1978, last bee...12.50
Cookie jar, Friar Tuck Monks, lg..........................85.00
Creamer, clown w/blk face figural, crown mk...............85.00
Creamer, Friar Tuck Monks, full bee mk, 4"................30.00
Creamer, Friar Tuck Monks, stylized mk, 5½"...............35.00
Creamer, Friar Tuck Monks, 2½"...........................25.00
Creamer, yellow daisy & bluebells, Crown mk, Lotte Sund.....18.00
Creamer & sugar, Friar Tuck Monks, full bee mk, 5", pr.....60.00
Creamer & sugar w/lid on tray, Friar Tuck Monks..........65.00
Decanter, Friar Tuck Monks, stout monk, full bee, 11".......80.00
Dresser box, soldier figural finial, 6½x5"................120.00
Egg cup, frowning boy's face, bee mk, WG..................26.00
Egg timer, Friar Tuck Monks, dbl, stylized bee mk..........25.00
Figurine, bird, 1960 mk...................................15.00
Figurine, brown spotted deer, standing, 1950s.............20.00
Figurine, colt, frolicking, terra cotta, 4¼".............50.00
Figurine, girl in pink dress w/HP florals, 7"............25.00
Figurine, goat, standing, terra cotta, 4¾"...............35.00
Figurine, Grumpy Dwarf, 1950s............................65.00
Figurine, honey bear, yel, wide crown mk, 4".............24.00
Figurine, kneeling angel, last bee mk, 2¾"...............30.00
Figurine, Madonna, 10"...................................75.00
Figurine, man & lady in ballroom, Victorian, slight damage, 8".100.00
Figurine, man offers lady ice cream, GM #503, 2½".........80.00
Figurine, nude girl, geese, terra cotta, Crown mk, R Unger, 9".400.00
Figurine, nude seated woman, terra cotta, 5½"............30.00
Figurine, nude w/partridge on outstretched hand, Crown mk...25.00
Figurine, praying angel kneeling on cloud, Crown mk.........35.00
Figurine, Praying Madonna, all white, eyes closed, HM 23......18.00
Figurine, rabbit, Deco style, wht/gold/blk, 4½"..........24.00
Figurine, Victorian lady sits on man's back, w/lamb, 2¾"....70.00
Figurine, Victorian man puts flower in lady's hair, w/lamb, 2"...75.00
Figurine, young goat, terra cotta, 4¾"...................40.00
Flower holder, orange tied bandanna, Crown mk, OH 26, 5½"..20.00
Liquor bottle, 10", w/6 liquor tots, Friar Tuck, current mk.....50.00
Mug, Friar Tuck Monks, 5"................................40.00
Mustard, Cardinal Tuck, 1956.............................35.00

Mustard, w/lid; Friar Tuck Monks.........................45.00
Perfume, Victorian lady, dbl crown mk, 4½"...............65.00
Perfume, Victorian lady, slender shaped body, pk dress........35.00
Perfume, Victorian woman, wide skirt w/flower decals.........35.00
Pin tray, Deco girl shape................................75.00
Pitcher, miniature, Cardinal Tuck........................25.00
Plaque, girl carrying water jars relief, sgn, in fr, 10".........295.00
Shaker, Friar Tuck Monks, w/red book, full bee mk, 3".......40.00
Shakers, boy in golfing suit and ball on golf club base, 3¾", pr.70.00
Shakers, Friar Tuck Monks, sm bee mk, pr.................22.00
Shakers, w/mustard and tray, Friar Tuck Monks, current mk, pr.28.00
Shakers on tray, Friar Tuck Monks, stylized bee, 'Foreign', pr...40.00
Sugar w/lid, Friar Tuck Monks, full bee mk...............35.00
Tea bag caddy, Cardinal Tuck.............................20.00
Toby jug, Mrs Gamp, full bee, 6".........................45.00
Toothpick, pussy willow branch w/rabbit along side, full B/V.....45.00
Vase, beige w/4 orange bands, ftd, 9½"...................25.00
Wall vase, orange heart, Crown mk, VP 44./1., 4¾"...........10.00
Wall vase, umbrella shape, beige w/orange hi-lights...........20.00

Bird figurine, 'Eagle', 1969, 9½" x 19½", $100.00.

Going-to-bed Lamps

Going-to-bed lamps, used for just that purpose, had a compartment for matches, a striker, and a socket to hold a burning match or a small taper. The match provided just enough illumination to enable one to find his way to bed after the oil lamp was extinguished.

Castle tower, turned ebony, ivory finial socket, screw lid, 3".....25.00
Hanging, treen w/blk transfer scenes, 4¾"..................55.00
Horn, threaded lid, 2⅛"..................................25.00
Lignum vitae, turned; brass socket, threaded lid, 2½".........35.00
Mahogany, turned; ivory socket, bottom unscrews, 2½".......10.00
Oak w/brass studs, age cracks, 3½".......................15.00
Stirling Castle, blk transfer on treen, ivory socket, 2¾".......22.50
Wood, decoupage 'McPherson' tartan, ivory socket, 2½".......15.00
Wood, turned/carved, threaded lid, G detail, 2¼"............25.00

Goldscheider

The Goldscheider family operated a pottery in Vienna for many generations before seeking refuge in the United States following Hitler's invasion of their country. They settled in Trenton, New Jersey, in the early 1940s, where they established a new corporation, producing objects of art and tableware items. In 1946 Marcel Goldscheider established a pottery in Staffordshire, where he manufactured bone china figures, earthenware, etc., marked with a stamp of his signature.

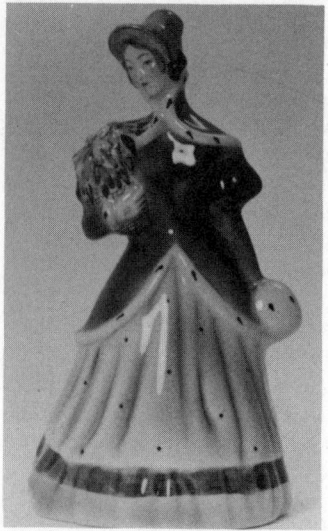

Figurine, lady in green, pink, and gray, 7", $40.00.

Bust, Black Madonna, artist sgnd, Austria, 5½"............750.00
Bust, Chinese heads, man & woman, artist sgnd, 7", pr......125.00
Bust, lady, brown w/turq curls, Austrian, sgnd..............350.00
Figurine, Blanche, artist sgnd, 5".........................50.00
Figurine, child in snow, alabaster, marble base, w/seal, 9½"....390.00
Figurine, Chinese Guitarist, 10¼" on 3" base, Everlast........40.00
Figurine, Chinese Princess, sgnd Barbara Loveday #270, 8¼"...75.00
Figurine, Christmas Lady, 1800s costume, w/Poinsettia, 7½"....75.00
Figurine, Colonial couple, USA, 9", pr...................125.00
Figurine, Colonial woman, flowers on hat, artist sgnd, 6½".....50.00
Figurine, dancing couple on base, man w/flowers, artist sgnd...140.00
Figurine, dog, American, 5"..............................25.00
Figurine, Japanese woman w/lantern, colorful, artist sgnd.....125.00
Figurine, Juliet with Doves, ¾ figure, deep purple dress, 12"...225.00
Figurine, lady at machine, Singer Sewing 100th Anniv, musical.275.00
Figurine, Lady Caller, artist sgnd, 5½"....................49.00
Figurine, lady dancing, plum floral skirt, Deco, Austria, 7".....375.00
Figurine, lady w/parasol, pk/navy/cream dress, 6½"..........60.00
Figurine, man & woman on base, pinks & grays, 9"..........140.00
Figurine, Siamese cat...................................40.00
Figurine, Southern woman, pk dress/blk hat, artist sgnd, 8".....65.00
Figurine, Terrier, orange, Deco, Austria....................45.00
Figurine, White Christmas, artist sgnd, 5½"................55.00
Figurine, woman, gr coat/pk hat & flowers, #912, 7" on 3" base.35.00
Figurine, Yankee Doodle Dandy, artist sgnd, 6"............55.00
Figurine, 18th century courtier, EX details, #255, 6".........18.00

Gonder

Lawton Gonder grew up a ceramist. By the time he opened his own pottery in December, 1941, he had a solid background in both production and management. Gonder Ceramic Arts, Inc., purchased the old Peters and Reed-Zane Pottery in South Zanesville, Ohio. There they turned out quality commercial ware with graceful shapes in both Oriental and contemporary designs. Their greatest achievements were the development of their superior glazes: flambe; 24k gold crackle; and Chinese crackle glazes in celadon, ming yellow, and blue. Most of the ware is marked with 'Gonder' impressed in script, and a mold number.

Candlesticks, ½ moon, aqua/pink mottle, 7", pr.............15.00
Ewer, Shell & Star, gr, 13"............................48.00

Figurine, cat, lime gr, 12¼" H...........................45.00
Figurine, Chinese man, kneeling; on ped, tan/red mottle, 5"....16.00
Figurine, elephant, trunk up, rose/gray, 10½" L............40.00
Pitcher, vertical rectangle/strap hdl/ice lip, dk gr/wht, #917...15.00
Temple jar, yellow, w/lid, 9½"...........................15.00
Vase, # H-79, 8", pr...................................12.00
Vase, aqua & br mottle w/pink interior, 7", pr..............15.00
Vase, fan shape, yellow, 11½"...........................35.00
Vase, gr/br swirled leaves, 6"............................9.00
Vase, w/hdls, pk & gray-bl mottle, #H5, 9¼"...............8.00
Vase, weeping willow, bl/wht............................18.00

Goofus Glass

Goofus was an inexpensive type of lustre-painted pressed glassware made by many companies during the first two decades of the 20th century. Bowls and trays are most common, and red and gold combinations are found more often than blues and greens.

Bowl, gold, lg clusters dogwood, 1 in center, ornate, 10x3", M..45.00
Bowl, gold lattice ground w/8 red roses, fluted rim, 2x7", NM...39.00
Bread tray, Last Supper, gold & red, orig paint, 7x11", NM....75.00
Card holder, gold w/red poppies, orig paint, 4x7", NM........17.00
Coaster, gold w/flowers, orig paint, 3", EX.................10.00
Decanter, allover relief roses, bulbous, orig stopper & paint.....55.00
Decanter, basketweave w/emb rose, rose on stopper, all orig.....45.00
Decanter w/tray, allover high relief roses, w/stopper, VG.......50.00
Perfume bottle, many raised tulips, orig stopper, 3½", VG......15.00
Plate, crackle ground shades gold to pink, 4 lg red roses, 7"....19.00
Plate, gold w/morning-glories, 12" dia, EX..................28.00
Plate, gold w/poppies, red center has 2 cupids, scalloped, 7"...37.00
Plate, gold w/4 double red roses, 1 rose in center, 9", NM......20.00
Plate, green w/3 lg poppies, 1 in center, sgnd Northwood, 7"...25.00
Powder box, relief allover roses, Gibson cameo on top, 3", VG..35.00
Salt & pepper, Cabbage Rose, milk glass w/orig paint & lids....37.00
Syrup, gold w/strawberries in relief, 75% orig paint, no lid.....25.00
Vase, Cabbage Rose, silver w/red roses, 12", NM............40.00
Vase, lg dogwood blossoms, bl/gold/red, orig paint, 15", EX.....48.00
Vase, relief iris front & back, 10", VG.....................60.00

Plate, gold with red mums, 11", $23.00.

Goss

The Goss Pottery was established in 1858 at Stoke-on-Trent in England. Their earliest products were quality porcelains, parian, and earthenware. Later, they also produced 'farings' -- small souvenir items decorated with decals that were sometimes over-painted by hand. The decals represented English landmarks, coats of arms, or scenes of historical significance. Early wares were marked 'W.H.G' or 'W.H. Goss'. After 1862, a falcon mark was used. The company was purchased in 1934 by Cauldon Potteries, Ltd.

Aberdeen Bronze Pot....................................20.00
Abergavenny Jar.......................................20.00
Alnwick Celtic Urn....................................25.00
Bagware, Torquay, sm..................................25.00
Bath Roman Ewer.......................................19.00
Bournemouth Bronze Urn................................31.00
Cambridge Pitcher.....................................15.00
Candle holder, Bettws-t-Coed..........................25.00
Canterbury Leather Bottle.............................20.00
Carlisle Salt Pot.....................................18.00
Chester Vase..25.00
Cup, 3 hdls, St George, Wiltshire, Calne..............20.00
Cup & saucer, Bag.....................................32.00
Devon Oak Pitcher.....................................20.00
Dickens bust, 8″......................................90.00
Dover Stone Vessel....................................20.00
Dragon Beerbowl.......................................40.00
Egyptian Water Jug....................................20.00
Ewer, Llanberis.......................................28.00
Foutain's Abbey Cup...................................25.00
Gibraltar Alcaraza....................................20.00
Glastonbury Vase, Arms of Wales.......................20.00
Greek lady bust, 8″...................................75.00
Guy's Porridge Pot....................................35.00
Hamworthy Lamp..22.00
Highland Cuash..20.00
Highland Milk Grogan..................................30.00
Hythe Cromwellian Mortar..............................20.00
Ilkeley Roman Ewer....................................18.00
Irish Mather..25.00
Irish Wooden Nogen....................................21.00
Japan Ewer..30.00
Kendall Jug...20.00
Litchfield Jug..25.00
Lobster Trap..35.00
Looe Ewer...18.00
Maltese Vase A Canard.................................40.00
Manz Pot..22.00
Norwich Urn...19.00
Ostend Tobacco Jar....................................24.00
Plate, Cambridge, 6″..................................15.00
Portland Vase...18.00
Seaford Urn...30.00
Sir Walter Scott bust, 5″.............................60.00
Southampton Pipkin....................................25.00
Southwold Jar...18.00
St Neats Urn..22.00
Staffordshire Tyg, 2 hdls.............................15.00
Swindon Vase..16.00
Swiss Vinegar Bottle..................................30.00
Tewkesbury Saxon Urn..................................20.00
Tray, Maidenhead, 10x12½″.............................75.00

Walmer Roman Vase.....................................18.00
Wareham Roman Bottle..................................16.00
Waterlooville Army Water Bottle.......................40.00
Weymouth Roman Vase...................................15.00

Gouda

Since the 18th century the main center of the pottery industry in Holland was in Gouda. One of its earliest industries, the manufacture of clay pipes, continues to the present day. The art ware so easily recognized by collectors today was first produced about 1885. It was decorated in the Art Nouveau manner. Stylized florals, birds, and geometrics were favored motifs; only rarely is the design naturalistic. The Nouveau influence was strong until about 1915. Art Deco was attempted, but with less success. Most of the workshops failed during the depression. Watch for the Gouda name, which is usually a part of the backstamp of the various manufacturers.

Candle lantern, orange, blue and yellow, 11¼″, $295.00.

Ash tray, bl-gr, cobalt on rim, mc w/in, house mk, 1¼x4″ dia...48.00
Ash tray, 4 rests, schoolhouse mk, 3½″ dia.................35.00
Bowl, Aurora, oval, 6¾″...................................85.00
Bowl, dk gr w/mc Rococo decor, 9½″ dia....................90.00
Candle holder, blk/bl/rust/mustard on ivory, house mk, 4″, pr...35.00
Candlestick, vine/flower/dots, Karata Rood, dia/house, 13″, pr.410.00
Chamberstick, very high hdl, Nouveau decor, house mk, 14½″.145.00
Compote, Art Nouveau stylized florals, house mk, 7½″........75.00
Compote, rust/gr/bl/blk, decor w/in, house mk Trudy, 6½x5½″..70.00
Ewer, mc Art Nouveau, high glaze, Zuid, Holland house mk, 9″.95.00
Ewer, Regina, 6″..25.00
Inkwell, attached under plate, Kelat House mk.............150.00
Inkwell, Dutch shoe figural, sgn Regina Rosario, 6½″......235.00
Inkwell, w/lid, house mk..................................70.00
Pipe, African Chieftan, sgn...............................35.00
Pipe, water; dancing people, Godenewaagen, Holland, 10″...145.00
Pitcher, blk/gold on red/bl, peacock eyes, Zward house mk, 2½″.30.00
Pitcher, schoolhouse mk, 5½″..............................65.00
Plate, Baden Powell in center, 1937, Royal Gouda, 5″......45.00
Teapot, Aladdin lamp shape, matt florals, sgn Hssel, 9½″..175.00
Vase, Art Nouveau decor, w/hdls, house mk, 3½″............65.00
Vase, dahlia, Royal Soedewahsen, 4″.......................38.00
Vase, hi-gloss florals w/crackle bk ground, Zuid, 3″, pr..85.00
Vase, pansies, 6 colors & blk, Plazuid, 6″................65.00

Vase, pitcher; stylized oak, leaf, & floral, 6 colors, early........75.00
Vase, Royal Pottery House of Zuid, 11", pr................125.00
Vase, scenic w/windmill/house/canal/boat, sgn Z/#68/412, 7¾"..125.00
Vase, sgn Flora Gouda Holland, 3"........................22.50
Vase, stick neck, florals w/windmill/house reserve, Zuid, 8½"....75.00
Vase, sunflowers, rust/bl/yel, Hava Plaziud, Holland, 8"........85.00
Vase, w/hdls, mc floral/blk w/bl bands, house mk Blaret, 5½"...55.00
Vase, windmill scene, figure w/wheelbarrow, sgn Zenith, 4¼"....85.00
Wall plaque, 1938.......................................45.00
Wall pocket, sgn, 11½x2"................................100.00

Graniteware

Graniteware, thin iron ware with an enamel coating, derives its name from its appearance. The speckled or mottled effect of the vari-colored enamels may look like granite -- but there the resemblance stops! It wasn't especially durable! Expect at least minor chipping if you plan to collect.

Graniteware was featured in 1876 at Phily's Expo. It was mass produced in quantity, and enough of it has survived to make at least the common items easily affordable. Color is an important consideration in evaluating an item; purple, brown, or green swirl is unusual, and thus are more expensive. Pieces with wire bales and wooden handles are premium -- so are decorated examples.

In recent months, magazine articles featuring decorating ideas with an emphasis on the 'country look' have caused the price of graniteware to escalate -- a trend which is likely to continue.

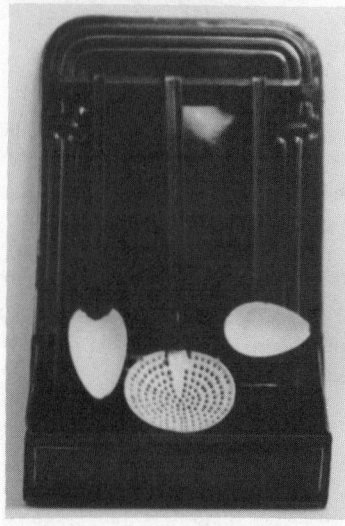

Utensil rack with spoon, ladle, and strainer, gray with gold trim, $195.00.

Basin, cream & gr, 9".....................................6.00
Bathroom sink, gray....................................185.00
Bedpan, gray speckled...................................6.50
Bowl, blue swirl, small.................................25.00
Bowl, custard; gray, 5" dia.............................20.00
Bowl, dough riser; tin vented lid, gray.................38.00
Bowl, mixing; large, gray..............................18.00
Bowl, soup; gray, stamped label N......................20.00
Bowl, turq swirl, small, EX............................22.00
Bread box, round, hinged, wht w/blue lines, 15" dia.....45.00
Bucket, beer; gray, tin lid............................29.00
Bucket, berry; blue swirled, w/lid & bail, 8x8¾".......65.00
Bucket, berry; gray, w/lid & bail, sgn, lg.............45.00
Bucket, berry; gray, w/lid & bail, unsgn...............38.00
Bucket, berry; shaded cobalt...........................30.00
Bucket, miniature, gray, wire bail, 3¼x3"..............45.00

Bucket, turq swirl, bail hdl, large, EX................65.00
Bucket, water; brown marbled...........................45.00
Bucket, water; child's, gray...........................65.00
Bucket, water; cobalt, bail hdl, wood grip.............50.00
Butter churn, blue/wht swirl, 18".....................400.00
Candlestick, gray......................................45.00
Candlestick, green.....................................15.00
Chamberstick, cobalt...................................19.50
Coffee biggin, wht, large..............................32.00
Coffee boiler, gray, tin lid, 1 gal....................35.00
Coffee pot, bl/wht checked body, pewter: top/spout/bottom.....165.00
Coffee pot, bl/wht speckled, 9"........................35.00
Coffee pot, blue & wht mottled.........................65.00
Coffee pot, brown, Manning & Bowman....................95.00
Coffee pot, camp; blue swirl...........................65.00
Coffee pot, cobalt swirl, 1 chip, tin lid, large.......85.00
Coffee pot, dk green swirl, enamel lid, EX.............95.00
Coffee pot, gray, pewter spout/lid/hdl, pat'd 1876....375.00
Coffee pot, gray, tin lid, lg..........................48.00
Coffee pot, gray & pewter, gooseneck spout............175.00
Coffee pot, gray w/unusual blk turned wooden hdl, M...100.00
Coffee pot, gray/wht mottled, w/tin lid, 10"...........40.00
Coffee pot, percolator, wht w/blk trim, 1940s, 9"......12.00
Coffee pot, solid gr w/bl hdl & trim...................30.00
Coffee pot, turq swirl, enamel lid, small, EX..........48.00
Coffee urn, gray......................................115.00
Colander, gray...14.00
Colander, shallow, gray, unusual, NM...................32.00
Colander, wht w/cobalt trim............................10.00
Combinet, blue/wht marbled, 15".......................40.00
Combinet, gray, 15"....................................25.00
Cooker, bl/wht...16.50
Cream can, gray, bail hdl, ½ gal.......................30.00
Cream pail, gray, tin lid, wire bale w/wood grip, qt...35.00
Creamer, gray, small...................................40.00
Creamer, gray & pewter.................................75.00
Cup, blue, tea size....................................20.00
Cup, cream & gr, hooked hdl, small, set of 4...........22.00
Cup, gray mottled, hdl open for hanging on lip of bucket......10.00
Cup, Nursery Rhyme, Little Polly Flanders, lt bl, dk bl rim.....37.00
Cup, solid cobalt exterior, wht interior, German, 4"...12.50
Cup & saucer, gray.....................................15.00
Cup & saucer, wht/bl w/scrolled band, miniature........30.00
Cuspidor, gray, small..................................20.00
Cuspidor, hotel; wht, salesman's sample................34.00
Custard, gray, triangle, sm............................50.00
Dipper, gray...18.00
Dipper, robin's egg blue, wht interior, long hdl, Elite stamp.....25.00
Dish pan, gray mottled, oval, 10x18x6"..................8.00
Double boiler, cream & green...........................15.00
Double boiler, gr & wht swirled, w/lid.................48.00
Double boiler, gray, sm, M.............................30.00
Double boiler, shaded blue.............................27.50
Egg poacher, cobalt & wht..............................40.00
Flask, dk blue...50.00
Funnel, gray, elliptical, 6"...........................35.00
Funnel, gray, very lg..................................19.00
Funnel, gray mottled, 7"...............................14.00
Funnel, wht, miniature.................................20.00
Funnel, wht w/blue trim, side hdl, 3"...................7.00
Kettle, cobalt bl & wht marbled, w/steam vent..........65.00
Kettle, preserve; gray.................................14.00
Ladle, gray, pierced...................................23.00
Ladle, maroon hdl, gray bowl...........................18.00

Lunch pail, blue & wht, bail hdl, tin lid, 6" high............50.00
Lunch pail, blue/wht marble, no lid, 6"................38.00
Lunch pail, miner's; oblong w/thermos top, gray.........45.00
Matchbox, French, Allumettes, wht/red checked............25.00
Measure, bl/wht, ¼ pt, USN.......................18.50
Measure, gray, riveted hdl & lip, sgn, 1 pt...........40.00
Measure, gray, 1 cup..........................40.00
Measure, speckled gray, 1 gal...................28.00
Meat grinder, wht decorated.....................25.00
Milk can, mottled gray, w/side hdl, quart............50.00
Mold, blue w/lt & dk blue swirl..................45.00
Mold, child's; fluted, gray & wht mottled............40.00
Mold, ice cream; turk's head, mottled gray, hang hook, 4x4"...49.00
Mold, melon shape, gray granite top w/tin bottom, 3½x5x6½"..35.00
Mold, pudding; gray, fluted, lg...................22.00
Mold, tube; cobalt, wht interior, swirl design, EX............70.00
Mold, wht, fluted, diamond shape, sm.................35.00
Mug, advertising Clover seeds, wht, 1 cup sz, chips on 1 side....40.00
Mug, gray............................12.00
Mug, miner's; dk gr & wht swirl...................50.00
Mug, turq swirl..........................15.00
Mustard pail w/spoon, gray/wht spatter..............60.00
Napkin holder, wall type, inscribed: Topflappen............28.00
Onion holder, solid sky blue, German..............65.00
Pan, blue swirl, 3¼x14" dia.....................35.00
Pan, cobalt swirl, 2¾x11¼".....................40.00
Pan, lady finger; navy blue/wht mottled, 6x12"...........145.00
Pan, loaf; gray, 5¼x10½x3", EX...................15.00
Pan, milk; turq swirl, 10", M....................30.00
Pan, muffin; gray, turk's head style, 12 hole............38.00
Pan, muffin; gray, 12 cup, ribbed, pretty mottling, EX.........85.00
Pan, muffin; gray, 8 cups, shallow.................30.00
Pan, pie; blue swirl.........................15.00
Pan, pie; child's, gray mottled, hole for hanging, 4x4¾".......35.00
Pan, pudding; gray, Chefette paper label, M............22.00
Pan, sauce; bl/wht swirl, finger grip/lid/bail............35.00
Pan, sauce; emerald swirl, w/lip & bail, 4x9¼".............55.00
Pan, sauce; gray, domed lid w/bail, 3x5"..............35.00
Pan, sauce; gray, miniature, w/lip & bail, 2x4½" dia...........30.00
Pan, strainer; gray, lg holes around side/bottom, Shaker type....37.00
Pitcher, blue & wht mottled, large.................75.00
Pitcher, gray, bulbous, 4 cup, 7".................22.00
Pitcher, gray, sgnd, 8".......................45.00
Pitcher, milk; blue........................65.00
Pitcher & bowl, wht, set.....................25.00
Plate, child's, gray........................20.00
Plate, dinner; cobalt & wht, 9" dia................30.00
Plate, dinner; cream & green, 9 " dia...............7.50
Plate, dinner; gray.........................12.00
Plate, soup; blue swirl......................20.00
Platter, meat; oval, wht w/cobalt trim...............7.50
Platter, turkey; gray.......................35.00
Pot, stock; gray, tall, has side hdls, tin lid............32.00
Potty, child's; mauve pink.....................12.00
Roaster, gray, self-basting, w/lid, rnd w/button ft, M........35.00
Roaster, gray/wht mottled, raised National on lid, 15".......22.00
Rolling pin, blk & wht......................185.00
Salt box, blue & wht, Seife lettered on front............42.00
Salt box, cobalt speckled.....................45.00
Saucer, cobalt, 6" dia......................12.00
Scoop, gray mottled, 7" long, granite hdl.............30.00
Scrub board, dk blue, primitive..................40.00
Skillet, blue/wht mottled.....................55.00
Skillet, gray, arched granite 8½" hdl, pour spout, 2x10" dia....32.00

Skillet, lav swirl, wht inside, turned hdl, iron pan, lg, EX......90.00
Skimmer, blue/wht swirl, 11" blk hdl...............50.00
Soap dish, blue mottled, blk trim, oval, 1x5¼x7"............68.00
Soap dish, sea-shell, wht.....................35.00
Soap dish, shell, scroll back plate, gray, sm flakes on edges....35.00
Soap dish, wht, 2 pc.......................15.00
Spatula, gray, 9" rack hdl, blade: 2¾x3¾".............20.00
Spatula, gray mottled, 7 drain holes in center, 12" long.......38.00
Spice set, 4 pc, rose pink, blk trim................125.00
Spoon, cobalt swirl, wht bowl, sm chips on hdl, 19"........24.00
Spoon, gray, 18".........................10.50
Spoon, gray, 9".........................15.00
Spooner, gray w/pewter trim, EX mottling, M...........185.00
Stove, child's; gray, electric, gray doors.............85.00
Stove, green & tan, gas......................225.00
Stove, table top kerosene, gr w/heart & gold design at rim, EX..85.00
Stove, toy Empire Electric, 2 burner/dbl oven w/booklet, 1927..150.00
Stove, 3 burner, wood, triangle shape, tan w/red tulips.......300.00
Sugar bowl, gray, matching lid..................75.00
Sugar shaker, wht........................55.00
Syrup pitcher, snow on mountain.................60.00
Table, alphabet, circus center/nursery rhyme corners, sm, M....115.00
Tea kettle, blue w/wht swirls, lg.................60.00
Tea set, child's; wht/red flowers, gr trim, 21 pcs..........175.00
Tea set, miniature, wht/bl w/gold bands, 10 pcs...........125.00
Tea steeper, gray, approx 3 cups.................40.00
Tea strainer, gray, w/round pierced designs in bowl, sm flakes...28.00
Tea strainer, gray mottled, hole to hang, screen bottom.......50.00
Teapot, blue, Manning & Bowman.................95.00
Teapot, blue/wht marbled.....................65.00
Teapot, gray, w/high tin domed lid................22.50
Teapot, gray & pewter......................175.00
Teapot, solid cobalt.......................29.00
Toothbrush holder, wht......................19.50
Tray, beer; round, wht inside...................16.00
Tray, child's; w/bonnet babies, wht w/blk trim..........135.00
Tray, gray, oval.........................40.00
Utensil rack, blk rack w/4 utensils, gray & blk hdl..........40.00
Water cooler, blue/wht swirl, brass spigot, 15" tall.........140.00

Green and Ivory

Green and ivory are the colors of a type of country pottery decorated with in-mold designs very similar to those of the more familiar blue and white wares. It is unmarked and was produced from about 1910 to 1935 by many manufacturers as part of their staple line of kitchenwares.

Bowl, Apricots, 9½" dia......................50.00
Bowl, cherries & rim design in gr, 4¼x9¼"............45.00
Bowl, Daisy & Waffle, 8" dia...................45.00
Bowl, Wedding Ring.......................35.00
Butter crock w/lid, Apricots & Honeycomb, bail hdl.........95.00
Butter crock w/lid, Daisy & Waffle................80.00
Custard, ribbed sides, 2½".....................20.00
Milk crock, Apricots, bail hdl, 10" dia..............65.00
Mug, Grapes, 4".........................35.00
Pitcher, Apricots, 8".......................110.00
Pitcher, Cow, 7¼".........................125.00
Pitcher, Cows, 6".........................75.00
Pitcher, milk; Grapes......................75.00
Pitcher, Pine Cone, 9".......................135.00
Pitcher, Swirl, 9".........................85.00

Pitcher, Wild Rose, 9" 125.00
Salt, hanging; incised trees & cabin 95.00
Spittoon, Cosmos, 5½" 75.00
Spittoon, salesman's sample, Waffle & Grape, 2" 65.00
Toothpick holder, Swan 25.00
Umbrella stand, Irises, 20" 225.00

Greenaway, Kate

Kate Greenaway was an English artist who lived from 1846 to 1901. She gained world-wide fame as an illustrator of children's books, drawing children clothed in the styles worn by proper English and American boys and girls of the very early 1800s. Her book, *Under the Willow Tree*, published in 1878, was the first of many. Her sketches appeared in leading magazines, and her greeting cards were in great demand. Manufacturers of china, pottery, and metal products copied her characters to decorate children's dishes, tiles, salt and pepper shakers, as well as many other items.

Match holder with striker, girl figural, 5¼", $65.00.

Autograph, orig pen & ink illustration, sgnd, mounted, 9x7" . . .400.00
Book, A Day in a Child's Life, Greenaway illus 90.00
Book, Alphabet 55.00
Book, Birthday Book For Children, Routhledge 75.00
Book, Language of the Flowers, 1880s, M 85.00
Book, Under the Window, Frederick Warne & Co, EX 150.00
Box, child laying on bear skin rug 250.00
Button, 2 figures on fence, lg 22.00
Cards, orig Four Seasons, full color, set of 4 in frame, M 125.00
Chocolate set, Sarreguemines 250.00
Fan, children playing Ring Around the Rosie, 10½" 40.00
Figurine, Grandpa/Grandma, sgn Germany, 7½", pr 90.00
Foot bath, child's; divided, open hdl grip, Sarreguemines 215.00
Mug, SP, Greenaway figures decor 75.00
Nodder, seated on chair, boy w/book, girl knitting, 5", pr 175.00
Plate, girl leaving home w/fruit basket, mc, Sarreguemines 60.00
Plate, little girls in relief around rim, 7¼" 65.00
Salt shaker, lady w/muff 45.00
Salt shaker, man in wht w/roses 65.00
Shakers, boy & girl, pr 100.00
Shakers, boy & girl peep out of barrels, pr 50.00
Spoon, child's; girl, Lucky Locket poem engraved on bowl 50.00
Toothpick holder, sea shell in bk, Greenaway girl, 5" 18.00
Tumbler, all around enameled figures on crystal, 3½" 25.00

Greentown Glass

Greentown glass refers to the product of the Indiana Tumbler and Goblet Company of Greentown, Indiana, ca. 1894 to 1903. Their earlier pressed glass patterns were #1, a pseudo-cut glass design; #137, Pleat Band; and #200, Austrian. Another line, Dewey, was designed in 1898. Many lovely colors were produced, in addition to crystal. Jacob Rosenthal, who was later affiliated with Fenton, developed his famous Chocolate glass in 1900. The rich shaded opaque brown glass was an overnight success. Two new patterns, Leaf Bracket and Cactus, were designed to display the glass to its best advantage, but previously existing molds were also used. In only three years, Rosenthal developed yet another important color formula, Golden Agate. The Holly Amber pattern was designed especially for its production. The figural Dolphin dish and cover, with fish finial, is perhaps the most and easily recognized piece ever produced. Other animal dishes were also made; all are highly collectible. There have been many repros -- not all are marked!

#11, compote, open, clear, 6½x6½" 35.00
#11, rose bowl, clear 22.00
#11, salt dip, individual 25.00
#11, toothpick, green 50.00
#11, tumbler, clear 10.00
#11, tumbler, clear w/trace of gold 18.00
#11, vase, celery,clear 30.00
#11, vase, green w/gold rim 65.00
Austrian, compote, clear, 8" 62.50
Austrian, cordial, vaseline 135.00
Austrian, goblet, clear 40.00
Austrian, pitcher 185.00
Austrian, punch cup, clear & gold .20.00
Austrian, spooner, table size, clear 36.00
Austrian, sugar, open, clear 27.00
Austrian, vase, clear, 8" 70.00
Austrian, wine, clear 25.00
Austrian, wine, vaseline 125.00
Beehive, goblet 65.00
Beehive, wine 45.00
Brazen Shield, goblet, clear 40.00
Brazen Shield, tumbler, blue 45.00
Cactus, bowl, chocolate, 6" 85.00
Cactus, butter w/cover, chocolate .250.00
Cactus, cake stand, chocolate 1,200.00
Cactus, compote, large, chocolate 225.00
Cactus, compote, small, chocolate 140.00
Cactus, cracker jar, chocolate 245.00
Cactus, creamer, chocolate 100.00
Cactus, cruet, chocolate, w/orig stopper 175.00
Cactus, mug, chocolate 75.00
Cactus, pitcher, chocolate 395.00
Cactus, spooner, chocolate 95.00
Cactus, sugar, chocolate 265.00
Cactus, sweetmeat, chocolate 420.00
Cactus, syrup w/lid, chocolate 85.00
Cactus, tumbler, chocolate 60.00
Cactus, tumbler, clear 45.00
Cord Drapery, bowl, clear, 10" 35.00
Cord Drapery, bowl, rectangular, amber 140.00
Cord Drapery, butter w/lid, clear .50.00
Cord Drapery, butter w/lid, green, lg 150.00
Cord Drapery, cake plate, low ft, clear 25.00
Cord Drapery, compote, open, clear, 6¼x8½" 50.00

Cord Drapery, cruet, clear..................................40.00
Cord Drapery, cup, clear....................................10.00
Cord Drapery, mug, clear...................................29.00
Cord Drapery, pitcher, clear...............................75.00
Cord Drapery, relish, amber...............................110.00
Cord Drapery, relish, clear, 9½″ oval.....................20.00
Cord Drapery, sauce, flat, clear............................10.00
Cord Drapery, sauce, footed, clear.........................20.00
Cord Drapery, shakers, clear, pr...........................40.00
Cord Drapery, sugar, clear.................................40.00
Cord Drapery, syrup w/lid, chocolate.....................150.00
Daisy, butter w/cover, chocolate..........................195.00
Dewey, berry bowl, clear...................................50.00
Dewey, bowl, canary, 8″ dia...............................65.00
Dewey, butter w/cover, green, lg..........................65.00
Dewey, butter w/cover, vaseline, ¼ lb.....................90.00
Dewey, cruet, clear..80.00
Dewey, frappe, chocolate..................................85.00
Dewey, mug, Gettysburg 1863, chocolate..................150.00
Dewey, mug, green...45.00
Dewey, pitcher, canary....................................185.00
Dewey, plate, canary......................................40.00
Dewey, plate, ftd, amber..................................40.00
Dewey, salt & pepper, green, pr...........................80.00
Dewey, sauce, canary......................................45.00
Dewey, serpentine tray, lg, amber.........................50.00
Dewey, table set, chocolate, 4 pc, small size............295.00
Dewey, table set, vaseline, 4 pc.........................225.00
Dewey, tumbler, canary....................................55.00
Dolphin, covered dish, beaded top, chocolate.............295.00
Dolphin, covered dish, sawtooth edge, chocolate..........175.00
Early Diamond, pitcher, clear.............................25.00
Early Diamond, pitcher, emerald green.....................85.00
Fleur-De-Lis, creamer, chocolate, large...................60.00
Herringbone Buttress, cup, clear..........................60.00
Herringbone Buttress, mug, chocolate......................55.00
Herringbone Buttress, pitcher, water.....................145.00
Holly, butter w/cover, clear.............................235.00
Holly, cruet, orig stopper, clear........................200.00
Holly, deep dish, rectangular, clear, 10x4″..............140.00
Holly, relish, clear......................................65.00
Holly Amber, berry bowl..................................625.00
Holly Amber, butter w/lid..............................1,000.00
Holly Amber, jelly compote, w/lid........................800.00
Holly Amber, mug, 4½″...................................485.00
Holly Amber, nappy, hdld.................................450.00
Holly Amber, relish......................................450.00
Holly Amber, tumbler.....................................500.00
Holly Amber, vase, 6″....................................500.00
Holly Amber, water pitcher.............................1,750.00
Holly Amber, water tray................................1,000.00
Leaf Bracket, berry set, all ftd, master +4 sauces, chocolate...200.00
Leaf Bracket, bowl, clear.................................38.50
Leaf Bracket, butter w/cover, chocolate..................150.00
Leaf Bracket, butter w/cover, clear......................110.00
Leaf Bracket, celery tray, chocolate.....................110.00
Leaf Bracket, creamer, clear..............................50.00
Leaf Bracket, creamer & sugar, chocolate, pr.............145.00
Leaf Bracket, nappy, chocolate, small.....................30.00
Leaf Bracket, nappy, clear................................25.00
Leaf Bracket, nappy, triangular, chocolate................40.00
Leaf Bracket, relish, chocolate...........................65.00
Leaf Bracket, table set, chocolate, 4 pc.................375.00
Leaf Bracket, tray, chocolate, 11″........................70.00

Pitcher, squirrel embossing, Chocolate glass, 9″, $400.00

Leaf Bracket, tumbler, chocolate..........................45.00
Leaf Bracket, water pitcher, chocolate...................250.00
Leaf Bracket, water pitcher, clear.......................175.00
Novelty, mitted hand, clear...............................40.00
Novelty, Uneeda Biscuit tumbler, chocolate...............120.00
Pitcher, Heron, chocolate................................350.00
Pitcher, Running Deer, chocolate.........................325.00
Pitcher, Squirrel, chocolate.............................400.00
Shuttle, cake stand, clear...............................120.00
Shuttle, cordial, clear...................................33.00
Shuttle, creamer, chocolate...............................62.50
Shuttle, creamer, clear...................................32.50
Shuttle, cup, chocolate...................................50.00
Shuttle, punch cup, chocolate.............................50.00
Shuttle, punch cup, clear.................................10.00
Shuttle, syrup, chocolate.................................70.00
Shuttle, tumbler, chocolate...............................60.00
Stein, Elves, Nile green..................................45.00
Stein, outdoor drinking scene w/castle, flared top, Nile green...125.00
Stein, Troubadore, Nile green, small......................58.00
Teardrop & Tassel, butter w/cover, green, some roughness.....140.00
Teardrop & Tassel, compote, no lid, clear.................35.00
Teardrop & Tassel, relish, green..........................35.00
Teardrop & Tassel, tumbler, cobalt blue...................45.00
Teardrop & Tassel, water pitcher, minor under spout roughness.35.00

Grueby

William Henry Grueby joined the firm of the Low Art Tile Works at the age of fifteen, and in 1894, after several years of experience in the production of architectural tiles, founded his own plant, the Grueby Faience Company, in Boston, Massachusetts. Grueby began experimenting with the idea of producing art pottery, and had soon perfected a fine glaze -- soft and without gloss -- in shades of blue, grey, yellow, brown, and his most successful, cucumber green. In 1900 his exhibit at the Paris Exposition Universelle won him three gold medals.

Grueby pottery was hand thrown and hand decorated in the Arts and Crafts style. Vertically thrust stylized leaves and flowers in relief were the most common decorative devices. Tiles continued to be an important product -- unique (due to the matt glaze decoration) as well as durable. Grueby tiles were often a full inch thick. Obviously incompatible with the Art Nouveau style, the art ware was discontinued soon after 1910.

The ware is always marked in one of several ways: 'Grueby Pottery, Boston, USA'; 'Grueby, Boston, Mass.'; or 'Grueby Faience'. The art ware is often artist signed.

Bowl, lt bl w/mottled leaves, sgn ER, minor chips, 6" dia......200.00
Lamp, pink beige, elongated neck, swollen cylinder, 25", VG...325.00
Paperweight, flying scarab, br relief on blue, no mk, 2½" dia..150.00
Paperweight, gold winged beetle on bl, sgn..............225.00
Tile, 'EPOS', red clay through yel glaze, 6x6"..............180.00
Tile, cherub w/ball in ea hand, tan on bl, 6x6"............180.00
Tile, figural relief, yellow on bl, no mk, 6"..............110.00
Tile, geometric star shape decor, bl/yellow/gr/wht, no mk, 3"....30.00
Tile, grapes, mc on tan, sgn, 6x6"....................340.00
Tile, landscape in gr/bl, sgn PS on side, 4⅛" sq............250.00
Tile, lt bl w/seagulls, sgn GM, 6" sq, VG.................125.00
Tile, mermaid w/mirror, red clay through yel glaze, sgn, 6x6"..275.00
Tile, monk, red clay through yel glaze, 6x6"..............180.00
Tile, stylized grape cluster, leaves 2 corners, 6x6"..........100.00
Tile, water lilies, mc on green, sgn, 6x6"................400.00
Vase, dk gr w/yel & gr buds, 4".....................450.00
Vase, gr leaves w/yel buds, 4½"....................495.00
Vase, gr w/gr leaves & plum buds, chips, #161, 12½".......950.00
Vase, leaf relief, gr, sgn MS, minor chips, 15"............700.00
Vase, lotus leaves, cylindrical form, gr glaze, mk, 9½".......660.00
Vase, slim leaves form 14 point top, gr/blk drips, Post, 6x7½".425.00
Vase, textured gr, no decor, 8½"....................300.00
Vase, thick gr matt, collar neck/wide body, 3¼x5½"........150.00
Vase, yellow, ovi-form, 4½".......................280.00
Vase, 2 color, 4"...............................425.00

Vase, upright lotus leafage, typical green glaze, signed with lotus mark, 9½", $660.00.

Gutta Percha

Gutta-percha is the plastic substance from the latex of several types of Malaysian trees. It resembles rubber but contains more resin. A patent for the use of this material in manufacturing an early type of plastic was issued in the 1850s, and it was used extensively for daguerreotype cases and picture frames.

Case, angel & cherub, br, 2½x3".....................45.00
Case, beehive w/grain border, LP & Co label, EX, 6th plate.....55.00
Case, Belt & Buckle, S Peck label w/in, VG, 6th plate.........45.00
Case, cherub & deer, minor chips, 4x4¾"................45.00
Case, eagle/scroll 'Constitution/Laws', 3¼x3¾"............35.00
Case, figure resting under tree, br, 2x2⅛"...............30.00
Case, fireman in ornate arch, br, 3¼x3¾", VG.............95.00
Case, grain & sickle, 2½x3".........................25.00

Case, grain/plow/anvil, rnd medallion fr w/in, 4x5"..........50.00
Case, Habana, monument/trees/ships, LP & Co, VG, ¼ plate...120.00
Case, knight & maiden, EX, 9th plate...................60.00
Case, lady in daguerrian gallery, EX, 6th plate.............85.00
Case, lyre, MB Brady sgn w/in design, w/dag of lady, 6th plate...60.00
Case, Mary & her lamb, LP & Co, VG, 9th plate............55.00
Case, Shield & Shells, by AP Critchlow & Co, EX, 6th plate....35.00
Case, strawberry/leaves in oval, blk, 2½x3".............60.00
Case, Washington Monument, good detail, 5x6¼"...........45.00
Case, window in top, inside w/rnd medallion fr, 2½x3".......135.00
Case, winged figure holding horns of deer, br, 3¼x3½".......75.00
Case, X cannons/flags/liberty cap, 3¼x3¾"...............75.00
Case, 2 peacocks at fountain, br, 2½x3"...............60.00
Cup, collapsible, dtd 1860.........................30.00
Hand mirror, dtd 1866, rpr, 11".....................35.00
Knife, figural shoe, 'Lorley', 5½"....................45.00
Manicure set, in box w/orig lining, portrait/medallion, 8x5".....55.00
Tray, woman's profile medallion, wood stem & insert, 12" dia..195.00

Case, sixteenth plate, embossed head of Indian, $165.00.

Haeger

In 1871 David Henry Haeger, a young son of German immigrants, purchased a brick factory at Dundee, Illinois, and began an association with the ceramic industry that his descendents have pursued to the present time. Soon their production was expanded to include drainage tile. By 1914 they had ventured into the field of commercial art ware. Vases, figurines, lamp bases, and gift items in a pastel matt glaze carried the logo of the company name written over the bar of an 'H'. From 1929 to 1933, they produced a line of dinnerware in solid colors -- blue, rose, green, and yellow -- which they marketed through Marshall Fields. Royal Haeger, their premium line designed in 1938 by Royal Hickman, and the Flower Ware line (1945 to 1950, marked 'RG' for Royal Garden), are especially desirable with collectors today. Ware produced before the mid-thirties sometimes is found with a paper label; these are also of special interest. A stylized script mark, Royal Haeger, was used during the forties; later a paper label in the shape of a crown was used.

The Macomb, Illinois plant, built in 1939, primarily made ware for the florist trade. A second plant, built there in 1969, produces lamp bases.

Ash tray, emb Texas w/emb oil well/star/hat/etc, #R1858........18.00
Ash tray, 1934 Century of Progress, green.................45.00
Box w/lid, impressed dots, brass knob, 7½" dia.............10.00
Clam shell w/silver overlay, lg......................75.00
Dish, shell, dk gr, mk Royal Haegar R-1822 USA, 6x14".......23.00
Flower frog, nude, blue, 12", w/matching bowl..............60.00
Jardiniere, golden hi-gloss, rounded, 10½x15", w/maple stand...85.00

Jardiniere, Signing of the Constitution, sgn Olsen/Rovelstad.....30.00
Planter, Aladdin lamp shape, bl..........................6.00
Planter, Madonna & Child, wht, 11½".....................9.00
Planter, old fashioned lady in bonnet w/basket, w/sticker, 6".....6.50
Planter, ped ft, lime, 5x5¼" dia..........................4.00
Vase, ball shape, gr, 5x6".................................5.00
Vase, bulbous w/twin spouts, #4001, Aztec Gold, 8x4".......20.00
Vase, chalet w/birds, pink/bl & turq.....................14.00
Vase, gazelle, brush bkground, #R707, 7".................45.00
Vase, lumberjack by tree trunk, Royal Hickman, R-600-9".....30.00
Vase, red, #3081..5.00
Vase, snail, dk br, 7x11½"................................8.00
Vase, w/hdls, dogwood decor, 8"..........................15.00
Vase, wht stem forms rnd br/tan/wht bulb at base, 10x4½".....15.00

Figural nude flower frog, blue glossy glaze, Royal Haeger, 12¾", $75.00.

Hair Weaving

A rather unusual craft became popular during the mid-1800s. Human hair was used to make jewelry -- rings, bracelets, lockets, etc. -- by braiding and interlacing fine strands of hair around hollow forms, with pearls and beads added for effect. Hair wreaths were also made, often using hair from deceased family members as well as the living. They were displayed in deep satin-lined frames along with mementoes of the weaver or her departed kin. The fad was abandoned before the turn of the century.

Bracelet, 6 circular strands, gold medallion w/hanging heart....185.00
Pin, 18k w/blk enamel, plaited pendant, 1¾" W.............150.00
Ring, gold w/decorative openings encased with hair..........110.00
Ring, tightly braided w/gold initialed mounting in center.......95.00
Watch chain, braided hair, EX.............................42.00
Watch chain, woven hair w/book fob.......................45.00

Hall

The Hall China Company of East Liverpool, Ohio, was established in 1903. Their earliest product was whiteware toilet seats, mugs, jugs, etc. By 1920, their restaurant-type dinnerware and cookingware had become so successful that Hall was assured of a solid future. They continue today to be one of the country's largest manufacturers of this type of product.

Hall introduced the first of their famous teapots in 1920; new shapes and colors were added each year until about 1948, making them the largest teapot manufacturer in the world. These and the dinnerware lines of the thirties through the fifties have become popular collectibles.

See also Autumn Leaf

Acacia, casserole & lid...................................20.00
Advertising, cheese dish, Kraft, red......................18.00
Advertising, punch set, Old Crow, complete...............225.00
Advertising, punch set, Old Crow, 1950s, MIB.............300.00
Advertising, sugar, Lipton, blk...........................8.50
Ash tray, w/match stand, blk..............................9.00
Ball jug, Forest, 2 qt...................................15.00
Ball jug, Sea Spray, 2 qt................................15.00
Banded, cookie jar, Indian Red...........................45.00
Banded, jug, Lettuce Green...............................18.00
Blue Blossom, casserole, w/cover.........................45.00
Blue Blossom, cookie jar, Banded........................100.00
Blue Blossom, leftover, loop hdl.........................40.00
Blue Blossom, pepper w/hdl...............................15.00
Blue Bouquet, bowl, salad................................12.00
Blue Bouquet, creamer.....................................6.00
Blue Bouquet, sugar w/lid.................................8.00
Blue Garden, casserole, #4, w/lid........................38.00
Cactus, cookie jar.......................................80.00
Cactus, drip-o-lator.....................................25.00
Cameo Rose, cup...4.00
Cameo Rose, saucer..3.00
Cameo Rose, shakers, pr..................................15.00
Cameo Rose, sugar w/lid..................................13.00
Candlestick, saucer base, dk bl/gr........................8.00
Chinese Red, ash tray.....................................5.00
Chinese Red, baker, fluted, lg...........................22.50
Chinese Red, baker, open, 8".............................22.50
Chinese Red, ball jug, #2................................15.00
Chinese Red, ball jug, #3................................18.00
Chinese Red, bean pot, tab hdld, 2 qt....................20.00
Chinese Red, bowl, mixing; set of 3, Straightside........35.00
Chinese Red, canister, Sunshine; Flour, Coffee, Sugar, each.....45.00
Chinese Red, casserole, Saf-Handle.......................30.00
Chinese Red, casserole, tab hdl..........................15.00
Chinese Red, creamer, Sani-Grid...........................7.00
Chinese Red, creamer & sugar, #2293, pr..................25.00
Chinese Red, jug, Doughnut...............................35.00
Chinese Red, jug, Sani-Grid, lg, 7½".....................15.00
Chinese Red, jug, Sani-Grid, medium, 6½".................11.00
Chinese Red, jug, Sani-Grid, small, 5¼"..................10.00
Chinese Red, jug, 1½ pint, 5¼"............................8.50
Chinese Red, mustard, hdl is spreader, sm................10.00
Chinese Red, shakers, loop handle, #1187, pr.............20.00
Chinese Red, shakers, Sani-Grid, pr......................18.00
Chinese Red, syrup, Banded...............................25.00
Coffee mug, Irish; blk....................................8.00
Coffee pot, Bigboy.......................................25.00
Coffee pot, Coffee Queen, blue...........................12.00
Coffee pot, Enterprise Drip-O-Lator, Panel, w/flower pots.......10.00
Coffee pot, Trellis, w/drip..............................34.00
Colonial, jug, Delphinium................................20.00
Colonial, jug, Lettuce Green, 6½"........................28.00
Crest, coffee pot..20.00
Crocus, bowl, mixing, 6"..................................9.00
Crocus, bowl, mixing, 7½"................................10.00
Crocus, bowl, mixing, 9".................................12.00
Crocus, bowl, salad......................................14.00
Crocus, bowl, 5½"...6.00

Crocus, casserole, covered, Sunshine........................25.00
Crocus, coffee dispenser, metal.....................15.00
Crocus, coffee pot, Banded........................25.00
Crocus, cup & saucer.............................9.00
Crocus, plate, 10″................................8.00
Crocus, platter, 11″.............................10.00
Crocus, salt & pepper, hdld, pr..................18.00
Crocus, soup tureen, w/lid.......................60.00
Crocus, soup tureen, w/lid, Big Lip..............85.00
Crocus, sugar w/lid, Art Deco....................12.00
Fantasy, casserole, Saf-Handle...................25.00
Flowerpot, syrup.................................35.00
Heather Rose, cup & saucer........................6.00
Heather Rose, jug, 4-pt, 6½″.....................15.00
Jug, #628, green.................................22.00
Jug, Loop Handle, Cadet..........................25.00
Jug, Loop Handle, Lettuce........................18.00
Monterrey, casserole, covered, round, hdld, w/gold Medallion....25.00
Morning Glory, bowl, Straightside, #4, Cadet.....12.00
Morning Glory, casserole w/lid...................27.50
Mt Vernon, bowl, covered vegetable...............30.00
Mt Vernon, bowl, fruit; 5″........................4.50
Mt Vernon, bowl, 9¼″ oval........................15.00
Mt Vernon, coffee pot............................40.00
Mt Vernon, creamer...............................6.50
Mt Vernon, cup...................................5.00
Mt Vernon, flat soup.............................8.50
Mt Vernon, gravy & under plate...................22.00
Mt Vernon, plate, 10″............................7.50
Mt Vernon, plate, 6″.............................2.50
Mt Vernon, plate, 7¼″............................4.50
Mt Vernon, plate, 9¼″............................6.00
Mt Vernon, platter, 15½″ oval....................20.00
Mt Vernon, sugar, open...........................5.00
Orange Poppy, baker, Flute........................9.00
Orange Poppy, bowl, deep, 10″ dia................12.00
Orange Poppy, bowl, salad........................12.00
Orange Poppy, bowls, nesting, set of 3...........35.00
Orange Poppy, cake plate.........................12.00
Orange Poppy, canister set, metal, 4 pcs, G pnt...35.00
Orange Poppy, coffee pot.........................25.00
Orange Poppy, cup & saucer.......................10.00
Orange Poppy, jug, Sunshine, 7″..................14.00
Orange Poppy, platter, 11″.......................10.00
Orange Poppy, pretzel jar, slight silver wear....35.00
Orange Poppy, sugar w/lid.........................8.00
Orange Poppy, teapot, Streamline.................45.00
Poppy & Wheat, bowl, mixing; 10½″x5½″............15.00
Poppy & Wheat, casserole.........................30.00
Poppy & Wheat, jug, Sunshine, 7″.................28.00
Primrose, bowl, 5¼″..............................6.50
Primrose, jug, 5¾″...............................15.00
Primrose, plate, 9″..............................8.50
Primrose, saucer.................................1.50
Radiant Ware, bowl, blue.........................17.50
Radiant Ware, bowl set, 4-pc.....................75.00
Red Poppy, bowl, cereal..........................6.50
Red Poppy, bowl, coupe; 9″........................6.00
Red Poppy, bowl, fruit............................4.00
Red Poppy, bowl, mixing; set of 3................35.00
Red Poppy, bowl, round vegetable; 9″.............15.00
Red Poppy, bowl, salad...........................10.00
Red Poppy, casserole, covered....................18.00
Red Poppy, coffee pot, Rickson, w/aluminum drip..35.00

Red Poppy, creamer & sugar w/lid.................15.00
Red Poppy, cup & saucer...........................6.00
Red Poppy, drip, w/lid, bowl shape...............12.00
Red Poppy, jug, Ball; #3.........................22.00
Red Poppy, jug, Sunshine; #5.....................20.00
Red Poppy, plate, cake...........................10.00
Red Poppy, plate, 6″..............................2.50
Red Poppy, plate, 9″..............................5.00
Red Poppy, platter, 11½″.........................14.00
Red Poppy, platter, 13″..........................14.00
Red Poppy, salt & pepper, Egg-Drop, pr...........12.00
Red Poppy, teapot, Aladdin.......................22.00
Red Poppy, teapot, New York......................32.00
Refrigerator Ware, Aristocrat, butter............12.00
Refrigerator Ware, Aristocrat, leftover, ivory...12.00
Refrigerator Ware, Aristocrat, water server, blue...35.00
Refrigerator Ware, Aristocrat, water server, brown....35.00
Refrigerator Ware, Emperor, leftover, Sunset.....13.00
Refrigerator Ware, Emperor, leftover w/lid, Canary............8.00
Refrigerator Ware, Emporer, water server, Garden Green......20.00
Refrigerator Ware, General Electric, leftover, gray/yellow.......12.50
Refrigerator Ware, Hot Point, leftover, Warm Yel, #3, lg round..20.00
Refrigerator Ware, King, roaster, open, Canary, Westinghouse....5.00
Refrigerator Ware, Montgomery Ward, leftover w/lid, Delphinium..8.00
Refrigerator Ware, Montgomery Ward, water server w/lid, blue...15.00
Refrigerator Ware, Patrician, leftover, Delphinium.........12.00
Refrigerator Ware, Patrician, water server, Delphinium.........28.00
Refrigerator Ware, Queen, roaster w/lid, Delphinium.........18.00
Refrigerator Ware, Sears, 3-section leftover set, Cadet Blue.....35.00
Rose Parade, bean pot, 2 qt......................22.50
Rose Parade, casserole w/cover, lg...............20.00
Rose Parade, jug, Sani-Grid, lg..................20.00
Rose Parade, salt & pepper, w/hdl, pr............15.00
Rose Parade, shakers, Sani-Grid, pr..............15.00
Rose White, jug, med.............................15.00
Rose White, salt & pepper shakers, Sani-Grid, pr...........15.00
Rose White, teapot, Sani-Grid, small.............15.00
Rose White, teapot, 3 cup, Sani-Grid.............18.00
Saf-Handle, casserole, Marine....................25.00
Sani-Grid, grease pot w/lid, plain hdl, blue.....12.00
Sani-Grid, jug, plain hdl, blue..................18.00
Sani-Grid, salt & pepper shakers, plain hdl, blue, pr..........15.00
Serenade, mixing bowl, 6″.........................7.00
Serenade, plate, 9⅛″ dia.........................8.00
Springtime, bowl, salad..........................12.00
Springtime, bowl, soup; 8½″.......................7.00
Springtime, bowl, 5½″.............................4.50
Springtime, bowl, 9″.............................14.00
Springtime, creamer & sugar......................16.00
Springtime, cup & saucer..........................5.50
Springtime, gravy boat...........................17.00
Springtime, plate, cake..........................10.00
Springtime, plate, 6¼″...........................3.00
Springtime, plate, 9¼″...........................5.00
Springtime, platter, 13½″.........................8.50
Springtime, salt & pepper, hdld..................15.00
Springtime, teapot, French.......................30.00
Taverne, bowl, fruit; 5⅝″........................10.00
Taverne, bowl, salad; 9″.........................18.00
Taverne, cake saver, wood bottom.................18.00
Taverne, casserole, covered, Colonial............30.00
Taverne, coffee pot, Banded......................32.50
Taverne, cookie jar w/lid........................70.00
Taverne, creamer, Colonial........................8.00

Basketball teapot, yellow with silver trim, 6¾", $250.00.

Taverne, French baker, fluted	16.00
Taverne, jug, Classic	55.00
Taverne, jug, Colonial, medium	18.00
Taverne, leftover, rectangular	25.00
Taverne, nappy, 5½"	4.00
Taverne, rolling pin	85.00
Taverne, salt & pepper, Banded	28.00
Taverne, salt & pepper, Colonial	28.00
Teapot, Airflow, Chinese Red	50.00
Teapot, Airflow, cobalt, gold decor, 6 cup	45.00
Teapot, Airflow, turquoise, gold decor	35.00
Teapot, Aladdin, blk w/gold, w/infuser	22.00
Teapot, Aladdin, cobalt, 6 cup	30.00
Teapot, Aladdin, Delph blue w/infuser, 6 cup	25.00
Teapot, Aladdin, Warm Yellow, w/infuser, 6 cup	25.00
Teapot, Albany, gr & gold decor, 6 cup	25.00
Teapot, Albany, turquoise w/gold	25.00
Teapot, Albert, Celadon, no gold, 6 cup	23.00
Teapot, Boston, Addison (lt gray), gold trim, 6 cup	27.00
Teapot, Boston, beige & gold, 6 cup	24.00
Teapot, Boston, cobalt, no gold, 2 cup	22.00
Teapot, Boston, Delphinium Blue	20.00
Teapot, Boston, Warm Yellow, w/gold, 6 cup	20.00
Teapot, Cleveland, cobalt	55.00
Teapot, Cleveland, green & gold decor, 6 cup	24.00
Teapot, Cube, green, 2 cup	35.00
Teapot, designed by Thorley, wht, decorated	45.00
Teapot, Disraeli, aqua, 6 cup	25.00
Teapot, Disraeli, pink, 6 cup	25.00
Teapot, French, Addison (lt gray), gold decor	25.00
Teapot, French, Cadet w/gold, 6 cup	25.00
Teapot, French, Dresden, gold flowers, 8 cup	30.00
Teapot, Gladstone, pink w/gold	30.00
Teapot, Hollywood, black w/gold, 6 cup	23.00
Teapot, Hollywood, ivory w/gold	22.00
Teapot, Hollywood, maroon	18.00
Teapot, Hollywood, Warm Yellow	25.00
Teapot, Hook Cover, Emerald	35.00
Teapot, Hook Cover, lt blue & gold, 6 cup	30.00
Teapot, Lipton, Canary Yellow, 3 pc	28.00
Teapot, Lipton, lt bl	15.00

Teapot, Lipton, Mustard Yellow	15.00
Teapot, Los Angeles, Canary w/gold	25.00
Teapot, Los Angeles, cobalt w/gold	38.00
Teapot, Los Angeles, Delphinium, no gold	25.00
Teapot, Los Angeles, Dresden	30.00
Teapot, Los Angeles, lt green & gold, 6 cup	34.00
Teapot, McCormick, dk gr w/infuser, 6 cup	24.00
Teapot, McCormick, maroon, w/infuser	20.00
Teapot, Moderne, Canary Yellow	20.00
Teapot, Moderne, Marine w/gold	40.00
Teapot, Nautilus, Canary Yellow w/gold, 6 cup	90.00
Teapot, Nautilus, green w/gold	100.00
Teapot, Nautilus, turquoise	90.00
Teapot, New York, blue/w gold, 2 cup	25.00
Teapot, New York, Chinese Red, 4 cup	35.00
Teapot, New York, green & gold, 6 cup	24.00
Teapot, New York, Lettuce Green w/gold, 2 cup	18.00
Teapot, New York, Warm Yellow, gold decor	25.00
Teapot, Parade, ivory, no gold	18.00
Teapot, Parade, yellow, much gold, 6 cup	38.00
Teapot, Philadelphia, blk w/gold	25.00
Teapot, Philadelphia, cobalt & gold decor, 4 cup	26.00
Teapot, Philadelphia, Delph Blue & gold, 8 cup	28.00
Teapot, Philadelphia, ivory w/gold	22.00
Teapot, Philadelphia, pink & gold, 6 cup	25.00
Teapot, Rhythm, Canary Yellow w/gold	60.00
Teapot, Sani-Grid, Chinese Red, #2294, sm	25.00
Teapot, Star, cobalt	45.00
Teapot, Star, dk gr	25.00
Teapot, Star, turq w/gold, 6 cup	32.00
Teapot, Streamline, Delph Blue, 6 cup, chip under lid	20.00
Teapot, Streamline, Emerald	45.00
Teapot, Streamline, Marine	45.00
Teapot, Twinspout, cobalt	48.00
Teapot, Windshield, Camellia (rose color), w/gold, 6 cup	25.00
Teapot, Windshield, ivory w/gold dots, much gold	20.00
Teapot, Windshield, maroon & gold, 6 cup	25.00
Tom & Jerry, mug, gold on blk gloss, set of 4	16.00
Tulip, coffee pot, Deca-plain	30.00
Tulip, custard	6.00
Tulip, fruit, 5¾"	4.00
Tulip, plate, breakfast	8.00
Tulip, platter	12.50
Wild Rose, mixing bowl, #4	7.00
Wildfire, bowl, cereal; 6"	3.50
Wildfire, bowl, fruit; 5½"	2.00
Wildfire, bowl, salad; 9"	15.00
Wildfire, cup	3.50
Wildfire, custard cup	3.25
Wildfire, drip jar w/cover	15.00
Wildfire, pie baker, 10"	10.00
Wildfire, plate, 9"	4.00
Wildfire, shakers, Sani-Grid, pr	20.00
Zeisel, celery, red/blk flower	12.00
Zeisel, coffee pot, Fantasy	35.00
Zeisel, cookie jar, Blue Daisy	35.00
Zeisel, cookie jar, gold pot	25.00
Zeisel, cookie jar, pink basket	35.00
Zeisel, cookie jar, Tri Color	55.00
Zeisel, cookie jar, turq/daisy	15.00
Zeisel, creamer, Fantasy	8.00
Zeisel, creamer & sugar w/lid, Harlequin	22.00
Zeisel, cup, Fantasy	7.00
Zeisel, gravy, red/blk flower	12.00

Zeisel, shakers, Tri Color, 3½", pr......................25.00
Zeisel, sugar w/lid, Fantasy................................12.00

Halloween

The origin of Halloween can be traced back to the ancient practices of the Druids of Great Britain who began their New Year on the 1st of November. The Druids were pagans, and their New Year's celebrations involved pagan rites and superstitions. They believed that as the old year came to an end, the Devil would gather up all the demons and evil in the world and take them back to Hell with him. Witches were women who had sold their souls to the Devil, and with their black cat in attendance, flew up through their chimneys riding their brooms. When the Roman Catholic Church came into power in 700 A.D., they changed the holiday into a religious event, called All Saints Day, or 'Allhallows'. The evening before, October 31, became 'Allhallow's Eve', or 'Halloween'.

Today Halloween is strictly a fun time, and Halloween items are fun to collect. Pumpkin head candy containers of papier mache or pressed cardboard, noise makers, postcards with black cats and witches, costumes, and decorations -- these are only a sampling of the variety available.

Candy box, hat box w/witch/cat/vegetable people, MIG, 1½x1¾".55.00
Candy container, blk cat, papier mache & fabric, head removes..85.00
Candy container, blk cat emerges from orange pumpkin, 6".....50.00
Candy container, blk cat w/arched bk on rnd cb box, MIG, 3"...35.00
Candy container, cat w/arched bk, blk papier mache, 3½".....18.50
Candy container, guitar w/pumpkin face, Germany, 6".........35.00
Candy container, pumpkin head, pnt face, Germany, 3½".......32.00
Fan, blk cat center, orange/blk, folds, MIG, 13½x8½".......15.00
Game, Chromomagica, wizard scene on box, McLoughlin Bros..95.00
Horn, cb w/cat in moon, jack-o-lantern, witch, etc, mk 1921.....10.00
Horn, Halloween scenes, cb w/wood mouthpiece, Germany, 11"...4.00
Jack-O'-Lantern, papier mache, menacing eyes, 6x8"..........20.00
Lantern, paper, blk & orange, devil/witch/owl/cat.............20.00
Mask, wizard, wire mesh, real hair, early...................110.00
Owl, papier mache, orange/blk w/yellow/blk glass eyes, 10½"....45.00
Owl, 3-D figure, pressed paper, Germany, 14"..............125.00
Place cards, uncut page, Ladies Home Journal, 1920...........8.00
Pumpkin man, sits, leaf on lap, candle holder atop, MIG, 4x6"..95.00
Rattle, frying pan w/witch/rats/crows/etc, metal, Germany, 6½"...4.00
Skeleton, die-cut, Germany, 27".........................32.00

Sheet music, The Black Cat Rag, orange and black, 14", $35.00.

Tambourine, tin, w/cats/pumpkins/witches, by Chein..........25.00
Tin container, Tindeco, Halloween decor....................35.00
Whirligig, witch, 1930s, red & mustard paint, M............155.00

Hampshire

The Hampshire Pottery Company was established in 1871 in Keene, New Hampshire, by James Scollay Taft. Their earliest products were redware and stoneware utility items such as jugs, churns, crocks, and flower pots. In 1878 they produced majolica ware which met with such success that they began to experiment with the idea of manufacturing art pottery. By 1883, they had developed a Royal Worcester type of finish which they applied to vases, tea sets, powder boxes, and cookie jars. It was also utilized for souvenir items that were decorated with transfer designs prepared from photographic plates.

Cadmon Robertson, brother-in-law of Taft, joined the company in 1904, and was responsible for developing their famous matt glazes. Colors included shades of green and brown, red and blue. Early examples were of earthenware, but eventually the body changed to semi-porcelain. Some of his designs were marked with an M in a circle as a tribute to his wife, Emoretta.

Robertson died in 1914, leaving a void impossible to fill. Taft sold the business in 1916 to George Morton, who continued to use the matt glazes that Robertson had developed. After a temporary halt in production during WWI, Morton returned to Keene and re-equipped the factory with the needed machinery to manufacture hotel china and floor tile. Because of the expense involved in transporting coal to fire the kilns, Morton found he could not compete with potteries of Ohio and New Jersey, who were able to utilize locally available natural gas. He was forced to close the plant in 1923.

Pitcher, deep green glaze, 4", $35.00.

Bowl, gr lotus leaf, mottled/striated/matt, early, 3x4¾"........75.00
Bowl, gr matt, geometric decor, 3x5".......................35.00
Bowl, incised lotus blossoms, sgn Robertson & artist, 2x5½"....70.00
Demitasse set, cream w/gr & gold trim, 7 pcs...............100.00
Lamp base, gr matt, w/hdls, ftd...........................125.00
Lamp base, incised circular design, matt gr, rim chips, 9½".....75.00
Lamp base, pond lilies, gr, sgn, 26" overall.................150.00
Lamp base, 5 loop hdls, stem & bud relief, green, 1910, 14"...200.00
Mug, snakeskin, w/designs................................70.00
Paperweight, 2 fish, gr matt, artist sgn, 3½".................45.00
Pitcher, snakeskin, w/designs, 7½"........................90.00
Stein, sailing boats, Royal Worcester, 5½".................60.00
Teapot, butterfly finial, Royal Worcester finish.............65.00
Vase, bl matt w/pink & blue drip, wide lobed rim, hairline, 8"...75.00
Vase, bl mottled/striated, matt, incised mk/#107, 9x6½".......95.00
Vase, blue, 7½"...65.00
Vase, blue-gr mottled, matt, scarab mk, 461/46933/#119, 6x5"...75.00

Vase, dragonflies/mottled/striated/matt, incised mk/#123, 6x5"..110.00
Vase, forest gr, mottled/striated, matt, incised MO/#33, 6x4"....70.00
Vase, matt gr w/dandelions in relief, 6x5½"..................95.00
Vase, mottled blue, swollen cylinder, ca 1920, 12", pr.......200.00
Vase, mottled blue design, 9½".............................110.00
Vase, thistles, gr mottled/striated/matt, incised mk/#464, 6"....110.00
Vase, yellow matt, incurvate rim/full body, 7¼"..............80.00

Handel Lamps

Philip Handel was best known for the art glass lamps he produced at the turn of the century. His work is similar to the Tiffany lamps of the same era. Handel made gas and electric lamps, with both leaded glass and reverse painted shades. He also produced 'chipped ice' shades, with a texture similar to overshot glass.

Base, bronze, ornate, lg signature......................250.00
Base, 3 sockets, Greek Key decor, M patina, sgn............350.00
Boudoir, red flowers & vines, shade sgn, #6771, KC.......1,125.00
Candlestick, pnt glass, Dutch scene/windmill, sgn, 8½", pr...1,100.00
Desk, brass, sgn Hubbell socket w/acorn pull..............175.00
Desk, rvpt oblong shade, C scroll support/curved std, 14½"....605.00
Desk, rvpt sunset scenic, bronze Deco base, 24"..........1,050.00
Desk, sgn, #6011, orig label on base......................685.00
Desk, 4 panel glass w/pnt metal leaves/berries, dbl sgn.......575.00
Hanging, birds of paradise, mc, unsgn, 12" dia...........1,200.00
Kerosene burner, orig CI bracket & font....................50.00
Ldgl 14½" shade, geometric w/jewels at rim, metal base, 20"..600.00
Ldgl 18" filigree poppy/brick-work border, simple std, 24"....1,100.00
Ldgl 18" shade w/5" floral border, sgn base...............950.00
Ldgl 19" shade, simple panels, irregular border, sgn, w/std.....700.00
Ldgl 20" shade on bronze Chinese urn base..............2,700.00
Miniature, winter landscape, tree trunk metal base, 14½"......660.00
Night lamp, chipped ice/parrots/flowers on egg form, gilt base..575.00
Palm tree, red sunset glass, metal overlay & std............1,500.00
Pnt w/out, pasture scene, 14" dia shade, metal std, sgn, 10"...825.00
Rvpt bulbous yellow shade w/trellis rose border, #3347, 20"....385.00
Rvpt dome w/lake scene on rust, #6741, metal/std, ea sgn....1,300.00
Rvpt 14" landscape, bronzed tree trunk base, sgn, 20".......550.00
Rvpt 14" umbrella w/sunset landscape, wht metal base, 22½"..400.00
Rvpt 14" windmill scene shade, sgn/#6497, w/orig base......1,525.00
Shade, opal ware, inside decor gr pnt/clear frosting..........340.00
Slag glass 18" shade w/8 panels, baluster leaf cap base, 24"...325.00
Wall, bronze w/clear & frosted panes, pr..................325.00
Woodland scene pnt on exterior, metal std, pat #s, 20½"....825.00
8 slag glass panels w/in gilt metal fr/leaf capped base, 24".....325.00

Harker

The Harker Pottery was established in East Liverpool, Ohio, in 1840. Their earliest product was yellowware and Rockingham produced from local clay. After 1800, whiteware was made from imported materials. The plant eventually grew to be a large manufacturer of dinnerware and kitchenware, employing as many as three hundred people. It closed in 1972, after it was purchased by the Jeanette Glass Company.

Perhaps their best known lines were their Cameo wares, decorated with white silhouettes in a cameo effect on contrasting solid colors. Floral silhouettes are standard, but other designs were also used. Blue and pink are the most often found background hues; a few pieces are found in yellow.

Bean pot, individual, Amy................................2.00
Bowl, covered vegetable; Petit Point......................15.00

Rolling pin, 'Shaggy Tulip' pattern, 15", $75.00.

Bowl, fruit; Colonial Lady...............................3.00
Bowl, mixing; Cameo Ware, pink.........................15.00
Cake lifter, Modern Tulip..............................15.00
Creamer & sugar, Petit Point, pr........................10.00
Creamer & sugar, White Clover, pr......................21.00
Custard cup, Deco Dahlia...............................4.50
Custard cup, Ruffled Tulip..............................5.00
Jar, tall, Petit Point..................................15.00
Pie baker, Amy..8.00
Plate, Cameo, blue, 6"..................................2.00
Plate, Cameo, duck w/umbrella, blue, child's.............10.00
Plate, chop; White Clover, 11".........................15.00
Plate, Colonial Lady, 6"................................2.00
Plate, dinner; Tulip, round.............................5.00
Plate, dinner; Tulip, square............................6.00
Plate, serving; Mallow & Pansy, 12"....................15.00
Plate, serving; Red Apple #1, 12"......................12.00
Plate, utility w/lifter; Petit Point.....................15.00
Platter, Cameo, blue, oval, 14x10½"....................10.00
Platter, Cameo, blue, rectangle, 14"....................8.00
Platter, Colonial Lady, oval.............................6.00
Rolling pin, Cameo Rose, pink..........................65.00
Rolling pin, Petit Point Rose, 3rd style.................70.00
Rolling pin, Silhouette, silver rings, cork..............85.00
Salad fork & spoon, Cameo, blue........................18.00
Salad fork & spoon, Petit Point Rose....................30.00
Salt & peppers, Cameo, bl/wht, range size, pr............8.00
Saucer, White Clover...................................2.50
Serving spoon, Modern Tulip...........................15.00
Sugar scoop, Amy......................................15.00
Teacup, White Clover...................................4.00
Teapot, Cameo, pink...................................15.00
Utility tray, Cameo, blue, 11¾"..........................9.00
Utility tray, Colonial Lady, sq.........................10.00
Water server, advertising, Kelvinator...................25.00

Harlequin

Harlequin dinnerware, produced by the Homer Laughlin China Company of Newell, West Virginia, was introduced in 1938. It was a light-weight ware, made in maroon, mauve blue, and spruce green, as well as all the Fiesta colors except ivory. (See Fiesta section) It was marketed exclusively by the Woolworth stores, who considered it to be their all-time best seller. For this reason, they contracted with Homer Laughlin to reissue Harlequin to commemorate their 100th anniversary in 1979. Although three of the original glazes were used in the reissue, the few serving pieces that were made have been restyled, and the new line offers no threat to the investment of collectors of old Harlequin.

The Harlequin animals, including a fish, lamb, cat, penguin, duck, and donkey, were made during the early 1940s, also for the dime-store trade. Today these are highly regarded by collectors of Homer Laughlin China.

Left: Marmalade, $42.00; Right: Novelty Creamer, $6.50.

'36s bowl	9.00
'36s oatmeal, 6½"	5.50
Animals, maverics	22.00
Animals, regular colors	45.00
Ash tray, basketweave	20.00
Ash tray, regular	18.00
Baker, oval, 9"	6.50
Butter w/cover	35.00
Candle holders, pr	32.00
Casserole w/lid	25.00
Coffee cup & saucer, demitasse	20.00
Coffee cup & saucer, demitasse, '50s colors	40.00
Cream soup	7.00
Creamer, novelty	6.50
Creamer, regular	4.00
Creamer, w/high lip	20.00
Cup, large tankard	40.00
Deep plate	10.00
Egg cup, double	7.00
Egg cup, individual	10.00
Fruit, 5½"	4.50
Jug, 22 oz	17.50
Jug, 22 oz, gray, chartreuse, dark & medium green	25.00
Marmalade	42.00
Nappy, 9"	9.00
Nut dish	6.00
Plate, 10"	5.50
Plate, 6"	2.50
Plate, 7"	3.00
Plate, 9"	4.50
Platter, 11"	6.50
Platter, 13"	9.00
Relish tray, 5 pc	45.00
Salad bowl, individual, 7"	7.50
Salt & pepper shakers, pr	7.00
Sauce boat	7.00
Saucer	1.50
Saucer/ash tray	25.00
Spoon rest, dk gr, red	135.00
Spoon rest, yel & turq	95.00
Sugar w/lid	5.00
Syrup	85.00
Teacup	4.50
Teapot	23.00
Tumbler, w/car decal	22.00

Hatpin Holders

Most hatpin holders were made from 1860 to 1920 to coincide with the period during which hatpins were popularly in vogue. The taller types were required to house the long hatpins necessary to secure the large bonnets that were in style from 1890 to 1914. They were usually porcelain, either decorated by hand or by transfer with florals or scenics, although some were clever figurals. Glass examples are rare, and those of slag or carnival glass are especially valuable.

Bristol glass, bl w/jewels, gold on brass, ftd, 6½"	95.00
Carnival glass, Grape & Cable, marigold	160.00
Carnival glass, Grape & Cable, purple	175.00
Carnival glass, Orange Tree, marigold	125.00
Geisha Girl, hexagonal, 3 legs	65.00
Germany, gr & br leaves on yel, feathery blossoms, wht flowers	48.00
Nippon, Airplane Series, HP	145.00
Nippon, hanging, roses & gold decor	135.00

Nippon, violets and moriage decor, 1½", $45.00.

Nippon, open top, light moriage, corset shape, violet decor	45.00
Nippon, violets, open top	25.00
Nippon, wall hanging cornucopia w/pk roses, gold trim	140.00
Parian type, 2 sides lady's face	55.00
Porcelain, slender tapered body, swirl relief, lines/roses	75.00
Royal Rudolstadt, gr w/wht poppies, sgn Hahn	52.00
RS Germany, bulbous w/wht roses, green mk	45.00
RS Germany, HP roses, gold trim, 4¾"	60.00
RS Germany, wht poppies on gr, green mk	65.00
RS Germany, yel w/wht roses, 6 sided, green mk	45.00
RS Germany, 4 molded ft, lg pk rose, sm yel rose; gr mk	60.00
RS Prussia, attached tray, lg pk/wht roses, red mk	175.00
RS Prussia, basket, hanging	125.00
RS Prussia, swan scene, 6 sided, red mk	225.00
RS Prussia, yel rose, 3 legs, red mk	165.00
Schafer & Vater, cameo heads, pink bisque w/bl trim	95.00
Schafer & Vater, gr jasperware w/relief wht roses	55.00
Schafer & Vater, seated Geisha holds fan, bisque	140.00
Torquay Motto Ware, bl/gr decor	45.00
Willet's Belleek, gold leaves, tiny bl flowers, red mk	95.00

Hatpins

A hatpin was used to securely fasten a hat to the hair and head of the wearer. Hatpins, measuring from 4" to 12" in length, were worn from approximately 1850 to 1920. During the Art Deco period, hatpins became ornaments rather than the decorative functional jewels that they had been. The hatpin period reached its zenith in 1913 just prior to World War I, which brought about a radical change in women's headdress and fashion. About that time, women began to scorn the bonnet and adopt 'the hat' as a symbol of their equality.

The hatpin was made of every natural and manufactured element, in a myriad of designs that challenge the imagination. They were contrived to serve every fashion need and compliment the milliner's art. Collectors often concentrate on a specific type: hand-painted porcelains, sterling silver, commemoratives, sporting activities, carnival glass, Art Nouveau and/or Art Deco designs, Victorian gothics with mounted stones, exquisite rhinestones, escutcheon engraved and brass mounted heads, gold and gems, or simply primitive types made in the Victorian parlor. Some collectors prefer the long pin-shanks while others select only those on tramblants or nodder type pin-shanks.

If you are interested in collecting or dealing in hatpins, you will find that authority Lillian Baker has several fine books available on the subject, including her most recent publication, *Hatpins and Hatpin Holders*, complete with beautiful color illustrations and current market values. She is listed in the Directory under 'California', as well as 'Clubs and Newsletters'.

Betty Boop, 1½" dia.................................35.00
Bird, brass w/turq stone..............................22.00
Blue center stone w/2 rings of rhinestones, 2" head, 11" shaft...35.00
Bone, gr tint, pocked, w/matching sm dangle, 4½"...........8.00
Bulldog figural, carved amethyst, bull's eye glass eyes........265.00
Butterfly w/horn wings, Peacock Eye head, 15 brilliants, 3¼" W.95.00
Carnival glass, butterfly, purple......................17.00
Carnival glass, flying bat............................32.00
Carnival glass, peacock, bl-gr........................32.00
Carnival glass, Top O' Morning, rooster................27.00
Crystal prism......................................10.00
Flat triangle of pave-set brilliants, ca 1895, 1¾"........25.00
Gold filled, reticulated sides, engraved top, 9"...........14.00
Gold filled flower w/lg rhinestone + 8 smaller on stamen, 9"....14.00
Gold filled lacy wire teardrop w/jade-like stone, 8¾".........16.00
Gold teardrop, 10k, 6¼"............................12.00
Large pearl drop cupped in sterling lilies & leaves, 1½".......45.00
Marbleized cobalt oval stone, metal lattice, w/9 sm brilliants.....12.00
Mercury glass, cased, elongated teardrop, 2¼"...........65.00
Mosaic, multicolor 'florals' on brass button mount, 1".........55.00
Ormolu, pierced, w/lg faceted emerald gr stone, 6"..........14.00
Peacock Eye, 1" oval head on 7½" steel pin, ca 1905........40.00
Pique draped, 1" head atop 12" steel pin, pr..............200.00
Rhinestones, ornate..................................6.00
Satsuma, sm floral, gold trim.........................56.00
Satsuma, 2 Geishas, ball shape........................95.00
Shield, mc enamel, people/pine tree/deer, Dirigo Maine, 8".....20.00
Silver alloy, 3-D grapes/leaves cup purple glass accent, 2¼".....35.00
Silver ball, 11" shaft................................30.00
Sterling, repousse w/purple stone, 6¾"..................15.00
Three curved brass straps w/scrolls & amethysts, 1 atop, 2½"...35.00
Topaz atop 3" pierced brass tube, 'topaz' in center swell, 3"....45.00
Wood ball, blk, 1½" dia, 7½" shaft.....................8.00

Right: Art Nouveau coral cabochon, 1", on 9¾" pin, sterling, $75.00.
Left: Art Nouveau coral plastic rose, 1", on 9" pin, circa 1900, $45.00.

Haviland

The Haviland China Company was organized in 1840 by David Haviland, a New York china importer. His search for a pure white, non-porous porcelain led him to Limoges, France, where natural deposits of suitable clay had already attracted numerous china manufacturers. The fine hand-painted china he produced there was translucent and meticulously decorated, with each piece fired in an individual sagger.

It has been estimated that as many as 60,000 chinaware patterns were designed, each piece marked with one of several company backstamps. 'H. & Co.' was used until 1890, when a law was enacted making it necessary to include the country of origin. Various marks have been used since that time including 'Haviland, France'; 'Haviland & Co. Limoges'; and 'Decorated by Haviland & Co.'.

Various associations with family members over the years have resulted in changes in management as well as company name. In 1892, Theodore Haviland left the firm to start his own business. Some of his ware was marked 'Mont Mery'. Later logos included a horseshoe, a shield, and various uses of his initials and name. In 1941, this branch moved to the United States. Wares produced here are marked 'Theodore Haviland, N.Y.' or 'Made In America'.

Though it is their dinnerware lines for which they are most famous, during the 1880s and 1890s they also made exquisite art pottery using a technique of underglaze slip decoration called 'Barbotine', which had been invented by Ernest Chaplet. In 1885 Haviland bought the formula and hired Chaplet to oversee its production. The technique involved mixing heavy white clay slip with pigments to produce a compound of the same consistency as oil paints. The finished product actually resembled oil paintings of the period, the texture achieved through the application of the heavy medium to the clay body in much the same manner as an artist would apply paint to his canvas. Primarily the body used with this method was a low-fired 'faience', though they also produced stoneware.

Bowl, bl w/pk dogwood, 1876 mk, shallow, 7½".............18.00
Bowl, ftd, scalloped, Drop Rose, gold trim, 11"...........90.00
Bowl, ftd, sm bl flowers, lg..........................55.00
Bowl, HP on lattice relief, scalloped, hdls, 6¼" dia.........175.00
Bowl, pk open rose on shaded ground, gold scallops, France, 9".30.00
Bowl, sauce; Clover, #98............................15.00
Bowl, vegetable; Autumn Leaf, France..................40.00
Bowl, vegetable; open, Cherbourgh, #667................30.00
Bowl, vegetable; Rosalinde, oval, Theo.................55.00
Butter pat, #432....................................6.50
Butter pat, #944, H&C mk............................8.00
Casserole, Clover #98..............................100.00
Casserole, wht w/gold trim, hdls, French, 7x11" L.........55.00
Charger, grape clusters in gr/rust/purple on pastel, 13½".....135.00
Chocolate pot, Cherbourgh, #667.....................110.00
Chocolate pot, pk rose sprays, gold hdl/trim/finial, scalloped....135.00
Chocolate pot, pk wild roses, ribbon hdls, #40............160.00
Chocolate pot, wht w/yel tulips, HP, dtd 1886, CF.........100.00
Cracker jar, pk wild roses, #40........................90.00
Cream soup, w/saucer, Chantilly, France................25.00
Cream soup, w/under plate, Mosaic, Theo...............28.00
Creamer, child's; chickens & bunnies, HP, Elite...........30.00
Cup, Rosalinde, Theo...............................15.50
Cup & saucer, #342................................15.00
Cup & saucer, #49.................................20.00
Cup & saucer, #944, H&C mk.........................12.00
Cup & saucer, Annette, Theo.........................28.00
Cup & saucer, Autumn Leaf, France....................25.00
Cup & saucer, bouillon; #559..........................8.50
Cup & saucer, Chantilly, France.......................32.00
Cup & saucer, chocolate; #146........................25.00

Ewer, stoneware with Barbotine decor, by Frederic Hexamer, circa 1882-1887, 13″, $2,200.00.

Cup & saucer, Clover #98.............................55.00
Cup & saucer, demitasse; Clover #98.....................30.00
Cup & saucer, Montabello............................30.00
Cup & saucer, Mosaic...............................28.00
Cup & saucer, Pasadena.............................20.00
Ewer, cylinder form, Barbotine decor, Damouse, 12″........1,500.00
Gravy boat, Autumn Leaf, France......................40.00
Gravy boat w/stand, Clover #98.......................85.00
Lobster dish, gold trim on scalloped edges, sgn/1888........125.00
Mustard, Chrysanthemum, w/attached under plate............75.00
Oyster plate, HP, gold rippled rim, shell/seaweed, pink/br......35.00
Oyster plate, pk florals.............................50.00
Oyster plate, wht w/allover gold, 8¼″..................60.00
Oyster plate, wht w/gold edge & center, 5 wells, Theo, 8½″.....35.00
Pancake dish, dome cover, pk roses, gold trim, ornate hdl, 9″...45.00
Pancake dish, pk roses/forget-me-nots, ¼″ buttons, Theo......70.00
Place setting, Berkley, Theo, France, 5 pc................105.00
Place setting, Pasadena, Theo, France, 5 pc..............105.00
Place setting, Pink Spray, Theo, France, 5 pc.............105.00
Place setting, Rosalinde, Theo, France, 5 pc..............105.00
Place setting, Trellis, Theo, France, 5 pc................125.00
Place setting, Windsor, Theo, France, 5 pc...............115.00
Plate, bird dog w/pheasant, artist sgn, 1885, lg............85.00
Plate, bread & butter; #488, 7½″, set of 4...............30.00
Plate, bread & butter; Autumn Leaf, France..............10.00
Plate, bread & butter; Chantilly, France.................12.00
Plate, bread & butter; Cherbourgh, #667, 7½″.............9.00
Plate, bread & butter; Clover #98, 7½″..................20.00
Plate, bread & butter; Drop Rose, 7¼″..................80.00
Plate, bread & butter; Varenne, France..................12.50
Plate, dessert; #488, pk roses & lt gr/gold cartouches at rim....7.50
Plate, dessert; Ranson, #24..........................14.50
Plate, dinner; #66.................................16.00
Plate, dinner; Annette, Theo.........................26.00
Plate, dinner; Autumn Leaf, France....................20.00
Plate, dinner; Chantilly, France.......................20.00
Plate, dinner; Clover #98, 9½″.......................32.00
Plate, dinner; Montabello, 9″........................12.50
Plate, dinner; Mosaic..............................20.00
Plate, lucheon; Drop Rose, 8½″.......................90.00

Plate, lucheon; pansies on pastel, 8½″..................35.00
Plate, luncheon; Norma, gold trim.....................16.50
Plate, napkin corner, HP flowers, H & Co, 8½″............15.00
Plate, salad; Chantilly, France........................15.00
Plate & egg cup, child's; HP chickens, Limoges............45.00
Platter, #146-E, 16″...............................45.00
Platter, #39-C, 14″................................28.00
Platter, Cherbourgh, 10″............................32.50
Platter, Clover #98, 16″............................110.00
Platter, Pasadena, 14″.............................30.00
Platter, Princess, 16½″.............................65.00
Platter, Rosalinde, w/well, Theo, 16″...................95.00
Platter, sm pk roses, gold trim, 16½″...................46.00
Shaving mug, rose garlands, sgn GD....................35.00
Soup, Clover #98, 7½″.............................25.00
Soup, flat, #944, H&C mk...........................9.00
Soup, pk roses, irregular gold edge, Theo, 7¼″, 12 for......175.00
Sugar, Clover #98................................65.00
Sugar, pink florals, gold trim, hdls, 4″.................35.00
Tea set, butterflies on 1 side; flowers bk, H&Co L France.....225.00
Tea set, pk wild roses, ribbon hdls, #30, 3 pcs............140.00
Teapot, Clover #98...............................85.00
Tray, #498, 18x18″...............................150.00
Tray, pin; 3 lg red cabbage roses in center, gilt sides, 5″......22.50

Hawkes

Thomas Hawkes established his factory in Corning, New York, in 1880. He developed many beautiful patterns of cut glass, two of which were awarded the Grand Prize at the Paris Exposition in 1889. By the end of the century, his company was renowned for the finest in cut glass production. The company logo was a trefoil form enclosing a hawk in each of the two bottom lobes, with a fleur-de-lis in the center.

Ash tray, yel w/gilt sterling overlay & center rest, 3½″ dia.....100.00
Basket, basketweave cutting, flared, 12½x10″.............350.00
Bell, amber w/crystal hdl, no clapper...................65.00
Bon bon, heart shaped, sgnd, miniature, 3″..............95.00
Bowl, Late Panel cutting, 1910, 8″.....................160.00
Bowl, Princess cutting, sgn, low, 9″ dia.................325.00
Bowl, salad; marquise shape, fans/vesicas/central hobstar, 12″..300.00
Bowl, sawtooth & pineapple plume, deep, 9″ sq............150.00
Bowl, sq, cut to pcs, hobstar pattern, 8½″...............375.00
Bowl, Venetian cutting, repousse sterling rim, 8″ dia........425.00
Bud vase, verre de soie, sgn, 14″.....................250.00
Butter tub, open applied hdl, cut & engraved, 3x5″ dia.......150.00
Candlestick, Delft Diamond w/full teardrop stem, 9″, pr......310.00
Candlestick, etched, w/sterling bases, set of 4...........2,700.00
Candy dish, strawberry pattern.......................160.00
Carafe, Venetian cutting, sgn........................125.00
Champagne, silver band on rnd ft & rim, 5¼″.............15.00
Cologne, Russian & Pillars, Gorham repousse top, 7½″.......425.00
Compote, Classic pattern, 5″........................165.00
Compote, garlands of intaglio florals, verre de soie, 5x7¼″...200.00
Cordial, Chelsea Rose, 4¾″..........................24.00
Creamer & sugar, Gravic Strawberries..................325.00
Creamer & sugar, Milton, 3¾″, pr.....................135.00
Cruet, cut glass stopper, silver overlay, sgn..............195.00
Cruet, oil/vinegar, floral teardrop stopper, dtd 1916, 7½″.....75.00
Cruet, silver stopper, sgn, 7½″.......................100.00
Dish, ice cream; Gravic, sawtooth edge, hobstars/X hatch, 6″...45.00
Dish, vesicas form octagonal flower, central hobstar rim, 8″....200.00
Goblet, Aquilla, sgn, 7″............................30.00
Goblet, Delft Diamond, 7″..........................47.50

Goblet, Patricia, 6½"................................32.50
Goblet, Ramsey, 6¼"...............................26.00
Goblet, Sierra, 7½"................................75.00
Goblet, Surrey, 6¾"...............................30.00
Goblet, Wild Rose, 6½".............................42.50
Ice bucket, etched, SP rim & hdl, sgn..............60.00
Jug, whiskey; eng log cabin in woods, moon on stopper, sgn...225.00
Loving cup, 3 hdls, Middlesex, 24 point hobstar base, 7¾"....900.00
Martini beaker, clear w/2 roosters decor, sgn, 16¼".........175.00
Nappy, Gravic Iris, sgn, 6" dia.....................16.00
Pitcher, Brunswick, triple notched hdl, sgn, 9".............500.00
Pitcher, milk; hobstar & pineapple blossom, air stem hdl, 5½".275.00
Plate, hobstar & silver thread pattern, sgn, 7"............125.00
Punch bowl, 2 part, cut, sgn, lg..................2,900.00
Salt, nailhead diamond, zipper, sgn.................30.00
Sherbet, Cornwall, 3½"............................37.50
Sherbet, Surrey, 5"...............................30.00
Sherbet, Wild Rose, 5".............................42.50
Tray, Chrysanthemum, folded corners, 14½x7½".........750.00
Tumbler, diamond & fan cutting......................35.00
Tumbler, Doris, 3½"...............................40.00
Tumbler, fans/straight line cuttings w/X hatch/stars.........35.00
Tumbler, flared rim, fluted body, stencil mk, 3¾", 10 for.....125.00
Tumbler, iced tea; cut & engraved, early, set of 4..........200.00
Tumbler, juice; Marquis of Waterford, 3½"..............26.00
Tumbler, juice; St George, 3¾"......................24.00
Vase, Brunswick, trumpet shape, 12"..................275.00
Vase, corset form, brilliant cut, sgn, 10".............350.00
Vase, fan shape, gr w/cut grape leaves, sgn, 7¼"..........85.00
Vase, lavender flashed, engraved dragon, Steuben blank, 8"....150.00
Vase, lavender w/bird decor, Steuben blank, 12".........265.00
Vase, panel cutting, 8"..........................1,800.00
Vase, pirate ship w/skull & crossbones, deep bl, 10½".......225.00
Vase, Shooting Star, 8½"...........................25.00
Vase, stick neck, engraved flowers, leaves, sgn, 8".........160.00
Vase, tea caddy shape, Oriental scene engraved, lid w/figures...200.00
Vase, trumpet form, Queens, faceted knob on stem, 10".......650.00
Vase, tubular floral cutting, sgn, 9¼"................50.00
Wine, Aquilla, star & starburst decor, set of 8..........275.00
Wine, diamond pattern, silver ped base, sgn, set of 6......175.00
Wine, Marquis of Waterford, 6½"....................40.00

Heisey

A.H. Heisey began his long career at the King Glass Company of Pittsburgh. He later joined the Ripley Glass Company which soon became Geo. Duncan and Sons. After Duncan's death, Heisey became half owner along with his brother-in-law, James Duncan. In 1895, he built his own factory in Newark, Ohio, starting production in 1896 and continuing until Christmas of 1957. At that time, Imperial Glass Corporation purchased some of the moulds. In 1968, they removed the old Diamond H from any moulds they put into use.

During their highly successful period of production, Heisey made fine hand-crafted tableware with simple yet graceful designs. Early pieces were not marked. After November 1901, the glassware was marked either with the 'Diamond H' or a paper label. Blown ware is often marked on the stem, never on the bowl or foot.

Today Heisey glass is highly collectible.

Animals

Airedale...550.00
Bull..1,200.00

Rooster vase, crystal glass, 6¼" x 6", $95.00.

Clydesdale......................................400.00
Colts, set of 3..................................320.00
Dolphin, candlesticks, pink, #110, pr..............400.00
Donkey...275.00
Duck, ash tray..................................110.00
Elephant, lg....................................325.00
Elephants, 3 grad sizes in set....................750.00
Fish, bookends, crystal, pr.......................200.00
Fish, candlestick................................200.00
Fish, match holder...............................150.00
Gazelle.......................................1,200.00
Geese, set of 3..................................450.00
Giraffe...170.00
Goose, cocktail..................................100.00
Goose, wings down................................300.00
Goose, wings half.................................75.00
Goose, wings up...................................75.00
Hen..425.00
Horse head, bookends, frosted, pr..................200.00
Horse head, cigarette box, crystal, #1489, 4¼x4".....65.00
Horse head, cocktail shaker.......................120.00
Kingfisher, flower block, moongleam...............200.00
Mallards, set of 3...............................400.00
Plug horse.......................................75.00
Pouter Pigeon...................................700.00
Rabbit, paperweight..............................165.00
Ringneck pheasant...............................145.00
Rooster, Fighting; 8"............................150.00
Rooster, vase, 6½"...............................95.00
Rooster, 5⅝"...................................425.00
Rooster head cocktail shaker, 1 qt.................95.00
Rooster stem, cocktail............................60.00
Scotty dog.....................................120.00
Setter, ash tray, flamingo, #1286..................40.00
Sparrow...65.00
Tropical Fish..................................1,000.00
Wood Duck......................................550.00

Dinnerware

African Tempo, cocktail, 3 oz......................30.00
Banded Flute, punch bowl w/stand & 10 cups, 14"......300.00

Banded Flute, toothpick holder............................40.00
Beaded Panel & Sunburst, punch cup.......................15.00
Beaded Panel & Sunburst, toothpick holder................80.00
Beaded Swag, toothpick holder, ruby flashed souvenir.........40.00
Beaded Swag, tumbler, opal w/flower decor................60.00
Beehive, moongleam; plate, #1238, 8"....................38.50
Coleport, ash tray, individual, #1486....................30.00
Coleport, bar glass, 2 oz...............................15.00
Coleport, cigarette holder, #1486.......................50.00
Colonial, cake stand...................................45.00
Colonial, creamer & sugar, individual, pr................38.00
Crystolite, ash tray w/box match holder, #1503½..........30.00
Crystolite, bon bon, 2 hdld, mkd........................16.00
Crystolite, candlestick, 1 lite, #1503, pr...............28.00
Crystolite, candlestick, 3 lite, pr.....................40.00
Crystolite, candy, shell, w/cover.......................30.00
Crystolite, candy w/lid, 3 ftd, 6"......................45.00
Crystolite, cheese, ftd, #1503.........................15.00
Crystolite, cigarette box, 3½".........................24.00
Crystolite, cigarette holder...........................15.00
Crystolite, cigarette holder, ftd, #1503................27.00
Crystolite, coaster...................................10.00
Crystolite, compote, #1503, 4½".......................18.00
Crystolite, creamer, oval, mkd.........................12.00
Crystolite, creamer, sugar & tray, individual, 3 pc.........55.00
Crystolite, creamer & sugar, individual, pr..............40.00
Crystolite, creamer & sugar, lg, mkd....................33.00
Crystolite, cruet w/stopper............................35.00
Crystolite, goblet, 12 oz, #5003.......................21.00
Crystolite, ice bucket, w/tongs........................67.50
Crystolite, jelly, 2 part, 2 hdld, 6", mkd..............15.00
Crystolite, mayonnaise, 3 pc..........................35.00
Crystolite, mustard, w/cover..........................25.00
Crystolite, nappy, mkd, 4½"............................8.00
Crystolite, nut dish, leaf shape, w/hdl.................15.00
Crystolite, nut dish, swan, individual, #1503...........15.00
Crystolite, plate, 14".................................25.00
Crystolite, plate, 2 hdld, 6½".........................12.00
Crystolite, relish tray, 3 part, 10" L..................28.00
Crystolite, sherbet...................................15.00
Crystolite, swan, lg..................................30.00
Crystolite, tumbler, ftd, 14 oz........................20.00
Crystolite, tumbler, juice, ftd, blown..................15.00
Diamond Optic, bowl, Empress etched, 5½"................8.00
Diamond Optic, cream soup w/liner, Empress etched.......10.00
Diamond Optic, cup & saucer, Empress etched.............25.00
Diamond Optic, goblet, 10 oz, Empress etched............20.00
Duquesne, tangerine; cocktail, 3 oz....................170.00
Duquesne, tangerine; soda, ftd, 12 oz..................135.00
Empress, alexandrite; ash tray, #1401..................210.00
Empress, alexandrite; plate, #1401, 7", set of 6........240.00
Empress, alexandrite; vase, dolphin ftd, EX color, 9".....375.00
Empress, crystal; creamer, ftd.........................16.00
Empress, crystal; cruet...............................55.00
Empress, crystal; cup.................................10.00
Empress, crystal; ice bucket w/tongs...................95.00
Empress, flamingo; creamer & sugar.....................85.00
Empress, green; muffin, 12"...........................60.00
Empress, sahara; candlestick, toed, 6", pr.............210.00
Empress, sahara; candy dish & cover...................125.00
Empress, sahara; compote, oval........................75.00
Empress, sahara; cream soup & liner, round.............25.00
Empress, sahara; creamer, dolphin ftd..................45.00
Empress, sahara; creamer & sugar, individual...........85.00

Empress, sahara; cup & saucer, #1401...................38.00
Empress, sahara; nappy, 4½"...........................15.00
Empress, sahara; nut dish, individual..................27.50
Empress, sahara; oil cruet, w/orig stopper, 4 oz........95.00
Empress, sahara; plate, dinner, square.................85.00
Empress, sahara; plate, square, #1401, 6"..............10.00
Empress, sahara; plate, square, #1401, 7"..............13.00
Empress, sahara; plate, square, #1401, 8"..............18.00
Empress, sahara; plate, 7" dia........................13.00
Empress, sahara; platter, oval........................65.00
Empress, sahara; saucer, round..........................9.00
Empress, sahara; saucer, square.......................12.00
Fancy Loop, crystal; compote, ruffled, 9½".............95.00
Fancy Loop, crystal; pickle tray, 7"...................22.50
Fancy Loop, crystal; punch cup, gold decor.............15.00
Fancy Loop, crystal; toothpick holder..................55.00
Fancy Loop, crystal; toothpick holder, heavy gold decor....75.00
Fancy Loop, emerald; toothpick holder, w/gold decor.....135.00
Fancy Loop, emerald; tumbler, gold decor...............60.00
Fern, mayonnaise, divided, handled.....................20.00
Flat Panel, creamer & sugar, individual, pr.............42.00
Flat Panel, cruet w/stopper, 6 oz......................45.00
Flat Panel, mustard w/lid, 2 sm hdls...................30.00
Gascony, tangerine; juice, 5 oz.......................225.00
Greek Key, almond.....................................22.00
Greek Key, cordial...................................250.00
Greek Key, ice tub, med...............................95.00
Greek Key, oil, 2 oz..................................80.00
Greek Key, plate, #433, 4½"...........................15.00
Heisey Rose, bowl, crimped, #1519, 12".................80.00
Heisey Rose, bowl, crimped, #1519, 9½".................50.00
Heisey Rose, compote, #1519, 6½".......................55.00
Heisey Rose, juice, ftd, 5 oz, #5072...................40.00
Heisey Rose, oil, ftd, w/stopper, #122, 3 oz...........175.00
Heisey Rose, plate, luncheon, orig sticker, 7"..........30.00
Heisey Rose, plate, torte, 14".........................90.00
Hotel, pink; creamer & covered sugar, #406.............35.00
Ipswich, cobalt; centerpiece vase w/crystal A prisms.....350.00
Ipswich, crystal; centerpiece vase w/crystal A prisms.....97.00
Ipswich, crystal; plate, 8"...........................12.50
Ipswich, crystal; sherbet, tall.......................13.50
Ipswich, crystal; tumbler, ftd, 8 oz...................12.00
Ipswich, sahara; sherbet, mkd.........................35.00
Ipswich, sahara; sugar, 2 hdld........................45.00
Jamestown, goblet, Kruth Cut, 9 oz.....................30.00
Kohinoor, juice, 5 oz.................................25.00
Lariat, ash tray.......................................9.00
Lariat, basket, 7"....................................95.00
Lariat, bowl, flared, 12".............................25.00
Lariat, candlestick, small round......................12.00
Lariat, candlestick, 2 light, pr......................45.00
Lariat, candlestick, 3 lite, #1540, pr.................70.00
Lariat, caramel dish, covered.........................40.00
Lariat, cheese compote................................17.50
Lariat, cheese dish w/lid, 5".........................37.50
Lariat, coaster..6.50
Lariat, creamer, sugar & tray, 3 pc....................55.00
Lariat, creamer & sugar, #1540........................36.00
Lariat, goblet, stemmed...............................18.50
Lariat, nut dish, individual..........................15.00
Lariat, plate, cupped, 9".............................15.00
Lariat, plate, 21", for punch bowl.....................55.00
Lariat, plate, 8½"....................................15.00
Lariat, punch cup......................................9.00

Lariat, salad dressing, divided.........................25.00
Lariat, vase, fan, moonglow cutting.....................45.00
Legionnaire, goblet, Arcadia cut, 10 oz.................25.00
Minuet, candle holder, 2 lite, pr......................150.00
Minuet, champagne sherbet..............................27.50
Narrow Flute, crystal; almond, ftd, individual.........12.50
Narrow Flute, crystal; creamer & sugar, individual, pr..38.00
Narrow Flute, crystal; salt dip........................12.50
Narrow Flute, flamingo; almond, ftd, individual........25.00
Narrow Flute, green; relish, divided, #473, pat 6/20/16........30.00
Narrow Flute, moongleam; almond, ftd, individual.......27.50
Octagon, flamingo; nut dish, individual................18.00
Octagon, green; rib celery, 12″, #1231.................18.00
Octagon, moongleam; ice bucket w/hdl, #500.............65.00
Octagon, moongleam; nut dish, individual...............20.00
Octagon, pink; bowl, 2 hdld, 6″........................12.00
Octagon, pink; tray, oblong, 6″........................16.00
Octagon, yellow; sugar.................................30.00
Old Colony, plate, 10½″ sq.............................60.00
Old Colony, plate, 9″..................................18.00
Old Dominion, sahara; champagne, Old Colony etching........30.00
Old Dominion, sahara; goblet, 8″.......................26.00
Old Glory, wine, Renaissance etch, 2 oz................25.00
Old Sandwich, crystal; ash tray, cut bottom, #1404.........12.00
Old Sandwich, crystal; bar glass, 1 oz.................22.00
Old Sandwich, crystal; catsup bottle w/stopper.............65.00
Old Sandwich, crystal; pitcher, ½ gal, no ice lip...........55.00
Old Sandwich, crystal; salt & peppers, pr..............35.00
Old Sandwich, crystal; tumbler, 10 oz...................8.00
Old Sandwich, flamingo; ash tray, #1404................48.00
Old Sandwich, green; candlesticks, 6″, #1404, pr.......200.00
Old Sandwich, moongleam; ash tray, individual, #1404........45.00
Old Sandwich, sahara; ash tray, individual, #1404..........30.00
Old Sandwich, sahara; candlesticks, #1404, pr..........185.00
Old Sandwich, sahara; creamer..........................45.00
Old Sandwich, sahara; shaker...........................50.00
Old Sandwich, sahara; sherbet, 5 oz....................18.00
Old Sandwich, sahara; tumbler, juice, 5 oz.............18.00
Old Williamsburg, compote, 5″..........................24.00
Old Williamsburg, nested bowls, set of 3...............70.00
Old Williamsburg, pitcher, water; straight scalloped top........80.00
Orchid, bon bon, ftd, mkd, #1519, 6½″..................40.00
Orchid, bowl, divided, 8″..............................30.00
Orchid, bowl, dressing; 2 part oval, 6″................34.00

Orchid, butter dish w/cover...........................139.00
Orchid, candlestick, 3 lite, pr.......................120.00
Orchid, cheese, Rococo, #1147..........................55.00
Orchid, compote, 3½x6¼″ dia............................40.00
Orchid, compote, 7″....................................97.00
Orchid, creamer & sugar, ftd, sgnd.....................52.00
Orchid, creamer & sugar, individual, pr................60.00
Orchid, cup & saucer...................................45.00
Orchid, ginger ale, 8 oz...............................37.00
Orchid, goblet, low, 10 oz.............................40.00
Orchid, goblet, water, tall, 10 oz.....................40.00
Orchid, honey, ftd, #1519, 6½″.........................40.00
Orchid, jelly, ftd, hdld, #1509, 6½″...................27.00
Orchid, mayonnaise, ftd, w/liner, sgnd ladle...........65.00
Orchid, mint bowl, dolphin, ftd, #1509.................37.00
Orchid, oil, ftd, w/stopper...........................122.00
Orchid, oyster cocktail................................42.00
Orchid, plate, #1519, 8″...............................20.00
Orchid, plate, demi-torte; #1519, 11″..................50.00
Orchid, plate, dinner; #1519...........................75.00
Orchid, plate, salad; #1519, 7″........................15.00
Orchid, plate, torte; #1519, 14″.......................50.00
Orchid, relish, 3 part, oblong, #1519, 11″.............62.00
Orchid, relish, 3 part, round, #1509...................45.00
Orchid, saucer champagne, 6 oz, mkd, #5025.............30.00
Orchid, server, center hdl, #1519, 14″................150.00
Orchid, shakers, #1519, pr.............................75.00
Orchid, shakers, #42, pr...............................75.00
Orchid, sherbet, low, #5025............................24.00
Orchid, sherry, 2 oz, #5025............................72.00
Orchid, soda, ftd, 12 oz, #5025........................35.00
Orchid, soda, ftd, 5 oz, #5025.........................32.00
Orchid, tumbler, juice, #2351, 5 oz....................40.00
Oxford, soda, 5 oz.....................................10.00
Peerless, toothpick holder.............................40.00
Pied Piper, sherbet, low...............................18.00
Pied Piper, tumbler, ftd, 12 oz, #3350.................22.00
Pineapple & Fan, crystal; salt & pepper, #3, sterling tops, pr....50.00
Pineapple & Fan, emerald; toothpick holder............135.00
Plain Band, toothpick holder...........................45.00
Plain Panel Recess, tumbler, EX cutting................50.00
Plantation, compote, covered, deep.....................60.00
Plantation, oil w/stopper, 3 oz........................75.00
Plantation, syrup, chrome lid & hdl....................65.00
Plantation, wine, ivy etch, 3 oz.......................22.50
Plateau, moongleam; rose bowl, 6″......................60.00
Pleat & Panel, crystal; pitcher, 1 qt, #1170...........70.00
Pleat & Panel, flamingo; comportier w/lid..............55.00
Pleat & Panel, green; bouillon.........................12.00
Pleat & Panel, green; cruet, w/stopper.................55.00
Pleat & Panel, green; lemon dish & cover...............37.50
Pleat & Panel, pink; cruet, w/stopper..................50.00
Pleat & Panel, pink; lemon, covered....................32.00
Priscilla, butter pat, #351............................15.00
Priscilla, toothpick holder............................40.00
Prison Stripe, punch cup...............................20.00
Punty Band, olive drab flashed; toy cream, #1220...........38.00
Punty Band, ruby flashed; toothpick holder, bead top souvenir...45.00
Puritan, 'Oil & Vinegar' w/stopper, late, #1489, 6 oz........25.00
Puritan, cocktail, #341, 3 oz..........................12.50
Puritan, cordial, #341, 1 oz...........................25.00
Puritan, creme de menthe, #341, 2½ oz..................25.00
Puritan, oil cruet w/stopper, #341, 2 oz...............40.00
Puritan, salt dip, #341................................15.00

Creamer and sugar, Empress, in rare 'Alexandrite', $400.00.

Puritan, sherbet, low, #341.............................12.00
Queen Ann, candelabra, 1 lite, A prisms, #1509, pr.........125.00
Queen Ann, mustard w/lid, sm.........................35.00
Queen Ann, nut dish, individual.......................18.00
Recessed Panel, candy, ½ lb, G gold....................40.00
Recessed Panel, candy, ¼ lb, EX gold....................50.00
Rib & Panel, crystal; oil w/stopper, 6 oz...............38.00
Rib & Panel, moongleam; bon bon, 2 hdld, mkd...........22.50
Ridgeleigh, ash tray, club only.......................20.00
Ridgeleigh, ash tray set, bridge, #1469................75.00
Ridgeleigh, bar glass, 1½ oz.........................25.00
Ridgeleigh, celery/olive, 12".........................24.00
Ridgeleigh, cigarette box w/lid, #1469, 4".............30.00
Ridgeleigh, cigarette holder, sq, #1469................15.00
Ridgeleigh, coasters, Zircon, #1467, set of 6..........275.00
Ridgeleigh, creamer & sugar, individual, pr............38.00
Ridgeleigh, nut, individual, hdld.....................12.00
Ridgeleigh, salts, 8 in box...........................75.00
Ridgeleigh, shakers, pr..............................35.00
Ridgeleigh, vase, 6".................................25.00
Spanish Stem, compote, cobalt/clear, 6x6" dia..........300.00
Triplex, moongleam; candlestick, #129.................75.00
Trojan, wine, 2½ oz, #3366...........................15.00
Twist, flamingo; ice bucket...........................75.00
Twist, green; bowl, 2 hdld, 6".........................20.00
Twist, green; mustard, w/lid..........................55.00
Twist, marigold; tumbler, 8 oz........................50.00
Twist, moongleam; ice tub, w/hdl......................85.00
Twist, moongleam; nut dish, individual.................22.50
Twist, moongleam; saucer..............................7.00
Twist, pink; bowl, 2 hdld, 7½".........................20.00
Twist, pink; cream soup w/liner.......................32.00
Twist, pink; nappy, 4"...............................12.00
Twist, pink; nut, ftd & hdld..........................25.00
Twist, pink; plate, hdld, 6"..........................15.00
Twist, pink; relish, 13".............................22.00
Twist, pink; tray, sgnd, 10"..........................20.00
Twist, sahara; dressing bottle........................75.00
Victorian, ash tray w/cigarette holder, silver ship, #1425...30.00
Victorian, custard cup, 5 oz, #1425, mkd...............9.00
Victorian, French dressing bottle.....................55.00
Victorian, goblet, ftd, 4¾"...........................15.00
Victorian, juice, flat, 5 oz, 4"......................12.00
Victorian, oil w/stopper, 3 oz........................50.00
Victorian, sherbet, ftd...............................8.00
Victorian, tray, 3 part, 12"..........................30.00
Victorian, tumbler, flat, 5½".........................15.00
Victorian, tumbler, flat, 8 oz, 4½"...................15.00
Warwick, crystal; candlestick, pr.....................35.00
Warwick, crystal; match holder, #1428.................20.00
Warwick, sahara; candle holder, double................75.00
Whirlpool, cheese, low ftd, #1506, 8".................17.00
Whirlpool, coaster....................................6.00
Whirlpool, creamer, sugar & tray, individual, 3 pcs....55.00
Whirlpool, punch cup, #79, 6 for......................40.00
Winged Scroll, emerald; creamer & sugar...............175.00
Winged Scroll, emerald; trinket box, gold decor........85.00
Winged Scroll, ivorina; toothpick holder, w/gold decor...110.00
Yeoman, crystal; creamer & sugar, cut/silver decor, ind, pr...52.00
Yeoman, green; cup & saucer, mkd......................20.00
Yeoman, green; plate, 8¼".............................8.50
Yeoman, moongleam; egg cup............................37.00
Yeoman, pink; compote, ftd, mkd.......................28.00
Yeoman, pink; plate, 10"..............................25.00

Miscellaneous

Ash tray, green, w/match holder.......................35.00
Bar glass, #2052, mermaids etching, 1½ oz.............125.00
Bar glass, #2052, tally-ho............................30.00
Bar glass, club drinking scene etch, 1½ oz............95.00
Basket, Butterfly & Floral cutting, #461, 9"..........150.00
Basket, pink, #417, 6"...............................135.00
Candlestick, #109, dolphin, flamingo Petticoat, 6", pr....300.00
Candlestick, #120, low, 1 lite, pr....................40.00
Candlestick, #1445, grape cluster, 1 lite, pr.........150.00
Candlestick, #1541, Athena, 2 lite, pr................90.00
Candlestick, #301, sahara, 2 lite, 10½", pr...........650.00
Candlestick, #301, 2 lite, low ftd, A prisms, pr......285.00
Candlestick, #31, toy, pr.............................70.00
Candlestick, #33, toy, pr.............................80.00
Candlestick, #5, toy, pr..............................80.00
Candlestick, New Era..................................35.00
Candy compote w/lid, etched elk, seahorse hdls, #1519...85.00
Cologne, #305, Punty & Diamond Point, sterling top.....75.00
Cologne, #516, flamingo w/moongleam stopper, 1 oz......125.00
Comportier, dolphin ftd, flamingo Petticoat, #109-1225...160.00
Cornucopia, crystal, #1428, 9¼".......................40.00
Cruet, Saturn, #1485.................................45.00
Lavender jar, clear, w/cover..........................46.50
Salt dip, #1183, Revere, flamingo.....................18.00
Salt dip, #429, Plain Panel Recess, ftd...............22.00
Stein, fox chase scene...............................140.00
Syrup, crystal.......................................35.00

Heubach

Gebruder Heubach is a German porcelain company that has been in operation since the 1800s producing quality figurines and novelty items. They are perhaps most famous for their doll heads and piano babies, most of which are marked with the circular rising sun device containing an 'H' superimposed over a 'C'.

Baby, crawling, in nightie, 4½".......................95.00
Baby, crawling, right ft up, off shoulder gown, sgn, 7"...225.00
Baby, crawling, right leg up, wht gown, sgn, 5".........125.00
Baby, flower child, hand to toes, pleated wht gown, hat, 5"....125.00
Baby, lying on bk, foot in air, 10" L.................400.00
Baby, on back touching toes, leg raised, wht gown, mk, 4"....95.00
Baby, on ball, 4"....................................90.00
Baby, on bk w/ft up, wht bonnet, 4"..................100.00
Baby, sitting, holding toes, sgn, 6¼x5½"..............225.00
Baby, sitting in tattered shoe, toes protruding.......300.00
Baby boy, left hand over left eye, nude w/br shoes, w/vase, 5"..150.00
Baby boy, sitting, legs Xd, throwing kisses, nude, mk, 5"...200.00
Black banjo player, 5¾x2¾"...........................400.00
Boy, doing handsprings, EX detail, sgn, 13"...........400.00
Boy, in beach suit w/sand pail, wire hdl, 9¼"........150.00
Boy, in gr suit, pockets pulled out, 10x4½"..........175.00
Boy, on stool, arms Xd/fez cap/glasses/cigar, bisque, 9½"....165.00
Boy, sitting on stool, fez cap/glasses/cigar, 7x2¾"....95.00
Boy, standing, holding rabbit to chest, bisque, sgn, 7"...145.00
Boy, standing w/rabbit in arms, decor bisque, 9½"......165.00
Boy, w/little girl riding dog, 8¾x3¾x7"...............165.00
Boy & girl, he w/snowballs, she w/muff to face, 13½"...375.00
Boy & girl, removable bubble pipes, sitting on benches, 8", pr..375.00
Children sitting on potties, 5¾x2¾", pr..............350.00
Dancing girl, floral base, tambourine at ft, holds skirt, 16½"...550.00

Dish, Indian w/shield & axe, wheat sheaves at rim, gr/wht.......60.00
Dog, sitting, wearing muzzle, bisque, wht/br, 3x4½".........85.00
Dogs, shaggy, wht glaze, sunburst mk, 4½", pr.............125.00

Figurine, dancing boy and girl, marked with the die stamp, 12½", $550.00.

Duck, wht, yel ft/bill, on 5" base, 6½"....................225.00
Dutch girl, holding wht pail, lav/peach/gr, 7x2¾"..........175.00
Girl, dancing, holding skirt wide, 11½x6½"................250.00
Girl, holding up pleated skirt, aqua/wht dress, 8".........85.00
Girl, in gown & night cap, 9"............................295.00
Girl, w/tambourine, sgn, 14½"...........................265.00
Inkwell, sailing ship relief, mc, sgn.....................45.00
Lady, shoes in hand, holding up skirts, ruffled bonnet, 11½"...220.00
Marchioness, from Old Curiosity Shop, 7½".................85.00
Mrs Bardell, from Pickwick Papers, 7"....................85.00
Plate, jasperware Indian, full face, triple swags beading, 6½"...125.00
Vase, emb Dutch girl, rising sun mk, 4"...................25.00
Vase, gold pebbled top, pk/lav flowers, bl border, sgn, 9½"....195.00
Vase, mermaid protrudes from top, 10"....................350.00
Vase, pate sur pate, celadon w/lav lady, gold trim, hdls, 4½"...175.00
Vase, pate sur pate, gourd shape, celadon w/lav putti, 3½"....140.00

Hobbs and Brockunier

Hobbs and Brockunier's South Wheeling Glass Works was in operation during the last quarter of the 19th century. They are most famous for their peachblow, amberina, Daisy and Button, and Hobnail pattern glass. The mainstay of the operation, however, was druggist items and plain glassware -- bowls, mugs, and simple footed pitchers with shell handles.
See also Francisware

Bowl, berry; Hobnail, vaseline opal, sq...................100.00
Celery vase, Hobnail, vaseline opal......................45.00
Creamer, Hobnail, cased canary, miniature, rare...........195.00
Cruet, Hobnail, opal.....................................115.00
Lamp, stand; wht opal snowflake, clear base, 8"..........165.00
Tankard, Poinsettia, vaseline opal, 13¼".................250.00
Tumbler, Hobnail, rubena verde, M........................160.00
Vase, Hobnail, rubena verde, 6½", M......................275.00

Hobnail

Barber bottle, blue, 4 rows of rings on neck.............110.00
Barber bottle, blue opal................................135.00

Bowl, blue opal, 9"......................................30.00
Bowl, ruffled, lt blue...................................18.00
Compote, clear, 9x9"....................................50.00
Creamer, ball ft, clear..................................25.00
Goblet, clear to opal....................................25.00
Juice set, squat pitcher, 6 tumblers, clear opal..........95.00
Pitcher, frosted, ruffled top, 7¾"......................45.00
Pitcher, frosted pk, bulbous w/sq mouth, frosted hdl, 7"...245.00
Pitcher, sq mouth, bulbous, rebena verde opal, 8x7".......295.00
Plate, ruffled, clear, 5"................................9.00
Rose bowl, vaseline opal.................................45.00
Tray, water; clear.......................................22.00
Tumbler, clear to opal, set of 5, old, M.................100.00
Tumbler, cranberry opal..................................110.00
Tumbler, milk glass......................................12.00
Tumbler, ruby stained....................................37.00
Tumbler, 10 row hobs, rubena.............................110.00
Vase, blue opal, 3½".....................................9.00
Vase, blue opal, 8"......................................16.00
Vase, flared, lt blue opal...............................18.00

Homer Laughlin

The Homer Laughlin China Company of Newell, West Virginia, was founded in 1871. The superior dinnerware they displayed at the Centennial Exposition in Philadelphia in 1876 won the highest award of excellence. From that time to the present, they have continued to produce quality dinnerware and kitchenware, many lines of which are becoming very popular collectibles. Their most famous pattern, Fiesta, is included in a separate section.

Most of the dinnerware is marked with the name of the pattern, and occasionally with the shape name as well. The 'HLC' trademark is usually followed by a number series, the first two digits of which indicate the year of its manufacture.

See also Fiesta; Harlequin; Riviera

Amberstone, cup & saucer.................................6.50
Amberstone, plate, bread & butter........................2.50
Amberstone, plate, dinner................................4.00
American Potter, plate, Artist, turq.....................18.00
American Provincial, bowl, cereal; 5½"...................3.00
American Provincial, bowl, 6¼"...........................3.00

Bowl, signed Laughlin Art China, grape transfer with gold trim, 11" dia, $90.00.

American Provincial, creamer...............................4.00
American Provincial, cup & saucer..........................3.50
American Provincial, plate, 7¼".............................2.00
American Provincial, sugar w/lid...........................5.00
Currier & Ives, plate, red, 7¼".............................1.50
Dogwood, cup & saucer, demitasse.........................10.00
Epicure, coffee pot, 10"..................................25.00
Epicure, cup & saucer......................................6.50
Epicure, gravy bowl, 7½"...................................9.00
Epicure, ladle, 5½".......................................11.00
Epicure, nappy, 8¾x3"......................................6.00
Epicure, plate, 10"..5.00
George & Martha Washington, bowl, soup.....................3.50
George & Martha Washington, creamer........................3.00
George & Martha Washington, cup & saucer...................3.00
George & Martha Washington, plate, 9"......................2.00
Hacienda, bowl, vegetable; 9"..............................8.00
Hacienda, cup & saucer.....................................8.00
Hacienda, deep plate, 8"...................................5.50
Hacienda, oatmeal, 6"......................................5.50
Hacienda, plate, 9"..4.00
Hacienda, platter w/oval well, 13½".......................10.00
Hacienda, sauce boat.......................................8.00
Jubilee, plate, 1954 calendar..............................8.00
King Charles, casserole w/lid, round......................13.00
King Charles, gravy boat...................................5.00
Mexicana, bowl, oval vegetable; 9".........................8.00
Mexicana, casserole w/lid, 8½"............................27.00
Mexicana, egg cup...10.00
Mexicana, lug soup, 4½"....................................8.00
Mexicana, plate, 9"..4.00
Mexicana, platter, 11".....................................6.00
Mexicana, teacup & saucer..................................7.50
Organdy, demitasse set, 4: cups/saucers/plates, cr/sug, pastel.....75.00
Priscilla, bowl, fruit; 5".................................3.00
Priscilla, bowl, soup; 8"..................................6.00
Priscilla, cake plate, Kitchen Kraft, 10".................15.00
Priscilla, casserole w/cover, Kitchen Kraft, 8½"..........17.00
Priscilla, cup & saucer, demitasse........................10.00
Priscilla, jug, open, Kitchen Kraft, 5½"..................18.00
Priscilla, pickle dish, 9¼"................................8.00
Priscilla, pie plate, Kitchen Kraft, 10"..................15.00
Priscilla, platter, 13¾"...................................8.00
Rhythm, footed cereal/chowder, 5½".........................3.50
Rhythm, plate, 10"...7.00
Rhythm, platter, 13½".....................................11.00
Rhythm, salt & pepper shakers, pr..........................5.00
Rhythm, teapot, 5½".......................................20.00
Rhythm Rose, cake plate, 10½"..............................8.00
Rhythm Rose, casserole, Kitchen Kraft, 8½"................14.00
Rhythm Rose, creamer & sugar w/lid........................10.50
Rhythm Rose, cup & saucer, demitasse.......................9.00
Rhythm Rose, Kitchen Kraft jug pitcher....................11.00
Rhythm Rose, plate, dinner; 9".............................3.50
Rhythm Rose, platter, 13"..................................6.50
Rhythm Rose, teapot.......................................22.00
Serenade, bowl, cereal.....................................2.50
Serenade, creamer..6.00
Serenade, flat soup..5.00
Serenade, open vegetable...................................6.00
Serenade, plate, bread & butter............................3.00
Serenade, plate, dessert...................................2.50
Serenade, plate, dinner....................................6.00
Serenade, saucer...1.50

Tango, creamer & sugar w/lid...............................9.00
Tango, cup & saucer..5.50
Tango, nappy, 8¾"..5.50
Tango, oval baker, 9"......................................5.50
Tango, plate, 9¼"..3.00
Teapot, wht w/Colonial lady in polychrome, 1930...........14.00
Tom & Jerry, mug...5.00
Virginia Rose, bowl, deep, 6¼".............................5.00
Virginia Rose, bowl, oval, 9¼".............................7.00
Virginia Rose, bowl, 5¼"...................................2.00
Virginia Rose, bowl, 6"....................................2.00
Virginia Rose, bowl, 8"....................................6.00
Virginia Rose, butter w/cover, ½ lb.......................35.00
Virginia Rose, cake plate, 11".............................8.00
Virginia Rose, cake server.................................7.00
Virginia Rose, casserole w/lid............................25.00
Virginia Rose, creamer.....................................5.00
Virginia Rose, cup...3.00
Virginia Rose, cup & saucer................................4.50
Virginia Rose, double egg cup..............................7.50
Virginia Rose, gravy......................................12.00
Virginia Rose, plate, 6"...................................2.00
Virginia Rose, plate, 9½"..................................4.00
Virginia Rose, platter, 11"................................8.00
Virginia Rose, shakers, pr................................25.00
Virginia Rose, sugar w/lid................................10.00
Zodiac, cup & saucer......................................35.00

Hull

The A.E. Hull Pottery was formed in 1905 in Zanesville, Ohio, and in the early years produced stoneware specialties. They expanded in 1907, adding a second plant, and employing over two hundred workers. By 1920 they were manufacturing a full line of stoneware, art pottery with both air-brushed and blended glazes, florist pots, and garden ware. They also produced toilet ware and kitchen items with a white semi-porcelain body. Although these continued to be staple products, after the stock market crash of 1929, emphasis was shifted to tile production. By the mid-thirties interest in art pottery production was growing, and over the next fifteen years, several lines of matt pastel floral decorated patterns were designed, consisting of vases, planters, baskets, ewers, and bowls in various sizes.

The Red Riding Hood cookie jar, patented in 1943, proved so successful that a whole line of figural kitchenware and novelty items were added. They continued to be produced well into the fifties.

Through the forties their floral art ware lines flooded the market, due to the restriction of foreign imports. Although best known for their pastel matt glazed ware, some of the lines were high gloss. Rosella, glossy coral on pink clay body, was produced for a short time only, and Magnolia, although offered in a matt glaze, was produced in gloss as well.

The plant was destroyed in 1950 by a flood which resulted in a devastating fire when the floodwater caused the kilns to explode. The company rebuilt and equipped their new factory with the most modern machinery. It was soon apparent that the matt glaze could not be duplicated through the more modern processes, however, and soon attention was concentrated on high gloss art ware lines such as Parchment and Pine, and Ebb Tide. Figural planters and novelties, piggy banks, and dinnerware were produced in abundance in the late fifties and sixties. By the mid-seventies dinnerware and florist ware were the mainstay of their business. The firm continues to operate.

Bank, Corky Pig, no mk, br, 5"...........................10.00
Bank, pig, emb floral, HP on wht, bow at neck, mkd USA, 14"..50.00
Basket, #56, 6¼"..20.00

Red Riding Hood butter dish, 6" x 6½", $135.00.

Basket, girl, #954, 8"..........................16.00
Basket, maroon, #71............................15.00
Basket, squirrel, #44, red/wht..................20.00
Blossomflite, basket, ruffled oval, T-8..........35.00
Blossomflite, console set, T-10 bowl, T-11 candle holders.......45.00
Blossomflite, pitcher, T-13.....................50.00
Bow Knot, basket, B-25, 6½"....................60.00
Bow Knot, console set, B-16, 13½" bowl & sticks.............90.00
Bow Knot, cornucopia, B-5, 7½"................40.00
Bow Knot, urn, B-18, 5¾".......................42.00
Bow Knot, vase, B-2, 5"........................30.00
Bow Knot, vase, B-4, 6½".......................38.00
Bow Knot, vase, B-7, 8½".......................48.00
Bow Knot, vase, B-8, 8½".......................45.00
Bow Knot, wall pitcher, B-26, 6"................40.00
Bow Knot, wall pocket, cup & saucer, B-24, 6"......40.00
Bow Knot, wall pocket, iron, no mk..............40.00
Bow Knot, wall pocket, whiskbroom, B-27, 8"......40.00
Butterfly, ash tray, heart shape, 7"............20.00
Butterfly, basket, bl lining, tri-hdl, 10½"......65.00
Butterfly, bowl, B-7, rectangular...............20.00
Butterfly, cornucopia, B-12, 10½"..............30.00
Butterfly, cornucopia, B-2, 6¼"................12.50
Butterfly, lavabo wall set, 2 pc, orig hanger......65.00
Butterfly, pitcher, bl lining, B-11.............30.00
Butterfly, pitcher, 5".........................10.00
Butterfly, vase, B-14, 3 ft, 10½"..............35.00
Calla Lily, cornucopia, #570-33, 8"............35.00
Calla Lily, vase, #501-33, 6½"................35.00
Calla Lily, vase, #510-33, 8".................45.00
Calla Lily, vase, #560-33, 10"................55.00
Calla Lily, vase, pillow; #530-33, 9x9".......85.00
Candy dish, covered, pink, #158...............16.00
Coffee server, yellow & br, #32, 11"..........24.00
Console set, wht swans: 1 large, 2 small; M......22.00
Cookie jar, Bouquet, yel/wht, mc flowers, Cinderella label.......40.00
Dancing girl, #955, 7"........................16.00
Dogwood, basket, #501, 7½"...................55.00
Dogwood, bowl, #521, 7".......................38.00
Dogwood, candle holders, #512, 3¾", pr........35.00
Dogwood, console bowl, #511, 11½"............65.00
Dogwood, cornucopia, #522, 4½"...............20.00
Dogwood, ewer, #520, 4¾".....................27.00

Dogwood, jardiniere, #514, 4".................20.00
Dogwood, pitcher, #505, 8½"...................35.00
Dogwood, vase, #503, 10½"....................40.00
Dogwood, vase, #513, 6½".....................36.00
Dogwood, vase, suspended; #502, 6½"..........45.00
Duck, bandana, gr, medium, #75...............15.00
Duck, snooty, green, lg, #69.................27.50
Early Art, flower pot, mk H, 4½"..............20.00
Early Art, jardiniere, orange tree decor, turq, 7"......35.00
Early Art, vase, brush stroke decor, #32, 8"......25.00
Early Art, vase, brush stroke decor, #40, 7"......25.00
Ebb Tide, basket, no mk, 6¼".................28.00
Ebb Tide, candle holder, E-13, 2¾", pr.......20.00
Ebb Tide, cornucopia, dbl fish & shell, 11¾"......30.00
Ebb Tide, vase, twin fish, E-2, 7"............15.00
Ebb Tide, vase, 6"...........................10.00
Granada, vase, Deco design, wht, #49, 9"......19.00
Iris, bud vase, #410, 7½"....................36.00
Iris, candle holder, #411, 5", pr............40.00
Iris, console bowl, #409, 12"................72.00
Iris, ewer, #401, 13½"......................125.00
Iris, jardiniere, #413, 5½"..................28.00
Iris, rose bowl, #412, 7"....................36.00
Iris, vase, #402, 7".........................35.00
Iris, vase, #402, 8½".......................45.00
Iris, vase, #403, 4¾".......................21.00
Iris, vase, #407, 7".........................35.00
Lavo bowl, blue spatter, orig hanger..........40.00
Leaf, low planter, #85, 13"..................15.00
Magnolia, glossy; console set, H-23 & 24, 13" bowl & sticks....38.00
Magnolia, glossy; double cornucopia, H-15, 12"......40.00
Magnolia, glossy; pitcher, H-3, 5½"..........18.00
Magnolia, glossy; vase, H-13, 10½"...........35.00
Magnolia, glossy; vase, H-2, 5½".............15.00
Magnolia, glossy; vase, H-5, 6½".............16.00
Magnolia, glossy; vase, H-6, 6½".............18.00
Magnolia, glossy; vase, H-7, 6½".............16.00
Magnolia, glossy; vase, H-8, 8½".............26.00
Magnolia, matt; console bowl, #26, 12½"......40.00
Magnolia, matt; console set, #26 & 27........65.00
Magnolia, matt; cornucopia, #19, 8½".........35.00
Magnolia, matt; creamer & sugar, #24 & 25, 3¾", pr......30.00
Magnolia, matt; double cornucopia, #6, 12"......42.00
Magnolia, matt; ewer, #18, 13½"..............90.00
Magnolia, matt; pitcher, #5, 7"..............35.00
Magnolia, matt; tea set, #23, 24 & 25, 6½", 3 pcs......85.00
Magnolia, matt; vase, #1, 8½"................33.00
Magnolia, matt; vase, #12, 6¼"..............22.00
Magnolia, matt; vase, #13, 4¾"..............14.00
Magnolia, matt; vase, #15, 6¼"..............16.00
Magnolia, matt; vase, #2, 8½"...............27.00
Magnolia, matt; vase, #3, 8½"...............27.50
Magnolia, matt; vase, #4, 6¼"...............19.00
Magnolia, matt; vase, #7, 8½"...............38.00
Magnolia, matt; vase, #8, 10½"..............44.00
Magnolia, matt; vase, #9, 10½"..............37.50
Mardi Gras, basket, #65, 8".................32.00
Mardi Gras, ewer, #66, 10"..................32.00
Mardi Gras, vase, #47, 9"...................18.50
Open Rose, basket, #107, 8".................65.00
Open Rose, cornucopia, #101, 8½"...........37.50
Open Rose, pitcher, #128, 4¾"..............25.00
Open Rose, planter, #113, 7"................35.00
Open Rose, swan, #118, 6¼".................30.00

Open Rose, vase, #102, 8½″.............................40.00
Open Rose, vase, #123, flat, 6½″....................35.00
Open Rose, vase, #130, 4¾″..........................18.00
Open Rose, vase, #131, 5″.............................20.00
Open Rose, vase, #136, 6¼″..........................32.00
Open Rose, vase, #138, 6¼″..........................30.00
Open Rose, vase, #515, 8½″..........................40.00
Orchid, candlestick, #315, pr........................40.00
Orchid, low bowl, #321, 7″............................40.00
Parchment & Pine, console set, S-9 & 10, 16″ bowl & sticks....50.00
Parchment & Pine, cornucopia, S-2, 7¾″............20.00
Parchment & Pine, planter, S-5, 10″.................25.00
Parchment & Pine, vase, 5″............................15.00
Pitcher, Alpine design, br, 5 pt.....................100.00
Planter, baby & pillow, pink w/gold trim............12.50
Planter, boat shape, maroon, #71....................15.00
Planter, daschund, br, 14″ L..........................40.00
Planter, double swans, #81............................20.00
Planter, duck, #104, 10½″.............................20.00
Planter, lamb, standing, wht, #965..................22.50
Planter, love birds, pink, #93........................16.00
Planter, madonna, wht, #417, 9½″....................20.00
Planter, madonna, yellow, #24, 7″...................16.00
Planter, parrot, #60, 9½″.............................20.00
Planter, poodle, green, #114..........................20.00
Planter, wishing well, orange/green, #101............10.00
Poppy, vase, #602, 6½″................................35.00
Poppy, vase, #611, 6¼″................................30.00
Poppy, vase, #612, 6½″................................30.00
Red Riding Hood, bank, standing....................195.00
Red Riding Hood, biscuit jar, w/decal, 8″..........135.00
Red Riding Hood, butter w/lid.......................135.00
Red Riding Hood, candy w/cover.....................150.00
Red Riding Hood, canister, coffee, w/lid............200.00
Red Riding Hood, cookie jar...........................70.00
Red Riding Hood, creamer.............................35.00
Red Riding Hood, creamer, side pour.................65.00
Red Riding Hood, marmalade.........................120.00
Red Riding Hood, mustard w/lid.....................125.00
Red Riding Hood, pitcher, milk......................100.00
Red Riding Hood, pitcher, top pour, 8″.............150.00
Red Riding Hood, planter..............................85.00
Red Riding Hood, salt & peppers, large..............30.00
Red Riding Hood, salt & peppers, small..............18.00
Red Riding Hood, sugar, flat, open skirt.............50.00
Red Riding Hood, syrup pitcher, large..............100.00
Red Riding Hood, tea caddy..........................150.00
Red Riding Hood, teapot..............................100.00
Red Riding Hood, wall pocket........................175.00
Regal, flamingo vase, #309, 8¾″......................17.50
Rosella, ewer, R-11, 7″................................35.00
Rosella, pitcher, R-9, 6½″.............................30.00
Rosella, vase, R-1, 5″.................................15.00
Rosella, vase, R-14, 8½″..............................40.00
Rosella, vase, R-5, 6¼″...............................30.00
Rosella, vase, R-7, 6¼″...............................30.00
Rosella, wall pocket, R-10, 6¼″......................35.00
Serenade, basket, S-14................................65.00
Serenade, covered casserole, blue....................35.00
Serenade, fruit bowl, blue, S-15......................25.00
Serenade, hat vase, S-4...............................25.00
Serenade, pitcher, S-21...............................40.00
Serenade, vase, S-1, 6″...............................18.00
Serenade, vase, S-11, gold trim......................50.00

Sunglow, basket, #84, 6½″............................17.50
Sunglow, wali pitcher, #81, 5½″......................20.00
Sunglow, wall pocket, iron............................30.00
Sunglow, wall pocket, whiskbroom...................20.00
Thistle, vase, #51, 6½″................................24.00
Thistle, vase, #52, 6½″................................24.00
Thistle, vase, #53, 6½″................................24.00
Tokay, basket, #6, 8″.................................25.00
Tokay, basket, lg moon shape.........................35.00
Tokay, candy on stem, covered, 8½″..................25.00
Tokay, cornucopia, 10″................................25.00
Tokay, leaf dish, #19, 13″.............................15.00
Tokay, urn, #5, 5½″...................................10.00
Tulip, basket, #102-33, 6″............................57.50
Tulip, bud vase, 6″...................................30.00
Tulip, jardiniere, #117-30, 5″.........................30.00
Tulip, pitcher, #109, 8″...............................40.00
Tulip, vase, #100-33, 6″..............................30.00
Tulip, vase, #101-33, 9″..............................45.00
Tulip, vase, #105-33, 8″..............................40.00
Tulip, vase, #107-33, 6″..............................32.50
Tulip, vase, #108-33, 6″..............................32.00
Tulip, vase, #111-33, 6″..............................30.00
Vase, #108, 8″..16.00

Bow Knot vase, B7-8½″, $40.00.

Vase, deer decor, wht w/red, #50, 10″...............20.00
Vase, double, orange, #103............................22.00
Vase, Mardi Gras/Granada design, wht, ribbed, USA, #218-9.....20.00
Vase, peacock, #73, 10½″.............................19.00
Wall pocket, goose, gold trim........................25.00
Wall pocket, mandolin, #84, 7″.......................20.00
Wall pocket, picture frame, oval, #611, 8½″..........22.00
Wall pocket, ribbon-tied package, #71, 6″............20.00
Wall pocket, stylized leaf w/berry, #112, 10½″.......18.00
Wall pocket, violin, #85, 7″..........................20.00
Water Lily, console bowl, L-21, 13½″.................65.00
Water Lily, cornucopia, L-7, w/label, 6½″............35.00
Water Lily, cornucopia, L-7, 6½″.....................28.50
Water Lily, ewer, L-3, 5½″............................28.00
Water Lily, jardiniere, L-23, 5½″.....................27.50
Water Lily, planter w/saucer, L-25, 5½″..............50.00
Water Lily, vase, L-1, 5½″............................25.00

Water Lily, vase, L-10, 9½″ 42.50
Water Lily, vase, L-13, 10½″ 50.00
Water Lily, vase, L-2, 5½″ 25.00
Water Lily, vase, L-4, 6½″ 25.00
Water Lily, vase, L-5, 6½″ 30.00
Wildflower, basket, W-16, 10½″ 85.00
Wildflower, console bowl, W-21, 12″ 42.00
Wildflower, cornucopia, W-10, 8½″ 27.50
Wildflower, cornucopia, W-7, 7½″ 24.00
Wildflower, pitcher, W-2, 5½″ 25.00
Wildflower, vase, W-1, 5½″ 17.50
Wildflower, vase, W-12, 9½″ 40.00
Wildflower, vase, W-13, 9½″ 42.50
Wildflower, vase, W-14, 10½″ 45.00
Wildflower, vase, W-15, 10½″ 47.50
Wildflower, vase, W-4, 6½″ 30.00
Wildflower, vase, W-5, 6½″ 28.00
Wildflower, vase, W-6, 7½″ 27.50
Wildflower, vase, W-8, 7½″ 27.50
Wildflower, vase, W-9, 8½″ 35.00
Woodland, glossy; basket, W-9, 8½″ 45.00
Woodland, glossy; console bowl, W-29 .... 42.00
Woodland, glossy; cornucopia, W-2, 5½″ 19.00
Woodland, glossy; double bud vase, W-15, 8½″ 25.00
Woodland, glossy; ewer, W-3, 5½″ 16.50
Woodland, glossy; pitcher, W-6, 6½″ 30.00
Woodland, glossy; planter, W-14 .... 20.00
Woodland, glossy; teapot, W-26 .... 45.00
Woodland, glossy; urn, W-7, 5½″ 30.00
Woodland, glossy; vase, W-4, 6½″ 16.00
Woodland, glossy; wall pocket, shell shape, 7½″ 35.00
Woodland, matt; cornucopia, W-10, 11″ 28.00
Woodland, matt; cornucopia, W-5, 6½″ 20.00
Woodland, matt; ewer, 5½″ 28.00
Woodland, matt; planter, W-14, 10″ 32.00
Woodland, matt; planter, W-19, 10½″ 35.00
Woodland, matt; vase, W-18, 10½″ 55.00
Woodland, matt; wall pocket, shell shape, W-13, 7½″ ... 40.00

Hummel

Hummel figurines were created through the artistry of Berta Hummel, a Franciscan nun called Sister M. Innocentia. The first figures were made about 1935 by Franz Goebel of Goebel Art Inc., Rodental, West Germany. Plates, plaques, and candy dishes are also produced, and the older, discontinued editions are highly sought collectibles.

Generally speaking, an issue can be dated by the trademark. The first Hummels, from 1934-1950, were either incised or stamped with the Crown 'WG' mark. The full bee in 'V' mark was employed with minor variations until 1959. At that time the bee was stylized and represented by a solid disc with symetrical angled wings completely contained within the confines of the 'V'. The three-line mark, 1964-1972, utilized the stylized bee, and included a three-line arrangement, 'c by W. Goebel, W. Germany'. Another change in 1970 saw the stylized bee in 'V' suspended between the vertical bars of the 'b' and 'l' of a printed 'Goebel, West Germany'. Collectors refer to this mark as the 'last bee mark' or 'Goebel bee'. The current mark in use since 1979 omits the bee in 'V'.

Key:
FB----Full Bee   SB--------Stylized Bee
GB---Goebel Bee

Accordion Boy, #185, FB 125.00
Adoration, #23/I, SB 200.00

Ring Around the Rosie, current mark, 6¾″ x 6½″, $1,100.00.

Angel Serenade w/Lamb, #83, FB, 5½″ 270.00
Angelic Song, #144, FB, 4″ 115.00
Apple Tree Boy, #141/V, GB, 10″ 350.00
Apple Tree Boy, #142/3/0, SB, 4″ 70.00
Apple Tree Girl, #141/I, tree trunk base, FB, 6″ 175.00
Ash tray, Happy Pastime, #62, SB 90.00
Ash tray, Let's Sing, #113, SB 100.00
Ash tray, Singing Lesson, #34, SB 75.00
Auf Wiedersehen, #153/0, sm SB, 5″ 130.00
Ba-Bee-Ring, #30/0/B, mkd Germany, 5″ dia 82.00
Baker, #128, SB, 4¾″ 85.00
Band Leader, #129, GB, 5″ 60.00
Band Leader, #129, incised crown & FB 143.00
Band Leader, #129, SB, 5″ 120.00
Barnyard Hero, #195/I, GB, 5½″ 85.00
Barnyard Hero, #195/I, SB, 5½″ 180.00
Barnyard Hero, #195/2/0, 3-line, 4″ 85.00
Be Patient, #197/I, GB, 6¼″ 70.00
Be Patient, #197/2/0, 3-line, 4¼″ 85.00
Begging His Share, #9, sm SB, no hole in cake, 6″ 160.00
Begging His Share, #9., Crown mk, hole in cake, 5¾″ . 450.00
Begging His Share, #9., FB, hole in cake 350.00
Begging His Share, #9., SB, hole in cake, 6″ 250.00
Bell, 1979, w/box 15.00
Bell, 1980, w/box 28.00
Bird Duet, #169, FB 135.00
Birthday Serenade, #218/0, FB, girl w/horn, 5″ 450.00
Birthday Serenade, #218/0, GB, 5″ 85.00
Birthday Serenade, #218/2/0, 3-line, 4″ 95.00
Bookends, Bookworm, #14/A&B, SB, 5″ 300.00
Bookworm, #3/I, sm SB, 5½″ 150.00
Bookworm, #3/II, GB, 8″ 350.00
Bookworm, #8, OS, red artist mk, Crown mk, 4½″ 200.00
Bookworm, #8, sm SB, 4″ 120.00
Boots, #143/0, sm SB, 5″ 70.00
Boy w/Horse, #117, SB 45.00
Boy w/Toothache, #217, SB, 5″ 105.00
Builder, #305, 3-line, 5½″ 100.00
Busy Student, #367, 3-line, 4¼″ 95.00
Calendar, 1960s 35.00
Calendar, 1980s 20.00

Candy bowl, Chick Girl, CE old style, SB...................200.00
Celestial Musician, #188, SB, 5¾".....................130.00
Chick Girl, #57, C, incised FB, 4"......................245.00
Chick Girl, #57/I, GB, 4¼"............................70.00
Chick Girl, #57/I, sm SB, 4¼"........................140.00
Chick Girl, #57/0, incised FB, 4"......................125.00
Chick Girl, #57/0, SB, 3½"..........................100.00
Chimney Sweep, #12/I, GB, 6".........................50.00
Chimney Sweep, #12/I, sm SB, 6".....................90.00
Christ Child, #18, sm SB, 5"...........................50.00
Cinderella, #337, GB, 4¾"...........................110.00
Confidentially, #314, GB, 6"...........................65.00
Congratulations, #17/0, no socks, SB, 5"..............150.00
Coquettes, #179, SB.................................150.00
Cow, #214/K, SB, 3½"................................45.00
Culprits, #56., decimal #, eyes open, hollow, Crown mk......375.00
Culprits, #56/A, SB, 6¼"............................150.00
Doctor, #127, SB, 5"................................100.00
Doll Bath, #319, 3-line, 5".........................110.00
Doll Mother, #67, SB...............................110.00
Donkey, #214/J, SB, 5"..............................45.00
Duet, #130, FB, 5".................................160.00
Duet, #130, GB, 5"..................................70.00
Duet, #130, SB, 5".................................100.00
Duet, #130., decimal #, notes ea side, Crown mk, 5".......375.00
Farewell, #65, GB, 4¾"..............................75.00
Farewell, #65/I, sm SB, 4¾".........................125.00
Farewell, #65/I, Western Germany, SB, 4¾"............155.00
Farm Boy, #66, SB, 5"..............................145.00
Farm Boy, #66, sm SB, 5"...........................120.00
Farm Boy, #66., FB, 5¼"............................200.00
Favorite Pet, #361, 3-line, 4¾".....................120.00
Feeding Time, #199/I, old style, SB..................150.00
Festival Harmony, #173/0, w/flute, GB, 8".............80.00
Festival Harmony, #173/0, w/flute, 3-line, 8".........150.00
Flower Madonna, #10/I, white, sm SB, 8"..............100.00
Flower Madonna, #101/I, color, FB, 9¾"..............195.00
Flower Vendor, #381, GB, 5"..........................65.00
Flying Angel, #366, 3-line, 3½".......................75.00
Font, Angel Cloud, #206, old style, c Goebel..........250.00
Font, Angelic Prayer, #75, sm SB......................30.00
Font, Worship, #164, SB, 4"...........................40.00
For Father, #87, GB, 5"...............................55.00
For Mother, #257, 3-line..............................65.00
Friends, #136/I, 3-line...............................85.00
Girl w/Fir Tree, #116, SB.............................45.00
Girl w/Nosegay, #115, FB.............................50.00
Globe Trotter, #79, basket yellow inside, FB..........180.00
Going to Grandma's, #52/0, SB.......................130.00
Good Friends, #182, old style, Crown mk, 4¼".........160.00
Good Friends, #182, old style, sm SB, 4".............95.00
Good Hunting, #307, 3-line..........................100.00
Good Shepherd, #42/0, FB...........................130.00
Goose Girl, #47/3/0, sm SB, 4".......................95.00
Happiness, #86, SB..................................80.00
Happy Birthday, #176, US Zone Germany, 5¾"..........600.00
Happy Days, #150/I, GB, 6¼".........................150.00
Happy Days, #150/0, GB, 5¼"..........................85.00
Happy Pastime, #69, SB, 3½".........................100.00
Happy Traveler, #109/0, SB...........................90.00
Hear Ye, Hear Ye, #15/I, brown mittens, Crown mk, 6½"......200.00
Hear Ye, Hear Ye, #15/I, GB, 7"......................65.00
Hear Ye, Hear Ye, #15/I, sm SB, 6"..................145.00
Hear Ye, Hear Ye, #15/II, GB, 7"....................135.00

Hear Ye, Hear Ye, #15/II, sm SB, 7".................165.00
Hear Ye, Hear Ye, #15/0, sm SB, 5"...................95.00
Heavenly Angel, #21/0/1/2, GB, 6½"...................50.00
Hello, #124/0, GB, 6¼"................................50.00
Hello, #124/0, green pants, SB, 6"...................100.00
Home From Market, #198, plain number, Crown mk, 6"......200.00
Home From Market, #198/2/0, 3-line, 4"................50.00
Infant, #214/A, SB, 1½"...............................40.00
Joseph, #214/B, in color, 3-line, 7".................85.00
Joseph, #214/B, SB, in color, 7"....................125.00
Joseph, #214/B, white, 3-line, 7"....................65.00
Joyful, #53, sm SB, 3"................................50.00
Just Resting, #122/3/0, SB, 4".......................85.00
King, kneeling, #214/M, SB, 5½"......................125.00
King, kneeling, #214/N, SB, 4".......................125.00
King, standing, #214/L, SB, 8".......................125.00
Kiss Me, #311, w/socks, SB, 6"......................360.00
Knitting Lesson, #256, GB, 7½".......................65.00
Lamb, #214/0, SB, 2"..................................20.00
Lamp, Culprits, #44/A, Crown mk, 9½".................195.00
Lamp, Out of Danger, #44/B, Crown mk, 9½"............195.00
Latest News, #184, sq base, Munchner Press, SB........250.00
Lets Sing, #110/I, GB, 4"............................50.00
Letter To Santa, #340, 3-line, 7"...................325.00
Little Bookkeeper, #306, 3-line, 5".................125.00
Little Cellist, #89/I, eyes open, gr staff, Crown mk, 6"......195.00
Little Drummer, #240, 3-line.........................55.00
Little Fiddler, #2/I, GB, 7".........................125.00
Little Fiddler, #2/I, sm SB, 7½".....................175.00
Little Fiddler, #4, sm SB, 5".........................65.00
Little Gabriel, #32/0, SB, 5½"........................65.00
Little Gardener, #74, raised flower oval base, SB, 4½"......125.00
Little Goat Herder, #200/0, SB, 4½".................100.00
Little Guardian, #145, SB, 4".........................75.00
Little Helper, #73, SB, 4"............................65.00
Little Hiker, #16/I, sm SB, 6"........................90.00
Little Pharmacist, #322, Rizinusol, GB, 6"............75.00
Little Pharmacist, #322, Vitamins, 3-line, 6".........115.00
Little Shopper, #96, sm SB, 4¼".......................50.00
Little Tailor, #308, GB, 5"...........................80.00
Lost Sheep, #68/2/0, 3-line, 4"......................50.00
Lullaby, #24/I, GB, 4"................................55.00
Madonna, #45/I, color, sm SB, 12"...................100.00
Madonna w/Halo, #45/I, Crown mk, 11¼"...............200.00
Mail Coach, #226, GB................................180.00
Mail Coach, #226, 3-line............................290.00
March Winds, #43, GB, 5".............................40.00
Max & Moritz, #123, FB..............................175.00
Meditation, #13/II, GB, 7"..........................125.00
Meditation, #13/0, GB, 5"............................50.00
Meditation, #13/0, SB, 5"............................95.00
Merry Wanderer, #11/0, 5 buttons, sm SB, 4¾".........100.00
Merry Wanderer, #7/II, GB, 9½".......................340.00
Mother's Darling, #175, sm SB.......................120.00
Mother's Helper, #133, FB, 5".......................165.00
Mountaineer, #315, GB, 5"............................65.00
Not For You, #317, 3-line.............................95.00
On Secret Path, #386, GB, 5".........................75.00
Out of Danger, #65B, SB.............................124.00
Photographer, #178, FB, 5"..........................165.00
Photographer, #178, SB, 5"..........................150.00
Plaque, Madonna, #48/V, Crown mk, rare.............1,200.00
Plaque, Mail Coach, #140, sm SB.....................110.00
Plaque, Merry Christmas, #323, GB....................40.00

Plaque, Quartet, #134, sm SB..........................200.00
Plaque, Retreat to Safety, #126, sm SB.................135.00
Plaque, Vacation Time, #125, 6 posts, Crown mk...........350.00
Playmates, #58/0, Crown mk, 4"........................125.00
Playmates, #58/0, sm SB, 4"............................75.00
Postman, #119, Crown mk, 5"...........................200.00
Prayer Before Battle, #20, SB.........................140.00
Puppy Love, #1, SB...................................120.00
Retreat To Safety, #201/I, 3-line, 5½"................145.00
Retreat To Safety, #201/2/0, SB, 4"....................80.00
Ring Around the Rosie, #348, 3-line, Oeslau, 7".......1,300.00
School Boy, #82/II, GB, 7"............................115.00
School Boy, #82/2/0, SB, 4"............................75.00
School Boys, #170, SB, 10"..........................1,600.00
School Girl, #81/2/0, pink blouse, SB, 4"..............75.00
Sensitive Hunter, #6/0, orange rabbit, GB, 5"..........50.00
Sensitive Hunter, #6/0, parallel straps, SB...........150.00
Serenade, #85/II, Crown mk, 7¾"......................550.00
Serenade, #85/II, GB, 7".............................115.00
Serenade, #85/II, sm SB, 6¾".........................130.00
Serenade, #85/0, sm SB, 4¾"...........................60.00
She Loves Me, She Loves Me Not, #174, eyes open, SB, 4¼"..150.00
She Loves Me, She Loves Me Not, #174, open eyes, FB, 5"...175.00
Shepherd, #214/G, 3-line, 4¾".........................70.00
Signs of Spring, #203, Crown mk, 5¼".................300.00
Signs of Spring, #203, FB, 5¼".......................300.00
Signs of Spring, #203/2/0, 3-line, 4".................75.00
Singing Lesson, #63, sm SB, 3".........................80.00
Sister, #98, Crown mk.................................99.00
Sister, #98, FB......................................99.00
Skier, #59, wooden poles, Crown mk, 5¾"..............200.00
Soloist, #135, Crown mk, 5"..........................110.00
Soloist, #135, FB, 5"................................110.00
Soloist, #135, sm SB, 5"..............................85.00
Spring Cheer, #72, GB, 5".............................35.00
Spring Cheer, #72, gr dress, sm SB....................95.00
Spring Cheer, #72, no flowers right hand/yellow dress, SB, 5"..150.00
Stitch in Time, #255, 3-line, 7".....................100.00
Stormy Weather, #71, SB, 6½".........................300.00
Stormy Weather, #71, split base, Crown mk, 6½".......425.00
Stormy Weather, #71, split base, FB, 6½".............425.00
Street Singer, #131, GB, 5"...........................45.00
Surprise, #94/3/0, SB.................................80.00
Sweet Music, #186, GB, 5½"............................55.00
Sweet Music, #186, sm SB, 5"..........................85.00
Telling Her Secret, #196/0, GB, 5"....................85.00
To Market, #49/0, GB, 5"..............................80.00
To Market, #49/0, sm SB, 5"...........................85.00
To Market, #49/3/0, sm SB, 4".........................65.00
Trumpet Boy, #97, FB................................125.00
Umbrella Boy, #152/II, sm SB, 8".....................525.00
Umbrella Girl, #152, SB, 8"..........................625.00
Village Boy, #51/I, GB, 7"............................65.00
Village Boy, #51/2/0, 3-line, 5"......................50.00
Village Boy, #51/3/0, sm SB, 4".......................45.00
Visiting An Invalid, #382, GB, 5".....................65.00
Volunteers, #50/0, GB, 6".............................80.00
Volunteers, #50/0, SB, 5½"...........................200.00
Volunteers, #50/2/0, sm SB, 5"........................85.00
Waiter, #154., decimal #, grey outfit, US Zone Crown mk, rare.850.00
Waiter, #154/0, FB, 5"...............................130.00
Wayside Devotion, #28/2, Arabic 2, FB, 7½"...........400.00
Wayside Devotion, #28/2, Arabic 2, SB, 6¼"...........230.00
We Congratulate, #220, SB, 4".........................95.00

Whitsuntide, #163., yellow candle, FB................600.00
Worship, #84/0, SB, 5"................................95.00

Hutschenreuther

Sources do not agree as to when the Carl Hutschenreuther factory was initially established in the Bavarian district of Germany. Most indicate a year near the middle of the 19th century. Carl's sons, Christian and Lorenz, later formed their own companies and operated independently until 1969. At that time Carl and Lorenz merged, and that firm is still in business today, producing limited edition plates, figurines, dinnerware, and other fine china.

Figurine, boy & girl dancing, sgn Tutter................265.00
Figurine, cherub standing on gold ball, plays horn, 4".....50.00
Figurine, kneeling lady, Deco, wht, sgn K Tuttle, #1814......225.00
Figurine, on sq tray, Pan playing flute on corner, Tutter, 5"...125.00
Figurine, polar bear, walking, 5x10¼".................195.00
Figurine, sparrow on branch, sgn K tutter, 6½".........120.00
Plate, Geo Washington; Martha Washington, 6", matched pr....75.00
Plate, HP forals, 24k border on floral loop design, 12"....40.00

Figural group, Three Stallions, 16" x 24", $500.00.

Imari

Imari is a generic term which covers a broad family of wares. It was made in more than a dozen Japanese villages, but the name is that of the port from whence it was shipped to Europe. There are several types of Imari. The most common features a design with panels of birds, florals, or people, surrounding a central basket of flowers. The colors used in this type are underglaze blue, with overglaze red, gold, and green enamels. The Chinese also made Imari wares, which differ from the Japanese type in several ways -- the absence of spur marks, a thinner type body, and a more consistent control of the blue. Imari type wares were copied on the continent by Meissen; and by English potters, among them Worcester, Derby, and Bow.

Bowl, bl/wht prunus on brick red, scalloped, shallow, 8½"......75.00
Bowl, blue & wht, good detail, shallow, 12" dia.............165.00
Bowl, figures in fields w/huts/trees, 1850s, 6" dia.........170.00
Bowl, floral/bird reserves in mc, 3½x8¾"..................125.00
Bowl, fluted, 3-color, 10"................................135.00
Bowl, gold/orange, Japanese, 1800s, 12"..................550.00
Bowl, good details, 3-color, 7½"..........................85.00
Bowl, hexagonal, 9" dia..................................400.00

Platter, 18½" long, $1,550.00.

Bowl, landscape medallion, bird/foliage/florals, 14"	175.00
Bowl, mc w/ornate scenic gold panels, scallop, 5¼" dia	48.00
Bowl, mc/gold, scallops/ribbed, scenic/brocade panels, 6" dia	65.00
Bowl, petal shape/scallops, alternate panels/florals, mc, 5¾"	50.00
Bowl, petal shape/scallops, stylize floral panels, shallow, 7"	45.00
Bowl, samurai helmet form w/kirin relief, w/lid, 1800s, 7½"	125.00
Bowl, scalloped, melon shape, panels w/decor, 4x9½"	145.00
Bowl, scenic & stork panels, brocade, mc/gold, shallow, 7" dia	65.00
Bowl, ship decor, Japanese, 1800s, 7¼" dia	175.00
Bowl, simple bl iris, red butterfly, gr/gold, shallow, 6½"	38.00
Bowl, 6 lobes, trees/flowers, Fuku mk on base, 1800, set of 10	250.00
Bowl w/lid, rice; mc figures, scenes, simple	38.00
Charger, birds/flowers/etc, EX detail, mc, 14"	325.00
Charger, bonsai medallion/dragon & scroll band, 1700s, 18"	600.00
Charger, gilt/iron red/cobalt, 18"	350.00
Charger, vignettes w/floral/branches, bl/wht, late 1800s, 22"	450.00
Charger, 4 vignettes w/scenes, centering palmette, 1800s, 18"	400.00
Cup & saucer, mc fancy florals, heavy gold, scalloped	45.00
Dish, fish shape, blue & wht, fish scale details, 1860s, 10"	190.00
Hibachi, bl/wht, 1800s, 10¾x15"	485.00
Jar, domed lid w/figure, reserve w/building, 37", G	1,100.00
Jardiniere, exotic birds in foliage, bl/wht, 10x12"	175.00
Plate, early 1800s, 8½"	100.00
Plate, flowering tree/birds/swan; cobalt, iron red, 9¾"	75.00
Plate, late, 8"	32.00
Plate, late, 8½"	38.00
Plate, scalloped, floral spray center/radiating panels, 11"	100.00
Platter, 3-color, with flowers, etc, old, oval, 11x14"	150.00
Punch bowl, vignettes w/men/birds w/in & w/out, 18" dia	275.00
Rice carrier, floral decor, 4-tier cylinder, blue/wht, 9"	90.00
Saki bottle, scalloped ft, scenic decor, blue/wht, 5½"	25.00
Saucer, demitasse; 3 chickens in center design	34.00
Sweetmeat, lid & base w/foliage/bats/birds, 6 parts, 7"	40.00
Vase, bird in reserves, mid 19th C, 11½", pr	450.00
Vase, phoenix/prunis motif, 1800s, 7½"	200.00

Imperial Glass

Although the Imperial Glass Company was organized in 1901, it was not until three years later that they began to manufacture glassware. Their early products were jelly glasses, hotel tumblers, etc., but by 1910 they were making a name for themselves by pressing quantities of Carnival Glass, the iridescent colored glassware that was popular during that time. From 1916 to 1920, they used the lustre process to make a line they called Imperial Jewels, now referred to as stretch glass. Opalescent glassware was introduced in the thirties and was made in Sea Foam, Harding Blue, Moss Green, and Burnt Almond. In contrast to these colored lines, Candlewick was a simple pattern in crystal glass, yet one for which the company is best known. All of these types are listed in specific sections of the book.

Free-Hand Ware, art glass made entirely by hand using no molds, was made for a short time only, from about 1923 to 1928. Nu-Cut was made to imitate cut glass; it was produced in crystal as well as color and was introduced in 1914.

The company closed in 1931, but soon reorganized and reopened as the Imperial Glass Corporation. In 1940 they bought the molds and assets of the Central Glass Works of Wheeling, West Virginia; and in 1958 they purchased molds from Cambridge and Heisey. Although Imperial later used these molds to reproduce the older pieces, they marked the reissues with the 'I' superimposed over a 'G' trademark used since 1951. The company sold out to Lenox in 1973, but continues today to make hand pressed giftware items.

See also Candlewick; Carnival Glass; Opalescent Glass

Bitters Bottle, Cape Cod	25.00
Bowl, Candlewick, caramel slag, 6"	15.00
Bowl, Colonial, crystal, 6½"	3.50
Bowl, red slag, ftd, 8½"	54.00
Candle holder, Cathay Dragon, figural, #5009, pr	280.00
Candle holder, Cathay Pillow Base, #5013, pr	100.00
Candle holder, Cathay Shen, #5020, jade green, pr	45.00
Candle holder, Cathay Wedding Lamp, #5027, pr	160.00
Candle holder, saucer type; Cape Cod	10.00
Candlestick, Diamond Quilted, black, #414, pr	25.00
Candlestick, free hand, irid dk bl w/wht loopings, 11"	150.00
Candlestick, Rubigold, 8½", pr	55.00
Champagne, saucer; Cape Cod, #1602	6.50
Compote, Nu Cut, ftd, 4½"	22.50
Compote, w/pr candle holders, cupid bases, custard, 3 pc	110.00
Console set, Cathay Shen, 3 pc: pr candle bases+box+bowl	135.00
Creamer, D'Angelo, crystal	6.00
Cruet, Cape Cod, pointed top	25.00
Dealer sign	150.00
Decanter, Cape Cod, cobalt, w/stopper	170.00
Dish w/lid, caramel slag, dog finial, sgn	25.00
Figurine, colt, caramel slag	20.00
Figurine, elephant, caramel slag	28.00
Figurine, mallard, wings up, caramel slag	20.00
Figurine, Sparky, caramel	20.00
Figurine, wood chuck, caramel slag	22.00
Figurine, wood duck, caramel slag	28.00
Goblet, water; Cape Cod, ball stem, crystal	9.00
Goblet, water; Cape Cod, red, #160	15.00
Jar w/lid, owl, caramel slag	30.00
Juice, ftd, Cape Cod, ball stem	7.50
Mayonnaise set, Cape Cod, 3 pc	18.00
Paperweight, w/logo	145.00
Plate, Cape Cod, 6"	3.50
Plate, Cape Cod, 8"	6.00
Plate, Diamond Quilted, blue, 8"	9.00
Relish, Cape Cod, 3 part	18.00
Relish, Cape Cod, 6 part w/covered marmalade & spoon, 11½"	55.00
Shakers, Huckabee, crystal, pr	12.00
Sherbet, Cape Cod, ball stem, tall	6.00
Sherbet, Diamond Quilted, blue	10.00
Sherbet, Diamond Quilted, pink	5.00

Sugar, Daisy J, green.....................................5.00
Swan, gr slag, open, lg...............................40.00
Swan, open neck, milk glass...........................20.00
Tankard, Heavy Diamond, crystal, pint...................12.00
Toothpick holder, caramel slag, 2 hdld................10.00
Tumbler, hobstar bottom, wide silver rim, dia cut border, 4½"..30.00
Vase, bl irid w/wht vines & leaf, 6".....................185.00
Vase, free hand, bl leaves & vines on clear, 10"..........150.00
Vase, free hand, cobalt w/lt bl pull-up, 10"..............200.00
Vase, free hand, flat rim, 3 knob body, irid bl loopings, 10"...120.00
Vase, free hand, marbleized cobalt/lt bl, irid orange w/in, 8"...125.00
Vase, free hand, tan w/wht loops, orange irid w/in, 11½".....225.00
Vase, King Tut decor, gr on opal w/gold interior, 9".........210.00
Vase, Nuart, irid cylinder w/red/bl/gold hi-lites, sgn, 7"......125.00
Vase, octagonal, frosted, sgn Virginia B Evans, 7½".........125.00
Vase, 3 swans, bl carnival...............................50.00
Whiskey, Cape Cod, cobalt...............................22.50
Whiskey, Cape Cod, crystal...............................20.00

Imperial Porcelain

The Blue Ridge Mountain Boys were created by cartoonist Paul Webb and translated into three dimension by the Imperial Porcelain Corporation of Zanesville, Ohio in 1947. These figurines decorated ash trays, vases, mugs, bowls, pitchers, planters, and other items. The Mountain Boys series were numbered 92 through 108, each with a different and amusing portrayal of mountain life. Imperial also produced American Folklore miniatures -- twenty-three tiny animals one inch or less in size -- and the All Capp Dogpatch series. Because of financial difficulties, the company closed in 1960.

Ash tray, hillbilly seated w/skunk, #103.....................65.00
Decanter, man in outhouse, Paul Webb.....................60.00
Figurine, cat, 1½"......................................40.00
Figurine, cow, 1¾", illus................................35.00
Figurine, elf, 1¾".....................................35.00
Figurine, hound dogs...................................30.00
Figurine, sow...30.00
Mug, Bearin' Down, sgn................................50.00
Mug, Maw hdl, Paul Webb...............................50.00
Mug, mountain boy hdl, #94, lg..........................50.00
Mug, Paw, mkd Paul Webb...............................45.00
Pitcher, #93, 1½ qt, rabbit hunting......................90.00
Planter, #104, Ma.....................................60.00
Vase, #101, Willie.....................................60.00

Bottle, Blue Ridge Mountain Boys, 7", $80.00.

Indian Tree

Indian Tree was a popular dinnerware pattern produced by various potteries since the early 1800s to recent times. Although backgrounds and borders vary, the Oriental theme is carried out with the gnarled brown branch of a pink blossomed tree. Among the manufacturers marks, you may find represented such notable firms as Coalport, S. Hancock and Sons, Soho Pottery, and John Maddock and Sons.

Bowl, bouillon; w/under plate, w/hdl.....................15.00
Bowl, ftd, Minton, 8½x11"..............................45.00
Bowl, Johnson Bros, 8" dia..............................11.00
Bowl, vegetable; Davison & Son, 10" oval..................35.00
Bowl, vegetable; Maddock, 9¾" oval.......................35.00
Bowl, vegetable; w/lid, oval, Nippon Noritake..............35.00
Creamer, Maddock, 3"..................................20.00
Creamer & sugar, covered, crown & wreath, Staffordshire.......22.00
Cup, demitasse; Coalport...............................22.50
Cup, Johnson Bros......................................7.50
Cup, Spode...20.00
Cup & saucer, demitasse; John Maddock Sons, Ltd.............22.50
Cup & saucer, demitasse; Nippon Noritake.................15.00
Cup & saucer, demitasse; Spode.........................27.00
Egg cup, Maddock, 4"...................................20.00
Gravy boat w/lid, Brownfield & Son, ca 1856...............30.00
Pitcher, bulbous, gold trim, Davison, 8"..................25.00
Plate, bread & butter; Johnson Bros........................2.50
Plate, bread & butter; Spode.............................15.00
Plate, Burgess & Leigh, 9".............................18.50
Plate, dinner; Johnson Bros..............................9.00
Plate, Maddock, 10"...................................16.00
Plate, Maddock, 8".....................................9.00
Plate, salad; Spode....................................20.00
Platter, Hancock, 11½".................................30.00
Platter, Maddock, 11"..................................10.00
Platter, Maddock, 12½".................................15.00
Platter, Maddock, 15"..................................20.00
Platter, Maddock, 16½".................................25.00
Platter, Nippon Noritake, 18"............................90.00
Soup, Johnson Bros......................................7.00
Soup, Myott..30.00
Teapot, Burgess & Leigh................................55.00
Teapot, Coalport......................................45.00
Teapot, creamer & sugar w/lid, Myott, M...................95.00

Inkwells

Ink, the fluid form as we know it today, was not developed until 1836. The inkwell was a natural follow-up. They were made in many materials -- glass the most common since it was non-porous and stain resistant. Pewter, silver, brass, and even gold was used, depending on the station and financial status of the owner. During the Victorian era, inkwells became more elaborate -- some had two wells, others trays and pen holders, and a few had a well or shaker for fine sand or steel powder to sift onto wet ink to blot up the excess. Cut glass inserts and ornate brass frames were popular.

With the development of the fountain pen, the inkwell's usefullness began to decline.

Abalone, hinged lid....................................20.00
Agate, red veined, beveled, hinged top, 2" sq..............95.00
Aladdin lamp shape, ornate, porcelain, Limoges.............50.00
Amber, beveled & cut, hinged, 4"........................175.00
Amethyst, sq, pewter star lid, 1840s.....................70.00

Barrel, exotic wood, glass insert...........................20.00
Benedictine liquor bottle, bronze patina, glass insert, 3".......45.00
Black boy's face, hat lifts, bronze patina on metal, 6x3"......225.00
Blk crystal, faceted lid, HP bees/butterflies in mc, sgn, 2½"...165.00
Blown, olive gr, 3 mold, 1½x2½"............................85.00
Bottle, 12 sides, aqua, flanged collar, Harrison's Columbia......45.00
Bottle, 12 sides, green, 'Ink', rough pontil, 2"...............16.00
Boy sleeping, br Rockingham glaze.........................245.00
Brass, bell form, lid removes, 3" dia.......................60.00
Bulldog, figural, silverplate..............................165.00
Camel, kneeling figural, br pnt metal, 9x6"..................85.00
Capitol Bldg, Washington DC, SP w/milk glass insert..........30.00
Champleve, w/3" attached saucer, glass insert...............335.00
China, dbl wells in tray, loose lids, dk bl w/red/wht, crown E...135.00
Clear glass, gutta percha insert, Sengbusch Self-Closing.......32.50
Cloisonne, dk bl w/mc designs.............................225.00
Compass on lid, applied figures, 6 sides, Chinese brass, 3"......40.00
Copper, hinged lid, 3½" dia...............................45.00
Counting House type, pewter, 3¼" dia......................85.00
Crab, figural, bronze, Art Deco, lg.........................55.00
Cranberry irid, brass hinged lid, artist sgn/dtd, 4½x4½".......265.00
Crystal, hexagonal, pewter top w/diapered design, 3½" dia......95.00
Crystal, sq w/faceted hinged glass lid, EX..................125.00
Cut glass, block, deep azure blue..........................140.00
Cut glass, dbl well, w/pyramid thermometer, blk base, 5½" L....55.00
Cut glass, hinged lid, 1¾" sq.............................45.00
Cut glass, sapphire bl block design, faceted top, 2½" sq......100.00
Cut glass, SP collar, cut top..............................75.00
Cut glass, star motif, w/sterling monogrammed hinged lid, 2⅛".135.00
Cut glass, 8 sides, pyramid top, 2½x3½"....................45.00
Double, crossed guns, bow & arrow, hinged glass bottles.......50.00
Double, w/3 Dutch children figures between wells, bronze......325.00
Eagle ftd, Nouveau style, cast brass........................35.00
Flint glass, clover design, pressed base, cut top, 4x2½" sq......45.00
French silver, retailed by Cartier, pierced gallery, dbl, 9"......660.00
Funnel type, br glaze over yellow clay.......................45.00
Glass w/brass hinged top & base, 3" dia.....................20.00
Globe Insurance, figural, 1923.............................35.00
Gold wash/brass w/cranberry wells, stamp box, cupid finial, 8"..225.00
Gremlin, CI, frog on hat, pnt G............................40.00
Horse's hoof, br glaze w/gold trim, McIntyre................135.00
Horseshoe, iron, 5¼".....................................40.00
Indian head, brass, sgn w/B/squiggle.......................575.00
Intaglio fish among reeds, rippling water; fancy Gorham lid...1,200.00
Jacobus, emerald gr glass w/clear glass dome................45.00
Kettle, cobalt, 8 sides, orig brass cap, collar spout, 2".......255.00
Lapis Lazuli, beveled, hinged Lapis top, 1½" sq..............75.00
Leather, travel well, oval.................................38.00
Lion's head, Bennington type br glaze.......................95.00
Loetz type, Art Nouveau, purple w/gold irid.................225.00
Mauchline, cup & saucer shape, wood w/village scene transfer...70.00
Mephistopheles, bronze figural, face is cover, 6"............85.00
Metal, knight w/shield & swords on hinged lid, 2½x4".........75.00
Millers emb, clear domed glass, brass pen holder, 4½" dia......40.00
Mountain goat head, blk horns, china well, German wht metal..60.00
Opaque blue, deep ribs, silver hinged lid, 2½" dia............95.00
Overshot, hinged mushroom lid, Sandwich, 4½x4"...........145.00
Owl figural, SP, glass insert, feather detail/glass eyes, 10¼"...140.00
Pairpoint, controlled bubbles, sterling lid, 2½" dia..........225.00
Petra Dura, glass insert, hexagonal, unusual, 4¼".............350.00
Pewter, 5 quill holders around saucer base, 3½x4¾"..........150.00
Pressed glass, bakelite cover, Sengbusch pat 1907............25.00
Redware, shoe figural, 2 holes, br glaze.....................95.00
Reindeer & sleigh, brass/copper, 6x11"....................135.00

Sapphire bl glass, hinged, 3¾"............................150.00
Sheffield, pad ft, beaded trim, crystal wells w/SP top, 7" L.....95.00
Shepherdess w/lambs reclines on ledge, bronze, C Korschann..550.00
Shoe, amber glass, w/lid..................................48.00
Silver emb metal, low flared ft, pen holders, swirl wells........60.00
Stag's head w/rack, pen wipe w/in lid, 12 sided well, mk pat...100.00
Standish, mother & child w/picture fr, Fr porcelain, 7½"......300.00
Sterling w/Celtic decor, English, ca 1930, 1¾x3½" dia........110.00
Tatums Standard, blk metal w/2 sq swirl inserts, attached lids...65.00
Tea kettle, cobalt glass, 8 sides, brass hinged spout..........235.00
Terrier head, w/in paperweight top, 3¼x2" sq................50.00
Thousand Eye, vaseline, w/orig glass lid.....................85.00
Traveling, blk leather cover, 2" dia.........................60.00
Traveling, br leather on cube, 1½" sq.......................50.00
Traveling, gutta percha, sq w/2 rnd screw lids, EX............95.00
Traveling, pewter base w/brass lid, 3" dia...................65.00
Vaseline glass on Art Nouveau stand, mk Geschutzt, Bronze...125.00
Wood, rnd w/glass inset, 2 quill holders, Silliman, 2½"........60.00
Yellowware, w/gold lustre dbl well, grape leaf tray, mk #12.....145.00

Figural lion reclines on lid, bronze, 3½" x 3½", $195.00.

Insulators

The telegraph was invented in 1844. The devices developed to hold the electrical transmission wires to the poles were called insulators. The telephone, invented in 1876, intensified their usefullness and by the turn of the century thousands of varieties were being produced in glass of various colors, pottery, and wood. Of the more than 3,000 types known to exist, today's collectors evaluate their worth by age and rarity of color. Aqua and green are the most common colors in glass, dark brown the most common in ceramic. Threadless insulators, made between 1850 and 1870, bring prices well into the hundreds.

In the listings that follow, the CD numbers are from an identification system developed in the late 1960s by N.R. Woodward. 'CD' refers to 'Consolidated Design'.

Agee, CD 121.2, purple, Australian........................15.00
AGM, CD 124.7, Australian, lt apple gr.....................10.00
Am Tel & Tel, CD 121, jade milk glass......................12.00
Armstrong #5, CD 164, crystal.............................5.00
Armstrong #51-C1, CD 167, purple.........................12.00
Armstrong #511-A, CD 272, amber..........................8.00
Armstrong DPI, CD 154, lemon yellow.......................9.00
Armstrong DPI, CD 155, smoke.............................6.00

B, CD 112, aqua 4.00

B, CD 145, emerald gr 7.00

Bar & Diamond, CD 102, royal purple 122.00

Beehive, porcelain, 2 tone caramel/yellow 10.00

Breakfield, CD 127.5, frosty aqua .7.00

Breakfield, CD 160, baby signal, aqua 5.00

Brookfield, CD 121, 7-Up green 8.00

Brookfield, CD 126, yellow-gr 7.00

Brookfield, CD 152, aqua 4.00

Brookfield, CD 157, aqua 10.00

Brookfield #41, CD 134, aqua 8.00

Brookfield #9, CD 190/191, 2 pc, ice bl 10.00

Brookfield Dauvet (Cauvet mispelled), w/3 dates, bl 13.00

Cable top, porcelain, double groove, wht 7.00

Cable top, porcelain, yellow 9.00

California, CD 121, blue 10.00

California, CD 145, purple 14.00

California, CD 152, lt gr 8.00

California, CD 152, purple 8.00

California, CD 152, smoke & straw 10.00

California, CD 161, lavender 100.00

California, CD 161, yellow-straw .30.00

California, CD 166, sage gr 12.00

California (A007), CD 121, purple 14.00

Can Pac RY, CD 143, lt lavender .12.00

Canada, CD 121, bl 7.00

Canada, CD 121, ice blue w/milky swirl 9.00

Canadian-Pacific, CD 143, sm beehive, ice bl 5.00

CCG, CD 130.7, purple, Australian 15.00

CGI Co, CD 102, smoke 7.00

Diamond, CD 190/191, 2 pc transposition, lt gr 17.00

Dominion #42, CD 154, w/drips, peach 7.00

Dwight-Pattern, CD 143, aqua 8.00

Gayner, CD 205, aqua-gr 10.00

Gayner #44, CD 154, aqua 6.00

Gayner #530, CD 205, lt aqua 8.00

Gayner #6-190, CD 162, signal, dk aqua 6.00

Gayner #90, CD 106, w/drips, lt aqua 7.00

GNW Tel Co, CD 145, w/drips, bl-aqua 9.00

H & G Co, CD 145, dk aqua 3.00

H & G Co, CD 145, jade milk glass 10.00

H & G Petticoat, CD 145, clear .12.00

H & G Petticoat, CD 151, w/drips, aqua 7.00

H & G Petticoat, CD 164, w/drips, aqua 5.00

H & G Standard, CD 133, aqua .6.00

Hawley, CD 102, aqua 9.00

Hemingray #10, CD 115, clear 3.00

Hemingray #10, CD 115, w/drips, dk aqua 5.00

Hemingray #109, CD 1070, spool, ice bl 8.00

Hemingray #19, CD 162, w/drips, ice blue 4.50

Hemingray #19, CD 162, w/drips, lt honey amber 40.00

Hemingray #20, CD 165, w/drips, clear 4.00

Hemingray #25, CD 175, bl 13.00

Hemingray #4, CD 124, w/drips, aqua 7.00

Hemingray #43, CD 213, w/drips, tall 8.00

Hemingray #43, CD 214, w/drips, gr-aqua 8.00

Hemingray #60, CD 257, w/drips, ice blue 15.00

Hemingray #60, CD 257, w/drips, Mickey Mouse type, gr tinge . . .15.00

Hemingray #670, CD 220, clear-straw 8.00

Hemingray #9, CD 106, w/drips, clear 2.00

Hemingray #9, CD 106, w/drips, jade milk glass 11.00

Hemingray #9, CD 106, w/drips, 7-Up Green 10.00

Hemingray #9, CD 107, w/drips, unusual shape, clear 3.00

Hemingray D-510, CD 168, dk aqua 7.00

Hemingray D-512, CD 230, smoky clear 5.00

Hemingray D-512, CD 230.1, extended skirt, bl-aqua 12.00

Hemingray D-990, CD 137, clear 7.00

Hemingray-Lowex, CD 219, root beer amber 11.00

Kimble #820, CD 231, smokey clear 6.00

Locke #14, CD 202, dk aqua 14.00

Locke #20 (Victor), CD 296, dk aqua 9.00

Lowex-512, CD 230, root beer amber 12.00

Lynchburg #2, CD 252, w/drips, lt aqua 11.00

Lynchburg #36, CD 162, yellow gr 10.00

Lynchburg #43, CD 145, w/drips, beehive, lt aqua 10.00

Maydwell, CD 122, w/drips, lemonade 8.00

Maydwell #14, CD 160, w/drips, straw 6.00

Maydwell #16, CD 122, w/drips, smoky 6.00

Maydwell #19, CD 162, w/drips, lemon yellow 12.00

Maydwell #19, CD 162, w/drips, lt lime-yellow 11.00

Maydwell #19, CD 162, w/drips, straw 7.00

Maydwell #20, CD 164, w/drips, lt purple 12.00

Maydwell #20, CD 164, w/drips, milk glass 10.00

Maydwell #20, CD 164, w/drips, straw-yellow 7.00

Maydwell #42, CD 154, w/drips, crystal 5.00

Maydwell #62, CD 252, w/drips, dk straw 15.00

Maydwell #62, CD 252, w/drips, EX cable, yellow-straw 14.00

McLaughlin #10, CD 115, w/drips, lt gr 5.00

McLaughlin #16, CD 121, w/drips, amber 10.00

McLaughlin #16, CD 121, w/drips, lt gr 6.00

McLaughlin #16, CD 121, w/drips, steel blue 8.00

McLaughlin #19, CD 162, Delft bl 7.00

McLaughlin #19, CD 162, w/drips, gr 6.00

McLaughlin #20, CD 164, w/drips, bright lime gr 9.00

McLaughlin #20, CE 164, w/drips, emerald gr 9.00

McLaughlin #62, CD 252, w/drips, lt aqua 10.00

McLaughlin #9, CD 106, w/drips, gr 5.00

McLaughlin #9, CD 106, w/drips, 7-Up Green 10.00

NEGM Co, CE 145, aqua 5.00

New England Tel & Tel, CD 104, aqua 6.00

New England Tel & Tel, CD 104, ice blue 6.00

No Name, CD 121, purple 12.00

No Name, CD 141, straight up, cross top, aqua 12.00

No 3 Cable, CD 254, gr 18.00

OVG Co, CD 145, lt gr 7.00

Pony, porcelain, single groove, br 3.00

Postal, CD 145, aqua 6.00

Postal Tel Co, CD 138, unusual shape, lt aqua 12.00

Purex-Sombrero, dk carnival 25.00

Pyrex, CD 128, clear 3.00

Pyrex #171, CD 320, clear 10.00

Pyrex #63, CD 234, lt yellow 8.00

Pyrex #661, CD 233, clear 5.00

Roman Helmet, porcelain, emb Thomas, terra cotta 7.00

SF, CD 102, moss gr 4.00

Star, CD 112, aqua 4.00

Star, CD 133, emerald gr 6.00

Star, CD 145, short style, gr 4.00

Star, CD 162, gr 5.00

Star, CD 164, w/drips, aqua 8.00

Sterling, CD 102, aqua 10.00

THE Co, CD 134, Pat Dec 19, 1871, bl 8.00

VMR Napoli, CD 1222, lt aqua 7.00

W Brookfield, CD 126.3, w/3 dates, lt aqua 9.00

WGM Co, CD 145, lavender, base chip 10.00

Whital Tatum #1, CD 154, extra dk purple 8.00

Whital Tatum #1, CD 154, peach 7.00

Whital Tatum #13, CD 113, clear 8.00

Whital Tatum #9, CD 109, clear..........................3.00
Whital Tatum #1, CD 154, dk smoky plum, unusual color......15.00
Whital Tatum #512-U, CD 216, amber......................7.00
Whital Tatum #9, CD 108, dk purple.....................120.00
Wm Brookfield, CD 162, name & date on dome, bl aqua.......6.00
WV 5-A, CD 126, dated, lt gr............................8.00
1678, CD 162.4, tall dome, yellow-straw...................10.00
2 Diamonds BTC-Can, CD 102, w/drips, bubbly ice bl.........10.00
2 Diamonds 2 Bars, CD 102, Canadian pony, lt lavender.......9.00

Irons

Irons come in all shapes and sizes; there are sadirons, fluting irons, and tailor's irons, to name but the most common. Hooded sadirons, patented about 1870, supposedly shielded the ironer's hand from the heat. Box irons from the late 1800s had hinged rear doors to accomodate heated slugs. Charcoal irons worked on the same principal, but removing the ashes was a nusiance! Even the gas irons of the early 20th century had drawbacks. Pressure on the tank controlled the flame. Too little meant no heat, too much could result in an accident! Denatured alcohol and boiling water were also used as heat sources. Electric irons, though invented around the turn of the century, were not used to any great extent until electricity became a commonplace commodity several decades later.

Box, brass, punch decor of flower on top, no slug, 4½x5".....110.00
Charcoal, CI, cut out designs, wood hdl, early 1900s, 7x6"......45.00
Charcoal, Vulcan head on damper, 1852....................55.00
Charcoal, w/lion's head finial...........................55.00
Child's, dtd 1893, 3¼x3½"...............................20.00
Child's, gas, all orig, 5½x7"............................75.00
Child's, Ober #1, Chadrintall SC, 2½x3½".................20.00
Coleman, gas, bl enamel, #4A, w/trivet/filler/cup/pump, in box...75.00
Easy Sad Iron, Foote Mfg, alcohol, iron w/SP, blk wood hdl....45.00
Fluting, Geneva Hand Fluter, hdl half circle & base, pat 1886...55.00
Fluting, hdld roller & corrugated base w/heater plate, pat '80....85.00
Fluting, hinged sadiron w/corrugated interior, pat 1860s........65.00
Millinery, brass flower design on stem w/wood hdl, 8" long......45.00
Monitor, gasoline powered, brass tank/wood hdl, Pat 1903, 9½".20.00
New Sensible #25, Manf'd by CI Co, Pottstown, nickel plate....20.00
Pleater, CI w/brass rollers, Star Pat Oct 19, 1875, 14" L......20.00
Sadiron, #50..17.50
Sadiron, ACW #7, CI, 6" L...............................10.00

Sadiron, cast base & hdl, then wrought together, 1800s........38.00
Sadiron, emb: Enterprise/Phila, star/Pat 1887; fluted hdl........35.00
Sadiron, forged w/forged iron hdl, 1700s, ¼" thick, 6" L......95.00
Sadiron, Mrs Pott's, EX.................................17.50
Sadiron, orig hdl replaced by smithy, 1830s, no mks..........35.00
Sadiron, small, w/open holes in hdl for cooling, #12 Ober....15.00
Sadiron, tailor's; heavy smithy twisted & forged-on hdl, 1800s...25.00
Sadiron, Turkish turned-up toe, beading on seperately cast hdl..35.00
Sadiron, wrought iron, primitive, 5½"....................18.00
Sadiron, wrought iron w/scroll hdl, 6½"..................85.00
Sadiron set, Mrs Potts, 2 sz irons/interchanging hdl, 1908......30.00
Slog, door opens to insert hot slog, wrought hdl, 1700s.......125.00
Tailor's, child's size, JC Morris Fdy Co....................28.00
Tailor's, large rectangle, smith twisted/forged-on hdl, 1810......45.00
Tailor's, rectangle w/angled front, twist/forged-on hdl, 1820s.....45.00
Tailor's, Sensible, removable hdl, 8"....................20.00

Ironstone

During the last quarter of the 18th century, English potters began experimenting with a new type of body that contained calcinated flint and a higher china clay content, intent on producing a fine durable white ware -- heavy, yet with a texture that would resemble porcelain. To remove the last trace of yellow, a minute amount of cobalt was added, often resulting in a bluish white tone. Wm. and John Turner of Caughley, and Josiah Spode II were the first to manufacture the ware successfully. Others, such as Davenport, Hicks and Meigh, and Ralph and Josiah Wedgwood, followed with their own versions. The latter coined the name 'Pearl' to refer to his product and incorporated the term into his trademark.

In 1813 a 14-year patent was issued to Charles James Mason, who called his ware Patented Ironstone. Francis Morley, G.L. Asworth, T.J. Mayer, and other Staffordshire potters continued to produce ironstone until the end of the century. While some of these patterns are simple to the extreme, many are decorated with in-mold designs of fruit, grains, and foliage on ribbed or scalloped shapes. In the 1830s, transfer printed designs in blue, mulberry, pink, green, and black became popular, and polychrome versions of Oriental wares were manufactured to compete with the Chinese trade.

Potpourri bowl and cover, Mason's Patented Ironstone, 1820-25, 12½" x 17½", auction estimate: $800.00.

Bowl, fruit; Bellflower, Edwards, sm.........................12.00
Bowl, ftd, red transfer, Mason's Pat, China Vista, 10½x6"......40.00
Bowl, Imari pattern, Mason's Pat, open, 10¼"................65.00
Bowl, mocha stripes in bl/blk/wht, minor wear, flakes, 3x6½"...35.00
Bowl, scalloped, lg......................................30.00

Flatiron, cast iron, 5½", $17.50.

Bowl, soup; Corn & Oats, Davenport & Wedgwood............20.00
Bowl, soup; Ribbed Raspberry w/Bloom, Meakin..............20.00
Bowl, vegetable, w/lid; Corn & Oats, Davenport & Wedgwood, lg.75.00
Bowl, vegetable, w/lid; Fuschia, Meakin....................45.00
Bowl, vegetable, w/lid; Lily shape, Burgess................95.00
Bowl, vegetable, w/lid; President, Edwards.................85.00
Bowl, vegetable, w/lid; Sydenham, Boote...................150.00
Bowl, vegetable, w/lid; Wheat & Blackberry, Meakin.........85.00
Bowl, vegetable; Atlantic, Boote, 1858....................85.00
Bowl & pitcher, Wheat & Blackberry, Meakin...............180.00
Butter dish, Athens, Podmore Walker, 1857.................75.00
Cake plate, on pedestal; Grenade, Boote, 1850s............65.00
Chamber pot, snake hdl, allover mc floral, Mason's, 6x9"...125.00
Chamber pot, vertical flutes & ribs, wht..................35.00
Chamber pot, w/hdl, ribbon finial.........................45.00
Charger, Am Marine, Mason's Pat, 15" dia..................55.00
Cigarette caddy, Mandarin, gold trim, Mason's, 2½".........14.00
Coffee pot, Alcock..80.00
Coffee pot, Baltimore, Brougham Mayer, 1850s.............115.00
Coffee pot, Gothic, Edwards..............................165.00
Coffee pot, Lily of the Valley, Shaw, rpr.................85.00
Coffee service, sugar & creamer, ea w/lid, Somerset Kensington..25.00
Creamer, Gothic, Alcock...................................45.00
Creamer, Memnon, Meir, 1857..............................50.00
Creamer, President, Edwards...............................40.00
Creamer, Wheat & Blackberry, Meakin......................50.00
Cup, Ceres, Forester.....................................32.00
Cup, Corn & Oats...15.00
Cup & saucer, Arms of States transfer, imp lion/Mellor, rpr....45.00
Ewer, Scalloped Decagon, Wedgwood.......................125.00
Gravy boat, Am Marine, attached liner, Mason's Pat........35.00
Pitcher, bl & wht floral under glaze, ornate hdl, gold, 12x8"...195.00
Pitcher, Jas Edwards & Son, 9"...........................65.00
Pitcher, Mandarin, Mason's Pat, 6".......................70.00
Pitcher, milk; Hyacinth, Wedgwood........................75.00
Pitcher, milk; Lily, Burgess, 1860s......................95.00
Pitcher, milk; Paneled Grape, Meakin.....................65.00
Pitcher, purple transfer w/enamel, man/tree, Mason's, 5½"...65.00
Pitcher, Regency, Mason's, 6¼"...........................50.00
Pitcher, snake hdl, mc floral, Mason's, 6"...............120.00
Pitcher, snake hdl, mc Oriental figures, Mason's, 5½".....120.00
Pitcher, Sterling China Co, 7½"..........................35.00
Pitcher, wash; Sydenham type, Meakin.....................85.00
Pitcher, water; Blackberry...............................65.00
Pitcher, water; Corn & Oats.............................125.00
Pitcher, water; gaudy decor, dolphin hdl, Mason's........295.00
Pitcher, water; Sydenham type, Barrow....................80.00
Pitcher, water; w/ice lip................................45.00
Pitcher, water; Wheat, Turner Goddard....................80.00
Plate, bl foliage rims, Elsmore & Forster, 9¾", set of 6...60.00
Plate, dinner; Corn & Oats, Davenport & Wedgwood.........17.00
Plate, dinner; New York shape, Clementson................20.00
Plate, dinner; Trent shape, Alcock.......................18.00
Plate, dinner; Wheat, Meakin.............................15.00
Plate, emb rim 'Our Union Forever--Centennial', Washington, 6"..45.00
Plate, Imari colors on cobalt, mk Ashworth Beal, 8½".....45.00
Plate, luncheon; Corn & Oats, Davenport & Wedgwood.......14.00
Plate, scroll rim, Berlin Ironstone/lion/unicorn mk, 9"...8.00
Plate, wht, James Edwards & Sons, 1851-82, 4", pr.........12.00
Platter, Corn & Oates, 13x9½"............................15.00
Platter, orange/pk flowers, mk Adams Tunstall, 10¾".......75.00
Platter, Ribbed Raspberry w/Bloom, Meakin................45.00
Platter, warming; orig stopper...........................90.00
Platter, wht, Meakin, 12"................................12.00

Platter, wht, 14"..16.00
Potty w/lid, Gothic, Meigh...............................90.00
Pudding mold, Cauliflower, Alcock, lg....................70.00
Pudding mold, Corn, med..................................55.00
Pudding mold, Grape, med.................................40.00
Pudding mold, Lion, Minton...............................75.00
Pudding mold, Poinsettia.................................55.00
Pudding mold, Shell, Edge Malkin.........................42.00
Punch bowl, w/hdls, Loop & Line, Parkhurst..............100.00
Sauce boat, Ceres, Forester..............................60.00
Sauce boat w/lid, Ribbed Raspberry w/Bloom, Meakin, 1860s..55.00
Soup tureen, Atlantic, Boote, 1858, 4 pc................375.00
Soup tureen, Canada, 1877, 3 pc.........................225.00
Soup tureen, Twin Leaves, Edwards, 1851, 4 pc...........275.00
Spittoon, lady's...50.00
Sugar bowl, Gothic, Ridgway..............................60.00
Sugar bowl, Grenade type.................................52.00
Teapot, Corn & Oats......................................75.00
Teapot, cr/sug, J&G Meakin, 3 pc........................135.00
Teapot, Gothic, Mayer...................................150.00
Teapot, St Louis, Edwards, 1850s.........................95.00
Toothbrush holder, Wheat & Blackberry....................44.00
Tureen, Atlantic shape, Boote, 1858, 4 pc...............375.00
Tureen, President shape, acorn finial on grape leaves, Edwards..85.00

Ispanky

Ispanky figurines, designed by Lazlo Ispanky, have been produced at his Pennington, New Jersey workshop since 1966.

Ballerina, ca 1967, limited edition........................412.00
Cinderella, ca 1972, 12" long.............................330.00
Dawn, ca 1970, #107/300, 14½".............................605.00
Easter Egg, 1st Annual....................................150.00
Mr & Mrs Otter, ca 1971, 13"..............................247.00
On the Trail, decorated.................................3,000.00
Peace, ca 1970, #95/100, 13"..............................209.00
Pioneer Women...500.00
Prudence, 9½"...165.00
Romeo & Juliet, ca 1967, limited edition, 12¾"............357.00
Secret, 10"...187.00
Spring, ca 1972, limited edition, 15¼"....................412.00
Susie, 7¼"..110.00

Ivory

Technically, true ivory is the substance composing the tusk of the elephant; the finest type comes from those of Africa. However, tusks and teeth of other animals -- the walrus, for instance, the hippopotamus, and the sperm whale -- are similar in composition and appearance and have also been used for carving. The Chinese have used this substance for centuries, preferring it over bone because of the natural oil contained in its pores, which not only renders it easier to carve, but also imparts a soft sheen to the finished product. Aged ivory usually takes on a soft caramel patina, but unscrupulous dealers sometimes treat new ivory to a tea bath to 'antique' it!

A bill passed in 1978 reinforced a ban on the importation of whale and walrus ivory.

Apple, carved w/in, pine tree/man on horse/bridge/etc, 2x4¼"..180.00
Chess set..275.00
Doctor's doll, movable bracelet, 4"......................75.00
Doctor's doll, reclining nude holding peony, 8".........180.00
Figure, farmer, holds rooster w/EX plumage/flowing tail, 28"..3,300.00

Figure, farmer weighs rooster, birds at feet, sgnd, 18" 220.00
Figure, Guanyin/flowers/peach sprig, phoenix, Qianlong, 40" . .3,630.00
Figure, sage leaning on staff, shades eyes w/hand, sgnd, 22" . .1,540.00
Figure, Shoulao w/staff, acolyte on deer beside, 37" 3,300.00
Figurine, Apollo w/lyre, English, early 1700s, 9½" 935.00
Figurine, Archangel Michael on Devil, Goanese, 1700, 9" 715.00
Figurine, armed general, chain mail garmet w/shield on bk, 8" . .275.00
Figurine, boy in ornate costume holds 2 chickens, Japan, 6" . . .600.00
Figurine, dragon w/flaming pearl/turq eyes, gods, 3½x14" 895.00
Figurine, fisherman w/pointed beard, lg hat, staff, 1850s, 12" . . .450.00
Figurine, foo lion, seated, removable head, jeweled collar, 5" . . .165.00
Figurine, Good Shepherd, on foliage bed, Goanese, 1700s, 7" . .935.00
Figurine, Han Xiangzi riding water buffalo, hardwood base, 6" . .110.00
Figurine, He Zianqu riding foo lion, hardwood base, 6" 130.00
Figurine, Lan Caihe seated on a stag, hardwood base, 6" 150.00
Figurine, Lu Dongbin on horseback, hardwood stand, 6¼" 90.00
Figurine, multi-armed goddess w/flowers, on lotus base, 5" 250.00
Figurine, Oriental maiden in kimono w/lg peony, 9" 275.00
Figurine, phoenix bird w/long tail on stump, openwork, 8½" . . .275.00
Figurine, seated girl musicians, 4", set of 4 . . . . .550.00
Figurine, seated Rakan, Japanese, tea stained, sgn, 5" 125.00
Figurine, set of 4 horses ea in various pursuits, ea 2½" L 140.00
Figurine, Vishnu & Shiva dancing, wood stand, 9" 270.00
Figurine, woman samurai w/lg hat & chain mail suit, cloak, 8" . .275.00
Figurine, Zhong Liquan on foo lion, hardwood base, 6¼" 130.00
Group, Diana & hound, cylinder socle, 11½" 1,100.00
Group, winged female/putto, cylinder socle, 13" 1,100.00
Inro, 3 compartments, silk cord, incised scene, sgn, 1½x1¾" . . .90.00
Okimono, elder seated on rock holds lg fish, boy at side, 3¾" .110.00
Okimono, immortal, pnt, 4" 55.00
Okimono, woman holding parrot, 4½" .50.00
Okimono, woman in kimono w/red sash, 4⅛" 55.00
Shrine, hexagon w/florals/sages, doors open, Buddha w/in, 24" .800.00
Table screen, Diana & 2 attendants before Cupid, 18" 2,200.00
Tankard, carved lion hunt, figural hdl & finial, 12" 3,960.00
Triptych, Lord Nelson in uniform w/telescope, rstr, 9" 440.00
Tusk, carved emperor & empress, curve retained, 15", pr 1,700.00

Mythological god of war atop a lion on a lotus pedestal, mounted before a chased silver lotus leaf studded with turquoise matrix and carnelian, 18th century, 19", $3,000.00.

Tusk, Chinese heroes/legendary figures relief, 72" 7,150.00
Tusk, 31" 315.00
Vase w/lid, cylinder, well carved w/frieze of figures, 15" 1,540.00
Watch chain, hand carved, 29" 30.00

Jack-in-the-Pulpit Vases

Popular novelties at the turn of the century, Jack-in-the-Pulpit vases were made in every type of art glass produced. Some were simple -- others elaborately appliqued and enameled. They were shaped to resemble the lily for which they were named.

Amber, applied rigaree, 8" 65.00
Amber w/applied flower, leaf & branch, Sturbridge 90.00
Blue opal, 6", pr 100.00
Blue w/silver flecks, cased w/beige, 5" .75.00
Cased, gr, wht w/out, clear ft, scalloped edge top, 6½x5½" 105.00
Cased, lavender, wht w/out, ruffled, 7½x6" 110.00
Cranberry, clear coiled stem & petal ft, 9¼" 115.00
Cranberry, ped ft, ruffled edge, clear base, 10¾x6" 100.00
Cranberry opal swirl w/clear overlay & base, vaseline rim, 11" . .150.00
Cranberry top, vaseline base, 6 ftd, gold/wht enamel, 5½" 145.00
Gunderson Burmese, 13" 65.00
Lime gr opal to clear gr, 7" 70.00
Opalescent, purple edge, fluted, 7" 60.00
Opalescent, purple shading to lt gr, ruffled, bulbous base, 6" 75.00
Opaque pink top, wht base, 4 applied ft, 6½" 85.00
Pink opal top, wht opal base, ribbed, 5" 70.00
Rose to pk to wht w/in, wht w/out, 5 gr petal ft, 7" 145.00
Rubena verde, vaseline applique & ft, 8¼" 100.00
Rubena verde opal, vaseline ft & body applique, 8x4" 100.00
Spangle glass, maroon/bl/cream, 8" 65.00
Spatter glass, pink & clear, ruffled, 7" .65.00
Turq opal, 8x5" 70.00
Vaseline opal, shell ft/ruffle, applied rigaree, 4¾x2" 60.00
Vaseline opal w/pink ruffled top & body applique, 7½" 90.00

Jackfield

Jackfield has come to be a generic term used to refer to wares with a red clay body and a high gloss black glaze. It originated at Jackfield, in Stropshire, England; however, it was also produced in the Staffordshire district as well. While some pieces are decorated with relief motifs or painted-on florals and gilting, many are unadorned. Teapots produced in the 18th century were known locally as 'black decanters'. These pots, and figural dogs and roosters, are the items most often found.

Creamer, emb florals, 4" 45.00
Dogs, seated, gilded detail, late, 9¼", pr 100.00
Dogs, Spaniels, old, 12x12", pr 350.00
Pitcher, gold floral spray, 6" 22.00
Pitcher, pewter lid, enamel decor 85.00
Pitcher, swirl mold, waisted neck/bulbous, 1760, 6½" 165.00

Jewelry

Jewelry as objects of adornment have always been regarded with special affection. Whether it be a trinket or a costly ornament of gold, silver, or enameled work, jewelry has personal significance to the wearer.

The art of the jeweler is valued as is any art object, and the names of Lalique or Faberge on collectible pieces bring prices demanded by the signed works of Picasso.

Once the province of kings and noblemen, jewelry now is a legacy of all strata of society. The creativity reflected in the jewelers' art has resulted in a myriad of decorative adornments for men and women, and the modern usage of 'lesser' gems and base metals has elevated the values and increased the demand for aristic merit on a par with instrinsic values. Luxuriously appointed pieces of Victorian splendor and Edwardian grandeur, now compete with the unique, imaginative renditions of jewelry produced in the exciting Art Nouveau period, as well as the adventurous translation of jewelry executed in man-made materials versus natural elements.

Today, prices for gems and gemstones crafted into antique and collectible jewelry, are based on artistic merit, personal appeal, pure sentimentality, and intrinsic values.

If you are interested in collecting or dealing in jewelry, you will find that authority Lillian Baker has several fine books available on the subject, complete with beautiful color illustrations and current market values. She is listed in the Directory under 'California', as well as 'Clubs & Newsletters'.

Key:

AD----Art Deco	gp----gold plated
AN----Art Nouveau	gw----gold washed
cab----cabochon	k----karat
comp----complementary	plat----platinum
dia----diamond	tw----total weight
dwt---penny weight	wg---white gold
gf----gold filled	yg----yellow gold
grad----graduated	

Bracelet, Georg Jensen, sterling flower-heads with green stone centers, $245.00.

Beads, amber, faceted ovals, 7mm to 19mm, 22" 75.00
Beads, amber & ivory, w/ivory pendant: monkey & baby, 17" . . .160.00
Beads, carved bone, gold separators, 20" 25.00
Beads, clear cherry amber, knotted, 31" .95.00
Beads, dbl, faceted crystals/blk rondells w/rhinestones 22.00
Beads, gr serpentine/lapis lazuli, 10mm, +amulet w/bird 175.00
Beads, lg red triangles of opaque glass, 34" 15.00
Beads, mc agate & carnelian, 36" 28.00
Beads, pink aurora borealis, 15"; w/cluster earrings 13.00
Beads, pressed pink glass, 30" 12.00
Beads, psuedo pearls 3.00
Beads, rose & jade quartz, 23 beads ea 13mm, w/pendant 120.00
Beads, salmon coral, 4 to 7 mm, gold clasp, 18" 30.00
Beads, 10mm aurora borealis on chain, brass lock 15.00
Beads, 120 ivory floral carved beads, 39" 90.00
Beads, 5 strands, graduated faceted crystals 35.00
Beads, 6mm rnd lapis lazuli, 14k clasp, 32" 90.00
Beads, 7.5mm carnelian, 34" 125.00
Beads, 8mm carved bone, 40" strand 28.00
Beads, 83 ruby beads, 4.50mm to 6.50mm, sterling clasp 200.00
Belt, sterling, geometric open links 35.00
Belt buckle, abalone on g/w wire work, Czechoslovakia 7.00
Belt buckle, brass, curved rectangle, engraved, 2" 10.00
Bracelet, bangle; engraved silver, opens, ¾" 8.00
Bracelet, bangle; hand carved elephant ivory, ½" 35.00

Bracelet, bangle; 18k, Cartier, wide bulbous band w/stars 425.00
Bracelet, cameo on wide gold mesh, fringed, adjusts, 1850s 200.00
Bracelet, double chain, w/ivory squares 20.00
Bracelet, five 18k links ea w/cluster sm dia/rubies/sapphires 375.00
Bracelet, Fr enamel 'rings' on rod, front 2 w/several pearls 975.00
Bracelet, g/f spring type mesh w/faceted continuous rectangles . . .34.00
Bracelet, g/p, China, 5 parts/openwork/enamel/15 cab amethysts . .95.00
Bracelet, g/w, 9 engraved links w/faux amethysts & turq, 1930s . .20.00
Bracelet, hammered aluminum, 5 sqs links/applied flowers, AD . . .18.00
Bracelet, link w/lg gr enamel rnds outlined in g/w, Ken Lane 10.00
Bracelet, Mexican sterling, ea flexible link w/18k Aztec decor 65.00
Bracelet, mosaic in g/w, 11 links 9.00
Bracelet, silver, 5 pierced rnds set w/marcasites & pearls 75.00
Bracelet, silver mt w/8 emerald cut quartz in ea flexible link 40.00
Bracelet, sterling, links of seahorses & pink moonstones 20.00
Bracelet, sterling w/10 charms, 1940s 65.00
Bracelet, sterling w/5 oval 10mm opals w/in 5 flowers 95.00
Bracelet, sterling w/5 pcs banded agates, Scotland 65.00
Bracelet, sterling w/8 flower links set w/marcasites 75.00
Bracelet, ten 10mm jade beads w/24 gold 3.8mm beads 110.00
Bracelet, 14k, 6 marquise jadeite cabs between pierced ovals . . .115.00
Bracelet, 14k bangle w/wheat motif, 2½" dia 170.00
Bracelet, 14k filigree w/3 sapphires & 2 dia 365.00
Bracelet, 14k pink heavy links, 8" 450.00
Bracelet, 14k slide; 11 mixed stones, heavy gold, ca 1890 . . . . .775.00
Bracelet, 15k Etruscan, 2¼" dia, ca 1900 . . . . .360.00
Bracelet, 2 joined flat rings, strip of sapphires/dia in front 975.00
Bracelet, 6 mosaic/gold ovals w/classical scenic decor 450.00
Brooch, blk jet w/2 jet leaves, rhinestone flowers, Weiss, lg 15.00
Brooch, brass w/cameo, 2" dia 12.00
Brooch, celluloid, HP violets 16.50
Brooch, crescent moon, vermeil fr w/20 rose cut garnets, 1¼" . . .65.00
Brooch, g/f, Art Deco, 3 tulips w/faux amethysts, 3¼" L 18.00
Brooch, g/f bar, emb/enamelled, bow w/sm opal atop, 2½" 18.00
Brooch, g/w silver Art Deco ½ moon, mc faceted stones, 2½" . . .10.00
Brooch, gilt metal, insect atop w/gr irid scarab, garnet eyes 35.00
Brooch, marcasites, 3 initials on metal, 1½" sq 12.00
Brooch, painting on porcelain, 14k yg fr 375.00
Brooch, porcelain, HP pink roses 22.00

Necklace, faceted amethyst beads; drop, clasp, and stations with brilliants in gold filigree, signed Miriam Haskell, $60.00.

Brooch, star form, w/drop earrings, silver mt w/garnets........110.00
Brooch, sterling, notched 1¼x1″ oval w/engraved leaves.......18.00
Brooch, sterling, Siamese dancer, pierced....................8.00
Brooch, sterling, 2 flowers w/gr stones, Art Deco...........15.00
Brooch, sterling bird w/gold overlay, Coro, 3½″............22.00
Brooch, triangular, marcasite initials on blk, 2½″...........15.00
Brooch, 14k, otter holding fire opal cabachon..............225.00
Brooch, 14k, 7 lapis lazuli ball flowers, gold leaves, stems.....100.00
Brooch, 14k feather w/25 sm sapphires, tw 10.80k..........250.00
Brooch, 18k, woodpecker & tree stump, ruby eyes..........175.00
Brooch, 2 Pharaohs, full figures, 2 heads, silver type finish......45.00
Brooch, 2 sterling hearts w/9k leaves & flowers, Mizpah/prayer...30.00
Brooch/pendant, carved coral man's head, 6 turq beads/chain...250.00
Brooch/pendant, 14k, enamel lady bug on 17 pearl 'grapes'....80.00
Brooch/pendant, 14k w/oval pierced carved jade, +earrings....250.00
Cameo, coral, scenic, engraved 10k frame, 1910........250.00
Cameo, lady w/roses in hair, gold mtd shell, 2¼″ L.........200.00
Cameo, mythological subject, 14k fr, att Giovani Goto........750.00
Cameo, silver bead mt, lady in high relief on lt pink, 1¾″...95.00
Cameo, silver rope border & foliage, lady on pink, sgnd, 1¼″...85.00
Chain, watch; g/f, 4 sided ½″ bars, engraved, 13″............23.00
Chain, watch; 14k, dbl flat link, 30″......................635.00
Chain, 14k, w/2 tone 10k deco flower lavaliere on leaf........90.00
Chain, 14k filigree, 30″................................210.00
Chain, 14k w/Edwardian carved carnelian 1½″ pendant......125.00
Chain, 14k w/six 4mm turq beads........................35.00
Chain, 14k w/14mm synthetic alexandrite heart pendant.....165.00
Charm, 10k, rnd disc, 'Graduate', 1940s...................20.00
Charm, 14k, birthday cake, candles pop up................45.00
Clip, brass, leaf w/turq stone decor......................8.00
Clip, g/w filigree on MOP, 1½″ dia.......................10.00
Clip, triangular w/6 lg faux topaz, 1½″....................5.00
Comb, pique work, paste stones, English, 1890s............113.00
Comb, tortoise shell w/solid gold inlaid & 3 rhinestones, 4x3″...75.00
Compact, enamel flowers, Art Deco, Volupte, 2¼″ sq.........10.00
Cuff buttons, 14k octagons w/engraved leaves..............75.00
Earrings, butterfly, gold & rhinestone, Weiss................8.00
Earrings, gold filigree w/aqua & seed pearl flowers, Czech......12.00
Earrings, mosaics, vermicelli, Italy, ovals..................7.00
Earrings, silver, 20mm, marcasites w/flower border..........40.00
Earrings, silver w/pink g/w, petals w/blk center & marcasites.....17.00
Earrings, sq w/pressed & faceted mc stones, Austria...........7.00
Earrings, sterling, lg rnd/engraved flower w/aqua spinel, Siam....40.00
Earrings, sterling, 5 drop chains w/rhinestones...............9.00
Earrings, wg flower form mt w/.15k ruby+6 dia, tw .18k......200.00
Earrings, wg rosette form mt ea w/.15k dia.................160.00
Earrings, ½ moons w/aurora borealis, Weiss................12.00
Earrings, 14k wg, 2 cultured pearls+8 dia on ea............325.00
Earrings, 6mm pearl studs.............................45.00
Lavaliere, 14k, 2.5k wht sapphire+pearl..................120.00
Lavaliere, 14k w/3mm ruby & pearl......................155.00
Locket, engraved allover w/leaves, roses, etc, bl enamelling......45.00
Locket, g/f engraved heart w/wht stone, g/f chain, ¾″........35.00
Locket, heart, g/f engraved bk, wht MOP w/gold cross front, ¾″.35.00
Locket, sterling in 9k yg fr, flower decor, 30″ dbl curb chain...130.00
Locket, 14k, lg heart................................120.00
Necklace, blk jet w/lg rnd clear glass drops in gold fr, 16″.....10.00
Necklace, branch coral, 18″............................35.00
Necklace, brass w/links & tassel drops of lg wht brilliants......35.00
Necklace, choker; dbl strand, brass beads..................7.00
Necklace, choker; 24 strands of tiny pearls, 1930s...........12.00
Necklace, choker; 7 fine strands: brass & wht pnt, 1920s......22.00
Necklace, engraved brass w/bead dangles, 16″..............10.00
Necklace, g/f 16″ chain w/five 8x10mm oval garnets..........40.00

Necklace, carved carnelian agate cameo, etruscan work, 18k gold chain, 1860s, cameo: 1¼″, $1,500.00.

Necklace, lg Austrian faceted crystals on brass chain..........35.00
Necklace, silver rope, 4 sqs w/flower petals & gr stones, Vict...100.00
Necklace, silver/Chinese turq/marcasites, lavaliere w/drops......50.00
Necklace, sm ivory beads w/7 ivory elephants, 19″............75.00
Necklace, sterling, 1¼″ linking leaves, Johnl, Denmark, 15½″...30.00
Necklace, sterling, 14 leaves, w/bracelets, Jewlart..............85.00
Necklace, sterling chain w/lg aqua pendant w/in rhinestones.....35.00
Necklace, tourmaline, pink/gr, 14k wg, long drop+2 ea side...425.00
Necklace, yg w/enamel, box links, 20″ L..................200.00
Necklace, 101 pearls, 7.5mm, w/14k w clasp w/pearl, matinee L.400.00
Necklace, 14k rope chain, shield slide w/6 sapphires/tassels....550.00
Necklace, 14k rope intertwined w/seed pearls..............350.00
Necklace, 14k wg pendant w/42 rnd/oval cab moonstones......550.00
Necklace, 58 bl/gray 6mm cultured pearls w/silver gilt clasp....100.00
Necklace, 91 grad cultured pearls, 3.5mm to 8.5mm.........150.00
Pendant, carved lavender jade on 14k bk, pierced, 1½″.......750.00
Pendant, Chinese vermeil, 24k over sterling filigree, 1½x2″.....20.00
Pendant, cross, blk pique w/ivory inlay, sm.................75.00
Pendant, cross, onyx w/seed pearls......................110.00
Pendant, crystal w/bust of girl, bronze rim/ring, Desprez, 3″....385.00
Pendant, enamel/glass icon w/carved wood reliquary, late 1800s..80.00
Pendant, floral carved amethyst cab, g/f bezel & chain.........50.00
Pendant, free form boulder opal, 1½x1¼″, silver chain........70.00
Pendant, g/p 3 tier fr, flowers w/87 garnets, 1.5mm to 3.5 mm..50.00
Pendant, heart, 18 pearl/36 sm dia, pin bk, 14k............525.00
Pendant, sterling filigree fr w/carved hematite, Mexico.........20.00
Pendant, yg fr Mexican 1959 ten pesos coin, rope twist rim....125.00
Pendant, 10k, flowers, 2.5mm sapphire+2 pearls, pearl drop....65.00
Pendant, 14k, ornate decor, lg.........................450.00
Pendant, 14k wg, 4 rnd drops w/4 dia tw .40k/billet link chain.130.00
Pendant, 14k yg, wg face, scroll triangle/2 rose dia/4mm pearl...35.00
Pendant, 14k/sterling, bicycle, 2″.......................15.00
Pendant, 35k sq cut aquamarine w/dia set bow atop........2,850.00
Pendant, 9k rose, pierced vase w/leaves & amethyst flower/drop..85.00
Pin, Art Deco, star shape w/'brilliants', 2″.................7.00
Pin, bar; g/f, engraved, mc stones, 2″ L..................22.00
Pin, bar; rolled gold, 3″...............................10.00
Pin, bar; silver filigree w/bl center stone.................12.00
Pin, bar; silver gunmetal w/faux diamonds.................12.00

Pin, marked Sterling, Norwegian, surrealistic motif, 1930s, 2″ square, $115.00.

Pin, bar; 10k wg filigree w/center dia+2 sapphires, Victorian...130.00
Pin, bar; 18k wg w/6.5mm amethyst, Belais, 2¼″ W..........75.00
Pin, bar; 2½″ curved gold filigree arrow w/6 mc stones.......10.00
Pin, brass, w/17 bl-gr stones, 3″ W.........................10.00
Pin, diamond crescent, Victorian, ¾k tw...................525.00
Pin, dk bl enamel w/wht dots, Weiss, 1940s.................5.00
Pin, dragonfly, 14k yg w/opal cabs down bk, dia on wings/eyes.575.00
Pin, faceted pink stones, Austria, 1½″....................10.00
Pin, g/f, rose w/leaves, 1¾″.............................12.00
Pin, gold filigree w/gr stones, Austria....................7.00
Pin, ivory, star flower, colored center, ¾″...............10.00
Pin, lizard, emerald set w/dia streak down bk.............875.00
Pin, marcasites, rectangle w/sq center opening, Art Deco, 1½″..17.00
Pin, plastic, swordfish, green.............................4.50
Pin, plastic mushroom, 1940s, 1″..........................6.00
Pin, plastic rose, foreign mk.............................4.00
Pin, plat AD rectangle, 1k dia center+tw 3½k sm dia.......3,800.00
Pin, plat w/4k dia+3k sapphires, AD design, converts to clips.5,500.00
Pin, rock crystal oval carved w/dancers, pearl trim, 14k, 1908..875.00
Pin, silver filigree w/lg topaz in center, 2″.............19.00
Pin, sq MOP w/Mother in g/f script, red stone, 1″.........12.00
Pin, sterling, Art Nouveau lily, 2″.......................15.00
Pin, sterling, butterfly, 2¾″.............................8.00
Pin, sterling, Danecraft flying goose.....................49.00
Pin, sterling, filigree butterfly, 1″.....................8.00
Pin, sterling, flowers w/faux amythest....................39.00
Pin, sterling, leaf, 3″...................................6.50
Pin, sterling, leaf & acorn, Jensen.......................80.00
Pin, sterling, leaf w/aquamarine, 4″......................12.50
Pin, sterling, maple leaf, 3 color enamel.................11.00
Pin, sterling, spoon, souvenir of Niagara Falls...........29.00
Pin, sterling, 2 acorns w/orange stones, 1½″..............10.00
Pin, sterling w/gold overlay bow w/center pearl, lg.......10.00
Pin, tan enamel w/cut out ½ moons, mk Hogan Bolas, 1″.....7.00
Pin, tortoise shell w/pique work, paste stones, small, 1920s.....85.00
Ring, carved moonstone satyr cameo & dia..................2,250.00
Ring, g/f, bl stone cluster...............................15.00
Ring, gold w/enameled porcelain oval, boy w/flute.........110.00
Ring, guard; plat, rosette engraved crown/beaded border...50.00
Ring, ivory w/mini painting, 18 mine cut dia, yg..........550.00
Ring, jade, full circle...................................12.50
Ring, man's; heavy 14k mt w/.08k dia......................115.00
Ring, man's; yg w/oval star sapphire cab flanked w/.80k tw dia..425.00
Ring, man's; 10k brushed mt w/pink star sapphire..........60.00
Ring, man's; 10k w/oblong cut amethyst....................60.00
Ring, man's; 14k Masonic, dbl head eagle w/mine cut .25k dia...90.00
Ring, man's; 14k w/bl scarab..............................200.00

Ring, plat, oval .75k sapphire w/6 sm single cut dia..........100.00
Ring, plat filigree w/1.20k dia...........................2,950.00
Ring, plat floral filigree, w/5mm iolite, ca 1920.............70.00
Ring, platinum w/3.20k dia in Art Deco mount.............3,250.00
Ring, scroll/pierced plat mt w/rnd 1.30k dia solitaire.......1,200.00
Ring, silver, wedding band set w/marcasites...................75.00
Ring, silver, 5mm garnet w/in six 4.5mm moonstones..........60.00
Ring, silver w/flower marcasite..............................25.00
Ring, sterling, hand holds bl stone between thumb & forefinger..22.50
Ring, sterling, marcasites w/gr onyx, oval mt................65.00
Ring, sterling, oval, lg rose surrounded by hearts...........75.00
Ring, sterling, Siamese dancers on twin fish, adjusts........25.00
Ring, sterling, 3 sm turq cabs...............................12.00
Ring, sterling filigree w/prong set topaz, 1940s.............40.00
Ring, sterling w/marcasites, twin flowers....................65.00
Ring, wg mt w/3k emerald+8 rose dia & 8 rnd dia.............500.00
Ring, yg, row of 3 sm opals..................................50.00
Ring, yg shank/cherubs w/wg flowers set w/47 sm single cut dia.500.00
Ring, yg w/oval carved cameo of maid, 4 dia surround........250.00
Ring, 10k, flower cluster opal, 5.2mm w/in 8--2mm surround...130.00
Ring, 10k, flower w/open petals, 3 bl sapphires in center....50.00
Ring, 10k, lg rectangle blk onyx with .6k center dia.........95.00
Ring, 10k oblong swirl design w/4 sm dia.....................60.00
Ring, 10k ribbon swirl w/cultured pearl......................35.00
Ring, 14k, .20k dia center/3 rubies in ea corner, Deco......315.00
Ring, 14k, .22k dia+five 2.5mm aquamarines, tree motif......350.00
Ring, 14k, angelskin coral cameo with .8k dia, ca 1900......260.00
Ring, 14k, Art Nouveau, male figure w/orange jade cab.......200.00
Ring, 14k, center garnet surrounded by 18, heavy............150.00
Ring, 14k, eleven 1.5mm emeralds+five .2½k dia..............210.00
Ring, 14k, emerald cut .60k emerald solitaire...............115.00
Ring, 14k, emerald cut tourmaline w/in 6 sm dia..............95.00
Ring, 14k, fire opal in oval swirl...........................80.00
Ring, 14k, flower spray mt w/amethyst cab...................125.00
Ring, 14k, lg amethyst flanked by 6 sm rubies...............210.00
Ring, 14k, rnd w/6 pt dia w/in 6 sapphires w/in 12 opals....195.00
Ring, 14k, row of three 4mm turq.............................7.00
Ring, 14k, row of two 3mm rose cut garnets...................65.00
Ring, 14k, row of two 5mm pearls ea side of 5.5mm pearl.....145.00
Ring, 14k, row of 2 rose cut garnets, forked shoulders.......65.00
Ring, 14k, row of 5.5mm tourmaline & two 5mm opals, 1890s...105.00
Ring, 14k, 2.5mm pearl w/in six 4mm tourmalines, flower motif.100.00
Ring, 14k, 4.5mm emerald+.16k dia & .8k dia set vertically...325.00
Ring, 14k, 40k amethyst w/in 14 three pt dia................850.00
Ring, 14k, 6.5mm citrine topaz..............................45.00
Ring, 14k cab cut 3mm carnelian, 1900.......................60.00
Ring, 14k emerald cut aquamarine, 1930s....................150.00
Ring, 14k filigree, leaf engraving, 7x9mm marquise garnet....60.00
Ring, 14k mt frames lg topaz surrounded by seed pearls......275.00
Ring, 14k open work wide band with .07k dia+.03k side dia....90.00
Ring, 14k oval garnet, two .3k dia ea side...................85.00
Ring, 14k rope mt w/oval garnet & sm dia.....................80.00
Ring, 14k rope twist crescent w/shaped angelskin coral crown..120.00
Ring, 14k rose, band, sq ruby w/2.5mm turq cab ea side.......60.00
Ring, 14k snake w/3mm emerald eyes, ca 1920..................85.00
Ring, 14k Tiffany set 5mm ruby...............................75.00
Ring, 14k Tiffany set 9.5mm garnet, engraved................145.00
Ring, 14k w/emerald gr jade, vertically set, 1930...........175.00
Ring, 14k w/row of 3mm opals, 1910..........................105.00
Ring, 14k wg, flip; 1 side with .4k dia in blk; 2nd w/cameo....245.00
Ring, 14k wg, rectangle profile cameo, open scroll work sides..110.00
Ring, 14k wg, three 6mm emerald cabs+three .12k dia, 1920s.295.00
Ring, 14k wg w/vertical row of 2 sq opals+2 dia, filigree mt...245.00
Ring, 14k with .75k garnet, basket mt........................80.00

Ring, 14k yg w/wht top, two 2mm gr tourmalines+sq sapphire...55.00
Ring, 14k 10.5mm moonstone w/inclusion, 1920............165.00
Ring, 14k 7mmx5mm blk sapphire solitaire.................50.00
Ring, 18k, basket type w/red stone.......................60.00
Ring, 18k filigree with .20k bl sapphire..................80.00
Ring, 18k filigree with .20k garnet......................90.00
Ring, 18k w/leaf ea side, marquise cut 1k jade..............70.00
Ring, 2 lg teardrop sapphires tw 3k ringed by 20 sm dia.....2,750.00
Ring, 9k rose, band w/Mizpah engraved on front, brite cut.....85.00
Ring, 9k rose, engraved band, mk Birmingham, 1872-73......25.00
Stickpin, g/f top w/piece of branch coral...................12.00
Stickpin, rnd top w/abalone & center brilliant..............10.00
Stickpin, 14k filigree octagon with .25k diamond............165.00
Tie tac, g/f, gray MOP button, Kromentz....................8.00
Watch bracelet, 18k, calibre sapphires, dbl rope w/buckle, AD..975.00
Watch fob, tortoise shell w/pique work, paste stones, 1890s.....97.00
Watch slide, g/f, dia shaped w/dia chip, eng sides, 24" chain....75.00
Watch slide, g/f, fancy slide w/12 seed pearls, 25" chain.......80.00
Watch slide, g/f, rnd slide eng clover, ruby center, 24" chain....80.00
Watch slide, g/f, 4 pearls & oval opal, 25" chain.............80.00

Jewelry Boxes

Jewelry boxes have been made from metals of every type, wood, ivory, glass and china, some adorned with 'jewels' themselves, porcelain inserts, filigree work, or figural forms. Jewelry boxes of a long rectangular form, usually on legs and designed in the Art Nouveau style, are called jewelry caskets. Today, these have become popular collectibles.

Birdcage, brass, bird swings, musical, drawer activated.........45.00
Blk amethyst, Mary Gregory style enamel, ormolu, 5½".......195.00
Blk amethyst, ovoid, enameled, ormolu mt, 6½"............115.00
Box, brilliant cutting, hinged lid, 5" dia..................165.00
Casket, brass ormolu, Louis XV, children/floral relief, 4½" L....70.00
Cupids/garlands/roses, SP, oval/ftd/lined, 8" L...............50.00
Heart shape w/filigree sides, engraved lid, SP................42.00
Hunting dog w/hare figural on lid, Meriden SP, ball ft, 6x7"...175.00
Leather w/brass trim, 8½x6½x5".........................145.00
Mary Gregory style, gr w/lady & harp, 7" W.................225.00
Nude w/scarf finial, cylinder w/3 drw, SP, ornate base/ft, 8"....195.00
Opaline, warrior, medallion w/lovers on lid, ormolu, 6½x5"....160.00
Porcelain, Rococo form, bl/wht under glaze decor, 2x5".......100.00
Porcelain w/elaborate relief decor, sgn Naples, 2½x3½" dia....200.00
Sand painting under glass lid, wood, Lost Art, 7x5x3".......225.00
Treasure chest, bronze/brass mts, relief florals, French, 4" L....75.00
Victorian, blk lacquer w/MOP inlay, doors over 6 drws, 11"...275.00

Metal box with ormolu trim, hand painted ivory insert, 4¼" wide, $225.00.

Judaica

The items listed below are representative of objects used in both the secular and religious life of the Jewish people. They are evident of a culture where silversmithing, painters, engravers, writers, and metal workers were highly gifted and skilled in their art. Most of the treasures shown in recently displayed exhibits of Judaica were confiscated during the late 1930s up to 1945; by then eight of their synagogues and fifty warehouses had been filled with Hitler's plunder.

Hungarian silver Seder plate, vignettes relating to Passover alternate with fruit clusters; Order of Seder in Hebrew in center, 1870s, 21", $1,870.00.

Ark lamp, hanging, chased w/floral swags, suspensions w/birds..700.00
Beaker w/lid, Holy Society, German silver, 1710, 5¾".....12,000.00
Buckle, Day of Atonement, Polish silver, 1840, 3".........1,100.00
Circumcision knife, parcel-gilt silver hdl, 1806, 6".........1,100.00
Esther scroll/ivory cased w/crown knop, 1700s, 7½"........1,250.00
Esther scroll/silver case w/scroll work/flowers, Vienna, 1846...2,250.00
Etrog container, Italian silver emb w/scrolls/flowers, 6".......600.00
Etrog container, Polish silver, octagon w/foliage/cherubs......600.00
Haggadah, commentary of Abarbanel, Furth, 1770, folio......605.00
Hanukah lamp, brass, arched w/emb rondels, inverted heart, 8".700.00
Hanukah lamp, Gothic revival pewter, pointed/pierced bk plate..550.00
Map, Canaan, Richard Blome, 1687, engraved w/cherubs/etc...605.00
Map, Jerusalem, Matthew Seutter, 1730, key in German to #s.3,300.00
Marriage casket, steel/brass pierced w/birds/scrolls, 5".........800.00
Plate, Hanukah; Alice & Celia Silverberg, NY, 1800s, 9½", G..600.00
Plate, marriage; brass w/Hebrew inscription of vows/birds, 6"...450.00
Plate, passover; pewter, center family scene, 15"...........1,000.00
Plate, Seder; German silver, Hebrew inscription/vignettes, 17".4,000.00
Ram's horn, leaf tip edge/Hebrew inscriptions, 12"..........2,200.00
Sabbath lamp, brass, hanging, 6 pointed star font, 14".......500.00
Spice box, deer form w/hinged antlers, German, 6"..........550.00
Spice box, stork w/chased leathers/red stone eyes, silver, 7"....750.00
Spice container, house/gabled roof/window/door, silver, 4½"....550.00
Spice tower, cubic mid-part w/eagles, set on stem, silver, 9½".1,200.00
Spice tower, cylinder, filigree mid-section, pennant atop, 10"...650.00
Spice tower, pierced flag/lid, cylinder chased w/vignettes, 6"..1,450.00
Spice tower, silver filigree, 4 presentation plaques, 12"......4,200.00
Torah finials, tapered hex form/pierced/hung w/bells, 19".....7,000.00

Jugtown

The Jugtown Pottery was started about 1920 by Juliana and Jacques Busbee, in Moore County, North Carolina. Ben Owen, a young descendant of a Staffordshire potter, was hired in 1923. He was the master potter, while the Busbees experimented with perfecting glazes and supervising design and modeling. Preferred shapes were those reminiscent of traditional country wares, and classic Oriental forms. Glazes were various: natural clay oranges, buffs, 'tobacco spit' brown, mirror black, white, 'frogskin' green, a lovely turquoise called Chinese blue, and the traditional cobalt decorated salt glaze. The pottery gained national recognition and as a result of their success, several other local potteries were established. Jugtown closed in 1959.

Bean pot, bright orange glaze, sm..........................10.00
Bean pot, w/lid, br/amber, imp Jugtown, rim damage, 6".......45.00
Bowl, Chinese Translation glaze, red/bl, 8"..................128.00
Bowl, hand thrown, flared, orange glaze.....................38.00
Bowl, speckled high glaze, cobalt design bottom, 7½" dia......48.00
Cat, bl, dbl sgnd, 5".......................................95.00
Creamer, stoneware w/incised lines, blue rim dots, imp mk, 3½".55.00
Creamer & sugar w/lid, bl glaze............................50.00
Jar, stoneware w/2 tone gr/gray glaze, shoulder ears, mkd, 6½"..40.00
Jar w/lid, 7x5½"...60.00
Jug, Chinese blue, miniature...............................50.00
Mug, pale yellow...75.00
Pie dish, deep...30.00
Pitcher, hand thrown, buckskin br, G shape, 4".............18.00
Plate, orange, 8½"...35.00
Plate, redware, pumpkin w/br specks, mk, glaze flake, 9".....45.00
Porridge bowl, w/lid, pumpkin..............................30.00
Tureen w/lid & hdl, 9" dia.................................65.00
Vase, Chinese glaze w/thick drip, turq/reds, wide shoulder, 6"..160.00
Vase, Chinese translation, gr-bl w/red-br/crystals/hdls, 11x9"....375.00
Vase, frogskin, 6"...55.00
Vase, frogskin lustre, 4 hdls, wide clay base strip, Owens, 8"...150.00
Vase, heavy bl drip over red clay, wide body, hairline, 5¾".....25.00

Pitcher, green glaze, hand thrown, 5¾", $58.00.

K.P.M. Porcelain

Under the tutelage of Frederick the Great, King of Prussia, porcelain manufacture was instituted in Berlin in 1751 by William K. Wegeley. In jealous competition with Meissen, hard paste porcelain was produced -- din-nerware, figurines, vases, etc. -- some of which were undecorated while other pieces were hand painted in Watteau scenes, landscapes, or florals. Never able to seriously compete, the King withdrew his support and the factory failed in 1757.

In 1761, Johann Ernst Gotzkowsky bought the rights and attempted a similar operation which soon failed due to financial difficulties. Still determined to gain the same recognition enjoyed by Meissen, the King bought the plant in 1763, and ruled the operation with an iron hand, often assuring his success by taking advantage of his position. The King died in 1786, but production has continued and quality tableware and decorative porcelains are still being made on a commercial basis.

Earliest marks were simply 'G' or 'W', followed by the sceptre mark. After 1830, 'K.P.M.' with an orb or eagle was adopted.

Plaque, girl in rose-colored gown, painted by Wagner, signed 'KPM' and sceptre mark, 9", $3,000.00.

Bust, Kaiser Freidrich III, unglazed, on glazed bl ped, 7½"....105.00
Figurine, Diane sitting by recumbent deer, 4½x5"............225.00
Pitcher, pear form/ruffled, HP cherubs, red mk, 12"..........100.00
Plaque, Christ in Temple, by Langhamer, in fr, 19x16"......4,125.00
Plaque, classic female in clouds w/cherub, sgn Chloris, 6x4"...550.00
Plaque, Guardian Angel, after Plockhorst, in fr, 16x10"......2,200.00
Plaque, Infant Jesus/St John the Baptist, by Vogt, 9½x6"......770.00
Plaque, lady musician standing before brook, 8x5"...........660.00
Plaque, Magdeline, after Corregio, reclining w/book, 5x7"......850.00
Plaque, Napoleon, after David, 19x12"....................3,850.00
Plaque, nude reclining on chaise w/book, by Chloris, 6x4"......600.00
Plaque, portrait artist's parent, after Rembrandt, 15x13", pr..3,850.00
Plaque, The Monkey's Feast, sgn, 12x15".................2,310.00
Plaque, 3 sleeping maidens in rocky landscape, 7½x4½"....1,760.00
Plate, fruit; set of 6, sceptre mark, 6½"..................132.00
Platter, floral relief, leaf hdls, gilt hi-lites, +11 plates........130.00
Tile, HP rustic scene w/9 figures, many children, 10x12".....1,400.00
Vase, HP lovers in winter landscape, hdls/lids/ped ft, 17", pr..1,430.00

Kaiser

Bell, painted Bird of Paradise, flowers, gold trim.............28.00
Bird, painted bisque, perched on natural foliage, 3"..........70.00
Figurine, nude, sitting, wht bisque, #429..................250.00

Kayserzinn Pewter

J.P. Kayser Sohn produced pewter decorated in the Art Nouveau manner in Germany during the late 1800s and into the 20th century. Examples are marked with 'Kayserzinn' and the mould number within an elongated oval reserve.

Bowl, #4245, water lily, dragonflies, scalloped, 10″ dia........95.00
Bowl, #4296, tulips, rim w/leaves, open work ea swirl, 11″.....85.00
Cake plate, #4134, lilies, 11″..............................80.00
Charger, #4364, forget-me-nots, 14″ dia...................130.00
Dish w/lid, #4556, oval, 2 open hdls, lily floral relief, 11″......135.00
Gravy boat, #4261, dbl spouts, attached tray, leaf form, 9¾″....60.00
Knife rest, dachshund...................................57.50
Lamp, Aladdin shaped, oil burning, 9″......................95.00
Pitcher, #4061, Mephistopheles, sm base rpr, 11″...........165.00
Plate, #4097, iris & shell relief, 10¼″ dia.................110.00
Platter, #4344, wild boar center, pea pods/pine rim, 21x16″ L..150.00
Platter, #4365, wild roses, deep, 17½x12″.................130.00
Platter, fish; #4128, water lilies, dragonfly, 24x11″..........250.00
Platter, fish; #4143, fish/lilies/cattails/crab, 21½x10¼″......160.00
Sauce boat, #4251, attached under plate, molded leaf, 9½″ L...65.00
Tray, clover & bee relief................................60.00
Tray, turkeys & vegetables, oval, 16x10½″................110.00
Vase, #4310, wheat & butterflies, 7¾″....................115.00
Vase, flowers in bold relief, 3½″ tapers to base, 8½″.........75.00
Vase, ped ft, tendrils, 5″...............................65.00

Inkwell and pen tray, relief face of man on lid, Nouveau florals, #4333, 5½″ x 7″, $500.00.

Keen Kutter

Keen Kutter was a brand name of E.C. Simmons Hardware, used from about 1870 until the mid-1930s. In 1923, Winchester merged with Simmons, but continued to produce Keen Kutter marked knives and tools. The merger dissolved and in 1940 the Simmons Company was purchased by Shapleigh Hardware. Older items are very collectible.

Axe, broad; Shapleigh Day marking, EX...................75.00
Axe, hand; boy's......................................15.00
Bottle, oil; glass w/cork stopper.........................18.00
Box, for double bit axes, wood, dovetailed, M..............20.00
Bush scythe, paper sticker in corner, 18″, M...............25.00
Calendar, wall; tin, pad type, boy w/litter of puppies..........65.00

Calendar, 1957, paper, w/store name & location, EX..........15.00
Carving set, 3-pc, stag hdl, EX..........................45.00
Child's wagon, ball bearing wheels, Keen Kutter Supreme......150.00
Chisel, cold; 1⅛″.....................................10.00
Chisel, wood; corner, ¾″...............................17.00
Cookbook, small, comes with food chopper, M...............15.00
Cork screw, self puller.................................19.00
Display case, large, EX................................275.00
Fan, fold up hand type, floral, reverse in logo..............35.00
File, half-round, 12″..................................12.00
File, three-square, 6″...................................7.00
Flashlight, 2 cell.....................................25.00
Floor/cabinet scraper, wood hdl.........................22.00
Food chopper, #11.....................................7.50
Gun holster, leather...................................25.00
Hammer, curved claw; 20 oz, round neck..................20.00
Hay fork..13.00
Horse clippers.......................................10.00
Kraut cutter, single blade, pat Oct 1904, mkd side/top, 26½″...35.00
Level, #KK40, brass bound/adjustable/brass side view, 30″, M...84.00
Level, Shapleigh Keen Kutter #53744GK, non-adjust, 28″, M....29.00
Mallet, wooden, w/double stamp.........................18.00
Nail clippers...10.00
Nail puller..25.00
Nail set, 5/32″..8.00
Paint brush, 1½″......................................10.00
Pinback lapel button, w/logo.............................7.00
Pipe cutter, No K2, three-wheel pattern from ½″ to 2″.........35.00
Pipe wrench, 12″.....................................25.00
Plane, #80, 22″, G....................................49.00
Plane, bench; #4, iron, smooth bottom, logo on blade/lever cap..30.00
Plane, scrub; #K240, 9½″...............................50.00
Plane, very early logo on wood base & blade................26.00
Pliers, 75 degree combination slip joint....................22.00
Plumb bob, 12 oz, hexagonal, steel, M....................17.00
Pocket knife, #K2884, ¾ white celluloid hdl, 2 blades, M......28.00
Pocket knife, #0214TK, red/blk glitter celluloid hdl, M.........65.00
Postcard, mother/daughter mower, NM....................25.00
Razor hone, No K20 Kombination, w/tin box................35.00
Rip saw blade, 8″, M w/orig carton.......................25.00
Rule, No K620, brass bound, folding, 2 foot................16.00
Saw, flooring; adjustable...............................55.00
Saw, keyhole..20.00
Scissors, bent trimmers, 7″..............................6.00
Scissors, ladies, 7″.....................................7.00
Screwdriver, large....................................20.00
Shoe rasp, 8″...7.00
Shovel, round point spade..............................12.00
Silverware, set w/orig oak dovetailed box, w/label, EC Simmons..45.00
Square, framing; No KC3, 16″ tongue, copper finish..........20.00
Square, sliding T-bevel, w/CI hdl, 9¾″ blade................30.00
Square, tri-square, logo on blade, 7½″....................17.50
Stropper, No K600 for safety razor, in orig box w/instructions...28.00
Tack claw..9.00
Thermometer, indoor/outdoor, 1¾x7½″...................30.00
Waffle iron, CI, 4 sections w/logo, EC Simmons emb on lid....150.00

Kelva

Kelva was a trademark of the C.F. Monroe Company of Meriden, Connecticut, used on an opaque mold blown glassware that was hand decorated with pastel florals and often set in ormolu holders. It was very similar to the company's other lines, Nakara and Wave Crest; only those pieces bearing the Kelva mark are listed here. All three types were in production from about 1900 until WWI.

Box, bl w/pk florals, silver ormolu rim, orig lining, 3¾" dia....200.00
Box, cigar; sgn..675.00
Box, collar & cuff; sgn...725.00
Box, gray w/pk flowers, hinged lid, 8" dia.........................675.00
Box, jewel; pk florals, oval...360.00
Box, pk w/wht, gray, bl & yel flowers, sgn, 3½x5½" dia......425.00
Sweetmeat, w/lid, sgn...320.00
Vase, florals, 8"...325.00
Vase, pk w/daisies in pk/rust, in dk bl reserve, 8¼".............375.00
Vase, pk/lav flowers, ftd, w/hdls, 14½x6"........................675.00

Humidor, hinged lid, green with pink florals, gold 'Cigars', 4¾", $525.00.

Kenton Hills

Kenton Hills Porcelain was established in 1940 in Erlanger, Kentucky by Harold Bopp, former Rookwood superintendent, and David Seyler, noted artist and sculptor. Native clay was used; glazes were very similar to those that were currently being used at Rookwood. The work was of high quality, but because of the restrictions imposed on needed material due to the onset of the war, the operation failed in 1942. Much of the ware is artist signed and marked with the Kenton Hill name and shape number.

Paperweight, lady's head figural, sgn David Seyler............145.00
Vase, bottle form, caramel gloss, 6½".............................30.00
Vase, heavy gloss glaze, leaf band, wht w/rust/bl, WH, 12"......90.00
Vase, wht w/blue, red allover floral, sgn Dickman, 8¼".......275.00

Kew Blas

Kew Blas was a trade name used by the Union Glass Company of Somerville, Massachusetts, for their iridescent art glass produced from 1890 until about 1920. The glass was made in imitation of Tiffany, and achieved notable success.

Bowl, gold irid, ribbed/flared, 5" dia.............................165.00
Sherbet, irid gold, sgn, 5"...200.00
Vase, zipper pattern in gr & gold, sgnd, 7¾"...................850.00
Vase, 2 folded sides, flared rim, 7¾"..............................650.00
Wine glass, gold, curving stem, 4¾"..............................135.00

King's Rose

King's Rose is a soft paste ware that was made in Staffordshire, England, from about 1820 to 1830. It is closely related to Gaudy Dutch in body type as well as the colors used in its decoration. The pattern consists of a large full blown orange-red rose with green, pink, and yellow leaves and accents.

Coffee pot, dome top, flakes on spout, prof rpr, 11".........275.00
Coffee pot, dome top, vine border, prof rpr hdl/lid/spout, 12"..300.00
Cup & saucer, handleless; line border, decor w/in only, VG.....40.00
Cup & saucer, handleless; line border, tiny flakes on cup ft.....75.00
Cup & saucer, Oyster, pink border, minor wear/scratches.......65.00
Cup & saucer, scalloped rim, M..................................145.00
Plate, ca 1800-1810, rare size, 5¼", NM.......................145.00
Plate, line border, imp Wood, minor enamel flaking, 6½"......75.00
Plate, line border, minor wear, imp Wood, 9¾"................95.00
Plate, pink border, worn/sm prof rim rpr, 10"..................75.00
Plate, pink border w/red swags, minor scratches, 10".........110.00
Plate, vine border, edge wear/enamel flaking, 6½"............35.00
Plate, vine border, minor scratches/flakes, 10"................55.00
Plate, vine border, soft paste, rim hairline, 8"................45.00
Saucer, vine border, VG...20.00
Soup plate, broken band border, 9¼", NM.....................135.00
Soup plate, Oyster, pink border, scratched, 10"................75.00
Toddy, vine border, soft paste, hairlines, 5¾"................35.00

Kitchen Collectibles

During the last half of the 1850s, mass-produced kitchen gadgets were patented at an astonishing rate. Most were ingeniously efficient. Apple peelers, egg beaters, cherry pitters, food choppers, and such were only the most common of hundreds of kitchen tools well designed to perform only specific tasks. Today all are very collectible.

Apple corer, hand held, tin, T hdl, sgn H ea end hdl............15.00
Apple corer & segmenter, CI, tin, pat'd 2/10/1869, 10"........55.00
Apple peeler, Bonanza, CI, elaborate, 16"......................45.00
Apple peeler, DH Whittemore, Worcester MA, clamp-on, CI.....75.00

Apple peeler, cast iron, #72, dated 1872, $45.00.

Apple peeler, Goodell, 4 pat dates.........................50.00
Apple peeler, Goodell Co, 4 gears, dtd 1898.............65.00
Apple peeler, hand held, hewn hdl, steel X blade, 1700s, 6½".. .85.00
Apple peeler, Hudson Parer Co, Mass, 1882, iron.......36.00
Apple peeler, Keen Kutter, 1898.......................60.00
Apple peeler, Keyes, iron, 1856.......................40.00
Apple peeler, Lockey, Howland, Turntable, CI, 1856.....40.00
Apple peeler, Monroe Bros, iron, 1856..................65.00
Apple peeler, pat dates, 1863, '69, '70................50.00
Apple peeler, Reading, PA, 4 gears.....................55.00
Apple peeler, Sinclair Scott Top Gear, iron............37.50
Apple peeler & corer, Goodell, 18".....................125.00
Apple peeler/corer/slicer, Bonanza, Goodell, 15x26".....260.00
Bake-O-Meter, oven top, enamel........................9.00
Berry washer, folding hdl, 1912........................750.00
Bottle, for kerosene, metal rim/hdl to fit onto cookstove.......12.00
Bread maker, Universal, 'Awarded Gold Medal St Louis Expo'...35.00
Cabbage cutter, Indpls Kraut Kutter, dtd 1905..............45.00
Cabbage cutter, Queen, blade adjusts, elaborate, in box, 1904..47.00
Cake pan, easy-lift, tin, Calumet......................8.00
Cake pan, Swansdown, tin 8" tube......................15.00
Cake plate, copper w/pewter trim, Betty Crocker award, 1949...50.00
Can opener, Delmonico, iron, 1890......................12.00
Can opener, Edmund Jr, red hdl turns on top.............5.00
Can opener, Pet Milk, rnd, fits over can................10.00
Cheese keeper, ½ lift top, mustard pnt, 9x22½" dia.........250.00
Cheese slicer, Dania #00, wood/iron....................75.00
Cherry pitter, Enterprise #1...........................22.50
Cherry pitter, Enterprise #16..........................25.00
Cherry pitter, Home, CI clamp, 1917....................45.00
Cherry pitter, Mt Joye, Rolling Mfg Co, clamp-on, CI......37.50
Cherry pitter, New Standard, clamp-on, CI...............40.00
Cherry pitter, Rollamn #3, table clamp, iron............15.00
Cherry pitter, 3 legged, pat 1863......................70.00
Chocolate grater, The Edgar, Nov 10 1896, 2¼x7".........180.00
Churn, Buffums Little Wonder, hdls/wood/tin/iron, 34".....115.00
Churn, metal/wood/CI, cream color, Dazey, pat'd 1877, 18"...85.00
Clothes wringer, Anchor Brand, wood, stencilled..........40.00
Combination tool, tongs/pie lift/stove lid lifter, iron, 1875.....35.00
Cooker/canner, Conservo, copper bottom, w/instructions, 1907...35.00
Cork sizer, CI, decorative embossing, 10" long...........45.00
Cream whip, spiral....................................6.00
Cream whip, Whippit A&J, rnd beater, wood hdl, 13½".....16.50
Dough scraper, wrought iron, 4½" blade.................19.00
Dutch oven, CI w/bail hld, 3 legs, flanged lid, late 1700s, 7"...375.00
Egg beater, A&J, dtd 1923, gr hdl.....................9.00
Egg beater, A&J, 1923, w/orig bowl & shield, EX.........30.00
Egg beater, Dover, dtd 1873...........................12.00
Egg beater, Dover, improved Taplin's, iron/tin, offset hdl....26.00
Egg beater, Dover, ivory w/sm corrugated blades, 1903.....18.00
Egg beater, Dover, sm blades, 1891.....................25.00
Egg beater, Dover, 1908..............................16.00
Egg beater, Dover #14, shelf-clamped hotel model, 17".....50.00
Egg beater, Family, emb iron, pat 1876.................35.00
Egg beater, Holts, iron, 1900.........................18.00
Egg beater, homemade, machined brass, wire whip, unique.....95.00
Egg beater, nickeled iron, tin, table clamps, manufactured.....35.00
Egg beater, pat appl for, Made in KC USA, rnd wire loops w/in..11.50
Egg beater, Pat'd Flare Dasher, iron & tin, ca 1899, 8¾".....35.00
Egg beater, Ram Beater, crown shape grip, ca 1930.........20.00
Egg beater, tin, w/advertising, 1894...................18.00
Egg beater, tin screw lid, rachet agitator, Jeannette glass.......20.00
Egg beater, Whip Well, simple drive gear, yellow hdls, ca 1920..24.00
Egg poacher, tin, Buffalo Steam Egg Poacher, 5 egg, ca 1900...35.00

Egg poacher, tin w/wire hdl, hdld spring lift remover, for 6.....45.00
Flour sifter, Androck Triple Sift, red hdl................18.00
Flour sifter, Calumet Baking Powder, dk tin, 2 cup.........11.00
Flour sifter, Red Top Flour, gr pntd, 2 cup..............8.50
Flour sifter/measure, 5 cup, Bromwell, red wood hdl.........5.00
Fly cover, wire screen, dome shaped, 9½x10½".............20.00
Food chopper, #1, 1897-1899...........................15.00
Food chopper, crescent blade, trn hdl, mkd, 12" W.........35.00
Food chopper, crescent blade w/wood hdl, 8" W............25.00
Food chopper, wood hdl, curved blade mk B Denton, Pat, 6½".25.00
Fork, meat; Rumford, 12"..............................8.00
Fork, 3 tine, Rumford................................15.00
Fruit press, Wearever aluminum, table clamp, lever, 1920s.....12.00
Fruit press, 1" wood slats/iron bands, base rotates, 7x7½".....30.00

Glassware

Bottle, water; dk green, 1 qt..........................9.00
Bowl, batter; green, 3 ftd............................25.00
Bowl, mixing; amber, 7¾"..............................4.75
Bowl, mixing; green, 6"...............................4.50
Bowl, mixing; jadite, tab hdl, 9½".....................6.50
Bowl, mixing; jadite, w/spout, 6½"....................5.00
Bowl, mixing; set of 3, yellow........................15.00
Bowl, stick hdl, green, 9"............................22.00
Canister, green, 40 oz...............................20.00
Casserole, individual, blue, w/lid.....................6.00
Churn, Dandy, tin top, wood paddle....................28.00
Cocktail shaker, green...............................22.00
Cookie jar, lt green, 1 gal..........................25.00
Cup, jadite, 16 oz...................................13.00
Egg cup, jadite, double.............................2.50
Egg separator, green................................65.00
Jug, blue...13.00
Knife, blue, 3 star, w/box..........................19.50
Measuring cup, blue, slight use, 8 oz.................12.00
Measuring cup, green, 3-spout........................13.00
Measuring cup, jadite, set of 4......................32.00
Measuring cup, jadite, ½ cup........................10.00
Pie plate, blue, 8".................................5.75
Platter, well & tree, bl tint, Pyrex.................12.00
Range set, white w/green letters.....................21.00
Refrigerator dish, yellow, 8x8".....................10.00
Rolling pin, amethyst blown glass...................100.00
Rolling pin, Columbus Flour Co, milk glass..........285.00
Rolling pin, custard glass, aluminum shaker cap.......80.00
Rolling pin, glass, painted wht, screw on metal cap, 14".....25.00
Sanitary Cheese Preserver, pat applied, w/lid.........28.00
Shaker, dk green, 8 oz, square......................5.50
Towel rod, jadite, 15"..............................23.00
Water dispenser, jadite, w/clear top................35.00

Grater, hanging, tin, 1876..........................8.00
Grater, Lorraine, revolving, table clamp............14.00
Ham boiler, copper w/tinned lid, CI hdls, 1870s, 12½" long...100.00
Ice grinder, Dazey, 1940............................24.00
Ice shaver, Enterprise, pat July 4, 1893, makes balls.....40.00
Ice tongs, brass hdl, mk FJ Hinkey, 14½"............45.00
Ironing board, New Improved, 1869...................250.00
Juice-o-mat, chrome................................18.00
Knife, bread; All Width Bread Slicer, Miller & Sons........12.00
Lemon squeezer, CI, screw down press, Landers, Frary & Clark..65.00

Lemon squeezer, Diamond Point, pat'd July 10, 1888.........32.00
Lemon squeezer, Dunlap, iron......................17.00
Lemon squeezer, metal, 1940.......................6.00
Lemon squeezer & slicer, wood/iron stand, 2 blades, 15" L....140.00
Measuring cup, Swansdown cake flour, emb ad..............10.00
Meat & juice press, Columbus #2, CI, 3 part...............25.00
Meat & juice press, Universal; Landers, Frary & Clark, 1880s...25.00
Meat grinder, Enterprise, 1888, clamp-on................11.00
Meat grinder, Larkin, heavily emb....................12.50
Meat grinder, Universal #12, table mount, wood hdl..........12.00
Meat tenderizer, all wood, red hdl, lg.................10.00
Meat tenderizer, pottery w/wood hdl, pat Dec 25, 1877, 10"....25.00
Meat tenderizer, wht porcelain w/EX turned maple hdl, 1890s...65.00
Noodle cutter, Teek One, sgn Germany, iron/wood/brass.......45.00
Noodle cutter, wood hdl.........................6.00
Nutmeg grater, CI, bellows shape, emb: decor/1870, brass clip..240.00
Nutmeg grater, ivory..........................250.00
Nutmeg grater, w/wheel & blk wood turning hdl & holding knob..65.00
Nutmeg grater, wood & tin, 'Common Sense', pat'd 7/23/1867...65.00
Nutmeg grater, wood/tin/wire, 'Edgar', pat'd 8/18/1891........65.00
Pan, bread; tin cylinder w/isinglass window, 1897...........35.00
Pancake turner, tin, side-flip......................8.00
Pastry blender, Androck, red hdl....................5.00
Pastry iron, CI, Griswold Co, heart shape #2..............15.00
Pastry roller, 3 carved decorations, iron frame w/wood hdl....135.00
Peach peeler, Sinclair Scott, Baltimore, heart design, 3 gears...65.00
Pliers, cast brass, rooster head jaws, 6"................15.00
Pot cleaner, iron mesh, handle.....................30.00
Pot scraper, Mt Penn advertising....................22.00
Potato baker, stove-top, tin, 1911...................28.00
Potato julienne curler, mechanical, clamp-on, CI, dtd 1877......75.00
Potato masher, wood, 10½"......................10.00
Raisin seeder, Everett, hand held, 1890................35.00
Raisin seeder, The Gem, 1895.....................35.00
Raisin seeder, 3 legs w/rotating gear, CI, 1870s, French......120.00
Rolling pin, clear glass, wooden dowel, pat 1879............125.00
Rolling pin, crockery, w/ad: Tulsa, Polar Bear Flour is King....150.00
Scoop, ceramic, ivory w/flowers....................12.00
Slicer, potato/vegetable, clamp-on, rnd disc w/4 blades, CI.....85.00
Slicer, US Slicing Machine Co #7, self sharpening, 1919.......360.00
Spoon, mixing; slotted, wood hdl, 1908................8.00
Spoon, slotted, wooden hdl, Rumford..................13.00
Sprinkler bottle, cat w/marble eyes..................25.00
Sprinkler bottle, Chinaman, wht/turq..................20.00
Sprinkler bottle, clothes pin, turquoise................22.50
Sprinkler bottle, elephant w/flowers..................20.00
Sprinkler bottle, iron w/ivy.......................18.00
Sprinkler bottle, iron w/rooster....................15.00
Sprinkler bottle, Sprinkle Plenty....................12.00
Strawberry huller, brass, 1894.....................20.00
Tin kitchen, sheet iron, wrought iron spit, late 1700s, 13¼"...400.00
Toaster, cook stove type........................10.00
Toaster, revolves, wrought iron/dbl arch design, early 1800s....175.00
Tool, combination, iron, pat 1875...................28.00
Vegetable slicer, Catawissa Spec, pat 1898, orig paper on bk....45.00
Wafer iron, CI w/wrought hdls, wreath w/instruments, 26" L....35.00
Waffle iron, CI, emb drum & fife players, long hdls, 24".......175.00
Waffle iron, Griswold, CI, heart pattern, pat May 1820........65.00
Waffle iron, Griswold #8, spiral wound hdl, 1908...........30.00
Waffle iron, Piqua-Ware, #8, rotates w/in rnd iron fr, w/hdls....25.00
Waffle iron, Wagner, 2 pc w/bail, 1910...............16.00
Washboard, blue porcelain, Capitol Line National...........30.00
Washboard, Little Queen.........................9.00
Washboard, National #801, brass....................8.00

Washboard, rockingham stoneware in rfn maple fr...........58.00
Washboard, roller; Mother Hubbard..................50.00
Washboard, Sani-steel..........................18.00
Washboard, zinc, Sanitary Cable....................40.00
Washer, plunger type, w/wood hdl...................8.00

Knives

Knife collecting as a hobby began in earnest during the 1960s when government regulations required for the first time that knife companies mark their product with the country of origin. The few collectors and dealers cognizant of this change at once began stockpiling the older knives made before this law was enacted. Another impetus to the growing interest in this area came with the Gun Control Act of 1968, which severely restricted gun trading. Frustrated gun dealers transferred their attention to knives. Today there are collectors clubs in many of the states.

The ones to look for are old bone handled knives in mint, unsharpened condition, pearl handles, Case doctor's knives, and large display models.

Pocket Knives

Case, Bradford, 62042, green bone..................85.00
Case, Coke bottle, green bone, WR Case & Sons...........250.00
Case, G5233, gold metal flake hdl, mk Tested, 2⅝".........145.00
Case, Muskrat, rough blk hdl, 1940s, mk XX, 3⅞".........195.00
Case, T2210, tortoise shell compo, 1930s, mk Tested, 3⅜"....195.00
Case, USA, 5299½............................125.00
Case, USA, 54025............................100.00
Case, USA, 6308.............................24.00
Case, XX 6279, red bone........................60.00
Case, XX 6333..............................35.00
Case, XX 82079.............................45.00
Case, X31048..............................30.00
Case, 2212L, walnut hdl, 1930s, mk Tested, 3⅝"..........68.00
Case, 3220, yel bone hdl, mk XX, 2¾"...............120.00
Case, 3220, yel compo hdl, 1940s, mk Tested, 2¾".........120.00
Case, 5202½, stag hdl, 1930s, mk Tested, 3⅜"..........195.00
Case, 52131, stag hdl, mk XX, 3⅝"................348.00
Case, 62009, br bone hdl, 1930s, mk XX, 3⅜"...........145.00
Case, 62009½, bone hdl, 1950s, mk XX, 3⅜"...........28.00
Case, 62019, gr bone hdl, mk Tested, 4⅛"............320.00
Case, 6205 RAZ, green bone hdl, 1950s, mk XX, 3¾".......145.00
Case, 6207, red bone hdl, 1940s, mk XX, 3½"..........49.00
Case, 62109X, rough blk hdl, 1940s, mk XX, 3⅛"........55.00
Case, 6216, gr bone hdl, 1940s, mk Tested, 3⅜"........116.00
Case, 6225½, gr bone hdl, mk Tested, 3".............170.00
Case, 6233, Tested...........................60.00
Case, 6235EO, gr bone hdl, mk Tested, 3¼"...........145.00
Case, 8220, pearl hdl, 1940s, mk Tested, 2¾"..........295.00
Case, 9201, cracked ice hdl, 1950s, 2⅝"............26.00
Case, 92024R, imitation pearl hdl, mk XX, 3".........34.00
Case, 92027, imitation pearl hdl, mk Tested, 2¾".......58.00
Case, 9233, cracked ice hdl, mk XX, 2⅝"...........45.00
Cattaraugus, 11709, stag hdl, shielded, brass lined, 4".......75.00
Cattaraugus, 12819, stag hdl, glaze finish, brass lined, 5⅜"....198.00
Cattaraugus, 20594, amber celluloid hdl, brass lined, 3¼".....54.00
Cattaraugus, 2249, stag hdl, brass lined, shielded, 4".......48.00
Cattaraugus, 2929, MOP hdl, crocus finish, 2 blades, 3".....172.00
Cattaraugus, 5003, MOP hdl, crocus finish, silver lined, 3¼"...135.00
German, hen & rooster, pearl hdl...................100.00
Ka Bar, 01103, fancy celluloid hdl, 3⅜"..............48.00
Ka Bar, 0111, pyraline hdl, Union Cut Co, 3⅞"..........72.00
Ka Bar, 11107LG, cream celluloid hdl, 5¼"............645.00

Ka Bar, 21106, genuine stag hdl, Union Cut Co, 5⅜".......800.00
Ka Bar, 2179-L Grizzly, genuine stag hdl, 5½"...........1,510.00
Ka Bar, 3170, redwood hdl, Union Cut Co, 4"..............95.00
Ka Bar, 6112, rough blk hdl, 4".........................38.00
Keen Kutter, K0195¾K, pearl bl celluloid hdl, 2 blades, ⅜"...42.00
Keen Kutter, K02736, smooth fibre hdl, 2 blades, 3".......50.00
Keen Kutter, K04527, stag hdl, 2 blades, 3¼".............115.00
Keen Kutter, K0814, nickel silver hdl, 2 blades, 3".......33.00
Keen Kutter, K1704, cocobola hdl, 1 lg spey blade, 3¾"....21.00
Keen Kutter, K3071F, stag hdl, 3 blades, 3⅜"............105.00
Keen Kutter, K3215¾G, gold celluloid hdl, 3 blades, 3⅜"..125.00
Keen Kutter, K33720R, iridescent celluloid hdl, 3 blades, 4"..88.00
Keen Kutter, K341, stag hdl, 3 blades, 3¼"...............84.00
Keen Kutter, K3430, genuine buffalo horn hdl, 3 blades, 4"..130.00
Keen Kutter, K3483, pearl hdl, 3 blades, 3⅛"...........1,210.00
Keen Kutter, K443, pearl hdl, 4 blades, 3¼".............124.00
Keen Kutter, K50K, red & blk hdl, crest shield, 2 blades, 3¼"..62.00
Keen Kutter, K51¾, ebony hdl, 2 blades, 3⅜".............43.00
Keen Kutter, K5738/S, skeleton pearl hdl, 3 blades, 3⅛"...65.00
Keen Kutter, K7WPC, pearl hdl, 2 blades, 3⅛"...........125.00
Keen Kutter, K711, curved pearl hdl, 2 blades, 2¾".......85.00
Keen Kutter, K72423, fibre hdl, 2 blades, 3¼"............68.00
Keen Kutter, K73265G, gold celluloid hdl, 3 blades, 3".....95.00
Keen Kutter, K7530J, gr & blk celluloid hdl, 3 blades, 3¼"..120.00
Keen Kutter, K8464¼, ivory hdl, 3 blades, 3⅝"..........138.00
Remington, R-S3333......................................70.00
Remington, R-1173....................................1,490.00
Remington, R-3056.....................................305.00
Remington, R-4605, acorn shield.........................85.00
Remington, R-995, waterfall hdls.......................100.00
Robeson, 126301.......................................110.00
Robeson, 128105, lifelong ebonized hdl, blk pyralin, 3"....32.00
Robeson, 222050, rosewood hdl, brass lining, 3⅞".......145.00
Robeson, 421200, wht pyralin hdl, steel lining, 3⅜".....98.00
Robeson, 533278, solid nickel silver hdl, 3⅜"...........28.00
Robeson, 622382, bone stag hdl, brass lining, 4⅛"......145.00
Robeson, 623505, bone stag hdl, 3¼"....................58.00
Robeson, 632838, horn pyralin hdl, brass lining, 3⅜".....43.00
Schrade, #2 blade Congress..............................45.00
Schrade, C3-186, cocobola hdl, pruning blade, 4⅞".......38.00
Schrade, 9464US, red/wht/blue celluloid hdl, 4 blades, 3⅝"..138.00
Shapleigh, 1S440¾C, fancy celluloid hdl, 5"............155.00
Shapleigh, 1S445, cocobola wood hdl, lg maize blade, 4"...58.00
Shapleigh, 2S377W, celluloid hdl, lg ink eraser, 3⅜"....545.00
Shapleigh, 2S432C, celluloid hdl, brass lining, 3".......128.00
Utica, goldstone whittler...............................45.00
Winchester, H2123P, fiber hdl, straight Jack pattern, 3⅛"..53.00
Winchester, H2951P, stag hdl, regular Jack pattern, 3½"..140.00
Winchester, H3342P, pearl hdl, lt cattle pattern, 3⅜"...255.00
Winchester, 1701, bone hdl, 1 lg spear blade, 3½".......195.00
Winchester, 1950, lockback, bone hdl, brass lining, 6¾"..1,205.00
Winchester, 2039, red & blk celluloid hdl, 2 blades, 3"....95.00
Winchester, 2057, varicolored finish celluloid hdl, 3⅜"..123.00
Winchester, 2087, shell celluloid hdl, 2 blades, 3".....128.00
Winchester, 2088, gray celluloid hdl, 2 blades, 3⅜"....115.00
Winchester, 2201, nickel silver skeleton hdl, 3¼".......65.00
Winchester, 2202, smooth fiber hdl, 2 blades, 3".........70.00
Winchester, 2629, ebony hdl, 2 blades, 3¼".............180.00
Winchester, 2850, stag hdl, 2 blades, 3¾"..............278.00
Winchester, 2910, stag hdl, 2 blades, spear & file, 3"....94.00
Winchester, 2928, stag hdl, 2 blades, 4"................205.00
Winchester, 3005, blk celluloid hdl, 3 blades, 3⅝".....210.00
Winchester, 3025, abalone blue celluloid hdl, 3½".......245.00
Winchester, 3376, pearl hdl, 3 blades, 4"...............270.00

Miscellaneous

Bowie, A Williams, German silver guard, 2 pc stag grip, 8½"....75.00
Bowie, Austin, forged bolster, stag grip, silver pommel, 19½"..400.00
Bowie, decorated blade/horn grip/steel mts/silver decor, 17"....300.00
Bowie, folding 7¼" blade mk Sheffield, #6, brass guard lockbk..50.00
Bowie, Geo Crookes, tip w/top logo, brass hilt, sheath, 10¾"..150.00
Bowie, German, brass guard, 1 pc horn grip, 1800s, 14".....300.00
Bowie, Gilpin & Whitehouse, brass guard/ferrule/cap, 16½"..350.00
Bowie, J Harrison, 1811, 1 pc stag horn, steel mts, 14"......185.00
Bowie, Lingard, hide-away, silver guard/hilt, orig sheath, 8¾"..140.00
Bowie, Rinley Cutls & Co, spearpoint, fancy silver mts, 10"..110.00
Bowie, Sheffield blade, stag horn hdl, leather sheath, 11¾"..75.00
Bowie, Smith & Son, 4½" clip point blade, silver guard, 8"..130.00
Bowie, Stacy, German silver mts, tooled leather sheath, 10"..150.00
Bowie, Thos Ibbotson, clip point, German silver guard, 9¾"....85.00
Bowie type, stag simulated bakelite grip, steel guard, 8¾".....20.00
Hunting, US Army, 1880, brass guard, Springfield...........100.00
Hunting, Western USAW, w/scabbard, 14¾"................50.00
Hunting, 6" dbl edge, Shapleigh, leather grip/brass pommel...25.00
Military, EGW WWII, USA...............................25.00
Pribyl Bros, take-apart, fork/spoon/corkscrew/blade, ivory hdl...150.00
Skinning, J Russel Green River, curved 6" blade, 10½".......50.00

Knowles, Taylor, Knowles

Isaac Knowles and Isaac Harvey operated a pottery in East Liverpool, Ohio, in 1853, where they produced both yellowware and Rockingham. In 1870, Knowles bought Harvey's interests and took as partners John Taylor and Homer Knowles. Their principal product was Ironstone china, but Knowles was confident that American potters could produce as fine a ware as the Europeans, and to prove his point hired Joshua Poole, an artist from the Belleek Works in Ireland. Poole quickly perfected a Belleek type china, but fire destroyed this portion of the company and before it could function again, their hotel china business had grown to the point that their full attention was required to meet market demands. By 1891 they were able to try again. They developed a bone china, as fine and thin as before, which they called Lotus. Henry Schmidt from the Meissen factory in Germany decorated the ware, often with lacy filigree applications, or with hand formed leaves and flowers to which he added further decoration with liquid slip applied by means of a squeeze bag. Due to high production costs, with so much of the fragile ware damaged in firing, and because of changes in tastes and styles of decoration, the Lotus Ware line was dropped in 1896. Some of the early ware was marked 'KT&K China'; later marks have a star and a crescent, with 'Lotus Ware' added.

Lotus Ware

Bowl, raised floral decor, filigree hdls, mkd, minor roughness...220.00
Creamer, HP rose decor, mkd...........................160.00
Pitcher, gold fishnet decor, HP, sgnd Dillingham 1898, mkd...400.00
Pitcher, wht w/wht fishnet decor, mkd, small...............160.00
Pitcher, wild rose HP decor, gold trim, mkd................200.00
Sugar, HP floral decor, mkd............................170.00
Vase, cylinder, gold floral panels, wht fishnet, ftd, mkd, 11"....500.00
Vase, floral decor, sgn, w/hdls, 7½".....................275.00
Vase, HP figures in panels, gold fishnet, mkd, chip on top rim.500.00
Vase, HP floral relief, dtd Aug 1896, 6", 1 small chip........150.00

Miscellaneous

Whiskey jug, advertising Pennsylvania Club Pure Rye, mkd......95.00
Whiskey jug, HP corn, Urban Club......................145.00

Kutani

Kutani, named for the Japanese village where it originated, was first produced in the 17th century. The early ware, Ko Kutani, was produced for only about thirty years. Several types were produced before 1800, but these are rarely encountered. In the 19th century, kilns located in several different villages began to copy the old Kutani wares. This later, more familiar type, has large areas of red with gold designs on a white ground decorated with warriors, birds, florals, etc., in controlled colors of red, gold, and black.

Beaker, orange, gold on wht, birds/florals, sgn, 4½"..........55.00
Bowl, butterflies & flowers on wht, gold blk border, 9".......125.00
Bowl, figures, flowers & landscapes on red, 1900, 3½x7"......250.00
Bowl, ladies by lake, gr/red/gold, 1½x5"..................75.00
Bowl, ribbed, 3 ftd, scalloped top, figures/florals, gold, 4".......12.00
Cat, sleeping, tan w/blk detail, enamel mc collar, 11½"........155.00
Creamer & sugar, men/women by lake, cobalt & gold trim.....200.00
Elephant, ash tray on bk, boxes ea side, Satsuma style, 6½"....42.00
Figurine, lady, seated, playing mandolin, Satsuma style, 6"......32.00
Ginger jar, 6"..85.00

Labels

Before the advent of the cardboard box, wooden crates were used for transporting products. Paper labels were attached to the crates to identify the contents and the packer. These labels often had colorful lithographed illustrations, covering a broad range of subjects. Eventually the cardboard box replaced the crate, and the art work was imprinted directly onto the carton. Today, these paper labels are becoming collectible, primarily for the art, but also for their advertising appeal.

Broom, Dixie, Black man on fence w/banjo, 1915, 3½x5¼"......2.00
Cigar, Admiral Gherardi, bust/Navy uniform, outer, 4x4" 15.00
Cigar, Admiration, lady w/mirror, 1936, 7x8"..............2.00
Cigar, Aida, sphinx & pyramids, early, inner lid, 6x9"..........20.00
Cigar, College Widow, Victorian woman/football game, outer....40.00
Cigar, Edsonia, pictures early Victrola, inner lid, 6x9".........68.00
Cigar, El Jaffe, mosque, emb & bronzed, outer label...........6.00
Cigar, Fifty Little Orphans, 1 is holding cigar, inner lid.........8.00
Cigar, First Cabinet, Washington & cabinet, inner lid..........11.00
Cigar, La Boda, Clear Havana, 1924, Colonial couple, 4½x6¾"..3.00
Cigar, Legal Tender, Schwencke, Lady Liberty w/coin, outer.....20.00
Cigar, Madrilena, Neuman, woman/much cleavage, salesman's....10.00
Cigar, Magnolia, deeply emb flower/flags/coins, inner lid.......13.00
Cigar, Mark Twain, w/portrait, 1920s, 7x9"..................4.50
Cigar, Pres McKinley Memorata, lady w/scroll, names..........7.50
Cigar, Rudolph Valentino portrait, end label, '20s............4.00
Cigar, Sherlock Holmes, 1920s, 7x8"......................4.50
Cigar, Sheyboygan, Indian on mtn, mc/gold trim, 6½x9".......2.00
Cigar, Swan, wht swan on pond, inner lid, 6x9".............5.50
Cigar, Yellow Jack, bee w/clover, early, inner lid, 6x9"........30.00
Fruit, Baby Turtle, baby riding turtle, Modesto..............2.00
Fruit, Black Joe, Lodi...................................2.50
Fruit, Camel, desert scene, Loomis.......................2.00
Fruit, Dixie Boy, Black boy eating grapefruit, Fla, 9x9".........3.00
Fruit, Owl, owl on branch, Sacramento....................2.00
Fruit, Peacock, Sacramento.............................2.00
Fruit, Pheasant, Visalia................................2.50
Fruit, Roseville Belle, lady in bell.......................2.00
Fruit, Thorobreads, Boxer dog, San Francisco...............1.50
Oranges, Airship, old 4 prop plane, blue ground, Fillmore.......8.00
Oranges, Annie Laurie..................................5.00
Oranges, Athlete, 3 runners at finish line, Claremont, 10x11"....5.00

Oranges, Avenue......................................4.00
Oranges, Blue Goose...................................4.00
Oranges, Daisy..4.00
Oranges, Endurance...................................15.00
Oranges, Golden Rod...................................3.00
Oranges, Handsum.....................................5.00
Oranges, Humming Bird................................17.00
Oranges, La Reina.....................................5.00
Oranges, Malibu......................................10.00
Oranges, Navajo......................................10.00
Oranges, Reindeer.....................................7.00
Oranges, Shamrock.....................................3.00
Oranges, Strength.....................................15.00
Oranges, Western Queen................................8.00
Syrup, Uncle Remus, dtd 1924, 6¾x20"......................8.00
Tobacco, Dan Patch Cut Plug, horse/harness racer on yellow.....1.00
Tobacco, landmark Cut Plug, windmill, blk/yellow.............1.00
Tobacco, Pep Cigarette Tobacco, man sprinting, orange.........1.50

Cigar box label, 'Call Again', white letters on red, $3.00.

Labino

Mr. Labino is currently producing glassware in Ohio. A ceramic engineer by trade, he was instrumental in developing the heat-resistant tiles used in space flights. His glass making shows his versatility in the art. While some of his designs are free-form and futuristic, others are reminiscent of the products of older glasshouses.

Candy bowl, orange amber, ftd, 1972, 6"...................225.00
Pitcher, ruby shaded to gr, melon ribbed, 1965, 5½"........350.00
Vase, bulbous, wht circles w/orange centers on rose amber, 6".250.00
Vase, copper schmeltz..................................325.00

Lace, Linens & Needlework

It has been recorded that lace was found in the tombs of ancient Egypt. Lace has always been a symbol of wealth and fashion. Italian laces are regarded as the finest ever produced, but the differences between them and the laces of France are nearly indistinguishable. In Munich a type of lace was woven, not by human fingers but by insects. Caterpillar lace was made by smearing a flat surface with an edible paste, over which the desired design was outlaid in oil. The caterpillars were repelled by the oiled areas, but ate the paste, all the while spinning their silken threads.

Needlework was revived during the middle of the 18th century, and became the favorite of feminine pastimes. Examples of many forms are readily available today -- tatting, embroidery, needlepoint, and crochet -- and although fragile in appearance have withstood the ravages of time with remarkable durability.

See also Samplers

Banner, linen, state seal of Mass w/Indian, 98x94".........100.00
Banquet cloth, Madeira ecru linen/lace/embroidery, +8 napkins.300.00
Bedspread, candlewicking, star/tulips, 1835.................500.00
Bedspread, crochet, candlewick, 100" sq...................200.00
Bedspread, crochet, 6 point stars, 3" fringe, full size.........175.00
Bib, homespun w/X stitch hearts/deer/flowers/1845, worn, 7x11".70.00
Chair back, crochet, Home Sweet Home, 27x20½".............25.00
Coverlet, crochet, cotton, popcorn stitch, 1880s, 66x80"......175.00
Coverlet, crochet, cotton, popcorn stitch, 1880s, 72x92"......185.00
Embroidery, linen panel, birds/flowering trees, lined, 30x80"....65.00
Homespun, bl/wht 12x22", +2 br/wht 6½x7" pcs............60.00
Homespun, gold/wht, 41x65", EX.........................125.00
Homespun, wht, 36x93"..................................22.00
Lace maker's pillow, 12 wood bobbins/paper pattern/etc, 9".....65.00
Lace strip, handmade, buildings/ladies/man, 6 colors, 55x8½"..145.00
Needlepoint, girl/dog by river, vine border, in fr, 25".........165.00
Needlepoint, petit point florals, stained, 15x24"..............25.00
Needlework, girl/tree/dog/bird/rabbit/verse/1846, 25".........250.00
Needlework on paper, florals, bird's eye veneer fr, 12x15".....80.00
Needlework on satin, castle/moat/trees/windmill/sheep, 24x32"..600.00
Needlework on satin, horseshoe/grain/flowers, mc, 24x30"......35.00
Needlework on silk, flower basket in satin stitch, 18" sq......225.00
Needlework on silk, lady in garden, water color features, 7"....115.00
Needlework on silk, lady/landscape/birds/verse, 18x20".......475.00
Picture, mourning, silk embroidery, weeping maid/tree, 10x13".385.00
Picture, stumpwork, Adam & Eve, silk/gilt/silver, 1600, 10x13".400.00
Picture, woolwork, flags surround circle w/ship, 23x25".......350.00
Pillow sham, embroidery cupid/floral, lace border, worn.......25.00
Runner, Battenburg & linen, 70x18", EX....................65.00
Runner, linen, stylized floral embroidery, 17x56"............40.00
Table cloth, Battenburg & linen, EX quality, 72x72", EX.....150.00
Table cloth, hand tatted, fine thread, 70x90", M............350.00
Table cloth, Portland Vase damask, 16½x7½ ft.............500.00
Table cloth, red linen w/wht fern design, 50x72"............60.00
Table cloth, red/gr, woven, w/fringe, 56x59"................50.00
Table cloth, red/wht linen/Greek key border/floral/fringe, 76"....50.00
Textile, copper plate, Apothesis of Franklin/Geo Washington...205.00
Textile, red/wht copper plate print, scalloped/quilted, 54x84"....65.00
Towel, linen, embroidery of birds/florals, 14½x21"...........30.00
Towel, show; homespun linen, X stitch w/flowers, 1816, 57".....90.00
Towel, tea; linen, red/wht w/red eagle, 18½x32"............25.00

Battenburg tablecloth, 67" diameter, $250.00.

Lacy Glassware

Lacy glass became popular in the late 1820s after the development of the pressing machine. It was decorated with allover patterns -- hearts, lyres, sheafs of wheat, etc. -- and backgrounds were completely stippled. The designs were intricate and delicate, hence the term 'lacy'. Although Sandwich produced this type of glassware in abundance, it was also made by other eastern glassworks, as well as in the midwest. By 1840, its popularity on the wane and a depressed economy forcing manufacturers to seek less expensive modes of production, lacy glass began to be phased out in favor of pressed pattern glassware.

Bowl, Daisy, minor edge chips, 10" dia....................145.00
Bowl, Daisy, 6¼"....................................25.00
Bowl, Princess Feather w/diamond motif, minor roughness, 10".145.00
Bowl & pitcher, rim chips, 3" dia........................105.00
Chamberstick, 1½x2"...............................150.00
Curtain tie back, opal glass, florals, pewter post, 3" dia, pr....55.00
Dish, Pineapple, cut rim, 6½x9".........................80.00
Dish, Pipes of Pan, ground spot on rim, 6¼x8¼"............50.00
Goblet, French, 5¾"..................................25.00
Honey dish, flower shape, 3¼".........................18.00
Honey dish, Paneled Scroll, 3½", pr......................15.00
Honey dish, Roman Rosette, sm rim chips, 4"..............10.00
Plate, flower center, stippled rim w/bull's eyes, 5¾".........18.00
Plate, Gothic arch rim, waffle center, sm rim chips, 6".......15.00
Plate, Heart, sm rim chips, 6¼".........................45.00
Plate, lyre & basket of fruit rim, minor rim flakes, 5".........15.00
Plate, pinwheel flower center, heavy, early, rim chips, 6".....17.50
Plate, Roman Rosette, clear, 5½".......................35.00
Plate, scalloped w/almond design, ribs w/dia point center, 6"....15.00
Plate, shield design, 6"...............................30.00
Sauce, Nectarine pattern, rim chips, 5¼".................10.00
Sauce, Paneled Scroll, 4½", pr.........................20.00
Sauce, Peacock Eye, 4¼"..............................15.00
Sauce, Prince of Wales feathered cap, 'Ich Dien . . .', 4¾"....10.00
Sauce, Princess Feather w/X swords, minor rim chips, 4½".....12.50
Sauce, Roman Rosette, minor rim flakes, 4"................11.00
Sauce, 11 hearts, minor rim flakes, 4¼"...................8.00

Lalique

Beginning his lengthy career as a designer and maker of fine jewelry, Rene Lalique at first only daubled in glass, making small panels of pate-de-vere (paste on paste) and cire perdue (wax casting) to use in his jewelry. He also made small flacons of gold and silver with his glass inlays, which attracted the attention of M.F. Coty, who commissioned Lalique to design bottles for his perfume company. The success of this venture resulted in the opening of his own glasshouse at Combs-la-Ville in 1909. In 1921, a larger factory was established at Wingen-sur-Moder, in Alsace-Lorraine. By the thirties, Lalique was world reknown as the most important designer of his time.

Lalique glass is lead based, either mold blown or pressed. Favored motifs during the Art Nouveau period were dancing nymphs, fish, dragonflies, and foliage. Characteristically the glass is crystal in combination with acid etched relief. Later, some items were made in as many as ten colors -- red, amber, and green among them -- and were occasionally accented with enameling. These colored pieces, especially those in black, are rare and highly prized by advanced collectors.

During the twenties and thirties, Lalique designed several vases and bowls reminiscent of American Indian art. He also developed a line in the Art Deco style decorated with stylized birds, florals, and geometrics. In addition to vases, clocks, automobile mascots, stemware, bottles, and many other useful objects were produced.

Items made before his death in 1945 were marked 'R. Lalique'; later the 'R' was deleted even though some of the original molds were still used. Numbers found on the bases of some pieces are catalogue numbers.

Key:

cl/f-----clear and frosted	RL-----signed R. Lalique
L-----signed Lalique	RLF-----signed R. Lalique, France
fr-----frosted	cl-----clear

Ash tray, Fauvette, triangles w/birds form rim, RL, 6¾" dia....295.00
Atomizer, Frosted Nudes, RL............................385.00
Blotter, Mures, frosted, mulberries motif, RLF, ca 1929, 6½"..895.00
Bottle, Nina Ricci display, dbl dove, wing span 13", 12" H...125.00
Bowl, Anges, opal, 8 pr kneeling angels, RL, 14¼" dia......2,375.00
Bowl, center; Armentiers, sgn RLF/#393, 10½".............650.00
Bowl, clear w/4 coiled amber opal serpants, LF............550.00
Bowl, Coquilles, opal, 4 molded seashells, RL, ca 1930, 5"....310.00
Bowl, fruit; stylized wheat, acid etched, RL, ca 1930, 5¼"....365.00
Bowl, Ondine, opal, 6 molded mermaids/spray, RL, ca 1920....560.00
Bowl, Pinsons, fr, molded songbirds/swirls, L, ca 1936, 10"....240.00
Bowl, Thistle, flared w/thistle relief, 10"..................300.00
Box, birds/grapes/vines, w/topaz glass cabochons, RL, 7" dia..1,945.00
Box, Isabelle, fr, 3 peacocks, RL, minor chip, 3½" dia.......633.00
Box, Mesanges, opal, molded sm birds, RL, ca 1930, 7" dia...633.00
Box, Primeveres, opal, relief flowers, RLF, ca 1929, 6½" dia.1,295.00
Brooch, enamel, woman & child, in gold & topaz fr, sgn L...9,500.00
Car mascot, Faucon, molded falcon, frosted hi-lites, RL, 6"...1,530.00
Car mascot, Sanglier, topaz, molded boar, RL, ca 1929, 3¾".1,775.00
Centerpiece, Trepid Sirene, opal, plate w/siren relief, 14½"....850.00
Chandelier, Coquilles, scallop shell relief, sgn, 11¾" dia.....1,430.00
Decanter, cl pyramid shape w/floral design stopper, RL, 12"....385.00
Figurine, Sirene, opal mermaid, RL, ca 1927, 4"............925.00
Figurine, Source de Fontaine, Oriental w/fish, RL, #841, 25".5,250.00
Figurine, Timide, cl/fr, sparrow/tail down, RLF #1151/RL, 5"...235.00
Fish, orig label, Lalique France, 6½x4"....................265.00
Flacon, perfume; Carre Hirondelles, relief swallows, RLF, 3¾".715.00
Hand mirror, fr leaf/vine/figures, silver backed, L, ca 1917....2,450.00
Inkwell, Nenuphar, frosted, water lilies, 3 pc, RL, 5¾".......540.00
Jardiniere, Saint Hubert, cl/fr, gazelle hdls, RLF, 5½".......1,275.00
Medallion, mistletoe relief, gr, 1912, 2¾"..................495.00
Necklace, beads: 6 sided w/molded fr floral/sm amethyst, 1920..855.00
Paperweight, 2 Aigles, cl/fr, eagles w/glass ball, RLF, ca '28..1,295.00
Pendant, Lilies, org/red, weeping lilies, dk enameling, unsgnd..395.00
Pendant, Wasps, electric bl, wasp motif, RL, ca 1927.......1,445.00
Perfume, blk, sq w/carved ladies ea corner, Ambre D'orsay, 5".450.00
Perfume, Couer Joie, for Nina Ricci, w/contents, 3¼".......250.00
Perfume, Couer Joie, for Nina Ricci, w/contents, 4".........350.00
Perfume, engraved classic figures, molded stopper, Coty, RL...857.00
Perfume, Fleurettes, rectangular, molded corner floral, L, 5"...400.00
Perfume, Le Jade, gr glass, orig case, sgn, 3"..............1,760.00
Perfume, Lunaria, cl, dk gray stain 'Honesty', RL, ca '20, 3½".575.00
Perfume, relief head of pan & garlands, RL, ca 1925, 5".....747.00
Pitcher, tray, 6 glasses, Bahia, yel w/molded leaf, RL, ca '30..3,080.00
Plate, opal, molded 6 mermaids & spray, RL, ca 1920, 11" dia.785.00
Ring dish, frosted madonna, #288, sgn RLF, 5x3¾".........195.00
Seal, Aigle, clear, eagle w/hunched wings, RL, ca '30, 3¾"...1,500.00
Seal, Tete d'Aigle, cl cylinder/bust of eagle, RL, ca '29, 3¼"...650.00
Tumbler, fr/cl, frenzied nudes design, RL, ca 1929, 5½".....145.00
Vase, Albert, smoke gr, sparrow-hawk heads at rim, RLF, 7".2,495.00
Vase, Aras, opal, molded birds/cherries, RL, ca '27, 9½"....2,325.00
Vase, Bali, bird relief, frosted w/br stain, 8"..............2,200.00
Vase, bl, elongated oviform, 9"..........................1,300.00
Vase, Chamarande, lug hdls w/thorn relief, charcoal gray, 8"...825.00
Vase, Chardons, cl, molded thistle, butterscotch stain, RL, 8".1,650.00
Vase, Cire Perdue, boldly molded leaf/stalk, brn wash, L, 10".9,250.00

Vase, Coqs et Plumes, fr/cl, molded rooster, RLS, 6"........550.00
Vase, Courges, molded electric bl w/gourds, L, ca 1925, 8"...3,995.00
Vase, Dentile, fr w/beaded vertical stripes, RLF, ca 1930, 7¾".925.00
Vase, Druides, fr, molded bl stain berry branches, RL, 7½"....469.00
Vase, Epicea, cylinder, clear w/relief hemlock, RL, ca '30, 9"...595.00
Vase, Escargot, molded, fr, lg snail shell, RL, ca '30, 9".......963.00
Vase, Eucalyptus, opal w/molded leaves/buds, RL, ca '20, 6½"..615.00
Vase, Fountainbleu, frost/bl, sgn, 7"......................1,870.00
Vase, fr w/bl stain, molded recumbent antelope at base, RL, 8".755.00
Vase, Gros Scarabees, amber spheroid/relief scarabs, RL, 12".7,225.00
Vase, Gui, lime gr, molded stylized leaves, RL, ca '30, 6¾"...1,055.00
Vase, Lievres, sphere, opal, relief band of hares, RLF, 5¾"....945.00
Vase, Lizards et Bleuets, slim ovoid/cone collar, blk, 13½"...2,300.00
Vase, lt amber glass, molded deer/foliage, LF, ca 1928, 7".....795.00
Vase, Meduse, cl, engraved/enamel spirals, RL, ca '27, 7"....1,100.00
Vase, Oran, fr, molded camellia leaves/blossoms, RLF, 10½".3,695.00
Vase, Ormeaux, leaf relief, frosted amber, #984, 6½".......750.00
Vase, Palissy, round, dk gray, raised snails, RL, ca '25, 6½"..1,155.00
Vase, Plumes, round, molded feathers, fr, RL, ca '30s, 8½"....604.00
Vase, Sauterelles, molded amber w/grasshopper, RL, '20, 11".3,190.00
Vase, Serpant, amber, high relief snake, RL, ca '23, 10½"...7,610.00
Vase, Violettes, trumpet, patina enamel, fr w/in, RLF, 6½"....775.00

Car mascots, molded charcoal gray, circa 1925, molded R. Lalique, France, #1135, 8", $550.00 each.

Lamps

The earliest known lamp was the primitive grease lamp, a small alabaster dish holding openly burning grease. An improved version, the Betty lamp introduced in the 18th century, made use of a lid and cloth wick. The development of the tubal wick by Swiss inventor Aime Argand in 1784 brought about a more sophisticated oil lamp, featuring a glass chimney. With the discovery of petroleum in 1859, new methods of producing artificial light were made possible, and bigger, heavier, and more elaborate lamps came into vogue.

The most popular of the kerosene lamps were the Aladdins, introduced in 1908 by the Mantle Lamp Company of America. Aladdin lamps were made in over eighteen models and more than one-hundred styles.

Banquet lamps were kerosene lighting devices with round glass globes, often with hand painted decorations. They were quite similar to the Gone

With the Wind lamps of the 1870s.

Other types of early lamps were 'spark lamps', small night-lights with limited illumination; and 'student lamps', useful for late-night reading. Gas lamps were used, especially for outdoor lighting.

With the invention of the electric bulb in 1879, oil lamps slowly became obsolete. The light from the electric bulb was so bright, ornamental shades were necessary to reduce the glare. Glassmaker Louis C. Tiffany devoted most of his career in the latter 1800s to producing original and elaborate glass and bronze lamps for the electric bulb.

See also Bradley and Hubbard; Frankart; Handel Lamps; Tiffany

Argon lamps, Empire bronze and crystal, paw feet, J. & I. Cox, New York, circa 1840-50, $1,300.00 for the pair.

Aladdin Lamps

Alacite, font, Model B, for bracket w/burner.................40.00
Alacite, G-2111, candelabra.............................100.00
Alacite, G-229, dbl....................................70.00
Alacite, G-233, flower lamp.............................30.00
Alacite, G-24, Alacite cupid...........................125.00
Alacite, G-34...20.00
Alacite, G-375, Alacite, Dancing Ladies Urn............475.00
Alacite, Hopalong Cassidy night lamp, gun in holster.........85.00
Alacite, TLD w/701A opal shade.........................130.00
Beehive, B-80, clear crystal, w/burner..................85.00
Beehive, B-81, green crystal, w/burner..................80.00
Beehive, B-81, green crystal, w/out burner..............55.00
Beehive, B-82, dk amber crystal, w/out burner...........90.00
Beehive, B-82, lt amber crystal, w/out burner...........75.00
Beehive, B-83, red, orig shade holder, orig/complete.........450.00
Beehive, B-83, ruby w/out burner.......................225.00
Caboose, Model B, w/shade.............................125.00
Caboose, wall, blk metal bracket........................30.00
Cathedral, B-110, wht moonstone, w/burner...............165.00
Cathedral, B-110, wht moonstone, w/out burner...........150.00
Cathedral, B-111, rose moonstone, w/out burner..........135.00
Colonial, #106, amber crystal, w/burner.................130.00
Corinthian, B-100, clear crystal w/burner................45.00
Corinthian, B-104, clear w/blk ft, w/burner..............60.00
Corinthian, B-105, clear font w/gr ft, w/burner..........55.00
Corinthian, B-105, clear font w/gr ft, w/out burner......40.00
Corinthian, B-116, rose moonstone, w/burner.............85.00
Corinthian, B-126, moonstone, wht w/rose ft, w/out burner.....80.00

Hanging lamp, #6, w/#215 shade........................275.00
Hanging lamp, #8, w/#3 ceiling extension.................385.00
Hanging lamp, #9......................................200.00
Hanging lamp, #9, w/shade.............................225.00
Lincoln Drape, Tall; B-75, alacite, w/burner..............75.00
Lincoln Drape, Tall; B-75, alacite, w/out burner..........65.00
Majestic, B-120, wht moonstone, w/out burner............100.00
Queen, B-97, gr moonstone, w/out burner.................95.00
Quilt, B-85, wht moonstone, w/out burner................90.00
Quilt, B-86, gr moonstone, w/burner....................100.00
Quilt, B-86, gr moonstone, w/out burner.................90.00
Quilt, B-91, moonstone, wht w/rose ft, w/out burner.........90.00
Shade, #201..125.00
Shade, #301..125.00
Shade, #415..175.00
Shade, #416..175.00
Shade, #501..100.00
Shade, #501-9..300.00
Shade, #550, Swiss scenic.............................525.00
Shade, #601..125.00
Shade, #701-A...70.00
Simplicity, B-26, Alacite w/decal, w/burner..............225.00
Simplicity, B-27, Alacite w/gold trim, w/burner..........225.00
Simplicity, B-28, rose, w/burner........................75.00
Simplicity, B-29, gr, w/out burner......................55.00
Simplicity, B-30, wht, w/burner........................120.00
Table lamp, #1248 Ebony Venetian Art-Craft..............95.00
Table lamp, #2, w/burner.............................450.00
Table lamp, #8, w/burner.............................175.00
Table lamp, Model #11 w/501 shade....................130.00
Table lamp, Model #12 w/601 shade....................120.00
Table lamp, Model #6 w/301 shade.....................150.00
Table lamp, woman leaning on burner, made in France......375.00
Table lamp, 70th Anniversary, orig carton...............200.00
Treasure, B-138, nickel, w/burner.......................75.00
Venetian, #102, pink, EX..............................130.00
Venetian, #103, rose, w/burner..........................90.00
Venetian, #99, clear, w/out burner.....................135.00
Vertique, B-88, yel moonstone.........................275.00
Washington Drape, B-40, gr, w/burner....................75.00
Washington Drape, B-40, gr, w/out burner................60.00
Washington Drape, B-41, amber, w/out burner.............60.00
Washington Drape, B-51, gr, w/out burner................60.00
Washington Drape, B-52, amber, w/burner.................85.00
Washington Drape, B-53, clear, w/burner.................60.00
Washington Drape, B-53 w/701 shade...................110.00
Washington Drape, B-53X, clear, w/burner................60.00
Washington Drape, B-55, amber, w/burner................75.00

Chandeliers

Brass, 2 tiers S curve arms w/12 sockets, eagle atop, 31x26"...800.00
Gilt bronze, 3 scrolling candle branches, 17" dia...........1,320.00
Gold irid orb shades on dbl scroll leaf caped arms, 24x36"....225.00
Louis XV gilt metal/crystal & amethyst pendants, 12 lite, 35".4,400.00
Trn urn center, 8 iron S curve arms, tin drip pans, 26" dia....160.00
Walnut, trn center/5 spindles/drip pans, brass tack trim, 27"...200.00

Crusie Lamps

Double, tin, simple tooling on round medallion, 9".........80.00
Double, tin, w/pick hanger, early.......................95.00
Double, wrought iron, cut-out dove crests, 9"+hanger........60.00
Double, wrought iron w/worn tin, dbl pinwheels, 7".........40.00

European, wrought iron, dbl, twisted hanger, 5¾"............35.00
Wrought iron w/tin plating, twist hanger, 6¾"...............45.00

Fairy Lamps

Baccarat, amberina, 4½"................................225.00
Baccarat, pinwheel, rose teinte, vase on saucer shape, 4½x5¼".245.00
Burmese, reversible, ruffled, Clarke cup, sgn Webb, 6¾" dia...595.00
Cranberry, Dia Quilt clear mk Clarke base, 3½"............95.00
Cranberry overshot, embossed, clear mk Clarke base, 4x3".....100.00
Cranberry verre moire, Clarke clear base, lg................235.00
Crown, royal bl overshot, clear mk Clarke pyramid base, 4½".195.00
Dia Quilt, med gr, emb rib, clear mk Clarke base, 5x4".......145.00
Frosted orange glass, emb dia, clear base, 4½x3"...........118.00
MOP Dia Quilt, bl, mk Tunnecliffe pottery base, 3¾"........265.00
MOP Dia Quilt, bl, sgn Clarke base, 3½x2½"................150.00
Overlay, pink stripe dome, ruffled, applied ft, 3 part, 5x4½"...365.00
Overshot, yellow, emb swirl, clear Clarke base, 3½x3".......125.00
Satin, gr/wht stripe, clear Clarke base, Stevens/Wms, 5"......175.00
Satin, rose w/wht swag stripes, clear base & holder mk Clarke..220.00

Gone-With-The-Wind

Blown out lion's heads, red satin, 11" dia, all orig, 23½".....700.00
Climax, HP iris on globe & font, 22".....................565.00
Egyptian HP scenes, emb lion's heads/Rococo scrolls, wired...245.00
Emb flowers on lavender globe & font, 19".................265.00
Pillar & Scroll, dk red satin, sgn Fostoria, dtd 1890, 25".....725.00
Puffy Cushion, red satin, Pittsburg, 11" dia, all orig, 25".....900.00
Roses, pk on pk & gr bkground, sgn Success, 23"...........285.00
Roses, yel on maroon, ornate brass base, shaped font........400.00
Ruffles & Roses, red satin.............................700.00
Swan & cottage scene, 9" globes, 23"....................450.00

Hanging Lamps

Brass, can top w/flared shade over chimney, English, dbl wick..195.00
Cottage, milk glass shade w/pnt floral, clear font, brass fr......240.00
Hall, blown, brass trim emb w/shells/floral/bird's heads, 22"....575.00
Hall, blown globe w/folded rim, frosted/florals, brass fitting....300.00
Hall, blown w/folded rim, emb brass/gilt scroll fittings, 9".....525.00
Moravian Star, glass reflectors.........................65.00

Kerosene Lamps

Almond Thumbprint font, stepped marble/brass base, 11"......40.00
Banquet, blown-out lion's heads, enamel desert scene, 28".....295.00
Bristol, finger lamp, bl w/enamel decor, w/chimney, 9½"......135.00
Clear glass pressed in 1 pc, hexagonal w/3 printie font, 9½"....55.00
Cranberry w/wht opal netting, brass collar, finger lamp, 8"....185.00
Cranberry w/wht opal netting, clear hdl, brass collar, 8"......185.00
Crown Milano, melon base, metal ft w/leaves/acorns, w/shade..550.00
Cut glass bun font, mahog cylinder std, ormolu mt plinth, 28"..325.00
Gimbal, tin, 7", G...................................45.00
Hamilton, electric bl, leaf pattern font/swirled brass stem.....250.00
Hobbs, #2, cranberry font/clear base....................450.00
Hobbs, #2, cranberry Snowflake........................500.00
Marble base, brass stem, clear font w/cut florals, 9"+burner....50.00
Match holder base, plain font, #1 burner.................80.00
Pattern font/cut foliage at top, stepped marble/brass base......95.00
Rayo, w/Fry glass shade..............................115.00
Sandwich, clear ribbed acorn font/bl pressed base/frost globe...375.00
Sandwich, opaque bl font/opaque wht pressed base/gr chimney..225.00
Sapphire bl, emb design, w/chimney, finger lamp, 9"..........125.00

USA, all brass, orig shade, brass burner, working...........175.00

Lanterns

Barn, hanging, cherry, handmade, 20th c, 11"...............55.00
Blown/engraved, mtd in brass w/swing hdl, 17".............250.00
Candle, tin, glass on 4 sides w/wire guards/pyramid top, 11"...95.00
Candle, tin, glass 3 sides, sliding tin door, pyramid top, 11"...70.00
Candle, tin, glass 3 sides, Universal Lantern, 10½"..........65.00
Candle, tin, hinge door/pyramid punched top/glass 3 sides, 13"..35.00
Candle, tin, 7 glass panels, pierced air holes, 11½".........125.00
Candle, tin w/glass guards & sliding door, 10½"............85.00
Carriage, Gem, pnt tin, red reflectors, in kerosene, 1880......60.00
Cast metal/etched glass, Federal, 1850, 26".................300.00
Coleman, dbl, rnd brass tank, student shades on burners.....250.00
Dietz #0, crystal, barn...............................65.00
Dietz US Tubular, brass, globe cast w/mfg name, pat dates, 13".90.00
Hubbard Spencer Bartlett, barn, OVB #2, copper/brass, 15"....85.00
Huhl Crown, barn, w/match holder & striker................65.00
Robb Moore & Neill, nautical, brass w/straight rib globe, 12"...95.00
Steven's Pat, 1875, litho tin & mesh, ribbon burner, red glass...75.00
Tin, kerosene, reflector/tubular base, mk Ham Mfg, 18".......40.00
Tin, 4 glass sides, 1 sliding; font removes, 10"............65.00
Whale oil, dbl burner, removable well, 'onion globe', 12"......280.00

Leaded Glass Lamps

Art Deco, gr w/pk border, 3 Hubbell sockets, 18"............525.00
Bigelow Kennard, brickwork, bronze figural athlete base.....2,310.00
Bigelow Kennard, lobed w/geometric tiles, 26".............715.00
Domed w/irregular border, floral, metal std, 25"..........1,210.00
Floor, flat domical shade w/flowers, irregular edge, 72"......5,775.00
Pointed devices w/in panels, bronze base w/figural, 27"......1,870.00

Miniature Lamps

Acanthus, gr.......................................55.00
Amethyst Twinkle...................................310.00
Banquet, ornate SP, emb open work, globe w/violets, 16".....295.00
Beaded Bulging Loop, milk glass........................45.00
Bristol, pink w/mc enamel flowers, 11½x4½"...............650.00
Bull's Eye, oil, cranberry & clear, w/burner & chimney........48.00

Mother of Pearl glass, 12½", $1,175.00.

Bull's Eye, ruby flashed.................................35.00
Buttercup, clear..65.00
Cased, yel w/clear overlay, applied hdl, shell ft, late 1800s...450.00
Christmas tree, clear...................................90.00
Clear pressed w/pewter collar & snuffer, single tube burner.....20.00
Cobalt bl glass, Handy base............................55.00
Delft, orig burner, 1800s..............................65.00
Eagle Co, Fleur de Lis, milk glass.....................295.00
Finger, cobalt, British Made on thumbscrew.............95.00
Gillinder, Uncle Sam's Night Lamp, milk glass..........300.00
Handy, clear, w/reflector..............................55.00
Handy, gr..75.00
Improved Banner, milk glass, w/orig burner & milk glass shade..85.00
LG Wright, cranberry opal dot, 7½"....................100.00
LG Wright, Fluted Ruby Toy, 9".........................82.00
LG Wright, Moon & Star, blue, w/umbrella shade, 8".....57.50
Lincoln Drape..75.00
Little Duchess, no saucer, cobalt......................125.00
Moon & Star, acorn burner, glass shade.................75.00
Moon & Star, amber, glass shade........................70.00
Nellie Bly, milk glass w/pk decor......................115.00
Swirl, blue..60.00
US Glass, Bull's Eye...................................50.00
US Glass, Daisy..85.00
Vapo Cresolene...40.00
Vaseline & pink spatter, base & orig burner only.......98.00
Vaseline opal, copper base w/3 ball ft, ruffled shade, 8".....200.00

Pattern Glass Lamps

Algion, finger lamp....................................35.00
Aquarius, amber w/amber chimney, #1 burner.............160.00
Aquarius, clear, #1 burner.............................65.00
Aquarius, finger lamp..................................45.00
Aries, finger lamp.....................................45.00
Atterbury, dated, finger lamp..........................35.00
Atterbury Loop, glass base.............................80.00
Atterbury Melon, finger lamp...........................45.00
Ava, flat hand...60.00
Barrel, #2...200.00
Basketweave w/Flower Medallion, finger on ped, blue....95.00
Belsize, finger lamp...................................45.00
Beveled Blocks, stand lamp.............................145.00
Bolton, finger lamp....................................40.00
Bolton, lg, squat......................................50.00
Bulging Waist, flat finger, cobalt.....................95.00
Bull's Eye, gr, #2.....................................200.00
Burne, stand lamp......................................160.00
Coin Dot, opal, flat hand..............................140.00
Columbia...45.00
Columbia Coin, milk glass, 10".........................145.00
Coolidge Drape, #2.....................................150.00
Coolidge Drape, cobalt, ftd............................225.00
Coolidge Drape, flat hand..............................90.00
Corn in Shield, flat hand..............................125.00
Cottage, #2 burner.....................................85.00
Curved Rib, #1...50.00
Depressed Jewel, finger lamp...........................60.00
Diamond Sunburst, flat hand............................65.00
Dominion Panel...50.00
Dorothy, flat hand.....................................60.00
Dorothy, ftd...70.00
Double Arch..75.00
Drape, cobalt, brass collar, 8½".......................145.00

Duncan Ribbed Band.....................................110.00
Ella, #2...40.00
Ellipse w/Thumbprint, flat hand........................65.00
Empress, gr..175.00
English Hobnail, amber, #1.............................125.00
Erin Fan, gr, #1.......................................145.00
Eyebrow, flat hand.....................................50.00
Fickle Block, flat finger, blue........................110.00
Frosted Star font......................................45.00
Greek Key, #2..75.00
Greek Key, finger lamp.................................45.00
Guardian Angel, finger, w/orig shades & burner, amber..95.00
Heart, flat finger, green custard......................215.00
Heart Stem, opaque gr..................................125.00
Janice...75.00
King Comet, flat hand..................................65.00
King Heart, #1...80.00
King Melon, #2...65.00
Late Petal, hand lamp..................................50.00
Lincoln Drape, finger on ped, cobalt...................195.00
Lomax, #1..70.00
Lomax, flat hand.......................................75.00
Moon & Star base, frosted bl font, minor chips, 10½"...30.00
Nosegay, flat hand.....................................85.00
Otis, ftd..40.00
Patented Safety Handle, finger lamp....................40.00
Peacock Feather, #1....................................75.00
Peacock Feather, #2 burner.............................55.00
Peacock Feather, bl, flat hand.........................95.00
Peacock Feather, bl, ftd...............................235.00
Peacock Feather, flat hand.............................55.00
Peacock Feather, ftd...................................65.00
Peanut, hand lamp......................................65.00
Petal & Bulging Loops, finger on ped, clinch collar, blue.....95.00
Pinwheel...70.00
Plume, #1..65.00
Pointed Panel..75.00
Prince Edward, #1......................................85.00
Prince Edward, finger on ped, green....................135.00
Princess Feather.......................................75.00
Prism & Diamond Band, milk glass cloverleaf base.......95.00
Prisms w/Plain Band, flat hand.........................65.00
Quartered Block, #2....................................85.00
Quartered Block, finger................................60.00
Queen Heart, clear, #2.................................150.00
Queen Heart, gr, #2....................................350.00
Rib & Bead Rings, #1...................................75.00
Rib & Plume, #2..45.00
Ripley, ftd..95.00
Ripley, sgn/dtd, finger lamp...........................80.00
Riven Ribs, stand lamp.................................145.00
Riverside Rib, finger lamp.............................45.00
Riverside's Fern, finger, green & clear, on pedestal...175.00
Rowena, finger lamp....................................35.00
Ruffled Bull's Eye, #2.................................55.00
Serrated Loop, #2, no chimney..........................80.00
Shield, clear, 1876, to brass collar: 6½"..............85.00
Shield, finger lamp....................................65.00
Stippled Fishscale Rib, finger lamp....................45.00
Swirl, flat finger, cranberry wash.....................95.00
Thousand Eye, bl base, amber font, #2..................200.00
Thousand Eye, hand lamp................................120.00
Thumbprint Panel, #2...................................50.00
Torch & Wreath...65.00

Turkey Foot, peacock blue, ftd............................225.00
Vintage font, opaque wht base, brass collar, pat 1870, 9".......40.00
Wild Rose, #2 burner..................................100.00
Wild Rose & Bowknot, #2...............................250.00
Zipper & Rib, flat hand.................................65.00
Zipper Loop, lg..85.00
Zipper Loop, marigold, #2.............................300.00
Zipper Loop, sm..75.00

Reverse Painted Lamps

Chipped ice 18" shade, pastel sailboats; bronze std, Classique.1,650.00
Florals, sgn twice, #d, Jefferson, 19" dia..................1,200.00
Jungle scenes, domed 14" shade; silvered base, Pittsburg, 20"..800.00

Reverse painted river scene with farmhouses in autumnal tones, American, 20th century, 24", $1,210.00.

Moe Bridges, boudoir, sgn base, rvpt scenic shade, 14".......350.00
Night scene w/teepee, metal base w/molded leaves, 22"........715.00
Swans & pond scene, metal std, Pittsburg, 16" dia...........850.00
Woodland scenic, 2 socket, Nouveau brass base, 15".........500.00

Student Lamps

Brass, burnished, 10" cased ribbed gr shade, Covell, 1877, 10".795.00
Brass, 2 lite, molded yellow glass shades, 21¼"..............225.00
Brass w/opaque wht shade, mk Berlin, old soldered rpr, 20"...210.00
Kaiser, German Student Lamp Co, brass w/wht shade, 20½"...175.00
Knapp Mfg, NY, orig gr cased shade, pat 1877, brass, wired...475.00
Miller's Ideal #2 burner, brass std, gr cased ribbed shade.....325.00

Whale Oil Lamps

Ball font, wafer connector, 3 rnd step base, free blown, 6½"...225.00
Blown/pressed, trumpet font/sq bell base, 9½"...............100.00
Blue/opaque wht, acanthus leaf mold, Sandwich, 11".........400.00
Brass, single, inverted cone font, 1800-35, 8¼".............275.00
Brass, single chamber w/lemon font, saucer base, carrying hdl..295.00
Flint, sq base/octagon baluster stem/hex star/punty font, 10"...110.00
Pressed base, blown pear font w/brass collar, 11¼"..........105.00
Pressed diamond pattern, scalloped ft, hex base, 10".........115.00
Pressed glass, molded sqs, flared ft, pewter collar, 1830, 9½"..140.00
Tin, saucer base, traces of old blk pnt, cap missing, 6¼".......65.00
Tin, saucer base, worn br japanning, 6¼"..................150.00
Tin, twin wick..200.00
Trunnion, brass, 5¾"...................................55.00

Miscellaneous

Betty lamp, wrought iron w/twisted hanger, 5"..............105.00
Ceiling, solid brass, Phoenix design, sgn Miller, 14" dia.......100.00
Cigar, cranberry globe on ornate brass base w/2 holders, 10"...225.00
Clay, lipped saucer, Egyptian, EX.........................65.00
Edison Incandescent, orig carbon filament, 1879, Menlo Park..150.00
Edison Incandescent, tungsten filament, produced at Menlo Park.75.00
Emeralite, desk, #8730.................................250.00
Emeralite, desk, brass base w/gr cased shade, EX............275.00
Emeralite, metal desk, pat May 11, 1909, all orig, M..........325.00
Emeralite Jr, boudoir table lamp..........................225.00
Figural, owl, br w/yellow eyes, wht opaque shade, 15"........400.00
Figural, owl, wht w/pink ruffled satin shade, 20½"...........575.00
Figural, owl head/glass eyes, burns candle, bisque, 3½".......145.00
Figural, owl head/glass eyes, burns candle, bisque, 4½".......165.00
Gimbal, brass, rpr, 6¼".................................50.00
Glass globe in tin joined to CI base w/hinge, 1864 pat, 11"....350.00
Kinnear, worn br japanning w/yel striping, lard oil, 6½"........35.00
Lacemaker's, cranberry overshot shade/polished brass base, 16".375.00
Marble/alabaster figural Egyptian maid by light support, 47"..3,300.00
Marriage, blue opal/pat DC Ripley & Co...................1,500.00
Miner's, CI, rnd font, on hooked rod w/swivel joint, 1850s.....165.00
Miner's cap lamp, coffee pot shape, hinged lid, Geo Anton......35.00
Peg, clear blown, brass collar, fluid burner, 5¾"............115.00
Peg, clear blown, 3 applied spouts, brass base ring, 5"........200.00
Rush light, forged iron, sleeve style, 9½"..................275.00
Sconce, mirrored tin w/hurricane shade, 9½", pr.............300.00
Skater's, tin/brass, 7".................................45.00
Spout lamp, ornate, SP..................................75.00
Torch, tin, ½ circle font w/2 spouts, ring hangers, 4x7¼"......40.00
Tumbler, clear glass insert, tin fr, conical top, 6½"..........150.00
Yellow dog, CI, 2 spouts, used in oil fields.................40.00

Lap Desks

Lap desks were popular during the last half of the 19th century and were often used by travelers who filled some of their lengthy travel time with correspondence. They provided a portable writing surface and were fitted with an inkwell and compartments for various writing accouterments.

Curly maple, line inlay/ivory tear drops & ½ circles..........600.00
Leather covered mahogany w/fitted interior, English, 10x14"...100.00
Mahog, tambour front encloses 3 bottles, 2 drw/frieze drw, 12".600.00

Victorian brass mounted and inlaid padouk wood campaign lap desk, cylinder tambour opening, fitted interior, 11" x 21", $800.00.

Oak, relief carved front/sides, fitted, edge damage, 10x22x17"..350.00
Papier mache, MOP inlay, floral medallion, mosaic frame......125.00
Rosewood, brass medallion & corners, secret drawer, 7x20x11".300.00
Satinwood w/marquetry inlay, tambour w/frieze drw, 12".......605.00
Victorian, Watson/Williams of London, well fitted, brass mts..1,100.00

Law Related Collectibles

Law enforcement efforts in this country began as early as the 1700s. Since then various groups such as the Texas Rangers and U.S. Marshalls, now defunct, have left a colorful legacy, of interest not only to those now involved in law enforcement but to others as well.

Badges, old photos, wanted posters, handcuffs, and firearms are but a few of the relics that are included in this field of collecting.

See also Badges

Burglar lamp, clear lens/whale oil burner, Dietz, Pat '88, 8".....35.00
Fingerprint camera, Folmer & Schwing, Eastman Camera Co...110.00
Handcuffs, iron, early 1800s, no key.........................35.00
Handcuffs, Peerless, early, in leather case..................125.00
Handcuffs, Peerless, 1940s, w/holster.......................35.00
Lie detector, 1950s..100.00
Mug shot, Carte de Visite, Michael Franks, forger, 1899........8.50
Postcard, Auburn prison electric chair......................15.00
Whistle, brass, City Police................................12.50

Le Verre Francais

Le Verre Francais was produced during the 1920s by Schneider, at Epinay-sur-Seine in France. It was a commercial art glass in the cameo style, composed of layered glass with the designs engraved by acid. Favored motifs were stylized leaves and flowers, or geometric patterns. It was marked with the name in script or with an inlaid filigrane.

Vase, bottle form, cameo, roses, rose/pk/gr, 11"............600.00
Vase, gr to orange leaves, mottled base, bulbous, 8".........275.00
Vase, pk w/amber ruffle, purple/pk floral, gold stem, 11"......275.00

Leeds

The Leeds Pottery was established in 1758 in Yorkshire, and under various managements produced fine creamware, often highly reticulated and transfer printed; shiny black glazed Jackfield wares; and figurines similar to those made in the Staffordshire area. Little of the early wares were marked; after 1775, the impressed 'Leeds Pottery' mark was used. From 1781 to 1820, the name 'Hartley Greens & Co.' was added. The pottery closed in 1898.

Bowl, bl feather edge, late 1700s, 10" dia..................55.00
Creamer, florals/leaves/swags in bl/orange/yellow, 5¼".......165.00
Creamer, paneled w/tulip & other flowers in 4 colors, 5½", G...85.00
Cup, handleless; gaudy floral in 4 colors, minor wear, mini......35.00
Cup & saucer, handleless; soft paste/bl florals, minor chips......55.00
Cup & saucer, handleless; 4 color bird/sponge foliage, mini, G..400.00
Pitcher, 4 color bird in branch/sponge foliage, sm flakes, 2"...300.00
Plate, Am eagle/shield, bl feather edge, 8", M..............395.00
Plate, gr feather edge/peafowl w/sponged foliage, 4 colors, 9"..350.00
Platter, bl emb feather edge, Leeds style, 1814-1832, 12x15"..120.00
Platter, gaudy bl/wht florals, feather edge, 15", VG.........375.00
Sugar bowl, bl/wht gaudy florals, tab hdls, 4¼", G...........75.00
Sugar bowl, soft paste w/fluted ribs/3 color floral, 4¾", G.....85.00
Teapot, soft paste w/HP flowers, 10".......................275.00

Legras

Legras and Cie was founded in St. Denis, France in 1864. Production continued until about 1914. In addition to their enameled wares, they made cameo art glass decorated with outdoor scenes and florals executed by acid cuttings through two to six layers of glass. Their work is signed 'Legras' in relief.

Centerpiece w/candlesticks, clear w/acid cut floral, enameling...500.00
Rose bowl, enamel winter scene, ruffled, 3x3"...............150.00
Rose bowl, wht w/internal br flecks, Deco cameo, 6".........200.00
Vase, allover enamel florals, wide mouth cylinder, 2¾".......100.00
Vase, blossoms, enamel/gilt, long neck/bulb body, 18".......300.00
Vase, boats, lake & mtns, cameo & enamel, 8½"..............450.00
Vase, cameo, acid finish, diamond sqs in amber, 8"..........300.00
Vase, cameo, branches w/apple blossoms, 5 color, 6".........440.00
Vase, enameled scenic decor, 11".........................375.00
Vase, enameled trees, snow capped mtns, 11"................350.00
Vase, flower branches, enamel/cameo, sgn, 19½".............1,250.00
Vase, red maple leaf decor, frosted ground, sgnd, 11½".......225.00
Vase, seaweed, br to tan cameo, 14"......................1,250.00
Vase, sm neck w/3 hdls, cameo, floral in 4 colors, 9".......1,200.00

Centennial glass vase, red-brown prunus blossoms on light frosted background, signed, 8", $400.00.

Lenox

Walter Scott Lenox, former art director at Ott and Brewer, and Jonathan Cox founded The Ceramic Art Company of Trenton, New Jersey, in 1889. By 1906, Lenox had formed his own company which he called Lenox, Inc. Originally he produced high quality ornamental art wares, but always striving for improvements, he imported two potters from the Belleek district of Ireland and became the first in America to produce the fine fragile chinaware known as Belleek. Because of this development, he began to concentrate on the superior dinnerware for which the company became famous. Since 1917, Lenox has been chosen the official White House china.

See also Collector Plates

Key: CAC----Ceramic Art Company

Alcohol burner, CAC......................................135.00
Atomizer, ivory w/gold trim/fleur de lis finial, DeVilbiss........50.00
Atomizer, penguin, w/felt wings, M.........................75.00
Berry set, 11" ftd 2 hdl bowl, wht w/M-139 gold etch, 7 pcs....95.00
Blotter holder, wht w/gold decor feather hdl.................65.00
Bottle, Rye, cobalt w/silver overlay; Scotch, gr w/overlay, pr....275.00
Bowl, console; yellow w/wht interior, for J McD & S Co, 13½"..95.00
Bowl, covered, Rose, round, w/hdls, 9"......................175.00

Bowl, Florida, 6″...12.50
Bowl, fruit; Avon.......................................15.00
Bowl, gray w/wht interior, platinum trim, gold mk, 7x6″.......22.00
Bowl, ornate gold scroll trim, shallow, 10½″.................35.00
Bowl, patriot's; 1976 Centennial........................150.00
Bowl, ribbed, Princess Occabot, gold trim, Bayuk Cigars, 8″....45.00
Box, blue w/sheaf of wheat, round, shape #514, green mark.....65.00
Box, cigarette; wht w/apple blossom decor, w/lid............25.00
Box, cigarette; wht w/gold wheat pattern..................25.00
Box, gr w/gold trim, wht feathery hdl, 7½″ L..............125.00
Box, Hattie Carnegie, w/lid.............................110.00
Box, heart shape, Romeo & Juliet, w/lid..................65.00
Box, Mystic, wht w/florals, #514, 7″ W...................75.00
Bust, cherub, wht, 5″..................................205.00
Bust, lady's head, Deco style, wht satin, #2138, 3x3½″.......125.00
Candlestick, Nouveau florals, gr/gilt/gray on ivory, 6″, pr.......75.00
Candlestick, Nouveau florals, mc on belleek, sgn, 6½″.......115.00
Casserole, Floral Fantasy, Temper Ware.................32.00
Cigarette urn, pink/wht, w/M-344 gold trim..............20.00
Cigarette urn, w/robin, sgn Fenzl, gr mk................25.00
Coaster, cobalt w/gold washed sterling overlay, 3″........75.00
Coffee pot, Lenox Rose................................125.00
Compote, lt bl stem/ft, fluted wht top, gr wreath mark, 5x7″...50.00
Cornucopia, all green, 5″..............................36.00
Cornucopia, blue w/wht hdl, 5″.........................36.00
Cornucopia, dbl, lt pk w/wht ring hdl, 5x7″..............52.50
Cornucopia, ped ft, gold decor, gr wreath mark, 8″, pr.......225.00
Cornucopia, wht, gr mk, 8¼″...........................35.00
Cornucopia, yellow w/wht hdl, 5″.......................40.00
Creamer, rnd w/florals, gold trimmed, CAC, 3½″..........100.00
Creamer & sugar, Floral Fantasy, Temper Ware...........35.00
Creamer & sugar, Ming, old style.......................75.00
Creamer & sugar, Olympia Platinum.....................55.00
Creamer & sugar, Quakertown, Temper Ware.............36.00
Creamer & sugar, ribbed gray, wht w/in hdls, gold, w/orig box...45.00
Creamer & sugar, Sprite, Temper Ware..................42.00
Cup & saucer, Arcadia, demitasse......................20.00
Cup & saucer, blue bird, HP, demitasse.................15.00
Cup & saucer, Celeste, demitasse......................20.00
Cup & saucer, Cinderella, platinum trim.................20.00
Cup & saucer, Coquette...............................28.00
Cup & saucer, Cynthia, P319..........................30.00
Cup & saucer, fluted shell, demitasse, blk mk............20.00
Cup & saucer, Golden Wreath.........................35.00
Cup & saucer, Imperial...............................32.50
Cup & saucer, in sterling holder, demitasse.............40.00
Cup & saucer, Lenox Rose............................35.00
Cup & saucer, Ming, demitasse........................36.00
Cup & saucer, Pine..................................32.00
Cup & saucer, Tuscany...............................40.00
Cup & saucer, Virginian..............................35.00
Cup & saucer, wht beleek, CAC........................35.00
Cup & saucer, Windsor...............................30.00
Dish, sm pink roses, HP, gold trim, 1x6″ dia.............35.00
Ewer, gray w/wht hdl & interior, platinum trim, 9″........36.00
Ewer, Lenox Rose, reticulated hdls, gold trim, gr mk, 6½″....45.00
Ewer, pink w/wht top, wht ornate hdl, 8″................41.00
Figurine, bird, tail down, wht, 2½″.....................18.00
Figurine, bird, tail up, cocoa brown, gold mk, 7″..........80.00
Figurine, bird, tail up, green, 3″.......................32.00
Figurine, blue bird, 6½″..............................105.00
Figurine, gr Jay, gr wreath mk, 4″......................65.00
Figurine, llama.....................................225.00
Figurine, St Teresa, decorated, 8″.....................300.00

Figurine, The Reader................................395.00
Figurine, wht bird, 6½″..............................75.00
Fondue pot, Fall Bounty, Temper Ware.................30.00
Gravy boat, Windsor................................65.00
Honey pot, beehive w/bees, gr mk.....................75.00
Jam pot, wht w/silver overlay.........................45.00
Jug, Scotch & Rye w/silver letters/hdl/stopper, CAC, 7¼″, pr...350.00
Lamp, bl w/stylized florals, 1930s, 11″, base............90.00
Lamp, 2 pc ivory oval w/hdls, slender neck, ped ft, 10½″ base..85.00
Mask, lady, Deco, wht, open back, 9″..................295.00
Mug, br w/monk scene, CAC wreath+Made for Tiffany, 5¾″...110.00
Mug, gooseberries, artist sgn, gr CAC mk, 5″............95.00
Mug, pearly gray w/wht hdl & lining, 5½″...............65.00
Mug, 3 hdl, monks in wine cellar in panel, silver rim, CAC, 6″.230.00
Nut dish, ped base, mc floral on wht irid, sgn, gold rim/hdls....40.00
Pen stand, gr & wht, for Sheaffer Pen Co, gilt metal pin, NM...95.00
Peppermill, Quakertown, Temper Ware.................35.00
Pitcher, cobalt w/silver overlay, w/lid, gr mk, 7″.........105.00
Pitcher, Indian portrait, full headdress, CAC, 13½x7″......420.00
Pitcher, mask, #64, all wht...........................70.00
Pitcher, mask, #64, lt bl.............................95.00
Pitcher, peanut, masked spout, powder blue & wht, 8″.....125.00
Place setting, Chalet, 5 pc...........................80.00
Place setting, Golden Wreath, 5 pc...................145.00
Place setting, Lenox Rose, 5 pc......................145.00
Planter, bird figural, open back, green, tail up, green mk, 7″...54.00
Plate, cake; ped base, HP floral/birds, gold rim, belleek, 10″...75.00
Plate, Coralton, dinner..............................22.50
Plate, Cynthia, P319, 9″.............................20.00
Plate, Essex, cobalt, salad...........................20.00
Plate, Golden Wreath, dinner........................33.00
Plate, HP fish by WH Morley, gold rim band, 9″, 12 for.....750.00
Plate, Lenox Rose, dinner............................32.00
Plate, Ming, old style, dinner........................35.00
Plate, Pavlova, dinner...............................25.00
Plate, Pheasant & Roach, Morley, gold banded, 9″, pr......78.00
Plate, Pine, bread & butter..........................14.00
Plate, Pine, dinner.................................24.00
Plate, Pine, salad..................................18.00
Plate, pk roses, shaped gold edge, pink CAC mk, 3¼″......25.00
Plate, portrait, sgn Nosek, 10¼″.....................750.00
Plate, Rose, dinner................................35.00
Plate, Rose, luncheon..............................25.00
Plate, Rose, 6″....................................18.00
Plate, silver overlay on wht, fruit design, 5″............12.00
Plate, Tuscany, dinner..............................28.00
Plate, Virginia pattern, 8¼″, set of 12................240.00
Plate, Windsor, dinner..............................20.00
Platter, Rose, 17x13″..............................125.00
Salesman's sample, place setting+teapot, coffee pot.......200.00
Salt, Swan, gr wreath mk...........................32.50
Salt & pepper, white bird figural, much gold trim, pr.......36.00
Salt & pepper mill, Pine, 5″, pr.......................40.00
Sauce boat, Fall Bounty, Temper Ware................30.00
Shaving mug w/inner soap shelf, palette mk.............70.00
Stein, blackberries & blossoms on shaded gr, CAC, 5½″....75.00
Stein, flowers & grapes, pewter lid, CAC..............125.00
Sugar, cobalt w/sterling overlay, CAC................55.00
Sugar, on ped base, Lenox Rose......................60.00
Swan, pink w/gold trim, green mk, 4½″................32.00
Swan, wht w/gold trim, old type, gr mk...............20.00
Tea set, ivory w/gold border & bl bands, pot 4½″........135.00
Teapot, Lenox Rose................................125.00
Toby jug, Geo Washington, fully decorated.............425.00

Tankard, brown with silver overlay, CAC unicorn mark, 7", $165.00.

Toby jug, Wm Penn, pk w/wht hdl, rare color...............160.00
Toby jug, Wm Penn, wht glaze, gr mk....................175.00
Vase, Black boy playing banjo, purple CAC mk, 11".........385.00
Vase, cylinder, pk w/blk & gold seahorse/seaweed pattern, 12"...63.00
Vase, florals w/in & w/out, gr palette mk, CAC, 8½".........250.00
Vase, ftd egg shape, wht w/gold trim, gr mk, 12".............40.00
Vase, geraniums & leaves on gr, gold trim, CAC, 11"........185.00
Vase, gold & wht, swan hdl, 11".........................60.00
Vase, gr & gold trim, birds/fountain design, late 1920s, 10½"..132.00
Vase, ltd issue, Walter Scott............................175.00
Vase, maiden, Cupid decor, plume hdls..................225.00
Vase, poppies & leaves on yel to br, sgn G Morley, 11¾".....325.00
Vase, red & wht roses, artist sgn, belleek, dtd 1903, CAC, 15"..350.00
Vase, shield shape, yel w/wht swan hdls, ped ft, 10x5½"......165.00
Vase, silver overlay by Rockwell, palette mk, 11¼".........195.00
Vase, tree trunk w/bird atop, 6 holes for flowers, wht, 5¾"....38.00
Vase, urn, flared top, 2 hdls, wht, 5½"....................19.00
Vase, urn, wht, bl hdls/base, slim classical shape, 9½", pr....158.00
Vase, w/hdls, flared rim, wht, gr mk, 5½x6"................30.00
Vase, wht, gray floriform top, platinum trim, gold mk, 9", pr....88.00
Vase, wht w/bl ring hdls, bl neck, 8"......................45.00
Vase, yellow, flared top, Lenox Opaque mk, 8"..............95.00
Vase, 4 finger, wht w/HP lav roses, gold leaves, CAC, 9".....290.00
Whiskey measure, pail w/gold pnt hdl.....................25.00

Letter Openers

Alligator head, good.................................12.00
Art Nouveau lady, full figure, bronze....................24.00
Bookmark/opener, sterling, squash racket & ball atop, 4".......35.00
Bronze, Art Nouveau, sgn Austria.......................12.00
Camel Cigarettes, advertising...........................5.00
Carved treen, figure of Alpine youth on hdl, 11¼"..........12.50
Coes Wrench Co, celluloid, monkey wrench shape...........16.50
DuPont-Hercules Powder, emb advertising.................45.00
Egyptian head paper clip at top, hanging hook, 11½".........65.00
Elephant head hdl, celluloid............................7.50
Feather & claw, bronze...............................20.00
Frank Mossberg & Co, w/factory........................18.00
Garden of Gods, Pikes Peak, carved ivory.................17.50
Geo Parker, Lucky Curve, 6"...........................18.00
Ice Cream Mfg, silver anniversary, Art Nouveau, w/sundae......28.00

Ivory, allover filigree, 5".............................50.00
Knowles & Moudry Doctor's Pharmacy...................22.00
Motor Trades Dealers Convention, 1919...................6.00
Opener/pager turner, figural man Japanese bronze..........135.00
Owl, full figure, bronze..............................28.00
Peters Cartridge Co, metal, hdl is .30 caliber bullet..........30.00
Prudential Life Insurance, Both Sexes, ornate scroll work......25.00
Rat, on ear of corn, brass............................60.00
Seagull, bronze....................................22.00
Ship hdl, solid brass, 8½"............................20.00
Souvenir, Kennedy Space Center, Florida.................15.00
Souvenir, Turkish dagger type w/dragon head hdl...........20.00
St Louis Expo, brass w/cupid hdl.......................50.00
ST McNight Co, w/Remington knife.....................25.00
Statesman Cigars, curved brass, w/lion head...............20.00
Sterling, solid ornate hdl & blade, in orig box, 7".............30.00
Sterling blade, MOP hdl..............................15.00
Sword, all brass, English, 7¼".........................6.50
Sword, sterling, repousse, S Kirk, 6"....................35.00
Uneeda Biscuit, slicker boy, G.........................40.00
Welsbach Lights, eagle & lamp, advertising...............25.00
Yale & Towne, padlock decor..........................45.00

Libbey

The New England Glass Company was established in 1818 in Boston, Massachusetts. In 1892, it became known as the Libbey Glass Company. At Chicago's Columbian Expo in 1893, Libbey set up a ten pot furnace and made glass souvenirs. The display brought them world wide fame. Between 1878 and 1918, Libbey made exquisite cut and faceted glass, considered today to be the best of the brilliant period glassware. The company is credited for several innovations -- the Owens bottle machine that made mass production possible, and the Westlake machine which turned out both electric light bulbs and tumblers automatically. They developed a machine to polish the rims of their tumblers in such a way that chipping was unlikely to occur. Their glassware carried the patented Safedge guarantee.

Libbey also made glassware in numerous colors -- cobalt, ruby, pink, green, and amber. In 1935, it was bought by Owens-Illinois, and remains a division of that company.

Bowl, boat shape, Thistle pattern, cut crystal, 11½" L........250.00
Bowl, brilliant cut, shallow, sgn, 8" dia..................145.00
Bowl, Colonna cutting, sgn, 8".........................150.00
Bowl, hobstar & dandelion cutting, stencil mk, early 1900s, 8".350.00
Bowl, strawberry diamond & fan cutting, shallow, sabre mk, 7"..75.00
Bowl, 3 cut bands of hobstars w/central hobstar, fan rim, 8"...165.00
Butter dish, Gloria cutting, orig pattern.................525.00
Candlestick, cut in plain flutes, teardrop stem, sgn, 6", pr.....300.00
Candlestick, lg teardrop in body, allover engraving, 12", pr....475.00
Champagne, engraved florals & fern, set of 9..............275.00
Champagne, twist stem, flared, thin gr stripes decor.........110.00
Claret, bear stem...................................150.00
Cocktail, kangaroo stem, camphor, sgn..................145.00
Cologne, amberina, orig paper label....................500.00
Compote, cut & etched allover; bulbous/swirled std, 4x7"....125.00
Compote, floral wheel engraved bowl & base, 3¾x6".......100.00
Compote, rare fuschia amberina, sgnd, 4¼".............575.00
Darner, peachblow, New England......................110.00
Decanter, Inverted Thumbprint, amberina, 14"..............85.00
Dish, floral engraved w/wheat sheaves, 6"................40.00
Finger bowl, grape & leaf cutting, sgn, 2½x4½"...........65.00
Finger bowl/under plate, amberina, EX coloring, sgn.........550.00
Goblet, Cornucopia series, 7¼", set of 8.................315.00

Intaglio carved vase, black with gray tulips, olive highlights, acid stamped 'Libbey' within a circle, circa 1925, 14", $2,530.00.

Goblet, water; opal cat stem, sgn...........................175.00
Maize, butter dish w/cover, custard w/gr leaves...............650.00
Maize, celery vase, cream w/gold leaves, 6½".................145.00
Maize, celery vase, wht opaque w/gr leaves, 6½"..............125.00
Maize, master berry, custard w/blue trim.....................175.00
Maize, pickle castor, gr leaves, SP frame....................500.00
Maize, spooner, custard......................................175.00
Maize, sugar shaker, custard w/yellow leaves.................175.00
Maize, sugar shaker, pearlized w/colored foliage, 5½"........225.00
Maize, sugar shaker, pearlized w/tan leaves, 5½".............210.00
Maize, syrup, wht w/yel leaves, pewter lid, 7½"..............235.00
Maize, toothpick, blue & gold husks, 2¼".....................275.00
Maize, tumbler, custard w/yel leaves outlined w/gold.........125.00
Paperweight, 1893 Expo, Michigan State Bldg, 2x4"............45.00
Pitcher, Harvard cutting, bulbous............................395.00
Pitcher, tankard; New Brilliant cutting, sgn, 8¼"............260.00
Pitcher, Thumbprint, amberina, 8½x7".........................300.00

Cut glass sweets comport, signed, 8" x 7", $250.00.

Plate, ice cream; Somerset pattern, 12" dia.................165.00
Plate, Santa Maria in sepia, sgn Libbey Cut Glass, 7¾".......375.00
Powder box, Florence cutting, hinged, 6" dia................425.00
Salt, ped base, allover cut, sgn.............................110.00
Shaker, egg shape, Columbian Exhibition, 1893...............95.00
Tray, ice cream, Senora pattern, 17½".......................990.00
Tray, ice cream; Iverina variant w/cut/flashed flowers, 16" L..795.00
Tray, ice cream; Kimberly cutting, 7½x14"...................250.00
Tumbler, Corinthian cutting, sgn, set of 4..................180.00
Vase, amberina, sgn, 10"....................................325.00
Vase, cut glass, Masonic, sgn, Zenobia, Toledo O, 5".........78.00
Vase, trumpet, Bull's Eye & Zipper cutting, sgn, 14".........300.00
Vase, trumpet, cut snowflakes, scalloped rim, 1920s, 8"......125.00
Wine, engraved stylized florals, panel cut stem, 4", set of 6....195.00
Wine, kangaroo, blk stem, sgn, 5¾"..........................150.00
Wine, opal monkey stem, sgn, 5".............................75.00
Wine, polar bear, opal stem.................................85.00

Limoges

From the mid-18th century, Limoges was the center of the porcelain industry of France, where at one time more than forty companies utilized the local kaolin deposits to make a superior quality china, much of which was exported to the United States. Various marks were used; some included the name of the American export company rather than the manufacturer, and 'Limoges'. After 1891 'France' was added.

Basket, pk rim & roses, gold hdl, irreg edge, Elite, 8x4¾"....45.00
Biscuit barrel, ivory w/peacock feathers, bamboo hdl, T&V, 7"..125.00
Bone dish, HP..8.00
Bouillon w/saucer, griffin hdls, HP roses, T&V...............30.00
Bowl, poppies, HP, 9" sq.....................................35.00
Bowl, scalloped/twisted rope edge, lg HP iris, sgn LUC, 10½"...48.00
Box, bl w/HP cupid, gold decor, 3x5" dia.....................90.00
Box, powder; w/lid, HP, sgn Walleau..........................28.00
Box, trinket; lg pk roses on gr lid, gr/rose base, sgn, 7" dia..82.00
Butter dish, wht w/gold trim, 7½"............................35.00
Butter pat, violets w/gold trim, L Strauss, 3"...............10.00
Cake plate, cobalt w/gold band, HP scene w/ducks in center, 9"..80.00
Cake plate, violets, 10"....................................12.00
Charger, Musee' de Versailles, Bataille D'Lena, 12½".........275.00
Charger, portrait of girl in lace snood, sgn R Comby, 13"....225.00
Charger, roses, T&V, 14"....................................85.00
Cheese & cracker, 2 tier, HP roses..........................75.00
Chocolate pot, HP floral, 14"...............................125.00
Chocolate pot+6 cups/saucers, pk/red flowers on wht.........185.00
Coffee server, ind; wht w/gold & floral bands, gold spout/hdl...30.00
Cracker jar, floral/gold stippling/bamboo finial, T&V.......125.00
Creamer & sugar, HP rose, gold decor, set...................75.00
Cup & saucer, demitasse; floral decor, much gold............16.50
Cup & saucer, tea; teapk roses, gr/gray, much gold, JP......18.00
Dresser set, florals & gold, 5 pcs on rectangle tray, sgn...45.00
Ewer, dogwood & bluebells, HP, much gold, 11"...............100.00
Fish set, yellow, shell decor, gold trim, platter & 6 plates..379.00
Humidor, cigarette pack decor...............................75.00
Humidor, pine cones & branches, sgn GDA.....................80.00
Ice cream set, 16x9" tray+8--6½" plates, sm floral, Elite...165.00
Match holder, attached saucer, florals......................48.00
Mustache cup & saucer, gr w/florals.........................45.00
Mustard w/lid, on tray; burgandy w/gold ribbons & flowers, HP..80.00
Pitcher, cider; HP pastel asters............................95.00
Pitcher, lemonade; cherries, HP.............................135.00
Plaque, fish, sgn Rosies, heavy gold border, mk Coronet, 13"..115.00

Charger, hand painted portrait, artist signed, 18″, $1,250.00.

Plaque, flying ducks, hunters in boat, gold rim, DuBois, 11½″.220.00
Plaque, nude portrait, sgn DuBois, gold Rococo border, 12″..235.00
Plaque, Victorian couple, wide gold Rococo border, sgn, 13½″.195.00
Plaque, woman & child at seaside, pate sur pate, 7¾″........85.00
Plate, bird in yel/rust/br/gr on mc, scalloped, Coronet, 9¾″....125.00
Plate, chop; gold relief border, Coronet, 12″.................45.00
Plate, clover, yel/pk w/gr leaves, D & Co, 7½″, pr............25.00
Plate, dessert; scalloped, gr w/lilac clusters, gold trim, T&V.....40.00
Plate, floral w/gold, scalloped, sgn AK, 7½″.................48.00
Plate, florals on satin finish, gold scalloped rim, 8½″, 12 for...175.00
Plate, fruit, sgn Brouillion, gold scroll rim, facing pr, 11½″....275.00
Plate, HP roses, gold relief irregular edge, 7¼″..............20.00
Plate, LaFayette Series, D'Arceau, set of 8..................210.00
Plate, pheasant & quail, scalloped gold borders, sgn, 10″, pr...250.00
Plate, pk florals, 6½″, set of 6..........................115.00
Plate, portrait: Marie Leczinske, cobalt bl w/heavy gold trim.....50.00
Plate, scroll/shell rim, w/cupids, mk Lanternier, 8½″, pr........45.00
Plate, Victorian lady portrait, heavy gold/beading, 8½″.......125.00
Plate, women & children watch ships at sea, Kreis, T&V, 12½″.95.00
Plate, 2 game birds in br/gray/yel, sgn L Coudert, 10¾″.......135.00
Plate, 3 groups currants w/X hatching, gold, sgn, T&V, 8¼″....48.00
Plate, ¾ view lady in garden, sgn LP Patten, in fr, 17½″.....800.00
Punch bowl, w/6 cups, fruit decor, 13″....................300.00
Punch bowl, wisteria w/gold trim, T&V, 1895, 5½x13″........195.00
Ramekin, w/saucer, pk floral, Elite........................16.00
Tankard, allover berry branch/vines/leaves, raised gold, 13″....225.00
Tankard, purple berries, br base & hdl, T&V, 11″............195.00
Tankard, silver leaves & grapes on pk/blk, 1909, 14″........200.00
Tankard, 3 color grapes, emb gold leaves, vine hdl, T&V, 16″..265.00
Tea set, sterling overlay, ornate hdls, D & Co..............180.00
Teapot, creamer & sugar w/lid, swirled, bl/lav floral, Gutherz....75.00
Tray, dresser; violets..................................45.00
Tray, ivory w/stars, pastel flowers, 13″ dia...............55.00
Vase, enamel/copper, girl lifts skirts, sgn Juan, 6″..........300.00
Vase, enamel/copper, silver mtd, landscape by Nory, 8″.......350.00

Lithophanes

Lithophanes are porcelain panels with relief designs of varying degrees of thickness and density. Transmitted light brings out the pattern in graduated shadings, lighter where the porcelain is thin, and shaded in the heavy areas.

They were cast from wax models prepared by artists, and depict views of life from the 1800s, religious themes, or scenes of historical significance. First made in Berlin about 1825, they were used as lamp shade panels, window plaques, or candle shields. Later, steins, mugs, and cups were made with lithophanes in their bases. Japanese wares were sometimes made with dragons or Geisha lithophanes.

See also Steins

Key:
bh-----brass hanger   rect------rectangular
fr----framed   tz--------trapezoid
hh----holes for hanging

Cast in stand, girl in meadow pets collie, scepter/KPM, 8x10″..375.00
Desk light, brass base w/framed litho/Sphinx ea side, 13x4½″..500.00
Lamp, Sandwich Glass base w/chimney shade of 5 lithos, 19″.1,350.00
Lamp, student; brass, 2 curved shades w/4″ pictures, 19″....1,600.00
Lamp, table; brass std emb w/floral, 5 trapezoidal panels, 15″.1,050.00
Panel, boy & girl play/wall, PR sickle, oval, 2½x3″...........85.00
Panel, boy w/dog, EX quality, KPM sceptor, rect 4¾x5¾″.....160.00
Panel, boys/dog playing, EX quality, PR sickle, oval 2½x3½″..85.00
Panel, castle, leaded self fr, bl glass fr/red corners, 8x9″.......350.00
Panel, child on lion pedestal, PPM #98, tz 5¼x3¼x5½″......150.00
Panel, child plays in open window, PR #1677, oval 2½x3½″....85.00
Panel, child/puppy at top of stairs, PR #1634, oval 2½x3½″....85.00
Panel, children w/Dutch door, EX quality, hh, PR #1326, 5x4″..185.00
Panel, children/lg tree/mountains, rounded ornate top, 8x4″....150.00
Panel, Falstaff, EX detail, PPM #484, rect 3¼x3¾″.........160.00
Panel, girl w/long hair cat, PR sickle, oval 2x3″, M..........87.00
Panel, hunters shoot turkey in tree, detailed, hh, 4½x5¼″.....175.00
Panel, Lord Nelson, deep sculpting, hh, rect 3½x5¼″, EX...195.00
Panel, lovers in garland swing, PR sickle #1674, oval 2½x3½″..85.00
Panel, lovers in woods/stream, PR sickle #1299, hh, rect 4x5″..175.00
Panel, lovers running in woods, PR #1673, oval 2½x3½″......85.00
Panel, milkmaid/suitor/dog/gun, PPM #186, rect 5x4¼″.......165.00
Panel, mother/girl in wedding veil scene, EX detail, PR, 4x6″..195.00
Panel, old man/children/dog in woods, PR #1678, oval 2½x3½″.85.00
Panel, rock house/sailboats/water wheel, curved ornate top, 8″..150.00
Panel, scene w/2 deer, colored, PPM #1190, EX detail, 4x5¼″.285.00
Panel, selling of Joseph into slavery, PPM #556, 4½x5½″.....185.00
Panel, semi-draped girl reading, self fr, #43, 5½″ round........95.00
Panel, sm girl holds bunny, ornate self fr, PPM #330, 3x3½″...85.00
Panel, Swiss chalet/people on path, rounded ornate top, 8x4″..150.00
Panel, town/steeples/mountains, #1873, rect 2¾x3¼″.........40.00
Panel, wayside shrine/mother/child/monk, KPM, ornate fr, 8x7″.250.00
Panel, woman holds child on table/flax spindle, #1387, 4½x4″.150.00
Panel, woman in tree swing, EX detail, KPM sceptor, rect 5x6″.165.00
Panel, woman scans hillside, KPM sceptor, rect 5x6″........160.00
Panel, women hold 2 children/garden, brass fr, PR #1739, 2x3″.83.00
Panel, women in doorway, brass fr, prongs for stand, 2½x3″....85.00
Panel, 2 girls/lamb/bridge, PR sickle/bh mkd Paris, rect 5x4″...150.00
Panel, 3 children/sled/snow, PR sickle/bh mkd Paris, rect 5x4″.150.00
Panel, 4 children in snow, PR sickle/bh mkd Paris, rect 5x4″..150.00
Panel, 4 sm children in snow, PR sickle mk, oval, 2½x3½″....82.00
Saki set, whistling bird on bottle, cups w/woman litho, ornate...85.00
Shade, 1 pc, 3 panels w/animals/3 panels w/scrolls, 10″ dia....500.00
Stein, tavern scene, German............................175.00
Tea set, figural dragon pot, geisha litho, 15 pc, very ornate....350.00
Tea warmer, pierced brass, 4 sq: 3 scenic/1 children, sgnd, M..185.00

Liverpool

In the late 1700s, Liverpool potters produced a creamy ivory ware, sometimes called Queen's Ware, which they decorated by means of the newly perfected transfer print. Made specifically for the American export trade, patriotic inscriptions, political portraits, or other States themes were applied in black with colors sometimes added by hand. (Obviously their loyalty to the crown did not stand in the way of their business success!) Before it lost favor in about 1825, other English potters made a similar product; today Liverpool is a generic term used to refer to all ware of this type.

Jug, Am ship, verso Hope/ship, 1804, Gabriel under hdl, 10".. .400.00
Jug, Washington in Glory, bk: ship w/flag, 9", G.............400.00
Pitcher, lover's poem, tribute to farmer, tools/heart, 5½", VG..250.00
Sugar bowl, cupid on teeter-totter, blk transfer, 1835.........200.00

Lladro

Lladro porcelains are currently being produced in Labernes Blanques, Spain. Their limited edition figurines are popular collectibles.

After The Dance, L-5092................................170.00
Anniversary Waltz, #1372................................200.00
Avoiding the Goose, #5033...............................125.00
Carnival Couple, #4822.................................110.00
Dancer, #5050..70.00
Feeding Her Daughter, #5140............................105.00
Feeding The Ducks, L-4849..............................165.00
Girl Kissing, L-4873....................................50.00
Girl Picking Flowers, #1172............................110.00
Girl w/cat, L-1187.....................................148.00
Girl w/Geese, L-4568...................................140.00
Girl w/Pails, matt finish, L-3512......................185.00
Group of Angels, #4542..................................75.00
Halloween, #5067.......................................270.00
Little Friskies, L-5023................................145.00
My Little Pet, L-4994...................................13.00
Naughty Dog, #4982.....................................100.00
Nuns, matt finish, L-2075..............................150.00
Pharmacist, #4833......................................140.00
Tennis Puppet, L-4966...................................85.00
The Car, ltd ed......................................8,000.00
Veterinarian, L-4825...................................155.00

Ballerina, #817, 10½", $150.00.

Lobmeyer

J. and L. Lobmeyer, contemporaries of Moser, worked in Vienna, Austria during the last quadrant of the 1800s. Most of the work attributed to them is decorated with distinctive enameling very similar to the decoration on the illustrated salt.

Goblet, paneled w/etched cavalier/lady in trees/foliage, 4½"....85.00
Tumbler, ftd, lady w/tumbler surrounded w/pastel florals.......350.00
Tumbler, w/rare signature, 3".........................550.00
Wine, floral and gold enamel, ruffled foot, 7"...............160.00

Salt, individual, enamel decor, 2¼", $65.00.

Locke Art

Champagne, Vintage, sgn, 4½"...........................110.00
Pitcher, concave shape, allover wild rose etching, 8¼".......275.00
Pitcher, concave shape, etched w/poppies, sgn, 8¼"..........275.00
Punch cup, poppy pattern, sgn...........................45.00
Sherbet, pineapple design w/grapes, sgn HR mono...........135.00
Sherbet, vintage, turned up base rim, 3x3¾"...............150.00
Tumbler, wild rose etching..............................60.00
Wine glass, grape & vine etched, sgn w/in the pattern, 4 for...400.00

Locks

The earliest type of lock in recorded history was the wooden cross bar used by ancient Egyptians and their contemporaries. The early Romans are credited with making the first key operated mechanical lock. The ward lock was invented during the Middle Ages by the Etruscans of Northern Italy; the lever tumbler and combination locks followed at various stages of history with varying degrees of effectiveness. In the 18th century, the first precision lock was constructed -- it was a device that utilized a lever tumbler mechanism.

Two of the best known of the early 19th century American lock manufacturers are Yale and Sargent. Today's collectors also value names such as Winchester and Keen Kutter. Other factors to consider are rarity, condition, and construction. Brass and bronze locks are generally priced higher than those of steel or iron.

ALPHA, emb iron, w/key, VG............................50.00
Ames Sword Co, Pat 1882, brass lever, UP on shackle........16.00
Barnes, Good Luck, horseshoe shape......................65.00
Bengal, eagle lock, w/raised tiger, brass, w/key...........15.00
BETA, emb iron, no key, VG..............................5.00
Bohannan, FWSY Co, iron switch, w/chain..................65.00
Box, J Carpenters Pat, iron w/brass knobs, no keeper, 4½x6"...25.00
Browne & Sons, London Lock Smith, brass, 6 lever, mk WF Co.40.00
Champion, brass, 6 lever, push key missing, EX.............20.00
CIPS Co, Fraim, brass heart switch, w/chain & key..........50.00
Cleveland, brass, 4 way, w/brass chain, no key, EX.........42.00
Corbin, brass, pin tumbler, XLCR, SO Co, w/key, VG.........20.00
Corbin, iron, 6 lever, Iron Clad, w/key, EX................8.00
Corbin, pin tumbler, push key missing....................15.00
Corbin Cabinet Lock Co, bronze padlock w/key & chain, 3¼"...25.00

Elbow box, wrought iron/brass plate on exterior level, 4x4½"...65.00
Excelsior, brass, 6 lever, push key missing, M..............35.00
Excelsior, brass, 6 lever, push key missing, VG.............15.00
FEC Slaymaker, w/chain & unmk key, 1956.................30.00
Ford, brass, pin tumbler, mk both sides, 2 mk keys.........20.00
Fraim, brass, pin tumbler, w/key, VG.......................5.00
Fraim, iron, 6 lever, for dbl barrel key, no key, EX..........8.00
Good Luck Horse Shoe, brass, w/key, G....................40.00
Harvard, brass, 4 lever, push key.........................35.00
Harvard, brass, 6 lever, w/push key, EX...................35.00
Hudson, brass, 6 lever, w/chain, push key missing............30.00
Keen Kutter, brass, swivel for chain, w/key, EC Simmons......65.00
Keystone, brass, 6 lever, push key missing.................20.00
Keystone, brass, 6 lever, w/push key, VG..................30.00
Loxem, iron, warded, rnd, w/key, VG......................15.00
MARS US, emb iron, no key...............................10.00
MW & Co, iron, smoke house, brass drop, no key, 2¾", EX....12.00
NAR cast on brass drop, iron body, chain swivel on hasp......35.00
Navy, pancake..24.00
Omeco, iron, 6 lever, no key..............................5.00
Omeco, iron w/red pnt, no key.............................5.00
Reese, iron, 6 lever, VG..................................6.00
Reg'd US Mail, brass, counter on side, VG.................75.00
Romer & Co, brass heart, w/key, VG......................15.00
RR ea side, brass, pat 1891, 1¾x2½"......................25.00
Rugby, emb iron, no key..................................8.00
S Ohio, brass, pin tumbler, w/key, VG.....................20.00
SAFE, brass, 6 lever, w/push key, VG......................30.00
Sampson, iron, warded, rnd, w/key........................10.00
Sargent, iron, brass shackle, pin tumbler, push key missing.....15.00
Sargent & Co, iron, smoke house, no key, 3½", VG..........10.00
Scandinavian, iron, w/key, 3½"...........................20.00
Seaboard Adlake, raised on drop, iron, no key, VG..........35.00
Sesamee, brass, combination.............................40.00
Slaymaker, brass, 1 seal, M..............................50.00
Slaymaker, pin tumbler, w/push key, EX...................20.00
Smith & Egge, brass, push key, no key, 1877...............15.00
St Louis, brass, 2x1½"...................................6.00
Switch, brass, heart, emb SAFE, w/key....................20.00
US Army, iron, warded, rnd..............................20.00
US Mail, brass, no key, 1½x2"............................15.00
W Mfg Co, iron, smoke house, brass drop, w/key, VG........10.00
WB Bell System, brass, pin tumbler, w/brass chain, EX.......15.00
WB-Iroquois Gas, brass, pin tumbler, no key...............15.00
Wilson Bohannan, brass heart w/key......................10.00
Yale, brass, pin tumbler, Ordinance Dept USA, VG...........12.00
Yale, brass, 6 lever, push key missing.....................30.00
Yale, Century, iron, 6 lever..............................8.00
Yale, iron, pin tumbler, no key............................5.00
Yale, iron, rnd, no key, 3¼".............................8.00

Loetz

The Loetz glassworks was established in Klostermule, Austria, in 1840. After Loetz's death, the firm was purchased by his grandson, Johann Loetz Witwe. Until WWII the operation continued to produce fine art ware, some of which made in the early 1900s bears a striking resemblance to Tiffany's, with whom Loetz was associated at one time. In addition to the iridescent Tiffany-style glass, he also produced threaded glass and some cameo. Signed pieces bring premium prices.

Basket, hat shape, clear hdl, gr irid.......................225.00
Bowl, 6 puffed out sections, gr, sgn, 4x6½"...............275.00
Compote, leaf, ribbed verre de soie, 6 prong ft, unsgn, 5"....325.00

Vase, pink with green threading, signed Loetz, Austria, 10½", $650.00.

Compote, ruffled/raindrop, gr/pink/purple, 4 ftd metal mt, 9"...340.00
Cuspidor, gr irid, melon rib, polished pontil, unsgn, 4½x5".....95.00
Inkwell, random threads on bl irid, w/insert, unsgn, 3" sq.....170.00
Mug, matt rose w/silver overlay, 3"........................250.00
Rose bowl, melon shape, allover threading, 5"..............125.00
Sweetmeat, wavy amber, pk/gr irid hi-lites, brass bail, sgn.....265.00
Syrup pitcher, irid bl w/silver top/hdl, sgn, 6½"............400.00
Vase, amber irid w/bl & gold hi-lites, pinched top, 7¼".......110.00
Vase, berry & leaf silver overlay on silver/gr irid, sgn, 9x6"....450.00
Vase, bl stripes on red, unsgn, 11".......................275.00
Vase, bl/gr tints, ruffled, sgn, 4¼"......................225.00
Vase, bl/silver bl spots, U form/vertical amber hdls, att, 7".....660.00
Vase, cobalt spatter, 3 hdls, sgn, 5¾"....................950.00
Vase, cobalt w/gold foliage, pinched sides, fluted top, 8"......285.00
Vase, ftd tubular, gr/optic rib/irid gold/wht waves/unsgn, 12"...425.00
Vase, gold, bulbous w/pinched sides, 7"...................285.00
Vase, gold, ruffled/long full neck/rnd pinch body, unsgn, 15"...225.00
Vase, gold oil spots, 4"..................................135.00
Vase, gold w/ovoid pinch body/taper neck/lacy rim, unsgn, 15"..225.00
Vase, gold/pink irid w/gr pulled decor, crimp top, unsgn, 10"...195.00
Vase, gourd form, mc irid swirl on gr, unsgn, 9½".........50.00
Vase, gr irid/gold dust, flower form opening, 3 dimples, 14x7"..350.00
Vase, gr w/combination gloss & irid finish, sgn, 8".........175.00
Vase, gr w/marbleized/swirl bl/purple/br, 4 lobe top, 9".......160.00
Vase, heavy overall threading, amethyst/red/gr, unsgn, 11".....175.00
Vase, in Nouveau pewter holder w/iris; pk irid, unsgn, 5x5"....95.00
Vase, irid bl mottle, red w/in, slender bottom ½, sgn, 10".....650.00
Vase, irid gr/amethyst, ruffled, sgn, 10"..................265.00
Vase, irid oil spots, wave & dot devices, att, 7"...........825.00
Vase, lakeside scene, in cameo, bulbous, waisted neck, 7".....675.00
Vase, mottle gold/pink, cobalt irid prunts, unsgn, lg........160.00
Vase, purple irid w/bl threading, sgn, 9".................300.00
Vase, rose w/silver blue irid, gourd shape, sgn, 13½".......935.00
Vase, silver bl drip over apricot laced w/gr, unsgn, 6¾"...1,320.00
Vase, wht mottle w/gr & gold irid 'basketry' & ft, 5¼".......245.00
Vase, yellow w/applied loops, irid, cylinder, sgn, 11½".......770.00
Vase, yellow/silver bl strings, applied br prunts, sgn, 6" dia...1,210.00
Vase, yellow/violet irid, flat amphora/4 neck hdls, sgn, 7"......825.00

Longwy

The Longwy workshops were founded in 1798, and continue today to produce pottery in the north of France near the Luxembourgh-Belgian border. The ware for which they are best known was produced during the Art Deco period, and decorated in bold color and geometric designs. Earlier wares made during the first quarter of the 19th century reflected the popularity of Oriental art, cloisonne enamels in particular. The designs were executed by impressing the pattern into the moist clay, and filling in the depressions with enamels. Examples are marked 'Longwy', either impressed or painted under glaze.

```
Bowl, bl w/out, floral on bl w/in, 3¾" dia...................30.00
Bowl, floral on burgandy, bl w/out, imp mk, 5½" dia.........58.00
Box, jewelry; br crackle, mc floral w/central star.............85.00
Candlestick, figural griffin base, 9½", pr...................400.00
Plaque, Dutch shoe, bl w/pk & wht flowers, pink w/in, 3x6"....135.00
Salt shaker, wht w/mc flowers, blue-gr border, orig lid, mkd.....48.00
Tile, ftd, geometrics, coat of arms, lion & castles, 8" sq......145.00
Vase, cylinder, dk blue w/blue & yel floral border, mkd, 7x3"..165.00
```

Powder boxes: reclining nude, Primavera, after Mattise, 3½", $375.00; vase and florals, after Magrette, 3½", $350.00; ram and mystic trees, 3½", $325.00.

Lonhuda

William Long was a druggist by trade, who combined his knowledge of chemistry with his artistic ability, in an attempt to produce a type of brown glazed slip-decorated art ware similar to that made by the Rookwood Pottery. He achieved his goal in 1889, after years of long and dedicated study. Three years later, he founded his firm, the Lonhuda Pottery Company. The name was coined from the first few letters of the last name of each of his partners, W.H. Hunter and Alfred Day. Laura Fry, formerly of the Rookwood company, joined the firm in 1892, bringing with her a license for Long to use her patented air brush blending process. Other artists of note, Sarah McLaughlin, Helen Harper, and Jessie Spaulding joined the firm and decorated the ware with nature studies, animals, and portraits, often signing their work with their initials. Three types of marks were used on the Steubenville Lonhuda ware. The first was a linear composite of the letters 'LPCO' with the name 'Lonhuda' impressed above it. The second, adopted in 1893, was a die stamp representing the solid profile of an Indian, used on ware patterned after pottery made by the American Indians. This mark was later replaced with an impressed outline of the Indian head, with 'Lonhuda' arching above it. Although the ware was successful, the business floundered due to poor management; in 1895, Long became a partner of Sam Weller and moved to Zanesville where the manufacture of the Lonhuda line continued. Less than a year later, Long left the Weller company.

```
Bowl vase, artist sgn Jessie Spaulding, 1895, 6"............350.00
Creamer & sugar, yellow roses, #41/42, creamer w/hairline.....130.00
Jug vase, bud & leaf decor, sm hdl, sgn, 5¾"...............125.00
Vase, br glaze w/lg orange/yellow mums, glaze scratches, 9".....90.00
Vase, floral artwork, loop hdls, Jessie Spaulding, 1893, 4x7"...425.00
```

Lu Ray Pastels

Lu Ray Pastels dinnerware was introduced in the early 1940s by Taylor, Smith, and Taylor of East Liverpool, Ohio. It was offered in assorted colors -- Persian Cream, Sharon Pink, Surf Green, Windsor Blue, and Gray -- in complete place settings as well as many service pieces. It was a successful line in its day and is once again finding favor with collectors of American dinnerware.

```
Bowl, fruit; 5½".........................................4.50
Bowl, mixing; green, rare, M............................30.00
Bowl, oval vegetable......................................6.50
Bowl, soup; tab hdld.....................................10.00
Butter, covered; ¼ lb, Sharon Pink.....................18.00
Casserole, covered; yellow..............................20.00
Coffee pot, demitasse; w/lid, ovoid, Windsor Blue.......25.00
Coffee pot, demitasse; w/lid, straight side.............40.00
Creamer, demitasse; ovoid, Sharon Pink..................10.00
Creamer, demitasse; straight side.......................15.00
Cup & saucer, demitasse; Persian Cream..................10.00
Egg cup, Sharon Pink....................................12.00
Gravy boat, Sharon Pink.................................12.00
Muffin cover, w/8" under plate, Surf Green..............45.00
Pitcher, juice; ovoid, Sharon Pink......................25.00
Pitcher, syrup; green, M, rare..........................40.00
Pitcher, water; footed, Windsor Blue....................25.00
Plate, cake; Sharon Pink................................15.00
Plate, calendar; 1959...................................10.00
Plate, grill............................................11.00
Plate, serving; tab hdl.................................15.00
Plate, 10"...............................................6.00
Plate, 7"................................................3.00
Plate, 7", Chatham Gray, rare color......................6.00
Plate, 8"................................................4.00
Salt & pepper, pr.......................................10.00
Sugar, w/lid, demitasse; ovoid, Windsor Blue............10.00
Sugar, w/lid, demitasse; straight side..................20.00
Teapot, w/lid, Windsor Blue.............................25.00
Tidbit, 2 tier, sgnd....................................18.00
Tumbler, juice; Persian Cream...........................10.00
Tumbler, water; Surf Green..............................12.00
```

Teapot, Windsor Blue, 5", $35.00.

Lunch Boxes

Early 20th century tobacco companies such as Union Leader, Tiger, and Dixie issued a series of square containers with flat metal carrying handles designed to be used for lunch boxes after the contents had been otherwise enjoyed. By 1930, oval lunch pails with colorful lithographed decorations on tin were being manufactured to appeal directly to children. These were made by Ohio Art, who in 1950 changed from the oval to the standard rectangular shape more often seen today. In 1950 the Aladdin Company issued the first of their character lunch boxes, decorated with pictures of Hopalong Cassidy, Trigger, Bozo, etc., fully fitted with matching thermos bottles.

Early boxes sometimes were die pressed so that the shape of the character stood out in relief. Character decals were applied to the corresponding embossed design. The thermos bottles, however, were lithographed and by the mid-fifties, so were the boxes.

Other companies -- ADCO Liberty; Landers, Frary & Clark; and American Thermos -- also produced character pails. Today collectors often tend to specialize in those dealing with a particular subject. Western, space, TV series, Disney movies, or cartoon characters are among the most popular.

Adam 12, 1972	5.00
Banquet Hall Little Cigars, tin container	20.00
Barbie & Francie, vinyl, dtd 1965	15.00
Batman, 1966	8.00
Beatles, bl portrait, w/thermos	85.00
Beatles Yellow Submarine	42.50
Bengal Little Cigars, tin container	20.00
Bobby Sherman	8.00
Brotherhood	85.00
Cameron & Cameron, red, humidor top	125.00
Central Union, rnd corners	45.00
Cinco	48.00
Custom House, cigar tin	85.00
Dan Patch, bail hdl	120.00
Disney, School Bus, dome top, Aladdin, EX	75.00
Dixie Kid, 4x7½x4"	225.00
Emilia Garcia, cigar tin	25.00
Evil Knievel, 1974	5.00
Family Affair, 1969	8.00
Fashion, tobacco	125.00
Gail & Ax Navy, VG	75.00
GI Joe, w/thermos	15.00
Green Turtle Cigars	125.00
Handbag, VG	60.00
Hopalong Cassidy, 1950, NM	45.00
It's About Time, 1967	10.00
Joe Palooka	40.00
Just Suits	65.00
Laredo, bail hdl	70.00
Mayos	35.00
Mickey Mouse, complete, WD Ent, EX	250.00
Mother Goose characters, tin litho, candy box	125.00
Oceanic	90.00
Pastora, cigar tin	85.00
Patterson's Seal Cut Plug, basketweave tin	38.00
Pedro Tobacco	95.00
Plow Boy	145.00
Postmaster, cigar tin, orange	30.00
Redicut, tobacco	95.00
Round Trip	35.00
Scooby Doo	8.00
Sensation, basketweave	25.00
Skookum, G	40.00
Summer Time, pail	40.00

Thermos, Barbie/Midge/Skipper, blk bkground	15.00
Tiger, lg	35.00
Tiger, sm	30.00
Tindeco, bl, Santa	45.00
Union Leader Cut Plug, eagle tin	45.00
US Marine, pictures Marine, VG	130.00
Warnick Brown	75.00
Welcome Back Kotter	8.00
Wild Fruit, 4½x7x4"	62.50
Winners, tobacco	125.00
Woody Woodpecker, 1972	6.00

Lustre Art Glass Co.

The Lustre Art Glass Company operated in Long Island, New York, from about 1920 until 1925, manufacturing iridescent lampshades similar to those of Durand and Quezal.

Shade, gold irid w/wht feathers w/gr outlines, 6 for	675.00
Shade, gold lily	175.00
Shade, gold threading on pulled feathers, gold w/in, set of 4	400.00
Shade, gold zipper over opal, ruffled rim, set of 4	600.00
Shade, pulled br feathers on irid gr, gold surround, sgn, pr	290.00
Shade, random gold spiderweb on wht/gold pulled feather	145.00
Shade, yel bands on opal, gold lined, set of 4	375.00

Lutz

Nicholas Lutz worked for the Boston and Sandwich Glass Company from 1869 to 1888, where he produced the threaded and striped art glass that was popular during that era. His works were not marked, and since many other glassmakers of the day made similar wares, the term Lutz has come to refer not only to his original works but to any of this type.

See also Threaded Glass

Cake plate, threaded, pink, 7" dia	100.00
Epergne, 3 lilies	225.00
Finger bowl w/under plate, clear applied baby face medallions	160.00
Plate, goldstone, rose shades to amber, ruffled, unsgn, 6"	80.00
Salt, clear w/bl & gold twists alternate w/wht latticinio	30.00
Tumbler, ftd, 6 strawberries/threading on wht latticinio, 3"	85.00
Vase, gr w/bl threading, 8¾"	110.00

Maastricht

Maastricht, Holland, was the site of the De Sphinx Pottery, founded in 1836 by Petrus Regout. They made earthenware decorated with transfer prints, as well as dinnerware with gaudy hand painted designs. Potteries are still working in this area today.

Bowl, bl/wht, 9½"	45.00
Bowl, porridge; Pompeii, P Regout	65.00
Cake plate, gaudy florals in red/bl/gr/blk, sgn, 12"	75.00
Cup & saucer, gaudy florals in bl/gr/ochre/red, mkd	20.00
Pitcher, Timor, Oriental scene, mc, 4½"	65.00
Plaque, Roosevelt portrait, gr wreath, 10"	30.00
Plate, Abbey, lustre trim, ca 1880, 8"	12.00
Plate, gaudy stick spatter, floral border, 7", pr	45.00
Soup plate, gaudy, rooster, foliage rim, 8½", pr	40.00

Magazines

Magazines are collected primarily for their cover prints, and for the information pertaining to defunct companies and their products that can be gleaned from the old advertisements.

See also Prints

Agricultural Digest, 1934, Nov, Parrish cover.................25.00
All Sports, 1942, May, Vol 2, #3.........................12.50
American, 1918, Sept..................................45.00
American, 1930, May..................................16.50
American, 1934, May...................................5.00
American, 1936, June..................................5.00
American Boy, 1920, Apr, Rockwell cover/ad............20.00
American Heritage, 1970, Dec..........................20.00
Arizona Highways, 1959, Sept..........................3.00
Atlantic, 1969, Nov, Death of the Post................15.00
Atlantic Monthly, 1921, June, Parrish ad..............25.00
Avant Garde, 1968, Jan, Vol 1, #1.....................9.00
Better Homes & Gardens, 1941, May.....................2.50
Booknews, 1896, Feb, Parrish cover...................40.00
Boy's Life, 1937, July, Howard Chandler Christy cover........12.00
Boy's Life, 1939, Feb, Rockwell cover................15.00
Boy's Life, 1963, Feb, Rockwell cover.................8.00
Business Week, 1968, June 8, Kennedy.................3.50
Century, 1898, Parrish art...........................17.50
Century, 1904, Parrish prints........................25.00
Century, 1921, July, Parrish ad......................20.00
Click, 1938, Dec, Shirley Temple article.............15.00
Click, 1940, June, Quints on cover in party dresses w/cake.....25.00
Collier's, 1905, Jan 7, Parrish art..................28.00
Collier's, 1905, May 6, Parrish cover................40.00
Collier's, 1908, June 6, Parrish cover...............35.00
Collier's, 1909, Mar 27, Parrish illus, blk/wht......7.50
Collier's, 1910, July 30, Parrish cover..............30.00
Collier's, 1913, May 17, Parrish cover...............30.00
Collier's, 1933, Dec 29..............................3.50
Collier's, 1933, June 10, Chicago World's Fair cover...........5.00
Collier's, 1939, Dec 26, Parrish cover...............40.00
Coronet, 1936, Nov, Vol 1, #1........................5.00
Cosmopolitan, 1908, Mar, Harrison Fisher cover.......4.00
Country Gentleman, 1919, Dec 27, Rockwell cover......22.00
Country Gentleman, 1921, July 2, Rockwell cover......19.00
Country Life, 1919, Aug, Parrish tire ad.............35.00
Daughters o/t Am Revolution, 1931, Feb..............4.00
Etude, 1937, Jan.....................................3.00
Fact, 1964, Vol 1, #s 1 & 2, both for................35.00
Family Circle, 1938, June 10, Shirley Temple.........15.00
Farm Journal, 1934, July 8...........................2.00
Fortune, 1933, Jan, Vol 7, #1, M.....................25.00
Fortune, 1935, Apr, Vol 11, #4, EX...................20.00
Fortune, 1936, Dec, Lipfert doll article w/Quints....18.00
Good Housekeeping, 1979, Oct, article on Dionne Quints........7.50
Harper's, 1901, Apr, The Cherubs, M Parrish..........18.00
Harper's Bazaar, 1895, Parrish cover.................50.00
Harper's Bazaar, 1922, Mar, Parrish ad...............25.00
Harper's Weekly, 1865, Lincoln Assassination, Booth cover.....45.00
Harper's Weekly, 1865, Lincoln Inauguration, EX.............40.00
Harper's Weekly, 1865, Sherman's march/burning of Atlanta, EX.40.00
Hearst's, 1912, Parrish cover.......................100.00
Hearst's, 1922, Parrish ad...........................35.00
Holiday, 1946, March, Vol 1, #1......................29.00
Illustrated London News, 1952, Oct, centerfold Royal Family.....5.00
Inland Printer, 1902, Nov, Seymour cover.............8.00

Ladies' Home Companion, 1938, Aug....................6.00
Ladies' Home Journal, 1901, Parrish cover............50.00
Ladies' Home Journal, 1904, Sept, Parrish cover......30.00
Ladies' Home Journal, 1912, July, Parrish cover......25.00
Ladies' Home Journal, 1916, Dec, Parrish ad..........45.00
Ladies' Home Journal, 1930, Mar, Parrish frontispiece.........35.00
Ladies' Home Journal, 1938, Dec......................3.00
Ladies' Home Journal, 1939, Feb......................4.00
Ladies' Home Journal, 1942, Apr......................4.00
Ladies' Home Journal, 1958, Sept, Rockwell ad........7.00
Ladies' World, 1915, Mar, Clarence Underwood cover........12.00
Le Samedi, 1935, Feb, Dionne Quints on cover.........20.00
Leslie's, 1917, Dec 22, Rockwell cover...............18.00
Leslie's, 1919, Mar 22, Rockwell cover...............16.00
Liberty, 1936, June 6, Quints on cover...............18.00
Liberty, 1941, Lindbergh, The Most Dangerous Man in America..6.50
Life, 1936, Nov 23, Vol 1, #1, Ft Peck Dam, EX, w/envelope..100.00
Life, 1936, Vol 1, #1, VG............................35.00
Life, 1937, Jan 4, Franklin Roosevelt, M.............25.00
Life, 1937, May 3, Harlow in Hollywood, M............15.00
Life, 1937, Sept 6, Harpo Marx, EX...................12.00
Life, 1938, Jan 3, A Lady on Ice, M..................12.00
Life, 1938, May 23, Errol Flynn, Glamor Boy, EX......10.00
Life, 1938, Oct 17, Carol Lombard, M.................12.00
Life, 1939, July 18, GWTW/NY Fair features, Vivien Leigh cover..8.50
Life, 1940, Apr 1, NY Giants rookie John Rooker on cover......5.00
Life, 1940, Oct 7, Gary Cooper in Western outfit.............7.00
Life, 1940, Sept 2, Dionne Quints, 1st communion............55.00
Life, 1941, Aug 11, Rita Hayworth cover..............9.00
Life, 1941, Jan 6, Katherine Hepburn.................7.50
Life, 1942, Mar 30, Shirley Temple...................10.00
Life, 1944, July 24, Jennifer Jones..................4.00
Life, 1945, Dec 3, Spencer Tracy, Rockwell bk cover.........10.00
Life, 1945, July 16, Audie Murphy cover..............9.00
Life, 1945, May 21, Winston Churchill................8.00
Life, 1945, Sept 24, Jimmy Stewart, Coke ad..........12.00
Life, 1948, Nov 22, Harry Truman cover...............9.00
Life, 1949, Aug 1, Joe Dimaggio......................5.50
Life, 1950, Aug 28, Gen Douglas MacArthur, Rockwell ad......10.00
Life, 1950, June 12, Hopalong Cassidy cover..........9.00
Life, 1958, Feb 3, Shirley Temple on cover...........8.00
Life, 1962, Aug, Marilyn Monroe......................6.00

Pictorial Review, December 1925, $6.00.

Life, 1970, Nov 13, If We All Like It, Is It Art.................3.50
Literary Digest, 1918, Nov 9.................22.00
Literary Digest, 1921, Aug 27.................20.00
Literary Digest, 1923, Dec 22.................19.00
Look, 1937, Dec 21, Shirley Temple entertains Santa.........22.00
Look, 1938, Oct 11, Dionne Quints.................25.00
Look, 1943, Nov 16, Shirley Temple cover.................12.00
Look, 1960, May 10, Princess Margaret; Catholic for President...4.00
Look, 1961, June 20, Doris Day cover, Kennedy's Decisions, EX..6.00
Look, 1961, Sept 12, Kennedy One Year Later, VG.............7.00
Look, 1964, July 14.................10.00
Look, 1966, June 14, Rockwell illus.................10.00
Look, 1967, Oct 3.................5.00
Look, 1968, June 25.................5.00
Look, 1969, July 15.................10.00
Look, 1971, Oct 19.................8.00
Master Detective, 1936, Jan, M.................6.50
McCall's, 1921, Jan, Howard Chandler Christy cover...........13.00
McCall's, 1922, Mar, Parrish cover.................40.00
McCall's, 1931, Sept, Lindbergh story w/Wyeth illus, G.........4.00
McCall's, 1934, June, w/Flagg illustrations.................4.00
McCall's, 1936, Aug, full page color Coke ad, VG.............3.00
McCall's, 1958, June, Rockwell ad.................7.00
McCall's, 1964, Dec, Rockwell cover.................16.00
McCall's, 1964, Nov.................5.00
Modern Maturity, 1976, Oct-Nov, Rockwell illus.................5.00
Modern Priscilla, 1927, May.................5.00
Mother Earth News, 1970, Jan.................8.00
Mother's Magazine, Jan-Dec 1844, 304 pgs, VG.................10.00
National Geographic, Vol 3 (1891/92), #1.................175.00
National Geographic, Vol 3 (1891/92), #4.................220.00
National Geographic, Vol 4 (1892/93), #2.................200.00
National Geographic, Vol 5 (1893/94), #1.................150.00
National Geographic, Vol 5 (1893/94), #4.................165.00
National Geographic, Vol 6 (1894/95), #1.................150.00
National Geographic, Vol 6 (1894/95), #2 through #5, each....165.00
National Geographic, 1896, Jan.................75.00
National Geographic, 1897, Mar.................60.00
National Geographic, 1898, May.................60.00
National Geographic, 1899, Dec.................60.00
National Geographic, 1899, Feb.................60.00
National Geographic, 1900, Aug.................35.00
National Geographic, 1906, June.................25.00
National Geographic, 1908, April.................20.00
National Geographic, 1910, Jan.................20.00
National Geographic, 1913, Feb.................17.00
National Geographic, 1917, Dog Issue.................15.00
National Geographic, 1919, July.................12.00
National Geographic, 1920, May.................11.00
National Geographic, 1921, January.................9.00
National Geographic, 1926, January.................5.00
National Observer, 1963, Nov 25.................5.00
Photoplay, 1958, May, Rick Nelson cover.................2.00
Pic, 1941, May 27, Veronica Lake cover.................4.50
Pic, 1945, Feb 13, Toni Steven cover.................3.50
Pictorial Review, 1912, Apr, Howard Chandler Christy cover.....6.00
Playboy, 1968, June, Girls of Scandanavia, EX.................8.00
Playboy, 1969, Apr, Bardot Pictorials, EX.................8.00
Post, 1959, Jan 31, Rockwell ad.................5.00
Post, 1960, Mar 26, kids building rocket, Rockwell ad.........5.00
Puck, 1895, Apr 10, political cartoons.................20.00
Reader's Digest, 1971, Apr, Norman Rockwell Album.................2.00
Red Cross, 1918, Nov, Rockwell illus story.................15.00
Red Cross, 1919, July, Rockwell cover.................22.00

Saturday Evening Post, 1908, Sept 26, NC Wyeth cover.........9.00
Saturday Evening Post, 1909, July 3, C Livingston Bull cover.....5.00
Saturday Evening Post, 1911, Feb 18, CF Underwood cover.....8.00
Saturday Evening Post, 1911, Mar 25, ZP Nikolaki cover.........6.00
Saturday Evening Post, 1911, Oct 28, Robert Robinson cover....8.00
Saturday Evening Post, 1912, June 8, Leslie Thrasher cover.....8.00
Saturday Evening Post, 1913, Aug 9, Boileau cover, ad bk......25.00
Saturday Evening Post, 1913, Nov 22.................10.00
Saturday Evening Post, 1918, Aug 10, Rockwell cover.........40.00
Saturday Evening Post, 1920, Jan 3.................7.00
Saturday Evening Post, 1921, Dec 3, Rockwell cover.........32.00
Saturday Evening Post, 1921, Oct 1, Rockwell cover.........30.00
Saturday Evening Post, 1922, Apr 8, Rockwell cover.........24.00
Saturday Evening Post, 1922, Aug 19, Rockwell cover, Coke ad.45.00
Saturday Evening Post, 1923, Sept 8, Rockwell cover.........22.00
Saturday Evening Post, 1924, Dec 27, Parrish ad.................12.00
Saturday Evening Post, 1926, Mar 27, Rockwell cover.........24.00
Saturday Evening Post, 1927, Mar 12, Rockwell cover.........22.00
Saturday Evening Post, 1928, Apr 14, Rockwell cover.........20.00
Saturday Evening Post, 1928, May 5, mailman/child by Rockwell.12.50
Saturday Evening Post, 1929, Dec 7, Rockwell cover.........22.00
Saturday Evening Post, 1931, Apr 18, Rockwell cover.........20.00
Saturday Evening Post, 1931, July 31, Rockwell cover.........20.00
Saturday Evening Post, 1933, Apr 8, Rockwell cover.........18.00
Saturday Evening Post, 1934, June 30, Rockwell cover, VG...35.00
Saturday Evening Post, 1935, Dec 21, Rockwell cover.........19.00
Saturday Evening Post, 1936, Feb 22, Rockwell illus.........10.00
Saturday Evening Post, 1938, Oct 24, Leyendecker cover, VG...25.00
Saturday Evening Post, 1938, Oct 8, Rockwell cover, VG......35.00
Saturday Evening Post, 1939, Sept 2, Rockwell cover.........19.00
Saturday Evening Post, 1941, Dec 20, Rockwell cover.........14.00
Saturday Evening Post, 1941, July 26, Rockwell cover.........15.00
Saturday Evening Post, 1941, Nov 29, Rockwell cover.........14.00
Saturday Evening Post, 1941, Oct 4, Rockwell cover.........12.00
Saturday Evening Post, 1942, July 25, Rockwell cover.........14.00
Saturday Evening Post, 1942, Mar 21, Rockwell cover.........15.00
Saturday Evening Post, 1944, Apr 29, Rockwell cover.........12.00
Saturday Evening Post, 1944, July 1, Rockwell cover.........12.00
Saturday Evening Post, 1945, Dec 15, Rockwell cover.........14.00
Saturday Evening Post, 1945, Nov 3, Rockwell cover.........10.00
Saturday Evening Post, 1945, Sept 15, Rockwell cover.........10.00
Saturday Evening Post, 1946, Aug 3, Rockwell cover.........10.00
Saturday Evening Post, 1947, Dec 27, Rockwell cover.........10.00
Saturday Evening Post, 1947, Jan 11, Rockwell cover.........10.00
Saturday Evening Post, 1947, Mar 22, Rockwell cover.........12.00
Saturday Evening Post, 1947, May 3, Rockwell cover.........10.00
Saturday Evening Post, 1948, Jan 24, Rockwell cover.........8.00
Saturday Evening Post, 1949, Mar 19, Rockwell cover.........11.00
Saturday Evening Post, 1950, Aug 19, Rockwell cover.........10.00
Saturday Evening Post, 1951, July 14, Rockwell cover.........8.00
Saturday Evening Post, 1953, Apr 4, Rockwell cover.........10.00
Saturday Evening Post, 1955, June 11, Rockwell cover.........10.00
Saturday Evening Post, 1955, Mar 12, Rockwell cover.........14.00
Saturday Evening Post, 1956, Oct 6, Rockwell cover.........8.00
Saturday Evening Post, 1957, Mar 2, Rockwell cover, Red Sox..21.00
Saturday Evening Post, 1957, May 25, Rockwell, After the Prom.19.00
Saturday Evening Post, 1957, Nov 30, Rockwell, Expense Acct..20.00
Saturday Evening Post, 1957, Sept 7, Rockwell, Missing Tooth..18.00
Saturday Evening Post, 1958, Mar 15, Rockwell, Dr's Office.....22.00
Saturday Evening Post, 1958, Nov 8, Rockwell, Elect Casey.....18.00
Saturday Evening Post, 1958, Sept 20, Rockwell, Jockey cover..20.00
Saturday Evening Post, 1959, June 6, Rockwell cover.........12.00
Saturday Evening Post, 1959, Oct 24, Rockwell cover.........14.00
Saturday Evening Post, 1967, Jan 14, Did Oswald Act Alone, EX.6.00

Scouting, 1944, Feb, Rockwell cover........................8.00
Scouting, 1960, Feb...................................7.00
Scribner's, 1899, Parrish cover.........................35.00
Scribner's, 1906, Apr, Parrish illus.......................15.00
Sportsman, 1934, May.................................5.00
St Nicholas, 1917, Jan, Rockwell illus story................10.00
St Nicholas, 1919, Aug, Rockwell Fisk Tire ad..............25.00
Stage, 1938, Sept, Rockwell sketch, Raymond Massey as Lincoln..8.00
True Detective, 1937, Jan, M...........................6.50
TV Guide, 1953, Vol 1, #1, April 3.....................190.00
TV Guide, 1953, Vol 1, #2............................40.00
TV Guide, 1953, Vol 1, #26, Superman, NM...............90.00
TV Guide, 1953, Vol 1, #3............................30.00
TV Guide, 1953, Vol 1, #37, NM.......................15.00
TV Guide, 1953, Vol 1, #4, VG.........................20.00
US Camera, 1944, Aug................................5.00
Woman's Day, 1965, June..............................3.00
Woman's Home Companion, 1918, Feb, Parrish ad..........40.00
Woman's Home Companion, 1938, Aug.....................4.00
Yank, 1944, June 2, Signal Corps in Newfoundland...........2.50
Yankee, 1968, Dec, Vermont Church, Parrish...............14.00
Youth's Companion, 1924, Jan 3, Parrish ad................42.00

Majolica

Majolica is a type of heavy earthenware, design molded, and decorated in vivid colors with either a lead or tin type of glaze. It reached its height of popularity in the Victorian era; examples from this period are found in only the lead glazes. Nearly every potter of note, both here and abroad, produced large majolica jardinieres, umbrella stands, pitchers with animal themes, leaf shapes, vegetable forms, and nearly any other nature theme that came to mind. Few, however, marked their ware. Among those who did were Minton, Wedgwood, and George Jones in England; Griffin, Smith and Hill (Etruscan) in Phoenixville, Pennsylvania; and Chesapeake Pottery (Avalon and Clifton) in Baltimore.

Authority Mariann K. Marks has compiled a lovely book, *Majolica Pottery, An Identification and Value Guide*, with many full-color photos; you will find her address in the Directory under 'Pennsylvania'.

Basket, Bamboo & Basketweave, English...................95.00
Basket, shell, lav/bl/gr w/br rope hdl, 8"................185.00
Basket, 3 branch hdls, floral encrusted, 3 birds, 18".......250.00
Biscuit jar, cobalt & floral, French, later period...........85.00
Biscuit jar, gr basketweave, red apples, wicker swing hdl....60.00
Bowl, cabbage leaf, luggage straps, turq, ftd.............200.00
Bowl, Classical Series, Etruscan.......................100.00
Bowl, floral pattern, turq lining, large..................350.00
Bowl, fruit; begonia basketweave, 3½x10"...............105.00
Bowl, fruit; lt bl shell w/3 dk bl shell ft, lav w/in, 9½x12"...85.00
Bowl, lg maple leaf in center, shallow, 10½"..............55.00
Bowl, Pond Lily, Holdcroft, ftd, 8½"...................120.00
Bowl, Shell & Seaweed, bird perched on edge.............275.00
Bowl, Shell & Seaweed, Etruscan, 3x8".................125.00
Bust, American Indian, 4½".............................68.00
Butter dish, Bamboo, Etruscan.........................225.00
Butter dish, Bamboo & Basketweave, sgn VPC, 8x4".......225.00
Butter pat, Begonia Leaf...............................22.00
Butter pat, Begonia Leaf variant, stem forms hdl, gr/gold....24.00
Butter pat, Pansy, Etruscan............................35.00
Cake plate, br basketweave, open hdls....................35.00
Cake plate, Geranium, Etruscan........................135.00
Cake plate, 11", +4 servers, grape leaves on yel texture, Zell...85.00
Cake platter, Bamboo & Basketweave.....................45.00
Cake stand, pink w/gr leaves, tree base, Etruscan, 9½", G....65.00

Cake stand, Pond Lily, George Jones....................195.00
Cheese keeper, Pond Lily, Holdcroft....................550.00
Chocolate pot, cr/sug, 4 mugs, br/yel w/gr orchids..........85.00
Clock, Avalon, sgn, orig works.........................185.00
Compote, molded cupid on flying lion, Etruscan, 4x9¾"......70.00
Compote, peacock/reticulated tail, Baroque base, Eichwald, 11".180.00
Creamer, Bamboo, Etruscan............................95.00
Creamer, Corn motif, Etruscan..........................95.00
Creamer, individual; yel basketweave w/gr bamboo leaves......32.00
Creamer, Pineapple, Bennington.........................65.00
Creamer, Robin on Branch, picket fence bkground...........32.00
Creamer, Shell & Seaweed, Albino, lt gr/pink/yellow trim, 4"....45.00
Creamer, Wild Rose, Etruscan, 4½".....................65.00
Cup & saucer, Bamboo, Etruscan......................120.00
Cup & saucer, Bamboo, orchid lining, Etruscan.............60.00
Cup & saucer, Shell & Seaweed, Carr...................67.50
Cup & saucer, Shell & Seaweed, Etruscan...............125.00
Cup & saucer, Shell & Seaweed, yel/br on cobalt, fish hdl....135.00
Cup & saucer, Water Lily..............................55.00
Cup w/Leaf & Flower formed saucer.....................35.00
Cuspidor, Raspberry pattern on yel basketweave, English reg mk.75.00
Dessert set, Lily Pad pattern, 5 pc, German...............85.00
Dessert stand, Choisy Le Roi, sgn, 4x8½"...............195.00
Figurine, Fr poodle, sitting on pillow, gray/wht, 3½".........35.00
Figurine, man/bouquet; lady/parasol; ea on wood chair, 7", pr..245.00
Flower frog, figural duck, #s on base, 2½x4"..............20.00
Jug, baseball & soccer, Etruscan, full color, sgn, rare.......1,200.00
Jug, baseball & soccer players, Etruscan, all brown, unsgn....175.00
Jug, baseball & soccer players, Etruscan, all cobalt, unsgn....225.00
Leaf dish, Etruscan, 12x9½"............................68.00
Match holder, man & woman figurals, 6½", pr..............95.00
Match holder, 2 Black boys, watermelon, cotton bale, 1884....85.00
Match/cigarette holder, striker; Black boy w/basket on wall....135.00
Mug, Acorn on br, Etruscan...........................125.00
Mug, Bamboo pattern, w/2 frogs inside...................75.00
Mug, Daisy & Bow...................................75.00
Oil lamp, Raspberry pattern, sgn Clifton Decor............150.00
Oyster plate, Fish decor, star shape.....................155.00
Pitcher, Albino tree trunk, br hdl, mc leaves/flowers, 5"......85.00
Pitcher, Basketweave w/Blackberry, English mk, 8½"........85.00
Pitcher, Blackberry, 6"................................65.00
Pitcher, Bow & Bamboo Stalks, bl bow, mc leaves/floral, 9"...145.00
Pitcher, cobalt, wht lilies relief at base/hdl, lav w/in, 10"....195.00
Pitcher, cobalt w/mc leafy branches in relief, English, 8".....85.00
Pitcher, crane & foliage, 9"............................85.00
Pitcher, dragon hdl, florals, 6".........................85.00
Pitcher, figural pig, Albino, 6½".........................75.00
Pitcher, fish, Morley, 8½".............................115.00
Pitcher, fish, 12½"...................................95.00
Pitcher, Fish on Waves, turq ground, 6"..................155.00
Pitcher, floral, sq top, br/yellow, English, 7"..............70.00
Pitcher, floral w/bow.................................25.00
Pitcher, gr leaves at base, rim & hdl, pink center, Wardel, 7"...75.00
Pitcher, hexagonal, pk roses, grs, yel hdl, Onnaing France, 8"...65.00
Pitcher, Honeysuckle & Hummingbirds, bright colors, 6¾".....75.00
Pitcher, hound hdl, ped ft, birds/fox/rabbit/etc, 10".........175.00
Pitcher, Nouveau florals, Frie Onnaing, 7½"...............75.00
Pitcher, outside tavern scene relief, Frie Onnaing, 8½".......120.00
Pitcher, ovoid, gr/br leaves, 8".........................65.00
Pitcher, palm tree, milk size...........................55.00
Pitcher, Pineapple, 6½"................................85.00
Pitcher, Robin, 6½"..................................95.00
Pitcher, Shell & Seaweed, Albino, tan trim, 6"............75.00
Pitcher, Shell & Seaweed, 6".........................175.00

Pitcher, sitting bear figural..................200.00
Pitcher, Sunflower, Etruscan, cobalt, EX glaze, 6", M.........225.00
Pitcher, w/7" plate, Bamboo & Fern, Wardel, 4"..........135.00
Pitcher, wheat, turq/gr on pk, yel border, Geo Jones, 6½".....85.00
Pitcher, wht swan top, gr/br cattails around base, 11"........275.00
Pitcher, Wild Rose, Albino, sq Greek Key top, basketweave, 9".110.00
Place setting, Classical, Albino, Etruscan..............195.00
Plaque, chalet, scenic in relief, pierced, Zell, 9¼".........55.00
Plate, Apple & Raspberry, Etruscan..................85.00
Plate, Bamboo, Etruscan, 8"......................80.00
Plate, Basketweave & Blackberry, Etruscan, 8½"..........70.00
Plate, Basketweave & Blackberry, 10".................45.00
Plate, Basketweave & Blackberry edge, mottled center, 7½"....35.00
Plate, bird, Wardel, 8".........................52.00
Plate, bread; wheat, table ring chips, 13".............80.00
Plate, Cauliflower, Etruscan, 8"...................72.00
Plate, Cauliflower, Etruscan, 9"..................100.00
Plate, cobalt & green leaf pattern, Holdcroft...........95.00
Plate, Deer & Hound, turq/br w/florals, 9"............50.00
Plate, dk br w/Greek family relief, openwork rim, 9½"......30.00
Plate, dk gr leaves, wht water lilies, Holdcroft...........52.00
Plate, dog chasing deer, 9¼"....................55.00
Plate, Dogwood pattern........................36.00
Plate, floral, small..........................20.00
Plate, grape leaf w/grapes, flowers & berries, 8".........35.00
Plate, leaf, Albino, open twig hdl, red/bl flowers, 9½"......60.00
Plate, leaf, Etruscan, 9".......................55.00
Plate, leaf on plate decor, 9"....................50.00
Plate, leaf pattern, George Jones..................90.00
Plate, leaves & ferns, reticulated rim, 8"..............60.00
Plate, Lotus pattern, George Jones.................150.00
Plate, Maple Leaf, 8½".......................29.00
Plate, melon, plums, blackberries, Wedgwood..........85.00
Plate, shaggy dog & house, scalloped, gr/br, 10½".......65.00
Plate, Shell & Fan, 10½"......................35.00
Plate, Shell & Seaweed, Etruscan, 6"...............60.00
Plate, yellow w/pink flowers, Wedgwood Eturia, 9"........48.00
Plate, 9"; cup & saucer, Albino Classical, w/enamel, Etruscan..235.00
Platter, apple & cherry motif, hdl.................155.00
Platter, begonia on bark, w/hdls, 12"...............88.00
Platter, Butterfly & Fan.......................120.00
Platter, fish figural, 13x21" L....................65.00
Platter, ftd, open hdls, bl weaving/lav morning-glories, 14".....65.00
Platter, gr w/2 br baskets, yel floral/leaves, Eng reg mk, 10"....60.00
Platter, large leaf pattern......................110.00
Platter, mc leaves & grapes, Wedgwood, 1883, 12"........65.00
Platter, Overlapping Leaves, red/bl flowers, twig hdl, 9½".....65.00
Platter, Rose & Rope, pk & gr, 2 hdls, minor damage, 11½"...55.00
Relish dish, Begonia Leaf......................15.00
Relish dish, Begonia Leaf, Etruscan, large............45.00
Relish dish, Pickle & Onion pattern, Wedgwood.........150.00
Sardine box, Bamboo & Lilies....................210.00
Sardine box, Basketweave & Shells.................150.00
Sardine box, Lily & Fish motif, Holdcroft.............200.00
Sardine box, yel/br basketweave, fish finial, 'Sardines'.......90.00
Shaving set, Avalon, grape decor pitcher, mug, soap w/lid.....165.00
Sugar w/lid, Wild Rose, Etruscan..................55.00
Sweetmeat dish, grapes/leaves, pk flowers, ear hdls, Wedgwood..95.00
Syrup, Bamboo, Etruscan......................250.00
Syrup, ferns on side, rope hdl, pewter lid, 4½".........110.00
Syrup, Sunflower, Albino, Etruscan................150.00
Syrup, Sunflower, wht ground, Etruscan.............175.00
Tea set, Geranium, sugar has been mended............250.00
Teapot, cobalt w/blue birds, rectangular.............200.00

Teapot, drum shaped w/high hdl..................160.00
Teapot, figural duck.........................175.00
Teapot, strawberry motif.......................125.00
Tobacco jar, frog w/pipe, 6"....................150.00
Toothbrush holder, New England Aster, ftd............72.00
Toothpick, old woman figural, EX quality.............85.00
Tray, bread; Pineapple pattern...................120.00
Tray, Fern, oval............................78.00
Tray, ice cream; shells, snails, seaweed, Wedgwood, 9x15"....550.00
Tray, leaf, Etruscan, gr w/yel, pk edges, open stem hdl, 9x12"...70.00
Tray, leaf w/snail figural, gr/bl/gray/tan, no mk, 2x7".........145.00
Tray, nude w/flowing hair, #8225, 4x6½".............35.00
Tureen, fish figural, 8x18" L....................75.00
Urn, griffin hdls, 4 panels w/lizards/vines, mk imp O w/X, 13"..350.00
Vase, Butterfly & Bouquet w/sand strip on beige, 2 hdls, 5"....18.00
Vase, daisies on leaves & bl bkground, #7259, Austrian, 12"...110.00
Vase, flower stem hdls end in daffodils on olive gr, 9"........42.00

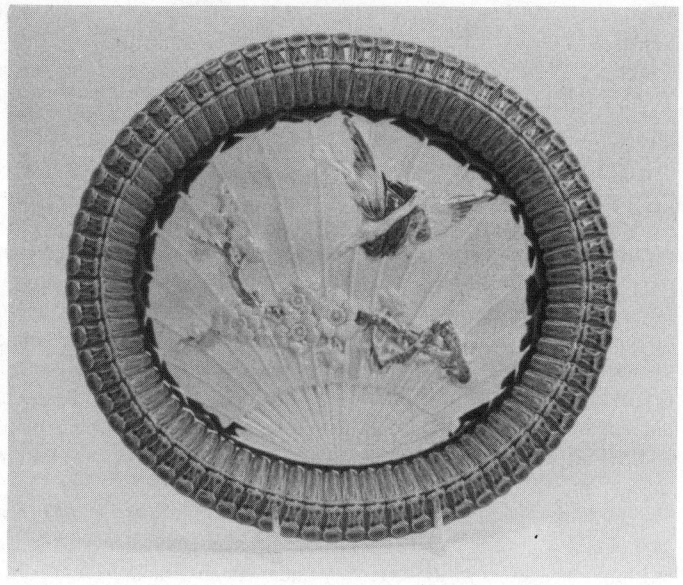

Plaque, crane and dogwood blossoms, wide brown rim, dated, 10/17/1879, $185.00.0

Malachite

Malachite is a type of art glass that exhibits strata-like layerings in shades of green -- similar to the mineral in its natural form.

Ash tray, floral, 4 ft, Moser, 4¼x2¾".................65.00
Figurine, rooster, 3¾"........................42.00
Lamp, floral relief, faceted sides, floral eng gr chimney, 9½"...125.00
Toothpick holder, Diamond Point, bulbous w/flared rim.......18.00
Vase, nudes, sgn Moser, 10"....................285.00
Vase, 6 nudes/grapes in relief, 12 sided ft, 5"............135.00

Maps and Atlases

Maps are highly collectible, not only for historical value, but also for their sometimes elaborate art work, legendary information, or data that has since been proven erroneous. There are many types of maps, including geographical, military, celestial, road, and railroad. The most valuable are those made before the mid-1800s.

Key: hc----hand colored

Alaska, from Alaska Steamship Co, 1936, 20x30″ 8.00
Arizona & New Mexico, dbl folio, colored, SA Mitchell, 1884 . . . .40.00
California, dbl folio, pub 1884, Wm Bradley, 22x14″ 60.00
Cherokee Nation, Indian Territory, RL McAlpine, 1900, 35x25″ .40.00
Chicago, street guide, parks are colored, Rand McNally, 1899 . . .20.00
Chief Part o/t Western States & Part of VA, 1939, hc, 16x24″ . . .55.00
Choctaw Nation, Indian Territory, full color, 36x32″ 40.00
Florida, Map of New Governments, 1757, 8½x11″ 110.00
Indian Reservations w/in US, DM Browning, color by Fetters 35.00
Indian Territory, folio, 1884, SA Mitchell, hc, 11x14″ 60.00
Indian Tribes w/in the US, Capt S Eastman, 1852, pub Grambo .55.00
Kentucky, att J Scott, Phila, 1795, foxing, engraved, 11x12″ 55.00
Kentucky, printed/hc, published 1838, 17x19″ 50.00
Kentucky from the Best Authorities, hc, 1800, in fr, 12x13¾″ . .65.00
Map o/t Middle States of Am, hc engraving, Russell, 1794, 26″ .150.00
New Map of Asia, Beft Authority, 1791, copperplate eng, 11x8″ .15.00
No Am, Alaska is Russian Possession, Gold Region, 1853, 5x7″ .12.00
North & South America, Pazzini Carli, 1780, floral cartouch . . .125.00
Oregon & Washington, dbl folio, 1884, WM Bradley, 22x14″ 10.00
Oregon Territoire aux Etats Unis, engraved, 1854, Paris, 8x10″ . .10.00
Oregon w/location of Indian Tribes, Eastman, 1852, 8x10″ 15.00
Outline Map of Indian Localities, 1833, pub 1876, 9x14½″ 50.00
Rand McNally Commercial Atlas of America, 1924, 640 pgs 75.00
So States, Smith, 1839, tinted, 18x11″ .30.00
Southeast N America, A Ortelius, 1584, hc, latin verse, 13x18″ .750.00
Texas, AJ Johnson, NY City, 1866, hc, ornate border, 17x22″ . . .70.00
US, Engraved for Modern Traveller, S Hall, 1930, 7½x7″ 25.00
Utah & Nevada, dbl folio, hc by SA Mitchell, c Bradley, 14x22″ .25.00
Virginia, West Virginia, Mitchell, hc, 1876, 12x15″ 11.00
West Indies & Mexican Gulf, Pierre Lapie, 1806, 20x30″, EX . .250.00
World, GV Magini, Venice, 1598, 6 wind gods, 5½x7″, EX 225.00
World, Mitchell School Atlas, hc, 9x11″ 10.00

Marblehead

What began as therapy for patients in a sanitarium in Marblehead, Massachusetts, has become recognized as an important part of the Arts and Crafts movement in America. Results of the early experiments under the guidance of Arthur E. Baggs in 1904 met with such success that by 1908 the pottery had been converted to a solely commercial venture. Simple vase shapes were often incised with stylized animal and floral motifs or sailing ships; some were decorated in low relief; many were plain. Simple matt glazes in soft yellow, gray, wisteria, rose, tobacco brown, and their most popular, Marblehead Blue, were used alone, or in combination. The Marblehead logo is distinctive -- a boat with full sail, and the letters 'M' and 'P'. The pottery closed in 1936.

Bowl, dk bl, low, 6″ dia 35.00
Bowl, dk gr w/incised red mushroom border, sgn AEB, 1¼x7″ .250.00
Bowl, gray w/bl flowers, bl w/in, 2¾x7¾″ 350.00
Bowl, w/flower frog, pink glaze, sm 65.00
Candlestick, bl matt, trumpet shape, 4½″, pr 95.00
Jardiniere, bl matt, 4x5″ 70.00
Match holder, w/lid, bl 75.00
Pitcher, cylindrical w/loop hdl, gr, stamped/labeled, 8″ 125.00
Planter, turq orange peel glaze, trial, sgn AEB-1934, 3½″ dia . .150.00
Vase, blue, classic shape, mkd, 6¾x4½″ 80.00
Vase, blue, flared rim, 4x7″ 75.00
Vase, blue, 4″ 40.00
Vase, dk bl, fan shape, 7x7¼″ 75.00
Vase, dk gr, slender body, 6¼″ 55.00
Vase, gray, 3½″ 38.00
Vase, gray w/bl speckles, 4″ 65.00

Vase, incurvate rim, bl matt, 8″ 110.00
Vase, lavender, 8″ 125.00
Vase, stem/leaf relief, tan on gray texture, Hannah Tutt, 12″ . . .600.00
Wall pocket, bean shape, fine ribbing, scalloped, 5″ 55.00
Wall pocket, blue matt 40.00
Wall pocket, mc, incised tree & bird, 7″ 250.00

Marbles

Marbles have been popular with children since the mid-1800s. They've been made in many types from a variety of materials. Among some of the first glass items to be produced, the earliest marbles were made from a solid glass rod broken into sections of the proper length, which were placed in a tray of sand and charcoal, and returned to the fire. As they were reheated, the trays were constantly agitated until the marbles were completely round. Other marbles were made of china, pottery, steel, and natural stones.

Below is a listing of the various types, along with a brief description of each. When size is not otherwise indicated, prices are listed for mint condition marbles of average size, ½″ to 1″.

Agates: stone marbles of many different colors, bands of color alternating with white usually encircle the marble, most are translucent.

Ballot Box: handmade (with pontils), opaque white or black, used in lodge elections.

Bloodstone: green chalcedony with red spots, a type of quartz.

China: with or without glaze, in a variety of hand painted designs -- parallel bands or bull's eye designs most common.

Clambroth: opaque glass with outer evenly spaced swirl of one or alternating colors.

Clay: one of the most common older types, some are painted, while others are not.

Comic Strip: a series of machine made marbles with faces of comic strip characters; Peltier Glass Factory, Illinois; 12 characters.

Crockery: sometimes referred to as Benningtons, most are either blue or brown, although some are speckled. The clay is shaped into a sphere, then coated with glaze and fired.

End of the Day: single pontil glass marbles, the colored part often appears as a multicolored blob or mushroom cloud.

Indian Swirls: usually black glass, with a colored swirl appearing on the outside next to the surface, usually irregular.

Latticinio Core Swirls: double pontil marble, with an inner area with net-like effects of swirls coming up around the center.

Lutz (goldstone): glass with colored or clear bands alternating with bands which contain copper flecks.

Micas: clear or colored glass with mica flecks which reflect as silver dots when marble is turned. Red is rare.

Onionskin: spiral type which are solidly colored instead of having individual ribbons or threads; multicolored.

Peppermint Swirls: made of white opaque glass with alternating blue and red outer swirls.

Ribbon Core Swirls: double pontil marble, center shaped like a ribbon with swirls that come up around the middle.

Rose Quartz: stone marble, usually pink in color, often with fractures inside and on outer surface.

Solid Core Swirls: double pontil marble, middle is solid with swirls coming up around the core.

Steelies: hollow steel spheres marked with a cross where the steel was bent together to form the ball.

Sulfides: generally made of clear glass with figures inside. Rarer types have colored figures or colored glass.

Tiger Eye: stone marble of golden quartz with inclusions of asbestos, dark brown with gold highlights.

Vaseline: machine made of yellowish-green glass with small bubbles.

Advertising, Poll Parrot Shoes, 5 marbles in box.............18.00
Agate, average size, new type, M.............5.00
Agate, average size, old type, M.............12.00
Banded Swirl, ¾".............10.00
Bennington, blue, 1½".............8.00
Bennington, brown, 1½".............12.50
Bennington, brown, 1⅞".............27.00
Bennington, 100 in orig box, small.............25.00
Bloodstone, average size, M.............25.00
China, glazed; 1".............35.00
China, glazed; 1¼".............70.00
Clambroth, bl/wht, ¾".............58.00
Clambroth, bl/wht, ⅝".............55.00
Clambroth, blk/wht, ⅝".............60.00
Clambroth, gr/wht, ¾".............95.00
Clambroth, red/bl/gr lines, ⅝".............65.00
Clambroth, red/wht, ¾".............65.00
Cloud, yellow & orange, lots of mica, rare, lg chip, 2¼".......125.00
Comic, Betty, clear & perfect.............45.00
Comic, complete set of 12, clear & perfect.............475.00
Comic, Emma or Koko, clear & perfect, each.............30.00
Comic, Herbie, Skeezix, or Sandy, clear & perfect, each.............40.00
Comic, Moon, clear & perfect.............75.00
Comic, Smitty, Andy, Bimbo, or Annie, clear & perfect, each....35.00
Coreless, pink cast, 1¼".............65.00
Crockery, lined, 1".............20.00
Crockery, lined, 1¼".............28.00
Double Ribbon, red/yel/wht; bl/wht, yel/wht strands, 1¾", G....65.00
End of Day, average size, M.............12.00
End of Day, mc clear & brite, 1¾".............60.00
End of Day, red/wht w/bl & yellow, 2¼", G.............100.00
End of Day, red/wht/bl, 1⅞".............75.00
End of Day, red/wht/bl/yel w/mica, 1⅞", NM.............100.00
Goldstone, blue, average size, M.............25.00
Goldstone, brown, average size.............20.00
Goldstone, no pontil, ⅝".............35.00
Handmade Opaque, average size, M.............12.00
Imitation sulfide, w/lion, 1¼".............8.00
Indian Swirl, average size, G.............20.00
Indian Swirl, average size, M.............35.00
Indian Swirl, 1".............85.00
Indian Swirl, ¾".............40.00
Indian Swirl, ⅞".............65.00
Late Swirl, 2¼".............35.00
Latticinio Swirl, average size.............8.00
Latticinio Swirl, wht core w/bl bands alternate w/yel, 1⅞".......100.00
Limestone, gray, 1½".............10.00
Lobed Core, polished, 1½".............80.00
Lutz, banded, average size, M.............40.00
Lutz type, blk w/much gold flaking, ¾".............95.00
Lutz type, gr w/allover gold flaked streaks, rare, 1⅞", G......350.00
Lutz type, 1 band of gold, ⅝".............45.00
Lutz type, 1⅞", M.............500.00
Lutz type, ⅝", M.............50.00
Machine made, amber slag, 1¼".............3.00
Malachite, average size, M.............40.00
Mica, average size, M.............10.00
Mica, deep purple, 1".............35.00
Mica, dk amber, 1".............20.00
Mica, dk bl, 1½", NM.............190.00
Mica, green, ¾".............15.00
Mica, polished, 1⅜".............60.00
Mica, 1 pontil, green, rare, lg chip, 2⅛".............260.00
One Pontil, amber slag, ¾", M.............12.50

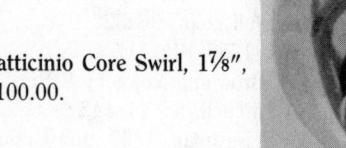

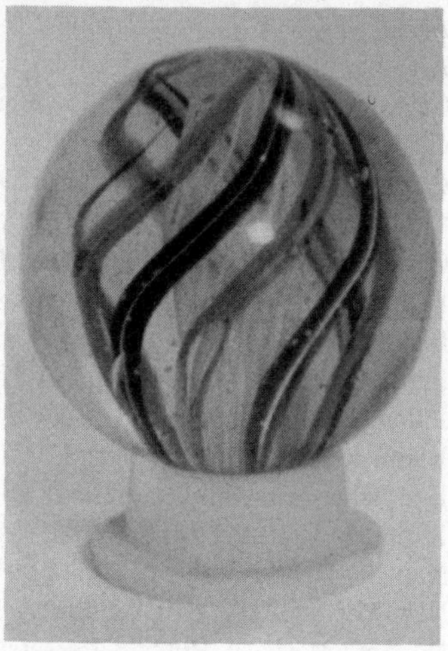

**Latticinio Core Swirl, 1⅞",
$100.00.**

One Pontil, gr slag, ⅞", M.............10.00
One Pontil, honey amber slag, ¾", M.............15.00
One Pontil, purple slag, 1".............8.00
Onionskin, bl/yellow, factory flaw, 1½", NM.............75.00
Onionskin, light color, 1⅞", NM.............80.00
Onionskin, polished, 1⅜".............35.00
Onionskin, rose & green, 2⅛", M.............375.00
Onionskin, 1⅛", NM.............55.00
Onionskin, 1⅝", NM.............75.00
Onionskin, 1⅞", M.............180.00
Onionskin, 2", M.............350.00
Onionskin w/mica, ⅝".............35.00
Onyx, banded, old, 2", M.............15.00
Open Core, bl/yel/red/wht center; 4 outer mc bands, 1½", NM..75.00
Open Core, 1¾", M.............110.00
Slag, purple, single pontil mk, 1¼".............20.00
Solid Core, 1⅞", NM.............110.00
Solid Core Swirl, average size.............10.00
Solid Opaque, blk, 1".............6.00
Solid Opaque, handmade, wht, ¾".............5.00
Solid Opaque, melon, ¾".............17.50
Sulfide, #2, 1⅝".............175.00
Sulfide, alligator, 1¾".............60.00
Sulfide, bear, polished, 1¼".............45.00
Sulfide, bear on all fours, 1⅛".............75.00
Sulfide, boy on stump, many tiny chips, 2".............100.00
Sulfide, boy w/horn, polished, 1⅝".............80.00
Sulfide, camel, 1½".............90.00
Sulfide, child sitting, polished, 1¼".............65.00
Sulfide, cow, glass M, figure w/crack, 2".............80.00
Sulfide, dog, begging; 1½".............80.00
Sulfide, dog, Irish gr glass, EX, 1⅛".............360.00
Sulfide, dog, looks like Nipper, 1⅝".............100.00
Sulfide, double eagle, very rare, 1¾".............275.00
Sulfide, eagle, 1½".............100.00
Sulfide, eagle, 1¼", EX.............60.00
Sulfide, fish, 1⅜", NM.............75.00
Sulfide, girl w/doll, 5¾" circumference, shallow chip.........185.00
Sulfide, goose, minor chips, 1⅞".............125.00
Sulfide, horse, 2¼".............160.00
Sulfide, lady in long dress, off center, polished, 2".............155.00
Sulfide, lamb, feeding, 1⅜", M.............50.00
Sulfide, lamb, standing, 1½" dia, EX.............85.00
Sulfide, lion, 1½", NM.............65.00
Sulfide, owl on perch, 1½", G.............75.00
Sulfide, pig, standing, 2¼".............160.00

Sulfide, pig, 1¼", NM.................................65.00
Sulfide, praying angel, polished, 1⅞"...................110.00
Sulfide, prehistoric man on stump, polished, 1⅜"............60.00
Sulfide, rabbit, 1½".................................60.00
Sulfide, ram, standing, 1¼", NM.......................65.00
Sulfide, rooster, silver figure, 1¾"...................110.00
Sulfide, sheep, 1⅞"..................................60.00
Sulfide, sheep, 2", M................................120.00
Sulfide, squirrel, 1¾"...............................60.00
Swirl, bl cast w/wht stripes w/in, stripes w/out, 1⅛"..........70.00
Swirl, clear sm line core w/in, mc stripes w/out, 1⅛".........65.00
Swirl, cobalt w/red & wht inner decor, polished, 1⅜".......200.00
Swirl, handmade, Germany, 1900, ½", M...................4.00
Tiger Eye, blue, average size, M.......................35.00
Tiger Eye, brown, average size.........................25.00
Vaseline, ¾"..15.00

Marine Collectibles

Alidade, US Navy telescopic, 13".......................28.00
Bell, ship's; w/hanging bracket, all original, 12x10½" dia......400.00
Binnacle, British Lifeboat Compass, 15/2/1951, brass/2 lantern..200.00
Book, New Am Practical Navigator, N Bowditch, 27th edition...55.00
Booklet, Outfits for a Whaling Voyage, 19th century..........175.00
Charts, bl/blk, North Pacific; English Channel, 2 for..........100.00
Clock, brass, w/outside bell, Seth Thomas.................600.00
Clock, brass case, 6" dial, Chelsea......................220.00
Clock, ship's wheel oak 14" case, 7" face, Seth Thomas......175.00
Compass, card, Ritchie, gimbaled, in orig case.............80.00
Compass, dry card, American...........................120.00
Compass, tell-tale, brass, w/bracket, 7" mica card, mk Boston..950.00
Compass, wood w/brass sight vanes, early.................425.00
Compass, wooden bowl, British, old, restored..............140.00
Diving helmet, Mark V, by Schraders of New York, VG......2,000.00
Fid, sailor's rope working tool, mahog, 17", G..............25.00
Gauges, pressure; Negretti & Zambra, cased pr.............45.00
Gimbal, brass, for oil lantern, lg size w/weighted base.........80.00
Instruments, drafting; in rosewood case...................80.00
Journal, Canadian whaleship, 1843-44, incomplete/poor cond...200.00

Ship's compass, copper, brass and beveled glass, oil lantern on side, U.S. Navy Bu. of Ships, Lionel Corp., NY, 10" x 7", $500.00.

Journal, log book of ship 'Mary', 1852...................6,000.00
Lamp, buoy; Dressel Mohawk, 8" fresnel lens, 23", pr........300.00
Lance, mtd to wood & roped together, 48".................60.00
Lantern, metal w/clear lenses, red/gr bulbs, 19" w/hdl, pr......95.00
Lantern, ship's; brass w/red/bl lens, Perko, 9"..............20.00
Lighthouse lamp filler can, brass w/funnel top, unusual, 16"....525.00
Octant, ebony & brass, ivory scales, 1800s, 12", w/case......550.00
Octant, ebony & brass, ivory scales, 1800s, 16", w/step case...600.00
Octant, handmade, wood, w/paper scale...................125.00
Painting, brigantine Josefa, oil, Stubbs (1842-'09), 24x36"....3,000.00
Painting, 2 boats w/flags & pennants, Flemish, 1800s, 15x20"..750.00
Panbone, pnt whaling scene, 10¾x20"...................4,500.00
Pennant, ship's; US, stars & stripes, 10 ft L...............45.00
Pin, belaying, brass, pr: 8½", 10½"....................45.00
Plaque, bronze, Naval w/Am eagle & Xd anchors, 10x8"........15.00
Porthole, brass, 17"................................100.00
Print, USS NY of the Great White Fleet, in fr, 23x16"........45.00
Quadrant, Jas Thirkell, ebony fr/brass fittings, ivory scales.....550.00
Roller rule, ebony & brass, cased, 18"...................145.00
Sailor's bag, macrame rope work over linen, inlaid closure......30.00
Sailor's valentine, octagon, star/scallop/rose, table mtd, 13"....880.00
Seam rubber, rosewood, w/Turk's-head knob...............90.00
Sector, ivory & brass, 1800s, 12", G....................100.00
Sextant, brass, inlaid silver scales, English; w/keystone case....675.00
Sextant, Bufs 3 upper East Smithfield, brass w/silver scale.....325.00
Sextant, Hezzanith Instrument Works, cased, G............200.00
Ship's wheel, CI w/wood hdls, Edison Mfg, old rpt, 24" dia....52.00
Ship's wheel, mahogany, brass hub & rims, 66" dia........1,100.00
Ship's wheel, wood/br pnt, 36".........................35.00
Stern board, carved American eagle/shield/flag, painted, 67" L..700.00
Still, water purification; Precision Scientific Co, 31".........125.00
Telegraph, brass, reproduction, 44"....................400.00
Telescope, brass, Bardou & Son--Paris; w/wood tripod (copy)..1,100.00
Tiller, wood w/brass fittings, 69".......................435.00

Martin Bros.

The Martin Bros. were studio potters who worked from 1873 until 1914, first at Fulham, and later at London and Southall. There were four brothers, each who excelled in their peculiar area. Robert, known as Wallace, was an experienced stonecarver. He modeled a series of grotesque bird and animal figural caricatures. Walter was the potter, responsible for throwing the larger vases on the wheel, firing the kiln, and mixing the clay. Edwin, an artist of stature, preferred more naturalistic forms of decoration. His work was often incised or with relief designs of seaweed, florals, fish, and birds. The fourth brother, Charles, was their business manager. Their work was incised with their name, place of production, and letters and numbers indicating month and year.

Ewer, etched comical faces, bulbous, 7"..................425.00
Imp on base, musical................................295.00
Pitcher, four dragons, matt glaze, 9½"..................325.00
Vase, allover incised Nouveau florals, 2 hdls, sgn, 1898, 11"...550.00
Vase, floral, 5"....................................100.00
Vase, hummingbirds, sgraffito decor, 9"..................250.00
Vase, incised fish, sq form, gr/gray, Southall 12-1911, 5"......170.00
Vase, terra cotta, Mr Pickwick, 1909, sgn, cabinet pc.........87.00

Mary Gregory

Mary Gregory glass, for reasons that remain obscure, is the namesake of a Boston and Sandwich Glass Company employee who worked for the company for only two years in the mid-1800s. Although the company's museum says no evidence exists to indicate that glass of this type was even produced there, the fine colored or crystal ware decorated with figures of children in white enamel is commonly referred to as Mary Gregory. The glass, in fact, originated in Europe, and was imported into this country where it was copied by several eastern glass houses. It was popular from the mid-1800s until the turn of the century.

Barber bottle, cranberry, wht figure & foliage, very large.......165.00
Barber bottle, gr w/boy in woodlands, 8"......................175.00
Biscuit jar, emerald gr, girl w/pk dress, lilies trim, 6¾".......225.00
Bowl, cranberry, girl picking fruit, deep, 9½"...............395.00
Bud vase, lt gr, boy w/hoop in wht.........................85.00
Carafe w/tumbler, sapphire bl, wht enamel, 8¼x4"...........225.00
Cruet, cranberry, gourd form, wht figure & foliage, w/stopper...220.00
Cruet, green, facing pr, boy/girl/trees, gold stripe, 6", pr......295.00
Decanter, clear, girl w/flower, tinted face..................125.00
Decanter, cranberry, 1 w/Colonial man; 1 w/lady/dog, 12", pr...300.00
Dresser set, cranberry, 6 pcs.........................1,000.00
Ewer, cranberry, twist hdl, ribbed, bulbous, 9½"............225.00
Ewer, cranberry w/clear hdl, girl & bushes, 10x3"...........190.00
Mug, amber, girl w/flag..................................75.00
Mug, blue, 1 w/boy, 1 w/girl, pewter hdl & rim, 4¾", pr......300.00
Mug, cranberry, boy, 3"..................................98.00
Mug, cranberry, girl, clear hdl, 3½".....................110.00
Pitcher, clear, melon ribbed, girl catching butterflies, 6"......125.00
Pitcher, cranberry, girl w/basket, 6"......................300.00
Pitcher, med bl, engraved w/name/date, 11".................150.00
Pitcher, tankard; amber, girl in garden, tinted features, 12¾"..225.00
Pitcher, tankard; honey amber ribbed, girl/house, tinted, 13"...275.00
Plate, blk, girl pulling dog on sleigh, reticulated, 8½".........65.00
Powder jar, slightly milky amethyst, w/boy & bird, 6", EX.....140.00
Tea warmer, cranberry, 3 scenic panels, SP/brass holder w/hdl..395.00
Tray, dresser; cranberry, girl hugs boy, 6½x9"..............245.00
Tray, dresser; cranberry, girl w/bunnies, 1¾x8x10½"........265.00
Tumbler, amber..55.00
Tumbler, gr, girl, 3¾"...................................58.00
Tumbler, lt gr, boy, 4"...................................60.00
Tumbler, marina blue, ribbed & bulbous, enamel boy..........70.00
Vase, amber, reed snail hdls, gold trim, boy in wht, 7x4¼"...165.00
Vase, blk amethyst, clowns on bicycles in wht, facing pr, 12"...275.00
Vase, blk amethyst, deer & foliage in wht, ftd, 13"...........130.00
Vase, cobalt, boy w/hat, ftd bottle form, 8"................110.00
Vase, cobalt, girl/fence, ftd/hi-waist/tall collar, 13½", pr......575.00

Stein, sapphire blue with boy and foliage, 5½", $125.00.

Vase, cranberry, boy, cylinder, 6¼"......................125.00
Vase, cranberry, boy on 1, girl on 2nd, facing pr, gold, 10x5"..300.00
Vase, cranberry, boy w/garland, 10".......................145.00
Vase, cranberry, EX detail wht enamel, 5x2¾".............135.00
Vase, cranberry, girl, flowers in apron, snail hdl, 13".........425.00
Vase, cranberry, girl w/lyre in ornate gold medallion, 10"......215.00
Vase, cranberry, ribbed, girl w/floral garland, 8"............200.00
Vase, cranberry, 1 w/boy, 1 w/girl, flattened ovoid, 5½", pr....125.00
Vase, cranberry w/clear ped ft, boy in wht enamel, 4¾x1½"...105.00
Vase, emerald gr, boy w/bicycle, clear trim ea side, 10½"......200.00
Vase, lime gr/clear ped ft, girl decor, 4½x1¾"..............90.00
Vase, lime opal satin, girl, flared/slim neck/bulbous, 8".......135.00
Vase, pink, boy w/hoop & stick, 9½"......................170.00
Vase, ruby flashed, girl w/flowers, 10x5½"................210.00
Vase, sapphire bl, boy w/hat, 9½x3"......................90.00
Vase, sapphire bl, EX gold, ribbed, girl w/foliage, ftd, 8".....115.00
Vase, sapphire bl, jack-in-pulpit shape, SP holder, 13"........295.00

Massier

Clement Massier was a French artist-potter who established a workshop at Golfe Jaun, France, in 1881, where he experimented with metallic lustre glazes. (One of his pupils was Jacques Sicardo, who brought the knowledge he had gained through his association with Massier to the Weller Pottery Company in Zanesville, Ohio). The lustre lines developed by Massier incorporated nature themes with allover decorations of foliage or flowers on shapes modelled in the Art Nouveau style. The ware was usually incised with the Massier name, his initials, or the location of the pottery. Massier died in 1917.

Jardiniere, vines w/fruit, gr/aqua/rose irid glaze, sgn, 12"......575.00
Toothpick, irid, sgn....................................130.00

Match Holders

Before the invention of the safety match in 1855, matches were kept in match boxes and carried in pocket size match safes because they ignited so easily. John Walker, an English chemist, invented the match more than one hundred years ago, quite by accident. Walker was working with a mixture of potash and antimony, hoping to make a combustible that could be used to fire guns. The mixture adhered to the end of the wooden stick he had used for stirring. As he tried to remove it by scraping the stick on the stone floor, it burst into flames. The invention of the match was only a step away! From that time to the present, match holders have been made in amusing figural forms as well as simple utilitarian styles, in a wide range of materials. Most were wall hanging; a few were table top models -- all designed to keep matches conveniently at hand.

Alligator, CI, blk/wht/red pnt, back opens, 12x3½x2½".......70.00
Baby in bl bed, rose decor blanket lifts off, Staffordshire......125.00
Box on ped base, lid w/reclining dog, CI, 4½"...............100.00
Boy, seated/smiling, monkey scratching boy's head, porcelain....75.00
Boy kneels by basket, lamb stands beside, porcelain...........75.00
Cat & barrel, pewter, table top, 3½x5"....................65.00
Ceresota Boy, EX......................................125.00
Child w/basket on bk, bisque, Victorian, 6"................60.00
Commemorative, 100th Anniv Battle of Lake Erie, cast bronze..20.00
Daisy & Button, sapphire bl, striker across front, 4x3"........65.00
DeLaval, separator shape................................45.00
Dockash Stove Factory, hanging, tin.......................35.00
Dogs stare at cat peaking out of house, china...............45.00
Double urn, orig floral decals, pat Jan 15, 1867, CI..........50.00
Eagle w/spread wings, wall hanging, CI, gilt/blk pnt, 4¾" W...55.00
Gnome smoking pipe, pottery, dbl, Germany, 5½x5"..........45.00

Molded metal figure of boy with brass pipe by barrel, 4", $135.00.

Hanging game, 2 pouches below, leaves atop, brass, 7½"......55.00
High top shoe on base w/striking surface, CI w/pnt, 5".........20.00
JC Stevens, G......65.00
Judson Whiskey, child serving father, wall mount............48.00
Juicy Fruit, G......60.00
Lucas Paint, VG......55.00
Michigan Stove, CI......60.00
Milk glass, emb butterfly, 3¼"......45.00
Porcelain box w/applied florals, striker under lid, 3x2"........75.00
Satsuma, hanging, orange/gold figure on pocket..............75.00
Sharples Separator, Pet of the Dairy, G litho..............80.00
Toleware, crimped crest, worn br japanning, 4½x7½".........55.00
Wall type, tin, lift lid, remains of old blue, pat 7/16/1878.......35.00
Wilson Bros Grinding Mills, emb CI, ornate.................48.50

Match Safes

Match safes, aptly named cases used to carry matches in the days before cigarette lighters, were used during the last half of the 19th century until about 1920. Some incorporated added features -- hidden compartments, cigar cutters, etc. -- some were figural, and others were used by retail companies as advertising give-aways. They were made from every type of material, but silverplated styles abound.

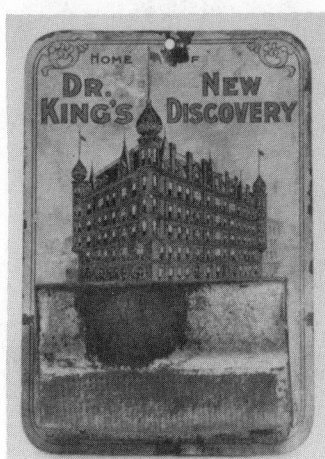

Advertising match safe, Dr. King's New Discovery, 5" x 3½", $150.00.

Arm & Hammer, gutta percha......50.00
Art Nouveau sterling, head of lady......65.00
Bowler B Brewers......50.00
Brass, pat 1884, w/old matches......40.00
Daniel Boone, brass, GAR 29th Nat'l Encpt, Louisville, 1895...350.00
Dewars, Whiskey of his Forefathers, emb......60.00
Diamond Match Co, tin, sm......15.00
Doctor's bag......110.00
Dog, standing on bk legs, silver w/red stone eyes, 3"........210.00
Dungarees w/suspenders hanging, wht metal, adv, pat 9/1896....50.00
GAR motif, troops & cannon on reverse, brass......125.00
Golfer, sterling repousse silver, dtd 1900......275.00
HJ Gaus, Beer & Ale Pumps, celluloid on metal, pat 1903......40.00
Hoof figural, brass......45.00
Horse in horseshoe, SP, Art Nouveau, 2"......32.00
Liberty, enamel......200.00
Mizpah ring, 18k gold, dtd 1899......100.00
Nude, dancing w/draped flowers & scrolls, Gorham sterling......95.00
Nude amidst waves, scrolls, sgn Unger Bros......165.00
O'Conner & Wittner, Syracuse, NY, emb stag, pat 1904........50.00
Owl, brass figural, hinged top, base striker, 2¼x1½".........100.00
Pig, brass figural......68.00
Pig, SP figural, hinged at head, base striker, 1½x1x2¾".......75.00
Pocket knife figural, brass......70.00
Pocket watch, brass......55.00
Queen Caroline Clear Habana Segars, w/portrait......75.00
Rooster head, mechanical......185.00
Thistle......110.00
Trousers figural......140.00
Valise shape, iron......20.00

McCoy

The third generation McCoy potter in the Roseville, Ohio, area was Nelson, who with the aid of his father, J.W., established the Nelson McCoy Sanitary Stoneware Company in 1910. They manufactured churns, jars and jugs, poultry fountains, and footwarmers. By 1925, they had expanded their wares to include majolica jardinieres and pedestals, umbrella stands and cuspidors, and an embossed line of vases and small jardiniers in a blended brown and green matt glaze. From the late twenties through the mid-forties a utilitarian stoneware was produced, some of which was glazed in the soft blue and white so popular with collectors today. They also used a dark brown mahogany color, and a medium to dark green -- both in a high gloss. In 1933, the company became known as the Nelson McCoy Pottery Company. They expanded their facilities in 1940, and began to make the novelty art wares, cookie jars, and dinnerware that today are synonomous with 'McCoy'. To date more than two hundred cookie jars of every theme and description have been produced. Some are very common. Mammy, the Clown, and the Bear, although very old, are easy to find; while the Dalmations, Christmas Tree, and Kangaroo, for instance, though not so old are harder to locate. The Indian and the Teepee, both made in the fifties, are two of the most popular and some of the most expensive!

More than a dozen different marks have been used by the company; nearly all incorporate the name 'McCoy', although some of the older items were marked 'NM USA'.

Cookie Jars

Animal Crackers......32.00
Apollo Age......140.00
Apple, 1950-64......22.00
Apple on Basketweave......22.00
Bananas......32.00

Barnum's Animals	35.00
Bear, cookie in vest	30.00
Black Kettle	18.00
Bobby Baker	20.00
Caboose	50.00
Chef	30.00
Chinese Lantern	30.00
Chipmunk	38.00
Christmas Tree	145.00
Circus Horse	60.00
Clown Bust	22.00
Clown in Barrel	30.00
Clyde Dog	22.00
Coalby Cat	28.00
Coffee Grinder	17.50
Coffee Mug	25.00
Colonial Fireplace	45.00
Cookie Barrel	28.00
Cookie Boy, aqua	75.00
Cookie Cabin	32.00
Cookie Log	16.00
Cookie Safe	25.00
Cookstove	20.00
Corn	75.00
Country Stove	20.00
Covered Wagon	30.00
Cylinder, w/red flowers	12.50
Dalmations in Rocking Chair	95.00
Dog on Basketweave	25.00
Drum	32.00
Duck on Basketweave, EX orig paint	32.00
Dutch Girl, boy on reverse	50.00
Dutch Treat Barn	25.00
Early American, Frontier Family	25.00
Early American Chest, Chiffoniere	50.00
Elephant	32.00
Elephant w/Split Trunk	60.00
Engine	50.00
Forbidden Fruit	32.00
Gingerbread Boy	22.00
Globe	35.00
Grandfather Clock	32.00
Granny	25.00
Hamm's Bear	40.00
Have a Happy Day	15.00
Hen on Nest	35.00
Hillbilly Bear	150.00
Hobby Horse	45.00
Honey Bear	28.00
House	65.00
Indian	125.00
Kissing Penguins	30.00
Kitten on Basketweave	25.00
Kittens on Ball of Yarn	34.00
Kookie Kettle	14.00
Lamb on Basketweave	30.00
Liberty Bell	20.00
Little Clown	32.00
Lollipop	30.00
Mac Dog	30.00
Mammy	45.00
Mammy w/Cauliflower	145.00
Mother Goose	75.00
Mr & Mrs Owl	32.00

Nabisco, Barnum's Animals	35.00
Oaken Bucket	12.00
Old Churn	12.00
Pears on Basketweave	25.00
Pelican	60.00
Picnic Basket	35.00
Pineapple	28.00
Pirates Chest	22.00
Pumpkin, Jack-O'-Lantern	40.00
Puppy	35.00
Quaker Oats	30.00
Rooster	35.00
Snow Bear	38.00
Spaceship, Friendship	38.00
Strawberry, 1955-57	24.00
Strawberry, 1971-75	14.00
Tepee	95.00
Tilt Pitcher, blk w/roses	26.00
Touring Car	35.00
Turkey	75.00
Upside Down Bear, panda	12.00
WC Fields	65.00
Wedding Jar	35.00
Windmill	40.00
Wishing Well	18.00
Woodsey Owl	40.00
Wren House	35.00
Yellow Bear	45.00
Yosemite Sam	16.00

Miscellaneous

Bank, hobo, #609	20.00
Bank, Replica, 1st Money Chest	15.00
Bank, State Federal Savings	15.00
Basket, oak leaf & acorn	15.00
Bookends, lily figural, pr	28.00
Bud vase, lily	10.00
Caddy, American eagle	18.00
Caddy, buffalo	18.00
Caddy, dog w/shoe spoon tail	18.00

Dalmations in Rocking Chair, $95.00.

Decanter, Apollo Series, astronaut.........................35.00
Decanter, Apollo Series, len.............................35.00
Decanter, Apollo Series, missile..........................18.00
Decanter, Pierce Arrow, Sport Phantom....................40.00
El Rancho Bar-B-Que, chuck wagon w/wheels...............65.00
El Rancho Bar-B-Que, coffee server, warmer & 4 mugs........60.00
El Rancho Bar-B-Que, ice tub............................22.00
El Rancho Bar-B-Que, iced tea server.....................45.00
El Rancho Bar-B-Que, salad bowl.........................22.00
El Rancho Bar-B-Que, sombrero serve-all..................45.00
Feeding dish, hunting dog...............................15.00
Fern box, Butterfly line..................................6.00
Pitcher, Seagrams, emb Highlanders, Blended Scotch Whiskey...28.00
Pitcher, WC Fields....................................28.00
Planter, Baa, Baa, Black Sheep...........................7.00
Planter, carriage, removable umbrella....................50.00
Planter, Chinese w/wheelbarrow...........................8.00
Planter, Coffee, Tea, Sugar, Salt........................25.00
Planter, convertible auto...............................12.00
Planter, cradle...8.00
Planter, dog w/cart.....................................9.00
Planter, double duck & egg..............................8.50
Planter, duck w/removable umbrella......................40.00
Planter, gondola.......................................12.00
Planter, hobby horse...................................10.00
Planter, Humpty Dumpty.................................8.00
Planter, old mill......................................12.00
Planter, orange figural.................................10.00
Planter, plow boy......................................14.00
Planter, pussy at the well..............................12.00
Planter, rabbit & stump.................................9.00
Planter, rocking chair..................................18.00
Planter, rodeo cowboy..................................22.00
Planter, rolling pin w/Blue Boy..........................20.00
Planter, scoop w/Mammy................................25.00
Planter, Springwood, ftd...............................12.00
Planter, squirrel.......................................9.00
Planter, Village Smithy.................................14.00
Planter, wishing well..................................10.00
Planter, zebra..14.00
Planter bookend, violin, pr.............................17.50
Shoes, twin...7.00
Strawberry jar w/bird..................................15.00
Tea set, Ivy, pot, creamer & sugar w/lid..................50.00
Turtle planter...10.00
Turtle sprinkler.......................................20.00
Vase, aqua-gr semi-matt, lizard hdl, 10"..................25.00
Vase, Butterfly line, 6"..................................9.00
Vase, ram's head......................................45.00
Vase, swan, 9"...8.00
Wall pocket, banana...................................12.00
Wall pocket, basketweave...............................10.00
Wall pocket, bellows...................................12.00
Wall pocket, clock.....................................20.00
Wall pocket, grapes....................................12.00
Wall pocket, lily......................................12.00
Wall pocket, orange...................................12.00
Wall pocket, owls on trivet.............................15.00
Wall pocket, pear.....................................12.00

McCoy, J. W.

The J.W. McCoy Pottery Company was incorporated in 1899. It operated under that name in Roseville, Ohio, until 1911, when McCoy entered into

a partnership with George Brush, forming the Brush-McCoy Company.

During the early years, McCoy produced kitchenwares, majolica jardinieres and pedestals, umbrella stands and cuspidors. By 1903, they had begun to experiment in the field of art pottery, and though never involved to the extent of some of their contemporaries, nevertheless produced several art lines of merit.

Their first line was Mt. Pelee, examples of which are very rare today. Two types of glazes were used, matt green and an iridescent charcoal gray. Though the line was primarily mold formed, some pieces evidence the fact that while the clay remained wet and pliable, it was pulled and pinched with the fingers to form crests and peaks, in a style not unlike George Ohr.

The company rebuilt in 1904, after being destroyed by fire, and other art ware was designed. Loy-Nel Art and Renaissance were standard brown lines, hand decorated under the glaze with colored slip. Shapes and art work were usually simple but effective. Olympia and Rosewood were relief molded brown glaze lines, decorated in natural colors with wreaths of leaves and berries or simple floral sprays. Although much of this ware was not marked, you may find examples with the die stamped 'Loy-Nel Art, McCoy' or an incised line identification.

Loy-Nel Art, bowl, florals, w/hdls, 8" dia.................60.00
Loy-Nel Art, bowl, ftd, 3x7"...........................135.00
Loy-Nel Art, jardiniere, pansies, 6"....................100.00
Loy-Nel Art, lamp base, pansy decor, 11½"...............95.00
Loy-Nel Art, spittoon, pansies, 4½"....................100.00
Loy-Nel Art, vase, cylinder w/florals, 12"...............150.00
Loy-Nel Art, vase, pansies, bulbous, 8".................125.00
Loy-Nel Art, vase, roses, 6"............................80.00
Olympia, jug vase, 7"..................................155.00
Olympia, punch bowl, grapes & vines...................375.00
Olympia, vase, Aladdin lamp shape, sgn.................130.00
Olympia, vase, corn motif, cylinder, 11".................185.00
Olympia, vase, leaves, w/hdls, 12"......................185.00
Rosewood, ewer, w/florals, sgn, 10"....................200.00
Rosewood, jardiniere, orange streaks on br glaze, 9".......60.00
Rosewood, vase, orange streaks on br glaze, 9"............50.00
Rosewood, vase, w/floral, #41, 5".......................100.00

Loy-Nel Art vase, floral on brown glaze, with handles, 8", $125.00.

McKee

McKee Glass was founded in 1853, in Pittsburg, Pennsylvania. Among their early products were tablewares of both the flint and non-flint variety.

In 1888 the company relocated to avail themselves of a source of natural gas, thereby founding the town of Jeanette, Pennsylvania.

One of their most famous colored dinnerware lines, Rock Crystal, was manufactured in the 1920s. During the thirties and forties, colored opaque dinnerware, Sunkist reamers, and 'bottoms up' cocktail tumblers were popular, as well as a line of black glass vases, bowls, and novelty items. All are popular items with today's collectors.

The company was purchased in 1916 by Jeanette Glass, under which name it continues to operate.

Bowl, custard w/fired-on gr stripe, 9"......................18.00
Bowl, delfite, 9"...10.50
Bowl, jadite kitchenware, w/lid, 5x8".......................12.00
Bowl, Laurel, jade, 9" round...............................12.00
Bowl, oval vegetable; Laurel, jade.........................12.00
Bowl, Snappy Apple, cut & pressed, pk, ftd, 7x9½"..........60.00
Clock, Tambour, amber.....................................375.00
Cup & saucer, Laurel, jade.................................12.00
Egg cup, jadite kitchenware, 4¼"............................7.00
Measuring pitcher, custard, 4-cup..........................24.00
Mug, milk glass, Serenade, M...............................25.00
Pitcher, milk; Tol-Tec, ca 1910, mkd Pres-Cut..............65.00
Plate, dinner; Laurel, jade.................................6.50
Plate, grill; Laurel, jade..................................6.00
Platter, Laurel, jade, oval................................12.00
Punch bowl & 12 cups, Tom & Jerry, custard.................75.00
Sherbet, Laurel, jade.......................................4.25
Sugar, ftd, Laurel, jade....................................7.00
Tumbler, ftd, custard, 4¼"..................................9.00
Tumbler, ftd, jadite, 4¼"...................................9.00

Medical Collectibles

The field of medical-related items encompasses a wide area, from the primitive bleeding bowl, to the X-ray machines of the early 1900s. Other closely related collectibles include apothecary and dental items. Many tools that were originally intended for the pharmacist found their way to the doctor's office, and often dentists used surgical tools when no suitable dental instrument was available. A trend in the late 1700s toward self-medication brought a whole new wave of home care manuals and 'patent' medical machines for home use. Commonly referred to as 'quack' medical gimmicks, these machines were usually ineffective, and occasionally dangerous.

Applicator, aluminum, knife shape, 'Apply Antiphogistine...'......4.00
Bleeder, lancet; brass/steel, orig box, 3"...................85.00
Book, Dr Chase's Last & Complete Receipt/household physician.35.00
Book, Medico-Legal Guide for Drs & Lawyers, Geo Field, 1887..35.00
Book, People's Medical Advisor, RV Pierce, 1909..............40.00
Book, Practical Obstetrics, TW Eden, 1915, 700 pgs...........5.00
Book, Slit-Lamp Microscopy of the Living Eye, Koby, 1930.....4.00
Book, Texas Druggist, Santa on cover, 1927, 124 pgs, 6x9"...15.00
Book, Therapeutics of Dry Hot Air, CE Skinner, 1916..........7.00
Booklet, Deafness & Ear Diseases Cured in 5 Hours, 16 pgs...12.50
Booklet, Swaim's Panacea, 1873, 42 pgs, 4x6".................8.50
Bottle w/stopper, cobalt, glass label, polished pontil, 8½"..85.00
Box, mahog, hinged top, 2 doors, fitted w/in, brass hdls, 11"..600.00
Broadside, Electric Brand Bitters, 9x12"....................35.00
Cabinet, Dr AD Daniels, veterinary medicine, oak...........525.00
Corkpress, CI, emb: S Lee/Taunton/Mass/pat 1863, ca 1880...100.00
Cupboard, apothecary; 9 drw, late wire nails, rpt/damage....85.00
Dentist kit, pocket size....................................15.00
Dose spoon, Bovinine, early plastic, 5½"....................10.00
Hearing aid, ear trumpet, hand size, blk over brass, 2x3"...85.00

Human skull, Dr's...150.00
Hypodermic, Codman & Shurteff, in case, 1¾x3½"............105.00
Kit, tin w/brass bale hdl, fitted w/in, orig pnt, 8¾x11½"..105.00
License, physician's; dtd 1897, in fr, 8¾x10¾"..............12.50
Machine, Beauty, Health & Strength, Renu Life Generator.....90.00
Machine, Davis/Kidder's Magneto Electric for Nerves, pat 1854.100.00
Machine, w/ray gun..125.00
Medicine, Foley's Catharitic Tablets, in box, 1x1x3".........4.00
Medicine tin, Gr Mt Asthma Cure, JH Guild, compound to burn.15.00
Medicine tin, St Joseph's Liver Regulator, blk/yellow, 3"...25.00
Microscope, Enst Leitz, Wetzlar, binocular/single scope, 12"...180.00
Microscope, Spencer Lens Co, blk enameled w/brass trim, 11"..200.00
Microscope, Spencer Lens Co, brass, mahog case.............205.00
Nasal douche, Bermingham, glass tube w/central funnel, in box...8.00
Newspaper, Hood's Holiday Herald, 1890, boy in diapers/EX ads.16.00
Print, engraving, opened cadaver showing organs, German, 1825.20.00
Saddle bags, doctor's; complete w/medicine & equipment, 1870.500.00
Sign, HGC For Colds, man in tuxedo, emb tin, 1890s, 7x10"...95.00
Sign, Jayne's Expectorant for Coughs/etc, metal, 6½x10" oval...55.00
Tonic cup, wood on ped, label w/directions, 4¼"............12.00
Tooth extractor, 4½".......................................30.00
Tray, medicine patented US 1900, nude children around bottle.125.00

Meissen

The Royal Saxon Porcelain Works was established in Meissen, Saxony, in 1710. Under the direction of Johann Freidrick Bottger, who in 1708 had developed the formula for the first true porcelain body, fine ceramic figurines with exquisite detail, and tableware of the highest quality were produced. Although every effort was made to insure the secrecy of Bottger's discovery, others soon began to copy his ware, and in 1731 Meissen adopted the famous crossed sword trademark to identify their own work. The term 'Dresden ware' is often used to refer to the Meissen porcelain, since Bottger's discovery and first potting efforts were in nearby Dresden.

See also Onion Pattern

Centerpiece, shell & reed, gilt decor, late 1800s, 11½" dia.....60.00
Clock, mantel; Jupiter surmount/allover florals/figures, 27"....4,400.00
Coffee set, gold trim, florals, X swords, 3 pcs...............600.00
Creamer & sugar, blue & wht floral...........................175.00

Covered vases, Oriental merchants in river landscapes reserved on pink ground, crossed swords mark, 15", $1,210.00 for the pair.

Cup & saucer, chocolate; 3 military officers w/map, 1813/1913..175.00
Cup & saucer, demitasse; wht w/heavy gold, bl X swords........65.00
Ewer w/figural milk maid seated alongside, 7½"............950.00
Figurine, boy & girl w/flower garlands, 1890, 3¾", pr, M.....880.00
Figurine, boy dressed as turk, turban/harem pants, 5"........800.00
Figurine, cherub w/heart, 6½"...............................295.00
Figurine, cherub w/heart on anvil, 7½".....................225.00
Figurine, Cupid Feathered, Rococo style base, 7"............240.00
Figurine, cupid piercing two hearts, M116, 20th C, 10½".....500.00
Figurine, Cybele on lion w/putti, X swords, 9".............935.00
Figurine, dog, sitting wht spaniel w/blk mks, X swords, 5½"..245.00
Figurine, emblematic, 1 of night/1 of day, X swords, 20", pr..2,420.00
Figurine, fishwife from Cries de Paris, #13, 5", EX........2,700.00
Figurine, girl in 18th century dress/birdcage, 4½".........1,100.00
Figurine, girl w/grapevine wreath & bird, marble ped, 5"....1,100.00
Figurine, lady, Bible under arm, crucifix, elaborate dress, 6"..1,100.00
Figurine, lioness, recumbent, teeth bared, 11¼" L..........990.00
Figurine, maid w/2 swains by pedestal, X swords #60, 12½"..1,045.00
Figurine, man in red coat/tri-con hat w/cane/sword/watch, 7½"..400.00
Figurine, monkey w/oboe/female monkey singer, 4½", pr......400.00
Figurine, mouse, tail curled over back, X swords, 1½x2½"..185.00
Figurine, nude in Oriental hat w/dragon at her feet, 1930, 10"..660.00
Figurine, pug dog w/bl collar, gold bells, X swords, 2¼".....265.00
Figurine, shepherd lovers w/2 other couples, tall tree, 18"....1,100.00
Figurine, songbird on wht stump, ca 1900..................350.00
Figurine, Spaniel, seated, wht w/blk mks, X swords, 5½"......245.00
Figurine, St Paul, on plinth base, late 19th C, 19"..........250.00
Figurine, waiter from Cries de Paris, 1800, 5½"...........3,200.00
Figurine, Winter, cherub draped in fur skates on pond, 1850s..375.00
Figurine, 6 gardeners on rock base, ea w/implements, 13"....880.00
Inkwell, wht, floral motif 2 sides, sq, acorn finial, X swords.....99.00
Master salt, w/mc harbor scene: men unload ships, lg.........95.00
Mirror, pk/bl w/cherubs, X swords, 10x12"..................300.00
Perfume, blanc de chine, floral encrusted, miniature..........45.00
Perfume, lady figural, curtsying, in leather case, 1¼"........170.00
Plate, emb figure border/cupids pnt in center, 9", G, 12 for....990.00
Slipper, Augustus Rex, yel, floral, Billingsley style, 6½".......100.00
Spoon, serving; ribbed hdl, fancy tip, deep oval bowl, 8"......145.00
Tureen w/under plate, putti finial, HP shepherd, bronze stand.3,025.00
Vase, dk bl/wht, flowers, bird, gold trim, X swords, 3¼x2¼"....55.00
Vase, florals/butterfly in gold/wht on aqua, X swords, 14x11"...400.00
Vase, snake hdls, leaf relief band, yel w/gilt, 1800s, 16".......325.00

Mercury Glass

Mercury glass was popular during the 1850s, and enjoyed a short revival at the turn of the century. It was made with two thin layers, either blown with a double wall or joined in sections, with the space between the walls of the vessel filled with a mixture of tin, lead, bismuth, and mercury. The opening was sealed to prevent air from dulling the bright silver color.

Candlesticks, 4", pr...45.00
Cup & saucer, etched......................................50.00
Curtain tie backs, pewter shanks w/screws, 3", pr............25.00
Drawer pulls, set of 6, 1¼" dia.............................20.00
Lightning rod ball, quilted relief..........................70.00
Reflector for wall lamp, 10"...............................20.00
Rose bowl, Czech...35.00
Rose bowl, no mk...8.00
Vase, bulbous, ped ft, 8¼", pr.............................30.00
Vase, 4", pr...15.00
Vase, 7"...8.00

Metlox

The Metlox Manufacturing Company was founded in 1927 in Manhattan Beach, California, but it was not until the forties that they began producing the dinnerware for which they have become famous.

California Ivy, berry, 4"....................................3.00
California Ivy, relish, 2 compartments.......................7.00
California Ivy, salt & pepper shakers........................6.00
California Ivy, sugar w/lid..................................7.00
Cookie jar, Pinocchio, w/orig label........................60.00
Provincial Fruit, covered sugar.............................6.00
Provincial Fruit, cup & saucer..............................5.00
Provincial Fruit, plate, dinner; 10½".......................6.00
Provincial Fruit, platter, 13½"...........................11.00
Rooster, creamer...15.00
Rooster, cup & saucer, oatmeal w/red/gr/yel rooster..........15.00
Rooster, plate, dinner....................................13.00
Rooster, plate, salad.....................................10.00
Rooster, platter, 12".....................................26.00
Rooster, sugar...19.00
Rooster, vegetable, 10" dia...............................27.00
Vase, lady w/stork, sgn Romanelli, 9".....................25.00
Vase, Poppytrail, fish decor, 14".........................20.00
Yorkshire Red, pitcher, chip on bottom of ft................10.00

Poppytrail dealer's sign, 6" x 7½", $35.00.

Mettlach

In 1836, Nicholas Villeroy and Eugene Francis Boch, both of whom were already involved in the potting industry, formed a partnership and established a stoneware factory in an old restored abbey in Mettlach, Germany. Decorative stoneware with in-mold relief was their specialty, steins in particular. Through constant experimentation, they developed innovative methods of decoration. One process, called chromolith, involved inlaying colorful mosaic designs into the body of the ware. Later, underglaze printing from copper plates was used. Their stoneware was of high quality, and their steins won many medals at the St. Louis Expo and early world's fairs. Most examples are marked with an incised castle and the name 'Mettlach'. The numbering system indicates size, date, stock number, and decorator. Production was halted by a fire in 1921 -- the factory was not rebuilt.

Key:
L-----liter
PUG-----painted underglaze
tl-----thumblift

Beaker, #2327, man playing fiddle decor, old mk............75.00
Beaker, #2327/1023, PUG, boy playing violin................50.00
Beaker, #2327/1024, PUG, boy playing flute.................50.00
Beaker, #2327/1025, PUG, girl w/pheasant on tray, ¼L.......50.00
Beaker, #2327/1141, PUG, man w/3-corner hat being served....85.00
Beaker, #2327/1214, Deco scene of woman smoking, w/hdl, ¼L.85.00
Beaker, #2327/1215, Deco scene of woman w/tray, hdl, ¼L, 85.00
Beaker, wht glazed w/red cherries, ¼L.....................35.00
Boot, #225, .75L, hairline crack.........................240.00
Candy dish, #3041, cameo, reclining figures, sm chips........325.00
Cigar holder, #464, figural gnome w/hollow branches, VG.....250.00
Flagon, #1690, equestrian scenic, 18½"................2,500.00
Flagon, #2128, 11".....................................325.00
Flower arranger, #3146, Deco style, 3¾x7x3¼"............100.00
Mayonnaise set, bl & tan Deco tree design, etched, 3 pc.....190.00
Mug, #1909, PUG, German beer advertising, Astra Bavaria, .3L..36.00
Mug, #2189, print over glaze, verse, ¼L, M.................43.00
Pipe, figural skull bisque bowl, 17" long, M...............237.00
Pitcher, #2076, ivory on blue, 4 panels/eagle & owl crests, 3L..394.00
Pitcher, green & cream, 4"................................130.00
Plaque, #1044-156, PUG, river scene of Coblenz, 14", M......325.00
Plaque, #1044-157, PUG, city of Coln, 14", M..............324.00
Plaque, #1044/1122, girl feeding swans, Heinrick Schlitt, 17"...664.00
Plaque, #1044/1123, PUG, girl feeds ducks, Heinrick Schlitt...664.00
Plaque, #1044/1142, PUG, outdoor feast, colorful, Schlitt, 17"..729.00
Plaque, #1044/129, Nurnberg, 12" dia, M...................243.00
Plaque, #1044/134, mountain road running along river, 14" dia.166.00
Plaque, #1044/135, mountains & seashore, 14" dia, M.......166.00
Plaque, #1044/162, PUG, Germania Monument, 14".........308.00
Plaque, #1044/304, Dutch children in water w/boat, 14" dia, M.156.00
Plaque, #1044/360, PUG, Oriental town scene, 12".........217.00
Plaque, #1044/5176, PUG, bl/wht detailed castle scene, 12"....196.00
Plaque, #1048/8, etched, battle scene, colorful border, 16"....351.00
Plaque, #1365, etched, castle & river scene, 17"..........1,090.00
Plaque, #167A, PUG, castle ruins, scalloped border, 18", M....540.00
Plaque, #167B, PUG, castle scene, scalloped border, 15", M....351.00
Plaque, #167B, PUG, castle scene, scalloped border, 18", M....540.00
Plaque, #1769, etched, Arnold Von Winkerbried, 14½", M...1,314.00
Plaque, #2011, etched, shield of Imperial Eagle............799.00
Plaque, #2071, etched, dogs attacking boar, sgn Stucke, 15½".659.00
Plaque, #2078, etched, cavalry men on horses, sgn Stucke, 15".972.00
Plaque, #2112, etched, dwarf w/bottles in nest, sgn, 16".....1,621.00
Plaque, #2195, etched, Rhinestein castle, fishing boats, 17½"..896.00
Plaque, #2196, castle & river scene, 17¼"................767.00
Plaque, #2322, etched, cavalier gets farewell kiss, 14½".....918.00
Plaque, #2361B, etched, Wartburg castle, 17", M..........990.00
Plaque, #2442, cameo, ship w/many figures, 19" dia, M......925.00
Plaque, #2443, cameo, scene w/many classical figures, 19", M..880.00
Plaque, #2534, etched, Drachenfels castle ruins, 17", M....1,360.00
Plaque, #3162, 2 cavaliers toasting, EX color/etching, 17½"..1,216.00
Plaque, lady w/plumed hat, bl/wht, HP, 19" dia, pr, M......1,150.00
Plaque, PUG, hunting dog pointing, 17" dia, M.............225.00
Plate, #1070, PUG, Oriental man & 'Kioutschou', 6½", M......80.00
Pokal, #2066, etched, man/barmaid, chips, crack rpr, 2.5L.....750.00
Pokal, #2110, etched, Gambrinus, cover chips, crack rpr, 2.5L.750.00
Punch bowl, #2843, figures/musicians/dancers, rim chip, 13½".500.00
Stein, #1000, relief, 3 crests, 3 panels cherub face inlay, ¼L..100.00
Stein, #1028, relief, man/woman bringing harvest in, inlay, ½L.234.00
Stein, #1132, etched, fiddler/crocodile/pyramids, ½L........540.00

Stein, #1163, glazed relief, Yale emblem, American tl, ½L.....395.00
Stein, #1180, relief, vines & verse, ½L....................111.00
Stein, #1265, relief, tree panels of shields, star inlay, ¼L......131.00
Stein, #1370, relief, couple around German verse, vines, ½L...180.00
Stein, #1379, etched panels depict architect, inlay lid, ½L.....648.00
Stein, #1403, etched, men bowl, others watch, sgn Warth, ½L.467.00
Stein, #1477, etched, gnomes/vineyard, inlay grapes, US tl, ½L.551.00
Stein, #1508, etched, many men in tavern, orig pewter lid, ½L.384.00
Stein, #1520, etched, 2 cavaliers surround German Eagle, ½L..490.00
Stein, #1526, HP fraternal crest w/insignia on lid, ½L........148.00
Stein, #1526/1101, PUG, barmaid & animals, dwarf tl, ½L.....189.00
Stein, #1526/1219, PUG, 3 students w/dice, dwarfs hdl, ½L....270.00
Stein, #1526/587, PUG, drinking cavalier, verse, ½L.........140.00
Stein, #1526/589, PUG, 2 men at table, German verse, ½L.....145.00
Stein, #1526/600, PUG, cavalier w/stein beside barrel, 1L......195.00
Stein, #1560/580, PUG, hunter/dog, sgn, floral inlay lid, ½L...243.00
Stein, #1641, etched, tapestry, cavalier pouring, Warth, ½L....302.00
Stein, #1645, etched, tapestry, mandolin player, sgn CW, 1L...352.00
Stein, #1647, etched, tapestry, innkeeper w/stein, ½L.........260.00
Stein, #1675, etched, City of Heidelberg, ½L...............442.00
Stein, #1742, etched, 150 Anniv Gottingen Univ, Warth, ½L...462.00
Stein, #1786, etched/glazed, Ft Florian/fire, dragon hdl, ½L...515.00
Stein, #1789, mosaic, floral, minor chip on hdl, ½L.........210.00
Stein, #1895, relief, cavalier/maiden embrace, vines, 1L......335.00
Stein, #1909/1009, PUG, 3 dwarfs at wine press, ½L........245.00
Stein, #1909/726, PUG, comical walking steins, sm chip, ½L...220.00
Stein, #1909/727, PUG, dwarfs bowling, sgn, 3" rpr line, ½L..178.00
Stein, #1909/942, PUG, nightwatchman & clothed rooster, ½L.180.00
Stein, #1909/993, PUG, 3 cavalier musicians, H Schlitt, ½L....210.00
Stein, #1932, etched, Swashbucklers toasting, inlay lid, ½L....464.00
Stein, #1947, etched, laborer w/cat, cat inlay, ½L...........486.00
Stein, #1998, etched, panel w/cavalier, castle inlay, gold, ½L...443.00
Stein, #2001A, lawyer's books, inlay lid, owl tl, ½L..........576.00
Stein, #2001K, banking books, inlay snakes, Mercury tl, ½L...546.00
Stein, #2002, etched, Munich Maid/city/German verse, ½L....388.00
Stein, #2005, etched, couples eat pheasant, inlay star, ½L....455.00
Stein, #2012, etched/mosaic, inlay: VB on Viking ship sail, ½L.418.00
Stein, #202, relief, scene of 5 carolers, inlay harp, ½L.......320.00
Stein, #2024, etched, shields of Berlin, city scenes, ½L......600.00
Stein, #2027, Gambrinus/animals, pewter relief, figural tl, 1L..1,026.00
Stein, #2035, etched, scene of Bacchus & revelers, .3L........337.00

Stein, #2035, etched design of cherubs feasting, 5¾", $365.00.

Stein, #2065, etched, man w/cane, barmaid/barrel, inlay, 14"..1,328.00
Stein, #2077, relief, 3 shield scenes, inlay lid, ½L...........174.00
Stein, #2082, etched, William Tell shoots apple on son, ½L..1,112.00
Stein, #2086, relief, 8 dancing people, inlay lid, ¼L.........179.00
Stein, #2090, etched, man at inn/wife with broom, sgn, .3L....352.00
Stein, #2092, etched, dwarf on ladder winds clock, sgn, ½L...620.00
Stein, #2093, etched, panels w/cards, inlay suits: lid/hdl, ½L...648.00
Stein, #2096, etched, ornately dressed man, 1½L, M........2,700.00
Stein, #2100, etched scene/Roman soldier/barbarian, sgn, ½L..500.00
Stein, #2123, etched, armored knight drinks, inlay, sgn, .3L....757.00
Stein, #2133, etched, gnome on branch, clay pipe in hat, ½L.1,728.00
Stein, #2134, etched, dwarf in nest, inlay rooster/sun, .3L.....720.00
Stein, #2140/993, PUG, bicyclist & train, bike inlay, ½L......405.00
Stein, #2181/958, PUG, cavalier w/horn, rabbits, sgn HS, ¼L..163.00
Stein, #2191, etched Etruscan, soldier hides girl, sgn, ½L.....875.00
Stein, #2231, etched, 4 drinking cavaliers scene, tall, ½L......540.00
Stein, #2261/1012, PUG, barbarian drinks from keg, 2L, 16"...567.00
Stein, #2271/1055, PUG, 2 drunks/monkeys, false bottom, ½L.295.00
Stein, #2382, etched, Thirsty Knight/3 scenes, conical lid, 1L..973.00
Stein, #2391, etched, Lohengrin walks the aisle/inlay swan, ½L.657.00
Stein, #2391, etched, Lohengrin wedding, swan/tower hdl, 1L.2,268.00
Stein, #24, relief, 4 panels w/hunters, inlay 3 shields, 1L.....351.00
Stein, #2401, etched, maiden/prince/cupids, inlay harp, 1L...1,030.00
Stein, #2440, relief figures all around, ½L..................503.00
Stein, #2455, scene from Lohengrin, 5 litre, minor rpr, 25"..2,200.00
Stein, #2520, etched, barmaid serves student, sgn HS, ½L.....513.00
Stein, #2583, etched, Egyptian scene/man eating, sgn, ½L...1,004.00
Stein, #2599, etched, 3 shooting scenes, chalice inlay lid, 1L...677.00
Stein, #2693, etched, cavaliers/barmaid in dark archway, ½L...575.00
Stein, #2720, etched, tailor occupational, ½L..............1,134.00
Stein, #2778, etched, men drink/mandolin player/jester, ¼L....919.00
Stein, #2784-6129, Rookwood type PUG, Mandolin Player, 3L..526.00
Stein, #2789/6134, PUG, man w/beret, ½L.................333.00
Stein, #2789/6145, PUG, man w/pipe & glass, ½L...........333.00
Stein, #2802, etched, Nouveau pattern w/wheat & hearts, ½L..298.00
Stein, #2824, castle atop, 15¾".......................4,000.00
Stein, #2886, etched, 5 men/table, verse/orig pewter lid, ½L...571.00
Stein, #2921, etched, men at campfire/German verse, 2.8L..1,150.00
Stein, #2936, etched, Elks Club, logo body & thumblift, ½L....423.00
Stein, #2939, etched, barmaid/wreath, inlay heart/fork lid, 1L..605.00
Stein, #3043, etched, shield of Munich, city scenes, ½L.....1,296.00
Stein, #3099, etched, Diogenes in barrel, Socrates inlay, 4L..2,160.00
Stein, #3220, etched, Alpine couple under archway, sgn, ½L...594.00
Stein, #485, relief, 5 musicians w/children, ornate vines, 1L....352.00
Stein, #5020, PUG, bulbous w/Munich Maid decor, 3.1L......626.00
Stein, #675, relief, barrel shape, ¼L......................118.00
Tobacco jar, #116, relief figures alternating panels, sm chips...220.00
Vase, #1875, etched mosaic, bl w/gr & br glaze, 9", M.......194.00
Vase, #2414, etched leaves, hdls akimbo, 2 base chips, 17"....217.00
Vase, floral incising, vertical hdls w/leaf attachment, 18".......415.00
Vase, relief, cherub scenes, 4½".........................65.00

Midwestern Glass

As early as 1814, blown glass was made in Ohio. By 1835, glass houses in Michigan were producing similar pattern- molded types that have long been highly regarded by collectors. During the latter part of the 19th century, all six of the states of the Northwest Territory were mass producing the pressed glass tableware patterns that were then in vogue. Various types of art glass were produced in the area until after the turn of the century. Items listed here are attributed to the Midwest by certain physical characteristics known to be indigenous to that part of the country.

See also Zanesville Glass; Findlay Onyx; Greentown Glass; Libbey Glass

Cruet, 16 vertical ribs slightly swirled at neck, 8", EX..........70.00
Cruet, 19 vertical ribs, applied hollow hdl, 7¾"..............45.00
Jar w/lid, aqua, 16 swirled ribs, folded rim, ball finial, 5½"....275.00
Sugar bowl, clear, lacy, sm edge chips, 6¼"................85.00
Sugar bowl, 24 swirled ribs, folded rim, aqua, finial chip, 5½"..150.00

Militaria

Because of the wide and varied scope of items available to collectors of militaria, most tend to concentrate mainly on the area or areas that interest them most, or that they can afford to buy. Some items represent a major investment, and because of their value have been reproduced. Extreme caution should be used when purchasing Nazi items. Every badge, medal, cap, uniform, dagger, and sword that Nazi Germany issued is being reproduced today. Some repros are crude and easily identified as fakes, while others are very well done and difficult to recognize as reproductions.

Purchases from WWII veterans are usually your safest buys. Reputable dealers or collectors will normally offer a money back guarantee on Nazi items purchased from them.

There are a number of excellent 3rd Reich reference books available in bookstores at a very reasonable price. Study them to avoid loosing a much larger sum spent on a reproduction!

Arm band, Nazi, Im Dienst Der Deutschen Wehrmacht.........10.00
Arm band, Nazi, NSDAP Swastika on red....................15.00
Arm band, Nazi, SA Sports..............................20.00
Arm band, Nazi, SS....................................50.00
Arm band, Nazi, Volkstrum.............................10.00
Artillery round, 75mm, WWI, copper case w/projectile point, 6¼".6.50
Badge, beret; English Parachute Regiment, metal, King's crown..15.00
Badge, Black Watch, gilt, Scottish, Queen's crown, 1953.......25.00
Badge, Border Guard's, Poland..........................40.00
Badge, breast; US Army, This We'll Defend, oval.............3.50
Badge, cap; Foot Guards, service chevron, 1 stripe, English.....2.00
Badge, cap; RAF Officer's, gold wire, King's crown...........25.00
Badge, CW, bandolier, brass w/eagle, 2½" dia..............25.00
Badge, Field Gendarmerie, silver # reverse, Poland..........125.00
Badge, Imperial German/'08 turnfest silver 2 pc/red/wht ribbon....8.00
Badge, Nazi, General Assault, EX.........................20.00
Badge, Nazi, Infantry Assault, EX........................25.00
Badge, Nazi, Luftwaffe Airgunner, EX....................150.00
Badge, Nazi, Luftwaffe Flak, EX.........................75.00
Badge, Nazi, Luftwaffe Flight Engineer, EX................150.00
Badge, Nazi, Luftwaffe Ground Assault, EX.................40.00
Badge, Nazi, Luftwaffe Pilot, EX........................200.00
Badge, Nazi, Navy Auxiliary Cruiser, EX..................150.00
Badge, Nazi, Navy Blockade Runners, EX..................125.00
Badge, Nazi, Navy Coast Artillery, EX.....................60.00
Badge, Nazi, Navy Destroyer, EX.........................75.00
Badge, Nazi, Navy E-Boat, 1st Pattern, EX................250.00
Badge, Nazi, Navy E-Boat, 2nd Pattern, EX................125.00
Badge, Nazi, Navy High Seas Fleet, EX...................125.00
Badge, Nazi, Navy Minesweeper, EX......................65.00
Badge, Nazi, Navy U-Boat, EX..........................125.00
Badge, Nazi, Panzer Assault, EX.........................30.00
Badge, Nazi, Paratrooper, EX...........................150.00
Badge, Nazi, Wound, black, EX..........................10.00
Badge, Nazi, Wound, gold, EX...........................30.00
Badge, Nazi, Wound, silver, EX..........................20.00
Badge, Order of St Vladimir, III Class, gold/enamel, 1875......575.00
Badge, peaked cap; Royal Marines, brass, King's crown........25.00
Badge, peaked cap; WWI, National Fire Service, English........6.00
Badge, Spanish Am War, fancy brass top: Dewey on celluloid.....4.00

Badge, US Marksman, bar Rifle, sterling, pin back............6.00
Badge, USAF fire protection, orig plastic box.................6.00
Badge, WWI, RWB motif, eagle/anchor/star..................3.00
Badge, WWI Navy Yard Workers, nickel on brass, anchor center..5.00
Banner, British Royal Engineer Corp, Geo VI cypher/crown, 22"..55.00
Bayonet, M8 for M16, 6½" blade, blk plastic grip, sheath......21.50
Bayonet, Nazi Fireman's, dress, 9¾" Eickhorn blade, scabbard..45.00
Bayonet, Nazi Infantry & Artillery, double etched............185.00
Bayonet, Nazi Infantry & Artillery, single etched............105.00
Bayonet, Nazi Luftwaffe, double etched....................225.00
Bayonet, Nazi Luftwaffe, single etched...................175.00
Belt, CW, brass US buckle/leather cap box/scabbard/CI bayonet..70.00
Belt, Indian War officer's sword; lg cast eagle buckle, EX.....100.00
Belt, US Army officer's Sam Brown, quartermaster proof dtd '25..9.00
Beret, WWII, Royal Tank Regiment, blk, w/King's crown, EX...20.00
Binoculars, Civil War, Fr made, brass trim & sun shade, EX....40.00
Blouse, battle dress, English, 1944......................15.00
Book, Guide Book to US Navy, 1942, 436 pgs.............4.50
Book, US Army Headgear to 1854, Horwell & Kloster.........40.00
Boots, US Army WWI Tanker, G.........................35.00
Bowl, soup; Nazi Army mess, eagle/swastika, dtd 1941.......22.50
Box, cartridge; Am Revolution, leather, tin w/in for 25 ctgs....200.00
Box, cartridge; Am War of 1812, belly box, w/belt, no block...115.00
Box, cartridge; CW, brass oval US plate, eagle plate on strap....50.00
Box, cartridge; CW, leather w/emb US on front flap, G........75.00
Box, cartridge; Revolutionary period, wood w/24 holes.......70.00
Box, w/label: Yankee Soap Shaving & Toilet, 7x5"............30.00
Bronze, presentation, Kaiser Wilhelm II, 1896, R Bellair, 18"..495.00
Buckle, belt; plain brass w/orig hooks, Confederate.........60.00
Buckle, belt; snake, Civil War...........................75.00
Buckle, CW, brass oval w/US relief.......................30.00
Buckle, Imperial German, Gott Mit Uns & crest, steel/iron......10.00
Buckle, Indian Wars, rectangular w/eagle, 1870s, EX..........30.00
Buckle, Indian Wars, US in oval on rectangle, Hagner, dug.....30.00
Buckle, London Scottish Volunteers, 2 pc interlocking........19.00
Buckle, rectangular w/eagle & wreath, 1890................35.00
Buckle, Spanish Am War, officer's, rectangular, eagle..........25.00
Buckle, sword belt; CW Officer's, US Eagle.................65.00
Bullet mold, Colt 44 cal, mk Colts Pat, G..................60.00
Bullet mold, Revolutionary War, V pattern for two 45 cal balls..48.00
Bullet mold, scissor type, Near Eastern, dbl 50 cal balls........65.00
Bust, bronze, Kaiser Wilhelm, 1 in Shako/1 hatless, pr, 9", 7"..250.00
Bust, bronze presentation, Kaiser Wilhelm II, Gladenbeck/Sohn.440.00
Button, CW, GAR, silvered brass, star w/friendship motif.......22.50
Button, CW, RI state seal, staff type......................3.00
Button, Mass Militia, Indian w/bow 'Mass', SP, infantry, 1800....12.00
Calitrop, 4 spiked weapon, iron, 1750s....................45.00
Cannon ball, Revolutionary, 12#, exploding, fuse hole.........68.00
Canteen, Confederate, cedar w/carved inscription, EX.........800.00
Canteen, Confederate, cedar w/leather strap & iron buckle.....400.00
Canteen, felt covered w/web carrier, 1937, English............15.00
Canteen, Nazi WWII, w/cup, EX.........................30.00
Cap, overseas military, dk gr w/CCC emblem, dtd 1941........25.00
Cap, visor; Nazi Army Officer's, silver chin cord, complete.....165.00
Cap, visor; Nazi Army Officer's Enlisted, blk leather cords.....125.00
Cap, visor; Nazi Luftwaffe Enlisted, blk leather chin cords.....135.00
Cap, visor; Nazi Luftwaffe Officer's, silver chin cords.........175.00
Cap, visor; Nazi Naval Officer's, blk leather chin cords.......250.00
Cap, visor; Nazi Waffen SS Enlisted, blk leather chin cords....300.00
Cap, visor; Nazi Waffen SS Officer's, silver chin cords........450.00
Cap, visor; Royal Artillery Officer's, khaki dress, EX..........25.00
Cap, visor; Welsh Guards, khaki, EX.....................20.00
Cartridge box plate, CSA, Civil War......................250.00
Catalog, US Stokes Kirk, firearms & military surplus, 1928......10.00

Chevron, Indian Wars Artillery Cpl, red felt w/blk edging, pr....10.00
Cigarette case, WWII, leather w/US Navy silver anchor insignia...6.50
Coat, CW Brigadier Gen, cotton/velvet trim/16 eagle buttons..1,500.00
Coat, frock; Foot Guards, English, 1900...................125.00
Coat, Indian War, RI militia officer's, 18 buttons, wool, EX....130.00
Coat, NH militia, wool w/piping decor/47 brass buttons, 1840s..350.00
Collar device, US Army 9th Inf Reg't WWI, brass, Keep Up Fire..3.50
Collar device, WWI Officer Infantry, Xd rifles...............7.50
Collar tabs, Waffen SS, velvet/hand embroidered oak leaves....300.00
Cover, Civil War Patriotic, naval theme, lot of 3.............25.00
Cover, Confederate, SC flag w/banner 'Southern Independence'..27.00
Cross, Conspicuous Service, NY issue, sterling by Tiffany, '17...55.00
Cross, Imperial Bavaria, 1866...........................10.00
Cross, Police Long Service, 25-yr, gold, 3rd Reich...........35.00
Cup, collapsible; German, carried by officers in WWI, in case....8.50
Dagger, Nazi Army Officer's, yel/wht or orange hdl, w/scabbard.135.00
Dagger, Nazi Hitler Youth Knife, no motto on blade, w/scabbard.40.00
Dagger, Nazi Hitler Youth Knife, w/motto on blade, w/scabbard.65.00
Dagger, Nazi Luftwaffe Officer's, 1st, chain hanger, scabbard...250.00
Dagger, Nazi Luftwaffe Officer's, 2nd model, w/scabbard......150.00
Dagger, Nazi Navy Officer's, plain or etch blade/gilt scabbard..250.00
Dagger, Nazi Police bayonet............................175.00
Dagger, Nazi Red Cross Enlisted Hewer, w/scabbard..........175.00
Dagger, Nazi Red Cross Officer's, w/scabbard...............350.00
Dagger, Nazi SA, br wood hdl, br scabbard.................130.00
Dagger, Nazi SS, blk wood hdl, blk scabbard...............300.00
Dish, wht stone, Nazi, w/eagle & swastika mk, dtd 1938........20.00
Dog tag, CW, steel disc, 1862...........................27.50
Drum, Am shield/eagle w/shield/X arrows/etc, Haynes, 18½"...200.00
Drum, US Infantry Crest, Civil War, rosewood sticks, 13"......385.00
Entrenching tool, US Army, 1880, w/leather scabbard..........100.00
Envelope, CW, patriotic, alligator: Old Secesh...............4.00
Envelope, CW, patriotic, Jefferson Davis hanging on gallows......4.00
Envelope, CW, patriotic, Map of US, Washington on battlefield...8.50
Fife, CW, dk wood, pat 1860, EX.........................50.00
Flag, framed segment, Imperial German Flag w/Iron Cross, 9x7".35.00
Flag, Imperial Russian, machine stitched, 8x11"..............32.50
Flag, Nazi Staff car fender, circular swastika, 12x8".........20.00
Flag, swastika, 12x8¼"................................10.00
Fork, folding; CW soldier's non-regulation brass w/bone scales...22.50
Fuse, wood, for mortar shell, Civil War....................25.00
Goblet, etched crystal commemorative of Wilhelm I/Fredrick III.145.00
Gorget, SA, nickel silver, standard bearer's................145.00
Gun case, for John Blanch & Son London shotgun, 32½" L...150.00
Hat, American Union Yankee............................30.00
Hat, glengarry; Perth Batt of Blk Watch, w/war badge, 1964....30.00
Hat, pillbox; Ghurka Regt, full dress, Hobson & Sons, 1940.....50.00
Hat, service; Span Am War, bl wool, flat visor, EX............35.00
Hat, Spanish Am, Naval Chief Petty Officer, soft top/visor......55.00
Hat, WWI, overseas, broad arrow & 1918 on sweatband, English.12.50
Hat, 19th C blk felt kepi w/dbl headed eagle/2 brass buttons....20.00
Hat insignia, Spanish Am War, Xd muskets, 19 over L, pin bk..6.50
Hat insignia, Spanish Am War, Xd muskets w/1 over C.........4.50
Hat insignia, WWI, Enlisted Garrison.....................6.50
Hat insignia, WWI, Norwich Univ, cavalry, eagle over crest......2.50
Hat insignia, WWI, officer's ROTC garrison, eagle w/ROTC.....4.50
Hat plate, CW US Marine, Am shield w/stars & stripes.........30.00
Hat wreath, brass, w/hooks, Civil War....................15.00
Haversack, Confederate, linsey-woolsey w/oil cloth cover, '63..1,300.00
Helmet, British army, 1840-1901.........................35.00
Helmet, Imp German Officer's Pickelhaube, spike/patent leather.130.00
Helmet, Mod 1870 US Infantry Officer's dress, felt/eagle plate..55.00
Helmet, Nazi Army, complete, EX........................70.00
Helmet, Nazi fireman's................................55.00

Helmet, Nazi Luftschutz, decal in front, complete, EX..........40.00	Medal w/ribbon, Nazi, Close Combat, silver, EX.............150.00
Helmet, Nazi Luftwaffe, complete, EX....................100.00	Medal w/ribbon, Nazi, Iron Cross, 1st Class, cased, EX.........60.00
Helmet, Nazi Navy, complete, EX........................150.00	Medal w/ribbon, Nazi, Iron Cross, 1st Class, EX.............40.00
Helmet, Nazi Police, complete, EX.......................60.00	Medal w/ribbon, Nazi, Iron Cross, 2nd Class, EX.............25.00
Helmet, Nazi Waffen SS, complete, EX...................200.00	Medal w/ribbon, Nazi, Luftwaffe Service, 4-yr, EX............30.00
Helmet, pith; British Officer's, insignia RASC................35.00	Medal w/ribbon, Nazi, Russian Front, EX...................15.00
Helmet, Prussian Officer's, blk leather/crest/banner, 1900-14....185.00	Medal w/ribbon, Nazi, SS Long Service, 4-yr, EX.............80.00
Helmet, Royal Artillery Officer's, bl cloth w/ornaments........225.00	Medal w/ribbon, Nazi, SS Long Service, 8-yr, EX............125.00
Helmet, US Mod 1870 Cavalry Officer's, horsehair plume, EX..105.00	Medal w/ribbon, Nazi, War Merit Cross, 1st Class, EX.........40.00
Helmet, WWI, American.............................20.00	Medal w/ribbon, Nazi, War Merit Cross, 2nd Class, EX.........15.00
Helmet, WWI, French...............................25.00	Medal w/ribbon, Nazi, Westwall, EX......................15.00
Helmet, WWI, German, Baden EM spike..................225.00	Medal w/ribbon, Vietnam Service........................8.00
Helmet, WWI, German, brass, pull top artillery.............240.00	Medal w/ribbon, WWI, Great War for Civilization, (+$5 per bar).10.00
Helmet, WWI, US Marine............................40.00	Medal w/ribbon, WWII, crown on wreath w/X swords, England...25.00
Helmet, WWII, American, M60 tankers....................20.00	Medal w/ribbon, WWII, Victory, US.......................7.00
Helmet, WWII, Paratrooper, steel, English.................50.00	Medallion, bronze, Memory of Service w/t CMTC, 1932, 2¼"....22.50
Helmet plate, Household Cavalry, 2 pc, pouch badge, brass.....45.00	Mess kit, CW, tin cup/plate/spoon/knife/fork, reunion of 1886..125.00
Helmet plate, spiked, Am; E Pluribus Unum bridge/eagle head...30.00	Mess tin, WWI, aluminum, mk US 1916/anchor/France, G.....10.00
Holster, CW, E Gaylord Chicopee Mass, w/stenciled name, G....90.00	Mold, 69 caliber rnd ball, cutter between hdls...............20.00
Horse rosette, round, copper w/hooks, Indian Wars...........10.00	Muster role, Co I, 12 Reg GA, official paper of CSA, 1864.....275.00
Insignia, collar; WWI Officer's, Dentist Cadusus...............5.00	Octant, Spencer, Browning & Rust; bl pnt w/eagle/Indian case..900.00
Insignia, sleeve; WWI, Navy 2nd class Medical Corp, red/wht/bl...4.00	Patch, WWI, 1st Army, blk A on khaki patch.................5.00
Jacket, CW private's Artillery Shell, 20 eagle buttons/piping....400.00	Patch, WWI, 4th Division, EX............................5.00
Jacket, CW Union private, bl fatigue w/4 eagle buttons........200.00	Payboard, wood, used to count out pay in 1899, dtd...........5.00
Jacket, English, bl wool, Firman & Sons, ca 1890............20.00	Pennant, dbl sided, for 5th SS Panzer Wiking...............100.00
Jacket, Indian Wars, fatigue, 5 eagle buttons, bl wool.........85.00	Pike, Confederate, swallow tail/hand forged/orig 96" oak shaft..150.00
Kilt, Seaforth Highlanders, dtd 1939....................110.00	Pike, naval boarding; CW, orig 7½ ft pole, W Honnor........150.00
Kit, WWII, US Field Surgeon's; w/9 chrome instruments.......55.00	Pin, lapel; Distinguished Service Artillary, 1881..............17.50
Lance cap, 12th Lancers, w/horsehair plume, chin chain, 1856.600.00	Pin, Nazi Party Membership.............................6.00
Letter, CW soldier's; from Camp Gen Casey, Fairfax Co, 1863....8.50	Pin, sweetheart; visored cap opens for photo, X rifles on top.....8.00
Letter, CW soldier's; very informing, facts/data, 4 pgs.........30.00	Pin, sweetheart; WWII, silver, eagle/chain/lieutenant's bar.......7.50
Letter & cover, Civil War, re parade, 1863, 8 pgs............25.00	Pin, WWI, celluloid w/colors of all Allies, 1914-1915 center......2.50
Machete, Cattaraugus Army Air Force, folding...............40.00	Pin, WWI, Victory, 1941 penny w/raised V center, helmet drop...3.50
Magazine, American Field, March 22, 1890..................4.00	Pin, WWII, Soviet Russian, star, cloisonne on brass............6.50
Map, Plan of Battle of Brandywine, 1777, colored, 16½x21"....15.00	Pipe, opium; Japanese, nickeled metal parts w/straight stem.....25.00
Medal, Anhalt Bernberg campaign, 1848-49................125.00	Plaque, bronze relief of Franz Josef, 9" dia..................85.00
Medal, Armed Forces Expeditionary.......................6.50	Plaque, copper relief, 3 Kaisers, sgn Lauterbach, 1888.........85.00
Medal, Army Reserve Achievement......................10.00	Plaque, wood, pnt eagle w/IV, Germany Imperial..............40.00
Medal, blk iron 40mm dtd 1916, Iron For Your Gold...........9.00	Plate, dinner; Nazi, wht ironstone, swords/sheaf/Stedingsehre...20.00
Medal, Centenary of Lenin's Birth......................125.00	Plate, dinner; Nazi Luftwaffe, wht ironstone w/eagle, Haviland...25.00
Medal, commemorative, 1940-43, Italy....................20.00	Platter, Nazi, dished oval wht ironstone w/eagle, 1941.........38.00
Medal, Congressional Medal of Honor, US.................375.00	Pocket knife, US Navy pilot survival kit, blk plastic hdl, 6".....15.00
Medal, Defense Dept Meritorious Service Medal..............15.00	Police club, British Military, WWI, 1 pc maple, w/crown/MP.....20.00
Medal, Earthquake, silver, Italy, 1915....................50.00	Postcard, WWI, French soldier photo......................1.50
Medal, Egypt, w/The Nile, 1884-85 bar..................150.00	Pouch, CW, leather/canvas strap & card, for 18th reunion 1883.55.00
Medal, Franz Joseph, bravery, silver, lg...................85.00	Presentation, Medal of Honor, Conn Vols Co E, by Gillmore...225.00
Medal, General Campaign, Austria-Hungary, 1873............15.00	Priming horn, Am Revolution, 13" L......................35.00
Medal, Hesse, general campaign, 1840....................42.00	Priming horn, Revolutionary, hinged measure on end...........45.00
Medal, Ifni-Sahara campaign, Spain......................45.00	Print, Andersonville Prison, J&R Klapp, 1903, 21x15" in fr....100.00
Medal, Imperial German, memorial bronze, Friedrich Deutscher..15.00	Print, Battle of Waterloo, pub 1816 in London, 10½x16½"....25.00
Medal, Imperial Service, in case of issue, Geo VI issue........65.00	Quadrant, Spencer, Browning & Rust; cased................625.00
Medal, Italy Star...................................10.00	Ring, Gold Is For Iron, German 1914, gold ring concealed w/in..50.00
Medal, Pakistan Independence, 1947.....................20.00	Ring, US Army, silver filled, bl stone.....................10.00
Medal, Southern Veteran, postwar, 1888..................37.50	Ring, US Marine Corps memorial, 19k gold filled w/red stone...20.00
Medal, Spanish Am War, California......................75.00	Saddle cover, Am Revolution, leopard skin, 2 side panels.....275.00
Medal, Spanish Campaign, USN, 3 ring type...............110.00	Scalpel, WWI, folding, mk Stainless, elongated triangle........16.00
Medal, US Women's Relief Corps, 1883...................27.50	Sea chest, slant front/bk, orig pnt, name/1771, 26"..........375.00
Medal, WWI, bronze 5 pc service, 1917-18, 3x2"............5.00	Seal, wax; Confederate States of Am, Treasury Dept, 2" dia.....30.00
Medal w/ribbon, Armed Forces Reserve....................8.00	Shako hat plume, red ostrich feathers, 1800s, in box..........30.00
Medal w/ribbon, CW, 5 pnt star, eagle top of ribbon.........35.00	Spoon, Spanish Am War, engraved name/dtd 1899............7.00
Medal w/ribbon, National Defense........................5.00	Spur, CW Union, brass, cavalry, iron rowel.................50.00
Medal w/ribbon, Nazi, Army Long Service, 4-yr, EX...........25.00	Spur, Nazi, unmk, blk finish, w/straps, pr..................20.00
Medal w/ribbon, Nazi, Close Combat, bronze, EX...........115.00	Spy glass, CW, monocular, American made.................75.00
Medal w/ribbon, Nazi, Close Combat, gold, EX.............175.00	Standard, Deutschland Erwache, wire swastika, wool fringe...2,500.00

Stick pin, Luftwaffe, 1st eagle design, silver finish, EX..........5.00
Sword, Ames, 1864 US, NCO, eagle leather scabbard, EX.....175.00
Sword, Nazi Army Officer's, dove pommel/etch blade, scabbard.300.00
Sword, Nazi Army Officer's, dove pommel/plain blade, scabbard.125.00
Sword, Nazi Army Officer's, lion pommel/etch blade, scabbard..350.00
Sword, Nazi Army Officer's, lion pommel/plain blade, scabbard..150.00
Sword, Nazi Luftwaffe Officer's, leather wrapped grip/scabbard..250.00
Sword, Nazi Navy Officer's, w/scabbard......................350.00
Sword, rooster hilt, stamped US & NC.......................285.00
Tam-O'-Shanter, Scottish Regimental Officer's, khaki..........30.00
Token, CW, Equestrian State of Washington, First in War/Peace..5.00
Token, CW, Indian head, Our Navy.............................5.00
Token, CW, Indian head, shield w/motto: Union Forever.........5.00
Tool set for officer's pistols, ebony w/ivory tips, 3 pc, 1800.....68.00
Tunic, Royal Artillery, full dress, private's, 1903.............50.00
Wings, Air Crew, sterling pin bk, LeVelle & Co...............25.00
Wings, RAF Pilot, service dress, cloth padded...............12.00
Wings, Royal Canadian Air Force, gold/silver wire............20.00
Wings, US Pilot w/star in wreath on top, sterling, pin back.....35.00

Milk Glass

Milk glass, so named because of its milky white color, has been produced since the 18th century. The early glass, made with cryolite, looks very much like true porcelain, and rings with a clear bell tone when tapped. It was made both here and in England.

Battleship, no name, rare size, 6"........................75.00
Battleship, twin stacks, 'Three Gun', side turrets, 7¾".......60.00
Bottle, dresser; Actress, 11"..............................65.00
Bottle, dresser; 10x6"...................................25.00
Bottle, Sawtooth.......................................18.00
Bowl, Apple Blossom, open lattice edge, Atterbury, 8".......48.00
Bowl, Basketweave w/Lattice, reticulated, 6½x9½"...........23.00
Bowl, closed lattice edge, flower center, 3x9".............38.00
Bowl, Crinkled Lacy Edge, oval.........................15.00
Bowl, Daisy & Tree of Life, 4x8".......................50.00
Bowl, H-Border, 7"....................................16.00
Bowl, Scroll & Eye, 7".................................16.00
Bowl, Wicket, 8"......................................10.00
Bowl, Wild Rose, closed lattice edge, Atterbury, 8"..........48.00
Box, dresser; sectional, Southern Belle top.................75.00
Box, emb chicken/nest/Easter greetings, 3x4"..............18.00
Box, powder; emb lady's head, ornate, ca 1860s.............75.00
Butter dish, Blackberry.................................75.00
Candle holder, inverted funnel shape, rope hdl, floral/gold.....35.00
Candlestick, crucifix, 12½"............................32.50
Candlestick, crucifix, 7"...............................15.00
Candlestick, Dolphin, hexagon base, 4", pr...............40.00
Card holder, Scroll....................................10.00
Celery, Sawtooth, flint................................85.00
Christmas light, quilted...............................18.00
Compote, Atlas, old, 9"................................80.00
Compote, Atlas, scalloped.............................80.00
Compote, Fleur-de-Lis, open edge, 4½x8"................50.00
Compote, Hexagonal C Scroll...........................65.00
Compote, Jenny Lind, 7½x8½" dia.......................150.00
Compote, lattice sides, cherry blossom transfer decor........45.00
Compote, Louis XV, blue...............................40.00
Compote, Scroll, tall standard, 6 sides..................50.00
Compote, Strawberry...................................95.00
Creamer, Blackberry...................................27.00
Creamer, Ceres..22.50
Creamer, Owl, w/glass eyes, detailed feathers, 3½".........25.00

Creamer, Swan & Cattails, w/lid.........................40.00
Creamer, Wheat..48.00
Creamer & sugar, Leaf & Cherries, beaded, pr..............45.00
Cruet, child's..12.00
Dish, covered; Dewey, tile base.........................45.00
Dish, relish; dual fish, dtd 1872.........................32.00
Dish, relish; ram's head either end, oval..................35.00
Figurine, Scottie dog, sitting, 4½".......................20.00
Flask, Klondyke.......................................45.00
Goblet, Blackberry, HB & Co, set of 6...................540.00

Westmoreland mustard jar, log cabin figural, coin slot in chimney, 4" x 3½", $70.00.

Goblet, Blackberry, no mk..............................35.00
Goblet, Dewberry, iridized..............................65.00
Humidor, monk on front, pipe on bk, brown, metal lid, Austria..45.00
Jar, dresser; HP blue Forget-Me-Nots on cover, gold, w/lid, 3"...22.00
Jar, Eagle & Shield, w/lid..............................165.00
Match holder, pipe, some gold..........................15.00
Mug, Bar & Swirl......................................10.00
Mug, birds, sq hdl.....................................14.00
Mustard, Bull's Head, w/ladle...........................85.00
Napkin ring..35.00
Pitcher, bottom half cross block, 7½"....................50.00
Pitcher, water; Dart Bar, med bl........................90.00
Pitcher, water; Guttate.................................65.00
Plaque, Lincoln bust relief, br stain, latticed, 8½x6¾".......185.00
Plate, Anchor & Yacht.................................20.00
Plate, Angel & Harp....................................18.00
Plate, Beaded Loop w/Indian Head, 7½"..................20.00
Plate, California Bear, 9½".............................110.00
Plate, Cherubs, reticulated, 9".........................15.00
Plate, Chrysanthemum, 6½"............................30.00
Plate, Columbus 1492-1892............................32.00
Plate, Cupid & Psyche..................................20.00
Plate, Ducklings, Scroll & Fleur-de-Lis openwork rim, 7½".....25.00
Plate, Eagle border, flag at top, dtd 1903.................22.00
Plate, Easter Greeting, chick/basket/eggs, open beaded rim, 7"..40.00
Plate, Flag/Eagle/Fleur-de-Lis, 7½", rare.................30.00
Plate, Forget-Me-Not border, 7¼"......................15.00
Plate, Frank Bros, Chicago, 7".........................35.00
Plate, Gothic, pasted picture of Dewey in center, 7½"........16.00
Plate, Hen w/chicks, 'No Easter Without Us'..............25.00
Plate, Indian portrait, sgn Geronimo, mc headdress, 12".......65.00
Plate, Niagara Falls....................................20.00

Plate, One Hundred One, 5".............................6.00
Plate, One Hundred One, 9".............................9.00
Plate, Owl Family, 7½".................................25.00
Plate, Serenade, Greentown, 6".........................38.00
Plate, Serenade, 8"....................................55.00
Plate, Square-S, 7"....................................10.00
Plate, Stubborn Mule in relief, Scroll & Fleur-de-Lis rim, 7½"...25.00
Plate, US Battleship Maine, openwork border, 7½"...........25.00
Platter, Retriever....................................115.00
Salt, w/lid; Sawtooth, flint...........................65.00
Shakers, GE Refrigerator, pr...........................26.00
Shakers, Scroll, orig brass tops, pr...................45.00
Shaving mug, bearded man's head relief, dtd 1867...........38.00
Spooner, Blackberry, pat Feb 1, 1870...................32.00
Spooner, Ceres..20.00
Spooner, Monkey, minor base chips, rare.................175.00
Spooner, Sawtooth, flint...............................42.00
Spooner, Swan...20.00
Straw hat, 4¼"...24.00
Sugar bowl, Apple Blossom, EX decor, Northwood...........95.00
Sugar bowl, Birch Leaf, flint..........................55.00
Sugar bowl, Block & Fan................................15.00
Sugar bowl, Dahlia....................................20.00
Sugar bowl, GE Refrigerator............................28.00
Sugar bowl, Swan......................................68.00
Sugar shaker, Creased Waist............................35.00
Sugar shaker, Ribbed..................................35.00
Syrup, Fishnet & Poppies..............................125.00
Syrup, Fishnet w/Acorns & Oak Leaves, unusual shape........85.00
Syrup, French Primrose.................................40.00
Syrup, Guttate..85.00
Syrup, Strawberry, applied hdl, pewter top, flint.............105.00
Table set, Wild Rose, 4 pc............................250.00
Toothpick, Negro boy's head, 1886......................125.00
Toothpick, Swans & Cattails............................22.00
Tray, Blackberry......................................12.00
Tray, dresser; Chrysanthemum, 7½x10"...................45.00
Tray, Ram's Head, oval, 5x9"...........................38.00
Tumbler, Fleur-de-Lis.................................10.00
Tumbler, LA Purchase, tall.............................20.00
Tumbler, Scroll.......................................22.00
Vase, HP roses w/gold trim, cylinder shaped, sgn, 9".........85.00
Vase, Poppy...25.00
Vase, Zipper & Diamond, 8½"............................17.00

Millefiori

Millefiori was a type of art glass produced during the late 1800s. Literally, the term means 'thousand flowers', an accurate description of its appearance. Canes, fused bundles of multicolored glass threads such as are often used in paperweights, were cut into small cross sections, arranged in the desired pattern, refired and shaped into articles such as cruets, lamps, and novelty items.

See also Paperweights

Bowl, w/hdls, pk/gr/wht canes, 2".......................50.00
Bowl, w/hdls, 4".....................................100.00
Cruet, applied camphor hdl & stopper, dk canes............110.00
Lamp, table; mushroom style, shaped std, electrified, 10"......425.00
Lamp, 9½"...160.00
Paperweight, Chinese, 1920s, 2½x1½".....................35.00
Punch set, child's; 1 pc ftd 9 oz bowl, 6 cups.............95.00
Rose bowl, crimp top, wht cased, 7"....................175.00

Tie tack, paperweight, yel/red/aqua & wht canes on gr, Gentile.125.00
Toothpick holder, w/hdls, 2½".........................100.00
Tumbler, 4"...50.00
Vase, fluted, long neck, bulbous bottom, clambroth base, 7"...165.00
Vase, w/hdls, yel w/red/bl/wht, broken pontil, 6"............50.00

Cup and saucer, predominately blue and yellow, 2½" cup; 4½" saucer, $150.00.

Miniatures

There is some confusion as to what should be included in a listing of miniature collectibles. Some feel the only true miniature is the salesman's sample. Common during the latter part of the 19th century, these were small-scale copies of a particular product. Other collectors consider certain small-scale children's toys to be appropriately referred to as miniatures, while yet others believe a miniature to be any small-scale item used to display the craftsmanship of its creator. For Salesman's Samples, see specific category; other types are listed below.

Bean pot, rockingham, minor edge chips & on hdl, 2½".......20.00
Bureau bookcase, Chinese export gilt/blk lacquer decor, 30"..1,150.00
Chamber pot, yellowware w/wht stripes, 3½"...............20.00
Chest, blanket; poplar, dvtl, trn ft, rpl, rfn, 8x10x15".......125.00
Chest, Empire type, serpentine sides, brass knobs, Hingham, 9".95.00
Chest of drw, cherry w/mahog flame grain veneer, Empire, 21".320.00
Chest of drw, inlaid mahog, bow front, Federal, 18x19"......900.00
Chest of drw, mahog, 4 dvtl drw w/locks, bracket ft, 9x7x5"....150.00
Chest of drw, walnut, late wire nail built, 4 drw, 15x14x8".....100.00
Chest of drw, Wm & Mary, walnut bow front, 1840, 3½", pr...935.00
Churn, stoneware w/Albany slip, wood lid & dasher replaced, 7".65.00
Churn, w/dasher & trn top, wood burned decor, Norwegian, 8".105.00
Churn, yellowware w/rockingham glaze, wood lid/dasher, 3".....65.00
Commode, Louis XV style, fruitwood/burl walnut/inlay, 12".....110.00
Cooking set, pewter, 11 pcs w/4 lids, largest 1¼"............50.00
Cooking utensils, in orig box, mfg by Wagner, CI............200.00
Cup, footed; pewter, 1", set of 4........................10.00
Desk, mahog w/ball ft/scallop apron/curved facade, 23x22".....850.00
Flatware, knife, fork, spoon, pewter, 4½" L................10.00
Flatware, knife & fork, steel w/ivory hdls, 3½"............12.00
Flatware set, w/bone hdls, 6 forks/6 knives, 4½" L..........50.00
Globe, mahog, Geo III, L Smith, London, 1818, 6½"........2,500.00
Graniteware, 6 pcs kitchenware, minor wear, largest, 5¼".....150.00
Jug, stoneware, br/blk glaze, base flakes, 2¾"..............8.00
Mug, canary lustre, silver resist of bird on branch, 2".........145.00
Napkin ring, pewter, ½" dia, set of 4....................18.00

Pan, sauce; copper, tinned w/in, sgn NY, 2".............20.00
Plate, pewter, 2" dia, set of 5............................40.00
Portrait on ivory, Anna of Austria after Rubens, 3x2½".......70.00
Portrait on ivory, bust length, lady, sgn, in ivory fr, 5x3½".....55.00
Portrait on ivory, gentleman in dk red coat, 1¾"..........200.00
Portrait on tin, ¾ length lady w/shawl, 5x3¾"..............175.00
Skillet, CI, 3 short ft & lid, 3½" dia, 3" hdl.................45.00
Stove, Eagle, CI, ornate..................................175.00
Tea set, pewter, emb florals, no lids, 7 pcs, largest 1"........50.00
Tea set, Queen Style, 2 pots, cr/sug, sterling, ¾"..........175.00

Minton

Thomas Minton established his firm in 1793 at Stoke on Trent, and within a few years began producing earthenware with blue printed patterns similar to the ware he had learned to decorate while employed by the Caughley Porcelain Factory. The Willow pattern was one of his most popular. Neither this nor the porcelain made from 1798 to 1805 was marked (except for an occasional number series), making identification often impossible.

After 1805 until about 1816, fine tea services, beehive shaped honey pots, trays, etc., were hand decorated with florals, landscapes, Imari-type designs, and neo-classic devices. These were often marked with crossed 'L's.

From 1816 until 1823, no porcelain was made. Through the twenties and thirties the ornamental wares with colorful decoration of applied fruits and florals, and figurines in both bisque and enamel were usually left unmarked. As a result, they have been erroneously attributed to other potters. Some of the ware that was marked bears a deliberate imitation of Meissen's crossed swords.

From the late twenties through the forties, Minton made a molded stoneware line -- mugs, jugs, teapots, etc. -- with florals or figures in high relief. These were marked with an embossed scroll with an 'M' in the bottom curve. Fine parian ware was made in the late 1840s, and in the fifties Minton perfected and produced a line of quality majolica which gained them widespread recognition.

During the Victorian era, M.L. Solon decorated pieces in the pate-sur-pate style, often signing his work; these examples are considered to be the finest of their type. After 1862, all wares were marked 'Minton' or 'Mintons', with an impressed year cypher.

Sherbet, lustre decoration, circa 1892 to 1902, 3½", $225.00.

Bird bath on stand, majolica, figural crane/flowers/shell bowl..3,860.00
Bowl, pnt w/birds on blue, 1900, 9½"....................2,200.00
China, Windmere pattern, 102 pc service for 12............880.00
Cream soup & liner, Eton.................................12.00
Cream soup & liner, Hampshire..........................22.50
Cup, toddy; dk blue Genevese pattern, ca 1830, 3½" dia....30.00
Cup & saucer, Ancestral.................................25.00
Cup & saucer, Lady Hamilton............................30.00
Cup & saucer, Lady Rodney.............................32.50
Cup & saucer, Pandora..................................25.00
Figurine, parrots, turq/rose/yel majolica, 9", pr...........175.00
Master salt, br transfer branches & leaves, 2 birds, Faisan......60.00
Pilgrim flask, bone china w/florals, flat disk w/hdls, 1873.....500.00
Plate, bread & butter; Elizabethan Oak.....................8.00
Plate, bread & butter; Greenwich.........................12.50
Plate, bread & butter; Lady Rodney.......................13.50
Plate, bread & butter; Pandora...........................10.00
Plate, dinner; Elizabethan Oak...........................20.00
Plate, dinner; Lady Rodney..............................22.50
Plate, dinner; Pandora...................................20.00
Plate, dinner; Roxburgh.................................25.00
Plate, HP landscapes, pierced gold borders w/6 ovals, 9", 12...500.00
Plate, salad; Greenwich..................................17.50
Plate, salad; Lady Hamilton..............................15.00
Plate, salad; Lady Rodney...............................17.50
Plate, salad; Meadow....................................16.50
Plate, salad; Pandora....................................15.00
Plate, Tree of Life, set of 6.............................108.00
Tazza, cabbage leaf w/2 rabbit supports, 1870, 9¾" L........550.00
Vase, pate sur pate, polychrome, cupids/flowers, 32".......12,000.00

Mirrors

The first mirrors were made in England in the 13th century of very thin glass backed with lead. Reverse painted glass mirrors were made in this country as early as the late 1700s, and remained popular throughout the next century. The simple hand painted panel was separated from the mirrored section by a narrow slat, and the frame was either the dark finished Federal style or the more elegant, often gilded Sheraton.

Mirrors changed with the style of other furnishings, but whatever type you purchase, as long as the glass sections remain solid, even broken or flaking mirrors are more valued than replaced glass. Careful resilvering is acceptable if excessive deterioration has taken place.

Key:
fr----frame   ped----pediment
mahog----mahogany   trn----turned

Architectural gilded Fed, rvpt panel w/eagle/cannon, 45x25"....125.00
Bird's eye veneer fr w/gilded liner, 21½x30½"................45.00
Cheval, mahog/ormolu, pr 2-lite candle arms, 75"...........990.00
Chpndl, elaborate fretwork, walnut fr, gold leaf trim, 20x12"...300.00
Chpndl, scroll, only top crest orig, parts rpl, 13x21".........175.00
Chpndl style, mahog w/gilt eagle, pendant w/shell, 31x37".....350.00
Courting, pine, QA, engraved/rvpt, shaped crest, 15½".......1,980.00
Decorated wood fr, rpt w/florals, old glass, 12x15½".........150.00
Decoupage fr, worn, 14½x18"..............................80.00
Deer head, antlers form oval frame, CI, 8¾"................30.00
Federal, convex, wood/gilt w/eagle/acanthus leaf, 24x42", VG...365.00
Gesso, carved/gilt, Queen Anne style, cartouch/scrolls, 39".....500.00
Gilt wood, carved scrolls/leafy cartouch surmount, 50x32"....5,000.00
Gilt wood, flower filled urn crest, Baroque fr, 49x26".......1,540.00
Gilt wood, Geo II style, over mantel, thrice divided, 42x57"...605.00
Gilt wood, Napoleon III, oval mirror/ornate scroll fr, 50x36"..1,430.00

Gilt wood, Regency, ball hung cornice/rvpt panel, 37x21″......440.00
Gilt wood/gesso, Emp, acanthus slip/leaf carve colonettes, 42″..200.00
Hand, silver w/jade hdl, inlaid gems, Oriental, 10¼″.........495.00
Hand, trn mahog fr w/delicate trn hdl, 6½″ dia, 12″ L, G......95.00
Mahog, Chpndl, gilt scroll crest w/floral/urn finial, 48″.......800.00
Mahog, Chpndl scroll, gilt foliage/phoenix, rpr, 19x35″.......250.00
Mahog, gilt Prince of Wales feathers/fruit/florals, 49″........2,500.00
Mahog, QA style, scroll crest w/Prince of Wales feathers, 58″..600.00
Mahog, scroll, rpl bottom ear, old rpr, old glass, 32x18″......225.00

Courting mirror, reverse glass painted panel with fruit in mahogany frame; with original pine carrying case, Continental, 18th century, 12½″ x 9½″, $550.00.

Mahog on pine, QA, scrolled crests/gilt liner & shell, 20x10″...350.00
Mahog/gilt wood, carved phoenix atop, 51″..............3,190.00
Mahog/gilt wood, Chpndl, eagle atop, acanthus fillets, 59″....3,080.00
Mahog/gilt wood/inlay, urn of flowers atop, rvpt, 59″.......4,400.00
Pier, gilt wood, Am Eastlake, w/console, 85x65″...........1,760.00
Pier, gilt wood, eagle finial/foliate crest/acanthus ped, 47″....1,025.00
Pier, Napoleon III, bronze/Sevres HP porcelain mtd, 96x66″..5,775.00
Queen Anne, pine w/scalloped crest w/carved shell, sm.......1,650.00
Rococo, tooled gesso on wood, early mirror, 9x15″...........75.00
Rvpt house/garden, fluted pine frame, mirror rpl, 19x11″.......55.00
Rvpt 2 part, mahog veneer fr, minor damage, 12x20″.........65.00
Rvpt 2 part, side wheel boat Washington, veneer, 12x22″......175.00
Rvpt 2 part, w/house, bevel mahog veneer fr, 12x20″, G........65.00
Scroll, mahog/line inlay, shell inlaid on crest, rpr, rpl, 23″.....150.00
Shaving, Federal bow front, mahog/pine, 3 dvtl drw, inlay, 20″.240.00
Shaving, inlaid mahog, Geo III, shield form/3 drw, 24x16″.....250.00
Shaving, tin w/emb rope/shell/fan, w/shelf, 9½x12″...........35.00
Victorian, plated CI, cameo & filigree frame, beveled mirror....125.00
Victorian, wall, brass plated filigree fr, sconces/prisms........165.00
Walnut/gilt wood, QA, shaped crest w/carved shell, 40″........990.00
Wrought iron, att Raymond Subes, hexagon/tassels, 20x61″....935.00

Mocha

Mocha was made in England from as early as 1780, in Scotland, Wales, and even America, until well after the turn of the 20th century. The term refers to the distinctive effect achieved by the slip decoration. Among the most common designs are worm, seaweed, cat's-eye, and marbling. These patterns resulted from colored slip being allowed to flow or drip onto the ware's surface as it was turned on a lathe. While the finished product partially reflected the skill of the turner, a second factor involved the reaction of the slip when sprinkled with drops of a chemical fluid. Although very little of this ware was ever marked, researchers believe that at least some mocha was made in America by J. Vodrey, George S. Harker, Edwin Bennett, and John Bell.

Today's collectors tend to prefer English and French made pieces on pearlware and creamware, made between 1780 and 1830.

Basin, gray, worm on band & w/in, age line, 4½x11″.........675.00
Bowl, br band w/wht wavy lines, tan stripes, 3¾x7½″, G......445.00
Bowl, gr emb rim, tan/bl/wht/br marble, hairlines/chips, 3x8″...115.00
Bowl, seaweed, emb rim, br/orange/gr, hairline, 2¾x5″.......155.00
Bowl, tan w/wht/bl/dk gr loops, hairlines, wear, 3x6½″........215.00
Bowl, wht/gray-bl band, blk stripes, bl/wht/blk worm, 3x5¾″, G.425.00
Jug, wide 'waves' band in center, pearlware, 1820s, chips, 9″...350.00
Mug, bl bands, Pub Ware.................................70.00
Mug, bl bands w/wht/br stripes, hairline in rim, Pub Ware, 5″...50.00
Mug, bl/gray bands w/wht stripes, hairline, 4″................85.00
Mug, seaweed, wht w/br/bl/tan bands, rib hdl, Imperial, 5″, EX.150.00
Mug, twig/cat's eye, br/bl/gray band, sienna ea side, 4½″, VG..600.00
Pepper castor, br/bl/orange/wht stripes, 3¾″, VG.............195.00
Pitcher, br seaweed on ochre, emb bl shoulder band, 7″, G....260.00
Pitcher, earthworm/wavy lines in bl/blk/wht/br, emb rim, 7″, G..375.00
Pitcher, emb surface, tan/wht bands/bl stripes, hairline, 6″.....125.00
Pitcher, gr emb base/rim bands/rust w/br stripes/trees, 8″, G...450.00
Pitcher, gr emb rim, tan/bl/br on wht marble, hairline, 7″.....305.00
Pitcher, gray/wht/bl top band, wide center bl band, Pub Ware...85.00
Pitcher, marbleized medallions, br stripes, emb rim, 5¼″, G...325.00
Pitcher, seaweed on bl bkground, 1 qt, Pub Ware, VG........195.00
Pitcher, wht w/lt gr/bl bands & stripes, 6″.................45.00
Salt, open; ftd, straight worm, orange band, br stripes, VG....305.00
Shaker, emb stripes w/br/wht & gr, 4″, G.................205.00
Shaker, worm, bl/wht/br/blk, old rpr, 4½″.................165.00
Shaker, worm in br/bl on bl & wht w/br stripes, rstr, 4¾″.....245.00
Spill, vellum, br/sienna/bl, band/incised leaves, chip, 5″, pr.....650.00

Molds

Food molds have become a popular collectible; not only for their value as antiques, but because they also revive childhood memories of elaborate ice cream Santas with candy trim, or barley sugar figurals adorning a Christmas tree. Ice cream molds were made of pewter and came in a wide variety of shapes and styles. Chocolate molds were made in fewer shapes, but were more detailed. They were usually made of tin, copper, and occasionally of pewter. Hard candy molds were usually metal, although the primitive maple sugar molds -- usually simple hearts, rabbits, and other animals -- were carved from wood. Cake molds were made of cast iron or cast aluminum, and were most common in the shape of a lamb, a rabbit, or Santa Claus.

Key: npci----nickel plated cast iron

Chocolate Molds

Basket, double; hinged, overall 5¼x7″.....................28.00
Blackpool tower, tin, 4 part, mk FW Kutscher Schwarzenberg...26.00
Bulldog, tin ½ mold, 3x4½″.............................10.00
Bunnies/chicks/hens on nest/eggs, flat, 85 cavities, 7½x15″.....45.00
Cat, sitting up, front view, tin, 2 part, 1¼x2¼″..............13.00
Chick, 2 part, hinged, 3¾x2¾″..........................40.00
Chicks, 3 wearing bonnets, hinged, overall 9x5″.............42.00
Child & boot, 'Be-be', npci, 6 in 7x4″ panel, mk Paris, 1900s...75.00

Cross, 3, w/flowers, hinged, overall 4½x8".....................29.00
Duck, w/briefcase, wears hat, tin, 2 part, 2½x5".............18.00
Easter mixture, flat, egg/hen on nest/chicken/rabbit, 13x28".....66.00
Easter mixture, tin, 2 pc, heavy frame, attached clips.........38.00
Eggs, 2, hinged, overall 5½x8"..............................20.00
Elephant, tin, 2 part, 2¼x2¾".............................12.00
Football, tin, 2 part, 3x4½".................................17.00
Girl & boot, 'Elegante', 6 in 7x4" npci panel, mk Paris, 1900s..75.00
Halloween mixture, flat, jack-o'-lanterns/owls/witches, 13x28"..66.00
Hearts, 3 in each of 3 rows, 10x11"..........................65.00
Hen on nest, tin, EX quality, 6x12"........................125.00
Hen on nest, tin, 7x7".......................................85.00
Hen on nest, 2 part w/base, mk Germany, 5¾"...............50.00
Horse, detailed, hinged, 5¼" L.............................45.00
Hunter, 'Chassuer', 6 in 7x4" npci panel, mk Paris, ca 1900....75.00
Lambs, 2 jumping over fence, hinged, overall 5x9½".........40.00
Man/riding attire, 'Jockey', 6 in 7x4" npci panel, Paris, 1900....75.00
Peafowl, 11x10"..125.00
Pelicans, 2, hinged, overall 6½x10".........................40.00
Puppy, tin, 2 part, 3x5"....................................16.00
Rabbit, in car, 2 in mold, hinged, 6x10½"...................60.00
Rabbit, on mushroom, tin, 8½x12".........................150.00
Rabbit, pulling cart, hinged, overall 4x8"....................38.00
Rabbit, w/pack, hinged, overall 7½x15".....................55.00
Rabbits, Disney Thumper, 2 in mold, tin, hinged, overall 7x12"..40.00
Rabbits, emb on ea of 6 eggs, Made in Germany, 6½".........20.00
Rabbits, pair on nest holding hands, tin ½ mold, 5x7".........24.00
Rabbits, 24 joined into one block, 13x11¼"..................45.00
Rooster, stylized, tin, 7x11½".............................115.00
Rooster, tin, 8½x10"..85.00
Rooster, 2 part, 6¼"...40.00
Roosters, 2 w/hats, hinged, overall 6x8½"...................40.00
Santa, standing, flat sheet, 7 rows w/15 each, overall 13x28"....66.00
Santa, 3, hinged, overall 6½x10"...........................70.00
Santa head, flat sheet, 4 rows w/4 each, stick indent, 13x28"....70.00
Squirrel, tin, 6½x10".......................................95.00
Turkey, tin, 2 part, 3½x4½"................................18.00
Valentine mixture, flat, hearts/arrows/cupids, 105 figures.......66.00

Ice Cream Molds

Acorn on leaf, S-385..25.00
Admiral Byrd, bust, E-1165.................................50.00
Airplane, E & Co, NY, 4¾"...................................45.00
Alligator, detailed, S-394...................................65.00
American shield, K-281......................................39.00
Asparagus, bunch, CC.......................................50.00
Aster, K-234..35.00
Baby, lying down, E-1020....................................35.00
Bale of cotton, E-1095......................................30.00
Banana, E & Co, NY, 6" L...................................25.00
Banjo, K-545..40.00
Baseball bat, E-1060..35.00
Basket, oval, K-203...24.00
Basket, scalloped, 5".......................................40.00
Basketball, E-1150..25.00
Battleship, E & Co, NY, 7¼"................................40.00
Bear, sitting, K-222...49.00
Beehive, K-251..42.00
Bell, New Year's, K-605.....................................22.00
Bicyclist, man, early 20th century clothing, S-551..........75.00
Bleeding Heart, K-448.......................................36.00
Book, Pat Apd for Des Coprd 1888, E & Co, NY, 4½".......35.00
Bottle of champagne, E-1092, miniature.....................45.00

Boy in sailboat, 4¾"...42.00
Bride, w/veil, E-1227..45.00
Brownie, #1031..70.00
Bunch of grapes, leaf back half, 5".........................28.00
Bunch of grapes, no leaves, mk Long, 4"....................22.50
Butterfly, S-181...52.00
Cabbage, small, S-162.......................................25.00
Cabin cruiser, 5½" L...50.00
Camel, E-681..75.00
Canary, E-540...45.00
Candlestick, K-207..34.00
Cannon, S-273..40.00
Carrots, bunch, S-305.......................................35.00
Cat, seated, good detail, head to left, 3½"..................50.00
Cauliflower, 3¾"..27.50
Cherries, four, E-340..28.00
Chestnut, S-131...30.00
Chicken, setting, 3¾" L.....................................35.00
Child of Spring, E-682.......................................70.00
Chinaman, 308..70.00
Christmas tree, small, E-1137...............................50.00
Christmas wreath, 4½x4½", E-1146.........................40.00
Chrysanthemum, K-589.......................................32.00
Cleopatra's needle, CC, rare................................55.00
Clover, 3 leaf, E & Co, NY, 5"..............................30.00
Clown head, E-1035...63.00
Clown w/rabbit, 5¼"..45.00
Coach, S-479..52.00
Colonial lady's skirt, E-1185................................27.00
Columbus, bust, S-312.......................................40.00
Conch shell, S-310..40.00
Convertible car, E & Co, NY, 4¾"...........................55.00
Corn in husk, K-270...30.00
Couple on garden bench on disk, 3¾" dia...................35.00
Cow, well detailed, head up, bell around neck, 4½".........100.00
Crab, S-174...45.00
Cradle, w/flowers, 3 part, S-470.............................45.00
Cricket player, K-525, very rare.............................70.00
Cross, E-1005...15.00
Cucumber, S-163..25.00
Cupid, standing, K-492......................................45.00
Cupid, w/anvil..70.00
Dahlia, full blown flowerhead, 4"...........................30.00
Dice, S-199...25.00
Diploma, K-633...25.00
Doe, 3½"...45.00
Dog, Pug, S-390..40.00
Dolphin, S-258...45.00
Donkey, K-630..42.00
Dove of Peace, wings outstretched, E-677...................50.00
Drum, 3 part, S-511..40.00
Duck, S-165..44.00
Dutch shoe, E-978..30.00
Eagle, w/US shield, S-239...................................85.00
Eastern Star, K-1178..40.00
Egg, sliced, E-946...30.00
Elephant, S-169...60.00
Elk head, 3 part, S-493......................................65.00
Engagement ring, 4¼" L.....................................20.00
Father Knickerbocker, K-504.................................70.00
Fire pumper, S & Co, 4¾"...................................65.00
Firecracker, E-1016..15.00
Fireman, with horn, early 20th century, S-340...............80.00
Fish, S-259...43.00

Flag, K-282...34.00

Flowers, row of 3, 4½".......................26.00

Football, E-1008................................25.00

Fox, S-179..68.00

Frog, on mushroom, S-180...................57.00

Geo Washington, S & Co, pewter, 3½x4"....85.00

Golf bag, w/clubs, K-622....................62.00

Guitar, K-456....................................40.00

Hand w/fan, K-304.............................55.00

Happy Easter plaque, w/bunny face, K-645...36.00

Harp, K-361......................................45.00

Hat, K-399..30.00

Heart w/cupid w/bow, 3".....................40.00

Hickory nut in shell, S-378..................30.00

Horn of plenty, E-1004.......................38.00

Horse, rearing, E-639.........................52.00

Horseshoe, E & Co, NY, 4¾"................35.00

Horseshoe, w/horse head, S-498............45.00

Jack of Diamonds, face card, K-439.......22.00

Jack-O'-Lantern w/cigar & hat, E & Co, NY, Pat Applied, 3½"..55.00

Kewpie, #1115...................................70.00

King of Clubs, face card, K-441............23.00

Lady Golfer, putting, early 20th century clothing, K-464......49.00

Lamb, E & Co, NY, 3¼".......................35.00

Liberty bell, 4th of July, 1776, S-473.....34.00

Lighthouse, S-565...............................50.00

Lincoln, bust, K-597............................52.00

Lion, K-166.......................................40.00

Lobster, small, K-330..........................48.00

Locomotive, K-477.............................65.00

Lovebirds on pie, 5"............................35.00

Man in top hat & tails, E & Co, NY, 5"...45.00

Mandolin, S-547.................................44.00

Martha Washington, K-461...................75.00

Masonic emblem, square & compass, E-948...22.00

Mikado, E-914...................................57.00

Monkey, E-542...................................47.00

Mother Hubbard, E-581......................45.00

Mother plaque, w/face, K-643...............38.00

Napoleon, S-426................................68.00

Nest, w/4 eggs, S-552.........................65.00

Opera glasses, K-483...........................44.00

Owl, K-175.......................................54.00

Pansies, makes three, E & Co, NY, 4½"...45.00

Parrot, S-359.....................................45.00

Pea pod, S-293...................................20.00

Peach, K-152.....................................14.00

Pears, row of 3, center inverted, 3½".....18.00

Pepper shaker, S-216...........................30.00

Petunia, S-238....................................31.00

Piece of pie, E-1097............................25.00

Pig, boar, E-647.................................44.00

Pig, seated, 3½".................................60.00

Pineapple, 3¾"...................................32.50

Pipe, K-374.......................................27.00

Poinsettia, K-403................................40.00

Policeman, S-405.................................50.00

Pomegranate, CC...............................30.00

Poodle, E-636....................................55.00

Pork chop, S-139................................35.00

Possum, S-616....................................48.00

Potato, K-154.....................................18.00

Pumpkin, S-600..................................15.00

Queen of Hearts, face card, K-434.........24.00

Question mark, S-288...........................35.00

Rabbit, sitting up, K-189......................37.00

Raspberries, row of 4, mk E & Co, NY, 4"...25.00

Roadster, E-1143................................85.00

Rooster, E-645...................................44.00

Roses, bunch, S-391............................40.00

Sailboat, S-553...................................65.00

Santa, w/basket & backpack, S & Co, 4½"...65.00

Shamrock, E-1039...............................32.00

Sheaf of wheat, E-200.........................45.00

Shriner crescent, E-1080......................22.00

Skull & crossbones medallion, S-608......45.00

Sleigh, 3 part, S-494...........................70.00

Slipper, 3 part, E-899A........................27.00

Snowman, K-601................................32.00

Sprinkling can, S-302..........................30.00

Squirrel, small, K-383.........................60.00

St Bernard dog, E-654.........................60.00

Star, E-1041......................................18.00

Steamer, 2 smokestacks, E & Co, NY, 7"...40.00

Stork, flying, K-631.............................50.00

Strawberries, cluster of 3 on leaf, K-195...37.00

Swan, CC..38.00

Sweet peas, dated 1893, K-375..............34.00

Tent, S-515..38.00

Thimble, S-372...................................30.00

Three flowerheads, E & Co, NY, 5".........20.00

Tomato, E-208....................................18.00

Tree stump..16.00

Tulip, E-352.......................................34.00

Turkey, E & Co, NY, 3¾".....................40.00

Turtle, S-176......................................54.00

Two dogs & bear, 4"............................40.00

Uncle Sam, Palmer Cox, S-407.............85.00

Valentine, w/stamp, K-506....................43.00

Vase of flowers, S-252.........................47.00

Violets, S-366.....................................45.00

Violin, S-544......................................50.00

Waffle, E-842.....................................32.00

Walnut in shell, S-130.........................25.00

Whale, S-602.....................................54.00

Wheelbarrow, K-480...........................30.00

Wishbone, S-322.................................40.00

Wishing well, 3 part, S-487...................54.00

Witch on broom, E-1153......................50.00

Wolf, E-669.......................................55.00

Yule log, E-987...................................19.00

Miscellaneous

Baking, recumbent lamb, CI, 12½"........65.00

Bread, tin, dbl, hinged, corrugated, late 1800s, 12x8½x4"......27.00

Bunt, CI, Griswold Mfg, fluted, #965-A65...65.00

Bunt, ribbed ceramic w/caramel glaze, 6½"...50.00

Cake, lamb, lying down, 2 part, CI, reproduction, ca 1950s.....35.00

Cake, lamb figural, lying down, 2 part, CI, ca 1880...........75.00

Cake, Santa full-figure, emb Hello Kiddies!!, CI, 2 part....135.00

Cake, turk's head, br glazed pottery, 7½" dia....65.00

Candy, CI, makes 3 hands, 3x4¾".........100.00

Candy, pine, ½ of fish, 3⅛x9".............100.00

Cast iron, fish, worn orig gold pnt, ca 1860s, 9x7x2"........75.00

Cheese, Pennsylvania heart, 3 ft, 4x4½"...110.00

Cheese, pierced rnd tin, Pennsylvania, 5½"...55.00

Cheese, wood, hand carved chickens, ca 1850s, 12" dia.......60.00

Cheese, wood, hand carved pigs, ca 1850s, 14″ dia...........70.00
Clay, buff w/gr clear glaze, Jonah & whale, 4½″ dia, G.........65.00
Cottage cheese, tin, 3 pc, PA tulip shape, 7x6″............1,000.00
Lady finger, EX shell design, buff clay, 5¼″ L............30.00
Maple sugar, house form, carved windows/door, wire nails......30.00
Maple sugar, rooster, wood, half missing, 7½x8½″.........125.00
Maple sugar, walnut w/28 round depressions, hdl/ped ft.......165.00
Maple sugar, wood w/carved hearts/diamond/spade, 17″........40.00
Pewter, 2 part, for chalk kissing doves, dents/losses, 10¼″.....140.00
Pudding, fluted sides, flower base, mk 1½L, late 1800s.......45.00
Pudding, forms pigs face, for souse, CI, all orig, M..........110.00
Redware, fish shape, amber glaze w/gr splotches, chip, 11¾″...150.00
Tin, bunch of grapes in top of oval, 7¼x6½″..............30.00
Tin/copper, hollow center, 2 tiered top, rpr, 5x7¼″.........100.00
Tin/copper, oval w/decorative geometric top, 3¼x5″.........105.00
Tin/copper, swirled top, 4x4″......................80.00
Turk's head, hammered copper, 10½″ dia................55.00
Yellowware, rabbit, chips on rim/ft, 4x6x9″..............50.00

Monmouth

The Monmouth Pottery Company was established in 1892 in Monmouth, Illinois. Their primary products were stoneware crocks, churns, and jugs, in saltglaze, Bristol, spongeware, and brown glaze. In 1906 they were absorbed by a conglomerate called the Western Stoneware Company. Monmouth became their #1 plant, and until 1930, continued to produce stoneware marked with their maple leaf logo. Items marked 'Monmouth Pottery Co.' were made before 1906; after the merger, 'Co.' was dropped, and 'Ill.' was substituted.

Bowl vase, w/hdl; spongy rust glaze...................40.00
Hanging planter, dk bl ball shape, w/orig sticker, 5″.........25.00
Jardiniere, brushware w/egret decor, 6″................30.00
Jug, br gloss, 5½″............................28.00
Mug, round handle...........................45.00

Egypto vase, brown glazed interior, 9¼″, $42.50.

Mont Joye

Mont Joye was a type of acid cut French cameo glass produced by Cristallerie de Pantin in Paris around the turn of the century.

Loving cup, goldfish/Art Nouveau on amethyst, 3 hdls, 6″.....110.00
Vase, floral, opal & enamel, str sides, sgn, 11″...........275.00

Vase, floral, wht/rose/lav/rust enamel, gold leaves/rim, 6½″.....575.00
Vase, frosted/textured surface, pnt leaves, gold stems, 4x3″....135.00
Vase, gold mums on gr, acid cut-back, 7½″.............185.00
Vase, green w/gold & silver Nouveau decor, 15″..........775.00
Vase, internally ribbed, flared, acid w/HP florals, 4x3″........95.00
Vase, lily form, ruffled top, enamel forget-me-nots, 10″.......650.00
Vase, violets, enameled, gr base, 14″................225.00
Vase, 4 sided, w/enameled mums...................185.00

Moorcroft

William Moorcroft was an English potter who established a workshop in Burslem, England, in 1913. He produced tablewares and a line of fine Art Nouveau vases, bowls, etc., which until 1919 were marked with the printed or impressed block lettered 'Moorcroft, Burslem'. After that, the patented 'W. Moorcroft' signature mark was used. Wm. Moorcroft died in 1945, and the work was continued by his son. Modern wares are marked 'Moorcroft', and 'Made In England'.

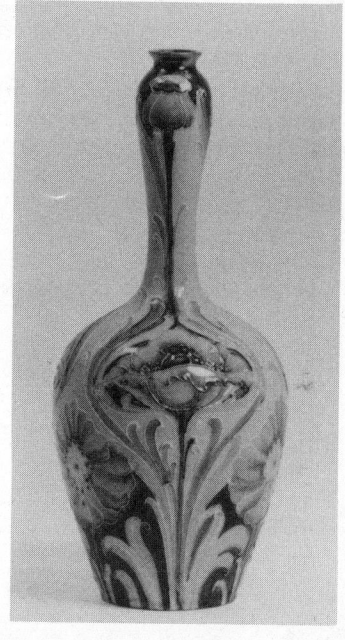

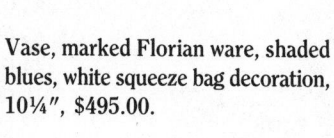
Vase, marked Florian ware, shaded blues, white squeeze bag decoration, 10¼″, $495.00.

Bowl, ftd, gr w/relief flower, 5½″ dia.................45.00
Bowl, ftd, pk flowers on gr bkground, 3½x7″............85.00
Bowl, ftd, poppies decor, 11″ dia..................150.00
Bowl, grape leaves, 8″ dia......................75.00
Bowl, orchids & wht flowers, 10″ dia................125.00
Bowl, pansies, 1920, 7½″ dia....................75.00
Bowl, pomegranates, 13″ dia....................175.00
Bowl, w/lid; cobalt w/mc floral, 7″ dia...............80.00
Bowl, wisteria, 1930, 9″ dia.....................95.00
Box, florals on bl, script sgn, 3½x5″................95.00
Candlestick, Florian, bl carnation on dk bl, 7½″, pr.........500.00
Candlestick, pk floral w/gr leaves, imp mk, 3½″, pr.........55.00
Creamer & sugar, poppies, red/ochre, pr..............225.00
Cup & saucer, bl on bl, gilded, Macintyre.............210.00
Goblet, bl w/gr lilac, gold trim, Macintyre, 5¾″..........550.00
Jar, cobalt, w/lid, 6½″.......................125.00
Jar, green, w/lid, 6½″.......................125.00
Plaque, autumn colors, 1930-40, 11½″...............185.00
Teapot, cr/sug, cobalt w/pk floral, 1930-40............225.00
Teapot, orchids, 8″.........................185.00

Vase, anemones, blue, Florian Ware, bulbous, 4".........200.00
Vase, cornflowers, blue, Florian Ware, 8"...............275.00
Vase, florals, Macintyre, 6".........................150.00
Vase, florals, 2½"...................................16.00
Vase, Florian Ware, irid, Dennis #55, 10"..............400.00
Vase, hibiscus, cobalt w/red, script sgn, 7½"...........165.00
Vase, Macintyre, 18th C pattern, 11"..................150.00
Vase, orange lustre, ca 1913, 9".....................120.00
Vase, peacock eyes, blue, Florian Ware, 6".............200.00
Vase, pomegranate, blk bkground, bulbous, 4¼"...........85.00
Vase, pomegranate, blk bkground, bulbous, 7"...........165.00
Vase, pomegranate, blk bkground, slender, 8"...........120.00
Vase, sang de bouef, red dahlias, 5¼".................175.00
Vase, tulips, Macintyre, 12".........................250.00
Vase, tulips, Macintyre, 8"..........................175.00
Vase, wisteria, 10".................................140.00

Moravian Pottery & Tile Works

Dr. Henry Chapman Mercer was an author, anthropologist, historian, collector, and artist. One of his diversified interests was pottery. In 1898, he established the Moravian Pottery and Tile Works in Doylestown, Pennsylvania, the name inspired by his study and collection of decorative stove plates made by the early Moravians. Because the red clay he used there proved unfit for tableware, he turned to the production of handmade tile which he himself designed. Though never allowing it to become more than a studio operation, the tile works was nevertheless responsible for some important commercial installations, one of which was in the capitol building at Harrisburg.

Mercer died in 1930. Business continued in the established vein under the supervision of Mercer's assistant, Frank Swain, until his death in 1954. Since 1968, the studio has been operated by The Bucks County Commission, and tiles are still fashioned in the handmade tradition. They are marked 'Mercer', and are dated.

Bowl, redware, worn yellow wavy line decor, hairline, 11" dia...150.00
Plate, lad & lass sharing muff, 'Time for a Thaw', Mercer, 9¾"..45.00
Tile, redware w/emb tulip, clear glaze, edge flakes, sgn, 6x7"....95.00
Tile, Santa Maria, br w/blue, 3¾"......................65.00
Tile, zodiac sign decor..............................56.00

Moriage

The term 'moriage' refers to certain Japanese wares decorated with applied slipwork designs. There are several methods used to achieve the characteristic relief effect. The decorative devices may be designed separately and applied to the vessel, piped on in narrow ribbons of clay (slip-trailed), or built up by brushing on successive layers of liquified slip.

See also Nippon

Chocolate pot, mc florals, 7¾".......................190.00
Coffee pot, demitasse; cr/sug w/lid, 4 c/s, dragons on gray.....150.00
Cracker jar, allover beading.........................200.00
Creamer & sugar, allover pk florals, heavy slip.........75.00
Creamer & sugar, allover slip trailing/jewels, scenics, 3 ftd......95.00
Cup & saucer, gray w/dragon, pearlized w/in............12.00
Dresser set, floral slip, SP hdls w/poppies, orig box, 3 pc.......85.00
Ewer, florals, turq beads, panels of roses, fancy hdl/lip, 6".....195.00
Powder jar, allover slip trailing/jewels, scenic atop, 4" dia......45.00
Salt & pepper, dragon relief, tall/slender, mk Japan...........10.00
Teapot, dragon ware, elephant figural, gold trim, 7x9½".......55.00

Ewer, white stylized flowers on green ground, 7", $195.00.

Teapot, dragon ware, gray, 2¼"........................6.00
Vase, allover mc slip, reserves ea side squirrels/grapes, 10"....180.00
Vase, birds & pagoda, 12¼"...........................95.00
Vase, dragon ware, 3"................................11.00
Vase, dragon ware, 6"................................19.00
Vase, dragon ware, 8"................................35.00
Vase, floral medallions, hdls, classical shape, 5½".......50.00
Vase, florals on yel, pk/gr trim, 2¾".................20.00
Vase, HP violets, lacy slip, dbl hdls, 9¼"............180.00
Vase, HP violets on bl, lacy slip allover, 14¼".........295.00
Vase, 3 hdls, orchids, fuchsia/orange/purple, 9½".........300.00
Vase, 3 hdls, purple/wht flowers, gr/wht applied leaves, 7"....275.00
Vase, 4 wht dancing skeletons w/fans/lantern on gray, 8½"....285.00
Wall pocket, dragon ware, 7x4".......................22.00

Mortar and Pestle

Mortars are bowl shaped vessels used for centuries for the purpose of grinding drugs to a powder or grain into meal. The masher or grinding device is called a pestle.

Bell metal, w/pestle, 3"............................30.00
Brass, late 1800s, w/pestle, 5½".....................75.00
Bronze, Gott Allein De Ehrr Anno 1642, dolphins, pestle, 5¾".690.00
Bronze, Lof Godt Van Al Ad 1665, florals, w/pestle, 4¾".......380.00
Cast iron, urn shape, late 1800s, 4".................50.00
Cast iron, urn shape, late 1800s, 6".................60.00
Cherry, w/pestle, 7"...............................110.00
Drug store type, ceramic, w/pestle, 14" dia...........90.00
Maple, American, w/pestle, 8".........................65.00
Stone, carved, w/pestle, 5x6".........................25.00
Tiger maple, turned, no pestle, 7½x5½"...............150.00
Tiger maple, w/pestle...............................220.00
Walnut, turned, w/pestle, 7¼".......................125.00

Morton Pottery

Six potteries operated in Morton, Illinois, at various times over a ninety-nine year period. Each traced its origin to six brothers who immigrated to

America to avoid forced military service in Germany. The Rapp brothers established their first pottery to make field tile, but soon branched out to include utility wares. Second and third generation potters, sons and nephews, either expanded the original operation, or started their own potteries where art ware and gift store items were produced. The last operating pottery, the Morton Pottery Company, closed its doors on September 8, 1976.

Mug, brown glaze with parrot on basketweave relief, $25.00.

Morton Pottery Works--Morton Earthenware Company (1877-1914)

Coffee pot, ornate decor, br Rockingham, applied hdl, 5 pt.....80.00
Fluted rice nappy, brown Rockingham glaze, 8" dia...........50.00
Pie baker, brown Rockingham glaze, 10" dia................22.00
Pie baker, yellowware, 10" dia.........................30.00
Tea set, individual; br Rockingham, pot, cr/sug+lid, spooner...100.00

Cliftwood Art Potteries, Inc. (1920-1939)

Dresser set, gr glaze, hair receiver & pill box on 10x8" tray.....60.00
Figurine, Lioness, head raised/roar position, br drip, 7x12".....50.00
Flower arranger, Lorelie, blue-mulberry drip glaze, 6½x4¼"....30.00
Pottery stand, br glaze, 1¼x3½" top dia...................5.00

Midwest Potteries, Inc. (1939-1944)

Figurine, Deco dancing lady, wht w/14k gold, w/label, 8½".....30.00
Figurine, eagle, applied wings, br/wht/yel, on stump, 8¾".......60.00
Figurine, polar bear, wht gloss, 6x10", on rectangular base.....30.00
Figurine, squirrel eating nut, br spray glaze over wht, 7"......25.00
Miniature, frog, gr w/yel ft, 1½x2"......................6.00
Miniature, sailboat, golden yel glaze w/bl & wht sail, 2x2".......5.00
Miniature, squirrel, wht glaze w/14k gold decor, 2x1½"........8.00
Miniature, turtle, gr & wht glaze, yel head & ft, 1x2½"........6.00

Morton Pottery Company (1922-1976)

Bank, country schoolhouse, br gloss glaze, 3x4", rare.........35.00
Bank, pig, hangs on wall, blue, 5x6"......................10.00
Beater jar & beater, spatter glaze: gr/br/yel, 5x4" dia.........80.00
Cookie jar, Panda, blk & wht, AFK mk on back..............22.50
Cookie jar, turkey w/chick on bk, br glaze on wht, red wattle....45.00

Incense burner, Oriental lady holds bowl, br gloss glaze, 5".....30.00
Jardiniere, tulip shape, emb leaves around sides, dk gr, 5x5"....18.00
Pitcher, milk; lt bl glaze, w/advertising, 4½"................22.00
Pitcher, milk; lt bl glaze, w/blank for advertising, 4½"........15.00
Plate, Santa, wht w/underglaze decor, hat cold-pnt red, 12".....30.00

American Art Potteries (1947-1961)

Bud vase, chartreuse spray glaze on wht, 4½x1" top dia........3.50
Creamer & sugar, blk spray glaze, lime w/in, orig labels, 3".....10.00
Planter, baby shoes, pk flowers/strings, 3½", on heart base.....14.00
Vase, gray, pk flowers, pk w/in, long neck/applied floral, 12"....16.00
Wall pocket, bulbous, plain, mauve, lt bl w/in, 5½x4½".........6.00

Mosaic Tile Co.

The Mosaic Tile Company was organized in Zanesville, Ohio, in 1894 by Herman Mueller and Karl Langenbeck, both of whom had years of previous experience in the industy. They developed a faster, less costly method of potting decorative tile, utilizing paper patterns rather than copper molds. By 1901 the company had grown and expanded, with offices in many major cities. Faience tile was introduced in 1918, greatly increasing their volume of sales. They also made novelty ash trays, figural boxes, bookends, etc., though not to any large extent. Until they closed during the 1960s, Mosaic used various marks that included the company name or their initials -- 'MT' superimposed over 'Co.' in a circle.

Ash tray, Airedale, mc.................................130.00
Ash tray, boomerang shape, green, large.................32.00
Ash tray & match box holder, hexagonal, gr, 4"...........10.00
Bookends, boy w/book, pr...:.........................85.00
Cookie jar, Mammy, gray, minor damage..................95.00
Cookie jar, Mammy, yellow, EX.........................95.00
Figurine, bear, blk, standing, 5x9"......................95.00
Figurine, dog, crouching, mk MTC on collar, 6x10"..........90.00
Soap dish, shallow turtle, bl, 4"........................35.00
Tile, floral & geometric, porcelain type, 6"...............10.00
Tile, Fortune & The Boy...............................35.00
Tile, General Pershing, oval cameo, bl jasperware, M..........40.00

Tile, Pennsylvania Dutch two-headed bird motif, signed U.S.A. on front, 6", $25.00.

Moser

Ludwig Moser founded the Moser Glassworks in Czechoslovakia in 1857. He produced Art Nouveau style glass -- cameo, intaglio cut, iridescent, and enameled ware. Most valued by collectors are items made between 1860 and 1920. The firm is still in operation.

Bowl, bride's basket; ruby cased, allover floral enameling......250.00
Bowl, emerald shading to clear, wide oval, sgn, 11".........250.00
Box, amethyst w/3 amber salamander ft, 1 on lid, 4½".......575.00
Candlestick, topaz w/gilded flat relief frieze band, 13", pr.....395.00
Cologne, babies & lovebirds, swirl, shaded gr, 5¾x4".........250.00
Cologne, nudes in relief, shaded gr, 9x6½"..................300.00
Cologne, pk opal w/gold/red/wht/bl enameling, sgn, 5".......350.00
Cologne, w/atomizer, gold spatter glass, 6"..................95.00
Cordial, engraved ducks & cattails.........................75.00
Cup, amber swirl w/applied hdl/ft, pnt flowers, ground pontil....65.00
Decanter, cranberry, gold etching, 16", pr.................1,250.00
Decanter, gr cut to clear, matching stopper, sgn, 8".........225.00
Dish, dresser; cobalt w/decor, 2 lilies/swivel bevel mirror.......310.00
Pokal, amber, floral in gold/enamels, applied prunts, 11".....850.00
Toothpick holder, cranberry fan form w/silver/gold foliage/ft...300.00
Tumbler, amber, clear/ruby floral overlay, 5 etch panels, 5½"..200.00
Tumbler, ornate gold, blue & wht enamel....................95.00
Vase, amethyst, gilt band, cut-back figures, 6½"............265.00
Vase, amethyst, gilt band, Etruscan warriors, ftd, 12x7"......550.00
Vase, bl w/amber ft, mc pnt grapes/bee, applied grapes, 5½"...325.00
Vase, cameo, foliage & bust of nude, 15"..................475.00
Vase, emerald gr, heavy gold & enamel, sgn, 11"...........225.00
Vase, fish/florals relief, aqua & gold on lt amber, unsgn, 5½"..275.00
Vase, knight in armor, enamel on amethyst, sgn, ftd, 11"......400.00
Vase, lav w/cut edges, acid etched girl/tree, MK/T in circle.....450.00
Vase, twist stem, pk opal, 3 openings atop w/jewels, 14"......350.00
Vase, 3 reed/scroll gold ft, mc oak leaves on pink opal, 8x7".1,250.00

Vase, cranberry with applied multicolor acorns and oak leaves, enameled bees, gold decor and handles, 13", $1,650.00.

Moss Rose

Moss Rose was a favorite dinnerware pattern of many Staffordshire and American potters from the mid-1800s. The Wheeling Pottery in West Virginia introduced their version in the 1880s, and it became one of their best sellers, remaining popular well into the nineties.

Bowl, oval vegetable; covered, Meakin, 11½x7", VG...........23.00
Bowl, square, open, Meakin, M.............................58.00
Box, oval, no mk..14.00
Butter pat, square, Meakin, EX............................15.00
Butter tub, w/lid; Japan..................................24.00

Cake plate, open hdls.....................................18.00
Cake plate, pink lustre trim, 9¾".........................22.00
Coaster, sterling rim, Rosenthal..........................10.00
Coffee mug & saucer, Meakin, M............................40.00
Creamer, Meakin, 5½", M..................................30.00
Creamer & sugar, no mk....................................20.00
Cup & saucer, Edwards Bros, M.............................24.00
Cup & saucer, handleless; Meakin, M.......................50.00
Cup & saucer, Haviland Limoges, 2½x3".....................15.00
Cup & saucer, Meakin, M...................................35.00
Demitasse set, pear shaped pot, cr/sug, 6 c/s; Japan.......75.00
Gravy boat, Green & Co, England, M........................20.00
Gravy boat, Knowles Taylor & Knowles, EX..................19.00
Gravy boat, Meakin, EX....................................25.00
Nappy, Edwards Bros, 4½", M...............................10.00
Plate, Edwards Bros, 8", M................................10.00
Plate, Meakin, 10", M.....................................20.00
Plate, Meakin, 8", EX.....................................16.00
Plate, pk trim, dbl mk Haviland, 8½"......................22.00
Plate, serving; 10", EX...................................20.00
Plate, soup; Meakin, 9", M................................16.00
Platter, Meakin, 10x14", M................................35.00
Platter, Meakin, 11x16"...................................58.00
Platter, Meakin, 12"......................................25.00
Saucer, Meakin, EX...7.00
Shaving mug, EX...35.00
Soup tureen, oblong, Edwards Bros.........................95.00
Sugar, bulbous, Meakin, 6½", sm chip inside rim...........45.00
Tea set, child's; in orig box............................100.00
Tea set, pot+5½" creamer+6¼" sugar, Meakin, M............190.00
Teapot, J&E Mayer, slight crazing.........................35.00
Teapot, pewter lid, sgn KTK...............................45.00
Teapot, textured basketweave/gold trim, T&V Limoges, 7x8½"..75.00
Tureen, w/lid, 8x5"; w/serving plate & 7½" ladle, Edwards, EX.100.00
Wash set, pitcher & bowl, EX.............................200.00
Wash set, 11" ewer; 12 sided bowl, 13½" dia..............230.00

Mother of Pearl

Mother-of-Pearl glass was a type of mold blown satin art glass popular during the last half of the 19th century. A patent for its manufacture was issued in 1886 to Frederick S. Shirley, and one of the companies which produced it was the Mt. Washington Glass Company of New Bedford, Massachusetts. Another was the English firm of Stevens and Williams.

Its delicate patterns were developed by blowing the gather into a mold with inside projections that left an intaglio design on the surface of the glass, then sealing the first layer with a second, trapping air in the recesses. Most common are the Diamond Quilted, Raindrop, and Herringbone patterns. It was made in several soft colors, the most rare and valuable is rainbow -- a blend of rose, light blue, yellow, and white. Occasionally it may be decorated with coralene, enameling, or gilt.

Bottle vase, Dia Quilt, peach, 8½x4½"....................150.00
Bowl, Dia Quilt, rainbow, sgn Patent, 9".................750.00
Cracker jar, Dia Quilt, rose, SP top/rim/hdl, 3x4¾".......365.00
Cruet, Dia Quilt, blue, no stopper.......................200.00
Cruet, Dia Quilt, yellow, 3 petal top, reed hdl, 7"......275.00
Ewer, Dia Quilt, pink, frosted thorn hdl, deep ruffles, 7"....135.00
Ewer, Dia Quilt, pk shaded/wht lining, ruffled, thorn hdl, 12"..425.00
Ewer, Dia Quilt, rainbow, frosted hdl, 6¾"...............850.00
Ewer, Herringbone, blue, ruffled, frosted hdl, 7¾x3¾".....195.00
Ewer, Herringbone, blue, 8"..............................175.00
Ewer, Herringbone, rainbow, ped base, 10"................750.00

Ewer, Herringbone, rainbow, satin, mk Patent, 10".........900.00
Fairy lamp, Dia Quilt, blue, sgn Clarke base, 3½x2½".......145.00
Rose bowl, Dia Quilt, ¾ rainbow, sgn Patent.............1,150.00
Rose bowl, Herringbone, lemon to lt lemon, 8 crimp, 5x5½"...275.00
Rose bowl, Pinwheel, lt to dk pink, 8 flute top, 5¾".........295.00
Scent bottle, Dia Quilt, blue, silver top, straight body, 4½"....225.00
Sweetmeat, Dia Quilt, pk w/wht lining, SP top/rim/hdl, 5¼"....295.00
Tumbler, Dia Quilt, blue...............................90.00
Tumbler, Dia Quilt, pink, 4"..........................85.00
Tumbler, Dia Quilt, yellow............................45.00
Tumbler, Herringbone, rubena satin, cased.................125.00
Vase, Dia Quilt, apricot, frosted edge, ruffled, thorn hdl, 8"...250.00
Vase, Dia Quilt, blue, gourd shape w/pleating, Webb, 9½".....400.00
Vase, Dia Quilt, clear gr over pink, melon shape, 8½".........350.00
Vase, Dia Quilt, coral, thorn hdls, bulb/slim shaped neck, 11"..190.00
Vase, Dia Quilt, gr/wht, ormolu ft/flowers, 10x4"............450.00
Vase, Dia Quilt, peachblow/cream/bulbous/stick neck, Webb, 7".400.00
Vase, Dia Quilt, rainbow, slim neck/dimpled body, 10½".....750.00
Vase, Dia Quilt, raspberry, wht w/lin, 4¾"................135.00
Vase, Dia Quilt, SP ftd mt, pk to rose w/enamel florals........165.00
Vase, Dia Quilt, yel, stick neck, bulbous base, 8½"..........150.00
Vase, Dia Quilt, yel/wht, 3 petal top, 6x3½"..............185.00
Vase, Federzeichnug, glossy brown, bulbous, 6x5".........1,650.00
Vase, Herringbone, blue, stick neck, bulbous base, 10½".....285.00
Vase, Herringbone, blue, 6".............................150.00
Vase, Herringbone, pink, 3 hdls, Webb....................350.00
Vase, Herringbone, wht to pink, 6¼"......................195.00
Vase, Moire, peach, thorn hdls, Mt Washington, 6"..........300.00
Vase, Raindrop, bl/wht, 7¾".............................250.00
Vase, Raindrop, lime green, 3 lobed ruffled top, 7"..........165.00

Vase, Drapery pattern in orange and gold, 4¼", $795.00.

Movie Memorabilia

Movie memorabilia covers a broad range of collectibles, from books and magazines dealing with the industry in general, to the various promotional materials which were distributed to arouse interest in a particular film. Many collectors specialize in a specific area -- posters, press books, stills, lobby cards, or souvenir programs (also referred to as premier booklets).

See also Autographs; Personalities

Key:
cp----photo in center of sheet
P-----producer
D-----director

Book, Gone w/t Wind, 1936, hard back, w/out dust jacket......21.00
Book, Gone w/t Wind, 1939-40 movie edition/paperbk/color illus.45.00
Button, blk/wht sketch, 'Just Spent an Eve w/Joan Crawford'...15.00
Costume, Barry Gibb, from Sergeant Pepper's Lonely...Band...137.00
Film cel, mk Chuck Jones, seals/cat/whale/etc, matted, 5 for..65.00
Film cel, Pinocchio w/Dutch marionettes, 1939.............770.00
Film cel, Three Caballeros, Jose Carioco, watercolor ground....203.00
Game, Scarlett O'Hara Marble Game, 1939, all orig, M.........25.00
Lobby card, Bedlam, 1946, Boris Karloff...................35.00
Lobby card, Black Friday, Realart release, Boris Karloff.......40.00
Lobby card, Captain January, 1936, Shirley Temple..........200.00
Lobby card, Glorifying the American Girl, 1929, F Ziegfield/P..100.00
Lobby card, Gone w/t Wind, re-release, w/movie scenes, 1968...50.00
Lobby card, Hunchback of Notre Dame, A Quinn, #2..........15.00
Lobby card, Island of Doomed Men, 1940, Peter Lorre.........15.00
Lobby card, Isle of the Dead, 1945, B Karloff, title card........75.00
Lobby card, Magnificent Obsession, 1935, Robert Taylor.......75.00
Lobby card, Man Who Shot Liberty Valance, 1962, J Stewart....15.00
Lobby card, My Neighbors Wife, 1925, H Rawlinson, repaired...40.00
Lobby card, Once Upon a Honeymoon, 1942, Grant & Rogers...15.00
Lobby card, Rear Window, 1945, Hitchcock/D, #7.............20.00
Lobby card, Return of Frank James, 1940, Tierney & Hull......25.00
Lobby card, Secret Life of Walter Mitty, 1947, D Kaye, #7......10.00
Lobby card, Shepherd of the Hills, 1955, John Wayne, #3......15.00
Lobby card, The Harvey Girls, 1945, Judy Garland, #7.........25.00
Lobby card, Treasure of Sierra Madre, 1948, Bogart, title......200.00
Lobby card, Wife vs Secretary, 1936, Myrna Loy............150.00
Magazine, Modern Screen, June 1939, Olivia DeHavilland......10.00
Magazine, Modern Screen, Sept 1936, Carol Lombard cover....15.00
Magazine, Screen Stories, Nov 1954, M Monroe cover, EX......15.00
Photo, Vivien Leigh, framed w/signed typed letter............200.00
Poster, A Man Betrayed, 1941, John Wayne, 81x81".........175.00
Poster, All About Eve, M Monroe, 1950, 36x14"............175.00
Poster, All in a Night's Work, 1961, Dean Martin, 27x41"......20.00
Poster, And the Angels Sing, 1944, D Lamour, cp, 27x41".....50.00
Poster, Any Number Can Play, 1949, Clark Gable, cp, 14x36"...40.00
Poster, Auntie Mame, 1958, Rosalind Russell, 27x41".........30.00
Poster, Babe Comes Home, 1927, Babe Ruth, cp, 27x41"....900.00
Poster, Bedlam, 1946, B Karloff, 27x41"..................140.00
Poster, Between Two Women, Van Johnson, 27x41"..........40.00
Poster, Black Magic, 1949, Orson Welles, 27x41"...........40.00
Poster, Boccaccio '70, 1962, Sophia Loren, 27x41"...........20.00
Poster, Breakfast at Tiffany's, 1961, A Hepburn, 27x41".......30.00
Poster, Bus Stop, M Monroe, 1952, 36x14"...............100.00
Poster, Butterfield 8, 1960, Elizabeth Taylor, 27x41".........30.00
Poster, Calcutta, 1946, Alan Ladd, 27x41"................65.00
Poster, Carmen, 1913, Marion Leonard, cp, 27x41".........350.00
Poster, Carrie, 1952, Laurence Olivier, 27x41".............30.00
Poster, Casey Jones, 1928, Ralph Lewis, cp, Ritchey litho, 41".175.00
Poster, Charlie Chan in Rio, 1941, Sidney Toler, cp, 14x36"...125.00
Poster, Clash By Night, M Monroe, 1952, 36x14"...........50.00
Poster, Confessions of a Nazi Spy, 1939, EG Robinson, 8x14"..65.00
Poster, Crossfire, 1947, R Young, cp, 27x41"..............35.00
Poster, Cry of the City, 1948, Victor Mature, cp, 27x41".......35.00
Poster, Deep Blue Sea, 1955, Vivien Leigh, 27x41"..........25.00
Poster, Desire Me, 1947, Greer Garson, 27x41"............50.00
Poster, Destination Tokyo, 1943, Cary Grant, 14x36".........50.00
Poster, Edward My Son, 1949, Spencer Tracy, cp, 27x41".....50.00
Poster, First Traveling Saleslady, 1956, Ginger Rogers, 27x41".25.00
Poster, Flying Deuces, 1939, Laurel & Hardy, 27x41"........400.00

Poster, Follow That Dream, 1962, Elvis Presley, 41x81".......45.00
Poster, Foreign Affair, 1948, M Dietrich, 81x81".............100.00
Poster, Go West, Young Lady; 1941, Glenn Ford, 27x41"......45.00
Poster, Gone w/t Wind, Italian, set of 3 posters + 3 lobbies...125.00
Poster, Gone w/t Wind, shows Clark Gable & Vivien Leigh.....85.00
Poster, Guide for the Married Man, 1967, W Matthau, 27x41"..15.00
Poster, Harvey, 1950, James Stewart, 14x36", minor tape stains.50.00
Poster, He Who Gets Slapped, 1924, Lon Chaney, Sr; 22x14"..275.00
Poster, Hidden Menace, 1927, C Hutchison, cp, 27x41".......150.00
Poster, His First Flame, 1927, H Langdon, Mack Sennett, 41".600.00
Poster, Hold That Kiss, 1938, Mickey Rooney, 14x36"........65.00
Poster, Inspector General, 1949, Danny Kaye, 27x41"........25.00
Poster, Island in the Sky, 1953, J Wayne, 41x81"............65.00
Poster, Jungle Man Eaters, 1954, J Weissmuller, cp, 27x41"....30.00
Poster, King of the Roaring '20s, 1961, Mickey Rooney, 27x41".15.00
Poster, Latin Lovers, 1953, Lana Turner, 27x41".............25.00
Poster, Mask of Diijon, 1946, Erich Von Stroheim, 27x41"....50.00
Poster, Mask of Dimitrios, 1944, Peter Lorre, 14x36".........50.00
Poster, Mr Ace, 1946, George Raft, cp, 27x41"...............60.00
Poster, My Favorite Brunette, 1947, Bob Hope, 27x41".......40.00
Poster, Raw Wind in Eden, 1958, E Williams, 27x41".........20.00
Poster, Shamus, 1973, Burt Reynolds, 27x41"................10.00
Poster, Story of Mankind, 1957, Marx Brothers, 27x41".......35.00
Poster, Tarzan & the Slave Girl, 1950, Lex Barker, 27x41".....25.00
Poster, Ten Tall Men, 1951, Burt Lancaster, 27x41"..........30.00
Poster, That Wonderful Urge, 1949, Tyrone Power, 27x41"....30.00
Poster, The Conspirators, 1944, Hedy Lamarr, 27x41"........65.00
Poster, The Farmer's Daughter, 1947, L Young, 27x41".......65.00
Poster, The Fly, 1958, Vincent Price, 14x36"................40.00
Poster, The Wife's Relations, 1928, Turpin, cp, 27x41"......350.00
Poster, This Property Is Condemned, 1966, R Redford, 27x41"..15.00
Poster, Vertigo, 1958, Hitchcock/D, Bass art, rolled, 40x60"...200.00
Poster, Wayward Wife, 1954, G Lollobrigida, rolled, 22x28"....15.00
Poster, Will Success Spoil Rock Hunter?, 1957, Mansfield, 41"..20.00
Poster, Wings of Eagles, 1957, John Wayne, 27x41".........40.00
Poster, Witness to Murder, 1954, Barbara Stanwyck, 27x41"....20.00
Poster, World of Henry Orient, 1964, Peter Sellers, 27x41".....15.00
Poster, Yellow Submarine, Italian, 47x63"...................35.00
Pressbook, A Fistful of Dollars, 1966, C Eastwood, 12 pgs......25.00
Pressbook, Anatomy of a Murder, 1959, James Stewart, 10 pgs..15.00
Pressbook, Caine Mutiny, 1954, Bogart, 20 pgs, cover loose.....60.00
Pressbook, Cannibal Attack, 1954, J Weissmuller, 6 pgs.......15.00
Pressbook, Hatari!, 1962, John Wayne, 32 pgs...............20.00
Pressbook, Hotel Imperial, 1939, Ray Milland, 24 pgs, sm tear..40.00
Pressbook, Key Largo/Treasure of Sierra Madre, 1953, 12 pgs..25.00
Pressbook, Meet John Doe, Goodwill release, G Cooper, 12 pgs..25.00
Pressbook, Ministry of Fear, 1944, Ray Milland, 20 pgs.......30.00
Pressbook, On the Riviera, 1951, Danny Kaye, 12 pgs........10.00
Pressbook, Poppy, 1936, British, WC Fields..................50.00
Pressbook, River of No Return, 1945, M Monroe, 16 pgs.......25.00
Pressbook, Scared to Death, 1947, B Lugosi, 12 pgs.........40.00
Pressbook, Some Like It Hot, 1959.......................65.00
Pressbook, Tarzan's Greatest Adventure, 1959, S Gordon, 8 pgs.10.00
Pressbook, The Alamo, 1961, John Wayne, 12 pgs...........10.00
Pressbook, The Good, The Bad & The Ugly; 1968, British......20.00
Pressbook, These Wilder Years, 1956....................15.00
Pressbook, To Kill A Mockingbird, 1963..................15.00
Pressbook, Treasure of Sierra Madre, 1948................175.00
Pressbook, You Only Live Twice, 1967...................50.00
Program, Ben Hur, 1960...............................10.00
Program, Gone w/t Wind, 1939, black back................75.00
Program, 2001: A Space Odyssey, 1968..................50.00
Promotional packet, Gone w/t Wind, posters/film info, VG.....650.00
Script, Gone w/t Wind, MGM vault copy, unbound...........350.00

Sheet music, Casablanca, 1941, Bogart & Bergman cover......25.00
Sheet music, From Here To Eternity, 1953, Never Again.......25.00
Sheet music, High Society, Grace Kelly on cover.............20.00
Sheet music, The Paleface, 1948, Buttons & Bows, Bob Hope...10.00
Sheet music, The Three Caballeros, 1944, Disney, You Belong..15.00
Sheet music, True Love, G Kelly/B Crosby/F Sinatra cover.....20.00
Standee, cardboard; A Lion In The Streets, Cagney, 1953, 60".100.00
Standee, cardboard; Donovan's Reef, 1963, J Wayne, 30x60"...75.00
Standee, cardboard; Goodbye Mr Chipps, 1968, 30x60"........15.00
Standee, cardboard; Love Nest, 1951, Marilyn Monroe, 30x60".150.00
Standee, cardboard; Storm Warning, 1951, Reagan, 30x60"....250.00
Standee, cardboard; Wild in the Country, 1961, Elvis, 30x60"..100.00
Still, A Place in the Sun, Taylor/Cliff/Winters, set of 6........65.00
Still, Cahill, US Marshall; J Wayne, color, 8x10", set of 8......30.00
Still, Hello Dolly!, 1969, B Streisand, b/w, 8x10", set of 19.....20.00
Still, Mighty Joe Young, 1949, shows Joe, b/w, 8x10"...........5.00
Window card, Asphalt Jungle, Marilyn Monroe, 1950, 14x22"...60.00
Window card, Let's Make It Legal, M Monroe, 1951, 14x22"....30.00
Window card, Love Nest, M Monroe, 1951, 14x22"............30.00
Window card, Monkey Business, M Monroe, 1952, 14x22".......40.00
Window card, O'Henry's Fullhouse, M Monroe, 1952, 14x22"...30.00
Window card, We're Not Married, M Monroe, 1952, 14x22"....30.00

Mt. Washington

The Mt. Washington Glass Works was founded in 1837 in South Boston, Massachusetts, but moved to New Bedford in 1869, after purchasing the facilities of the New Bedford Glass Company. Frederick S. Shirley became associated with the firm in 1874. Two years later the company reorganized and became known as the Mt. Washington Glass Company. In 1894, it merged with the Pairpoint Manufacturing Company, a small Brittania works nearby, but continued to conduct business under its own title until after the turn of the century. The combined plants were equipped with the most modern and varied machinery available, and boasted a working force with experience and expertise rival to none in the art of blowing and cutting glass.

In addition to their fine cut glass, they are recognized as the first American company to make cameo glass, an effect they achieved through acid cutting methods. In 1885, Shirley was issued a patent to make Burmese, the yellow glassware tinged with a delicate pink blush. Another patent issued in 1886 allowed them the rights to produce Rose Amber, or amberina, a transparent ware shading from ruby to amber. Pearl Satin Ware and Peachblow, so named for its resemblance to a rosy peach skin, were patented the same year. One of their most famous lines, Crown Milano, was introduced in 1893. It was an opal glass either free blown or pattern molded, tinted a delicate color and decorated with enameling and gilt. Royal Flemish was patented in 1894, and is considered the most rare of the Mt. Washington art glass lines. It was decorated with raised gold enameled lines dividing the surface of the ware in much the same way as lead lines divide a stained glass window. The sections were filled in with one or several transparent colors, and further decorated in gold enamel with florals, foliage, beading, and medallions.

See also specific types, such as Crown Milano, Burmese, Royal Flemish, etc.

Biscuit jar, cream w/HP flowers, scroll relief, SP lid/bale.......225.00
Biscuit jar, ovoid w/swirl ribs, pink w/daisies................395.00
Bride's bowl, pk/wht cameo cut w/birds/flowers, gold wash fr...950.00
Celery vase, amberina Dia Quilt...........................375.00
Condiment, salt/pepper/cruet, amberina, Pairpoint fr.........475.00
Creamer, satin w/HP florals, SP rim/hdl....................55.00
Flower frog, mushroom shape, beige satin w/mc leaves, 2¾"...125.00

Bride's basket, Napoli glass, $750.00.

Jar, melon rib, lav irid outlined leaves on pale florals, 5½".....275.00
Lamp, Delft globe & base, 9¼"...........................585.00
Lamp, melon rib shade w/enamel florals on beige, 6"........500.00
Mustard, columned ribs, lav/bl/gr floral on wht opaque, SP top..65.00
Plate, chimney; horses in meadow, HP, 1890................125.00
Plate, winter scene, turned-up edge, orig paper label, 11¾"....425.00
Rose bowl, rose to pk satin, lg...........................110.00
Rose bowl, satin w/cherub decor, lg.......................250.00
Salt shaker, Columbian Expo, egg shape....................80.00
Salt shaker, Delft......................................145.00
Salt shaker, pewter lid, rnd w/enamel flowers, 2"...........50.00
Salt shaker, 5 lobed, pk/wht w/bl flowers..................40.00
Shakers, egg shape w/floral, Pairpoint SP holder, pr.........285.00
Shakers, melon, orig top, pr..............................75.00
Shakers, rib barrel, peach to lt yel, floral, Pairpoint fr, pr......225.00
Sugar shaker, egg shape, peach satin to lt yel w/gr floral.....200.00
Sugar shaker, straw/dia cutting, egg shape, M.............375.00
Tumbler, pink to salmon satin, floral decor................110.00
Tumbler, satin, salmon cased, w/enamel decor.............135.00
Vase, bl/wht MOP, swirl pull-up, wht cased, 7".............475.00
Vase, jack-in-the-pulpit, lusterless wht, 10½"...............285.00
Vase, Lava, flared/squat w/circle shoulder hdls, disk ft, 3½"...950.00
Vase, Verona, page boy in court regalia on rose bkground, 16".750.00

Mulberry China

Mulberry china was made by many of the Staffordshire area potters from about 1830 until the 1850s. It is a transfer printed earthenware or ironstone named for the color of its decorations, a purplish brown resembling the juice of the mulberry. Shades vary; some pieces look almost gray, with only a hint of purple. Some of the patterns, Corean, Jeddo, Pelew, and Formosa for instance, were also produced in Flow Blue ware. Others seem to have been used exclusively with the mulberry color.

Abbey Ruins, plate, T Mayer, 10½".....................35.00
Abbey Ruins, soap dish w/lid & matching insert............95.00

Adelaide's Bower, plate, 10½"..........................35.00
Allegheny, plate, Goodfellow, 9".......................45.00
Athens, cup, handleless................................50.00
Athens, plate, W Adams, 10½"..........................35.00
Athens, sauce dish, Meigh.............................28.00
Bochara, gravy boat...................................40.00
Bochara, plate, 10½"..................................35.00
Bochara, plate, 9"....................................30.00
Bochara, platter, 14".................................100.00
Bochara, sugar w/lid.................................100.00
Bochara, vegetable dish w/cover, large..................150.00
Bosphorus, plate, Marshall, 7½".......................25.00
Calcutta, plate, 9¾"..................................30.00
Chariot, soup plate, w/rim, 9¼".......................35.00
Chusan, cup plate....................................40.00
Chusan, platter, 15x11½".............................95.00
Corean, coffee pot, octagonal body, 9½"................195.00
Corean, creamer......................................95.00
Corean, cup & saucer, handleless......................45.00
Corean, cup plate....................................40.00
Corean, plate, PW & Co, 9½"..........................45.00
Corean, platter, oval, 16x12¾".......................185.00
Corean, platter, 12x15".............................160.00
Corean, platter, 18"................................250.00

Vegetable bowl, Chepstow pattern, marked Woods and Sons, Manufacturers, 2" deep, 9¾" long, $50.00.

Cornflower, platter, Stoke on Trent, 10"................35.00
Cypress, coffee pot, Davenport.......................155.00
Cypress, plate, 9"...................................35.00
Cypress, platter, 13¾x10½"...........................95.00
Cypress, sauce......................................25.00
Cypress, wash bowl..................................150.00
Eagle, cup & saucer, Podmore & Walker................75.00
Eagle, plate, 9¾"....................................40.00
Etruscan Vase, plate, Wedgwood, 10¼"................45.00
Gazelle, cup & saucer, handleless; Adams..............95.00
Genoa, cup & saucer w/handle, Davenport, 1852........40.00
Jeddo, creamer & sugar, Adams........................90.00
Jeddo, cup & saucer, handleless.......................50.00
Jeddo, cup plate....................................40.00
Jeddo, pitcher, 8"..................................125.00
Jeddo, plate, 9¼"...................................42.50
Jeddo, platter, 12x15½", Adams......................125.00
Jeddo, sauce tureen w/under plate, oval...............150.00
Jeddo, teapot......................................175.00

Jeddo, vegetable w/lid, octagonal, Wm Adams & Son.........125.00
Kyber, cup & saucer, handleless; early Meir mk..............65.00
Kyber, plate, 10"...55.00
Madras, plate, W&B, 8"..25.00
Milan, relish, 6 sided, w/hdl......................................38.00
Moss Rose, butter dish w/lid.....................................125.00
Moss Rose, plate, 10"..38.00
Ning Po, cup & saucer...40.00
Ning Po, milk pitcher, R Hall.....................................100.00
Ning Po, plate, 10½"..24.00
Ning Po, plate, 7½"..16.00
Ning Po, plate, 9½"..20.00
Ning Po, shaving mug...85.00
Ning Po, vegetable, 9¼"..50.00
Pagoda, plate, Enoch Wood, 10"..................................50.00
Pelew, coffee pot..150.00
Pelew, cup & saucer, handleless..................................48.00
Pelew, deep dish, E Challinor, 9½" dia............................50.00
Pelew, gravy boat..85.00
Pelew, pitcher, milk; rope handle, 8"............................95.00
Pelew, plate, 10½"..70.00
Pelew, posset cup, E Challinor...................................32.50
Pelew, relish, shell shape, E Challinor...........................50.00
Peruvian, plate, 10"...45.00
Peruvian, teapot..225.00
Rhone Scenery, plate, 9½", TJ & J Mayer.....................30.00
Rhone Scenery, platter, 15½"....................................145.00
Shapoo, teapot...95.00
Soup, Hartford, CT; Jackson, 10½", M...........................75.00
Susa, plate, 7", Meigh & Son......................................28.00
Susa, sauce tureen & under tray, minor damage............200.00
Tavoy, creamer...95.00
Temple, bowl, 12" dia...85.00
Temple, cup & saucer, handleless................................70.00
Temple, gravy boat..95.00
Temple, pitcher, 7"..150.00
Temple, plate, 10"...60.00
Temple, sauce dish..20.00
Temple, teapot...235.00
Tonquin, platter, Heath & Co, ca 1830s, 12½x9½".........125.00
Vincennes, pitcher, 9½", J Alcock..............................135.00
Vincennes, platter, 10½x8"...50.00
Vincennes, platter, 15½"...125.00
Vincennes, tureen, w/cover, octagonal.........................125.00
Washington Vase, creamer, 5½"...................................80.00
Washington Vase, cup & saucer...................................40.00
Washington Vase, plate, 9"..35.00
Washington Vase, plate, 9¾".......................................38.00
Washington Vase, vegetable, octagonal w/cover.............150.00
Zoological, plate, Wood & Brownfield..........................45.00

Muller Freres

Henri Muller established a factory in 1900 at Croismare, France. He produced fine cameo art glass decorated with florals, birds, and insects in the Art Nouveau style. The work was accomplished by acid engraving and hand finishing. Usual marks were 'Muller', 'Muller Croismare', or 'Croismare, Nancy'.

In 1910, Henri and his brother Deseri formed a glassworks at Luneville. The cameo art glass made there was nearly all produced by acid cuttings of up to four layers, with motifs similar to those favored at Croismare. A good range of colors were used, and some pieces were gold flecked. Handles and decorative devices were sometimes applied by hand. To commemorate

Lindbergh's first flight, they designed a series of vases with cameo scenes featuring the monoplane. A second familiar type of ware they produced was an acid finished glass of bold mottled colors in the Deco style. Examples were signed 'Muller Freres' or 'Luneville'.

Chandelier, vine fixture, orange/bl mottled shades, sgn........650.00
Vase, cameo, river scene w/trees, 3 cuttings, 8¼x4½".......700.00
Vase, canal w/boats & windmill, in cameo, 12½"............450.00
Vase, chinoiserie decor w/phoenix, in cameo, 6¼"..........550.00
Vase, ferns & ladybugs, cameo & enamel, 6¾".............300.00
Vase, floral cameo, br/citron, sgn, 6½"......................900.00
Vase, gold w/br scenic cameo, 2 cuttings, 4¾x4"...........650.00
Vase, red orchid cameo on wht w/gr/br, 3 cuts, 8"..........785.00
Vase, shepherd & sheep, cameo, 9"........................1,195.00

Muncie

The Muncie Clay Products Company was founded in 1922 in Muncie, Indiana, by Charles Benham. By 1939 it had closed -- a casualty of the Great Depression. Little is known about the ware they manufactured. Only an occasional piece was marked with the name of the company; others bear only an 'A', '1A', '2A', or '3A'. The body of the ware is heavier than that of most of their contemporaries; the style of their vases is sturdy and simple. Glazes are varied; you will find subdued matt solids, mottled effects, and a drip glaze similar to Roseville's Carnelian.

Basket, rose w/gr over-drip, high loop hdl, mk E4, 11¾".......60.00
Ginger jar, pk/gr mottle, w/lid...................................40.00
Vase, blue, pinched top, 6"..15.00
Vase, cylinder, bl on bl drip glaze, ftd, full mk, 8"...........20.00
Vase, flat oval, panels, scalloped, gr over rose, 9½x9x2".....25.00
Vase, 4 finger, 3 hdls, 5"...35.00
Vase, 4 scallops, 2 wide/2 narrow, gr over lav, hdls, 6"......20.00

Bookends, mottled blue and beige glossy glaze, no mark, 6", $75.00.

Musical Instruments

The field of automatic musical instruments covers many different categories ranging from tiny dolls and trinkets concealing musical movements to huge organs and orchestrions which weigh many tons. Music boxes, first made in the late 18th century by Swiss watchmakers, were produced in both disc and cylinder models. The latter type employs a cylinder studded with tiny projections. As the cylinder turns, these projections lift the tuned teeth in the 'music comb' and the melody results. The value of the instrument depends upon the length of the cylinder and the quality of workmanship, though other factors must also be considered. Those in ornate cabinets or with extra features such as bells, mechanical birds, etc., often sell for much more. Units built into matching tables sell for about twice the amount they would bring otherwise. While small and medium size units are still being made today, most of the larger ones date from the 19th century.

Disc type music boxes utilize interchangeable steel discs with projecting studs, which by means of an intervening 'star wheel' cause a music comb to play. There are many different variations and mechanisms. Most were made in Germany, but some were produced in the United States. Among the most popular makes are Polyphon, Symphonion, and Regina. The latter was made in Rahway, New Jersey, from about 1894 through 1917.

Player pianos were made in a wide variety of styles. Early varieties consisted of a mechanism which pushed up to a piano and played on the keyboard by means of felt tipped fingers. These use sixty-five note rolls. Later models have the playing mechanisms built in. At first these also used sixty-five note rolls, but those produced from about 1908 until 1940 use eighty-eight note rolls.

Coin-operated electric pianos are deluxe versions of player pianos. These incorporate expression mechanisms so that by using special-made rolls they can play the hand recorded rolls of famous pianists. Popular makes include Ampico, Duo-Art, and Welte.

Roll operated organs were made in many forms, ranging from table-top models to large foot pumped versions. Of the latter, the Aeolian Orchestrelle is considered to be one of the best.

Unless noted, prices given are for instruments in fine condition, playing properly, with cabinets or cases in well preserved or refinished condition. In all instances, unrestored instruments sell for much less, as do pieces with broken parts, damaged cases, and the like. On the other hand, particularly superb examples in especially ornate case designs, and pieces which have been particularly well restored often will command more.

Banjo, 4 string, Tango, Vega Co, mk Fairbanks, 1920 . . . . 800.00
Banjo, 5 string, JC Haynes, in case, 35½" L 250.00
Banjo, 5 string, LB Gatcomb, pearl inlays to fingerboard, 35" . . 350.00
Box, Baker Troll Swiss, 17½" cylinder/12 tune, inlaid, EX . . 2,000.00
Box, Bremond Bells in View, 15" cylinder/10 airs/9 bells, 26" . 2,090.00
Box, Capital, Style A, interchangeable cuff, 1896, 7x15x11" . . 2,850.00
Box, Helvetia, 12" disc, stripped of veneer 1,000.00
Box, JH Heller Organocleide Piccolo Harpe, 19" cylinder 2,750.00
Box, Kalliope, 13¼" disc/single comb, walnut/orig picture 1,400.00
Box, keywind, 13" cylinder, brass bedplate, side door/3 levers . 1,600.00
Box, keywind, 2 tune 4" cylinder, 1840s, 3½x4x8½" 800.00
Box, Mermod Freres, four 13" 8 tune cylinders, inlay case . . . 2,600.00
Box, Mermod Freres, 8 tunes/5½" cylinder, coin-op, 6x9x17" . . 900.00
Box, Mermod Freres Ideal Sublime Harmonie, 4 cylinders 2,200.00
Box, Mira, 15½" duplex comb, 13x27x20", VG orig 2,400.00
Box, Mojon Manger Soprano Bells in View, 13" cylinder/12 air . 990.00
Box, Nicole Freres Overture, 9" cylinder, rosewood/inlay, 17" . 3,500.00
Box, Pillard Vaucher Fils, 13" cylinder/10 airs/zither, 22" 600.00
Box, Polyphon #104, 19½" disc, coin-op, case lacks gallery . . 2,500.00
Box, Polyphon #42D, 11" dbl comb, inlaid lid, M rstr 1,800.00
Box, Polyphon Excelsior, 15½" disc, single comb 2,000.00
Box, Regina, single comb/crank, mahog case 1,430.00
Box, Regina, 15½"/single comb, cherry case, EX orig 1,850.00
Box, Regina #11, 15½" disc, carved mahog case/stand, 42" . . . 2,200.00
Box, Regina #26, mahog w/cupola, 20¾", zither, M 4,900.00
Box, Stella, 17" disk, mahog w/burl walnut decor, drw, 28½" . 2,800.00
Box, Swiss, jewel movement, plays 8 songs, 1890 . . . . 1,700.00
Box, Swiss, 15" cylinder/12 airs, lever wind, rosewood/inlay . . . 800.00
Box, Symphonion, 19⅛" disc, upright table, coin op, 40x22" . 4,000.00
Box, 9" cylinder plays 8 Germany hymns, inlay, 6x20x8½" . . 1,800.00
Cello, Nicholas des Croies des Petits Champs a Paris, 1806 . . 2,750.00
Cornet, Antoine Courtois & Mille, SP, w/mute/case, 1870 . . . . 275.00
Cornet, silverplate, Curtois & Mille, Paris, 1878, in case 195.00
Disc, Regina, 15½", 9 for 50.00

Flute, Boehm, cocuswood, ca 1880, in case 350.00
Flute, Boehm, silver/gold, eng Karl Mendler/Muchen, 23½" . . 2,310.00
Flute, boxwood w/ivory mounts, 1810 . . . . 140.00
Flute, 6 keyed, boxwood, Astor & Co, ivory mounts, 1880 . . . . 375.00
Flute, 8 keyed, Tebaldo Monzani, silver mts/keys, case, 1825 . . 325.00
Guitar, harp; Gibson Co, Style V, 1910, pearly inlay, case . . . 1,150.00
Harp, Neoclassical style, gilt wood, 1800s 1,650.00
Mandolin, Ferrari, Naples, 1900 . . . . 100.00
Mandolin, Giovanni de Meglio, Naples, 1897 . . . . 115.00
Music desk, mahog, dbl, height adjusts, fluted support, 1900 . . 600.00
Nickelodeon, Cremona, Style A, art glass case, rfn/rstr 9,000.00
Nickelodeon, Nelson-Wiggen Style 3, art glass/walnut, orig . . 7,400.00
Oboe, Geo Miller, boxwood w/ivory mt, brass keys, 23" 2,200.00
Oboe, Mollenhauer & Sons, 14 nickel keys, ivory mount 450.00
Orchestrion, Seeburg L, art glass case, M rstr 39,500.00
Orchestrion, Wurlitzer BX, w/flute pipes 13,500.00
Orchestrion, Wurlitzer CX, auto changer/wonder lite, VG . . . 27,500.00
Organ, Aeolian Orchestrelle, 58 note, 72x69x54", rstr 5,000.00
Organ, Aeolian Orchestrelle F, M rstr 22,500.00
Organ, Aeolian Orchestrelle Y, 100" ornate oak case, rstr . . 10,500.00
Organ, band; North Tonawanda, Style 146, G orig 9,750.00
Organ, lap; button type, Bartlett, 1846, rosewood w/bird's eye . 500.00
Organ, Mirocourt, 17" barrel/10 airs, 51 pipes, walnut, 36" . . 1,650.00
Organ, parlor; 1 barrel/51 pipes/3 stops/10 tunes, 32x21", G . 1,250.00
Organ, pipe; Aeolian, 116 note, 2 manual player only 1,400.00
Organ, pipe; Wurlitzer residence, w/blower & bench, part rstr . 2,600.00
Organ, pump; extra octave, ornate solid oak, Williams, EX orig . 475.00
Organ, reed; Bridgeport, ornate, w/mirror, tall 500.00
Organ, walnut piano type case, EP Carpenter, rstr/rfn 800.00
Organ harp, Moller-Deagan, 37 note, lg 700.00
Organette, Ariston, 13" paper disc, ebony case, 9x15x15" 675.00
Organette, floor model, 21½" rolls, 47x34", G orig 2,500.00
Organette, Herophon, w/8 discs, lg, unrstr 650.00
Organette, McTammany, 7x14x13", EX orig 550.00
Piano, Berry Wood, auto-electric coin-op, bevel glass, 1900 . . 2,000.00
Piano, Duo Art Steinway, 73", rstr/rfn 4,900.00
Piano, grand; Steinway, Rococo carved rosewood, 1866, 102" . 4,950.00
Piano, Kingsbury upright w/pianocorder, walnut case 4,250.00
Piano, Marshall & Wendell Ampico A, 60" mahog grand, rstr . 5,750.00
Piano, street; 1¢ operated, 10 tune, maple, English, 1915, rst . 2,500.00
Piano, Tel-Electric, brass rolls 600.00
Piano, Weber Duo-Art, 68" walnut case, 1920s, VG orig 3,000.00
Recordo, Cable-Nelson upright grand, rstr/rfn 7,500.00
Roll, A La Bien Aimee, Schutt, played by Fannie Zeisler, lg 8.50
Roll, Duo Art, Nocturne, by Adler 7.50
Roll, Heart of My Heart, 88 note 3.50
Roll, 5th Nocturne, Leybach, played by Laura Danziger, lg 8.50
Saxophone, mk GC Conn, USA, in case 510.00
Tenor viol, Josephus Contreras, 1744 . . . . 2,250.00
Viola, David Tecchler Liuiaro/1703, br varnish, 2 bows/case . . 950.00
Viola, Leon Jolly/Luthier, French, length of back, 16" 1,100.00
Violano, double; Mills, rfn/rstr 27,500.00
Violin, David Rittner, Vienna, 1850 . . . . 315.00
Violin, Eugen Meinel, 1928, w/bow & case, 14" 700.00
Violin, Jokobos Stainer, yellow/red varnish, w/bow & case 300.00

Mustache Cups

Mustache cups were popular items during the late Victorian period, designed specifically for the man with the mustache! They were made in silverplate as well as china and ironstone. Decorations ranged from simple transfers to elaborately applied and gilded florals. To properly position the 'mustache bar', special cups were designed for the 'lefties' -- these are the rare ones!

Cup and saucer, rust-orange and cobalt with enamel daisies and gold encrusted decoration, $65.00.

Aurora SP, minor wear, Victorian	38.00
Bird & floral in gold on pk/yellow, scrolls/ribbed, w/saucer	40.00
Blue/gold flowers across front, #s on bottom, short, mug, NM	42.00
German, vertical ribs, hp roses/cornflowers, 'Present from...'	45.00
Gold flowers hang from rim, lower ½: red roses & leaves, NM	33.00
Green leaves, yel flowers, mug shape, NM	42.00
Off-wht china w/gold floral decor, ½: gold scroll on purple	31.00
Poppies on shaded gr to rose, ornate hdl, Bavaria, w/saucer	35.00
Red/bl flowers, gr leaves, tan lower ⅓, mug shape, NM	31.00
RS Prussia, florals	90.00

Nailsea

Nailsea is a term referring to clear or colored glass decorated in contrasting spatters, swirls, or loops. These are usually white, but may also be pink or blue. It was first produced in Nailsea, England, during the late 1700s, but was made in other parts of Britain and Scotland as well. Originally used for decorative novelties only, by 1845 pitchers, tumblers, and other practical items were being made from Nailsea glass.

Bellows bottle, on stand, wht w/red & bl loops, rigaree, 13¼"	625.00
Bottle, figural boot, clear w/wht loops, tooled mouth, 9¼"	130.00
Bowl, cranberry, satin finish, tri-con, 7"	350.00
Carafe, clear w/wht loops, applied ft & shoulder rings, 10"	200.00
Cruet, bl w/wht looping, clear hdl & ft, orig stopper, 8"	80.00
Flask, clear w/pink & tan loops, teardrop shape, 6¾"	100.00
Flask, clear w/pink & wht spiral stripes, ovoid, 7¼"	120.00
Flask, clear w/red & wht loops, blue mouth, teardrop, 9¼"	140.00
Flask, cobalt w/overlapped wht loops, teardrop shape, 6¾"	525.00
Flask, yel-gr w/wide wht spiral band, teardrop shape, 7"	170.00
Gemel bottle, wht w/blue loops, sheared mouth, 9"	130.00
Powder horn, lt bl-gr w/wht loops, applied body rings, 12¼"	160.00
Powder horn on stand, clear w/wht loops, applied rings, 12¼"	180.00
Rolling pin, clear w/ruby loops, 14"	115.00
Rolling pin, wht w/cranberry loops, 15"	125.00
Vase, red & wht, w/blk amethyst base & ears, 10½"	165.00

Nakara

Nakara was an opaque glassware made soon after the turn of the century by the C.F. Monroe Company. Though shapes were plainer and colors deeper, it was very similar to their famous Wave Crest line. Boxes of all sizes, pin trays, and dresser items of every sort were decorated with delicate hand painted florals, and 'squeeze bag' lace reserves transfer printed with portraits of classical figures, birds, or Victorian ladies. Ormolu handles, bases, and collars, and scented satin box linings added opulence to the already elegant ware.

The C.F. Monroe Company closed in 1916.

Box, Bishop's Hat, apricot w/HP bl dogwood, no lining, 5½"	475.00
Box, Bishop's Hat, bl w/pk flowers, orig lining, hinged, 3¾"	395.00
Box, bl w/pk, pk flowers, wht dots, 4½"	350.00
Box, bl w/pk & wht flowers, sgn, 3½x3½"	325.00
Box, bl w/pk floral, wht beading, 5"	375.00
Box, glove; shades of blue, lid w/allover florals	850.00
Box, gr w/wht clover on top, portrait w/in, 4¾" W	375.00
Box, hinged lid, mirror w/in, pk to yel w/enameling, 3½x6"	675.00
Box, match; bl & pk lilies, round	325.00
Box, ring; portrait, pk, 2½"	350.00
Candle holder, cherub on gr, ormolu mt	190.00
Dresser dish, pink floral, ormolu hdls, sgn	85.00
Hair receiver, little girls at outdoor tea in dia reserve	385.00
Humidor, frog reading paper, Nakara headline, 6¾"	700.00
Jar, rose w/angels playing in haystack, sgn, 6" dia	565.00
Tray, crown mold, pk w/wht florals, sgn, 6½" dia	275.00
Vase, cobalt w/florals in reserve, ormolu mt & ft, 9½x6½"	1,800.00
Vase, florals & beading on gr, ftd, 14"	875.00

Napkin Rings

Napkin rings became popular during the late 1800s. They were made from various materials. Among the most popular were the silverplated figural types, many of which are listed below. For other types, see specific materials.

Angel pushing ring w/butterfly on top	160.00
Angel writing on heart	95.00
Bambi, emb, mk WDP 800	42.00
Barrel, branch & leaf ft	45.00
Bird w/long tail on leaf, Meriden	75.00
Boston Terrier w/large fan ea side of ring, Pairpoint	125.00
Boy, standing w/ring on shoulder, Rogers Bros	165.00
Boy in floppy hat, books under arm, feeding begging dog	275.00
Boy in hat, sleeves rolled up, pushing barrel ring	145.00
Boy pulling boot	120.00
Boy pulling fancy cart, wheel revolves	195.00
Boy sitting on ftd base w/drumstick, Pairpoint	175.00
Boy w/cookie on ftd oval base, sgn, 3" figure	105.00
Boy w/drum in uniform stands at attention	235.00
Branch w/flowers & leaves at top holds ring, Meriden	65.00
Bug by ring, Shiebler	75.00
Bulldog beside ring	45.00
Bulldog sits chained to dog house, Simpson, Hall & Miller	275.00
Cat atop ring spits at dog w/paws on ring, Meriden	215.00
Cat on hind legs, one paw on ring, Knickerbocker	135.00
Cat on pillow w/tail in air	97.50
Cherries & leaves hang from ring, leaf base, ball ft, gold	165.00
Cherub, ring on bk, standing on oval base, ornate, Middletown	110.00
Cherub playing mandolin, 6¾"	75.00
Cherub standing on oval base w/leaves/scrolls/quilting	135.00
Cherubs ea side of ring, Victor Silver Co	60.00
Cherubs support ornate ring	85.00
Chick on wish bone, 'Best Wishes', Derby	72.00
Chinese Mandarin, head shaved/pigtail/robes/daisy at feet	275.00
Cow beside ring, round base	185.00
Cupid atop ring, dog w/front paws on ring	125.00

Cupid leans on ring w/ornate branch & flower 115.00
Cupid peers around ring, heart-shape base on wishbone, ft 135.00
Cupid standing by ring 125.00
Cupids, ea side of ring, scalloped base, Wilcox, #1536 . . . . 100.00
Dog chasing bird on ring 80.00
Dog w/glass eyes, ring forms center of body, 3" 125.00
Eagles, carrying ring, Rogers Bros, 2" 65.00
Eagles, 2 small w/wings spread, ea side of ring, Meriden 65.00
Fans on side, butterfly below, sq base, 4 ball ft, Meriden, 3" 95.00
Flower & leaf sprays hold ring, rnd base, Pairpoint 75.00
Fox & the grapes, ornate, full figure 145.00
Good Luck horseshoe on lg leaf base, finger grip hdl 75.00
Griffin sits atop ring, ornate base, Meriden 195.00
Hickory chair w/barrel ring 120.00
Kangaroo beside ring, EX 75.00
Kate Greenaway, boy & girl either side of ring 225.00
Kate Greenaway, boy holds ring w/right hand 185.00
Kate Greenaway, boy lying on tummy, hand under chin 190.00
Kate Greenaway, boy on foot stool base holds rope in hands . . . 225.00
Kate Greenaway, condiment set, S&P, napkin ring 260.00
Kate Greenaway, girl, long coat, muff, Meriden 210.00
Kate Greenaway, girl sits w/ring to her back 225.00
Kate Greenaway, girl w/dog 150.00
Kate Greenaway, girl w/dog ea side of ring 195.00
Kate Greenaway, girl w/goat, oval base, Meriden 225.00
Kate Greenaway, girls in coats w/hats & muffs, backs to ring . . . 245.00
Kate Greenaway, lady w/dog, ring in front, Wilcox 235.00
Koala bear figural, Australia, 2x3" dia 65.00
Kookaburra bird figural, 2½" 75.00
Lady waters flowers, barefoot, Eureka 275.00
Lily bud w/ring on leaf base, Meriden 60.00
Lion, rampant, on base mk Rogers, 3¼" 125.00
Lion, w/ring on back, crouching on rectangle base, dtd 1887 . . . 115.00
Lion pulling fancy cart, wheels revolve 195.00
Mickey Mouse, early 75.00
Monkey, dressed, missing cane 135.00
Ostrich on 1 side, kangaroo on other, leaf base, eng name 105.00
Peacock on perch, ea side of ring, ornate base, no mk 115.00
Pear & leaves hang from ring, leaf base, gold washed 165.00
Rabbit standing by ring 75.00
Seal beside ring, EX 95.00
Soldiers w/bugles ea side of ring 95.00
Squirrel eating nut beside ring, Barbour Silver, EX 48.00
Squirrel on hind legs w/large tail, beside ring, Wilcox 115.00
Turtle, ring on bk 65.00

Goat and cart with revolving wheels, 3" x 4¾", $300.00.

Nash

A. Douglas Nash founded the Corona Art Glass Company in 1929, in Long Island, New York. He produced tableware, vases, flasks, etc., using delicate artistic shapes and forms. After 1933, he worked for the Libbey Glass Company.

Bowl, opalescent rays, w/under tray, cranberry rims, 4¾" dia . . . 130.00
Champagne, threaded, twisted stem 40.00
Compote and candlesticks, red chintz, #RD89/#RD652, 3 pcs . . 850.00
Cordial, bl & gr chintz, 4" 55.00
Cordial, bl & gr chintz, 5½" 70.00
Rose bowl, icing glass, vaseline, reticulated, dimpled, 4½" 45.00
Tumbler, threaded 60.00
Vase, gold irid vertical stripes, blk herringbone between, 9½" . . 265.00
Vase, optic rib, irid, 12" 275.00
Vase, red w/silver chintz, EX shape, sgn/#d, 5¾" 625.00
Wine, pk & gr chintz, 6" 75.00

Netsukes

Netsukes are miniature Japanese carvings made with holes, either channeled or within the carved design, that allow it to be threaded onto a waist cord and worn with the kimono. Although most are of ivory, others were made of wood, metal, porcelain, or semi-precious stones. Some were inlayed or lacquered. They are found in many forms, but figurals are the most common and desirable. They range in size from 1" to 2", with a few up to 5". Prime considerations are condition, workmanship, subject matter, and material.

Horse and horsefly, signed, $50.00.

Abalone shell, crab w/2nd shell, shells form himotoshi, wood . . . 200.00
Amber w/carving 250.00
Blind Masseur, crouches/lifts stone, wood/ivory inlay, Gyokkei . . . 660.00
Buddah w/mirror, sgn, 2" 125.00
Cat, sleeping on leaf, wood 375.00
Daikoku, wood, sgn Gyokuyosai 525.00
Dessicated salmon, well depicted in dk sea pine, 1800s 770.00
Dragon, coiling around jewels, wood, sgn, 1800s 415.00
Fish, three, wood 675.00
Fisherwoman, child on bk, red/yellow fish 87.50
Fox god on hind legs, rests forepaws on celestial jewel, 1700s . . 550.00
Goat, seated, kid on bk, boxwood/horn inlay, sgn Itsuo 880.00
Group of shishi, lg dog holds ball/movable ball in mouth, sgn . 1,045.00
Hanasaka Jiji, on tree trunk, scatters ashes, wood/inlay, sgn . . . 700.00
Hotei, group of boys carrying him w/in his sack, inlaid, sgn . . . 605.00
Hotei, seated, rests on sack, glazed porcelain, sgn Masakazu . . 415.00
Hotei, sgn w/seal 375.00
Karako, seated, spilling toys from basket, sgn Komin 660.00
Kylin, reclining, mouth open, teeth bared, sgn, 1x1¼x1¾" 50.00
Legend Maiden & octopus 110.00
Lotus fruit, agate 225.00

Man, elder, w/basket, gr pants & hat on bk	125.00
Man, elder, w/staff, animal on bk, sgn	95.00
Man, scroll in 1 hand, knife in other, basket to left, sgn	95.00
Man, shaving wood, sgn Mitsukiyo	600.00
Man, turning head, mask face	95.00
Man, w/box, wood, sgn Abe Noseinei	375.00
Man, w/fan, wood, sgn	275.00
Man, w/gr frog	95.00
Manju w/shishimai mask, lacquered, metal rims, 2 part, 1800s	220.00
Mask box, opens to Noh stage w/actors, ivory inset, Jumasa	825.00
Mask cluster, 7 Noh w/red/blk details, sgn Gyokuyosai	465.00
Monkey, reclining atop catfish, holding gourd, 1700s, unsgn	660.00
Mushroom cluster, wood, 1800s	495.00
Musician, w/drum, kneeling, ivory/inlaid horn, sgn Gyokuyosai	465.00
New Year's study, Jorojin as rice cake, 1781, sgn Hidemasa	605.00
Nio, stern expression, sits atop sandal, wood, sgn Gyokuyosai	550.00
Noh preformer, kneeling w/fan before him, inlaid horn, Yausaki	465.00
Octopus, clutching edge of broken pot, inlay eyes, Kogetsu	990.00
Oni, trapped in box, wood	475.00
Quail, two, joined atop 2 millet stalks, inlaid eyes, Okatomo	465.00
Rabbit, ceramic, sgn	375.00
Sage, head on arms, reclines on shishi, 1800s, sgn	275.00
Sambaso mask, ivory, Mitsukiyo	500.00
Sarumuwashi, lying on side, monkey takes fruit from basket	990.00
Scholar w/fan, wood, Masakazu	650.00
Sennin, on rocks, shishi seated alongside, 1700s, unsgn	415.00
Shaft w/butterflies, fruit; vine ivory	250.00
Shishi, blk ebony	325.00
Shishi head, wood, Jin Gord	675.00
Shrine, wood; ivory figure w/in, Fukurokuju	375.00
Tea jar, wrapped at top w/tied cloth, lacquered, 1800s	495.00
Tiger, seated, head to left, wood/brass eyes, sgn Minko	990.00
Tobasaku, elaborate hair/dress, 3 peaches in basket, 1700	880.00
Turtle, w/3 babies on bk, sgn, 1½x1¾"	60.00
Wild beast, Baku, turtle in paws, rabbit in rear, sgn, 2¼" L	60.00
Wild boar, wood	275.00
Winged horse, 1800s	148.00
Woman, kneeling, wood, Urashenia	575.00
Woman, w/fan	65.00
Woman, w/lg pot, 2"	65.00
Wrestlers, 2 figure, pop-eye	145.00

New Hall

The New Hall Company was established in the early 1780s in the Shelton district of England. In the early years, they produced hard paste dinnerware typically decorated with simple floral sprays, often assigning a number rather than a name to their patterns. By 1812, a bone china body was favored and styles revised to suit the fashion. Decorations became more elaborate. Much of the ware was unmarked and is often attributed to Worcester. Occasionally a piece was marked 'New Hall' within a double circle. Production ceased by 1835.

Cup & saucer, handleless; polychrome fruit/foliage	45.00
Sugar w/cover, gilt decor, 1790, 4" dia	220.00
Teapot, silver form, mkd, 1770s	575.00

New Martinsville

The New Martinsville Glass Company took its name from the town in West Virginia where it began operations in 1901. In the beginning years, pressed tablewares were made in crystal as well as colored opalescent glass. Considered an innovator, the company was known for their imaginative applications of the medium in creating lamps made entirely of glass, vanity sets, figural decanters, and novelty figures. The company was purchased by Viking Glass in 1944. It is still in production; current wares are marked 'Viking' or 'Rainbow Art'.

Candle holder, Moondrops, green flat	4.50
Cocktail shaker, Moondrops, dk green	20.00
Compote, Ancestral #14, crystal	7.00
Compote, Moondrops, ruby, 4"	35.00
Console bowl, w/wings, Moondrops, amber, 13"	15.00
Console set, swan & pr swan candlesticks, amber	45.00
Creamer, Moondrops, ruby, lg	14.00
Creamer & sugar, individual, Moondrops, ruby	28.00
Cup, Moondrops, amber	6.00
Cup, Moondrops, dk gr	7.50
Cup, Moondrops, ruby	9.00
Cup & saucer, Janice, lt blue	10.00
Cup & saucer, Moondrops, amber	10.00
Cup & saucer, Moondrops, dk gr	10.00
Decanter, Moondrops, amber	28.00
Figurine, baby bear, crystal	45.00
Figurine, baby bear, satin finish	45.00
Figurine, police dog	48.00
Figurine, rooster	50.00
Figurine, seal, lg	55.00
Figurine, squirrel, crystal, w/base	40.00
Figurine, tiger	90.00
Goblet, water; Mt Vernon, ruby	14.00
Plate, luncheon; Janice, lt blue, 8"	10.00
Plate, luncheon; Moondrops, dk gr	5.00
Platter, Moondrops, pink	20.00
Sherbet, Ancestral #14, crystal	3.50
Swan, emerald, 7½"	18.00
Swan, Prelude etch	35.00
Tumbler, Moondrops, amber, 9 oz, 4¾"	5.00
Tumbler, Moondrops, dk gr, 4¾"	10.00
Tumbler, Moondrops, ftd, amber, 5¼"	10.00
Vase, cornucopia, #650	25.00
Vase, Radiance, flared, blue, 10"	20.00
Wine, Moondrops, ruby, 4 oz, 4¼"	17.00

Newcomb

The Newcomb College of New Orleans, Louisianna, established a pottery in 1895 to provide the students with first-hand experience in the fields of art and ceramics. Using locally dug clays -- red and buff in the early years, white burning by the turn of the century -- potters were employed to throw the ware which the ladies of the college decorated.

Until about 1910, a glossy glaze was used on ware decorated by slip painting or incising. After that, a matt glaze was favored. Soft blues and greens were used almost exclusively, and the decorative themes were chosen to reflect the beauty of the South. 1930 marked the end of the matt glaze period, and the art pottery era.

Various marks used by the pottery include an 'N' within a 'C', sometimes with 'HB' added to indicate a 'hand-built' piece. The potter often incised his initials into the ware, and the artists were encouraged to sign their work. Among the most well known artists were Sadie Irvine, Henrietta Bailey, and Fannie Simpson.

Bowl, carved daffodils on bl, sgn JM/AFS, 5¾" dia	300.00
Bowl, dogwood/yel centers/gr leaves, Sadie Irvine, 2¾"	285.00
Bowl, flowers at top edge, #263, PZ 75, 8" dia	500.00
Bowl, iris band at top on bl matt, H Bailey, 4¾x6¼"	500.00
Bowl vase, floral, Anna F Simpson, JM, 5½" dia	450.00

Vase, white florals on blue, signed Henrietta Bailey, 8", $750.00.

Bud vase, lilies, Henrietta Bailey, 8"......................485.00
Candlestick, blue w/many magnolias, sgn AFS...............400.00
Coaster, pk floral on bl.................................325.00
Creamer, gr matt, 4¾"...................................250.00
Inkwell, Sadie Irvine, 3 pcs.............................700.00
Vase, bl w/band of wht narcissus, sgn Anne F Simpson, 3½"...300.00
Vase, bl w/long gr stems/wht flowers, sgn, rpr hairline, 6½"....325.00
Vase, buttress, incised geometrics, gr crystalline, 3½".........260.00
Vase, daylight scene, mossy trees, Sadie Irvine, 3¼".........625.00
Vase, florals, bl/yel centers, gr leaves, bulbous, Irvine, 4".....375.00
Vase, florals, incised, bl-gr w/cream, Sadie Irvine, 1910, 6"....525.00
Vase, florals, long leaves, Sadie Irvine, 4½"................450.00
Vase, florals, pk on lavender-bl, Sadie Irvine, 2¾"...........265.00
Vase, florals, sgn HM, #22, 3½".........................475.00
Vase, florals in relief on purple, orig label, 5"..............200.00
Vase, gr crystalline decor, 3½".........................240.00
Vase, irises w/orange centers, yellow tracings, HLB/JM, 10½"..700.00
Vase, landscape, Henrietta Bailey, incised banyan trees, 6", G..800.00
Vase, moon shines through mossy trees, Sadie Irvine, 2¼x2½".525.00
Vase, moon through trees w/moss, sgn AFS, matt gr, 10x7"....950.00
Vase, moon/moss, Sadie Irvine, 5"........................675.00
Vase, oleander, bl matt, H Bailey, full body, paper label, 5"....625.00
Vase, pink w/aubergine channels, sgn Sadie Irvine, 5".........330.00
Vase, sunset scenic, AFS/FH, 5¾".......................700.00
Vase, wht lilies/gr stems on bl, sgn AFS, 6"...............500.00
Vase, 4 pendant cartouches, bl w/rose, Irvine, 3", EX........250.00

Newspapers

Newspapers are primarily collected for their news content. Those reporting important political or military events in the history of our country are usually of greater value.

Key:
fs----folio size   qs----quarto size
lr----letter   ss----single sheet
omh----ornate masthead   wc----wood cut

Adventurer, 1752, Vol 1/#1, London; popular paper, 6 pgs, EX..16.00
Adventurer, 1753, London; discussion of topics, omh, 6 pgs, EX..5.00
Athenian Mercury, 1692, London; question/answer style, ss, 12".20.00

Boston Evening Transcript, Apr 16, 1912; Titanic's Survivors....35.00
Boston Gazette, Nov 1770; P Rever wc in mh, thick paper, EX..59.00
Boston Gazette & Country Journal, 1769; omh, fs, EX.........48.00
Boston Weekly Messenger, Dec 15, 1825; Pres message, sgn.....8.00
Bucks County Patriot, 1827, Pennsylvania; Gen Jackson, VG.....4.00
Buxton Blade, 1882, Vol 1/#1, Dakota Territory; rare.........125.00
California Farmer, 1855; farm & other news, omh, VG..........7.50
Carlisle Republican, 1820, PA; speech: Gov DeWitt Clinton, G....6.00
Carolina Spartan, Oct 25, 1860; Anti-Slavery Government, G.....8.00
Carolina Spartan, 1864, Spartanburg, SC; war news, ss, VG.....35.00
Chicago Daily Tribune, 1881; Billy t/Kid shot, James brothers...55.00
Chicago Tribune/Daily News, 1927, Paris edition; Lindbergh.....55.00
Christian Sun, 1856, Virginia; typical Southern religious.........7.00
City Gazette & Daily Advertiser, Jan 1977, Charleston, SC; omh.37.00
Colorado Miner, 1872, Colo Territory; typical news, rag paper...30.00
Columbian Centinel, Mar 11, 1809; Embargo Act/Jefferson, EX..32.00
Columbian Centinel, 1802; long joke tribute to US judiciary......5.00
Columbian Centinel, 1807, Boston; Burr's Prosecution, G........7.00
Connecticut Courant, Jan 1, 1787; American Revolution, ss, VG.11.00
Connoisseur, 1756, London; discusses various topics, 6 pgs......5.50
Courier, June 1862, Natchez, Miss; brown paper, war news, ss..125.00
Courier, 1812, London; To The People of KY, by WH Harrison..4.00
Daily Advertiser, 1794, NY; lg ad for G Washington's dentist....12.00
Daily Alta California, 1857; news, shipping ads, lg size.........12.00
Daily Arizona Citizen, 1879, Vol 1; John Clum publisher, VG....23.00
Daily Crimson, 1866; by students of Harvard U, 4 pgs, qs, EX....4.00
Daily Georgian, 1840; ads: Van Buren for President, slaves, VG...7.50
Daily Herald, July 5, 1863; Extra, Mass; Battle of Gettysburg...185.00
Daily Picayune, Aug 2, 1862, New Orleans; Union occupation, ss.22.00
Desert Evening News, 1876, Utah Territory; Indian Wars.......12.00
Freeman's Journal, 1782, Phila; Justice wc/mh, anti-Tories, EX..60.00
Guardian, 1713, London; editorial-type, ss, VG...............12.50
Hampshire Gazette, Jan 8, 1800; Washington's death in detail...85.00
Harper's Weekly, Jan 9, 1869; Winslow Homer full pg print.....26.00
Heraclitus Ridens, 1681, London; 'dialogue of Jest & Earnest'...28.00
Herald--Gazette for t/Country, 1796, NY; Anniv of Independence.11.00
Honolulu Advertiser, Dec 8, 1941; lg headline re: start of war...90.00
Independent Chronicle, May 30, 1805; very displayable omh, EX..9.00
Independent Chronicle, 1790, Boston; Congress of America, VG.11.00
Independent Chronicle, 1805, Boston; Thomas Paine lr, omh.....9.00
Lloyds of London, 1862; US Civil War news, estimated costs....25.00
London Gazette, Dec 1667; Capt Lightfoot Guilty, New World...34.00
London Gazette, 1674; ss printed both sides, VG.............14.00
Military Monitor, Aug 1812, Vol 1/#1, New York; war news, qs..26.00
Military Monitor & American Register, 1813; Madison inaugural..23.00
Mirror, 1779, London; literary type, front pg letter to author....5.00
Misc Scrap Book, 1834, Vol 1/#1, Hartford; unusual, VG......15.00
Montana Mining Journal, 1891; mining scene wc in mh, 8 pgs....8.00
National Anti-Slavery Standard, 1845, NY; slavery discussed......5.50
National Intelligencer, Aug 23, 1814; last pre Brit invasion.....325.00
National Intelligencer, 1818; Pres Monroe re: Cherokee treaty...13.00
National Intelligencer, 1845; Capt Fremont's Report on West....12.00
New England Chronicle, Oct 12, 1775; reports of Bunker Hill..550.00
New Observer, 1691, London; interesting dialogue, ss, 8x12"....38.00
New York Herald, Nov 8, 1860; Lincoln elected, charts, etc.....57.00
New York Observer, Dec 23, 1848; details of CA gold rush......5.00
New York Observer, 1853; religous reporting, lg sz, VG.........3.00
New York Tribune, Oct 19, 1865; Andersonville trials..........10.00
Nippon Times, Nov 1945, Tokyo; in English, re: reconstruction...5.00
NY Herald, Apr 8, 1862; The National Tax, new gas rates, etc...4.00
NY Herald, Dec 23, 1863; articles on Ulysses S Grant, EX.......5.00
NY Herald Tribune, Oct 12, 1934; Lindbergh kidnapping trial...14.00
NY Herald Tribune, 1934; Crowd Jeers Hitler in Munich, 24 pgs.12.00
NY Mirror, 1833; literature & fine arts, qs, EX...............3.50

NY Times, Apr 2, 1864; Lynch Law In Nevada, few stains.......4.50
NY Times, April 19, 1865; Lincoln assassination/blk border, VG.19.00
NY Times, 1864; Success of Gen Custer's Cavalry, Civil War.....8.00
NY Tribune, Aug 23, 1865; Trial of Wirz, Pleads Not Guilty....10.00
NY Tribune, Aug 5, 1865; map showing cable across Atlantic, VG.4.00
NY Tribune, July 7, 1865; assassination prisoners guilty, VG....26.00
Oakland Tribune, Apr 22, 1906; SF Earthquake & Fire, 10 pgs.17.00
Observator, 1681, London; dialogue, old style type, ss, 8x12"...12.50
Oxford Gazette, 1665, #6; later became London Gazette, ss, VG.99.00
Patriot Union, July 13, 1865, Harrisburg; Conspirator Trial.....24.00
Pennsylvania Ledger, 1778; Tory paper in British occupation...168.00
Pennsylvania Packet, Aug 1782; lr reflects on Cornwallis, omh...39.00
Penny Whistle, 1891, Oakland, CA; 8 pgs, very sm: 4x5½".......4.00
Phila Inquirer, July 27, 1861; Battle of Bull Run, w/maps, EX...38.00
Pioneer & Democrat, 1860; Washington Territory, Pony Express.15.00
Pioneer & Democrat, 1860; Washington Territory, Pres message.13.00
Porcupine's Gazette, 1798, Phila; porcupine wc in mh, VG.....10.00
Port Folio, July 14, 1804, Phila; death of Alex Hamilton, qs....66.00
Puck, 1885, New York; full pg Mark Twain...Best Humorist, EX.22.00
Puget Sound Daily Courier, 1874; Washington Territory, omh...13.00
Repertory, 1807, Boston; news of the day, fs, G.............4.00
Sacramento Daily Record-Union, July 1876; Custer's Last Stand..75.00
Salem Gazette, Nov 7, 1820; Gov calls for day of Thanksgiving..4.00
Salem Gazette, 1796; 6 EX wc of ships on front pg, EX.........9.00
San Francisco Examiner, Dec 8, 1941; US-Jap War! 28 pg......85.00
San Francisco Examiner, Dec 8, 1941; 2nd Hawaii Raid, photos.40.00
Stockton Daily Record, June 6, '44/6 AM Extra; Invasion Begins.27.00
Tatler, 1710, London; social/literary/misc, ss, 12x7", VG.......12.00
The Age, 1849, Augusta, Maine; Admission of CA as State......5.00
The War, 1812, New York; war reports, 4 pgs, qs, VG........21.00
Warren Ledger, 1864, Pennsylvania; Civil War, eagle mh.......4.00
Weekly Messenger, Sept 1814, Boston; Capture of Washington...8.00
World, 1756, London; 'humorous exposure of follies of the age'..5.50
Zion's Herald, Jan 28, 1824, Boston; mostly religious, omh......4.00

Niloak

Benton, Arkansas, was an area rich with natural clay, high in quality and easily accessible. During the last half of the 1800s, a dozen potteries flourished there, but by 1898, the only one remaining was owned by Charles Dean Hyten. In 1909 he began to experiment, trying to preserve in his finished ware the many colors of the native clay. By 1912 he had perfected a method that produced the desired effect. He obtained a U.S. patent for his hand crafted Niloak Mission pottery, characterized by swirling layers of browns, blues, red, and buff clays. Only a few early pieces were glazed both inside and out; these are extremely rare. After the process was perfected, only the interior was glazed. The ware was marked 'Niloak', the backward spelling of Kaolin, a type of fine porcelain clay. No sooner had production began than the pottery burned, but Hyten rebuilt, and added a stoneware line called Eagle Pottery. Hywood, an inexpensive novelty ware, was introduced in 1929 -- an attempt to boost sales during the onset of the depression years. Until 1934, when the management changed hands, the line was marked 'Hywood-Niloak'. After that, 'Hywood' no longer appeared on the ware.

Hyten left the pottery in 1941; in 1946 the operation closed.

Values listed below are average show prices. Our Niloak experts advise us, however, that in certain areas, prices may yet be from 20% to 30% under the norm.

Candle holders, Mission Ware, sgn, 4", pr.................130.00
Candlestick, Mission Ware, 6".............................80.00
Candlestick, Mission Ware, 9¾x6".........................195.00
Jug, matt blue, w/stopper, 7".............................55.00
Match holder, Howitzer, bl.................................35.00
Mug, Mission Ware, bl/cream, pat pend....................85.00

Pitcher, bl, unusual shape, sgn, 5"........................20.00
Pitcher, wht w/lt gr shading, 4"...........................12.00
Pitcher, 3"...8.00
Planter, br matt, sgn, 5".................................21.00
Planter, bullfrog figural, 4x5"...........................16.00
Planter, deer in grass, green.............................12.50
Planter, doe & fawn, glossy lt bl, 7".....................15.00
Planter, elephant, green..................................22.00
Planter, fox, recumbent, sgn.............................18.00
Planter, leaping fawn, turq/rose/gr blend, 9".............18.00
Planter, polar bear.......................................25.00
Planter, seal...18.00
Planter, squirrel, gr, 6".................................25.00
Planter, swan..12.00
Planter, wishing well, green..............................22.00
Vase, bulbous, ftd/hdls, rose w/gray shading, 4"..........15.00
Vase, med blue, 2 hdls, 7½"..............................19.00
Vase, Mission Ware, ball shape, old colors, 1½" opening, 4½"..55.00
Vase, Mission Ware, bl/cream, lg mouth w/lip, 6"..........42.00
Vase, Mission Ware, blue & tan, 4½".......................35.00
Vase, Mission Ware, br/bl/cream, angle mid point, 3½".......35.00
Vase, Mission Ware, br/bl/cream, curving sides, 9½"..........90.00
Vase, Mission Ware, br/bl/cream, tight swirl, 6½"............45.00
Vase, Mission Ware, EX colors, 10"......................125.00
Vase, Mission Ware, EX colors, 4½".......................40.00
Vase, Mission Ware, flared rim, 4½".......................35.00
Vase, Mission Ware, tight swirls, no mk, 5½"..............30.00
Vase, Mission Ware, top folds in, paper label, 6¼"........50.00
Vase, Mission Ware, 3½"..................................35.00
Vase, pine trees in high relief, blue, sgn Hywood, 5½".....45.00
Vase, 5 openings, yellow, 7".............................16.00

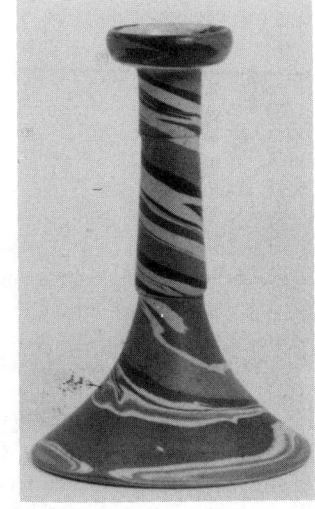

Mission Ware candlestick, 8", $95.00.

Nippon

Nippon generally refers to Japanese wares made during the period from 1891 to 1921, although the Nippon mark was also used to a limited extent on later wares. Nippon, meaning Japan, identified the country of origin to comply with American importation restrictions. After 1921, 'Japan' was an acceptable alternative. The term does not imply a specific type of product, and may be found on items other than porcelains. In the listings that follow, the numbers refer to these specific marks:

1. China E-OH   5. Rising Sun
2. M in Wreath   6. Royal Kinran
3. Cherry Blossom   7. Maple leaf
4. Double T Diamond in circle

For wares marked 'Noritake Nippon', see Noritake section.

Authority Joan Van Patton has compiled a lovely series, *The Collector's Encyclopedia of Nippon Porcelain*, with many full-color photos and current prices; you will find her address in the Directory under 'New York'.

Ash tray, boy figural sits on edge.............................400.00
Ash tray, br w/3 horses, hexagonal, gr #2.................135.00
Ash tray, lt bl band, tan w/pk floral/ho-ho bird, 3 rests, 4½"....65.00
Ash tray, moriage dragon, 3 rests, gr #2..................135.00
Ash tray, pipe in center, rnd w/3 rests, gr #2............95.00
Ash tray, red sailing ships, 2 jeweled rests...............95.00
Ash tray, red w/Egyptian scene/camels, 3 rests, gr #2....110.00
Ash tray, swans, blue tones, crown mk.....................85.00
Ash tray, w/Fatima holder...................................65.00
Ash tray, windmills, 4 jeweled rests, sq..................95.00
Asparagus set, 10½x7½" server+6 plates.................180.00
Basket, floral decor, gold hdl, 8½" L......................160.00
Berry set, mc florals w/gr borders, E-OH mk, 7 pcs.......75.00
Berry set, windmill scene in lavenders, gold decor, 7 pcs.....85.00
Boat dish, florals w/moriage decor, #5....................40.00
Bon bon dish, bisque, sailboat on water, br trim & hdls.....25.00
Bowl, azalias, open hdls, #5, 10" dia......................60.00
Bowl, basketweave hdls & w/in, HP chestnuts, 6" dia.......50.00
Bowl, bird of paradise, pastels & blk, w/hdls, 9".........65.00
Bowl, blown-out strawberries, bark bkground, w/hdls, 9" dia...250.00
Bowl, boat shape, scenic interior, gr #2, 13" long.......145.00
Bowl, br/lav scenic, E-OH mk, 9½" dia....................45.00
Bowl, cobalt w/florals & gold, 10".......................175.00
Bowl, florals, gold beading, 3 hdls, 8"...................30.00
Bowl, florals, 7" sq......................................25.00
Bowl, gold rim, lt bl border, pk/bl floral/butterfly w/in, 7½"....30.00
Bowl, gold rim/leaves, pk flowers, 2 turned in hdls, #5, 5".....15.00
Bowl, hexagonal, wht w/wht dots, pk/lav florals, gr #2, 5".....25.00
Bowl, lg blk traced pk roses, gold scalloped, blue #7, 8".....105.00
Bowl, molded peanuts, earth tones/leaves/vines, gr #2, 10"....100.00
Bowl, peanut/walnut/acorn/leaves on scenic bkground, 10".....80.00
Bowl, ped ft, gaudy florals on yellow, cobalt/gold bird, 14"....150.00
Bowl, poppies decor, 8"...................................75.00
Bowl, portrait of Gibson girl in center, ornate border, 6½"....165.00
Bowl, scalloped, 3 gold ft, rnd reserves, allover gold, 9".....85.00
Bowl, scenic center, gold/jeweled trim, crimped, gr #2......65.00
Bowl, scenic w/walnut relief, jeweled hdls, diamond shape, 10"...75.00
Bowl, shallow w/hdls, orange flowers, much gold, 5½".....15.00
Bowl, sq, gr w/spring florals, gold beading, rose borders, 10"...55.00
Bowl, sq/scalloped/ftd, tree of life motif, gr #2, 9½".....45.00
Bowl, w/under plate, rose & gold decor, reticulated, 7¾"....140.00
Bowl, windmill, jeweled beading...........................70.00
Box, cigarette; gold on beige, lid w/scenic, gold rim, gr #2....150.00
Box, patch; lt gr w/pk trumpet flowers/gold beading, 1⅞" sq....20.00
Box, powder; allover gold/turq/pink jewels, 3x3½".......46.00
Box, powder; 3 ft, wht w/gold rim, top: gold flowers/3 birds....30.00
Box, stamp; w/lid, sailing ships..........................75.00
Box, triangular, w/lid, ships/windmill, 3½"...............40.00
Box, 4 curved gold ft, allover gold/turq/pk jewels, w/lid, 3¾"....45.00
Bread tray, gaudy, gr/gold w/pink asters.................150.00
Bread tray, scenic, hdls/scalloped ft, 11"................55.00
Butter dish, rose on wht, HP Nippon, 3 pc................50.00
Cake plate, lake w/trees, lavender & br, gr #2............60.00
Cake plate, notched edges, gold border/floral, #6, 11".....80.00
Cake plate, pk/bl florals w/gold trim, #5, 10½"..........33.50
Cake plate, plain w/beaded hdls & trim, bisque...........30.00
Cake plate, portrait of Madonna and Child, hdls, 6 for.....300.00
Cake plate, scenic w/swans, relief gold border, gr #2, 11".....80.00
Cake plate, sm roses w/heavy gold relief, 10"............58.00

Cake plate, wht w/band of pk flowers, hdls, bl #5, 11".....30.00
Cake plate, wht w/2 robins & bl florals, hdls, crown mk, 9½"...25.00
Cake set, gold stenciled grapes, spoke mk, 7 pc.........115.00
Cake set, pk flowers in ivory, br/bl trim, 7 pc..........125.00
Cake set, raised wht daisies on blk border, 7 pc.........65.00
Candlestick, Arab on camel, 8"...........................135.00
Candlestick, Dutch lady & child, bunnies/chicks border, 8"....75.00
Candlestick, geometric design, 6½", pr..................225.00
Candlestick, Gouda type decor, sq base, 7"...............75.00
Candlestick, ivory w/gold floral relief, 8"...............85.00
Candlestick, paneled, deer & trees, 8"...................85.00
Candlestick, swirl, gr w/red floral, gold decor, scalloped, 7"....34.00
Candlestick, triangular, bisque w/flowers, 7¾".........65.00

Footed bowl with squirrel in high relief, very rare, 8¾", $850.00.

Candy box, w/lid, dk rose floral w/gold relief, clover mk, 5½"...50.00
Candy dish, clover shape, elk in lake....................35.00
Candy dish, lake w/swans, turq/br rim & hdl beading, rnd.....45.00
Candy dish, leaf form, red/pink roses, gold scalloped rim, hdl....48.00
Candy dish, 4 sections, floral enameling, gold hdls & trim.....30.00
Celery dish, mc wild roses, gr #2, 12"...................40.00
Celery set, master w/6 salts, violets on lav/br bkground.....85.00
Celery set, pastel flowers, gold beading & trim, 7 pc, RC mk....120.00
Charger, 2 dogs molded in relief, 15" W................1,950.00
Cheese dish, butterflies on bl, gold hdl, #2.............75.00
Cheese dish, Wedgwood bl decor, slanted, gr #2..........325.00
Chocolate pot, cobalt rim/hdl, roses on cr, gold trim.....65.00
Chocolate pot, Deco design, gold trim, 10"..............142.00
Chocolate pot, woodland scene, green mk, 9".............225.00
Chocolate pot+4 c/s, cobalt/gold, swans on lake, #7.....395.00
Chocolate pot+4 c/s, gold ground w/yel roses, gr #2.....215.00
Chocolate pot+4 c/s, moriage dragons...................200.00
Chocolate pot+6 c/s, berries, gold, ornate.............250.00
Chocolate pot+6 c/s, Deco shape, aqua, blk & wht stripes....200.00
Chocolate pot+6 c/s, wht w/gold decor..................175.00
Coaster set, ho-ho bird design, 6 pc....................80.00
Coffee pot, cobalt trim, red roses, gold, #2............100.00
Coffee pot, individual; desert scene top/base, bl #7.....95.00
Cologne, yellow flowers, gold trim, matching stopper, 4"....75.00
Compote, boat scene, 7" dia.............................90.00

Compote, gold traced pk roses in red reserves, w/hdls..........90.00
Compote w/matching 6" candlesticks, blk/gold scenic on wht...225.00
Console set, lakeside sunset w/goose, 8" bowl+pr 3½" sticks..200.00
Cracker jar, barrel, red/pk rose clusters, cobalt trim, bl #7.....199.00
Cracker jar, cobalt & roses w/heavy gold decor..............275.00
Cracker jar, gr w/roses, inlay design, gold lacing/hdls/knob.....215.00
Creamer, Wedgwood type, ped base, cut-out decor hdl, 3¼"....30.00
Creamer & sugar, glass eyes in dragons................65.00
Creamer & sugar, lt bl/cobalt border w/pastel floral, gold, #2...85.00
Creamer & sugar, wht w/bl bird on branch/yel florals/butterfly...40.00
Creamer & sugar, wild flowers w/gold tracing..............26.00
Cup & plate, blown-out child's face....................65.00
Cup & saucer, house near water....................20.00
Cup & saucer, Oriental decor......................22.00
Demitasse set, 12 pcs on tray.......................250.00
Dish, beaded gold rose medallion, scroll on wht, 5½" sq.......10.00
Dish, child's; heart shaped, blown-out child's face, #5, 5"......85.00
Dish, side hdls, bl rim w/lg roses, gr #2, 6"...............18.00
Dish, w/hdl, Gouda type decor....................45.00
Dresser set, cobalt w/florals, red #2, 5 pcs..............185.00
Dresser set, floral decor, beaded gold, 6 pcs..............95.00
Dresser set, roses w/blk & gold, gr #2, 5 pcs.............235.00
Dresser tray, bl w/violets, gold beads, bl #7, 8x10".........20.00
Egg cup, rose & lattice.........................20.00
Egg warmer, pink roses & gold on wht, #5..............105.00
Egg warmer, wht w/roses & lav flowers, 5½" dia..........115.00
Ewer, floral w/gold trim, 8½"....................175.00
Ewer, rose & gold, gold hdl, gr #7, 4½"................95.00
Hair receiver, cobalt/wht w/relief gold overlay, bl #7.........60.00
Hair receiver, pink dogwood/gold on wht, bl #2............55.00
Hair receiver, pk roses/gr leaves/gold trim, gr #2, 4" wide......60.00
Hair receiver, wht/yellow base; palm trees/souvenir top, #5......30.00
Hatpin holder, cobalt rim/base w/gold emb, apple blossom, 4½".42.00
Hatpin holder, rnd w/flared base, pk/bl floral band on gr, 4¾"..25.00
Humidor, allover rose & florals w/moriage Queen Ann's lace...450.00
Humidor, blown-out lion, gr #2.....................750.00
Humidor, playing cards, 6".......................465.00
Humidor, 7 ducks on shore, swirling sky & water, Nouveau....325.00
Inkwell, Egyptian scene........................165.00
Inkwell, w/insert, stylized rooster, lg................185.00
Inkwell, w/insert & pen tray, bisque, riding scene on gr.......250.00
Jam jar w/under plate, lav/br scenic w/turq beading, gr #2......50.00
Jug, chickens by water, bl moriage wreath, 6½"...........400.00
Jug, whiskey; house/lake scenic, moriage trim, w/stopper.....450.00
Jug, whiskey; palm trees, matching stopper, moriage........450.00
Jug, whiskey; stag in forest, w/stopper, in basket, moriage.....450.00
Lazy susan set w/7 bowls, bl w/swans/prunus, in orig box......75.00
Lemonade pitcher, wht w/gold rim, lavender violets, #1........65.00
Lemonade pitcher+4 mugs, strawberries/etc.............120.00
Lemonade pitcher+6 mugs, Dutch sailing ships w/windmill....175.00
Luncheon set, mc florals, orange rims, red #3, 21 pcs........45.00
Mayonnaise bowl, ftd; under plate & ladle, 2 gold iris/buds.....65.00
Mug, barrel shape, allover scenic, jeweled hdl, 5"..........165.00
Mug, child's; children playing on wht.................50.00
Mug, ruins, gold hdl.........................150.00
Mug, stag in forest, moriage leaves/trim, jewel hdl, 4½".......125.00
Mustard, floral decor, w/handle....................25.00
Mustard w/attached under plate/spoon, gold geometrics........50.00
Napkin holder, relief holly, gold trim w/gold dots...........50.00
Napkin ring, owl on stump figural, 4".................450.00
Nappy, floral & gold design, 3½"...................13.50
Nappy w/hdl, scenic w/jewels & beading, gr #2............40.00
Nut bowl, blown-out leaves w/acorns, #2...............75.00
Nut set, bisque leaves & acorns on ivory, all w/sm ft, #2......120.00

Nut set, ivory w/gold florals, ftd, 6" dia, 5 pcs.............65.00
Nut set, leaves & acorns design, 7 pc.................147.00
Nut set, ped ft, hdld, wild flowers, EX gold, 7 pc...........150.00
Nut set, 3 pointed lobes, shell molding/HP chestnuts, 7 pcs....150.00
Pancake server, roses w/geometric turq/br beading, #5.......90.00
Pancake server, wht w/pink & blue floral, 8¾" dia..........100.00
Pansy bowl, lid w/holes, gr w/HP pansies, bl #7, 5½" dia.....140.00
Perfume, bulbous, pk/yel flowers, gold neck, magenta #2, 4"...95.00
Pin tray, house/tree/lake, souvenir, gr #2...............18.00
Pincushion, heart shape, florals/gold.................40.00
Pitcher, leaves, autumn colors, heavy outline beading, 5½".....80.00
Pitcher, melon rib, cream w/pk roses/gold leaves/beads, 7½"...175.00
Pitcher, roses in bl reserves, gold medallions, 9".........110.00
Pitcher, tankard; gr w/roses, 13"...................350.00
Planter, Deco design, 8" L......................127.00
Planter, ruffled, allover moriage Aztec decor, 7"..........125.00
Planter, scenic w/house/woods, bl marbleized trim/gold, sq....125.00
Planter, sq/ftd, bl florals, mc beading, #5, 6"............85.00
Planter, w/insert, blown-out purple grape hdls, Gouda decor....275.00
Planter, w/insert, Egyptian decor, gold trim, 3 sides........140.00
Plaque, church w/steeple by lake, ornate enamel border, 9"...175.00
Plaque, desert scene, 10" dia....................237.00
Plaque, Egyptian boat & palm trees, 7½"...............75.00
Plaque, English hunt scene, 10"...................325.00
Plaque, floral/fruit in wicker basket, 11½", pr...........295.00
Plaque, orange w/orange poppies, gold traced, matt finish.....225.00
Plaque, scenic, pk border, gold relief trim, gr #2, 8"........85.00
Plate, boat in water, br trim, 7½"..................25.00
Plate, center: 4 lg orchids; scalloped, cobalt/gr/gold, 11½"....250.00
Plate, fish decor, gold border, 8½".................105.00
Plate, gold beads/pk jewels, roses center, bl #7, 10" dia......145.00
Plate, house/lake/man in canoe, dk colors, 8½"...........110.00
Plate, Indian in canoe shooting deer, 1" Indian border, 7½"...100.00
Plate, lobster, gold trim, 7"....................105.00
Plate, orchids, pk/rose on pastel, gold relief rim, 10".......110.00
Plate, poppies & daisies, gold filigree, 7½".............55.00
Potpourri jar, hexagonal, relief gold, florals............80.00
Reamer, allover gold/mc florals, gold hdl & top...........125.00
Reamer, wht w/florals, 2 pcs, gr #2.................85.00
Relish, blk/gold scenic on wht, gr #2................25.00
Relish, center ring hdl, Nile, boat, gold/blk palms, #2, 6¾"....90.00
Relish, divided; lg center hdl, wht w/florals, bl #7, 7½"......40.00
Relish, 2 houses/trees, center hdl, crown mk, 8"..........25.00
Ring tree, gold swags & beading, 2½"...............55.00
Salt & pepper shakers, cobalt w/red roses/gold decor, Chikusa..25.00
Salt & pepper shakers, ftd, flowers/leaves, HP Nippon, 3", pr....20.00
Salt & pepper shakers, Oriental lake scene, Nagoya mk, pr....21.50
Salt & pepper shakers, w/hdls, sm yellow flowers, bl #5, 2½"...15.00
Shaving mug, Indian in canoe, 4"..................167.00
Shaving mug, overall scenic, enamel decor, jeweled hdl, gr #2..130.00
Shaving mug, pink florals on wht, #5................75.00
Smoke set, ho-ho bird, tray/cig holder/ash tray/match holder...185.00
Smoke set, horsehead medallion, Indian designs, 4 pc, gr #2...450.00
Soap dish, ribbed, florals on wht..................75.00
Spittoon, lady's; violets, turq beading, moriage..........275.00
Stickpin holder, attached tray, pk flowers/leaves, gr #2, 2½"...100.00
Sugar cube holder, double, florals, gold trim, gr #2, 7" long....85.00
Sugar shaker, barrel form, mc bkground w/pansies, 4½".......87.50
Sugar shaker, roses & gold relief decor, gr #2...........42.50
Sugar w/lid, house on lake, jeweled hdls..............25.00
Syrup w/under plate, yellow w/scenic design, 4"..........77.00
Tea set, Egyptian design, much raised gold/beads, 3 pc, bl #7..125.00
Tea set, ivory bands, gold encrusted florals, gr #2, 15 pcs.....125.00
Tea set, ribbed melon shapes, lg roses, 11 pc, #1.........250.00

Tea set, wht w/bands of bl & gold flowers, 15 pcs............150.00
Tea strainer, floral design/gold trim, 2 pc, gr #2, 6″ long.......85.00
Teapot, Flying Turkey, blue & wht....................55.00
Teapot, gold trim, yellow/ivory bands, HP florals, red #2, 4¼″...14.00
Tidbit tray w/center hdl, florals, gold trim, bl #7............56.00
Toothpick, barrel shape, scenic....................30.00
Toothpick, floral w/sepia trim, 2 hdls..................35.00
Toothpick, florals/gold, 2 hdls.....................40.00
Toothpick, gr dragon, 4 sides.....................45.00
Toothpick, palm trees/pyramids, 3 ball ft...............45.00
Toothpick, ped ft, lt gr w/pink flowers.................40.00
Toothpick, 3 ftd, hdls, souvenir of Wash DC, 2¼″..........40.00
Toothpick, 3 gold hdls & rim, bl #5..................25.00
Tray, blk w/gold filigree, gr #2, 12″ dia................70.00
Trivet, blk medallions w/pk flowers, 6″ sq...............42.00
Trivet, stylized rooster, sq, gr #2...................45.00
Urn, floral, gold swags & jewels, double hdls, 13″..........385.00
Urn, floral bkground w/gold relief & red/gr jewels, w/lid, 6½″..135.00
Urn, jeweling/gold, portrait in center medallion, w/lid, 14½″..525.00
Urn, lake w/2 geese, hdls, gold trim/beading, #7, 8x9½″.....550.00
Urn, scenic reserve front/bk, allover gold, w/lid & hdls, 15″..475.00
Urn, 2 pc, ped/hdls/heavy moriage/floral, Royal Moriage, 10½″.475.00
Vase, bisque, w/windmills, gr #2, 9″.................100.00
Vase, blk w/mc florals, gr #2, 12″..................180.00
Vase, blown-out leaves & acorns, gr/gold, 7″............635.00
Vase, bluebirds in flight, 3″ top border, Imperial mk, 10½″....160.00
Vase, brown bark ground w/red cloisonne flowers, 8″........325.00
Vase, cottage scene w/water/trees/gaudy borders, 13″.......145.00
Vase, cream w/dk rose florals, gold overlacing, ftd/hdls, 6″....110.00
Vase, dbl hdls, oxen scenic, dk tones, artist sgn, #7, 10½″....325.00
Vase, dbl hdls, reserves w/red roses/gold overlay, gr #2, 9″....165.00
Vase, dk gr w/dk red roses, moriage flowers/leaves, 10″......200.00
Vase, dk gr w/pk flowers, raised gold, ring hdls, bl #7, 7″....145.00
Vase, Egyptian decor, triangular, gr #2, 5″..............125.00
Vase, famille noire w/mc phoenix in peony bush, seal mk, 10″..225.00
Vase, florals in fuschia/lavender, moriage in gr, 9½″.........185.00
Vase, gr matt w/scenic reserves/gold filigree, ftd/hdls, 9½″....265.00
Vase, gr w/allover gold, scenic reserves front/bk, 14″........385.00
Vase, hexagonal, lt pk w/roses/gold, top: gold/wht, hdls, 12″...225.00
Vase, jeweled at top & on elephant hdls, sailing ship, bisque...225.00
Vase, lake/tree/house, top/base blk w/gold filigree, hdls, 13″...200.00
Vase, lt gr w/florals, 11″.......................85.00
Vase, lt gr w/overall violets, moriage trim, hdl, 9½″.........135.00
Vase, medallion w/2 deer w/in moriage leaves, hdls, 7½″.....200.00
Vase, melon ribbed, red & pk roses, gold trim, bl #7, 10″.....150.00
Vase, melon shape, bl/pk, w/cerise flowers, gold decor, #6, 7″..245.00
Vase, moriage dragonfly/hydrangeas, spiderweb, rim/hdls, 10½″.260.00
Vase, orange/gray, 2 birds on lg wht/gold branch, Nishiki, 12″..175.00
Vase, orchids design, gold trim/beads/legs, gr #2, 9½″.......145.00
Vase, pk roses on dk gr, much moriage decor, gr #7, 8″......250.00
Vase, poppies/daisies, gold filigree top/base, 3 ft/hdls, 14″....400.00
Vase, reserve w/forest/deers 4 sides, gray w/gold allover, 13″..525.00
Vase, river w/owl in tree top, pillow form w/2 self hdls.......185.00
Vase, roses w/gold beading, hdls, 5½x6½″...............80.00
Vase, rust to yel, yel flowers/gold beads/jewels/side hdls, 8″...110.00
Vase, scenic beyond trees, much gold, 9″..............165.00
Vase, swans on lake w/house/trees, gold at top, 7″..........70.00
Vase, swans/trees/lake; maple leaves above, hdls, #2, 11½″....275.00
Vase, tapestry, pk & yel roses, shaded gr ground, 7½″.......375.00
Vase, tapestry w/red/pk roses, 2 hdls, bl #2, 7½″..........400.00
Vase, violets w/much gold & green, slender form, 12″........100.00
Vase, wht, blue flowers w/gold outline, gr #2, 8″...........165.00
Vase, wild roses w/geometric beading, Imperial mk, w/hdls, 12″.160.00
Vase, winter scene, 8½″.......................165.00

Vase, 6 sides, bisque, cascading roses, EX jeweling/enamel, 9″..150.00
Wall pocket, molded dog w/florals, 6″.................112.00

Nodders

So called because of the nodding action of their head and hands, nodders originated in China where they were used in temple rituals to represent deity. Early in the 18th century, the idea was adapted by Meissen and by French manufacturers who produced not only china nodders but bisque as well. Most nodders are individual -- couples are unusual. The idea remained popular until the end of the 19th century, and was used during the Victorian era by toy manufacturers.

Black boy, nude on alligator, gold earrings, straw hat removes...30.00
Black musicians, 1 playing sax, 1 w/banjo, Germany, pr.......125.00
Black pickaninny girl, bisque, 7″...................175.00
Couple, old man & old woman riding pigs, bisque, pr.........195.00
Daddy Warbucks, bisque........................100.00
Elf musicians, German bisque, set of 6.................275.00
Herbie, bisque, mk Germany......................45.00
Indian dancing girl, 4 parts, 11″....................90.00
Indian w/fruit, 5½″..........................125.00
Monkey musician, sticks out tongue, Occupied Japan, bisque....85.00
Oriental, man sits X-legged, holds hands up, Germany, 4½″....135.00
Oriental, woman sits X-legged, fan behind head, Germany, 4½″.200.00
Oriental figure, bronzed white metal, German made, 5½″.....110.00
Rachel, bisque, mk Germany.....................80.00
Turkish girl, bisque, EX features, wht relief beading, 6x6″.....300.00
Uncle Walt, bisque, mk Germany..................60.00

Oriental with fish, 3¾″, $50.00.

Noritake

The Noritake Company was first registered in 1904 as Nippon Gomei Kaisha. In 1917, the name became Nippon Toki Kabushiki Toki. The 'M' in wreath mark is that of the Morimura Brothers, distributors with offices in New York. It was used until 1941. The tree crest mark is the crest of the Morimura family.

The Noritake Company has produced fine porcelain dinnerware sets and occasional pieces decorated in the delicate manner for which the Japanese are noted. Their Azalea pattern was produced exclusively for the Larkin Company, who gave the lovely ware away as premiums to club members and their home agents.

From 1916 through the thirties, Larkin distributed the fine china which was decorated in pink Azaleas on white with gold tracing along edges and handles. Early in the thirties, six pieces of crystal hand painted with the same design were offered: candle holders, a compote, a tray with handles, a scalloped fruit bowl, a cheese and cracker set, and a cake plate. All in all, seventy different pieces of Azalea were offered. Some, such as the fifteen piece child's set, bulbous vase, china ash tray, and the pancake jug, are quite rare. Marks varied over the years; the earliest was the blue rising sun Nippon mark, followed by the Noritake M in wreath with variations. Later, the ware was marked 'Noritake, Azalea, hand painted, Japan'.

Cracker jar, yellow ground with tree by lake scene, gold trim, green M in wreath mark, 7", $100.00.

Azalea

Basket, mint; Dolly Varden, #193	90.00
Bon bon, #184, 6¼"	35.00
Bowl, deep, #310	45.00
Bowl, divided, #439	175.00
Bowl, oval vegetable; #101, 10½"	35.00
Bowl, salad; round, #12, 10" dia	26.00
Butter chip, #312, 3¼"	55.00
Butter tub, w/insert, #54	26.00
Butter w/cover, #314, 6¼"	85.00
Casserole, covered, gold finial, #372	350.00
Casserole, covered, regular, #16	60.00
Celery dish, #444, 10"	205.00
Child's set, 15 pc	1,350.00
Coffee pot, #182	450.00
Compote, #170	65.00
Condiment set, 5 pc, #14	35.00
Cream soup, 2 hdl, #363, 5½"	75.00
Creamer & sugar, gold finial, #401	120.00
Creamer & sugar, individual, scalloped, #449	320.00
Creamer & sugar shaker set, #122	100.00
Cruet, #190	165.00
Cup & saucer, #2	12.00
Cup & saucer, bouillon; #124, 5¼"	15.00
Cup & saucer, demitasse; #183	85.00
Egg cup, #120	30.00
Glass ware, cake plate, 10½"	50.00
Glass ware, candlesticks, #114, pr	30.00
Glass ware, cheese & cracker set, 2 pc, 10"	65.00
Glass ware, sandwich tray, 10"	50.00
Gravy boat, #40	30.00

Jam jar set, 3 pc, #125	85.00
Jug, milk; #100	140.00
Mayonnaise set, scalloped, 3 pc, #453	385.00
Mustard, hdl, #191	35.00
Plate, breakfast; #98, 8½"	15.00
Plate, cake; #10, 9¾"	28.00
Plate, dinner; M	17.00
Plate, grill; 3 sections, #338, 10¼"	90.00
Plate, lemon	15.00
Plate, square, #315, 7¾"	38.00
Platter, #17, 14"	38.00
Platter, #186, 16"	3.00
Platter, #311, 10¼"	140.00
Platter, #56, 12"	34.00
Refreshment set, 2 pc, #39	35.00
Relish, oval, #194, 7¼"	55.00
Relish, twin section, #171, 8¼x4¾"	38.00
Relish, twin w/loop hdl, #450	220.00
Relish, 4 section, #119, 10"	95.00
Salt & pepper, bulbous, #89, 3"	22.00
Salt & pepper, individual, #126, 2½"	14.00
Salt & pepper, tapered, #11, 3½"	20.00
Sauce, 5½"	8.00
Spoon holder, #189, 8"	65.00
Syrup pitcher, w/under plate, #97	75.00
Teapot, gold finial, #400	360.00
Teapot, regular, #15	75.00
Teapot tile, #169, 6"	30.00
Tobacco jar, #313	450.00
Toothpick holder, #192	70.00
Vase, bulbous, #452	700.00
Vase, fan, ftd, #187	120.00

Miscellaneous

#16034, White & Gold; basket, ruffle border, gr wreath mk	65.00
#16034, White & Gold; demitasse cup & saucer, gr wreath mk	20.00
#16034, White & Gold; plate, dinner; gr wreath mk, 9¾"	16.00
#16034, White & Gold; platter, gr wreath mk, 16"	60.00
#16034, White & Gold; serving dish, square, hdl, gr wreath mk	55.00
#16034, White & Gold; spooner, gr wreath mk	50.00
#16034, White & Gold; sweetmeat set, 7 pc in lacquered box	100.00
#5693, creamer & sugar w/lid	15.00
#5693, cup & saucer	3.50
#5693, gravy boat, w/attached under tray	20.00
#5693, platter, 12x8¼"	15.00
Ash tray, acorns & pine cones	35.00
Ash tray, pelican figural	145.00
Asparagus set, platter: 11¾"; 6 plates: 7¾"	120.00
Basket, molded leaves & figural blossom, w/hdl, 7x3"	25.00
Bowl, blown-out peanuts w/in, 3 ball ft, 5 sides, 7" W	50.00
Bowl, Deco design, 3 ftd, 6¾" dia	35.00
Bowl, floral decor, 10½"	37.00
Bowl, pierced hdl, apricot lustre w/flower basket, 6¾" dia	14.00
Bread tray, fruit decor, lustre finish, 11" long	57.00
Bud vase, tree stump w/butterflies	95.00
Butter dish, roses & geometric designs	50.00
Cake plate, roses decor, 9½"	50.00
Candle holder, scenic, raised gold, M, pr	60.00
Candlestick, lustre ground w/butterflies, 5½", pr	110.00
Celery set, ruffled, lustre/MOP apricot w/mc & bl floral, 5 pc	26.00
Chocolate set, wht w/floral decor, 9½" pot, 9 pc	192.00
Cologne, gentleman wearing cape, Deco, lustre finish, 6¾"	125.00
Creamer & sugar shaker, house by lake pattern	40.00

Dealer's sign..50.00
Demitasse set, eggshell, pk/wht/blk Deco lines, sgn, 15 pc.....110.00
Dresser set, scenic decor, 7 pc on 12½" L tray.............230.00
Egg cup, double, small floral design, 3½".................25.00
Egg warmer, pink rim w/flowers, 5½" W.................65.00
Ferner, triangular, floral decor, 6" W................92.00
Game set, ornate, w/gold trim, 16" platter + 8 plates........575.00
Honey pot, log cabin w/applied bumble bees..............75.00
Humidor, lion & python, blown-out..................625.00
Humidor, owl design molded in relief.................445.00
Humidor w/tray, triangular shape, aqua, Furness Studio mk....90.00
Inkwell, owl figural................................210.00
Jam jar, w/under plate, floral finial, lustre finish, 5¼".........58.00
Lamp base, candlestick; scenic w/swan, 6½"................25.00
Lemon dish, house by lake pattern, ring hdl................10.00
Luncheon set, floral, 10½" server, six 7" plates, cr/sug.......88.00
Mug, decal of children playing, child size, 2½"...............45.00
Mustache cup w/saucer, scenic decor, 5¾" dia saucer.........70.00
Napkin ring, floral decor, 2¼".........................25.00
Nut, individual; allover gold enamel, scalloped, 2½" sq.........8.00
Plate, apricot lustre w/long stemmed flowers/butterfly, 7½".....18.00
Plate, Venetian scene, 9½".............................14.00
Potpourri jar, lt bl w/floral decor, 6"....................85.00
Powder puff box, Deco clown decoration, 4" W............85.00
Punch bowl, red ground w/Oriental scene, 16" dia..........375.00
Sandwich server, floral decor, 9¾"....................35.00
Sauce, w/under plate & ladle, floral decor, 3¼"............35.00
Snack set, Art Deco.................................50.00
Spooner, Deco design, 8" L...........................35.00
Sugar shaker, Art Deco blk silhouettes/plants/winged figure.....24.00
Syrup, bands of bl lustre & relief gold leaves/beading, 4".......26.00
Syrup, w/under plate, scenic design, 4¼"................45.00
Tea caddy, scenic decor, 3¾".........................160.00
Tea set, child's; pk, w/blk & wht border trim, 15 pc.........145.00
Tea tile, canted corners, lustre w/sailing ship/seagull, 5" sq....15.00
Tea tile, Deco style lady, 6½" dia.......................55.00
Toast rack, 2 slice..................................25.00
Urn, covered, red, scenic medallion center, 12" high........195.00
Vase, boat scene, 2 hdls, 8½".........................110.00
Vase, fan shape, floral decor, 6½".....................85.00
Vase, gold hdls, florals in blues, bl/yel phoenix bird, 11½".....275.00
Vase, jack-in-the-pulpit shape, 7¾"....................95.00
Vase, wht w/floral design, 8".........................98.00
Waffle set: muffineer & syrup; tree in meadow.............70.00
Wall plaque, floral decor, 8½" dia.....................105.00
Wall plaque, 3 dogs molded in relief, 10½" W............550.00
Wall pocket, bird decor, 8½" L........................45.00

Norse

The Norse Pottery was established in 1903 in Edgerton, Wisconsin, by Thorwald Sampson and Louis Ipson. A year later it was purchased by A.W. Wheelock and moved to Rockford, Illinois. The ware they produced was inspired by ancient bronze vessels of the Norsemen. Designs were often incised into the red clay body, dragon handles and feet were favored decorative devices, and they achieved a semblance of patina through the application of metallic glazes. The ware was marked with a stylized 'N' containing a vertical arrangement of the remaining letters of the name. Production ceased after 1913.

Bowl, simulated bronze, 8 owls in relief, round ft, mk, 4x6"....110.00
Jar, fossil-like leaf impressions, blk/gr/gold, 9x9½".........200.00
Mug, #51, 5"...85.00

Vase, encircling arrowhead design, tapered shape, mk, 8¾"....135.00
Vase, high relief ferns, copper underglaze, 4 hdls, #24, 9x10"..275.00
Vase, 3 ft, 2 snake hdls, incised decor, #70, 4x7"...........110.00

North Dakota School of Mines

The School of Mines of the University of North Dakota was established in 1890, but due to a lack of funding, it was not until 1898 that Earle J. Babcock was appointed as Director and efforts were made to produce ware from the native clay he had discovered several years earlier. The first pieces were made by firms in the east from the clay Babcock sent them. Some of the ware was decorated by the manufacturer; some was shipped back to North Dakota to be decorated by native artists. By 1909, students at the University of North Dakota were producing utilitarian items -- tile, brick, shingles, etc. -- in conjunction with a ceramic course offered through the Chemistry Department. By 1910, a ceramic department had been established, supervised by Margaret Kelly Cable. Under her leadership, fine art ware was produced. Native flowers, grains, buffalo, cowboys, and other subjects indigenous to the state were incorporated into the decorations. Some pieces have an Art Nouveau-Art Deco style easily attributed to her association with Frederick H. Rhead, with whom she studied in 1911. During the twenties the pottery was marketed on a limited scale through gift and jewelry stores in the state. From 1927 until 1949, when Miss Cable announced her retirement, a more widespread distribution was maintained, with sales branching out into other states. The ware was marked in cobalt with the official seal -- 'Made at School of Mines, N.D. Clay, University of North Dakota, Grand Forks, N.D.' -- in a circle. Very early ware was sometimes marked 'U.N.D.' in cobalt by hand.

Lamp, incised & carved cowboys on horseback.............500.00
Mug, hand thrown, br glaze...........................30.00
Paperweight, Rebekan design..........................65.00
Tile/trivet, seahorse, artist sgn, 6"....................85.00
Vase, aqua w/rings of red clay exposed at top, 2½x3½"........55.00
Vase, bl drip, 1925, 5".................................50.00
Vase, brown, ribbed, 3"...............................40.00
Vase, buff shading to bl-gray, bulbous, 5¾"................65.00
Vase, floral, green glaze, sgn, 4".......................135.00
Vase, green, Cable, 7"...............................100.00
Vase, horizontal wheat motif on gr, sgn Huck, 4½"..........125.00
Vase, HP cactus allover, bulbous, sgn Huck, 5¼"...........135.00
Vase, incised cowboys & Indians, sgn Mattson, 1935, 9".......200.00
Vase, incised daffodils, sgn Mattson, 5½"................140.00
Vase, incised girls, 2 colors, Cable......................160.00

Vase, black and white sawtooth, blue bottom, 4" x 6½", $185.00.

Vase, incised oak leaves, 2 colors, sgn Cable, 7"............225.00
Vase, incised rings, Cable, 7x6"..........................95.00
Vase, leaves/floral relief, gr matt, mk, 7"................180.00
Vase, ribbed, yellow, 2"...................................40.00
Vase, squat shape, blue, sgn A Osmundson, 5"..............45.00
Vase, turkeys, brown, 3x4"................................175.00
Vase, turq, sgn Cable, 7½".................................95.00

Northwood

The Northwood Company was founded in 1896 in Indiana, Pennsylvania, by Harry Northwood, whose father, John, was the art director for Stevens and Williams, an English glassworks. Harry Northwood joined the National Glass Company in 1899, but in 1901 again became an independent contractor, and formed the Harry Northwood Glass Company of Wheeling, West Virginia. He marketed his first carnival glass in 1908, and it became his most popular product. His company was also famous for its custard, goofus, and pressed glass. Northwood died in 1923, and the company closed.

See also Carnival; Custard; Goofus; Opalescent; Pattern Glass

Banana Dish, Alaska, green..............................35.00
Berry set, Royal Ivy, rubena frosted, master+4 sm.........210.00
Bowl, Fluted Scrolls, ftd, sapphire bl, 4x3"...............35.00
Bowl, red slag, Wheeling.................................40.00
Butter dish, Royal Ivy, rubena clear......................315.00
Candlestick, dolphin petticoat, blue opal, pr..............130.00
Chandelier, Paneled Poppies, custard glass, 30x16".........500.00
Cruet, Royal Ivy, rubena frosted.........................435.00
Jar, Paneled Sprig, cranberry, ribbed, pnt florals, gold, 4"...125.00
Pitcher, Cherry Lattice, gold trim, w/6 tumblers...........325.00
Pitcher, water; Royal Ivy, frosted........................95.00
Pitcher, water; Royal Ivy, rubena frosted.................275.00
Pitcher, water; Royal Oak, rubena frosted.................350.00
Rose bowl, on frosted wishbone ft, bl satin w/loopings, 3x2"...110.00
Rose bowl, Royal Ivy, cranberry..........................95.00
Rose bowl, Royal Ivy, yel/pk spatter, acid finish..........110.00
Spooner, Cherry & Plum..................................55.00
Sugar, Royal Ivy, frosted rubena, w/lid...................130.00
Sugar shaker, Royal Ivy, rubena frosted..................175.00
Sugar shaker, Royal Oak, milk glass, EX decor..............35.00

Cracker jar, Leaf Umbrella, cranberry with white spatter, 8½", $450.00

Sweetmeat, Strawberry & Cable...........................55.00
Sweetmeat, yel/wht/br/aqua loops, wht w/in, silver rim/lid/hdl....270.00
Tankard w/6 glasses, Oriental Poppy, emerald w/gold.........275.00
Tumbler, Golden Peach, emerald...........................25.00
Vase, pulled feathers, box pleat top, bl/yel w/in, mk Pat, 6½".1,350.00
Water set, gr w/enamel decor, bulbous, pleated top, 7 pc......250.00
Water set, Narcissus Spray, amethyst w/gr & gold, 5 pc.......190.00

Nutcrackers

The nutcracker, though a strictly functional tool, is a good example of one to which man has applied ingenuity, imagination, and engineering skills. Though all were designed to accomplish the same end, hundreds of types exist in almost every material sturdy enough to withstand sufficient pressure to crack the nut. Figurals are popular collectibles, as are those with unusual design and construction.

Cast iron dog, tail handle, 5" x 12", $45.00.

Antelope head, glass eyes, solid wood, hand carved, 9x3½".....70.00
Columbia, lizard & star on side..........................34.00
Dog, CI w/chrome plate, FA Altkoff Co, Chicago.............65.00
Dog, nickeled iron, pat 1863, England.....................40.00
Dog on scrolled base, cast steel, 12" L...................25.00
Dog's head, dtd 1820....................................62.00
Easy Cracker, Sapulpa, Okla, CI, worn bl pnt, wood hdl, 4½"...32.50
Elephant, CI, orig pnt, 1920s, 5x10".....................70.00
Fist holding cup, carved of wood, intricate detail, 7½".......105.00
Lady's legs, brass, well modeled, 4½"....................35.00
Lady's legs, CI...75.00
Lady's legs, mahogany, 7" L.............................30.00
Parrot, brass..25.00
Perfection, #28, table top attachment, turn screw...........17.00
Pheasant, dore bronze..................................90.00
Punch & Judy, brass....................................90.00
Rooster head, brass, lg.................................15.00
Skull & cross bones, iron, 6"...........................85.00
Squirrel Cracker, pat 1913, Tyler, Tex/Chicago, iron.........20.00
Squirrel on branch, bronze..............................40.00
Squirrel sitting on leaf, CI.............................35.00
St Bernard, brass, w/stoneware bowl, unusual..............125.00
St Bernard, iron, EX...................................65.00
Waco, table mounted...................................30.00

Occupied Japan

Items marked 'Occupied Japan' have become popular collectibles in the last few years. They were produced during the period from the end of World War II until April 18, 1952, when the occupation ended. By no means was all of the ware exported during that time marked 'Occupied Japan' -- some was marked 'Japan', or 'Made In Japan'. It is thought that because of the natural resentment felt by the Japanese toward the occupation, only a fraction of these wares were marked 'Occupied Japan'. Even though you may find identical 'Japan' marked items, because of the limited use of the 'Occupied' mark only these are being collected to any great extent.

This year we were assisted in our listings by the Occupied Japan Club, whose mailing address may be found in the Directory under 'Clubs, Newsletters, and Catalogues'.

Ash tray, w/Black boy...........................22.00
Ash tray, 3 elephants, br.......................25.00
Bowl, lacquer, Yoshida, 9¾" dia................22.00
Bust, Hiawatha, chalkware, 20"................115.00
Candy dish, bisque, lady in high relief on lid.................40.00
Cheese dish, cover in form of country cottage..............25.00
Cigarette lighter, Buick.......................25.00
Cigarette set, cowboy boots, one is lighter, other is holder.....20.00
Compote w/lid, Andrea portrait, 5½x7".......32.00
Creamer & sugar, honeycomb, w/bee finial....25.00
Creamer & sugar, Toby figural, 3½".........20.00
Cup & saucer, demitasse; Capo di Monte style, mk SGK....20.00
Cup & saucer, demitasse; flowers ea pc........15.00
Cup & saucer, pk dogwood, gr leaves, gold trim..........28.00
Cup & saucer, Shofu China....................35.00
Demitasse pot, cr/sug, 6 c/s, wht & bl w/gold..............125.00
Dish, ceramic, br w/mc floral relief, hdls, 8¾x7".........15.00
Doll, bisque baby, clothed, 2¾"................20.00
Doll, celluloid, 9"............................13.50
Figurine, accordian player, 8½"...............18.00
Figurine, baby on butterfly, bisque.............35.00
Figurine, bee, spread wings, 4"................14.00
Figurine, boy w/back pack; girl w/bandana, 4¾", pr..........25.00
Figurine, boy w/dog & horn, Hummel type, 4¼"..........12.50
Figurine, bride & groom, 4", pr................15.00
Figurine, cat playing saxaphone, bisque, 5"....25.00
Figurine, Colonial lady holding skirt, 3½".....8.50
Figurine, Colonial man, standing, 3½".........7.00
Figurine, Colonial man playing sousaphone, 3"............8.50
Figurine, Colonial man w/cape, 3½"............8.50
Figurine, Colonial pair on single base, lady seated, 4".........15.00
Figurine, Dutch girl w/flower, Delft blue, 4¼"..............21.00
Figurine, Dutch lady carrying buckets, 3¼".....7.50
Figurine, girl w/banjo, Hummel type, 4¼".....15.00
Figurine, girl w/umbrella, pup beside her, 3"..8.50
Figurine, Indian chief, 6½"...................17.50
Figurine, lady, bisque, 11"...................38.00
Figurine, man w/accordion, 4"................10.00
Figurine, man w/flute, 7"....................18.00
Figurine, mountain climbers, carved wood......25.00
Figurine, Oriental man, 4½"..................10.00
Figurine, seaman, Delft blue, 5"..............17.00
Figurine, stork, celluloid, 6"................25.00
Figurine, swan, cobalt w/florals..............18.00
Figurine, Victorian lady, 7".................22.50
Figurine, 2 hugging pandas, 2½"..............15.00
Figurine, 3 frog musicians, 2½", set..........35.00
Incense burner, Indian, 4"...................15.00
Incense burner, Oriental figure, 4"...........15.00

Jewelry casket, enamel top w/pheasant.........20.00
Lamp, Colonial man, w/shade..................25.00
Lighter, cigarette; camera on tripod...........25.00
Lighter, cigarette; horse head, metal, 3¼".....12.00
Liquor set, skeleton figural, w/stopper & 6 skull shots, Shofu....95.00
Match & cigarette holder, Black boy peeking between laundry...25.00
Match holder, 2" Colonial man sitting by vase, w/striker.......12.00
Mirror, wire stand, orig box, 6¼x4¾"..........15.00
Mug, Black man w/beard, winking, animal hdl, 5"...........40.00
Mug, Gen McArthur toby, 3½".................50.00
Mug, Indian bust, mc.........................31.00
Nativity figures, angel/Mary/Joseph/wise men/donkey, VG, all.....28.00
Nodder, dog, celluloid windup.................35.00
Nodder, monkey musician, sticks out tongue, bisque..........85.00
Pencil box, wood w/mc decor...................22.50
Pincushion, shoe, china, 2½"...................6.00
Pincushion, SP heart...........................7.00
Pitcher, applied flower, 2¼"...................5.00
Pitcher, toby; full figure....................19.00
Planter, cowboy boot, tan/wht, 4x3"...........15.00
Planter, donkey pulling cart, 8" L.............10.00
Planter, elephant, raised trunk, 3x4½".........21.50
Planter, pot belly stove, 4x2¼"...............16.00
Planter, spotted deer, 4½"...................12.00
Plaque, boat scene, Sieloff, 6" dia............18.00
Plate, trees, water, grass, mtns, HP, sgn Frunabashi, 9"........28.00
Shakers, dog figural, pr.......................9.00
Shakers, lemon figural, yellow, pr.............8.00
Shakers, polar bear cubs, pr..................15.00
Shakers, tomato, 4", pr......................15.00
Tape measure, cat figural, celluloid, 2½".....20.00
Tea set, tomato figural, 7 pc, lg size.........60.00
Teapot, porcelain, gold, miniature............12.00
Toothpick holder, dog w/basket, 2¾"..........10.00
Toy, dog, key wind, celluloid.................27.00
Tray, lacquer ware, gold decor, 16x22"........58.00
Vase, emb flowers on side, 2½".................8.00
Vase, portrait Oriental lady in relief, Moriyama, 8x4¾"........40.00
Vase, reticulated neck, full figure peacock on side, 6½".......22.00
Wall plaques, Colonial figures, pr............30.00

Ohr, George

George Ohr established his pottery around 1893 in Biloxi, Mississippi. The unusual style of the ware he produced, and his flamboyant personality earned him the dubious title of 'the mad potter of Biloxi'. Though acclaimed by some of the critics of his day to be perhaps the most accomplished thrower in the history of the industry, others overlooked the eggshell thin walls of his vessels, each a different shape and contortion, and saw only that their 'tortured' appearance contradicted their own sedate preferences.

Ohr worked by himself with only minimal help from his son. His work was typically pinched and pulled, pleated, crumpled, dented, and folded. Lizards and worms were often applied to the ware, each with detailed, expressive features. He was well recognized, however, for his glazes, especially those with a metallic patina.

The ware was marked with his name, alone or with 'Biloxi' added. Ohr died in 1918.

Bowl, crimped, shallow body, angle shoulder, olive gr, 6½"....120.00
Mug, clay coil w/in, stamped mk, 2¼x3"................130.00
Mug, rectangular hdl+1 scroll hdl, gr glaze, script mk, 5".....210.00
Penny bank, unglazed lt tan, pear shape, break to open, sgn...125.00
Vase, blk matt, straight flared sides, 3½"..................55.00

Vase, br goldstone glaze, crimped top, 5"................350.00
Vase, bulbous/everted lip, dk gr/gun metal w/in, sgn, 6"......220.00
Vase, cucumber green, classic shape, sgn Geo Ohr, 3½"......150.00
Vase, gr/blk gloss, collar on wide bell, sgn Biloxi, 4", VG.....100.00
Vase, gunmetal glaze, flattened bottle form, 4¾"...........245.00
Vase, pinched sides, mottled gr/blk, 3¼"..................200.00
Vase, pitcher form, crimped neck, br speckled, imp mk, 4"....300.00

Old Ivory

Old Ivory dinnerware was produced during the late 1800s in Selesia. The patterns are referred to by the numbers stamped on the bottom of each piece. The mark sometimes includes a crown, and the name 'Silesia'.

Berry set, #84, 9½" master, 5¼" serving, 7 pc.............195.00
Berry set, Eglantine, 9½" bowl+4 sm berries.............150.00
Bowl, #15, Silesia Clairon, 2½x10¼" dia...................70.00
Bowl, #15, Silesia Clairon, 2¼x9¼" dia....................60.00
Bowl, #16, 10"...80.00
Bowl, #28, 9¾"..68.00
Cake plate, #11, pierced hdls, 10½".........................75.00
Cake plate, #120..65.00
Cake plate, #15, hdl, 10".................................75.00
Cake plate, #33, hdl, Silesia, 10¼".......................65.00
Cake plate, #73, pierced hdls, 10½" dia...................70.00
Cake plate, #75, open hdls, 10"...........................55.00
Cake plate, #84, open hdls, 10"...........................65.00
Cake plate, #16, w/hdls, 10"..............................90.00
Charger, #15, Silesia Clairon, 13" dia...................128.00
Cookie jar, #84, 5½x7"...................................375.00
Creamer, VIII, 3½x4"......................................40.00
Creamer, XVI, Clarion.....................................40.00
Creamer & sugar, #15......................................95.00
Creamer & sugar, #16.....................................130.00
Creamer & sugar, #39......................................75.00
Creamer & sugar, #84.....................................110.00
Cup & saucer, #15...48.00
Cup & saucer, #202..30.00
Cup & saucer, #84...55.00
Mustard jar, #84..80.00
Mustard jar, Holly, #22..................................130.00
Nappy, #16..52.50
Nappy, hdls, VII..45.00
Pickle dish, #83, rectangular, 6¼".........................40.00

Plate, #15, 7½"...24.00
Plate, #16, 7"..28.00
Plate, #16, 7¾"...30.00
Plate, #200, 8¼"..28.00
Plate, #41, 8"..35.00
Plate, #84, 7½"...25.00
Relish, #15, oval, open hdld..............................50.00
Relish, #202, 4 sided, 8¼x4¾".............................45.00
Saucer, #16, set of 6....................................100.00
Saucer, VII...25.00
Shakers, #84, pr...110.00
Sugar w/lid, La Touraine, Striegan, gold encrusted.........48.00
Teapot, La Touraine, Striegan, gold encrusted.............95.00
Toothpick holder, #84.....................................95.00
Tray, #84, 12x7"...180.00
Waste bowl, #16..110.00

Old Paris

Old Paris porcelains were made from the late 18th century until about 1900. Seldom marked, the term refers to the area of manufacture rather than a specific company. In general, the ware was of high quality, and characterized by classic shapes, colorful elegant decoration, and gold application.

Apothecary jar, w/HP flowers & eagles, gold striping, 10", pr...325.00
Cup & saucer, handleless; pk florals, set of 8..............200.00
Dessert set, 12 plates, 2 tureens, crest/lion/crown, mk Maison.1,045.00
Lamp, plum stripes on wht, neck/base w/gilt garland, 36", pr...275.00
Vase, cobalt w/heavy gold Art Nouveau leaves, 6½", pr........65.00
Vase, pear form, HP reserves w/lovers on bl ground, 17", pr...225.00
Vase, portrait of maiden HP in panel, 15½", pr...........4,385.00
Vase, profile portrait, ca 1815, 6½"......................80.00
Vase, rose, floral/scroll/wedding scene; christening, 14", pr.....450.00
Vase, rose w/wht/gold floral, wedding or christening, 11", pr...350.00
Vase, scenic, ornate hdls, applied devices, ftd, 43", damage...3,000.00
Vase, 4 gold leaves at base, floral bouquet, gr/wine, 10¾".....100.00

Old Sleepy Eye

Old Sleepy Eye was a Sioux Indian Chief who was born in Minnesota in 1780. His name was used for the name of a town, as well as a flour mill. The Sleepy Eye Milling Company, of Sleepy Eye, Minnesota, contracted the Weir Pottery Company of Monmouth, Illinois, to make steins, vases, salt crocks, and butter tubs which the company gave away to their customers in each bag of their flour. A bust profile of the old Indian and his name decorated each piece of the blue and gray stoneware. In addition to these four items, the Minnesota Stoneware Company of Red Wing made a mug with a verse which is very scarce today.

In 1906, Weir Pottery merged with six others to form the Western Stoneware Company in Monmouth. They produced a line of blue and white ware using a lighter body, but these pieces were never given as flour premiums. This line consisted of pitchers (five sizes), steins, mugs, sugar bowls, vases, trivets, and mustache cups. These pieces turn up only rarely in other colors and are highly sought by advanced collectors.

Advertising items, such as trade cards, pillow tops, thermometers, paperweights, letter openers, postcards, cookbooks, and thimbles are considered very valuable.

The original ware was made sporadically until 1937. Brown steins and mugs were produced in 1952.

Sugar and creamer, $125.00 for the pair.

Pillow top, audience with President Monroe at Washington, $550.00.

Apron, clothespin...650.00
Calendar, 1906, M..250.00
Cookbook, loaf of bread......................................185.00
Cookbook, portrait on front, 95 pgs..........................225.00
Egg carton, paper, 'We Sell Sleepy Eye Flour'................175.00
Fan..165.00
Label, 30 doz eggs, w/Indian, hops on feathers...............17.50
Letter opener, bronze..900.00
Mirror, advertising, 1940s....................................15.00
Mug, bl/wht, convention issue, dated.........................125.00
Mug, br, 1952..400.00
Mug, wht/cobalt, 5", M.......................................200.00
Paperweight, bronze plated, rare.............................450.00
Pillow top, Monroe at Washington, M..........................550.00
Pillow top, pictures lg trademark head in center, colorful...550.00
Pitcher, #1..175.00
Pitcher, #2..200.00
Pitcher, #3..225.00
Pitcher, #4..250.00
Pitcher, #5..295.00
Pitcher, all gr, ½ gal.......................................500.00
Pitcher, br/gr, ½ gal..550.00
Pitcher, yel w/bl decor, 1 qt, 6¼"...........................990.00
Salt crock, M..500.00
Sign, cardboard, w/litho, 1905, 15" dia......................500.00
Sign, tin, 19x13¼"..1,000.00
Stein, all blue..750.00
Stein, all wht...600.00
Stein, bl/gray...450.00
Stein, bl/wht..500.00
Stein, br/wht..775.00
Stein, brown, 1952...360.00
Stein, dk green..950.00
Stein, yel/br, M...850.00
Sugar bowl...500.00
Thimble..350.00
Vase, bl/gray..300.00
Vase, bl/wht...350.00

O'Neill, Rose

Rose O'Neill's Kewpies first became popular in 1909, when they were used to conclude a story in the December issue of *Ladies' Home Journal*. They were an immediate success, and soon Kewpie dolls were being produced world-wide. German manufacturers were among the earliest, and also used the Kewpie motif to decorate chinaware as well as other items. The Kewpie is still popular today, and can be found on products ranging from Christmas cards and cake ornaments to fabrics and wallpaper.

Bank, chalk Kewpie, 12", EX...................................25.00
Bell, Kewpie figural, brass...................................45.00
Book, Kewpies' Health Book, O'Neill, 1929....................22.50
Booklet, Jello Girl Entertains...............................25.00
Booklet, Jello Girl Gives a Party, O'Neill illus.............25.00
Bowl, child's; w/Kewpie.....................................100.00
Bowl, 6 Kewpies, bl jasperware, sgn.........................275.00
Box, jasperware, bl, ftd, sgn, 3½x2¾".......................140.00
Calendar, Kewpies, 1916, Campbell Art Co, Kleverkard, 5½"....32.00
Calendar, official, 13 pictures, 1975, M.....................30.00
Card holder, Kewpie..25.00
Charm, Kewpie figural, ivory, ¾".............................50.00
Charm, sterling, Kewpie......................................25.00
Christmas ornament, Kewpie, cloth............................12.00
Clock, jasperware w/Kewpies, Germany, sgn, 3½x4½"...........300.00
Coloring book, Kewpies, licensed edition, Saalfield, 1962....12.50
Cradle, for Kewpie..125.00
Creamer, bl jasperware w/frolicking Kewpies, sgn O'Neill, 2½"..195.00
Creamer, Kewpie decor, sgn, Royal Rudolstadt, 3¾"...........125.00
Creamer & sugar, allover action Kewpies, lustre ware, sgn...265.00
Cup, wht w/gr trim, Kewpie decor, sgn, 2" dia................50.00
Cup & saucer, Action Kewpies, Royal Rudolstadt, sgn O'Neill..100.00
Door knocker, Kewpie, brass..................................70.00
Felt...18.00
Giggles, M..375.00
Greeting card, Kewpie..16.00
Hair receiver, blue jasperware, 10 action Kewpies, sgn......250.00
Hat pin, Kewpie, bronze, 5"..................................15.00
Kewpie, bean bag, Cameo......................................50.00
Kewpie, bisque, jtd arms, mk on ft, 4½".....................150.00
Kewpie, bisque, jtd arms, sgn, 9"...........................285.00
Kewpie, bisque, jtd arms, w/heart sticker, sgn, 5"..........135.00
Kewpie, bisque, jtd arms, 4".................................65.00
Kewpie, bisque, jtd arms, 5".................................85.00
Kewpie, bisque, jtd arms & hips, 5".........................400.00
Kewpie, bisque, sitting w/fly on ft, German, 3½", EX........275.00
Kewpie, bisque, sucking thumb, M.............................55.00
Kewpie, bisque, 6½", Nippon..................................90.00
Kewpie, bl wings, movable arms, orig stickers, sgn on ft, 6"..285.00
Kewpie, blk bisque, bent limb baby, jtd arms, tufted hair, 4½"..35.00
Kewpie, blk celluloid, 3"...................................135.00
Kewpie, brass figure...85.00
Kewpie, Cameo, 1968, dressed, 12", MIB.......................80.00
Kewpie, celluloid, emerging from egg, jtd arms, 2¼"..........45.00
Kewpie, celluloid, Hawaiian, 4"..............................15.00
Kewpie, celluloid, Occupied Japan, standing, jtd arms........22.50
Kewpie, celluloid, orig pk ribbon bow & ring, w/label, 4¾"...85.00
Kewpie, celluloid, w/hat, 2¼"................................40.00
Kewpie, celluloid, 2½".......................................10.00
Kewpie, compo, orig bride's dress, stickers chest & ft, 9", NM..135.00
Kewpie, crawling, sgn O'Neill, 4½"..........................150.00
Kewpie, Happifat Girl.......................................200.00
Kewpie, hard plastic, jtd, sleep eyes, 13", NM..............400.00
Kewpie, sitting, holding rose, 2"...........................265.00

Kewpie, sitting, thumb in mouth, bisque, mk KW #228, 5".....75.00
Kewpie, sitting, vinyl face, red stuffed body, 10".............35.00
Kewpie, sitting in chair, wht, NM..........................60.00
Kewpie Bride & Groom, bisque, Nippon, pr..................90.00
Kewpie Bride & Groom, celluloid, Occupied Japan, 2½", pr....40.00
Kewpie Bride & Groom, celluloid, 1920s, 3½"................30.00
Kewpie Bride & Groom, orig outfits, O'Neill, all bisque, 4½"...275.00
Kewpie Cowboy, Cowgirl, pnt bisque/glass eyes, 8", pr........125.00
Kewpie Doodle Dog, sgn, 3".................................385.00
Kewpie Ho-Ho, brass.......................................45.00
Kewpie Ho-Ho, sgn, lg.....................................85.00
Kewpie Ho-Ho, sgn, sm.....................................35.00
Kewpie Hot-n'-Tot, Cameo, MIB.............................65.00
Kewpie Huggers, bisque, sgn, 3½", pr......................225.00
Kewpie Huggers, w/sticker, 'Rose O'Neill, 1913, Made in Japan'.100.00
Kewpie Indian, hard plastic................................6.00
Kewpie Nun, celluloid.....................................15.00
Kewpie Preacher, bisque...................................25.00
Kewpie Santa, cardboard, 1913, 11"........................45.00
Kewpie Sleeper, Cameo, MIB................................40.00
Kewpie Thinker, bisque, no mk, 5".........................65.00
Kewpie Thinker, bisque, sgn, 6"...........................250.00
Kewpie Thinker, chalk, sgn O'Neill, Germany...............125.00
Kewpie Thinker, vinyl, sgn O'Neill, Cameo, 4".............15.00
Kewpie Traveler, heart sticker, Japan, 2½"................135.00
Lamp, chalkware Kewpie, orig shade........................200.00
Lamp, metal, w/Kewpies, sgn...............................525.00
Lapel button, Kewpie, sgn, 2½"............................175.00
Letter opener, Kewpie figural, sgn, pewter.................65.00
Magazine page from June 1927 Ladies' Home Joural, Kewpieville.12.00
Marble puzzle, Kewpie......................................4.50
Mayonnaise jar, Kewpie on label & lid......................30.00
Mug, w/Kewpies, sgn O'Neill, Royal Rudolstadt, 2½".........80.00
Mug, w/Kewpies, sgn O'Neill, Royal Rudolstadt, 3¾".........125.00
Name plate, Kewpie holding open book, stamped C............350.00
Perfume bottle, bisque Kewpie.............................325.00
Pin, enamel Kewpie, The Cook..............................150.00
Pitcher, playing leapfrog/butterflies, sgn, 4½"............130.00
Planter, heart shaped w/Kewpie.............................45.00
Planter, Kewpie by stump...................................35.00
Planter, Thinker Kewpie....................................65.00

Plaque, bl jasper, Wedgwood...............................70.00
Plate, 7 Kewpies, Royal Rudolstadt, sgn, 7¾"..............125.00
Postcard, Kewpies w/sled, sgn.............................20.00
Poster, sgn, w/Kewpie, lg.................................30.00
Print, Kewpie eating sundae, 1920s, 16x12"................20.00
Ragsie, red, mk Ragsie, sm................................35.00
Ring, Kewpie, sterling....................................75.00
Salt, Kewpie w/turkey, china..............................250.00
Scootles, bisque, sgn, Japan, 6½".........................125.00
Scootles, brass...100.00
Shakers, SP, Kewpies, sgn, pr.............................200.00
Soap, Kewpie figural, MIB.................................85.00
Song sheet, sgn cover.....................................15.00
Spoon, baby's; sterling w/Kewpie, mk P&B..................150.00
Stickpin, blk celluloid Kewpie, 1¼".......................65.00
Talcum powder, celluloid Kewpie/red heart, blk/wht sticker, 8".125.00
Tea set, doll's, china w/Kewpie decor, sgn Rose O'Neill....85.00
Teapot, Kewpie, sgn.......................................200.00
Teapot, 4 c/s, cr/sug w/lid, Action Kewpies, wht w/pk lustre....475.00
Thimble, military Kewpie, mk Kewpie.......................35.00
Toothpick holder, unusual bisque Kewpie, open mouth, reclining.85.00
Transfer sheet, 28 different designs, Germany, 1913, 7x13"....95.00
Whistle, brass Kewpie.....................................25.00

Onion Pattern

The familiar pattern known to collectors as Onion acquired its name through a case of mistaken identity. Designed in the early 1700s by Johann Haroldt of the Meissen factory in Germany, the pattern was a mixture from earlier Oriental designs. One of its components was a stylized peach, which was mistaken to be an onion, causing the pattern to become known by that name. Usually found in blue, an occasional piece is also found in pink. The pattern is commonly associated with Meissen, but it has been reproduced by many others including Villeroy and Boch, and Royal Copenhagen.

Bowl, shaped, X swords front & bk, 1½x7½x6"................65.00
Butter dish w/lid, Vienna Woods...........................27.50
Candy dish, loop hdl, Vienna Woods........................14.50
Canister w/lid, barrel shape, Coffee, 8"..................75.00
Canister w/lid, spice; barrel shape, Allspice, no mk......45.00
Cheese board, 'Guten Appetit', hanging, Meissen, 5x8".....140.00
Compote, X swords, Meissen, 8½"...........................165.00
Cup & saucer, demitasse; oval mk, Meissen.................35.00
Cup & saucer, X swords, Meissen...........................65.00
Funnel, wood hdl, unsgn Meissen, 4".......................78.00
Funnel, wood hdl, unsgn Meissen, 4¾"......................95.00
Funnel, wood hdl, unsgn Meissen, 5½"......................110.00
Gravy boat w/attached under plate, 2 hdls, X swords, Meissen..130.00
Hot plate, mk Bonn..50.00
Knife rest..75.00
Ladle, wood hdl, unsgn Meissen, 4x2"......................135.00
Masher, wood hdl, unsgn Meissen...........................135.00
Meat tenderizer...135.00
Pitcher, milk; Vienna Woods...............................27.50
Plate, reticulated border, X swords, Meissen, 8"..........300.00
Plate, X swords, Meissen, 10".............................100.00
Plate, X swords, Meissen, 9"..............................70.00
Plate, 7"..18.00
Platter, England, 18x13"..................................125.00
Platter, Villeroy & Boch, 15¼x11".........................65.00
Platter, X swords, Meissen, 10" L.........................125.00
Platter, X swords, Meissen, 11½"..........................150.00
Platter, X swords, Meissen, 19"...........................225.00

Cloverleaf tray, green jasperware with pink Kewpies, signed 'Rose O'Neill, Kewpies, Germany', 7" wide, $335.00.

Platter, very rare bowknot handles, signed with the crossed swords, 16″ long, $600.00.

Platter, X swords, Meissen, 21x10″	300.00
Relish dish, scalloped, Meissen, 11¾x7¼″	85.00
Rolling pin, w/wooden hdls, 15″ L	150.00
Scoop/strainer	95.00
Soup, X swords, Meissen	70.00
Spoon rest, X swords, Meissen	175.00
Tea strainer, all china	65.00
Tea strainer, wood hdl, unsgn Meissen	90.00
Tenderizer, wood hdl, unsgn Meissen, 3″, EX	125.00
Trivet	120.00
Vase, X swords in design on front, Meissen, 4″	42.00

Opalescent Glass

First made in England in 1870, opalescent glass became popular in America around the turn of the century. Its name comes from the milky white opalescent trim that defines the lines of the pattern. It was produced in table sets, novelties, toothpick holders, vases, and lamps.

Buttons and Braids, pitcher, blue, 10″, $125.00.

Alaska, banana boat, vaseline	275.00
Alaska, bowl, berry; clear, small	25.00
Alaska, bowl, berry; flat, blue, Northwood	45.00
Alaska, butter w/cover, blue, decorated	250.00
Alaska, creamer, blue	75.00
Alaska, creamer, clear	35.00
Alaska, creamer, vaseline	65.00
Alaska, cruet, blue, w/orig stopper	200.00
Alaska, pitcher, water; vaseline	285.00
Alaska, sauce, blue	45.00
Alaska, sauce, clear	28.00
Alaska, sauce, vaseline	45.00
Alaska, sugar w/lid, blue, no show inner rim chip	95.00
Alaska, tray, celery; vaseline	185.00
Arabian Nights, pitcher, water; cranberry	325.00
Arabian Nights, tumbler, cranberry	85.00
Argonaut Shell, creamer, blue	72.00
Astro, bowl, ruffled, blue	40.00
Astro, bowl, ruffled, gr, 9″	40.00
Ball, bowl, ftd, blue	37.50
Basketweave, bowl, reticulated, blue	30.00
Basketweave, candlesticks, low, green, pr	40.00
Bead & Bark, vase, blue	40.00
Beaded Cable, bowl, green, ruffled, 3 ft	22.50
Beatty Honeycomb, creamer, individual; blue	45.00
Beatty Honeycomb, tumbler, clear	25.00
Beatty Rib, celery vase, blue	35.00
Beatty Rib, master salt, blue	40.00
Beatty Rib, toothpick, clear	28.00
Beatty Swirl, butter w/cover, blue	140.00
Beatty Swirl, pitcher, water; blue	140.00
Blocked Thumbprint & Beads, bowl, blue, 5″	15.00
Bubble Lattice, syrup, canary, orig top	85.00
Bubble Lattice, tumbler, blue	45.00
Button Panels, rose bowl	45.00
Buttons & Braids, pitcher, water; blue	125.00
Buttons & Braids, pitcher, water; green	135.00
Buttons & Braids, tumbler, blue	25.00
Chrysanthemum Base, tumbler, cranberry	95.00
Chrysanthemum Base Swirl, mug, cranberry	75.00
Chrysanthemum Base Swirl, punch cup, clear	25.00
Circled Scroll, berry set, blue, 7 pc	350.00
Circled Scroll, bowl, berry; blue, small	32.00
Circled Scroll, bowl, master berry; green	65.00
Circled Scroll, butter w/cover, green	175.00
Circled Scroll, pitcher, water; green	245.00
Circled Scroll, sauce, ftd, blue, 4¼″ dia	25.00
Circled Scroll, table set, blue, 4 pc	750.00
Circled Scroll, table set, green, 4 pc	575.00
Circled Scroll, water set, blue, 7 pc	700.00
Coin Spot, pitcher, amberina, clear reeded applied hdl, 8″	325.00
Coin Spot, pitcher, water; bl, ruffled opal top, bulbous, 9½″	120.00
Coin Spot, pitcher, water; bl w/ribbed handle, early Hobb's	145.00
Coin Spot, pitcher, water; clear w/rope handle	90.00
Coin Spot, pitcher, water; cranberry, ruffled top	145.00
Coin Spot, pitcher, water; green	90.00
Coin Spot, syrup, blue	95.00
Coin Spot, tumbler, blue crackle glass, Baby Coinspot	45.00
Coin Spot, tumbler, blue opal	35.00
Coin Spot, tumbler, cranberry opal	45.00
Daisy & Fern, pitcher, water; clear	120.00
Daisy & Fern, tumbler, blue	32.00
Daisy & Fern, tumbler, cranberry	45.00
Daisy & Fern, water set, cranberry, sq ruffled top, 5 pc	255.00

Beatty Swirl, pitcher, clear, by Tiffin, 8", $125.00

Diamond Spearhead, butter dish, vaseline.................175.00
Diamond Spearhead, creamer, individual; green.............45.00
Diamond Spearhead, jelly compote, vaseline...............110.00
Diamond Spearhead, mug, dk blue..........................45.00
Dolly Madison, spooner, green............................45.00
Drapery, bowl, berry; blue, w/gold, small, Northwood.........30.00
Drapery, celery, opal/clear w/ruffle cranberry rim, blown mold....55.00
Drapery, sauce, blue.....................................13.00
Drapery, tumbler, blue...................................27.00
Everglades, berry set, blue, 7 pc.......................395.00
Everglades, bowl, master berry; blue....................110.00
Everglades, butter w/cover, blue........................280.00
Everglades, compote, blue................................50.00
Everglades, compote, jelly; vaseline.....................95.00
Everglades, creamer, clear w/gold........................40.00
Everglades, pitcher, water; vaseline....................425.00
Everglades, sauce, blue..................................30.00
Everglades, sauce, vaseline..............................35.00
Everglades, spooner, blue................................85.00
Everglades, spooner, clear w/good gold...................40.00
Everglades, spooner, vaseline, w/EX gold.................75.00
Everglades, sugar w/lid, blue...........................145.00
Everglades, table set, blue, w/EX gold, 4 pc............685.00
Everglades, tumbler, blue................................65.00
Everglades, tumbler, vaseline............................75.00
Eyelets & Flowers, pitcher, blue........................350.00
Fluted Scroll, butter w/cover, vaseline.................165.00
Fluted Scroll, creamer, blue.............................58.00
Fluted Scroll, creamer, clear............................20.00
Fluted Scroll, creamer, vaseline.........................50.00
Fluted Scroll, pitcher, water; clear.....................65.00
Fluted Scroll, pitcher, water; vaseline.................195.00
Fluted Scroll, puff box, vaseline........................55.00
Fluted Scroll, sauce, vaseline...........................25.00
Fluted Scroll, spooner, blue.............................50.00
Fluted Scroll, spooner, vaseline.........................45.00
Fluted Scroll, table set, clear.........................200.00
Fluted Scroll, tumbler, vaseline.........................40.00
Frosted Leaf & Basketweave, spooner, blue................90.00
Gonterman Swirl, spooner, clear w/amber rim.............110.00
Grape & Cable, bowl, ftd, large, clear..................110.00
Grapevine Cluster, vase, green...........................45.00
Guttate, butter w/cover, clear w/some gold...............80.00

Hobnail & Paneled Thumbprint, spooner, blue...............65.00
Hobnail & Paneled Thumbprint, spooner, vaseline...........45.00
Hobnail & Paneled Thumbprint, table set, blue, 4 pc......425.00
Hobnail & Paneled Thumbprint, table set, vaseline........385.00
Hobnail Fan, vase, vaseline..............................42.00
Honeycomb & Clover, bowl, blue, 8½" dia..................38.00
Intaglio, berry set, blue, 7 pc.........................400.00
Intaglio, bowl, ruffled, ftd, vaseline...................45.00
Intaglio, creamer, blue..................................43.00
Intaglio, sauce, ftd, blue...............................22.50
Intaglio, table set, blue, 4 pc.........................850.00
Intaglio, table set, clear, 4 pc........................245.00
Intaglio, water set, blue, 7 pc.........................725.00
Inverted Fan & Feather, tumbler, blue....................50.00
Inverted Fan & Feather, water set, EX gold, 7 pc........450.00
Iris w/Meander, butter w/cover, blue....................365.00
Iris w/Meander, compote, blue............................38.00
Iris w/Meander, compote, jelly; vaseline.................30.00
Iris w/Meander, creamer, blue...........................125.00
Iris w/Meander, sauce, vaseline..........................25.00
Iris w/Meander, toothpick, green.........................55.00
Jackson, butter dish, vaseline..........................165.00
Jackson, creamer, blue...................................40.00
Jackson, spooner, blue...................................23.00
Jackson, tray, card; clear...............................10.00
Jackson, tumbler, blue...................................14.00
Jewel & Fan, bowl, oval, green, 7".......................25.00
Jewel & Fan, bowl, round, green, 6¼".....................25.00
Jewel & Flower, spooner, clear w/gold & red..............25.00
Jewel & Flower, sugar w/lid, clear w/gold & red..........35.00
Jewel & Flower, table set, blue, 4 pc...................425.00
Jewel & Flower, tumbler, clear w/gold & red..............45.00
Jewelled Heart, creamer, blue............................60.00
Jewelled Heart, tumbler, green...........................35.00
Leaf Chalice, sugar, ped, green..........................55.00
Leaf w/Basketweave, spooner, blue.......................115.00
Many Loops, bowl, trefoil, green.........................25.00
Meander, bowl, deep, 3 legs, blue........................40.00
Palisades, vase, blue....................................25.00
Palm & Scroll, bowl, green, 9"...........................14.00
Palm Beach, berry set, blue, 7 pc.......................285.00
Palm Beach, berry set, vaseline, 7 pc...................295.00
Palm Beach, butter w/cover, vaseline....................275.00
Palm Beach, pitcher, water; blue........................395.00
Palm Beach, spooner, vaseline............................95.00
Palm Beach, sugar w/lid, blue...........................175.00
Palm Beach, table set, blue, 4 pc.......................650.00
Palm Beach, water set, vaseline, 7 pc...................695.00
Paneled Holly, butter w/cover, blue, no decor...........200.00
Pearl Flowers, bowl, 3 ftd, green........................25.00
Plume & Flowers, bowl, blue..............................35.00
Poinsettia, tankard, blue...............................195.00
Poinsettia, tumbler, green, blown........................30.00
Poinsettia, water set, blue, 7 pc, molded tumblers......375.00
Regal, butter w/cover, blue, Northwood..................150.00
Regal, butter w/cover, green............................135.00
Regal, butter w/cover, green w/gold, Northwood..........175.00
Regal, celery vase, blue.................................95.00
Regal, compote, blue.....................................63.00
Regal, sauce, blue.......................................18.00
Regal, spooner, blue, Northwood..........................65.00
Regal, spooner, green....................................45.00
Regal, sugar, blue, Northwood............................95.00
Reverse Swirl, cruet, vaseline..........................165.00

Reverse Swirl, pitcher, water; tankard......................85.00
Reverse Swirl, pitcher, water; vaseline....................150.00
Reverse Swirl, tumbler, cranberry.........................40.00
Reverse Swirl, tumbler, vaseline..........................45.00
Ribbed Lattice, celery vase, cranberry....................85.00
Ribbed Spiral, bowl, vaseline.............................37.00
Ribbed Spiral, compote, jelly; blue.......................40.00
Roulette, bowl, ftd, green, 8½" dia.......................25.00
Ruffles & Rings, bowl, green, 9"..........................13.00
Ruffles & Rings, bowl, scroll legs........................35.00
Scroll w/Acanthus, compote, blue..........................28.00
Scroll w/Acanthus, compote, jelly; green..................30.00
Scroll w/Acanthus, creamer, blue..........................55.00
Scroll w/Acanthus, creamer, vaseline......................50.00
Sea Spray, nappy, green, round hdl........................15.00
Sea Spray, olive, hdl, green..............................25.00
Shell, creamer, blue......................................75.00
Shell, creamer, clear.....................................30.00
Shell, creamer, green, Northwood-Dugan....................60.00
Shell, spooner, blue......................................85.00
Shell, sugar w/lid, blue.................................105.00
Shell & Dogwood, bowl, open lattice border, green.........21.00
Shell & Wild Rose, bowl, blue, 8½"........................13.00
Spanish Lace, pitcher, vaseline, 80 oz...................145.00
Squirrel & Acorn, vase, green, 9".........................85.00
Stars & Bars, tumbler, cranberry..........................30.00
Stars & Stripes, barber bottle, blue.....................195.00
Sunburst on Shield, sugar, breakfast; blue................25.00
Swag w/Brackets, berry set, blue.........................250.00
Swag w/Brackets, butter w/cover, vaseline................195.00
Swag w/Brackets, compote, green...........................37.50
Swag w/Brackets, compote, jelly; open, blue...............40.00
Swag w/Brackets, spooner, green...........................45.00
Swag w/Brackets, table set, vaseline, 4 pc...............450.00
Swag w/Brackets, tumbler, blue............................70.00
Swirl, barber bottle, blue, polished pontil..............145.00
Swirl, barber bottle, tall round shape, clear, polished pontil....135.00
Swirl, pitcher, water; blue, sq crimped top, Burlington mk.....155.00
Swirl, pitcher, water; cranberry, square top.............210.00
Swirl, pitcher, water; square neck, cranberry, Burlington mk....235.00
Swirl, tumbler, blue......................................30.00
Swirl, tumbler, cranberry.................................32.00
Swirl, vase, cranberry....................................40.00
Tokyo, berry set, blue...................................285.00
Tokyo, bowl, green, 4x9"..................................50.00
Tokyo, compote, green.....................................33.00
Tokyo, creamer, blue......................................85.00
Tokyo, doughnut stand, apple green w/EX opal..............48.00
Tokyo, pitcher, water; green.............................135.00
Tokyo, sugar, blue.......................................125.00
Tokyo, table set, blue, 4 pc.............................475.00
Vintage, plate, blue, footed..............................25.00
Water Lily & Cattails, bowl, ruffled, amethyst, 9"........35.00
Wild Bouquet, berry set, green...........................325.00
Wild Bouquet, creamer, blue...............................90.00
Wild Bouquet, creamer, green..............................50.00
Wild Bouquet, spooner, blue...............................75.00
Wild Bouquet, spooner, green..............................65.00
Windows, barber bottle, clear............................110.00
Windows Swirl, pitcher, water; clear......................95.00
Windows Swirl, tumbler, clear.............................25.00
Wooden Pail, table set, vaseline.........................200.00
Wreath & Shell, berry set, blue, 6 pc....................250.00
Wreath & Shell, butter w/cover, vaseline.................185.00

Wreath & Shell, dish, 3 ftd, blue.........................50.00
Wreath & Shell, spooner...................................50.00
Wreath & Shell, table set, vaseline......................450.00
Wreath & Shell, water set, vaseline, 7 pc................625.00
Wreathed Shell, tumbler, blue.............................32.00

Openers

Around the turn of the century, manufacturers began to seal bottles with a metal cap that required a new type of bottle opener. Now the screw cap and the flip top are making bottle openers nearly obsolete.

There are many variations, some in combination with other tools. Many openers were used as means of advertising a product. Various materials were used, including silver and brass.

A figural bottle opener is defined as a figure designed for the sole purpose of lifting a bottle cap. The actual opener must be an integral part of the figure itself. The major producers of iron figurals were Wilton Products; John Wright, Inc.; Gadzik Sales; and L & L Favors. Openers may be freestanding three-dimensional, wall hung, or flat. They can be made of cast iron (often painted), brass, bronze, or aluminum.

Bottle Openers

Alligator, #124.......................................25.00
Alligator, #125.......................................65.00
Alligator, blk, on ash tray...........................65.00
Auto jack...35.00
Bear..40.00
Bully, bull's head, CI, 6½"...........................25.00
Canada goose, brass...................................50.00
Cappy, brass..45.00
Century of Progress, figural nude Egyptian lady hdl, iron........8.00
Cliquot Club, Eskimo figural..........................75.00
Clown...25.00
Cockatoo..55.00
Cocker dog..15.00
Corn, brass...15.00
Cowboy..45.00
Crab..15.00
Crab, brass...20.00
Dachshund, brass......................................55.00
Dolphin, brass..25.00
Donkey, brass...25.00
Donkey, iron..35.00
Elephant..20.00
Fireman's hat, iron, G................................20.00
Fish, #127..25.00
Fish, #130..65.00
Fish, brass & abalone shell...........................15.00
Flamingo..30.00
Foundrymen, aluminum..................................25.00
Four eyed lady..25.00
Four eyed man...25.00
Frontier gun, brass...................................35.00
Geisha girl, iron.....................................65.00
Goat, sitting, CI.....................................45.00
Graef & Schimdt, ivory slab hdl, plated opener, ca 1900........5.00
Green River Whiskey, w/corkscrew.......................15.00
Hammer..15.00
Handyhands on ash tray................................50.00
Hanging drunk...35.00
Iron, engraved hdl, pierced, pat but no date, ca 1900........7.00
Iroquois Indian, aluminum.............................75.00

Lamp signpost drunk, Dalecraft, EX rare, on ash tray........225.00
Lamppost drunk, brass....................20.00
Lamppost drunk, iron....................15.00
Lobster, #132....................35.00
Lobster, #133....................20.00
Lobster, #134....................15.00
Lock....................35.00
Mademoiselle....................45.00
Mademoiselle w/sign....................25.00
Mallard....................25.00
No legend, #150....................45.00
Nude, brass....................50.00
Nude, Canada on wreath, chrome....................75.00
Nude, reclining, chrome, unlisted....................35.00
Nude, reclining, copper color, unlisted....................35.00
Nude on bell, brass....................35.00
Nude on duck, brass....................30.00
Nude w/wreath....................50.00
Palm tree drunk....................25.00
Parrot, lg....................25.00
Parrot, sm....................45.00
Parrot w/can punch....................45.00
Pelican, #116....................25.00
Pheasant, brass....................35.00
Pink elephant....................45.00
Pixie, brass/steel, English reg mk, 1920s....................20.00
Rooster....................20.00
Sailor....................15.00
Sam Weller, figural....................12.00
Seagull....................25.00
Seahorse, brass, unlisted....................65.00
Setter dog....................22.00
Shark, aluminum....................25.00
Signpost drunk....................15.00
Silverman's Strand Theatre, leg w/ft opener....................7.00
Straw hat signpost....................85.00
Tennis racket....................30.00
Top hat man....................25.00
Wolf head, mouth is opener, chrome, ½ moon hdl....................32.00

Corkscrews

Boar tusk, SP end, English, turned shaft, 8¼"....................85.00
Boar tusk hdl w/sterling butt, fancy faceted shaft, 1900, 9½"...180.00
Cherrywood trn hdl w/ring & brush, rnd steel shaft, 1860........35.00
Combination cap lifter/measure-funnel, sterling & plate, 3 pc....80.00
Eagle, outspread wings, cast brass....................25.00
Elephant, cast brass, wire helix tail, 1920, 3"....................15.00
Folding, harp, steel, 1890, 2¾x2½"....................20.00
Green River, Whiskey w/o Headache, Pat June 27 '05/July 3 '06.35.00
Horn hdl, long rnd steel shaft, ca 1890....................35.00
James Heeley & Sons, pat 6006 dbl lever, copper finish, 1880s.125.00
Key, CI w/copper finish, unscrews, 3" shaft & worm, 8"........45.00
Man's head, carved wood/orig pnt....................10.00
Mother of pearl hdl, scent bottle, silver ferrule, 3¾"....................25.00
Revolver, metal w/silver finish, ca 1940, 4½"....................22.00
Souvenir, Jenny Jones, brass, ca 1930, English....................20.00
Staghorn hdl w/sterling end, trn plated shaft, 1910....................130.00
Steel, 3 finger straight pull oval ring, ca 1900, 2" worm........20.00
Sterling, fancy T hdl, Walker patent bell, ca 1900....................100.00
Surprise, English, ball bearing trn mechanism, plated steel......25.00
Syroco, waiter's head, 1930s....................25.00
Weir's Pat 12804/35 Sept/1884 Heeley & Son Makers, EX.....150.00
Wht brass, champagne tap, ca 1910....................30.00

Williamson, trn wood hdl, plated shaft cover, open bell, 1895...20.00
Williamson's New Century, bottle hdl, #1900, 2½"....................35.00
Wood hdl, tapered wire shaft, ca 1900....................10.00
Wood hdl, trn/banded, Colonial American....................22.50
2 Faced Senator Volstead, SP, measure/cap lifter/spoon, 1925..135.00

Opera Glasses

Chevalier, Paris, cast metal/brass/nickel w/birds relief, 2¾".....38.00
Folding, 'Le Petit fabricant Paris 1923', wine leather cover.....32.00
French, enameled romantic scenes on body & long hdl........300.00
French, smokey MOP, w/case, EX....................45.00
J Gall & Co, classical scenes in gold on transparent blue......250.00

Opera glasses, copper with gold florals, marked 'Mermod Jaccard Jewelry Co', 3", $110.00.

Optical Items

Collectors of Americana are beginning to appreciate the charm of antique optical items, and those involved in the related trade find them particularly fascinating. Anyone, however, can appreciate the evolution of technology apparent when viewing a collection of old eye wear, and at the same time admire the primitive ingenuity involved in their construction.

Case, carved ivory w/shield & florals, German, 1800s..........70.00
Case, tin, pat 9/20/1864, JL Harlem....................10.00
Case, tin w/brass spectacles, rpr, 4¾"....................10.00
Lorgnette, gold, heavily engraved hdl & cover..............725.00
Lorgnette, Hungarian niello w/griffins....................225.00
Lorgnette, sterling vermeil, overall reticulation, 5" L.........135.00
Lorgnette, tortoise shell....................100.00

Case, ivory with carved horse in recessed reserve, French, ca 1860 to 1880, 5½" x 3", $1,500.00.

Spectacles, Ben Franklin type, aqua lens..................16.00
Spectacles, granny, extension type, orig leather case..........12.00
Spectacles, granny, rnd, 14k gold........................65.00
Spectacles, granny, 1 pc folding pince-nez, orig leather case......8.00
Spectacles, ladies', gold filled, chain & hairpin...............17.50
Sunglasses, Georgian, folding, sun shields ea side...........135.00

Orientalia

The art of the Orient is an area of collecting that has recently enjoyed a surge of interest, not only in those examples that are truly 'antique', but in the 20th century items as well. Auction prices seem to well exceed their estimates with a regularity not apparent in many other collectible fields.

Because of the many aspects involved in a study of Orientalia, we can only try through brief comments to acquaint the reader with some of the more readily available examples and suggest specialized reference sources for detailed information.

Celadon, introduced during the Chin Dynasty, is a green glazed ware developed in an attempt to imitate the color of jade. Designs are often incised or painted on over glaze in heavy enamel applications.

Chinese export ware was designed to appeal to Western tastes, and was often made to order. During the 18th century, vast amounts were shipped to Europe and on westward. Many of these dinnerwares were given specific pattern names -- Rose Mandarin, Fitzhugh, Rose Medallion, Canton, and Armorial are but a few of the more familiar.

Cinnabar is carved lacquer work, often involving hundreds of layers built one at a time on a metal or wooden base. Later pieces are red; older examples tend to darken.

See also Canton; Champleve; Cloisonne; Geisha Girl; Imari; Ivory; Kutani; Moriage; Netsuke; Nippon; Noritake; Peking Glass; Rose Medallion; Satsuma; Snuff Bottles; Soapstone

Banko

Mug, applied decor, scholar & cat on red, drip glaze neck/hdl...70.00
Teapot, animals, reed hdl, early.........................225.00
Vase, 2 applied robed animals play board game on red/gr, 12".150.00
Vase, 4 boys climbing mtn, orange/blk, bl/red top, 10".......200.00

Blue & White Porcelain

Bowl, bird/floral decor, 1860, 16" dia.....................250.00
Bowl, dbl ogee, lotus meander/ruyi heads band, Yongzheng, 7".495.00
Bowl, reticulated, scenic rondels, diaper band, Kangxi, 3½"....250.00
Dish, dragons/clouds, Arita, 1700s, 7½" dia................300.00
Dish, heaped/piled effect, lotus meander, Ming style, 5½".....220.00
Dish, jard of flowers, pomegranate vine border, 1600s, 21"...1,100.00
Dish, medallion w/branch of finger citrons, Yongzheng, 8".....440.00
Dish, petal form/fluted, bird on rock medallion, late Ming, 8"...65.00
Fish bowl, panels of carp, 16" dia, pr....................600.00
Jar, Qianlong, 4 warriors, scroll/floral neck, 12".............475.00
Jar w/lid, prunus on bl wash, rstr, Kangxi Period, 8¾".......605.00
Mizusashi, cylinder w/waisted ft, landscape/dragon, 10".......200.00
Nanking, platter/strainer, bl/wht Willow variant, 1790, 15"....275.00
Nanking, vegetable dish/cover, Willow variant, 1790, 13½"....350.00
Plate, pagoda in river landscape in center, octagonal, 9", 12...450.00
Saucer, garden of 3 Friends, cloud panels, Qianlong, 6", pr....550.00
Tea caddy, prunus blossoms, 5¼".........................35.00
Tureen, rabbit head hdls/pomegranate finial, scenic, 1780, 13".750.00
Vase, baluster form, Taoist symbols/bats/clouds, 16½".......175.00
Vase, crackleware, continuous scenes w/warriors, 1800s, 9¼"....75.00
Vase, dbl gourd/lobed, flying horse/floral panels, Wanli, 11".1,430.00

Vase, Yenyen, courtiers in pavilion/priest, waisted neck, 17"..1,210.00
Wine pot, peach form, allover shou characters, Kangxi, 5½"...440.00

Bowl, Nanking, quatrefoil/scalloped, 4¾x9½x10⅛"..........525.00
Bowl, rice; blanc de chine, ftd/Greek key border/medallion, 5"...35.00
Bowl, Shufu-type, flared sides, florals w/in, lt bl, Song, 4½"....440.00
Bowl, Yingqing, carved med/cloud whirls w/in, lt bl, Song, 7"..990.00
Bowl, Yingqing, wedge ft, carved band of petals, bl, Song, 6"..660.00
Bowl w/lid, pewter, twig form hdl, 4 clusters grapes/rats, 12"..125.00
Box, Masonic devices/Vitruvian scroll border, 1790, 11"......550.00
Box, seal; bl/wht soft paste, scenic, w/lid, Kangxi, 2¾".......525.00

Bronze

Bowl, waisted rnd ft, wave form stand, flaring rim, 7x12".....100.00
Buddha, seated, flowing robes, Thai, 40"..................1,650.00
Censer, oval w/steep sides, 4 ft, dragon handles, 1800s, 11"....330.00
Censer, ovoid w/reticulated clouds/phoenix hdls, 16"..........350.00
Censer, 4 part, emb deities/samurai/dragon, Miyao, 94".....11,000.00
Dish, lily pad on stem work support, Japanese, 3½x9"........60.00
Equestrian guardian, parcel gilt, Chinese, 6"................40.00
Guanyin, seated on lotus ped, holding vial, 1600s, 13".......660.00
Hand of Buddha, on carved wood stand, Tibet, 1700s, 9½"....100.00
Incense burner, dragon boat form base w/snail form lid, 6¾"...100.00
Incense burner, sq ftd base w/2 children, lid w/foo dog, 5¾"...100.00
Jardiniere, pierced lip, bamboo sides, br on gr, raised ft......200.00
Mirror, 4 emb lions galloping around central knob, Tang, 4½".770.00
Pheasant figural, mk Masatsune, late 1800s, 34" L..........1,320.00
Plaque of Vairocana, late Muromachi period, 12¾" dia........440.00
Rooster, gilt, red lacquer stand, 32".....................2,420.00
Socket axe, flared blade/circular socket, Shang Dynasty, 5½"...165.00
Sword, incised w/5 pictograms, emb masks, 300-200 BC, 18".1,100.00
Vase, cloud base/applied dragon, relief dragon sides/hdls, 14"..600.00
Vase, grass sheaves form w/birds/wind chimes, 12½"..........200.00
Vase, 3 applied oni, 1 on neck looking down, 1800s, 15".....475.00
Vase w/enamel silver grasshopper figural, sgn, 8¾"..........825.00
Wenshu seated on lion, wears crown w/Buddah, Ming, 9½"....770.00

Celadon

Bowl, incised scrolling foliage underglaze w/in, 6¼"..........80.00
Dish, Zhejiang, florals w/in, olive gr/orange base ring, 9½"....550.00
Dog, seated, fringed cloth collar, Kutani, 1900, 5½".........350.00
Plate, ftd, calligraphy medallion w/bl floral/cloud, 11½"........75.00
Toddy jug w/lid, birds/butterflies/flowers, enamel/gilt, 11".....300.00
Vase, Ku-form, animals/florals, enamel/gilt, 1800s, 13".......450.00
Vase w/lid, rows of carved petals, bud finial, Song, 11"......1,100.00

Chinese Paintings

Album, erotica, 12 leaves, silk, 1800s, ea 9x8".............1,650.00
Album, 12 landscapes, on silk, 1 sgn Tang Yin, ea: 9x11½"..1,650.00
Birds in Landscape, silk scroll/ink/color, Cui Bo, 14x95".....3,025.00
Calligraphy in Xing Shu, paper scroll, Wang Wenzhi, 53x14"...660.00
Dragon & Sun, att Gao Qipei, paper fan/ink & color, 7x21"..1,870.00
Flowers, hanging scroll/ink & color on silk, Yun Bing, 59x15"..495.00
Landscape, paper fan/ink & color, Sheng Dashi, 7x20".......500.00
Lohans, bl paper scroll/gold ink, sgn Shang Xi, dtd, 165x11"..825.00
Palace scene, set of 12, silk scroll/ink & color, 67x271".....7,700.00

Copper, incense burner, ftd lotoid bow w/long hdl, Japan, 12"..150.00
Cream pot w/lid, Nanking, beak spout, 1810, M.............265.00
Creamer, helmet; iron red urn & florals, late 19th C, 5½".....65.00
Creamer, helmet; mc kissing doves, 5½"...................125.00
Dish, diaper ground w/panels of flowers, underglaze bl/red, 6"..550.00
Dish, petal form/barbed & lobed rim, crane/pond, Tianqui, 6"..440.00
Famille rose, basin, Mandarins on terrace/dragon rim, 16".....450.00
Famille rose, garden seat, rnd hex/lotus on turq, pierced, 18"..750.00
Famille rose, jardiniere, dragons/flowers on yellow, 12", pr..1,320.00
Famille rose, jardiniere, red w/petal molded sides, 10" W, G...385.00
Famille rose, noblemen in court/flowers, lion hdls, 30"......1,100.00
Famille rose, plate, Allegorical of Earth, 1745, 9"..........1,540.00
Famille rose, plate, retic, pheasant/birds/flowers, 8", 6 for......715.00
Famille rose, vase, baluster, scenes w/figures, lion hdls, 32"....330.00
Famille rose, vase, enamel panels of Immortals on pewter, 25".715.00
Famille rose, vase, turq, birds/florals in oval, 1850, 14", pr...1,800.00
Famille rose, vase, 2 pr dragons/lotus scroll, dragon hdls, 7"....440.00
Famille rose, warriors in combat, ovoid, Qianlong, 18", pr.....495.00
Famille verte, jar w/lid, exotic birds/flowering trees, 23"......1,800.00
Famille verte, jar w/lid, warriors in combat, lion finial, 30"...1,500.00
Famille verte, jardiniere, warriors, blk bkground, 16", pr.....1,760.00
Famille verte, peacock on rock w/florals, Chien Lung, 14½"...165.00
Famille verte, vase, bird w/in chrysanthemum on rocks, 15"....550.00
Fan dish, landscape beyond wisteria, earthenware, 1900, 18" L.495.00
Figure, Buddha, on dbl lotus ped, gilt-copper, Qianlong, 12".1,650.00
Figure, demon guardians, glazed tilework, Ming, rstr, 19", pr.2,200.00
Figure, Guanyin, lotus in hand, glazed pottery, Ming, 30", G.1,320.00
Figure, horse, tassels on saddle cloth, straw glazed, Sui, 13"..3,300.00
Figure, hound, head raised, pottery, Tang, 3¾"............660.00
Figure, Kannon, wht robes/gr clouds/gold jewels, 1800s, 23"..2,000.00
Figure, official, glazed pottery tilework, Ming, rstr, 25".....1,650.00
Figure, ram, lavender w/olive br streaks, 1800, 7½", pr.......770.00
Figure, scholar in flowing robes w/book, mc, metal base, 17"....75.00
Figure, seated girl, bl bib w/famille rose decor/yel dog, 9".....325.00
Figure, soldier, red pottery w/wht slip, Tang, 15¼".........1,045.00
Figure, warrior on horse, glazed pottery tileworks, 18"......1,540.00
Fruit basket w/stand, after Meissen, putti/tree trunk, 15".....1,000.00
Garden seat, Chinese style, brick red glazed pottery, 17", pr...250.00

Hardstone Carvings

Crystal, vase/lid, chimera/rocks/taotie mask, loose hdls, 12"...1,980.00
Crystal, vase/lid, rocky base/foo dog/ball/birds, 5½", pr......1,430.00
Jade, dk gr, hexagonal bowl, lotus/ring hdls w/bats, 4 ft, 16".2,310.00
Jade, gr wht mottle, mountain w/Shoulao/deer/trees/etc, 5" L.1,100.00
Jade, gr/gray, phoenix w/vase on back, EX carving, 6¾".....1,430.00
Jade, gray, recumbent ram w/incised details, 2½" L.........1,155.00
Jade, lt gr, Bodhisattva, seated, on dk gr base, 6½"........1,980.00
Jade, lt gr/wht, belt buckle, camel w/shrew atop figural, 3½"...990.00
Jade, lt gray/wht, box w/lid, quadrilobed, birds/lotus/ftd, 5"....550.00
Jade, mottled, elephant w/man atop, Ming style, 4¾".........550.00
Jade, wht, belthook w/praying mantis/peony, horse, 4½".......990.00
Jade, yellow/wht, incense burner/lid, 3 paw legs/masks, 5" W...770.00
Jadeite, gr, vase/lid, herons/waves, ram loose ring hdl, 9"....1,650.00
Jadeite, gr/gray, Meriren holding basket, 1 hand up, 4¾"......715.00
Jadeite, vase, lion's masks/rings/scenics/foo dog knop, 12".....275.00
Jadeite, wht/gr mottle, pendant, form of axe w/dragons, 2½"...660.00
Turquoise, unicorn, recumbent, 3x4".....................350.00

Headdress, kingfisher feathers/hardstones/jade/pearl/etc, 10"....685.00
Hot water dish, br/gilt w/carnation sprig center, 1790, 11".....210.00
Incense burner w/cover, bird finial, gray pottery, N Wei, 3"....660.00

Inro, 3 case, lacquer, grasshoppers/foliage, MOP/pewter inlay...800.00
Inro, 3 case, lacquer, inlaid dancers, sgn Toyo..............770.00
Inro, 4 case, lacquer, grazing horse, MOP inlay, late 1600s....605.00
Inro, 5 case, lacquer, mtd falconer w/bow & arrow, Yoyusai...1,320.00

Japanese Paintings

Genji Scenes, pr 6 fold screens, ink/color/gold paper, 68x25".6,600.00
Landscape After Nican, paper scroll/ink, Okada Hanko, 50x11".550.00
Monkeys & White Rabbit, scroll, silk w/ink/colors, 45x26"....2,750.00
River Gorge, scroll, ink/minimal red/paper, Hyakusen, 42x9"...440.00
Scattered Fans, pr 6 fold screens, ink/color/foil, ea 66x24"...7,975.00
Spring Landscape, paper scroll/ink/color, Yo Shukuya, 52x12"..385.00
Tiger & Bamboo, scroll/ink on silk, sgn Gantai, 14x22".......900.00
Two Monkeys/Berry Vines, scroll, ink & color, Sosen, 46x20".1,100.00
Two Sages, pr of hanging scrolls ink/paper, Shohaku, 52x21".1,200.00
Jar, gr glazed red pottery, lobed, 10th century, 5½".........770.00
Jar, Henan br glaze, ivory over wht w/out, Song/Yuan, 4".....880.00
Jardiniere & stand, Empress Dowager, dragons/foliage, 7", G...600.00
Jug, Valentine, altar/doves/dogs/shepherd's crook, 1750, 11"...935.00
Jug w/lid, armorial/florals, gilt scroll work, 1760, 16".......1,870.00
Koro, phoenix/paulowia medallion/diaper borders, 6", G......550.00
Koro w/lid, 2 oni creating havoc in village, earthenware, 11"..2,475.00
Koro w/retic lid, emb chrysanthemum, earthenware, 4½"......385.00

Lacquer

Bowl w/lid, cinnabar, landscape/figures/floral medallions, 12"...225.00
Box, allover gold/speckled foil leaves, 9" L, 3" W...........800.00
Box w/lid, Guri, red/blk w/allover ruyi motif, 1600s, 7" dia....770.00
Box w/lid, village scene top/sides/cinnabar/lobed, 1800s, 12"..1,100.00
Cigarette box, nautillus shell/starfish, takamakie/nashiji, 5".....100.00
Dish, courtiers in gold/red reserves on blk, 10" dia, pr........50.00
Lamp, panels of figures lotus meander ground, cinnabar, 29"...990.00
Table, dk on cinnabar, tree scenic/people, 12x12x5".........800.00

Libation cup, rhinoceros horn, allover carving, 1700s, 3½"...1,100.00
Libation cup, rhinoceros horn, carved/pierced/figures, 25" L.3,410.00
Mineral plant, florals in agate/quartz/serpentine, 26", pr......825.00
Mystery ball, 6 layers carved ivory, ped w/3 elephants, 4"......80.00
Needlework, export, eagle & shield on silk, in fr, 20x25".......95.00

Ojime

Cast silver Daruma doll w/shakudo face/gilt eyes, 1800s.......440.00
Horse, head to left, horn eyes, sgn Kaigyoku...............7,150.00
Ovoid, pierced/hollow, 2 sages w/in bamboo grove/tiger......247.00
Ovoid, snail confronting beetle decor, unsgn................275.00
Round, 12 zodiac animals w/horn eyes, 1800s..............770.00
Round bead w/gold lacquered flowering branch, 1800s........495.00
Round w/allover octopi, horn inlaid eyes, sgn Ichiraku.......1,100.00

Pipe, opium; brass relief cranes, reed stem, 1800s, 8".........85.00
Plate, Aesop's Fables, fox attacking rooster, 1810, 9¾".......475.00
Plate, Fitzhugh, br/gr w/florals/insects, 1800-20, 9½", G.....450.00
Plate, Judgement of Paris, 1775, 9".....................440.00
Plate, Tobacco Leaf, scalloped rim, 9" dia, 1770, pr........1,150.00
Platter, armorial/flowers, 1770, 11½"...................360.00
Platter, boy w/bird & lady in garden, polychrome, 1760, 18"...465.00

Black Mandarin robe, silk 'Forbidden' stick floral embroidery with ornate cuffs, flowers and butterflies, ca 1900, $300.00.

Platter, Fitzhugh, gr/wht, late 1700s, 21x18".............800.00
Pot de creme w/lid, Orange Fitzhugh, eagle decor, 1800, 3½"..800.00
Reverse painting on glass, European figures/landscape, 14x11".460.00
Reverse painting on glass, lady/son in study, 1880s, 18x23"....550.00
Rose Mandarin, hexagonal baluster, salamander/squirrels, 24"..450.00
Rose Mandarin, punch bowl, w/gilt metal stand, 1785, 14"...2,600.00
Sauce tureen, Pseudo Tobacco Leaf, rabbit hdls, no lid, 7"....330.00
Screen, 4 fold, Coromandle, noblemen pavilion/dragons, 72"..2,750.00
Soup plate, armorial, motto/florals, 1802, 9¾", set of 6......2,860.00

Sumida Gawa

Bowl, 2 people lean over side look at man by house w/in, 4x6".395.00
Mug, w/tiger & cheetah, Poo, 5".........................200.00
Pitcher & 4 mugs, applied Oriental men, lg size pitcher.......800.00

Tea bowl & saucer, Nanking, 1810......................135.00
Tea caddy, festival procession, rpr lid, sgn Kinkozan, 5"......550.00
Tea ceremony set, travelling, 7 pc+silk bags & basket, 6x4x4"..525.00
Teapot, drum form, roses in sepia/gold, late 1700s, 5½"......150.00
Teapot, lichee form, branch spout/hdl, aubergine/gr, rstr, 3½"...300.00
Teapot, Yixing, red-br clay/wht speckled peach form, 6½"......330.00
Teapot, 2 lg cartouches w/figures by river, 1700s.............210.00

Textiles

Embroidered panel, interlocking floral mon/gr brocade, 73x57".275.00
Robe, contrasting blk/turq borders, embroidered/florals, 53"..1,320.00
Robe, embroidered, dragons/cloud/peach/peonies on bl, 1700s.1,100.00
Robe, figured w/floral medallions, purple/blk, late 1800s, 51"...700.00
Robe, finely woven w/flowers in lt bl/gr, stained, 1900, 57".....770.00
Robe, informal, satin stitched w/hydrangeas, late 1800s, 55"..550.00
Robe, worked w/gold dragons/shou characters, maroon, 1890s..770.00

Tureen, pig form w/howdah/jeweled headdress, export.......1,600.00
Tureen on stand, 14 figures on terrace/hen/rooster, 1780, 15"..465.00
Vase, blanc de chine, priest in landscape relief, chop mk, 7"...400.00
Vase, clobberware, dragon/flowers/gilt field, early 1700s, 8"....300.00
Vase, copper red, unglazed base, Qianlong, 7½"............440.00
Vase, faceted pear w/elephant hdls, turq glaze, Kangxi, 5½"..275.00
Vase, flambe glaze, wht w/in, glaze crack, 1700s, 7".........415.00
Vase, flambe w/milky & lavender flecks, Qianlong, 14½"......825.00
Vase, hexagon, mums/landscape/bird panels, sgn Minzan, 3½"..415.00
Vase, incised insects/peony/bamboo, wht glaze, 7½".........440.00

Vase, ovoid w/lid, 2 karako support, pnt Immortals, rstr, 20"...990.00
Vase, palace; birds on branch reserve, ruffled rim/ovoid, 22"..1,100.00
Vase, panels of figures w/in landscape, polychrome, 1780, 14"..900.00
Vase, panels of Immortals in garden on millefleur, 25½"....1,320.00
Vase, procession of travellers, mk Kinkozan, 5".............935.00
Vase, relief carved w/turtles by lily pond, earthenware, 13"...1,100.00
Vase, sang de boeuf, baluster, lamp mount, w/shade: 36"......350.00
Vase, sang de boeuf, bulbous w/long neck, 2¾"..............65.00
Vase, women/children w/birds/etc, ovoid, Hankinzan, 4"......250.00
Vase, Yenyen, turq/aubergine/bl-purple, elephant hdls, 15".....440.00
Vase, 2 panels Immortals/children/dragon, dragon relief, 17"..1,540.00
Vase, 3 rnd reserves w/goats, florals on yellow/red, 8½", pr....250.00
Vegetable w/lid, armorial, rectangle, lioness/florals, 9½"......715.00
Water dropper, lotus form, molded petals, w/inscription, 8"...495.00
Wine pot, peach w/applied turq/yellow leaves on aubergine, 6"..495.00

Tobacco Leaf oval platter, circa 1775, 15" long, $1,200.00.

Orrefors

Orrefors glassworks was founded in the early 1900s in the Swedish province of Smaaland. Utilizing the expertise of designers such as Lindquist and Gate, it produced quality art glass. Various techniques were used in achieving the decoration; some were wheel engraved, and others blown through a unique process that formed controlled bubbles or air pockets resulting in unusual patterns and shapes.

Bowl, Ravenna, by Sven Palmqvist, bl/yel decor, 13" dia.....1,785.00
Cologne, melon rib, crystal................................45.00
Comport, Grall, opal bl w/maroon swirls, Gate/Bergqvist, 10".2,750.00
Decanter, Diana w/bow, animals, engraved, sgn/#d, 11½"......300.00
Decanter, fish & bubbles, cut & etched, artist sgn, 9".........175.00
Decanter, Susanna & the Elders, Edvard Haald, etched, 9"....440.00
Figurine, elephant......................................85.00
Paperweight, owl, sgn, 3"................................65.00
Perfume, Eve & the serpent, etch/inlaid w/dk base, 5".........250.00
Tazza, internal 'stained glass' decor, Jan Johansson, 5" dia....330.00
Vase, Ariel, by Ingeborg Lundin, geometrics, bl/br, 6½".....1,450.00
Vase, Ariel, by Ingeborg Lundin, striations & waves, 6".......775.00
Vase, Ariel, Edvin Ohrstrom, thick walls, internal decor, 8"..1,350.00
Vase, Ariel, stylized profiles, aubergine/lt blue, Lundin, 7"....2,400.00
Vase, Ariel, thick walls w/air trap oxblood cowboy/horse, 8¾".7,150.00
Vase, engraved w/South Sea Island, by Londberg, 1939, 7"....140.00
Vase, skiers on slopes front & bk, engraved, 4x9"...........180.00

Vase, internal fish and seaweed decor, signed Edvard Haald, 1950s, 5¼", $475.00.

Ott and Brewer

The partnership of Ott and Brewer began in 1865 in Trenton, New Jersey. By 1876 they were making decorated graniteware, parian, and 'ivory porcelain' -- similar to Irish belleek, though not as fine and of different composition. In 1883, however, experiments toward that end had reached a successful conclusion and a true belleek body was introduced. It came to be regarded as the finest china ever produced by an American firm. The ware was decorated by various means -- hand painting, transfer printing, gilding, and lustre glazing. The company closed in 1893, one of many that failed during that depression.

In the listings below, the ware is belleek unless noted otherwise.

Cup, Echinus pattern.....................................55.00
Cup & saucer, cream pearlized, w/thin gold rims.............145.00
Cup & saucer, gold florals, monogram, belleek..............130.00
Demitasse pot, cr/sug, 2 c/s (1 pk w/in), twig hdl, belleek......650.00
Nut cup, shell shape, 2 shell ft, wht lustre, belleek, 2"........95.00
Pitcher, tapioca design, gold filigree/hdl, belleek, 5".........235.00
Potpourri, water lily, girl's head finial, retic top, 3 pc, 6".....1,800.00
Sugar, Cactus pattern, ornate gold decor twig hdl, no lid......275.00
Teapot, Cactus pattern, heavy gold decor twig hdls..........395.00

Overbeck

The Overbeck Studio was established in 1911 in Cambridge City, Indiana, by four Overbeck sisters. It survived until the last sister died in 1955. Early wares were often decorated with carved designs of stylized animals, birds, or florals with the designs colored to contrast with the background. Others had tooled designs filled in with various colors for a mosaic effect. After 1937, Mary Frances, the last remaining sister, favored handmade figurines with somewhat bizarre features in fanciful combinations of color. Overbeck ware is signed 'OBK'.

Figurine, dog, pink/bl/wht/blk, 2x3½"......................110.00
Figurine, gentleman w/beard/cane/hat, bl/pinks, glossy, 6"......200.00
Figurine, long eared spaniel, wht/bl/yellow, 2¼x4"...........160.00
Figurine, Victorian lady, wht/pink/bl gloss, 4¾".............175.00
Plate, floral/chick band and center design, bl/yel/wht, 9½".....275.00

Vase, carved medallions w/flying geese, 3 color, sgn EH, 6½"..800.00
Vase, geometric design, green & brown, 4x2"...............250.00
Vase, 3 carved Art Nouveau panels, sgn E/F, 6x20".........600.00

Overlay Glass

Ewer, wht/clear, mc enamel florals, 10½"..................250.00
Pitcher, cobalt/wht/clear, floral & band cuttings, 4½".........300.00
Pitcher, cream w/enamel roses, pk lined, cranberry hdl, 10½"..295.00
Rose bowl, pk, gold prunus blossoms, Whitehouse Glass, 3"...300.00
Vase, red/wht/clear, Nouveau cutting, 10"..................435.00
Vase, tall trumpet neck on ovoid, wht/cranberry/mc floral, 12"..175.00

Overshot

Overshot glass is characterized by the beaded or craggy appearance of the surface. Earlier ware was irregularly textured, while 20th century examples tend to be more uniform.

Basket, vaseline, clear applied hdl/bottom, pk applied florals....175.00
Dish, canary to cranberry, crimped edge, flint, 6¼".........120.00
Pitcher, cranberry w/clear reed hdl, bulbous, 6½"...........120.00
Pitcher, pk/wht spatter, ruffled top, 8"...................175.00
Pitcher, rubena, swirled, 8".............................175.00
Pitcher, tankard; cranberry w/clear reed hdls, 10½"..........185.00
Rose bowl, cranberry, 6x5"..............................120.00
Rose bowl, cranberry w/wht overshot, 2¾"..................65.00
Rose bowl, rubena, 6x6"................................110.00
Tumbler, rubena..135.00
Vase, stick neck/pyramid base, irid gold/silver florals, 8"........65.00
Vase, yel, melon ribs, 6"...............................65.00

Owens Pottery

J.B. Owens founded his company in Zanesville, Ohio, in 1891, and until 1907, when the company decided to exert most of its energies in the area of tile production, made several quality lines of art pottery. His first line, Utopian, was a standard brown ware with underglaze slip decoration of nature studies, animals, and portraits. A similar line, Lotus, utilized lighter background colors. Henri Deux, introduced in 1900, featured incised Art Nouveau forms inlaid with color. Other important lines were Opalesce, Rustic, Feroza, Cyrano, and Mission, examples of which are rare today.

The factory burned in 1928, and the company closed shortly thereafter.

Bowl, Aborigine, w/peace sign, 3".........................50.00
Candle holder, Utopian, sgn Decores Harvey, 6¾"..........145.00
Ewer, Utopian, yellow roses, 6½".........................145.00
Jardiniere, Cyrano, imp Cyrano mk, 8½", VG...............150.00
Jardiniere, Henry Deux, tight hairline, 8x10"...............200.00
Jardiniere, Matt Utopian, sgn Haubrich, 8½x13"...........1,200.00
Jug, Utopian, yellow florals, Owensart die stamp............175.00
Lamp base, Sudanese, blk gloss w/red florals, gold decor, 13"..240.00
Lamp base, Sudanese, trees, cream/gold, sgn Lessell, 13¾"....225.00
Letter holder, Utopian, florals, F Ferrell, torch mk, 5½x6"....225.00
Mug, Utopian, raspberries by Tot Steele, #1035, 5".........200.00
Mug, Utopian, yellow berries, sgn, 5¼"...................135.00
Pitcher, Lotus, age lines in bottom, 8¾".................140.00
Pitcher, orange berries, T Steel, 12"....................180.00
Pitcher, Utopian, orange floral, wide mouth, 3 ft, 5¾"......120.00
Umbrella stand, Matt Utopian, br irid, 3 chips inside, 20"....220.00
Vase, Aqua Verdi, incised bats, 11½x9".................325.00
Vase, Aqua Verdi, incised Indian design, matt gr, 5¾"........80.00

Vase, Feroza, gr/molded decor, sm neck/wide shoulder/hdls, 6"..70.00
Vase, Feroza, metallic purple, w/hdls, chip on edge, 9x4"......100.00
Vase, flowers/girls' faces relief, bl/yellow/gr/red drip, 12"....130.00
Vase, Henri Deux, br w/lady's face, red roses, wide base, 8"....400.00
Vase, Henri Deux, w/hdls, 9½x6½".........................450.00
Vase, Lotus, floral, sgn, 9", EX...........................200.00
Vase, Lotus, sgn Ferrell, 12½"............................250.00
Vase, lt gr/wht matt, fruit, trumpet top/ovoid body, rst, 18"....275.00
Vase, Matt Gr, wide cone/hdls, waves/fish relief, #1104, 15x6"..425.00
Vase, Matt Gr, 4 sq incurved vertical ft/floral mold, #823, 9"....60.00
Vase, Matt Utopian, gr/rust w/floral, sgn, twisted, 12".........180.00
Vase, Matt Utopian, 3 hdls, florals, sgn CJ, #826, 7".........345.00
Vase, Sudanese, blk w/gold moose/trees, 13", rpr...........170.00
Vase, Sudanese, Indian woman portrait, sgn Williams, 10"....2,000.00
Vase, Utopian, florals, top bulge, sgn, 10".................75.00
Vase, Utopian, gr/yellow florals, factory flaw, 8¾"..........60.00
Vase, Utopian, leaf decor, EX art, MS, 3¼"................100.00
Vase, Utopian, man's portrait, artist sgn/Millet, 16", rstr......350.00
Vase, Utopian, orange florals, artist sgn, bell form, 8"........70.00
Vase, Utopian, orange florals, short collar/cylinder body, 10"....80.00
Vase, Utopian, pansy decor, #144, 3"......................70.00
Vase, Utopian, pillow, cherries, 4 ftd, 5"...................90.00
Vase, Utopian, roses, flared rim, waisted neck, sgn ST, 13¾"..175.00
Vase, Utopian, spiral shape, violets by H Smith, #1080, 5".....150.00
Vase, Utopian, twisted, orange poppies/buds, #015, 14".......175.00
Vase, Utopian, w/hdls, pansies, Frank Ferrell, torch mk, 5½"..225.00
Wall pocket, Matt Gr, free form 'gourd', 9"..................50.00

Pacific Clay Products

The Pacific Clay Products Company, founded in 1881, had several locations in southern California that were involved in the production of yellowware and red clay products such as brick and tile. By 1936, however, they had developed a full line of products, including a low-fired pastel glazed dinnerware called 'Coralitos'. About the same time, they designed a dinnerware in the more vivid hues to compete with the highly successful Fiesta, by Homer Laughlin, and Ring, made by the Bauer Company. With the onset of WWII, the company began to manufacture insulators for radio equipment, and the dinnerware lines were discontinued.

Bowl, mixing; green, small...............................10.00
Bowl, salad; orange....................................22.00
Butter, green..18.00
Butter, orange.......................................35.00
Coaster, green..3.00
Coaster, orange.......................................4.50
Creamer, green..9.00
Cup, coffee; green.....................................7.50
Cup, orange...12.00
Pitcher, water; orange.................................55.00
Plate, dinner; green....................................9.00
Plate, dinner; orange..................................12.00
Plate, salad; orange....................................8.00
Platter, orange.......................................30.00
Punch bowl, orange...................................55.00
Saucer, green...3.00
Saucer, orange..4.00
Soup, green..6.00
Soup, orange...9.00
Sugar w/lid, green....................................12.50
Tray, green..30.00
Tray, orange...45.00
Tumbler, water; orange.................................15.00

Paden City

The Paden City Glass Company began operations in 1916, in Paden City, West Virginia. The company's early lines consisted largely of the usual pressed tablewares, but by the 1920s production had expanded to include colored wares, in crystal as well as opaque glass, and in a variety of patterns and styles. The company maintained its high standards of handmade perfection until 1949, when under new management, much of the work formerly done by hand was replaced by automation.

The Paden City Glass Company closed in 1951, and its earlier wares, the colored patterns in particular, are becoming very collectible.

Bowl, oval vegetable; Crow's Foot, amber square..............12.00
Bowl, oval vegetable; Crow's Foot, red square................25.00
Candlestick, cobalt ped base, square top, 3¼"...............37.50
Candlestick, Crow's Foot, amber, 5", pr....................50.00
Candlestick, Crow's Foot, ruby, 5", pr.....................50.00
Cream soup, Crow's Foot, red square.......................14.00
Creamer & sugar, Cupid & Venus, round, green...............75.00
Cup & saucer, #411, ebony..............................11.00
Cup & saucer, #411, red................................12.50
Cup & saucer, Lucy, red................................12.00
Cup & saucer, Maya, ruby...............................12.50
Cup & saucer, Party Line, lt green........................9.00
Cup & saucer, Penny, ruby..............................12.50
Cup & saucer, Wotta Line, red...........................12.00
Plate, #411, 8" square, red..............................8.00
Plate, Maya, ruby, dinner..............................16.00
Plate, Wotta Line, ruby, 8½"............................4.00
Plate, Wotta Line, ruby, 9½"............................6.00
Platter, oval, Crow's Foot, amber square...................12.00
Pouter pigeon..55.00
Server, center hdl; #411, pink, Ardith etched................22.50
Server, center hdl; #411, red............................25.00
Server, center hdl; Crow's Foot, amber square...............13.00
Tumbler, Penny Line, flat, ruby, 2¾".......................3.00
Tumbler, Penny Line, flat, ruby, 4".........................4.00
Tumbler, Penny Line, flat, ruby, 5¼".......................5.00
Vase, Crow's Foot, red square, 8".........................35.00

Pairpoint

The Pairpoint Manufacturing Company was built in 1880 in New Bedford, Massachusetts. It was primarily a metalworks, whose chief product was coffin fittings. Next door, the Mt. Washington Glassworks made quality glasswares of many varieties. (See Mt. Washington for more information concerning their art ware lines.) By 1894 it became apparent to both companies that a merger would be to their best interest.

From the late 1890s until the 1930s, lamps and lamp accessories were an important part of Pairpoint's production. There were three main types of shades, all of which were blown: puffy -- blown-out reverse painted shades (usually floral designs); ribbed -- also reverse painted; and scenic -- reverse painted with scenes of land or seascapes (usually executed on smooth surfaces, although ribbed scenics may be found occasionally). Cut glass lamps and those with metal overlay panels were also made.

Scenic shades were sometimes artist signed, and although many are unmarked, some are stamped 'Pairpoint Corp.' Blown-out shades may be marked 'Pat July 9, 1907'. Bases were made from bronze, copper, brass, silver, or wood, and are always signed.

Because they produced only fancy handmade art ware, the company's sales lagged seriously during the depression, and as time and tastes changed, their style of products was less in demand. As a result, they never fully recovered and consequently part of the buildings and equipment were sold in 1938.

The company reorganized in 1939 under the direction of Robert Gunderson, and again specialized in quality hand blown glassware. Isaac Babbit regained possession of the silver departments, and together they established Gunderson Glassworks, Inc. After WWII, during which sales made a sharp decline, it again became necessary to reorganize. The Gunderson-Pairpoint Glassworks was formed, and the old line of cut, engraved art ware was reintroduced.

The company moved to East Wareham, Massachusetts, in 1957, but business continued to suffer, and the firm closed only one year later. In 1970, however, new facilities were constructed in Sagamore under the direction of Robert Bryden, sales manager for the company since the 1950s.

In 1974, the company began to produce lead glass cup plates which were made on commission as fund raisings for various churches and organizations. These are signed with a 'P' in diamond, and are becoming quite collectible.

Cup Plates

Arms of Dexter, clear	15.00
Cape Cod Light House, amethyst	42.00
City of New Bedford, City Seal, amethyst	15.00
Dead Whale or a Stove Boat, cobalt	55.00
Edaville RR, yellow	11.00
Evening Grosbeak, amethyst	10.00
First Congregational Church, Yarmouthport, cobalt	45.00
Flying Horses, Dragon Chariot, dk amber	13.00
Grandfather Frog, cobalt	100.00
Hidden Fireplace, amber	300.00
Honeybee, amber	30.00
King House, clear	35.00
Lafayette w/'SM', gr opal	45.00
Little Joe Otter, ice blue	20.00
Millicent Library, cobalt	95.00
Mother Goose, teal	40.00
NBGM, Drummer Boy, Christmas 1979, turquoise	75.00
NBGM, Santa, smoky amber	95.00
NBGM, Snowflake, Christmas, 1980, violet	25.00
NBGM, 1977 Rotch-Rodman, cobalt	60.00
NBGM, 1977 Rotch-Rodman, wht opal	75.00
Nye Homestead, script y, #68A, clear	85.00
Osterville Cat Boat, yellow	15.00
Peter Rabbit, auroria, rare color	20.00
Puss n' Boots, copper blue	18.00
Sandwich Glass Museum, #123, clear	20.00
Smiling Pool, 1981, clear	30.00
St Andrew's Episcopal Church, clear	20.00
Study Gallery, The; teal	15.00
Swan, #80A, teal	11.00
We Teach The Children, amethyst	20.00

Lamps

Brass, reticulated brass shade	675.00
Cut glass, 12" dome shade, baluster base, cut prisms, 18½"	850.00
Hanging, Courting Cherubs/blown-out Vellon, pnt decor/pk	1,250.00
Hurricane, chipped ice/coralene scenic, wood base, 20½", pr	675.00
Puffy, roses/daisies, rvpt w/cartouches w/baskets, sgn twice	2,420.00
Puffy, 12" iris, red/gr/mc shade; tree trunk base, sgn, 21"	2,650.00
Puffy, 13" irregular dome w/red poppies; SP eng ftd base	1,750.00
Puffy, 13" rose blossom shade; base w/poppies, 21"	2,090.00
Puffy, 15½" shade w/mc floral swags/yel drapery; 4 arm base	2,250.00
Puffy, 5" purple lilac, yel butterfly shade; silver base	1,650.00

Biscuit jar, melon ribbed, green with gold florals, signed 'PMC', 7" x 6½", $595.00.

Puffy, 5" rose bouquet shade, red/yel on lt ground; w/base	1,750.00
Puffy, 8" gingham w/dogwood border shade; brass base	1,800.00
Puffy, 8" Papillon/rose atop, 4 bouquets/butterflies; on std	2,500.00
Puffy, 9¼" floral shade; metal base, 14"	1,000.00
Rvpt 15" New Bedford waterfront w/ships; trn wood/brass ft	1,800.00
Rvpt 16" scroll band/roses irregular border shade, metal base	1,300.00
Rvpt 17½" waisted shade w/birds, sgn, 23"	715.00
Rvpt 17¾" flared cylinder, trees; base lions/cornucopias	100.00
Rvpt 18" scene of woods/mtns, sgn C Durand, sgn base, 22"	750.00
Rvpt 19½" seagull shade, artist sgn, mk, w/base, EX	3,000.00

Miscellaneous

Bowl, berry; SP stand w/3 figural heads, cut crystal bowl	85.00
Bowl, centerpiece; amber w/silver overlay, roll-down rim, lg.	225.00
Bowl, centerpiece; Kentwood, bubble ball ped, 5x12¼"	140.00
Bowl, centerpiece; Wilton, bubble ball ped, 5x12¼"	170.00
Bowl, console; 12", w/pr 3" sticks, ruby/clear bubble ball	195.00
Bowl, quadruple plate, ftd, florals, 2 hdls, 3x7½"	125.00
Bowl, swan hdls, gr, Gunderson	100.00
Candlestick, blown, baluster form w/wide ft, 16", pr	100.00
Candlestick, brass, Gothic pattern, B6147, 4¾", pr	150.00
Canister, brass, figural enamel rooster finial, commemorative	75.00
Cocktail glass, rouge flambe, long stemmed, pr	225.00
Cocktail glass, w/tray, rouge flambe, w/silver overlay	175.00
Comb holder, SP, acorn pattern, bulldog on base under tray	85.00
Compote, amber w/clear bubble ball stem, 7½"	110.00
Compote, Canaria w/eng grapes, bubble ball connector, 7x8"	125.00
Compote, clear w/amber ft, intaglio floral bowl & ft, 6x5"	85.00
Compote, gr w/silver overlay garlands/bubble ball, mk Rockwell	215.00
Compote, ruby w/clear controlled bubble ball stem, 4x5¾"	95.00
Cornucopia vase, lt gr w/clear bubble ball base	115.00
Cornucopia vase, ruby w/clear bubble base, 8", pr	160.00
Creamer & sugar, Colias cutting, butterfly in web	115.00
Creamer & sugar basket, rope border, engraved flowers, SP	65.00
Figurine, crystal swan, large	30.00
Inkwell, ovoid, gr glass 'jade cabs' w/in bronze fr, sgn, 3¾"	575.00
Jewel box, quadruple plate, ornate openwork, ftd	135.00
Ladle, eng hdl, SP, 13"	35.00
Perfume, triple ball, bl florals topper, Gunderson, 9½"	250.00

Pitcher, purple, Bryden, 3".............................35.00
Plate, intaglio Grecian Urn & Flame, 1900, 10"...........185.00
Plate, Wren pattern on clear, 8½" dia, 6 for.............100.00
Sherbet, Adelaide cutting, Gunderson, set of 6............150.00
Swan, amberina...25.00
Swan, rosaria, crystal neck, largest size, M.............450.00
Syrup pitcher, quadruple plate...........................75.00
Vase, amethyst, vintage engraving, 15x5½"...............195.00
Vase, black, trumpet, w/clear controlled bubble connector, 16".195.00
Vase, brass base, w/3 cupids holding 10" ruffled crystal lily....135.00
Vase, bubble ball connector, flared, ruby, Gunderson, 12".....190.00
Vase, bubbled base, emerald gr, 10x9"...................150.00
Vase, butterfly/floral/fern cutting, 12"................195.00
Vase, chalice; Canaria, eng grapes, bubble ball connector, 12"..250.00
Vase, cranberry, clear bubble ball std, Gunderson, 8".........110.00
Vase, gourd shape, student glass, gr, 7½"................50.00
Vase, gr w/bubble ball stem, ped base, 11"...............85.00
Vase, Tavern Glass, #d pontil............................88.00
Vase, trumpet, Canaria, grape/leaves, ball connector, 10"......110.00

Paper Dolls

Our Dollies Model Book, McLoughlin Bros., #239, 1909, $45.00.

No one knows quite how or when paper dolls originated. One belief is that they began in Europe as 'pantins' (jumping jacks) and were frequently worn as part of the costume. By the late 1790s, they were being mass-produced.

During the 19th century, most paper dolls portrayed famous dancers and opera stars such as Fanny Elssler and Jenny Lind. In the late 1800s, the Raphael Tuck Publishers of England produced many series of beautiful paper dolls. Also about this time, retail companies used them as advertisements to further the sale of their products. Around the turn of the century many popular women's magazines began featuring a page of paper dolls.

Most familiar to today's collectors are the books with dolls on cardboard covers, and clothes on the inside pages. These made their appearance in the late 1920s and early thirties. The most collectible of these, and the most valuable, are those representing celebrities, movie stars, and comic strip characters of the thirties and forties.

Paper doll books in their original, uncut condition will, of course, demand higher prices than those with missing, bent, or torn parts.

Authority Mary Joung has compiled an informative book *Collector's Guide to Paper Dolls*, with current prices; you will find her address in the Directory under 'Ohio'.

Advertising, Elsie Dinsmore, Walton/Spencer, 1919, uncut......35.00
Advertising, McLaughlin Coffee, Queen, complete set..........25.00
All Star Movie, 1934, Whitman, M.........................50.00
Ann Sheridan, Whitman #986, 1944, cut set, VG..............75.00
Ann Southern, Saalfield #301, 1943, cut set, EX.............25.00
Annie Laurie/Little Women/5 Peppers, Lowe #1030, uncut.....125.00
Annie Oakley, Whitman #2043:15, 1954, uncut...............50.00
Annie Oakley w/Tagg & Lofty, Whitman #1960, 1956, uncut....50.00
Army Nurse & Doctor, Merrill #3425, 1942, 10 dolls, EX......42.00
Baby Dolls, Whitman #969, 1945, by Queen Holden, EX........48.00
Baby Dolls, Whitman #971, 1944, 4 babies/toys/clothing, EX....17.00
Baby Mine, Merrill #4860, 1944, by Louise Rumely, EX........38.00
Barbie Boutique, book, 1973, uncut........................6.00
Becky & Betsy, Merrill #3452, 1952, EX...................14.00
Betsy McCall, Golden Book #559, 1965, Betsy & Sandy, uncut..25.00
Betty Field, Saalfield #2462, 1943, 8 pgs, uncut, EX.........48.00
Betty Grable, Whitman #976, 1943, VG.....................75.00
Blondie, Saalfield #1334, TV version, comic characters too.....25.00
Blondie, Whitman #987, 1945, whole Bumstead family, EX.....40.00
Bobbsey Twins, Lowe #1257, twins/brother/sister, uncut........25.00

Boot's & Her Buddies, Saalfield #330, 1953, uncut...........45.00
Buffy, Whitman #1995, from Family Affair, w/Mrs Beasley, uncut.25.00
Captain Marvel Jr Ski Jump, in orig package, 1945.............7.50
Carolyn Lee, Whitman #997, 1943, by Queen Holden, uncut EX.78.00
Chitty Chitty Bang Bang, Whitman #1982, 1968, uncut.........35.00
Claudette Colbert, Saalfield #2451, 1943, 8 pgs, EX..........70.00
Connie Francis, Whitman #1956, 1965, uncut................35.00
Coronation, Saalfield #4450, 1953, by B&C Bailey, uncut......35.00
Coronation Story, by Dean, made in England, 1950s, uncut.....65.00
Cuddles & Rags, Bonnie Books #2738, 1950s, uncut...........35.00
Diana Lynn, Saalfield #2611, 1953, J Stang portrait, uncut.....25.00
Dinah Shore, Whitman #1963, 1958, uncut..................65.00
Dodie from My Three Sons, Artcraft #5115, 1971, uncut.......25.00
Doris Day, Whitman #1952, 1956, uncut, VG................45.00
Doris Day, Whitman #210325, 1952, uncut in folder...........65.00
Dress-A-Doll, Dennison #512, 2 dolls: girl & boy, EX..........8.00
Ed Kookie Byrnes, Whitman #2085, 1959, uncut, EX...........75.00
Elaine Stewart, Whitman #2048, cut set, incomplete, VG.......25.00
Elly May, Watkins/Strathmore #1819A, uncut, 8 pgs clothes.....45.00
Evelyn Rudie, Saalfield #1795, 4 dolls, 4 pgs clothes, uncut....25.00
Evelyn Rudie, Saalfield #4425, 1958, hard cover, M..........14.00
Fairy Tale Princess, Lowe #2787, reprint of Cinderella, uncut...25.00
Flying Captain Marvel, dtd 1944, in orig package, M..........10.00
Four Mothers, Whitman #968, 1941, cut set, VG.............65.00
Gale Storm, #2061, 1958, 2 dolls, uncut...................45.00
Gigi Perreau, Saalfield #1542, 1951, 4 doll set, uncut.........25.00
Gina Gillespie, Saalfield #1347, 1962, by J Volez, uncut.......25.00
Gisele MacKenzie, #4425, 1958, uncut.....................35.00
Good Neighbor, Saalfield #324, 1944, uncut, VG.............25.00
Haley Mills in That Darn Cat, Whitman #1955, 1965, uncut.....45.00
Jane Powell, Whitman #2085, 1957, uncut..................75.00
Jane Withers, Whitman #989, 1940, uncut, VG..............140.00
Janet Leigh, Leigh-Mor Inc #2733, 1958, uncut in folder.......65.00
Jimmy & Jane Visit Gene Autry, Whitman #1184115, uncut.....65.00
June & Stu Erwin w/Jacke & Joyce, Trouble w/Father, uncut....45.00
June Allyson, Whitman #1173:15, 1953, uncut...............75.00
June Allyson, Whitman #1190:15, 1950, uncut...............75.00
June Allyson, Whitman #2089, 1957, uncut.................75.00
Kim Novak, Saalfield #4459, 1957, uncut..................60.00
Lana Turner, Whitman #988, 1942, 8 pgs, EX...............78.00
Lennon Sisters, Whitman #1995, 1963, uncut in tri-folder......50.00

Let's Play House, Whitman #W968B, 1932, uncut, EX........50.00
Let's Play Store, Saalfield #971, 1933, grocery store, uncut.....75.00
Lucille Ball, Saalfield #338, 1945, uncut, EX................50.00
Lucille Ball (Madam Pompadour set), Saalfield #2475, 1944, VG.65.00
Lucille Ball & D Arnez w/Little Ricky, Whitman #2116, uncut...65.00
Lucy, Whitman #1963, 1964, uncut.....................35.00
Lucy & Her TV Family, Whitman #1991, 1963, 5 dolls, uncut...50.00
Margaret O'Brien, Whitman #970, 1944, EX................70.00
Marge & Gower Champion, Whitman #1966, 1959, uncut.......75.00
Mary Martin, Saalfield #368, 1944, 6 pgs clothes, uncut........60.00
Mary Martin, Saalfield #448, 1942, set, VG..................55.00
Multi-Head Paper Dolls, 4 bodies, 6 heads, 1933, uncut, EX...150.00
My Little Margie, #1954, Gale Storm, cover sgn Aralo, uncut....35.00
National Velvet, Whitman #1948, 1962, uncut................35.00
National Velvet, Whitman #1958, TV show, uncut folder, VG....25.00
Navy Girls & Marines, Merrill #4855, 1943, 8 dolls, VG.......38.00
Navy Scouts, Merrill #1942, 1942, cut set.................45.00
Nora Drake, Radio Star; Lowe #989, 1952, uncut............25.00
Nurse & Doctor, Saalfield #2777, by Betty Campbell, uncut....35.00
Oklahoma, Whitman #1954, G MacRae/S Jones, 1956, uncut....75.00
Paper Doll Patsy & Her Friends, Saalfield #1600, 1954, uncut..20.00
Paper Dolly Fun, Saalfield #345, 1944, uncut, EX............25.00
Pat Boone, Whitman #1968, 2 statuette dolls in folder, uncut...35.00
Patience & Prudence, Abbott #1807, 1959, uncut............35.00
Patty Duke, Whitman #1991:59, 1956, uncut................50.00
Petticoat Junction, Whitman #1954, 1964, uncut, EX.........50.00
Pinocchio, 1939, uncut................................250.00
Raggedy Ann & Andy, Saalfield #4409, EH Simms, uncut......25.00
Ricky Nelson, Whitman #2081, 1959, uncut, EX.............50.00
Rock Hudson, Whitman #2087, 1957, uncut................45.00
Roy Rogers & Dale Evans, Whitman #1950, 1954, uncut folder..50.00
Sandra Dee, Saalfield #4417, 1959, uncut.................45.00
Seven & Seventeen, Merrill #3441, 1945, sisters, EX artwork....22.00
Sheree North, Saalfield #1728, 1957, uncut................50.00
Shirley Temple, #1765, 1936, uncut, 34".................150.00
Shirley Temple, #2425, 1942...........................40.00
Shirley Temple, Dolls & Dresses, #1761, 1937, uncut........100.00
Shirley Temple, Dolls & Dresses, #2112, 1934, uncut........100.00
Shirley Temple, Gabriel #300, statuette, snap-on clothes, cut....25.00
Shirley Temple, Saalfied #5110, 18½" statuette, 1958, cut.....45.00
Shirley Temple, Saalfield #4440, folio type, uncut, EX........45.00
Shirley Temple, Snap on Paperdolls, box set, 1958, G.........45.00
Shirley Temple, Standing Dolls, #1715, 1935, uncut.........100.00
Shirley Temple, Whitman book #1986, w/tote bag, uncut......10.00
Square Dance, Saalfield #2717-15, 1950, die-cut book, uncut...25.00
Stand-Ups, Alice in Wonderland; Saal #964, uncut...........75.00
Star Trek, Saalfield #C2272, 1975......................10.00
Sun Bonnet Sue, Lowe #L521, 1943, uncut................35.00
That Girl, Saalfield #1379, 1967, uncut..................15.00
Three Dolls In One, Trudy, ART Publishing, partly cut, 1947...50.00
Three Flying Marvels, Capt/Mary/Jr, flying dolls, 1945, M......11.00
Three Little Sisters, Whitman #979, 1943, G...............17.00
Tricia Nixon, Wht House Tour Game/Saalfield #4248, '70, uncut.15.00
Twiggy, Whitman #1999:100, 1967, uncut................35.00
Walt Disney's Mary Poppins, Whitman #1982:59, 1964, uncut...45.00
Walt Disney's 101 Dalmations, Whitman #1993:59, uncut/folder..65.00
War Girls, Lowe #529, 1943, uncut, EX..................35.00
Watch Me Grow, Merrill #4857, 1944, 12 girls ages 1-12, EX...38.00

Paperweights

The term 'paperweight' technically refers to any small, heavy object used to hold down loose papers. They have been made from a broad range of materials; many have been sold as souvenirs or given away by retail com-panies as advertising premiums. But today, those attracting the most in-terest are the glass collector weights.

During the mid-1800s the interest in these paperweights reached a high point, during which three major French factories were in close competi-tion. The St. Louis, Baccarat, and Clichy companies were among the first to produce paperweights as a commercial venture, and their products are among the most valued. In the late 1860s, an unexplained decrease in their popularity caused the market for paperweights to diminish, and all three major companies eventually discontinued production.

The manufacture of paperweights in the United States, which began in the 1850s, did not experience this decline, and they have continued in production to the present time. The most valued antique American weights are from the New England, Sandwich, and Milleville companies. In 1954 a renewed surge of interest resulted in the organization of collectors clubs and an exciting new era of paperweight production. Because of this, the manufacture of weights by St. Louis and Baccarat was resumed, and con-temporary artists such as Kaziun, Stankard, and Ysart are bringing their own ingenuity to this rediscovered art form.

Key:

cl-----clear	latt----latticinio
fct----faceted	mc-----multicolor
gar----garland	mill----millefiori
grd----ground	o/l----overlay
jsp----jasper	

Ayotte, Rick

Eastern Phoebe, w/grapes...........................400.00
Falcon, on branch, clear grd, 2½" dia.................350.00
Great White Heron, w/frog, lt blue grd, 1981...........350.00
Marsh Wren, w/nest, 1981..........................350.00
Marsh Wren, wht ground, 2½" dia....................350.00
Meadowlark, on stump, clear ground, 2½" dia..........275.00
Seagull, on log, clear ground, 2½" dia................250.00

Baccarat, Antique

Close pack, dtd B1848, w/4 silhouette canes, 2½" dia.......1,350.00
Concentric mill, 3 rings mc canes, cl grd, 2" dia..........300.00
Interlacing gar, center cane & 2 concentric rows, green grd..1,100.00
Millefiori mushroom, bl/wht torsade, star cut base, EX quality.1,125.00
Pansy & bud, bull's eye central cane, star cut base..........400.00
Pansy & bud, w/gr leaves & stem, cl grd, star cut base, 3" dia..450.00
Pansy bud, star cut base, 2½" dia....................550.00
Spaced millefiori, w/10 silhouette canes, dtd B1848, 2½" dia.1,350.00

Baccarat, Modern

Basket of fruit, 1976..............................310.00
Concentric, blue & wht, 1972.......................125.00
Double Clematis, wht, w/bud, 1974...................200.00
Flower, yellow & wht, 5 petals, 1972..................200.00
Flowers, 2 pink & wht, each w/5 square petals, 1973........200.00
Gr & wht star cane carpet grd, w/zodiac silhouettes, 1968.....250.00
Grapes, 1975...................................310.00
Gridel Doves, 1976, 3⅝" dia........................200.00
Gridel Stag, 1976, 3¼" dia.........................200.00
Gridel Stork, 1977, 3¼" dia........................200.00
Lizard, on yel & gr jsp grd, 1972, 2¾" dia..............450.00
Sulfide, Ben Franklin, overlay.......................750.00
Sulfide, Coronation, clear, fan cut base................250.00
Sulfide, Coronation, overlay........................300.00
Sulfide, Dwight Eisenhower.........................225.00
Sulfide, Eleanor Roosevelt, overlay...................150.00

Sulfide, John Kennedy...175.00
Sulfide, Martin Luther..150.00
Sulfide, Mount Rushmore, overlay.........................300.00
Sulfide, Napolean Bonapart, overlay....................:...175.00
Sulfide, Will Rogers..75.00
Sulfide, Winston Churchill...................................600.00
Tulips, on latt, 1975...310.00

Banford, Bob

Blue flowers, on trellis, cranberry grd, 2¾"..............350.00
Striped snake, w/flower, on yel grd, 2½" dia.............350.00

Caithness

Arctic Night..95.00
Embryo..95.00
Floral Fountain..175.00
Ice Fountain...95.00
Nucleus...95.00
Ocean Springs..95.00
Three Wise Men...150.00
Veiltail..100.00

Clichy, Antique

C scroll, sodden snow grd, mill set-up, 3⅝" dia..........2,100.00
Central red/gr rose, surrounded by 2 intertwining gar, 3" dia...900.00
Chequer, w/central red & gr rose plus wht & gr rose, 2½"...1,500.00
Mushroom, 6 roses, lined w/wht staves, fct, 3¼" dia.......2,850.00
Scattered, w/wht rose, cl ground, 2" dia..................300.00
Scattered mill, 30+ canes including 2 roses, cl grd, 3" dia....750.00
Spaced concentric, w/10 pk & gr roses, fct, 2".............425.00
Spaced concentric, w/10 pk & wht roses in outer row, 2"......450.00
Spaced mill, central cluster w/outer gar, 3 roses, moss canes...750.00
Spaced mill, w/pk & gr rose, 1¾" dia.....................290.00
Swirl, pk & wht, w/bl & wht complex center cane, 3" dia....1,200.00

D'Albret

Audubon, John J..50.00
Columbus, Christopher..90.00
Da Vinci, overlay...125.00
Gandhi, two color...60.00
Hemingway, Ernest..50.00
Jones, John Paul..40.00
Kennedy, John F & Mrs..60.00
King, Martin Luther; tri-color...............................60.00
Lindbergh..40.00
MacArthur, Douglas..55.00
Roosevelt, Franklin...55.00
Twain, Mark; overlay...125.00

J Glass

Bloom In May, 1980, 2¼" dia.................................125.00
Old Fashion Rose, fct, 2⅝" dia..............................220.00
Patterned millefiori, 2¼" dia...............................125.00
Solya on amethyst grd, 1980, 2¼" dia.......................125.00
Wild Rose, 1981, 2¼" dia....................................160.00

Kaziun, Charles

Cuff links, red rose/gr leaves/interspersed gold stone, pr.......160.00

Lily, lavender, gr leaves, turq & gold grd, pedestal, 1¼" H....350.00
Lily, orange on wht latt cushion, cobalt ground, on ped, 2½"..500.00
Lily, red; orange & yel center, 4 leaves, gr & goldstone grd....350.00
Lily, wht on gold speckled bl, on ped, 2".................275.00
Lily, yel w/gr leaves, amethyst & gold grd, ped, 1¼" H.......350.00
Lily, yellow on gold speckled pink ground, on ped, 2"........300.00
Lily, yellow/orange on gold speckled gr ground, on ped, 2"....325.00
Lily on turq & gold flecked ground, on ped, 1¾"............275.00
Rose, dk pk on amethyst, bl/wht muslin entwined torsade, 2¼".700.00
Sandwich rose, yel w/pk/wht torsade, turq grd, ped, 2¼" H...700.00
Striped morning-glory, convulvous, w/bud, gold foil bee, sgn..1,200.00

Manson, William

Silhouette swan, ring of bl/wht complex canes, fct...........240.00
Summer Rose, 1980, 2¾" dia.................................240.00
Swan, 5 & 1 fct, 1979, 3" dia..............................180.00
3 candles, gr adventurine leaves/ribbon, mill gar, 3".......150.00

Perthshire

Bouquet, w/2 3-D flowers & 3 sm flowers, star cut base, fct....345.00
Christmas, angel & stars on blue, 1979.....................175.00
Christmas bells, on cranberry, 1977........................175.00
Cruciform, 1978...137.00
Mill butterfly, w/garland, on red grd, 1978................250.00
Mill garland, w/center colored flower silhouette, 1974......110.00
Pattern mill, w/garlands, 1978.............................140.00
Pattern mill, 1979...245.00
Scottish bluebells, fct, 1978..............................170.00
Sunflower, on golden amber base, w/gar of gr leaves & canes...195.00
Tropical fish, fct, 1980...................................395.00

St. Louis, Antique

Nosegay, fct, 3¼" dia......................................650.00
Panel, central honeycomb cane/6 florettes, jsp grd, 2½" dia....325.00
Scrambled canes & ribbons, 3" dia..........................225.00
Scrambled muslin & ribbons, 3" dia.........................225.00

St. Louis, Modern

Basket of fruit, on latt grd, 1979.........................390.00
Blue & wht carpet grd, w/9 concentric rows, 1972, 2¾" dia....200.00
Carpet grd, w/6 millefiori clusters, 1972, 3" dia..........225.00
Clematis, red, on dk grd, 1970.............................210.00
Coronation sulfide, fct, 1953..............................225.00
Coronation sulfide, garland, 1953..........................275.00
Flat bouquet, w/3 Clematis type flowers, 1972, 3⅛" dia......250.00
Flat bouquet, 3 flowers on wht grd, fct, 1971..............250.00
Fruit, on wht latt, 1980, miniature........................320.00
Garland, w/star cut base, 1979.............................290.00
Gold incrustation of G Washington on horse, w/overlay, 1976..350.00
Gold incrustation of G Washington on horse, 1976...........230.00
Hand cooler, red, wht & blue 'crown', 1976.................200.00
Hourglass, 1980..900.00
Lizard, gilded & coiled, pk & wht double overlay, 1980......1,000.00
Looped mill garland, on red grd, 1973......................200.00
Millefiori, doily patterned, 1972, 3" dia..................210.00
Pansy, on lace, special fct, 1980..........................450.00
Sulfide, Amour/Cupid, w/5 bl flowers, pk grd, fct, 1979.....385.00
Sulfide, Carter, overlay, 1977.............................145.00
Sulfide, DeGaulle, overlay, 1977...........................145.00
Tutankhomun 24 karat gold medallion, on blue grd, 1979....375.00

Wht flower, on orange grd, 1973........................170.00
Wht flower w/11 petals, blue grd, 1963.....................300.00
Yellow 'Clichy' roses, on blue grd, 1976...................300.00

Stankard, Paul

Clintonia Borealis, 2 yel blossoms w/center stamens, roots.....600.00
Lady Slipper, #48 of 50, 1972, 2½″ dia...................550.00
White Marsh Gentian, translucent wine grd, 1975...........800.00

Trabucco, Victor

Bouquet, violets/buttercups/etc, 9 + bud, fct, 3″ dia..........700.00
Cherries, w/blossoms, cl grd, 2½″ dia......................300.00
Forget-Me-Nots, bl flowers/buds, cl grd, fct, 1980, 2½″.......250.00
Hand cooler, bl flower/yel stamens & bud, 3″ high...........200.00
Jack-In-The-Pulpit, pk/wht flowers & buds w/yel stamens, 3″....350.00
Orange butterfly & daisies, cl grd, 3″ dia.................350.00
Violet bouquet, on cl grd, fct, 1980, 2½″ dia..............300.00
Violets, 3, w/bud & foliage................................300.00
Yellow butterfly, over daisies/bluebells, Nature in Ice.........450.00

Whittemore, Francis D.

Bl rose w/wht tips, wine o/l, early, 2″.....................450.00
Blue flower & bud, wht grd, fct, early......................325.00
Clear w/pink rose petals, gr leaves, 2½″...................150.00
Holly on wht jsp grd, 2½″ dia.............................245.00
Pk & wht rose, ftd ped, early, 2¾″ H......................400.00
Scottish rose on blue grd, 2″ dia..........................350.00
Tilted pk/wht rose, ftd ped, early.........................450.00
Violet on gr grd, 2″ dia...................................325.00

Ysart, Paul

Bouquet, multicolored, on intricate latt, dk red cushion, 3″....550.00
Butterfly, on radiating latt w/mill garland, sgn PY, 3″ dia......600.00
Coiled snake, on gr grd, 2¾″ dia.........................650.00
Lg cane heart, in intricate latt basket, PY cane, 3″...........500.00
Purple flower, radiating latt, mill gar, cobalt grd, PY cane.....600.00
Single floating fish, PY cane, 3″ dia......................650.00

Miscellaneous

Advertising, celluloid, w/semi w/route map on bk.............12.50
Advertising, Smith Bros, cast iron.........................45.00
Antique New England, blown pear on cl circular 2½″ dia base.525.00
Antique Sandwich, Cross, coakwheel cane, 2⅝″ dia.........700.00
Antique Sandwich, Weedflower, complex mill center cane, 2¾″.700.00
Antique Sandwich, 10-petal Poinsettia, Lutz rose center cane...590.00
Child pulling cat's tail, cast bronze, 2¾″..................20.00
Deer, recumbent; CI, worn gold pnt, late 1800s, 3½x3x2″......35.00
Deer, recumbent; full rack, head to side, 4¾″ L............95.00
Deer, resting on plinth, CI, black, 5″.....................40.00
Dog, resting on plinth, CI, blk, 5¼″......................30.00
Hansen, Ron; butterfly on pink cushion, etched sgn, 2¼″.....100.00
Hansen, Ron; mc bouquet/lav, 6 punties on curve/1 atop, 2″...100.00
Kosta, Alan B Shepard, Jr................................70.00
Kosta, Albert Schweitzer.................................70.00
Lutz, Wes; blue rose, cl grd, ped, 2½″ H.................130.00
Photo on porcelain, 2 girls on book shape, J Schiffner........45.00
Scotia, snowman, not sgn, paper label, 2¾″ dia............75.00
Sulfide, obelisk, bust of Madonna w/in, spiked dia bk, 6½″...660.00
Tarsitano, Debbie; bouquet w/9 flowers, cobalt grd, 2″ dia....225.00

Whitefriars, Butterfly, mill canes frame & capture butterfly.....195.00
Whitefriars, Circular Garden, concentric mill, 2⅜″ dia........115.00
Whitefriars, Rings of Roses, concentric mill w/claret grd.......150.00

Papier Mache

The art of papier mache was mainly European. It originated in Paris around the middle of the 18th century, and became popular in America during Victorian times. Small items, such as boxes, trays, inkwells, frames, etc., as well as extensive ceiling moldings and larger articles of furniture were made. The process involved building layer upon layer of paper soaked in glue, coaxed into shape over a wood or wire form. When dry, it was painted or decorated with gilt or inlays. Inexpensive 20th century 'notions' were machine processed and mold pressed.

Advertising pc, duck on oval base, Victor Duck Decoys, 5¾″....75.00
Bank, Amish boy & Amish girl, pr..........................20.00
Bank, General MacArthur, 7x4″.............................95.00
Box, Russian, decor w/portrait of scholar, 4½″ dia...........40.00
Box, sulfide insert w/4 allegorical women, 1700s, 2¾″........385.00
Bull dog, on wood wheels, glass eyes, barks, 12x21″, VG.....250.00
Dog, recumbent, 20th century folk art, minor damage, 7½″.....16.00
Milliner's model, French, scrolls on bodice, lace cap, worn.....525.00
Parrot, standing, in old pnt, early 1900s, 10x10x4¾″.........45.00
Pencil box, w/pewter inlay, 7¾x2″.........................28.00
Puppet head, alligatored pnt, 3½″.........................45.00
Rabbit, spring ears, mk Germany, 6½″......................35.00
Tray, Austrian, rectangular, 1800s, 12x16¼″................40.00
Tray, oval w/floral border on blk, Victorian, 25″ L...........150.00
Whisk broom holder, cat's head, velvet cover/glass eyes, 11″...150.00

Parian Ware

Parian is hard paste unglazed porcelain made to resemble marble. First made in the mid-1800s by Staffordshire potters, it was soon after produced in the United States by the U.S. Pottery at Bennington, Vermont. Busts and statuary were favored, but plaques, vases, mugs, and pitchers were also made.

Ewer, pink and white, lady with mirror in cameo-like reserve, 6½″, $75.00.

Bottle, Venus De Milo figure, Perfect Love Goddess of Liqueurs .60.00
Bust, Grecian lady, 8"....................................25.00
Bust, Grecian lady w/laurel wreath, 10½".................60.00
Bust, Homer, mk J & TB, 9"...............................25.00
Bust, lady, garland in hair, fluted column base, 24", rstr.....250.00
Bust, lady in lace headdress, roses drape shoulder, 10¾".....155.00
Bust, Scott, imp J & TB, 10½"............................75.00
Bust, Shakespeare, sgn R & L, 7¾".......................125.00
Creamer, emb decor, mk Argyle, WB, Cobridge, 5"..........20.00
Ewer, snake hdl, florals, 6¾"............................35.00
Figurine, Colonial boy, bone in upraised hand, w/dog, 9½".....75.00
Figurine, nude seated atop lioness, 15", VG..............125.00
Figurine, Rebecca at Well, 14"..........................145.00
Figurine, semi nude holds flame aloft, Cupid over left arm, 9"..145.00
Figurine, woman seated on stump, bird on arm, Copeland, 13".285.00
Lamp, 3 faces w/glass eyes, owl/cat/bulldog, needs burner, 4"...115.00
Match box, cat w/fiddle, mc enamel, 5"...................35.00
Nut dish, Cupid......................................22.50
Pitcher, bl w/wht florals, leaves, Alcock, 1840s, 7½".....100.00
Pitcher, British subdue Napoleon, battle scene, lav/wht, 5¼"...135.00
Pitcher, emb cherubs & vintage, mk Copeland, 6¼".........45.00
Pitcher, emb florals, mk WB in rope, 8¾"................75.00
Pitcher, emb leaves/grain, WB, Cobridge, Fern, 7"........70.00
Pitcher, emb lilies, hinged pewter lid, 6¾".............35.00
Pitcher, emb musical instruments, mk Copeland, 6½".......75.00
Pitcher, Naomi & daughters-in-law, lav relief/hdl, Alcock, 9"...150.00
Pitcher, ribbed & stippled, ivy relief, rope hdl, 6".....32.00
Pitcher, water lilies, lav relief, branch hdl, Alcock, 7½".....150.00
Plaque, Seal of NC Smoking Tobacco, w/2 women, 12" sq fr...185.00
Plaque, 3 nude Cupids in relief, mk Enoret, B&G, 13" dia.....160.00
Vase, figural warrior/chariot/horses, 7½"................75.00
Vase, monkeys & applied grapes, bl/wht, ca 1850, 10".....245.00

Pate-Sur-Pate

Pate-sure-pate, literally paste on paste, is a technique where relief decorations are built up on a ceramic body by layering several applications of slip, one on the other until the desired result is achieved. Usually only two colors are used, and the value of a piece is greatly enhanced as more color is added.

Plate, fruit/basket medallion, wht/bl, att Newhall, 1815, 8½"...100.00
Vase, cameo full length figure, lustre finish, Germany, 5¾"....195.00
Vase, Cupid & Psyche, bronze mt, duck hdls, Sevres, 30"....5,500.00
Vase, lady in relief, irid gr on mauve medallion, sgn, 5¾".....225.00
Vase, Pandora in relief, sgn, 5¾"......................180.00
Vase, putti rising from sea, 4 colors, Meissen, #105, 8¾"....1,100.00

Pattern Glass

The process for making mold pressed glassware was perfected in the 1820s. Many early glass houses produced tableware in hundreds of patterns and variations. In the early years, flint glass was used. This type of glass contained lead, which gave the ware resonance and clarity of color. Through the remaining years of the century until about 1915 when glassware of this type lost favor, soda lime was used to replace the lead. Glass of this type is referred to as non-flint.

Though in the past, collectors have tended to ignore all but the early flint glass, today there are many who appreciate the later glass as well, and prices within the last few years reflect this attitude. There are several important non-flint patterns. The rare portrait goblet and the American Coin pattern are both non-flint, as are the States series made by U.S. Glass Com-

pany which are enjoying a new-found popularity.

In the listing that follows, if color is not noted, the glass is clear.

Acorn, butter w/cover....................................25.00
Acorn, compote, covered.................................60.00
Acorn, goblet...30.00
Acorn, spooner..18.00
Actress, bowl, 5".......................................25.00
Actress, bread platter..................................55.00
Actress, butter w/cover.................................75.00
Actress, cake stand....................................150.00
Actress, celery vase, Pinafore.........................155.00
Actress, cheese dish...................................195.00
Actress, compote, covered, tall standard, 13".........159.00
Actress, compote, covered, 7".........................110.00
Actress, compote, covered, 8".........................120.00
Actress, compote, low standard, open, all clear, 6"....55.00
Actress, compote, open, Adelaide Nielsen, 7x7" dia.....45.00
Actress, creamer..45.00
Actress, goblet, Maud Granger...........................55.00
Actress, jam jar w/lid..................................85.00
Actress, relish, 'Loves Request Is Pickles'.............40.00
Actress, sauce, 5"......................................28.00
Actress, spooner..65.00
Actress, sugar, open....................................60.00
Actress, sugar w/lid....................................85.00
Admiral Dewey, see Greentown Glass, Dewey
Alabama, bowl, master berry.............................40.00
Alabama, bowl, rectangular..............................20.00
Alabama, creamer..28.00
Alabama, relish, oval...................................12.00
Alaska, creamer...20.00
Alaska, creamer, green..................................35.00
Alaska, cruet, gr w/enamel, w/clear stopper............225.00
Alaska, sauce, emerald gr w/enameled forget-me-nots/leaves.....45.00
Alaska, spooner, clear..................................28.00
Alaska, sugar w/cover, clear............................40.00
Alligator Scales, celery................................17.00
Alligator Scales w/Spearpoint, see Alligator Scales
Almond Thumbprint, compote, covered, flint, M...........45.00
Almond Thumbprint, goblet, barrel.......................19.00
Almond Thumbprint, wine.................................16.00
Amazon, creamer...30.00
Amazon, goblet, etched..................................20.00
Amazon, spooner, etched.................................29.00
Amazon, sugar w/lid.....................................55.00
Amazon, wine..22.00
Amberette, spooner......................................50.00
American Beauty, creamer, green w/gold..................18.00
American Beauty, water set, green w/gold, 7 pc.........185.00
American Shield, creamer...............................100.00
Anthemion, plate, 10¼"..................................22.00
Apollo, goblet..40.00
Apollo, plate, sq, lg...................................65.00
Apollo, sauce, ftd, 3¼" dia.............................20.00
Apollo, tray, water.....................................29.00
Aquarium, pitcher, water...............................180.00
Arched Fleur-de-Lis, bowl, 8"...........................15.00
Arched Fleur-de-Lis, plate, 7¼" square..................13.00
Arched Fleur-de-Lis, spooner............................18.00
Arched Grape, goblet....................................30.00
Arched Ovals, creamer...................................30.00
Arched Ovals, goblet....................................18.00
Arched Ovals, tumbler, gold trim........................10.00

Arched Ovals, wine....................................25.00
Argus, champagne, blown, flint.............................35.00
Argus, egg cup.......................................23.00
Argus, spill holder, (not spooner), flint.....................95.00
Argus, tumbler, water.................................45.00
Argus, whiskey, handled, flint............................95.00
Art, banana stand....................................85.00
Art, goblet...25.00
Art, pitcher, milk; ruby stained.........................120.00
Ashburton, ale glass, flint, 6½"........................55.00
Ashburton, bar bottle, qt, flint.........................40.00
Ashburton, champagne, flint............................45.00
Ashburton, claret, low stem, flint.......................40.00
Ashburton, cordial, vaseline...........................140.00
Ashburton, egg cup, barrel.............................23.00
Ashburton, egg cup, double, flint.......................95.00
Ashburton, egg cup, flared.............................23.00
Ashburton, flip glass, flint, 5¾".......................95.00
Ashburton, goblet, etched grapes/leaves/tendrils, flint........175.00
Ashburton, goblet, flint, flared sides....................60.00
Ashburton, honey dish, flint, 3½"........................8.00
Ashburton, whiskey, handled, flint......................67.50
Ashburton, wine, flint................................32.00
Ashburton, wine, non-flint.............................24.00
Ashland, sauce, handled, flat............................7.00
Atlanta (Tarantum's), see Royal Crystal
Atlas, cake stand, 8".................................18.00
Atlas, creamer, flat, etched...........................21.00
Atlas, goblet.......................................28.00
Atlas, pitcher, 10"..................................25.00
Atlas, toothpick....................................18.00
Atlas, water set, clear to cranberry w/gold, 7 pc, Northwood....250.00
Atlas, wine..18.00
Atlas Ball & Swirl, cake stand, ftd......................95.00
Aurora, decanter, orig stopper, 6 wines, tray, ruby stained.....350.00
Aurora, tray, water..................................18.00
Austrian, creamer, individual, canary....................50.00
Austrian, Finecut Medallion, wine, canary................110.00
Austrian, tumbler...................................25.00
Austrian, wine.....................................30.00
Aztec, cruet.......................................35.00
Aztec, punch cup.....................................6.50
Aztec, wine..25.00
Bagware, creamer....................................18.00
Bagware, ketchup bottle, amber, w/orig top................85.00
Bagware, table set, amber............................225.00
Ball & Swirl, creamer................................22.50
Ball & Swirl, pitcher, water; tankard....................35.00
Ball & Swirl, spooner................................15.00
Baltimore Pear, creamer...............................20.00
Baltimore Pear, goblet................................55.00
Baltimore Pear, goblet, early repro......................22.00
Baltimore Pear, pitcher..............................100.00
Baltimore Pear, sugar, open............................20.00
Banded Beaded Grape Medallion, goblet...................27.00
Banded Beaded Grape Medallion, goblet, design on ft........38.00
Banded Buckle, creamer...............................80.00
Banded Buckle, spooner...............................24.00
Banded Buckle, sugar, open............................30.00
Banded Diamond Rosette, goblet.........................20.00
Banded Icicle, celery................................40.00
Banded Portland, butter, covered, maiden blush...........165.00
Banded Portland, celery, flat..........................17.50
Banded Portland, cologne, w/orig stopper, 9½"............45.00

Banded Portland, compote, jelly; w/cover.................24.50
Banded Portland, creamer, breakfast; w/maiden's blush........35.00
Banded Portland, dresser jar, w/gold....................27.00
Banded Portland, pitcher..............................75.00
Banded Portland, relish, maiden's blush, 6½".............15.00
Banded Portland, relish, maiden's blush, 8"..............25.00
Banded Portland, ring tree, good gold....................40.00
Banded Portland, shakers, orig top, maiden's blush, pr........75.00
Banded Portland, shakers, pr...........................30.00
Banded Portland, tumbler, EX gold.......................29.00
Banded Portland, vase, 6".............................15.00
Banded Portland, vase, 9".............................17.00
Banded Portland, water bottle..........................80.00
Banded Portland, wine................................32.00
Banded Raindrops, sugar w/lid, large....................35.00
Banded Star, creamer.................................25.00
Banded Stippled Starflower, goblet......................15.00
Banner, butter w/cover, minor chips....................110.00
Bar & Diamond, see Kokomo
Bar w/Flute, butter w/cover, ruby flashed................85.00
Bar w/Flute, creamer, ruby flashed......................30.00
Bar w/Flute, spooner, ruby flashed......................30.00
Barberry, pitcher, water; w/applied hdl..................75.00
Barberry, spooner...................................22.50
Barley, compote, open, 8½" dia.........................22.00
Barley, creamer.....................................20.00
Barley, goblet.....................................27.50
Barley, pitcher, water................................30.00
Barley, wine.......................................23.00
Barred Forget-Me-Not, compote.........................33.00
Barred Forget-Me-Not, goblet...........................23.00
Barred Forget-Me-Not, wine............................23.00
Barred Hobnail, wine.................................25.00
Barred Ovals, tray, relish; lg, ruby stained..............55.00
Barrel Huber, see Huber
Bartlett Pear, goblet................................30.00
Basketweave, goblet..................................23.00
Basketweave, goblet, vaseline..........................25.00
Basketweave, pitcher, amber............................45.00
Basketweave, tray, condiment; blue......................85.00
Basketweave, tray, water; w/scenic center, vaseline........50.00
Beaded Acorn Medallion, goblet.........................34.00
Beaded Acorn Medallion, goblet, w/leaf band..............38.00
Beaded Acorn Medallion, plate, 6".......................17.00
Beaded Band, doughnut stand, 7½".......................17.00
Beaded Band, relish..................................18.00
Beaded Band, spooner.................................16.00
Beaded Band, sugar w/lid..............................28.00
Beaded Band, wine...................................18.00
Beaded Bull's Eye & Drape, see Alabama
Beaded Frog's Eye, goblet.............................25.00
Beaded Grape, butter w/cover, green.....................95.00
Beaded Grape, butter w/cover, green w/gold..............110.00
Beaded Grape, cake stand, green........................75.00
Beaded Grape, compote, ftd, clear......................35.00
Beaded Grape, creamer, green..........................25.00
Beaded Grape, egg cup................................16.00
Beaded Grape, pickle.................................20.00
Beaded Grape, pitcher, green.........................135.00
Beaded Grape, plate, 8¼".............................25.00
Beaded Grape, tray, bread; green.......................45.00
Beaded Grape, wine..................................30.00
Beaded Grape, wine, green w/gold.......................65.00
Beaded Grape Medallion, goblet.........................22.00

Beaded Grape Medallion, spooner.............................25.00
Beaded Loop, celery...29.00
Beaded Loop, goblet...30.00
Beaded Loop, pitcher, milk..................................39.00
Beaded Loop, pitcher, water.................................42.00
Beaded Loop, sugar w/lid, ruby flashed......................45.00
Beaded Loop, whiskey carafe.................................50.00
Beaded Medallion, goblet....................................30.00
Beaded Medallion, pitcher, water; green....................110.00
Beaded Medallion, spooner...................................23.00
Beaded Medallion, tumbler, green, Findlay...................40.00
Beaded Mirror, see Beaded Medallion
Beaded Panels, celery.......................................28.00
Beaded Swirl, berry set, green w/EX gold, 7 pc.............175.00
Beaded Swirl, creamer, green................................38.00
Beaded Swirl, creamer, green/gold...........................60.00
Beaded Swirl, mug, electric blue, ca 1905, M................25.00
Beaded Swirl, tumbler, ruby stained, rare...................45.00
Beaded Swirl, wine..30.00
Beaded Tulip, bowl, oval, 9½"...............................20.00
Beaded Tulip, goblet..32.00
Beaded Tulip, relish..22.50
Bearded Man, sugar bowl w/lid...............................55.00
Beautiful Lady, candy dish..................................16.00
Beautiful Lady, compote, square.............................25.00
Beautiful Lady, creamer.....................................23.00
Beautiful Lady, vase, 6½"...................................13.00
Bellflower, bowl, scalloped rim, ftd, flint, 8".............35.00
Bellflower, celery vase....................................150.00
Bellflower, champagne, flint................................75.00
Bellflower, decanter, flint................................160.00
Bellflower, goblet, fine rib, banded, flint, amethyst tinted......75.00

Bellflower, goblet, flint glass, $45.00.

bellflower, goblet, flint...................................45.00
Bellflower, honey dish, flint...............................12.00
Bellflower, sauce, flint....................................12.00
Bellflower, sugar, open, double vine, flint.................46.00
Bellflower, tumbler, flint..................................70.00
Bellflower, wine, flint.....................................65.00
Belted Worchester, goblet, flare top, flint, 1850s..........25.00
Belted Worchester, tumbler, flint...........................40.00
Bent Buckle, see New Hampshire

Berry Cluster, creamer......................................25.00
Berry Cluster, wine...22.00
Bethlehem Star, compote, jelly; w/cover.....................38.00
Bethlehem Star, creamer.....................................29.00
Bethlehem Star, pitcher.....................................60.00
Bethlehem Star, relish......................................15.00
Bethlehem Star, sauce.......................................10.00
Bethlehem Star, wine..23.00
Bevelled Diamond & Star, creamer............................20.00
Bevelled Diamond & Star, cruet w/orig stopper...............22.00
Bevelled Diamond & Star, tray, water; no harm smooth........15.00
Bevelled Diamond & Star, wine decanter, ruby stained........65.00
Bird & Fern, see Hummingbird
Bird & Strawberry, cake stand...............................60.00
Bird & Strawberry, compote, open, scalloped-ruffled rim, 6x8"..110.00
Bird & Strawberry, creamer..................................45.00
Bird & Strawberry, pitcher, water..........................185.00
Bird & Strawberry, punch cup................................20.00
Bird & Strawberry, table set...............................335.00
Bird & Strawberry, water set, clear w/pink & blue, 7 pc....395.00
Bird & Strawberry, wine.....................................40.00
Bird in Ring, celery..35.00
Birds at Fountain, goblet...................................40.00
Blackberry, egg cup, double.................................32.50
Blackberry, goblet..35.00
Blackberry, master salt.....................................32.00
Blackberry, spooner...50.00
Bleeding Heart, bowl, covered...............................65.00
Bleeding Heart, goblet......................................32.00
Bleeding Heart, spooner.....................................29.50
Block, tumbler, amber.......................................25.00
Block, wine...24.00
Block & Circle, creamer, ped................................25.00
Block & Circle, sauce, flat..................................9.00
Block & Circle, spooner, ped................................25.00
Block & Fan, celery...30.00
Block & Fan, goblet...45.00
Block & Fan, ice bucket.....................................45.00
Block & Fan, pitcher, milk..................................35.00
Block & Fan, rose bowl, large...............................25.00
Block & Jewel, wine...28.00
Block & Lattice, butter w/cover, amber stain................85.00
Block & Lattice, celery vase, ruby stained..................65.00
Block & Lattice, creamer, ruby stained......................55.00
Block & Lattice, pitcher, water; bulbous, ruby stained.....150.00
Block & Lattice, sugar w/lid, amber stain...................70.00
Block & Lattice, table set, amber & clear, 4 pc............235.00
Block & Lattice, water set w/tankard pitcher, amber, 5 pc..175.00
Block & Thumbprint, tumbler.................................35.00
Block & Thumbprint, wine.....................................9.00
Blue Jay, see Cardinal Bird
Bluebird, see Bird & Strawberry
Bosworth, celery..15.00
Bosworth, creamer...20.00
Bosworth, relish..12.00
Bow Tie, butter pat...25.00
Bow Tie, cake stand, minor wear marks, no chips, 9" dia.....45.00
Bow Tie, goblet...36.00
Bow Tie, marmalade jar, w/lid...............................46.00
Boy & Goose, compote.......................................135.00
Bradford Grape, champagne...................................57.50
Bradford Grape, goblet......................................49.50
Bradford Grape, goblet, flint...............................65.00
Bradford Grape, sugar w/lid.................................75.00

Brazilian, spooner, green...............................50.00
Brazilian, tumbler, green..............................25.00
Brilliant, creamer & sugar, etched.....................60.00
Britannic, pitcher, water; ruby stained................95.00
Broken Column, banana dish, ftd, 9"....................80.00
Broken Column, basket, w/applied handle...............160.00
Broken Column, bowl, berry; sm.........................18.00
Broken Column, bowl, covered vegetable.................80.00
Broken Column, bowl, 6"................................25.00
Broken Column, bowl, 8½"...............................31.00
Broken Column, butter w/cover..........................45.00
Broken Column, cake plate, ftd.........................70.00
Broken Column, carafe..................................60.00
Broken Column, compote, covered, 10x5" square..........55.00
Broken Column, compote, covered, 11" to finial, 6" dia.....60.00
Broken Column, compote, open, 6".......................38.00
Broken Column, compote, open, 7½x7½"...................55.00
Broken Column, cracker jar, w/cover....................70.00
Broken Column, creamer.................................34.00
Broken Column, cruet...................................65.00
Broken Column, decanter, wine; lapidary stopper........95.00
Broken Column, goblet..................................50.00
Broken Column, honey dish...............................6.00
Broken Column, jam jar, w/cover........................57.00
Broken Column, pitcher................................110.00
Broken Column, plate, 5"...............................25.00
Broken Column, plate, 8"...............................30.00
Broken Column, relish, oval, 11x5".....................22.00
Broken Column, relish, oval, 7½x4".....................20.00
Broken Column, relish, rectangular, 7½x5"..............15.00
Broken Column, spooner.................................30.00
Broken Column, sugar w/lid.............................75.00
Broken Column, tumbler.................................45.00
Broken Column w/Red Notches, plate, 7¼" dia............75.00
Broken Column w/Red Notches, sauce, 4¼" dia............35.00
Buck & Doe, goblet, etched.............................90.00
Buckle, compote, covered, very lg......................95.00
Buckle, egg cup..20.00
Buckle, goblet...24.00
Buckle, sauce...6.00
Buckle, sugar, open, flint.............................40.00
Buckle, tumbler..30.00
Buckle w/English Hobnail, sugar........................20.00
Buckle w/English Hobnail, vase, ftd, 6"................15.00
Buckle w/Star, goblet..................................28.00
Buckle w/Star, pickle..................................12.50
Budded Ivy, creamer, clear.............................22.50
Budded Ivy, spooner....................................22.00
Bull's Eye, celery vase, flint.........................32.00
Bull's Eye, punch cup, ftd, ruby stained...............45.00
Bull's Eye, wine, flint, knob stem.....................37.50
Bull's Eye & Bar, goblet, flint.......................135.00
Bull's Eye & Daisy, decanter w/stopper, clear w/pink eyes......50.00
Bull's Eye & Daisy, goblet, clear w/gold & gr eyes.....18.00
Bull's Eye & Daisy, spooner, gold eyes, EX gold........28.00
Bull's Eye & Daisy, tumbler, gold eyes.................17.00
Bull's Eye & Daisy, wine, gold eyes....................21.00
Bull's Eye & Diamond Point, spill, flint...............40.00
Bull's Eye & Fan, see Daisies in Oval Panels
Bull's Eye & Spearhead, cologne bottle, orig stopper...22.50
Bull's Eye & Spearhead, wine...........................15.00
Bull's Eye in Heart, see Heart w/Thumbprint
Bull's Eye Variant, see Texas Bull's Eye
Bungalo, compote, open, etched, 8".....................54.00

Bungalo, goblet, etched................................34.00
Butterfly, mug...21.00
Butterfly & Fan, celery vase...........................20.00
Butterfly & Fan, tumbler...............................15.00
Butterfly w/Spray, mug, amber..........................35.00
Button Arches, compote, 4½" high.......................48.00
Button Arches, creamer, ruby stained...................40.00
Button Arches, goblet, ruby stained....................35.00
Button Arches, pitcher, milk; ruby stained.............55.00
Button Arches, pitcher, water; tall tankard, ruby stained......125.00
Button Arches, spooner, gold band......................25.00
Button Arches, wine, ruby flashed......................24.50
Button Arches w/Clear Band, spooner, ruby stained......25.00
Button Arches w/Frost Band, water set, ruby stain & gold, 7 pc.....265.00
Button Band, cordial...................................28.00
Cabbage Rose, celery...................................39.00
Cabbage Rose, champagne................................55.00
Cabbage Rose, creamer..................................52.00
Cabbage Rose, goblet...................................35.00
Cabbage Rose, spooner..................................32.00
Cabbage Rose, tumbler..................................35.00
Cabbage Rose, wine.....................................45.00
Cable, decanter, bar-lip, quart.......................125.00
Cable, goblet, flint...................................58.00
Cable, master salt.....................................45.00
Cable, spooner...35.00
Cable, wine, flint.....................................75.00
Cable w/Ring, sugar w/lid, flint.......................85.00
Cadmus, creamer & open sugar, large....................26.00
Cadmus, creamer & sugar, individual....................22.00
Cadmus, plate, 8½".....................................15.00
Cambridge Feather, wine................................25.00
Canadian, compote, covered, high standard, 7" dia.....125.00
Canadian, goblet.......................................45.00
Canadian, pitcher, water...............................60.00
Canadian, wine...40.00
Cane, creamer..20.00
Cane, goblet...20.00
Cane, goblet, apple green..............................58.00
Cane, pitcher, water; blue.............................60.00
Cane, plate, apple green, 4½"..........................10.00
Cane, plate, toddy; amber, 4½" dia.....................12.00
Cane, tumbler, blue....................................22.00
Cane & Rosette, creamer................................30.00
Cane Column, see Panelled Cane
Cape Cod, goblet.......................................35.00
Cardinal, see Cardinal Bird
Cardinal Bird, creamer.................................37.50
Cardinal Bird, goblet..................................32.50
Cardinal Bird, sauce, flat, 4" dia.....................12.00
Carnation, bowl, master berry; ruby stained, w/gold....48.00
Carolina, creamer......................................19.50
Carolina, pitcher......................................55.00
Carolina, plate, 7½"...................................12.00
Carolina, sauce, ped, gilt rim & violet flowers........15.00
Cartridge Belt, wine...................................16.00
Casco, wine..14.00
Cat & Dog, pitcher, water.............................270.00
Cat's Eye & Block, see Cut Log
Catawba Grape, goblet..................................20.00
Cathedral, bowl, berry; vaseline, 3x8" dia.............25.00
Cathedral, bowl, ruffled, w/ruby flashing, 5"..........26.00
Cathedral, butter w/cover..............................40.00
Cathedral, compote, open, amber........................38.00

Cathedral, compote, scalloped top, blue, 9½"................65.00
Cathedral, goblet, amber.................................40.00
Cathedral, spooner......................................24.00
Cathedral, sugar, open..................................25.00
Cathedral, sugar w/lid, ruby stained....................65.00
Cathedral, tumbler, ruby stained........................32.00
Cathedral, wine...29.00
Cathedral, wine, blue...................................55.00
Centennial, see Liberty Bell
Centennial Shield, see American Shield
Chain, spooner..24.00
Chain, wine...25.00
Chain & Shield, creamer.................................16.00
Chain & Shield, goblet..................................22.00
Chain & Shield, platter, oval...........................30.00
Chain & Star Band, cake stand...........................35.00
Chain & Star Band, goblet...............................20.00
Chain w/Star, cake stand, 10½"..........................30.00
Chain w/Star, cake stand, 8¾"...........................27.00
Chain w/Star, compote, open, high standard, 8"..........25.00
Chain w/Star, creamer...................................22.00
Chain w/Star, plate, 7".................................14.00
Chain w/Star, sugar w/lid...............................27.00
Chain w/Star, wine......................................18.00
Champion, rose bowl.....................................25.00
Champion, wine..10.00
Chandelier, butter w/cover..............................58.00
Chandelier, creamer.....................................40.00
Chandelier, finger bowl.................................16.00
Chandelier, goblet, etched..............................35.00
Chandelier, inkwell.....................................75.00
Chandelier, tumbler.....................................30.00
Checkerboard, celery vase...............................32.00
Checkerboard, creamer, diagonal lines are gold flashed........40.00
Checkerboard, water set, ruby stained, 5 pc............210.00
Cherry, goblet..30.00
Cherry & Cable, creamer, tinted, fair gold, sgn Northwood......50.00
Cherry & Cable, punch cup, on ped, clear................18.00
Cherry & Cable, sugar w/lid, tinted, Northwood..........40.00
Cherry w/Thumbprint, bowl, berry........................15.00
Cherry w/Thumbprint, butter dish........................95.00
Cherry w/Thumbprint, celery vase, tall..................87.00
Cherry w/Thumbprint, creamer............................28.00
Cherry w/Thumbprint, pitcher, water; mint stain, Northwood....110.00
Cherry w/Thumbprint, pitcher, water; no decor...........70.00
Cherry w/Thumbprint, spooner............................32.50
Cherry w/Thumbprint, tumbler............................30.00
Chrysanthemum Leaf, see Curled Leaf
Church Windows, see Tulip Petals
Classic, celery, color base.............................95.00
Classic, celery, open log feet.........................195.00
Classic, spooner, collar base...........................95.00
Classic Medallion, bowl, ftd, 3½x6¾"....................38.00
Classic Medallion, creamer..............................25.00
Classic Medallion, spooner..............................24.00
Clear Block, creamer, tall..............................15.00
Clear Block, punch cup...................................8.00
Clear Diagonal Band, berry set, 6 pc....................48.00
Clear Diagonal Band, creamer............................20.50
Clear Diagonal Band, goblet.............................20.00
Clear Diagonal Band, wine...............................15.00
Clear Panels w/Cord Band, see Rope Bands
Clear Roman Key, creamer, w/applied hdl.................37.00
Clear Roman Key, goblet.................................13.00

Clear Roman Key, goblet, flint..........................32.00
Clear Stork, creamer....................................35.00
Clematis, goblet..25.00
Clematis, spooner.......................................20.00
Clover & Daisy, goblet..................................15.00
Coarse Zigzag, wine.....................................22.00
Coat of Arms, pitcher, water............................35.00
Coin Glass, see US Coin
Colonial, celery, Heisey................................50.00
Colonial, creamer, applied handle, flint...............120.00
Colonial, sherbet, Higbee...............................55.00
Colonial, tumbler, flint................................45.00
Colonial w/Diamond Band, goblet, flint..................35.00
Colorado, berry set, green w/EX gold, 7 pc.............165.00
Colorado, bowl, berry; green w/EX gold, small...........22.00
Colorado, bowl, blue w/good gold, 5"....................35.00
Colorado, butter w/cover, blue w/gold..................225.00
Colorado, butter w/cover, clear/no gold.................65.00
Colorado, creamer, blue w/gold, table size..............95.00
Colorado, creamer, green, small.........................25.00
Colorado, creamer, green, table size....................40.00
Colorado, creamer, green w/gold, small..................35.00
Colorado, creamer, green w/gold, table size.............60.00
Colorado, nappy, tri-cornered...........................20.00
Colorado, pitcher, milk; green..........................42.00
Colorado, pitcher, water; dk blue, no gold.............115.00
Colorado, pitcher, water; green & gold.................175.00
Colorado, salver, blue, no gold, 8".....................60.00
Colorado, sauce, ftd, blue w/gold, 4½"..................25.00
Colorado, sauce, ftd, ruffled, blue w/gold, 4½".........30.00
Colorado, sherbet, blue w/gold..........................35.00
Colorado, sherbet, green w/gold.........................30.00
Colorado, spooner, green w/gold.........................65.00
Colorado, sugar, individual; clear......................20.00
Colorado, tray, card; ftd, emerald green................19.00
Colorado, tray, green w/EX gold, 4½"....................28.00
Colorado, tumbler, green................................25.00
Colorado, vase, blue w/EX gold, 12½"....................95.00
Colorado, wine, green w/gold............................30.00
Columbian Coin, berry set, gilded, 7 pc................295.00
Columbian Coin, claret, clear & frosted................145.00
Columbian Coin, creamer................................225.00
Columbian Coin, pitcher, milk tankard..................135.00
Columbian Coin, spooner.................................40.00
Columbian Coin, sugar w/lid, clear......................95.00
Columbian Coin, syrup..................................145.00
Columbian Coin, table set, clear w/EX gold, 4 pc.......350.00

Colorado, basket, 3" x 7½", $30.00.

Columbian Exposition, goblet............................30.00
Comet, goblet, flint....................................68.00
Compact, see Snail
Coral, see Fishscale
Corcoran, wine..25.00
Cord & Tassel, creamer................................25.00
Cord & Tassel, goblet.................................32.00
Cord & Tassel, wine...................................25.00
Cord Drapery, bowl, berry; small......................11.00
Cord Drapery, bowl, candy; blue, 5x8".................50.00
Cord Drapery, cruet...................................90.00
Cord Drapery, cup.....................................14.00
Cord Drapery, pitcher.................................59.00
Cord Drapery, wine....................................25.00
Cordova, compote, stemmed.............................35.00
Cordova, inkwell......................................75.00
Cordova, pitcher, milk................................28.00
Cordova, syrup jug...................................125.00
Cornucopia, cordial...................................25.00
Cornucopia, pitcher, water............................80.00
Cornucopia, wine......................................23.00
Corona, see Sunk Honeycomb
Corrigan, wine..15.00
Cottage, cake stand, 9"...............................28.00
Cottage, compote, jelly...............................19.00
Cottage, creamer......................................22.00
Cottage, goblet.......................................22.00
Cottage, spooner......................................20.00
Cradled Prisms, goblet................................18.00
Cradled Prisms, sugar w/lid...........................23.00
Crescent & Fan, decanter..............................47.00
Crescent & Fan, wine..................................18.00
Croesus, bowl, berry; purple w/EX gold................35.00
Croesus, butter w/cover, green.......................180.00
Croesus, compote, jelly; amethyst....................250.00
Croesus, creamer, green w/gold, 5¼"...................85.00
Croesus, pitcher, water; purple & gold, heat check on hdl top..160.00
Croesus, relish, amethyst.............................75.00
Croesus, spooner, gr w/gold...........................58.00
Croesus, sugar, breakfast; gr w/gold..................65.00
Croesus, sugar w/lid, green w/EX gold................135.00
Croesus, toothpick, gr w/gold.........................70.00
Croesus, tumbler, green & gold, set of 4.............200.00
Croesus, water set, gr w/gold, 6 pc..................425.00
Crossed Block, see Roman Cross
Crossed Ovals, wine...................................22.00
Crossed Pressed Leaf, spooner.........................28.00
Crowfoot, creamer.....................................35.00
Crystal Ball, see Atlas
Crystal Wedding, banana stand........................160.00
Crystal Wedding, cake stand...........................35.00
Crystal Wedding, compote, covered, clear & frosted, 9¾x6" sq..65.00
Crystal Wedding, compote, covered, ruby stained, 10" high.....45.00
Crystal Wedding, compote, scalloped, 6"...............65.00
Crystal Wedding, goblet...............................60.00
Crystal Wedding, saucer, 3"...........................14.00
Crystal Wedding, spooner, clear & frosted.............35.00
Crystal Wedding, tumbler, clear.......................35.00
Cube, goblet, plain stem..............................11.00
Cube & Diamond, see Milton
Cube w/Fan, see Holbrook
Cupid & Venus, butter w/cover.........................50.00
Cupid & Venus, celery.................................40.00
Cupid & Venus, champagne..............................85.00

Cupid & Venus, compote, covered, low standard, 7".....55.00
Cupid & Venus, compote, open, low standard, 8½" wide.......25.00
Cupid & Venus, creamer................................35.00
Cupid & Venus, goblet.................................52.00
Cupid & Venus, marmalade, w/cover.....................62.00
Cupid & Venus, mug, 2"................................20.00
Cupid & Venus, mug, 3½"...............................25.00
Cupid & Venus, pitcher, milk..........................45.00
Cupid & Venus, pitcher, milk; amber..................190.00
Cupid & Venus, plate, large...........................28.00
Cupid & Venus, sauce, ftd, 3½" dia.....................7.50
Cupid & Venus, spooner................................35.00
Cupid's Hunt, berry set, compote w/ped + 5 bowls......80.00
Cupid's Hunt, relish..................................26.00
Cupid's Hunt, sauce, ftd, 4"..........................10.00
Curled Leaf, creamer..................................32.50
Curled Leaf, nappy, handled...........................20.00
Curled Leaf, sauce, large.............................12.50
Curled Leaf, spooner..................................22.00
Curled Leaf, tumbler..................................20.00
Currant, goblet.......................................74.00
Currier & Ives, compote, open.........................50.00
Currier & Ives, cup & saucer..........................35.00
Currier & Ives, goblet................................24.00
Currier & Ives, pitcher, milk.........................35.00
Currier & Ives, pitcher, water; ca 1890, Bellaire.....75.00
Currier & Ives, sauce, flat............................4.00
Currier & Ives, tray, Balking Mule on RR Tracks, 12"..68.00
Currier & Ives, wine..................................16.00
Cut Log, bowl, master berry; large....................25.00
Cut Log, cake stand, 9"...............................56.00
Cut Log, celery.......................................40.00
Cut Log, compote, jelly; w/cover......................65.00
Cut Log, compote, open, 10" dia.......................30.00
Cut Log, mug..14.00
Cut Log, nappy..17.00
Cut Log, pitcher, tankard.............................75.00
Cut Log, relish.......................................20.00
Cut Log, wine...22.00
Dahlia, egg cup, double...............................45.00
Dahlia, pitcher, water................................40.00
Dahlia, wine..30.00
Daisies in Oval Panels, compote, 5x7¼"................18.00
Daisies in Oval Panels, goblet, non-flint.............13.00
Daisies in Oval Panels, lemonade set, cranberry/gold, 7 pc.....225.00
Daisies in Oval Panels, relish, oval, clear, 12"......18.00
Daisies in Oval Panels, spooner, w/gold...............20.00
Daisies in Oval Panels, wine, some gold...............15.00
Daisy & Button, bowl, ice cream; vaseline.............65.00
Daisy & Button, bowl, triangular, green, early, 7"....22.00
Daisy & Button, bowl, triangular, vaseline, early, 8"..........26.00
Daisy & Button, butter or ice tub, 2 hdls, early, vaseline........29.00
Daisy & Button, butter w/cover, square, amber top, clear base...35.00
Daisy & Button, carafe, mold blown, early.............35.00
Daisy & Button, compote, deep scallop bowl/sawtooth base, 8"..40.00
Daisy & Button, creamer, applied hdl, 4"..............15.00
Daisy & Button, pitcher, ftd, 6 oz, canary............35.00
Daisy & Button, pitcher, water; w/reeded handle.......85.00
Daisy & Button, sauce, round, scalloped, amber, 6" dia.........25.00
Daisy & Button, spooner, w/amber panels...............40.00
Daisy & Button, tray, water; triangular, hdld, vaseline..46.00
Daisy & Button in Oval Panels, wine...................15.00
Daisy & Button w/Amber Panel, see Amberette
Daisy & Button w/Crossbar, celery.....................30.00

Daisy & Button w/Crossbar, creamer, amber..................38.00
Daisy & Button w/Crossbar, goblet..........................22.00
Daisy & Button w/Crossbar, sauce, amber....................12.00
Daisy & Button w/Crossbar, wine............................30.00
Daisy & Button w/Narcissus, pitcher........................50.00
Daisy & Button w/Narcissus, tumbler, clear w/gold & pink......12.00
Daisy & Button w/Narcissus, wine, ruby flashed.............22.00
Daisy & Button w/Thumbprint, goblet........................12.00
Daisy & Button w/Thumbprint, goblet, crystal w/blue..........35.00
Daisy & Button w/Thumbprint, pitcher, water; clear w/bl......65.00
Daisy & Button w/Thumbprint, tumbler, green................16.00
Daisy & Button w/Thumbprint, wine, apple green.............22.00
Daisy & Button w/V Ornament, celery, canary...............65.00
Daisy & Button w/V Ornament, compote......................25.00
Daisy & Button w/V Ornament, creamer, amber...............28.00
Daisy & Scroll, wine, flared...............................22.00
Daisy in Oval Panels, butter w/cover, green w/EX gold........75.00
Daisy Whorl, tumbler.......................................18.00
Daisy-in-Square, celery....................................25.00
Dakota, butter w/cover.....................................52.00
Dakota, cake stand, etched, 10".............................85.00
Dakota, celery vase, etched................................42.00
Dakota, compote, covered, etched, sm.......................65.00
Dakota, compote, covered, etched, 12x8" dia.................98.00
Dakota, compote, jelly.....................................35.00
Dakota, compote, open, etched, 8x7¾" dia...................38.00
Dakota, creamer..25.00
Dakota, creamer & sugar, ruby stained......................25.00
Dakota, goblet...30.00
Dakota, goblet, ruby flashed & etched......................65.00
Dakota, lamp..175.00
Dakota, salver, etched, 10".................................85.00
Dakota, spooner, etched....................................33.00
Dakota, sugar w/lid..45.00
Dakota, sugar w/lid, etched fern & berry...................65.00
Dakota, wine, etched.......................................38.00
Dakota, wine, ruby stained.................................50.00
Dart, spooner..17.00
Dart, sugar w/lid..30.00
Deer & Dog, goblet...45.00
Deer & Dog, pitcher, milk; 9", rare.......................165.00
Deer & Pine Tree, goblet...................................55.00
Deer & Pine Tree, pitcher, water..........................110.00
Deer & Pine Tree, sauce, ftd...............................27.00
Delaware, bowl, berry; boat shape, gr w/gold, small........28.00
Delaware, bowl, master berry; green w/gold.................65.00
Delaware, bowl, oval, rose, good gold, in silver holder......45.00
Delaware, bowl, rose, 8"...................................85.00
Delaware, butter w/cover, green...........................125.00
Delaware, celery vase.....................................115.00
Delaware, creamer, rose....................................42.00
Delaware, custard cup, rose w/gold.........................20.00
Delaware, pitcher, tankard; clear w/cranberry & gold, EX.....110.00
Delaware, pitcher, tankard; gr w/EX gold..................110.00
Delaware, pitcher, tankard; rose w/EX gold................175.00
Delaware, punch cup, rose w/EX gold........................30.00
Delaware, tumbler..12.00
Delaware, tumbler, green & gold............................30.00
Delaware, tumbler, rose....................................32.00
Delaware, vase, green w/gold, 8"...........................55.00
Delaware, vase, rose w/EX gold, 5½x3".......................70.00
Dew & Raindrop, cordial....................................19.00
Dew & Raindrop, pitcher, water.............................65.00
Dew & Raindrop, wine.......................................25.00

Dewdrop, goblet..16.00
Dewdrop, goblet, blue......................................25.00
Dewdrop in Points, compote, open, 8".......................25.00
Dewey, see Greentown Glass, Dewey
Diagonal Band, butter w/cover..............................28.00
Diagonal Band, celery vase.................................22.00
Diagonal Band, goblet......................................20.00
Diagonal Band w/Fan, goblet................................22.00
Diagonal Band w/Fan, plate, 7".............................10.00
Diagonal Band w/Fan, plate, 8".............................12.00
Diagonal Band w/Fan, spooner...............................24.00
Diamond & Long Sunburst, see Champion
Diamond & Sunburst, spooner................................21.00
Diamond Cut w/Leaf, goblet.................................15.00
Diamond Cut w/Leaf, sugar w/lid, amber.....................35.00
Diamond Cut w/Leaf, wine...................................19.00
Diamond Horseshoe, see Aurora
Diamond Lattice, see Chesterfield
Diamond Medallion, butter w/cover..........................45.00
Diamond Medallion, cake stand, 10".........................20.00
Diamond Medallion, goblet..................................18.00
Diamond Medallion, pitcher, 9".............................30.00
Diamond Medallion, spooner.................................22.50
Diamond Medallion, sugar w/lid.............................37.50
Diamond Medallion, wine....................................35.00
Diamond Point, egg cup, flint..............................30.00
Diamond Point, frappe, flint...............................65.00
Diamond Point, sugar w/lid, flint..........................65.00
Diamond Point, tumbler, flint..............................65.00
Diamond Point, whiskey, hdld, flint........................65.00
Diamond Point, wine..16.00
Diamond Point, wine, plain stem............................12.00
Diamond Point Discs, spooner...............................26.50
Diamond Point Loop, creamer, amber.........................30.00
Diamond Point Loop, sauce, green............................8.50
Diamond Point w/Panels, see Hinoto
Diamond Prisms, compote....................................30.00
Diamond Quilted, champagne.................................21.00
Diamond Quilted, creamer, amethyst.........................30.00
Diamond Quilted, goblet, blue..............................35.00
Diamond Quilted, goblet, vaseline..........................35.00
Diamond Quilted, mug, hdld, amethyst.......................30.00
Diamond Quilted, sauce, flat, amber, 4" dia................10.00
Diamond Quilted, sauce, ped, vaseline......................22.00
Diamond Quilted, sugar w/lid, canary yellow................45.00
Diamond Quilted, wine......................................19.00
Diamond Quilted, wine, lt blue.............................38.00
Diamond Sunburst, compote, jelly; open.....................12.00
Diamond Sunburst, goblet...................................11.00
Diamond Thumbprint, butter w/cover, flint.................200.00
Diamond Thumbprint, goblet, flint.........................325.00
Diamond Thumbprint, tumbler, water; flint..................95.00
Diamonds in Oval, see Prism Arc
Dinner Bell, see Cottage
Divided Block w/Sunburst, spooner..........................12.00
Divided Stem, celery, etched...............................54.00
Dogwood, spooner, ruby stained.............................40.00
Dolphin, celery, frosted & clear, 9" high..................45.00
Doric, see Feather
Dot & Dash, compote w/cover................................50.00
Dot & Dash, goblet...16.00
Dot & Dash, sugar w/lid....................................40.00
Dotted Loop, wine..20.00
Double Band Forget-Me-Not, wine............................17.00

Double Beetle Band, pitcher...........................25.00
Double Beetle Band, wine, blue....................50.00
Double Daisy, goblet................................25.00
Double Daisy, pitcher, water; etched..............48.00
Double Daisy, spooner, ruby stained..............47.00
Double Leaf & Dart, see Leaf & Dart
Double Loop, see Ribbon Candy
Double Loop & Dart, goblet.........................25.00
Double Loop & Dart, wine..........................30.00
Double Red Block, see Hexagon Block, w/red flashing
Double Ribbon, goblet, clear & frosted...........38.00
Double Snail, cup, frosted..........................18.00
Double Snail, pitcher, frosted.....................85.00
Double Spear, creamer..............................27.00
Double Spear, sugar, frosted......................28.00
Doyle's Shell, creamer..............................18.00
Doyle's Shell, mustard w/cover....................12.50
Doyle's Shell, tumbler..............................18.00
Drapery, creamer...................................24.00
Drapery Variant, see Tidy
Early Panelled Grape Band, creamer, ornate applied hdl.......48.00
Early Thumbprint, goblet, baluster stem..........46.00
Early Thumbprint, tumbler, ftd, flint.............39.00
Egg in Sand, goblet................................29.00
Egg in Sand, spooner, amber......................55.00
Egg in Sand, sugar w/lid...........................28.00
Egg in Sand, tumbler...............................35.00
Egyptian, compote, covered, sphinx on base, 12½x8″ dia.....120.00
Egyptian, relish....................................25.00
Eight-O-Eight, wine................................30.00
Emerald Green Herringbone, see Green Herringbone
Empress, bowl, ice cream; fluted top, gr w/EX gold, 2¾x8½″...45.00
Empress, cruet tray, vaseline w/EX gold..........45.00
Empress, sugar, gold trim..........................45.00
Empress, water set, green & gold, 7 pc, Riverside...........365.00
English Hobnail Cross, see Klondike
Esther, bowl, berry................................27.00
Esther, butter w/cover, amber stained............95.00
Etched Dakota, see Dakota
Euclid, see Rexford
Eureka, creamer, ruby stained....................45.00
Eureka, goblet, flint...............................25.00
Excelsior, spillholder, flint, 1850................75.00
Excelsior, wine....................................42.00
Excelsior w/Maltese Cross, goblet, flint..........36.00
Fagot, compote, open, frosted, large.............40.00
Fairfax Strawberry, see Strawberry
Fan w/Diamond, creamer...........................25.00
Fan w/Diamond, goblet.............................29.00
Fancy Diamonds, goblet...........................18.00
Fancy Loop, celery.................................39.50
Fancy Loop, creamer, individual; clear w/gold....20.00
Fancy Loop, tumbler, green w/some gold..........38.00
Feather, compote, covered, high standard, 12x8½″ dia.......125.00
Feather, cruet....................................30.00
Feather, goblet...................................45.00
Feather, relish, oval, clear w/amber, 8¼″ long...45.00
Feather, sauce, ped...............................20.00
Feather, spooner, green...........................60.00
Feather, sugar w/lid, large........................30.00
Feather, tumbler..................................35.00
Feather, wine.....................................35.00
Feather, wine, clear w/cranberry stain...........42.00
Feather Duster, pitcher, water....................45.00

Feather Duster, water set, 6 pc, green............95.00
Fern Garland, compote, low........................18.00
Festoon, bowl, master berry.......................25.00
Festoon, pickle dish...............................15.00
Festoon, plate, 9¼″...............................29.00
Festoon, table set.................................185.00
Festoon, tumbler..................................20.00
Figure Eight, see Ribbon Candy
Fine Cut, creamer, blue...........................40.00
Fine Cut, plate, 10½″.............................21.00
Fine Cut, plate, 6″................................5.00
Fine Cut & Block, celery dish.....................26.50
Fine Cut & Block, creamer, blue & clear..........60.00
Fine Cut & Block, creamer, w/pink blocks.........65.00
Fine Cut & Block, egg cup.........................25.00
Fine Cut & Block, sauce, ftd, clear w/amber......16.00
Fine Cut & Block, sugar w/lid, yellow blocks.....125.00
Fine Cut & Panel, compote, open, high ped, amber...45.00
Fine Cut & Panel, wine, dk blue...................70.00
Fine Cut Medallion, butter, sm....................35.00
Fine Rib, compote, flint, 6x7″ dia................45.00
Fine Rib, goblet, flint.............................45.00
Fine Rib, wine, flint..............................38.00
Fishscale, butter w/cover..........................45.00
Fishscale, cake stand..............................27.00
Fishscale, compote, open..........................25.00
Fishscale, goblet..................................25.00
Fishscale, pitcher, milk...........................28.00
Fishscale, salt & pepper w/under tray............35.00
Fishscale, sauce..................................6.00
Flamingo Habitat, goblet..........................33.00
Flat Diamond, spooner............................26.50
Flat Panel, see Pleating
Fleur-de-Lys, cake plate...........................24.00
Fleur-de-Lys & Drape, sugar w/lid................32.50
Fleur-de-Lys & Drape, tray, water; round, 12″ dia...22.50
Flora, see Opposing Pyramids
Florida, bowl, green, 7¾″.........................20.00
Florida, spooner, green............................43.00
Florida, sugar w/lid, green........................50.00
Florida Palm, goblet..............................19.00
Flower & Quill, sugar.............................25.00
Flower Flange, see Greentown Glass, Dewey
Flower Pot, spooner...............................22.00
Flying Birds, goblet...............................40.00
Flying Robin, see Hummingbird
Forget-Me-Not in Scroll, spooner.................22.00
Four Petal Flower, see Delaware
Fox & Crow, pitcher, water........................175.00
Frosted Circle, butter w/cover, clear & frosted...55.00
Frosted Circle, creamer...........................35.00
Frosted Circle, salt & pepper, pr.................40.00
Frosted Circle, spooner...........................30.00
Frosted Eagle, creamer............................42.00
Frosted Fruits, compote, covered, clear, 6½x4¼″ dia.......35.00
Frosted Leaf, egg cup, flint.......................95.00
Frosted Ribbon, compote, open, 8″...............60.00
Frosted Ribbon, spooner..........................26.00
Frosted Stork, creamer............................45.00
Frosted Stork, goblet.............................45.00
Gaelic, butter w/cover............................85.00
Gaelic, compote, 4½x4¾″ dia.....................20.00
Galloway, butter w/cover, maiden's blush w/gold...125.00
Galloway, champagne.............................45.00

Galloway, pitcher.....................52.50

Galloway, pitcher, water; maiden's blush..................125.00

Galloway, relish, w/gold.....................18.00

Galloway, salt & peppers, pr.....................50.00

Galloway, syrup can.....................65.00

Galloway, wine.....................43.50

Garden Fruits, compote, covered, etched, 8″.....................58.00

Garden of Eden, pitcher.....................125.00

Garfield Drape, celery vase.....................40.00

Garfield Drape, creamer.....................37.50

Garfield Drape, pitcher, water.....................72.00

Garfield Drape, relish, oval.....................18.00

Gathered Knot, wine.....................22.00

Gem, see Nailhead

Geneva, pitcher, water; green w/gold.....................70.00

Geneva, water set, green, 7 pc.....................225.00

Georgia, see Peacock Feather

Giant Baby Thumbprint, see Early Thumbprint

Gibson Girl, butter w/cover.....................265.00

Gibson Girl, pitcher, water.....................185.00

Gibson Girl, pitcher, water; clear w/frosted heads.....................225.00

Gibson Girl, sauce.....................25.00

Gibson Girl, tumbler.....................65.00

Gloved Hand, see Coat of Arms

Good Luck, see Horseshoe

Gooseberry, mug.....................25.00

Gothic, goblet, flint.....................50.00

Gothic, spooner, flint.....................40.00

Grace, creamer.....................29.50

Grape & Festoon, goblet.....................27.00

Grape & Festoon w/Shield, creamer.....................35.00

Grape & Festoon w/Shield, goblet.....................40.00

Grape & Gothic Arches, pitcher, water; gr w/gold.....................85.00

Grape & Gothic Arches, water set, gr w/EX gold, 7 pc.......265.00

Grape Band, relish.....................18.00

Grasshopper, creamer, no insect.....................22.00

Grasshopper, pitcher.....................65.00

Grasshopper, sauce, ftd.....................10.00

Grated Ribbon, spooner.....................25.00

Greek Key, pitcher, water; ruby stain.....................115.00

Green Herringbone, bowl, master berry.....................35.00

Green Herringbone, cruet, orig stopper.....................95.00

Green Herringbone, table set, 4 pc.....................175.00

Green Herringbone, wine.....................45.00

Guttate, butter, cranberry.....................80.00

Guttate, water set, wht/gold, 7 pc.....................235.00

Haley's Comet, goblet.....................30.00

Haley's Comet, spooner.....................35.00

Haley's Comet, tumbler, etched.....................27.00

Hamilton, egg cup, flint.....................34.00

Hamilton, pitcher, water; flint, 7¼″.....................175.00

Hamilton w/Leaf, spooner, flared rim.....................32.00

Hand, celery vase.....................40.00

Hand, goblet.....................37.00

Hand, pickle jar, w/lid, hand finial.....................40.00

Harp, butter w/cover, flint.....................100.00

Harp, spooner.....................60.00

Hartley, goblet.....................17.50

Harvard Yard, pitcher, water.....................40.00

Heart, creamer, stemmed.....................35.00

Heart & Spades, see Medallion

Heart w/Thumbprint, bowl, master berry.....................28.00

Heart w/Thumbprint, celery vase.....................45.00

Heart w/Thumbprint, creamer, individual.....................18.00

Heart w/Thumbprint, goblet, EX gold.....................45.00

Heart w/Thumbprint, mustard, green, plated lid.....................95.00

Heart w/Thumbprint, plate, clear, 6″.....................25.00

Heart w/Thumbprint, punch cup, green w/gold.....................45.00

Heart w/Thumbprint, tray, card; clear w/gold, folded sides.....................20.00

Heavy Drape, berry set, gold/cranberry flashed.....................125.00

Heavy Gothic, tumbler.....................20.00

Heavy Panelled Fine Cut, compote, covered, 10x7″ sq.....................35.00

Heck, celery vase.....................19.00

Heisey's Colonial, pitcher.....................60.00

Henrietta, celery, ped, scalloped top.....................35.00

Heron, celery.....................32.00

Heron, creamer.....................47.00

Heron, pitcher, water.....................145.00

Herringbone, spooner.....................20.00

Hexagon Block, berry set, EX red flashed, 7 pc.....................135.00

Hexagon Block, compote, open.....................50.00

Hexagon Block, creamer, ruby stain.....................48.00

Hexagon Block, spooner, ruby stain.....................48.00

Hickman, cake plate.....................30.00

Hickman, compote, open, 7½x8″ wide.....................34.00

Hickman, sugar w/lid, green, lg.....................50.00

Hickman, vase, 12″.....................26.00

Hinoto, wine, flint.....................48.00

Hobb's Block, creamer, frost w/amber.....................65.00

Hobnail, pitcher, milk; ruby band top/ruby thumbprint at base...50.00

Hobnail, tumbler, amber, 7 rows.....................15.00

Hobnail, wine.....................24.50

Hobnail in Squares, celery.....................28.00

Hobnail w/Fan, bowl.....................22.00

Hobnail w/Thumbprint Base, butter w/cover, blue.....................65.00

Hobnail w/Thumbprint Base, pitcher, milk; lg, ruby stained.....................55.00

Hobnail w/Thumbprint Base, pitcher, water; old, 7¾″, M.....................50.00

Holbrook, punch cup.....................5.00

Holly, butter dish.....................150.00

Holly, cake stand, 5″ high.....................55.00

Holly, egg cup.....................65.00

Holly, goblet.....................95.00

Holly, pitcher, water.....................170.00

Holly, table set, 4 pc.....................450.00

Holly Band, celery.....................60.00

Honeycomb, decanter, allover pattern, flint, w/stopper, qt.......70.00

Honeycomb, goblet, flint.....................25.00

Honeycomb, spooner, flint.....................20.00

Honeycomb, whiskey, hdld, flint.....................45.00

Honeycomb, wine, non-flint.....................16.00

Honeycomb w/Flower Rim, creamer, amber.....................27.00

Hooks & Eyes, goblet.....................25.00

Hops & Barley, see Wheat & Barley

Horizontal Oval Frames, master salt, ped, flint.....................55.00

Horn of Plenty, bar tumbler.....................85.00

Horn of Plenty, celery, flint.....................140.00

Horn of Plenty, compote, open, high standard, flint, 8″.......90.00

Horn of Plenty, goblet.....................70.00

Horn of Plenty, wine.....................125.00

Horse, Cat, & Rabbit, goblet, etched.....................225.00

Horsehead Medallion, spooner.....................40.00

Horseshoe, bowl, oval vegetable; large.....................16.00

Horseshoe, cake stand, 8″.....................35.00

Horseshoe, celery.....................40.00

Horseshoe, creamer.....................37.00

Horseshoe, goblet, ornate stem.....................35.00

Horseshoe, goblet, regular stem.....................32.00

Horseshoe, pitcher.....................110.00

Horseshoe, pitcher, milk............................58.00
Horseshoe, spooner................................35.00
Horseshoe, waste bowl.............................40.00
Horseshoe, wine...................................125.00
Hotel Thumbprint, goblet, non-flint...............15.00
Huber, goblet, barrel, flint......................22.00
Huber, wine, non-flint............................14.00
Huckle, see Feather Duster
Hummingbird, butter w/cover.......................60.00
Hummingbird, creamer, amber.......................40.00
Hummingbird, creamer, blue........................40.00
Hummingbird, goblet, amber........................52.00
Hummingbird, pitcher, milk........................49.00
Hummingbird, pitcher, water; blue.................95.00
Humpty Dumpty/Tom Thumb, mug, handled, novelty of 1880s...35.00
Hundred Eye, goblet...............................15.00
Hunting Dog, pitcher, water.......................260.00
Iceburg, see Polar Bear
Icicle w/Chain Band, goblet.......................60.00
Idaho, see Snail
Indian Tree, see Sprig
Indiana, see Cord Drapery
Indiana Swirl, see Feather
Intaglio, pitcher, water; green w/gold, M.........150.00
Intaglio, spooner, green w/good gold..............40.00
Intaglio Sunflower, pitcher, water; very lg.......60.00
Interlocked Hearts, creamer.......................20.00
Interlocked Hearts, spooner.......................18.00
Interlocking Crescents, compote, open, scalloped edge........20.00
Inverted Fan & Feather, berry set, gr w/gold, 7 pc..........295.00

Inverted Fan and Feather, berry set, green and gold, 7 pieces, $295.00.

Inverted Thistle, berry set, green w/gold, 6 pc.............95.00
Inverted Thistle, pitcher, water; gr w/gold................70.00
Inverted Thistle, water set, green w/gold, 5 pc............165.00
Inverted Thumbprint, creamer, blown, amber, 4x4"...........20.00
Inverted Thumbprint, tray, water; amber....................42.00
Inverted Thumbprint, tumbler, cranberry....................32.00
Inverted Thumbprint, wine, amber...........................38.00
Inverted Thumbprint, wine, apple green.....................40.00
Inverted Thumbprint, wine, blue............................46.00
Inverted Thumbprint, wine, blue w/clear stem...............22.00
Inverted Thumbprint, wine, vaseline........................40.00
Inverted Thumbprint & Star, goblet, vaseline...............30.00
Iowa, sugar, sm..20.00
Iowa, wine...36.00
Iris w/Meander, pitcher, water; green......................85.00
Irish Column, see Broken Column
Ivy in Snow, celery..25.00
Ivy in Snow, mug...21.00
Ivy in Snow, relish..16.50

Ivy in Snow, tumbler.......................................25.00
Jacob's Coat, creamer, green...............................50.00
Jacob's Ladder, celery.....................................49.00
Jacob's Ladder, compote, open, low standard, 10"...........30.00
Jacob's Ladder, creamer....................................32.00
Jacob's Ladder, pickle.....................................15.00
Jacob's Ladder, plate, 6½".................................25.00
Jacob's Ladder, wine.......................................31.00
Jasper, relish...13.50
Jersey Swirl, cruet w/stopper..............................20.00
Jersey Swirl, plate, amber, 10"............................16.00
Jersey Swirl, wine...12.00
Jewel & Dewdrop, see Kansas
Jewel & Festoon, see Loop & Jewel
Jewelled Band, bread plate.................................35.00
Jewelled Heart, creamer....................................30.00
Jewelled Heart, tumbler....................................22.00
Jewelled Heart, tumbler, blue w/NM gold....................40.00
Jewelled Rosettes, see Tennessee
Jewelled w/Moon & Star, see Shrine
Job's Tears, see Art
Jubilee, cake stand, 9"....................................22.00
Jubilee, creamer...20.00
Jubilee, sugar w/lid.......................................25.00
Kansas, bowl, master berry.................................42.00
Kansas, compote, open, high standard.......................75.00
Kansas, goblet, clear......................................38.00
Kansas, mug..19.00
Kansas, pitcher, milk......................................48.00
Kansas, pitcher, water.....................................55.00
Kansas, sauce..15.00
Kayak, goblet..17.00
Kentucky, pitcher..55.00
Kentucky, wine, green......................................40.00
King Arthur, pitcher, water................................32.00
King Arthur, punch bowl, 2 pc..............................60.00
King's Crown, cake stand, 9"...............................85.00
King's Crown, compote, jelly; open.........................20.00
King's Crown, compote, 7½".................................60.00
King's Crown, goblet, citrine rim..........................32.00
King's Crown, goblet, silver flashed rim...................19.00
King's Crown, goblet, w/gr eyes............................35.00
King's Crown, goblet, w/purple eyes........................28.00
King's Crown, pitcher, tankard; 12"........................95.00
King's Crown, punch bowl w/11 cups, Indiana Glass Co.......75.00
King's Crown, salt dip, individual; rectangular............12.00
King's Crown, tumblers, cobalt, Indiana Glass Co, set of 6......75.00
King's Crown, wine...14.00
King's Curtain, goblet.....................................18.00
King's 500, tumbler, cobalt w/good gold....................30.00
Klondike, butter w/cover, ca 1885, Beatty Co...............300.00
Klondike, pitcher, water; amber stain......................545.00
Klondike, sugar w/lid, frosted & gold......................250.00
Klondike, tumbler, frosted clear w/amber flashed cross, 4"......135.00
Knobby Bull's Eye, goblet..................................17.00
Knobby Bull's Eye, punch bowl on stand, gr eyes & good gold..80.00
Knobby Bull's Eye, toothpick holder, lay-down type.........20.00
Knobby Bull's Eye, wine....................................20.00
Knobby Bull's Eye, wine, w/gold............................27.00
Kokomo, creamer..18.00
Kokomo, goblet, non-flint..................................20.00
Kokomo, spooner..18.00
La Clede, see Hickman
Lacy Daisy, creamer..19.50

Leaf Medallion, water set, cobalt and gold, 7 pieces, $750.00.

Lacy Daisy, spooner....................................18.00
Lacy Daisy, sugar w/lid................................24.50
Lacy Medallion, see Princess Feather
Lady Hamilton, see Peerless
Lakewood, goblet.......................................12.00
Late Block, pitcher, water; ruby stained.............65.00
Late Butterfly, pitcher, milk.........................40.00
Late Butterfly, pitcher, water........................60.00
Late Butterfly, wine..................................22.00
Late Moon & Star, see Priscilla
Late Sawtooth, see Zipper
Late Thistle, see Inverted Thistle
Lattice, goblet..20.00
Lattice, wine..32.00
Lattice & Oval Panels, butter w/cover.................95.00
Lattice & Oval Panels, creamer, w/applied handle....125.00
Lattice & Oval Panels, goblet, flint.................105.00
Lattice & Oval Panels, sauce...........................9.00
Lattice & Oval Panels, sugar w/lid, high standard, flint.......125.00
Laverne, celery..50.00
Lawrence, see Bull's Eye
Leaf & Dart, egg cup...................................27.00
Leaf & Dart, goblet....................................21.00
Leaf & Dart, pitcher & 5 ftd tumblers................290.00
Leaf & Dart, sugar w/lid...............................42.00
Leaf & Flower, tumbler, clear & frosted...............25.00
Leaf & Star, see Tobin
Leaf Bracket, see Greentown Glass, Leaf Bracket
Leaf Medallion, berry set, cobalt & gold, 5 pc.......250.00
Leaf Medallion, bowl, berry; cobalt, sm...............20.00
Leaf Medallion, bowl, master berry; green w/EX gold...........85.00
Leaf Medallion, butter w/cover, amethyst w/gold.............225.00
Leaf Medallion, creamer, amethyst, good gold, Northwood......75.00
Leaf Medallion, creamer, green, Northwood.............70.00
Leaf Medallion, jelly, green w/gold...................65.00
Leaf Medallion, sauce, green w/EX gold................25.00
Leaf Medallion, spooner, amethyst, good gold, Northwood......65.00
Leaf Medallion, spooner, green, Northwood.............70.00
Leaf Medallion, water set, cobalt/gold...............750.00
Leaf Mold, berry set, satin spatter, 6 pc............195.00
Leaf Mold, water set, satin spatter, 7 pc............650.00
Leaf Umbrella, bowl, master berry; spatter...........75.00
Leaf Umbrella, pitcher, water; blue cased............285.00
Leaf Umbrella, pitcher, water; cranberry.............285.00
Leaf Umbrella, pitcher, water; cranberry spatter.....295.00
Lens & Star, celery, ½ frosted, etched...............35.00

Leverne, pickle dish....................................9.75
Leverne, relish, oval, 5¼x7¼".........................12.00
Leverne, sauce, ftd, 4¼"...............................6.00
Liberty, see Cornucopia
Liberty Bell, creamer, applied hdl....................80.00
Liberty Bell, plate, 6"...............................35.00
Liberty Bell, plate, 8"...............................45.00
Liberty Bell, relish tray.............................40.00
Liberty Bell, sauce...................................22.00
Lily of the Valley, goblet, Sandwich, 1870s..........40.00
Lily of the Valley, wine..............................70.00
Lion, butter w/cover, frosted, sm....................175.00
Lion, celery, frosted.................................75.00
Lion, compote, open, 7¼x5¾"...........................65.00
Lion, compote, oval, frosted & clear, 8" high.......115.00
Lion, creamer, frosted base...........................63.00
Lion, goblet, frosted.................................65.00
Lion, marmalade jar w/cover, clear & frosted..........65.00
Lion, sauce, ftd, frosted..............................8.50
Lion, spooner...47.00
Lion's Leg, see Alaska
Locket on Chain, bowl, berry; small...................18.00
Locket on Chain, wine................................110.00
Locust, see Grasshopper
Log & Star, goblet....................................15.00
Log Cabin, creamer....................................90.00
Log Cabin, sugar w/lid...............................130.00
Loganberry & Grape, goblet............................19.00
Long Spear, see Grasshopper
Loop, see Seneca Loop
Loop & Block, goblet, ruby stained....................38.00
Loop & Block, sauce, ruby stained.....................18.00
Loop & Block, tumbler, ruby stained...................30.00
Loop & Dart, celery...................................32.00
Loop & Dart, tumbler, ftd.............................25.00
Loop & Dart w/Diamond Ornament, butter w/cover........38.00
Loop & Dart w/Diamond Ornament, buttermilk............25.00
Loop & Dart w/Diamond Ornament, goblet................22.00
Loop & Dart w/Diamond Ornament, spooner...............25.00
Loop & Dart w/Round Ornament, creamer, w/applied handle....45.00
Loop & Dart w/Round Ornament, dish, oval, 9x6".......25.00
Loop & Dart w/Round Ornament, goblet, non-flint.......30.00
Loop & Dart w/Round Ornament, pitcher, water; applied hdl....90.00
Loop & Dart w/Round Ornament, spooner.................24.00
Loop & Dart w/Round Ornament, tumbler.................30.00
Loop & Dart w/Round Ornament, wine, barrel shape......35.00
Loop & Dart w/Round Ornament, wine, non-flint.........30.00
Loop & Fan, relish....................................16.50
Loop & Jewel, relish..................................20.00
Loop & Jewel, spooner.................................22.50
Loop & Jewel, sugar w/lid.............................30.00
Loop & Noose, goblet..................................38.00
Loop & Pyramids, goblet...............................19.00
Loop & Pyramids, tumbler..............................16.00
Loop w/Fisheye, goblet, non-flint.....................18.00
Loop w/Stippled Panels, see Texas
Louis XV, creamer, gr w/gold..........................45.00
Louis XV, sauce, gr w/gold............................25.00
Louis XV, table set, gr..............................385.00
Louisiana, goblet.....................................30.00
Louisiana, pitcher....................................65.00
Louisiana, tumbler....................................25.00
Louisiana Purchase, tumbler...........................50.00
Lucerne, wine...30.00

Magna, wine..22.00
Magnet & Grape, compote, open, tall, frosted leaf, flint........65.00
Magnet & Grape, goblet, flint.............................62.00
Magnet & Grape, wine.....................................40.00
Magnet & Grape (Stippled Leaf), sugar w/lid................80.00
Maiden Blush, see Banded Portland
Maine, compote, open, green, 9"...........................35.00
Maine, compote, open, 7½" wide..........................20.00
Majestic, see Divided Block w/Sunburst
Maltese, see Jacob's Ladder
Manhattan, bowl, scalloped, 8¼"..........................20.00
Manhattan, plate, 10¾".....................................20.00
Manhattan, plate, 6"...6.50
Manhattan, punch bowl....................................125.00
Manting, tumbler, flint.....................................40.00
Maple Leaf, bowl, oval, lg, vaseline.......................35.00
Maple Leaf, goblet, vaseline...............................125.00
Maple Leaf, platter, bread; vaseline........................35.00
Maple Leaf, waste bowl, vaseline..........................45.00
Maple Leaf Band, goblet....................................35.00
Marquisette, celery..38.50
Marquisette, goblet..23.00
Marquisette, spooner.......................................26.00
Martha's Tears, goblet, amber.............................20.00
Martha's Tears, wine.......................................25.00
Maryland, goblet...18.00
Maryland, relish..16.50
Maryland, sugar, open......................................25.00
Maryland, tumbler..25.00
Mascotte, butter w/cover, etched..........................48.00
Mascotte, goblet...23.00
Mascotte, pitcher, water; tankard..........................35.00
Mascotte, sauce, ftd, etched...............................15.00
Mascotte, spooner...20.00
Mascotte, sugar, open......................................17.00
Mascotte, sugar w/lid, etched..............................38.00
Mascotte, wine..24.00
Masonic, pitcher, water; tankard w/silverplated lip.........45.00
Massachusetts, decanter, w/orig stopper...................115.00
Massachusetts, pitcher, water.............................175.00
Massachusetts, rum jug, 1898 era, US Glass...............100.00
McKinley, tumbler, Protection & Plenty....................25.00
Medallion, goblet, amber..................................29.00
Medallion, spooner, green.................................45.00
Medallion Sunburst, berry set, 8 pc.......................120.00
Medallion Sunburst, bowl, 8¼" square.....................27.00
Medallion Sunburst, bowl, 9¼" round.....................30.00
Medallion Sunburst, butter pat..............................5.00
Medallion Sunburst, cake stand, 10½"......................35.00
Medallion Sunburst, compote, open, high standard, 8" dia.....25.00
Medallion Sunburst, cruet, clear...........................20.00
Medallion Sunburst, goblet.................................22.00
Medallion Sunburst, mug, 3¼"..............................18.00
Medallion Sunburst, punch cup..............................9.00
Medallion Sunburst, relish.................................10.00
Medallion Sunburst, spooner...............................20.00
Medallion Sunburst, vase, 9½".............................32.50
Mellor, wine...20.00
Melrose, celery..25.00
Melrose, plate, cake.......................................30.00
Melrose, tray, water.......................................45.00
Memphis, berry set, green w/EX gold, 7 pc.................125.00
Memphis, creamer, green & gold...........................25.00
Memphis, pitcher, water....................................75.00

Memphis, punch bowl, 2 pc................................85.00
Memphis, spooner, green w/gold...........................35.00
Memphis, water set, gr/gold, pitcher/4 tumblers, Northwood....185.00
Mephistopheles, goblet, frosted............................30.00
Michigan, butter w/cover, maiden blush & gold, EX..........90.00
Michigan, celery vase, 6"...................................30.00
Michigan, compote, open, 9¼" dia.........................65.00
Michigan, creamer..18.00
Michigan, creamer, maiden blush & gold, EX................50.00
Michigan, goblet...30.00
Michigan, parfait, 6½".....................................30.00
Michigan, pitcher, water; 8"................................50.00
Michigan, punch cup, 2½"..................................12.00
Michigan, spooner, maiden blush & gold, EX................55.00
Michigan, sugar, open, maiden blush & gold, EX.............50.00
Michigan, water carafe....................................155.00
Michigan, water set, clear w/pink carnation, souvenir, 5 pc.....235.00
Millard, creamer, ruby stained..............................55.00
Millard, creamer & sugar w/lid, ruby stained..............145.00
Millard, pitcher, water; ruby stained, w/etching...........125.00
Milton, goblet...22.00
Milton, pitcher, water; tankard............................48.00
Minerva, bowl, berry..9.00
Minerva, bowl, rectangular, 2x9x6".........................45.00
Minerva, goblet, water.....................................75.00
Minerva, sauce, ftd, 4"....................................18.00
Minerva, sherbet...15.00
Minerva, spooner..35.00
Minnesota, cup, clear & gold...............................18.00
Minnesota, goblet..26.00
Minnesota, mug, hdld, fair gold on rim.....................25.00
Minnesota, relish, oval, 8¾x6¾"...........................12.50
Minnesota, sugar w/lid.....................................28.00
Minor Block, see Mascotte
Mioton, goblet, plain stem.................................10.00
Mirror, goblet, flint..35.00
Mississippi, pitcher..75.00
Missouri, cake stand.......................................30.00
Missouri, spooner, green...................................48.00
Missouri, sugar w/lid, green...............................55.00
Missouri, wine...30.00
Mitered Diamond, condiment set, 5 pc, clear...............65.00
Mitered Diamond, goblet, w/gold...........................10.00
Mitered Diamond, tumbler, amber..........................25.00
Mitered Diamond, water set, blue, 6 pc...................180.00
Mitered Diamond, wine, amber.............................45.00
Mitered Diamond Point, see Zig-Zag
Mitered Prisms, goblet.....................................24.00
Moesser, see Overall Lattice
Monkey, mug, amethyst....................................80.00
Monkey, spooner..130.00
Moon & Star, compote, covered, 6¼" dia..................55.00
Moon & Star, compote, w/frosted band, 7½x8½" dia.........55.00
Moon & Star, creamer, w/reeded handle....................42.00
Moon & Star, goblet, frosted...............................45.00
Moon & Star w/Waffle Stem, see Shrine
Moon & Stork, see Ostrich Looking at the Moon.
Nail, butter w/cover, etched................................35.00
Nail, creamer, ruby stained.................................65.00
Nail, salver, clear...50.00
Nailhead, cake stand, 9½".................................30.00
Nailhead, pitcher, water; ruby stained......................65.00
Nailhead, plate, 7" square..................................15.00
Nailhead, plate, 9"..10.00

Nailhead, sugar w/lid................................25.00
Nailhead, wine.....................................17.00
Narcissus Spray, goblet.............................18.00
Near Cut, nappy, ftd, hdl...........................15.00
Nellie Bly, platter................................150.00
Nelly, wine..18.00
Nemesis, spooner...................................25.00
Nestor, creamer, gr w/EX enameling & gold...........40.00
Nestor, spooner, amethyst...........................48.00
Nestor, spooner, blue w/wht enameling, good gold....55.00
Nestor, wine, blue w/enamel.........................25.00
Netted Roses, bowl, ruffle edge, green, Northwood, 8".....35.00
Nevada, spooner....................................29.00
New England Centennial, goblet, flint..............125.00
New England Pineapple, creamer, applied hdl, flint...155.00
New England Pineapple, goblet, flint................60.00
New England Pineapple, master salt..................45.00
New England Pineapple, plate........................90.00
New England Pineapple, spooner......................35.00
New England Pineapple, sweetmeat, covered..........225.00
New England Pineapple, wine........................150.00
New Hampshire, cake stand, high std, 8¼"............20.00
New Hampshire, creamer, small.......................30.00
New Hampshire, pitcher, EX gold.....................70.00
New Hampshire, pitcher, water; w/ice lip............40.00
New Hampshire, sugar, individual; w/maiden's blush..25.50
New Hampshire, syrup w/pewter top...................25.00
New Hampshire, tumbler..............................16.50
New Hampshire, wine.................................16.00
New Jersey, butter, EX gold.........................78.00
New Jersey, creamer, gold flashed...................30.00
New Jersey, creamer & open sugar, clear.............38.00
New Jersey, goblet..................................38.00
New Jersey, jelly dish, open........................16.00
New Jersey, pitcher, water..........................65.00
New Jersey, pitcher, water; G gold..................80.00
New Jersey, sauce...................................10.00
New Jersey, sugar w/lid, gold flashed...............35.00
New Jersey, water set, pitcher & 6 tumblers, w/gold...190.00
New Jersey, wine....................................41.00
New York Honeycomb, mug, applied hdl, flint.........22.50
Niagara, wine.......................................18.00
North Pole, see Polar Bear
Notched Rib, see Broken Column
Oak Leaves, see Willow Oak
Oaken Bucket, see Wooden Pail
Oasis, compote, jelly...............................29.00
Odd Fellow, goblet..................................30.00
Ohio, pitcher.......................................65.00
Ohio Inverted Thumbprint, goblet, amber.............14.00
Old Man, see Bearded Man
Old Man of the Mountain, see Bearded Man
Old Man of the Woods, see Bearded Man
One Hundred One, plate, 7"..........................17.00
One Hundred One, sauce, ftd.........................15.00
One Hundred One, spooner............................42.00
One Hundred One, sugar, open........................25.00
Open Rose, egg cup..................................20.00
Open Rose, spooner..................................20.00
Opposing Pyramids, goblet...........................28.50
Opposing Pyramids, sugar w/lid......................30.00
Opposing Pyramids, water set, green & gold, 7 pc...250.00
Opposing Pyramids, wine.............................15.00
Oregon, butter w/cover, ruby stained................70.00

Oregon, compote, ruby flashed, 7x4½"................55.00
Oregon, goblet......................................35.00
Oregon, pitcher, milk; US Glass Co, ca 1906.........35.00
Oregon, sugar w/lid, ruby stained...................65.00
Oriental, butter w/cover............................58.00
Oriental, creamer...................................40.00
Oriental, creamer & open sugar, 3 legged............70.00
Oriental, sugar w/lid...............................65.00
Oriental, table set................................125.00
Oriental, tumbler...................................20.00
Orion, see Cathedral
Orion Inverted Thumbprint, plate, large.............20.00
Ostrich Looking at the Moon, goblet.................65.00
Oval Loop, celery vase..............................25.00
Overall Lattice, creamer............................10.00
Owl & Possum, goblet................................50.00
Owl in Fan, see Parrot & Fan
Paisley, creamer, w/green eyes......................20.00
Paisley, tumbler, gold eyes..........................8.00
Paling, creamer.....................................16.00
Palm Leaf Fan, bowl, low ftd, 9½"...................20.00
Palm Leaf Fan, cruet................................23.00
Palm Leaf w/Scroll, pitcher, 7".....................37.00
Palm Stub, goblet...................................18.00
Palmette, spooner...................................35.00
Panelled Acorn Band, goblet.........................25.00
Panelled Apple Blossoms, goblet.....................18.00
Panelled Cane, creamer..............................19.00
Panelled Cane, goblet...............................16.00
Panelled Cherry, pitcher, water; clear cherries & cable...62.00
Panelled Daisy, cake stand, 11½"....................45.00
Panelled Daisy, celery..............................29.00
Panelled Daisy, pickle..............................12.00
Panelled Daisy, pitcher, water......................43.00
Panelled Daisy, tray, water.........................33.00
Panelled Daisy & Button, see Queen
Panelled Dewdrop, creamer...........................25.00
Panelled Diamond Cut & Fan, see Hartley
Panelled Diamond Point, wine........................25.00
Panelled Diamonds & Flowers, goblet.................23.00
Panelled Dogwood, see Dogwood
Panelled Fern, goblet, flint........................50.00
Panelled Forget-Me-Not, butter w/cover..............38.00
Panelled Forget-Me-Not, cake stand..................35.00
Panelled Forget-Me-Not, celery......................30.00
Panelled Forget-Me-Not, compote, covered, high standard...52.00
Panelled Forget-Me-Not, sauce, ftd..................12.00
Panelled Forget-Me-Not, spooner.....................22.00
Panelled Grape, butter w/cover......................25.00
Panelled Grape, pitcher, water; trunk hdl...........35.00
Panelled Grape Band, spooner........................18.00
Panelled Heather, compote...........................25.00
Panelled Heather, wine..............................30.00
Panelled Herringbone, wine..........................20.00
Panelled Hobnail, plate, 7"..........................6.00
Panelled Honeycomb, pitcher, milk...................35.00
Panelled Iris, wine.................................20.00
Panelled Ivy, goblet................................26.00
Panelled Jewels, goblet.............................20.00
Panelled Jewels, wine...............................30.00
Panelled Jewels, wine, vaseline.....................55.00
Panelled Julep, goblet..............................23.00
Panelled Lattice, wine..............................22.00
Panelled Nightshade, goblet.........................22.00

Panelled Nightshade, wine.........................28.00
Panelled Palm, pitcher, water; clear w/pink & EX gold........95.00
Panelled Potted Flower, goblet.....................25.00
Panelled Smocking, berry set, w/blue & wht enamel, 7 pc......35.00
Panelled Sprig, see Sprig
Panelled Star & Button, see Sedan
Panelled Strawberry, tumbler.......................16.00
Panelled Sunflower, goblet.........................11.00
Panelled Sunflower, sugar w/lid....................25.00
Panelled Thistle, plate, ftd, 10¼".................25.00
Panelled Thistle, wine.............................27.00
Panelled Wild Daisy, goblet........................15.00
Panelled 44, tumbler, lemonade; w/silver...........26.50
Pangyric, see Prism & Crescent
Parrot & Fan, goblet...............................30.00
Pathfinder, bowl, flat, 7".........................15.00
Pathfinder, compote, 7"............................30.00
Pathfinder, tumbler................................15.00
Pathfinder, wine...................................18.00
Pattee Cross, pitcher..............................50.00
Pavonia, cake stand, 9"............................35.00
Pavonia, finger bowl...............................30.00
Pavonia, goblet, etched............................32.00
Pavonia, pitcher, lemonade; non-souvenir, 11½".....125.00
Pavonia, pitcher, water; tankard, etched...........63.00
Pavonia, tumbler...................................15.00
Pavonia, tumbler, maple leaf etching...............20.00
Pavonia, waste bowl, etched, ruby stained..........102.00
Pavonia, wine, etched..............................35.00
Pea Pods, wine, ruby stained.......................35.00
Peacock Eye, see Peacock Feather
Peacock Feather, bowl, master berry; 8½"...........27.50
Peacock Feather, pitcher, water....................55.00
Pecorah, goblet....................................17.00
Pecorah, sauce, ftd.................................9.00
Pecorah, wine......................................18.00
Peerless, wine.....................................26.00
Pennsylvania, creamer..............................27.00
Pennsylvania, cruet, orig stopper..................22.00
Pennsylvania, goblet...............................16.00
Pennsylvania, punch cup.............................8.50
Pennsylvania, syrup................................42.00
Pennsylvania, wine.................................16.00
Pennsylvania, wine, green..........................37.50
Pennsylvania, wine, green w/gold...................45.00
Persian, goblet....................................20.00
Petal & Loop, compote, loops on base, 6x9".........70.00
Philadelphia, goblet...............................10.00
Philadelphia Centennial, goblet....................26.00
Picket, compote, covered, large, M.................125.00
Picket, creamer....................................35.00
Picket, sauce......................................16.00
Pillar, goblet, flint..............................50.00
Pillar & Bull's Eye, goblet........................50.00
Pillar & Bull's Eye, relish........................25.00
Pillar & Bull's Eye, sauce.........................10.00
Pillar & Bull's Eye, wine, flint...................60.00
Pillow Encircled, bowl, master berry; ruby stained.........45.00
Pillow Encircled, celery vase, etched, ruby stained........55.00
Pillow Encircled, creamer, ruby stained............30.00
Pillow Encircled, sauce, ruby stained..............18.00
Pillow Encircled, spooner, etched..................27.00
Pillow Encircled, spooner, ruby stained............55.00
Pineapple & Fan, rose bowl.........................10.00

Pineapple & Fan, spooner...........................15.00
Pineapple & Fan, tumbler...........................15.00
Pineapple Stem, see Pavonia
Pinwheel, sugar w/lid, mkd 1896 & WS Co............20.00
Pioneer, see Westward Ho
Pioneer's Victoria, butter w/cover, ruby stained...........95.00
Pioneer's Victoria, creamer, ruby stained..........55.00
Pioneer's Victoria, wine............................9.00
Pitcairn, wine.....................................16.00
Pittsburgh Centennial, goblet......................75.00
Pittsburgh Tree of Life, compote, open, hand stem, 8½" high...65.00
Pittsburgh Tree of Life, creamer...................38.50
Plaid, goblet......................................10.00
Pleat & Panel, goblet..............................24.00
Pleat & Panel, pitcher, water......................45.00
Pleat & Panel, plate, 6" square....................15.00
Pleat & Panel, plate, 7"...........................15.00
Pleat & Panel, spooner.............................24.00
Pleating, pitcher, water; ruby stained.............100.00
Pleating, tumbler, red flashed.....................18.00
Plume, butter w/cover..............................50.00
Plume, cake stand..................................35.00
Plume, compote, crimped, 7"........................25.00
Plume, goblet......................................25.00
Plume, sugar, open, ruby stained...................35.00
Plume & Block, see Feather & Block
Pointed Panel, see Queen
Pointed Panel Daisy & Button, see Queen
Pointed Thumbprint, see Almond Thumbprint
Polar Bear, tray, water; frosted, w/seals, sgn CG Co.........175.00
Popcorn, creamer, w/ears...........................50.00
Popcorn, goblet, Sandwich..........................46.00
Popcorn, spooner...................................32.00
Portland, basket, applied hdl......................35.00
Portland, bowl, 4½".................................8.00
Portland, cruet, orig stopper......................22.00
Portland, jam dish, maiden's blush, w/SP frame, cover, & spoon.95.00
Portland, sugar, no lid............................25.00
Portland, tumbler..................................20.00
Portland Tree of Life, celery vase, in metal holder, 9½".......35.00
Portland Tree of Life, goblet......................45.00
Portland Tree of Life, goblet, knob stem, flint, sgn.......85.00
Portland Tree of Life, pitcher.....................65.00
Portland Tree of Life, plate, amber, 6¼"...........35.00
Portland Tree of Life, tumbler, cranberry..........65.00
Portland w/Diamond Point Band, see Banded Portland
Post, celery.......................................38.00
Post, salt dip......................................8.00
Prayer Rug, see Horseshoe
Pressed Diamond, spooner, vaseline.................45.00
Pressed Leaf, goblet...............................22.00
Pressed Leaf, spooner..............................18.00
Pressed Leaf Band, see Hops Band
Primrose, plate, amber, 4½"........................12.00
Primrose, plate, clear, 4½"........................10.00
Primrose, sauce, ped, blue.........................25.00
Primrose, tray, water; amber.......................32.00
Primrose, tray, water; clear.......................25.00
Primrose, wine, amber..............................40.00
Prince's Feather, see Feather
Princess Feather, creamer, green & gold............25.00
Princess Feather, creamer, individual; green.......18.00
Princess Feather, mug, green.......................30.00
Princess Feather, spooner..........................25.00

Princess Feather, tumbler, green & gold.....................25.00
Printed Hobnail, pitcher, 1880s............................45.00
Printed Hobnail, tumbler.................................18.00
Printed Hobnail, waste bowl..............................20.00
Priscilla, bowl, berry; straight sides, small...............10.00
Priscilla, butter w/cover................................40.00
Priscilla, cake stand, 9½x5½"...........................60.00
Priscilla, compote, open, slightly flared sides, 8¾x9¾".......60.00
Priscilla, doughnut stand, 9x5¾".........................60.00
Priscilla, goblet..45.00
Priscilla, sauce, flared sides, clear......................6.00
Priscilla, spooner, small...............................28.00
Priscilla, table set, 4 pc..............................185.00
Prism, bowl, 7¼" dia.....................................8.00
Prism, compote, covered, high standard....................25.00
Prism & Crescent, goblet, flint..........................55.00
Prism & Crescent, wine, flint............................45.00
Prism & Flute, wine......................................18.00
Prism Arc, wine, amber...................................26.00
Prism Bars, goblet......................................10.00
Prism w/Loops, goblet...................................10.00
Prize, butter w/cover....................................55.00
Prize, celery vase, ruby stained.........................85.00
Prize, wine...30.00
Prophet, see Bearded Man
Psyche & Cupid, creamer..................................45.00
Psyche & Cupid, goblet...................................48.00
Psyche & Cupid, spooner..................................35.00
Psyche & Cupid, sugar w/lid..............................55.00
Purple Block Portland, see Barred Ovals
Pygmy, see Torpedo
Pyramid, see Mitered Diamond
Queen, goblet...18.00
Queen, goblet, amber.....................................29.00
Queen, wine...25.00
Queen Anne, see Bearded Man
Queen's Necklace, dresser bottle, w/matching stopper, 7½".....50.00
Queen's Necklace, wine...................................23.00
Question Mark, see Oval Loop
Radiant, goblet...20.00
Radiant, wine...28.00
Radiant Daisy & Button, see Isis
Ray, bowl, ftd, 3¼"......................................12.00
Rayed Flower, compote, open, 6½" dia......................25.00
Recessed Ovals, goblet..................................18.00
Recessed Pillar Thumbprint Band, see Nail
Recessed Pillared Red Top, see Nail
Red Block, creamer, individual...........................35.00
Red Block, goblet.......................................35.00
Red Block, pitcher, water...............................100.00
Red Block, sugar w/lid...................................75.00
Red Block, tumbler, ruby stain...........................25.00
Red Block, water set, ruby stained, 7 pc.................245.00
Red Top, see Button Arches
Regal Block, wine.......................................16.00
Regent, see Leaf Medallion
Reverse Torpedo, compote, jelly..........................40.00
Reverse Torpedo, compote, 8".............................65.00
Rexford, goblet...18.00
Rexford, pitcher, sm....................................35.00
Ribbed Acorn, butter w/cover, ftd........................50.00
Ribbed Acorn, compote, covered, flint, 7" high............75.00
Ribbed Forget-Me-Not, creamer, individual................18.00
Ribbed Forget-Me-Not, mustard w/lid......................30.00

Ribbed Grape, goblet, flint..............................30.00
Ribbed Ivy, sauce.......................................12.00
Ribbed Ivy, wine, flint..................................48.00
Ribbed Palm, goblet, flint...............................32.00
Ribbon, goblet, clear & frosted..........................25.00
Ribbon, spooner, clear & frosted.........................35.00
Ribbon, wine, clear & frosted, Bakewell, Pears & Co.......110.00
Ribbon Candy, creamer....................................17.00
Ribbon Candy, spooner....................................22.00
Ripple Band, see Ripple
Rising Sun, goblet, green suns...........................22.00
Rising Sun, pitcher, water...............................95.00
Rising Sun, water set, clear w/gold, 7 pc................105.00
Rising Sun, wine..19.00
Riverside, pitcher, water; vaseline w/gold...............85.00
Roanoke, see Sawtooth
Roanoke Star, wine......................................20.00
Rochelle, see Princess Feather
Roman Key, goblet, flint.................................40.00
Roman Key, goblet, non-flint.............................20.00
Roman Rosette, butter w/cover............................50.00
Roman Rosette, compote, jelly............................20.00
Roman Rosette, creamer...................................30.00
Roman Rosette, sauce, red flashed........................12.00
Roman Rosette, water set, 7 pc..........................195.00
Romeo, see Block & Fan
Rope & Thumbprint, creamer, amber........................25.00
Rope & Thumbprint, pitcher, milk; 6¼"....................48.00
Rope Bands, creamer......................................19.00
Rope Bands, goblet.......................................18.00
Rope Bands, plate, 7¼"...................................10.00
Rope Bands, wine..15.00
Rose & Sunbursts, see American Beauty
Rose in Snow, compote, covered, low base, clear..........75.00
Rose in Snow, creamer....................................29.50
Rose in Snow, double pickle dish.........................75.00
Rose in Snow, goblet....................................33.00
Rose in Snow, plate, 6"..................................17.50
Rose in Snow, plate, 7"..................................19.50
Rose in Snow, relish, 8½"................................15.00
Rose in Snow, tumbler....................................35.00
Rose Leaves, goblet.....................................26.00
Rose Point Band, creamer, flat...........................16.00
Rose Point Band, relish..................................15.00
Rose Point Band, sauce, ftd..............................11.00
Rose Point Band, tumbler.................................18.00
Rose Point Band, wine....................................19.00
Rose Sprig, cake stand, high standard, square, blue.......47.50
Rose Sprig, compote, covered, high standard, lg...........75.00
Rose Sprig, nappy, hdld, 6" sq...........................18.00
Rose Sprig, pitcher, ftd, 1 qt, canary...................65.00
Rose Sprig, relish, boat shape, vaseline.................30.00
Rosette, cake stand, 8½".................................17.00
Rosette, creamer..20.00
Rosette, goblet...24.00
Rosette, pitcher, water; ca 1891, Bryce..................65.00
Rosette, sugar w/lid.....................................20.00
Rosette & Palms, cake stand, 4½x9½" dia...................27.00
Rosette & Palms, goblet..................................22.00
Rosette & Palms, pitcher.................................45.00
Rosette & Palms, wine....................................24.00
Rosette Medallion, see Feather Duster
Royal Crystal, plate, 10¼"...............................24.00
Royal Crystal, tumbler...................................18.00

Royal Ivy, berry set, rainbow cracquelle......................295.00
Royal Ivy, bowl, berry; frosted rubena, small, EX color........35.00
Royal Ivy, bowl, master berry; rainbow cracquelle satin.......125.00
Royal Ivy, butter, cranberry..................................175.00
Royal Ivy, creamer, clear frosted..............................55.00
Royal Ivy, pitcher, water; frosted rubena, EX color...........275.00
Royal Lady, creamer..18.00
Royal Lady, pitcher..50.00
Royal Oak, butter w/cover, frosted............................175.00
Royal Oak, butter w/cover, frosted rubena.....................210.00
Royal Oak, creamer, frosted rubena............................150.00
Royal Oak, spooner, rubena & clear.............................75.00
Royal Oak, sugar shaker, frosted rubena, w/orig lid...........165.00
Royal Oak, sugar w/lid, frosted rubena........................180.00
Royal Oak, table set, frosted rubena, excellent color.........625.00
Ruby Thumbprint, bowl, belled scalloped top, red flashed, 4½"..14.00
Ruby Thumbprint, celery..60.00
Ruby Thumbprint, compote, high standard, 5"....................55.00
Ruby Thumbprint, cup...20.00
Ruby Thumbprint, pitcher, milk.................................90.00
Ruby Thumbprint, salt & peppers, etched, pr....................65.00
Ruby Thumbprint, sauce, 4½"....................................18.00
Ruby Thumbprint, spooner, etched, ruby stained.................60.00
Ruby Thumbprint, spooner, ruby & clear.........................35.00
Ruffled Eye, pitcher, water; amber............................135.00
S-Repeat, butter w/cover, green w/EX gold.....................135.00
S-Repeat, carafe, water; amethyst w/good gold..................80.00
S-Repeat, tray, water; green...................................60.00
S-Repeat, wine, green..70.00
Sandwich Ivy, compote, jelly...................................45.00
Sandwich Loop, see Hairpin
Sandwich Star, spill holder....................................29.00
Sandwich Star, spooner, flint..................................30.00
Sawtooth, bowl, ruby stained, 5"................................8.00
Sawtooth, champagne, knob stem, flint..........................35.00
Sawtooth, cordial, ruby stained................................38.00
Sawtooth, goblet, knob stem, flint.............................40.00
Sawtooth, pitcher, water; applied hdl..........................85.00
Sawtooth, pitcher, water; ruby stained........................120.00
Sawtooth, spooner, flint.......................................35.00
Sawtooth, spooner, non-flint...................................14.00
Sawtooth, wine, flint..24.00
Sawtooth, wine, non-flint.......................................7.00
Sawtooth Band, see Amazon
Sawtoothed Honeycomb, tumbler, ruby stain......................35.00
Scalloped Daisy Red Top, see Button Arches
Scalloped Lines, goblet..20.00
Scarab, goblet, flint..85.00
Scroll, buttermilk...15.00
Scroll, goblet, non-flint......................................19.00
Scroll, tumbler, ftd...22.00
Scroll w/Acanthus, tumbler, apple green w/gold & enamel........12.00
Scroll w/Cane Band, butter dish, amber stain...................60.00
Scroll w/Cane Band, spooner, ruby stained......................65.00
Scroll w/Cane Band, sugar, ruby stained........................85.00
Scroll w/Cane Band, tumbler....................................18.00
Scroll w/Flowers, creamer......................................40.00
Scroll w/Flowers, egg cup, 2 hdl...............................15.00
Scroll w/Flowers, goblet.......................................22.50
Scroll w/Flowers, spooner......................................20.00
Scroll w/Flowers, sugar w/lid..................................35.00
Scroll w/Flowers, wine, amber..................................35.00
Seashell, wine...35.00
Sedan, creamer...22.00

Sedan, wine..18.00
Seneca Loop, compote, covered, w/cable edge, 9¼x9" dia.........65.00
Seneca Loop, goblet..30.00
Seneca Loop, spooner, flint....................................22.00
Seneca Loop, wine, non-flint...................................20.00
Serrated Prism, goblet, clear w/gold...........................18.00
Sharp Oval & Diamond, see Louisiana
Sheaf & Block, tumbler, ruby stain.............................28.00
Sheaf & Diamonds, cake stand, 9½"..............................15.00
Shell & Jewel, cake stand, 10".................................50.00
Shell & Jewel, pitcher...30.00
Shell & Jewel, tumbler, blue...................................35.00
Shell & Jewel, tumbler, green..................................35.00
Shell & Jewel, water set, blue, 7 pc..........................310.00
Shell & Scroll, see Geneva
Shell & Spike, see Shell & Tassel
Shell & Tassel, bowl, oval, ftd, 12"...........................85.00
Shell & Tassel, celery vase....................................55.00
Shell & Tassel, oyster plate..................................160.00
Shell & Tassel, sauce, ftd, 4½" square.........................15.00
Shell & Tassel, spooner, square................................37.00
Shell & Tassel, table set.....................................325.00
Sheraton, celery...26.00
Sheraton, compote, open, 10"...................................45.00
Sheraton, goblet...25.00
Sheraton, pitcher, water; clear................................34.00
Sheraton, wine...30.00
Shields, see Tape Measure
Shoshone, banana stand...28.00
Shoshone, bowl, fruit; on ped ft, ruby trim, 5½x8½" dia........88.00
Shoshone, syrup, squatty, ruby stained, orig top..............135.00
Shrine, butter w/cover...45.00
Shrine, carafe...35.00
Shrine, celery...45.00
Shrine, creamer..30.00
Shrine, goblet...45.00
Shrine, pitcher, large, 2-gallon..............................110.00
Shrine, shaker...22.00
Shrine, spooner..25.00
Shrine, tumbler, lemonade......................................35.00
Shuttle, wine..16.00
Singing Birds, spooner, 2 hdl..................................50.00
Six Panel Fine Cut, goblet, amber stained, etched..............35.00
Six Panel Fine Cut, wine.......................................30.00
Skilton, see Oregon
Smocking Band, see Double Beetle Band
Snail, celery..30.00
Snail, celery, etched..65.00
Snail, individual salt dip.....................................15.00
Snail, pitcher..135.00
Snake Drape, goblet..18.00
Snakeskin & Dot Band, goblet...................................18.50
Snow Band, see Puffed Bands
Souvenir w/Red Panels, see Millard
Spearheads, goblet...12.00
Spearpoint Band, compote, jelly; open, ruby trim,4 1/4x5¼" dia 55.00
Spearpoint Band, sauce, ruby stained, EX gold..................15.00
Spearpoint Band, spooner, ruby stained.........................50.00
Spiral Diamond Point, plate, 10¼"..............................15.00
Spirea Band, creamer, amber....................................35.00
Spirea Band, goblet..18.00
Spirea Band, goblet, etched....................................26.00
Spirea Band, sauce, amber......................................12.00
Spirea Band, spooner, amber....................................25.00

Spirea Band, sugar, open, amber..................22.00
Spirea Band, wine, amber.......................25.00
Sprig, bowl, ftd, 8".............................42.00
Sprig, celery...................................35.00
Sprig, compote, covered, 10½"...................60.00
Sprig, compote, open, low base..................30.00
Sprig, creamer.................................29.50
Sprig, pitcher, water...........................48.00
Sprig, sauce, flat...............................8.00
Sprig, wine....................................35.00
Square Panes, see Post
Squirrel, pitcher, water; 1 digging, 1 on branch...........165.00
Squirrel, sauce................................15.00
Stamen, see Tidy
Star & File, bowl, 2 hdl, 4½"...................10.00
Star Band, see Bosworth
Star Flower Band, see Stippled Star Flower
Star in Bull's Eye, butter dish, good gold..............32.00
Star in Honeycomb, see Leverne
Star of David, tumbler..........................12.00
Starred Block, table set, 4 pc..................135.00
Starred Cosmos, water set, 6 pc.................85.00
Starred Scroll, wine.............................7.00
Stars & Bars, cruet set, salt/pepper/tray..........35.00
Stars & Bars, goblet............................20.00
Stars & Stripes, cordial........................15.00
Stars & Stripes, tumbler, clear w/gold, McKee.............14.00
States, bowl, 3 hdl.............................27.00
States, creamer, individual.....................19.50
States, relish w/lid, lt gr rim, silver holder & spoon, 4".......125.00
States, spooner................................20.00
States, tumbler................................27.00
States, wine...................................32.00
Steele, see Priscilla
Stippled Chain, spooner.........................28.00
Stippled Cherry, plate, 9½".....................13.00
Stippled Cherry, tumbler........................22.00
Stippled Daisy, tumbler.........................18.00
Stippled Double Loop, sugar w/lid...............24.00
Stippled Double Loop, tumbler...................30.00
Stippled Forget-Me-Not, cake stand, high standard, 9" dia.....29.50
Stippled Forget-Me-Not, salt, master; oval.........35.00
Stippled Fuschia, goblet........................26.00
Stippled Grape & Festoon, spooner...............25.00
Stippled Ivy, goblet............................25.00
Stippled Loop, goblet...........................20.00
Stippled Panelled Flower, see Maine
Stippled Peppers, goblet........................25.00
Stippled Sandbur, compote, 4"...................40.00
Stippled Sandbur, compote, 6"...................50.00
Stippled Star, celery, Gillinder.................30.00
Stippled Star, spooner..........................25.00
Straight Banded Worcester, goblet, flint, 1850s...........28.00
Strawberry, spooner............................30.00
Strawberry, tumbler............................45.00
Strawberry & Cable, creamer, Northwood.............70.00
Strawberry & Cable, water set, 7 pc, EX stain, Northwood....275.00
Strawberry w/Checkerboard, compote, jelly; w/lid..........22.00
Strawberry w/Roman Key Band, spooner...............25.00
Strawberry w/Roman Key Band, tumbler...............85.00
Style, wine....................................18.00
Sunbeam, champagne, ftd, green w/gold..............12.00
Sunbeam, wine, green...........................50.00
Sunburst, celery...............................30.00

Sunk Honeycomb, pitcher, water; tankard, ruby stained.......95.00
Sunken Buttons, see Mitered Diamond
Sunken Primrose, bowl, berry; clear & frosted.............20.00
Swan, pitcher.................................130.00
Swan, sauce, ftd...............................15.00
Swan, sugar w/lid, swan finial..................55.00
Swirl, see Jersey Swirl
Swirl w/Star Base, pitcher, water...............35.00
Tacoma, carafe, clear w/ruby stain..............85.00
Tacoma, pitcher, water; tankard, ruby stain, 9", EX.........195.00
Tacoma, tumbler, ruby stained...................30.00
Tacoma, wine...................................18.00
Tandem Bicycle, wine...........................32.00
Tape Measure, spooner..........................28.00
Tarentum's Victoria, sugar w/lid, green............30.00
Tarentum's Victoria, water set, emerald gr w/M gold, 7 pc.....265.00
Teardrop, creamer, cobalt.......................45.00
Teardrop, goblet...............................40.00
Teardrop, wine.................................15.00
Teardrop & Diamond Thumbprint, see Art
Teardrop & Tassel, relish, oval, green.............40.00
Teardrop & Tassel, sugar w/lid..................50.00
Teardrop & Tassel, tumbler......................30.00
Teardrop & Thumbprint, see Teardrop
Teasel, wine...................................11.50
Tennessee, compote, open........................35.00
Tennessee, pitcher.............................65.00
Tennessee, relish..............................22.00
Texas, bowl, oval..............................24.00
Texas, creamer, individual......................17.00
Texas, relish..................................22.00
Texas, sauce, flat, round, 4½"..................14.00
Texas, vase, 7"................................18.00
Texas, wine....................................72.00
Texas Bull's Eye, goblet........................18.00
Texas Bull's Eye, wine..........................21.00
Texas Star, see Swirl w/Star Base
Thistle, see Pillar & Bull's Eye
Thistle Shield, goblet, blue....................30.00
Thousand Eye, compote, open, apple green............35.00
Thousand Eye, egg cup, vaseline.................65.00
Thousand Eye, goblet, blue......................50.00
Thousand Eye, hand lamp.......................120.00
Thousand Eye, spooner..........................30.00
Thousand Eye, sugar w/lid, plain stem..............38.00
Three Face, cake stand, 11"....................165.00
Three Face, cake stand, 8".......................95.00
Three Face, cake stand, 9"......................120.00
Three Face, champagne, saucer shape.............125.00
Three Face, claret............................125.00
Three Face, compote, clear & frosted, 6x7½"............60.00
Three Face, compote, covered, high standard, old, 9½" dia....225.00
Three Face, creamer, clear w/frosted stem & base...........110.00
Three Face, goblet.............................55.00
Three Face, goblet, clear w/frosted stem & base, etched.......85.00
Three Face, spooner............................65.00
Three Face, spooner, etched.....................95.00
Three Face, sweetmeat, clear & frosted.............55.00
Three Panel, berry set, 7 pc, amber, ftd w/scalloped rims.....108.00
Three Panel, compote, blue......................32.00
Three Panel, compote, open, low ped, vaseline............35.00
Three Panel, goblet, amber......................32.00
Three Panel, goblet, blue.......................40.00
Three Panel, mug, amber........................35.00

Three Panel, spooner, clear...................................15.00
Three Panel, sugar w/lid, vaseline.........................57.00
Three Presidents, goblet...................................225.00
Three Row Baby Thumbprint, goblet..........................15.00
Three-In-One, compote......................................18.00
Thumbprint, berry bowl, boat shape, small, ruby stained.......30.00
Thumbprint, celery vase, ruby stained......................45.00
Thumbprint, cheese dish, ruby stained, 7" round............55.00
Thumbprint, compote, low standard, short rim, plain base, 3x7".42.00
Thumbprint, compote, ruby stained, 6"......................45.00
Thumbprint, cup..20.00
Thumbprint, finger bowl, amberina..........................95.00
Thumbprint, match holder, ruby stained.....................20.00
Thumbprint, pickle dish, ruby stained......................55.00
Thumbprint, pitcher, water; bulbous, ruby stained..........145.00
Thumbprint, tumbler, ruby stained..........................35.00
Thumbprint, wine, ruby stained.............................28.00
Thumbprint Block, wine.....................................30.00
Thunderbird, see Hummingbird
Tiny Fine Cut, wine..18.00
Tiny Fine Cut, wine, green.................................35.00
Tiny Lion, creamer & open sugar............................50.00
Tobin, goblet..14.00
Toltec, pitcher, water.....................................36.00
Torpedo, bowl, berry; ruby stained, small..................25.00
Torpedo, butter w/cover....................................85.00
Torpedo, celery vase.......................................40.00
Torpedo, creamer...40.00
Torpedo, goblet..49.00
Torpedo, pitcher, tankard..................................85.00
Torpedo, spooner...35.00
Torpedo, sugar, open.......................................28.00
Torpedo, sugar w/lid.......................................65.00
Torpedo, waste bowl..48.00
Tree of Life w/Hand, compote, hand holds bowl, ftd, bl, 8x8"..110.00
Tree of Life w/Hand, compote/frosted stem, Pittsburg, 10x10"..75.00
Tree of Life w/Hand, creamer, w/frosted hand ped, lg.........70.00
Triangular Prism, compote, flint, 7½x5"....................30.00
Triple Triangle, butter w/cover, clear.....................40.00
Triple Triangle, goblet, ruby stained......................37.00
Triple Triangle, sugar w/lid, ruby stained, lg.............75.00
Triple Triangle, tumbler...................................24.50
Triple Triangle, tumbler, ruby stained.....................30.00
Triple Triangle, wine, ruby stained........................45.00
Truncated Cube, wine.......................................22.00
Tulip, sugar...25.00
Tulip Petals, wine, gold flashing on rim...................15.00
Tulip w/Sawtooth, goblet, flint............................35.00
Tulip w/Sawtooth, master salt, flint.......................25.00
Tulip w/Sawtooth, vase, flint, 10¼"........................45.00
Turkey Track, see Crowfoot
Twin Leaves, creamer, pedestaled...........................30.00
Twinkle Star, pitcher......................................30.00
Two Band, compote, covered, 7½x7" dia......................35.00
Two Panel, bowl, oval, apple green, 9".....................35.00
Two Panel, creamer...16.00
Two Panel, creamer, blue...................................35.00
Two Panel, sauce, ftd, vaseline............................19.00
Two Panel, spooner, amber..................................28.00
Two Panel, spooner, vaseline...............................27.00
Two Panel, wine, blue......................................37.50
Two Panel, wine, vaseline..................................25.00
US Coin, bowl, oval, 8"....................................250.00
US Coin, cake stand, frosted 25¢ & $1......................450.00

US Coin, compote, quarters & dimes, 5½"....................250.00
US Coin, salt shaker, 1892 quarters, orig top..............150.00
US Coin, spooner, clear 25¢................................200.00
US Coin, sugar, w/lid, traces of gold......................275.00
US Coin, toothpick...180.00
Valencia Waffle, celery....................................40.00
Valencia Waffle, creamer, ruby stained.....................35.00
Valencia Waffle, goblet....................................12.00
Valencia Waffle, goblet, amber.............................35.00
Valentine, goblet..85.00
Valentine, pitcher, water..................................185.00
Vermont, tray, handled basket, green.......................45.00
Victor, see Shell & Jewell
Viking, compote, covered, low standard.....................60.00
Viking, creamer, clear.....................................35.00
Virginia, see Galloway
Waffle, celery, flint......................................48.00
Waffle, sugar w/lid, on high standard, flint...............75.00
Waffle & Star Band, wine...................................16.00
Waffle & Thumbprint, frappe, flint.........................55.00
Waffle & Thumbprint, goblet, flint.........................65.00
Waffle & Thumbprint, whiskey, hdl, flint...................85.00
Waffle w/Fan Top, tray, water; blue........................55.00
Washington Centennial, egg cup, clear......................45.00
Washington Centennial, goblet..............................40.00
Washington Centennial, platter, Independence Hall/bear paw hdl.95.00
Washington Centennial, spooner.............................35.00
Washington Centennial, wine................................45.00
Wedding Bells, wine, clear w/pink blush....................40.00
Wedding Bells, wine, gold panels...........................21.00
Wedding Ring, goblet, flint................................45.00
Wellington, wine...18.00
Westmoreland, celery vase, ped.............................25.00
Westward Ho, butter dish...................................180.00
Westward Ho, compote, 6"...................................125.00
Westward Ho, creamer.......................................80.00
Westward Ho, goblet..75.00
Westward Ho, pitcher, milk.................................175.00
Westward Ho, pitcher, water................................210.00
Westward Ho, sugar w/lid...................................175.00
Wheat & Barley, compote, covered...........................42.00
Wheat & Barley, goblet.....................................25.00
Wheat & Barley, goblet, amber..............................32.00
Wheat & Barley, salt & pepper, pr..........................35.00
Wheat & Barley, spooner....................................22.50
Wheat & Barley, tumbler, amber.............................38.00
Wheat Sheaf, pitcher, water................................47.50
Wheeling, boat, covered....................................70.00
Whitton, see Heavy Gothic
Wildflower, butter w/cover.................................34.00
Wildflower, butter w/cover, blue, collared base............50.00
Wildflower, cake stand, blue, 9½"..........................87.00
Wildflower, celery...23.00
Wildflower, creamer, vaseline..............................35.00
Wildflower, goblet...24.50
Wildflower, goblet, apple green............................35.00
Wildflower, goblet, vaseline...............................20.00
Wildflower, pitcher, water; amber..........................42.00
Wildflower, plate, blue, square, 10".......................38.00
Wildflower, platter, bread; apple green....................25.00
Wildflower, relish dish, apple green.......................16.50
Wildflower, sauce, blue....................................18.00
Wildflower, sauce, flat, apple green.......................7.50
Wildflower, sauce, flat, square, amber.....................15.00

Wildflower, sauce, flat, vaseline...........................16.00
Wildflower, spooner, yellow..............................35.00
Wildflower, sugar w/lid, green...........................50.00
Wildflower, table set, amber, 4 pc.....................135.00
Wildflower, tray, deep, vaseline.........................45.00
Wildflower, tray, oblong, vaseline.......................43.50
Wildflower, tray, water; amber..........................39.00
Wildflower, tray, water; apple green....................50.00
Wildflower, tumbler.....................................25.00
Wildflower, tumbler, amber.............................45.00
Wildflower, tumbler, apple green........................29.00
Wildflower, tumbler, blue...............................29.00
Wildflower, tumbler, vaseline...........................20.00
Wildrose & Bowknot, water set, frosted on clear, 7 pc........65.00
Willow Oak, butter w/cover, amber......................50.00
Willow Oak, celery, ped ft, serrated rim................50.00
Willow Oak, compote, open, scalloped edge..............20.00
Willow Oak, creamer....................................26.00
Willow Oak, pitcher....................................50.00
Willow Oak, plate, large...............................22.50
Willow Oak, plate, w/closed handles, blue, 9″...........28.00
Willow Oak, plate, 9″..................................22.00
Willow Oak, sugar w/lid, amber.........................68.00
Willow Oak, tray, water................................25.00
Windflower, goblet.....................................35.00
Winona, see Barbed Hobnail
Wisconsin, bowl, 4½x6¼″ dia...........................28.00
Wisconsin, cake stand, 9½″ dia.........................55.00
Wisconsin, celery tray, 10½x5½″........................45.00
Wisconsin, creamer.....................................25.00
Wisconsin, pitcher.....................................65.00
Wisconsin, sugar w/lid.................................25.00
Wisconsin, tumbler.....................................38.00
Wisconsin, wine..55.00
Wishbone, see Interlocked Hearts
Wooden Pail, creamer, vaseline.........................35.00
Wooden Pail, pitcher, water; amethyst.................145.00
Wooden Pail, sugar w/lid, blue.........................48.00
Wooden Pail, sugar w/lid, vaseline.....................45.00
Wreath & Bars, goblet..................................21.00
Wyoming, cake stand....................................60.00
Wyoming, pitcher, water................................68.00
Wyoming, relish..11.00
X-Logs, see Prism Arc
X-Ray, berry set, green w/gold, 7 pc..................165.00
X-Ray, compote, jelly; amethyst w/gold.................65.00
X-Ray, creamer, green & gold...........................55.00
X-Ray, sauce, green w/M gold...........................12.50
X-Ray, sugar, open, individual, green w/gold............20.00
X-Ray, sugar w/lid, amethyst...........................88.00
Yale, see Crowfoot
Yolked Loop, compote, 3½x7″...........................20.00
Yolked Loop, goblet, flint.............................20.00
York Colonial, tumbler, flint..........................40.00
York Herringbone, goblet, etched.......................35.00
York Herringbone, table set, red flashed, 4 pc.........235.00
Yuma Loop, goblet......................................18.00
Zig-Zag, cordial.......................................25.00
Zipper, creamer, w/ornate applied hdl..................38.00
Zipper, goblet...14.00
Zipper, pitcher, milk; canary..........................50.00
Zipper Slash, spooner, amber stained & etched...........45.00
Zippered Block, see Iowa
Zippered Swirl, see Kokomo

Paul Revere Pottery

The Saturday Evening Girls were a social group of young Boston ladies who met to pursue various activities, among them pottery making. Their first kiln was bought in 1906, and within a few years it became necessary to move to a larger location. Because their new quarters were near the historical Old North Church, they chose the name Paul Revere Pottery. With very little training, the girls produced only simple ware. Until 1915, the pottery operated at a deficit. Then a new building with four kilns was constructed on Nottingham Road. Vases, miniature jugs, children's tea sets, tiles, dinnerware, and lamps were produced, usually in soft matt glazes with simple stylized nature decorations often incised on the ware. Occasional examples in a dark high gloss may also be found.

Several marks were used: 'P.R.P.'; 'S.E.G.'; or the circular device, 'Boston, Paul Revere Pottery' with the horse and rider.

The pottery continued to operate, and even though their product sold well, the high production costs of the handmade ware caused the pottery to fail in 1946.

Bowl, blue semi-gloss, artist sgn, 2½x6″.................35.00
Bowl, blue semi-gloss, SEG, 3½x6¼″...................50.00
Bowl, cream lotus blossoms on turquoise, sgn, 12½″ dia.....150.00
Bowl, gr band w/swans on bl, SEG/DHK/Aug 5-12, rpr, 5¾″...150.00
Bowl, yellow lotus & wht band on yellow, sgn EM, 8½″.......125.00
Calendar holder, trees/river, sgn/dtd 11/21, SEG, base chip.....90.00
Candlestick, gun metal, sgn, 6″, pr.....................80.00
Candlestick, lt bl/gr floral bands on bl, sgn PRP/LS/41, 2x4½″.110.00
Creamer, child's; wht w/bl band w/rabbits, sgn JG/4/15, SEG...100.00
Creamer, sky, mountains, trees, SEG, 3½″................100.00
Creamer, wht w/band of trees, cracked, 4¼″.............65.00
Cup, wht, gr band w/yellow flowers, SEG, 1¾″...........50.00
Cup & saucer, wht, bl/gr tree band, sgn Edith Brown, 5 for....325.00
Cup & saucer, yellow...................................38.50
Mug, yellow..43.00
Plate, cream w/band of rabbits on orange, SEG, 7½″......125.00
Plate, heavy blue glaze w/maroon shading, 8″............40.00
Plate, hills/trees, 5 colors, EX detail, SEG/AM/5-19, 8½″......150.00
Plate, rabbit center, 5 colors, sgn, SEG...............115.00
Sugar, child's; wht w/bl band w/rabbits, LE/11/19, SEG........95.00
Tea tile, wht geometrics on yellow, SEG, FL, 1917, 5¼″ sq...125.00
Tile, blue, SEG..35.00
Tile, mustard yellow, dtd 1920, SEG, 5½″ dia...........32.00
Vase, blue, SEG, 10″...................................85.00
Vase, br gloss w/scenic 3 color band, mk SEG 11/21 EG, 6″...240.00
Vase, bud; cylinder w/base swell, yel w/daffodils, SEG/FL, G....250.00
Vase, glossy deep blue, 4½″............................40.00
Vase, gray gloss, SEG, 13¾″...........................100.00
Vase, gun metal blk, wide base, dtd 4/23, 8½″..........60.00
Vase, lt blue drip over dk blue, embossed mk, 4¼x4¾″.......50.00
Vase, scenic band, SEG, 3/21/EG, 6½″...................325.00

Peachblow

Peachblow, made to imitate the colors of the Chinese Peachbloom porcelain, was made by several glass houses in the late 1800s. Among them were New England Glass, Mt. Washington, Webb, and Hobbs Brockunier and Company. Its pink shading was achieved through action of the heat on the gold content of the glass. While New England Peachblow shades from pink to cool white, Mt. Washington's tends to shade from peach to ivory. Although usually glossy, a satin finish was also produced, and many pieces were enameled and gilded.

Biscuit jar, floral and peacock decoration, New England, 7", $675.00.

Bottle, fine rib w/floral, bl stopper, Mt Washington, 5".......600.00
Box, dore lid, raspberry to blue, Gunderson, 5x6½".........350.00
Celery vase, crimp top, New England.....................795.00
Chalice, Gunderson, 8¾"...............................275.00
Claret, silver neck band, faceted amber stopper, Wheeling, pr.5,200.00
Compote, flower form, EX color, acid finish, Gunderson, 6x7"..375.00
Compote, magenta to wht, satin, crimped, SP ft, Webb, 5½x7".245.00
Creamer, applied hdl, acid finish, Gunderson................345.00
Creamer, cream/dk red, pk/wht cased, pink hdl, 5¼".........275.00
Creamer, ribbed, New England............................300.00
Cruet, acid w/amber stopper & hdl, Wheeling, 7½".........1,350.00
Cruet, shiny, teardrop shape, Wheeling, 7½"...............1,350.00
Cup, punch; New England, 2½"...........................350.00
Cup & saucer, wht reed hdl, Gunderson....................165.00
Darning egg, New England................................150.00
Ewer, cased/enamel decor, applied rib hdl pnt yel, Webb, 5½".325.00
Fairy lamp, ruffled edge, Gunderson.......................150.00
Finger bowl, glossy, fluted, New England, 2¼x5¼"..........325.00
Finger bowl, Wheeling....................................450.00
Goblet, bl/wht forget-me-nots, sgn Kiluk, Pairpoint, 6¾".......90.00
Jar, w/lid, cylinder shape, decor, Webb, 4½"..............650.00
Mustard dish, shiny finish, SP top, Wheeling, 3"...........500.00
Pear, blown figural, 1893, New England, VG................195.00
Pear, New England, 6", M...............................350.00
Perfume, gold prunus/butterfly, acid, spherical, Webb, 4¾"....495.00
Pitcher, applied amber hdl, Wheeling, 8"................1,500.00
Rose bowl, decorated, 4½" dia..........................140.00
Rose jar, hawthorn decor in gold, wht lined, 3½" dia........130.00
Spoon holder, sq ruffled top, satin, New England, 4½".......425.00
Sweetmeat, gold prunus, silver top/rim/hdl, acid, Webb, 4½"...395.00
Tumbler, deep raspberry color, good shading, acid finish, NE...345.00
Tumbler, New England, 3¾"..............................250.00
Vase, applied cream florals, acid finish, Webb, 5"..........395.00
Vase, applied decor, glossy, Gunderson, 3"................365.00
Vase, cameo carved flowers, sgn Webb, 4½x3".............1,650.00
Vase, gold florals/butterfly, Webb, 8x3"..................495.00
Vase, Jack-in-the-Pulpit, by Babbit of Pairpoint............325.00
Vase, Morgan, plastic amber griffin holder, Wheeling, 8".....1,350.00
Vase, narrow tri-lobe top/bulbous base, Webb, 10x4½".......550.00
Vase, stick neck, satin, Webb, 9¾".......................220.00

Peking Glass

The first glass house to be established in Peking in 1680 produced glassware made in imitation of porcelain, a more desirable medium to the Chinese. By 1725, multi-layered carving with a cameo effect resulted in a wider range of shapes and colors. The factory was closed from 1736 to 1795, but glass made in Po-shan and shipped to Peking for finishing continued to be called Peking glass.

Twentieth century ware is usually decorated in soft frosted colors on relief molded designs.

Bottle, snuff; cameo, bl to clear, w/spoon, no stopper, 2¾"....150.00
Bowl, amethyst, shaped rim, fluted body, mid 1700s, 13", pr..190.00
Bowl, ftd, amethyst, late 1800s, 9"......................130.00
Cup & saucer, handleless; 2¼x3¾".......................85.00
Floral bouquet, pk/wht/tan peonies in celadon pot, 16x20".....165.00
Jar, bl cut to wht flowering thorn branches, 4".............200.00
Vase, bl cut to wht flowering branches, rim nick, bulbous, 6"..350.00
Vase, br/red cut to wht flowering branches, 7", pr...........475.00
Vase, bright yel, 8 sided/stick neck, teak stand, 5½".........375.00
Vase, gr cameo over wht honeycomb, 8"..................140.00
Vase, gr cut to wht, cranes/peonies, Ching Dynasty, 14".......650.00
Vase, red cut to wht, birds in flowering branches, 10", pr.....550.00
Vase, red cut to wht, ducks/lotus, dbl neck ring, 8½x5½".....325.00
Vase, red cut to wht, narcissus/prunus branches, 9", pr.......550.00

Peloton

Peloton glass was first made by Wilhelm Kralik in Bohemia in 1880. This unusual art glass was produced by rolling colored threads onto the transparent or opaque glass gather as it was removed from the furnace. Usually, more than one color of threading was used, and some items were further decorated with enameling. It was made with both shiny and acid finishes.

Sugar bowl w/under plate, melon rib, satin w/wht filaments.....135.00
Sweetmeat, mc filaments, SP lid & bail....................350.00
Vase, bulb w/ruffled fan top, lav-pk w/pastel strings, 5x4".....300.00
Vase, bulb/tri-con top, wht case/ribs, pastel strings, 4¾x4"....300.00
Vase, ftd, cranberry threads, 7½".......................150.00
Vase, mauve, cased, mc confetti string, clear ft, ribbed, 6x4"...295.00
Vase, opal to clear, clear rim/ft, 8"......................465.00
Vase, stick neck, yel w/pastel strings, 7x3"...............250.00

Pennsbury

New in the collectibles' market, Pennsbury Pottery is drawing quite a following! Established in the 1950s in Morrisville, Pennsylvania, by Henry Below, the company produced dinnerware and novelty items, much of which was sold in gift shops along the Pennsylvania Turnpike. Some of their ware was hand painted in blue on white, some in multicolors on a light orange-brown. Pennsylvania Dutch motifs, Amish couples, and barbershop singers were among their most popular decorative themes. Sgraffito, or hand incising, was used extensively.

The company marked their wares 'Pennsbury Pottery' or 'Pennsbury Pottery, Morrisville, PA.' They closed during the early 1970s.

Cake plate, ped ft, 4 Amish figures, 11"...................35.00
Cookie jar, couple carrying platter, incised/HP both sides, mk...65.00
Figurine, bluebird #103...................................25.00
Figurine, rooster & hen, wht/red combs/dk bl trim, 11x7", pr..250.00

Mug, barbershop quartet decor, 4¾".....................20.00
Pitcher, Amish man & woman, 8"......................50.00
Plate, Amish man & lady, 9".........................30.00
Plate, Christmas 1970, w/angel, 'Noel', 8".............22.50
Snack set, 3 buckets, each w/hdl & barbershop quartet decor...35.00

Beverage set, incised barbershop singers decor; pitcher, 7", 9 piece set, $185.00.

Pens and Pencils

The first metallic writing pen was patented in 1809 and soon machine produced pens with steel nibs gradually began replacing the quill. The first fountain pen was invented in 1830, but due to the fact that a suitable metal for the tips had not yet been developed, they were not manufactured commercially until the 1880s. The first commercial producers were Waterman in 1884, and Parker with the Lucky Curve in 1888.

The self-filling pen, in 1890, featured the soft interior sack which filled with ink as the metal bar on the outside of the pen was raised and lowered. Variations of the pumping mechanism were tried until 1932 when Parker introduced the Vacumatic, a sackless pen with an internal pump.

Key:

AF-----aeromatic filler	GPT----gold plated trim
BF-----button filler	I--------initialed
cartr-----cartridge	LF------lever filler
CPT-----chrome plated trim	NPT----nickel plated trim
ED------eyedropper filler	TD------touchdown filler
GFM----gold filled metal	VF-----vacumatic filler

Fountain Pens

Accurate, green...6.50
Century, Durapoint, 1928, red mottled hard rubber, EX.......115.00
Chas N Ingersol, 1928, green marbled, needs sac otherwise M...24.00
Conklin, #50, blk.......................................65.00
Conklin, Endura, 1928, sapphire bl marbled, GPT, LF, EX....105.00
Conklin, Endura Senior, blk.............................110.00
Conklin, red woodgrain.................................110.00
Conklin, 1929, green, gold plated trim, LF, G..............12.00
Crocker Inktite, blk....................................55.00
Dunn Dreadnaught, see thru..............................75.00
Eversharp, blk..2.50
John Holland, Hatchet Filler, 1916, blk chased hard rubber, EX.40.00
Moore, L-83, 1923, blk chased hard rubber, M.............22.00
Moore, 1934, scarlet pearl marbled, G....................57.00
Moore, 56-X, 1928, blk & pearl, M........................45.00
Parker, Blue Diamond Maxima, 1939, emerald striped, GPT, I..225.00
Parker, Blue Diamond Maxima, 1940, gold striped, VF, EX....195.00

Parker, Blue Diamond 51, 1944, gray, aluminum cap, VF, G....18.00
Parker, Duofold, Big Red, 1928, GPT, BF, EX..............85.00
Parker, Duofold, 1931, black, BF, G......................29.00
Parker, Duofold, 1935, emerald, gold plated trim, BF, EX....260.00
Parker, Duofold Jr, orange/blk...........................14.50
Parker, Duofold Sr, 1927, solid blue, BF, M..............795.00
Parker, Duofold Sr, 1928, mandarin yel, GPT, BF, EX.......275.00
Parker, Lady Duofold, 1928, lapis blue, initialed, BF, EX......45.00
Parker, Lady Duofold, 1929, red hard rubber, BF, M.........49.00
Parker, Lady Duofold, 1931, lapis blue, BF, EX.............45.00
Parker, Super 21, 1956, blk w/stainless cap, CPT, AF, M......10.00
Parker, Vacumatic, 1933, gr-blk striped, early edition, VF, M...85.00
Parker, Vacumatic, 1935, gold striped, VF, EX.............20.00
Parker, Vacumatic, 1947, blue striped, VF, EX.............20.00
Parker, 21 Special, 1949, blk w/stainless cap, CPT, AF, M.....12.00
Parker, 51, 1948, gray w/Lustraloy cap, AF, M.............20.00
Parker, 61, 1960, blk w/Lustraloy cap, CPT, med nib, M.......32.00
Parker, 61 Demonstrator, 1957, cl Lucite, Lustraloy, CPT, M..195.00
Presto, #8...50.00
Schnell's Combo..75.00
Sheaffer's, #2, GFM....................................85.00
Sheaffer's, Lifetime, 1934, emerald, G...................60.00
Sheaffer's, Lifetime, 1939, blk w/pearl inlay, G...........26.00
Sheaffer's, Lifetime, 1939, emerald striped, G.............62.00
Sheaffer's, Snorkel, 1953, blue, TD, M...................10.00
Sheaffer's, Snorkel, 1954, green, chrome cap, TD, M........15.00
Sheaffer's, White Dot Imperial, 1972, cartr set in blk, M.....20.00
Sheaffer's, White Dot Snorkel Triumph, 1953, maroon, TD, EX.22.00
Sheaffer's, White Dot Triumph TM, 1951, blk, TD, EX........22.00
Sheaffer's, 500 Cartridge, 1971, green, M.................9.00
Swan, #192/33, 1925, blk, gold plated trim, LF, EX.........19.00
Swan, #44 ETN, blk....................................60.00
Swan, #54 ETN, 1926, red mottled, gold plated trim, LF, G...20.00
Swan, Eternal #46 ETN, 1928, blk, EX...................100.00
Swan, Eternal #46 ETN, 1932, red-blk marble, GPT, LF, G....160.00
Swan, 1905, blk hard rubber, under-over feed, ED, EX.......85.00
Wahl, #2, 1921, blk chased hard rubber, M................18.00
Wahl-Eversharp, Coronet, 1936, GFM, blk Pyrolin insets, G....200.00
Wahl-Eversharp, Executive Skyliner, 1941, blk, GPT, LF, EX..120.00
Wahl-Eversharp, Skyline, 1942, black, G..................10.00
Wahl-Eversharp, Skyline Executive Giant, 1942, bl, striped cap.215.00
Wahl-Eversharp, Skyline Executive Giant, 1942, blk, G.......140.00
Wahl-Eversharp, 1931, green jade marbled, EX.............22.00
Waterman's, #22, blk..................................85.00
Waterman's, #46, blk.................................250.00
Waterman's, #55, orange..............................150.00
Waterman's, Commando, 1948, black, EX..................14.00
Waterman's, Ideal #0552, 1925, gold filled metal, EX.......140.00
Waterman's, Ideal #12, 1904, red mottled hard rubber, ED, EX.18.00
Waterman's, Ideal #55, 1923, blk chased hard rubber, NPT..1,150.00
Waterman's, Ideal #56, 1923, blk chased hard rubber, NPT, M.165.00
Waterman's, Ideal #58, 1924, blk chased hard rubber, NPT....250.00
Waterman's, Ideal 3-V, 1935, scarlet marbled, NPT, G.......12.00
Waterman's, Lady Taperite, 1948, black, stainless cap, EX.....14.00
Waterman's, Patrician, onyx...........................300.00
Waterman's, Patrician, 1930, gr marbled, GPT, LF, NM......615.00
Waterman's, Patrician, 1932, moss agate, GPT, LF, EX......620.00
Waterman's, Patrician, 1939, turq, GPT, LF, final edition, M...625.00
Waterman's, Waterman CF, '54, blk, gold filled cap, cartr, M....26.00
Waterman's, 0512½, filigree............................95.00
Waterman's, 100 Year Ideal.............................40.00
Waterman's, 1942, silver marbled, EX....................10.00
Waterman's, 1948, red w/bronze & silver cap, M............18.00
Waterman's, 414, Art Nouveau.........................150.00

Mechanical Pencils

Eversharp, 1923, GFM, EX..............................10.00
Eversharp, 1924, sterling, G...........................16.00
Parker, Duofold, 1930, jade green marbled, EX..............29.00
Parker, Vacumatic Repeater, 1939, emerald striped, EX, rare....69.00
Parker, 51, 1945, black, GFM cap, G.....................12.00
Parker, 51, 1952, blue, GFM cap, M.....................20.00
Sheaffer's, 1971, black, GFM cap, M....................10.00
Wahl-Eversharp, Fifth Ave Repeater, 1943, blk, GFM cap, M....18.00
Wahl-Eversharp, Repeater, 1936, blk, GPT, EX..............35.00
Wahl-Eversharp, 1927, blk chased hard rubber, EX...........36.00
Waterman's, Ideal, 1924, GFM filigree, EX...............165.00
Waterman's, Ideal, 1937, turquoise, G..................45.00
Webster, 1928, red mottled hard rubber, EX................67.00

Sets

Conklin, Endura, 1928, gold marbled, GPT, LF, EX.........145.00
Conklin, 1929, pearl & blk, gold plated trim, LF, EX.........45.00
Eversharp, Command Performance, 1944, 14k gold, LF, MIB...625.00
Morrison, 1926, sterling filigree, pen EX, pencil G............37.00
Parker, Duofold Sr, 1929, mandarin yel, GPT, BF, EX.......525.00
Parker, Duofold Sr, 1929, streamlined, red, M w/stickers.....460.00
Parker, 51 Demi-Size, 1948, gray w/Lustraloy caps, CPT, AF, M.20.00
Swan, Eternal #46 ETN, 1931, blk lined pearl, GPT, LF, EX..185.00
Wahl-Eversharp, Skyline Gold Award, '45, GFM/sterling, M.....235.00
Waterman's, #5506, filigree, 2 pc........................500.00

Personalities, Fact & Fiction

One of the largest and most popular areas of collecting today, if tradepaper ads and articles be any indication, is character related memorabilia. Everyone has a favorite or favorites, whether they be comic strip personalities or true life heroes.

The earliest comic strip dealt with the adventures of the Yellow Kid, the smiling, bald headed Oriental boy always in a nightshirt. He was introduced in 1895, a product of the imagination of Richard Fenton Outcault. Today, though very hard to come by, items relating to the Yellow Kid bring premium prices.

In 1902, Buster Brown and Tige, his dog and constant companion, another of Outcault's progenies, made it big in the comics as well as in the world of advertising. Shoe stores appealed to the younger set through merchandising displays that featured them both; today, the items from their earlier years are very collectible.

Other early comic figures were Moon Mullins, created in 1923 by Frank Willard; Little Orphan Annie, by Harold Gray in 1923; Buck Rogers by Philip Nowlan in 1928; and Betty Boop, the round-faced, innocent-eyed, chubby-cheeked Boop-Boop-a-Doop girl of the early 1930s. Bimbo was her dog, and KoKo her clown friend.

Tarzan, created around 1930 by Edgar Rice Burroughs; and Captain Midnight, by Robert Burtt and Willfred G. Moore are popular heroes with today's collectors. During the days of radio, Sky King of the Flying Crown Ranch (also created by Burtt and Moore) thrilled boys and girls of the mid-1940s. Hopalong Cassidy, Red Rider, Tom Mix, and The Lone Ranger were only a few of the other 'good guys' always on the side of law and order.

But of all the fictional heroes and comic characters collected today, probably the best loved and well known is Mickey Mouse. Created in the late 1920s by Walt Disney, Micky (as his name was first spelled) became an instant success with his film debut, Steamboat Willie. His popularity was parlayed through windup toys, watches, figurines, cookie jars, puppets, clothing, and numerous other saleables.

Donald Duck celebrated his fiftieth birthday this year, arriving in his hometown, Disneyland U. S. A., by means of his own private jet, 'Duck One.' The star of more than 170 animated films, daily comic strips, and comic books was greeted by a ticker tape parade and thousands of fans, and after reviewing the troops at El Toro Marine Base, was made an honorary Marine.

Not all personalities being collected today are fictional, however. Shirley Temple, the child star who danced and sang her way to fame and fortune, was imortalized by doll companies who attempted to reproduce her long curls, dimples, and movie costumes; by music companies whose sheet music carried her pictures, and by paper dolls manufacturers who faithfully followed her career. Shirley Temple 12 oz. pitchers were a premium offered in the early 1930s by the General Mills Company. They were free inside boxes of their cereal. All in all, over 10,000 were produced by the U.S. Glass Company of Pittsburgh. Four more items were added later -- an 8 oz. mug, 6 and 6½" bowls, and a 4" nappy; these are more difficult to find. Look for a well preserved decal!

Enjoying a birthday this year -- their fiftieth -- the Dionne Quintuplets, who won the hearts of America as well as their native country, continue to be very much in the spotlight, at least as far as collectors of their abundantly produced memorabilia is concerned. And twenty years ago, the boys from Liverpool, England, first toured the United States, making 1984 an 'anniversary' year for fans of the fantastic foursome of rock and roll, The Beatles.

Related areas include Autographs and Movie Memorabilia. See also specific items, such as: Banks; Big Little Books; Cartoon Books; Comic Books; Cookie Jars; Dolls; Paper Dolls; Posters; Toys.

Alice in Wonderland, billfold, 1950s........................12.00
Alice in Wonderland, cup & saucer, bone china, English.......50.00
Alice in Wonderland, marionette in box, Mad Hatter..........40.00
Alice in Wonderland, wrist watch, animated, w/Mad Hatter.....185.00
Amos & Andy, cardboard stand up, Pepsodent................17.00
Amos & Andy, display sign, Rexall.......................15.00
Amos & Andy, map of Weber City, mtd on cb................28.00
Amos & Andy, match holder, chalk.......................75.00
Andy Gump, nodder, bisque, Germany, 1930s, 4", VG.........75.00
Andy Gump & Min, toothbrush holder, bisque................75.00
Babe Ruth, digital clock...............................250.00
Babe Ruth, wrist watch, Exacta Time Corp, 1949............175.00
Barney Google, costume, FKS 1936, M.....................40.00
Barney Google, hand puppet, King Features.................18.00
Batman, bicycle ornament, full figure, 1966................10.00
Batman, ice cream carton, M.............................7.00
Batman & Robin, clock, talking, emb figures, Janex Corp, 1974.15.00
Beatles, alarm clock, Yellow Submarine...................325.00
Beatles, banjo......................................600.00
Beatles, carrying case, blue...........................145.00
Beatles, Danish stockings, M, in pkg.....................15.00
Beatles, diary, 1965.................................15.00
Beatles, fan, 1964..................................22.00
Beatles, figures, bobbing head, set, ea 8"................250.00
Beatles, figures, composition, complete w/instruments, set MIB..250.00
Beatles, figures, vinyl, complete w/instruments, set..........210.00
Beatles, game, Flip Your Wig...........................30.00
Beatles, guitar pin, inset photo of Paul...................20.00
Beatles, gum card wrapper.............................10.00
Beatles, hair brush, M...............................15.00
Beatles, lunchbox, Yellow Submarine.....................25.00
Beatles, Lux Soap, sealed box w/inflatable adv, 1967.........150.00
Beatles, model, Yellow Sub, in box......................145.00
Beatles, movie poster, 'Help'..........................85.00
Beatles, mug......................................18.00
Beatles, music, Hard Days Night, 1 sheet.................125.00
Beatles, music, Yellow Submarine, 1 sheet................125.00

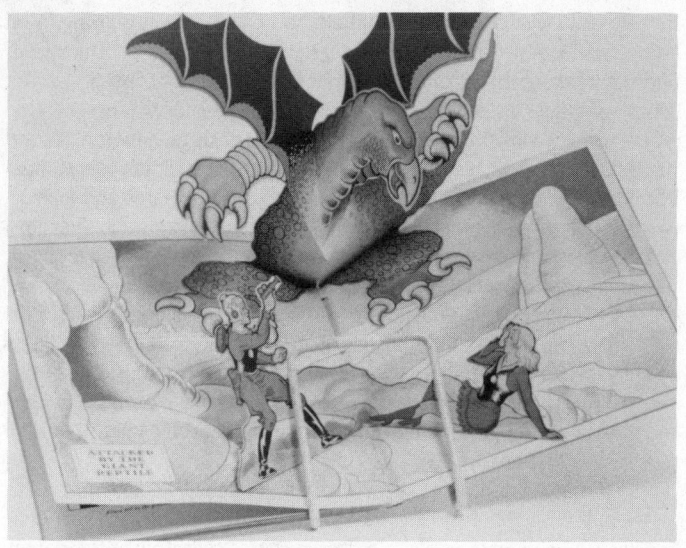

Buck Rogers pop-up book, Spider Ship Adventures, in mint condition, $350.00; in average used condition, $175.00.

Beatles, Paul McCartney blow up doll......................35.00
Beatles, pendant, 1964 record..........................10.00
Beatles, pillow......................................85.00
Beatles, pin, pictures, names in filigree, lg...............40.00
Beatles, pin-back, 1964................................5.00
Beatles, plate, English...............................175.00
Beatles, pocket book.................................165.00
Beatles, pressbook, Let It Be..........................20.00
Beatles, Quiz Book, 1964.............................20.00
Beatles, ring, pictures all four, Hems Ent Ltd.............20.00
Beatles, souvenir, Yellow Submarine....................20.00
Beatles, thermos....................................30.00
Beatles, 45 record case, cardboard.....................145.00
Ben Casey, jigsaw puzzle..............................10.00
Betty Boop, ash tray, w/Bimbo, Japan lustre..............95.00
Betty Boop, bisque figure, playing orange instrument, 3½"....75.00
Betty Boop, book, The Fleischer Story, by Leslie Caraga.....50.00
Betty Boop, pin, enamel...............................45.00
Betty Boop, sheet music, Natwick autograph..............175.00
Betty Boop, socks, pr................................45.00
Betty Boop, wall pocket, lustre ware...................125.00
Betty Boop, wood figure, jtd, 4½".....................100.00
Betty Boop & Mr Boop, perfume, glass figural/paper heart, pr...50.00
Bing Crosby, game, Call Me Lucky.......................45.00
Bing Crosby, game, Mouse Trap, w/box...................12.00
Bing Crosby, photo, Woodbury Radio.....................10.00
Bing Crosby, recipe book, TV Special, Kraft...............9.00
Blondie & Dagwood, game, Westinghouse premium, 1940, MIB..45.00
Bobby Benson, book, Tunnel of Gold, Hecker H-O premium....20.00
Bobby Benson, card game, H-Bar-O Ranch, instructions.......65.00
Bobby Benson, cereal bowl.............................12.00
Buck Jones, folder, BJ Club, courtesy Grape Nuts Flakes, 1937..15.00
Buck Rogers, Big Big Book, Planetoid Eros, 1934...........75.00
Buck Rogers, booklet, Kellogg premium, 1933 letter mailer....175.00
Buck Rogers, early 1931 full pg Sunday strip, XX85 ships.....22.50
Buck Rogers, inlaid puzzle.............................35.00
Buck Rogers, paint book, 1935, 11x18"...................95.00
Buck Rogers, pencil box, EX illustrations, 1930s, VG..........35.00
Buck Rogers, pocket knife..............................45.00
Buck Rogers, radio premium, Chemical Lab, Gropper, 1937....350.00
Buck Rogers, rubber band gun, color cardboard punch-out, '40..75.00

Buck Rogers, rug, blue w/mc, English, 40x27"............400.00
Buck Rogers, Solar Scouts pin..........................30.00
Buck Rogers, Strato Kite...............................35.00
Buck Rogers, telescope, Scientific Labratory..............185.00
Buck Rogers, Tootsie Toy Rocket Ships, 4 in box, 1937, MIB..650.00
Buffalo Bill, story book, #164..........................12.00
Buffalo Bill, story book, #65...........................18.00
Bugs Bunny, clock, other characters on dial, Warner Bros.....250.00
Bugs Bunny, pin-back button, Looney Tunes, red/bl/gray, 1¼"..20.00
Bugs Bunny, Quaker Comics giveaway set in orig mailer........25.00
Buster Brown, bank, CI, w/Tige........................135.00
Buster Brown, belt & buckle, embossed, w/Tige.............22.50
Buster Brown, book, muslin, BB Plays Indian..............40.00
Buster Brown, card game, BB at the Circus, w/Yellow Kid.....225.00
Buster Brown, counter sign.............................35.00
Buster Brown, dictionary, 324 pgs, 1927.................32.50
Buster Brown, drawing book, Ringer Stoves Co, 1905.........25.00
Buster Brown, face mask, paper, 1920s...................16.00
Buster Brown, iron figure in cart pulled by iron dog, 1900.....420.00
Buster Brown, knife, leg shaped........................55.00
Buster Brown, periscope, w/Tige........................12.00
Buster Brown, Pin the Bowtie Game, 1902, 24x29".........1,000.00
Buster Brown, pin-back, Buster Brown bread...............35.00
Buster Brown, pitcher, w/alphabet......................95.00
Buster Brown, plate, scene/name, wht china, 7¼"..........50.00
Buster Brown, playing cards............................50.00
Buster Brown, pocket mirror, 1946......................12.00
Buster Brown, postcard/Over...Bounding Main, w/Yellow Kid, '03.15.00
Buster Brown, printing ad blocks.......................135.00
Buster Brown, wrist watch, w/Tige......................55.00
Captain Hawks, Sky Patrol pin..........................12.00
Captain Marvel, club membership button, Fawcett Pub, 1941....10.00
Captain Marvel, dime bank.............................68.00
Captain Marvel, picture puzzle, ca 1945, MIB...............7.50
Captain Midnight, decoder, VG.........................23.00
Captain Midnight, decoder & manual, w/orig mailer.........70.00
Captain Midnight, mug, M.............................30.00
Captain Midnight, spinner, Medal of Membership, 1940.......25.00
Casper, rubber figure, 9".............................20.00
Charlie Chaplin, balance toy, rides bike, tin litho, EX action...325.00
Charlie Chaplin, clockwork toy, litho tin w/cane, 1920, 9".....550.00
Charlie Chaplin, plastic mechanical figure, Italy, 1950s.......95.00
Charlie Chaplin, stick pin, metal, 2"....................25.00
Charlie McCarthy, book, Grosset & Dunlop, 1938, 48 pgs.....20.00
Charlie McCarthy, paint book...........................15.00
Charlie McCarthy, pencil sharpener, M....................60.00
Charlie McCarthy, pin, enameled, in tux.................28.00
Charlie McCarthy, Radio Party Game....................26.00
Charlie McCarthy, spoon, figural.......................19.00
Chester Gump, nodder, bisque, Germany, 1930s, 2½", NM....50.00
Cinderella, book, pop-up, 8 scenes, German, taped spine.......25.00
Cinderella, watch, animated, Swiss......................20.00
Cinderella, watch, US Time, orig slipper from box..........65.00
Cinderella, watch, w/glass slipper, Disney, MIB............110.00
Cinderella, watch, WDP...............................25.00
Cisco Kid, ring, brass, 1950...........................25.00
Daddy Warbucks, nodder, bisque, Germany, 1930s, 3½", M....95.00
Daisy Duck, wrist watch, US Time, orig band G............150.00
Dale Evans, wrist watch, Ingraham Co, #55...............65.00
Dan Patch, bottle, shape of horseshoe w/DP, sulky & driver....35.00
Dan Patch, cloth pouch...............................10.00
Dan Patch, sheet music...............................30.00
Dan Patch, stop watch, 7 jewel........................750.00
Dan Patch, tobacco tin...............................28.00

Davy Crockett, belt, leather..................12.00
Davy Crockett, game, Tennessee-Alamo Radar, in box, 1955...15.00
Davy Crockett, gum card set, green, complete.............90.00
Davy Crockett, gum card set, orange, complete............65.00
Davy Crockett, holster set, MIB..................42.00
Davy Crockett, rubber figure, w/bear, boxed set, 1950s........30.00
Davy Crockett, signal siren flashlight, MIB..............30.00
Davy Crockett, tumblers, w/name, dates, scenes, 4", set of 8...28.00
Davy Crockett, wallet & western tie, in pkg, M, pr..........20.00
Davy Crockett, wrist watch, w/orig display box, Bradley........70.00
Dick Tracy, Aurora model kit....................25.00
Dick Tracy, badge pin-back, Detective Club, brass shield, 2"....14.00
Dick Tracy, Detective Set, orig box.................15.00
Dick Tracy, flashlight, 1940s....................20.00
Dick Tracy, pocket knife, 3", EX...................30.00
Dick Tracy, pop-up book, VG....................65.00
Dick Tracy, rubber stamp, 1930s..................20.00
Dick Tracy, suspender set.....................15.00
Dick Tracy, table lamp, chalk figural base, orig shade........250.00
Dick Tracy, target & gun, Marx, MIB................45.00
Dick Tracy, watch, metal band...................125.00
Dick Tracy, watch, MIB......................175.00
Dionne Quintuplets, ad for Quaker Oats chromium bowl, mailer.125.00
Dionne Quintuplets, bib type apron, Quints on stairs, sgn, 20"..50.00
Dionne Quintuplets, book, DQ Play Mother Goose, Dell 1938...35.00
Dionne Quintuplets, cake plate, Niagara Falls w/Quints, 12"....300.00
Dionne Quintuplets, calendar, 1937, 4x9"..............25.00
Dionne Quintuplets, calendar, 1953, M, in wrapper..........15.00
Dionne Quintuplets, cereal bowl, metal...............24.00
Dionne Quintuplets, fan, cardboard, playing in sand, 1936.....25.00
Dionne Quintuplets, fan, School Days, adv St Paul Milk.......16.50
Dionne Quintuplets, game, Can You Feed Quintuplets.........50.00
Dionne Quintuplets, handkerchief showing various activities....37.50
Dionne Quintuplets, photo, 8x10", w/Mdme Lebel autograph...35.00
Dionne Quintuplets, Pictorial Story of DQ, authorized, 1935....20.00
Dionne Quintuplets, playing cards, aqua w/Quints...........50.00
Dionne Quintuplets, porcelain Kewpies, MIB.............80.00
Dionne Quintuplets, set of dolls, NM................725.00
Dionne Quintuplets, soap dolls, in orig box.............110.00
Dionne Quintuplets, thermometer, cb, adv Hallett & Hallett.....50.00
Disney, book, School Days in Disneyville, 1939, VG..........15.00
Disney, book, Tortoise & Hair, 1935, 40 pgs, VG...........40.00
Disney, Delivery Wagon, Pluto drives tricycle w/cart, MIB.....295.00
Disney, Disneyland News, Vol 1/#1, July, 1955............25.00
Disney, Fantasia program, 28 pgs, 1940...............50.00
Disney, Official School Tablet, 1960................18.00
Disney, sand pail, Gulliver's Travels, 3"...............25.00
Disney, sand pail, Treasure Island.................55.00
Donald Duck, bank, as sailor by lifesaver, composition, 1938...125.00
Donald Duck, bisque figure, fishing.................50.00
Donald Duck, bisque figure, in military uniform, 3"..........85.00
Donald Duck, bisque figure, long bill, hand on shoulders, 3¼"..50.00
Donald Duck, bisque figure, long bill, hands on hips, 1¾".....50.00
Donald Duck, bisque figure, long bill, mk WD, Japan, 1935.....35.00
Donald Duck, bisque figure, pedals scooter, 3½"..........110.00
Donald Duck, camera.......................45.00
Donald Duck, charms, celluloid, pr.................15.00
Donald Duck, Coke bottle, 7 oz, 2 decals, 1950s...........20.00
Donald Duck, compo figure, windup, 12"..............525.00
Donald Duck, doll, cloth/oilskin, stuffed, 1930s, 14½".......485.00
Donald Duck, figure, hard rubber, Seiberling Co, 5".........95.00
Donald Duck, floating squeeze toy, DD in boat, Dell.........25.00
Donald Duck, hair brush, MIB...................85.00
Donald Duck, Home Movie, Hollywood, CA, c WDP, MIB.....15.00

Donald Duck, paint box, 1938...................20.00
Donald Duck, perfume bottle...................25.00
Donald Duck, puppet, papier mache, 9"..............60.00
Donald Duck, sand sifter, tin litho w/nephews/Pluto, '40s.......50.00
Donald Duck, sprinkler can, tin..................37.50
Donald Duck, Sunoco blotter, 1942, shows DD driving car......7.50
Donald Duck, Sunshine straws, box w/straws, 1950s.........15.00
Donald Duck, wallpaper border, 12 ft roll..............25.00
Dopey, figural, Castile Soap...................12.00
Dopey, valentine, mechanical; w/candle, 1938, NM..........15.00
Dr Kildare, nodder figure.....................20.00
Dr Seuss, Hanky Bird figure...................16.00
Dumbo, hand puppet, Disney...................12.50
Elvis Presley, billfold, w/color saddle, M..............100.00
Elvis Presley, hat w/tag, orig...................100.00
Elvis Presley, Life, 8/27/56, w/9 pg article: The Impact of EP....25.00
Elvis Presley, souvenir menu, Sahara Tahoe, 1970, 8½x11"......9.00
Felix the Cat, composition doll, large...............385.00
Felix the Cat, in cowboy outfit, 1920s, 14"............375.00
Felix the Cat, stuffed jointed doll, English, 1930s, 12".......135.00
Felix the Cat, wood jtd figure, Pat Sullivan, 1925, 4".........95.00
Ferdinand the Bull, bisque, mk Japan, 1939.............27.50
Ferdinand the Bull, book, linen-like, Whitman, 12 pgs, EX.....20.00
Fibber McGee & Molly, record set, complete............25.00
Flash Gordon, Jet Propelled Kite, orig box.............20.00
Flash Gordon, water pistol, MIB..................95.00
Frank Buck, sun watch pin....................35.00
G-Man, fingerprinting set, MIB..................20.00
Gene Autry, bicycle horn, metal, gun shaped............25.00
Gene Autry, book, punch-out figures................65.00
Gene Autry, cap pistol, EX....................37.00
Gene Autry, cowboy outfit, MIB.................125.00
Gene Autry, guitar, Emenee, plastic chord player & case.......65.00
Gene Autry, guitar, wood, orig carrying case............185.00
Gene Autry, rain boots......................65.00
Gene Autry, wrist watch, moving 6 gun, orig box.........225.00
Goldilocks, pop-up book, 1934..................75.00
Goofy, blotter, Sunoco, 1939...................15.00
Herb Shriner, harmonica, 1950s..................15.00
Hopalong Cassidy, alarm clock, US Time, blk metal.........80.00
Hopalong Cassidy, baby boots, w/picture, MIB...........75.00
Hopalong Cassidy, bedside matt, chenille, M............70.00
Hopalong Cassidy, book, hardbk, HC & 2 Young Cowboys, '51..12.50
Hopalong Cassidy, camera....................30.00
Hopalong Cassidy, coloring book, Abandoned Mine.........15.00
Hopalong Cassidy, cowboy outfit, for boy or girl, MIB, ea......85.00
Hopalong Cassidy, Dairylea milk bottle, 1 qt............35.00
Hopalong Cassidy, dental kit, M..................45.00
Hopalong Cassidy, ear muffs...................65.00
Hopalong Cassidy, Hair Trainer, M................45.00
Hopalong Cassidy, hat, M....................65.00
Hopalong Cassidy, horseshoe, plastic, M..............12.50
Hopalong Cassidy, lamp, Bar 20 Ranch, revolving cylinder, '49.115.00
Hopalong Cassidy, mug, glass, wht/gr...............8.00
Hopalong Cassidy, paper cups, 6 in package, 1950s.........12.50
Hopalong Cassidy, radio, Arvin, 1946, 5x8x4"...........130.00
Hopalong Cassidy, roller skates..................45.00
Hopalong Cassidy, television set #352, w/4 strips, in box......175.00
Hopalong Cassidy, waste can, simulated leather cover.........55.00
Hopalong Cassidy, watch, girl's, on saddle, MIB..........125.00
Hopalong Cassidy, watch, orig band, working............50.00
Howdy Doody, band, ceramic...................65.00
Howdy Doody, hot mug, Ovaltine premium, 1950s..........35.00
Howdy Doody, Palmolive cardboard premium figure.........15.00

Howdy Doody, puzzles, set of 3 in orig box, Milton Bradley.....10.00
Howdy Doody, sewing cards, 4 seasons, MIB.................25.00
Howdy Doody, T-shirt, VG...............................12.50
Howdy Doody, tumbler, Welch grape juice...................20.00
Ingatz Mouse, figure, wood jointed, 5½".....................45.00
Jack Armstrong, flashlight..............................25.00
Jack Armstrong, Hike-O-Meter, for Wheaties..............15.00
Jack Armstrong, Magic Answer Box, w/mailer, NM...........75.00
Jack Armstrong, Pedometer.............................15.00
Jack Armstrong, Shooting Plane, radio premium, orig box.....65.00
Jack Webb, game, Dragnet.............................15.00
James Bond, game, Message from M, in box, 1966...........95.00
James Bond, poster, 007 Goldfinger, 22x28"...............80.00
James Dean, necklace, 1955, rare.......................875.00
Jeff, button, mc pin-back, w/cigar/top hat, Hassan premium......5.00
Jiggs, chalk statue, HP, 1930s, 9".........................55.00
Jiggs, figurine, bisque, standing, Japan, 1930s, 3½", VG.......35.00
Jiminy Cricket, wood figure, jtd, 9".......................75.00
Kayo, cane head, china................................25.00
Li'l Abner, mixed up sqs picture puzzle on key chain, '50s......8.00
Lindbergh, pencil box, w/decals of plane & Lindy............40.00
Lindbergh, plane erector set, sgn........................30.00
Lone Ranger, chalk statue, 15", 1940s....................55.00
Lone Ranger, coloring contest entry picture, uncolored, 1950...12.00
Lone Ranger, flashlight, MIB............................40.00
Lone Ranger, knife, silver bullet on side/LR Hi-Ho Silver, '47...55.00
Lone Ranger, pedometer...............................20.00
Lone Ranger, pencil box, gr cardboard, gold horse/rider relief..28.50
Lone Ranger, puzzle, Guarding Gold Panners..............22.50
Lone Ranger, ring w/film..............................50.00
Lone Ranger, scarf mask, LR & horse ea end...............29.00
Lone Ranger, siren/flashlight...........................22.50
Lone Ranger, toothbrush holder, 1938...................20.00
Lone Ranger & Silver, Hartland Figures, MIB..............75.00
Lone Ranger & Silver, Lucky Horseshoe..................12.50
Maggie & Jiggs, shakers, china, pr......................45.00
Marilyn Monroe, calendar, salesman's sample.............100.00
Marilyn Monroe, tip tray..............................19.00
Marilyn Monroe, 2 decks of cards+4 tip trays, orig velvet box.145.00
Mickey, Donald & Goofy, band concert, bisque, M..........100.00
Mickey, Donald & Goofy, music box, bisque, 1967..........400.00
Mickey, Minnie & Pluto, bank, metal canister, 1930s........125.00
Mickey & Donald, Merry Christmas, 1948 Firestone giveaway...300.00
Mickey & Goofy, music box, bisque, 1976................350.00
Mickey & Minnie Mouse, bisque figures, 2¾", pr...........95.00
Mickey & Minnie Mouse, celluloid figures, 1930s, 3½", pr.....115.00
Mickey & Minnie Mouse, dolls, McCall pattern, pr..........300.00
Mickey & Minnie Mouse, handkerchief...................12.00
Mickey & Minnie Mouse, Inkograph pen & pencil set, WDP....150.00
Mickey & Minnie Mouse, Knickerbocker, papier mache shoes.1,100.00
Mickey & Minnie Mouse, on party horn by Marx Bros.........45.00
Mickey & Minnie Mouse, pencil box, w/drawer, 8½x5¼"......150.00
Mickey & Minnie Mouse, pin-back, Yoo-Hoo, dtd 1930, 3½"....45.00
Mickey & Pluto, bisque figure, MM riding P, 2¼", EX.........75.00
Mickey Mouse, acrobat, wood squeeze toy.................35.00
Mickey Mouse, alarm clock, Bradley.....................40.00
Mickey Mouse, alarm clock, head moves, arms point, Ingersoll..290.00
Mickey Mouse, bank, plastic, WDP/Play Pal Plastics, 12".......8.00
Mickey Mouse, bisque figure, in hat w/cane, 4¼", EX.........75.00
Mickey Mouse, bisque figure, playing sax, minor pnt wear, 3¼"..30.00
Mickey Mouse, blackboard, 1939........................38.00
Mickey Mouse, book, Alphabet Book, 1936................65.00
Mickey Mouse, book, MM & Friends, linen, Disney Ent, 1936...35.00
Mickey Mouse, book, MM Crusoe, 1938..................65.00

Mickey Mouse, book, MM Never Fails, 1939................55.00
Mickey Mouse, book, MM Sees USA, 138 pgs, 1944..........15.00
Mickey Mouse, book, MM Stories, #2, McKay, 1934..........75.00
Mickey Mouse, book, The Adventures of, #1, McKay, 1931, NM475.00
Mickey Mouse, bookends, pnt, CI, WDP, EX................25.00
Mickey Mouse, booklets, 3-D, set of 6 w/glasses, 1953.........75.00
Mickey Mouse, brush, child's; sterling, 1940s...............50.00
Mickey Mouse, camera, figural head, WDP, Child Guidance.....35.00
Mickey Mouse, carnival chalk figure, 1930s, 9¾"............95.00
Mickey Mouse, celluloid windup, w/whirling umbrella.........450.00
Mickey Mouse, comic book, Wheaties, Magic Mtn, 1951.......10.00
Mickey Mouse, corn popper, 1930s, rare..................185.00
Mickey Mouse, doll, cloth w/felt clothes, weighted shoes, 12½".525.00
Mickey Mouse, doll, Steiff, 11".........................375.00
Mickey Mouse, figure, hard rubber, Seiberling Co, 6½".......125.00
Mickey Mouse, figure, wood, jointed, mk Micky on front, 4½"...95.00
Mickey Mouse, game, cloth, pin on tail, uncut in box, 1930s...170.00
Mickey Mouse, gum cards, By Gum, Inc, #26, M.............12.00
Mickey Mouse, hanky w/paper label......................28.00
Mickey Mouse, house, cardboard, in orig envelope, 30".......250.00
Mickey Mouse, jam jar, metal screw top w/coin slit, emb........80.00
Mickey Mouse, map, enterprise, w/stamp..................145.00
Mickey Mouse, marionette, WDP, 1930s, MIB..............75.00
Mickey Mouse, Mickey Mouseketooner....................35.00
Mickey Mouse, MM Newsreel w/sound, 3 records, 6 slides, 1956.65.00
Mickey Mouse, night light, battery op.....................95.00
Mickey Mouse, pencil, mechanical, w/head of Mickey..........55.00
Mickey Mouse, pencil box, early, red.....................38.00
Mickey Mouse, pencil holder figural, by Dixon, Disney pat.....125.00
Mickey Mouse, penny book, At Carnival, Whitman, 1934, 40 pgs.15.00
Mickey Mouse, penny book, Wins Race, Whitman, 1934, 40 pgs.15.00
Mickey Mouse, pin, globetrotter, Eat Freihofer's Perfect Loaf....35.00
Mickey Mouse, pin-back button, Emerson Radio.............65.00
Mickey Mouse, pocket watch, Ingersoll, fob/mice on 2nd hand..350.00
Mickey Mouse, pop-up book, Babes In Woods, '33, EX........120.00
Mickey Mouse, pop-up book, 1933, M.....................175.00
Mickey Mouse, porringer, SP...........................85.00
Mickey Mouse, race car, tin windup, in orig box............225.00
Mickey Mouse, radio, 4 figures w/instruments in relief, M.....2,500.00

Mickey and Minnie Mouse, pie-eyed; cloth, composition, and wood shoes, ca 1930s, 11", $195.00 for the pair.

Mickey Mouse, ring, sterling, 1930s........................300.00
Mickey Mouse, sand sifter w/tools, metal.....................95.00
Mickey Mouse, spoon, by Post-O cereal......................25.00
Mickey Mouse, squeeze toy, Mickey as acrobat...............35.00
Mickey Mouse, telephone, 1930s............................225.00
Mickey Mouse, Tool Chest, w/Pluto & camping scenes, 1936....80.00
Mickey Mouse, toothbrush holder, bisque, lg head, arms move..250.00
Mickey Mouse, toy chest, 1930s............................150.00
Mickey Mouse, typewriter, Mouseketeer, w/box...............80.00
Mickey Mouse, umbrella, celluloid, full figure on hdl.........150.00
Mickey Mouse, wallpaper border, 12 ft roll...................25.00
Mickey Mouse, Wilbur Chocolate Bar, M.....................90.00
Mickey Mouse, wrapping paper sheet........................40.00
Mickey Mouse, wrist watch, Ingersoll.......................200.00
Mickey Mouse, wrist watch, Timex electric, 1970............100.00
Minnie Mouse, bisque figure, in hat w/umbrella, 4½", EX......75.00
Minnie Mouse, bisque figure, plays accordian, 3¼", EX.......30.00
Minnie Mouse, bisque figure, red ruffle top/hat, 1st aid kit......65.00
Minnie Mouse, cane head, china.............................30.00
Minnie Mouse, doll, English, Deans Rag Book Co, 1930s, 7"...350.00
Minnie Mouse, Halloween costume..........................125.00
Minnie Mouse, marionette, hi-heel papier mache shoes, 12"....100.00
Minnie Mouse, stuffed doll, compo shoes, 1930s, 12"........200.00
Minnie Mouse, toothbrush holder, lg head/arms move, 5"......250.00
Moon Mullins, wood figure, jtd, 5½".........................80.00
Mortimer Snerd, hair growing figure.........................25.00
Mutt & Jeff, Mutt cigarette lighter, head removes.............35.00
Mutt & Jeff, still bank....................................110.00
Olive Oyl, wood figure, jtd, 5".............................50.00
Orphan Annie, book, pop-up................................75.00
Orphan Annie, doll, segmented wood, 5".....................55.00
Orphan Annie, figurine, bisque, standing, Japan, 3½".........35.00
Orphan Annie, manual w/mailer, 1934.......................35.00
Orphan Annie, nodder, bisque, Germany, 1930s, 3½".........75.00
Orphan Annie, radio, decoder, brass pin-back, 1937, 2".......30.00
Orphan Annie, stove......................................40.00
Orphan Annie, toothbrush holder, bisque.....................65.00
Orphan Annie & Sandy, ash tray, lustre ware................100.00
Orphan Annie & Sandy, wall pocket, china...................125.00
Our Gang, plaster mold set, orig box........................250.00
Peanuts, watch, cartoon animated, 1958......................35.00
Peter Rabbit, bank..45.00
Peter Rabbit, candy pail, oval..............................55.00
Peter Rabbit, fork, brass, rabbit/watering can/alphabet.......140.00
Peter Rabbit, highchair tray...............................150.00
Peter Rabbit, lunch tin, Kandies for the Kiddies, 4x6".........65.00
Peter Rabbit, peanut butter pail............................90.00
Peter Rabbit, ruler.......................................100.00
Peter Rabbit, tin plate, Radio Party........................80.00
Phineas T Bluster, puppet, plastic, 4½".......................8.00
Pinocchio, bank, composition, Crown Co, 1940................75.00
Pinocchio, book, giveaway from Coco Malt, 1939, 8½x11", VG..20.00
Pinocchio, book, 1939, 9x14"..............................55.00
Pinocchio, lunch pail, rnd tin w/characters, 1940.............50.00
Pinocchio, mask, Gillette giveaway, 5 story character masks.....75.00
Pinocchio, Merry Puppet Game, orig box, 10x22".............75.00
Pinocchio, paint book, story of Pinocchio, 1939, NM..........40.00
Pinocchio, postcards, French, w/scenes from movie, set of 24...150.00
Pinocchio, soap figure, in box, 1939........................25.00
Pinocchio, writing paper, 1939.............................30.00
Pluto, bisque figure, sitting w/head forward, 2¾", EX.........50.00
Pluto, book, Story of Pluto the Pup, 1938, Whitman...........35.00
Pluto, pencil sharpener, celluloid...........................20.00
Pluto, wood figure, 1930s, 3".............................60.00

Pluto, wood jointed figure, 6".............................85.00
Popeye, Big Big Book, Thimble Theatre, 1935................55.00
Popeye, blocks, cylindrical, nesting.........................85.00
Popeye, cereal bowl, 1935.................................45.00
Popeye, checkers...35.00
Popeye, Christmas light shades, orig box, 1929...............55.00
Popeye, crayons...8.00
Popeye, door stop, CI, King Features, 1929, 9", EX..........550.00
Popeye, figure, rubber, 1940s, Cameo KFS, 13½"............125.00
Popeye, handkerchief, allover picture........................22.00
Popeye, Intelligence Test, cased glass puzzle, 5x3½".........15.00
Popeye, Magic Playground.................................55.00
Popeye, mechanical pencil, Eagle, dtd 1929, 11", MIB........25.00
Popeye, mirror, metal, EX 2½" decal, early, VG overall.......45.00
Popeye, Paint-O-Graf, lg..................................75.00
Popeye, picture puzzles, 4 in orig box, 1932.................65.00
Popeye, picture record, 1948..............................25.00
Popeye, pistol, KFS, 1929, MIB...........................120.00
Popeye, playing cards, orig box, 1934.......................35.00
Popeye, pocket knife, advertising, w/Popeye.................60.00
Popeye, sand pail, Popeye at the Beach, tin, lg...............65.00
Popeye, sparkler, 1930s, good working condition.............175.00
Popeye, target game, in orig box...........................28.00
Popeye, target sign, w/Popeye & friends, 1936, 23x14"......120.00
Popeye, wood jtd figure, 'Poppy Memorial Day' label..........68.00
Popeye, wood jtd figure, Chein Co, 1930s, 11".............325.00
Popeye, wood jtd figure, 1930s, 5½".......................65.00
Popeye, wood jtd figure on blocks, 1940, 6".................75.00
Popeye & Sweetpea, clock, animated, in box................275.00
Porky Pig, bank, bisque, 4½".............................135.00
Porky Pig, wrist watch, MIB..............................175.00
Red Rider, Good Luck token, brass coin, JC Penny, '42........6.50
Red Rider, target game, orig box...........................10.00
Red Riding Hood, bisque figure, w/wolf, 6", M...............65.00
Red Riding Hood, pop-up book, 1934.......................18.00
Red Riding Hood, spoon & wolf fork, sterling, European......100.00
Red Riding Hood, 7½" bowl, 7¾" plate, US Zone Germany....45.00
Rin-Tin-Tin, book, Little Folks Story of RTT, Whitman, 1927...35.00
Rin-Tin-Tin, game, Transogram, 1955.......................15.00
Roy Rogers, belt & guns, fancy dbl holsters..................35.00
Roy Rogers, book, Golden Book, 1953.......................18.00
Roy Rogers, book, My Favorite Christmas Story, by RR, 1960...10.00
Roy Rogers, boot, metal w/copper finish, horseshoe base, 5¾"..26.00
Roy Rogers, branding iron ring w/orig Quaker Oat box ad......55.00
Roy Rogers, button, photo on yellow, pin-back, 1¼"...........3.00
Roy Rogers, cartridge belt, leather/38 chrome buttons, 40" L...30.00
Roy Rogers, harmonica, metal/plastic, 'Roy Rogers Riders', NM..18.00
Roy Rogers, horseshoe set, MIB...........................28.00
Roy Rogers, lantern, Ohio Art, battery op....................30.00
Roy Rogers, neckerchief slide..............................25.00
Roy Rogers, pajamas, child's...............................30.00
Roy Rogers, raincoat.....................................100.00
Roy Rogers, ring, magnifier, premium, ca 1949, EX...........19.95
Roy Rogers, Rodeo Ranch, M..............................45.00
Roy Rogers, toby mug, King o/t Cowboys/plastic, Quaker Oats...15.00
Roy Rogers, View Master reel, Holdup, 1953.................10.00
Roy Rogers, wrist watch, Ingrahm, orig expansion band........65.00
Roy Rogers & Dale Evans, Double R Bar Ranch, thermos/cork..15.00
Roy Rogers & Trigger, figure & horse........................50.00
Scrappy, compo head/hands/ft, stuffed body, orig clothes, 14"..450.00
Seven Dwarfs, books, Whitman, story of ea, 24 pgs, 7 book set.350.00
Sgt Preston, Totem Pole set, orig papers....................60.00
Shirley Temple, book, Birthday Book, 1935, #1735...........60.00
Shirley Temple, book, Christmas Book, 1937, #1770..........65.00

Shirley Temple, book, Drawing & Coloring; #1724...........45.00
Shirley Temple, book, Fairyland, 1958....................12.00
Shirley Temple, book, Films of ST, Windeler, 1978..........15.00
Shirley Temple, book, How I Raised ST, 1935...............25.00
Shirley Temple, book, Little Miss Broadway, M...............25.00
Shirley Temple, book, Poor Little Rich Girl, #1723, EX.......25.00
Shirley Temple, book, Sing w/ST, 1935....................45.00
Shirley Temple, book, ST's Favorite Songs, 1937...........45.00
Shirley Temple, book, Stowaway........................22.00
Shirley Temple, book, This Is My Crayon Book, 1935, #1711...45.00
Shirley Temple, books, Five Books About Me, in orig box, EX..85.00
Shirley Temple, bowl, cobalt w/wht picture, glass, EX.........47.50
Shirley Temple, creamer, cobalt w/wht picture, glass...........35.00
Shirley Temple, doll trunk.............................45.00
Shirley Temple, dress, Cinderella, pk, M..................40.00
Shirley Temple, embroidery set........................30.00
Shirley Temple, figural soap bar, 5"......................75.00
Shirley Temple, figurine, salt glaze, pink..................15.00
Shirley Temple, figurine, salt glaze, wht/silver trim, 4½".......15.00
Shirley Temple, full page ad, Quaker Puffed Wheat...........10.00
Shirley Temple, hat, red, orig tag.......................50.00
Shirley Temple, Magnetic TV Theatre, 1950s.............125.00
Shirley Temple, mirror, w/photo on pink, dtd 1935, 1¾".......55.00
Shirley Temple, mug, cobalt w/wht picture, glass, EX.........52.00
Shirley Temple, photo, color giveaway, 8x10"..............13.00
Shirley Temple, pin, doll.............................35.00
Shirley Temple, pin-back, sgn, Genuine ST Doll, Ideal, 1¼"....45.00
Shirley Temple, pitcher, cobalt w/wht picture, glass, EX........37.00
Shirley Temple, playing cards, dbl deck, in box, US PC Co....100.00
Shirley Temple, poster, Stowaway, ST in Chinese outfit, 18x24".10.00
Shirley Temple, purse w/ivory dog, tagged inside, w/picture.....125.00
Shirley Temple, ring, child's; sterling w/picture of ST.........150.00
Shirley Temple, scrapbook, authorized ed #1714, unused.......20.00
Shirley Temple, sheet music, On Good Ship Lollipop..........16.00
Shirley Temple, stick pin, gold filled.....................20.00
Shirley Temple, tablet cover, holds 2 dolls, 1930s............10.00
Skeezix, figurine, bisque, standing, Japan, 1930s, 3¾", M.....35.00
Skeezix, nodder, bisque, Germany, 1930s, 2¾", M...........75.00
Skeezix, toothbrush holder, tin, Listerine, 6", EX............35.00
Sky King, Spy Detecto Writer..........................47.00
Sky King, TV ring...................................25.00
Smitty, figurine, bisque, standing, Japan, 1930s, 3½", NM....35.00
Smitty, nodder, bisque, Germany, 1930s, 3½", VG............50.00
Snow White, pencil shapener, celluloid, WDP...............25.00
Snow White, sheet music, Whistle While You Work, 1937, M...15.00
Snow White, song book, 50 illus pgs, songs from movie, 1938..50.00
Snow White, watch.................................25.00
Snow White & 7 Dwarfs, bisque, 3½", 2½", Japan, MIB.....200.00
Snow White & 7 Dwarfs, book, linen-like, McKay, 1938, EX...30.00
Snow White & 7 Dwarfs, bracelet, Brier Mfg, 1938, EX.......20.00
Snow White & 7 Dwarfs, cereal bowl, milk glass, 1938........20.00
Snow White & 7 Dwarfs, charm bracelet, 8 figures, 1938, EX...50.00
Snow White & 7 Dwarfs, game, orig box, 10x22"...........75.00
Snow White & 7 Dwarfs, picture plaque, Snow White........10.00
Snow White & 7 Dwarfs, premium stamp, Armour, M.........50.00
Snow White & 7 Dwarfs, rubber figures, 2½", set............42.00
Snow White & 7 Dwarfs, rug, 1930s, 40x22", EX...........30.00
Snow White & 7 Dwarfs, sand pail, 1930s, 4".............45.00
Snow White & 7 Dwarfs, Sleepy mechanical valentine.........15.00
Soupy Sales, marionette, rubber face/compo body, 1966, 12"...25.00
Sparkle Plenty, soap figure, MIB.......................45.00
Spike Jones, Sax-o-Fun, orig box.......................40.00
Spiro Agnew, watch.................................65.00
Straight Arrow, handkerchief, Natn'l Biscuit Co, 1949..........55.00

Straight Arrow, ring..................................25.00
Superman, alarm clock, animated, 1940.................550.00
Superman, club membership certificate, decoder, letter, M.....30.00
Superman, coloring book, 1955........................20.00
Superman, Crusader ring, NM.........................125.00
Superman, figure, flying, orig card......................20.00
Superman, film viewer, w/3 films, orig box, 1946............25.00
Superman, kiddie swim fins, official, MIB..................25.00
Superman, picture set, Touch of Velvet, in box, 1966.........10.00
Superman, wood jtd figure, Ideal, 1940s, 13"..............345.00
Tarzan, book, Tarzan o/t Apes, Burroughs, McClurg, 1st ed..4,500.00
Tarzan, movie jigsaw puzzle, Pippins cigars premium, M.......35.00
Three Little Pigs, ash tray, figural......................75.00
Three Little Pigs, bisque figure, 1, plays violin on stump, 3"....30.00
Three Little Pigs, plate, divided, wht china, WDE, 8"..........75.00
Three Little Pigs, toothbrush holder, bisque, laying bricks......45.00
Three Little Pigs, toothbrush holder, bisque, playing piano.....75.00
Three Little Wolves, book, linen, 1937, 10x15"..............67.00
Tom Corbett, Automic Pistol flashlight...................95.00
Tom Corbett, binoculars.............................20.00
Tom Corbett, space cadet signal siren flashlight, 6½".........35.00
Tom Mix, compass..................................20.00
Tom Mix, Golden Tone Birdcall.........................20.00
Tom Mix, magnet ring...............................25.00
Tom Mix, movie, paper film, Rustler's Roundup, in Ralston box.75.00
Tom Mix, paint book, 1935, unused.....................90.00
Tom Mix, periscope.................................80.00
Tom Mix, ring, sliding whistle..........................25.00
Tom Mix, Secret Writing Manual.......................20.00
Tom Mix, siren badge, Dobie County....................25.00
Tom Mix, song book, Tom on cover, picture centerfold, 1935...35.00
Tom Mix, 6 gun decoder badge.........................28.00
Uncle Bim, figurine, bisque, standing, Japan, 1930s, 4", M.....40.00
Uncle Bim, nodder, bisque, Germany, 1930s, 4", NM.........75.00
Uncle Walt & Skeezix, toothbrush holder, bisque, 1930s.......75.00
Uncle Wiggily, bowl, Find the Bottom, Ralston Co...........45.00
Uncle Willie & Emmie, toothbrush holder, bisque, 1930s.......75.00
Wild Bill Hickock, badge..............................15.00
Wild Bill Hickock, cap pistol, EX.......................28.00
Will Rogers, Wiley Post, lamp, no shade..................65.00
Wimpy, wood figure, jtd, 4"...........................45.00
Woody Woodpecker, alarm clock, animated, Wood's Cafe......175.00
Woody Woodpecker, drawing set, 1959...................10.00
Wyatt Earp, marshal's outfit, in box, 1950s................35.00
Yellow Kid, button, cigarette..........................12.00
Yellow Kid, gum card, Adams Co, 1896, 1½x4"............38.00
Yellow Kid, paper doll, 1896, 6".......................25.00
Yellow Kid, pin-back, #6.............................35.00
Yellow Kid, pin-back, I Am Goin Ter Paint NY Red, #15, 1¼"..30.00

Orphan Annie bisque nodder,
with Sandy, 2½", $125.00.

Yellow Kid, pin-back, Wot Do Ye Tink of Me Suit, 1¼"......30.00
Yellow Kid, postcard, 1910 calendar & hardware advertising, M..96.00
Yellow Kid, tobacco cutter, 1890s, VG....................2,000.00
Yellow Kid, toy cart, CI/metal goat drawn, pnt VG, 8".......385.00
Yellow Kid & Buster Brown, postcard, Outcault lecture souvenir. 97.50

Peters and Reed

John Peters and Adam Reed founded their pottery in Zanesville, Ohio, just before the turn of the century, using the local red clay to produce a variety of wares.

Moss Aztec, introduced about 1912, has an unglazed exterior with designs molded in high relief, and the recesses highlighted with a green wash. Only the interior is glazed to hold water. Pereco, named for Peters, Reed and Company, is glazed in semi-matt blue, maroon, or cream. Orange was also used very early, but such examples are rare. Shapes are simple with in-mold decoration, sometimes borrowed from the Moss Aztec line.

Wilse Blue is a line of high gloss medium blue with dark specks on simple shapes. Landsun, characterized by its soft matt multicolor or blue and gray combinations, is decorated either by dripping or by hand brushing, in an effect sometimes called Flame or Herringbone. Chromal, in much the same colors as Landsun, may be decorated with a realistic scenic, or the swirling application of colors may merely suggest one.

Shadow ware is a glossy, multicolor drip over a harmonious base color. When the base is black, the effect is often iridescent.

Perhaps the most desirable line is the brown high glaze art ware with the 'sprigged' type designs. Although research has uncovered no positive proof, it is generally accepted as having been made by Peters and Reed. It is interesting to note that many of the artistic shapes in this line are recognizable as those made by Weller, Roseville, and other Zanesville area companies.

Other lines include Mirror Black, Persian, and an unidentified line which collectors call Mottled Colors. In this high gloss line, the red clay body often shows through the splashed-on multicolors.

In 1922, the company became known as the Zane Pottery. Peters and Reed retired, and Harry McClelland became president. Charles Chilcote designed new lines, and production of many of the old lines continued. The body of the ware after 1922 was light in color.

Marks include the impressed logo or ink stamp 'Zaneware' in a rectangle.

Vase, Chromal, impressionistic landscape in brown, blue, yellow, and green, 5½", $175.00.

Chromal

Vase, scenic, EX color, slightly concave sides, 5¾x4¾".......130.00
Vase, scenic house/trees/etc, 8x7"........................200.00
Vase, scenic w/browns & blues, thick collar/full body, 8".......200.00

High Glaze Brown Ware

Jug, bl grapes at shoulder, 7½"............................75.00
Jug, ear of corn decor, 7"................................285.00
Jug, grapes & leaves in relief, ball shape, 6¼"..............75.00
Pitcher, tankard; grapes & leaves relief, 12"..............150.00
Vase, Aladdin lamp, dbl loop hdls, garlands on shoulder, 5x8".100.00
Vase, sprigged floral, 10"..................................60.00
Vase, wreath w/cherubs decor, 12½".........................75.00

Landsun

Bowl, 3" dia...20.00
Bud vase, gr/bl/br, 10¼"...................................55.00
Vase, tan/bl/gr, mk Zaneware, 3¾"..........................20.00
Vase, 10½"...40.00

Marbleized

Ginger jar, multicolored, 6x4" dia........................100.00
Vase, multicolored, flared lip, 7".........................65.00

Moss Aztec

Bowl, pine cones, sgn Ferrell, 6¼" dia.....................50.00
Bud vase, tapered, 10x3½"..................................40.00
Console bowl, flowers, 3½x8"...............................28.00
Cuspidor, flowers...58.00
Hanging basket, basketweave, w/chains......................40.00
Hanging basket, flowers, w/chains..........................25.00
Hanging basket, sm..15.00
Jardiniere, pine cones....................................50.00
Jardiniere, roses, 10x12".................................75.00
Jardiniere, women in allover relief, 9"...................65.00
Umbrella stand, flowers, sgn Ferrell, 17".................150.00
Vase, flowers, sgn Ferrell, 6¾"...........................45.00
Vase, flowers, 6"...35.00
Vase, flowers & acorns, 8"................................40.00
Vase, flowers & berries, 12"..............................65.00
Vase, pansy decor, #412...................................18.00
Vase, pine cones, 10".....................................55.00
Wall pocket, dk red/gr branches, 8¼"......................50.00
Wall pocket, flowers & berries, sgn Ferrell, 10"..........70.00
Wall pocket, grapes, sgn Ferrell, 8"......................55.00
Window box, Homer w/nudes, sgn Ferrell, 13" L.............125.00

Pereco

Bowl, #612..20.00
Bowl, #9, 3½x8"...30.00
Bowl, butterfly decor, green, 5"..........................20.00
Bowl, gr w/bronze tones, nailhead decor recessed band, 4¾"....30.00
Bowl, lattice w/flower band at top, 4¾"...................25.00
Vase, green, 11½"...20.00

Shadow Ware

Ginger jar, gr/blk, w/lid, 6"..............................90.00

Vase, bl/br drip over tan, 9"............................75.00

Miscellaneous

Bud vase, double; wht w/HP floral decor, mk Zane............35.00
Vase, gr/bl glaze, tube neck/wide shoulder/full body, 8"........50.00

Pewabic

The Pewabic Pottery was formally established in Detroit, Michigan, in 1907, by Mary Chase Perry Stratton and Horace James Caulkins. The two had worked together since 1903, firing their ware in a small kiln Caulkins had designed especially for use by the dental trade. Always a small operation which relied upon basic equipment and the skill of the workers, they took pride in being commissioned for several important architectural tile installations.

Some of the early art ware was glazed a simple matt green; occasionally other colors were added, sometimes in combination, one over the other in a drip effect. Later, Stratton developed a lustrous crystalline glaze.

The body of the ware was highly fired and extremely hard. Shapes were basic, and decorative modeling, if used at all, was in low relief. Mary Stratton kept the pottery open until her death in 1961. In 1968, it was purchased and reopened by the Michigan State University.

Several marks were used over the years: a triangle with 'Revelation Pottery' (for a short time only), 'Pewabic' with five maple leaves, and the impressed circle mark.

Ash tray, turq over yel-gr high glaze.......................125.00
Bottle vase, gold lustre over turq, 2¾".....................150.00
Bowl, irid, lava glaze, 4x6½".............................400.00
Bowl, undulating lines & balls at rim, br matt, early, 2x4¾"...250.00
Bowl vase, bl runs on yel-gr, high lustre, 4x5½"............335.00
Dish, burgandy irid w/in, gr/gold w/out, triangular, 4".......70.00
Tile, bl florals on wht, 3"................................85.00
Tile, bl w/tan rabbit, 3".................................125.00
Tile, red, bird of paradise, lustre glaze, 3" sq..............95.00
Tile, red, horseshoe crab, lustre glaze.....................95.00
Tile, red, seahorse, lustre glaze, 3"......................95.00
Vase, bl w/some crystals, angle shoulder, script sgn, 3½x5½"..300.00
Vase, gr irid, sgn Pewabic, Detroit, 5x4½".................350.00
Vase, high lustre copper, 2¼x2¾".........................140.00
Vase, irid, bulbous, 7x7"................................395.00
Vase, irid gr, ribbed, metalic encrusted shoulders, label, 22"..2,500.00
Vase, lavender irid lava, sgn/paper label, 2x3½"............200.00

Pitcher, flat black glaze, 3", $100.00.

Vase, lustrous bl-gr w/gold hi-lites, 10¾"..................495.00
Vase, metallic bl lustre, hand thrown, angle shoulder, 7"......375.00
Vase, metallic bl lustre, squat/bulbous, 1910, 3x3½".........110.00
Vase, metallic glaze, mk AA, 1923, 3¾x5½"................180.00
Vase, mottled royal bl, high lustre, ball shape, 4½".........335.00
Vase, peacock bl w/red/gr splotches on dk gray, 3¼".........180.00
Vase, pink/lav/gr irid, sm top/angle shoulder, 6½", VG.......280.00
Vase, thick bl glaze, squat pear form, early mk, 4¾".........265.00

Pewter

Pewter is a metal alloy of tin combined with small amounts of lead, copper, or brass. It has been used since the days of Ancient Rome, and was imported to this country from England by the American Colonists. Much of the Colonial pewter was melted during the American Revolution to make bullets, which accounts to some extent for the scarcity of examples from this period. Production of pewter in the United States reached its peak after the Revolution.

Basin, American, no mk, cleaned/polished, 2x8"..............90.00
Basin, angel touch mk, Johann Georg Klingling, 1785, 2½x12".165.00
Basin, phoenix touch mk, 2¼x9¼".........................55.00
Basin, Townsend, London, 3½x13".........................175.00
Beaker, minor battering, rpr, 2¾".........................47.00
Bottle, threaded cap w/ring hdl, 3¼x11½"..................55.00
Bowl, bleeding; indistinct mks, battered/cleaned/polished, 11"...85.00
Bowl, Continental touch mk, side hdls, 3¾x11¾"............85.00
Bowl, footed, out-folded rim, EX patina, early 1800s, 2½x5"...165.00
Bowl, Fr touch mks on rim, hammered, 12¼"................45.00
Bowl, ftd, no mk, 4½x5"..................................55.00
Bowl, Liberty Tudric, bl enamel insert, 11x8"...............185.00
Bowl, phoenix touch mk, w/1845, 1¼x8½"..................35.00
Bowl, S Rothhan, Fien Zinn, lg open rim hdls, 9½"...........45.00
Bowl, 3x10½"...50.00
Box, hinged lid, mk Best Britannia Metal, ¾x3½x5".........20.00
Candlestick, Cincinnati, no mk, 10"........................175.00
Candlestick, Cincinnati, w/push-up, 9½"....................95.00
Candlestick, crown mk w/1709/crown/WH, mid drip, 7½", pr...850.00
Candlestick, Rosewell Gleason, cup removes, 8½", pr.........360.00
Candlestick, uniformed guard figural, X hammer insignia, 9½"...35.00
Candlestick, w/push-up, rope twist trim, 9½", pr............230.00
Candlestick, weighted base, push-up, 6½", pr...............145.00
Castor frame, touch mk R Dunham, no bottles, 9"............155.00
Chalice, communion; att Boardman, worn SP, 7"..............125.00
Chalice, communion; att Boardman, 4¾", pr................230.00
Chalice, communion; worn SP, 7"...........................125.00
Chalice, hand chased, American, 1700s......................275.00
Chalice, minor battering, 5½", pr..........................150.00
Chalice, Reed & Barton, 7", pr............................190.00
Chamber pot, cleaned & polished, 4x8½"...................40.00
Charger, American, no mk, minor wear, 11½"................155.00
Charger, angel touch w/RA, worn/sm splits, polished, 15".....95.00
Charger, crowned rose touch mk, rpr, 15"...................135.00
Charger, crowned rose touch mk, worn, 13¾"................125.00
Charger, Edgar Curtis & Co, sm rpr, 12⅛"..................135.00
Charger, English touch mk, 'London', slightly battered, 12¼"..125.00
Charger, English touch mk, hammered, rim split, 20".........365.00
Charger, good touch mks w/London/antelope/RB, polished, 15".155.00
Charger, oval touch mks, rpr split, 15" dia..................75.00
Charger, phoenix touch mk, rim engraved AMR, 1853, 11¾"...70.00
Charger, rose touch mk, worn/slightly battered, 12".........100.00
Charger, rpr, worn, 14"...................................115.00
Charger, rpr split, bk corroded, worn, 15" dia..............145.00

Charger, Samuel Hamlin, sm split in rim, 15″ dia............425.00
Charger, scalloped, knife scratches, 11½″...................95.00
Charger, Tietje Schweidnity, eng foliage/X cannon/1817, 13″...135.00
Charger, Townsend & Compton, 13¼″ dia.................165.00
Charger, 2 oval touch mks w/'1805 & Froesler'..............65.00
Coffee pot, L Reed & Barton, ftd, paneled w/wood hdl, 10″.....90.00
Coffee pot, octagonal gourd, scrolled hdl, ftd, 13¼″.........100.00
Coffee pot, pear form, lion touch mk, Boardman, rpr, 11″.....125.00
Coffee pot, R Gleason, tip of spout slightly battered, 12½″....260.00
Creamer, Dixon & Son, hinged lid, minor hdl damage, 5″......40.00
Creamer, ear hdl, soldered rpr, 5″.........................75.00
Desk set, English mk, 2 wells w/inserts, lids & caps, 6x9″.....150.00
Flagon, acorn thumb piece, 5½″...........................25.00
Flagon, communion; att Boardman, EX hdl, 10¼″..........150.00
Flagon, communion; no mk, 13¾″..........................75.00
Flagon, communion; SP, mk Reed & Barton, 14½″..........55.00
Flagon, communion; Waters & Thorp, incomplete finial, 12½″.225.00
Flagon, communion; Waters & Thorp, sm hole/damage, 12½″..150.00
Flagon, engraved rigglework of leaves & LV 1803, finial, 11″...238.00
Flagon, engraved rigglework of leaves/flowers, JAD 1795, 12″..332.00
Flagon, European, hexagonal, simple florals/hearts, 13″......175.00
Flagon, European, 11″, pr, G.............................170.00
Flagon, German, heart motif engraving, scroll hdl, 1763, 15½″.660.00
Flagon, no mk, cast interior rose center of base, polished, 9″..85.00
Flagon, Reed & Barton, 10¼″.............................250.00
Flagon, well shaped hdl, 10¼″............................150.00
Footwarmer, sgn H Heinord.............................325.00
Fork, 6¾″, set of 4.....................................35.00
Funnel, no mk, 5½x4½″..................................45.00
Funnel, wine; removable strainer, slightly battered, 8¼″......135.00
Grape scissors, butterfly hinge, shell atop ea hdl, 1880, 6½″...75.00
Hot water dish, Samuel Cocks, w/bl transfer plate, 10″.......140.00
Inkwell, wide flat base, ceramic insert, quill holes, 3x9″......115.00
Jar, American, hinged lid, cast flower finial, 4½″............75.00
Ladle, crowned rose touch mk, cleaned/polished, 13¾″.......25.00
Ladle, Shaw & Fisher, 6½″, pr............................30.00
Lamp, American, no mk, whale oil burner, 8¼″..............140.00
Lamp, Ostrander & Norris, saucer base/hdl, fluid burning, 10″..450.00
Lamp, single spout, minor dents, 10¾″.....................65.00
Lamp, sparking; matching burner w/brass single tube spout, 4″.120.00
Lamp, sparking; single spout burner w/old wicking, 4x4″, G.....45.00
Lamp, weighted base, orig brass & pewter burner, rpr, 8½″....105.00
Lamp, whale oil, Smith & Co, 8½″, pr......................450.00
Lamp, whale oil burner, 4½″..............................115.00
Measure, baluster, mk ½ Pint, minor dents, 3½″............40.00
Measure, tankard; Barclay, Perkins & Cos, mk 'Quart', 6″.....85.00
Measure, tankard; English, 'Pint', 5″.......................40.00
Measure, tankard; engraved monogram, pub name, 'Pint', 4½″.120.00
Measure, tankard; James Yates, 'Pint', bellied, 5⅛″..........80.00
Measure, tankard; James Yates, 1 qt, minor dents, 6″.........85.00
Measure, tankard; mk 'Pint', glass bottom, 4½″..............20.00
Measure, tankard; R Gleason, rpr, hdl battered, 4½″.........185.00
Measure, tankard; RJ Thorpe, 'Half Pint', 3½″..............55.00
Mug, mid-1800s, English, ½ pint.........................55.00
Mug, scroll hdl, base/rim flakes, 4″.......................65.00
Pan, eagle mk (Boardman), screw off hdl, battered, 10½″.....200.00
Pen box, hinged lid, recessed ring hdl, 7″..................35.00
Pie plate, 1½x9½″......................................40.00
Pitcher, Austrian, mk Wien, Fein Zinn, 12″.................80.00
Pitcher, emb tulip, 6½″..................................35.00
Pitcher, hinged lid, minor dents, rpr spout, 6″..............105.00
Pitcher, lion touch mk w/Boardman, hinged lid, 9¾″........500.00
Plate, angel touch mk, Beindorf Block Zinn, 9″..............35.00

Plate, crowned rose/E Brown, 8¾″........................90.00
Plate, crowned X touch mk, worn, 9″ dia, pr...............100.00
Plate, Edmound Dolbeare, rare mk, 1671-1711, 7″........3,740.00
Plate, John Townsend, 8½″...............................75.00
Plate, no mk, engraved initials on rim, heavy, 9″............55.00
Plate, no mk, 8½″.......................................60.00
Plate, RA, Boston, surface wear, 8″.......................195.00
Plate, Reed & Barton, 10″, pr............................235.00
Plate, Thomas, Townsend & Co, 8″........................50.00
Plate, touch mks w/London, battered, 8½″..................45.00
Plate, 3 crowned heads touch mk, '95', 9″..................40.00
Platter, tree/well/hot water compartment, Shaw & Fisher, 23″..135.00
Porringer, att to Lee, minor surface wear, 5″...............175.00
Porringer, Reed & Barton, 4½″...........................35.00
Porringer, TD & SB in rectangle, EX hdl, 4″...............425.00
Riding crop, bamboo w/pewter hounds head hdl.............40.00
Salt, wide base engraved GF, beaded rim, 1½x3″............32.50
Shakers, att Thomas Danforth, pear form, screw-in plugs, 5¾″.145.00
Shakers, mk TC (Townsend & Compton), 4¾″, pr...........85.00
Snuff box, emb florals w/urn & pr of hawks, cleaned, 2x3½″....15.00
Soup plate, Angel of Justice mk, A DeGiuli, Paderborn, 9″.....45.00
Soup plate, primitive rim engraving, minor dents, wear, 8½″...70.00
Soup plate, 3 simple quatrefoil mks, worn/scratched, 9¼″.....80.00
Spoon, crowned rose touch mk, rnd bowls, 6½″, 5 for........50.00
Spoon, floral cast hdls, late, 8″, 3 for.....................18.00
Spoon, Hall & Bailey, shell on bk of bowl, 7″...............28.00
Spoon, indistinct mk, elongated deep bowl, 7½″.............10.00
Spoon, John Yates, dents, 8¾″, pr........................40.00
Spoon, serving; J Ozenne, 12¼″..........................20.00
Spoon, soup; BDK & crowned rose mk, set of 6, 7″ L........75.00
Spoon, tablespoon, one mk J Sabadie, 8″ L, 3 for...........30.00
Spoon rack, crowned rose mk, scalloped/cut-out, 8x12″......250.00
Spoon rack, hanging, engraved flowers, 1840, w/3 spoons, 4½″.150.00
Sundial, dtd 1702, trn wood base, 6″......................265.00
Syrup, well shaped hdl, soldered rpr, 6″....................95.00
Tall pot, American, no mk, spout reattached, 11½″...........105.00
Tall pot, D Curtiss, minor dents/rpr, 10¾″.................150.00
Tall pot, HB Ward in rectangle, blk pnt hdl, 11¼″...........285.00
Tall pot, James Dixon & Sons, paneled, wood hdl/finial, 12¼″.105.00
Tall pot, WW Lyman Pat 1867, copper base, finial, 10″.......105.00

Teapot, unsigned, 9½″, $125.00.

Tankard, English, 'Gill', hdl resoldered, 4".................100.00
Tankard, Glas-67 'Imperial Gill', shell thumb piece, 4"........165.00
Tankard, mk James Yates, unusual spout on left, qt, 1800-40...160.00
Tankard, mk James Yates, w/spout, quart, ca 1800-1840.......140.00
Tankard, mk Yates & Birch, no spout, quart, ca 1800-1840....120.00
Tankard, no spout, quart, 2 unidentified mks, ca 1800-1840...100.00
Tankard, simple engraved heart/flowers, minor dents, 7¾".....145.00
Tea set, child's size, 7¾" teapot, creamer & sugar............80.00
Teapot, American, no mk, sm rpr, 8"........................75.00
Teapot, att Dixon, footed base, wood hdl & finial, 10"........75.00
Teapot, E Smith, several old soldered rprs, 9¾"..............250.00
Teapot, eagle touch mk, Boardman Warranted, ft splits, 7½"...160.00
Teapot, eagle w/JB Woodbury, 7¼"..........................350.00
Teapot, EC Delavan, wood hdl & finial, ball ft, 7"...........105.00
Teapot, G Richardson, sm rpr, 7¼".........................180.00
Teapot, Gleason, ovoid w/panel sides, leaf form ft, 9"........200.00
Teapot, James Dixon & Sons, ftd, paneled, full body, rpr, 9"....95.00
Teapot, Leonard Reed & Barton, wood hdl/finial, 10".........175.00
Teapot, lion touch mk Boardman, scroll hdl, 9"...............85.00
Teapot, Putnam, minor dents, 8¼"..........................125.00
Teapot, R Gleason, Jacobs #147, 6¾".......................275.00
Tobacco jar, acorn finial, 9".............................105.00
Wine, 4½"...55.00

Phoenix Bird

Blue and white Phoenix Bird china has been produced by various Japanese potteries from the early 1900s. With slight variations the design features the Japanese bird of paradise and scroll-like vines of Kara-Kusa, or Chinese grass. Although some of their earlier ware is unmarked, the majority is marked in some fashion. More than forty different stamps have been reported, with 'Made in Japan' the one most often found. Newer items, if marked at all, carry a paper label. Compared to the older ware, the coloring of the new is whiter and the blue more harsh; the design is sparse, with more ground area showing. Although collectors buy even 'new' pieces, the older is of course more highly prized and valued.

Bowl, rice...12.50
Bowl, sauce..9.50
Bowl, 5½"..12.00
Bowl, 7¼"..20.00
Butter dish w/lid & liner, gold detail.......................85.00
Butter pat..15.00
Coffee pot, demitasse....................................45.00
Cream soup...25.00
Creamer, sm..9.00
Creamer & sugar, ea w/lid; pr.............................48.50
Creamer & sugar w/lid, lg, pr.............................40.00
Cup & saucer..12.50
Cup & saucer, demitasse..................................15.50
Cup & saucer, green, rare color...........................15.00
Egg cup, large...20.00
Egg cup, 2¼"...10.00
Hot plate...65.00
Ice bowl..55.00
Lamp, 11"..110.00
Marmalade, round, open..................................55.00
Match holder, wall hanging................................55.00
Mustard pot...25.00
Pitcher, milk; 6"...65.00
Plate, 6"..7.50
Plate, 7"..10.00
Plate, 8¼"...13.50

Plate, 9½"...15.00
Platter, 12½"...22.00
Salt & pepper, ball, sm, pr................................12.00
Salt & pepper, tall, pr....................................28.50
Sugar w/lid, 3"..12.00
Tumbler, 2¾"...16.50

Phoenix Glass

Established in the 1880s, the Phoenix Glass Company of Beaver, Pennsylvania, originally manufactured commercial glassware such as bottles, beakers, and lighting fixtures. However, during the thirties and into the early fifties they produced a line of sculptured vases and bowls with naturalistic insects, flowers, birds, etc., as well as some decorated with figures of dancing nymphs. These are becoming highly collectible.

Vase, salmon with white lustre flowers, 7", $95.00.

Bowl, allover leaves, leaf ft, clear/frost, 11¼" dia............45.00
Bowl, ftd, hummingbirds & lilies, purple, 3x6" dia...........75.00
Centerpiece, boat shape, custard w/lt br love birds, 15x8"....110.00
Lamp, berries/foliage, aqua/orange on wht, 22"..............75.00
Pitcher, gr, cased, ½ gal, #507, 1931.....................150.00
Plate, red, bronze holder, fruit/berry motif.................135.00
Vase, allover floral embossing, gr ground, 10½".............95.00
Vase, berries & leaves, wht, 9¼"..........................48.00
Vase, berries & leaves, wht w/turq/red, 10"................85.00
Vase, berries on vine, frosted/clear, 10"...................65.00
Vase, birds, tree branches, gr frosted, 7".................75.00
Vase, birds & foliage, milk glass, rectangular, 6½x5½".......45.00
Vase, bittersweet, 3 colors on wht, 9½x5½"...............140.00
Vase, cattails & dragonflies, all green, 6"..................35.00
Vase, dragonflies & cattails, gold on wht, 6"...............40.00
Vase, dragonfly relief, lavender, 6".......................65.00
Vase, floral, yel w/gr leaves, 6½"........................70.00
Vase, flowers, custard w/high lustre decor, 10½"...........190.00
Vase, flying geese, frost wht, 12x10".....................150.00
Vase, flying geese, pillow form, br/custard, paper label, 9½"...195.00
Vase, frolicking nudes, br w/tan & wht, 11½"..............375.00
Vase, goldfish, pk w/bl, 8x9"............................95.00
Vase, grasshoppers, clear/frost, 8½".....................45.00
Vase, grasshoppers, tan on lt gr, 7x8"....................85.00

Vase, grasshoppers & vines, turq w/frosted relief, 8x8″ top W...75.00
Vase, leaves, wht on bl, 12″..............................95.00
Vase, lovebirds, wht w/turquoise & salmon, 10½x9″.........150.00
Vase, lovebirds, yel/pk/gr, 7″............................75.00
Vase, lovebirds & floral, wht on wht, 5½″ W...............65.00
Vase, Madonna in relief front & bk on cream, 10¼″.........215.00
Vase, poppies & foliage, all yellow, 12″..................135.00
Vase, praying mantis, custard w/copper irid insects, 8¼″......95.00
Vase, praying mantis, lt yel frost/clear, oval, 7x9″ dia.........85.00
Vase, rose, aqua on wht, 9½″..............................90.00
Vase, thistles, milk glass, 18″...........................200.00

Phonographs

The phonograph, invented by Thomas Edison in 1877, was later manufactured by various companies who incorporated their own variations with the original Edison model. Those with the large morning-glory horns are especially desirable.

Key:
mg------morning-glory
rpd------reproducer

Aeolian Vocalion, ornate case, Graduola control.............200.00
Apollophone, piano w/phono, M rstr......................7,000.00
Aretino, front mount, w/records..........................725.00
Berliner, Canadian top brake auto grand rpd, brass bell.....1,550.00
Berliner, side brake, blk cone horn, US trademark model....2,250.00
Busy Bee, front mount, all orig, morning-glory horn.........400.00
Cameraphone...120.00
Carilon, metal case, lid reflects sound....................100.00
Carola, disc...140.00
Columbia, 2-4 min reproducer, morning-glory horn, all orig....795.00
Columbia AB, orig 2″ & 5″ mandrels....................1,200.00
Columbia AG, Concert...................................995.00
Columbia AT..350.00
Columbia B, Eagle......................................350.00
Columbia BG, long mandrel w/mahog case..................500.00
Columbia BS, coin-op cylinder, all orig..................2,000.00
Columbia BV..345.00
Columbia BY, mahog horn, serpentine case...............1,400.00
Columbia Commercial Electric............................350.00
Columbia EE..325.00
Columbia Improved Imperial, nickel horn...................550.00
Columbia Peerless, BF, cylinder, EX orig...................500.00
Columbia Q, metal base, replacement horn..................275.00
Columbia S, cylinder coin-op, oak table model w/curved glass.2,400.00
Edison, official laboratory model #250, Wm/Mary cabinet......400.00
Edison Amberola #30, oak table model, Dia C rpd...........275.00
Edison Amberola #50....................................325.00
Edison Amberola #75....................................300.00
Edison Amberola Model III, oak cabinet, opera works......1,200.00
Edison Amberola Model V, oak table model, Dia B rpd.......325.00
Edison DD, 3-C, long play, w/two 10″ records............1,300.00
Edison Diamond Disc, Chippendale lowboy, M...............300.00
Edison Fireside, Combination K...........................400.00
Edison Fireside, 2/4 min, H reproducer, orig 2 pc horn, NM...550.00
Edison Fireside, 2/4 min, H rpd/M scrolls/10 panel cygnet horn.750.00
Edison Gem, A, petaled horn.............................450.00
Edison Gem, blk, 2 min, C rpd, crank, sm mg horn/crane.....450.00
Edison Gem, maroon, K rpd, sm old maroon mg horn not orig.700.00
Edison Home, metal cygnet horn.........................600.00
Edison Home, 2 min, C reproducer........................300.00
Edison Home, 4 min, 14″ horn...........................425.00

Edison Home C, C reproducer, 11 panel lg Home mg horn....385.00
Edison Home E, Diamond B rpd, rpt 10 panel cygnet horn....575.00
Edison Opera, oak case, Concert plate, all orig, VG.........3,500.00
Edison Standard, B, banner decal, C rpd, ICS repeater.......380.00
Edison Standard, C reproducer...........................210.00
Edison Standard, complete, no horn.......................240.00
Edison Standard, D, H reproducer, orig 10 panel cygnet horn..600.00
Edison Standard, lg nickel horn...........................460.00
Edison Standard, 2 & 4 min cylinder, cygnet horn...........500.00
Edison Suitcase Standard, automatic reproducer, no horn......350.00
Edison Triumph, A......................................575.00
Edison Triumph, B......................................500.00
Eldridge R Johnson, Model C, M orig....................2,000.00
Excelda, miniature......................................175.00
G&T Monarch, all brass horn, German...................1,450.00
HMV Gramaphone #7, lg fluted Victor mahog horn, cabinet..1,250.00
Kalamazoo Duplex, w/decal............................1,800.00
Kalamazoo Multiphone, cylinder, 'Jukebox', ornate, 1905....20,000.00
Kalamazoo Multiphone, w/25 cylinder records, needs rstr.....9,000.00
Maestrophone, German, mahogany, lg horn.................750.00
Pathe, coin-op, disc, floor model.......................1,100.00
Pathe Actvelle...400.00
Perophone, disc, outside horn, lg blk horn.................350.00
Regina Hexaphone, coin-op, 6 cylinder positions, w/ad sign...6,200.00
Reginaphone, #240 floor model, serpentine case w/dragons...5,000.00
Silvertone, 36″ W......................................500.00
Sonora, Chippendale console, wood arm....................850.00
Standard Phonograph Co, Model A, rear mt, mg horn.......500.00
Standard Phonograph Co, Model AU, open works...........375.00
Standard Phonograph Co, Model X, black bell horn, all orig...450.00
Standard Phonograph Co, Model X, morning glory horn......450.00
Victor C, front mt, metal top, concert rpd, brass bell........900.00
Victor D, fancy oak case, wood horn, EX orig.............1,200.00
Victor D, style L horn, 23½″ brass bell, plain case.........850.00
Victor E, front mt, complete, orig.........................750.00
Victor E, front mt, 14″ brass bell horn....................550.00
Victor I, 8″ turntable, sm blk petal horn, EX...............600.00
Victor II, humpback....................................640.00
Victor II, w/brass belled horn, M.........................750.00
Victor II, 10″ turntable, std blk petal horn, EX.............600.00
Victor III, 10″ turntable, brass bell horn..................700.00
Victor III, 10″ turntable, std blk petal horn, EX............700.00
Victor IV, mahog cabinet w/orig brass bell horn, M..........650.00
Victor IV, sm mahog horn, rfn.........................1,100.00
Victor Jr, sm blk bell horn, all orig......................650.00
Victor M, front mt, brass bell horn.......................700.00
Victor M, rigid tone arm, blk/brass horn, EX orig.........1,500.00
Victor MS, front mt, all brass horn, concert reproducer......1,450.00
Victor MS, nickel plated petal horn, concert reproducer, EX..1,250.00
Victor O, amber color horn, EX orig......................650.00
Victor Orthophonic, coin-op/deluxe, 10″/12″ discs, 50″...1,400.00
Victor P, bottom mt motor, brass bell.....................550.00
Victor R, front mt, EX...................................600.00
Victor Schoolhouse, no horn, early version, EX.............950.00
Victor V, lg oak case, orig lg blk petal horn, NM..........1,100.00
Victor V, rear mt, lg oak case, matching lg Victor oak horn..1,800.00
Victor V, 24″ 11 petal nickel plated horn, 1908..........1,200.00
Victor VI, lg mahog cabinet, gold metal parts, brass bell horn.2,000.00
Victor VV100, disk, walnut case, EX......................350.00
Victor VV50, suitcase, wood.............................150.00
Victrola, style 16, flared out, upright....................185.00
Victrola Orthophonic #1050, deluxe console, mahog, EX rstr.1,250.00
Zonophone, all brass horn, rstr..........................725.00
Zonophone, glass sides................................2,000.00

Photographica

Photographic collectibles include not only the cameras and equipment used to 'freeze' special moments in time, but also the photographic images produced by a great variety of processes that have evolved since the daguerrean era of the mid-1800s.

Among the earliest cameras was the box-like view camera with a sliding lens. The lens slid in and out of a protective wooden 'drawer' which was replaced on later models with leather bellows. These were the forerunners of the multi-lens cameras developed in the late 1870s, which were capable of recording many small portraits on a single plate. Double lens cameras produced stereo images which, when viewed through a device called a stereoscope, achieved a 3-dimensional effect. In 1888, George Eastman introduced his box camera, the first to utilize roll film. This greatly simplified the process, making it possible for the amateur to enjoy photography as a hobby. Detective cameras, those disguised as books, handbags, etc., are among the most sought after by today's collectors.

Many processes have been used to produce photographic images: daguerrotypes – the most valued examples being the full plate which measures 6½″ x 8½″; ambrotypes, produced by an early wet-plate process whereby a faint negative image on glass is seen as positive when held against a dark background; and tintypes, contemporaries to ambrotypes, but produced on japanned iron, and not as easily damaged.

Other collectible images include cartes de visites, known as CDVs, which are portraits printed on paper, and produced in quantity. The CDV fad of the 1800s enticed the famous and the unknown alike to pose for these cards, which were circulated among the public to the extent that they became known as 'publics'. When the popularity of CDVs began to wane, a new fascination developed for the cabinet photo, a larger version measuring about 4½″ x 6½″.

Stereo cards, photos viewed through a device called a stereoscope, are another popular collectible. The glass stereo plates of the mid-1800s and photo prints produced in the darkroom are among the most valued.

In the following listings, cameras are in case unless noted otherwise.

Albums and Cases

Carte de visite, leather w/magnifying glass/holder, Oppermann. .135.00
Case, Bazaros, Holmes, Booth & Hayden, brown, ¼ plate 225.00

Album, girl's portrait on cover, 10½″ x 8½″, $30.00.

Case, Bouquet of Flowers, S Peck & Co, 4½x3″ 60.00
Case, geometrics, thermoplastic, Critchlow, 1/9 plate, VG 27.50
Case, Golden Medallion, blk w/gilt center, ¼ plate, chip 75.00
Case, Sir Henry Havelock, ¼ plate, EX 165.00
Musical, 'On' switch in clasp, good movement 225.00
Musical, 2 tunes, mother/child/rose garden, Victorian, EX 200.00

Ambrotype

1/2 plate, lad w/thoughtful expression w/book, drape/bkdrop 65.00
1/2 plate, 12 ladies in print dresses, matt/preserver/no case 160.00
1/4 plate, ornate house w/gingerbread trim/trees, full case 85.00
1/4 plate, young mother w/2 daughters, by RH Vance 240.00
1/4 plate, 4 boys, 1 w/violin & bow, ½ case 85.00
1/6 plate, boy in yellow shirt/bl pants w/lg gilt horn, ½ case 65.00
1/6 plate, horizontal, boy w/dog, girl w/flowers, leather case 150.00
1/6 plate, houses/carriage w/men before Clothing Store 85.00
1/6 plate, man w/rare bike, camera/tripod in bkground, ½ case .400.00
1/6 plate, young village cooper, ¾ view, w/adz, full case 195.00
1/6 plate, 2 bearded men in red/wht/bl striped suits, in case 225.00
1/9 plate, well accoutred soldier w/Burnside carbine, EX frame . .225.00
1/9 plate, ¾ length standing infantry soldier, cased 40.00

Cabinet Photo

At The Grave of Osceola, Sullivan's Island, by Leidoff, 1880s 50.00
Bandsman in fancy uniform w/baritone horn 22.50
Black Rock & Antelope Island, Salt Lake, albumen, CR Savage . .15.00
Circus horse, 18 ft tail, 14 ft mane, by Wendt, G 8.00
Corn Palace, 1890, w/crowd of people, Hamilton & Co, VG 13.00
Elephantine Colossus, NY, specifications on reverse, VG 20.00
Girl in bonnet & plaid jacket w/spaniel dog, Stevens & Johnson . . .7.00
Indian Papoose In Cradleboard, Hatch Studio, Bath, Maine 18.00
JJ Corbet, boxing stance, albumen by Newsboy, NY, EX 22.50
Lone Star Harry, Wild West Show performer, by Wendt 40.00
Louis Agassiz, naturalist, in chair w/book, 1868, sgn, Sonrel 35.00
Mines in Eagle River Canon, D & RG RR, Jackson, 5x8″ mt 10.00
Occupational, lady blacksmith w/corncob pipe, Jefferson, VG 9.00
Photography, 2 girls & donkey before studio, Kasson, VG 15.00
Pikes Peak From Garden o/t Gods, albumen, WH Jackson, EX . .14.00
Rainbow Falls, Ute Pass, #407, w/men on rock, WH Jackson 8.00
Sitting Bull w/Peace Pipe, by Palmquist & Jurgens, EX 165.00
Two ponies on studio floor w/lady sitting between, VG 13.00
Unca, Araphoe, warrior w/rifle, by Chas Weitfle 180.00
Ute Pass, #786, albumen, WH Jackson, VG 8.00
Vulcans Anvil, Monument Park, by Wheeler, EX 9.00
WF Cody, Buffalo Bill, in beaver fur hat/buckskin shirt 50.00
WF Cody, Buffalo Bill, in overcoat, 1875, VG 110.00
Wild West Show, female in corn husk dress, Kortright & Graven .95.00

Cameras

Agfa view camera, Ica lens, fine wood/bellows, 3x4″ 125.00
Agfa-Ansco, folding bellows, 616 film, 1913 . . . . .8.00
Ansco #6, Model C, for use w/Vidil film 45.00
Birdland, reflex w/2 lenses, 9 plate holders, mk IN Dracopoli . .725.00
Birdland, Sanders & Crowhurst, 1890, VG 500.00
Contessa Nettel Tropical, teak, ¼ plate, 1920, w/tripod, EX 675.00
Coronet Midget, 16mm bakelite, brown, orig instructions, EX 85.00
Coronet Midget, 16mm bakelite, red, orig box, EX 125.00
Darlot 12 lens, polished wood w/ground glass screen/holder . . .3,500.00
E Mazo Stereo, mahog, Thornton Pickard shutter/Mazo lenses . .750.00
Elgy, Lumiere & Co, 24x36mm on 35mm cassette film, 1937 . . . .90.00
Eureka Detective, WW Rouch & Co, 1888, mahog sliding box . .500.00

Expo De Luxe, by Int'l, in orig carton w/instructions, EX......165.00
Expo Watch, w/lens cap & chain, orig box/instructions, 1905...125.00
French Sliding Box, by Caillard, early 1850s...............3,200.00
Giroux Replica, ⅓ scale, 5x7" base, working model..........125.00
Graflex, series D, revolving back...........................95.00
Kodak, #1, 100 exposure, 2½" size photo, in orig case......700.00
Kodak, #1 Brownie improved, hinged bk/view finder detaches....95.00
Kodak, #1-A, Gift; Art Deco, w/cedar presentation box, EX....275.00
Kodak, #2 Beau Brownie, pink, no hdl, EX....................95.00
Kodak, #2 Brownie, Anniversary, premium from 1930, MIB.....95.00
Kodak, #2-A Beau Brownie, br/tan, no hdl, w/case, VG........55.00
Kodak, Pocket; #102 roll film/rnd view finder/built in shutter...150.00
Kookie Kamera, Ideal, developer/flash cube/accessories/in box..65.00
Korona II, 4x5", EX...95.00
Mystic Button, self contained/developing, w/instructions.......345.00
National Graflex, SLR, 10 exposures on 120 roll, in case/book..145.00
Photo Jumelle Box, binocular style, Carpentier, 1890s, EX.....285.00
Photosphere, Campagnie Francaise de Photographie, 1890...1,750.00
Pocket Obsura, Hahn Hanover & Co, blk tin w/gold striping...250.00
Pocket Zar, Western Camera, magazine premium #531, w/box..165.00
Potenza, shaped like rubber car tire, MIB...................30.00
ROC New Model Improved view camera w/brass ROC lens, case.150.00
Schaeffner's Photo Carnet, book; w/plates, EX.............2,850.00
Secret Sam Attache Case & Camera, 1965...................135.00
Shew Xit, all wood, brass B&L lens w/WH stops ring, EX......275.00
Shur-Shot, Robert Ingersoll Bros, wood, lg version, 6½x4x3¾".325.00
Student Field, ¼ plate, brass barrel lens, rotating disc stops...225.00
T Ottewill, folding-sliding wet plate, ivory label, 1853, EX....4,200.00
Taschenbuck, book; Dr R Krugener, inoperative, orig case...2,750.00
Tourist Multiple, New Idea Mfg Co, 35 mm, 2 cassettes, VG..2,200.00
Tropical UNA, ½ plate, mahog/brass bound, case...........1,600.00
Victor Tintype, aluminum, self developing tank, no shutter.....950.00
Voightlander Avus, Skopar lens.............................45.00

Carte De Visite

Admiral David D Porter, albumen, Anthony/Brady mk on mt....27.50
Andrew Jackson, engraving, VG..............................4.00
Andrew Johnson, vignetted albumen, pub Anthony, VG.........25.00
Boy on rocking horse, Howard & Co, EX......................7.00
Brig Gen William Rosecrans, albumen, Anthony/Brady mk on mt.22.50
Capt Myles W Keogh, vignette bust, EX.....................200.00
Chippewa Wedding, Taken at Chippewa Agency, by Upton......45.00
Civil War, 1st Lieut, frock buttoned at top/epaulettes..........16.00
Col Ulric Dahlgreen, vignetted albumen, pub Anthony, EX.....32.50
Cut Nose, albumen, by JE Whitney, 1862.....................50.00
Gen GA Custer, by M Brady, sepia albumen full length, 1865...400.00
Gen GA Custer, imprint M Brady front/bk, vignette portrait....250.00
Gen GA Custer, in full dress uniform, post CW, Mora........325.00
Gen GA Custer, Indian war uniform, albumen image.........250.00
General Grant, vignetted albumen, mt mk Brady, revenue stamp.25.00
Gideon Wells, albumen, pub Anthony, revenue stamp, EX......25.00
Henry Clay, vignetted albumen, pub Anthony, VG.............18.00
Jefferson Davis, vignette bust view, Pratt bkmark, G..........28.00
Major Gen Alfred Pleasonton, albumen, Anthony/Brady mk, EX..25.00
Old Abe, War Eagle, w/history printed on bk, VG.............10.00
Post mortem, baby in shroud in cradle, holding flowers.........8.50
Union Captain, frock coat/epaulettes/mustache, Brady on face...21.00
Union soldier, ¾ standing, Brady on face/bkstamp...........23.00

Daguerreotypes

Stereo, statuary, lady w/goose, from 1855 Paris Expo, orig mt..160.00
Whole plate, gentleman, ¾ length, by Appleby, VG...........950.00

Whole plate, Niagara Falls w/6 people, sgn Babbitt..........1,000.00
1/2 plate, distinguished gentleman, VG......................95.00
1/4 plate, family before home, picket fence, in full case.......325.00
1/4 plate, Federal House, 2 story, winter scene, ½ case......325.00
1/4 plate, mother w/bonnet & girl in tinted bl dress, EX......65.00
1/4 plate, occupational, man in top hat holds sextant, Thayer.1,000.00
1/6 plate, Blk gent in 3 pc suit & gold finger ring, in case.....365.00
1/6 plate, copy of engraving, pirate, lovely lady, skull, EX.....125.00
1/6 plate, group of 4 children, full case, EX..................75.00
1/6 plate, man holding wide brimmed hat...................55.00
1/6 plate, post mortem of young man draped w/coverlet, cased...90.00
1/6 plate, young child, dress off one shoulder, tinted, cased....80.00
1/6 plate, 2 girls, 1 w/concertina, ½ case, VG................80.00
1/9 plate, occupational, carpenter in smock w/hammer, in case..225.00
1/6 plate, occupational, man in hat w/iron worker's hammer....500.00
1/6 plate, woman with baby, portrait.......................53.00

Photos

Albumen, Bridal Veil Falls, Carleton Watkins, 12x8", VG.......50.00
Albumen, Calcutta Cathedral, Friths Series, 7¾x6"...........22.50
Albumen, Santa Barbara Mission, mk Taber, 7½x4¾".........22.50
Albumen, Taber, 2 views of Yosemite, 1880, 15x20", pr.....1,300.00
Apache Indian (A little ancient) #92, Cockrell, EX............55.00
Colorado Colorow Ute Chief, Detroit Photo Co, Kirkland.......65.00
Edward Curtis, A Mat Lodge, Umatilla, on tissue, Van Gelder...60.00
Edward Curtis, Cayuse Type, portrait on tissue...............65.00
Edward Curtis, Gyalkum, Kosimo, on tissue..................55.00
Edward Curtis, Paqusilahl, Qagyuhl, on tissue...............50.00
Edward Curtis, Ready For The Cast, Qagyuhl, on tissue........65.00
Edward Curtis, Saguaro Fruit Gatherers, Maricopa, lg folio....200.00
Edward Curtis, Sentinel, San Ildefonso, folio, 1925...........125.00
Edward Curtis, Wisham Child, portrait on tissue..............70.00
Edward Curtis, Wisham Female Type, portrait, tissue/Van Gelder.70.00
Graves of Soldiers Killed at Wounded Knee, WR Cross........225.00
Kit Carson's Scout, National Press Assoc Wash DC, 7x5".......55.00
Orabi, AZ, Thanksgiving Dance, Detroit Photo, color..........30.00
Photogravure, Peaceful Camp, JK Dixon, 1913, 10x7".........40.00
Photogravure, Swirl of Warriors, JK Dixon, 1913, 10x7".......45.00
Sepia, Boise, Idaho, CR Savage, 11½x5", VG.................20.00
Sepia, 4 men before log cabin & tent/horse/camera, 8x5".......25.00

Edward S. Curtis print, 'Oasis in Badlands', signed and numbered, in frame, 12½" x 16", $700.00.

Sepia platinum, Flathead brave in beaded vest/headdress.......40.00
Silver print, Albert Einstein, #27, Philippe Halsman.........300.00
Silver print, Arapahoe Girl, ca 1890, 6½x4½"..............25.00
Silver print, Grace Kelly, #15, Philippe Halsman, 11x14".....200.00
Silver print, La Dame Indignee, Robert Doisneau, 12x9½"....300.00
Utes, Jose Romero & Family, color/red mt, Detroit Photo.......70.00

Stereoscopic Views

Airplane, 1st air rail trip, 1929, Keystone, #32372.............15.00
Alaskan Indian & his abode, CH Graves, Universal Photo, 1902..15.00
Amputation scene at Gettysburg, by WH Tipton...............28.00
An Oats Field in Tanana Valley, Keystone, #37499.............13.00
Apache scouts, 10 in military uniforms, Wilson & Haven, G.....75.00
Arrival of Heroes from the Front, U&U #14184, gray mount....6.00
At the Cliff House, San Francisco, by Tabler, orange mt, VG....15.00
Avalon at Santa Catalina Island, by Underwood & Underwood...11.00
Battery of the Famous 270 Mortars, U&U #12305, gray mount..12.00
Battle of Bull Run, McCullum & Butterworth, before disbanding.35.00
Bear, #13, by Wm Bell, albumen on yellow, EX...............17.50
Bird's Eye View of St Augustine, Fla, Bloomfield Guide series....8.00
Blackfoot Indian Chief, by RA Waugh, 1890.................25.00
Blacks Picking Cotton in Field, LA, U&U, 1892, tan mount......6.00
Booker T Washington, by FW Kelley, Presko Binocular Co.....25.00
Brighton, England; early street scene, by WH Mason..........7.00
Butterfly Collection, tinted, Kilburn, #89..................15.00
Camp Cooking, Army o/t Potomac, Anthony, albumen on orange.42.50
Cat-O-Graph-ic, kittens crawling on lg camera, John P Soule....37.00
Chester Illustrated, English, lot of 5, by Francis Bedford.......26.00
Cheyenne Indians at Grave of Gen Custer, Keystone..........50.00
Chicago after the Great Fire, Mich Ave Hotel, Hendricks, #201..12.00
Chicago Fire, PB Greene, orange mount....................13.00
Chief Black Hawk, Wife Green Cloud Family, Keystone, #23095.18.00
Col Lindbergh, Keysone, #32062.........................15.00
Colorado locomotive, diamond-stacked narrow-gauge, C Weitfle..95.00
Colossi o/t Plain, Statues of Memmon, #377, Frith, glass......45.00
Curtain & Silver Cascades, #7, Prof Towler, MD.............27.50
Deck of US Battleship Pennsylvania, Keystone #19147........11.00
Deep-sea diver, by BW Kilburn..........................40.00
Dr Anna Howard Shaw, suffrage leader, close portrait.........22.00
Eclipse of Sun, Alfred Bros, dtd 1867, EX.................85.00
Egypt, set of 100, orig guidebook & boxes, Underwood.......220.00
Eye-exercise cartoon, 20 views, by Keystone View Co.........19.00
Ft Sumner o/t Chickahominy, VA, Anthony, albumen on orange.32.50
Granite Quarry, #280, Watkins New Series, albumen on orange..20.00
Great Johnstown Flood, 1889, Woodvale jail, RK Bonine #16...10.00
Holland House, England, interior view, by William England.....11.00
Hutchin's Hotel w/Sentinel Rock in Distance, 1860s...........10.00
Hydraulic Mining, Alaska, Keystone, #37502...............20.00
India, lot of 30 scenes, by Stereo-Travel Co, 1908...........42.00
Ireland, view of Rope Bridge, Carrick-A-Rede, VG............7.00
JA French's photo wagon, in New Hampshire................36.00
Japan, early view, 1860, by F Beato.......................30.00
Japan, lot of 15, by CH Graves, published by Stereal Travel Co..21.00
JK Mortimer, full length studio portrait, In NY, E&H Anthony...60.00
John Burns, Hero of Gettysburg; published by E&H Anthony....38.00
John D Rockefeller, close portrait, by Keystone View Co.......38.00
Johnstown Flood, lot of 12 views, by RK Bonine.............26.00
Kiowa Apache, 9 warriors in full dress, Wilson/Haven, 1870s, G..75.00
LAW Championship Bicycle Race, 1890....................26.00
Locomotive, by Charles Weitfle..........................155.00
Logging views, lot of 2, by Underwood & Underwood.........28.00
Los Angeles, scarce later view by Keystone View Co..........16.00
Men of Fighting 27th Arrive in Hobeken, U&U #14226, gray mt..9.00

Mid-season on Beach at Atlantic City, Universal #4396, gray mt..10.00
Miniature steam train at Central Park, Underwood & Underwood.21.00
Mining Camp in Klondyke, #12725, c 1898 BW Kilburn, sepia..13.00
Mining scene, southwest Colorado, by Luke & Wheeler, 1879..130.00
Oregon, Cape Horn, Columbia River, Watkins, #1232, VG......9.00
Paris, France; informal street scene, by London Stereoscopic....16.00
Photo camp in White Mountains, John P Soule's, 1860s........50.00
Photographer working high above 5th Ave, U&U.............27.00
Pres McKinley in Cabinet Room, U&U, gray mount...........12.00
Pres Roosevelt's Journey through the West, U&U, 1903, gray mt.18.00
Redlands from Smiley Heights, CA, Keystone, #13549, 1903....10.00
Ruins of Acropolis, glass view, ca 1864, by Ferrier...........31.00
San Francisco, Jewish Synagogue, T Houseworth, #235.........50.00
Self-portrait, AJ Russell.............................105.00
Seth Kingman, California trapper, studio portrait............100.00
Short Point Stab, Keystone, #V19219, gray mount............8.00
Soldiers winter quarters, Army o/t Potomac, by JC Taylor, VG...20.00
State Capitol at Sacramento, CA; stairway view, JJ Reilly.......20.00
Strictly Confidential, girl on tiptoe whispering to mother, VG.....9.00
Svengali, close portrait, by BW Kilburn...................36.00
Swallow Cave, #80, EO Beaman, albumen on yellow, EX.......11.00
Ten Million Dollar Ead's Bridge over MS, Keystone #V26506....10.00
Terrible Destruction of City Hall from Market St, White #8712..13.00
Terrible Lode, Rocky Mtn Scenery View, WG Chamberlain, #263.9.00
Texas railroad passenger car, interior view.................155.00
The Moon, 1860s view, VG.............................20.00
Thomas Edison, portrait...............................105.00
Union Street, Sunk by Great Earth Convulsion, U&U #8224....16.00
View of Mission Carmel, by CWJ Johnson, California..........15.00
War for the Union, Maj Gen McClellan & Staff, Brady, #2344...48.50
Whaleback Freighters in Canal at Sault Ste Marie, U&U #7994...8.00
Yosemite, CA; lot of 7 scenes, by John P Soule.............28.00
Zeppelin Wrecked & Burned, Keystone, #18632.............12.00
14th St Circle from Portland Circle, Washington DC, HL Roberts.8.00

Tintypes

Baby, in gutta percha case w/foliage decor, 1858, 3½x4".......65.00
CDV size, barman/barmaid w/steins, G....................35.00
CDV size, Mountain Man, w/hat/coat/powder horn/rifle/bird.....75.00
Girl, striped stockings, w/spaniel dog, 2½x3½"..............6.00
Hunter w/game bag & musket, dog on chair, 2x3¼", G.........8.00
Lady, in painted studio prop of early biplane, paper matt, 3¾"..15.00
Man, head posed in prop, drives donkey cart, sgn, 2½x3¾"....14.00
Man & wife, ea about 5x7", orig 8x10" beveled matts, pr.......18.50
US Indian scout in military uniform, 3½x2½", EX............80.00
Western carriage maker, 1870s, 4x2½"....................90.00
Whole plate, close-up of Black baby in spindled crib..........35.00
Whole plate, girl in fancy wht dress/hat w/rosary, tinted.......12.00
1/2 plate, huge St Bernard, matt/preserver, EX..............47.50
1/4 plate, Am sailor in uniform, bkdrop w/warships, G........100.00
1/4 plate, boy w/drum decorated w/13 star flag, tinted, EX.....50.00
1/4 plate, Union soldier, seated in caped overcoat, full case....55.00
1/4 plate, Western pioneers, 1 w/pipe, 1 w/measuring stick.....25.00
1/4 plate, 3 uniformed Indian War soldiers w/infantry insignia..30.00
1/4 plate, 5 Union soldiers before martial bkdrop w/flag.......65.00
1/6 plate, Civil War officer w/sword, seated, 1864, G case.....130.00
1/6 plate, Civil War soldier w/bayonetted rifle, tinted, cased...145.00
1/6 plate, young Civil War soldier in uniform/cap/kepi, tinted...145.00

Viewers and Slides

Brewster, burl wood, unusual shape, mirrored flap, EX........225.00
Brewster, emb SG & Co, mahog/ground glass bk, EX........145.00

Graphoscope, blk w/carved flowers, lens mt rpr, age crack, VG..145.00
ICA Stereospekt, mahog cabinet style for 6x13cm glass slides...285.00
ICA Stereospekt, table model, w/100 glass slides, 20x10"......300.00
Lantern slide, counter rotating kaleidoscope, 4½x7"..........45.00
Lantern slide, mechanical, Snow Storm, Carpenter & Westley....85.00
Lantern slide, monkey stabbing fish, side bar moves his arm....45.00
Lantern slides, Mickey Mouse, early 1920s, set of 12..........75.00
Le Minimus, w/changing mechanism, 6½", EX..............400.00
Magic lantern, Lantern Magique, blued tin, kerosene lamp, VG.145.00
Magic lantern, TH McAllister pat 4/6/1886, w/slides..........600.00
Metascope, Unis, taxiphote style, mahog, w/counter, 2 trays....595.00
Midget Movies, Reel Movie Show, hand crank/4 flip books.....125.00
Parlour Graphoscope, burl wood/ornate fretwork, 12x24", EX..265.00
Sliding Box, hand held, rack/pinion focus/locking device, EX...185.00
Smith, Beck & Beck; burl wood w/brass fittings, orig mirrors...375.00
Travelscope, for 1934 Century of Progress by Keystone, EX.....45.00
Uncle Sam's projector+9 rolls color film, 1934..............250.00
Vautier, tin litho, cigarette advertising, w/47 views, EX........55.00

Miscellaneous

Advertisement, Kodak, 4 tipped-on photos of ships/children....160.00
Bank, Kodak, CI box Brownie, w/orig key, 1903.............325.00
Book, Bloomfield's Illustrated Guide to St Augustine..........53.00
Book, Treatise...Differential Equations, 1873, stereo views......52.50
Flash pistol gun, Chelsea, hdl shaped as gun stock, early.....275.00
Permit, Columbian Expo, allowed bearer to use camera/dk room.47.50
Photo postcard, Gen Pancho Villa, Ortega & Medina, Horne....40.00
Pillow, w/photo of girl in flag costume, 1880s................65.00
Salt & pepper, in shape of folding roll film camera............35.00
Stanhope, binoculars, bone, view of Niagara ea side..........25.00
Stanhope, ring, brass w/emerald gr stone, view of nude........85.00
Stanhope, television, 14k charm w/3 views of NYC...........85.00
Store display, Kodak, man w/camera, 1920s.................150.00
Wall plaque, 2 girls photo on porcelain, J Schiffner, 3x4½".....45.00

Piano Babies

A familiar sight in Victorian parlors, piano babies languished atop shawl covered pianos in a variety of poses: crawling, sitting, on their tummies, or on their backs playing with their toes. Some babies were nude and some wore gowns. Sizes ranged from about 3" up to 12". The most famous manufacturer of these bisque darlings was the Heubach Brothers of Germany who nearly always marked their product; see Heubach for more listings. Watch for reproductions.

Baby, cat eating from bowl, w/doll, 8".....................195.00
Baby w/apple, molded bonnet/clothes, intaglio eyes, bsk, 11"...450.00
Boy in socks & shorts, holding gray dog, bisque, 8½x5"......65.00
Child in high chair, puppy in lap, taking off bib, 11".........250.00
Crawling, nightshirt open, 2¾"...........................55.00
Crawling, wht gown w/gr bows, bisque, 5½"................75.00
Holds up left leg w/left hand, wht gown w/bl, German, 3¼"....85.00
Laying on side holding fruit, sgn GH, 9x5"................200.00
On back, playing with toes, quality bisque, 7"..............95.00
On stomach w/pillow, dog w/pacifier, bl gown, German, 6".....125.00
Sits w/1 leg over 2nd, leaning, holds ball, intaglio eyes, 5½"...225.00
Sitting, floral nightie, butterfly on leg, Canta-Boehm, 10x10½".400.00
Sitting, holding bonnet, wht gown/pk bows, mk GH, 6¾".....250.00
Sitting, holding toes, sgn Heubach, 6¼x5½"...............200.00
Sitting, holds shoe in air, Canta-Boehm, 7¼x6½".........250.00
Sitting w/rattle, sgn Canta-Boehm, 7¼x6½"..............200.00

Pickard

Founded in 1897 in Chicago, Illinois, the Pickard China Company was originally a decorating studio, importing china blanks from European manufacturers. Some of these early pieces bear the name of those companies as well as Pickard's. Trained artists decorated the wares with hand painted studies of fruit, florals, birds, and scenics, and often signed their work. In 1915, Pickard introduced a line of 23k gold over a dainty floral etched ground design.

In the 1930s, they began to experiment with the idea of making their own ware, and by 1938 had succeeded in developing a formula for fine translucent china. Since 1976 they have issued an annual limited edition Christmas plate. They are now located in Antioch, Illinois.

The company has used various marks: 'Pickard' with double circles; the crown mark; 'Pickard' on a gold maple leaf; and the current mark, the lion and shield.

Bowl, fruit; deserted garden, sgnd Nessey, hdld.............180.00
Bowl, gold w/HP fruits in center, sgn Yeschek, Limoges, 10"...245.00
Bowl, gooseberries, rust/yel, sgn, scalloped, TV Limoges, 11"....95.00
Bowl, orchard/tree & fruit, open hdls, 1915, mk Nippon, 8½"..150.00
Bowl, 3 hdls, poppies, tri-lobe dimpled top, sgn, 8" dia......165.00
Cake plate, Dutch scenic border, sgn, 11"..................120.00
Candlestick, Aura Argenta, artist sgn, circle mk, 5", pr........115.00
Candlestick, etched gold, 1½" HP band fruits/florals, 9"......150.00
Candlestick, irid gr w/red flowers, gold, sgn Tolley, 7".......235.00
Candy dish, allover gold etched floral, scalloped, 6½"........32.00
Candy dish, pierced gold hdls, wht/gold/pastel nosegays, 5¾"....22.00
Coffee pot, allover gold floral w/inset band w/basket..........80.00
Coffee pot, ped ft, cobalt w/encrusted gold, Chinese enamel....225.00
Coffee set, demitasse; pot, 8 c/s, HP br/gold iris............70.00
Compote, allover gold w/heavily chased gold top, 2½x6"......75.00
Creamer & sugar, allover gold etched floral, 1930s, lg.........43.50
Creamer & sugar, birds/butterflies/floral, sgn, leaf mk........135.00
Creamer & sugar, Deco shape, floral sprays, E Challinor, pr.....30.00
Creamer & sugar, Deserted Garden, artist sgn Maker........250.00
Creamer & sugar, gold/floral bouquet in center/rim, sgn......145.00
Creamer & sugar, octagonal, gold etched, mk RS Germany.....45.00
Creamer & sugar, wht w/gold etching, maple leaf mk..........70.00
Cup & saucer, poppies, sgn.............................90.00
Jug, ear of corn, artist sgn, 6".........................190.00
Marmalade jar, strawberries, sgn Yeschek..................135.00
Mustard pot w/attached under plate, wht w/heavy gold floral.....38.00
Nappy, ring hdl, applied rim, gold trim, tree scenic, sgn, 7½"...68.00
Pitcher, Aura Argenta Linear decor, artist sgn..............325.00
Pitcher, cider; sgn Beuttich, 1908........................175.00
Pitcher, floral in bl/tan, blk/tan/gold bands, Hessler, 8".......335.00
Pitcher, lemonade; yel/orange tulips, gold, sgn Schoner, '05....280.00
Pitcher, milk; bl/gold bands & flowers, heavy gold, squat, 6½".170.00
Pitcher, pk/bl flowers, heavy gold, Nippon blank, leaf mk, 4½"..60.00
Pitcher, plums/gold top & hdl, Carriage Barn mk, Reury, 4½"..185.00
Pitcher, sm HP florals, heavy gold, maple leaf mk, 5".........65.00
Pitcher, tankard; poppies, heavy gold, sgn Fuchs, 1905, 10½"..470.00
Plate, birch trees/lake/tower, sgn Challinor, 7"..............90.00
Plate, bl violets, sgn Mark, gold border, 7½"...............60.00
Plate, daisies, artist sgn, maple leaf mk, 8½"...............60.00
Plate, encrusted gold, 3 HP birds, 8½"....................65.00
Plate, gold over bl borders w/floral centers, 10¾"...........35.00
Plate, gold traced floral, Beutlich, GDA France blank, 7½"....50.00
Plate, irises/Nile fronds, much gr/gold tracing, sgn, 7½"......70.00
Plate, marsh scene, gold band, E Challinor, Limoges, 8½".....90.00

Plate, open hdls, heavy gold & florals, 12".................175.00
Plate, orange poppy, scalloped gold border, gold, Limoges, 7"...85.00
Plate, purple violets, sgn, 8¾"............................65.00
Plate, red berries, rust/br leaves, gold rim, sgn Reller, 8½"....130.00
Plate, sgn Osborne, 23k gold, 8½".........................80.00
Plate, shamrocks & heavy gold, maple leaf mk, 8½"..........70.00
Plate, water lilies & cattails, artist sgn, 9"..............65.00
Plate, wht w/bl Hall of Science, Century of Progress, 9½".....22.00
Platter, scenic w/roses, sgn Marker, 12½".................125.00
Punch bowl, gold bkground/desert garden, 6 sides, Vonral, 15".650.00
Relish, HP pk/gr leaves, heavy gold, open hdls, leaf mk, 9x5"..70.00
Relish, much gold, pk/bl floral, open hdls, late, 8½x5".......35.00
Relish, wood violets, heavy gold, Krisney, 8x3"............95.00
Shaker, metallic grape, slight gold wear on rim............65.00
Shakers, allover gold etched floral, tall, pr...............28.00
Shakers, allover gold etched floral, 3", pr................12.00
Shakers, Aura Argenta, artist sgn, pr....................38.00
Stein, Elk Lodge, gold elk/clock on purple, sgn Coufal.......225.00
Teapot, bl tassels, much gold, mk Nippon, 1905............125.00
Teapot, cr/sug, sm HP pk/bl floral, B&Co Limoges, leaf mk...175.00
Tray, allover gold etched floral, 16¾x10½"................70.00
Tray, pastel temple scene, lg gold hdls, sgn Yeschek, 14x5"...195.00
Vase, allover gold etched floral, gr w/in, 5¾".............35.00
Vase, blk w/purple grapes, heavy gold, sgn Hessler, 1898, 9"...285.00
Vase, deep red w/floral design, sgn Challinor, 1890s, 7¼".....325.00
Vase, florals, heavy gold, sgn Platt, 1908, 9"............175.00
Vase, Indian Tree, gold etched, sgn, lion shield mk, 7½".....70.00
Vase, pastel scenic, blue mk, sgn, early, 12"..............375.00
Vase, scenic, sgn Marker, matt glaze, gold base/neck/hdls, 9¾".450.00
Vase, spring scenic, w/hdls, sgn Challinor, leaf mk, matt, 6"....300.00
Vase, violets, gold/gr/blk Deco decor, 6".................65.00
Vase, wht, gold double hdls, pink floral trim, 7½".........58.00
Vase, wildwood pattern, sgn James, bisque, 1912, 8¼".....395.00

Pickle Castors

The pickle castor is a novel item made popular during the Victorian period. It consists of a glass insert, usually a type of colored art glass, contained in a decorative metal frame. A pickle fork or tongs are usually hung from the frame.

Light green opaline insert with enameled florals, elaborate frame with fork, 11½", $130.00.

Amber, ornate high ft fr, w/fork...........................115.00
Amber w/Bow Tie pattern, EX fr w/tongs..................165.00
Beatty Rib, blue opal; SP holder.........................225.00
Beatty Rib, blue; elephant trunk ft, cupid figural holds tongs...325.00
Blue, multi-faceted; emb floral/nymphs on base, tongs........165.00
Blue w/enamel floral, plated fr..........................185.00
Bristol, blue w/enamel floral; ornate SP frame.............300.00
Cane & Fan on clear insert, SP fancy fr w/tongs............100.00
Clear, Block & Fan insert, SP fr w/claw tongs, EX...........75.00
Clear, Dia Quilt; quadruple plate, w/tongs, 10"............95.00
Clear, SP fr w/emb birds & flowers, bud lid finial...........65.00
Clear, Zipper panel, ribs at base; retic fr w/tongs, Meriden......95.00
Cranberry, enamel florals...............................285.00
Cranberry, Inverted Thumbprint; enameled decor, complete....225.00
Cranberry, Inverted Thumbprint; London SP fr w/ornaments...195.00
Cranberry, Inverted Thumbprint; Middletown fr w/tongs......225.00
Cranberry, Optic, pnt daffodils; Tufts fr w/side hdl & tongs....250.00
Cranberry opal, in Barbour Bros fr on tall slim std, w/fork....295.00
Daisy & Button, apple green; SP holder...................185.00
Daisy & Button, clear; SP Victorian holder w/birds, claw tongs..120.00
Daisy & Button, sapphire; Rogers fr w/tongs...............250.00
Daisy & Button, vaseline; Tufts SP fr w/tongs.............145.00
Daisy & Fern, Apple Blossom mold, blue; ftd ornate fr/tongs...250.00
Dbl, clear; Meriden fr w/emb masks, center hdl.............135.00
Dbl, diamond pattern; ornate ftd fr w/tongs & fork.........175.00
Dbl, frosted w/floral cutting; fancy ftd fr w/tongs, Webster......160.00
Dbl, pattern glass; Meriden fr w/center hdl................155.00
Festoon, in Forbes SP holder w/bird finial.................110.00
Frosted glass, claw tongs, SP fr..........................75.00
Frosted gold floral insert; Pairpoint ftd holder & tongs.......135.00
Leaf Mold, cranberry satin; w/ornate SP holder w/tongs......350.00
Mother of Pearl, Dia Quilt, blue; silver trim..............275.00
Mother of Pearl, Dia Quilt, red; SP frame................375.00
Nailsea, blue w/opal loopings; SP frame..................200.00
Near Cut, SP frame w/ornate top, sgn Amsterdam, w/tongs & lid.65.00
Opalescent insert; SP frame w/tongs, 4"..................145.00
Panelled Sprig, cranberry, enameled florals; ornate SP fr......265.00
Panelled Sprig, cranberry & clear; SP holder..............240.00
Peachblow, cased; footed frame.........................350.00
Pigeon blood, SP fr....................................225.00
Rubena, enamel daisies; Aurora SP fr....................225.00
Ruby insert, ornate fr w/cut-out birds, Meriden, 14".........125.00
Satin, pink w/floral enamel; ornate SP frame w/tongs.........350.00
Satin, pink; SP Pairpoint frame.........................375.00
Slag, purple; SP frame.................................375.00
Stippled glass w/3 scenic medallions; Hartford fr w/tongs......85.00
Stork in Rushes, Webster tongs.........................75.00

Pie Birds

Pie birds or vents were used around 1930 to prevent pies from boiling over in the oven. When the juices began to bubble and expand, they were contained within the hollow form; as the pie cooled, the juices drained back into the pie.

Benny the Baker, w/orig box.............................22.00
Bird, black & wht, 2 pc, Royal Worcester..................18.00
Bird, blue & yellow, 4½".................................8.00
Bird, turq/yel/rose/blue on cream, 5"....................10.00
Black bird, Royal Worcester, in box......................20.00
Black chef w/spoon, underglaze color, 4¼"................18.00
Black girl holding spoons...............................40.00

Chick, wht w/pk & gr, 5½"............................12.00
Elephant, gray...45.00
Rooster, Blue Willow..................................12.00

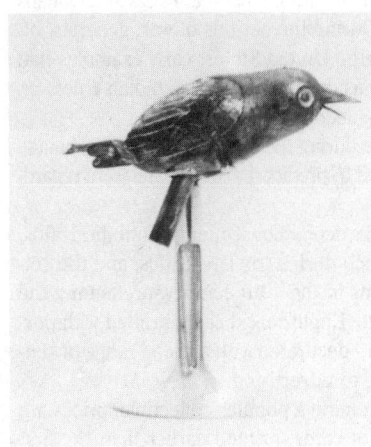

Unusual brass pie bird, 3" long, $55.00.

Pigeon Blood

Pigeon blood glass, produced in the late 1800s, may be distinguished from other dark red glass by its distinctive orange tint.

Celery vase, Torquay, silverplate collar....................110.00
Pitcher, milk; 8 sides, gold leaves, strap hdl................125.00
Pitcher, water; Torquay..................................245.00
Shakers, Ada, orig tops, pr.............................125.00
Tankard, Diamond Quilted...............................185.00
Vase, gilt/wht enamel decor, classic shape, 8"..............70.00

Pink Lustre Ware

Pink lustre was produced by nearly every potter in the Staffordshire district in the 18th and 19th centuries. The application of gold lustre on white or light colored backgrounds produced pinks, while the same over dark colors developed copper. The wares ranged from hand painted plaques to transfer printed dinnerware.

Pitcher, hand painted rose decor, 6", $50.00.

Cup, child's; girl at stove w/cat, German...................20.00
Cup & saucer, floral, wishbone hdl, 3½" dia...............32.50
Cup & saucer, schoolhouse pattern.......................65.00
Mug, child's; pink/purple house decor, soft paste, 2¼".........35.00
Mug, red rose transfer w/blue squiggles, edge wear, 4".........45.00
Pitcher, jug type, buildings/rural landscapes/acorns/etc, 7¾"....400.00
Plaque, iris decor, open rim hdls, 11"......................65.00
Plate, house pattern, 6½".................................35.00
Plate, pyramid & ferns, 8¼"..............................30.00
Plate, scallops/scroll relief, HP lustre decor, gr dots, 9½".......35.00
Plate, sprig decor, 9"; w/cup & saucer.....................75.00
Teapot, Rebecca at the Well, mc decor, 8".................50.00
Vase, flared lip, ped ft, house decor, edge flakes, 6"..........40.00
Wall plaque, Prepare to Meet Thy God....................125.00

Pisgah Forest

The Pisgah Forest Pottery was established near Mount Pisgah in Arden, North Carolina, by Walter B. Stephen in 1914. Stephen is best known for his cameo ware which he decorated by hand in the pate-sur-pate style with scenes portraying covered wagons and other subjects related to the pioneer days. He also produced a turquoise crackled ware, and developed a fine crystalline glaze, examples of which are highly prized by today's collectors. The ware was marked 'Pisgah Forest', often with a potter at the wheel. Stephen died in 1961, but the work was continued by his associates.

Vase, ivory with crystals, signed, 5½", $225.00.

Bowl, Cameo, wagon train/mtns/cabin/people, Stephen, 1951...275.00
Creamer, bl/gr w/out, pink w/in, 1950, 4"..................28.00
Jug, purple/blue glaze, dtd 1940, 6".......................35.00
Pitcher, aqua crackle, 1938, 5"...........................40.00
Pitcher, aqua crackle, 1940 (?), sgn Stephen 3½"............35.00
Pitcher, Cameo, wht/gr, lime glaze below, Stephen, 1951, 5"...180.00
Pitcher, turq w/out, pink w/in, crackle glaze, 9"............47.50
Teapot, Cameo, covered wagon/oxen, etc, sgn Stephen........550.00
Teapot, Cameo, gr w/br flecks, wht wagon train, 5¾".........200.00
Vase, aqua, pink w/in, bulbous, 1938, 3"...................40.00
Vase, bl/wht crystalline, pink w/in, trumpet shape, 5½"........165.00
Vase, cream/bl/wht w/bl/gr crystals, EX example, 6¾".........185.00
Vase, ivory, pink w/in, bulbous, 1940, potter facing left, 3".....35.00
Vase, lt gr celadon, mkd, 1927, 11x6".....................90.00
Vase, lt gr/wht w/gr/cream crystals, factory pitting, 5½".......150.00

Vase, lt sea gr, celadon glaze, mk & 1927, 11x6".............90.00
Vase, moss gr, pink w/in, 1950, 3¾"......................30.00
Vase, rose, tapered form, sgn SB Stephen, 4"..............35.00
Vase, turquoise, dtd 1939, 5"............................25.00
Vase, wht to cream w/out w/cream/bl crystals, pink w/in, 5½"..165.00

Pittsburg

As early as 1797, utility window glass and hollow ware were being produced in the Pittsburgh area. Coal had been found in abundance, and it was there that it was first used instead of wood to fuel the glass furnaces. Because of this, as many as 150 glass companies operated there at one time. However, most failed due to the economically disasterous effects of the War of 1812. By the mid-1850s, those that remained were producing a wide range of flint glass items including pattern-molded and free-blown glass, cut and engraved wares, and pressed tableware patterns.

Bar bottle, 8 panels, bulbous lip, sapphire bl, 11"...........495.00
Bottle vase on ped ft, opal loops/clear, rings/rigaree, 13"......260.00
Compote, baluster stem/bowl, 12 ribs, folded rim, 5x6".......180.00
Compote, loop (leaf) pattern, lead glass, ca 1860, 7¾x10½"...225.00
Compote, pillar mold, 8 ribs, baluster stem/rnd ft, 7½x8"......225.00
Compote, pillar mold, 8 ribs, 8¾x10½"....................475.00
Creamer, applied flared ft, folded rim, cobalt, 5½"..........600.00
Creamer, from 9 panel tumbler mold, wear/scratches, 4"......205.00
Cruet, swirl pillar mold, hollow hdl, some residue, 8¼"......115.00
Cruet, 14 vertical ribs, applied ft/hdl/ring, pewter cap, 8"......100.00
Decanter, pillar mold, pewter jigger top, applied hdl, 10½"....235.00
Decanter, thick molded lip/pyriform body/vertical ribs, 11".....150.00
Food cover, applied hdl, folded rim, 10½x14¼"..............155.00
Hat, golden amber, 5½x7".................................75.00
Pitcher, clear w/opal looping, applied hdl, pontil chip, 5½"....400.00
Sugar bowl, folded rim on lid, applied ft, 6½".............380.00
Syrup, pressed, 6 panels, applied hollow hdl, 7"............30.00
Tumbler, panels at base, sapphire bl, 3"...................40.00
Tumbler, 8 panels, cobalt, 3½"...........................55.00
Whiskey taster, cobalt, 8 panel..........................175.00
Whiskey taster, sapphire blue, w/hdl, 2½"................55.00
Whiskey taster, sapphire blue, 2¼".......................45.00

Covered compote, fluted, 9" x 7", $125.00.

Playing Cards

Playing cards can be an enjoyable way to trace the course of history. The art, literature, and politics of an era can be gleaned from a study of its playing cards. When royalty lost favor with the people, Kings and Queens were replaced by common people. During the periods of war, generals, officers, and soldiers were favored. In the United States, early examples had portraits of Washington and Adams as opposed to Kings, Indian chiefs instead of Jacks, and goddesses for Queens.

Tarot cards were used in Europe during the 1300s as a game of chance, but by the 15th century they were used to predict the future, and were regarded with great reverence.

The backs of cards were of no particular consequence until the 1800s. The marble design used by the French during the late 1800s, and the colored wood-cut patterns of the Italians in the 19th century, are among the first attempts at decoration. Later, the English used cards printed with portraits of royalty. Eventually cards were decorated with a broad range of subjects from reproductions of fine art to advertising.

Although playing cards are becoming a popular collectible, prices are still relatively low. Complete decks of cards, printed earlier than the first postage stamp, can still be purchased for less than $100.

Periodic auction catalogs are available from 'Full House' Antique Playing Cards and Gambling Memorabilia. See the Directory under 'Clubs, Newsletters and Catalogs' for their address.

Key:

C------complete	hc------hand colored
cts-----courts	sz------size

Advertising

Dewar's White Label, wide, 1920s, Goodall, bk: Scotsman, MIB..20.00
DuPont Explosives, wide, ca 1900, 52+, G.................20.00
Edison Mazda Lamps, Parrish bk: The Waterfall, 52, w/box, G..50.00
Ford V8, ca 1930, made in Holland, Aces w/car & plant, 52, EX.25.00
Gold Medal Flour, wide, ca 1910, 52+, MIB...............25.00
Gordon's Dry Gin, wide, ca 1900, 52, EX.................12.00
Kramer's Music House, 1916, wide, USPC, pinochle, 48, MIB...20.00
Neiman Marcus, 1961, K's & J's: cowboys, Q's: barmaids, M....25.00
NY State Bankers, 1907, wide, USPC, gold edges, 52+, MIB....20.00
Pickwick Coffee, in orig box, G...........................7.00
Pippins 5¢ Cigars, ca 1900, colorful bks, 52, orig box, EX......20.00
RonRico Rum, narrow, ea face has bottle, sealed, MIB........15.00
Wayne Dog Food, narrow, ca 1950, B&B, 52+, w/orig box, EX..5.00
5A Horse Blankets, ca 1900, wide, gold edges, 52+, MIB......75.00

France and Belgium

Belgium, by DuBois, Gatteaux, 1811, eagle watermk, EX......675.00
Ciel de France, by Miro, Draeger Freres, 1950s, MIB..........10.00
French Costume, by Gibert, delicate coloring, 1840s, 52C, M...275.00
Guerre Mondiale I, Brepols, Allied leaders/war scenes, 1919, M..75.00
Jeu des Copains, Le Triboulet, courts/singing stars, 1965, MIB...10.00
Jeu Louis XV, Grimaud, 1895, gold edges, orig wrapper/box, M.100.00
Pre-Revolution French Std/LeBrun, hc woodblocks, 1750, M...200.00
Salvador Dali, unusual designs, 1969, Fourn #50, M..........50.00

Games

Baseball, pat June 19, 1917, 48+umpire+score card, MIB......16.00
Bookie, made in Belgium for England, 1930, horse racing, MIB..15.00
Japanese Aircraft & Ships, ca 1942, for US Navy, 53 cards, VG..15.00
Mayflower #1121, Cincinnati Co, 1897, 52+, w/orig box, VG....12.00
Moth & The Flame, 1906, stars of Broadway show, 40, MIB....22.00

Germany and Austria

Aluminum PC, Hauserman, Vienna/1920s, 100% aluminum, EX..65.00
German, anonymous, 1890s, stencilled color/pips, plaid bk, EX..40.00
Prussian Doppelbild, by ASS Altenburg, '20s, 32+Schweinblatt J.12.00
Timon Schroeter's Neue Deutche Spielkarten, Fritche, 1883....225.00

Great Britain

Boudoir, linen grained, Goodall, 1910s, orig wrapper, MIB......10.00
Coronation, DeLaRue, dbl deck, full length Elizabeth/Philip, M..40.00
Exportation Ace, Stopforth/Son, 1809, Geo III, 1 way cts, VG..175.00
Goodall, seals of 22 Oxford colleges, 1910s, orig box, EX.....10.00
Goodall, Victorian, Queen Elizabeth/Blk Prince courts, 1897...100.00
Queen Victoria Diamond Jubilee, 52C, a few damaged cards....30.00
What the Butler Saw, nudes/bk: butler w/camera, 1940s, MIB...20.00
Worshipful Co, bl border Cricket on Village Green, w/orig case..30.00
Worshipful Co, 1893, gold edges, 52+blank, in wrapper, MIB..200.00

Italy, Spain and Latin America

A Todos Alumbria, Spanish suits, 1878, 40C, orig wrapper, M...18.00
American Civil War, 1961, 100th Anniv, original dbl deck, M...40.00
Carte por Baccarat/Whist, Armanino, stamp dtd 1943, 52C, MIB..8.00
Cuajo Filipino, Fournier, 1930, special deck: 112, wrapper, M...20.00
Flor de Cadiz, by J Roura, Barcelona, 1926, 48C, orig wrap, M...20.00
Real Fabrica de Madrid, dtd 1849, hc woodblock, 46 of 48, G...50.00

Miniatures

Delands Tiny Playing Cards, 6½x9mm, rare.................100.00
Gold Lady, by A.S.S., 1950s, dbl deck: ea 52+, w/orig case, M....6.00
Grimaud, 1890s tax stamp, odd color, dbl deck: 52C, VG+box..25.00
LP Holmblad, 1860s, Spielkort for Born, cts: children, hc, M...125.00

Tarot and Fortune Telling

Deutches Original Tarot, 1930s, small sz, 78C, M w/orig box....25.00
Military Fortune, HV Loring, 1918, bells/hearts/stars/doves, M...20.00
Piemontese Tarot, A Viassone, tax stamp dtd 1900, 78C, worn..40.00

Transformations

Comic Karte, Fromann & Bunte, 1860s, 48 of 52, orig box....150.00
Hustling Joe #61, by USPC, 1895, 52+J, ½ orig box, VG.....300.00
Murphy Varnish, 52+J, previously mtd, EX w/orig box, rare....750.00

Transportation, Railroad, Sea and Air

Anchor Line, Goodall, 1920s, reversible 3 stack ship, 52, MIB...25.00
Cotton Belt Route, RR, 1903, 52+J, w/orig box, EX........175.00
Essberger, special for Hamburg Shipping/1939, unusual cts, MIB.35.00
P&O British SS Line, 'Eastern Highway', 1930s, 52, w/box, VG..25.00
Pacemaker, New York Central System, 1940s, Arrco, w/box, EX.15.00
Shaw & Savill Line, dbl deck, 1940, ea w/orig tax wrapper, MIB.35.00
Swedish American Line, ca 1926, bk: reversible SS on red, MIB.35.00
Union Pacific, wide souvenir deck, orig box, EX.............45.00
100th Anniv Soo Line RR, 1883-1983, ltd ed, dbl deck, MIB....16.00

United States

A Dougherty, no indices/ornate red bk/round corner/2 way cts..116.00
Amercanische Gaigel, USPC, 1890, German suits, 48C, VG.....35.00
American Beauties, drawn by Elvgren, 1950s, 52+, MIB........15.00

American Red Cross, government use only, 1944, in box......20.00
Apache, wide name, Indian on horse, 1916, gold edge, MIB.....40.00
Avoid, Non Revoke, orange Diamonds/purple Clubs, 52+J, EX..25.00
Celluloid by Piroxloid Corp, 1928, 52, EX w/box.............40.00
Contentment, wide name, gr tones, pinochle, 48C, EX w/box...15.00
Currier & Ives, Fireman, 1939, Western PCC, 52+, EX w/box...10.00
Dionne Quintuplets, in garden, 1937, by B&B, 52+, EX......50.00
Discus, Arrow PCC, 1930, Deco bks, gold edge, 52+, EX w/box.12.00
Holland, Congress, 1903, wide name, 52+Holland joker, M.....35.00
Jeffries, 1909, ea: fighter or fight scene, 52+, EX w/box......150.00
Kennedy Kards, MIB.................................25.00
Laugh In, 1969, cts: Rowan/Martin, 52+, MIB..............20.00
Lawrence & Cohen, 1860s, Owen Jones: Ace of Spades, 52, G.100.00
National Rambler #22, ca 1885, unusual Ace of Spades, 52, EX.35.00
Ripley's Believe It Or Not, 1963, each w/cartoon, 52+, MIB....15.00
Roodles, 1912, wishbone/shamrock/swastika/horseshoe, 56+, EX.20.00
Royal, NYCC for Paris Expo, 1878, illuminated pips, 52+, EX.225.00
Stag Party, 1953, cartoon deck, 52, MIB..................15.00
Stage Stars, for Craddock's Soap, 1890s, 52+, w/box, EX.....75.00
Union/Civil War, 1862, 52C, orig box, EX.................225.00
Victory, K's: Uncle Sam, J's: Hitler/Mussolini, 52+, EX w/box...45.00
Votes for Women, Suffrage, 1908, 52+, orig box, VG.........60.00

World's Fair and Souvenir Decks

California, souvenir, 1911............................30.00
Century of Progress, 1933, Arrco, bk: Belgian Village, 52, VG...10.00
Clark's Columbian Expo, 1893, 52+J+Blank, orig box, EX....65.00
Jamestown Expo, 1907...............................50.00
Lost Channel/1000 Islands, scenic, 1930s, Santway Photo, EX...22.00
Maine, scenic, ca 1900, Chisholm, gold edges, 52+, MIB.......55.00
Nation's Capitol, souvenir, 1925.......................35.00
Nation's Capitol, 1909, USPC, gold edges, 52+, MIB.........40.00
NY World's Fair, 1964-5, scenic, B&B, M..................6.00
O'Callaghan's, Chicago, 1930, odd faces, 52+, MIB, rare......100.00
Pan-American Expo, 1901............................30.00
Paris Expo, 1900, Tom Jones/USPC, gold edges, 52+, box, EX.75.00
Peking, The Forbidden City; 52+, orig box, VG, rare.........100.00
Pittsburg, Gilmore, 1901, 52+Father Pitt Joker+Map, box, VG..35.00
South Dakota, narrow scenic, 1950s, MIB.................10.00
St Joseph, Missouri; wide scenic, 1907, 52, ½ orig box, VG.....65.00
St Louis, narrow scenic, dbl deck, 1950s, B&B, 54 views, MIB..12.00
1st Panama Canal, wide scenic, 1908, gold edges, 52+, MIB....50.00

Miscellaneous

Adolph Wulff, Copenhagen ca 1890 tax stamp, 52C, EX........40.00
National Leader, for India by Belgium, 1931, bk: Ghandi, MIB...20.00
Russian, Slavonic #501, ca 1928, silver edges, 52+, MIB.......45.00
Russian anti-religious, 1930, ridicules 4 religions, 52+, MIB....200.00
Sweden, 1860, A Boman, Stockholm, stenciled/pips, 52C, EX..135.00
Swiss, Scenic Ages, 1915 by J Muller, 36C, EX..............18.00

Political Entourage

The most valuable political items are those from any period which relate to a political figure whose term was especially significant or marked by an important event, or one whose personality was particularly colorful. Posters, ribbons, badges, photographs, and pin-back buttons are but a few examples of the items popular with collectors of political memorabilia.

Political campaign pin-back buttons were first mass-produced and widely distributed in 1896 for the president-to-be William McKinley and for the first of three unsuccessful attempts by William Jennings Bryan. Pin-back buttons have been used during each presidential campaign ever since and are collected by many people. The scarcest ones are those used in the presidential campaigns for James Davis in 1924 and for James Cox in 1920.

See also Autographs

Key:

bk----back   ft----front

Ad, Quaker Bitters, Cleveland/Hendricks 'litho, orig 5x7" sheet..18.50
Ad, Teddy Roosevelt, for re-election, 1904, 11x16"............12.00
Ad, Van Heusen shirts, Ronald Reagan, 1953, 11x14".........35.00
Badge, Chicago Republican Convention guest, 1908...........45.00
Badge, GOP Convention, Iowa, 1912.......................19.00
Badge, Loyal Temperance Legion, incised letters, 1890-1900....12.00
Ballot, Lincoln/Johnson, 1864..........................150.00
Banner, Nixon, red/silver/bl/wht aluminum, 1972, 5x30".........5.00
Bill of Fare, Abraham Lincoln inaugural, 5½x10½"............180.00
Book, Authentic Life Pres McKinley, salesman's sample.......17.00
Book, campaign songs; Garfield/Arthur, 1880...............18.00
Book, children's; Heroic Life of Wm McKinley, 1902, 48 pgs....22.00
Book, Garfield Album, sm pleated chromolitho on assasination...20.00
Book, The Presidents, pub 1908 by Gravure Co Am, 16x20"....35.00
Booklet, Terrible Tragedy at Washington, Pres Lincoln, 116 pgs.55.00
Bookmark, FDR, cut-out profile on thin silver metal, 1x2"......8.00
Bookmark, Lincoln, woven, eagle/flag/shield/quote, 12".......30.00
Bottle, Pres Cleveland figural, frosted/clear glass, 10".......135.00
Bumper sticker, Ike & Dick, license plate shape, blk/orange......4.00
Bust, Wilkie, frosted glass, 10"........................145.00
Button, Adlai Stevenson, Our Next President, w/picture........8.00
Button, Alfred E Smith................................18.00
Button, All the way with LBJ, 3" photo changes w/angle........5.00
Button, Bryan & Kern jugate, 1¼".....................135.00
Button, Carter, Ohio For Carter, photo in flag, 1776-1976, 4"...10.00
Button, Carter, Vote For Tennessee's Delegates, May 24, 3"...10.00
Button, Carter & Mondale, 'orange', leaves at top, 3½".........7.00
Button, Chas Evans Hughes for Pres.....................24.00
Button, Eisenhower, Man o/t Hour, w/ribbon & elephant pendant.4.00
Button, Goldwater, I'm A Teenager For Barry, 3½"..........10.00
Button, Goldwater & Miller America Needs, photo, oval, 4".....50.00
Button, HH Humphrey, 2½"............................30.00
Button, Hoover & Curtis, jugate........................100.00
Button, Jimmy Walker.................................16.00
Button, John F Kennedy, memorial, flasher.................2.00
Button, Johnson for President, For Leadership We Need, photo..8.00
Button, Kennedy & Johnson, America Needs, w/photos.........6.00
Button, LBJ, w/ribbon: Welcome Pres LBJ, Inauguration '65....10.00
Button, McKinley & Hobart, presidential campaign, M..........45.00
Button, Nixon & Lodge, Best Choice for '60, photos, 3½".....10.00
Button, Parker & Davis, 1¾"..........................60.00
Button, Roosevelt & Curley, paper, sm nick on shield.........85.00
Button, Roosevelt & Wallace, jugate.....................22.00
Button, Smith For President, w/photo, ¾"..................15.00
Button, Taft & Sherman jugate, blk/wht, 1¼"..............130.00
Button, Teddy Roosevelt, celluloid, sepia pic, ⅝"...........10.00
Button, Uncle Sam hangs Hitler/Let's Pull Together, mechanical.50.00
Button, Vote for Wallace, 3½".........................5.00
Button, Vote Truman in '48............................30.00
Button, Warren Harding................................24.00
Button, Wilkie & FDR, jugate, salesman's safety pin..........25.00
Button, Wilkie & McNary, jugate........................65.00
Button, Wilson, celluloid, Am flag, Peace & Preparedness, 1912.12.00
Carte de visite, Grover Cleveland........................8.00
Cartoon, Horace Greeley, Thos Nast, Greely w/Boss Tweed.....10.00
Cartoon, WWII, Uncle Sam w/Nazis, W Engright/Miami Herald..85.00
Cigar box, Rough Riders, w/Teddy.......................95.00

Bronze plaque, profile of Roosevelt, 'Aggressive fighting for the right is the noblest sport the world affords', $1,000.00.

Collar box, Handcock, gutta percha w/bust of Hancock, 4¾"...110.00
Cup & saucer, relief scene: When Roosevelt Came...Okla, 1900..45.00
Document, sgn Roosevelt, dtd 1904, appointing PMaster Gen...150.00
Engraving, Warren Harding, 9x12"...................,....20.00
Ferrotype, Grant & Colfax.............................140.00
Ferrotype, Lincoln/Hamlin, token, 1860, 23mm..............50.00
Ferrotype, McClellan & Pendleton, brass, 1", M............150.00
Ferrotype, McClellan for President, 1864..................125.00
Game, Dewey Game, cards, w/Dewey portrait ribbon, in box.....50.00
Handkerchief, Bryan/Sewell campaign, silk, free coinage/eagle....50.00
Handkerchief, Eisenhower, lg............................20.00
Handkerchief, Harrison/Morton, blue, lg...................95.00
Handkerchief, McKinley, various flags, portrait, lg..........115.00
Handkerchief, Parker/Davis, 1904, lg....................110.00
Handkerchief, Progressive Party, w/moose, 1912, lg..........70.00
Handkerchief, Roosevelt, Progressive battle, w/flag, 1912, lg....95.00
Handkerchief, Tippecanoe, Morton Too, Protection, Home, G...25.00
Handkerchief, Washington/Eisenhower.....................12.00
Handkerchief, WH Harrison, equestrian, 1840, lg..........1,000.00
Handkerchief, Woodrow Wilson, Allied Nations' flags/portraits...25.00
Magazine, Life, JFK in Memoriam.........................25.00
Magazine, Souvenir Pres McKinley's Visit to Boston, 1899.......8.00
Magazine cover, Puck, 1912, cartoon: T Roosevelt in tutu, EX..45.00
Medal, GAR Vets, EX..................................12.50
Medalet, Henry Harrison presidential election, 1840, copper.....75.00
Medalet, James Buchanan presidential election, 1865..........50.00
Mirror, field; pewter, 'Georgus Washington' w/profile, 1844.....200.00
Money, New Deal, 1936................................10.00
Mug, McKinley, pressed glass, picture/motto, flared rim, 3½"....40.00
Mug, Taft/Sherman, porcelain w/mc portrait/flags/eagle, 5".....60.00
Newspaper, Austin American, JFK Assassinated, Nov 23, 1963...50.00
Newspaper, Austin American, LBJ Becomes President, Nov 23...50.00
Newspaper, extra, Austin American, Death of JFK, Nov 22.....100.00
Pamphlet, Communist Manifesto, pub Intn'l, NY, '30s, 5x7"......5.00
Paperweight, Roosevelt/Fairbanks, glass...................150.00
Photo, Franz Josef of Austria & his court, 13x17"...........220.00
Photo, Hohenzollern family, 2 w/enamel fr, coat of arms, 10"..300.00
Picture, John Honey Fitzgerald, for Mayor of Boston, celluloid..100.00
Pin, Cox, rooster shape................................90.00
Pin, Hoover/Curtis, wht enamel elephant...................25.00
Pitcher, Al Smith, toby w/smiling face, signature, 7".........50.00
Plate, commemorative, Kaiser Wilhelm II, 1914, set of 3......65.00
Plate, For President, Grover Cleveland, ironstone, 8".........30.00
Plate, James Garfield, porcelain w/blk transfer/signature, 9"....38.00
Plate, McKinley/Roosevelt, milk glass/br jugate, open rim, 5½"..32.00
Plate, Pres & Mrs Eisenhower, china w/mc picture/florals, 6"....10.00
Plate, Ulysses Grant, br transfer: eagle/flags/dates 1869-77.....60.00
Plate, US Grant administration, floral center, gold band, 8½"..500.00

Pop can, Goldwater, top cut out.............................5.00
Postcard, mechanical; Taft, elephant w/string tail.............15.00
Postcard, Wilson, Temperance Prohibition/bottle labeled Wilson..5.00
Postcard, Wilson's 1916 campaign, Wilson in wreath w/flag......5.00
Postcard, WJ Bryan, color portrait, last campaign.............8.00
Postcard, Women's Suffrage, New Woman, 1919...............4.50
Poster, FDR's 1933 campaign, flowers/eagle/flags/FDR, 18x24"..35.00
Poster, James Garfield for Pres, dtd 1800...................100.00
Poster, Landon/Knox, 20½x14".........................15.00
Poster, WM J Bryan for Pres, w/picture....................90.00
Print, Dewey's Battle of Manila, c 1898 by Muller, Luschinger..50.00
Print, FDR, dtd 1933, 17x21".........................19.00
Program & invitation, inaugural Gov Green, Ill, 1941.........10.00
Puzzle, Playing Possum w/Taft, paper on wood, in box........80.00
Puzzle, The Administration, Blaine/Harrison, block game.....100.00
Record, A Campaign Talk by Pres Calvin Coolidge, 1924......30.00
Record, Edison cylinder; Ideal Republic, Wm J Bryan.........100.00
Record, Edison cylinder; Roosevelt Policies, by Taft, M.......100.00
Ribbon, Harrison/Morton, Protector for Am Labor, woven silk...65.00
Ribbon, Lincoln, mourning, bust in oval, Our Martyred Father...50.00
Ribbon, Lincoln, mourning, bust in wreath/eagle/shield, France..65.00
Ribbon, Lincoln memorial, eagle/flags/weeping Liberty, Swiss...130.00
Ribbon, Lincoln memorial, silver portrait/eagle, Carquillet......40.00
Ribbon, McKinley/Hobart, yellow w/oval portraits/motto, 7".....30.00
Ribbon, Tammany Hall, Cleveland/Stevenson Inauguration, 1893.80.00
Roster, Whig Convention, 1848.........................45.00
Sheet music, Grant/Colfax, Our Nation's Choice.............40.00
Sheet music, We Want Wilkie, Republican campaign, 1940.....10.00
Sign, porc, Uncle Sam/I Want You, by Flagg, 2 sides, WW2"..895.00
Sign, 2 board w/pnt message, Cleveland vs Harrison, 74x22"..260.00
Statue, Teddy Roosevelt, frosted glass....................150.00
Stereocard set, McKinley's Assassination, 5 for.............20.00
Stick pin, Wm Jennings Bryan, paper, dingy................13.50
Stud button, Teddy Roosevelt, campaign hat w/animal face......20.00
Ticket, Democratic National Convention, 1920, Wilson portrait...9.00
Ticket, Republican Nat'l Convention, June 19th, 1900, complete.19.00
Tile, Coolidge, American Encaustic, lt bl...................45.00
Tile, Woodrow Wilson portrait, sgn Cartlidge, 1916...........150.00
Tip tray, Democratic Nat'l Convention, Baltimore, 1912........60.00
Token, Harrison, 1888.................................9.00
Token, Hoover, Good for 4 yrs prosperity, brass, 1928, 1".......5.50
Top hat, Harrison & Reid campaign, felt, 1892...............70.00
Tote bag, canvas w/pic Reagan, 'Colorado Reagan Country', M..30.00
Tumbler, Wm J Bryan, milk glass........................35.00
Watch fob, Our Choice Taft.............................16.00
Watch fob, Parker/Davis, brass, 1904....................125.00
Watch fob, Roosevelt/Fairbanks, brass, 1904..............85.00
Watch fob, Taft/Sherman, Good Luck, 1908, w/strap..........20.00
Watch fob, Wilson, celluloid............................60.00
Wrist watch, American flag on face, 17 jewels, emb JFK profile.175.00

Pomona

Pomona glass was patented in 1885 by the New England Glass works. Its characteristics are an etched background of crystal lead glass decorated with simple designs painted on with metallic stains of amber or blue. The etching was first achieved by hand cutting through an acid resist. This method, called first grind, resulted in an uneven feather-like frost effect. Later, to cut production costs, the hand cut process was discontinued in favor of an acid bath, which effected an even frosting. This method is called second grind.

Bowl, 1st grind, ruffled/crimped rim, ftd, cornflowers, 6" dia...110.00
Bowl, 2nd grind, cornflowers, crimped rim, 3½x8"...........275.00

Celery, 2nd grind, blueberry decor, 6½"....................225.00
Creamer, 2nd grind, pansy & butterfly, no color, 4"..........80.00
Cruet, 1st grind, w/light amber neck.....................450.00
Cup, 1st grind, clear amber above fancy border.............135.00
Pickle castor, cornflower decor; SP frame..................400.00
Pitcher, tankard; 2nd grind, dbl row bl cornflowers, 12"......895.00
Pitcher, 1st grind, plain, 4½".........................165.00
Pitcher, 1st grind, sq mouth, cornflower decor, 6¼".........290.00
Pitcher, 1st grind, w/6 tumblers, gold stain................750.00
Pitcher, 2nd grind, cornflower decor, sq top, 5"............225.00
Punch cup, 1st grind...................................95.00
Punch cup, 2nd grind, cornflower decor...................85.00
Rose bowl, 2nd grind, amber stain, crimp top, 3 legs, 2½x4"..150.00
Toothpick, 1st grind, tri-lobe top.......................235.00
Toothpick, 2nd grind, tri-lobe top......................165.00
Tumbler, 2nd grind, cornflower decor....................85.00
Tumbler, 2nd grind, scalloped band under amber rim band, 4"..95.00
Vase, lily form, w/cornflowers..........................225.00

Bowl, first grind, cornflower decoration, 5", $150.00.

Popcorn and Peanut Machines

The popcorn and peanut machines that were a popular sight a century ago were often elaborately decorated. Some were designed with special attention-getting features, such as a small clown to turn the peanut roaster, or a fascinating steam engine placed where curious onlookers could watch it power the rotating corn popper. The vendor hoped that should the enticing aroma of his wares go unnoticed, the appeal of his machine would capture the attention of those passing by!

Peanut roaster, Bartholomew, ca 1910, converted to gas.....2,500.00
Peanut roaster, Bartholomew, spring wound, 1900, M rstr....3,500.00
Peanut roaster, Bartholomew, 1928, professionally rstr.......2,450.00
Peanut roaster, Holcom Hoke/counter Fresh Butter Kist, rstr...350.00
Popcorn wagon, Stutsman, 4 wheel kerosene, red, EX......3,500.00

Post Cards

A German by the name of Von Stephan is credited for inventing the postcard, first printed in Austria in 1869. They were eagerly accepted by the Continentals and the English alike, who saw them as a more economical way to send written messages. Three years later postcards were introduced in America.

The first to be printed in the United States were plain U.S. postal cards. Photo cards, first sold here in the 1880s, were made in Germany by order of the Leighton Company of Portland, Maine. But the Columbian Exposition in 1893 was the spark that ignited the postcard phenomenon. Souvenir cards by the millions were sent to folks back home -- Expo scenes, transportation themes, animals, birds, and advertising messages became popular. There were patriotic themes, Black themes, and cards for every occasion.

In 1907, the Payne-Aldrich Bill placed such a high tariff on imported cards that dealers began to turn to American printers and lithographers. Some of the earliest postcard publishers were Raphael Tuck, Gibson Art, and Nister and Gabriel. Early 20th century illustrators such as Winsch, Brundage, Rose O'Neill, and Clapsaddle designed cards that are especially valued today.

Though the postcard rage waned at the onset of WWI, they rank today among the most sought after paper collectibles.

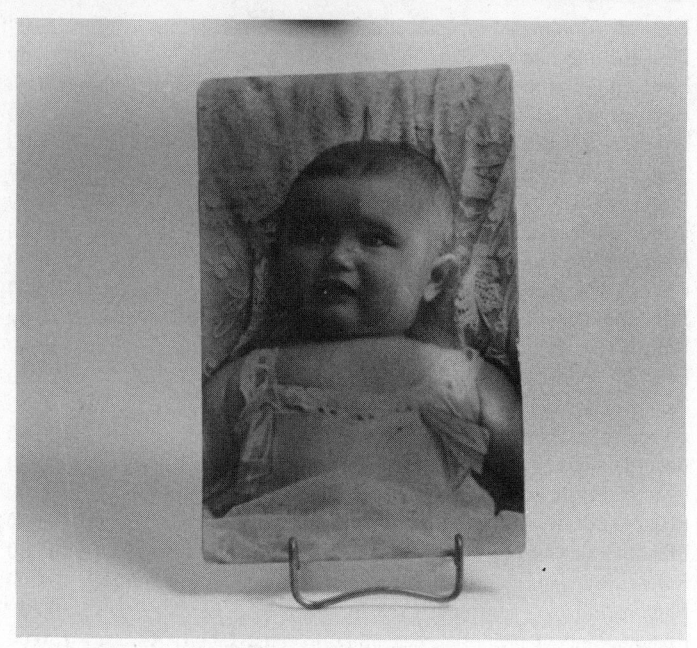

Baby photo, squeeker inside, made in Germany, Pittle Supply Co., 5½" x 3½", $30.00.

Adolph Hitler, sgn Schindler, printed in Germany, G..........45.00
Advertising, Allentown Adpostal, lady w/umbrella, NM.........40.00
Advertising, Campbell's Kids #1, Thrive on..., unused........15.00
Advertising, Coca-Cola, lady w/lg hat, sgn Hamilton King, EX..525.00
Advertising, Coffee Culture, set of 16, unused, EX...........32.00
Advertising, Dental Flossy, lady using product, unused, M....12.00
Advertising, Happy Thought: the American Flyer, unused, VG....8.00
Advertising, Hood's Sarsaparilla: Lab, Lowell, MA, used, G......4.00
Advertising, JI Case: Steam Roller, Country Roads, unused, G....5.00
Advertising, RJ Reynolds, Winston, Camel, Prince Albert, NM....4.00
Advertising, Texaco, Back on the Air Again, Ed Wynn, 1933, G.10.00
Advertising, Walkover Shoes, Going to Church, used, EX.......4.00
Advertising, Walkover Shoes, set of 9, in delft, unused, EX.....27.00
Advertising, Warner Rust Proof Corsets, A Mucha illus, unused.215.00
Asti, full-bosomed lady, unused, NM.........................10.00
Asti-type ladies, set of 3, BB London series #2402, NM........18.00
Attwell, Mabel Lucie; Valentine's series #745, I Loves..., G.......8.00
Benito Mussolini, Ballerini e Fratini, Firenze #125, used, G.....20.00
Black Liberation, 150th Anniv French Revolution/1939, set of 5.20.00
Brundage, F; New Year, clock w/child emerging, PM 1914, EX..12.00
Busy Bears, Days of Week, set of 7, Ullman Series 79, Wall....80.00
Charles Lindbergh, set of 17, Excelsior Supply Co, Chicago, NM.68.00
Christy, F Early; College Girls, Princeton, Ullman series #93....15.00
Clappsaddle, Easter child, used, G............................4.00
Clappsaddle, New Year, boy w/suitcase, emb, International......17.00
Clappsaddle, Santa/girl/telephone, unused, NM................10.00
Clappsaddle, St Patrick's, boy w/knickers & top hat, used, G....5.00
Clappsaddle, Valentine, To The One I Love, little girl, used, G...5.00
Colby Cats & Dogs, set of 3, unused, VG....................12.00
Commemorative, CA's welcoming the fleet, 1908, Briggs Co.....25.00
Cupid & Nude Lady, set of 4, wht & gold against dk blue, M....24.00
Dog Seller, Berliner Typen, artist sgn, unused, EX............20.00
Erika/Fantasy Lady, portrait & artistic masks, ca 1902, G......10.00
Fisher, Harrison; Anticipation, series #101, Reinthal/Newman....10.00
Fisher, Harrison; Chums, girl w/cat, Cosmo Series #970, NM...100.00
Fisher, Harrison; Farewell, R&N #773, M....................12.50
Fisher, Harrison; Moments of Girl's Life, 6 in orig frame......70.00
Gassaway, child mailing letter, unused, EX....................6.00
Gassaway, children & geese, used, G..........................5.00
Gods & Goddesses, Apollo & the Muses, set of 10, b/w, NM....25.00
Gods & Goddesses, set of 9 different pictures, colorful, NM.....54.00
Golay, Mary; still life, set of 6, unused, M...................15.00
Heal Bears, Days of the Week, set of 7, Wm S Heal, 1907, NM.84.00
Hermann Goring, sgn Karl Bauer, #852, Fingerle & Co, VG.....25.00
Hold-to-light, die-cut view of White House, Cupples...........32.00
Hold-to-light, Donaldson Glass Block, Minneapolis, unused.....20.00
Hold-to-light, garlands form '1908', portraits inside #s, VG.....30.00

Hold-to-light, St Louis Expo 1904, Inside Inn, Expo cancel, G..135.00
Hold-to-light, State Street/Chicago, Joseph Koehler #2401, EX...40.00
HSM Money Card, Russia, unused, NM........................20.00
Installment set, Her Name was Maud, set of 4, G...............32.00
Japanese Art, set of 6, by Hokusai, M in orig wrapper.........15.00
Kaiser Wilhelm II, set of 4, 1 with his wife, G.................40.00
Kewpie, Was Glad To Get That Letter, Gartner/Bender, VG......5.00
Kewpies, Nipped in the Bud, Blk boy/Wht girl, Czechoslavakia...10.00
Kewpies, You Are Invited, easel cars Klever Kard, O'Neill, NM...35.00
L'Entolage, set of 6 w/wrapper, sgn Edouard Bernard, all M....600.00
Ladies & Lg Hats, set of 3, gold border, used, G..............12.00
Langsdorf, College Girls, silk, Vassar, emb, unused, VG........20.00
Langsdorf, Lovers, 'Surrender', from Christmas set, emb, NM....20.00
Langsdorf, Military, Corporal-US Cavalry, #14, emb, VG........15.00
Langsdorf, State of Michigan girl, embossed, unused, VG........15.00
Langsdorf, State of Ohio girl, embossed, unused, G.............12.00
Leap Year, Come Birdie Come To Me, S Gabriel, sgn DWIG......7.00
Lewin, Blk boy & girl, Comique Series, I Hab Lost One..., VG....6.00
MacArthur Patriotic Poster Card, portrait on back, unused, M....15.00
McGill, Donald; naked Blk boy, I Can't Hide..., unused, NM......6.00
Mechanical, Clock Tower, DRGM, German litho, unused VG....15.00
Mechanical, girl mails letter, 2 movements rotate month/day.....22.00
Mechanical, water wheel, vivid color, M.......................25.00
Mermaid, being sung to by frog, EX early German litho, NM....20.00
Metamorphic, A Sport, ladies seen in face, b/w, unused, NM....50.00
Metamorphic, Napoleon, soldiers seen in face, b/w, VG.........50.00
Military, British Army WWI, King at Front, set of 6/sepia, M....36.00
Military, set of 12, sgn Archie Gunn, illustrated PC Co, M......72.00
Military, set of 6, sgn Wall, illustrated PC Co, M..............30.00
Miracle of Bernadette, set of 10 cards form lg picture, 10 for...100.00
New Year's, luck symbols, L Schnug, Philipp/Kramer--Vienna...125.00
Novelty, bear w/honey: glass eyes rotate, used, G..............4.00
Novelty, booklet card: MOP, unused, NM.....................5.00
Novelty, celluloid fan: silk covered, unused, G.................6.00
Novelty, pincushion: lady on bike, unused, VG................12.00
Novelty, 3 celluloid flowers, EX.............................6.00
Ottmat Zieher Children's Band, unused, VG...................10.00
Ottmat Zieher Stamp Card, Brazil, #38, unused, NM...........18.00
Ottmat Zieher Vegetable Heads, set of 4, unused, NM.........48.00

Otto Von Bismark, real photo, taken in Bad Kissingen, 1890, M.15.00
Panama Canal Poster Card, emb map, unused, EX............20.00
PFB Co, Lord's Prayer, Forgive Us, Series #7070, unused, VG...6.00
PFB Co, lovers in rowboat, set of 5, #6009, unused, M......20.00
PFB Co, mother-in-law: The Threatening..., used, EX..........7.00
PFB Co, proposal: Oh Sir! this is so sudden, used VG.........6.00
PFB Co, proposal: Saunter through Life, used, VG............6.00
PFB Co, Thanksgiving Greetings, turkey, Series #7721, used, NM.5.00
PFB Co, To My Valentine, 3 cherubs playing, M.............13.00
Playing Card Queens, set of 4, c 1909, Moffat/Yard/Gross, NM..240.00
Pour D'Or, set of 6, nude girl, sgn Josef Hart, all VG........480.00
Powell, Lyman; Eventful Days, set of 4, in orig frame, M......80.00
Queen Elizabeth II, set of 3, R Tuck & Sons, England, M.....18.00
Roosevelt Bears, #1, At Home, NM.......................25.00
Roosevelt Bears, #12, Take an Auto Ride, M...............10.00
Roosevelt Bears, #16, At The Circus, M..................10.00
Roosevelt Bears, #18, 4th of July, M....................10.00
Roseland, H; Teacup Fortune Telling, Blk's portrait, 1903, NM..10.00
Salon Des Beaux Arts Nude, #4378, blk/wht, unused, M.......20.00
Sunbonnet, Days of the Week, set of 7, Ullman, c 1905, NM....84.00
Sunbonnet, emb, pk ribbon, Richard Behrendt/SG, c 1902, VG..15.00
Sunbonnet, Hours of the Day, 10 AM/Mowing Time, Wall, G....10.00
Sunbonnet, Nobody's Lookin', sgn Wall, series #189, Ullman, G..6.00
Sunbonnet, Nursery Rhyme, set of 4, Mary...Lamb, G.........32.00
Sunbonnet, Paying Toll, sgn Dixon, Ullman, c 1905, G........10.00
Sunbonnet, Quotations, A Good Book..., sgn Wall, Ullman, G...10.00
Sunbonnet, Reasons, set of 4, Ullman, sgn Wall, c 1906, NM...48.00
Tempest, D; Black Looks Never Got Anybody Anywhere, VG.....6.00
Tuck, British Fish, set of 6 Tuck Oilette #1544, unused, M.....36.00
Tuck, Fantasy Egg Faces: man & lady in rain, used, G.........8.00
Tuck, Fantasy Masked Faces: lovers/wine glass, EX...........10.00
Tuck, Greeting from the Seaside, children at beach, M.........10.00
Tuck, Happy Little Coon, Dearest Friend, Oilette series IV, VG..15.00
Tuck, Happy Little Coons/A Man, Oilette series #9227, VG.....15.00
Tuck, Happy Little Coons/Quite the Lady, series #9049, G.....12.00
Tuck, Homes of US Presidents, set of 25..................100.00
Tuck, Knocks Witty & Wise, sgn DWIG, Don't Try to Build..., M.5.00
Tuck, Rulers of England, Cromwell, Series 616, unused, NM....15.00
Tuck, Rulers of England, Stephen, Series 614, unused, M......15.00
Tuck, School Days/Figures Never Lie, series #170, unused, VG...6.00
Tuck, 23-Skidoo: Love Tribunes, #5, used, G...............5.00
Twelvetrees, boy playing soldier, unused, VG...............5.00
Twelvetrees, boy working, unused, VG....................5.00
Ulrich, men, women & autos, set of 4, M.................60.00
US Stamp Card, flat printing, eagle & shield, unused, EX......23.50
Wain, Louis; I Had A Lovely Time, animals, unused, NM......40.00
Wiener Werkstaette, lady sitting/moon, sgn O Kokoscka, M...1,000.00
Wiener Werkstaette, New Year's, #37, anonymous design, 1914.100.00
Winsch, John; Halloween, unsigned Schmucker, used, G.......15.00
Winsch, John; Thanksgiving, unsigned Schmucker, used, VG....15.00
Women's Suffrage, Campbell Art #310, unused, M............32.00
Zodiac-Constellations, set of 8, wrapper, unused, M..........20.00

Posters

Advertising posters by such French artists as Monet and Toulouse-Lautrec were used as early as the mid-1800s. Color lithography spurred their popularity. The circus, movies, and patriotic causes are popular categories with poster collectors today. Works of noted artists such as Fox, Parrish, and Herrick bring high prices. Other considerations are good color, interesting subject matter, and of course, condition.

See also Circus Collectibles; Movie Memorabilia; Political Entourage
Key: lm----linen mounted

Advertising

Aux Travailleurs, turn of century lady/child, 58"............300.00
Brandy, Deco design of M Chevalier w/bottle, 1930..........425.00
Columbia Chainless Cycles, goddess, 1897, lm, 83"..........975.00
El Principal Cigars, 2 fold-out stands, paper/cb.............50.00
Fap Anis, flapper w/fan, by Delval, 1925, 48x63"...........350.00
Humber Bicycles, French, by Camis, 39x50"...............425.00
Mantalo Liqueur, woman/Cupid pours drink, 1905...........350.00
Moretti's, man on umbrella, French, 1920s, 44x55".........350.00
Raphaelle Liquor, shows airplane, Rosetti, 1908............450.00

Magic

Alexander, 10-color portrait holding crystal ball, 47x78", M....200.00
Carter Beats the Devil, Carter & Devil at poker, 14x22", EX....75.00
Dr Ormond's Great Sunflower Coterie, 1890s, 26x34", NM....225.00
Karmi, Shoots Cracker From Man's Head, Donaldson, 30x40"..100.00
Magic, Great Dayton Show, lady being levitated, 1915, 20x30"..135.00
Magic, Kassner The Magician, ghostly elephant, 1925, 38x55"..280.00
Newman the Great, Soiree Fantastiques, Newman & imp, 20x30"110.00

Minstrel

Al G Fields, parade of performers, Courier, 1907, lm, 30x40"..295.00
Bryant's, stars & stripes letters, banjo/guitar, 1869.............85.00
Johnson & Slavin's, Nautical Spectacular Clog Dance, 1890, lm.200.00
The Great Original New Orleans, orchestra on stage, early, b/w.150.00
Vogel's, man in blackface, 1903, 28x40"..................325.00

Theatrical

A Modern Cinderella, man/chorus line, 1900s, Ackermann, VG..75.00
Beautiful Indian Maidens, ornate lithograph, 1890s, lm, 20x30".100.00
Bringing Up Father, McManus Comedy w/Music, 1915, lm, 20x30"70.00
Cat & the Canary, woman & evil cat, blk/yel, 1910s, lm, 20x30".65.00
Erma the Elf/Surprise Infernal, devil costume, '90s, 14x28".....65.00
Fantasies of 1929, Vaudeville Burlesque, 28x40".............125.00
Gamblers of the West, comedic bad man, 1906, lm, 20x30", M.190.00
Jessie James, The Missouri Outlaw, 1910s, Donaldson, 20x30"..80.00
Katzenjammer Kids, 1911 musical, 29x40", EX.............150.00
La Farandole, Cheret, 1884, lm, 20x28", M...............285.00
La Houppa, Faye, mid-1930s, lm, 45x62", NM..............495.00
La Regina, for French Opera: The Queen, 22x32"...........150.00
Les Fetards, Pal, 1890s, lm, 23x30", M..................345.00
Sapho, L'Opera Comique, by Pal, 1897, 38x51", lm, M.......500.00
To Die At Dawn, turn of century lady, 1901, 43x79"........350.00

Transportation

Airline, United Over San Francisco, plane over bridge, 16x21".150.00
Canadian Scenic Dome Route Across Canada, train scene, 1951.75.00
Clear Road Ahead, English RR, interior locomotive, 1940s, EX.225.00
Moteur Romain, couple in Voiturette, sgn Duzolle, ca 1900....435.00
Railroad, Night Freight, British RR, Condor Locomotive, 1946.225.00
Speed Along Germany's Reichsautobahn, silvery highway, EX...100.00
Steamship, Cunard New Steamers, lg ship, Thomas, 1920s, M..350.00
Steamship, Red Star Line, steamer/vignette, Cassiers, orig fr....750.00
Steamship, Titanic, for a German film, ship sinking, late 40's...125.00

Travel

Bray Dunes (France), Beach/Sea, 1930s, lm, 29x41", M......275.00
Marseille (France), steamship, R Broders, 1925, lm, 30x43", M.475.00

Patzcuaro, Mexican State RR, men w/baskets, 1930s, 27x37"...175.00
Snowdonia, LMS RR/England, mountain scene, Tryfan, 40x50".180.00
State Railways Excursions to Brittany, Dorival, 1920s, 29x42"..225.00
Travel, Monte Carlo Beach, Le Paradis Retrouve, sgn SEM, 1930325.00
Wales, scenic, AB Webb, 1935, 40x50", lm, M.............165.00
Yorkshire Coast, G Brown, 1920s, village scene, lm, 40x50", M.250.00

War

A Careless Word/A Needless Loss, sailor on beach, AO Fisher...35.00
A Cent Cinquante Metres Au Dessus De La Bataille, 14x24"....12.50
Americans All! Victory Liberty Loan, Christy, 40x27", EX......60.00
And They Said We Couldn't Fight, Forsythe, 41x20½", EX.....45.00
Army recruiting, There Is No Peace, Civil War, 21x23½".....225.00
Avenge Dec 7th, angry man/Pearl Harbor, B Perlin, 28x40"....100.00
Avez-Vous Place Dans Votre Coeur Pour Nous? WWI, De Maris.60.00
Award For Careless Talk, hand w/Iron Cross, 20x30", EX.....85.00
Battlewise Infantryman is careful of what he says..., WWII.......9.50
Beat Back the Hun, Strothmann, trooper/bayonet, 30x20", G....50.00
Before Sunset, Buy A Liberty Bond, Statue of Liberty, EX......65.00
Blood or Bread, soldier helps another amid battle, 20x30", EX..50.00
Clear the Way, Buy Bonds, Christy, 29x20", EX.............100.00
Come On, Marine over fallen Hun, 20x30"..................75.00
Defeat the Kaiser & His U-Boats, rat-Kaiser, 14x22", M.......100.00
Don't Wait For The Draft, Uncle Sam/stars/stripes, 28x40", M..200.00
E-E-E-Yah Yip Yip, Marine charges, CB Falls, 20x30", NM.....65.00
Extra War Bonds, lg broom & weapons, J Atherton, 14x20"....40.00
Feed A Fighter, soldier in trench, W Morgan, 20x30", EX......70.00
Fight Or Buy Bonds, Columbia, HC Christy, 20x30", EX.......125.00
Food Will Win War, immigrants/ship, Riesenberg, 20x30", EX..75.00
For Every Fighter A Woman Worker, A Treidler, 40x30", VG...45.00
For Home & Country, AE Orr, soldier/wife/child, EX..........25.00
For Your Boy, AW Brown, 30x20", EX.....................25.00
Give 'Em Both Barrels, soldier & worker, J Carlu, lm, EX.....200.00
Give or We Perish, WT Benda, Alco-Gravure, NY, 33x22", EX..60.00
Greatest Mother In World, nurse/soldier, Red Cross, 20x30"....50.00
Halt The Hun, doughboy/woman/child, 20x30", EX............60.00
He's Home Over There, Herter, 41x28", EX................30.00
Help Him Win, Am Litho, serviceman w/boy & girl, 30", EX....30.00
Help Stop This, monster-Hun, A Triedler, 20x30", M.........120.00
Hey Fellows!, Sheridan, 1918, 30x20"....................30.00
Hunger, gaunt woman & child, expressionist design, 20x30", EX.50.00
I Am Telling You, WSS Enlistment, 30x20", EX..............135.00
Jewish Welfare Board, 'Civilian', S Riesenberg, 33x22", EX....45.00
Joan of Arc Saved France, Coffin, US Print & Litho, EX.......50.00
June 28th, National War Savings Day, simulated bank note.....15.00
Keep 'Em Smiling, ML Bracher, 42x28"....................70.00
Keep Him Free, CL Bull, Am bald Eagle/biplanes, 30x20".....75.00
Le Grande Pavois des Allies, flags of Allies, 14x24".........12.50
Look Who's Listening, rat-like Big 3, Seagram's Distilling.......50.00
Loose Lips Might Sink Ships, sinking ship, 20x30", EX........95.00
Men Wanted For Army, Hazleton, charging troops, 1914, VG...95.00
Men Wanted For Army, MP Whelen, Cavalry bugler, lm, EX...150.00
Motherless Fatherless Starving, Cirsp, 27x20½", VG..........30.00
My Daddy Bought Me a Government Bond, US Printing Co, 30".30.00
Navy, Gee! I Wish I Were A Man, girl in blue, Christy, 1918...600.00
Our Next Boss?, Japanese character, General Motors, 30x40"...80.00
President Wilson to People of US, 32x22", EX...............20.00
Put Fighting Blood In Your Business, marine scene, 20x30", M..75.00
Red Cross volunteer w/Am flag, Fisher, 40x30", EX.........105.00
Remember Belgium, E Young, German & girl, 30x20", EX....30.00
Remember The Flag Of Liberty, immigrant/ship, 20x30", EX...70.00
Right Down Our Alley, bowling/Hitler pins, General Motors.....65.00
Road To France/He Is Keeping It Open, Flagg, 25x19", EX....50.00

Victory Liberty Loan, signed Christy, 40", $60.00.

Share In The Victory, H Coffin, shows Columbia, 1918, 30"...150.00
Sow Seed Of Victory, Columbia throws seeds, Flagg, 20x30"...100.00
Tell That To The Marines, man/newspaper, Flagg, 30x40", EX.250.00
The Buzzard Waits For Waste, buzzard on branch, 18x24", EX.50.00
The Dead Cry Halt, bizarre battle scene, 1930s, lm, 20x26", M.100.00
The Hun/His Mark/Blot It Out, bloody hand, 20x30", EX......40.00
They Kept Sea Lanes Open, LA Shafer, 29x40", EX..........150.00
They Shall Not Perish, Douglas Volk, 40x28", EX............75.00
They're Fighting Harder Than Ever..., 1943, 20x30"...........9.50
Third Red Cross Roll Call, nurse, H Fisher design, 20x30", EX..75.00
This Is The Enemy, Nazi dagger in Bible, 28x40", EX........95.00
Together, soldier & Wave portrait, O Shepard, Wrigley's Gum..150.00
Trained To Defend Your Country?, Plattsburg, doughboy, EX...75.00
United We Are Strong, cannons w/flag of Allies, 20x30"........9.50
Uphold Your Honor, Join Army/Navy/Marines, Columbia/flag...125.00
US Marines/Soldiers of the Sea, Leyendecker, beach, 30x40"...100.00
Weapons For Liberty, Columbia/Boy Scout, Leyendecker, lm...160.00
Wings Over America, eagle/planes, Enlist/US Army, Woodburne..35.00
Women, Help America's Sons Win; wht-haired mom, 20x30"....80.00
Workers, Lend Your Strength, Gil Spear, 27x20", EX.........20.00
YMCA/YWCA, United We Serve, WWI, 30x20", EX.........15.00
4 Years In Flight, Women Of France, Jonas, 42x28", EX......50.00

Miscellaneous

Anti-war, Keep Our Boys At Home, Columbia, 1938, lm, 14x22".75.00
Anti-war, Peace/The Better Way, ML Bracker art, 1935, lm....250.00
Anti-war, You Can't Win In War, skull/helmets, 1936, 17x22"..135.00
Circus, see Circus Collectibles
French, bistro; Deco, girl drinking, DeMonnier, 1931, 48x63"..325.00
Movie, see Movie Memorabilia
Mucha, Alphonse; Reverie, lithographic, 1896, 22½x18".......550.00
Mucha, Alphonse; Societe Populaire des Beaux-Arts, 23x17"..1,500.00

Pot Lids

Pot lids were pottery covers for containers that were used for hair dressing, potted meats, etc. The most desirable were decorated with colorful transfer prints under the glaze in a variety of themes, animal and scenic. The first and probably the largest company to manufacture these lids was F and R Pratt of Fenton, Staffordshire, established in the early 1800s. The name or initials of Jesse Austin, their designer, may sometimes be found on exceptional designs. Although few pot lids were made after the 1880s, the firm continued into the 20th century.

A Pair, Pratt type, 4″ .575.00
Battle of the Nile, ebonized oak fr, Fenton Pratt, 4″ 250.00
Belle Vue Pegwell Bay, ebonized fr, Fenton Pratt, 5¼″ 250.00
Belle Vue Tavern, Fenton Pratt, 4¾″ 140.00
Church of Holy Trinity, Stratford on Avon, Pratt type, 4¾″ 450.00
City street scene, soldier, women & church, Pratt type, 4½″ . . .100.00
Dangerous, drawing by Jesse Austin, Pratt, 2⅞″ 325.00
Dr Johnson, Pratt type, 4⅛″ .375.00
Four Shrimpers at Pegwell Bay, ebonized fr, Fenton Pratt, 4″ . .320.00
Hamlet & His Father's Ghost, ebonized fr, Fenton Pratt, 4⅛″ . .410.00
His Royal Highness Prince of Wales Washington Tomb, Pratt . .175.00
I See You My Boy, Pratt, 4¼″ 65.00
Late Prince Consort, portrait of Prince Albert, Pratt, 4″ dia 145.00
Ning Po River, drawing by Jesse Austin, Pratt type, 4⅛″ 225.00
On Guard, Pratt, in frame 65.00
Peace, drawing by Jesse Austin, Pratt type, 4″ 600.00
Pegwell Bay, flat surface, Pratt type, 3½″ 425.00
Pegwell Bay Established 1760, walnut fr, Fenton Pratt, 3½″ . . .250.00
Queen Victoria, England's Pride, crest/motto, Pratt, M 125.00
Royal Harbour Ramsgate, mahogany fr, 4″ 250.00
Shakespeare's House Henley St Stratford, Pratt type, 4¼″ 600.00
Soldier & women in city park, edge flakes, Pratt, 4½″ 65.00
Strasburg, Pratt type, 4½″ 475.00
Strathfieldsaye, Seat of Duke of Wellington, Pratt type, 4¾″ . . .425.00
Tam-O'-Shanter & Souter Jonny, Pratt type, 4″ 275.00
The Enthusiast, drawing by Jesse Austin, Pratt type, 4⅛″ 470.00
War, sgn Jesse Austin, oblong jar w/lid, Fenton, 5½″ L 200.00

Potschappel

Figurine, boy in sleigh, fur hat & hatchet, Carl Thieme, 5¼″ . . .160.00
Vase, w/lid, on stand, Diana & companion HP, rstr, 41″ 4,950.00
Vase, w/lid, on stand, scenic, gilding, X line/T mk, 18″ 1,540.00
Vase, 3 reserves on front, 3 w/floral, 1 w/seascapes, 8½″ 150.00

Powder Horns and Flasks

Flask, Batty, eagle/clasped hands/US in shield, 1854, 7½″ 250.00
Flask, brass/copper, hunting dog/pheasants embossed, 6″ 60.00
Flask, Colt type, brass emb eagle/shield/gun ea side, 3½″ 60.00
Flask, copper, Civil War era, emb decor X flags/cannons 105.00
Flask, copper, emb peacocks, old rpr, 6¾″ 25.00
Flask, copper, 13 stars, eagle w/shield, garland, X swords, 4″ 85.00
Flask, copper w/brass fittings, emb Rococo designs, 9″ 55.00
Flask, copper/brass, emb eagle/hands w/26 stars, US, 1846, 9″ .175.00
Flask, relief Liberty or Death w/patriotic scene, 9″ 180.00
Flask, w/dispenser, copper, G & JW Hawksley, Sheffield, 7″ 65.00
Flask, w/dispenser, copper, star & circle, Dixon, 6½″ 90.00
Horn, Black Hawk, eagle w/motto, Indian, deer, 1822, 8¾″ 625.00
Horn, brass base & measuring spout, 7¼″ 85.00
Horn, brass cap, carved top, 8″ 40.00
Horn, brass tip, wood stopper, simple carving, 9″ L 60.00
Horn, carved top, carved wood end, 12″ 55.00
Horn, copper & brass, James Dixon & Sons, 7x2½″ 255.00

Horn, lion & unicorn, name, 1812, sailor/lion/verse, 14″ 375.00
Horn, lion/unicorn crest/house/dog/hunter/deer, sgn Moore, 10″ .700.00
Horn, trees, boat, anchor, harpoon & house, simple eng, 12½″ .125.00
Horn, trn wood cap, 9½″ 30.00
Horn, verse/map/sgn/1783, w/provenance/military record, 14½″ .800.00
Horn, w/wood plug, early 1800s, 14″ 30.00
Horn, wood horn shape w/silver spout, leather covered, 24″ L . . .50.00

Powder horn, inscribed 'Thos Moore / York Co. Militia 5th Batln / Cap Gerhart Graeff Co., 1777'; verso with cityscape inscribed 'York', 11″, $400.00.

Pratt

Prattware is a type of relief molded earthenware with polychrome decoration. Scenic motifs with figures were popular; sometimes captions were added. Jugs are most common, but teapots, tableware, even figurines were made. The term 'Pratt' refers to Wm. Pratt of Lane Delph, who is credited with making the first of this type, though similar wares were made later by other Staffordshire potters.

Candlestick, emb classic decor, 5 colors, rpr, flakes, 5″ 105.00
Cottage, wht bricks, blue trim, roof panes in yel, 1820s, 3½″ . .260.00
Cup & saucer, child's; royal children in open carriage w/goat . . .150.00
Figurine, Autumn w/cornucopia & sheaf, 5 colors, 11½″, G 175.00
Figurine, lady w/fan, 5 colors, minor wear, old rpr, 5¼″ 100.00
Figurine, lady w/harp 275.00
Figurine, man w/basket of flowers, hairline, rpr in base, 5½″ 75.00
Figurine, Pug w/br spots & eyes, on gr cushion, 1790, 3¼″ 800.00
Ink stand, sm dog on footstool, ca 1800, 1¾″, EX 400.00
Jug, hunting scene, mask hdl, dtd 1856, 6½″ 150.00

Plaque, lions in relief, ca 1790 to 1810, 12½″, $715.00.

Pitcher, Juno/Minerva/Petroclus/horses, 5½" 95.00
Plaque, emb blacksmith scene, 6 colors, chip/wear, 8x9" 250.00
Plaque, 2 recumbent lions, clouds, after Wood, 1790, 12" 700.00
Pot lid, see Pot Lids
Snuff jar, bl w/tan & blk transfer men & animals 30.00
Tea caddy, comical relief, 2 men/lady, 5 colors, no lid, 5" 325.00
Toby jug, tricorn hat, holding jug, pipe at feet, 1790, 10", G . . . 450.00
Vase, 5 finger w/emb leaves, 5 color floral, extensive rpr, 8" . . . 85.00

Pre-Columbian Artifacts

The term 'pre-Columbian' loosely refers to some time prior to 1492, when Columbus arrived in America. In particular, it indicates pre-1492 artifacts of Central and South America, some of which can be dated as early as 4000 B.C. Artifacts representing the cultures of the Inca, Maya, and Aztec Indians are avidly sought by the collector. These may be made of precious metals and hardstones, or of pottery. Some were used in rituals and religious rites; some such as bowls and other utensils, though strictly utilitarian, nevertheless convey through form and decoration the craftsmanship of these early tribes.

Beaker, silver cylinder emb w/crouching figure, Chimu, 11" . . . 3,500.00
Bird vessel, pierced eyes, rear spout, pnt, Vicus, 8" 400.00
Bowl, carved w/feathers, brown w/red, Mayan, AD 550-950, 6" . . 600.00
Bowl, Colima, wht on red, 3 legs, AD 300, 1 leg rpl, 6" dia 60.00
Bowl, mc/frieze of 2 stylized condors, Tiahuanaco, 7" 1,200.00
Bowl vase, pnt center band of 6 birds in flight, Nicoya, 8" . . . 1,250.00
Canteen, Peru, dk br/cream, checkerboard/dia, AD 1000, 4" 45.00
Dipper, rattle hdl w/cat head, Mixtec, AD 1200-1500, 15" 250.00
Dog, seated, incised features, Colima 100 BC-AD 250, 14" . . . 1,500.00
Earrings, gold ½ circles w/flat terminals, Tairona, 1" dia 800.00
Enthroned dignitary/Mayan molded/wht pigment/AD 550-950 . . . 850.00
Female figure w/bowl, Nayarit, 100 BC-AD 250, 18" 1,650.00
Female w/braids, ochre/red pigment, Tlatilco BC 1150-550, 4" . . 600.00
Flute, pottery, pnt red/br, Nazca, AD 200-700, 16" L 550.00
Funerary mask, hooked nose, copper, Mochica AD 200-700, 7" . . 800.00
Hacha, stone monkey, Veracruz, AD 550-950, 10" 5,000.00
Head, well formed, pnt, Olmec, BC 1150-550, 2½" 800.00
Jaguar figure, stone, block like form, Classic, AD 250-950, 5" . 1,500.00
Male figure, sits, wears jewelry, Manabi 500 BC-AD 500, 10" . . 600.00
Monkey, stone, lozenge device in paws, Rio Blass, 4½" 800.00
Necklace, irregular gr/gray & gr jade, Mayan, AD 550-950, 9" . 1,650.00
Projectile points, Vera Cruz, 12 for 20.00
Standing canine, rust br pnt, Colima, ca BC 100-AD 250, 12" . . 950.00
Tumis, copper, mushroom form, Peru, AD 1200, 13" 200.00
Vessel, female surmounted by jaguar, mc, Mochica, 7" 3,000.00
Vessel, pnt br/rust/cream/warriors, Middle Mochia, 12" 1,100.00
Vessel, pnt frieze, priest on throne, Mayan, AD 550-950, 8" . . 8,500.00

Primitives

Like the mouse that ate the grindstone, so has collectible interest in primitives increased, a little bit at a time, until demand is taking bites instead of nibbles into their availability. Although the term 'primitives' once referred to those survival essentials contrived by our American settlers, it has recently been expanded to include objects needed or desired by succeeding generations -- items representing the cabin-n'-cornpatch existence as well as examples of life on larger farms and in towns. Through popular usage, it also respectfully covers what are actually 'country collectibles'.

From the 1600s into the latter 1800s, factories employed carvers, blacksmiths, and other artisans, whose hand work contributed to turning out quality items. When buying, 'touchmarks' -- a company's name and/or

location, and maker's or owner's initials -- are exciting discoveries.

Primitives are uniquely individual. Following identical forms, results more often than not show typically personal ideas. Using this as a guide, combined with circumstances of age, condition, desire to own, etc., should lead to a reasonably accurate evaluation. For items not listed, consult comparable examples.

In business for profit, a dealer cannot reach the buying level of emotional evaluations which a seller of inherited artifacts might expect, nor can he pay retail prices, but may instead be able to offer only 50% of retail due to his considerable expenses. To continue to read and visit exhibits is the best approach toward knowledgeable purchasing.

Authority Kathryn McNerney has compiled several lovely books on primitives and related topics: *Primitives, Our American Heritage; Collectible Blue and White Stoneware*; and *Antique Tools, Our American Heritage*. You will find her address in the Directory under 'Florida'.

See also Butter Molds and Stamps; Copper; Farm Collectibles; Fireplace Implements; Kitchen Collectibles; Molds; Tinware; Woodenware

Footwarmer, hand pierced tin sides and door, ca 1830s, 6" x 9" x 8", $120.00.

Bed warmer, brass/copper, trn hdl, floral engraving, 11x43" 235.00
Bed warmer, copper w/florals, wood hdl, 12" dia, 32" hdl 150.00
Bed warmer, copper w/rooster engraving, polished/dents, 36" L . 145.00
Bed warmer, round brass, punch design, 1850s 135.00
Box, hanging; pine, truncated, circular crest, sq nails, 13" 75.00
Box, hanging; pine w/heart cut-out, 2 compartments, 26x15" . . . 400.00
Box, hanging; poplar, crest w/side ears, pnt, no lid, 16" W 135.00
Box, knife scouring; pine, hanging, 5x17" 120.00
Box, knife scouring; poplar w/old red pnt, wire nails, 18x9x4" . . 165.00
Box, spice, hanging; poplar, dvtl, ½ rnd crest, slant top, 12" . . . 175.00
Box, spice, hanging; 8 drw, wire nails, worn, 16x10x5" 115.00
Box, spice, hanging; 8 drw, inset porcelain knobs, wire nails . . . 105.00
Box, spice, hanging; 8 drw, wire nails, rfn, 15x10x5" 110.00
Buggy step, CI, emb designs 24.00
Butter worker, pine w/old red, orig roller pestle, 19" 110.00
Candle box, hanging; pine, scalloped edges, worn rpt, 12½" 80.00
Candle box, hanging; pine w/pnt, cut-out scallop bk, 12x10x6" . 185.00
Candle box, hanging; poplar, 2 trays, scalloped, 16x12" 210.00
Candle drying rack, wood, 4 pegs on triangle base, rpt 45.00
Candle mold, pine w/24 pewter tubes, 18x6x22½" 495.00
Candle mold, 1 tube, single handle, hanging type 80.00
Candle mold, 12 tube, tin, good hdl, 10½" 80.00
Candle mold, 12 tube, 10¾" 65.00
Candle mold, 16 tube, 11" 95.00
Candle mold, 18 tube, rpr, 10½" 155.00
Candle mold, 24 tube, tin, dbl strap hdls, 1860s 150.00

Candle mold, pewter tubes in dovetailed pine frame, signature carved in wood, 11″ x 9″, $450.00.

Candle mold, 36 tube, tin, dbl hdls, 12″.......................200.00
Candle mold, 36 tube, tin, in wood frame, 25x16″...........300.00
Candle mold, 4 tube, 10½″...............................55.00
Candle mold, 6 tube, w/hdl..............................65.00
Candle mold, 8 tube, tin, 10¾″..........................70.00
Cheese press, heavily constructed, all wood, worn red, 46x43″...85.00
Cheese strainer, buff clay, round w/sm ft, br mottle, 3½x5″.....15.00
Cheese strainer, punched tin, heart shape, 13½x5¾x6″.......125.00
Cheese strainer, woven cane, heart shape, minor wear, 2¼x5x5″.75.00
Crock stand, 3 tier, semi-circular shelves, rfn poplar, 44x36″...150.00
Curd breaker, slant side hopper/crank hdl/wood roller w/teeth..150.00
Curd knife, pistol grip hdl, 1 pc hand carved wood, 25″........75.00
Dipper, hammered brass bowl, wrought iron hdl, 20″ L........70.00
Dough box, pine, chip carved detail, H stretcher, 2 board top..215.00
Dough box, pine, trn legs, old grpt, 17x46x27″..............350.00
Dough box, pnt poplar, trn legs/orig dividing board, 28x15x36″.300.00
Dough box, poplar w/rpt of birds/eagle/tulips, 9x30x13″........35.00
Dough scraper, iron, 3½″ W..............................25.00
Drying rack, pine, 3 sections ea 38x54″ w/4 bars............70.00
Drying rack, 3 section folding w/mortised bars, rpr, 56x55″.....40.00
Feather bed fluffer, wood, carved decor, 21″...............145.00
Feather bed fluffer, wood paddle.........................50.00
Food chopper, wrought steel, wide blade/wood hdl, 8½″ W.....20.00
Foot warmer, punched tin, mortised fr, trn posts, 8x9x6″......120.00
Hatchel, chip carved, dvtl cover, 4x17″...................110.00
Hatchel, iron on wood base, 6x27½″.......................18.00
Hearth broom, birch splint, ca 1810, 41″ L................150.00
Hearth broom, handmade, hickory, 1800s, 30″...............55.00
Ice tongs, chain hdl...................................14.00
Knife box, pine, 2 part, sq nails, old finish, 5x7x13″..........45.00
Knife box, walnut dvtl, divided w/cut-out heart, worn, rpr......135.00
Knife box, 2 section, scallop sides/heart cut-out hdl, 9x14″....135.00
Kraut cutter, butternut, slanted blade, cut-out top, 7x20″.......25.00
Kraut cutter, cut-out hdl, old red pnt, 19x7x2″..............68.00
Kraut cutter, poplar, G detail w/cut-out heart, 7x20″.........165.00
Kraut cutter, walnut, heart cut-out, orig finish, crack, 8x20″....125.00
Kraut cutter, 3 wrought iron blades/handmade bolts/w/hdl, 25″..40.00
Ladle, wrought iron & brass, 15″........................50.00
Measure, bentwood w/CI hdls, worn red pnt, cracked, 7½x14″...45.00
Noise maker, wood, 16″ L..............................25.00
Pastry cutter, all wood, 5½″...........................30.00
Pastry cutter, trn hdl, wheel made from 1811 Liberty penny.....45.00

Peel, smithy made, iron, short rattail hdl..................65.00
Pegboard, pine, 7 hooks, 83″ L.........................150.00
Pegboard, poplar w/7 whittled hooks, no finish/patina, 46″ L....85.00
Quilting frame, folding base, 8 ft L.......................15.00
Quilting frame, tapered splay legs mortised into fr...........25.00
Roaster, apple; 2 tier tin w/hdl, EX orig condition...........350.00
Roaster, bird; tin, w/hdl, 2 rows hooks, drip pan............195.00
Roaster, chestnut; wrought iron/pierced brass lid, 10″ dia......60.00
Roasting kitchen, tin, w/crank hdl spit, 19″ L..............230.00
Rug beater, wood hdl/wire beater, 45″ L..................15.00
Salamander, iron w/long hdl, spade end, 1830..............65.00
Salt box, hanging hole in crest, walnut, dvtl, rpr crack, 9″ W..125.00
Salt box, hanging; poplar, dvtl/shaped crest/hinged lid, 9x13″...150.00
Scouring board, pine, area for scouring brick, 8x18″..........68.00
Scrubbing stick, 1 pc wood, corrugated, 29″................150.00
Skimmer, sheet brass bowl, wrought iron hdl, 20″ L..........55.00
Skimmer, wrought iron & brass, 17¾″ L..................50.00
Smoothing board, 1 pc wood, open D hdl, 28½″ L...........150.00
Stocking stretcher, wood, adjusts, 19½″ L................15.00
Stove leveler, imp John Bell, buff clay w/br glaze, hairline.....105.00
Taster, wrought iron & copper, hanging hook, 10″ L.........110.00
Taster, wrought iron/brass, well flared hdl, 15″.............60.00
Toaster, hearth; wrought iron, rotating, twisted arches, 1700s..325.00
Towel bar, gr pnt over orig bl, mortised/pinned joints, 24″ W..295.00
Towel rack, walnut, 7 bars, shoe ft, rpr, 27½x25″...........275.00
Warming pan, brass/wrought iron, resting ft on hdl, 19″ L......35.00
Washboard, National #801, 23½x12½″.....................15.00
Washboard, wood w/sewer pipe insert, rfn, 7x13½″..........165.00
Wick trimmer, scissors, iron w/tin tray....................25.00

Prints

The term 'print' may be defined today as almost any image printed on paper by any available method. Examples of collectible old 'prints' are Norman Rockwell magazine covers and Maxfield Parrish posters and calendars. 'Original print' refers to one achieved through the efforts of the artist, or under his direct supervision. A 'reproduction' is a print produced by an accomplished print maker, who reproduces another artist's print or original work.

Thorough study is required on the part of the collector to recognize and appreciate the many variable factors to be considered in evaluating a print. Prices vary from one area of the country to another, and are dependent upon new findings regarding the scarcity or abundance of prints as such information may arise. Although each collector of old prints may have their own varying criteria by which to judge condition, for those who deal only rarely in this area, or newer collectors, a few guidelines may prove helpful. Staining, though unquestionably detrimental, is nearly always present in some degree, and should be weighed against the rarity of the print. Professional cleaning should improve its appearance and at the same time help to preserve it. Avoid tears that affect the image; minor margin tears are another matter, especially if the print is a rare one. Moderate 'foxing' (brown spots caused by mold or the fermentation of the rag content of old paper) and light stains from the old frames are not serious unless present in excess. Margin trimming was a common practice, but look for at least ¾″ to 1½″ margins, depending on print size.

Audubon, John J.

Audubon is the best known of American and European wildlife artists. His first series of prints, 'Birds of America', was produced by Robert Havell of London. They were printed on Whitman watermarked paper, bearing dates of 1826 to 1838. The Octavo Edition of the same series was printed in three editions, the first by J.T. Bowen under Audubon's direction. There were seven volumes of prints, each 11" x 7", the first five bearing the J.J. Audubon and J.B. Chevalier mark, the last two, J.J. Audubon. They were produced from 1840 through 1871. The Bien Edition prints were full size, made under the direction of Audubon's son and daughter in the late 1850s. Due to the onset of the Civil War, only 105 plates were finished. These are considered to be the most valuable of the reprints of the 'Birds of America' series.

In the 1950s New York Graphics reproduced the full color prints through photolithography; and in 1971 the complete set was reprinted by Johnson Reprint Corp. of New York, and Theaturm Orbis Terrarum of Amsterdam. Examples of the latter bear the watermark G. Schut and Zonen.

Although Audubon is best known for his portrayal of birds, one of his less familiar series, 'Viviparous Quadrupeds of North America', portrayed various species of animals. Assembled in corroboration with John Bachman from 1839 until 1851, these prints are 28x22" in size.

American Water Ouzel, CCCLXX, Havell, 1837	900.00
Baltimore Oriole, XII, Havell, 1833	5,000.00
Barn Owl, CLXXII, Havell, 1833	7,000.00
Barn Swallow, CLXXIII, Havell, 1833	1,400.00
Black Vulture/Carrion Crow, CVI, Havell, 1831	2,000.00
Black-Bellied Darter, CCCXVI, Havell, 1836	5,000.00
Bonapartian Gull, CCCXXIV, Havell, 1836	1,600.00
Brown Creeper/California Nut-Hatch, CCCCXV, Havell, 1838	900.00
Brown Headed Worm Eating Warbler, CXCVIII, Havell, 1834	1,000.00
Canada Warbler, CIII, Havell, 1834	1,000.00
Canadian Titmouse, CLCIV, Havell, 1834	1,000.00
Common Cormorant, CCLXVI, Havell, 1835	3,000.00
Florida Jay, LXXXVII, Havell, 1833	3,500.00
Frigate Pelican, CCLXXI, Havell, 1835	4,000.00
Golden-Eye Duck, CCCCIII, Havell, 1838	1,800.00
Greenshank, View St Augustine, CCLXIX, Havell	2,200.00
Hooping Crane, CCLXI, Havell, 1835	10,000.00
Hudsonian Godwit, CCLVIII, Havell, 1835	800.00
Kentucky Warbler, XXXVIII, Havell, 1833	1,100.00
King Duck, CCLXXVI, Havell, 1835	3,200.00
Large Billed Puffin, CCXCII, Havell, 1836	1,200.00
Little Owl, CXCIX, Havell, 1834	1,500.00
Lousiana Hawk, CCCXCII, Havell, 1837	2,450.00
Meadow Lark, CXXXVI, Havell, 1832	6,000.00
Passenger Pigeon, LXII, Havell, 1833	5,000.00
Prothonotary Warbler, III, Havell, 1833	1,200.00
Raven, CI, Havell, 1834	2,500.00
Rough-Legged Falcon, CLXVI, Havell, 1833	3,200.00
Salt Water Marsh Hen, CCIV, Havell, 1834	1,800.00
Sea-Side Finch, XCIII, Havell, 1833	25,000.00
Sharp-Tailed Finch, CXLIX, Havell, 1832	1,350.00
Shore Lark, CC, Havell, 1834	600.00
Stormy Petrel, CCLXX, Havell, 1835	700.00
Swallow-Tailed Hawk, LXXII, Havell, 1833	4,000.00
Towhe Buntin, XXIX, Havell, 1833	1,250.00
Townsend's Sandpiper, CCCCXXVII, Havell, 1838	1,000.00
Tufted Auk, CCXLIX, Havell, 1835	1,400.00
Turn-Stone, CCCIV, Havell, 1836	1,100.00
Vigors's Warbler, XXX, Havell, 1833	1,250.00
Western Duck, CCCCXXIX, Havell, 1838	1,800.00
White-Crowned Pigeon, CLXXVII, Havell, 1833	4,000.00
White-Fronted Goose, CCLXXXVI, Havell, 1836	3,500.00
White-Headed Eagle, CXXVI, Havell, 1831	4,000.00
Yellow-Billed Cuckoo, II, Havell, 1833	2,250.00
Yellow-Crown Warbler, CLIII, Havell, 1832	850.00
Yellow-Throated Warbler, LXXXV, Havell, 1833	900.00
Zenaida Dove, CLXII, Havell, 1833	3,800.00

Baillie, Coronation of the Virgin	40.00
Baillie, Family Register	40.00
Baillie, Good Shepherd	40.00
Baillie, Young Mother, in mahog veneer fr	45.00
Bartlett, Wm Henry; Landing on the American Side	20.00
Becker, Charlotte; baby in laundry basket w/teddy	18.00
Benton, Thos Hart; Jesse James, sgn in pencil, 16x22"	2,500.00
Bodmer, Carl; Ft Mackenzie, hc steel engraving, 9x5", 1850s	55.00
Bodmer, Carl; Saukie & Fox Indians, hc steel engraving, 9x5"	60.00

Boileau, Philip

Philip Boileau (1864-1917) was well known for his illustrations of women, particularly those painted during the early 20th century. He did three dozen covers for *The Saturday Evening Post*, dozens of postcard subjects, and many other illustrations.

Chums, framed	185.00
Peggy, large, in frame	275.00
With Care For None	125.00

Cassells, Ducks, England, matted, 11¾x14"	27.00
Cassells, Hunt Scene, horse, rider, dog	30.00
Cassells, Thoroughbred Mare and Foal	28.00
Catlin, George; Dance o/t Chiefs, 5x7"	50.00
Catlin, George; Pe-Toh-Pee-Kiss, 5x7"	50.00
Chappel, L; lady in wht dress, red shawl, dancing, 35x29"	125.00
Cousen, J; after JMW Turner, Calais Pier, matt, 15x13¾"	50.00

Currier and Ives

Nathaniel Currier was in business by himself until the late 1850s when he formed a partnership with James Merrit Ives. Currier is given credit for being the first to use the medium to portray newsworthy subjects; and the Currier and Ives views of 19th century American culture are familiar to us all.

Winter Scene in the Country, A Cold Morning, large folio, $2,500.00.

Abraham Lincoln, Nation's Martyr, Assassinated 1865, sm	110.00
Adelaide, N Currier, sm folio	55.00
Africa, N Currier, sm folio	55.00

Amelia, N Currier, sm folio	60.00
American Beauty, sm folio	60.00
American Brook Trout, sm folio	250.00
American Champion Yacht Puritan, sm folio	295.00
American Farm Yard Evening, lg folio	900.00
American Fruit Piece, lg folio	1,500.00
American Homestead, Autumn, sm folio	275.00
American Homestead, Summer, sm folio	250.00
American Homestead, Winter, sm folio	500.00
American Whaler, N Currier, sm folio	800.00
Among the Pines, sm folio	250.00
April Shower, med folio	150.00
Assassination of Pres Lincoln at Ford's Theatre, sm folio	95.00
Autumn on Lake George, sm folio	175.00
Base Hit, sm folio	200.00
Battle of Antietam, MD, Oct 17, 1862, sm folio	175.00
Battle of Cedar Mountain, sm folio	175.00
Battle of Chancellorsville, VA, May 3, 1863, sm folio	175.00
Battle of Coal Harbor, VA, June 1, 1864	175.00
Battle of Corinth, MI, Oct 4, 1862, sm folio	175.00
Battle of Fair Oaks, VA, lg folio	500.00
Battle of Fair Oaks, VA, May 31, 1862, sm folio	175.00
Battle of Gettysburg, PA, July 3, 1863, sm folio	250.00
Battle of Malvern Hill, VA, July 1, 1862, sm folio	175.00
Battle of Pea Ridge, AR, Mar 8, 1862, sm folio	175.00
Battle of Williamsburg, VA, lg folio	500.00
Beatrice Cenci, sm folio	35.00
Beauty of the Atlantic, sm folio	55.00
Between Two Fires, sm folio	225.00
Birth-Place of Washington, sm folio	275.00
Bombardment and Capture of Fredericksburg, sm folio	175.00
Bombardment and Capture of Ft Henry, TN, sm folio	175.00
Bombardment of Fort Sumter, Charleston Harbor...1861, sm	200.00
Bouquet, The; N Currier, sm folio	95.00
Bouquet of Roses, sm folio	80.00
Bridge at the Outlet, Lake Memphremagog, sm folio	180.00
Brilliant Naval Victory on Mississippi River, Ft Wright, sm	285.00
Brook Trout, Just Caught, med folio	320.00
Brush for the Lead, lg folio, G	1,000.00
Burning of Chicago, sm folio	275.00
Burning of Steamship Golden Gate, sm folio	265.00
Burning of the Clipper Ship Golden Light, N Currier, sm folio	275.00
Camping Out, Some of the Right Sort, lg folio	1,800.00
Capture of Andre, 1780, N Currier, sm folio	175.00
Carrier Dove, sm folio	55.00
Celebrated Trotting Stallion Patron, sm folio	250.00
Celebrated Winning Horses, Jockeys of American Turf, CLZ, lg	800.00
Champions of the Union, med folio	250.00
Charles, N Currier, sm folio	100.00
Clipper Ship Great Republic, sm folio	350.00
Clipper Ship Sweepstakes, N Currier, FF Palmer, 1853, lg	5,000.00
Clipper Ship 3 Brothers, Formerly Steamship Vanderbilt, sm	400.00
Col Frank P Blair, 1st Reg't Missouri Vol, sm folio	75.00
Col Michael Corcoran at Battle of Bull Run, sm folio	75.00
Cooling Stream, med folio	350.00
Cornwallis is Taken, sm folio	350.00
Cottage Life, Summer, med folio	200.00
Cromwell's Bridge, Glengariff, Ireland, sm folio	45.00
Crowd that Scooped the Pools, sm folio	175.00
Darktown Fire Brigade, Chief on Duty, sm folio	200.00
Dawn of Love, sm folio	45.00
Death of Gen Lyon at Head of His Troops, sm folio	75.00
Death of Major Ringgold, N Currier, sm folio	75.00
Death of Pres Lincoln at Washington, sm folio	125.00
Death of Stonewall Jackson, sm folio	75.00
Declaration Committee, sm folio	200.00
Deer in the Woods, sm folio	150.00
Don't You Want Another Baby, sm folio	95.00
Dotty Dimple, sm folio	70.00
Easter Morning, sm folio	50.00
Easter Offering, sm folio	40.00
Eastern Beauty, sm folio	55.00
Echo Lake, White Mountains, med folio	300.00
Elizabeth, sm folio	60.00
Emeline, N Currier, sm folio	50.00
Emma, sm folio	75.00
English Winter Scene, sm folio	275.00
Evangeline, sm folio	50.00
Evening Star, sm folio	50.00
Fall of Richmond, VA, lg folio	500.00
Falls Des Chats, Ottawa River, Canada, sm folio	250.00
Farmer's Friends, sm folio	125.00
Father and Child, sm folio	55.00
Father's Pride, sm folio	55.00
Favorite Pony, N Currier, sm folio	90.00
First Care, Young Mother, sm folio	45.00
First Fight Between Iron-clad Ships of War, sm folio	400.00
First Ride, sm folio	50.00
First Trot of the Season, lg folio	1,000.00
Flower Vase, N Currier, sm folio	100.00
Fording the River, N Currier, med folio	250.00
Fort Pickens, Pensacola Harbor, FL, sm folio	175.00
Four Seasons of Life, Middle Age, lg folio	700.00
Fox Hunting, The Death, med folio	700.00
Friends of Fruit, sm folio	50.00
Frontier Lake, sm folio	175.00
Fruit & Flower Piece, med folio	275.00
Fruits of Temperance, sm folio	150.00
Fruits of the Seasons, sm folio	95.00
Gallant Charge of 69th on Rebel Batteries at...Bull Run, sm	175.00
Gems of American Scenery, sm folio	250.00
Gen Franz Siegel, At Battle of Pea Ridge, sm folio	95.00
Gen George Washington, Father of His Country, N Currier, sm	75.00
Gen Grant & Family, blk/wht, sm folio	75.00
Gen Meagher at Battle of Fair Oaks, VA, sm folio	125.00
Gen Shields at Battle of Winchester, sm folio	125.00
Gen US Grant, Nation's Choice for Pres, blk/wht, sm folio	50.00
Geo Washington, blk/wht, sm folio	60.00
Georgianna, N Currier, sm folio	50.00
Gertrude, N Currier, sm folio	50.00
Getting a Hoist, Bad Case of the Heaves, sm folio	185.00
Good Send Off, lg folio	1,000.00
Gracie, sm folio	50.00
Grand Horse St Julien, King of Trotters, sm folio	250.00
Grand National Whig Banner, Onward, N Currier, sm folio	150.00
Grandpapa's Cane, sm folio	60.00
Grant & His Generals, med folio	190.00
Great Eastern, sm folio	250.00
Great Fire at Boston, sm folio	275.00
Great Mississippi Steamboat Race, sm folio	400.00
Great Pole Mares Belle Hamlin & Justina, sm folio	250.00
Great Victory in Shenandoah Valley, Sept 19, 1864, sm folio	175.00
Great West, sm folio	700.00
Halt by the Wayside, sm folio	175.00
Harbor for the Night, sm folio	250.00
Hard Road to Travel, Thos Worth on stone, sm folio	180.00
Harvest, sm folio	250.00
Haunted Castle, sm folio	85.00

He is Saved, blk/wht, sm folio............................60.00
Hiawatha's Departure, lg folio...........................400.00
High Bridge at Harlem, NY, sm folio......................400.00
Home in the Country, med folio...........................400.00
Home of the Deer, Morning in Adirondacks, lg folio, G.....3,000.00
Home of Washington, med folio............................250.00
Home on the Mississippi, sm folio........................375.00
Homeward Bound, sm folio.................................400.00
Hues of Autumn, On the Racquet River, sm folio...........375.00
Hundred Leaf Rose, sm folio..............................95.00
In the Mountains, sm folio...............................200.00
Indian Lake, Sunset, lg folio............................800.00
Interior of Fort Sumter During Bombardment, sm folio.......235.00
Inundation, The; sm folio...............................100.00
Ivy Bridge, sm folio....................................125.00
James Madison, 4th Pres US, N Currier, sm folio...........125.00
John J Dwyer, Champion of America, med folio.............300.00
Jolly Hunters, sm folio.................................150.00
Julia, sm folio...50.00
Kiss Me Quick, sm folio.................................175.00
Lake Memphremagog, Owl's Head, sm folio.................200.00
Lakes of Killarney, sm folio............................75.00
Lakeside Home, med folio................................350.00
Last Ditch of Chivalry, med folio.......................175.00
Laying Back Stiff for a Brush, sm folio.................200.00
Lexington of 1861, sm folio.............................200.00
Life & Age of Man, Stages of Life..., N Currier, sm folio......125.00
Life of a Fireman, Night Alarm, N Currier, lg folio.........1,850.00
Life of a Fireman, The Fire, N Currier, lg folio...........1,800.00
Life of a Fireman, The Race, N Currier, lg folio...........2,000.00
Life of a Sportsman, Coming Into Camp, sm folio..........250.00
Lincoln Family, blk/wht, sm folio.......................75.00
Little Beauty, med folio................................85.00
Little Brother, sm folio................................60.00
Little Brothers, sm folio...............................70.00
Little Caroline, sm folio...............................60.00
Little Charlie, sm folio................................60.00
Little Daisy, sm folio..................................55.00
Little Dot, sm folio....................................55.00
Little Flora, sm folio..................................55.00
Little Jennie, sm folio.................................55.00
Little Julia, sm folio..................................60.00
Little Lizzie, sm folio.................................55.00
Little Playfellow, N Currier, sm folio..................50.00
Little Sisters, sm folio................................70.00
Little Thoughtful, sm folio.............................50.00
Little Willie, sm folio.................................60.00
Longfellow, (thoroughbred), sm folio....................300.00
Look at Mamma, sm folio.................................50.00
Looking Down the Yo-Semite, sm folio....................300.00
Loss of Steamship Arctic Off Cape Race, N Currier, sm folio...200.00
Lottie, sm folio..60.00
Lucy, sm folio..50.00
Lydia, N Currier, sm folio..............................60.00
Magic Lake, med folio...................................80.00
Maiden Rock, Mississippi River, sm folio................300.00
Maj Gen Benjamin F Butler of Massachusetts, sm folio........85.00
Maj Gen Geo B McClellan, sm folio.......................95.00
Maj Gen Geo C Meade at Battle of Gettysburg, sm folio.....125.00
Maj Gen John C Fremont, sm folio........................95.00
Maj Gen Philip H Sheridan, sm folio.....................95.00
Maj Gen Philip Sheridan Rallying His Troops, Cedar Creek, sm.110.00
Mambrino, Sire of Imported Messenger, sm folio...........225.00
Mammoth Iron Steamship Laviathan, sm folio..............225.00

Margaret, sm folio......................................60.00
Maria, sm folio...65.00
Marriage Morning, The; sm folio.........................75.00
Martha Washington, blk/wht, sm folio....................50.00
Melrose Abbey, sm folio.................................70.00
Midnight Race o/t Mississippi, Memphis & James Howard, sm...400.00
Minute Men of the Revolution, Spirit of '76, sm folio........350.00
Moonlight Promenade, sm folio...........................65.00
Moosehead Lake, sm folio................................200.00
Morning Star, sm folio..................................50.00
Mountain Ramble, sm folio...............................130.00
Mule Train on an Upgrade, sm folio......................200.00
My Little White Kitties, Playing Dominoes, sm folio..........75.00
My Sweetheart, sm folio.................................60.00
My Three White Kitties, sm folio........................75.00
Narrows, From Ft Hamilton, N Currier, sm folio...........275.00
New England Homestead, N Currier, sm folio..............175.00
New York Bay, From Bay Ridge, LI, med folio.............875.00
New York Clipper Ship Challenge, N Currier, sm folio.........400.00
Niagara Falls From the Canada Side, sm folio............150.00
Night by the Campfire, med folio........................325.00
No You Don't, sm folio..................................60.00
Noontide, A Shady Spot, sm folio........................130.00
Nova Scotia Scenery, med folio..........................300.00
Odd Fellows Chart, med folio............................125.00
Old Blandford Church, Petersburg, VA, sm folio..........165.00
Old Ford Bridge, sm folio...............................165.00
Old Homestead, med folio................................300.00
Old Oaken Bucket, sm folio..............................175.00
Old Ruins, sm folio.....................................100.00
On the Owago, sm folio..................................175.00
On the St Lawrence, Indian Encampment, sm folio..........275.00
Outlet of Niagara River, sm folio.......................200.00
Pair of Nutcrackers, sm folio...........................130.00
Papa's Pet, sm folio....................................60.00
Part of the Battle of Shiloh, sm folio..................175.00
Partridge Shooting, N Currier, med folio................2,000.00
Patriot of 1776 Defending His Homestead, sm folio..........200.00
Phebe, N Currier, sm folio..............................60.00
Pickerel, c 1872..180.00
Pilot Boat in a Storm, sm folio.........................375.00
Playmates, The; N Currier, sm folio.....................65.00
Prairie Hens, sm folio..................................275.00
Presidents of the US, Washington to Polk, sm folio.........100.00
Pride of the South, sm folio............................60.00
Quails, N Currier, sm folio.............................225.00
Queen of Beauty, sm folio...............................50.00
Race on the Mississippi, Steamboats Eagle and Diana, sm folio.350.00
Rafting on the St Lawrence, med folio...................350.00
Reconciliation, The; N Currier, sm folio................60.00
Record for Birth and Baptism, sm folio..................50.00
Rival Roses, sm folio...................................95.00
Roadside Cottage, med folio.............................350.00
Roadside Mill, sm folio.................................175.00
Robert Burns and His Highland Mary, sm folio............60.00
Rose, The; sm folio.....................................90.00
Rose of Beauty, sm folio................................60.00
Rubber, The; sm folio...................................225.00
Rural Lake, med folio...................................325.00
Rush for the Pole, J Cameron on stone, sm folio.........175.00
Sale of the Pet Lamb, blk/wht, N Currier, lg folio.........450.00
Saratoga Lake, sm folio.................................175.00
Saratoga Springs, sm folio..............................180.00
Scene on the Susquehanna, sm folio......................250.00

Season of Joy, sm folio..............................80.00
Sherman and His Generals, Distinguished Commanders..., med.200.00
Silver Cascade, White Mountains, sm folio...............175.00
Single, N Currier, sm folio.............................95.00
Sinking of Steamship Oregon, Cunard Line/Long Island, med...400.00
Sinking of the Steamship Ville du Havre, sm folio...........225.00
Snipe Shooting, N Currier, lg folio...................3,500.00
Snipe Shooting, sm folio..............................500.00
Soldier's Memorial, sm folio...........................95.00
Soldier's Memorial, 133rd Reg't Co B PA, med folio.........150.00
Soldier's Return, N Currier, sm folio....................75.00
Southern Rose, sm folio...............................55.00
Spendthrift, sm folio................................275.00
Spring, rural scene, sm folio..........................175.00
Spring Flowers, med folio............................300.00
Squirrel Shooting, sm folio...........................375.00
Star of the Night, sm folio............................50.00
Steam Yacht Namouna, Property of James G Bennett, lg/oil....850.00
Steamship Oceanic, White Star Line, sm folio.............225.00
Stratford on Avon, sm folio...........................50.00
Summer Night, sm folio..............................150.00
Summer Ramble, med folio............................300.00
Sunny Side, Residence of Late Washington Irving, lg folio....700.00
Sunrise on Lake Saranac, lg folio....................1,750.00
Surrender of Port Hudson, LA, July 8th, 1863, sm folio......175.00
Susie, sm folio......................................50.00
Sylvan Lake, sm folio...............................150.00
Take Care!, sm folio.................................55.00
Tick, Tick, Tickle!, sm folio...........................50.00
To the Rescue, sm folio...............................50.00
Tomb of Washington, med folio........................190.00
Trotters on the Snow, sm folio........................500.00
Trying It On, blk/wht, sm folio........................150.00
Under Cliff, On the Hudson, sm folio...................200.00
United American--Patriotism, Charity, Harmony; N Currier, sm...80.00
Valley Falls, sm folio................................150.00
Vase of Flowers, sm folio.............................110.00
View Near Highbridge, Harlem River, NY, med folio.........750.00
View of the Park Fountain and City Hall, NY, sm folio.......350.00
View on Hudson River, From Ruggle's House, Newburg, sm....275.00
View on the Rondout, med folio........................325.00
Warwick Castle on the Avon, med folio..................110.00
Washington, First in War, First in Peace, N Currier, sm folio....65.00
Washington At Princeton, N Currier, sm folio.............325.00
Washington Crossing the Delaware, sm folio..............175.00
Washington Family, blk/wht, sm folio....................50.00
Watkins Glen, sm folio...............................275.00
Wedding Day, N Currier, sm folio.......................60.00
Well Bred Setter, sm folio............................225.00
Will You Be True, sm folio.............................55.00
William Henry Harrison, 9th President of US, N Currier, sm...100.00
Winter, (girl's head), sm folio.........................55.00
Winter Scene in the Country, lg folio..................2,500.00
Woodcock Shooting, N Currier, lg folio................3,000.00
Woodcock Shooting, sm folio..........................400.00
Woodlands in Winter, sm folio.........................300.00
Wreck of the Atlantic, sm folio........................175.00
Year After Marriage, Mother's Jewel, sm folio.............50.00
Yo-Semite Falls, CA, sm folio.........................250.00
Young Cavalier, N Currier, sm folio.....................50.00

D Appleton & Co, City of St Louis, 1872, 9x12".............20.00
D Appleton & Co, Phila from Belmont, West Park, 9x12".......20.00

Dali, Salvador; Plaza de Toros, #228, pencil sgn, 29½x21"....120.00
DeLongpre, Paul; Study of Roses, yard long, 1895...........65.00
Der Bazar, 2 ladies in 1883 dress, 9x12¾"................10.00
Devorss, girl in gr jacket, yel blouse/gloves, ca 1940s, 10"......35.00
Fashion, Delineator, Mar 1916, w/matt..................26.00
Fashion, Godey; lady w/parasol; 1 w/spyglass, dtd 1849, EX fr...45.00
Fashion, Out Door Toilettes, 1897......................20.00
Fashion, Spring Millinery, Apr 1898.....................20.00

Fisher, Harrison

Harrison Fisher (1875-1934) was America's most highly paid illustrator circa 1910 when he earned $50,000 a year. He did nearly one hundred covers for *The Saturday Evening Post*, over two hundred covers for *Cosmopolitan*, as well as covers for many other magazines. He also did postcards, prints, and other illustrations, among them several large books including *The Harrison Fisher Book, A Dream of Fair Women, Maidens Fair, American Belles,* and *A Girl's Life and Other Pictures.* Many of the 'prints' seen today are pages removed from these books. These have value, but not as much as individual prints issued as such.

Book, American Beauties..............................185.00
Book, Bachelor Belles.................................75.00
Book, Hiawatha.....................................85.00
Bookplate, Bachelor Bells, 1908, ea.....................20.00
Bookplate, lady in pk dress w/gent in wht pants/racquet.......18.00
Match Play, 19½x16"................................40.00
Modern Eve, 19½x16"................................40.00

Fox, R. Atkinson

Blossom Time......................................32.00
Dreamland, #8601, stone steps w/florals, yel urn, 8x12".......45.00
Garden scene, Midsummer Magic, #8603, Morris/Bendien, 12"...45.00
Glorious Vista......................................65.00
Indian Summer, lg, ornate gold scalloped fr...............90.00
Lady sitting on railing...............................35.00
Loves Paradise.....................................38.00
Spirit of Spring, orig fr, 8x14".........................45.00

Gibson, Charles Dana; mother w/child look at pictures........15.00
Goodwin, Philip R; 2 hunters w/canoe, distant animal, 10½x15".50.00
Gould, Budytes Flave...............................150.00
Gould, Calobates Sulphurea, Summer Plumage.............150.00
Gould, Crex Pratensis...............................170.00
Gould, Syrrhaptes Paracloxus.........................180.00
Gould, Trochalopteron Variegatum.....................165.00
Grant, Gordon; Aquarium, pencil sgn, Assoc Am Artists, 9x12".100.00

Gutmann, Bessie Pease

Awakening..18.00
Butterfly..30.00
Contentment, oval fr................................38.00
Happy Dreams, lg...................................75.00

Hacker, lady in boat, garden & steps, swan, fountain, 14x22"...85.00
Hare, J Knowles; bust portrait, lady w/red hair, bl gown, 22"....65.00
Harlow, LK; Anne Hathaway's Cottage from the Brook, 6½x9"..15.00
Harlow, LK; Stratford on Avon, w/matt & fr, 15x18"..........18.00

Haskell, FM; Great Republic, side-wheeler, 17x21"............65.00
Hassam, Childe; Home o/t Hummingbird, 1894, 5x4".........75.00
Hassam, Childe; Poppy Bank in Early Morning, 5x4".........40.00
Hassam, Childe; Sunset & Pinafore, 1894................45.00
Hintermeister, Hy; Indian man on rocks by water, 9x7".......28.00

Homer, Winslow

Bivouac Fire on the Potomac, Harper's Weekly, 1861..........50.00
Eight Bells, etching, 1887, 19x24".................2,500.00
Fly Fishing, Saranac Lake, etching, 1889, sgn/#d, 14x20½".22,000.00
Sheet music, Minnie Clyde by Bufford, litho cover, sgn WH, G.200.00
Sheet music, Polka Mazurkas, by Bufford, ballroom scene litho.275.00

Icart, Louis

Louis Icart was a French artist who immortalized the French woman through his etchings, which were widely produced during the 1920s. Most of his post-1920 etchings carry a U.S. copyright notice in the margin, as well as Icart's personal intaglio seal.

Bathers (Les Baigneuses), 1926/Estampe Moderne, sgn, in fr...550.00
Bird Seller (Marchande D'oiseaux), 1929/L Icart, Campbell, fr..440.00
Blue Alcove & Pink Alcove, 1929/L Icart, sgn/stamp, in fr, pr..770.00
Blue Buddha, 1924/les Graveurs Modernes, sgn, fr/matt......375.00
Blue Butterflies, oval, c 1922, sgn, 19½x14"...............550.00
Bubbles, sgn/stamp, ca 1930, 18x13½"..................5,500.00
Cinderella, 1927/les Artistes Modernes, sgn/stamp, foxing/fr....385.00
Colette Willy, L'Ingenue Libertine, #d ed, w/22 etchings......660.00
Coursing III, 1930/L Icart, sgn/stamp, darkened, in fr........935.00
Farewell (Au Revoir), 1927/les Graveurs Modernes, sgn, in fr...250.00
Faust & Tosca, 1928/L Icart, Paris, stamp, trimmed/in fr, pr...770.00
French Dolls, oval, windmill seal, sgn, 14x18"..............495.00
Grand Eve, pencil sgn/blindstamp, 1934, 31x20"...........3,500.00
Green Screen, 1928/L Icart, Paris, stamped, foxed, in fr.......220.00
Joy of Life (Joie De Vivre), 1929/L Icart, Paris, creased, fr...495.00
Leda & Swan, pencil sgn/blindstamp, lacquer, 1934, 20x30"..2,900.00
Montmartre, 1928/L Icart, Paris, sgn/stamp, imp Campbell, fr...385.00
Nude Figure on Pillows, tagged H Levasseur, ca 1930, in fr....495.00
Orchids, 1937/L Icart Society, sgn/stamp, trimmed, in fr.......990.00
Papillon II, Open Wings, 1936/Icart Society, sgn, stamped, fr.1,320.00
Papillon III, Woman in Wings, gr/bl wings, 1936, 6½x8¾"...1,000.00
Smoke (Fumee), 1926/les Graveurs Modernes, sgn, trimmed, fr..605.00
Speed, sgn, windmill seal, 1933, 15x24½"..............1,100.00
Sweet Enigma (Doux Mystere), 1935/Icart Society, sgn, in fr....935.00
The Sofa, 1937/Louis Icart Society, sgn, stamped, in fr.....1,650.00
Two Women & Monkey, 1922 FH Bresler, sgn, fr/matt.......385.00

Friends, young girl and terrier, drypoint and etching, 21" x 22", $600.00.

Untitled, pr of ovals, ladies in long gowns w/dogs, ea 9x11"....660.00
Venus, 1928/L Icart, Paris, sgn, stamped, matt/in fr..........880.00
Woman at Well, 1925/les Graveurs Modernes, sgn, in fr.......365.00
Woman in Evening Dress, 1925/les Graveurs Modernes, sgn, fr.385.00
Zest, sgn, windmill seal, 1928, 19x14"..................770.00

Kellogg, Battle of Chattanooga, TN, Nov 24, 1863..........150.00
Kellogg, Death of Zachary Taylor.....................100.00
Kellogg, Flowers & Fruit..............................90.00
Kellogg, Lady of the Lake............................65.00
Kellogg, Perry's Victory on Lake Erie, dbl matt, 16x22"......425.00
Kellogg, The Floral Car..............................95.00
Kellogg, Thos Wildey, Father of the Order of Odd Fellows.....50.00
Kellogg, Washington's Reception by the Ladies at Trenton, NJ..80.00
Kellogg & Comstock, Lady of the Lake.................40.00
Kellogg & Thayer, Household Pets.....................32.00
Kellogg & Thayer, Hyde Park, Hudson River, in fr, 16½x21"...45.00
Kenyon, Zula; girl on window sill, trees/2 bluebirds, 5x4½"....15.00
Keulemans, J; Gray-Lag Goose, matted, 12x14½"...........57.50
Kollner, August; Baltimore, Washington's Monument #2......285.00
Kollner, August; New York, Grace Church.................200.00
Kollner, August; Saratoga, United States Hotel, #26.........350.00

Kurz and Allison

Louis Kurz founded the Chicago Lithograph Company in 1833. Among his most notable works were a series of thirty-six Civil War scenes and one hundred illustrations of Chicago architecture. His company was destroyed in the Great Fire of 1871, and in 1880 Kurz formed a partnership with Alexander Allison, an engraver. Until both retired in 1903, they produced hundreds of lithographs, in color as well as black and white.

Assault of Fort Sanders, lg folio.........................150.00
Battle of Atlanta, lg folio..............................185.00
Battle of Bunker Hill, lg folio..........................200.00
Battle of Chancellorsville, lg folio......................150.00
Battle of Chattanooga, lg folio.........................170.00
Battle of Five Forks, lg folio...........................170.00
Battle of Fort Donelson, lg folio........................150.00
Battle of Franklin, lg folio.............................150.00
Battle of La Quasina, Near Santiago De Cuba, lg folio........150.00
Battle of Lookout Mountain, lg folio.....................150.00
Battle of Monmouth, blk/wht, med folio..................25.00
Battle of Nashville, lg folio............................150.00
Battle of New Orleans, lg folio.........................240.00
Battle of Williamsburg, lg folio.........................170.00
Declaration of Independence, lg folio....................130.00
Destruction of Battleship Maine, In Havana Harbor, sm folio....60.00
Die Hermann's Schlacht, 25x38"........................130.00
Fall of Petersburg, lg folio............................150.00
Fort Pillow Massacre, lg folio..........................190.00
Great Intn'l Naval Review, NY, April 27, 1893, lg folio........225.00
John Paul Jones Captures Countess and Serapis, blk/wht, med...25.00
Landing of Columbus, lg folio..........................130.00
Mammoth Hot Springs, Yellowstone Park, blk/wht, lg folio.....115.00
Perry's Victory on Lake Erie, lg folio....................245.00
Presidents of the US, Washington to Harding, blk/wht, lg.......55.00
Rubio Canyon Falls, Mt Lowe, CA, blk/wht, lg folio..........115.00
Sgt Jasper Recovers the Flag at Charleston, SC, blk/wht, med...25.00
Siege of Vicksburg, lg folio............................190.00
Storming of Fort Wagner, lg folio.......................150.00
Storming Stony Point, blk/wht, med folio.................25.00

Transporting Munitions From Concord, blk/wht, med folio......25.00
Washington Entering Trenton, Way to Inauguration, med.......45.00

McKenney and Hall

A-Mis-Quam, lg folio, Bowen litho, 20x13".................75.00
Appanoosee, 1836, 14x20", no fr.........................150.00
Hunting the Buffalo, octavo, Bowen litho.................85.00
Ka-Ta-Wa-Be-Da, lg folio, Bowen litho...................85.00
Ma-Ka-Tai-Me-She-Kia-Kaih, Saukie Brave.................50.00
Me-Na-Wa, Creek Warrior, octavo, Bowen litho............35.00
Opothle Yohole, Creek Chief, 1837, 14x20"..............170.00
Paddy Carr, Creek Chief, 14x20", no fr.................145.00
Stum-Ma-Nu, lg folio, Bowen litho.......................95.00
Tah-Ro-Hon, lg folio, Bowen litho......................115.00
Thayendanega, Capt of 6 Nations, 7x9"...................90.00
Timpoechee Barnard, Yushi Chief, 14x20" no fr..........150.00
Tshi-Zun-Hau-Kau, lg folio, Bowen litho................145.00
Wa-Pel-La, Musquakee Chief..............................80.00
Wat-Che-Mon-No, Ioway Chief, 1836, 14x20".............170.00
Yehole Micco, Creek Chief, 14x20", no fr...............170.00

Nutting, Wallace

Adorable Maids, 16x13"..................................85.00
Affectionately Yours, in fr.............................80.00
Along the River, 9½x4", in fr...........................32.00
An Absorbing Tale, in 15x18" fr.........................70.00
An Elaborate Dinner, 15x12".............................70.00
An Old Drawing Room, in old fr, 7½x10"..................60.00
An Overflowing Creek....................................50.00
Apple Tree Bend, 7x9½", w/fr............................30.00
Autumn Processional, 7½x9½", in fr......................30.00
Birch Bend..50.00
Birch Tree Top, 7x13", w/fr.............................35.00
Bonny Dale, 9½x7", w/fr.................................35.00
Book Settle, The; 16½x10"...............................70.00
Brides Maid of the Woods, 13x10½".......................35.00
Call of the Country, 6½x4½", in fr......................30.00
Cove Landing, 9½x7½", in fr.............................30.00
Garden of Larkspur, 8¼x10½".............................30.00
Golden Birches..40.00
Goose Chase Pattern.....................................70.00
Hollyhock Cottage, 6x4", in fr..........................30.00
Honeymoon Blossoms, 11x13", w/fr........................32.00
Ladies in White Satin...................................45.00
Lady putting dishes into corner hutch, 9½x7½"...........50.00
Lady reads book at table, fireplace, vase of flowers, 10½x9"....65.00
Lady reads letter before fire, table/highboy/etc, 12x9".....65.00
Lady sets out tea set from corner hutch onto table, 12x9"......60.00
Larkspur, 6½x4½"..30.00
Larkspur, 7½x9½", w/fr..................................35.00
Lined with Petals, 9¼x7¼", w/fr.........................30.00
Lingering Waters, in fr, 13x17".........................35.00
Little River with Mt Washington, 6x9", w/fr.............32.00
Maple Sugar Cupboard, 15x13"............................60.00
Nearing the Crest, 9½x4", w/fr..........................30.00
New Hampshire Birches, 6½x4½", w/fr.....................35.00
Obstructed Brook, 9½x7½", in fr.........................30.00
Old Settee, in gilt fr, 11½x17".........................95.00
Old Story, #28595.......................................80.00
Overflowing Cup, 6½x4½", in fr..........................30.00
Patience on a Chippendale, 12¾x10¾".....................75.00
Peep at the Hills, 9x4", in fr..........................35.00

Pinning the Lace, in old fr, 18½x15½"...................75.00
Purity and Grace, in fr.................................40.00
Sallying of Sally, The; 18½x16".........................85.00
Sea Ledges, 7¼x9½", w/fr................................50.00
Spring in the Berkshires, 9x7", in fr...................35.00
Stitch in Time, 12¾x10½"................................80.00
Swimming Pool, 12x18", w/fr.............................28.00
Warm Spring Day, 18x14".................................65.00
Way Through the Orchard, 7x9", in fr....................35.00
Westfield Water, 13x5", in fr...........................35.00

Parrish, Maxfield

Maxfield Parrish was a painter and illustrator who began his career in the last decade of the 19th century. His work remained prominent until the early 1940s. His most famous painting, *Daybreak*, was published in print form and sold nearly two thousand copies between 1910 and 1930. Prices are for unsigned prints, unframed unless noted.

Advertising, Edison Mazda, Ladies' Home Journal, 1918, 10x16".45.00
Advertising, Fisk Tires, w/Mother Goose, 1919, 9½x14"........35.00
Advertising, Florentine Fete, 1920, 10x15½".................40.00
Advertising, Jack Pratt ham, 1921, 10½x14".................50.00
Air Castles, orig fr, 13x17"...............................100.00
And Night Is Fled, Edison Mazda, card deck, MIB...........180.00
Arizona, magazine illus, 1930...............................30.00
Arizona, orig fr..45.00
Book, Golden Treasury.......................................75.00
Book, Knickerbockers History of New York...................110.00
Book, Poems of Childhood....................................50.00
Brazan Boatmen, bookplate...................................65.00
Broodmoor Hotel, The; Edison Mazda, 1921, orig fr, 16x20"...200.00
Cadmus, orig fr, 7x9½"......................................42.00
Canyon, Edison Mazda, EX fr, 1924, 12x15"..................135.00
Christmas card, Evening #2...................................7.50
Circes Palace, Edison Mazda, 1908, EX frame, 9x11".........25.00
Cleopatra, orig fr, 17½x9½"................................325.00
Cleopatra, Reinthal Newman, 15x16"........................200.00
Contentment, Edison Mazda, calendar, in fr................100.00
Daybreak, Edison Mazda, EX fr, 1922, 18x30"...............225.00
Daybreak, orig fr, 13½x21"................................110.00
Daybreak, orig fr, 22x34".................................210.00
Daybreak, Reinthal Newman, 18x30".........................200.00

Daybreak, in ornate Art Nouveau blue and gold frame, published by House of Art for Reinthal and Newman in 1922, excellent color, mint condition, 18" x 30", at auction: $385.00.

Dinkey Bird, Poems of Childhood, 5x7"......35.00
Djer-Kiss, ad, 1916......68.00
Djer-Kiss, ad, 1918......68.00
Djer-Kiss, in fr, 14½x18"......70.00
Dreaming, orig fr, 12x20"......225.00
Dreamlight, Edison Mazda, calendar, in fr......100.00
Ecstasy, calendar top, sm, M......95.00
Enchantment, Edison Mazda, in fr, 1926, 7x11"......100.00
End, The; orig fr, 12x14"......45.00
Evening, Brown & Bigelow, calendar, complete, 1947, in fr....150.00
Evening, orig fr, 14x17"......100.00
Evening Shadows #2, Brown & Bigelow, orig fr, 18x22½"....265.00
Fisherman and Geni, The; orig fr, 13x11"......65.00
Garden of Allah, Edison Mazda, 1918, w/frame, 9x18"......100.00
Garden of Allah, orig bl/gold fr, 9x18"......85.00
Garden of Allah, orig fr, 17x32"......225.00
Garden of Allah, Reinthal Newman, med......75.00
Giant and Boy with Sword, Poems of Childhood cover......15.00
Giant Seated by Castle, oil on paper, sgn/dated, 22x16½"....275.00
Golden Hours, Edison Mazda, 1929, 8½x13"......85.00
Golden Reveries......150.00
Hiawatha, bookplate......100.00
Hilltop, Edison Mazda, in fr, 1927, 12x18"......175.00
Hilltop, orig fr, 14x23"......265.00
Hilltop, orig fr, 21x33"......350.00
Hires Gnomes, orig fr......45.00
Ink blotter, VT Assoc for Billboard Restriction......50.00
Interlude, orig fr, 14½x18"......115.00
Jell-O ad, King & Queen being served, in fr, 11x15½"......65.00
Jell-O ad, Polly Put the Kettle On, in fr, 6x8"......35.00
Jell-O booklet, 1924......22.00
King and Chancellor, orig fr, 12x14"......40.00
Lute Players, The; House of Art, 6x10"......50.00
Lute Players, The; 18x30"......300.00
Morning Light, Brown & Bigelow, 1957, 9x10"......35.00
Morning Light, lg......150.00
New Day, A; Brown & Bigelow, orig fr, 12½x15"......125.00
New Moon, Brown & Bigelow, 1958, 8x8"......35.00
New Moon, Brown & Bigelow, 1981, 11x14"......8.50
Old Romance, orig fr, 7x10"......45.00
Old Romance, Scribner's, 1907......12.00
Page, The; orig fr, 12x14"......75.00
Peaceful Valley, Brown & Bigelow, 1936, 8x11"......70.00
Perfect Day, A; Brown & Bigelow, calendar, complete, 22x48"....325.00
Pied Piper......200.00
Potpourri, orig fr, 6x8"......42.00
Prince, The; Reinthal Newman, 10x12"......110.00
Prince Codadad, bookplate......65.00
Prometheus, Edison Mazda calendar, in fr......195.00
Royal Gorge, minor foxing......300.00
Rubiayat, lg......275.00
Rubiayat, med w/verse......125.00
Rubiayat, sm......70.00
Sandman, The; orig fr, 7x10"......45.00
Sheltering Oaks, Brown & Bigelow, 1960, 6x7"......10.00
Sing a Song of Sixpence, Century Magazine, 1911, 9x3½"......12.00
Sing a Song of Sixpence, orig fr, 6x11"......42.00
Singing Tree, The; orig fr, 11x13"......85.00
Stars, lg......600.00
Stars, med......375.00
Sugar Plum Tree, Scribner, Grignard, 1905, in fr......110.00
Summer, bookplate......75.00
Thy Rocks & Rills, Brown & Bigelow, 1972, 12x16"......15.00
Thy Templed Hills, Brown & Bigelow, 1942, 8x11"......75.00

Twilight, Brown & Bigelow, winter scene, 1972, 12x16"......150.00
Twilight, Brown & Bigelow, 1937, 8x11"......70.00
Waterfall, calendar top, M......325.00
White Birch, orig fr......40.00
Wild Geese, orig fr, 13x16"......100.00
Wild Geese, Reinthal Newman, 12x15"......125.00
Wynken, Blinken and Nod, Poems of Childhood, 11x16"......100.00

Prang, Louis

American Beauty, sm folio......40.00
American Homestead, Summer, sm folio......235.00
Battle of Kenesaw Mountain, Am Litho Co, 17½x25"......80.00
Battle of Shiloh, Hornet's Nest, Prang's Aquarelle Facsimille...235.00
Bay of Annapolis, Nova Scotia, sm folio......165.00
Buffon's Natural History, shells, matted, 8x11"......22.00
California Scenery, Seal Rock, Point Lobos, sm folio......200.00
Carnations and Mignonette, 7½x10¾"......15.00
Chickens I, 12½x10", in walnut fr w/gold liner......60.00
Cocker & Woodcock, 9x11½", walnut fr w/gold liner......45.00
Daisies, 7½x10¾"......15.00
Dog's Head II, 11½x9"......20.00
Harvest, North Conway White Mountains, in EX walnut fr......65.00
Late Autumn in White Mountains, in VG fr......65.00
Maurandia, 7½x10¾"......15.00
Mock Orange or Syringa, 7½x10½"......12.00
Monument, 1st Battle of Bull Run......35.00
Monument, 2nd Battle of Bull Run, EX, in G frame......50.00
Mother's Care, 8½x12", walnut fr w/gold liner......45.00
Pansies, 7½x10½"......15.00
Piper and Pair of Nutcrackers, 6x8", no fr......15.00
Sea Lions, Animate Creations......28.00
Sheridan's Ride, L Prang & Co......200.00
Spirea, 7½x10½"......12.00
Sunlight in Winter, 16x24", in walnut fr w/gold liner......165.00
Sunset, California Scenery, 12½x18½", walnut fr w/gold liner...80.00
Windmill, Long Island, 6x16", w/matt......30.00

Remington, Frederic

Abandoned, cover engraving Harper's Weekly, 1886......50.00
Antelope Hunting, orig card mt, 18x24"......75.00
Apache War-Indian Scouts on Geronimo's Trail, wood engraving.40.00
Apaches Are Coming, full pg wood engraving, Harper's, 1886...45.00
Bell Mare, matted/framed, c 1903, 19x13"......50.00
Travaux Pony, steel engraving, matt/fr, 7x4¾"......65.00
Wild Geese Shooting, orig card mt, 18x24"......75.00

Sarony, Major & Knapp, Cotton Wood Grove, 9x12"......12.00
Sarony, Major & Knapp, Head of 1st Canon of Grand River......12.00
Sarony & Major, Kate, floral margins......40.00
Sarony & Major, Washington, The Patriot, Statesman, Warrior..32.00
Smith, Jessie Wilcox; A Friendly Game, 1908, Collier's......23.00
Stanfield, C; Looking Toward Treport......14.00
Studor, Jacob H; Baltimore Oriole......48.00
Studor, Jacob H; Cinereous Coot......45.00
Studor, Jacob H; Fish Hawk......50.00
Studor, Jacob H; Rail, The......45.00
Studor, Jacob H; White Headed or Bald Eagle......55.00
Taber Prang Art Co, Fire Lightning/Rushing Eagle, 1907, pr...75.00
Underwood, Clarence; lady & gent in shop, w/matt, 11x14"......20.00

Underwood, Clarence; man & lady sailing, w/matt, 11x14".....22.00
Varin, R; Chicago in 1833, pub Ackermann 1932, aqua tint..1,200.00
Varin, R; 1st House in Chicago, 1827, pub Ackerman, 1930..1,200.00
Ward, Joseph; Death of Lieutenant Col Henry Clay, Jr........40.00
Waugh, Ida; baby girl in wht bonnet, pk dress...............25.00
Weinmann, Johann Wilhelm; Brassica Caulorapa Prolifera.....225.00
Weinmann, Johann Wilhelm; Granata Seu Malus...............250.00
Wolf, Joseph; Bird of Prey, Eagle, matted, 11x14"...........30.00
Wolf, Joseph; Bird of Prey, Falcon, matted, 11x14"..........30.00
Wood, Grant; Seed Time & Harvest, litho, 1937, 7½x12"....1,600.00
Wood, Grant; Tree Planting Group, litho, 1937, 8½x11"....2,400.00
Yard long, Roses...42.00
Zogbaum, Rufus; Cheyenne Scouts At Drill, cover engraving.....15.00
Zogbaum, Rufus; Modern Ship o/t Plains, full pg wood engraving.45.00
Zogbaum, Rufus; Prairie Letter Box, cover illus wood engraving..20.00

Purses

A popular new collectible, one that seems to have captured the attention of many, is metal mesh and beaded bags. They are found in floral beaded velvets that represent the tastes of the turn of the century, or in styles recalling the flapper era. Deco styling is also represented, and these are usually made from metal mesh in a gold or silver finish. Some of the mesh bags are enameled with florals or birds, and some are fitted inside with mirrors and compacts. All are very collectible, and prices reflect their popularity.

Beaded, allover beading, drawstring closure, 8½x4½"..........35.00
Beaded, bl & cream w/ornate fr w/birds, 4x7"................55.00
Beaded, blk envelope clutch, made in France, 5x8"...........45.00
Beaded, box style, allover sm wht beads, 7x4x3".............40.00
Beaded, boy & girl, fountain, trees, jeweled fr, 7½x10¾"......150.00
Beaded, checkerboard effect, bl/gr/wht, fringe, Czech, 7x9".....70.00
Beaded, clutch style, blk beads in butterfly pattern, 9x5".......38.00
Beaded, egg shape, rose, tassel at bottom, 5x8¾"............60.00
Beaded, gourd shape, 3 tulips, 4½x9¼"......................50.00
Beaded, hunter w/dogs shooting birds, gilt brass mts, 1870......45.00
Beaded, irid navy clutch, 'diamonds' in ball closure...........40.00
Beaded, jet blk allover beading, rnd w/tassels, 7x4"...........35.00
Beaded, jet w/bead fringe, silver fr & chain, 1920s............33.50
Beaded, mc geometrics, 4x7"................................65.00
Beaded, mountain village scene, sterling fr, 7x12"...........225.00
Beaded, peacock bl allover beading, rnd w/2" fringe, 6" dia.....35.00
Beaded, peacock on fence, potted flower, fringe, 8x12".......100.00
Beaded, ribbon drawstring, openwork beading, 4½x13".........35.00
Beaded, sm blk diamond pattern, shaped, chain hdl, 8x4".......50.00
Beaded, tortoise shell fr w/metal trim, florals..............75.00
Beaded, wht/cream stripes, gold washed fr, 5x7"............35.00
Beaded, 5 rows looped steel gray beads, drawstring, 4x7½".....36.00
Chain mail, wide SP fr, mk German silver....................35.00
Chatelain, fancy links, ornate silver fr, mk G Silver..........23.50
Chiffon w/wht beading, embroidered flowers.................25.00
Crochet, blk w/blk beads in checkerboard, German silver fr.....65.00
Crochet flowers & metal beading, ornate fr, France..........125.00
Cut steel beads, gold/silver, brocade design, fringe, France......55.00
Enameled, turq border w/wht center & flowers, 2½x2½".......50.00
Faille, Art Nouveau metal cupids in panel, 4½x5½"...........35.00
Mesh, bl/wht w/blk trim, fringe, Whiting & Davis.............45.00
Mesh, bl/wht w/silver top, compact in top w/bl glass clasp......60.00
Mesh, blue rectangle w/diamond, Whiting & Davis, 3½x7".....45.00
Mesh, brass; fancy chain hdl, lacy fr, scrolls/facet stones........60.00
Mesh, daisies & roses, zigzag bottom, Whiting & Davis, 6x9¾"..85.00
Mesh, flower center, V bottom, fringe, Mandalian, 3½x6½".....45.00

Mesh, flowers in diamonds, green, Whiting & Davis, 4½x7".....65.00
Mesh, German silver, fringe, pierced florals on fr, medallion.....95.00
Mesh, portrait of man, Whiting & Davis, 3¾x6¼"........250.00
Mesh, red/wht, Mandalian Mfg Co, lg....................17.50
Mesh, rnd w/inside mirror & decorative hdl, Armor...........40.00
Mesh, roses, lg/med/sm, Mandalian, 5x8¼"..................85.00
Mesh, silver w/Art Nouveau clasp...........................20.00
Mesh, silver w/bl jeweled clasp, Bliss......................35.00
Mesh, sterling, ball drops, sgn, 3½x2"......................42.00
Mesh, sterling, sapphire cabs in clasp, Whiting & Davis, 4x4½".130.00
Mesh, style El Sah enameled, Whiting & Davis, 6½x3½"......150.00
Needlepoint, tortoise shell fr, br bkground, lg...............35.00
Sequin & pearl, mc, w/hdl, 10x5"...........................24.00
Silk, petit point roses, fancy brass fr w/48 stones, France.....125.00
Tapestry, allover beaded except for floral forms, wht..........50.00
Tapestry, beaded floral border & village scene, fringe, 7x11"...125.00
Tapestry, courting couple & sheep, jeweled fr, 7¼x8¼"......200.00
Tapestry pouch in sterling fr w/marcasites, chain hdl..........32.00
Velvet, accordian top, silver over brass, 'amethysts'..........27.50
Velvet, blk w/facing figural crayfish fr, Germany, 9½x9".......150.00
Velvet, sterling fr/clasp/loop, scroll/heads/King/Queen, 5".....85.00
Velvet, w/chain & long tassel, Victorian, 8x13".............15.00
Velvet, wht w/beaded front, peacock in design...............45.00

Quezal

The Quezal Art Glass and Decorating Company of Brooklyn, New York, was founded in 1901 by Martin Bach. A former Tiffany employee, Bach's glass closely resembled that of his former employer. Most pieces were signed 'Quezal', a name taken from a Central American bird. After Bach's death in 1920, his son-in-law, Conrad Vohlsing, continued to produce a Quezal-type glass in Elmhurst, New York, which he marked 'Lustre Art Glass'.

Bottle, teardrop form, gr w/lav/mc hi-lites/feathering, 9"......1,850.00
Bowl, gold irid, ribbed, 5x12"............................300.00
Chandelier, dbl bowl, 3 shades, gold leaves on wht, gold w/in...500.00
Cologne, soft gold, Deco design, sgn Q and Melba, 7½"......195.00
Lamp, domed opal shade & base, amber irid waves, 24½"...2,200.00
Nut dish, irid, ruffled, sgn, 3".............................135.00
Salt, aurene w/mc hi-lites, ribbed, sgn.....................175.00
Shade, bridge lamp, domical, gold threads/gr leaves, 2x10" dia..900.00
Shade, gold, bl/purple hi-lites, lily form, sgn................250.00
Shade, gold lustre, sgn, 4", pr.............................275.00
Shade, gold w/in, wht/gr/gold pulled feathers, pr............600.00
Shade, gold w/wht feathers, gr outlines, sgn, pr.............275.00
Shade, pulled feather, opal w/gr edge on gold ribs, sgn, 3 for..375.00
Shade, pulled feather on calcite/threaded/scalloped, set of 4....625.00
Shade, ribbed, calcite w/out, gold w/in.....................160.00
Shade, waisted bell form, optic rib, gold net w/bl irid, 4 for....785.00
Toothpick holder, gold irid, ribbed, sgn & #d................225.00
Vase, bl/gold allover swirls on opal, gold lining, 5½x5½"......550.00
Vase, floriform, flared/ruffled, opaque, gr feathers, irid, 6"....550.00
Vase, floriform, gold irid, rare shape, sgn, 12x3"............750.00
Vase, floriform, gold/wht feathers, unsgn, 9"...............550.00
Vase, floriform, trefoil lip, opal w/gr feathers, irid, 10½"......880.00
Vase, gold, fine rib fluted top, 2".........................275.00
Vase, gold w/gr pulled feathers, thin w/flare/wide base, 6"......900.00
Vase, irid gold & orange designs on opaque wht, 10½"......1,200.00
Vase, lattice: irid gr/bl/ruby; ivory case/silver overlay, 6½"....3,000.00
Vase, petal top, gr/yel, pulled feathers, sgn, 5½x6½"........495.00
Vase, shades of bl irid, swirled, sgn, 7"....................425.00

Quilts

Quilts, while made out of necessity, nevertheless represent an art form which expresses the character and the personality of the designer. During the 17th and 18th centuries, quilts were considered a necessary part of a bride's hope chest -- the traditional number required to be properly endowed for marriage was a 'baker's dozen'! Quilts were used not only for bed coverings, but for curtains, extra insulation, and mattresses as well. The early quilts were made from pieces salvaged from cloth items that had outlived their original usefulness, and from bits left over from sewing projects. Regardless of shape, these scraps were fitted together following no organized lines. The resulting hodge-podge design was called a crazy quilt.

In 1793, Eli Whitney developed the cotton gin, and as a result, textile production in America became industrialized. Soon inexpensive fabrics were readily available, and ladies were able to choose from colorful prints and solids to add contrast to their work. Both pieced and appliqued work became popular -- pieced quilts were considered utilitarian, while appliqued work was shown with pride of accomplishment at the fair. Today many collectors prize pieced quilts and their intricate geometric patterns above all other types. Many of these designs were given names: Daisy and Oak Leaf, Grandmother's Flower Garden, Log Cabin, and Ocean Wave are only a few. Appliqued quilts involved stitching one piece, carefully cut into a specific form such as a leaf, a flower, or a stylized device, onto either a large one piece ground fabric or an individual block. Often the background fabric was quilted in a decorative pattern.

Amish women scorned printed calicos as 'worldly', and instead used colorful blocks set with black ground fabrics to produce a stunning pieced effect.

During the Victorian era, the crazy quilt was revived, but the ladies of the 1870s used plush velvets, brocades, silks, and linen patches and embroidered along the seams with feather or chain stitches.

Another type of quilting, highly prized and rare today is trapunto. These quilts were made by first stitching the outline of the design onto a solid sheet of fabric which was backed with a second having a much looser weave. White was often favored, but color was sometimes used for accent. The design (grapes, flowers, leaves, etc.) was padded through openings made by separating the loose weave of the underneath fabric; a backing was added and the three layers quilted as one.

Besides condition, value is judged on intricacy of pattern, color effect, and craftsmanship.

Key: dia----diamond   embr----embroidery

Amish

Checkerboard, dk fabrics w/blk border, youth size, 48x60".....150.00
Comforter, Log Cabin in red/blk/gray, knotted, 74x69"........200.00
Crib, Around the World, bl/purple/br/blk....................550.00
Crib, lg & sm sqs, maroon/purple/bl/br/blk, 40x49"..........325.00
Diamonds w/sqs ea corner & center, embroidered initials, lg....210.00
Double T, on dia blocks, cable quilted border, 1920s, VG.....675.00
Friendship, gr/bl/blk on maroon, embroidered initials........475.00
Hand quilted tulips/ocean waves, pieced in sqs, 71x82".......550.00
Hole In Barn Door Variation, maroon on blk diamonds.......550.00
Johnny In The Corner In Garden Maze, never washed........375.00
Medallions, bl/tan/br/gray/red on tan, 1890, faded, 62x87".....700.00
Nine Patch, cotton/linsey woolsey, 1930, 30x44"............415.00
Nine Patch, wools, deep rich colors, PA, EX quilting........600.00
Nine 8-ptd stars in bl & gold strips on gr, scalloped, 1930s....175.00
One Patch, jewel tones, light weight wools/flannel bk, faded....175.00
Patches of sm sqs divided by frame of maroon, 1930, 80"....685.00
Picture Frame, plain center, EX quilting, EX................250.00
Simple arrangements of sqs, mostly crepe, 43x48"..........165.00
Solid color w/elaborate wht hand quilting, stars/tulips, etc......160.00

Star designs in maroon/lavender/magenta/lt bl, contemporary...150.00
Streak of Lightning pattern in dark colors, rpr, 74x84"......225.00
Sunshine & Shadow, bl/gr/br/gray/blk, 1940s, 64x77"........775.00
Tumbling Blocks, deep colors/blk border, dtd 1965..........550.00
Tumbling Blocks in gr/navy/peach, unused, 80x92"..........520.00
24 stylized basket squares, floral meandering quilted border....200.00

Appliqued

Blossom & Bud, calico, leaf & sprig quilted, 92x104"........880.00
Bold floral w/leaves & buds, minor wear, 70x88"............225.00
Butterflies applied w/blk embroidery, 1920s.................75.00
Dahlias, wht/yel/dk blue/med blue, 20th century, 84x87"......525.00
Double Heart & Spade, line quilting, 80x80"................415.00
Floral circle medallions, gr/salmon on wht homespun, 86" G...225.00
Floral design, red/gr calico, stained/worn, 54x82"..........75.00
Flowers, crazy silk/satin ground, embroidery/feather stitching...225.00
Flowers in solid colors allover, central bouquet, scalloped.....350.00
Grapevine Wreath, hand quilted/machine applique, pre 1900, M.475.00
Iris Garden, mc/gr/wht, 20th century, 81x98"...............410.00
Morning Glories, reds/greens/wht, 20th century, 76x91"......400.00
Pinwheel designs in red/gr, overall wear, 90" sq............200.00
Pinwheels w/star centers, well quilted, 76x82".............245.00
Poppies, yel/gr/brn/wht, 20th century, 66x86"..............300.00
Poppies w/leaves ea corner & toward center, recent, M.......375.00
Princess Feather, gr/gold/wht, 20th century, 78x79".........450.00
Princess Feather, pieced border, 1900, 84x92".............495.00
Rose of Sharon, 1890, 48" sq............................100.00
Stylized florals & border, embroidery flower centers, 86" sq....450.00
Tree of Life, turq/gr/brn/wht, 20th century, 75x94".........500.00
Tulip Wreath, lime gr/yel/red/wht, 20th century, 69x72"......275.00
Tulips, pk/yel/red/gr/wht, 20th century, 69x93".............275.00
Tulips on pieced work, 4 colors, unused, 85x102"...........400.00
12 baskets of flowers, scalloped border, 82x96"............300.00
16 medallions ea w/8 stylized tulips, vining border, red/ecru....325.00
20 floral designs ea w/3 stylized flowers, dtd 1914..........185.00
25 baskets of flowers, meandering feather border, worn/stained.350.00
4 Am eagles centering star, sawtooth border, PA, 1800s......825.00
4 devices w/stylized tulips/leaves, late 1800s, 84x80".......550.00
4 rows of 4 alternate plain sqs w/star/leaf device, homespun....500.00
4 stylized floral medallions, 66x78".......................175.00
5 devices of stylized flowers/stems/buds in 4 colors, 84x88"....300.00
5 rows of 4 repeats: facing birds centered by single flower.....300.00
6 rows ea way, stylized oak leaves, calico/homespun, worn, 90".175.00
9 devices w/oak leaves or wreaths, ea sgn, floral stitching......400.00
9 devices w/4 rosebuds, 1 in ea corner, leaves in center.......195.00
9 medallions ea w/4 stylized flowers, machine applique border..225.00

Pieced

Baskets, calico, VG quilting patterns, 1900, VG.............250.00
Baskets of triangles w/goldenrod hdls, 73x81".............265.00
Blazing Star, feather wreath/diagonal line quilting, 84x88"....825.00
Bow Tie, mc prints, hand stitched w/machine stitched binding...90.00
Broken Star, G..300.00
Broken Star, 1930s, EX..................................435.00
Checkerboard sqs in crazy quilt type piecing, 76x78".........75.00
Checkerboard w/wht/mc prints in 2" sq, contempory, 66x80"...165.00
Churn Dash, old calicos, 3 bar border, VG.................225.00
Comforter, Log Cabin, multicolor prints, 70x80"............65.00
Crazy, embroidery/printed train fireman memorabilia, 1913....325.00
Crazy, good variety in size of patches & colors, 80x86".......180.00
Crazy, hand embroidery, 2nd place winner 1885 fair, 70x61"...465.00
Crazy, mostly wool w/feather stitch, wool batting, G.........100.00

Diagonals of 3 rows sm squares, calico/homespun, 76x74″, G...275.00
Diamond checkerboard w/4 tulips in ea, on dyed homespun bk.245.00
Diamond in the Square, cube/floral/cable quilting, PA, 1800s.1,210.00
Double Irish Chain, red/gold on wht, EX quilting, 88″ sq......135.00
Double Irish Chain w/floral/feather quilting, contemporary.....225.00
Double Monkey Wrench, cable/leaf quilted, 76x100″.........425.00
Feathered Stars, Civil War era, M........................650.00
Flower Baskets, 1930s prints on wht, EX quilting patterns, VG.225.00
Flower Garden design, bright colors, 84x86″................125.00
Flowerheads w/in 3 line bars, checkerboard intersections, worn.130.00
German friendship, red/yellow calico, dtd 1860, 80x96″.......215.00
Irish Chain, lt bl/wht, chain border.......................275.00
Irish Chain, navy calico on wht, new binding, 68x84″........200.00
Lattice design, red/wht, machine stitched binding, 80″ sq.....145.00
Lattice designs of diamonds, br on wht calico, worn, 78x82″...285.00
Log Cabin, good sawtooth lattice, paisley back, minor wear....295.00
Log Cabin Barn Raising, wool/cotton/silk, old, EX...........300.00
Lone Star, dia pieces w/rainbow colors, EX graphics, later.....325.00
Lone Star, pastels on wht, new binding, 76x80″.............250.00
Monkey Wrench, rich colors/wht print blocks in dia, early.....450.00
Nine Patch, diagonal line quilted, 1800s, 84x92″...........330.00
Nine Patch, mc prints on wht, 1920s, VG.................165.00
Nine Patch, red/navy calico w/flannel bk, M...............350.00
Patch, ea 18″ part sgn by different maker, 1890s, EX........250.00
Pineapple, old calicos, bk stained, o/w EX................500.00
Pink & wht bars, 72x76″.............................135.00
Rail Fence, old calicos, red/gr w/br bk, never washed........285.00
Red blocks alternate w/sqs of multicolor prints/blk, 76x78″...145.00
Red X center ea sq formed by 4x4″ sm sqs on diagonal, 67x84″.90.00
Sawtooth design, red/wht, some wear, 84x86″...............185.00
Sawtooth Sq, star corners, circle/dia quilted, 68x88″.........605.00
Schoolhouse, w/diagonal line quilting....................350.00
Simple baskets in colored prints, wht homespun bk, 84x103″...175.00
Sixteen Patch, calicos, PA, M.........................365.00
Sm sqs form diagonals/geometric shapes, calico, 83x84″......350.00
Snowball, design in center w/wide border, EX stitching, 90″...275.00
Star design, all calico, 68x78″.........................135.00
Star designs in pink/bl/wht, 70x88″.....................105.00
Star designs in red/bl/wht, fine quilting, day bed size........425.00
Star of Bethlehem, feather/circle quilted, scalloped, 1930.....495.00
Star w/in star designs, 4½ in ea of 5 rows, EX quilting.......465.00
Stylized trees, red/gr w/stripe border, dtd 1880, worn, 76″....375.00
Sunshine & Shadow, all calico, red/yellow/gr/bl, 80x82″......425.00
Texas Stars, mc w/red star centers, w/in hexagons...........165.00
Turkey Tracks w/Flying Geese border, on new backing........250.00
Variable Star in navy calico on wht, stains/wear, 74x82″......150.00
Wandering Foot, wht w/2 shades of rose & gr calico, M......285.00
Wedding Ring, 70x78″...............................75.00
Wht lattice encloses sm sqs of 2 triangles, calico, minor wear...250.00
Wild Goose Chase w/Stars, minor overall wear, 76x78″.......375.00
12 compass stars w/machine appliqued vining border, 86x109″.275.00
16 medallions, bl/wht, embroidered names, minor wear, 68″...125.00
20 star medallions, w/4 diamond points, zigzag border, 76x86″.250.00
30 stars in mc prints, red bars between, faded, 68x76″........150.00
32 point stars/lg sqs, calico/homespun, worn, 77x79″........425.00
42 baskets of multicolored prints on dia checkerboard, 70x78″.175.00
56 bl pinwheels on wht, 76x84″.......................165.00
8 rows of 7 alternate plain sqs w/stylized stars, calicos.......175.00
9 patch, red floss quilting, machine stitched binding, 72x76″...110.00

Trapunto

Trapunto cherries w/applied leaves, red/gr/wht, EX quilting...2,000.00
Trapunto leaves in border & pineapples in pieced diamonds, G.325.00

Quimper

Quimper is a type of pottery produced in Quimper, France. A tin enamel glazed earthenware pottery with hand painted decoration, it was first produced in the 1600s by the Bousquet and Caussy Factories. Little of this early ware was marked.

By the late 1700s, three factories were operating in the area, manufacturing the same type of pottery. The Grande Maison de HB, a company formed because of a marriage joining the Hubaudiere and Bousquet families, was a major producer of Quimper pottery. They marked their wares with various forms of the 'HB' logo, but of the pottery they produced, collectors value examples marked with the 'HB' within a triangle most highly.

Francois Eloury established another pottery in Quimper in the late 1700s. Under the direction of Charles Porquier, the ware was marked simply 'P'. Adolph Porquier replaced Charles in the 1850s, marking the ware produced during that period with an 'AP' logo.

Jule Henriot began operations in 1886, using molds he had purchased from Porquier. His mark was 'HR', and until the 20th century he was in competition with The Grande Maison de HB. In 1926 he began to mark his wares 'Henriot Quimper'.

In 1968, the two factories merged. They are still in operation under the name Les Faenceries de Quimper.

The factory sold in the fall of 1983 to Sarah and Paul Janssens, from the United States, making it the first time the owners were not French.

Ash tray, peasant woman....................................30.00
Bookend, seated babies, artist Berthe Savigny, HB, pr........425.00
Bowl, peasant man, spatter rim, 1½x4¾″....................35.00
Bowl, woman & floral wreath, HB, 6″.......................37.50
Butter pat, abstract design................................12.50
Candlestick, chamber type, fleur-de-lis shape, HR............200.00
Candlestick, horse figural, yel w/br trim/floral, rare..........250.00
Cheese dish, w/lid, HB..................................185.00
Condiment set, figural, peasant couple, HB, pr..............225.00
Cruet, dbl; peasant man & woman, HB, M...................65.00
Cup & saucer, girl figure, HB Q France, RZ on cup, saucer: 4″.30.00
Cup & saucer, octagonal, HB.............................30.00
Cup plate, peasant man, Henriot..........................22.00
Dish, lady's head, beige/gr, HB, 2½x3¾″...................45.00

Bookends, peasant man and woman, signed 'HB France, Bouvier', 9″ x 6″ x 4″, $400.00 for the pair.

Figurine, 'Les Trois Commeres', artist Nicot, Henriot, 15".....750.00
Figurine, lady w/sheaves of wheat, HR, 9"................275.00
Figurine, Le Grandpere de Plugestal, HQ, 7"................300.00
Figurine, Ste Vierge & Child, Premier Empire era, unsgn, 8"...325.00
Figurine, Ste Vierge Hen, Quimper Fr, 11¼"................185.00
Figurine, Ste Vierge w/dove, Keraluc, 7½"................115.00
Figurine, Yann & Naikiss, sgn HQ, 3½", pr................300.00
Flower pot, ruffled, PB mk, 5¾x3¾"................350.00
Hors d'oeuvre dish, swan hdls, decor riche, sgn HR, late 1900s.395.00
Inkwell, double; cashew shape, Henriot....................185.00
Oyster plate, peasant, florals, Malicorne, sgn PBX, 11" dia.....225.00
Pitcher, cider; HQ France, 6¼"..........................90.00
Pitcher, lady w/cobalt dress & ink apron, figural, 2½".......85.00
Pitcher, miniature, Breton woman's head, HB, 2¼"..........50.00
Pitcher, peasant woman, pinch lip, spongeware hdl, 5"........85.00
Plaque, base relief/mother holding child, 19th C, PB mk, 15"..450.00
Plaque, man w/rake, Provence, 4½"......................30.00
Plate, bl sponge border, basket of flowers, Henriot, 9½".......40.00
Plate, lady, wreath border, B on front, 9"................95.00
Plate, lg bird decor, Henriot, 10"........................125.00
Plate, man figural, HB, 9¼".............................85.00
Plate, peasant girl center, mk Porquier Beau, 10"...........300.00
Plate, peasant lady, AP mk, 9"..........................135.00
Plate, peasant lady, yel/bl bands, Henriot, 9¾"............95.00
Plate, peasant man/peasant lady, 10½", pr................95.00
Plate, peasant woman & sheep on yel, HB Quimper mk, 9½"...55.00
Plate, woman w/umbrella, ca 1880, 9½"...................90.00
Plate, yel w/cobalt rooster, rust/gr floral, HB France, 8".......68.00
Salt, dbl, boat shape, sgn, HB...........................65.00
Salt, dbl, Dutch shoes shape, HR........................55.00
Snuff bottle, geometric pattern, unsgn....................125.00
Teapot, child size, peasant figures, Henriot................80.00
Trivet, fisherwoman, decor riche border, ftd, sgn HB, 8" sq....145.00
Vase, emb man & lady, Sevellec, 3x5"....................150.00
Vase, florals, mk HB Q, 24H, CC, 6"......................65.00
Vase, Sevellec, Art Deco...............................175.00
Vase, tulip shape, milkmaid decor, Henriot, 5½"............95.00
Wall pocket, cone shape, peasant men, Henriot.............90.00
Wall pocket, peasant lady, flowers, HR, 10½".............255.00

Radford Jasper

The Jasperware listed below was made in Zanesville, Ohio, at the A. Radford Pottery Company incorporated there in 1903. This type of ware was first designed and produced in 1896 when Albert Radford worked in Tiffin, Ohio. The Zanesville Jasper, in contrast to the original line, was decorated with Wedgwood type cameos in relief that were not applied, but were formed within the general mold. The only mark found on the ware is a two digit shape number. The Tiffin Jasper, though not always marked, is sometimes impressed 'Radford Jasper'.

After only a few months Radford sold the plant to Arc-En-Ciel and moved his works to West Virginia. In addition to the regular line of utility wares, several art ware lines were also produced there. Among them were Ruko, a standard brown underglaze decorated line; Thera, matt glazed with slip decoration; and Radura, usually done in matt green glazes.

Jardiniere, Ruko, floral, fluted rim, 10"..................250.00
Mug, Jasper, grapes decor, #25, 5"......................150.00
Pitcher, Jasper, grapes decor, Old Man Winter hdl, #17, 9"....600.00
Vase, Jasper, flat, lady w/flowers, grapes on bk, #59, 4".......150.00
Vase, Jasper, Grecian man w/spear, #52, 6"...............150.00
Vase, Jasper, lady beneath grape arch, #58, 5½"...........150.00
Vase, Jasper, lady beside fire, grapes on bk, #55, 3½"......100.00

Vase, Jasper, lady in flowing robe w/arm raised, #19, 9"......600.00
Vase, Jasper, lady kneels w/bird in hand, bark trim, #24, 9"....600.00
Vase, Jasper, lion & children both sides; bark trim, #15, 7"....300.00
Vase, Jasper, w/Lincoln bust, eagle on bk, bark trim, #12, 7"..300.00
Vase, Jasper, 3 horses & chariot in clouds, bark trim, #16, 7"..300.00
Vase, Radura, gr matt, 4 lily pad top, 4 lg base hdls, 10".......70.00
Vase, Ruko, portrait of lg stork, unmkd, unsgn, restored, 22".850.00
Vase, Ruko, tulip decor, 16"............................525.00
Vase, Velvety, dk gr bisque w/red tulip, sgn AH, 12½".......175.00

Radios

Vintage radios represent a field of collecting that is becoming very popular. There were thousands of styles and types produced, the most popular of which today are the breadboard and the cathedral. Consoles are usually considered less saleable since their size makes them hard to display and store.

AC Dayton XL20.......................................85.00
Arborphone, 2 dial, TRF, curved front....................87.50
Atwater Kent, #10B, breadboard.........................350.00
Atwater Kent, #20, lg...................................75.00
Atwater Kent, #20, sloping front panel, sm................125.00
Atwater Kent, #30, EX orig..............................60.00
Atwater Kent, #30, in console Pooley case.................200.00
Atwater Kent, #35, copper band.........................50.00
B Kennedy #5, exposed tubes on slant front panel...........235.00
Bremer Tully Counterphase, 7 tube, battery................75.00
Case, 6 tube, 2 dial TRF................................65.00
Chelsea Super Five, 3 dial TRF..........................175.00
Coronado, #813, wood..................................13.00
Crosley, #169, beehive, sm..............................98.00
Crosley, #429, EX orig..................................90.00
Crosley, #51..100.00
Crosley, #51S...100.00
Crosley, #52, w/clock & Fillmore horn speaker..............125.00
Crosley Pup..100.00
Crosley X, early 1920s...................................55.00
Crosley XJ..180.00
De Forrest Radiophone, D-10, VG.........................400.00
De Forrest Radiophone, 1924, VG.........................500.00
Edison, C4, Radiophono................................650.00
EH Scott, #800B.......................................150.00
Federal Jr, crystal, w/earphones.........................180.00
Freed Eisemann, #30....................................90.00
Freed Eisemann, FE15...................................75.00
Freed Eisemann, NR7...................................75.00
Freshman Masterpiece, 3 dial TRF........................90.00
Grebe Synchrophase....................................235.00
Jubilee, crystal, NM....................................100.00
Magnavox, 1 dial, drawer type...........................85.00
Marshall, cathedral, silver, M...........................300.00
Pearson, 3 dial, TRF....................................65.00
Philco, #18, cathedral, finish poor.......................100.00
Philco, #38, cathedral...................................70.00
Philco, #45..30.00
Philco, #70, cathedral, M...............................245.00
Philco, #90, cathedral, M...............................275.00
Philco, PT-87, electric/battery, suitcase style..............50.00
Philco Jr, cathedral.....................................95.00
Radiola, #100..20.00
Radiola, #100A...20.00
Radiola, #16...75.00
Radiola, #17...40.00
Radiola, #17, w/speaker.................................85.00

Radiola, #20..95.00
Radiola, #25, w/loop................................130.00
Radiola, #3, w/balanced amplifier, M.....................185.00
Radiola, #48, AC console...........................80.00
Radiola, #60......................................30.00
Radiola, AK20.....................................40.00
Radiola, AK33.....................................40.00
Radiola, III......................................65.00
RCA Superhet, portable..............................75.00
RCA Victor #224, 6 leg console.....................160.00
Silvertone, #1809, amateur/foreign, planes/ships, Deco style.....35.00
Silvertone, #4408, airplane dial, farm set................20.00
Sparton #79, AC.....................................7.50
Sparton #79, console...............................75.00
Sparton Trolian, AC, 18 tube, 3 speakers................110.00
Stewart Warner, #950, metal chasis, early electric..........15.00
Telemonic 5 tube TRF...............................75.00
Transamerica, 3 dial, TRF..........................87.50
Vitrodyne, 3 dial TRF..............................65.00
Westinghouse Areola Sr, battery op.....................85.00
Zenith, #75-633R...................................35.00

Railroadiana

As evidenced by the growing number of ads in the trade papers today, collecting railroad related memorabilia is fast becoming one of America's most popular hobbies. The range of collectible items available is almost endless, considering the fact that there are more than 175 different railroad lines represented.

Some collectors prefer to specialize in one railroad in particular, while others attempt to collect at least one item from every railway line that is known to have existed. For the advanced collector, there is the challenge of locating rarities from short-lived railroads; for the novice there are abundant keys, buttons, passes, and playing cards. Among the most popular specializations are dining car collectibles -- flatware, glassware, dinnerware, etc. -- in a wide variety of patterns and styles.

Key:

BS------bottom stamp	SM------side mark
RR----railroad	TM--------top mark

Cup and saucer, Baltimore and Ohio, Shenango, 150th year commemorative, $50.00.

Dinnerware

Ash tray, C&O, Geo Washington, SM, Buffalo, 7x3"..........85.00
Baked apple dish, ATSF, Membreno, full BS, M.............65.00
Bowl, berry; UPRR, Challenger, EX....................15.00
Bowl, berry; UPRR, Harriman Blue, NM..................15.00
Bowl, berry; Vicksburg Route, top logo, average wear.......155.00
Bowl, cereal; ATSF, Adobe, BS, EX....................40.00
Bowl, cereal; ATSF, Mimbreno, BS, 7"..................85.00
Bowl, cereal; B&O, Centennial........................25.00
Bowl, cereal; UPRR, Challenger, M....................30.00
Bowl, cereal; Wabash, Banner, flag logo, 6"............85.00
Bowl, dessert; ACL, Flora of the South, BS, Buffalo......45.00
Bowl, GN, Glory of the West, BS, 6"..................40.00
Bowl, salad; N&W RY, Yellowbird......................25.00
Bowl, soup; B&O RR, Centennial, 9"...................40.00
Bowl, Uintah Railway, 8" oval, EX...................335.00
Butter pat, ATSF, Membreno, full Membreno BS............40.00
Butter pat, CB&Q, Violets & Daisies, M.................18.00
Butter pat, UPRR, Challenger, 3½"....................12.00
Butter pat, UPRR, Streamliner, M.....................15.00
Celery dish, B&O RR, Centennial, oval..................35.00
Celery dish, Milwaukee RY, Galatea, no BS, M............40.00
Celery dish, MoPac, St Albans, BS, OP Syracuse, 1915......85.00
Celery dish, UPRR, Blue & Gold, no BS, NM...............8.00
Celery dish, UPRR, Streamliner, M....................20.00
Chocolate pot, ATSF, California Poppy, BS...............85.00
Creamer, Canadian Pacific, w/logo, ca 1910..............20.00
Creamer, Pullman, Calumet, TM, 8 oz....................80.00
Creamer, Pullman, Indian Tree, no hdl..................35.00
Creamer, SP, individual, bl logo......................16.50
Cup, CB&Q, Violets & Daisies, mug type.................20.00
Cup & saucer, coffee; ATSF, Adobe, no BS, NM............50.00
Cup & saucer, coffee; ATSF, Membreno..................95.00
Cup & saucer, coffee; B&O, Lamberton Scammell, BS........85.00
Cup & saucer, coffee; CM St P&P, Olympian, w/gold Limoges..100.00
Cup & saucer, coffee; CNW, Rose, M....................100.00
Cup & saucer, coffee; SP, Prairie Mtn Wildflower, BS......100.00
Cup & saucer, coffee; UPRR, Challenger, EX.............50.00
Cup & saucer, coffee; UPRR, Harriman Blue, M............60.00
Cup & saucer, coffee; UPRR, Winged Streamliner motif......50.00
Cup & saucer, demitasse; ATSF, Membreno, M............165.00
Cup & saucer, demitasse; CB&O, Violets & Daisies.........55.00
Cup & saucer, demitasse; Milwaukee Traveler, M..........40.00
Cup & saucer, demitasse; Rio Grande, Prospector, NM......55.00
Cup & saucer, demitasse; UPRR, Streamliner, BS, M........35.00
Egg cup, double; UPRR, Desert Flower, BS, M.............30.00
Egg cup, double; UPRR, Streamliner, M..................12.00
Egg cup, single; UPRR, Harriman Blue, M................35.00
Egg cup, single; UPRR, Streamliner, M..................10.00
Grapefruit dish, UPRR, Desert Flower, BS, M.............17.00
Gravy boat, UPRR, Streamliner, M.....................35.00
Ice cream shell, ATSF, Black Chain, BS, M..............75.00
Ice cream shell, UPRR Streamliner, M..................20.00
Mustard stand, ATSF, Poppy, M........................40.00
Plate, Atlantic Coast Line, Palmetto, BS, Shenango, 1910, 7"...95.00
Plate, ATSF, Adobe, BS, dinner sz, EX..................80.00
Plate, ATSF, Adobe, BS, salad sz, EX..................40.00
Plate, ATSF, Black Chain, BS, dinner sz, EX............150.00
Plate, ATSF, Bleeding Blue, fine top logo, dinner sz......165.00
Plate, ATSF, Membreno, BS, dinner sz.................100.00
Plate, ATSF, Membreno, full Membreno BS, salad sz........35.00
Plate, B&O, Centennial, Lamberton Scammell, BS, 10¼".....70.00
Plate, B&O, Centennial, Lamberton Scammell, 1927, BS, 8¼"..100.00

Plate, B&O, Centennial, Scammels Lamberton, bread sz, M.....30.00
Plate, C RI&P, El Reno, RI mono, sectioned, 11½".........225.00
Plate, C RI&P, La Salle, RI mono, BS, Albert Pick, 9".......250.00
Plate, CB&Q, Aristocrat, dinner sz, average wear...........160.00
Plate, CB&Q, Spider Mums, no BS, salad sz, M..............80.00
Plate, CB&Q, Violets & Daisies, 7", VG....................10.00
Plate, D&RGW, TM Rio Grande, Prospector, 9"...............75.00
Plate, GN, Glory of the West, dinner sz, average wear........95.00
Plate, GN, Glory of the West, salad sz, EX.................30.00
Plate, GN, Mountains & Flowers pattern, dinner sz...........75.00
Plate, IC, Pirate, BS, Syracuse, 10".....................150.00
Plate, IC Miss Valley in red, OP Co, 4 tracks/train, Syracuse...500.00
Plate, Milwaukee RY, Galatea, no BS, 9", EX...............60.00
Plate, MKT, Old Abbey, red band, no BS, 10", NM.........135.00
Plate, MKT, Old Abbey, Texas Centennial, '36, Buffalo, 10"...250.00
Plate, MoPac, Bismark, TM/BS, OP Co Syracuse, 1900, 9"....150.00
Plate, MoPac, diesel streamliner w/state capitols, service sz.....350.00
Plate, MoPac, St Albans, BS, 8½"......................150.00
Plate, MoPac, steam train w/state flowers, service sz..........250.00
Plate, MoPac, TM Eagle/BS full name; Syracuse, 10½" oval....80.00
Plate, NP, goat overlooking mtns, Glory to West, 9½".........85.00
Plate, NYC, Mohawk, dinner, EX.........................40.00
Plate, NYNH, BS, Shenango, 9".........................70.00
Plate, SOO Line, Logan, dinner sz, NM...................110.00
Plate, Southern Ry, Peach Blossom, BS, 10½"..............90.00
Plate, SP, Prairie Mtn Wildflower, dinner sz, BS.............80.00
Plate, UPRR, blue & gold, no BS, dinner sz, EX.............32.00
Plate, UPRR, Challenger, dinner sz, EX...................40.00
Plate, UPRR, Challenger, salad sz, EX....................20.00
Plate, UPRR, Desert Flower, BS, 10", NM.................75.00
Plate, UPRR, Harriman Blue, BS, 7".....................30.00
Plate, UPRR, Harriman Blue, dinner sz, EX................25.00
Plate, UPRR, Harriman Blue, dinner sz, NM...............40.00
Plate, UPRR, Harriman Blue, salad sz, M.................20.00
Plate, UPRR, Streamliner, dinner sz, M..................35.00
Plate, UPRR, Streamliner, salad sz, M...................15.00
Platter, ATSF, Black Chain, BS, 9", M...................85.00
Platter, ATSF, Membreno, BS, Syracuse, 4 fish in circle, 11½".280.00
Platter, C&S Railway, top logo: some wear, 9", G...........175.00
Platter, CNW, Rose, 9", M.............................30.00
Platter, D&RGW, Exposition, stripes, no logo, 13½".........50.00
Platter, D&RGW, Prospector, 11", M....................45.00
Platter, D&RGW, Prospector, 9", M.....................40.00
Platter, GN, Glory of the West, 7½"....................30.00
Platter, Milwaukee RY, Galatea, no BS, 12", EX............70.00
Platter, Milwaukee RY, Galatea, no BS, 7", NM............60.00
Platter, Nickle Plate, gold name, TM, Ft Wayne, 11¼".......295.00
Platter, OSL Railway, top logo, 9", VG..................300.00
Platter, Salt Lake Route, top logo, 12", EX...............285.00
Platter, SP, sunset logo, gr floral border, Onandaga, 12½"....85.00
Platter, SR, Peach Blossom, TM, logo/motto, Buffalo........195.00
Platter, T&P, TM Eagle, BS, Syracuse, 12x8½"............165.00
Platter, UPRR, Columbine, 8", M......................115.00
Platter, UPRR, Harriman Blue, BS, 11" oval...............35.00
Platter, UPRR, Harriman Blue, BS, 12½x6"...............100.00
Platter, UPRR, Harriman Blue, 9" oval, EX................25.00
Platter, UPRR, Overland, 8", M.......................136.00
Platter, UPRR, Streamliner, 11" oval, M..................45.00
Platter, Vicksburg Rt, TM, 9½x6¼"....................325.00
Saucer, coffee; CB&Q, Chuck Wagon, M..................40.00
Saucer, coffee; Milwaukee, Galatea, no BS, NM............25.00
Saucer, coffee; Rock Island, LaSalle, TM, M..............30.00
Saucer, coffee; UPRR, Harriman Blue, BS, 6".............25.00
Saucer, coffee; UPRR, Portland Rose....................15.00

Saucer, demitasse; D&RGW, Exposition, stripes, no logo......50.00
Saucer, demitasse; D&RGW, Prospector..................50.00
Saucer, demitasse; Milwaukee RY, Galatea, no BS, M........30.00
Saucer, demitasse; N&W RY, Yellowbird.................18.00
Sherbet, CNW, Rose, ftd, M...........................30.00
Soup, CNW, wide flange, Rose, M......................30.00
Soup, D&RGW, wide flange, Prospector, 7", M.............32.00
Soup, UPRR, wide flange, Desert Flower, BS, M............25.00
Sugar bowl, Milwaukee RY, Galatea, no BS, NM............80.00
Sugar bowl, UPRR, Streamliner, M......................35.00
Teapot, MoPac, buzz saw logo, cobalt w/gold, Hall.........145.00
Teapot, UPRR, Streamliner, 16 oz, M....................37.50
Teapot, UPRR, Streamliner, 32 oz, M....................45.00
Underliner, Frisco, Denmark, 5½"......................34.00
Underliner, UPRR, Harriman Blue, BS, 7"................15.00
Vegetable dish, UPRR, Harriman Blue, BS, 6".............17.00

Glassware

Ash tray, Denver Zephyr, blk, orange chuckwagon/brands......35.00
Ash tray, UPRR in shield, blk onyx glass/gold shields, '50s.....16.50
Stein, Amtrak, logo in color, 5¼".......................10.00
Water glass, NYC, 20th C Limited, 50th Anniv, gold letters, 5"..20.00

Linens

Blanket, Pullman, standard pink berth, wool...............45.00
Blanket, UP shield, Pendleton, gray wool w/blk letters........175.00
Hand towel, California Zephyr, red stripe.................15.00
Hand towel, Pullman, blue pin stripe, M..................7.50
Laundry bag, California Zephyr, wht duck, lg..............10.00
Napkin, NYC w/logo..................................4.50
Napkin, SP, in script, Dayliner logo....................24.00
Pillowcase, Pullman logo, pr...........................9.00
Table cloth, California Zephyr, w/logo in center, 48" sq.......15.00
Table cloth, Rock Island logo, 52x60", EX................15.00

Silver, Flatware

Fork, condiment; Rock Island, BM, stainless, 6"...........15.00
Fork, dinner; CB&Q, Belmont..........................10.00
Fork, dinner; D&RG, Clarendon, Reed & Barton, 1890.......20.00
Fork, dinner; GM&O, Broadway, TM.....................17.50
Fork, dinner; GN Ry, Hutton...........................8.00
Fork, dinner; IC, Dartmouth, TM.......................18.00
Fork, dinner; Milwaukee CM St P&P, Ambassador...........8.00
Fork, dinner; Seaboard, Cromwell, 1912..................15.00
Fork, dinner; Seaboard, Zephyr, TM....................17.50
Fork, dinner; SR, Century.............................15.00
Fork, dinner; UPRR..................................15.00
Fork, dinner; UPRR, Savoy.............................4.00
Fork, oyster; UPRR, Savoy.............................5.00
Fork, pickle; IC, Dartmouth, TM.......................18.00
Knife, butter; ACL, Zephyr, TM........................15.00
Knife, butter; GN Ry, Hutton..........................10.00
Knife, butter; PRR, Century, TM.......................15.00
Knife, dinner; CB&Q, Belmont.........................10.00
Knife, dinner; CM St P&P, Broadway, TM................15.00
Knife, dinner; GM&O, Broadway........................10.00
Knife, dinner; IC, Dartmouth, TM......................18.00
Knife, dinner; Milwaukee CM St P&P, Ambassador...........8.00
Knife, dinner; MK&T, Dartmouth, TM...................15.00
Knife, dinner; MK&T, Elmwood, TM....................15.00
Knife, dinner; Northern Pacific, Silhouette...............10.00

Knife, dinner; Santa Fe, Albany, TM.....................15.00
Knife, dinner; SR, #1 Century, International...................8.00
Knife, dinner; SR, Century, TM.......................15.00
Knife, dinner; SR, Sierra, Reed & Barton.....................12.00
Knife, dinner; UPRR, Savoy............................4.00
Knife, dinner; UPRR, Savoy, TM.......................18.00
Knife, dinner; WP, Hutton, TM.......................17.50
Ladle, NYC, Century, TM............................25.00
Spoon, bouillon; MP Lines, Century....................15.00
Spoon, bouillon; WP, Hutton, TM.....................18.00
Spoon, bouillon; Milwaukee CM St P&P, Ambassador.........10.00
Spoon, bouillon; UPRR, Savoy..........................4.00
Spoon, demitasse; UPRR Savoy.......................12.00
Spoon, demitasse; WP, Hutton, TM....................20.00
Spoon, grapefruit; CM St P&P........................20.00
Spoon, grapefruit; SR, Vassar, TM....................20.00
Spoon, ice cream; Fred Harvey, Harrison & Howson Bros, TM..20.00
Spoon, ice tea; ACL, Zephyr, TM.....................15.00
Spoon, ice tea; MP Lines, Century....................18.00
Spoon, ice tea; PRR, Century, TM....................15.00
Spoon, ice tea; UPRR, Savoy...........................4.00
Spoon, sauce; N&W Ry, R Wallace....................12.00
Spoon, serving; UPRR, Savoy..........................6.00
Spoon, soup; IC, Dartmouth, TM.....................18.00
Spoon, soup; Seaboard, Century, TM...................15.00
Spoon, table; ATSF, Cromwell..........................8.00
Spoon, table; CB&Q, Belmont.........................10.00
Spoon, table; GN Ry, Hutton...........................8.00
Spoon, table; Milwaukee CM St P&P, Ambassador...........8.00
Spoon, table; MP Lines, Century.....................15.00
Spoon, table; N&W RY, #5 Dartmouth, Wallace Mfg, script mk..20.00
Spoon, table; Santa Fe, Cromwell, TM, 1912.............18.00
Spoon, table; SCL, Zehpyr............................8.00
Spoon, table; Seaboard, Zephyr.........................8.00
Spoon, table; SOO Line, TM.........................20.00
Spoon, table; UPRR, Sierra............................8.00
Spoon, table; WP, Hutton............................18.00
Spoon, teaspoon; ACL, #4 Cromwell, w/logo..............25.00
Spoon, teaspoon; ACL, Zephyr, TM....................15.00
Spoon, teaspoon; C&O RY, Flemish, Rogers, 1894.........35.00
Spoon, teaspoon; CZ, Century, International, BS...........10.00
Spoon, teaspoon; Fred Harvey, Cromwell................18.00
Spoon, teaspoon; Fred Harvey, Priscilla, TM, 1900........20.00
Spoon, teaspoon; GN, TM...........................15.00
Spoon, teaspoon; Gulf, Mobile & Ohio, TM w/logo.........10.00
Spoon, teaspoon; IC, Dartmouth, TM..................18.00
Spoon, teaspoon; ICRR, unlisted pattern, Albert Pick.......18.00
Spoon, teaspoon; MCRR.............................20.00
Spoon, teaspoon; Milwaukee CM St P&P, Ambassador......10.00
Spoon, teaspoon; MoPac, BM.........................12.00
Spoon, teaspoon; MP Lines, Century...................15.00
Spoon, teaspoon; PRR, keystone, Kings, 1888.............12.00
Spoon, teaspoon; PRR, Kings, TM, 1888................30.00
Spoon, teaspoon; Santa Fe, Cromwell, TM, 1912..........15.00
Spoon, teaspoon; Seaboard, Cromwell, 1912.............15.00
Spoon, teaspoon; Seaboard, Zephyr....................15.00
Spoon, teaspoon; SR, Century, TM....................18.00
Spoon, teaspoon; UPRR, Westfield, 1903................18.00

Silver, Hollow Ware

Bouillon cup, GN Ry, Oriental, M......................40.00
Bouillon cup holder, MPR, BS full name, International........55.00
Bud vase, side mk 'Eagle', BS Texas & Pacific, Int'l, 1953, 7"..140.00

Butter chip, GN, TM/BS, International, 3½"...............35.00
Cakestand, GN, BS, ftd/bead & lattice rim, Meridian Brittannia.195.00
Castor stand w/2 cruets, GN, SM/BS, International.........150.00
Coffee pot, C&NW RY, BS in script, International, 14 oz.....100.00
Coffee pot, NYC, BS, International, 1950.................75.00
Coffee pot, Rio Grande Western...in dia; Reed & Barton, 1900.395.00
Coffee pot, SOO Line, SM logo, ⅞ pt goose neck, Gorham....150.00
Coffee pot, SOO Line, 8 oz...........................75.00
Coffee pot, Texas & Pacific, International, 1947, 8 oz........110.00
Compote, Texas & Pacific, BS, Reed & Barton, 4½x7"......180.00
Cover, toast; Rio Grande, dtd 1947, 6¼"................35.00
Creamer, Canadian National, SM, Int'l, w/logo.............55.00
Creamer, Canadian National w/maple leaf logo, Int'l, 4 oz......60.00
Creamer, MoPac & Iron Mtn, Wallace, 6 oz, BS..........100.00
Crumber, CZ, MS, Century, International.................40.00
Crumber, IC, logo TM on hdl.........................75.00
Ice cream dish, CM St P&P, International, 1947...........35.00
Ice cream dish, UPRR, International, 1951...............35.00
Meat cover, NYC, International, w/center hdl, 1950.........115.00
Menu holder, CZ, BS, ½ moon shape w/Deco stripes, ftd......50.00
Menu holder, UPRR, w/2 pencil holders.................37.50
Money tray, Rio Grande Western, BS dia logo, Reed & Barton.125.00
Mustard pot holder w/cover/hdl, RI, R Wallace.............80.00
Platter, C&EI RR, BS, Gorham, 1892 mk...............100.00
Salt & pepper in castor, ATSF, BS, florals, 1923.........125.00
Steak cover, T&P, SM Eagle & logo, 1946, 10½".........55.00
Steak tray, CZ, International, 3 stripes at rim, 9½x6½"......45.00
Sugar bowl, B&M RR, w/lid, 6 oz.....................65.00
Sugar bowl, Burlington, SM/dbl line sq, Reed & Barton, 8 oz..140.00
Sugar bowl, GN Ry, Oriental, M.......................80.00
Sugar bowl, ICRR, SM mono, International, w/lid, 6 oz.......100.00
Sugar bowl, MoPac, BS, w/hdls, Wallace, 1910, w/lid.......120.00
Sugar bowl, SM&N, BS Albert Pick, silver on nickel, hdls....180.00
Sugar tongs, MoPac, Empire by International, 1921...........65.00
Syrup pitcher, UPRR, BS, attached tray, Reed & Barton......80.00
Teapot, C&NW, script BS Reed/Barton, Silver Banquet, 1 pt...145.00
Teapot, I&GN, BS, R Wallace, florals on spout & hdl base/top.220.00
Teapot, UPRR, BS, Reed & Barton, dtd 1947, 1 pt..........90.00
Toothpick holder, GN, SM, International, 1951..............45.00

Miscellaneous

Ash tray, Burlington, floor standing......................250.00
Badge, B of RT 20 yr, red enamel on gold, ⅝x⅜"..........16.00
Badge, breast; US Mail, Railway Mail Service, standard........65.00
Badge, cap; Baggage Agent, early Gothic lettering...........8.00
Badge, cap; Burlington Brakeman, silver color, 3½".........28.00
Badge, cap; C&O RY Brakeman, standard, old, silver w/blk.....20.00
Badge, cap; CB&Q Brakeman, nickel plate/blk enamel, 3½x¾"..45.00
Badge, cap; D&H CO/Trainman, ornate oval/silver/blk enamel...40.00
Badge, cap; Freight Conductor, Gothic lettering.............6.00
Badge, cap; Freight Conductor, older, Roman lettering.........9.00
Badge, cap; PRR Keystone/Trainman, gold w/red/blk, 1940s.....25.00
Badge, cap; Pullman/Conductor, gold pebbled, ornate, EX......35.00
Badge, cap; Santa Fe Brakeman, nickel w/blk letters & logo...22.50
Badge, cap; Southern RY Flagman, silver & blk, 1900........45.00
Badge, cap; Southern RY over Conductor, gold sq, old style....35.00
Badge, cap; Trainman, block letters......................7.00
Badge, cap; Vandalia/Baggage Master, ornate, silver w/blk......95.00
Badge, lapel; D&RGW, silver color letters, 1⅜"...........15.00
Badge, lapel; IC, silver color, screw bk...................7.00
Badge, lapel; Santa Fe, brass dbl screw bk/bl enamel logo, 1"...18.00
Bell, steam loco; bronze, w/yoke and stand................950.00
Book, guide; Southern Pacific, Overland Trail...............10.00

Book, Handbook of Ports Served by MoPac.................5.00
Book, Rail Oddities, 1957.............................15.00
Book, Oregon Short Line Yardmen's Schedule, UP logo, '29....10.00
Book, The Empire That MoPac Serves, 352 pgs..............4.00
Book, Virginian RW, Rates & Rules, 1915................15.00
Bottle, milk; MoPac, dtd 1946........................12.50
Brake club, N&W RY Link on side, old..................15.00
Broadside, ET & WNC RR CO, 1899......................75.00
Brochure, Outdoor Life in the Rockies, 1925, 4½x8".........25.00
Brochure, Overland logo emb, California, 47 pgs, 1932, 7x12"..10.00
Builder's plate, Baldwin, 1914, bronze, 9¼" dia............150.00
Button, coat; MoPac, silver, push-over type..............2.00
Button, coat; Santa Fe, cross logo emb, gold color, lg........4.00
Calendar, C&O RR, advertising, 1960..................15.00
Calendar, flying Rio Grande, Utah Centennial Monument, 1947..17.00
Calendar, MoPac, perpetual, picture of steam train...........75.00
Calendar, MoPac, perpetual wall, diesel, NM.............150.00
Can, DL&W RY, engineer's long spout oiler can............35.00
Can, kerosene; ATSF RY.............................18.50
Can, kerosene; D&RGW, Eagle Handlan, 1 gal, tin.........18.00
Can, kerosene; GN Ry..............................10.00
Can, kerosene; Ill Central RR, hinged lid, 11x7".........16.00
Can, kerosene; NYCS...............................17.50
Can, water; NP, side emb, 14".........................15.00
Can, water; Wabash (Wab), Handlan, tin................18.00
Card holder, Union Sta, Kansas City, metal, Indian head, 4x6"..37.50
Case, tin, no mk, conductor's, pnt....................15.00
Catalog, Morton Co RR Parts, illus, 1927...............50.00
Chandelier, dining car, dbl brass, oil burning, Adlake, 26".....750.00
Clock, wall; Postal Telegraph, #12, Brichronous, Hammond....150.00
Coal scuttle, B&O RR emb on side, tin, EX..............15.00
Dater, Boston & Maine RR/Laconia NH, Centennial, 1879.....95.00
Dater, UP System & Bancroft, IDA, Hill's Model A, rstr.......95.00
Diary, MKT, Lady Katy on cover, pocket size, 1912.........37.50
Dinner pail, Missouri Pacific, 6x8"....................12.00
Envelope, ticket; C&S, heavy tan stock, logo, 6x3½".........2.00
Fire extinguisher, CNS&M, emb brass, 14½"..............55.00
Flag, RR classification, bl...........................5.00
Flag case, passenger flagman's; no mk, pnt, EX orig..........15.00
Gauge, journal; Pratt & Whitney......................5.00
Gauge, steam; C&EI RR, brass plate rim, Kewanee, 6¼" dia....25.00
Gauge, tread wear; Pratt & Whitney, steel, 1¼x5¾".........5.00
Gauge, wheel coupler; Pratt & Whitney, steel, 2½x5".........9.00
Globe, cobalt, for Dietz car inspector's lamp, Corning, M.......45.00
Globe, DL&W RR, clear etched, Vesta, M.................8.00
Globe, MP, clear cast, 5⅜"..........................35.00
Globe, Southern, clear etched, 5⅜", Corning, M...........35.00
Hammer, B&O.....................................10.00
Hammer, CCC & ST L, shop forged, pick type, cast-in lettering..15.00
Hatchet, N&W RR Express Agency, Phila Tool Co, broad, old...60.00
Key, switch; ACL, Adlake, service #, light pocket wear........17.50
Key, switch; AE RR, Adlake, w/serial #, old, pocket worn......50.00
Key, switch; B&O, FS/Keystone, long barrel, service #, worn....17.50
Key, switch; B&O, Slaymaker, service #, pocket wear........12.00
Key, switch; C&NW, Adlake........................12.00
Key, switch; D&RGW, Adlake, pocket wear..............15.00
Key, switch; DM&N RR, A&W, brass, ca 1900, pocket wear.....45.00
Key, switch; Erie, Fraim, brass, VG..................18.00
Key, switch; Erie CT, Fraim, brass..................40.00
Key, switch; Frisco, S, Slaymaker...................13.50
Key, switch; GN RY, Fraim, serial #, brass, 1950s...........18.00
Key, switch; IT RR, Adlake, service #, big barrel...........25.00
Key, switch; LS&MS, 'steel', oiler...................25.00
Key, switch; NEO, FS, brass.........................45.00

Flares, left: Baltimore and Ohio, 10", $20.00; right: unmarked, 9", $14.00.

Key, switch; NY&LB, brass..........................15.00
Key, switch; P&PU, Adlake, service #..................20.00
Key, switch; So Ry, brass...........................20.00
Key, switch; SSW, Adlake, solid brass, sm.............25.00
Key, switch; TRRA, Adlake, service #.................15.00
Key, switch; UP Caboose, solid barrel, brass............15.00
Key, switch; VGN, FS in diamond....................40.00
Key, switch; W&StP RR, S Wilson, Bohannan, brass, 1880s.....75.00
Lamp, berth; brass, bulb in door lid, pat 7/5/04, pr..........150.00
Lamp, berth; Pullman, electric, w/shade, wall mt...........45.00
Lamp, caboose; C&O RY, Handlan #79 Markers, dbl mk, pr....225.00
Lamp, caboose; Erie/Adlake Non-Sweating, 2 gr/1 red lens, 15"..125.00
Lamp, caboose; iron, wall mtd, outside................45.00
Lamp, caboose; Star Headlight, flasher, electric 12 volt, pr.....40.00
Lamp, caboose; wall, Adams & Westlake, metal, 10" chimney...35.00
Lamp, gauge; Dietz Backhead steam loco, kero burner, 1940s...35.00
Lamp, marker; C&O RY, Handlan #79, oil, older style, EX, pr.240.00
Lamp, semaphore; Handlan, single lens, rnd body, M.........50.00
Lamp, semaphore; NYO&W RR, clear 6" single lens, Dressel...160.00
Lamp, semaphore; RI Lines, Adlake rnd top, gr/clear lens, oil..150.00
Lamp, switch; Adlake bell bottom/sq top, full oil interior.......75.00
Lamp, switch; Armspear, bulged, snow hoods, full int/oil parts...85.00
Lamp, switch; B&O RR, Adlake, rnd top/glass lens/snow hoods.125.00
Lamp, switch; C&O, glass lens/snow hoods/oil int, dbl mk, rstr..125.00
Lamp, switch; Seaboard, SM, Armspear, 5⅜" lenses, oil, 1915..125.00
Lamp, switch; TP&W, Adlake Non-Sweating, 1 gr/2 red lens...100.00
Lantern, B&M RR, Adlake Reliable, mk fr & 5⅜" clear globe...60.00
Lantern, B&O RR, A&W Adams, mk Dietz 5⅜" clear globe, G..55.00
Lantern, B&O RR, Adlake Reliable, mk fr & 5⅜" clear globe...55.00
Lantern, B&O RR, circle/dome, Adlake 200 Kero, clear globe...35.00
Lantern, B&O RR, Dressel, 3¼" clear globe, dome top, VG...25.00
Lantern, BR, Adlake Kero 3-41, clear globe..............30.00
Lantern, BR&P RY emb on lid/tall globe, bell bottom.........125.00
Lantern, Burlington, Reliable, tall 5⅜" clear cast globe, '08.....85.00
Lantern, C&A RR, A&W Adams, 5⅜" clear globe, 1909, EX....75.00
Lantern, C&A RR, Adlake Reliable, mk fr & 5⅜" clear globe...54.00
Lantern, C&NW RY, Adlake Kero 3-53, clear globe, M.......30.00

Lantern, C&NW RY raised on lid & globe, wire bottom, kero...75.00
Lantern, C&NW RY raised on lid/etched on short globe, kero...30.00
Lantern, C&O, dome, A&W, clear etched globe, EX...........30.00
Lantern, CCC & STL cast in 5⅜" clear globe, Handlan rnd top.55.00
Lantern, CM & STP RY, Handlan, 5⅜" clear globe, EX.......62.50
Lantern, CM & STP RY, Handlan, 5⅜" clear globe, pnt, VG....52.00
Lantern, CM St P&P RR, Adlake Kero 4-43, clear globe, EX....30.00
Lantern, CNR, Hiram Piper Ltd, 3¼" clear globe, EX........30.00
Lantern, Conger, battery, MIB....................15.00
Lantern, CUT CO, Adlake Kero, 3¼" red fresnel globe, EX...35.00
Lantern, D&RG RR, Handlan, clear etched barrel, EX.......125.00
Lantern, Dietz #39 Steel Clad, 5⅜" clear globe, EX...........34.00
Lantern, Dietz #39 Vulcan, 5⅜" red globe, EX.............34.00
Lantern, Erie RR, ERR Co on 5⅜" clear globe, Armspear, EX..65.00
Lantern, Genesy, KC MO Pat 1922, brass electric battery......25.00
Lantern, GM&O RR, Dietz Vesta, red globe, 1954, M........45.00
Lantern, GN RY, Adlake Reliable, mk fr & 5⅜" clear globe....85.00
Lantern, ICRR, Adlake Kero, 3¼" clear globe, pnt blk, M.....32.50
Lantern, ICRR, cast on 5⅜" clear globe, Handlan squat top....65.00
Lantern, ICRR, Dietz Vulcan #39, dbl guard, clear globe, EX..80.00
Lantern, IHB, Adlake Kero, lg lid letters....................30.00
Lantern, inspector's; PRR, Keystone on hdl, Dietz, heavy iron...75.00
Lantern, inspector's; Rock Island Lines, Dietz heavy iron body...85.00
Lantern, inspector's; Trackwalker, Dietz heavy iron body.......95.00
Lantern, KCT RY CO, Dressel, 3¼" clear globe, VG..........30.00
Lantern, L&N RR, Handlan, 3¼" clear globe, EX...........30.00
Lantern, LS&MS RY, Adlake Reliable, 5⅜" clear globe, VG....85.00
Lantern, LVRR, Adlake Kero, lg lid lettering, clear globe......35.00
Lantern, LVRR, Armspear, tall clear cast 5⅜" globe, 1889....120.00
Lantern, MC RR Adlake #200 Kero, 3¼" clear globe, VG......42.50
Lantern, MK&T RR fr & etched 5⅜" clear globe...........67.50
Lantern, Monon, Adlake Kero, 3¼" red globe, Dressel fount....50.00
Lantern, MoPac, Handlan, 4¼" clear globe, EX............35.00
Lantern, N&W RY, Adlake Kero, lg lettering, red etched globe..35.00
Lantern, N&W RY, Casey w/wick & fount device, gr globe, EX.150.00
Lantern, N&W RY fr & 5⅜" clear globe, Adlake Reliable, '22...75.00
Lantern, NY O&W, Dietz Vesta, USA on 4¼" clear globe, VG..50.00
Lantern, NYC, Dietz Vesta, tall 4¼" clear globe, VG.........25.00
Lantern, NYC, on fr/clear 6" globe, Dietz #6 bell bottom, 1890..80.00
Lantern, NYCL, Dietz Vesta, 4¼" clear globe, VG...........25.00
Lantern, NYCL, Handlan, 4½" clear globe, Dressel font, VG....25.00
Lantern, P RR, Keystone, insert pot/burner, clear globe, 1902..45.00
Lantern, PA Lines, Adlake Reliable 1913, clear cast globe......65.00
Lantern, PC, Dresell, 3¼" clear globe, EX.................27.00
Lantern, PE RY, Adlake Kero, sm letters/clear Safety 1st globe..40.00
Lantern, PE RY, Adlake Kero 2-36, sm letters, red etch globe...45.00
Lantern, RF&P RR, Dietz Vesta, 4¼" clear globe, EX........38.00
Lantern, S RY, Armspear, clear S RY globe, 1925..........40.00
Lantern, SP CO, dome, Adlake #250 Kero, red globe, M.......30.00
Lantern, SP CO on fr & 5⅜" clear globe, Adlake Reliable, VG..62.00
Lantern, TRRA, Handlan, Pat 12/12, EX................65.00
Lantern, UP, Adlake Kero 4-47, red etched UPRR globe.......50.00
Lantern, UP, dome, A&W Kero 1-39, clear etched UPRR globe.42.00
Lantern, UP, dome, Handlan w/3¼" etch globe, EX.........35.00
Lantern, VGN RY, Adlake Kero 2-57, clear globe...........110.00
Lantern, VRR, Handlan Buck, 5⅜" clear globe, G...........65.00
Lantern, Wabash RY, Dietz Acme Inspector, clear, mk fr, G....52.00
Lantern, Wabash RY, Handlan, flat top, 5⅜" clear, EX.......80.00
Lantern, WT CO, Adlake Kero, post-WWII, clear globe, EX.....30.00
Lantern, WT CO, Dressel, 3¼" blue globe, EX.............35.00
Letter opener, NP, bronze, Route Great Big Baked Potato......35.00
Letter opener, souvenir from Union Station, KS, MO, 6".......4.00
Lock, car; NYC, brass heart/iron hasp, GOEWEY/ALBANY/185?.65.00
Lock, general; Am Exp Co, iron, Corbin, G................25.00

Lock, general; B&O RT, iron Slaymaker, w/chain & mk key.....35.00
Lock, general; BH RR, iron heart, no dust cover or chain......45.00
Lock, general; BR&P RR cast in brass, padlock style, no key....25.00
Lock, general; CCC & St L, iron ET Fraim w/#d key..........30.00
Lock, general; L&N RR, iron Fraim w/chain & mk key, 1929..20.00
Lock, general; N&W, Fraim, 6 lever, iron/brass rivets........22.00
Lock, general; NYCS, iron, Corbin, w/chain & key..........25.00
Lock, general; SP Co, iron Fraim w/chain, mkd brass key.......10.00
Lock, general; SW S Ry W Sys, Adlake, iron, w/key iron, EX...35.00
Lock, general; TCRR SW, iron slaymaker, tab w/chain, 1959....35.00
Lock, mail bag; US Mail, for canvas mail bags, steel, no key...15.00
Lock, signal; AT&SF, Rayco w/star, brass................15.00
Lock, signal; DL&W, brass, 'Remove Key'...............20.00
Lock, signal; ICRR, emb, w/key, EX....................15.00
Lock, signal; L&N RR, brass heart, Yale, G...............20.00
Lock, signal; MK&T, Yale, iron w/brass hasp, emb letters......25.00
Lock, signal; N&W RY, brass padlock, mk Signal Dept, flat key.15.00
Lock, signal; NC & StL, brass padlock w/flat key...........30.00
Lock, signal; RRS Co, A&W, brass, w/chain..............35.00
Lock, signal; SO RY, brass heart, emb, w/chain, no key, EX....45.00
Lock, signal; Southern Pacific, cast logo, brass............35.00
Lock, switch; A&WP RR, brass heart, no chain/key, Climax, VG.40.00
Lock, switch; B&M RR, iron heart, Bohannon w/Slaymaker key..50.00
Lock, switch; B&M RR, steel heart, Sherbourne Co, VG.......35.00
Lock, switch; B&O RR, brass heart, w/chain, T on drop.......40.00
Lock, switch; B&O RR incised, F-S HDWE, brass heart.......40.00
Lock, switch; BCR&M RR on shackle, brass heart, 1870s......100.00
Lock, switch; CH 1941, w/chain, no key, EX..............10.00
Lock, switch; CN RR, brass heart w/key, EX..............35.00
Lock, switch; CRI & PRR, brass heart w/chain, Hansl, G......25.00
Lock, switch; CRI&P, Adlake, steel....................8.50
Lock, switch; D&E RR, Adlake, brass, w/chain & RR/mk key...60.00
Lock, switch; GA RR, Climax, brass, w/unmk key & chain......65.00
Lock, switch; JHW Climax Co, brass heart w/WUT SO key.....20.00
Lock, switch; L&N RR on hasp, iron heart, EX.............35.00
Lock, switch; MC RR, A&W, brass, w/key & chain..........80.00
Lock, switch; MoPac, Keen Kutter, br/iron, 'Don't use oil...'....150.00
Lock, switch; N&W RY cast across back, brass heart, 1952.....55.00
Lock, switch; NC & StL RY, iron slaymaker, center tab w/chain..20.00
Lock, switch; NC & StL RY, iron w/chain & mkd brass key.....35.00
Lock, switch; NP RR cast on back, heart shape, brass, 1911...100.00
Lock, switch; So Pacific, brass, cast letters, w/chain.........75.00
Lock, switch; So Ry, Yale, iron banjo, w/chain, EX...........25.00
Lock, switch; StP M&M cast on back, brass heart, 1880s.......150.00
Lock, switch; Union Pacific on bk, Aldake, brass heart, NM.....50.00
Lubricator, from steam loco cab, brass, Detroit............45.00
Magazine, Railway Age, from the 1920s.................4.00
Mainline sounder, WU TEL CO, 30 ohms, VG.............30.00
Map, wall; MoPac..............................35.00
Matchsafe, MKT, CI, Katy logo shape..................150.00
Maul, heavy iron w/wood hdl, 1860s...................25.00
Maul, track spike, SO RY, emb, forged, twist head..........20.00
Medallion, IC Centennial, 1951, cast bronze, M............30.00
Monkey wrench, Santa Fe, 12"......................17.00
Monkey wrench, Wabash..........................18.00
Newspaper, Rock Island 'Western Trail', 4 pgs, 1887.........15.00
Oil can, tin w/28" spout..........................20.00
Oiler, engineer's; M&O RR, longspout, tin, EX.............45.00
Oiler, engineer's; N&W RY, tin, base mk, pnt.............20.00
Oiler, engineer's; tin w/nickel plate, longspout gravity flow.....35.00
Oiler, engineer's; VGN, tin, longspout, side mk/emb tag, pnt....35.00
Oiler, tin, longspout, no mk.........................15.00
Order hoop, bent-wood hdl, EX orig...................20.00
Paperweight, BCR&N, metal medallion, Albert Lea Route, 1890s.50.00

Paperweight, KCS Golden Spike Anniv, 1947, bronze rectangle . . 35.00
Pass, Burlington & Lamoille RR, 1884, plain 15.00
Pass, C&EI RR CO, 1895 . . . . 8.50
Pass, Chicago & Alton, 1929 . . . . 3.00
Pass, Chicago & Alton RR, 1865, eagles & flags 45.00
Pass, CP & StL RY CO, 1895 . . . . 8.00
Pass, Erie Railway, 1874, picturesque 20.00
Pass, Great Northern Railway, 1911, plain 7.00
Pass, IB&W, 1877, annual 25.00
Pass, IC System, 1929 . . . . 4.00
Pass, J & StL, 1899 . . . . 8.50
Pass, Manistee & Northeastern, 1896, train/lake steamer/map 18.00
Pass, Missouri Pacific Railway, 1920, plain 4.00
Pass, StLA & TH RR, 1895 . . . . 8.50
Pencil, mechanical; Missouri-Ill 7.00
Pendant, key chain, Cotton Belt, gold, track walker on bk, '70 . . 22.00
Pendant, ORT 25 Yr Veteran 24.00
Photo, color, Colorado Rockies Reached by MoPac, w/girl, 31" . . 75.00
Photo, color, Market in Mexico Reached by MoPac, 30x22" fr . . 27.50
Pin, B of LE, Loyal Member 40 yr service, bl enamel on gold . . . 19.00
Pin, B of LF&E, 25 yrs, gold screw bk, red/wht/gr enamel, ¾" . . 17.00
Pin, Brotherhood of Railway Trainmen, 10k gold, M 10.00
Pin, Cotton Belt, logo, 20 yr service, silver/bl/blk enamel 16.00
Pin, MoPac Booster club 20.00
Pin, Norfolk, celluloid w/5 scenes, Whitehead/Hoag, 1896 . . . . . 50.00
Pin, Norfolk & Western Railway Veteran, sterling, M 25.00
Pin, NYC Employee's Organization, wht/bl w/gold letters 8.00
Pin, Railway Carmen of America, logo, gold, sm 7.50
Pin, UP logo, shield shape w/blue stone in 10k 22.50
Playing cards, Frisco, double deck, M 25.00
Playing cards, Frisco, single deck 8.00
Playing cards, GM&O, single deck 12.00
Playing cards, Illinois Central, single deck, M 10.00
Playing cards, Milwaukee Road, gr backs, Pinochle, MIB 18.00
Playing cards, Milwaukee Road, single deck, M 10.00
Playing cards, Norfolk & Western, dbl, used 20.00
Playing cards, RI Lines, single deck, M 12.00
Playing cards, Southern Pacific, Daylight, single deck, EX 15.00
Print, C&O, Black porter finds Chessie under berth, 14" 55.00
Punch, conductor's; nickel plated, M 15.00
Ruler, Burlington, tin 8.00
Scales, Chatillion Express, 50#, countertop, ornate, VG 85.00
Schedule, C&O, w/maps, 23 pgs, folded, 1920 . . . . 15.00
Scratch pad, Northern Pac 1.00
Scratch pad holder, SOO Line 12.00
Seal press, AM RY EX, CI/lead w/blk enamel, 11" 40.00
Sign, Railway Express Agency, exterior depot sign, 12x72" 135.00
Sign, REA, Pkg Received Here, dbl sided porcelain 150.00
Sign, REA Express, porcelain, diamond shape, 14" 35.00
Spittoon, L&N RR, Jim Crow style, bl enamel letters, rstr 40.00
Spittoon, N&W, CI, standard style, rpt 85.00
Spittoon, N&W, office, lg, cast SM 75.00
Stapler, Rio Grande 10.00
Station logo, RI Lines, metal, in fr 45.00
Stepbox, ICRR, Morton Mfg 150.00
Stepbox, Pullman, TM, Morton Co, pnt, rstr 125.00
Stepbox, SR, SM, Morton Co, light metal, riveted emblem, EX . 125.00
Stepbox, Union Pacific, Morton, passenger car 135.00
Stove poker, caboose; Seaboard, mkd 15.00
Tag, ID; Burlington Rt, silver/bl w/logo, 1¾" dia 7.00
Tallow pot, B&O, tin 15.00
Tallow pot, Eagle Mfg, no RR, tin 12.50
Tallow pot, Oregon Wash RR & Navigation Co, side emb 30.00
Tallow pot, Rock Island Lines, teapot style 25.00

Telegraph key, Bunnell & Co NY, GN RY 65.00
Telegraph peg board, 6 line, brass on wood 150.00
Ticket, Oregon Short Line, gr excursion stub, 1903 . . . . 3.00
Ticket, Rocky Mtn Ry, 1908 . . . . 2.00
Ticket punch, Omberg & Co, Chigago 9.00
Ticket punch, Poole Bros, Chicago, L shape 9.00
Ticket punch, ½ shape, half fare 9.00
Timetable, Burlington Route, 7-8/1930, stapled booklet type 6.00
Timetable, CB&Q, Employees, 1954 . . . . 5.00
Timetable, Denver & Rio Grande, 9/1893, folder type 25.00
Timetable, Fitchburg, 12/1884, pictorial fold-out sheet 35.00
Timetable, Harlem Extension, 5/29/1871, cut-out train 65.00
Timetable, Lake Shore & Mich Southern, 3/31/1857, plain card . . 50.00
Timetable, public; Queen & Crescent Rt, Mar 1911 . . . . 25.00
Timetable, SOO Line, 3/17/1915, folder type 15.00
Timetable, Western Pacific, 4/29/1951 . . . . 3.00
Tip tray, Frisco Line, train running by waterfall 65.00
Tongs, rail lifting; hand forged CI, Civil War period 45.00
Torch, locomotive; brass, top screws off, 12" 35.00
Torch, N&W RY shop, conical, blk pnt on tin 15.00
Torch, shop; C&O RY, tin, conical, pnt 10.00
Trade card, Erie, Time And Erie Wait For No Man, 1890s 20.00
Watch fob, MoPac, red enamel 45.00
Wax seals, see Seals
Whistle, cab; brass peanut single chime, polished 10.00
Whistle, steam; brass, ornate finial, 14x3" dia 75.00
Whistle, steam; brass, triple chimer 150.00

Razors

The razor has gone through several substantial changes since the first primitive, hand-hammered steel variety. Those models made before 1800, though very collectible because of their antique value, were very plain, with little etching or engraving. During the 1800s, the competition between English and German manufacturers brought about many innovations. Prior to 1820, most blades were marked 'Cast Steel'. M. Farraday discovered the process of adding silver to cast steel in 1820, and blades made from this material were marked 'Silver Steel'. During this same period, it became a common practice to stamp the blade with the initials of the current sovereign along with the cutler's marks, which is sometimes helpful when determining age and origin.

The hollow ground blade was another important development of the 19th century, and tangs became much more detailed. By the mid-1800s, etched blades and fancy handles were becoming popular. The elaborate styles of this period are most treasured by the collector.

Key:
bl------blade   pt------point

A Schaefer's Sons, real bone hdl, very clean blade, New York 9.00
American, semi-wedge blade, cast metal hdl w/raised scrolls 65.00
Atadross Best, celluloid, raised cockatoo/branches, rounded 30.00
Ator, imitation ivory wrapped rope hdl w/raised semi-nude 24.00
B&S Trade Mark, corn razor, rounded bone hdl 25.00
Beardsley & Alvord, etched blade, horn w/inlaid silver shield . . . 18.00
Bow trademark on tang, celluloid, raised semi-nude male/flower . . 68.00
Cast Steel Warranted, Sheffield, clear horn hdl, 1850s 19.00
Cattaraugus, imitation ivory/German silver ends/inlaid Indian 30.00
Centaur Corn Razor, pearl hdl, etched blade 60.00
Challenge Co, imitation tortoise shell, raised owl/scrolls, EX 15.00
Challenge Co, imitation tortoise shell bamboo pattern 22.00
Clark & Hall, Sheffield, horn w/inlaid escutcheon plate, 1810s . . 25.00
Clauss Fremont, imitation ivory w/beaded edge, raised scrolls . . . 6.00

Collins Safety Razor, round head, w/ornate lined case, M......140.00
Cosmo Mfg Co, silver steel, ivory celluloid, nude/grapes, M......90.00
Curtin & Clark, imitation ivory, raised windmill/trees/boat......27.00
CV Heljestrand Eskilstuna, Sweden, grained ivory hdl, 1870s, M..24.00
CV Heljestrand Eskilstuna, Sweden, tortoise shell hdl, MIB.....85.00
Doidge Blackpool, blade etched: Corn Razor, blk celluloid hdl...15.00
Eagle Razor Co, etched blade: Improved Eagle Razor/eagle, M..11.00
Electric Cutlery Co, celluloid, raised geometrics 2 sides........25.00
FA Koch Co, ivory celluloid, ptd oak leaves/deer, Germany, M...48.00
Frederick Reynolds, Sheffield, etched blade: G Washington......21.00
G Baker & Sons, celluloid, raised windmill/boat, etched blade...70.00
Garland Cutlery, blk horn, inlaid German silver/pearl chips, M..65.00
Golden Rule Cutlery, imitation ivory, raised gr/bl peacock, NM...60.00
Gould Mverinder St Pauls, ivory hdl, narrow bl/round pt, 1825..24.00
GW Ruff's Peerless Razor, ivory hdl, hollow ground blade, pr...32.00
H Boker & Co, etched: 1893 Columbian Expo scene/detailed....12.00
H Boker & Co, etched ship scene, blk celluloid hdl, EX.......35.00
Hamburg Concave, celluloid: nude w/red flowers, Quick Cutter..36.00
Hamon Fabricant Paris, blk horn hdl, NM blade, 1860, small, pr.35.00
Hamon Fabricant Paris, blk horn hdl w/pointed ends, elegant...17.00
Henkel Corn Razor, pearl hdl, slightly rounded, EX...........54.00
Herman Greiger's Improved, pat 1888, celluloid/German silver...48.00
Hibbard Spencer & Barlett, celluloid/raised pine cones & bark...27.00
Hope Cutlery Co, ivory celluloid, deer grazing on mountain.....25.00
Hub Corn Razor, imitation ivory hdl, Hub on blade, EX.......25.00
Imperial Razor Warranted, etched bicycle for 2/Imperial, horn...32.00
Imperial Razor Warranted, etched blade: early auto/driver......35.00
J Nowill & Sons, Sheffield, blk horn hld stamped Boston Razor..50.00
JH Hall, Sheffield, blk horn hdl w/inlaid MOP escutcheon, EX...52.00
John B Hobson, bone/ivory hdl, all orig, w/fitted box, ca 1830..119.00
Joseph Elliot, For Barbers Use, blk horn hdl, very lg, 1835....76.00
Joseph Rodgers & Sons, monkey tang, blk horn hdl, very small.14.00
Joseph Rodgers & Sons, Sheffield, ornate pressed horn hdl....227.00
Joseph Smith & Son, etched blade/soldier/flags, horn hdl.......67.00
Magnetic, imitation ivory, raised cowboy w/lasso & rifle, EX.....72.00
Marshes & Shepherd, Sheffield, fully etched Cornucopia blade...71.00
Najeeb Malluk Co, etched blade: The Orient Razor/symbols......9.00
National, celluloid, 2 semi-nude photos each side, EX.........37.00
New England Razor Co, etched blade, blk celluloid hdl........22.00
Nowill & Sons, Sheffield, glossy ivory hdl, 1860s.............21.00
Rogers Cutlery, blk celluloid, metal engraved bird, scrolls.......10.00
Sam'l Osborn & Co, Sheffield, etched Gold Medal, ivory hdl, M..11.00
Schnefer Bros, corn razor, imitation ivory hdl, NM blade.......25.00
Sheffield Steel, etched blade, bevelled MOP, ornate, 1890s, EX.117.00
Shumate, ivory celluloid, ribbed full length, tulip shape ends....16.00
Simon Au Havre, aged ivory hdl, semi-round blade point, 1830s.27.00
Slater Bros, Sheffield, etched blade: The Saloon Razor.........17.00
Southington, celluloid, eagle's head 1 end, claw 1 end, EX.....100.00
Southington, celluloid, nude holds robe, red flowers...........36.00
Superior Eisanach, etched Feinster Dramantstahl, horn hdl, sm..15.00
Thos Turner, Sheffield, etched bl: beaver/MD Canada.........17.00
Thos Turner, Sheffield, rounded ivory, etched blade, 1870, M...22.00
TR Cadman & Sons, Sheffield, clear horn hdl, clean blade......16.00
Union Razor Cutlery Co, celluloid Ear of Corn hdl, EX detail...43.00
W Harrison, Sheffield, horn w/inlaid brass escutcheon, ca 1815..71.00
Wade & Butcher, etched blade: train scene, clear horn hdl, EX..43.00
Wade & Butcher, Sheffield, etched: Celebrated Hollow Ground..21.00
Wade & Butcher, Sheffield, etched blade/Union...Preserved, M..208.00
Wade & Butcher, Sheffield, etched horse/wagon on blade......62.00
Wade & Butcher, Sheffield, etched You Lather Well..., horn hdl.42.00
Wade & Butcher, Sheffield, horn w/eng inlaid ornaments, M....15.00
Wadsworth Razor Co, celluloid, relief stork eating bird, EX.....34.00
Warranted, crude cut straight bone hdl, wedge blade, 1810s, sm.32.00
Warranted, Sheffield, travelling, sm wedge bl/bone hdl, 1810...177.00

Waterville Cutlery, celluloid w/fully scrolled raised pattern.......12.00
Wm Elliot Co, blk celluloid w/German silver & pearl inlay.....40.00
Wm Elliot Co, celluloid, raised deer scene/scroll/flowers.......40.00
Wm Elliot Co, imitation ivory, raised castle scene/sailboat.......36.00
Yankee Magnetized, celluloid, raised nude/long hair/lily pad.....52.00

Reamers

Reamers have been made in hundreds of styles and colors, and by as many manufacturers. Their purpose is to extract the juices from lemons, oranges, and grapefruits.

The largest producer of glass reamers was McKee, who pressed their products from many types of glass -- custard; delphite and Chalaine blue; opaque white; Skokie green; black; caramel and white opalescent; Seville yellow; and transparent pink, green, and clear. Among these, the black and the caramel opalescent are the most valuable.

The Fry Glass Company also made reamers that are today very collectible. Their vaseline glass juicers with embossed lettering, both the straight sided and ruffled top models, are valued at well over $200. The Hazel Atlas Crisscross orange reamer in pink often brings in excess of $175; the same in blue, $150.00. Hocking produced a light blue orange reamer and, in the same soft blue, a 2-pc reamer and measuring cup combination. Both are considered rare and very valuable, with $350 and up for the 1-pc and $400 and up for the 2-pc currently quoted estimates.

In addition to the colors mentioned, red glass examples -- transparent or slag -- are rare and costly. Regarded as one of the most valuable reamers ever made, the Cambridge bottom beaded 'Pat Jan. 6, 1909', in cobalt blue is worth from $1,000 to $1,250.00.

Hall Pottery Co., Colonial, red and ivory, 7" diameter, $250.00.

California Fruit Growers, Sunkist, crystal.....................18.00
Clown, gr suit, lg wht ruffle, porcelain figural, 2 pc...........65.00
Clown, lt yel, ceramic, 7"...................................35.00
Clown, pitcher & reamer, blk/cream w/flowers, ceramic.........40.00
Cottage, ceramic...45.00
Dazey, wall mtd, aluminum, pat applied for, 3 pc.............22.00
Duck, comical pouring beak, mc, china.......................38.00
Duck, yel lustre, ceramic....................................35.00
Easley, improved patent, March 6, 1900, crystal...............8.00
Federal, plain side, tab handle, amber.......................190.00
Federal, plain side, tab handle, green........................6.00
Federal, ribbed, embossed Sunkist in bottom, loop hdl, crystal..225.00
Federal, ribbed, loop handle, not embossed Sunkist, crystal.....2.50
Federal, ribbed, loop handle, pink............................20.00
Federal, ribbed, tab handle, seed dam, pink...................80.00
Fleur-de-Lis, red slag, loop hdl.............................250.00
Fry, Blue Goose embossed, opalescent.......................175.00
Fry, ruffled top, opalescent, embossed, loop handle............33.00

German porcelain, figural toby, 1 pc, #d, 5"..................65.00
Good Morning, ceramic, 2 pc pitcher w/reamer top...........25.00
Hall, Lettuce..250.00
Hand reamer, 'Little handy lemon squeezer', crystal..........40.00
Hazel Atlas, crisscross, orange reamer, loop hdl, cobalt blue...145.00
Hazel Atlas, crisscross pattern, tab handle lemon reamer, gr......8.00
Hazel Atlas, 2 quart pitcher & reamer, white w/red trim........30.00
Hazel Atlas, 32 oz pitcher & reamer, transparent green........20.00
Hazel Atlas, 32 oz pitcher & reamer, yellow................250.00
Hocking, loop hdl, orange reamer, emb, milk glass, Vitrock.....20.00
Hocking, orange reamer, blue, 1 pc......................375.00
Hocking, qt pitcher w/reamer top, fruit juice, green w/decal.....20.00
Hocking, ribbed, orange reamer, loop hdl, flashed-on black.....10.00
Hocking, tab hdl, lemon reamer, milk glass, Vitrock...........20.00
Jeannette, delfite blue, small loop hdl....................45.00
Jeannette, Hex Optic, bucket reamer, green.................40.00
Jeannette, Jennyware, ultra-marine, loop handle.............55.00
Jeannette, large loop hdl, transparent green, lg.............12.00
Jeannette, lt jadite, tab hdl, lg........................12.00
Jeannette, pink, tab hdl, lg...........................25.00
Jeannette, pitcher w/reamer, dk jadite...................50.00
Jenkins Glass Co, tab hdl, green.......................50.00
Los Angeles Fruit Growers, purple tint...................45.00
McKee, custard, footed, embossed McK, small..............30.00
McKee, delphite blue, footed, emb McK, small.............175.00
McKee, gr milk glass, grapefruit reamer.................140.00
McKee, gr opaque, footed, emb McK, small...............45.00
McKee, Sunkist, apple green..........................35.00
McKee, Sunkist, black..............................325.00
McKee, Sunkist, custard.............................35.00
McKee, Sunkist, opaque yel, slight rim roughness...........38.00
McKee, yellow, grapefruit reamer, minor flakes............185.00
Meriden silverplate.................................75.00
Orange, ceramic figural, wht top, 2 pc...................45.00
Orange Juice Extractor, tab handle, crystal................23.00
Paden City, shaker type w/metal insert, pink...............45.00
Paden City, 2 qt pitcher, etched, w/reamer top, complete, gr...110.00
Pear, ceramic, 3 pc................................25.00
Saunders, pointed cone, loop hdl, jadite.................450.00
US Glass, cup pitcher w/stick hdl & reamer top, turquoise.....80.00
Valencia, gr, EX..................................100.00
Valencia embossed, milk glass, loop hdl.................58.00

Records

Records of interest to collectors are generally not the million-selling hits by 'superstars'; very few records by Bing Crosby, for example, are of any more than nominal value, and those that are valuable usually don't even have his name on the label! Collectors today are most interested in records that were made in limited quantities, early works of a performer who later became famous, and those issued in special series or aimed at a limited market -- these are bringing prices well in excess of their original cost. The most widely collected categories are Jazz, Dance Bands, Celebrity, Blues, Rhythm and Blues, Country and Western, Hillbilly, Rockabilly, and Rock and Roll.

This year we were assisted in our listings by L.R. Docks, author of *American Premium Record Guide*, which lists 50,000 records by over 6,000 artists; you will find his address in the Directory under 'Texas'.

Key:

Bro----Broadway	Orch----Orchestra
Bru----Brunswick	Para----Paramount
Ch-----Champion	Va------Variety
Col----Columbia	Vi------Victor

Edi----Edison	Vo------Vocalion
Ha-----Harmony	Me-----Meritt

Adams, Woodrow & 3 B's; Pretty Baby Blues, Checker, 45 rpm.20.00
Aladdins, The; All Of My Life, Aladdin 3314, 45 rpm..........25.00
Allen Brothers, Salty Dog Blues, Col 15175-D...............25.00
Allison's Sacred Harp Singers, Gennett 6583................17.00
Anderson, Ivie & Boys From Dixie; All God's Chillun, Variety....9.00
Andrews, Lee & The Hearts; Maybe You'll Be There, Riviera....88.00
Anka, Paul; Diana, ABC Paramount, 78 rpm................18.00
Arkansas Woodchopper, In The Jailhouse Now, Gennett 7036...18.00
Armstrong, Louis; Gut Bucket Blues, Okeh 8261.............40.00
Arnold, Kokomo; Milk Cow Blues, Decca 7026..............17.50
Ashley, Clarence; Old John Hardy, Col 15654-D.............25.00
Austin, Don & The Sensational Dellos; Why Did You Leave Me.75.00
Austin's Serenaders, Jackass Blues, Bro 1018...............63.00
Avalon, Frankie; De De Dinah, Chancellor 1011, 78 rpm......16.00
Baltimore Bellhops, The; Hot And Anxious, Col 2449-D.......18.00
Banjo Joe, Jazz Gypsy Blues, Paramount 12604.............50.00
Barbecue Joe & Hot Dogs, Up The Country Blues, Ch 16127...69.00
Baxter, Phil & His Orch; Honey Child, Vi V-40204...........40.00
Bennett, Eloise; Sting Me Mr Strange Man, Black Patti 8006....50.00
Berry, Chuck; Little Queenie, Chess 1722, 78 rpm...........13.00
Black Boy Shine, Grey With Worry Blues, Vo 03613..........15.00
Blind Blake, Skeedle Loo Doo Blues, Para 12413............43.00
Blue Smitty & His String Men, Sad Story, Chess 1522........10.00
Blythe's Blue Boys, There'll Come A Day, Ch 15344.........90.00
Bogan, Lucille, Brunswick 7186........................59.00
Bond, Luther & His Emeralds; He Loves You Baby, Fed 12279.10.00
Boswell Sisters, Holiday Greetings..., special Edison pressing....46.00
Boswell Sisters, Vi 19639, their 1st record................27.50
Bowen, Jimmy; I'm Sticking With You, Roulette 4001, 78 rpm...10.00
Bragg, Dobby & C McFadden; Fire Detective Blues, Para 12827.90.00
Brown, Buster; The New King Of The Blues, Fire (LP) 102.....42.00
Brown, Dusty; Please Don't Go, Bandera 2503...............7.00
Brown, Richard 'Rabbit'; James Alley Blues, Vi 20578........45.00
Buccaneers, The; The Stars Will Remember, Rama 21, 45 rpm.125.00
Bumble Bee Slim, Greasy Greens, Vo 1719................30.00
Burbank, Jack & Jim; Try Not To Forget, Superior 2741.......25.00
Burnette, Johnny; JB & Rock 'N Roll Trio, Coral (LP) 57080..105.00
Burston, Clara; Try That Man O'Mine, Ch 16125............40.00
Buster & Jack, Guitar Duet Blues, Vi 23257................35.00
Butterbeans & Susie, Construction Gang, Okeh 8163..........35.00
Cadillacs, The; Gloria, Josie 765, 45 rpm.................35.00
Calicott, Joe; Fare Thee Well Blues, Bru 7166..............88.00
Calloway, Blanche & Joy Boys; Lazy Woman Blues, Okeh 8279..35.00
Candullo, Joe & His Orch; Spanish Mama, Buddy 8052........15.00
Cannon, Freddy; Solid Gold Hits, Swan (LP) 505............25.00
Cannon's Jug Stompers, Goin' To Germany, 5413............14.00
Carolina Peanut Boys, Spider's Nest Blues, Vi 23319.........95.00
Carter, Benny & His Orch; Blue Lou, Okeh 41567............18.00
Carter, Bo & Walter Jacobs; Pussy Cat Blues, Col 14661-D....35.00
Carter, King & His Royal Orch; Blue Rhythm, Col 2504 D.....13.00
Carter Family, Keep On The Sunny Side, Bluebird 5006........7.00
Carter Family, Two Sweet Hearts, Vi 23791................45.00
Casa Loma Orch, When I Take My Sugar To Tea, Bru 6085.....8.50
Chavis, Boozoo; Forty One Days, Folk Star 1201............18.00
Childress, Buddy; My Lovin' Arms, Dub 2838...............7.00
Chiles, Buddy; Jet Black Woman, Gold Star 660............28.00
Chips, The; Rubber Biscuit, Josie 803...................14.00
Chocolate Dandies, The; Loveless Love, Vo 1610............65.00
Church, Blind Clyde; Number Nine Blues, Vi 23271..........43.00
Clifford's Louisville Jug Band, Dancing Blues, Okeh 8221.......30.00
Cline's Collegians, test pressing, 78 rpm.................135.00

Collins, Sam; Lead Me All The Way, Gennett 6291............89.00
Cooper, Robert; West Dallas Drug, Bluebird 5459............18.00
Corsairs, The; Goodbye Darling, Hytone 110...............100.00
Count Basie & His Orch, One O'Clock Jump, Decca 1363......8.50
Crayton, Pee Wee; Every Dog Has Day, Imperial 5288, 45 rpm..13.00
Crosby, Bing; Goodnight Sweetheart, Bru 6203..............8.50
Crystals, The; God Only Knows, De Luxe 6077..............40.00
Cupp, Pat; Do Me No Wrong, RPM 461, 45 rpm.............20.00
Daddy Stovepipe & Mississippi Sarah, Depression, Bluebird 6023.42.00
Dalhart, Vernon; Edison 52307...........................31.00
Danny & The Juniors, At The Hop, Singular 711............25.00
Darin, Bobby & The Jaybirds; That's All, Atco (LP) 104.......18.00
Davis, Link; Sixteen Chicks, Starday 235..................12.00
De Faut, Voltaire; Wolverine Blues, Autograph 623..........165.00
De Troit, Johnny & New Orleans Jazz; Panama, Okeh 40240....20.00
Deberry, Jimmy; Take A Little Chance, Sun 185, 45 rpm......82.00
Delaney, Mattie; Tallahatchie River Blues, Vo 1480..........25.00
Denson, Lee; High School Bop, Kent 306..................17.00
Devotions, The; Rip Van Winkle, Delta 1001...............18.00
Dial, Harry & His Blusicians; Poison, Vo 1594.............202.00
Dixie String Band, Soldier's Joy, Silvertone 3516............9.00
Dixieland Jug Blowers, Garden Of Joy Blues, Vi 21126........15.00
Dixon, Bob; There Ain't No Man In The Moon, Vi 23752......40.00
Dixon's Chicago Serenaders, Monte Carlo Joys, Black Patti 8010.75.00
Dominoes, The; Have Mercy Baby, Federal 12068............35.00
Donaldson Quartet, Hannah From Panama, Vi 23788..........9.00
Dorsey, Mattie; Stingaree Blues, Para 12554...............35.00
Dudads; I Heard You Call Me Dear, De Luxe 6083, 45 rpm.....17.00
Dukes, Willie; Snake Hip Twirl, Ch 16126.................18.00
Dupree's Rome Boys, Cat Rag Breakdown, Okeh 45356.......13.00
Ebonaires; 3 O'Clock In The Morning, Aladdin 3211, 45 rpm...17.00
Echoes, The; My Little Honey, Combo 128.................13.00
Edwards, Big Boy; Hoodoo Blues, Vo 02932...............10.00
Edwards, Piano Kid; Piano Kid Special, Para 13051...........95.00
El Capris, Your Star, Fee Bee 216, 45 rpm................18.00
Elgar's Creole Orch, Brotherly Love, Vo 15478.............25.00
Ellington, Duke; Animal Crackers, Buddy 8063.............50.00
Embers, The; Paradise Hill, Herald 410, red plastic, 45 rpm....40.00
Erby, John; Lonesome Jimmy Blues, Col 14151-D...........14.00
Erickson, Wally & His Coliseum Orch; Hard Luck, Vo 15778..66.00
Evans' Old Timers, No Low Down Hanging Around, Ch 16709.123.00
Ezell, Will; Pitchin' Boogie, Para 12855..................59.00
Farm Hands, The Old Hayloft Waltz, Para 3294............13.00
Ferguson, Ben; Please Don't Holler Mama, Vi 23297.........33.00
Five Chances, The; Gloria, States 156....................35.00
Five Satins, In The Still Of The Night, Standard 1005, 45 rpm..65.00
Flames, Together, 7-11 2107............................25.00
Floyd County Ramblers, Sunny Tennessee, Vi 3037..........18.00
Fontaine, Eddie; Goodness It's Gladys; Chancellor 1018, 45 rpm..8.00
Fort Worth Doughboys, Nancy Jane, Bluebird 5257..........74.00
Foster, Jim; Dark Cloudy Blues, Champion 15397...........80.50
Foster, Rudy; Corn Trimmer Blues, Para 12981............110.00
Four Buddies, Simply Say Goodbye, Savoy 823, 45 rpm......70.00
Four Tunes, Cool Water, RCA Victor 3967..................7.00
Fox, Curley; Yum Yum Blues, Decca 5185..................7.00
Frankie & Jazz Devils; Creeping Sneaking Blues, Perfect 107...14.00
Freezone, Indian Squaw Blues, Para 12803................50.00
Frisco Syncopators, Buddy's Habits, Puritan 11244..........10.00
Fruit Jar Guzzlers, Cripple Creek, Para 3116..............25.00
Gaddy, Bob; Little Girl's Boogie, Jax 308, 45 rpm..........18.00
Garner, Gabby; Smokin' Heart, Erald 2052................25.00
Gates, Dave & Accents; Lovin' At Night, Robbins 1008, 45 rpm.13.00
Georgia Yellow Hammers, Pass Around The Bottle, Vi 20550....7.00
Gibson, Clifford; Morgan Street Blues, QRS 7090...........80.00

Gilley, Mickey; Ooh Wee Baby, Minor 106, 45 rpm.........125.00
Gitfiddle Jim, Paddlin' Blues, Vi 23268...................88.00
Glaze, Ruby & Hot Shot Willie; Rollin' Mama Blues, Vi 23328..68.00
Golden Melody Boys, The Cross Eyed Butcher, Para 3068......8.00
Goodman, Benny & His Orch; Breakfast Ball, Col 2927-D.....14.00
Goodman, Benny & His Orch; Music Hall Rag, Col 3011-D....19.00
Goofers, The; Flip Flop & Fly, Coral 61383.................8.00
Gordon, Tommy & His Corn Huskers; Wild Hog In The Woods.25.00
Graves, Blind Roosevelt & Brother; Staggerin' Blues, Par 12891.50.00
Green, Vernon & Medallions; Magic Mountain, Dooto, 45 rpm...12.00
Greer, Sonny; Oh! How I Love My Darling; Blu-Disc 1003....185.00
Haggett, Jimmy; All I Have Is Love, Caprock 107, 45 rpm.....7.00
Haggett, Jimmy; They Call Our Love A Sin, Sun 236, 45 rpm..125.00
Haley, Bill; Green Tree Boogie, Holiday 108, 45 rpm.........90.00
Happy Harmonists, The; Baptistown Crawl, Gennett 5402......25.00
Harlem Footwarmers, The; Lazy Duke, Okeh 8760...........30.00
Harry's Reckless Five, Wailing Blues, Bro 1355.............50.00
Hazel, Monk & His Bienville Roof Orch; Git-Wit-It, Bru 4182..25.00
Heartbreakers, Why Don't I, RCA Victor 4662, 45 rpm.......70.00
Helms, Bud & His Band; Pee Wee Blues, Ch 15285..........40.00
Henderson, Fletcher & His Orch; Linger Awhile, Edison 51277..18.00
Herwin Hot Shots, Salty Dog, Herwin 93015...............89.00
Hill Top Inn Orch, Choose Your Pal, Ch 15031.............17.00
Hodgin, Willard; Girl That Lived On Polecat Creek, Edi 52243..15.00
Holiday, Billie & Her Orch; Billie's Blues, Vo 3288..........10.00
Hopkins, Lightnin'; Henny Penny Blues, Gold Star 640........18.00
Horsey's Hot Five, Weeping Blues, Gennett 6722............42.00
Hot Dogs, The; Hot Mustard, Silvertone 3560.......,......30.00
Howard, Bob & His Orch; I'll Never Change, Decca 439........10.00
Howell, Peg Leg & E Anthony; Turkey Buzzard Blues, Col 1438231.00
Hunter's Serenaders, Sensational Mood, Vo 1621............35.00
Imperials, You'll Never Walk Alone, Great Lakes 1212, 45 rpm..90.00
Inspirators, If Loving You Is Wrong, Treat 502, 45 rpm.......50.00
Jackson, Jim; My Monday Woman Blues, Vi 21236...........16.00
Jackson, Lulu; Lost Lover Blues, Vo 1242.................14.00
James, Corky & His Blackbirds; Bugahoma Blues, Bell 1182...251.00
James, Frank; Frank's Lonesome Blues, Ch 16809............67.00
James, Harry & His Orch; Texas Chatter, Bru 8067...........8.50
James, Jelly & His Fewsicians; Georgia Bo Bo, Gennett 6045....67.00
James, Skip; Drunken Spree, Para 13111.................200.00
Jazz Harmonists, The; Riverboat Shuffle, Claxtonola 40339.....66.00
Jefferson, Blind Lemon; Rabbit Foot Blues, Para 12454........35.00
Jelly Belly & Slim Seward, Sorry Woman Blues, Apollo 412......9.00
Jennings, Waylon; Jole Blond, Bru 55130.................25.00
Jimmie's Joys, Bugle Call Rag, Golden 1865...............40.00
Johnson, Blanche; Galveston Blues, Herwin 90216...........89.00
Johnson, Charlie's Paradise Band; Walk That Thing, Vi 21712..13.00
Johnson, JC & 5 Hot Sparks; Red Hot Hottentot, QRS 7064...100.00
Johnson, Louise; All Night Long Blues, Para 12992...........75.00
Jolson, Al; Little Wonder 20, credited anonymously...........37.00
Jones, Alberta; Shake A Little Bit, Gennett 6439............30.00
Jones, Isham & His Orch; Vi 24395.....................12.50
Jordan, Luke; Cocaine Blues, Vi 21076...................50.00
Jungle Band, The; Tiger Rag, Bru 4238..................15.00
Kansas City Frank & Footwarmers; Wailing Blues, Para 12898..80.00
Kentucky Jazz Babies, Old Folks Shake, Vi 38616........50,000.00
Keynotes, Wish You Were Here, Apollo 493, 45 rpm.........23.00
King Oliver's Jazz Band, Chattanooga Stomp, Col 13003-D....41.00
King Oliver's Jazz Band, Snake Rag, Okeh 4933............166.00
Kings Men, Don't Say You're Sorry, Club-51 108, 45 rpm.....89.00
La Vizzo, Thelma; The Stomps, Para 12250...............65.00
Lee, Winthrop & Orch; Daniel's Blues, Parlophone PNY-34148..15.00
Lewis, Smiley; It's So Peaceful, Imperial 5208.............35.00
Lumpkin, Guy; Decatur Street Rag, QRS 7078.............75.00

Lyrics, Every Night, Rhythm 127, 45 rpm.....................45.00
Mack, Baby; What Kind Of Man Is You?, Okeh 8313.........25.00
Marshall Brothers, Just Because, Savoy 828, 45 rpm.........100.00
Martin, Blind George; Southern Rag, Bro 5053..............30.00
McCoy, Violet; Lonesome Daddy Blues, Ajax 17010.........23.00
McKenzie, Red; There'll Be Some Changes Made, Okeh 40893..25.00
McKinney's Cotton Pickers, She's My Secret Passion, Vi 22628...6.00
McPhail, Black Bottom; Mix That Thing, Vo 1690..........43.00
Medallions, I Know, Essex, 45 rpm......................65.00
Melody Four, The; I'm Crazy 'Bout My Baby, Vi 23289.......23.00
Memphis Jug Band, Snitchin' Gambler Blues, Vi 21524.......131.00
Miller, Glen & His Orch; I Got Rhythm, Bru 7915...........10.00
Miller, Mae Belle; Long Tall Man Blues, Para 12985........50.00
Moore, Alice; My Man Blues, Para 12868..................70.00
Mosby, Curtis & Dixieland Blue Blowers; Tiger Stomp, Col 1192.19.00
Nelson, Ozzie & His Orch; Dream A Little Of Me, Bru 6060....12.00
Night Owls, The; Pump Tillie, Silvertone 3549.............25.00
Nighthawks, The; Jackson Town Gal, Aristocrat 413.........25.00
Nowlin, Sam; So What, Ch 16828.......................10.00
Oakie, Jack; Melotone 35-10-1.........................26.00
Original Dixieland Five, Clarinet Marmalade, Vi 25525......10.00
Ory's Sunshine Orch; Ory's Creole Trombone, Sunshine 3003..175.00
Pickett-Parham Apollo Syncopators, Mojo Strut, Para 12441...87.00
Platters, Give Thanks, Federal 12153...................50.00
Pollack, Ben & His Orch; Vi 24284.....................20.00
Porter, Flossie; Got Nobody To Grind My Coffee, Ch 15101.....30.00
Presley, Elvis; Baby Let's Play House, Sun 217, 78 rpm.......125.00
Presley, Elvis; Elvis' Christmas Album, RCA Victor LOC-1035..100.00
Presley, Elvis; Good Rockin' Tonite, Sun 210, 78 rpm.......105.00
Presley, Elvis; Heartbreak Hotel, RCA Victor 20-6420, 78 rpm...22.00
Presley, Elvis; I Beg Of You, RCA Victor 20-7150, 78 rpm.....23.00
Presley, Elvis; Love Me Tender, RCA Victor 20-6643, 78 rpm...16.00
Presley, Elvis; Milkcow Blues Boogie, Sun 215, 45 rpm......195.00
Presley, Elvis; Mystery Train, RCA Victor 20-6357, 78 rpm....19.00
Presley, Elvis; RCA Victor 47-7000, 45 rpm, w/picture sleeve...35.00
Presley, Elvis; RCA Victor 47-7740, 45 rpm, w/picture sleeve...15.00
Presley, Elvis; That's All Right, Sun 209, 78 rpm.........125.00
Quintones When My Sugar Walks Down The Street, Vo 5172...15.00
Randall, Duke & His Boys; Squeeze Me, Ch 15491...........95.00
Red Onion Jazz Babies; Terrible Blues, Gennett 5607.......146.00
Redman, Don & His Orch; I Heard, Bru 6233..............14.00
Reeves, Jim; I've Never Been So Blue, Macy's 132..........50.00
Reeves, Reuben 'River' & His River Boys; River Blues, Vo 1292.19.00
Revere, Paul & Raiders; Like Long Hair, Gardena 1000 (LP)....40.00
Richie, Bud & His Boys; Slappin' The Bass, Ch 16109........18.00
Robechaux, Joseph & New Orleans Rhythm Boys; Zola, Vo 2646.16.00
Rodgers, Jimmie; Moonlight And Skies, Vi 23574...........42.00
Rorer, Posey & His NC Ramblers; As We Sat...Hill, Edi 52414..55.00
Russell, Luis; Saratoga Drag, Vo 1579..................50.00
Savoy Bearcats, Bearcat Stomp, Vi 20307...............35.00
Scare Crow, The; Gennett 7297.......................137.00
Scruggs, Irene; My Back To The Wall, Ch 16148...........40.00
Sh-Booms, The; Could It Be, Cat 117....................7.00
Shreveport Sizzlers, You've Got To Be Modernistic, Okeh 41561.25.00
Smith, Bessie Mae; St Louis Daddy, Para 12922............65.00
Smith, Bessie; Beale Street Mama, Col A-3877............10.00
Snooks & His Memphis Ramblers; Kissable Baby, Vi 22813....10.00
Sons Of The Pioneers, Wagons West, Camden (LP) 413........11.00
State Street Ramblers, There'll Come A Day, Gennett 6249....80.00
Swallows, My Baby, After Hours 104, 45 rpm.............175.00
Sykes, Roosevelt; Boot That Thing, Okeh 8702...........87.50
Tomlin, Kingfish Bill; Dupree Blues, Para 13057...........89.00
Valentino, Rudolph; Kashmiri Song, Special Record.........35.00
Walker, Eddie & His Band; Mandy, Supertone 9486.........333.00

Walker, Eddie & His Band; West End Blues, Supertone 9368...61.00
Wallace, Sippie; Devil Dance Blues, Okey 8206.............61.00
Waller, Fats & His Buddies; Lookin' Good..., Vi V-38086......33.00
Washboard Sam, Down At The Old Village Store, Bluebird 7526.16.00
Washboard Serenaders, Teddy's Blues, Vi 38610............30.00
Washington, Lizzie; Mexico Blues, Black Patti 8054.........50.00
Wheatstraw, Peetie; Doin' The Best I Can, Decca 7007.......15.00
Whistler & His Jug Band, Pig Meat Blues, Okeh 8816.........35.00
Whistlin' Rufus, Sweet Thing, Bluebird 5360...............8.00
Williams & Memphis Stompers; Lotta Sax Appeal, Vo 1453.....43.00
Williamson, Sonny Boy; Sugar Mama Blues, Bluebird 2059.....18.00
Wilson & Reed, France Blues, Ch 15264.................45.00
Wrens, I Won't Come To Your Wedding, Rama 184, 45 rpm....90.00

Red Wing

The Red Wing Stoneware Company, founded in 1878, took its name from its location in Red Wing, Minnesota. In the 1920s, the name was changed to the Red Wing Union Stoneware Company after a merger with several of the other local potteries. For the most part, they produced utilitarian wares such as flowerpots, crocks, and jugs. In about 1930, their catalogues offered a line of art pottery vases in colored glazes, some of which featured handles modeled after swan's necks, snakes, or female nudes. Other examples were quite simple, often with classic styling. After the addition of their dinnerware lines in the early thirties, 'Stoneware' was dropped from the name, and the company became known as Red Wing Potteries, Inc. They closed in 1967.

Brushware

Bowl vase, acorns & leaves, w/hdls, sgn.....................26.00
Flowerpot, sgn...12.00
Mug, 4 for...110.00
Pitcher...60.00
Umbrella stand...85.00
Vase, cylinder, birds, cattails, no mk....................22.00
Vase, floral sprays, sgn Union Stoneware, 11".............55.00
Vase, gr w/ivy, 10".....................................60.00

Commercial Art Ware

Ash tray, cream to br....................................15.00
Ash tray, wing shape, 'Red Wing Potteries', 7¼" L..........40.00
Bookends, polar bears, gray, pr..........................60.00
Bowl, br w/people & florals, 11".........................45.00
Bowl, oval, free form, rolled-in w/leaf, gold/br, #B2014, 14"....40.00
Carafe, Gypsy Trail, #565, turq.........................12.00
Console bowl, ivory w/deer for flowers in center..........25.00
Ewer, funnel shape, gr, 6½".............................20.00
Figurine, Spanish dancers, 10", pr.......................65.00
Gopher on football figural, dtd 1939....................135.00
Hanging basket, br glaze w/in, fleur-de-lis, 5x7".........20.00
Pitcher, burnt orange, ball shape, 5½"...................20.00
Pitcher, w/lid; bl w/wood & copper hdl...................26.00
Planter, #11687..7.00
Planter, elephant, pink..................................7.50
Planter, flower cart, metal hdl, #M-1531, 5½x9½x8½".......31.00
Vase, #177, 9"...25.00
Vase, #341, 6x3¼".....................................20.00
Vase, ball w/3 holes, fire orange, 5½"...................35.00
Vase, fan flared, gr, #416-12...........................25.00
Vase, Nokomis glaze, 6"................................20.00

Vase, ovoid w/long neck, daubed glaze, #195, mkd, 9".........27.00
Vase, peacock in relief, yellow, 7½x3", pr..................125.00
Vase, ped ft, lt gr, 10"..............................10.00
Vase, pk w/leaf design, #1155, 10x7"...................20.00
Vase, ribbed, yellow, 12".............................20.00

Cookie Jars

Brown w/cattails.....................................100.00
Chef, yellow...36.00
Jack Frost on the Pumpkin, w/label...................75.00
Katrina, any color...................................36.00
King of Hearts, EX coloring..........................75.00
Monk, blue...38.00

Jack Frost on the Pumpkin, marked with foil 'Red Wing' label, 12", $75.00.

Dinnerware

Black Rose Anniversary, divided dish....................12.00
Bob White, bowl, berry..................................3.00
Bob White, bowl, divided vegetable.....................20.00
Bob White, bowl, oval cereal; w/birds...................8.50
Bob White, bowl, salad; 12"............................50.00
Bob White, bowl, vegetable.............................13.50
Bob White, casserole, 2 qt.............................25.00
Bob White, casserole, 4 qt, in copper fr...............42.00
Bob White, cookie jar..................................55.00
Bob White, creamer & sugar w/lid.......................18.00
Bob White, cup & saucer................................10.00
Bob White, hors d'oeuvre bird..........................35.00
Bob White, plate, 10½".................................8.00
Bob White, platter, 13"................................17.50
Bob White, shakers, bird, pr...........................16.00
Bob White, shakers, tall, pr...........................15.00
Bob White, sugar w/lid..................................9.00
Bob White, teapot......................................30.00
Bob White, tumbler.....................................50.00
Bob White, water pitcher, 60 oz........................25.00
Capistrano, bowl, divided vegetable....................10.00
Capistrano, bowl, serving...............................8.50
Capistrano, platter, 13"...............................12.00

Fondosa, batter pitcher, pink, w/lid...................25.00
Fondosa, syrup jar, pink, w/lid........................22.00
Labrigo, French casserole..............................25.00
Lexington, bowl, 8".....................................7.00
Lexington, creamer......................................7.00
Lexington, cup & saucer.................................8.00
Lexington, plate, 10"...................................6.00
Lexington, plate, 11"...................................8.00
Lexington, plate, 6"....................................4.00
Lexington, plate, 7"....................................5.00
Lexington, platter, lg..................................8.50
Lexington, sugar w/lid..................................9.00
Lotus, bowl, 8½"...6.00
Lotus, casserole w/lid.................................14.00
Lotus, cup..4.00
Lotus, gravy w/attached plate...........................8.00
Lotus, onion soup w/lid.................................8.50
Lotus, salt & pepper....................................6.00
Lotus, sugar & creamer.................................10.00
Magnolia, cup & saucer..................................8.00
Magnolia, plate, 10"....................................6.00
Morning Glory, plate, 10"...............................7.00
Normandie, creamer & sugar.............................15.00
Normandie, cup & saucer.................................8.00
Normandie, plate, dinner................................9.00
Orleans, bowl, 5½".......................................2.00
Orleans, bowl, 8¾".......................................5.00
Orleans, casserole w/lid...............................15.00
Orleans, creamer..5.00
Orleans, cup & saucer...................................4.00
Orleans, plate, 10".....................................3.00
Orleans, salt & pepper..................................6.00
Orleans, sugar w/lid...................................10.00
Orleans, teapot..12.00
Random Harvest, bowl, cereal............................4.50
Random Harvest, bowl, vegetable; divided................7.50
Random Harvest, cup & saucer............................5.50
Random Harvest, plate, dinner...........................4.50
Random Harvest, plate, 11"..............................7.50
Random Harvest, platter, 13"...........................10.00
Random Harvest, shakers, pr.............................5.00
Tampico, bowl, dessert..................................4.00
Tampico, creamer & sugar w/lid.........................20.00
Tampico, cup & saucer...................................9.00
Tampico, pitcher, ice lip..............................24.00
Tampico, plate, 10".....................................7.00
Tampico, plate, 6½".....................................3.00

Stoneware

Bean pot, w/lid; br glaze, Minnesota Stoneware, 8" dia.........45.00
Beater jar, advertising HL Sander, sgn Saffron Ware..........85.00
Beater jar, no adv, 1 bl band...........................40.00
Bowl, advertising, deep bl, Ewald Bros Dairy, 4½x6".....50.00
Bowl, rust/bl spongeware, Wisc ad w/in, dtd 1926, 4½x7"......95.00
Bowl, saffron sponge, Iowa advertising, 9½".............75.00
Bowl, spongeware, bl/tan, 4¾x7½", EX....................40.00
Bowl, spongeware w/panels, 10"..........................75.00
Bowls, nesting; spongeware, 6½"; 7½"; 8½"..............250.00
Butter jar, advertising, Moland Co-op, 5x7".............70.00
Butter jar, bl w/in & w/out, w/tie ring, unsgn, ½ lb....22.50
Butter jar, Fresh Butter, Model Dairy, in blk, 4½x5¾"........45.00
Butter jar, Return to North Star Creamery, 5x6¾", EX........65.00
Canning jar, 1 qt, dtd 1899............................95.00

Casserole, Gray Line, lg.................................140.00
Casserole, Gray Line, 4½".............................250.00
Casserole, sponge, Wisconsin advertising, hairline, 7".........65.00
Churn bottom w/lid, 4 gal, lg wing.....................110.00
Crock, bl bands, red wing 1 side, Minn advertising, 7".......165.00
Crock, lg red wing, verso: SD ad, 1½ qt.................185.00
Crock, w/lid, wing mk, 20 gal..........................125.00
Crock, w/lid, 2 gal, birch leaves, Union on front/Minn on base..100.00
Crock, 15 gal, w/big wing..............................100.00
Crock, 2 gal, w/birch leaves, transitional, 2 RW companies......90.00
Custard cup, Spongeband, mk Made in Red Wing, 2½x3¼"....37.00
Fruit jar, Mason, Union Stoneware, 1 qt.................90.00
Fruit jar, Mason, ½ gal...............................150.00
Jar, apple sauce; w/lid & clamp, sgn w/Red Wing, 5 gal......145.00
Jug, water; 15 gal, EX................................245.00
Jug, ½ gal, emb Minnesota Stoneware Co, wht glaze, 1896-1906.50.00
Jug, 4 gal, sm wing...................................35.00
Jug, 5 gal, lg wing...................................35.00
Pantry jar, wht w/bl, Minn adv, wing on reverse, w/lid, 5#......310.00
Pitcher, allover sponging, RWUS Co, Hull, Iowa ad, bulbous...285.00
Pitcher, Cherry Band, bl/red sponge, w/advertising, 'Peterson'..400.00
Pitcher, Cherry Band, bl/wht, Minn advertising, EX mold, lg...210.00
Pitcher, Cherry Band, dtd 1914, Iowa advertising, medium.....135.00
Pitcher, gr gloss, flowers, #179, 9½"...................22.00
Pitcher, Saffron, N Dakota ad, sm.....................105.00
Pitcher, Spongeband, Iowa ad, sm, M...................170.00
Pitcher, Spongeband, w/ad, lg.........................150.00
Pitcher & mug, Century of Progress, transportation, 1933.....225.00
Platter, oval w/lid, ca 1920...........................45.00
Poultry fount, Ko-rec.................................55.00
Rolling pin, flowers, orig hdls, w/Minn advertising, M........225.00

Normandy, plate, 10", $9.00; cup and saucer, $8.00; creamer and sugar, $15.00 for the pair.

Rolling pin, orange band, advertising....................140.00
Salt crock, Spongeband, w/advertising, dtd 1934, hairline.....300.00
Salt shaker, Spongeband, rare, M......................250.00
Water cooler, w/lid, wing mk, 5 gal....................200.00
Water cooler bottom, 8 gal............................250.00

Miscellaneous

Christmas tree holder.................................295.00
Hot plate, Centennial issue............................35.00
Mug, Hamm's Krug Klub...............................65.00

Pig, M...300.00
Sewer pipe...40.00
Shoes, miniature, sgn Minn RW Co, M..................45.00

Redware

The term redware refers to a type of simple earthenware produced by the Colonists as early as the 1600s. The red clay used in its production was abundant throughout the country, and during the 18th and 19th centuries redware was made in great quantities. Intended for utilitarian purposes such as everyday tableware, or use in the dairy, redware was simple in design and decoration. Glazes of various colors were used, and a liquid clay referred to as 'slip' was sometimes applied in patterns such as zigzag lines, daisies, or stars. With such decorations it is referred to as 'slip ware'.

Birdhouse, unglazed/tooled, chimney damaged, early 1900s, 8"..35.00
Bottle, donut form, mottled blk/gr glaze, 10½"............125.00
Bottle, form of woman in long dress, parts missing, 12".......525.00
Bottle, gentlemen figural, prof rpr, 15½"................250.00
Bottle, wht slip w/gr glaze, sgraffito inscription, 1887, 8".....40.00
Bowl, gr/clear glaze, 3½x8¾"...........................45.00
Bowl, milk; rim spout, gr w/orange spots, 3¼x8½".........125.00
Bowl, wavy & straight lines in br & wht on olive, 3x9¾".......55.00
Bowl, yellow scalloped slip decor, 2¾x8½"..............400.00
Bowl, yellow slip w/sgraffito tulips/vines, coggled, 2¼x12".....200.00
Candlestick, dk gr gloss, hdl reattached, flakes, 5".........45.00
Canteen, keg shape w/hdl/spout, slip florals, flakes, 10"......185.00
Canteen, yellow slip w/sgraffito decor, European, 8¼"........45.00
Charger, notched rim, bold combed slip trailings, 13", G......770.00
Charger, notched rim, Temperance/Health/Wealth in slip, 14".4,950.00
Charger, notched rim, opposing M-like slip trails, 13".......1,650.00
Charger, sgraffito fife & drum player, Breininger 1976, 13"....105.00
Charger, sgraffito lady on horse, Breininger, 1976, 12½"......85.00
Charger, swirled center, clear w/gr, imp Jugtownware, rpr, 15"..65.00
Collander, yellow slip rim decor, 2 of 3 ft missing, 5x12½"....150.00
Creamer, 2 tone w/yellow slip, clear glaze, 3¾"...........110.00
Cup, dk br, very thin, flared lip, rim flake, 2½"...........30.00
Cup, good detail, rich br, att Swank pottery, sm rim flakes......50.00
Dish, clear glaze w/bittersweet color, 7¾" dia.............65.00
Dish, clear w/good dk red color, old edge flakes, 7½".......45.00
Dish, dk metallic glaze, old gr w/in, edge flakes, 6".........30.00
Dish, primitive bird in yellow slip, coggled edge, 2x8½", G....525.00
Dish, sponge decor on rust, incised rim line, 1840, 8"......220.00
Dish, straight & wavy lines in yellow, hairlines, 1¾x7¾".......85.00
Dish, 3 line crow's ft in yellow, coggled edge, 7¼".........155.00
Figurine, bird on branch, applied birds & flowers on base, 9"..440.00
Figurine, dog, wht splotches, clear glaze, sm flakes, 8", pr...390.00
Figurine, man's head, br/blk glaze, 4¾"..................55.00
Flower pot, attached saucer, running br, rim hairline, 6".......35.00
Flower pot, finger crimped rim, gr/br glaze, edge chips, 9½"....65.00
Flower pot, flared rim, attached saucer, amber w/gr, 5½", G....35.00
Jar, apple butter; glazed w/in, 6½"......................35.00
Jar, canning; att Galena, mottled amber/orange/gr w/wht drips..325.00
Jar, Galena, shiny orange amber, pitted/edge wear, 9½".......85.00
Jar, ovoid, clear w/br flecked glaze, base flake, 5¾".........25.00
Jar, ovoid, glazed w/in, imp John Bell, minor rim flakes, 8¾"...35.00
Jar, ovoid, good color, hairlines, 10"....................55.00
Jar, ovoid, imp John Bell, dk olive gr, 5¼"..............145.00
Jar, ovoid, Swank pottery, yellow/blk slip, flaking, 5¾".......45.00
Jar, ovoid, tooled at shoulder, 2 unglazed circles, dk br, 9"....35.00
Jar, pouring spout/hdl, amber/orange, 7"................100.00

Jar, pouring spout/lid, sponged br, base has cracks, 8"........150.00
Jar, red/wht w/gr brushed leaf decor, imp W Burshnell, 6½", G.260.00
Jar, w/hdl, Conic NH glaze, gr w/orange spots, edge flakes.....195.00
Jar, w/lid, incised lines, ovoid, br splotches, hairline, 11"......250.00
Jug, grotesque face, sgn Lanier Meaders, 10"...............415.00
Jug, ovoid, gr/orange color, G wide strap hdl, minor wear, 6"..225.00
Jug, ovoid, imp John Bell, dk orange color, 7", G............95.00
Jug, ovoid, tooled bands, strap hdl, orange/br, 7½".........255.00
Jug, unusual yellow & pink blush, 1850s, 8"...............85.00
Loaf pan, coggled edge, 3 line slip decor, 17"..............425.00
Loaf pan, yellow wavy lines in lattice, coggled, 13x15¾", G....175.00
Milk pan, molded lip w/trails of gr/br slip, sponge decor, 13".1,210.00
Milk pan, rust w/slip zigzag/3 ring border, spoke center, 14"..1,320.00
Miniature chest, scalloped apron/4 drw/applied decor, 14x13"..575.00
Mold, cookie; bunch of grapes, unglazed, 4" L...............55.00
Mold, gr/amber, scalloped w/emb fruit/flowers, 3 ft, 2x3½x4½"..75.00
Mold, Turk's head; gr w/orange spots, edge chips, 3½x10¼"....95.00
Mold, Turk's head; yel glaze, imp John Bell, cracks, 9".......85.00
Mold, Turk's head; yel slip rim w/dots of dk gr, worn, 9", G...85.00
Pepper shaker, clear glaze, dk br color, chips on flange, 4"....25.00
Pie plate, coggled edge, yellow slip lattice, flaking, 8½".......65.00
Pie plate, sgraffito urn w/tulips, yellow/gr/br, crimped, 8".....850.00
Pie plate, swirled yellow slip, coggled edge, 9¼"...........300.00
Pie plate, yellow slip lines, coggled edge, rim crack, 11"......105.00
Pie plate, 3 repeats of 4 wavy lines in yellow, hairline, 10½"...110.00
Pitcher, chicken w/beak spout, E Paulo, 12¾"..............85.00
Pitcher, Shenandoah, cream slip/clear w/br & gr runs, 6", G...170.00
Pitcher, Shenandoah, wht slip/clear/gr/green drips, 11", G....375.00
Pitcher, strap hdl, dk orange, hairline/spout chip, 4¾".......45.00
Pitcher, tooling, applied hdl, br splotches, base flake, 5½"......40.00
Pitcher, yellow slip foliage, clear glaze, edge flakes, 8".........65.00
Pitcher, 2 tone/sgraffito florals, J Mahoney, Wm Pottery, 10"....65.00
Plate, coggled edge, basketweave br/gr lines over wht, 8", G....95.00
Plate, coggled edge, slip decor, early 20th century, 9¾".......325.00
Plate, notched rim, 2 slip devices of 3 joined wavy lines, 10"...715.00
Plate, slip pinwheels, gr/yellow on rust, sgn Womelsdorf, 8"..1,650.00
Plate, stylized slip tulip ea side & center of 4 strokes, 11½"...990.00
Pot, interior glaze, imp Henshaw Motor Co, 3"..............18.00
Pot, primitive, incised wavy lines, inscription: Parsley, 3".......20.00
Pot, strap hdl, rim spout, w/lid, tooled, 6½", G.............400.00
Puzzle jug, sgraffito flowers/foliage, 'R+C pusle pot, 1844'......45.00
Tray, notched rim, 3 rows wavy slip lines, emb parrot, 14½".1,760.00
Tray, X-hatching of yellow slip, 11x14"...................495.00
Vase, bulbous, narrow neck, flared rim, att Galena, 12"........85.00
Washboard, clear w/gr splotches, wood fr damaged, 15x19½"..100.00
Washbowl, Shenandoah, applied soap dish, ornament, 13", G..245.00
Water jug, ovoid, blk/amber/tan mottle, sm spout/hole/hdl, 9"..150.00
Whistle, bird, unglazed, att to Bell family, 2¼".............200.00

Religious Items

Altar vase, pewter, urn w/scroll hdl, 1742, Continental, 8".....467.00
Cross, processional; gilt copper w/applied figures, 1500s, 30".2,310.00
Figure, Bishop Saint, polychrome wood, Spanish, 1400s, 21"...550.00
Figure, St Anthony, walnut, Flemish, late 1500s, 29".......1,500.00
Figure, St Sebastian, silver gilt, coral tree, 1600s, 6¾".....1,320.00
Figure, The Virgin, walnut, crowned/veiled, rpr, 1400s, 61"..2,200.00
Group, Marys & St Elizabeth, alabaster, Flemish, 1500s, 10".1,210.00
Group, Virgin & Child, polychrome oak, Spanish, 1500s, 27".1,320.00
Group, Virgin & Child, polychrome wood, early 1500s, 4¾"....770.00
Wood engraving, paths to Heaven & Hell w/PA German message.35.00

Russian icon, Christ Pantocrator, gilded silver oclade with enamel halo, mark of District Control Administration, 12" x 10½", $4,000.00.

Reverse Painting on Glass

Verre eglomise is the technique of painting on the underside of glass. Dating back to the early 1700s, this art became popular in the 19th century when German immigrants chose historical figures and beautiful women as subjects for their reverse glass paintings. Advertising mirrors of this type came into vogue at the turn of the century.

Virgin Mary and Infant Jesus; Holy Family -- Spanish, late 18th/early 19th century, initialed F.M.F., 10" x 7", $385.00 for the pair.

Bouquet of flowers on blk, tinsel, gilt fr, 10½x12¾"..........45.00
Bust of Grand Duchess of Saxony, oval, crown surmount, 3x2".140.00
Checkerboard, in mahog shadow box fr, minor flaking, 22" sq...55.00
Doublet, clergyman & son, ovals, coat of arms, dtd 1791, 5½".330.00
Gent in bl coat w/rust collar, gr ground, 'Wolf', early 1800.....625.00

Gentleman w/long wig, very flaked, after Charles II, 7x9"......115.00
Geo Washington portrait, 1900s, 8x9½"....................30.00
Goethe contemplating tomb of friend, Brion, 3¾x2¾".......350.00
Lady & gentleman play chess, mk Lie Lind Matt! Meinn Herr!..358.00
Lady in blk on silver leaf, gilt jewelry, oval brass fr, 2¼"......125.00
Lady w/bl bonnet, gr ribbon, salmon dress, 'Spaniolin', 11x15".275.00
Lady w/flowers in hair, 'Portugeserin', in fr, 8½x10¾".......300.00
Lady w/lg red bow in hair, yellow dress, 'Joseffina', 12x9½"..475.00
Man & lady at writing table, rosewood fr, Chinese, 22½x16"...225.00
Man plays harpsichord lady looks on, sgn Koehler, 10x7".....600.00
Marriage portrait, 2 ovals, facing, joined by eagle, 3x4".......250.00
Pennsylvania German inscription, mc tinsel, 18x20"..........30.00
Sign, advertising, mc on silver flecked ground, 18½x26".......70.00
Silhouette of young boy in oval vignette, 1700s, 5¾"........275.00

Rhead

Associated with many companies during his career -- Weller, Vance Avon, Arequipa, A.E. Tile, and finally Homer Laughlin China -- Frederick Hurten Rhead organized his own pottery in Santa Barbara, California, in about 1913. Admittedly more of a designer than a potter, Rhead hired help to turn the pieces on the wheel, but did most of the decorating himself. The process he favored most involved sgraffito designs inlaid with enameling; Egyptian and Art Nouveau influences were evidenced in much of his work. The ware he produced there was often marked with a logo incorporating the potter at the wheel and 'Santa Barbara'.

Vase, bisque, Los Angeles, 7½".........................150.00
Vase, gray matt w/incised geometrics, 8"..................950.00
Vase, ovoid, gr blistered glaze, 4½"......................375.00
Vase, yel/br glaze, Santa Barbara, 4½x1½"................325.00
Wall pocket, advertising Santa Barbara Mission, rare.........175.00

Richard

Richard, who at one time worked for Galle, made cameo art glass in France during the 1920s. His work was often multi-layered and acid cut with florals and scenics in lovely colors. The ware was marked with his name in relief.

Atomizer, floral cameo, purple shades, 7"..................525.00
Vase, autumn scenic cameo, lavender cut to orange, sgn, 17¾".700.00
Vase, houses/trees, 3 cuttings, 8¼x4¼"...................360.00
Vase, landscape/dwellings on full base, long neck w/trees, 18"..700.00
Vase, oasis w/palm trees, river; base plugged, 16"...........400.00
Vase, pine tree cameo w/enameling, sgn, 5"................350.00

Ridgway

As early as 1792, the Ridgway brothers, Job and George, produced fine quality earthenwares in Shelton, Staffordshire, marking their product 'Ridgway, Smith & Ridgway', and later, 'Job & George Ridgway'. About 1800, the brothers split and each had his own firm, both in Shelton. They were joined in the business by various members of the Ridgway family, and in fact their descendents still operate there today.

The two firms created by the split were the Bell Works and the Cauldon Pottery. Bell produced stone china and earthenware decorated with blue transfer printing. Their mark was 'J. & W. Ridgway' or 'J. & W.R.', until 1848 when 'William Ridgway' was used.

The Cauldon Pottery made earthenware, stone china, and high quality porcelains fine enough to win them the distinction of being appointed potters to the Queen. From 1830, their wares attest to this fact, bearing the

Royal Arms mark with 'J.R.' within the crest. In 1840, '& Co.' was added.

Most examples of Ridgway's wares found today are transfer printed historical scenes.

See also Staffordshire, Historical; Flow Blue

Ash tray, Coaching Days, Fresh Teams.....................26.00
Biscuit jar, Coaching Days, Racing Mail, self lid/wicker hdl.....135.00
Bowl, Coaching Days, Eloped, scalloped silver rim, 10"........65.00
Bowl, Coaching Days, 2¾x4¾" dia........................50.00
Box w/lid, Coaching Days, 2¼x4¼x5½".....................110.00
Cup & saucer, Coaching Days, Mother Goose Rhymes, rare.....50.00
Cup & saucer, handleless; Chusan.........................25.00
Mug, Coaching Days, 2 hdls, 4½".........................95.00
Mug, Coaching Days, 4¾"................................40.00
Pitcher, Coaching Days, lt gr w/lustre rim, scarce color, 5".....110.00
Pitcher, Coaching Days, platinum wash rim & hdl, 2½"........45.00
Pitcher, Coaching Days, 3½x3½".........................55.00
Pitcher, Coaching Days, 9½"............................120.00
Pitcher, hot milk; ivory w/gold leaves, pewter top, July 1881....110.00
Pitcher, Tam-O'-Shanter, lt bl, dtd 1835, 11x9½"............165.00
Pitcher, tankard; Coaching Days, w/six ½ pt mugs............275.00
Pitcher, tankard; Coaching Days, 6x4"......................65.00
Plaque, Coaching Days, Taking Up the Mails, 12" dia.........95.00
Plate, India Jar, bl transfer, 10", set of 6.................185.00
Plate, Lynton, 9¾"....................................10.00
Plate, Niagara, br transfer, 9".........................22.50
Platter, Lynton, 14"...................................35.00
Teapot, Coaching Days, Eloped, sgn, 4½x4½"................95.00

Plate, Charles Dickens Series, Mr. Pickwick Under Arrest, flow blue transfer, 10", $95.00.

Riviera

Riviera was a line of dinnerware introduced by the Homer Laughlin China Company in 1938. It was sold exclusively by the Murphy Company through their nationwide chain of dime stores. Riviera was unmarked, light weight, and inexpensive. It was discontinued sometime prior to 1950. Colors are mauve blue, red, yellow, light green, and ivory. On rare occasions dark blue pieces are found, but this was not a standard color.

Baker, oval, 9".................................6.50
Batter set, complete............................110.00
Butter, covered................................45.00
Casserole w/lid................................42.00
Creamer, regular...............................5.00
Cup & saucer..................................6.50
Fruit, 5½".....................................4.00
Jug, covered...................................45.00
Jug, juice, yellow..............................45.00
Nappy, 8¼"...................................8.50
Plate, deep, 8"................................6.50
Plate, 10"....................................6.50
Plate, 6".....................................2.50
Plate, 7".....................................3.50
Plate, 9".....................................4.50
Plate, 9", red.................................5.75
Platter, 11"..................................9.00
Platter, 12"..................................10.50
Salt & peppers, pr.............................6.00
Sauce boat....................................8.00
Sugar w/lid...................................6.50
Syrup w/lid...................................50.00
Teapot.......................................35.00
Tumbler, juice................................22.00
Tumbler, w/handle.............................38.00

Robertson

Fred H. Robertson, clay expert for the Los Angeles Brick Company, and son of Alexander Robertson of the Roblin Pottery, experimented with crystalline glazes as early as 1906. In 1934, Fred and his son George established their own works in Los Angeles, but by 1943 they had moved operations to Hollywood. Though most of their early wares were turned by hand, some were also molded in low relief. Fine crackle glazes and crystallines were developed. The ware was marked with 'Robertson', 'F.H.R.', or 'R.', with the particular location of its manufacture noted. The small pottery closed in 1952.

Tile, HP purple flowers, matt bl ground, mkd, 6x9"..........35.00
Vase, Chinese blue gloss, ovoid w/stick neck, 3½"...........50.00
Vase, crystalline, bl/br/gr, Los Angeles, minor base chips, 7"...375.00
Vase, wht bisque, sm neck/bulbous, 4½".....................75.00
Vase, yellow crackle, sgn R, 3½".........................60.00

Robinson Clay Products

In the early 1900s, Whitemore, Robinson and Company merged with the E.H. Merrill Company to form Robinson Clay Products of Akron, Ohio. They produced stoneware, fine glazed Rockingham, and yellowware until 1915, when the emphasis was shifted to bricks, tile, etc. In 1920 the company merged with the Ransbottom Brothers Pottery Company of Roseville, and was thereafter known as the Robinson Ransbottom Company. (See Robinson Ransbottom)

Cooler, emb flowers, oval w/woman at well, sgn, no spigot, 14".205.00
Flower pot, emb cattails, attached saucer, br glaze, worn, 7"....15.00
Jardiniere, emb swirls in cobalt & brown, 1902, 8½" dia.......45.00
Mug, emb acanthus decor, dk br on wht clay, 4¾", 6 for......50.00
Mug, emb flat iron bldg/woman on reverse, bl/wht, 6 for......300.00
Mug, emb medallion of drinking monk, bl/wht, 4½"..........35.00
Mug, emb scenes of golfers, bl/wht, sm base flake, 5½".......115.00
Mug, Windy City...................................110.00

Pitcher, emb flat iron building/woman reverse, bl/wht, rpr, 8"..165.00
Pitcher w/6 mugs, emb acanthus leaves, wht w/tan............65.00

Pitcher, blue and gray Flemish Ware, 8¾", $235.00.

Robinson Ransbottom

In 1900 the four Ransbottom brothers founded the Ransbottom Bros. Pottery Company in Ironspot, Ohio, very close to Roseville. They produced utilitarian stoneware products until 1920, when they merged with the Robinson Clay Products Company of Akron. Production was broadened to include kitchenwares, and 'Early American' accessories. Cookie jars were an important line from the 1930s until recent times. The company is still in operation in Roseville, Ohio. Items made after the merger were marked 'RRP CO' (for Robinson Ransbottom Pottery Company), 'Roseville'. The green and brown streaky glazed flowerpots, jardinieres, and pedestals which they produce today are often mistaken for older products of the Roseville Pottery Company, which operated there until the 1950s.

Chicken fountain, wht w/blue label, 7¼"...................25.00
Cookie jar, Cookie Stories.............................30.00
Cookie jar, Cow Jumped Over Moon......................43.00
Cookie jar, Owl...................................15.00
Cookie jar, Peter Pumpkin Eater.........................50.00
Cookie jar, Sailor, Navy uniform........................40.00
Cookie jar, Sheriff Pig...............................35.00
Cookie jar, World War II Soldier.........................40.00
Spittoon, br glaze, 4½x7½", RR USA, Roseville, Ohio........25.00

Roblin

In the late 1800s, Alexander W. Robertson and Linna Irelan established a pottery in San Francisco, combining parts of their respective names to coin the name Roblin. Robertson was responsible for potting and firing the ware, which often reflected his taste for classic styling. Mrs. Irelan did much of the decorating, utilizing almost every method, but favoring relief modeling. Mushrooms and lizards were her favorite subjects. Vases were a large part of their production, all of which were made from native California red, buff, and white clays. The ware was well marked with the firm name or the outline of a bear. Roblin Pottery was destroyed in the earthquake of 1906.

Bowl vase, wht salt glaze, 3¼x5¼"..........................100.00
Tile, floral, artist sgn, 6"................................595.00
Tile, scenic, artist sgn..................................675.00
Vase, br semi-gloss, beaded, 3½".........................120.00
Vase, dk br, 2½"...140.00

Rockingham

In the early part of the 19th century, American potters began to favor brown and buff burning clays over red because of their durability. The glaze favored by many was Rockingham, which varied from a dark brown mottling to a sponged effect sometimes called tortoise shell. It consisted in part of manganese and various metallic salts, and was used by many potters until well after the 20th century.

Bank, ewe on oval base, 3¼"..............................85.00
Bedpan, mk Brookville Works, 14½"........................10.00
Bottle, book form; br/yellow on cream, 5½"...............85.00
Bottle, peasant woman w/scarf & guitar figural, 5¼".....75.00
Bowl, emb rim, minor base flakes, 4x7"...................85.00
Bowl, minor surface wear, 1¾x8¼".........................40.00
Bowl, mixing; minor wear, flakes on ft, 4¾x10"..........45.00
Bowl, oblong, canted corners, minor wear, 10" L........115.00
Bowl, oval, 2¼" deep, 9" L...............................40.00
Bowl, rich color, minor rim flakes, 6¾" dia.............45.00
Bowl, scalloped sides, smooth rim, 9½".................155.00
Bowl, shallow, embossed rim, 7¼" dia....................55.00
Bowl, 2⅛x7½"...55.00
Creamer, emb medallion, mk W in circle, 5¾".............35.00
Creamer, 3 rows beads at top edge, sm ft flakes, 4½"....40.00
Cuspidor, emb shell top, 8" dia.........................20.00
Cuspidor, octagonal panels, 4½x8".......................30.00
Cuspidor, Peacock at the Fountain, brick base design, lg......85.00
Figurine, cat, open front ft, EX detail, base/ear rpr, 11¼"....525.00
Figurine, dog, open front legs, tooling on ft & tail, 10"......195.00
Inkwell, seated dog on oval base, 5½"..................275.00
Jar, canning; drip glaze, sm inner rim flakes, 6".......55.00
Jar, emb leaves & vines, sm hdl flake, 1½"..............45.00
Jar, lid w/knob, hairline in base & lid, flakes, 8x8¾"..90.00
Jug, paper label 'Bon Ton Cologne, Smith & Martin', 2½".....75.00
Mold, Turk's head, sm size, 6½".........................85.00
Mold, Turk's head, 10½".................................85.00
Mold, Turk's head, 8½" dia..............................40.00
Mug, ear hdl, minor wear, 3½"..........................105.00
Mug, glaze bubbled, 3¼"..................................60.00
Mug, ring ft, sm rim flake, 3"..........................50.00
Mug, scrolled hdl, G color, 3"..........................90.00
Mug, vertical ribs, 3"..................................55.00
Pie plate, minor wear, 11"..............................85.00
Pie plate, worn, surface chips, 1¼x10½".................55.00
Pie plate, 1¼x10".......................................85.00
Pie plate, 1¼x11"......................................115.00
Pie plate, 1¼x9".......................................80.00
Pig bank, emb initials 'JA', 5½"........................30.00
Pig bank, wht clay, 6" L................................45.00
Pitcher, blackberry, American Pottery Co, 1860s, 6".....65.00
Pitcher, emb foliage & game, mk on base: emb lady's leg, 8½"..65.00
Pitcher, emb Geo Washington bust w/pnt hi-lites.........95.00
Pitcher, emb neck band, 7½".............................60.00
Pitcher, emb Peacock at the Fountain...................125.00
Pitcher, hound hdl, emb hunt scene, vintage rim, 11"...260.00
Pitcher, vintage & cherubs emb, minor glaze flakes, 7½"...85.00
Pitcher, w/lid, emb gent by lecturn, minor rim flakes, 9"....300.00

Plate, 8½", EX...110.00
Platter, emb rim, minor wear, oval, 12¾" L..............65.00
Platter, octagonal, minor wear, 11" L.................125.00
Platter, 13½" oval....................................150.00
Soap dish, emb foliage, dia in base, 4¼x6", G..........95.00
Soap dish, rings in bottom, 2½x6" dia..................85.00
Soap dish, 3½x5½" dia..................................70.00
Wash bowl, 12 sides, flakes on rim/ft, 4x12¾"..........85.00

Rockwell, Norman

Norman Rockwell began his career in 1911 at the age of seventeen doing illustrations for a children's book entitled *Tell Me Why Stories*. A few short years later in 1916, he produced the *Saturday Evening Post* cover that made him one of America's most beloved artists. Though not well accepted by the professional critics of his day who did not consider his work to be art but 'merely' commercial illustration, Rockwell's popularity grew to the extent that today there is an overwhelming abundance of examples of his work, or those related to the theme of one of his illustrations.

See also Collector Plates; Magazines

Ad, Edison Mazda, College of the Lighted Lamp, 11/3/20, SEP...8.00
Ad, Fisk Bicycle Tires, American Boy, Aug 1919, ½ pg blk/wht...4.00
Ad, Orange Crush, Like Lemon, in color, American Boy, 7/21....8.00
Ad, Post Bran Flakes, 1920s.............................6.00
Blotter, American Oil, 1939............................15.00
Calendar, 1953, Four Seasons, Brown & Bigelow, 15½x23"....18.00
Calendar, 1954, Boy Scouts of America, Scout is Reverent, 14"...15.00
Calendar, 1956, Four Seasons..........................20.00
Calendar top, Boy Scouts of America, 1938, 11x17"......12.50
Christmas figurine, Checking His List, Rockwell Museum, 1st Ed.75.00
Christmas ornament, ball, 1975, First Edition..........25.00
Christmas ornament, Caroler, 1978, First Edition.......40.00
Cover, Country Gentleman, July 31, 1920................18.00
Cover, Literary Digest, Mar 25, 1922...................20.00
Cover, Saturday Evening Post, Aug 10, 1918.............42.00
Cover, Saturday Evening Post, Aug 19, 1950, EX.........10.00
Cover, Saturday Evening Post, Aug 5, 1933, M...........25.00
Cover, Saturday Evening Post, Dec 9, 1916, M..........100.00
Cover, Saturday Evening Post, July 26, 1941............15.00
Cover, Saturday Evening Post, May 26, 1923, EX.........30.00
Cover, Saturday Evening Post, May 26, 1928, EX.........30.00
Cover, Saturday Evening Post, Nov 5, 1949, EX..........10.00
Cover, Saturday Evening Post, Oct 8, 1938, EX..........10.00
Figurine, Bedtime, Rockwell Museum.....................75.00
Figurine, Big Decision, Gorham........................150.00
Figurine, Choosing Up, Gorham.........................150.00
Figurine, Christmas Dancers, Gorham, Ltd Ed...........130.00
Figurine, Country Pedlar, Hoyle Salesman..............165.00
Figurine, Discovery, Grossman.........................125.00
Figurine, Drum for Tommy, Grossman.....................70.00
Figurine, First Smoke, Grossman, Tom Sawyer...........175.00
Figurine, Fishing, Gorham.............................100.00
Figurine, For a Good Boy, Rockwell Museum..............65.00
Figurine, God Rest Ye Merry Gentlemen, Gorham.......1,200.00
Figurine, Independence, Gorham........................170.00
Figurine, Jolly Coachman, Gorham Ltd Ed................90.00
Figurine, Lazybones, Grossman.........................225.00
Figurine, Leapfrog, Grossman..........................450.00
Figurine, Leapfrog, Grossman, Ltd Ed, lg..............650.00
Figurine, Lighthouse Keeper's Daughter, Rockwell Museum..65.00
Figurine, Lost in the Cave, Grossman, Tom Sawyer......150.00
Figurine, Love Letter, Grossman........................45.00

Color lithograph, Boy on Stilts, artist proof pencil signed and framed, including certificate of authenticity, 25¾" x 20", $1,400.00.

Coming to the Parson................................325.00
Council of War.....................................850.00
Fetching the Doctor................................750.00
Nominated in the Band..............................300.00
The Balcony.......................................800.00
Uncle Ned's School.................................650.00
We Boys...500.00
Wounded to the Rear, One More Shot, rpt.............500.00

Figurine, Memories, Rockwell Museum.....................65.00
Figurine, Missed, Gorham...............................150.00
Figurine, Missing Tooth, Gorham.........................72.00
Figurine, No Swimming, Grossman, Ltd Ed, lg............350.00
Figurine, Redhead, Grossman.............................90.00
Figurine, Schoolmaster, Grossman.......................225.00
Figurine, See American First, Grossman, Ltd Ed, lg.....350.00
Figurine, Springtime 1933, Grossman.....................75.00
Figurine, Take Your Medicine, Grossman, Tom Sawyer.....175.00
Figurine, Teacher's Pet, Grossman.......................80.00
Figurine, The Cobbler, Rockwell Museum..................65.00
Figurine, The Oculist, Gorham..........................175.00
Figurine, The Toymaker, Rockwell Museum.................65.00
Figurine, Tiny Tim, Gorham..............................75.00
Figurine, Weighing In, Gorham...........................80.00
Figurine, White Wash, Grossman, Tom Sawyer.............225.00
Figurine, Young Artist, Grossman, Rockwell Club, 1981...95.00
Figurine, Young Doctor, Grossman.......................150.00
Inaugural program, mailing envelope, Eisenhower/Nixon, 1957...45.00
Magazines, see Magazines
Poster, Boy Scouts of America, Growth of a Leader, 13x20"....18.00
Print, SEP cover reproduction, sgn, Art Critic, 22x25".......150.00
Print, SEP cover reproduction, sgn, Before & After, 22x25"...150.00
Print, SEP cover reproduction, sgn, Family Tree, 22x25"......250.00
Print, SEP cover reproduction, sgn, Homecoming, 22x25".......150.00
Print, SEP cover reproduction, sgn, Road Block, 22x25".......150.00
Print, SEP cover reproduction, sgn, Walking To Church.......150.00
Print, SEP cover reproduction, sgn, Weighing In, 22x25"......175.00
Sheet music, Over There................................17.50
Sheet music, Over Yonder Where Lilies Grow, war edition, 1918.25.00
Stein, Looking Out To Sea, Rockwell Museum, First Edition...150.00

Rogers, John

John Rogers (1829-1904) was a machinist from Manchester, New Jersey, who turned his hobby of sculpting into a financially successful venture. From the originals he meticulously fashioned of red clay, he had bronze master molds made from which plaster copies were cast. He specialized in five different categories: theatrical, Shakespeare, Civil War, everyday life, and horses. His large detailed groupings portrayed the life and times of the period between 1859 and 1892.

Charity Patient....................................700.00
Checkers at the Farm...............................425.00

Council of War, illustrated in bronze, auction estimate: $7,000 to $10,000; in plaster: $850.00.

Rookwood

The Rookwood Pottery Company was established in 1879, in Cincinnati, Ohio. Its founder was Maria Longworth Nichols Storer, daughter of a wealthy family who provided the backing necessary to make such an enterprise possible. Mrs. Storer hired competent ceramic workers who through constant experimentation developed many lines of superior art pottery. While in her employ, Laura Fry invented the airbrush blending process for which she was issued a patent in 1884. From this, several lines were designed that utilized blended backgrounds.

One of their earlier lines, Standard, was a brown ware decorated with underglaze slip painted nature studies, animals, portraits, etc. Iris and Sea Green were introduced in 1894, and Vellum, a transparent matt glaze line, in 1904. Other lines followed: Ombroso in 1910, and Soft Porcelain in 1915. Many of the early art ware lines were signed by the artist.

Soon after the turn of the 20th century, Rookwood manufactured 'production' pieces that relied mainly on molded designs and forms, rather than freehand decoration, for their esthetic appeal.

The Depression brought on financial difficulties from which the pottery never recovered. Though it continued to operate, the quality of the ware deteriorated, and the pottery was forced to close in 1967.

Unmarked Rookwood is only rarely encountered. Many marks may be found, but the most familiar is the reverse 'RP' monogram. First used in 1886, a flame point was added above it for each succeeding year until 1900. After that, a Roman numeral added below indicated the year of manufacture. Impressed letters that related to the type of clay utilized for the body were also used -- G for ginger, O for olive, R for red, S for sage green, W for white, and Y for yellow.

Art ware must be judged on an individual basis. Quality of the art work is the prime factor to consider. Portraits, animals, and birds are worth more than florals; and pieces signed by a particularly reknowned artist are highly prized.

Incised Matt

Bowl, inlaid matt, CST, 1916, 2½x9″ 70.00
Cup, 3 hdls, florals, A Pons, 1907, Xd but M, 5x6″ 275.00
Vase, blue w/wht/gr glossy florals, bl drip, W Rehm, 1944, 12″.325.00
Vase, fern decor on solid dk gr, S Toohey, 1905, 8½″ 130.00
Vase, inlaid, bl/gr/rust, floral w/bl center, Todd, 1912, 11″ 250.00
Vase, rust/gr w/red flowers, Lincoln, 1920, 5½″ 140.00

Iris

Bust of Madonna, 1959, #6949, 10″ 295.00
Creamer, blue sailing ship, 1926, 3½″ 95.00
Creamer, wht fruit blossoms, Ed Abel, 1891, 2x3″ sq 200.00
Flower basket, w/roses/asters/etc, artist sgn, 1920, 10½″ 900.00
Mug, clover decor in mug & on silver overlay hdl, 1905, 5½″ . .850.00
Platter, blue sailing ship, 1926, 12″ 195.00
Sugar bowl, blue sailing ships on wht, 1926, 3¼x3¼″ 125.00
Vase, all around floral, ET Hurley, 1948, #922D, 7¾″ 685.00
Vase, bl/br on wht, sgn Jens Jensen, 1945, 6½x3″ 275.00
Vase, Black-Eyed Susan, R Fecheimer, 1902, 9″ 625.00
Vase, bronze overlay w/floral, top/sides/hdl, Diers, 1900, 4¾″.1,100.00
Vase, carved, wht w/gr/bl leaves top/base, Wareham, 1899, 13″.900.00
Vase, daisies, Grace Young, 1905, 6″ 650.00
Vase, florals, EX art, Ed Diers, 1902, 7″ 900.00
Vase, florals, H Wilcox, #532, 1896, 9½″ 825.00
Vase, gondola/Venice, Maria L Storer, 1894, #589, 7″ 2,250.00
Vase, gr/br w/gypsy girl/trees, HW Wilcox, 1900, Xd/M, 8½″.1,850.00
Vase, gray w/pink flowers, EX art, VB Demarest, 1902, 7″ 550.00
Vase, gray/gr/wht w/yellow/wht pansy, Sara Sax, 1902, Xd, 7½″.500.00
Vase, gray/wht w/gr & wht, bottle form, R Fecheimer, Xd, 6″ . .160.00
Vase, gypsy girl w/tambourine, sgn HE Wilcox, 1900, 8½″ . . .1,850.00
Vase, pink floral on bl, C Steinle, 1909, 6½″ 875.00
Vase, wht clover blossoms/leaves, LN Lincoln, 1910, 7x3½″ 825.00
Vase, wht/gr/pink w/yellow florals, Sara Sax, 1899, 6¾″ 575.00
Vase, wht/gr/yel daisies on gray/wht/pink, C Steinle, '06, 7″ . . .600.00
Vase, wht/lav/blk, wht mum, classic form, Bishop, 1903 . . . . . .1,500.00
Vase, wht/pink at top, pink floral, Sara Sax, 1906, Xd, 8″, M . .500.00
Vase, wht/pink/gray, pink/purple floral, CA Baker, 1910, 5½″ . .600.00
Vase, wht/yellow/gray w/yellow floral, J Zettel, 1902, 6″ 475.00
Vase, yellow floral, sm pillow form, Ed Diers, 1903, 5½″ 475.00
Vase, yellow pine cones on yellow/gr, R Fechheimer, 1901 . . . .625.00
Vase, 7 butterflies, Carl Schmidt, 1899, #762C, 5½x6½″ 3,000.00

Limoges

Plate, crane in marsh, crimped/gold, NJ Hirschfeld, 1882, 6½″ .900.00
Plate, wht buds on mahog, gold crimp rim, Wilcox, 1887, 6½″.225.00
Ramekin, birds fly over marsh, AR Valentien, 1883 . . . . .325.00
Ramekin, butterfly, red clay, Martin Rettig, 1883, 4½″ 585.00

Matt

Bowl, reticulated fern, yellow, Shirayamadani, 1910, 2¼x7½″ . .105.00
Centerpiece bowl, female hdl ea end, wht/bl w/in, Abel, '34 . . . .170.00
Tray, br w/leaves/acorns/rook, 1922, 2½x10½″ 100.00
Vase, gr, 1927, 3½″ 25.00
Vase, pink w/gr drip, molded stylized florals, 1914, 7¾″ 50.00
Vase, yellow, grape relief, 1920, 10″ 40.00
Wall pocket, bl w/lily relief, 1920, 11½″ 70.00
Wall pocket, iris relief, bl, 1924, 13x8″ 190.00

Porcelain

Bowl, florals, wide bell form, L Epply, 1929, 5x8″ 175.00
Bowl, Jewell, lavender, 1916, 2¾x6½″ 90.00
Bud vase, Jewell, wht, 1944, 7¼x2″ 25.00
Vase, bands of bl collar & base, mc florals, Barrett, 1948, 8″ . .300.00
Vase, bl leaves/wht flowers/butterflies, K Van Horn, 1918, 9″ . .750.00
Vase, bl/pink/lt br floral, inverted bell form, KS, 1946, 7½″ 675.00
Vase, bl/wht/wht bellflowers, sq/4 sm ft, KS, 1946, 6½″ W 375.00
Vase, blk bands w/rust decor, glossy, Jens Jensen, 1946, 6½″ . .300.00
Vase, Jewell, incised band of daisies, yellow, 1950, 5½″ 95.00
Vase, Jewell, peacock feathers/blk glaze, Sara Sax, 1923, 6½″ . .800.00
Vase, Jewell, pnt/sgraffito floral, ET Hurley, 1944, 6½″ 300.00
Vase, molded w/3 female figures, wht/rust/gray, Xd, 1918, 7½″.160.00
Vase, wht gloss w/bl florals, 2 bl birds, K Ley, 1945, 12″ 1,125.00
Vase, wht gloss w/bl/gr foliage/2 birds, L Epply, 1928, 7¾″ 330.00
Vase, wht w/bl birds/flowers, EX art, K Ley, 1945, 5¾″ 410.00
Vase, wht w/pink floral, gray bottom, fish hdls, LH, 1949, 10″.325.00

Sea Green

Ewer, panels of fish, Harriet Wenderoth, 1882, 11¾″ 1,150.00
Vase, bl flowers/gr leaves, R Fecheimer, 1900, mk G, 6″ 1,050.00
Vase, incised/pnt yellow tulips/gr leaves, Laurence, 1901, 9″ . .1,500.00
Vase, 4 catfish, wide mouth/bulbous, S Laurence, 1901, 4″ . . .1,900.00

Standard

Ash tray/match holder, 1 pc, yellow clover, C Steinle, 6″ W 275.00
Bowl, yellow floral, S Markland, 1893, 2x4″ 160.00
Bud vase, crocus, Ed Diers, 1889, 7″ 285.00
Butter pat, floral on lt br, AR Valentien, 1887, 3¼″ 190.00
Chocolate pot, yellow/bl iris ea side, JD Wareham, 1894, 9¾″ . .875.00
Creamer, berries, E Diers, 1899, 2½″ 90.00
Ewer, allover silver overlay scrolls, Nourse, 1897, rstr, 11″ 950.00
Ewer, cherry branches, AM Valentien, #415B, 1892, 7¾″ 330.00
Ewer, EX Gorham silver overlay, floral, C Baker, 1892, 9½″.3,000.00
Ewer, floral, bottle form, K Hickman, 6¼″ 300.00
Ewer, floral, Josephine Zettle, 1893, #584C, 5½″ 325.00
Ewer, holly leaves & berries, Artus Van Briggle, 1892, 8¼″ 650.00
Ewer, holly leaves & berries, L Lincoln, paper label, 7¾″ 260.00
Ewer, Indian portrait, OG Pinney Reed, #564D, 1898, 9″ 1,760.00
Ewer, orange floral, bottle form, L Van Briggle, 1900, Xd, 8″ . .350.00
Ewer, orange floral, EX art, M Foglesong, 1899, 7½″ 400.00
Ewer, orange floral, L Lincoln, 1899, 11″ 375.00
Ewer, orange poppy, R Fecheimer, 1900, 6¼″ 320.00
Ewer, wht florals, EX art, O Geneva Red, 1894, #715E, 5½″ . .780.00
Ewer, yellow primroses, Katherine Hickman, 1895, 6½″ 675.00
Ewer, 4 tan maple leaves, Rose Fecheimer, 1898, 7x3½″ 470.00
Humidor, pipes/cigar/leaves, ruffled, LN Lincoln, 1898, 6½″ . . .750.00
Inkwell, holly berries/leaves, E Lindenfelter, 1897, 5½″ 200.00
Inkwell, lily pads/flowers, C Steinle, 1897, no lid, 2½″ 90.00
Inkwell, nasturtium, Sally Coyne, 1898, 6½″ 200.00
Jard, blueberries, yellow/gr leaves, F Rothenbush, w/hdls, 5¼″ . .425.00
Jug, corn, L Van Briggle, 1901, top rstr, 6½″ 100.00
Mug, cavalier portrait, EX art, WP McDonald, 1893, 5″ 550.00
Mug, cavalier portrait, Sally Toohey, #791, 6½″ 1,250.00
Mug, yellow wheat, EX art, LN Lincoln, 1900, 5¼″ 350.00
Pitcher, floral, C Steinle, 1897, 4½″ 200.00
Pitcher, floral, HA Straffer, 1894, #S1150, 7½x4½″ 450.00
Pitcher, fruit laden branch, Harriet Wilcox, #525S, 1889, 7½″.280.00
Pitcher, orange/gr floral, butterfly hdl, sgn, 1890, 4″ 240.00
Pitcher, yellow florals, Grace Young, 1898, Xd-scratch, 12″ 425.00
Pitcher, 4 bees & floral, M Perkins, 1888, spots in glaze, 4½″ .250.00

Vase, porcelain body with thick butterfat glaze, white with brown and touches of green; Iris decoration by Jensen, 1934, marked S, 6½", $2,000.00.

Punch bowl, berries/leaves, R Valentien, #162T/W/A, 16"....1,500.00
Vase, autumn leaves, Ed Hurley, #657C, 1899, 8x4".........595.00
Vase, berry/leaves, squat/slim neck, S Markland/L, 1893, 3"....350.00
Vase, br clover on br/gr, I Bishop, 1902, 6½"..............190.00
Vase, br/yellow w/yellow berries, Grace Young, 1889, 6¾".....375.00
Vase, bursting seed pods, S Coyne, sm neck/bulbous, 1900, 6".400.00
Vase, dk gr iris, br w/yel shading, AM Valentien, 1898, 11"..1,125.00
Vase, floral, C Steinle, 1907, 6½"........................180.00
Vase, floral, Ed Diers, 1897, 3½".........................175.00
Vase, floral, 2 hdls, silver mts, Ed Abel, 1894, 8".........1,980.00
Vase, flowers/vines, wide shoulder, C Steinle, 1898, 7".......525.00
Vase, holly, bottle form, MLP, 1896, 8½"..................400.00
Vase, leaf decor, ½ hdls, C Schmidt, 1898, 4¾"...........180.00
Vase, lg orange mums, classic form, M Mitchell, 1902, 8".....325.00
Vase, lg orange/yellow leaf around body, S Coyne, 1903, 10"...400.00
Vase, magnolia, cylinder form, MA Daly, #506S, 1890, 13½".1,100.00
Vase, orange florals, shaded ground, L Van Briggle, 1902, 6"..350.00
Vase, orange/br w/flowers, EX art, H Altman, 1903, 5½".....300.00
Vase, pansy decor, L Lincoln, 1896, 5"...................280.00
Vase, pine cone, gr/yellow on br, L Asbury, EX art, 1902, 9¾".500.00
Vase, portrait, after Van Dyke, Grace Young, 1903, Xd, 14"..1,575.00
Vase, rnd/flat/4 sm ft, berries, HR Straffer, 1895, 7½x8", VG.355.00
Vase, silver overlay/hdls, yellow nasturtium, HR Straffer, 4¾".2,550.00
Vase, tiger eye, lily pad/floral/insect, Shirayamadani, 7", VG....525.00
Vase, wht primroses, w/hdls, Anna M Valentien, 1892, 5½"....490.00
Vase, yellow daffodils, EX art, C Steinle, 1902, 6".........375.00
Vase, yellow dogwood, pinched sides, E Abel, 1895, 9"......450.00
Vase, yellow floral, akimbo rim hdls, Sally Toohey, 1890, 6"...180.00
Vase, yellow florals, C Steinle, 1896, 6¾"................275.00
Vase, yellow fruit, inverted teardrop form, L Van Briggle, 8"..350.00
Vase, yellow water lily, bottle form, EX art, Epply, 1898, 6"..250.00
Vase, yellow/gr iris, bottle form, E Diers, 6¼".............375.00
Vase, 4 birds in flight, J Zettel, 1900, Xd-bubbles, 11".......290.00
Vase, 4 palm leaves all over, EX art, LN Lincoln, 1903, 7"...300.00

Vellum

Box, gr/bl w/red floral top, K Van Horn, 1910, sgn GV, 3¼"...650.00
Plaque, An April Day, M Denzler, 1914, 9x5"..............850.00
Plaque, Birch Trees, E Diers, uncrazed, orig fr, 7x11".....1,300.00
Plaque, moon over lake, 'Moonlight', SE Coyne, 1922, 8x6"..1,200.00
Plaque, trees ea side stream, ET Hurley, 1927, 5x10".......1,950.00
Plaque, Winter Eve, EF McDermott, '18, orig fr, 15½x21"...6,000.00
Vase, all around woodland, Ed Diers, 1913, #2039C, 11½"..1,285.00
Vase, bl w/branches/red berries/red w/in, L Asbury, 1922, 9½".525.00
Vase, bl/pk/wht/gr/carved dogwood at base, L Epply, 1910, 7".190.00
Vase, blk/wht band/pink flowers/pink w/in, A Cravens, 1918, 8".350.00
Vase, dk bl bands/scene w/birch trees, ET Hurley, 1918, 11".1,200.00

Vase, floral, yellow tint overglaze, L Asbury, 1922, 8"........435.00
Vase, forest at dawn, Lenore Asbury, 1920, #1664D, 11"....1,500.00
Vase, gr w/yellow roses, ET Hurley, 1909, 7"..............160.00
Vase, gray/pk w/6 gray geese, ET Hurley, 1907, Xd but M, 10".800.00
Vase, hills/roads/trees/house, EX art, ET Hurley, 1930, 12"...2,800.00
Vase, lavender bands/multi-lavender art, C McLaughlin, '15, 8".775.00
Vase, lg orchid w/strong outlines, AMV, 1905, 10½"........1,300.00
Vase, lg trees, heavy slip in gr/bl, E Diers, 1909, 9¾".......800.00
Vase, lg trees, impressionistic, F Rothenbush, 1929, rstr, 17".1,250.00
Vase, night scenic in dk bl/lt gr, ET Hurley, 1909, 9¾"......460.00
Vase, pastoral scene w/trees, Ed Diers, 1919, 7½x3½".......490.00
Vase, pink/gray w/wht/gray florals, LN Lincoln, 1905, 5¾"....250.00
Vase, pond w/lily pads/flowers/grass, Ed Diers, 1908, 8¼"....1,025.00
Vase, river scene, F Rothenbush, #295D, 1922, 9½"........1,210.00
Vase, river w/tree-lined banks, ET Hurley, 1946, mk S, 8"..1,200.00
Vase, sailing vessels, Carl Schmidt, #2032D, 1924, 9½".....1,900.00
Vase, scenic, bl top/base bands, McLaughlin, 1914, 8¾".....800.00
Vase, scenic, EX art, sgn E, 1919, 14x8".................1,550.00
Vase, scenic, L Asbury, 1929, 9¼".......................1,075.00
Vase, scenic, Lorinda Epply, 1915, #808, 8x3½"...........495.00
Vase, scenic w/bl/gr, L Asbury, full body, uncrazed, '29, 9"..1,075.00
Vase, scenic w/trees, EX art/good color, Ed Diers, 1913, 11½".700.00
Vase, scenic w/trees, F Rothenbush, 1919, 7¾"............775.00
Vase, snowy landscape, Sally Coyne, 1919, 7¾"...........950.00
Vase, tree-lined river shore, Sarah E Coyne, 1920, 7½".....1,250.00
Vase, trees, EX art, E Diers, 1914, 7¾".................750.00
Vase, trees, Lorinda Epply, 1915, #808, 8".................595.00
Vase, trees around lake, EX art, Carl Schmidt, cylinder, 9½".1,100.00
Vase, trees in pastels, F Rothenbush, 1914, 7¾"...........725.00
Vase, water scenic w/reeds, Charles McLaughlin, 1913, 8"...525.00
Vase, wht geese at top on gr/gray/pink, L Asbury, 1908, 7¾".725.00
Vase, wooded scenic, L Asbury, 1915, pear shape, 11¼".....1,200.00
Vase, yellow w/bl/br florals/3 birds, P Conant, 1916, 6x6".....575.00
Vase, 2 panels gr w/lav florals, Sally Coyne, 1908, 8¼".....290.00
Vase, 6 geese, gray/pink, ET Hurley, 1907, 10".............800.00

Wax Matt

Bowl, geometrics, flared rim, EX art, E Barrett, Xd/M, 5x8"...225.00
Vase, bl, ovoid, L Abel, 1926, 4¾"......................220.00
Vase, bl w/bl floral, C Klinger, 6 sided, 1930, 5¾"...........170.00
Vase, bl/br zebras, handmade, W Rehm, '46, rstr drilling, 13".405.00
Vase, br/mc flowers/bl top, angle shoulder, Tischler, '22, 6"...250.00
Vase, carved w/peacock feathers, CS Todd, 1905, 10", rstr.....240.00
Vase, daffodil, EX art, K Shirayamadani, 1932, uncrazed, 8½".675.00
Vase, floral, band of geometrics, LN Lincoln, 1923, 14".....525.00
Vase, floral, bl w/br, br/blk gloss w/in, C Zanetta, 1946, 9"....220.00
Vase, floral, Shirayamadani, 1938, drilled for lamp, 11".......300.00
Vase, gr w/br lines/circles, E Barrett, 1929, 6¼"...........250.00
Vase, impressionistic grapes, dk bl, S Coyne, 1924, 7"........180.00
Vase, mc abstract, Jensen, 1930, Xd, 8¼", M..............250.00
Vase, Nouveau violets/leaves, Shirayamadani, 1938, mk S, 6½".495.00
Vase, pink w/red florals/lg leaves, L Lincoln, 1930, 8½".....360.00
Vase, pink/wht, lg wht florals, Shirayamadani, 1943, 7¼"....900.00
Vase, purple to pink w/purple flowers, U form, KS, 1944, 6½".375.00
Vase, red to purple w/floral top band, CS Todd, 1915, 8¾"...200.00
Vase, rust w/br top, red florals, LN Lincoln, 1930, 6¼".......160.00
Vase, wht to pink w/blue top, florals, KS, 6¾".............575.00
Vase, yellow/br/gr vertical streaks, E Barrett, 1930, 5¾".....110.00

Miscellaneous

Advertising sign, 1900, bl matt triangle, rare, 6½x7¼"........140.00
Advertising sign, 1915, Rookwood Soft Porcelain in floral sq...330.00

Advertising sign, 1947, name/rectangle/ribbon scrolls, 13″, VG..575.00
Apple, 1933, w/lid, dk br, red goldstone glaze, 3″............110.00
Ash tray, 1932, shell, goldstone red glaze, 1½x5″............85.00
Ash tray, 1944, gr tiger eye, shield w/dolphins/eagle/US CARP..200.00
Ash tray, 1944, owl on side, lt gr gloss, 4¼x7″...............75.00
Ash tray, 1946, rose gloss, 9x8″..........................110.00
Ash tray, 1949, rook on edge, #1139, lt gr, 4½x8″............120.00
Ash tray, 1951, fish, lt blue gloss, 5½″.....................35.00
Ash tray, 1952, owl on edge, dk gr gloss, 4¼x7″............110.00
Ash tray/paperweight, 1951, face w/gaping mouth, ear hdls, EX..50.00
Bookends, 1928, rooks, bl matt, McDonald.................110.00
Bookends, 1929, Sphynx holding books, gr/bl matt..........220.00
Bookends, 1934, Spanish galleons, Wm P McDonald, wht matt.200.00
Bookends, 1941, elephant, gr matt.......................140.00
Bookends, 1944, rooks, wht matt, McDonald...............100.00
Bowl, 1890, Cameo, peach w/wht flowers, S Toohey, 3x9½″...525.00
Bowl, 1931, red gloss coramandel tiger eye, #966, 3½x4″.....225.00
Box, 1905, grapes, Z glaze, gr matt, w/lid, Shirayamadani, 5½″.190.00
Box, 1924, acorn finial, 6 sided, br, 4x4½″.................60.00
Cup & saucer, 1890, Cameo, peach/wht floral, Ed Abel, #4-121.475.00
Dish, 1890, Cameo, peach/gr w/wht florals, log shaped, 5″ L...115.00
Ewer, red clay/tiger eye, lg angle hdl/1 sm, leaf, L Fry, 11″...825.00
Figurine, cock pheasant, K Shirayamadani, #2832, 9x16″.....880.00
Figurine, 1935, donkey/baskets on bk, gr gloss, 4″...........80.00
Figurine, 1945, deer, lt gr, 4¾″...........................90.00
Figurine, 1946, leopard, tan glaze, McDonald, 3x6½″........135.00
Figurine, 1954, deer, gray/br gloss, 5¼″....................80.00
Figurine, 1954, horse head, sgn, 6½″.....................185.00
Flower frog, 1925, nude on flower w/frog, wht matt, 5½″......100.00
Honey jug, 1882, bl flowers on gr, sgn JH, 5″...............485.00
Honey jug, 1882, tan semi-matt/incised gold florals, MEB, 5″...195.00
Honey jug, 1883, blk reeds/birds, gold hi-lites, M Rettig, 4¾″..375.00
Honey jug, 1883, reeds/birds/gold, red clay, M Rettig, 5″.....400.00
Honey jug, 1883, tan bisque/incised cover, H Wendroth,.......140.00
Jard, 1882, imp brocade/swallows/grass, A Valentien, 6″.....1,700.00
Jard, 1886, smear glaze w/floral, #131Y, 5½x8″.............375.00
Jug, 1882, crane wading, mahogany bkground, #61, 5x2¼″....650.00
Jug, 1884, bisque, top hdl/2 spouts/reeds/butterflies, ARV, 9″.1,300.00
Jug, 1884, gray bisque, incised br leaf/berry, ARV, 8½″......600.00
Nut dish, 1886, ½ shell form, br bisque/florals, AMB, 6″ L....100.00
Paperweight, 1918, rook, dk bl matt porcelain, 2½x4″.......130.00
Paperweight, 1921, rook, br ombroso glaze, 2½x4″..........110.00
Paperweight, 1922, elephant/2 clowns, br gloss, McDonald, 4″.140.00
Paperweight, 1924, dog, cream glaze, #2777..............110.00
Paperweight, 1926, sitting nude, wht matt, Abel, 4½″.......100.00
Paperweight, 1927, elephant, wht matt, McDonald, 3½″.......80.00
Paperweight, 1930, beagle dog, Louise Abel, 3½x5½″.......155.00
Paperweight, 1930, monkey, gr gloss, 4″..................125.00
Paperweight, 1931, rabbit, wht gloss.....................120.00
Paperweight, 1933, squirrel, yellow/wht matt, S Toohey, 4¼″..110.00
Paperweight, 1935, donkey, wht ombroso, 6″...............130.00
Paperweight, 1935, donkey, yellow gloss, 4¼″...............75.00
Paperweight, 1937, duck, wht matt, L Abel, 3¾″.............85.00
Paperweight, 1941, rabbit, gr/bl, 3″......................85.00
Paperweight, 1943, nude, blue gloss, L Abel, 4¼″..........115.00
Paperweight, 1943, rooster, matt glaze, W McDonald, 5″.....170.00
Paperweight, 1946, bird, HP, sgn DH, 5x6″................140.00
Paperweight, 1946, elephant, wht matt, 3¾″................75.00
Paperweight, 1947, bird, yellow gloss, 4″..................55.00
Paperweight, 1949, yellow w/CWBC on front, ¾x3″..........20.00
Paperweight, 1955, rabbit, blk gloss, 3¼″.................160.00
Paperweight, 1958, Scottie dog, blk, imp mk, 5″...........120.00
Pitcher, 1887, blue gloss w/wht florals, ARV, hairline, 7″....275.00
Pitcher, 1887, w/lid, natural pine cones on bl/wht, ARV, 10″...600.00

Plaque, 1904, cameo portrait of Menzel, AM Valentien, 9¾″...200.00
Plate, 1885, fox/bird, Uncle Remus, Ed Pope Cranch, 6½″..1,500.00
Rose jar w/lid, 1887 crystal glaze/primrose, G Young, 8½″....575.00
Salad plate/cup, 1887, Cameo, peach/wht florals, AMV, 8″ dia..360.00
Sugar bowl, Cameo, wht/peach, E Abel, 1891, 3x4″ sq......275.00
Tea caddy, 1882, mahog w/storks, Hirschfeld, imp anchor mk.2,675.00
Teapot, 1880, bl bisque/gold band/floral/birds, L McL, rpr.....450.00
Teapot, 1923, lobed, gray clay, bl w/wht floral, Epply, 6″.....675.00
Tile, brownish matt, 6¼″, in fr..........................15.00
Tile, faience, mc experimental glaze, sgn, 4″ sq............85.00
Tile, high relief red apples against gr leaves, 8x8″, M.......175.00
Tile, pink/br matt, heavy glaze, 6¼″ sq, in fr..............15.00
Tray, 1948, nude on side, blue gloss, 4¼″.................55.00
Tray, 1951, nude on side, gr gloss, 4½″..................50.00
Vase, 1882, crystal glaze w/kingfisher, Matt Daly, 5x2½″.....800.00
Vase, 1882, quail in woods, beige w/gilt, ML Nichols, 18″..2,750.00
Vase, 1885, asters/geraniums on pk bisque, A Van Briggle, 5″..750.00
Vase, 1886, bisque w/pink florals, AR Valentien, 13½″......1,595.00
Vase, 1886, bl bisque, blk leaves/birds, gold top, M Daly, 11″.1,500.00
Vase, 1888, roses in pastels, Shirayamadani, #345W, 10″.....450.00
Vase, 1891, gr/pink bisque w/pink floral, hdls, Ed Abel, 6¼″..390.00
Vase, 1892, lt gr/br w/lg orange poppies, Matt Daly, 5¼x11″.1,000.00
Vase, 1912, unglazed banded scenic, mk G/V, L Asbury, 9″...975.00
Vase, 1914, sq, wht gloss w/br/wht flowers, E Barrett, 7¼″...210.00
Vase, 1917, pink/gr, geometrics, sq/lines, 10¼″............60.00
Vase, 1917, winter scenic, bl/wht, EF McDermott, 7½″......275.00
Vase, 1918, lt/dk pink w/bl floral/berry, L Epply, 6¾″, VG.....100.00
Vase, 1919, pink matt w/seahorse relief, 7″...............40.00
Vase, 1921, berries & leaves relief, pink matt, 4″...........30.00
Vase, 1923, blk gloss, 3″..............................60.00
Vase, 1932, crystalline gray/bl drip, 7″...................50.00
Vase, 1935, red tiger eye, horn shape, 9″.................290.00
Vase, 1945, allover flowers/bl birds, K Ley, 12″..........1,125.00
Vase, 1945, sq, lt bl/wht gloss w/wht dogwood, sgn KS, 7½″...430.00
Vase, 1946, bl gloss w/girl & stars relief, hdls, 9″..........45.00
Vase, 1946, sq, 4 ft, yel/bl w/pink floral, Shirayamadani, 6″....475.00

Rose Medallion

   Rose Medallion is one of the patterns of Chinese export produced from the early 1800s until the first part of the 20th century. It is
decorated in rose colors with panels of florals, birds, and butterflies that
form reserves containing Chinese figures. Earlier examples were decorated
with gold tracery; some were heavily reticulated.
   Key: MIC----Made In China

Basket w/tray, ea pc reticulated, 4x10½″; 9½x11″..........625.00
Bowl, border w/four 3¼″ floral medallions, 3½x9″.........250.00
Bowl, figures, birds & flowers, no mk, 9″.................265.00
Bowl, fruit; ftd oval, genre center, 1840, 3½x14½″ dia......525.00
Bowl, interior wear, 2¼x4¾″...........................55.00
Bowl, MIC, deep, 7½″.................................75.00
Brush pot, cylindrical, 10x4½″.........................275.00
Butter pat, canted corners, 3″ sq.......................45.00
Butter pat, 3″ dia....................................45.00
Candlestick, 8½″....................................245.00
Chamber pot w/lid, 9″................................485.00
Creamer, bulbous, ca 1800............................195.00
Creamer & sugar w/lid, people on porch/butterflies, MIC, 5½″..275.00
Cup & saucer, 'C' in rnd gold medallion.................105.00
Cup & saucer, demitasse; MIC.........................50.00
Cup & saucer, hexagonal, China.......................40.00
Dish w/lid, almond shape, 'C' in gold medallion, 4½x8¾x11¼″.425.00

Punch bowl, 1860s, 15¾″, $1,000.00.

Dish w/lid, fruit finial, 'C' in rnd gold medallion, 4½x5½″.....235.00
Fish bowl, vignettes of court figures/butterfly border, 18x20″..2,100.00
Jar, pomade; w/lid, no mk, early, 2¼x1⅞″....................75.00
Knife rest, scroll shape, flat top, 4″........................300.00
Leaf dish, 8½x6½″...145.00
Plate, hexagonal, mk MIC, 8″...............................45.00
Plate, MIC, 6″..35.00
Plate, MIC, 7½″...45.00
Plate, MIC, 9½″...55.00
Plate, no mk, early, 8½″...................................85.00
Platter, ca 1800, 11x8½″..................................650.00
Platter, ca 1875, orange peel bk, 9″......................125.00
Platter, fish; w/drainer, gold rim, 18½″..................900.00
Punch bowl, early 1800s, 15½″...........................1,400.00
Punch bowl, minor chips, late 1800s, 16″.................650.00
Sauce boat, rose/butterfly w/in; household scenes w/out, 4¼″...130.00
Saucer, China..20.00
Soup bowl w/lid & under plate, no mk......................50.00
Soup plate, 2⅛x9″...45.00
Spoon...15.00
Sugar bowl, bulbous, MIC.................................175.00
Sugar bowl, fruit finial, twist hdls, 4⅛″.................105.00
Teapot, bulbous, no mk, 7″................................300.00
Teapot, individual; bell shape, 4″........................185.00
Teapot, pear form, 3¼″...................................150.00
Teapot, rnd, 3 ft...350.00
Teapot, w/2 cups, in wicker basket w/brass mts, ca 1890.....375.00
Teapot, wide shoulder, floral/butterfly/bird, late 1800s, 9″.....400.00
Teapot, 5½″..245.00
Tureen w/lid, oval, 1800s, minor crack, 15″ L.............1,320.00
Tureen w/tray, early 1800s, tray, 14½″ L.................2,600.00
Vase, applied lions & dragons in gold, wood base, 11¾″.....350.00
Vase, 7″, pr...250.00

Rosemeade

Rosemeade was the name chosen by Whapeton Pottery Company of Whapeton, North Dakota, to represent their product. The founders of the company were Laura Meade Taylor and R.J. Hughes, who organized the firm in 1940. It is most noted for small bird and animal figural designs, either in high gloss or a Van Briggle-like matt glaze. The ware was marked 'Rosemeade' with an ink stamp, or carried a 'Prairie Rose' sticker. The pottery closed in 1961.

Ash tray, DeKalb Chix, w/chicken.........................30.00
Bowl, scalloped, metallic br, 2x7¼″.......................13.00
Figurine, Am bison, 3″....................................35.00

Figurine, elephant, sitting, rose, paper label, 4″............42.50
Figurine, pheasant, 7x13″...............................165.00
Flower frog, bird...14.00
Planter, swan figural, rose glaze, 5″......................12.00
Shakers, duck figural, w/label, pr.........................25.00
Shakers, Paul Bunyan, pr.................................12.00
Shakers, pheasants, pr...................................12.00
Shakers, skunks, pr......................................16.00
Toothpick, corn shape, 2″.................................6.50
Vase, swan, pk, 5″.......................................18.00
Wall pocket, modeled deer, lt pink, 5x3¼″.................19.50

Donkey figurine, rust glaze, 4½″ x 4½″, $25.00.

Rosenthal

In 1879, Phillip Rosenthal established the Rosenthal Porcelain Factory in Selb, Bavaria. Its earliest products were figurines and fine tablewares. The company has continued to operate to the present decade, manufacturing limited edition plates.

See also Collector Plates

Bowl, gold/silver butterflies, hdls, Donatello, sgn Selb, 11″.....185.00
Bowl, HP cherries, gold trim, hdls, artist sgn, 10″...........85.00
Cake plate, Chippendale, pierced hdls, 12½″................39.00
Figurine, ballerina, sgn D Charol, 11½″....................325.00
Figurine, Blackamoor, sgn H Meisel, 7″, pr.................300.00
Figurine, bulldog, standing, 3½x6″.........................195.00
Figurine, cat, reclining, sgn Heidenreich, blk w/yel eyes, 5″.....30.00
Figurine, duck, artist sgn, 4¼″............................45.00
Figurine, German short-haired setter, gray/wht, 11½″ L......250.00
Figurine, kneeling nude, wht porcelain, sgn Wenck, 7x7″.....195.00
Figurine, nude child holding baby goat, 8″.................125.00
Figurine, nude child on gray goat, ped base, Selb Bavaria.....200.00
Figurine, panther, 2¼″....................................30.00
Figurine, pekingese, wht/br, sgn Diller, 3¼″...............150.00
Figurine, polar bear, 1½″.................................30.00
Figurine, pouter pigeon, 6″...............................110.00
Figurine, redheaded woodpecker, artist sgn.................95.00
Figurine, Russian wolfhound, recumbent, gray/blk/wht........270.00
Figurine, snail, Caasmann, 3¼″ L.........................145.00
Plate, mc floral medallion, pink border w/gold design........50.00
Plate, wht w/heavy gold tooled border, 1920s, 10¾″........95.00

Ring tree, sgn, Donatello.................................38.00
Tea set, pine needles, sgn, 3 pc.........................92.00
Vase, exotic birds, pear form, 12".......................100.00

Roseville

The Roseville Pottery Company was established in 1892 by George F. Young in Roseville, Ohio. Finding their facilities inadequate, the company moved to Zanesville in 1898, erected a new building and installed the most modern equipment available. By 1900 Young felt ready to enter into the stiffly competitive art pottery market.

Roseville's first art line was called Rozane. Similar to Rookwood's Standard, Rozane featured dark blended backgrounds with slip painted underglaze art work of nature studies, portraits, birds, and animals.

Azurean, developed in 1902, was a blue and white underglaze art line on a blue blended background. Egypto (1904) featured a matt glaze in a soft shade of old green and was modeled in low relief after examples of ancient Egyptian pottery. Mongol (1904) was a high gloss oxblood red line after the fashion of the Chinese Sang de Boeuf. Mara (1904), an iridescent lustre line of magenta and rose with intricate patterns developed on the surface or in low relief, successfully duplicated Sicardo's work.

These early lines were followed by many others of highest quality: Fudjiyama and Woodland (1905-06) reflected an Oriental theme; Crystalis (1906) was covered with beautiful frost-like crystals.

Their most famous was Della Robbia, introduced in 1906, which was decorated with designs ranging from florals, animals, and birds, to scenes of Viking warriors and Roman gladiators. These designs were accomplished by sgraffito with slip painted details.

Very limited but of great importance to collectors today, Rozane Olympic (1905) was decorated with scenes of Greek mythology on a red ground.

Pauleo (1914) was the last of the art ware lines. It was varied -- over two hundred glazes were recorded -- and some pieces were decorated by hand, usually with florals.

During the second decade of the century until the plant closed forty years later, new lines were added regularly, each reflecting the tastes of its time. Some of the more popular of the middle period lines were Donatello, 1915; Futura, 1928; Pine Cone, 1931; and Blackberry, 1933. The floral lines of the later years have become highly collectible. Pottery from every era of Roseville production -- even its utility ware -- attest to an unwavering dedication to quality and artistic merit.

Examples of the fine art pottery lines present the greatest challenge to evaluate. Scarcity is a prime consideration. The quality of art work varied from one artist to another -- some pieces show fine detail and good color, and naturally this influences their value. Studies of animals and portraits bring higher prices than the floral designs. Artist's signatures often increase the value of any item, especially if the artist is one who is well recognized.

Apple Blossom

Basket, 8½x8"...60.00
Bookends, blue, pr.......................................85.00
Bud vase, #379-7".......................................35.00
Console, 8"...35.00
Hanging basket, blue, 8"................................65.00
Jardiniere, #302-8".....................................115.00
Jardiniere, 6"..50.00
Tea set...125.00
Teapot..75.00
Vase, #387-9"...45.00
Vase, #389-10"..55.00
Wall pocket...75.00
Window box, pk, 12" L...................................48.00

Artwood

Planter, #1055-9".......................................30.00
Vase, #1054-8½"...32.00
Vase, #1059-10", thistle................................35.00
Vase, circle, #1053-8", gray/maroon.....................35.00

Aztec

Pitcher, deep blue, 5"..................................250.00
Vase, cylinder w/wider can top, blue w/stylized hearts, 11½"...300.00
Vase, tan, waisted w/flared rim, 11"....................300.00
Vase, wide shoulder narrows to base, gray-blue w/wht, 8".....225.00

Azurean

Chocolate pot, sailboat scenic, no mk, sm glaze flakes, 9½"...500.00
Tankard, Dutch scene, 14"...............................1,350.00
Vase, floral decor, sgn B Myers, trumpet form, #856, 18"....1,000.00
Vase, simple leafage, w/hdl, V Adams, 4½"...............450.00

Baneda

Console bowl, 12".......................................85.00
Jardiniere, gr, 4x5½"...................................65.00
Vase, black/silver label, 9"............................85.00
Vase, collar on straight sided body, rim hdls, 7".......60.00
Vase, cone body on disk ft, long base hdls, 12".........145.00
Vase, inverted funnel, sm rim hdls, 4½".................50.00
Vase, red, can top/rnd body, hdls, paper label, 6"......55.00
Vase, sm hdl ea side can neck, green, 9¼"...............95.00
Vase, stepped sides, D hdls at base, 8".................105.00
Wall pocket, 8"...185.00

Bittersweet

Basket, #808-6", gr.....................................45.00
Basket, #811-10", gr....................................65.00
Candle holder, #851-3", pr..............................30.00
Cornucopia, #882-8", gold...............................45.00
Hanging basket..80.00
Vase, 16"...175.00
Wall pocket, gray.......................................52.00

Blackberry

Bowl, oval, 13"...185.00
Hanging basket..300.00
Jardiniere, 4x5½".......................................145.00
Jardiniere & pedestal, 28"..............................1,200.00
Jug vase, 5"..145.00
Vase, can neck, ear hdls at waist, 8¼".................165.00
Vase, can top ½, rnd bottom, side hdls, 5".............125.00
Vase, sides flare, tiny rim hdls, 5¼"..................110.00
Vase, 12"...450.00
Vase, 4"..120.00
Vase, 9"..300.00
Wall pocket...345.00

Bleeding Heart

Basket, 12"...110.00
Bowl, #382-10"..40.00
Ewer, 10"...85.00

Flower frog, #40 . . . . .35.00
Vase, #360-10″ 80.00
Vase, #964-6″ 50.00

Burmese

Bookends, figural, gr, pr 150.00
Planter, #90B-10″ 30.00
Planter, wht, ftd, #91B-9″ 23.00
Wall pocket, #72-B, black 150.00

Bushberry

Ash tray 65.00
Basket, #369-6½″ 50.00
Basket, #379-8″ 55.00
Basket, 12″ 98.00
Bowl, #1-10″ 42.00
Bowl, #657-3″ 30.00
Candlestick, 2½″, pr 18.00
Console bowl, #385-10, bl, 13″ 50.00
Cornucopia, bl, 6″ 32.00
Hanging basket, gr, 7″ 85.00
Mug 55.00
Planter, #383-6″ 30.00
Vase, #28-4″, br 28.00
Vase, #29-6″, blue 38.00
Vase, #36-9″, blue 48.00
Vase, 10″ 75.00

Capri, Royal Capri

Basket, #509-8″, green 60.00
Bowl, blue, 7″ 35.00
Dish, leaf; #531-14″, wht 25.00
Vase, #527-7″, Royal Capri 250.00
Vase, C-1004-9″, tan 32.00

Carnelian I

Candle holder, 3¼″, pr 28.00
Double bud vase 24.00
Loving cup, bl 45.00
Urn, 7″ 45.00
Vase, bl-gr, 18″ 135.00
Vase, bl/gray on beige, w/hdls, 14½″ 95.00
Vase, blue, 5″ 25.00
Wall pocket, bl drip, 8″ 55.00
Wall pocket, gr tones, 9½″ 60.00

Carnelian II

Bowl vase, angled sides, short flare neck band, w/hdls, 5″ 40.00
Double bud vase 35.00
Planter, on platform w/hdls, 3x8″ 30.00
Urn, sides w/low angle bulge, large ornate hdls, 8″ 60.00
Vase, low swell, waist to base hdl, 10″ 55.00
Vase, ovoid w/wide flare rim, straight hdls rim to body, 12″ 100.00

Cherry Blossom

Bowl, 4x5½″ 135.00
Console bowl, 11″ 155.00
Jardiniere, brown, 4″ 95.00

Jardiniere, brown, 5″ 115.00
Jardiniere & pedestal, 25½″ .900.00
Jug vase, 6″ 110.00
Lamp base 325.00
Vase, br, 7″ 125.00
Vase, brown, 4″ 95.00
Vase, sm hdls ea side wide top/bulbous, 5″ 110.00
Vase, tiny rim hdls, full body, rust, 7″ 150.00
Vase, w/hdls, silver sticker, 10½″ 175.00
Vase, 12″ 250.00

Chloron

Candlestick, reticulated base, 8″ 85.00
Vase, Art Nouveau style, relief berries, scroll hdls, 9″ 325.00
Wall sconce, 17″, VG 465.00

Clemana

Bowl, #281-5, 4½″ 65.00
Flower arranger, 4½″ 48.00
Vase, full body, sm akimbo shoulder hdls, br, 10½″ 150.00

Clematis

Candlestick, #1159-4½″, pr 38.00
Cookie jar 100.00
Ewer, #18 . . . . .125.00
Hanging basket 50.00
Tea set, gr 145.00
Vase, #110-10″, brown 52.00
Vase, #281-5″ 30.00
Vase, #457-8″, aqua 40.00
Wall pocket, 8″ 55.00

Columbine

Basket, #365-7″ 55.00
Basket, 12″ 95.00
Bowl, #402-8″, tan 35.00

Columbine, vase, 16½″, $160.00.

Candle holder, #1145-2½", pr........................25.00
Candle holder, #15, br, 7", pr........................65.00
Ewer, #18-7", blue........................50.00
Vase, #22-9", tan........................52.00
Vase, #26-14"........................135.00
Vase, #30-8", tan........................48.00
Vase, 6"........................25.00
Wall pocket, blue........................85.00

Corinthian

Jardiniere, 10"........................100.00
Jardiniere & pedestal, 24"........................375.00
Jardiniere & pedestal, 30½"........................400.00
Umbrella stand, 20"........................375.00
Vase, 10"........................65.00
Vase, 7½"........................50.00
Vase, 8"........................45.00
Wall pocket, 8"........................65.00

Cosmos

Basket, 12"........................115.00
Bowl, #376-6", tan........................52.00
Console bowl, #374-14", blue........................65.00
Ewer, #955, 10"........................85.00
Vase, #195-7"........................35.00
Vase, #649-3"........................19.00
Vase, #905-8", aqua........................48.00
Vase, #944-4"........................22.00
Vase, w/hdls, 6½"........................35.00
Wall pocket, dbl........................75.00

Creamware

Ash tray, K of P........................54.00
Ash tray, seascape scene, Fatima shape........................120.00
Candlestick, Good Night, shield back........................285.00
Dresser set, Forget-Me-Not, 6 pc........................275.00
Mug, Cornell Jr Law Smoker, w/orange decor, 1906........................75.00
Mug, FOE........................85.00
Mug, Knights of Pythias........................125.00
Mug, Shrine emblem, Feb 14, 1916, 5"........................125.00
Smoker Set, Indian........................425.00
Stein, Knights of Pythias, 5"........................185.00
Tankard, FOE w/eagle, 10½"........................275.00
Tankard, Howdy Pap, 11½"........................265.00
Tray, powder box & ring holder, Medallion........................180.00
Tumbler, conventional........................40.00

Cremona

Candle holders, 4", pr........................40.00
Console bowl, square, 9"........................45.00
Vase, fan on disc ft, 5"........................25.00
Vase, flared flange on incurvate neck, sides taper, pink, 10"....50.00
Vase, green, 12"........................65.00
Vase, sq, pink, 10¼"........................50.00

Dahlrose

Bowl, oblong, 4"........................40.00
Bowl, 10"........................40.00
Bud vase, single, 8"........................60.00

Hanging basket........................100.00
Jardiniere, 4"........................40.00
Jardiniere, 6"........................62.50
Vase, w/hdls, 8"........................40.00
Wall pocket, 10¼"........................95.00

Dawn

Bookends, #4-5", pr........................115.00
Ewer, #834, 16"........................175.00
Vase, #828, 8"........................55.00
Vase, #833, 12"........................90.00
Vase, yellow, 7"........................35.00

Della Robbia

Mug, band w/Dutch children, 4"........................500.00
Vase, bulbous, tan w/br shoulder band w/wht florals, 8½"...1,550.00
Vase, narrow neck, bulbous, daisy rings, leaves at base, 8"...1,550.00
Vase, reticulated rolled in top w/repetitive daffodils, 12".....2,600.00

Dogwood I

Hanging basket........................95.00
Jardiniere, 8"........................115.00
Wall pocket........................90.00

Dogwood II

Basket, 10"........................55.00
Basket, 6"........................45.00
Basket, 8x4¾"........................35.00
Basket, 8x8½"........................65.00
Jardiniere, 8½x8"........................55.00
Wall pocket, dbl........................75.00

Donatello

Bowl, 2½x6"........................35.00
Candlestick, 8"........................65.00
Compote, 5"........................45.00
Compote, 9½x7½"........................85.00
Double bud vase........................150.00
Jardiniere, 6"........................85.00
Jardiniere & pedestal, 28½"........................375.00
Pitcher, bulbous, 6½"........................125.00
Plate, 8"........................225.00
Vase, cylinder, 12"........................130.00
Vase, straight sides, 8½"........................55.00
Vase, thin trumpet form, 8"........................45.00
Vase, 3 grad stacked disk top, vertical hdls, 6¾"........................120.00
Wall pocket, 9"........................95.00

Dutch

Mug, 4"........................45.00
Sugar bowl, 2½x4¼"........................55.00
Tobacco jar, boy & girl, comp Hotel Olympia, Boston........................200.00
Toothbrush holder........................45.00

Earlam

Bowl, 3x11½"........................35.00
Candlesticks, 1½", pr........................42.00

Strawberry pot 75.00
Vase, short collar on rnd body, lg hdls, lt br/bl, 6″ 40.00
Vase, 4″ 38.00

Early Pitchers

Boy w/Horn 175.00
Bridge 65.00
Cow, no horns, 7½″ 100.00
Golden Rod, NM 100.00
Grapes 100.00
Landscape 50.00
Poppy, full body, cream w/orange, 9″ 130.00
Tulip 55.00
Windmill, rare 150.00

Egypto

Dish, 3 hdls, 3½x8½″ 85.00
Ewer, 10¾″ 350.00
Inkwell, In Hoc Signo Vinces 210.00
Pitcher, w/seal mk, 4″ 125.00
Vase, can neck w/relief bands, rim to width hdls, wafer mk, 9″.170.00
Vase, can neck/base flares/molded bands/metal liner/hdl, 11″...120.00

Elsie the Cow

Bowl, #B3 . . . . .70.00
Mug, #B1 . . . . .70.00
Plate, #B2, 7½″ 85.00

Falline

Bowl, w/hdls, 2½x10½″ 85.00
Vase, bulbous/stepped neck, lg shoulder hdls, 7½″ 175.00
Vase, corrugated bottom, lg side hdls, 9½″ 200.00
Vase, egg shape w/lg ear hdls, 6¼″ 150.00
Vase, 12″, blue 300.00

Ferella

Bowl, 5″ 225.00
Bowl vase, br, 4¼″ 210.00
Vase, br, 10½″ 225.00
Vase, close side hdls, br, 10″ 200.00
Vase, red, 4¼″ 155.00
Vase, red, 9¼″ 225.00
Vase, shape #506-8″ 190.00
Vase, top/ft flares, fuller at center, side hdls, red, 9″ 200.00
Vase, trumpet shape, hdls, br, 5x6½″ 195.00
Vase, U shape, ftd, long hdls, brown, 5¼″ 160.00

Florane

Bowl, #63-10″ 29.00
Bud vase, dbl 32.00
Pot, #73-6″ 40.00
Vase, #3-8″, tan/br 40.00
Wall pocket, 9″ 68.00

Florentine

Basket, cream bkground, 9″ .120.00
Basket, 9″ 85.00

Bowl, 2x6″ 28.00
Hanging basket 110.00
Jardiniere, #130-4″ 37.50
Umbrella stand, ivory 285.00
Vase, catalog #231-8″ 65.00
Vase, catalog #232-10″ 75.00
Vase, catalog #254-6″, brown 34.00
Wall pocket, 7″ 40.00
Wall pocket, 9½″ 65.00

Foxglove

Basket, #373-8″ 50.00
Cornucopia, 6″ 20.00
Ewer, 15″ 125.00
Hanging basket 75.00
Urn, #418-4″ 40.00
Vase, #43-6″, blue 30.00
Vase, #51-10″ 75.00
Vase, #659-3″, pink 22.00

Freesia

Basket, #390-7″ 55.00
Basket, high sides, 10½″ 55.00
Bud vase, bl, bulb base, akimbo hdls, 7¼″ 20.00
Ewer, #20-10″ 75.00
Ewer, 6″ 45.00
Planter box, #1392, oblong, br, 9″ 50.00
Tea set 145.00
Vase, #126-10″ 60.00
Vase, #20-7″ 40.00
Vase, #55-14″ 150.00
Vase, bl, 6″ 30.00
Wall pocket, #1296, 8″ 55.00

Fuschia

Bowl, #364-4″ 37.00
Bowl vase, 3″ 30.00
Candlestick, #1133-5″, pr 85.00
Ewer, #902-10″ 65.00
Jardiniere, 7″ 75.00
Vase, #896-8″ 55.00
Vase, #904-15″ 135.00
Vase, #989-8″ 50.00

Futura

Bowl, catalog #187-8″ 110.00
Candlestick, flat top, akimbo hdls, pointed panels, 4″, pr 155.00
Hanging basket 140.00
Vase, acorn resting in 4 vertical stepped ft, gr/bl, 7¾″ 160.00
Vase, ball on stilts, gr w/mc disks, 8½″ 225.00
Vase, beehive, mottle tan, bl/gr leaves, 8¼″ 195.00
Vase, bottle w/stacked neck, pink/gr, 8¼″ 110.00
Vase, cylinder w/stacked top/base, sq side hdls, rust/gr, 6″ . . .75.00
Vase, flat sided fan w/rectangle rim, bl w/gr, 6x9¼″ 72.50
Vase, pink w/bl/gr/gray, hexagon twist, 8⅛″ 150.00
Vase, rim ring/4 stepped bands to bulbous mid point, bl/br, 7″.150.00
Vase, seagulls 360.00
Vase, short collar, 3 rings mid point, bl floral, bl/tan, 8″ 150.00
Vase, star shaped rim, conforming sides, gr/pink hi-gloss, 8″...120.00
Vase, stepped tube on wide body w/mid angle, angle hdls, 9x9″.190.00

Vase, V shape on sq ped w/rod ft, gr/br/bl, 4x5"............65.00
Vase, vertical hdls top of stacked neck to low angle width, 7"...80.00
Wall pocket, overlapping angle panels, akimbo hdls, 8½".....180.00

Gardenia

Basket, #608-8", brown............................60.00
Ewer, #617-10"..................................65.00
Hanging basket, brown...........................65.00
Jardiniere, #601-6".............................45.00
Tray, 14"......................................45.00
Vase, #684-8", green............................45.00
Vase, #686-10".................................55.00

Imperial I

Basket, catalog #9, 10".........................65.00
Basket, straight top, inverted U hdl, 10½".........50.00
Bud vase, flared base w/hdls, 9"..................30.00
Console, hdls, 9" dia...........................45.00
Dish, w/hdls, 2¾x6½"...........................24.00
Jardiniere, 7".................................40.00
Wall pocket, 2 openings, 9½"....................75.00

Imperial II

Basket, flat, low, 6¼x7"........................65.00
Bowl vase, deep, round base, yellow/mauve drip, 4½".........70.00
Candlestick, orange/gr..........................75.00
Pot w/flared top, tan w/gr 'moss', 6".............90.00
Vase, bl/gr/lav drip from top, flared sides/ring band, 5".......45.00
Vase, bulbous body, flaring w/incised rings, 7".......150.00
Vase, flaring tumbler shape, irregular incised lines, 8".......90.00
Vase, sm hi shoulder hdls, narrowing w/ring band, 8".......90.00
Wall pocket, br w/gr 'moss'.....................185.00
Wall pocket, U-shape, 6½".......................265.00

Iris

Vase, #917-6", blue............................45.00
Vase, #929-15", blue...........................115.00
Vase, rose bowl shape, tan, 4"...................25.00
Vase, 3"......................................20.00
Wall pocket, #1284-8"..........................125.00
Wall shelf....................................135.00

Ivory II

Candlestick, Topeo shape, dbl, paper label, pr.............35.00
Vase, Carnelian shape, 10".......................50.00
Vase, Russco design, 7½"........................40.00
Vase, Savona shape, 6"..........................60.00

Ixia

Jardiniere, #387-6", pink.........................45.00
Vase, #854-7".................................40.00
Vase, #857-8½", aqua...........................45.00
Vase, tan, 10"................................50.00

Jonquil

Basket, catalog #323-7½"........................140.00
Basket, catalog #324-8".........................135.00

Bowl, attached frog, #89, label, 10"...............120.00
Bowl, catalog #524-4", w/hdls....................42.00
Bowl, label, 3x6".............................70.00
Bud vase.....................................52.00
Candlesticks, catalog #1082, w/label, 4", pr.........125.00
Console bowl, 12".............................70.00
Jardiniere, 4"................................40.00
Jardiniere, 7"................................100.00
Jardiniere & pedestal, 29"......................900.00
Strawberry pot, catalog #95, 6½".................225.00
Vase, U-form w/low hdls, 7".....................80.00
Vase, 4".....................................38.00
Vase, 7".....................................70.00
Vase, 8".....................................75.00
Vase, 9½"....................................125.00

Juvenile

Bowl, chicks, 5½".............................40.00
Chamber, w/chicks............................265.00
Cup & saucer, chicks..........................60.00
Dish, Sunbonnet Babies, orange band, RV...........50.00
Egg cup, rabbit head, single, 3"..................135.00
Milk pitcher, standing rabbit.....................45.00
Mug, rabbit, matt glaze, 3".......................42.00
Mug, rabbit w/jacket...........................60.00
Plate, Baby's Plate, rolled edge w/chicks, 6½".......45.00
Plate, Old Woman, rolled edge, sm.................55.00
Plate, rabbit in jacket.........................60.00
Plate, Sunbonnet Baby, flat.....................35.00

Juvenile, Santa Claus plate, green band, 8", $175.00.

La Rose

Bowl, low, 6" dia.............................50.00
Candle holders, 4", pr.........................45.00
Hanging basket...............................140.00
Jardiniere & pedestal, 24½".....................400.00
Vase, full body, 10"...........................80.00
Vase, 5".....................................25.00
Wall pocket, fan shape, 7½".....................70.00

Landscape

Casserole....................................175.00
Creamer, 3"..................................45.00

Laurel

Vase, #668-6″, rust.............................45.00
Vase, brown, 6½″..............................42.50
Vase, brown, 7″...............................40.00
Vase, gold, 7″................................60.00
Vase, gold, 8″................................60.00
Vase, gr/tan, 9″..............................75.00
Vase, green, 9½″..............................70.00
Vase, red, 6″.................................45.00
Vase, silver sticker, 12″.....................95.00
Vase, sm closed hdl ea side short collar, yellow/blk, 6¼″.......45.00
Vase, yellow/blk, 8½″.........................50.00

Lombardy

Jardiniere, footed, 6½″......................150.00
Vase, wht glaze, 6″..........................150.00
Wall pocket, straight top, 8″................185.00

Lotus

Candle holder, bl/wht, 2½″, pr................60.00
Planter, L-7, br/peach, 10½″.................125.00
Planter, L-9, tan............................85.00
Vase, bl/cream, 10″.........................125.00
Wall pocket, 7½″............................175.00

Luffa

Console bowl w/flower frog....................75.00
Jardiniere, brown, 7″........................95.00
Jardiniere, 6″...............................70.00
Vase, full body, sm akimbo rim hdls, 7″......60.00
Vase, w/hdls, 8½″............................68.00

Magnolia

Ash tray, #28, green.........................40.00
Basket, #383-7″..............................45.00
Basket, #384-10″.............................85.00
Basket, #384-8″..............................50.00
Bowl, #459-10″...............................38.00
Bowl, #665-5″................................25.00
Candle holders, #1157, 4½″, pr...............25.00
Cider pitcher...............................110.00
Conch shell, #453-6″.........................35.00
Cookie jar, blue............................125.00
Cornucopia, #185-8″, tan.....................35.00
Creamer & sugar..............................35.00
Ewer, green, 6″..............................40.00
Flower frog, #49.............................30.00
Jardiniere, 3″...............................18.00
Mug, br......................................35.00
Tea set, tan................................145.00
Vase, #446-4″, green.........................30.00
Vase, #453-6½″...............................35.00
Vase, #89-7″.................................35.00
Wall pocket..................................55.00

Mayfair

Cornucopia, #127-6″, brown, pr...............60.00
Planter, #1111, round, tan, 5″...............25.00

Planter, w/under plate, #1117, round, tan....30.00
Wall pocket, corner, brown...................42.00

Ming Tree

Basket, #508-8″, blue........................75.00
Basket, #508-8″, wht.........................55.00
Basket, #510-14″, blue......................120.00
Ewer, #516, blue.............................85.00
Vase, #572-6½″, white........................60.00
Window box...................................60.00

Mock Orange

Bowl, #941-5″, w/hdls........................26.00
Coffee pot, #971-P...........................50.00
Ewer, #916, 6″...............................45.00
Planter, pink................................25.00
Vase, #956-8″................................40.00
Vase, #986-18″..............................225.00

Moderne

Compote, #295, 5″............................55.00
Lamp, #799, 9″..............................100.00
Triple candle holder, #112, 6″...............45.00
Urn vase, blue, 6″...........................40.00
Vase, rose, 6″...............................30.00

Monticello

Basket, can top on wide bottom, pointed hdl, 6½″..........180.00
Console bowl.................................95.00
Vase, hdls from rim to mid-point width, orange, 9″.......90.00
Vase, tapering cylinder, hdls at bottom, 10½″.............105.00
Vase, w/hdls, 6½″............................50.00
Vase, w/hdls, 8½x5″..........................70.00
Vase, 4″.....................................45.00
Vase, 5″.....................................54.00

Morning Glory

Candlestick, wht, 5″, pr....................110.00
Vase, ball shape w/shoulder hdl, vivid color, paper label, 6″....160.00
Vase, green, squat, 4″......................125.00

Morning-Glory, vase, white with lavender and green flowers and leaves, 8½″ x 7″, $160.00.

Vase, pillow shape, w/low hdls, green, 7"....................145.00
Vase, teardrop shape w/hdls, wht, 10½", M................270.00
Vase, U-shape on disk ft, side hdls, green, 5"............150.00
Vase, w/hdls, 12"..300.00
Vase, white, 6"..150.00
Vase, wht, inverted bell form, disk ft w/sm hdls, 8½".......160.00
Vase, wht, squat, 4".......................................100.00
Wall pocket, wht...300.00

Moss

Bowl, #292-8", pink...38.00
Candle holder, #1109-2", pink, pr...........................32.00
Console bowl, #293-10".....................................45.00
Jardiniere & pedestal, 25".................................400.00
Urn vase, w/hdls, #779-8"..................................45.00
Vase, #290-6"..50.00
Vase, #775-6", blue..60.00
Vase, #781-8"..60.00
Vase, #783-9", blue..80.00

Mostique

Bowl, gray w/pk/gr/yel/cobalt, 3½x9¼".......................30.00
Bowl, tan, 7" dia..25.00
Bowl, unusual decor, 3x5"..................................40.00
Jardiniere, stylized flowers, 10" H........................125.00
Planter, arrowhead, 8½x10".................................85.00
Vase, arrowhead, 10".......................................40.00
Vase, arrowhead, 12".......................................45.00
Vase, arrowhead, 6"..25.00
Vase, arrowhead, 8"..30.00
Wall pocket, gray, 10½"....................................60.00

Olympic

Pitcher, Ulysses at the Table of Circle, 7"..............1,800.00
Vase, Persia & Ionia-Xesxes, bullet form w/blk ft, 14½".....3,500.00
Vase, 3 toed, straight slightly flared sides, 13"........2,750.00

Orian

Compote, #272-10"..65.00
Vase, close-to-body hdls shoulder to disk ft, yellow/gr, 10½"....90.00
Vase, long can neck/angle sides below, waist hdls, gr/bl, 8".....70.00
Vase, red, 10½"..90.00
Vase, tan, 7"...60.00
Vase, trumpet form, long vertical hdls, red/gr, 7½"........50.00
Vase, w/hdls, 10½"...95.00

Panel

Bowl, floral, gr, 7½"......................................48.00
Candle holder, 8½", pr.....................................100.00
Lamp base w/nude, 10"......................................245.00
Urn w/lid, br, 10"...265.00
Vase, fan; gr w/wht nude, 8"...............................175.00
Vase, floral, brown, 7½"...................................52.00
Wall pocket, nude, brown...................................250.00

Pauleo

Vase, ovoid, short neck, no decor, 9½x6½"..................600.00
Vase, shoulder, ivory & lav w/iris, 19"..................1,200.00

Peony

Ash tray, #27, gold..40.00
Basket, #376-7"..50.00
Basket, #379-12"...80.00
Bowl, #661-3", green.......................................22.00
Conch shell, 9½"...50.00
Dish, #428-6"..22.50
Ewer, #7-6"..40.00
Ewer, yellow, 10"..65.00
Hanging basket...65.00
Vase, #168-6", gold..50.00
Vase, #69-15", gold..115.00

Persian

Creamer, 3"..75.00
Humidor...335.00
Jardiniere, ftd, 6x9x7"....................................95.00
Teapot, 4½"...160.00
Wall pocket, 11½"...385.00

Pine Cone

Ash tray, #499, br...35.00
Ash tray, #499, green......................................25.00
Ash tray, ftd, blue..55.00
Basket, disk ft, gnarled branch hdl, br, 10x8"............130.00
Boat dish, #427-8", green..................................50.00
Bud vase, rnd ft, pine cone & needles on side, gr, 7½".....35.00
Candle holder, triple, br, pr.............................135.00
Cornucopia, #126-6", gr....................................24.00
Cornucopia, #422-8", brown.................................65.00
Dish, #497, brown..35.00
Dish, 3 legs, #432-12", brown..............................75.00
Ewer, br, 10"..60.00
Hanging basket, green.....................................125.00
Pitcher, #708, 9½"...200.00
Planter, #456-6", brown....................................35.00
Tray, #430-12"...60.00
Tray, dbl, gr..75.00
Tumbler, brown...95.00

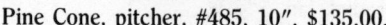

Pine Cone, pitcher, #485, 10", $135.00.

Vase, #261-6″, br..50.00
Vase, #485-10″, w/hdls, green.....................75.00
Vase, #711-10½″, gr...................................80.00
Vase, #712-12″..95.00
Vase, #745-7″..55.00
Vase, #747-10″, br......................................85.00
Vase, #838-6″, w/hdls.................................40.00
Vase, #845-8″, pillow shape........................70.00
Vase, urn shape, gnarled twig shoulder hdls, brown, 8″.......85.00
Wall pocket, br, U-shape w/cone & needle device at top, 9″....175.00

Poppy

Basket, #348-12″, pink...............................95.00
Bowl, #336-7″..30.00
Jardiniere & pedestal, lg...........................550.00
Vase, w/hdls, #370-8″.................................42.00

Primrose

Vase, #763-7″..36.00
Vase, w/hdls, 6¾x4½″.................................30.00
Vase, 6″...30.00
Vase, 9″...40.00

Raymor

Butter w/cover, wht.....................................30.00
Coffee pot, paper label, no stand................125.00
Cup...14.00
Mustard, wht, 3½″.......................................26.00
Pitcher, #189, br...55.00
Plate, bread & butter....................................5.00
Plate, dinner...12.00
Plate, luncheon...8.00
Ramekin...18.00
Relish tray..25.00
Salt & peppers, wht, pr...............................20.00
Saucer..4.00
Vegetable bowl..25.00

Rosecraft

Bowl, blue...35.00
Vase, yellow, sm rim hdl, 8″.........................45.00
Wall pocket, blue, sides curve to point at bottom, 9″.........65.00

Rosecraft Black

Compote, 4x11″..125.00
Ginger jar w/lid..180.00
Vase, high shoulder, 13½″...........................150.00
Vase, rnd ft, very lg rim to shoulder hdls, 15¾″...........210.00

Rosecraft Hexagon

Bud vase, double, 5″...................................65.00
Vase, 8″..100.00
Wall pocket, 8½″.......................................115.00

Rosecraft Vintage

Bowl, w/frog, 9″ dia....................................70.00
Dish, 2½x6½″..25.00

Jardiniere, 5x6″...45.00
Vase, br, 6″...60.00
Vase, 10″...110.00
Vase, 12½″...150.00
Vase, 4″...85.00
Wall pocket, 9″..80.00
Window box...125.00

Rozane

Bud vase, leafage decor, #862, hdl rim to low swell, 4″.......150.00
Ewer, florals, #905, 7½″.............................165.00
Ewer, leaves & berries, bulb bottom, complex hdl, 7″.......350.00
Ewer, yellow holly berries, sgn AM, wafer mk, 9¼″.......175.00
Jardiniere, florals, 3 ball ft, ball shaped body, 9½″.......175.00
Jug, blackberries, sgn, wafer, 6″..................220.00
Tankard, blackberries, sgn CF, #821, 10½″......265.00
Tankard, corn, EX art, gr/br/orange, 14″.........400.00
Tankard, grapes, EX art, W Myers, wafer mk, 14″.......330.00
Vase, clover decor, long slim neck, flared rim, 8″.......160.00
Vase, delicate florals, Pillsbury, inverted trumpet, 8″.......160.00
Vase, dog portrait, Dunlavy, ovoid form, 8″...1,900.00
Vase, dog portrait, Mitchell, 12″..................350.00
Vase, floral, 'butterfly' hdls at slim neck, pulled ovoid, 8½″.....90.00
Vase, wide squat body, sm neck, silver overlay, no mk, 2½″...850.00
Vase, yellow clover, slender shape, wafer mk, artist sgn, 9″....110.00
Vase, yellow clover, twisted w/crimped top, 10½″.........90.00
Vase, yellow/orange floral, sgn SC, RP Co, 6¼″...........155.00

Rozane, 1917

Basket, blue..70.00
Basket, yellow, 7½″.....................................80.00
Bowl, 8″...32.00
Candlestick, 7″, pr......................................45.00
Compote, ivory, 10″....................................55.00
Jardiniere, 7x5″...40.00

Rozane Light

Pitcher, pansies, gray on gray w/wht beading, M Pierce, 7″....800.00
Teapot, chicks, sgn Rhead, complex hdl, #60, 8″...........1,100.00
Vase, berries, twisted/4 lobed top, M Timberlake, 10½″......225.00
Vase, blackberries, gray/wht on gray/wht, slender, Myers, 10″...350.00
Vase, floral on slightly ribbed body, J Imlay, 10¾″.........225.00
Vase, gr/wht w/EX yellow floral, sgn Myers, 14¾″............460.00
Vase, nasturtiums on gray, gourd shape, M Timberlake, 8″.....200.00

Russco

Candle holder, 4½″, pr.................................35.00
Vase, flared U, lt gr/yellow w/crystals, 8x6″......110.00
Vase, full body, ped base, angle hdls, crystalline, 7½x7½″.....90.00
Vase, rust, 12½″...90.00

Silhouette

Ash tray, red...25.00
Basket, #708-6″...30.00
Basket, #710-10″, wht w/gr trim.....................55.00
Bowl, 3¼x6″..35.00
Candlestick, #751-3″, wht, pr........................22.00
Cigarette box, red......................................50.00
Ewer, aqua, 6″...35.00

Vase, #779-5″, brown...................................19.00
Vase, #780-6″...24.00
Vase, #781-6″...20.00
Vase, #783-7″, w/nude..................................135.00
Vase, #784-8″, wht..30.00
Vase, #785-9″, w/nude..................................135.00
Vase, #788-12″, wht.......................................40.00

Snowberry

Basket, BK-7″..55.00
Basket, BK-8″..60.00
Basket, green, 10″...60.00
Bookends, pr...65.00
Bowl, 1BL1-10″..40.00
Bowl, 6x9″..28.00
Bud vase, 7″...28.00
Candle holder, CS1, pr....................................25.00
Candlestick, #1652-4½″, pr..............................38.00
Cornucopia, ICC-8″...38.00
Ewer, 10″...60.00
Hanging basket, blue, 8½″................................55.00
Jardiniere, 5″..25.00
Jardiniere & pedestal.....................................350.00
Planter w/saucer...45.00
Tea set..95.00
Vase, #201-7″, blue..35.00

Sunflower

Bowl, w/hdls, 4″...60.00
Vase, cylindrical w/slight taper, sm rim hdls, 6″.....110.00
Vase, sm hdls, full body, 5¼″............................60.00
Vase, U-form, rim to base hdls, 5″......................50.00
Vase, w/hdls, blk sticker, 10½″.........................140.00
Vase, wide mouth, round body, sm rim hdls, 4″.......45.00

Teasel

Candle holder, #113, pr...................................25.00
Console bowl w/frog, pr candleholders..................90.00
Vase, blue, 4″...25.00
Vase, 12½″..75.00
Vase, 2 hdls, #889-15″....................................125.00

Thornapple

Basket, #365-7″...50.00
Vase, #808-4″..28.00
Vase, #810-6″, pink..35.00
Vase, #822-10″, pink.......................................75.00
Vase, #825-5″..32.00

Topeo

Bowl, console; blue, lg....................................70.00
Bowl vase, bl/gr, 6″..65.00
Vase, can top on rnd body, blue, 7″.....................75.00
Vase, red, 6½″..145.00
Vase, red glaze, 9½″......................................175.00

Tourmaline

Planter, blue, 12″ L..48.00

Vase, #613-8″..30.00
Vase, bl gloss drip, rnd/divided band of rings top, 6½x5″.......55.00
Vase, blue, 9″..60.00
Vase, pillow form, w/hdls, blue, 6″......................45.00
Vase, simple shape, 7¼″...................................40.00

Tuscany

Console bowl, 15″...50.00
Flower arranger vase, gray...............................20.00
Vase, can neck/full body, pink w/gr leaf hdls, 9″.....45.00
Vase, pink, w/hdls, 12″....................................75.00
Vase, w/hdls, 6″..38.00
Wall pocket, gray, 8″......................................50.00

Velmoss

Cornucopia, catalog #115-7″, gr.........................40.00
Urn, catalog #265-6″.......................................60.00
Vase, catalog #119-10″....................................75.00
Vase, catalog #720, gr, 10″..............................65.00
Vase, w/hdls, 11″...68.00
Vase, wide brimmed lip, 7″...............................38.00
Wall pocket, 8½″...240.00

Velmoss Scroll

Flower pot..50.00
Vase, 10″...70.00
Vase, 5″..45.00

Victorian Art Pottery

Bowl vase, floral & beetle band, 4″.....................85.00
Jar, bulbous, br w/beetles & stylized florals, 10″....235.00
Jar w/lid, blue w/band of berries at shoulder, 8″....265.00
Vase, floral & beetle band, 6″..........................100.00
Vase, incurvate rim, gray w/band of berries/leaves, 8¼″.......150.00

Vista

Basket, 9½″...115.00
Jardiniere, 8½″...145.00
Jardiniere & pedestal, 28″...............................140.00
Wall pocket, 9½″...165.00

Volpato

Bud vase..50.00
Candlestick, 3½″..25.00
Pot w/saucer, 6″..65.00
Window box, 2½x9″..30.00

Water Lily

Basket, #381-10″..68.00
Cookie jar...110.00
Vase, #77-8″, aqua...48.00
Vase, #78-9″...55.00
Vase, #81-12″..75.00

White Rose

Basket, #363-10″..65.00

Bowl, #389, w/hdls..............................22.00
Candle holder, pr..............................42.00
Creamer......................................20.00
Ewer, #981-6"..................................45.00
Jardiniere, 6".................................45.00
Pitcher, #1324, pk/gr...........................60.00
Teapot w/lid, blue.............................85.00
Vase, #653-11"................................70.00
Vase, #985-7".................................45.00
Vase, #992-15"...............................125.00
Vase, 8".....................................50.00
Wall pocket, #1288-6"..........................58.00
Wall pocket, 8"...............................60.00
Window box...................................48.00

Wincraft

Basket, #209-12", tan..........................50.00
Bookends, #259-6", tan, pr......................38.00
Console bowl, #229-14".........................35.00
Cornucopia, #2CC-8"...........................30.00
Ewer, #217-6".................................32.00
Hanging basket................................95.00
Tea set, #271.................................85.00
Teapot, #2TP.................................60.00
Vase, #241-6"................................25.00
Vase, #274-7".................................40.00
Vase, #281-6", bl w/ivory flowers................30.00
Vase, #289-18"...............................175.00
Wall pocket, gr, 8½"...........................75.00
Wall pocket, round, 5".........................65.00
Window box, #268-12".........................35.00

Windsor

Basket, very low hdl, disk ft, 4½".............175.00
Console bowl, 2 hdls; w/flower frog, silver sticker.............90.00
Vase, bl w/geometrics, 6x6½"...................85.00
Vase, geometrics on br, no hdls, 6".............95.00
Vase, w/ferns, hdls, silver sticker, 7½".........145.00
Vase, w/ferns, hdls, silver sticker, 9½".........175.00

Wisteria

Bowl, catalog #243-12"........................85.00
Bowl, catalog #629-4".........................55.00
Hanging basket...............................285.00
Jardiniere, brown, 8".........................175.00
Jardiniere, 5x6½"..............................75.00
Jardiniere, 8"...............................250.00
Vase, #633-8".................................95.00
Vase, blue, 6"................................75.00
Vase, full body, narrow mouth, sm shoulder hdls, br, 7½"..80.00
Vase, narrow can neck w/akimbo hdls, bulbous body, 9".....120.00
Vase, ovoid, incurvate rim w/sm hdls, blue, 5¼".....70.00
Vase, sides flare to full mid point, sm angle hdls, 4¼".....55.00
Vase, straight sides, rim hdls, 10"............150.00
Vase, w/hdls, 7½".............................65.00
Vase, wide top, sides flare slightly, sm rim hdls, 8½".....90.00

Woodland

Vase, floral, Rozane seal, 6".................600.00
Vase, floral, shoulder bulge widens to base, 7¾"......900.00

Vase, 4-scallop top, simple floral, no neck, 9"........800.00

Zephyr Lily

Basket, #394-8"..............................58.00
Bookends, green, pr...........................50.00
Bowl, #474-8", blue...........................40.00
Compote, #8-10", blue.........................45.00
Ewer, #23-10"................................75.00
Jardiniere, #571-8"............................85.00
Tea set, brown..............................105.00
Vase, #139-12", green.........................58.00
Vase, #394-8", w/hdls, blue....................45.00

Miscellaneous

Bank, cat's head, no mk, 4"...................150.00
Bank, orange figural, slot in top, 3¼x3½".......80.00
Bank, Uncle Sam.............................100.00
Bottle, monkey figural, yel w/sponging, 6".....150.00
Mug, pink/wht/gold, oval reserve w/transfer of girl, 5½"......75.00
Tankard, pink/wht/gold, oval reserve w/transfer of girl, 12¾"...140.00

Rowland and Marsellus

Though the impressive back stamp seems to insist otherwise, Rowland and Marsellus Company were not Staffordshire potters, but American importers who commissioned various English companies to supply them with the blue printed historical ware that had been a popular import item since the early 1800s. Plates, cups and saucers, pitchers, and platters were sold as souvenirs from 1890 to 1920. The mark may be in full or 'R. & M.' in a diamond.

Dish, Souvenir of Yale, brick row center, halls at rim, 10½"....45.00
Pitcher, straight sides, Landing of Columbus, 3 qt, EX........375.00
Plate, Albany, NY, bl/wht, rolled rim..........................40.00
Plate, Bunker Hill Monument, flat, 10".........................40.00
Plate, Capture of Vincennes...................................45.00
Plate, City Hall, Worcester, rolled rim.........................40.00
Plate, Grand Union Hotel, Saratoga, NY.......................45.00

Plate, American Poets, blue and white transfer, 10", $75.00.

Plate, Hartford, Conn, capitol, bl/wht, rolled rim..............40.00
Plate, Homestead Fairbanks Family.........................45.00
Plate, Landing at Hendrick, Hudson, bl/wht, rolled rim........40.00
Plate, Mohawk Trail thru Berkshires, bl/wht, flat, 9¼".........40.00
Plate, Mt Vernon, flat....................................32.00
Plate, New Capitol, Albany, NY, flat.......................40.00
Plate, Old Boston Theatre................................40.00
Plate, Old Feather Store, Boston, flat......................45.00
Plate, Old South Church, Boston...........................40.00
Plate, Robert Burns, rolled rim............................50.00
Plate, Teddy Roosevelt commemorative, bl/wht, 9¾"..........45.00
Plate, Thos Jefferson center, rolled edge....................50.00
Plate, Washington in Prayer at Valley Forge, flat, 10½".......50.00
Plate, 1000 Islands, rolled rim............................40.00
Tumbler, views of Washington, bl transfer..................30.00

Royal Bayreuth

Founded in 1794 in Tettau, Bavaria, the Royal Bayreuth firm originally manufactured fine dinnerwares of superior quality. In more recent times,
they have produced lines of dinnerware and accessory items such as humidors,
vases, ash trays, and boxes in patterns called Rose Tapestry, Sunbonnet
Babies, Beach Babies, and Devil and Cards. These are highly sought by
today's collectors. Figural creamers, sugar bowls, and shakers in the shape
of tomatoes, grapes, shells, and animals were made in abundance.

Pitcher, black poodle, orange interior, blue mark, 5", $345.00.

Ash tray, clown..160.00
Ash tray, Devil's head, red, sgn...........................130.00
Ash tray, elk..125.00
Ash tray, heart form, man w/lyre courts lady, scenic, 5¼".....55.00
Ash tray, mountain goat..................................235.00
Ash tray, Murex shell, Deponiert, 4½".....................35.00
Ash tray, Rose Tapestry, 4" square.........................85.00
Ash tray, Tryolean men on bench w/flute & violin, 4" dia.......45.00
Ash tray & match holder, Devil & Cards....................200.00
Basket, oyster & pearl figural, irid, sgn, 4¾".................225.00
Bell, Sunbonnet Babies, washing & hanging, no mk..........325.00
Biscuit jar, pearlized wht grapes w/lav/gold leaves, lg..........210.00
Biscuit jar, poppy, wht MOP, blue mk......................500.00
Bowl, banana; pearlized lav grapes w/wht/gold leaves, 5x9".....210.00
Bowl, finger; Murex shell.................................55.00

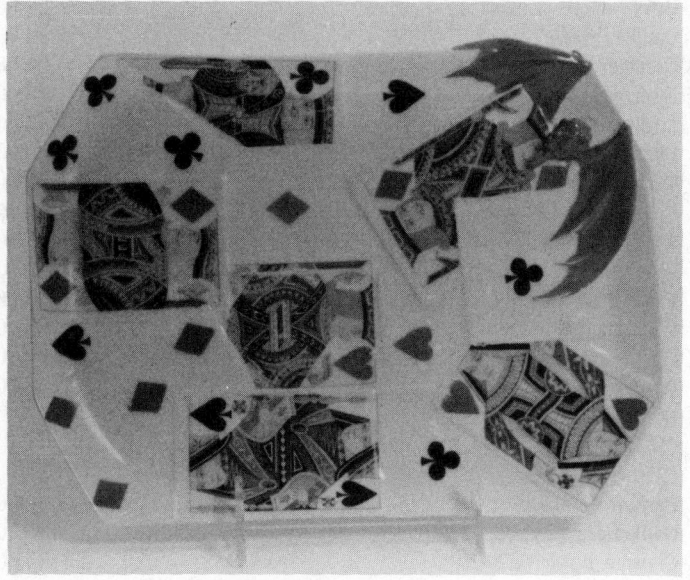

Tray, Devil and Cards, blue mark, 10" x 7", $350.00.

Bowl, lettuce, 10"......................................145.00
Bowl, tapestry, man & lady, 5½".........................75.00
Box, jewel; Ivory Rose, blue mk..........................85.00
Box, lady on horse, fox hounds, blue mk, 2x3½"...........80.00
Box, pin; narrow chain pk/wht flowers, gold outline, 2½" sq....58.00
Box, pin; pk/wht flowers, blue mk, 2½" sq.................65.00
Box, pin; Rose Tapestry, pk roses, pinched-in sides, w/lid, sm..160.00
Box, powder; Rose Tapestry, ftd.........................200.00
Box, tomato, large, 3½x4½" dia.........................38.00
Candlestick, attached saucer/hdl, yel w/blk/wht birds, 5".......140.00
Candlestick, Bo-Peep...................................98.00
Candlestick, Corinthian, blue mk.........................60.00
Candlestick, elk, 8"....................................350.00
Candlestick, hunting scene, blue mk, 4¼".................125.00
Candlestick, peasant & turkeys, ring hdl, souvenir, 5".........60.00
Candlestick, shield bk w/hdl, pk roses/bl leaves, 4½x3¾".......95.00
Candlestick, Sunbonnet Babies..........................195.00
Candlestick, Sunbonnet Babies, cleaning, hooded, w/hdl, bl mk.325.00
Cereal set, Nursery Rhymes, six 1⅞" mugs & dishes, cr/sug....695.00
Chamberstick, sheep scene..............................75.00
Cheese dish, slant top, blue mk, miniature.................110.00
Chocolate pot, boy seated on log, 2 donkeys, blue mk........195.00
Chocolate pot, Brittany girl, blue mk......................180.00
Chocolate pot, hunter w/bird dog decor, 1900..............195.00
Chocolate pot, pastel roses, wht satin, reticulated base, ftd.....250.00
Chocolate pot, Rose Tapestry, 3 color roses, blue mk, M......900.00
Chocolate pot, Snow Babies, bl mk, 6"....................225.00
Chocolate set, poppy, MOP, blue mk, 13 pc..............1,375.00
Clock, Rose Tapestry, EX...............................350.00
Creamer, alligator......................................165.00
Creamer, apple, blue mk................................75.00
Creamer, Arab & 2 horses, 2 hdls, blue mk, 3".............48.00
Creamer, bird of paradise, blue mk.......................205.00
Creamer, black cat.....................................140.00
Creamer, bull, blk......................................140.00
Creamer, bull, brown...................................135.00
Creamer, bull, gray; blue mk............................125.00
Creamer, cat figural hdl, wht on gr.......................170.00
Creamer, cavaliers drinking & smoking, 3¾"...............45.00
Creamer, cherries & leaves, gr to rose, 3¾"...............40.00
Creamer, chickens & peasant w/scythe, 3½"...............60.00

Creamer, chrysanthemum, sgnd.........................135.00
Creamer, clown.....................................170.00
Creamer, coachman.................................195.00
Creamer, conch shell, pearlized, w/red lobster figural..........35.00
Creamer, conch shell, tall, diagonal ribs, twig hdl.............80.00
Creamer, cow, black................................95.00
Creamer, cow, brown...............................145.00
Creamer, crow.....................................125.00
Creamer, dachshund................................130.00
Creamer, Devil, red; no mk.........................275.00
Creamer, donkey boy...............................95.00
Creamer, duck, blue mk.............................175.00
Creamer, elk, blue mk, 4½".........................75.00
Creamer, farmer & 5 chickens, green, blue mk...........55.00
Creamer, French poodle, gray; blue mk.................165.00
Creamer, frog, green, blue mk.......................135.00
Creamer, frog, no mk...............................65.00
Creamer, girl w/basket.............................175.00
Creamer, goats, long haired, 6x3¾"...................85.00
Creamer, goose girl................................85.00
Creamer, grape, pink MOP; sgn DEP & Germany..........110.00
Creamer, grape, yellow, no mk.......................65.00
Creamer, hunting scene.............................35.00
Creamer, Jack & Beanstalk, bulbous, blue mk, 4".........95.00
Creamer, Jack & Jill, blue mk, 6"....................145.00
Creamer, Kewpie, Jasperware, blue, fully sgn...........185.00
Creamer, lady on horse, peasants, pk/cream to gr at base, 4¾"..55.00
Creamer, lady shielding candle flame w/hand, 3¾".........55.00
Creamer, lemon....................................85.00
Creamer, lettuce leaf & red lobster, good color..........80.00
Creamer, moose....................................65.00
Creamer, mountain goat, blue mk.....................275.00
Creamer, Old Man of the Mountain, Tettau..............65.00
Creamer, owl......................................235.00
Creamer, pansy, blue mk............................165.00
Creamer, parakeet, blue mk..........................165.00
Creamer, peasant w/turkeys, 6¾x5"....................75.00
Creamer, perch....................................165.00
Creamer, pheasant, blue mk..........................210.00
Creamer, pig, Deponiert............................200.00
Creamer, platypus, blue mk, 4"......................165.00
Creamer, poppy, MOP lavender, blue mk................170.00
Creamer, poppy, red, blue mk........................125.00
Creamer, poppy, yellow, sgn.........................95.00
Creamer, robin, no mk..............................88.00
Creamer, rooster, bl mk, M..........................110.00
Creamer, Rose Tapestry, 3 color roses, pinch spout, 4".....275.00
Creamer, Rose Tapestry, 4½".........................165.00
Creamer, seal, gray, 4", M..........................180.00
Creamer, shell w/coral hdl, no mk....................50.00
Creamer, shell w/lobster hdl, low, sgn................52.00
Creamer, St Bernard, sgn...........................165.00
Creamer, Sunbonnet Babies, washing windows & floors, 4"....125.00
Creamer, trees & long haired sheep, blue mk, 6".........55.00
Creamer, washer woman.............................55.00
Creamer, water buffalo, blk w/red detail...............120.00
Creamer, 3 cows on shades of gr, 2 hdls, blue mk, 4".....40.00
Creamer, 3 storks, sq body, 4½".....................45.00
Creamer, 4 turkeys & farmer, mc, blue mk..............65.00
Creamer & sugar, grapes, bl w/gr leaves, 4", pr..........95.00
Creamer & sugar, lobster............................65.00
Creamer & sugar, poppy, wht MOP....................280.00
Creamer & sugar, Rose Tapestry, blue mk..............325.00
Creamer & sugar, Snow Babies, blue mk...............125.00

Creamer & sugar, tomato, gr leaf......................95.00
Creamer & sugar, wht w/gold & pk rose band, 4½", pr........75.00
Cruet, purple grapes figural, gr leaf & branch hdl, gr stopper....45.00
Cup, child's; Sand Babies............................42.00
Cup, demitasse; pastoral scene w/cows.................23.00
Cup, demitasse; Sunbonnet Babies, fishing, gold trim, sgn.....85.00
Decanter, musician scene, w/hdl, 7"...................125.00
Dish, child's; cherubs, blue mk......................125.00
Dish, child's; Sand Babies, 7".......................95.00
Dish, child's; Sunbonnet Babies, blue mk, M............250.00
Dish, clover leaf; Rose Tapestry, 3 color, ring hdl, blue mk....150.00
Dish, heart form, Jack & Jill, nursery rhyme border, 5½"......65.00
Dish, lettuce leaf; stem forms loop hdl, blue mk, 6¾".........28.00
Dish, maple leaf; Little Bo Peep, blue mk..............115.00
Dish, sauce; grape, yellow, sgn......................50.00
Dish, Sunbonnet Babies, washing & hanging, w/hdl, blue mk...145.00
Dish, w/lid; egg shape, girl w/geese, 5½"..............135.00
Dish, w/lid; pastoral scene, sgn, oval.................46.00
Dish, 3 cows, gr/br to red, w/hdls, 3x3½".............45.00
Hair receiver, boy w/donkey.........................75.00
Hair receiver, tapestry, daisies, gold ft, blue mk........150.00
Hair receiver, white roses decor.....................95.00
Hair receiver & powder box, pink roses, ftd, rnd, tall, pr......80.00
Hatpin holder, poppy, blue mk.......................180.00
Hatpin holder, Rose Tapestry, no mk..................225.00
Hatpin holder, Sunbonnet Babies, washing, blue mk.........425.00
Humidor, Devil & Cards.............................285.00
Match holder, clown, blue mk........................190.00
Match holder, Murex shell, wall hanging, Deponiert.........75.00
Match holder, red Devil head, blue mk.................165.00
Match striker/holder, boats at sunset, no mk.............32.00
Mug, Devil & Cards, blue mk........................175.00
Mush set, Sunbonnet Babies, cleaning & hanging, bl mk, 3 pc..310.00
Mustard, Corinthian, black..........................75.00
Mustard, grape, pink MOP...........................95.00
Mustard, lobster, red, hdl, w/lid.....................47.00
Mustard, poppy....................................50.00
Mustard, shell, pearlized...........................65.00
Mustard, tomato...................................65.00
Pitcher, Art Nouveau lady, water, blue mk, M...........850.00
Pitcher, bass, milk, blue mk.........................165.00
Pitcher, cavaliers/tavern scene, green, sgn Dixon, blue mk, 6"..125.00
Pitcher, clown, milk...............................245.00
Pitcher, coachman, milk, blue mk.....................300.00
Pitcher, Corinthian, wht figures on blk, salmon throat, 8".....130.00
Pitcher, Devil & Cards, blue mk, 4½".................200.00
Pitcher, Devil & Cards, sgn, 7½"....................365.00
Pitcher, Eagle, milk...............................245.00
Pitcher, elk, blue mk, 5"...........................145.00
Pitcher, fish head, milk, blue mk.....................185.00
Pitcher, fisherman decor, blue mk, 6".................125.00
Pitcher, grape, milk, wht, MOP......................125.00
Pitcher, grape, water..............................275.00
Pitcher, hunting scene at top on gr, blue mk, 4".........125.00
Pitcher, Little Boy Blue, 3½".......................115.00
Pitcher, lobster, milk..............................105.00
Pitcher, lobster, water.............................200.00
Pitcher, man w/turkeys decor, 7½"...................150.00
Pitcher, man w/2 horses, flat bk/sides, 9".............350.00
Pitcher, parakeet, milk.............................155.00
Pitcher, parrot figural, no mk, 4¾"...................135.00
Pitcher, roses decor, much gold, sgn, 6¾"..............86.00
Pitcher, sailboat in storm, 3"........................75.00
Pitcher, Snow Babies, 6"...........................185.00

Pitcher, storks, wht enamel on gr w/blk, sq shape, blue mk, 5"..65.00
Pitcher, Sunbonnet Babies, milk, washing/ironing, bulbous, lg..210.00
Pitcher, Ye Old Lantern, 5½".............................70.00
Planter, Corinthian................................55.00
Planter, Rose Tapestry, 3 color, bulbous base, hdls, miniature..185.00
Plaque, hunting scene, scalloped gold border, blue mk, 9½"...120.00
Plaque, Rose Tapestry, 4 colors, blue mk, 9½"..............375.00
Plate, cabbage leaf, 8"............................35.00
Plate, cake; Rose Tapestry, w/hdls, 10"...................175.00
Plate, cake; Sunbonnet Babies, washing & ironing, open hdl, lg.250.00
Plate, clam shell.................................30.00
Plate, fishermen & boat scene, 'B53' on sail, 9"............75.00
Plate, goose girl, 6"..............................60.00
Plate, grapes, purple/gr/wht on gr, Rococo border, bl mk, 10½".75.00
Plate, Jack & the Beanstalk, blue mk, 7"..................50.00
Plate, leaf; loop hdl, w/7 yel flowers, 5¼"................17.00
Plate, leaf; w/embossed tomato, 7½"....................75.00
Plate, lemon; lettuce leaf, ring hdl, sm..................25.00
Plate, Little Bo Peep, blue mk, 6¼" dia..................75.00
Plate, Little Miss Muffet...........................85.00
Plate, poppy, wht MOP, 6", blue mk, set of 6.............300.00
Plate, Rose Tapestry, 7¾".........................165.00
Plate, roses, pink w/gr leaves, open hdls, gold rays, 10½".....60.00
Plate, Snow Babies, blue mk, 6"......................70.00
Plate, Sunbonnet Babies, cleaning, 6¼"................125.00
Plate, Sunbonnet Babies, ironing, 7½".................190.00
Potpourri, boats at sunset, w/lid, blue mk................65.00
Relish, elk.....................................170.00
Relish, Rose Tapestry, blue mk......................145.00
Rose bowl, peasant girl w/geese, house & trees, 3x4½".......32.00
Rose bowl, Sunbonnet Babies.......................190.00
Shakers, elk figural, pr...........................125.00
Shakers, grapes, bl w/gr leaf bases, 3", pr...............100.00
Shakers, plum, pr................................40.00
Shakers, tomato, pr..............................40.00
Shoe, black, right & left, pr........................130.00
Shoe, man's high top.............................95.00
Shoe, Rose Tapestry.............................325.00
Stickpin holder, w/attached tray, scenic, blue mk..........150.00
String holder, rooster, blue mk......................165.00
Sugar, grape, wht satin...........................105.00
Sugar, lobster..................................125.00
Sugar, pansy...................................175.00
Sugar, Rose Tapestry, no lid.......................125.00
Sugar w/under plate, lobster, lg, w/lid..................70.00
Tankard, girl on stairs w/candle.....................145.00
Tankard, musicians decor..........................165.00
Tea tile, Sunbonnet Babies, washing & ironing, flat/rnd, bl mk..120.00
Teapot, boy standing, 2 donkeys, 3 cup size, blue mk.......150.00
Teapot, grapes, mc, pearlized.......................175.00
Teapot, ivory shaded to bl w/red & pk roses, 5½"...........55.00
Teapot, man w/donkey scenic, 3 cup, blue mk............145.00
Teapot, pansy, blue mk...........................450.00
Tile, girl with dog...............................85.00
Toothpick, elk, blue mk...........................110.00
Toothpick, lobster...............................40.00
Toothpick, Rose Tapestry, 2 hdls....................275.00
Tray, celery; pk roses, blue mk, 12¾"..................115.00
Tray, dresser; Ring Around the Rosie..................195.00
Tray, dresser; Rose Tapestry.......................250.00
Tray, dresser; tapestry, w/pastoral scene, 11x8"..........345.00
Tray, Dutch girl w/shoulder yoke, flowers in pails, 4½x4"....38.50
Tray, horseshoe w/twig atop, hunting scene in bottom, 4¾"...45.00
Tray, lettuce leaf, w/hdl, gr, 6".....................22.50

Chocolate pot, Sunbonnet Babies, blue mark, 5¾", $585.00.

Tray, pin; Sunbonnet Babies, mending; club shape, 4¾".......85.00
Tray, pond lily leaf w/pk flowers in center, 6x5"............27.50
Tray, tapestry scenic, blue mk, 8x11".................325.00
Tray, 2 cavaliers w/mandolin & wine glasses, 5x3¾"..........45.00
Tumbler, Rose Tapestry w/portrait of lady in pk gown, 3¾"....235.00
Vase, Arab scene, silver rim, w/hdls, blue mk, 4"...........45.00
Vase, birds of paradise, w/hdls, blue mk, 3"..............28.00
Vase, children w/dog & rabbits, silver rim, w/hdls, 3½".......150.00
Vase, cow scene, 2 hdls, 4½".......................75.00
Vase, Dutch girl, 3 hdls, sterling rim, blue mk, 3½".........55.00
Vase, men in sail boat, HP, 2 hdls, silver collar, 3½".........45.00
Vase, mountain goats, trees, mountains, 5½"..............65.00
Vase, portrait, sgn Muller, Art Nouveau, 15½"............795.00
Vase, sheep scene, bulbous, no mk, 6".................85.00
Vase, steamship decor, w/hdls, sterling rim, blue mk........75.00
Vase, tapestry, deer/Grecian temple, 4 sm ft/hdls, 4".......195.00
Wall pocket, grape, yellow, sgn......................150.00
Wall pocket, strawberry, 9"........................250.00
Watering can, tapestry, swan scene, no mk...............275.00

Royal Bonn

Royal Bonn is a fine-paste porcelain, ornately decorated with scenes, portraits, or florals. The factory was established in the mid-1800s in Bonn,

Vase, white 'lace work' over hand painted florals, gold trimmed, artist signed, 8", $165.00.

Germany; however most pieces found today are from the latter part of the century.

Biscuit jar, tan w/floral, SP lid & bail........................85.00
Clock, pink w/florals...................................395.00
Ewer, pink/yel/blue/gold flowers on cream ground, 12".......175.00
Figurine, fox, head high, 5½"..............................135.00
Figurine, polar bear on bk, paws in air, #729, 2½x4¼".......90.00
Loving cup, 3 hdls, ped base, 11"..........................95.00
Vase, acanthus leaf twist hdl, florals, sgn Mehlen, 13¼"......175.00
Vase, florals w/gold relief tracing, dbl hdls, imp mk, 11", pr....325.00
Vase, girls dancing, wht, 1920, 9"..........................150.00
Vase, maiden bust portrait, sgn, 1895, 13".................450.00
Vase, rooster/hen/chicks/inscription, sgn, 6½"............145.00

Royal Copenhagen

The Royal Copenhagen Manufactory was established in Denmark in about 1775 by Frantz Henrich Muller. When bankruptcy threatened in 1779, the Crown took charge, and the fine dinnerware and objects of art produced after that time carries the familiar logo, the crown over three wavy lines.
See also Collector Plates

Bowl, gray crackle glaze, 5½"..............................55.00
Coffee server, snail on hdl, blue, fluted, 9¾"..............125.00
Cruet, bl/wht, sgn...95.00
Figurine, Boxer dog, #1238, 5½x5½".......................190.00
Figurine, boy & sow, #848.................................130.00
Figurine, boy w/lunchbox, #865............................145.00
Figurine, chicken, 5¾".....................................60.00
Figurine, cobbler, #2228..................................135.00
Figurine, gibbon, 5".......................................75.00
Figurine, goat on rock, #4760, 4x3½".....................120.00
Figurine, goose girl, #527, 9"............................275.00
Figurine, knight & maiden, by Christensen, 20"............700.00
Figurine, leopard cub, artist sgn...........................95.00
Figurine, Pan w/rabbit, #439..............................125.00
Figurine, penguins, 3¾"....................................65.00
Figurine, polar bear attacks sea lion, #1108, 9x14".......200.00
Figurine, salesman, man w/bolt of cloth, 8"...............125.00
Figurine, sea bird, 5" L....................................45.00
Figurine, shepherdess, #694...............................135.00
Figurine, sleeping pigs, #683, 2½x4½x4"..................165.00
Figurine, swan, #755, 4x6½"...............................110.00
Planter, Cocker Spaniel head...............................12.00
Plate, see Collector Plates
Vase, cactus, 4¼"..35.00
Vase, crackle ware, Art Deco, 6"...........................50.00
Vase, crackle ware, gold fish & ship decor, 12x7½".........345.00
Vase, crackle ware, turq w/gold trim, 3¼x4"................35.00
Vase, gray flowers on wht, sgn, 5½"........................65.00
Vase, w/lid, putti w/shield surmount, florals/gilt, 1800s, 11"....300.00
Wall pocket, apple...10.00
Wall pocket, spaniel.......................................15.00

Royal Copley

Royal Copley is a decorative type of pottery made by the Spaulding China Company in Sebring, Ohio, from 1939 to 1960. In addition to the Royal Copley mark, some pieces were also marked with the company's name.

Ash tray, heart shape w/figural pair of birds, 5½"............5.50
Bank, pig, standing, w/blue & white stripe shirt, 6"........18.00

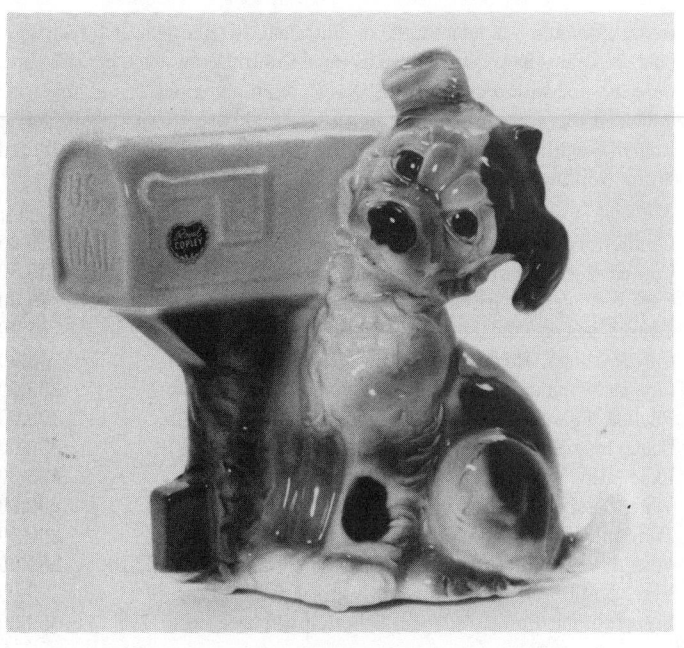

Planter, dog and mailbox, 8", $13.00.

Bank, rooster, 'Chicken Feed', coin slot at top of tail, 7½".....16.00
Bank, teddy bear, sitting, bow around neck, 7½".............18.00
Bud vase, parrot on branch, yellow, 5"......................5.00
Creamer & sugar, leaf, yellow w/pink hdls, pr................6.50
Figurine, cockatoo, blue, wings out, 7¼"...................18.00
Figurine, Cocker Spaniel, sitting, looking up, 6¼"...........9.00
Figurine, double wren-like birds on branch, blue............12.00
Figurine, kitten w/ball of yarn, w/paper label, 6½"........15.00
Pitcher, daffodil..13.00
Planter, angel kneeling, blue gown, 8".....................15.00
Planter, birdhouse w/bird on roof, 8"......................25.00
Planter, coach figural, teal blue, 3¼x6"....................5.00
Planter, Colonial old man & old woman busts, each 8", pr.....35.00
Planter, dancing lady, 8"..................................15.00
Planter, deer & fawn.......................................15.00
Planter, Dutch boy w/bucket; Dutch girl w/bucket, 6", pr.....15.00
Planter, farm boy w/fishing pole, green & rose, 6½".........6.00
Planter, kitten & boot, 7½"................................13.00
Planter, mailbox w/baby duck sitting beneath, 6¾".........20.00
Planter, mailbox w/dog sitting beside, 7¾"................13.00
Planter, mallard duck beside stump, 8"....................14.00
Planter, Oriental boy kneeling w/basket on back, 8".......12.00
Planter, pigtail girl bust, 7".............................8.00
Planter, pirate head, 8"...................................15.00
Planter, ram head, 6½".....................................9.00
Planter, rooster, 7¼"......................................6.50
Planter, rooster pushing wheelbarrow, rare, 8"............24.00
Planter, teddy bear w/concertina, 7½".....................19.00
Planter, teddy bear w/sucker, 8"...........................17.00
Smoking set, mallards, 3" cigarette holder, two 2" trays.....13.50
Vase, cornucopia, floral decal, gold trim, 8¼", pr..........14.00
Vase, dogwood, 8¼"...7.00
Vase, horse head w/mane, 8"................................12.00
Vase, yellow w/roses in relief, sgn, 7"....................11.00
Wall pocket, girl in lg blue hat...........................13.50

Royal Crown Derby

In the latter years of the 1870s, a new firm, the Derby Crown Porcelain Company Ltd. began operations in Derby, England. Since 1890, when they were appointed Manufacturers of Porcelain to Her Majesty, their fine porcelain wares have been known as Royal Crown Derby. Their earliest wares were marked with a crown over 'Derby'; often a complicated dating code indicated the year of manufacture. After 1890, the 'Royal Crown Derby, England' mark was employed; in 1921, 'Made In England' was substituted in the wording. 'Bone China' was added after 1945.

Candle holder, hammered copper, 2 pc, 1½x4½"............30.00
Cup & saucer, Derby Panel, green.........................38.50
Cup & saucer, Imari pattern #1128........................75.00
Cup & saucer, Midako, blue, 1928.........................45.00
Cup & saucer, Royal Antoinette...........................48.50
Jam jar w/under plate, Imari, 1911, 5¼"..................285.00
Pitcher, Imari, octagonal w/dragon hdl, ca 1855, 7".......300.00
Plate, Imari, 10½", set of 8.............................550.00
Plate, King's pattern, 1850s, 10¼" dia, set of 6..........425.00
Plate, Tissinton Spires by E Trowsell, jewel border, 9"....200.00
Toby pitcher, snuff taker, mc enamel, rpr hat, 4".........300.00
Vase, blue iris on cream, ca 1873, top of vase also mkd, 10"...285.00
Vase, bottle; red w/gold florals, Nouveau neck decor, 8½"....225.00
Vase, wht/gilt florals on rose, spherical w/foliate neck, 7½"....350.00

Royal Dux

The Duxer Porzellan Manufactur was established by E. Eichler in 1860. Located in what is now Duchcov, Czechoslovakia, the area was known as Dux, Bohemia, until WWI. Several marks have been used over the years, all variations of the acorn mark -- Eichel in German meaning 'acorn'. The Art Nouveau figurines and decorative wares were imported into the United States at the turn of the century, and were marketed at moderate prices.

Bust, lady w/orchids in hair & bodice, #507, 21"..........1,760.00
Bust, young girl, iris in long hair, mk E in oval, 20".......1,045.00
Centerpiece, lady sits aside bowl, flower in hand, 13½" L.....665.00
Centerpiece, shell bowl on wave, female figures aside, 16½" L..750.00
Figurine, African Crane, pink triangle mk, 13"...............70.00
Figurine, bathing girl, scarf on head, pk triangle mk, 22"....2,000.00
Figurine, boy on donkey, pink triangle mk, 15x11"...........235.00
Figurine, boy walking dog, stick/coat over shoulder, 13".......185.00
Figurine, cockatoo, 7".....................................85.00
Figurine, dancing couple, pk triangle mk, 9x6½x4"..........150.00
Figurine, Deco lady, blue irid satin dress/gr hat, 9", pk mk....265.00
Figurine, Deco lady, skirt bk, leg exposed, sgn Kunnert, 9¾"..275.00
Figurine, elephant, tusks up, pk triangle mk, 10x11½".......150.00
Figurine, fairy sitting on lily pad, pk triangle mk, 6½x9"......400.00
Figurine, fisherman w/seaweed/knife, wife in apron, 21".......750.00
Figurine, girl, bucket in hand, by cow, wht.................450.00
Figurine, Greek male w/scroll, gr/gold drape, grassy base, 13"..195.00
Figurine, Hunter, The; pk/gr/lt gold, 14"...................400.00
Figurine, Irish Setter w/bird, pink triangle mk, 9x18".......125.00
Figurine, lady, gray dress/shoes/hat, hands raised, 1920s, 9"...95.00
Figurine, lady in blue dress, 1920, 10"....................115.00
Figurine, lady in drapery w/bowl of fruit, pk triangle, 15".....300.00
Figurine, mother holds young boy w/ea hand, pk triangle, 16"..795.00
Figurine, parrot, pk triangle mk, 9x16"....................95.00
Figurine, pr of dogs, Setter & Pointer, pk triangle mk, 16" L..375.00
Figurine, princess, seated, ruffled dress, pk triangle, 10x13"..210.00
Figurine, semi-nude, cobalt bl/gold, 9¾x3¼"...............450.00
Figurine, sleeping deer, head left, resting on bk, pk mk......150.00
Figurine, stalking tiger, pk triangle mk, 18"................185.00
Figurine, Tom Sawyer & dog, pink triangle mk, 13x11".......250.00
Figurine, young girl on gold bench, 1900..................250.00

Figurine, zebra, pink triangle mk, 3x4"....................25.00
Figurine, 2 boys pulling lambs, pink triangle mk, 9x9".......175.00
Planter, shell ea side, scroll hdls ea end, 17x11x5½".......385.00
Vase, applied flowers & fruit, orange/br, 5"...............65.00
Vase, applied orange poppies on gr, sgn, 15"..............100.00
Vase, columns, emb flowers, medallions w/ladies' heads, 8"....115.00
Vase, heavy relief leaves, openwork, 1900, 14"............200.00

Figural palace vases, Arab with mandolin and woman with water jug, 36", $1,500.00.

Royal Flemish

Royal Flemish was made from the late 1880s, and was patented in 1894 by the Mt. Washington Glass Company. Transparent glass was enameled with one or several colors, and the surface divided by a network of raised lines suggesting leaded glass work. Some pieces were further decorated with enameled florals, birds, or Roman coins.

Cracker jar, apple blossoms decor.......................3,000.00
Cracker jar, sgn Mt Washington.........................1,200.00
Ewer, heraldic shields/sectioned/swirl devices, ball form, 8½"..1,800.00
Ewer, rope hdl, gold lines & spiral intersections, 9".........3,950.00
Pitcher, random panels w/silver flowers, applied centers, 7"...2,000.00
Vase, gold coins, cup rim, bottle form, w/hdl, 12¼".........1,850.00
Vase, shield w/gold scrolled leaves; coat of arms, 10".......3,750.00

Royal Rudolstadt

The hard paste porcelain that has come to be known as Royal Rudolstadt was produced in Thuringia, Germany, in the early 18th century. Various names and marks have been associated with this pottery – one of the earliest was a hay fork symbol associated with Johann Frederich von Schwarzburg-Rudolstadt, one of the first founders. Variations, some that included an 'R', were also used.

In 1854, Earnst Bohne produced wares that were marked with an anchor and the letters 'EB'. Wares commonly found today are those made during the late 1800s and early 20th century. These are usually marked with an 'RW' within a shield under a crown, and the words 'Crown Rudolstadt'. Items marked 'Germany' were made after 1890.

Bowl, wht roses, HP, 5", set of 4..........................72.00
Children's dishes, Happifats decor, service for 6, 23 pc......500.00
Creamer & sugar, cream w/pansies, ornate..................75.00
Creamer & sugar, lavender classical design, gr shading.......165.00
Ewer, pastel w/flowers, 1890, 5"..........................25.00
Figurine, elderly peasants, 6", pr........................100.00

Hair receiver, yel roses on shaded yel, Prussia/crown, 4¼"......95.00
Inkwell, attached saucer, mc flowers on ivory, 3½x6".........58.00
Plate, forget-me-nots, 8½"................................35.00
Plate, lilies, sgn Kahn, 6", pr...........................45.00
Plate, wht/lav pansies, gold border, 8¼" dia.................60.00
Relish, HP flowers, artist sgn, oval, 8¾"....................24.00
Server, 2 tier, 9" & 5" dish on std, Deco, mc, crown mk.......35.00
Vase, tapestry, bulbous/br loop hdls, wht w/bl floral, RW, 7½".250.00
Vase, yel/beige w/florals, hdls, 10½x7"......................80.00
Violet bowl, cream w/HP florals, gold trim, wht w/in, 3".......24.00

Figurine, Napoleonic lady in Empire gown, 17", $750.00.

Royal Worcester

The Worcester Porcelain Company was deeded in 1751. During the first, or Dr. Wall period (so called for one of its proprietors), porcelain reflecting an Oriental influence was decorated in underglaze blue. Useful tablewares represented the largest portion of production, but figurines and decorative items were also made. Very little of the earliest wares were marked, and can only be identified by a study of forms, glazes, and the porcelain body which tends to transmit a greenish cast when held to light. Late in the fifties a crescent mark was in general use, and rare examples bare a facsimile of the Meissen crossed swords. The first period ended in 1783 and the company went through several changes in ownership during the next eighty years. The years from 1783-1792 are referred to as the Flight period. Marks were a small crescent, a crown with 'Royal', or an impressed 'Flight'. From 1792-1807 the company was known as Flight and Barr, and used the trademark 'F&B' or 'B', with or without a small cross. From 1807-1813 the company was under the Barr, Flight, and Barr management; this era is recognized as having produced porcelain of the highest quality of artistic decoration. Their mark was 'B.F.B.'.

From 1813-1840 many marks were used, but the most usual was 'F.B.B.' under a crown, to indicate Flight, Barr and Barr. In 1840 the firm merged with Chamberlain; and in 1852 they were succeeded by Kerr and Binns. The firm became known as Royal Worcester in 1862.

Since 1930, Royal Worcester has been considered one of the leaders in the field of limited edition plates and figurines.

Basket, Pine Cone, open reedwork, twist hdls, 8½" L.........300.00
Basket, Pine Cone, reticulated, twist hdls, bl/wht, 1770, 10"...425.00
Biscuit barrel w/under plate, beige w/florals, 6x3½"...........325.00
Biscuit barrel w/under plate, melon ribbed, floral sprays, 8"....350.00

Bowl, covered vegetable; Valencia...........................65.00
Bowl, cream soup w/under plate; Bacchanal....................30.00
Bowl, Pine Cone, scalloped border, 10" dia..................550.00
Bowl, underglaze bl w/mc florals in reserves, sq fret mk, 7"....575.00
Bowl, vegetable; Bacchanal.................................35.00
Bowl, vegetable; Valencia..................................40.00
Butter tub, cover & stand, 3 Flowers, bl/wht, 1770-75.........750.00
Butter tub w/cover, blue scale, cartouches of branches, 5¾"...500.00
Cake plate, wht, gold HP decor, on standard, pre WWI, 3x10".145.00
Candle snuffer, nun, 1930s, 3½"...........................115.00
Candlestick, child by dog, arms about candle, 1876, 5"......375.00
Candlestick, sq base, embossed twisted design, 12x4", pr.....330.00
Cigarette holder, plum colored, scene on each, pr............55.00
Cornucopia, scroll base, florals, 1898, 7x4x6"..............325.00
Creamer, fruit decor by Walter Austin, 1923, 4¼"...........225.00
Creamer & open sugar, Mansfield Blue.......................50.00
Creamer & sugar, Bacchanal................................40.00
Cup & saucer, Bacchanal...................................35.00
Cup & saucer, demitasse; beige w/florals, gold traced, ca 1887...43.00
Cup & saucer, demitasse; Oriental scenes in orchid, purple mk..30.00
Cup & saucer, fruit, sgn William Hale, 1926, gold worn, 1½"..150.00
Cup & saucer, handleless; bl border/gold vines, 1775.........98.00
Cup & saucer, pk to violet, miniature, Worcester Shot Enamel..35.00
Demitasse set, printed w/florals, cobalt/gilt, orig box, 1890s....250.00
Ewer, bamboo hdl, pink/bl/rust florals/gold, 1889, 10¼".....250.00
Ewer, bird hdl, bulbous w/narrow neck, wht w/flowers, 7x5½"..220.00
Ewer, flat bk, fluted gold hdl, tan w/florals, 3½"...........120.00
Ewer, flat bk, fluted gold hdl, tan w/florals, 5"............135.00
Ewer, horn hdl, wht w/florals, gold trim, 6½x3"............175.00
Ewer, lobed form w/pierced foliate decor, gilt details, 5".....275.00
Ewer, reticulated top, cream w/gr/gold, grouse medallion, 12"..825.00
Ewer, tan w/floral, 4 lobed, gold thorn hdl, 1896, 8".........275.00
Ewer, wht texture w/flowers, gold hdl, 14x6"................250.00

Urn, sheep scene, artist signed, gold trimmed, 10", $1,250.00.

Figurine, Beswick Wren, Doughty........................1,200.00
Figurine, dolphin, R Van Ruychevelt, 11½"..................550.00
Figurine, Flying Fish, R Van Ruychevelt, 7¾"...............440.00
Figurine, Goldcrest, Doughty............................2,100.00
Figurine, Golden Retriever, #3309, Lindner, rare............150.00

Figurine, June, boy w/his dog, FG Doughty, 6½"............75.00
Figurine, mallard family, decor/bisque....................1,375.00
Figurine, Mischief, purple mk, ca 1941....................115.00
Figurine, mockingbirds, Doughty.........................100.00
Figurine, Old Goat Woman, by Phoebe Stabler, 1930........125.00
Figurine, pansy, 3"....................................285.00
Figurine, Wednesday's Child, 7"........................110.00
Figurine, woodpecker, #3248, 7".......................145.00
Flower arranger, shaded peach & ivory, ftd, dtd 1907, 2½x4¼".75.00
Gravy, Valencia.......................................45.00
Jug, Cabbage Leaf, bl/wht, bell shaped, mask spout, rpr, 10½".600.00
Leaf dish, molded as two overlapping leaves, 1756, 8½" L....350.00
Mug, dbl hdls, scrolls/crests/flowers, Chamberlain's, 7x6"......660.00
Nut dish, triangular, mc leaf design, gold scalloped edges.......50.00
Perfume, bl/wht w/gilt & florals, 4¾"...................220.00
Perfume, lay-down; robin & flowers on wht, 1875, 3¾"......150.00
Pitcher, acanthus relief, mask spout, bl florals, Dr Wall, 9"....550.00
Pitcher, Sabrina Ware, bl-gr w/acorn & leaf, 1906, 5¾".......185.00
Planter, wall; wht w/seashell coral trim, dtd 1885, 11"......150.00
Plate, bird, sgn Jas Stinton...........................110.00
Plate, bread & butter; Bacchanal........................12.50
Plate, bread & butter; Ferncroft, pink....................8.50
Plate, bread & butter; Valencia.........................12.50
Plate, dinner; Bacchanal...............................18.50
Plate, dinner; Valencia................................20.00
Plate, HP flowers & border, dtd, early, 9"................75.00
Plate, leaf, HP yel florals/asters/gold traced, dtd 1890, 7"......45.00
Plate, luncheon; Bacchanal............................16.50
Plate, salad; Valencia.................................15.00
Platter, Bacchanal, 14"...............................48.00
Platter, Bacchanal, 16"...............................58.00
Platter, Valencia, 16".................................60.00
Rose bowl, 4 lobed, beige w/flowers, 3x3¼"...............95.00
Sugar, cream w/mc floral sprays/gold vein leaves, w/lid, 3½"....135.00
Sugar, open; fruit decor by Horace Price, 1923, 2".........225.00
Sweetmeat dish, Blind Earl, 1760-65, 6½" W..............700.00
Tea caddy, egg shaped, ribbed, multifloral, 1775, 4¾".......350.00
Teapot, cream w/mc floral sprays/gold veined leaves, purple mk.325.00
Teapot, Mansfield Blue................................65.00
Toothpick, beige w/gold, bamboo knuckle, 2½"............65.00
Toothpick, cream bark ground, ornate gold base & leaf decor..110.00
Urn, w/lid, reticulated hdls & top, HP bird on wht, 12x5".....965.00
Vase, bamboo, sgn/#1049, 2¼".........................60.00
Vase, beige w/floral, gold trim, 1902, 8¼"...............165.00
Vase, beige w/sepia florals, Hadley, 4x3"................135.00
Vase, cattle/river/castle/emb gold florals, Granger, 1891, 8"...325.00
Vase, floral sprays, stick neck, 1886, 6½"...............130.00
Vase, Highland cattle, HP Stinton, 1905, 8½".............275.00
Vase, off-wht w/florals, 2 sm rnd hdls, 6½x4"............185.00
Vase, pink w/florals, artist sgn, 7½x4"..................185.00
Vase, wht, fabulous birds, 2 applied hdls, 7x3½".........200.00
Vase, wht w/fruit, HP, dtd 1957, 3½x3".................85.00

Roycroft

Near the turn of the century, Elbert Hubbard established the Roycroft Printing Shop in East Aurora, New York. Named in honor of two 17th century printer-bookbinders, the print shop was just the beginning of a community called Roycroft, which came to be known world-wide. Hubbard became a popular personality of the early 1900s, known for his talents in a variety of areas, from writing and lecturing to manufacturing. The Roycroft community became a meeting place for people of various capabilities, and included shops for the production of furniture, copper, leather items, and

a multitude of other wares which were marked with the Roycroft symbol, an 'R' within a circle below a stylized cross. Hubbard lost his life on the Lucitania in 1915; production in the community continued until the Depression.

Ash tray, hammered, silver finish, 3½"..................22.00
Book, Concerning Slang, 1923.........................15.00
Book, Little Journeys, Elbert Hubbard, leather, set of 14, M...120.00
Book, Message to Garcia, Hubbard, red suede covers.........20.00
Book, Pig Pen Pete, tooled leather bound, 1914............40.00
Book, Queen of the Porch, 1923.......................15.00
Book, Selected Writings, Elbert Hubbard, leather, set of 14.....50.00
Book, Time & Chance, Elbert Hubbard, G................10.00
Book, Wm Morris, hand illuminated, 1900...............15.00
Book, 29 mini leather bound volumes, w/orig Roycroft bookends.50.00
Book rack, oak, 2 shelves w/exposed tenons, shoe ft base, 27".225.00
Bookcase, 5 shelves over open drw, cut-out base, w/logo, 65"..750.00
Bookends, hammered copper, Roycrofter's Hallmark, lg, pr.....50.00
Bookends, hammered copper, w/monogram, 5", pr...........25.00
Bowl, hammered copper, Deco flowers in center, sgn, 8" dia....75.00
Bud vase, glass tube, copper holder, 6"..................75.00
Candlestick, SP copper, hollow can/disk base, 9½", pr........130.00
Catalog, Some Books For Sale at Our Shop, 40 pgs, G........17.00
Cigarette urn, hammered copper.......................20.00
Crumb set, hammered copper, Art Deco, sgn..............70.00
Desk organizer, drawer w/orig appointment calendar, 4x11½"...80.00
Hubbard's scrapbook, 1923, NM.......................10.00
Inkwell, hammered copper, dk patina, sgn, 3⅛" dia..........90.00
Jug, br stoneware....................................20.00
Lamp, copper, 4 panels w/4 lower mica panels, inscription, 15".660.00
Letter opener, hammered copper.......................30.00
Magazine pedestal, oak, 5 shelves widen at base, 48".........800.00
Napkin ring, pewter..................................10.00
Pen tray, hammered copper, 11".......................28.00
Plate, copper, 6"....................................25.00
Postcard...3.00
Rocker, oak, 6 vertical bk slats, straight arms, logo, 39x36"....375.00
Tray, copper, rnd, sm................................35.00
Vase, hammered brass, 5".............................25.00
Vase, hammered copper, 8½"..........................150.00

Rubena

Rubena glass was made by several firms in the late 1800s. It is a blown art glass that shades from clear to red.

Celery vase, enameled floral decor, w/SP holder, 1880s........235.00
Cheese dome cover, 5¾"..............................45.00
Mustard, enamel flowers, Baby Thumbprint, SP lid............95.00
Mustard, Inverted Thumbprint, enamel flowers, pewter top......65.00
Pitcher, Hobb's Hobnail, 5"..........................250.00
Pitcher, water; threaded.............................185.00
Tumbler, sculptured overshot.........................135.00
Vase, flared, ribbed w/in, gold trim, pnt floral, 12½".........105.00

Rubena Verte

Rubena Verte glass was introduced in the late 1800s by Hobbs, Brockunier and Company, of Wheeling, West Virginia. Its transparent colors shade from red to clear to green.

Lamp shade, Shell pattern, lg.........................375.00
Sweetmeat, vaseline shell trim & rim, SP basket fr, 5¾"......115.00

Tumbler, 10 row Hobnail, 4"............................225.00
Vase, mc florals/bl ribbon, ribbed/ruffled, 10"..............280.00
Vase, peony top, 13½".................................195.00
Vase, stick on raised base, applied clear rigaree, 10"........125.00
Vase, swirl, sq opening, 12x6"..........................180.00

Vase, leaf-form feet, ruffled top, 7¾", $80.00.

Ruby Stained Souvenirs

Ruby flashed or stained glass was made by the application of a thin layer of color over clear. It was used in the manufacture of some early pressed tableware and from the Victorian era well into the 20th century for souvenir items which were often engraved on the spot with the date, location, and buyer's name.

Basket, enamel decor, Palisades Park, NJ.................30.00
Bowl, heart shape, Norwich, NY..........................12.00
Coal bucket w/bail, Iowa................................30.00
Creamer, Button Arches, South Dakota....................20.00
Creamer, individual; Ruby Thumbprint....................42.00

Cruet, gold trim, faceted stopper, 6", $125.00.

Cruet, Tiny Thumbprint, w/orig stopper..................125.00
Decanter & 4 wines, Double Block, 1892..................175.00
Goblet, challice, 'Thy Kingdom Come'....................25.00
Goblet, Ruby Thumbprint, Niagara Falls...................20.00
Letter holder, Bailey, Mich.............................40.00
Mug, Beaded Swag, tall.................................18.00
Mug, Button Arches, Revere Beach, Mass, 1905.............25.00
Mustard pot, Ruby Thumbprint, World's Fair, 1893.........125.00
Pitcher, milk; Button Arches, 'Mother'...................55.00
Salt shaker, Sunk Honeycomb............................12.00
Toothpick, Harvard, ruby stained, Atlantic City, 1899.......35.00
Toothpick, Heart Band..................................35.00
Toothpick, Shamrock, Providence, Rhode Island............30.00
Tumbler, Button Arches, 'Mother', 1905...................31.00
Wine, Bull's Eye Band..................................18.00
Wine, King's Crown, Buffalo Center, Iowa.................20.00

Rugs

Key:
comp----complimentary   med----medallion
dia-----diamond   s/a----semi-antique
gb--------guard border

Hooked

Hooked rugs are treasured today for their folk art appeal. It was a craft that was introduced to this country in about 1830 and flourished its best in the New England states. The prime consideration is not age, but artistic appeal. Scenes with animals, buildings, and people; patriotic designs; or whimsical themes are preferred. Condition is, of course, also a factor. Marked examples bearing the stamps of 'Frost and Co.', 'Abenakee', 'C.R.', and 'Ouia' are highly prized.

American hooked rug, Cow Jumped Over the Moon theme, contemporary, 28" x 44", $440.00.

Mat, rag, dog team/driver, good detail, Grenfell label, 12x23"...300.00
Rag, bird on flowering branch, leaf border, dtd 1920, 52x26"..250.00
Rag, Boston Bulldogs, facing, on gray w/bl border, 25x48".....150.00
Rag, central design w/multicolored flowers & scrolls, 30x50"....50.00
Rag, colorful sqs, 20x31"...............................55.00
Rag, dog, recumbent; roses in border, rebacked, 18x40"......325.00
Rag, dog, very large; standing, 3 flowers in corner...........750.00
Rag, floral design w/dk colors on olive, rpr, 28x42".........70.00
Rag, geometric design w/blk border, 21x38"................100.00
Rag, geometrics, minor edge wear, 27x39".................60.00
Rag, geometrics in blk & dk colors, rebound, 27x43".........75.00

Rag, horse, primitive, stylized bkground, 1916, worn, 18x36"...175.00
Rag, lg peacock w/flowers, stand w/urn at side.............340.00
Rag, scene of cabin w/stylized sky/lake/foliage, 24x48".......525.00
Rag, semi-circle, cat, kitten, flowers & Welcome, 27x40".....510.00
Rag, stripes/checkerboard in br/wht/gr, rpr, 19x36"...........40.00
Rag, stylized deer (button eyes) in cattails, worn rpr, 26x43"....65.00
Rag, stylized floral in intricately shaped reserve, 39x64".......90.00
Rag, stylized floral in lg oval, velvet border, 18x36"..........35.00
Rag, stylized vase of flowers, faded/worn, 23x39".............35.00
Rag, tulips, folk design, some wear, 23x39"................65.00
Rag, urn w/ferns & flowers in lg reserve..................575.00
Rag, 2 children on teeter-totter, 1 child is Black, 39x31"......325.00
Rag, 2 rabbit-ear donkeys, primitive, edge stripes, 19x33".....95.00
Runner, rag, 5 leaf medallions on stripes, little worn, 19x75"....45.00
Table rug, on burlap, Tree of Life, 1880s, blk border, 14x20"...125.00
Yarn, single red poinsettia on blk, 25x31".................35.00

Oriental

The Oriental and Eastern rug market has enjoyed a renewal of interest in recent years, as collectors have become aware of the fact that some of the semi-antique rugs (those sixty to one hundred years old) may be had at a price within the range of the average buyer.

Akstaf, bl w/multi star med, crab border, 9¾x4 ft..........3,850.00
Akstaf, dk bl w/hooked devices/boteh/florals/cocks, 10x4 ft.....300.00
Akstaf, prayer, wht mihrab w/hooked motif trellis, 5½x3 ft...1,760.00
Bakitari, grid work of bouquets, palmette/comp gb, 12x9 ft...3,025.00
Bakshaish, prayer, center tree w/flanking willows, 5x4½ ft....3,960.00
Belouchistan, bagface, 2½x2½ ft.....................2,530.00
Belouchistan, lobed med/flanking bird/floral border, 5½x3 ft...880.00
Belouchistan, red w/wht/bl octagon guls, star border, 6½x4 ft.3,500.00
Bergamo, bl/red/yellow, center floral med/spandrels, 3x3 ft....1,750.00
Bergamo, 2 lg octagon med w/bl/gr radiating panels, 7x5 ft.....9,000.00
Bergamo, 3 pumpkin med on ivory, vine border, 4x3 ft......3,250.00
Beshir, bl/br w/florals/center med, 8x4 ft.................2,250.00
Beshir, cloud band/florals, rstr, 9x5 ft..................6,600.00
Beshir, prayer, ivory/bl/red, center head/shoulders, 5½x3½ ft.6,000.00
Bidjar, herati in floral med, floral borders, 15½x12 ft......3,850.00
Bidjar, herati w/center med & comp spandrels, 12x8½ ft....1,750.00
Bidjar, mat, bl/ivory, cartoon w/lions/florals, 2x1½ ft........1,320.00
Bidjov, bl w/ivory/turq/br/red overscale palmettes, 9x3½ ft....600.00
Bordjalou Kazak, prayer, red dia med w/geometrics, 4x3½ ft..1,650.00
Caucasian, blue w/floral lozenges/tendril motifs, 9x8 ft......3,300.00
Central Anatolian Kilm, ruby/ivory, stepped dia med, 12x5 ft..1,100.00
Chi Chi, bl w/med/rows of arrows, 5½x3 ft................990.00
Chi Chi, br/bl, lattice center of sm med w/florals, 5x4 ft......3,850.00
Chinese, Art Deco, floral cartouch/vine border, 1925, 9x12 ft.1,100.00
Chinese, beige w/peony/vines design, bl border, 7¾x5 ft....2,970.00
Chinese, center flowering bush w/birds/florals, 11½x9 ft....2,420.00
Chinese, oval, landscape mirage design, 9½x8½ ft.........770.00
Chinese, pillar, bl w/2 monks blowing conch shells, 8x4¾ ft..2,200.00
Chinese, seascape of village/mtns, 11½x9 ft.............4,675.00
Chinese, throne, dragons w/in border of symbols, 2x2¼ ft....275.00
Chinese, throne, tan w/dragon/cloud motif, 2¾x3 ft........2,250.00
Demirdjik Kula, prayer, mihrab w/tree, inscribed, 4x3½ ft....3,500.00
Ersari, ivory/bl, lg S motif in gul med border, 3½x3 ft.......2,250.00
Ersari Torba, red/bl, gul med/flowerhead border, 2x5½ ft.....2,500.00
Gendje, gold/bl, palmette trellis, flower/vine gb, 8½x3½ ft....2,750.00
Heriz, med w/spandrels, 10x6½ ft....................3,080.00
Heriz, red w/serrated lozenges/leaves/humans, 14½x4 ft....2,500.00
Isphahab, silk warp, ca 1945, 7½x4½ ft................8,800.00
Joshagan, garden design w/tree filled cartouches, 14x10 ft...8,525.00
Karachopt Kazak, gr w/ivory/yellow reserves, 8x5½ ft......6,000.00

Karagashli, bl/yellow, latchhooks/rosettes, 7½x3½ ft........10,000.00
Kashan, center med w/arabesque/floral spandrels, 11½x8½ ft.9,350.00
Kashan, med w/floral meander spandrels, 11x8¾ ft........11,550.00
Kazak, prayer, bl-gr mihrab w/angular motifs, arch, 6x4 ft....1,870.00
Kazak, prayer, dbl niche, latchhook/stars, 13x4½ ft.........2,250.00
Khotan, coral/bl/gr, rosettes/gul, wave motif gb, 5x3 ft......1,100.00
Kirman, floral cartouches w/center med, 18x12 ft..........14,850.00
Kizil Ayak, rust/ivory, 4 rows/12 guls, latchhook gb, 7x6½ ft..2,500.00
Konagkend, bl/blk w/ivory angular trellis, 5x3¾ ft.........4,200.00
Konya, red w/2 ivory latchhook med, 9x4 ft.............9,000.00
Kuba, bl/red/wht, florals w/in barber pole border, 4½x4 ft...41,250.00
Kuba, prayer, br/bl mihrab, animal motifs, 2x1 ft..........2,090.00
Lesghi, bl/ivory/gr/turq, stars w/in octagon border, 5x4 ft.....3,200.00
Melas, prayer, red mihrab w/3 dia latchhooks, 4x3½ ft......5,000.00
Northwest Persian, blue w/allover florals, 10½x4 ft.........1,750.00
Perpedil, prayer, ram horns, barber pole border, 6x4½ ft.....3,410.00
Perpedil, red w/ivory/bl ram horn, floral/trefoil gb, 4x3 ft....2,090.00
Qashqa'i, bagface, bl/wht/red/yellow, floral med, 2¼x2½ ft...1,100.00
Qashqa'i, bl allover stylized botehs, red spandrels, 5½x4 ft...5,000.00
Qashqa'i, bl w/repetitive boteh, flowerhead border, 9½x5 ft..2,250.00
Qashqa'i, bl w/three 4-armed med w/ivory spandrels, 6x4 ft..2,640.00
Qashqa'i, red dia med on bl w/palmettes, 7x4¼ ft.........6,050.00
Sarouk, center flowering vine/4 stylized bouquets, 6½x4 ft..2,310.00
Serab, br w/red med/horsemen/birds, 12x3½ ft...........1,870.00
Serab, camel w/meandering trellis, dk bl gb, 12x3½ ft......1,320.00
Serab, trellis of rosettes/flowerheads, geometrics, 15x3½ ft..2,750.00
Shirvan, bl w/exotic animals/men, silk hi-lites, 5x4 ft........3,300.00
Shirvan, bl w/floral rosettes, dragon border, 5x4 ft.........2,640.00
Shirvan, bl/blk w/trellis of ivory cartouches, 4½x3½ ft......2,200.00
Shirvan, prayer, ca 1875, 2x2 ft.....................3,190.00
Shirvan, yellow/red/bl, rows box flowers, crab border, 5x4 ft..5,200.00
Shirvan Marasali, female portrait, 3 sm figures, 5x4 ft......7,700.00
Shulaver Kazak, geometric latchhook/florals, 8½x3¾ ft.....1,870.00
Soumac, bagface, center octagon med w/striped gb, 2x2 ft....605.00
Tabriz, hexagonal herati-filled med w/in comp spadrels, 6x4 ft.3,250.00
Tabriz, red w/fawn/gr med, comp spandrels, 11x8 ft........9,900.00
Turkish Kilim, bl/ochre/tan, serrated dia, serrated gb, 8x6 ft..2,200.00
Veramin, bl w/lattice of floral sprays, 11½x4 ft............2,250.00
Yomud, asmalyk, 4½x2¾ ft........................5,500.00
Yomud, dense Dyrnak guls, ram horn skirts, 6½x4½ ft......3,200.00
Ziegler Sultanabad, oversize flowerheads/palmettes, 7x7 ft...3,850.00

Miscellaneous

Felt penny rug, Liberty Bell design, mc on blk, 30x45".......115.00
Felt penny rug, mc w/dia edge border, early 1900s, 39x20", M..85.00
Rag carpet, Pennsylvania, stripes, minor wear, 41"x56 ft.......500.00

Rumrill

During the early 1930s, the Red Wing Union Stoneware Company of Red Wing, Minnesota, produced pottery for George Rumrill of Little Rock, Arkansas. Rumrill not only designed the ware, but marketed it as well. In 1938 when the Shawnee Pottery Company of Zanesville, Ohio, submitted a lower bid, he awarded the contract to them, and they continued to manufacture decorative pottery for Rumrill until the early forties. His designs can be identified by the 'RumRill' mark or label.

Bookend, fan & scroll, gold wing RumRill sticker, #391, pr.....15.00
Candle holder, orange w/3 rows of beads, 3¼", pr...........23.00
Jug, maroon, w/stopper..........................10.00
Pitcher, ice lip, round tilt type, #547..................20.00
Planter, rectangle w/relief grapes, semi-gloss wht, #623........8.00

Vase, bulbous w/long neck, matt bl, imp #308. . . . . .15.00
Vase, Deco nudes, 10″. 55.00
Vase, fan shape, Deco, wht/blk decor. 15.00
Vase, fan shape, turq, 6½x6″. 14.00
Vase, swirl decor, base hdls, matt turq, #I-24. . . . . .18.00
Vase, w/hdls, 11½″. 35.00
Vase, white, 8″. 6.00
Vase, 2 hdls, green & rose, sgn, 7″. .30.00

Russel Wright Dinnerware

Russel Wright, one of America's foremost industrial engineers, also designed several lines of ceramic dinnerware which are today becoming popular collectibles. His first line, American Modern, was manufactured by Steubenville Pottery Company from 1939 until 1959. It was produced in a variety of solid colors, in assortments chosen to stay attune with the times.

In 1944, he designed his Iroquois line. Due in part to its thick and heavy styling, it is more easily found today than American Modern which was prone to easy damage. The earlier examples of Iroquois were heavily mottled, while later pieces were smoothly glazed. The ware was marked with Wright's signature and 'China by Iroquois'. It was marketed in fine department stores throughout the country. After 1950, the line was restyled and marked 'Iroquois China by Russel Wright'.

American Modern

Bowl, covered vegetable; Chartreuse Curray. 18.00
Bowl, divided vegetable; Cedar Green. 35.00
Bowl, divided vegetable; Chartreuse Curray. 30.00
Bowl, salad; Cedar Green. 35.00
Bowl, salad; Chartreuse Curray. 16.00
Bowl, vegetable; Black Chutney. 18.00
Bowl, vegetable; Chartreuse Curray. .15.00
Casserole, Chartreuse Curray. 24.00
Celery dish, Bean Brown. 22.00
Celery dish, Chartreuse Curray. 15.00
Creamer, Chartreuse Curray. 5.00
Creamer, Granite Gray. 5.00
Cup, Black Chutney. 10.00
Cup, Chartreuse Curray. 5.00

Goblet, water. 17.50
Gravy boat, Cedar Green. 18.00
Gravy boat, Chartreuse Curray. 7.00
Hostess set w/cup, Chartreuse Curray. 20.00
Lug fruit. 5.00
Lug soup. 3.00
Mug, Black Chutney. 30.00
Pitcher, water; Black Chutney. 52.00
Pitcher, water; Chartreuse Curray. 40.00
Plate, chop; Chartreuse Curray. 10.00
Plate, dinner; Chartreuse Curray. 3.50
Plate, dinner; Granite Gray. 5.00
Plate, salad; Chartreuse Curray. 3.00
Platter, Chartreuse Curray. 15.00
Platter, Granite Gray. 14.00
Shakers, Chartreuse Curray, pr. 5.00
Sherbet, stemmed. 17.00
Sugar, Chartreuse Curray, w/lid. 6.00
Tumbler, juice. 10.00
Wine, Granite Gray. 16.50

Highlight

Bowl, vegetable. 16.00
Cup. 10.00
Plate, bread & butter. 3.00
Plate, dinner. 8.00
Plate, salad. 6.00

Iroquois

Bowl, divided covered vegetable; avacado. 32.00
Bowl, 5″, brown. 3.50
Butter w/cover, yellow. 35.00
Gumbo, nutmeg, blue, or yellow. 10.00
Stack cream, brown. 5.00
Stack sugar, brown. 6.00

Sterling

Bouillon. 7,00
Bowl, fruit. 4.00
Coffee bottle. 30.00
Creamer. 6.00
Pitcher, water. 25.00
Plate, bread & butter; 6¼″. 2.00
Plate, 10¼″. 5.00
Plate, 11½″. 6.00
Plate, 7½″. 3.00
Plate, 9″. 4.00
Platter, 11¾″. 10.00
Platter, 7⅛″. 6.00
Saucer. 2.00
Soup. 8.00
Teapot. 22.00

Russian Art

Before the Revolution in 1917, many jewelers and craftsmen created exquisite marvels of their arts, distinctive in the extravagant detail of their enamel work, jeweled inlays, and use of precious metals. These treasures aptly symbolized the glitter and the romance of the glorious days under the reign of the Tsars of Imperial Russia.

The most famous of these master jewelers was Peter Carl Faberge.

Iroquois, wine carafe, light pink glaze, 10″, $60.00.

Following the tradition of his father, he took over the Faberge workshop in 1870 at the age of twenty-four. His specialties were enamel work, clockwork automated figures, carved animal and human figures of precious or semiprecious stone, and his best known creations, the Imperial Easter Eggs, each of an entirely different design.

By the turn of the century, his influence had spread to other countries, and his work was revered by royalty and the very wealthy. The onset of the war marked the end of the era.

Bowl, porcelain, Kuznettsoff, 6¾"............................75.00
Box, lacquered, w/Prince & Princess, sgn, w/lid, 5x4x2"......275.00
Carving, chickadee, agate/crockery base, ruby eyes, 3¼".......350.00
Caviar scoup, mc enamel on gold, sgn Faberge, 4¾x1½".....795.00
Ceremonial cup, samovar shape, w/lid, porcelain............195.00
Charm, silver, egg in basket, ⅝"..........................125.00
Cigarette box, lacquered, winter Troika scene................150.00
Cigarette box, mc enamel on gold, sgn Faberge, 3¾x3"....1,195.00
Cuff links, crown w/laurel wreath, gold/diamond/ruby, Faberge.2,800.00
Dish, porcelain, ram w/bl/wht coat, gilded horns, 7" L........95.00
Egg, enamel scenes of Christ & angels, 3", pr..............120.00
Egg, porcelain, bl w/pk florals, 5½"......................300.00
Egg, Resurrection, HP, gold tablets on bk, hanging..........250.00
Figurine, bisque, father, girl on shoulders, doe; Gardner, 12".1,200.00
Figurine, dancing figure w/bottle, mk Faberge, silver/nephrite.1,000.00
Figurine, peasant woman in blk apron/bl jacket, 1800s, 10½"..225.00
Jardiniere, silver/gilt/enamel floral/crest, Ruckert, 3¾".......2,800.00
Kovsh, bird form hdl, angels/knights in reserve, 1883, 6½"..4,000.00
Kovsh, enamel silver/nephrite, Imperial Crest, Faberge, 3¼"..1,600.00
Napkin ring, silver/enamel floral..........................200.00
Pendant, silver gilt/diamond/builloche, Faberge, 1¼".......1,300.00
Salt, open; matching spoon, sgn 1895 GK, Moscow mk........350.00
Spoon, bl/red florals, silver gilt, twist hdl w/mc, #84, 5"......250.00
Spoon, mc enamel on gold, 7" L, 2½" dia bowl, Faberge.....495.00
Spoon, pierced silver bowl, geometric/floral, 88 std/AK, 5¾"...300.00
Spoon, silver/enamel floral, mk 84 std, 7½"................400.00
Stanhope, carved bone cross, picture: head of Russian church...70.00
Tea strainer, gold washed, Nikolay Dubroven, ornate, 1838....150.00
Vodka cup, mc enamel on gold, sgn Faberge, 2x1¾" dia......450.00
Vodka cup, plique a jour/silver, scrolls/florals, Ovchinnikov...1,600.00

Enamel and silver gilt kovsh, circular reserves with angels each side of large central reserve with mounted knight, bird form handle; marked with Ovchinnikov in Cryillic, Imperial Crest and 88 standard, testers mark and date 1883, 6½", $4,000.00.

Sabino

Sabino art glass was produced by Marius-Ernest Sabino in France during the 1920s and thirties. It was made in opalescent, frosted, and colored glass, and was designed to reflect the Art Deco style of that era. In 1960, using molds he modeled by hand, Sabino once again began to produce art glass using a special formula he himself developed that was characterized by a golden opalescence. Although the family continued to produce glassware for export after his death in 1971, they were never able to duplicate Sabino's formula.

Butterfly, large...183.00
Cat, sitting; sgn, 2¼".....................................28.00
Collie dog, 2"...42.00
Cologne, Petalia, orig stopper, 5½".......................145.00
Dragonfly..85.00
Fish, large, St Yves.......................................64.00
Knife rest, figural squirrel on log.........................75.00
Napkin ring, birds around edge, sgn.......................37.50
Nude silhouette, Art Deco, 7".............................140.00
Nude w/Pouter Pigeons....................................365.00
Owl..67.00
Tray, Thistle..36.00
Vase, Art Deco, topaz, 12"................................475.00
Vase, basketweave geometric, globular, early 1900s, 7".....70.00
Vase, Beehive, bulbous....................................235.00
Vase, Wisteria, serrated leaf rim, amethyst on frost, 5½x8"...250.00

Salesman's Samples

Axe head, wood, paper label, Collins Co...................27.00
Brick, Buffalo, w/emb buffalo..............................40.00
Canoe, fishing; aluminum, EX detail, 42" L................75.00
Canoe, Old Town..475.00
Clock, mantel; fancy brass face ring, 6½"................140.00
Damper motor, instructional, Blue Coal Co................65.00
Egg beater, Betty Taplin, 5½"............................17.50
Furnace, Sunbeam, in case w/brochure, 1935..............350.00
Hat, Stetson, soft hat in small box.......................22.00
Horse-drawn wagon's 5th wheel, oak/iron..................45.00
Ice cream freezer, Wht Mountain Jr.......................195.00
Meat grinder, CI, JP Co, NY...............................30.00
Mixing bowl, tan stoneware w/br lining, 3½"..............20.00
Paddle, wood, Beaver Brand Paddles......................18.00
Rocker, oak, caned bk & seat..............................55.00
Rubber glove, Wilson Rubber, miniature...................15.00
Shoe, Florsheim, golden chalkware, 3½"...................35.00
Shotgun case, leather, Nott Maker, 13½"..................75.00
Sleigh, lifts off w/stakes for hauling, 46"................650.00
Stove, Charter Oak #503, reservoir lid gone...............960.00
Stove, gas heating, Schneider & Trend Kamp...............375.00
Stove, six lids, reservoir, stove pipe, old, 16x10x16", M.....600.00
Table, Shaker harvest, 3 drw, 7x15".......................50.00
Tire, Bunting, Puncture Proof, rubber, 8".................20.00
Tub, bath; CI & enamel, on 4 legs.........................35.00
Tub, wash; metal, US Steel................................40.00
Washer, Paramount Steam, 1 gal sz, pat 1925..............275.00
Washer, Speed Queen, in box..............................85.00
Washer, Wolverine Deluxe, metal/plastic lid...............120.00
Whisk broom, Union Made, 1893...........................16.00
Wicker, table/chair/loveseat...............................47.00

Saloon Memorabilia

The period between the Civil War and the onset of the prohibition era in 1919 furnishes the most charming and collectible examples of early saloon memorabilia. Photographs of early establishments, beer steins, advertising signs, and 'bar room nude' portraits are only a few of the varied items from the Golden Age of saloons that are popular with today's collectors.

Bottle, back bar; cut/gold Belle of Kentucky, fully ribbed, NM...98.00
Bottle, back bar; cut/gold Brook Hill, beveled glass neck, NM...65.00
Bottle, back bar; cut/gold Westminster Rye, cylinder, M, 11"....65.00
Bottle, back bar; emb wht Paul Jones, fluted neck...........100.00
Bottle, back bar; raised wht letters, lg cut stopper............65.00
Bottle, back bar; red over gold Solo Rye, neck/base fluted, 9"..115.00
Hatchet, metal, w/Carrie Nation cut-out, motto, orig pnt, 11½".100.00
Shot glass, Democratic Happy Days..........................7.50
Shot glass, Jack Daniel's Whiskey...........................7.50
Table, heavy CI base, rnd marble top, ornate...............200.00

Salt Glaze

As early as the 1600s, potters used common salt to glaze their stoneware. This was accomplished by heating the salt, and introducing it into the kiln at maximum temperature. The resulting gray-white glaze was a thin, pitted surface that resembled the peel of an orange.

Creamer, wht, intricate embossing, mk Pub Nov 1, 1839, Meigh.65.00
Creamer, wht, melon rib, emb vintage, Havelock, pewter lid, 5"..55.00
Pitcher, bl/wht, Nouveau devices, imp Copeland, 7¼".........55.00
Pitcher, emb cherubs, English reg mk, 11"..................85.00
Pitcher, Good Samaritan relief, violet tint, mk Pat, 4¼".....135.00
Pitcher, lt gr, emb cattails, English reg mk, 4"..............55.00
Pitcher, lt gr, hound hdl, emb hanging game, base flake, 7¼"...70.00
Pitcher, profile of Napoleon ea side, 6"...................125.00
Pitcher, putty, hound hdl, emb hounds & deer, 5"............40.00
Pitcher, wht, bl classical figures/dancers, hairlines, 6¾".......55.00
Syrup jug, fuschia in allover relief, 7½"....................30.00
Syrup jug, James Dixon & Sons, reg mk, 1868, 8"..........185.00

Salts

Before salt became refined, processed, and 'free-flowing' as we know it today, it was necessary to serve it in a 'cellar'. An innovation of the early 1800s, the master salt cellar was placed by the host and passed from person to person. Smaller 'individual' salts were a part of each place setting. A small silver spoon was used to sprinkle it onto the food.

The screw top salt shaker was invented by John Mason in 1858. In 1871, when salt became more refined, some ceramic shakers were molded with pierced tops. 'Christmas' shakers, so called because of their December 25, 1877, patent date, were fitted with a rotary agitator designed to break up any lumps in the salt. They were produced by the Boston and Sandwich Glass Company in various colors.

Open Salts

In the listing below, the numbers refer to *Pressed Glass Salt Dishes*, by L.W. and D.B. Neal.

Acorn, master, flint.......................................20.00
Almond Thumbprint, ftd, sm flakes on lid, 4¼"...............65.00

Amethyst flashed, 10 panels.............................10.00
Apollo, master, flat....................................25.00
Argus Variant, clear flint, 2¾", G.......................18.00
Banded Paneled Stippled Bowl, master, flat................24.00
Basket, Bull's Eye & Diamond Point, Sandwich............100.00
Basket, lacy, opal, minor flakes, 3⅛"....................105.00
Bellflower, master, flint...............................35.00
Birch Leaf, opaque white, flint.........................30.00
Bird w/cherry in mouth, amber...........................5.00
Bleeding Heart, master, oval...........................45.00
Blown, cobalt, applied ft, 19 vertical ribs swirl at top, 3⅛"....145.00
Blown 3 mold, applied hdl, 2x3¼"......................115.00
Buckle, master, flint...................................25.00
Buckle w/Star, master, ped ft...........................25.00
Bulging Bull's Eye, master..............................8.00
Bull's Eye w/Fleur-de-lis, petal foot, flint, 2½".............40.00
Butterfly, master, ped ft, flint.........................42.00
Buttressed Loop, master, on 4 ft........................15.00
Cambridge, plain w/rayed bottom, ped ft, 1½"..............6.00
Canterbury, Duncan & Miller............................5.00
Cloisonne, gr w/in & w/out w/wht & lav flowers on side, China...35.00
Colonial, #2570, Cambridge, ind, 1⅞"....................6.50
Colorado, bowl, ftd, 7"................................15.00
Cut glass, ped ft, diamond points, 2½x2½"................20.00
Cut glass, rnd w/narrow panels of straight cuts & notches......12.50
Cut glass, rnd w/6 panels, star in base...................8.00
Daisy & Button, tub, blue, 1x2".........................25.00
Diamond Point Discs, ftd, scalloped.....................10.00
Diamond Rosettes, master, flat.........................13.50
Diamond Sunburst, master, ped ft.......................14.00
Duralex, Made in France, ind, clear w/concentric circles........3.50
Early Thumbprint, master, flint.........................45.00
Eureka, master, flint..................................25.00
Excelsior, clear flint, ftd, minor edge flakes, 2¼"...........18.00
Excelsior w/Maltese Cross, master, flat, flint, no harm chip....22.00
Flattened Sawtooth, flint, clear, 2½x3½"..................25.00
Flint, hexagonal w/panel ft & petal top, 3⅛"...............65.00
Fluted sides, rayed bottom, pressed glass, sm, rnd...........6.00
Frosted Roman Key, master, flint........................35.00
Gothic Arch, flint, sm edge flakes, 3"....................15.00
Grasshopper, master, ftd..............................12.00
Green, ftd, ribbing around bowl.........................38.00
Hairpin, master, cover chipped..........................65.00

French enamel holder and spoon, glass insert, 2¼" diameter, $67.50.

Hamilton, master, ped ft................................25.00
Harp, clear flint, ftd, 2".............................10.00
Hexagonal Urn, clear flint, ftd, minor edge flakes, 3¼".......18.00
Hexagonal w/Oval Bull's Eyes, clear flint, ftd, 3", G..........18.00
Hinoto, master, flint................................35.00
Hobnail, master, clear, rnd...........................10.00
Horizontal Oval Frames, master, ped ft, flint...............55.00
Horn of Plenty, master, oval...........................69.50
Horseshoe design, ftd w/lid, minor roughness, 4"...........25.00
Inverted Fern, master, flint...........................35.00
King's Crown, ind, rectangular.........................12.00
Lacy, Neal-BS-3, opal, scarce, 3⅛"......................60.00
Lacy, Neal-BT-4d, violet bl w/opal mottle, crack in bow, 3½"...325.00
Lacy, Neal-CD-2, clear w/lid, minor flakes, 3¼".............75.00
Lacy, Neal-EE, scarce, 3¼"............................70.00
Lacy, Neal-EE-1a, chip on lip, 3".......................30.00
Lacy, Neal-EE-7, rare, chip on rim, 3¾"..................160.00
Lacy, Neal-EE-8a, crack in rim, very rare, 2x3"............75.00
Lacy, Neal-HN-8, sm edge flakes, scarce, 3¼"..............65.00
Lacy, Neal-LE-1a, clear, rare, 3⅛".....................65.00
Lacy, Neal-OL-12a, base chips, scarce, 3½"...............25.00
Lacy, Neal-OL-16, scarce, 3¼".........................40.00
Lacy, Neal-OO-25, minor flakes, scarce, 4"...............20.00
Lacy, Neal-OP-2, sm rim flakes, scarce, 3½"..............50.00
Lacy, Neal-PO-5, mold did not completely fill, 4"...........35.00
Lacy, Neal-PP-3, rim flakes, 2x3¼".....................45.00
Lacy, Neal-RP-18, rim & base flakes, scarce, 1¾x3"........45.00
Lacy, Neal-SD-12, cobalt, 3", G........................45.00
Lacy, Neal-SD-14, clear, 2¾".........................10.00
Lacy, Neal-SD-15b, clear, very rare, rim chips, 2¾".........22.50
Lacy, Neal-SL-1, very rare, 3", VG.....................80.00
Lady & Cupid, reclining, pk w/intaglio cutting, jeweled basket...38.00
Lily of the Valley, clear pressed, ftd w/lid, 4"............45.00
Magnet & Grape w/Frosted Leaf, master, flint..............50.00
Mercury glass, master, ped ft..........................25.00
Milk glass, ind, dia ped ft, serrated top w/stars in diamonds.....10.00
Milk glass, ind, ped ft, fluted on bowl & ft................10.00
Mirror, master, flint, w/cover.........................95.00
Monet Stumpf, Pantin, France, cranberry opal, orig label.....125.00
Nordic boat w/dragon head ends, crystal/silver, #830 European..45.00
Oak Leaf Band, master, ped ft.........................22.00
Pairpoint, master, clear w/controlled bubbles..............75.00
Pavonia, ind, clear...................................6.50
Petal & Loop, clear flint, ftd, 3¼", G...................22.00
Pewter, master, mk Tudric, #01072, w/cobalt liner...........30.00
Picket, master, oblong...............................35.00
Porcelain, ind, allover gold, 3 ft.......................10.00
Portland Tree of Life, master, 3" dia....................45.00
Pressed Block, clear flint, ftd, 2¾", G..................12.00
Pressed Leaf, master, ped ft, flint......................20.00
Reverse 44, master, ftd..............................12.00
Ribbed Bell Flower, sm flakes on ft, 2¾"................35.00
Ribbed Ivy, clear flint, ftd, 2½".......................20.00
Ribbed Palm, master, flint............................35.00
RS Germany, 2 hdls, gold trim on wht....................38.00
Russian enamel, mc w/silver gilt interior, 3 ft............245.00
Sawtooth, flint, ftd w/lid, minor chips on lid, 5⅛".........20.00
Sawtooth, opaque wht, ftd w/lid, minor edge flakes, 5".......55.00
Sawtooth & Circle, master, ped ft, flint..................30.00
Sedan, master, flat..................................12.50
Silver overlay, floral design, 1½x2"....................65.00
Silverplate, hunting scene w/dog & bird in base, James Tufts...20.00
Silverplate, 4 ft, mk MIE for BA & Co....................8.00
Snail, ind..25.00

Sterling, reticulated holder, cobalt liner.................35.00
Sterling, 6 sides w/amethyst liner, +ind pepper & spoon......52.00
Sterling holder w/str panel sides, cobalt liner, star in base.....25.00
Stippled Swag, master, ped ft.........................15.00
Sunburst & Bar, Hobbs, Brockunier, master...............16.50
Swan figural, opal glass, 3½".........................40.00
Three Row Argus, master, flint........................30.00
Thumbprint, clear flint, ftd, minor edge flakes, 2¼".........18.00
Thumbprint, 8 around, rayed base.......................4.00
Torpedo, 1½" dia...................................12.00
Tree of Life, master, flint............................30.00
Tulip & Sawtooth, master, flint........................40.00
Twelve Diamond, blown, applied foot, 3", G...............35.00
Two Panel, master, blue..............................16.00
Vaseline, applied shells, master......................140.00
Waffle & Thumbprint, master..........................25.00
Washington Centennial, master.........................30.00
Waterford, master, high ped ft, rolled rim, 4"............65.00
Westmoreland, master, flat............................23.00
Zipper, ind, Pitkins & Brooks, 1½".......................8.00

Shakers

In the following listing, prices are for single shakers unless noted 'pair'.

Acorn, pink to wht, pr...............................65.00
Ada..12.00
Barreled Block.....................................12.00
Beaded Dahlia, pink, pr.............................65.00
Beaded Vertical, wht................................12.00
Block & Panel......................................12.00
Bulging Loop, yellow cased, pr........................70.00
Bulging Petal, wht..................................25.00
Burmese, ribbed, glossy, Mt Washington, 4".............140.00
Butterfly, wht.....................................30.00
Button Block.......................................12.00
Cane Woven, blue, pr................................38.00
Christmas, cobalt, pewter lid, 2½"....................42.50
Christmas Panel, agitator, dtd lid, amber...............75.00
Chrysanthemum Sprig, custard, pr.....................100.00
Circle Scroll, gr opal...............................70.00
Clematis & Scroll...................................10.00
Cone, blue opaque, tall, pr...........................40.00
Corn, custard, pr...................................95.00
Corn Bulging, wht..................................35.00
Cotton Bale, blue, pr................................42.00
Cotton Bale, gr opaque..............................19.00
Creased Neck, flower decor...........................12.00
Creased Waist, wht w/flowers.........................25.00
Croesus, emerald green, base roughness.................30.00
Curved Body, 'S'...................................25.00
Custard, bulbous, souvenir SD........................40.00
Diamond Base, wht...................................8.00
Diamond Point & Leaf, blue...........................55.00
Diamond Point & Leaf, wht...........................50.00
Diamond w/Double Fan...............................12.00
Dogwood Paneled....................................15.00
Doodad...18.00
Double Crossroads, amber, pr.........................30.00
Dwarf...8.00
Elongated Drops, wht w/flowers.......................25.00
Empress, green & gold, pr...........................150.00
Fan Band Double, wht................................15.00
Feather, long......................................35.00

Fig, cranberry satin w/EX enamel decor, orig lid............115.00
Fig, wht w/floral decor, pr.................................130.00
Fine Cut Flattened, amber...................................18.00
Fine Cut Paneled...12.00
Fishscale..25.00
Flower Band, red satin w/enameling, pr....................125.00
Flower Footed, wht...12.00
Fluted Scroll, blue opal...................................35.00
Foggy Bottom, vaseline.....................................80.00
Forget-Me-Not, regular, wht................................27.00
Forget-Me-Not, tall, wht...................................35.00
Frazier, cranberry flashed/enamel, MOP/metal top, pr......39.00
Fruit Band...18.00
Gaelic...12.00
Galloway...12.00
Guttate, pink satin..45.00
Guttate, wht...35.00
Half Cone, pink cased......................................65.00
Hand & Fishscale...18.00
Heart, milk glass, orig lid................................22.00
Intaglio, w/green & gold, old lid..........................95.00
Inverted Fan & Feather, custard, EX gold & enamel, orig lid...175.00
Inverted Thumbprint, blue w/enameled flowers, pr...........75.00
Iowa, w/gold...18.00
Iris w/Meander, gold trim, pr..............................40.00
Jackson, blue opal...35.00
Jewel & Flower, clear opal.................................65.00
Klondike, frosted & gold, pr..............................195.00
Leaf, twisted, pink cased..................................19.00
Leaf & Flower, amber stain.................................29.00
Leaf Berry, milk glass, 4 ft,..............................90.00
Leaf Cornered Base, wht....................................15.00
Leaf Mold, blue opaque, pr.................................85.00
Leaf Mold, vaseline spatter................................55.00
Leaf Overlapping, blue.....................................45.00
Leaf Palm, blue opaque.....................................19.00
Liberty Bell, orig pewter top..............................55.00
Lobe Five, wide base.......................................45.00
Louis XV, custard w/trace of gold, pr.....................165.00
Maize, custard, w/yellow leaves............................90.00
Melon Ribbed, wht w/flower.................................18.00
Mt Washington, egg, floral decor...........................40.00
Mt Washington, tomato, shaded wht satin/EX decor/orig lid, pr.125.00
Net & Scroll, blue opaque, pr..............................45.00
Paneled Teardrop, green custard, old tops, pr..............65.00
Pineapple, figured, green opaque, pr.......................49.00
Pineapple & Fan, clear, w/sterling lid.....................20.00
Pressed Diamond, blue......................................30.00
Quilted Phlox..19.00
Reverse Swirl, vaseline opal...............................25.00
Rib Scrolled, wht..20.00
Ribbed Base, wht w/flower..................................15.00
Rose Viking, amber...18.00
Royal Oak, frosted rubena, pair...........................150.00
Ruby Thumbprint, w/fern & berry etching....................30.00
Satin, w/enamel tulip......................................20.00
Sawtooth & Thin Line, wht w/flowers........................15.00
Sawtooth Bulbous, amber....................................22.00
Scroll, low, green...30.00
Scroll Tapered, wht w/flowers..............................15.00
Scrolled Panel, milk glass, old tops, pr...................50.00
Shell Overlapping, pink....................................30.00
Shrine...25.00
Spanish Lace, clear opal...................................45.00

Split Rib, wht/yellow......................................12.00
Squatty Lobes..86.00
Stripe Vertical, opalescent canary.........................28.00
Sunk Honeycomb, red flashed, orig lid......................30.00
Sunrise, pink opaque.......................................22.00
Sunset, wht..25.00
Swirl, clear opal..45.00
Tassel, wht..15.00
Three Face, clear & frosted, old tops, pr..................65.00
Toltec...10.00
Tree of Life, green, tall style, pr........................75.00
Truncated Cube, ruby stained, old top......................18.00
Vine w/Flower, wht...15.00
Wild Rose w/Bow Knot.......................................15.00
Windows Swirl, cranberry opal, Hobb's, pr.................125.00
Wisconsin, clear, orig lids, pr............................45.00
X-Ray, pr..87.00

Samplers

American samplers were made as early as the colonial days; even earlier examples from 17th century England still exist today. Changes in style and decorative motif are evident down through the years. Verses were not added until the late 17th century. By the 18th century, samplers were used not only for sewing experience but as an educational tool. Young ladies who often signed and dated their work embroidered numbers and characters of the alphabet, as well as fancy stitches. Fruits and flowers were added for borders; birds, animals, and Adam and Eve were popular subjects. Later, houses and other buildings were included. By the 19th century, the American Eagle and the little red schoolhouse had made their appearance.

Alphabet, homespun linen, dtd 1819, 10x12"................135.00
Alphabet, vining border, urn of flowers, linen, w/provenance....600.00
Alphabet at top upside down, florals, homespun, 17x24"......150.00
Alphabets, crowns, linen homespun, faded, 1790, 9½x19".....215.00
Alphabets, flower baskets, faded, dtd 1787, 9½x17".........195.00
Alphabets, flowering border, stylized pots, verse, 1825, 20"....270.00
Alphabets, flowers, sgn 1844, homespun, holes, 18x19".......200.00
Alphabets, house, trees, birds, man, lady, 1784, 12x13"....525.00
Alphabets, house, vines, dtd 1817, linen homespun, 10½x15"..175.00
Alphabets, landscape, florals, 1811, 18¾" sq.............1,000.00
Alphabets, red w/gr dividing design, 1813, homespun, 10x12"..250.00
Alphabets, stars, homespun, faded, in cherry fr, 10½" sq....225.00
Alphabets, trees, animals, moralistic verse, 1824, fr, 16"....275.00
Alphabets, vines, flowers, 1815, linen homespun, 14x16"....275.00
Alphabets, vining border, name/1831, unfinished, 18" sq....200.00
Alphanumerics, crowned lions/woman/trees, no date, 17x17½"..250.00
Alphanumerics, house/trees/vines, homespun, 1826, 19x20"...395.00
Alphanumerics, trees/birds, silk/wool on linen, 1837, 19x16"..465.00
Alphanumerics, vining border, deer, sgn/dtd 1820, fr, 18x15"..260.00
Alphanumerics, vining floral border, 1817, homespun, 24" sq..400.00
Birds/pots of flowers/meandering vine, fine work, 1827, 30x33".990.00
Building/trees/birds/animals/people/poem, in fr, 21" sq....350.00
Family record, roses/flowering vines/trees, 1843, 17¾x18¾"..475.00
Family record, 3 columns, EX close work, 1843, 18x19"......400.00
Farm scene w/house/sheep/fence/birds, 1840s, 17x21"......2,090.00
Flowers, 3 panels poetry, sgn, homespun, in fr, 15x18", G..225.00
Flowers center panel w/flower basket/plaited trees, 1793, 22"..850.00
House/shepherdess/9 sheep/dog/squirrel, EX detail, 1794, 20".3,100.00
House/trees/animals, 2 verses, 1822, linen.................875.00
Lovebirds/flowers/etc on linen handkerchief, 1802, holes...175.00
Meadow w/sheep/shepherd/maid/lg brick house, 1812, 20x24"..625.00
Miniature, alphanumerics & name, no fr, 7½x9½".............175.00

Needlepoint, birds, building/animals, 1855, 19x20"...........550.00
Needlepoint, mc florals/baskets/shepherd w/flock/cottage, 25"...400.00
Open weave border, record, 1788, many designs, 17", EX.....750.00
Verse, alphabet, bird decor, dated 1820, 16½x17½"..........295.00
Verse, angels/flowers/house/fence/trees, 1836, bird's eye fr.....575.00
Verse, house/animals/angels/flowers, 1845, framed, 13x17".....250.00
Verse, panel w/deer/lg bird/flowering trees, EX work, 23x26".1,325.00
Verse, rose border w/birds/baskets, 1822, incomplete, 24x28"..450.00
Verse, strawberry border, flowers, people, homespun, 11x14"...250.00
Verses, alphanumerics, animals/birds, 1818, English, fr, 12"....275.00
Verses, florals above house, vine border, 1800s, 16x13".......275.00

Shepherdess, sheep, dog, squirrel, deer, angels, doves, building; signed and dated 1794, finely executed on homespun, 16" x 20", $3,100.00.

Sandwich Glass

The Boston and Sandwich Glass Company was founded in 1820 by Deming Jarves in Sandwich, Massachusetts. Their first products were simple cruets, salts, half pint jugs, and lamps. They were attributed as being one of the first to perfect a method for pressing glass, a step toward the manufacture of the 'lacy' glass, which they made until about 1840. Many other types of glass were made there -- cut, colored, snakeskin, hobnail, and opalescent among them.

After the Civil War, profits began to dwindle due to the keen competition of the Western factories who were situated in areas rich in natural gas and more suitable coal and sand resources. The end came with an unreconcilable wage dispute between the workers and the company, and the factory closed in 1888.

In the following listings, the use of the 'G' to denote 'good condition', takes into account the minor flakes that often occur in Sandwich glass.

See also specific types of glass.

Bank, bird finial, knob stem/coins embedded, clear/bl rigaree...700.00
Bowl, lacy, stippled, scalloped w/scroll & rosette bands, 8"......75.00

Candlestick, crucifix, canary, 11½", pr.....................150.00
Candlestick, crucifix, peacock gr, 10", pr....................375.00
Candlestick, dolphin base, canary, petal socket, 10½", G......175.00
Candlestick, hex base, petal socket, clambroth, 7½", G.......145.00
Candlestick, loop base, olive gr, 7", pr......................500.00
Candlestick, loop base, petal top, canary, sm flakes, 6½".....115.00
Candlestick, petal top/hex base, med bl, 7½", pr............525.00
Celery vase, Sandwich Loop, canary........................295.00
Cologne, amethyst, pewter cap.............................60.00
Cologne, hexagon, cut stopper, deep canary, ground lip/top, 5".165.00
Cologne, hexagon w/Bull's Eye/Punty, apple gr, cut stopper, 5".510.00
Cologne, Star & Punty, canary.............................300.00
Covered dish, hen on nest, clambroth, 5½x7½"..............225.00
Creamer, lacy, miniature....................................95.00
Decanter, bar lip, Sandwich Star, qt, pr....................175.00
Decanter, bar lip, Waffle & Bull's Eye, canary, 12"..........900.00
Lamp, cobalt/clear overlay, pear font, 11"...................550.00
Lamp, whale oil, 3 Punty Block, sm inside base chip.........135.00
Pitcher, Hobnail, peachblow, clear frosted reed hdl, 6".......310.00
Plate, lacy, stippled, scalloped, shield/anchor, 8"............60.00
Plate, Scotch Plaid, ca 1840, 8"............................45.00
Pomade jar, bear, bl opaque, polished base.................175.00
Pomade jar, bear, clambroth, FB Strouse, rim & ft flake, 3¾"..215.00
Salt, boat, opal, sm rim & base flakes, 3¾"..................185.00
Spill holder, Bull's Eye & Punty, electric bl, 4½", VG.......425.00
Spill holder, Bull's Eye & Punty, opal, 5".....................270.00
Spill holder, Dia Quilt, 3 dia w/Bull's Eye, amethyst, 4½"....480.00
Spill holder, Dia Quilt, 3 dia w/Bull's Eye, canary, 4½".......275.00
Spill holder, Sandwich Star, canary, ground pontil...........400.00
Spill holder, Sandwich Star, deep electric bl, 5⅛".........575.00
Sugar bowl, Gothic Arch, canary, VG.......................700.00
Toothpick, Baby Mine, camphor glass........................85.00
Tray, Butterfly, lacy, 8x5½"...............................195.00
Tray, Scroll & Fleur-de-lis, 6".............................45.00
Tumbler, paneled, footed, canary, 4¼", G...................60.00
Vase, hex w/circle/ellipse bowl/ruffled rim, canary, 7½", G......75.00
Vase, hex w/3 Punty & Block bowl, ruffled, canary, 9½", G....100.00
Vase, rnd ft w/hex bowl, dbl punty, ruffled, canary, 6"........200.00
Vase, tulip, emerald gr, 9½".............................450.00
Vase, tulip, violet bl, minor ft flakes, 10¼"..............500.00
Whiskey taster, canary....................................145.00

Sarreguemines

Sarreguemines, France, is the location of Utzschneider and Company, founded in 1770, producers of transfer printed dinnerware, figurines, and novelty ware, usually marked 'Sarreguemines'.

Basket, w/domed fruit lid, majolica, 8½x7"..................75.00
Compote, pastel floral sprigs on ivory, 5x8½"..............47.00
Creamer, row of ducks, frog, flower border, 5".............45.00
Pitcher, children in trees in high relief....................110.00
Pitcher, happy face reverses to frown on bk, 8¾"...........75.00
Pitcher, man's face figural, majolica, sgn, 7½"............75.00
Plate, 'Cluny', cobalt & gold trim, 9¾"....................25.00
Plate, apples, majolica, 7½"..............................25.00
Plate, boy & girl in doorway, 8½".........................35.00
Plate, cobalt, wide etched lacy gold border & center, 8".......20.00
Plate, Foreign Legionnaires, pr...........................50.00
Plate, oyster; peach & gray, sgn..........................40.00
Plate, pk lattice edge, wht woven center w/2 lg gr leaves, 8½"...10.00
Plate, St Joan, various scenes, set of 4...................100.00
Plate, strawberries, plums, grapes, majolica, 12"...........85.00

Satin Glass

Satin glass is simply glassware with a velvety matt finish achieved through the application of an acid bath. This procedure has been used by many companies since the 19th century both here and abroad, on many types of colored and art glass.

Pitcher, white with enameled beetles and thistle plants, 9″, $125.00.

Bowl, beige w/gold roses & leaves, crimp/fluted rim, 10½″.....150.00
Bowl, bl/cased, sheaves of wheat, crimped top, 6x4½″.........65.00
Bowl, w/lid; vaseline, 3 applied ft, light ribbing, roses, 3½″....125.00
Cracker jar, bl, bulbous w/swirls, SP rim/lid/bale.............160.00
Cracker jar, Open Heart Arches, red, enamel florals, SP trim...165.00
Creamer, Beaded Drape, lime gr.........................85.00
Ewer, bl cased w/wht, floral, 9¼″.........................85.00
Ewer, lime gr cased w/wht, floral, 9″, pr...................150.00
Ewer, pearl shading to rose, cased, camphor thorn hdl, 13″....235.00
Ewer, pink cased w/wht, bird decor, 10″....................85.00
Pitcher, rose, Florette pattern, camphor hdl, 7″.............200.00
Rose bowl, bl, ped base, 5″.............................90.00
Rose bowl, bl shaded, wht cased, 3¾″.....................95.00
Rose bowl, bl/wht w/in, 8 crimp top, frosted ft, pnt daisy, 4″...135.00
Rose bowl, egg shape, ftd, bl/wht w/in, floral/butterfly, 5½″....135.00
Rose bowl, pk w/enamel flowers, artist sgn, 4″..............95.00
Rose bowl, pk w/wht florals, maroon foliage, 5x5½″.........175.00
Rose bowl, rose to pk/wht w/in, emb florals, 8 crimps, 3½x4″..120.00
Rose bowl, wht shading to lemon, 4″......................75.00
Rose bowl, yel shading to cream, 6x6″....................95.00
Tumbler, beige w/gold & enamel decor....................65.00
Tumbler, bl w/wht lining, peacock feather pattern, 2x3¾″......38.00
Vase, bl/wht verre moire w/wht loopings, fluted, 3¾x3½″......135.00
Vase, cased shaded pk/wht, gold decor, scalloped, 9″.........195.00
Vase, Nouveau lady w/flowing hair in enamel/silver on gr......400.00
Vase, orange striations, cased, 9x5″......................130.00
Vase, peach w/decor, ruffle/cone on fluted body/3 ftd, 9″, pr...225.00
Vase, pk, decorated, applied camphor glass hdls, 6½″.........95.00
Vase, pk, w/enamel yel rose, ruffled, 10½″.................165.00
Vase, shaded pk, wht w/in, floral enamel, melon rib/hdls, 5½″..195.00
Vase, shaded rose, wht pnt flowers, gold foliage, 7x4½″.......195.00
Vase, tan, thorn overlay, crimped, camphor ft, pk w/in, 14″....295.00
Vase, yel shade to wht, folded & ruffled, 9½″...............150.00
Water set, Cone, yel, 7 pc............................265.00

Satsuma

Satsuma is a type of fine cream crackle-glaze pottery or earthenware made in Japan as early as the 17th century. The earliest wares, made at the original kiln in the Satsuma province, were enameled with only simple florals. By the late 18th century a floral brocade, or nishikide, design was favored, and similar wares were being made at other kilns under the direction of the Lord of Satsuma. In the early part of the 19th century, a diaper pattern was added to the florals. Gold and silver enameling was used for accents by the latter years of the century.

During the 1850s, as the quantity of goods made for export to the Western world increased and the style of decoration began to evolve toward becoming more appealing to the Westerners, human forms such as Arhats, Kannon, Geisha girls, and Samurai warriors were added.

Today the most valuable pieces are those marked 'Kinkozan', 'Shuzan', 'Ryuzan', and 'Kozan'. The genuine Satsuma 'mon' or mark is an 'X' within a circle -- it may appear anywhere on the ware.

Bottle, gold on wht, florals, gourd shape, 5″...............475.00
Bottle, Nishikide diapering/mums/butterflies, dbl gourd, 6″.....165.00
Bowl, diapered border w/figures, florals, gold trim, 10″.......125.00
Bowl, wisteria/butterflies, Kinkozan, late 19th C, 5″.........195.00
Box, canted corners, children/swans, scenes w/in, 3½″........450.00
Box, Thousand Butterflies, sgn, 4″ dia....................400.00
Buttons, florals, geisha girls, set of 6....................45.00
Censer w/lid, mc/gilt landscape w/pavilions/maples, 3½″........60.00
Chalice, mc butterlies w/in, mc florals w/out, silver base, 6″...1,500.00
Compote, Arhats raised w/halos, dragon on stand, 4¾x7″.....250.00
Creamer & sugar, birds & flowers, sgn, 1880................75.00
Dish, scalloped, 3 boys on terrace w/tutors, 9½″ dia.........150.00
Ewer, mums w/gold tracing/scrolls, allover jewels on rose, 11″..125.00
Ewer, Thousand Faces, dragon spout, sgn, 1900, 12″, G......700.00
Figurine, man sitting on 2 barrels, br/yel/gold, 2¾x1¾″.......60.00
Ginger jar, inner & outer lid, good decor, 9″...............110.00
Ginger jar, men/bluebird/heron, red & bl, 5″...............650.00
Jar w/lid, Orientals in garden scene, stylized dragon hdls, 9″...275.00
Jardiniere, pastel mums/diaper borders/gold trim, ca 1900, 6¾″.135.00
Koro w/cover, foo dog motif, purple/gold, 15″..............135.00
Lamp, blk w/figures in high relief, much gold, lg............875.00
Plate, Kinkozan style florals, gold, red mk, 7¼″.............45.00

Vase, human forms, gold trim, 24½″, $950.00.

Plate, wisteria, scenic in circle, much gold, 7¼".............45.00
Powder jar, allover slip trail/jewels, squirrels/grapes, 9¾"......110.00
Shakers, rust/bl florals, gold tops, pr......................22.00
Tankard, lake w/beauties, pagoda in gold/enamel, Awata, 13"...285.00
Tankard, trumpet flowers/bird/wisteria, 4 character mks, 5".....45.00
Teapot, children play ball in garden, mc floral, sgn, 3x4".....725.00
Teapot, cr/sug, 6 c/s; wisteria on cream, gold decor, 1920s.....275.00
Teapot, mums, butterflies, mc, ca 1800s....................95.00
Teapot, pnt cranes/flowers, butterfly finial, Kinkozan, 6½".....125.00
Teapot, 4 c/s; Arhat & Kwannon in bl enamel, 1850s........600.00
Urn, warrior/flowers, foo dog hdls & finials, 1900s, 10", pr...290.00
Vase, bamboo hdls, bl w/butterflies, wht/pk lily, Awata, 10½"...125.00
Vase, beige crackle w/wisteria in red/purple, red mk/crest, 6"...385.00
Vase, bird, lt bl/gold flowers on cream, 10¼"...............75.00
Vase, bl bk, panels: ladies, lg lotus; dragon hdls, 1900, 25"....450.00
Vase, bl w/3" beige top band w/wht mums, gold scrolls, '25, 8"..50.00
Vase, bl/wht w/florals, hdls/ped base, Awata, 1880, 16".......250.00
Vase, haloed Arhats/Kwannon, ca 1915, 12½"...............225.00
Vase, haloed Arhats/Kwannon, red/orange/bl/gold, 1920s, 9½"...145.00
Vase, high quality Bamboo pattern, ca 1910, mini, 2½".......95.00
Vase, ladies in medallions, much cobalt & gold, 6½", pr......695.00
Vase, mc florals, sgn, 2½"................................50.00
Vase, pear shape w/hdls, ped base, florals, Awata, 1880, 16½".255.00
Vase, pk/wht floral, gold ring hdls/trim, Nishikide decor, 10"...125.00
Vase, rectangular figural reserves on brocade ground, 19", pr.425.00
Vase, rust lilies/bud/stems, twist shoulder hdls, EX gold, 14"...175.00
Vase, scaly dragon/gilt figures in landscapes, 1800s, 10"....350.00
Vase, shi-shi hdls w/ring tassels, phoenix panels, Awata, 15"..350.00
Vase, tapestry relief, red/turq/br on beige, EX detail, 3x1¾"...375.00
Vase, Thousand Butterflies, sgn, 6"........................400.00
Vase, wisteria in red/purple on beige crackle, ca 1840, 6", pr..350.00
Vase, 2 lg+2 sm panels of women at temple/samurai, 7"......770.00
Vase, 7 war lords, circled X of gold, 1860s, 7".............375.00
Wall vase, lady in relief enamel, gold outline, 1930s, 7½".....30.00

Scales

In today's world of pre-measured and pre-packaged goods, it is hard to imagine the days when such products as sugar, flour, soap, and candy first had to be weighed by the grocer. The variety of scales used at the turn of the century was highly diverse; at the Philadelphia Exposition in 1876, one company alone displayed over three hundred different weighing devices. Among those found today, brass and iron models are the most common.

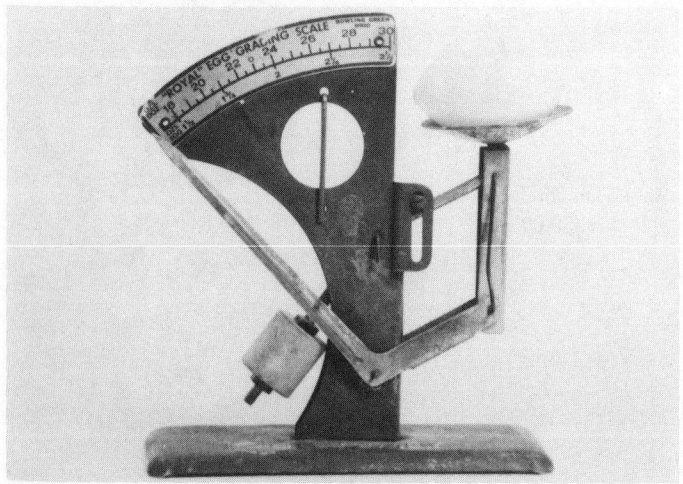

Egg scales, made in Bowling Green, Ohio; 6¾" x 6" x 2", $20.00.

Acme, egg grading, ca 1924....................16.00
Am Cutlery Co, kitchen, rnd brass dial, openwork daisy.......70.00
Balance, platform, crimped tin oval pan, w/weights, miniature....65.00
Brass, 6 ft CI columns, accurate to 22000 lbs...............275.00
Caille, Geo Washington, 1¢ coin operated................2,000.00
Candy, emb: Enterprise Mfg, tin scoop, brass slide.........135.00
Candy, needle eye fan, Exact Wt, brass base, side mt weights..210.00
Candy, 1 lb, orig red & gold stenciling, brass pan..........125.00
Chatillon, #2, spring balance, brass, 1892.................15.00
Chatillon, milk, 120 lb..................................80.00
Chatillon, spring, brass face, pat 1867.....................9.00
Chicago Scale Co, CI/brass w/orig blk pnt, red/gold decor, 12"..30.00
Christian Becker Chainomatic, jeweler's balance & weights.....225.00
Coin operated, CI, w/marquee, 5¢, G....................100.00
Dayton Computing, #120, rare.........................450.00
Dayton Computing, #144, grocery store type, G............350.00
Dayton Computing, #166, candy, 2 lb, brass trim/scoop.......125.00
Dayton Computing, barrel, EX..........................225.00
Dayton Computing, mirrors on sides, ornate brass, pat 1895..1,495.00
Detector, 2 metal plates, brass bar, iron teardrop slide, 23"...35.00
Dodge, #210, CI/brass & marble, roller wheel type..........325.00
Guitnea, folding, wooden.............................155.00
Hanging, brass face, 60 lbs...........................35.00
Hanson, dairy, wht face, dbl row measure, 2 arrows, bird logo...25.00
Hanson, hanging scale w/hook, 100 lb capacity, brass dial.....35.00
Hanson, produce, hanging scale w/pan...................30.00
IBM, #146, electric, ruby glass, barrel type, ornate trim.......400.00
IBM, #250, fan type grocery, ornate trim..................150.00
IBM, candy, ornate, brass trimmed......................175.00
Jennings Lollipop, w/etched glass dial, M.................400.00
Johan Peter Braselmann, goldsmith's, iron balance, in case....385.00
Landers, spring balance, tole tray......................70.00
Landers Improved #2, hanging balance, brass face............8.50
Meat, nickel trimmed, upright, Canadian Govt seal dtd 1898...150.00
National, #4 fan, store, ornate, plated, brass scoop, 1901......350.00
National, candy, porcelain w/nickel, eagle, cherub decal, 1911..250.00
National, Indian head decal, Wall Walla Gum Co, 10".......500.00
Pelouze, dairy, wht face..............................12.00
Pelouze, 25#, tin w/porcelain top, 1898..................30.00
Perfection, scoop scale...............................195.00
Postal, lighthouse, brass.............................175.00
Postal, Parnell, pendulum.............................75.00
Postal, postage in ¢s to 20 lbs by oz, 1906...............18.00
Postal, Reliance, 2 drws, 2 inkwells, pen rack.............65.00
Postal, Sav-A-Stamp, quadrant........................65.00
Sargent & Co, Improved Circular Spring Balance, brass, 12" L..35.00
Standard Computing, #9759-B, wht porcelain, M...........250.00
Steelyard, iron, 3 hooks & weights, 1700s, 36" L............50.00
Store, brass face, eagle on sides, 1898, EX................85.00
Sweden, CI w/porcelain dial, ornate Victorian, 1885.........85.00
Toledo, #0891, platform, 125#, store model, VG...........250.00
Toledo, #3 fan, candy, brass trim & scoop, 1903, EX........225.00
Toledo, #3 fan, candy, wht porcelain w/platform, 1920s.......125.00
Triner, Airmail Accuracy, enamel steel/brass, 1940..........48.00
Triner Magestic, candy, brass pan......................140.00
Winchester, grain, brass, pat 1877.....................250.00
Wm Ainsworth & Sons, analytical balance, metal case, 19½"....75.00

Schafer and Vater

Schafer and Vater operated in Volkstadt, Germany, from the last decade of the 1800s until about 1920. They produced novelties such as figural bottles, flasks, vases, etc., marked with an 'R' within a star device.

Bottle, comical man bowling figural, 6⅛"............115.00
Box, bl jasper, Priscilla/John Alden, 2½x3¼"..............40.00
Box, child figural, hands over head, balance scales side, 6½"...42.00
Box, dog in doghouse, cat on roof, bisque, 3½x4¼".........95.00
Chamberstick, faces in relief, sgn........................55.00
Creamer, bear's head w/overcoat & muff, 3½"...............50.00
Creamer, clown w/mandolin figural, 3".....................80.00
Creamer, comical Black man............................125.00
Creamer, Dutch housekeeper figural, w/basket/pitcher, 3½".....68.00
Creamer, goat figural, bl, 5"...........................42.50
Creamer, kneeling witch, bl/wht, 4"......................50.00
Creamer, maid w/fan, kneeling, bl, 4¼"...................70.00
Creamer, standing girl figural, basket on bk, pitcher in hands...60.00
Creamer, tortoise shell w/in, 2 jasper inserts w/maidens, 4".....50.00
Hair receiver, triangular w/lady's face & jewels on bisque.......90.00
Hatpin holder, gr jasper, relief wht roses.................55.00
Hatpin holder, seated geisha holds fan, bisque.............140.00
Mug, Van Houtens Hot Chocolate, emb Dutch boy & girl, 1908..65.00
Planter, Cupid & Psyche, jasper w/bisque liner.............75.00

Schlegelmilch Porcelain

Key:
BM-----blue mark   SM-----steeple mark
GM-----green mark

E.S. Germany

Fine chinaware marked 'E.S. Germany' or 'E.S. Prov. Saxe' was produced by E.S. Schlegelmilch at his Suhl Factory in the Thuringia region of Prussia from the turn of the century until about 1925.

Bowl, portrait Nouveau lady, gold emb border, Prov Saxe, 9½".265.00
Box, violin shape, Indian decal, gold trim, sm..............125.00
Chocolate pot, pk peonies, relief enamel, Prov Saxe.........88.00
Chocolate pot, roses decor, 9¼"........................95.00
Chocolate pot, 4 c/s; bl/gr/tan ferns....................300.00
Pin dish w/hdls, emb grapes, rose/gold leaves, Prov Saxe, 7"....48.00
Plate, Josephine portrait, ornate, sgn Royal Saxe, 8"........75.00

Vase, green with gold, portrait reserve, 8", $275.00.

Plate, orange poppies, orange rim, 8½"...................45.00
Sugar, yel w/bl rim/lid band, pk primroses, gold, Prov Saxe.....45.00
Tray, dresser; long stem pk/peach tulips..................48.00
Tray, dresser; roses decor............................55.00
Tray, pin; oblong, molded rim, dainty florals..............40.00
Vase, burgundy lustre/relief gold, lady & Cupid in reserve, 8"...165.00
Vase, florals, sgn, Prov Saxe, 12"......................68.00
Vase, portrait, encrusted gold, sgn, 7".................225.00
Vase, portrait, lady w/doves, gold w/turq beads, 6".........195.00
Vase, portrait, Royal Saxe, 1 hdl, 6½"..................210.00
Vase, 4 portraits, gold & Tiffany finish, 4¾x3¾"..........250.00

E.S. Prussia

E.S. Prussia was a mark used by the Erdmann Schlegelmilch porcelain manufactory established in 1861 in the Prussian province in Saxony, Germany. Most examples seen today date from the early 1900s until the factory closed in the 1920s.

Bouillon, ped saucer, Kauffmann scene...................95.00
Bowl, classical scene, handles, 6¼"....................50.00
Ewer, portrait of lady, 6½"...........................45.00
Pin dish, portrait, winged shape, gold trim, 7" wide.........85.00
Pitcher, lemonade; roses decor, 8"....................125.00
Plate, Indian portrait, red rim, 7½"....................65.00
Tea strainer, florals.................................95.00
Tray, dresser; roses & gr leaf ground, gr eagle mk, 11x8".....105.00
Vase, cartouch w/birds, mk: bird in circle w/Frederick, 8"......150.00

R.S. Germany

In 1869, Reinhold Schlegelmilch began to manfacture porcelain in Tillowitz, in upper Silesia. He had formerly worked with his brother, Erdmann, in his factory in Suhl, in the German province of Thuringia. Both areas were rich in resources necessary for the production of hard paste porcelain. Wares marked with the name 'Tillowitz' and the accompanying 'R.S. Germany' phrase, are attributed to Reinhold. The most common mark is a wreath and star in a solid color, under the glaze. Items marked 'R.S. Germany' are usually more simply decorated than R.S. Prussia. Some reflect the Art Deco trend of the 1920s. Certain hand painted floral decorations and hand painted themes such as 'Sheepherder', 'Man with Horses', and 'Cottage' are especially valued by collectors -- those with a high gloss finish or on Art Deco shapes in particular.

Not all hand painted items were painted at the factory. Those with an artist's signature, but no 'Hand Painted' mark, indicate that the blank was decorated outside the factory.

Ash tray, Dutch scenic...............................35.00
Basket, shaded pk w/yel roses, scalloped rim/hdl, BM, 3"......35.00
Berry set, calla lily decor, 7 pc.......................200.00
Berry set, cottage scene, shaded gr, 7 pc, GM.............400.00
Berry set, gr w/stylized wht florals, gold enameling, 5 pc......250.00
Bouillon cup & saucer, roses decor.....................45.00
Bowl, cabbage leaf shape, wht florals, silver-gr lustre, 10"....325.00
Bowl, orange poppies decor, ftd, 6"....................55.00
Bowl, oval, stippled floral edge mold/florals/gold, SM, 12".....110.00
Bowl, scenic, cottage & cattle, Deco shape, gold trim, 4x6"....250.00
Bowl, scenic, woman & ox, 7".........................95.00
Bowl, Sheepherder II scene, hand enameling, sgn Kleft, 10"..1,200.00
Bowl, stippled floral mold, pk/yel roses center, 12" long......135.00
Bowl, wht poppies, 3 hdls, satin finish, 6¾"..............38.00
Cake plate, pk roses decor, 11" dia....................150.00
Cake set, cotton plant, open hdl, 7 pc..................250.00
Cake set, florals, BM, 7 pc..........................150.00

Candy dish, florals, gold trim, sgn, 9"........................40.00
Candy dish, poppies, gold leaves, w/hdls, 4 ball ft, GM, 5".....55.00
Candy dish, sq, scallops, gray-gr w/orange roses, gold, 7"......42.50
Cheese & cracker dish, roses decor............................45.00
Cheese & cracker dish, snowballs & roses decor, 10" dia.......70.00
Chocolate pot, shaded bl w/stylized wht tulips, 9"............125.00
Chocolate pot, w/4 c/s; roses decor..........................255.00
Compote, floral decor, ped base...............................55.00
Cracker jar, pk & wht roses decor............................150.00
Cracker jar, red & wht tulips decor..........................115.00
Cracker jar, yel & wht floral decor..........................115.00
Creamer, roses & snowballs decor..............................50.00
Creamer & sugar, iris decor...................................45.00
Creamer & sugar, pk roses decor, satin finish.................67.00
Creamer & sugar, ½ irid gr, ½ spattered yel, blk trim.........38.00
Creamer & sugar on oval hdl tray, hexagonal, rose decor......145.00
Cup & saucer, blown-out, ruffled, wht dogwood/lt br trim, BM...55.00
Cup & saucer, blown-out swirl, dogwood blossoms, gold ft, BM..62.00
Cup & saucer, demitasse; brn & gr w/open wht lilies, GM.......32.00
Cup & saucer, demitasse; rose decor, ftd......................35.00
Dresser set, w/ring tree, wht w/florals, cobalt/gold trim.....85.00
Ferner, w/insert, bl ground w/wht roses, BM...................70.00
Gravy boat, w/under plate, lilacs decor.......................50.00
Hair receiver, pansies decor..................................30.00
Hair receiver, poppy & gardenia decor.........................35.00
Hair receiver, rose & gold leaves, GM.........................65.00
Hatpin holder, calla lilies decor.............................75.00
Hatpin holder, pussy willow decor.............................45.00
Hatpin holder, 4 molded ft, lg pk rose, sm yel rose, GM.......55.00
Inkwell, lily of the valley decor.............................50.00
Inkwell, w/liner, yel/gold/gr leaves, SM.....................185.00
Jam jar w/under plate, morning-glory decor....................60.00
Lamp, fairy; owl...250.00
Match holder, barrel shape, striker base, pk roses, 1¾"......75.00
Match holder, figural pipe on tray............................45.00
Mayonnaise set, floral, 3 pc..................................50.00
Mug, coffee; dk pk roses, 3".................................45.00
Mustard w/lid & spoon, roses decor............................58.00
Nappy, gr w/wht hydrangeas, gold border, 3 hdls, 3 sided, BM...52.00
Pin dish w/lid, clover shaped.................................45.00
Pin tray, bl-gray lustre w/mixed florals......................40.00
Pin tray, open hdl, oblong, 2 long stem roses, pk/yel, GM.....40.00
Pin tray, pierced ends, orange/wht tulips on gray, oval, 8"...35.00
Pitcher, lemonade; pk roses decor, 6½".......................200.00
Pitcher, milk; lt bl w/yel & pk roses, M......................75.00
Plate, calla lilies, BM, 10".................................55.00
Plate, icicle mold, bl & gr floral/shadow foliage, hdls, 10½"...125.00
Plate, lav/gold leaf rim, rust/floral center, open hdls, 10½"...100.00
Plate, lg wht/pk bell flowers, gold rim, GM, 8¼"..............20.00
Plate, man w/horses, 8".....................................195.00
Plate, molded floral border/pk roses/gold trim, SM, 9".......150.00
Plate, orange poppies, gold rim, w/hdls, GM, 10"..............48.00
Plate, peacocks, Art Deco, bl border w/gold decor, 6½".......38.00
Plate, pk & orange nasturtiums, open hdls, GM, 9½"...........52.00
Plate, pk/wht carnations, open hdls, 10".....................55.00
Plate, poppies decor, 6" dia.................................10.00
Plate, roses, gold rim, 8¼".................................25.00
Powder box, gr w/pk flowers, scalloped, beads, gold, 8 ft, GM...75.00
Relish, bl w/bird on blossom branch, open hdls, 7½" long.....145.00
Relish, gr pearl lustre w/pk roses decor, 9" long.............60.00
Relish, ivory-yel, mc poppies & daisies, pierced, gold rim, GM...32.00
Relish, swan scenes in each section, hdls, 8½" long..........125.00
Sauce boat w/liner, gr w/wht florals..........................45.00
Shaving mug, tan/br/gr w/lg wht snowballs.....................65.00

Syrup w/under plate, covered, hydrangeas decor................78.00
Syrup w/under plate, 6".......................................55.00
Teapot, bl to cream, w/shaded pk full blown roses.............65.00
Toothbrush holder, pk rose decor, wall hanging, sgn..........130.00
Tray, bread; roses, 10x6½"....................................38.00
Tray, celery; roses, open hdls, 12"...........................45.00
Tray, fuschias, artist sgn, 7x10½"............................85.00
Tray, leaf shape, gold hdl, gr w/pk roses.....................35.00
Vase, nightwatch scene, 10¾x4½".............................350.00
Vase, pansy; bulbous, wht w/gold decor, 3½x3½"................12.00

R.S. Poland

'R.S. Poland' is a mark attributed to Reinhold Schlegelmilch's Tillowitz, Silesia Factory.

Cake plate, roses, watered silk finish, open hdls............135.00
Candlestick, pk/wht floral decor, gr lustre finish, pr.......145.00
Dresser set, blk w/pk roses, tray/hatpin holder/hair receiver....310.00
Dresser set, gr w/peach & wht roses, 5 pc....................265.00
Jardiniere, peach roses, satin finish, miniature, 5".........225.00
Mug, pk floral...75.00
Mug, shaving; gr to wht ground, orchid florals...............90.00
Shaker, talcum; poppies decor...............................165.00
Sugar w/lid, scalloped shoulder, angle hdls, pk roses, gold..125.00
Vase, cottage scene, 4".....................................110.00
Vase, florals, Deco shoulder hdl, RM, 12½"..................195.00

Ewer, cavaliers and ladies on shaded green, gold trim 6¼", $725.00.

R.S. Prussia

Art porcelain bearing the mark 'R.S. Prussia' was manufactured by Erdmann and Reinhold Schlegelmilch from the late 1870s to the early 1900s in a Germanic area known until the end of WWI as Prussia. The vast array of mold shapes in combination with a wide variety of decorations is the basis for R.S. Prussia's appeal. Themes can be categorized as figural (usually based on a famous artist's work), birds, florals, portraits, scenics, and animals.

Berry set, lt gr w/gr leaves, RM, 7 pc.......................210.00
Berry set, 8 point 11" bowl, lime w/purple/wht floral, 7 pc.....275.00
Bowl, applied fleur-de-lis ft, roses, mold #704, RM, 5½".....129.00
Bowl, apricot roses, trailing leaves, hdls, sm...............20.00
Bowl, aqua rims, rose festoons below, RM, 10"................75.00
Bowl, bluebirds & water lilies, 11".........................300.00

Bowl, carnation mold, pk & wht roses, bl/wht carnations, 9½"..230.00
Bowl, carnation mold, pk/wht roses on yel-gr, 9½".........220.00
Bowl, Countess Flora, Tiffany border w/cherubs, no mk, 10"..1,200.00
Bowl, cream & yel w/lilies, 5½"...........................40.00
Bowl, Easter lilies mold, bl to lav, RM, 10", M............235.00
Bowl, floral w/cobalt trim, rare mold, no mk...............140.00
Bowl, molded poppy edge, beaded rim, poppies in center, 9¼".195.00
Bowl, Old Man in Mountain, icicle mold, RM, 11"...........850.00
Bowl, rounded scallops border, pk wild roses & foliage, RM, 9"..125.00
Bowl, stag scene, foliage/flowers, scalloped/ruffled, 5" dia......295.00
Bowl, swans/bl ground/water lilies, shadow border, 11", VG....250.00
Bowl, Winter, ftd, RM.....................................700.00
Bowl, 8 molded 3" tan & floral rim panels, gr w/peonies, 10"..180.00
Bowl w/in bowl, fleur-de-lis mold, pk/yel roses, RM, 10"......195.00
Cake plate, dogwood, scalloped, high lustre, open hdls, 12"....115.00
Cake plate, gr/wht blown irises w/gold centers, RM, 9½"......195.00
Cake plate, icicle mold, 4 swans, 9¾"....................400.00
Cake plate, jewel & ribbon mold, roses/hydrangeas, 10½".....250.00
Cake plate, Melon Eaters, ripple mold, high lustre, RM, 10½"..875.00
Cake plate, pk w/roses, satin, scalloped, open hdl, RM, 12"....135.00
Cake plate, poppy, br scalloped rim, gold gadroon border, 9½"..85.00
Cake plate, Spring, portrait, open hdls...................1,300.00
Cake plate, 4 molded jeweled flowers, pk roses, open hdls, 11".215.00
Celery tray, cabbage roses, satin finish, open hdl, 11½"......180.00
Celery tray, hidden image mold, icicle/iris edge............250.00
Celery tray, stippled floral mold, pk/yel roses, artist sgn......125.00
Celery tray, swan scenic, satin finish, RM, 12x6".........290.00
Centerpiece, w/pr attached rings, satin w/pk/wht roses, 4x9½"..275.00
Chocolate pot, floral, ftd, ornate........................300.00
Chocolate pot, lilac decor, RM...........................310.00
Chocolate pot, pk roses/wht daisies, reflected in water, 9".....215.00
Chocolate pot, roses, RM................................175.00
Coffee cup, Melon Boy, RM..............................350.00
Cracker jar, farmyard, RM..............................1,200.00
Cracker jar, lav/purple/pk, pearl button finish, RM..........250.00
Cracker jar, pearl, shell rim/ft, lily of the valley, RM........150.00
Cracker jar, poppies on lt gr, gold relief, satin, RM.........345.00
Creamer, Melon Boy, jewel mold, gr/wht/gold w/opal jewels.....600.00
Creamer, pheasant & pine tree, 4"......................250.00
Creamer & sugar, castle scene, rare mold, RM.............500.00
Creamer & sugar, cottage scene, br tints, gold paw ft, RM.....625.00
Creamer & sugar, roses decor, matt finish, ca 1890.........125.00
Creamer & sugar, swallows, turkeys, rooster, swans, RM.....1,200.00
Creamer & sugar, yel & wht florals, gold trim, satin, RM.....229.00
Cup & saucer, stippled floral mold, rose on yel, gr/wht body....95.00
Hair receiver, floral, ftd...............................110.00
Hair receiver, gr w/pk & red roses, lacy ruffle, ornate, M......175.00
Hair receiver, red flowers, gold trim, clover mold...........110.00
Hair receiver, swans w/evergreens, lustre glaze, RM, 7½"......350.00
Hatpin holder, violets on gr, RM, 4½"....................75.00
Muffineer, ped ft, dbl hdls, roses decor...................250.00
Mustard jar, clematis on gr/wht, 3½"....................95.00
Pin dish, leaf form w/lilac decor, RM, 5½"................50.00
Pitcher, lemonade; poppy decor on gr/beige w/berries, RM, 10".450.00
Pitcher, tankard; Easter lilies, ferns, RM.................285.00
Pitcher, tankard; floral decor, 14".......................750.00
Pitcher, tankard; Winter, ftd, no mk, 13"...............1,150.00
Pitcher, 4 red diamonds, gold beads at top, pearlized, RM, 4"..95.00
Plate, delicate florals on satin, RM, set of 4..............265.00
Plate, Fall, keyhole mold, RM........................1,500.00
Plate, Fall, Royal Vienna colors, RM, 6½"................650.00
Plate, iris mold, pk poppies center, gold trim, RM, 10".......185.00
Plate, Melon Boy, 2 boys/dog/melon, cable edge, RM, 8½"....525.00
Plate, Melon Boy, 3 boys/dog/dice, cable edge, RM, 8½", M..525.00

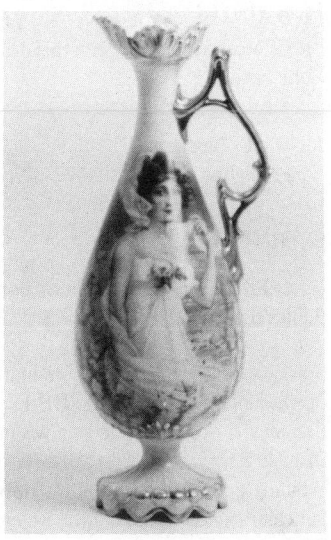

Ewer, portrait of lady, artist signed, red mark, 9", $1,500.00.

Plate, mill scene, br, RM, 6"............................135.00
Plate, pk/golds on wht, sunflower mold, no mk, w/hdls, 9½"....85.00
Plate, roses decor, RM, 8½"..............................78.00
Plate, scalloped ruffled edge mold, 2 lg primroses, gold, 7".....82.00
Plate, Spring portrait, keyhole mold, 9"................1,200.00
Plate, swallows, turkeys, swans, RM, 8½"...............1,200.00
Plate, water lilies, icicle mold, open hdls................200.00
Plate, Winter, blown iris, satin, RM, 9".................750.00
Plate, 6 medallion mold, pk poppies & daisies center, RM, 11".175.00
Powder box, ftd; jeweled, w/Recamier portrait, RM.........950.00
Relish, swan scene, icicle mold, 2 open hdls, RM, 4½x9½"....175.00
Relish, 4 cherub portraits, unmarked, 9¼"................100.00
Relish, 4-circle/medallion mold, roses/lilies of valley..........80.00
Salt & pepper, bl/yel, mc flowers, gold vine, barrel shape.......68.00
Shaving mug, floral/gr shading/gold, side mirror, RM.........325.00
Shaving mug, LeBrun self portrait, Tiffany, RM.............475.00
Spoon holder, floral, no mk, 14".........................275.00
Sugar, dogwood, scalloped, beaded rim, gold trim............70.00
Sugar, single rosebud decor, RM..........................95.00
Sugar, 4 scallop mold, hanging basket decor, pk/yel, RM......140.00
Sugar shaker, floral, 2 hdls, RM.........................125.00
Syrup w/under plate, roses, carnation mold................175.00
Talcum shaker, roses, w/hdls, RM, 5"....................225.00
Tea set, cream & br w/red roses, ped, RM.................375.00
Teapot, cr/sug, open, Winter girl, Tiffany color, gold ball ft...1,850.00
Teapot, cr/sug w/lid, cream to wht, gold/wht/red flowers, RM...225.00
Tray, daisy mold, orchids, bl border/gold tracery, hdls, 12x8"..185.00
Tray, dresser; carnation mold, satin finish, w/roses...........375.00
Tray, dresser; floral, RM................................75.00
Tray, dresser; Winter, RM, 22½x7½"...................1,300.00
Tray, roses, open hdls, 9x12¾".........................150.00
Vase, cartouch form, roses on wht/lav, gold hdls, RM, 9¾"....450.00
Vase, castle scene, cylindrical shape, RM, 7".............625.00
Vase, castle scene, RM, 4".............................200.00
Vase, Dice Throwers, jeweled, w/hdls, RM, 9"...........1,800.00
Vase, florals, 6½x6"..................................225.00
Vase, hanging basket decor on lav satin, RM, 11¾"..........425.00
Vase, hummingbird, no mk, 4"...........................500.00
Vase, loving cup, Melon Eaters, jeweled, miniature, 7".......900.00
Vase, loving cup, roses, RM, 11".........................400.00
Vase, Melon Boy, RM, 6"...............................550.00
Vase, mill scene, bulbous, RM, 6½".......................325.00
Vase, mill/cottage/florals on bl, bulbous, 5½"...............250.00
Vase, olive gr w/pk roses, RM, 13".......................425.00
Vase, portrait on red, ped ft, hdls, LeBrun, 9½".............500.00

R.S. Suhl

Porcelains marked with this designation are attributed to Schlegelmilch's Suhl factory.

Jar w/lid, Tapestry, 7"...................................135.00
Vase, Nightwatch, br shades, sgn Rembrandt, 7½"...........350.00

R.S. Tillowitz

R.S. Tillowitz marked porcelains are attributed to Reinhold Schlegelmilch's Tillowitz, Silesia factory.

Bowl, roses & violets on lt gr matt, 4 leaf ft, open hdls, 8".....95.00
Bowl, ruffled, 4 molded ft, HP lilies, gold, 2½x6"............48.00
Creamer & sugar, shaded gr w/wht lilies...................175.00
Dish, 2 tier, mocha w/lg apricot roses......................65.00
Mustard pot w/ladle, forget-me-nots, gold hdl/finial, HP........55.00
Pancake server w/insert, wht w/gold trim, 4x7½".............35.00
Pitcher, poppies..85.00
Plate, cherries decor, 11"...............................23.00
Plate, 2 parrots on yel, HP, open hdls, 7".................45.00
Relish, florals..25.00
Relish, pierced hdls, azaleas/foliage on yel/br, 10½"..........32.00

Schneider

The Schneider Glass Company was founded in 1914 at Epinay-sur-seine, France. They made many types of art glass, some of which sandwiched designs between layers. Other decorative devices were applique and carved work. These were marked 'Charder', or 'Schneider'.

During the twenties, commercial art ware was produced with Deco motifs, cut by acid through two or three layers, and signed 'LeVerre Francais' in script or with a section of inlayed filigrane.

See also Le Verre Francais

Tazza, green bowl, amethyst base, signed, 5¾", $350.00.

Candle holder, paperweight, clematis, bubble dew drops, sgn...250.00
Charger, pk w/mottle amethyst, sgn Ovington, 16"...........235.00
Compote, amethyst base, wht stem, orange mottle center, 7"...195.00
Compote, orange/yel mottle/blk stem/metal ped w/glass berries..265.00
Compote, purple w/orange center, 7¼".....................175.00
Pitcher, orange mottled body, amethyst hdl, unsgn, 7".......275.00

Vase, orange, amethyst & wht mottled colors, 7½"...........295.00
Vase, orange/br w/bl hi-lites, sgn, 9½"....................105.00
Vase, rose/yel marbleized w/amethyst base, 7"..............375.00

Schoolhouse Collectibles

Schoolhouse collectibles bring to mind memories of a bygone era when the teacher rang her bell to call the youngsters to class in a one-room schoolhouse -- where often both the 'hickory stick' and an apple occupied a prominent position on her desk.

Bell, bell metal, trn wood hdl, 9".........................25.00
Bell, brass w/cherry hdl, used in Shaker school, 8¾".........35.00
Book, calligraphic accounts & exercises, 1700s, 13x8".......300.00
Book, Illustrated Primer/Child's First Book, early 1800s........50.00
Book, McGuffey's Fifth Eclectic Reader, 1866, Van Antwerp.....12.50
Book, McGuffey's Third Eclectic Reader....................10.00
Book, Primary Standard Speaker, E Sargent, illustrated, 1857...20.00
Calligraphy, bird w/banner, inscription/sgn, in fr, 10½x12".....85.00
Calligraphy, leaping deer, in fr, 26x32"..................135.00
Calligraphy, stag pursued by hunting dogs, fr, 21x25"........400.00
Calligraphy chart, chain of states, historical info, in fr........250.00
Certificate, Spencerian, pen/ink, eagle/fish/etc, 1846, 22x17"...155.00
Classroom Printer, rubber stamps, letters/#s/animals, in chest....85.00
Desk, maple & cast iron, lift top, 1800s, 23½".............75.00
Desk, pine/poplar, w/seat, from row......................95.00
Desk, teacher's; pine/poplar, mortised apron, slant top........90.00
Desk, teacher's; walnut, fitted w/in, primitive, 45x30"........350.00
Pencil box, litho on paper, US eagle & shield...............18.00
Pencil box, wood, dvtl, 1 divider, dog & sheep decor, 8" L.....12.50
Pencil sharpener, US Automatic, 1907, table mt, crank/drw, 5"..75.00
Slate, dbl, etched lines 1 side, 13x18", VG.................25.00
Slate, dbl, w/red wool bound wood fr, 6¾x8¾"..............20.00
Slate, wood fr, 14x10"...................................8.50
Thrashing flail, hickory, 1850s, 48".......................46.00
Workbook, Fulton's steamboat on cover, handwritten, 1829.....40.00

Scouting Collectibles

Scouting was founded in England in 1907 by a retired Major General, Lord Robert Baden-Powell. Its purpose is the same today as it was then -- to help develop physically strong, mentally alert boys who were taught basic fundamentals of survival and leadership. The movement soon spread to the United States, and in 1910 a Chicago publisher, William Boyce set out to establish Scouting in America. The first World Scout Jamboree was held in 1911 in England. Baden-Powell was honored as the Chief Scout of the World. In 1926, he was awarded the Silver Buffalo Award in the United States. He was knighted in 1929 for distinguished military service, and for his scouting efforts. Baden-Powell died in 1941.

Award, Silver World, globe w/silver on blue enamel, old type...450.00
Bank, Girl Scout, copper/bronze, full figure on base, 7"........15.00
Belt buckle, 1967 World Jamboree Official Buckle.............8.00
Box, has paper doll Girl Scouts/orig uniforms, uncut, 1930s.....35.00
Bugle, Boy Scout, brass mouthpiece attached w/chain.........47.00
Button, celluloid, 1937 BSA National Jamboree, I'm Going......13.00
Calendar, 1912, Boy Scouts of America, complete, 16x30", EX..88.00
Calendar, 1925, Boy Scouts of America, 1st Rockwell, complete..59.00
Calendar, 1945, Boy Scouts of America, Rockwell: Oath, NM....11.00
Canteen, Girl Scout, mc plaid cloth over metal, MIB..........15.00

Flag, 1950 Boy Scout Jamboree, New Jersey Troop, red/wht....115.00
Flag, 1964 BSA National Jamboree, miniature................18.00
Handbook, For Boys, 2nd ed, May 1927, dk olive cover.......25.00
Handbook, For Boys, 2nd ed, Oct 31, 1914, silver cover.......75.00
Handbook, For Scoutmaster, 1st ed/5th print, 1913, hard cover..47.00
Handbook, For Scoutmaster, 2nd ed/15th print, 1930, red cover.17.50
Handbook, Official...For Boys, 1st ed, Mar 3, '14, red cover.....60.00
Knife, pocket; Boy Scout, Remington, 4 blades, brown bone hdl.42.00
Knife, pocket; Girl Scout Kutmaster, 4 blade, plastic w/emblem...6.50
License plate, 1957 National Boy Scout Jamboree, Michigan, #1.30.00
Magazine, Life, July 24, 1950, National Jamboree issue.........10.00
Manual, BSA Official, 1910, original ed, hard bound, VG.....185.00
Manual, Seton's Forester's, 1912, 2nd series................150.00
Match safe, 1964 BSA National Jamboree, Bucktail Council/glass..5.00
Medal, Sprints, runner crouched, gold color, w/ribbon, 1920s....15.00
Medal, WWI Service, Boy Scouts, Victory Liberty Loan.........45.00
Medal, WWI War Savings Service, Boy Scouts, pin-back button...8.00
Medal, WWII War Loan Gallant Ribbon Bar, Boy Scouts.......12.00
Neckerchief, 1950 BSA National Jamboree, rayon-silk.........22.00
Neckerchief, 1950 National Jamboree, emblem on silk triangle...27.00
Paperweight, Girl Scout feeding rabbit, case metal, blk, 1920s...22.00
Paperweight, pewter w/3¢ Boy Scout stamp on marble base, 1948.7.50
Patch, Girl Scout Jamboree, Senior Round-Up, 1965...........10.00
Patch, Junior Assistant Scoutmaster, 1937 series.............10.00
Patch, Ranger, round back patch, yel twill, 1969.............26.00
Patch, Segment-Mountainman, yel twill/blk musket, 1950s......45.00
Patch, Segment-Naturalist, bl twill/br mesa/gr tree, 1950s.......9.00
Patch, staff back patch, USA form, bl twill/yel cut edge, 1953..130.00
Patch, 50-Miler Award, mule skin w/stamped design, '40's.......10.00
Pennant, 1937 Girl Scout Jamboree, large..................45.00
Pillow case, silk, w/scene of 1957 BSA National Jamboree......14.00
Poster, 1957 BSA National Jamboree, promotional, large.......20.00
Ring, 1957 BSA National Jamboree, sterling, w/logo...........10.00
Sardine can, 1957 National Boy Scout Jamboree, unopened, M..14.00
Sash, Order of the Arrow, 1924 Ordeal, wht felt/red felt arrow...39.00
Souvenir book, 1953 BSA National Jamboree, w/logo..........7.50
Statue, Cub & Dog, Norman Rockwell, plastic-type, 10½"......25.00
Statue, Moody Scout, plaster w/carved wood staff, 1911, 12"....49.00
T-shirt, 1950 BSA National Jamboree, official, M w/package.....20.00
Uniform, Boy Scout, 1935, official hat, fur felt, M...........19.00
Uniform, Brownie Scouts, dress, pocket patch, hat, belt, 1950s..15.00
Uniform, Girl Scout, 1927, coat style dress, official buttons......35.00
Yearbook, Boy Scouts, 1928............................12.00
Yearbook, Boy Scouts, 1931, w/Norman Rockwell dust jacket....20.00

Scrimshaw

The most desirable examples of the art of scrimshaw can be traced back to the first half of the 19th century, to the heyday of the whaling industry. Some voyages lasted for several years, and conditions on board were often dismal. Sailors filled the long hours by carving or engraving designs in whale or walrus ivory. Using the tools of their trade, they created animal figures, boxes, pie crimpers, etc., often emphasizing the lines of their carvings with ink or berry stain.

Eskimos also made scrimshaw, sometimes borrowing designs from the sailors who traded with them.

Baby rattle, whalebone, 4¾".............................190.00
Block, whalebone, dbl whale tooth ivory sheaves/brass pins, 3".250.00
Bodkin, pair: 1 ends in fist, other in die...................60.00
Busk, 10" baleen w/arrows, hearts & flowers...............175.00
Busk, 13¼" baleen w/pinwheel & flowers..................125.00
Busk, 7¼" ivory w/whales & flowers, recent................75.00

Sperm whale tooth, whaling ship under full sail, signed Clyde King, 6", $1,650.00.

Fid, whalebone, engraved whaling scene, 11¾"..............200.00
Flax wheel, intricate detail, 3½".........................225.00
Game, alphabet set, whalebone, in mahogany box............200.00
Game, jackstraws, ivory, in walnut box....................95.00
Inkwell, pewter inside a walrus tusk base..................200.00
Jagging wheel, fish form w/crenellated wheel at tail, 5½"......150.00
Mirror, carved ivory, 20x32".............................300.00
Pipe, whalebone bowl & stem, 9".........................250.00
Pipe tamp, whalebone, fist, 2¼".........................150.00
Pipe tamp, whalebone, plain, 2½"........................45.00
Seam rubber, whalebone, simple, 4"......................150.00
Swift, whalebone ribs, hand-form clamp, floral engraved, 22½".675.00
Swift, whalebone/ivory, wood shaft, 1800s, 21".............700.00
Tool, for rubbing wax into seams of sail, whalebone, 4½".....105.00
Tusk, ship, scene of dying whale, Am eagle/banner, 20".....3,200.00
Whale stamp, 2", pr...................................215.00
Whale tooth, eagle/flags/shields/cannons, w/color, 3¾"........550.00
Whale tooth, lg sailing ship ea side, deep engraving, 6½"...1,200.00
Whale tooth, monument w/Am flag, naval ship, polychrome, 5".330.00
Whale tooth, panoramic whaling scene/naval battle, color, 8".2,300.00
Whale tooth, sailor on rope coil w/anchor holds flag, 6".....1,950.00
Whale tooth, ship in storm, octopus grasping harpoons, 7"...1,300.00
Whale tooth, ship/patriotic engraving, EX work, 9".........2,400.00
Whale tooth, ship/scene: Apothecary on wht horse, etc, 8"...1,400.00
Whale tooth, Victorian couple, 4½".......................350.00
Whale tooth, whale ship & eagle, 6½".....................250.00
Whale tooth, whales/eagle/ship/sailor w/harpoon/flags, sgn, 6".2,500.00
Whale tooth, young lady of 18th century, 4½"..............125.00
Woman figural, arms are ear diggers/feet are toothpicks, 3".....80.00

Seals and Sealing Wax

A seal is used to affix a stamp or emboss either on an official paper or on wax such as was once used on correspondence. The sealing wax was first melted, then allowed to drip on the seam of the envelope or the writing paper. The imprint of the seal on the wax was an easily identifiable device, or the writers monogram.

Adams Express, heavy lead toad stool hdl, ornate border.......85.00
Adams Express Co, w/station name.......................85.00
American Ry Express, rnd matrix, tall wood hdl..............35.00
American Ry Express, 1 pc cast brass, hollow bulb hdl........35.00
European, 4 lobed/inscription border/coat of arms/eagle, 1600s.110.00
Ivory & brass, crested, 1700s, 3½"......................145.00
Montreal & Champlain Junction, brass, dtd 1820............20.00
Official, city, ornate cast steel.........................20.00
R Lalique, nude, frosted opal, circle base w/monogram, 2½"...215.00

Railway Express Agency, w/station name..................30.00
Script engraving, brass, trn hdl, 1¼x3½"..................10.00
Southern Express Co, w/station name..................65.00
Wax sealer, Nat'l Express Co, ornate, solid bulb, oval........150.00
Wells Fargo Express, Bement, Ill, Depot..................125.00
Wood, geometric design, 2"..................20.00

Sebastians

Sebastian miniatures were first produced in 1938 by Prescott W. Baston, in Marblehead, Massachusetts. Since then, he has modeled more than four hundred. These figurines have been sold through gift shops all over the country, primarily in the New England states. In 1976, Baston withdrew his 'Sebastians' from production. Under an agreement with the Lance Corporation of Hudson, Massachusetts, one hundred designs were selected to be produced by that company under Baston's supervision. Those remaining were discontinued. In the short time since then, the older figurines have become very collectible.

Boy and Girl, Skating Pair, 1st Edition, 1978, green label, $45.00.

Abraham Lincoln, 1947..................90.00
Alco Wrap, pen stand, 1959..................700.00
Alexander Smith, Weaver, 1959..................400.00
Anne Boleyn, 1963..................575.00
Audiovox Dachshund, 1954..................450.00
Ben & Deborah Franklin, 1939..................170.00
Ben Franklin, pewter, 1972..................100.00
Betsy Ross, pewter, 1970..................100.00
Blacksmith, pewter, 1970..................210.00
Christopher Columbus, 1951..................290.00
Coronado & Senora, 1946..................190.00
Dahl's Fisherman, 1947..................160.00
Daniel & Mrs Boone, 1940..................210.00
Davy Crockett, 1955..................230.00
Democratic Victory, 1948..................375.00
Down East, 1952..................280.00
Emmett Kelly, 1949..................215.00
Eustace Tilley, 1949..................475.00
Expansion, plate, pewter, 1977..................105.00
Falstaff & Mistress Ford, 1947..................210.00
First House, Plimoth, 1952..................210.00

Gabriel & Evangeline, 1946..................220.00
Gem Crib & Cradle Co, 1953..................225.00
George & Martha Washington, 1946..................140.00
George Washington, pewter, 1970..................105.00
Glen Raven Panti Legs Girl, 1965..................375.00
Grocery Store, initials, 1960..................325.00
Harvey Girl, 1948..................270.00
Henry VIII, 1963..................670.00
Henry VIII & Ann Boleyn, 1947..................245.00
Horn of Plenty, 1940..................325.00
James & Elizabeth Monroe, 1946..................145.00
James Madison, bell, 1974..................90.00
James Madison, pewter, 1973..................80.00
Jean Lafitte & Catherine, 1946..................250.00
Jesus Nativity, wall hanging, 1940..................200.00
John Adams, bell, 1974..................120.00
John Alden & Priscilla, 1939..................160.00
John Hancock, 1949..................200.00
John Smith & Pocahontas, 1946..................225.00
Jolly Green Giant, 1956..................650.00
Jordan Marsh Observer, 1948..................230.00
Jordan Marsh Observer & Dame, 1951..................425.00
Judge Pyncheon, 1951..................180.00
King George Hotel Diving Board, 1956..................400.00
Lexington Minuteman, 1968..................440.00
Lost in the Kitchen, Jell-O, 1952..................300.00
Mark Antony, 1950..................195.00
Mayflower, 1957..................120.00
Merchants Warren Sailor, 1961..................225.00
Metropolitan Tower, pen stand, 1960..................825.00
Moose, Jell-O, 1954..................450.00
Mr & Mrs Beacon Hill, 1947..................185.00
Mr & Mrs John Harvard, 1940..................200.00
Mr Obocel, 1950..................200.00
Nathaniel Hawthorne, 1948..................265.00
National Diaper Service, 1950..................280.00
Naumkeag Indian, bronze, 1964..................165.00
New England Little Wanderers, 1965..................1,000.00
Old Lady & Shoe, Jell-O, 1955..................450.00
Old Powder House, 1952..................375.00
Old Put Takes A Licking, 1953..................350.00
Our Lady of LeLeche, 1954..................275.00
Parade Rest, 1953..................105.00
Paul Revere Plaque, Grant, 1966..................350.00
Peter & Annie Stuvvesant, 1940..................250.00
Pilgrims, 1947..................105.00
Romeo & Juliet, 1947..................220.00
Royal Worcester Blacksmith, 1973..................550.00
Royal Worcester Cabinetmaker, 1973..................300.00
Royal Worcester Clockmaker, 1975..................500.00
Royal Worcester Potter, 1973..................250.00
Sales Demonstrator, mounted on wood base, 1952..........1,250.00
Sebastian dealer plaque, 1951..................310.00
Shaker Man & Lady, 1946..................230.00
Shawmut Indian, painted, 1947..................180.00
Son of the Desert, Allepo, 1961..................275.00
Son of the Desert, 1960..................270.00
Spirit of '76, Marblehead Bank, 1959..................225.00
Spirit of '76, pewter, 1975..................575.00
Spirit of '76, plate, pewter..................130.00
Spirit of '76, Rotary Club, 1961..................250.00
St Joan of Arc, bronze, 1954..................275.00
St Jude Thaddeus, 1961..................550.00
St Sebastian, ivory, 1956..................290.00

Stearns' Chestnut Hill Mall, 1953.....................350.00
Stork, Jell-O, 1952...............................625.00
Supp-Hose Lady, 1960.............................350.00
Swan Boat Brooch, 1954...........................450.00
Swedish Boy and Girl, 1948.........................495.00
Weighing the Baby, 1952..........................230.00
William & Hannah Penn, 1946......................220.00
William Penn, 1954...............................375.00
Williamsburg Governor & Lady, 1946................145.00

Sevres

Fine quality porcelains have been made in Sevres, France, since the early 1700s. Rich ground colors were decorated with hand painted portraits, scenics and florals, transfer printing or decalcomania, and were often embellished with heavy gold. These wares are the most respected of all French porcelain. Their style and designs have been widely copied.

Bowl, cupids w/dove, verso: florals, ornate bronze mt, 22″ L..2,200.00
Box, Napoleon & military by Dauchet, bronze mt, 15½″ L...2,200.00
Box, oval w/dome lid, maroon w/florals/gold scrolls, 6½x9″....265.00
Box, scenic top/sides HP by Frane, shaped, bronze mt, 9″ L.1,210.00
Bust, Marie Antoinette, on waisted socle/ped, bisque, 13½″....200.00
Clock, mantel; 4 columns, HP panels, leaf crest, 1910, 16″ L..650.00
Plate, Henriette le Bourbon-Conti, sgn J Georget, cobalt rim...225.00
Plate, Mme De Pompadour, sgn, yellow/gold border, 9½″.....225.00
Table, Louis XVI portrait surrounded by 6 smaller, 19″ dia...1,320.00
Tete-A-Tete, portrait panels on blue, 18″ tray+7 pcs........1,540.00
Urn, cobalt & gold, 9″..................................145.00
Urn, Napoleonic scenes/castle scenes, sgn Guy, 19″, pr......3,350.00
Vase, blue, oval w/riding party, interlaced L's mk, 30″.......1,650.00
Vase, blue w/gilt floral swags/ped/swan neck hdls/cap, 20″, pr..550.00
Vase, landscapes, scrolled gilt/jewel borders, rstr, 15″, pr.....1,430.00
Vase, portrait panels, bronze hdls w/female figurals, lid, 28″..2,250.00
Vase, w/lid, Battle of Denain in oval, bronze mt, rstr, 32″....3,300.00
Vase, w/lid, game of chess, verso: garden, Lucot, rstr, 31″....3,025.00
Vase, w/lid, romantic scene in oval, foliate hdls, ped ft, 18″....550.00
Vase, w/lid, seaport, bl w/much gilt, 34″, G...............1,980.00

Center bowl, gilt-bronze mountd, shepherd lovers in landscape, signed L. Morin, 15″ diameter, $1,760.00.

Sewer Tile

Whimsies, advertising novelties, and other ornamental items were sometimes made in potteries where the primary product was simply tile.

Fish, slab form with hand tooled details, 10″, $100.00.

Ash tray, imp ROMIG Uhricksville, O; sm base flakes, 4″ dia....10.00
Bank, pig, br/gr/gray mottle, wood insert, 10″...............475.00
Bank, seated dog, tooled face, minor chips, 9″..............175.00
Bell tile trap, mk Nat'l Sewer Pipe Co, Akron, 4″ L..........20.00
Desk set, handmade, dog/4 stumps/2 snakes, hand tooled, 4x9″.220.00
Desk set, 3 open stumps w/bird's nest, chips, 2¼x5″.........18.00
Dish, imp Adams, Allison & Co, Mfg; 3″ dia................20.00
Fish bowl ornament, castle tower, 1927, minor base chips, 3½″.40.00
Hot plate, 3¾″ thick, 9½″ dia.........................18.00
Jug, hand formed, primitive, dtd 1911, 6″..................25.00
Lamp, tree & 2 stumps, dtd 1929, glued base break, 8″........25.00
Lamp, tree trunk w/3 open stems, nude lady & lion, 1928, 14″.575.00
Paperweight, bell tile on beveled base, Crown Co, 3x4½″.......22.50
Paperweight, Minerva head, imp Nelsonville SP Co, 4½″.......25.00
Pipe, 4 part, imp HB Camp Co, minor flakes, 4″ L...........10.00
Pitcher, primitive, applied hdl, brushed surface, 6¼″...........35.00
Pitcher, tooled tree trunk hdl, applied branches/leaves, 7½″....95.00
Planter, 5 protruding branches, minor chips, 36″............350.00
Plaque, 2 roses in relief, 16″ dia.........................15.00
Shaving mug, wht clay, mottled br/blk, sgraffito, 1879, 3″, VG...65.00
String holder, funny man's head, hand tooled features, 7x6″...225.00
Vase, stump, 11¼″.................................70.00
Whimsey, baby shoe, 3¾″ L...........................20.00
Whimsey, chicken, tooled detail, edge flakes, 2½″.............10.00
Whimsey, cowboy boot, hand tooled, 3¼″..................15.00
Whimsey, dog, open front legs, EX detail, ruby eyes, 13″......250.00
Whimsey, dog, seated, hand tooled face & collar, G glaze, 12″.225.00
Whimsey, dog, seated, rectangular base, sm edge chips, 5¾″...115.00
Whimsey, dog, seated, tooled face, collar & ft, 11″..........215.00
Whimsey, frog, hand tooled features, goggle eyes, 6″.........150.00
Whimsey, frog, 3¾″ L..............................35.00
Whimsey, horseshoe/bell tile/brick, advertising sample, 7x10″....40.00
Whimsey, Indian, hand tooled, holes for feathers, 10″........275.00
Whimsey, pig, tooled face, base chips, 8¾″.................205.00

Sewing Items

In the early colonial days, the teaching of needlework skills was considered an important part of a young girl's education. The Victorians developed many curious yet functional sewing accessories. One of these is the sewing bird. Made of brass, wood, or iron, these figural tools were designed to be clamped onto the top of the worktable. Through the lever action of the tail, the beak would open and close to hold the fabric in the proper position for hand sewing. A velvet pincushion often topped it off.

The first mechanical sewing machine was invented by Thomas Paint, an Englishman, in 1790. The first American patent went to Elias Howe in 1840 -- but Howe took his invention to England! Not until 1846, when the Wheeler Wilson Mfg. Company was founded, were there any truly functional home sewing machines. The first electric machine was developed by Isaac Singer in 1889.

Thimbles have long been collectible. Some were made of silver -- a few in gold. Many were embossed with scrolls, engraved, and occasionally jeweled! Hallmarked examples are especially valuable.

Sewing caddy, English, turned wood, brass eyes, 10″ x 8½″, $75.00.

Basket, ash splint, rnd top/sq base, hdl/lid, orig pnt, 16x10″....85.00
Basket, wicker, tufted interior.....35.00
Bodkin, engraved florals & etc, ½″.....20.00
Bodkin, sterling, fancy embossed florals, ⅜″ W.....22.00
Booklet, Fancy Needlework, 1843, 3¼x5″.....12.00
Booklet, Singer Sewing Library, 1930, 4 in case.....10.00
Box, Chinese, w/coins & glass beads, 5¾″ W.....18.50
Box, mahog, trn ft & ivory finial, line inlay/2 drw/mirror, 9″....185.00
Box, satinwood w/orig ivory lace-making tools/2 birds, 1825..1,250.00
Box, thread; Brooks, HP Victorian lady atop, 3½x4″.....25.00
Box, tiny oak table w/drawer, cushion top, 1910, 4½″.....30.00
Box, wool w/scissor holder, emb brass, girl/flowing hair, 3x4″....70.00
Button hole cutter, wrought iron, wood hdl, 2 sizes, early, 7″...95.00
Darning egg, blown, bl glass.....30.00
Darning egg, dtd Nov 8, 1907.....15.00
Darning egg, ebony, ornate sterling mk hdl.....25.00
Darning egg, walnut, very lg.....16.00
Display case, bl/wht tin, Boyles needles.....45.00
Kit, celluloid fish, 6″.....15.00
Kit, leather, w/Belding thread, thimble, etc.....10.00
Machine, Gateway, Jr Model NP-1, pat pending, operable.....35.00
Machine, Kayanee, Berlin, US Zone Germany.....30.00
Machine, Singer For Girls, japanned finish, gold stripes, 1920..175.00
Machine, Wheeler & Wilson, pat 1850, treadle w/2 foot shapes.750.00
Needle box, ivory, 1½″.....22.00
Needle case, book, allover beading, roses/lyre, dtd 1838.....95.00
Needle case, brass w/MOP, engraved designs, early 1700s, 4″...580.00
Needle case, hand holding umbrella, ivory, China Trade, 4½″...75.00
Needle case, paper, Aunt Jemima.....15.00
Needle case, paper, Our Presidents, 1926.....5.00
Needle case, parasol figural, ivory, 4¼″ long.....125.00
Needle case, pea pod figural, ivory.....175.00
Needle case, sterling, mk Victoria Mexico.....20.00
Needle case, vegetable ivory, intricate shape/carved, 4x1¼″ dia.70.00
Needle case/thread holder, 3 grooved channels, tape measure....55.00
Needle threader, tin, Coats & Clark.....20.00
Oil can, Singer, in script.....4.00
Pincushion, bisque cherub on shell, German.....25.00
Pincushion, Black doll, worn, 6″.....35.00
Pincushion, carved wooden shoe, 5½″.....30.00
Pincushion, decorated bucket, lift-off top, mirror w/in, 2″.....65.00
Pincushion, Dutch wooden shoe w/silver decor, 4½″.....65.00
Pincushion, metal, clamp-on, Victorian, rnd.....45.00
Pincushion, red velvet, Indian beaded, heart shaped, 1895, 5″...35.00
Pincushion, Sta-Flat advertising.....8.00

Pincushion, tin flat iron w/wood hdl, tape pulls from side.....8.00
Pincushion, treen, table clamp, plush pad, 2½″ L.....60.00
Pincushion/pin box, Collingbourne's Pure Silk for Mending.....16.00
Ruler, silver w/roses relief on hdl, S Kirk, 4″.....48.00
Scissors, Cut Your Costs, Buy CWS Goods.....14.00
Scissors, embroidery; sterling hdl, fancy engraving.....25.00
Scissors, man on 1 hdl, lady on other, SP, 10¼″, VG.....85.00
Scissors, tailor's; Clauss.....22.00
Sewing bird, brass, clamp-on, 5″.....75.00
Sewing bird, bronzed steel figural bird, complete, early.....135.00
Sewing case, pnt celluloid, thimble top.....25.00
Sewing clamp, carved ivory, red silk cushion, Victorian, 2¼″....50.00
Sewing clamp, w/mirror, thimble holder.....85.00
Stand, 4 tier walnut, pincushion top/bobbin/thread holder, 10″..35.00
Tape measure, 'Lucky Joy Germ', celluloid.....75.00
Tape measure, barrel, celluloid.....65.00
Tape measure, barrel w/native, celluloid.....70.00
Tape measure, basket of flowers, celluloid.....65.00
Tape measure, boat, celluloid.....15.00
Tape measure, cat, celluloid, Occupied Japan.....24.00
Tape measure, chicks in basket, celluloid, Germany, 2″.....35.00
Tape measure, clock, works.....50.00
Tape measure, clown head w/hat, celluloid.....95.00
Tape measure, coronation coach, brass w/red windows, 2½x1½″.35.00
Tape measure, cow, celluloid.....110.00
Tape measure, Dixie Lye, bl/wht celluloid, w/lye can.....20.00
Tape measure, dog in captain's hat, binoculars, wht celluloid....80.00
Tape measure, elephant, mc/china.....20.00
Tape measure, Fab box, celluloid.....19.00
Tape measure, fish, celluloid, 'Asbury Park', 4¾″.....17.50
Tape measure, fishing reel, wooden.....60.00
Tape measure, Frigidare man.....25.00
Tape measure, girl w/mandolin.....35.00
Tape measure, high shoe.....55.00
Tape measure, Hill Top Poultry Medicines.....20.00
Tape measure, Jamestown Expo, celluloid case, 1908.....25.00
Tape measure, John Deere.....32.00
Tape measure, kangaroo, celluloid.....27.00
Tape measure, Mark Twain, celluloid.....100.00
Tape measure, monkey w/celluloid head.....14.00
Tape measure, Nouveau, sterling, dtd 1891.....160.00
Tape measure, pig, brass.....55.00

Tape measure, pig, pewter..............................28.00
Tape measure, pig, silver...............................35.00
Tape measure, pig, wht celluloid.........................15.00
Tape measure, pig, wht celluloid w/HP flowers, 2"........25.00
Tape measure, pirate ship, red celluloid, Japan..............28.00
Tape measure, rabbit, celluloid........................120.00
Tape measure, Red Goose, advertising.....................38.00
Tape measure, rooster, tape pulls from beak, pin tray below......8.50
Tape measure, sadiron, metal...........................45.00
Tape measure, Sears, Roebuck, Bradley Plows, celluloid........30.00
Tape measure, ship, celluloid...........................55.00
Tape measure, souvenir, Hotel Aspinwall, library, 1¾" dia......25.00
Tape measure, spiked helmet, blk tin/gold trim/pnt cross, 1914..80.00
Tape measure, stanhope, bone barrel, view: Herod's Palace.....55.00
Tape measure, Stromberg Carburetors.....................30.00
Tape measure, terrier, celluloid.........................90.00
Tape measure, toucan, celluloid.........................75.00
Tape measure, tulip, celluloid..........................40.00
Tape measure, wash basket, celluloid.....................70.00
Tape measure, windmill, brass, mechanical..................45.00
Tatter, sterling......................................20.00
Thimble, aluminum w/advertising.........................12.00
Thimble, gold plated, engraved flowers & initials, sgn.........30.00
Thimble, porcelain, bird on branch, artist sgn, 1934, English...190.00
Thimble, sterling, agate top, dtd 1899...................140.00
Thimble, sterling, Charles Horner, dtd 1900................45.00
Thimble, sterling, Dorcas..............................45.00
Thimble, sterling, etched scene.........................50.00
Thimble, sterling, fancy engraved gold edge, size 8..........40.00
Thimble, sterling, mk Simons, egg & dart base, lg size........50.00
Thimble, sterling, overall relief scroll & floral, mk..........25.00
Thimble, sterling, scenic/house/lake, mk..................25.00
Thimble, sterling, shot cup, Only A Thimble Full............75.00
Thimble, sterling, w/tiny rubies, colored glass top, engraved....125.00
Thimble, sterling, wide band w/scrolls....................30.00
Thimble, 10k, double row engraving......................85.00
Thimble, 14k, band w/script mono, 1800s.................200.00
Thimble, 14k, engraved band, beading....................90.00
Thimble, 14k, engraved band, monogram..................95.00
Thimble, 14k, harbor scene, sgn.........................75.00
Thimble, 14k, Simmons...............................135.00
Thimble, 14k, wide scrolled band, house scene, unmk........115.00
Thimble, 14k, 12 sided, size 12.........................95.00
Thimble holder, kitten on rectangular base, Pairpoint SP.......55.00
Thimble holder/pincushion, 1933 World's Fair, wooden shoe, 4".20.00
Thread holder, brass, enamel decor.......................20.00
Thread holder, ivory, barrel shape, interior spool, 2"x1" dia....80.00
Thread waxer, cylinder, inlaid wood top & base, Victorian......75.00
Threader, sterling fish................................25.00
Travel kit, enamel/sterling, opal glass top thimble/scissors.....125.00

Thimble holder, sterling silver filigree, hinged lid, 1¼", $135.00.

Shaker Items

The Shaker community was founded in America in 1776 at Niskeyuna, New York, by a small group of English 'Shaking Quakers'. The name referred to a group dance which was part of their religious rites. Their leader was Mother Ann Lee.

By 1815 their membership had grown to more than one thousand in eighteen communities as far west as Indiana and Kentucky. But in less than a decade, their numbers began to decline, until today only a handful remain.

Their furniture is prized for its originality, simplicity, workmanship, and practicality. Few pieces were signed. Some were carefully finished to enhance the natural wood; a few were painted.

Although other methods were used earlier, most Shaker boxes were of oval construction with overlapping 'fingers' at the seams to prevent buckling as the wood aged. Boxes with original paint fetch double the price of an unpainted box; size and number of fingers should also be considered.

Although the Shakers were responsible for weaving a great number of baskets, their methods are not easily distinguished from those of their outside neighbors, and it is nearly impossible without first-hand knowledge to specifically attribute one to their manufacture. They were involved in various commercial efforts other than cabinetmaking -- among them sheep and dairy farming, sawmills, and pipe and brick making. They were the first to raise crops specifically for seed, and to market their product commercially. They perfected a method to recycle paper, and were able to produce wrinkle-free fabrics.

Apple picker, cherry w/wrought iron fork, blade gone, 10x14"...65.00
Basket, berry; fancy cut-out split wood sides, tin base, 4x4½"...65.00
Basket, miniature kitten head, rpr, 3½"...................475.00
Basket, primitive woven splint, worn, shellacked, 8x14"........75.00
Basket, split poplar filled w/cone of pinhead 'berries', 2¾".....20.00
Basket, woven cane w/dbl hinged lids, minor wear, 7½x10x14"..70.00
Basket, woven grass, melon ribbed, slight wear, 3½x7½".......32.50
Basket, woven splint, worn/weathered, 9"+hdlx15"............75.00
Bevel gauge, att Enfield, NH, wood, 8" L..................22.50
Book, The Manifesto, pub Shaker Village, NH, 1886, 6x9".....35.00
Book strap, worn orig tape, rpr, 6¼" W...................40.00
Bottle, apothecary, blown w/pressed stopper, printed label, 8"...45.00
Bottle, apothecary, clear pressed w/label, cork stopper, 7"......20.00
Bottle, aqua, Shaker Pickles, Portland EDP & Co, sickness, 9"..75.00
Bottle, emb Fluid Extract Valerian, aqua, pontiled, 3½"........40.00
Bowl, wood w/end hdls, worn finish, 3½x21x10½"............95.00
Box, gathering; wood w/leather shoulder strap, gr pnt, 1910....125.00
Box, lift lid/drw, pine w/dvtl sides, rfn, 12x18x12"............225.00
Box, seed; label Choice Vegetable Seeds, incomplete, 22x9"....75.00
Box, sewing; geometric decor in inlaid wood on lid, 4x8x11", G.55.00
Box, sewing; mahog w/bird's eye inlay, tray missing, 8x11"......65.00
Box, wood; poplar, hinged lid, old rpt, porcelain knob, 25x22".180.00
Box, writing; walnut, simple fitted interior, 3½x8x11"..........70.00
Box, 1 finger, copper tacks, for spices, set of 3.............435.00
Box, 1 finger, copper tacks, traces of old paint, 6¼" oval.....115.00
Box, 1 finger, natural, minor break, oval, 5½"..............225.00
Box, 1 finger, worn bl pnt, lid damage, oval, 5"............250.00
Box, 1 finger, worn flame graining, oval, 3x4".............275.00
Box, 1 finger, worn varnish, oval, 2½x4¾x6"...............170.00
Box, 2 fingers, Candied Flag Root, prepared at Enfield, 3½"...550.00
Box, 2 fingers, old patina, 8" dia.......................250.00
Box, 2 fingers, old red, 11¾".........................250.00
Box, 2 fingers, orig red/br, lid chips, oval, 5¼x7"..........195.00
Box, 3 fingers, copper tacks, natural, oval, 2¼x4x6".........235.00
Box, 3 fingers, mustard wash, 8½" dia..................700.00
Box, 3 fingers, red stained, 9¼"......................275.00
Box, 3 fingers, varnished, oval, 11½"...................450.00
Box, 4 fingers, tiger maple/pine, 13½"..................600.00

Brush, horsehair, trn hdl, 10″ L............................25.00
Bucket, sap; wood staves w/metal bands, yellow varnish........45.00
Bucket, sugar; wood staves, copper tacks, gray pnt, 15″......155.00
Bucket, sugar; wood staves, copper tacks, green pnt, 14x14″...215.00
Bucket, sugar; wood staves, copper tacks, rpr, rfn, 10x8½″.....45.00
Bucket, sugar; wood staves, copper tacks, 10½″.............70.00
Bucket, sugar; wood/copper tacks, CA Wilder, orig bl pnt, 14″.285.00
Carpet beater, bent willow w/trn beech hdl, minor break, 42″...75.00
Carrier, 4 fingers, 10¾″....................................125.00
Case, sewing; bronzed leather/velvet/silk, 5½″...............50.00
Clothespins, whittled, 2 w/tin bands, 4¾″ to 6″, 3 for.......115.00
Coffee pot, tin, wide spout, hinged lid, wood hdl w/bale, 10″....45.00
Comb, shampoo...68.00
Commode, butternut, cut-out legs, paneled doors, rfn, rpr......325.00
Corn cutter, 5½x11″..50.00
Corn planter, orig gr pnt worn, blk Shaker label, trn hdl, 32″...75.00
Corn sheller, 2 planks w/sq nail teeth, trn hdl, red stain.......60.00
Dipper, tin, 6½″ L...50.00
Dipper strainer, trn wood bowl & inserted hdl, 13″...........45.00
Dough scraper, wrought iron, 4½″...........................35.00
Drying rack, mortised, 1 spindle broken, 20x23″.............350.00
Drying rack, 2 part mortised pine, burlap hinges, 30x72″......105.00
Dust pan, tin, slightly battered, 8x15″......................40.00
Embroidery hoop, trn table clamp, age cracks, 7½″ dia........65.00
Furniture, see Furniture
Glove stretcher, 11″ L......................................65.00
Gout stool, folding, made from several sizes of dowels, 12x21″..45.00
Herb rake, primitive, Union Village, 49½″...................110.00
Inkwell, black stone, primitive carved heart/X-hatch, 2″ sq.....35.00
Kneeling bench, pine w/old pnt, Canterbury, 7½x25″ L.......115.00
Kraut cutter, poplar/pine, rectangle top, short ft, 4x9x18″......65.00
Ladle, wood, wide hdl, good wear & patina, 9″...............80.00
Marking ink cup, tin, wood ball, 5″ dia w/4″ hdl.............35.00
Measure, bentwood, rfn, new nails in rim, 7x11¼″ dia........25.00
Measure, bentwood w/strap iron band, rpt, 5x9½″............40.00
Mixer, trn wood lid-like top fits crock, trn crank, 13½″.......45.00
Mold, wax; trn wood, 3 for.................................35.00
Noodle cutter, wood, 12¼″ L..............................50.00
Pamphlet, medical; Shakers' Manual, worn, 6x9″..............5.00
Peg rail, pine, beaded edge & 4 trn maple pegs, 23″..........45.00
Pegboard, pine, beaded edge, 7 trn maple pegs, 54″, EX......200.00
Pegboard, 8 trn pegs, bl pnt, rpl, 30½″....................165.00
Pincushion, sgn Sabbath Day, Maine.........................42.50
Pincushion, treen, table clamp, plush pad, 5″...............75.00
Pincushion, trn wood base w/wire pins for spools, w/label, 6″...65.00
Pincushion, velvet, 5½″ dia.................................8.00
Plane, for cutting spills, mk LH, 11½″......................115.00
Rake, wood w/worn bl pnt, well constructed, 76″.............145.00
Rolling pin, maple, rfn, surface scars, 15″..................40.00
Rolling pin, trn wood, 14″ L................................30.00
Sander, turned wood, Mt Lebanon, 3½″.....................70.00
Seed box, orig yel pnt, label: '...Vegetable Seed', 9x22″......415.00
Sieve, bentwood w/horsehair, stains & wear, 7″ dia...........65.00
Sleeve board, cherry, 24½″ L...............................40.00
Sock stretcher, wood, 26″ L................................15.00
Spinning wheel, mk JA, 1751-1829, old splits, 61x45″ dia.....175.00
Stirrer for open kettle, S-form agitator w/old split, 18x19″.....35.00
Stove, CI w/wrought detail, Mt Lebanon, rpr crack in side, 19″.225.00
Stove pipe shelves w/adjustable clamp, sheet metal, 16x25″.....85.00
Swift, table clamp, orig yellow varnish, rpr, staves rpl, 24″....95.00
Table scarf, red/wht, w/tassels, 18″.........................65.00
Tailor's worktable, mortised legs fold, scarred, rpl, 60″ L......400.00
Tool, leather working; hand wrought, trn hdls/brass ferrule......20.00
Towel bar, cherry, removable bar for continuous towel, 22″....105.00

Trestle, folding, mortised construction, old patina, 29x48″.....65.00
Weaver's stool, trn front ft, rpl paper rush seat, 30″.........200.00
Yarn reel, trn column/legs, top mount clock hand counter, 46″.130.00

Shaving Mugs

In the 1860s it became a popular practice for every shaving man to have his own shaving mug. Mugs belonging to men who frequented the barber shop for their tonsorial services were often personalized with their owner's name, and kept on display on the barber's shelf. Occupational shaving mugs became the high point of individualism during this period. China mugs, mostly made in France, Germany, and Austria, were imported by American barber supply companies where artists hand painted the occupation, fraternal or sports affiliation of its customer on the mug, and adding the name, usually in gold. The mug was then fired in a kiln for later use and displayed in the local barber shop. Because of sanitary rules and restrictions imposed around 1915, they were eventually taken off the barbers' shelves.

Today, occupational shaving mugs are the most valuable of all the decorated mugs. Although some are valued by the excellence of the artist, most are priced by the rarity of the subject matter.

The John Hudson Moore Company produced a line of Sportsman mugs in 1953 and 1954.

Advertising, HP elk.......................................60.00
Aluminum, very old & simple...............................75.00
Ben Hur..90.00
Civil War, HP Am flag facing left, Union Forever............135.00
Clambroth, pressed 'Robin & Wheat', soap divider...........100.00
Copper lustre, blue bands, large............................85.00
CT Germany, floral, mc....................................30.00
Eagle, two 25 star flags, name.............................180.00
Floral, HP, gold name & trim...............................60.00
Floral, HP, w/name, gold edge, dtd 1925....................65.00
Floral & grapes, scrolled relief, divided top, drain holes........30.00
Fraternal, BPOE, elk head center, gold top/bottom, mc, NM....78.00
Fraternal, GAR, w/name, owl & moon.......................90.00
Fraternal, Improved Order of Red Men, eagle & shields, T&V...75.00
Fraternal, Knights Templar insignia, gold hdl/base, mk Germany.55.00
Fraternal, Order of Eagles, symbol in color, gold name........110.00
Germany, rose decor, ftd, scalloped rim/ornate hdl, soap shelf...25.00
Germany, roses, mk 3 Crown China.........................22.00
Germany, spread eagle/Am flag & shield/English flag, NM......110.00
Medallions w/colorful flowers, lt bl ground, gold/rim, NM.......38.00
Milk glass, pressed 'Robin & Wheat', ped, soap divider, 1870s..100.00
Occupational, accountant, roll-top desk.....................200.00
Occupational, artist, pallette & brushes w/name, NM..........110.00
Occupational, bartender, men in bar, name in gold............125.00
Occupational, boxcar.....................................100.00
Occupational, butcher, steer w/carving tools, gold bands, NM...150.00
Occupational, carpenter, tools/saw/plane/chisel, gold scroll.....150.00
Occupational, dentist.....................................110.00
Occupational, farmer w/horses & plow, gold name, EX........165.00
Occupational, gamebird in grass...........................115.00
Occupational, horse head, horseshoe & flowers, name..........65.00
Occupational, metal worker................................175.00
Occupational, musician, trombone w/name, T&V Limoges, NM..125.00
Occupational, railroad, Masonic............................200.00
Occupational, railroad, woodburning locomotive, Limoges......175.00
Occupational, salesman, shoe store scene, Made In Burma.....105.00
Occupational, skull & crossbones, Dr Melville................135.00
Occupational, telegraph operator, VG.......................175.00
Occupational, tinsmith w/snips & hammer....................105.00
Occupational, trolley, BL RR...............................200.00

RS Germany, floral, emb scroll/sq/scalloped/divided w/drain......48.00
RS Prussia, gr w/pk & yel roses.........................110.00
Scrolls, 'Father', in gold.............................45.00
Sterling, bulbous shape, dtd 1891, monogram..............150.00
Violets, HP, in relief on gr melon rib, fancy soap drain........35.00
Will & Finck, pk w/bl & red flowers & fan w/name, bulbous....297.00

Shawnee

The Shawnee Pottery Company operated in Zanesville, Ohio, from 1937 to 1961. They produced inexpensive novelty ware -- vases, flowerpots, and figurines -- as well as a very successful line of figural cookie jars. These cookie jars and their dinnerware, the Corn Line, are very popular with today's collectors.

Ash tray, orange w/silver & gold spots, #219.................7.00
Ash tray, woven decor, pink............................3.00
Ash tray/coaster, playing card decor, #411.................4.50
Bean pot, handled, gray w/wht lid, red lobster, Kenwood, #907..12.00
Bookends, flying geese, pr............................25.00
Bowl, pink & black, Kenwood, #2112.....................10.00
Bud vase, #1014, blue w/gray lines......................8.00
Bud vase, #1402, green & black........................10.00
Candle holder, pink & black, #2113, pr...................12.00
Candle holder, w/hdl, tan, #3026, 2¼x6¼"...............12.00
Candy dish, blue, #154...............................6.00
Cookie jar, Dutch Boy, blue pants......................35.00
Cookie jar, Dutch Boy, blue pants w/patches, gold trim........75.00
Cookie jar, Dutch Boy, yellow pants....................35.00
Cookie jar, Dutch Girl, gold trim.......................60.00
Cookie jar, Dutch Girl, tulip decor.....................35.00
Cookie jar, Elephant, #60............................35.00
Cookie jar, Fruit Basket, lg...........................35.00
Cookie jar, Lucky Elephant, blue scarf, black eyes & trim......45.00
Cookie jar, Mugsey, gold trim.........................65.00
Cookie jar, Owl, decorated...........................40.00
Cookie jar, Owl, gold trim............................75.00
Cookie jar, Owl, plain...............................38.00
Cookie jar, Puss 'n Boots, decorated....................50.00
Cookie jar, Puss 'n Boots, plain.......................35.00

Cookie jar, Winnie Pig, blue daisies on white, $50.00.

Cookie jar, Sailor Boy, decorated.......................45.00
Cookie jar, Sailor Boy, plain..........................30.00
Cookie jar, Smiley Pig, (bank/cookie) brown...............75.00
Cookie jar, Smiley Pig, (bank/cookie) salmon..............75.00
Cookie jar, Smiley Pig, pink bib, flower, gold trim...........60.00
Cookie jar, Smiley Pig, tulip decor.....................40.00
Cookie jar, Winnie Pig, (bank/cookie) brown...............75.00
Cookie jar, Winnie Pig, little decor.....................50.00
Corn, bowl, #6.....................................14.00
Corn, bowl, #94....................................15.00
Corn, butter dish...................................30.00
Corn, casserole, ind................................30.00
Corn, casserole, lg.................................35.00
Corn, cookie jar w/lid...............................60.00
Corn, creamer.....................................15.00
Corn, cup, #90....................................12.50
Corn, cup & saucer.................................18.00
Corn, fruit dish, #92................................12.00
Corn, mug..18.00
Corn, plate, #68...................................14.50
Corn, platter, #96..................................24.50
Corn, popcorn set in orig box........................135.00
Corn, relish, #79...................................16.00
Corn, shakers, 3½", pr..............................15.00
Corn, shakers, 5½", pr..............................20.00
Corn, sugar w/lid...................................25.00
Corn, teapot, 1 cup, #65.............................75.00
Creamer, elephant..................................10.00
Creamer, Puss 'n Boots..............................15.00
Creamer, Puss 'n Boots, #85, EX color & detail............20.00
Creamer, Smiley Pig, yellow w/blue scarf, #86, 4½".........18.00
Figurine, teddy bear................................16.00
Flower pot, bowknot, maroon, attached saucer..............4.00
French casserole, lobster, Kenwood, #900.................10.00
Jam jar w/lid, fruit basket............................45.00
Lamp, covered wagon................................30.00
Mug, hammered copper lustre, #990, 5¾"................20.00
Pitcher, Bo-Peep, gold trim & decals, 8"..................38.00
Pitcher, Bo-Peep, multicolor..........................35.00
Pitcher, Chanticleer.................................25.00
Pitcher, elephant....................................9.00
Pitcher, fruit, tilt..................................35.00
Pitcher, Smiley Pig, pnt detail w/gold....................40.00
Planter, basketweave, #1317..........................10.00
Planter, black/wht, Kenwood, #2112....................10.00
Planter, bloodhound, #610.............................6.00
Planter, bowl, #181..................................6.50
Planter, boy by stump, #533............................5.00
Planter, boy w/chopsticks by yellow bamboo, gold decor, #702...12.50
Planter, bull, black & pink............................27.00
Planter, Cameo, #2506................................9.00
Planter, car, #506...................................6.50
Planter, cherub.....................................6.00
Planter, clock, maroon face, #530......................16.00
Planter, clown, #619.................................8.50
Planter, clown, gold trim, #607........................12.00
Planter, cockatiel, tan/brown, #523......................8.50
Planter, cocker spaniel w/house, gold trim................14.00
Planter, Coolie with cart, #539.........................6.00
Planter, covered wagon, #514..........................6.50
Planter, deer, #752..................................6.50
Planter, doe, gold trim, #624..........................12.00
Planter, doe & fawn figural, #669......................12.50
Planter, donkey & cart, #538...........................7.50

Planter, Dutch children, #710 . . . . .12.50
Planter, Dutch girl 14.00
Planter, elephant, black 25.00
Planter, elf, gold trim, #536 . . . . .6.50
Planter, elf by box, #566 . . . . .5.00
Planter, fawn, #737 . . . . .12.00
Planter, fawn figural, wht/gray, #624 . . . . .15.00
Planter, fawn lying before log, #766 . . . . .18.00
Planter, fish, #845 . . . . .5.00
Planter, gazelle, USA #613 . . . . .5.50
Planter, girl at fence, USA #581 .4.50
Planter, girl w/book, #574 . . . . .6.50
Planter, girl w/flowers, #616 . . . . .16.00
Planter, girl w/parasol, #701 . . . . .8.50
Planter, globe, #635, 7½″ 15.00
Planter, green/wht, #2503, 10″ 15.00
Planter, grist mill, #769 . . . . .16.00
Planter, man pushing cart, #621 . . . . .10.00
Planter, morning-glory, #181 . . . . .6.50
Planter, Polynesian girl, #896 .12.50
Planter, pump 10.00
Planter, rooster, #503 . . . . .15.00
Planter, shell, mk USA 3.00
Planter, squirrel on tree stump, #664 . . . . .6.00
Planter, Touche, ftd, #1024 . . . . .10.00
Planter, 2 Orientals carrying basket, #537 . . . . .6.00
Shakers, baskets of fruit, large .22.50
Shakers, baskets of fruit, 2½″, pr 8.00
Shakers, cats, 2½″, pr 8.00
Shakers, Chanticleer, 5″, pr 13.00
Shakers, chefs, gold trim, pr 12.00
Shakers, chefs, no gold, pr 7.00
Shakers, dogs, 2½″, pr 8.00
Shakers, dogs, 5″, pr 15.00
Shakers, Dutch boy & girl, 5″, pr 20.00
Shakers, Farmer Pig w/shovel, 2½″, pr 8.00
Shakers, Farmer Pig w/shovel, 5″, pr 12.00
Shakers, flower pots, 2½″, pr 8.00
Shakers, milk cans, pr 8.00
Shakers, Mugsey, 5″ 37.00
Shakers, owls, gold & decorated 25.00
Shakers, owls, 2½″, pr 10.00
Shakers, Puss 'n Boots, sm, pr 10.00
Shakers, Sailor boy & girl, pr .12.00
Shakers, Smiley Pig, blue, 2½″, pr 10.00
Shakers, Swiss children, gold decor, pr 15.00
Shakers, water cans 14.00
Shakers, Winnie Pig, 2½″, pr .12.00
Shakers, Winnie Pig & Farmer Pig 18.00
Sugar, lobster, Kenwood, #907 . . . . .10.00
Sugar, water bucket 22.00
Teapot, flower decor, ribbing at base 18.00
Teapot, Granny Anne, pink apron 38.00
Teapot, Granny Anne, w/basket gold detail & decals 70.00
Teapot, rose in relief, ribbed, USA 18.00
Teapot, Tom, Tom, the Piper's Son; no gold, #44 . . . . .38.00
Train, 4 pc 60.00
Vase, Arcature, green w/yellow deer, #850 . . . . .12.50
Vase, blue & pink, #1013 . . . . .8.00
Vase, bowknot, yellow, USA #819 . . . . .6.50
Vase, Cameo, blue w/cream, fluted top, #2505, 5½″ 12.50
Vase, cornucopia, red, #865 . . . . .10.00
Vase, dolphin, #828 . . . . .13.00
Vase, fan; USA #1264 . . . . .6.50

Vase, ivy, yellow, #805, 6″ 10.00
Vase, swan, yellow, #806, 6¼″ .12.50
Vase, wood grain, #868 . . . . .8.00
Wall pocket, red birds w/birdhouse, #830 . . . . .10.00
Watering can, red flowers, blue bands, 3½″ 6.50

Shearwater Pottery

Ash tray, gray w/blk/wht abstract, 5½″ 45.00
Pitcher, bulbous, 6″ 17.00
Pitcher, gray w/blk/br/wht abstract, squat, 5½″ 100.00
Vase, turquoise, 5″ 35.00

Sheet Music

Sheet music is often collected more for the colorful lithographed covers rather than for the music itself. Transportation songs which have pictures or illustrations of trains, ships, and planes; ragtime tunes which feature popular entertainers such as Al Jolson; or those with Disney characters are among the most valuable.

A-M-E-R-I-C-A Means I Love You, Liberty w/sword, 1917, lg sz . . .7.00
Aba Daba Honeymoon, Debbie Reynolds, large format, 1914 . . . . .5.50
ABC Boogie, Haley/Comets, 1954 . . . . .14.00
Alcoholic Blues, drunken owl w/top hat on moon w/cat, 1919, VG .5.00
All Mixed Up, Dionne Quints in Alpine costumes, 1938 . . . . . . .20.00
America First, by Callahan/Gray, lg G Washington, 1918, lg sz . . .8.00
At A Georgia Camp Meeting, by K Mills, shows Blk folks, 1897 . .10.00
At The High Brown Babies' Ball, Blk couple dancing, 1919, VG . .6.00
Because He Did His Duty, photo Sophie Tucker, 1913, lg sz, VG .8.00
Beginning Of The USA, Betsy Ross sews flag & map, 1916, VG . .4.00
Best Things Happen While You're Dancing, B Crosby, 1953, M . . .7.00
Brotherly Love, photo Lew Dockstader, 1906, lg sz, VG 8.00
Buy A Bale Of Cotton For Me, couple in cotton field, 1914, VG . .8.00
Celebratin' Day In Tennessee, photo Emma Carcus, 1914, lg, VG .8.00
Disillusion, Erich Von Stroheim looks at Jeanne Bates, 1946 . . . .8.00
Don't Be Cruel, Elvis Presley, EP Music, RCA, 1956 . . . . .15.00
El Rancho Rock, Champs, Challenge Records, 1958 . . . . .5.00
Estrallita, full figure of Harry James, 1914, G 5.00
Everything's Been Done Before, Jean Harlow, Art Jarrett, 1935 . .10.00
Farewell Daisy Bell, soldier w/sweetheart, 1905, lg sz, VG 4.00
Fatal Shot, Pres McKinley in casket, 1901, VG 20.00
Fifty Chubby Tiny Toes, Dionne Quints as babies, tinted, 1935 . .10.00
Five Minutes More, shows young Frank Sinatra, 1946 . . . . .3.50
Flying Down To Rio, from movie same title, Fred Astaire, 1933 . . .6.00
For You A Rose, Harrison Fisher illustration, 1910 . . . . .18.00
Freckles, Hess/Ager, pictures Nora Bayes, 1919, VG 5.00
Giant, E Taylor & R Hudson, also sm James Dean photo, 1956 . . .5.00
Girl Of Mine, Rolf Armstrong .12.00
Give Me A Little Kiss, Will You Huh?, full cover D Durbin, '45 . .12.50
Go Way Back & Sit Down, Blk man at rear of restaurant, 1901 . .10.00
Good Morning Glory, from Sitting Pretty, Ginger Rogers 8.00
Heart Of Wetona, pictures Norma Talmadge, 1919, VG 5.00
Heartbreak Hotel, Elvis Presley, Tree Pub Co, 1956 . . . . .15.00
How Lovely Is Christmas, gr cover, B Crosby w/hat & pipe, 1957 .6.00
Hush-A-Bye Island, from Smash Up, Susan Hayward, 1946 . . . . .6.00
I Don't Like No Cheap Man, photo McIntyre & Heath, 1897, lg .10.00
I Want To Shimmie, Brooks/Clarke, pictures Bee Palmer, 1919 . . .5.00
I Wonder Where My Easy Rider's Gone?, S Tucker, 1913 . . . . . .5.00
If I'm Not At The Roll Call, Boyden, soldiers in trenches, '18 . . . .4.00
In Caliente, Dolores Del Rio, yellow cover, 1935, NM 15.00
In My Merry Oldsmobile, couple in red convertible, 1905, EX 6.00

In The City Of Broken Hearts, lg photo Theda Bara, 1916, lg...10.00
In The Gloaming Mother Darling, mother/son/angel, 1918, lg sz..6.00
In The Wildwood Where Bluebells Grew, forest scene, 1907, lg...4.00
Ireland Never Seemed So Far Away, lass by brick wall, 1912, lg..4.50
Is Your Mother In, Molly Malone; man peeks in window, 1903, lg.7.00
It's All Gone Now, shows Press Eldridge: Blk performer, 1894....8.00
Jezebel, red cover, Bette Davis in red gown, 1938, EX........25.00
Joan Of Arc They're Calling You, troops illus, 1917, lg sz, VG...2.00
Johnny's In Town, Yellen/Olman, comic soldier, 1919, VG......4.00
Kiss Me Kid, pushy girl & bashful boy, 1909, lg sz, VG........4.50
Lady In Red, full figure Dolores Del Rio in red gown, 1935.....8.00
Let's Choo Choo Choo To Idaho, Esther Williams, M...........6.00
Love Is Love Anywhere, EX portrait Ann Southern, 1933.......4.00
Love With A Capital 'You', Martha Raye portrait photo, 1939, M.6.00
Lovin' Sam The Shiek Of Alabam, photo Al Harman, 1922, VG...4.00
Lullaby Of The Bells, N Eddy/S Foster, WWII war bonds stamp..6.00
Magic Is The Moonlight, E Williams/Skelton/X Cugat, lg format...3.00
Moon Is In Tears Tonight, Bette Davis in green gown, 1937....25.00
Muchacha, yellow cover w/Dolores Del Rio, 1935............12.50
Oh Doctor, men wait for alcohol prescription at Dr's, 1920, EX..10.00
Oh! Ebenezer!, pictures Blk couple, 1897, lg sz, VG.........10.00
Oh! How I Hate To Get Up In The Morning, E Cantor, 1918....5.50
Old Man, from White Christmas, Bing Crosby, 1952..........10.00
Only A Memory Of By Gone Days, H Hutt illus: girl w/hat, 1918..5.00
Poor Pauline, photo Pearl White of Perils of Pauline, 1914, lg...6.00
Ragging The Chopsticks, 2 kids at piano, 1919, VG..........5.00
Rhode Island Clambake, Blk crowd round fire, 1900, lg sz, VG..15.00
Rock Around the Clock, Haley/Comets, Myers, Deca, 1953.....24.00
Salvation Lassie Of Mine, Salvation Army girl, 1919, VG........4.00
Sheik of Araby, Sheik holding girl, 1921, VG...............2.50
Sipping Cider Thru A Straw, 3 photos Fatty Arbuckle, 1919, VG.10.00
Six Women, from George Whites Scandals, Alice Faye.........15.00

Solace, A Mexican Serenade; by S Joplin, couple by wall, 1909..20.00
South Rampart Street Parade, Andrews Sisters, Bing Crosby, '52..4.50
Sweetheart Waltz, from College Holiday, Martha Raye, EX.......5.00
Take A Tip From The Tulip, from Radio City Revels, Ann Miller.5.50
Tammy, Debbie Reynolds in pigtails, Universal, 1957...........3.00
Ten Pins In The Sky, Judy Garland, Freddie Bartholomew, 1938.13.50
That Christmas Feeling, B Crosby w/Santa hat, photos of sons...10.00
Three Bells, lg Andrews Sisters portrait.....................350.00
Thrill Of A Lifetime, B Grable/B Crabbe/D Lamour, 1937, M....25.00
Too Much, Elvis Presley, EP Music Inc, RCA, 1956...........15.00
Uncle Joe's Hail Columbia, Henry Work, 1862................23.00
Warmin' Up In Dixie, Blk folk dancing around fire, 1899, VG...25.00
We Have Much To Be Thankful For, I Berlin, 1913, lg sz, EX..20.00
We'll Sing To Victory, Dionne Quints in uniform, 1942........10.00
We're All Americans, lg Kate Smith portrait, 1940............4.00
Web Of Love, from The Great Gabbo, Erich Von Stroheim......5.50
When I'm Alone I'm Lonesome, I Berlin, 1911, lg sz, VG.......15.00
When The Robert E Lee Arrives, Blk folk/paddle boat, 1918, VG.5.00
When You Come Back, lg photo GM Cohan, 1918, lg sz, VG...10.00
Where Do We Go From Here, Pfeiffer pic of strolling couple, lg..4.50
Who's Afraid, graphic faces of E Taylor/R Burton, 1966.......6.00
Whoa January, drunk looks in closed saloon, 1919, EX........10.00
Will You Be My Teddy Bear, woman holding bear, 1907, VG....10.00
You Can't Beat American Love, 1910, Fisher................20.00
You're Slightly Terrific, from Pigskin Parade, J Garland, 1936....4.50
Ziegfield Follies, 1931.................................25.00

Shelley

Founded in Stoke-on-Trent in 1892 as Wileman and Company, the firm became known as Shelley Potteries, Ltd. in 1925. They produced fine bone china marked with the name of the firm in a shield with 'England' below. In 1967, Shelley was absorbed by the Royal Doulton group.

Ash tray, Rose Spray, straight edge.........................25.00
Ash tray, Shell, Quebec...................................25.00
Box, Rosebud, sm, rnd....................................57.50
Butter dish w/lid, Rose & Red Daisy, 6 flutes.................85.00
Butter dish w/lid, Stocks, 6 flutes.........................82.50
Butter pat, Regency, 6 flutes, 3¾".........................20.00
Cake plate, Hedgerow, w/hdls, 8¾".........................65.00
Cake plate, Hollyhocks, 6".................................45.00
Candle holder, Harmony, 2½"...............................20.00
Candy dish, Begonia, 4" sq.................................25.00
Candy dish, Pansy, 6" dia..................................30.00
Candy dish, Rose & Red Daisy..............................30.00
Casserole w/lid, Rising Sun, 8½" sq.........................65.00
Chamberstick, Shamrock, brass holder in center, 6" dia........30.00
Chocolate pot, Blue Rock, 6 flutes, 8"......................160.00
Chocolate set, Begonia, pot, cr/sug, 6 c/s...................150.00
Cigarette holder, Primrose, 6 flutes, 2"......................32.50
Cigarette holder, Rose Spray, 6 flutes, 2"....................28.00
Coffee pot, Blue Rock, 6 flutes, 6".........................125.00
Coffee pot, wht w/green & gold bands, 7"....................75.00
Creamer, Begonia, 6 flutes.................................25.00
Creamer, Hawick Crest.....................................16.00
Creamer, Stocks, 6 flutes...................................25.00
Creamer & sugar, Begonia, 6 flutes..........................50.00
Creamer & sugar, Dainty Blue, 6 flutes......................55.00
Creamer & sugar, DuBarry, wine............................42.00
Creamer & sugar, Rambler Rose, 6 flutes.....................50.00
Creamer & sugar, Rose Spray, 6 flutes.......................40.00

Montmartre Rose, written by Tommy Lyman, $10.00.

Coffee pot, Dainty Blue, 8″, $135.00.

Creamer & sugar, Rosebud, gr trim, 6 flutes	40.00
Creamer & sugar, Stocks	65.00
Creamer & sugar, Sunrise, blk trees, 8 sided	60.00
Creamer & sugar, Wild Anemone, 6 flutes	38.00
Creamer & sugar, Wild Flowers	40.00
Creamer & sugar on tray, Pansy, wht w/purple	65.00
Creamer & sugar on tray, Regency, 6 flutes	65.00
Cup, Loch Lomond	20.00
Cup & saucer, Begonia, 6 flutes	37.50
Cup & saucer, birds, HP	42.00
Cup & saucer, Blue Rock	38.00
Cup & saucer, bouillon; Wildman, 1888	38.00
Cup & saucer, Canada, maple leaf, C Wildman	25.00
Cup & saucer, Daffodil	42.50
Cup & saucer, Dainty Pink, 6 flutes	40.00
Cup & saucer, demitasse; Begonia, 16 flutes	35.00
Cup & saucer, demitasse; Blue Rock, 16 flutes	38.00
Cup & saucer, demitasse; Celadine, 6 flutes	32.00
Cup & saucer, demitasse; Charm, bl	35.00
Cup & saucer, demitasse; Charm, yel	40.00
Cup & saucer, demitasse; Daffodil	37.50
Cup & saucer, demitasse; Dainty Green, 6 flutes	40.00
Cup & saucer, demitasse; Heather	35.00
Cup & saucer, demitasse; Indian Peony, gr/wht	25.00
Cup & saucer, demitasse; Lily of the Valley, 16 flutes	38.00
Cup & saucer, demitasse; Melody, gold trim	38.00
Cup & saucer, demitasse; Regency, 6 flutes	25.00
Cup & saucer, demitasse; Rose & Red Daisy, 6 flutes	35.00
Cup & saucer, demitasse; Rose Pansy FMN, 16 flutes	37.50
Cup & saucer, demitasse; Rose Pansy FMN, 6 flutes	38.00
Cup & saucer, demitasse; Rosebud, 6 flutes	40.00
Cup & saucer, demitasse; Summer Glory, pk	38.00
Cup & saucer, demitasse; Woodland	35.00
Cup & saucer, DuBarry, bl	40.00
Cup & saucer, Duchess	45.00
Cup & saucer, gr, flowers w/in	54.00
Cup & saucer, gr w/gold scroll border	40.00
Cup & saucer, maple leaves & roses, gold trim, Royalty	25.00
Cup & saucer, mini; pk floral w/purple & red grapes	50.00
Cup & saucer, mini; Primrose Chintz	60.00

Cup & saucer, mini; Rambler Rose	65.00
Cup & saucer, mini; Rose Spray	60.00
Cup & saucer, mini; Rosebud	55.00
Cup & saucer, mini; Serenity	65.00
Cup & saucer, mini; Shamrock	60.00
Cup & saucer, Oleander, 6 flutes	38.00
Cup & saucer, Pansy	38.00
Cup & saucer, pk roses, yel/bl floral, pk hdl	40.00
Cup & saucer, pk w/dk pk roses	38.00
Cup & saucer, Primrose Chintz	38.00
Cup & saucer, Rambler Rose	15.00
Cup & saucer, Rock Garden, pk	40.00
Cup & saucer, Rose Spray, pk/gr border, notched	40.00
Cup & saucer, Rosebud, 6 flutes	35.00
Cup & saucer, Shell, American Brooklime	40.00
Cup & saucer, Shell, Harebell	40.00
Cup & saucer, Shell, Rosebud w/in, pk w/out, scalloped	40.00
Cup & saucer, Shell, Summer Glory inside, lav w/out	40.00
Cup & saucer, Stocks, 6 flutes	38.00
Cup & saucer, Thistle	40.00
Cup & saucer, Wild Flowers, notched, bl trim	35.00
Cup & saucer, Wind Flower, 16 flutes	38.00
Cup & saucer, yel, blk border	40.00
Cup & saucer, 3 blk & 3 gold flutes	45.00
Dish, serving; Blue Rock, 13″	80.00
Egg cup, Bridal Rose, sm	24.00
Egg cup, Bridal Rose, 6 flutes, lg	45.00
Egg cup, Harebell, 6 flutes	30.00
Egg cup, Regency, 6 flutes, 2½″	45.00
Egg cup, Rose Spray, 6 flutes, lg	40.00
Egg cup, Rosebud, sm	24.00
Egg cup, Stocks, 6 flutes, lg	40.00
Jam jar w/lid & under plate, Maytime, 4″	70.00
Jam jar w/lid & under plate, red/purple roses, 4″	65.00
Mustard jar w/lid, Rose & Red Daisy, 3″	45.00
Mustard jar w/lid & under plate, Blue Rock, rnd	70.00
Mustard jar w/lid & under plate, Campanula	60.00
Nappy, Rose & Red Daisy, 6 flutes	20.00
Pitcher, ribbed, bl decor, 8″	75.00
Plate, Begonia, 11″	52.00
Plate, Begonia, 6″	25.00
Plate, Begonia, 6 flutes, 10″	45.00
Plate, Blue Rock, 6 flutes, 11″	55.00
Plate, Blue Rock, 6 flutes, 8″	35.00
Plate, Bridal Rose, 6 flutes, 6″	10.00
Plate, Crochet, 8″	25.00
Plate, Dainty White, 6″	15.00
Plate, dk bl w/wht floral, gold trim, 8″	30.00
Plate, DuBarry, wine, 8″	16.00
Plate, English Collage, 4½″ sq	20.00
Plate, Lakeland, 5½″ sq	15.00
Plate, Melody, gr trim, notched, 6″	20.00
Plate, Morning Glory, 6 flutes, 8″	25.00
Plate, orange & yel asters, 5½″	15.00
Plate, Rose & Red Daisy, 6 flutes, 7″	18.00
Plate, Rose & Red Daisy, 6 flutes, 8″	25.00
Plate, Rosebud, 6 flutes, 11″	40.00
Plate, serving; Melody, 8″ sq	30.00
Plate, serving; Rose Spray, 6 flutes, 8″	40.00
Plate, Stocks, fluted, 8″	20.00
Plate, wht, gr dots, 6 flutes, 8″	20.00
Platter, DuBarry, wine, 12x14″	50.00
Pudding mold, star, 5″	25.00
Reamer, bl & cream dripware, sm	55.00

Saucer, Briar Rose.......................................6.00
Saucer, demitasse; Begonia, 6 flutes..........................5.00
Saucer, mini; gr w/roses...................................20.00
Set, 3 pc; Campanula, 6 flutes.............................67.50
Set, 3 pc; Daffodil.......................................67.50
Set, 3 pc; Dainty White, 6 flutes...........................40.00
Set, 3 pc; English Lakes...................................65.00
Set, 3 pc; Georgian.......................................70.00
Set, 3 pc; Heather..65.00
Set, 3 pc; pk w/dk pk roses................................65.00
Set, 3 pc; Primrose Chintz, gold trim........................65.00
Set, 3 pc; Rambler Rose, 6 flutes...........................50.00
Set, 3 pc; Regency, 6 flutes................................57.50
Set, 3 pc; Rosebud, orig pattern............................40.00
Set, 3 pc; Wild Anemone, 16 flutes..........................65.00
Set, 3 pc; Wildflower, 6 flutes.............................45.00
Snack set, Regency, cup w/indented 8" plate..................28.00
Strainer, orange/tan, 3 ft, 2½".............................55.00
Sugar bowl, Dainty White...................................16.00
Sugar bowl, Quebec, Wildman................................9.00
Sugar bowl, Rose & Red Daisy, 6 flutes.......................25.00
Sugar bowl, Rose Spray, 6 flutes............................23.50
Sugar bowl, wht w/gold trim, 3".............................30.00
Tea & toast, floral border, gold trim, 8" plate...............40.00
Tea & toast, Regency, 6 flutes..............................45.00
Tea & toast, Rose Spray....................................45.00
Tea set, Begonia, pot, cr/sug.............................160.00
Tea set, Hibiscus, pot, cr/sug............................180.00
Tea set, Stocks, pot, cr/sug, 6 flutes.....................200.00
Teapot, Blue Rock, 6 flutes, 6"...........................155.00
Teapot, mushroom; Mabel Lucie Attwell.......................87.50
Teapot, Rose & Red Daisy, 6 flutes..........................85.00
Teapot, Wild Flowers, 4½".................................125.00
Toast rack, 3¼x7½"..55.00
Tray, Morning Glory, 5x8".................................27.50

Ship Models

Cruiser, Brooklyn, Marklin, pnt tin, 1904, 28"............9,900.00
Half hull, laminated, orig backboard, fine details, 10½x46"....650.00
Lusitania, pnt wood, by HL Wheeler, 1930, on wood base, 49".605.00
Prisoner of war, HMS Juno, bone, in mahog case: 30x24x12".7,500.00
Racing cutter, Madge, Stephen Pinney, complete hull/rigging...800.00
Robert E Lee, cased, 24" L................................950.00
Schooner, Currier, 2 masted w/sails, EX detail, 1800s, 53" L.2,300.00
Shadow box, tugboat, Maren-New York, 6½x12x31"...........175.00
Ship, Lightening, blk hull/completely rigged, EX detail, 46" L.2,800.00

Silhouettes

Silhouette portraits were made by positioning the subject between a bright light and a sheet of white drawing paper, the resulting shadow traced and cut out. The paper was mounted over a contrasting color and framed. The process was simplified by an invention called the Physiog-notrace, a device that allowed tracing and cutting to be done in one operation.

Experienced silhouette artists could do full length figures, scenics, ships, or trains. Some of the most famous of these artists were Charles Peale Polk, Charles Willson Peale, James Elsworth, and William King.

Boy, hollow cut, rpl bk mk Henry C Bosler, 1806, 5½x7½"....45.00
Boy & dog, identified, simple ink ground, 1840, 9½x11½"....650.00
Boy w/walking stick, in ink, pine fr, 11x9"................175.00

Child, detail/gilded hi-lites/coral necklace/penciled lace, 5".....350.00
Couple seated on open porch, ink scenic, Maydell, 20x24"....275.00
Family, ea w/wht hi-lites, inked bkground, sgn Turner, 13x16"..850.00
Group of 5, celebrities identified, ink drape, Brougham, 17"...900.00
Lady, hollow cut, turned wood fr cracked, 5"..................50.00
Lady in bonnet, rvpt glass, emb label: Peale, 4½x5½"........105.00
Lady in bonnet & muff on blk fabric, full length, 6½x10".....160.00
Lady in fancy bonnet, rvpt matt, oval fr, 6x4¾"..............65.00
Man, hollow cut, oval fr, on bk: Sanborn Blake, 5½"..........55.00
Man, ink ground, sgn Sam'l Metford, 1843, 13x9"..........1,125.00
Man w/hat & cane, standing, 11x13".........................105.00
Man w/walking stick, full length, ink & ink wash, 9½x7¾".....185.00
Plaster of a gentleman, EX detail, by J Miers, 1805, rvpt lens..150.00
Pr, ladies in facing chairs, sgn Weston, 1831, 9½x12"........575.00
Pr, man & lady, hollow cut heads, watercolor costumes, 5x4"..250.00
Pr, man dtd 1800, lady 1799, fancy reverse gilding, blk bk, 7".270.00
Pr, man/lady, busts, inscription: Cut w/out hands, 1847, 4x5"..480.00
Pr, young men, busts, hollow cut, trn frames, 4¾" dia........290.00
Pr, ¾ busts of man & lady, bird's eye fr, 4x2¾"..............150.00

Depicting 'Benjamin Disraeli' signed William Powell Frith, 1855, hand colored, in rosewood frame, 11½" x 8", $250.00.

Silver

Silver flatware is being collected today, either to replace missing pieces of heirloom sets, or in lieu of buying new patterns, by those who admire and appreciate the style and quality of the older ware. Prices vary from dealer to dealer; some pieces are harder to find and are therefore more expensive. Items such as olive spoons, cream ladles, lemon forks, etc., once thought a necessary part of a silver service, may today be slow to sell, and as a result dealers may price them low and make up the difference on items that sell more readily. Many factors enter into evaluation -- popular patterns may be high due to demand, even though easily found, while scarce patterns may be passed over by collectors who find them difficult to reassemble.

Key: FH----flat handle   HH----hollow handle

Flatware

Amaryllis, salad fork.....................................20.00
American Classic, cold meat fork...........................40.00
American Classic, cream soup spoon.........................19.00
American Classic, gravy ladle..............................38.00
American Classic, luncheon fork............................22.00
American Classic, place spoon..............................20.00
American Victorian, butter, HH.............................12.00
American Victorian, sugar shell............................18.00
Angelique, butter, HH.....................................12.00
Angelique, luncheon fork..................................27.00

Angelique, serving spoon.................................40.00	Carolina, demitasse spoon.........................8.00
Angelique, teaspoon....................................15.00	Carollton, teaspoon..................................15.00
Arcadia, master butter................................22.00	Cascade, butter, FH.................................16.00
Arcadia, salad fork....................................20.00	Cascade, cake server................................25.00
Autumn Leaves, butter, HH.........................12.00	Cascade, gravy ladle................................40.00
Autumn Leaves, cocktail fork.....................13.00	Cascade, lemon fork.................................13.00
Autumn Leaves, flat server, pierced.............45.00	Cascade, salad fork..................................20.00
Autumn Leaves, salad fork.........................20.00	Cascade, sugar spoon................................20.00
Ballet, butter, FH.....................................15.00	Castle Rose, cold meat fork.......................40.00
Ballet, cream soup spoon............................18.00	Castle Rose, gravy ladle............................40.00
Ballet, luncheon fork.................................24.00	Celeste, luncheon fork, 7½".......................24.00
Ballet, teaspoon.......................................14.00	Celeste, pickle fork..................................12.00
Belle Rose, cold meat fork.........................45.00	Celeste, serving spoon...............................40.00
Belle Rose, cream soup spoon.....................20.00	Celeste, teaspoon.....................................15.00
Belle Rose, salad fork...............................20.00	Chantilly, bouillon spoon, 5".....................15.00
Belle Rose, sauce ladle..............................25.00	Chantilly, butter, FH...............................14.00
Belle Rose, serving spoon, pierced...............50.00	Chantilly, dinner fork, 7½".......................32.00
Blossom Time, gravy ladle..........................36.00	Chantilly, jelly......................................23.00
Blossom Time, luncheon fork, 7¼"...............26.00	Chantilly, teaspoon..................................15.00
Blossom Time, place spoon..........................22.00	Chapel Bells, butter, FH...........................16.00
Blossom Time, sugar shell...........................20.00	Chapel Bells, iced tea spoon......................18.00
Bostonian, fish fork..................................20.00	Chapel Bells, master butter.......................20.00
Bostonian, iced tea spoon...........................18.00	Chapel Bells, pierced bon bon....................20.00
Bostonian, sauce ladle...............................23.00	Chapel Bells, salad serving spoon................55.00
Brandon, dessert fork................................25.00	Charlemagne, luncheon fork, 7½"................36.00
Brandon, teaspoon....................................13.00	Charlemagne, oval spoon...........................32.00
Breton Rose, luncheon knife.......................15.00	Charlemagne, salad fork............................30.00
Breton Rose, serving spoon.........................40.00	Charlemagne, teaspoon..............................22.00
Burgundy, cold meat fork...........................55.00	Charles II, cold meat fork.........................50.00
Burgundy, dessert spoon.............................35.00	Charles II, cream soup spoon......................23.00
Burgundy, dinner fork, 7⅞".......................52.00	Charles II, luncheon fork..........................30.00
Burgundy, place spoon...............................27.00	Charles II, teaspoon.................................19.00
Burgundy, salad fork.................................24.00	Chased Diane, lemon fork..........................13.00
Burgundy, serving spoon, pierced.................60.00	Chased Diane, pickle fork..........................13.00
Buttercup, luncheon fork............................25.00	Chelmsford, teaspoon................................14.00
Buttercup, luncheon knife...........................20.00	Cherry Blossom, teaspoon..........................15.00
Buttercup, oval soup spoon, 7"....................28.00	Cinderella, iced tea spoon.........................10.00
Buttercup, teaspoon..................................15.00	Cinderella, serving spoon...........................40.00
Cabot, cold meat fork................................35.00	Cinderella, sugar shell..............................18.00
Cameo, master butter................................23.00	Classic Rose, carving set...........................50.00
Candlelight, butter, FH.............................14.00	Classic Rose, pastry server........................30.00
Candlelight, cake server.............................22.00	Classic Rose, salad fork............................21.00
Candlelight, cheese knife............................16.00	Classic Rose, serving spoon........................45.00
Candlelight, cocktail fork...........................11.00	Clermont, buffet fork...............................40.00
Candlelight, cream soup spoon.....................20.00	Clermont, 5 o'clock spoon..........................11.00
Candlelight, dinner fork, 7¾".....................30.00	Clovelly, ice cream fork............................22.00
Candlelight, dinner knife............................16.00	Clovelly, sauce ladle.................................22.00
Candlelight, gravy ladle.............................40.00	Colonial, sauce ladle................................22.00
Candlelight, jelly server.............................19.00	Colonial Shell, baby spoon, monogram...........9.00
Candlelight, lemon fork.............................13.00	Columbia, ice cream fork, monogram.............18.00
Candlelight, luncheon knife.........................13.00	Columbia, teaspoon..................................14.00
Candlelight, roast carving set......................40.00	Commonwealth, cocktail fork......................14.00
Candlelight, salad fork..............................19.00	Concord, luncheon fork.............................24.00
Candlelight, serving spoon, pierced...............45.00	Concord, teaspoon...................................15.00
Candlelight, steak carving set......................35.00	Contessina, luncheon fork..........................25.00
Candlelight, sugar shell..............................18.00	Contessina, teaspoon................................15.00
Candlelight, teaspoon................................14.00	Contour, cream soup spoon.........................20.00
Candlelight, 5 o'clock spoon........................15.00	Contour, flat server.................................55.00
Carillion, luncheon fork, 7⅜".....................23.00	Contour, iced tea spoon.............................19.00
Carillion, salad fork.................................20.00	Contour, salad fork..................................22.00
Carillion, serving spoon.............................40.00	Corsage, luncheon knife.............................15.00
Carillion, sugar spoon...............................20.00	Corsage, oval soup...................................19.00
Carillion, teaspoon...................................15.00	Corsage, 5 o'clock spoon............................14.00
Carnation, place spoon..............................28.00	Country Manor, luncheon knife....................15.00

Courtship, luncheon fork . . . 20.00
Courtship, master butter . . . 22.00
Courtship, sugar shell . . . 18.00
Courtship, teaspoon . . . 15.00
Craftsman, bon bon . . . 15.00
Craftsman, luncheon knife . . . 15.00
Craftsman, salad fork . . . 19.00
Crest of Arden, salad serving fork . . . 75.00
Crest of Arden, serving spoon . . . 60.00
Crown Princess, cold meat fork . . . 45.00
Crown Princess, gravy ladle . . . 45.00
Crown Princess, jelly . . . 22.00
Crown Princess, serving spoon . . . 38.00
Crown Princess, teaspoon . . . 15.00
Da Vinci, luncheon fork, 7½″ . . . 25.00
Da Vinci, sugar shell . . . 25.00
Damask Rose, butter, FH . . . 15.00
Damask Rose, cocktail fork . . . 13.00
Damask Rose, coffee spoon . . . 20.00
Damask Rose, dinner fork, 7⅞″ . . . 28.00
Damask Rose, iced tea spoon . . . 18.00
Debutante, baby spoon . . . 10.00
Debutante, cheese, HH . . . 16.00
Debutante, cold meat fork . . . 38.00
Debutante, pickle fork . . . 16.00
Debutante, pierced serving spoon . . . 45.00
Debutante, place spoon . . . 22.00
Della Robbia, bon bon . . . 18.00
Della Robbia, chowder . . . 25.00
Della Robbia, cold meat fork . . . 38.00
Della Robbia, teaspoon . . . 15.00
Dolly Madison, butter, FH . . . 15.00
Dolly Madison, jelly server . . . 18.00
Dolly Madison, luncheon knife . . . 15.00
Dolly Madison, 5 o'clock spoon . . . 13.00
Dominique, butter, FH . . . 14.00
Dominique, luncheon fork . . . 23.00
Dominique, teaspoon . . . 15.00
Dorian, serving spoon . . . 40.00
Dresden Scroll, gravy ladle . . . 48.00
Dresden Scroll, salad fork . . . 20.00
Dresden Scroll, sugar shell . . . 20.00
Du Barry, dinner fork, 7⅞″ . . . 39.00
Du Barry, luncheon fork, 7⅜″ . . . 35.00
Du Barry, place spoon, 7″ . . . 40.00
Du Barry, serving spoon, pierced . . . 65.00
Du Barry, teaspoon . . . 22.00
Elaine, berry spoon . . . 60.00
Eloquence, carving fork . . . 20.00
Eloquence, luncheon knife . . . 22.00
Eloquence, teaspoon . . . 18.00
Empire, teaspoon . . . 15.00
Empire, 5 o'clock spoon . . . 13.00
Enchantress, butter, FH . . . 14.00
Enchantress, sugar shell . . . 19.00
Esplande, flat server, 6⅛″ . . . 30.00
Esplande, jelly server . . . 25.00
Etiquette, bouillon spoon . . . 14.00
Evening Rose, master butter . . . 23.00
Evening Rose, salad fork . . . 20.00
Evening Rose, sugar shell . . . 20.00
Fanevil, demitasse spoon . . . 10.00
Fanevil, dinner fork . . . 30.00
Fanevil, luncheon fork . . . 26.00
Fanevil, luncheon knife . . . 18.00
Festival, cheese knife . . . 14.00
Festival, cream soup . . . 19.00
Festival, salad fork . . . 20.00
Fleetwood, cream soup spoon . . . 20.00
Fleetwood, luncheon fork . . . 23.00
Fleetwood, teaspoon . . . 15.00
Flemish, dinner fork . . . 38.00
Flemish, iced tea spoon . . . 22.00
Flemish, salad fork . . . 28.00
Fleur-De-Lis, place spoon . . . 24.00
Florentine Lace, teaspoon . . . 17.00
Fontana, bouillon spoon . . . 17.00
Fontana, cheese knife . . . 13.00
Fontana, cheese server . . . 14.00
Fontana, place spoon . . . 23.00
Fontana, salad fork . . . 20.00
Fontana, steak carving set . . . 40.00
French Provincial, butter, HH . . . 15.00
French Provincial, gravy ladle . . . 50.00
French Provincial, salad fork . . . 21.00
French Provincial, sugar shell . . . 20.00
French Provincial, teaspoon . . . 15.00
French Renaissance, dinner fork . . . 38.00
French Renaissance, place spoon . . . 32.00
French Renaissance, serving spoon . . . 55.00
French Renaissance, teaspoon . . . 16.00
Gadroonette, cocktail fork . . . 13.00
Gadroonette, gravy ladle . . . 35.00
Gadroonette, iced tea spoon . . . 20.00
Gadroonette, sauce ladle . . . 22.00
Gadroonette, 5 o'clock spoon . . . 12.00
George & Martha, butter, FH . . . 15.00
George & Martha, cold meat fork . . . 50.00
George & Martha, dessert spoon . . . 25.00
George & Martha, flat server . . . 42.00
George & Martha, jelly server . . . 22.00
George & Martha, luncheon knife . . . 16.00
George & Martha, salad fork . . . 18.00
Grand Baroque, luncheon fork, 7½″ . . . 40.00
Grand Baroque, youth fork . . . 25.00
Grand Baroque, 5 o'clock teaspoon . . . 18.00
Grand Regency, lemon fork . . . 13.00
Grand Regency, oval soup spoon . . . 30.00
Grand Regency, place spoon . . . 25.00
Hampton Court, place spoon . . . 25.00
Hampton Court, teaspoon . . . 16.00
Heiress, gravy ladle . . . 38.00
Heiress, iced tea spoon . . . 15.00
Heiress, teaspoon . . . 14.00
Hunt Club, luncheon fork, 7¼″ . . . 23.00
Hunt Club, oval soup spoon . . . 15.00
Hunt Club, serving spoon . . . 40.00
Hunt Club, sugar shell . . . 23.00
Impresario, luncheon knife . . . 18.00
Impresario, pie/cake server . . . 25.00
Impresario, place spoon . . . 22.00
Impresario, salad fork . . . 20.00
Ivy, serving spoon . . . 40.00
Ivy, teaspoon . . . 15.00
Joan of Arc, dinner fork, 7⅝″ . . . 33.00
Joan of Arc, dinner knife . . . 21.00
Joan of Arc, teaspoon . . . 18.00
Joan of Arc, youth fork, 6¼″ . . . 35.00

John & Priscilla, cream soup	18.00
John & Priscilla, master butter	23.00
John & Priscilla, place spoon	21.00
John & Priscilla, salad fork	19.00
Julianna, luncheon fork	22.00
Julianna, master butter	23.00
Julianna, sugar shell	20.00
King Albert, gravy ladle	35.00
King Albert, pastry server	22.00
King Christian, cake cutter	18.00
King Christian, salad fork	19.00
King Christian, salad serving spoon	48.00
Lace Point, butter, HH	13.00
Lace Point, cheese	15.00
Lace Point, iced tea spoon	18.00
Lady Mary, luncheon fork	20.00
Lady Mary, sugar shell	18.00
Lafayette, ice cream fork	24.00
Lafayette, serving spoon	48.00
Lancaster, berry spoon, monogram	40.00
Lancaster, pie fork	16.00
Lancaster, sugar tong, monogram	25.00
Lancaster, teaspoon	14.00
Lancaster, 5 o'clock spoon	11.00
Madam Morris, luncheon fork, 7⅝″	25.00
Madam Morris, teaspoon	15.00
Madeira, butter, HH	12.00
Madeira, flat server	50.00
Madeira, place spoon	23.00
Mansion House, cake server	25.00
Mansion House, cold meat fork	40.00
Mansion House, dinner fork, 7¾″	30.00
Mansion House, dinner knife	16.00
Margaret Rose, grill knife, 8½″	15.00
Margaret Rose, salad serving spoon, 8½″	45.00
Marie Antoinette, berry spoon, 9″	70.00
Marie Antoinette, fruit spoon	20.00
Modern Victorian, cream soup spoon	20.00
Modern Victorian, jelly	23.00
Modern Victorian, luncheon fork, 7¼″	24.00
Modern Victorian, serving spoon	45.00
Mount Vernon, fruit spoon	18.00
Mount Vernon, gravy ladle	35.00
Mount Vernon, meat fork	20.00
Mount Vernon, sugar tongs	25.00
Nancy Lee, luncheon fork, 7¼″	24.00
Nancy Lee, luncheon knife	16.00
Nancy Lee, teaspoon	15.00
Nocturne, flat server	45.00
Nocturne, salad fork	20.00
Nocturne, sugar shell	25.00
Norfolk, bouillon spoon, 7⅛″	14.00
Norfolk, ice cream fork	18.00
Norfolk, salad fork	20.00
Old Atlanta, dinner fork, 7½″	30.00
Old Atlanta, oval soup spoon	20.00
Old Atlanta, sauce ladle	22.00
Old Colonial, butter, HH	16.00
Old Colonial, luncheon fork, 7″	35.00
Old Colonial, serving spoon, 8½″	65.00
Old Colonial, teaspoon	20.00
Old Lace, butter, FH	16.00
Old Lace, luncheon knife, 8⅝″	16.00
Primrose, dinner fork, 7½″	28.00
Primrose, jelly server	25.00
Primrose, sugar tong	20.00
Primrose, teaspoon	16.00
Princess Patricia, bouillon spoon	16.00
Princess Patricia, dinner fork, 7¾″	24.00
Princess Patricia, ice cream fork	20.00
Princess Patricia, jelly	18.00
Princess Patricia, pie server	20.00
Processional, cream soup spoon	20.00
Processional, gravy ladle	40.00
Processional, luncheon knife	16.00
Processional, master butter	19.00
Queen Lace, butter, FH	16.00
Queen Lace, dinner fork, 7¾″	24.00
Queen Lace, jelly server	20.00
R.S.V.P., cream soup spoon	20.00
R.S.V.P., dinner fork, 7½″	26.00
R.S.V.P., teaspoon	16.00
Radiant Rose, salad fork	18.00
Radiant Rose, teaspoon	15.00
Rambler Rose, cheese server	20.00
Rambler Rose, cream soup	20.00
Rambler Rose, gravy ladle	45.00
Rambler Rose, luncheon fork, 7⅜″	24.00
Romance of the Stars, luncheon knife, 9″	16.00
Romance of the Stars, salad fork	20.00
Rose Cascade, lemon fork	13.00
Rose Cascade, serving spoon, pierced	55.00
Rose Cascade, sugar shell	25.00
Rose Cascade, teaspoon	15.00
Rose Tiara, butter, HH	13.00
Rose Tiara, iced tea spoon	18.00
Rose Tiara, salad fork	20.00
Rose Tiara, serving spoon	45.00
Sea Rose, cheese server	20.00
Sea Rose, place spoon	22.00
Sea Rose, serving spoon, pierced	50.00
Sea Rose, sugar spoon	20.00
Shenandoah, luncheon knife	16.00
Shenandoah, olive spoon	14.00
Shenandoah, salad fork	20.00
Silhouette, cheese knife	16.00
Silhouette, dinner knife	20.00
Silhouette, pie server	25.00
Silver Surf, bon bon	20.00
Silver Surf, cheese knife	14.00
Silver Surf, gravy ladle	40.00
Silver Surf, luncheon knife	16.00
Silver Surf, sugar	20.00
Snowflake, dinner fork, 7¾″	26.00
Snowflake, dinner knife	16.00
Snowflake, salad fork	21.00
Snowflake, teaspoon	16.00
Southern Grandeur, cold meat fork	45.00
Southern Grandeur, demitasse spoon	10.00
Southern Grandeur, master butter	25.00
Southern Grandeur, place spoon	24.00
Southern Grandeur, teaspoon	15.00
Spring Glory, butter, FH	16.00
Spring Glory, dinner knife	16.00
Spring Glory, gravy ladle	40.00
Spring Glory, luncheon fork, 7¼″	24.00
Strasbourg, coffee spoon	14.00
Strasbourg, dinner fork, 7⅝″	34.00

Strasbourg, place spoon................................30.00
Strasbourg, teaspoon.................................15.00
Strasbourg, youth fork...............................15.00
Summer Song, cold meat fork..........................40.00
Summer Song, salad fork..............................19.00
Summer Song, serving spoon...........................40.00
Summer Song, sugar shell.............................25.00
Torchlight, luncheon fork, 7⅛".......................24.00
Torchlight, luncheon knife...........................16.00
Torchlight, salad fork...............................19.00
Torchlight, teaspoon.................................15.00
Trianon, butter, FH..................................15.00
Trianon, cocktail fork...............................13.00
Trianon, cold meat fork..............................40.00
Trianon, flat server.................................22.00
Twilight, butter, HH.................................12.00
Twilight, cold meat knife............................35.00
Twilight, gravy ladle................................35.00
Twilight, luncheon knife.............................15.00
Twilight, serving spoon..............................35.00
Twilight, sugar......................................16.00
Vespera, cold meat fork..............................40.00
Vespera, cream soup..................................18.00
Vespera, pickle fork.................................13.00
Vespera, sauce ladle.................................30.00
Victorian, buffet fork...............................24.00
Victorian, butter, FH................................16.00
Victorian, cake server...............................25.00
Victorian, dinner knife..............................16.00
Victorian, sugar.....................................22.00
Virginia, chowder spoon..............................24.00
Virginia, gravy ladle................................45.00
Virginia, luncheon fork, 7⅛".........................24.00
Virginia, salad fork.................................21.00
Vision, cream soup spoon.............................21.00
Vision, luncheon knife...............................20.00
Vision, serving spoon................................60.00
Vision, teaspoon.....................................18.00
Waltz of Spring, luncheon fork, 7¼"..................28.00
Waltz of Spring, luncheon knife......................18.00
Wedding Bells, butter, FH............................16.00
Wedding Bells, luncheon fork, 7¼"....................26.00
Wedding Bells, master butter.........................20.00
Wedding Bells, salad fork............................20.00
Wedgewood, butter, FH................................14.00
Wedgewood, luncheon fork, 7¼"........................30.00
Wedgewood, serving spoon.............................45.00
Wild Rose, berry spoon, 9¼"..........................60.00
Wild Rose, cocktail fork.............................12.00
Wild Rose, demitasse.................................10.00
Wild Rose, place spoon...............................28.00
Wild Rose, salad fork................................20.00
William & Mary, flat server, pierced.................40.00
William & Mary, master butter........................22.00
William & Mary, place spoon, 7¼".....................24.00
William & Mary, 5 o'clock spoon, 5½".................14.00
Wishing Star, butter, HH.............................14.00
Wishing Star, gravy ladle............................35.00
Wishing Star, serving spoon..........................42.00
Wishing Star, teaspoon...............................15.00
Wreath, sugar..22.00
Wreath, teaspoon.....................................15.00
1810, butter, HH.....................................12.00
1810, place spoon....................................25.00

1810, salad serving set.............................110.00
1810, sauce ladle....................................25.00

Hollow Ware

Until the middle of the 19th century, the silverware produced in America was custom made on order of the buyer directly from the silversmith. With the rise of industrialization, factories sprung up that manufactured silverware for retailers who often added their trademark to the ware. Silver ore was mined in abundance, and demand spurred production. Changes in style occurred at the whim of fashion. Repousse decoration (relief work) became popular about 1885, reflecting the ostentatious taste of the Victorian era. Later in the century, Greek, Etruscan, and several classic styles found favor. Today, the Art Deco styles of this century are very popular with collectors.

In the listing that follows, manufacturer's name or trademark is noted first; in lieu of that information, listings are by item.

AB, att Alexander Barnet, marrow scoop, 1766-67...........250.00
AD, wine taster, twin snake hdl, 1800, 3".................495.00
AD w/standing bird in diamond mk, meat dish, oval, 22" L..605.00
Alexander Birkl, 6" demitasse set w/2 cups/saucers & tray....880.00
Anthony Nelme, coffee pot, cylinder, Queen Anne, 9½".....1,650.00
Augustin Le Sage, tea urn, armorials, acorn finial, 15"......1,500.00
Bahlsen, cake basket, wire work, pierced foliate border, 12"...450.00
Ball, Black & Co, coffee pot, emb architectural scenes, 13"....935.00
Benjamin Smith III, leaf dish, veined & matted, 9½"......660.00
CG, beaker, Louis XVI, tulip form/flat chased florals, 4½"....715.00
Charles Kander II, tea tray, leaf capped hdls, 25".........1,800.00
Charles Wright, coffee pot, shell decor spout, bud finial, 11"...880.00
Chinese export, teapot, scenes ea side, dragon hdl/finial, 7"..1,100.00
Cradock & Reid, sauce boat, leaf/paw ft, reed hdls, 7½", pr..1,485.00
Crichton Bros, punch bowl, 1916, 6½x10½"................725.00
CS, sugar chest, band of engraving on hinged lid, 1828, 5½"..990.00
CS Harris & Son, tea caddy, oval, pineapple finial, 6¾".......850.00
CSH & S, tankard, 3 lion ft foliate capped, chased, 7½".....880.00
D&J Welby, teapot, inverted pear w/chased shoulder, 6½".....440.00
Daniel Fischbacher, beaker, granulated finish, gilt, 4"......1,320.00
Daniel Piers, sauce boat, dbl lip, scroll hdls, 4½" dia.......1,375.00
Daniel Smith & Robert Sharp, salver, 4 supports, 15" L.....1,250.00
Danzig, spirit cup, spiral rib/chased w/floral pendants, 5 for...2,090.00
DH Buell, hors d'oeuvre bowl, boat form w/shell hdls, 22 oz...880.00
Dominick & Haff, cup, hammered w/copper insect, 2 hdls, 5½"..550.00
Dominick & Haff, salt & pepper, emb butterflies, gilt, 3"......200.00
Dutch, cow creamer, fly capped lid, ruby glass eyes, 6½".....495.00
Ebenezer Coker, taperstick, Geo III, hex base w/shells, 5"....935.00
Edme Pierre Balzac, coffee pot, pear form/ebony hdl, 3".....2,310.00
Edward Farrell, cake basket, scroll legs, pierced, 15" L......1,750.00
Edward Farrell, emb/chased 4 various scenes, bird hdls, 8½"..2,225.00
EH, claret jug, flowerheads/vines/crest, w/cut glass body, 10"...605.00
Elizabeth Jones, tea tray, reeded border, leaf cap hdls, 22"..2,640.00
English, nutmeg grater, engraved lid w/initials, 2½"..........135.00
Erasmus Cope, tea set, engraved foliage, paw ft, 3 pc.......1,430.00
FD, sauce boat, Empire, eagle head hdl, armorials, 1800, 7"...700.00
FGL, wine taster, Louis XV, coiled snake hdl, 3"...........1,045.00
Figurine, sitting Retriever dog wearing collar, 3½x4".........220.00
Francis Crump, tankard, Geo II, armorials, 6"................825.00
Francis Spilsbury, tankard, cylindrical, rpr, 7"............2,750.00
Franz Heinrich Hannover, snuffers tray, engraved/4 legs, 8" L..550.00
Frederick Elkington, 5-lite candelabra, gilt, figural, 20", pr...3,500.00
French, sauce boat, swan head hdl/armorials, 11½", pr......1,540.00
Garrards, candelabra, 7-lite, putti stds/shaped base, 29", pr..13,750.00
GC, bowl, spiral lobed/fluted, openwork spoon brackets, 1760.1,045.00
Geo Shiebler, bowl, 2 hdls, emb/chased leaves/grapes, 10¾"..1,045.00
Geo Shiebler, inverted pear, Nouveau poppies, ped ft, 20"....1,980.00

Viennese stirrup cup, Wurbel and Czokally, Wein, Austria; presentation inscription, stag head, cloven hoof feet, 33.6 oz., 8″, $800.00.

Georg Jensen, candelabra, scroll arms w/leaves/grapes, 8″, pr.4,500.00
Georg Jensen, tazza, spiral stems, grapevine under bowl, 6″....550.00
German, beaker, cylinder, flat chased at collar, 3½″.........880.00
German, centerpiece bowl w/lid, allover pierced/chased, 19″..3,740.00
German, coffee pot, cockerel form body, chased, 9″.........1,870.00
German, cup/cover, figural stem/putti finial, 16¾″...........825.00
German, figurine, prancing horse, 17½″ L................1,210.00
German, nautilus shell cup w/female finial, 14½″...........1,980.00
German, presentation cup/lid/stand, Victory finial, 25″......2,090.00
German, sauce boat, cannon figural, 10½″, pr.............2,090.00
German, sideboard dish, emb w/medieval battle scene, 32″ L.2,250.00
German, tazza/cover, allover chased/applied masks/fruit, 10″..1,320.00
German, wager cup, girl figural w/full skirt, late 1800s, 8½″....605.00
Gorham, basket, oval/pierced/chased w/scrolls/lattice, 15 oz.....300.00
Gorham, centerpiece bowl, rim w/floral/masks, female bust, 12″.440.00
Gorham, pitcher, cut glass w/silver mt, daffodils, 10½″......1,430.00
Gorham, platter, gadrooned border/engraved armorial, 14″ dia..450.00
Gorham, sweetmeat, shallow oval, 4 ft, Nouveau, 8½″ L.......935.00

Gorham, tazza, lion masks/foliage stem, 1871, 10½″.........415.00
Gorham, tazza, Nouveau poppies/leaves, lobed ft, 4″, pr.....1,540.00
Gorham, tea service w/urn, pear form/cottage in woods, 6 pc..2,800.00
Gorham, tea/coffee, florals on shoulder, rnd form, 6 pc......3,000.00
Gorham, tray, openwork ribbon-tied swags/columns, 27 oz, 9″..440.00
Gorham, vase, triple lily, realistically chased as lilies, 3¾″.....495.00
Gorham, water pitcher, band w/medallions, mask hdl, 12″.....990.00
Gustavus Byrne, waiter, reeded rim/engraved crest, 4 ft, 10″....500.00
H Lambert, tea tray, engraved armorials, 4 supports, 17½″...3,410.00
Hayden & Gregg, julep cup, engraved, 1843, 3½″...........605.00
Henry Chawner, teapot, Geo III, octagon/brite-cut armorial, 6″..715.00
Hester Bateman, caster, pear form on ped/pierced/engraved, 5″.440.00
Hester Bateman, creamer, Geo III, helmet form, 3.6 oz.......725.00
Hester Bateman, mustard pot, brite-cut/pierced ribbon work, 4″.715.00
Hester Bateman, salt, claw/ball ft, floral pierced, 3″, pr.........715.00
Hester Bateman, sugar urn, circle ped base, initialed, 9″.....1,100.00
Hester Bateman, teapot, oval cylinder, beaded borders, 6″....1,100.00
Humphrey Payne, coffee pot, armorial/crest, chased, 9″......1,430.00
ICB, sugar box, bombe w/4 paw ft, domed cover, 5½″........990.00
IMK, hot water jug, pear form/ivory hdl, 1775, 8½″.........1,540.00
Indian, tea set, Colonial, elephant finials/hdls/spouts, 4 pc....1,595.00
IVC in heart, sideboard dish, repousse/courtesan at table, 12″..770.00
J Hoyland & Co, wine coaster, pierced gallery/loop hdl, 5″, pr..550.00
James Fray, soup tureen, Geo II type, shell/paw ft, crest, 12″.7,000.00
James Hamilton, salver, scroll/leaf rim, chased/armorials, 20″.2,310.00
James Stamp, salver, Geo III, armorials, 4 claw/ball ft, 14″...1,100.00
Japanese, dish, chased/applied dragons, hammered, 1900, 12″..715.00
Jean-Baptiste Claude Odiot, vegetable dish w/lid, 8″ dia......2,475.00
John East, tankard, cylinder, Queen Anne, 7″...............660.00
John H Conner, tea set, ped ft, foliate/shell borders, 3 pc....1,100.00
John Lloyd, salver, swag/ram head border, 4 claw/ball ft, 17″.1,540.00
John McMullin, water pitcher w/lid, vine band/clusters, 12″...1,155.00
John Schuppe, cow creamer, Geo III, textured hide/fly, 6″....4,500.00
John Scofield, jug w/lid, pear form/crests/motto, 12″.........2,200.00
John Swift, tankard, Geo II, cylindrical, 2 cartouches, 8″.....1,100.00
John Swift, waiter, shell/scroll rim, 3 hoof ft, 9″ dia.........600.00
Joseph & John Angell, coffee pot, octagon, engraved, 11″....1,125.00
Jost Leschhorn, beaker, taper cylinder/engraved figures, 4½″.1,340.00
Kalo Shop, water pitcher, hammered, inverted pear form, 10″..715.00
Kirkpatrick, dresser set, floral chased, 6 pc.................605.00
KR, tazza, bowl on 5 bead-top rods set in tulip std, ped, 5½″..500.00
Lapar, tea set, 4 paw ft, acanthus leaf/shell, gilt w/in, 3 pc.....745.00
London & Newcastle, cup, inverted pear/ped ft/reed border, pr..750.00
Loring Andrews Co, bowl, emb/chased w/flowers/scrolls, 10″ dia.900.00
Lotus Co, bowl w/ped, 6 emb stylized foliate motifs, 11″ dia...275.00
Marshall & Sons, hot water jug, flat chased neck, 9″.........825.00
Mauser, bowl, 5 seagulls in flight at rim, on ped ft, 6¾″......385.00
Mauser, vase, Nouveau floral rim/ball base, w/hdls, 22″......1,540.00
Michael Plummer, tea caddy, Geo III, bombe form, 6¼″.......800.00
MML, salver, pierced/chased gallery, 4 panel supports, 13″...1,320.00
Odiot, centerpiece, boat form/Egyptian motif, 27″ L.........2,750.00
Parker & Wakelin, hot water jug, pear form/armorials, 10″.....550.00
Patrick Robertson, goblet, bell form, gilded w/in, 6″, pr.......715.00
Paul Storr, centerpiece bowls, Geo III, shells/acanthus, 9½″..1,100.00
Paul Storr, meat dish, Geo III/gadroon/shell rim, crest, 12″...1,540.00
Paul Storr, platter, well & tree, gadroon/leaf rim, 20″.......6,600.00
Paul Storr, sauce tureen/cover, acanthus/ring hdls, 9″, 4 for.11,000.00
Persian, samovar, allover chased w/bird/foliate design, 18″....2,310.00
Peruvian, incense burner, turkey form, filigree, 6½″.........440.00
Peruvian, water pitcher, baluster w/foliate scroll hdls, 12″....1,210.00
Peter & Jonathan Bateman, creamer, engraved helmet form, 6″.800.00
Peter & Jonathan Bateman, mustard pot, pierced foliate sides..900.00
Peter Archambo, salver, shells/masks, ornate cartouch, 17″...4,950.00
Philip Rundell, chamber candlestick, Geo IV, 5½″..........440.00

Soup tureen, E., J. and W. Barnard, London, 1846, bombe form with cast C-scroll and leafage border, presentation dated 1890, 115.6 oz., 12″ diameter, $3,100.00.

Philip Rundell, coursing cup, Geo IV, engraved dogs, 7"......4,500.00
Philip Rundell, dish covers, armorials, lion finials, set of 3....1,750.00
Preizyd, Grodno, teapot, grapevine borders, cluster finial, 6"...465.00
PT, Paris, hot water pot/stand, gadroon/shell border, 4".......715.00
Puiforcat, bowl w/liner on stand, flat chased border, 8", pr...1,210.00
R Blackinton, bowl w/hdls, emb/chased acanthus, 3"..........330.00
Redlich, compote, lobed/ftd, relief daisies, 14½" dia.......1,210.00
Reed & Barton, coffee service, Nouveau florals, pot 9", 3 pc...660.00
Reed & Barton, tea set, inverted paneled cones, 4 pc........715.00
Richard Bayley, coffee pot, armorials in cartouch, 9".......2,860.00
Richard Cooke, serving dish, gadroon rim, armorial, 13" dia..2,750.00
Robert Garrard, plate, engraved armorials, 9¾", 8 for.......6,000.00
Robert Garrard, 2nd course dish, lobed rim/engraved crest, 10".600.00
S Herbert & Co, dish cross, pear shaped lamp, shell cap ft...1,045.00
S Kirk, hot water urn, chinoiserie figures/birds, 19½".......2,400.00
S Kirk & Son, bread tray, emb/chased w/flowers, hdls, 15"....715.00
Scandinavian, coffee service emb/chased floral cartouch, 3 pc...400.00
Simpson, Hall, Miller, coffee service, Nouveau poppies, 3 pc..2,250.00
Starr & Marcus, vase, figural putti hdls, flat chased, 10"......605.00
Sven Dahlstrom, beaker, parcel gilt/engraved w/plants, 7".....350.00
T Fletcher, water pitcher, pear form, repousse vintage decor..1,000.00
TH Schumacher, coffee pot, 800/1000, 8".................200.00
Thomas Keeden, lemon strainer, Geo I, 6" L..............330.00
Thos Gilpin, coffee pot, chased florals, shell/swan spout, 9"....990.00
Thos Jones, cup, bell form/engraved crest, 6¾"............450.00
Thos Von Holten, bowl, flying multi-scroll hdls, 11" W......4,950.00
Turkish, goblet, tulip form/chased border/cartouch, 4½", 4....990.00
Turkish, traveling flask, baluster form, late 1800s, 9½".......770.00
Ulrich Schnell, sweetmeat, scalloped/chased/scroll hdls, 4"....715.00
Wakelin & Taylor, sauce tureen, boat shape/reed hdls, 8¾"....500.00
Wakley & Wheeler, goblet, gilt, floral chased/masks, 7½", 6..2,750.00
West & Son, hot water jug, emb/chased w/scrolls/flowers, 9"...900.00
Whiting, demitasse pot, tapered cylinder/emb bird, 11 oz, 9"...605.00
Whiting, tea service, Japanese style, copper birds, 6 pc......8,800.00
Whiting, vase, trumpet, flat chased w/florals/cartouch, 30"....2,750.00
Whiting, water pitcher, repousse/chased w/flowers, 7".......550.00
Whiting Dey, tea/coffee service, floral chased, 6 pc, 9" pot...4,500.00
William Allanson & Co, soup tureen w/lid, 4 scroll/foliate ft...4,400.00
William Bond, snuffers tray, boat shape/brite-cut, 10½".......375.00
William Forbes, creamer & covered sugar urn, 1795........1,650.00
William Frisbee, cup w/lid, ped ft, chased, eagle finial, 13"....850.00
William Holmes, coffee urn, ped base/bead rims/armorials, 14".715.00
William Partis, coffee pot, emb/chased florals, 11".........1,750.00
WK Vanderslice, straining pan, ivory hdl, 6½" dia...........825.00
Wm Bateman, gravy urn, Geo III, vase form w/2 hdls, 42 oz...950.00
Wm Cripps, mug, baluster w/leaf cap dbl scroll hdl, 6½".....1,100.00
Wm Cripps, tankard, Geo III, dbl scroll hdl/cartouches, 7¾"...880.00
Wm Pitts & Joseph Preedy, table temple, Apollo figural, 24".3,850.00

Silver Overlay

The silver overlay glass made during the 1800s was decorated with a cut-out pattern of sterling silver applied to the surface of the ware.

Bar bottle, amber, engraved leaves/thistles, neck overlay, 12"...165.00
Basket, cobalt, Nouveau floral overlay, 4½x5"...........165.00
Perfume, clear, Alvin mk silver scrolls & florals, 3½x3¼".....110.00
Perfume, clear, ground stopper, sterling screw cap, sm.........35.00
Perfume, clear, mk Fine Silver overlay, ball finial, 3¾".........75.00
Perfume, gr w/stopper, silver top, 2½"................100.00
Vase, clear, engraved Nouveau floral, Gorham mk, 14".......335.00
Vase, gr, fluted, ornate floral overlay, 7¼"..............450.00
Vase, gr, silver dogwood/vines, 4", pr................200.00
Vase, gr, simple stylized silver leaves/vines, 7½".........200.00

Silver Plate

Silver plated flatware is fast becoming the focus of attention for many of today's collectors. In the listings that follow, prices are for pieces in like-new condition with no monogram. Worn pieces or those with monograms will be substantially less. It is generally not profitable to restore worn pieces, except those from the very valuable patterns.

Flatware

Adoration (1939), butter server...........................7.00
Adoration (1939), sugar spoon...........................7.00
Affection (1960), dinner knife, hollow handle.................7.00
Affection (1960), gravy ladle............................12.00
Affection (1960), pierced tablespoon......................10.00
Affection (1960), serrated grapefruit spoon..................7.00
Affection (1960), tablespoon............................9.00
Affection (1960), youth fork............................5.00
Aloha (1959), cold meat fork............................14.00
Aloha (1959), salad fork...............................8.00
Aloha (1959), soup spoon, oval bowl.......................7.00
Aloha (1959), tablespoon..............................10.00
Ambassador (1919), cocktail fork.........................9.00
Ambassador (1919), cold meat fork........................14.00
Ambassador (1919), gravy ladle..........................16.00
Ambassador (1919), ice cream fork........................13.00
Ambassador (1919), tablespoon..........................9.00
Ambassador (1919), teaspoon...........................7.00
American Beauty Rose, berry spoon........................25.00
American Beauty Rose, master butter.......................15.00
American Beauty Rose, meat fork..........................25.00
American Beauty Rose, sugar spoon........................15.00
Angelica, cake fork..................................39.00
Anniversary Rose (1962), berry spoon......................14.00
Anniversary Rose (1962), cold meat fork....................12.50
Anniversary Rose (1962), dessert server....................12.50
Anniversary Rose (1962), teaspoon........................5.00
April (1950), luncheon fork.............................7.00
April (1950), teaspoon................................5.00
Ballad (1953), butter server............................6.00
Ballad (1953), dessert server...........................12.50
Ballad (1953), dinner fork.............................7.00
Ballad (1953), dinner knife, hollow handle..................8.00
Ballad (1953), salad fork..............................7.00
Baroque Rose (1967), berry spoon........................16.00
Baroque Rose (1967), butter spreader......................7.00
Baroque Rose (1967), salad fork.........................7.00
Baroque Rose (1967), steak knife, hollow handle..............12.00
Baroque Rose (1967), tablespoon.........................8.00
Beloved, dinner knife, hollow handle.......................7.00
Beloved, sugar spoon.................................7.00
Beloved, teaspoon...................................7.00
Betsy Ross, berry spoon...............................9.00
Betsy Ross, cold meat fork.............................9.00
Bird of Paradise, berry spoon...........................25.00
Bird of Paradise, tablespoon............................9.00
Bridal Wreath II (1950), cold meat fork....................11.00
Bridal Wreath II (1950), dinner knife, hollow handle...........7.00
Bridal Wreath II (1950), salad fork.......................6.00
Bridal Wreath II (1950), teaspoon........................4.00
Bright Future (1954), berry spoon........................14.00
Bright Future (1954), jelly server........................10.00
Bright Future (1954), soup spoon, round bowl................7.00
Bright Future (1954), sugar spoon........................6.00

Bright Future (1954), teaspoon	5.00
Brittany Rose (1948), dinner knife, hollow handle	7.00
Brittany Rose (1948), gravy ladle	12.50
Brittany Rose (1948), pierced pie server	12.50
Brittany Rose (1948), sugar spoon	7.00
Brookwood (1950), butter server	6.00
Brookwood (1950), dinner fork	7.00
Brookwood (1950), iced tea spoon	8.00
Brookwood (1950), soup spoon, round bowl	7.00
Camelot (1964), fruit spoon	6.00
Capri (1935), butter spreader, individual	7.00
Capri (1935), cold meat fork	12.50
Capri (1935), iced tea spoon	8.00
Carnation, berry spoon	25.00
Carnation, cocktail fork	12.00
Carnation, strawberry fork	15.00
Chalice (1958), cold meat fork	9.00
Chalice (1958), dinner knife, hollow handle	7.00
Chalice (1958), youth set, 3 pc, w/orig box	24.00
Coronation (1936), butter server	7.00
Coronation (1936), soup spoon, oval bowl	7.00
Coronation (1936), sugar spoon	7.00
Coronation (1936), tablespoon	10.00
Countess (1969), dinner fork	8.00
Countess (1969), dinner knife, hollow handle	9.00
Countess (1969), tablespoon	10.00
Countess (1969), teaspoon	6.00
Daffodil (1950), berry spoon	22.00
Daffodil (1950), cold meat fork	16.00
Daffodil (1950), fruit spoon	8.00
Daffodil (1950), pickle fork	14.00
Daffodil (1950), salad fork	8.00
Daffodil (1950), sugar tongs	25.00
Daffodil (1950), teaspoon	6.00
Daffodil (1950), tomato server	25.00
Danish Princess (1938), butter server	7.00
Danish Princess (1938), dessert/cereal spoon	7.00
Danish Princess (1938), dinner knife, hollow handle	9.00
Danish Princess (1938), teaspoon	6.00
Del Mar (1939), cocktail fork	9.00
Del Mar (1939), gravy ladle	12.50
Del Mar (1939), sugar spoon	6.00
Del Mar (1939), teaspoon	5.00
Empress (1969), dessert server	14.00
Empress (1969), gravy ladle	14.00
Empress (1969), iced tea spoon	9.00
Empress (1969), pierced tablespoon	12.00
Empress (1969), teaspoon	6.00
Enchantment (1952), dinner fork	7.00
Enchantment (1952), salad fork	7.00
Enchantment (1952), soup spoon, oval bowl	6.00
Enchantment (1952), teaspoon	5.00
Esperanto (1967), berry spoon	12.00
Esperanto (1967), dessert server	11.00
Esperanto (1967), dinner fork	6.00
Esperanto (1967), dinner knife, hollow handle	7.00
Esperanto (1967), salad fork	6.00
Eternally Yours (1941), butter server	7.00
Eternally Yours (1941), sugar spoon	7.00
Evening Star (1950), cold meat fork	14.00
Evening Star (1950), soup spoon, round bowl	8.00
Exquisite (1940), butter server	6.00
Exquisite (1940), dinner knife, hollow handle	8.00
Exquisite (1940), tablespoon	9.00
Fantasy (1941), cold meat fork	6.00
Fantasy (1941), teaspoon	5.00
First Love, cold meat fork	19.00
First Love, demitasse spoon	7.00
First Love, lg carving set	49.00
First Love, tomato server	27.00
Flair (1956), dessert/cereal spoon	7.00
Flair (1956), dinner knife, hollow handle	9.00
Flair (1956), teaspoon	6.00
Flight (1963), soup spoon, oval bowl	6.00
Flight (1963), teaspoon	5.00
Flirtation (1959), cold meat fork	12.50
Flirtation (1959), sugar spoon	6.00
Flower De Luce, berry spoon	28.00
Flower De Luce, individual butter spreader	16.00
Flower De Luce, salad serving fork	35.00
Garland (1965), demitasse spoon	8.00
Garland (1965), dinner fork	8.00
Garland (1965), iced tea spoon	9.00
Garland (1965), teaspoon	6.00
Grand Elegance (1959), cocktail fork	9.00
Grand Elegance (1959), sauce ladle	12.50
Grand Heritage (1968), berry spoon	16.00
Grand Heritage (1968), dessert server	14.00
Grand Heritage (1968), teaspoon	6.00
Grecian (1915), cocktail fork	6.00
Grecian (1915), pickle fork	8.00
Grecian (1915), tablespoon	6.00
Grenoble, cocktail fork	15.00
Grenoble, gravy ladle	29.00
Hanover, berry spoon	29.00
Hanover, ladle, 10″	79.00
Happy Anniversary (1960), berry spoon	14.00
Happy Anniversary (1960), dessert/cereal spoon	6.00
Happy Anniversary (1960), pierced tablespoon	10.50
Happy Anniversary (1960), teaspoon	5.00
Heritage (1953), dinner fork	8.00
Heritage (1953), salad fork	8.00
Heritage (1953), soup spoon, oval bowl	7.00
Heritage (1953), tablespoon	10.00
Invitation (1940), butter server	7.00
Invitation (1940), gravy ladle	14.00
Invitation (1940), jelly server	12.00
Invitation (1940), salad fork	8.00
Invitation (1940), teaspoon	6.00
Isabella, pickle fork, long	9.00
Isabella, soup spoon, round	5.00
King Frederick (1969), berry spoon	16.00
King Frederick (1969), demitasse spoon	8.00
King Frederick (1969), dinner knife, hollow handle	9.00
King Frederick (1969), pierced tablespoon	12.00
King Frederick (1969), sugar spoon	7.00
Lady Caroline (1930), butter server	7.00
Lady Caroline (1930), salad fork	8.00
Lady Caroline (1930), soup spoon, oval bowl	7.00
Lady Fair (1957), cocktail fork	8.00
Lady Fair (1957), dessert/cereal spoon	5.00
Lady Fair (1957), iced tea spoon	7.00
Lady Fair (1957), pickle fork	8.00
Lady Fair (1957), pierced tablespoon	9.00
Lady Fair (1957), teaspoon	4.00
Lady Hamilton (1932), iced tea spoon	9.00
Lady Hamilton (1932), sugar spoon	7.00
Laurel Mist (1966), berry spoon	16.00

Laurel Mist (1966), bon bon server........................12.00
Laurel Mist (1966), cold meat fork........................14.00
Laurel Mist (1966), dinner fork...........................8.00
LaVigne, cocktail fork...................................16.00
LaVigne, demitasse spoon................................12.00
LaVigne, orange spoon...................................19.00
LaVigne, tablespoon......................................8.00
Leilani (1961), butter spreader...........................6.00
Leilani (1961), cold meat fork...........................12.00
Leilani (1961), dessert/cereal spoon......................7.00
Leilani (1961), gravy ladle..............................12.00
Leilani (1961), pie server...............................9.00
Leilani (1961), teaspoon.................................6.00
Lilac Time (1957), butter server..........................6.00
Lilac Time (1957), dessert server........................12.50
Lilac Time (1957), dinner fork...........................7.00
Lilac Time (1957), dinner knife, hollow handle.............8.00
Lilac Time (1957), tablespoon............................9.00
Love (1970), dinner fork.................................7.00
Love (1970), dinner knife, hollow handle..................8.00
Love (1970), tablespoon..................................9.00
Lovely Lady (1937), teaspoon.............................4.00
Lufberry (1915), berry spoon.............................7.00
Lufberry (1915), cold meat fork..........................7.00
Lufberry (1915), salad fork..............................4.00
Lufberry (1915), tablespoon..............................4.00
Magic Rose (1963), berry spoon..........................16.00
Magic Rose (1963), dessert server........................14.00
Magic Rose (1963), dinner fork...........................8.00
Magic Rose (1963), pierced tablespoon....................12.00
Magic Rose (1963), salad fork............................8.00
Magic Rose (1963), tomato server........................14.00
Masterpiece (1956), pierced relish spoon..................7.00
May Queen (1951), berry spoon...........................16.00
May Queen (1951), iced tea spoon.........................9.00
May Queen (1951), soup spoon, oval bowl..................7.00
Memory (1937), dinner knife, hollow handle................8.00
Milady (1940), butter server.............................7.00
Milady (1940), cold meat fork...........................14.00
Milady (1940), dinner knife, hollow handle................9.00
Milady (1940), sugar spoon...............................7.00
Morning Rose (1960), butter server.......................7.00
Morning Rose (1960), sugar spoon.........................7.00
Morning Star (1948), butter server.......................7.00
Morning Star (1948), dinner knife, hollow handle...........9.00
Morning Star (1948), iced tea spoon......................9.00
Morning Star (1948), soup spoon, oval bowl................7.00
Morning Star (1948), soup spoon, round bowl...............8.00
Morning Star (1948), tablespoon.........................10.00
Muscatel, gravy ladle...................................10.00
Mystic (1903), bouillon..................................7.50
Mystic (1903), cocktail fork.............................8.00
Mystic (1903), dinner knife, hollow handle................12.00
Mystic (1903), fruit spoon..............................12.00
Mystic (1903), pastry fork..............................12.00
Narcissus, demitasse spoon..............................11.00
Narcissus, meat fork....................................25.00
Narcissus, teaspoon.....................................6.00
New Elegance (1947), dinner fork.........................8.00
New Elegance (1947), luncheon fork.......................8.00
New Elegance (1947), teaspoon............................6.00
Orleans (1964), baby set, 2 pc, w/box....................12.00
Orleans (1964), berry spoon.............................16.00
Orleans (1964), cocktail fork............................7.00

Orleans (1964), dessert server..........................12.50
Orleans (1964), gravy ladle.............................16.00
Orleans (1964), pierced tablespoon.......................10.00
Orleans (1964), sugar spoon..............................6.00
Orleans (1964), teaspoon.................................7.00
Persian, mustard ladle..................................22.00
Persian, pastry fork....................................15.00
Persian, teaspoon.......................................7.00
Precious Mirror (1954), butter server.....................5.00
Precious Mirror (1954), sugar spoon.......................5.00
Precious Mirror (1954), teaspoon..........................4.00
Proposal (1954), butter spreader, individual...............7.00
Proposal (1954), cocktail fork............................9.00
Proposal (1954), dinner fork..............................7.00
Proposal (1954), luncheon knife...........................8.00
Proposal (1954), salad fork...............................7.00
Raphael, soup spoon, oval................................8.50
Reflection (1959), berry spoon...........................12.00
Reflection (1959), dessert server........................11.00
Reflection (1959), dinner knife, hollow handle.............7.00
Reflection (1959), fruit spoon............................6.00
Reflection (1959), tablespoon.............................8.00
Remembrance (1948), cocktail fork.......................10.00
Remembrance (1948), fruit spoon..........................8.00
Remembrance (1948), iced tea spoon.......................9.00
Reverie (1937), demitasse spoon..........................5.00
Reverie (1937), iced tea spoon............................6.00
Reverie (1937), soup spoon, round.........................6.00
Reverie (1937), sugar spoon..............................5.00
Rhythmic (1957), berry spoon............................14.00
Rhythmic (1957), cold meat fork.........................12.50
Rhythmic (1957), dessert/cereal spoon.....................6.00
Rhythmic (1957), pierced tablespoon......................10.50
Rhythmic (1957), sugar spoon.............................6.00
Rhythmic (1957), teaspoon................................5.00
Roman, gravy ladle.....................................12.00
Romance, pierced olive..................................12.00
Romance II (1952), butter spreader, individual.............7.00
Romance II (1952), iced tea spoon.........................8.00
Romance II (1952), soup spoon, oval bowl..................6.00
Romance II (1952), tablespoon............................9.00
Rose Song (1964), butter server..........................5.00
Rose Song (1964), dinner fork............................6.00
Rose Song (1964), pierced tablespoon......................9.00
Rose Song (1964), teaspoon...............................4.00
Royal Lace (1973), berry spoon..........................12.00
Royal Lace (1973), cocktail fork..........................8.00
Royal Lace (1973), dessert server........................11.00
Royal Lace (1973), dinner knife, hollow handle.............7.00
Royal Lace (1973), salad fork............................6.00
Royal Lace (1973), sugar spoon...........................5.00
Scotia (1915), fruit spoon................................5.00
Scotia (1915), pie/cake server, hollow handle.............12.00
Scotia (1915), soup ladle, 10½".........................35.00
Sheraton, ice cream fork................................10.00
Sheraton, iced tea spoon.................................7.00
Silver Artistry (1965), pierced tablespoon................10.50
Silver Artistry (1965), salad fork.........................7.00
Silver Artistry (1965), soup spoon, oval bowl..............6.00
Silver Fashion (1957), cocktail fork.......................9.00
Silver Fashion (1957), iced tea spoon......................8.00
Silver Fashion (1957), tomato server.....................12.50
Silver Flowers (1960), dinner fork........................6.00
Silver Flowers (1960), sugar spoon........................5.00

Silver Flowers (1960), teaspoon.....................4.00
Silver Lace (1968), bon bon server.................12.00
Silver Lace (1968), cocktail fork..................10.00
Silver Lace (1968), teaspoon.......................6.00
Silver Sands (1966), cocktail fork.................9.00
Silver Valentine (1973), dessert server...........12.50
Silver Valentine (1973), dinner knife, hollow handle....8.00
Silver Valentine (1973), teaspoon..................5.00
Song of Autumn (1960), dessert/cereal spoon........6.00
Song of Autumn (1960), dinner knife, hollow handle....8.00
Song of Autumn (1960), salad fork..................7.00
South Seas (1955), butter spreader, individual.....6.00
South Seas (1955), dinner fork.....................6.00
South Seas (1955), soup spoon, oval bowl...........5.00
Spanish Crown (1970), berry spoon.................14.00
Spanish Crown (1970), cold meat fork..............12.50
Spanish Crown (1970), pierced tablespoon..........10.50
Spanish Crown (1970), salad fork...................7.00
Spanish Crown (1970), teaspoon.....................5.00
Spring Flower (1956), baby fork....................4.00
Spring Garden (1949), berry spoon.................16.00
Spring Garden (1949), sugar spoon..................7.00
Spring Garden (1949), tablespoon..................10.00
Springtime (1957), butter server...................6.00
Springtime (1957), cold meat fork.................12.50
Springtime (1957), fruit spoon.....................7.00
Tangier, cocktail fork.............................9.00
Tangier, iced tea spoon............................8.00
Tangier, salad fork................................7.00
Tangier, sauce ladle..............................12.50
Tangier, soup spoon, oval bowl.....................6.00
Triumph (1968), berry spoon.......................16.00
Triumph (1968), dessert server....................14.00
Triumph (1968), dinner knife, hollow handle........9.00
Triumph (1968), teaspoon...........................6.00
Twilight (1956), cold meat fork...................11.00
Twilight (1956), dinner fork.......................6.00
Twilight (1956), teaspoon..........................4.00
Wakefield (1965), berry spoon.....................14.00
Wakefield (1965), dinner fork......................7.00
Wakefield (1965), teaspoon.........................5.00
White Orchid, dinner fork..........................8.00
White Orchid, meat fork...........................22.00
White Orchid, salad fork...........................9.00
Woodland Rose (1955), demitasse spoon..............6.00
Woodsong (1958), berry spoon......................12.00
Woodsong (1958), cold meat fork...................11.00
Woodsong (1958), dessert/cereal spoon..............5.00
Woodsong (1958), gravy ladle......................11.00
Woodsong (1958), pierced tablespoon................9.00
Woodsong (1958), teaspoon..........................4.00
Woodsong (1958), tomato server....................11.00
Youth (1940), cold meat fork......................12.50
Youth (1940), dinner knife, hollow handle..........8.00
Youth (1940), jelly server........................10.00
Youth (1940), teaspoon.............................5.00

Hollow Ware

Bacon server, chased dome lid, foliate legs, claw/ball ft, 14"....385.00
Basket, bail hdl, fluted rim, gadrooned border, paw ft, 12½"....80.00
Butter dish, butterflies/flowers, ½" border, rnd, Hartford, 6"....60.00
Candelabra, Elkington, figural gnarled oak/shepherd, 33", pr.1,100.00
Candelabra, Sheffield, trn std/gadroon borders/3 arms, 16", pr..600.00

Candelabra, 3 socle, relief shell/plume/acanthus, 20x19½", pr..325.00
Candlestick, Sheffield, chased w/foliage, 1825, set of 4.......550.00
Coffee urn, bun form, mask decor, paw ft, repousse floral, 18".575.00
Creamer, floral & scrolls decor, ftd, Lee & Wigfiell...........75.00
Cup & saucer, Christofle, forked floral hdls, gilt w/in, 5 for....275.00
Decanter caddy, w/2 gr glass decanters, lion masks/paw ft, 12"..385.00
Entree dish, cartouch w/dbl hdls, reticulated/ftd, 1¾x3"......385.00
Entree dish, leaf legs/scroll ft, hdls, 14", pr...............305.00
Entree dish, Sheffield, lobed dome cover, paw ft, 13½"........450.00
Entree dish, Sheffield, octagonal, gadroon borders/crests, 14"..175.00
Entree dish, Sheffield/Waterhouse/Hadfield, scroll rim, 13"....300.00
Entree dish/cover/warmer, Sheffield, paw ft/armorials, 12", pr...330.00
Epergne, grape arbor std w/3 scroll arms, stag on base, 24"...900.00
Meat cover, w/heraldic crest, 12½", pr.........................90.00
Muffineer, shell form, ornate stand, 9½".....................220.00
Pitcher, Bacchic head w/gaping mouth figural, 8"..........1,400.00
Platter cover, beaded edge & hdl, domical, lg................110.00
Punch bowl, ftd, repousse foliate band, w/12 cups, 14" dia....300.00
Salver, Sheffield, reed border/engraved armorials/ball ft, 18"....700.00
Sauce boat, loop hdls, beaded borders, cartouches, sm, pr.....110.00
Sauce tureen, Sheffield, 4 paw ft, bud finials/lion masks, 6½"..325.00
Soup tureen, ped base, Derby #3707, 24 scenes, rope hdls......65.00
Tea set, paneled melon form, flower relief, foliate hdls, 4 pc...605.00
Tea urn, basketweave banding, loop/ring/mask hdls, paw ft, 17"..550.00
Tea urn, ornate chased decor, ped ft, English, 17"...........190.00
Tea urn, Sheffield, gadroon/shell/foliate rim, paw ft, 17".....1,430.00
Tea urn, Sheffield, rectangular w/lower lobed body, 1810, 19"..600.00
Tea urn, spherical tank, ring hdls, fluted legs/paw ft, 18".....440.00
Teapot, Egyptian head, Deco; Simpson, Hall & Miller..........40.00
Teapot, oval w/wood hdl, wreath/floral band engraving, 9½"....50.00
Tray, figural dragon hdls, Tufts #4000, 21x11"...............85.00
Vegetable dish w/lid, 11x11½".................................25.00
Vegetable w/cover/warmer, Sheffield, twig hdls/engraved, 14"...425.00
Waiter w/gallery, Sheffield, chased cartouch on scrolls, 22"....175.00
Wine cooler, dbl hdls, gadroon border, crest, metal liner, 8½".300.00
Wine cooler, Sheffield, compana form, w/liner, mk I/Iw/Co, 12".500.00
Wine cooler, Sheffield, ped base, cornucopia hdls, 9", pr....1,320.00
Wine cooler, Sheffield, tub shape w/lobed bottoms/masks, 8"...850.00

Silver Resist

The process for decorating pottery with the silver resist method involved first coating the design, or that portion of the pattern that was to be left unsilvered, with a water soluble solution. The lustre was applied to the entire surface of the vessel, and allowed to dry. Before the final firing the surface was washed, removing only the silver from the coated areas. This type of ware was produced early in the 1800s, by many English potteries, Wedgwood included.

Creamer, birds & flowers, unusual hdl, 6".....................150.00
Jug, vintage decor on band w/turq/gr/red enamel, 5½"..........325.00
Mug, leaf & vine decor w/red enamel, embossed, 4½".............75.00
Pitcher, hound hdl, Wedgwood, 4"..............................30.00

Sinclaire

In 1904, H.P. Sinclaire and Company was founded in Corning, New York. For the first sixteen years of production, Sinclaire used blanks from other glassworks for his cut and engraved designs. In 1920, he established his own glass blowing factory in Bath, New York. His most popular designs utilize fruits, flowers, and other forms from nature. Most of Sinclaire's glass is unmarked.

Bowl, rose & star pattern, 2½x8x10"......................325.00
Cake stand, intaglio vintage cutting, scalloped, Gorham base...600.00
Candlestick, amber, hollow twist stem, no mk, 8½"............65.00
Candlestick, celeste bl, hourglass stem/twist rib, 10", pr.......235.00
Celery, geometric cut w/hobstars, scalloped, flared-up ends.....225.00
Compote, amber w/bl ped ft, hollow twist stem, rim cut, 12"...225.00
Compote, topaz, engraved floral medallions, garlands, 4x8"....110.00
Console bowl, wide rim, w/pr 10" sticks, honey amber, sgn....185.00
Decanter, on ped, gr enamel on sterling stopper.............450.00
Dish, ftd, flared, brilliant cut, 3½x6".....................160.00
Ginger jar, blk glass, blown by Steuben, 8"................150.00
Nappy, brilliant cutting, w/hdl, sgn......................170.00
Rose bowl, engraved rock crystal, mums decor.............140.00
Teapot, ball form, floral cutting, sgn, 5½"..............3,000.00
Tumbler, copper wheel cut & etched.....................37.50
Vase, Adam cutting, sgn, 10¼"..........................310.00
Vase, engraved flowers & foliage, sgn, 12"................110.00
Vase, Nubian Black, wht rim, 5½".......................55.00

Sitzendorf

Candelabra, 5-lite, woman on base, applied fruit/flowers, 23"...400.00
Centerpiece, reticulated w/applied florals/maids on base, 20"...400.00
Compote, 2 winged Cupids, floral encrusted, 13".............700.00
Figurine, boy w/wheelbarrow, movable wheel, flowers, 6x8½"...260.00
Figurine, monkey band, 9 pc, tallest: 5"..................750.00
Figurine, shepherd & shepherdess, minor rpr, 7", pr.........225.00
Planter, 2 cats climbing out, porcelain...................125.00

Slag Glass

Slag glass is a marbleized opaque glassware made by several companies from about 1870 until the turn of the century. It is usually found in purple, or in caramel, though other colors were also made. Pink is rare and very expensive.

Caramel, bowl, Chrysanthemum Leaf, 4"...................120.00
Caramel, bowl, Geneva, oval, ftd, 10½"...................450.00
Caramel, bowl, Geneva, oval, ftd, 8½"....................135.00
Caramel, bowl, 6-fluted, 4"............................225.00
Caramel, carafe, Chrysanthemum Leaf...................2,200.00
Caramel, compote, Melrose.............................225.00
Caramel, creamer, Strigal, tankard.......................75.00
Caramel, hatpin holder, Orange Tree, EX.................235.00
Caramel, mug, Serenade...............................125.00
Caramel, nappy, Masonic...............................85.00
Caramel, pitcher, water; Geneva.........................600.00
Caramel, pitcher, water; Heron.........................450.00
Caramel, pitcher, water; Paneled, small hairline............225.00
Caramel, plate, Serenade...............................85.00
Caramel, powder jar, Venetian, no lid....................190.00
Caramel, vase, Beaded Triangle, minor damage.............65.00
Pink, sauce dish, Inverted Fan & Feather, ball ft, 2½x4½"....225.00
Pink, tumbler, Inverted Fan & Feather...................250.00
Purple, bowl, Beaded Rib, w/lid, 6x6x4½"................70.00
Purple, bowl, Dart Bar, 8"..............................45.00
Purple, bowl, Leaf Paneled, pat 4/22/78..................135.00
Purple, bowl, Raindrop pattern, 8¾"......................38.00
Purple, cake stand, plain design.........................75.00
Purple, celery vase, Fluted, ped base, scalloped, 8¼".........95.00
Purple, celery vase, Jewel.............................125.00

Purple, compote, Flute, w/lid, 9" dia.....................245.00
Purple, compote, Jenny Lind, 7½x8½"...................350.00
Purple, creamer, Scroll w/Acanthus......................55.00
Purple, creamer, Sunflower............................65.00
Purple, dish w/lid, cherry & leaf decor, 3 part, 7½" dia......60.00
Purple, dish w/lid, cow on tub.........................42.50
Purple, mug, rabbit..................................65.00
Purple, pitcher, water; Dart Bar........................95.00
Purple, plate, Closed Lattice Edge, 10½" dia..............100.00
Purple, salt, master; 2½x4"............................45.00
Purple, spooner, Flower & Panel.......................65.00
Purple, spooner, Flute................................80.00
Purple, spooner, Scroll w/Acanthus.....................55.00
Purple, sugar w/lid, Flute, tall........................200.00
Purple, toothpick, Ringed Urn.........................30.00
Purple, vase, grapes, 3 reticulated twigs, leaf base, 6", pr.....125.00
Purple, vase, novelty, Beads & Bark....................35.00
Purple, vase, novelty, Maple Leaf, chalice................35.00
Purple, vase, twig hdls, leaf base, grape decor, 6"..........45.00
Red, basket bowl, relief ovals, knobs for woven hdl..........85.00

Smith Bros.

Alfred and Harry Smith founded their glassmaking firm in New Bedford, Massachusetts. They had been formerly associated with the Mt. Washington Glass Works, working there from 1871 to 1875 to aid in establishing a decorating department.

Smith glass is valued for its excellent enameled decoration on satin or opalescent glass. Pieces were often marked with a lion in a red shield.

Biscuit jar, sq swirl, beige w/florals, rampant lion mk.........695.00
Bowl, bl/violet pansies, beaded rim, melon rib, 3x5½"........260.00
Bowl, in sgn Pairpoint ped holder, ornate hdls, 1½x8½"......165.00
Planter, melon rib, cream satin w/br floral, SP insert, 8" dia...260.00
Rose bowl, Queen's design on moire, beaded edge, 4¼".....285.00
Salt, master; gold/beaded rim, gr/lav floral w/beading, 1½x3"....65.00
Sugar shaker, melon rib, floral enamel, silver top............175.00
Vase, crane, HP, 4½"................................60.00
Vase, wht w/blk/wht heron/gr foliage, SP holder, no mk, 5½"...95.00

Snow Babies

Early in the 1800s, snow babies -- little figurals in white snowsuits -- originated in Germany. They were made of sugar candy and were often used as decorations for Christmas trees. Later on, they were made of marzipan, a confection of crushed almonds, sugar, and egg whites. Eventually, porcelain manufacturers began making them in bisque. They were popular until WWII. Some reproductions are now found on the market.

Admiral Perry & Byrd................................150.00
Babies, on snow covered ledge, mk Germany, 2¼"............95.00
Babies, w/snow covered igloo & penguin, mk Germany, 2".....95.00
Babies, 2 on sled...................................55.00
Baby, arms extended, Germany, 3x2½", M................110.00
Baby, arms extended, sm.............................25.00
Baby, bisque head, mache body, rabbit fur covered, 1913, 12"..175.00
Baby, cloth body, 8"................................225.00
Baby, holds gold hoop, Germany, 1½", M.................75.00
Baby, on brooch, 1¼"...............................40.00
Baby, on polar bear, 2¾"............................95.00
Baby, on snowball, sm...............................40.00
Baby, rides early prop plane, Germany, 1½x2½"...........125.00
Baby, sitting, one leg tucked under, Germany, sm............20.00

Baby, sitting, arms extended, Germany, 3", $175.00.

Baby, w/ball, mk Germany, 2"...........................95.00
Baby, w/dog, Germany, lg.............................125.00
Baby, w/penguin, Germany.............................65.00
Baby, w/sled, sgn Germany............................60.00
Baby, 1 arm extended/other holds early camera, Germany, 1½"..85.00
Bear, Germany, 1¼"...................................45.00
Mermaid, w/porpoise..................................75.00
Santa, on polar bear, mk Germany, 1¾"...............150.00
Snowman, 2"...30.00

Snuff Bottles, Boxes, and Jars

The Chinese were introduced to snuff in the 17th century, and their carved and painted snuff bottles typify their exquisite taste and workmanship. These tiny bottles, seldom measuring over 2½", were made of amber, jade, ivory, and cinnabar, and often had tiny spoons attached to their stoppers. By the 18th century, some were being made of porcelain, others were of glass with delicate designs tediously reverse painted with tiny brushes sometimes containing a single hair. Copper and brass were used, but to

Snuff bottle netsuke, head removes, tiny spoon attached, 3", $95.00.

no large extent.

By the early 19th century, the use of snuff had spread to Europe and America. It was used by both the gentlemen and the ladies alike, and expensive snuff boxes and bottles were the earmark of the genteel. Some were of silver or gold set with precious stones or pearls, while others contained music boxes.

Bottle, carved turq w/birds among peach branches, on stand....75.00
Bottle, Chinese mc porcelain, figures in landscape relief........90.00
Bottle, lapis lazuli, carved as dbl gourd tied w/sash...........50.00
Bottle, lt olive gr glass, 4¼"..............................18.00
Bottle, Peking glass overlay, red/snowflake, lion/bat/box/hawk...100.00
Bottle, quartz, gourd form, lav/clear leaf/gr stopper, China.....130.00
Bottle, rvpt scenes, ladies in garden/interior scenes, 4½"......160.00
Box, birch bark w/press-carved children/goat, 4½" L...........45.00
Box, bl w/sailing vessel, French enamel, 2" dia..............385.00
Box, burl, all wood including hinge, miniature................155.00
Box, cobalt, Lawyer & His Agent, English enamel, 2¼".......415.00
Box, cobalt, paneled lid w/female bust/florals, enamel, 2¼"....220.00
Box, demi cartouch, bl enamel, lid w/lady/bird, 2"...........165.00
Box, gr w/wht lattice, French enamel, courting scene, 3" L....350.00
Box, horn w/brass fittings, floral/bird engraving, 4"..........125.00
Box, paper/glass/cb, blk/wht, woman/tomb/willow, 2½"........60.00
Box, papier mache, blk w/orig HP girl w/ewer, cracks, 2x3½"..145.00
Box, papier mache, decoupage engraving, Dutch man, 3½"......45.00
Box, papier mache, engraving 'Prisonniers francais...', 3½".....55.00
Box, papier mache, engraving of David Porter Esq, 3½" dia...155.00
Box, papier mache, engraving of goat milking scene, 3½" dia, G.35.00
Box, papier mache, gold decor on lid, 2" L..................35.00
Box, papier mache, HP comic scene of tooth pulling, 3½", G...80.00
Box, papier mache, HP lady w/fan on lid, 2¼"...............30.00
Box, papier mache, Indian Chief Black Hawk lid, 1800s.......100.00
Box, pewter, engraved hawks/foliage/compote of flowers, 3¼"...85.00
Box, pnt all sides w/scenics, export porcelain, 1789, 2¾"......300.00
Box, puce w/in, wht lid w/florals, porcelain, 1½".............165.00
Box, puce w/scene of lady w/flower basket on lid, enamel......250.00
Box, serpentine, puce w/bird/branches/emb scrolls, enamel, 2"..275.00
Box, trn boxwood, engraved silver fittings, 3¾".............85.00
Box, walnut form, porcelain, 1¾".........................330.00
Box, wht/br, A New Year's Gift for 1758, English enamel, 2½".415.00

Soapstone

Soapstone is a soft talc in rock form with a smooth, greasy feel, from whence comes its name. In colonial times, it was extracted from out-croppings in large sections with hand saws, carted by oxen to mills, and fashioned into useful domestic articles such as footwarmers, cooking utensils, inkwells, etc. During the early 1800s it was used to make heating stoves and kitchen sinks. Most familiar today are the carved vases, bookends, and boxes made in China during the Victorian era.

Ash tray, leaf shape, scalloped, floral carving, 3x4"...........20.00
Buddha, lotus base, Sino-Tibetan, 1800s, 20"................150.00
Buddha, on lotus throne, conical flame, 5½x10½"............50.00
Camel, blk, 7"......................................125.00
Candle holder, 3 hole, long...............................90.00
Elder w/peach seated by young attendant, 3¾"...............40.00
Foo lion, female w/pup; male w/ball, 5½x6½", pr............80.00
Foo lion, standing in clouds, flames at front, 8½x9"..........75.00
Horse, full-figure, heavy, blk, 8".........................200.00
Horse, rearing, rock plinth, teeth bared, 9½x12"...........150.00
Incense burner, elephant decor, blk........................85.00
Incense burner, tripod ogre-head ft, foo lion hdls, 7½x9".......90.00
Match holder, figural monkey feeding bird...................35.00

Double vase, woody platform with florals and foliage, 6″ x 6½″, $48.00.

Parrot, long tail, perched on flowering branch, glass eyes, 8″....45.00
Peacock, 2½″...9.00
Screen, rnd plaque w/pk/blk goldfish, tan seaweed, 7¼x5½″....30.00
Screen, 5 color carving of 2 peacocks, peony flowers, 5½x6″....35.00
Seal, sq plinth surmounted w/foo dog, 6½″, pr..............110.00
Squirrel after fruit from trees, 6½x9″......................85.00
Standish, w/lg lizard, snakes & frogs, polychrome, 12″ L.......50.00
Toothpick holder, 3 monkeys, reddish-br, 2¼x1½″............25.00
Village, carved scene, 12″................................95.00

Soda Fountain Collectibles

As the neighborhood ice cream parlor becomes a thing of the past, soda fountain memorabilia, from fancy backbars to ice cream advertising, is becoming a popular field of collecting. One area of interest is the glassware used to serve the more elaborate ice cream concoctions. A sundae glass is familiar to us all, but there was also a 'mondae' glass, narrow at the bottom and flaring to a top dimension equal to one scoop! And a 'tuesday' glass with a rim wide enough to accommodate two scoops of ice cream side by side! At least part of their appeal is due to the mouth watering memories they revive.

Back bar, mahogany & cherry, mirror top, 1880, 22x9 ft, G..7,000.00
Book, Soda Water Dispenser Book, sundae recipes, 1909.......52.50
Bottle, back bar; emb 'Orange', early, 8″...................30.00
Canister, aluminum, Van Houten's, emb boy w/soda..........50.00
Dispenser, for Eskimo Pie, 3 Eskimos as feet, VG...........275.00
Dispenser, hot drink; Am Metalware, 'Hot Drinks', 18″.......200.00
Ice crusher, Alaska #1...................................150.00
Mixer, Hamilton Beach, gr porcelain, single, 1919...........135.00
Mixer, Hamilton Beach, marble base, brass.................135.00
Scoop, 'G' in finial, cone shaped tin......................24.00
Scoop, Fry dispenser...................................175.00
Scoop, Geer Co, cone shape wood hdl, pat 1906.............28.00
Scoop, Gilchrist #31, polished, EX........................55.00
Scoop, Gilchrist #33, cone shape wood hdl.................35.00
Scoop, Icy Pi Automatic Cone Co, brass, EX...............125.00
Scoop, Indestructo #4..................................45.00
Scoop, Indestructo #5, EX...............................52.00
Scoop, Nuroll, 1 pc metal................................8.00
Soda glass, ftd, heavy glass..............................3.00

Straw holder, cut glass, floral, needs top & insert.............95.00
Straw holder, glass w/nickel top & insert, 11″...............95.00
Straw holder, green, w/domed lid, ornate, EX..............295.00
Tray, Imperial Ice Cream, shows strawberry sundae, VG........38.00

Scoop, marked Gilchrist #30, 10″, original finish, $32.00.

Soft Paste

Soft paste refers to a low fired, granular type of porcelain that must be glazed to retain water.

Basket, almond shape, bl/wht, hairlines/damage, 32x7x9½″.....85.00
Cup & saucer, blk Oriental design, VG......................35.00
Cup & saucer, handleless; blk transfer country scenes.........55.00
Cup & saucer, handleless; blk transfer florals w/enamel........45.00
Cup & saucer, handleless; Queen's Rose w/ribbon border, G.....45.00
Figurine, lion reclining on wht rectangle plinth, 5½″, pr.......50.00
Plate, bl feather edge, Rogers, 9¾″.......................30.00
Plate, emb rim w/purple lustre/gr, rose center is red/gr, 6½″....65.00
Punch bowl, rim pnt w/turq/yel floral, Furnivals, 14″..........65.00
Sugar, mc florals, bl trim................................55.00
Toddy, emb rim w/bl stripe, Elijah Fed By Ravens, 5½″.......35.00
Toddy, emb rim w/purple lustre & polychrome enamel, hairlines.30.00
Window sash rest, cherubs, arched top w/sun face, 5″, pr, G....75.00

South Jersey Glass

As early as 1739, Caspar Wistar established a factory in Salem County, taking advantage of the large beds of sand suitable for glass blowing, and abundant forests available for fueling his furnaces. Scores of glassworks followed, many of which were short-lived. It is generally conceded that aside from the early works of Wistar and the Harmony Glass Works, which emerged from the Glassboro factory originally founded by the Stangers, the finest quality glassware was blown after 1800. In the 1850s, coal was substituted for the wood as fuel. Though a more efficient source of heat, the added cost of transporting the coal inland proved to be the downfall of many of the smaller factories. By the 1880s, many had failed.

Glassware can be attributed to this area through the study of colors, shapes, and decorative devices that were favored there; but because techniques were passed down through generations of South Jersey glass blowers, without specific documentation it is usually impossible to identify the specific factory that produced it.

Candlestick, amber, ribbed/waisted stem, late 1700s, 3½", pr...560.00
Cologne, clear pressed swirl w/ground stopper, 6"..............20.00
Creamer, blk-olive gr, applied top, thick base, ear hdl, 4".....435.00
Cuspidor, lady's; clear pressed swirl, 3¾"...................95.00
Hat, blk, free blown, pontil...........................120.00
Ink bottle, wht lilies w/mc mottling, facet in stopper, 8", EX...200.00
Ink bottle, wht lily w/red/bl/gr coloring, Rhulander, rpr, 9"....300.00
Jug, blk w/wht looping, tooled top, globular, 5"..............400.00
Paperweight, ftd; wht lily w/red/bl/gr, Rhulander, 3¾"........200.00
Paperweight, wht lily w/red/bl/gr/pk/yel, Millville, 3½"........200.00
Perfume, wht mushroom w/bl/red/gr coloring, Rhulander, 4x2"..100.00
Pitcher, amber, tooled top/pinch spout/crimp base, 10½".....385.00
Pitcher, aqua w/wht looping, base crack, 7⅛"..............400.00
Pitcher, att Wistarberg, amber, 7½x5½"..................800.00
Pitcher, cobalt, mold blown, 3 ring base, whittle mold, 8½"...495.00
Pitcher, lily pad, amber, minor rpr, 8"..................1,200.00
Pitcher, lily pad, aqua, threaded neck, thumb rest hdl, 6", VG..300.00
Pitcher, lt gr, gourd, left swirl, Hall, Pancoast & Craven, 8"...245.00
Vial, Wistarberg, 2¾x2½".............................160.00
Wig stand, cone center w/mc tree-like internal decor, 8".....300.00

Spangle Glass

Spangle glass, also known as Vasa Murrhina, is cased art glass characterized by the metallic flakes imbedded in its top layer. It was made both abroad and in the United States during the latter years of the 19th century, and it was reproduced in the 1960s by the Fenton Art Glass Company.

Vasa Murrhina was a New England distributor who sold glassware of this type manufactured by a Dr. Flower of Sandwich, Massachusetts. Flower had purchased the defunct Cape Cod Glassworks in 1885 and used the facilities to operate his own company. Since none of the ware was marked, it is very difficult to attribute specific examples to his manufacture.

Pitcher, bulbous, br/rust/wht, cased, clear hdl, 5¾"...........85.00
Pitcher, yel w/wht & metallic flakes in casing, tricon top, 9"....135.00
Rose bowl, rose w/silver mica in pattern, wht w/in, 3¾x3¾"...100.00
Rose bowl, satin finish, bl w/mica, crimped, 4½".............40.00
Rose bowl, 8 crimp top, heavy mica w/wht lining, 3½x3½"....100.00
Vase, apricot, much silver mica, 8".......................55.00
Vase, cranberry w/applied swirled rigaree, 10½"............165.00
Vase, lily; ruffled, bl w/wht casing, 5½".................100.00
Vase, melon rib, pk w/wht interior, 6"...................60.00

Pitcher, caramel and brown with gold spangles, white casing, amber handle, 8¼", $225.00.

Spatter Glass

Spatter glass, characterized by its multicolor 'spatters', has been made from the late 19th century to the present by American glass houses as well as those abroad. Although it was once thought to have been made entirely by workers at the 'end of the day' from bits and pieces of left-over scrap, it is now known that it was a standard line of production.

Box, egg form, 3 gold ft, yel w/leaves & branches, 7½" H.....245.00
Box, ormolu decor, 8"...............................115.00
Candlestick, gr/maroon/wht/gold, wht cased, 9", pr..........110.00
Decanter, cranberry/wht, cut stopper, 10"...............42.00
Jar w/lid, clear ft & finial, 6½x3¾"...................75.00
Jar w/lid, yel w/forget-me-nots, clear finial, 6¼x3½"........65.00
Pitcher, cranberry & wht, trefoil ruffled rim, 5½".........95.00
Pitcher, cranberry/yel/gr/wht cased, cloverleaf top, water sz....150.00
Pitcher, Inverted Thumbprint, maroon/wht, 5¾"..........110.00
Pitcher, mc, long neck, wht cased, water sz..............115.00
Pitcher, Reverse Swirl, bl satin, water sz...............150.00
Pitcher, ruffled top, rose/pk/yel & gr, wht lined, 7x3".......65.00
Rolling pin, red/bl, 14".............................120.00
Vase, pastels, 1880, 10½"...........................55.00
Vase, pk/gr/blk/wht, fluted, cased, 9"...................65.00

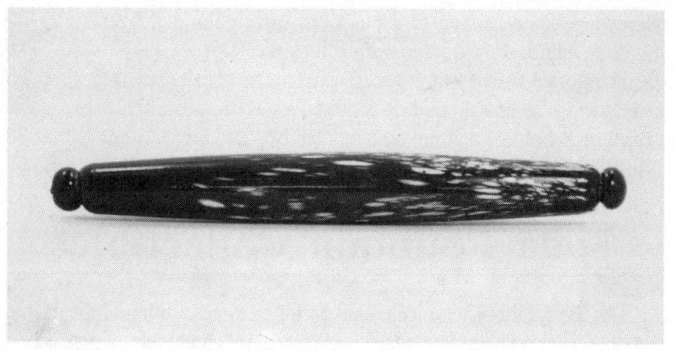

Rolling pin, late 18th century, 17", $135.00.

Spatterware

Spatterware is a general term referring to a type of decoration used by English potters beginning in the late 1700s. Using a brush or stick, brightly colored paint was 'dabbed' onto the soft paste earthenware items, achieving a 'spattered' effect which was often used as a border. Because much of this type of ware was made for export to the United States, some of the subjects in the central design, the schoolhouse and the eagle patterns, for instance, reflect American tastes. Yellow, green, and black spatterware is scarce and highly valued by collectors.

Bowl, red, peafowl in 4 colors, hairlines, 5x6¾".............115.00
Bowl, red/bl/gr/blk w/foliage, flower & fruit, 4x13".........65.00
Bowl, red/br/gr vining florals, blk mk Staffordshire, 3x6½"....20.00
Butter pat, yel w/red schoolhouse.....................200.00
Chamber pot, bl, rose in red/gr/blk, hdl chip/rpr, 6x8½".....250.00
Chamber pot w/lid, bl/wht, Meakin mk WM Co, 9½".......100.00
Creamer, bl, rooster in red/bl/yel/blk, hairlines, chips.......65.00
Creamer, br, rose in red/gr, minor rim hairline, 4".........130.00
Creamer, gr, vine/berry in red/yel, hairline in hdl, 3½".....525.00
Creamer, gr/blk rainbow, stripe effect, hairline, 4¼".......235.00
Creamer, purple/gr rainbow, flakes on spout, 3¾".........105.00
Cup, handleless; bl, parrot in red/gr/blk, old rim chips......95.00
Cup, handleless; red/bl, center has sm red/gr flower........25.00

Cup & saucer, blk, oversize...............85.00
Cup & saucer, br, miniature...............60.00
Cup & saucer, gaudy florals, mk Wm Adams, miniature, 4 for..100.00
Cup & saucer, gr w/bl/yel/red peafowl, child size...........175.00
Cup & saucer, handleless; bl, flowers red/gr/blk, minor wear....145.00
Cup & saucer, handleless; bl, fort on cup, mismatch, wear.....200.00
Cup & saucer, handleless; bl, memorial tulip in 3 colors, G....215.00
Cup & saucer, handleless; bl, paneled, center bl dot..........50.00
Cup & saucer, handleless; bl, surface wear, miniature.........55.00
Cup & saucer, handleless; bl/bl flower, Davenport, prof rpr.....30.00
Cup & saucer, handleless; clover in red/gr, hairline, flakes...165.00
Cup & saucer, handleless; dk bl spatter, miniature............55.00
Cup & saucer, handleless; gr w/red & yel dots, worn..........175.00
Cup & saucer, handleless; purple.........................115.00
Cup & saucer, handleless; rainbow, red/gr w/rose, edge flakes....65.00
Cup & saucer, handleless; rainbow, red/gr/bl..............185.00
Cup & saucer, handleless; rainbow, red/yel w/thistle, G.......225.00
Cup & saucer, handleless; red, bull's eye center, flakes........40.00
Cup & saucer, handleless; red, peafowl in 4 colors, rpr.......115.00
Cup & saucer, handleless; red, 3 color tulip cup only, Adams....65.00
Cup & saucer, handleless; red/gr X-hatching, edge flakes.....155.00
Cup & saucer, handleless; yel, thistle red/gr, ring flake.......375.00
Cup & saucer, handleless; yel w/bl dots...................210.00
Cup & saucer, peafowl, gr w/3 color bird..................225.00
Cup & saucer, underglaze flow bl w/red/gr, flakes on cup.....105.00
Cup plate, purple, eagle/arrows transfer in bl, 1840, 4", pr.....770.00
Cup plate, red, peafowl in red/bl/gr, sgn Adams.............150.00
Custard, bl coarse spatter, applied flatiron hdl, 12 sides.......55.00
Egg cup, bl, rose in red/bl/gr/blk, hairline, 2½".............525.00
Mug, red/bl/gr, orig lid, hairlines, 4¾"....................95.00
Mustard, purple, vine decor in red/gr/blk, no lid, 2¼".......245.00
Pitcher, bl, fort pattern, hairlines/chipped hdl, 8"...........150.00
Pitcher, bl, paneled, peafowl in red/gr/bl/blk, 8", G..........175.00
Pitcher, bl, vining foliage band in red/blk/gr, 9", G..........150.00
Pitcher, br, paneled, 4 petal flower in bl/red/blk, 8", G.......175.00
Pitcher, purple, gr spatter tree w/blk trunk, damaged, 9".....175.00
Pitcher, rainbow, red/bl/gr, scalloped rim, flakes, 8".........565.00
Pitcher, red, peafowl in ochre/bl/gr/blk, hairlines/wear, 6½"....150.00
Plate, bl, bl eagle & shield, rim hairline, 10½".............125.00
Plate, bl, fort design in gr/blk/red, rim hairline, wear, 9".....105.00
Plate, bl, peafowl in red/ochre/gr/blk, 8¾", G..............135.00
Plate, bl, star in red/bl/gr, stains, edge flakes, 8"...........65.00
Plate, bl, tulip in red/yel/gr, imp Cotton & Barlow, 9".......125.00
Plate, bl border, br transfer of flying eagle, 9"............195.00
Plate, bl/gr, rose in red/gr/blk, stained, 8½".............65.00
Plate, bl/gr/yel rim decor, stains/flakes, 8¾".............15.00
Plate, dk red/bl, br transfer of eagle, mk Walker, 8½".......325.00
Plate, gr & red clover w/blk vines, 9½", M...............375.00
Plate, gr rosette border, floral center, Harvey, 8½".........165.00
Plate, gr/red/bl floral rim; frog & 3 rabbits, late 1800s, 9".....155.00

Plate, purple rim, bl/gr bands, transfer tiger hunt/elephants.....70.00
Plate, purple rim, transfer of eagle/shield, stains/flakes, 6"......55.00
Plate, rainbow, bull's eye, blk/wht/purple, prof rpr, 9"........225.00
Plate, rainbow, bull's eye, red/yel, minor flakes, 9½".........245.00
Plate, rainbow, gr/bl, gaudy florals, minor flakes, 8½".......125.00
Plate, rainbow, red/bl, brushed X in center, 8¾"............405.00
Plate, rainbow loop in gr/purple/yel/blk, minor wear, 8"......775.00
Plate, red, castle pattern, rim flakes/wear, 8½".............300.00
Plate, red, peafowl in red/bl/gr/blk, imp Adams, flakes, 8¾"....205.00
Plate, red, primrose in gr/purple/yel/blk, 9¾", G...........205.00
Plate, red, schoolhouse in red/gr/br, primitive rpr, 7½".......85.00
Plate, red, swags/foliage in bl/red/gr/yel, 8½"..............45.00
Plate, red/bl/gr stylized leaves, stained, 9"................60.00
Plate, red/bl/gr/yel floral, mk Wild Flower, 9".............45.00
Plate, red/gr floral, imp Clementson Bros, minor wear, 9½".....25.00
Plate, red/gr/yel rows of daubs, imp Edge Malkin, 8½".......50.00
Plate, yel, morning-glory in bl/blk/gr, minor damage, 8¾".....225.00
Platter, blk transfer rabbits at rim, gaudy floral center, 15"....225.00
Platter, rainbow, bl/purple, hairlines/flakes, 12x16".........85.00
Saucer, bl, peafowl w/long tail in 4 colors, stains, 5¾"........45.00
Saucer, bl w/bl transfer of Chinaman......................35.00
Saucer, bl/ochre/gr/red, cottage w/gr sponged trees, Mayer, 6"..225.00
Saucer, gr, peafowl in red/bl/ochre/blk, primitive............45.00
Soup plate, bl border, 13 point star in center, 8½", M........145.00
Sugar bowl, bl, minor flakes on inside lid flanges, 5".........60.00
Sugar bowl, gr, peafowl in red/bl/gr/blk, stain/chip, 4½".....100.00
Sugar bowl, gr, peafowl in red/ochre/bl/blk, no lid, 2¾".......95.00
Sugar bowl, rainbow, red/bl w/rose in red/gr/blk, 5", G......200.00
Sugar bowl, rainbow drape, red/bl, rpr hole in bottom, 5".....150.00
Sugar bowl, red w/blk stripes, good hdls, minor flakes, 5".....105.00
Teapot, bl, minor ft flakes, stains, 6"......................95.00
Teapot, red, transfer of bl eagle & shield, glued rpr, 9".......325.00
Wash bowl, bl/purple rainbow, 12 sided, rim crack, 14" dia....125.00
Wash set, bl, eagle & shield...........................1,200.00
Waste bowl, florals at rim w/overlay of spatter, Adams.........45.00

Spelter

Spelter figurines are cast from commercial zinc and coated with a metallic patina. The result is a product very similar to bronze in appearance, yet much less expensive.

Crusader, bronzed, sword/lily, mtd on marble, 6½x4".........42.00
Dog, Golden Retriever Pointer, in pointing position, 3x15"......90.00
Dog, Scotty Terrier, standing at edge of metal bowl, 6x6½".....32.00
Elephant, trumpeting, on marble slab, 8½x5½".............125.00
Girl, 'Good Fairy', sgn JMR, dtd 1916, 10¾"...............85.00
Golfer in swing position, knickers, EX detail, base: 5½x3¾"...150.00
Lady w/sword, medieval attire, ivorene face, w/pen holder, 5"....75.00
Lamp, woman w/sheaf, man w/axe, Busheron, 19", pr........250.00
Maiden, wine ewer in arm, wine press at side, wood plinth, 21".140.00
Paperweight, Shriner wearing fez/tie/coat, Moores Metal, 5" L...32.00

Spode-Copeland

The Spode Works were established in 1770 and continued to operate under that title until 1843. Their earliest products were typical underglaze blue printed patterns, though basalt was also made. After 1790 a translucent porcelain body was the basis for a line of fine enamel decorated dinnerware. Stone china was introduced in 1805, often in patterns reflecting an Oriental influence.

In 1833 Wm. Taylor Copeland purchased the company, continuing business in much the same tradition. During the last half of the 19th cen-

Purple spatter rim, transfer of eagle clasping arrows, shield with thirteen stars in blue, cup plates, $500.00, pair; saucers, $600.00, pair.

tury, Copeland produced excellent parian figures and groups with such success that many other companies attempted to reproduce his work. He employed famous painters to decorate plaques, vases, and tablewares, many examples of which were signed by the artist. Most of the Copeland wares are marked with one of several variations that incorporate the firm name.

Biscuit jar, wht w/florals, SP lid & bail........................85.00
Bowl, Imari, w/lid, 10″ dia................................325.00
Bowl, Rosebriar, vegetable.................................32.50
Bowl, Spode's Tower Blue, cereal, old, M......................9.00
Bowl, Spode's Tower Blue, rimmed soup, old, M................12.00
Butter pat, Spode's Tower Blue, old, M.......................8.50
Child's set, flow blue w/animals, ca 1860s, 17 pc, EX........335.00
Cream soup w/under plate, Spode's Tower Blue, old, M.........16.50
Creamer, blue w/classical figures, wht hdl/spout, ca 1900....25.00
Cup & saucer, Chelsea Garden...............................22.50
Cup & saucer, Heath Rose, demitasse........................15.00
Cup & saucer, Reynolds.....................................17.50
Egg cup, Spode's Tower Blue, old, M........................10.00
Pitcher, Churchill commemorative, Copeland, 6¾″............150.00
Plate, Chelsea Garden, bread & butter.......................8.50
Plate, Cowslip, dinner.....................................22.50
Plate, Florence, dinner....................................22.50
Plate, Romney, salad.......................................13.50
Plate, Rosebriar, luncheon.................................10.00
Plate, Sorrento, dinner....................................15.00
Plate, Spode's Tower Blue, dinner, old, M..................15.00
Platter, City of Corinth, imp mk, Spode, 13″...............110.00
Platter, Gothic castle, bl/wht, very early, 20½″...........180.00
Platter, Imari, ironstone, well & tree, 18½″...............225.00
Platter, Principal Entrance o/t Harbor on Cacamo, bl, 15″..150.00
Platter, Spode's Tower Blue, old, 14″, M....................55.00
Soup tureen w/stand, Newstone, #3875, 1810.................650.00
Teapot/tea tile, allover florals, animal finial, reg mk....135.00

Teapot, Meadowbrook, $50.00.

Spongeware

Spongeware is a type of factory-made earthenware that was popular during the last quarter of the 19th century. It was decorated by dabbing color onto the drying ware with a sponge, leaving a splotched design at random or in simple patterns. Sometimes a solid band of color was added. The vessel was then covered with a clear glaze and fired at a high temperature. Blue on white is the most preferred combination, but green and ivory, orange on white, or those colors in combination may also occasionally be found.

Batter jug, bl/wht, orig lid, 7″, EX.......................175.00
Bowl, bl/br/wht, 4¼x6¼″....................................45.00

Bowl, bl/putty on gray, molded, late 1800s, 4x10½″.........60.00
Bowl, bl/rust/cream, advertising, 8½″......................72.00
Bowl, bl/rust/cream, 4x6½″.................................45.00
Bowl, bl/wht, mk Roseville, O; 4x8″........................75.00
Bowl, bl/wht, surface & edge flakes, 5½x12″................95.00
Bowl, bl/wht, 2x5½″, EX....................................70.00
Bowl, bl/wht, 7½″ dia......................................90.00
Bowl, bl/wht, 7x14″, M....................................195.00
Bowl, br on yel, 4½x10½″...................................85.00
Bowl, br/bl/wht/red on cream, 5¼″ dia......................45.00
Bowl, gr/br on cream, 9″...................................36.00
Bowl, mixing; gr/wht, 4½x10″ dia...........................85.00
Bowl, pudding; bl/wht, tin bail hdl, 1880s, 5x11½″ dia....140.00
Bowl, rust/bl on cream, paneled, 11″ dia..................150.00
Bowl set, nesting; bl/rust on cream, 6″ through 11″, M, 6 for..550.00
Casserole, ind; br/yel, 2x5″ dia, set of 6................140.00
Cat, seated; bl/wht, chips on ears, hairlines, 7″..........65.00
Chamber pot, bl/wht..95.00
Creamer, br/bl on wht, 3″..................................20.00
Creamer, cow w/milker, bl/blk/tan sponge, prof rpr, 7″ L..1,150.00
Crock, bl/tan, 'Bread', emb pine trees, huge..............325.00
Crock, bl/wht, 12 gal.....................................385.00
Crock w/lid, gr/wht, flake on inside lid flange, 5½″.......95.00
Crock w/lid & wire hdl, bl/wht, sliver off top edge, 6″...110.00
Cup, handleless; bl/wht, sm................................30.00
Cup & saucer, bl/wht, 3½″ cup; 6½″ saucer.................125.00
Custard cup, yel/gr/br, 3½″................................24.00
Dish, bl/wht, shallow, rectangular, 8x12″.................175.00
Gypsy kettle w/lid, bl/wht, no hdl, 4¾″....................65.00
Jardiniere, bl/wht w/gr rim flecked w/gold, 8x11″..........75.00
Jardiniere, br on cream, 7½″...............................55.00
Kettle, bl/wht, no lid, 7x11″ dia.........................295.00
Kettle, bl/wht, orig bail & clips, 1870s, 4½x8½″..........215.00
Kettle, bl/wht w/blk striping on lid, 1870s, 7x11″ dia, VG..325.00
Mug, bl/wht, mk Imperial...................................95.00
Mug, bl/wht, 3¼″..95.00
Mug, br on cream, base flake, 3″...........................15.00
Pig bank, br/bl on wht, minor roughness, 3½″...............85.00
Pitcher, batter; br/gr/yel, bulbous, 2 spouts..............85.00
Pitcher, bl on yel w/emb floral, 7½″......................115.00
Pitcher, bl sponge band top, molded flying duck ea side, 11″..85.00
Pitcher, bl/br on cream, emb corn, 5½″.....................95.00

Pitcher, blue and white with embossed leaf and flowers, 10″, $200.00.

Pitcher, bl/br on cream, molded top & base designs, 9"......145.00
Pitcher, bl/wht, bulbous, emb diamonds, lg.................140.00
Pitcher, bl/wht, emb medallion of child & dog, 9"..........160.00
Pitcher, bl/wht, sq hdl, 7"...............................135.00
Pitcher, bl/wht, 11".....................................160.00
Pitcher, bl/wht w/bl stripe, 12"...........................95.00
Pitcher, br/bl/red/wht on cream, 5".........................95.00
Pitcher, br/gr on wht, blk transfer Alpha Grain Co, 4½"......45.00
Pitcher, gr/br on cream, 4½"...............................45.00
Pitcher, gr/tan, straight sided, 6", EX....................40.00
Pitcher, gr/wht, minor rim flakes, 7"......................105.00
Pitcher, gr/yel/br, barrel pattern, 8½".....................75.00
Plate, bl/wht, 5½"..95.00
Platter, bl/wht, early, 15x10½"...........................275.00
Salt box, hanging; bl/br on cream, hinged walnut top, 6".....195.00
Sauce dish, Virginia, cut sponge decor, 5½"................90.00
Soap dish, bl/tan on wht.................................130.00
Spittoon, bl/wht, brass top...............................195.00
Spittoon, gr on cream w/gold traces.......................225.00
Teapot, br/gr on yel, minor flakes, 5½"....................65.00
Toothbrush holder, bl/wht.................................45.00
Vase, bl/wht, 3¾"...55.00

Spoons

Souvenir spoons have been popular remembrances since the 1890s. The early handwrought examples of the silversmith's art are especially sought and appreciated for their fine craftsmanship. Commemorative, personality related, advertising, those with Indian busts, and those with floral designs are only a few of the many types of collectible spoons.

In the following listing, spoons are entered by state, character, or occasion.

Key:	
B----bowl	FF----full figure
BR----bowl reverse	GW----gold wash
emb----embossed	H----handle
eng----engraved	HR----handle reverse

Alamo, San Antonio, emb in B; H: Davy Crocket & FF, 1836...55.00
Alaska, eng in shell B; H: cornucopia w/fruit, dtd '92, 4"......42.50
Alaska, Ketchikan, fish/name on H.........................17.50
Alaska, on HR, H: enamel flowers & bear....................45.00
Alaska, totem pole, seal, view, cabin on H; HR man w/dog.....25.00
Apostle, European, 4⅛"...................................12.50
Askansas, Hot Springs, eng B; FF Indian on H, HR w/FF miner.37.50
Atlantic City, seal/pier H, HR: man/lady/stroller/lighthouse.....18.00
Aztec, calendar in B; H: emb Aztec motif..................32.00
Baby's head on loop H; B: emb chickens....................35.00
Bear, figure in high relief atop twisted H; GW bowl, tsp......46.00
Bermuda, Hamilton, cut-out/fr harbor view H, 5½".........13.50
Boston, Old North Church in B; H: emb church/library/P Revere.32.00
Boston, St House emb B; H: pot of beans/spoon/fork, 5½"....17.50
BPOE on H; B: moose head & clock.........................22.50
Brownie, enameled figure in demitasse....................29.00
Busch Gardens & FF parrot on H, bowl plain.................37.50
California, eng in GW bowl; H: figural palm tree, 4".........45.00
California, H: lady/enamel seal; HR: eagle/flag; B: GW, bldg.....65.00
California, Los Angeles, curved H w/angel; mission in B.......27.50
California, Los Angeles, HR: Spaniard/priest, H: flower, GW....25.00
California, Oakland, eng oak tree, B w/name, GW.............25.00
California, Pasadena, lg flower on H; B: etch name...........28.50
California, seal/miner/grapes, B w/emb Golden Gate, tsp, 5½"...16.50
Canada, enamel crest w/beaver, branch H; 4¼".............14.00

Canada, enamel cut-out crest; Montreal in B, 3½"..........12.50
Canada, flag & Knight of the Carter crest emb on H, demi.....20.00
Canada, Toronto, beaver figure on branch H; B w/name, 5¼"...25.00
Cape Cod, cut-out of fisherman, 5½".......................16.00
Catalina Island w/view eng in GW bowl; H: FF tuna, shell, net...65.00
Chicago, Century of Progress & bldgs emb on H.............46.00
Chicago, Electrical Bldg, etched view in B, dtd 1893.........22.00
Chicago, emb 1832 view in B; H: Indians/children, Gorham, 6"..35.00
Christmas, star top of H, enamel holly band, Gorham, 1971.....32.50
Colorado, Denver, cut-out capitol view on H...............18.50
Colorado, Denver, name & view on H.......................15.00
Colorado, Denver, seal/tools/burro H; B: Auditorium, mk SSMC..15.00
Colorado, Denver, statue of lady H; B: etched capitol.........22.50
Colorado, Pike's Peak, floral H; B: emb train at summit.......36.00
Connecticut, eng Harkeness Tower in B; emblem on H; 4½"....10.00
Connecticut, seal w/eagle below, eng Litchfield School, Watson..16.00
Cupid figural on H, B: emb farm scene, 4¾"................16.50
Eagle w/US shield, full figure atop ornate H; GW bowl........95.00
Easter in B; H: sun, angel, bell, cross & lilies.............12.50
Florida, eagle top H w/crest below, 5¾"...................16.00
Florida, Jacksonville, in GW bowl; FF cut-out alligator on H...40.00
Florida, Jacksonville/floral eng GW B; H: boy/alligator/etc....65.00
Franz Joseph portrait emb on H, bowl plain.................45.00
Georgia, Black boy on hdl, demitasse.....................22.00
Glacier National Park & FF Indian on H, plain bowl..........47.50
Hartford, Charter Oak, Durgin; fruit 5¾".................26.00
High School, Omaha, Nebraska.............................27.50
Illinois, Chicago, B: etched government bldg...............16.50
Illinois, eagle/corn on H; HR eagle/flag; B: Effingham, P&B....18.50
Illinois, Springfield, B: etched Lincoln Monument...........18.50
Indiana, eagle, view, cabin, Who's Here, corn, monument H, 4".45.00
Indiana, emb capitol in B; H: buffalo, 5½"................16.50
Indiana, Gary, eng B w/steel mills, emb...................32.50
Indiana, Marion, corn/wheat/view on H; B: etched courthouse...20.00
Indiana, seal & name on H; GW bowl.......................30.00
Iowa, seal/hawk/eye H; B: emb ear of corn, tsp, 5½".........15.00
Iowa, Sigourney, seal/hawk/eye on H; HR w/eagle; B: eng school.15.00
Kansas, Topeka, sunflower H; B w/etched capitol, GW.........22.50
Longfellow's home emb in B; H: picture of Longfellow........60.00
Louisianna, New Orleans, St Louis Cathedral, emb hdl/bowl.....32.50
Louisianna, Shreveport, in B; H: twist w/FF alligator.........36.50
Maine, Bayville, boats, lighthouse emb in B; H: oar, FF fish....46.00
Maryland, Baltimore, in GW bowl; H: twist, cut-out flower/leaf...40.00
Massachusetts, Boston, 3 views on H; B: etched Public Library..20.00
Massachusetts, Concord, cut-out Minute Man on H; B: plain.....42.50
Massachusetts, Haverhill, Whittier's B'place, Durgin, 5½".......25.00
Massachusetts, Plymouth, cut-outs of John Alden/Priscilla on H..42.50
Michigan, Detroit, Riverfront, scenic bowl.................29.00
Michigan, Lansing, capitol etched in GW bowl...............20.00
Michigan, state seal emb on H; bk decorated...............25.00
Minnesota, eagle atop, state seal, 5¾"....................17.50
Minnesota, St Paul, GW bowl; H: tree w/2 FF bears...........40.00
Minnesota, State Prison, etched in GW bowl................20.00
Missouri, Kansas City, flower cut-out H; B w/name...........20.00
Missouri, St Louis, Union Station, openwork hdl.............39.00
Missouri, St Louis, Union Station etched in B...............12.00
Missouri, St Louis, w/FF statue of St Louis on H............32.00
Mohawk Trail, FF Mokawk Indian chief on H................46.50
Montana, swastika on H; B: emb capitol bldg, 5¼"..........22.50
Montreal eng in B; enameled crest on H....................25.00
Montreal eng in B; H: enameled maple leaves...............32.00
Mr Peanut, figural......................................18.00
Mt Vernon emb in B; H: emb view, Geo & Martha, demi.......45.00
Mt Vernon emb in B; H: Geo & Martha; Wilcox & Evertsen, 6".27.50

Independence Hall, Philadelphia; sterling 5¼", $17.50.

Navada City in shell B; H: FF eagle w/outspread wings, GW, 4".65.00
New Jersey, Cape May, eng, heart B; H: FF fish, starfish, etc....42.00
New Mexico, Alvarado, shows hotel, emb hdl/bowl............32.50
New Orleans, city seal emb H............................25.00
New Orleans, 3 views on H, 4 on HR; B: view Canal St.......27.50
New York, Albany, seal emb on H; B: capitol bldg, bk decorated.30.00
New York, Binghamton, Ins bldg in B; lily hdl, Watson-Newell...25.00
New York, Brooklyn Bridge etched in B...................20.00
New York, Buffalo, buffalo/Indian H; B: emb tower, BR: falls....28.50
New York, cut-out Empire St Bldg w/Am eagle atop............32.00
New York, eagle/seal below; B: eng Schenectady, 5¾"........18.50
New York, Kingston, goldenrod H; B w/eng Senate House, 5⅛".14.50
New York, Lower NY skyline...........................45.00
New York, Post Office, Auburn eng in B, H w/scrolls, 5½".....18.50
New York, views in B; simple H, tsp....................25.00
Niagara Falls, buffalo figural on column H; B: emb view, 5½"...28.50
Niagara Falls, Indian w/cut-out feathers/bow/arrows on H; 4"....18.50
Niagara Falls, view in B; FF Indian w/bow, etc, on H.........45.00
North Carolina, Southern Pines, full figure Indian, arms up.....45.00
Notre Dame Cathedral etched in B, beaver on branch.........12.00
Ohio, Cleveland, in GW bowl; H: twist w/cut-out FMN flowers...42.50
Oregon, Pendleton, cut-out cowboy on rearing horse on H......47.50
Panama Pacific Expo, bear figural/symbol/eagle, CMR, 5¾".....20.00
Panama Pacific Expo, eng San Fransisco on shaped H........30.00
Pennsylvania, Harrisburg, floral H; B: emb capitol bldg........40.00
Pennsylvania, Philadelphia, Masonic signs H; B etched temple..22.50
Pennsylvania, Pittsburg, Carnegie Library etched in B.........14.00
Pennsylvania, Pittsburg, City Hall etched in B..............22.50
Pennsylvania, Pittsburg, eng B; H: emb scroll, miner cut-out....40.00
Philadelphia, Indp Hall GW bowl; H: FF Wm Penn, bell, shield..75.00
Rhode Island, Providence, emb Quaker w/book on H, 4".......38.00
San Francisco Fire, fancy cut hdl, 1906, rare..............150.00
South Carolina, seal/plants on H; B: emb Ft Sumter, 5½"......15.00
South Dakota, cut-out miners, pan w/nuggets, shovel, mule on H.48.50
Stagecoach & horses w/in leaf form hdl, 4½"...............15.00
Statue of Liberty, figural, emb rnd bowl, Gorham............50.00
Stork w/baby on H; B: clock, Reed & Barton...............36.50
Syracuse, GW bowl; Greek letters/coin/Pallas on H, Gorham....82.00
Tennessee, Memphis, Tenn & view on H; GW bowl w/Memphis..20.00
Texas, cut-out saddle, twist on H; bowl plain, 4"............45.00
Tionesta, steamship emb B; H: anchor/dolphin, Wilcox-Evertsen.26.50
Utah, Salt Lake City, Mormon Temple etched in bowl.........16.00
Utah, Salt Lake City, Temple, emb hdl/bowl...............32.50
Vermont, B: Manchester in Mtns, H: seal, Towle, 5½"........16.00
Vermont, emb Ethan Allen Monument in B; H: pine trees/florals.18.50

Virginia, Roanoke, eng in heart B; H: arrow, flowers, leaves.....50.00
Virginia, seal/views on H; B: plain, demi..................25.00
Washington, DC, eagle, US Capitol in B...................16.00
Washington, Seattle, Mt Rainier B; H: totem pole/Chief Seattle..30.00
WC Fields, figural.................................18.00
Wisconsin, Superior; Indian H/HR......................65.00
Wyoming, Cheyenne, cut-out cowboy on rearing horse on H....35.00
Yellowstone Natn'l Park eng in GW bowl; H: cut-out buffalo....40.00

Sporting Goods

Baseball, Casey Stengel autograph, in clear sealed holder.......65.00
Baseball bat, Jackie Robinson, Hutchinson Bros, 30½".......24.00
Book, Baseball Record, 1950..........................7.00
Book, Everlast Boxing Record, 1930.....................20.00
Book, Knapp & Spaulding, Bicycles & Sundries, 1897........25.00
Book, Major League Baseball, Ethan Allen, 1st printing, 1938...30.00
Book, Who's Who in American Sports, 1928, 964 pgs.........35.00
Bottle, Coke; Paul 'Bear' Bryant commemorative, w/contents....15.00
Clock, Babe Ruth.................................200.00
Folder, 8 pgs, pictures Milwaukee Braves, Go Greyhound, 1954..13.50
Guide, football; Spaulding, 1926.......................20.00
Lamp, bicycle; carbide, Admiral Comb, bracket.............50.00
Lamp, bicycle; carbide, English Dazzler..................60.00
Lamp, bicycle; carbide, Globe, fork mt w/bracket............60.00
Lamp, bicycle; carbide, Silver King.....................75.00
Lamp, bicycle; carbide, Solar, brass w/jeweled sides, 1896.....95.00
Lamp, motorcycle; carbide, Old Sol, Hawthorne, brass........85.00
Pennant, Hank Aaron Home Run King...................20.00
Pennant, Maryland Orange Bowl, 1954, lg................18.00
Pennant, World Champion Mets, 1973...................20.00
Photo, high wheel bicycles & club members...............40.00
Photo, World's Champions Canton Bull Dogs, football, 1922....80.00
Pin-back, Baseball Stars, 1950........................10.00
Pin-back, Football for Spectator, Walter Camp, Yale, 1911......35.00
Plate, golfer w/knickers, HP, Mason's, dtd 1933, 8½", pr......150.00
Program, All Star Game DC stadium, National/Am League, '62...5.00
Program, Boston Braves, 1947.........................6.00
Program, Olympics, 1932, M.........................50.00
Program, St Mary's vs California, 15th annual, Oct 5, 1929.....16.00
Program, Yankees, 1961.............................6.00
Program insert, Lou Brock Day, Sept 26, 1979, 4 pgs..........3.00
Record, Joe E Brown, How to Play Baseball, two 78s..........85.00
Record, Mickey Mantel's Farewell to Baseball, in orig sleeve.....15.00
Sign, Professional Golfers Assoc, rvpt, ball & clubs, 1920......120.00
Skates, Dutch, acorn tip............................65.00
Sled, oak w/metal tipped runners, primitive, 13x49"..........35.00
Sleigh, wood, decorative carved runner finials, very worn, 50"..185.00
Snow shoes, wood fr lashed w/rawhide, early, 51" L, pr......40.00
Target ball, amber glass, checked design, Bogardus, pat 1877..200.00
Tricycle, all wood w/metal wheel rims, orig pnt/fringe, 35x52"..900.00
Watch fob, Babe Ruth.............................100.00
Wrist watch, Natn'l Invitational Tournament souvenir, 1968.....65.00
Yearbook, Pittsburgh Steelers, 1979, 48 pgs of facts..........3.00
Yearbook, Spaldings Golf Guide, 1927...................9.00

Staffordshire

Scores of potteries sprang up in England's Staffordshire district in the early 18th century; several remain to the present time. Some of the larger companies as well as specific types of ware are listed in other sections of this book.

Figurines and groups were made in great numbers; dogs were favorite subjects. Often they were made in pairs, each a mirror image of the other. They varied in heights from 3″ or 4″ to the largest, measuring 16″ to 18″.

The Historical ware listed here was made throughout the district; some collectors refer to it as Staffordshire Blue ware. It was produced as early as 1820, and because much was exported to America, it was very often decorated with transfers depicting scenic views of well-known American landmarks. Early examples were printed in a deep cobalt. By 1830, a softer blue was favored, and within the next decade, black, pink, red, and green prints were used. Although sometimes careless about adding their trademark, many companies used their own border designs that were as individual as their names.

Key:
blk----black	l/b----light blue
gr----green	m/b----medium blue
d/b----dark blue	m-d/b----medium dark blue

Historical

Bidet, Moore & Co, bl transfer	385.00
Bowl, Landing of LaFayette, d/b, Clews, 7½″	400.00
Bowl, man in sleigh, d/b, 6¼″	250.00
Bowl, Near Hudson/Junction of Scandaga/Hudson, br, 8¾″	150.00
Bowl, Pains Hill Surrey, d/b, Hall, beaded rim, 9½″	275.00
Creamer, Boston Harbor, d/b, M	480.00
Creamer, Crows Nest From Bull Hill, blk, Ridgway, 6½″	75.00
Creamer, Indian Encampment on St Lawrence, l/b, Morley	115.00
Creamer, LaFayette at Franklin's Tomb, d/b, Wood	450.00
Cup, handleless; Univ of Maryland, d/b, stains/hairlines	305.00
Cup & saucer, Boston State House, m-d/b, Rogers, EX	225.00
Cup & saucer, Cadmus/Fulton's Steamboat, blk w/pk border	125.00
Cup & saucer, eagle on rock, Wood	150.00
Cup & saucer, handleless; Boston State House, m/b, prof rpr	85.00
Cup & saucer, handleless; City Hall NY, m/b, sm flake	185.00
Cup & saucer, handleless; Priory, l/b, Challinor	40.00
Cup & saucer, LaFayette at Franklin's Tomb, d/b, Wood, M	275.00
Cup & saucer, milking cows, d/b, stains	40.00
Cup & saucer, sleigh scene, d/b, imp Wood, saucer hairline	75.00
Cup & saucer, Wadsworth Tower, d/b, lg	300.00
Cup & saucer, Washington at Tomb, w/scroll, d/b, flakes	205.00
Custard cup, Select Views, bl, Halls, w/hdls	75.00
Ladle, d/b, Stevenson's wild rose border, 12″	250.00
Pitcher, Albany, l/b, 8¾″, EX	180.00
Pitcher, Harbor Scene, m-d/b, Rogers, shell & seaweed, 9″	385.00
Pitcher, NY City Hall/NY Hospital, d/b, Stevenson, 6″, rpr	400.00
Pitcher, Water Girl, d/b, Clews, 5¾″	265.00
Plate, America & Independence, d/b, states rim, 10½″, VG	275.00
Plate, America & Independence, d/b, states rim, 8¾″, VG	250.00
Plate, Arched Stone Bridge, d/b, Adams, 8¾″	75.00
Plate, Armitage Park, d/b, Wood's grapevine border, 5½″	80.00
Plate, Arms o/t US, Hammersley, 7¾″, M	85.00
Plate, Arms of New York, d/b, Mayer, 10″, EX	500.00
Plate, Arms of New York, d/b, Mayer, 10″, M	650.00
Plate, Arms of South Carolina, d/b, Mayer, 7″	485.00
Plate, Baker's Falls, Hudson River, blk, Clews, 9″	85.00
Plate, Bank o/t United States, m/b, Stubb's eagle rim, 10″	300.00
Plate, Battery & C, gr, Jackson, American Scenery, 7¾″	75.00
Plate, Beehive, d/b, Stevenson, 8½″	75.00
Plate, Boston Hospital, untitled, d/b, Stevenson, 9⅛″	250.00
Plate, Boston State House, m-d/b, Wood, 7″, M	135.00
Plate, Boston State House, untitled, m/b, imp Wood, 10″	150.00
Plate, Castle of Furstenfel, d/b, Henshall, 8¾″	90.00
Plate, Catskill House, Hudson, d/b, Wood, 6½″	350.00
Plate, City Hall, NY, m-d/b, chips on table ring, 9¾″	85.00
Plate, City Hall, NY, m/b, hairline, 10″	145.00
Plate, City Hotel, NY, d/b, Stevenson, acorn/oak leaf rim, 8¾″	250.00
Plate, City of Albany, State of NY, d/b, Wood, shell rim, 10″	350.00
Plate, Commodore MacDonnough's Victory, d/b, Wood, 10¼″	325.00
Plate, Commodore MacDonnough's Victory, d/b, Wood, 7½″	250.00
Plate, Court House, Baltimore, d/b, 8½″, M	250.00
Plate, cup; Battery, d/b, Wood, trefoil border, 3⅝″	250.00
Plate, cup; Boreham House Essex, d/b, 4½″	100.00
Plate, cup; Cadmus, d/b, trefoil border, Wood, 3½″	170.00
Plate, cup; Cottage in Woods, d/b, trefoil border, Wood, 3½″	140.00
Plate, cup; frigate, ½ sail, d/b, Wood's shell border, 4″	325.00
Plate, cup; Ft Ticonderoga, purple, Jackson, 5″	200.00
Plate, cup; Large Cottage w/People, d/b, Adams, 3⅞″	75.00
Plate, cup; View of Newburgh, l/b, Jackson, 4″	170.00
Plate, Dalguise, Perthshire, d/b, grapevine border, Wood, 10″	110.00
Plate, Dam & Waterworks, m-d/b, 10″	325.00
Plate, Don Quixote & Sancho Panza, d/b, 6¾″, M	140.00
Plate, Don Quixote & Sancho Panza, d/b, 9″, M	165.00
Plate, Downing College, m-d/b, Ridgway, 6″	75.00
Plate, Dr Syntax Reading His Tour, d/b, 9″, M	165.00
Plate, Eashing Park, Surrey, m-d/b, R Hall, 7½″	45.00
Plate, Esholt House, Yorkshire, d/b, grapevine rim, Wood, 10″	55.00
Plate, Fairmount, Near Phila, d/b, Stubb's eagle border, 10¼″	175.00
Plate, Ghaut of Cutwa, d/b, Hall & Sons, 8¾″, set of 5	150.00
Plate, Gilpin's Mill on Brandywine Creek, d/b, Wood, 9½″	325.00
Plate, Havard College, m-d/b, minor stains, 10″	185.00
Plate, Highlands, North River, Stubbs, eagle border, 10″, M	850.00
Plate, Hudson River, d/b, Wood's shell border, 5¼″, EX	275.00
Plate, Junction of Sacandaga & Hudson Rivers, blk, 6¾″, M	75.00
Plate, Junction of Sacandaga & Hudson Rivers, l/b, Clews, 7″	70.00
Plate, Kingsweston, Gloucestershire, d/b, Riley, 9″, M	55.00
Plate, LaGrange, Residence of LaFayette, d/b, Wood, 10″, M	150.00
Plate, Landing o/t Fathers at Plymouth, m-d/b, Wood, 10″, M	140.00
Plate, Landing o/t Fathers at Plymouth, m-d/b, Wood, 8½″, M	125.00
Plate, Landing of LaFayette, d/b, Clews, 10″, M	275.00
Plate, Landing of LaFayette, d/b, Clews, 9″	175.00
Plate, Library Philadelphia, m-d/b, 8⅛″	175.00
Plate, Mahomedan Mosque & Tomb, d/b, Hall, Oriental, 9″	75.00
Plate, Man Shooting Fox, d/b, Wood, Zoological Series, 8½″	65.00
Plate, Marine Hospital, d/b, Wood, minor scratches, 9″	300.00
Plate, marine view, Shannon, m-d/b, Rogers' seaweed rim, 10″	150.00
Plate, Monuments & Urns, blk, 8¾″	65.00
Plate, Near Calcutta, d/b, Wood's irregular shell, 6½″, M	230.00
Plate, Near Fishkill, d/b, Clews, Cities Series, 7¾″	225.00
Plate, Near Fishkill, Hudson River, blk, Clews, 10½″, M	85.00
Plate, Near Sandy Hill, Hudson River, purple, 7¾″, M	45.00
Plate, New York City Hall, blk, Jackson, 10″	85.00
Plate, Pagoda, d/b, Clews, 8¾″	65.00
Plate, Pass in the Catskills, d/b, Wood's shell border, 7½″	275.00
Plate, Picturesque Views Baker's Falls, br, Clews, 9″	40.00
Plate, Pittsfield Elm, d/b, Clews, 8½″	235.00
Plate, Pittsfield Elm, d/b, 6¾″	230.00
Plate, Presidents House, Washington, Jackson, blk, 10½″	45.00
Plate, Residence o/t late Richard Jordan, NJ, br, 10½″	125.00
Plate, Shannondale Springs, VA, red transfer, Adams, 8″	85.00
Plate, Shelter'd Peasants, m-d/b, Hall, 10″	55.00
Plate, Shelter'd Peasants, m/b, 8½″	30.00
Plate, Shirley House Surrey, d/b, Wood's grapevine border, 6½″	65.00
Plate, St Paul's School Regents Park, d/b, Adams, 7½″	85.00
Plate, St Philip's Chapel, London Views, d/b, Wood, 10¼″	80.00
Plate, steamboat, Chief Justice Marshall Troy, m-d/b, 8″, G	275.00
Plate, steamboat, Diorama Series, d/b, 10″, M	300.00
Plate, steamboat, Union Line, d/b, Wood's irregular shell, 10″	300.00
Plate, The Valentine, d/b, Clews, Wilkie Series, 9″, M	165.00
Plate, toddy; Boston State House, d/b, Ridgway, 5″, M	350.00
Plate, toddy; Ft Edwards, Hudson River, blk, 5″, M	55.00

Plate, Transylvania Univ, d/b, Wood, 9¼"..................385.00
Plate, Transylvania Univ, m-d/b, imp Wood, minor wear, 9¼"..250.00
Plate, Troy from Mount Ida, blk, 10½", M..................95.00
Plate, Upper Ferry Bridge, d/b, Stubbs, 8¾"..............250.00
Plate, Utica Tribute, Erie Canal Inscription, d/b, 7½", M...350.00
Plate, View from Ruggles House, blk, Ridgway, 10", M........45.00
Plate, View from Ruggles House, l/b, Ridgway, 10¼"........60.00
Plate, View Near Conway, NH, pk, Adams, 9"...............65.00
Plate, View of Trenton Falls, man, d/b, Wood's, shell rim, 6½".250.00
Plate, View of Trenton Falls, 3 people, d/b, Wood, 7¾"......250.00
Plate, View on Road to Lake George, d/b, Stevenson, 8¾", EX.500.00
Plate, Villa in the Regents Park, d/b, Adams, 9"...........95.00
Plate, Village of Little Falls, NY, sepia, Meigh, 8"..........40.00
Plate, Warleigh House, m-d/b, Hall's Select Views, 8", flake....50.00
Plate, Washington, d/b, Clews, Cities Series, 7¾"..........250.00
Plate, West Point, Hudson River, blk or br, Clews, 8"........55.00
Plate, Wm Penn's Treaty, blk, 8½"........................35.00
Platter, Alms House, NY, d/b, Ridgway, 16½", M...........530.00
Platter, American Marine, purple, 13x10½"...............85.00
Platter, Arms of NC, d/b, imp T Mayer, prof rpr, 11½x14¾".2,000.00
Platter, Boston State House, bl, Stubbs, 14½"............550.00
Platter, Boston/Bunker Hill, slate bl, well/tree, Ridgway, 19"...275.00
Platter, British Views, d/b, fruit/flower rim, Henshall, 17".....325.00
Platter, Broke Hall, d/b, 10¾"...........................265.00
Platter, Catskill Mountains, d/b, Wood, 10½", EX...........635.00
Platter, Columbus, Ohio, d/b, City series, 14½", M........2,400.00
Platter, Columbus, red transfer, Adams, 15"..............175.00
Platter, Dorney Court, reticulated lattice border, Wood, 8x10"..265.00
Platter, Fairmount near Philadelphia, d/b, Stubbs, 20".......650.00
Platter, Harper's Ferry, WV, pk, Adams, 17½"............185.00
Platter, Hudson, Hudson River, blk, 13¼"................180.00
Platter, Iron Works at Saugerties, blk, Jackson, 13½".......240.00
Platter, Lake George, d/b, Woods's shell border, 16¾", M.....725.00
Platter, Landing of LaFayette, Clews, d/b, 12"............600.00
Platter, Landing of LaFayette, d/b, 17"..................690.00
Platter, Little Falls at Luzerne, blk, Clews, 17½".........260.00
Platter, Millenium, br transfer, 16¾x13¾"...............240.00
Platter, Millenium, pk, Stubbs, 17".....................250.00
Platter, Narrows From Fort Hamilton, l/b, Ridgway, 17½"....250.00
Platter, New Vesuvius, bl, floral/cherub border, 18"..........170.00
Platter, Newburgh, Hudson River, br, 15½", M............165.00
Platter, Niagara Falls From American Side, d/b, Wood, 14½".1,150.00
Platter, Palestine, bl/wht, floral border, 15"...............80.00
Platter, Pennsylvania Hospital, d/b, Ridgway, 18½".........550.00
Platter, Pittsfield Elm, d/b, wht rim, Clews, 16½", EX.......500.00
Platter, St George's Chapel Regents St, d/b, Wood, 17".......425.00
Platter, Tappan Zee, Greensburgh, d/b, Wood's shell rim, 9¾".950.00
Platter, Teresa Panza & Messenger, d/b, 14¾", M..........445.00
Platter, View of Greenwich, m/b, minor wear, 15"...........90.00
Relish dish, Don Quixote, gr, Brameld, 11½", EX...........95.00
Sauce boat, Fort Ticonderoga, ftd, br, prof rpr.............135.00
Sauce boat, Hoboken in NJ, d/b, Stubb's eagle border, 7", M..380.00
Sauce boat, Picturesque Scenery, d/b, Hall...............175.00
Sauce boat, State House, d/b, Ridgway, Beauties of Am, 7", M.380.00
Sauce tureen, lid/ladle/under tray, Hudson Views, l/b, Clews....450.00
Sauce tureen, lid/tray, dog/rabbit/fox/chicken, rose finial......450.00
Sauce tureen, w/lid, Bramber Church, d/b, Hall's Select Views..265.00
Sauce tureen, w/lid, Gubbins, Hertfordshire, d/b, Wood, 8"....250.00
Sauce tureen, w/under tray, Hindu Village, bl..............500.00
Soup, Albany, d/b, Clews, Cities Series, 9¾"..............250.00
Soup, Baltimore & Ohio, on level, d/b, Wood, 10", M.......550.00
Soup, Biddulph Castle, d/b, Hall's Select Views, 10"..........85.00
Soup, Boston State House, untitled, l/b, 10"..............145.00
Soup, Castle Views, Gates of Sebastion, m/b, Spode, 9¾"......55.00

Plate, Landing of LaFayette, marked Clews, warranted Staffordshire, 1818-1834, 6¾", $145.00.

Soup, Chateau Ermenonville, d/b, Wood, 10¼"..............150.00
Soup, Columbus, men/ships/animal border, lav, 10½".........50.00
Soup, Guy's Cliff, d/b, grapevine border, Wood, 10"..........55.00
Soup, Hannibal, l/b, elephants/mtns, Adams, 10¼"..........60.00
Soup, Hartford, CT, pk, Jackson, 10½"...................75.00
Soup, Harvard College, m-d/b, Stevenson, acorn/oak leaf, 10"..350.00
Soup, LaFayette at Tomb of Washington, d/b, rare, 9¾", M...450.00
Soup, Millenium, m/b, 10½" M..........................65.00
Soup, States, d/b, Clews, 10", M........................275.00
Soup, Table Rock Niagara, d/b, Wood, 10".................325.00
Soup, The Capitol, Washington, sepia, Godwin, 10½"........65.00
Soup, Wistow Hall, Leicestershire, m-d/b, 9"..............70.00
Soup, Wm Penn's Treaty, gr, 9½".......................25.00
Sugar bowl, Cupid Imprisoned, beehive finial/barrel form, 4"...325.00
Sugar bowl, eagle over panel, d/b, M....................370.00
Sugar bowl, LaFayette at Franklin's Tomb, d/b, Wood.......495.00
Sugar bowl, Mt Vernon, seat of...Washington, d/b, 5¾", G.....320.00
Sugar bowl, Wadsworth Tower, d/b, Wood, rectangular........400.00
Sugar bowl, Washington w/Scroll in Hand, d/b, Wood........550.00
Tankard, English Manor House, d/b, ½ pt.................165.00
Teapot, LaFayette at Franklin's Tomb, d/b, Wood, EX.......485.00
Teapot, Mt Vernon, m-d/b, rpr lid/spout, lid flange chip, 7"....400.00
Tray, hdls, Boston From...Dorchester, l/b, Meigh, 11½".......150.00
Vegetable dish, Catskill Mountains, d/b, Wood, 9¾", EX.....400.00
Vegetable dish, Enville Hall, dk/b, A Stevenson, 9¾"........265.00
Vegetable w/lid, Meredith, NH/Ruggles House, l/b, Ridgway...275.00
Vegetable w/lid, States, d/b, Clews....................1,750.00
Warming dish w/tin base & lid, Ruggle's House, bl, 10" W....250.00
Wash basin, Ontario, l/b, Heath.........................75.00

Miscellaneous

Box, money; Derbyshire souvenir, bell shaped, 1870s, 7".......65.00
Box, pin; child & angel w/open book, 3¼", G...............40.00
Box, pin; child in large chair, 4¼"......................50.00
Box, recumbent fox on lid, base w/foliage & landscape, 3½x6".160.00
Box, trinket; angel on clock w/dog, wht bisque, gold trim.......75.00
Bust, gentleman w/long br hair, mc, marbleized base, 7¼"......65.00
Bust, Geo Washington, mc enamel, 8"...................265.00
Castle, turreted, clock face, flowers, coleslaw grass, 8½".......130.00

Cottage ornament, saltglaze with slipware roof, circa 1790, 4¾", $325.00.

Chamber pot w/lid, gr transfer scenic, ca 1830s...............75.00
Compote, children at play transfer, bl/gr, 9¾x9"............65.00
Cottage, bank, br/yel roof, gr grass, 5"........................95.00
Cottage, bank, children in windows, parents ea side, 4½", EX..300.00
Cottage, pastille burner, removable roof, encrustations, 1820...750.00
Cottage, pastille burner, 6"..............................325.00
Cottage, peaked roof, 5"..................................250.00
Cottage, roof lifts, 2 inkwells w/in, baskets/butter churn, 4"...850.00
Cottage, Tudor; wht w/blk beams, 4 sm rnd ft, 1810, 4½"....600.00
Creamer, pk transfer, gazelle.............................40.00
Creamer, pk/copper lustre w/cobalt, Oriental scene, 3¾".....145.00
Cup & saucer, handleless; gaudy wreath decor...............30.00
Cup & saucer, handleless; Lombardy, l/b transfer............28.00
Cup & saucer, handleless; red transfer of eagle on rock, G....175.00
Cup & saucer, handleless; red transfer of NY, mk w/eagle......75.00
Cup & saucer, handleless; shell pattern, purple transfer........40.00
Cup & saucer, handleless; Venetian Temple, red transfer......30.00
Cup plate, child's; snail/ABC book & watering can decor......32.50
Dish, baby chicks emerge from shell, basketweave base, 5x6"...350.00
Egg, allover br transfer of girls playing, 2½x5½"............65.00
Figurine, bearded Bacchic musician, 1850s, 9"..............75.00
Figurine, Bonnie Prince, mc, 1800s, 11½"...................175.00
Figurine, cat on orange cushion, sponge decor, gold ribbon, 7"..85.00
Figurine, cobbler, 1890, 7"................................45.00
Figurine, couple in boat w/lighthouse/cottage, 6¾"..........160.00
Figurine, cupid, sitting, 1850s, 10".......................75.00
Figurine, David Garrick, Richard III, 1850.................125.00
Figurine, dog, br glass eyes, gold chain, 13"...............145.00
Figurine, dog, gr lustre trim, 12".........................175.00
Figurine, dog, poodle, seated w/2 pups, sanded coats, 7"......135.00
Figurine, dog, rust/wht w/blk/gold, wear/flakes, 2¾"..........45.00
Figurine, dog, spaniel, seated, russet/wht coat, 1875, 9½"....125.00
Figurine, dog, spaniels, 1 sits on barrel, 2nd along side, 8".....85.00
Figurine, dog, spaniels, 1800s, 12", pr.....................250.00
Figurine, dog, split legs w/gold chains & lockets, 9", pr......400.00
Figurine, Dog Tray, blk/wht dog w/master, tree trunk, 13".....495.00
Figurine, female dancer, 1850s, 10"........................85.00
Figurine, Garibaldi, hand on sword w/Liberte flag, 13".......95.00
Figurine, girl on lg dog w/purple lustre fur, 5½"............45.00
Figurine, girl w/pk tunic, 1850s, 7".......................45.00
Figurine, goose on basket, w/gosling, EX colors, 7x8x11".....235.00
Figurine, Gordon-Cummings, w/dog/gun/game pouch, 1860, 14"..115.00
Figurine, Highlander, 1850s, 12"..........................100.00

Figurine, Hope, 1800, 7"..................................125.00
Figurine, lady & gent, mc/cobalt, 12"......................145.00
Figurine, man by spring, cobalt, 1850s, 9"..................80.00
Figurine, Milton, ca 1875, 10½"...........................175.00
Figurine, Minerva, early, hollow, 8½".......................325.00
Figurine, Prince & Princess of Wales, w/palominos, 15", pr....995.00
Figurine, Queen Victoria, 1800s, 10½"......................130.00
Figurine, Queen Victoria & Prince Albert, late 1800s, 7½"....130.00
Figurine, ram, standing, 2¼x2½"...........................135.00
Figurine, red squirrel eating nut, ca 1800, 3¼".............550.00
Figurine, sailor & lass, 1850, 8"..........................85.00
Figurine, Scottish couple/bird, 1860s, 11".................175.00
Figurine, Scottish couple/clock, mc/cobalt, 13"..............145.00
Figurine, swan, oval gr base, ca 1800, 3½", EX..............210.00
Figurine, woman & dog, polychrome on soft paste, rpr, 5¾"...100.00
Figurine, Young Widow, memorial...........................65.00
Figurine, youth in courting posture w/tipped hat/bouquet, 7½".135.00
Flask, reform; stoneware, Duke of York, 1830, 8"...........165.00
Flask, spirit; Lord Brougham, 1800, 8"....................140.00
Hen on basketweave base, bisque w/blk/wht/gray, 7½x6½x8"..395.00
Inkwells, recumbent Whippets, 1890, pr....................275.00
Jug, Charlie Chaplin character, Art Deco, 9"...............150.00
Jug, saltglaze w/enamel floral branches/diaper work, 1775, 7"..300.00
Jug, satyr; pearlware, mc enamels/pk lustre decor, 5"........295.00
Mug, child's; children playing, blk transfer/mc enamel, 2¾"....45.00
Mug, Oriental scenery, l/b, 6"..............................80.00
Pitcher, ear of corn, bone china, 1867, 7½"................75.00
Pitcher, gaudy florals, minor wear & crazing, 8"............50.00
Pitcher, purple transfer birds/flowers, gr/yel enamel, 10½"....55.00
Plate, Athena, gray/gr, 10½"...............................40.00
Plate, bl transfer, Archery, 5½"...........................15.00
Plate, Canova, lav transfer, 10½"..........................32.00
Plate, Cologne, br transfer, J&G Alcock, 7¼", 11 for........165.00
Plate, Imari design, bl/yel/orange, 10½"...................65.00
Plate, Persian, bl transfer, Ridgway, 5¼"..................12.00
Plate, Trentham Castle, wall hanging, 1880.................75.00
Plate, Venus, polychrome on ironstone, 9".................38.00
Sauce tureen w/lid, under plate, ladle; Sicillian, br transfer.....175.00
Spill, Burns & His Mary, 1850, 12".........................150.00
Spill, girl w/rabbit, 1860s, 11"...........................100.00
Spill, huntsman w/dog, 1850s, 14".........................140.00
Teapot, bk bl transfer hound & stag, Stone China, worn/chips...85.00
Teapot, jester face, 1890s.................................65.00
Toddy, emb florals, blk transfer of children by stream, 5".....25.00
Toddy, floral emb rim, transfer He That by the Plough, 5¼"....35.00
Tureen w/lid, landscape, lion head hdls, floral border, 12x7"...250.00
Vase, Victorian lady/man, fancy dress, bl/wht, 4", pr.........45.00
Whistle, bird, wht/br/gr, chipped, 1¾".....................35.00
Wine barrel, stoneware, w/English Coat of Arms, 1840, 10½"..125.00

Stanford

Corn line, canister, 6½".....................................14.00
Corn line, cookie jar, 9½"...................................27.00
Corn line, creamer & sugar w/lid.............................12.00
Corn line, shakers, pr......................................10.00
Corn line, teapot, 7".......................................24.00

Stangl

In 1913 the Fulper Pottery was acquired by J. Martin Stangl, who had previously been employed there as superintendent of the technical division.

Under Stangl's direction, the production of dinnerware was initiated. In addition to the art wares already being made, figurines -- most notably the Audubon birds modeled after the *Birds of America* series -- became a large part of their output. These birds have become very popular with collectors in recent years. They are easily identified by the 'Stangl' mark on the base. Stangl pottery was produced until Martin Stangl's death in 1972.

Birds

Allen Hummingbird, #3634, MRF, 3½"	60.00
Audubon Warbler, #3755, MW, 4¼"	90.00
Bird of Paradise, #3408	70.00
Blue-headed Vireo, #3448, MH, 4¼"	50.00
Bluebird, #3276S	50.00
Broadtail Hummingbird, #3627	125.00
Cardinal, #3444, pk, VMF, revised edition, 6½", M	35.00
Cardinal, #3444, sample	80.00
Carrier Pigeon, wht, #3518D	350.00
Cerulean Warbler, #3456, ES, 4¼"	30.00
Chestnut Back Chickadee, #3811	45.00
Chickadees, #3581, mk Rae F, 5½x8½"	80.00
Cliff Swallow, #3852	55.00
Cock Pheasant, #3492, gr/br, IFF, 6¼x11"	120.00
Cockatoo, #3405, MW, pk, 6"	20.00
Cockatoo, #3580, VR, 9"	65.00
Cockatoos, #3405D, MK, revised edition, gr branch, 9½"	55.00
Evening Grosbeak, #3813	95.00
Flying Duck, #3443	250.00
Goldfinch, #3849	95.00
Goldfinches, #3635	165.00
Gray Cardinal, #3596	42.00
Hen, #3446	65.00
Hen Pheasant, #3491, FF, 6¼x11"	130.00
Hummingbirds, #3599D	200.00
Indigo Bunting, #3589, MW, 3¼"	20.00
Kentucky Warbler, #3598, sgn, 3"	30.00
Key West Quail Dove, #3454, LJ, 9", M	85.00
Lovebird, #3400, EBF, 4"	25.00
Lovebirds, #3400D, old base, rare bl crackle glaze	125.00
Nuthatch, #3593, MW, 2½"	45.00
Oriole, #3402, revised edition, VF, 3¼"	30.00
Orioles, #3402D, TVF, revised edition, 5½", M	45.00
Painted Bunting, #3452, sgn, 5"	45.00
Parakeets, #3582, VMF, 7"	110.00
Parrot w/Worm, #3449	125.00
Parula Warbler, #3583, MW, 4¾"	25.00
Penguin, #3274	275.00
Prothonatary Warbler, #3447, MV, 5"	45.00
Red Faced Warbler, #3594, JW, 3"	40.00
Redstarts, #3590D	125.00
Rivoli Hummingbird, #3627	125.00
Rooster, #3445	75.00
Rufous Hummingbird, #3585, MMF, 3"	50.00
Western Bluebird, #3815	125.00
White Crown Pigeons, #3518D	450.00
Wren, #3401	45.00
Yellow Warbler, #3850	60.00

Miscellaneous

Apple Tree, cake stand, 3 tier	20.00
Ash tray, Canada Goose	15.00
Ash tray, flower figural, HP	3.00
Bella Rosa, server, center hdl	15.00
Bittersweet, plate, 8¼"	4.00

Baby plate and cup, #3947, 10" plate, $55.00.

Blueberry, plate, 8"	5.00
Blueberry, saucer	2.00
Bowl, bl, oval, #3094, 6¼"	7.50
Bowl, gr, oval, scalloped, #3227, 9½"	12.00
Camellia, ash tray, 5" plate	12.00
Camellia, cigarette box w/lid	12.00
Candle holder, calla lily, wht/bl leaf, #3428, 6", pr	16.00
Candle warmer, openwork sides, mottled gr, #3412, 4½"	8.00
Carafe w/stopper, ribbed, yel/bl, HP, #1388, 7¾"	15.00
Casserole warmer, terra cotta, #3412	12.50
Child's dish, train decor, 3 part	15.00
Cigarette box, wht w/HP daisies, br w/in, 4x6"	8.00
Colonial, plate, 10¼"	4.50
Colonial, plate, 12½"	7.00
Colonial, syrup pitcher, #1388	6.50
Colonial Rose, plate, 6"	2.00
Dahlia, plate, pierced for hanging, 6"	4.50
Dish, pear shape w/curled leaves at stem end for hdl, #3783	8.00
Dish, 3 scallop shells, #3781, 11½"	10.00
Dogwood, plate clock	55.00
Fruit, cup	6.00
Fruit, saucer	2.00
Fruit & Flowers, plate, 6¼"	2.50
Golden Blossom, plate, 8"	5.00
Golden Harvest, creamer	6.00
Golden Harvest, cup	5.00
Golden Harvest, egg cup	4.00
Golden Harvest, gravy boat	12.00
Golden Harvest, lug soup	5.00
Golden Harvest, pickle dish	12.00
Golden Harvest, plate, 10"	7.00
Golden Harvest, plate, 6"	1.50
Golden Harvest, shakers, pr	10.00
Jug, tilting; high gloss yel, ice lip, swirl relief, #1388	28.00
Magnolia, coffee warmer	17.00
Magnolia, plate, 8"	5.00
Orchard Song, sandwich plate w/center hdl, 10"	8.00
Planter, female head figural, bl hairnet & bodice, #3418, 6½"	18.00
Rustic Garden, plate, 6"	2.00
Star Flower, plate, 10"	5.00
Star Flower, plate, 6"	2.50
Star Flower, saucer	2.00
Sugar w/lid, bluebell & daisy on wht, red body, #3434	8.00
Teapot, #1000, yel	15.00
Terra Rose, bowl, #3606, 10"	8.00
Terra Rose, bowl, irregular leaf hdl, #3784	6.00

Terra Rose, bowl w/lid, bl, 4x7″ 12.00
Terra Rose, cake stand, 4x8¼″ 15.00
Terra Rose, candle warmer, #3412, 4½x4½x3¼″ 12.50
Terra Rose, cigarette box w/ash tray leaf form lid, 3¼x4″ 12.00
Terra Rose, cloverleaf, 3 part, 8″ 8.00
Terra Rose, cornucopia, #2056, 6x8″ 8.00
Terra Rose, cornucopia, #3563, 7x8″ 8.00
Terra Rose, cornucopia, #3612, 8½″ 10.00
Terra Rose, dish, freeform, ruffled, #2356, 5″ 5.00
Terra Rose, dish, heart shape, #3785EW, 1¾x6″ 6.00
Terra Rose, dish, 3 part cloverleaf, 2x8″ .6.00
Terra Rose, dish w/lid, #3676, 3x5½″ 10.00
Terra Rose, vase, #3442, 6x2½x6″ 8.00
Terra Rose, vase, milk can, 7″ 8.00
Terra Rose, vase, pillow; sunflower, #3502, bl lustre, 12x12″ 30.00
Thistle, creamer, wht w/out, br w/in, 2½″ 5.00
Thistle, milk pitcher, 4½″ 12.50
Thistle, plate, 10″ 7.00
Thistle, plate, 8″ 5.00
Thistle, salad bowl, 12″ 35.00
Thistle, salt & peppers, pr 8.00
Thistle, soup, flat 7.00
Thistle, tidbit server, brass center hdl, 10″ dia 14.00
Trivet, octagonal, HP cherries, etc 6.00
Unid Rose, plate, w/cup indent, 8¼″ 4.00
Vase, cornucopia, #3502, tan 10.00
Vase, ftd, shoulder hdls, turq, B116, 5½″ 7.00
Vase, hdls, turq, #3103, 7¼″ 8.00
Vase, head of lovely lady, wht 125.00
Vase, leaf shape, glossy bl/terra cotta, #3442, 6¼″ 9.00
Vase, overlapping leaves, S204945, 11″ .12.00
Vase, pillow; sunflower, turq w/gold, gold mk, #5134, 7½″ 20.00
Vase, reeded, scalloped, ftd, side hdl, bl to yel, #3170, 7″ 13.00
Vase, scroll leaf, satin wht, 9x4½″ 20.00
Vase, shoulder hdl, gr w/in, orange/br/gold w/out, #2019, 4x3″ . .12.00
Vase, 3 hdls, gr gloss, thrown, paper label 19.00
Wall pocket, nautilus shell, #3238, 8x5½″ 12.00
Water set, horizontal ribs, bl, S1902, 2 qt pitcher+4 tumblers . . .30.00
Wild Rose, divided vegetable, 10½x7″ 15.00
Wild Rose, plate, 10″ 7.00

Statuary

Alabaster, semi-nude seated on wall w/lute, 33″ 660.00
Marble, bust, mother & child, French, sgn, w/base: 18″ 850.00

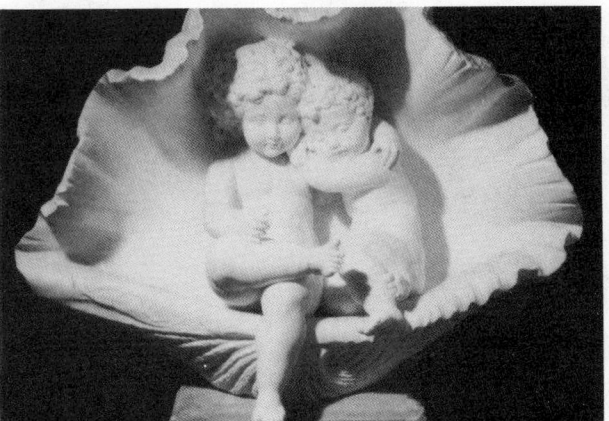

Carved marble group of two putti in a shell, Italian, late 19th century, 36″ long, $4,675.00.

Marble, bust of a senator, Italian, inscribed Seneca, 24″ 700.00
Marble, L'Enfant a L'oiseau Derobe, after Jean-Baptise Pigalle . .935.00
Marble, nude clutching drape to waist, J Vavra, 1900, 24″ 385.00
Marble, seated child on tree stump, in glass dome, 13″ 450.00
Stone, Cupid playing lute, Italian, 1900, 28½″ 990.00

Steins

Steins have been made from pottery, pewter, glass, stoneware, and porcelain, from very small up to the four liter size. They are decorated by etching, in-mold relief, decals -- and occasionally they are even hand painted. Some porcelain steins have lithophane bases. Collectors often specialize in a particular type -- faience, regimental, or figural -- while others limit themselves to the products of only one manufacturer.

See also Mettlach

Key:
tl------thumb lift   L------liter

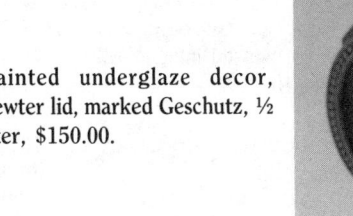

Painted underglaze decor, pewter lid, marked Geschutz, ½ liter, $150.00.

Character, ape head, impressed anchor mk, bisque, ½L, M . . .1,488.00
Character, barrel w/monkey on lid, fish hdl, Musterschutz 902.00
Character, bowling ball, ram hdl, man on pig lid, 3 ftd, ½L 251.00
Character, cat w/hangover, wrapped head, Musterschutz, ½L . . .385.00
Character, drunken monkey, Musterschutz, ½L 432.00
Character, face, Hops lady, 'Prosit', pottery/pewter lid, ½L 244.00
Character, Gaudeamus skull, pottery, ½L, 5½″ 265.00
Character, man's face, bug on head, pottery, ½L 325.00
Character, monk in brown w/litho of Alpine couple, porcelain . .222.00
Character, Munich Maid w/3 steins/radishes, HB on front, 1L . . .259.00
Character, nun, lithophane base, porcelain, ½L, 6¾″ 345.00
Character, nun in brown w/litho of 2 men & maiden at table 222.00
Character, Nuremberg Tower w/Hans Sach & city, ½L, VG 168.00
Character, owl, saltglaze stoneware, ½L 250.00
Character, pig w/pipe, porcelain, Musterschutz, rpr hdl, ½L 205.00
Character, radish, mk Musterschutz Bismark, ½L, 6¾″ 395.00
Character, ram head, cream color, Musterschutz, ½L, M 848.00
Character, sad radish, radish/sausage tl, Musterschutz, ½L 451.00
Character, skull, bisque, .4L 288.00
Character, standing alligator, repaired jaw, Musterschutz, ½L . . .489.00
Character, student frog stands on book, music box, ½L, M . . .1,253.00
Character, Turkish man, ½ figure, Musterschutz, ½L, M 950.00

Copper over pottery, relief scene: monks drinking, 1L 185.00
Faience, tin glaze, dog w/bone, ceramic lid, French, 1900, ½L . 280.00
German, lithophane, tavern scene 175.00
Glass, amber w/man & horse enameling, pewter lid, 15″ 656.00
Glass, blown, enamel verse & seal, pewter lid, .3L, M 86.00
Glass, blown, fluted, enamel Germania monument, prism lid, ¼L . 87.00
Glass, blown, hobnail, ram w/beaker tl, relief scenes lid, .3L . . . 170.00
Glass, blown, pink-red w/clear hdl, ribbed, pewter rim, ½L 335.00
Glass, blown w/applied mc prunts, glass inlay lid/dwarf tl, 12″ . . 459.00
Glass, blown/etched flower basket, bubble base, 1820s, ½L, M . . 298.00
Glass, clear w/green bull's eyes, name/1906, enamel cat, 4½″ . . . 245.00
Glass, pressed, enamel birds/flowers/heart, ornate lid, ½L 93.00
Lithophane, blue windmill scenes, inlay windmill lid, ½L 303.00
Lithophane, Edelweiss floral design, German saying, ½L 125.00
Lithophane, girl watches boat on lake, verse, ½L 89.00
Lithophane, Lindau shore town scenes, ½L 89.00
Lithophane, men at table w/serving girl, ornate pewter lid, 1L . . 178.00
Lithophane, Munich Maid w/master stein, heavy lid, 1L 165.00
Lithophane, polychrome naval scene, sailor finial, 11″ 100.00
Pewter, German finial fights Frenchman on hdl, 1861, ½L 875.00
Pewter, hand hammered, Nouveau woman & design, ½L, M . . . 135.00
Pewter, Nurnberg Tower, relief side scenes, Gooseman tl, ½L . 432.00
Pewter, 3 lg ball feet/matching tl, Sweden, 1913, 1L 216.00
Porcelain, rust/gr/bl/wht/gold, brass lid/tl, Munich, 8″ 495.00
Pottery, after bronze statue/mermaid hdl/nude man finial, 10″ . . 297.00
Pottery, children center panel, mc, HP, heavy pewter, ½L 85.00
Pottery, etched Alpine pair/country scene, cavalier inlay, 1L . . . 150.00
Pottery, etched couple/stone wall, Gerz, inlay verse lid, ½L 131.00
Pottery, etched dancing couples, Alpine men lid inlay, ¼L 118.00
Pottery, hand holding 4 suits of cards, HP, ¼L 77.00
Pottery, Munich Maid, HP, 2L, 15″, M 178.00
Pottery, relief: ancient warrior drinks by barrel, German, 8″ 70.00
Pottery, relief: German verse & flowers, ½L 66.00
Pottery, relief: maid/castle/dragon, conical turret inlay lid 180.00
Pottery, relief: Rheinstein Castle, 1L 197.00
Pottery, relief: soldiers drinking, EX detail, ½L 185.00
Pottery, relief: tavern scene, pewter top, German, 13″ 80.00
Pottery, relief: 7 Vikings at feast, ½L 147.00
Pottery, transfer Brewery Occupation Scenes, mc, verse, 1L . . . 189.00
Pottery, transfer coach/town scene, German verse, 1L 71.00
Regimental, cannon finial, military scenes, top unscrews, EX . . . 375.00
Regimental, glass/pewter Shako lid, commemorative of 1890 . . . 275.00
Regimental, prism lid, lion shield tl, Ingolstadt 1910-12 . . . . . . 299.00
Regimental, soldiers shake hands finial, dove tl, ULM 1903-05 . . 348.00
Regimental, tree trunk hdl/body, lion tl, man/lion finial 337.00
Regimental, 120 Prussian Inft, eagle tl, .4L 216.00
Saltglaze, enameled girl w/bouquet, Merkelbach/Wick, 1L 138.00
Saltglaze, enameled man carries turkey dinner, sgn FQ, 1L 145.00
Saltglaze, mosaic relief, German verse, 3L, M 86.00
Saltglaze, relief Gambrinus on barrel, porcelain inlay lid, 1L . . . 121.00
Saltglaze, transfer of Munich child, twin towers tl, ¼L 71.00
Saltglaze, transfer soldier silhouette sgn Mavder, ½L 101.00
Silver, elaborate war scenes, etc; touchmks, mid-1800s, 9″ . . . 2,431.00
Silverplate, ped ft, lion finial, ornate, inscribed/1886, 11″ 240.00
Silverplate, relief decor, eagle tl, hops bud finial, ¼L, M 504.00
Stoneware, Nouveau style, lead glaze, Rosskopf/Gerz, #832, 1L . 65.00
Stoneware, relief drunken marching band, EX pewter lid/tl, 1L . 287.00
Stoneware, w/cobalt, applied relief, dtd 1735, Westerwald, ½L . . 677.00
Wood, engraved cavalier & verse, dtd 1907, rpr hdl, 22″ 125.00

Steuben

The Steuben Glass Works of Corning, New York, was founded in 1903 by Frederick Carder and Thomas Hawkes. They made art glass of high quality similar to some of Tiffany's work. One of their earliest types of art glass was aurene, a lustrous metallic gold or blue. They also made verre de soie, rosaline, and silverene. In 1918, Steuben became a branch of Corning Glass Works.

See also Aurene; Verre de Soie

Ash tray, dk bl crystal, 3 open corners, applied hdl, #7026 . . . . 135.00
Ash tray, rosaline w/alabaster ring 75.00
Bowl, centerpiece; bristol yel, ftd, #3080, fleur-de-lis sgn 500.00
Bowl, centerpiece; rolled rim, crystal/bubbles/gr threading 85.00
Bowl, centerpiece; yel swirl stem, aquamarine, 5½x10″ 110.00
Bowl, dbl etch, Chinese symbols, flowers, bl overlay, 10″ dia . . . 660.00
Bowl, gold top, gr base, ftd, 4x6″ dia 135.00
Bowl, gr jade, diagonal ribbed, 6 sides, alabaster ped, #6241 . . . 165.00
Bowl, ivorene, grotesque, sgn, 6x6x12″ 330.00
Bowl, lotus; gr crystal, sgn F Carder, 2¾x5″ 140.00
Bowl, rosaline, #2851, 10″ dia 125.00
Bowl, rosaline, stem ft, sgn F Carder, 6x6″ 325.00
Bowl, shaded clear to ruby, Grotesque, 4x4″ 110.00
Bowl, silver mica & random bubbles, oval, sgn, 6x4″ 250.00
Bowl, verre de soie, 8″ 60.00
Bowl, w/under plate; gold ruby w/clear ped ft, swirled 65.00
Bud vase, blk glass ring above base, F Carder, 7″ 200.00
Cake tray, ped ft, celeste bl, folded rim, 10″ dia 75.00
Canape/sandwich server, crystal, 13″ 395.00
Candlestick, aurene on calcite, mushroom shape, pr 500.00
Candlestick, dk gr crystal, twist stem, 12″ 75.00
Candlestick, gold/purple, 7″, pr 280.00
Candlestick, jadite, alabaster knobs in stem, 10″, pr 290.00
Candlestick, topaz, swirl rib base & cup, #6270, 10″, pr 190.00
Candlestick, topaz domed ft/drip pan, bl rib ball stem, 12x7½″ . 165.00
Candlestick, verre de soie, dbl ball center, 10″, pr 250.00
Charger, ruby red, stenciled sgn in fleur-de-lis, 17½″ 550.00
Cologne, swirled, bristol yel, threaded stopper, 5″ 115.00
Compote, amethyst, ball stem, 10x6″ 135.00
Compote, celeste bl, twist stem 75.00
Compote, cobalt cut to clear, #7501 . . . . 375.00
Compote, dk amethyst, ribbed, clear stem, #3234, 3x7″ 80.00
Compote, gold aurene on calcite, unsgn, 8¼″ 225.00
Compote, gr crystal, sgn, 6x6½″ 70.00
Compote, gr w/bubbles/threading, 8″ 95.00
Compote, Oriental poppy, twist gr stem, 7″ 650.00
Compote, selenium ruby, twist stem, 7x6″ 195.00
Compote, topaz w/cobalt rim trimming & base prunts, 5½″ 120.00
Compote, w/lid, lt gr jade, alabaster stem & ft, 5¾x4½″ 245.00
Compote, yel w/bl rim & stem accent, 6½″ 250.00

Figure of a swan, unsigned, circa 1935, 8½″ long, $2,860.00.

Darner, spatter glass, blown, early, 7".....................150.00
Dresser set, clear w/gr threading & faceted stoppers, 3 pc......250.00
Ewer, helmet shape, clear, sgn, 9".....................125.00
Figurine, elephant, trunk raised, sgn, 5½x7".............425.00
Figurine, horse heads, #779, pr.......................300.00
Figurine, Koala bear, sgn, Lloyd Atkins, 5¾".............250.00
Figurine, songbird, sgn.............................225.00
Finger bowl w/under plate, jade/alabaster................60.00
Flower block, w/lady Buddha insert, alabaster.............275.00
Goblet, bristol yel crystal, #6476, 6"....................55.00
Goblet, celeste bl.................................150.00
Goblet, crystal w/pk reeding, swirl optic stem, #6278, 8½".....150.00
Goblet, jade, spindle stem, ½ globe/trumpet form bowl, 7½"...165.00
Goblet, jade, twisted alabaster stem, M.................125.00
Goblet, teardrop stem, rnd ped base, sgn, set of 12.........400.00
Goblet, wine; clear, teardrop stem, rnd ped base, set of 12.....400.00
Jar, acid cut-back rosaline to alabaster, symbols/florals, 6"....1,000.00
Lemonade set, gr jade w/blk hdls, pitcher/4 mugs..........660.00
Lemonade set, gr swirl, pitcher w/lid #6435, goblets w/no hdls..250.00
Lemonade set, Mat-Su-Noke, clear w/gr applied, pitcher/6 mugs.575.00
Liqueur glasses, #8055, set of 6......................400.00
Mug, topaz w/cerise bl hdl, unsgn, miniature..............50.00
Perfume, melon rib, gr jade, long alabaster dipper, 4¾".......180.00
Perfume, verre de soie, #1988, 8".....................135.00
Perfume, verre de soie, melon rib, bl melon rib stopper, 4½"...110.00
Pitcher, rosaline, applied alabaster hdl, 6x7¾"............400.00
Plate, celeste bl, sgn, 8½", set of 10..................395.00
Plate, jade, sgn, 8¾"...............................45.00
Plate, rosaline, sgn, 8¼"............................75.00
Salt, ped base, topaz crystal, sgn......................85.00
Shade, aurene w/calcite interior, ribbed................125.00
Shade, calcite w/gold lining..........................75.00
Shade, gr feather around base, gold inner lining & trim.......165.00
Sherbet, bl jade/alabaster...........................285.00
Sherbet, calcite, ribbed, platinum lining, 4x4"............115.00
Sherbet, Oriental poppy, 4½".........................250.00
Sherbet, rosaline, wht ft & stem......................120.00
Sherbet w/under plate, amethyst, sgn F Carder............130.00
Sherbet w/under plate, aquamarine....................60.00
Sherbet w/under plate, celeste bl, threaded...............65.00
Sherbet w/under plate, gold aurene on calcite.............175.00
Sherbet w/under plate, yel stem & rim, sgn...............78.00
Sugar & creamer, clear w/applied leaves, made for Pyrex......65.00
Vase, acid cut-bk, floral bouquets, 9"..................715.00
Vase, acid cut-bk geese/trees, lav/rose w/purple, w/hdls, 13"....275.00
Vase, acid etch acanthus/lozenges/commas, unsgn, 10"......2,420.00
Vase, amber, bulbous/ped ft, sgn F Carder, 11x8½".........275.00
Vase, aurene, millefiori decor, sgn, #661, 3"............1,300.00
Vase, bl threaded top, minor losses, 9¾"................150.00
Vase, blk jade, platinum hi-lites, #938, 5"................250.00
Vase, chrysanthemum acid cut, jade gr, rectangular, 9".......330.00
Vase, Cintra, stripe decor in yel/rose, blk zigzags, 10".....1,200.00
Vase, Cintra acid cut-bk, gr w/sculptured decor, sgn, 15"....2,000.00
Vase, clear, 3 prong, sgn Steuben, 10½"................355.00
Vase, clear w/bubbles, bl reeding around top, 3 tier, 8".......110.00
Vase, crystal, flared cylinder, leaf decor base, 14".........320.00
Vase, crystal/ivory/jet floriform w/ped base, 6"...........415.00
Vase, Dia Quilt, bl threading, 5¾"......................95.00
Vase, dk bl jade, sgn F Carder, inverted top hat shape, 8"...1,200.00
Vase, etched piper, Henri Matisse, 1940, 14¾", EX........3,200.00
Vase, fan shape, ball stem w/gold mica, ribbed, 10x6".......95.00
Vase, fan shape, Fr bl, ball stem, #6287, 8½"..............75.00
Vase, fan shape, gr rib top, eng w/florals, topaz stem/ft, 11"...175.00
Vase, fan shape, ivorene, 6".........................225.00

Vase, fan shape, ribbed crystal w/pk applied threads, 8½".....115.00
Vase, fan shape, vertically ribbed, gr, fleur-de-lis mk, 8¼x7"...120.00
Vase, flared cylinder, leaf decor base, sgn, 14"...........320.00
Vase, gold ruby, optic ribbed, scalloped, sgn, 8x4".........165.00
Vase, gr jade, amphora form, 9¾".....................415.00
Vase, gr jade, amphora form w/applied milky hdls, 10½".....660.00
Vase, gr jade, applied alabaster ft & rings, 6x3"...........275.00
Vase, gr jade & alabaster, ribbed, #7316, 9x5"............235.00
Vase, Grotesque, ruby, fleur-de-lis mk, 7"...............325.00
Vase, Grotesque, shaded clear to pomona gr, 4½x3".........110.00
Vase, irid bl, ribbed, curled lip, short waisted ft, 5"........275.00
Vase, ivorene, sgn, #7564, 6x6¼"....................325.00
Vase, ivorene, sgn, 8x6"............................385.00
Vase, ivorene, trumpet w/2 side lilies, sgn, 12".........1,100.00
Vase, opal w/amber irid hearts & vines, unsgn, 6".........605.00
Vase, ovoid, amethyst w/bubbles, pulled lily pads, 6½".......85.00
Vase, pomona gr, #6030, 7".........................125.00
Vase, topaz, shadow ribbed, #7411, unsgn, 4½"...........65.00
Vase, topaz diagonal ribs, wafer above ped ft, #3143, 8".....115.00
Vase, verre de soie, bulbous, aquamarine, flared rim, 6¾"....145.00
Wine, bl w/bubbles, sgn.............................65.00
Wine, clear w/gr threading, 6x3½", set of 6.............235.00
Wine, gold ruby, swirl top, clear twist stem, 6"............55.00
Wine, gr w/bubbles/threading, 7½".....................55.00
Wine, jade, #7169..................................75.00
Wine, lt bl jade, alabaster stem & ft, 6¼"...............200.00
Wine, rosaline....................................225.00

Stevengraph

A Stevengraph is a small picture made of woven silk, resembling an elaborate ribbon, created by Thomas Stevens in England in the latter half of the 1800s. They were matted and framed by Stevens, usually with his name appearing on the matt, or more commonly the trade announcement on the back of the matt. He also produced silk bookmarks, all of which have 'Stevens' woven in silk on one of the mitered corners.

Bookmark, A Blessing.............................42.00
Bookmark, Abraham Lincoln, eagle/shield/assassination date, 9".55.00
Bookmark, Centennial of USA, The Father of Our Country.....95.00
Bookmark, Discovery of Am & World's Columbian Expo......55.00
Bookmark, Forget-Me-Not, w/palm....................60.00
Bookmark, Home Sweet Home........................75.00
Bookmark, Hope, the Anchor of the Soul................35.00
Bookmark, Marriage of Prince & Princess of Wales, 1863.....125.00
Bookmark, May Your Birthday Be Happy................65.00
Bookmark, old arm chair...........................50.00
Bookmark, Red Riding Hood.........................85.00
Bookmark, Seymour & Blair, w/portraits, 1868, 6½".......150.00
Bookmark, To Mother, EX..........................55.00
Bookmark, Unchanging Love.........................42.00
Bookmark, Wish You Merry Christmas, Happy New Year......65.00
Hunt scene, mtd on fancy paper box...................95.00
Queen Victoria & her Premiers, orig matt/label, old fr, 15x12".165.00
Right Honorable WE Gladstone, MP, in orig matt, no fr......225.00
Robert Burns, orig matt, titles on bk, in fr...............365.00
The Meet...165.00
The Present Time, orig matt, titles on bk, 2 way fr..........425.00

Stevens and Williams

Stevens and Williams glass was produced at the Brierly Hill Glassworks in Stourbridge, England, for nearly a century, beginning in the 1830s. They were credited with being among the first to develop a method of manufacturing a more affordable type of cameo glass. Other lines were also made -- silver deposit, alexandrite, and engraved rock crystal to name but a few.

Basket, peppermint swirl, clear hdl & ruffle, 5½x4"..........145.00
Basket, peppermint swirl, clear thorn hdl, 7x6"..............195.00
Bowl, gr w/clear fish & shells, 4x7"........................135.00
Bowl, sea shells, coral, sea grasses in cameo, red/wht, 3½"...1,100.00
Bowl, threaded, clear berry pontil, dia motif, ft/ruffle, 5½"......85.00
Cologne, red/gr swirl w/swirled sterling cap, ball shape, 6".....650.00
Ewer, Dia Quilt clear cased w/opal to apricot, ruffled, 6½".....235.00
Finger bowl w/under plate, rosaline, sgn, 2½x5¼", set of 3....275.00
Perfume, yel-gr w/wht loopings, silver cap/collar/chain, 4"......150.00
Rose bowl, box pleated top, bl opal swirl, 3½x4½"............195.00
Rose bowl, wht w/applied flowers, leaves & vines, 6½x6"......145.00
Vase, applied plums, 4"...................................150.00
Vase, aqua, applied amber fluted rim/legs, bulbous, 13½"......165.00
Vase, Arboresque, cranberry frost/wht crackle, 3-D leaves, 6"...110.00
Vase, cameo, peachblow/wht, passion flower/butterfly, 6".....1,100.00
Vase, clear w/pk vertical bands, crimped rim, applied ft, 7"....150.00
Vase, MOP, orange & gold, aqua w/in, bulbous, 5"..........490.00
Vase, MOP, ribbon swirl, lav/rose, slim neck/sphere, 7½"......750.00
Vase, peachblow w/wht case, applied florals/etc, ruffled, 8".....285.00
Vase, vaseline opal w/applied flower/stem/leaf, 9"............195.00
Vase, wht w/amber hdl/branch/plum, pk leaf & sq top, 8x3½"..160.00
Vase, wht w/applied amber ruffled top & flowers, 7½x3½".....165.00
Vase, wht w/applied cherries, amber rim ruffle, 4¾x3".......145.00
Vase, wht w/bl case, applied pk/amber nut/leaves, ruffled, 10"..225.00

Basket, applied florals, amber foot and handle, 12½", $950.00.

Stiegel

Baron Henry Stiegel produced glassware in Pennsylvania as early as 1760, very similar to glass being made concurrently in Germany and England. Without substantiating evidence, it is impossible to positively attribute a specific article to his manufacture. Although he made other types of glass, today the term Stiegel generally refers to any very early enamel decorated glassware -- however, it is generally conceded that most glass of this type is of European origin.

Bottle, amethyst w/mc bird & flowers, pewter top.............45.00
Bottle, ½ post, applied top, enameled tools/boot/1787, 5½"...165.00

Jar with lid, floral decor, 10", $375.00.

Creamer, cobalt, 16 vertical ribs, applied ft/hdl, 4⅛".........420.00
Flask, deep amethyst, swirl, 7¼"...........................700.00
Flask, expanded dia, clear, 4½", EX.........................50.00
Flip, clear w/floral engraving, 7⅛x6".......................320.00
Flip, enamel flowers, Stiegel type, 4½"......................75.00
Flip, 20 panels, engraved leaf/tendril border, 4¾".............175.00
Salt, cobalt, 11 diamond mold markings indistinct............235.00
Scent bottle, cobalt w/24 swirled ribs, 2¼".................100.00
Wine, ribbed ft, peacock gr, 3"............................175.00

Stocks and Bonds

Scripophily (scrip-awfully) -- the collecting of 'worthless' old stocks and bonds -- gained recognition as a serious collectible around the mid-1970s. Today, there are an estimated 5,000 collectors in the United States and 15,000 world-wide. Collectors who come from numerous business fields mainly enjoy the hobby aspect, though there are those who consider scripophily an investment.

Some collectors like the historical significance that certain certificates have. Others prefer the beauty of older stocks and bonds that were printed in beautiful colors with fancy art work and ornate engravings. Even autograph collectors are found in this field, on the lookout for signed certificates.

Many factors help determine the collector value: autograph value, age of the certificate, the industry represented, whether it is issued or not, its attractiveness, condition, and collector demand.

Certificates from the mining, energy, and railroad industries are the most popular with collectors. Other industries or special collecting fields include banking, automobiles, aircraft, and territorials.

Adventure Consolidated Copper, vignette w/Mich seal, 1899.....12.00
American Smokeless Coal Co, bond, issued 1901, uncancelled....6.00
Baltimore & Ohio, Imlay Coach vignette, certificate, 1900.......20.00
Baltimore & Ohio SW, issued certificate/preferred shares, 1890..25.00
Baltimore & Yorktown Turnpike, issued certificate, 1880s, Hoen.80.00
Baltimore Consolidated RR, unissued certificate, ca 1890.......15.00
Bank of America, eagle/ships vignette, 1930.................16.00
Bergen Neck Rwy, Jersey City; vignette w/steam train, 1880s....22.00
Cambrian Oil Co, issued certificate, gushers/eagle, 1920, lg.....23.00

Charleston City RR, issued certificate, trolley, 1890s 45.00
Chicago & Alton RR, $1000 bond/coupons, train, 1899, ABNCO . 50.00
Choctaw, OK & Gulf RR; Indians & train, 3 sheets coupons 32.00
City of Jersey City, NJ; $1000 gold school bond, 1917 . . . . 12.50
City of Providence, RI; $10,000 bond, pink w/4 scenes, 1868 . . . . 38.00
Colt Patent Firearms, issued certificate, rampant horse, 1940s . . . 15.00
Comstock Tunnel Co, issued $1000 bond/2 pgs coupons, 1889 . . 65.00
Deming Sierra Madre & Pacific RR, issued $1000 bond, 1889 . . 125.00
Durant Motors Inc, issued certificate, 2 allegoricals, 1925 . . . . . . 85.00
Ford Motor Co, stock, early auto, 1977 . . . . 5.00
Frankford & Southwark, Phila; passenger rwy, vignettes, 1889 . . . 25.00
Germania Fire Insurance Co, issued certificate, goddess, 1880 . . . 10.00
Germantown Passenger Rwy, Phila; 3 vignettes, 1929 . . . . 28.00
Great Northern RR, $1000 bond w/coupons, train scene, 1955 . . 15.00
Hudson Motor Car Co, issued certificate, 3 vignettes, 1950s 20.00
Int'l Grand Trunk RR Co, NM Terr; unissued certificate, 1880s . . 80.00
Little Rock Oil & Gas, oil field vignette, 1917 . . . . 12.00
Omega Mining Co, Territory of AZ; issued certificate, 1906 . . . . . 10.00
Pabst Brewing Co, issued certificate, sgn by Pabst, 1905 . . . . 65.00
Pacific RR, $1000 gold bond/revenue stamp/coupons, CA, 1865 . 495.00
Phila & Lancaster Turnpike, sgn Bingham, Pres, 1795 . . . . 400.00
Puget Sound Commercial Co, unissued certificate/stub, 1877 . . . . 95.00
Realty Syndicate, bond, California, 1898 . . . . 9.00
Seaboard Airline RR, issued certificate, orange, 1940s 12.00
Utica & Mohawk RR, unissued certificate, horse trolley, 1880s . . . 20.00
Waltham Watch Co, certificate, eagle vignette, 1920s-40s 10.00
William Whitman Co, orange vignette w/2 ladies, 1922 . . . . 5.00
Willys Motor Corp, certificate of deposit for 5 shares, 1921 . . . . . . 7.00

Stoneware

There are three broad periods of time that collectors of American pottery can look to in evaluating and dating the stoneware and earthenware in their collections.

Among the first permanent settlers in America were English and German potters who found a great demand for their individually turned wares. The early pottery was produced from red and yellow clays scraped from the ground at surface levels. The earthenware made in these potteries was fragile and coated with lead glazes that periodically created health problems for the people who ate or drank from it.

There was little stoneware available for sale until the early 1800s because the clays used in its production were not readily available in many areas and transportation was prohibitively expensive. The opening of the Erie Canal and improved roads brought about a dramatic increase in the accessibility of stoneware clay, and many new potteries began to open in New York and New England.

Collectors have difficulty today locating earthenware and stoneware jugs produced prior to 1840, because few have survived intact. These ovoid or pear shaped jugs were designed to be used on a daily basis. When cracked or severely chipped, they were quickly discarded.

The value of hand crafted pottery is often determined by the cobalt decoration it carries. Pieces with elaborate scenes (a chicken pecking corn, a bluebird on a branch, a stag standing near a pine tree, a sailing ship, or people) may easily bring $600-$3,000 at auction.

After the Civil War, there was a need and a national demand for stoneware jugs, crocks, canning jars, churns, spittoons, and a wide variety of other pottery items. The competition among the many potteries reached the point where only the largest could survive. To cut costs, most potteries did away with all but the simplest kinds of decoration on their wares. Time-consuming brush-painted birds or flowers quickly gave way to more simply executed swirls or numbers and stenciled designs. The coming of home refrigeration and Prohibition in 1919 effectively destroyed the American stoneware industry.

Investment possibilities:

Early nineteenth century stoneware with elaborate decorations and a potter's mark is expensive and will continue to rise in price, though not as rapidly as in the past few years.

Late nineteenth century hand thrown stoneware with simple cobalt swirls or numbers is still reasonably priced and a good investment.

Mass produced stoneware (ca. 1890-1920) is available in large quantities, inexpensive, and will slowly increase in price over the decade of the 1980s.

At this point, reproductions or 'fakes' are not a major concern. Much of the reproduction stoneware is dated on the bottom of the piece. The Beaumont Pottery of York, Maine, which produced the 'finest reproduction stoneware of the twentieth century', scratched the date into each piece.

In the following listing, 'c/s' means 'cobalt on saltglaze'; all decoration described before this abbreviation is in cobalt.

See also Bennington

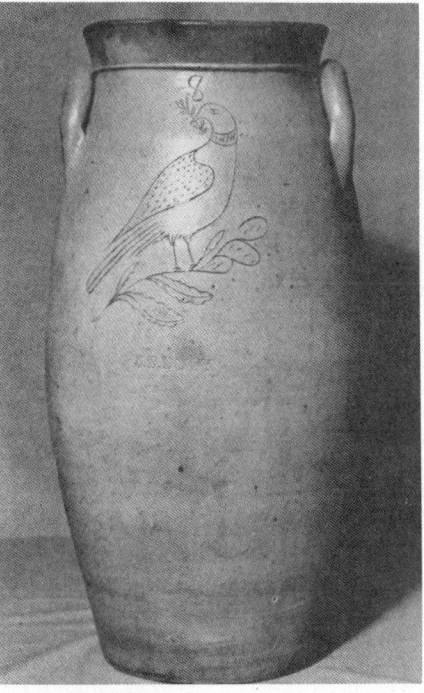

Churn, incised bird on branch, impressed label 'J.D. Doty', hairlines in base, rim chips; wood dasher and turned lid, 22", $1,225.00.

Batter jug, flower on front & spout, c/s, 1 gal, M 275.00
Batter jug, spout/hdls outlined, c/s, 1 gal, M 220.00
Bed pan, squiggle around ring & spout, c/s, M 225.00
Beehive, unglazed, 12½" 80.00
Bottle, imp M Streng, paneled, base chips 20.00
Cake crock, bird on twig, c/s, 3 gal, EX 225.00
Cake crock, flower, stylized; McKean & Boyle adv, 2 gal, M 200.00
Cake crock, leaf, c/s, Penn Yan, 2 gal, sm side hairline 150.00
Cake crock, leaf (revolving), c/s, ½ gal, M 375.00
Cake crock, leaf (revolving), squiggles under hdls, c/s, 1 gal 375.00
Cake crock, squiggle (revolving), c/s, ½ gal, M 225.00
Canteen, emb sunflower decor, pat Aug 11, 1891, ½ gal, M 100.00
Chicken fountain, olive br glaze, emb label & pr of doves, 10" . . 35.00
Churn, bird on branch, #3, c/s, minor chips, hairline, 15½" . . . 375.00
Churn, birds, 2 crossed; c/s, Ottman Bros & Co, 3 gal, EX 700.00
Churn, birds in flight w/in heart, c/s, N White & Co, 5 gal, G . . 575.00
Churn, fish w/polka dots, #3, c/s, ovoid, wood dasher, 15" 600.00
Churn, flourish in quillwork/6, c/s, lid, no dasher, 17" 65.00
Churn, flower, stylized; c/s, NY Stoneware, 2 gal, M 250.00
Churn, flowers in squiggle 'basket', c/s, 6 gal, 19" 250.00
Churn, gooney bird, covers front, c/s, Cortland, 5 gal, G 1,600.00
Churn, heart w/1887, dots, hdls, c/s, EW Farrington, 8 gal, VG . 500.00

Churn, incised bird/twig, c/s, wood lid, imp JD Doty, 22"....1,225.00
Churn, lion w/heavy mane, lg tree, c/s, J Burger, 8 gal, VG...4,500.00
Churn, tree, fancy; c/s, T Harrington, 4 gal, hairline........1,200.00
Colander, incised LM Wentz, Albany slip w/saltglaze, 5x10".....75.00
Container, bell tile shape, imp Compliments of Nat'l SP Co, 2"..15.00
Cooler, bands top & center, spout, c/s, barrel shape, EX.....275.00
Cooler, flower, c/s, dbl hdl, ovoid, 3 gal, EX..............500.00
Cooler, flower w/leaf (revolving), c/s, 5 gal, line/chips.........525.00
Cooler, flowers/Cold Water/1850, verso flower/bird, c/s, EX....675.00
Cooler, impression from butter print ea side, no lid, rpr, 14"..900.00
Cooler, Masonic decorations applied, M Tyler, 17½".......3,300.00
Figurine, poodle, Albany slip, molded, 9"...............155.00
Figurine, seated cat, gray w/amber, Albany interior, rpr, 14"..1,050.00
Flowerpot, attached base, flowers, triple, front/bk, c/s, G......125.00
Flowerpot, leaf (revolving), c/s, minor rim chip............175.00
Flowerpot, New Geneva, gray w/brushed br florals, 5½"......110.00
Flowerpot, red clay/Albany slip, tooled, 2 vases ea side, 8".....450.00
Foot warmer, diamonds front & sides, c/s, hdl glued.........250.00
Hot water bottle, stenciled John M Deane, c/s, 9½"..........65.00
Inkwell, imp Vitreous Bottles, Boss Bros, 2¼"..............135.00
Jar, #1 enclosed w/leaf, c/s, Lyons, 1 gal, EX..............225.00
Jar, #2 w/elaborate swirl, c/s, T Harrington Lyons, 2 gal, M...300.00
Jar, applied tulip, 2 toned br, 5 gal, EX..................50.00
Jar, bands top/bottom, swags in center, c/s, 1 gal, hairline.....100.00
Jar, bird, lg/dotted, on twig; c/s, OL & AK Ballard, 5 gal.....425.00
Jar, bird on branch w/polka dots, c/s, Bangor Stoneware, 11"..250.00
Jar, bird on fancy twig, c/s, Haxstun, Ottman & Co, 5 gal.....275.00
Jar, bird on fancy twig, c/s, 4 gal, M..................225.00
Jar, bird on leafy branch, fancy; c/s, Haxstun & Co, 2 gal.....425.00
Jar, bird on stump, c/s, FT Wright & Son, 3 gal, M.........400.00
Jar, bird on stump, c/s, 5 gal, EX......................300.00
Jar, bird on twig, c/s, 4 gal, EX......................275.00
Jar, bird w/fantail, c/s, Whites Utica, 2 gal, M............200.00
Jar, bird w/paddle tail, c/s, NA White & Son, 4 gal, crack.....450.00
Jar, birds on branches, crossed; c/s, Troy, NY, 4 gal, G.....450.00
Jar, birds w/flowers, c/s, Whites Utica, ovoid, 6 gal, EX.......550.00
Jar, brushed decor at shoulder, c/s, ovoid, 6¼"............160.00
Jar, canning; AP Donaghho, c/s, 8¼".....................45.00
Jar, canning; apple, c/s, 9"..........................250.00
Jar, canning; flower, c/s, ovoid/narrow neck, 9"............185.00
Jar, canning; foliage/stripes, c/s, 9½"..................85.00
Jar, canning; imp Lewis, base chip, 8"..................40.00
Jar, canning; imp Rich, narrow mouth, rim flake, 10½".......35.00
Jar, canning; imp S Boutson, Wooster, O, base flake, 9½".....55.00
Jar, canning; imp script Lenis, 10"....................28.00
Jar, canning; imp TA Packer, 1875-85, w/lid, 8¾".........95.00
Jar, canning; narrow mouth, gr/br glaze, 9"...............15.00
Jar, canning; paneled, imp EH Merrill, base flake, 7".........30.00
Jar, canning; stenciled AP Donaghho, 10"................65.00
Jar, canning; stenciled Williams & Reppert, c/s, 10".........85.00
Jar, canning; wavy lines, lines of stars, c/s, 9¾"..........200.00
Jar, canning; 3 dabs cobalt on shoulder, c/s, 10¼".........20.00
Jar, canning; 4 stripes, c/s, 1 qt, EX..................150.00
Jar, chicken pecking, c/s, Haxstun & Co, 5 gal, EX..........375.00
Jar, dog, reclining on dotted ground, c/s, 3 gal, EX.........525.00
Jar, dog, reclining on dotted ground w/stump, c/s, 4 gal, EX...700.00
Jar, eagle, imp; c/s, Charlestown, 2 gal, rear rim chip.......150.00
Jar, eagle & shield stencil, imp LC & CF Brown, c/s, 3 gal....145.00
Jar, eagle w/banner, c/s, Darrow & Sons, 4 gal, G..........550.00
Jar, fancy squiggle, c/s, Worcester, 2 gal, EX.............200.00
Jar, feather design ea side of #3, c/s, Curger/Lang, 10½", G...95.00
Jar, finger line decor, c/s, 1½ gal, EX..................85.00
Jar, fish, 2 crossed; c/s, HM Whitman, Havana, 1 gal, M.....4,600.00
Jar, flamingo, bent neck; c/s, Whites Utica, 1 gal, M.........275.00

Jar, flamingo, c/s, Whites Utica, 1 gal, M................225.00
Jar, flourish & 10, c/s, 10 gal, 18"....................75.00
Jar, flower, c/s, imp Cowden & Wilcox, edge flakes, 6½x8½"..155.00
Jar, flower, c/s, imp JF Hart, 9¼", EX..................115.00
Jar, flower, c/s, imp label, ovoid, flakes, 13½"............160.00
Jar, flower, c/s, imp OL & AK Ballard, orig lid, 10¾".......215.00
Jar, flower, c/s, Orcutt Humiston & Co, ovoid, 3 gal, M......150.00
Jar, flower, c/s, SS Perry West Troy, ovoid, 2 gal, EX.......100.00
Jar, flower, c/s, stylized, Haxstun & Co, 2 gal, M..........120.00
Jar, flower, c/s, tooled lip, ovoid, minor flakes, 8".........95.00
Jar, flower, dk c/s, NA White & Son, Utica, 2 gal, M........150.00
Jar, flower, dotted; c/s, Wm E Warner, W Troy, 2 gal, EX....150.00
Jar, flower, drooping; c/s, Cowden & Wilcox, 1 gal, rim chips..170.00
Jar, flower, fancy; c/s, Burger & Lang, 3 gal, minor flaking....150.00
Jar, flower & bow tie, c/s, ½ gal, M...................150.00
Jar, flower spray, c/s, Whites Utica, minor line, 7".........105.00
Jar, flower w/leaf, dbl; KW, c/s, Brown Bros, 1½ gal, EX.....200.00
Jar, flower w/leaf, fancy; c/s, Burger & Lang, 3 gal, M.......275.00
Jar, flower w/stem, c/s, Whites Utica, 3 gal, M............150.00
Jar, flower wreath, dtd 1868, c/s, Troy, NY, 2 gal, 12", EX....450.00
Jar, flowers, c/s, C Hart & Son, 3 gal, M................150.00
Jar, flowers, c/s, imp FB Norton, Worcester, Mass..........195.00
Jar, flowers, c/s, NA White & Son, chip under hdl, 7"........85.00
Jar, flowers, double w/leaf; c/s, Lyons, 2 gal, EX...........150.00
Jar, flowers, double; c/s, White & Wood, 2 gal, M..........85.00
Jar, flowers, elaborate; c/s, PH Smith, 16 gal, ovoid, EX......525.00
Jar, flowers, fancy/dbl; c/s, John Burger, 6 gal, hairline......1,450.00
Jar, flowers, stylized/elaborate; c/s, W Troy, 2 gal, EX.......225.00
Jar, flowers, T Harrington, Lyons, 3, c/s, rolled rim.........200.00
Jar, flowers, three simple; c/s, imp 1½, rim flake, 10½".......65.00
Jar, flowers w/leaf, #3, c/s, Geddes, NY, 3 gal, blue burned...160.00
Jar, flowers w/stems, triple/dotted, c/s, Whites Utica, 6 gal.....175.00
Jar, horses, 2 facing, tree in center, c/s, 6 gal, EX.........1,700.00
Jar, imp #2 & stenciled handshake, c/s, 11½" dia..........190.00
Jar, imp IM Meade & Co, c/s, ovoid, minor rim flakes, 11½"...125.00
Jar, imp L Marsilliot, Ohio, 2, brushed w/cobalt, damage, 13"..750.00
Jar, imp S Purdy, #3, cobalt splashed, ovoid, 12"..........130.00
Jar, imp S Routson, Wooster, O, dk olive, sm flakes on lip, 9"..75.00
Jar, leaf, c/s, ovoid, 2 gal, EX.......................80.00
Jar, leaf, dotted; c/s, 1½ gal, EX....................150.00
Jar, leaf (revolving), c/s, 1 gal, M....................160.00
Jar, man's head w/cowboy hat, c/s, 2 gal, hairlines..........425.00
Jar, One/flourish, c/s, base flake, 9½".................85.00
Jar, orchid, c/s, NA White & Son, Utica, 2 gal, EX..........250.00
Jar, orchid, dbl; c/s, Whites Utica, 2 gal, M.............200.00
Jar, ovoid, saltglaze, 18¼"........................55.00
Jar, parrot, plumes ea side, c/s, FB Norton, Mass, 4 gal, G....350.00
Jar, parrot on dotted plume, FB Norton, Worcester, 3 gal, M..550.00
Jar, plume, fancy/tied; c/s, T Harrington Lyons, 2 gal, M......300.00
Jar, ribbed exterior, br/amber glaze, 7½"................18.00
Jar, shaking hands, stencil, c/s, 2 gal, M................150.00
Jar, slightly ovoid, brushed florals/wavy lines, c/s, 11".......80.00
Jar, squiggle front & rear, c/s, 1½ gal, minor rim chips.......100.00
Jar, stenciled Williams & Reppert, brush lines, #2, c/s, 12"....115.00
Jar, tornado, c/s, FA Gale, 2 gal, M...................375.00
Jar, tornado, fancy; c/s, J Burger, 2 gal, EX..............140.00
Jar, tulip, large; c/s, imp A DeHaven, ovoid, no lid, 12".......450.00
Jar, tulip (revolving) w/leaf, c/s, ovoid, 1½ gal, EX.........425.00
Jar, tulips front & bk, hdl/lid decor, c/s, 4 gal, VG.........180.00
Jar, w/lid, gray glaze, wire bale hdl rpl, hairline, 10".........20.00
Jar, wreath, 1885, c/s, Ft Edward Stoneware, 5 gal, VG......170.00
Jar, 1871, 6 & quillwork flourish, c/s, 6 gal..............95.00
Jug, #2 encircled by 2 leaves, c/s, John Burger, 2 gal, EX.....120.00
Jug, #2 w/leaf, c/s, ovoid, 2 gal, EX..................150.00

Jug, 'John', c/s, S Hart, 1 gal, M..........................275.00

Jug, Albany slip, Ripley pottery, 9"........................25.00

Jug, bird, large; c/s, Harts, 4 gal, spout chip..............425.00

Jug, bird on branch, lg; c/s, 2 gal, EX.....................250.00

Jug, bird on flowering branch, c/s, White & Son, 16"........465.00

Jug, bird on ledge, flower/ship w/Am flag, incised, c/s, 1 gal..1,300.00

Jug, bird on ledge, incised, c/s, I Seymour & Co, 2 gal, VG....200.00

Jug, bird on twig, c/s, West Troy, 1 gal, M.................250.00

Jug, bird on twig, c/s, Whites Utica, 2 gal, 13¼"...........300.00

Jug, bird w/fantail, lg; c/s, EL Lewis adv, 2 gal, EX.........175.00

Jug, brush stroke decor, c/s, Jacob Caire, 1 gal, EX.........150.00

Jug, daubs, c/s, I Seymour, Troy, ovoid, 2 gal, EX..........100.00

Jug, daubs, c/s, SS Perry, Troy, ovoid, 1 gal, EX............75.00

Jug, diamond stencil, c/s, HF Cowden, 2 gal, EX.............75.00

Jug, dog w/basket in mouth, grass, c/s, S Hart, Fulton, 2 gal...350.00

Jug, dtd 1838, c/s, ovoid 2 gal, minor age lines............200.00

Jug, eagle/shield/23 stars/arrows, verso w/decor, c/s, 1 gal....4,750.00

Jug, emb FW Weeks, clear glaze, wire bail, wood hdl, 6".......25.00

Jug, emb O Stoneware Co, Akron, O, br/gray saltglaze, 11"....30.00

Jug, emb tavern scene/acanthus leaves/rope twist hdl, 1858, 7".145.00

Jug, fish, incised; c/s, ovoid, 4 gal, EX, minor base line......1,000.00

Jug, fish w/flower, imp; c/s, ovoid, 2 gal, pock mks..........300.00

Jug, flower, #2, c/s, ovoid, imp IM Meade, 14".............340.00

Jug, flower, c/s, A Lobdell & Co, 2 gal, spout chip..........175.00

Jug, flower, c/s, C Hart & Co, 3 gal, EX...................160.00

Jug, flower, c/s, imp J Mantell, 2 gal.....................155.00

Jug, flower, c/s, imp John Burger, ovoid, minor chips, 14"....285.00

Jug, flower, c/s, J Burger, Jr, 2 gal, M...................275.00

Jug, flower, c/s, lid chip, 13".............................95.00

Jug, flower, c/s, N White Utica, 1 gal, EX.................135.00

Jug, flower, c/s, NA White & Son, 5 gal, rim chip..........175.00

Jug, flower, c/s, ovoid, 2 gal, EX.........................100.00

Jug, flower, c/s, Roberts, 1 gal, M.......................225.00

Jug, flower, c/s, 2 gal, EX...............................100.00

Jug, flower, dk c/s, Worcester, 1 gal, base chip.............85.00

Jug, flower, drooping; #3, c/s, AO Whitmore, 3 gal, EX......175.00

Jug, flower, elaborate; c/s, CE Argersinger, 2 gal, M........375.00

Jug, flower, fancy; c/s, Harrington & Burger, 2 gal, EX......185.00

Jug, flower, fancy; c/s, Whites Binghamton, 1 gal, M........250.00

Jug, flower, fancy; striped hdl, c/s, W Roberts, 2 gal, EX.....225.00

Jug, flower, fancy/dotted, w/leaf, c/s, Martin Crafts, 2 gal.....175.00

Jug, flower, lg/stylized; c/s, Walker & Co adv, 5 gal, EX......225.00

Jug, flower, looped; c/s, D Weston, 2 gal, EX...............100.00

Jug, flower, potted w/2 bees; c/s, Somerset, 2 gal, base line....150.00

Jug, flower, quillwork, c/s, Mfg/sold by S James McKee, 15"...265.00

Jug, flower, stylized; c/s, Haxstun & Co, 2 gal, EX..........140.00

Jug, flower, stylized; c/s, Ithaca, NY, 1 gal, M............120.00

Jug, flower, triple; c/s, FA Plaisted & Co, 2 gal, EX.........100.00

Jug, flower, 6 petal, c/s, F Stetzenmeyer, ovoid, 2 gal, G.....375.00

Jug, flower & 3, c/s, sm flakes, 14".......................160.00

Jug, flower w/leaf, c/s, AE Allen, 3 gal, M................180.00

Jug, flower w/leaf, c/s, C Hart & Son, 4 gal, EX............170.00

Jug, flower w/leaf, c/s, Cowden & Wilcox, 3 gal, EX.........190.00

Jug, flower w/leaf, c/s, NA White & Son, Utica, 2 gal, M.....150.00

Jug, flowers, drooping; c/s, DP Shenfelder, 2 gal, EX........100.00

Jug, foliage, c/s, imp G Baird, 1 gal......................130.00

Jug, Fruehlich Bros & F in diamond under hdl, c/s, 1 gal, EX..125.00

Jug, harp, dotted w/tree atop, c/s, 2 gal, rim chips.........175.00

Jug, harvest; applied man & boy, Albany w/sgraffito, 11", G....350.00

Jug, harvest; twist rope hdl/root attachments, sgraffito, 12"...1,000.00

Jug, imp Boston, c/s, ovoid, lip flake, 13½"...............150.00

Jug, imp EH Merrill & Co, 9".............................45.00

Jug, imp J Bennage & JA Sutherland, cobalt splashed ovoid....135.00

Jug, imp N Terry 2, c/s, ovoid, 2 gal, 14".................65.00

Jug, imp S Purdy 3, c/s, ovoid, base drilled, 16"...........95.00

Jug, imp SH Sonner, mottled gray surface, 9"...............65.00

Jug, incised wings, imp Goodwin & Webster, c/s, ovoid, 17", G.400.00

Jug, leaf, c/s, CE Pharis & Co, 1 gal......................100.00

Jug, leaf, c/s, FB Norton, Worcester, Mass, 1 gal, M.........110.00

Jug, leaf, c/s, Whites Utica, 1 gal, EX....................140.00

Jug, leaf, lg; c/s, C Boyton & Co, 1 gal, EX...............125.00

Jug, leaf & #2, c/s, Lyons, dbl stamped, 2 gal, EX..........150.00

Jug, leafy vine in pot w/loops around reeded neck, c/s, 2 gal...140.00

Jug, M Sheehan advertising, c/s, 3 gal, EX.................100.00

Jug, ovoid, saltglaze, 1 pt, M.............................80.00

Jug, parrot on leaf, c/s, West Troy, 2 gal, EX..............375.00

Jug, pheasant in grass, incised; c/s, EP Gray, 1½ gal, dbl hdl..800.00

Jug, pine tree decor, c/s, NA White & Son, Utica, EX........120.00

Jug, rabbit, running, 3 leaves, c/s, ovoid, 2 gal, EX.........800.00

Jug, star, dotted; c/s, Somerset Potters, 1 gal, base chip......150.00

Jug, stenciled John Weaver, c/s, 11".......................75.00

Jug, stenciled L Sternberger, Wines & Liquors, c/s, 9".......125.00

Jug, swan (stamped in), c/s, Gardinere Stoneware Co, 12½"...100.00

Jug, tree between 2 flowers, c/s, Whites Utica, 1 gal, EX......175.00

Jug, turkey-like bird, c/s, 2 gal, 13".....................525.00

Jug, wreath encircling N Clark, c/s, ovoid, 1 gal, M.........125.00

Jug, 2 tone, emb Ohio Stoneware Co, 11"..................12.50

Jug, 2 tone, English, imp Slaney & Son, wht/amber, 12½".....25.00

Match holder, bands top & base, c/s, M...................150.00

Meat tenderizer, pat Dec 25, 1877, EX.....................85.00

Milk pan, F Stetzenmeyer, 1 gal, hairline in bk.............80.00

Mug, cobalt hdl on saltglaze, M...........................55.00

Mug, 2 bands, c/s, M....................................45.00

Pitcher, applied & tooled leaves/flowers, Albany slip, 11".....135.00

Pitcher, bird w/song note, c/s, fancy spout/neck, 2 gal, EX....625.00

Pitcher, flower, c/s, base hairlines, 8¾"..................145.00

Pitcher, flower, fancy; c/s, John Burger, 1 gal, base spider....325.00

Pitcher, flower, lg/bold; c/s, J Burger, 1 gal, EX...........550.00

Pitcher, flower, revolving line/dot at neck, incised, c/s, qt....625.00

Pitcher, flower, stylized; c/s, Satterlee & Mory, 1½ gal, EX...450.00

Pitcher, flower w/leaves, c/s, 1 gal, EX...................200.00

Pitcher, flowering branch, imp 1½, c/s, hdl prof rpr, 12".....500.00

Pitcher, gr amber glaze, old base flakes, 7"................55.00

Pitcher, imp #1, 7"......................................75.00

Pitcher, imp US Stoneware Co, Akron, 8"..................25.00

Crock, advertising 'Sure Shot Cigars, C. Riester and Co., Wholesale Dealer', gallon size, 12", $375.00.

Pitcher, New Geneva, br clay/brushed florals in dk br, 9¼"....575.00
Pitcher, New Geneva, gray clay/dk br stripe/dashes/stencil, 9"...500.00
Pitcher, New Geneva, red clay/brushed florals in br, 6½"....340.00
Pitcher, olive br, sgraffito bird, inscription, 1896, 9½", G.....235.00
Pitcher, star, c/s, 2 gal, EX......................................225.00
Pitcher, tulip, hdl stripes, c/s, imp H Purdy #4, 16".........575.00
Turkey feeder, leaves at hood/hdls & rear, knob, c/s, 2 gal....275.00
Umbrella stand, applied hdls, NY state, EX......................180.00
Whistle, bird w/bl base/legs/wings/tail, darker neck/head, EX....500.00

Store

Perhaps more than any other yester-year establishment, the country store evokes the most nostalgic feelings for folks old enough to remember its charms -- barrels for coffee, crackers, and big green pickles; candy in a jar for the grocer to weigh on shiny brass scales; beheaded chickens in the meat case outwardly devoid of nothing but feathers. Today, mementos from this segment of Americana are being collected by those who 'lived it' as well as those less fortunate.

Account file, McCaskey..................................185.00
Barrel, pickle; glass, lg all around ridges, 17x12"............55.00
Barrel, root beer; oak.....................................225.00
Bill holder, eight 12x18" sections, McCaskey, pat 1913.......100.00
Bin, tea; slant top, tin, lg...............................135.00
Box, Am Biscuit shipping & display, parrot labels, 11x23"......55.00
Box, Ferry Seeds label in lid, dvtl corners..................28.00
Box, Lenox Soap, dvtl corners, no lid, G.....................45.00
Broom holder, holds 24, rnd/revolving........................75.00
Canister, spice; Wheeler Stevens Co, lift top front w/cylinder...110.00
Canister, tea; Schluetter & Sons, Chicago, hammered brass, 15".35.00
Cash drawer, pine/raised slant top for book, rfn, 10x15x15"....65.00
Cheese safe, counter top; slide-out inner shelf..............135.00
Coffee bin, wood w/blk pnt Jersey Coffee 120#, 32x22½x18"...325.00
Cookie display, 4 hinged glass doors, floor model............95.00
Counter scale, CI, brass arm to 15 lbs, red/yel japanned.......65.00
Dispenser, Chero Crush, cherry shape & color.............1,320.00
Display, Jade-ite free w/bag of Town Crier Flour, w/6 bowls....49.00
Display case, Adams Gum...................................250.00
Display case, counter; advertising garters, glass............220.00

Boye Hook case, 9" x 8", $35.00.

Display case, counter; metal frame, 36"......................150.00
Display form, for men's coat, blk silk surface, walnut base......75.00
Display rack, for CI skillet lids, metal......................95.00
Display rack, National Biscuit, wood........................495.00
Egg crate, Cummer Mfg, wood slats w/wire bail & hdl, 6 doz....30.00
Grain counter, roll front, 8 ft.............................330.00
Jar, embossed elephant...................................125.00
Lamp, brass, hanging, Victorian, ornate.....................415.00
Mannequin, counter top; wood/cloth w/Treso corset, CI mt, 26".200.00
Meat slicer, American, non-electric, CI fly wheel.............895.00
Rack, paper sack; metal, #8 size...........................95.00
Rack, paper sack; orig stenciling, pat 1884, ¼ circle, 16".....275.00
Refrigerator, oak, 3 door, fancy...........................575.00
Scoop, tin, 1865, EX......................................55.00
Spool cabinet, Clarks.....................................250.00
Spool cabinet, Merrick, cotton thread, 6 drw................660.00

Stoves

Parlor stoves range from the simple to the very ornate. Many were obviously relative to a specific style of furnishing -- Rococo, Gothic, or Greek, for instance. This is due to the fact that they were first designed in wood, carved and constructed by cabinetmakers who transferred to them the decorative devices they routinely used on furniture. The wooden stove that resulted was then used as a basis for the mold.

Bangor Foundry, Comfort #23, parlor, urn/blk foot rail, oval...150.00
Barstow, The Gem #3, parlor, oven under dome, 1892, 30x27".275.00
Barstow #137 Orient 1886, coal fireplace, 7 tiles ea side, urn...900.00
Barstow CI Parlor Cottage, w/urn, cast bottom/top, 45".......100.00
C Williams, Forest #19, parlor, urn, ornate, 33x24"..........300.00
Culter & Proctor, Peoria, horizontal can form, urn, EX ornate..800.00
Detroit Stove Work, Emerald Jewel #14, parlor, coal, w/urn..1,400.00
E Eaton #23, box parlor, schoolhouse type, cathedral panels...350.00
Favorite #30, 1880s, brass urn, elaborate scrolls, mica doors..1,600.00
Fireplace, nickel top trim/foot rail, gr/red/wht tiles, 32x37".....200.00
GW Eddy, Forest Parlor #3, ornate parlor, emb design, w/urn..225.00
Ilion #3, parlor, pat 1853, urn atop, rnd w/rnd door, claw ft...500.00
J Petree, Excelcior, parlor heater, w/urn, emb bowl of fruit.....200.00
Low & Hicks, Gothic Parlor #4, ornate CI parlor, pierced front.350.00
Low & Hicks, Revere Air Tight, CI parlor, cathedral door, 29".275.00
McArthur & Co, Moonlight Cottage, parlor, 1858, rstr........450.00
Modern Glenwood Wood Parlor, nickel front/top rail & dome..275.00
Monitor #20, oil cookstove, dtd 1887, 29x23"...............100.00
Moores Air Tight Heater #420B, parlor, coal, sq, 1883........750.00
Noyes & Nutter, Kineo #15, fireplace, CI, 1870s, ornate front..150.00
Oven Parlor #7, pat 1855, 2 top doors w/oven, ornate, 34x27".200.00
Parlor box, corrugated sides w/ornate top panel, 1830s, 25x32".450.00
PP Stewart L'Hiver #17, parlor, coal, sq, emb cherub/maiden...450.00
Pratt & Perkins, Organ #2, parlor, ornate CI, 1852, 36x25"...275.00
Pratt & Weeks, De Soto Parlor #1, ornate CI, scroll legs, 42"..550.00
Queen Atlantic, CI cookstove, 1930s, bk shelf...............275.00
Rural #21, fireplace, lady's head medallion, oval urn, 37x29"...100.00
Standard Lighting Co, Globe Incandescent, kerosene parlor, 29".75.00
Tyson Furnace, CI, relief ships, 1839, 17x23"...............175.00
Vanderhecht, Bruxelles, #2160, ornate brass doors, 32x40x12".425.00
Walker & Pratt, Village Crawford Royal, cookstove, 1900-18...600.00
Wilson Co, CI fireplace, emb panels, brass balls atop, 29".....250.00

Strawberry Lustre Ware

Strawberry lustre is a general term for creamware decorated with hand painted strawberries, vines and tendrils, and pink lustre trim. It was made by many manufacturers in England in the 19th century, most of whom never marked their ware.

Cup & saucer, handleless; minor wear......................200.00
Plate, incised Adams, 8½".........................25.00
Plate, 1820-40, 10½"..................................125.00
Sauce dish, Elsmore Forster & Co, 1855.................22.50
Sugar, covered, S-shape, very early......................175.00
Teapot, 6x10"...450.00
Waste bowl, very early, 4¼x6½"......................125.00

Stretch Glass

Stretch glass, produced from the early 1900s until after 1930, was made in an effort to emulate the fine art glass of Tiffany and Carder. The glassware was sprayed with a special finish while still hot, and a reheating process caused the coating to contract, leaving a striated, crepe-like iridescence. Northwood, Imperial, Fenton, and the United States Glass Company were the largest manufacturers of this type of glass.

Bowl, amber, ftd, 2¾x8¾".............................32.00
Bowl, amberina, 5½x12".................................200.00
Bowl, blue opaque, 3½x7½"............................40.00
Bowl, pinched sides, marigold irid, Imperial, 9½" sq.........95.00
Bowl, vaseline, ftd, 2¾x8".................................34.00
Bowl, vaseline, gilt pheasants around edge, 10".............45.00
Bowl, vaseline, rolled edge, 10¾"......................32.00
Bowl, Velva Rose, Imperial, 5x9".........................45.00
Candlestick, blue irid, Imperial, 8", pr....................85.00
Candy jar w/lid, topaz, Fenton, #636.....................75.00
Compote, clear, 5x5"......................................30.00
Nut cup, gold/green, Northwood..........................50.00
Sherbet, blue...22.00
Sherbet, red shading to amber, ftd.......................65.00
Vase, excellent irid, 4" bulbous top to 2" base, Imperial.......85.00
Vase, fan form, pink, #857, Fenton......................25.00
Vase, fan form, Velva Rose, Imperial, 8"..................40.00

Candlestick, light green, 9½", $50.00 for the pair.

String Holders

Today, if you want to wrap and secure a package, you have a variety of products to choose from: cellophane tape, staples, etc. But in the 1800s,

string was about the only available binder; thus the string holder -- either the hanging or counter type -- was a common and practical item found in most homes and businesses.

Advertising, Legion Soap, tin container, English.............175.00
Apple, chalkware..15.00
Baby, chalkware..35.00
Beehive, CI, fluted edge, grooved 'hive', bolts to counter.......25.00
Beehive, CI, ornate 'hive' has wrapped rope design, pat 1860....75.00
Bird on nest, ceramic.....................................18.00
Bunch of grapes, chalkware...............................22.00
Cat, ceramic..18.00
Cat on ball of yarn, ceramic..............................15.00
Chef, chalkware..15.00
Cone, early style, vertical cone holds string, CI arm............30.00
Dome shape w/intersecting arches, CI, 5"..................35.00
Dutch girl, chalkware.....................................12.00
Lady, Art Deco...45.00
Lady in apron, chalkware..................................15.00
Lady in chair, ceramic....................................35.00
Mammy, ceramic...55.00
Mexican man, chalkware..................................25.00
Pig head, 3 dimensional, glass eyes, ceramic, 5½" sq.........95.00
Puppy, ceramic..25.00
Reticulated dome to accomodate cone of string, CI, 8½".......30.00
Reticulated sphere, hanging, w/worn floral decor, CI, 4¼".....40.00
Reticulated sphere, on triangular base, CI w/rpt, 6½".........25.00
Scotty dog, chalkware....................................45.00
Strawberry, chalkware....................................15.00
Wall mount, Pat Oct 21, 1893, CI, simple pocket for ball, 5"...15.00
Wire, 2 spindle, country store type.......................80.00

Sugar Shakers

Sugar shakers, or muffineers as they were also called, were used during the Victorian era to sprinkle sugar and spice onto breakfast muffins, toast, etc. They were made of art glass, in pressed patterns, and in china.

Acorn, EX decor..95.00
Argus Swirl, cranberry....................................135.00
Banded Portland, w/orig lid...............................45.00
Beatty Rib, blue opal.....................................85.00
Block & Fan..35.00
Bubble Lattice, blue satin opal, orig lid..................135.00
Bulging Loops, blue cased, glossy, orig top................145.00
Challinor's Blue Forget-Me-Not...........................140.00
Cherries & leaves decor, porcelain, gold ftd................50.00
Chrysanthemum Base Swirl, blue..........................120.00
Clear Circle..45.00
Cone, lt green opaque....................................90.00
Daisy & Fern, blue opal, Northwood.......................125.00
Daisy & Fern, cranberry opal, w/orig lid, Northwood.........135.00
Etched Apollo, orig lid....................................25.00
Fleurette, pink satin glass, orig brass top, 3¼"............125.00
Flower & Pleat...65.00
Horseshoe, amber..25.00
Inverted Thumbprint, rubena w/enamel daisies, SP 2-part top...125.00
Inverted Thumbprint, vaseline, orig top....................47.00
Lattice, blue opal, ribbed, tall...........................95.00
Lattice, cranberry opal, small............................90.00
Leaf Mold, green...150.00
Leaf Umbrella, cranberry.................................145.00
Midwestern Pomona......................................35.00

Paneled Daisy...35.00
Paneled Diamond Block..............................30.00
Peach colored flowers, HP, china....................45.00
Question Mark.......................................35.00
Reverse Swirl, blue opal............................110.00
Reverse Swirl, clear opal............................95.00
Ribbed Lattice, cranberry opal.....................125.00
Royal Ivy, satin spatter crackle....................225.00
Royal Ivy, spatter, cased..........................150.00
Royal Oak, frosted rubena, w/orig lid...............165.00
Satin, apple blossom decor, orig lid, Mt Washington..........125.00
Spanish Lace, blue opal.............................68.00
Venetian Diamonds, cranberry........................80.00
Windermere's Fan, milk glass, pink & yellow decor, M........40.00
Windows, blue opal.................................150.00

Sunderland Lustre

Sunderland lustre was made by various potters in the Sunderland district of England during the 18th and 19th centuries. It is characterized by a splashed-on application of the pink lustre, which results in an effect sometimes referred to as the 'cloud' pattern. Some pieces are transfer printed with scenes, ships, florals, or portraits.

Chalice, EX mottle, knob stem, early 1800s, 5½".............175.00
Cup, saucer & 6" under plate; Chas Allerton.................25.00
Pitcher, 'Success... Volunteers', w/poem, etc...............185.00
Pitcher, Dickens Days....................................50.00
Pitcher, Drunkard's Arms, view of bridge/verse, 8½".........390.00
Pitcher, mariner's rhyme, View of Iron Bridge in reserve, 9½"..500.00
Plaque, blk transfer of RR in polychrome, 'Express', rpr, 8x9"..175.00
Plate, 7¼"..24.00
Shell dish, coach & horses transfer, copper lustre rim, 1½x5"...32.00

Mug, 3", $65.00.

Swastika Keramos

Swastika Keramos was a line of art ware made by the Owens China Co., of Minerva, Ohio. It was produced around 1902-1904, and is characterized by a 'coralene' type of decoration, similar to the Opalesce line made by the J.B. Owens Pottery Company of Zanesville.

Vase, cylinder w/tiny neck, gold/red/gr gloss w/dripping, 6"......65.00
Vase, red gloss w/red iris/gold leaves, slim w/flared top, 12".....70.00
Vase, shiny scenic, purple 'clouds', waisted w/ear hdls, 8".......80.00
Vase, tall bell form, gold w/red flowers, 6¾".................90.00

Vase, three handles, allover coralene-like surface, marked 'Keramos', 7½", $125.00.

Syracuse

Syracuse was a line of fine dinnerware which was made for nearly a century by the Onondaga Pottery Company of Syracuse, New York. Collectors of American dinnerware are focusing their attention on reassembling some of their many lovely patterns. In 1966, the firm became officially known as the Syracuse China Company in order to better identify with the name of their popular chinaware. By 1971, dinnerware geared for use in the home was discontinued, and the company turned to the manufacture of hotel, restaurant, and other types of commercial tableware.

Alpine, plate, bread & butter..............................7.00
Apple Blossom, cream soup...............................12.00
Apple Blossom, cream soup w/stand.......................18.50
Apple Blossom, cup & saucer.............................18.50
Apple Blossom, plate, dinner.............................15.00
Apple Blossom, plate, luncheon..........................12.00
Apple Blossom, plate, salad.............................10.00
Apple Blossom, platter, 14".............................38.00
Apple Blossom, platter, 16½"............................45.00
Apple Blossom, rimmed soup.............................15.00
Belcanto Platinum, creamer..............................15.00
Bracelet, cup & saucer, demitasse.......................18.50
Briarcliff, salad...8.50
Candlelight, plate, dinner...............................16.00
Compote w/9½" under plate, floral, ladies in medallions, 7".....18.00
Corabel, creamer & sugar, pr............................25.00
Corabel, gravy boat w/attached under tray..................85.00
Corabel, platter, oval, 16".............................80.00
Corabel, vegetable, open, oval, 10"......................45.00
Cup & saucer, roses & leaves, gold spray, OP Co............8.00
Old Ivory, cup & saucer................................22.00
Old Ivory, plate, bread & butter.........................6.00
Old Ivory, plate, dinner................................20.00
Place setting, Appleton, 5 pc...........................75.00
Place setting, Dogwood, 5 pc...........................75.00
Place setting, Suzanne, 5 pc...........................125.00
Romance, creamer & sugar, maroon.......................35.00
Romance, cup & saucer, maroon..........................15.00

Romance, fruit, maroon	7.00
Romance, plate, dinner; maroon	12.00
Romance, plate, salad; maroon	8.00
Romance, platter, maroon, 14″	35.00
Romance, vegetable, rnd; maroon	30.00
Romance, vegetable w/lid, maroon	45.00
Shell Edge, plate, dinner	10.00
Sherwood, cup & saucer	36.00
Sherwood, plate, 10″	22.00
Sherwood, plate, 6¼″	10.00
Sonata, cup & saucer	15.00
Westminster, plate, bread & butter	7.00

Syrups

Acorn, green	110.00
Acorn, opaque pink blending to white	110.00
Alabama	65.00
Bellflower, flint, w/metal lid	495.00
Bellflower, 10 panel, tin top, ca 1850	330.00
Block Band, amber stain, enamel floral	75.00
Blocked Arches, domed top	32.50
Box in Box, floral etched, w/orig lid	22.00
Broken Column, ruby flashed	380.00
Bull's Eye w/Diamond Point, honeycomb neck, tin lid	45.00
China, Quimper-like country people, browns/blues/yellow, M	50.00
Chrysanthemum Base Speckled, blue glass	210.00
Chrysanthemum Base Swirl, frosted cranberry opal	200.00
Clear Circle	42.00
Coin Dot, blue, w/blue hdl, metal cover	85.00
Coin Spot, clear opal, M	50.00
Coin Spot Swirl, blue opal	78.00
Columbian Coin	105.00
Cord Drapery, amber	310.00
Cord Drapery, chocolate	210.00
Crown Milano, burmese bkground w/HP blue floral, melon rib	600.00
Crown Milano, glossy, sgn circular wreath #1724	320.00
Daisy & Button, amber, double panel, pewter top	45.00
Daisy & Button w/Thumbprint Panels, amber, w/orig top	145.00
Daisy & Fern, blue opal, orig lid	120.00
Daisy & Fern, cranberry opal, Northwood	245.00
Early Star & Punty, w/applied strap handle, orig lid	45.00
Erie Twist, Wavecrest, florals, Helmschmeid shape	200.00
Findlay Onyx, platinum inlay design, dtd Aug 26/81; Mar 28/82	410.00
Flat Flower, green fiery opal, w/applied hdl	95.00
Flora, clear w/EX heavy gold, orig lid	165.00
Galloway, w/orig top	65.00
Gonterman Swirl, amber top/clear opal base	320.00
Guttate, pink cased, 7x4¼″	145.00
Heart & Thumbprint, w/orig top	75.00
Hercules Pillar, blue, w/orig lid	145.00
Klondike, amber stained	500.00
Late Block, clear w/ruby stain, orig top	145.00
Late Pathfinder	45.00
Leaf Flower, clear w/amber stain, orig top	165.00
Leaf Mold, cased cranberry spatter	330.00
Leaf Mold, milk glass, M	55.00
Leaf Mold, vaseline satin spatter	325.00
Leaf Umbrella, yellow cased, glossy	275.00
Maize, custard w/gold leaves, Libbey	280.00
Milk glass, 6 panels, beaded, dtd 1871, pewter top	75.00
Nine Panel Coin Spot, blue opal	90.00
Optic, blue, w/enameling	75.00
Pennsylvania, clear	35.00

Swirl, blue opalescent, pewter lid, 6½″, $195.00.

Polka Dot, cranberry opal	220.00
Reverse Swirl, cranberry opal, orig lid	235.00
Reverse Swirl, speckled cranberry spatter	250.00
Reverse Swirl, vaseline satin speckled, thumb press missing	185.00
Royal Ivy, cranberry & clear, heat check in hdl	225.00
Sawtooth & Star	35.00
Smith Bros, enamel florals, sgn/#d	260.00
Smith Bros, melon rib, satin w/pansy decor, rampant lion mk	400.00
Spanish Lace, cranberry	97.50
Star & Oval Bull's Eye Panel, clear/applied hdl/pewter lid, 6″	25.00
Swirl, blown, vaseline opal	125.00
Swirled Windows, blue opal	175.00
The Prize, clear w/ruby stain, orig top	225.00
Thumbprint, amberina, SP throat/lid/hdl/tray, Tufts, #1954	600.00
Torpedo	80.00
Truncated Cube	35.00
US Coin, frosted 1892 coins	475.00

Tapestries

Tapestries are woven textiles with elaborate pictorial designs in rich colors. As early as the 15th century they were produced in Oudennarde in Belgium. Mythological and biblical figures were preferred, as well as verdures (landscapes); the quality of these early tapestries, however, was inferior to the fine work done there by the 17th century. Brussels was another important weaving center. It was reknown for producing some of the finest tapestries ever made. By the late 18th century, most of the mills had closed.

Biblical, Virgins & saints, Brussels, 1500s, 5½x11 ft	9,500.00
Biblical, 2 men in greeting, Flemish, 1575, 10½x15 ft	1,540.00
Floral, urn of flowers w/in arch, Flemish, 1600s, 7x4½ ft	2,420.00
Historical, Pandora & Epimetheus, Aubusson, 1750, 7x7 ft	2,310.00
Historical, scene from Trojan war, Flemish, 1550, 10½x9½ ft	2,200.00
Hunting scene, very detailed, Flemish, 1800s, 7x7½ ft	6,850.00
Panel, castle scenic, Aubusson, 1750, 6x4 ft	1,760.00
Panel, concerning life of Queen Guinevere, 1400s, 35x15″	2,090.00
Panel, Enghien, 1500s, 9½x3½ ft	2,200.00
Panel, florals w/floral border, Franco-Flemish, 1500s, 4½x7 ft	5,500.00
Panel, flowering tree, Aubusson, 1700s, 8x4½ ft	2,750.00

Panel, game park scenic, Brussels, 1500s, 10½x12 ft........3,025.00
Panel, mythological, Flemish, 1500s, 52x41"................440.00
Panel, parrot/lg flowers, Franco-Flemish Chouxfleur, 39x53"..2,090.00
Panel, scenic w/bird/trees, Flemish Verdure, 1650, 9x6½ ft..3,630.00
Panel, scenic w/lake, Flemish Verdure, 1700s, 6½x4 ft.....1,870.00
Scenic, lake & trees, Brussels Verdure, 1700s, 10x6½ ft.....1,870.00
Valance, castle/garden, English, late 1500s, 16x68"........3,025.00

Tapestry, signed 'd'apres Rubens', 76" x 54", $300.00.

Tea Caddies

Because tea was once regarded as a precious commodity, special boxes called caddies were used to store the tea leaves. They were made from various materials: porcelain, carved and inlaid woods, and metals ranging from painted tin or tole to engraved silver.

Apple form, fruitwood, late Geo III, 7"....................950.00
Blackthorn/boxwood/ebony inlay walnut, claw/ball ft, 7½" L..3,000.00
Chinese pewter, peach form, w/shou/bat decor, 5".............55.00
Dutch silver, Rococo repousse floral, cherubs' heads, 1850, 6".200.00
German porcelain, bl/wht florals, att Meissen, 1800s, 5¾"......50.00
Mahog, marquetry inlay, Geo III, hinged lid, 3 part, 12" L.....950.00
Quill work, hexagonal, gilded/inlaid wood dividers & glass, 5"..325.00
Sterling, Chester plate w/village scene in relief, 1906, 3x3".....135.00
Tortoise shell, casque form, 2 compartments, 5½x7".........385.00
Tortoise shell, silver inlay, Geo III, Pagoda form, 6½".......800.00
Tortoise shell, silver mts/inlay, oval/brass ball ft, 6"..........800.00
Walnut w/inlay, dome top, 5½x9x4½"......................50.00
Walnut w/inlay, octagonal, English, 5¼x5½x4¾"............75.00

Tea Leaf Ironstone

Tea Leaf Ironstone became popular in the 1880s, when the American middle class housewives became bored with the plain white Stone china that English potters had been exporting to this country for nearly a century. The original design has been credited to Anthony Shaw of Longport, who decorated the plain Ironstone with a hand painted copper lustre design of bands and leaves. Originally known as Lustre Band and Sprig, the pattern has since come to be known as Tea Leaf Lustre. It was produced with minor variations by many different firms, both in England and the United States.

By the early 1900s, it had become so commonplace that it had lost much of its appeal.

Bacon rasher, Meakin.......................................40.00
Baker, A Meakin, oblong, 5½x3¾"...........................35.00
Bone dish, gold lustre, no mk, some wear...................20.00
Bone dish, half moon shape, Meakin........................65.00
Bone dish, ruffled, Meakin.................................65.00
Bowl, fluted, 9½"..40.00
Bowl, Furnival, oval, 7½x10½".............................35.00
Bowl, vegetable (nappy), ind; sq, Wilkinson................24.00
Bowl, vegetable w/lid; Bamboo, Meakin, sq.................95.00
Bowl, vegetable w/lid; Cable, Shaw........................125.00
Bowl, vegetable w/lid; Wedgwood...........................95.00
Bowl, vegetable w/lid; 6 sides, A Shaw....................145.00
Bowl, vegetable; rectangular, open, Furnival...............30.00
Bowl, vegetable; rnd, open, Burgess........................45.00
Bread plate, Fish Hook, Meakin............................50.00
Butter dish, w/cover & insert, Mellor Taylor..............150.00
Butter dish, w/cover & insert, Shaw, sq...................140.00
Butter dish, w/cover & insert, Wedgwood...................140.00
Butter pat, Meakin...12.00
Cake plate, Meakin...48.00
Cake plate, oval, Mellor Taylor............................58.00
Chamber pot w/lid, Meakin.................................175.00
Coffee pot, Mellor Taylor.................................150.00
Creamer, Bamboo, Meakin..................................115.00
Creamer, Cable, rectangular, Shaw.........................125.00
Cup, child's; VG...85.00
Cup & saucer, handleless; Shaw............................95.00
Cup & saucer, Lily-of-the-Valley..........................85.00
Cup & saucer, Meakin.......................................60.00
Cup & saucer, Mellor Taylor................................60.00
Cup & saucer, Wedgwood.....................................60.00
Doughnut stand, Shaw......................................325.00
Gravy boat...45.00
Mug, child's; 2½"...135.00
Pickle dish, Meakin, 4½x8½"...............................35.00
Pitcher, Bamboo, Meakin, 8"...............................175.00
Pitcher, Bamboo, Meakin, 9"...............................265.00
Pitcher, Bamboo, 7".......................................150.00
Pitcher, Cable, 8"..175.00
Pitcher, Fish Hook, Meakin, 7¼"...........................165.00
Pitcher, Powell Bishop, 8½"................................85.00
Pitcher, rectangular, Wedgwood, 7".........................115.00
Pitcher, wash; Wedgwood, without bowl, 12"................185.00
Pitcher & bowl, AJ Wilkinson..............................375.00
Plate, Anthony Shaw, Lily-of-the-Valley border, 9¾"........32.50
Plate, Davenport, dessert; pk lustre.......................18.00
Plate, Davenport, dinner; pk lustre........................28.00
Plate, Furnival, 7"...10.00
Plate, Furnival, 9¼".......................................12.00
Plate, Meakin, luncheon....................................10.00
Plate, Meakin, 6"..10.00
Plate, Meakin, 9"..20.00
Platter, Meakin, oval, 12".................................30.00
Platter, Meakin, 9½x13"....................................32.00
Platter, Shaw, oval, 16"...................................45.00
Platter, Wilkinson, 9x13"..................................45.00
Sauce tureen, w/ladle/lid/under plate; Bamboo, Meakin.....425.00
Sauce tureen, w/ladle/lid/under plate; Fish Hook, Meakin...425.00
Sauce tureen, w/lid & under plate; Cable, Shaw, 3 pc......195.00
Saucer...5.00
Shaving mug, Meakin.......................................125.00

Shaving mug, Shaw...125.00
Soap dish w/lid & insert, Wedgwood.......................135.00
Soup, flanged; Meakin, 8¾"....................................24.00
Soup, flanged; Wilkinson, 8¾"................................24.00
Spittoon, gargoyle heads at sides, EX....................750.00
Sugar bowl, Bamboo...65.00
Teapot, Burgess, 9½"...150.00
Teapot, Lily-of-the-Valley...................................200.00
Teapot, Meakin..150.00
Toothbrush holder, Cable.....................................155.00
Toothbrush holder, no mk.....................................130.00
Wash bowl, 14"..85.00
Waste bowl, Cable...65.00
Waste bowl, Lily-of-the-Valley...............................85.00

Teco

Teco art ware was made by the American Terra Cotta and Ceramic Company, located near Chicago, Illinois. The firm was established in 1886 and until 1901 produced only brick, sewer tile, and other redware. Their early glaze was inspired by the matt green made popular by Grueby. 'Teco green' was made for nearly ten years. It was similar to Grueby's, yet with a subtle silver-gray cast.

The company was one of the first in the United States to perfect a true crystalline glaze. The only decoration used was through the modeling and glazing techniques; no hand painting was attempted. Favored motifs were naturalistic leaves and flowers.

The company broadened their lines to include garden pottery, faience tiles and panels. New matt glazes -- browns, yellows, blue, and rose -- were added to the green in 1910. By 1922, the art ware lines were discontinued; the company closed in 1920.

Teco is usually marked with a vertical impressed device comprised of a large 'T' to the left of the remaining three letters.

Bowl, blown-out drapery, 9½" dia.........................300.00
Bowl, grapevine decor, gr matt, low, 9"..................175.00
Candlestick, gr matt w/Nouveau silver overlay, 16½".....400.00
Chamberstick, metallic gray on gr, low, pr...............95.00
Table lamp, inverted trumpet, frog climbs body, gr matt, 16".1,650.00
Vase, gr matt, abstract relief, 9".......................135.00
Vase, gr matt, angular, 5"................................45.00

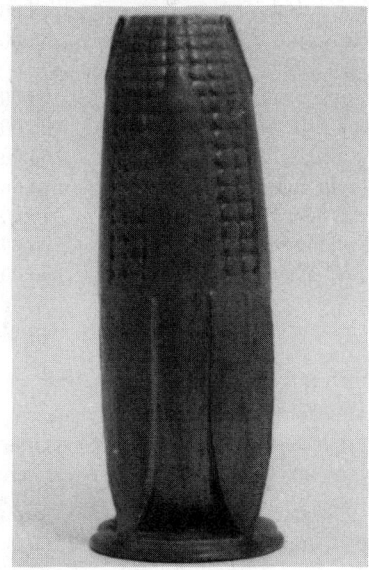

Vase, stylized ear of corn, green matt glaze, 14½", $1,200.00.

Vase, gr matt, bulbous, 4½x5¼".............................68.00
Vase, gr matt, flowers on stem relief, base chips, 20"..1,210.00
Vase, gr matt, full body, 4"...............................45.00
Vase, gr matt, 4 hdls, 6½"................................200.00
Vase, lt gr matt, 4".......................................55.00
Wall vase, decorated, 8x10"...............................265.00
Wall vase, emb decor, gr matt.............................125.00

Teddy Bear Collectibles

The story of Teddy Roosevelt's encounter with the bear cub has been oft recounted -- with varying degrees of accuracy -- so it will suffice to say that it was as a result of this incident in 1902 that the Teddy Bear got his name.

These appealing little creatures are enjoying renewed popularity with collectors today. To one who has not yet succumbed to their obvious charms, one bear seems to look very much like another. How to tell the older ones? Look for long snouts, jointed limbs, large feet and felt paws, long curving arms, and glass or shoe button eyes. Most old bears have a humped back and are made of mohair stuffed with straw or excelsior. Cute expressions, original clothes, and, off course, good condition add to their value.

Bears

Arrow Novelty, jtd arms/legs, hump back, orig tag & collar, 6"..95.00
Bell Hop, mohair, blue pants, red shirt, fully jtd, 14½"......295.00
Bicycle rider, fully jtd, mk PW, 5".........................120.00
Bully Bear, w/certificate, MIB...............................85.00
Chad Valley, musical, fully jointed, 15"....................125.00
Chad Valley, w/label, '30s dress, 15".......................185.00
Clockworks, automation, 1800s...............................450.00
Clockworks, real wht fur, glass eyes, EX....................600.00
Cloth, early, 3½"..50.00
Fully jtd, chocolate br, ca 1920, 11".......................185.00
Fully jtd, except for neck; long yellow hair, 9½"............95.00
Fully jtd, except for neck; plush, glass eyes, worn, 5"......45.00
Fully jtd, glass eyes, 1920s, 11½"..........................160.00
Fully jtd, glass eyes, 1920s, 18"...........................175.00
Fully jtd, glass eyes, 1930s, 6½"............................75.00
Fully jtd, humpback, gold plush, 1915, 20"..................310.00
Fully jtd, humpback, gold plush, 1920, worn, 11"............145.00
Fully jtd, long arms & paws, ca 1920, 12"...................185.00
Fully jtd, long haired, gold, 1940, 22".....................285.00
Fully jtd, mohair, golden, glass eyes, hump, 1910, 12"......250.00
Fully jtd, mohair, golden, 3¾"...............................65.00
Fully jtd, mohair, silver, baby, 1920, 12"...................85.00
Fully jtd, mohair, swivel head shows compo child's face, 17½"..100.00
Fully jtd, mohair, w/hump, 18"..............................225.00
Fully jtd, mohair, yellow, velvet pads, glass eyes, '30s, 21"..250.00
Fully jtd, mohair plush, button eyes, 13½".................100.00
Fully jtd, movable head, wire in tail control, early, 19"...410.00
Fully jtd, outside button joints, button eyes, lg hump, 21"..110.00
Fully jtd, plush, golden, glass eyes/embroidered features, 14"..130.00
Fully jtd, plush, golden, 14"...............................125.00
Fully jtd, small hump, glass eyes, 1920s, 12"...............175.00
Fully jtd, squealer, tan mohair/felt pads, glass eyes, 14½"..165.00
Fully jtd, straw filled, dressed, 21".......................225.00
Fully jtd, wht plush, long arms, embroidered features, 10"..105.00
Fully jtd, 1930s, 15".......................................125.00
Growler, fully jtd, blue mohair, 19"........................300.00
Growler, fully jtd, brown, 1940s, 22".......................225.00
Growler, fully jtd, plush, maize, straw stuffed, 16"........400.00
Growler, fully jtd, straw stuffed, early, 16"...............250.00

Teddy, fully jointed, plush, glass eyes, circa 1900, 24″, $450.00.

Growler, fully jtd, w/hump, straw stuffed, 19″.............185.00
Growler, fully jtd, 42″......................................230.00
Growler, grizzly, fully jtd, beige, 21″.....................85.00
Growler, on wheels, br mohair, 19x27″.......................600.00
Hermann Prince growler, wht mohair, jtd.....................85.00
Keywind, sitting, w/milk bottle, shoe button eyes, '20s, 5½″.....65.00
Merrythought, fully jtd, 15″................................125.00
Schuco, fully jointed, mohair, 2½″..........................130.00
Steiff, see Toys, Steiff

Miscellaneous

Baby bottle, emb Teddy, 1920s..............................45.00
Bank, w/children, toys & bear, Limoges.....................60.00
Book, Teddy Bears Come to Life, 1907.......................20.00
Booklet, advertising; Bears Baking School..................45.00
Cup, child's; SP, Teddies in swings in relief..............95.00
Cup & saucer, china, Roosevelt Bear decor..................45.00

Perfume bottle, head screws off, jointed legs and arms, in well-loved condition, 5″, $300.00.

Cup & saucer, Teddies playing leapfrog, English.............28.00
Dish, fork & spoon, child's; Feeding Teddy, MIB............45.00
Doll, flour sack, Bewley's Milk............................45.00
Figurine, chalkware, sitting girl holds Teddy bear.........35.00
Figurine, china, Teddy, sitting, looking at fly on bk, 3½″.....65.00
Figurine, CI teddy w/cap, advertising Parker Vises, 3″.........45.00
Fork & spoon, Teddies on hdl; ABCs on bk, pr..............65.00
Match holder, Teddy by hat, ceramic........................75.00
Mug, bear & Buddy Tucker, china............................20.00
Mug, Teddies at play, colorful, German porcelain...........32.00
Mush set, bowl & creamer, Teddies, dolls, horses on wheels.....60.00
Paperweight, dbl sided, sterling, 2¾″......................130.00
Pin-back, Won't You Be My Teddy............................45.00
Pitcher, majolica type, figural sitting bear, HP, old, 8″, M.....65.00
Plate, milk glass w/Roosevelt Bears........................40.00
Plate, tin, Teddies & kids on border, girl center, 1907.......50.00
Puppet, Herman, br mohair/stitched nose, w/orig tag.........50.00
Rattle, sterling silver Teddy, MOP hdl, 4″.................225.00
Tea set, Teddies at play, Japan, 15 pcs....................400.00
Teapot, creamer, honey pot w/lid, s/p; figurals, br pottery.....125.00
Toothpick holder, Teddy & His Bear, porcelain, souvenir.......95.00
Tray, advertising w/Roosevelt Bears........................60.00
Valise, round, tin hdl, mamma/pappa/baby bear, 1920s........35.00

Telephones

Since Alexander Graham Bell's first successful telephone communication, the phone itself has undergone a complete evolution in style as well as efficiency. Early models, especially those wall types with ornately carved oak boxes, are of special interest to collectors. Also of value are the candlestick phones from the early part of the century.

AT&T, candlestick, 1920, EX orig..........................95.00
Candlestick phone, brass, 1 button intercom................65.00
Cradle phone, sq, w/oak box................................65.00
Electrical Goods Mfg, candlestick..........................925.00
Federal Telephone & Telegraph, intercom cradle, nickel plate..200.00
Green Telephone & Electric Mfg, oak wall w/cathedral top, 25″.215.00
Kellogg, candlestick, w/oak wall box.......................145.00
Kellogg, candlestick, 1904.................................50.00
Kellogg, candlestick w/nickeled top........................100.00
Kellogg, wall hanging, Leadville, Colorado, EX.............230.00
Kellogg, wall hanging, orig................................155.00
Keystone, candlestick......................................45.00
Leich, cranker, wall type, complete........................265.00
Montgomery Ward Co, wall type, oak, 20″....................175.00
Pay phone, blk, w/keys.....................................100.00
Stromberg Carlson, candlestick, bell box, brass trim, 1909....125.00
Western Electric, dial candlestick type....................155.00
Western Electric, oak wall 3 slot coin collector, pat 1897, VG..375.00
Western Electric, scissors type extension, M...............175.00
Western Electric, Spacesaver wall phone w/ringer box, 1937.....75.00
Western Electric, wall phone, wood, 1900...................250.00

Telescopes

Old telescopes are still appreciated for the quality of the workmanship and materials that went into their production. Some of the more elaborate styles were covered in leather or ebony and the 'draws' or extensions were often brass.

Brass, macrame-type covering, single draw, 24″.............160.00
Brass, simulated wood finish, single draw, 15½″ extended.....100.00

Four draw, encased in leather, brass cap, early 19th century, original carrying case, 41″ extended, $385.00.

Brass, 4 draw, w/leather barrel, 33″......................150.00
Brass, 4 draw, 36″......................................225.00
Captain's, 5 sections, 20 power, w/case, 1900s, 42″..........275.00
Civil War officer's non-issue, brass/leather, 4 draw/sun hood....125.00
Field, brass w/leather covered barrel, 2 draw, 23″............45.00
Field, wood/brass, 3 draw, ca 1830-50.....................135.00
Leather barrel, single draw...............................170.00
Naval, Civil War period, 1 draw, leather, 17″................105.00
PH Steward, 4 draw, woven cord cover, knotted band........127.50
Ship's, brass, 56″ L; on table-top tripod, 22″, recent.........350.00
Ship's, long glass: 44″ extended, wood/sailcloth/brass, 1790s...350.00
Wood barrel w/brass fittings & draw tube, single draw, 23″....175.00

Teplitz

Teplitz, in Czechoslovakia, was an active art pottery center at the turn of the century. The Amphora Pottery Works was only one of the firms that operated there. (See Amphora.) Art Nouveau and Art Deco styling was favored, and much of the ware was hand decorated, with the primary emphasis on vases and figurines. Items listed here are marked 'Teplitz' or 'Turn', a nearby city.

Bust, lady's torso, lavender/cream w/gold trim, 1890, 17″, pr..1,150.00
Ewer, bulbous/straight neck, gold/pk/lav flowers, 10″..........140.00
Ewer, off-wht w/yel flowers, gold trim, retic, 11¼x4″..........225.00
Ewer, wedding; inlay cameos of bride/groom, stars/jewels, 8½″..175.00
Jardiniere, elaborate gilt & florals, open hdls, 8½x11″........175.00
Pitcher, Dutch boy decor in gr, sgn, 3½″....................35.00
Pitcher, Goose Girl, Stellmacher, open hdl, 6½″..............70.00
Tobacco jar, Roman scene, 4½″...........................100.00
Vase, bl poppies, #545-26, red crown mk, 4 hdls, 7½″, pr.....150.00
Vase, cavaliers, mc on gray, 3 hdls, Stellmacher mk, 8″........95.00
Vase, floral, dk gr, w/hdls, sgn, 9″........................70.00
Vase, goats/children relief, cobalt, Stellmacher, 7″...........325.00
Vase, incised mc figure/3-sided crimped rim/3 hdls, 8″........135.00
Vase, lady's face, jeweled headdress, long hair, 11″..........325.00
Vase, retic top, dragon coils body, #669/41, 20″.............990.00
Vase, retic top, stem hdls, enamel floral, gold trim, 8″.......150.00
Vase, retic top/hdls, gold trees/leaves, opal berries, sgn, 7″....200.00
Vase, scenic, yel w/relief bl florals, w/hdls, Stellmacher, 7″....115.00
Vase, seated child points at moon, mc on gray, bulbous base, 6″..75.00
Vase, sunbonnet baby decor, gr w/gr bkground, 4½″........145.00

Terra Cotta

Terra cotta is a type of earthenware or clay used for statuary, architectural facings, or domestic articles. It is unglazed, baked to durable hardness, and is characterized by the color of the body, which may range from brick red to buff.

Architectural ornaments, classical heads, chips, 9″, pr.........25.00
Bust, Diana, Samson Bros Am Art Clay Works, 11″.........550.00
Mural tile, couples at tennis/swimming, by Henry V Poor.....600.00
Pitcher, dragon wrapped about, claw/body hdl, Japanese, 11″...275.00
Statue, lady w/mandolin, Made in Athens, Greece, 1880.......400.00
Syrup pitcher, pewter lid................................95.00

Thermometers

Though the collecting of advertising thermometers has been popular for years, only recently have decorative thermometers come into their own as bona fide items of interest and value.

Indoor and outdoor decorative models have been manufactured for hundreds of years, yet their relative scarcity enhances their value and interest for the collector. Most American thermometers manufactured early in the 20th century were produced by Taylor (Tycos), and today their thermometers remain the most plentiful on the market. They also serve as the price standards for most historical thermometers.

Insofar as sheer beauty, uniqueness, and scientific accuracy, decorative thermometers are far superior to the ordinary and inexpensive versions which carry advertising. Decorative thermometers run the gamut from plain tin household varieties to the highly ornate creations of Tiffany and Bradley and Hubbard. They have been manufactured from nearly every conceivable material – oak, sterling, brass, and glass being the favorites -- and have tested the artistry and technical skills of some of America's finest craftsmen. Ornamental models can be found in free-hanging, wall-mounted, or desk/mantle versions.

Thermometer prices, for the most part, have hovered around the $25 level for the last five years, although those with mercury tubes, figural designs, or in short supply have fetched somewhat higher prices. Items with damaged or missing parts bring greatly reduced prices.

Virtually all American-made thermometers available today as collector items were made between 1875 and 1940. The Golden Age of decoratives ended in the early 1940s as modern manufacturing processes and materials robbed them of their natural distinctiveness. European thermometers, while of comparable beauty and craftsmanship, have not yet migrated to this country in any great numbers; those produced in America still dominate the buy/sell market.

Thermometer collectors who might be interested in forming a club are welcome to contact Warren D. Harris, who is listed in the Directory under 'California'.

A Heiligman, rosewood back, wht emb scale, mercury, 10x1⅜″..37.00
AB Co, pot metal Greek child, brass scale, permacolor, 4½″....35.00
Alexander, folding; Fahrenheit & Reamur scales, mercury, 1850s.54.00
American Thermometer, outdoor; steel & porcelain, mercury..25.00
Bargess Reversible Box, brass scale, oak case, mercury, 5½″...35.00
Bradley & Hubbard, bronze Colonial figure/scale, mercury, 11″..30.00
Bradley & Hubbard, engraved gold plate on iron, mercury, 15″..60.00
Bradley & Hubbard, iron w/gold plate, non-engraved back, 15″.450.00
Bradley & Hubbard, scroll back, steel/cardboard, mercury, 8″..850.00
Brannan, brass case, F&C stainless scales, mercury, 1932......38.00
Brown & Bigelow, desk; 'The Poker Fleet', 3x4″ ped, dial.....125.00
Bubkes, oversize brass scale, -40 to 120, bl spirit, MIG, 2x7″....40.00
C Wilder Co, bear & billboard figural brass, mercury, 6½″......45.00
C Wilder Co, Buffalo Incubator Co, mercury, hanging model....85.00

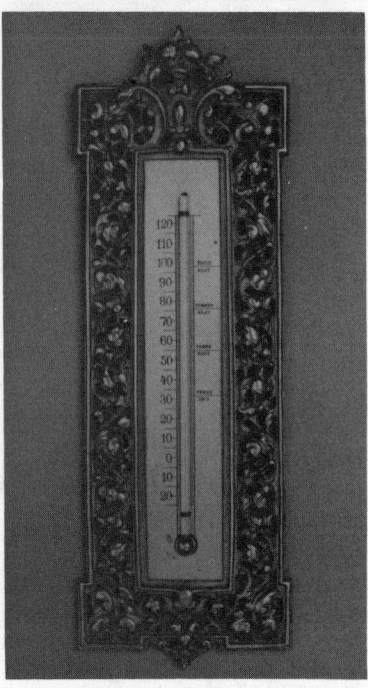

Bradley & Hubbard, engraved gold plate on iron, mercury, 15″, $60.00.

CE Large, The Modern Thermometer, kitchen; tin, permacolor.150.00
Chester, desk; stainless scale, sterling bezel, mercury, 2x6″.....95.00
Cloister, inkwell, stainless back & base w/side angels, 1901...1,050.00
Compton, silverplate flowers/butterflies, on ped, mercury, 4½″...24.00
CTT, cottage barometer, brass plate, bl spirit, 1¾x5″.........38.00
Dr Forbes, bath; wood w/glass tube, paper scale, 10″.........20.00
E Berman Co, desk; brass/filigree/top scroll work, mercury, 8″...75.00
Freeborn, desk; bronze w/lead decor/brass scale, mercury, 8″....39.00
G Barnes, oak fold-out box, plastic scale, mercury, 2½″.......400.00
G Cooper, desk; bell shape w/cupola, sterling, dial, 2x3″.......40.00
Golub, hanging; mahog/brass bulb cap/lg scale/red spirit, 9x2″...50.00
H Lauramark, hanging; gold stipple on boxwood, 0-120, mercury.60.00
Health, wht metal w/blk oxidize, permacolor, #T5106S, 5″......15.00
Helmut, desk; scroll edge, stainless & plastic, easel ped, 6″.....30.00
Hiergelsell Bros, cabinet/oak back, blue liquid, indoor, #159....40.00
Hiergelsell Bros, cabinet/oak back, blue liquid, outdoor, #159...35.00
Hiergelsell Bros, cold storage, tin case, permacolor, #147.......15.00
Hiergelsell Bros, self-registering, magnet, permacolor, #153....150.00
Hiergelsell Bros, spiral tube cabinet, red liquid, #160..........70.00
Hohmann Maurer Co, steel F&C scales & back, mercury, 12″...27.00
Hygro Autometer, 2 magnifying tubes w/stand, mercury, #T5558.45.00
Jedseth Ltd, desk; Mercury figure w/base filigree, mercury, 7″...80.00
LC Tower, Weather Prognosticator, cherry/brass scale, mercury..18.00
Moeller Instrument Co, metal w/brass scale, permacolor, 12″....20.00
Negretti & Zambra, desk; wht bakelite/mahog, blk spirit, 8x3½″.68.00
Orchard, iron case, brass face, w/glass intact, 14″.............25.00
Pace Mfg Co, cottage barometer, storm glass, permacolor, 8½″..25.00
Pahrenheit, indoor, oak w/brass scale, permacolor, 1889, 7″....45.00
R&G, Battleax, 4″ stainless scale, mercury, 1904, 18″.........550.00
S Mitzutani, alabaster ped, top candle figural, mercury, 15″....120.00
Samuel Sloan & Co, boiler, blk steel Deco top, permacolor....650.00
Souche, desk; alabaster ped, paper scale inset, mercury, 8x2½″..75.00
Standard Co, hanging; ivory scale, flower pattern, mercury, 9″..25.00
Standard Co, hanging; rnd, brass rim, -40 to 150, dial........35.00
Taylor, Comfortmeter, brass scale on gr back, permacolor, 7″..23.00
Taylor, hanging; pnt wood, red spirit, 6x24″................20.00
Tiffany, stainless, bevelled serving tray, mercury, 6″..........790.00
Tycos, maxi/minimum, japanned tin/brass, mercury, #T5452, 8″..25.00
Vogue, desk; gr pot metal, Deco curved top, dial, 6x3″........18.00
V3, hanging; brass clip, spiral tube, mercury, 1913, 3x3″......45.00

Threaded Glass

Threaded glass has been made both here and abroad since the 1870s. The procedure was done entirely by hand until about 1876 when a machine was developed to apply the fine threads to the glass automatically.

Cruet, liqueur; lime gr to clear, melon rib, pewter mts, 9″.....100.00
Decanter, 6 wines, 13″ tray; cranberry, blown, pewter top.....650.00
Finger bowl, cranberry w/gold threading around ruffled rim.....75.00
Sweetmeat jar, allover gr & bl random threads, SP lid/bail, 4″..245.00

Pitcher, rubena glass, 8½″, $300.00.

Tiffany

Louis Comfort Tiffany was born in 1848, to Charles Lewis and Harriet Young Tiffany of New York. By the time he was eighteen, his father's small dry goods and stationery store had grown and developed into the world reknowned Tiffany and Company.

Preferring the study of art to joining his father in the family business, Louis spent the next six years under the tutelage of noted artists. He returned to America in 1870, and until 1875 painted canvases that focused on European and North African scenes. Deciding the more lucrative approach was in the application of industrial arts and crafts, he opened a decorating studio called Louis C. Tiffany and Co., Associated Artists. He began seriously experimenting with glass, and eschewing traditionally painted-on details, he instead learned to produce glass with qualities that could suggest natural textures and effects. His experiments broadened and he soon concentrated his efforts on vases, bowls, etc., that came to be considered the highest achievements of the art. Peacock feathers, leaves and vines, flowers and abstracts were developed within the plane of the glass as it was blown. Opalescent and metallic lustres were combined with transparent color to produce stunning effects. Tiffany called his glass Favrile, meaning handmade.

In 1900 he established Tiffany Studios and turned his attention full time to producing art glass, leaded glass lamp shades, and household wares with metal components. He also designed a complete line of jewelry which was sold through his father's store. He became proficiently accomplished in silver work and produced such articles as hand mirrors embellished with peacock feather designs set with gems, and candlesticks with Favrile glass inserts.

Tiffany's work exemplified the Art Nouveau style of design and decoration, and through his own flamboyant personality and business acumen he perpetrated his tastes onto the American market to the extent that his name became a household word. Tiffany Studios continued to prosper until the second decade of this century when due to changing tastes his influence began to diminish. By 1920 the company had closed.

Serial numbers were assigned to much of Tiffany's work, and letter prefixes indicated the year of manufacture: A-N for 1896-1900; P-Z for 1901-1905. After that the letters followed the numbers with A-N in use from 1906-1912; P-Z from 1913-1920. O-marked pieces were made especially for friends or relatives; X indicated pieces not made for sale.

Glassware

Berry set, scroll ft, pale yel w/gold-gr bands, 8" master......1,100.00
Bowl, amber irid, flared, in bronze mt w/enameling, 9½" dia...715.00
Bowl, amber irid, ribbed, 8" dia.........................330.00
Bowl, amber irid, ruffled, sgn/#d, 5" dia, pr...............250.00
Bowl, bl, petal form edge, 8 stem-like ribs, 2½x6".........525.00
Bowl, bl irid, paneled, swirled, 10" dia..................550.00
Bowl, bl irid, swirled, sgn/#d, 7" dia...................495.00
Bowl, floriform, irid gold, dtd, 4¾"....................425.00
Bowl, free-form edge, gold irid, 2½x7"..................385.00
Bowl, gold, wide swirl ribs, sgn, 6¾"...................200.00
Bowl, irid gold w/gr leaves & vines, #1466J, 8" dia.........950.00
Bowl, oyster w/yel feathers, bronze base, 12"..............825.00
Bowl, purple w/peacock bl irid, swirl rib, sgn, 3½x8".......2,850.00
Bowl, yel, #583, 2½x4½"...............................140.00
Bud vase, cylindrical bl stem on bronze base, 9¾".........525.00
Bud vase, gold w/gr vines & ivy, 6½"...................650.00
Bud vase, gr/gold, feathered, mk LCT; gold Dore base mk TS..200.00
Bud vase, trumpet form, opal sides w/amber irid feathers, 10"..385.00
Candlestick, gold lustre, sgn, 7", pr...................750.00
Compote, floriform, amber irid, flared & ruffled, 5½".......470.00
Compote, floriform, bl irid, ruffled, deep on short std, 5"......685.00
Compote, floriform, stretch gold irid, sgn/#d, 4¼x5".........495.00
Compote, gold w/in & ft, 2" gr top edge, 3x5½"............685.00
Compote, gold w/intaglio leaves & vines w/in, scalloped, 6x3"..485.00
Compote, lt bl w/stretched edge, sgn, 2x5½"...............225.00
Compote, opal w/gr feathering, cylinder std, #2924H, 4½".....770.00
Compote, ribbed bl/violet on irid opal ped ft, 3x6½".........295.00
Cordial, gold w/long thin stem, 4½"....................175.00
Decanter, matching stopper, sgn, 10½"..................375.00
Decanter, Victoria pattern, yel irid, 10"...............1,000.00
Finger bowl w/under tray, amber irid, ruffled, 5" dia.........240.00
Goblet, clear yel, hollow stem, sgn....................300.00
Parfait, bl pastel, sgn..............................300.00
Plate, amethyst w/wht ribbing, sgn, 12".................385.00
Punch cup, rose bowl shape, applied hdl, gold w/gr leaves.....295.00
Salt dip, bl irid, ruffled, EX color & shape, sgn............225.00
Salt dip, gold w/pulled hdls, sgn, 1x2".................140.00
Salt dip, paperweight, allover pulled swirls, sgn, 1x1¾".......195.00
Sherbet, gold, spreading hollow ped stem, 3½"............140.00
Sherbet, opal irid ped & stem, irid gold yel at top..........225.00
Tumbler, faceted irid bottom, gold w/platinum bands/swirls, 3"..225.00
Vase, amber irid, dbl gourd, sgn, #1014-1768, 2½".........225.00
Vase, amber irid, free-form w/irregular honeycombing, 7"......550.00
Vase, amber irid w/gr foliage, baluster form, #8257E, 7".....1,100.00
Vase, bl irid, bulging cylinder, ribbed, conical ft, 13".......825.00
Vase, bl irid, gold/gr leaves, #618E, 7½"...............850.00
Vase, bl irid, ribbed, flared/faceted lip, w/in bronze fr, 17"..1,045.00
Vase, bl irid, round top, sq bottom, 4 lg dimples, sgn, 4"....275.00
Vase, bl irid shaded in amber, ribbed expanding cylinder, 9"...470.00
Vase, blk w/band of irid bl waves, R8639, 6½"..........1,540.00
Vase, blk w/dbl row gold hooked pulls, 3¾"............1,275.00
Vase, br w/vertical gold 'stripes', 8x4"................1,760.00

Vase, calyx, gr petals/stalk w/opal panels/irid rim, 13"......1,650.00
Vase, cameo morning-glories, purple/gr on frost, #3072C, 10"..2,300.00
Vase, caramel w/amber irid vertebrae, gourd shape, 8½".....2,640.00
Vase, dk peacock bl, sgn, 4½x5".......................725.00
Vase, floriform, amber irid, knopped std, 10¾"...........575.00
Vase, floriform, amber irid, ruffled/ribbed, short std, 13".....605.00
Vase, floriform, bl, ribbed, sgn, 13½"................1,760.00
Vase, floriform, bl irid, beetle carving, 11"...........2,500.00
Vase, floriform, dk bl irid, ribbed, waisted neck, ftd, 15".....950.00
Vase, floriform, gold, circle ft/ribbed bowl, 12".........1,320.00
Vase, floriform, gold, ped ft, knob stem, scalloped, 7".......575.00
Vase, floriform, gold, ribbed, sgn, 11¼"................950.00
Vase, floriform, gold, ribs, short stem/ped ft, sgn/#d, 3¾"....395.00
Vase, floriform, gold, waisted neck, paneled, 6½"..........825.00
Vase, floriform, gold w/in & ft, wht w/gr pulled leaves, 5x5½"..880.00
Vase, floriform, gr/amber sides w/feathers, ruffled, ftd, 15"...1,045.00
Vase, floriform, irid crimp bowl/gr leaves on gr stem, 14"....1,700.00
Vase, floriform, milky w/lime gr pulled feathers, 11"........1,045.00
Vase, floriform, orange irid, crimped, striated gr leaves, 14"..1,700.00
Vase, floriform, ruffled lip cup in opal, gr feathering, 14"....2,200.00
Vase, floriform, waisted neck/ruffled, opal ribbed sides, 10"...825.00
Vase, floriform, wht to pk/ribbed leaves/petal base, LCT, 11"..2,000.00
Vase, gold, bl hi-lites, chain decor on shoulder, 6".........800.00
Vase, gold, classical, sgn LC Tiffany-Favrile, 10½".........500.00
Vase, gold, ruffle rim/rnd taper body, domed ft, sgn, 4¾"....200.00
Vase, gold, ruffle/stretch rim, 4 pulled ft, sgn, 4".........550.00
Vase, gold w/applied feathers, straight sides, sgn, 12x4".....595.00
Vase, gr hooked feathers on gold, deep ruffles, 3½".........575.00
Vase, gr irid vines twist around wide gold body, sm neck, 6"...775.00
Vase, gr w/gold pulls at base & neck, opal collar, 4¼".....1,175.00
Vase, leaves on irid wht, pineapple base, bronze mt, 11".....795.00
Vase, lt bl to violet irid, yel trails, dimpled, K795, 4".......575.00
Vase, mc glass enamel over metal, sterling base sgn, 7".....1,000.00
Vase, opal w/gold chain decor, sgn, 9"................1,870.00
Vase, orchid pattern cut crystal, silver floral rim, 1890, 12"..900.00
Vase, paperweight, yel florals at top, pulled leaves, 10¾"...3,960.00
Vase, purple morning-glories/gr foliage on frost, cameo, 10"..2,300.00
Vase, Solefleur, wht leaf spears w/irid, bronze base, 13".....600.00
Vase, trumpet form, clear w/opal optic rib, aqua irid top, 10"..440.00
Vase, trumpet form, dk bl, sgn, 15"..................1,430.00
Vase, trumpet form, gold, sgn, 7x2½".................435.00
Vase, trumpet form, gold w/decor, sgn, 12¼"...........1,210.00
Wine, gold irid, engraved grapes/vine, hollow stem, sgn, 3½"..155.00
Wine, gold w/intaglio cherries/leaves, sgn.............345.00
Wine, long stem, bl pastel, sgn......................300.00

Jewelry

Pin, 18k gold & diamond butterfly.....................650.00
Pin, 18k gold maple leaf............................140.00
Ring, dinner; Art Deco, platinum w/3 diamonds, sgn.........650.00
Sweater clip, heart shaped, pr........................25.00

Lamps

Base, baluster amber irid w/gr trailing vines, bronze mts, 15"..660.00
Base, oil; pierced Islamic-inspired gr opal glass, 17".......2,200.00
Base, oil; spherical, amber irid/purple scrolls/lappets, 10"....440.00
Base, opal gr glass w/bl irid feathers, gilt mts, 20".........600.00
Base, 6 sockets, std adjusts, leaf mold base, 6 ft, 29".....1,980.00
Bridge, cased irid bl/gr ribbonwork on tripod base, 55".....2,200.00
Bridge, cased shade w/concentric waves, pendant shade......2,310.00
Bridge, counter balance, shade w/medial motif, 52".........2,200.00
Candle, amber irid flared shade, silvered metal std, 15".....650.00

Dragonfly shade on peacock base, signed Tiffany Studios, New York, 24" high, 20½" diameter, $14,000.00.

Candle, amber irid ruffled/quilted shade, 10½"..............770.00
Candle, floriform, red/bl irid ruffled/stretched 5½" shade.....1,050.00
Candle, gold irid glass base, 2 pt dome shade apricot/filigree..1,225.00
Candle, swirl rib base, stretched & ruffled shade, sgn, 13".....750.00
Candle, 2 floriform shades; tri-ftd base, w/snuffer, #174......1,350.00
Ceiling, circular bronze mt hung w/amber prisms/chains, 14".3,080.00
Ceiling, turtle-bk tiles over dome, 6 pendant lilies, 17" dia...3,630.00
Ceiling, turtle-bk tiles/stained glass & bronze fr.............1,900.00
Chandelier, brickwork/turtle-bk tile border; strap cap, 22"....5,775.00
Chandelier, gr glass tile panels, lower drop border, 24" dia...7,150.00
Chandelier, ldgl 12" brickwork/turtle-bk tiles; strapwork cap.6,050.00
Chandelier, ldgl 18" deep dome w/3 rows red turtle-bk tiles.25,000.00
Chandelier, ldgl 28" autumn leaf band, shallow dome........1,980.00
Desk, caramel on wht, silvery striations; harp std, petal base..1,650.00
Desk, cased gr shade w/amber irid damascening; 3 arm support.990.00
Desk, geometric border shade; panel base, flared ft, 18½".....605.00
Desk, gilt base in Zodiac set w/amber turtle-bk tiles/plaque...1,100.00
Desk, gr wave 7" shade on bell form frame, sgn, #418, 12"..1,300.00
Desk, oval dome, 2 turtle-bk tiles; base w/16 irid stones, 15".4,500.00
Floor, counter balance, 10" shade gold/br swirl w/bl irid, 55".3,800.00
Floor, ldgl 24½" geometric panels; leaf mold base, 4 ft.....13,200.00
Globe, ldgl, spherical w/central butterfly band, 13½", pr.....2,200.00
Lily, 3 amber irid shades on scrolled stems, 13"............1,980.00
Lily, 7-lite, amber floriform shades, sgn, 1 w/minor crack.....4,400.00
Shade, ldgl, panels of gr tiles, medial band, acorns, 16".....1,980.00
Shade, stalactite inverted teardop in amber irid/feathered, 4..2,200.00
Student, brass overlay shades, twisted wire decor...........2,000.00
Table, cased irid gr/wht w/bl ribbonwork; C-scroll std, 12"....2,090.00
Table, gr/gold shade; gold swirl base/opal std w/gr flame, 17".1,850.00
Table, ldgl, Fleur-de-Lis, bulbous base, all orig, M.........5,700.00
Table, ldgl 12" apple blossom shade; base imp 28639, 18"...4,950.00
Table, ldgl 14" brickwork shade; decorated Grueby base, 6"..2,200.00
Table, ldgl 16" acorn shade; brass bullet body w/4 legs, 21"..5,900.00
Table, ldgl 16" apple blossom shade; Grueby base, 18"......5,500.00
Table, ldgl 16" Black-Eyed Susan; tree trunk base, 21"......7,000.00
Table, ldgl 16" crocus shade; ovoid base w/4 legs/sq ft, 21".7,150.00
Table, ldgl 16" ivy leaves/brickwork; quatraped base, 26"....2,640.00

Table, ldgl 16" tulip; bronze base, scrollwork, 4 pad ft, 21"..5,100.00
Table, ldgl 16" w/band of circles, amphora base w/3 supports.2,800.00
Table, ldgl 17" dragonfly shade; base #394, 22½"........10,450.00
Table, ldgl 20" acorn shade; base w/4 leaf form ft, 27".....6,875.00
Table, ldgl 20" daffodil #1497 shade; base #667, 24"......9,000.00
Table, ldgl 20" daffodil; bronze std #532, 27".........7,000.00
Table, ldgl 22" peony; bronze openwork; 4 ft, #7342, 26½"..2,800.00
Table, ldgl 22" 9 dragonfly; 4 part std w/paw ft #391, 29"..50,000.00
Table, ldgl 24" sunflower shade; bronze base, 29".........3,100.00
Table, ldgl 24" wisteria; bronze tree trunk base, unsgn, 29"..2,400.00
Table, 18" paneled amber linenfold glass; geometric std, 25".3,000.00
Table, 4 lily, 3 inverted/1 up, gold lustre, all sgn, 20"......5,000.00

Metal Work

Bill spindle, Grapevine pattern, silvered bronze & wht glass....130.00
Blotter, rocker; American Indian, copper finish, #1191.......200.00
Blotter corners, Zodiac pattern, set..................150.00
Bookends, bronze w/gold finish, bl center medallion, #2028, pr.150.00
Bookends, emb horse's head, pr......................200.00
Bookends, gold dore, #1614, pr......................450.00
Box, copper, sgn Tiffany Studio, NY, #1114..............125.00
Candelabra, bronze 4 finger std w/4 pulled feather socles, pr..2,100.00
Candlestick, bronze, dbl, #1230......................795.00
Card receiver, gold dore, bl enamel, sgn, #413, 8" dia........225.00
Clock, gilt bronze boy balances on ball w/clock face, 17"......550.00
Desk set, Adams, 7 pc, all sgn.......................750.00
Desk set, Modeled Design pattern, sgn/#d, 5 pc.............715.00
Desk set, Zodiac pattern, gilt bronze, 9 pc................935.00
Dish, dore bronze, abstract border design, #1707, 9" dia......80.00
Dish, dore bronze, Oriental border, center monogram, sgn, 9"...75.00
Dish, lacquered brass w/allover acid etching, MOP discs, 9"....525.00
Dressing table set, 18k gold, engine turned reeding, 10 pc....4,730.00
Frame, Chinese pattern, sgn, 8½x7¼"...................300.00
Frame, Grapevine, gold/wht/caramel glass, 12x14"...........425.00
Inkwell, abalone shell discs on body, sgn, 3½x3½"..........150.00
Inkwell, Bookmark pattern, dore bronze, octagonal...........400.00
Inkwell, bronze, hinged lid, #864, sgn...................315.00
Inkwell, Chinese, double.........................325.00
Inkwell, Chinese, pyramid, lg......................450.00
Inkwell, Modeled pattern, w/pen tray, Tiffany patina.........250.00
Inkwell, ovoid, gr glass 'jade cabs' w/in bronze fr, sgn, 3¾"....575.00
Letter opener, Zodiac...........................135.00
Magnifying glass, 19th century, #1619.................220.00
Paper clip tray, Zodiac, 3x4"......................75.00
Paperweight, bronze tiger........................350.00
Paperweight, cat playing w/ball figural, bronze, sgn..........225.00

Inkwell, green glass blown into bronze frame, resembling jade cabachons, signed Tiffany Studios, New York, 3¾", $575.00.

Pen tray, Bookmark pattern, #1055, gold finish.............150.00
Pen tray, Pine Needles, #1004, 9¾" L....................110.00
Pen tray, Zodiac pattern, br finish.......................125.00
Plate, bronze w/red enamel border, floral/leaf, #1612, 10"....175.00
Plate, gold dore on bronze, #1749, 7¾"..................100.00
Stamp box, American Indian pattern, br finish, #1184........225.00
Stamp box, Zodiac...................................200.00

Pottery

Bowl, leaves & ferns in relief, ivory glaze, w/lid, 3½x6".......475.00
Teapot, floriform, bud hdl, gr semi-gloss...................380.00
Vase, bl/purple crystals/incised bands/wide body/3 hdls, 9"....450.00
Vase, mossy gr & br, red w/in, ovoid, 6"................1,700.00

Silver

Bottle cap..15.00
Bowl, centerpiece, ped base, emb flowers/leaves, 12" dia......825.00
Bowl, dessert; retic scalloped rim chased w/strawberries, 15"..2,300.00
Bowl, openwork, ca 1920, 13" dia.....................1,200.00
Bowl, ornate berry border, shallow 6"....................100.00
Charger, scalloped, bead & shell motif, 12" dia.............320.00
Coffee service, wavy flutes/harp hdls, ivory supports, 5 pc....3,960.00
Compote, Chrysanthemum, engraved, 9" dia, pr...........2,200.00
Compote, part openwork scrolls/shells, 3 foliate ft, 10".......500.00
Demitasse spoon, Olympian pattern, w/serving spoon, 13 pc....660.00
Dessert set, parcel gilt, Grapevine pattern, 15 pc, 20 oz......1,760.00
Entree dish, Chrysanthemum, oval, 10", pr..............1,870.00
Ewer, putti frolic w/in vines, figural atop hdl, 21"..........4,600.00
Fork & spoon, ea w/tapered hdl w/lady's profile medallion.....190.00
Ladle, Chrysanthemum pattern...........................90.00
Nutpicks, Chrysanthemum pattern, ca 1890, 11 oz, set of 12...495.00
Oil can, sterling, Tiffany & Co, 4"........................175.00
Pencil, telescopic lead, w/mono, ring for chain, 4½".........75.00
Perfume bottle on keychain, sterling, 3½" L...............125.00
Porringer, tab hdl w/pierced Deco decor, 4½" dia..........130.00
Salad set, Grapevine, parcel gilt, 2 pc...................495.00
Tablespoon, Beekman..................................55.00
Tazza, openwork rims w/cloverleaf, trumpet base, 7½", pr.....715.00
Tea/coffee service w/28" tray; molded flowers, 8 pc.........6,000.00
Vase, sq baluster/beaded sq base, quilted/applied leaves, 10"...495.00

Miscellaneous

Eye shade, ldgl & bronze dragonfly form, 10" L.............1,540.00
Window, ldgl, brook/trees/grass, in fr, losses/damage, 53x16".6,050.00
Window, ldgl, purple wisteria/br vines on yel, 15x40", G.....1,100.00

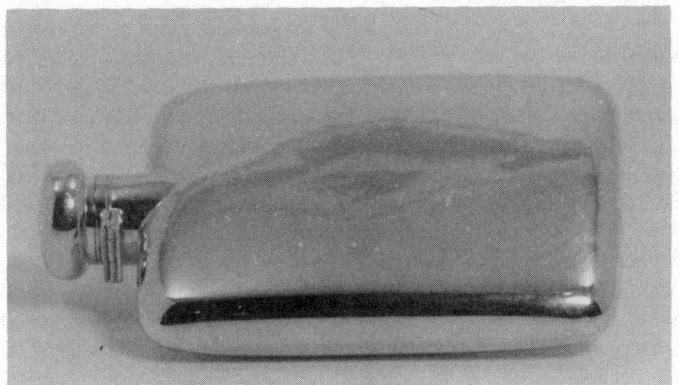

Flask, hinged lid, 18k gold, ca 1900, signed, 4", $2,000.00.

Tiffin Glass

The Tiffin Glass Company was founded in 1887 in Tiffin, Ohio, one of the many factories composing the U.S. Glass Company. Its early wares consisted of tablewares and decorative items such as lamps and globes. Among the most popular of all Tiffin products was the black satin glass produced there during the 1940s. In 1959 U.S. Glass was sold, and in 1962 the factories were closed. The plant was re-opened in 1963 as the Tiffin Art Glass Company. Products from this period were tableware, hand blown stemware, and other decorative items.

Basket, black satin, 11"................................50.00
Bell, goblet, Cherokee Rose.............................25.00
Bowl, centerpiece, June, topaz, 11".......................50.00
Bowl, rolled-in rim, burnt orange, 2x6½"..................65.00
Bowl, Velva, blue satin, open lace edge....................20.00
Candlestick, June, topaz, 3½"..........................22.50
Champagne, #024, pink, 6¼".............................16.00
Champagne, Cadena, yellow, 6½"........................27.00
Champagne, Cherokee Rose, reeded stem.................16.00
Champagne, June Night.................................13.00
Claret, Cherokee Rose, 6¼".............................16.00
Cocktail, Athlone......................................13.50
Cocktail, Cherokee....................................15.00
Cocktail, Flying Nun, green stem, crystal bowl..............22.00
Cocktail, Rosalind, topaz...............................17.50
Console set, blue satin, 9" bowl, 9½" rope candlesticks.......85.00
Creamer & sugar, Cherokee Rose........................39.00
Creamer & sugar, Sylvan, green.........................35.00
Finger bowl & under plate, June Night....................22.00
Goblet, champagne; Argenta.............................10.00
Goblet, champagne; Canterbury, pink or amber.............12.50
Goblet, champagne; Midnight Mood......................12.50
Goblet, water; #024, pink, 8¼"..........................19.00
Goblet, water; Cherokee Rose, reeded stem, 8¼"...........19.00
Goblet, water; Flanders, yellow..........................22.00
Goblet, water; Fontaine, blue............................20.00
Goblet, water; June Night...............................20.00
Goblet, wine; #024, pink, 6"............................22.00
Goblet, wine; June Night................................22.00
Goblet, wine; Midnight Mood............................15.00
Iced tea, Cherokee Rose, #17399........................18.00
Iced tea, Le Fleur, 6".................................24.00
Juice, Athlone.......................................10.50
Juice, June Night.....................................12.00
Liqueur, Athlone......................................13.50
Parfait, June Night....................................20.00
Pitcher, Tea Rose, silver trim, ice lip, 80 oz...............70.00
Plate, Flanders, crystal, 8"..............................11.00
Plate, June Night, 8"..................................15.00
Plate, Le Fleur, 7½"....................................5.00
Relish, Cherokee Rose, 3 part, 12½".....................45.00
Relish, Cherokee Rose, 3 part, 6½"......................25.00
Rose bowl, clear.....................................38.00
Sherbet, Cherokee Rose, low...........................12.00
Sherbet, June Night...................................15.00
Sundae, Cordelia, Mandarin & Cream, #067................8.00
Sundae, Flanders, pink.................................15.00
Swan, plum...45.00
Tumbler, Athlone, iced tea.............................17.50
Tumbler, Cordelia, Mandarin & Cream, 8 oz, #067.........10.00
Tumbler, Dancing Girl, ftd, pink, 5"......................10.00
Tumbler, Fuchsia, ftd, crystal, 6½"......................12.00
Vase, black satin, #16261, Tiffin sticker, 8½".............40.00

Tiles

Though originally strictly functional, tiles were being produced in various colors and used as architectural highlights as early as the Ancient Roman Empire. By the 18th century, Dutch tiles were decorated with polychrome landscapes and figures. During the 19th century, there were over a hundred companies in England involved in the manufacture of tile. By the Victorian era, the use of decorative tiles had reached its peak. Special souvenir editions, compaign and portrait tiles, and Art Nouveau motifs with lovely ladies and stylized examples from nature were popular. Today, all of these are very collectible.

Alice Cranston Fenner, w/title & #, dtd 1949, 8″ sq, pr........45.00
BFAT Co, Beaver Falls, PA; Sensation, br head of dog, 6½″...75.00
Calendar, 1895, Wedgwood for Jones McDuffie..............75.00
Calendar, 1908, Wedgwood for Jones McDuffie..............65.00
Calendar, 1922, Wedgwood for Jones McDuffie..............62.50
Low, cherubs w/banner in relief, Nouveau, 6x18″, set of 3.....180.00
Low, floral, br to amber, 7x7¾″..........................65.00
Low, gr floral, Nouveau, 6x6″.............................40.00
Low, lady w/turban, Nouveau, gr glaze, artist sgn.............120.00
Low, Olympia, dtd 1881, in fr, 12½x12½″..................140.00
Low, sunflower, br glaze, 4x4″............................25.00
Low, 2 figures w/pipes, dk gr, sgn Arthur Osborne, 6x11½″...395.00
Low, 4 Seasons, bl/gr gloss, sgn, 5½x7¼″, set of 4.........425.00
Minton, beige & br florals................................30.00
Providential, raspberries, 6x6″..........................20.00
Stoke-On-Trent, pr cherubs frolicking in reeds, turq, 8¼″ sq...95.00
Trent Art, gargoyle w/wings, br glaze, 9¼x6¼″.............75.00
Trent Art, stylized florals, 6x6″.........................20.00
US Encaustic, Indianaplis, IN, lady w/fire wood; King Lear, pr...75.00
W Yale, HP mc landscapes, continuous pr, 1800s, 6x12″......150.00
Wheeling, dk bl w/slip Masonic emblems, sgn XMX FU 24, 6″...55.00
Woman's portrait, Nouveau, artist sgn MLM, ca 1905, 3½″....300.00

Tinware

In the American household of the 17th and 18th centuries, tinware items could be found in abundance, from food containers to footwarmers and mirror frames. Although the first settlers brought much of their tinware with them from Europe, by 1798 sheets of tin plate were being imported from England for use by the growing number of American tinsmiths.

Tinwares were often decorated, either by piercing or painted designs, which were both free-hand and stenciled. (See Toleware) By the early 1900s, many homes had replaced their old tinware with the more attractive aluminum and graniteware.

Baking pan, heart shaped, 3½x9x11½″...................65.00
Box, candle, w/3″ hangers, 13½x5″.....................220.00
Box, lift top, orig gr w/blk border, 9¾x5⅛″, EX..........85.00
Box, pantry; oval, orig dk br pnt, 4⅛x5½″................295.00
Bucket, w/lid & wire hdl, 6x7½″ dia......................15.00
Bucket, wire hdl, 4x5″..................................12.50
Candlestick, heavy tin, drip plate, applied figure hdl, 1830......85.00
Coffee pot, broad body, 8″..............................35.00
Coffee pot, side spout, 12″.............................45.00
Comb case, emb w/diamond mirror & 2 pockets, pnt, 7¾x7″....25.00
Cookie cutter, bear, 4¾″................................28.00
Cookie cutter, bear cub, 3¼″............................25.00
Cookie cutter, bird, flying, 3″.........................17.50
Cookie cutter, bird w/crimped wings & tail, 5″...........70.00
Cookie cutter, bird w/large tail, 4¾″...................35.00
Cookie cutter, boot, 3¼″................................22.50

Candleholder, porcelain insert, signed Perry and Son, 5″ x 9″ long, $78.00.

Cookie cutter, church steeple, 5″.......................35.00
Cookie cutter, cross w/crimped edges, 4½″................15.00
Cookie cutter, deer, good stylized form, 5x5½″...........245.00
Cookie cutter, dog, 4″..................................30.00
Cookie cutter, duck, 2¾″................................40.00
Cookie cutter, Dutch woman, 5¼″.........................20.00
Cookie cutter, Dutchman, 5″.............................20.00
Cookie cutter, eagle, simple & primitive, 4″............35.00
Cookie cutter, eagle w/spread wings, 4½″................32.50
Cookie cutter, fireman, good stylized detail, 6¼″.......450.00
Cookie cutter, fish, 4½″................................17.50
Cookie cutter, gingerbread man, handmade, heavy, 9x5x1¼″....65.00
Cookie cutter, hobby horse, 5¼″.........................35.00
Cookie cutter, horse, straight base, 5¾″ L..............50.00
Cookie cutter, horse, stylized form, 7x10″..............75.00
Cookie cutter, lion, 4″.................................12.50
Cookie cutter, man in top hat on horseback..............260.00
Cookie cutter, moon & star, 2¾″ dia.....................20.00
Cookie cutter, pig w/long snout, 5″.....................75.00
Cookie cutter, pitcher, 3¾″.............................80.00
Cookie cutter, pony, 4¾″................................77.50
Cookie cutter, rooster, good detail, 4″.................55.00
Cookie cutter, Vict lady/feathered hat; man, tail coat, 7½″.....80.00
Cookie cutter, whale, 3¾″...............................25.00
Cookie cutter, woman, stylized form, 4¼″................17.50
Creamer, pewter hdl & rim, 3¼″..........................32.00
Lamp, betty; dbl burners, open font, cylinder stem, 6½″......75.00
Lamp, cone base, cylinder stem w/hdl, tube wick support, 5½″.115.00
Lamp, conical base w/wire stem/candle arm w/2 sockets, 15″...135.00
Lighting shelf, hanging, scalloped reflector, rpr, damage, 10″....35.00
Lighting shelf w/3 candle sockets & betty lamp bar hanger......45.00
Nutmeg grater, wood hdl, 5¼″............................35.00
Sconce, crimped pan, sunburst ribbed reflector, 9x10″.......215.00
Sconce, ribbed reflector, half circle crimp crests, 12″, pr......300.00
Sconce, round reflector back, 7¾″, pr...................170.00
Sconce, shield shaped w/oval reflector, scrolled arms, 15″, pr...250.00
Sieve, cottage cheese, heart shape, 4½x6″...............95.00
Spittoon, japanned, dk red, 4x7½″.......................50.00
Toy, pump, orig bl pnt w/blk transfers, minor dents, 5″........65.00
Tray, coffin shaped, red/mustard sponge decor, 12½x18″......195.00
Wash tub, japanned, hdls ea side, 6½x17″................65.00

Tobacciana

Tobacciana is the generally accepted term used to cover that field of collecting that includes smoking pipes, cigar molds, cigarette lighters, humidors -- in short, any article having to do with the practice of using tobacco in any form.

Tobacco tin-tags, strips of metal attached to a plug of tobacco for means of brand identification, are becoming popular collectibles, especially those featuring animals or political and patriotic themes. It is estimated that over 12,000 brands were produced.

Perhaps the most valuable variety of pipes is the Meerschaum -- hand carved from a clay-like medium formed by the action of the water on disintegrating seashells on the ocean floor. These figural bowls often portray an elaborately carved mythological character, an animal, or a historical scene. Amber is often used for the stem. Other collectible pipes are corncob (Missouri Meerschaum) and Indian peace pipes of clay or catlinite. (See American Indian Artifacts.)

Chosen because it was the Indians who first introduced the white man to smoking, the cigar store Indian was a symbol used to identify tobacco stores in the 19th century. The majority of them were hand carved between 1830 and 1900, and are today recognized as some of the finest examples of early wood sculptures. When found, they command very high prices.

Ash tray, bronze elephant head...........................35.00
Box, brass, engraved decor, Dutch, early 1800s, 6" L........130.00
Box, cigar; Cheroots, Black man's face w/in & w/out..........40.00
Case, cigarette; sterling, engraved, 4½ oz..................85.00
Cigar box opener, Dolly Madison.............................25.00
Cigar box opener/bottle opener, El Dallo....................28.00
Cigar clipper, Equity 5¢ Cigars, 1 ea side of ad...........200.00
Cigar clipper, Havana Cigars, clockwork, mfg Brunhoff.......225.00
Cigar clipper, New Currency, Ft Pitt/steamship, glass/wood/CI...135.00
Cigar clipper/match dispenser, Yankee, automatic, VG........325.00
Cigar holder, carved rosewood, figural thistle..............20.00
Cigar holder, meerschaum, amber stem, orig case.............18.00
Cigar holder, meerschaum, carved horse atop, lion on bowl...75.00
Cigar holder, wood, corncob carving..........................9.00
Cigar press, CI, EX detail w/leafy base, dog on hdl, 9½"....30.00
Cigar store Indian, elaborate feathers, late 1800s, 6 ft....9,500.00
Cigarette card, camera shape w/pretty lady, 2"..............22.00
Cigarette felt, Egyptienne Straights, w/rabbit..............10.00
Cigarette holder, Fatima, advertising......................50.00
Cigarette holder, ivory, carved eagle's claw...............35.00
Cigarette holder, ivory, carved rose band..................20.00
Cigarette silk, animal w/flag of its country................2.00
Cigarette silk, baseball, 2x3".............................10.00
Cigarette silk, flags of the world..........................2.00
Cigarette silk, Indian Chief...............................20.00
Cigarette silk, Queens......................................5.00
Cigarette silk, Syracuse University, sportsman, 3½x5½".......3.00
Cutter, cigar, counter; Betsy Ross, 5¢, CI, orig picture...385.00
Cutter, cigar, counter; Boston Trader.....................185.00
Cutter, cigar, counter; pig, Great Ohio 5¢ Cigar, CI......425.00
Cutter, cigar, desk; bone hdl, 4½".........................70.00
Cutter, cigar, desk; ivory w/engraved monkeys, 4½"........220.00
Cutter, cigar, desk; stag w/sterling ornament, 5".........70.00
Cutter, cigar, desk; sterling, bear relief cutter both ends...80.00
Cutter, cigar, desk; sterling, monogram, cutter both ends, 5½"...110.00
Cutter, cigar, pocket; arrowhead, silver & enamel.........135.00
Cutter, cigar, pocket; ballerina, scissor action..........75.00
Cutter, cigar, pocket; base w/bell & ring, gold filled, 1½"...28.00
Cutter, cigar, pocket; bottle w/advertising, brass.........65.00
Cutter, cigar, pocket; brass oval disc w/cutter in center...25.00
Cutter, cigar, pocket; bullet, brass & sterling............50.00

Cutter, cigar, pocket; girl on potty, brass................85.00
Cutter, cigar, pocket; guillotine, sterling, dtd 12/9/02...34.00
Cutter, cigar, pocket; helmet w/chain, brass..............225.00
Cutter, cigar, pocket; horseshoe, silver/brass, scissor action...85.00
Cutter, cigar, pocket; jester, SP, scissor action.........185.00
Cutter, cigar, pocket; Liberty coin........................45.00
Cutter, cigar, pocket; loving cup, sterling, inscribed, blk case...275.00
Cutter, cigar, pocket; man w/moving arms, chrome...........85.00
Cutter, cigar, pocket; poodle, brass......................175.00
Cutter, cigar, pocket; revolver, brass, w/blk onyx hdl, 3½"...160.00
Cutter, cigar, pocket; round box, SP, relief design........40.00
Cutter, cigar, pocket; scissors w/etching, silver..........29.00
Cutter, cigar, pocket; slipper, 14k gold..................225.00
Cutter, cigar, pocket; trick lock w/advertising............35.00
Cutter, cigar, pocket; violin case, brass.................160.00
Cutter, cigar, table, Dachshund, rocking blade, CI.........58.00
Cutter, cigar, table; brass 6" bird in ash tray, dtd 1920...85.00
Cutter, cigar, table; bulldog bust in coat/hat/vest, metal, 6"...560.00
Cutter, cigar, table; cat in dish, metal, 6x5"............110.00
Cutter, cigar, table; dog, brass, 7½x3½".................110.00
Cutter, cigar, table; dog w/top hat in mouth, metal, 11x3½"...115.00
Cutter, cigar, table; elephant, metal, w/match holder......60.00
Cutter, cigar, table; man squats over pot, pewter, 5".....465.00
Cutter, cigar, table; mariner's wheel, brass & wood, 6½"...110.00
Cutter, cigar, table; rowboat/chair/jug, sterling, 8x2".....11.00
Cutter, cigar; Gentleman's Preference, El Santo, w/glass base...105.00
Cutter, tobacco; battle axe...............................210.00
Cutter, tobacco; Enterprise, Pat 1885......................38.00
Cutter, tobacco; Enterprise #6............................125.00
Cutter, tobacco; Good Cheer, Good Luck, Call Again........125.00
Cutter, tobacco; imp......................................150.00
Cutter, tobacco; little boy thumbing nose..................85.00
Cutter, tobacco; Lorillard's, w/tin tag....................75.00
Cutter, tobacco; Prize, S Lee, cutter/corkpress/nutcracker...95.00
Cutter, tobacco; Spearhead, CI, PJ Sorg, 16x5x4½".........105.00
Cutter, tobacco; Star, Save the Tags.......................75.00
Cutter, tobacco; Wilson & McCallay, crank operated........225.00
Cutter, tobacco; wood block/steel blade, 7½x12"...........50.00
Cutter, tobacco; Yankee #0.................................36.00
Dispenser, cigarette; Art Deco, pigskin/plastic, Rolinx.....30.00
Dispenser, cigarette; elephant, blk, CI, 5½x9"............60.00
Dispenser, cigarette; mule, crank ear to release...........17.50
Display, CI Grecian figure w/pronged plate for cigars, pat '60...75.00
Humidor, barrel, lid w/3" bust of Black boy in cap/shirt/tie...170.00
Humidor, Briar Root Smoking Tobacco, majolica, gr, 7x6½"...70.00
Humidor, golfer w/knickers on lid, Wilcox SP, 9¾".........225.00
Humidor, lady w/turban, pottery, sgn BR/#d, 5¾"...........110.00
Humidor, LaPalina Senators, brass..........................48.00
Humidor, mandarin, papier mache figural, sgn...............60.00
Humidor, pig smoking pipe figural..........................65.00
Humidor, pipe figural, Deco flowers, majolica..............65.00
Humidor, rabbit w/gr head in bl overcoat, Germany, 5"......60.00
Humidor, skull on book, mc cap, Germany, 4½"..............60.00
Humidor, standing man figural, visor cap, vest, Germany, 5½"...80.00
Humidor, top hat, head of grotesque animal, rat, hoof, Austria...80.00
Humidor, 2 dogs on bl & br, pnt glass, sgn Bavry, Handel lid...350.00
Lighter, cigar; figural man w/Masonic hat, 1929............65.00
Lighter, cigar; Midland Jump Spark, oak base..............175.00
Lighter, cigar; Victorian lady, 2 lighters, cobalt bl globe...425.00
Lighter, cigarette; musical, Nestles, in box...............40.00
Lighter, cigarette; pot bellied stove, USA.................14.00
Lighter, cigarette; sterling, Nouveau styling, Zippo.......58.00
Lighter, cigarette; w/ash tray, Spirit of St Louis, CI.....65.00
Lighter, copper & chrome globe on stand, Art Deco, 5".......35.00

Cigar cutter, counter top, advertising Peter Schuyler Cigars, 7½" tall, $185.00.

Lighter, Elgin American, antelope decor on case, orig box......25.00
Lighter, fire extinguisher, engraved shield/frame, Bowers.......12.00
Lighter, Happy Joe, lights from top of hat, 1931..............60.00
Lighter, man w/branding iron, Conoco ad, Rolex..............30.00
Lighter, MOP, figural brass steam whistle over wick...........70.00
Lighter, Sir Walter Raleigh tobacco can.....................75.00
Lighter, table; chrome airplane, EX.........................35.00
Lighter, table; Deco nude figure, battery-op, Parker of London..40.00
Lighter, table; globe, HP flowers, iron base, 9½".............185.00
Lighter, table; silver tankard shape, Dunhill................40.00
Pipe, carved wood, SP fittings, 5" L.......................10.00
Pipe, majolica, lady's head, Nouveau......................125.00
Pipe, meerschaum, amber curved stem, in formed leather case...45.00
Pipe, meerschaum, Black man's face, amber stem, in case.....245.00
Pipe, meerschaum, curved stem+1 w/str, cigarette/cigar holders..80.00
Pipe, meerschaum, dog figure, amber stem, orig leather case...60.00
Pipe, meerschaum, eagle claw holds bowl....................35.00
Pipe, meerschaum, Negress, cream colored, 8"..............900.00
Pipe, meerschaum, plain, leather stem, alligator case..........20.00
Pipe, meerschaum, seated maid/roses, amber stem, in case, 8"..185.00
Pipe, meerschaum, semi-nude, full figure relief, lg............225.00
Pipe, meerschaum, standing elk, orig case, 3x2⅛"............60.00
Pipe, meerschaum, sultan's head, amber stem, leather case, M..275.00
Pipe, porcelain w/figural man & keg, brass hinges, long stem....65.00
Pipe, porcelain w/HP stag, burl/sapling/horn/antler stem.......12.50
Pipe, porcelain 2 part bowl w/mc German officer, 1914, 9¾"....50.00
Pipe, pottery, decorated w/rough briar stem.................145.00
Pipe, pottery, wht/blk glazed cat on bowl, 3½".............20.00
Pipe, primitive, long branch stem..........................8.00
Pipe, terra cotta w/incised decor, rough briar stem, 18".......165.00
Pipe & cigar holder, meerschaum, horse & lion, carved.......55.00
Pipe case, mahog, trn stem, stylized bird head, w/pipe.......155.00
Pipe holder, F Jones Ales advertising......................50.00
Spittoon, ceramic, HP cigar/pipe/matches, ca 1890s..........60.00
Store card, Buecher's Corn Cob Pipes, 25¢, w/6 orig pipes.....45.00
Tobacco card, Godfrey Phillips, How to Make...Wireless, 25 for..75.00
Tobacco card, Helmar Turkish, Coat of Arms, Countries of World.5.00
Tobacco card, Helmar Turkish, seals o/t United States.........5.00
Tobacco card, John Player/Sons, Struggle for Existence, 25 for..75.00

Tobacco card, Murad Cigarettes, College Series...............6.00
Tobacco card, Phillips Famous Minors, set of 50..............5.00
Tobacco card, Players Army Corps-Divisional Signs, set of 50....18.00
Tobacco card, Players Cries of London, set of 25.............7.50
Tobacco card, Players miniatures, set of 25.................7.00
Tool, cigar box; CI/SP woman ship's head figure, Zorns, PA...45.00
Trade stimulator, counter, Earl Clarenden Cigars, dome/dice...325.00

Toby Jugs and Mugs

The delightful drinking mug known as the Toby dates back to the 18th century, when factories in England produced them for export to the American colonies. Named for the character Toby Philpot in the song *The Little Brown Jug*, the Toby was fashioned in the form of a jolly fellow, usually holding a jug of beer and a glass. Some were seated, while others were full-bodied figurals. The earlier examples were made with strict attention to details such as fingernails and teeth. Originally representing only a non-entity, a trend developed to portray well known individuals such as George II, Napoleon, and Ben Franklin. Among the most valued Tobies are those produced by Ralph Wood I in the late 1700s. By the mid-1830s, Tobies were being made in America.

Jug, copper lustre trimmed, mc, Allerton's, 6¾".............20.00
Jug, D Whittington & cat, Staffordshire....................35.00
Jug, Father Neptune, Crown Devon, Shorter, England, 3½".....75.00
Jug, Hearty Good Fellow, Wood & Sons, England, 6½"........55.00
Jug, leatherjack, orig horn liner, 1700s, rare..............1,575.00
Jug, man, bl luster coat w/jug/tri-con hat, Staffordshire, 9"....150.00
Jug, Mrs Gamp, HP, mc, Japan, 4½".......................7.50
Jug, Mrs Toby, purple mk, 1931, Royal Worcester, rare........95.00
Jug, Rockingham, pot belly, hands are spout, 9½"...........185.00
Jug, Rockingham glaze, 6".............................95.00
Jug, seated, Torquay, 2".............................35.00
Jug, seated, wart on nose, att Cheslea, no mk, 4x5".........150.00
Jug, snuff taker, mc enamel, Royal Crown Derby, rpr hat, 4¼".300.00
Jug, Tony Weller, #281, Beswick.........................60.00
Jug, Town crier, Wedgwood & Co, 1900...................75.00
Jug, Uncle Sam, HP, Wesley China, 3"...................18.00
Jug, Winston Churchill, cigar in mouth, seated, Copeland, 8½".110.00
Miniature, Francis Drake, 1½".........................22.00
Miniature, HP, full figure, Germany, 1½".................8.50
Mug, Cabby, 1850, Righton, England....................50.00
Salt, full figure, bl transfer base, hat is dish, 5¼"...........135.00

Toby jug, flowing blue on white porcelain, Germany, marked 0926, 5½", $55.00.

Toleware

The term 'toleware' originally came from a French term meaning 'sheet iron'. Today it is used to refer to paint decorated tin items. The earliest toleware was hand painted; by the 1820s, much of it was decorated by means of a stencil. Among the most collectible today are those items painted by the Pennsylvania Dutch in the 1800s.

Beaker, orig japanning w/striping & foliage band, 3″, EX......230.00
Bird cage, wire bars, trn acorn finial, worn pnt, 17″..........55.00
Bowl, rpt w/stenciled gold/red decor, 10″...................35.00
Box, cylindrical, hinged lid, orig florals worn, 6x7″.........135.00
Box, deed; blk w/lt br slashes w/mc swags, worn, 8″...........85.00
Box, deed; dome top, orig florals G, 9″ L..................175.00
Box, deed; dome top, rpt, blk w/red/yel, 8½″...............45.00
Box, deed; fruit/leafage, mc on br, 4½x8½″, EX............275.00
Box, deed; orig br japanning w/yel decor/florals, 9¾″, EX....300.00
Box, deed; orig japanning w/striping/foliage on wht, 8″ L......75.00
Box, deed; orig japanning w/3 color florals on wht band, 7¾″..110.00
Box, deed; recessed hdl in lid, orig florals worn, 5x8x12″......65.00
Box, spice; emb lid, orig japanning w/stripes, 6 sm boxes w/in...55.00
Candlestick, saucer base, w/hdl, push-up, 1800s.............55.00
Canister, orig pnt w/stenciled Coffee, minor wear, 6″..........25.00
Coffee pot, floral roundels ea side, mc, early, 8½″, EX.....1,870.00
Coffee pot, goose neck, orig florals worn, rpl finial, 11″......450.00
Coffee pot, orig decor bird/fruit, side spout, rpr, 9″.........475.00
Creamer, blk w/florals, worn & touched up, 4¼″.............120.00
Cuspidor, cast paw ft, bl/wht smoked decor w/red trim, 3¼x8¼″.65.00
Jardiniere, cylindrical w/chinoiserie motif, 1800s, 7″, pr.....415.00
Match holder, crimped crest, worn br japanning, 4½x7½″......55.00
Needle case, very worn orig red w/yel decor, 9½″...........105.00
Scissor wick trimmers & tray, old rpt w/roses on blk, 9″.......35.00
Sugar bowl, old rpt w/fruit, etc, 4¼x3½″, EX..............235.00
Teapot, orig florals on worn br japanning ea side, 9″.........300.00
Tray, apple; rpt w/floral band, worn, 7x12″.................65.00
Tray, crystallized gold panel center w/leaf border, 8¾″, pr....825.00
Tray, flowers & leafage, stencil/free-hand, 12¾″ L..........605.00
Tray, leafage, mc on br, octagonal, PA, 1800s, 12″ L........495.00
Tray, Oriental lacquer, birds/floral/fan, mc/gold on blk, 29″...110.00
Tray, orig simple florals worn & touched up, octagonal, 8x12″..125.00
Tray, reticulated sides, worn pear on blk decor, 4x8x13½″.....65.00

Tools

Before the Civil War, tools for the most part were handmade. Some were primitive to the point of crudeness, while others reflected the skill of those who took pride in their trade. Increasing demand for quality tools and the dawning of the age of industrialization resulted in tools that were mass produced.

Factors important in evaluating antique tools are scarcity, usefulness, and portability. Those with a manufacturer's mark are worth more than unmarked items.

Adze, bowl; 3½″ blade, wrought 4½″ w/short hdl............60.00
Adze, gutter; polled, sm..................................80.00
Adze, hand; Connecticut style, w/orig scrolled wooden hdl.....110.00
Adze, ship scupper; deeply cupped, 8″ bit..................105.00
Anvil, 18th century toe...................................200.00
Auger, shipbuilder's; cage head, 2 post cage, 48″ overall......450.00
Auger bits, single twist w/wimble hdl, Sanford 1847, set of 6....45.00
Axe, bearded; decorated both sides, w/touch mk, early........145.00
Axe, broad; offset hdl, 12″...............................55.00
Axe, broad; 9″ blade has stamped signature, hdl rpl..........35.00

Axe, goose-wing; mk MP w/in heart, incised decor, 10″........55.00
Axe, goose-wing; mk w/3 crowns, EX hdl, 14″ blade.........275.00
Axe, Marble's Camp Axe #10, Gladstone, MI, w/leather sheath..125.00
Axe head, goose-wing; mk AP w/in heart, 15¼″ blade........180.00
Axe mortise chisel, wrought, mkd J Bung, touch mk, 17″ blade.350.00
Bitstock, fixed bit, dk beech, Marples/Sheffield/Hibernia, 14″...250.00
Blacksmith's bellows, wrought/CI fittings, CL English, 76″.....105.00
Blacksmith's carry-all, dvtl pine w/dvtl drw, tray top w/hdl.....105.00
Blacksmith's cone, solid, 1700s, 36″......................190.00
Blacksmith's cone, 1700s, 24″............................150.00
Blacksmith's screw plate, 6 graduated holes, includes 3 taps.....49.00
Brace, adjustable wrench; P Lowentraut, Neward, 1877 pat.....110.00
Brace, chair maker's; spoon bit, dk mellow beech, 13″ overall..175.00
Brace, gentleman's; polished steel/ornate head, Peugeot Freres..65.00
Brace, lady's; dk beech & coca bola head/brass, Sheffield......195.00
Brace, piano maker's; wood/brass, w/rosewood head, 11¾″....350.00
Brace, Ultimatum, Marples & Sons Hibernia Works, ebony......375.00
Brace, unplates, beech, Sheffield style, lignum vitae head......55.00
Brace, wagon builder's; all iron/wrought, 4½″ head/14″ overall..95.00
Brace, 2-post cage head..................................175.00
Calipers, brass, w/screw locking adjustment, 11x5½″..........49.00
Calipers, dbl; hand forged, 18″...........................85.00
Calipers, log; brass hardware, walking wheel, sgn W Greenlief..425.00
Calipers, log; brass slide window slot, iron jaws, G...........95.00
Calipers, slide; wood, decorated brass plates/tip, Page, 21″.....75.00
Calipers, wheelwright's; apple shaped, hand forged, EX........55.00
Clamp, cabinetmaker's; curly maple/hickory, 15″.............65.00
Clamp, wood, curved jaws, violin makers, set of 4............55.00
Cobbler's bench, whittled legs, leather seat, 48″.............225.00
Divider, cherry w/decorative brass quadrant/nuts/ferrules, 18″...175.00
Divider, oak, brass tips/ferrules/wing nut, 1¾x24″..........125.00
Drill, bow; brass ferrules/fruitwood/orig cord, M Falls chuck....295.00
Drill, pump; steel shaft & flywheel, beech cross arm, 12x12″....89.00
Farrier's worktable, pine, octagon top w/slots for tools........205.00
Gauge, circle cutting; mk J Cossey/AS Beeny, mahog/brass.....40.00
Gauge, dbl marking; mahogany w/polished brass, owner sgn.....60.00
Gauge, mortise; dk rosewood, polished brass.................55.00
Gauging rod, cooper's, boxwood, brass tips, single fold, 20″.....65.00
Graining assortment: combs, 11 rollers, compo/wood, in box...200.00
Hammer, bill poster's; 1 joint, both brass clips intact, sgn......85.00
Hammer, log marking; wrought, orig hdl, lg marker: GN........45.00
Hammer, saw maker's; mk 2¼ lbs, orig hdl, 5″ head.........89.00
Hatchet, butterfly shape, w/old hdl, 9″ across...............45.00
Hatchet, cooper's; goose-wing style........................35.00
Hatchet, mahogany, well carved hdl, 13¼″ L...............10.00
Jack, mitre; dk mahogany w/dk beech screw, 22″ overall, EX....95.00
Leather cutter, steel crescent blade mk HG Gomph & Co, 6½″..15.00
Leather worker's vice, wood w/iron screw, 25″...............10.00
Mallet, carpenter's; burl w/hickory hdl, rfn, 16″ L............15.00
Mortise scribe, mahog/brass fittings, mk S Hawks/W Johnson, 8″.22.00
Pick, prospector's; wrought, file work decor, early, 18″........150.00
Plane, axle; wheelwright's, old finish/3 line decor, orig, 18″....250.00
Plane, block; dbl end, Union #137, VG.....................33.00
Plane, block; wood, mk JM Snider, Ohio Tool Co, 16″.........18.00
Plane, box; cast brass core, dk beech hdl, 1⅞-2⅝″ wings....150.00
Plane, cast brass, wood tote/knob, H Foster both sides, 3x18″..285.00
Plane, coach maker's radius plow; walnut/slide arm fence, 13″..385.00
Plane, fore; beech, EX carved, ivory eagle head fore knob, 19″.550.00
Plane, grooving; iron, 3/16″ cut, wood hdl/knob, #23, 9½″.....45.00
Plane, hand forged skate, rivets to cut 3″ groove, early........35.00
Plane, jack; dk beech, carved florals sides & top, early, 17″....110.00
Plane, jointer; iron, corrugated bottom/checkered hdl, Siegley..150.00
Plane, Live Oak, tote: carved 1 pc/wedge: Phillip Walker, 23″..110.00
Plane, plow; Auburn Tool Co, rosewood hdl..................450.00

Plane, plow; center-wheel, Sandusky.....................3,500.00
Plane, Sargent #3415, 15", VG............................45.00
Plane, sash; Israel White, screw-arm/sgn/mk w/tools..........205.00
Plane, smooth; Bailey #2, tall knob, most of orig label, EX....150.00
Plane, Stanley #S5, jack; steel, rosewood hdl/knob, 14", G.....175.00
Plane, Stanley #100.....................................45.00
Plane, Stanley #100½....................................85.00
Plane, Stanley #101.....................................20.00
Plane, Stanley #113.....................................95.00
Plane, Stanley #13.....................................110.00
Plane, Stanley #239, w/out fencing, pre-1925, G.............145.00
Plane, Stanley #46, VG..................................65.00
Plane, Stanley #55, in case w/instruction book, EX..........300.00
Plane, Stanley #55, w/4 boxes of cutters...................225.00
Plane, Stanley #74, floor................................250.00
Plane, Stanley #75.....................................35.00
Plane, Stanley #90.....................................135.00
Reaping hook, early style w/long sweep, mk I Long............25.00
Router, bronze, right & left bead, 11".....................33.00
Router, coach maker's offset dbl, beech hdls, unusual, 17"...110.00
Rule, folding; boxwood/German silver, architect scale, 2 foot...125.00
Rule, Masonic, ivory.................................1,050.00
Rule, octagonal cane/brass ends, Doyle's Log Tables, #48½, 36".95.00
Rule, parallel; ebony w/brass, 6" long.....................20.00
Rule, parallel; rolling, solid brass, pat #160100, 'Harling'......85.00
Rule, Stanley #34¼, 12"..................................7.00
Rule, Stanley #81, boxwood, arch joint, 2 foot..............35.00

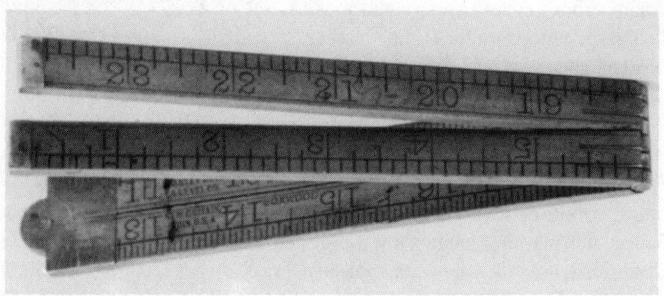

Stanley ruler, boxwood with brass mountings, folding, 2 ft in length, $35.00.

Saw, bucksaw w/blade, old dk patina, cord & lever rpl, 33" L...45.00
Saw, hand; brass label H Disston & Sons, 28½"..............32.00
Saw, salt; heavy copper blade mk T&S, 20" overall...........72.00
Saw, 2-man cross-cut; 5 ft blade, etched Victor/trademk, NM....38.00
Scale, crab; w/brass quadrant, complete...................72.00
Scorp, closed, 3" blade, 10" overall, VG...................45.00
Scraper, Stanley #112, G................................65.00
Shingle splitter, 2 pc, blade & beetle, 13½"................20.00
Sighting rule, boxwood, slide isinglass window, J Cail, 20"....85.00
Splitting froe, old hdl, 12" blade.........................30.00
Square, brass & steel, A McKenzie pat 1857 Boston, 12" blade..79.00
Square, dk oak/mortised/wood pins, lead bob, early, 18x24"....165.00
Square, rosewood/brass/steel blade, 5½x9".................10.00
Stake, tinsmith's; candle mold, good surface, 24"...........65.00
Straight edge, wallpaperer's, laminated lt/dk wood, brass, 72"...65.00
Stump blaster, touch hole for setting off blk powder, 9x2" dia..22.00
Swage block, ladle on 1 side, tire welding depression on other..250.00
Tool cabinet, hanging; blk walnut/basswood, 2 doors w/drws....95.00
Trammel, brass w/bird's head, late 1800s, 16¾".............125.00
Trammel point, Stanley #1, emb brass w/iron tips, pr.........42.00
Transit, surveyor's; K&E, 1905, M.......................545.00
Twibil, European style, wrought iron, 44" wide, G............225.00
Twibil, mk DIVAL, 47"..................................225.00

Vise, hand; PS Stubbs, w/bracket for ft strap sgn J Field.......18.00
Wheelwright's traveler, wrought w/wood hdl, 7" dia/15" overall..35.00
Wheelwright's traveler, 8ths stamped to 24", cast brass........210.00
Wrench, buggy; adjusts, iron w/wood crank hdl, Oliver Co, 19"..55.00
Wrench, hand ratchet, ¾" square drive, 9" long.............22.00

Toothpick Holders

Toothpick holders have been popular table accessories since the Victorian era. They were made in pressed glass patterns as well as in all types of art glass and china.

Alabama, clear.......................................60.00
Atlas...13.00
Aztec, McKee..17.00
Banded Portland, clear.................................18.50
Banded Portland, clear w/gold...........................25.00
Banded Portland, maiden blush...........................45.00
Bead Swag, opalescent, worn souvenir.....................60.00
Beaded Oval in Sand, lt green, decorated...................75.00
Beatty Honeycomb, blue opal.............................55.00
Beatty Rib, clear opal..................................20.00
Beatty Waffle, clear opal................................30.00
Bird & Wishbone, figural, SP, mk Warren NY/QSP, 2".........50.00
Bird on Stump, amber...................................30.00
Boot, amber..30.00
Brazilian..30.00
Bulging Loops, green...................................75.00
Bull's Eye & Fan......................................18.00
Button & Star Panel, clear...............................18.00
Button Arches, ruby stained.............................25.00
Cactus, chocolate, Greentown............................65.00
Cambridge Colonial, cobalt..............................30.00
Cat on Pillow, amber...................................40.00
Chrysanthemum Base Swirl, cranberry.....................95.00
Chrysanthemum Leaf, clear..............................30.00
Colorado, blue w/EX gold................................55.00
Colorado, green.......................................28.00
Colorado, green & gold.................................35.00
Continental, clear, Heisey...............................75.00
Croesus, green..78.00
Cross Cut Diamond, hat shape, clear, 2½x3¾".............18.00
Cross Cut Diamond, hat shape, milk glass..................15.00
Cupid & Hat, figural, SP, MSP Co, 3½"...................65.00
Cut glass, Icicle.......................................25.00
Daisy & Button, amber, flared rim.......................35.00
Daisy & Button, amber, metal rim........................20.00
Daisy & Button, amberina, old, tiny nick on 1 ft...........175.00
Daisy & Button, Coal Hod, blue..........................20.00
Daisy & Button, Gypsy Kettle w/lid & hdl, ftd, blue.........30.00
Daisy & Button w/Fan Brim, hat shape, blue................45.00
Darwin, vaseline......................................45.00
Delaware, green w/EX gold..............................85.00
Diamond Peg, custard..................................50.00
Diamond Spearhead, blue opal...........................70.00
Diamond Spearhead, green opal..........................60.00
Double Dahlia w/Lens, decor, EX.........................40.00
Double Eye Hobnail, amber..............................28.00
Elephant, howdah on bk, frosted, rare....................42.00
Elephant Head, amber, rare.............................50.00
Esther, green w/EX gold.................................75.00
Fan, amber...19.00
Fancy Loop, clear, Heisey...............................40.00

Fancy Loop, clear w/gold, Heisey	53.00
Finecut, hat shape, amber, 2½"	22.00
Flower & Pleat, clear & frosted	50.00
Gaelic	15.00
Gatling Gun	15.00
Geneva, chocolate, EX	175.00
Georgia Gem, custard, souvenir	25.00
Georgia Gem, custard, w/gold, not souvenir	55.00
Gold Band, vaseline	60.00
Guttate, blue satin glass	45.00
Guttate, peachbloom satin glass	45.00
Harvard, custard	35.00
Harvard, custard, green	55.00
Hat shape, clear blown w/polished pontil, 2½x3¼"	25.00
Hat shape, Mt Washington, satin w/pk casing, enameling	175.00
Hat shape, threaded, vaseline, 2½"	18.00
Heartband, green w/gold, trace of souvenir	38.00
Hobb's Hobnail, amber	30.00
Hobb's Hobnail, vaseline	35.00
Hobnail, amber	20.00
Hobnail Hat, clear opal	18.00
Horse w/Cart	28.00
Horseradish Jar, vaseline, sm chips on horse ears	41.00
Horseshoe & Clover, milk glass	30.00
Inverted Church Windows	15.00
Iowa, clear	20.00
Iris w/Meander, amethyst, w/gold	55.00
Iris w/Meander, blue opal	90.00
Iris w/Meander, green opal	65.00
Jefferson Optic, custard, souvenir	75.00
Kettle, purple slag	30.00
King's Crown	20.00
Lacy Medallion, green, souvenir	15.00
Lacy Medallion, green w/gold	25.00
Long Buttress	22.00
Manhattan, clear	28.00
Manhattan, w/gold	30.00
Medallion Sprig, decorated milk glass	30.00
Michigan, w/gold	43.00
Minnesota	20.00
Monkeys on Stump, milk glass	45.00
New Hampshire	23.00
New Jersey, clear w/gold	45.00
New Jersey, no gold	38.00
One-O-One, pink	50.00
Overall Hobnail, blue opal	40.00
Owl on Stump, blue	35.00
Panelled Cherry	12.00
Panelled Daisy, amber opal, ftd	25.00
Pansy, amber, 3 hdl	15.00
Pansy, green opaque	35.00
Peekaboo, amber	30.00
Plain Band, clear, Heisey	75.00
Pleating, w/grape & leaf etching, red flashed	45.00
Portland	20.00
Prince of Wales Plume, clear w/EX gold, Heisey	125.00
Reverse Swirl, blue opal	55.00
Rexford, clear	18.00
Ribbed Lattice, blue opal	68.00
Ribbed Spiral, vaseline, Northwood	40.00
Ring Band, custard, souvenir	50.00
Ring Base, amber w/EX decor	75.00
Rings & Beads, custard, souvenir	38.00
Rising Sun, gold flashed	25.00

Royal Ivy, rubena	75.00
Royal Ivy, rubena satin	110.00
Royal Oak, rubena	95.00
Ruby Thumbprint	30.00
Scalloped Panel, plain, green	35.00
Scroll Shell, milk glass	30.00
Spearhead, green opal	50.00
Squirrel & Stump, blue	35.00
Stars and Stripes	15.00
States, The; rectangular, clear	30.00
Sunbeam, green	65.00
Sunk Daisy	12.00
Sunset, opaque blue	36.00
Tapered Block, hat shape, blue, 2¼"	25.00
Teepee	30.00
Texas, clear	35.00
Texas, w/gold top	30.00
Tiny Thumbprint, blue to amber, ruffled top, M	150.00
Tramp's Shoe, milk glass	38.00
Trophy, green	20.00
Trophy, green, souvenir	22.00
US Rib, green w/gold, M	35.00
Venetian Diamond, amberina, square top, good color, M	150.00
Vermont, amber	25.00
Vermont, green w/EX gold	35.00
Virginia, emerald	20.00
Wedding Bells, clear w/gilded swirls	33.00
Zipper Swirl	14.00

Torquay Ware

Torquay is a unique type of pottery made in the South Devon area of England from the 1870s. At the height of productivity, at least a dozen companies flourished there, producing simple folk pottery from the area's natural red clay. The ware was both wheel-turned and molded, and decorated under the glaze with heavy slip resulting in low relief nature subjects or simple scroll work.

Three of the best known of these potteries were: Watcombe (1870-1900); Aller Vale (in operation from the mid-1800s, producing domestic ware and architectural products); and Longpark (1890 until 1957). Watcombe and Aller Vale merged in 1901 and operated until 1962 under the name of Royal Aller Vale and Watcombe Art Pottery.

Perhaps the most famous type of ware potted in this area was Motto Ware, so called because of the verses, proverbs, and quotations that decorated it. This decor was achieved by the sgraffito technique -- scratching the letters through the slip to expose the red clay underneath. The most popular decorative devices were cottages, stylized daisies, and a scroll work pattern called Sandringham.

Aller Vale ware may sometimes be found marked 'H.H. and Company,' a firm who assumed ownership from 1897 to 1901. 'Watcombe Torquay' was an impressed mark used from 1884 to 1895.

Ash tray, Cottage, rectangle, MIE, 'Soft words win...heart'	20.00
Ash tray, House, rectangle, Watcombe, 'Who burnt the t'cloth'	20.00
Basket, Cockerel, oval, 'Homemade preserves', 5"	28.00
Bowl, Cottage, square, 'Waste not, want not', 2x2¼"	22.00
Bowl, Dartmouth, 'Go aisy wi' it now', 4¼"	24.00
Bowl, Scandy, fluted, 'dinna take 2 bites o'a cherry', 3½" W	30.00
Bowl, Scandy, hat shape, Aller Vale, motto, 2½x7"	45.00
Bowl, Scandy, scalloped rim, Longpark, motto, 3x3½"	45.00
Bowl, Watcombe, 'Dont get discouraged...', 3x5¼"	42.00
Butter, Scandy, clover shape, Watcombe, 'Take a little butter'	28.00
Candlestick, Cockerel, Longpark, motto, 4¼"	27.50

Candlestick, Scandy, 'Many are called...', 3½".............25.00
Chamberstick, Scandy, Aller Vale, 'Good night...', 2".........35.00
Chamberstick, Scandy, deep bowl, Longpark, 'Last in bed...'....36.50
Cheese dish, Cottage, rectangle top, motto, 5¼x6½".......40.00
Coffee pot, Cottage, 'Do the work that's nearest...', 6¾".....57.50
Coffee pot, Cottage, Royal Watcombe, motto, 6"...........55.00
Coffee pot, Scandy, Aller Vale, 'May we be kind...'........38.50
Cream & sugar, Watcombe, 'Hope on--hope ever...', pr...32.00
Creamer, Cockerel, 'Help yerzel ter cream', 2¼"...........22.00
Creamer, Cottage, barrel shape, Watcombe, motto, 3".......20.00
Creamer, Cottage, Longpark, 'Help yourself to cream'.........25.00
Creamer, Cottage, MIE, 'Fine words will not fill...'........20.00
Creamer, Cottage, MIE, 'Fresh from the Dairy'..............18.00
Creamer, Cottage, Watcombe, 'Say little but think much', lg...28.50
Creamer, Sailboat, 'Arnheg o Gaergybi', lg................28.50
Creamer, Scandy, Aller Vale, 'Straight from the cow'........22.00
Creamer, Scandy, Aller Vale, 'Tak a little craim'...........20.00
Creamer, sunset & sailboats, 'Du'll be aisy'................20.00
Creamer, Thistle, Longpark, 'Frae Portobello', lg............28.00
Cup & saucer, Cockerel.................................28.00
Cup & saucer, Cottage, Dartmouth, motto, 5½" cup, 8½"....54.00
Cup & saucer, tea; Two-story Cottage, Watcombe, motto......26.00
Egg cup, pedestal......................................20.00
Egg cup, saucer shape...................................25.00
Egg cup, small, plain, w/design..........................15.00
Hair receiver, Scandy, Turmumun ware, 3"................30.00
Hatpin holder, Scandy, 'Guid folks are scare...'...........52.00
Hatpin holder, Scandy, Longpark, 'Keep me on...table', lg....55.00
Hot water pot, Watcombe, MIE, 'Remember the kindness...'....48.50
Ink pot, Scandy, 'pen is mightier than the sword', no mk......28.50
Ink pot, Scandy, w/stopper, 'Jist a scrape o'yer pen'..........35.00
Ink pot, Scandy-type, Exeter, 'Send us a scrape o'yer pen'.....32.00
Ink pot, Shearer, Glasgow, 'Dinna be aye ettlin' but write'.....32.50
Ink pot, Tormohun Ware, 'Blot out my faults...'.............32.00
Jam, Cottage, MIE, 'It's better to wear out than rust out'......32.00
Jam, Cottage, Watcombe Devon, 'No road is long...', 4½".....35.00
Jam, Scandy, sq w/pointed scallops, Longpark, 'Be aisy...'.....27.50
Jam dish w/hdl, Cockerel, 'Be aisy with the jam'.............30.00
Jug, Cockerel, motto, 2"................................22.00
Jug, heather flowers, pinched, 4½"......................27.50
Jug, no decor, pinched spout, Aller Vale, motto............25.00
Jug, puzzle; sunset & sailboats, 'More haste, less speed'.......32.00
Jug, ship, hdl thru top, Hastings, 'Make hay...'............31.50
Jug, side spout, bl w/cream/br decor, Hart Moist, motto, 3½"...32.00
Match holder, 'Strike me & I'll light', small...............32.00
Match holder, Watcombe, 'Strike me & I'll light', large........40.00
Match striker, Cockerel, 'A match for any man', 3¼".........40.00
Match striker, Scandy, 'A match for any man'..............30.00
Match striker, ships in sunset...........................40.00
Mug, Cottage, Dartmouth, 'Do not stain today's blue sky', 5"...30.00
Mug, Cottage, Longpark, ruffled rim, 'Help yerzel to jam'.....27.50
Mug, Cottage, Watcombe, 'Help yourself', medium size........32.50
Mug, Cottage, Watcombe, 'Take a little drink', large.........35.00
Perfume, Scotch Heather Bouquet, unopened...............25.00
Pin tray, Cottage, w/sunset, ruffled, Torquay, England, 5"....26.00
Pitcher, Cockerel, 'Better do one thing...', 4¼"...........40.00
Pitcher, Cottage, Watcombe, 'Heaven send thee...'..........42.00
Pitcher, house, blue dots, tadpoles, 4".....................35.00
Pitcher, sailboats/sunset, 'kindness is never lost', 5"........35.00
Pitcher, Scandy, 'Wishes never filled the bag', 3¼".........25.00
Pitcher, Scandy, hdl through top, Aller Vale, motto, 4"........32.00
Pitcher, Scandy, Longpark, 'Tis deeds alone...', 4½".........40.00
Pitcher, Watcombe, 'Every blade of grass...', 4½"..........32.00
Planter, Scandy, 'never say die', 3".......................22.00

Plate, Cottage, 'To thine own sel be true', 8¼".............30.00
Plate, Cottage, Dartmouth, motto, 10"....................35.00
Plate, Cottage, Royal Watcombe, 7".......................27.50
Plate, Cottage, Watcombe, motto, 6½"....................28.00
Plate, Scandy, 'Truth like cork never sinks', 5"............25.00
Salt, peacock...15.00
Salt & peppers, pr......................................22.00
Sugar, Cottage, Dartmouth, 'Do you take sugar?'...........20.00
Sugar, Cottage, lg/ped ft, 'elp yerzel to sugar'............32.00
Sugar, Scandy, Aller Vale, 'Take a little sugar'............22.00
Sugar, Scandy, ftd, 'Dunn'ee be afraid o't now', 3½".......20.00
Sugar, Scandy, Watcombe, 'sweeten to your liking'..........20.00
Sugar, seagull, Dartmouth...............................22.00
Sugar, Thistle, lg/ped bowl, ruffled rim, Longpark..........32.00
Sugar & creamer, bird in panel, 'To greet you...', pr........40.00
Sugar & creamer, Thistle, Longpark, motto................40.00
Sugar bowl, Cockerel, Longpark, 'Be aisy with the sugar'.....17.50
Sugar bowl, seagull, Dartmouth, 4"......................15.00
Tea set, Cottage, MIE, 'Remembered joys...', 4½" pot.......62.00
Teapot, Cockerel, 'Du'll mak yerzels at 'ome', 3¼".........40.00
Teapot, Cockerel, motto, 6".............................45.00
Teapot, Cottage, Watcombe, 'I cum from Lynton'...........50.00
Toast rack, Cottage, 3 rails, motto.......................30.00
Tumbler, Scandy, 'Every blade of grass...', 3¾"...........28.00
Vase, bird & tree, Royal Torquay, no motto, 7½"...........40.00
Vase, Cockerel, wavy rim, cone shape, Longpark, motto, 3½"...25.00
Vase, dolphin, 3 ft, Watcombe Torquay, 3½x2¾", pr.........80.00
Vase, motto ware, sailboat & people, 5½"..................55.00
Vase, Scandy, ovoid w/2 dimples, 'pound of pluck...', 6".....35.00
Vase, Scandy, scalloped, 'stitch in time...', 4¼" W.........30.00
Vase, Scandy, 2 hdls, 'Good wishes speed you...', 3½".......25.00
Vase, Scandy, 2 hdls, Aller Vale, motto, 3½"..............32.00
Vase, Scandy, 2 hdls, waisted, Longpark, verse, 4½".........30.00
Vase, Scandy, 3 hdls, 'Drink like a fish water only', 3¼".....30.00
Vase, sunset & sailboats, 2 dimples, motto, 6½"...........30.00
Vase, Thistle, 3 spouts, Longpark, motto, 5½".............32.00
Vase, 4 finger, seagulls, Barton.........................42.50

Tortoise Shell Glass

By combining several shades of glass -- brown, clear, and yellow -- glass manufacturers of the 19th century were able to produce an art glass that closely resembled the shell of the tortoise. Some of this type of glassware was manufactured in Germany. In America it was made by several firms, the most prominent of which was the Boston and Sandwich Glass Works.

Bowl, squared top, rolled in, floral gilt, 6" dia...............85.00
Cruet, amber stopper & hdl.............................150.00
Pitcher, applied amber hdl, att Sandwich, 8"...............50.00
Pitcher, applied amber hdl, 9½".........................65.00
Plate, blown, 10" dia...................................30.00
Urn, neoclassic form, 15", pr...........................500.00
Vase, paneled, English, 1910, 8".........................85.00
Vase, ruffled fan top, stick neck, bulbous bottom, 6".........40.00
Vase, 4 stacked bun sections, gilt flowers, French, 7¼".......85.00

Toys

Toys, obviously, are fun to collect. But especially those made before WWII also have sound investment potential. Lithograph-printed mechanical toys, for instance, are especially popular with today's collectors, and steadily continue to increase in value year after year. Condition of any type of toy is critical -- they were made for children to play with, and many that have survived to the present are in a well-played-with state, which only serves to enhance the value of those that remain in excellent condition. In the listings below, toys are listed by manufacturer's name when at all possible, otherwise by type.

Key: w/up----windup

Cast Iron

Cast iron toys were made from shortly before the Civil War until the beginning of the 20th century. They are evaluated to a large extent by scarcity, complexity, design, and detail.

American Stove, w/pots & pans, 8½".......................100.00
Cannon, back opens, sm wick hole, gold on spoke wheels, 16"..55.00
Car, Austin, old bl pnt, iron wheels, 3½"....................40.00
Car, orig pnt, rubber wheels, 1936, 1¾x4½"..................50.00
Chester Gump in cart pulled by horse, 1905.................350.00
Circus chariot, w/separate female driver, 3 horses, 1900......450.00
Coal wagon, rpt, 16"......................................90.00
Columbus Landing, bell ringer, 1893.....................375.00
Dump truck, rubber tires, 1940, 7".......................135.00
Fire engine steam pumper, #330, 1893, red/wht/gold/blk, 21" L.350.00
Fire truck, pumper w/driver, 1920s, 9½"..................175.00
Fire wagon w/ladders pulled by 2 horses, 2 fireman, 27"......385.00
Gasoline truck, 'Gasoline' ea side, resembles '20s Mack, 5" L...85.00
Goat cart, pnt CI, rpt, 13"...............................50.00
Horse, prancing on round base, wht/red/blk worn pnt, 5".......50.00
Hose reel, pnt, 13", VG..................................100.00
Ice wagon, pnt, some rpt, 13½".............................60.00
Speedboat w/driver, 1930s, 5½"............................65.00
Stake wagon, bl w/yel rider, 1 blk/1 wht horse, 1890s, 15" L...200.00
Train engine, CI, w/cowcatcher, blk w/red wheels, 1880s, 6"....65.00
Wild Mule Jack, bell ringer, figure rides jack rabbit...........450.00
Wrecker truck w/crane, 1940, 8"..........................150.00
Yellow Taxi Cab, 1920s, 5", scarce size....................350.00

Company or Country of Manufacturer

American Flyer, cyclist balancing toy, tin litho, 11", EX.......210.00
Arcade, Andy Gump 348 Car, pnt CI, rstr, 7"................400.00
Arcade, Chester Gump In Cart, pnt CI, 7½", EX...........1,000.00
Arcade, Chester Gump In Cart, pnt CI, 7½", VG...........300.00
Arcade, coupe, CI, bl w/wht rubber tires, sticker, 8", VG......300.00
Arcade, dump truck, Intn'l Harvester, w/driver, 1925, 10½"....275.00
Arcade, truck cab & trailer w/2 cars & trucks, 15"............375.00
Arnold, Howdy Doody Trapeze, tin litho/cloth/compo, 10", VG.350.00
Arnold, man gets on & off motorcycle.....................350.00
Asahi, violin, tin, orig box, 12" L...........................25.00
Automatic Toy Co, Captain Marvel Lightning Racing Cars, G...210.00
B&R Co, boy riding tricycle, w/up, 1920s..................250.00
B&R Co, Kid Flyer, boy on soap box scooter, w/up, 1920s.....250.00
B&R Co, Kids Special, boy on tricycle, w/up................250.00
Baldwin, Little Red Hen, w/2 orig wooden eggs, in orig box.....35.00
Bavaria, sedan, blk tin w/driver, w/up....................240.00
Bing, garage, tin litho, some rust, 4½x6½"..................80.00
Bing, Limousine, key wind, tin litho, G orig, 9½"............340.00
Bing, Model T convertible, key wind rear wheels, lady driver..4,000.00
Bing, Model T limousine, key wind, tin, no driver, 1920......140.00
Bing, touring car, tin litho w/up, 6", VG..................400.00
Bissell, Midget carpet sweeper, all wood, EX................45.00
Bliss, circus cart w/rider, paper litho on wood, 9½", VG......275.00

Bliss, Noah's ark, w/7 litho paper cb figures, 11", G..........160.00
Bliss, Noah's ark, 9 animals, sgn, 13", G..................400.00
Buddy L, dump truck, pressed steel/rubber tires, '30s, 22½"...165.00
Bush, kaleidoscope, hand held, oil colors in glass tubes, 9"....275.00
Bush, kaleidoscope, paper/glass/brass/wood, ftd std, 14"......570.00
Carette, limousine, tin litho w/up, glass windshield only, 16"..5,700.00
Carter Toy Co, Chinaman pulls cart, 1910, w/up............150.00
Champion, gasoline truck, CI, 8".........................200.00
Chein, Aquaplane, MIB, 9"...............................100.00
Chein, Barnacle Bill the Sailor, w/up walker, 1930s..........175.00
Chein, boat, mk Peggy Jane, orig box, 14½" L, VG..........40.00
Chein, Clown in Barrel, 7½", EX..........................110.00
Chein, Happy Hooligan, tin w/up, 6¼", EX.................250.00
Chein, Happy Hooligan, tin w/up, 6¼", VG.................170.00
Chein, penguin, lithographed tin w/up....................140.00
Chein, Popeye, w/up walker, 1930s.......................250.00
Chein, Popeye hits punching bag on platform, 1930.........550.00
Chein, Popeye in Barrel, w/up walker, 1930s...............250.00
Chein, sand bucket & shovel, elephants/boats/pigs/etc.........15.00
Chein, Three Little Pigs washer............................85.00
Chein, Walking Teddy Bear, tin, 5", G.....................35.00
Chein, Yellow Taxi, Main 7570, 6", VG....................140.00
Chime Toy Products, Jitter Bug, 2 Blk dancers, orig box......175.00
Clown Toy Mfg, Bo Jangle Dances Again, 9".................35.00
Converse, Roosevelt stock farm, stained/pnt wood, 18", VG....320.00
Courtland Mfg, Ice Cream Scooter, orig box, EX............140.00
CR Co, French bus w/driver, w/up, 1929...................375.00
Cragstan, Mr Atomic Robot, tin litho/plastic, battery op, 10"..1,000.00
Cragstan, Mr Robot, tin litho/plastic, battery op, 11", VG.....400.00
Crown Toy, Ferdinand the Bull, wood/composition...........38.00
Daiya Japan, rearing horse, tin litho w/up, 1950s, 8" L........50.00
Dayton Toy Co, fire truck w/extension ladders & driver, 18"...295.00
Dean Ragbrook Co, donkey on wheels, iron fr...............70.00
DJ Germany, convertible w/driver, tin litho, weight prop, 7½"..300.00
Empire, steam engine, horizontal plated boiler, electric fire.....85.00
English, auto w/long front end, driver, w/up, 1920s..........195.00
English, Donald Duck on tricycle, celluloid/metal w/up.......450.00
English, Mickey & Minnie Mouse play hurdy gurdy, pot metal..200.00
Fallows, carriage, pnt tin/wire/cloth fold top, w/8" doll, 14"...1,600.00
Fisher, Toonerville Trolley, Cracker Jack size, EX............325.00
Fisher, Toonerville Trolley, tin litho w/up, EX..............600.00
Franmonia, lady bug, metal w/up, 5¾x4½"..................35.00
French, acrobatic clown, compo w/glass eyes, 1920, 16".......550.00
French, clown in ball, spiral tower, tin litho, 13½", VG.......350.00
French, Horse Race, 4 lead horses w/riders, w/cover, 1890s, 8".150.00
French, piano player, tin litho/cloth, w/up, 6", VG...........375.00
French, zeppelin w/3" prop, moves in circle when twirled, 1900.175.00
Fun-E-Flex, Mickey Mouse figure, large....................150.00
Geo Brown, circus acrobat on horse, early, minor rstr, 6½"....475.00
Geo Brown, girl ringing bell on cart w/horse, tin, 15½".......2,200.00
German, Am Yellow Cab, Lenox 530, doors open............275.00
German, Balking Mule, w/cart & clown driver, 1924, 7".......100.00
German, bear w/cup & bottle, drinking, w/up, 7", EX.........125.00
German, beetle, push toy, legs move, tin litho, 3"............25.00
German, billiard player, shoots pool, w/up, 1910............250.00
German, biplane, pnt tin, clockwork, tin litho pilot, 12".....4,500.00
German, biplane w/rider, penny toy, tin litho, losses.........550.00
German, black cat squeeze toy, tin litho/wood, 4½", EX......120.00
German, blocks, wood/paper, children/ABC/soldiers...........90.00
German, cat chases mouse, w/up, 1920....................275.00
German, Charlie Chaplin, tin w/up, CI ft, 9", VG............650.00
German, clown, #504, elephants on wheels, w/up, 16x4½".....265.00
German, Comical Kat, w/up walker, 1920s..................150.00
German, cowboy twirls lasso on horse, 1930s, MIB..........195.00

German, Distler roadster, pnt tin clockwork, 1940s, 9½"......250.00
German, Donald Duck, plastic/plush, w/up, orig box, 8½", NM.170.00
German, man in speedboat, tin friction, minor wear, 12".......95.00
German, monkey wearing clothes plays drum, w/up, 1920.....350.00
German, motor scooter, litho/decal, tin w/up, 11", EX.........110.00
German, motorcycle/sidecar w/rider, Indian, tin litho w/up, 5"..180.00
German, Powerful Katrinka, tin litho w/up, 5½", EX........1,250.00
German, Powerful Katrinka, tin litho w/up, 5½", VG..........900.00
German, rolly polly, good orig pnt, 12"....................105.00
German, Torpedo touring car, tin litho w/up, 11¼".........2,800.00
German, touring car, tin litho w/up, 6", EX.................160.00
German, woman sweeping, tin w/up, 1920s, 7½".............600.00
GFN Germany, tanker, pnt/litho tin w/up, 20"...............900.00
Gibbs, Never Stop Seesaw, pnt tin, 1903, 14½", VG..........90.00
Gibbs, pony pulling 2 wheeled cart, wood/tin/paper litho, 7x4"..100.00
Gibbs, rocking horse, pnt/litho paper on wood, 9", VG........85.00
Gilbert, Erector set, #7½.................................45.00
Girard, Captain Kid's Sand Pail Boat, orig box, 10½", EX.....75.00
Hercules, Mack dump truck, tin litho, mechanical, 20" L.....130.00
Hercules, rumble seat roadster, 18", VG...................190.00
Hoge Mfg, Popeye in Row Boat, steel/tin, w/up, rpl oars, 14".1,500.00
Huber, road roller, pnt/nickeled CI, 7½", G................250.00
Hubley, airplane, P-38...................................45.00
Hubley, Foxy Grandpa, The Nodders, pnt CI, 6", VG.........150.00
Hubley, grasshopper, movable legs, on wheels, 1920s, EX.....400.00
Hubley, Mr Magoo Car, tin/plastic/cloth, battery op, in box...120.00
Hubley, Parcel Post Harley Davidson w/rider, CI/rubber, 9"...500.00
Hull & Stafford, lamb, tin pull toy on wheels, 1880s, 5x3½"..190.00
Japan, Astronaut, tin litho w/up, 7½", EX.................375.00
Japan, Atomic Robot Man, 5", VG.........................300.00
Japan, boy feeds rooster from pan, 1910, w/up.............265.00
Japan, Calypso Joe the Drummer, tin/paper, w/up, orig box....295.00
Japan, Charley Weaver Bartender, battery op, orig box, 12"....30.00
Japan, Chief Robot Man, tin litho/plastic, battery op, 12".....465.00
Japan, Clown on Roller Skates, tin/cloth w/up, orig box, 6"...235.00
Japan, dog w/bootie in mouth, blk fur, tail spins, head bobs....26.00
Japan, duck & 3 ducklings on wheels, tin w/up, worn, 12".....10.00
Japan, Emergency Service Tow Truck, tin, battery op, in box....85.00
Japan, Frankenstein Monster, tin/plastic/cloth, in box, 13½"...180.00
Japan, gray squirrel w/nut, w/up, EX......................35.00
Japan, Happy Band Trio, tin/plush/paper, orig box, 11".......285.00
Japan, Jolly Drummer Monkey, MIB........................45.00
Japan, Louis Armstrong, tin/plastic/cloth, w/up, orig box, 10"..210.00
Japan, Merry Go Round Truck, tin, battery op, in box, 11"....185.00
Japan, Mickey Mouse Locomotive, battery op, in box, 9", NM...60.00
Japan, Mickey the Magician, tin/plastic/cloth, battery op......500.00
Japan, Monkey Batter, tin w/up, orig box, 6", EX............90.00
Japan, Monkey Sheriff, TN mark, w/up.....................40.00
Japan, pink bunny, w/up................................22.50
Japan, Robby Robot, tin litho, battery op, orig box, 13½"...1,100.00
Japan, Rotate-O-Matic Super Astronaut, orig box, 11½", NM...40.00
Japan, San Francisco Cable Car, #514, 1950s...............30.00
Japan, skunk, w/up, G..................................30.00
Japan, Space Patrol, R-10, tin litho/plastic, battery op, 12"...410.00
Japan, Travelling Sam, Peace Corps Man, tin w/up, 7", EX....110.00
Japan, Video Robot, battery op, orig box..................50.00
Japan, Walking Mickey Mouse, celluloid w/up, ft cracked, 7½"..75.00
Jar Mar Co, Little King comic strip wood toy, pull string, MIB..125.00
Jensen, steam engine/piston/flywheel, burns alcohol, #35.......40.00
Kallus, Pete the Pup, wood jtd, 11".......................135.00
Kenton, Bakery Wagon, pulled by horse, 1910, 13".........425.00
Kenton, double decker bus, CI, 1930s, 6½"................250.00
Kenton, elephant pulling clown in chariot, pnt CI, G.........260.00
Kenton, Jaeger cement mixer truck, CI, mechanical, 1930, 9"..650.00

Kenton, Tige pulling Buster Brown in cart, pnt CI/steel, VG....370.00
Keystone, Ride 'Em Power Shovel, pressed steel, crank hdl, 20".85.00
Keystone, truck loader, pnt pressed steel, 17"..............190.00
Kilgore, Arctic Ice Cream Truck, CI, 6½".................250.00
Kilgore, Arctic Ice Cream Truck, CI, 8"..................250.00
Kingsbury, '37 Ford 2 door sedan, gr w/chrome grill/lights, VG.250.00
Kingsbury, Bus #788, pnt tin w/up, 16"...................385.00
Kingsbury, zeppelin Little Jim, tin litho clockwork, 20½"....1,300.00
Knickerbocker, donkey, stuffed, leather harness, 1930, MIB....125.00
Lehmann, Bucking Bronco, pat 1906, w/up, litho/HP tin, EX...465.00
Lehmann, Climbing Miller, orig box.......................400.00
Lehmann, Daredevil, Black man on cart pulled by zebra, w/up...350.00
Lehmann, gallop racing car, 1913, 5½", EX................500.00
Lehmann, Going to the Fair, pnt/litho tin.................650.00
Lehmann, Kadi, 2 Chinamen carry tea chest................550.00
Lehmann, Kamerun, Black man on mail cart pulled by ostrich..350.00
Lehmann, Masuyama, tin litho w/up, minor rust, 7".........775.00
Lehmann, Naughty Boy, tin litho w/up, 4½", VG...........375.00
Lehmann, New Century cycle, pnt/litho tin, 5"..............330.00
Lehmann, Quack Quack, goose pulls cart w/baby geese, w/up...250.00
Lehmann, seal, w/up....................................150.00
Lehmann, Tut Tut, man drives auto, plays horn.............750.00
Lehmann, zeppelin, w/up, 7½"..........................350.00
Lindstrom, Betty, tin litho w/up, 7½", EX.................130.00
Lindstrom, pecking bird, tin litho w/up....................20.00
Lindstrom, Skeeter Bug, #60, 8", MIB.....................85.00
Lindstrom, Sweeping Lady, 8", EX........................140.00
Linemar, Bubble Blowing Popeye, tin, battery op, 12".........300.00
Linemar, Casper the Ghost, mechanical tank...............100.00
Linemar, Disneyland Fire Truck, tin litho, battery op, 18".....400.00
Linemar, Donald Duck Climbing Fireman, tin w/up, 5", EX....200.00
Linemar, Donald Duck Drummer, w/up....................250.00
Linemar, Drummer Boy, tin litho w/up, 9".................75.00
Linemar, Mechanical Hopping Rabbit, #J-1836, in orig box.....25.00
Linemar, Mickey Mouse Xylophone Player, orig box, NM......475.00
Linemar, Minnie Mouse knits in rocker, w/up...............225.00
Linemar, Nutty Nibs, tin, battery op, in box, 12"............350.00
Linemar, Pluto w/movable head pulls cart, friction, 1950s......130.00
Linemar, Popeye balances Olive Oil in chair................850.00
Linemar, Popeye on roller skates, tin litho w/up, 6½".........450.00
Linemar, Popeye shoots basketball through goal, w/up........850.00
Linemar, R-35 robot, tin litho, battery op, remote, 7½".......500.00
Linemar, Smoking Popeye, tin, battery op, orig box, 9".......500.00
Lionel, Donald Duck Hand Car, pnt papier mache/tin, 11", VG.550.00
Lionel, electric range, #455, 1932, 33"...................220.00
Lionel, Mickey Mouse Hand Car, pnt papier mache/tin, 8", EX.550.00
Lionel, Peter Rabbit Chick Mobile, w/up..................450.00
Lorraine, table basketball game, orig box..................16.00
M Drolet & Co, Joy Wash Machine.......................325.00
M&K, Zeppelin Roundabout, pnt tin w/up, 11½", VG........425.00
Mamod, steam engine, horizontal brass boiler/2 cylinder........72.50
Marklin, side-wheeler gunboat, pnt tin, 1904, 31", G........4,070.00
Marklin, truck, HP tin clockwork, 1930s, 16"..............900.00
Martin Co, drunk, cloth/wood/tin litho w/up, 8", G..........350.00
Martin Co, Indian w/bow & arrow, HP, 1900...............250.00
Martin Co, man plays piano, musical, 1900.................650.00
Marx, Amos & Andy, walking figures, stationary eyes, pr.....1,100.00
Marx, Amos & Andy Fresh Air Taxi, MIB..................750.00
Marx, Amos & Andy Fresh Air Taxi, 1930, EX.............650.00
Marx, Beat It, The Komikal Kop, VG......................150.00
Marx, Blondie's Jalopy, tin w/up, 16", G..................300.00
Marx, BO Plenty, w/up, orig box, 8½", EX................160.00
Marx, Buck Rogers Space Ship, 12", G....................190.00
Marx, Bunny Express, tin litho, orig box, NM..............400.00

Marx, Cat & Ball, tin, 2½x5½", M.........................40.00

Marx, Charleston Trio, 1921, 9", EX.....................560.00

Marx, Charlie McCarthy, Benzine Buggy, 1930s.............275.00

Marx, Charlie McCarthy & Mortimer Snerd Private Car, 16"....525.00

Marx, Charlie McCarthy Drummer Boy, tin w/up, orig box, VG..550.00

Marx, Coke truck, wood wheels.........................35.00

Marx, College Crazy Car, EX...........................90.00

Marx, Coo Coo Crazy Car w/driver.....................165.00

Marx, Dagwood the Driver, wood/tin, orig box, 8", EX.......350.00

Marx, Dagwood's Solo Flight, tin w/up, 12", EX............270.00

Marx, Dapper Dan, Carter's Coon Jigger, 1910............250.00

Marx, Dick Tracy Police Station, in box, VG.............100.00

Marx, Dick Tracy Siren Squad, w/up, orig box, 11", EX......120.00

Marx, Dippy Dumper, celluloid/tin litho w/up, EX.........250.00

Marx, Disney Dipsy Car, Mickey driving, w/up, NM.........250.00

Marx, Donald Duck Duet, orig box, EX...................350.00

Marx, Drummer Boy, 9", VG............................120.00

Marx, Farmer in Cart, tin, pnt chipped, 6x10"............55.00

Marx, Harold Lloyd, w/up walker, tin litho, 11".........350.00

Marx, Honeymoon Special, tin w/up train, 6".............20.00

Marx, Hootin' Hollow Haunted House, tin/plastic, battery op...250.00

Marx, Hopalong Cassidy, 11¼", EX......................140.00

Marx, Joy Rider, tin, 7", G...........................100.00

Marx, Let Drummer Boy Play, M.........................165.00

Marx, Lone Ranger, w/up, in orig carton, 7½"............150.00

Marx, Main Street, orig box, 24", EX...................175.00

Marx, Merry Makers Mouse Band, EX.....................650.00

Marx, Mickey Mouse Crazy Car, plastic/tin w/up, EX.........160.00

Marx, Mickey Mouse Express, tin litho w/up, orig box, 9", VG..400.00

Marx, Mighty King, tin/plastic/plush/battery op remote, MIB....200.00

Marx, Milton Berle Car, EX............................170.00

Marx, Moon Mullins & Kayo handcar, litho/tin clockwork, 6"...450.00

Marx, Mortimer Snerd Crazy Car, tin litho w/up, 8".........350.00

Marx, Mortimer Snerd Drummer Boy, 9", EX...............450.00

Marx, Mortimer Snerd Tricky Auto, in orig box, EX.........450.00

Marx, Motorcycle Cop, #3, siren, runs in circle, 8½x6".......70.00

Marx, Mysterious Pluto, metal w/up, orig box.............150.00

Marx, Nutty Mad Indian w/war whoop, battery op, orig box....125.00

Marx, Officer 666, walking figure, w/up..................395.00

Marx, Orphan Annie skips rope; Sandy holds valise, 1930, pr...950.00

Marx, Patrolman, 11½", EX............................400.00

Marx, piggy, tin litho w/up...........................25.00

Marx, Popeye & Olive Oyl on the Roof, 10", EX............600.00

Marx, Popeye Eccentric Airplane, orig carton, EX.........410.00

Marx, Popeye Express, tin litho w/up, EX................260.00

Marx, Porky Pig, orig box, EX.........................170.00

Marx, Range Rider, Lone Ranger, VG.....................80.00

Marx, Red Cap Porter, Negro Carries Baggage, 1930s.........195.00

Marx, Sam the Gardener, plastic/tin litho w/up, 8", VG......95.00

Marx, Siren Fire Chief, sheet metal, friction, 5x14".........40.00

Marx, Solo Flight, Dagwood in airplane, 1935............300.00

Marx, Sparkling Rocket Fighter Ship, orig box, 12½", VG....200.00

Marx, Superman, flat metal figure pushes tank over, 1940....200.00

Marx, Tidy Tim the Clean-Up Man, tin litho, 8x8½".........175.00

Marx, Tom Corbett Sparkling Space Ship, orig box, 12½", VG.375.00

Marx, Toy Town Dairy, tin litho w/up, 1937.............75.00

Marx, Turnover Tank, 4", EX...........................200.00

Marx, Uncle Wiggily Car, tin w/up, 1930s, orig box, EX......375.00

Marx, Whoopee Car, EX...............................175.00

Marx, Wonder Cyclist, tin litho w/up, 9x8"..............285.00

Marx, WWI Tank, soldier w/gun/flag pops up.............125.00

Marx, Yeti, tin/plastic/plush, battery op remote, in box, 11"....285.00

Matchbox, 1911 Maxwell Roadster......................15.00

Matchbox, 1919 Open Coupe...........................15.00

Mavco, Mickey Mouse Scooter-Jockey, plastic/metal, w/up, 6"...200.00

Metalcraft Corp, Shell Motor Oil truck, pressed steel, 12", VG...75.00

Modern Toys, fire engine pumper, tin litho, friction, 5x4", VG...40.00

Mohawk Toys, Playgas gas pump, tin litho/glass/string, 8", EX.245.00

Newton, Aero Circus, zeppelin toy w/2 planes & tower.......650.00

Nifty, Barney Google & Spark Plug, not working, 7½", G.....750.00

Nifty, Buttercup & Spare Ribs pull toy, 7½", VG............450.00

Nifty, Felix on scooter, tin, 7½", VG...................200.00

Nifty, Maggie & Jiggs, tin w/up, 7½", VG................750.00

Nifty, Snowflake Riding Spark Plug, tin, G...............850.00

Nifty, Toonerville Trolly, 1922........................550.00

NY Lint Toy Co, Howdy Doody steers '20s cart, 1950s........175.00

Occupied Japan, Black Dancer Lenox Ave at 125th St, 8½"...170.00

Occupied Japan, Chevrolet w/back motion, MIB.............65.00

Occupied Japan, Donald Duck/whirligig/cart, celluloid/metal....475.00

Occupied Japan, Lucky Sledge, MIB.....................65.00

Occupied Japan, mother/daughter celluloid skaters, 5½".......60.00

Occupied Japan, Zoot-suit Jigger, metal/celluloid, 1945........195.00

Ohio Art, doll stroller, tin/pnt children, 20", EX...........25.00

Ohio Art, Mickey Mouse drum.........................45.00

Ohio Art, Mickey Mouse mechanical washer, tin............150.00

Ohio Art, watering can, tin, Dutch children..............17.00

Orobr, double-decker bus w/driver, 1920s, German, 6".......250.00

Orobr, Model T, door open, tin litho w/up, 6¼", VG.........250.00

Parker Bros, Toy Town Grocery Store, w/accessories, 8x12x17".130.00

Pat Sullivan, Felix the Cat, stuffed cloth w/up, orig card......650.00

Plastimarx, Jalopy, key wind rear wheels, Archie/Veronica/etc...340.00

Ranger Steel, Pool Players, #850, in orig box, NM..........200.00

Reed, Floating Palace, litho paper on wood, G.............900.00

Risdon Mfg, water whistle, brass, 1923, bird whistles..........15.00

Russell, steam engine, portable 8 hp, 1890, G............4,500.00

Schuco, bird, w/up, w/key, 4", M.......................75.00

Schuco, boy playing violin, w/key, 4½", EX..............100.00

Schuco, bulldog, mohair, movable head, 1930s.............275.00

Schuco, Chef, tin litho w/up, 6½", EX..................200.00

Schuco, Chip, c WDE, 1950, MIB, 9".....................65.00

Schuco, clown w/suitcase, tin litho/felt, 4½", VG..........100.00

Schuco, Donald Duck, long bill, orig felt coat, 5", EX........400.00

Schuco, girl drinking from porcelain mug, w/key, 4½", EX....150.00

Schuco, Hor-Zu, dressed, 1950, 11", MIB................125.00

Schuco, Mickey & Minnie Mouse, felt/plush/plastic, in box, pr..250.00

Schuco, Molly, dressed, mohair, 1950, 11½", MIB...........65.00

Schuco, mouse, w/up, 4", VG..........................145.00

Schuco, mouse in clothes lifts sm mouse in grass skirt, 1930s..110.00

Schuco, Packard Hawk, tin/plastic, battery op, 10½".........250.00

Schuco, pig, dressed, mohair, 1950, 10".................75.00

Schuco, Studebaker, tin/plastic, battery op, radio, 10".......265.00

Schuco, Tambo Tiger, mohair, 1950, 10", MIB.............65.00

Schuco, Yes/No Cat, 8"..............................110.00

SG Co, fire truck, pumper type w/3 fireman, w/up, 1920s.....375.00

Smith Miller, truck, pressed steel, Bank of Am decal, 14" L...165.00

Smitty, aerial ladder truck #3, 6 wheel tractor w/trailer, 34"....240.00

Steelcraft, Fire Truck City Fire Dept, sheet iron, 11x27", EX..270.00

Steelcraft, Good Year Zeppelin, pnt pressed steel, 31", VG....400.00

Strauss, Flying Air Ship, #1017 Gray Zeppelin, EX...........350.00

Strauss, Flying Air Ship, #1017 Gray Zeppelin, MIB.........450.00

Strauss, Ham & Sam, musicians at piano, 1921, NM..........450.00

Strauss, Ham & Sam, orig box, NM.....................500.00

Strauss, Interstate double-decker bus, 1920s..............350.00

Strauss, Jazzbo Jim dances on cabin, plays banjo, 1921.......250.00

Strauss, Kraka-Jack, man in 4 wheeled cart, MIB...........325.00

Strauss, Leaping Lena, w/up, 8½", EX..................200.00

Strauss, man drives 1915 auto, w/up....................225.00

Strauss, Tip Top, Black man pushing cart, 1920s...........175.00

Strauss, Tombo, Alabama Coon Jigger, 1910..............295.00
Strauss, Yell-O-Taxi, tin litho w/up, 8″, EX...............300.00
Structo, car, all orig w/decal, 7x16″......................350.00
Structo, cattle truck, sheet metal, all orig, 7½x21″...........45.00
TFS Co, Long Haulage Truck, tin litho, 11½″, VG..........220.00
Tip Top Toy Co, Giant Flyer airplane, 22½″...............225.00
Tonka, fire truck, sheet metal, all orig, 6x17″..............25.00
Tootsie Toy, Beechcraft Bonanza.......................13.00
Tootsie Toy, Corvette, 1954...........................25.00
Tootsie Toy, Dairy Truck, cab w/3 trailers................125.00
Tootsie Toy, Ford convertible, 1949.....................20.00
Tootsie Toy, Ford sedan, 1949.........................20.00
Tootsie Toy, Ford station wagon, 1938...................25.00
Tootsie Toy, Ford Trimotor...........................65.00
Tootsie Toy, GMC Greyhound Scenic Cruiser Bus, 1954.......13.00
Tootsie Toy, Graham Sedan...........................30.00
Tootsie Toy, Herbie & Smitty on Motorcycle...............195.00
Tootsie Toy, Herbie on Cycle w/sidecar, 1930s.............195.00
Tootsie Toy, La Salle w/rumble seat....................100.00
Tootsie Toy, Mack..................................25.00
Tootsie Toy, Moon Mullins Police Patrol, w/action camera, EX.140.00
Tootsie Toy, Offenhouser Racer, 1947...................15.00
Tootsie Toy, Pennsylvania loco freight train, 1939, 6 pcs.......55.00
Tootsie Toy, Railway Express Truck.....................75.00
Tootsie Toy, Uncle Walt drives roadster..................195.00
Tootsie Toy, Wrecker................................35.00
TPS Japan, hobo clown on roller skates, w/up, 1950s.........225.00
Tri-ang, dump truck, sheet iron w/orig red pnt/decal, 17x19″...140.00
Unique Art, Finnegan, tin litho w/up, orig box, 13½″, EX.....160.00
Unique Art, GI Joe & His Jouncing Jeep, VG................80.00
Unique Art, Hee Haw, tin litho w/up, 10½″, EX.............55.00
Unique Art, Howdy Doody & Bob Smith Piano, EX..........435.00
Unique Art, Kiddy Cyclist, boy rides tricycle, G.............125.00
Unique Art, Li'l Abner Dog Patch Band, EX...............350.00
Unique Art, Li'l Abner Dog Patch Band, MIB..............400.00
Unique Art, Rodeo Joe, G............................70.00
Unique Art, Sky Ranger, orig box, EX....................175.00
Unique Art, Unique Artie, orig box, EX..................125.00
Unitrol, Mad Hatter marionette, orig box, EX..............10.00
US Zone Germany, camel & driver, tin w/up, MIB, 6″.........120.00
USA, jigger, motor in chest, Oriental & Black features, 7″.....195.00
Vor Bonnet & Cie Succ, dump truck w/driver, w/up, 1910....350.00
Wells of London, Opera car, tin litho w/driver, w/up.........300.00
Welsotoys, Vauxhall, #101, battery op, MIB...............35.00
Wheeden, steam engine, horizontal brass boiler, 1 cylinder.....95.00
Wheeden, steam engine w/piston & fly wheel, electric, 6x6x6″...80.00
Wheeden, steam launch, Glouster, pntd tin, 3 blade prop, 19″..770.00
Wilkins, goat cart, pnt CI, 6½″, VG.....................210.00
Wilkins, tandem cart, pnt CI, 9″, EX....................80.00
Wolverine, Captain Sandy Andy, #63C, orig box, EX..........35.00
Wolverine, Drum Major, #27, 14″......................100.00
Wolverine, jet roller coaster, tin/pressed steel litho, 21″ L.....85.00
Wolverine, Sandy Andy Merry Go Round, #108, MIB........150.00
Wyandotte, Speed King, boy peddles handmade scooter, 1930s.225.00

Cranks and Windups

Bear drinking milk, sits on 'Farm Milk' carton, w/up, 6″, EX....75.00
Bico Bus to Joyville, tin, dbl decker bus w/passengers.........380.00
Bird, w/up, pecks ground, mk Dec 1927, 6 litho colors, 5½″....15.00
Black man on donkey, mechanical w/up pull toy, 20x27″.....2,000.00
Car, yellow/blk w/red stripes, V grill, open/close doors, 8″.....400.00
Cat, pnt tin, clockwork, pushes cage w/rats, late 1800s, 6½″...675.00
Charlie Chaplin, carrying luggage, celluloid w/up, 7″..........75.00

Charlie Chaplin, compo/metal, walks, w/up, 1920s, 11″.......650.00
Charlie Chaplin, tin/lead/cloth suit, holds cane/tips hat, 8″.....650.00
Chicken, pecking, tin litho w/up............................28.00
Children on teeter-totter, plastic, '30s, 7″ L..................35.00
Circus truck w/lion that jumps for tamer, w/up...............350.00
Clown dances w/dog on turntable, w/up, 1920s...............275.00
Clown plays xylophone, cloth & HP metal, 1900, w/up..........450.00
Coast to Coast, double decker bus, 1930s, w/up...............175.00
Cymbal player, compo head, key wind, early, 9½″.............200.00
Dirigible, aluminum w/up, prop spins, taxies, '30s, 11″.........350.00
Dog, tan fur, tail whirls, bends & straightens, 5″, VG...........25.00
Elf, w/up, 6″, VG......................................35.00
Fleet Flyer Sunny Andy #26, pressed steel/tin w/up............105.00
Geo Washington on horseback, tin litho, w/up, 6½″, EX.....325.00
Happy Hooligan, dances on drum, tin crank, 1930s...........650.00
Henry, celluloid w/up figure on metal trapeze, 1930s.........250.00
Hi-Way Henry, tin litho w/up, rpl, rpr..................2,000.00
Mickey Mouse, celluloid w/up walker, 7½″...............1,350.00
Monkey in clothes drives railroad handcar, HP, 1890s........350.00
Mother Bear pulling 2 baby bears, w/up, EX.................95.00
Popeye, celluloid w/up figure, movable arms/neck/head, 8½″...395.00
Prince & Princess dancing, w/up...........................75.00
Roadster, metal, CI driver, w/up, 1920s, 10½″..............250.00
Spic & Span, Black musicians............................650.00
Truck, North Am Van Lines, pressed steel w/up, 1940s, 14″ L.100.00
WWI German soldier crawls w/rifle, HP, 1915, rare, NM......400.00
1915 Stutz, front-end crank w/up.........................250.00
3 mice pull wheeled mechanism while doing somersaults, w/up..150.00

Farm Toys

Allis Chalmers, tractor, Am Precision Prod Co, 1940s.........150.00
Allis Chalmers, tractor, D17..............................110.00
Case, tractor, #1030, MIB...............................145.00
Case, tractor, #1370....................................40.00
Case, tractor, Spirit of '76...............................75.00
Ford, 1922 C Cab truck.................................900.00
Gehl, skid loader......................................100.00
Int'l Harvester, tractor, #1466............................70.00
Int'l Harvester, tractor, #450.............................160.00
Int'l Harvester, tractor, #5288, 1st Ed KC, 9-81.............130.00
Int'l Harvester, tractor, #560.............................50.00
Int'l Harvester, tractor, #806, round fenders................100.00
Int'l Harvester, tractor, #856, wide front...................65.00
John Deere, baler, #14T................................120.00
John Deere, combine, #12A, very good repaint...............75.00
John Deere, combine, #30...............................180.00
John Deere, combine, #6600.............................190.00
John Deere, corn picker, #60, 2 row mounted................90.00
John Deere, crawler, #1020..............................170.00
John Deere, manure loader, #60...........................75.00
John Deere, spreader, model R...........................107.50
John Deere, tractor, #60................................275.00
John Deere, tractor, #620...............................330.00
John Deere, tractor, #620, MIB...........................450.00
John Deere, tractor, #7020, 4-wheel rugged.................200.00
John Deere, tractor, Arcade A............................150.00
John Deere, tractor, high post A...........................95.00
Massey Harris, tractor, by Rehull, repaint..................295.00
New Idea, picker.......................................95.00
Oliver, combine, VG....................................80.00
Oliver, tractor, #1800...................................50.00
Oliver, tractor, #1850...................................45.00
Oliver, tractor, #77.....................................85.00

White, tractor, #2-155...........................60.00
White, tractor, #4-210, silver decals.........................80.00

Friction

Auto, 1910, metal w/CI driver, HP.........................175.00
Battleship, HP metal, 1910, 15″.........................135.00
Boy rides sled, 1900, 9″.........................150.00
Locomotive engine, sheet metal/CI wheels/wood trim, rpt, 14″...45.00
Toy horse pulls man in chariot, 1910.....................225.00

Guns

Though toy guns were patented as early as the 1850s, the cap pistol was not invented until 1870, when paper caps that were primarily developed to detonate muzzleloaders became available. Some of the earlier models were very ornate, and were occasionally decorated with figural heads. Most are marked with the name of their manufacturer – Ace, Daisy, Bulldog, Victor, and Excelsior are the most common.

Cap bomb, Bozo, pnt CI.........................65.00
Cap bomb, Dewey, nickeled CI, lg.........................65.00
Cap bomb, Indian, japanned CI.........................80.00
Cap bomb, Ives Squatting Negro, japanned CI...............85.00
Congo Fire Bug, japanned CI, cap shooter, orig box, NM.....450.00
Crack host dart pistol #37, w/dart, Wyandotte, in orig box.....20.00
Daisy, BB gun, 1901.........................125.00
Gene Autry, CI & plastic, G.........................25.00
Hubley, lock w/key shape, animated, late '40s, 4½x3¼″.......55.00
Humpty Dumpty, japanned CI, recast.........................20.00
King Air Rifle, 500 shot carbine, Markham Co, 1908........125.00
Kit Carson, Kilgore, cap pistol, MIB.........................18.00
Lion, pat June 21, 1887, 5½″.........................145.00
Lock Pistol, Hubley, die-cast, VG.........................200.00
Red Ryder, BB, Daisy, wood stock.........................32.50
Red Ryder carbine, 36″ L, orig box, G.........................25.00
Repeater, National, USA, pat 6/29/03, CI, shoots caps, 4x3″....35.00
Royal Pistol, nickeled CI & pnt wood.........................80.00
Shootin' Shell Fanner, Mattel, 1956, MIB.................20.00
Tom Corbett Official Space Pistol, Marx, tin clicker, 10″......135.00

Pedal Toys and Ride-On Toys

Boat, wood, Moncano, 17x41″.........................390.00
Car, Boycraft, 1934, rstr.........................1,000.00
Car, Peerless, 1910, rstr.........................1,100.00
Car, the 'Duke', sheet iron, 30″.........................60.00
Car, Torpedo, all orig pnt, 22x38″.........................75.00
Snail, Mobo, orig pnt, 26″.........................15.00
Train engine, pnt Cannonball Express, Casey Jones, sheet metal.45.00
Tricycle, tin mechanical horse, working, 39″...............270.00
Velocipede, G orig, 55″.........................245.00

Penny Toys

Auto.........................110.00
Biplane w/rider, tin litho, ½ prop missing.................200.00
Church w/steeple bank, G orig pnt, 3½x2½″.................60.00
Clown chasing donkey, German, tin litho, EX...............180.00
Coach, CR, France, orig pnt, 3″.........................80.00
Doll in carriage, wire pc hdl missing, made in Germany, 3″....120.00
Fire truck, pumper w/fireman.........................125.00
Girl feeding rooster, German, mechanical.................190.00
Man in cart pulled by 3-D horse, G orig color, 4″...........110.00

Man shoots pool, mechanical.........................85.00
Mother pushing baby in chair, German, litho tin, EX.........240.00
Train engine, friction drawn, G orig pnt, 5½″...............80.00
Train set, CKO, German, loco/tender/2 cars, orig box.........150.00
Truck w/driver, German, tin litho, EX.....................100.00

Pipsqueaks

Pipsqueak toys were popular among the Pennsylvania Germans. The earliest had bellows made from sheepskin. Later, cloth replaced the sheepskin, and finally paper bellows were used.

Bird in cage, compo w/flocking, wire cage battered, silent, 8″...45.00
Birds, facing, animated, tin, box torn but working, 3″.........75.00
Cardinal, bellows rpr, 5″.........................160.00
Cardinal, on sm bellows, working, 1870s, 5x2½x2″...........140.00
Cat, sitting, touched-up orig pnt, cloth box torn, 6″...........75.00
Chicken in topcoat, 8″.........................325.00
Chicken on nest, wings flap, 6″.........................250.00
Dog, 3½″, G orig.........................150.00
Dog w/tin watch around neck, 4½″, G orig.................300.00
Elephant, tip of trunk rpr, 4½″.........................180.00
Parrot, compo, orig pnt, some flaking, working, 7″...........175.00
Parrot on perch in wood birdcage, compo/felt w/feather tail....165.00
Rooster, compo body/orig pnt decor, cloth squeak box, 10½″...360.00
Rooster, compo/mc paint, leather bellows, rpr, 9½″.........150.00
Rooster, papier mache, worn orig pnt, paper bellows, 9″......150.00
Rooster & hen in cage, compo birds w/feathers, silent, 5½″.....70.00
Two face, 1 side man, other lady, 3″.........................340.00
Two face, 1 side smiling, 1 frowning, 2½″ dia................310.00

Pull Toys

Boy on tricycle, wood w/simple trn wood parts, worn pnt, 10″...40.00
Chick in hiking outfit, pressed chromolitho cardboard, 6x4x2″...85.00
Child & lion, tin w/orig bl/blk/gold/br, gr base, 3½″.........300.00
Cow on wheels, hide covered, 6½x9″.....................150.00
Dog, walking, composition w/worn br/blk pnt, 10″ L...........15.00
Elephant, gray felt/straw stuffing, ivory tusks, 1890s, 12x10″...250.00
Elephant, tin, trunk down, CI wheels, 1800, 6¼x5x2½″.....175.00
Goat, wood/compo/angora, glass eyes, voice box, 8¾″ L.......115.00
Horse, cloth over wood, CI wheels, all orig, 11x9″...........190.00
Horse, felt w/tin wheels, early Victorian, all orig, 8x7″.......210.00
Horse, hide covered, cast wheels, wood fr, all orig, 8″........160.00
Horse, nodder, compo/wood/flocked coat/paper blanket, 5″......60.00
Horse, wood & papier mache, 9″.........................105.00
Horse, wood/compo, dapple gray pnt G, no saddle/mane/tail, 7″..80.00
Horse, wood/papier mache, dappled wht/blk w/red saddle, 7″, G.55.00
Horse & cart, tin w/orig gold japanning on cart, 8⅛″.........160.00
Horse & rider, animated, tin w/orig pnt, 4½″...............525.00
Horse & wagon, tin w/orig red/wht/blk pnt, battered/rpr, 10″...295.00
Lamb, lambskin/wood base/metal wheels, baas, brass bell, 15″..950.00
Lion, tin w/orig yellow pnt, gr base, minor wear, 4⅛″.........150.00
Lion w/raised paw, tin w/orig yel pnt w/gr base, 4½″, VG......125.00
Locomotive & tender, tin, worn blk pnt w/gold stripe, 12″ L....30.00
Man on horse, tin, worn orig pnt, 3¼″.....................125.00
Peacock, mother & 2 babies, tin w/mc japanning, 4¼″; 7½″...300.00

Schoenhut

From 1872 to 1933, Schoenhut produced toys, dolls, games, and puzzles. Their circus toys were made as early as 1903 and are the most highly prized examples of their work. They also made a similar series of farm pieces, as well as several comic characters. Though they were never marked, Schoenhut figures are easily recognized by their jointed wood bodies, strung together with elastic cords. Early examples were made with glass eyes, and are more valuable than the later ones with painted eyes.

Airplane, in box...................................35.00
Alligator, pnt eyes, rpl leather ft, G orig pnt, 12½"...........140.00
Alligator, pnt eyes, 12½", EX.................225.00
Barney Google & Sparkplug, w/sticker, yellow coat, pr.......950.00
Bed, tester; orig canopy, hangings & lace/silk coverlet, 6½"...225.00
Black Man, colorful outfit, leather hat, 8"..................200.00
Book, Humpty Dumpty Circus, G.................45.00
Buffalo, pnt eyes, leather horns, 7½", EX.................170.00
Camel, 2 hump, orig pnt, 9"..................160.00
Catalogue, M.................................60.00
Circus, tent, 6 animals w/pnt eyes/3 people/4 accessories, VG...800.00
Circus, 16 pnt eye animals/7 people/20 accessories, EX......2,150.00
Clown, pnt eyes, rpl clothing, 8"..................125.00
Cow, pnt eyes, leather horns, 8½", EX.................185.00
Dirigible, builder, c 1929, orig box, unused.................375.00
Donkey, glass eyes, 7".......................140.00
Donkey, pnt eyes, 9½"........................50.00
Felix, blk/wht pnt, leather ears, rpt, 7½".................225.00
Felix, 4", M.................................75.00
Giraffe, pnt eyes, orig pnt, 11"..................150.00
Goat, pnt eyes...............................100.00
Gorilla, pnt eyes, leather ears, slight touch up, 8"..........410.00
Happy Hooligan, syndicate sticker on ft, EX.............1,400.00
Hippopotamus, glass eyes, 9½", EX.................260.00
Hobo, reg size..............................125.00
Horse w/platform............................60.00
Kangaroo, pnt eyes, orig pnt, 9"..................300.00
Lady bareback rider, bsk head/pnt eyes/hair, outfit G, 7½"....450.00
Leopard....................................100.00
Lion, cloth mane, reg size....................425.00
Mary & lamb, reg size.......................650.00
Monkey, pnt eyes/body, red felt hat & suit, 8", G.........120.00
Mule, rpl tail..............................100.00
Ostrich, pnt eyes, 9", EX.....................240.00
Piano, grain pnt decor, early 1900s, 6¼x8½x5"............45.00
Piano, 29 keys, pnt & decor G.................175.00
Piano, 6 keys, orig red finish, some rpr, 6x8"...............58.00
Piano stool, doll's, revolving top, 9".................65.00
Pig, orig pnt, 6½"...........................185.00
Poodle, glass eyes..........................115.00
Ringmaster, bisque head, 7"...................150.00
Roly Dolly Clown, pk top hat, w/umbrella.................150.00
Teddy Roosevelt, spring jointed, w/helmet/ammunition belt, 8"..440.00
U-Build House, in box, sm.....................75.00

Steiff

Margaret Steiff began making her felt stuffed toys in 1800, in Germany. The animals she made were tagged with an elephant in a circle. Her first teddy bear, made in 1903, became such a popular seller that she changed her tag to a bear. Felt stuffing was replaced with excelsior and wool, and when it became available, foam was used. In addition to the tag, look for the 'Steiff' ribbon, and the button inside the ear.

Bat, Eric, 8"...............................250.00
Bat, w/button, 3½"..........................125.00
Bear, Anniversary, MIB w/certificate..................350.00
Bear, Cosy Orsi, 7x8".......................85.00
Bear, Cosy Teddy, w/tag & button, 12".................95.00

Hen, mohair, with tag, 7" x 5½", $110.00.

Bear, Cosy Teddy, w/tag & button, 8"..................85.00
Bear, fully jtd, w/button, 9"...................150.00
Bear, Zotty, fully jtd, paws down, mohair, w/squeaker, 11".....145.00
Bear, Zotty, fully jtd, paws down, mohair, 9½".................110.00
Bear, Zotty, fully jtd, w/squeaker, 11"..................85.00
Bear, Zotty, w/squeaker, well loved condition, 9".............125.00
Beaver, jtd head, w/button, 7"..................65.00
Bison, mohair, w/tag, 6x9"....................125.00
Cat, Lizzy, w/tag & button, 6½"..................70.00
Cat, Lizzy, w/tag & button, 7½"..................80.00
Chimpanzee, Jocko, mohair, 5 jtd, 20", M.................140.00
Cow, Cosy Kalble, blk/wht, w/collar & bell, tag & button, 10"..125.00
Crocodile, w/button, 21½" L....................110.00
Deer, Bambi, mohair, lying, w/button, 8x16".................125.00
Deer, Bambi, w/tag & button, copyright Walt Disney, 6".......75.00
Dinosaur, w/button & tag, 53", 15 ft long.................700.00
Dog, Arco, mohair, w/collar & tag, 6½x11".................95.00
Dog, Cocker Spaniel, jtd head, w/collar & button, 10x12".....125.00
Dog, Floppy Cocki, w/tag & button, 7".................47.50
Dog, Hexie, Dachshund, jtd head, w/button/collar/squeak, 7x11".95.00
Dog, Peky, Pekinese, jtd head, w/tag & button, 5x6".........75.00
Dog, Peky, Pekinese, jtd head, w/tag & button, 9x12".........125.00
Dog, poodle, blk, jtd legs, w/collar & button, 5½".............55.00
Doll, Cappy, w/tag & button, 12", M.................95.00
Doll, Sandy, w/tag & button, 12", M.................95.00
Donkey, riding; open iron wheels, ear button, 1910, 30".....725.00
Duck, jtd head, w/tag & button, 8"..................65.00
Dwarf, Gucki, w/tag & button, 12", M.................150.00
Dwarf, Gucki, w/tag & button, 7", M.................75.00
Dwarf, Lucki, w/tag, 7", M....................65.00
Dwarf, Lucki, w/tag & button, 12", M.................150.00
Dwarf, Pucki, w/tag, 7", M....................65.00
Elephant, Jumbo, sitting, w/EX bells, w/tag & button, 15".....150.00
Elephant, w/bells, w/tag & button, 10"..................135.00
Elephant, w/bells, w/tag & button, 8"..................110.00
Fish, Flossy, w/tag & button, 5"..................35.00
Frog, mohair, w/button, 10½"...................125.00
Gazelle, 55x58"............................750.00
Giraffe, mohair, w/button, 13"..................95.00
Giraffe, mohair w/straw stuffing, 1960s, 59".................1,000.00
Hedgehog, w/button, 2½"......................15.00

Horse, w/button, 6x6½".............................85.00
Jocko, hand puppet, w/tag & button, M....................48.00
Lamb, w/bell & button, 8"............................85.00
Lion, Leo, lying, w/tag, 6x11"..........................95.00
Lion, Leo, standing, w/tag & button, 13".................125.00
Lion, Leo, w/tag & button, 3½x4½".......................45.00
Mickey Mouse, velvet/felt, button in ear, 12½", EX........500.00
Mole, mohair, felt nose, w/shovel, button, 4".............45.00
Monkey, on handcar, w/tag & button......................195.00
Mouse, mohair, felt paws & ears, w/button, 3".............45.00
Neander, primitive man, tooth necklace, rubber, w/tag, 5¼"....65.00
Owl, Wittie, w/tag & button, 10".........................125.00
Owl, Wittie, w/tag & button, 6"..........................75.00
Pelican, mohair, 6½"...................................85.00
Penguin, Peggy, tag & button, 9".........................85.00
Pig, felt, gr felt tux, red/gr/bl on wht checked pants, 16".....85.00
Pony, w/button, 6½"...................................75.00
Rabbit, Bunny, mohair, jtd head, w/button, 5"............55.00
Rabbit, mohair, jtd head, w/button, 4½"..................65.00
Rabbit, orig Vario, mohair, 3 jtd, working voice, w/tag, EX....150.00
Rabbit, Ossi, w/tag & button, 10½"......................85.00
Ram, Snucki, w/tag & button, 8".........................85.00
Rooster, w/button, 12".................................125.00
Rooster, w/tag & button, 7"............................95.00
Shepherd, felt clothes, jtd head & arms, w/tag & button, 8½"...85.00
Snake, 6 ft long......................................595.00
Squirrel, Perri, w/tag, copyright Walt Disney, 5".........65.00
Tiger, Bengal, working voice, 1960, 72".................635.00
Tiger, standing, w/tag, 3x7"...........................45.00
Tiger, standing, w/tag & button, 10"....................55.00
Turtle, mohair w/rubber shell, w/button, 7½".............45.00
Turtle, velvet w/rubber shell, w/button, 11".............85.00
Wolf, hand puppet, w/button, M.........................48.00
Zebra, mohair, w/button, 8"............................65.00

Toy Soldiers

Toy soldiers were popular playthings with children of the 19th century. They were made by many European manufacturers in various sizes until 1848, when a standard size of approximately 1⅓" was established. The most collectible of all toy soldiers were made in England by Britains Ltd. from 1893 to 1966. In America, some of the important manufacturers were Barclay, Manoil, Grey, and All-Nu.

Barclay, cameraman...................................25.00
Barclay, mechanic w/engine............................25.00
Barclay, parachutist..................................15.00
Barclay, rangefinder..................................15.00
Battles of Yesteryear, British Line Infantry, lead, 20 pc, 1"....60.00
Battles of Yesteryear, Russian Line Infantry, lead, 20 pc, 1"....65.00
Berdou, Marshall Davout on horseback, sgn 1960..........450.00
Blenheim, Band of the Line, #s B45 & B46................100.00
Britains, Austrian Foot Guards, marching at slope, #178.....300.00
Britains, Bahamas Police Band, #2186, 26 pc...........2,800.00
Britains, Band o/t Life Guards, State Dress, #101, 12 pc....300.00
Britains, Band o/t Royal Scots Greys, #1720, orig box.....135.00
Britains, Band of Royal Marines, #1622, minor chips......550.00
Britains, Bene, 4 policemen on motorcycles, #239, very rare...440.00
Britains, Boer Infantry, marching at shoulder arms, #26....800.00
Britains, Chinese Infantry, advancing, pre WWII, #241, in box..300.00
Britains, Circus set figures, 17 pc......................275.00
Britains, Coldstream Guard Band Set, #37, 21 pc.........500.00
Britains, Devonshire Regiment, marching at trail, #110....400.00
Britains, Drum & Pipe Band o/t Irish Guards, #9428, orig box..300.00
Britains, Egyptian Cavalry lancers/officers, #115, orig box....135.00

Britains, Gordon Highlanders & Scots Guards, 22 for......220.00
Britains, Guard Room, #1734...........................950.00
Britains, Heavy Duty Dorry w/driver, #1641, orig box.....300.00
Britains, Heavy Duty Underslung Army Lorry, #1641, rare....175.00
Britains, Imperial Yeomanry, mounted at trot, #105.......300.00
Britains, Infanteria Espanola, #92, in orig box..........145.00
Britains, Infantry, Marines, West Point Cadets, #232, orig box..220.00
Britains, Parachute Regiment, #2092, orig box...........140.00
Britains, Prussian Infantry marching at slope, #154, 1908, box..500.00
Britains, Royal Air Force, #240, in orig box.............145.00
Britains, Royal Air Force Monoplane, #433, w/4 extra....1,100.00
Britains, Royal Army Medical Corps, #137, chips/wear....250.00
Britains, Royal Horse Artillery in review order, #39......140.00
Britains, Royal Navy, #35, in orig box..................135.00
Britains, Royal Sussex Regiment, marching at slope, 42 for...250.00
Britains, Serbian Infantry, charging, #173, 1935.........500.00
Britains, Snow White/7 Dwarfs, #1654..................240.00
Britains, Spanish Infantry, marching at slope, #92........400.00
Britains, State Coach, #1470, orig box..................300.00
Britains, State Open Landau, #2094, orig box............420.00
Britains, Sudanese Infantry, marching at trail, #116......325.00
Britains, United States Military Band, #2110, 25 pc.....1,100.00
Britains, 1st Bengal Lancers & Skinners' Horses, 10 for....150.00
Britains, 21st Empress of India's Lancers at gallop, #94....400.00
Courtenay, Sir John Pateshull, attacking w/battleaxe, #7, sgn...375.00
Courtenay, Sir Robert Holland, sword/shield, #14, sgn....350.00
Elastolin, bear, standing, brown, #6230.................20.00
Elastolin, Indian, walking w/tomahawk, D/6825..........19.00
Elastolin, lion, sitting, #6216.........................14.00
Elastolin, policeman on horse, papier mache, 1920s, 6"....55.00
Elastolin, tiger, standing, #6218......................19.00
Elastolin, totem pole, #6790..........................19.00
Elastolin, trapper standing firing rifle, #6866..........19.00
Manoil, Black eating watermelon, M142.................75.00
Manoil, digging trench...............................25.00
Manoil, farmer at pump, M167.........................18.50
Manoil, Navy deck gunner, M76........................16.50
Manoil, observer w/periscope..........................15.00
Manoil, paymaster, rare..............................125.00
Manoil, soldier in poncho, M189.......................36.50
Manoil, standing sniper, long rifle, M48...............14.00
SA Sculptured Models, French infantry, 8 pc, orig box....125.00
SA Sculptured Models, Germany field gun team, #6499, 17 pc..110.00
Wood cut-out w/chromolithographic paper cover, 14", pr....25.00

Trains

Electric trains were produced as early as the late 19th century. Names to look for are Lionel, Ives, and American Flyer.

American Flyer, engine & tender, mk Penn #312...........50.00
Austin, HO, brass A-6 Atlantic 4-4-2 w/brass oil tender, EX....235.00

New York Central, #5207, handmade tin, coal and cabin hood, 12" high, 39" long, $225.00.

Bing, #1425, loco, tender, 3 coaches, pnt/litho tin, O ga......320.00
Bing, #5103 mini RR system, NYC & HR, orig box..........235.00
Buddy L, locomotive & tender, orig labels, pnt steel, G.......450.00
Lionel, Don Duck rail car, pnt papier mache/steel, not working.450.00
Lionel, engine #10, standard gauge, 11", G............110.00
Lionel, engine #248/observation car #630/pullman #629/track...195.00
Lionel, engine #390-E, standard gauge, 11", G.............200.00
Lionel, locomotive, #708, 0-72 gauge.....................550.00
Lionel, Mickey Mouse Handcar, #1100, orig box............750.00
Lionel, Peter Rabbit Chick Mobile, handcar, 1930s..........500.00
Lionel, Santa Handcar, Santa w/Mickey Mouse on pack......1,250.00
Lionel, set #347, Olive Inc, Lionel City station, bridges, etc....495.00
Marx, Stream Line, steam type electric, 6 parts, orig box.......65.00

Miscellaneous

Barnyard, 22 animals & farm accessories, paper..............25.00
Clockwork, stage w/clock, pig, weight lifter, 1895, 12x14"....1,250.00
Clown roly poly, papier mache, HP, early 1900s, 10"........125.00

Steel auto with electric lights, 5" x 14½", $300.00.

Dutch Village, paper, uncut, Bradley by Lulu Mard Chance......10.00
Horse, leather covered, on wheels, also fits rockers, 48".......500.00
Piano/xylophone, paper litho over wood, 15x14x7", 1890s.....140.00
Play Merry Go Round, 4 panoramas, paper, Schilling Co, 1944..25.00

Early stuffed horse, button eyes, 10" x 10½", $65.00.

Puppet, papier mache, orig clothes, wood hands/ft, 1800s......85.00
Rocking horse w/jockey, tin w/orig litho transfer, 3¾".......175.00
Stuffed, Bambi, tin eyes, straw filled, 14"...................40.00
Stuffed dog, glass eyes/leather collar, straw filled, 12x15"......45.00
Stuffed donkey, handmade, felt/MOP eyes/yarn tail, 1920s, 12"..38.00
Stuffed elephant, shoe button eyes, ISA Animated Toys, 7x9"...40.00
Stuffed rabbit, cotton/glass button eyes, sawdust w/in, 9".......38.00

Trade Signs

Trade signs were popular during the 1800s. They were usually made in an easily recognizable shape that one could mentally associate with the particular type of business it was to represent, especially appropriate in the days when many customers could not read!

Barber shop, wood, 32"....................................85.00
Beauty shop, neon sign w/name of proprietor................135.00
Bootmaker's, worn orig red/blk on yel, 2 boots/shoe, 14x38"...135.00
Boots, Shoes, pnt on curved sheet zinc, wood fr, 12x18½".....65.00
Butcher, cleaver/knife/saw forms base for sm steer atop, metal..350.00
Dairy, applied wood letters & bottles on masonite oval, 32x15".235.00
Dentist, glass w/pointing hand.............................65.00
Dentist, tin w/yel arrow: Painless Dentist, 19"...............45.00
Eyes Examined, glasses fitted, Reg Optometrist, rvpt, lights...375.00
Harness maker, horse head, tin, ca 1900, sm rpr, 13".......235.00
House & Sign Painting, mask/scrolls, old rpt, 27x24"........175.00
Jewelry, watch repair; pocket watch, porcelain, dbl face.......195.00

Wrought iron with heavy sheet iron top hat, worn old red and black paint, 36" x 38", $750.00.

Key figural, hollow metal................................165.00
Mortar & pestle, jeweled, w/lamp, 4 ft, EX.................1,250.00
Pocket watch, plated CI fr/sheet metal face/pnt hands, 11x16"...65.00
Riding boot, sheet metal, wrought iron fr, 36"...............275.00
Saw, wood/sheet metal, orig pnt, 'Saw Filling', 45"..........275.00
School of Dancing, Private Lessons, pnt wood, rpt, 39x19"....120.00
Shears, all wood, gr pnt, 38" L...........................155.00
Shoe store, curved sheet zinc on wood fr, blk/gold pnt, 12x18"..65.00
Tailor & Costumier, wood w/picture fr mold, rpt/worn, 20x25"...50.00
24 Hour Grill, neon sign..................................145.00

Tramp Art

Today considered a type of American folk art, tramp art was made from the late 1800s until after the turn of the century. Often produced by 'tramps' and 'hobos' from wooden materials which could be scavenged -- crates and cigar boxes for instance -- articles such as jewelry boxes and picture frames were usually decorated by chip-carving and then stained.

Box, chip carved facade, 6 drw, 11x12x6″	45.00
Box, chip carved/scalloped, 3 drw w/glass pulls, 15x7″	45.00
Box, drawer, flattened pyramid top, 5x7x10″	25.00
Box, hanging; chip carved heart/circles, 8x15″	85.00
Box, ped base, diamond shape, 6x5x5″	40.00
Box, very ornate, 10x7½″	37.50
Box, 2 ped base, good old finish, minor hinge damage, 10″ W	80.00
Doll's dresser w/mirror	30.00
Frame, geometric/heart, multi-layers, 47x40″, pr	522.00
Frame, H-shape superstructure, easel bk, 16x8″, pr	60.00
Frame, layers of chip carved wood, 6½x8½″	35.00
Frame, porcelain button corners, elaborate, 5x7″, pr	130.00
Frame, shadow box, 7x9″	35.00
Frame, 5 point star ea centered w/RR nailhead, 1915	37.50
Frame, 8x10½″	55.00
Inkwell, wood man w/pen holder, stamp box & glass insert, 5½″	75.00
Match safe	20.00
Mirror, irregular edge w/8 heart cut-outs, 22″ dia	200.00
Plant stand, worn br graining, 28½x12½x15½″	45.00
Plaque, chip carved pine, birds/butterflies, pnt decor, 12x14″	20.00
Shaving mirror, drw/tall crest, much chip carved applique, 33″	300.00

Traps

Though of interest to collectors for many years, trap collecting has gained in popularity over the past ten years in particular, causing prices to appreciate rapidly. Traps are usually marked on the pan as to manufacturer, and the condition of these trademarks are important when determining their value. Grading is as follows:

    Good: 1/2 of pan legible
    Very Good: legible in entirety, but light
    Fine: legible in entirety, with strong lettering
    Mint: in like-new, shiny condition
    Prices listed here are for traps in fine condition.

Aldrich Spring Loaded Snare	10.00
Alligator Game Trap #2	125.00
Arrow #0 Under Spring	65.00
Austin Humane Killer #2	50.00
Black Cat, plastic, 4 hole, mousetrap	4.50
Blake & Lamb #40 Double Under Spring	25.00
Bullock Jump	180.00
Champion #4 Long Spring	65.00
Champion Multi Trigger Los Angeles	189.00
Courtland #0, w/teeth	135.00
Davenport Killer	75.00
Dearborne Long Spring #3	250.00
Destro, metal, mousetrap	15.00
Diamond #51, coil	45.00
Eclipse #3, folding trap	45.00
Epp Chain Trap	125.00
Escape Proof #1, one hole pan	18.00
Fenn MK-3, English rodent trap	18.00
Gibbs #0 King Bee	15.00

Gibbs #2, sod pan w/teeth	20.00
Gibbs Gladiator, rattrap	35.00
Gibbs Hawk Trap	65.00
Goodhousekeeper, mousetrap	12.00
Goodluck #0	45.00
Hector #1 Long Spring	8.00
Hercules #1½ Dogless	75.00
Herters Kodiak Bear	225.00
Hold Fast #1 Jump	8.00
Hopper PS&W Co #2	50.00
IMBRA, English	30.00
Katch Kwik, mousetrap	15.00
KIDD'S Mouser, fruit jar mousetrap	30.00
Kliflock Killer #1	32.00
Kompact #3 Jump	30.00
Kwik Grip #1	6.00
Lic Lure, metal rattrap	6.00
Louisiana Special 'Victor' #1	16.00
Master Grip #34 Triumph Coil	135.00
Montgomery #2 Digger	20.00
Nelson Boode #2	85.00
Never Miss, mousetrap	10.00
Newhouse #0 Onieda Community, riveted pan	32.00
Newhouse #114 Animal Trap Co	100.00
Newhouse #15 Animal Trap Co, bear trap	295.00
Newhouse #150 Animal Trap Co, bear trap	275.00
Newhouse #21½ Onieda Community, NY	22.00
Newhouse #24 Clutch Trap	575.00
Newhouse #4½ Wolf Trap	125.00
Newhouse #5 Community NY, bear trap	370.00
Newhouse #6 Community NY, bear trap	1,200.00
Oneida 'Star Trap' #1	22.00
Pendulum Game Trap	130.00
Prott #1½	15.00
PS Mfg Co #2 Long Spring	30.00
PSW & Co 'Victoria'	70.00
Rittenhouse, mole trap	15.00
Rival, mousetrap	12.00
Runway, mousetrap	15.00
Sargent #21 Long Spring	120.00
Sargent #23 Long Spring	190.00
Sargent Cast Pan #0	25.00
Sav-A-Leg #110	45.00
Sheine Coil #2	40.00
Snappy, mousetrap	10.00
Sterling #4, 1st model	40.00
Taylor Runway	30.00
Trailzend #7	500.00
Triumph #1½, T-cut in pan	40.00
Union Hardware #2	65.00
Verbail Leg Snare	95.00
Victor #0 Jump	2.50
Victor #10, rabbit trap	40.00
Victor #12 Jump, w/teeth	30.00
Victor #40 Double Trap	70.00
Victor Special #11	12.00
Wigginton, mousetrap, glass	18.00

Trivets

Although strictly a decorative item today, the original purpose of the trivet was much more practical. They were used to protect table tops from hot serving dishes; and irons, heated on the kitchen range, were placed on trivets during the pressing process to protect work surfaces. The first patent date was 1869, and many of the earliest trivets bore portraits of famous people or patriotic designs. Florals, birds, animals, and fruit were also used.

Cat's head, EX detail, CI, 5th leg adjusts for tilt, 8¾"........145.00
Curving lattice design, cast brass, 8½"....................10.00
Eagle & heart in laurel wreath, CI, 8¾"...................35.00
Ferro Steel, Cleveland, CI, 6"............................7.50
Foliage scroll design, CI, 9"............................20.00
Girl w/dog retrieving hat, CI, 11½"......................40.00
Heart, detailed penny ft, wrought iron w/trn wood hdl, 12".....95.00
Heart in hand & Odd Fellows insignia, CI, 8¼".............25.00
Hearth warming, hanging, hand forged, 2 hangers, 1750s......160.00
Hearth warming, pennyfoot, hand wrought, 1710, 9½x14x9"...200.00
Hex sign w/good detail, CI, 9¾"..........................25.00
Horseshoe w/eagle, clasped hdls & 'Good Luck', CI, 6½".......30.00
Leafy foliage, English, cast brass, sm break in metal, 6¾"......15.00
Masonic, cast brass......................................75.00
Miniature, CI, flatiron, 3"..............................25.00
Pennyfoot, hand wrought, used under iron, 1800, 10"........60.00
Pinwheel design, cast brass, heavy, 9¾"..................25.00
Railroad, CI, Seaboard Coast Line, train hdl..............10.00
Scroll work, cast brass, 7¼"............................15.00
Scroll work, scroll hdl, cast bronze, 9".................15.00
Scroll work/sun face, CI, mk Muster Geshutz, worn plating, 12".20.00
Scrolled design w/central interlocked medallion, brass, 7½".....40.00
Sheet brass, cut-out star & clover, trn ft, 9"............70.00
Sheet brass w/iron ft, simple cut-out design, 9".........55.00
Tree & quadruped, cast brass, sm break...................35.00
Wrought iron, good detail, twisted hanging loop on hdl, 7"....30.00
Wrought iron, rnd, 4 scrolls around center circle, 4 tall legs...165.00
Wrought iron, rnd w/3 curved arm supports, 7x13½" dia.......25.00
Wrought iron, rnd w/3 simple bars, 7" hdl, 7" dia...........75.00
Wrought iron, triangular, scrolled ft, 8"................30.00

Brass, handmade, 19th century, 1¼" high, 10¾" long, $57.50.

Trolls

The modern day version of the troll was designed in 1952 by Helena and Marti Kuuskoski, of Tampere, Finland. Those made by DAM and those marked with a horseshoe are among the most valuable, since both are made from the original Kuuskoski design. Many copies have been produced, the best of which are the Wishniks, made by the Uneeda Doll Company. These were first marketed in 1979 and are currently still available.

Troll animals are scarce, and values are rising rapidly.

Authority Susan Miller has compiled an amusing and informative book, *The Troll Book*, with many photos and current prices; you will find her address in the Directory under 'Indiana'.

Baseball Player, Wishnik, 5½".............................15.00
Bear, 7"..50.00
Boy, gr hair, felt suit, 7".............................20.00

Cow, marked DAM, 6¼" x 5", $75.00.

Boy bank, Dam..15.00
Cave Man, Dam, med.....................................65.00
Cloth body, vinyl head, lg.............................35.00
Clown, Dam...50.00
Cow, Dam, sm...25.00
Cow, Dam, 1960s, lg....................................75.00
Donkey, Dam, sm..25.00
Elephant, Dam, sm......................................25.00
Fox, sm..15.00
Giraffe, Dam, 1960s, lg................................75.00
Girl, blk ponytail, red color over 1 eye, 3".............6.50
Hula Girl, Wishnick, 5½"...............................25.00
Lion, Dam, 1960s, lg..................................115.00
Man, Art Troll, 9½"....................................45.00
Mandy..15.00
Old lady w/stick, 7½"..................................27.50
Pirate, Dam, 7"..28.00
Playboy Bunny, Dam, all orig, 12".....................125.00
Raincoat bank..28.00
Santa, Dam, 7"...65.00
Susy Sunshine..15.00
Turtle, Dam..60.00
Two headed, Wishnick, 3"...............................18.00
Viking, Dam, medium....................................65.00
White hair, blk body, Design Dam, 1964, 2¾"..............8.50

Trunks

In the days of steamboat voyages, stage coach journeys, and railroad travel, trunks were used to transport clothing and personal belongings. Some, called 'dome top' or 'turtle backs' were rounded on top to better accomodate milady's finery. Today, some of the more interesting examples are used in various ways in home decorating. For instance, a flat topped trunk may become a coffee table, while a smaller dome style may be 'home' for antique dolls or a teddy bear collection.

Chinese export, brass bound leather, brass hdls, 18x36"......250.00
Dome top, dvtl pine, worn graining, edge damage/losses, 20x39".55.00
Dome top, hide cover w/brass studs, iron stud 'RS', 20" L......35.00
Dome top, hide/brass tacks, iron hdls/clasp, 1860s, 10x24x14".115.00
Dome top, iron bound pine, rosemauling, 1790, 17x38".......650.00

Dome top, wrought iron strap work, plaque: 1750, 27x47″.....600.00
Leatherized paper, iron band w/brass studs, 14x27″, G........40.00
Poplar, orig grain pnt flame mahog w/X band inlay, 14x33x15″.305.00
Steamer, Louis Vuitton, fitted w/in w/5 drw & hanging racks...400.00

Tuthill

The Tuthill Glass Company operated in Middletown, New York, from 1902 to 1923.

Butter dish, blown blank, cut to pieces in hobstar prism/etc....475.00
Cake stand, Rosemere, sgn, 8″ dia.......................600.00
Celery dish, Primrose & Hobstar Vesica, 11″................350.00
Compote, cut, 9x7½″....................................495.00
Creamer & sugar, Rosaceae, cut & engraved...............425.00
Powder box, engraved primroses, Gorham top.............165.00
Sherbet w/under plate, stone cut, floral swags/line/circles.......125.00
Vase, Primrose cutting, 16″, pr...........................875.00
Vase, Vintage w/Hobstar Chain, sq sides, 10x4″............575.00
Water set, flowers & brilliant cut, 9¾″ pitcher+6 tumblers....550.00

Typewriters

The first commercially successful typewriter was the Sholes and Glidden, introduced in 1874. By 1882 other models appeared, and by the 1890s dozens were on the market. At the time of the First World War, the ranks of typewriter makers thinned, and by the 1920s only a few survived.

Collectors informally divide typewriter history into the pioneering period, up to about 1890; the classic period, from 1890 to 1920; and the modern period, since 1920.

There are two broad classifications of early typewriters: (1) Keyboard machines, in which depression of a key prints a character, and, via a shift-key, prints up to three different characters per key. (2) Index machines, in which a chart of all the characters appears on the typewriter, the character is selected by a pointer or dial, and is printed by operation of a lever or other device. Even though index typewriters were simpler and more primitive than keyboard machines, they were none-the-less a later development, designed to provide a cheaper alternative to the standard keyboard models that were selling for upwards of $100. Eventually second-hand keyboard typewriters supplied the low-price customer and index typewriters vanished except as toys. Both classes of typewriters appeared in a great many designs.

It is difficult, if not impossible, to assign standard market prices to early typewriters. Unlike collectors of postage stamps, carnival glass, etc., few people collect typewriters -- so there is no active marketplace from which to establish prices. Also, condition is a very important factor, and typewriters can vary infinitely in condition. A third factor to consider is that an early typewriter achieves its value mainly through the skill, effort, and time of the collector who restores it to its original condition, in which case its purchase price is insignificant. Some unusual looking early typewriters are not at all rare or valuable, while some very ordinary looking ones are scarce and could be quite valuable. No general rules apply.

For a free appraisal of any early typewriter you may send a description (a photo is helpful) and a stamped, self-addressed envelope to Paul Lippman, 1216 Garden Street, Hoboken, New Jersey, 07030.

Blickensderfer #5, oak case...............................95.00
Blickensderfer #7½, wood case...........................75.00
Corona #3, w/case.....................................30.00
Hammond Multiplex, w/case.............................75.00
O'Dell #4...65.00
Oliver #5, orig & complete................................55.00
Oliver #9, working......................................50.00
Postal, w/case...95.00

Remington, portable, 1929................................22.50
Underwood #25, orig wood box, 1929......................65.00

Uhl Pottery

Founded in Evansville, Indiana, in 1854 by German immigrants, the Uhl Pottery was moved to Huntingburg, Indiana, in 1908 because of the more suitable clay available there. They produced stoneware -- Acorn Ware jugs, crocks, and bowls -- which were marked with the acorn logo and 'Uhl Pottery.' They also made mugs, pitchers, and vases in simple shapes and solid glazes marked with a circular ink stamp containing the name of the pottery and 'Huntingburg, Indiana.' The pottery closed in the mid-1940s.

Pitcher, red clay with brown and green glaze, very early, marked Uhl, 8″, $95.00.

Bean pot, br/cream, w/lid & hdl, sgn, 1 qt...................40.00
Casserole, lt yel, w/lid & hdls, 8″..........................35.00
Crock, bl acorn logo, 2 gal...............................30.00
Jug, acorn shape, 'Acorn Wares' emb on side, 3″............65.00
Pitcher, bl/wht stoneware, Grape Cluster on Trellis, set of 4....550.00
Pitcher, Edelweiss, beaded ground, 'Prosit', metal th'rest, 9″...200.00
Pitcher, Flemish Figures, grapes/leaves band, tulip band, 9½″..500.00
Pitcher, head of Lincoln, deep bl, 10″.....................400.00
Pitcher, head of Lincoln, deep bl, 4¾″.....................135.00
Pitcher, head of Lincoln, deep bl, 6″......................225.00
Pitcher, head of Lincoln, deep bl, 7″......................235.00
Pitcher, head of Lincoln, deep bl, 8″......................250.00

Unger Brothers

The Art Nouveau silver produced by the Unger Brothers, who operated in Newark, New Jersey, from the early 1880s until 1909, is fast becoming very popular on today's collectibles market. In addition to tableware, they also made brushes, mirrors, powder boxes and the like for milady's dressing table, as well as jewelry and small personal accessories such as match safes and flasks. They often marked their products with a circle seal containing an intertwined 'UB.'

Carving set, lg fork/knife, ornate flowers, heavy chasing, M.....150.00
Flask, emb profile of woman, smoke rings, 6¼″............750.00

Grape shears, sgn...95.00
Lorgnette...175.00
Match safe, nude amidst waves, scroll decor, sgn............150.00

Universal

Universal Potteries Incorporated operated in Cambridge, Ohio, from 1934 to 1956. Many lines of dinnerware and kitchen items were produced, in both earthenware and semi-porcelain. In 1956 the emphasis was shifted to the manufacture of floor and wall tiles, and the name was changed to the Oxford Tile Company, Division of Universal Potteries. The plant closed in 1976.

Ballerina, creamer..4.00
Ballerina, cup..4.00
Ballerina, gravy boat.....................................6.00
Ballerina, lug soup.......................................4.50
Ballerina, relish...5.00
Ballerina, saucer...1.50
Ballerina, sugar..7.50
Ballerina Mist, bowl, mixing; set w/1 qt, 2 qt, 3 qt sizes.......20.00
Ballerina Mist, bowl, salad..............................10.00
Ballerina Mist, cup & saucer..............................5.00
Ballerina Mist, grease jar w/lid..........................7.50
Ballerina Mist, plate, dinner; bl w/silver rim............5.00
Bowl, refrigerator; covered, red, 6¼"....................10.00
Bowl, utility; red, 4"....................................4.00
Calico Fruit, bowl, 8"....................................7.50
Calico Fruit, cake plate, hdld, 11¾".....................15.00
Calico Fruit, casserole, covered.........................25.00
Calico Fruit, pitcher....................................12.00
Calico Fruit, pitcher w/lid..............................29.00
Calico Fruit, plate, 9"...................................4.50
Canister, red, 16 oz.....................................10.00
Cattail, bowl, tab hdl, 6"................................3.00
Cattail, bowl; round vegetable, 9".........................8.00
Cattail, butter dish.....................................25.00
Cattail, casserole w/lid, 8½"............................15.00
Cattail, cookie jar......................................40.00
Cattail, creamer..3.00
Cattail, cup & saucer.....................................5.00
Cattail, plate, grill.....................................6.00
Cattail, plate, 10".......................................5.50
Cattail, plate, 9½".......................................4.00
Cattail, platter, 11½"....................................9.00
Cattail, syrup, 6".......................................37.50
Cattail, water jug w/stopper.............................12.00
Jug, milk; red, quart....................................12.00
Ridgleigh, ice tub liner, hdl............................15.00
Ridgleigh, plate, 7¾".....................................8.50
Salt & pepper, red, pr....................................6.00
Upico, water server, tip-top, maroon......................8.50
Vase, ribbed, br, 3".....................................35.00
Vase, ribbed, yel, 2"....................................35.00
Woodvine, pie baker......................................10.00
Woodvine, salt & pepper shakers...........................7.00

Val St. Lambert

Since its inception in Belgium at the turn of the 19th century, the Val St. Lambert Cristalleries has been involved in the production of high quality glass, specializing in cameo.

Boat dish, purple overlay acid & wheel cut floral, 11" L......375.00
Dish w/lid, diamond pattern, metal pineapple finial, 5" dia......18.00
Drink mixer, pouring spout, cutting around center, sgn.........75.00
Plate, wide rim w/frieze of gulls in flight & waves, 11¾".......55.00
Vase, floral cameo on cobalt/cobalt w/in, bronze overlay, 12"....485.00
Vase, roll top/prunts/tendrils in cobalt on crystal quilt, 5"......135.00
Vase, ruby overlay/X cut to clear, cameo carved, 10"........660.00

Valentines

Pagan ritual once held that on Valentine's Day the birds of the air elected to choose their mates; and as this premise was eagerly adopted by the homo sapien species, romantic poems became a familiar expression of one's intentions. By the mid-1800s, comical hand colored lithographic and wood block prints were mass produced both here and abroad. At the turn of the century, the more romantic, often mechanical German imports forced many American companies out of business. Today's collectors often specialize: comic, postcards, mechanical, Victorian, Kewpies, Greenaway characters, or those signed by a specific artist are among many well established categories.

Addenbrooke, lace edge, emb, HP florals, 4¼x3"............45.00
Addenbrooke, lace edge, w/2 sm central flower cages, 10x8"....75.00
American, hand colored floral, verse, dtd 1800, 3¾x4½"......75.00
Boy Scout, mechanical, German..............................12.00
Clown riding St Bernard, mechanical, German, 7½x6½".......15.00
Despondent Lover series, hand colored litho, 8x10"..........25.00
English, beehive type, emb lace edge paper w/Nash watermk...100.00
English, emb lace edge, pink paper, pnt/applied florals/motto....35.00
Flower cage, hand colored, on J Whatman 1825 paper, 9x7¼"..75.00
German, mechanical, 1700s, 3x4", lot of 7..................75.00
Heart shaped, Mother, satin ribbon, lace edge, sm...........3.00
Paper lace/gilt leaves/tinted cherub/verse, 11½x13¼".........55.00
Park, comic lithos, English, 1840, 9x7", lot of 6...........75.00
Penny, Blk lady all dressed up, full color, VG..............15.00
Rebus type, color printed, 9¼x7¼".........................50.00
Tuck, chromolitho, boy holds heart, straw hat removes, 7"......12.00
Tuck, chromolitho, girl/basket of roses/movable umbrella, 7"....12.00
Tuck, girl w/goo-goo eyes, mechanical.......................9.00
Unrequited Love series, aquatints/hand colored, 1840s, 14 for..500.00

Fold-out gazebo, marked 'Beistle, made in U.S.', 1920s, 9½", $20.00.

Vallerysthal

Fine glasswares have been made in Vallerysthal, France, since the middle of the 19th century.

Box w/lid, bl opaque, pig/grasses/pen on lid, 3x4½" dia	60.00
Candlesticks, Joseph & Mary figurals, sgn, pr	200.00
Compote, sq topped, allover lacy decor, bl milk glass, 6x6"	140.00
Ice cream dish w/under plate, aqua, petal shape	12.00
Jam jar w/lid, bl w/grapes, sgn	35.00
Salt, open, ram's head, ftd, cobalt	35.00
Vase, cameo branches, enamel insects, frost/ruby, 9½"	605.00

Van Briggle

The Van Briggle Pottery of Colorado Springs, Colorado, was established in 1901 by Artus Van Briggle, whose early career had been shaped by such notables as Karl Langenbeck and Maria Nichols Storer. His quest for several years had been to perfect a completely flat matt glaze, and upon accomplishing his goal, he opened his pottery. His wife, Anne, worked with him, and they, along with George Young, were responsible for the modeling of the wares. Their work typified the flow and form of the Art Nouveau movement, and the shapes they designed played as important a part in their success as their glazes. Some of their most famous pieces were Despondency, Lorelei, and Toast Cup.

Increasing demand for their work soon made it necessary to add to their quarters as well as their staff. Although much of the ware was eventually made from molds, each piece was carefully trimmed and refined before the glaze was sprayed on. Their most popular colors were rose, blue, green, and gray.

Van Briggle died in 1904, but the work was continued by his wife. New facilities were built and by 1908, in addition to their art ware, tiles, garden ware, and commercial lines were added.

By the twenties, the emphasis had shifted from art pottery to novelties and commercial wares. As late as 1970, reproductions of some of the early designs continued to be made.

Until about 1920, most pieces were marked with the date and shape number. Before Van Briggle's death, Roman numerals identified the artist: 'I' for Anne, 'II' for Harry Bangs, and 'III' for Van Briggle. The 'AA' mark was the earliest mark; 'Colorado Springs, Colorado' was used after 1920; and 'USA' was added from 1922 to 1930.

Ash tray, spiral interior, mk CS, 5½"	22.00
Ash tray, trapezoid, turq, mk CS, 6¾"	18.00
Bookend, owls, Persian rose, 5", pr	145.00
Bowl, AA & Van Briggle mks, 2" dia	22.00
Bowl, band of berries/leaves, matt pink/lt gr, 1908-11, #678	150.00
Bowl, leaf/flowers, lt bl matt, clay shows through, 1906, #283	160.00
Bowl, leaves at top, golden br matt, 1917, 2x4¼"	80.00
Bowl, leaves in relief, rose, #681, 2½x3¼"	20.00
Bowl, leaves in relief, turq, #681, mk CS, 2x3"	15.00
Bowl, oval, w/frog, sgn PL, CS & AA mk	35.00
Bowl, Persian rose, dtd 1915	70.00
Bowl, w/figural seashell girl, wht	60.00
Bowl, w/frog, tulips, turq, mk CS, 8¼x5¾"	32.00
Bowl vase, allover leaves, #858, Persian rose, 1911, 3½x6"	135.00
Bowl vase, leaves in relief, br w/gr, 4½x7½"	30.00
Bowl vase, yucca leaves, turq, #747, mk CS, 4½x5½"	28.00
Bunny, turq, 3"	35.00
Candle holder, bl, 3 legs	30.00
Candlestick, 7 sides, mk CS, 10¼x5½"	35.00
Console w/Goose Girl flower frog, turq	200.00
Creamer, turq, hexagonal, mk CS, 2⅛"	10.00
Dog, floppy ears, turq, 3"	35.00

Console bowl with figural female flower frog, blue matt glaze, 15" bowl, 9" tall figure, $200.00.

Donkey, turq, 3¾x4"	40.00
Elephant, trunk upraised, turq, mk CS, 4x3"	30.00
Elephant, yel/br gloss, 3"	25.00
Flower frog, acorns on leaf base, turq/bl veining, 3x6"	25.00
Flower frog, turtle, Persian rose, dtd 1914	75.00
Jar w/lid, bl/rose, knob finial, 1917, 5½"	75.00
Lamp base, kneeling woman w/jug on shoulder	195.00
Paperweight, duck, bl, 3½x4"	30.00
Pitcher, bl matt, 3¾"	17.50
Pitcher, lt bl matt, squat, 1908-11, 3½"	150.00
Vase, aqua, AA mk, 6½"	27.00
Vase, arrow design, wide base, '08-11, gr, 5¼"	135.00
Vase, bird of paradise, turq, mk CS, 8¼"	20.00
Vase, br w/thin turq drizzle over leaves, #851, 1921-22 mk, 5"	60.00
Vase, butterflies, rose, CS, #688, 4x4"	30.00
Vase, copper/br gloss w/gr drippings, CS, 4x4"	30.00
Vase, crocus & roots, turq, CS, 5"	35.00
Vase, dk bl matt glaze, incised mk, 1913, 5½x3¾"	175.00
Vase, dk red w/leaf & stem, 1919, 2"	45.00
Vase, dragonfly relief, shades of bl, 7"	20.00
Vase, gr/red matt, flaring rim, '08-11, 7¼"	50.00
Vase, heart shaped leaves, rose glaze, mk CS, 5¼"	30.00
Vase, high glaze copper flake on br/gr lip, CS, 4x4"	45.00
Vase, leaf design, red/bl, collar w/teardrop base, 1920, 8¼"	50.00
Vase, leaf mold, dk maroon/bl touches, rolled in rim, 1919, 5"	60.00
Vase, leaf relief, bl/gr, cylinder shape, 7¼"	20.00
Vase, leaf relief, bulbous neck/wide base, gr, dtd 1915, 6½"	165.00
Vase, leaf/fleur-de-lis relief, bl, '08-11, 2⅛"	55.00
Vase, leaf/floral relief, rose glaze, '08-11, 7½"	65.00
Vase, leaf/vine, gr/bl matt, 1915, #695, 4"	80.00
Vase, leaves & violets, br, #645, 4¼"	20.00
Vase, line forms 3 branches at base, bl/gr mottle, 1906, 5¾"	225.00
Vase, lines at top, circles w/spider/etc, blk, dtd 1902, 5"	850.00
Vase, long leaves in relief, rose glaze, #863, 8x2½"	35.00
Vase, Lorelei, blk matt, 10½"	158.00
Vase, lt lime w/blk flecks, #349, 1905, sm chip, 5½"	75.00
Vase, lt/dk bl matt, swirled, mk 33 1/3, minor pitting, 7"	30.00
Vase, maroon, molded leaves, dated 1916, 8"	110.00
Vase, maroon, 5 indentations, dated 1918, 6"	95.00
Vase, Ming turq, Van Briggle CS, 3¾x5½"	30.00
Vase, mustard, poppies, crazed, dated 1904, 10"	650.00
Vase, plum matt glaze, incised Van Briggle 9, 4½x3½"	150.00

Vase, plum matt glaze, incised 1916, 7¼x5¼"............200.00
Vase, red matt, arrow leaves, balls on stems at top, dtd, 5".....50.00
Vase, red w/bl butterfly, 1921, 2¾".................60.00
Vase, red w/butterflies, touches of bl, spherical, 3"...........42.50
Vase, red w/molded poppy touched w/bl, 8¼"................85.00
Vase, red/bl, drape & circle relief, 4"...................30.00
Vase, relief at base, bl, '08-11, #661, 7½".............125.00
Vase, rose to bl w/floral decor, dtd 1918, 6"...............55.00
Vase, spiderwort, turq, mk USA, #841................38.00
Vase, stylized leaves & flowers, lt bl, #661, 1908-11.........200.00
Vase, turq, dk clay, mk AA & VB, #684.................35.00
Vase, vertical stylized florals, gr w/red specks, '08-11, 12"....350.00
Vase, vine/flowers twisted around vase, red w/gr drip, '16, 5"....70.00
Vase, yucca leaves, Persian rose, #747, '22-'29, 4½".........85.00
Vase, 3 flamingos in relief, shades of bl, 20", VG............150.00
Vase, 3-Faced Indian, mulberry.........................165.00

Vance Avon

Although pottery had been made in Tiltonville, Ohio, since about 1880, the ware manufactured there was of little significance until after the turn of the century, when the Vance Faience Company was organized for the purpose of producing quality art ware. By 1902 the name had been changed to the Avon Faience Company, and late in the same year it and three other West Virginia potteries incorporated to form the Wheeling Potteries Company. The Avon branch operated in Tiltonville until 1905, when production was moved to Wheeling. Art pottery was discontinued.

From the beginning, only skilled craftsmen and trained engineers were hired. Wm. P. Jervis and Frederick Hurten Rhead were among the notable artists responsible for designing some of the early art ware. Some of the ware was slip decorated under glaze, while other pieces were molded with high relief designs. Examples with squeeze bag decoration by Rhead are obviously forerunners of the Jap Birdmal line he later developed for Weller. Ware was marked 'Vance F. Co.;' 'Avon F. Co., Tiltonville;' or 'Avon W. Pts. Co.'

Mug, barrel, gr/cream bands, 'Sandusky, O' in gold, Wheeling...30.00
Pitcher, lotus, squeezebag decor, Rhead, 5¼"...............250.00
Vase, relief decor, 4 shoulder openings, gr/br, #117, 10¾".....70.00
Vase, 5 holes, chains of ivy relief, high gloss, early, 11½".....300.00

Vaseline

Vaseline, a greenish yellow colored glass produced by adding uranium oxide to the batch, was made in large quantities during the Victorian era. It was used for pressed glass tablewares, vases, and souvenir items.

Boot, Cane pattern, on flat base, 5½"....................55.00
Candlestick, baluster w/bell base, chipped ice finish, 8", pr......68.00
Compote, opal, blown, early 1800s....................95.00
Creamer, Pressed Diamond..........................35.00
Creamer, Ransom, w/gold..........................45.00
Goblet, Daisy & Button, 6"..........................27.50
Hat, Daisy & Button, 1¾".............................25.00
Mug, Thousand Eye, 2½"............................25.00
Plate, scalloped.................................10.00
Salt, double, ribbed, w/metal handle....................35.00
Sugar w/lid, Pressed Diamond.........................45.00
Vase, chalice, crimped & folded top, opal.................27.00
Vase, hand holding vase, acorn & leaves decor, flint, 8".......85.00
Water set, Basketweave, pitcher/5 goblets/tray.............195.00

Venetian Glass

Venetian glass is a thin, fragile ware, usually made in colors, with an iridescence similar to that of Carnival glass. It was produced on the island of Murano, near Venice, from the 13th century to the early 1900s.

Bowl, covered, candy striped, lg...........................175.00
Candy dish, ftd, lattice stripes, pk/gold swirl, flower hdl........75.00
Centerpiece, kneeling page, bl/gold.....................85.00
Compote, applied fruit drops, orange w/wht rim/base edge, 10".150.00
Lamp, swirl, pink w/gilt flecked lavender trim, 24½".........35.00
Plate, swirl, lt gr, sgn Venini, 12"......................100.00
Salt, lt irid gr, bl dolphin hdls, ftd, 2½" wide.............42.00
Vase, cranberry, dolphin shape, 7"......................150.00
Vase, yel w/wht streaks, ruffled, clear shoulder hdls, 9"........50.00

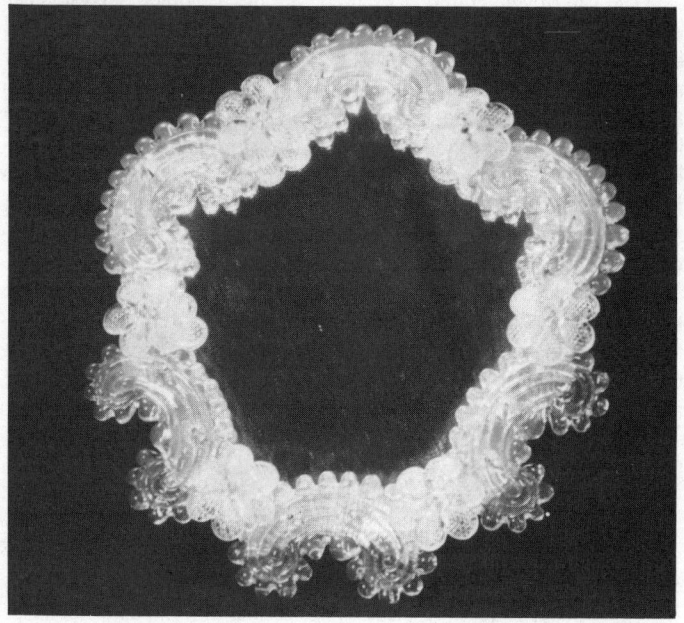

Mirror, floral and scroll frame, 10", $75.00.

Verlys

Verlys art glass, produced in France after 1931 by the Holophane Company of Verlys, was made in crystal with acid finished relief work in the Art Deco style. Colored and opalescent glass were also used.

In 1935 an American branch was opened in Newark, Ohio. Wares manufactured there were very similar, but less expensive.

Both factories signed their wares 'Verlys' -- the American branch by etching, the French with a molded signature.

Ash tray, sgn, shallow, 4½x3½"..........................20.00
Bowl, birds & bees, American, 11½".....................175.00
Bowl, butterfly, script sgn, 13½".......................110.00
Bowl, child & sheep in relief, clear, 13½".................50.00
Bowl, Cupid w/bow & hearts, 6"........................65.00
Bowl, doves, opal glass, sgn, 4½x12¾"..................150.00
Bowl, emb dahlias, smoky topaz, France..................165.00
Bowl, flying geese, unsgn, 13".........................68.00
Bowl, flying geese & fish, frost/clear, sgn in mold, 13½".....110.00
Bowl, flying geese & fish, sapphire bl, shallow, 13"..........190.00
Bowl, pine cone, bl, sgn.............................95.00
Bowl, pine cone, dusty rose, sgn.......................110.00
Bowl, pine cone, topaz..............................95.00
Bowl, pine cone, 6½"...............................65.00

Bowl, Poissons, clear etched, sgn, 19½″ L 300.00
Bowl, poppies, clear etched, sgn, 14″ 135.00
Bowl, tassel, directoire bl, 11″ 215.00
Bowl, tassel, 11¾″ 110.00
Bowl, thistle, bl, sgn twice, 3x8½″ 190.00
Bowl, thistle, frosted, script sgn, 3x9″ 60.00
Bowl, water lily, frosted, 13″ 175.00
Candlestick, frosted leaves, lily center, script sgn, 2½″ 28.00
Dish, duck figural, frosted, sgn in mold 85.00
Dresser jar, lovebirds 42.00
Fish bowl, amber, 19″ 225.00
Planter, chrysanthemum, clear, 10⅛″ 80.00
Vase, Lance, 8″ 75.00
Vase, mandarin & florals in relief, script sgn, 9½x5″ 185.00
Vase, Oriental man w/scenes in relief, frosted, 9¼″ 160.00
Vase, seasons, sgn Carl Schmitz, 1940, each 265.00

Vase, frosted panels of wheat, etched American mark, 9½″, $150.00.

Vernon Kilns

Vernon Potteries Ltd. was established by Fay G. Bennison in Vernon, California, in 1931. The name was later changed to Vernon Kilns, and until it closed in 1958, dinnerware and figurines were their primary products. Among its wares most sought by collectors today are items designed by such famous artists as Rockwell Kent and Walt Disney.

Authority Maxine Nelson has compiled a lovely book, *Versatile Vernon Kilns*, with full-color photos and current prices; you will find her address in the Directory under 'California.'

Ash tray, Petrified Forest 15.00
Beverly, chop plate, 12″ 12.00
Bowl, serving; Moby Dick, Rockwell Kent 40.00
Brown Eyed Susan, cup & saucer 5.00
Casual California, coffee server, mahogany br, 10 cup 25.00
Chintz, cup & saucer 10.00
Early California, bowl, vegetable; oval, 9″ 10.00
Early California, creamer 7.00
Early California, cup & saucer 9.00
Early California, cup & saucer, demitasse 15.00
Early California, plate, orange, 10″ 12.00
Early California, plate, orange, 6″ 4.00

Early California, plate, 10″ 10.00
Early California, plate, 6″ 4.00
Early California, platter, oval, orange, 14″ 18.00
Early California, salt 5.00
Early California, salt, orange 6.00
Figurine, Preston Foster, 1941 Movie Star 250.00
Fruitdale, plate, 7″ 5.00
Gingham, plate, 10½″ 4.50
Gingham, plate, 6½″ 2.50
Gingham, torte plate, 2 tiered 20.00
Hawaiian Flowers, Don Blanding, chop plate, blue, 12″ 50.00
Hawaiian Flowers, Don Blanding, plate, pink, 9″ 20.00
Heavenly Days, set, 20 pc 90.00
Heyday, creamer 3.50
Heyday, cup & saucer 5.00
Heyday, gravy boat 6.00
Heyday, plate, 10½″ 3.50
Heyday, plate, 7½″ 2.50
Heyday, salt & pepper, pr 6.00
Heyday, sugar w/lid 5.00
Homespun, bowl, round, 9″ 8.50
Homespun, coffee server 20.00
Homespun, cup 5.00
Homespun, egg cup 10.00
Homespun, pitcher, Streamline, 8½″ 10.00
Homespun, pitcher, ½ pt 12.00
Homespun, plate, bread & butter 3.00
Homespun, plate, salad 4.00
Homespun, plate, 12″ 10.00
Homespun, platter, oval 12.00
Homespun, salt & pepper shakers, pr 7.00
Homespun, sauce boat 12.50
Homespun, torte plate, 2 tiered 20.00
Joy, Don Blanding, platter, 12″ 14.00
Lei Lani, bowl, serving; Ultra shape, 9″ 27.50
Lei Lani, coupe soup 25.00
Lei Lani, demitasse cup 24.00
Lei Lani, plate, Ultra shape, 10½″ 27.00
Lei Lani, plate, Ultra shape, 6¼″ 10.00
Lei Lani, plate, Ultra shape, 7½″ 15.00
Lei Lani, saucer, Ultra shape 8.00
Linda, cup & saucer, demitasse 18.00
Mayflower, butter w/lid 28.00
Mayflower, cup & saucer 10.00
Mayflower, plate, 6″ 4.00
Mayflower, plate, 7″ 5.00
Mayflower, platter, oval, 14″ 20.00
Mayflower, vegetable, 10″ dia 12.00
Mayflower, vegetable, 12″ dia 14.00
Modern California, chop plate, 12″ 6.00
Modern California, coffee server w/lid 9.00
Modern California, teapot 25.00
Modern California, vegetable, round, 9″ 12.00
Native California, platter, 13¾″ 23.00
Native California, sauce boat 18.00
Organdie, bowl, 9″ 9.50
Organdie, bowl; vegetable 6.00
Organdie, chop plate, 12″ 8.00
Organdie, chop plate, 14″ 10.00
Organdie, coffee cup 4.50
Organdie, coffee server 35.00
Organdie, creamer & sugar w/lid 15.00
Organdie, creamer & sugar w/lid, individual 12.00
Organdie, cup & saucer, demitasse 6.50

Organdie, pitcher, 2 qt IL Streamline.....................16.00
Organdie, plate, 7½".....................................2.00
Organdie, plate, 9½".....................................3.50
Organdie, salt & pepper, pr..............................9.00
Organdie, saucer, jumbo..................................3.00
Organdie, soup, flat....................................10.00
Organdie, torte plate, 2 tiered.........................20.00
Organdie, tumbler, 16 oz, 5½"............................7.00
Our America, plate, brown, 10½".........................45.00
Our America, plate, brown, 12"..........................75.00
Our America, plate, brown, 14"..........................82.00
Our America, plate, brown, 7½"..........................27.00
Our America, plate, brown, 8½"..........................30.00
Our America, plate, brown, 9½"..........................36.00
Plate, Baker Chocolate 175th Anniversary, 1941..........27.00
Plate, Bits of the Old South, Cotton Patch..............19.50
Plate, Bits of the Old South, Down on Levee.............19.50
Plate, Bits of the Old South, The Old Mill..............19.50
Plate, California, w/map, brown..........................8.00
Plate, Carlsbad Caverns.................................13.00
Plate, Deep in the Heart of Texas.......................10.00
Plate, FDR 1st Ed, sgn Goode............................35.00
Plate, French Opera, Faust..............................14.50
Plate, French Opera, Guillaume Tell.....................14.50
Plate, George Washington................................15.00
Plate, Indiana Eastern Star 1849-1949, commemorative....15.00
Plate, MacArthur, Corregidor............................25.00
Plate, Montana..10.00
Plate, Palm Springs, for Reid's Pottery, maroon..........8.00
Plate, Postmaster.......................................15.00
Plate, Texas..10.00
Plate, University of Alabama............................18.00
Plate, 2nd Presidential.................................12.00
Raffia, butter w/cover..................................15.00
Raffia, pitcher, water..................................15.00
Raffia, sauce boat......................................15.00
Tam-O'-Shanter, chop plate, 12"..........................8.00
Tam-O'-Shanter, coffee cup...............................4.50
Tam-O'-Shanter, creamer..................................4.50
Tam-O'-Shanter, pitcher, Streamline w/ice lip, 3 qt.....25.00
Tam-O'-Shanter, pitcher, 2 qt...........................18.00

Tam-O'-Shanter, plate, 9½"...............................4.00
Tam-O'-Shanter, tumbler, 5½"............................10.00
Tickled Pink, bowl, cereal; 5½"..........................6.00
Tickled Pink, bowl, 9"..................................12.00
Tickled Pink, creamer....................................6.00
Tickled Pink, cup & saucer...............................7.50
Tickled Pink, plate, 10".................................7.50
Tickled Pink, plate, 7½".................................4.00
Tickled Pink, platter, oval, 13½".......................15.00
Tickled Pink, sugar w/lid................................8.50
Tweed, coffee server w/lid..............................20.00
Tweed, creamer...8.00
Tweed, pitcher, ½ pt, Streamline........................10.00
Ultra California, bowl, mixing; blue, 7"................10.00
Ultra California, bowl, mixing; yellow, 8"..............14.00
Ultra California, bowl, vegetable; red, 9¼".............10.00
Ultra California, chop plate, pink, 12½".................6.50
Ultra California, cup & saucer, blue....................12.00
Ultra California, cup & saucer, demitasse...............15.00
Vernon Rose, sauce boat w/attached under plate..........25.00

Verre de Soie

Literally meaning glass of silk, this type of glass is named for its lovely, almost pearl-like lustre.

Bowl, flared w/triple threaded fluted rim, 3½x4½".......75.00
Bowl, pearl, shallow w/4 cylindrical stds, flat base, 8" dia.....385.00
Cracker jar, enameled flowers, plated lid..............110.00
Cruet, Steuben, Hawkes floral engraving, engraved stopper, 7"..125.00
Perfume, gr, unsgn Steuben.............................125.00
Perfume, gr flame stopper, Steuben.....................250.00
Rose bowl, gr, 5x4".....................................85.00
Sherbet w/under plate, sgn Steuben......................80.00
Vase, gr threading, #3033, Steuben, 6".................275.00
Vase, trumpet, stretched ruffle top, ped ft, Steuben, 10"......125.00
Vase, wht w/rainbow irid, polish pontil, bulbous, ruffled, 7"....125.00

Vienna

In 1719, Claude Innocentius de Paquier established a hard paste porcelain factory in Vienna where he produced highly ornamental wares similar to the type produced at Meissen. Early wares were usually unmarked, but after 1744, when the factory was purchased by the Empress, the Austrian shield (often called 'beehive') was stamped on underglaze.

Charger, Europa & Bull/attendants, HP on claret, 15".......715.00
Charger, figures before flaming cup, by Baershneider, 14"....550.00
Charger, lovers/putti, printed/pnt, 15"....................605.00
Charger, maid sitting on bench/Cupid, Weiner, 13¾" dia.....550.00
Dish, nymphs w/Cupid, lavender border, oval, 14½" L........880.00
Ewer, military scenic, by Bauer, 15½"....................1,760.00
Jardiniere, lovers w/in oval, transfer print, 12½", pr.....660.00
Plaque, Belshazzar's Feast, by Richter, claret border, 19"..1,540.00
Plaque, Hero & Leander, Temple of Venus, by Leiner, 19½"..1,870.00
Plaque, King Steven, HP w/purple/claret border, 20".......3,575.00
Plaque, Venus & Vulcan's Forge, by Tager, 19½"...........1,320.00
Plate, Lorelei, by Wagner, purple border, 14" dia........1,650.00
Plate, maiden & angel w/lute, cobalt/gold border, artist sgn....350.00
Plate, Mother & Child, by Lieb, Sr, ivory border, 10½"....225.00
Plate, Napoleon at the bedside of Marshall Bernadotte, Wagner.350.00
Plate, Napoleon w/troops, by Wagner, blue border, 9½", pr....880.00

Plate, marked 'Salamina', designed by Rockwell Kent, 10½", $65.00.

Plate, portrait, brunette w/lilacs, gold/gr border, 9¾".........155.00
Plate, portrait, by Wagner, claret border w/gilt, 9½", 3 for.....605.00
Plate, roses, HP, Greek Key border, beehive mk, 9½".......125.00
Plate, Solitude, by Wagner, blue w/jeweled rim, 9½"...1,100.00
Plate, various maidens, by Wagner, cobalt border, 9½", 5 for.3,300.00
Plate, w/classical scenes, RV, 6", pr......................60.00
Platter, Departure of Hector, by Leber, oval, 20" L........1,210.00
Platter, Flirtation, mk for A Lamm, oval, 20" L............1,540.00
Table top, center portrait+14 sm plaques w/in gilt wood, 27".4,950.00
Tray, Cupid/Psyche at river, HP on bl, lozenge form, 11"......605.00
Vase, coronation of Marie de Medici, by Gust, 1900, 21¾"...2,750.00
Vase, nude & cherub, cobalt/gilt border, pierced lid/hdls, 13"..200.00
Vase, portrait, by A Valk, gr ground w/gilt florals, 10".......605.00
Vase, w/lid, on stand, continuous scenic frieze, 15".........2,200.00
Vase, w/lid, on stand, mythological figures, 13½", pr.......1,870.00
Vase, w/lid, on stand, scenes from Vulcan's Forge, 24"......5,225.00
Vase, w/lid, portrait of Josephine, by Wagner, rpr, 21"......1,650.00
Vase, 3 scroll hdls/paw ft, HP w/3 classic titled scenes, 7½"...250.00

Apothecary crock, wht ironstone, 7x6"......................42.00
Bowl, divided, bl floral, Dresden, 11"......................125.00
Cup & saucer, dk gray floral, Jardene.......................45.00
Jug, beige w/gr leaves, twig hdl, 2½".......................35.00
Plaque, seascape, bl/wht, 9"...............................75.00
Plate, birds & flowers, bl transfer, 8"......................20.00
Plate, bl thistle, mercury mk, 9½"..........................30.00
Plate, gaudy florals in red/bl/gr/yel/purple, stains, 10".......25.00
Tray, child's; 3 sections, bl/wht, 7½"......................25.00
Tumbler, girl holding pitcher, peacock on tray, #1025.........60.00
Vase, Delft style, scenic................................85.00
Vase, gray, ornate hdls, silver lustre leaves, 7½"............55.00
Vase, teardrop shape, bl/wht, Lilo, 9½"....................48.00

Mug, white with flowing blue brushed-on floral, marked, 3¾", $50.00.

Vase, portrait of lady in reserve on green, gold lace applications, inscribed 'Summer,' #07259, marked with gold 'beehive,' 8½", $1,250.00.

Viennese Enameled Ware

Clock, miniature, pierced/scroll engraved, garden scene, 4"...1,590.00
Coin purse, w/chain & belt hook, pnt both sides, 1800s.......550.00
Compact, silver w/geometric stripes in blk, Wiener Werkstatte..440.00
Table & chair, mc w/girl dancing in garden, musicians, 3½"...650.00

Villeroy and Boch

The firm of Villeroy and Boch, located in Mettlach, Germany, was brought about by the 1841 merger of three German factories -- the Wallerfangen factory, founded by Nicholas Villeroy in 1787; the Mettlach factory, founded by Jean Francis Boch in 1809; and his father's factory in Septfontaines, established in 1767. Villeroy and Boch produced many varieties of wares, including earthenware with printed underglaze designs, and the famous Mettlach steins. The company made use of a variety of marks, including the castle mark with the name 'Mettlach.'
See also Mettlach

Vistosa

Vistosa was produced from about 1938 through the early forties. It was Taylor, Smith and Taylor's answer to the very successful Fiesta line of their nearby competitor, Homer Laughlin. Vistosa was made in four solid colors -- mango red, cobalt blue, light green, and deep yellow. 'Pie crust' edges and a dainty five-petal flower on handles and lid finials made for a very attractive yet never-the-less commercially unsuccessful product.

Teapot, 6-cup, mango red, $45.00.

Chop plate, 11".................................16.00
Creamer.......................................12.50
Cup & saucer, demitasse.........................20.00
Egg cup.......................................18.00
Pitcher, ball shape.............................35.00
Plate, 9".......................................8.50
Salt shaker.....................................8.00
Sugar w/lid...................................14.00

Volkmar

Charles Volkmar established a workshop in Tremont, New York, in 1882. He produced art ware decorated under the glaze in the manner of the early barbotine work done at the Haviland factory in Limoges, France. He relocated in 1888 in Menlo Park, New Jersey, and together with J.T. Smith established the Menlo Park Ceramic Company for the production of art tile. The partnership was dissolved in 1893.

From 1895 until 1902, Volkmar located in Corona, New York, first under the name Volkmar Ceramic Company, later as Volkmar and Cory, and for the final six years as Crown Point. During the latter period he made art tile, blue underglaze Delft-type wares, and colorful polychrome vases, etc. The Volkmar Kilns were established in 1903 in Metuchen, New Jersey, by Volkmar and his son.

Wares were marked with various devices consisting of the Volkmar name, initials, or 'Crown Point Ware.'

Plaque, bl/wht, 11"...............................250.00
Vase, dk br, thrown, ca 1910, 5x6".................450.00
Vase, hand thrown, purple gloss, concave sides, 10"........65.00
Vase, hand thrown, purple gloss, concave sides, 4/23, 8½"....60.00
Vase, limoges style, HP nude on red clay, mk CV, rpr hdl, 13".775.00

Plate, Mt. Vernon, DAR, blue and white with gold trim, dated 1896, 11", $385.00.

Volkstadt

The Volkstadt Porcelain Factory was established in Thuringia, Germany about 1760. They continue to operate to the present, often marking their wares with a 'crossed hayfork' device used since the late 1700s.

Figurine, butterfly, mc, 2¼".......................45.00
Figurine, French Hussar, 1910, 9".................95.00

Figurine, frog, gr/blk, wears gold crown, Ens mk, 2".....65.00
Figurine, man offers flowers to lady, both seated, 6½".....250.00
Figurine, 2 bl herons, 13½".......................225.00
Figurine, 3 ladies seated at tea, sgn, 7x5".............575.00

Walley

The Walley Pottery operated in West Sterling, Massachusetts, from 1898 to 1919. Never more than a one man operation, Walley himself hand crafted all his wares from local clay. The majority of his pottery was simple and unadorned, and usually glazed in matt green. On occasion, however, you may find high- and semi-gloss green, as well as matt glazes in blue, cream, brown, and red. The most rare and desirable examples of his work are those with applied or carved in relief decorations.

Some pieces are marked 'WJW.'

Bowl, bulbous/inverted rim, matt gr, applied leaves, MJW, 5" H.375.00
Bowl, inverted lip, matt br, gr hi-lites, drip glaze, 3½x6".....300.00
Bowl, thick matt gr glaze, MJW, 1x3" dia.................100.00
Bud vase, gr w/oxblood, 5"........................200.00
Candlestick, vegetative semi-gloss gr, carved relief, MJW, 8"....350.00
Vase, bulbous, semi-gloss gr/br drip, applied leaves, MJW, 6"...450.00
Vase, dk br w/gr drips, heavy glossy glaze, 3¼"............130.00
Vase, gr, high glaze, carved, 7¼"....................525.00
Vase, matt bl glaze, MJW, 4".......................200.00
Vase, wide mouth on squat bulb, mottled matt gr, 3x4"......200.00

Walrath

Fredrick Walrath was a studio potter who worked from around the turn of the century until his death in 1920. He was located in Rochester, New York, until 1918, when he became associated with the Newcomb Pottery in New Orleans, Louisiana.

Bowl, lavender, 2½x8" diameter.......................125.00
Bowl w/nude centerpiece, gr matt/nude flesh tones, sgn, 6x7½".230.00
Bowl w/nude holding water jug, lt matt gr, 11".............475.00
Flower frog, child figural...........................225.00
Paperweight, nude curled in fetal position, gr/flesh, 4½"......160.00
Paperweight, scarab, gr matt, 3¾".....................125.00

Flower frog, swan figural, light green, 3¾" x 4½", $225.00.

Wannopee

The Wannopee Pottery, established in 1892, developed from the reorganization of the financially insecure New Milford Pottery Company of New Milford, Connecticut. They produced a line of mottled glaze pottery called 'Dutchess', and a similar line in porcelain. Both were marked with the impressed sunburst 'W', with 'Porcelain' added to indicate that particular body type.

In 1895, semi-porcelain pitchers in three sizes were decorated with relief medallion cameos of Beethoven, Mozart, and Napoleon. Lettuce-leaf ware was first produced in 1901, and used actual leaves in the modeling. Scarabronze, made in 1895, was their finest art ware. It featured simple Egyptian shapes with a coppery glaze. It was marked with a scarab, either impressed or applied.

Production ceased in 1903.

Chamberstick, gr, 2"...75.00
Ewer, blown, tan flambe glaze, 4"...........................50.00
Oil lamp, shade, orig font, 3 feet, br glaze, #79, 20½".....200.00
Planter, mottled br & gold, signed, 4x8"....................150.00
Vase, br cream, gr, 10x7½x2½"................................75.00
Vase, mirror blk w/gr flambe at top, low bulb, 7½".........250.00

Candle holder, blue, yellow and green running glaze colors, 4¼" x 6", $60.00.

Warwick

The Warwick China Company operated in Wheeling, West Virginia, from 1887 until 1951. They produced both hand painted and decaled plates, vases, tea and coffee pots, pitchers, bowls, and jardiniers featuring lovely florals or portraits of beautiful ladies done in luscious colors. Backgrounds were usually blendings of brown and beige, but ivory was also used.

Various marks were employed, all of which incorporate the Warwick name.

Bowl, 3-ftd, gr ground w/rose decor, 3½" tall................85.00
Humidor, barrel shape, br/crabapple decor, pewter lid, 5⅜"...110.00
Humidor, bulbous bottom, br w/fisherman, matching lid, 5¼"..125.00
Humidor, bulbous bottom, br w/Indian, matching lid, 5¼".....150.00
Humidor, bulbous bottom, br w/monk, matching lid, 5¼".......95.00
Humidor, bulbous bottom, charcoal w/nude, matching lid, 5¼".175.00
Humidor, pouch shape, br/crabapple decor, lid/ring hdl, 5¼".115.00
Jardiniere, br w/Beck dog scene, flat top, 12¼"............300.00
Jardiniere, br w/fisherman, flat top, 12¼".................250.00
Jardiniere, br w/Indian, flat top, 12¼"....................295.00

Tankard and mugs, portrait of monk on pink to green background, 10½" tankard, 4" mugs, $1,200.00 for the 7 piece set.

Jardiniere, br w/monk, flat top, 12¼".......................200.00
Jardiniere, br w/portrait, flat top, 12¼"...................275.00
Marmalade jar, br to yel, poppy decor, ornate hdls, w/lid, 4"....55.00
Mug, br w/bulldog, sq hdl, imp VP, 4½"......................85.00
Mug, br w/Dickens character, sq hdl, imp VP, 4½"............80.00
Mug, br w/eagle, sq hdl, imp VP, 4½".........................55.00
Mug, br w/elk, sq hdl, imp VP, 4½"..........................55.00
Mug, br w/fisherman, sq hdl, imp VP, 4½"....................60.00
Mug, br w/Gibson Girl, sq hdl, imp VP, 4½"..................95.00
Mug, br w/Indian, sq hdl, imp VP, 4½".......................90.00
Mug, br w/monk, sq hdl, imp VP, 4½".........................55.00
Mug, br w/portrait, sq hdl, imp VP, 4½".....................85.00
Mug, matt, tan to bl, Osiris desert scene, sq hdl, imp VP, 4½"..95.00
Mug, matt, w/fisherman, sq hdl, imp VP, 4½".................75.00
Mug, matt, w/monk, sq hdl, imp VP, 4½"......................65.00
Mug, pedestal; br to yel w/grapes, round hdl, 5½"...........70.00
Mug, pedestal; br w/bulldogs, round hdl, 5½"................85.00
Mug, pedestal; br w/fisherman, round hdl, 5½"...............80.00
Mug, pedestal; br w/Indian, round hdl, 5½"..................90.00
Mug, pedestal; br w/monk, round hdl, 5½"....................80.00
Mug, pedestal; br w/opera scenes, round hdl, 5½"............90.00
Mug, pedestal; red w/fisherman, round hdl, 5½"..............85.00
Mug, red w/fisherman, sq hdl, imp VP, 4½"...................75.00
Mug, shaving; br tones, floral decor, ring hdl..............75.00
Pitcher, beer; Tobio, br w/bulldogs, 7"....................110.00
Pitcher, beer; Tobio, br w/cardinal monk, 7"................80.00
Pitcher, beer; Tobio, br w/fisherman, 7"....................95.00
Pitcher, beer; Tobio, br w/fruit, 7".........................75.00
Pitcher, beer; Tobio, br w/Indians, 7"......................105.00
Pitcher, beer; Tobio, br w/monk, 7".........................75.00
Pitcher, beer; Tobio, charcoal w/floral, 7"................125.00
Pitcher, beer; Tobio, gr w/floral, 7"......................135.00
Pitcher, beer; Tobio, matt tan to br w/cardinal monk, 7"...130.00
Pitcher, beer; Tobio, matt tan to br w/fisherman, 7".......130.00
Pitcher, beer; Tobio, matt tan to br w/monk, 7"............120.00
Pitcher, beer; Tobio, red w/cardinal monk, 7"...............95.00
Pitcher, beer; Tobio, red w/fisherman, 7"...................95.00
Pitcher, beer; Tobio, red w/floral, 7"......................80.00
Pitcher, beer; Tobio, red w/monk, 7"........................90.00
Pitcher, beer; Tobio, wht w/floral, 7"......................135.00
Pitcher, bulbous, fluted top, br w/floral, ornate hdl, 10"..110.00
Pitcher, bulbous, fluted top, br w/fruit, ornate hdl, 10"...125.00
Pitcher, bulbous, fluted top, red w/floral, ornate hdl, 10".120.00

Pitcher, bulbous, fluted top/wht to gr/floral, ornate hdl, 10"....125.00
Pitcher, cider; br w/fruit decor, round hdl, 6¼"..............150.00
Pitcher, lemonade; br w/fruit, fluted top, ornate hdl, 6½".....100.00
Pitcher, lemonade; br w/portrait, fluted top/ornate hdl, 6½"...150.00
Pitcher, lemonade; pink w/portrait, fluted top/ornate hdl, 6½"..285.00
Pitcher, lemonade; wht w/fruit, fluted top, ornate hdl, 6½"....165.00
Plate, br w/eagle, 9½".....................................100.00
Plate, br w/elk, 9½".......................................100.00
Plate, br w/Indian, 9½"....................................130.00
Plate, br w/monk, 9½".....................................110.00
Plate, calendar; 1910, girl w/horse, 8"......................85.00
Plate, children's nursery rhyme, 7¼".........................30.00
Plate, coaching scene, wht background, 3" blk border, 10½"...65.00
Plate, flow blue w/castle scene, 10½"........................85.00
Plate, flow blue w/maple leaf pattern, 10½"..................65.00
Plate, flow blue w/windmill scene, 10½".....................90.00
Plate, fraternal, Masons, wht w/double gold rim, 8"...........35.00
Plate, hunting scene border on wht ground, 9"................40.00
Plate, Lincoln's picture on wht background, 9"..............120.00
Plate, portrait, wht background, double gold rim, 6¼".........65.00
Plate, portrait, wht background, fluted gold rim, 12".........135.00
Plate, red w/Indian, 9½"...................................140.00
Plate, red w/monk, 9½"....................................120.00
Plate, White House, wht background, 10½"...................120.00
Punch set, br tones w/poppy decor, bowl on ped + 12 cups...525.00
Spittoon, man's; br tones, no decal, emb on body, 6¾".......150.00
Spittoon, woman's; lt br w/wht center & floral decor, 7¼".....150.00
Stein, curved hdl, br w/BPOE, 13".........................185.00
Stein, curved hdl, br w/bust portrait of monk, 13".........165.00
Stein, curved hdl, br w/full figure of monk, 13"...........190.00
Stein, curved hdl, br w/Gibson Girl, 13"...................225.00
Stein, sq hdl, br w/bulldog, 10½".........................195.00
Stein, sq hdl, br w/Dickens character, 10½"................160.00
Stein, sq hdl, br w/elk, 10½".............................125.00
Stein, sq hdl, br w/fisherman, 10½".......................150.00
Stein, sq hdl, br w/Indian, 10½"..........................150.00
Stein, sq hdl, br w/monk, 10½"............................145.00
Stein, sq hdl, br w/nude, 10½"............................260.00
Stein, sq hdl, charcoal w/full figured nude, 10½"..........250.00
Stein, sq hdl, charcoal w/monk, 10½"......................200.00
Stein, sq hdl w/support bar, br w/FOE, 10½"................148.00
Stein, sq hdl w/support bar, br w/monk, 10½"...............145.00
Stein, sq hdl w/support bar, pink to gray/cardinal monk, 10½"..650.00
Vase, Bouquet, br w/floral decor, twig hdl, 10½"............95.00
Vase, Bouquet, br w/monk, twig hdl, 10½"..................140.00
Vase, Bouquet, br w/nude, twig hdl, 10½"..................160.00
Vase, Bouquet, br w/pine cone, twig hdl, 10½".............115.00
Vase, Bouquet, br w/portrait, twig hdl, 10½"...............135.00
Vase, Bouquet, charcoal w/floral decor, twig hdl, 10½".....115.00
Vase, Bouquet, charcoal w/nude, twig hdl, 10½"............320.00
Vase, Bouquet, charcoal w/portrait, twig hdl, 10½"........230.00
Vase, Bouquet, gr w/lg red/pink/wht roses, twig hdl, 10½"...280.00
Vase, Bouquet, matt finish w/beechnuts, twig hdl, 10½".....215.00
Vase, Bouquet, pink w/portrait, twig hdl, 10½".............325.00
Vase, Bouquet, red w/floral decor, twig hdl, 10½"..........105.00
Vase, Bouquet, red w/portrait, twig hdl, 10½".............150.00
Vase, Bouquet, rose color w/floral decor, twig hdl, 10½"...295.00
Vase, Bouquet, rose color w/portrait, twig hdl, 10½".......300.00
Vase, Bouquet, white w/birds, twig hdl, 10½"..............215.00
Vase, Carnation, br w/floral, bulbous w/narrow neck, 10½"...80.00
Vase, Carnation, gr w/floral, bulbous w/narrow neck, 10½"...95.00
Vase, Carnation, pink w/portrait, bulbous/narrow neck, 10½"..280.00
Vase, Carol, br w/portrait, bulbous top & bottom, 8½".......225.00
Vase, Carol, matt w/pine cones, bulbous top & bottom, 8½"...195.00

Vase, Carol, pink w/portrait, bulbous top & bottom, 8½".....325.00
Vase, Maria, br w/floral, narrow w/bulbous top, sq hdls, 10"...200.00
Vase, Maria, br w/portrait, narrow w/bulbous top, sq hdl, 10"...250.00
Vase, Maria, pink w/portrait, narrow/bulbous top/sq hdls, 10"...350.00
Vase, Maria, red w/portrait, narrow w/bulbous top/sq hdls, 10"..275.00
Vase, Maria, wht w/birds, narrow w/bulbous top, sq hdls, 10"...350.00
Vase, Verona, charcoal w/nude, ring hdl, 11¼"..............285.00
Vase, Verona, red w/floral, ring hdl, 11¼".................125.00
Vase, Verona, wht w/birds, ring hdl, 11¼".................225.00

Wash Sets

Before the days of running water, bedrooms were standardly equipped with a wash bowl and pitcher as a matter of necessity. A 'toilet set' was comprised of the pitcher and bowl, toothbrush holder, covered commode, soap dish, shaving dish and mug. Some sets were even more elaborate. Through everyday usage, the smaller items were often broken, and today it is unusual to find a complete set.

Porcelain sets decorated with florals, fruits, or scenics were produced abroad by Limoges in France, and some were imported from Germany and England. During the last quarter of the 1800s and until after the turn of the century, American-made toilet sets were manufactured in abundance. Tin and graniteware sets were also made.

Canton pattern, pitcher/bowl/jar/tb holder/sm pitcher, English...395.00
Flow blue, Sylvia, 12½" pitcher, 16" dia bowl...............325.00
Gaudy ironstone, flow blue floral w/red/gr, Middlesbro, 2 pc....470.00
KT&K, child's size, wht w/gold trim, bowl & pitcher.........95.00
Old Hall Earthenware, Excelsior, schooner in circle, 7 pc.....320.00
Sponge spatter, bl & gr on wht, bl bands, 12" dia bowl/pitcher.325.00
Sponge spatter, bl & wht, 11" pitcher, 14" dia bowl.........275.00
Taunton, Stoke, English, gr w/roses, bowl & pitcher.........225.00
US Pottery, wht w/bl thistles, Champion, bowl & pitcher.....250.00
Villeroy & Boch, wht w/gold band, bowl & pitcher...........110.00

Wedgwood, mid-19th century, pair of covered pails, bowl, pitcher, soap dish, hair bowl, and toothbrush holder, $500.00 for the 7 piece set.

Watch Fobs

Watch fobs have been popular since the last quarter of the 19th century. They were often made by retail companies to advertise their products. Souvenir, commemorative, and political fobs were also produced -- all are popular collectibles today.

Adamant Suit, Rosenthal Bros, boy in knickers on box, w/pants..20.00
Adams Road Machinery...................................15.00

Advance Rumely, silver metal, factory/man w/flag............60.00
Am Legion, Paul Revere's Ride, Boston, 1930..............40.00
Angelica Jacket Co, chef in wht porcelain uniform..........53.50
Arkansas Brick & Mfg Co, Little Rock, red celluloid, w/factory..12.50
Armour, pig figural, Fargo, ND.........................65.00
Armour Meats.......................................25.00
Armour's Simon Pure Lard............................40.00
Aultman Taylor, starred chicken......................75.00
Avery, bulldog......................................90.00
Avery Tractor.......................................75.00
Banigan Rubbers, lion, emb brass.....................20.00
Banker's Ass'n, brass, Oklahoma Indian Territory, 1907......35.00
Battle Ax Shoes, silver metal, w/ax & shoe..............25.00
Ben Franklin Rye, Delaney & Murphey, brass, bust of Franklin..45.00
Bryan, political, w/face.............................90.00
Buescher True Tone, silver metal, bell/trumpet, Elkhart, IN....28.50
Buffalo Bill, Pawnee Bill............................75.00
Bull Durham...5.00
California Mission Bell, FS, 1915, shell insert..........20.00
Case, steel lug farm tractor..........................50.00
Caterpillar Holt, brass, EX.........................200.00
Central States Life Ins, brass w/eagle, bl enamel.........22.00
Chapman Drug Co, White Lion Drugs, silver metal, lions....21.00
Clyde Grade Machinery, upright steam engine cast on 1 side...125.00
Cyrus McCormick Centennial..........................28.00
Dr Pepper, billiken.................................75.00
Dr Pepper, w/factory, oblong........................62.50
Eagle on newspapers, Sold Out.......................15.00
Eagle w/flag shield, bronze..........................15.00
Earnest Machine Prod, blk diamond plow bolt............45.00
Emerson, Baltimore, MD, brass turtle..................15.00
Euclid..14.00
Fifteenth Masons, adv St Louis jeweler on bk............20.00
Fireman's, w/truck, axes & hats......................35.00
Firestone, w/picture of tire.........................60.00
Fordson Tractor, cut-out.............................85.00
German Stove Co, pictures hard coal heater.............50.00
Geuaga Co Sugar Camp, celluloid on brass, w/log cabin....15.00
Gipps Amberlin Beer, porcelain, minor crack............85.00
Green River Whiskey.................................25.00
Hamilton Brown Shoes...............................50.00
Hardware Co, figural padlock........................125.00
Harley Davidson Cycles..............................30.00
Heinz 57 Varieties..................................55.00
Indian in headdress, brass...........................24.00
Ingersoll-Rand, construction worker w/jackhammer........35.00
Intn'l Harvester, dbl globe, cornstalks, brass...........43.50
Intn'l Harvester, dbl globe, cornstalks, wht............100.00
Intn'l Harvester Reaper, brass, w/reaper & C McCormick, 1931..30.00
Intn'l Harvester Spreaders, brass, w/horse-drawn spreader....22.00
Intn'l Life of St Louis, enameled world w/eagle atop........26.00
Jamestown Expo, arrowhead...........................27.00
John Deere, dk bl oval, porcelain.....................85.00
John Yordy, Union Line, 5 pt star center, eagle/steam engine....75.00
Kaiser Wilhelm & Uncle Sam.........................38.00
Keen Kutter, strap type.............................75.00
Kellogg's Toasted Corn Flakes, brass/enamel............70.00
Kraemer Pathfinder Compass, Indian bust in headdress, brass...43.50
Leisey Brewing Co, red porcelain L on brass............45.00
Lincoln, The Great Compeer, emb brass................18.00
Lions International Convention, 1953...................22.50
Livestock Remedy Co, hog/sheep/rooster/box, celluloid......58.50
Magcobar Mud, brass bag, Houston....................12.50
Malleable Ranges....................................35.00

Marion, steam shovel, oval, brass.....................45.00
Masonic, brass & porcelain...........................50.00
Masonic, dtd 1906..................................30.00
Masonic, rnd 2 tone yel gold/bl enamel, gold plated chain....45.00
Massachusetts Christian Endeavor, brass, witch on broom, 1916.18.00
Massey-Ferguson, key chain type......................30.00
McCormick Deering Farm Machines, bl enamel, H/C in red....45.00
Mickey Mouse.......................................35.00
Military Order of Serphentis..........................20.00
Miners Institute, silver metal w/celluloid center, w/institute......20.00
Minnesota Dairymen's Assoc, Northfield, 1913............40.00
Mohawk Trail, brass, emb elk on boulder................24.00
Munising Bond, colored porcelain......................35.00
National Quartet Contest, brass, R&W, enamel barber pole.....15.00
Natn'l Rifle Meet...................................40.00
Natn'l Sportsman....................................35.00
Norseman, figural Norseman carrying sign...............30.00
Northwest Shovel, Denver, Colorado....................22.00
Oakland Car, bl/wht porcelain........................150.00
Ohio state seal, brass................................9.00
Oklahoma Indian Territory Bankers Ass'n, 1907, brass.......48.50
Old Dutch Cleanser, Dutch Girl, bl/wht on yel porcelain.....44.00
Old Reliable Coffee.................................40.00
Panama, w/RR steam shovel, SP.......................50.00
Pepsi, Delicious Pepsi Cola Healthful, emb eagle w/bottle....125.00
Peters' Weatherbird Shoes, picture, red/wht enamel on brass....60.00
Peters' Weatherbird Shoes, wishbone, silver metal.........35.00
Phoenix Fire Co, Hollidaysburg, PA, ornate, 1971.........12.50
Pioneer Coal & Timber Co, emb brass buffalo............53.50
Polar Bear Flour, wht porcelain polar bear..............48.50
Poll Parrot Shoes, celluloid w/PP/Star Brand Shoes Are Better..50.00
Porter, hay carrier..................................95.00
Racine, WI, 1909...................................25.00
Red Diamond Overalls, w/RR man......................40.00
Red Goose Shoes, enameled..........................100.00
Reo motor car.......................................75.00
Rock Island American Legion, airplane shape, 1929.........30.00
Roosevelt, 1904.....................................31.00
Rumley 6...56.00
Sal Vet, brass......................................45.00
Saxon, pop-out.....................................85.00
Sept Morn..35.00
SGLIOOF, corn/cotton/wheat/oil/gas/coal, celluloid, w/oil well....48.50

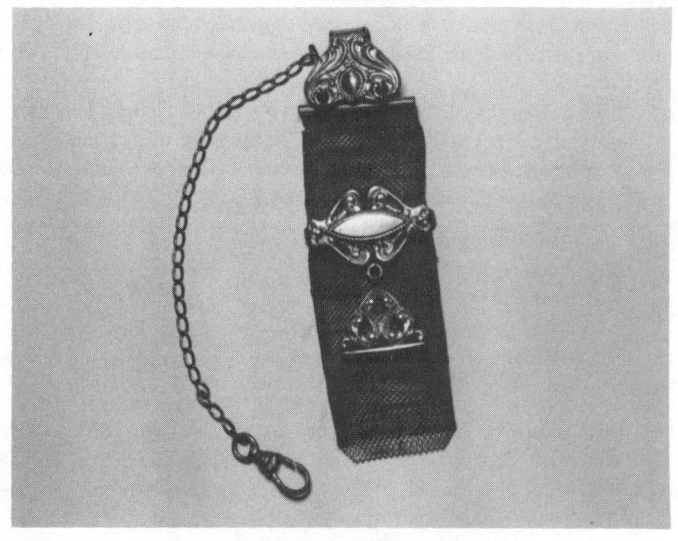

Art Nouveau styling, gold filled, 4½", $35.00.

Shapleigh Diamond Edge.........................55.00
Shield w/warships & plane, sterling.......................15.00
Sportsman's Digest, hunting scene.......................35.00
St Louis Livestock Remedy Co, celluloid on brass, animals/box..48.50
Studebaker.................................90.00
Sugar Glen, canned in Memphis, emb dog & can.............35.00
Swastika Coal & Coke, red porcelain swastika on silver metal....45.00
Taft.....................................20.00
Troop Train..................................10.00
US Steel, 5 Yrs Service...........................18.00
Western Bank, Ft Worth...........................35.00
William J Bryant................................60.00

Watch Stands

Watch stands were decorative articles designed with a hook from which to hang a watch. Some displayed the watch as the face of a grandfather clock, or as part of an interior scene with figures in period costumes and contemporary furnishings. They were popular products of Staffordshire potters and silver companies as well.

Banjo shape, brass & glass, hinged, tufted w/in, 7¾".........95.00
Birds, pewter figural, ormolu branch & leaves, brick base, 7"...125.00
Brass horseshoe, incised decor, 1800s....................85.00
Castle, Staffordshire, 10½".........................100.00
Rapp Brothers Pottery, Morton, Ill, in relief on arch..........60.00
Tufts silverplate, simulated campfire, twigs, branches.........105.00

Watches

First made in the 1500s in Germany, early watches were actually small clocks, suspended from the wrist or belt. By 1700 they had become the approximate shape and size we find today. The first watches produced in America were made in 1810. The well-known Waltham Watch Company was established in 1850, and their inexpensive 'Waterbury' models were produced by the thousands.

Open face and hunting case watches of the 1890s were solid gold or gold-filled and were often elaborately designed with several colors of gold. Gold watches became a status symbol in this decade, and were worn by both men and women on chains with fobs or jeweled slides. Ladies sometimes fastened them to their clothing with pins often set with jewels. The chatelaine watch was worn at the waist, only one of several items such as scissors, coin purses, or needle cases, each attached to small chains. During this period, movements and cases could be purchased separately, so inexpensive cases may sometimes be found containing well-jeweled movements, or the contrary may be true.

Most turn of the century watch cases were gold-filled, and these are plentiful today. 18k cases are rare, and 22k cases are very valuable! Sterling cases, though interest in them is on the increase, are not in great demand.

Key:
d/s----double sunk dial	RR----railroad
h/c----hunter case	s----size
j----jewel	s/s------single sunk dial
k----karat face	w/g/f------white gold filled
mvt----movement	y/g/f------yellow gold filled
o/f----open face	

Am Watch Co, RR, 18s, 15j, silver o/f, key wind/key set, 1870..400.00
Am Watch Co, 18s, 11j, sterling h/c, key wind, rpr...........200.00
Am Watch Co, 18s, 15j, silverine o/f, Fogg's Pat, key wind.....125.00
Appleton-Tracy, yellow gold hunting case, 4 oz...........325.00
Appleton-Tracy, 10s, 18k w/blk enamel, h/c, fancy..........585.00
Appleton-Tracy, 18s, 15j, nickel damaskeen y/g/f h/c, d/s.....180.00

Aurora, 18s, 15j, g/f, h/c..........................300.00
Ball, 16s, 19j, 20 yr y/g/f o/f, Official RR standard...........400.00
Blinn, 24j RR.................................650.00
Bulova, 10s, 17j, rolled gold plate o/f, s/s...............80.00
Bunn, Special Ill, 18s, 24j, y/g/f h/c..................645.00
Bunn, 16s, 21j, 60 hr, g/f Bunn case, d/s................250.00
Bunn, 18s, fancy silver h/c, adjusted Ill................900.00
Buren, 10s, 7j, thin o/f, s/s........................55.00
Buren, 10s, 7j, y/g/f o/f d/s metal dial, Imperial............50.00
Burlington, 16s, 21j, bridge model, y/g/f h/c.............125.00
Burlington, 16s, 21j, RR..........................145.00
BW Raymond, 16s, 21j, mk case, RR..................170.00
Cornell, 18s, o/f silverode, key wind, JC Adams.............350.00
Crawford, 14s, 17j, wht o/f, s/s......................50.00

Elgin, 17 jewel adjusted, decorative multicolor dial, gold filigree hands, 10k gold lift-out case, $900.00.

Cummings & Son, 6s, 15j, y/g/f, h/c, s/s, lever set...........215.00
Deuber case, 18s, coin silver, o/f.....................50.00
Dudley, Masonic series 3, y/g/f display case.............1,500.00
E Howard, 17j, 14k g/f, h/c, #17729...................225.00
Elgin, 0s, 7j, 20 yr y/g/f h/c, s/s.....................130.00
Elgin, 10s, 15j, 20 yr y/g/f o/f, metal dial, s/s, gold #s.........70.00
Elgin, 10s, 17j, wht 14k, s/s, o/f.....................285.00
Elgin, 10s, 17j, 20 yr y/g/f, o/f, s/s...................65.00
Elgin, 10s, 7j, w/g/f, o/f, s/s.......................50.00
Elgin, 10s, 7j, y/g/f, o/f, s/s.......................55.00
Elgin, 10s, 7j, 20 yr y/g/f h/c w/birds.................65.00
Elgin, 12s, 15j, rose g/f case & dial, porcelain dial, thin.......30.00
Elgin, 12s, 15j, 25 yr, o/f, s/s......................145.00
Elgin, 12s, 17j, y/g/f, GM Wheeler...................35.00
Elgin, 12s, 7j, o/f, y/g/f.........................35.00
Elgin, 12s, 7j, 14k, EX..........................200.00
Elgin, 16s, o/f, mc dial/silverode case, fancy.............55.00
Elgin, 16s, 17j, g/f o/f, d/s.......................105.00
Elgin, 16s, 17j, h/c, w/lake scene, d/s.................185.00
Elgin, 16s, 17j, sterling, engraved o/f.................100.00
Elgin, 16s, 17j, 3 finger bridge model, y/g/f h/c, d/s.........80.00
Elgin, 16s, 21j, BW Raymond, w/g/f..................95.00
Elgin, 16s, 21j, BW Raymond RR....................170.00
Elgin, 16s, 21j, BW Raymond 20 yr y/f/g o/f, s/s...........180.00
Elgin, 16s, 21j, orig o/f, lever set, Montgomery dial..........180.00

Elgin, 16s, 21j, y/g/f, Father Time	100.00
Elgin, 18s, h/c, o/f silverode, gold/silver dial, GM Wheeler	55.00
Elgin, 18s, o/f, expose balance cut-out sgn Normal Univ/silver	200.00
Elgin, 18s, o/f, silver, key wind, RR, BW Raymond	3,650.00
Elgin, 18s, 15j, ore silver case, o/f	60.00
Elgin, 18s, 17j, h/c, nickel mvt, gold/yellow dial	80.00
Elgin, 18s, 17j, o/f, silverode, h/c works, lever set	125.00
Elgin, 18s, 17j, o/f BWR/mc d/s Gibraltar w/Knights of Malta X	395.00
Elgin, 18s, 17j, 20 yr y/g/f o/f, nickel plate, lever set, d/s	90.00
Elgin, 18s, 21j, Father Time RR, #8833454, engraved train	245.00
Elgin, 18s, 21j, y/g/f, h/c, d/s, EX	225.00
Elgin, 18s, 23j, o/f, d/s, y/g/f, Vertias	200.00
Elgin, 18s, 7j, silverode o/f, lever set, 'Sun Dial'	125.00
Elgin, 18s, 7j, y/g/f/ h/c, convertible, engraved inscription	125.00
Elgin, 18s, 7j, 20 yr y/g/f h/c, fancy hands, s/s	130.00
Elgin, 2/0s, 7j, 25 yr y/g/f o/f, s/s, w/monogram	75.00
Elgin, 6s, 15j, w/g/f, h/c, scalloped, w/monogram, s/s	150.00
Elgin, 6s, 15j, 20 yr y/g/f h/c, s/s	150.00
Elgin, 6s, 7j, 14k h/c, s/s, EX	385.00
Elgin, 6s, 7j, 20 yr, y/g/f h/c, s/s, pendant watch	100.00
Elgin Nat'l, g/f h/c, florals & landscape engravings	100.00
English, Fusee Birmingham, CH sterling case, ca 1852, 2″ dia	165.00
Fournemenne A Charleroi, cylindre 10 rubies, silver o/f	210.00
FS Chadwick, 16s, 15j, g/f screw bk o/f	140.00
Gruen Verithin, 12s, 17j, y/g/f case	65.00
Hamilton, #23 chronograph, 19j, o/f	200.00
Hamilton, #3950, 16s, 21j, 20 yr y/g/f o/f, d/s, motor barrel	465.00
Hamilton, #4992, 16s, 22j, nickel, 2nd hand, military	165.00
Hamilton, #910, 12s, 17j, orig 25 yr o/f, s/s	70.00
Hamilton, #910, 12s, 17j, 20 yr y/g/f o/f, s/s	90.00
Hamilton, #910, 12s, 17j, 25 yr y/g/f o/f orig case, d/s	85.00
Hamilton, #910, 21s, 17j, 25 yr orig o/f w/monogram, s/s	110.00
Hamilton, #912, 10s, 17j, 14k w/g/f, triad, o/f emb s/s dial	195.00
Hamilton, #912, 12s, 17j, w/g/f o/f, s/s gray metal dial	70.00
Hamilton, #912, 12s, 17j, w/g/f orig o/f, floral emb dial	80.00
Hamilton, #914, 12s, 17j, 10k rolled gold plate, o/f, d/s	80.00
Hamilton, #917, 10s, 17j, 14k mk Hamilton case, EX	220.00
Hamilton, #917, 12s, 17j, rose g/f o/f, metal dial	45.00
Hamilton, #918, presentation, 14k w/20 diamonds, orig box	450.00
Hamilton, #920, 12s, 21j, 14k o/f	225.00
Hamilton, #921, 10s, 21j, y/g/f Hamilton case, M	155.00
Hamilton, #921, 12s, 21j, 14k g/f, o/f, s/s	150.00
Hamilton, #922 Masterpiece, 12s, 14k o/f	365.00
Hamilton, #922-B, 16s, 21j, g/f, Montgomery RR Special dial	220.00
Hamilton, #925, 18s, 17j, y/g/f h/c, s/s, lever set	80.00
Hamilton, #936, 18s, 17j, nickel o/f swing out, d/s	100.00
Hamilton, #940, 18s, 21j, o/f, y/g/f, d/s, engineer on dial	225.00
Hamilton, #940, 18s, 21j, 25 yr o/f, y/g/f, masonic engraving	165.00
Hamilton, #941, 18s, 21j, o/f glass h/c	100.00
Hamilton, #944, 17j, d/s, y/g/f, o/f	165.00
Hamilton, #946, 18s, 23j, y/g/f, J Boss, o/f, d/s Montgomery	700.00
Hamilton, #950, 16s, 23j, o/f, y/g/f	300.00
Hamilton, #950, 19j, d/s, o/f, y/g/f	165.00
Hamilton, #972, 16s, 17j, y/g/f o/f, d/s	100.00
Hamilton, #974, 16s, 17j, silveroid, o/f	80.00
Hamilton, #974, 16s, 17j, Special, Montgomery dial, RR	125.00
Hamilton, #974, 16s, 17j, 20 yr y/g/f, o/f, s/s	140.00
Hamilton, #974, 16s, 17j, 25 yr y/g/f o/f	100.00
Hamilton, #975, 16s, 17j, 20 yr y/g/f h/c, s/s	180.00
Hamilton, #987, 16s, 17j, g/f o/f swing out w/masonic emblems	125.00
Hamilton, #992, 16s, 21j, Montgomery dial, d/s, y/g/f	110.00
Hamilton, #992B, 16s, RR, cross bow y/g/f case w/logo	235.00
Hamilton, #992B, 16s, 21j, y/g/f raised dot RR case	160.00
Hamilton, #992B, 21j, stainless	135.00
Hampden, 10s, 15j, #306, w/g/f, o/f	70.00
Hampden, 12s, 17j, h/c, s/s, lever set, Gen Stark	180.00
Hampden, 16s, 17j, 20 yr y/g/f o/f d/s, lever set, Wm KcKinley	160.00
Hampden, 16s, 21j, RR Primus, d/s, y/g/f, o/f	140.00
Hampden, 18s, 15j, 4 oz silveroid, o/f, mc dial	110.00
Hampden, 18s, 21j, nickel swing out case, d/s, John Hancock	170.00
Hampden, 18s, 21J, RR, o/f, damaskeened, nickel movement	155.00
Hampden, 18s, 7j, silverode o/f, s/s, nickle plate, Champion	80.00
Hampden, 3/0s, 7j, y/g/f o/f, d/s, Molly Sark, pendant	70.00
Hirsch Espint, 12//0s, 7j, 10 yr y/g/f o/f, s/s, pendant	35.00
Howard, series I, key wind, key set, silver h/c	1,500.00
Howard, 12j, 18k orig case	775.00
Howard, 12s, 17j, w/g/f, Howard case, metal dial	130.00
Howard, 12s, 17j, y/g/f o/f, w/sm mono, Keystone	90.00
Howard, 14s, 17j, orig w/g/f o/f, d/s	180.00
Howard, 16s, 21j, series II, y/g/f	175.00
Howard, 18k, Muir case, key wind, series III, h/c	1,675.00
Howard, 18s, 17j, 25 yr y/g/f o/f	250.00
Illinois, 10s, 17j, 25 yr y/g/f o/f, d/s, Autocrat	70.00
Illinois, 10s, 21j, 14k y/g/f o/f	100.00
Illinois, 10s, 21j, 25 yr y/g/f o/f, d/s, Abe Lincoln	130.00
Illinois, 12j, 18k y/g/f Bunn Special RR, 60 hr, #4818500	275.00
Illinois, 12s, 14k, w/g/f, Federal, Art Deco	70.00
Illinois, 12s, 17j, y/g/f o/f, engraved	40.00
Illinois, 12s, 17j, 25 yr hinged bk, o/f, JA Garfield, s/s	95.00
Illinois, 12s, 17j, 25 yr y/g/f o/f, Time King, brass s/s dial	95.00
Illinois, 12s, 19j, 10 yr y/g/f o/f, d/s metal dial, Elite	80.00
Illinois, 12s, 21j, w/g/f, s/s, Garland	165.00
Illinois, 16s, y/g/f, h/c, engraved decor	110.00
Illinois, 16s, 11j, 25 yr y/g/f, h/c, s/s, lever set	110.00
Illinois, 16s, 11j, ¾ plate o/f, y/g/f	70.00
Illinois, 16s, 15j, 25 yr y/g/f o/f, hunting works, d/s	100.00
Illinois, 16s, 17j, y/g/f o/f, d/s, Belmont	95.00
Illinois, 16s, 17j, 20 yr y/g/f h/c, d/s	130.00
Illinois, 16s, 17j, 20 yr y/g/f o/f, d/s	95.00
Illinois, 16s, 19j, 25 yr y/g/f swing out, d/s	95.00
Illinois, 16s, 21j, Santa Fe Special, o/f, y/g/f	170.00
Illinois, 16s, 21j, w/f/g, Bunn Special, Bunn case, metal dial	170.00
Illinois, 16s, 21j, wht metal, o/f Bunn Special, Montgomery	210.00
Illinois, 16s, 21j, 20 yr y/g/f o/f, d/s, lever set	160.00
Illinois, 16s, 21j, 60 hr Bunn Special, o/f, y/g/f, Montgomery	325.00
Illinois, 18s, mc dial w/roses	270.00
Illinois, 18s, o/f, silverine, key wind, Deuber case	35.00
Illinois, 18s, 11j, silver ore o/f, hunting works, d/s, lever	200.00
Illinois, 18s, 15j, coin silver h/c, key wind	235.00
Illinois, 18s, 15j, Fahys #1 h/c, d/s, Negley, lever set	285.00
Illinois, 18s, 17j, nickeloid o/f w/loco engraving	100.00
Illinois, 6s, 17j, g/f, RR	90.00
Illinois Stewart, h/c, g/f, wht enamel face	100.00
Ingersol, 16s, 0j, Yankee	100.00
Ingersol, 16s, 7j, wht base metal, Reliance	55.00
Ingersol Jr, 10s, 0j, nickel case, s/s	50.00
Ingraham, 16s, 0j, o/f, 2nd hand, Sentinel	40.00
Iowa Watch Co, 18s, key wind, silverode w/chain/key, Ill	190.00
Iowa Watch Co, 18s, silverode h/c, key wind/set, Ill mvt	90.00
J Ritter, 18s, 15j, coin silver h/c, full brass plate, s/s	115.00
Jay Gould, RR King Columbus, 18s, o/f, y/g/f	425.00
JH Winslow, Civil War soldier w/tent engraving, key wind, G	175.00
Lapel, Elgin, 14k gf, hc, engraved engine trn, presentation	200.00
London, 16s, fusee works, o/f, sterling, key wind	195.00
Longines, 10s, 17j, y/g/f o/f	50.00
Lonville Extra, 16s, 17j, y/g/f, rolled gold plate o/f, d/s	70.00
Marcle, 10s, 6j, 25 yr y/g/f o/f, silver dial	60.00
Marlboro Goering, 16s, 7j, 10 yr y/g/f o/f, brushed dial	70.00

Medora, 15j, wht base o/f d/s............................70.00
MJ Tobias, 18s, full jewel, detached lever, KW/KS...........260.00
Nashua, Am Watch Co, Wm Ellery, sgn 4 oz silver case, 1879..275.00
National Watch Co, 18s, 15j, coin silver h/c, key wind........165.00
New York Std, 10s, 15j, 20 yr y/g/f o/f, s/s metal, Keystone.....65.00
New York Std, 16s, mc dial..............................40.00
New York Std, 18s, h/c, y/g/f, logger's dial..................120.00
New York Std, 18s, 7j, sterling h/c w/gold inlay, gr/wht dial....400.00
New York Std, 18s, 7j, 10 yr y/g/f h/c, lever set.............130.00
New York Std, 6s, 7j, 10 yr y/g/f h/c, gr/wht dial, Columbia.....95.00
Orvin, 16s, 17j, o/f, nickel, s/s.........................50.00
Pima, 14s, 21j, o/f, 10k rolled gold plate, d/s..............60.00
Regin, 17j, o/f, g/f...................................30.00
Rexas, 16s, 15j, o/f, silver...........................55.00
Rhiga, 4s, 11j, sterling o/f, lever set, pendant...............70.00
Robert Roskell, 18k, o/f, pat lever, engraved costal village.....250.00
Robert Ward, fusee, hallmarks for 1773, wht enamel dial, 2"...475.00
Rockford, 15j, mk Extra on mvt, key wind, early #, y/g/f h/c...110.00
Rockford, 16s, 21j, 515, y/g/f.........................320.00
Rockford, 18s, y/g/f h/c, Paragon.....................400.00
Rockford, 18s, 11j, y/g/f h/c..........................160.00
Rockford, 18s, 17j, silverode w/mc dial, fancy mvt/hands.......225.00
Rockford, 18s, 19 rubies, y/g/f h/c, d/s, key wind, last run....2,500.00
Rockford, 18s, 7j, coin silver h/c, key wind................175.00
Rockford, 18s, 7j, silveroid, o/f, key wind.................100.00
Ruxton RR, 16s, 17j, Montomery, rolled gold plate, key wind...100.00
San Francisco Cornell, 18s, 15j, silver h/c, key wind.........1,900.00
Sanagamo Special, 21j, w/g/f stiff bow case...............350.00
Seth Thomas, 18s, 7j, y/g/f h/c w/inlaid fleur-de-lis...........155.00
Seth Thomas, 6s, 7j, y/g/f h/c, s/s, lever set...............160.00
Seth Thomas, 6s, 7j, yel 25 yr h/c, ornate engraving, s/s.......235.00
Solar Watch Co, 18s, o/f, sgn Chicago, silverode w/mc dial......90.00
South Bend, RR, silver case, engraved steam locomotive........95.00
South Bend, 12s, 21j, Studebaker, orig o/f, d/s.............200.00
South Bend, 16s, 15j, mc gold dial w/fancy hands, h/c, o/f......70.00
South Bend, 16s, 15j, o/f silverode w/hunter mvt, mc dial.......70.00
South Bend, 16s, 17j, #211, 20 yr y/g/f o/f, d/s..............95.00
South Bend, 16s, 19j, #219, 20 yr y/g/f o/f, d/s..............95.00
South Bend, 16s, 9j, #209, 25 yr y/g/f h/c, s/s.............140.00
Studebaker, 12s, 21j, o/f, y/g/f........................80.00
Swiss, 10/0, 18k, very ornate.........................265.00
Swiss, 10s, 15j, Longines Grand Prix, sterling o/f............425.00
Swiss, 3/0s, 11j, .80 silver o/f, pen set..................60.00
Swiss King, 18s, 15j, wht nickel o/f, s/s.................70.00
Tacy Admiral, 12s, 7j, 10 yr y/g/f o/f, d/s................80.00
Tiffany, 3/0s, 15j, 18k o/f, swing out...................400.00
Vanguard, 16s, 23j, y/g/f Bunn Special o/f, up/down movement..365.00
Vanguard, 18s, 21j, 92 model Waltham y/g/f case............100.00
Waltham, sterling, h/c, #175635.......................145.00
Waltham, 0s, red/silver/gold dial, fancy..................100.00
Waltham, 10s, 15j, wht o/f base w/hunting works, s/s..........55.00
Waltham, 10s, 15j, 20 yr y/g/f h/c, s/s..................155.00
Waltham, 10s, 17j, 14k o/f, s/s........................75.00
Waltham, 10s, 17j, 14k swing out, wht metal s/s dial.........365.00
Waltham, 10s, 7j, 20 yr y/g/f o/f w/hunting works, s/s.........55.00
Waltham, 12s, 15j, o/f, metal dial/Star Watch case/base metal...25.00
Waltham, 12s, 17j, IWCCO w/g/f o/f, Riverside.............35.00
Waltham, 12s, 17j, y/g/f o/f, s/s.......................65.00
Waltham, 12s, 21j, 10k y/g/f o/f, d/s, Riverside............100.00
Waltham, 14s, 17j, 20 yr y/g/f Riverside, s/s...............85.00
Waltham, 16s, 15j, h/c y/g/f, s/s.......................85.00
Waltham, 16s, 15j, sterling h/c w/inlaid rose, y/g deer head...235.00
Waltham, 16s, 17j, royal nickel case, d/s.................80.00
Waltham, 16s, 17j, 14k o/f, d/s gold metal dial.............500.00

Waltham, 16s, 17j, 20 yr y/g/f o/f, d/s...................85.00
Waltham, 16s, 19j, 14k w/g/f o/f, Ball Official RR Standard....375.00
Waltham, 16s, 21j, 25 yr Cresant hinged case, o/f, d/s........150.00
Waltham, 16s, 23j, rolled gold plate o/f, lever set, Vanguard...150.00
Waltham, 16s, 7j, 20 yr y/g/f o/f, s/s...................125.00
Waltham, 18s, 15j, coin silver h/c, s/s, lever set, Chas Henn...210.00
Waltham, 18s, 15j, gold filled open face, porcelain dial........85.00
Waltham, 18s, 15j, silverode o/f, Appleton Tracy, d/s.........130.00
Waltham, 18s, 15j, silverode o/f w/hunting works, nickel plate..100.00
Waltham, 18s, 15j, y/g/f o/f, full brass plate, s/s...........135.00
Waltham, 18s, 15j, 20 yr y/g/f h/c Appleton Tracy KW/KS.....300.00
Waltham, 18s, 17j, silverode o/f, hunting works, d/s.........125.00
Waltham, 18s, 17j, 25 yr y/g/f o/f, s/s, PS Bartlett...........185.00
Waltham, 18s, 7j, coin silver h/c, s/s, lever set.............95.00
Waltham, 18s, 7j, silveroid o/f, key wind.................100.00
Waltham, 18s, 7j, sterling o/f, Bond Street, pen set..........160.00
Waltham, 3/0s, 7j, h/c...............................160.00
Waltham, 6s, 7j, Deuber Special h/c, s/s.................185.00
Waltham, 6s, 7j, y/g/f h/c...........................100.00
Waltham, 6s, 7j, 14k h/c, s/s.........................700.00
Wrist, Benrus, lady's, 17j, 14k w/g w/6 sm diamonds.........180.00
Wrist, Bulova Accutron, man's, 14k, y/g/f band.............285.00
Wrist, Elgin, 5-0s, 15j, 14k flex strap, 2nd hand, 1925........350.00
Wrist, Hamilton, 17j men's, w/g/f Ill Special case, 2nd hand....70.00
Wrist, Jules Jergensen, Quartz, men's, day/date, leather band...150.00
Wrist, Lady Elgin, 10/0s, 15j, 18k w/g, Model Z............140.00
Wrist, Omega, man's, stainless, automatic................160.00
Wrist, Swiss, 14k lady's, w/bl stone....................185.00

Waterford

The Waterford Glass Company operated in Ireland from the late 1700s until 1851 when the factory closed. One hundred years later, in 1951, another Waterford glassworks was instituted that produced glass similar to the 18th century wares -- crystal glass, usually with cut decoration. Today, Waterford is a generic term referring to the type of glass first produced there.

Compote, blown & cut, engraved on base: 1928, 6¼".........70.00
Cruet, polished pontil, rayed stars, faceted stopper, 7½".......40.00
Decanter, allover geometric cutting, 15"..................110.00
Decanter, Colleen pattern, w/stopper, 14"................105.00
Goblet, Curraghmore................................38.00
Goblet, engraved coat of arms, 8".....................90.00

Decanter with dolphin handle and six cordials on silverplated tray, $225.00 for the set.

Goblet, etched thistles, 7¼″...50.00
Vase, Christmas: The Magi, sgn/#d ltd edition, 1971, 10″....1,075.00
Vase, cut crystal, 12″...45.00
Wine rinser, cut crystal, 1860, 4¾″ dia, pr.................80.00

Watt Pottery

The Watt Pottery Company was incorporated on July 5, 1922, in Perry County, Crooksville, Ohio. Their early products were stoneware jars, jugs, milk pans, Dutch pots, mixing bowls (white with blue bands), churns, preserve jars, and chicken waterers, all marked in cobalt with their trademark, 'Acorn.' In 1935, these items were discontinued, and the company began to make free-hand decorated kitchen and oven ware items such as 'Banded' and 'Decorated' mixing bowls, 'Spaghetti' bowls, canister sets, covered casseroles, nappies, cookie jars, ice buckets, pitchers, handled French casseroles, bean pots, salad sets, and dog dishes. Bold brush strokes of red and green contrasted with the natural buff color of the glazed body; several patterns were produced: 'Red Apple,' 'Star Flower,' 'Rooster,' 'Autumn Foliage,' 'Morning Glory,' and 'Tulip.' Other lines were 'Basket Weave' (made in solid colors), 'Wood Grain' (a brown glazed line), and 'Royal Danish' dinnerware.

Fire destroyed the entire manufacturing plant on October 4, 1965.

Because of the country flavor of the hand decorated yellowware pieces, Watt Pottery is fast becoming a favorite collectible. Much of the ware was made for advertising premiums and is often found stenciled with the name of a retail company.

Bean pot w/lid, sgn.......................................25.00
Bowl, Apple, w/advertising, 10″...........................24.00
Bowl, mixing; Apple, 6″....................................7.00
Bowl w/lid, Rooster, 6″ H.................................35.00
Cookie jar, Apple..30.00
Cookie jar, Goodies......................................20.00
Cookie jar, Peidecco.....................................23.00
Hot plate, Apple, electric...............................30.00
Mug, Grapes, mk Esmond...................................20.00
Pitcher, Apple, advertising, 5″..........................15.00
Pitcher, Apple, no mk, lg................................25.00
Pitcher, Rooster, 6″.....................................30.00
Pitcher, Tulips, red & bl, 6″............................25.00
Pitcher, w/br bands, 4″..................................15.00
Shakers, Apple, hourglass shape, 4″, pr..................15.00
Spooner, Apple, 2 hdls, 4″...............................25.00
Wall pocket, blended br & yel, 8″ dia....................15.00

Pitcher, hand painted rooster decoration, 8″, $40.00.

Wave Crest

Wave Crest is the trademark used on a line of creamy opaque glassware manufactured by the C.F. Monroe Company of New York, who operated there from 1892 until 1916. Vases, boxes, tablewares, and humidors in swirled and blown-out shapes were either hand painted or transfer printed with florals, scenics, or portraits. Many pieces were enhanced with ornately scrolled ormolu handles, feet, or rims. Several marks were used: the black mark, 'Trade Mark Wave Crest'; the Red Banner mark; and the paper label, 'Wave Crest Ware, Patented Oct. 4, 1892'.

Box, Rococo mold, hand painted daisies, 2½″ x 3″, $220.00.

Biscuit jar, bl w/florals, Puffy lid, cut-out SP hdl............400.00
Biscuit jar, moon & stars in lt pk & bl.......................500.00
Biscuit jar, pk apple blossoms/ornate scrolls, CFM in cover.....345.00
Bon bon, w/bail hdl, scroll relief, blown-out flowers, 6″.......225.00
Box, Baroque Shell, lt bl, heavy beading, 7″...................625.00
Box, Baroque Shell lid, lt bl w/floral, brass collar, 3x4″ dia....250.00
Box, bl mums/enamel dots, relief decor, hinged lid, 3¼″ sq....250.00
Box, blown-out pansy on lid, bronze to yel shading, 4½″.....380.00
Box, blue, blown heart corners, decor w/silver tracing, 3x7″....675.00
Box, cherubs, 3¼x5½″ dia......................................525.00
Box, cigarette; banner mk....................................325.00
Box, Collars & Cuffs, ftd, red banner mk.....................885.00
Box, country road scenic top, HP, 3¾″........................225.00
Box, Cupid on lid, HP, 2½″...................................295.00
Box, Cupids & florals, oblong, 5¼″ L.........................495.00
Box, emb rope edges & HP florals top & base, 7½″ dia.......625.00
Box, handkerchief; Swirl, ormolu ft & collar, florals, 6½x7″....750.00
Box, hex base, rnd top, orchids/lg scrolls, Spindrift mold, 9″.1,200.00
Box, octagonal, pk w/enamel flowers, bl dots, 4″............225.00
Box, oval, bl scroll, enamel flowers, 5½″...................385.00
Box, pk & bl floral, emb, ormolu collar, 5″ dia.............450.00
Box, pk w/brass collar, floral decor, 2½x4½″................235.00
Box, pk w/wht scrolls, bl astors, ormolu, ftd, 9½x6x5½″.....1,200.00
Box, Puffy, dk gr w/wht cartouch top & sides w/pk roses, 7″...850.00
Box, Rococo, brass ped ft, 3x4″, M...........................250.00
Box, Rococo, orig lining, sgn, 7½″ dia.......................595.00
Box, Swirl, floral, 7¼″......................................575.00
Box, Swirl, florals, brass collar, 2½x3½″...................200.00
Box, Swirl, gr tones, EX detail, 6″..........................345.00
Box, wht/emb/floral decor top/base, ormolu mt/ft, 3¾x3″.....250.00
Box, 2 Cupids, 3″..495.00
Creamer, Swirl, yel daisies, silver collar/hdl...............110.00
Creamer & sugar, Swirl, floral panels, gold dots, silver fr......360.00
Ferner, Puffy, allover pk decor, brass collar/insert, 3½x7″.....265.00

Humidor, Cigars; shell lid, sgn..........................475.00
Humidor, tobacco, Egg Crate, ormolu trim, 5½" dia.........425.00
Jar, pomade; forget-me-nots.............................185.00
Lamp base, oil; Rococo relief, florals....................195.00
Letter holder, Puffy, bl floral, wht beading, ormolu rim, 5½"...300.00
Letter holder, scroll relief, floral decor, brass fitting..........245.00
Paperweight, angel w/cymbal............................450.00
Photo holder, pk to wht, lion's feet......................675.00
Pin tray, Rococo, w/hdls, sgn red banner mk, 4½"..........125.00
Pin tray, shell relief, florals, brass rim, lined, 2¾"..........135.00
Powder jar, pk/wht roses, bl/wht flower spray, orig puff.......450.00
Salt dip, pr..75.00
Shakers, pink scrolls w/violet center, pr...................80.00
Shakers, tulip, 1 w/cat & spider, 1 w/orchids, pr.............90.00
Sugar w/lid; Swirl, shasta daisies, silver collar/lid/hdl........195.00
Tray, jewel; ftd, oval hdls, orig lining, 5¾x3½".............275.00
Urn, ornate pewter top & bottom, 13"....................175.00

Wax

The craft of wax modeling flourished after a very successful showing in 1851 at the Great London Exhibition, and continued to be of interest throughout the century. Many painstaking hours were put into each article. Instruction in the craft was published in the book *Handbook of Modeling Wax*. Upon completion, the project was often framed in glass for protection.

Figurine, Virgin Mary, 1840...........................200.00
Portrait bust, Charles Dickens, hand colored, convex lens, 6"..155.00
Portrait bust, gent in long wig, mk Tassie Fecit, 1825, 6".....300.00
Portrait bust, man/young lady, G detail, oval fr, 6½x7½", pr...110.00
Portrait bust, officer, sgn Pool, on velvet matt, 8x9¼"........65.00
Portrait bust, possibly Louis XIV, velvet matt, mahog fr, 9½"..155.00

Weapons

Among the varied areas of specialization within the broad category of weapons, guns are by far the most popular. Muskets are among the earliest firearms; they were large-bore shoulder arms, usually firing black powder, with separate loading of powder and shot. Some ignited the charge by flintlock or caplock, while later types used a firing pin with a metallic cartridge. Side arms, referred to as such because they were worn at the side, include pistols and revolvers. Pistols range from early single-shot and multiple barrels to modern types with cartridges held in the handle. Revolvers were supplied with a cylinder that turned to feed a fresh round in front of the barrel breech. Other firearms include shotguns, which fired round or conical bullets and had a smooth inner barrel surface, and rifles, so named because the interior of the barrel contained spiral grooves (rifling) which increased accuracy.

Key:
bbl------barrel   ga-------gauge
cal------caliber   hdw------hardware
conv-----conversion   mag-----magazine
f/l-----flintlock   p/b----patch box
f/s----full stock   perc----percussion

Bayonet, German WWII mauser, ground blade...............15.00
Bayonet, Indian Wars, metal/leather scabbard/brass US insignia..35.00
Bayonet, Revolutionary War, 15" blade & socket, orig scabbard.45.00
Bayonet, US Civil War Springfield, leather scabbard...........35.00
Bayonet, US Model 1816................................17.50
Bayonet, US 45-70 type...............................17.50
Blunderbus, f/l, brass inlay, 1800s......................220.00

Bullet mold, Colt, dbl cavity, conical & round, mk #36/1851....25.00
Bullet mold, KY rifle, 31 cal, 6".........................10.00
Carbine, CW Burnside single shot, 4th model w/#10627.....450.00
Carbine, Joslyn 1864 single, 52 cal rimfire 22" rnd bbl.......325.00
Carbine, Remington split breech, single shot, saddle ring....600.00
Carbine, Sharps saddle ring single shot, 50 cal 22" rnd bbl...675.00
Carbine, Sharps 1863 saddle ring single, 52 cal, 22" rnd bbl..625.00
Carbine, US Springfield trapdoor single, saddle ring, 45-70.....285.00
Cutlass, CW naval, Model 1860, Ames, dtd 1862, w/scabbard...250.00
Dagger, curved, Damascus steel, dbl edge, damascened, Persian.550.00
Dagger, gentleman's, spear point, horn grip, 1800s, 9¼"......150.00
Dagger, Indian jade carved w/leaves & flowers, 10"..........330.00
Dagger, neillo silver hilt/scroll/foliage decor, 1800s, 11"....200.00
Dagger, Unwin & Rodgers, silver hilt, orig sheath, 10¾"......140.00
Derringer, Colt #3, brass fr, single, 41 cal rimfire, 2½" bbl...260.00
Derringer, Colt #3, brass fr, spur trigger, 41 cal rimfire.......300.00
Derringer, Colt #3, single, eng spur trigger, 41 cal rimfire.....365.00

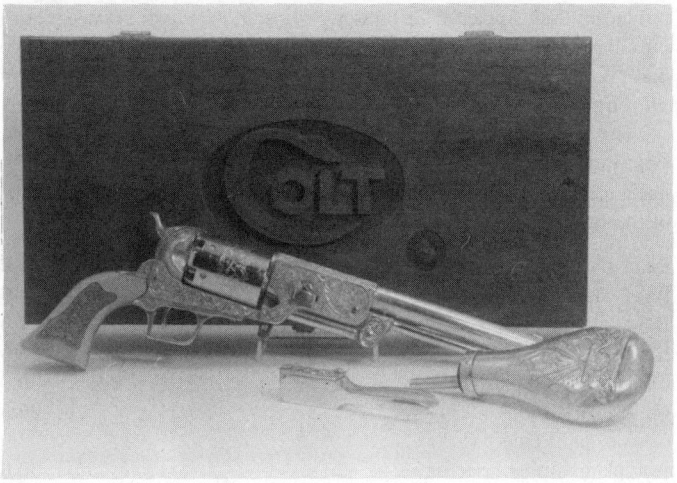

Colt Dragoon, six cylinder Cavalry revolver, presentation piece, silverplated flask and .44 bullet mold, 1850s, all original, $40,000.00.

Derringer, Nat'l, eng brass fr, single shot #1, 41 cal rimfire....450.00
Derringer, Philadelphia, dbl mk, 5½".....................685.00
Katar, gold damascene hdl, Indian, 1800s, in velvet case, 1700.465.00
Lantaka, stepped rnd barrel, heart cast on top, 44½"........1,000.00
Lantaka, ½ rnd, ½ octagon barrel, 1¼" bore, 43½".........900.00
Musket, Blunt-Enfield perc f/s single, 58 cal 39" bbl, w/eagle...325.00
Musket, Flobert single shot f/s 30 cal rimfire 27½" rnd bbl.....85.00
Pepperbox, Mariette 8 Damascus barrels, chased, 1830, in case.935.00
Pistol, English percussion cap, damascened/engraved, 1810, pr.935.00
Pistol, English percussion cap, Ezekiel Baker, 1800s..........605.00
Pistol, F Wesson 1862 2nd type brass fr, single shot, 22 cal....90.00
Pistol, f/l, brass barrel/walnut stock/checker grip, 14½", pr....400.00
Pistol, f/l, f/s, brass hdw/silver inlay, Arabian, 15½"..........60.00
Pistol, f/l horse, full stock, 15¾" barrel, w/ram rod............80.00
Pistol, Fr percussion cap duelling, engraved, 1845, pr.......1,430.00
Pistol, German f/l, carved/inlaid walnut stock, 1700s, pr......1,430.00
Pistol, KY percussion, curly maple/silver inlay, ca 1835, 14½"..550.00
Pistol, Laroche, f/l f/s, single, 8" bbl, eng brass hdw, pr.....1,750.00
Pistol, octagonal barrels/folding triggers, walnut grip, 1800.....125.00
Pistol, percussion, mahog stock w/brass trim, 8" barrel, 14" L..200.00
Pistol, Protector, 21 cal, 1¾" rnd bbl, blk grips............500.00
Pistol, Robbins/Lawrence ring trigger/28 cal pepperbox/5 shot..225.00
Pistol, Scottish all steel f/l Highlander's, chased, 1775.......1,210.00
Pistol, silver mtd officer's 1700s, Ketland & Co, 8" barrel.....400.00
Pistol, US Army 1862 perc single, brass fr, 1¾" bbl.........400.00

Pistol, US model 1842 Aston perc single shot, 54 cal, 8½" bbl.525.00
Revolver, Adams percussion, pat #, 1850s, in case...........605.00
Revolver, American Std Tool, brass fr, bottom-break, 7 shot....60.00
Revolver, Colt Cloverleaf, brass fr/spur trigger 4 shot 41 cal....500.00
Revolver, Colt Frontier single action 6 shot, 45 cal 7½" bbl...900.00
Revolver, Colt New Line, 5 shot, 38 cal rimfire, 2¼" bbl......245.00
Revolver, Colt 1849, stage coach hold-up on cylinder.........350.00
Revolver, Colt 1849 Hartford pocket perc 5 shot, 31 cal 4" bbl.425.00
Revolver, Colt 1860 Army perc 6 shot, 44 cal, 8" rnd bbl.....465.00
Revolver, Colt 1860 Army perc 6 shot, 44 cal, 8" rnd bbl, eng.525.00
Revolver, Colt 1861 Navy perc 6 shot, 36 cal, 7½" rnd bbl....700.00
Revolver, Colt 1861 rnd barrel Navy 36 cal, low #, VG.......850.00
Revolver, Fr service model 1873, 6 shot, cal 11mm, orig bbl...145.00
Revolver, Harrington Richardson 7 shot spur trigger, 32 cal....140.00
Revolver, Hopkins & Allen Army XL#8 lg single action 6 shot..825.00
Revolver, Manhattan perc 5 shot, 36 cal, 4" oct bbl, eng......365.00
Revolver, Manhattan perc 5 shot, 36 cal, 5" oct bbl, plain.....295.00
Revolver, Marlin #32 Std 1875 5 shot spur trigger, 32 cal.....100.00
Revolver, Nepperhan, pocket model, 5 shot, 31 cal, orig 5" bbl.300.00
Revolver, Remington #4, 5 shot, 38 cal rimfire, 2½" bbl......200.00
Revolver, Remington Army perc 6 shot, 44 cal, 8" oct bbl.....650.00
Revolver, Remington Iroquois, 7 shot, 22 cal 2¼" rnd bbl.....225.00
Revolver, Remington New Model 1858, unfired, EX.........1,250.00
Revolver, Smith & Wesson dlb action Frontier top-break 6 shot.550.00
Rifle, Allin conv 1865 single, 58 cal rimfire 29½" bbl........250.00
Rifle, Ballard, Ball & Williams, lever, single shot 38 cal......325.00
Rifle, curly maple f/s, 13 silver inlay, engraved brass box.....475.00
Rifle, curly maple f/s f/l copy of JP Beck, EX inlay, Buchele..1,600.00
Rifle, KY, curly maple f/s, f/l, silver inlay eagles/lion, 54".....800.00
Rifle, KY, curly maple f/s, f/l oct/rnd barrel w/inlay..........450.00
Rifle, KY, curly maple f/s percussion, B Samples, 59"........800.00
Rifle, KY, curly maple f/s percussion lock, 54½".............425.00
Rifle, KY, curly maple ½ stock, mk Golcher, Masonic inlay....375.00
Rifle, KY, curly maple ½ stock perc, 23 silver inlays, EX....1,800.00
Rifle, KY, curly maple ½ stock perc lock, brass patch box.....400.00
Rifle, KY, curly maple ½ stock perc lock, 5 silver inlays.......350.00
Rifle, KY, maple ½ stock/perc lock, silver inlay man/deer......485.00
Rifle, long; maple ½ stock w/silver star/dia inlay, 52".........275.00
Rifle, Marlin 1894 lever action, 32-20 cal, orig 26" rnd bbl....275.00
Rifle, Marlin 1895 lever action, 40-82 cal, 26" oct bbl........500.00
Rifle, Persian Miquelet, gold damascene, burl walnut inlay....2,200.00
Rifle, Persian Miquelet Lock, burl stock w/silver inlay, 1800s...330.00
Rifle, Persian Miquelet Lock, octagon, gold damascene/inlay..1,980.00
Rifle, Persian Miquelet Lock, silver damascene steel, inlay....1,210.00
Rifle, Remington #1 single shot, 32 cal rimfire, 26" oct bbl....265.00
Rifle, Sharps 1852 percussion breech load..................605.00
Rifle, Sharps 1874 single, 44 cal 26" oct bbl, pewter fore tip.1,500.00
Rifle, Siamese Mauser bolt action military, 8x52 cal...........85.00
Rifle, Spencer, 3 barrel bands, 1st mod w/out Stabler cut-off...400.00
Rifle, Spencer Mod 1865 w/Stabler cut-off, Burnside, 2 bands..350.00
Rifle, US Springfield trapdoor f/s, single, 45-70, 32½" bbl....425.00
Rifle, Wheelock, lg octagon barrel, EX engraving, 1750.....3,850.00
Rifle, Winchester 1st 1876 lever, open top, w/out dust cover..1,200.00
Rifle, Winchester 1873 lever/22 cal short/24" rnd bbl/full mag..800.00
Rifle, Winchester 1892, lever, 38-40 cal, orig 24" octagon bbl..785.00
Sabre, gilt/niello on silver, Caucasian, 31".................770.00
Sabre, US Model 1840 artillery, mk US/ADK, Ames Mfg.......185.00
Shotgun, English perc cap, dbl barrel, walnut/silver mts.......660.00
Shotgun, mk London, f/l dbl bbl, 14 ga, 34½" side by side....825.00
Shotgun, Winchester 1887, lever action 12 ga, 30" bbl.......300.00
Shotgun, Winchester 1887, lever action 12 ga, 32" bbl.......400.00
Shotgun, ½ octagon, ½ round, silver inlay, 1844, Am perc....400.00
Sword, chased/pierced/damascened hilt, 32" blade engraved, Fr.935.00
Sword, curved blade w/gold damascene, Indian, 1800s, 27"....137.00

Sword, CW non-regulation, cut-out Am Eagle on brass guard...125.00
Sword, CW non-regulation, foot officer's, brass mt scabbard.....90.00
Sword, damascene war trophies on steel hilt, 32" blade.......935.00
Sword, foreign w/carved lion head hdl, w/scabbard............25.00
Sword, Fr Artillery, steel blade/brass hilt, leather scabbard......60.00
Sword, from Pacific Southsea, carved hdl, 1890, 22".........30.00
Sword, Indian, dbl handed, w/brass knobs, 1800s, 62"........465.00
Sword, Japanese police w/36" blade, w/scabbard/sword knot.....35.00
Sword, Marine officer's Model 1875, ivory Mameluke grip, 38"..150.00
Sword, Model 1742 British Infantry hanger, 24" blade.........70.00
Sword, Model 1850 Militia NCO, fluted ivory grip, w/scabbard...50.00
Sword, Model 1940 light artillery sabre w/blued scabbard, Ames.150.00
Sword, Nazi Army officer's, Eickhorn, w/scabbard/sword knot...140.00
Sword, NCO Model 1840 variant w/29" blade mk Phila, G......40.00
Sword, Phillipine, leather scabbard, G......................30.00
Sword, US Militia, bone grip, etched 26" blade, 1st ½ 19th C..125.00
Sword, wavy blade kris w/brass hdl & 25" blade.............35.00
Sword, 1730 period hanger, 26" straight blade, 32", G........70.00
Sword, 18th C infantry hanger, 24½" curved blade, English....100.00

Weathervanes

The earliest weathervanes were of handmade wrought iron and were generally simple angular silhouettes with a small hole suggesting an eye. Later, copper, zinc, and polychromed wood with features in relief were fashioned into more realistic forms. Ships, horses, fish, Indians, roosters, and angels were popular motifs.

In the 19th century, silhouettes were often made from sheet metal. Wooden figures became highly carved and were painted in vivid colors. E.G. Washburne and Company in New York was one of the most prominent manufacturers of weathervanes during the last half of the century.

Two dimensional sheet metal weathervanes are increasing in value due to the already heady prices of the full-bodied variety. Originality, strength of line, and patination help to determine value.

Cow, copper, CI head, worn pnt, battered, bullet holes, 28" L..200.00
Cow, copper, molded/orig pnt good, 16x28"...............2,500.00
Cow, figure only, emb zinc on brass rod, blk pnt, 15" L.......75.00
Cow, low relief, sheet metal ears, cast horns, 18x25", G......550.00
Cow, pressed tin/CI, CI 30" arrow, G orig pnt/gold leaf, 15" L.165.00
Deer, leaping, copper/full rack of CI antlers, EX detail, 30"..3,250.00
Duck, hand carved, wood eyes, New England, 16x17½".......135.00
Eagle, copper/gilt, full body, on orb w/directionals, 37" W..2,500.00
Eagle, copper/gilt, full body, wings out, perched on orb, 29"..1,045.00
Eagle, copper/gilt, on ball, spread wing, arrow w/feather, 18"..375.00
Eagle, emb copper, full figure, arrow/CI directionals, 33" W....250.00
Fighting cock, copper w/cast zinc head, battered/holes, 23"....650.00
Fish, figure only, wood w/metal fins/tail, pnt, 37"............425.00
Goat, running, figure only, molded copper, 11".............200.00
Horse, Black Hawk, copper w/cast zinc head, has holes, 28" L.600.00
Horse, figure only, full body, simple, old pnt, 14"...........105.00
Horse, flying, sheet copper head/body, cut-out mane/tail, 31".2,750.00
Horse, prancing, CI, full body, sheet iron tail, 26x39".......5,500.00
Horse, running, copper, molded head/tail, pnt/gilt, 22x37"....880.00
Horse, running, copper w/cast zinc head, rpt, rpr, 32".......175.00
Horse, running, EX detail, copper w/gold pnt, 29"..........1,000.00
Horse & jockey, CI/copper, on rod, 34" L.................2,900.00
Horse & rider, stylized, gilt on sheet copper, 1800s, 26x25"..5,000.00
Pig, copper, full figure, contemporary, rod/directionals, 32"....300.00
Pig, zinc on CI arrow, bullet holes, 22" L.................140.00
Rooster, copper/zinc, J Howard, bullet holes, 31x26"........3,080.00
Rooster, figure only, handmade, copper w/gr patina, 25½".....300.00
Rooster, figure only, sheet metal w/worn pnt, 18½".........150.00

Rooster, figure only, zinc, good emb detail, 14".............115.00
Rooster, galvanized tin, early 1900s, 9", on 25" L arrow.......95.00
Rooster, on arrow, primitive sheet metal part galvanized, 39"...100.00
Rooster, sheet iron, torch-cut, 22"........................100.00
Rooster, stylized 3-D body, ribbed head/tail, tin, pnt, 27", G...275.00
Rooster, tin, stylized w/some dimension, rpt/rpr, 14½" L.....375.00

Weaving

Early Americans used a variety of tools and a great amount of time to produce the material from which their clothing was made. Soaked and dried flax was broken on a flax brake to remove waste material. It was then tapped and stroked with a scutching knife. Hackles further removed waste and separated the short fibers from the longer ones. Unspun fibers were placed on the distaff of the spinning wheel for processing into yarn. The yarn was then wound around a reel for measuring. Three tools used for this purpose were the niddy-noddy, the reel yarn winder, and the click reel. After it was washed and dyed, the yarn was transferred to a barrel-cage or squirrel-cage swift and fed onto a bobbin winder.

Today, flax wheels are more plentiful than the large wool wheels, since they were small and could be more easily stored and preserved. The distaff, an often discarded or misplaced part of the wheel, is very scarce. French spinners from the Quebec area painted their wheels. Many have been stripped and refinished by those unaware of this fact. Wheels may be very simple or have a great amount of detail, depending upon the owner's ethnic background and the maker's skill.

Flax wheel, trn legs/posts, chip carved block, 20" wheel, G....175.00
Hatchel, wrought iron spikes, pine board w/heart cut-out, 25"...65.00
Hatchel on cut-out poplar board, old patina, 8½x24".........15.00
Loom shuttle, canoe shape, 10½"...........................6.50
Niddy-noddy, good sculptural detail, 10" L.................105.00
Shuttles, wood w/simple chip carving, 11", 3 for............30.00
Spindle box, wood, 7x16½".................................15.00
Spinning wheel, G trn w/sm ivory around bobbin fr, 12" dia....300.00
Spinning wheel, oak/cherry, G trn details, 48".............275.00
Swift, maple, 22"...110.00
Tape loom, maple, cut-out crest w/heart & initials, 11x22".....245.00
Wool carder, wood, 1920s, EX, pr..........................15.00
Yarn winder, all wood w/geared counter, trn legs, chip carving...85.00
Yarn winder, gear counter intact but not working, 25x22½"....75.00
Yarn winder, poplar X member ft/chestnut spindle, 34".........90.00

Webb

Thomas Webb and Sons have been making fine art glass in Stourbridge, England, since 1837. Besides their fine cameo glass, they have also made enameled ware, and pieces heavily decorated with applied glass ornaments. The butterfly is a motif that has been so often featured that it tends to suggest Webb as the manufacturer.

Bowl, turq overlay, gold prunus/butterfly, crimped, 4 ft, 3".....275.00
Bowl vase, yel satin w/gold prunus, butterfly, 3½x4¼".......325.00
Bowl w/5" under tray, cameo, wht/bl/red, floral/butterflies....1,300.00
Compote, crystal Inverted T'print, 6x5", set of 4...........275.00
Cup & saucer, cameo, wht/yellow, vines/floral/butterflies, pr.....500.00
Cup & saucer, demitasse; cut glass........................65.00
Decanter, cut glass, sgn, 11¾"...........................100.00
Dresser bottle, cameo, wht & gr, fruit/blossoms/butterfly, 5"...750.00
Finger bowl/under plate, cameo, raspberry/bl/wht, floral, sgn..1,700.00
Muffineer, bl satin w/oval design, SP top, sgn, 5"...........125.00

Left: three-color cameo glass footed bowl, blue overlaid in white and violet, florals, butterfly on reverse, unsigned, ca 1895, 7" dia, $1,980.00.

Right: three-color cameo glass vase, blue overlaid in deeper blue and white, iris on front, butterfly on reverse, impressed signature, ca 1895, 9½" , $2,530.00.

Perfume, cameo, yel w/wht flowers, sterling top, 2½".........485.00
Perfume, Ivorine, ball w/sterling top, wheel cut flowers, 4".....560.00
Pitcher, cameo, frosted w/gr leaves/cattails, cameo sgn, 10"...1,150.00
Pitcher, cameo, red/clear, oak leaves, 5"...................1,375.00
Pitcher, cameo, wht on red, leaves & flowers, unsgn, 7¾"....2,400.00
Rose bowl, shaded br satin, gold prunus/butterfly/8 crimps, sm..345.00
Salt, cameo, wht to bl, leaf & tassel, top band, 1⅝x2⅛".....395.00
Sweetmeat, coralene, seaweed decor, SP lid/bail.............325.00
Vase, allover pnt florals, 8½"............................200.00
Vase, apricot w/gold prunus, waisted, mk Giles & Rowe, 5½"..250.00
Vase, bronze finish w/gr irid, bulbous, sgn, 9".............500.00
Vase, bronze finish w/purple irid, 14"....................500.00
Vase, butterflies/Murrhina/intaglio/internal decor, 7".........750.00
Vase, cameo, bl/wht, crocus/florals, top/base bands, 5½".....1,400.00
Vase, cameo, bl/wht flowers/butterfly, elongated teardrop, 7"..1,800.00
Vase, cameo, bl/wht leaves, simple neck/base trim, 8".......1,100.00
Vase, cameo, citron w/wht flowers & butterflies, 6".........1,600.00
Vase, cameo, citron/pk/wht, florals/butterfly, sgn, 6¼".....2,000.00
Vase, cameo, dk red w/wht florals, 3½"...................850.00
Vase, cameo, red w/wht foxglove flowers, sm neck, 13".....2,200.00
Vase, cameo, red/wht florals/fancy band, 4½x3½".........1,250.00
Vase, cameo, royal bl/cream, foliage, miniature, 2".........435.00
Vase, cameo, wht/lav/bright bl, floral spray, sgn, 7".......2,200.00
Vase, cameo, wht/pink/yellow florals, 4¼"................1,195.00
Vase, cameo, yellow/pink/wht magnolia/butterfly, sgn, 5¼"....1,100.00
Vase, cameo, yellow/wht, poppies/butterfly, full body, 7¾"....1,430.00
Vase, cameo, yellow/wht lily-of-the-valley, 7".............500.00
Vase, cased rainbow swirl, coin gold on top, 7"............675.00
Vase, cut, alternating panels, T'print & stars/prisms, 10".....195.00
Vase, gold cased w/bl plums, gold leaves, 6½"............165.00
Vase, MOP satin, butterscotch Diamond Quilted, 7¾".......240.00
Vase, MOP satin, cranberry/wht mottle, florals, prop mk, 8"...450.00
Vase, Optic Swirl, amethyst, ftd, sgn, 5¼"................45.00
Vase, rose shaded satin w/gold flowers/branches, 11x4½", pr..600.00
Vase, ruffled, floral enamel, peachblow/pink lining, 11", pr..1,495.00
Vase, wht irid on wht case, gr irid hand threading, 4½".....285.00
Water set, yel satin cased, Herringbone, 5 pcs.............650.00

Wedgwood

Josiah Wedgwood established his pottery in Burslem, England, in 1759. He produced only molded utilitarian earthenwares until 1770, when new facilities were opened at Etruria. It was there he introduced his famous Basalt and Jasperware. Jasperware, an unglazed fine stoneware decorated with classic figures in white relief, was usually produced in blues, but it was also made in ground colors of green, lilac, yellow, black, or white. Occasionally, three or more colors were used in combination. It has been in continuous production to the present day, and is the most easily recognized of all the Wedgwood lines.

Though his Jasperware was highly acclaimed, on a more practical basis his creamware was his greatest success. Due to the ease with which it could be potted, and because its lighter weight significantly reduced transportation expenses, Wedgwood was able to offer 'china' ware at affordable prices. Queen Charlotte was so pleased with the ware that she allowed it to be called 'Queen's Ware'. Most creamware was marked simply 'Wedgwood.' ('Wedgwood & Co.' and 'Wedgeood' are marks of other potters.)

From 1769 to 1780, Wedgwood was in partnership with Thomas Bently; art wares of the highest quality bear the mark indicating this partnership.

Moonlight lustre, an allover splashed-on effect of pink intermingling with gray, brown, or yellow, was made from 1805 to 1815. Porcelain was made, though not to any great extent, from 1812 to 1822. Both of these types of wares were marked 'Wedgwood'.

Stone china and Pearl ware were made from about 1820 to 1875. Examples of either may be found with a mark to indicate their body type.

During the late 1800s, Wedgwood produced some fine Parian and Majolica. Creamware, hand painted by Emile Lessore, was sold from about 1860 to 1875.

Nearly all of Wedgwood's wares are clearly marked. 'Wedgwood' was used before 1891, after which time 'England' was added. Most examples marked 'Made In England' were made after 1910. 'Wedgwood' in sans serif type was used after 1929. A detailed study of all marks is recommended for accurate dating.

Key: WW----Wedgwood   WWE----Wedgwood England

Ash tray, Jasper, dk bl, Pegasus, 3½", WW 20.00
Biscuit barrel, Jasper, dk & lt bl/wht, WW 550.00
Biscuit barrel, Jasper, dk bl, MIE, 5½" 230.00
Biscuit barrel, Jasper, dk bl, straight sides, WW, 6x5" 300.00
Biscuit barrel, Jasper, lilac, WW, 6x5" 395.00
Bottle, water; Tosso Antico, WW, 11" 235.00
Bottle w/lid, Jasper, gr/lilac/wht, 10½" 1,550.00
Bowl, Butterfly Lustre, cobalt w/in, flame w/out, 6½" 375.00
Bowl, Butterfly Lustre, ped, mottled orange w/in, 4" dia 190.00
Bowl, commemorating independence of US, 8" 30.00
Bowl, Dragon Lustre, K'ang Hsi, 3½x7¼" 650.00
Bowl, Dragon Lustre, octagonal, orange/dk red, WWE, 6½" 550.00
Bowl, Fairyland Lustre, leap-frogging elves, birds, WW, 2x4" . . .850.00
Bowl, Fairyland Lustre, Mizami pattern, EX color, 4½" 650.00
Bowl, Jasper, dk bl, MIE, 9½" 180.00
Bowl, Jasper, dk bl, WW, 2¾x5" 130.00
Bowl, Jasper, dk bl, WWE, 2x3" 75.00
Bowl, Jasper, lt bl, MIE, 2x4¾" 110.00
Bowl, vegetable, Newport, 10½" oval .15.00
Box, Jasper, blk, heart shape w/lid, MIE 45.00
Box, Jasper, lt bl, mk WW, 4x4" 230.00
Box, letter; brass w/jasper cameos, 7½x5x4" 575.00
Box, powder; Jasper, lt bl, Elizabeth Arden puff, 5" dia 235.00
Bud vase, Jasper, blk, Arcadian, ca 1965, pr 170.00
Cameo, Jasper, bl, 'Hope', WW, 1" dia 200.00
Candle holder, Jasper, dk bl, brass, sgn W Dia Reg mk, pr 395.00
Coffee pot, Basalt, acanthus decor on hdl, WW, 10¾" 500.00

Coffee pot, Bellefleur 58.00
Compote, Fairyland Lustre, Woodland Elves II, DMJ, 5½x8" . . .880.00
Creamer, Basalt, emb rose, harp, shamrock, etc, WW, 3x4" 95.00
Creamer, Jasper, lt bl, MIE, 2" 75.00
Cup & saucer, Ashford Grey 30.00
Cup & saucer, Avon, demitasse 21.00
Cup & saucer, Basalt, cameo decor, WWE 100.00
Cup & saucer, Basalt, Niagara Falls, gr border, MIE 130.00
Cup & saucer, Medina Beige 28.00
Dish, Creamware, children in meadow by Emile Lessore, 13" L . 850.00
Easter egg, duck on lid, ca 1979 . . . . .40.00
Ecuelle, cover/stand, Jasper, bl, florals, mk WW, 6" dia 400.00
Figurine, bulldog, Basalt, 2¾x4½" 365.00
Figurine, Cupid & Psyche, rnd plinths, WW, 8½", pr 1,800.00
Figurine, monkey & baby, Creamware, J Skeaping 350.00
Flower pot, Jasper, lt bl, Grecian, MIE, 4½x4¾" 125.00
Honey pot, Basalt, Capri, WW, 5x6" 565.00
Jar, Fairyland Lustre, end of rainbow, Z4968, w/lid, 9¼" 1,900.00
Jar, Hummingbird Lustre, gr, w/lid, 9½" 725.00
Jardiniere, Jasper, dk bl, MIE, 4½x5" 130.00
Jardiniere, Jasper, dk bl, WW, 5½x6" 230.00
Jug, Creamware, leaf decor, 6½" 190.00
Jug, Jasper, dk bl, trefoil spout, 2½" 130.00
Jug, Rosso Antico, Capri, mc florals, WW, 5½" 465.00
Knife, steak; Jasper, lt bl 50.00
Loving cup, Jasper, lt gr, 3 hdls, WWE 165.00
Medallion, Basalt, Maximinius, 2¼x1x1½" 130.00
Medallion, Jasper, med bl, in wood plaque w/brass, WW, 10" . . .180.00
Pitcher, hound hdl, cream colored, 4½" 65.00
Pitcher, Jasper, gr, MIE, 8" 200.00
Pitcher, Stoneware, gr/wht, Franklin/Washington cameo, 8½" . .500.00
Pitcher, tankard; Jasper, dk bl, MIE, 4" 75.00
Pitcher, tankard; Jasper, dk bl, WW, 5½" 160.00
Plaque, Basalt, Marriage of Bacchus & Ariadne, in fr, 8¼x6" . .465.00
Plaque, Fairyland Lustre, Picnic by River, WWE, 4¾x10¾" . .3,250.00
Plaque, Jasper, blk, Dancing Hours, 2¾x8½" 230.00
Plaque, Jasper, Elizabeth II/Philip Coronation, pr 465.00
Plate, Avon, luncheon 15.00
Plate, Bicentennial, NY, 9¼" 20.00
Plate, Creamware, dinner; ribbon edge 70.00
Plate, Creamware, HP Little Red Riding Hood, WW, 10" 225.00
Plate, Imari, octagonal, WW, 6¾" 50.00
Plate, Jasper, dk bl, 2½" miniature 130.00
Plate, Jasper, lt bl, President Kennedy profile, 4½" 35.00
Plate, Kruger Nat'l Park, 1st ed, 10½" 50.00
Plate, Majolica, mc leaves & grapes, 8¾" 45.00
Plate, Medina Beige, dinner 24.00
Plate, Medina Beige, salad 20.00
Plate, Pearlware, California, bl transfer, WW, 6¾" 50.00
Plate, Pearlware, shell form w/ribbon hdl, 1882, 8½", 12 for . . .550.00
Plate, Shakespeare Characters, World's a Stage, mc, 10" 50.00
Plate, shell relief, 2 women, by Emile Lessore, 8½" 600.00
Platter, Creamware, br transfer rim, WW, 18x13" 60.00
Platter, Newport, scalloped, 14" 20.00
Posy pot, Jasper, lilac, seasons, ca 1960, 3½" 230.00
Smoke set, Jasper, gr, 2 ash trays/lighter/cig jar, MIE 100.00
Sugar, Basalt, trn body, Battlement rim, MIE, 4½" 200.00
Sugar, Jasper, dk bl, MIE 125.00
Tea set, Jasper, lt gr 325.00
Teacup & saucer, Caneware, Vintage pattern, WW 350.00
Teapot, Basalt, Sybil finial, WW, 4¾" 250.00
Teapot, Caneware, spaniel finial, WW 465.00
Teapot, lt bl, WW, 3½x6" 150.00
Tile, calendar, 1898 . . . . .85.00

Tile, calendar, 1906...........................85.00
Urn, Queen's Ware, classical, wht w/gr emb, 2 hdls, 6½", pr....75.00
Vase, Basalt, Canada, coat of arms, mk Etruria, 4"...........95.00
Vase, Dragon Lustre, lt bl w/gold, WWE, 8½".............575.00
Vase, Jasper, bl, Muses, urn form w/hdls & lid, WW, 11½"....875.00
Vase, Jasper, blk, copy, imp WW, 10".................800.00
Vase, Stoneware, wht w/bl acanthus, WW, 6½"...........600.00

Weller

The Weller Pottery Company was established in Zanesville, Ohio, in 1882, the outgrowth of a small one-kiln log cabin works Sam Weller had operated in Fultonham. Through an association with Wm. Long, he entered the art pottery field in 1895, producing the Lonhuda ware Long had perfected in Steubenville, six years earlier. His famous Louwelsa line was merely a continuation of Lonhuda, and was made in at least five hundred different shapes until 1924.

Many fine lines of art ware followed under the direction of Charles Babcock Upjohn, art director from 1895 to 1904: Dickens Ware (1st line), underglaze slip decorations on dark backgrounds; Turada, featuring applied ivory bands of delicate openwork on solid dark brown backgrounds; and Aurelian, similar to Louwelsa, but with a brushed-on rather than blended ground.

One of their most famous lines was 2nd Line Dickens, introduced in 1900. Backgrounds, characteristically caramel shading to turquoise matt, were decorated by sgraffito with animals, golfers, monks, Indians, and scenes from Dickens novels. The work is often artist signed.

Sicardo, 1903, was a metallic lustre line in tones of flame, rose, blue, green, or purple, with flowing Art Nouveau patterns developed within the glaze.

Frederick Hurten Rhead, who worked for Weller in 1903 to 1904, created the prestigious Jap Birdimal line, decorated with geisha girls, landscapes, storks, etc., accomplished through application of heavy slip forced through the tiny nozzle of a squeeze bag. Other lines to his credit are L'Art Nouveau, produced both in high gloss brown and matt pastels, and 3rd Line Dickens, often decorated with Cruikshank's illustrations in relief.

Other early art ware lines were Eocean, Floretta, Hunter, Perfecto, Dresden, Etched Matt, and Etna.

In 1920 John Lessel was hired as Art Director, and under his supervision several new lines were created. LaSa, LaMar, Marengo, and Besline attest to his expertise with metallic lustres.

The last of the art ware lines and one of the most sought after by collectors today is Hudson, first made during the early 1920s. Hudson, a semi-matt glazed ware, was beautifully artist decorated on shaded backgrounds with florals, animals, birds, and scenics. Notable artists often signed their work, among them Hester Pillsbury, Dorothy England Laughead, Ruth Axline, Claude Leffler, Sarah Reid McLaughlin, E.L. Pickens, and Mae Timberlake.

During the thirties, Weller produced a line of garden ware and naturalistic life sized figures of dogs, cats, swans, geese, and playful gnomes.

The depression brought a slow steady decline in sales, and by 1948, the pottery was closed.

Alvin

Bud vase, yel w/fruit on branches, paper label..............75.00
Vase, fan; crimped, 5½"..............................35.00
Vase, fan; 5 hole, 8"................................45.00

Ardsley

Candle holders, 3", pr................................50.00
Console bowl, 17", w/9" Kingfisher flower frog.............255.00
Vase, corner; iris, 7".................................90.00

Vase, double, 9½"...................................45.00
Vase, fan; cattails, 8"..............................55.00
Vase, 10½"...85.00
Wall pocket, double, 12".............................85.00

Aurelian

Mug, hunting dog, silver lid, sgn K, 7"...............1,400.00
Pitcher, florals, 3 ft, #503, 5x6"...................185.00
Vase, bulbous/sm neck/3 toed, yel pansy, sgn EA, 4½"........85.00
Vase, dahlias, Albert Haubrich, 18".................595.00
Vase, floral, EX art, sgn K, rim to shoulder hdls, 10¾"......230.00
Vase, floral, slender shape, 7"......................80.00
Vase, pillow; 4 ft, floral, Karl Kappes, 5x6½".........335.00
Vase, roses, wide shoulder, artist sgn, 12½".........475.00

Baldin

Jardiniere & pedestal..............................585.00
Umbrella stand.....................................360.00
Vase, 13"..225.00
Vase, 9"...140.00

Barcelona

Vase, floral medallion, 14½".........................200.00
Vase, ruffled & pinched, w/hdls, 8"..................120.00
Vase, tumbler shape, stylized flower, 7".............85.00

Blo' Red

Vase, tassel hdls, 3½"...............................50.00
Vase, 7"...70.00
Vase, 9½"..135.00

Blossom

Cornucopia, double; 6"..............................25.00
Cornucopia, 8½".....................................30.00
Vase, gr w/pk/wht/bl flowers, 8"....................22.00

Blue and Decorated

Vase, gr fern fronds, pk & wht pendant floral, sgn, 10"......200.00
Vase, wht band, florals allover front, 8¾"...........150.00
Vase, 4 sided, pk/gr leaf at top edge, 9¼"...........220.00

Blue Drapery

Bowl, 2x5½"...28.00
Bowl, 3x5½"...35.00
Candlestick/lamp base, 9½"..........................35.00
Lamp, 12"..100.00
Vase, 8"...45.00

Blue Ware

Jardiniere, classic figure, 10".....................100.00
Vase, ladies/bands of flowers, straight sides, 11"........130.00

Bonito

Bowl, high gloss finish, 7".........................35.00
Bowl vase, ornate hdls, 6x8"........................55.00

Bowl vase, 4x5″ 48.00
Vase, ped ft, 2 hdls, 4″ 40.00
Vase, w/hdls, 12″ 150.00
Vase, 10½″ 130.00

Bouquet

Bowl, console; B-12, 5x12½″ 37.50
Pitcher, B-18, 9½″ 60.00
Vase, gr w/wht cosmos, B-3, 4½x5″ 20.00

Brighton

Figurine, bird on perch, mc, 8″ 295.00
Figurine, woodpecker, 5″ 75.00
Flower frog, swan, 5″ 145.00

Burntwood

Bowl, fish decor, 2¼x3⅜″ 35.00
Bowl, swimming ducks, 3x3″ 45.00
Jardiniere, seagull, continuous ocean scene, 9x11″ 175.00
Vase, birds & flower, 11¾x5½″ 120.00
Vase, floral incising, 5¼x5″ 75.00

Cactus

Camel, seated 85.00
Cat 75.00
Horse 85.00
Monkey 85.00

Cameo

Basket, ftd, gr w/wht pansies, 7½″ 30.00
Cornucopia, bl, 6¾″ 20.00
Ewer, ftd, gr w/wht roses, 10″ 35.00
Vase, bl, 9x9½″ 30.00
Vase, ftd, tan, sgn DL, 11¼″ 37.50
Vase, sq, bl, 8½″ 25.00

Chase

Ginger jar, w/paper label, 6x5½″ .235.00
Vase, bl, ftd, 10½x5¾″ 250.00
Vase, hunter jumping fence w/dog, bl/wht, 6½″ 150.00

Chengtu

Ash tray, 3 pigs figural, 4x5″ 125.00
Jar, flat cover, 3½″ 60.00
Vase, 4 panels, 8″ 70.00

Classic

Bowl, goose boy flower frog, 14½″ dia 185.00
Bowl, 11″ dia 50.00
Vase, fan; wide top, 5″ 55.00
Wall pocket, very wide, 6″ 80.00

Claywood

Bowl, flowers, flared rim, 3¾x4¾″ 35.00
Mug, 5 petal flower, 5″ 75.00

Spittoon, spiderwebs, 3½x4½″ 40.00
Vase, pine cones, wide base, 6½″ .50.00

Coppertone

Candle holder, turtle w/water lily on bk, 3¼″ 110.00
Console bowl, frog & lily on hdl, 10½″ 175.00
Frog, 7″ 225.00
Pitcher, fish hdl, lily pad around spout, 7¾″ 235.00
Vase, 2 frogs for hdls, 8½x7¾″ 175.00

Coppertone vase, figural frog handles, 8½″ x 8″, $175.00.

Cornish

Candle holder, 3½″, pr 30.00
Vase, bl, tab hdls, 6½″ 26.00
Vase, orange, 8½″ 30.00

Darsie

Bowl, bl, 3½x7½″ 22.00
Vase, bl, 7½″ 22.00
Vase, 7x6½″ 25.00

Delsa

Basket, 7″ 35.00
Ewer, 7″ 25.00
Pitcher, #10, 7″ 32.00

Dickens, 1st Line

Umbrella stand, relief masks at top, HP birds by Abel, 26″, VG . 375.00
Vase, berries, lg rim-to-width loop hdls w/silver overlay, 5″ 700.00
Vase, Indian portrait, A Daugherty, tiny base chip, 10″ 350.00

Dickens, 2nd Line

Humidor, Captain, 7″ 600.00
Humidor, Chinaman, 6″ 850.00
Humidor, skull, 5½″ 1,175.00
Jug, swirling body w/2 fish, 5¾″ .300.00
Mug, Indian Chief, 2 feather headdress, LPE '04, St Louis 600.00
Mug, Indian in full headdress 575.00
Vase, Dombey & Son, 9½″ 700.00
Vase, golfer, 7½″ 375.00
Vase, Indian Bald Eagle, EL Pickens, 9¼″ 1,600.00
Vase, lady golfer, flask shape, 7½″ 480.00
Vase, pillow form; Dutch girl, sgraffito, 4x6″ 425.00
Vase, two fish, seaweed, bulbous w/hdls, sgn, 9½″ 2,400.00

Dickens, 3rd Line

Creamer, Charles Dickens on disk, 4"......................350.00
Inkwell, Income 20#, Expenditure 19-6, sgn R, 2½".........500.00
Mug, 2 hdls, cavalier w/pipe, 4¼"......................475.00
Vase, King, 11"......................450.00
Vase, Wilker Mcawber, David Copperfield, sgn LS, 10½"......600.00

Dupont

Bowl, straight sides, 3"......................50.00
Planter, sq, 3½"......................50.00
Vase, cylinder, 10"......................125.00

Eocean

Mug, charcoal/gr w/pk carnations, 4¼"......................90.00
Mug, lg red rose, 5"......................100.00
Vase, charcoal/lt gr w/red rasberry decor, 6½"......................125.00
Vase, florals, artist sgn, mk Eocean Rose, 6¼"......................175.00
Vase, lilies, Leffler, mk Eocean Rose, 17¾"......................420.00
Vase, nasturitum narrow rim, wide body, 4½"......................80.00
Vase, purple berries, 9¼"......................250.00
Vase, red/pk florals & leaves top to base, full body, 8"......................260.00
Vase, 2 toned gray w/red raspberries, artist sgn, 4"......................70.00

Eocean, Late Line

Bud vase, cherries, 7"......................80.00
Bud vase, 6"......................75.00
Vase, allover primroses, 13"......................350.00
Vase, lg pk/wht floral on bl smear colors, 10¾x8½"......................350.00

Etna

Jard, lg red roses, 7½x9"......................140.00
Jard, purple iris, sgn on side, 7¾x10"......................140.00
Mug, cherries, lt to dk gr......................125.00
Mug, gray/wht w/pk florals, 5½"......................90.00
Pitcher, lg pk flowers, sgn bottom & side, 10¼"......................200.00
Vase, figural lizard, br/gray gloss, 4½x3"......................225.00
Vase, gray w/florals, hdls near top, 12"......................185.00
Vase, gray/pk w/dk pink flowers, 4½"......................55.00
Vase, pulled ovoid, gray/wht purple florals, 7"......................90.00

Etna vase, shaded gray ground with hand painted grapes in magenta, 15", $245.00.

Fairfield

Vase, br/wht blended, 10"......................30.00
Wall pocket, 11"......................120.00
Wall pocket, 9"......................40.00

Flasks

All's Well, 4"......................140.00
BPOE, w/elk, 4½"......................90.00
F.O.E., 5½"......................90.00
Never Dry, 6"......................135.00
Old Kentucky, 5"......................145.00
Take a Plunge, 6"......................140.00

Flemish

Inkwell, facing birds in floral arch, 4½x7"......................425.00
Jardiniere, fruit relief at top, 4 ft, 8½"......................130.00
Planter, floral & lily pad relief at bottom, 3 toed, 6"......................95.00
Planter, tub shape, w/hdls, 4"......................50.00
Vase, br, 16"......................190.00
Vase, U shape, red apples on tan, 7"......................90.00
Wall pocket, 9½"......................55.00

Fleron

Batter pitcher, 11½"......................135.00
Bowl, 3x7½"......................35.00
Vase, w/hdls, 19½"......................165.00

Floral

Console bowl, tan w/lav/bl flowers, 6x5x10½"......................25.00
Vase, bl w/pk flowers, 9¼"......................30.00
Vase, cream, flared/ruffled, bl flowers, 7¾x5"......................25.00

Floretta

Tankard, matt, bl/tan, 10½"......................135.00
Vase, br w/orange flowers, cylinder w/low bulge, 9¾"......................80.00
Vase, purple grapes on wht/gr w/shaped top, 14"......................135.00
Vase, yel cherry decor on br, shaped top/teardrop, 11¾"......................100.00

Florenzo

Basket, 5½"......................55.00
Planter, 4 ft, 5" sq......................35.00
Vase, 7"......................55.00
Window box......................35.00

Forest

Basket, sides taper to disk ft, 9½"......................115.00
Bowl, 3x7"......................60.00
Hanging basket, 10"......................145.00
Jardiniere & pedestal, 26"......................500.00
Vase, fan; 8"......................65.00
Window box, 5¼x14½"......................200.00

Fruitone

Bowl, gr/br, 3x5¾"......................30.00
Bud vase, 11½"......................90.00

Vase, gr/br w/shoulder hdls, 4½″ 30.00
Wall pocket, 5½″ 80.00

Glendale

Candle holder, 5½″, pr. 75.00
Vase, birds/butterfly/flowers, 12″ 300.00
Vase, 2 birds on branch, 8½″ 200.00
Wall vase, dbl bud, 7″ 125.00

Glendale vase, birds and nest with wall and trees in background, 8¾″, $200.00.

Gloria

Ewer, gr, G-12, 9″ 50.00
Vase, dbl, 4½″ 25.00
Vase, 12½″ 85.00

Greenbriar

Ewer, dbl hdl, 11½″ 165.00
Vase, full body, 6½″ 85.00
Vase, wine w/gr drip, 3½″ 20.00

Greora

Strawberry pot, sgn B, 5″ 60.00
Strawberry pot, 8¾″ 110.00
Vase, triangular, 3 ft, 4½″ 50.00
Vase, fan. 32.00

Hobart

Bowl, 3x9½″ 45.00
Flower frog, girl w/bouquet, turq matt, ped base, 8½″ 85.00
Nude, between tree stump vases, flower arch above, 10″ 125.00

Hudson

Candlestick, bl to gray, bl flowers at base, sgn AP, 9″ 120.00
Vase, bl grapes/vines top to base on bl ground, HP, 10½″ 325.00
Vase, bl/rose w/yel/br roses all around, sgn Kennedy, 8¾x4½″ .300.00
Vase, florals, dk gr/pk w/bl, MT, cylinder, flared top, 8″ 240.00
Vase, florals, EX art, sgn Hunter, pk/wht on pk to gr, 8¾″ 220.00

Vase, gnarled tree trunk/branches, Timberlake, 9½″, EX 775.00
Vase, gr/pk w/EX florals, S Timberlake, loving cup form, 8″ 180.00
Vase, gray to pk w/pk flowers, gr pads, sgn DL, 6″ 120.00
Vase, gray w/pk & wht flowers, 5½″ 70.00
Vase, gray w/wht daisies, 7″ 90.00
Vase, lav to wht w/wht florals, EX detail, 10″ 200.00
Vase, lg dogwood, lav to cream ground, hexagonal, 11″ 160.00
Vase, lily-of-the-valley, lav/wht on shaded ground, 7″ 125.00
Vase, pk/gr ground w/dogwood at top, Pillsbury, 7¼″ 135.00
Vase, pk/gr/bl w/pk/bl dogwood, EX art, M Ansel, 9″ 325.00
Vase, pk/red dogwood, EX art, H Pillsbury, 13″ 270.00
Vase, raspberries on pastel, 10¾″ 160.00
Vase, trees all around, EX art, sm rstr base flake, 6″ 200.00
Vase, wht red flowers in heavy slip on bl, Timberlake, 12″ 750.00
Vase, wht/bl, lg water lily, can top/bulb base, 7″ 80.00
Vase, wht/gray w/lg pk/purple flowers, 10″ 120.00
Vase, wht/red roses on bl/lt bl, Pillsbury, 8″ 210.00
Vase, yel/wht daffodils on wht, EX art, 8½″ 300.00
Vase, 2 birds on limb, dk bl w/bl flowers/mc birds, 8½″ 575.00
Vase, 5 gr/gray geese around width, pk/gr, Pillsbury, 11½″ ...1,475.00

Hudson Perfecto

Vase, grapes & leaves at shoulder, glossy, F Dedonatis, 6x6″ ...210.00
Vase, pine cones, very bulbous, sgn Leffler, 10″ 450.00
Vase, spider mums, bulbous, sgn Leffler, 9½″ 360.00

Hunter

Pillow vase, butterflies on br glaze, 7½″ 600.00
Pillow vase, woodcock in marsh on br glaze, 4¾″ 600.00
Vase, flying gulls on br glaze, 7½″ 600.00
Vase, head & front quarter of deer with antlers, hdls, 6½″ 650.00

Ivoris

Console set, 14″ ftd bowl & pr 7″ 2 branch sticks. 50.00
Powder box, pointed lid finial, 4″ 50.00
Vase, cuspidor shape w/shoulder hdls, 5¾x3¾″ 25.00
Vase, ornate hdls, 6″ 30.00

Ivory

Jardiniere, Knifewood type, pheasants & oak leaves relief, 10″ ..165.00
Jardiniere & ped, 10x13″ jard, 18½″ ped, EX. 335.00
Wall pocket, Orris shape, 9½″ 60.00

Jap Birdimal

Mug, geisha girl, sgn Rhead. 680.00
Vase, gray w/wht goose, 3 ft, sgn VMH, 5″ 215.00
Vase, Oriental w/lantern, facing away, CMM, very bulbous, 7″ ..925.00
Vase, peacock feather in pk, sgn VMH, 5½″ 250.00

Jewel

Mug, 6½″ 250.00
Vase, stylized trees w/jewels, 10½″ 190.00
Vase, 4 vertical shoulder posts & neck band, 9½″ 160.00

Knifewood

Jar w/lid, bl bird, matt glaze, 8″ 350.00
Jardiniere, daisies & butterflies, 8″ 125.00

Vase, daisies on textured ground, 7″.......................125.00
Wall pocket, mc daisies, 9½″............................120.00

L'Art Nouveau

Pitcher, matt, nude, flowers/grapes in panels, ornate hdl, 12″...120.00
Vase, matt, stems/orange flowers at flared top/lobed base, 15″..140.00
Vase, sq, 4 panels w/lady/flowers/fruit, gr/pink bisque, 13½″....135.00

LaSa

Vase, castle among trees, pear form, 10″.................350.00
Vase, lake, trees, mtns; 7x4″..........................325.00
Vase, round form, w/trees, G color, 3¾″.................150.00
Vase, scenic, 13″, M...................................475.00

Lavonia

Console bowl w/frog, candlesticks, lav....................145.00
Vase, slender bottom w/3 vertical hdls, 9″.................65.00
Vase, thistles, 10″....................................85.00

Lido

Cornucopia, turq, ftd, 7¼x4¾″.........................20.00
Hanging basket, w/attached plate, 6″....................18.00
Planter, 2x9″..25.00
Vase, fan; 7½″.......................................25.00

Lorbeek

Bowl, gr, gold w/in, paper label, silver sticker, 10½″..........55.00
Candlesticks, pr......................................30.00
Vase, fan; 7″...65.00
Wall pocket, 8½″.....................................65.00

Louella

Bowl, 3x5″..35.00
Bowl, 8½″...55.00
Hair receiver, 3″.....................................55.00
Vase, 9″...90.00

Louwelsa

Clock, lg mantel, w/roses decor........................600.00
Ewer, flattened, yel/orange berries, artist sgnd, 3″...........85.00
Ewer, yel florals, ruffled, curving hdl, 7″..................130.00
Jug, corn decor, artist sgn, 7¾″........................220.00
Jug, corn decor, sgn Claude Leffler, #374, 6x5″............225.00
Mug, Indian portrait, EX art, LJ Burgess, 6″..............800.00
Mug, mulberries, Levi Burgess, 5″......................100.00
Pitcher, orange floral, sgn, squat, 3½″..................130.00
Punch bowl, sgn Lybarger, 7x13½″....................495.00
Tankard, ¾ Indian Chief in profile, sgn Levi J Burgess, 13″..1,100.00
Vase, astors, 3¼x2¾″.................................95.00
Vase, floral, artist sgn, 7″.............................160.00
Vase, heart shaped, clock in center, floral decor...........375.00
Vase, kitten w/bl ribbon, pillow form, H Pillsbury, 7½″, EX..1,950.00
Vase, lion portrait, EX art, sgn, 2 restorations, 14½″........750.00
Vase, orange florals, sgn E, twisted, 13¾″...............150.00
Vase, orange poppies, EX art, classic shape, 14″...........180.00
Vase, St Bernard portrait, L Blake, 10½″.................700.00
Vase, yel floral, sm rim/bulbous, 8½″....................85.00

Louwelsa-Blue

Pitcher, wht holly, EX art, HP, 3 ft, circle hdl, 5″...........675.00
Vase, bl florals on shaded ground, mk w/circle seal, 10¾″....850.00
Vase, detailed wht floral, sm ring neck, straight sides, 11″....1,275.00
Vase, florals in dk bl, 11″..............................900.00
Vase, lt/dk w/bl/wht roses & leaves, cylinder, 9″............800.00

Luxor

Bud vase, 7½″.......................................30.00
Vase, concave sides, 9″................................45.00
Vase, 11″..55.00

Malvern

Basket, 8x6″...55.00
Bud vase, bulbous base, 8″.............................35.00
Console bowl w/frog, 10″...............................70.00
Planter, basket shape w/rim hdls, 4x6″..................25.00
Vase, shoulder hdls, 6x5½″............................35.00
Vase, shoulder hdls, 7″................................40.00

Mammy Line

Cookie jar, 11″.......................................200.00
Creamer, 3½″..140.00
Syrup pitcher, 6″.....................................165.00
Teapot, 8″...190.00

Marbleized

Bowl, w/frog, 10″ dia..................................60.00
Bud vase, 12″..150.00
Vase, br/cream, 4½″..................................35.00
Vase, wide can shape, br w/ivory, 9½″...................175.00
Vase, wide mouth, low flare, 4½″......................100.00

Marvo

Bud vase, dbl; gr.....................................30.00
Jardiniere, 7x6½″.....................................20.00
Vase, 9″...68.00
Wall pocket, 8½″.....................................40.00

Melrose

Basket, grapes, 10″...................................180.00
Pitcher, pk/gray w/grapes & vines, 10½″.................125.00
Vase, severe mold, apple branch hdls, 7″.................135.00
Vase, slim, severe mold, bl berries, 8½″.................100.00

Modeled Etched Matt

Planter, ftd..60.00
Vase, cylindrical, lt gr w/yel roses, 8½″..................185.00
Vase, rose, square shape, 10″..........................200.00
Vase, 6½″..10.00

Muskota

Fence, 5″..140.00
Fishing boy, sitting, 6½″...............................110.00

Inkwell, turtle w/pottery insert, lid w/frog finial, 3x7"..........260.00
Nude, leaning on driftwood, flower frog, 8"..................130.00
Woman, kneeling......................................140.00

Noval

Basket, 9"...45.00
Bowl, 3½x9½"..65.00
Candle holder, 9½", pr................................125.00
Vase, 8"..60.00

Orris

Bowl, leaf medallion, 2x6"............................40.00
Umbrella stand, lotus & misc flowers, 19x10"..........200.00
Vase, flared w/floral relief, 12x7"...................95.00

Panella

Bowl, bl, 3x12½"......................................30.00
Pitcher, bl/turq w/magnolia, 9".......................32.50
Vase, pansies, scalloped, 5"..........................20.00
Vase, scalloped top, yel, 5"..........................20.00

Patricia

Bowl, 4 geese w/necks entwined, wht, 4¾x10"...........100.00
Bowl, 6 geese, long necks, 8".........................220.00
Planter, pelican, 5"..................................95.00
Vase, duck head hdls, 4"..............................30.00

Pearl

Basket, 6½"...135.00
Bowl, console; 3x10"..................................65.00
Candle holders, 8½", pr...............................120.00
Vase, 4 hdls, 9½".....................................115.00
Wall pocket, 8½x4½"...................................85.00

Perfecto (Matt Louwelsa)

Tankard, ear of corn, gray/yel, sgn A Haubrich, 12"..........750.00
Vase, grapes/vines in pk/br on pk/yel, Lybarger, 14".........385.00
Vase, lt pk/gr w/pk florals, sgn Perfecto, LJB, 11"..........200.00
Wall pocket, florals, on bl/gray, sgn HP, 7"................165.00

Pierre

Bowl, mixing; gr, 5½x10½".............................32.00
Creamer, lav, 2½x4"...................................20.00
Sugar...15.00
Teapot, 8½"...60.00

Pumila

Bowl, 3½"...25.00
Console plate, 3x12"..................................50.00
Vase, flared rim, 9½".................................50.00
Wall pocket, 7".......................................65.00

Roba

Bowl, triangular, bl w/pk dogwood, 3½x7"..............30.00
Pitcher, 11"..70.00

Vase, w/hdls, 13".....................................90.00
Wall pocket, gr, 10"..................................60.00

Roma

Bowl, ped ft, water lilies, 5¾x6½"....................45.00
Candlestick lamp, 9¾".................................45.00
Planter, fruit clusters, 4x4½"........................30.00
Planter, medallions w/lady's head, 4x4½" sq...........55.00
Vase, cylinder, 2 bands of leaves & roses, 7½"........45.00
Wall pocket, red roses, bl ribbon, 8x8"...............60.00

Roma door stop, basket of flowers, soft matt glaze colors, $95.00.

Rosemont

Jardiniere, bluebird, flowering branch, 6½"..................175.00
Jardiniere, octagonal, 5¾x4½"...............................150.00
Vase, bluebird, flowering branch, 10".......................300.00
Vase, 2 lg br/orange birds on flowered branches, butterfly, 8"..285.00

Rudlor

Cornucopia, yel w/apple blossoms, 8½".................25.00
Vase, #19, 13¼".......................................70.00
Vase, gr, 8½"...22.00

Sabrinian

Bowl, scallop shells, gr fish ft at corners, 4x5¼"..........55.00
Console set, 2½x9" bowl+2" sticks...........................110.00
Pitcher, 10½"..165.00
Wall pocket, 8½"..60.00

Senic

Double vase, tree in landscape, gr, 6¼x8¾x3½".........45.00
Vase, gr w/lake scene, 3 ft, 5¼"......................25.00
Vase, pillow shape, #S-11, 7½"........................40.00

Sicardo

Vase, clover, rim hdls/shaped body widens to base, sgn, 5½"...300.00
Vase, cylinder, lt gr/bl, 5½"..................................195.00
Vase, maple leaves, sgn, 6"..................................400.00
Vase, orchids on bl/gr/magenta, sgn, 6x5"..................700.00

Silvertone

Basket, grapes in relief, 12½"..............................165.00
Basket, pk florals, 8½x7"...................................100.00
Console bowl w/flower holder................................125.00
Vase, calla lillies, trumpet form, sgn C, 15"..............190.00
Vase, sgn HP, 9x5"...95.00
Vase, twist hdls, 7½"..85.00
Vase, w/hdls, 8½"..120.00

Softone

Bud vase, dbl; 9"...30.00
Hanging basket, 10"...55.00
Planter, 3 ft, pk, oval, 10"..................................30.00
Vase, flared top, pk, 6½".....................................22.00

Souevo

Hanging basket..85.00
Pot, brick red/ivory, narrow rim, wide flared body, 6½x8"....150.00
Tobacco jar, tan/buff/blk designs, 6x5"......................150.00
Vase, blk geometrics on wide band, ovoid w/narrow rim, 4½"..100.00
Wall pocket, brick red/ivory, C motif in blk, 9½"............65.00

Sydonia

Cornucopia, gr..25.00
Vase, dbl; 7½"..65.00
Vase, fan; 9½"..90.00
Wall pocket, bl, 9"...50.00

Tivoli

Basket, 8"..50.00
Vase, wht, funnel shape, 6"...................................60.00
Vase, 8"..65.00

Turada

Bowl, 3½x8"..165.00
Jar w/lid, sgn, 7x6"...400.00
Lamp base, blk w/enamel band, 10"............................200.00
Mug, 6"..275.00
Umbrella stand, 21"..750.00

Turkis

Vase, full body, lg hdls, 14"................................135.00
Vase, sq, cylinder w/ring hdls, 7"............................80.00
Vase, 3½"...35.00

Tutone

Vase, cylinder, 5"..25.00
Vase, 12"..100.00
Wall pocket, 10½"...55.00

Warwick

Console bowl, 10½"...100.00
Planter, 1 hdl, 3 ft, 3½".....................................60.00
Vase, cylinder, 9½"...55.00
Vase, dbl; 4½"..45.00

White and Decorated

Vase, berries on bl band, 6x6½"..............................165.00
Vase, br bird watches bee/pk & red florals, 7"...............625.00
Vase, lg red/wht roses, 13"..................................365.00
Vase, 4 sided flare, trailing florals from rim band, 9¾"....100.00

Wild Rose

Basket, gr, 6"..22.00
Candle holder, triple, pr.....................................50.00
Console bowl, 6x18"...47.00
Cornucopia, pk, 6"..20.00
Ewer, 7"..25.00
Tankard, gr, 12"..40.00
Vase, ftd, side hdls, gr, 7¾".................................25.00
Vase, tab hdls, ftd, gr, 6½"..................................20.00

Woodcraft

Bowl, squirrel w/in branch reserve, 3½"......................80.00
Bud vase, dbl; 8"...55.00
Bud vase, 7½"...30.00
Bud vase, 9"..35.00
Flower holder, tree stump.....................................35.00
Tankard, 3 foxes in stump....................................485.00
Vase, stemmed, twigs support upper ½, paper label, 9".........55.00
Wall pocket, figural squirrel w/nut, 9¼"....................100.00
Wall pocket, owl in den, 10½".................................95.00

Woodrose

Bowl, 2½x8½"..45.00
Jardiniere, 7"...115.00
Vase, bucket form, 4x4".......................................28.00
Vase, 7x4"..35.00
Wall pocket, 5½"..65.00

Zona

Bowl, rabbit & bird decor, 5½"................................30.00
Comport, florals on stippling, mc/ivory, 5½".................75.00
Pitcher, band of red florals in ivory, 7½"..................110.00
Pitcher, lg mums, 7½"...98.00
Plate, child's; duck decal, rolled lip, 7½"..................42.00
Platter, 12"..30.00
Vase, apple decor, 8"...80.00

Miscellaneous

Besline, candlestick, 10½"...................................150.00
Cameo, planter, integral legs, reticulated, 4x8½"............30.00
Clarmont, candle holder, 8", pr.............................165.00
Copra, basket, rust/orange/gr flowers, 11"..................190.00
Delta, vase, iris decor, bl on bl, 15"......................925.00
Dresden, vase, dimpled sides, JLB/MAH, crazed, 10½".........275.00
Dresden, vase, mk Matt Weller/LJB, Dutch girls/etc, rstr, 13"...500.00

Euclid, wall pocket, mirror blk w/HP roses...................65.00
Evergreen, vase, ftd, Deco shape, turq, 9x4½".............30.00
Green Matt, vase, incised wht flower spray, 5"..............60.00
Jard, matt w/incised Dutch mother/child/ships, 9x9½"........275.00
Jewell Scenic, vase, house/foliage, matt glaze, 17", rstr.......250.00
Juvenile, pitcher, duck decor, 4"........................32.50
Kenova, vase, 8½".....................................110.00
LaMar, vase, lake & trees, 9½x4"........................600.00
Majolica, jardiniere, Forest mold, 8½x10"..................100.00
Majolica, 2 dragons in relief, 7½x9"......................80.00
Man, vase, 6"...75.00
Manhattan, umbrella stand, 18".........................120.00
Manhattan, vase, relief band of leaves at base, br matt, 6½"....15.00
Monochrome, candle holder, 11½".........................55.00
Neiska, vase, yel, 6".....................................20.00
Olla, water set, red.....................................28.00
Paragon, vase, deep red w/molded florals, oval, 7¼"..........58.00
Stellar, vase, wht w/bl stars, 6".........................110.00
Teapot, pumpkin, 6"....................................85.00
Utility bowl, blk/wht, 3x12".............................30.00
Vase, mistletoe relief, line/dot decor, purple gloss/gr, 5¾"......50.00
Velva, vase, br, 10½"...................................50.00

Western Americana

Relics from the era of the Western Frontier to the age of the cowboys hold a fascination for many. Leather items, such as holsters, saddles, and chaps, are often elaborately hand tooled and sometimes bear the mark of their makers. 'California' spurs were ornate, sometimes inlaid with silver work, and are considered very desirable among today's collectors. So are those stamped 'McChestney,' 'Kelly,' 'G.A. Bischoff and Co.,' and 'J.O. Bass.'

Sheriff's badges, old photographs, Express memorabilia, and barbed wire -- in short, anything from the Old West is being collected!

See also Badges

Autograph, Ned Buntline, in ink, Buntline & Judson............30.00
Autograph, WF Cody, Buffalo Bill, ink on show program, 1908.160.00
Bit, Garcia, silver mounted..............................325.00
Bit, iron, single chain, 11½"..............................4.00
Bit, spade; silver mounted w/copper roller in mouthpiece.....325.00
Bit, US Army shoemaker, G..............................125.00
Book, Jesse James Narrow Escape/Ensnared by Woman Detective.9.50
Branding iron, intertwined initials, wrought iron, 14" L........20.00
Branding iron, 2 brass letters, 5½x4", 11" hdl..............16.00
Business card, JW Hardin/attorney at law, pre-1895, w/letter....220.00
Cart de visite, Kit Carson, hand on J Freemont's arm, sgn...1,500.00
Cartridge belt, 2½" leather w/11 loops, iron buckle, 1889......20.00
Chaps, batwing, blk leather w/nickel plated conchos..........200.00
Chaps, batwing, leather heavily brass studded, pr............275.00
Chaps, leather, shotgun style, pr........................150.00
Chaps, wht wooly, shotgun style, pr......................275.00
Chuck wagon pan, smithy-made, pouring corners, sheet iron....45.00
Cuffs, full beaded buckskin, from Wild West show, 8¾" L.....450.00
Gauntlets, cowhide, pr.................................150.00
Gauntlets, wolfskin, pr.................................175.00
Harness, neck; horse team, brass balls atop................45.00
Holster, fold-over Mexican type, basketweave/tooling..........75.00
Jack, for Conestoga wagon, dtd 1865, sgn CB, EX............185.00
Letter, seeking safe passage through Indian territory, 1886......60.00
Lithographs, CA gold rush, after Cooper/Taylor, lot of 4........80.00
Magazine, Western Story, Sept 12, 1931, Max Brand/Damon/etc..3.50
Oil lamp, rnd, brass w/hook, hung from covered wagon train....65.00
Postcard, cowboys playing cards/going for guns, color, ca 1900..19.00
Poster, Montana Frank, mc litho, cowboy/horse, 1910, 24x15"..45.00

Boot mold, copper over tin, 12¾" tall, $85.00.

Print, Nighthawk, Olaf Wieghorst, sgn.....................165.00
Print, Range Chuck, Olaf Wieghorst, sgn...................195.00
Print, Range Ponies, Olaf Wieghorst, sgn...................195.00
Program, Buffalo Bill Wild West Show & Circus, 1917.........35.00
Rug, lg buffalo including head, wood backed, 8½ ft L........300.00
Saddle, brass rosettes, steer head on saddle horn, VG.........185.00
Saddle, Cavalry, leather/brass trim, US 1st BN, TN 104 PA, sm.185.00
Saddle, McClellan.....................................375.00
Saddle, mule, Army issue, brass horn, 1913.................600.00
Saddle, side; California style, red velvet seat................450.00
Saddle bags, leather, 9½x10½"...........................45.00
Spurs, lady leg, silver/gold/copper inlay, sgn Hall, pr.........350.00
Statue, Buffalo Bill on horse, CI w/copper wire lasso, 9x8x3"....85.00
Tar bucket, Conestoga wagon, wood/tar/mud/animal hair, 1820s..70.00
Way bill, Am Express Co, Wells Fargo, 1899.................10.00
Way bill, Maine Central RR Co, w/logo, 1899................10.00
Wrist cuffs, leather, pr.................................75.00

Wheatley, T.J.

In 1880, after a brief association with the Coultry Works, Thomas J. Wheatley opened his own studio in Cincinnati, Ohio, claiming to have been the first to discover the secret of underglaze slip decoration on an unbaked clay vessel. He applied for and was granted a patent toward that end. Demand for his ware increased to the point that several artists were hired to decorate the ware. The company incorporated in 1880 as the Cincinnati Art Pottery, but until 1882, it continued to operate under Wheatley's name. Ware from this period is marked 'T.J. Wheatley,' or 'T.G.W. and Co.,' and it may be dated.

Vase, flattened oval, limoges, heavy slip florals, 1880s, 12".....650.00
Vase, leopard skin glaze, 8"............................165.00
Vase, limoges, wht/bl/red w/yel florals, dtd 1879, chip, 8"......330.00
Vase, pillow; bl w/daisies, artist sgn, 1885, 8½"............350.00

Whieldon

Thomas Whieldon was regarded as the finest of the Staffordshire potters of the mid-1700s. He produced marbled and black Egyptian wares, as well as tortoise shell, a mottled brown glazed earthenware accented with touches of blue. In 1754 he became a partner of Josiah Wedgwood.

Bowl, mottle br w/gr & orange splotches, crack, 2½x5½"......325.00
Cup & saucer, sprigged floral decor......................1,254.00
Plate, br/gr/sepia/tan mottle, 9¼"........................325.00
Plate, tortoise shell glaze, Tudor rose shape, 1760, 9¼"......125.00
Sugar bowl, mottled br w/gr splotches, rpr crack, 3¾x4½"......350.00
Teapot, pineapple form, 18th C...........................715.00

Wicker

Wicker is the basket-like material used in many types of furniture and accessories; it may be made from bamboo cane, rattan, reed, or artificial fibers. It is airy and lightweight, and very popular in hot regions.

Imported from the Orient in the 18th century, it was first manufactured in the United States in about 1850. The elaborate, closely woven Victorian designs belong to the mid-to-late 1800s, and the simple styles with coarse reedings usually indicate a post-1900 production. Art Deco styles followed in the twenties and thirties.

The most important consideration in buying wicker is condition -- it can be restored, but only by a professional. Age is an important factor, but be aware that 'Victorian-look' furniture is being manufactured today.

Armchair, Nouveau styling, Heywood Bros/Wakefield, 1920s....450.00
Armchair, twisted paper, barrel bk, uphl seat, 1920s..........90.00
Basket, pet carrying; arched hdl, door w/peg & hasp, 1840s.....95.00
Basket, rolled edge, wicker loop hdl.......................50.00
Basket, sewing; ornate weave, lift lid, on legs, w/base shelf....300.00
Basket, sewing; tufted lining, brass/enamel thread holder.......20.00
Basket, wall hanging, rattan, simple weave, 8x8½"...........45.00
Birdcage, wicker base, std & hanger arm & cage, pntd........300.00
Buggy, doll's; 26".....................................120.00
Buggy, simulated fretwork, metal/wood wheels, parasol, 1890s..800.00
Chair, child's; open weave bk section & front apron, roll arms..150.00
Chair, corner; tight weave fan bk/apron, curved legs, str arms..150.00
Chair, occasional; armless, oval bk, deep apron, 1890s, 42"....375.00
Chair, photographer's; 1 arm, triangle bk, very fancy, 44".....500.00
Chair, rnd bk w/fancy panel, fretwork, fancy scroll legs, 32"...245.00
Chair, side; ornate fan bk, pressed seat, fancy apron..........175.00
Chair, side; very simple, no apron, 36"....................85.00
Chaise, wicker legs, open weave apron, simple design........385.00
Coffin, adult size....................................200.00
Coffin, baby..100.00
Console set, tray w/tab hdls, +pr 6" candle holders..........150.00
Cradle, doll's; tight weave, w/hood, ca 1920s, lg...........250.00
Cradle, doll's; very open weave, 1920s, 16x15"............90.00
Desk, reed, oak top, caned side panels & bk rail, w/chair......425.00
Etagere, 4 wood shelves, fretwork wicker crest, trn legs, 42"...225.00
Footstool, deep open weave aprons, uphl top, 20" sq.........140.00
Footstool, mushroom top, 4 legs.........................175.00
Footstool, sq base, rnd top w/uphl insert, 9½x12"..........100.00
Go-cart, armchair seat, metal wheels, 1920s, 36"...........225.00
Go-cart, elaborate scrolls, uphl seat, w/parasol, 1890s.......1,000.00
Highchair, Victorian, woven braid trim, simple design........150.00
Lamp, floor; wicker std, 26" dia shade w/fringe, simple weave..365.00
Lamp, floor; woven base & shade, wood std...............450.00
Lamp, table; rnd wicker base, wood std, open weave shade, 15".90.00
Lamp, table; vase shaped base, dome shade, 22"...........150.00
Magazine rack, reed, open weave sides, bentwood hdl........125.00
Mattress smoother...................................30.00
Pie caddy, 2 tier, woven grass, 27".......................80.00
Plant stand, reed, sq flaring pedestal, bowl top, 30½"........135.00
Plant stand, simple design, str legs, 25x32" L.............125.00

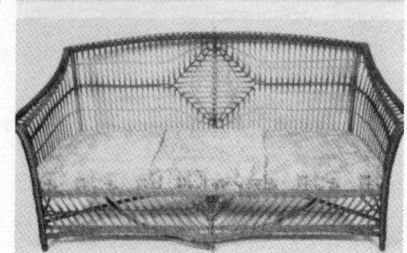

Five piece set, two rockers, one chair, one side table, and one six foot settee, diamond backs, $700.00.

Plant stand, wood legs, open weave receptacle & apron, sq....100.00
Plant stand w/hanging birdcage in center, open weave, 64"....375.00
Porch swing..500.00
Rocker, armless, simple fiber weave, uphl seat, 30".........150.00
Rocker, camel bk w/arms, Deco design, slip seat, 36".......200.00
Rocker, child's; arms & ½ bk loose weave, ca 1915, 20½"....135.00
Rocker, child's; continuous reed flange around bk/seat, 26"....300.00
Rocker, fretwork & wicker, fancy turnings, 40".............500.00
Rocker, high bk, arms & apron very elaborate, 1890s, 38"....675.00
Rocker, open weave bk, sides & apron; tighter crest/arm band..250.00
Rocker, platform; cane seat, 'cane' woven bk; arms, 1880s, 35"..350.00
Rocker, sewing; 32"..................................150.00
Rocker, w/arms, barrel back, Lloyd Loom Products label, 32"..175.00
Rocker, wide curving bk, very ornate design, fancy legs, 40"...325.00
Settee, fiber, allover tight weave, barrel back, 60" L.........285.00
Settee, open arms, simple weave, str lines, 41" W..........300.00
Settee, w/arms, heart scroll bk, sides & legs; 58".........365.00
Sofa, barrel bk, slip seats, shaped apron, Lloyd Looms, 72"...300.00
Sofa, child's; allover even weave, rolled out arms, 40" W.....200.00
Sofa, open arms, uphl bk & seat cushions, simple weave, 75"..190.00
Table, coffee; wicker legs & top, open weave apron, 37" L.....90.00
Table, lamp; simple weave, str legs, base shelf.............100.00
Table, oval wood 46x25" top, deep apron, fancy stretcher.....225.00
Table, oval 27x20" top, curving legs, tight weave, X brace.....125.00
Table, sewing; lift-top, bamboo legs, 1885................125.00
Table, wood insert top, wide flat woven legs, 30" dia........235.00
Table, 2 tier, wood top, wide lower apron, 30" dia..........180.00
Tea cart, 2 tier, simple weave, wood frame, 30x36" L........350.00

Willets

The Willets Manufacturing Company of Trenton, New Jersey, produced a type of belleek porcelain during the late 1880s and 1890s. Examples were often marked with a coiled snake that formed a 'W,' with 'Willets' below, and 'Belleek' above.

In the listings below, all items are belleek unless noted otherwise.

Basket, spaghetti strand weave, 10½".....................1,200.00
Bouillon, floral decor, w/under tray.......................85.00
Bowl, fold-over rim, HP, 4x11"..........................200.00
Chalice, gr to rose w/HP grapes & leaves, br mk, 11".........210.00
Compote, mauve lustre w/in, gold edge/hdls, red mk, 3½".....90.00
Compote, roses around rim, gold ft/trim, oval, 6"...........85.00
Creamer & sugar, melon shape, gold filigree, factory decor.....95.00
Cup & saucer, gold decor on irid wht, red mk..............88.00

Ewer, claret; silver overlay dragon hdl/grapes, on wht, 9½"....475.00
Hatpin holder, gold & bl flowers.............................75.00
Hatpin holder, gold leaves w/tiny bl flowers, red belleek mk.....95.00
Humidor, cavalier w/pipe, pipe finial, sgn Schindler, 7".......425.00
Jug, wht, plain, w/hdl, 7"..................................40.00
Mug, dragon hdl, artist sgn, blk mk.........................200.00
Mug, grapes, HP, 4¼".......................................125.00
Mug, Oriental girl w/lanterns, belleek, 4¼"..................245.00
Mug, vines & leaves, factory decor, 5¼".....................125.00
Pitcher, irid gr overall, br mk, 4¼"..........................65.00
Pitcher, tankard; man eating & drinking, 15"................250.00
Plate, grape leaves & cluster, sgn Marsh, scalloped rim, 8½"....85.00
Plate, roses in pk/red/yel, gold scroll edge, br mk, 7½".......45.00
Salt dip, ftd, gold/jeweled, snake mk........................22.50
Teapot, creamer & sugar; Aladdin............................245.00
Vase, birds & florals, belleek, blk mk, 9"...................185.00
Vase, dk gr w/red cabbage roses, bulbous, 12"...............350.00
Vase, lovebirds on belleek, cylinder shape, 13"..............300.00
Vase, scenic, belleek, artist sgn, 8".........................90.00

Cup and saucer, Allerton's, small, $20.00.

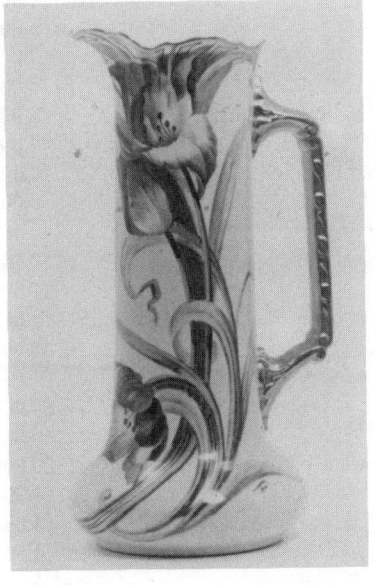

Tankard, yellow shaded to green with orange tulips, gold handle and trim, artist signed, 13½", $450.00.

Willow Ware

Willow Ware, inspired no doubt by the numerous patterns of the blue and white Nanking imports, has been popular since the late 18th century, and has been made in as many variations as there were manufacturers. English transfer wares by such notable firms as Allerton and Ridgway are the most sought after and the most expensive. Japanese potters have been producing Willow patterned dinnerware since the late 1800s and American manufacturers have followed suit. Although blue is the color most commonly used, mauve, black, and even multicolor Willow Ware may be found. Complimentary glassware, tinware, and linens have also been made.

In addition to 'Allerton' and 'Ridgway', both companies used the possessive form of their names in marking their wares (i.e. Allerton's, Ridgway's).

Ash tray, fish novelty, Japan, 1950s, MIB....................8.00
Ash tray, Royal Doulton, 6" sq.............................25.00
Baking dish, Hall, 4 pattern repeats, 3x9".................15.00
Baking dish, Oven Proof, Japan, 2½x5".....................15.00
Batter jug, Hazel Atlas, frosted glass, 8½"................25.00
Bone dish, Minton, pattern in oval reserve, 8¼"............25.00

Bowl, Adams, Staffordshire, 9"............................22.00
Bowl, bread; no mk, pattern on rim, sm repeat 4 sides, 15"....125.00
Bowl, cereal; Homer Laughlin..............................5.00
Bowl, cereal; Japan, blk mk, 1½x6".........................5.00
Bowl, cereal; Japan, pink.................................5.00
Bowl, Clews Warranted Staffordshire, mk #919, 1¼x10"......40.00
Bowl, Homer Laughlin, no mk, 7x9".........................7.50
Bowl, Homer Laughlin, 8½" dia............................10.00
Bowl, Japan, no mk, 10"..................................20.00
Bowl, Japan, 5¼"...3.00
Bowl, red transfer, no mk, 5½"............................3.50
Bowl, Royal, center pattern, 10" dia......................45.00
Bowl, Royal Grafton, bone china, oval, 10x8"..............45.00
Bowl, vegetable w/lid, Allertons, 1930s-40s, 8½x10"........75.00
Bowl, vegetable w/lid, Wood & Son, w/hdl, 11" dia.........100.00
Bowl, wht opaque glass, 4 pattern repeats, 2½x5"..........10.00
Butter dish, Allerton, allover pattern, 7½"................85.00
Butter dish, Japan, no mk, sq, 7x4½".......................25.00
Butter dish, Moyott & Sons, rnd w/willow band.............75.00
Butter pat, Allertons, 1930s-40s..........................15.00
Butter pat, England, 3"..................................15.00
Butter warmer, no mk, bent iron 3 leg fr, cup & candle holder..22.00
Cake plate, flow blue, mk Balmoral w/lion, 10" sq..........35.00
Cake stand, English, no mk, 2½x8½".......................125.00
Candle holder, Coalport, ca 1960s, w/Willow candle, 5½", pr..110.00
Canisters, Japan, hexagonal w/hex base, 10½"; 9½"; 8½"......80.00
Canisters, no mk, Flour, Coffee, Tea, sq, 8½"; 6"; 5".......100.00
Carafe & warmer, mk Japan, 10" overall...................150.00
Cereal, Allertons, 1930s-40s.............................15.00
Charger, Allerton, 13"...................................45.00
Child's cake plate, Made in Japan, 5".....................12.00
Child's creamer, 2½".....................................12.50
Child's cup, 2¾"...9.00
Child's cup & saucer, Made in Japan, 2½" cup; 3¾" dia......12.00
Child's cup & saucer, 4" saucer; 2" cup...................12.50
Child's dinner service, gr, mk Bisto, England, 18 pcs, VG.....330.00
Child's grill plate, Made in Japan, 4½"....................8.50
Child's luncheon set, bl/wht, 23 pcs.....................125.00
Child's plate, dbl border, rare, 4½".......................20.00
Child's plate, Made in Japan, 3⅝".........................7.50
Child's plate, Made in Japan, 4⅜"........................10.00

Child's plate, tin, no mk, 1½″..............................5.00
Child's plate, 5″..............................15.00
Child's platter, Made in Japan, 3½x6″..............................17.50
Child's platter, Occupied Japan, 4x6¼″..............................20.00
Child's saucer, Made in Japan, 3¾″..............................3.00
Child's saucer, 3½″..............................2.50
Child's tea set, Made in Japan, flat sided, 3 pcs..............................50.00
Chocolate pot w/lid & warmer, Japan..............................75.00
Clock, mk Smith's, Made in Great Britain..............................80.00
Coaster, advertising, Schweppes Indian Tonic, 4½″..............................15.00
Coaster, advertising, Yorkshire Relish, English, 4″..............................15.00
Coffee can, English, no mk, 2½″..............................18.00
Coffee mug, restaurant ware, thick hdl, 3½″, set of 4..............................20.00
Coffee pot, demitasse; Burgess & Leigh, scroll/flower border.....90.00
Coffee server, no mk, bulbous, 1940s, 10″..............................85.00
Compote, Cambridge Glass Co, no mk, 3x5½″..............................50.00
Cookie jar, McCoy Pottery, pitcher form, 9″..............................30.00
Cream soup, Ridgways, ca 1927, w/6″ saucer; 2½″..............................35.00
Creamer, Homer Laughlin..............................5.00
Creamer & sugar, Allertons, 1930s-40s, 4″, pr..............................85.00
Creamer & sugar, Booths, 1912, 4″; 5″; pr..............................90.00
Creamer & sugar, Haupton, pattern around body, spout, pk, 4″..75.00
Creamer & sugar, Japan, stacking..............................15.00
Creamer & sugar, Royal, pr..............................15.00
Cup, demitasse; Arabia, Made in Finland, 2½″..............................12.00
Cup, demitasse; Booths A8025, gold trim..............................7.00
Cup, farmers'; mk Japan, 4″..............................12.00
Cup, Homer Laughlin..............................5.00
Cup & saucer, Allertons, 1930s-40s, lg..............................23.00
Cup & saucer, decor on hdl & w/in, Japan..............................7.50
Cup & saucer, demitasse; Johnson Bros, after 1912..............................20.00
Cup & saucer, Homer Laughlin..............................8.00
Cup & saucer, Japan..............................6.00
Cup & saucer, Japan, pink..............................9.00
Cup & saucer, Japan, red transfer, design in cup..............................5.00
Cup & saucer, Royal..............................5.00
Drainer, meat; mk Iron Stone China, English, 10x7¼″..............................50.00
Egg cup, Buffalo China script mk, flat bottom, single, 2½″..............................20.00
Egg cup, Japan, double..............................15.00
Egg cup, no mk, double, 4″..............................15.00
Egg cup, no mk, ftd, 2″..............................12.00
Ginger jar, Mason's Ironstone, scroll/flower border, 7½″..............................70.00
Gravy boat, Dudson, Wilcox & Till, 2½x6″..............................45.00
Gravy boat w/9″ under plate, Allerton, 1930s-40s, 4x8″..............................60.00
Gravy tureen w/lid & ladle, Japan, MIB..............................23.00
Honey dish, WR Midwinter, 4″..............................16.00
Jar, 'Instant Coffee', Japan, 6″..............................20.00
Juice tumbler, Burgess & Leigh, 3½″..............................20.00
Juice tumbler, mk Japan, 3½″..............................12.00
Lamp, candle; cylinder base w/pattern, clear globe, 11½″..............................20.00
Mug, Royal, stacking..............................4.00
Mug, USA, Japan birds, 3½x3½″..............................6.00
Mustard jar w/attached under plate, no mk, 3″..............................55.00
Nappy, red transfer, Japan, 5¾″..............................4.00
Oil & vinegar cruets, Japan, 6″, pr..............................25.00
Piggy bank, 3-tier, Japan, 1950s, MIB..............................20.00
Pitcher, Adderley Ware, ca 1929, dk bl, 2 temples, 6″..............................30.00
Pitcher, Edge, Malkin & Co Ltd, dagger border, 5″..............................55.00
Pitcher, no mk, English, polychrome, 12″..............................145.00
Pitcher set, sm cream, med milk, lg juice, Japan, 1950s, MIB....26.00
Plate, Alfred Meakin, Old Willow, 9½″..............................10.00
Plate, Allertons, 1890, butterfly border, 9″..............................25.00
Plate, Allertons, 1930s-40s, luncheon..............................17.50

Plate, Booths A8025, gold trim, 6″..............................5.00
Plate, chop; Cook China, 12″..............................15.00
Plate, Copeland, Mandarin II, ca 1883, ribbed edge, 9″..............................15.00
Plate, Cronin Casuals, ovenware, 24k gold pattern, 9″..............................10.00
Plate, Dudson Wilcox & Hill, 8″..............................6.50
Plate, grill; Maastricht, 11″..............................15.00
Plate, grill; Made in USA, bridal veil border, 11″..............................8.00
Plate, grill; Mfg Imperial Royale, Nimy, 10″..............................18.00
Plate, grill; NY Grill, Carr China, 10″..............................10.00
Plate, grill; SM Willow, MIE, 10¾″..............................15.00
Plate, Homer Laughlin, 6″..............................4.00
Plate, Homer Laughlin, 9″..............................7.00
Plate, House of Blue Willow, Japan, 9″..............................4.00
Plate, Japan, pink, 9″..............................8.00
Plate, Japan, 6″..............................3.00
Plate, John Steventon, 6″..............................5.00
Plate, Johnson Bros, 8″..............................7.50
Plate, Maastricht, 9″..............................15.00
Plate, Made in Japan, good color, 6″..............................4.00
Plate, Midwinter, England, 8″..............................6.50
Plate, Ridgway, 9″..............................12.50
Plate, rolled edge, no mk, 10″..............................5.00
Plate, rolled edge, no mk, 7¼″..............................3.00
Plate, rolled edge, no mk, 9″..............................4.00
Plate, rolled edge, Willow Ware by Royal China, 10″..............................5.00
Plate, Royal, 9″..............................5.00
Plate, Samuel Radford Ltd, fishtail birds, ca 1928, 4″..............................10.00
Plate, Shenango, 9½″..............................6.00
Plate, WS George, fluted, center pattern, 9″..............................20.00
Platter, Crown Clement, gr transfer, 12¼″..............................17.50
Platter, Homer Laughlin, 9x12″..............................17.50
Platter, Japan, 12½″..............................12.00
Platter, Johnson Bros, 11x14″..............................30.00
Platter, no mk, red transfer, 11¼″..............................9.00
Platter, no mk, traditional border & center, lg..............................60.00
Platter, Wedgwood, Eturia, 7x10¼″..............................80.00
Punch bowl, no mk, rim border w/in, pattern front/bk, 6x9″...130.00
Salad fork & spoon, Japan, porcelain/wood, 11″..............................8.50
Sauce dish, Homer Laughlin, 5″..............................4.00
Sauce dish, Johnson Bros, 5″..............................4.00
Saucer, Allerton, 5¾″..............................4.00
Saucer, Allerton, 6¼″..............................5.00
Saucer, Homer Laughlin..............................2.00
Saucer, Japan, pk, 6¾″..............................7.50
Shakers, Japan, pagoda shape, pr..............................17.50
Shakers, Japan, rnd shape, 3¼″, pr..............................17.50
Shakers, ped base, scroll hdl, ca 1950s, 4″, pr..............................15.00
Shaving mug, scuttle; Burgess & Leigh, 4″..............................55.00
Soap pad holder w/lid, Japan, 1950s, MIB..............................20.00
Soup, Homer Laughlin, flat, 8″..............................8.00
Spice set, Japan, book form, set of 6..............................50.00
Sugar, Royal, open..............................4.00
Sugar w/lid, no mk..............................8.00
Syrup w/4½″ under plate, no mk, rnd body w/ornate hdl, 4″....30.00
Tea caddy, Rington Limited, 8″..............................150.00
Tea tile, Wiltshaw & Robinson, 4¾″..............................60.00
Teapot, GL Ashworth, 6″..............................60.00
Teapot, no mk, musical..............................50.00
Tid bit stand w/wooden post, 2 tier, earthenware, unmk Japan...20.00
Toothpick holder, English, 2½″..............................30.00
Tray, brass hdls, wood fr, red/blk on natural cloth, 1940, 18″...25.00
Tureen, English, no mk, w/ladle, 6x9″..............................300.00
Wash set, Doulton & Co, 1890-1902..............................600.00

Winchester

The Winchester Repeating Arms Company lost their important government contract after WWI, and of necessity turned to the manufacture of sporting goods, hardware items, tools, etc., to augment their gun production. Between 1920 and 1931, over 7,500 different items, each marked 'Winchester Trademark U.S.A.', were offered for sale by thousands of Winchester Hardware stores throughout the country. After 1931 the firm became Winchester-Western.

Axe, camp; w/sheath, both mkd, fair condition..............62.00
Axe, orig hdl, VG..45.00
Barrel reflector, brass.....................................50.00
Baseball bat, #2425, well mkd, EX..........................125.00
Belt & buckle, issue of 180 made for engineers in 1966......745.00
Book, Blue Book of Game Laws & Guides, 1917, VG........117.00
Bottle, oil; etched 'Winchester', EX.......................18.00
Bullet mold, #2520..30.00
Bullet mold, #31165...30.00
Bullet mold, #44..30.00
Butcher steel...25.00
Calendar, 1920, father/son unloading ducks, w/matt, 25x40"...375.00
Calendar, 1929, store, framed, all pads, M.................250.00
Calendar, 1930, framed, w/all pads, M......................355.00
Calendar, 1933, framed, w/all pads, NM.....................360.00
Carving set, stag hdl, 2 pc, w/bag/box/tape all mkd Winchester..86.00
Casting rod, bamboo...70.00
Catalog, salesman's; leather/gold emb, 1909 items/prices, VG...155.00
Catalog, 1892, October, NM.................................200.00
Catalog, 1909, 182 pgs, EX.................................135.00
Catalog, 1931, fishing tackle, pocket size..................40.00
Change mat, 1930s, framed, M...............................135.00
Christmas card, scarce......................................20.00
Copper heater..150.00
Counter felt, red & white...................................65.00
Display, cb of wooden Indian w/gun barrels, 1967..........100.00
Display, cb stand-up of metal 12 gauge shotgun, 8x11".......15.00
Drill bit, #1305, VG..18.00
Fishing plug, wood...100.00
Flashlight..10.00
Flashlight, new Havien mks, 2 cell, MIB.....................55.00
Floor mat, red rubber, EX...................................43.00
Fly rod, orig pouch, double tip, gr metal box..............250.00
Golf club, mashie, wood hdl, EX............................114.00
Golf clubs, lady's set: mashie/mid-iron/driver/putter......425.00
Hammer, ball peen, VG.......................................22.00
Hammer, claw..55.00
Hoe, garden...35.00
Hone stone, round...25.00
Knife, grapefruit; EX.......................................19.50
Letter on letterhead, 1919, EX...............................9.00
Level, wood, 14"..70.00
Level, wood, 26"..75.00
Loading tool, 32S & W Pat Nov 7, 1888.......................35.00
Magazine, Store News, 1927, Winchester ads & articles.......62.00
Medal, Jr Rifle Corps, bronze, Pro-Marksman, M..............30.00
Padlock, 6 lever, no key, rusty but good condition..........27.00
Pamphlet, baseball equipment, EX............................45.00
Paperweight, red, dated 1910, VG............................68.00
Pellet gun, boy-size, .177, EX..............................63.00
Pellet gun, man-size, .177, VG..............................62.00
Pin, Junior Rifle Corps, M..................................24.00
Plane, #4...70.00
Playing cards, red, WRA.....................................30.00

Pliers, lineman's...30.00
Pocket protector, plastic w/advertising......................5.00
Postcard, from Winchester Museum, in color..................40.00
Putty knife, #2364, VG......................................22.00
Rake..35.00
Reel, bait casting, #1321, VG...............................40.00
Roller skates...12.00
Safety razor..16.00
Scissors, #9010, VG...21.00
Screwdriver, wood hdl, 5½", VG..............................19.00
Shell, 1 pound, dated 1918, EX..............................13.00
Shooting glasses..25.00
Square, carpenter's, 7", VG.................................31.00
Target, back advertises steel air rifle shot Kopperklad, 4½".....4.00
Target, back pictures 22 single shot musket, 7x5"...........15.00
Whet stone..10.00
Wood brace, #10...85.00
Wrench, #1130...45.00
Wrench, pipe; 10"...75.00
Yard stick, wood, Winchester Store, 1920....................50.00

Windmill Weights

Windmill weights were used to protect the windmill's plunger rod from damage during high winds by adding weight that slowed down the speed of the blades.

Bull, Fairbury, name cast on 1 side, 38 lbs, old pnt, #16, 18"..650.00
Bull, Fairbury, tail indented both sides, 38 lbs, old pnt, #17....650.00
Bull, Hanchett, 24 lbs, #22, in the round, old pnt, 12½".....650.00
Chicken, Elgin, 22 lbs, #30, on ½ base, 12x17".............475.00
Chicken, Elgin, 64 lbs, 4 tail feathers, U-base, old pnt, 19½"..695.00
Chicken, Hummer cast on tail, 28 lbs, old pnt, 14x16½".....550.00
Chicken, Hummer Model L, 8 lbs, rusty iron patina, 10x9"...375.00
Horse, bobtail, CI, concrete base not orig, 18¼"...........165.00
Horse, CI, 16½"...155.00
Horse, Dempster, short tail, 13 lbs, 16½x17"...............350.00
Moon, eclipse, 18 lbs, 6½x10"...............................155.00
Rooster, CI, full bodied, G detail, 20"....................475.00
Rooster, emb: Hummer E 184; 9 lbs, 1800s, orig pnt.........400.00
Squirrel, stylized silhouette, CI, blk pnt, 14½"...........475.00

Wire Ware

Basket, fruit; flared top, ornate design on sides, hdl, lg.........85.00
Basket, oval, w/ped, ornate top hdl, small..................50.00
Basket, twisted wire, looped edge, 3 curled ft, hdl, miniature....65.00
Compote, twisted wire, ftd..................................85.00
Cruet holder, twisted wire, cup shape/center loop/wire ft.......50.00
Egg stand, twisted wire, 2 tier, loop center hdl, 8 ft, old........85.00
Pie carrier, drum shape w/wire fastener, wire bail hdl.........45.00
Soap dish, hanging; ornate, w/toothbrush holder at top........60.00
Soap dish, hanging; twisted wire, curlique wire decor, ornate....55.00
Sponge holder, hanging; twisted wire, ornate................55.00
Trivet, unusual flower shape, twisted wire, looped round ft......40.00
Trivet, 8 round wire ft, 14" dia............................40.00
Vegetable washer, oval, clamps in center w/2 oval hdls, lg.......45.00

Witch Balls

Witch balls were a Victorian fad touted to be meritorious toward ridding the house of evil spirits and thus warding off sickness and bad luck.

Folklore would have it that by wiping the dust and soot from the ball the spirits were exorcised. It is much more probable, however, considering the fact that such beautiful art glass was used in their making, that the ostensus Victorians perpetrated the myth rather tongue-in-cheek while enjoying them as lovely decorations for their homes.

Amber, blown, 4¼″ dia...............................45.00
Amberina, ribbed, lg.................................65.00
Cobalt bl, coin imp on inside.........................150.00
Opaque wht w/transparent red/pk/yel/bl/gr spots, blown.......325.00
W/vase, clear w/pink & wht loopings, Pittsburg, 9½″, pr......700.00
W/vase, clear w/wht loops, Pittsburg, 12¾″, pr............1,500.00

Wood Carvings

Wood sculptures represent an important section of American folk art. Wood carvings were made not only by skilled woodworkers, such as cabinet-makers, carpenters, etc., but by amateur 'whittlers' as well. They take the form of circus-wagon figures, carousel animals, decoys, busts, figurines, and cigar store Indians. Oriental artists show themselves to have been as proficient with the medium of wood as they were with ivory or hardstone.

Amish woman w/vase of flowers, PA, 20th century, 12″........200.00
Bird, long neck, weathered gray w/wht spots, primitive, 8½″....45.00
Bird, simple detail, orig pnt, sgn, early 1900s, rpr, 11″.......145.00
Black man in sulky, bobtailed horse w/metal harness, 15″.....440.00
Chicken, X hatch detail, no finish, glued break, 5½″..........55.00
Dog, recumbent, nose lifted, tail curled around, walnut, 10x4″..235.00
Eagle, intricate feather carving, detailed talons, rpr, 42″ W....650.00
Geo Washington bust, primitive, G detail, pnt, 5½″, G........100.00
Italian villa, w/balustrades/balconies/terraces, 10½″..........225.00
Leopard, stalking, primitive, 14½″, G.....................55.00
Oxen, pr in yoke, orig pnt, 5½″..........................50.00
Pegasus, relief carved & chip carved base, 6″................40.00
Plaque, w/fish, alligatored polychrome pnt, 6¾x17″..........285.00
Rooster w/top hat, stylized silhouette, orig red pnt, 15¾″....4,500.00
Staff, w/smiling snake w/brass tack eyes entwined w/2nd snake..880.00
Waiter carries tray of wine 'Wino Blanco' pnt, W Hedstrom, 9″.190.00

Horse, artist signed, 4½″, $50.00.

Wood, Enoch and Sons

Enoch Wood began his own business in Burslem, England, about 1784. By 1790 he was in partnership with James Caldwell, and until 1818 he was best known for his busts and plaques.

From 1818 to 1846, the firm was known as Enoch Wood and Sons. They produced the underglaze blue transfer printed dinnerware, much of which was specifically designed for export to America.

Bulb pot/liner, crescent form, pnt landscape panels, 1800, 6″.1,200.00
Cup & saucer, English harvest fruit cluster, EW Ltd/unicorn mk.60.00
Figurine, lady, arms outstretched, 1810, 7″................275.00
Plate, Grecian scenery, med bl scenic, rope rim, 10½″, EX.....68.00

Pitcher, Sylvan pattern, signed, 8½″, $55.00.

Woodenware

Woodenware, or treenware as it is sometimes called, generally refers to those wooden items used in the preparation of food, such as spoons, bowls, food molds, etc. Common during the 18th and 19th centuries, these wares were designed from a strictly functional viewpoint, and were used on a day-to-day basis. With the advent of the Industrial Revolution bringing new materials and products, many of the old woodenwares were simply discarded. Today, original hand-crafted American woodenwares are extremely difficult to find.

Barrel, stave construction w/wood bands/lid, rpt, 30x18″........65.00
Bowl, ash burl, bottom worn through to applied ft, 3x6½″......95.00
Bowl, ash burl, EX figure, G color, age cracks, 5½x15″.......455.00
Bowl, ash burl, G figure, age cracks, 4¾x11″...............295.00
Bowl, baker's; turned, flared rim, putty filled cracks, 8x24″....110.00
Bowl, burl, cherry finish, 2x7″..........................45.00
Bowl, burl, EX close figure, sm rim rpr, 4¾x11½″..........425.00
Bowl, burl, trn detail, 2¾x7″...........................155.00
Bowl, burl, 2¾x8½″..................................300.00
Bowl, carved ridges in bottom, 3 ft, worn/hole, 28x15″........45.00
Bowl, chestnut, primitive hdls, made in 1 pc, 20½x46½″......270.00
Bowl, dough; maple, oval w/closed hdls ea end, 1865, 16x9″....90.00
Bowl, hand hewn, rfn, 4x11½x19½″.....................95.00
Bowl, hewn from 1 pc of poplar, rfn, 7¾x18x44¾″.........135.00
Bowl, long oval, worn old finish, 5½x13x25″................75.00

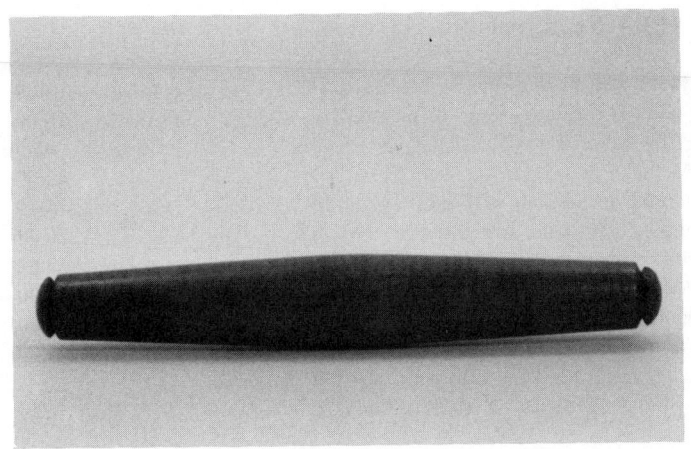

Rolling pin, curly maple, 18th century, 18½", $125.00.

Bowl, poplar, worn blue pnt w/out, chip, 12½x18½".........135.00
Bowl, well shaped ends, dk old finish, crack wired, 11x32".....85.00
Bowl, 1 pc wood w/open hdls, gouge carving, 3½x12x5"......125.00
Box, apple w/large stem, 1900s, 6".........................30.00
Box, burl, trn, filled in age crack in lid, 2x4¾".............85.00
Box, cylinder on ped ft, inlaid mosaic in mc woods, 17½".....300.00
Box, good detail, ped base, lid finial, miniature, 1¾".........75.00
Box, on ft, G turned detail, 2¾"...........................45.00
Box, trn ft/lid, by Pease, 3".............................95.00
Box, trn poplar, orig red/yel grpt good, 8¼"...............525.00
Bread board, curly maple, carved rim/flowers/inscribed, 9" dia...55.00
Bread board, pine, hinge pins, legs fold, pnt 1 side, 20x34"....105.00
Bucket, stave constructed, tin bands/wire bale, pnt, 4½x5½"....35.00
Bucket, stave constructed, wire bands/wood hdl/wire bale, 6x8"...25.00
Butter carrier, wood w/wood pinned flat bail.................120.00
Butter paddle, curly maple, well shaped bowl/hdl, 12½" L.....135.00
Butter paddle, maple, peacock head hdl, edge wear, 9½"......275.00
Butter paddle, maple, well carved stylized bird head hdl, 6¼"..345.00
Butter paddle, maple/some curl, stylized animal head hdl, 9½"..40.00
Butter paddle, scrubbed finish, 11" L.......................25.00
Butter paddle, stylized bird head hdl, worn finish, 10".......200.00
Butter scoop, maple, well made, good color, 7".............125.00
Candlesticks, well trn figured mahog, open dbl spiral stds, 8"...110.00
Canteen, trn, concentric circles ea side, spout, 1696, 10½"...350.00
Case, maple burl/bird's eye, 4 parts fold, wood hinges, 3x3½"..200.00
Chalice, turned walnut, 5"...............................40.00
Churn, stave/interlocking finger bands, sm lid hdl, 21".......600.00
Container, stave constructed, carved rim, heart cut-outs, 17"..325.00
Cookie board, basket of fruit/foliage, oval/thin, 6½x4½", G...185.00
Cookie board, cherry, G detail, Indian, papoose on bk, 8x3½"..345.00
Cookie board, dog/windmill; full length lady on bk, 18"......125.00
Cookie board, ea side w/lady in long dress w/fan, crack, 15x7"..295.00
Cookie board, ea side well carved w/people/birds/etc, 5½x10"..335.00
Cookie board, oval w/flowers/2 hearts/Fr inscription, 8x6½"...175.00
Cookie board, Renaissance lady; jester on bk, 22x8".........350.00
Cookie board, Renaissance Queen in long dress, 12½x6"......175.00
Cookie board, sheep w/Christian banner, 3 sizes, crack, 14x12".150.00
Cookie board, 3 part, flag, fox & flower, 20th century, 2x6½"..25.00
Cookie board, 4 connecting dia w/heart/foliage, 11½x7½", G...75.00
Cookie board, 4 part w/fruit & 2 horses, 3½x4¾".............70.00
Cookie board, 5 carvings: ship/couple/man/animals, 4x23½"....175.00
Cookie board, 6 animals/people ea side, rpr, 4¼x18½".......225.00
Cookie board, 6 designs on poplar, deer/cornucopia/etc, 3x6"...55.00
Cutting board, pine, round crest w/chip carving, inlaid, 9x24"..165.00
Dipper, curved hdl, thin bowl, 11½".......................70.00
Dipper, pouring spout, well made, 12".....................175.00

Dipper, trn hdl, 1900s, 12" L.............................60.00
Firkin, stave constructed, brass/iron bands, hdl, 8x10½"......105.00
Firkin, stave constructed, old rpt, 9¼".....................45.00
Firkin, stave constructed w/2 ears for hdl, pnt, 4x5".........80.00
Funnel, maple, 1 pc.....................................75.00
Game ball, burl, 3¼"....................................95.00
Inkwell, turned, glass insert, pnt w/gilt decor/caduceus, 2½"....70.00
Inkwell, turned, glass insert/cork stopper, grpt, S Silliman......85.00
Jar, birch bark w/pine lid, made 1827, pntd 1938, 8".........125.00
Jar, ftd w/lid, good turnings, made by Pease, 5¼"...........115.00
Jar, poplar, turned, well shaped ft & lid, rfn, 7¼"...........35.00
Jar, turned, maple w/good color & detail, age crack, 8x8".....155.00
Jar, turned ft/lid, natural finish, by Pease, 3"..............85.00
Jar, wire bale & wood hdl, by Pease, rare lg size, 11x14"....2,750.00
Keg, burl, vertical grooves suggest staves, glued lid, 5½"......40.00
Keg, stave constructed, brass band/hdl, English, 17".........40.00
Keg cover, orig br grain w/'Crackers' on hdl, 20" dia.........75.00
Knife, cut-out hole in hdl................................15.00
Knife tray, bird's eye maple, cut-out hdl, 9x12"............70.00
Kraut stomper, trn oak, wht scrubbed, 24"...................8.00
Ladle, burl w/some curl in bowl, dog's head on hdl, 9½", VG..275.00
Measure, bentwood, metal trim, old red, 6½x11¾"...........35.00
Noggin, age crack, 7¾".................................65.00
Noggin, minor age crack, 8¾"............................65.00
Paddle, burl, EX figure, 8¾"............................235.00
Paddle, butter palette; walnut, rectangular, 9x16"...........75.00
Paddle, geometric carving on blade, 16½"..................45.00
Plate, edge & surface wear, good color, age cracks, 6½", pr...210.00
Plate, nice wear & patina, 6x6¼".........................100.00
Porringer, bird's eye burl, 2 hdls, lacquer finish, 1¾x3½".....200.00
Porringer, 1 pc w/hdl, 1700s............................175.00
Rolling pin, lignum vitae, 17½"...........................30.00
Salt, burl, ftd, varnish finish, 2x2¾"......................165.00
Salt, burl, VG trn detail, 3x4"...........................200.00
Salt, turned, worn br patina, 1¾x3¼"......................50.00
Sander, figured wood, G trn detail, branded S Davis, 3".......80.00
Sander, turned boxwood, 2½"............................40.00
Scoop, apple butter; pine, 1 pc, open hdl..................150.00
Scoop, beech w/worm holes, 16½".........................35.00
Scoop, curly maple, 10½"................................85.00
Scoop, walnut w/some burl, sq shape, 1900s, 9"............105.00
Skimmer, cream; shell shaped, tab, brass pierced filter center...160.00
Skimmer, tallow; pierced wood, long hld, 24"...............110.00
Snuff box, burl, all wood including hinge, miniature..........155.00
Soap dish, twined, 2x4¾"................................35.00
Spoon, ash, no finish, 16" L.............................35.00
Spoon, hasty pudding, pine, hand hewn, crook in shaft, 18" L...45.00
Spoon, well shaped, 7½".................................10.00
Stirrer, long hdl, minor age cracks, 33"....................45.00
Stocking stretchers, 17" L, pr............................30.00
Taster, G detail, 4¾"....................................40.00
Tobacco jar, quarter sawed soft wood, hexagon, whittle hdl, 7"..50.00
Trencher, pine, tab hdls, hand hewn, 4x14x24".............260.00
Wick pick, trn, 4¼".....................................35.00

World's Fairs and Expos

Since 1851 and the Crystal Palace Exhibition in London, World's Fairs and Expositions have taken place at a steady pace, except during wartime. These events have been the source of tens of thousands of souvenirs, and collectors today find the possibility of locating representative examples an exciting challenge.

Key: T/P----Trylon & Perisphere

Pan-clock, 'Cold Handle, Acme, NYSCO.,' copyright 1899 by Pan American Expo Co. for 1901 fair, keywind, 25″ x 13″, $500.00.

1876 Centennial, Philadelphia

Bookmark, woven cloth, Women's Pavilion, fringed, 4x3½″, VG.40.00
Paperweight, glass.....................................38.00
Pin, Liberty Bell figural, enameled red/wht/bl.................20.00
Print, Machinery Hall, Thos Hunter Lithographers, color, 7x11″.15.00

1893 Columbian, Chicago

Beer foam scraper, wood, Machinery Hall scene, 10½″, EX.....35.00
Bell, clear glass, frosted: florals & twist hdl; LE Clark, EX......75.00
Belt buckle, brass, emb scene, mkd Official Souvenir/Tiffany.....45.00
Book, Samantha at the World's Fair........................6.00
Book, Story of Columbus & World's Columbian Expo.........35.00
Candle holder, 2 pc, hdld, 18 mc jewels, ornate filigree......145.00
Candy dish, fine porcelain...............................27.00
Envelope, unused......................................13.00
Kerchief, gold silk, Machinery Building, etc; M...............45.00
Match holder, sterling, engraved '1492 Columbia 1892'........65.00
Official guide & map...................................15.00
Paperweight, clear glass w/Utah State Building, Libbey Co, EX..45.00
Photo, ferris wheel, in fr, 20x24″.......................80.00
Plate, Horticultural Bldg, bl/wht, Wedgwood Etruria..........45.00
Ring, sterling, describes Expo in Spanish..................150.00
Souvenir book, The Best Things To Be Seen, 182 pgs........11.00
Stereo cards, 7 different...............................21.00
Stick pin, 'World's Columbian Expo 1893', face of Columbus....35.00
Sugar/creamer, shell design, gold edge & hdl, Coalport......150.00
Tumbler, amber glass, allover leaves, 'World's Fair 1893'......35.00
Tumbler, cranberry border, clear bottom, 'World's Fair 1893'....45.00

1898 Omaha

Button, celluloid, 2 sided, 2″...........................40.00
Spoon, Administration Bldg/canal/boats, detailed, demitasse.....15.00

1901 Pan American

Coin purse, pig skin, buffalo in relief/lettering/date............24.00
Playing cards...40.00
Poster, diamond shape, by Rafael Beck, official, 13x13″.......145.00
Tumbler, etched, Manufacturers & Liberal Arts Building.......45.00
Tumbler, etched, Temple of Music......................45.00

1904 St. Louis

Book, Samantha at the St Louis Expo.....................5.00
Book, The Kilties, songs & pictures......................10.00
Dish, metal, Electric Building, 6″........................8.50
Hatchet, glass..45.00
Inkwell, metal crab w/10 legs...........................75.00
Jewelry box, w/lid, metal filigree.......................20.00
Mug, Administration Bldg, china, 4″......................45.00
Pocket mirror, hdld, gold beveled glass..................40.00
Spoon, silverplate....................................22.00
Vase, Palace of Liberal Arts, wht metal, 3½″...............45.00

1909 Alaska Yukon Pacific

Fruit crate label, Sunkist, w/Expo scene..................6.00
Tray, metal, highly emb scenes w/gilt outline, 7″ dia, VG......27.50

1915 Panama Pacific

Album of Views, 25 separate cards, full color, EX............25.00
Bookmark, celluloid, red carnation top, Carnation Milk, 5½″....22.00
Cloth, woven silk, Tower of Jewels, colorful, 12x14″, VG......15.00
Liberty Bell, suspended from 13 star flag w/shield, metal, 5½″...35.00
Match safe, cannon design, Are You Ready/1915/Panama, VG...20.00
Napking ring, SP, some wear, markings clear................12.50
Skillet, copper, emb scene of California Building, 4″ long......15.00
Spoon, eagle/flag hdl w/map at top, view of SF Bay, 5½″......15.00

1933 Chicago

Ash tray, metal, small.................................4.50
Cocktail shaker, Deco.................................40.00
Marbles, colorful agate, 28 in Century of Progress bag, M......45.00
Picture, Midget City, shows complete cast, sgnd by Capt Doyle...50.00
Plate, 'Black Forest', wht w/gr, emb border, Pickard, 11″.......15.00
Plate, pierced border w/Chicago scenes, set of 4.............16.50
Playing cards, scenes of fair, COP design on back, w/orig case...30.00
Souvenir booklet, 1893-1933, 30 pgs.....................8.50
Umbrella, Japanese...................................22.50

1939 New York

Belt buckle, goldtone, enameled T/P, dtd 1939, 1½″ sq, EX....20.00
Booklet, Official Guide Book............................12.00
Bottle, Perisphere Perfume, attached brass T/P tag, 2″.........15.00
Bracelet, 16 enameled flags, emb names of nations, EX.......27.50
Coaster, tin, mc scene of Aviation Building, EX...............10.00
Compact, brass, mc Administration Building, 3″ sq, NM.......25.00
Globe, silver lustre, on black glass base, dated 1940..........15.00
Newspaper, Today At The Fair..........................2.00
Paperweight, Scotty dog, metal.........................20.00
Pin, brass, oval w/cut-out design of T/P, 1¼x1″, EX..........12.50
Pin-back button, bl on wht, T/P, American Banking Day, 1¼″..15.00
Plate, 150th Anniv/Washington's Inaug, F Murphy, w/gold seal...55.00
Postcards, various exhibits, each.........................2.00
Program, American Jubilee..............................5.00
Program, Aquacade, w/ticket...........................10.00
Spoon, silverplate....................................12.50
Tie bar...10.00
Tobacco pouch, leather, embossed T/P...................12.50
Tumbler, glass, red & blue design & lettering, 5″, mkd.........12.50
Vase, glass, bulbous, clear & cranberry, gold T/P design, 4″....20.00
Viewer, w/orig box...................................45.00

1939 San Francisco

Blanket, M...75.00
Kerchief, pink...9.00
Knife, pink depression glass fruit, orig red carton............26.50

Wrought Iron

Until the middle of the 19th century, almost all the iron hand forged in America was made in a material called wrought iron. When wrought iron rusts, it appears grainy, while the mild steel that was used later shows no grain, but pits to an orange peel surface. This is an important aid in determining the age of an ironwork piece.

Bird, good detail/tooling, perched on bar, 22x27"............225.00
Buggy step, rnd plate w/compass star punching, 7¾" L........30.00
Candle holder, on spring, punched crescent brass reflector.....375.00
Candle holder, sawtooth trammel hanger, EX detail, 27".....805.00
Dough scraper, 3½" W.....................................35.00
Fork, tooling above 3 tines, shaped hdl, 16½" L..............25.00
Fork, well shaped hdl, 10" L..............................50.00
Fork, 2 tines, edges of hdl curve downward, 9¾"............65.00
Fork, 2 tines, good cast detail on hdl, 18"................75.00
Fork, 2 tines, sgn J Schmidt, 1841, worn, 18".............100.00
Frying pan, 10" hdl mk Whitfield, 9" dia...................30.00
Gate, simple w/scrolled arch top, 23x49"..................125.00
Latch, tooled & dated 1824, New England, 17".............170.00
Nail rake, 3 prongs, hanging loop, 10½"...................45.00
Pastry cutter, faceted finial on hdl, handmade, 7"..........65.00
Peel, flat flared hdl w/hanging hole, worn, 42"............45.00
Peel, ram's horn finial, 47"..............................85.00
Peel, ram's horn hdl, 33" L..............................55.00
Rush light holder w/candle socket counter balance, 9¾"......155.00
S hooks, set of 4, 6" L..................................40.00
Skimmer, trowel shaped bowl, short twist hdl & ring, 15".......85.00
Spatula, stamped designs, 8¾"...........................60.00
Spatula, twist hdl, simple tooling, European, 9¼"..........22.00

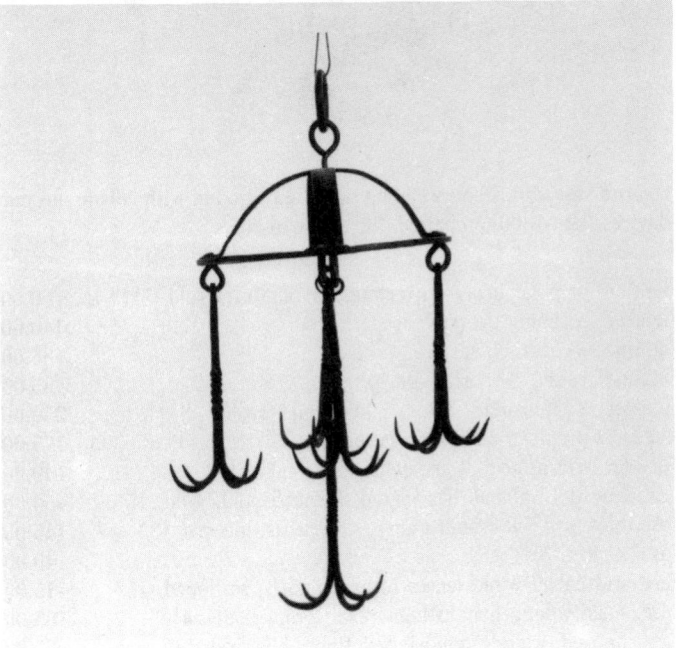

Dutch crown, used to hang game, early 1700s, 22", $295.00.

Spatula, 20" L...15.00
Stake, heart top, 40½"...................................65.00
Strap hinges, worn wht pnt, 24" L, set of 4................70.00
Taster, primitive, w/tooling, European, 8"................12.00
Thumb latch w/leaf form plates, no thumb piece, 12".........35.00
Torchere, adjustable sawtooth stem, adjusts from 54"........110.00
Trammel, sawtooth, cut-out finial, adjust from 39"..........175.00
Utensil rack, 7 hooks, scrolled/twisted crest, 13½x33".......105.00
Wafer iron, geometric florals, initials, good detail, 29"........45.00

Yellowware

Yellowware is an inexpensive, plain type of earthenware, so called because of the color of the clay used in its manufacture. Pieces may vary from buff to yellow to nearly brown; the glaze itself is clear. Some yellowware was decorated with blue, white, brown, or black bands; only seldom was it relief molded.

Yellowware was made to a large extent in East Liverpool, Ohio, but other Ohio potteries, as well as some in Pennsylvania and Vermont also produced it. English yellowware has a harder body composition. Because it was not often marked, it is almost impossible to identify the manufacturer.

There is a growing interest in this type of pottery, and consequently, prices are continually increasing.

Set of five kitchenware nested bowls, in-mold relief decoration on outside, brown bands, $125.00.

Bank, hen on nest, br base, clear glaze hen w/spots, 3½"......95.00
Bottle, fish form, 10¾".................................145.00
Bowl, bl seaweed, br/wht bands, 6x12¾".................100.00
Bowl, bl sponge spatter, exterior w/amber over bl, 2x7½"......45.00
Bowl, br sponging, 2x4½"...............................20.00
Bowl, br sponging, 4¼x9¼"..............................40.00
Bowl, mixing; tan/wht stripes, minor wear, 7x14¾"..........50.00
Bowl, mixing; tan/wht stripes, 6½x14"...................45.00
Bowl, mixing; wht band w/br stripes & bl seaweed, 5½x12", G..85.00
Bowl, mixing; wht band w/br stripes & bl seaweed, 5½x12", M.135.00
Bowl, tan w/wht stripes, 5¼" dia........................20.00
Chamber pot, bl seaweed, blk/wht bands, rpr, mini, 2".........35.00
Chamber pot, wht/bl seaweed/blk stripes, mini, 2", M.........60.00
Chamber pot, wht/bl seaweed/blk stripes/rpr lid, mini, 2".......20.00
Compote, running blue glaze around rim, 8x10½"...........155.00
Creamer, emb dk br checkerboard decor, stains/chips, 3½"......15.00

Creamer, emb dk br Checkerboard decor, 3½", M..........40.00
Dish, oval, bk mk E Liverpool, Nagle, 2½x8¾x11½"........100.00

Figurine, lion, recumbent, oval base, emb detail, 8x15".......700.00
Jar w/lid, wht bands, br stripes, edge flakes, 5x6½"..........85.00
Jar w/lid, wht bands, br stripes, 7½"....................105.00
Mold, pineapple, fluted sides, 4¾x7"....................135.00
Mold, 6 petal flower, 3" dia.............................35.00
Mug, sand finish, bl bands.............................75.00

Mug, wht band w/unusual gr decor of floral outline..........245.00
Pepper shaker, yellowware w/bl seaweed band, rpr, 4¼".......65.00
Pie plate, coggled edge, glazed w/in, edge & bk unglazed, 8"....45.00
Pie plate, gr/br sponged decor, misshapen, 10"............55.00
Pie plate, sm rim hairline, 11" dia......................25.00
Pie plate, 11" dia, M..................................50.00
Pitcher, splashes of running bl, 6¼"....................45.00
Plaque, bust of Washington in wht, oval, 5x5¼"............30.00
Rolling pin, trn wood hdls, 15" L......................130.00
Salt, wht band w/br seaweed decor, ftd, hairlines, 2x3" dia.....55.00
Teapot, Rebecca at the Well, bl mottled, spout flake, 9"......125.00

Zanesville Art Pottery

Prior to 1900, this company was known as The Zanesville Roofing Tile Company; then it was reorganized, and production shifted to the manufacture of art pottery. Their most familiar line, La Moro, was made in the standard brown glaze as well as in a matt version very similar to Owens' Matt Utopia.

Bud vase, La Moro, sgn AD, 6½"........................110.00
Pitcher, floral on br glaze, La Moro, 6¼"................125.00
Vase, La Moro, matt glaze, artist sgn CD, 9¾"............215.00
Vase, standard w/florals, sgn La Moro, 10½"..............135.00

Zanesville Glass

Glassware was produced in Zanesville, Ohio from as early as 1815 until 1851. Two companies produced clear and colored hollowware pieces in five characteristic patterns: (1) diamond faceted, (2) broken swirls, (3) vertical swirls, (4) perpendicular fluting, (5) un-patterned with scalloped or fluted rims and strap handles. The most readily identified product is perhaps the whiskey bottles made in the vertical swirl pattern, often called globular swirls because of their full round body. Their necks vary in width -- some have a ringed rim and some are collared. They were made in several colors: amber, light green, and light aquamarine are the most common.

Bottle, club, aqua, 24 rib broken swirl, minor sickness, 8"......75.00
Bottle, globular, aqua, 24 swirl ribs, sick, 7½"............155.00
Bottle, globular, deep golden amber, 24 swirled ribs, 8", EX...475.00
Bottle, globular, golden amber, 24 swirled ribs, 7¼".........325.00
Bottle, globular, golden amber, 24 swirled ribs, 8".........350.00
Compote, applied ft/baluster stem, golden amber, 4x5½"......450.00
Flask, chestnut, deep golden amber, 10 diamond, 5¼".......375.00
Flask, chestnut, yellow gr, 24 vertical ribs, wear/residue, 5"...475.00
Flask, chestnut; gold amber/grandfather/24 vertical ribs, 8½"...900.00
Flask, chestnut; golden amber, 24 swirled ribs, 5", G........175.00
Inkwell, 24 vertical ribs, aqua, 2¾"....................140.00
Pan, 10 dia, folded rim, aqua, 1¾x4¾"..................725.00
Pan, 24 ribs, folded rim, golden amber, 1½x5½"...........650.00
Salt, 24 ribs w/folded rim, 1½x2½", pr..................130.00

Zsolnay

Zsolnay pottery has been made in Hungary since the mid-1800s. Early wares were highly ornamental -- some with high relief Art Nouveau motifs, others depending on surface decoration for their appeal. Today, the firm produces figurines with an iridescent glaze which are becoming very collectible.

Bowl, heart shape, fish, flowers, red/bl/gr, 4x8" L...........410.00
Bowl, oval, double-wall, pierced flowers..................350.00
Bowl, up-curving 'horns' 2 sides, retic, florals, 12" L.........475.00
Figurine, feeding hen, gr/gold..........................50.00
Figurine, French poodle, gr/gold, 4" L...................45.00
Figurine, giraffe, head erect, gr/gold, 7½"................60.00
Figurine, girl, sitting holding basket, gr/gold, 3"...........35.00

Pilgrim vase and cover, wedding party, gilt ground with cobalt and puce devices, late 1800s, repaired, 32", $2,640.00.

Figurine, pr polar bears on rectangular plinth, gr/gold, 7½" L...60.00
Figurine, reclining deer, artist sgn.....................140.00
Figurine, Trojan horse................................88.00
Figurine, young girl, irid, sgn, 4"......................35.00
Figurine, 2 Hungarian maids, 1 kneeling/1 reclining, 9", pr....250.00
Mug, irid purple/gr/gold, emb grapes, mk 5 steeples/Pecs/6303..175.00
Tumbler, irid gr/gold, 4 maidens, castle mk, 6½"..........140.00
Urn, retic dbl wall/ball base/flared ft, much gold, w/lid, 15"...450.00
Vase, bl-gr irid, blown-out tadpoles, raised castle mk, 13"....145.00
Vase, gr irid, 5½".....................................40.00
Vase, irid cobalt w/red leaves in base panels, scalloped, 11"...115.00
Vase, maid w/long hair in high relief, gr/gold, 9¼x4½".....185.00
Vase, on ped, w/nude removing clothing, bl/gr/irid, 11".......265.00
Vase, openings ea side, top closed, retic designs, 14½".......575.00
Vase, retic, raised flowers, gold tracing, colorful, 9".........150.00

Directory of Contributors

California

Baker, Lillian
15237 Chanera Ave., Gardena, 90249
Author Collector Books on jewelry, hatpins & hatpin holders

Benjamin, Scott
920 N. Kings Rd. #110
Los Angeles, 90069; 213-656-5794
Specializes in gasoline pump globes

Chamberlain, Jackie
1520 Foothill Blvd., La Canada, 91011
818-790-5416
Specializes in holiday collectibles, antique reference books, teddy bears

Harris, Warren D.
6130 Rampart Dr., Carmichael, 95608
Specializes in thermometers

Long, Jennie D.
P.O. Box 552, Kingsburg, 93631
209-897-5077
Author of *An Album of Candy Containers Volumes I & II* Privately published by: Thomas O. & Jennie D. Long

The Willow Society
Misiewicz, Lois K.
2062 Trevino, Oceanside, 92056
619-757-2062
Specializes in Willow Ware

Oliphant, Steve
5255 Alott Ave., Van Nuys, 91401;
818-789-2339
Specializes in phonographs

Pardini, Dick
3107 N. El Dorado St.
Stockton, 95204; 209-466-5550
Specializes in California Perfume Company items: buyer & information center

Richard, Marty Atwell
2701 Second Ave. #103
San Diego, 92103; 619-232-1638
Wanted to buy: blue & white Pennsbury Pottery

Connecticut

Bondhus, Sandra V.
P.O. Box 203, Watertown, 06795
203-274-1064
Author of *Quimper: A French Folk Art Faience*
Specializes in Quimper Pottery

Bull, Don
64 October Lane, Trumbull, 06661
Buy & sell corkscrews with beer & brewery advertising
SASE for ordering info re: book on corkscrews

Mechanical Music Center, Inc.
Edgerton, William H., President
25 Kings Highway North, Box 88
Darien, 06820; 203-655-9510
Specializes in mechanical musical instruments

Florida

Lipschutz, Jeffrey
952 Versailles Circle, Maitland, 32751
Collects Peters & Reed

McNerney, Kathryn
Northwoods Apt II, #221, 4051 Olive Road
Pensacola, 32504
Author Collector Books on Blue & White, primitives, tools

Georgia

Geode Ltd.
Glenn, Walter
3393 Peachtree Rd., Atlanta, 30326
404-261-9346
Specializes in contemporary jewelry & Frankart

Illinois

Beckham, Margaret
Greenup, 62428
Collects Bluebird China

Danis, John
2929 Sunnyside Dr. B327, Rockford, 61111
815-877-6098
Specializes in R. Lalique

Hospice House Antiques
Durham, William & Galaway, William
9633 Beaver Valley Rd., Belvidere, 61008
815-547-5128
Specializes in Tea Leaf Ironstone & White Ironstone

Griffith, Woody
4107 White Ash Rd., Crystal Lake, 60014
815-459-7808
Specializes in Jewel-T, Noritake, Hall

Everett & Goldie
Grist, Everett
Charleston, 61920; 217-345-7238
Specializes in marbles

B & B Antiques
Hall, Doris & Burdell
210 W. Sassafras Dr., Morton, 61550
Authors of *Morton's Potteries: 99 Years*
Specializes in Morton Pottery, American dinnerware, early American pattern glass, historical items, small primitives

Hoffmann, Pat & Don, Sr.
1291 N. Elmwood Dr., Aurora, 60506
312-859-3435
Specializes in Warwick China

The Basement Door
Kocmoud, Jean & Jim
4222 Deyo Ave., Brookfield, 60513
312-485-7317
Specializes in dinnerware & art pottery

Larry's Antiques
Lafary, Larry
2316 N. Knoxville, Peoria, 61604
309-686-0100
Specializes in pottery, tools & advertising

Raycraft, Don
RR 8, Normal, 61761
Author Collector Books on stoneware & baskets

Antiques Unique
Walsh, Shirley & David
100 Kansas, Frankfort, 60423; 815-469-2741
Specializes in jewelry, stained glass, furniture

Weldi, Frank & Skinner, Mary
1736 W. Farragut, Chicago, 60640
312-728-7750
Specializes in American dinnerware & art pottery

Angel's Roost Antiques
Wolfe, Rev. Leslie
Box 66, Villa Grove, 61956; 217-832-8073
Author of *Royal Copley, Royal Windsor, and Spaulding*

Indiana

Buchanan, James III
3758 N. Pennsylvania, Indianapolis, 46307
317-923-4548
Specializes in jewelry & general line

Beth's Antiques
Conrad, Beth
US 421 South, Monticello, 47960
219-583-5133
Specializes in cut & art glass, fine china, primitives

Edwards, Bill
423 N. Main, Rushville, 46173
Author Collector Books on carnival glass

Frey, Judy & Dick
716 4th St., Covington, 47932
Specializes in bottles and art pottery

Frey, Virginia
715 4th St., Covington, 47932
Specializes in majolica, Tea Leaf Ironstone, miscellaneous

Hoosier Peddler
Harris, Dave
5400 S. Webster, Kokomo, 46902
317-453-6172
Specializes in advertising & toys

Ted's Treasures
Haun, Ted
2426 N. 700 East, Kokomo, 46901
317-628-3640
Specializes in American pottery and china with emphasis on designer ware

Summer Kitchen
Maddox, Glenn
Wolfe St., Oaktown, 47561; 812-745-4771
Specializes in primitives and country items

Mary's Antiques
Indianapolis
Specializes in art glass, cut glass and jewelry

Scowden, Virgil
303 Lincoln, Williamsport, 47993
317-762-3408
Antiques museum, general line, tours

Marnette Antiques
Stofft, Marvin & Jeanette
812-547-5707
Ohio art pottery, cut glass, R.S. Prussia, buy & sell

Wetzel, Mary M.
P.O. Box 594, Notre Dame, 46556
Secretary of Michigan Assoc. of Candlewick Collectors
Author of *Candlewick, the Jewel of Imperial*

Iowa

Main Street Antiques & Art
110 W. Main, Box 340, West Branch, 52358
319-643-2065
Folk art, country Americana, the unusual

Nichols, Harold & Ruth
632 Agg Ave., Ames, 50010
Buy & sell American art pottery

Shawnee Man
1517 Grove, Burlington, 52601; 319-753-2450
Specializes in Shawnee & Kenwood

Williams, Don
Ottumwa, 52501
Specializes in art glass

Kansas

Robison, Joleen A.
502 Lindley Dr., Lawrence, 66044
Author Collector Books on advertising dolls

Tinsley's Antiques
Tinsley, Mrs. Dan
105 15th St., Osawatomie, 66064
Specializes in primitives, kitchen, farm, graniteware, textiles, tools & miscellaneous

Kentucky

American Crown Antiques
Louisville

Florence, Gene
Box 7186H, Lexington, 40522
Author Collector Books on Depression, Occupied Japan

Maryland

Banks, Bob
18901 Gold Mine Court, Brookeville, 20833
Wanted: American flags, old or unusual

Humphrey, George C.
4932 Prince George Ave.
Beltsville, 20705; 301-937-7899
Specializes in John Rogers groups

Massachusetts

Adams, Charles & Barbara
Middleboro, 617-947-7277
Specializes in Bennington (brown only)

Rudisill's Alt Print Haus
Rudisill, John & Barbara
3 Lakewood, Medfield, 02052; 617-359-2261
Specializes in Currier & Ives

Toke, Bob; Wilson, Roger
41 Park Dr. Penthouse, Boston, 02215
Specializes in S.E.G., decorated Marblehead, Grueby, W.J. Walley, Merrimac, Hampshire

Michigan

Lucinda's Loot (co-operative)
Dunn, Gail M.
117 Main St., Blissfield, 49228; 517-486-4607
General line from furniture to jewelry

Haas, Barbara & Norman 264 Clizbe Rd.,
Quincy, 49082; 517-639-8537
Specializes in American art pottery

Modern Times
Lopez, Andrew
P.O. Box 1294, Jackson, 49204; 517-782-9910

Nedry, Boyd W.
728 Buth Dr., Comstock Park, 49321
616-784-1513
Specializes in traps & trap related items

Oswald, Bob & Bernie
440 Ridge Dr., Reading, 49274; 517-283-2763
General line

Grandma's Antiques
Robinson, Lucille
RR 2, 13200 Cambria Rd., Camden, 49232
517-368-5822
Specializes in glass, china and primitives

R.F. Willis Gallery
Willis, Robert F.
Grand Rapids, 616-456-8400
Specializes in antique jewelry, jade, paintings, Oriental rugs

Minnesota

Knutson, Debra K.
8434 Park Ave. South, Bloomington, 55420
612-888-3291
Specializes in Goebel

Marcheschi, Cork
2418 Steven Ave. So., Minneapolis, 55404
Longwy, Keith Murray, Boch, Carlton, Cowan, Futura, Deco pottery

Missouri

Whetstone Antiques
Beth, Edward
Williamsburg, 314-254-3597
Specializes in American dinnerware & general line

Kansas City Tradewinds
Bosworth, Wauneta, David & Dick
7307 N.W. 75th St., Kansas City, 64152;
816-741-7745
Specializes in American art pottery

Buchheit, Terry
214 S. Moulton, Perryville, 63775
314-547-2617
Collector of Coca-Cola items

Country-Side Antiques
Roberts, Brenda
Rt. 2, Marshall, 65340
Specializes in Hull Pottery & general line
Author Collector Books on Hull Pottery

Smith, Pat
Independence
Author Collector Books doll book series

Blue Budda Antiques
Stratton, Bill
1862 Boonville, Springfield, 65803
417-862-4212
Miscellaneous pottery

New Hampshire

Marden, Richard G.
Box 524, Elm St., Wolfeboro, 03894
603-569-3209

New Jersey

Hochman, Gene
29 Hampton Terrace, Livingston, 07039
201-992-0084
Playing cards--will date and price any, include SASE

Rago, David
P.O. Box 3592, Station E, Trenton, 08629
609-585-2546
Specializes in Arts & Crafts, American art pottery

Warns, Peter
59 Ross Ave., Emerson, 07630; 201-265-5220
Specializes in antique cash registers

New Mexico

Berryman, Jan
203 Country Road, Hobbs, 88240
505-392-3301
Specializes in American dinnerware, California pottery

New York

Bittner, Marvin A.
74-10 35th Ave., Jackson Heights, 11372
212-898-3396
Rookwood, Pewabic, Overbeck, Brouwer, Clewell, Ott & Brewer, Union Porcelain Works

Fenner's Antiques
2611 Ave. S., Brooklyn, 11229
SASE for lists: jewelry, glass, European china, books, porcelain, and pottery

F.T.S. Inc.
Fox, Ron
416 Throop St., N. Babylon, 11704
516-669-7232
Specializes in steins

Moses, John
192 6th Ave., New York, 10013; 212-431-5059
Specializes in American dinnerware, art pottery, Black memorabilia 1925-55

Mood Indigo
Petipas, Diane
172 Prince St., New York, 10012
212-925-7591
Specializes in Fiesta Ware, Hall china, Art Deco accessories

U.S. Games Systems, Inc.
38 East 32nd St., New York, 10016
212-685-4300
Specializes in antique unusual playing cards

Ruth & Dale Van Kuren Antiques
Van Kuren, Ruth
5990 Goodrich Rd., Clarence Center, 14032
716-741-2606
Specializes in Buffalo Pottery, general line

Van Patten, Joan
c/o Collector Books, Box 3009
Paducah, KY, 42001
Author Collector Books on Nippon

Ohio

Gretchen's Collections
Armstrong, Gretchen
3584 Ridgewood Road, Toledo, 43606
419-536-9155
Specializes in country furniture & accessories, children's furniture & accessories

Bettinger, Lewis & Alice
Canton, 44780; 216-454-4863
Specializes in American pottery

Golden Apple Antiques
Blair, Betty
403 Chilicothe, Jackson, 45640
General line, pottery, furniture, silver

Town & Country Antiques
Clark, Joe R. & Wilma
7770 Rodebaugh Rd., Reynoldsburg, 43068
614-863-2637
Specializes in clocks & watches

Cousino, Carol
5414 302nd St., Toledo, 43611; 419-726-4513
Specializes in jewelry

Coyle, Robert H.
P.O. Box 982, Newark, 43055; 614-349-7362
General line, shows & mail order only

Red Barn Antiques
DeLuca, Mary A.
5510 W. Lakeshore Dr., Port Clinton, 43452
419-635-2045
General line -- 2 buildings

Dunn's Antiques
Dunn, Gail M.
6742 Maplewood Ave., Sylvania, 43560
419-882-7093

Wayside Antiques
Ferguson, Maxine
2290 E. Pike, Zanesville, 43701
General line, furniture, dolls, pottery, glass

Hermes, Amy
5664 W. Harbor Rd., Port Clinton
Specializes in trolls & dolls

Hermes, Mrs. Joe
5664 W. Harbor Rd., Port Clinton; 634-2495
Specializes in glass

Hopfinger, Jackie
208 E. 6th St., P.O. Box 284,
Port Clinton, 43452; 419-732-3268
Specializes in Hummel figurines

Lustre Pitcher Antiques
Kao, Fern
P.O. Box 312, Bowling Green, 43402
419-352-5928
Specializes in Shelly China, small antiques

The Golden Acorn
Kile, Elizabeth
127 Kilbourne St.
Bellevue, 44811; 419-483-7376
Specializes in primitives

Kitchen, Lorrie; Tucker, Dan
Toledo, 43612; 419-478-3815
Specializes in depression era glass, Hall China, Fiesta, Blue Ridge, Shawnee

Kline, (Mr. & Mrs.) Jerry & Gerry
604 Orchard View Dr., Maumee, 43537
419-893-1226
Specializes in collecting Torquay Pottery, coordinators of Torquay Pottery Collectors' Society

Laskey, Jane
5559 Steffins Rd., Toledo, 43623; 474-4189
Specializes in glass, china, jewelry

The Hitching Post
McDaniel, Doris
7467 S.R. 88, Ravenna, 216-296-3686
General line

Messenger, Patty
331 Pearl, Bowling Green, 43402
419-352-8602
Buying Greentown Glass

Wooden Squirrel Antiques
Moore, Carolyn
1017 N. Main St., Bowling Green, 43402
419-352-7879
Specializes in primitives, yellowware, graniteware

Osborne, Ruth
Higginsport, 45131; 513-375-6605

Zanes Trace Antiques
Rees, Debbie & Bill
3630 East Pike, Zanesville, 43701
614-452-4481
Buying & selling cookie jars, Roseville, Watt Pottery, Steiff, Blue & White stoneware

Rose, Sandra
555 Wyman, Toledo, 43603; 419-382-8448

Stagecoach Antique Mall
Rt 40½ mile west of I-70, Norwich Exit 16
7527 East Pike, Norwich, 43767

Calico Cat
St. John, D. M.
1635 Circular Rd., Toledo, 43614
Specializes in fine glassware, kitchen, & vintage clothes

Treadway, Don
P.O. Box 8924, Cincinnati, 45208
Buy & sell Newcomb, Grueby, Pewabic, Overbeck

Walker, Bunny
Box 502, Bucyrus, 44820; 419-562-8355
Specializes in dolls, teddy bears, cookie jars, art pottery

Watt, Bryce & Cheryl
7990 Fultonrose Rd., Roseville, 43777
Specializes in Watt Pottery

The Bird of Paradise
Wilkins, Juanita
Box 1884, Lima, 45802; 419-227-2163
Specializes in R.S. China, Old Ivory, art pottery, antique jewelry

Oklahoma

Bess, Phyllis & Tom
14535 E. 13th, Tulsa, 74108; 918-437-7776
Authors of *Frankoma Treasures*

Willis, Ron L.
2110 Fox Ave., Moore, 73160
Specializes in militaria

Pennsylvania

Atkinson, Phil & Karol
903 Apache Trail, Mercer, 16137;
412-475-2490
Specializes in antique advertising & country store collectibles

Cohen, Bea
P.O. Box 825, Easton, 18042; 215-252-1098
Specializes in spatterware, Gaudy Dutch, mocha, chalkware, Dedham and spongeware

DLK Antiques
2778 Richland St., Johnstown, 15904
Buy & sell: animated clocks, pre-1890 sewing machines, space toys, pre-prohibition items, Occupied Japan

Jancuska, Joseph
P.O. Box 176, Luzerne, 18709
Specializes in coin operated machines

The Kelly Collection
Kelly, Jim & Kathy
1621 Princess Ave., Pittsburgh, 15216
412-561-6064
Specializes in Depression Glass, American pottery & china

Maier, Clarence & Betty
Mail order: The Burmese Cruet
P.O. Box 432, Montgomeryville, 18936
215-855-5388
Specializes in Victorian art glass, circa 1880-1910

Marks, Mariann
1416 N. Main Street, Honesdale, 18431
717-253-1923
Author Collector Books on Majolica pottery

Rhode Island

Dumont, Louise
591 Old Main St., Coventry, 02816
401-828-2799
Specializes in cookie jars; pottery: Hull, Gonder, Abingdon, Shawnee, McCoy; Black Americana

Tennessee

Railroad Antiques
Price, Gene
P.O. Box 278, Erwin, 37650
Specializes in Railroadiana

Texas

Shellac Shack
Docks, L.R. 'Les'
P.O. Box 32924, San Antonio, 78216
512-492-6021
Author of *American Premium Record Guide*
Specializes in vintage records

Washington

Antonation, Linda
P.O. Box 1551, Bellevue, 98009
206-822-0678
Buy & sell Black Americana, quarterly catalogues of items for sale

Wisconsin

Continental Hobby House
P.O. Box 193, 1616 N. 3rd St.,
Sheboygan, 53081
Meissen, KPM porcelain, gambling devices, slot machines

Cowen, Robert & Deloris
Box 843, Appleton, 54912; 414-734-0847
Specializes in Cowan pottery

Fortney, Dan
Suite 713, Chalet at the River
823 N. 2nd St., Milwaukee, 53203
Specializes in china & glass

Clubs, Newsletters and Catalogues

American Graniteware Association
Box 605, Downers Grove, IL 60515
312-852-2960 or 968-1393

Avon Collectors Club
for info contact Dick Pardini
3107 N. El Dorado St., Stockton, CA 95204

The Coin Slot
Joseph S. Jancuska, Publisher/Editor
P.O. Box 176, Luzerne, PA 18709

The Cola Clan
Alice Fischer, Treasurer
2084 Continental Drive, N.E.,
Atlanta, GA 30345

Depression Glass Daze
12135 N. State St., Otisville, MI 48463

Don Treadway
American Art Pottery Auction catalogues
P.O. Box 8924, Cincinnati, OH 45208

Elephant Collectors Newsletter
Richard Massiglia, Box CY-7, Boston, MA 02215

Fenton Art Glass Collectors of America
P.O. Box 2441, Appleton, WI 54913

Fiesta Collectors Association
Dan Anderson
P.O. Box 100582, Nashville, TN 37210

Figural Bottle Opener Collectors
Barbara Rosen, President
6 Shoshone Trail, Wayne, NJ 07470

Full House Antique Playing Cards & Gambling Memorabilia
29 Hampton Terrace, Livingston, NJ 07039
Mail auction catalogs; will date & price cards--include SASE

Geisha Girl Porcelain Newsletter
P.O. Box 925, Orange, NJ 07051

The Glaze, Pottery Collectors Newsletter
535 E. Normal, Springfield, MO 65807

Hall China Newsletter
B&B Collectibles
Benjamin Moulton
RR 21, Box 103, Terre Haute, IN 47802
Send SASE for info

Heisey Collectors of America, Inc.
National Heisey Glass Museum
Sixth & Church Streets, P.O. Box 27
Newark, OH 43055; 614-345-2932

International Club for Collectors of Hatpins & Holders
Lillian Baker, founder
15237 Chanera Ave., Gardena, CA 90249

National Autumn Leaf Collectors Clubs
c/o Woody Griffith
4107 White Ash Rd., Crystal Lake, IL 60014

National Reamer Collectors
112 S. Center, Lacon, IL 61540; 309-246-8996

Occupied Japan Club
Sissie Jackson
4908 Old Heady Rd., Louisville, KY 40299

Occupied Japan Collectors Club
Robert Gee, founder
18309 Faysmith Ave., Torrance, CA 90504
Buy, sell, aid with info re: items marked MIOJ

Pen Fancier's Club
1169 Overcash Dr., Dunedin, FL 33528
Publishes monthly magazine of pens & mechanical pencils

Postcard Auctions
Sally Carver
179 S. St., Chestnut Hill, ME 02167
SASE for info

Red Wing Collectors Society
David A. Newkirk
Rt 3, Box 141, Monticello, MN 55362

Roberta Etter, Box 22, Oradell, NJ 07649
$3 for sample: Photographic Catalogue, illustrated quarterly, 32 pg, daguerreotypes, cameras, stereo views

Thimble Collectors International
134 W. Prairie St., Columbus, WI 53925

The Torquay Pottery Collectors' Society
c/o Jerry & Gerry Kline, Coordinators
604 Orchard View Dr., Maumee, OH 43537

Auction Houses

We wish to thank the following auction houses for allowing us to reproduce photographs from their fine catalogues:

C.E. Guarino
Box 49, Denmark, ME 04022

C.G. Sloan & Co., Inc.
919 E. St. N.W., Washington, DC 20004

Col. Doug Allard
P.O. Box 460, St. Ignatius, MT 59865

Continental Auctions
Div. of Continental Hobby House
P.O. Box 193, Sheybogan, WI 53081

Daniel F. Kelleher Co., Inc.
Ten Post Office Square, Boston MA 02109

Doyle, Auctioneers & Appraisers
98 Main St., Fishkill, NY 12524

Du Mouchelles
409 Jefferson Ave., Detroit, MI 48226

Early Auction Company
123 Main St., Milford, OH 45150

Garths Auctions Inc.
2690 Stratford Rd., Box 369
Delaware, OH 43015

Jack Sellner Auctioneer
P.O. Box 113, Scottsdale, AZ 85252

James D. Julia
P.O. Box 210, Showhegan Rd.   ME
Fairfield, ME 04937

Lloyd Ralston Toys
447 Stratford Rd., Fairfield, CT 06432

Maritime Auctions
RR 2, Box 45A, York, ME 03909

Mortons Auction Exchange
P.O. Box 30380, New Orleans, LA 70190

New England Auction Gallery
Box 682, Methuen, MA 01844

Phillips
406 E. 79th St., New York City, NY 10021

Roan, Inc.
Box 118, RD 3, Cogan Station, PA 17728

Robert C. Eldred Co., Inc.
East Dennis, MA 02641

Sotheby Parke Bernet Inc.
980 Madison Ave., New York City, NY 10021

Weschler's, Adam A. Weschler & Son
905 E. St. N.W., Washington, DC 20004

Willis Henry Auctions
22 Main St., Marshfield, MA 02050

Advisory Board

Charles & Barbara Adams
Middleboro, Massachusetts

American Graniteware Association
Downers Grove, Illinois

Scott Benjamin
Los Angeles, California

Phyllis & Tom Bess
Tulsa, Oklahoma

Edward Beth
Williamsburg, Missouri

Marvin A. Bittner
Jackson Heights, New York

Sandra V. Bondhus
Watertown, Connecticut

Terry Buchheit
Perryville, Missouri

Jackie Chamberlain
La Canada, California

Joe R. & Wilma Clark
Reynoldsburg, Ohio

Bea Cohen
Easton, Pennsylvania

Robert & Deloris Cowan
Appleton, Wisconsin

John Danis
Rockford, Illinois

L. R. 'Les' Docks
San Antonio, Texas

Louise Dumont
Coventry, Rhode Island

Delores Dunsker

William Durham
Belvidere, Illinois

William H. Edgerton
Darien, Connecticut

Fenton Art Glass Collectors of America
Appleton, Wisconsin

Daniel Fortney
Milwaukee, Wisconsin

Ron Fox
North Babylon, New York

William Galaway
Belvidere, Illinois

Walter Glenn
Atlanta, Georgia

Woody Griffith
Crystal Lake, Illinois

Doris & Burdell Hall
Morton, Illinois

Dave Harris
Kokomo, Indiana

Warren D. Harris
Carmichael, California

Heisey Collectors of America, Inc.
Newark, Ohio

Pat & Don Hoffman
Aurora, Illinois

George C. Humphrey
Beltsville, Maryland

Mr. & Mrs. Jerry & Gerry Kline
Maumee, Ohio

Jeffrey Lipschutz
Maitland, Florida

Jennie D. Long
Kingsburg, California

Clarence & Betty Maier
Montgomeryville, Pennsylvania

Richard G. Marden
Wolfeboro, New Hampshire

Mariann K. Marks
Honesdale, Pennsylvania

Carolyn Moore
Bowling Green, Ohio

Boyd Nedry
Comstock Park, Michigan

Occupied Japan Club
Louisville, Kentucky

Ruth Osborne
Higginsport, Ohio

Dick Pardini
Stockton, California

Pen Fancier's Club
Dunedin, Florida

Gene Price
Erwin, Tennessee

David Rago
Trenton, New Jersey

Debbie & Bill Rees
Zanesville, Ohio

Brenda Roberts
Marshall, Missouri

John & Barbara Rudisill
Medfield, Maryland

Pat Smith
Independence, Missouri

Bob Toke
Boston, Massachusetts

Ruth Van Kuren
Clarence Center, New York

Peter Warns
Emerson, New Jersey

Roger Wilson
Boston, Massachusetts

Don Williams
Ottumwa, Iowa

Ron L. Willis
Moore, Oklahoma

Our primary goal being to supply our readers with accurate information, up-to-date market dealing and full coverage of both the established fields of antiques and the 'new' collectibles as well, we felt that we should enlist the advise of the experts. Listed above are those who graciously agreed to work with us this year in helping us achieve that end.

May we, the editors and the staff of Schroeder's Antiques Price Guide, take this opportunity to acknowledge their kind cooperation and assistance with a most sincere 'Thank You'.

Of our nearly six hundred categories there are many for which we still have no advisors. If you have a special interest and would like to contribute to our next edition, contact us at 1202 7th St., Covington, Indiana 47932.

The Editors

Photos on the following pages have been reproduced by kind permission of Sotheby Parke Bernet, Inc. from their auction catalogues copyright 1984: 22,37,38,41, 69,109,110,116,129,132,133,142,194,198, 200,201,202,203,218,242,269,293,299,342, 416,428,454,460,480,494,518,540,597.

Books on Antiques & Collectibles

Most of the following books are available from your local book seller or antique dealer, or on loan from your public library. If you are unable to locate certain titles in your area you may order by mail from COLLECTOR BOOKS, P.O. Box 3009, Paducah, KY 42001. Add $1.00 for postage for the first book ordered and $.65 for each additional book. Include item number, title, and price when ordering. Allow 14 to 21 days for delivery. **All books are well illustrated and contain current values.**

Item #	Title & Author	Price
	Books On Glass & Pottery	
1444	Coll. Ency of Depression Glass, 6th Ed.	$17.95
1542	Depression Glass Pocket Guide, 4th Ed.	9.95
1443	Kitchen Glassware of the Depression, 2nd Ed.	19.95
1368	Standard Ency. of Carnival Glass, Edwards	24.95
1365	World of Salt Shakers, Lechner	9.95
1396	Elegant Glassware of the Depression, Florence	17.95
1379	Coll. Ency. of Glass Candlesticks, Archer	19.95
1443	Children's Glass Dishes, China, & Furniture	17.95
1435	Children's Dishes, Whitmyer	9.95
1438	Oil Lamps II, Thuro	19.95
1311	Coll. Ency. of R.S. Prussia, Gaston	24.95
1033	Coll. Ency. of Weller Pottery, Huxford	24.95
1034	Coll. Ency. of Roseville Pottery, Huxford	19.95
1035	Coll. Ency. of Roseville Pottery II	19.95
1039	Coll. Ency. of Nippon Porcelain, Van Patten	19.95
1350	Coll. Ency. of Nippon Porcelain II	19.95
1358	Coll. Ency. of McCoy Pottery, Huxford	19.95
1276	Coll. Ency. of Hull Pottery, Roberts	19.95
1210	Coll. Ency. of Limoges Porcelain, Gaston	19.95
1512	Coll. Ency. of Fiesta, Fifth Ed., Huxford	9.95
1312	Coll. Blue & White Stoneware, McNerney	9.95
1346	Decorated Country Stoneware, Raycraft	5.95
1373	Coll. Ency. of Am. Dinnerware, Cunningham	24.95
1425	Cookie Jars, Westfall	9.95
1440	Red Wing Stoneware, DePasquale	9.95
1432	Blue Willow, Gaston	9.95
1439	Coll. Ency. of Flow Blue China, Gaston	19.95
1447	Coll. Ency. of Noritake, Van Patten	19.95
	Books On Dolls	
1066	Coll. Ency. of Half-Dolls, Marion & Werner	29.95
1067	Madame Alexander Coll. Dolls, Smith	19.95
1068	Madame Alexander Coll. Dolls II	19.95
1069	Price Guide only for Madame Alexander	3.95
1076	Antique Coll. Dolls, Smith	17.95
1077	Antique Coll. Dolls II, Smith	17.95

Item #	Title & Author	Price
1079	Modern Coll. Dolls, Smith	17.95
1080	Modern Coll. Dolls II, Smith	17.95
1081	Modern Coll. Dolls III, Smith	17.95
1082	Modern Coll. Dolls IV, Smith	17.95
1375	Effanbee Dolls, Smith	19.95
1089	Patricia Smith's Doll Values	9.95
1090	Patricia Smith's Doll Values, Series II	9.95
1446	Patricia Smith's Doll Values, Series III	9.95
1430	World Of Barbie Dolls, Manos	9.95
	Other Collectibles	
1212	Marketplace Guide to Oak Furniture	17.95
1283	Marketplace Guide to Victorian Furniture	17.95
1279	Victorian Furniture, McNerney	8.95
1118	Antique Oak Furniture, Hill	7.95
1124	Primitives, Our American Heritage, McNerney	8.95
1437	Coll. Guide to Country Furniture, Raycraft	8.95
1457	Coll. Guide to Oak Furniture, McNerney	9.95
1278	Art Nouveau & Art Deco Jewelry, Baker	9.95
1128	Bottle Pricing Guide, 3rd Ed., Cleveland	7.95
1427	American Beer CAn Ency., 1983-1984 Ed	9.95
1154	Antique Tools, Our American Heritage	8.95
1539	Modern Guns, Revised 5th Ed. Quertermous	11.95
1277	Silverplated Flatware, Hagan	14.95
1181	100 Years of Collectible Jewelry, Baker	9.95
1374	Antique Purses, Holiner	9.95
1377	Elvis Collectibles, Cranor	12.95
1524	Collectible & Antique Marbles, Grist	9.95
1514	Character Toys & Collectibles, Longest	19.95
1516	Modern Collector's Dolls V, Smith	19.95
1513	Teddy Bears & Steiff Animals, Mandel	9.95
1442	Creative & Collectible Miniatures, Baker	9.95
1426	Indian Arrowheads & Projectile Points, Hothem	7.95
1441	Collectors Guide to Post Cards, Wood	9.95
1436	Antique Iron, McNerney	7.95
1465	Haviland Collectibles & Art Objects	19.95

Schroeder's INSIDER and Price Update

A monthly newsletter published for the antiques and collectibles marketplace.

The "INSIDER", as our subscribers have fondly dubbed it, is a monthly newsletter published for the antiques and collectibles marketplace. It gives the readers timely information as to trends, price changes, new finds, and market moves both upward and downward. Our writers are made up of a panel of well-known experts in the fields of Glass, Pottery, Dolls, Furniture, Jewelry, Country, Primitives, Oriental and a host of other fields in our huge industry. Our subscribers have that "inside edge" that makes them more profitable. Each month we explore 8-10 subjects that are "in", and close each discussion with a random sampling of current values that are recorded at press time. Thousands of subscribers eagerly await each monthly issue of this timely 16-page newsletter. A sample copy is available for $3.00 postpaid. Subscriptions are $24.00 for 12 months; 24 months for $45.00; 36 months for $65.00, all postpaid. A sturdy 3-ring binder to store your **Insider** is available for $5.00 postpaid. This newsletter contains NO paid advertising and is not available on your newsstand. It may be ordered by sending your check or money order to Collector Books, P. O. Box 3009, Paducah, KY 42001.